COLLINS
FRENCH
DICTIONARY
Plus GRAMMAR

COLLINS
FRENCH
DICTIONARY
Plus GRAMMAR

HarperCollins*Publishers*

first published in this edition 1997

© HarperCollins Publishers 1997

latest reprint 1998

HarperCollins Publishers
P.O. Box, Glasgow G4 0NB, Great Britain

ISBN 0 00 472100-4

HarperCollins Publishers, Inc.
10 East 53rd Street, New York, NY 10022
ISBN 0-06-276056-4

First HarperCollins edition published 1998

Library of Congress Card Number: 98-070452

98 99 00 01 02 CIBM 10 9 8 7 6 5 4 3 2

Dictionary text typeset by Morton Word Processing Ltd, Scarborough
Grammar text typeset by Tradespools Ltd, Frome, Somerset

A catalogue record for this book is available from the British Library

Printed and bound in Great Britain by
Caledonian International Book Manufacturing Ltd, Glasgow, G64

Pierre-Henri Cousin, Lorna Sinclair, Lesley A. Robertson
Jean-François Allain, Catherine E. Love

editorial team
Megan Thomson, Cécile Aubinière-Robb, Harry Campbell
Keith Foley, Janet Gough, Jean-Benoît Ormal-Grenon
Elspeth Anderson, Susan Dunsmore, Christine Penman
Val McNulty, Caitlin McMahon

series editor
Lorna Sinclair

editorial management
Vivian Marr

INTRODUCTION

You may be starting French for the first time, or you may wish to extend your knowledge of the language. Perhaps you want to read and study French books, newspapers and magazines, or perhaps simply have a conversation with French speakers. Whatever the reason, whether you're a student, a tourist or want to use French for business, this is the ideal book to help you understand and communicate. This modern, user-friendly dictionary gives priority to everyday vocabulary and the language of current affairs, business, computing and tourism, and, as in all Collins dictionaries, the emphasis is firmly placed on contemporary language and expressions.

HOW TO USE THE DICTIONARY

Below you will find an outline of how information is presented in your dictionary. Our aim is to give you the maximum amount of detail in the clearest and most helpful way.

Entries

A typical entry in your dictionary will be made up of the following elements:

Phonetic transcription

Phonetics appear in square brackets immediately after the headword. They are shown using the International Phonetic Alphabet (IPA), and a complete list of the symbols used in this system can be found on pages viii and ix.

Grammatical information

All words belong to one of the following parts of speech: noun, verb, adjective, adverb, pronoun, article, conjunction, preposition, abbreviation. Nouns can be singular or plural and, in French, masculine or feminine. Verbs can be transitive, intransitive, reflexive or impersonal. Parts of speech appear in *italics* immediately after the phonetic spelling of the headword. The gender of the translation also appears in *italics* immediately following the key element of the translation.

Often a word can have more than one part of speech. Just as the English word **chemical** can be an adjective or a noun, the French word **rose** can be an adjective ("pink") or a feminine noun ("rose"). In the same way the verb **to walk** is sometimes transitive, ie it takes an object ("to walk the dog") and sometimes intransitive, ie it doesn't take an object ("to walk to school"). To help you find the meaning you are looking for quickly and for clarity of presentation, the different part of speech categories are separated by a black lozenge ◆.

Meaning divisions

Most words have more than one meaning. Take, for example, **punch** which can be, amongst other things, a blow with the fist or an object used for making holes. Other words are translated differently depending on the context in which they are used. The transitive verb **to roll up**, for example, can be translated by "rouler" or "retrousser" depending on *what* it is you are rolling up. To help you select the most appropriate translation in every context, entries are divided according to meaning. Different meanings are introduced by an "indicator" in *italics* and in brackets. Thus, the examples given above will be shown as follows:

> **punch** *n* (*blow*) coup *m* de poing; (*tool*) poinçon *m*

> **roll up** *vt* (*carpet, cloth, map*) rouler; (*sleeves*) retrousser

Likewise, some words can have a different meaning when used to talk about a specific subject area or field. For example, **bishop**, which we generally use to mean a high-ranking clergyman, is also the name of a chess piece. To show English speakers which translation to use, we have added "subject field labels" in capitals and in brackets, in this case (*CHESS*):

bishop *n* évêque *m*; (*CHESS*) fou *m*

Field labels are often shortened to save space. You will find a complete list of abbreviations used in the dictionary on pages vi and vii.

Translations

Most English words have a direct translation in French and vice versa, as shown in the examples given above. Sometimes, however, no exact equivalent exists in the target language. In such cases we have given an approximate equivalent, indicated by the sign ≈. An example is **National Insurance**, the French equivalent of which is "Sécurité Sociale". There is no exact equivalent since the systems of the two countries are quite different:

National Insurance *n* (*BRIT*) ≈ Sécurité Sociale

On occasion it is impossible to find even an approximate equivalent. This may be the case, for example, with the names of types of food:

mince pie *n sorte de tarte aux fruits secs*

Here the translation (which doesn't exist) is replaced by an explanation. For increased clarity the explanation, or "gloss", is shown in *italics*.

It is often the case that a word, or a particular meaning of a word, cannot be translated in isolation. The translation of **Dutch**, for example, is "hollandais(e), néerlandais(e)". However, the phrase **to go Dutch** is rendered by "partager les frais". Even an expression as simple as **washing powder** needs a separate translation since it translates as "lessive (en poudre)", not "poudre à laver". This is where your dictionary will prove to be particularly informative and useful since it contains an abundance of compounds, phrases and idiomatic expressions.

Levels of formality and familiarity

In English you instinctively know when to say **I don't have any money** and when to say **I'm broke** or **I'm a bit short of cash**. When you are trying to understand someone who is speaking French, however, or when you yourself try to speak French, it is important to know what is polite and what is less so, and what you can say in a relaxed situation but not in a formal context. To help you with this, on the French-English side we have added the label (*fam*) to show that a French meaning or expression is colloquial, while those meanings or expressions which are vulgar are given an exclamation mark (*fam!*), warning you they can cause serious offence. Note also that on the English-French side, translations which are vulgar are followed by an exclamation mark in brackets.

Key words

Words labelled in the text as *KEYWORDS*, such as **be** and **do** or their French equivalents **être** and **faire**, have been given special treatment because they form the basic elements of the language. This extra help will ensure that you know how to use these complex words with confidence.

Cultural information

Entries which appear separated from the main text by a line above and below them explain aspects of culture in French and English-speaking countries. Subject areas covered include politics, education, media and national festivals, for example **Assemblée nationale, baccalauréat, BBC** and **Hallowe'en**.

ABRÉVIATIONS

ABBREVIATIONS

abréviation	*ab(b)r*	abbreviation
adjectif, locution adjective	*adj*	adjective, adjectival phrase
administration	*ADMIN*	administration
adverbe, locution adverbiale	*adv*	adverb, adverbial phrase
agriculture	*AGR*	agriculture
anatomie	*ANAT*	anatomy
architecture	*ARCHIT*	architecture
article défini	*art déf*	definite article
article indéfini	*art indéf*	indefinite article
automobile	*AUT(O)*	the motor car and motoring
aviation, voyages aériens	*AVIAT*	flying, air travel
biologie	*BIO(L)*	biology
botanique	*BOT*	botany
anglais de Grande-Bretagne	*BRIT*	British English
chimie	*CHIMIE, CHEM*	chemistry
cinéma	*CINÉ, CINE*	cinema
langue familière (! emploi vulgaire)	*col(!)*	colloquial usage (! particularly offensive)
commerce, finance, banque	*COMM*	commerce, finance, banking
informatique	*COMPUT*	computing
conjonction	*conj*	conjunction
construction	*CONSTR*	building
nom utilisé comme adjectif, ne peut s'employer ni comme attribut, ni après le nom qualifié	*cpd*	compound element: noun used as an adjective and which cannot follow the noun it qualifies
cuisine, art culinaire	*CULIN*	cookery
article défini	*def art*	definite article
déterminant: adjectif démonstratif, indéfini etc	*dét*	determiner: demonstrative etc.
économie	*ECON*	economics
électricité, électronique	*ELEC*	electricity, electronics
exclamation, interjection	*excl*	exclamation, interjection
féminin	*f*	feminine
langue familière (! emploi vulgaire)	*fam (!)*	colloquial usage (! particularly offensive)
emploi figuré	*fig*	figurative use
(verbe anglais) dont la particule est inséparable du verbe	*fus*	(phrasal verb) where the particle cannot be separated from the main verb
dans la plupart des sens; généralement	*gén, gen*	in most or all senses; generally
géographie, géologie	*GEO*	geography, geology
géométrie	*GEOM*	geometry
histoire	*HIST*	history
article indéfini	*indef art*	indefinite article
informatique	*INFORM*	computing
invariable	*inv*	invariable
irrégulier	*irrég, irreg*	irregular
domaine juridique	*JUR*	law
grammaire, linguistique	*LING*	grammar, linguistics
masculin	*m*	masculine
mathématiques, algèbre	*MATH*	mathematics, calculus
médecine	*MÉD, MED*	medical term, medicine

masculin ou féminin, suivant le sexe	**m/f**	either masculine or feminine depending on sex
domaine militaire, armée	**MIL**	military matters
musique	**MUS**	music
nom	**n**	noun
navigation, nautisme	**NAVIG, NAUT**	sailing, navigation
nom non comptable: ne peut s'utiliser au pluriel	**no pl**	collective (uncountable) noun: is not used in the plural
nom ou adjectif numéral	**num**	numeral adjective or noun
	o.s.	oneself
péjoratif	**péj, pej**	derogatory, pejorative
photographie	**PHOT(O)**	photography
physiologie	**PHYSIOL**	physiology
pluriel	**pl**	plural
politique	**POL**	politics
participe passé	**pp**	past participle
préposition	**prép, prep**	preposition
psychologie, psychiatrie	**PSYCH**	psychology, psychiatry
temps du passé	**pt**	past tense
quelque chose	**qch**	
quelqu'un	**qn**	
religions, domaine ecclésiastique	**REL**	religions, church service
	sb	somebody
enseignement, système scolaire et universitaire	**SCOL**	schooling, schools and universities
singulier	**sg**	singular
	sth	something
subjonctif	**sub**	subjunctive
sujet (grammatical)	**su(b)j**	(grammatical) subject
techniques, technologie	**TECH**	technical term, technology
télécommunications	**TEL**	telecommunications
théâtre	**THÉÂT, THEAT**	theatre
télévision	**TV**	television
typographie	**TYP(O)**	typography, printing
anglais des USA	**US**	American English
verbe	**vb**	verb
verbe ou groupe verbal à fonction intransitive	**vi**	verb or phrasal verb used intransitively
verbe ou groupe verbal à fonction transitive	**vt**	verb or phrasal verb used transitively
zoologie	**ZOOL**	zoology
marque déposée	®	registered trademark
indique une équivalence culturelle	≈	introduces a cultural equivalent
pas de liaison devant h aspiré	'	no liaison before aspirate h

TRANSCRIPTION PHONÉTIQUE

Consonnes

Consonants

NB. p, b, t, d, k, g sont suivis d'une aspiration en anglais.

NB. p, b, t, d, k, g are not aspirated in French.

poupée	p	puppy
bombe	b	baby
tente thermal	t	tent
dinde	d	daddy
coq qui képi	k	cork kiss chord
gag bague	g	gag guess
sale ce nation	s	so rice kiss
zéro rose	z	cousin buzz
tache chat	ʃ	sheep sugar
gilet juge	ʒ	pleasure beige
	tʃ	church
	dʒ	judge general
fer phare	f	farm raffle
valve	v	very rev
	θ	thin maths
	ð	that other
lent salle	l	little ball
rare rentrer	ʀ	
	r	rat rare
maman femme	m	mummy comb
non nonne	n	no ran
agneau vigne	ɲ	
	ŋ	singing bank
hop!	h	hat reheat
yeux paille pied	j	yet
nouer oui	w	wall bewail
huile lui	ɥ	
	x	loch

Divers

Miscellaneous

pour l'anglais: le r final se prononce en liaison devant une voyelle	*	
pour l'anglais: précède la syllabe accentuée	'	in French transcription: no liaison before aspirate h

En règle générale, la prononciation est donnée entre crochets après chaque entrée. Toutefois, du côté anglais-français et dans le cas des expressions composées de deux ou plusieurs mots non réunis par un trait d'union et faisant l'objet d'une entrée séparée, la prononciation doit être cherchée sous chacun des mots constitutifs de l'expression en question.

PHONETIC TRANSCRIPTION

Voyelles

NB. La mise en équivalence de certains sons n'indique qu'une ressemblance approximative.

Vowels

NB. The pairing of some vowel sounds only indicates approximate equivalence.

ici v_ie_ l_y_re	i iː	h_ee_l b_ea_d
	ɪ	h_i_t p_i_ty
jou_er_ ét_é_	e	
l_ai_t jou_et_ m_e_rci	ɛ	s_e_t t_e_nt
pl_a_t _a_mour	a æ	b_a_t _a_pple
b_a_s p_â_te	ɑ ɑː	_a_fter c_a_r c_a_lm
	ʌ	f_u_n c_ou_sin
l_e_ pr_e_mier	ə	_o_ver _a_bove
b_eu_rre p_eu_r	œ	
p_eu_ d_eu_x	ø əː	_ur_n f_er_n w_or_k
_o_r h_o_mme	ɔ	w_a_sh p_o_t
m_o_t _eau_ g_au_che	o ɔː	b_or_n c_or_k
gen_ou_ r_ou_e	u	f_u_ll s_oo_t
	uː	b_oo_n l_ew_d
r_ue_ _u_rne	y	

Diphtongues

Diphthongs

	ɪə	b_eer_ t_ier_
	ɛə	t_ear_ f_air_ th_ere_
	eɪ	d_a_te pl_ai_ce d_ay_
	aɪ	l_i_fe b_uy_ cry
	au	_ow_l f_ou_l n_ow_
	əu	l_ow_ n_o_
	ɔɪ	b_oi_l b_oy_ _oi_ly
	uə	p_oor_ t_our_

Nasales

Nasal Vowels

mat_in_ pl_ein_	ɛ̃
br_un_	œ̃
s_ang_ _an_ d_ans_	ɑ̃
n_on_ p_ont_	ɔ̃

In general, we give the pronunciation of each entry in square brackets after the word in question. However, on the English-French side, where the entry is composed of two or more unhyphenated words, each of which is given elsewhere in this dictionary, you will find the pronunciation of each word in its alphabetical position.

FRENCH VERB FORMS

1 Participe présent *2* Participe passé *3* Présent *4* Imparfait *5* Futur *6* Conditionnel *7* Subjonctif présent

acquérir *1* acquérant *2* acquis *3* acquiers, acquérons, acquièrent *4* acquérais *5* acquerrai *7* acquière

ALLER *1* allant *2* allé *3* vais, vas, va, allons, allez, vont *4* allais *5* irai *6* irais *7* aille

asseoir *1* asseyant *2* assis *3* assieds, asseyons, asseyez, asseyent *4* asseyais *5* assiérai *7* asseye

atteindre *1* atteignant *2* atteint *3* atteins, atteignons *4* atteignais *7* atteigne

AVOIR *1* ayant *2* eu *3* ai, as, a, avons, avez, ont *4* avais *5* aurai *6* aurais *7* aie, aies, ait, ayons, ayez, aient

battre *1* battant *2* battu *3* bats, bat, battons *4* battais *7* batte

boire *1* buvant *2* bu *3* bois, buvons, boivent *4* buvais *7* boive

bouillir *1* bouillant *2* bouilli *3* bous, bouillons *4* bouillais *7* bouille

conclure *1* concluant *2* conclu *3* conclus, concluons *4* concluais *7* conclue

conduire *1* conduisant *2* conduit *3* conduis, conduisons *4* conduisais *7* conduise

connaître *1* connaissant *2* connu *3* connais, connaît, connaissons *4* connaissais *7* connaisse

coudre *1* cousant *2* cousu *3* couds, cousons, cousez, cousent *4* cousais *7* couse

courir *1* courant *2* couru *3* cours, courons *4* courais *5* courrai *7* coure

couvrir *1* couvrant *2* couvert *3* couvre, couvrons *4* couvrais *7* couvre

craindre *1* craignant *2* craint *3* crains, craignons *4* craignais *7* craigne

croire *1* croyant *2* cru *3* crois, croyons, croient *4* croyais *7* croie

croître *1* croissant *2* crû, crue, crus, crues *3* croîs, croissons *4* croissais *7* croisse

cueillir *1* cueillant *2* cueilli *3* cueille, cueillons *4* cueillais *5* cueillerai *7* cueille

devoir *1* devant *2* dû, due, dus, dues *3* dois, devons, doivent *4* devais *5* devrai *7* doive

dire *1* disant *2* dit *3* dis, disons, dites, disent *4* disais *7* dise

dormir *1* dormant *2* dormi *3* dors, dormons *4* dormais *7* dorme

écrire *1* écrivant *2* écrit *3* écris, écrivons *4* écrivais *7* écrive

ÊTRE *1* étant *2* été *3* suis, es, est, sommes, êtes, sont *4* étais *5* serai *6* serais *7* sois, sois, soit, soyons, soyez, soient

FAIRE *1* faisant *2* fait *3* fais, fais, fait, faisons, faites, font *4* faisais *5* ferai *6* ferais *7* fasse

falloir *2* fallu *3* faut *4* fallait *5* faudra *7* faille

FINIR *1* finissant *2* fini *3* finis, finis, finit, finissons, finissez, finissent *4* finissais *5* finirai *6* finirais *7* finisse

fuir *1* fuyant *2* fui *3* fuis, fuyons, fuient *4* fuyais *7* fuie

joindre *1* joignant *2* joint *3* joins, joignons *4* joignais *7* joigne

lire *1* lisant *2* lu *3* lis, lisons *4* lisais *7* lise

luire *1* luisant *2* lui *3* luis, luisons *4* luisais *7* luise

maudire *1* maudissant *2* maudit *3* maudis, maudissons *4* maudissait *7* maudisse

mentir *1* mentant *2* menti *3* mens, mentons *4* mentais *7* mente

mettre *1* mettant *2* mis *3* mets, mettons *4* mettais *7* mette

mourir *1* mourant *2* mort *3* meurs, mourons, meurent *4* mourais *5* mourrai *7* meure

naître *1* naissant *2* né *3* nais, naît, naissons *4* naissais *7* naisse

offrir *1* offrant *2* offert *3* offre, offrons *4* offrais *7* offre

PARLER *1* parlant *2* parlé *3* parle, parles, parle, parlons, parlez, parlent *4* parlais, parlais, parlait, parlions, parliez, parlaient *5* parlerai, parleras, parlera, parlerons, parlerez, parleront *6* parlerais, parlerais, parlerait, parlerions, parleriez, parleraient *7*

1 Participe présent **2** Participe passé **3** Présent **4** Imparfait **5** Futur **6** Conditionnel **7** Subjonctif présent

parle, parles, parle, parlions, parliez, parlent *impératif* parle! parlez!

partir *1* partant *2* parti *3* pars, partons *4* partais *7* parte

plaire *1* plaisant *2* plu *3* plais, plaît, plaisons *4* plaisais *7* plaise

pleuvoir *1* pleuvant *2* plu *3* pleut, pleuvent *4* pleuvait *5* pleuvra *7* pleuve

pourvoir *1* pourvoyant *2* pourvu *3* pourvois, pourvoyons, pourvoient *4* pourvoyais *7* pourvoie

pouvoir *1* pouvant *2* pu *3* peux, peut, pouvons, peuvent *4* pouvais *5* pourrai *7* puisse

prendre *1* prenant *2* pris *3* prends, prenons, prennent *4* prenais *7* prenne

prévoir *like voir* *5* prévoirai

RECEVOIR *1* recevant *2* reçu *3* reçois, reçois, reçoit, recevons, recevez, reçoivent *4* recevais *5* recevrai *6* recevrais *7* reçoive

RENDRE *1* rendant *2* rendu *3* rends, rends, rend, rendons, rendez, rendent *4* rendais *5* rendrai *6* rendrais *7* rende

résoudre *1* résolvant *2* résolu *3* résous, résout, résolvons *4* résolvais *7* résolve

rire *1* riant *2* ri *3* ris, rions *4* riais *7* rie

savoir *1* sachant *2* su *3* sais, savons, savent *4* savais *5* saurai *7* sache

impératif sache, sachons, sachez

servir *1* servant *2* servi *3* sers, servons *4* servais *7* serve

sortir *1* sortant *2* sorti *3* sors, sortons *4* sortais *7* sorte

souffrir *1* souffrant *2* souffert *3* souffre, souffrons *4* souffrais *7* souffre

suffire *1* suffisant *2* suffi *3* suffis, suffisons *4* suffisais *7* suffise

suivre *1* suivant *2* suivi *3* suis, suivons *4* suivais *7* suive

taire *1* taisant *2* tu *3* tais, taisons *4* taisais *7* taise

tenir *1* tenant *2* tenu *3* tiens, tenons, tiennent *4* tenais *5* tiendrai *7* tienne

vaincre *1* vainquant *2* vaincu *3* vaincs, vainc, vainquons *4* vainquais *7* vainque

valoir *1* valant *2* valu *3* vaux, vaut, valons *4* valais *5* vaudrai *7* vaille

venir *1* venant *2* venu *3* viens, venons, viennent *4* venais *5* viendrai *7* vienne

vivre *1* vivant *2* vécu *3* vis, vivons *4* vivais *7* vive

voir *1* voyant *2* vu *3* vois, voyons, voient *4* voyais *5* verrai *7* voie

vouloir *1* voulant *2* voulu *3* veux, veut, voulons, veulent *4* voulais *5* voudrai *7* veuille *impératif* veuillez

For additional information on French verb formation, see pp. 6-131 of Grammar section.

LES NOMBRES

NUMBERS

un (une)	1	one
deux	2	two
trois	3	three
quatre	4	four
cinq	5	five
six	6	six
sept	7	seven
huit	8	eight
neuf	9	nine
dix	10	ten
onze	11	eleven
douze	12	twelve
treize	13	thirteen
quatorze	14	fourteen
quinze	15	fifteen
seize	16	sixteen
dix-sept	17	seventeen
dix-huit	18	eighteen
dix-neuf	19	nineteen
vingt	20	twenty
vingt et un (une)	21	twenty-one
vingt-deux	22	twenty-two
trente	30	thirty
quarante	40	forty
cinquante	50	fifty
soixante	60	sixty
soixante-dix	70	seventy
soixante et onze	71	seventy-one
soixante-douze	72	seventy-two
quatre-vingts	80	eighty
quatre-vingt-un (-une)	81	eighty-one
quatre-vingt-dix	90	ninety
quatre-vingt-onze	91	ninety-one
cent	100	a hundred
cent un (une)	101	a hundred and one
trois cents	300	three hundred
trois cent un (une)	301	three hundred and one
mille	1 000	a thousand
un million	1 000 000	a million

LES NOMBRES

NUMBERS

premier (première), 1er	first, 1st
deuxième, 2e *or* 2ème	second, 2nd
troisième, 3e *or* 3ème	third, 3rd
quatrième	fourth, 4th
cinquième	fifth, 5th
sixième	sixth, 6th
septième	seventh
huitième	eighth
neuvième	ninth
dixième	tenth
onzième	eleventh
douzième	twelfth
treizième	thirteenth
quatorzième	fourteenth
quinzième	fifteenth
seizième	sixteenth
dix-septième	seventeenth
dix-huitième	eighteenth
dix-neuvième	nineteenth
vingtième	twentieth
vingt-et-unième	twenty-first
vingt-deuxième	twenty-second
trentième	thirtieth
centième	hundredth
cent-unième	hundred-and-first
millième	thousandth

L'HEURE

THE TIME

quelle heure est-il?
il est ...

what time is it?
it's ...

minuit
midnight

une heure (du matin)
one o'clock (in the morning) , one (am)

une heure cinq
five past one

une heure dix
ten past one

une heure et quart
a quarter past one, one fifteen

une heure vingt-cinq
twenty-five past one, one twenty-five

une heure et demie, une heure trente
half past one, one thirty

deux heures moins vingt-cinq, une heure trente-cinq
twenty-five to two, one thirty-five

deux heures moins vingt, une heure quarante
twenty to two, one forty

deux heures moins le quart, une heure quarante-cinq
a quarter to two, one forty-five

deux heures moins dix, une heure cinquante
ten to two, one fifty

midi
twelve o'clock, midday, noon

deux heures (de l'après-midi)
two o'clock (in the afternoon), two (pm)

sept heures (du soir)
seven o'clock (in the evening), seven (pm)

à quelle heure?

at what time?

à minuit
at midnight

à sept heures
at seven o'clock

à une heure
at one o'clock

dans vingt minutes
in twenty minutes

il y a dix minutes
ten minutes ago

LA DATE

THE DATE

aujourd'hui
today

demain
tomorrow

après-demain
the day after tomorrow

hier
yesterday

avant-hier
the day before yesterday

la veille
the day before, the previous day

le lendemain
the next *or* following day

le matin	morning
le soir	evening
ce matin	this morning
ce soir	this evening
cet après-midi	this afternoon
hier matin	yesterday morning
hier soir	yesterday evening
demain matin	tomorrow morning
demain soir	tomorrow evening
dans la nuit du samedi au dimanche	during Saturday night, during the night of Saturday to Sunday
il viendra samedi	he's coming on Saturday
le samedi	on Saturdays
tous les samedis	every Saturday
samedi passé *ou* dernier	last Saturday
samedi prochain	next Saturday
samedi en huit	a week on Saturday
samedi en quinze	a fortnight *or* two weeks on Saturday
du lundi au samedi	from Monday to Saturday
tous les jours	every day
une fois par semaine	once a week
une fois par mois	once a month
deux fois par semaine	twice a week
il y a une semaine *ou* huit jours	a week ago
il y a quinze jours	a fortnight *or* two weeks ago
l'année passée *ou* dernière	last year
dans deux jours	in two days
dans huit jours *ou* une semaine	in a week
dans quinze jours	in a fortnight *or* two weeks
le mois prochain	next month
l'année prochaine	next year
quel jour sommes-nous?	*what day is it?*
le 1er/24 octobre 1996	the 1st/24th of October 1996, October 1st/24th 1996
en 1996	in 1996
mille neuf cent quatre-vingt seize	nineteen ninety-six
44 av. J.-C.	44 BC
14 apr. J.-C.	14 AD
au XIXe (siècle)	in the nineteenth century
dans les années trente	in the thirties
il était une fois ...	once upon a time ...

A a

A, a [ɑ] *nm inv* A, a ♦ *abr* = **anticyclone, are**; (= *ampère*) amp; (= *autoroute*) ≈ M (*BRIT*); **A comme Anatole** A for Andrew (*BRIT*) *ou* Able (*US*); **de a à z** from a to z; **prouver qch par a + b** to prove sth conclusively.
a [a] *vb voir* **avoir.**

à [a] (*à + le* = **au,** *à + les* = **aux**) *prép* **1** (*endroit, situation*) at, in; **être ~ Paris/au Portugal** to be in Paris/Portugal; **être ~ la maison/~ l'école** to be at home/at school; **~ la campagne** in the country; **c'est ~ 10 km/~ 20 minutes (d'ici)** it's 10 km/20 minutes away
2 (*direction*) to; **aller ~ Paris/au Portugal** to go to Paris/Portugal; **aller ~ la maison/~ l'école** to go home/to school; **~ la campagne** to the country
3 (*temps*): **~ 3 heures/minuit** at 3 o'clock/midnight; **au printemps** in the spring; **au mois de juin** in June; **au départ** at the start, at the outset; **~ demain/la semaine prochaine!** see you tomorrow/next week!; **visites de 5 heures ~ 6 heures** visiting from 5 to *ou* till 6 o'clock
4 (*attribution, appartenance*) to; **le livre est ~ Paul/~ lui/~ nous** this book is Paul's/his/ours; **donner qch ~ qn** to give sth to sb; **un ami ~ moi** a friend of mine; **c'est ~ moi de le faire** it's up to me to do it
5 (*moyen*) with; **se chauffer au gaz** to have gas heating; **~ bicyclette** on a *ou* by bicycle; **~ la main/machine** by hand/machine; **~ la télévision/la radio** on television/the radio
6 (*provenance*) from; **boire ~ la bouteille** to drink from the bottle
7 (*caractérisation, manière*): **l'homme aux yeux bleus** the man with the blue eyes; **~ la russe** the Russian way; **glace ~ la framboise** raspberry ice cream
8 (*but, destination*): **tasse ~ café** coffee cup; **maison ~ vendre** house for sale; **problème ~ régler** problem to sort out
9 (*rapport, évaluation, distribution*): **100 km/unités ~ l'heure** 100 km/units per *ou* an hour; **payé ~ l'heure** paid by the hour; **cinq ~ six** five to six

10 (*conséquence, résultat*): **~ ce qu'il prétend** according to him; **~ leur grande surprise** much to their surprise; **~ nous trois nous n'avons pas su le faire** we couldn't do it even between the three of us; **ils sont arrivés ~ 4** 4 of them arrived (together).

Å *abr* (= *Angstrom*) A *ou* Å.
A2 *abr* (= *Antenne 2*) *French TV channel.*
AB *abr* = **assez bien.**
abaissement [abɛsmɑ̃] *nm* lowering; pulling down.
abaisser [abese] *vt* to lower, bring down; (*manette*) to pull down; (*fig*) to debase; to humiliate; **s'~** *vi* to go down; (*fig*) to demean o.s.; **s'~ à faire/à qch** to stoop *ou* descend to doing/to sth.
abandon [abɑ̃dɔ̃] *nm* abandoning; deserting; giving up; withdrawal; surrender, relinquishing; (*fig*) lack of constraint; relaxed pose *ou* mood; **être à l'~** to be in a state of neglect; **laisser à l'~** to abandon.
abandonné, e [abɑ̃dɔne] *adj* (*solitaire*) deserted; (*route, usine*) disused; (*jardin*) abandoned.
abandonner [abɑ̃dɔne] *vt* to leave, abandon, desert; (*projet, activité*) to abandon, give up; (*SPORT*) to retire *ou* withdraw from; (*céder*) to surrender, relinquish; **s'~** *vi* to let o.s. go; **s'~ à** (*paresse, plaisirs*) to give o.s. up to; **~ qch à qn** to give sth up to sb.
abasourdir [abazuʀdiʀ] *vt* to stun, stagger.
abat [aba] *etc vb voir* **abattre.**
abat-jour [abaʒuʀ] *nm inv* lampshade.
abats [aba] *vb voir* **abattre** ♦ *nmpl* (*de bœuf, porc*) offal *sg* (*BRIT*), entrails (*US*); (*de volaille*) giblets.
abattage [abataʒ] *nm* cutting down, felling.
abattant [abatɑ̃] *vb voir* **abattre** ♦ *nm* leaf, flap.
abattement [abatmɑ̃] *nm* (*physique*) enfeeblement; (*moral*) dejection, despondency; (*déduction*) reduction; **~ fiscal** ≈ tax allowance.
abattis [abati] *vb voir* **abattre** ♦ *nmpl* giblets.
abattoir [abatwaʀ] *nm* abattoir (*BRIT*), slaughterhouse.
abattre [abatʀ(ə)] *vt* (*arbre*) to cut down, fell; (*mur, maison*) to pull down; (*avion, personne*)

to shoot down; (_animal_) to shoot, kill; (_fig: physiquement_) to wear out, tire out; (_: moralement_) to demoralize; **s'~** _vi_ to crash down; **s'~ sur** (_suj: pluie_) to beat down on; (_: coups, injures_) to rain down on; **~ ses cartes** (_aussi fig_) to lay one's cards on the table; **~ du travail** _ou_ **de la besogne** to get through a lot of work.

abattu, e [abaty] _pp de_ **abattre** ♦ _adj_ (_déprimé_) downcast.

abbatiale [abasjal] _nf_ abbey (_church_).

abbaye [abei] _nf_ abbey.

abbé [abe] _nm_ priest; (_d'une abbaye_) abbot; **M l'~** Father.

abbesse [abɛs] _nf_ abbess.

abc, ABC [abese] _nm_ alphabet primer; (_fig_) rudiments _pl_.

abcès [apsɛ] _nm_ abscess.

abdication [abdikasjɔ̃] _nf_ abdication.

abdiquer [abdike] _vi_ to abdicate ♦ _vt_ to renounce, give up.

abdomen [abdɔmɛn] _nm_ abdomen.

abdominal, e, aux [abdɔminal, -o] _adj_ abdominal ♦ _nmpl_: **faire des abdominaux** to do exercises for the stomach muscles.

abécédaire [abesedɛR] _nm_ alphabet primer.

abeille [abɛj] _nf_ bee.

aberrant, e [abeRɑ̃, -ɑ̃t] _adj_ absurd.

aberration [abeRasjɔ̃] _nf_ aberration.

abêtir [abetiR] _vt_ to make morons (_ou_ a moron) of.

abêtissant, e [abetisɑ̃, -ɑ̃t] _adj_ stultifying.

abhorrer [abɔRe] _vt_ to abhor, loathe.

abîme [abim] _nm_ abyss, gulf.

abîmer [abime] _vt_ to spoil, damage; **s'~** _vi_ to get spoilt _ou_ damaged; (_fruits_) to spoil; (_tomber_) to sink, founder; **s'~ les yeux** to ruin one's eyes _ou_ eyesight.

abject, e [abʒɛkt] _adj_ abject, despicable.

abjurer [abʒyRe] _vt_ to abjure, renounce.

ablatif [ablatif] _nm_ ablative.

ablation [ablasjɔ̃] _nf_ removal.

ablutions [ablysjɔ̃] _nfpl_: **faire ses ~** to perform one's ablutions.

abnégation [abnegasjɔ̃] _nf_ (self-)abnegation.

aboie [abwa] _etc vb voir_ **aboyer**.

aboiement [abwamɑ̃] _nm_ bark, barking _no pl_.

aboierai [abwajoRe] _etc vb voir_ **aboyer**.

abois [abwa] _nmpl_: **aux ~** at bay.

abolir [abɔliR] _vt_ to abolish.

abolition [abɔlisjɔ̃] _nf_ abolition.

abolitionniste [abɔlisjɔnist(ə)] _adj, nm/f_ abolitionist.

abominable [abɔminabl(ə)] _adj_ abominable.

abomination [abɔminasjɔ̃] _nf_ abomination.

abondamment [abɔ̃damɑ̃] _adv_ abundantly.

abondance [abɔ̃dɑ̃s] _nf_ abundance; (_richesse_) affluence; **en ~** in abundance.

abondant, e [abɔ̃dɑ̃, -ɑ̃t] _adj_ plentiful, abundant, copious.

abonder [abɔ̃de] _vi_ to abound, be plentiful; **~ en** to be full of, abound in; **~ dans le sens de** qn to concur with sb.

abonné, e [abɔne] _nm/f_ subscriber; season ticket holder ♦ _adj_: **être ~ à un journal** to subscribe to _ou_ have a subscription to a periodical; **être ~ au téléphone** to be on the (tele)phone.

abonnement [abɔnmɑ̃] _nm_ subscription; (_pour transports en commun, concerts_) season ticket.

abonner [abɔne] _vt_: **s'~ à** to subscribe to, take out a subscription to.

abord [abɔR] _nm_: **être d'un ~ facile** to be approachable; **être d'un ~ difficile** (_personne_) to be unapproachable; (_lieu_) to be hard to reach _ou_ difficult to get to; **de prime ~**, **au premier ~** at first sight; **d'~** _adv_ first; **tout d'~** first of all.

abordable [abɔRdabl(ə)] _adj_ (_personne_) approachable; (_marchandise_) reasonably priced; (_prix_) affordable, reasonable.

abordage [abɔRdaʒ] _nm_ boarding.

aborder [abɔRde] _vi_ to land ♦ _vt_ (_sujet, difficulté_) to tackle; (_personne_) to approach; (_rivage etc_) to reach; (_NAVIG: attaquer_) to board; (_: heurter_) to collide with.

abords [abɔR] _nmpl_ surroundings.

aborigène [abɔRiʒɛn] _nm_ aborigine, native.

Abou Dhabî, Abu Dhabi [abudabi] _nm_ Abu Dhabi.

aboulique [abulik] _adj_ totally lacking in willpower.

aboutir [abutiR] _vi_ (_négociations etc_) to succeed; (_abcès_) to come to a head; **~ à/dans/sur** to end up at/in/on.

aboutissants [abutisɑ̃] _nmpl voir_ **tenants**.

aboutissement [abutismɑ̃] _nm_ success; (_de concept, projet_) successful realization; (_d'années de travail_) successful conclusion.

aboyer [abwaje] _vi_ to bark.

abracadabrant, e [abRakadabRɑ̃, -ɑ̃t] _adj_ incredible, preposterous.

abrasif, ive [abRazif, -iv] _adj, nm_ abrasive.

abrégé [abReʒe] _nm_ summary; **en ~** in a shortened _ou_ abbreviated form.

abréger [abReʒe] _vt_ (_texte_) to shorten, abridge; (_mot_) to shorten, abbreviate; (_réunion, voyage_) to cut short, shorten.

abreuver [abRœve] _vt_ to water; (_fig_): **~ qn de** to shower _ou_ swamp sb with; (_injures etc_) to shower sb with; **s'~** _vi_ to drink.

abreuvoir [abRœvwaR] _nm_ watering place.

abréviation [abRevjasjɔ̃] _nf_ abbreviation.

abri [abRi] _nm_ shelter; **à l'~** under cover; **être/se mettre à l'~** to be/get under cover _ou_ shelter; **à l'~ de** sheltered from; (_fig_) safe from.

Abribus [abRibys] _nm_ ® bus shelter.

abricot [abRiko] _nm_ apricot.

abricotier [abRikɔtje] _nm_ apricot tree.

abrité, e [abRite] _adj_ sheltered.

abriter [abRite] _vt_ to shelter; (_loger_) to accommodate; **s'~** to shelter, take cover.

abrogation [abʀɔgasjɔ̃] nf (JUR) repeal, abrogation.

abroger [abʀɔʒe] vt to repeal, abrogate.

abrupt, e [abʀypt] adj sheer, steep; (ton) abrupt.

abruti, e [abʀyti] nm/f (fam) idiot, moron.

abrutir [abʀytiʀ] vt to daze; (fatiguer) to exhaust; (abêtir) to stupefy.

abrutissant, e [abʀytisɑ̃, -ɑ̃t] adj (bruit, travail) stupefying.

abscisse [apsis] nf X axis, abscissa.

absence [apsɑ̃s] nf absence; (MÉD) blackout; (distraction) mental blank; **en l'~ de** in the absence of.

absent, e [apsɑ̃, -ɑ̃t] adj absent; (chose) missing, lacking; (distrait: air) vacant, faraway ♦ nm/f absentee.

absentéisme [apsɑ̃teism(ə)] nm absenteeism.

absenter [apsɑ̃te]: **s'~** vi to take time off work; (sortir) to leave, go out.

abside [apsid] nf (ARCHIT) apse.

absinthe [apsɛ̃t] nf (boisson) absinth(e); (BOT) wormwood, absinth(e).

absolu, e [apsɔly] adj absolute; (caractère) rigid, uncompromising ♦ nm (PHILOSOPHIE): **l'~** the Absolute; **dans l'~** in the absolute, in a vacuum.

absolument [apsɔlymɑ̃] adv absolutely.

absolution [apsɔlysjɔ̃] nf absolution; (JUR) dismissal (of case).

absolutisme [apsɔlytism(ə)] nm absolutism.

absolvais [apsɔlvɛ] etc vb voir **absoudre**.

absorbant, e [apsɔʀbɑ̃, -ɑ̃t] adj absorbent; (tâche) absorbing, engrossing.

absorbé, e [apsɔʀbe] adj absorbed, engrossed.

absorber [apsɔʀbe] vt to absorb; (gén MÉD: manger, boire) to take; (ÉCON: firme) to take over, absorb.

absorption [apsɔʀpsjɔ̃] nf absorption.

absoudre [apsudʀ(ə)] vt to absolve; (JUR) to dismiss.

absous, oute [apsu, -ut] pp de **absoudre**.

abstenir [apstəniʀ]: **s'~** vi (POL) to abstain; **s'~ de qch/de faire** to refrain from sth/from doing.

abstention [apstɑ̃sjɔ̃] nf abstention.

abstentionnisme [apstɑ̃sjɔnism(ə)] nm abstaining.

abstentionniste [apstɑ̃sjɔnist(ə)] nm abstentionist.

abstenu, e [apstəny] pp de **abstenir**.

abstiendrai [apstjɛ̃dʀe], **abstiens** [apstjɛ̃] etc voir **abstenir**.

abstinence [apstinɑ̃s] nf abstinence; **faire ~ to** abstain (from meat on Fridays).

abstint [apstɛ̃] etc vb voir **abstenir**.

abstraction [apstʀaksjɔ̃] nf abstraction; **faire ~ de** to set ou leave aside; **~ faite de ...** leaving aside ....

abstraire [apstʀɛʀ] vt to abstract; **s'~ vi: s'~ (de)** (s'isoler) to cut o.s. off (from).

abstrait, e [apstʀɛ, -ɛt] pp de **abstraire** ♦ adj abstract ♦ nm: **dans l'~** in the abstract.

abstraitement [apstʀɛtmɑ̃] adv abstractly.

abstrayais [apstʀɛjɛ] etc vb voir **abstraire**.

absurde [apsyʀd(ə)] adj absurd ♦ nm absurdity; (PHILOSOPHIE): **l'~** absurd; **par l'~** ad absurdio.

absurdité [apsyʀdite] nf absurdity.

abus [aby] nm (excès) abuse, misuse; (injustice) abuse; **~ de confiance** breach of trust; (détournement de fonds) embezzlement; **~ de pouvoir** abuse of power.

abuser [abyze] vi to go too far, overstep the mark ♦ vt to deceive, mislead; **s'~** vi (se méprendre) to be mistaken; **~ de** vt (force, droit) to misuse; (alcool) to take to excess; (violer, duper) to take advantage of.

abusif, ive [abyzif, -iv] adj exorbitant; (punition) excessive; (pratique) improper.

abusivement [abyzivmɑ̃] adv exorbitantly; excessively; improperly.

AC sigle f (= appellation contrôlée) guarantee of quality of wine.

acabit [akabi] nm: **du même ~** of the same type.

acacia [akasja] nm (BOT) acacia.

académicien, ne [akademisjɛ̃, -ɛn] nm/f academician.

académie [akademi] nf (société) learned society; (école: d'art, de danse) academy; (ART: nu) nude; (SCOL: circonscription) ≈ regional education authority; **l'A~ (française)** the French Academy.

The **Académie française** was founded by Cardinal Richelieu in 1635 during the reign of Louis XIII. It consists of forty elected scholars and writers who are known as "les Quarante" or "les Immortels". One of the Académie's functions is to regulate the development of the French language and its recommendations are frequently the subject of lively public debate. It has produced several editions of its famous dictionary and also awards various literary prizes.

---

académique [akademik] adj academic.

Acadie [akadi] nf: **l'~** the Maritime Provinces.

acadien, ne [akadjɛ̃, -ɛn] adj Acadian, of ou from the Maritime Provinces.

acajou [akaʒu] nm mahogany.

acariâtre [akaʀjɑtʀ(ə)] adj sour(-tempered) (BRIT), cantankerous.

accablant, e [akɑblɑ̃, -ɑ̃t] adj (témoignage, preuve) overwhelming.

accablement [akɑbləmɑ̃] nm deep despondency.

accabler [akɑble] vt to overwhelm, overcome; (suj: témoignage) to condemn, damn; **~ qn d'injures** to heap ou shower abuse on sb; **~ qn de travail** to overburden sb with work; **accablé de dettes/soucis** weighed down with debts/cares.

accalmie [akalmi] *nf* lull.

accaparant, e [akaparã, -ãt] *adj* that takes up all one's time *ou* attention.

accaparer [akapaʀe] *vt* to monopolize; (*suj: travail etc*) to take up (all) the time *ou* attention of.

accéder [aksede]: ~ **à** *vt* (*lieu*) to reach; (*fig: pouvoir*) to accede to; (: *poste*) to attain; (*accorder: requête*) to grant, accede to.

accélérateur [akseleʀatœʀ] *nm* accelerator.

accélération [akseleʀasjɔ̃] *nf* speeding up; acceleration.

accéléré [akseleʀe] *nm*: **en** ~ (*CINÉ*) speeded up.

accélérer [akseleʀe] *vt* (*mouvement, travaux*) to speed up ♦ *vi* (*AUTO*) to accelerate.

accent [aksã] *nm* accent; (*inflexions expressives*) tone (of voice); (*PHONÉTIQUE, fig*) stress; **aux** ~**s de** (*musique*) to the strains of; **mettre l'**~ **sur** (*fig*) to stress; ~ **aigu/grave/ circonflexe** acute/grave/ circumflex accent.

accentuation [aksãtyasjɔ̃] *nf* accenting; stressing.

accentué, e [aksãtye] *adj* marked, pronounced.

accentuer [aksãtye] *vt* (*LING: orthographe*) to accent; (: *phonétique*) to stress, accent; (*fig*) to accentuate, emphasize; (: *effort, pression*) to increase; **s'**~ *vi* to become more marked *ou* pronounced.

acceptable [akseptabl(ə)] *adj* satisfactory, acceptable.

acceptation [akseptasjɔ̃] *nf* acceptance.

accepter [aksepte] *vt* to accept; (*tolérer*): ~ **que qn fasse** to agree to sb doing; ~ **de faire** to agree to do.

acception [aksepsjɔ̃] *nf* meaning, sense; **dans toute l'**~ **du terme** in the full sense *ou* meaning of the word.

accès [aksɛ] *nm* (*à un lieu, INFORM*) access; (*MÉD*) attack; (: *de toux*) fit, bout ♦ *nmpl* (*routes etc*) means of access, approaches; **d'**~ **facile/malaisé** easily/not easily accessible; **donner** ~ **à** (*lieu*) to give access to; (*carrière*) to open the door to; **avoir** ~ **auprès de qn** to have access to sb; **l'**~ **aux quais est interdit aux personnes non munies d'un billet** ticket-holders only on platforms, no access to platforms without a ticket; ~ **de colère** fit of anger; ~ **de joie** burst of joy.

accessible [aksesibl(ə)] *adj* accessible; (*personne*) approachable; (*livre, sujet*): ~ **à qn** within the reach of sb; (*sensible*): ~ **à la pitié/l'amour** open to pity/love.

accession [aksesjɔ̃] *nf*: ~ **à** accession to; (*à un poste*) attainment of; ~ **à la propriété** home-ownership.

accessit [aksesit] *nm* (*SCOL*) ≈ certificate of merit.

accessoire [akseswaʀ] *adj* secondary, of secondary importance; (*frais*) incidental ♦ *nm*

accessory; (*THÉÂT*) prop.

accessoirement [akseswaʀmã] *adv* secondarily; incidentally.

accessoiriste [akseswaʀist(ə)] *nm/f* (*TV, CINÉ*) property man/woman.

accident [aksidã] *nm* accident; **par** ~ by chance; ~ **de parcours** mishap; ~ **de la route** road accident; ~ **du travail** accident at work; industrial injury *ou* accident; ~**s de terrain** unevenness of the ground.

accidenté, e [aksidãte] *adj* damaged *ou* injured (in an accident); (*relief, terrain*) uneven; hilly.

accidentel, le [aksidãtɛl] *adj* accidental.

accidentellement [aksidãtɛlmã] *adv* (*par hasard*) accidentally; (*mourir*) in an accident.

accise [aksiz] *nf*: **droit d'**~**(s)** excise duty.

acclamation [aklamasjɔ̃] *nf*: **par** ~ (*vote*) by acclamation; ~**s** *nfpl* cheers, cheering *sg*.

acclamer [aklame] *vt* to cheer, acclaim.

acclimatation [aklimatasjɔ̃] *nf* acclimatization.

acclimater [aklimate] *vt* to acclimatize; **s'**~ *vi* to become acclimatized.

accointances [akwɛ̃tãs] *nfpl*: **avoir des** ~ **avec** to have contacts with.

accolade [akɔlad] *nf* (*amicale*) embrace; (*signe*) brace; **donner l'**~ **à qn** to embrace sb.

accoler [akɔle] *vt* to place side by side.

accommodant, e [akɔmɔdã, -ãt] *adj* accommodating, easy-going.

accommodement [akɔmɔdmã] *nm* compromise.

accommoder [akɔmɔde] *vt* (*CULIN*) to prepare; (*points de vue*) to reconcile; ~ **qch à** (*adapter*) to adapt sth to; **s'**~ **de** to put up with; (*se contenter de*) to make do with; **s'**~ **à** (*s'adapter*) to adapt to.

accompagnateur, trice [akɔ̃paɲatœʀ, -tʀis] *nm/f* (*MUS*) accompanist; (*de voyage*) guide; (*de voyage organisé*) courier; (*d'enfants*) accompanying adult.

accompagnement [akɔ̃paɲmã] *nm* (*MUS*) accompaniment; (*MIL*) support.

accompagner [akɔ̃paɲe] *vt* to accompany, be *ou* go *ou* come with; (*MUS*) to accompany; **s'**~ **de** to bring, be accompanied by.

accompli, e [akɔ̃pli] *adj* accomplished.

accomplir [akɔ̃pliʀ] *vt* (*tâche, projet*) to carry out; (*souhait*) to fulfil; **s'**~ *vi* to be fulfilled.

accomplissement [akɔ̃plismã] *nm* carrying out; fulfilment (*BRIT*), fulfillment (*US*).

accord [akɔʀ] *nm* (*entente, convention, LING*) agreement; (*entre des styles, tons etc*) harmony; (*consentement*) agreement, consent; (*MUS*) chord; **donner son** ~ to give one's agreement; **mettre 2 personnes d'**~ to make 2 people come to an agreement, reconcile 2 people; **se mettre d'**~ to come to an agreement (with each other); **être d'**~ to agree; **être d'**~ **avec qn** to agree with sb; **d'**~! OK!, right!; **d'un commun** ~ of one accord; ~ **parfait** (*MUS*) tonic chord.

accord-cadre, *pl* **accords-cadres** [akɔʀkɑdʀ(ə)] *nm* framework *ou* outline agreement.

accordéon [akɔʀdeɔ̃] *nm* (*MUS*) accordion.

accordéoniste [akɔʀdeɔnist(ə)] *nm/f* accordionist.

accorder [akɔʀde] *vt* (*faveur, délai*) to grant; (*attribuer*): ~ **de l'importance/de la valeur à qch** to attach importance/value to sth; (*harmoniser*) to match; (*MUS*) to tune; **s'**~ to get on together; (*être d'accord*) to agree; (*couleurs, caractères*) to go together, match; (*LING*) to agree; **je vous accorde que** ... I grant you that ....

accordeur [akɔʀdœʀ] *nm* (*MUS*) tuner.

accoster [akɔste] *vt* (*NAVIG*) to draw alongside; (*personne*) to accost ♦ *vi* (*NAVIG*) to berth.

accotement [akɔtmɑ̃] *nm* (*de route*) verge (*BRIT*), shoulder; ~ **stabilisé/non stabilisé** hard shoulder/soft verge *ou* shoulder.

accoter [akɔte] *vt*: ~ **qch contre/à** to lean *ou* rest sth against/on; **s'**~ **contre/à** to lean against/on.

accouchement [akuʃmɑ̃] *nm* delivery, (child)birth; (*travail*) labour (*BRIT*), labor (*US*); ~ **à terme** delivery at (full) term; ~ **sans douleur** natural childbirth.

accoucher [akuʃe] *vi* to give birth, have a baby; (*être en travail*) to be in labour (*BRIT*) *ou* labor (*US*) ♦ *vt* to deliver; ~ **d'un garçon** to give birth to a boy.

accoucheur [akuʃœʀ] *nm*: (**médecin**) ~ obstetrician.

accoucheuse [akuʃøz] *nf* midwife.

accouder [akude]: **s'**~ *vi*: **s'**~ **à/contre/sur** to rest one's elbows on/against/on; **accoudé à la fenêtre** leaning on the windowsill.

accoudoir [akudwaʀ] *nm* armrest.

accouplement [akupləmɑ̃] *nm* coupling; mating.

accoupler [akuple] *vt* to couple; (*pour la reproduction*) to mate; **s'**~ to mate.

accourir [akuʀiʀ] *vi* to rush *ou* run up.

accoutrement [akutʀəmɑ̃] *nm* (*péj*) getup (*BRIT*), outfit.

accoutrer [akutʀe] (*péj*) *vt* to do *ou* get up; **s'**~ to do *ou* get o.s. up.

accoutumance [akutymɑ̃s] *nf* (*gén*) adaptation; (*MÉD*) addiction.

accoutumé, e [akutyme] *adj* (*habituel*) customary, usual; **comme à l'**~**e** as is customary *ou* usual.

accoutumer [akutyme] *vt*: ~ **qn à qch/faire** to accustom sb to sth/to doing; **s'**~ **à** to get accustomed *ou* used to.

accréditer [akʀedite] *vt* (*nouvelle*) to substantiate; ~ **qn (auprès de)** to accredit sb (to).

accro [akʀo] *nm/f* (*fam*: = *accroché(e)*) addict.

accroc [akʀo] *nm* (*déchirure*) tear; (*fig*) hitch, snag; **sans** ~ without a hitch; **faire un** ~ **à** (*vêtement*) to make a tear in, tear; (*fig: règle etc*) to infringe.

accrochage [akʀɔʃaʒ] *nm* hanging (up); hitching (up); (*AUTO*) (minor) collision; (*MIL*) encounter, engagement; (*dispute*) clash, brush.

accroche-cœur [akʀɔʃkœʀ] *nm* kiss-curl.

accrocher [akʀɔʃe] *vt* (*suspendre*): ~ **qch à** to hang sth (up) on; (*attacher: remorque*): ~ **qch à** to hitch sth (up) to; (*heurter*) to catch; to hit; (*déchirer*): ~ **qch (à)** to catch sth (on); (*MIL*) to engage; (*fig*) to catch, attract ♦ *vi* to stick, get stuck; (*fig: pourparlers etc*) to hit a snag; (*plaire: disque etc*) to catch on; **s'**~ (*se disputer*) to have a clash *ou* brush; (*ne pas céder*) to hold one's own, hang on in (*fam*); **s'**~ **à** (*rester pris à*) to catch on; (*agripper, fig*) to hang on *ou* cling to.

accrocheur, euse [akʀɔʃœʀ, -øz] *adj* (*vendeur, concurrent*) tenacious; (*publicité*) eye-catching; (*titre*) catchy, eye-catching.

accroire [akʀwaʀ] *vt*: **faire** *ou* **laisser** ~ **à qn qch/que** to give sb to believe sth/that.

accroîs [akʀwa], **accroissais** [akʀwasɛ] *etc vb voir* **accroître**.

accroissement [akʀwasmɑ̃] *nm* increase.

accroître [akʀwatʀ(ə)] *vt*, **s'**~ *vi* to increase.

accroupi, e [akʀupi] *adj* squatting, crouching (down).

accroupir [akʀupiʀ]: **s'**~ *vi* to squat, crouch (down).

accru, e [akʀy] *pp de* **accroître**.

accu [aky] *nm* (*fam*: = *accumulateur*) accumulator, battery.

accueil [akœj] *nm* welcome; (*endroit*) reception (desk); (: *dans une gare*) information kiosk; **comité/centre d'**~ reception committee/centre.

accueillant, e [akœjɑ̃, -ɑ̃t] *adj* welcoming, friendly.

accueillir [akœjiʀ] *vt* to welcome; (*loger*) to accommodate.

acculer [akyle] *vt*: ~ **qn à** *ou* **contre** to drive sb back against; ~ **qn dans** to corner sb in; ~ **qn à** (*faillite*) to drive sb to the brink of.

accumulateur [akymylatœʀ] *nm* accumulator, battery.

accumulation [akymylɑsjɔ̃] *nf* accumulation; **chauffage/radiateur à** ~ (night-)storage heating/heater.

accumuler [akymyle] *vt* to accumulate, amass; **s'**~ *vi* to accumulate; to pile up.

accusateur, trice [akyzatœʀ, -tʀis] *nm/f* accuser ♦ *adj* accusing; (*document, preuve*) incriminating.

accusatif [akyzatif] *nm* (*LING*) accusative.

accusation [akyzɑsjɔ̃] *nf* (*gén*) accusation; (*JUR*) charge; (*partie*): **l'**~ the prosecution; **mettre en** ~ to indict; **acte d'**~ bill of indictment.

accusé, e [akyze] *nm/f* accused; (*prévenu(e)*)

defendant ♦ *nm*: ~ **de réception** acknowledgement of receipt.

accuser [akyze] *vt* to accuse; *(fig)* to emphasize, bring out; *(: montrer)* to show; **s'~** *vi* *(s'accentuer)* to become more marked; ~ **qn de** to accuse sb of; *(JUR)* to charge sb with; ~ **qn/qch de qch** *(rendre responsable)* to blame sb/sth for sth; **s'~ de qch/d'avoir fait qch** to admit sth/having done sth; to blame o.s. for sth/for having done sth; ~ **réception de** to acknowledge receipt of; ~ **le coup** *(aussi fig)* to be visibly affected.

acerbe [asɛrb(ə)] *adj* caustic, acid.

acéré, e [asere] *adj* sharp.

acétate [asetat] *nm* acetate.

acétique [asetik] *adj*: **acide** ~ acetic acid.

acétone [asetɔn] *nf* acetone.

acétylène [asetilɛn] *nm* acetylene.

ACF *sigle m* (= *Automobile Club de France*) ≈ AA *(BRIT)*, ≈ AAA *(US)*.

ach. *abr* = *achète*.

acharné, e [aʃarne] *adj* *(lutte, adversaire)* fierce, bitter; *(travail)* relentless, unremitting.

acharnement [aʃarnəmɑ̃] *nm* fierceness; relentlessness.

acharner [aʃarne]: **s'~** *vi*: **s'~ sur** to go at fiercely, hound; **s'~ contre** to set o.s. against; to dog, pursue; *(suj: malchance)* to hound; **s'~ à faire** to try doggedly to do; to persist in doing.

achat [aʃa] *nm* buying *no pl*; *(article acheté)* purchase; **faire l'~ de** to buy, purchase; **faire des ~s** to do some shopping, buy a few things.

acheminement [aʃminmɑ̃] *nm* conveyance.

acheminer [aʃmine] *vt* *(courrier)* to forward, dispatch; *(troupes)* to convey, transport; *(train)* to route; **s'~ vers** to head for.

acheter [aʃte] *vt* to buy, purchase; *(soudoyer)* to buy, bribe; ~ **qch à** *(marchand)* to buy *ou* purchase sth from; *(ami etc: offrir)* to buy sth for; ~ **à crédit** to buy on credit.

acheteur, euse [aʃtœr, -øz] *nm/f* buyer; shopper; *(COMM)* buyer; *(JUR)* vendee, purchaser.

achevé, e [aʃve] *adj*: **d'un ridicule** ~ thoroughly *ou* absolutely ridiculous; **d'un comique** ~ absolutely hilarious.

achèvement [aʃɛvmɑ̃] *nm* completion, finishing.

achever [aʃve] *vt* to complete, finish; *(blessé)* to finish off; **s'~** *vi* to end.

achoppement [aʃɔpmɑ̃] *nm*: **pierre d'~** stumbling block.

acide [asid] *adj* sour, sharp; *(ton)* acid, biting; *(CHIMIE)* acid(ic) ♦ *nm* acid.

acidifier [asidifje] *vt* to acidify.

acidité [asidite] *nf* sharpness; acidity.

acidulé, e [asidyle] *adj* slightly acid; **bonbons ~s** acid drops *(BRIT)*, ≈ lemon drops *(US)*.

acier [asje] *nm* steel; ~ **inoxydable** stainless steel.

aciérie [asjeri] *nf* steelworks *sg*.

acné [akne] *nf* acne.

acolyte [akɔlit] *nm* *(péj)* associate.

acompte [akɔ̃t] *nm* deposit; *(versement régulier)* instalment; *(sur somme due)* payment on account; *(sur salaire)* advance; **un ~ de 100 F** 100 F on account.

acoquiner [akɔkine]: **s'~ avec** *vt* *(péj)* to team up with.

Açores [asɔr] *nfpl*: **les ~** the Azores.

à-côté [akote] *nm* side-issue; *(argent)* extra.

à-coup [aku] *nm* *(du moteur)* (hic)cough; *(fig)* jolt; **sans ~s** smoothly; **par ~s** by fits and starts.

acoustique [akustik] *nf* *(d'une salle)* acoustics *pl*; *(science)* acoustics *sg* ♦ *adj* acoustic.

acquéreur [akerœr] *nm* buyer, purchaser; **se porter/se rendre ~ de qch** to announce one's intention to purchase/to purchase sth.

acquérir [akerir] *vt* to acquire; *(par achat)* to purchase, acquire; *(valeur)* to gain; *(résultats)* to achieve; **ce que ses efforts lui ont acquis** what his efforts have won *ou* gained (for) him.

acquiers [akjɛr] *etc vb voir* **acquérir**.

acquiescement [akjɛsmɑ̃] *nm* acquiescence, agreement.

acquiescer [akjese] *vi* *(opiner)* to agree; *(consentir)*: ~ **(à qch)** to acquiesce *ou* assent (to sth).

acquis, e [aki, -iz] *pp de* **acquérir** ♦ *nm* (accumulated) experience; *(avantage)* gain ♦ *adj* *(voir acquérir)* acquired; gained; achieved; **être ~ à** *(plan, idée)* to be in full agreement with; **son aide nous est ~e** we can count on *ou* be sure of his help; **tenir qch pour ~** to take sth for granted.

acquisition [akizisjɔ̃] *nf* acquisition; *(achat)* purchase; **faire l'~ de** to acquire; to purchase.

acquit [aki] *vb voir* **acquérir** ♦ *nm* *(quittance)* receipt; **pour ~** received; **par ~ de conscience** to set one's mind at rest.

acquittement [akitmɑ̃] *nm* acquittal; payment, settlement.

acquitter [akite] *vt* *(JUR)* to acquit; *(facture)* to pay, settle; **s'~ de** to discharge; *(promesse, tâche)* to fulfil *(BRIT)*, fulfill *(US)*, carry out.

âcre [ɑkr(ə)] *adj* acrid, pungent.

âcreté [ɑkrəte] *nf* acridness, pungency.

acrimonie [akrimɔni] *nf* acrimony.

acrobate [akrɔbat] *nm/f* acrobat.

acrobatie [akrɔbasi] *nf* *(art)* acrobatics *sg*; *(exercice)* acrobatic feat; ~ **aérienne** aerobatics *sg*.

acrobatique [akrɔbatik] *adj* acrobatic.

acronyme [akrɔnim] *nm* acronym.

Acropole [akrɔpɔl] *nf*: **l'~** the Acropolis.

acrylique [akrilik] *adj*, *nm* acrylic.

acte [akt(ə)] *nm* act, action; *(THÉÂT)* act; **~s** *nmpl* *(compte-rendu)* proceedings; **prendre ~**

de to note, take note of; **faire ~ de présence** to put in an appearance; **faire ~ de candidature** to submit an application; **~ d'accusation** charge (*BRIT*), bill of indictment; **~ de baptême** baptismal certificate; **~ de mariage/naissance** marriage/birth certificate; **~ de vente** bill of sale.

acteur [aktœR] *nm* actor.

actif, ive [aktif, -iv] *adj* active ◊ *nm* (*COMM*) assets *pl*; (*LING*) active (voice); (*fig*): **avoir à son ~** to have to one's credit; **~s** *nmpl* people in employment; **mettre à son ~** to add to one's list of achievements; **l'~ et le passif** assets and liabilities; **prendre une part active à qch** to take an active part in sth; **population active** working population.

action [aksjɔ̃] *nf* (*gén*) action; (*COMM*) share; **une bonne/mauvaise ~** a good/an unkind deed; **mettre en ~** to put into action; **passer à l'~** to take action; **sous l'~ de** under the effect of; **l'~ syndicale** (the) union action; **un film d'~** an action film *ou* movie; **~ en diffamation** libel action; **~ de grâce(s)** (*REL*) thanksgiving.

actionnaire [aksjɔnɛR] *nm/f* shareholder.

actionner [aksjɔne] *vt* to work; to activate; to operate.

active [aktiv] *adj f voir* **actif**.

activement [aktivmɑ̃] *adv* actively.

activer [aktive] *vt* to speed up; (*CHIMIE*) to activate; **s'~** *vi* (*s'affairer*) to bustle about; (*se hâter*) to hurry up.

activisme [aktivism(ə)] *nm* activism.

activiste [aktivist(ə)] *nm/f* activist.

activité [aktivite] *nf* activity; **en ~** (*volcan*) active; (*fonctionnaire*) in active life; (*militaire*) on active service.

actrice [aktRis] *nf* actress.

actualiser [aktɥalize] *vt* to actualize; (*mettre à jour*) to bring up to date.

actualité [aktɥalite] *nf* (*d'un problème*) topicality; (*événements*): **l'~** current events; **les ~s** (*CINÉ*, *TV*) the news; **l'~ politique/sportive** the political/sports *ou* sporting news; **les ~s télévisées** the television news; **d'~** topical.

actuel, le [aktɥɛl] *adj* (*présent*) present; (*d'actualité*) topical; (*non virtuel*) actual; **à l'heure ~le** at this moment in time, at the moment.

actuellement [aktɥɛlmɑ̃] *adv* at present, at the present time.

acuité [akɥite] *nf* acuteness.

acupuncteur, acupuncteur [akypɔ̃ktœR] *nm* acupuncturist.

acuponcture, acupuncture [akypɔ̃ktyR] *nf* acupuncture.

adage [adaʒ] *nm* adage.

adagio [ada(d)ʒjo] *adv*, *nm* adagio.

adaptable [adaptabl(ə)] *adj* adaptable.

adaptateur, trice [adaptatœR, -tRis] *nm/f* adapter.

adaptation [adaptasjɔ̃] *nf* adaptation.

adapter [adapte] *vt* to adapt; **s'~ (à)** (*suj: personne*) to adapt (to); (*: objet, prise etc*) to apply (to); **~ qch à** (*approprier*) to adapt sth to (fit); **~ qch sur/dans/à** (*fixer*) to fit sth on/into/to.

addenda [adɛ̃da] *nm inv* addenda.

Addis-Ababa [adisababa], **Addis-Abeba** [adisababa] *n* Addis Ababa.

additif [aditif] *nm* additional clause; (*substance*) additive; **~ alimentaire** food additive.

addition [adisjɔ̃] *nf* addition; (*au café*) bill.

additionnel, le [adisjɔnɛl] *adj* additional.

additionner [adisjɔne] *vt* to add (up); **s'~** *vi* to add up; **~ un produit d'eau** to add water to a product.

adduction [adyksjɔ̃] *nf* (*de gaz, d'eau*) conveyance.

ADEP *sigle f* (= *Agence nationale pour le développement de l'éducation permanente*) *national body which promotes adult education.*

adepte [adɛpt(ə)] *nm/f* follower.

adéquat, e [adekwa, -at] *adj* appropriate, suitable.

adéquation [adekwasjɔ̃] *nf* appropriateness; (*LING*) adequacy.

adhérence [adeRɑ̃s] *nf* adhesion.

adhérent, e [adeRɑ̃, -ɑ̃t] *nm/f* (*de club*) member.

adhérer [adeRe] *vi* (*coller*) to adhere, stick; **~ à** (*coller*) to adhere *ou* stick to; (*se rallier à: parti, club*) to join; to be a member of; (*: opinion, mouvement*) to support.

adhésif, ive [adezif, -iv] *adj* adhesive, sticky ◊ *nm* adhesive.

adhésion [adezjɔ̃] *nf* (*à un club*) joining; membership; (*à une opinion*) support.

ad hoc [adɔk] *adj* ad hoc.

adieu, x [adjø] *excl* goodbye ◊ *nm* farewell; **dire ~ à qn** to say goodbye *ou* farewell to sb; **dire ~ à qch** (*renoncer*) to say *ou* wave goodbye to sth.

adipeux, euse [adipø, -øz] *adj* bloated, fat; (*ANAT*) adipose.

adjacent, e [adʒasɑ̃, -ɑ̃t] *adj*: **~ (à)** adjacent (to).

adjectif [adʒɛktif] *nm* adjective; **~ attribut** adjectival complement; **~ épithète** attributive adjective.

adjectival, e, aux [adʒɛktival, -o] *adj* adjectival.

adjoignais [adʒwanɛ] *etc vb voir* **adjoindre**.

adjoindre [adʒwɛ̃dR(ə)] *vt*: **~ qch à** to attach sth to; (*ajouter*) to add sth to; **~ qn à** (*personne*) to appoint sb as an assistant to; (*comité*) to appoint sb to, attach sb to; **s'~** *vt* (*collaborateur etc*) to take on, appoint.

adjoint, e [adʒwɛ̃, -wɛ̃t] *pp de* **adjoindre** ◊ *nm/f* assistant; **directeur ~** assistant manager.

adjonction [adʒɔ̃ksjɔ̃] *nf* (*voir adjoindre*) attaching; addition; appointment.

adjudant [adʒydɑ̃] *nm* (*MIL*) warrant officer;

~-**chef** ≈ warrant officer 1st class (*BRIT*), ≈ chief warrant officer (*US*).

adjudicataire [adʒydikatɛʀ] *nm/f* successful bidder, purchaser; (*pour travaux*) successful tenderer (*BRIT*) *ou* bidder (*US*).

adjudicateur, trice [adʒydikatœʀ, -tʀis] *nm/f* (*aux enchères*) seller.

adjudication [adʒydikɑsjɔ̃] *nf* sale by auction; (*pour travaux*) invitation to tender (*BRIT*) *ou* bid (*US*).

adjuger [adʒyʒe] *vt* (*prix, récompense*) to award; (*lors d'une vente*) to auction (off); **s'**~ *vt* to take for o.s; **adjugé!** (*vendu*) gone!, sold!

adjurer [adʒyʀe] *vt*: ~ **qn de faire** *ou* beg sb to do.

adjuvant [adʒyvɑ̃] *nm* (*médicament*) adjuvant; (*additif*) additive; (*stimulant*) stimulant.

admettre [admɛtʀ(ə)] *vt* (*visiteur, nouveau-venu*) to admit, let in; (*candidat: SCOL*) to pass; (*TECH: gaz, eau, air*) to admit; (*tolérer*) to allow, accept; (*reconnaître*) to admit, acknowledge; (*supposer*) to suppose; **j'admets que ...** I admit that ...; **je n'admets pas que tu fasses cela** I won't allow you to do that; **admettons que ...** let's suppose that ...; **admettons** let's suppose so.

administrateur, trice [administʀatœʀ, -tʀis] *nm/f* (*COMM*) director; (*ADMIN*) administrator; ~ **délégué** managing director; ~ **judiciaire** receiver.

administratif, ive [administʀatif, -iv] *adj* administrative ♦ *nm* person in administration.

administration [administʀɑsjɔ̃] *nf* administration; **l'A**~ ≈ the Civil Service.

administré, e [administʀe] *nm/f* ≈ citizen.

administrer [administʀe] *vt* (*firme*) to manage, run; (*biens, remède, sacrement etc*) to administer.

admirable [admiʀabl(ə)] *adj* admirable, wonderful.

admirablement [admiʀabləmɑ̃] *adv* admirably.

admirateur, trice [admiʀatœʀ, -tʀis] *nm/f* admirer.

admiratif, ive [admiʀatif, -iv] *adj* admiring.

admiration [admiʀɑsjɔ̃] *nf* admiration; **être en** ~ **devant** to be lost in admiration before.

admirativement [admiʀativmɑ̃] *adv* admiringly.

admirer [admiʀe] *vt* to admire.

admis, e [admi, -iz] *pp de* **admettre**.

admissibilité [admisibilite] *nf* eligibility; admissibility, acceptability.

admissible [admisibl(ə)] *adj* (*candidat*) eligible; (*comportement*) admissible, acceptable; (*JUR*) receivable.

admission [admisjɔ̃] *nf* admission; **tuyau d'**~ intake pipe; **demande d'**~ application for membership; **service des** ~**s** admissions.

admonester [admɔnɛste] *vt* to admonish.

ADN *sigle m* (= *acide désoxyribonucléique*) DNA.

ado [ado] *nm/f* (*fam*: = *adolescent(e)*) adolescent, teenager.

adolescence [adɔlesɑ̃s] *nf* adolescence.

adolescent, e [adɔlesɑ̃, -ɑ̃t] *nm/f* adolescent, teenager.

adonner [adɔne]: **s'**~ **à** *vt* (*sport*) to devote o.s. to; (*boisson*) to give o.s. over to.

adopter [adɔpte] *vt* to adopt; (*projet de loi etc*) to pass.

adoptif, ive [adɔptif, -iv] *adj* (*parents*) adoptive; (*fils, patrie*) adopted.

adoption [adɔpsjɔ̃] *nf* adoption; **son pays/sa ville d'**~ his adopted country/town.

adorable [adɔʀabl(ə)] *adj* adorable.

adoration [adɔʀɑsjɔ̃] *nf* adoration; (*REL*) worship; **être en** ~ **devant** to be lost in adoration before.

adorer [adɔʀe] *vt* to adore; (*REL*) to worship.

adosser [adose] *vt*: ~ **qch à** *ou* **contre** to stand sth against; **s'**~ **à** *ou* **contre** to lean with one's back against; **être adossé à** *ou* **contre** to be leaning with one's back against.

adoucir [adusiʀ] *vt* (*goût, température*) to make milder; (*avec du sucre*) to sweeten; (*peau, voix, eau*) to soften; (*caractère, personne*) to mellow; (*peine*) to soothe, allay; **s'**~ *vi* to become milder; to soften; to mellow.

adoucissement [adusismɑ̃] *nm* becoming milder; sweetening; softening; mellowing; soothing.

adoucisseur [adusisœʀ] *nm*: ~ **(d'eau)** water softener.

adr. *abr* = **adresse, adresser**.

adrénaline [adʀenalin] *nf* adrenaline.

adresse [adʀɛs] *nf* (*voir adroit*) skill, dexterity; (*domicile, INFORM*) address; **à l'**~ **de** (*pour*) for the benefit of.

adresser [adʀese] *vt* (*lettre: expédier*) to send; (: *écrire l'adresse sur*) to address; (*injure, compliments*) to address; ~ **qn à un docteur/bureau** to refer *ou* send sb to a doctor/an office; ~ **la parole à qn** to speak to *ou* address sb; **s'**~ **à** (*parler à*) to speak to, address; (*s'informer auprès de*) to go and see, go and speak to; (: *bureau*) to enquire at; (*suj: livre, conseil*) to be aimed at.

Adriatique [adʀijatik] *nf*: **l'**~ the Adriatic.

adroit, e [adʀwa, -wat] *adj* (*joueur, mécanicien*) skilful (*BRIT*), skillful (*US*), dext(e)rous; (*politicien etc*) shrewd, skilled.

adroitement [adʀwatmɑ̃] *adv* skilfully (*BRIT*), skillfully (*US*), dext(e)rously; shrewdly.

AdS *sigle f* = *Académie des Sciences*.

aduler [adyle] *vt* to adulate.

adulte [adylt(ə)] *nm/f* adult, grown-up ♦ *adj* (*personne, attitude*) adult, grown-up; (*chien, arbre*) fully-grown, mature; **l'âge** ~ adulthood; **formation/film pour** ~**s** adult training/film.

adultère [adyltɛʀ] *adj* adulterous ♦ *nm/f* adulterer/adulteress ♦ *nm* (*acte*) adultery.

adultérin, e [adylteʀɛ̃, -in] *adj* born of adultery.

advenir [advǝniʀ] vi to happen; **qu'est-il adve-nu de?** what has become of?; **quoi qu'il ad-vienne** whatever befalls ou happens.

adventiste [advɑ̃tist(ǝ)] nm/f (REL) Adventist.

adverbe [advɛʀb(ǝ)] nm adverb; ~ **de manière** adverb of manner.

adverbial, e, aux [advɛʀbjal, -o] adj adver-bial.

adversaire [advɛʀsɛʀ] nm/f (SPORT, gén) oppo-nent, adversary; (MIL) adversary, enemy.

adverse [advɛʀs(ǝ)] adj opposing.

adversité [advɛʀsite] nf adversity.

AE sigle m (= adjoint d'enseignement) non-certificated teacher.

AELE sigle f (= Association européenne de libre-échange) EFTA (= European Free Trade Asso-ciation).

AEN sigle f (= Agence pour l'énergie nucléaire) ≈ AEA (= Atomic Energy Authority).

aérateur [aeʀatœʀ] nm ventilator.

aération [aeʀɑsjɔ̃] nf airing; (circulation de l'air) ventilation; **conduit d'~** ventilation shaft; **bouche d'~** air vent.

aéré, e [aeʀe] adj (pièce, local) airy, well-ventilated; (tissu) loose-woven; **centre ~** outdoor centre.

aérer [aeʀe] vt to air; (fig) to lighten; **s'~** vi to get some (fresh) air.

aérien, ne [aeʀjɛ̃, -ɛn] adj (AVIAT) air cpd, aer-ial; (câble, métro) overhead; (fig) light; **com-pagnie ~ne** airline (company); **ligne ~ne** airline.

aérobic [aeʀɔbik] nf aerobics sg.

aérobie [aeʀɔbi] adj aerobic.

aéro-club [aeʀɔklœb] nm flying club.

aérodrome [aeʀodʀɔm] nm airfield, aero-drome.

aérodynamique [aeʀodinamik] adj aerody-namic, streamlined ♦ nf aerodynamics sg.

aérofrein [aeʀofʀɛ̃] nm air brake.

aérogare [aeʀogaʀ] nf airport (buildings); (en ville) air terminal.

aéroglisseur [aeʀoglisœʀ] nm hovercraft.

aérogramme [aeʀogʀam] nm air letter, aero-gram(me).

aéromodélisme [aeʀomodelism(ǝ)] nm model aircraft making.

aéronaute [aeʀonot] nm/f aeronaut.

aéronautique [aeʀonotik] adj aeronautical ♦ nf aeronautics sg.

aéronaval, e [aeʀonaval] adj air and sea cpd ♦ nf: **l'A~e** ≈ the Fleet Air Arm (BRIT), ≈ the Naval Air Force (US).

aéronef [aeʀonɛf] nm aircraft.

aérophagie [aeʀofaʒi] nf aerophagy.

aéroport [aeʀopɔʀ] nm airport; ~ **d'embarquement** departure airport.

aéroporté, e [aeʀopɔʀte] adj airborne, air-lifted.

aéroportuaire [aeʀopɔʀtɥɛʀ] adj of an ou the airport, airport cpd.

aéropostal, e, aux [aeʀopɔstal, -o] adj airmail cpd.

aérosol [aeʀɔsɔl] nm aerosol.

aérospatial, e, aux [aeʀospasjal, -o] adj aero-space ♦ nf the aerospace industry.

aérostat [aeʀosta] nm aerostat.

aérotrain [aeʀotʀɛ̃] nm hovertrain.

AF sigle fpl = **allocations familiales** ♦ sigle f (Suisse) = Assemblée fédérale.

AFAT [afat] sigle m (= Auxiliaire féminin de l'armée de terre) member of the women's army.

affabilité [afabilite] nf affability.

affable [afabl(ǝ)] adj affable.

affabulateur, trice [afabylatœʀ, -tʀis] nm/f storyteller.

affabulation [afabylɑsjɔ̃] nf invention, fanta-sy.

affabuler [afabyle] vi to make up stories.

affacturage [afaktyʀaʒ] nm factoring.

affadir [afadiʀ] vt to make insipid ou tasteless.

affaiblir [afebliʀ] vt to weaken; **s'~** vi to weak-en, grow weaker; (vue) to grow dim.

affaiblissement [afeblismɑ̃] nm weakening.

affaire [afɛʀ] nf (problème, question) matter; (criminelle, judiciaire) case; (scandaleuse etc) affair; (entreprise) business; (marché, transac-tion) (business) deal, (piece of) business no pl; (occasion intéressante) good deal, bargain; **~s** nfpl affairs; (activité commerciale) busi-ness sg; (effets personnels) things, belong-ings; **tirer qn/se tirer d'~** to get sb/o.s. out of trouble; **ceci fera l'~** this will do (nicely); **avoir ~ à** (comme adversaire) to be faced with; (en contact) to be dealing with; **tu auras ~ à moi!** (menace) you'll have me to contend with!; **c'est une ~ de goût/d'argent** it's a question ou matter of taste/money; **c'est l'~ d'une minute/heure** it'll only take a minute/an hour; **ce sont mes ~s** (cela me concerne) that's my business; **toutes ~s ces-santes** forthwith; **les ~s étrangères** (POL) foreign affairs.

affairé, e [afeʀe] adj busy.

affairer [afeʀe]: **s'~** vi to busy o.s., bustle about.

affairisme [afeʀism(ǝ)] nm (political) racket-eering.

affaissement [afɛsmɑ̃] nm subsidence; col-lapse.

affaisser [afese]: **s'~** vi (terrain, immeuble) to subside, sink; (personne) to collapse.

affaler [afale]: **s'~** vi: **s'~ dans/sur** to collapse ou slump into/onto.

affamé, e [afame] adj starving, famished.

affamer [afame] vt to starve.

affectation [afɛktɑsjɔ̃] nf (voir affecter) allot-ment; appointment; posting; (voir affecté) af-fectedness.

affecté, e [afɛkte] adj affected.

affecter [afɛkte] vt (émouvoir) to affect, move; (feindre) to affect, feign; (telle ou telle forme *etc*) to take on, assume; ~ **qch à** to allocate *ou* allot sth to; ~ **qn à** to appoint sb to; (*diplomate*) to post sb to; ~ **qch de** (*de coefficient*) to modify sth by.

affectif, ive [afɛktif, -iv] *adj* emotional, affective.

affection [afɛksjɔ̃] *nf* affection; (*mal*) ailment; **avoir de l'~ pour** to feel affection for; **prendre en** ~ to become fond of.

affectionner [afɛksjɔne] *vt* to be fond of.

affectueusement [afɛktɥøzmã] *adv* affectionately.

affectueux, euse [afɛktɥø, -øz] *adj* affectionate.

afférent, e [afeRã, -ãt] *adj*: ~ **à** pertaining *ou* relating to.

affermir [afɛRmiR] *vt* to consolidate, strengthen.

aff. étr. *abr* (= *Affaires étrangères*) *voir* **affaire.**

affichage [afiʃaʒ] *nm* billposting, billsticking; (*électronique*) display; "~ **interdit**" "stick no bills", "billsticking prohibited"; ~ **à cristaux liquides** liquid crystal display, LCD; ~ **numérique** *ou* **digital** digital display.

affiche [afiʃ] *nf* poster; (*officielle*) (public) notice; (*THÉÂT*) bill; **être à l'~** (*THÉÂT*) to be on; **tenir l'~** to run.

afficher [afiʃe] *vt* (*affiche*) to put up, post up; (*réunion*) to put up a notice about; (*électroniquement*) to display; (*fig*) to exhibit, display; **s'~** (*péj*) to flaunt o.s.; **"défense d'~"** "stick no bills".

affichette [afiʃɛt] *nf* small poster *ou* notice.

affilé, e [afile] *adj* sharp.

affilée [afile]: **d'~** *adv* at a stretch.

affiler [afile] *vt* to sharpen.

affiliation [afiljasjɔ̃] *nf* affiliation.

affilié, e [afilje] *adj*: **être** ~ **à** to be affiliated to ♦ *nm/f* affiliated party *ou* member.

affilier [afilje] *vt*: **s'~** **à** to become affiliated to.

affiner [afine] *vt* to refine; **s'~** *vi* to become (more) refined.

affinité [afinite] *nf* affinity.

affirmatif, ive [afiRmatif, -iv] *adj* affirmative ♦ *nf*: **répondre par l'affirmative** to reply in the affirmative; **dans l'affirmative** (*si oui*) if (the answer is) yes ..., if he does (*ou* you do *etc*) ....

affirmation [afiRmasjɔ̃] *nf* assertion.

affirmativement [afiRmativmã] *adv* affirmatively, in the affirmative.

affirmer [afiRme] *vt* (*prétendre*) to maintain, assert; (*autorité etc*) to assert; **s'~** to assert o.s.; to assert itself.

affleurer [aflœRe] *vi* to show on the surface.

affliction [afliksjɔ̃] *nf* affliction.

affligé, e [afliʒe] *adj* distressed, grieved; ~ **de** (*maladie, tare*) afflicted with.

affligeant, e [afliʒã, -ãt] *adj* distressing.

affliger [afliʒe] *vt* (*peiner*) to distress, grieve.

affluence [aflyãs] *nf* crowds *pl*; **heures d'~** rush hour *sg*; **jours d'~** busiest days.

affluent [aflyã] *nm* tributary.

affluer [aflye] *vi* (*secours, biens*) to flood in, pour in; (*sang*) to rush, flow.

afflux [afly] *nm* flood, influx; rush.

affolant, e [afɔlã, -ãt] *adj* terrifying.

affolé, e [afɔle] *adj* panic-stricken, panicky.

affolement [afɔlmã] *nm* panic.

affoler [afɔle] *vt* to throw into a panic; **s'~** *vi* to panic.

affranchir [afRãʃiR] *vt* to put a stamp *ou* stamps on; (*à la machine*) to frank (*BRIT*), meter (*US*); (*esclave*) to enfranchise, emancipate; (*fig*) to free, liberate; **s'~ de** to free o.s. from; **machine à** ~ franking machine, postage meter.

affranchissement [afRãʃismã] *nm* franking (*BRIT*), metering (*US*); freeing; (*POSTES: prix payé*) postage; **tarifs d'~** postage rates.

affres [afR(ə)] *nfpl*: **dans les** ~ **de** in the throes of.

affréter [afRete] *vt* to charter.

affreusement [afRøzmã] *adv* dreadfully, awfully.

affreux, euse [afRø, -øz] *adj* dreadful, awful.

affriolant, e [afRijɔlã, -ãt] *adj* tempting, enticing.

affront [afRɔ̃] *nm* affront.

affrontement [afRɔ̃tmã] *nm* (*MIL, POL*) clash, confrontation.

affronter [afRɔ̃te] *vt* to confront, face; **s'~** to confront each other.

affubler [afyble] *vt* (*péj*): ~ **qn de** to rig *ou* deck sb out in; (*surnom*) to attach to sb.

affût [afy] *nm* (*de canon*) gun carriage; **à l'~ (de)** (*gibier*) lying in wait (for); (*fig*) on the look-out (for).

affûter [afyte] *vt* to sharpen, grind.

afghan, e [afgã, -an] *adj* Afghan.

Afghanistan [afganistã] *nm*: **l'~** Afghanistan.

afin [afɛ̃]: ~ **que** *conj* so that, in order that; ~ **de faire** in order to do, so as to do.

AFNOR [afnɔR] *sigle f* (= *Association française de normalisation*) industrial standards authority.

a fortiori [afɔRsjɔRi] *adv* all the more, a fortiori.

AFP *sigle f* = *Agence France-Presse.*

AFPA *sigle f* = *Association pour la formation professionnelle des adultes.*

africain, e [afRikɛ̃, -ɛn] *adj* African ♦ *nm/f*: **A~, e** African.

afrikaans [afRikã] *nm*, *adj inv* Afrikaans.

Afrikaner [afRikaner] *nm/f* Afrikaner.

Afrique [afRik] *nf*: **l'~** Africa; **l'~ australe/du Nord/du Sud** southern/North/South Africa.

afro [afRo] *adj inv*: **coupe** ~ afro hairstyle ♦ *nm/f*: **A~** Afro.

afro-américain, e [afRoameRikɛ̃, -ɛn] *adj* Afro-American.

afro-asiatique [afRoazjatik] *adj* Afro-Asian.

AG *sigle f* = *assemblée générale.*

ag. *abr* = **agence.**

agaçant, e [agasã, -ãt] *adj* irritating, aggravating.

agacement [agasmã] *nm* irritation, aggravation.

agacer [agase] *vt* to pester, tease; (*involontairement*) to irritate, aggravate; (*aguicher*) to excite, lead on.

agapes [agap] *nfpl* (*humoristique: festin*) feast.

agate [agat] *nf* agate.

AGE *sigle f* = assemblée générale extraordinaire.

âge [aʒ] *nm* age; **quel ~ as-tu?** how old are you?; **une femme d'un certain ~** a middle-aged woman, a woman who is getting on (in years); **bien porter son ~** to wear well; **prendre de l'~** to be getting on (in years), grow older; **limite d'~** age limit; **dispense d'~** special exemption from age limit; **troisième ~** (*période*) retirement; (*personnes âgées*) senior citizens; **l'~ ingrat** the awkward *ou* difficult age; **~ légal** legal age; **~ mental** mental age; **l'~ mûr** maturity, middle age; **~ de raison** age of reason.

âgé, e [aʒe] *adj* old, elderly; **~ de 10 ans** 10 years old.

agence [aʒãs] *nf* agency, office; (*succursale*) branch; **~ immobilière** estate agent's (office) (*BRIT*), real estate office (*US*); **~ matrimoniale** marriage bureau; **~ de placement** employment agency; **~ de publicité** advertising agency; **~ de voyages** travel agency.

agencé, e [aʒãse] *adj*: **bien/mal ~** well/badly put together; well/badly laid out *ou* arranged.

agencement [aʒãsmã] *nm* putting together; arrangement, laying out.

agencer [aʒãse] *vt* to put together; (*local*) to arrange, lay out.

agenda [aʒɛ̃da] *nm* diary.

agenouiller [aʒnuje]: **s'~** *vi* to kneel (down).

agent [aʒã] *nm* (*aussi*: **~ de police**) policeman; (*ADMIN*) official, officer; (*fig: élément, facteur*) agent; **~ d'assurances** insurance broker; **~ de change** stockbroker; **~ commercial** sales representative; **~ immobilier** estate agent (*BRIT*), realtor (*US*); **~ (secret)** (secret) agent.

agglo [aglo] *nm* (*fam*) = **aggloméré.**

agglomérat [aglɔmeʀa] *nm* (*GÉO*) agglomerate.

agglomération [aglɔmeʀasjɔ̃] *nf* town; (*AUTO*) built-up area; **l'~ parisienne** the urban area of Paris.

aggloméré [aglɔmeʀe] *nm* (*bois*) chipboard; (*pierre*) conglomerate.

agglomérer [aglɔmeʀe] *vt* to pile up; (*TECH: bois, pierre*) to compress; **s'~** *vi* to pile up.

agglutiner [aglytine] *vt* to stick together; **s'~** *vi* to congregate.

aggravant, e [agʀavã, -ãt] *adj*: **circonstances ~es** aggravating circumstances.

aggravation [agʀavasjɔ̃] *nf* worsening, aggravation; increase.

aggraver [agʀave] *vt* to worsen, aggravate; (*JUR: peine*) to increase; **s'~** *vi* to worsen; **~ son cas** to make one's case worse.

agile [aʒil] *adj* agile, nimble.

agilement [aʒilmã] *adv* nimbly.

agilité [aʒilite] *nf* agility, nimbleness.

agio [aʒjo] *nm* (bank) charges *pl*.

agir [aʒiʀ] *vi* (*se comporter*) to behave, act; (*faire quelque chose*) to act, take action; (*avoir de l'effet*) to act; **il s'agit de** it's a matter *ou* question of; it is about; (*il importe que*): **il s'agit de faire** we (*ou* you *etc*) must do; **de quoi s'agit-il?** what is it about?

agissements [aʒismã] *nmpl* (*gén péj*) schemes, intrigues.

agitateur, trice [aʒitatœʀ, -tʀis] *nm/f* agitator.

agitation [aʒitasjɔ̃] *nf* (hustle and) bustle; (*trouble*) agitation, excitement; (*politique*) unrest, agitation.

agité, e [aʒite] *adj* (*remuant*) fidgety, restless; (*troublé*) agitated, perturbed; (*journée*) hectic; (*mer*) rough; (*sommeil*) disturbed, broken.

agiter [aʒite] *vt* (*bouteille, chiffon*) to shake; (*bras, mains*) to wave; (*préoccuper, exciter*) to trouble, perturb; **s'~** *vi* to bustle about; (*dormeur*) to toss and turn; (*enfant*) to fidget; (*POL*) to grow restless; **"~ avant l'emploi"** "shake before use".

agneau, x [aɲo] *nm* lamb; (*toison*) lambswool.

agnelet [aɲlɛ] *nm* little lamb.

agnostique [agnɔstik] *adj, nm/f* agnostic.

agonie [agɔni] *nf* mortal agony, death pangs *pl*; (*fig*) death throes *pl*.

agonir [agɔniʀ] *vt*: **~ qn d'injures** to hurl abuse at sb.

agoniser [agɔnize] *vi* to be dying; (*fig*) to be in its death throes.

agrafe [agʀaf] *nf* (*de vêtement*) hook, fastener; (*de bureau*) staple; (*MÉD*) clip.

agrafer [agʀafe] *vt* to fasten; to staple.

agrafeuse [agʀaføz] *nf* stapler.

agraire [agʀɛʀ] *adj* agrarian; (*mesure, surface*) land *cpd*.

agrandir [agʀãdiʀ] *vt* (*magasin, domaine*) to extend, enlarge; (*trou*) to enlarge, make bigger; (*PHOTO*) to enlarge, blow up; **s'~** *vi* to be extended; to be enlarged.

agrandissement [agʀãdismã] *nm* extension; enlargement; (*photographie*) enlargement.

agrandisseur [agʀãdisœʀ] *nm* (*PHOTO*) enlarger.

agréable [agʀeabl(ə)] *adj* pleasant, nice.

agréablement [agʀeabləmã] *adv* pleasantly.

agréé, e [agʀee] *adj*: **concessionnaire ~** registered dealer; **magasin ~** registered dealer('s).

agréer [agʀee] *vt* (*requête*) to accept; **~ à** *vt* to please, suit; **veuillez ~ ...** (*formule épistolaire*) yours faithfully.

agrég [agʀɛg] *nf* (*fam*) = **agrégation.**

agrégat [agʀega] *nm* aggregate.
agrégation [agʀegɑsjɔ̃] *nf* highest teaching diploma in France.

The **agrégation**, colloquially known as the **agrég**, is a prestigious competitive examination for the recruitment of secondary education teachers in France. The number of candidates always far exceeds the number of posts available. Most teachers of **classes préparatoires** and university lecturers hold the agrégation; see also **CAPES**.

agrégé, e [agʀeʒe] *nm/f* holder of the *agrégation*.
agréger [agʀeʒe]: **s'~** *vi* to aggregate.
agrément [agʀemɑ̃] *nm* (*accord*) consent, approval; (*attraits*) charm, attractiveness; (*plaisir*) pleasure; **voyage/jardin d'~** pleasure trip/garden.
agrémenter [agʀemɑ̃te] *vt*: ~ **(de)** to embellish (with), adorn (with).
agrès [agʀɛ] *nmpl* (gymnastics) apparatus *sg*.
agresser [agʀese] *vt* to attack.
agresseur [agʀesœʀ] *nm* aggressor.
agressif, ive [agʀesif, -iv] *adj* aggressive.
agression [agʀesjɔ̃] *nf* attack; (*POL*, *MIL*, *PSYCH*) aggression.
agressivement [agʀesivmɑ̃] *adv* aggressively.
agressivité [agʀesivite] *nf* aggressiveness.
agreste [agʀɛst(ə)] *adj* rustic.
agricole [agʀikɔl] *adj* agricultural, farm *cpd*.
agriculteur, trice [agʀikyltœʀ, -tʀis] *nm/f* farmer.
agriculture [agʀikyltyʀ] *nf* agriculture; farming.
agripper [agʀipe] *vt* to grab, clutch; (*pour arracher*) to snatch, grab; **s'~ à** to cling (on) to, clutch, grip.
agro-alimentaire [agʀɔalimɑ̃tɛʀ] *adj* farming *cpd* ♦ *nm*: **l'~** agribusiness.
agronome [agʀɔnɔm] *nm/f* agronomist.
agronomie [agʀɔnɔmi] *nf* agronomy.
agronomique [agʀɔnɔmik] *adj* agronomic(al).
agrumes [agʀym] *nmpl* citrus fruit(s).
aguerrir [ageʀiʀ] *vt* to harden; **s'~ (contre)** to become hardened (to).
aguets [agɛ]: **aux ~** *adv*: **être aux ~** to be on the look-out.
aguichant, e [agiʃɑ̃, -ɑ̃t] *adj* enticing.
aguicher [agiʃe] *vt* to entice.
aguicheur, euse [agiʃœʀ, -øz] *adj* enticing.
ah [ɑ] *excl* ah!; ~ **bon?** really?, is that so?; ~ **mais ...** yes, but ...; ~ **non!** oh no!
ahuri, e [ayʀi] *adj* (*stupéfait*) flabbergasted; (*idiot*) dim-witted.
ahurir [ayʀiʀ] *vt* to stupefy, stagger.
ahurissant, e [ayʀisɑ̃, -ɑ̃t] *adj* stupefying, staggering, mind-boggling.
ai [e] *vb voir* **avoir**.
aide [ɛd] *nm/f* assistant, help ♦ *nf* assistance, help; (*secours financier*) aid; **à l'~ de** with the help

ou aid of; **aller à l'~ de qn** to go to sb's aid, go to help sb; **venir en ~ à qn** to help sb, come to sb's assistance; **appeler (qn) à l'~** to call for help (from sb); **à l'~!** help!; ~ **de camp** *nm* aide-de-camp; ~ **comptable** *nm* accountant's assistant; ~ **électricien** *nm* electrician's mate; ~ **familiale** *nf* mother's help, ≈ home help; ~ **judiciaire** *nf* legal aid; ~ **de laboratoire** *nm/f* laboratory assistant; ~ **ménagère** *nf* ≈ home help; ~ **sociale** *nf* (*assistance*) state aid; ~ **soignant, e** *nm/f* auxiliary nurse; ~ **technique** *nf* ≈ VSO (*BRIT*), ≈ Peace Corps (*US*).
aide-mémoire [ɛdmemwaʀ] *nm inv* (key facts) handbook.
aider [ede] *vt* to help; ~ **à qch** to help (towards) sth; ~ **qn à faire qch** to help sb to do sth; **s'~ de** (*se servir de*) to use, make use of.
aie [ɛ] *etc vb voir* **avoir**.
aïe [aj] *excl* ouch!
AIEA *sigle f* (= *Agence internationale de l'énergie nucléaire*) IAEA (= *International Atomic Energy Agency*).
aïeul, e [ajœl] *nm/f* grandparent, grandfather/ grandmother; (*ancêtre*) forebear.
aïeux [ajø] *nmpl* grandparents; forebears, forefathers.
aigle [ɛgl(ə)] *nm* eagle.
aiglefin [ɛgləfɛ̃] *nm* = **églefin**.
aigre [ɛgʀ(ə)] *adj* sour, sharp; (*fig*) sharp, cutting; **tourner à l'~** to turn sour.
aigre-doux, -douce [ɛgʀədu, -dus] *adj* (*fruit*) bitter-sweet; (*sauce*) sweet and sour.
aigrefin [ɛgʀəfɛ̃] *nm* swindler.
aigrelet, te [ɛgʀəlɛ, -ɛt] *adj* (*taste*) sourish; (*voix, son*) sharpish.
aigrette [ɛgʀɛt] *nf* (*plume*) feather.
aigreur [ɛgʀœʀ] *nf* sourness; sharpness; ~**s d'estomac** heartburn *sg*.
aigri, e [egʀi] *adj* embittered.
aigrir [egʀiʀ] *vt* (*personne*) to embitter; (*caractère*) to sour; **s'~** *vi* to become embittered; to sour; (*lait etc*) to turn sour.
aigu, ë [egy] *adj* (*objet, arête*) sharp, pointed; (*son, voix*) high-pitched, shrill; (*note*) high(-pitched); (*douleur, intelligence*) acute, sharp.
aigue-marine, *pl* **aigues-marines** [ɛgmaʀin] *nf* aquamarine.
aiguillage [eguijaʒ] *nm* (*RAIL*) points *pl*.
aiguille [eguij] *nf* needle; (*de montre*) hand; ~ **à tricoter** knitting needle.
aiguiller [eguije] *vt* (*orienter*) to direct; (*RAIL*) to shunt.
aiguillette [eguijɛt] *nf* (*CULIN*) aiguillette.
aiguilleur [eguijœʀ] *nm* (*RAIL*) pointsman; ~ **du ciel** air traffic controller.
aiguillon [eguijɔ̃] *nm* (*d'abeille*) sting; (*fig*) spur, stimulus.
aiguillonner [eguijɔne] *vt* to spur *ou* goad on.
aiguiser [egize] *vt* to sharpen, grind; (*fig*) to stimulate; (*: esprit*) to sharpen; (*: sens*) to excite.

aiguisoir [egizwaʀ] *nm* sharpener.
aïkido [ajkido] *nm* aikido.
ail [aj] *nm* garlic.
aile [ɛl] *nf* wing; (*de voiture*) wing (*BRIT*), fender (*US*); **battre de l'~** (*fig*) to be in a sorry state; **voler de ses propres ~s** to stand on one's own two feet; **~ libre** hang-glider.
ailé, e [ele] *adj* winged.
aileron [ɛlʀɔ̃] *nm* (*de requin*) fin; (*d'avion*) aileron.
ailette [ɛlɛt] *nf* (*TECH*) fin; (: *de turbine*) blade.
ailier [elje] *nm* (*SPORT*) winger.
aille [aj] *etc vb voir* **aller**.
ailleurs [ajœʀ] *adv* elsewhere, somewhere else; **partout/nulle part ~** everywhere/ nowhere else; **d'~** *adv* (*du reste*) moreover, besides; **par ~** *adv* (*d'autre part*) moreover, furthermore.
ailloli [ajɔli] *nm* garlic mayonnaise.
aimable [ɛmabl(ə)] *adj* kind, nice; **vous êtes bien ~** that's very nice *ou* kind of you, how kind (of you)!
aimablement [ɛmabləmɑ̃] *adv* kindly.
aimant [ɛmɑ̃] *nm* magnet.
aimant, e [ɛmɑ̃, -ɑ̃t] *adj* loving, affectionate.
aimanté, e [ɛmɑ̃te] *adj* magnetic.
aimanter [ɛmɑ̃te] *vt* to magnetize.
aimer [eme] *vt* to love; (*d'amitié, affection, par goût*) to like; (*souhait*): **j'aimerais ...** I would like ...; **s'~** to love each other; to like each other; **je n'aime pas beaucoup Paul** I don't like Paul much, I don't care much for Paul; **~ faire qch** to like doing sth, like to do sth; **aimeriez-vous que je vous accompagne?** would you like me to come with you?; **j'aimerais (bien) m'en aller** I should (really) like to go; **bien ~ qn/qch** to like sb/sth; **j'aime mieux Paul (que Pierre)** I prefer Paul (to Pierre); **j'aime mieux** *ou* **autant vous dire que** I may as well tell you that; **j'aimerais autant** *ou* **mieux y aller maintenant** I'd sooner *ou* rather go now; **j'aime assez aller au cinéma** I quite like going to the cinema.
aine [ɛn] *nf* groin.
aîné, e [ene] *adj* elder, older; (*le plus âgé*) eldest, oldest ♦ *nm/f* oldest child *ou* one, oldest boy *ou* son/girl *ou* daughter; **~s** *nmpl* (*fig*: *anciens*) elders; **il est mon ~ (de 2 ans)** he's (2 years) older than me, he's 2 years my senior.
aînesse [ɛnɛs] *nf*: **droit d'~** birthright.
ainsi [ɛ̃si] *adv* (*de cette façon*) like this, in this way, thus; (*ce faisant*) thus ♦ *conj* thus, so; **~ que** (*comme*) (just) as; (*et aussi*) as well as; **pour ~ dire** so to speak, as it were; **~ donc** and so; **~ soit-il** (*REL*) so be it; **et ~ de suite** and so on (and so forth).
aïoli [ajɔli] *nm* = **ailloli**.
air [ɛʀ] *nm* air; (*mélodie*) tune; (*expression*) look, air; (*atmosphère, ambiance*): **dans l'~** in the air (*fig*); **prendre de grands ~s (avec qn)** to give o.s. airs (with sb); **en l'~** (up) into

the air; **tirer en l'~** to fire shots in the air; **paroles/menaces en l'~** idle words/threats; **prendre l'~** to get some (fresh) air; (*avion*) to take off; **avoir l'~ triste** to look *ou* seem sad; **avoir l'~ de qch** to look like sth; **avoir l'~ de faire** to look as though one is doing, appear to be doing; **courant d'~** draught (*BRIT*), draft (*US*); **le grand ~** the open air; **mal de l'~** air-sickness; **tête en l'~** scatterbrain; **~ comprimé** compressed air; **~ conditionné** air-conditioning.
airbag [ɛʀbag] *nm* air bag.
aire [ɛʀ] *nf* (*zone, fig, MATH*) area; (*nid*) eyrie (*BRIT*), aerie (*US*); **~ d'atterrissage** landing strip; landing patch; **~ de jeu** play area; **~ de lancement** launching site; **~ de stationnement** parking area.
airelle [ɛʀɛl] *nf* bilberry.
aisance [ɛzɑ̃s] *nf* ease; (*COUTURE*) easing, freedom of movement; (*richesse*) affluence; **être dans l'~** to be well-off *ou* affluent.
aise [ɛz] *nf* comfort ♦ *adj*: **être bien ~ de/que** to be delighted to/that; **~s** *nfpl*: **aimer ses ~s** to like one's (creature) comforts; **prendre ses ~s** to make o.s. comfortable; **frémir d'~** to shudder with pleasure; **être à l'~** *ou* **à son ~** to be comfortable; (*pas embarrassé*) to be at ease; (*financièrement*) to be comfortably off; **se mettre à l'~** to make o.s. comfortable; **être mal à l'~** *ou* **à son ~** to be uncomfortable; (*gêné*) to be ill at ease; **mettre qn à l'~** to put sb at his (*ou* her) ease; **mettre qn mal à l'~** to make sb feel ill at ease; **à votre ~** please yourself, just as you like; **en faire à son ~** to do as one likes; **en prendre à son ~ avec qch** to be free and easy with sth, do as one likes with sth.
aisé, e [eze] *adj* easy; (*assez riche*) well-to-do, well-off.
aisément [ezemɑ̃] *adv* easily.
aisselle [ɛsɛl] *nf* armpit.
ait [ɛ] *vb voir* **avoir**.
ajonc [aʒɔ̃] *nm* gorse *no pl*.
ajouré, e [aʒuʀe] *adj* openwork *cpd*.
ajournement [aʒuʀnəmɑ̃] *nm* adjournment; deferment, postponement.
ajourner [aʒuʀne] *vt* (*réunion*) to adjourn; (*décision*) to defer, postpone; (*candidat*) to refer; (*conscrit*) to defer.
ajout [aʒu] *nm* addition.
ajouter [aʒute] *vt* to add; (*INFORM*) to append; **~ à** *vt* (*accroître*) to add to; **s'~ à** to add to; **~ que** to add that; **~ foi à** to lend *ou* give credence to.
ajustage [aʒystaʒ] *nm* fitting.
ajusté, e [aʒyste] *adj*: **bien ~** (*robe etc*) close-fitting.
ajustement [aʒystəmɑ̃] *nm* adjustment.
ajuster [aʒyste] *vt* (*régler*) to adjust; (*vêtement*) to alter; (*arranger*): **~ sa cravate** to adjust one's tie; (*coup de fusil*) to aim; (*cible*) to aim at; (*adapter*): **~ qch à** to fit sth to.

ajusteur [aʒystœʀ] *nm* metal worker.
al *abr* = **année-lumière**.
alaise [alɛz] *nf* = **alèse**.
alambic [alɑ̃bik] *nm* still.
alambiqué, e [alɑ̃bike] *adj* convoluted, over-complicated.
alangui, e [alɑ̃gi] *adj* languid.
alanguir [alɑ̃giʀ]: **s'~** *vi* to grow languid.
alarmant, e [alaʀmɑ̃, -ɑ̃t] *adj* alarming.
alarme [alaʀm(ə)] *nf* alarm; **donner l'~** to give *ou* raise the alarm; **jeter l'~** to cause alarm.
alarmer [alaʀme] *vt* to alarm; **s'~** *vi* to become alarmed.
alarmiste [alaʀmist(ə)] *adj* alarmist.
Alaska [alaska] *nm*: **l'~** Alaska.
albanais, e [albanɛ, -ɛz] *adj* Albanian ♦ *nm* (*LING*) Albanian ♦ *nm/f*: **A~, e** Albanian.
Albanie [albani] *nf*: **l'~** Albania.
albâtre [albɑtʀ(ə)] *nm* alabaster.
albatros [albatʀos] *nm* albatross.
albigeois, e [albiʒwa, -waz] *adj* of *ou* from Albi.
albinos [albinos] *nm/f* albino.
album [albɔm] *nm* album; **~ à colorier** colouring book; **~ de timbres** stamp album.
albumen [albymɛn] *nm* albumen.
albumine [albymin] *nf* albumin; **avoir** *ou* **faire de l'~** to suffer from albuminuria.
alcalin [alkalɛ̃, -in] *adj* alkaline.
alchimie [alʃimi] *nf* alchemy.
alchimiste [alʃimist(ə)] *nm* alchemist.
alcool [alkɔl] *nm*: **l'~** alcohol; **un ~** a spirit, a brandy; **~ à brûler** methylated spirits (*BRIT*), wood alcohol (*US*); **~ à 90°** surgical spirit; **~ camphré** camphorated alcohol; **~ de prune** *etc* plum *etc* brandy.
alcoolémie [alkɔlemi] *nf* blood alcohol level.
alcoolique [alkɔlik] *adj, nm/f* alcoholic.
alcoolisé, e [alkɔlize] *adj* alcoholic.
alcoolisme [alkɔlism(ə)] *nm* alcoholism.
alco(o)test [alkɔtɛst] *nm* ® (*objet*) Breathalyser ®; (*test*) breath-test; **faire subir l'~ à qn** to Breathalyze ® sb.
alcôve [alkov] *nf* alcove, recess.
aléas [alea] *nmpl* hazards.
aléatoire [aleatwaʀ] *adj* uncertain; (*INFORM, STATISTIQUE*) random.
alémanique [alemanik] *adj*: **la Suisse ~** German-speaking Switzerland.
ALENA [alena] *sigle m* (= *Accord de libre-échange nord-américain*) NAFTA (= *North American Free Trade Agreement*).
alentour [alɑ̃tuʀ] *adv* around (about); **~s** *nmpl* surroundings; **aux ~s de** in the vicinity *ou* neighbourhood of, around about; (*temps*) around about.
Aléoutiennes [aleusjɛn] *nfpl*: **les (îles) ~** the Aleutian Islands.
alerte [alɛʀt(ə)] *adj* agile, nimble; (*style*) brisk, lively ♦ *nf* alert; warning; **donner l'~** to give the alert; **à la première ~** at the first sign of trouble *ou* danger; **~ à la bombe** bomb scare.
alerter [alɛʀte] *vt* to alert.
alèse [alɛz] *nf* (*drap*) undersheet, drawsheet.
aléser [aleze] *vt* to ream.
alevin [alvɛ̃] *nm* alevin, young fish.
alevinage [alvinaʒ] *nm* fish farming.
Alexandrie [alɛksɑ̃dʀi] *n* Alexandria.
alexandrin [alɛksɑ̃dʀɛ̃] *nm* alexandrine.
alezan, e [alzɑ̃, -an] *adj* chestnut.
algarade [algaʀad] *nf* row, dispute.
algèbre [alʒɛbʀ(ə)] *nf* algebra.
algébrique [alʒebʀik] *adj* algebraic.
Alger [alʒe] *n* Algiers.
Algérie [alʒeʀi] *nf*: **l'~** Algeria.
algérien, ne [alʒeʀjɛ̃, -ɛn] *adj* Algerian ♦ *nm/f*: **A~, ne** Algerian.
algérois, e [alʒeʀwa, -waz] *adj* of *ou* from Algiers ♦ *nm*: **l'A~** (*région*) the Algiers region.
algorithme [algɔʀitm(ə)] *nm* algorithm.
algue [alg(ə)] *nf* (*gén*) seaweed *no pl*; (*BOT*) alga (*pl* -ae).
alias [aljas] *adv* alias.
alibi [alibi] *nm* alibi.
aliénation [aljenasjɔ̃] *nf* alienation.
aliéné, e [aljene] *nm/f* insane person, lunatic (*péj*).
aliéner [aljene] *vt* to alienate; (*bien, liberté*) to give up; **s'~** *vt* to alienate.
alignement [aliɲmɑ̃] *nm* alignment, lining up; **à l'~** in line.
aligner [aliɲe] *vt* to align, line up; (*idées, chiffres*) to string together; (*adapter*): **~ qch sur** to bring sth into alignment with; **s'~** (*soldats etc*) to line up; **s'~ sur** (*POL*) to align o.s. with.
aliment [alimɑ̃] *nm* food; **~ complet** whole food.
alimentaire [alimɑ̃tɛʀ] *adj* food *cpd*; (*péj: besogne*) done merely to earn a living; **produits ~s** foodstuffs, foods.
alimentation [alimɑ̃tasjɔ̃] *nf* feeding; supplying, supply; (*commerce*) food trade; (*produits*) groceries *pl*; (*régime*) diet; (*INFORM*) feed; **~ (générale)** (general) grocer's; **~ de base** staple diet; **~ en feuilles/en continu/en papier** form/stream/sheet feed.
alimenter [alimɑ̃te] *vt* to feed; (*TECH*): **~ (en)** to supply (with), feed (with); (*fig*) to sustain, keep going.
alinéa [alinea] *nm* paragraph; **"nouvel ~"** "new line".
aliter [alite]: **s'~** *vi* to take to one's bed; **infirme alité** bedridden person *ou* invalid.
alizé [alize] *adj, nm*: **(vent) ~** trade wind.
allaitement [alɛtmɑ̃] *nm* feeding; **~ maternel/au biberon** breast-/bottle-feeding; **~ mixte** mixed feeding.
allaiter [alete] *vt* (*suj: femme*) to (breast-)feed, nurse; (*suj: animal*) to suckle; **~ au biberon** to bottle-feed.

allant [alɑ̃] *nm* drive, go.

alléchant, e [aleʃɑ̃, -ɑ̃t] *adj* tempting, enticing.

allécher [aleʃe] *vt:* ~ **qn** to make sb's mouth water; to tempt sb, entice sb.

allée [ale] *nf (de jardin)* path; *(en ville)* avenue, drive; ~**s et venues** comings and goings.

allégation [alegasjɔ̃] *nf* allegation.

alléger [aleʒe] *vt (voiture)* to make lighter; *(chargement)* to lighten; *(souffrance)* to alleviate, soothe.

allégorie [alegɔri] *nf* allegory.

allégorique [alegɔrik] *adj* allegorical.

allègre [alɛgr(ə)] *adj* lively, jaunty *(BRIT)*; *(personne)* gay, cheerful.

allégresse [alegrɛs] *nf* elation, gaiety.

allegretto [al(l)egrɛt(t)o] *adv, nm* allegretto.

allegro [al(l)egro] *adv, nm* allegro.

alléguer [alege] *vt* to put forward (as proof *ou* an excuse).

Allemagne [aləmaɲ] *nf:* l'~ Germany; l'~ **de l'Est/Ouest** East/West Germany; l'~ **fédérale (RFA)** the Federal Republic of Germany (FRG).

allemand, e [almɑ̃, -ɑ̃d] *adj* German ♦ *nm (LING)* German ♦ *nm/f:* A~, e German; A~ **de l'Est/l'Ouest** East/West German.

aller [ale] *nm (trajet)* outward journey; *(billet):* ~ **(simple)** single *(BRIT) ou* one-way ticket; ~ **(et) retour (AR)** *(trajet)* return trip *ou* journey *(BRIT)*, round trip *(US)*; *(billet)* return *(BRIT) ou* round-trip *(US)* ticket ♦ *vi (gén)* to go; ~ **à** *(convenir)* to suit; *(suj: forme, pointure etc)* to fit; **cela me va** *(couleur)* that suits me; *(vêtement)* that suits me; that fits me; *(projet, disposition)* that suits me, that's fine *ou* OK by me; ~ **à la chasse/pêche** to go hunting/fishing; ~ **avec** *(couleurs, style etc)* to go (well) with; **je vais le faire/me fâcher** I'm going to do it/to get angry; ~ **voir/chercher qn** to go and see/look for sb; **comment allez-vous?** how are you?; **comment ça va?** how are you?; *(affaires etc)* how are things?; **ça va? — oui (ça va)!** how are things? — fine!; **ça va (comme ça)** that's fine (as it is); **il va bien/mal** he's well/not well, he's fine/ill; **ça va bien/mal** *(affaires etc)* it's going well/not going well; **tout va bien** everything's fine; **ça ne va pas!** *(mauvaise humeur etc)* that's not on!, hey, come on!; **ça ne va pas sans difficultés** it's not without difficulties; ~ **mieux** to be better; **il y a de leur vie** their lives are at stake; **se laisser** ~ to let o.s. go; **s'en** ~ *vi (partir)* to be off, go, leave; *(disparaître)* to go away; ~ **jusqu'à** to go as far as; **ça va de soi, ça va sans dire** that goes without saying; **tu y vas un peu fort** you're going a bit (too) far; **allez!** go on!; come on!; **allons-y!** let's go!; **allez, au revoir** right *ou* OK then, bye-bye!

allergène [alɛrʒɛn] *nm* allergen.

allergie [alɛrʒi] *nf* allergy.

allergique [alɛrʒik] *adj* allergic; ~ **à** allergic to.

allez [ale] *vb voir* **aller**.

alliage [aljaʒ] *nm* alloy.

alliance [aljɑ̃s] *nf (MIL, POL)* alliance; *(mariage)* marriage; *(bague)* wedding ring; **neveu par** ~ nephew by marriage.

allié, e [alje] *nm/f* ally; **parents et** ~**s** relatives and relatives by marriage.

allier [alje] *vt (métaux)* to alloy; *(POL, gén)* to ally; *(fig)* to combine; **s'~** to become allies; *(éléments, caractéristiques)* to combine; **s'~ à** to become allied to *ou* with.

alligator [aligatɔr] *nm* alligator.

allitération [aliterasjɔ̃] *nf* alliteration.

allô [alo] *excl* hullo, hallo.

allocataire [alɔkatɛr] *nm/f* beneficiary.

allocation [alɔkasjɔ̃] *nf* allowance; ~ **(de) chômage** unemployment benefit; ~ **(de) logement** rent allowance; ~**s familiales** ≈ child benefit *no pl*; ~**s de maternité** maternity allowance.

allocution [alɔkysjɔ̃] *nf* short speech.

allongé, e [alɔ̃ʒe] *adj (étendu):* **être** ~ to be stretched out *ou* lying down; *(long)* long; *(étiré)* elongated; *(oblong)* oblong; **rester** ~ to be lying down; **mine** ~**e** long face.

allonger [alɔ̃ʒe] *vt* to lengthen, make longer; *(étendre: bras, jambe)* to stretch (out); *(sauce)* to spin out, make go further; **s'~** *vi* to get longer; *(se coucher)* to lie down, stretch out; ~ **le pas** to hasten one's step(s).

allouer [alwe] *vt:* ~ **qch à** to allocate sth to, allot sth to.

allumage [alymaʒ] *nm (AUTO)* ignition.

allume-cigare [alymsigar] *nm inv* cigar lighter.

allume-gaz [alymgɑz] *nm inv* gas lighter.

allumer [alyme] *vt (lampe, phare, radio)* to put *ou* switch on; *(pièce)* to put *ou* switch the light(s) on in; *(feu, bougie, cigare, pipe, gaz)* to light; *(chauffage)* to put on; **s'~** *vi (lumière, lampe)* to come *ou* go on; ~ **(la lumière** *ou* **l'électricité)** to put on the light.

allumette [alymɛt] *nf* match; *(morceau de bois)* matchstick; *(CULIN):* ~ **au fromage** cheese straw; ~ **de sûreté** safety match.

allumeuse [alymøz] *nf (péj)* tease *(woman)*.

allure [alyr] *nf (vitesse)* speed; *(: à pied)* pace; *(démarche)* walk; *(maintien)* bearing; *(aspect, air)* look; **avoir de l'~** to have style *ou* a certain elegance; **à toute** ~ at top *ou* full speed.

allusion [alyzjɔ̃] *nf* allusion; *(sous-entendu)* hint; **faire** ~ **à** to allude *ou* refer to; to hint at.

alluvions [alyvjɔ̃] *nfpl* alluvial deposits, alluvium *sg*.

almanach [almana] *nm* almanac.

aloès [alɔɛs] *nm (BOT)* aloe.

aloi [alwa] *nm:* **de bon/mauvais** ~ of genuine/doubtful worth *ou* quality.

=== *MOT-CLÉ*

alors [alɔʀ] *adv* **1** (*à ce moment-là*) then, at that time; **il habitait** ~ **à Paris** he lived in Paris at that time; **jusqu'**~ up till *ou* until then
2 (*par conséquent*) then; **tu as fini?** ~ **je m'en vais** have you finished? I'm going then
3 (*expressions*): ~**? quoi de neuf?** well *ou* so? what's new?; **et** ~**?** so (what)?; **ça** ~**!** (well) really!
~ **que** *conj* **1** (*au moment où*) when, as; **il est arrivé alors que je partais** he arrived as I was leaving
2 (*pendant que*) while, when; ~ **qu'il était à Paris, il a visité ...** while *ou* when he was in Paris, he visited ...
3 (*tandis que*) whereas, while; ~ **que son frère travaillait dur, lui se reposait** while his brother was working hard, HE would rest.

alouette [alwɛt] *nf* (sky)lark.
alourdir [aluʀdiʀ] *vt* to weigh down, make heavy; **s'**~ *vi* to grow heavy *ou* heavier.
aloyau [alwajo] *nm* sirloin.
alpaga [alpaga] *nm* (*tissu*) alpaca.
alpage [alpaʒ] *nm* high mountain pasture.
Alpes [alp(ə)] *nfpl*: **les** ~ the Alps.
alpestre [alpɛstʀ(ə)] *adj* alpine.
alphabet [alfabɛ] *nm* alphabet; (*livre*) ABC (book), primer.
alphabétique [alfabetik] *adj* alphabetic(al); **par ordre** ~ in alphabetical order.
alphabétisation [alfabetizasjɔ̃] *nf* literacy teaching.
alphabétiser [alfabetize] *vt* to teach to read and write; (*pays*) to eliminate illiteracy in.
alphanumérique [alfanymeʀik] *adj* alphanumeric.
alpin, e [alpɛ̃, -in] *adj* (*plante etc*) alpine; (*club*) climbing.
alpinisme [alpinism(ə)] *nm* mountaineering, climbing.
alpiniste [alpinist(ə)] *nm/f* mountaineer, climber.
Alsace [alzas] *nf*: **l'**~ Alsace.
alsacien, ne [alzasjɛ̃, -ɛn] *adj* Alsatian.
altercation [altɛʀkasjɔ̃] *nf* altercation.
alter ego [altɛʀego] *nm* alter ego.
altérer [alteʀe] *vt* (*faits, vérité*) to falsify, distort; (*qualité*) to debase, impair; (*données*) to corrupt; (*donner soif à*) to make thirsty; **s'**~ *vi* to deteriorate; to spoil.
alternance [altɛʀnɑ̃s] *nf* alternation; **en** ~ alternately; **formation en** ~ sandwich course.
alternateur [altɛʀnatœʀ] *nm* alternator.
alternatif, ive [altɛʀnatif, -iv] *adj* alternating ♦ *nf* alternative.
alternativement [altɛʀnativmɑ̃] *adv* alternately.
alterner [altɛʀne] *vt* to alternate ♦ *vi*: ~ (**avec**) to alternate (with); (**faire**) ~ **qch avec qch** to alternate sth with sth.

Altesse [altɛs] *nf* Highness.
altier, ière [altje, -jɛʀ] *adj* haughty.
altimètre [altimɛtʀ(ə)] *nm* altimeter.
altiport [altipɔʀ] *nm* mountain airfield.
altiste [altist(ə)] *nm/f* viola player, violist.
altitude [altityd] *nf* altitude, height; **à 1 000 m d'**~ at a height *ou* an altitude of 1000 m; **en** ~ at high altitudes; **perdre/prendre de l'**~ to lose/gain height; **voler à haute/basse** ~ to fly at a high/low altitude.
alto [alto] *nm* (*instrument*) viola ♦ *nf* (*contr*)alto.
altruisme [altʀɥism(ə)] *nm* altruism.
altruiste [altʀɥist(ə)] *adj* altruistic.
aluminium [alyminjɔm] *nm* aluminium (*BRIT*), aluminum (*US*).
alun [alœ̃] *nm* alum.
alunir [alyniʀ] *vi* to land on the moon.
alunissage [alynisaʒ] *nm* (moon) landing.
alvéole [alveɔl] *nm ou f* (*de ruche*) alveolus.
alvéolé, e [alveɔle] *adj* honeycombed.
AM *sigle f* = **assurance maladie**.
amabilité [amabilite] *nf* kindness; **il a eu l'**~ **de** he was kind *ou* good enough to.
amadou [amadu] *nm* touchwood, amadou.
amadouer [amadwe] *vt* to coax, cajole; (*adoucir*) to mollify, soothe.
amaigrir [amegʀiʀ] *vt* to make thin *ou* thinner.
amaigrissant, e [amegʀisɑ̃, -ɑ̃t] *adj*: **régime** ~ slimming (*BRIT*) *ou* weight-reduction (*US*) diet.
amalgame [amalgam] *nm* amalgam; (*fig: de gens, d'idées*) hotch-potch, mixture.
amalgamer [amalgame] *vt* to amalgamate.
amande [amɑ̃d] *nf* (*de l'amandier*) almond; (*de noyau de fruit*) kernel; **en** ~ (*yeux*) almond *cpd*, almond-shaped.
amandier [amɑ̃dje] *nm* almond (tree).
amanite [amanit] *nf* (*BOT*) mushroom of the genus Amanita; ~ **tue-mouches** fly agaric.
amant [amɑ̃] *nm* lover.
amarre [amaʀ] *nf* (*NAVIG*) (mooring) rope *ou* line; ~**s** *nfpl* moorings.
amarrer [amaʀe] *vt* (*NAVIG*) to moor; (*gén*) to make fast.
amaryllis [amarilis] *nf* amaryllis.
amas [ama] *nm* heap, pile.
amasser [amase] *vt* to amass; **s'**~ *vi* to pile up, accumulate; (*foule*) to gather.
amateur [amatœʀ] *nm* amateur; **en** ~ (*péj*) amateurishly; **musicien/sportif** ~ amateur musician/sportsman; ~ **de musique/sport** *etc* music/sport *etc* lover.
amateurisme [amatœʀism(ə)] *nm* amateurism; (*péj*) amateurishness.
Amazone [amazɔn] *nf*: **l'**~ the Amazon.
amazone [amazɔn] *nf* horsewoman; **en** ~ sidesaddle.
Amazonie [amazɔni] *nf*: **l'**~ Amazonia.
ambages [ɑ̃baʒ]: **sans** ~ *adv* without beating about the bush, plainly.
ambassade [ɑ̃basad] *nf* embassy; (*mission*): **en**

~ on a mission.

ambassadeur, drice [ɑ̃basadœʀ, -dʀis] *nm/f* ambassador/ambassadress.

ambiance [ɑ̃bjɑ̃s] *nf* atmosphere; **il y a de l'**~ everyone's having a good time.

ambiant, e [ɑ̃bjɑ̃, -ɑ̃t] *adj* (*air, milieu*) surrounding; (*température*) ambient.

ambidextre [ɑ̃bidɛkstʀ(ə)] *adj* ambidextrous.

ambigu, ë [ɑ̃bigy] *adj* ambiguous.

ambiguïté [ɑ̃bigɥite] *nf* ambiguousness *no pl*, ambiguity.

ambitieux, euse [ɑ̃bisjø, -øz] *adj* ambitious.

ambition [ɑ̃bisjɔ̃] *nf* ambition.

ambitionner [ɑ̃bisjɔne] *vt* to have as one's aim *ou* ambition.

ambivalent, e [ɑ̃bivalɑ̃, -ɑ̃t] *adj* ambivalent.

amble [ɑ̃bl(ə)] *nm*: **aller l'**~ to amble.

ambre [ɑ̃bʀ(ə)] *nm*: ~ **(jaune)** amber; ~ **gris** ambergris.

ambré, e [ɑ̃bʀe] *adj* (*couleur*) amber; (*parfum*) ambergris-scented.

ambulance [ɑ̃bylɑ̃s] *nf* ambulance.

ambulancier, ière [ɑ̃bylɑ̃sje, -jɛʀ] *nm/f* ambulanceman/woman (*BRIT*), paramedic (*US*).

ambulant, e [ɑ̃bylɑ̃, -ɑ̃t] *adj* travelling, itinerant.

âme [ɑm] *nf* soul; **rendre l'**~ to give up the ghost; **bonne** ~ (*aussi ironique*) kind soul; **un joueur/tricheur dans l'**~ a gambler/cheat through and through; ~ **sœur** kindred spirit.

amélioration [ameljɔʀɑsjɔ̃] *nf* improvement.

améliorer [ameljɔʀe] *vt* to improve; **s'**~ *vi* to improve, get better.

aménagement [amenaʒmɑ̃] *nm* fitting out; laying out; development; ~**s** *nmpl* developments; **l'**~ **du territoire** ≈ town and country planning; ~**s fiscaux** tax adjustments.

aménager [amenaʒe] *vt* (*agencer: espace, local*) to fit out; (*: terrain*) to lay out; (*: quartier, territoire*) to develop; (*installer*) to fix up, put in; **ferme aménagée** converted farmhouse.

amende [amɑ̃d] *nf* fine; **mettre à l'**~ to penalize; **faire** ~ **honorable** to make amends.

amendement [amɑ̃dmɑ̃] *nm* (*JUR*) amendment.

amender [amɑ̃de] *vt* (*loi*) to amend; (*terre*) to enrich; **s'**~ *vi* to mend one's ways.

amène [amɛn] *adj* affable; **peu** ~ unkind.

amener [amne] *vt* to bring; (*causer*) to bring about; (*baisser: drapeau, voiles*) to strike; **s'**~ *vi* (*fam*) to show up, turn up; ~ **qn à qch/à faire** to lead sb to sth/to do.

amenuiser [amənɥize]: **s'**~ *vi* to dwindle; (*chances*) to grow slimmer, lessen.

amer, amère [amɛʀ] *adj* bitter.

amèrement [amɛʀmɑ̃] *adv* bitterly.

américain, e [ameʀikɛ̃, -ɛn] *adj* American ♦ *nm* (*LING*) American (English) ♦ *nm/f*: **A**~, **e** American; **en vedette** ~**e** as a special guest (star).

américaniser [ameʀikanize] *vt* to Americanize.

américanisme [ameʀikanism(ə)] *nm* Americanism.

amérindien, ne [ameʀɛ̃djɛ̃, -ɛn] *adj* Amerindian, American Indian.

Amérique [ameʀik] *nf* America; **l'**~ **centrale** Central America; **l'**~ **latine** Latin America; **l'**~ **du Nord** North America; **l'**~ **du Sud** South America.

Amerloque [amɛʀlɔk] *nm/f* (*fam*) Yank, Yankee.

amerrir [ameʀiʀ] *vi* to land (on the sea); (*capsule spatiale*) to splash down.

amerrissage [ameʀisaʒ] *nm* landing (on the sea); splash-down.

amertume [amɛʀtym] *nf* bitterness.

améthyste [ametist(ə)] *nf* amethyst.

ameublement [amœbləmɑ̃] *nm* furnishing; (*meubles*) furniture; **articles d'**~ furnishings; **tissus d'**~ soft furnishings, furnishing fabrics.

ameuter [amøte] *vt* (*badauds*) to draw a crowd of; (*peuple*) to rouse, stir up.

ami, e [ami] *nm/f* friend; (*amant/maîtresse*) boyfriend/girlfriend ♦ *adj*: **pays/groupe** ~ friendly country/group; **être (très)** ~ **avec qn** to be (very) friendly with sb; **être** ~ **de l'ordre** to be a lover of order; **un** ~ **des arts** a patron of the arts; **un** ~ **des chiens** a dog lover; **petit** ~/**petite** ~**e** (*fam*) boyfriend/girlfriend.

amiable [amjabl(ə)]: **à l'**~ *adv* (*JUR*) out of court; (*gén*) amicably.

amiante [amjɑ̃t] *nm* asbestos.

amibe [amib] *nf* amoeba (*pl* -ae).

amical, e, aux [amikal, -o] *adj* friendly ♦ *nf* (*club*) association.

amicalement [amikalmɑ̃] *adv* in a friendly way; (*formule épistolaire*) regards.

amidon [amidɔ̃] *nm* starch.

amidonner [amidɔne] *vt* to starch.

amincir [amɛ̃siʀ] *vt* (*objet*) to thin (down); **s'**~ *vi* to get thinner *ou* slimmer; ~ **qn** to make sb thinner *ou* slimmer.

amincissant, e [amɛ̃sisɑ̃, -ɑ̃t] *adj* slimming.

aminé, e [amine] *adj*: **acide** ~ amino acid.

amiral, aux [amiʀal, -o] *nm* admiral.

amirauté [amiʀote] *nf* admiralty.

amitié [amitje] *nf* friendship; **prendre en** ~ to take a liking to; **faire** *ou* **présenter ses** ~**s à qn** to send sb one's best wishes; ~**s** (*formule épistolaire*) (with) best wishes.

ammoniac [amɔnjak] *nm*: **(gaz)** ~ ammonia.

ammoniaque [amɔnjak] *nf* ammonia (water).

amnésie [amnezi] *nf* amnesia.

amnésique [amnezik] *adj* amnesic.

Amnesty International [amnɛsti-] *n* Amnesty International.

amniocentèse [amnjosɛtɛz] *nf* amniocentesis.

amnistie [amnisti] *nf* amnesty.

amnistier [amnistje] *vt* to amnesty.

amocher [amɔʃe] vt (fam) to mess up.
amoindrir [amwɛ̃dʀiʀ] vt to reduce.
amollir [amɔliʀ] vt to soften.
amonceler [amɔ̃sle] vt, **s'~** vi to pile ou heap up; (fig) to accumulate.
amoncellement [amɔ̃sɛlmɑ̃] nm piling ou heaping up; accumulation; (tas) pile, heap; accumulation.
amont [amɔ̃]: **en ~** adv upstream; (sur une pente) uphill; **en ~ de** prép upstream from; uphill from, above.
amoral, e, aux [amɔʀal, -o] adj amoral.
amorce [amɔʀs(ə)] nf (sur un hameçon) bait; (explosif) cap; (tube) primer; (: contenu) priming; (fig: début) beginning(s), start.
amorcer [amɔʀse] vt to bait; to prime; (commencer) to begin, start.
amorphe [amɔʀf(ə)] adj passive, lifeless.
amortir [amɔʀtiʀ] vt (atténuer: choc) to absorb, cushion; (bruit, douleur) to deaden; (COMM: dette) to pay off, amortize; (: mise de fonds, matériel) to write off; **~ un abonnement** to make a season ticket pay (for itself).
amortissable [amɔʀtisabl(ə)] adj (COMM) that can be paid off.
amortissement [amɔʀtismɑ̃] nm (de matériel) writing off; (d'une dette) paying off.
amortisseur [amɔʀtisœʀ] nm shock absorber.
amour [amuʀ] nm love; (liaison) love affair, love; (statuette etc) cupid; **un ~ de** a lovely little; **faire l'~** to make love.
amouracher [amuʀaʃe]: **s'~ de** vt (péj) to become infatuated with.
amourette [amuʀɛt] nf passing fancy.
amoureusement [amuʀøzmɑ̃] adv lovingly.
amoureux, euse [amuʀø, -øz] adj (regard, tempérament) amorous; (vie, problèmes) love cpd; (personne): **~ (de qn)** in love (with sb) ♦ nm/f lover ♦ nmpl courting couple(s); **tomber ~ de qn** to fall in love with sb; **être ~ de qch** to be passionately fond of sth; **un ~ de la nature** a nature lover.
amour-propre, pl **amours-propres** [amuʀpʀɔpʀ(ə)] nm self-esteem.
amovible [amɔvibl(ə)] adj removable, detachable.
ampère [ɑ̃pɛʀ] nm amp(ere).
ampèremètre [ɑ̃pɛʀmɛtʀ(ə)] nm ammeter.
amphétamine [ɑ̃fetamin] nf amphetamine.
amphi [ɑ̃fi] nm (SCOL fam: = amphithéâtre) lecture hall ou theatre.
amphibie [ɑ̃fibi] adj amphibious.
amphibien [ɑ̃fibjɛ̃] nm (ZOOL) amphibian.
amphithéâtre [ɑ̃fiteatʀ(ə)] nm amphitheatre; (d'université) lecture hall ou theatre.
amphore [ɑ̃fɔʀ] nf amphora.
ample [ɑ̃pl(ə)] adj (vêtement) roomy, ample; (gestes, mouvement) broad; (ressources) ample; **jusqu'à plus ~ informé** (ADMIN) until further details are available.
amplement [ɑ̃pləmɑ̃] adv amply; **~ suffisant** ample, more than enough.

ampleur [ɑ̃plœʀ] nf scale, size; extent, magnitude.
ampli [ɑ̃pli] nm (fam: = amplificateur) amplifier, amp.
amplificateur [ɑ̃plifikatœʀ] nm amplifier.
amplification [ɑ̃plifikasjɔ̃] nf amplification; expansion, increase.
amplifier [ɑ̃plifje] vt (son, oscillation) to amplify; (fig) to expand, increase.
amplitude [ɑ̃plityd] nf amplitude; (des températures) range.
ampoule [ɑ̃pul] nf (électrique) bulb; (de médicament) phial; (aux mains, pieds) blister.
ampoulé, e [ɑ̃pule] adj (péj) pompous, bombastic.
amputation [ɑ̃pytasjɔ̃] nf amputation.
amputer [ɑ̃pyte] vt (MÉD) to amputate; (fig) to cut ou reduce drastically; **~ qn d'un bras/ pied** to amputate sb's arm/foot.
Amsterdam [amstɛʀdam] n Amsterdam.
amulette [amylɛt] nf amulet.
amusant, e [amyzɑ̃, -ɑ̃t] adj (divertissant, spirituel) entertaining, amusing; (comique) funny, amusing.
amusé, e [amyze] adj amused.
amuse-gueule [amyzgœl] nm inv appetizer, snack.
amusement [amyzmɑ̃] nm (voir amusé) amusement; (voir amuser) entertaining, amusing; (jeu etc) pastime, diversion.
amuser [amyze] vt (divertir) to entertain, amuse; (égayer, faire rire) to amuse; (détourner l'attention de) to distract; **s'~** vi (jouer) to amuse o.s., play; (se divertir) to enjoy o.s., have fun; (fig) to mess around; **s'~ de qch** (trouver comique) to find sth amusing; **s'~ avec** ou **de qn** (duper) to make a fool of sb.
amusette [amyzɛt] nf idle pleasure, trivial pastime.
amuseur [amyzœʀ] nm entertainer; (péj) clown.
amygdale [amidal] nf tonsil; **opérer qn des ~s** to take sb's tonsils out.
amygdalite [amidalit] nf tonsillitis.
AN sigle f = Assemblée nationale.
an [ɑ̃] nm year; **être âgé de** ou **avoir 3 ~s** to be 3 (years old); **en l'~** 1980 in the year 1980; **le jour de l'~, le premier de l'~, le nouvel ~** New Year's Day.
anabolisant [anabɔlizɑ̃] nm anabolic steroid.
anachronique [anakʀɔnik] adj anachronistic.
anachronisme [anakʀɔnism(ə)] nm anachronism.
anaconda [anakɔ̃da] nm (ZOOL) anaconda.
anaérobie [anaeʀɔbi] adj anaerobic.
anagramme [anagʀam] nf anagram.
ANAH sigle f = Agence nationale pour l'amélioration de l'habitat.
anal, e, aux [anal, -o] adj anal.
analgésique [analʒezik] nm analgesic.
anallergique [analɛʀʒik] adj hypoallergenic.
analogie [analɔʒi] nf analogy.

analogique [analɔʒik] *adj* (*LOGIQUE*: *raisonnement*) analogical; (*calculateur, montre etc*) analogue; (*INFORM*) analog.

analogue [analɔg] *adj*: ~ **(à)** analogous (to), similar (to).

analphabète [analfabɛt] *nm/f* illiterate.

analphabétisme [analfabetism(ə)] *nm* illiteracy.

analyse [analiz] *nf* analysis; (*MÉD*) test; **faire l'~ de** to analyse; **une ~ approfondie** an indepth analysis; **en dernière ~** in the last analysis; **avoir l'esprit d'~** to have an analytical turn of mind; ~ **grammaticale** grammatical analysis, parsing (*SCOL*).

analyser [analize] *vt* to analyse; (*MÉD*) to test.

analyste [analist] *nm/f* analyst; (*psychanalyste*) (psycho)analyst.

analyste-programmeur, euse, *pl* **analystes-programmeurs, euses** [analist-prɔgramœr, -øz] *nm/f* systems analyst.

analytique [analitik] *adj* analytical.

analytiquement [analitikmɑ̃] *adv* analytically.

ananas [anana] *nm* pineapple.

anarchie [anarʃi] *nf* anarchy.

anarchique [anarʃik] *adj* anarchic.

anarchisme [anarʃism(ə)] *nm* anarchism.

anarchiste [anarʃist(ə)] *adj* anarchistic ♦ *nm/f* anarchist.

anathème [anatɛm] *nm*: **jeter l'~ sur, lancer l'~ contre** to anathematize, curse.

anatomie [anatɔmi] *nf* anatomy.

anatomique [anatɔmik] *adj* anatomical.

ancestral, e, aux [ɑ̃sɛstral, -o] *adj* ancestral.

ancêtre [ɑ̃sɛtr(ə)] *nm/f* ancestor; (*fig*): **l'~ de** the forerunner of.

anche [ɑ̃ʃ] *nf* reed.

anchois [ɑ̃ʃwa] *nm* anchovy.

ancien, ne [ɑ̃sjɛ̃, -ɛn] *adj* old; (*de jadis, de l'antiquité*) ancient; (*précédent, ex-*) former, old ♦ *nm* (*mobilier ancien*): **l'~** antiques *pl* ♦ *nm/f* (*dans une tribu etc*) elder; **un ~ ministre** a former minister; **mon ~ne voiture** my previous car; **être plus ~ que qn dans une maison** to have been in a firm longer than sb; (*dans l'hiérarchie*) to be senior to sb in a firm; ~ **combattant** ex-serviceman; ~ **(élève)** (*SCOL*) ex-pupil (*BRIT*), alumnus (*US*).

anciennement [ɑ̃sjɛnmɑ̃] *adv* formerly.

ancienneté [ɑ̃sjɛnte] *nf* oldness; antiquity; (*ADMIN*) (length of) service; seniority.

ancrage [ɑ̃kraʒ] *nm* anchoring; (*NAVIG*) anchorage; (*CONSTR*) anchor.

ancre [ɑ̃kr(ə)] *nf* anchor; **jeter/lever l'~** to cast/weigh anchor; **à l'~** at anchor.

ancrer [ɑ̃kre] *vt* (*CONSTR*) to anchor; (*fig*) to fix firmly; **s'~** *vi* (*NAVIG*) to (cast) anchor.

andalou, ouse [ɑ̃dalu, -uz] *adj* Andalusian.

Andalousie [ɑ̃daluzi] *nf*: **l'~** Andalusia.

andante [ɑ̃dɑ̃t] *adv, nm* andante.

Andes [ɑ̃d] *nfpl*: **les ~** the Andes.

Andorre [ɑ̃dɔr] *nf* Andorra.

andouille [ɑ̃duj] *nf* (*CULIN*) sausage made of chitterlings; (*fam*) clot, nit.

andouillette [ɑ̃dujɛt] *nf* small andouille.

âne [ɑn] *nm* donkey, ass; (*péj*) dunce, fool.

anéantir [aneɑ̃tir] *vt* to annihilate, wipe out; (*fig*) to obliterate, destroy; (*déprimer*) to overwhelm.

anecdote [anɛkdɔt] *nf* anecdote.

anecdotique [anɛkdɔtik] *adj* anecdotal.

anémie [anemi] *nf* anaemia.

anémié, e [anemje] *adj* anaemic; (*fig*) enfeebled.

anémique [anemik] *adj* anaemic.

anémone [anemɔn] *nf* anemone; ~ **de mer** sea anemone.

ânerie [ɑnri] *nf* stupidity; (*parole etc*) stupid *ou* idiotic comment *etc*.

anéroïde [anerɔid] *adj voir* **baromètre**.

ânesse [ɑnɛs] *nf* she-ass.

anesthésie [anɛstezi] *nf* anaesthesia; **sous** ~ under anaesthetic; ~ **générale/locale** general/local anaesthetic; **faire une ~ locale à qn** to give sb a local anaesthetic.

anesthésier [anɛstezje] *vt* to anaesthetize.

anesthésique [anɛstezik] *adj* anaesthetic.

anesthésiste [anɛstezist(ə)] *nm/f* anaesthetist.

anfractuosité [ɑ̃fraktɥozite] *nf* crevice.

ange [ɑ̃ʒ] *nm* angel; **être aux ~s** to be over the moon; ~ **gardien** guardian angel.

angélique [ɑ̃ʒelik] *adj* angelic(al) ♦ *nf* angelica.

angelot [ɑ̃ʒlo] *nm* cherub.

angélus [ɑ̃ʒelys] *nm* angelus; (*cloches*) evening bells *pl*.

angevin, e [ɑ̃ʒvɛ̃, -in] *adj* of *ou* from Anjou; of *ou* from Angers.

angine [ɑ̃ʒin] *nf* sore throat, throat infection; ~ **de poitrine** angina (pectoris).

angiome [ɑ̃ʒjom] *nm* angioma.

anglais, e [ɑ̃glɛ, -ɛz] *adj* English ♦ *nm* (*LING*) English ♦ *nm/f*: **A~, e** Englishman/woman; **les A~** the English; **filer à l'~e** to take French leave; **à l'~e** (*CULIN*) boiled.

anglaises [ɑ̃glɛz] *nfpl* (*cheveux*) ringlets.

angle [ɑ̃gl(ə)] *nm* angle; (*coin*) corner; ~ **droit/obtus/aigu/mort** right/obtuse/acute/dead angle.

Angleterre [ɑ̃glətɛr] *nf*: **l'~** England.

anglican, e [ɑ̃glikɑ̃, -an] *adj, nm/f* Anglican.

anglicanisme [ɑ̃glikanism(ə)] *nm* Anglicanism.

anglicisme [ɑ̃glisism(ə)] *nm* anglicism.

angliciste [ɑ̃glisist(ə)] *nm/f* English scholar; (*étudiant*) student of English.

anglo... [ɑ̃glo] *préfixe* Anglo-, anglo(-).

anglo-américain, e [ɑ̃gloamerikɛ̃, -ɛn] *adj* Anglo-American ♦ *nm* (*LING*) American English.

anglo-arabe [ɑ̃glɔarab] *adj* Anglo-Arab.

anglo-canadien, ne [ɑ̃glɔkanadjɛ̃, -ɛn] *adj* Anglo-Canadian ♦ *nm* (*LING*) Canadian English.

anglo-normand, e [ɑ̃glɔnɔrmɑ̃, -ɑ̃d] *adj*

Anglo-Norman; **les îles ~es** the Channel Islands.

anglophile [ɑ̃glɔfil] *adj* anglophilic.

anglophobe [ɑ̃glɔfɔb] *adj* anglophobic.

anglophone [ɑ̃glɔfɔn] *adj* English-speaking.

anglo-saxon, ne [ɑ̃glɔsaksɔ̃, -ɔn] *adj* Anglo-Saxon.

angoissant, e [ɑ̃gwasɑ̃, -ɑ̃t] *adj* harrowing.

angoisse [ɑ̃gwas] *nf*: **l'~** anguish *no pl*.

angoissé, e [ɑ̃gwase] *adj* anguished; (*personne*) full of anxieties *ou* hang-ups (*fam*).

angoisser [ɑ̃gwase] *vt* to harrow, cause anguish to ♦ *vi* to worry, fret.

Angola [ɑ̃gɔla] *nm*: **l'~** Angola.

angolais, e [ɑ̃gɔlɛ, -ez] *adj* Angolan.

angora [ɑ̃gɔra] *adj, nm* angora.

anguille [ɑ̃gij] *nf* eel; **~ de mer** conger (eel); **il y a ~ sous roche** (*fig*) there's something going on, there's something beneath all this.

angulaire [ɑ̃gylɛr] *adj* angular.

anguleux, euse [ɑ̃gylø, -øz] *adj* angular.

anhydride [anidrid] *nm* anhydride.

anicroche [anikrɔʃ] *nf* hitch, snag.

animal, e, aux [animal, -o] *adj, nm* animal; **~ domestique/sauvage** domestic/wild animal.

animalier [animalje] *adj*: **peintre ~** animal painter.

animateur, trice [animatœr, -tris] *nm/f* (*de télévision*) host; (*de music-hall*) compère; (*de groupe*) leader, organizer; (*CINÉ: technicien*) animator.

animation [animɑsjɔ̃] *nf* (*voir animé*) busyness; liveliness; (*CINÉ: technique*) animation; (*activité*): **~s** *nfpl* activities; **centre d'~** ≈ community centre.

animé, e [anime] *adj* (*rue, lieu*) busy, lively; (*conversation, réunion*) lively, animated; (*opposé à inanimé, aussi LING*) animate.

animer [anime] *vt* (*ville, soirée*) to liven up, enliven; (*mettre en mouvement*) to drive; (*stimuler*) to drive, impel; **s'~** *vi* to liven up, come to life.

animosité [animozite] *nf* animosity.

anis [ani] *nm* (*CULIN*) aniseed; (*BOT*) anise.

anisette [anizɛt] *nf* anisette.

Ankara [ɑ̃kara] *n* Ankara.

ankyloser [ɑ̃kiloze]: **s'~** *vi* to get stiff, ankylose.

annales [anal] *nfpl* annals.

anneau, x [ano] *nm* ring; (*de chaîne*) link; (*SPORT*): **exercices aux ~x** ring exercises.

année [ane] *nf* year; **souhaiter la bonne ~ à qn** to wish sb a Happy New Year; **tout au long de l'~** all year long; **d'une ~ à l'autre** from one year to the next; **d'~ en ~** from year to year; **l'~ scolaire/fiscale** the school/tax year.

année-lumière, *pl* **années-lumières** [anelymjɛr] *nf* light year.

annexe [anɛks(ə)] *adj* (*problème*) related; (*document*) appended; (*salle*) adjoining ♦ *nf* (*bâtiment*) annex(e); (*de document, ouvrage*) annex, appendix; (*jointe à une lettre, un dossier*) enclosure.

annexer [anɛkse] *vt* to annex; **s'~** (*pays*) to annex; **~ qch à** (*joindre*) to append sth to.

annexion [anɛksjɔ̃] *nf* annexation.

annihiler [aniile] *vt* to annihilate.

anniversaire [anivɛrsɛr] *nm* birthday; (*d'un événement, bâtiment*) anniversary ♦ *adj*: **jour ~** anniversary.

annonce [anɔ̃s] *nf* announcement; (*signe, indice*) sign; (*aussi*: **~ publicitaire**) advertisement; (*CARTES*) declaration; **~ personnelle** personal message; **les petites ~s** the small *ou* classified ads.

annoncer [anɔ̃se] *vt* to announce; (*être le signe de*) to herald; (*CARTES*) to declare; **je vous annonce que ...** I wish to tell you that ...; **s'~ bien/difficile** to look promising/difficult; **~ la couleur** (*fig*) to lay one's cards on the table.

annonceur, euse [anɔ̃sœr, -øz] *nm/f* (*TV, RADIO: speaker*) announcer; (*publicitaire*) advertiser.

annonciateur, trice [anɔ̃sjatœr, -tris] *adj*: **d'un événement** presaging an event.

Annonciation [anɔ̃sjasjɔ̃] *nf*: **l'~** (*REL*) the Annunciation; (*jour*) Annunciation Day.

annotation [anɔtasjɔ̃] *nf* annotation.

annoter [anɔte] *vt* to annotate.

annuaire [anɥɛr] *nm* yearbook, annual; **~ téléphonique** (telephone) directory, phone book.

annuel, le [anɥɛl] *adj* annual, yearly.

annuellement [anɥɛlmɑ̃] *adv* annually, yearly.

annuité [anɥite] *nf* annual instalment.

annulaire [anɥlɛr] *nm* ring *ou* third finger.

annulation [anɥlasjɔ̃] *nf* cancellation; annulment; quashing, repeal.

annuler [anɥle] *vt* (*rendez-vous, voyage*) to cancel, call off; (*mariage*) to annul; (*jugement*) to quash (*BRIT*), repeal (*US*); (*résultats*) to declare void; (*MATH, PHYSIQUE*) to cancel out; **s'~** to cancel each other out.

anoblir [anɔblir] *vt* to ennoble.

anode [anɔd] *nf* anode.

anodin, e [anɔdɛ̃, -in] *adj* harmless; (*sans importance*) insignificant, trivial.

anomalie [anɔmali] *nf* anomaly.

ânon [anɔ̃] *nm* baby donkey; (*petit âne*) little donkey.

ânonner [anɔne] *vi, vt* to read in a drone; (*hésiter*) to read in a fumbling manner.

anonymat [anɔnima] *nm* anonymity; **garder l'~** to remain anonymous.

anonyme [anɔnim] *adj* anonymous; (*fig*) impersonal.

anonymement [anɔnimmɑ̃] *adv* anonymously.

anorak [anɔrak] *nm* anorak.

anorexie [anɔrɛksi] *nf* anorexia.

anorexique [anɔrɛksik] *adj, nm/f* anorexic.

anormal, e, aux [anɔʀmal, -o] *adj* abnormal; (*insolite*) unusual, abnormal.

anormalement [anɔʀmalmɑ̃] *adv* abnormally; unusually.

ANPE *sigle f* (= *Agence nationale pour l'emploi*) *national employment agency* (*functions include job creation*).

anse [ɑ̃s] *nf* handle; (*GÉO*) cove.

antagonisme [ɑ̃tagɔnism(ə)] *nm* antagonism.

antagoniste [ɑ̃tagɔnist(ə)] *adj* antagonistic ♦ *nm* antagonist.

antan [ɑ̃tɑ̃]: **d'~** *adj* of yesteryear, of long ago.

antarctique [ɑ̃taʀktik] *adj* Antarctic ♦ *nm*: **l'A~** the Antarctic; **le cercle A~** the Antarctic Circle; **l'océan A~** the Antarctic Ocean.

antécédent [ɑ̃tesedɑ̃] *nm* (*LING*) antecedent; **~s** *nmpl* (*MÉD etc*) past history *sg*; **~s professionnels** record, career to date.

antédiluvien, ne [ɑ̃tedilyvjɛ̃, -ɛn] *adj* (*fig*) ancient, antediluvian.

antenne [ɑ̃tɛn] *nf* (*de radio, télévision*) aerial; (*d'insecte*) antenna (*pl* -ae), feeler; (*poste avancé*) outpost; (*petite succursale*) sub-branch; **sur l'~** on the air; **passer à/avoir l'~** to go/be on the air; **2 heures d'~** 2 hours' broadcasting time; **hors ~** off the air; **~ chirurgicale** (*MIL*) advance surgical unit.

antépénultième [ɑ̃tepenyltjɛm] *adj* antepenultimate.

antérieur, e [ɑ̃teʀjœʀ] *adj* (*d'avant*) previous, earlier; (*de devant*) front; **~ à** prior *ou* previous to; **passé/futur ~** (*LING*) past/future anterior.

antérieurement [ɑ̃teʀjœʀmɑ̃] *adv* earlier; (*précédemment*) previously; **~ à** prior *ou* previous to.

antériorité [ɑ̃teʀjɔʀite] *nf* precedence (*in time*).

anthologie [ɑ̃tɔlɔʒi] *nf* anthology.

anthracite [ɑ̃tʀasit] *nm* anthracite ♦ *adj*: **(gris) ~ charcoal** (grey).

anthropologie [ɑ̃tʀɔpɔlɔʒi] *nf* anthropology.

anthropologue [ɑ̃tʀɔpɔlɔg] *nm/f* anthropologist.

anthropomorphisme [ɑ̃tʀɔpɔmɔʀfism(ə)] *nm* anthropomorphism.

anthropophage [ɑ̃tʀɔpɔfaʒ] *adj* cannibalistic.

anthropophagie [ɑ̃tʀɔpɔfaʒi] *nf* cannibalism, anthropophagy.

anti... [ɑ̃ti] *préfixe* anti....

antiaérien, ne [ɑ̃tiaeʀjɛ̃, -ɛn] *adj* anti-aircraft; **abri ~** air-raid shelter.

antialcoolique [ɑ̃tialkɔlik] *adj* anti-alcohol; **ligue ~** temperance league.

antiatomique [ɑ̃tiatɔmik] *adj*: **abri ~** fallout shelter.

antibiotique [ɑ̃tibjɔtik] *nm* antibiotic.

antibrouillard [ɑ̃tibʀujaʀ] *adj*: **phare ~** fog lamp.

antibruit [ɑ̃tibʀɥi] *adj inv*: **mur ~** (*sur autoroute*) sound-muffling wall.

antibuée [ɑ̃tibɥe] *adj inv*: **dispositif ~** demister; **bombe ~** demister spray.

anticancéreux, euse [ɑ̃tikɑ̃seʀø, -øz] *adj* cancer *cpd*.

anticasseur(s) [ɑ̃tikɑsœʀ] *adj*: **loi/mesure ~** law/measure against damage done by demonstrators.

antichambre [ɑ̃tiʃɑ̃bʀ(ə)] *nf* antechamber, anteroom; **faire ~** to wait (for an audience).

antichar [ɑ̃tiʃaʀ] *adj* antitank.

antichoc [ɑ̃tiʃɔk] *adj* shockproof.

anticipation [ɑ̃tisipasjɔ̃] *nf* anticipation; (*COMM*) payment in advance; **par ~** in anticipation, in advance; **livre/film d'~** science fiction book/film.

anticipé, e [ɑ̃tisipe] *adj* (*règlement, paiement*) early, in advance; (*joie etc*) anticipated, early; **avec mes remerciements ~s** thanking you in advance *ou* anticipation.

anticiper [ɑ̃tisipe] *vt* to anticipate, foresee; (*paiement*) to pay *ou* make in advance ♦ *vi* to look *ou* think ahead; (*en racontant*) to jump ahead; (*prévoir*) to anticipate; **~ sur** to anticipate.

anticlérical, e, aux [ɑ̃tikleʀikal, -o] *adj* anticlerical.

anticoagulant, e [ɑ̃tikɔagylɑ̃, -ɑ̃t] *adj, nm* anticoagulant.

anticolonialisme [ɑ̃tikɔlɔnjalism(ə)] *nm* anticolonialism.

anticonceptionnel, le [ɑ̃tikɔ̃sɛpsjɔnɛl] *adj* contraceptive.

anticonformisme [ɑ̃tikɔ̃fɔʀmism(ə)] *nm* nonconformism.

anticonstitutionnel, le [ɑ̃tikɔ̃stitysjɔnɛl] *adj* unconstitutional.

anticorps [ɑ̃tikɔʀ] *nm* antibody.

anticyclone [ɑ̃tisiklon] *nm* anticyclone.

antidater [ɑ̃tidate] *vt* to backdate, predate.

antidémocratique [ɑ̃tidemɔkʀatik] *adj* antidemocratic; (*peu démocratique*) undemocratic.

antidérapant, e [ɑ̃tideʀapɑ̃, -ɑ̃t] *adj* nonskid.

antidopage [ɑ̃tidɔpaʒ], **antidoping** [ɑ̃tidɔpiŋ] *adj* (*lutte*) antidoping; (*contrôle*) dope *cpd*.

antidote [ɑ̃tidɔt] *nm* antidote.

antienne [ɑ̃tjɛn] *nf* (*fig*) chant, refrain.

antigang [ɑ̃tigɑ̃g] *adj inv*: **brigade ~** commando unit.

antigel [ɑ̃tiʒɛl] *nm* antifreeze.

antigène [ɑ̃tiʒɛn] *nm* antigen.

antigouvernemental, e, aux [ɑ̃tiguvɛʀnəmãtal, -o] *adj* antigovernment.

Antigua et Barbude [ɑ̃tigaebaʀbyd] *nf* Antigua and Barbuda.

antihistaminique [ɑ̃tiistaminik] *nm* antihistamine.

anti-inflammatoire [ɑ̃tiɛ̃flamatwaʀ] *adj* antiinflammatory.

anti-inflationniste [ɑ̃tiɛ̃flasjɔnist(ə)] *adj* antiinflationary.

antillais, e [ɑ̃tijɛ, -ɛz] *adj* West Indian.

Antilles [ɑ̃tij] *nfpl*: **les ~** the West Indies; **les**

Grandes/Petites ~ the Greater/Lesser Antilles.
antilope [ɑ̃tilɔp] *nf* antelope.
antimilitarisme [ɑ̃timilitaʀism(ə)] *nm* antimilitarism.
antimilitariste [ɑ̃timilitaʀist(ə)] *adj* antimilitarist.
antimissile [ɑ̃timisil] *adj* antimissile.
antimite(s) [ɑ̃timit] *adj, nm*: **(produit)** ~ mothproofer, moth repellent.
antinucléaire [ɑ̃tinykleɛʀ] *adj* antinuclear.
antioxydant [ɑ̃tiɔksidɑ̃] *nm* antioxidant.
antiparasite [ɑ̃tipaʀazit] *adj* (*RADIO, TV*) anti-interference; **dispositif** ~ suppressor.
antipathie [ɑ̃tipati] *nf* antipathy.
antipathique [ɑ̃tipatik] *adj* unpleasant, disagreeable.
antipelliculaire [ɑ̃tipelikylɛʀ] *adj* antidandruff.
antiphrase [ɑ̃tifʀɑz] *nf*: **par** ~ ironically.
antipodes [ɑ̃tipɔd] *nmpl* (*GÉO*): **les** ~ the antipodes; (*fig*): **être aux** ~ **de** to be the opposite extreme of.
antipoison [ɑ̃tipwazɔ̃] *adj inv*: **centre** ~ poison centre.
antipoliomyélitique [ɑ̃tipɔljɔmjelitik] *adj* polio *cpd*.
antiprotectionniste [ɑ̃tipʀɔtɛksjɔnist(ə)] *adj* free-trade.
antiquaire [ɑ̃tikɛʀ] *nm/f* antique dealer.
antique [ɑ̃tik] *adj* antique; (*très vieux*) ancient, antiquated.
antiquité [ɑ̃tikite] *nf* (*objet*) antique; **l'A**~ Antiquity; **magasin/marchand d'**~**s** antique shop/dealer.
antirabique [ɑ̃tiʀabik] *adj* rabies *cpd*.
antiraciste [ɑ̃tiʀasist(ə)] *adj* antiracist, antiracialist.
antireflet [ɑ̃tiʀəflɛ] *adj inv* (*verres*) antireflective.
antirépublicain, e [ɑ̃tiʀepyblikɛ̃, -ɛn] *adj* antirepublican.
antirides [ɑ̃tiʀid] *adj* (*crème*) antiwrinkle.
antirouille [ɑ̃tiʀuj] *adj inv*: **peinture** ~ antirust paint; **traitement** ~ rustproofing.
antisémite [ɑ̃tisemit] *adj* anti-Semitic.
antisémitisme [ɑ̃tisemitism(ə)] *nm* anti-Semitism.
antiseptique [ɑ̃tisɛptik] *adj, nm* antiseptic.
antisocial, e, aux [ɑ̃tisɔsjal, -o] *adj* antisocial.
antispasmodique [ɑ̃tispasmɔdik] *adj, nm* antispasmodic.
antisportif, ive [ɑ̃tispɔrtif, -iv] *adj* unsporting; (*hostile au sport*) against sport, antisport.
antitétanique [ɑ̃titetanik] *adj* tetanus *cpd*.
antithèse [ɑ̃titɛz] *nf* antithesis.
antitrust [ɑ̃titʀœst] *adj inv* (*loi, mesures*) antimonopoly.
antituberculeux, euse [ɑ̃titybɛʀkylø, -øz] *adj* tuberculosis *cpd*.
antitussif, ive [ɑ̃titysif, -iv] *adj* antitussive,

cough *cpd*.
antivariolique [ɑ̃tivaʀjɔlik] *adj* smallpox *cpd*.
antivol [ɑ̃tivɔl] *adj, nm*: **(dispositif)** ~ antitheft device; (*pour vélo*) padlock.
antonyme [ɑ̃tɔnim] *nm* antonym.
antre [ɑ̃tʀ(ə)] *nm* den, lair.
anus [anys] *nm* anus.
Anvers [ɑ̃vɛʀ] *n* Antwerp.
anxiété [ɑ̃ksjete] *nf* anxiety.
anxieusement [ɑ̃ksjøzmɑ̃] *adv* anxiously.
anxieux, euse [ɑ̃ksjø, -øz] *adj* anxious, worried; **être** ~ **de faire** to be anxious to do.
AOC *sigle f* (= *Appellation d'origine contrôlée*) guarantee of quality of wine.

> **AOC** is the highest French wine classification. It indicates that the wine meets strict requirements concerning the vineyard of origin, the type of vine grown, the method of production, and the volume of alcohol present; *see also* **VDQS**.

aorte [aɔʀt(ə)] *nf* aorta.
août [u] *nm* August; *voir aussi* **juillet**; **Assomption**.
aoûtien, ne [ausjɛ̃, -ɛn] *nm/f* August holiday-maker.
AP *sigle f* = **Assistance publique**.
apaisant, e [apezɑ̃, -ɑ̃t] *adj* soothing.
apaisement [apezmɑ̃] *nm* calming; soothing; (*aussi POL*) appeasement; ~**s** *nmpl* soothing reassurances; (*pour calmer*) pacifying words.
apaiser [apeze] *vt* (*colère*) to calm, quell, soothe; (*faim*) to appease, assuage; (*douleur*) to soothe; (*personne*) to calm (down), pacify; **s'**~ *vi* (*tempête, bruit*) to die down, subside.
apanage [apanaʒ] *nm*: **être l'**~ **de** to be the privilege *ou* prerogative of.
aparté [apaʀte] *nm* (*THÉÂT*) aside; (*entretien*) private conversation; **en** ~ *adv* in an aside (*BRIT*); (*entretien*) in private.
apartheid [apaʀtɛd] *nm* apartheid.
apathie [apati] *nf* apathy.
apathique [apatik] *adj* apathetic.
apatride [apatʀid] *nm/f* stateless person.
Apennins [apɛnɛ̃] *nmpl*: **les** ~ the Apennines.
apercevoir [apɛʀsəvwaʀ] *vt* to see; **s'**~ **de** *vt* to notice; **s'**~ **que** to notice that; **sans s'en** ~ without realizing *ou* noticing.
aperçu, e [apɛʀsy] *pp de* **apercevoir** ♦ *nm* (*vue d'ensemble*) general survey; (*intuition*) insight.
apéritif, ive [apeʀitif, -iv] *adj* which stimulates the appetite ♦ *nm* (*boisson*) aperitif; (*réunion*) (pre-lunch *ou* -dinner) drinks *pl*; **prendre l'**~ to have drinks (before lunch *ou* dinner) *ou* an aperitif.
apesanteur [apəzɑ̃tœʀ] *nf* weightlessness.
à-peu-près [apøpʀɛ] *nm inv* (*péj*) vague approximation.
apeuré, e [apœʀe] *adj* frightened, scared.

aphasie [afazi] *nm* aphasia.

aphone [afɔn] *adj* voiceless.

aphorisme [afɔʀism(ə)] *nm* aphorism.

aphrodisiaque [afʀɔdizjak] *adj, nm* aphrodisiac.

aphte [aft(ə)] *nm* mouth ulcer.

aphteuse [aftøz] *adj f*: **fièvre** ~ foot-and-mouth disease.

à-pic [apik] *nm* cliff, drop.

apicole [apikɔl] *adj* beekeeping *cpd*.

apiculteur, trice [apikyltœʀ, -tʀis] *nm/f* beekeeper.

apiculture [apikyltyʀ] *nf* beekeeping, apiculture.

apitoiement [apitwamã] *nm* pity, compassion.

apitoyer [apitwaje] *vt* to move to pity; ~ **qn sur qn/qch** to move sb to pity for sb/over sth; **s'~ (sur qn/qch)** to feel pity *ou* compassion (for sb/over sth).

ap. J.-C. *abr* (= *après Jésus-Christ*) AD.

APL *sigle f* (= *aide personnalisée au logement*) *type of loan for house purchase.*

aplanir [aplaniʀ] *vt* to level; (*fig*) to smooth away, iron out.

aplati, e [aplati] *adj* flat, flattened.

aplatir [aplatiʀ] *vt* to flatten; **s'~** *vi* to become flatter; (*écrasé*) to be flattened; (*fig*) to lie flat on the ground; (: *fam*) to fall flat on one's face; (: *péj*) to grovel.

aplomb [aplɔ̃] *nm* (*équilibre*) balance, equilibrium; (*fig*) self-assurance; (: *péj*) nerve; **d'~** *adv* steady; (*CONSTR*) plumb.

apocalypse [apɔkalips(ə)] *nf* apocalypse.

apocalyptique [apɔkaliptik] *adj* (*fig*) apocalyptic.

apocryphe [apɔkʀif] *adj* apocryphal.

apogée [apɔʒe] *nm* (*fig*) peak, apogee.

apolitique [apɔlitik] *adj* (*indifférent*) apolitical; (*indépendant*) unpolitical, non-political.

apologie [apɔlɔʒi] *nf* praise; (*JUR*) vindication.

apoplexie [apɔplɛksi] *nf* apoplexy.

a posteriori [apɔsteʀjɔʀi] *adv* after the event, with hindsight, a posteriori.

apostolat [apɔstɔla] *nm* (*REL*) apostolate, discipleship; (*gén*) evangelism.

apostolique [apɔstɔlik] *adj* apostolic.

apostrophe [apɔstʀɔf] *nf* (*signe*) apostrophe; (*appel*) interpellation.

apostropher [apɔstʀɔfe] *vt* (*interpeller*) to shout at, address sharply.

apothéose [apɔteoz] *nf* pinnacle (of achievement); (*MUS etc*) grand finale.

apothicaire [apɔtikɛʀ] *nm* apothecary.

apôtre [apotʀ(ə)] *nm* apostle, disciple.

Appalaches [apalaʃ] *nmpl*: **les** ~ the Appalachian Mountains.

appalachien, ne [apalaʃjɛ̃, -ɛn] *adj* Appalachian.

apparaître [apaʀɛtʀ(ə)] *vi* to appear ♦ *vb avec attribut* to appear, seem.

apparat [apaʀa] *nm*: **tenue/dîner d'~** ceremonial dress/dinner.

appareil [apaʀɛj] *nm* (*outil, machine*) piece of apparatus, device; (*électrique etc*) appliance; (*politique, syndical*) machinery; (*avion*) (aero)plane (*BRIT*), (air)plane (*US*), aircraft *inv*; (*téléphonique*) telephone; (*dentier*) brace (*BRIT*), braces (*US*); ~ **digestif/reproducteur** digestive/reproductive system *ou* apparatus; **l'~ productif** the means of production; **qui est à l'~?** who's speaking?; **dans le plus simple** ~ in one's birthday suit; ~ **(photographique)** camera; ~ **24 x 36** *ou* **petit format** 35 mm camera.

appareillage [apaʀɛjaʒ] *nm* (*appareils*) equipment; (*NAVIG*) casting off, getting under way.

appareiller [apaʀeje] *vi* (*NAVIG*) to cast off, get under way ♦ *vt* (*assortir*) to match up.

appareil-photo, *pl* **appareils-photos** [apaʀɛjfɔto] *nm* camera.

apparemment [apaʀamã] *adv* apparently.

apparence [apaʀɑ̃s] *nf* appearance; **malgré les** ~**s** despite appearances; **en** ~ apparently, seemingly.

apparent, e [apaʀɑ̃, -ɑ̃t] *adj* visible; (*évident*) obvious; (*superficiel*) apparent; **coutures** ~**es** topstitched seams; **poutres** ~**es** exposed beams.

apparenté, e [apaʀɑ̃te] *adj*: ~ **à** related to; (*fig*) similar to.

apparenter [apaʀɑ̃te]: **s'~ à** *vt* to be similar to.

apparier [apaʀje] *vt* (*gants*) to pair, match.

appariteur [apaʀitœʀ] *nm* attendant, porter (*in French universities*).

apparition [apaʀisjɔ̃] *nf* appearance; (*surnaturelle*) apparition; **faire son** ~ to appear.

appartement [apaʀtəmã] *nm* flat (*BRIT*), apartment (*US*).

appartenance [apaʀtənɑ̃s] *nf*: ~ **à** belonging to, membership of.

appartenir [apaʀtəniʀ]: ~ **à** *vt* to belong to; (*faire partie de*) to belong to, be a member of; **il lui appartient de** it is up to him to.

appartiendrai [apaʀtjɛ̃dʀe], **appartiens** [apaʀtjɛ̃] *etc voir* **appartenir**.

apparu, e [apaʀy] *pp de* **apparaître**.

appas [apɑ] *nmpl* (*d'une femme*) charms.

appât [apɑ] *nm* (*PÊCHE*) bait; (*fig*) lure, bait.

appâter [apɑte] *vt* (*hameçon*) to bait; (*poisson, fig*) to lure, entice.

appauvrir [apovʀiʀ] *vt* to impoverish; **s'~** *vi* to grow poorer, become impoverished.

appauvrissement [apovʀismã] *nm* impoverishment.

appel [apɛl] *nm* call; (*nominal*) roll call; (: *SCOL*) register; (*MIL: recrutement*) call-up; (*JUR*) appeal; **faire** ~ **à** (*invoquer*) to appeal to; (*avoir recours à*) to call on; (*nécessiter*) to call for, require; **faire** *ou* **interjeter** ~ (*JUR*) to appeal, lodge an appeal; **faire l'~** to call the roll; to call the register; **indicatif d'~** call sign; **numéro d'~** (*TÉL*) number; **produit**

d'~ (COMM) loss leader; **sans ~** (fig) final, irrevocable; **~ d'air** in-draught; **~ d'offres** (COMM) invitation to tender; **faire un ~ de phares** to flash one's headlights; **~ (téléphonique)** (tele)phone call.

appelé [aple] nm (MIL) conscript.

appeler [aple] vt to call; (TÉL) to call, ring; (faire venir: médecin etc) to call, send for; (fig: nécessiter) to call for, demand; **~ au secours** to call for help; **~ qn à l'aide** ou **au secours** to call to sb for help; **~ qn à un poste/des fonctions** to appoint sb to a post/assign duties to sb; **être appelé à** (fig) to be destined to; **~ qn à comparaître** (JUR) to summon sb to appear; **en ~ à** to appeal to; **s'~: elle s'appelle Gabrielle** her name is Gabrielle, she's called Gabrielle; **comment ça s'appelle?** what is it ou that called?

appellation [apelɑsjɔ̃] nf designation, appellation; **vin d'~ contrôlée** "appellation contrôlée" wine, wine guaranteed of a certain quality.

appelle [apel] etc vb voir **appeler**.

appendice [apɛ̃dis] nm appendix.

appendicite [apɑ̃disit] nf appendicitis.

appentis [apɑ̃ti] nm lean-to.

appert [apɛʀ] vb: **il ~ que** it appears that, it is evident that.

appesantir [apzɑ̃tiʀ]: **s'~** vi to grow heavier; **s'~ sur** (fig) to dwell at length on.

appétissant, e [apetisɑ̃, -ɑ̃t] adj appetizing, mouth-watering.

appétit [apeti] nm appetite; **couper l'~ à qn** to take away sb's appetite; **bon ~!** enjoy your meal!

applaudimètre [aplodimɛtʀ(ə)] nm applause meter.

applaudir [aplodiʀ] vt to applaud ♦ vi to applaud, clap; **~ à** vt (décision) to applaud, commend.

applaudissements [aplodismɑ̃] nmpl applause sg, clapping sg.

applicable [aplikabl(ə)] adj applicable.

applicateur [aplikatœʀ] nm applicator.

application [aplikɑsjɔ̃] nf application; (d'une loi) enforcement; **mettre en ~** to implement.

applique [aplik] nf wall lamp.

appliqué, e [aplike] adj (élève etc) industrious, assiduous; (science) applied.

appliquer [aplike] vt to apply; (loi) to enforce; (donner: gifle, châtiment) to give; **s'~** vi (élève etc) to apply o.s.; **s'~ à** (loi, remarque) to apply to; **s'~ à faire qch** to apply o.s. to doing sth, take pains to do sth; **s'~ sur** (coïncider avec) to fit over.

appoint [apwɛ̃] nm (extra) contribution ou help; **avoir/faire l'~** (en payant) to have/give the right change ou money; **chauffage d'~** extra heating.

appointements [apwɛ̃tmɑ̃] nmpl salary sg, stipend (surtout REL).

appointer [apwɛ̃te] vt: **être appointé à**

l'année/au mois to be paid yearly/monthly.

appontage [apɔ̃taʒ] nm landing (on an aircraft carrier).

appontement [apɔ̃tmɑ̃] nm landing stage, wharf.

apponter [apɔ̃te] vi (avion, hélicoptère) to land.

apport [apɔʀ] nm supply; (argent, biens etc) contribution.

apporter [apɔʀte] vt to bring; (preuve) to give, provide; (modification) to make; (suj: remarque) to contribute, add.

apposer [apoze] vt to append; (sceau etc) to affix.

apposition [apozisjɔ̃] nf appending; affixing; (LING): **en ~** in apposition.

appréciable [apʀesjabl(ə)] adj (important) appreciable, significant.

appréciation [apʀesjɑsjɔ̃] nf appreciation; estimation, assessment; **~s** nfpl (avis) assessment sg, appraisal sg.

apprécier [apʀesje] vt to appreciate; (évaluer) to estimate, assess; **j'apprécierais que tu ...** I should appreciate (it) if you ....

appréhender [apʀeɑ̃de] vt (craindre) to dread; (arrêter) to apprehend; **~ que** to fear that; **~ de faire** to dread doing.

appréhensif, ive [apʀeɑ̃sif, -iv] adj apprehensive.

appréhension [apʀeɑ̃sjɔ̃] nf apprehension.

apprendre [apʀɑ̃dʀ(ə)] vt to learn; (événement, résultats) to learn of, hear of; **~ qch à qn** (informer) to tell sb (of) sth; (enseigner) to teach sb sth; **tu me l'apprends!** that's news to me!; **~ à faire qch** to learn to do sth; **~ à qn à faire qch** to teach sb to do sth.

apprenti, e [apʀɑ̃ti] nm/f apprentice; (fig) novice, beginner.

apprentissage [apʀɑ̃tisaʒ] nm learning; (COMM, SCOL: période) apprenticeship; **école** ou **centre d'~** training school ou centre; **faire l'~ de qch** (fig) to be initiated into sth.

apprêt [apʀɛ] nm (sur un cuir, une étoffe) dressing; (sur un mur) size; (sur un papier) finish; **sans ~** (fig) without artifice, unaffectedly.

apprêté, e [apʀete] adj (fig) affected.

apprêter [apʀete] vt to dress, finish; **s'~** vi: **s'~ à qch/à faire qch** to prepare for sth/for doing sth.

appris, e [apʀi, -iz] pp de **apprendre**.

apprivoisé, e [apʀivwaze] adj tame, tamed.

apprivoiser [apʀivwaze] vt to tame.

approbateur, trice [apʀɔbatœʀ, -tʀis] adj approving.

approbatif, ive [apʀɔbatif, -iv] adj approving.

approbation [apʀɔbɑsjɔ̃] nf approval; **digne d'~** (conduite, travail) praiseworthy, commendable.

approchant, e [apʀɔʃɑ̃, -ɑ̃t] adj similar, close; **quelque chose d'~** something similar.

approche [apʀɔʃ] nf approaching; (arrivée, attitude) approach; **~s** nfpl (abords) surroundings; **à l'~ du bateau/de l'ennemi** as the ship/enemy approached ou drew near; **l'~ d'un problème** the approach to a problem; **travaux d'~** (*fig*) manoeuvrings.

approché, e [apʀɔʃe] *adj* approximate.

approcher [apʀɔʃe] *vi* to approach, come near ♦ *vt* (*vedette, artiste*) to come close to, approach; (*rapprocher*): ~ **qch (de qch)** to bring *ou* put *ou* move sth near (to sth); ~ **de** *vt* to draw near to; (*quantité, moment*) to approach; **s'~ de** *vt* to approach, go *ou* come *ou* move near to; **approchez-vous** come *ou* go nearer.

approfondi, e [apʀɔfɔ̃di] *adj* thorough, detailed.

approfondir [apʀɔfɔ̃diʀ] *vt* to deepen; (*question*) to go further into; **sans** ~ without going too deeply into it.

appropriation [apʀɔpʀijasjɔ̃] *nf* appropriation.

approprié, e [apʀɔpʀije] *adj*: ~ **(à)** appropriate (to), suited to.

approprier [apʀɔpʀije] *vt* (*adapter*) adapt; **s'~** *vt* to appropriate, take over.

approuver [apʀuve] *vt* to agree with; (*autoriser: loi, projet*) to approve, pass; (*trouver louable*) to approve of; **je vous approuve entièrement/ne vous approuve pas** I agree with you entirely/don't agree with you; **lu et approuvé** (read and) approved.

approvisionnement [apʀɔvizjɔnmɑ̃] *nm* supplying; (*provisions*) supply, stock.

approvisionner [apʀɔvizjɔne] *vt* to supply; (*compte bancaire*) to pay funds into; ~ **qn en** to supply sb with; **s'~** *vi*: **s'~ dans un certain magasin/au marché** to shop in a certain shop/at the market; **s'~ en** to stock up with.

approximatif, ive [apʀɔksimatif, -iv] *adj* approximate, rough; (*imprécis*) vague.

approximation [apʀɔksimasjɔ̃] *nf* approximation.

approximativement [apʀɔksimativmɑ̃] *adv* approximately, roughly; vaguely.

appt *abr* = **appartement**.

appui [apɥi] *nm* support; **prendre** ~ **sur** to lean on; (*objet*) to rest on; **point d'~** fulcrum; (*fig*) something to lean on; **à l'~ de** (*pour prouver*) in support of; **à l'~** *adv* to support one's argument; **l'~ de la fenêtre** the windowsill, the window ledge.

appuie [apɥi] *etc vb voir* **appuyer**.

appui-tête, appuie-tête [apɥitɛt] *nm inv* headrest.

appuyé, e [apɥije] *adj* (*regard*) meaningful; (*: insistant*) intent, insistent; (*excessif: politesse, compliment*) exaggerated, overdone.

appuyer [apɥije] *vt* (*poser*): ~ **qch sur/contre/ à** to lean *ou* rest sth on/against/on; (*soutenir: personne, demande*) to support, back (up) ♦ *vi*: ~ **sur** (*bouton, frein*) to press, push; (*mot, détail*) to stress, emphasize; (*suj: chose: peser sur*) to rest (heavily) on, press against; **s'~ sur** *vt* to lean on; (*compter sur*) to rely on;

s'~ sur qn to lean on sb; ~ **contre** (*toucher: mur, porte*) to lean *ou* rest against; ~ **à droite** *ou* **sur sa droite** to bear (to the) right; ~ **sur le champignon** to put one's foot down.

apr. *abr* = **après**.

âpre [ɑpʀ(ə)] *adj* acrid, pungent; (*fig*) harsh; (*lutte*) bitter; ~ **au gain** grasping, greedy.

après [apʀɛ] *prép* after ♦ *adv* afterwards; **2 heures** ~ 2 hours later; ~ **qu'il est parti/ avoir fait** after he left/having done; **courir** ~ **qn** to run after sb; **crier** ~ **qn** to shout at sb; **être toujours** ~ **qn** (*critiquer etc*) to be always on at sb; ~ **quoi** after which; **d'~** *prép* (*selon*) according to; **d'~ lui** according to him; **d'~ moi** in my opinion; ~ **coup** *adv* after the event, afterwards; ~ **tout** *adv* (*au fond*) after all; **et (puis)** ~? so what?

après-demain [apʀɛdmɛ̃] *adv* the day after tomorrow.

après-guerre [apʀɛgɛʀ] *nm* post-war years *pl*; **d'~** *adj* post-war.

après-midi [apʀɛmidi] *nm ou nf inv* afternoon.

après-rasage [apʀɛʀazaʒ] *nm inv*: **(lotion)** ~ after-shave (lotion).

après-ski [apʀɛski] *nm inv* (*chaussure*) snow boot; (*moment*) après-ski.

après-vente [apʀɛvɑ̃t] *adj inv* after-sales *cpd*.

âpreté [ɑpʀəte] *nf* (*voir âpre*) pungency; harshness; bitterness.

à-propos [apʀopo] *nm* (*d'une remarque*) aptness; **faire preuve d'~** to show presence of mind, do the right thing; **avec** ~ suitably, aptly.

apte [apt(ə)] *adj*: ~ **à qch/faire qch** capable of sth/doing sth; ~ **(au service)** (*MIL*) fit (for service).

aptitude [aptityd] *nf* ability, aptitude.

apurer [apyʀe] *vt* (*COMM*) to clear.

aquaculture [akwakyltyʀ] *nf* fish farming.

aquaplanage [akwaplanaʒ] *nm* (*AUTO*) aquaplaning.

aquaplane [akwaplan] *nm* (*planche*) aquaplane; (*sport*) aquaplaning.

aquaplaning [akwaplaniŋ] *nm* aquaplaning.

aquarelle [akwaʀɛl] *nf* (*tableau*) watercolour (*BRIT*), watercolor (*US*); (*genre*) watercolo(u)rs *pl*, aquarelle.

aquarelliste [akwaʀelist(ə)] *nm/f* painter in watercolo(u)rs.

aquarium [akwaʀjɔm] *nm* aquarium.

aquatique [akwatik] *adj* aquatic, water *cpd*.

aqueduc [akdyk] *nm* aqueduct.

aqueux, euse [akø, -øz] *adj* aqueous.

aquilin [akilɛ̃] *adj m*: **nez** ~ aquiline nose.

AR *sigle m* (= *accusé de réception*): **lettre/paquet avec** ~ ≈ recorded delivery letter/parcel; (*AVIAT, RAIL etc*) = **aller (et) retour** ♦ *abr* (*AUTO*) = **arrière**.

arabe [aʀab] *adj* Arabic; (*désert, cheval*) Arabian; (*nation, peuple*) Arab ♦ *nm* (*LING*) Arabic ♦ *nm/f*: **A~** Arab.

arabesque [aʀabɛsk(ə)] *nf* arabesque.

Arabie [aʀabi] *nf*: l'~ Arabia; l'~ **Séoudite** *ou* **Séoudite** Saudi Arabia.

arable [aʀabl(ə)] *adj* arable.

arachide [aʀaʃid] *nf* groundnut (plant); (*graine*) peanut, groundnut.

araignée [aʀɛɲe] *nf* spider; ~ **de mer** spider crab.

araser [aʀaze] *vt* to level; (*en rabotant*) to plane (down).

aratoire [aʀatwaʀ] *adj*: **instrument** ~ ploughing implement.

arbalète [aʀbalɛt] *nf* crossbow.

arbitrage [aʀbitʀaʒ] *nm* refereeing; umpiring; arbitration.

arbitraire [aʀbitʀɛʀ] *adj* arbitrary.

arbitrairement [aʀbitʀɛʀmɑ̃] *adv* arbitrarily.

arbitre [aʀbitʀ(ə)] *nm* (*SPORT*) referee; (: *TENNIS, CRICKET*) umpire; (*fig*) arbiter, judge; (*JUR*) arbitrator.

arbitrer [aʀbitʀe] *vt* to referee; to umpire; to arbitrate.

arborer [aʀbɔʀe] *vt* to bear, display; (*avec ostentation*) to sport.

arborescence [aʀbɔʀesɑ̃s] *nf* tree structure.

arboricole [aʀbɔʀikɔl] *adj* (*animal*) arboreal; (*technique*) arboricultural.

arboriculture [aʀbɔʀikyltyʀ] *nf* arboriculture; ~ **fruitière** fruit (tree) growing.

arbre [aʀbʀ(ə)] *nm* tree; (*TECH*) shaft; ~ **à cames** (*AUTO*) camshaft; ~ **fruitier** fruit tree; ~ **généalogique** family tree; ~ **de Noël** Christmas tree; ~ **de transmission** (*AUTO*) driveshaft.

arbrisseau, x [aʀbʀiso] *nm* shrub.

arbuste [aʀbyst(ə)] *nm* small shrub, bush.

arc [aʀk] *nm* (*arme*) bow; (*GÉOM*) arc; (*ARCHIT*) arch; ~ **de cercle** arc of a circle; **en** ~ **de cercle** *adj* semi-circular.

arcade [aʀkad] *nf* arch(way); ~**s** *nfpl* arcade *sg*, arches; ~ **sourcilière** arch of the eyebrows.

arcanes [aʀkan] *nmpl* mysteries.

arc-boutant, pl arcs-boutants [aʀkbutɑ̃] *nm* flying buttress.

arc-bouter [aʀkbute]: **s'**~ *vi*: **s'**~ **contre** to lean *ou* press against.

arceau, x [aʀso] *nm* (*métallique etc*) hoop.

arc-en-ciel, pl arcs-en-ciel [aʀkɑ̃sjɛl] *nm* rainbow.

archaïque [aʀkaik] *adj* archaic.

archaïsme [aʀkaism(ə)] *nm* archaism.

archange [aʀkɑ̃ʒ] *nm* archangel.

arche [aʀʃ(ə)] *nf* arch; ~ **de Noé** Noah's Ark.

archéologie [aʀkeɔlɔʒi] *nf* arch(a)eology.

archéologique [aʀkeɔlɔʒik] *adj* arch(a)eological.

archéologue [aʀkeɔlɔg] *nm/f* arch(a)eologist.

archer [aʀʃe] *nm* archer.

archet [aʀʃɛ] *nm* bow.

archétype [aʀketip] *nm* archetype.

archevêché [aʀʃəveʃe] *nm* archbishopric; (*palais*) archbishop's palace.

archevêque [aʀʃəvɛk] *nm* archbishop.

archi... [aʀʃi] *préfixe* (*très*) dead, extra.

archibondé, e [aʀʃibɔ̃de] *adj* chock-a-block (*BRIT*), packed solid.

archiduc [aʀʃidyk] *nm* archduke.

archiduchesse [aʀʃidyʃɛs] *nf* archduchess.

archipel [aʀʃipɛl] *nm* archipelago.

archisimple [aʀʃisɛ̃pl(ə)] *adj* dead easy *ou* simple.

architecte [aʀʃitɛkt(ə)] *nm* architect.

architectural, e, aux [aʀʃitɛktyʀal, -o] *adj* architectural.

architecture [aʀʃitɛktyʀ] *nf* architecture.

archive [aʀʃiv] *nf* file; ~**s** *nfpl* archives.

archiver [aʀʃive] *vt* to file.

archiviste [aʀʃivist(ə)] *nm/f* archivist.

arçon [aʀsɔ̃] *nm voir* **cheval**.

arctique [aʀktik] *adj* Arctic ♦ *nm*: **l'A~** the Arctic; **le cercle A~** the Arctic Circle; **l'océan A~** the Arctic Ocean.

ardemment [aʀdamɑ̃] *adv* ardently, fervently.

ardent, e [aʀdɑ̃, -ɑ̃t] *adj* (*soleil*) blazing; (*fièvre*) raging; (*amour*) ardent, passionate; (*prière*) fervent.

ardeur [aʀdœʀ] *nf* blazing heat; (*fig*) fervour, ardour.

ardoise [aʀdwaz] *nf* slate.

ardu, e [aʀdy] *adj* arduous, difficult; (*pente*) steep, abrupt.

are [aʀ] *nm* are, 100 square metres.

arène [aʀɛn] *nf* arena; (*fig*): **l'**~ **politique/littéraire** the political/literary arena; ~**s** *nfpl* bull-ring *sg*.

arête [aʀɛt] *nf* (*de poisson*) bone; (*d'une montagne*) ridge; (*GÉOM etc*) edge (*where two faces meet*).

arg. *abr* = **argus**.

argent [aʀʒɑ̃] *nm* (*métal*) silver; (*monnaie*) money; (*couleur*) silver; **en avoir pour son** ~ to get value for money; **gagner beaucoup d'**~ to earn a lot of money; ~ **comptant** (hard) cash; ~ **liquide** ready money, (ready) cash; ~ **de poche** pocket money.

argenté, e [aʀʒɑ̃te] *adj* silver(y); (*métal*) silver-plated.

argenter [aʀʒɑ̃te] *vt* to silver(-plate).

argenterie [aʀʒɑ̃tʀi] *nf* silverware; (*en métal argenté*) silver plate.

argentin, e [aʀʒɑ̃tɛ̃, -in] *adj* (*son*) silvery; (*d'Argentine*) Argentinian, Argentine ♦ *nm/f*: **A~, e** Argentinian, Argentine.

Argentine [aʀʒɑ̃tin] *nf*: **l'**~ Argentina, the Argentine.

argile [aʀʒil] *nf* clay.

argileux, euse [aʀʒilø, -øz] *adj* clayey.

argot [aʀgo] *nm* slang.

Initially argot was the jargon of the criminal underworld, characterized by colourful images and distinctive intonation and designed to confuse the outsider. Some French authors write in argot and contribute to its diffusion and de-

velopment. More generally, the special vocabulary used by any social or professional group is also known as argot.

argotique [aʀgɔtik] *adj* slang *cpd*; (*très familier*) slangy.

arguer [aʀgɥe]: ~ **de** *vt* to put forward as a pretext *ou* reason; ~ **que** to argue that.

argument [aʀgymɑ̃] *nm* argument.

argumentaire [aʀgymɑ̃tɛʀ] *nm* list of sales points; (*brochure*) sales leaflet.

argumentation [aʀgymɑ̃tasjɔ̃] *nf* (*fait d'argumenter*) arguing; (*ensemble des arguments*) argument.

argumenter [aʀgymɑ̃te] *vi* to argue.

argus [aʀgys] *nm* guide to second-hand car etc prices.

arguties [aʀgysi] *nfpl* pettifoggery *sg* (*BRIT*), quibbles.

aride [aʀid] *adj* arid.

aridité [aʀidite] *nf* aridity.

arien, ne [aʀjɛ̃, -ɛn] *adj* Arian.

aristocrate [aʀistɔkʀat] *nm/f* aristocrat.

aristocratie [aʀistɔkʀasi] *nf* aristocracy.

aristocratique [aʀistɔkʀatik] *adj* aristocratic.

arithmétique [aʀitmetik] *adj* arithmetic(al) ♦ *nf* arithmetic.

armada [aʀmada] *nf* (*fig*) army.

armagnac [aʀmaɲak] *nm* armagnac.

armateur [aʀmatœʀ] *nm* shipowner.

armature [aʀmatyʀ] *nf* framework; (*de tente etc*) frame; (*de corset*) bone; (*de soutien-gorge*) wiring.

arme [aʀm(ə)] *nf* weapon; (*section de l'armée*) arm; ~**s** *nfpl* weapons, arms; (*blason*) (coat of) arms; **les** ~**s** (*profession*) soldiering *sg*; **à** ~**s égales** on equal terms; **en** ~**s** up in arms; **passer par les** ~**s** to execute (by firing squad); **prendre/présenter les** ~**s** to take up/present arms; **se battre à l'**~ **blanche** to fight with blades; ~ **à feu** firearm.

armé, e [aʀme] *adj* armed; ~ **de** armed with.

armée [aʀme] *nf* army; ~ **de l'air** Air Force; **l'**~ **du Salut** the Salvation Army; ~ **de terre** Army.

armement [aʀməmɑ̃] *nm* (*matériel*) arms *pl*, weapons *pl*; (: *d'un pays*) arms *pl*, armament; (*action d'équiper: d'un navire*) fitting out; ~**s** **nucléaires** nuclear armaments; **course aux** ~**s** arms race.

Arménie [aʀmeni] *nf*: **l'**~ Armenia.

arménien, ne [aʀmenjɛ̃, -ɛn] *adj* Armenian ♦ *nm* (*LING*) Armenian ♦ *nm/f*: **A**~, **ne** Armenian.

armer [aʀme] *vt* to arm; (*arme à feu*) to cock; (*appareil-photo*) to wind on; ~ **qch de** to fit sth with; (*renforcer*) to reinforce sth with; ~ **qn de** to arm *ou* equip sb with; **s'**~ **de** to arm o.s. with.

armistice [aʀmistis] *nm* armistice; **l'A**~ ≈ Remembrance (*BRIT*) *ou* Veterans (*US*) Day.

armoire [aʀmwaʀ] *nf* (tall) cupboard; (*pende-* *rie*) wardrobe (*BRIT*), closet (*US*); ~ **à pharmacie** medicine chest.

armoiries [aʀmwaʀi] *nfpl* coat of arms *sg*.

armure [aʀmyʀ] *nf* armour *no pl*, suit of armour.

armurerie [aʀmyʀʀi] *nf* arms factory; (*magasin*) gunsmith's (shop).

armurier [aʀmyʀje] *nm* gunsmith; (*MIL*, *d'armes blanches*) armourer.

ARN *sigle m* (= *acide ribonucléique*) RNA.

arnaque [aʀnak] *nf*: **de l'**~ daylight robbery.

arnaquer [aʀnake] *vt* to do (*fam*), swindle; **se faire** ~ to be had (*fam*) *ou* done.

arnaqueur [aʀnakœʀ] *nm* swindler.

arnica [aʀnika] *nm*: (**teinture d'**)~ arnica.

aromates [aʀɔmat] *nmpl* seasoning *sg*, herbs (and spices).

aromathérapie [aʀɔmateʀapi] *nf* aromatherapy.

aromatique [aʀɔmatik] *adj* aromatic.

aromatiser [aʀɔmatize] *vt* to flavour.

arôme [aʀom] *nm* aroma; (*d'une fleur etc*) fragrance.

arpège [aʀpɛʒ] *nm* arpeggio.

arpentage [aʀpɑ̃taʒ] *nm* (land) surveying.

arpenter [aʀpɑ̃te] *vt* to pace up and down.

arpenteur [aʀpɑ̃tœʀ] *nm* land surveyor.

arqué, e [aʀke] *adj* arched; (*jambes*) bow *cpd*, bandy.

arr. *abr* = **arrondissement.**

arrachage [aʀaʃaʒ] *nm*: ~ **des mauvaises herbes** weeding.

arraché [aʀaʃe] *nm* (*SPORT*) snatch; **obtenir à l'**~ (*fig*) to snatch.

arrache-pied [aʀaʃpje]: **d'**~ *adv* relentlessly.

arracher [aʀaʃe] *vt* to pull out; (*page etc*) to tear off, tear out; (*déplanter: légume*) to lift; (: *herbe, souche*) to pull up; (*bras etc: par explosion*) to blow off; (: *par accident*) to tear off; **s'**~ *vt* (*article très recherché*) to fight over; ~ **qch à qn** to snatch sth from sb; (*fig*) to wring sth out of sb, wrest sth from sb; ~ **qn à** (*solitude, rêverie*) to drag sb out of; (*famille etc*) to tear *ou* wrench sb away from; **se faire** ~ **une dent** to have a tooth out *ou* pulled (*US*); **s'**~ **de** (*lieu*) to tear o.s. away from; (*habitude*) to force o.s. out of.

arraisonner [aʀɛzɔne] *vt* to board and search.

arrangeant, e [aʀɑ̃ʒɑ̃, -ɑ̃t] *adj* accommodating, obliging.

arrangement [aʀɑ̃ʒmɑ̃] *nm* arrangement.

arranger [aʀɑ̃ʒe] *vt* to arrange; (*réparer*) to fix, put right; (*régler*) to settle, sort out; (*convenir à*) to suit, be convenient for; **s'**~ (*se mettre d'accord*) to come to an agreement *ou* arrangement; (*s'améliorer: querelle, situation*) to be sorted out; (*se débrouiller*): **s'**~ **pour que ...** to arrange things so that ...; **je vais m'**~ I'll manage; **ça va s'**~ it'll sort itself out; **s'**~ **pour faire** to make sure that *ou* see to it that one can do.

arrangeur [aʀɑ̃ʒœʀ] *nm* (*MUS*) arranger.

arrestation [arɛstɑsjɔ̃] *nf* arrest.

arrêt [arɛ] *nm* stopping; (*de bus etc*) stop; (*JUR*) judgment, decision; (*FOOTBALL*) save; **~s** *nmpl* (*MIL*) arrest *sg*; **être à l'~** to be stopped, have come to a halt; **rester** *ou* **tomber en ~ devant** to stop short in front of; **sans ~** without stopping, non-stop; (*fréquemment*) continually; **~ d'autobus** bus stop; **~ facultatif** request stop; **~ de mort** capital sentence; **~ de travail** stoppage (of work).

arrêté, e [arete] *adj* (*idées*) firm, fixed ♦ *nm* order, decree; **~ municipal** ≈ bylaw, byelaw.

arrêter [arete] *vt* to stop; (*chauffage etc*) to turn off, switch off; (*COMM: compte*) to settle; (*COUTURE: point*) to fasten off; (*fixer: date etc*) to appoint, decide on; (*criminel, suspect*) to arrest; **s'~** *vi* to stop; (*s'interrompre*) to stop o.s.; **~ de faire** to stop doing; **arrête de te plaindre** stop complaining; **ne pas ~ de faire** to keep on doing; **s'~ de faire** to stop doing; **s'~ sur** (*suj: choix, regard*) to fall on.

arrhes [ar] *nfpl* deposit *sg*.

arrière [arjɛr] *nm* back; (*SPORT*) fullback ♦ *adj inv*: **siège/roue ~** back *ou* rear seat/wheel; **~s** *nmpl* (*fig*): **protéger ses ~s** to protect the rear; **à l'~** *adv* behind, at the back; **en ~** *adv* behind; (*regarder*) back, behind; (*tomber, aller*) backwards; **en ~ de** *prép* behind.

arriéré, e [arjere] *adj* (*péj*) backward ♦ *nm* (*d'argent*) arrears *pl*.

arrière-boutique [arjɛrbutik] *nf* back shop.

arrière-cour [arjɛrkur] *nf* backyard.

arrière-cuisine [arjɛrkɥizin] *nf* scullery.

arrière-garde [arjɛrgard(ə)] *nf* rearguard.

arrière-goût [arjɛrgu] *nm* aftertaste.

arrière-grand-mère, *pl* **arrière-grand-mères** [arjɛrgrɑ̃mɛr] *nf* great-grandmother.

arrière-grand-père, *pl* **arrière-grands-pères** [arjɛrgrɑ̃pɛr] *nm* great-grandfather.

arrière-grands-parents [arjɛrgrɑ̃parɑ̃] *nmpl* great-grandparents.

arrière-pays [arjɛrpei] *nm inv* hinterland.

arrière-pensée [arjɛrpɑ̃se] *nf* ulterior motive; (*doute*) mental reservation.

arrière-petite-fille, *pl* **arrière-petites-filles** [arjɛrpətitfij] *nf* great-granddaughter.

arrière-petit-fils, *pl* **arrière-petits-fils** [arjɛrpətifis] *nm* great-grandson.

arrière-petits-enfants [arjɛrpətizɑ̃fɑ̃] *nmpl* great-grandchildren.

arrière-plan [arjɛrplɑ̃] *nm* background; **d'~** *adj* (*INFORM*) background *cpd*.

arriérer [arjere]: **s'~** *vi* (*COMM*) to fall into arrears.

arrière-saison [arjɛrsɛzɔ̃] *nf* late autumn.

arrière-salle [arjɛrsal] *nf* back room.

arrière-train [arjɛrtrɛ̃] *nm* hindquarters *pl*.

arrimer [arime] *vt* to stow; (*fixer*) to secure, fasten securely.

arrivage [arivaʒ] *nm* arrival.

arrivant, e [arivɑ̃, -ɑ̃t] *nm/f* newcomer.

arrivée [arive] *nf* arrival; (*ligne d'arrivée*) finish; **~ d'air/de gaz** air/gas inlet; **courrier à l'~** incoming mail; **à mon ~** when I arrived.

arriver [arive] *vi* to arrive; (*survenir*) to happen, occur; **j'arrive!** (I'm) just coming!; **il arrive à Paris à 8 h** he gets to *ou* arrives in Paris at 8; **~ à destination** to arrive at one's destination; **~ à** (*atteindre*) to reach; **~ à** (*faire*) **qch** (*réussir*) to manage (to do) sth; **~ à échéance** to fall due; **en ~ à faire** to end up doing, get to the point of doing; **il arrive que** it happens that; **il lui arrive de faire** he sometimes does.

arrivisme [arivism(ə)] *nm* ambition, ambitiousness.

arriviste [arivist(ə)] *nm/f* go-getter.

arrogance [arogɑ̃s] *nf* arrogance.

arrogant, e [arogɑ̃, -ɑ̃t] *adj* arrogant.

arroger [aroʒe]: **s'~** *vt* to assume (without right); **s'~ le droit de ...** to assume the right to ....

arrondi, e [arɔ̃di] *adj* round ♦ *nm* roundness.

arrondir [arɔ̃dir] *vt* (*forme, objet*) to round; (*somme*) to round off; **s'~** *vi* to become round(ed); **~ ses fins de mois** to supplement one's pay.

arrondissement [arɔ̃dismɑ̃] *nm* (*ADMIN*) ≈ district.

arrosage [arozaʒ] *nm* watering; **tuyau d'~** hose(pipe).

arroser [aroze] *vt* to water; (*victoire etc*) to celebrate (over a drink); (*CULIN*) to baste.

arroseur [arozœr] *nm* (*tourniquet*) sprinkler.

arroseuse [arozøz] *nf* water cart.

arrosoir [arozwar] *nm* watering can.

arrt *abr* = **arrondissement**.

arsenal, aux [arsənal, -o] *nm* (*NAVIG*) naval dockyard; (*MIL*) arsenal; (*fig*) gear, paraphernalia.

arsenic [arsənik] *nm* arsenic.

art [ar] *nm* art; **avoir l'~ de faire** (*fig: personne*) to have a talent for doing; **les ~s** the arts; **livre/critique d'~** art book/critic; **objet d'~** objet d'art; **~ dramatique** dramatic art; **~s martiaux** martial arts; **~s et métiers** applied arts and crafts; **~s ménagers** home economics *sg*; **~s plastiques** plastic arts.

art. *abr* = **article**.

artère [artɛr] *nf* (*ANAT*) artery; (*rue*) main road.

artériel, le [arterjɛl] *adj* arterial.

artériosclérose [arterjoskleroz] *nf* arteriosclerosis.

arthrite [artrit] *nf* arthritis.

arthrose [artroz] *nf* (*degenerative*) osteoarthritis.

artichaut [artiʃo] *nm* artichoke.

article [artikl(ə)] *nm* article; (*COMM*) item, article; (*INFORM*) record, item; **faire l'~** (*COMM*) to do one's sales spiel; **faire l'~ de** (*fig*) to sing the praises of; **à l'~ de la mort** at the point of death; **~ défini/indéfini** definite/indefinite article; **~ de fond**

(*PRESSE*) feature article; ~**s de bureau** office equipment; ~**s de voyage** travel goods *ou* items.

articulaire [aʀtikylɛʀ] *adj* of the joints, articular.

articulation [aʀtikylɑsjɔ̃] *nf* articulation; (*ANAT*) joint.

articulé, e [aʀtikyle] *adj* (*membre*) jointed; (*poupée*) with moving joints.

articuler [aʀtikyle] *vt* to articulate; **s'**~ **(sur)** (*ANAT, TECH*) to articulate (with); **s'**~ **autour de** (*fig*) to centre around *ou* on, turn on.

artifice [aʀtifis] *nm* device, trick.

artificiel, le [aʀtifisjɛl] *adj* artificial.

artificiellement [aʀtifisjɛlmɑ̃] *adv* artificially.

artificier [aʀtifisje] *nm* pyrotechnist.

artificieux, euse [aʀtifisjø, -øz] *adj* guileful, deceitful.

artillerie [aʀtijʀi] *nf* artillery, ordnance.

artilleur [aʀtijœʀ] *nm* artilleryman, gunner.

artisan [aʀtizɑ̃] *nm* artisan, (self-employed) craftsman; **l'**~ **de la victoire/du malheur** the architect of victory/of the disaster.

artisanal, e, aux [aʀtizanal, -o] *adj* of *ou* made by craftsmen; (*péj*) cottage industry *cpd*, unsophisticated.

artisanalement [aʀtizanalmɑ̃] *adv* by craftsmen.

artisanat [aʀtizana] *nm* arts and crafts *pl*.

artiste [aʀtist(ə)] *nm/f* artist; (*THÉÂT, MUS*) artist, performer; (*: de variétés*) entertainer.

artistique [aʀtistik] *adj* artistic.

artistiquement [aʀtistikmɑ̃] *adv* artistically.

aryen, ne [aʀjɛ̃, -ɛn] *adj* Aryan.

AS *sigle fpl* (*ADMIN*) = **assurances sociales** ♦ *sigle f* (*SPORT*: = *Association sportive*) ≈ FC (= *Football Club*).

as *vb* [a] *voir* **avoir** ♦ *nm* [ɑs] ace.

a/s *abr* (= *aux soins de*) c/o.

ASBL *sigle f* (= *association sans but lucratif*) non-profit-making organization.

asc. *abr* = **ascenseur**.

ascendance [asɑ̃dɑ̃s] *nf* (*origine*) ancestry; (*ASTROLOGIE*) ascendant.

ascendant, e [asɑ̃dɑ̃, -ɑ̃t] *adj* upward ♦ *nm* influence; ~**s** *nmpl* ascendants.

ascenseur [asɑ̃sœʀ] *nm* lift (*BRIT*), elevator (*US*).

ascension [asɑ̃sjɔ̃] *nf* ascent; climb; **l'A**~ (*REL*) the Ascension; (*: jour férié*) Ascension (Day); **(île de) l'A**~ Ascension Island.

La fête de l'**Ascension** *is a public holiday in France. Falling on a Thursday, usually in May, the holiday provides the opportunity for many French people also to take Friday off work and enjoy a long weekend; see also faire le* **pont**.

---

ascète [aset] *nm/f* ascetic.

ascétique [asetik] *adj* ascetic.

ascétisme [asetism(ə)] *nm* asceticism.

ascorbique [askɔʀbik] *adj*: **acide** ~ ascorbic acid.

ASE *sigle f* (= *Agence spatiale européenne*) ESA (= *European Space Agency*).

asepsie [asɛpsi] *nf* asepsis.

aseptique [asɛptik] *adj* aseptic.

aseptiser [asɛptize] *vt* to sterilize; (*plaie*) to disinfect.

asexué, e [asɛksɥe] *adj* asexual.

asiatique [azjatik] *adj* Asian, Asiatic ♦ *nm/f*: **A**~ Asian.

Asie [azi] *nf*: **l'**~ Asia.

asile [azil] *nm* (*refuge*) refuge, sanctuary; (*POL*): **droit d'**~ (political) asylum; (*pour malades, vieillards etc*) home; **accorder l'**~ **politique à qn** to grant *ou* give sb political asylum; **chercher/trouver** ~ **quelque part** to seek/find refuge somewhere.

asocial, e, aux [asɔsjal, -o] *adj* antisocial.

aspect [aspɛ] *nm* appearance, look; (*fig*) aspect, side; (*LING*) aspect; **à l'**~ **de** at the sight of.

asperge [aspɛʀʒ(ə)] *nf* asparagus *no pl*.

asperger [aspɛʀʒe] *vt* to spray, sprinkle.

aspérité [asperite] *nf* excrescence, protruding bit (of rock *etc*).

aspersion [aspɛʀsjɔ̃] *nf* spraying, sprinkling.

asphalte [asfalt(ə)] *nm* asphalt.

asphyxiant, e [asfiksjɑ̃, -ɑ̃t] *adj* suffocating; **gaz** ~ poison gas.

asphyxie [asfiksi] *nf* suffocation, asphyxia, asphyxiation.

asphyxier [asfiksje] *vt* to suffocate, asphyxiate; (*fig*) to stifle; **mourir asphyxié** to die of suffocation *ou* asphyxiation.

aspic [aspik] *nm* (*ZOOL*) asp; (*CULIN*) aspic.

aspirant, e [aspirɑ̃, -ɑ̃t] *adj*: **pompe** ~**e** suction pump ♦ *nm* (*NAVIG*) midshipman.

aspirateur [aspiratœʀ] *nm* vacuum cleaner, hoover ®.

aspiration [aspirasjɔ̃] *nf* inhalation; sucking (up); drawing up; ~**s** *nfpl* (*ambitions*) aspirations.

aspirer [aspire] *vt* (*air*) to inhale; (*liquide*) to suck (up); (*suj: appareil*) to suck *ou* draw up; ~ **à** *vt* to aspire to.

aspirine [aspirin] *nf* aspirin.

assagir [asaʒiʀ] *vt*, **s'**~ *vi* to quieten down, sober down.

assaillant, e [asajɑ̃, -ɑ̃t] *nm/f* assailant, attacker.

assaillir [asajiʀ] *vt* to assail, attack; ~ **qn** (*questions*) to assail *ou* bombard sb with.

assainir [aseniʀ] *vt* to clean up; (*eau, air*) to purify.

assainissement [asenismɑ̃] *nm* cleaning up; purifying.

assaisonnement [asɛzɔnmɑ̃] *nm* seasoning.

assaisonner [asɛzɔne] *vt* to season; **bien assaisonné** highly seasoned.

assassin [asasɛ̃] *nm* murderer; assassin.

assassinat [asasina] *nm* murder; assassination.

assassiner [asasine] *vt* to murder; (*surtout POL*) to assassinate.

assaut [aso] *nm* assault, attack; **prendre d'~** to (take by) storm, assault; **donner l'~ (à)** to attack; **faire ~ de** (*rivaliser*) to vie with *ou* rival each other in.

assèchement [aseʃmɑ̃] *nm* draining, drainage.

assécher [aseʃe] *vt* to drain.

ASSEDIC [asedik] *sigle f* (= *Association pour l'emploi dans l'industrie et le commerce*) *unemployment insurance scheme.*

assemblage [asɑ̃blaʒ] *nm* assembling; (*MENUISERIE*) joint; **un ~ de** (*fig*) a collection of; **langage d'~** (*INFORM*) assembly language.

assemblée [asɑ̃ble] *nf* (*réunion*) meeting; (*public, assistance*) gathering; assembled people; (*POL*) assembly; (*REL*): **l'~ des fidèles** the congregation; **l'A~ nationale (AN)** the (French) National Assembly.

The **Assemblée nationale** *is the lower house of the French parliament, the upper house being the* **Sénat**. *It sits at the Palais Bourbon in Paris and consists of about 580* **députés** *elected every five years; see also* **élection**.

---

assembler [asɑ̃ble] *vt* (*joindre, monter*) to assemble, put together; (*amasser*) to gather (together), collect (together); **s'~** *vi* to gather, collect.

assembleur [asɑ̃blœʀ] *nm* assembler, fitter; (*INFORM*) assembler.

assener, asséner [asene] *vt*: **~ un coup à qn** to deal sb a blow.

assentiment [asɑ̃timɑ̃] *nm* assent, consent; (*approbation*) approval.

asseoir [aswaʀ] *vt* (*malade, bébé*) to sit up; (*personne debout*) to sit down; (*autorité, réputation*) to establish; **s'~** *vi* to sit (o.s.) up; to sit (o.s.) down; **faire ~ qn** to ask sb to sit down; **~ qch sur** to build sth on; (*appuyer*) to base sth on.

assermenté, e [asɛʀmɑ̃te] *adj* sworn, on oath.

assertion [asɛʀsjɔ̃] *nf* assertion.

asservir [asɛʀviʀ] *vt* to subjugate, enslave.

asservissement [asɛʀvismɑ̃] *nm* (*action*) enslavement; (*état*) slavery.

assesseur [asesœʀ] *nm* (*JUR*) assessor.

asseyais [asɛje] *etc vb voir* **asseoir**.

assez [ase] *adv* (*suffisamment*) enough, sufficiently; (*passablement*) rather, quite, fairly; **~!** enough!, that'll do!; **~/pas ~ cuit** well enough done/underdone; **est-il ~ fort/rapide?** is he strong/fast enough *ou* sufficiently strong/fast?; **il est passé ~ vite** he went past rather *ou* quite *ou* fairly fast; **~ de pain/livres** enough *ou* sufficient bread/books; **vous en avez ~?** have you got enough?; **en avoir ~ de qch** (*en être fatigué*) to have had enough of sth; **travailler ~** to work sufficiently (hard), work (hard) enough.

assidu, e [asidy] *adj* assiduous, painstaking; (*régulier*) regular; **~ auprès de qn** attentive towards sb.

assiduité [asidɥite] *nf* assiduousness, painstaking; regularity; attentiveness; **~s** *nfpl* assiduous attentions.

assidûment [asidymɑ̃] *adv* assiduously, painstakingly; attentively.

assied [asje] *etc vb voir* **asseoir**.

assiégé, e [asjeʒe] *adj* under siege, besieged.

assiéger [asjeʒe] *vt* to besiege, lay siege to; (*suj: foule, touristes*) to mob, besiege.

assiérai [asjeʀe] *etc vb voir* **asseoir**.

assiette [asjɛt] *nf* plate; (*contenu*) plate(ful); (*équilibre*) seat; (*de colonne*) seating; (*de navire*) trim; **~ anglaise** assorted cold meats; **~ creuse** (soup) dish, soup plate; **~ à dessert** dessert *ou* side plate; **~ de l'impôt** basis of (tax) assessment; **~ plate** (dinner) plate.

assiettée [asjete] *nf* plateful.

assignation [asiɲasjɔ̃] *nf* assignation; (*JUR*) summons; (: *de témoin*) subpoena; **~ à résidence** compulsory order of residence.

assigner [asiɲe] *vt*: **~ qch à** to assign *ou* allot sth to; (*valeur, importance*) to attach sth to; (*somme*) to allocate sth to; (*limites*) to set *ou* fix sth to; (*cause, effet*) to ascribe *ou* attribute sth to; **~ qn à** (*affecter*) to assign sb to; **~ qn à résidence** (*JUR*) to give sb a compulsory order of residence.

assimilable [asimilabl(ə)] *adj* easily assimilated *ou* absorbed.

assimilation [asimilasjɔ̃] *nf* assimilation, absorption.

assimiler [asimile] *vt* to assimilate, absorb; (*comparer*): **~ qch/qn à** to liken *ou* compare sth/sb to; **s'~** *vi* (*s'intégrer*) to be assimilated *ou* absorbed; **ils sont assimilés aux infirmières** (*ADMIN*) they are classed as nurses.

assis, e [asi, -iz] *pp de* **asseoir** ♦ *adj* sitting (down), seated ♦ *nf* (*CONSTR*) course; (*GÉO*) stratum (*pl* -a); (*fig*) basis (*pl* bases), foundation; **~ en tailleur** sitting cross-legged.

assises [asiz] *nfpl* (*JUR*) assizes; (*congrès*) (annual) conference.

assistanat [asistana] *nm* assistantship; (*à l'université*) probationary lectureship.

assistance [asistɑ̃s] *nf* (*public*) audience; (*aide*) assistance; **porter** *ou* **prêter ~ à qn** to give sb assistance; **A~ publique (AP)** *public health service*; **enfant de l'A~ (publique)** (*formerly*) child in care; **~ technique** technical aid.

assistant, e [asistɑ̃, -ɑ̃t] *nm/f* assistant; (*d'université*) probationary lecturer; **les ~s** *nmpl* (*auditeurs etc*) those present; **~e sociale** social worker.

assisté, e [asiste] *adj* (*AUTO*) power assisted ♦ *nm/f* person receiving aid from the State.

assister [asiste] *vt* to assist; **~ à** *vt* (*scène, évé-*

nement) to witness; (*conférence, séminaire*) to attend, be (present) at; (*spectacle, match*) to be at, see.

association [asɔsjasjɔ̃] *nf* association; (*COMM*) partnership; ~ **d'idées/images** association of ideas/images.

associé, e [asɔsje] *nm/f* associate; (*COMM*) partner.

associer [asɔsje] *vt* to associate; ~ **qn à** (*profits*) to give sb a share of; (*affaire*) to make sb a partner in; (*joie, triomphe*) to include sb in; ~ **qch à** (*joindre, allier*) to combine sth with; **s'~** *vi* to join together; (*COMM*) to form a partnership ♦ *vt* (*collaborateur*) to take on (as a partner); **s'~ à** to be combined with; (*opinions, joie de qn*) to share in; **s'~ à** *ou* **avec qn pour faire** to join (forces) *ou* join together with sb to do.

assoie [aswa] *etc vb voir* **asseoir**.

assoiffé, e [aswafe] *adj* thirsty; (*fig*): ~ **de** (*sang*) thirsting for; (*gloire*) thirsting after.

assoirai [aswaʀe], **assois** [aswa] *etc vb voir* **asseoir**.

assolement [asɔlmɑ̃] *nm* (systematic) rotation of crops.

assombrir [asɔ̃bʀiʀ] *vt* to darken; (*fig*) to fill with gloom; **s'~** *vi* to darken; (*devenir nuageux, fig: visage*) to cloud over; (*fig*) to become gloomy.

assommer [asɔme] *vt* (*étourdir, abrutir*) to knock out, stun; (*fam: ennuyer*) to bore stiff.

Assomption [asɔ̃psjɔ̃] *nf*: **l'~** the Assumption.

> La fête de l'**Assomption**, *or more commonly* Le 15 août *on August 15 is a national holiday in France. Traditionally, large numbers of holidaymakers set out on this date, frequently causing chaos on French roads; see also* faire le pont.

assorti, e [asɔʀti] *adj* matched, matching; **fromages/légumes** ~**s** assorted cheeses/vegetables; ~ **à** matching; ~ **de** accompanied with; (*conditions, conseils*) coupled with; **bien/mal** ~ well/ill-matched.

assortiment [asɔʀtimɑ̃] *nm* (*choix*) assortment, selection; (*harmonie de couleurs, formes*) arrangement; (*COMM: lot, stock*) selection.

assortir [asɔʀtiʀ] *vt* to match; **s'~** to go well together, match; ~ **qch à** to match sth with; ~ **qch de** to accompany sth with; **s'~ de** to be accompanied by.

assoupi, e [asupi] *adj* dozing, sleeping; (*fig*) (be)numbed; (*sens*) dulled.

assoupir [asupiʀ]: **s'~** *vi* (*personne*) to doze off; (*sens*) to go numb.

assoupissement [asupismɑ̃] *nm* (*sommeil*) dozing; (*fig: somnolence*) drowsiness.

assouplir [asupliʀ] *vt* to make supple, soften; (*membres, corps*) to limber up, make supple; (*fig*) to relax; (: *caractère*) to soften, make

more flexible; **s'~** *vi* to soften; to limber up; to relax; to become more flexible.

assouplissement [asuplismɑ̃] *nm* softening; limbering up; relaxation; **exercices d'~** limbering up exercises.

assourdir [asuʀdiʀ] *vt* (*bruit*) to deaden, muffle; (*suj: bruit*) to deafen.

assourdissant, e [asuʀdisɑ̃, -ɑ̃t] *adj* (*bruit*) deafening.

assouvir [asuviʀ] *vt* to satisfy, appease.

assoyais [aswaje] *etc vb voir* **asseoir**.

ASSU [asy] *sigle f* = **Association du sport scolaire et universitaire.**

assujetti, e [asyʒeti] *adj*: ~ **(à)** subject (to); (*ADMIN*): ~ **à l'impôt** subject to tax(ation).

assujettir [asyʒetiʀ] *vt* to subject, subjugate; (*fixer: planches, tableau*) to secure, fix securely; ~ **qn à** (*règle, impôt*) to subject sb to.

assujettissement [asyʒetismɑ̃] *nm* subjection, subjugation.

assumer [asyme] *vt* (*fonction, emploi*) to assume, take on; (*accepter: conséquence, situation*) to accept.

assurance [asyʀɑ̃s] *nf* (*certitude*) assurance; (*confiance en soi*) (self-)confidence; (*contrat*) insurance (policy); (*secteur commercial*) insurance; **prendre une ~ contre** to take out insurance *ou* an insurance policy against; ~ **contre l'incendie** fire insurance; ~ **contre le vol** insurance against theft; **société d'~**, **compagnie d'~s** insurance company; ~ **maladie (AM)** health insurance; ~ **au tiers** third party insurance; ~ **tous risques** (*AUTO*) comprehensive insurance; ~**s sociales (AS)** ≈ National Insurance (*BRIT*), ≈ Social Security (*US*).

assurance-vie, *pl* **assurances-vie** [asyʀɑ̃svi] *nf* life assurance *ou* insurance.

assurance-vol, *pl* **assurances-vol** [asyʀɑ̃svɔl] *nf* insurance against theft.

assuré, e [asyʀe] *adj* (*victoire etc*) certain, sure; (*démarche, voix*) assured, (self-)confident; (*certain*): ~ **de** confident of; (*ASSURANCES*) insured ♦ *nm/f* insured (person); ~ **social** ≈ member of the National Insurance (*BRIT*) *ou* Social Security (*US*) scheme.

assurément [asyʀemɑ̃] *adv* assuredly, most certainly.

assurer [asyʀe] *vt* (*COMM*) to insure; (*stabiliser*) to steady, stabilize; (*victoire etc*) to ensure, make certain; (*frontières, pouvoir*) to make secure; (*service, garde*) to provide, operate; ~ **qch à qn** (*garantir*) to secure *ou* guarantee sth for sb; (*certifier*) to assure sb of sth; ~ **à qn que** to assure sb that; **je vous assure que non/si** I assure you that that is not the case/is the case; ~ **qn de** to assure sb of; ~ **ses arrières** (*fig*) to be sure one has something to fall back on; **s'~** (*COMM*) to insure o.s. (against); **s'~ de/que** (*vérifier*) to make sure of/that: **s'~ (de)** (*aide* *de qn*) to secure; **s'~ sur la vie** to take out a life insurance; **s'~ le concours/la collaboration de qn** to secure sb's aid/collaboration.

assureur [asyRœR] *nm* insurance agent; (*société*) insurers *pl*.

Assyrie [asiRi] *nf*: **l'~** Assyria.

assyrien, ne [asiRjɛ̃, -ɛn] *adj* Assyrian ♦ *nm/f*: **A~**, **ne** Assyrian.

astérisque [asteRisk(ə)] *nm* asterisk.

astéroïde [asteRɔid] *nm* asteroid.

asthmatique [asmatik] *adj* asthmatic.

asthme [asm(ə)] *nm* asthma.

asticot [astiko] *nm* maggot.

asticoter [astikɔte] *vt* (*fam*) to needle, get at.

astigmate [astigmat] *adj* (*MÉD: personne*) astigmatic, having an astigmatism.

astiquer [astike] *vt* to polish, shine.

astrakan [astRakɑ̃] *nm* astrakhan.

astral, e, aux [astRal, -o] *adj* astral.

astre [astR(ə)] *nm* star.

astreignant, e [astRɛɲɑ̃, -ɑ̃t] *adj* demanding.

astreindre [astRɛ̃dR(ə)] *vt*: **~ qn à qch** to force sth upon sb; **~ qn à faire** to compel *ou* force sb to do; **s'~ à** to compel *ou* force o.s. to.

astringent, e [astRɛ̃ʒɑ̃, -ɑ̃t] *adj* astringent.

astrologie [astRɔlɔʒi] *nf* astrology.

astrologique [astRɔlɔʒik] *adj* astrological.

astrologue [astRɔlɔg] *nm/f* astrologer.

astronaute [astRɔnot] *nm/f* astronaut.

astronautique [astRɔnotik] *nf* astronautics *sg*.

astronome [astRɔnɔm] *nm/f* astronomer.

astronomie [astRɔnɔmi] *nf* astronomy.

astronomique [astRɔnɔmik] *adj* astronomic(al).

astrophysicien, ne [astRɔfizisjɛ̃, -ɛn] *nm/f* astrophysicist.

astrophysique [astRɔfizik] *nf* astrophysics *sg*.

astuce [astys] *nf* shrewdness, astuteness; (*truc*) trick, clever way; (*plaisanterie*) wisecrack.

astucieusement [astysjøzmɑ̃] *adv* shrewdly, cleverly, astutely.

astucieux, euse [astysjø, -øz] *adj* shrewd, clever, astute.

asymétrique [asimetRik] *adj* asymmetric(al).

AT *sigle m* (= *Ancien Testament*) OT.

atavisme [atavism(ə)] *nm* atavism, heredity.

atelier [atəlje] *nm* workshop; (*de peintre*) studio.

atermoiements [atɛRmwamɑ̃] *nmpl* procrastination *sg*.

atermoyer [atɛRmwaje] *vi* to temporize, procrastinate.

athée [ate] *adj* atheistic ♦ *nm/f* atheist.

athéisme [ateism(ə)] *nm* atheism.

Athènes [atɛn] *n* Athens.

athénien, ne [atenjɛ̃, -ɛn] *adj* Athenian.

athlète [atlɛt] *nm/f* (*SPORT*) athlete; (*costaud*) muscleman.

athlétique [atletik] *adj* athletic.

athlétisme [atletism(ə)] *nm* athletics *sg*; **faire de l'~** to do athletics; **tournoi d'~** athletics

meeting.

Atlantide [atlɑ̃tid] *nf*: **l'~** Atlantis.

atlantique [atlɑ̃tik] *adj* Atlantic ♦ *nm*: **l'(océan) A~** the Atlantic (Ocean).

atlantiste [atlɑ̃tist(ə)] *adj*, *nm/f* Atlanticist.

Atlas [atlɑs] *nm*: **l'~** the Atlas Mountains.

atlas [atlɑs] *nm* atlas.

atmosphère [atmɔsfɛR] *nf* atmosphere.

atmosphérique [atmɔsfeRik] *adj* atmospheric.

atoll [atɔl] *nm* atoll.

atome [atom] *nm* atom.

atomique [atɔmik] *adj* atomic, nuclear; (*usine*) nuclear; (*nombre, masse*) atomic.

atomiseur [atɔmizœR] *nm* atomizer.

atomiste [atɔmist(ə)] *nm/f* (*aussi*: **savant, ingénieur** *etc* **~**) atomic scientist.

atone [atɔn] *adj* lifeless; (*LING*) unstressed, unaccented.

atours [atuR] *nmpl* attire *sg*, finery *sg*.

atout [atu] *nm* trump; (*fig*) asset; (*: plus fort*) trump card; "**~ pique/trèfle**" "spades/clubs are trumps".

ATP *sigle f* (= *Association des tennismen professionnels*) ATP (= *Association of Tennis Professionals*) ♦ *sigle mpl* (= *arts et traditions populaires*): **musée des ~** ≈ folk museum.

âtre [ɑtR(ə)] *nm* hearth.

atroce [atRɔs] *adj* atrocious, horrible.

atrocement [atRɔsmɑ̃] *adv* atrociously, horribly.

atrocité [atRɔsite] *nf* atrocity.

atrophie [atRɔfi] *nf* atrophy.

atrophier [atRɔfje]: **s'~** *vi* to atrophy.

atropine [atRɔpin] *nf* (*CHIMIE*) atropine.

attabler [atable]: **s'~** *vi* to sit down at (the) table; **s'~ à la terrasse** to sit down (at a table) on the terrace.

attachant, e [ataʃɑ̃, -ɑ̃t] *adj* engaging, likeable.

attache [ataʃ] *nf* clip, fastener; (*fig*) tie; **~s** *nfpl* (*relations*) connections; **à l'~** (*chien*) tied up.

attaché, e [ataʃe] *adj*: **être ~ à** (*aimer*) to be attached to ♦ *nm* (*ADMIN*) attaché; **~ de presse/d'ambassade** press/embassy attaché; **~ commercial** commercial attaché.

attaché-case [ataʃekɛz] *nm inv* attaché case (*BRIT*), briefcase.

attachement [ataʃmɑ̃] *nm* attachment.

attacher [ataʃe] *vt* to tie up; (*étiquette*) to attach, tie on; (*souliers*) to do up ♦ *vi* (*poêle, riz*) to stick; **s'~** (*robe etc*) to do up; **s'~ à** (*par affection*) to become attached to; **~ qch à** to tie *ou* fasten *ou* attach sth to; **~ qn à** (*fig: lier*) to attach sb to; **~ du prix/de l'importance à** to attach great value/attach importance to.

attaquant [atakɑ̃] *nm* (*MIL*) attacker; (*SPORT*) striker, forward.

attaque [atak] *nf* attack; (*cérébrale*) stroke; (*d'épilepsie*) fit; **être/se sentir d'~** to be/feel on form; **~ à main armée** armed attack.

attaquer [atake] *vt* to attack; (*en justice*) to

bring an action against, sue; (*travail*) to tackle, set about ♦ *vi* to attack; **s'~ à** to attack; (*épidémie, misère*) to tackle, attack.

attardé, e [atarde] *adj* (*passants*) late; (*enfant*) backward; (*conceptions*) old-fashioned.

attarder [atarde] **s'~** *vi* (*sur qch, en chemin*) to linger; (*chez qn*) to stay on.

atteignais [atɛɲɛ] *etc vb voir* **atteindre.**

atteindre [atɛ̃dʀ(ə)] *vt* to reach; (*blesser*) to hit; (*contacter*) to reach, contact, get in touch with; (*émouvoir*) to affect.

atteint, e [atɛ̃, -ɛ̃t] *pp de* **atteindre** ♦ *adj* (*MÉD*): **être ~ de** to be suffering from ♦ *nf* attack; **hors d'~e** out of reach; **porter ~e à** to strike a blow at, undermine.

attelage [atlaʒ] *nm* (*de remorque etc*) coupling (*BRIT*), (trailer) hitch (*US*); (*animaux*) team; (*harnachement*) harness; (: *de bœufs*) yoke.

atteler [atle] *vt* (*cheval, bœufs*) to hitch up; (*wagons*) to couple; **s'~ à** (*travail*) to buckle down to.

attelle [atɛl] *nf* splint.

attenant, e [atnɑ̃, -ɑ̃t] *adj*: ~ **(à)** adjoining.

attendant [atɑ̃dɑ̃]: **en ~** *adv* (*dans l'intervalle*) meanwhile, in the meantime.

attendre [atɑ̃dʀ(ə)] *vt* to wait for; (*être destiné ou réservé à*) to await, be in store for ♦ *vi* to wait; **je n'attends plus rien (de la vie)** I expect nothing more (from life); **attendez que je réfléchisse** wait while I think; **s'~ à (ce que)** (*escompter*) to expect (that); **je ne m'y attendais pas** I didn't expect that; **ce n'est pas ce à quoi je m'attendais** that's not what I expected; ~ **un enfant** to be expecting a baby; ~ **de pied ferme** to wait determinedly; ~ **de faire/d'être** to wait until one does/is; ~ **que** to wait until; ~ **qch de** to expect sth of; **faire ~ qn** to keep sb waiting; **se faire ~** to keep people (*ou* us *etc*) waiting; **en attendant** *adv voir* **attendant.**

attendri, e [atɑ̃dʀi] *adj* tender.

attendrir [atɑ̃dʀiʀ] *vt* to move (to pity); (*viande*) to tenderize; **s'~ (sur)** to be moved *ou* touched (by).

attendrissant, e [atɑ̃dʀisɑ̃, -ɑ̃t] *adj* moving, touching.

attendrissement [atɑ̃dʀismɑ̃] *nm* (*tendre*) emotion; (*apitoyé*) pity.

attendrisseur [atɑ̃dʀisœʀ] *nm* tenderizer.

attendu, e [atɑ̃dy] *pp de* **attendre** ♦ *adj* long-awaited; (*prévu*) expected ♦ *nm*: **~s** *reasons adduced for a judgment*; ~ **que** *conj* considering that, since.

attentat [atɑ̃ta] *nm* (*contre une personne*) assassination attempt; (*contre un bâtiment*) attack; ~ **à la bombe** bomb attack; ~ **à la pudeur** (*exhibitionnisme*) indecent exposure *no pl*; (*agression*) indecent assault *no pl*.

attente [atɑ̃t] *nf* wait; (*espérance*) expectation; **contre toute ~** contrary to (all) expectations.

attenter [atɑ̃te]: ~ **à** *vt* (*liberté*) to violate; ~ **à**

la vie de qn to make an attempt on sb's life; ~ **à ses jours** to make an attempt on one's life.

attentif, ive [atɑ̃tif, -iv] *adj* attentive; (*soin*) scrupulous; (*travail*) careful; ~ **à** paying attention to; (*devoir*) mindful of; ~ **à faire** careful to do.

attention [atɑ̃sjɔ̃] *nf* attention; (*prévenance*) attention, thoughtfulness *no pl*; **mériter ~** to be worthy of attention; **à l'~ de** for the attention of; **porter qch à l'~ de qn** to bring sth to sb's attention; **attirer l'~ de qn sur qch** to draw sb's attention to sth; **faire ~ (à)** to be careful (of); **faire ~ (à ce) que** to be *ou* make sure that; **~!** careful!, watch!, watch *ou* mind (*BRIT*) out!; **~, si vous ouvrez cette lettre** (*sanction*) just watch out, if you open that letter; **~, respectez les consignes de sécurité** be sure to observe the safety instructions.

attentionné, e [atɑ̃sjɔne] *adj* thoughtful, considerate.

attentisme [atɑ̃tism(ə)] *nm* wait-and-see policy.

attentiste [atɑ̃tist(ə)] *adj* (*politique*) wait-and-see ♦ *nm/f* believer in a wait-and-see policy.

attentivement [atɑ̃tivmɑ̃] *adv* attentively.

atténuant, e [atenɥɑ̃, -ɑ̃t] *adj*: **circonstances ~es** extenuating circumstances.

atténuer [atenɥe] *vt* to alleviate, ease; (*diminuer*) to lessen; (*amoindrir*) to mitigate the effects of; **s'~** *vi* to ease; (*violence etc*) to abate.

atterrer [ateʀe] *vt* to dismay, appal.

atterrir [ateʀiʀ] *vi* to land.

atterrissage [ateʀisaʒ] *nm* landing; ~ **sur le ventre/sans visibilité/forcé** belly/blind/forced landing.

attestation [atɛstasjɔ̃] *nf* certificate, testimonial; ~ **médicale** doctor's certificate.

attester [atɛste] *vt* to testify to, vouch for; (*démontrer*) to attest, testify to; ~ **que** to testify that.

attiédir [atj̃ediʀ]: **s'~** *vi* to become lukewarm; (*fig*) to cool down.

attifé, e [atife] *adj* (*fam*) got up (*BRIT*), decked out.

attifer [atife] *vt* to get (*BRIT*) *ou* do up, deck out.

attique [atik] *nm*: **appartement en ~** penthouse (flat (*BRIT*) *ou* apartment (*US*)).

attirail [atiʀaj] *nm* gear; (*péj*) paraphernalia.

attirance [atiʀɑ̃s] *nf* attraction; (*séduction*) lure.

attirant, e [atiʀɑ̃, -ɑ̃t] *adj* attractive, appealing.

attirer [atiʀe] *vt* to attract; (*appâter*) to lure, entice; ~ **qn dans un coin/vers soi** to draw sb into a corner/towards one; ~ **l'attention de qn** to attract sb's attention; ~ **l'attention de qn sur qch** to draw sb's attention to sth; ~ **des ennuis à qn** to make trouble for sb;

s'~ des ennuis to bring trouble upon o.s., get into trouble.

attiser [atize] *vt* (*feu*) to poke (up), stir up; (*fig*) to fan the flame of, stir up.

attitré, e [atitʀe] *adj* qualified; (*agréé*) accredited, appointed.

attitude [atityd] *nf* attitude; (*position du corps*) bearing.

attouchements [atuʃmɑ̃] *nmpl* touching *sg*; (*sexuels*) fondling *sg*, stroking *sg*.

attractif, ive [atʀaktif, -iv] *adj* attractive.

attraction [atʀaksjɔ̃] *nf* attraction; (*de cabaret, cirque*) number.

attrait [atʀɛ] *nm* appeal, attraction; (*plus fort*) lure; **~s** *nmpl* attractions; **éprouver de l'~ pour** to be attracted to.

attrape [atʀap] *nf voir* **farce**.

attrape-nigaud [atʀapnigo] *nm* con.

attraper [atʀape] *vt* to catch; (*habitude, amende*) to get, pick up; (*fam: duper*) to take in (*BRIT*), con.

attrayant, e [atʀɛjɑ̃, -ɑ̃t] *adj* attractive.

attribuer [atʀibɥe] *vt* (*prix*) to award; (*rôle, tâche*) to allocate, assign; (*imputer*): **~ qch à** to attribute sth to, ascribe sth to, put sth down to; **s'~** *vt* (*s'approprier*) to claim for o.s.

attribut [atʀiby] *nm* attribute; (*LING*) complement.

attribution [atʀibysjɔ̃] *nf* (*voir attribuer*) awarding; allocation, assignment; attribution; **~s** *nfpl* (*compétence*) attributions; **complément d'~** (*LING*) indirect object.

attristant, e [atʀistɑ̃, -ɑ̃t] *adj* saddening.

attrister [atʀiste] *vt* to sadden; **s'~ de qch** to be saddened by sth.

attroupement [atʀupmɑ̃] *nm* crowd, mob.

attrouper [atʀupe]: **s'~** *vi* to gather.

au [o] *prép + dét voir* **à**.

aubade [obad] *nf* dawn serenade.

aubaine [obɛn] *nf* godsend; (*financière*) windfall; (*COMM*) bonanza.

aube [ob] *nf* dawn, daybreak; (*REL*) alb; **à l'~** at dawn *ou* daybreak; **à l'~ de** (*fig*) at the dawn of.

aubépine [obepin] *nf* hawthorn.

auberge [obɛʀ3(ə)] *nf* inn; **~ de jeunesse** youth hostel.

aubergine [obɛʀ3in] *nf* aubergine (*BRIT*), eggplant (*US*).

aubergiste [obɛʀ3ist(ə)] *nm/f* inn-keeper, hotel-keeper.

auburn [obœʀn] *adj inv* auburn.

aucun, e [okœ̃, -yn] *dét* no, *tournure négative +* any; (*positif*) any ♦ *pron* none, *tournure négative +* any; (*positif*) any(one); **il n'y a ~ livre** there isn't any book, there is no book; **je n'en vois ~ qui** I can't see any which, I (can) see none which; **~ homme** no man; **sans ~ doute** without any doubt; **sans ~e hésitation** without hesitation; **plus qu'~ autre** more than any other; **plus qu'~ de ceux qui ...** more than any of those who ...; **en ~e façon**

in no way at all; **~ des deux** neither of the two; **~ d'entre eux** none of them; **d'~s** (*certains*) some.

aucunement [okynmɑ̃] *adv* in no way, not in the least.

audace [odas] *nf* daring, boldness; (*péj*) audacity; **il a eu l'~ de ...** he had the audacity to ...; **vous ne manquez pas d'~!** you're not lacking in nerve *ou* cheek!

audacieux, euse [odasjø, -øz] *adj* daring, bold.

au-dedans [odədɑ̃] *adv, prép* inside.

au-dehors [odəɔʀ] *adv, prép* outside.

au-delà [odla] *adv* beyond ♦ *nm*: **l'~** the hereafter; **~ de** *prép* beyond.

au-dessous [odsu] *adv* underneath; below; **~ de** *prép* under(neath), below; (*limite, somme etc*) below, under; (*dignité, condition*) below.

au-dessus [odsy] *adv* above; **~ de** *prép* above.

au-devant [odvɑ̃]: **~ de** *prép*: **aller ~ de** to go (out) and meet; (*souhaits de qn*) to anticipate.

audible [odibl(ə)] *adj* audible.

audience [odjɑ̃s] *nf* audience; (*JUR: séance*) hearing; **trouver ~ auprès de** to arouse much interest among, get the (interested) attention of.

audimat [odimat] *nm* (*taux d'écoute*) ratings *pl*.

audiogramme [odjɔgʀam] *nm* audiogramme.

audio-visuel, le [odjɔvizɥɛl] *adj* audio-visual ♦ *nm* (*équipement*) audio-visual aids *pl*; (*méthodes*) audio-visual methods *pl*; **l'~** radio and television.

auditeur, trice [oditœʀ, -tʀis] *nm/f* (*à la radio*) listener; (*à une conférence*) member of the audience, listener; **~ libre** unregistered student (*attending lectures*), auditor (*US*).

auditif, ive [oditif, -iv] (*mémoire*) auditory; **appareil ~** hearing aid.

audition [odisjɔ̃] *nf* (*ouïe, écoute*) hearing; (*JUR: de témoins*) examination; (*MUS, THÉÂT*: épreuve) audition.

auditionner [odisjɔne] *vt, vi* to audition.

auditoire [oditwaʀ] *nm* audience.

auditorium [oditɔʀjɔm] *nm* (*public*) studio.

auge [o3] *nf* trough.

augmentation [ɔgmɑ̃tasjɔ̃] *nf* (*action*) increasing; raising; (*résultat*) increase; **~ (de salaire)** rise (in salary) (*BRIT*), (pay) raise (*US*).

augmenter [ɔgmɑ̃te] *vt* to increase; (*salaire, prix*) to increase, raise, put up; (*employé*) to increase the salary of, give a (salary) rise (*BRIT*) *ou* (pay) raise (*US*) to ♦ *vi* to increase; **~ de poids/volume** to gain (in) weight/volume.

augure [ɔgyʀ] *nm* soothsayer, oracle; **de bon/mauvais ~** of good/ill omen.

augurer [ɔgyʀe] *vt*: **~ qch de** to foresee sth (coming) from *ou* out of; **~ bien de** to augur well for.

auguste [ɔgyst(ə)] *adj* august, noble, majestic.

aujourd'hui [oʒuʀdɥi] *adv* today; ~ **en huit/ quinze** a week/two weeks today, a week/two weeks from now; **à dater** *ou* **partir d'**~ from today('s date).

aumône [omon] *nf* alms *sg* (*pl inv*); **faire l'**~ (**à qn**) to give alms (to sb); **faire l'**~ **de qch à qn** (*fig*) to favour sb with sth.

aumônerie [omonʀi] *nf* chaplaincy.

aumônier [omonje] *nm* chaplain.

auparavant [oparavã] *adv* before(hand).

auprès [opʀɛ]: ~ **de** *prép* next to, close to; (*recourir, s'adresser*) to; (*en comparaison de*) compared with, next to; (*dans l'opinion de*) in the opinion of.

auquel [okɛl] *prép + pron voir* **lequel.**

aurai [ɔʀe] *etc vb voir* **avoir.**

auréole [ɔʀeɔl] *nf* halo; (*tache*) ring.

auréolé, e [ɔʀeɔle] *adj* (*fig*): ~ **de gloire** crowned with *ou* in glory.

auriculaire [ɔʀikylɛʀ] *nm* little finger.

aurore [ɔʀɔʀ] *nf* dawn, daybreak; ~ **boréale** northern lights *pl.*

ausculter [ɔskylte] *vt* to sound.

auspices [ɔspis] *nmpl*: **sous les** ~ **de** under the patronage *ou* auspices of; **sous de bons/ mauvais** ~ under favourable/unfavourable auspices.

aussi [osi] *adv* (*également*) also, too; (*de comparaison*) as ♦ *conj* therefore, consequently; ~ **fort que** as strong as; **lui** ~ (*sujet*) he too; (*objet*) him too; ~ **bien que** (*de même que*) as well as.

aussitôt [osito] *adv* straight away, immediately; ~ **que** as soon as; ~ **enyoyé** as soon as it is (*ou* was) sent; ~ **fait** no sooner done.

austère [ɔstɛʀ] *adj* austere; (*sévère*) stern.

austérité [ɔsteʀite] *nf* austerity; **plan/budget d'**~ austerity plan/budget.

austral, e [ɔstʀal] *adj* southern; **l'océan A**~ the Antarctic Ocean; **les Terres A**~**es** Antarctica.

Australie [ɔstʀali] *nf*: **l'A**~ Australia.

australien, ne [ɔstʀaljɛ̃, -ɛn] *adj* Australian ♦ *nm/f*: **A**~, **ne** Australian.

autant [otã] *adv* so much; (*comparatif*): ~ (**que**) as much (as); (*nombre*) as many (as); ~ (**de**) so much (*ou* many); as much (*ou* many); **n'importe qui aurait pu en faire** ~ anyone could have done the same *ou* as much; ~ **partir** we (*ou* you *etc*) may as well leave; ~ **ne rien dire** best not say anything; ~ **dire que ...** one might as well say that ...; **fort** ~ **que courageux** as strong as he is brave; **il n'est pas découragé pour** ~ he isn't discouraged for all that; **pour** ~ **que** *conj* assuming, as long as; **d'**~ *adv* accordingly, in proportion; **d'**~ **plus/mieux (que)** all the more/the better (since).

autarcie [otaʀsi] *nf* autarky, self-sufficiency.

autel [otɛl] *nm* altar.

auteur [otœʀ] *nm* author; **l'**~ **de cette remarque** the person who said that; **droit d'**~

copyright.

auteur-compositeur [otœʀkɔ̃pozitœʀ] *nm/f* composer-songwriter.

authenticité [otãtisite] *nf* authenticity.

authentifier [otãtifje] *vt* to authenticate.

authentique [otãtik] *adj* authentic, genuine.

autiste [otist] *adj* autistic.

auto [oto] *nf* car; ~**s tamponneuses** bumper cars, dodgems.

auto... [oto] *préfixe* auto..., self-.

autobiographie [otɔbjɔgʀafi] *nf* autobiography.

autobiographique [otɔbjɔgʀafik] *adj* autobiographical.

autobus [otɔbys] *nm* bus.

autocar [otɔkaʀ] *nm* coach.

autocensure [otosãsyʀ] *nf* self-censorship.

autochtone [otɔktɔn] *nm/f* native.

autocollant, e [otɔkɔlã, -ãt] *adj* self-adhesive; (*enveloppe*) self-seal ♦ *nm* sticker.

auto-couchettes [otokuʃɛt] *adj inv*: **train** ~ **car** sleeper train, motorail ® train (*BRIT*).

autocratique [otɔkʀatik] *adj* autocratic.

autocritique [otɔkʀitik] *nf* self-criticism.

autocuiseur [otɔkɥizœʀ] *nm* (*CULIN*) pressure cooker.

autodéfense [otɔdefãs] *nf* self-defence; **groupe d'**~ vigilante committee.

autodétermination [otɔdeteʀminasjɔ̃] *nf* self-determination.

autodidacte [otɔdidakt(ə)] *nm/f* self-taught person.

autodiscipline [otɔdisiplin] *nf* self-discipline.

autodrome [otɔdʀom] *nm* motor-racing stadium.

auto-école [otoekɔl] *nf* driving school.

autofinancement [otɔfinãsmã] *nm* self-financing.

autogéré, e [otɔʒeʀe] *adj* self-managed, managed internally.

autogestion [otɔʒɛstjɔ̃] *nf* joint worker-management control.

autographe [otɔgʀaf] *nm* autograph.

autoguidé, e [otɔgide] *adj* self-guided.

auto-immun, e [otoimɛ̃, -yn] *adj* auto-immune.

automate [otɔmat] *nm* (*robot*) automaton; (*machine*) (automatic) machine.

automatique [otɔmatik] *adj, nm* automatic; **l'**~ (*TÉL*) ≈ direct dialling.

automatiquement [otɔmatikmã] *adv* automatically.

automatisation [otɔmatizasjɔ̃] *nf* automation.

automatiser [otɔmatize] *vt* to automate.

automatisme [otɔmatism(ə)] *nm* automatism.

automédication [otɔmedikasjɔ̃] *nf* self-medication.

automitrailleuse [otɔmitʀajøz] *nf* armoured car.

automnal, e, aux [otɔnal, -o] *adj* autumnal.

automne [otɔn] *nm* autumn (*BRIT*), fall (*US*).

automobile [otɔmɔbil] *adj* motor *cpd* ♦ *nf* (motor) car; **l'~** motoring; (*industrie*) the car *ou* automobile (*US*) industry.

automobiliste [ɔtɔmɔbilist(ə)] *nm/f* motorist.

autonettoyant, e [ɔtɔnɛtwajɑ̃, -ɑ̃t] *adj*: **four ~** self-cleaning oven.

autonome [ɔtɔnɔm] *adj* autonomous; (*INFORM*) stand-alone; **(en mode) ~** off line.

autonomie [ɔtɔnɔmi] *nf* autonomy; (*POL*) self-government, autonomy; **~ de vol** range.

autonomiste [ɔtɔnɔmist(ə)] *nm/f* separatist.

autoportrait [ɔtɔpɔʀtʀɛ] *nm* self-portrait.

autopsie [ɔtɔpsi] *nf* post-mortem (examination), autopsy.

autopsier [ɔtɔpsje] *vt* to carry out a post-mortem *ou* an autopsy on.

autoradio [ɔtɔʀadjo] *nf* car radio.

autorail [ɔtɔʀaj] *nm* railcar.

autorisation [ɔtɔʀizɑsjɔ̃] *nf* permission, authorization; (*papiers*) permit; **donner à qn l'~ de** to give sb permission to, authorize sb to; **avoir l'~ de faire** to be allowed *ou* have permission to do, be authorized to do.

autorisé, e [ɔtɔʀize] *adj* (*opinion, sources*) authoritative; (*permis*): **~ à faire** authorized *ou* permitted to do; **dans les milieux ~s** in official circles.

autoriser [ɔtɔʀize] *vt* to give permission for, authorize; (*fig*) to allow (of), sanction; **~ qn à faire** to give permission to sb to do, authorize sb to do.

autoritaire [ɔtɔʀitɛʀ] *adj* authoritarian.

autoritarisme [ɔtɔʀitaʀism(ə)] *nm* authoritarianism.

autorité [ɔtɔʀite] *nf* authority; **faire ~** to be authoritative; **~s constituées** constitutional authorities.

autoroute [ɔtɔʀut] *nf* motorway (*BRIT*), expressway (*US*); **~ de l'information** (*TEL*) information highway.

autoroutier, ière [ɔtɔʀutje, -jɛʀ] *adj* motorway *cpd* (*BRIT*), expressway *cpd* (*US*).

autosatisfaction [ɔtɔsatisfaksjɔ̃] *nf* self-satisfaction.

auto-stop [ɔtɔstɔp] *nm*: **l'~** hitch-hiking; **faire de l'~** to hitch-hike; **prendre qn en ~** to give sb a lift.

auto-stoppeur, euse [ɔtɔstɔpœʀ, -øz] *nm/f* hitch-hiker, hitcher (*BRIT*).

autosuffisant, e [ɔtɔsyfizɑ̃, -ɑ̃t] *adj* self-sufficient.

autosuggestion [ɔtɔsyɡʒɛstjɔ̃] *nf* autosuggestion.

autour [otuʀ] *adv* around; **~ de** *prép* around; (*environ*) around, about; **tout ~** *adv* all around.

═══════════════════════════ *MOT-CLÉ*

autre [otʀ(ə)] *adj* **1** (*différent*) other, different; **je préférerais un ~ verre** I'd prefer another *ou* a different glass; **d'~s verres** different glasses; **se sentir ~** to feel different; **la difficulté est ~** the difficulty is *ou* lies else-

where

2 (*supplémentaire*) other; **je voudrais un ~ verre d'eau** I'd like another glass of water

3: **~ chose** something else; **~ part** somewhere else; **d'~ part** on the other hand

♦ *pron* **1**: **un ~** another (one); **nous/vous ~s** us/you; **d'~s** others; **l'~** the other (one); **les ~s** the others; (*autrui*) others; **l'un et l'~** both of them; **ni l'un ni l'~** neither of them; **se détester l'un l'~/les uns les ~s** to hate each other *ou* one another; **d'une semaine/minute à l'~** from one week/minute *ou* moment to the next; (*incessamment*) any week/minute *ou* moment now; **de temps à ~** from time to time; **entre ~s** among other things

2 (*expressions*): **j'en ai vu d'~s** I've seen worse; **à d'~s!** pull the other one!

autrefois [otʀəfwa] *adv* in the past.

autrement [otʀəmɑ̃] *adv* differently; (*d'une manière différente*) in another way; (*sinon*) otherwise; **je n'ai pas pu faire ~** I couldn't do anything else, I couldn't do otherwise; **~ dit** in other words; (*c'est-à-dire*) that is to say.

Autriche [otʀiʃ] *nf*: **l'~** Austria.

autrichien, ne [otʀiʃjɛ̃, -ɛn] *adj* Austrian ♦ *nm/f*: **A~, ne** Austrian.

autruche [otʀyʃ] *nf* ostrich; **faire l'~** (*fig*) to bury one's head in the sand.

autrui [otʀɥi] *pron* others.

auvent [ovɑ̃] *nm* canopy.

auvergnat, e [ovɛʀɲa, -at] *adj* of *ou* from the Auvergne.

Auvergne [ovɛʀɲ(ə)] *nf*: **l'~** the Auvergne.

aux [o] *prép + dét voir* **à**.

auxiliaire [ɔksiljɛʀ] *adj, nm/f* auxiliary.

auxquels, auxquelles [okɛl] *prép + pron voir* **lequel**.

AV *sigle m* (*BANQUE*: = *avis de virement*) *advice of bank transfer* ♦ *abr* (*AUTO*) = **avant**.

av. *abr* (= *avenue*) Av(e).

avachi, e [avaʃi] *adj* limp, flabby; (*chaussure, vêtement*) out-of-shape; (*personne*): **~ sur qch** slumped on *ou* across sth.

avais [avɛ] *etc vb voir* **avoir**.

aval [aval] *nm* (*accord*) endorsement, backing; (*GÉO*): **en ~** downstream, downriver; (*sur une pente*) downhill; **en ~ de** downstream *ou* downriver from; downhill from.

avalanche [avalɑ̃ʃ] *nf* avalanche; **~ poudreuse** powder snow avalanche.

avaler [avale] *vt* to swallow.

avaliser [avalize] *vt* (*plan, entreprise*) to back, support; (*COMM, JUR*) to guarantee.

avance [avɑ̃s] *nf* (*de troupes etc*) advance; (*progrès*) progress; (*d'argent*) advance; (*opposé à retard*) lead; being ahead of schedule; **~s** *nfpl* overtures; (*amoureuses*) advances; **une ~ de 300 m/4 h** (*SPORT*) a 300 m/4 hour lead; **(être) en ~** (to be) early; (*sur un programme*) (to be) ahead of schedule; **on n'est**

pas en ~**!** we're kind of late!; **être en** ~ **sur qn** to be ahead of sb; **d'**~**, à l'**~**, par** ~ in advance; ~ **(du) papier** (INFORM) paper advance.

avancé, e [avɑ̃se] adj advanced; (travail etc) well on, well under way; (fruit, fromage) overripe ♦ nf projection; overhang; **il est** ~ **pour son âge** he is advanced for his age.

avancement [avɑ̃smɑ̃] nm (professionnel) promotion; (de travaux) progress.

avancer [avɑ̃se] vi to move forward, advance; (projet, travail) to make progress; (être en saillie) to overhang; to project; (montre, réveil) to be fast; (: d'habitude) to gain ♦ vt to move forward, advance; (argent) to advance; (montre, pendule) to put forward; (faire progresser: travail etc) to advance, move on; **s'**~ vi to move forward, advance; (fig) to commit o.s.; (faire saillie) to overhang; to project; **j'avance (d'une heure)** I'm (an hour) fast.

avanies [avani] nfpl snubs (BRIT), insults.

avant [avɑ̃] prép before ♦ adv: **trop/plus** ~ too far/further forward ♦ adj inv: **siège/roue** ~ front seat/wheel ♦ nm front; (SPORT: joueur) forward; ~ **qu'il parte/de partir** before he leaves/leaving; ~ **qu'il (ne) pleuve** before it rains (ou rained); ~ **tout** (surtout) above all; **à l'**~ (dans un véhicule) in (the) front; **en** ~ adv forward(s); **en** ~ **de** prép in front of; **aller de l'**~ to steam ahead (fig), make good progress.

avantage [avɑ̃taʒ] nm advantage; (TENNIS): ~ **service/dehors** advantage ou van (BRIT) ou ad (US) in/out; **tirer** ~ **de** to take advantage of; **vous auriez** ~ **à faire** you would be well-advised to do, it would be to your advantage to do; **à l'**~ **de qn** to sb's advantage; **être à son** ~ to be at one's best; ~**s en nature** benefits in kind; ~**s sociaux** fringe benefits.

avantager [avɑ̃taʒe] vt (favoriser) to favour; (embellir) to flatter.

avantageux, euse [avɑ̃taʒø, -øz] adj attractive; (intéressant) attractively priced; (portrait, coiffure) flattering; **conditions avantageuses** favourable terms.

avant-bras [avɑ̃bʀɑ] nm inv forearm.

avant-centre [avɑ̃sɑ̃tʀ(ə)] nm centre-forward.

avant-coureur [avɑ̃kuʀœʀ] adj inv (bruit etc) precursory; **signe** ~ advance indication ou sign.

avant-dernier, ière [avɑ̃dɛʀnje, -jɛʀ] adj, nm/f next to last, last but one.

avant-garde [avɑ̃gaʀd(ə)] nf (MIL) vanguard; (fig) avant-garde; **d'**~ avant-garde.

avant-goût [avɑ̃gu] nm foretaste.

avant-hier [avɑ̃tjɛʀ] adv the day before yesterday.

avant-poste [avɑ̃pɔst(ə)] nm outpost.

avant-première [avɑ̃pʀəmjɛʀ] nf (de film) preview; **en** ~ as a preview, in a preview show-ing.

avant-projet [avɑ̃pʀɔʒe] nm preliminary draft.

avant-propos [avɑ̃pʀɔpo] nm foreword.

avant-veille [avɑ̃vɛj] nf: **l'**~ two days before.

avare [avaʀ] adj miserly, avaricious ♦ nm/f miser; ~ **de compliments** stingy ou sparing with one's compliments.

avarice [avaʀis] nf avarice, miserliness.

avaricieux, euse [avaʀisjø, -øz] adj miserly, niggardly.

avarié, e [avaʀje] adj (viande, fruits) rotting, going off (BRIT); (NAVIG: navire) damaged.

avaries [avaʀi] nfpl (NAVIG) damage sg.

avatar [avataʀ] nm misadventure; (transformation) metamorphosis (pl -phoses).

avec [avɛk] prép with; (à l'égard de) to(wards), with ♦ adv (fam) with it (ou him etc); ~ **habileté/lenteur** skilfully/slowly; ~ **eux/ces maladies** with them/these diseases; ~ **ça** (malgré ça) for all that; **et** ~ **ça?** (dans un magasin) anything ou something else?

avenant, e [avnɑ̃, -ɑ̃t] adj pleasant ♦ nm (ASSURANCES) additional clause; **à l'**~ adv in keeping.

avènement [avɛnmɑ̃] nm (d'un roi) accession, succession; (d'un changement) advent; (d'une politique, idée) coming.

avenir [avniʀ] nm: **l'**~ the future; **à l'**~ in future; **sans** ~ with no future, without a future; **carrière/politicien d'**~ career/politician with prospects ou a future.

Avent [avɑ̃] nm: **l'**~ Advent.

aventure [avɑ̃tyʀ] nf: **l'**~ adventure; **une** ~ an adventure; (amoureuse) an affair; **partir à l'**~ to go off in search of adventure; (au hasard) to go where one's fancy takes one; **roman/film d'**~ adventure story/film.

aventurer [avɑ̃tyʀe] vt (somme, réputation, vie) to stake; (remarque, opinion) to venture; **s'**~ vi to venture; **s'**~ **à faire qch** to venture into sth.

aventureux, euse [avɑ̃tyʀø, -øz] adj adventurous, venturesome; (projet) risky, chancy.

aventurier, ière [avɑ̃tyʀje, -jɛʀ] nm/f adventurer ♦ nf (péj) adventuress.

avenu, e [avny] adj: **nul et non** ~ null and void.

avenue [avny] nf avenue.

avéré, e [aveʀe] adj recognized, acknowledged.

avérer [aveʀe]: **s'**~ vb avec attribut: **s'**~ **faux/coûteux** to prove (to be) wrong/expensive.

averse [avɛʀs(ə)] nf shower.

aversion [avɛʀsjɔ̃] nf aversion, loathing.

averti, e [avɛʀti] adj (well-)informed.

avertir [avɛʀtiʀ] vt: ~ **qn (de qch/que)** to warn sb (of sth/that); (renseigner) to inform sb (of sth/that); ~ **qn de ne pas faire qch** to warn sb not to do sth.

avertissement [avɛʀtismɑ̃] nm warning.

avertisseur [avɛʀtisœʀ] nm horn, siren; ~

(d'incendie) (fire) alarm.

aveu, x [avø] *nm* confession; **passer aux ~x** to make a confession; **de l'~ de** according to.

aveuglant, e [avœglɑ̃, -ɑ̃t] *adj* blinding.

aveugle [avœgl(ə)] *adj* blind ♦ *nm/f* blind person; **les ~s** the blind; **test en (double) ~** (double) blind test.

aveuglement [avœgləmɑ̃] *nm* blindness.

aveuglément [avœglemɑ̃] *adv* blindly.

aveugler [avœgle] *vt* to blind.

aveuglette [avœglɛt]: **à l'~** groping one's way along; (*fig*) in the dark, blindly.

avez [ave] *vb voir* **avoir**.

aviateur, trice [avjatœʀ, -tʀis] *nm/f* aviator, pilot.

aviation [avjɑsjɔ̃] *nf* (*secteur commercial*) aviation; (*sport, métier de pilote*) flying; (*MIL*) air force; **terrain d'~** airfield; **~ de chasse** fighter force.

aviculteur, trice [avikyltœʀ, -tʀis] *nm/f* poultry farmer; bird breeder.

aviculture [avikyltyʀ] *nf* (*de volailles*) poultry farming.

avide [avid] *adj* eager; (*péj*) greedy, grasping; **~ de** (*sang etc*) thirsting for; **~ d'honneurs/ d'argent** greedy for honours/money; **~ de connaître/d'apprendre** eager to know/learn.

avidité [avidite] *nf* eagerness; greed.

avilir [aviliʀ] *vt* to debase.

avilissant, e [avilisɑ̃, -ɑ̃t] *adj* degrading.

aviné, e [avine] *adj* drunken.

avion [avjɔ̃] *nm* (aero)plane (*BRIT*), (air)plane (*US*); **aller (quelque part) en ~** to go (somewhere) by plane, fly (somewhere); **par ~** by airmail; **~ de chasse** fighter; **~ de ligne** airliner; **~ à réaction** jet (plane).

avion-cargo [avjɔ̃kaʀgo] *nm* air freighter.

avion-citerne [avjɔ̃sitɛʀn(ə)] *nm* air tanker.

aviron [aviʀɔ̃] *nm* oar; (*sport*): **l'~** rowing.

avis [avi] *nm* opinion; (*notification*) notice; (*COMM*): **~ de crédit/débit** credit/debit advice; **à mon ~** in my opinion; **je suis de votre ~** I share your opinion, I am of your opinion; **être d'~ que** to be of the opinion that; **changer d'~** to change one's mind; **sauf ~ contraire** unless you hear to the contrary; **sans ~ préalable** without notice; **jusqu'à nouvel ~** until further notice; **~ de décès** death announcement.

avisé, e [avize] *adj* sensible, wise; **être bien/ mal ~ de faire** to be well-/ill-advised to do.

aviser [avize] *vt* (*voir*) to notice, catch sight of; (*informer*): **~ qn de/que** to advise *ou* inform *ou* notify sb of/that ♦ *vi* to think about things, assess the situation; **s'~ de qch/que** to become suddenly aware of sth/that; **s'~ de faire** to take it into one's head to do.

aviver [avive] *vt* (*douleur, chagrin*) to intensify; (*intérêt, désir*) to sharpen; (*colère, querelle*) to stir up; (*couleur*) to brighten up.

av. J.-C. *abr* (= *avant Jésus-Christ*) BC.

avocat, e [avɔka, -at] *nm/f* (*JUR*) ≈ barrister (*BRIT*), lawyer; (*fig*) advocate, champion ♦ *nm* (*CULIN*) avocado (pear); **se faire l'~ du diable** to be the devil's advocate; **l'~ de la défense/partie civile** the counsel for the defence/plaintiff; **~ d'affaires** business lawyer; **~ général** assistant public prosecutor.

avocat-conseil, *pl* **avocats-conseils** [avɔkakɔ̃sɛj] *nm* ≈ barrister (*BRIT*).

avocat-stagiaire, *pl* **avocats-stagiaires** [avɔkastaʒjɛʀ] *nm* ≈ barrister doing his articles (*BRIT*).

avoine [avwan] *nf* oats *pl*.

MOT-CLÉ

avoir [avwaʀ] *nm* assets *pl*, resources *pl*; (*COMM*) credit; **~ fiscal** tax credit

♦ *vt* **1** (*posséder*) to have; **elle a 2 enfants/une belle maison** she has (got) 2 children/a lovely house; **il a les yeux bleus** he has (got) blue eyes

2 (*éprouver*): **qu'est-ce que tu as?, qu'as-tu?** what's wrong?, what's the matter?; *voir aussi* **faim, peur** *etc*

3 (*âge, dimensions*) to be; **il a 3 ans** he is 3 (years old); **le mur a 3 mètres de haut** the wall is 3 metres high

4 (*fam: duper*) to do, have; **on vous a eu!** you've been done *ou* had!

5: en ~ contre qn to have a grudge against sb; **en ~ assez** to be fed up; **j'en ai pour une demi-heure** it'll take me half an hour; **n'~ que faire de qch** to have no use for sth

♦ *vb aux* **1** to have; **~ mangé/dormi** to have eaten/slept; **hier je n'ai pas mangé** I didn't eat yesterday

2 (*avoir +à +infinitif*): **~ à faire qch** to have to do sth; **vous n'avez qu'à lui demander** you only have to ask him; **tu n'as pas à me poser des questions** it's not for you to ask me questions

♦ *vb impers* **1**: **il y a** (+ *singulier*) there is; (+ *pluriel*) there are; **qu'y a-t-il?, qu'est-ce qu'il y a?** what's the matter?, what is it?; **il doit y avoir une explication** there must be an explanation; **il n'y a qu'à ...** we (*ou* you *etc*) will just have to ...; **il ne peut y en ~ qu'un** there can only be one

2 (*temporel*): **il y a 10 ans** 10 years ago; **il y a 10 ans/longtemps que je le connais** I've known him for 10 years/a long time; **il y a 10 ans qu'il est arrivé** it's 10 years since he arrived.

avoisinant, e [avwazinɑ̃, -ɑ̃t] *adj* neighbouring.

avoisiner [avwazine] *vt* to be near *ou* close to; (*fig*) to border *ou* verge on.

avons [avɔ̃] *vb voir* **avoir**.

avortement [avɔʀtəmɑ̃] *nm* abortion.

avorter [avɔʀte] *vi* (*MÉD*) to have an abortion; (*fig*) to fail; **faire ~** to abort; **se faire ~** to have an abortion.

avorton [avɔʀtɔ̃] *nm* (*péj*) little runt.
avouable [avwabl(ə)] *adj* respectable; **des pensées non ~s** unrepeatable thoughts.
avoué, e [avwe] *adj* avowed ♦ *nm* (*JUR*) ≈ solicitor (*BRIT*), lawyer.
avouer [avwe] *vt* (*crime, défaut*) to confess (to) ♦ *vi* (*se confesser*) to confess; (*admettre*) to admit; **~ avoir fait/que** to admit *ou* confess to having done/that; **~ que oui/non** to admit that that is so/not so; **s'~ vaincu** to admit defeat.
avril [avʀil] *nm* April; *voir aussi* **juillet**.

The traditional prank on April 1 in France involves placing a cut-out paper fish, known as a **poisson d'avril**, *on the back of one's victim, without being caught.*

---

axe [aks(ə)] *nm* axis (*pl* axes); (*de roue etc*) axle; (*prolongement*): **dans l'~ de** directly in line with; (*fig*) main line; **~ routier** trunk road, main road.
axer [akse] *vt*: **~ qch sur** to centre sth on.
axial, e, aux [aksjal, -o] *adj* axial.
axiome [aksjom] *nm* axiom.
ayant [ɛjɑ̃] *vb voir* **avoir** ♦ *nm*: **~ droit** assignee; **~ droit à** (*pension etc*) person eligible for *ou* entitled to.
ayons [ɛjɔ̃] *etc vb voir* **avoir**.
azalée [azale] *nf* azalea.
Azerbaïdjan [azɛʀbaidʒɑ̃] *nm* Azerbaijan.
azerbaïdjanais, e [azɛʀbaidʒanɛ, -ɛz] *adj* Azerbaijani ♦ *nm* (*LING*) Azerbaijani ♦ *nm/f*: **A~, e** Azerbaijani.
azimut [azimyt] *nm* azimuth; **tous ~s** *adj* (*fig*) omnidirectional.
azote [azɔt] *nm* nitrogen.
azoté, e [azɔte] *adj* nitrogenous.
AZT *sigle m* (= azidothymidine) AZT.
aztèque [aztɛk] *adj* Aztec.
azur [azyʀ] *nm* (*couleur*) azure, sky blue; (*ciel*) sky, skies *pl*.
azyme [azim] *adj*: **pain ~** unleavened bread.

B b

B, b [be] *nm inv* B, b ♦ *abr* = **bien**; **B comme Bertha** B for Benjamin (*BRIT*) *ou* Baker (*US*).
BA *sigle f* (= bonne action) good deed.
baba [baba] *adj inv*: **en être ~** (*fam*) to be flabbergasted ♦ *nm*: **~ au rhum** rum baba.
babil [babi] *nm* prattle.
babillage [babijaʒ] *nm* chatter.
babiller [babije] *vi* to prattle, chatter; (*bébé*) to babble.

babines [babin] *nfpl* chops.
babiole [babjɔl] *nf* (*bibelot*) trinket; (*vétille*) trifle.
bâbord [babɔʀ] *nm*: **à ou par ~** to port, on the port side.
babouin [babwɛ̃] *nm* baboon.
baby-foot [babifut] *nm inv* table football.
Babylone [babilɔn] *n* Babylon.
babylonien, ne [babilɔnjɛ̃, -ɛn] *adj* Babylonian.
baby-sitter [babisitœʀ] *nm/f* baby-sitter.
baby-sitting [babisitiŋ] *nm* baby-sitting.
bac [bak] *nm* (*SCOL*) = **baccalauréat**; (*bateau*) ferry; (*récipient*) tub; (*: PHOTO etc*) tray; (*: INDUSTRIE*) tank; **~ à glace** ice-tray; **~ à légumes** vegetable compartment *ou* rack.
baccalauréat [bakalɔʀea] *nm* ≈ GCE A-levels *pl* (*BRIT*), ≈ high school diploma (*US*).

In France the **baccalauréat** *or* **bac** *is the school-leaving certificate taken at a lycée at the age of seventeen or eighteen after seven years of secondary education. A variety of subject combinations is available, although in all cases a broad range of subjects is studied. Holders of the certificate are entitled to go on to university.*

---

bâche [baʃ] *nf* tarpaulin, canvas sheet.
bachelier, ière [baʃəlje, -jɛʀ] *nm/f* holder of the baccalauréat.
bâcher [baʃe] *vt* to cover (with a canvas sheet *ou* a tarpaulin).
bachot [baʃo] *nm* = **baccalauréat**.
bachotage [baʃotaʒ] *nm* (*SCOL*) cramming.
bachoter [baʃote] *vi* (*SCOL*) to cram (for an exam).
bacille [basil] *nm* bacillus (*pl* -i).
bâcler [bakle] *vt* to botch (up).
bacon [bekɔn] *nm* bacon.
bactéricide [bakteʀisid] *nm* (*MÉD*) bactericide.
bactérie [bakteʀi] *nf* bacterium (*pl* -ia).
bactérien, ne [bakteʀjɛ̃, -ɛn] *adj* bacterial.
bactériologie [bakteʀjɔlɔʒi] *nf* bacteriology.
bactériologique [bakteʀjɔlɔʒik] *adj* bacteriological.
bactériologiste [bakteʀjɔlɔʒist(ə)] *nm/f* bacteriologist.
badaud, e [bado, -od] *nm/f* idle onlooker, stroller.
baderne [badɛʀn(ə)] *nf* (*péj*): **(vieille) ~** old fossil.
badge [badʒ(ə)] *nm* badge.
badigeon [badiʒɔ̃] *nm* distemper; colourwash.
badigeonner [badiʒɔne] *vt* to distemper; to colourwash; (*péj: barbouiller*) to daub; (*MÉD*) to paint.
badin, e [badɛ̃, -in] *adj* light-hearted, playful.
badinage [badinaʒ] *nm* banter.
badine [badin] *nf* switch (*stick*).
badiner [badine] *vi*: **~ avec qch** to treat sth lightly; **ne pas ~ avec qch** not to trifle with

sth.

badminton [badmintɔn] *nm* badminton.

BAFA [bafa] *sigle m* (= *Brevet d'aptitude aux fonctions d'animation*) *diploma for youth leaders and workers.*

baffe [baf] *nf* (*fam*) slap, clout.

Baffin [bafin] *nf*: **terre de** ~ Baffin Island.

baffle [bafl(ə)] *nm* baffle (board).

bafouer [bafwe] *vt* to deride, ridicule.

bafouillage [bafujaʒ] *nm* (*fam: propos incohérents*) jumble of words.

bafouiller [bafuje] *vi, vt* to stammer.

bâfrer [bɑfʀe] *vi, vt* (*fam*) to guzzle, gobble.

bagage [bagaʒ] *nm*: ~**s** luggage *sg*, baggage *sg*; ~ **littéraire** (stock of) literary knowledge; ~**s à main** hand-luggage.

bagarre [bagaʀ] *nf* fight, brawl; **il aime la** ~ he loves a fight, he likes fighting.

bagarrer [bagaʀe]: **se** ~ *vi* to (have a) fight.

bagarreur, euse [bagaʀœʀ, -øz] *adj* pugnacious ♦ *nm/f*: **il est** ~ he loves a fight.

bagatelle [bagatɛl] *nf* trifle, trifling sum (*ou* matter).

Bagdad, Baghdâd [bagdad] *n* Baghdad.

bagnard [baɲaʀ] *nm* convict.

bagne [baɲ] *nm* penal colony; **c'est le** ~ (*fig*) it's forced labour.

bagnole [baɲɔl] *nf* (*fam*) car, wheels *pl* (*BRIT*).

bagout [bagu] *nm* glibness; **avoir du** ~ to have the gift of the gab.

bague [bag] *nf* ring; ~ **de fiançailles** engagement ring; ~ **de serrage** clip.

baguenauder [bagnode]: **se** ~ *vi* to trail around, loaf around.

baguer [bage] *vt* to ring.

baguette [bagɛt] *nf* stick; (*cuisine chinoise*) chopstick; (*de chef d'orchestre*) baton; (*pain*) stick of (French) bread; (*CONSTR: moulure*) beading; **mener qn à la** ~ to rule sb with a rod of iron; ~ **magique** magic wand; ~ **de sourcier** divining rod; ~ **de tambour** drumstick.

Bahamas [baamas] *nfpl*: **les (îles)** ~ the Bahamas.

Bahrein [baʀɛn] *nm* Bahrain *ou* Bahrein.

bahut [bay] *nm* chest.

bai, e [bɛ] *adj* (*cheval*) bay.

baie [bɛ] *nf* (*GÉO*) bay; (*fruit*) berry; ~ (**vitrée**) picture window.

baignade [bɛɲad] *nf* (*action*) bathing; (*bain*) bathe; (*endroit*) bathing place.

baigné, e [bɛɲe] *adj*: ~ **de** bathed in; (*trempé*) soaked with; (*inondé*) flooded with.

baigner [bɛɲe] *vt* (*bébé*) to bath ♦ *vi*: ~ **dans son sang** to lie in a pool of blood; ~ **dans la brume** to be shrouded in mist; **se** ~ *vi* to go swimming *ou* bathing; (*dans une baignoire*) to have a bath; **ça baigne!** (*fam*) everything's great!

baigneur, euse [bɛɲœʀ, -øz] *nm/f* bather ♦ *nm* (*poupée*) baby doll.

baignoire [bɛɲwaʀ] *nf* bath(tub); (*THÉÂT*)

ground-floor box.

bail, baux [baj, bo] *nm* lease; **donner** *ou* **prendre qch à** ~ to lease sth.

bâillement [bɑjmɑ̃] *nm* yawn.

bâiller [bɑje] *vi* to yawn; (*être ouvert*) to gape.

bailleur [bajœʀ] *nm*: ~ **de fonds** sponsor, backer; (*COMM*) sleeping *ou* silent partner.

bâillon [bɑjɔ̃] *nm* gag.

bâillonner [bɑjɔne] *vt* to gag.

bain [bɛ̃] *nm* (*dans une baignoire, PHOTO, TECH*) bath; (*dans la mer, une piscine*) swim; **costume de** ~ bathing costume (*BRIT*), swimsuit; **prendre un** ~ to have a bath; **se mettre dans le** ~ (*fig*) to get into (the way of) it *ou* things; ~ **de bouche** mouthwash; ~ **de foule** walkabout; ~ **de pieds** footbath; (*au bord de la mer*) paddle; ~ **de siège** hip bath; ~ **de soleil** sunbathing *no pl*; **prendre un** ~ **de soleil** to sunbathe; ~**s de mer** sea bathing *sg*; ~**s(-douches) municipaux** public baths.

bain-marie, *pl* **bains-marie** [bɛ̃maʀi] *nm* double boiler; **faire chauffer au** ~ (*boîte etc*) to immerse in boiling water.

baïonnette [bajɔnɛt] *nf* bayonet; (*ÉLEC*): **douille à** ~ bayonet socket; **ampoule à** ~ bulb with a bayonet fitting.

baisemain [bɛzmɛ̃] *nm* kissing a lady's hand.

baiser [beze] *nm* kiss ♦ *vt* (*main, front*) to kiss; (*fam!*) to screw (*!*).

baisse [bɛs] *nf* fall, drop; (*COMM*): *"*~ **sur la viande"** "meat prices down"; **en** ~ (*cours, action*) falling; **à la** ~ downwards.

baisser [bese] *vt* to lower; (*radio, chauffage*) to turn down; (*AUTO: phares*) to dip (*BRIT*), lower (*US*) ♦ *vi* to fall, drop, go down; **se** ~ *vi* to bend down.

bajoues [baʒu] *nfpl* chaps, chops.

bal [bal] *nm* dance; (*grande soirée*) ball; ~ **costumé/masqué** fancy-dress/masked ball; ~ **musette** dance (*with accordion accompaniment*).

balade [balad] *nf* walk, stroll; (*en voiture*) drive; **faire une** ~ to go for a walk *ou* stroll; to go for a drive.

balader [balade] *vt* (*traîner*) to trail around; **se** ~ *vi* to go for a walk *ou* stroll; to go for a drive.

baladeur [baladœʀ] *nm* personal stereo.

baladeuse [baladøz] *nf* inspection lamp.

baladin [baladɛ̃] *nm* wandering entertainer.

balafre [balafʀ(ə)] *nf* gash, slash; (*cicatrice*) scar.

balafrer [balafʀe] *vt* to gash, slash.

balai [balɛ] *nm* broom, brush; (*AUTO: d'essuie-glace*) blade; (*MUS: de batterie etc*) brush; **donner un coup de** ~ to give the floor a sweep; ~ **mécanique** carpet sweeper.

balai-brosse, *pl* **balais-brosses** [balɛbʀɔs] *nm* (long-handled) scrubbing brush.

balance [balɑ̃s] *nf* (*à plateaux*) scales *pl*; (*de précision*) balance; (*COMM, POL*): ~ **des comptes** *ou* **paiements** balance of payments; (*signe*): **la B**~ Libra, the Scales; **être de la B**~ to be Libra; ~ **commerciale** balance of trade; ~ **des forces** balance of power; ~ **romaine** steelyard.

balancelle [balɑ̃sɛl] *nf* garden hammock-seat.

balancer [balɑ̃se] *vt* to swing; (*lancer*) to fling, chuck; (*renvoyer, jeter*) to chuck out ♦ *vi* to swing; **se** ~ *vi* to swing; (*bateau*) to rock; (*branche*) to sway; **se** ~ **de qch** (*fam*) not to give a toss about sth.

balancier [balɑ̃sje] *nm* (*de pendule*) pendulum; (*de montre*) balance wheel; (*perche*) (*balancing*) pole.

balançoire [balɑ̃swaʀ] *nf* swing; (*sur pivot*) seesaw.

balayage [balɛjaʒ] *nm* sweeping; scanning.

balayer [baleje] *vt* (*feuilles etc*) to sweep up, brush up; (*pièce, cour*) to sweep; (*chasser*) to sweep away *ou* aside; (*suj: radar*) to scan; (: *phares*) to sweep across.

balayette [balɛjɛt] *nf* small brush.

balayeur, euse [balɛjœʀ, -øz] *nm/f* roadsweeper ♦ *nf* (*engin*) roadsweeper.

balayures [balɛjyʀ] *nfpl* sweepings.

balbutiement [balbysimɑ̃] *nm* (*paroles*) stammering *no pl*; ~**s** *nmpl* (*fig: débuts*) first faltering steps.

balbutier [balbysje] *vi, vt* to stammer.

balcon [balkɔ̃] *nm* balcony; (*THÉÂT*) dress circle.

baldaquin [baldakɛ̃] *nm* canopy.

Bâle [bɑl] *n* Basle *ou* Basel.

Baléares [baleaʀ] *nfpl*: **les** ~ the Balearic Islands.

baleine [balɛn] *nf* whale; (*de parapluie*) rib; (*de corset*) bone.

baleinier [balenje] *nm* (*NAVIG*) whaler.

baleinière [balenjɛʀ] *nf* whaleboat.

balisage [balizaʒ] *nm* (*signaux*) beacons *pl*; buoys *pl*; runway lights *pl*; signs *pl*, markers *pl*.

balise [baliz] *nf* (*NAVIG*) beacon, (*marker*) buoy; (*AVIAT*) runway light, beacon; (*AUTO, SKI*) sign, marker.

baliser [balize] *vt* to mark out (with beacons *ou* lights *etc*).

balistique [balistik] *adj* (*engin*) ballistic ♦ *nf* ballistics.

balivernes [balivɛʀn(ə)] *nfpl* twaddle *sg* (*BRIT*), nonsense *sg*.

balkanique [balkanik] *adj* Balkan.

Balkans [balkɑ̃] *nmpl*: **les** ~ the Balkans.

ballade [balad] *nf* ballad.

ballant, e [balɑ̃, -ɑ̃t] *adj* dangling.

ballast [balast] *nm* ballast.

balle [bal] *nf* (*de fusil*) bullet; (*de sport*) ball; (*du blé*) chaff; (*paquet*) bale; (*fam: franc*) franc; ~ **perdue** stray bullet.

ballerine [balʀin] *nf* ballet dancer; (*chaussure*) pump, ballerina.

ballet [balɛ] *nm* ballet; (*fig*): ~ **diplomatique** diplomatic to-ings and fro-ings.

ballon [balɔ̃] *nm* (*de sport*) ball; (*jouet, AVIAT, de bande dessinée*) balloon; (*de vin*) glass; ~ **d'essai** (*météorologique*) pilot balloon; (*fig*) feeler(s); ~ **de football** football; ~ **d'oxygène** oxygen bottle.

ballonner [balɔne] *vt*: **j'ai le ventre ballonné** I feel bloated.

ballon-sonde, *pl* **ballons-sondes** [balɔ̃sɔ̃d] *nm* sounding balloon.

ballot [balo] *nm* bundle; (*péj*) nitwit.

ballottage [balɔtaʒ] *nm* (*POL*) second ballot.

ballotter [balɔte] *vi* to roll around; (*bateau etc*) to toss ♦ *vt* to shake *ou* throw about; to toss; **être ballotté entre** (*fig*) to be shunted between; (: *indécis*) to be torn between.

ballottine [balɔtin] *nf* (*CULIN*): ~ **de volaille** meat loaf made with poultry.

ball-trap [baltʀap] *nm* (*appareil*) trap; (*tir*) clay pigeon shooting.

balluchon [balyʃɔ̃] *nm* bundle (of clothes).

balnéaire [balneɛʀ] *adj* seaside *cpd*.

balnéothérapie [balneɔteʀapi] *nf* spa bath therapy.

BALO *sigle m* (= *Bulletin des annonces légales obligatoires*) ≈ Public Notices (*in newspapers etc*).

balourd, e [baluʀ, -uʀd(ə)] *adj* clumsy ♦ *nm/f* clodhopper.

balourdise [baluʀdiz] *nf* clumsiness; (*gaffe*) blunder.

balte [balt] *adj* Baltic ♦ *nm/f*: **B**~ native of the Baltic States.

baltique [baltik] *adj* Baltic ♦ *nf*: **la (mer) B**~ the Baltic (Sea).

baluchon [balyʃɔ̃] *nm* = **balluchon**.

balustrade [balystʀad] *nf* railings *pl*, handrail.

bambin [bɑ̃bɛ̃] *nm* little child.

bambou [bɑ̃bu] *nm* bamboo.

ban [bɑ̃] *nm* round of applause, cheer; **être/mettre au** ~ **de** to be outlawed/to outlaw from; **le** ~ **et l'arrière-**~ **de sa famille** every last one of his relatives; ~**s (de mariage)** banns, bans.

banal, e [banal] *adj* banal, commonplace; (*péj*) trite; **four/moulin** ~ village oven/mill.

banalisé, e [banalize] *adj* (*voiture de police*) unmarked.

banalité [banalite] *nf* banality; (*remarque*) truism, trite remark.

banane [banan] *nf* banana.

bananeraie [bananʀɛ] *nf* banana plantation.

bananier [bananje] *nm* banana tree; (*bateau*) banana boat.

banc [bɑ̃] *nm* seat, bench; (*de poissons*) shoal; ~ **des accusés** dock; ~ **d'essai** (*fig*) testing ground; ~ **de sable** sandbank; ~ **des témoins** witness box; ~ **de touche** dugout.

bancaire [bɑ̃kɛʀ] *adj* banking, bank *cpd*.

bancal, e [bɑ̃kal] *adj* wobbly; (*personne*) bow-legged; (*fig: projet*) shaky.

bandage [bɑ̃daʒ] *nm* bandaging; (*pansement*) bandage; ~ **herniaire** truss.

bande [bɑ̃d] *nf* (*de tissu etc*) strip; (*MÉD*) bandage; (*motif, dessin*) stripe; (*CINÉ*) film; (*INFORM*) tape; (*RADIO, groupe*) band; (*péj*): **une ~ de** a bunch *ou* crowd of; **par la ~** in a roundabout way; **donner de la ~** to list; **faire ~ à part** to keep to o.s.; **~ dessinée (BD)** strip cartoon (*BRIT*), comic strip; **~ magnétique** magnetic tape; **~ perforée** punched tape; **~ de roulement** (*de pneu*) tread; **~ sonore** sound track; **~ de terre** strip of land; **~ Velpeau** ® (*MÉD*) crêpe bandage.

---

*The **bande dessinée** or **BD** enjoys a huge following in France amongst adults as well as children, with the strip cartoon being accorded both literary and artistic status. An international show takes place at Angoulême at the end of January every year. Astérix, Tintin, Lucky Luke and Gaston Lagaffe are among the most famous cartoon characters.*

---

bandé, e [bɑ̃de] *adj* bandaged; **les yeux ~s** blindfold.
bande-annonce, *pl* **bandes-annonces** [bɑ̃dɑ̃nɔ̃s] *nf* (*CINÉ*) trailer.
bandeau, x [bɑ̃do] *nm* headband; (*sur les yeux*) blindfold; (*MÉD*) head bandage.
bandelette [bɑ̃dlɛt] *nf* strip of cloth, bandage.
bander [bɑ̃de] *vt* to bandage; (*muscle*) to tense; (*arc*) to bend ♦ *vi* (*fam!*) to have a hard on (*!*); **~ les yeux à qn** to blindfold sb.
banderole [bɑ̃dʀɔl] *nf* banderole; (*dans un défilé etc*) streamer.
bande-son, *pl* **bandes-son** [bɑ̃dsɔ̃] *nf* (*CINÉ*) soundtrack.
bande-vidéo, *pl* **bandes-vidéo** [bɑ̃dvideo] *nf* video tape.
bandit [bɑ̃di] *nm* bandit.
banditisme [bɑ̃ditism(ə)] *nm* violent crime, armed robberies *pl*.
bandoulière [bɑ̃duljɛʀ] *nf*: **en ~** (slung *ou* worn) across the shoulder.
Bangkok [bɑ̃ŋkɔk] *n* Bangkok.
Bangladesh [bɑ̃gladɛʃ] *nm*: **le ~** Bangladesh.
banjo [bɑ̃(d)ʒo] *nm* banjo.
banlieue [bɑ̃ljø] *nf* suburbs *pl*; **lignes/quartiers de ~** suburban lines/areas; **trains de ~** commuter trains.
banlieusard, e [bɑ̃ljøzaʀ, -aʀd(ə)] *nm/f* suburbanite.
bannière [banjɛʀ] *nf* banner.
bannir [baniʀ] *vt* to banish.
banque [bɑ̃k] *nf* bank; (*activités*) banking; **~ des yeux/du sang** eye/blood bank; **~ d'affaires** merchant bank; **~ de dépôt** deposit bank; **~ de données** (*INFORM*) data bank; **~ d'émission** bank of issue.
banqueroute [bɑ̃kʀut] *nf* bankruptcy.
banquet [bɑ̃kɛ] *nm* (*de club*) dinner; (*de noces*) reception; (*d'apparat*) banquet.
banquette [bɑ̃kɛt] *nf* seat.
banquier [bɑ̃kje] *nm* banker.

banquise [bɑ̃kiz] *nf* ice field.
bantou, e [bɑ̃tu] *adj* Bantu.
baptême [batɛm] *nm* (*sacrement*) baptism; (*cérémonie*) christening, baptism; (*d'un navire*) launching; (*d'une cloche*) consecration, dedication; **~ de l'air** first flight.
baptiser [batize] *vt* to christen; to baptize; to launch; to consecrate, dedicate.
baptismal, e, aux [batismal, -o] *adj*: **eau ~e** baptismal water.
baptiste [batist(ə)] *adj*, *nm/f* Baptist.
baquet [bakɛ] *nm* tub, bucket.
bar [baʀ] *nm* bar; (*poisson*) bass.
baragouin [baʀagwɛ̃] *nm* gibberish.
baragouiner [baʀagwine] *vi* to gibber, jabber.
baraque [baʀak] *nf* shed; (*fam*) house; **~ foraine** fairground stand.
baraqué, e [baʀake] *adj* well-built, hefty.
baraquements [baʀakmɑ̃] *nmpl* huts (*for refugees, workers etc*).
baratin [baʀatɛ̃] *nm* (*fam*) smooth talk, patter.
baratiner [baʀatine] *vt* to chat up.
baratte [baʀat] *nf* churn.
Barbade [baʀbad] *nf*: **la ~** Barbados.
barbant, e [baʀbɑ̃, -ɑ̃t] *adj* (*fam*) deadly (boring).
barbare [baʀbaʀ] *adj* barbaric ♦ *nm/f* barbarian.
Barbarie [baʀbaʀi] *nf*: **la ~** the Barbary Coast.
barbarie [baʀbaʀi] *nf* barbarism; (*cruauté*) barbarity.
barbarisme [baʀbaʀism(ə)] *nm* (*LING*) barbarism.
barbe [baʀb(ə)] *nf* beard; (**au nez et**) **à la ~ de qn** (*fig*) under sb's very nose; **quelle ~!** (*fam*) what a drag *ou* bore!; **~ à papa** candy-floss (*BRIT*), cotton candy (*US*).
barbecue [baʀbəkju] *nm* barbecue.
barbelé [baʀbəle] *nm* barbed wire *no pl*.
barber [baʀbe] *vt* (*fam*) to bore stiff.
barbiche [baʀbiʃ] *nf* goatee.
barbichette [baʀbiʃɛt] *nf* small goatee.
barbiturique [baʀbityʀik] *nm* barbiturate.
barboter [baʀbɔte] *vi* to paddle, dabble ♦ *vt* (*fam*) to filch.
barboteuse [baʀbɔtøz] *nf* rompers *pl*.
barbouiller [baʀbuje] *vt* to daub; (*péj: écrire, dessiner*) to scribble; **avoir l'estomac barbouillé** to feel queasy *ou* sick.
barbu, e [baʀby] *adj* bearded.
barbue [baʀby] *nf* (*poisson*) brill.
Barcelone [baʀsəlɔn] *n* Barcelona.
barda [baʀda] *nm* (*fam*) kit, gear.
barde [baʀd(ə)] *nf* (*CULIN*) piece of fat bacon ♦ *nm* (*poète*) bard.
bardé, e [baʀde] *adj*: **~ de médailles** *etc* bedecked with medals *etc*.
bardeaux [baʀdo] *nmpl* shingle *no pl*.
barder [baʀde] *vt* (*CULIN: rôti, volaille*) to bard ♦ *vi* (*fam*): **ça va ~** sparks will fly, things are going to get hot.
barème [baʀɛm] *nm* scale; (*liste*) table; **~ des**

salaires salary scale.
barge [baʀʒ] *nf* barge.
barguigner [baʀɡiɲe] *vi*: **sans** ~ without (any) humming and hawing *ou* shilly-shallying.
baril [baʀil] *nm* (*tonneau*) barrel; (*de poudre*) keg.
barillet [baʀijɛ] *nm* (*de revolver*) cylinder.
bariolé, e [baʀjɔle] *adj* many-coloured, rainbow-coloured.
barman [baʀman] *nm* barman.
baromètre [baʀɔmɛtʀ(ə)] *nm* barometer; ~ **anéroïde** aneroid barometer.
baron [baʀɔ̃] *nm* baron.
baronne [baʀɔn] *nf* baroness.
baroque [baʀɔk] *adj* (*ART*) baroque; (*fig*) weird.
baroud [baʀud] *nm*: ~ **d'honneur** gallant last stand.
baroudeur [baʀudœʀ] *nm* (*fam*) fighter.
barque [baʀk(ə)] *nf* small boat.
barquette [baʀkɛt] *nf* small boat-shaped tart; (*récipient: en aluminium*) tub; (: *en bois*) basket.
barracuda [baʀakyda] *nm* barracuda.
barrage [baʀaʒ] *nm* dam; (*sur route*) roadblock, barricade; ~ **de police** police roadblock.
barre [baʀ] *nf* (*de fer etc*) rod, bar; (*NAVIG*) helm; (*écrite*) line, stroke; (*DANSE*) barre; (*niveau*): **la livre a franchi la** ~ **des 10 frs** the pound has broken the 10 frs barrier; (*JUR*): **comparaître à la** ~ to appear as a witness; **être à** *ou* **tenir la** ~ (*NAVIG*) to be at the helm; **coup de** ~ (*fig*): **c'est le coup de** ~! it's daylight robbery!; **j'ai le coup de** ~! I'm all in!; ~ **fixe** (*GYM*) horizontal bar; ~ **de mesure** (*MUS*) bar line; ~ **à mine** crowbar; ~**s parallèles/asymétriques** (*GYM*) parallel/ asymmetric bars.
barreau, x [baʀo] *nm* bar; (*JUR*): **le** ~ the Bar.
barrer [baʀe] *vt* (*route etc*) to block; (*mot*) to cross out; (*chèque*) to cross (*BRIT*); (*NAVIG*) to steer; **se** ~ *vi* (*fam*) to clear off.
barrette [baʀɛt] *nf* (*pour cheveux*) (hair) slide (*BRIT*) *ou* clip (*US*); (*REL*: *bonnet*) biretta; (*broche*) brooch.
barreur [baʀœʀ] *nm* helmsman; (*aviron*) coxswain.
barricade [baʀikad] *nf* barricade.
barricader [baʀikade] *vt* to barricade; **se** ~ **chez soi** (*fig*) to lock o.s. in.
barrière [baʀjɛʀ] *nf* fence; (*obstacle*) barrier; (*porte*) gate; **la Grande B**~ the Great Barrier Reef; ~ **de dégel** (*ADMIN*: *on roadsigns*) no heavy vehicles - road liable to subsidence due to thaw; ~**s douanières** trade barriers.
barrique [baʀik] *nf* barrel, cask.
barrir [baʀiʀ] *vi* to trumpet.
baryton [baʀitɔ̃] *nm* baritone.
BAS *sigle m* (= *bureau d'aide sociale*) ≈ social security office (*BRIT*), ≈ Welfare office (*US*).
bas, basse [bɑ, bɑs] *adj* low; (*action*) low, ig-

noble ♦ *nm* (*vêtement*) stocking; (*partie inférieure*): **le** ~ **de** the lower part *ou* foot *ou* bottom of ♦ *nf* (*MUS*) bass ♦ *adv* low; (*parler*) softly; **plus** ~ lower down; more softly; (*dans un texte*) further on, below; **la tête basse** with lowered head; (*fig*) with head hung low; **avoir la vue basse** to be short-sighted; **au** ~ **mot** at the lowest estimate; **enfant en** ~ **âge** infant, young child; **en** ~ down below; at (*ou* to) the bottom; (*dans une maison*) downstairs; **en** ~ **de** at the bottom of; **de** ~ **en haut** upwards; from the bottom to the top; **des hauts et des** ~ ups and downs; **un** ~ **de laine** (*fam*: *économies*) money under the mattress (*fig*); **mettre** ~ *vi* to give birth; **à** ~ **la dictature!** down with dictatorship!; ~ **morceaux** (*viande*) cheap cuts.
basalte [bazalt(ə)] *nm* basalt.
basané, e [bazane] *adj* tanned, bronzed; (*immigré etc*) swarthy.
bas-côté [bakote] *nm* (*de route*) verge (*BRIT*), shoulder (*US*); (*d'église*) aisle.
bascule [baskyl] *nf*: (**jeu de**) ~ seesaw; (**balance à**) ~ scales *pl*; **fauteuil à** ~ rocking chair; **système à** ~ tip-over device; rocker device.
basculer [baskyle] *vi* to fall over, topple (over); (*benne*) to tip up ♦ *vt* (*aussi*: **faire** ~) to topple over; to tip out, tip up.
base [baz] *nf* base; (*POL*): **la** ~ the rank and file, the grass roots; (*fondement, principe*) basis (*pl* bases); **jeter les** ~**s de** to lay the foundations of; **à la** ~ **de** (*fig*) at the root of; **sur la** ~ **de** (*fig*) on the basis of; **de** ~ basic; **à** ~ **de café** *etc* coffee *etc* -based; ~ **de données** (*INFORM*) database; ~ **de lancement** launching site.
base-ball [bɛzbol] *nm* baseball.
baser [baze] *vt*: ~ **qch sur** to base sth on; **se** ~ **sur** (*données, preuves*) to base one's argument on; **être basé à/dans** (*MIL*) to be based at/in.
bas-fond [bɑfɔ̃] *nm* (*NAVIG*) shallow; ~**s** *nmpl* (*fig*) dregs.
BASIC [bazik] *nm* BASIC.
basilic [bazilik] *nm* (*CULIN*) basil.
basilique [bazilik] *nf* basilica.
basket(-ball) [basket(bol)] *nm* basketball.
baskets [baskɛt] *nfpl* (*chaussures*) trainers (*BRIT*), sneakers (*US*).
basketteur, euse [baskɛtœʀ, -øz] *nm/f* basketball player.
basquaise [baskɛz] *adj f* Basque ♦ *nf*: **B**~ Basque.
basque [bask(ə)] *adj, nm* (*LING*) Basque ♦ *nm/f*: **B**~ Basque; **le Pays** ~ the Basque country.
basques [bask(ə)] *nfpl* skirts; **pendu aux** ~ **de qn** constantly pestering sb; (*mère etc*) hanging on sb's apron strings.
bas-relief [baʀɔljɛf] *nm* bas-relief.
basse [bɑs] *adj f, nf voir* **bas**.

basse-cour, *pl* **basses-cours** [baskuʀ] *nf* farmyard; (*animaux*) farmyard animals.

bassement [bɑsmɑ̃] *adv* basely.

bassesse [bɑsɛs] *nf* baseness; (*acte*) base act.

basset [basɛ] *nm* (*ZOOL*) basset (hound).

bassin [basɛ̃] *nm* (*cuvette*) bowl; (*pièce d'eau*) pond, pool; (*de fontaine, GÉO*) basin; (*ANAT*) pelvis; (*portuaire*) dock; ~ **houiller** coalfield.

bassine [basin] *nf* basin; (*contenu*) bowl, bowlful.

bassiner [basine] *vt* (*plaie*) to bathe; (*lit*) to warm with a warming pan; (*fam: ennuyer*) to bore; (: *importuner*) to bug, pester.

bassiste [basist(ə)] *nm/f* (double) bass player.

basson [bɑsɔ̃] *nm* bassoon.

bastide [bastid] *nf* (*maison*) country house (*in Provence*); (*ville*) walled town (*in SW France*).

bastingage [bastɛ̃gaʒ] *nm* (ship's) rail.

bastion [bastjɔ̃] *nm* (*aussi fig, POL*) bastion.

bas-ventre [bɑvɑ̃tʀ(ə)] *nm* (lower part of the) stomach.

bât [bɑ] *nm* packsaddle.

bataille [bataj] *nf* battle; **en** ~ (*en travers*) at an angle; (*en désordre*) awry; ~ **rangée** pitched battle.

bataillon [batajɔ̃] *nm* battalion.

bâtard, e [bɑtaʀ, -aʀd(ə)] *adj* (*enfant*) illegitimate; (*fig*) hybrid ♦ *nm/f* illegitimate child, bastard (*péj*) ♦ *nm* (*BOULANGERIE*) ≈ Vienna loaf; **chien** ~ mongrel.

batavia [batavja] *nf* ≈ Webb lettuce.

bateau, x [bato] *nm* boat; (*grand*) ship ♦ *adj inv* (*banal, rebattu*) hackneyed; ~ **de pêche/à moteur** fishing/motor boat.

bateau-citerne [batositɛʀn(ə)] *nm* tanker.

bateau-mouche [batomuʃ] *nm* (passenger) pleasure boat (*on the Seine*).

bateau-pilote [batopilɔt] *nm* pilot ship.

bateleur, euse [batlœʀ, -øz] *nm/f* street performer.

batelier, ière [batəlje, -jɛʀ] *nm/f* ferryman/woman.

bat-flanc [baflɑ̃] *nm inv* raised boards for sleeping, in cells, army huts etc.

bâti, e [bɑti] *adj* (*terrain*) developed ♦ *nm* (*armature*) frame; (*COUTURE*) tacking; **bien** ~ (*personne*) well-built.

batifoler [batifɔle] *vi* to frolic *ou* lark about.

batik [batik] *nm* batik.

bâtiment [bɑtimɑ̃] *nm* building; (*NAVIG*) ship, vessel; (*industrie*): **le** ~ the building trade.

bâtir [bɑtiʀ] *vt* to build; (*COUTURE: jupe, ourlet*) to tack; **fil à** ~ (*COUTURE*) tacking thread.

bâtisse [bɑtis] *nf* building.

bâtisseur, euse [bɑtisœʀ, -øz] *nm/f* builder.

batiste [batist(ə)] *nf* (*COUTURE*) batiste, cambric.

bâton [bɑtɔ̃] *nm* stick; **mettre des ~s dans les roues à qn** to put a spoke in sb's wheel; **à ~s rompus** informally; ~ **de rouge (à lèvres)** lipstick; ~ **de ski** ski stick.

bâtonnet [bɑtɔnɛ] *nm* short stick *ou* rod.

bâtonnier [bɑtɔnje] *nm* (*JUR*) ≈ President of the Bar.

batraciens [batʀasjɛ̃] *nmpl* amphibians.

battage [bataʒ] *nm* (*publicité*) (hard) plugging.

battant, e [batɑ̃, -ɑ̃t] *vb voir* **battre** ♦ *adj*: **pluie ~e** lashing rain ♦ *nm* (*de cloche*) clapper; (*de volets*) shutter, flap; (*de porte*) side; (*fig: personne*) fighter; **porte à double** ~ double door; **tambour** ~ briskly.

batte [bat] *nf* (*SPORT*) bat.

battement [batmɑ̃] *nm* (*de cœur*) beat; (*intervalle*) interval (*between classes, trains etc*); ~ **de paupières** blinking *no pl* (of eyelids); **un** ~ **de 10 minutes, 10 minutes de** ~ 10 minutes to spare.

batterie [batʀi] *nf* (*MIL, ÉLEC*) battery; (*MUS*) drums *pl*, drum kit; ~ **de cuisine** kitchen utensils *pl*; (*casseroles etc*) pots and pans *pl*; **une** ~ **de tests** a string of tests.

batteur [batœʀ] *nm* (*MUS*) drummer; (*appareil*) whisk.

batteuse [batøz] *nf* (*AGR*) threshing machine.

battoir [batwaʀ] *nm* (*à linge*) beetle (*for laundry*); (*à tapis*) (carpet) beater.

battre [batʀ(ə)] *vt* to beat; (*suj: pluie, vagues*) to beat *ou* lash against; (*œufs etc*) to beat up, whisk; (*blé*) to thresh; (*cartes*) to shuffle; (*passer au peigne fin*) to scour ♦ *vi* (*cœur*) to beat; (*volets etc*) to bang, rattle; **se** ~ *vi* to fight; ~ **la mesure** to beat time; ~ **en brèche** (*MIL: mur*) to batter; (*fig: théorie*) to demolish; (: *institution etc*) to attack; ~ **son plein** to be at its height, be going full swing; ~ **pavillon britannique** to fly the British flag; ~ **des mains** to clap one's hands; ~ **des ailes** to flap its wings; ~ **de l'aile** (*fig*) to be in a bad way *ou* in bad shape; ~ **la semelle** to stamp one's feet; ~ **en retraite** to beat a retreat.

battu, e [baty] *pp de* **battre** ♦ *nf* (*chasse*) beat; (*policière etc*) search, hunt.

baud [bo(d)] *nm* baud.

baudruche [bodʀyʃ] *nf*: **ballon en** ~ (toy) balloon; (*fig*) windbag.

baume [bom] *nm* balm.

bauxite [boksit] *nf* bauxite.

bavard, e [bavaʀ, -aʀd(ə)] *adj* (very) talkative, gossipy.

bavardage [bavaʀdaʒ] *nm* chatter *no pl*; gossip *no pl*.

bavarder [bavaʀde] *vi* to chatter; (*indiscrètement*) to gossip; (: *révéler un secret*) to blab.

bavarois, e [bavaʀwa, -waz] *adj* Bavarian ♦ *nm ou nf* (*CULIN*) bavarois.

bave [bav] *nf* dribble; (*de chien etc*) slobber, slaver (*BRIT*), drool (*US*); (*d'escargot*) slime.

baver [bave] *vi* to dribble; to slobber, slaver (*BRIT*), drool (*US*); (*encre, couleur*) to run; **en** ~ (*fam*) to have a hard time (of it).

bavette [bavɛt] *nf* bib.

baveux, euse [bavø, -øz] *adj* dribbling; (*omelette*) runny.

Bavière [bavjɛʀ] *nf*: **la ~** Bavaria.
bavoir [bavwaʀ] *nm* (*de bébé*) bib.
bavure [bavyʀ] *nf* smudge; (*fig*) hitch; blunder.
bayer [baje] *vi*: **~ aux corneilles** to stand gaping.
bazar [bazaʀ] *nm* general store; (*fam*) jumble.
bazarder [bazaʀde] *vt* (*fam*) to chuck out.
BCBG *sigle a* (= *bon chic bon genre*) ≈ preppy.
BCG *sigle m* (= *bacille Calmette-Guérin*) BCG.
bcp *abr* = **beaucoup**.
BD *sigle f* = **bande dessinée**; (= *base de données*) DB.
bd *abr* = **boulevard**.
b.d.c. *abr* (*TYPO*: = *bas de casse*) l.c.
béant, e [beã, -ãt] *adj* gaping.
béarnais, e [beaʀnɛ, -ɛz] *adj* of *ou* from the Béarn.
béat, e [bea, -at] *adj* showing open-eyed wonder; (*sourire etc*) blissful.
béatitude [beatityd] *nf* bliss.
beau (bel), belle, beaux [bo, bɛl] *adj* beautiful, lovely; (*homme*) handsome ♦ *nf* (*SPORT*) decider ♦ *adv*: **il fait ~** the weather's fine ♦ *nm*: **avoir le sens du ~** to have an aesthetic sense; **le temps est au ~** the weather is set fair; **un ~ geste** (*fig*) a fine gesture; **un ~ salaire** a good salary; **un ~ gâchis/rhume** a fine mess/nasty cold; **en faire/dire de belles** to do/say (some) stupid things; **le ~ monde** high society; **~ parleur** smooth talker; **un ~ jour** one (fine) day; **de plus belle** more than ever, even more; **bel et bien** well and truly; (*vraiment*) really (and truly); **le plus ~ c'est que ...** the best of it is that ...; **c'est du ~!** that's great, that is!; **on a ~ essayer** however hard *ou* no matter how hard we try; **il a ~ jeu de protester** *etc* it's easy for him to protest *etc*; **faire le ~** (*chien*) to sit up and beg.
beauceron, ne [bosʀɔ̃, -ɔn] *adj* of *ou* from the Beauce.

===================== *MOT-CLÉ*

beaucoup [boku] *adv* **1** a lot; **il boit ~** he drinks a lot; **il ne boit pas ~** he doesn't drink much *ou* a lot
2 (*suivi de plus, trop etc*) much, a lot, far; **il est ~ plus grand** he is much *ou* a lot *ou* far taller
3: **~ de** (*nombre*) many, a lot of; (*quantité*) a lot of; **pas ~ de** (*nombre*) not many, not a lot of; (*quantité*) not much, not a lot of; **~ d'étudiants/de touristes** a lot of *ou* many students/tourists; **~ de courage** a lot of courage; **il n'a pas ~ d'argent** he hasn't got much *ou* a lot of money; **il n'y a pas ~ de touristes** there aren't many *ou* a lot of tourists
4: **de ~** by far
♦ *pron*: **~ le savent** lots of people know that.

beau-fils, *pl* **beaux-fils** [bofis] *nm* son-in-law;

(*remariage*) stepson.
beau-frère, *pl* **beaux-frères** [bofʀɛʀ] *nm* brother-in-law.
beau-père, *pl* **beaux-pères** [bopɛʀ] *nm* father-in-law; (*remariage*) stepfather.
beauté [bote] *nf* beauty; **de toute ~** beautiful; **en ~** *adv* with a flourish, brilliantly.
beaux-arts [bozaʀ] *nmpl* fine arts.
beaux-parents [bopaʀɑ̃] *nmpl* wife's/husband's family *sg ou pl*, in-laws.
bébé [bebe] *nm* baby.
bébé-éprouvette, *pl* **bébés-éprouvette** [bebeepʀuvɛt] *nm* test-tube baby.
bec [bɛk] *nm* beak, bill; (*de plume*) nib; (*de cafetière etc*) spout; (*de casserole etc*) lip; (*d'une clarinette etc*) mouthpiece; (*fam*) mouth; **clouer le ~ à qn** (*fam*) to shut sb up; **ouvrir le ~** (*fam*) to open one's mouth; **~ de gaz** (street) gaslamp; **~ verseur** pouring lip.
bécane [bekan] *nf* (*fam*) bike.
bécarre [bekaʀ] *nm* (*MUS*) natural.
bécasse [bekas] *nf* (*ZOOL*) woodcock; (*fam*) silly goose.
bec-de-cane, *pl* **becs-de-cane** [bɛkdəkan] *nm* (*poignée*) door handle.
bec-de-lièvre, *pl* **becs-de-lièvre** [bɛkdəljɛvʀ(ə)] *nm* harelip.
béchamel [beʃamɛl] *nf*: (**sauce**) **~** white sauce, bechamel sauce.
bêche [bɛʃ] *nf* spade.
bêcher [beʃe] *vt* (*terre*) to dig; (*personne: critiquer*) to slate; (*: snober*) to look down on.
bêcheur, euse [beʃœʀ, -øz] *adj* (*fam*) stuck-up ♦ *nm/f* fault-finder; (*snob*) stuck-up person.
bécoter [bekɔte]: **se ~** *vi* to smooch.
becquée [beke] *nf*: **donner la ~ à** to feed.
becqueter [bɛkte] *vt* (*fam*) to eat.
bedaine [bədɛn] *nf* paunch.
bédé [bede] *nf* (*fam*: = *bande dessinée*) strip cartoon (*BRIT*), comic strip.
bedeau, x [bədo] *nm* beadle.
bedonnant, e [bədɔnɑ̃, -ɑ̃t] *adj* paunchy, potbellied.
bée [be] *adj*: **bouche ~** gaping.
beffroi [befʀwa] *nm* belfry.
bégaiement [begɛmɑ̃] *nm* stammering, stuttering.
bégayer [begeje] *vt, vi* to stammer.
bégonia [begɔnja] *nm* (*BOT*) begonia.
bègue [bɛg] *nm/f*: **être ~** to have a stammer.
bégueule [begœl] *adj* prudish.
beige [bɛʒ] *adj* beige.
beignet [bɛɲɛ] *nm* fritter.
bel [bɛl] *adj m voir* **beau**.
bêler [bele] *vi* to bleat.
belette [bəlɛt] *nf* weasel.
belge [bɛlʒ(ə)] *adj* Belgian ♦ *nm/f*: **B~** Belgian.

> **La fête nationale belge**, *on July 21, is the anniversary of Leopold of Saxe-Coburg Gotha becoming King Leopold I in 1831.*

Belgique [bɛlʒik] *nf*: **la ~** Belgium.

Belgrade [bɛlgʀad] *n* Belgrade.

bélier [belje] *nm* ram; (*engin*) (battering) ram; (*signe*): **le B~** Aries, the Ram; **être du B~** to be Aries.

Bélize [beliz] *nm*: **le ~** Belize.

bellâtre [bɛlɑtʀ(ə)] *nm* dandy.

belle [bɛl] *adj f, nf voir* beau.

belle-famille, *pl* **belles-familles** [bɛlfamij] *nf* (*fam*) in-laws *pl*.

belle-fille, *pl* **belles-filles** [bɛlfij] *nf* daughter-in-law; (*remariage*) stepdaughter.

belle-mère, *pl* **belles-mères** [bɛlmɛʀ] *nf* mother-in-law; (*remariage*) stepmother.

belle-sœur, *pl* **belles-sœurs** [bɛlsœʀ] *nf* sister-in-law.

belliciste [belisist(ə)] *adj* warmongering.

belligérance [beliʒeʀɑ̃s] *nf* belligerence.

belligérant, e [beliʒeʀɑ̃, -ɑ̃t] *adj* belligerent.

belliqueux, euse [belikø, -øz] *adj* aggressive, warlike.

belote [bəlɔt] *nf* belote (*card game*).

belvédère [bɛlvedeʀ] *nm* panoramic view-point (*or small building there*).

bémol [bemɔl] *nm* (*MUS*) flat.

ben [bɛ̃] *excl* (*fam*) well.

bénédiction [benediksjɔ̃] *nf* blessing.

bénéfice [benefis] *nm* (*COMM*) profit; (*avantage*) benefit; **au ~ de** in aid of.

bénéficiaire [benefisjɛʀ] *nm/f* beneficiary.

bénéficier [benefisje] *vi*: **~ de** to enjoy; (*profiter*) to benefit by *ou* from; (*obtenir*) to get, be given.

bénéfique [benefik] *adj* beneficial.

Bénélux [benelyks] *nm*: **le ~** Benelux, the Benelux countries.

benêt [bənɛ] *nm* simpleton.

bénévolat [benevɔla] *nm* voluntary service *ou* work.

bénévole [benevɔl] *adj* voluntary, unpaid.

bénévolement [benevɔlmɑ̃] *adv* voluntarily.

Bengale [bɛ̃gal] *nm*: **le ~** Bengal; **le golfe du ~** the Bay of Bengal.

bengali [bɛ̃gali] *adj* Bengali, Bengalese ♦ *nm* (*LING*) Bengali.

Bénin [benɛ̃] *nm*: **le ~** Benin.

bénin, igne [benɛ̃, -iɲ] *adj* minor, mild; (*tumeur*) benign.

bénir [beniʀ] *vt* to bless.

bénit, e [beni, -it] *adj* consecrated; **eau ~e** holy water.

bénitier [benitje] *nm* stoup, font (*for holy water*).

benjamin, e [bɛ̃ʒamɛ̃, -in] *nm/f* youngest child; (*SPORT*) under-13.

benne [bɛn] *nf* skip; (*de téléphérique*) (cable) car; **~ basculante** tipper (*BRIT*), dump *ou* dumper truck.

benzine [bɛ̃zin] *nf* benzine.

béotien, ne [beɔsjɛ̃, -ɛn] *nm/f* philistine.

BEP *sigle m* (= *Brevet d'études professionnelles*) *school-leaving diploma, taken at approx. 18*

years.

BEPA [bepa] *sigle m* (= *Brevet d'études professionnelles agricoles*) *school-leaving diploma in agriculture, taken at approx. 18 years.*

BEPC *sigle m* (= *Brevet d'études du premier cycle*) *former school certificate (taken at approx. 16 years).*

béquille [bekij] *nf* crutch; (*de bicyclette*) stand.

berbère [bɛʀbɛʀ] *adj* Berber ♦ *nm* (*LING*) Berber ♦ *nm/f*: **B~** Berber.

bercail [bɛʀkaj] *nm* fold.

berceau, x [bɛʀso] *nm* cradle, crib.

bercer [bɛʀse] *vt* to rock, cradle; (*suj: musique etc*) to lull; **~ qn de** (*promesses etc*) to delude sb with.

berceur, euse [bɛʀsœʀ, -øz] *adj* soothing ♦ *nf* (*chanson*) lullaby.

BERD [bɛʀd] *sigle f* (= *Banque européenne pour la reconstruction et le développement*) EBRD.

béret (basque) [beʀɛ(bask(ə))] *nm* beret.

bergamote [bɛʀgamɔt] *nf* (*BOT*) bergamot.

berge [bɛʀʒ(ə)] *nf* bank.

berger, ère [bɛʀʒe, -ɛʀ] *nm/f* shepherd/shepherdess; **~ allemand** (*chien*) alsatian (dog) (*BRIT*), German shepherd (dog) (*US*).

bergerie [bɛʀʒəʀi] *nf* sheep pen.

bergeronnette [bɛʀʒəʀɔnɛt] *nf* wagtail.

béribéri [beʀibeʀi] *nm* beriberi.

Berlin [bɛʀlɛ̃] *n* Berlin; **~-Est/-Ouest** East/West Berlin.

berline [bɛʀlin] *nf* (*AUTO*) saloon (car) (*BRIT*), sedan (*US*).

berlingot [bɛʀlɛ̃go] *nm* (*emballage*) carton (*pyramid shaped*); (*bonbon*) lozenge.

berlinois, e [bɛʀlinwa, -waz] *adj* of *ou* from Berlin ♦ *nm/f*: **B~, e** Berliner.

berlue [bɛʀly] *nf*: **j'ai la ~** I must be seeing things.

bermuda [bɛʀmyda] *nm* (*short*) Bermuda shorts.

Bermudes [bɛʀmyd] *nfpl*: **les (îles) ~** Bermuda.

Berne [bɛʀn(ə)] *n* Bern.

berne [bɛʀn(ə)] *nf*: **en ~** at half-mast; **mettre en ~** to fly at half-mast.

berner [bɛʀne] *vt* to fool.

bernois, e [bɛʀnwa, -waz] *adj* Bernese.

berrichon, ne [beʀiʃɔ̃, -ɔn] *adj* of *ou* from the Berry.

besace [bəzas] *nf* beggar's bag.

besogne [bəzɔɲ] *nf* work *no pl*, job.

besogneux, euse [bəzɔɲø, -øz] *adj* hardworking.

besoin [bəzwɛ̃] *nm* need; (*pauvreté*): **le ~** need, want; **le ~ d'argent/de gloire** the need for money/glory; **~s** (*naturels*) nature's needs; **faire ses ~s** to relieve o.s.; **avoir ~ de qch/faire qch** to need sth/to do sth; **il n'y a pas ~ de (faire)** there is no need to (do); **au ~, si ~ est** if need be; **pour les ~s de la cause** for the purpose in hand.

bestial, e, aux [bɛstjal, -o] *adj* bestial, brutish ♦ *nmpl* cattle.
bestiole [bɛstjɔl] *nf* (tiny) creature.
bétail [betaj] *nm* livestock, cattle *pl*.
bétaillère [betajɛʀ] *nf* livestock truck.
bête [bɛt] *nf* animal; (*bestiole*) insect, creature ♦ *adj* stupid, silly; **les ~s** (the) animals; **chercher la petite ~** to nit-pick; **~ noire** pet hate, bugbear (*BRIT*); **~ sauvage** wild beast; **~ de somme** beast of burden.
bêtement [bɛtmɑ̃] *adv* stupidly; **tout ~** quite simply.
Bethléem [bɛtleɛm] *n* Bethlehem.
bêtifier [betifje] *vi* to talk nonsense.
bêtise [betiz] *nf* stupidity; (*action, remarque*) stupid thing (to say *ou* do); (*bonbon*) *type of mint sweet* (*BRIT*) *ou candy* (*US*); **faire/dire une ~** to do/say something stupid.
béton [betɔ̃] *nm* concrete; (**en**) **~** (*fig: alibi, argument*) cast iron; **~ armé** reinforced concrete; **~ précontraint** prestressed concrete.
bétonner [betɔne] *vt* to concrete (over).
bétonnière [betɔnjɛʀ] *nf* cement mixer.
bette [bɛt] *nf* (*BOT*) (Swiss) chard.
betterave [bɛtʀav] *nf* (*rouge*) beetroot (*BRIT*), beet (*US*); **~ fourragère** mangel-wurzel; **~ sucrière** sugar beet.
beugler [bøgle] *vi* to low; (*péj: radio etc*) to blare ♦ *vt* (*péj: chanson etc*) to bawl out.
Beur [bœʀ] *adj, nm/f* second-generation Arab immigrant.

Beur *is the term used to refer to a person born in France of North African immigrant parents. It is not a racist term and is often used by the media, anti-racist groups and second-generation North Africans themselves. The word itself comes from verlan.*

---

beurre [bœʀ] *nm* butter; **mettre du ~ dans les épinards** (*fig*) to add a little to the kitty; **~ de cacao** cocoa butter; **~ noir** brown butter (sauce).
beurrer [bœʀe] *vt* to butter.
beurrier [bœʀje] *nm* butter dish.
beuverie [bœvʀi] *nf* drinking session.
bévue [bevy] *nf* blunder.
Beyrouth [beʀut] *n* Beirut.
Bhoutan [butɑ̃] *nm*: **le ~** Bhutan.
bi... [bi] *préfixe* bi..., two-.
Biafra [bjafʀa] *nm*: **le ~** Biafra.
biafrais, e [bjafʀɛ, -ɛz] *adj* Biafran.
biais [bjɛ] *nm* (*moyen*) device, expedient; (*aspect*) angle; (*bande de tissu*) piece of cloth cut on the bias; **en ~, de ~** (*obliquement*) at an angle; (*fig*) indirectly.
biaiser [bjeze] *vi* (*fig*) to sidestep the issue.
biathlon [bjatlɔ̃] *nm* biathlon.
bibelot [biblo] *nm* trinket, curio.
biberon [bibʀɔ̃] *nm* (feeding) bottle; **nourrir au ~** to bottle-feed.
bible [bibl(ə)] *nf* bible.

bibliobus [biblijɔbys] *nm* mobile library van.
bibliographie [biblijɔgʀafi] *nf* bibliography.
bibliophile [biblijɔfil] *nm/f* book-lover.
bibliothécaire [biblijɔtekɛʀ] *nm/f* librarian.
bibliothèque [biblijɔtɛk] *nf* library; (*meuble*) bookcase; **~ municipale** public library.
biblique [biblik] *adj* biblical.
bicarbonate [bikaʀbɔnat] *nm*: **~ (de soude)** bicarbonate of soda.
bicentenaire [bisɑ̃tnɛʀ] *nm* bicentenary.
biceps [bisɛps] *nm* biceps.
biche [biʃ] *nf* doe.
bichonner [biʃɔne] *vt* to groom.
bicolore [bikɔlɔʀ] *adj* two-coloured (*BRIT*), two-colored (*US*).
bicoque [bikɔk] *nf* (*péj*) shack, dump.
bicorne [bikɔʀn(ə)] *nm* cocked hat.
bicyclette [bisiklɛt] *nf* bicycle.
bidasse [bidas] *nm* (*fam*) squaddie (*BRIT*).
bide [bid] *nm* (*fam: ventre*) belly; (*THÉÂT*) flop.
bidet [bidɛ] *nm* bidet.
bidirectionnel, le [bidiʀɛksjɔnɛl] *adj* bidirectional.
bidoche [bidɔʃ] *nf* (*fam*) meat.
bidon [bidɔ̃] *nm* can ♦ *adj inv* (*fam*) phoney.
bidonnant, e [bidɔnɑ̃, -ɑ̃t] *adj* (*fam*) hilarious.
bidonville [bidɔ̃vil] *nm* shanty town.
bidule [bidyl] *nm* (*fam*) thingamajig.
bielle [bjɛl] *nf* connecting rod; (*AUTO*) track rod.
biélorusse [bjelɔʀys] *adj* Belarussian ♦ *nm/f*: **B~** Belarrussian.
Biélorussie [bjelɔʀysi] *nf* Belorussia.

=================================== *MOT-CLÉ*

bien [bjɛ̃] *nm* **1** (*avantage, profit*): **faire le ~** to do good; **faire du ~ à qn** to do sb good; **ça fait du ~ de faire** it does you good to do; **dire du ~ de** to speak well of; **c'est pour son ~** it's for his own good; **changer en ~** to change for the better; **le ~ public** the public good; **vouloir du ~ à qn** (*vouloir aider*) to have sb's (best) interests at heart; **je te veux du ~** (*pour mettre en confiance*) I don't wish you any harm
2 (*possession, patrimoine*) possession, property; **son ~ le plus précieux** his most treasured possession; **avoir du ~** to have property; **~s (de consommation** *etc*) (consumer *etc*) goods; **~s durables** (consumer) durables
3 (*moral*): **le ~** good; **distinguer le ~ du mal** to tell good from evil
♦ *adv* **1** (*de façon satisfaisante*) well; **elle travaille/mange ~** she works/eats well; **aller or se porter ~** to be well; **croyant ~ faire, je/il ...** thinking I/he was doing the right thing, I/he ...
2 (*valeur intensive*) quite; **~ jeune** quite young; **~ assez** quite enough; **~ mieux** (very) much better; **~ du temps/des gens** quite a time/a number of people; **j'espère ~** ~

y aller I do hope to go; **je veux ~ le faire** (*concession*) I'm quite willing to do it; **il faut ~ le faire** it has to be done; **il y a ~ 2 ans** at least 2 years ago; **il semble ~ que** it really seems that; **peut-être ~** it could well be; **aimer ~** to like; **Paul est ~ venu, n'est-ce pas?** Paul HAS come, hasn't he?; **où peut-il ~ être passé?** where on earth can he have got to?

3 (*conséquence, résultat*): **si ~ que** with the result that; **on verra ~** we'll see; **faire ~ de ...** to be right to ...

♦ *excl* right!, OK!, fine!; **eh ~!** well!; **(c'est) ~ fait!** it serves you (*ou* him *etc*) right!; **~ sûr!, ~ entendu!** certainly!, of course!

♦ *adj inv* **1** (*en bonne forme, à l'aise*): **je me sens ~, je suis ~** I feel fine; **je ne me sens pas ~, je ne suis pas ~** I don't feel well; **on est ~ dans ce fauteuil** this chair is very comfortable

2 (*joli, beau*) good-looking; **tu es ~ dans cette robe** you look good in that dress

3 (*satisfaisant*) good; **elle est ~, cette maison/secrétaire** it's a good house/she's a good secretary; **c'est très ~ (comme ça)** it's fine (like that); **ce n'est pas si ~ que ça** it's not as good *ou* great as all that; **c'est ~?** is that all right?

4 (*moralement*) right; (: *personne*) good, nice; (*respectable*) respectable; **ce n'est pas ~ de ...** it's not right to ...; **elle est ~, cette femme** she's a nice woman, she's a good sort; **des gens ~** respectable people

5 (*en bons termes*): **être ~ avec qn** to be on good terms with sb.

bien-aimé, e [bjɛ̃neme] *adj, nm/f* beloved.

bien-être [bjɛ̃nɛtʀ(ə)] *nm* well-being.

bienfaisance [bjɛ̃fəzɑ̃s] *nf* charity.

bienfaisant, e [bjɛ̃fəzɑ̃, -ɑ̃t] *adj* (*chose*) beneficial.

bienfait [bjɛ̃fɛ] *nm* act of generosity, benefaction; (*de la science etc*) benefit.

bienfaiteur, trice [bjɛ̃fɛtœʀ, -tʀis] *nm/f* benefactor/benefactress.

bien-fondé [bjɛ̃fɔ̃de] *nm* soundness.

bien-fonds [bjɛ̃fɔ̃] *nm* property.

bienheureux, euse [bjɛ̃nœʀø, -øz] *adj* happy; (*REL*) blessed, blest.

biennal, e, aux [bjenal, -o] *adj* biennial.

bien-pensant, e [bjɛ̃pɑ̃sɑ̃, -ɑ̃t] *adj* right-thinking ♦ *nm/f*: **les ~s** right-minded people.

bien que [bjɛ̃k(ə)] *conj* although.

bienséance [bjɛ̃seɑ̃s] *nf* propriety, decorum *no pl*; **les ~s** (*convenances*) the proprieties.

bienséant, e [bjɛ̃seɑ̃, -ɑ̃t] *adj* proper, seemly.

bientôt [bjɛ̃to] *adv* soon; **à ~** see you soon.

bienveillance [bjɛ̃vɛjɑ̃s] *nf* kindness.

bienveillant, e [bjɛ̃vɛjɑ̃, -ɑ̃t] *adj* kindly.

bienvenu, e [bjɛ̃vny] *adj* welcome ♦ *nm/f*: **être le ~/la ~e** to be welcome ♦ *nf*: **souhaiter la ~e à** to welcome; **~e à** welcome to.

bière [bjɛʀ] *nf* (*boisson*) beer; (*cercueil*) bier; **~ blonde** lager; **~ brune** brown ale; **~ (à la) pression** draught beer.

biffer [bife] *vt* to cross out.

bifteck [biftɛk] *nm* steak.

bifurcation [bifyʀkɑsjɔ̃] *nf* fork (*in road*); (*fig*) new direction.

bifurquer [bifyʀke] *vi* (*route*) to fork; (*véhicule*) to turn off.

bigame [bigam] *adj* bigamous.

bigamie [bigami] *nf* bigamy.

bigarré, e [bigaʀe] *adj* multicoloured (*BRIT*), multicolored (*US*); (*disparate*) motley.

bigarreau, x [bigaʀo] *nm* type of cherry.

bigleux, euse [biglø, -øz] *adj* (*fam: qui louche*) cross-eyed; (: *qui voit mal*) short-sighted; **il est complètement ~** he's as blind as a bat.

bigorneau, x [bigɔʀno] *nm* winkle.

bigot, e [bigo, -ɔt] (*péj*) *adj* bigoted ♦ *nm/f* bigot.

bigoterie [bigɔtʀi] *nf* bigotry.

bigoudi [bigudi] *nm* curler.

bigrement [bigʀəmɑ̃] *adv* (*fam*) fantastically.

bijou, x [biʒu] *nm* jewel.

bijouterie [biʒutʀi] *nf* (*magasin*) jeweller's (shop) (*BRIT*), jewelry store (*US*); (*bijoux*) jewellery, jewelry.

bijoutier, ière [biʒutje, -jɛʀ] *nm/f* jeweller (*BRIT*), jeweler (*US*).

bikini [bikini] *nm* bikini.

bilan [bilɑ̃] *nm* (*COMM*) balance sheet(s); (*annuel*) end of year statement; (*fig*) (net) outcome; (: *de victimes*) toll; **faire le ~ de** to assess; to review; **déposer son ~** to file a bankruptcy statement; **~ de santé** (*MÉD*) checkup; **~ social** statement of a firm's policies towards its employees.

bilatéral, e, aux [bilateʀal, -o] *adj* bilateral.

bilboquet [bilbɔkɛ] *nm* (*jouet*) cup-and-ball game.

bile [bil] *nf* bile; **se faire de la ~** (*fam*) to worry o.s. sick.

biliaire [biljɛʀ] *adj* biliary.

bilieux, euse [biljø, -øz] *adj* bilious; (*fig: colérique*) testy.

bilingue [bilɛ̃g] *adj* bilingual.

bilinguisme [bilɛ̃gɥism(ə)] *nm* bilingualism.

billard [bijaʀ] *nm* billiards *sg*; (*table*) billiard table; **c'est du ~** (*fam*) it's a cinch; **passer sur le ~** (*fam*) to have an (*ou* one's) operation; **~ électrique** pinball.

bille [bij] *nf* ball; (*du jeu de billes*) marble; (*de bois*) log; **jouer aux ~s** to play marbles.

billet [bijɛ] *nm* (*aussi:* **~ de banque**) (bank)note; (*de cinéma, de bus etc*) ticket; (*courte lettre*) note; **~ à ordre** *ou* **de commerce** (*COMM*) promissory note, IOU; **~ d'avion/de train** plane/train ticket; **~ circulaire** round-trip ticket; **~ doux** love letter; **~ de faveur** complimentary ticket; **~ de loterie** lottery ticket; **~ de quai** platform ticket.

billetterie [bijɛtʀi] *nf* ticket office; (*distribu-*

teur) ticket dispenser; *(BANQUE)* cash dispenser.

billion [biljɔ̃] *nm* billion *(BRIT)*, trillion *(US)*.

billot [bijo] *nm* block.

BIMA *sigle m* = *Bulletin d'information du ministère de l'agriculture.*

bimbeloterie [bɛ̃blɔtʀi] *nf (objets)* fancy goods.

bimensuel, le [bimɑ̃sɥɛl] *adj* bimonthly, twice-monthly.

bimestriel, le [bimɛstʀijɛl] *adj* bimonthly, two-monthly.

bimoteur [bimɔtœʀ] *adj* twin-engined.

binaire [binɛʀ] *adj* binary.

biner [bine] *vt* to hoe.

binette [binɛt] *nf (outil)* hoe.

binoclard, e [binɔklaʀ, -aʀd(ə)] *(fam) adj* specky ♦ *nm/f* four-eyes.

binocle [binɔkl(ə)] *nm* pince-nez.

binoculaire [binɔkylɛʀ] *adj* binocular.

binôme [binom] *nm* binomial.

bio... [bjɔ] *préfixe* bio....

biochimie [bjɔʃimi] *nf* biochemistry.

biochimique [bjɔʃimik] *adj* biochemical.

biochimiste [bjɔʃimist(ə)] *nm/f* biochemist.

biodégradable [bjɔdegʀadabl(ə)] *adj* biodegradable.

biodiversité [bjodivɛʀsite] *nf* biodiversity.

bioéthique [bjoetik] *nf* bioethics *sg.*

biographe [bjɔgʀaf] *nm/f* biographer.

biographie [bjɔgʀafi] *nf* biography.

biographique [bjɔgʀafik] *adj* biographical.

biologie [bjɔlɔʒi] *nf* biology.

biologique [bjɔlɔʒik] *adj* biological.

biologiste [bjɔlɔʒist(ə)] *nm/f* biologist.

biomasse [bjɔmas] *nf* biomass.

biopsie [bjɔpsi] *nf (MÉD)* biopsy.

biosphère [bjɔsfɛʀ] *nf* biosphere.

biotope [bjɔtɔp] *nm* biotope.

bipartisme [bipaʀtism(ə)] *nm* two-party system.

bipartite [bipaʀtit] *adj (POL)* two-party, bipartisan.

bipède [bipɛd] *nm* biped, two-footed creature.

biphasé, e [bifaze] *adj (ÉLEC)* two-phase.

biplace [biplas] *adj, nm (avion)* two-seater.

biplan [biplɑ̃] *nm* biplane.

bique [bik] *nf* nanny goat; *(péj)* old hag.

biquet, te [bikɛ, -ɛt] *nm/f:* **mon ~** *(fam)* my lamb.

BIRD [biʀd] *sigle f* (= *Banque internationale pour la reconstruction et le développement)* IBRD.

biréacteur [biʀeaktœʀ] *nm* twin-engined jet.

birman, e [biʀmɑ̃, -an] *adj* Burmese.

Birmanie [biʀmani] *nf:* **la ~** Burma.

bis, e [bi, biz] *adj (couleur)* greyish brown ♦ *adv* [bis]: **12 ~ 12a** *ou* **A** ♦ *excl, nm* [bis] encore ♦ *nf (baiser)* kiss; *(vent)* North wind.

bisaïeul, e [bizajœl] *nm/f* great-grandfather/great-grandmother.

bisannuel, le [bizanɥɛl] *adj* biennial.

bisbille [bisbij] *nf:* **être en ~ avec qn** to be at loggerheads with sb.

Biscaye [biske] *nf:* **le golfe de ~** the Bay of Biscay.

biscornu, e [biskɔʀny] *adj* crooked; *(bizarre)* weird(-looking).

biscotte [biskɔt] *nf* (breakfast) rusk.

biscuit [biskɥi] *nm* biscuit *(BRIT)*, cookie *(US)*; *(gateau)* sponge cake; **~ à la cuiller** sponge finger.

biscuiterie [biskɥitʀi] *nf* biscuit manufacturing.

bise [biz] *adj f, nf voir* **bis.**

biseau, x [bizo] *nm* bevelled edge; **en ~** bevelled.

biseauter [bizote] *vt* to bevel.

bisexué, e [bisɛksɥe] *adj* bisexual.

bisexuel, le [bisɛksɥɛl] *adj, nm/f* bisexual.

bismuth [bismyt] *nm* bismuth.

bison [bizɔ̃] *nm* bison.

bisou [bizu] *nm (fam)* kiss.

bisque [bisk(ə)] *nf:* **~ d'écrevisses** shrimp bisque.

bissectrice [bisɛktʀis] *nf* bisector.

bisser [bise] *vt (faire rejouer: artiste, chanson)* to encore; *(rejouer: morceau)* to give an encore of.

bissextile [bisɛkstil] *adj:* **année ~** leap year.

bistouri [bisturi] *nm* lancet.

bistre [bistʀ(ə)] *adj (couleur)* bistre; *(peau, teint)* tanned.

bistro(t) [bistʀo] *nm* bistro, café.

BIT *sigle m* (= *Bureau international du travail)* ILO.

bit [bit] *nm (INFORM)* bit.

biterrois, e [bitɛʀwa, -waz] *adj* of *ou* from Béziers.

bitte [bit] *nf:* **~ d'amarrage** bollard *(NAUT).*

bitume [bitym] *nm* asphalt.

bitumer [bityme] *vt* to asphalt.

bivalent, e [bivalɑ̃, -ɑ̃t] *adj* bivalent.

bivouac [bivwak] *nm* bivouac.

bizarre [bizaʀ] *adj* strange, odd.

bizarrement [bizaʀmɑ̃] *adv* strangely, oddly.

bizarrerie [bizaʀʀi] *nf* strangeness, oddness.

blackbouler [blakbule] *vt (à une élection)* to blackball.

blafard, e [blafaʀ, -aʀd(ə)] *adj* wan.

blague [blag] *nf (propos)* joke; *(farce)* trick; **sans ~!** no kidding!; **~ à tabac** tobacco pouch.

blaguer [blage] *vi* to joke ♦ *vt* to tease.

blagueur, euse [blagœʀ, -øz] *adj* teasing ♦ *nm/f* joker.

blair [blɛʀ] *nm (fam)* conk.

blaireau, x [blɛʀo] *nm (ZOOL)* badger; *(brosse)* shaving brush.

blairer [blɛʀe] *vt:* **je ne peux pas le ~** I can't bear *ou* stand him.

blâmable [blɑmabl(ə)] *adj* blameworthy.

blâme [blɑm] *nm* blame; *(sanction)* reprimand.

blâmer [blɑme] *vt (réprouver)* to blame; *(réprimander)* to reprimand.

blanc, blanche [blɑ̃, blɑ̃ʃ] *adj* white; (*non imprimé*) blank; (*innocent*) pure ♦ *nm/f* white, white man/woman ♦ *nm* (*couleur*) white; (*linge*): **le** ~ whites *pl*; (*espace non écrit*) blank; (*aussi:* ~ **d'œuf**) (egg-)white; (*aussi:* ~ **de poulet**) breast, white meat; (*aussi:* **vin** ~) white wine ♦ *nf* (*MUS*) minim (*BRIT*), half-note (*US*); (*fam: drogue*) smack; **d'une voix blanche** in a toneless voice; **aux cheveux** ~**s** white-haired; **le** ~ **de l'œil** the white of the eye; **laisser en** ~ to leave blank; **chèque en** ~ blank cheque; **à** ~ *adv* (*chauffer*) white-hot; (*tirer, charger*) with blanks; **saigner à** ~ to bleed white; ~ **cassé** off-white.

blanc-bec, *pl* **blancs-becs** [blɑ̃bɛk] *nm* greenhorn.

blanchâtre [blɑ̃ʃɑtʀ(ə)] *adj* (*teint, lumière*) whitish.

blancheur [blɑ̃ʃœʀ] *nf* whiteness.

blanchir [blɑ̃ʃiʀ] *vt* (*gén*) to whiten; (*linge, fig: argent*) to launder; (*CULIN*) to blanch; (*fig: disculper*) to clear ♦ *vi* to grow white; (*cheveux*) to go white; **blanchi à la chaux** whitewashed.

blanchissage [blɑ̃ʃisaʒ] *nm* (*du linge*) laundering.

blanchisserie [blɑ̃ʃisʀi] *nf* laundry.

blanchisseur, euse [blɑ̃ʃisœʀ, -øz] *nm/f* launderer.

blanc-seing, *pl* **blancs-seings** [blɑ̃sɛ̃] *nm* signed blank paper.

blanquette [blɑ̃kɛt] *nf* (*CULIN*): ~ **de veau** veal in a white sauce, blanquette de veau.

blasé, e [blaze] *adj* blasé.

blaser [blaze] *vt* to make blasé.

blason [blazɔ̃] *nm* coat of arms.

blasphémateur, trice [blasfematœʀ, -tʀis] *nm/f* blasphemer.

blasphématoire [blasfematwaʀ] *adj* blasphemous.

blasphème [blasfɛm] *nm* blasphemy.

blasphémer [blasfeme] *vi* to blaspheme ♦ *vt* to blaspheme against.

blatte [blat] *nf* cockroach.

blazer [blazɛʀ] *nm* blazer.

blé [ble] *nm* wheat; ~ **en herbe** wheat on the ear; ~ **noir** buckwheat.

bled [blɛd] *nm* (*péj*) hole; (*en Afrique du Nord*): **le** ~ the interior.

blême [blɛm] *adj* pale.

blêmir [blemiʀ] *vi* (*personne*) to (turn) pale; (*lueur*) to grow pale.

blennorragie [blenɔʀaʒi] *nf* blennorrhoea.

blessant, e [blɛsɑ̃, -ɑ̃t] *adj* hurtful.

blessé, e [blese] *adj* injured ♦ *nm/f* injured person, casualty; **un** ~ **grave, un grand** ~ a seriously injured *ou* wounded person.

blesser [blese] *vt* to injure; (*délibérément: MIL etc*) to wound; (*suj: souliers etc, offenser*) to hurt; **se** ~ to injure o.s.; **se** ~ **au pied** *etc* to injure one's foot *etc*.

blessure [blesyʀ] *nf* injury; wound.

blet, te [blɛ, blɛt] *adj* overripe.

blette [blɛt] *nf* = **bette**.

bleu, e [blø] *adj* blue; (*bifteck*) very rare ♦ *nm* (*couleur*) blue; (*novice*) greenhorn; (*contusion*) bruise; (*vêtement: aussi:* ~**s**) overalls *pl* (*BRIT*), coveralls *pl* (*US*); **avoir une peur** ~**e** to be scared stiff; **zone** ~**e** ≈ restricted parking area; **fromage** ~ blue cheese; **au** ~ (*CULIN*) au bleu; ~ (**de lessive**) ≈ blue bag; ~ **de méthylène** (*MÉD*) methylene blue; ~ **marine/nuit/roi** navy/midnight/royal blue.

bleuâtre [bløɑtʀ(ə)] *adj* (*fumée etc*) bluish, blueish.

bleuet [bløɛ] *nm* cornflower.

bleuir [bløiʀ] *vt, vi* to turn blue.

bleuté, e [bløte] *adj* blue-shaded.

blindage [blɛ̃daʒ] *nm* armo(u)r-plating.

blindé, e [blɛ̃de] *adj* armoured (*BRIT*), armored (*US*); (*fig*) hardened ♦ *nm* armoured *ou* armored car; (*char*) tank.

blinder [blɛ̃de] *vt* to armour (*BRIT*), armor (*US*); (*fig*) to harden.

blizzard [blizaʀ] *nm* blizzard.

bloc [blɔk] *nm* (*de pierre etc, INFORM*) block; (*de papier à lettres*) pad; (*ensemble*) group, block; **serré à** ~ tightened right down; **en** ~ as a whole; wholesale; **faire** ~ to unite; ~ **opératoire** operating *ou* theatre block; ~ **sanitaire** toilet block; ~ **sténo** shorthand notebook.

blocage [blɔkaʒ] *nm* (*voir bloquer*) blocking; jamming; freezing; (*PSYCH*) hang-up.

bloc-cuisine, *pl* **blocs-cuisines** [blɔkkɥizin] *nm* kitchen unit.

bloc-cylindres, *pl* **blocs-cylindres** [blɔksilɛ̃dʀ(ə)] *nm* cylinder block.

bloc-évier, *pl* **blocs-éviers** [blɔkevje] *nm* sink unit.

bloc-moteur, *pl* **blocs-moteurs** [blɔkmɔtœʀ] *nm* engine block.

bloc-notes, *pl* **blocs-notes** [blɔknɔt] *nm* note pad.

blocus [blɔkys] *nm* blockade.

blond, e [blɔ̃, -ɔ̃d] *adj* fair; (*plus clair*) blond; (*sable, blés*) golden ♦ *nm/f* fair-haired *ou* blond man/woman; ~ **cendré** ash blond.

blondeur [blɔ̃dœʀ] *nf* fairness; blondness.

blondin, e [blɔ̃dɛ̃, -in] *nm/f* fair-haired *ou* blond child *ou* young person.

blondinet, te [blɔ̃dinɛ, -ɛt] *nm/f* blondy.

blondir [blɔ̃diʀ] *vi* (*personne, cheveux*) to go fair *ou* blond.

bloquer [blɔke] *vt* (*passage*) to block; (*pièce mobile*) to jam; (*crédits, compte*) to freeze; (*personne, négociations etc*) to hold up; (*regrouper*) to group; ~ **les freins** to jam on the brakes.

blottir [blɔtiʀ]: **se** ~ *vi* to huddle up.

blousant, e [bluzɑ̃, ɑ̃t] *adj* blousing out.

blouse [bluz] *nf* overall.

blouser [bluze] *vi* to blouse out.

blouson [bluzɔ̃] *nm* blouson (jacket); ~ **noir** (*fig*) ≈ rocker.

blue-jean(s) [bludʒin(s)] *nm* jeans.
blues [bluz] *nm* blues *pl*.
bluet [blyɛ] *nm* = **bleuet**.
bluff [blœf] *nm* bluff.
bluffer [blœfe] *vi*, *vt* to bluff.
BN *sigle f* = *Bibliothèque nationale.*
BNP *sigle f* = *Banque nationale de Paris.*
boa [bɔa] *nm* (*ZOOL*): ~ **(constricteur)** boa (constrictor); (*tour de cou*) (feather *ou* fur) boa.
bobard [bɔbaʀ] *nm* (*fam*) tall story.
bobèche [bɔbɛʃ] *nf* candle-ring.
bobine [bɔbin] *nf* (*de fil*) reel; (*de machine à coudre*) spool; (*de machine à écrire*) ribbon; (*ÉLEC*) coil; ~ **(d'allumage)** (*AUTO*) coil; ~ **de pellicule** (*PHOTO*) roll of film.
bobo [bobo] *nm* (*aussi fig*) sore spot.
bob(sleigh) [bɔb(slɛg)] *nm* bob(sleigh).
bocage [bɔkaʒ] *nm* (*GÉO*) bocage, *farmland criss-crossed by hedges and trees*; (*bois*) grove, copse (*BRIT*).
bocal, aux [bɔkal, -o] *nm* jar.
bock [bɔk] *nm* (beer) glass; (*contenu*) glass of beer.
bœuf [bœf, *pl* bø] *nm* ox (*pl* oxen), steer; (*CULIN*) beef; (*MUS*: *fam*) jam session.
bof [bɔf] *excl* (*fam*: *indifférence*) don't care!; (: *pas terrible*) nothing special.
Bogota [bɔgɔta] *n* Bogotá.
bogue [bɔg] *nf* (*BOT*) husk ♦ *nm* (*ORDIN*) bug.
Bohème [bɔɛm] *nf*: **la** ~ Bohemia.
bohème [bɔɛm] *adj* happy-go-lucky, unconventional.
bohémien, ne [bɔemjɛ̃, -ɛn] *adj* Bohemian ♦ *nm/f* gipsy.
boire [bwaʀ] *vt* to drink; (*s'imprégner de*) to soak up; ~ **un coup** to have a drink.
bois [bwa] *vb voir* **boire** ♦ *nm* wood; (*ZOOL*) antler; (*MUS*): **les** ~ the woodwind; **de** ~, **en** ~ wooden; ~ **vert** green wood; ~ **mort** deadwood; ~ **de lit** bedstead.
boisé, e [bwaze] *adj* woody, wooded.
boiser [bwaze] *vt* (*galerie de mine*) to timber; (*chambre*) to panel; (*terrain*) to plant with trees.
boiseries [bwazʀi] *nfpl* panelling *sg*.
boisson [bwasɔ̃] *nf* drink; **pris de** ~ drunk, intoxicated; ~**s alcoolisées** alcoholic beverages *ou* drinks; ~**s non alcoolisées** soft drinks.
boit [bwa] *vb voir* **boire**.
boîte [bwat] *nf* box; (*fam*: *entreprise*) firm, company; **aliments en** ~ canned *ou* tinned (*BRIT*) foods; ~ **de sardines/petits pois** can *ou* tin (*BRIT*) of sardines/peas; **mettre qn en** ~ (*fam*) to have a laugh at sb's expense; ~ **d'allumettes** box of matches; (*vide*) matchbox; ~ **de conserves** can *ou* tin (*BRIT*) (of food); ~ **crânienne** cranium; ~ **à gants** glove compartment; ~ **aux lettres** letter box, mailbox (*US*); (*INFORM*) mailbox; ~ **à musique** musical box; ~ **noire** (*AVIAT*) black box; ~ **de nuit** night club; ~ **à ordures** dustbin

(*BRIT*), trash can (*US*); ~ **postale (BP)** PO box; ~ **de vitesses** gear box.
boiter [bwate] *vi* to limp; (*fig*) to wobble; (*raisonnement*) to be shaky.
boiteux, euse [bwatø, -øz] *adj* lame; wobbly; shaky.
boîtier [bwatje] *nm* case; (*d'appareil-photo*) body; ~ **de montre** watch case.
boitiller [bwatije] *vi* to limp slightly, have a slight limp.
boive [bwav] *etc vb voir* **boire**.
bol [bɔl] *nm* bowl; (*contenu*): **un** ~ **de café** *etc* a bowl of coffee *etc*; **un** ~ **d'air** a breath of fresh air; **en avoir ras le** ~ (*fam*) to have had a bellyful.
bolée [bɔle] *nf* bowlful.
boléro [bɔleʀo] *nm* bolero.
bolet [bɔlɛ] *nm* boletus (mushroom).
bolide [bɔlid] *nm* racing car; **comme un** ~ like a rocket.
Bolivie [bɔlivi] *nf*: **la** ~ Bolivia.
bolivien, ne [bɔlivjɛ̃, -ɛn] *adj* Bolivian ♦ *nm/f*: **B~, ne** Bolivian.
bolognais, e [bɔlɔɲɛ, -ɛz] *adj* Bolognese.
Bologne [bɔlɔɲ] *n* Bologna.
bombance [bɔ̃bɑ̃s] *nf*: **faire** ~ to have a feast, revel.
bombardement [bɔ̃baʀdəmɑ̃] *nm* bombing.
bombarder [bɔ̃baʀde] *vt* to bomb; ~ **qn de** (*cailloux, lettres*) to bombard sb with; ~ **qn directeur** to thrust sb into the director's seat.
bombardier [bɔ̃baʀdje] *nm* (*avion*) bomber; (*aviateur*) bombardier.
bombe [bɔ̃b] *nf* bomb; (*atomiseur*) (aerosol) spray; (*ÉQUITATION*) riding cap; **faire la** ~ (*fam*) to go on a binge; ~ **atomique** atomic bomb; ~ **à retardement** time bomb.
bombé, e [bɔ̃be] *adj* rounded; (*mur*) bulging; (*front*) domed; (*route*) steeply cambered.
bomber [bɔ̃be] *vi* to bulge; (*route*) to camber ♦ *vt*: ~ **le torse** to swell out one's chest.

============================ *MOT-CLÉ*

bon, bonne [bɔ̃, bɔn] *adj* **1** (*agréable, satisfaisant*) good; **un** ~ **repas/restaurant** a good meal/restaurant; **être** ~ **en maths** to be good at maths
2 (*charitable*): **être** ~ **(envers)** to be good (to), to be kind (to); **vous êtes trop** ~ you're too kind
3 (*correct*) right; **le** ~ **numéro/moment** the right number/moment
4 (*souhaits*): ~ **anniversaire** happy birthday; ~ **voyage** have a good trip; **bonne chance** good luck; **bonne année** happy New Year; **bonne nuit** good night
5 (*approprié*): ~ **à/pour** fit to/for; ~ **à jeter** for the bin; **c'est** ~ **à savoir** that's useful to know; **à quoi** ~ **(...)?** what's the point *ou* use (of ...)?
6 (*intensif*): **ça m'a pris 2 bonnes heures** it

took me a good 2 hours; **un** ~ **nombre de** a good number of

7: ~ **enfant** *adj inv* accommodating, easygoing; **bonne femme** (*péj*) woman; **de bonne heure** early; ~ **marché** cheap; ~ **mot** witticism; **pour faire** ~ **poids** ... to make up for it ...; ~ **sens** common sense; ~ **vivant** jovial chap; **bonnes œuvres** charitable works, charities; **bonne sœur** nun

♦ *nm* **1** (*billet*) voucher; (*aussi:* ~ **cadeau**) gift voucher; ~ **de caisse** cash voucher; ~ **d'essence** petrol coupon; ~ **à tirer** pass for press; ~ **du Trésor** Treasury bond

2: **avoir du** ~ to have its good points; **il y a du** ~ **dans ce qu'il dit** there's some sense in what he says; **pour de** ~ for good

♦ *nm/f:* **un** ~ **à rien** a good-for-nothing

♦ *adv:* **il fait** ~ it's *ou* the weather is fine; **sentir** ~ to smell good; **tenir** ~ to stand firm; **juger** ~ **de faire** ... to think fit to do ...

♦ *excl* right!, good!; **ah** ~? really?; ~, **je reste** right, I'll stay; *voir aussi* **bonne.**

bonasse [bɔnas] *adj* soft, meek.
bonbon [bɔ̃bɔ̃] *nm* (boiled) sweet.
bonbonne [bɔ̃bɔn] *nf* demijohn; carboy.
bonbonnière [bɔ̃bɔnjɛʀ] *nf* sweet (*BRIT*) *ou* candy (*US*) box.
bond [bɔ̃] *nm* leap; (*d'une balle*) rebound, ricochet; **faire un** ~ to leap in the air; **d'un seul** ~ in one bound, with one leap; ~ **en avant** (*fig: progrès*) leap forward.
bonde [bɔ̃d] *nf* (*d'évier etc*) plug; (*: trou*) plughole; (*de tonneau*) bung; bunghole.
bondé, e [bɔ̃de] *adj* packed (full).
bondieuserie [bɔ̃djøzʀi] *nf* (*péj: objet*) religious knick-knack.
bondir [bɔ̃diʀ] *vi* to leap; ~ **de joie** (*fig*) to jump for joy; ~ **de colère** (*fig*) to be hopping mad.
bonheur [bɔnœʀ] *nm* happiness; **avoir le** ~ **de** to have the good fortune to; **porter** ~ (**à qn**) to bring (sb) luck; **au petit** ~ haphazardly; **par** ... fortunately.
bonhomie [bɔnɔmi] *nf* goodnaturedness.
bonhomme [bɔnɔm], *pl* **bonshommes** [bɔ̃zɔm] *nm* fellow ♦ *adj* good-natured; **un vieux** ~ an old chap; **aller son** ~ **de chemin** to carry on in one's own sweet way; ~ **de neige** snowman.
boni [bɔni] *nm* profit.
bonification [bɔnifikasjɔ̃] *nf* bonus.
bonifier [bɔnifje] *vt*, **se** ~ *vi* to improve.
boniment [bɔnimɑ̃] *nm* patter *no pl*.
bonjour [bɔ̃ʒuʀ] *excl, nm* hello; (*selon l'heure*) good morning (*ou* afternoon); **donner** *ou* **souhaiter le** ~ **à qn** to bid sb good morning *ou* afternoon.
Bonn [bɔn] *n* Bonn.
bonne [bɔn] *adj f voir* **bon** ♦ *nf* (*domestique*) maid; ~ **à tout faire** general help; ~ **d'enfant** nanny.

bonne-maman, *pl* **bonnes-mamans** [bɔnmamɑ̃] granny, grandma, gran.
bonnement [bɔnmɑ̃] *adv:* **tout** ~ quite simply.
bonnet [bɔnɛ] *nm* bonnet, hat; (*de soutiengorge*) cup; ~ **d'âne** dunce's cap; ~ **de bain** bathing cap; ~ **de nuit** nightcap.
bonneterie [bɔnɛtʀi] *nf* hosiery.
bon-papa, *pl* **bons-papas** [bɔ̃papa] *nm* grandpa, grandad.
bonsoir [bɔ̃swaʀ] *excl* good evening.
bonté [bɔ̃te] *nf* kindness *no pl*; **avoir la** ~ **de** to be kind *ou* good enough to.
bonus [bɔnys] *nm* (*assurances*) no-claims bonus.
bonze [bɔ̃z] *nm* (*REL*) bonze.
boomerang [bumʀɑ̃g] *nm* boomerang.
boots [buts] *nfpl* boots.
borborygme [bɔʀbɔʀigm(ə)] *nm* rumbling noise.
bord [bɔʀ] *nm* (*de table, verre, falaise*) edge; (*de rivière, lac*) bank; (*de route*) side; (*de vêtement*) edge, border; (*de chapeau*) brim; (**monter**) **à** ~ (to go) on board; **jeter pardessus** ~ to throw overboard; **le commandant de** ~/**les hommes du** ~ the ship's master/crew; **du même** ~ (*fig*) of the same opinion; **au** ~ **de la mer/route** at the seaside/roadside; **être au** ~ **des larmes** to be on the verge of tears; **virer de** ~ (*NAVIG*) to tack; **sur les** ~**s** (*fig*) slightly; **de tous** ~**s** on all sides; ~ **du trottoir** kerb (*BRIT*), curb (*US*).
bordage [bɔʀdaʒ] *nm* (*NAVIG*) planking *no pl*; plating *no pl*.
bordeaux [bɔʀdo] *nm* Bordeaux ♦ *adj inv* maroon.
bordée [bɔʀde] *nf* broadside; **une** ~ **d'injures** a volley of abuse; **tirer une** ~ to go on the town.
bordel [bɔʀdɛl] *nm* brothel; (*fam!*) bloody (*BRIT*) *ou* goddamn (*US*) mess (*!*) ♦ *excl* hell!
bordelais, e [bɔʀdəlɛ, -ɛz] *adj* of *ou* from Bordeaux.
border [bɔʀde] *vt* (*être le long de*) to border, line; (*garnir*): ~ **qch de** to line sth with; to trim sth with; (*qn dans son lit*) to tuck up.
bordereau, x [bɔʀdəʀo] *nm* docket, slip.
bordure [bɔʀdyʀ] *nf* border; (*sur un vêtement*) trim(ming), border; **en** ~ **de** on the edge of.
boréal, e, aux [bɔʀeal, -o] *adj* boreal, northern.
borgne [bɔʀɲ(ə)] *adj* one-eyed; **hôtel** ~ shady hotel; **fenêtre** ~ obstructed window.
bornage [bɔʀnaʒ] *nm* (*d'un terrain*) demarcation.
borne [bɔʀn(ə)] *nf* boundary stone; (*aussi:* ~ **kilométrique**) kilometre-marker, ≈ milestone; ~**s** *nfpl* (*fig*) limits; **dépasser les** ~**s** to go too far; **sans** ~(**s**) boundless.
borné, e [bɔʀne] *adj* narrow; (*obtus*) narrow-minded.
Bornéo [bɔʀneo] *nm:* **le** ~ Borneo.
borner [bɔʀne] *vt* (*délimiter*) to limit; (*limiter*)

bosniaque – bougeoir

to confine; **se ~ à faire** to content o.s. with doing; to limit o.s. to doing.

bosniaque [bɔznjak] *adj* Bosnian ♦ *nm/f:* **B~** Bosnian.

Bosnie [bɔsni] *nf* Bosnia.

bosnien, ne [bɔznjɛ̃, -ɛn] *adj* Bosnian ♦ *nm/f:* **B~, ne** Bosnian.

Bosphore [bɔsfɔʀ] *nm:* **le ~** the Bosphorus.

bosquet [bɔskɛ] *nm* copse (*BRIT*), grove.

bosse [bɔs] *nf* (*de terrain etc*) bump; (*enflure*) lump; (*du bossu, du chameau*) hump; **avoir la ~ des maths** *etc* to have a gift for maths *etc*; **il a roulé sa ~** he's been around.

bosseler [bɔsle] *vt* (*ouvrer*) to emboss; (*abîmer*) to dent.

bosser [bɔse] *vi* (*fam*) to work; (*: dur*) to slog (hard) (*BRIT*), slave (away).

bosseur, euse [bɔsœʀ, -øz] *nm/f* (hard) worker, slogger (*BRIT*).

bossu, e [bɔsy] *nm/f* hunchback.

bot [bo] *adj m:* **pied ~** club foot.

botanique [bɔtanik] *nf* botany ♦ *adj* botanic(al).

botaniste [bɔtanist(ə)] *nm/f* botanist.

Botswana [bɔtswana] *nm:* **le ~** Botswana.

botte [bɔt] *nf* (*soulier*) (high) boot; (*ESCRIME*) thrust; (*gerbe*): **~ de paille** bundle of straw; **~ de radis/d'asperges** bunch of radishes/asparagus; **~s de caoutchouc** wellington boots.

botter [bɔte] *vt* to put boots on; (*donner un coup de pied à*) to kick; (*fam*): **ça me botte** I fancy that.

bottier [bɔtje] *nm* bootmaker.

bottillon [bɔtijɔ̃] *nm* bootee.

bottin [bɔtɛ̃] *nm* ® directory.

bottine [bɔtin] *nf* ankle boot.

botulisme [bɔtylism(ə)] *nm* botulism.

bouc [buk] *nm* goat; (*barbe*) goatee; **~ émissaire** scapegoat.

boucan [bukɑ̃] *nm* din, racket.

bouche [buʃ] *nf* mouth; **une ~ à nourrir** a mouth to feed; **les ~s inutiles** the non-productive members of the population; **faire du ~ à ~ à qn** to give sb the kiss of life (*BRIT*), give sb mouth-to-mouth resuscitation; **de ~ à oreille** confidentially; **pour la bonne ~** (*pour la fin*) till last; **faire venir l'eau à la ~** to make one's mouth water; **~ cousue!** mum's the word!; **~ d'aération** air vent; **~ de chaleur** hot air vent; **~ d'égout** manhole; **~ d'incendie** fire hydrant; **~ de métro** métro entrance.

bouché, e [buʃe] *adj* (*flacon etc*) stoppered; (*temps, ciel*) overcast; (*carrière*) blocked; (*péj: personne*) thick; (*trompette*) muted; **avoir le nez ~** to have a blocked(-up) nose.

bouchée [buʃe] *nf* mouthful; **ne faire qu'une ~ de** (*fig*) to make short work of; **pour une ~ de pain** (*fig*) for next to nothing; **~s à la reine** chicken vol-au-vents.

boucher [buʃe] *nm* butcher ♦ *vt* (*pour colmater*)

to stop up; to fill up; (*obstruer*) to block (up); **se ~** (*tuyau etc*) to block up, get blocked up; **se ~ le nez** to hold one's nose.

bouchère [buʃɛʀ] *nf* butcher; (*femme du boucher*) butcher's wife.

boucherie [buʃʀi] *nf* butcher's (shop); (*métier*) butchery; (*fig*) slaughter, butchery.

bouche-trou [buʃtʀu] *nm* (*fig*) stop-gap.

bouchon [buʃɔ̃] *nm* (*en liège*) cork; (*autre matière*) stopper; (*fig: embouteillage*) holdup; (*PÊCHE*) float; (*doseur*) measuring cap.

bouchonner [buʃɔne] *vt* to rub down ♦ *vi* to form a traffic jam.

bouchot [buʃo] *nm* mussel bed.

bouclage [buklaʒ] *nm* sealing off.

boucle [bukl(ə)] *nf* (*forme, figure, aussi INFORM*) loop; (*objet*) buckle; **~ (de cheveux)** curl; **~ d'oreilles** earring.

bouclé, e [bukle] *adj* curly; (*tapis*) uncut.

boucler [bukle] *vt* (*fermer: ceinture etc*) to fasten; (*: magasin*) to shut; (*terminer*) to finish off; (*: circuit*) to complete; (*budget*) to balance; (*enfermer*) to shut away; (*: condamné*) to lock up; (*: quartier*) to seal off ♦ *vi* to curl; **faire ~** (*cheveux*) to curl; **~ la boucle** (*AVIAT*) to loop the loop.

bouclette [buklɛt] *nf* small curl.

bouclier [buklije] *nm* shield.

bouddha [buda] *nm* Buddha.

bouddhisme [budism(ə)] *nm* Buddhism.

bouddhiste [budist(ə)] *nm/f* Buddhist.

bouder [bude] *vi* to sulk ♦ *vt* (*chose*) to turn one's nose up at; (*personne*) to refuse to have anything to do with.

bouderie [budʀi] *nf* sulking *no pl*.

boudeur, euse [budœʀ, -øz] *adj* sullen, sulky.

boudin [budɛ̃] *nm* (*CULIN*) black pudding; (*TECH*) roll; **~ blanc** white pudding.

boudiné, e [budine] *adj* (*doigt*) podgy; (*serré*): **~ dans** (*vêtement*) bulging out of.

boudoir [budwaʀ] *nm* boudoir; (*biscuit*) sponge finger.

boue [bu] *nf* mud.

bouée [bwe] *nf* buoy; (*de baigneur*) rubber ring; **~ (de sauvetage)** lifebuoy; (*fig*) lifeline.

boueux, euse [bwø, -øz] *adj* muddy ♦ *nm* (*fam*) refuse (*BRIT*) *ou* garbage (*US*) collector.

bouffant, e [bufɑ̃, -ɑ̃t] *adj* puffed out.

bouffe [buf] *nf* (*fam*) grub, food.

bouffée [bufe] *nf* puff; **~ de chaleur** (*gén*) blast of hot air; (*MÉD*) hot flush (*BRIT*) *ou* flash (*US*); **~ de fièvre/de honte** flush of fever/shame; **~ d'orgueil** fit of pride.

bouffer [bufe] *vi* (*fam*) to eat; (*COUTURE*) to puff out ♦ *vt* (*fam*) to eat.

bouffi, e [bufi] *adj* swollen.

bouffon, ne [bufɔ̃, -ɔn] *adj* farcical, comical ♦ *nm* jester.

bouge [buʒ] *nm* (*bar louche*) (low) dive; (*taudis*) hovel.

bougeoir [buʒwaʀ] *nm* candlestick.

bougeotte [buʒɔt] *nf*: **avoir la ~** to have the fidgets.

bouger [buʒe] *vi* to move; (*dent etc*) to be loose; (*changer*) to alter; (*agir*) to stir ♦ *vt* to move; **se ~** (*fam*) to move (oneself).

bougie [buʒi] *nf* candle; (*AUTO*) spark(ing) plug.

bougon, ne [bugɔ̃, -ɔn] *adj* grumpy.

bougonner [bugɔne] *vi, vt* to grumble.

bougre [bugʀ(ə)] *nm* chap; (*fam*): **ce ~ de ...** that confounded ....

boui-boui [bwibwi] *nm* (*fam*) greasy spoon.

bouillabaisse [bujabɛs] *nf* type of fish soup.

bouillant, e [bujɑ̃, -ɑ̃t] *adj* (*qui bout*) boiling; (*très chaud*) boiling (hot); (*fig: ardent*) hotheaded; **~ de colère** *etc* seething with anger *etc*.

bouille [buj] *nf* (*fam*) mug.

bouilleur [bujœʀ] *nm*: **~ de cru** (home) distiller.

bouillie [buji] *nf* gruel; (*de bébé*) cereal; **en ~** (*fig*) crushed.

bouillir [bujiʀ] *vi* to boil ♦ *vt* (*aussi*: **faire ~**: *CULIN*) to boil; **~ de colère** *etc* to seethe with anger *etc*.

bouilloire [bujwaʀ] *nf* kettle.

bouillon [bujɔ̃] *nm* (*CULIN*) stock *no pl*; (*bulles, écume*) bubble; **~ de culture** culture medium.

bouillonnement [bujɔnmɑ̃] *nm* (*d'un liquide*) bubbling; (*des idées*) ferment.

bouillonner [bujɔne] *vi* to bubble; (*fig*) to bubble up; (*torrent*) to foam.

bouillotte [bujɔt] *nf* hot-water bottle.

boulanger, ère [bulɑ̃ʒe, -ɛʀ] *nm/f* baker ♦ *nf* (*femme du boulanger*) baker's wife.

boulangerie [bulɑ̃ʒʀi] *nf* bakery, baker's (shop); (*commerce*) bakery; **~ industrielle** bakery.

boulangerie-pâtisserie, *pl* **boulangeries-pâtisseries** [bulɑ̃ʒʀipɑtisʀi] *nf* baker's and confectioner's (shop).

boule [bul] *nf* (*gén*) ball; (*pour jouer*) bowl; (*de machine à écrire*) golf ball; **roulé en ~** curled up in a ball; **se mettre en ~** (*fig*) to fly off the handle, blow one's top; **perdre la ~** (*fig: fam*) to go off one's rocker; **~ de gomme** (*bonbon*) gum(drop), pastille; **~ de neige** snowball; **faire ~ de neige** (*fig*) to snowball.

bouleau, x [bulo] *nm* (silver) birch.

bouledogue [buldɔg] *nm* bulldog.

bouler [bule] *vi* (*fam*): **envoyer ~ qn** to send sb packing; **je me suis fait ~** (*à un examen*) they flunked me.

boulet [bulɛ] *nm* (*aussi*: **~ de canon**) cannonball; (*de bagnard*) ball and chain; (*charbon*) (coal) nut.

boulette [bulɛt] *nf* ball.

boulevard [bulvaʀ] *nm* boulevard.

bouleversant, e [bulvɛʀsɑ̃, -ɑ̃t] *adj* (*récit*) deeply distressing; (*nouvelle*) shattering.

bouleversé, e [bulvɛʀse] *adj* (*ému*) deeply distressed; shattered.

bouleversement [bulvɛʀsəmɑ̃] *nm* (*politique, social*) upheaval.

bouleverser [bulvɛʀse] *vt* (*émouvoir*) to overwhelm; (*causer du chagrin à*) to distress; (*pays, vie*) to disrupt; (*papiers, objets*) to turn upside down, upset.

boulier [bulje] *nm* abacus; (*de jeu*) scoring board.

boulimie [bulimi] *nf* bulimia; compulsive eating.

boulimique [bulimik] *adj* bulimic.

boulingrin [bulɛ̃gʀɛ̃] *nm* lawn.

bouliste [bulist(ə)] *nm/f* bowler.

boulocher [bulɔʃe] *vi* (*laine etc*) to develop little snarls.

boulodrome [bulɔdʀɔm] *nm* bowling pitch.

boulon [bulɔ̃] *nm* bolt.

boulonner [bulɔne] *vt* to bolt.

boulot [bulo] *nm* (*fam: travail*) work.

boulot, te [bulo, -ɔt] *adj* plump, tubby.

boum [bum] *nm* bang ♦ *nf* party.

bouquet [bukɛ] *nm* (*de fleurs*) bunch (of flowers), bouquet; (*de persil etc*) bunch; (*parfum*) bouquet; (*fig*) crowning piece; **c'est le ~!** that's the last straw!; **~ garni** (*CULIN*) bouquet garni.

bouquetin [buktɛ̃] *nm* ibex.

bouquin [bukɛ̃] *nm* (*fam*) book.

bouquiner [bukine] *vi* (*fam*) to read.

bouquiniste [bukinist(ə)] *nm/f* bookseller.

bourbeux, euse [buʀbø, -øz] *adj* muddy.

bourbier [buʀbje] *nm* (quag)mire.

bourde [buʀd(ə)] *nf* (*erreur*) howler; (*gaffe*) blunder.

bourdon [buʀdɔ̃] *nm* bumblebee.

bourdonnement [buʀdɔnmɑ̃] *nm* buzzing *no pl*, buzz; **avoir des ~s d'oreilles** to have a buzzing (noise) in one's ears.

bourdonner [buʀdɔne] *vi* to buzz; (*moteur*) to hum.

bourg [buʀ] *nm* small market town (*ou* village).

bourgade [buʀgad] *nf* township.

bourgeois, e [buʀʒwa, -waz] *adj* (*péj*) ≈ (upper) middle class; bourgeois; (*maison etc*) very comfortable ♦ *nm/f* (*autrefois*) burgher.

bourgeoisie [buʀʒwazi] *nf* ≈ upper middle classes *pl*; bourgeoisie; **petite ~** ≈ middle classes.

bourgeon [buʀʒɔ̃] *nm* bud.

bourgeonner [buʀʒɔne] *vi* to bud.

Bourgogne [buʀgɔɲ] *nf*: **la ~** Burgundy ♦ *nm*: **b~** burgundy (wine).

bourguignon, ne [buʀgiɲɔ̃, -ɔn] *adj* of *ou* from Burgundy, Burgundian; **bœuf ~** bœuf bourguignon.

bourlinguer [buʀlɛ̃ge] *vi* to knock about a lot, get around a lot.

bourrade [buʀad] *nf* shove, thump.

bourrage [buʀaʒ] *nm* (*papier*) jamming; **~ de**

crâne brainwashing; (*SCOL*) cramming.
bourrasque [buʀask(ə)] *nf* squall.
bourratif, ive [buʀatif, -iv] *adj* filling, stodgy.
bourre [buʀ] *nf* (*de coussin, matelas etc*) stuffing.
bourré, e [buʀe] *adj* (*rempli*): ~ **de** crammed full of; (*fam: ivre*) pickled, plastered.
bourreau, x [buʀo] *nm* executioner; (*fig*) torturer; ~ **de travail** workaholic, glutton for work.
bourrelé, e [buʀle] *adj*: **être** ~ **de remords** to be racked by remorse.
bourrelet [buʀlɛ] *nm* draught (*BRIT*) *ou* draft (*US*) excluder; (*de peau*) fold *ou* roll (of flesh).
bourrer [buʀe] *vt* (*pipe*) to fill; (*poêle*) to pack; (*valise*) to cram (full); ~ **de** to cram (full) with, stuff with; ~ **de coups** to hammer blows on, pummel; ~ **le crâne à qn** to pull the wool over sb's eyes; (*endoctriner*) to brainwash sb.
bourricot [buʀiko] *nm* small donkey.
bourrique [buʀik] *nf* (*âne*) ass.
bourru, e [buʀy] *adj* surly, gruff.
bourse [buʀs(ə)] *nf* (*subvention*) grant; (*porte-monnaie*) purse; **sans** ~ **délier** without spending a penny; **la B~** the Stock Exchange; ~ **du travail** ≈ trades union council (regional headquarters).
boursicoter [buʀsikɔte] *vi* (*COMM*) to dabble on the Stock Market.
boursier, ière [buʀsje, -jɛʀ] *adj* (*COMM*) Stock Market *cpd* ♦ *nm/f* (*SCOL*) grant-holder.
boursouflé, e [buʀsufle] *adj* swollen, puffy; (*fig*) bombastic, turgid.
boursoufler [buʀsufle] *vt* to puff up, bloat; **se** ~ *vi* (*visage*) to swell *ou* puff up; (*peinture*) to blister.
boursouflure [buʀsuflyʀ] *nf* (*du visage*) swelling, puffiness; (*de la peinture*) blister; (*fig: du style*) pomposity.
bous [bu] *vb voir* **bouillir**.
bousculade [buskylad] *nf* (*hâte*) rush; (*poussée*) crush.
bousculer [buskyle] *vt* to knock over; to knock into; (*fig*) to push, rush.
bouse [buz] *nf*: ~ **(de vache)** (cow) dung *no pl* (*BRIT*), manure *no pl*.
bousiller [buzije] *vt* (*fam*) to wreck.
boussole [busɔl] *nf* compass.
bout [bu] *vb voir* **bouillir** ♦ *nm* bit; (*extrémité: d'un bâton etc*) tip; (: *d'une ficelle, table, rue, période*) end; **au** ~ **de** at the end of, after; **au** ~ **du compte** at the end of the day; **pousser qn à** ~ to push sb to the limit (of his patience); **venir à** ~ **de** to manage to finish (off) *ou* overcome; ~ **à** ~ end to end; **à tout** ~ **de champ** at every turn; **d'un** ~ **à l'autre, de** ~ **en** ~ from one end to the other; **à** ~ **portant** at point-blank range; **un** ~ **de chou** (*enfant*) a little tot; ~ **d'essai** (*CINÉ etc*) screen test; ~ **filtre** filter tip.

boutade [butad] *nf* quip, sally.
boute-en-train [butɑ̃tʀɛ̃] *nm inv* live wire (*fig*).
bouteille [butɛj] *nf* bottle; (*de gaz butane*) cylinder.
boutiquaire [butikɛʀ] *adj*: **niveau** ~ shopping level.
boutique [butik] *nf* shop (*BRIT*), store (*US*); (*de grand couturier, de mode*) boutique.
boutiquier, ière [butikje, -jɛʀ] *nm/f* shopkeeper (*BRIT*), storekeeper (*US*).
boutoir [butwaʀ] *nm*: **coup de** ~ (*choc*) thrust; (*fig: propos*) barb.
bouton [butɔ̃] *nm* (*de vêtement, électrique etc*) button; (*BOT*) bud; (*sur la peau*) spot; (*de porte*) knob; ~ **de manchette** cuff-link; ~ **d'or** buttercup.
boutonnage [butɔnaʒ] *nm* (*action*) buttoning(-up); **un manteau à double** ~ a coat with two rows of buttons.
boutonner [butɔne] *vt* to button up, do up; **se** ~ to button one's clothes up.
boutonneux, euse [butɔnø, -øz] *adj* spotty.
boutonnière [butɔnjɛʀ] *nf* buttonhole.
bouton-poussoir, *pl* **boutons-poussoirs** [butɔ̃puswaʀ] *nm* pushbutton.
bouton-pression, *pl* **boutons-pression** [butɔ̃pʀesjɔ̃] *nm* press stud, snap fastener.
bouture [butyʀ] *nf* cutting; **faire des** ~**s** to take cuttings.
bouvreuil [buvʀœj] *nm* bullfinch.
bovidé [bɔvide] *nm* bovine.
bovin, e [bɔvɛ̃, -in] *adj* bovine ♦ *nm*: ~**s** cattle.
bowling [bɔliŋ] *nm* (tenpin) bowling; (*salle*) bowling alley.
box [bɔks] *nm* lock-up (garage); (*de salle, dortoir*) cubicle; (*d'écurie*) loose-box; **le** ~ **des accusés** the dock.
box(-calf) [bɔks(kalf)] *nm inv* box calf.
boxe [bɔks(ə)] *nf* boxing.
boxer [bɔkse] *vi* to box ♦ *nm* [bɔksɛʀ] (*chien*) boxer.
boxeur [bɔksœʀ] *nm* boxer.
boyau, x [bwajo] *nm* (*corde de raquette etc*) (cat) gut; (*galerie*) passage(way); (narrow) gallery; (*pneu de bicyclette*) tubeless tyre ♦ *nmpl* (*viscères*) entrails, guts.
boycottage [bɔjkɔtaʒ] *nm* (*d'un produit*) boycotting.
boycotter [bɔjkɔte] *vt* to boycott.
BP *sigle f* = **boîte postale.**
BPAL *sigle f* (= *base de plein air et de loisir*) open-air leisure centre.
BPF *sigle* (= *bon pour francs*) *printed on cheques before space for amount to be inserted.*
brabançon, ne [bʀabɑ̃sɔ̃, -ɔn] *adj* of *ou* from Brabant.
Brabant [bʀabɑ̃] *nm*: **le** ~ Brabant.
bracelet [bʀaslɛ] *nm* bracelet.
bracelet-montre [bʀaslɛmɔ̃tʀ(ə)] *nm* wristwatch.
braconnage [bʀakɔnaʒ] *nm* poaching.

braconner [bʀakɔne] *vi* to poach.

braconnier [bʀakɔnje] *nm* poacher.

brader [bʀade] *vt* to sell off, sell cheaply.

braderie [bʀadʀi] *nf* clearance sale; (*par des particuliers*) ≈ car boot sale (*BRIT*), ≈ garage sale (*US*); (*magasin*) discount store; (*sur marché*) cut-price (*BRIT*) *ou* cut-rate (*US*) stall.

braguette [bʀagɛt] *nf* fly, flies *pl* (*BRIT*), zipper (*US*).

braillard, e [bʀajaʀ, -aʀd] *adj* (*fam*) bawling, yelling.

braille [bʀaj] *nm* Braille.

braillement [bʀajmã] *nm* (*cri*) bawling *no pl*, yelling *no pl*.

brailler [bʀaje] *vi* to bawl, yell ♦ *vt* to bawl out, yell out.

braire [bʀɛʀ] *vi* to bray.

braise [bʀɛz] *nf* embers *pl*.

braiser [bʀeze] *vt* to braise; **bœuf braisé** braised steak.

bramer [bʀame] *vi* to bell; (*fig*) to wail.

brancard [bʀãkaʀ] *nm* (*civière*) stretcher; (*bras, perche*) shaft.

brancardier [bʀãkaʀdje] *nm* stretcher-bearer.

branchages [bʀãʃaʒ] *nmpl* branches, boughs.

branche [bʀãʃ] *nf* branch; (*de lunettes*) side(-piece).

branché, e [bʀãʃe] *adj* (*fam*) switched-on, trendy ♦ *nm/f* (*fam*) trendy.

branchement [bʀãʃmã] *nm* connection.

brancher [bʀãʃe] *vt* to connect (up); (*en mettant la prise*) to plug in; ~ **qn/qch sur** (*fig*) to get sb/sth launched onto.

branchies [bʀãʃi] *nfpl* gills.

brandade [bʀãdad] *nf* brandade (*cod dish*).

brandebourgeois, e [bʀãdəbuʀʒwa, -waz] *adj* of *ou* from Brandenburg.

brandir [bʀãdiʀ] *vt* (*arme*) to brandish, wield; (*document*) to flourish, wave.

brandon [bʀãdɔ̃] *nm* firebrand.

branlant, e [bʀãlã, -ãt] *adj* (*mur, meuble*) shaky.

branle [bʀãl] *nm*: **mettre en** ~ to set swinging; **donner le** ~ **à** to set in motion.

branle-bas [bʀãlba] *nm inv* commotion.

branler [bʀãle] *vi* to be shaky, be loose ♦ *vt*: ~ **la tête** to shake one's head.

braquage [bʀakaʒ] *nm* (*fam*) stick-up, hold-up; (*AUTO*): **rayon de** ~ turning circle.

braque [bʀak] *nm* (*ZOOL*) pointer.

braquer [bʀake] *vi* (*AUTO*) to turn (the wheel) ♦ *vt* (*revolver etc*): ~ **qch sur** to aim sth at, point sth at; (*mettre en colère*): ~ **qn** to antagonize sb, put sb's back up; ~ **son regard sur** to fix one's gaze on; **se** ~ *vi*: **se** ~ (**contre**) to take a stand (against).

bras [bʀa] *nm* arm; (*de fleuve*) branch ♦ *nmpl* (*fig: travailleurs*) labour *sg* (*BRIT*), labor *sg* (*US*), hands; ~ **dessus** ~ **dessous** arm in arm; **à** ~ **raccourcis** with fists flying; **à tour de** ~ with all one's might; **baisser les** ~ to

give up; ~ **droit** (*fig*) right hand man; ~ **de fer** arm-wrestling; **une partie de** ~ **de fer** (*fig*) a trial of strength; ~ **de levier** lever arm; ~ **de mer** arm of the sea, sound.

brasero [bʀazeʀo] *nm* brazier.

brasier [bʀazje] *nm* blaze, (blazing) inferno; (*fig*) inferno.

Brasilia [bʀazilja] *n* Brasilia.

bras-le-corps [bʀalkɔʀ]: **à** ~ *adv* (a)round the waist.

brassage [bʀasaʒ] *nm* (*de la bière*) brewing; (*fig*) mixing.

brassard [bʀasaʀ] *nm* armband.

brasse [bʀas] *nf* (*nage*) breast-stroke; (*mesure*) fathom; ~ **papillon** butterfly(-stroke).

brassée [bʀase] *nf* armful; **une** ~ **de** (*fig*) a number of.

brasser [bʀase] *vt* (*bière*) to brew; (*remuer: salade*) to toss; (*: cartes*) to shuffle; (*fig*) to mix; ~ **l'argent/les affaires** to handle a lot of money/business.

brasserie [bʀasʀi] *nf* (*restaurant*) bar (*selling food*), brasserie; (*usine*) brewery.

brasseur [bʀasœʀ] *nm* (*de bière*) brewer; ~ **d'affaires** big businessman.

brassière [bʀasjɛʀ] *nf* (baby's) vest (*BRIT*) *ou* undershirt (*US*); (*de sauvetage*) life jacket.

bravache [bʀavaʃ] *nm* blusterer, braggart.

bravade [bʀavad] *nf*: **par** ~ out of bravado.

brave [bʀav] *adj* (*courageux*) brave; (*bon, gentil*) good, kind.

bravement [bʀavmã] *adv* bravely; (*résolument*) boldly.

braver [bʀave] *vt* to defy.

bravo [bʀavo] *excl* bravo! ♦ *nm* cheer.

bravoure [bʀavuʀ] *nf* bravery.

BRB *sigle f* (*POLICE*: = *Brigade de répression du banditisme*) ≈ serious crime squad.

break [bʀɛk] *nm* (*AUTO*) estate car (*BRIT*), station wagon (*US*).

brebis [bʀəbi] *nf* ewe; ~ **galeuse** black sheep.

brèche [bʀɛʃ] *nf* breach, gap; **être sur la** ~ (*fig*) to be on the go.

bredouille [bʀəduj] *adj* empty-handed.

bredouiller [bʀəduje] *vi, vt* to mumble, stammer.

bref, brève [bʀɛf, bʀɛv] *adj* short, brief ♦ *adv* in short ♦ *nf* (*voyelle*) short vowel; (*information*) brief news item; **d'un ton** ~ sharply, curtly; **en** ~ in short, in brief; **à** ~ **délai** shortly.

brelan [bʀəlã] *nm*: **un** ~ three of a kind; **un** ~ **d'as** three aces.

breloque [bʀəlɔk] *nf* charm.

brème [bʀɛm] *nf* bream.

Brésil [bʀezil] *nm*: **le** ~ Brazil.

brésilien, ne [bʀeziljɛ̃, -ɛn] *adj* Brazilian ♦ *nm/ f*: **B~, ne** Brazilian.

bressan, e [bʀesã, -an] *adj* of *ou* from Bresse.

Bretagne [bʀətaɲ] *nf*: **la** ~ Brittany.

bretelle [bʀətɛl] *nf* (*de fusil etc*) sling; (*de vêtement*) strap; (*d'autoroute*) slip road

(*BRIT*), entrance *ou* exit ramp (*US*); ~s *nfpl* (*pour pantalon*) braces (*BRIT*), suspenders (*US*); ~ **de contournement** (*AUTO*) bypass; ~ **de raccordement** (*AUTO*) access road.

breton, ne [brətɔ̃, -ɔn] *adj* Breton ♦ *nm* (*LING*) Breton ♦ *nm/f*: **B~, ne** Breton.

breuvage [brœvaʒ] *nm* beverage, drink.

brève [brɛv] *adj f*, *nf voir* **bref**.

brevet [brəvɛ] *nm* diploma, certificate; ~ (**d'invention**) patent; ~ **d'apprentissage** certificate of apprenticeship; ~ (**des collèges**) *school certificate, taken at approx. 16 years*.

breveté, e [brəvte] *adj* patented; (*diplômé*) qualified.

breveter [brəvte] *vt* to patent.

bréviaire [brevjɛr] *nm* breviary.

BRGM *sigle m* = *Bureau de recherches géologiques et minières.*

briard, e [brijar, -ard(ə)] *adj* of *ou* from Brie ♦ *nm* (*chien*) briard.

bribes [brib] *nfpl* bits, scraps; (*d'une conversation*) snatches; **par** ~ piecemeal.

bric [brik]: **de** ~ **et de broc** *adv* with any old thing.

bric-à-brac [brikabrak] *nm inv* bric-a-brac, jumble.

bricolage [brikɔlaʒ] *nm*: **le** ~ do-it-yourself (*jobs*); (*péj*) patched-up job.

bricole [brikɔl] *nf* (*babiole, chose insignifiante*) trifle; (*petit travail*) small job.

bricoler [brikɔle] *vi* to do odd jobs; (*en amateur*) to do DIY jobs; (*passe-temps*) to potter about ♦ *vt* (*réparer*) to fix up; (*mal réparer*) to tinker with; (*trafiquer: voiture etc*) to doctor, fix.

bricoleur, euse [brikɔlœr, -øz] *nm/f* handyman/woman, DIY enthusiast.

bride [brid] *nf* bridle; (*d'un bonnet*) string, tie; **à** ~ **abattue** flat out, hell for leather; **tenir en** ~ to keep in check; **lâcher la** ~ **à, laisser la** ~ **sur le cou à** to give free rein to.

bridé, e [bride] *adj*: **yeux** ~**s** slit eyes.

brider [bride] *vt* (*réprimer*) to keep in check; (*cheval*) to bridle; (*CULIN: volaille*) to truss.

bridge [bridʒ(ə)] *nm* bridge.

brie [bri] *nm* Brie (*cheese*).

brièvement [brijɛvmɑ̃] *adv* briefly.

brièveté [brijɛvte] *nf* brevity.

brigade [brigad] *nf* squad; (*MIL*) brigade.

brigadier [brigadje] *nm* (*POLICE*) ≈ sergeant; (*MIL*) bombardier; corporal.

brigadier-chef, *pl* **brigadiers-chefs** [brigadjeʃɛf] *nm* ≈ lance-sergeant.

brigand [brigɑ̃] *nm* brigand.

brigandage [brigɑ̃daʒ] *nm* robbery.

briguer [brige] *vt* to aspire to; (*suffrages*) to canvass.

brillamment [brijamɑ̃] *adv* brilliantly.

brillant, e [brijɑ̃, -ɑ̃t] *adj* brilliant; bright; (*luisant*) shiny, shining ♦ *nm* (*diamant*) brilliant.

briller [brije] *vi* to shine.

brimade [brimad] *nf* vexation, harassment *no pl*; bullying *no pl*.

brimbaler [brɛ̃bale] *vb* = **bringuebaler**.

brimer [brime] *vt* to harass; to bully.

brin [brɛ̃] *nm* (*de laine, ficelle etc*) strand; (*fig*): **un** ~ **de** a bit of; **un** ~ **mystérieux** *etc* (*fam*) a weeny bit mysterious *etc*; ~ **d'herbe** blade of grass; ~ **de muguet** sprig of lily of the valley; ~ **de paille** wisp of straw.

brindille [brɛ̃dij] *nf* twig.

bringue [brɛ̃g] *nf* (*fam*): **faire la** ~ to go on a binge.

bringuebaler [brɛ̃gbale] *vi* to shake (about) ♦ *vt* to cart about.

brio [brijo] *nm* brilliance; (*MUS*) brio; **avec** ~ brilliantly, with panache.

brioche [brijɔʃ] *nf* brioche (bun); (*fam: ventre*) paunch.

brioché, e [brijɔʃe] *adj* brioche-style.

brique [brik] *nf* brick; (*fam*) 10,000 francs ♦ *adj inv* brick red.

briquer [brike] *vt* (*fam*) to polish up.

briquet [brikɛ] *nm* (*cigarette*) lighter.

briqueterie [briktri] *nf* brickyard.

bris [bri] *nm*: ~ **de clôture** (*JUR*) breaking in; ~ **de glaces** (*AUTO*) breaking of windows.

brisant [brizɑ̃] *nm* reef; (*vague*) breaker.

brise [briz] *nf* breeze.

brisé, e [brize] *adj* broken; ~ (**de fatigue**) exhausted; **d'une voix** ~**e** in a voice broken with emotion; **pâte** ~**e** shortcrust pastry.

brisées [brize] *nfpl*: **aller** *ou* **marcher sur les** ~ **de qn** to compete with sb in his own province.

brise-glace(s) [brizglas] *nm inv* (*navire*) icebreaker.

brise-jet [brizʒɛ] *nm inv* tap swirl.

brise-lames [brizlam] *nm inv* breakwater.

briser [brize] *vt* to break; **se** ~ *vi* to break.

brise-tout [briztu] *nm inv* wrecker.

briseur, euse [brizœr, -øz] *nm/f*: ~ **de grève** strike-breaker.

brise-vent [brizvɑ̃] *nm inv* windbreak.

bristol [bristɔl] *nm* (*carte de visite*) visiting card.

britannique [britanik] *adj* British ♦ *nm/f*: **B~** Briton, British person; **les B~s** the British.

broc [bro] *nm* pitcher.

brocante [brɔkɑ̃t] *nf* (*objets*) secondhand goods *pl*, junk; (*commerce*) secondhand trade; junk dealing.

brocanteur, euse [brɔkɑ̃tœr, -øz] *nm/f* junkshop owner; junk dealer.

brocart [brɔkar] *nm* brocade.

broche [brɔʃ] *nf* brooch; (*CULIN*) spit; (*fiche*) spike, peg; (*MÉD*) pin; **à la** ~ spit-roasted, roasted on a spit.

broché, e [brɔʃe] *adj* (*livre*) paper-backed; (*tissu*) brocaded.

brochet [brɔʃɛ] *nm* pike *inv*.

brochette [brɔʃɛt] *nf* skewer; ~ **de décorations** row of medals.

brochure [bʀɔʃyʀ] *nf* pamphlet, brochure, booklet.

brocoli [bʀɔkɔli] *nm* broccoli.

brodequins [bʀɔdkɛ̃] *nmpl* (*de marche*) (lace-up) boots.

broder [bʀɔde] *vt* to embroider ♦ *vi*: ~ **(sur des faits** *ou* **une histoire)** to embroider the facts.

broderie [bʀɔdʀi] *nf* embroidery.

bromure [bʀɔmyʀ] *nm* bromide.

broncher [bʀɔ̃ʃe] *vi*: **sans** ~ without flinching, without turning a hair.

bronches [bʀɔ̃ʃ] *nfpl* bronchial tubes.

bronchite [bʀɔ̃ʃit] *nf* bronchitis.

broncho-pneumonie [bʀɔ̃kɔpnømɔni] *nf* broncho-pneumonia *no pl.*

bronzage [bʀɔ̃zaʒ] *nm* (*hâle*) (sun)tan.

bronze [bʀɔ̃z] *nm* bronze.

bronzé, e [bʀɔ̃ze] *adj* tanned.

bronzer [bʀɔ̃ze] *vt* to tan ♦ *vi* to get a tan; **se** ~ to sunbathe.

brosse [bʀɔs] *nf* brush; **donner un coup de** ~ **à qch** to give sth a brush; **coiffé en** ~ with a crewcut; ~ **à cheveux** hairbrush; ~ **à dents** toothbrush; ~ **à habits** clothesbrush.

brosser [bʀɔse] *vt* (*nettoyer*) to brush; (*fig: tableau etc*) to paint; to draw; **se** ~ to brush one's clothes; **se** ~ **les dents** to brush one's teeth; **tu peux te** ~! (*fam*) you can sing for it!

brou [bʀu] *nm*: ~ **de noix** (*pour bois*) walnut stain; (*liqueur*) walnut liqueur.

brouette [bʀuɛt] *nf* wheelbarrow.

brouhaha [bʀuaa] *nm* hubbub.

brouillage [bʀujaʒ] *nm* (*d'une émission*) jamming.

brouillard [bʀujaʀ] *nm* fog; **être dans le** ~ (*fig*) to be all at sea.

brouille [bʀuj] *nf* quarrel.

brouillé, e [bʀuje] *adj* (*fâché*): **il est** ~ **avec ses parents** he has fallen out with his parents; (*teint*) muddy.

brouiller [bʀuje] *vt* to mix up; to confuse; (*RADIO*) to cause interference to; (: *délibérément*) to jam; (*rendre trouble*) to cloud; (*désunir: amis*) to set at odds; **se** ~ *vi* (*ciel, vue*) to cloud over; (*détails*) to become confused; **se** ~ **(avec)** to fall out (with); ~ **les pistes** to cover one's tracks; (*fig*) to confuse the issue.

brouillon, ne [bʀujɔ̃, -ɔn] *adj* disorganized, unmethodical ♦ *nm* (first) draft; **cahier de** ~ rough (work) book.

broussailles [bʀusaj] *nfpl* undergrowth *sg.*

broussailleux, euse [bʀusajø, -øz] *adj* bushy.

brousse [bʀus] *nf*: **la** ~ the bush.

brouter [bʀute] *vt* to graze on ♦ *vi* to graze; (*AUTO*) to judder.

broutille [bʀutij] *nf* trifle.

broyer [bʀwaje] *vt* to crush; ~ **du noir** to be down in the dumps.

bru [bʀy] *nf* daughter-in-law.

brucelles [bʀysɛl] *nfpl*: (*pinces*) ~ tweezers.

brugnon [bʀyɲɔ̃] *nm* nectarine.

bruine [bʀɥin] *nf* drizzle.

bruiner [bʀɥine] *vb impers*: **il bruine** it's drizzling, there's a drizzle.

bruire [bʀɥiʀ] *vi* (*eau*) to murmur; (*feuilles, étoffe*) to rustle.

bruissement [bʀɥismɑ̃] *nm* murmuring; rustling.

bruit [bʀɥi] *nm*: **un** ~ a noise, a sound; (*fig: rumeur*) a rumour (*BRIT*), a rumor (*US*); **le** ~ noise; **pas/trop de** ~ no/too much noise; **sans** ~ without a sound, noiselessly; **faire du** ~ to make a noise; ~ **de fond** background noise.

bruitage [bʀɥitaʒ] *nm* sound effects *pl.*

bruiteur, euse [bʀɥitœʀ, -øz] *nm/f* sound-effects engineer.

brûlant, e [bʀylɑ̃, -ɑ̃t] *adj* burning (hot); (*liquide*) boiling (hot); (*regard*) fiery; (*sujet*) red-hot.

brûlé, e [bʀyle] *adj* (*fig: démasqué*) blown; (: *homme politique etc*) discredited ♦ *nm*: **odeur de** ~ smell of burning.

brûle-pourpoint [bʀylpuʀpwɛ̃]: **à** ~ *adv* point-blank.

brûler [bʀyle] *vt* to burn; (*suj: eau bouillante*) to scald; (*consommer: électricité, essence*) to use; (*feu rouge, signal*) to go through (without stopping) ♦ *vi* to burn; (*jeu*): **tu brûles** you're getting warm *ou* hot; **se** ~ to burn o.s.; to scald o.s.; **se** ~ **la cervelle** to blow one's brains out; ~ **les étapes** to make rapid progress; (*aller trop vite*) to cut corners; ~ **(d'impatience) de faire qch** to burn with impatience to do sth, be dying to do sth.

brûleur [bʀylœʀ] *nm* burner.

brûlot [bʀylo] *nm* (*CULIN*) flaming brandy; **un** ~ **de contestation** (*fig*) a hotbed of dissent.

brûlure [bʀylyʀ] *nf* (*lésion*) burn; (*sensation*) burning *no pl*, burning sensation; ~**s d'estomac** heartburn *sg.*

brume [bʀym] *nf* mist.

brumeux, euse [bʀymø, -øz] *adj* misty; (*fig*) hazy.

brumisateur [bʀymizatœʀ] *nm* atomizer.

brun, e [bʀœ̃, -yn] *adj* brown; (*cheveux, personne*) dark ♦ *nm* (*couleur*) brown ♦ *nf* (*cigarette*) *cigarette made of dark tobacco*; (*bière*) ≈ brown ale, stout.

brunâtre [bʀynɑtʀ(ə)] *adj* brownish.

brunch [bʀœntʃ] *nm* brunch.

Brunei [bʀynei] *nm*: **le** ~ Brunei.

brunir [bʀyniʀ] *vi* (*aussi*: **se** ~) to get a tan ♦ *vt* to tan.

brushing [bʀœʃiŋ] *nm* blow-dry.

brusque [bʀysk(ə)] *adj* (*soudain*) abrupt, sudden; (*rude*) abrupt, brusque.

brusquement [bʀyskəmɑ̃] *adv* (*soudainement*) abruptly, suddenly.

brusquer [bʀyske] *vt* to rush.

brusquerie [bʀyskəʀi] *nf* abruptness, brusqueness.

brut, e [bʀyt] *adj* raw, crude, rough; (*diamant*) uncut; (*soie, minéral, INFORM: données*) raw; (*COMM*) gross ♦ *nf* brute; **(champagne)** ~ brut champagne; **(pétrole)** ~ crude (oil).

brutal, e, aux [bʀytal, -o] *adj* brutal.

brutalement [bʀytalmɑ̃] *adv* brutally.

brutaliser [bʀytalize] *vt* to handle roughly, manhandle.

brutalité [bʀytalite] *nf* brutality *no pl*.

brute [bʀyt] *adj f, nf voir* **brut**.

Bruxelles [bʀysɛl] *n* Brussels.

bruxellois, e [bʀysɛlwa, -waz] *adj* of *ou* from Brussels ♦ *nm/f*: B~, e inhabitant *ou* native of Brussels.

bruyamment [bʀɥijamɑ̃] *adv* noisily.

bruyant, e [bʀɥijɑ̃, -ɑ̃t] *adj* noisy.

bruyère [bʀɥijɛʀ] *nf* heather.

BT *sigle m* (= *Brevet de technicien*) *vocational training certificate, taken at approx. 18 years*.

BTA *sigle m* (= *Brevet de technicien agricole*) *agricultural training certificate, taken at approx. 18 years*.

BTP *sigle mpl* (= *Bâtiments et travaux publics*) *public buildings and works sector*.

BTS *sigle m* (= *Brevet de technicien supérieur*) *vocational training certificate taken at end of 2-year higher education course*.

BU *sigle f* = *Bibliothèque universitaire*.

bu, e [by] *pp de* **boire**.

buanderie [bɥɑ̃dʀi] *nf* laundry.

Bucarest [bykaʀɛst] *n* Bucharest.

buccal, e, aux [bykal, -o] *adj*: **par voie ~e** orally.

bûche [byʃ] *nf* log; **prendre une ~** (*fig*) to come a cropper (*BRIT*), fall flat on one's face; ~ **de Noël** Yule log.

bûcher [byʃe] *nm* pyre; bonfire ♦ *vi* (*fam: étudier*) to swot (*BRIT*), grind (*US*) ♦ *vt* to swot up (*BRIT*), cram.

bûcheron [byʃʀɔ̃] *nm* woodcutter.

bûchette [byʃɛt] *nf* (*de bois*) stick, twig; (*pour compter*) rod.

bûcheur, euse [byʃœʀ, -øz] *nm/f* (*fam: étudiant*) swot (*BRIT*), grind (*US*).

bucolique [bykɔlik] *adj* bucolic, pastoral.

Budapest [bydapɛst] *n* Budapest.

budget [bydʒɛ] *nm* budget.

budgétaire [bydʒetɛʀ] *adj* budgetary, budget *cpd*.

budgétiser [bydʒetize] *vt* to budget (for).

buée [bɥe] *nf* (*sur une vitre*) mist; (*de l'haleine*) steam.

Buenos Aires [bwenɔzɛʀ] *n* Buenos Aires.

buffet [byfɛ] *nm* (*meuble*) sideboard; (*de réception*) buffet; ~ **(de gare)** (station) buffet, snack bar.

buffle [byfl(ə)] *nm* buffalo.

buis [bɥi] *nm* box tree; (*bois*) box(wood).

buisson [bɥisɔ̃] *nm* bush.

buissonnière [bɥisɔnjɛʀ] *adj f*: **faire l'école ~** to play truant (*BRIT*), skip school.

bulbe [bylb(ə)] *nm* (*BOT, ANAT*) bulb; (*coupole*) onion-shaped dome.

bulgare [bylgaʀ] *adj* Bulgarian ♦ *nm* (*LING*) Bulgarian ♦ *nm/f*: B~ Bulgarian, Bulgar.

Bulgarie [bylgaʀi] *nf*: **la ~** Bulgaria.

bulldozer [buldozœʀ] *nm* bulldozer.

bulle [byl] *adj, nm*: **(papier)** ~ manil(l)a paper ♦ *nf* bubble; (*de bande dessinée*) balloon; (*papale*) bull; ~ **de savon** soap bubble.

bulletin [byltɛ̃] *nm* (*communiqué, journal*) bulletin; (*papier*) form; (: *de bagages*) ticket; (*SCOL*) report; ~ **d'informations** news bulletin; ~ **météorologique** weather report; ~ **de naissance** birth certificate; ~ **de salaire** pay slip; ~ **de santé** medical bulletin; ~ **(de vote)** ballot paper.

buraliste [byʀalist(ə)] *nm/f* (*de bureau de tabac*) tobacconist; (*de poste*) clerk.

bure [byʀ] *nf* homespun; (*de moine*) frock.

bureau, x [byʀo] *nm* (*meuble*) desk; (*pièce, service*) office; ~ **de change** (foreign) exchange office *ou* bureau; ~ **d'embauche** ≈ job centre; ~ **d'études** design office; ~ **de location** box office; ~ **de placement** employment agency; ~ **de poste** post office; ~ **de tabac** tobacconist's (shop), smoke shop (*US*); ~ **de vote** polling station.

bureaucrate [byʀokʀat] *nm* bureaucrat.

bureaucratie [byʀokʀasi] *nf* bureaucracy.

bureaucratique [byʀokʀatik] *adj* bureaucratic.

bureautique [byʀotik] *nf* office automation.

burette [byʀɛt] *nf* (*de mécanicien*) oilcan; (*de chimiste*) burette.

burin [byʀɛ̃] *nm* cold chisel; (*ART*) burin.

buriné, e [byʀine] *adj* (*fig: visage*) craggy, seamed.

Burkina(-Faso) [byʀkina(faso)] *nm*: **le ~** Burkina Faso.

burlesque [byʀlɛsk(ə)] *adj* ridiculous; (*LITTÉRATURE*) burlesque.

burnous [byʀnu(s)] *nm* burnous.

Burundi [buʀundi] *nm*: **le ~** Burundi.

BUS *sigle m* = *Bureau universitaire de statistiques*.

bus *vb* [by] *voir* **boire** ♦ *nm* [bys] (*véhicule, aussi INFORM*) bus.

busard [byzaʀ] *nm* harrier.

buse [byz] *nf* buzzard.

busqué, e [byske] *adj*: **nez ~** hook(ed) nose.

buste [byst(ə)] *nm* (*ANAT*) chest; (: *de femme*) bust; (*sculpture*) bust.

bustier [bystje] *nm* (*soutien-gorge*) long-line bra.

but [by] *vb voir* **boire** ♦ *nm* (*cible*) target; (*fig*) goal, aim; (*FOOTBALL etc*) goal; **de ~ en blanc** point-blank; **avoir pour ~ de faire** to aim to do; **dans le ~ de** with the intention of.

butane [bytan] *nm* butane; (*domestique*) calor gas ® (*BRIT*), butane.

buté, e [byte] *adj* stubborn, obstinate ♦ *nf* (*ARCHIT*) abutment; (*TECH*) stop.

buter [byte] *vi*: ~ **contre** *ou* **sur** to bump into; (*trébucher*) to stumble against ♦ *vt* to antagonize; **se** ~ *vi* to get obstinate, dig in one's heels.

buteur [bytœʀ] *nm* striker.

butin [bytɛ̃] *nm* booty, spoils *pl*; (*d'un vol*) loot.

butiner [bytine] *vi* to gather nectar.

butor [bytɔʀ] *nm* (*fig*) lout.

butte [byt] *nf* mound, hillock; **être en** ~ **à** to be exposed to.

buvable [byvabl(ə)] *adj* (*eau, vin*) drinkable; (*MÉD: ampoule etc*) to be taken orally; (*fig: roman etc*) reasonable.

buvais [byve] *etc vb voir* **boire**.

buvard [byvaʀ] *nm* blotter.

buvette [byvɛt] *nf* refreshment room *ou* stall; (*comptoir*) bar.

buveur, euse [byvœʀ, -øz] *nm/f* drinker.

buvons [byvɔ̃] *etc vb voir* **boire**.

BVP *sigle m* (= *Bureau de vérification de la publicité*) *advertising standards authority*.

Byzance [bizɑ̃s] *n* Byzantium.

byzantin, e [bizɑ̃tɛ̃, -in] *adj* Byzantine.

BZH *abr* (= *Breizh*) Brittany.

C c

C, c [se] *nm inv* C, c ♦ *abr* (= *centime*) c; (= *Celsius*) C; **C comme Célestin** C for Charlie.

c' [s] *dét voir* **ce**.

CA *sigle m* = **chiffre d'affaires, conseil d'administration, corps d'armée** ♦ *sigle f* = **chambre d'agriculture**.

ca *abr* (= *centiare*) $1 m^2$.

ça [sa] *pron* (*pour désigner*) this; (*: plus loin*) that; (*comme sujet indéfini*) it; ~ **m'étonne que** it surprises me that; ~ **va?** how are you?; how are things?; (*d'accord?*) OK?, all right?; ~ **alors!** (*désapprobation*) well!, really!; (*étonnement*) heavens!; **c'est** ~ that's right.

çà [sa] *adv*: ~ **et là** here and there.

cabale [kabal] *nf* (*THÉÂT, POL*) cabal, clique.

caban [kabɑ̃] *nm* reefer jacket, donkey jacket.

cabane [kaban] *nf* hut, cabin.

cabanon [kabanɔ̃] *nm* chalet; (*country*) cottage.

cabaret [kabaʀɛ] *nm* night club.

cabas [kaba] *nm* shopping bag.

cabestan [kabɛstɑ̃] *nm* capstan.

cabillaud [kabijo] *nm* cod *inv*.

cabine [kabin] *nf* (*de bateau*) cabin; (*de plage*) (beach) hut; (*de piscine etc*) cubicle; (*de camion, train*) cab; (*d'avion*) cockpit; ~ **(d'ascenseur)** lift cage; ~ **d'essayage** fitting room; ~ **de projection** projection room; ~ **spatiale** space capsule; ~ **(téléphonique)** call *ou* (tele)phone box, (tele)phone booth.

cabinet [kabinɛ] *nm* (*petite pièce*) closet; (*de médecin*) surgery (*BRIT*), office (*US*); (*de notaire etc*) office; (*: clientèle*) practice; (*POL*) cabinet; (*d'un ministre*) advisers *pl*; ~**s** *nmpl* (*w.-c.*) toilet *sg*, loo *sg* (*fam BRIT*); ~ **d'affaires** business consultants' (bureau), business partnership; ~ **de toilette** toilet; ~ **de travail** study.

câble [kɑbl(ə)] *nm* cable; **le** ~ (*TV*) cable television, cablevision (*US*).

câblé, e [kɑble] *adj* (*fam*) switched on; (*TECH*) linked to cable television.

câbler [kɑble] *vt* to cable; ~ **un quartier** (*TV*) to put cable television into an area.

câblogramme [kɑblɔgʀam] *nm* cablegram.

cabosser [kabɔse] *vt* to dent.

cabot [kabo] *nm* (*péj: chien*) mutt.

cabotage [kabɔtaʒ] *nm* coastal navigation.

caboteur [kabɔtœʀ] *nm* coaster.

cabotin, e [kabɔtɛ̃, -in] *nm/f* (*péj: personne maniérée*) poseur; (*: acteur*) ham ♦ *adj* dramatic, theatrical.

cabotinage [kabɔtinaʒ] *nm* playacting; third-rate acting, ham acting.

cabrer [kabʀe]: **se** ~ *vi* (*cheval*) to rear up; (*avion*) to nose up; (*fig*) to revolt, rebel; to jib.

cabri [kabʀi] *nm* kid.

cabriole [kabʀijɔl] *nf* caper; (*gymnastique etc*) somersault.

cabriolet [kabʀijɔlɛ] *nm* convertible.

CAC [kak] *sigle f* (= *Compagnie des agents de change*): **indice** ~ ≈ FT index (*BRIT*), ≈ Dow Jones average (*US*).

caca [kaka] *nm* (*langage enfantin*) pooh; (*couleur*): ~ **d'oie** greeny-yellow; **faire** ~ (*fam*) to do a pooh.

cacahuète [kakaɥɛt] *nf* peanut.

cacao [kakao] *nm* cocoa (powder); (*boisson*) cocoa.

cachalot [kaʃalo] *nm* sperm whale.

cache [kaʃ] *nm* mask, card (for masking) ♦ *nf* hiding place.

cache-cache [kaʃkaʃ] *nm*: **jouer à** ~ to play hide-and-seek.

cache-col [kaʃkɔl] *nm* scarf (*pl* scarves).

cachemire [kaʃmiʀ] *nm* cashmere ♦ *adj*: **dessin** ~ paisley pattern; **le C**~ Kashmir.

cache-nez [kaʃne] *nm inv* scarf (*pl* scarves), muffler.

cache-pot [kaʃpo] *nm inv* flower-pot holder.

cache-prise [kaʃpʀiz] *nm inv* socket cover.

cacher [kaʃe] *vt* to hide, conceal; ~ **qch à qn** to hide *ou* conceal sth from sb; **se** ~ to hide to be hidden *ou* concealed; **il ne s'en cache pas** he makes no secret of it.

cache-sexe [kaʃsɛks] *nm inv* G-string.

cachet [kaʃɛ] *nm* (*comprimé*) tablet; (*sceau: du roi*) seal; (*: de la poste*) postmark; (*rétribution*)

fee; (fig) style, character.
cacheter [kaʃte] vt to seal; **vin cacheté** vintage wine.
cachette [kaʃɛt] nf hiding place; **en** ~ on the sly, secretly.
cachot [kaʃo] nm dungeon.
cachotterie [kaʃɔtʀi] nf mystery; **faire des** ~**s** to be secretive.
cachottier, ière [kaʃɔtje, -jɛʀ] adj secretive.
cachou [kaʃu] nm: **pastille de** ~ cachou (sweet).
cacophonie [kakɔfɔni] nf cacophony, din.
cacophonique [kakɔfɔnik] adj cacophonous.
cactus [kaktys] nm cactus.
c-à-d abr (= c'est-à-dire) i.e.
cadastre [kadastʀ(ə)] nm land register.
cadavéreux, euse [kadaveʀø, -øz] adj (teint, visage) deathly pale.
cadavérique [kadaveʀik] adj deathly (pale), deadly pale.
cadavre [kadavʀ(ə)] nm corpse, (dead) body.
Caddie [kadi] nm ® (supermarket) trolley.
cadeau, x [kado] nm present, gift; **faire un** ~ **à qn** to give sb a present ou gift; **faire** ~ **de qch à qn** to make a present of sth to sb, give sb sth as a present.
cadenas [kadna] nm padlock.
cadenasser [kadnase] vt to padlock.
cadence [kadɑ̃s] nf (MUS) cadence; (: rythme) rhythm; (de travail etc) rate; ~**s** nfpl (en usine) production rate sg; **en** ~ rhythmically; in time.
cadencé, e [kadɑ̃se] adj rhythmic(al); **au pas** ~ (MIL) in quick time.
cadet, te [kadɛ, -ɛt] adj younger; (le plus jeune) youngest ♦ nm/f youngest child ou one, youngest boy ou son/girl ou daughter; **il est mon** ~ **de deux ans** he's 2 years younger than me, he's 2 years my junior; **les** ~**s** (SPORT) the minors (15 - 17 years); **le** ~ **de mes soucis** the least of my worries.
cadrage [kadʀaʒ] nm framing (of shot).
cadran [kadʀɑ̃] nm dial; ~ **solaire** sundial.
cadre [kadʀ(ə)] nm frame; (environnement) surroundings pl; (limites) scope ♦ nm/f (ADMIN) managerial employee, executive ♦ adj: **loi** ~ outline ou blueprint law; ~ **moyen/supérieur** (ADMIN) middle/senior management employee, junior/senior executive; **rayer qn des** ~**s** to discharge sb; to dismiss sb; **dans le** ~ **de** (fig) within the framework ou context of.
cadrer [kadʀe] vi: ~ **avec** to tally ou correspond with ♦ vt (CINÉ, PHOTO) to frame.
cadreur, euse [kadʀœʀ, -øz] nm/f (CINÉ) cameraman/woman.
caduc, uque [kadyk] adj obsolete; (BOT) deciduous.
CAF sigle f (= Caisse d'allocations familiales) family allowance office.
caf abr (= coût, assurance, fret) cif.
cafard [kafaʀ] nm cockroach; **avoir le** ~ to be

down in the dumps, be feeling low.
cafardeux, euse [kafaʀdø, -øz] adj (personne, ambiance) depressing, melancholy.
café [kafe] nm coffee; (bistro) café ♦ adj inv coffee cpd; ~ **crème** coffee with cream; ~ **au lait** white coffee; ~ **noir** black coffee; ~ **en grains** coffee beans; ~ **en poudre** instant coffee; ~ **tabac** tobacconist's or newsagent's also serving cᴏffee and spirits; ~ **liégeois** coffee ice cream with whipped cream.
café-concert, pl cafés-concerts [kafekɔ̃sɛʀ] nm (aussi: **caf'conc'**) café with a cabaret.
caféine [kafein] nf caffeine.
cafétéria [kafeteʀja] nf cafeteria.
café-théâtre, pl cafés-théâtres [kafeteatʀ(ə)] nm café used as a venue by (experimental) theatre groups.
cafetier, ière [kaftje, -jɛʀ] nm/f café-owner ♦ nf (pot) coffee-pot.
cafouillage [kafujaʒ] nm shambles sg.
cafouiller [kafuje] vi to get in a shambles; (machine etc) to work in fits and starts.
cage [kaʒ] nf cage; ~ **(des buts)** goal; **en** ~ in a cage, caged up ou in; ~ **d'ascenseur** lift shaft; ~ **d'escalier** (stair)well; ~ **thoracique** rib cage.
cageot [kaʒo] nm crate.
cagibi [kaʒibi] nm shed.
cagneux, euse [kaɲø, -øz] adj knock-kneed.
cagnotte [kaɲɔt] nf kitty.
cagoule [kagul] nf cowl; hood; (SKI etc) cagoule.
cahier [kaje] nm notebook; (TYPO) signature; (revue): ~**s** journal; ~ **de revendications/doléances** list of claims/grievances; ~ **de brouillons** roughbook, jotter; ~ **des charges** specification; ~ **d'exercices** exercise book.
cahin-caha [kaɛ̃kaa] adv: **aller** ~ to jog along; (fig) to be so-so.
cahot [kao] nm jolt, bump.
cahoter [kaɔte] vi to bump along, jog along.
cahoteux, euse [kaɔtø, -øz] adj bumpy.
cahute [kayt] nf shack, hut.
caïd [kaid] nm big chief, boss.
caillasse [kajas] nf (pierraille) loose stones pl.
caille [kaj] nf quail.
caillé, e [kaje] adj: **lait** ~ curdled milk, curds pl.
caillebotis [kajbɔti] nm duckboard.
cailler [kaje] vi (lait) to curdle; (sang) to clot; (fam) to be cold.
caillot [kajo] nm (blood) clot.
caillou, x [kaju] nm (little) stone.
caillouter [kajute] vt (chemin) to metal.
caillouteux, euse [kajutø, -øz] adj stony; pebbly.
cailloutis [kajuti] nm (petits graviers) gravel.
caïman [kaimɑ̃] nm cayman.
Caïmans [kaimɑ̃] nfpl: **les** ~ the Cayman Islands.
Caire [kɛʀ] nm: **le** ~ Cairo.
caisse [kɛs] nf box; (où l'on met la recette) cash-

box; (: *machine*) till; (*où l'on paye*) cash desk (*BRIT*), checkout counter; (: *au supermarché*) checkout; (*de banque*) cashier's desk; (*TECH*) case, casing; **faire sa** ~ (*COMM*) to count the takings; ~ **claire** (*MUS*) side *ou* snare drum; ~ **éclair** express checkout; ~ **enregistreuse** cash register; ~ **d'épargne (CE)** savings bank; ~ **noire** slush fund; ~ **de retraite** pension fund; ~ **de sortie** checkout; *voir* **grosse**.

caissier, ière [kɛsje, -jɛʀ] *nm/f* cashier.

caisson [kɛsɔ̃] *nm* box, case.

cajoler [kaʒɔle] *vt* to wheedle, coax; to surround with love and care, make a fuss of.

cajoleries [kaʒɔlʀi] *nfpl* coaxing *sg*, flattery *sg*.

cajou [kaʒu] *nm* cashew nut.

cake [kɛk] *nm* fruit cake.

CAL *sigle m* (= *Comité d'action lycéen*) *pupils' action group seeking to reform school system*.

cal [kal] *nm* callus.

cal. *abr* = **calorie**.

calamar [kalamaʀ] *nm* = **calmar**.

calaminé, e [kalamine] *adj* (*AUTO*) coked up.

calamité [kalamite] *nf* calamity, disaster.

calandre [kalɑ̃dʀ(ə)] *nf* radiator grill; (*machine*) calender, mangle.

calanque [kalɑ̃k] *nf* rocky inlet.

calcaire [kalkɛʀ] *nm* limestone ♦ *adj* (*eau*) hard; (*GÉO*) limestone *cpd*.

calciné, e [kalsine] *adj* burnt to ashes.

calcium [kalsjɔm] *nm* calcium.

calcul [kalkyl] *nm* calculation; **le** ~ (*SCOL*) arithmetic; ~ **différentiel/intégral** differential/integral calculus; ~ **mental** mental arithmetic; ~ **(biliaire)** (gall)stone; ~ **(rénal)** (kidney) stone; **d'après mes** ~**s** by my reckoning.

calculateur [kalkylatœʀ] *nm*, **calculatrice** [kalkylatʀis] *nf* calculator.

calculé, e [kalkyle] *adj*: **risque** ~ calculated risk.

calculer [kalkyle] *vt* to calculate, work out, reckon; (*combiner*) to calculate; ~ **qch de tête** to work sth out in one's head.

calculette [kalkylɛt] *nf* (pocket) calculator.

cale [kal] *nf* (*de bateau*) hold; (*en bois*) wedge, chock; ~ **sèche** *ou* **de radoub** dry dock.

calé, e [kale] *adj* (*fam*) clever, bright.

calebasse [kalbas] *nf* calabash, gourd.

calèche [kalɛʃ] *nf* horse-drawn carriage.

caleçon [kalsɔ̃] *nm* pair of underpants, trunks *pl*; ~ **de bain** bathing trunks *pl*.

calembour [kalɑ̃buʀ] *nm* pun.

calendes [kalɑ̃d] *nfpl*: **renvoyer aux** ~ **grecques** to postpone indefinitely.

calendrier [kalɑ̃dʀije] *nm* calendar; (*fig*) timetable.

cale-pied [kalpje] *nm inv* toe clip.

calepin [kalpɛ̃] *nm* notebook.

caler [kale] *vt* to wedge, chock up; ~ (**son moteur/véhicule**) to stall (one's engine/vehicle); **se** ~ **dans un fauteuil** to make o.s.

comfortable in an armchair.

calfater [kalfate] *vt* to caulk.

calfeutrage [kalføtʀaʒ] *nm* draughtproofing (*BRIT*), draftproofing (*US*).

calfeutrer [kalføtʀe] *vt* to (make) draughtproof (*BRIT*) *ou* draftproof (*US*); **se** ~ to make o.s. snug and comfortable.

calibre [kalibʀ(ə)] *nm* (*d'un fruit*) grade; (*d'une arme*) bore, calibre (*BRIT*), caliber (*US*); (*fig*) calibre, caliber.

calibrer [kalibʀe] *vt* to grade.

calice [kalis] *nm* (*REL*) chalice; (*BOT*) calyx.

calicot [kaliko] *nm* (*tissu*) calico.

calife [kalif] *nm* caliph.

Californie [kalifɔʀni] *nf*: **la** ~ California.

californien, ne [kalifɔʀnjɛ̃, -ɛn] *adj* Californian.

califourchon [kalifuʀʃɔ̃]: **à** ~ *adv* astride; **à** ~ **sur** astride, straddling.

câlin, e [kɑlɛ̃, -in] *adj* cuddly, cuddlesome; tender.

câliner [kɑline] *vt* to fondle, cuddle.

câlineries [kɑlinʀi] *nfpl* cuddles.

calisson [kalisɔ̃] *nm* diamond-shaped sweet or candy made with ground almonds.

calleux, euse [kalø, -øz] *adj* horny, callous.

calligraphie [kaligʀafi] *nf* calligraphy.

callosité [kalozite] *nf* callus.

calmant [kalmɑ̃] *nm* tranquillizer, sedative; (*contre la douleur*) painkiller.

calmar [kalmaʀ] *nm* squid.

calme [kalm(ə)] *adj* calm, quiet ♦ *nm* calm(ness), quietness; **sans perdre son** ~ without losing one's cool *ou* calmness; ~ **plat** (*NAVIG*) dead calm.

calmement [kalməmɑ̃] *adv* calmly, quietly.

calmer [kalme] *vt* to calm (down); (*douleur, inquiétude*) to ease, soothe; **se** ~ to calm down.

calomniateur, trice [kalɔmnjatœʀ, -tʀis] *nm/f* slanderer; libeller.

calomnie [kalɔmni] *nf* slander; (*écrite*) libel.

calomnier [kalɔmnje] *vt* to slander; to libel.

calomnieux, euse [kalɔmnjø, -øz] *adj* slanderous; libellous.

calorie [kalɔʀi] *nf* calorie.

calorifère [kalɔʀifɛʀ] *nm* stove.

calorifique [kalɔʀifik] *adj* calorific.

calorifuge [kalɔʀifyʒ] *adj* (heat-)insulating, heat-retaining.

calot [kalo] *nm* forage cap.

calotte [kalɔt] *nf* (*coiffure*) skullcap; (*gifle*) slap; **la** ~ (*péj: clergé*) the cloth, the clergy; ~ **glaciaire** icecap.

calque [kalk(ə)] *nm* (*aussi*: **papier** ~) tracing paper; (*dessin*) tracing; (*fig*) carbon copy.

calquer [kalke] *vt* to trace; (*fig*) to copy exactly.

calvados [kalvados] *nm* Calvados (*apple brandy*).

calvaire [kalvɛʀ] *nm* (*croix*) wayside cross, calvary; (*souffrances*) suffering, martyrdom.

calvitie [kalvisi] *nf* baldness.

camaïeu [kamajø] *nm*: **(motif en)** ~ monochrome motif.

camarade [kamaʀad] *nmf* friend, pal; (*POL*) comrade.

camaraderie [kamaʀadʀi] *nf* friendship.

camarguais, e [kamaʀgɛ, -ɛz] *adj* of *ou* from the Camargue.

Camargue [kamaʀg] *nf*: **la** ~ the Camargue.

cambiste [kɑ̃bist(ə)] *nm* (*COMM*) foreign exchange dealer, exchange agent.

Cambodge [kɑ̃bɔdʒ] *nm*: **le** ~ Cambodia.

cambodgien, ne [kɑ̃bɔdʒjɛ̃, -ɛn] *adj* Cambodian ♦ *nmf*: **C~, ne** Cambodian.

cambouis [kɑ̃bwi] *nm* dirty oil *ou* grease.

cambré, e [kɑ̃bʀe] *adj*: **avoir les reins** ~**s** to have an arched back; **avoir le pied très** ~ to have very high arches *ou* insteps.

cambrer [kɑ̃bʀe] *vt* to arch; **se** ~ to arch one's back; ~ **la taille** *ou* **les reins** to arch one's back.

cambriolage [kɑ̃bʀijɔlaʒ] *nm* burglary.

cambrioler [kɑ̃bʀijɔle] *vt* to burgle (*BRIT*), burglarize (*US*).

cambrioleur, euse [kɑ̃bʀijɔlœʀ, -øz] *nmf* burglar.

cambrure [kɑ̃bʀyʀ] *nf* (*du pied*) arch; (*de la route*) camber; ~ **des reins** small of the back.

cambuse [kɑ̃byz] *nf* storeroom.

came [kam] *nf*: **arbre à** ~**s** camshaft; **arbre à** ~**s en tête** overhead camshaft.

camée [kame] *nm* cameo.

caméléon [kameleɔ̃] *nm* chameleon.

camélia [kamelja] *nm* camellia.

camelot [kamlo] *nm* street pedlar.

camelote [kamlɔt] *nf* rubbish, trash, junk.

camembert [kamɑ̃bɛʀ] *nm* Camembert (*cheese*).

caméra [kameʀa] *nf* (*CINÉ*, *TV*) camera; (*d'amateur*) cine-camera.

caméraman [kameʀaman] *nm* cameraman/woman.

Cameroun [kamʀun] *nm*: **le** ~ Cameroon.

camerounais, e [kamʀunɛ, -ɛz] *adj* Cameroonian.

caméscope [kameskɔp] ® *nm* camcorder ®.

camion [kamjɔ̃] *nm* lorry (*BRIT*), truck; (*plus petit, fermé*) van; (*charge*): ~ **de sable/ cailloux** lorry-load (*BRIT*) *ou* truck-load of sand/stones; ~ **de dépannage** breakdown (*BRIT*) *ou* tow (*US*) truck.

camion-citerne, *pl* **camions-citernes** [kamjɔ̃sitɛʀn(ə)] *nm* tanker.

camionnage [kamjɔnaʒ] *nm* haulage (*BRIT*), trucking (*US*); **frais/entreprise de** ~ haulage costs/business.

camionnette [kamjɔnɛt] *nf* (small) van.

camionneur [kamjɔnœʀ] *nm* (*entrepreneur*) haulage contractor (*BRIT*), trucker (*US*); (*chauffeur*) lorry (*BRIT*) *ou* truck driver; van driver.

camisole [kamizɔl] *nf*: ~ **(de force)** straitjacket.

camomille [kamɔmij] *nf* camomile; (*boisson*) camomile tea.

camouflage [kamuflaʒ] *nm* camouflage.

camoufler [kamufle] *vt* to camouflage; (*fig*) to conceal, cover up.

camouflet [kamuflɛ] *nm* (*fam*) snub.

camp [kɑ̃] *nm* camp; (*fig*) side; ~ **de nudistes/ vacances** nudist/holiday camp; ~ **de concentration** concentration camp.

campagnard, e [kɑ̃paɲaʀ, -aʀd(ə)] *adj* country *cpd* ♦ *nmf* countryman/woman.

campagne [kɑ̃paɲ] *nf* country, countryside; (*MIL*, *POL*, *COMM*) campaign; **en** ~ (*MIL*) in the field; **à la** ~ in/to the country; **faire** ~ **pour** to campaign for; ~ **électorale** election campaign; ~ **de publicité** advertising campaign.

campanile [kɑ̃panil] *nm* (*tour*) bell tower.

campé, e [kɑ̃pe] *adj*: **bien** ~ (*personnage, tableau*) well-drawn.

campement [kɑ̃pmɑ̃] *nm* camp, encampment.

camper [kɑ̃pe] *vi* to camp ♦ *vt* (*chapeau etc*) to pull *ou* put on firmly; (*dessin*) to sketch; **se** ~ **devant** to plant o.s. in front of.

campeur, euse [kɑ̃pœʀ, -øz] *nmf* camper.

camphre [kɑ̃fʀ(ə)] *nm* camphor.

camphré, e [kɑ̃fʀe] *adj* camphorated.

camping [kɑ̃piŋ] *nm* camping; **(terrain de)** ~ campsite, camping site; **faire du** ~ to go camping; **faire du** ~ **sauvage** to camp rough.

camping-car [kɑ̃piŋkaʀ] *nm* caravanette, camper (*US*).

campus [kɑ̃pys] *nm* campus.

camus, e [kamy, -yz] *adj*: **nez** ~ pug nose.

Canada [kanada] *nm*: **le** ~ Canada.

canadair [kanadɛʀ] *nm* ® fire-fighting plane.

canadien, ne [kanadjɛ̃, -ɛn] *adj* Canadian ♦ *nmf*: **C~, ne** Canadian ♦ *nf* (*veste*) fur-lined jacket.

canaille [kanaj] *nf* (*péj*) scoundrel; (*populace*) riff-raff ♦ *adj* raffish, rakish.

canal, aux [kanal, -o] *nm* canal; (*naturel*) channel; (*ADMIN*): **par le** ~ **de** through (the medium of), via; ~ **de distribution/télévision** distribution/television channel; ~ **de Panama/Suez** Panama/Suez Canal.

canalisation [kanalizasjɔ̃] *nf* (*tuyau*) pipe.

canaliser [kanalize] *vt* to canalize; (*fig*) to channel.

canapé [kanape] *nm* settee, sofa; (*CULIN*) canapé, open sandwich.

canapé-lit, *pl* **canapés-lits** [kanapeli] *nm* sofa bed.

canaque [kanak] *adj* of *ou* from New Caledonia ♦ *nmf*: **C~** native of New Caledonia.

canard [kanaʀ] *nm* duck.

canari [kanaʀi] *nm* canary.

Canaries [kanaʀi] *nfpl*: **les (îles)** ~ the Canary Islands, the Canaries.

cancaner [kɑ̃kane] *vi* to gossip (maliciously); (*canard*) to quack.

cancanier, ière [kɑ̃kanje, -jɛʀ] *adj* gossiping.

cancans [kɑ̃kɑ̃] *nmpl* (malicious) gossip *sg*.
cancer [kɑ̃sɛʀ] *nm* cancer; (*signe*): **le C~** Cancer, the Crab; **être du C~** to be Cancer; **il a un ~** he has cancer.
cancéreux, euse [kɑ̃seʀø, -øz] *adj* cancerous; (*personne*) suffering from cancer.
cancérigène [kɑ̃seʀiʒɛn] *adj* carcinogenic.
cancérologue [kɑ̃seʀɔlɔg] *nm/f* cancer specialist.
cancre [kɑ̃kʀ(ə)] *nm* dunce.
cancrelat [kɑ̃kʀəla] *nm* cockroach.
candélabre [kɑ̃delabʀ(ə)] *nm* candelabrum; (*lampadaire*) street lamp, lamppost.
candeur [kɑ̃dœʀ] *nf* ingenuousness, guilelessness.
candi [kɑ̃di] *adj inv*: **sucre ~** (sugar-)candy.
candidat, e [kɑ̃dida, -at] *nm/f* candidate; (*à un poste*) applicant, candidate.
candidature [kɑ̃didatyʀ] *nf* candidacy; application; **poser sa ~** to submit an application, apply.
candide [kɑ̃did] *adj* ingenuous, guileless, naïve.
cane [kan] *nf* (female) duck.
caneton [kantɔ̃] *nm* duckling.
canette [kanɛt] *nf* (*de bière*) (flip-top) bottle; (*de machine à coudre*) spool.
canevas [kanva] *nm* (*COUTURE*) canvas (for tapestry work); (*fig*) framework, structure.
caniche [kaniʃ] *nm* poodle.
caniculaire [kanikylɛʀ] *adj* (*chaleur, jour*) scorching.
canicule [kanikyl] *nf* scorching heat; midsummer heat, dog days *pl*.
canif [kanif] *nm* penknife, pocket knife.
canin, e [kanɛ̃, -in] *adj* canine ♦ *nf* canine (tooth), eye tooth; **exposition ~e** dog show.
caniveau, x [kanivo] *nm* gutter.
cannabis [kanabis] *nm* cannabis.
canne [kan] *nf* (walking) stick; **~ à pêche** fishing rod; **~ à sucre** sugar cane; **les ~s blanches** (*les aveugles*) the blind.
canné, e [kane] *adj* (*chaise*) cane *cpd*.
cannelé, e [kanle] *adj* fluted.
cannelle [kanɛl] *nf* cinnamon.
cannelure [kanlyʀ] *nf* fluting *no pl*.
canner [kane] *vt* (*chaise*) to make *ou* repair with cane.
cannibale [kanibal] *nm/f* cannibal.
cannibalisme [kanibalism(ə)] *nm* cannibalism.
canoë [kanɔe] *nm* canoe; (*sport*) canoeing; **~ (kayak)** kayak.
canon [kanɔ̃] *nm* (*arme*) gun; (*HIST*) cannon; (*d'une arme: tube*) barrel; (*fig*) model; (*MUS*) canon ♦ *adj*: **droit ~** canon law; **~ rayé** rifled barrel.
cañon [kaɲɔ̃] *nm* canyon.
canonique [kanɔnik] *adj*: **âge ~** respectable age.
canoniser [kanɔnize] *vt* to canonize.
canonnade [kanɔnad] *nf* cannonade.
canonnier [kanɔnje] *nm* gunner.

canonnière [kanɔnjɛʀ] *nf* gunboat.
canot [kano] *nm* boat, ding(h)y; **~ pneumatique** rubber *ou* inflatable ding(h)y; **~ de sauvetage** lifeboat.
canotage [kanɔtaʒ] *nm* rowing.
canoter [kanɔte] *vi* to go rowing.
canoteur, euse [kanɔtœʀ, -øz] *nm/f* rower.
canotier [kanɔtje] *nm* boater.
Cantal [kɑ̃tal] *nm*: **le ~** Cantal.
cantate [kɑ̃tat] *nf* cantata.
cantatrice [kɑ̃tatʀis] *nf* (opera) singer.
cantilène [kɑ̃tilɛn] *nf* (*MUS*) cantilena.
cantine [kɑ̃tin] *nf* canteen; (*réfectoire d'école*) dining hall.
cantique [kɑ̃tik] *nm* hymn.
canton [kɑ̃tɔ̃] *nm* district (*consisting of several communes*); (*en Suisse*) canton.

> In France the **canton** is the administrative division represented by a councillor in the **Conseil général**. It comprises a number of **communes** and is, in turn, a subdivision of the **arrondissement**. In Switzerland the cantons are the 23 sovereign political divisions comprising the Swiss confederation.

cantonade [kɑ̃tɔnad] *nf*: **à la ~** *adv* to everyone in general; (*crier*) from the rooftops.
cantonais, e [kɑ̃tɔnɛ, -ɛz] *adj* Cantonese ♦ *nm* (*LING*) Cantonese.
cantonal, e, aux [kɑ̃tɔnal, -o] *adj* cantonal, ≈ district.
cantonnement [kɑ̃tɔnmɑ̃] *nm* (*lieu*) billet; (*action*) billeting.
cantonner [kɑ̃tɔne] *vt* (*MIL*) to billet (*BRIT*), quarter; to station; **se ~ dans** to confine o.s. to.
cantonnier [kɑ̃tɔnje] *nm* roadmender.
canular [kanylaʀ] *nm* hoax.
CAO *sigle f* (= conception assistée par ordinateur) CAD.
caoutchouc [kautʃu] *nm* rubber; **~ mousse** foam rubber; **en ~** rubber *cpd*.
caoutchouté, e [kautʃute] *adj* rubberized.
caoutchouteux, euse [kautʃutø, -øz] *adj* rubbery.
CAP *sigle m* (= Certificat d'aptitude professionnelle) vocational training certificate taken at secondary school.
cap [kap] *nm* (*GÉO*) cape; headland; (*fig*) hurdle; watershed; (*NAVIG*): **changer de ~** to change course; **mettre le ~ sur** to head *ou* steer for; **doubler** *ou* **passer le ~** (*fig*) to get over the worst; **Le C~** Cape Town; **le ~ de Bonne Espérance** the Cape of Good Hope; **le ~ Horn** Cape Horn; **les îles du C~ Vert** (*aussi*: **le C~-Vert**) the Cape Verde Islands.
capable [kapabl(ə)] *adj* able, capable; **~ de qch/faire** capable of sth/doing; **il est ~ d'oublier** he could easily forget; **spectacle/livre ~ d'intéresser** show/book liable *ou* likely to be of interest.

capacité [kapasite] nf (*compétence*) ability; (*JUR, INFORM, d'un récipient*) capacity; ~ **(en droit)** basic legal qualification.

caparaçonner [kaparasɔne] vt (*fig*) to clad.

cape [kap] nf cape, cloak; **rire sous** ~ to laugh up one's sleeve.

capeline [kaplin] nf wide-brimmed hat.

CAPES [kapɛs] sigle m (= *Certificat d'aptitude au professorat de l'enseignement du second degré*) secondary teaching diploma.

> The **CAPES** is a competitive examination for the recruitment of French secondary school teachers. It is taken after the **licence**. Successful candidates become fully-qualified teachers (*professeurs certifiés*); see also **agrégation**.

capésien, ne [kapesjɛ̃, -ɛn] nm/f person who holds the CAPES.

CAPET [kapɛt] sigle m (= *Certificat d'aptitude au professorat de l'enseignement technique*) technical teaching diploma.

capharnaüm [kafaʀnaɔm] nm shambles sg.

capillaire [kapilɛʀ] adj (*soins, lotion*) hair cpd; (*vaisseau etc*) capillary; **artiste** ~ hair artist ou designer.

capillarité [kapilaʀite] nf capillary action.

capilliculteur [kapilikyltœʀ] nm hair-care specialist.

capilotade [kapilɔtad]: **en** ~ adv crushed to a pulp; smashed to pieces.

capitaine [kapitɛn] nm captain; ~ **des pompiers** fire chief (*BRIT*), fire marshal (*US*); ~ **au long cours** master mariner.

capitainerie [kapitɛnʀi] nf (*du port*) harbour (*BRIT*) ou harbor (*US*) master's (office).

capital, e, aux [kapital, -o] adj major; of paramount importance; fundamental; (*JUR*) capital ♦ nm capital; (*fig*) stock; asset ♦ nf (*ville*) capital; (*lettre*) capital (letter) ♦ nmpl (*fonds*) capital sg, money sg; **les sept péchés capitaux** the seven deadly sins; **peine** ~**e** capital punishment; ~ **(social)** authorized capital; ~ **d'exploitation** working capital.

capitaliser [kapitalize] vt to amass, build up; (*COMM*) to capitalize ♦ vi to save.

capitalisme [kapitalism(ə)] nm capitalism.

capitaliste [kapitalist(ə)] adj, nm/f capitalist.

capiteux, euse [kapitø, -øz] adj (*vin, parfum*) heady; (*sensuel*) sensuous, alluring.

capitonnage [kapitɔnaʒ] nm padding.

capitonné, e [kapitɔne] adj padded.

capitonner [kapitɔne] vt to pad.

capitulation [kapitylɑsjɔ̃] nf capitulation.

capituler [kapityle] vi to capitulate.

caporal, aux [kapɔʀal, -o] nm lance corporal.

caporal-chef, pl **caporaux-chefs** [kapɔʀalʃef, kapɔʀo-] nm corporal.

capot [kapo] nm (*AUTO*) bonnet (*BRIT*), hood (*US*) ♦ adj inv (*CARTES*): **être** ~ to lose without taking a single trick.

capote [kapɔt] nf (*de voiture*) hood (*BRIT*), top (*US*); (*de soldat*) greatcoat; ~ **(anglaise)** (*fam*) rubber, condom.

capoter [kapɔte] vi to overturn; (*négociations*) to founder.

câpre [kɑpʀ(ə)] nf caper.

caprice [kapʀis] nm whim, caprice; passing fancy; ~**s** nmpl (*de la mode etc*) vagaries; **faire un** ~ to throw a tantrum; **faire des** ~**s** to be temperamental.

capricieux, euse [kapʀisjø, -øz] adj capricious; whimsical; temperamental.

Capricorne [kapʀikɔʀn] nm: **le** ~ Capricorn, the Goat; **être du** ~ to be Capricorn.

capsule [kapsyl] nf (*de bouteille*) cap; (*amorce*) primer; cap; (*BOT etc, spatiale*) capsule.

captage [kaptaʒ] nm (*d'une émission de radio*) picking-up; (*d'énergie, d'eau*) harnessing.

capter [kapte] vt (*ondes radio*) to pick up; (*eau*) to harness; (*fig*) to win, capture.

capteur [kaptœʀ] nm: ~ **solaire** solar collector.

captieux, euse [kapsjø, -øz] adj specious.

captif, ive [kaptif, -iv] adj, nm/f captive.

captivant, e [kaptivɑ̃, -ɑ̃t] adj captivating.

captiver [kaptive] vt to captivate.

captivité [kaptivite] nf captivity; **en** ~ in captivity.

capture [kaptyʀ] nf capture, catching no pl; catch.

capturer [kaptyʀe] vt to capture, catch.

capuche [kapyʃ] nf hood.

capuchon [kapyʃɔ̃] nm hood; (*de stylo*) cap, top.

capucin [kapysɛ̃] nm Capuchin monk.

capucine [kapysin] nf (*BOT*) nasturtium.

Cap-Vert [kabvɛʀ] nm: **le** ~ Cape Verde.

caquelon [kaklɔ̃] nm (*ustensile de cuisson*) fondue pot.

caquet [kakɛ] nm: **rabattre le** ~ **à qn** to bring sb down a peg or two.

caqueter [kakte] vi (*poule*) to cackle; (*fig*) to prattle.

car [kaʀ] nm coach (*BRIT*), bus ♦ conj because, for; ~ **de police** police van; ~ **de reportage** broadcasting ou radio van.

carabine [kaʀabin] nf carbine, rifle; ~ **à air comprimé** airgun.

carabiné, e [kaʀabine] adj violent; (*cocktail, amende*) stiff.

Caracas [kaʀakas] n Caracas.

caracoler [kaʀakɔle] vi to caracole, prance.

caractère [kaʀaktɛʀ] nm (*gén*) character; **en** ~**s gras** in bold type; **en petits** ~**s** in small print; **en** ~**s d'imprimerie** in block capitals; **avoir du** ~ to have character; **avoir bon/mauvais** ~ to be good-/ill-natured ou tempered; ~ **de remplacement** wild card (*INFORM*); ~**s/seconde (cps)** characters per second (cps).

caractériel, le [kaʀakteʀjɛl] adj (*enfant*) (emotionally) disturbed ♦ nm/f problem child; **troubles** ~**s** emotional problems.

caractérisé, e [kaʀakteʀize] *adj*: **c'est une grippe/de l'insubordination** ~**e** it is a clear(-cut) case of flu/insubordination.

caractériser [kaʀakteʀize] *vt* to characterize; **se** ~ **par** to be characterized *ou* distinguished by.

caractéristique [kaʀakteʀistik] *adj*, *nf* characteristic.

carafe [kaʀaf] *nf* decanter; carafe.

carafon [kaʀafɔ̃] *nm* small carafe.

caraïbe [kaʀaib] *adj* Caribbean; **les C**~**s** *nfpl* the Caribbean (Islands); **la mer des C**~**s** the Caribbean Sea.

carambolage [kaʀɑ̃bɔlaʒ] *nm* multiple crash, pileup.

caramel [kaʀamɛl] *nm* (*bonbon*) caramel, toffee; (*substance*) caramel.

caraméliser [kaʀamelize] *vt* to caramelize.

carapace [kaʀapas] *nf* shell.

carapater [kaʀapate]: **se** ~ *vi* to take to one's heels, scram.

carat [kaʀa] *nm* carat; **or à 18** ~**s** 18-carat gold.

caravane [kaʀavan] *nf* caravan.

caravanier [kaʀavanje] *nm* caravanner.

caravaning [kaʀavaniŋ] *nm* caravanning; (*emplacement*) caravan site.

caravelle [kaʀavɛl] *nf* caravel.

carbonate [kaʀbɔnat] *nm* (*CHIMIE*): ~ **de soude** sodium carbonate.

carbone [kaʀbɔn] *nm* carbon; (*feuille*) carbon, sheet of carbon paper; (*double*) carbon (copy).

carbonique [kaʀbɔnik] *adj*: **gaz** ~ carbon dioxide; **neige** ~ dry ice.

carbonisé, e [kaʀbɔnize] *adj* charred; **mourir** ~ to be burned to death.

carboniser [kaʀbɔnize] *vt* to carbonize; (*brûler complètement*) to burn down, reduce to ashes.

carburant [kaʀbyʀɑ̃] *nm* (motor) fuel.

carburateur [kaʀbyʀatœʀ] *nm* carburettor.

carburation [kaʀbyʀasjɔ̃] *nf* carburation.

carburer [kaʀbyʀe] *vi* (*moteur*): **bien/mal** ~ to be well/badly tuned.

carcan [kaʀkɑ̃] *nm* (*fig*) yoke, shackles *pl*.

carcasse [kaʀkas] *nf* carcass; (*de véhicule etc*) shell.

carcéral, e, aux [kaʀseʀal, -o] *adj* prison *cpd*.

carcinogène [kaʀsinɔʒɛn] *adj* carcinogenic.

cardan [kaʀdɑ̃] *nm* universal joint.

carder [kaʀde] *vt* to card.

cardiaque [kaʀdjak] *adj* cardiac, heart *cpd* ♦ *nm/f* heart patient; **être** ~ to have a heart condition.

cardigan [kaʀdigɑ̃] *nm* cardigan.

cardinal, e, aux [kaʀdinal, -o] *adj* cardinal ♦ *nm* (*REL*) cardinal.

cardiologie [kaʀdjɔlɔʒi] *nf* cardiology.

cardiologue [kaʀdjɔlɔg] *nm/f* cardiologist, heart specialist.

cardio-vasculaire [kaʀdjɔvaskylɛʀ] *adj* cardio-

vascular.

cardon [kaʀdɔ̃] *nm* cardoon.

carême [kaʀɛm] *nm*: **le C**~ Lent.

carence [kaʀɑ̃s] *nf* incompetence, inadequacy; (*manque*) deficiency; ~ **vitaminique** vitamin deficiency.

carène [kaʀɛn] *nf* hull.

caréner [kaʀene] *vt* (*NAVIG*) to careen; (*carrosserie*) to streamline.

caressant, e [kaʀɛsɑ̃, -ɑ̃t] *adj* affectionate; caressing, tender.

caresse [kaʀɛs] *nf* caress.

caresser [kaʀese] *vt* to caress, stroke, fondle; (*fig: projet, espoir*) to toy with.

cargaison [kaʀgɛzɔ̃] *nf* cargo, freight.

cargo [kaʀgo] *nm* cargo boat, freighter; ~ **mixte** cargo and passenger ship.

cari [kaʀi] *nm* = **curry**.

caricatural, e, aux [kaʀikatyʀal, -o] *adj* caricatural, caricature-like.

caricature [kaʀikatyʀ] *nf* caricature; (*politique etc*) (satirical) cartoon.

caricaturer [kaʀikatyʀe] *vt* (*personne*) to caricature; (*politique etc*) to satirize.

caricaturiste [kaʀikatyʀist(ə)] *nm/f* caricaturist; (satirical) cartoonist.

carie [kaʀi] *nf*: **la** ~ (**dentaire**) tooth decay; **une** ~ a bad tooth.

carié, e [kaʀje] *adj*: **dent** ~**e** bad *ou* decayed tooth.

carillon [kaʀijɔ̃] *nm* (*d'église*) bells *pl*; (*de pendule*) chimes *pl*; (*de porte*): ~ (**électrique**) (electric) door chime *ou* bell.

carillonner [kaʀijɔne] *vi* to ring, chime, peal.

caritatif, ive [kaʀitatif, -iv] *adj* charitable.

carlingue [kaʀlɛ̃g] *nf* cabin.

carmélite [kaʀmelit] *nf* Carmelite nun.

carmin [kaʀmɛ̃] *adj inv* crimson.

carnage [kaʀnaʒ] *nm* carnage, slaughter.

carnassier, ière [kaʀnasje, -jɛʀ] *adj* carnivorous ♦ *nm* carnivore.

carnation [kaʀnasjɔ̃] *nf* complexion; ~**s** *nfpl* (*PEINTURE*) flesh tones.

carnaval [kaʀnaval] *nm* carnival.

carné, e [kaʀne] *adj* meat *cpd*, meat-based.

carnet [kaʀnɛ] *nm* (*calepin*) notebook; (*de tickets, timbres etc*) book; (*d'école*) school report; (*journal intime*) diary; ~ **d'adresses** address book; ~ **de chèques** cheque book (*BRIT*), checkbook (*US*); ~ **de commandes** order book; ~ **de notes** (*SCOL*) (school) report; ~ **à souches** counterfoil book.

carnier [kaʀnje] *nm* gamebag.

carnivore [kaʀnivɔʀ] *adj* carnivorous ♦ *nm* carnivore.

Carolines [kaʀɔlin] *nfpl*: **les** ~ the Caroline Islands.

carotide [kaʀɔtid] *nf* carotid (artery).

carotte [kaʀɔt] *nf* (*aussi fig*) carrot.

Carpates [kaʀpat] *nfpl*: **les** ~ the Carpathians, the Carpathian Mountains.

carpe [kaʀp(ə)] *nf* carp.

carpette [kaʀpɛt] *nf* rug.
carquois [kaʀkwa] *nm* quiver.
carre [kaʀ] *nf* (*de ski*) edge.
carré, e [kaʀe] *adj* square; (*fig: franc*) straightforward ♦ *nm* (*de terrain, jardin*) patch, plot; (*NAVIG: salle*) wardroom; (*MATH*) square; (*CARTES*): ~ **d'as/de rois** four aces/kings; **élever un nombre au** ~ to square a number; **mètre/kilomètre** ~ square metre/kilometre; ~ **de soie** silk headsquare *ou* headscarf; ~ **d'agneau** loin of lamb.
carreau, x [kaʀo] *nm* (*en faïence etc*) (floor) tile; (wall) tile; (*de fenêtre*) (window) pane; (*motif*) check, square; (*CARTES: couleur*) diamonds *pl*; (*: carte*) diamond; **tissu à** ~**x** checked fabric; **papier à** ~**x** squared paper.
carrefour [kaʀfuʀ] *nm* crossroads *sg*.
carrelage [kaʀlaʒ] *nm* tiling; (tiled) floor.
carreler [kaʀle] *vt* to tile.
carrelet [kaʀlɛ] *nm* (*poisson*) plaice.
carreleur [kaʀlœʀ] *nm* (floor) tiler.
carrément [kaʀemã] *adv* (*franchement*) straight out, bluntly; (*sans détours, sans hésiter*) straight; (*nettement*) definitely; **il l'a** ~ **mis à la porte** he threw him straight out.
carrer [kaʀe]: **se** ~ *vi*: **se** ~ **dans un fauteuil** to settle o.s. comfortably *ou* ensconce o.s. in an armchair.
carrier [kaʀje] *nm*: **(ouvrier)** ~ quarryman, quarrier.
carrière [kaʀjɛʀ] *nf* (*de roches*) quarry; (*métier*) career; **militaire de** ~ professional soldier; **faire** ~ **dans** to make one's career in.
carriériste [kaʀjeʀist(ə)] *nm/f* careerist.
carriole [kaʀjɔl] *nf* (*péj*) old cart.
carrossable [kaʀosabl(ə)] *adj* suitable for (motor) vehicles.
carrosse [kaʀos] *nm* (horse-drawn) coach.
carrosserie [kaʀosʀi] *nf* body, bodywork *no pl* (*BRIT*); (*activité, commerce*) coachwork (*BRIT*), (car) body manufacturing; **atelier de** ~ (*pour réparations*) body shop, panel beaters' (yard) (*BRIT*).
carrossier [kaʀosje] *nm* coachbuilder (*BRIT*), (car) body repairer; (*dessinateur*) car designer.
carrousel [kaʀuzɛl] *nm* (*ÉQUITATION*) carousel; (*fig*) merry-go-round.
carrure [kaʀyʀ] *nf* build; (*fig*) stature.
cartable [kaʀtabl(ə)] *nm* (*d'écolier*) satchel, (school)bag.
carte [kaʀt(ə)] *nf* (*de géographie*) map; (*marine, du ciel*) chart; (*de fichier, d'abonnement etc, à jouer*) card; (*au restaurant*) menu; (*aussi:* ~ **postale**) (post)card; (*aussi:* ~ **de visite**) (visiting) card; **avoir/donner** ~ **blanche** to have/give carte blanche *ou* a free hand; **tirer les** ~**s à qn** to read sb's cards; **jouer aux** ~**s** to play cards; **jouer** ~**s sur table** (*fig*) to put one's cards on the table; **à la** ~ (*au restaurant*) à la carte; ~ **bancaire** cash card; ~ **à circuit imprimé** printed circuit; ~ **à puce**

smartcard; ~ **de crédit** credit card; ~ **d'état-major** ≈ Ordnance (*BRIT*) *ou* Geological (*US*) Survey map; **la** ~ **grise** (*AUTO*) ≈ the (car) registration document; ~ **d'identité** identity card; ~ **jeune** young person's railcard; ~ **perforée** punch(ed) card; ~ **de séjour** residence permit; ~ **routière** road map; **la** ~ **verte** (*AUTO*) the green card; **la** ~ **des vins** the wine list.
cartel [kaʀtɛl] *nm* cartel.
carte-lettre, *pl* **cartes-lettres** [kaʀtəlɛtʀ(ə)] *nf* letter-card.
carte-mère, *pl* **cartes-mères** [kaʀtəmɛʀ] *nf* (*INFORM*) mother board.
carter [kaʀtɛʀ] *nm* (*AUTO: d'huile*) sump (*BRIT*), oil pan (*US*); (*: de la boîte de vitesses*) casing; (*de bicyclette*) chain guard.
carte-réponse, *pl* **cartes-réponses** [kaʀt(ə)ʀepõs] *nf* reply card.
cartésien, ne [kaʀtezjɛ̃, -ɛn] *adj* Cartesian.
Carthage [kaʀtaʒ] *n* Carthage.
carthaginois, e [kaʀtaʒinwa, -waz] *adj* Carthaginian.
cartilage [kaʀtilaʒ] *nm* (*ANAT*) cartilage.
cartilagineux, euse [kaʀtilaʒinø, -øz] *adj* (*viande*) gristly.
cartographe [kaʀtɔgʀaf] *nm/f* cartographer.
cartographie [kaʀtɔgʀafi] *nf* cartography, map-making.
cartomancie [kaʀtɔmãsi] *nf* fortune-telling, card-reading.
cartomancien, ne [kaʀtɔmãsjɛ̃, -ɛn] *nm/f* fortune-teller (*with cards*).
carton [kaʀtõ] *nm* (*matériau*) cardboard; (*boîte*) (cardboard) box; (*d'invitation*) invitation card; (*ART*) sketch; cartoon; **en** ~ cardboard *cpd*; **faire un** ~ (*au tir*) to have a go at the rifle range; to score a hit; ~ (**à dessin**) portfolio.
cartonnage [kaʀtɔnaʒ] *nm* cardboard (packing).
cartonné, e [kaʀtɔne] *adj* (*livre*) hardback, cased.
carton-pâte [kaʀtõpɑt] *nm* pasteboard; **de** ~ (*fig*) cardboard *cpd*.
cartouche [kaʀtuʃ] *nf* cartridge; (*de cigarettes*) carton.
cartouchière [kaʀtuʃjɛʀ] *nf* cartridge belt.
cas [kɑ] *nm* case; **faire peu de** ~/**grand** ~ **de** to attach little/great importance to; **le** ~ **échéant** if need be; **en aucun** ~ on no account, under no circumstances (whatsoever); **au** ~ **où** in case; **dans ce** ~ in that case; **en** ~ **de** in case of, in the event of; **en** ~ **de besoin** if need be; **en** ~ **d'urgence** in an emergency; **en ce** ~ in that case; **en tout** ~ in any case, at any rate; ~ **de conscience** matter of conscience; ~ **de force majeure** case of absolute necessity; (*ASSURANCES*) act of God; ~ **limite** borderline case; ~ **social** social problem.
Casablanca [kazablãka] *n* Casablanca.

casanier, ière [kazanje, -jɛʀ] *adj* stay-at-home.

casaque [kazak] *nf* (*de jockey*) blouse.

cascade [kaskad] *nf* waterfall, cascade; (*fig*) stream, torrent.

cascadeur, euse [kaskadœʀ, -øz] *nm/f* stuntman/girl.

case [kɑz] *nf* (*hutte*) hut; (*compartiment*) compartment; (*pour le courrier*) pigeonhole; (*de mots croisés, d'échiquier*) square; (*sur un formulaire*) box.

casemate [kazmat] *nf* blockhouse.

caser [kaze] *vt* (*mettre*) to put; (*loger*) to put up; (*péj*) to find a job for; to marry off; **se ~** (*personne*) to settle down.

caserne [kazɛʀn(ə)] *nf* barracks.

casernement [kazɛʀnəmɑ̃] *nm* barrack buildings *pl*.

cash [kaʃ] *adv*: **payer ~** to pay cash down.

casier [kazje] *nm* (*à journaux etc*) rack; (*de bureau*) filing cabinet; (: *à cases*) set of pigeonholes; (*case*) compartment; pigeonhole; (: *à clef*) locker; (*PÊCHE*) lobster pot; **~ à bouteilles** bottle rack; **~ judiciaire** police record.

casino [kazino] *nm* casino.

casque [kask(ə)] *nm* helmet; (*chez le coiffeur*) (hair-)dryer; (*pour audition*) (head-)phones *pl*, headset; **les C~s bleus** the UN peacekeeping force.

casquer [kaske] *vi* (*fam*) to cough up, stump up (*BRIT*).

casquette [kaskɛt] *nf* cap.

cassable [kɑsabl(ə)] *adj* (*fragile*) breakable.

cassant, e [kɑsɑ̃, -ɑ̃t] *adj* brittle; (*fig*) brusque, abrupt.

cassate [kasat] *nf*: (**glace**) **~** cassata.

cassation [kɑsɑsjɔ̃] *nf*: **se pourvoir en ~** to lodge an appeal; **recours en ~** appeal to the Supreme Court.

casse [kɑs] *nf* (*pour voitures*): **mettre à la ~** to scrap, send to the breakers (*BRIT*); (*dégâts*): **il y a eu de la ~** there were a lot of breakages; (*TYPO*): **haut/bas de ~** upper/lower case.

cassé, e [kɑse] *adj* (*voix*) cracked; (*vieillard*) bent.

casse-cou [kɑsku] *adj inv* daredevil, reckless; **crier ~ à qn** to warn sb (*against a risky undertaking*).

casse-croûte [kɑskʀut] *nm inv* snack.

casse-noisette(s) [kɑsnwazɛt], **casse-noix** [kɑsnwa] *nm inv* nutcrackers *pl*.

casse-pieds [kɑspje] *adj, nm/f inv* (*fam*): **il est ~, c'est un ~** he's a pain (in the neck).

casser [kɑse] *vt* to break; (*ADMIN: gradé*) to demote; (*JUR*) to quash; (*COMM*): **~ les prix** to slash prices; **se ~** *vi* to break; (*fam*) to go, leave ♦ *vt*: **se ~ la jambe/une jambe** to break one's leg/a leg; **à tout ~** fantastic, brilliant; **se ~ net** to break clean off.

casserole [kɑsʀɔl] *nf* saucepan; **à la ~** (*CULIN*)

braised.

casse-tête [kɑstɛt] *nm inv* (*fig*) brain teaser; (*difficultés*) headache (*fig*).

cassette [kasɛt] *nf* (*bande magnétique*) cassette; (*coffret*) casket; **~ numérique** digital compact cassette.

casseur [kɑsœʀ] *nm* hooligan; rioter.

cassis [kasis] *nm* blackcurrant; (*de la route*) dip, bump.

cassonade [kasɔnad] *nf* brown sugar.

cassoulet [kasulɛ] *nm* sausage and bean hot-pot.

cassure [kɑsyʀ] *nf* break, crack.

castagnettes [kastaɲɛt] *nfpl* castanets.

caste [kast(ə)] *nf* caste.

castillan, e [kastijɑ̃, -an] *adj* Castilian ♦ *nm* (*LING*) Castilian.

Castille [kastij] *nf*: **la ~** Castile.

castor [kastɔʀ] *nm* beaver.

castrer [kastʀe] *vt* (*mâle*) to castrate; (*femelle*) to spay; (*cheval*) to geld; (*chat, chien*) to doctor (*BRIT*), fix (*US*).

cataclysme [kataklism(ə)] *nm* cataclysm.

catacombes [katakɔ̃b] *nfpl* catacombs.

catadioptre [katadjɔptʀ(ə)] *nm* = **cataphote.**

catafalque [katafalk(ə)] *nm* catafalque.

catalan, e [katalɑ̃, -an] *adj* Catalan, Catalonian ♦ *nm* (*LING*) Catalan.

Catalogne [katalɔɲ] *nf*: **la ~** Catalonia.

catalogue [katalɔg] *nm* catalogue.

cataloguer [kataloge] *vt* to catalogue, list; (*péj*) to put a label on.

catalyse [kataliz] *nf* catalysis.

catalyser [katalize] *vt* to catalyze.

catalyseur [katalizœʀ] *nm* catalyst.

catalytique [katalitik] *adj* catalytic.

catamaran [katamaʀɑ̃] *nm* (*voilier*) catamaran.

cataphote [katafɔt] *nm* reflector.

cataplasme [kataplasm(ə)] *nm* poultice.

catapulte [katapylt(ə)] *nf* catapult.

catapulter [katapylte] *vt* to catapult.

cataracte [kataʀakt(ə)] *nf* cataract; **opérer qn de la ~** to operate on sb for a cataract.

catarrhe [kataʀ] *nm* catarrh.

catarrheux, euse [kataʀø, -øz] *adj* catarrhal.

catastrophe [katastʀɔf] *nf* catastrophe, disaster; **atterrir en ~** to make an emergency landing; **partir en ~** to rush away.

catastropher [katastʀɔfe] *vt* (*personne*) to shatter.

catastrophique [katastʀɔfik] *adj* catastrophic, disastrous.

catch [katʃ] *nm* (all-in) wrestling.

catcheur, euse [katʃœʀ, -øz] *nm/f* (all-in) wrestler.

catéchiser [kateʃize] *vt* to indoctrinate; to lecture.

catéchisme [kateʃism(ə)] *nm* catechism.

catéchumène [katekymɛn] *nm/f* catechumen, *person attending religious instruction prior to baptism.*

catégorie [kategɔʀi] *nf* category; (*BOUCHERIE*):

morceaux de première/deuxième ~ prime/
second cuts.
catégorique [kategɔʀik] *adj* categorical.
catégoriquement [kategɔʀikmɑ̃] *adv* cat-
egorically.
catégoriser [kategɔʀize] *vt* to categorize.
caténaire [katenɛʀ] *nf* (RAIL) catenary.
cathédrale [katedʀal] *nf* cathedral.
cathéter [katetɛʀ] *nm* (MÉD) catheter.
cathode [katɔd] *nf* cathode.
cathodique [katɔdik] *adj*: **rayons ~s** cathode
rays; **tube/écran ~** cathode-ray tube/
screen.
catholicisme [katɔlisism(ə)] *nm* (Roman)
Catholicism.
catholique [katɔlik] *adj, nm/f* (Roman) Catholic; **pas très ~** a bit shady *ou* fishy.
catimini [katimini]: **en ~** *adv* on the sly, on the
quiet.
catogan [katɔgɑ̃] *nm* bow (*tying hair on neck*).
Caucase [kokaz] *nm*: **le ~** the Caucasus
(Mountains).
caucasien, ne [kokazjɛ̃, -ɛn] *adj* Caucasian.
cauchemar [koʃmaʀ] *nm* nightmare.
cauchemardesque [koʃmaʀdɛsk(ə)] *adj* night-
marish.
caudal, e, aux [kodal, -o] *adj* caudal, tail *cpd*.
causal, e [kozal] *adj* causal.
causalité [kozalite] *nf* causality.
causant, e [kozɑ̃, -ɑ̃t] *adj* chatty, talkative.
cause [koz] *nf* cause; (*JUR*) lawsuit, case;
brief; **faire ~ commune avec qn** to take
sides with sb; **être ~ de** to be the cause of; **à
~ de** because of, owing to; **pour ~ de** on account of; owing to; **(et) pour ~** and for (a
very) good reason; **être en ~** (*intérêts*) to be
at stake; (*personne*) to be involved; (*qualité*)
to be in question; **mettre en ~** to implicate;
to call into question; **remettre en ~** to challenge, call into question; **c'est hors de ~** it's
out of the question; **en tout état de ~** in any
case.
causer [koze] *vt* to cause ♦ *vi* to chat, talk.
causerie [kozʀi] *nf* talk.
causette [kozɛt] *nf*: **faire la** *ou* **un brin de ~** to
have a chat.
caustique [kostik] *adj* caustic.
cauteleux, euse [kotlø, -øz] *adj* wily.
cautériser [koteʀize] *vt* to cauterize.
caution [kosjɔ̃] *nf* guarantee, security; deposit; (*JUR*) bail (bond); (*fig*) backing, support;
payer la ~ de qn to stand bail for sb; **se
porter ~ pour qn** to stand security for sb;
libéré sous ~ released on bail; **sujet à ~**
unconfirmed.
cautionnement [kosjɔnmɑ̃] *nm* (*somme*)
guarantee, security.
cautionner [kosjɔne] *vt* to guarantee; (*soutenir*) to support.
cavalcade [kavalkad] *nf* (*fig*) stampede.
cavale [kaval] *nf*: **en ~** on the run.
cavalerie [kavalʀi] *nf* cavalry.

cavalier, ière [kavalje, -jɛʀ] *adj* (*désinvolte*)
offhand ♦ *nm/f* rider; (*au bal*) partner ♦ *nm*
(*ÉCHECS*) knight; **faire ~ seul** to go it alone;
allée *ou* **piste cavalière** riding path.
cavalièrement [kavaljɛʀmɑ̃] *adv* offhandedly.
cave [kav] *nf* cellar; (*cabaret*) (cellar) night-
club ♦ *adj*: **yeux ~s** sunken eyes; **joues ~s**
hollow cheeks.
caveau, x [kavo] *nm* vault.
caverne [kavɛʀn(ə)] *nf* cave.
caverneux, euse [kavɛʀnø, -øz] *adj* cavern-
ous.
caviar [kavjaʀ] *nm* caviar(e).
cavité [kavite] *nf* cavity.
Cayenne [kajɛn] *n* Cayenne.
CB [sibi] *sigle f* (= *citizens' band, canaux bana-
lisés*) CB.
CC *sigle m* = **corps consulaire, compte courant**.
CCI *sigle f* = **Chambre de commerce et
d'industrie**.
CCP *sigle m* = **compte chèque postal**.
CD *sigle m* (= *chemin départemental*) secondary
road, ≈ B road (*BRIT*); (= *compact disc*) CD;
(= *comité directeur*) steering committee;
(*POL*) = **corps diplomatique**.
CDD *sigle m* (= *contrat à durée déterminée*)
fixed-term contract.
CDF, CdF *sigle mpl* (= *Charbonnages de France*)
national coal board.
CDI *sigle m* (= *Centre de documentation et
d'information*) school library; (= *contrat à du-
rée indéterminée*) permanent *ou* open-ended
contract.
CD-I *sigle m* (= *compact disc interactif*) CD-I®.
CD-Rom [sedeʀɔm] *nm inv* (= *Compact Disc Read
Only Memory*) CD-Rom.
CDS *sigle m* (= *Centre des démocrates sociaux*)
political party.
CE *sigle f* (= *Communauté européenne*) EC;
(*COMM*) = **caisse d'épargne** ♦ *sigle m* (*INDUS-
TRIE*) = **comité d'entreprise**; (*SCOL*) = **cours
élémentaire**.

━━━━━━━━━━━━━━ *MOT-CLÉ*

ce, cette [sə, sɛt] (*devant nm* **cet** + *voyelle ou h
aspiré*; *pl* **ces**) *dét* (*proximité*) this; these *pl*;
(*non-proximité*) that; those *pl*; **cette maison(-
ci/là**) this/that house; **cette nuit** (*qui vient*) tonight; (*passée*) last night
♦ *pron* **1**: **c'est** it's, it is; **c'est petit/grand/un
livre** it's *ou* it is small/big/a book; **c'est un
peintre** he's *ou* he is a painter; **ce sont des
peintres** they're *ou* they are painters; **c'est
le facteur** *etc* (*à la porte*) it's the postman
etc; **qui est-ce?** who is it?; (*en désignant*) who
is he/she?; **qu'est-ce?** what is it?; **c'est toi
qui lui as parlé** it was you who spoke to him
2: **c'est que**: **c'est qu'il est lent/qu'il n'a pas
faim** the fact is, he's slow/he's not hungry
3 (*expressions*): **c'est ça** (*correct*) that's it,
that's right; **c'est toi qui le dis!** that's what
YOU say!; *voir aussi* **c'est-à-dire; -ci; est-ce**

que; n'est-ce pas.
4: ~ **qui**, ~ **que** what; (*chose qui*): **il est bête,** ~ **qui me chagrine** he's stupid, which saddens me; **tout** ~ **qui bouge** everything that *ou* which moves; **tout** ~ **que je sais** all I know; ~ **dont j'ai parlé** what I talked about; ~ **que c'est grand!** it's so big!

CEA *sigle m* (= *Commissariat à l'énergie atomique*) ≈ AEA (= *Atomic Energy Authority*) (*BRIT*), ≈ AEC (= *Atomic Energy Commission*) (*US*).
CECA [seka] *sigle f* (= *Communauté européenne du charbon et de l'acier*) ECSC (= *European Coal and Steel Community*).
ceci [səsi] *pron* this.
cécité [sesite] *nf* blindness.
céder [sede] *vt* to give up ♦ *vi* (*pont, barrage*) to give way; (*personne*) to give in; ~ **à** to yield to, give in to.
CEDEX [sedɛks] *sigle m* (= *courrier d'entreprise à distribution exceptionnelle*) *accelerated postal service for bulk users.*
cédille [sedij] *nf* cedilla.
cèdre [sɛdʀ(ə)] *nm* cedar.
CEE *sigle f* (= *Communauté économique européenne*) EEC.
CEG *sigle m* (= *Collège d'enseignement général*) ≈ junior secondary school (*BRIT*), ≈ junior high school (*US*).
CEI *sigle f* (= *Communauté des États indépendants*) CIS.
ceindre [sɛ̃dʀ(ə)] *vt* (*mettre*) to put on, don; (*entourer*): ~ **qch de qch** to put sth round sth.
ceinture [sɛ̃tyʀ] *nf* belt; (*taille*) waist; (*fig*) ring; belt; circle; ~ **de sauvetage** lifebelt (*BRIT*), life preserver (*US*); ~ **de sécurité** safety *ou* seat belt; ~ **(de sécurité) à enrouleur** inertia reel seat belt; ~ **verte** green belt.
ceinturer [sɛ̃tyʀe] *vt* (*saisir*) to grasp (round the waist); (*entourer*) to surround.
ceinturon [sɛ̃tyʀɔ̃] *nm* belt.
cela [səla] *pron* that; (*comme sujet indéfini*) it; ~ **m'étonne que** it surprises me that; **quand/où** ~? when/where (was that)?
célébrant [selebʀɑ̃] *nm* (*REL*) celebrant.
célébration [selebʀɑsjɔ̃] *nf* celebration.
célèbre [selɛbʀ(ə)] *adj* famous.
célébrer [selebʀe] *vt* to celebrate; (*louer*) to extol.
célébrité [selebʀite] *nf* fame; (*star*) celebrity.
céleri [sɛlʀi] *nm*: ~**(-rave)** celeriac; ~ **(en branche)** celery.
célérité [seleʀite] *nf* speed, swiftness.
céleste [selɛst(ə)] *adj* celestial; heavenly.
célibat [seliba] *nm* celibacy; bachelor/spinsterhood.
célibataire [selibatɛʀ] *adj* single, unmarried ♦ *nm/f* bachelor/unmarried *ou* single woman; **mère** ~ single *ou* unmarried mother.

celle, celles [sɛl] *pron voir* **celui**.
cellier [selje] *nm* storeroom.
cellophane [selɔfan] *nf* ® cellophane.
cellulaire [selylɛʀ] *adj* (*BIO*) cell *cpd*, cellular; **voiture** *ou* **fourgon** ~ prison *ou* police van; **régime** ~ confinement.
cellule [selyl] *nf* (*gén*) cell; ~ **(photoélectrique)** electronic eye.
cellulite [selylit] *nf* cellulite.
celluloïd [selylɔid] *nm* ® Celluloid.
cellulose [selyloz] *nf* cellulose.
celte [sɛlt(ə)], **celtique** [sɛltik] *adj* Celt, Celtic.

════════════════════════ *MOT-CLÉ*

celui, celle [səlɥi, sɛl] (*mpl* **ceux**, *fpl* **celles**) *pron*
1: ~**-ci/là, celle-ci/là** this one/that one; **ceux-ci, celles-ci** these (ones); **ceux-là, celles-là** those (ones); ~ **de mon frère** my brother's; ~ **du salon/du dessous** the one in (*ou* from) the lounge/below
2: ~ **qui bouge** the one which *ou* that moves; (*personne*) the one who moves; ~ **que je vois** the one (which *ou* that) I see; (*personne*) the one (whom) I see; ~ **dont je parle** the one I'm talking about
3 (*valeur indéfinie*): ~ **qui veut** whoever wants.

──────────────────────────

cénacle [senakl(ə)] *nm* (literary) coterie *ou* set.
cendre [sɑ̃dʀ(ə)] *nf* ash; ~**s** (*d'un foyer*) ash(es), cinders; (*volcaniques*) ash *sg*; (*d'un défunt*) ashes; **sous la** ~ (*CULIN*) in (the) embers.
cendré, e [sɑ̃dʀe] *adj* (*couleur*) ashen; (*piste*) ~**e** cinder track.
cendreux, euse [sɑ̃dʀø, -øz] *adj* (*terrain, substance*) cindery; (*teint*) ashen.
cendrier [sɑ̃dʀije] *nm* ashtray.
cène [sɛn] *nf*: **la** ~ (Holy) Communion; (*ART*) the Last Supper.
censé, e [sɑ̃se] *adj*: **être** ~ **faire** to be supposed to do.
censément [sɑ̃semɑ̃] *adv* supposedly.
censeur [sɑ̃sœʀ] *nm* (*SCOL*) deputy-head (*BRIT*), vice-principal (*US*); (*CINÉ, POL*) censor.
censure [sɑ̃syʀ] *nf* censorship.
censurer [sɑ̃syʀe] *vt* (*CINÉ, PRESSE*) to censor; (*POL*) to censure.
cent [sɑ̃] *num* a hundred, one hundred; **pour** ~ **(%)** per cent (%); **faire les** ~ **pas** to pace up and down.
centaine [sɑ̃tɛn] *nf*: **une** ~ **(de)** about a hundred, a hundred or so; (*COMM*) a hundred; **plusieurs** ~**s (de)** several hundred; **des** ~**s (de)** hundreds (of).
centenaire [sɑ̃tnɛʀ] *adj* hundred-year-old ♦ *nm/f* centenarian ♦ *nm* (*anniversaire*) centenary.
centième [sɑ̃tjɛm] *num* hundredth.
centigrade [sɑ̃tigʀad] *nm* centigrade.

centigramme [sɑ̃tigʀam] nm centigramme.
centilitre [sɑ̃tilitʀ(ə)] nm centilitre (BRIT), centiliter (US).
centime [sɑ̃tim] nm centime.
centimètre [sɑ̃timɛtʀ(ə)] nm centimetre (BRIT), centimeter (US); (ruban) tape measure, measuring tape.
centrafricain, e [sɑ̃tʀafʀikɛ̃, -ɛn] adj of ou from the Central African Republic.
central, e, aux [sɑ̃tʀal, -o] adj central ♦ nm: ~ **(téléphonique)** (telephone) exchange ♦ nf: ~**e d'achat** (COMM) central buying service; ~**e électrique/nucléaire** electric/nuclear power station; ~**e syndicale** group of affiliated trade unions.
centralisation [sɑ̃tʀalizasjɔ̃] nf centralization.
centraliser [sɑ̃tʀalize] vt to centralize.
centralisme [sɑ̃tʀalism(ə)] nm centralism.
centraméricain, e [sɑ̃tʀameʀikɛ̃, -ɛn] adj Central American.
centre [sɑ̃tʀ(ə)] nm centre (BRIT), center (US); ~ **commercial/sportif/culturel** shopping/sports/arts centre; ~ **aéré** outdoor centre; ~ **d'apprentissage** training college; ~ **d'attraction** centre of attraction; ~ **de gravité** centre of gravity; ~ **d'enfouissement des déchets** landfill site; ~ **hospitalier** hospital complex; ~ **de tri** (POSTES) sorting office; ~**s nerveux** (ANAT) nerve centres.
centrer [sɑ̃tʀe] vt to centre (BRIT), center (US) ♦ vi (FOOTBALL) to centre the ball.
centre-ville, pl **centres-villes** [sɑ̃tʀəvil] nm town centre (BRIT) ou center (US), downtown (area) (US).
centrifuge [sɑ̃tʀify3] adj: **force** ~ centrifugal force.
centrifuger [sɑ̃tʀify3e] vt to centrifuge.
centrifugeuse [sɑ̃tʀify3øz] nf (pour fruits) juice extractor.
centripète [sɑ̃tʀipɛt] adj: **force** ~ centripetal force.
centrisme [sɑ̃tʀism(ə)] nm centrism.
centriste [sɑ̃tʀist(ə)] adj, nm/f centrist.
centuple [sɑ̃typl(ə)] nm: **le** ~ **de qch** a hundred times sth; **au** ~ a hundredfold.
centupler [sɑ̃typle] vi, vt to increase a hundredfold.
CEP sigle m = **Certificat d'études (primaires)**.
cep [sɛp] nm (vine) stock.
cépage [sepa3] nm (type of) vine.
cèpe [sɛp] nm (edible) boletus.
cependant [səpɑ̃dɑ̃] adv however, nevertheless.
céramique [seramik] adj ceramic ♦ nf ceramic; (art) ceramics sg.
céramiste [seramist(ə)] nm/f ceramist.
cerbère [sɛʀbɛʀ] nm (fig: péj) bad-tempered doorkeeper.
cerceau, x [sɛʀso] nm (d'enfant, de tonnelle) hoop.
cercle [sɛʀkl(ə)] nm circle; (objet) band, hoop; **décrire un** ~ (avion) to circle; (projectile) to

describe a circle; ~ **d'amis** circle of friends; ~ **de famille** family circle; ~ **vicieux** vicious circle.
cercler [sɛʀkle] vt: **lunettes cerclées d'or** gold-rimmed glasses.
cercueil [sɛʀkœj] nm coffin.
céréale [seʀeal] nf cereal.
céréalier, ière [seʀealje, -jɛʀ] adj (production, cultures) cereal cpd.
cérébral, e, aux [seʀebʀal, -o] adj (ANAT) cerebral, brain cpd; (fig) mental, cerebral.
cérémonial [seʀemɔnjal] nm ceremonial.
cérémonie [seʀemɔni] nf ceremony; ~**s** nfpl (péj) fuss sg, to-do sg.
cérémonieux, euse [seʀemɔnjø, -øz] adj ceremonious, formal.
CERES [seʀɛs] sigle m (= Centre d'études, de recherches et d'éducation socialiste) (formerly) intellectual section of the French Socialist party.
cerf [sɛʀ] nm stag.
cerfeuil [sɛʀfœj] nm chervil.
cerf-volant [sɛʀvɔlɑ̃] nm kite; **jouer au** ~ to fly a kite.
cerisaie [səʀize] nf cherry orchard.
cerise [səʀiz] nf cherry.
cerisier [səʀizje] nm cherry (tree).
CERN [sɛʀn] sigle m (= Centre européen de recherche nucléaire) CERN.
cerné, e [sɛʀne] adj: **les yeux** ~**s** with dark rings ou shadows under the eyes.
cerner [sɛʀne] vt (MIL etc) to surround; (fig: problème) to delimit, define.
cernes [sɛʀn(ə)] nfpl (dark) rings, shadows (under the eyes).
certain, e [sɛʀtɛ̃, -ɛn] adj certain; (sûr): ~ **(de/que)** certain ou sure (of/ that) ♦ dét certain; **d'un** ~ **âge** past one's prime, not so young; **un** ~ **temps** (quite) some time; **sûr et** ~ absolutely certain; ~**s** pron some.
certainement [sɛʀtɛnmɑ̃] adv (probablement) most probably ou likely; (bien sûr) certainly, of course.
certes [sɛʀt(ə)] adv admittedly; of course; indeed (yes).
certificat [sɛʀtifika] nm certificate; **C**~ **d'études (primaires) (CEP)** former school leaving certificate (taken at the end of primary education); **C**~ **de fin d'études secondaires (CFES)** school leaving certificate.
certifié, e [sɛʀtifje] adj: **professeur** ~ qualified teacher; (ADMIN): **copie** ~**e conforme (à l'original)** certified copy (of the original).
certifier [sɛʀtifje] vt to certify, guarantee; ~ **à qn que** to assure sb that, guarantee to sb that; ~ **qch à qn** to guarantee sth to sb.
certitude [sɛʀtityd] nf certainty.
cérumen [seʀymɛn] nm (ear)wax.
cerveau, x [sɛʀvo] nm brain; ~ **électronique** electronic brain.
cervelas [sɛʀvəla] nm saveloy.
cervelle [sɛʀvɛl] nf (ANAT) brain; (CULIN)

brain(s); **se creuser la** ~ to rack one's brains.

cervical, e, aux [sɛʀvikal, -o] *adj* cervical.

cervidés [sɛʀvide] *nmpl* cervidae.

CES *sigle m* (= *Collège d'enseignement secondaire*) ≈ (junior) secondary school (*BRIT*), ≈ junior high school (*US*).

ces [se] *dét voir* **ce**.

césarienne [sezaʀjɛn] *nf* caesarean (*BRIT*) *ou* cesarean (*US*) (section).

cessantes [sɛsɑ̃t] *adj fpl*: **toutes affaires** ~ forthwith.

cessation [sɛsasjɔ̃] *nf*: ~ **des hostilités** cessation of hostilities; ~ **de paiements/ commerce** suspension of payments/trading.

cesse [sɛs]: **sans** ~ *adv* continually, constantly; continuously; **il n'avait de** ~ **que** he would not rest until.

cesser [sese] *vt* to stop ♦ *vi* to stop, cease; ~ **de faire** to stop doing; **faire** ~ (*bruit, scandale*) to put a stop to.

cessez-le-feu [seselfø] *nm inv* ceasefire.

cession [sɛsjɔ̃] *nf* transfer.

c'est [sɛ] *pron + vb voir* **ce**.

c'est-à-dire [sɛtadiʀ] *adv* that is (to say); (*demander de préciser*): ~**?** what does that mean?; ~ **que** ... (*en conséquence*) which means that ...; (*manière d'excuse*) well, in fact ....

CET *sigle m* (= *Collège d'enseignement technique*) (*formerly*) *technical school*.

cet [sɛt] *dét voir* **ce**.

cétacé [setase] *nm* cetacean.

cette [sɛt] *dét voir* **ce**.

ceux [sø] *pron voir* **celui**.

cévenol, e [sevnɔl] *adj* of *ou* from the Cévennes region.

cf. *abr* (= *confer*) cf, cp.

CFAO *sigle f* (= *conception de fabrication assistée par ordinateur*) CAM.

CFC *sigle mpl* (= *chlorofluorocarbures*) CFC.

CFDT *sigle f* (= *Confédération française démocratique du travail*) *trade union*.

CFES *sigle m* = **Certificat de fin d'études secondaires**.

CFF *sigle m* (= *Chemins de fer fédéraux*) *Swiss railways*.

CFL *sigle m* (= *Chemins de fer luxembourgeois*) *Luxembourg railways*.

CFP *sigle m* = *Centre de formation professionnelle* ♦ *sigle f* = *Compagnie française des pétroles*.

CFTC *sigle f* (= *Confédération française des travailleurs chrétiens*) *trade union*.

CGC *sigle f* (= *Confédération générale des cadres*) *management union*.

CGPME *sigle f* = *Confédération générale des petites et moyennes entreprises*.

CGT *sigle f* (= *Confédération générale du travail*) *trade union*.

CH *abr* (= *Confédération helvétique*) CH.

ch. *abr* = **charges, chauffage, cherche**.

chacal [ʃakal] *nm* jackal.

chacun, e [ʃakœ̃, -yn] *pron* each; (*indéfini*) everyone, everybody.

chagrin, e [ʃagʀɛ̃, -in] *adj* morose ♦ *nm* grief, sorrow; **avoir du** ~ to be grieved *ou* sorrowful.

chagriner [ʃagʀine] *vt* to grieve, distress; (*contrarier*) to bother, worry.

chahut [ʃay] *nm* uproar.

chahuter [ʃayte] *vt* to rag, bait ♦ *vi* to make an uproar.

chahuteur, euse [ʃaytœʀ, -øz] *nm/f* rowdy.

chai [ʃɛ] *nm* wine and spirit store(house).

chaîne [ʃɛn] *nf* chain; (*RADIO, TV*) channel; (*INFORM*) string; ~**s** *nfpl* (*liens, asservissement*) fetters, bonds; **travail à la** ~ production line work; **réactions en** ~ chain reactions; **faire la** ~ to form a (human) chain; ~ **alimentaire** food chain; ~ **compacte** music centre; ~ **d'entraide** mutual aid association; ~ **(haute-fidélité** *ou* **hi-fi)** hi-fi system; ~ **(de montage** *ou* **de fabrication)** production *ou* assembly line; ~ **(de montagnes)** (mountain) range; ~ **de solidarité** solidarity network; ~ **(stéréo** *ou* **audio)** stereo (system).

chaînette [ʃɛnɛt] *nf* (small) chain.

chaînon [ʃɛnɔ̃] *nm* link.

chair [ʃɛʀ] *nf* flesh ♦ *adj*: **(couleur)** ~ flesh-coloured; **avoir la** ~ **de poule** to have goose-pimples *ou* gooseflesh; **bien en** ~ plump, well-padded; **en** ~ **et en os** in the flesh; ~ **à saucisses** sausage meat.

chaire [ʃɛʀ] *nf* (*d'église*) pulpit; (*d'université*) chair.

chaise [ʃɛz] *nf* chair; ~ **de bébé** high chair; ~ **électrique** electric chair; ~ **longue** deckchair.

chaland [ʃalɑ̃] *nm* (*bateau*) barge.

châle [ʃal] *nm* shawl.

chalet [ʃalɛ] *nm* chalet.

chaleur [ʃalœʀ] *nf* heat; (*fig*) warmth; fire, fervour (*BRIT*), fervor (*US*); heat; **en** ~ (*ZOOL*) on heat.

chaleureusement [ʃalœʀøzmɑ̃] *adv* warmly.

chaleureux, euse [ʃalœʀø, -øz] *adj* warm.

challenge [ʃalɑ̃ʒ] *nm* contest, tournament.

challenger [ʃalɑ̃ʒɛʀ] *nm* (*SPORT*) challenger.

chaloupe [ʃalup] *nf* launch; (*de sauvetage*) lifeboat.

chalumeau, x [ʃalymo] *nm* blowlamp (*BRIT*), blowtorch.

chalut [ʃaly] *nm* trawl (net); **pêcher au** ~ to trawl.

chalutier [ʃalytje] *nm* trawler; (*pêcheur*) trawlerman.

chamade [ʃamad] *nf*: **battre la** ~ to beat wildly.

chamailler [ʃamaje]: **se** ~ *vi* to squabble, bicker.

chamarré, e [ʃamaʀe] *adj* richly brocaded.

chambard [ʃɑ̃baʀ] *nm* rumpus.

chambardement [ʃɑ̃baʀdəmɑ̃] *nm*: **c'est le grand** ~ everything has been (*ou* is being) turned upside down.

chambarder [ʃãbaʀde] *vt* to turn upside down.

chamboulement [ʃãbulmã] *nm* disruption.

chambouler [ʃãbule] *vt* to disrupt, turn upside down.

chambranle [ʃãbʀãl] *nm* (door) frame.

chambre [ʃãbʀ(ə)] *nf* bedroom; (*TECH*) chamber; (*POL*) chamber, house; (*JUR*) court; (*COMM*) chamber; federation; **faire ~ à part** to sleep in separate rooms; **stratège/ alpiniste en ~** armchair strategist/ mountaineer; **~ à un lit/deux lits** single/ twin-bedded room; **~ pour une/deux personne(s)** single/double room; **~ d'accusation** court of criminal appeal; **~ d'agriculture** *body responsible for the agricultural interests of a département*; **~ à air** (*de pneu*) (inner) tube; **~ d'amis** spare *ou* guest room; **~ de combustion** combustion chamber; **~ de commerce et d'industrie (CCI)** chamber of commerce and industry; **~ à coucher** bedroom; **la C~ des députés** the Chamber of Deputies, ≈ the House (of Commons) (*BRIT*), ≈ the House of Rep- resentatives (*US*); **~ forte** strongroom; **~ froide** *ou* **frigorifique** cold room; **~ à gaz** gas chamber; **~ d'hôte** ≈ bed and breakfast (*in private home*); **~ des machines** engine-room; **~ des métiers (CM)** *chamber of commerce for trades*; **~ meublée** bedsit(ter) (*BRIT*), furnished room; **~ noire** (*PHOTO*) dark room.

chambrée [ʃãbʀe] *nf* room.

chambrer [ʃãbʀe] *vt* (*vin*) to bring to room temperature.

chameau, x [ʃamo] *nm* camel.

chamois [ʃamwa] *nm* chamois ♦ *adj*: **(couleur) ~** fawn, buff.

champ [ʃã] *nm* (*aussi INFORM*) field; (*PHOTO*): **dans le ~** in the picture; **prendre du ~** to draw back; **laisser le ~ libre à qn** to leave sb a clear field; **~ d'action** sphere of operation(s); **~ de bataille** battlefield; **~ de courses** racecourse; **~ d'honneur** field of honour; **~ de manœuvre** (*MIL*) parade ground; **~ de mines** minefield; **~ de tir** shooting *ou* rifle range; **~ visuel** field of vision.

Champagne [ʃãpaɲ] *nf*: **la ~** Champagne, the Champagne region.

champagne [ʃãpaɲ] *nm* champagne.

champenois, e [ʃãpənwa, -waz] *adj* of *ou* from Champagne; (*vin*): **méthode ~e** champagne-type.

champêtre [ʃãpɛtʀ(ə)] *adj* country *cpd*, rural.

champignon [ʃãpiɲɔ̃] *nm* mushroom; (*terme générique*) fungus (*pl* -i); (*fam: accélérateur*) accelerator, gas pedal (*US*); **~ de couche** *ou* **de Paris** button mushroom; **~ vénéneux** toadstool, poisonous mushroom.

champion, ne [ʃãpjɔ̃, -ɔn] *adj, nm/f* champion.

championnat [ʃãpjɔna] *nm* championship.

chance [ʃãs] *nf*: **la ~** luck; **une ~** a stroke *ou*

piece of luck *ou* good fortune; (*occasion*) a lucky break; **~s** *nfpl* (*probabilités*) chances; **avoir de la ~** to be lucky; **il a des ~s de gagner** he has a chance of winning; **il y a de fortes ~s pour que Paul soit malade** it's highly probable that Paul is ill; **bonne ~!** good luck!; **encore une ~ que tu viennes!** it's lucky you're coming; **je n'ai pas de ~** I'm out of luck; (*toujours*) I never have any luck; **donner sa ~ à qn** to give sb a chance.

chancelant, e [ʃãslã, -ãt] *adj* (*personne*) tottering; (*santé*) failing.

chanceler [ʃãsle] *vi* to totter.

chancelier [ʃãsəlje] *nm* (*allemand*) chancellor; (*d'ambassade*) secretary.

chancellerie [ʃãsɛlʀi] *nf* (*en France*) ministry of justice; (*en Allemagne*) chancellery; (*d'ambassade*) chancery.

chanceux, euse [ʃãsø, -øz] *adj* lucky, fortunate.

chancre [ʃãkʀ(ə)] *nm* canker.

chandail [ʃãdaj] *nm* (thick) jumper *ou* sweater.

Chandeleur [ʃãdlœʀ] *nf*: **la ~** Candlemas.

chandelier [ʃãdəlje] *nm* candlestick; (*à plusieurs branches*) candelabra.

chandelle [ʃãdɛl] *nf* (tallow) candle; (*TENNIS*): **faire une ~** to lob; (*AVIAT*): **monter en ~** to climb vertically; **tenir la ~** to play gooseberry; **dîner aux ~s** candlelight dinner.

change [ʃãʒ] *nm* (*COMM*) exchange; **opérations de ~** (foreign) exchange transactions; **contrôle des ~s** exchange control; **gagner/ perdre au ~** to be better/worse off (for it); **donner le ~ à qn** (*fig*) to lead sb up the garden path.

changeant, e [ʃãʒã, -ãt] *adj* changeable, fickle.

changement [ʃãʒmã] *nm* change; **~ de vitesse** (*dispositif*) gears *pl*; (*action*) gear change.

changer [ʃãʒe] *vt* (*modifier*) to change, alter; (*remplacer, COMM, rhabiller*) to change ♦ *vi* to change, alter; **se ~** to change (o.s.); **~ de** (*remplacer: adresse, nom, voiture etc*) to change one's; (*échanger, alterner: côté, place, train etc*) to change + *npl*; **~ d'air** to get a change of air; **~ de couleur/direction** to change colour/direction; **~ d'idée** to change one's mind; **~ de place avec qn** to change places with sb; **~ de vitesse** (*AUTO*) to change gear; **~ qn/qch de place** to move sb/sth to another place; **~ (de train etc)** to change (trains *etc*); **~ qch en** to change sth into.

changeur [ʃãʒœʀ] *nm* (*personne*) moneychanger; **~ automatique** change machine; **~ de disques** record changer, autochange.

chanoine [ʃanwan] *nm* canon.

chanson [ʃãsɔ̃] *nf* song.

chansonnette [ʃãsɔnɛt] *nf* ditty.

chansonnier [ʃãsɔnje] *nm* cabaret artist (*spe-*

cializing in political satire); (*recueil*) song book.

chant [ʃɑ̃] *nm* song; (*art vocal*) singing; (*d'église*) hymn; (*de poème*) canto; (*TECH*): **posé de** *ou* **sur ~** placed edgeways; **~ de Noël** Christmas carol.

chantage [ʃɑ̃taʒ] *nm* blackmail; **faire du ~** to use blackmail; **soumettre qn à un ~** to blackmail sb.

chantant, e [ʃɑ̃tɑ̃, -ɑ̃t] *adj* (*accent, voix*) singsong.

chanter [ʃɑ̃te] *vt, vi* to sing; **~ juste/faux** to sing in tune/out of tune; **si cela lui chante** (*fam*) if he feels like it *ou* fancies it.

chanterelle [ʃɑ̃tʀɛl] *nf* chanterelle (*edible mushroom*).

chanteur, euse [ʃɑ̃tœʀ, -øz] *nm/f* singer; **~ de charme** crooner.

chantier [ʃɑ̃tje] *nm* (building) site; (*sur une route*) roadworks *pl*; **mettre en ~** to start work on; **~ naval** shipyard.

chantilly [ʃɑ̃tiji] *nf voir* **crème**.

chantonner [ʃɑ̃tɔne] *vi, vt* to sing to oneself, hum.

chantre [ʃɑ̃tʀ(ə)] *nm* (*fig*) eulogist.

chanvre [ʃɑ̃vʀ(ə)] *nm* hemp.

chaos [kao] *nm* chaos.

chaotique [kaɔtik] *adj* chaotic.

chap. *abr* (= *chapitre*) ch.

chapardage [ʃapaʀdaʒ] *nm* pilfering.

chaparder [ʃapaʀde] *vt* to pinch.

chapeau, x [ʃapo] *nm* hat; (*PRESSE*) introductory paragraph; **~!** well done!; **~ melon** bowler hat; **~ mou** trilby; **~x de roues** hub caps.

chapeauter [ʃapote] *vt* (*ADMIN*) to head, oversee.

chapelain [ʃaplɛ̃] *nm* (*REL*) chaplain.

chapelet [ʃaplɛ] *nm* (*REL*) rosary; (*fig*): **un ~ de** a string of; **dire son ~** to tell one's beads.

chapelier, ière [ʃapəlje, -jɛʀ] *nm/f* hatter; milliner.

chapelle [ʃapɛl] *nf* chapel; **~ ardente** chapel of rest.

chapellerie [ʃapɛlʀi] *nf* (*magasin*) hat shop; (*commerce*) hat trade.

chapelure [ʃaplyʀ] *nf* (dried) breadcrumbs *pl*.

chaperon [ʃapʀɔ̃] *nm* chaperon.

chaperonner [ʃapʀɔne] *vt* to chaperon.

chapiteau, x [ʃapito] *nm* (*ARCHIT*) capital; (*de cirque*) marquee, big top.

chapitre [ʃapitʀ(ə)] *nm* chapter; (*fig*) subject, matter; **avoir voix au ~** to have a say in the matter.

chapitrer [ʃapitʀe] *vt* to lecture, reprimand.

chapon [ʃapɔ̃] *nm* capon.

chaque [ʃak] *dét* each, every; (*indéfini*) every.

char [ʃaʀ] *nm* (*à foin etc*) cart, waggon; (*de carnaval*) float; **~ (d'assaut)** tank.

charabia [ʃaʀabja] *nm* (*péj*) gibberish, gobbledygook (*BRIT*).

charade [ʃaʀad] *nf* riddle; (*mimée*) charade.

charbon [ʃaʀbɔ̃] *nm* coal; **~ de bois** charcoal.

charbonnage [ʃaʀbɔnaʒ] *nm*: **les ~s de France** the (French) Coal Board *sg*.

charbonnier [ʃaʀbɔnje] *nm* coalman.

charcuterie [ʃaʀkytʀi] *nf* (*magasin*) pork butcher's shop and delicatessen; (*produits*) cooked pork meats *pl*.

charcutier, ière [ʃaʀkytje, -jɛʀ] *nm/f* pork butcher.

chardon [ʃaʀdɔ̃] *nm* thistle.

chardonneret [ʃaʀdɔnʀɛ] *nm* goldfinch.

charentais, e [ʃaʀɑ̃tɛ, -ɛz] *adj* of *ou* from Charente ♦ *nf* (*pantoufle*) slipper.

charge [ʃaʀʒ(ə)] *nf* (*fardeau*) load; (*explosif, ÉLEC, MIL, JUR*) charge; (*rôle, mission*) responsibility; **~s** *nfpl* (*du loyer*) service charges; **à la ~ de** (*dépendant de*) dependent upon, supported by; (*aux frais de*) chargeable to, payable by; **j'accepte, à ~ de revanche** I accept, provided I can do the same for you (in return) one day; **prendre en ~** to take charge of; (*suj: véhicule*) to take on; (*dépenses*) to take care of; **~ utile** (*AUTO*) live load; (*COMM*) payload; **~s sociales** social security contributions.

chargé [ʃaʀʒe] *adj* (*voiture, animal, personne*) laden; (*fusil, batterie, caméra*) loaded; (*occupé: emploi du temps, journée*) busy, full; (*estomac*) heavy, full; (*langue*) furred; (*décoration, style*) heavy, ornate ♦ *nm*: **~ d'affaires** chargé d'affaires; **~ de cours** ≈ lecturer; **~ de** (*responsable de*) responsible for.

chargement [ʃaʀʒəmɑ̃] *nm* (*action*) loading; charging; (*objets*) load.

charger [ʃaʀʒe] *vt* (*voiture, fusil, caméra, INFORM*) to load; (*batterie*) to charge ♦ *vi* (*MIL etc*) to charge; **se ~ de** *vt* to see to, take care of; **~ qn de qch/faire qch** to give sb the responsibility for sth/of doing sth; to put sb in charge of sth/doing sth; **se ~ de faire qch** to take it upon o.s. to do sth.

chargeur [ʃaʀʒœʀ] *nm* (*dispositif: d'arme à feu*) magazine; (*: PHOTO*) cartridge; **~ de batterie** (*ÉLEC*) battery charger.

chariot [ʃaʀjo] *nm* trolley; (*charrette*) waggon; (*de machine à écrire*) carriage; **~ élévateur** fork-lift truck.

charisme [kaʀism(ə)] *nm* charisma.

charitable [ʃaʀitabl(ə)] *adj* charitable; kind.

charité [ʃaʀite] *nf* charity; **faire la ~** to give to charity; to do charitable works; **faire la ~ à** to give (something) to; **fête/vente de ~** fête/sale in aid of charity.

charivari [ʃaʀivaʀi] *nm* hullabaloo.

charlatan [ʃaʀlatɑ̃] *nm* charlatan.

charlotte [ʃaʀlɔt] *nf* (*CULIN*) charlotte.

charmant, e [ʃaʀmɑ̃, -ɑ̃t] *adj* charming.

charme [ʃaʀm(ə)] *nm* charm; **~s** *nmpl* (*appas*) charms; **c'est ce qui en fait le ~** that is its attraction; **faire du ~** to be charming, turn on the charm; **aller** *ou* **se porter comme un ~** to be in the pink.

charmer [ʃaʀme] *vt* to charm; **je suis charmé**

de I'm delighted to.

charmeur, euse [ʃaRmœR, -øz] *nm/f* charmer; ~ **de serpents** snake charmer.

charnel, le [ʃaRnɛl] *adj* carnal.

charnier [ʃaRnje] *nm* mass grave.

charnière [ʃaRnjɛR] *nf* hinge; (*fig*) turning-point.

charnu, e [ʃaRny] *adj* fleshy.

charogne [ʃaRɔɲ] *nf* carrion *no pl*; (*fam!*) bastard (*!*).

charolais, e [ʃaRɔlɛ, -ɛz] *adj* of *ou* from the Charolais.

charpente [ʃaRpɑ̃t] *nf* frame(work); (*fig*) structure, framework; (*carrure*) build, frame.

charpenté, e [ʃaRpɑ̃te] *adj*: **bien** *ou* **solidement** ~ (*personne*) well-built; (*texte*) well-constructed.

charpenterie [ʃaRpɑ̃tRi] *nf* carpentry.

charpentier [ʃaRpɑ̃tje] *nm* carpenter.

charpie [ʃaRpi] *nf*: **en** ~ (*fig*) in shreds *ou* ribbons.

charretier [ʃaRtje] *nm* carter; **de** ~ (*péj: langage, manières*) uncouth.

charrette [ʃaRɛt] *nf* cart.

charrier [ʃaRje] *vt* to carry (along); to cart, carry ♦ *vi* (*fam*) to exaggerate.

charrue [ʃaRy] *nf* plough (*BRIT*), plow (*US*).

charte [ʃaRt(ə)] *nf* charter.

charter [tʃaRtœR] *nm* (*vol*) charter flight; (*avion*) charter plane.

chasse [ʃas] *nf* hunting; (*au fusil*) shooting; (*poursuite*) chase; (*aussi*: ~ **d'eau**) flush; **la** ~ **est ouverte** the hunting season is open; **la** ~ **est fermée** it is the close (*BRIT*) *ou* closed (*US*) season; **aller à la** ~ to go hunting; **prendre en** ~, **donner la** ~ **à** to give chase to; **tirer la** ~ (**d'eau**) to flush the toilet, pull the chain; ~ **aérienne** aerial pursuit; ~ **à courre** hunting; ~ **à l'homme** manhunt; ~ **gardée** private hunting grounds *pl*; ~ **sous-marine** underwater fishing.

châsse [ʃas] *nf* reliquary, shrine.

chassé-croisé, pl chassés-croisés [ʃasekRwaze] *nm* (*DANSE*) chassé-croisé; (*fig*) mix-up (*where people miss each other in turn*).

chasse-neige [ʃasnɛʒ] *nm inv* snowplough (*BRIT*), snowplow (*US*).

chasser [ʃase] *vt* to hunt; (*expulser*) to chase away *ou* out, drive away *ou* out; (*dissiper*) to chase *ou* sweep away; to dispel, drive away.

chasseur, euse [ʃasœR, -øz] *nm/f* hunter ♦ *nm* (*avion*) fighter; (*domestique*) page (boy), messenger (boy); ~ **d'images** roving photographer; ~ **de têtes** (*fig*) headhunter; ~**s alpins** mountain infantry.

chassieux, euse [ʃasjø, -øz] *adj* sticky, gummy.

châssis [ʃasi] *nm* (*AUTO*) chassis; (*cadre*) frame; (*de jardin*) cold frame.

chaste [ʃast(ə)] *adj* chaste.

chasteté [ʃastəte] *nf* chastity.

chasuble [ʃazybl(ə)] *nf* chasuble; **robe** ~ pinafore dress (*BRIT*), jumper (*US*).

chat [ʃa] *nm* cat; ~ **sauvage** wildcat.

châtaigne [ʃatɛɲ] *nf* chestnut.

châtaignier [ʃatɛɲe] *nm* chestnut (tree).

châtain [ʃatɛ̃] *adj inv* chestnut (brown); (*personne*) chestnut-haired.

château, x [ʃato] *nm* castle; ~ **d'eau** water tower; ~ **fort** stronghold, fortified castle; ~ **de sable** sandcastle.

châtelain, e [ʃatlɛ̃, -ɛn] *nm/f* lord/lady of the manor ♦ *nf* (*ceinture*) chatelaine.

châtier [ʃatje] *vt* to punish, castigate; (*fig: style*) to polish, refine.

chatière [ʃatjɛR] *nf* (*porte*) cat flap.

châtiment [ʃatimɑ̃] *nm* punishment, castigation; ~ **corporel** corporal punishment.

chatoiement [ʃatwamɑ̃] *nm* shimmer(ing).

chaton [ʃatɔ̃] *nm* (*ZOOL*) kitten; (*BOT*) catkin; (*de bague*) bezel; stone.

chatouillement [ʃatujmɑ̃] *nm* (*gén*) tickling; (*dans le nez, la gorge*) tickle.

chatouiller [ʃatuje] *vt* to tickle; (*l'odorat, le palais*) to titillate.

chatouilleux, euse [ʃatujø, -øz] *adj* ticklish; (*fig*) touchy, over-sensitive.

chatoyant, e [ʃatwajɑ̃, -ɑ̃t] *adj* (*reflet, étoffe*) shimmering; (*couleurs*) sparkling.

chatoyer [ʃatwaje] *vi* to shimmer.

châtrer [ʃatRe] *vt* (*mâle*) to castrate; (*femelle*) to spay; (*cheval*) to geld; (*chat, chien*) to doctor (*BRIT*), fix (*US*); (*fig*) to mutilate.

chatte [ʃat] *nf* (she-)cat.

chatterton [ʃatɛRtɔn] *nm* (*ruban isolant: ÉLEC*) (adhesive) insulating tape.

chaud, e [ʃo, -od] *adj* (*gén*) warm; (*très chaud*) hot; (*fig: félicitations*) hearty; (*discussion*) heated; **il fait** ~ it's warm; it's hot; **manger** ~ to have something hot to eat; **avoir** ~ to be warm; to be hot; **tenir** ~ to keep hot; **ça me tient** ~ it keeps me warm; **tenir au** ~ to keep in a warm place; **rester au** ~ to stay in the warm.

chaudement [ʃodmɑ̃] *adv* warmly; (*fig*) hotly.

chaudière [ʃodjɛR] *nf* boiler.

chaudron [ʃodRɔ̃] *nm* cauldron.

chaudronnerie [ʃodRɔnRi] *nf* (*usine*) boiler-works; (*activité*) boilermaking; (*boutique*) coppersmith's workshop.

chauffage [ʃofaʒ] *nm* heating; ~ **au gaz/à l'électricité/au charbon** gas/electric/solid fuel heating; ~ **central** central heating; ~ **par le sol** underfloor heating.

chauffagiste [ʃofaʒist(ə)] *nm* (*installateur*) heating engineer.

chauffant, e [ʃofɑ̃, -ɑ̃t]: **couverture** ~**e** electric blanket; **plaque** ~**e** hotplate.

chauffard [ʃofaR] *nm* (*péj*) reckless driver; roadhog; (*après un accident*) hit-and-run driver.

chauffe-bain [ʃofbɛ̃] *nm* = **chauffe-eau**.

chauffe-biberon [ʃofbibRɔ̃] *nm* (baby's) bottle

warmer.

chauffe-eau [ʃofo] *nm inv* water heater.

chauffe-plats [ʃofpla] *nm inv* dish warmer.

chauffer [ʃofe] *vt* to heat up, warm up; (*trop chauffer: moteur*) to overheat; **se** ~ (*se mettre en train*) to warm up; (*au soleil*) to warm o.s.

chaufferie [ʃofʀi] *nf* boiler room.

chauffeur [ʃofœʀ] *nm* driver; (*privé*) chauffeur; **voiture avec/sans** ~ chauffeur-driven/self-drive car.

chauffeuse [ʃoføz] *nf* fireside chair.

chauler [ʃole] *vt* (*mur*) to whitewash.

chaume [ʃom] *nm* (*du toit*) thatch; (*tiges*) stubble.

chaumière [ʃomjɛʀ] *nf* (thatched) cottage.

chaussée [ʃose] *nf* road(way); (*digue*) causeway.

chausse-pied [ʃospje] *nm* shoe-horn.

chausser [ʃose] *vt* (*bottes, skis*) to put on; (*enfant*) to put shoes on; (*suj: soulier*) to fit; ~ **du 38/42** to take size 38/42; ~ **grand/bien** to be big-/well-fitting; **se** ~ to put one's shoes on.

chausse-trappe [ʃostʀap] *nf* trap.

chaussette [ʃosɛt] *nf* sock.

chausseur [ʃosœʀ] *nm* (*marchand*) footwear specialist, shoemaker.

chausson [ʃosɔ̃] *nm* slipper; (*de bébé*) bootee; ~ **(aux pommes)** (apple) turnover.

chaussure [ʃosyʀ] *nf* shoe; (*commerce*): **la** ~ the shoe industry *ou* trade; ~**s basses** flat shoes; ~**s montantes** ankle boots; ~**s de ski** ski boots.

chaut [ʃo] *vb*: **peu me** ~ it matters little to me.

chauve [ʃov] *adj* bald.

chauve-souris, *pl* **chauves-souris** [ʃovsuʀi] *nf* bat.

chauvin, e [ʃovɛ̃, -in] *adj* chauvinistic; jingoistic.

chauvinisme [ʃovinism(ə)] *nm* chauvinism; jingoism.

chaux [ʃo] *nf* lime; **blanchi à la** ~ whitewashed.

chavirer [ʃaviʀe] *vi* to capsize, overturn.

chef [ʃɛf] *nm* head, leader; (*patron*) boss; (*de cuisine*) chef; **au premier** ~ extremely, to the nth degree; **de son propre** ~ on his *ou* her own initiative; **général/commandant en** ~ general-/commander-in-chief; ~ **d'accusation** (*JUR*) charge, count (of indictment); ~ **d'atelier** (shop) foreman; ~ **de bureau** head clerk; ~ **de clinique** senior hospital lecturer; ~ **d'entreprise** company head; ~ **d'équipe** team leader; ~ **d'état** head of state; ~ **de famille** head of the family; ~ **de file** (*de parti etc*) leader; ~ **de gare** station master; ~ **d'orchestre** conductor (*BRIT*), leader (*US*); ~ **de rayon** department(al) supervisor; ~ **de service** departmental head.

chef-d'œuvre, *pl* **chefs-d'œuvre** [ʃɛdœvʀ(ə)] *nm* masterpiece.

chef-lieu, *pl* **chefs-lieux** [ʃɛfljø] *nm* county town.

cheftaine [ʃɛftɛn] *nf* (guide) captain.

cheik(h) [ʃɛk] *nm* sheik.

chemin [ʃəmɛ̃] *nm* path; (*itinéraire, direction, trajet*) way; **en** ~, ~ **faisant** on the way; ~ **de fer** railway (*BRIT*), railroad (*US*); **par** ~ **de fer** by rail; **les** ~**s de fer** the railways (*BRIT*), the railroad (*US*); ~ **de terre** dirt track.

cheminée [ʃəmine] *nf* chimney; (*à l'intérieur*) chimney piece, fireplace; (*de bateau*) funnel.

cheminement [ʃəminmɑ̃] *nm* progress; course.

cheminer [ʃəmine] *vi* to walk (along).

cheminot [ʃəmino] *nm* railwayman (*BRIT*), railroad worker (*US*).

chemise [ʃəmiz] *nf* shirt; (*dossier*) folder; ~ **de nuit** nightdress.

chemiserie [ʃəmizʀi] *nf* (gentlemen's) outfitters'.

chemisette [ʃəmizɛt] *nf* short-sleeved shirt.

chemisier [ʃəmizje] *nm* blouse.

chenal, aux [ʃənal, -o] *nm* channel.

chenapan [ʃənapɑ̃] *nm* (*garnement*) rascal; (*péj: vaurien*) rogue.

chêne [ʃɛn] *nm* oak (tree); (*bois*) oak.

chenet [ʃənɛ] *nm* fire-dog, andiron.

chenil [ʃənil] *nm* kennels *pl*.

chenille [ʃənij] *nf* (*ZOOL*) caterpillar; (*AUTO*) caterpillar track; **véhicule à** ~**s** tracked vehicle, caterpillar.

chenillette [ʃənijɛt] *nf* tracked vehicle.

cheptel [ʃɛptɛl] *nm* livestock.

chèque [ʃɛk] *nm* cheque (*BRIT*), check (*US*); **faire/toucher un** ~ to write/cash a cheque; **par** ~ by cheque; ~ **barré/sans provision** crossed (*BRIT*)/bad cheque; ~ **en blanc** blank cheque; ~ **au porteur** cheque to bearer; ~ **postal** post office cheque, ≈ giro cheque (*BRIT*); ~ **de voyage** traveller's cheque.

chèque-cadeau, *pl* **chèques-cadeaux** [ʃɛkkado] *nm* gift token.

chèque-repas, *pl* **chèques-repas** [ʃɛkʀəpa], **chèque-restaurant**, *pl* **chèques-restaurant** [ʃɛkʀɛstɔʀɑ̃] *nm* ≈ luncheon voucher.

chéquier [ʃekje] *nm* cheque book (*BRIT*), checkbook (*US*).

cher, ère [ʃɛʀ] *adj* (*aimé*) dear; (*coûteux*) expensive, dear ♦ *adv*: **coûter/payer** ~ to cost/pay a lot ♦ *nf*: **la bonne chère** good food; **cela coûte** ~ it's expensive, it costs a lot of money; **mon** ~, **ma chère** my dear.

chercher [ʃɛʀʃe] *vt* to look for; (*gloire etc*) to seek; (*INFORM*) to search; ~ **des ennuis/la bagarre** to be looking for trouble/a fight; **aller** ~ to go for, go and fetch; ~ **à faire** to try to do.

chercheur, euse [ʃɛʀʃœʀ, -øz] *nm/f* searcher, research worker; ~ **de** seeker of; hunter of; ~ **d'or** gold digger.

chère [ʃɛʀ] *adj f*, *nf voir* **cher**.

chèrement – chier

chèrement [ʃɛʀmã] adv dearly.
chéri, e [ʃeʀi] adj beloved, dear; **(mon)** ~ **darling**.
chérir [ʃeʀiʀ] vt to cherish.
cherté [ʃɛʀte] nf: **la** ~ **de la vie** the high cost of living.
chérubin [ʃeʀybɛ̃] nm cherub.
chétif, ive [ʃetif, -iv] adj puny, stunted.
cheval, aux [ʃəval, -o] nm horse; (AUTO): ~ **(vapeur) (CV)** horsepower no pl; **50 chevaux (au frein)** 50 brake horsepower, 50 b.h.p.; **10 chevaux (fiscaux)** 10 horsepower (for tax purposes); **faire du** ~ to ride; **à** ~ on horseback; **à** ~ **sur** astride, straddling; (fig) overlapping; ~ **d'arçons** vaulting horse; ~ **à bascule** rocking horse; ~ **de bataille** charger; (fig) hobby-horse; ~ **de course** race horse; **chevaux de bois** (des manèges) wooden (fairground) horses; (manège) merry-go-round.
chevaleresque [ʃəvalʀɛsk(ə)] adj chivalrous.
chevalerie [ʃəvalʀi] nf chivalry; knighthood.
chevalet [ʃəvalɛ] nm easel.
chevalier [ʃəvalje] nm knight; ~ **servant** escort.
chevalière [ʃəvaljɛʀ] nf signet ring.
chevalin, e [ʃəvalɛ̃, -in] adj of horses, equine; (péj) horsy; **boucherie** ~**e** horse-meat butcher's.
cheval-vapeur, pl **chevaux-vapeur** [ʃəvalvapœʀ, ʃəvo-] nm voir **cheval**.
chevauchée [ʃəvoʃe] nf ride; cavalcade.
chevauchement [ʃəvoʃmã] nm overlap.
chevaucher [ʃəvoʃe] vi (aussi: **se** ~) to overlap (each other) ♦ vt to be astride, straddle.
chevaux [ʃəvo] nmpl voir **cheval**.
chevelu, e [ʃəvly] adj with a good head of hair, hairy (péj).
chevelure [ʃəvlyʀ] nf hair no pl.
chevet [ʃəvɛ] nm: **au** ~ **de qn** at sb's bedside; **lampe de** ~ bedside lamp.
cheveu, x [ʃəvø] nm hair ♦ nmpl (chevelure) hair sg; **avoir les** ~**x courts/en brosse** to have short hair/a crew cut; **se faire couper les** ~**x** to get ou have one's hair cut; **tiré par les** ~**x** (histoire) far-fetched.
cheville [ʃəvij] nf (ANAT) ankle; (de bois) peg; (pour enfoncer une vis) plug; **être en** ~ **avec qn** to be in cahoots with sb; ~ **ouvrière** (fig) kingpin.
chèvre [ʃɛvʀ(ə)] nf (she-)goat; **ménager la** ~ **et le chou** to try to please everyone.
chevreau, x [ʃəvʀo] nm kid.
chèvrefeuille [ʃɛvʀəfœj] nm honeysuckle.
chevreuil [ʃəvʀœj] nm roe deer inv; (CULIN) venison.
chevron [ʃəvʀɔ̃] nm (poutre) rafter; (motif) chevron, v(-shape); à ~**s** chevron-patterned; (petits) herringbone.
chevronné, e [ʃəvʀɔne] adj seasoned, experienced.
chevrotant, e [ʃəvʀɔtã, -ãt] adj quavering.
chevroter [ʃəvʀɔte] vi (personne, voix) to quaver.
chevrotine [ʃəvʀɔtin] nf buckshot no pl.
chewing-gum [ʃwiŋgɔm] nm chewing gum.

═══════════════════════ *MOT-CLÉ*

chez [ʃe] prép **1** (à la demeure de) at; (: direction) to; ~ **qn** at/to sb's house ou place; ~ **moi** at home; (direction) home
2 (à l'entreprise de): **il travaille** ~ **Renault** he works for Renault, he works at Renault('s)
3 (+profession) at; (: direction) to; ~ **le boulanger/dentiste** at ou to the baker's/dentist's
4 (dans le caractère, l'œuvre de) in; ~ **les renards/Racine** in foxes/Racine; ~ **les Français** among the French; ~ **lui, c'est un devoir** for him, it's a duty
♦ nm inv: **mon** ~ **moi/ton** ~ **toi** etc my/your etc home ou place.

chez-soi [ʃeswa] nm inv home.
Chf. cent. abr (= chauffage central) c.h.
chiadé, e [ʃjade] adj (fam: fignolé, soigné) wicked.
chialer [ʃjale] vi (fam) to blubber; **arrête de** ~! stop blubbering!
chiant, e [ʃjã, -ãt] adj (fam!) bloody annoying (BRIT!), damn annoying; **qu'est-ce qu'il est** ~! he's such a bloody pain! (!).
chic [ʃik] adj inv chic, smart; (généreux) nice, decent ♦ nm stylishness; **avoir le** ~ **de** ou **pour** to have the knack of ou for; **de** ~ adv off the cuff; ~! great!, terrific!
chicane [ʃikan] nf (obstacle) zigzag; (querelle) squabble.
chicaner [ʃikane] vi (ergoter): ~ **sur** to quibble about.
chiche [ʃiʃ] adj (mesquin) niggardly, mean; (pauvre) meagre (BRIT), meager (US) ♦ excl (en réponse à un défi) you're on!; **tu n'es pas** ~ **de lui parler!** you wouldn't (dare) speak to her!
chichement [ʃiʃmã] adv (pauvrement) meagrely (BRIT), meagerly (US); (mesquinement) meanly.
chichi [ʃiʃi] nm (fam) fuss; **faire des** ~**s** to make a fuss.
chicorée [ʃikɔʀe] nf (café) chicory; (salade) endive; ~ **frisée** curly endive.
chicot [ʃiko] nm stump.
chien [ʃjɛ̃] nm dog; (de pistolet) hammer; **temps de** ~ rotten weather; **vie de** ~ dog's life; **couché en** ~ **de fusil** curled up; ~ **d'aveugle** guide dog; ~ **de chasse** gun dog; ~ **de garde** guard dog; ~ **policier** police dog; ~ **de race** pedigree dog; ~ **de traîneau** husky.
chiendent [ʃjɛ̃dã] nm couch grass.
chien-loup, pl **chiens-loups** [ʃjɛ̃lu] nm wolfhound.
chienne [ʃjɛn] nf (she-)dog, bitch.
chier [ʃje] vi (fam!) to crap (!), shit (!); **faire** ~

qn (*importuner*) to bug sb; (*causer des ennuis à*) to piss sb around (*!*); **se faire ~** (*s'ennuyer*) to be bored rigid.

chiffe [ʃif] *nf*: **il est mou comme une ~, c'est une ~ molle** he's spineless *ou* wet.

chiffon [ʃifɔ̃] *nm* (piece of) rag.

chiffonné, e [ʃifɔne] *adj* (*fatigué: visage*) worn-looking.

chiffonner [ʃifɔne] *vt* to crumple, crease; (*tracasser*) to concern.

chiffonnier [ʃifɔnje] *nm* ragman, rag-and-bone man; (*meuble*) chiffonier.

chiffrable [ʃifʀabl(ə)] *adj* numerable.

chiffre [ʃifʀ(ə)] *nm* (*représentant un nombre*) figure; numeral; (*montant, total*) total, sum; (*d'un code*) code, cipher; **~s romains/arabes** roman/arabic figures *ou* numerals; **en ~s ronds** in round figures; **écrire un nombre en ~s** to write a number in figures; **~ d'affaires (CA)** turnover; **~ de ventes** sales figures.

chiffrer [ʃifʀe] *vt* (*dépense*) to put a figure to, assess; (*message*) to (en)code, cipher ♦ *vi*: **~ à, se ~ à** to add up to.

chignole [ʃiɲɔl] *nf* drill.

chignon [ʃiɲɔ̃] *nm* chignon, bun.

chiite [ʃiit] *adj* Shiite ♦ *nm/f*: **C~** Shiite.

Chili [ʃili] *nm*: **le ~** Chile.

chilien, ne [ʃiljɛ̃, -ɛn] *adj* Chilean ♦ *nm/f*: **C~, ne** Chilean.

chimère [ʃimɛʀ] *nf* (wild) dream; pipe dream, idle fancy.

chimérique [ʃimeʀik] *adj* (*utopique*) fanciful.

chimie [ʃimi] *nf* chemistry.

chimio [ʃimjɔ], **chimiothérapie** [ʃimjɔteʀapi] *nf* chemotherapy.

chimique [ʃimik] *adj* chemical; **produits ~s** chemicals.

chimiste [ʃimist(ə)] *nm/f* chemist.

chimpanzé [ʃɛ̃pɑ̃ze] *nm* chimpanzee.

chinchilla [ʃɛ̃ʃila] *nm* chinchilla.

Chine [ʃin] *nf*: **la ~** China; **la ~ libre, la république de ~** the Republic of China, Nationalist China (*Taiwan*).

chine [ʃin] *nm* rice paper; (*porcelaine*) china (vase).

chiné, e [ʃine] *adj* flecked.

chinois, e [ʃinwa, -waz] *adj* Chinese; (*fig: péj*) pernickety, fussy ♦ *nm* (*LING*) Chinese ♦ *nm/f*: **C~, e** Chinese.

chinoiserie(s) [ʃinwazʀi] *nf(pl)* (*péj*) red tape, fuss.

chiot [ʃjo] *nm* pup(py).

chiper [ʃipe] *vt* (*fam*) to pinch.

chipie [ʃipi] *nf* shrew.

chipolata [ʃipɔlata] *nf* chipolata.

chipoter [ʃipɔte] *vi* (*manger*) to nibble; (*ergoter*) to quibble, haggle.

chips [ʃips] *nfpl* (*aussi*: **pommes ~**) crisps (*BRIT*), (potato) chips (*US*).

chique [ʃik] *nf* quid, chew.

chiquenaude [ʃiknod] *nf* flick, flip.

chiquer [ʃike] *vi* to chew tobacco.

chiromancie [kiʀɔmɑ̃si] *nf* palmistry.

chiromancien, ne [kiʀɔmɑ̃sjɛ̃, -ɛn] *nm/f* palmist.

chiropracteur [kiʀɔpʀaktœʀ] *nm*, **chiropraticien, ne** [kiʀɔpʀatisjɛ̃, -ɛn] *nm/f* chiropractor.

chirurgical, e, aux [ʃiʀyʀʒikal, -o] *adj* surgical.

chirurgie [ʃiʀyʀʒi] *nf* surgery; **~ esthétique** cosmetic *ou* plastic surgery.

chirurgien [ʃiʀyʀʒjɛ̃] *nm* surgeon; **~ dentiste** dental surgeon.

chiure [ʃjyʀ] *nf*: **~s de mouche** fly specks.

ch.-l. *abr* = **chef-lieu**.

chlore [klɔʀ] *nm* chlorine.

chloroforme [klɔʀɔfɔʀm(ə)] *nm* chloroform.

chlorophylle [klɔʀɔfil] *nf* chlorophyll.

chlorure [klɔʀyʀ] *nm* chloride.

choc [ʃɔk] *nm* impact; shock; crash; (*moral*) shock; (*affrontement*) clash ♦ *adj*: **prix ~** amazing *ou* incredible price/prices; **de ~** (*troupe, traitement*) shock *cpd*; (*patron etc*) high-powered; **~ opératoire/nerveux** postoperative/nervous shock; **~ en retour** return shock; (*fig*) backlash.

chocolat [ʃɔkɔla] *nm* chocolate; (*boisson*) (hot) chocolate; **~ à cuire** cooking chocolate; **~ au lait** milk chocolate; **~ en poudre** drinking chocolate.

chocolaté, e [ʃɔkɔlate] *adj* chocolate *cpd*, chocolate-flavoured.

chocolaterie [ʃɔkɔlatʀi] *nf* (*fabrique*) chocolate factory.

chocolatier, ière [ʃɔkɔlatje, -jɛʀ] *nm/f* chocolate maker.

chœur [kœʀ] *nm* (*chorale*) choir; (*OPÉRA, THÉÂT*) chorus; (*ARCHIT*) choir, chancel; **en ~** in chorus.

choir [ʃwaʀ] *vi* to fall.

choisi, e [ʃwazi] *adj* (*de premier choix*) carefully chosen; select; **textes ~s** selected writings.

choisir [ʃwaziʀ] *vt* to choose; (*entre plusieurs*) to choose, select; **~ de faire qch** to choose *ou* opt to do sth.

choix [ʃwa] *nm* choice; selection; **avoir le ~** to have the choice; **je n'avais pas le ~** I had no choice; **de premier ~** (*COMM*) class *ou* grade one; **de ~** choice *cpd*, selected; **au ~** as you wish *ou* prefer; **de mon/son ~** of my/his *ou* her choosing.

choléra [kɔleʀa] *nm* cholera.

cholestérol [kɔlesteʀɔl] *nm* cholesterol.

chômage [ʃomaʒ] *nm* unemployment; **mettre au ~** to make redundant, put out of work; **être au ~** to be unemployed *ou* out of work; **~ partiel** short-time working; **~ structurel** structural unemployment; **~ technique** lay-offs *pl*.

chômer [ʃome] *vi* to be unemployed, be idle; **jour chômé** public holiday.

chômeur, euse [ʃomœʀ, -øz] *nm/f* unemployed person, person out of work.

chope [ʃɔp] nf tankard.

choquant, e [ʃɔkɑ̃, -ɑ̃t] adj shocking.

choquer [ʃɔke] vt (offenser) to shock; (commotionner) to shake (up).

choral, e [kɔʀal] adj choral ♦ nf choral society, choir.

chorégraphe [kɔʀegʀaf] nmf choreographer.

chorégraphie [kɔʀegʀafi] nf choreography.

choriste [kɔʀist(ə)] nmf choir member; (OPÉRA) chorus member.

chorus [kɔʀys] nm: **faire ~ (avec)** to voice one's agreement (with).

chose [ʃoz] nf thing ♦ nm (fam: machin) thingamajig ♦ adj inv: **être/se sentir tout ~** (bizarre) to be/feel a bit odd; (malade) to be/feel out of sorts; **dire bien des ~s à qn** to give sb's regards to sb; **parler de ~(s) et d'autre(s)** to talk about one thing and another; **c'est peu de ~** it's nothing much.

chou, x [ʃu] nm cabbage ♦ adj inv cute; **mon petit ~** (my) sweetheart; **faire ~ blanc** to draw a blank; **feuille de ~** (fig: journal) rag; **~ à la crème** cream bun (made of choux pastry); **~ de Bruxelles** Brussels sprout.

choucas [ʃuka] nm jackdaw.

chouchou, te [ʃuʃu, -ut] nmf (SCOL) teacher's pet.

chouchouter [ʃuʃute] vt to pet.

choucroute [ʃukʀut] nf sauerkraut; **~ garnie** sauerkraut with cooked meats and potatoes.

chouette [ʃwɛt] nf owl ♦ adj (fam) great, smashing.

chou-fleur, pl choux-fleurs [ʃuflœʀ] nm cauliflower.

chou-rave, pl choux-raves [ʃuʀav] nm kohlrabi.

choyer [ʃwaje] vt to cherish; to pamper.

CHR sigle m = Centre hospitalier régional.

chrétien, ne [kʀetjɛ̃, -ɛn] adj, nmf Christian.

chrétiennement [kʀetjɛnmɑ̃] adv in a Christian way ou spirit.

chrétienté [kʀetjɛ̃te] nf Christendom.

Christ [kʀist] nm: **le ~** Christ; **c~** (crucifix etc) figure of Christ; **Jésus ~** Jesus Christ.

christianiser [kʀistjanize] vt to convert to Christianity.

christianisme [kʀistjanism(ə)] nm Christianity.

Christmas [kʀistmas] nf: **(l'île) ~** Christmas Island.

chromatique [kʀɔmatik] adj chromatic.

chrome [kʀom] nm chromium; (revêtement) chrome, chromium.

chromé, e [kʀome] adj chrome-plated, chromium-plated.

chromosome [kʀɔmozom] nm chromosome.

chronique [kʀɔnik] adj chronic ♦ nf (de journal) column, page; (historique) chronicle; (RADIO, TV): **la ~ sportive/théâtrale** the sports/theatre review; **la ~ locale** local news and gossip.

chroniqueur [kʀɔnikœʀ] nm columnist; chronicler.

chrono [kʀɔno] nm (fam) = chronomètre.

chronologie [kʀɔnɔlɔʒi] nf chronology.

chronologique [kʀɔnɔlɔʒik] adj chronological.

chronologiquement [kʀɔnɔlɔʒikmɑ̃] adv chronologically.

chronomètre [kʀɔnɔmɛtʀ(ə)] nm stopwatch.

chronométrer [kʀɔnɔmetʀe] vt to time.

chronométreur [kʀɔnɔmetʀœʀ] nm timekeeper.

chrysalide [kʀizalid] nf chrysalis.

chrysanthème [kʀizɑ̃tɛm] nm chrysanthemum.

CHU sigle m (= Centre hospitalo-universitaire) ≈ (teaching) hospital.

chu, e [ʃy] pp de **choir**.

chuchotement [ʃyʃɔtmɑ̃] nm whisper.

chuchoter [ʃyʃɔte] vt, vi to whisper.

chuintement [ʃɥɛ̃tmɑ̃] nm hiss.

chuinter [ʃɥɛ̃te] vi to hiss.

chut excl [ʃyt] sh! ♦ vb [ʃy] voir **choir**.

chute [ʃyt] nf fall; (de bois, papier: déchet) scrap; **la ~ des cheveux** hair loss; **faire une ~ (de 10 m)** to fall (10 m); **~s de pluie/neige** rain/snowfalls; **~ (d'eau)** waterfall; **~ du jour** nightfall; **~ libre** free fall; **~ des reins** small of the back.

Chypre [ʃipʀ] nm: **le ~** Cyprus.

chypriote [ʃipʀiɔt] adj, nmf = **cypriote**.

-ci, ci- [si] adv voir **par, ci-contre, ci-joint** etc ♦ dét: **ce garçon-ci/-là** this/that boy; **ces femmes-ci/-là** these/those women.

CIA sigle f CIA.

cial abr = **commercial**.

ciao [tʃao] excl (fam) (bye-)bye.

ci-après [siapʀɛ] adv hereafter.

cibiste [sibist(ə)] nm CB enthusiast.

cible [sibl(ə)] nf target.

cibler [sible] vt to target.

ciboire [sibwaʀ] nm ciborium (vessel).

ciboule [sibul] nf (large) chive.

ciboulette [sibulɛt] nf (small) chive.

ciboulot [sibulo] nm (fam) head, nut; **il n'a rien dans le ~** he's got nothing between his ears.

cicatrice [sikatʀis] nf scar.

cicatriser [sikatʀize] vt to heal; **se ~** to heal (up), form a scar.

ci-contre [sikɔ̃tʀ(ə)] adv opposite.

CICR sigle m (= Comité international de la Croix-Rouge) ICRC.

ci-dessous [sidəsu] adv below.

ci-dessus [sidəsy] adv above.

ci-devant [sidəvɑ̃] nmf inv aristocrat who lost his/her title in the French Revolution.

CIDEX sigle m (= Courrier individuel à distribution exceptionnelle) system which groups letter boxes in country areas, rather than each house having its letter box at its front door.

CIDJ sigle m (= Centre d'information et de documentation de la jeunesse) careers advisory *service.*

cidre [sidʀ(ə)] *nm* cider.

cidrerie [sidʀəʀi] *nf* cider factory.

CIDUNATI [sidynati] *sigle m* (= *Comité interprofessionnel de défense de l'union nationale des artisans et travailleurs indépendants*) union of self-employed craftsmen.

Cie *abr* (= *compagnie*) Co.

ciel [sjɛl] *nm* sky; (*REL*) heaven; **~s** *nmpl* (*PEINTURE etc*) skies; **cieux** *nmpl* sky *sg*, skies; (*REL*) heaven *sg*; **à ~ ouvert** open-air; (*mine*) opencast; **tomber du ~** (*arriver à l'improviste*) to appear out of the blue; (*être stupéfait*) to be unable to believe one's eyes; **C~!** good heavens!; **~ de lit** canopy.

cierge [sjɛʀʒ(ə)] *nm* candle; **~ pascal** Easter candle.

cieux [sjø] *nmpl voir* **ciel**.

cigale [sigal] *nf* cicada.

cigare [sigaʀ] *nm* cigar.

cigarette [sigaʀɛt] *nf* cigarette; **~ (à) bout filtre** filter cigarette.

ci-gît [siʒi] *adv* here lies.

cigogne [sigɔɲ] *nf* stork.

ciguë [sigy] *nf* hemlock.

ci-inclus, e [siɛkly, -yz] *adj, adv* enclosed.

ci-joint, e [siʒwɛ̃, -ɛ̃t] *adj, adv* enclosed; **veuillez trouver ~** please find enclosed.

cil [sil] *nm* (eye)lash.

ciller [sije] *vi* to blink.

cimaise [simɛz] *nf* picture rail.

cime [sim] *nf* top; (*montagne*) peak.

ciment [simɑ̃] *nm* cement; **~ armé** reinforced concrete.

cimenter [simɑ̃te] *vt* to cement.

cimenterie [simɑ̃tʀi] *nf* cement works *sg*.

cimetière [simtjɛʀ] *nm* cemetery; (*d'église*) churchyard; **~ de voitures** scrapyard.

cinéaste [sineast(ə)] *nm/f* film-maker.

ciné-club [sineklœb] *nm* film club; film society.

cinéma [sinema] *nm* cinema; **aller au ~** to go to the cinema *ou* pictures *ou* movies; **~ d'animation** cartoon (film).

cinémascope [sinemaskɔp] *nm* ® Cinemascope ®.

cinémathèque [sinematɛk] *nf* film archives *pl ou* library.

cinématographie [sinematɔgʀafi] *nf* cinematography.

cinématographique [sinematɔgʀafik] *adj* film *cpd*, cinema *cpd*.

cinéphile [sinefil] *nm/f* film buff.

cinérama [sinerama] *nm* ®: **en ~** in Cinerama ®.

cinétique [sinetik] *adj* kinetic.

cing(h)alais, e [sɛ̃galɛ, -ɛz] *adj* Sin(g)halese.

cinglant, e [sɛ̃glɑ̃, -ɑ̃t] *adj* (*propos, ironie*) scathing, biting; (*échec*) crushing.

cinglé, e [sɛ̃gle] *adj* (*fam*) crazy.

cingler [sɛ̃gle] *vt* to lash; (*fig*) to sting ♦ *vi* (*NAVIG*): **~ vers** to make *ou* head for.

cinq [sɛ̃k] *num* five.

cinquantaine [sɛ̃kɑ̃tɛn] *nf*: **une ~ (de)** about fifty; **avoir la ~ (âge)** to be around fifty.

cinquante [sɛ̃kɑ̃t] *num* fifty.

cinquantenaire [sɛ̃kɑ̃tnɛʀ] *adj, nm/f* fifty-year-old.

cinquantième [sɛ̃kɑ̃tjɛm] *num* fiftieth.

cinquième [sɛ̃kjɛm] *num* fifth.

cinquièmement [sɛ̃kjɛmmɑ̃] *adv* fifthly.

cintre [sɛ̃tʀ(ə)] *nm* coat-hanger; (*ARCHIT*) arch; **plein ~** semicircular arch.

cintré, e [sɛ̃tʀe] *adj* curved; (*chemise*) fitted, slim-fitting.

CIO *sigle m* (= *Comité international olympique*) IOC (= *International Olympic Committee*).

cirage [siʀaʒ] *nm* (shoe) polish.

circoncis, e [siʀkɔ̃si, -iz] *adj* circumcized.

circoncision [siʀkɔ̃sizjɔ̃] *nf* circumcision.

circonférence [siʀkɔ̃feʀɑ̃s] *nf* circumference.

circonflexe [siʀkɔ̃flɛks(ə)] *adj*: **accent ~** circumflex accent.

circonlocution [siʀkɔ̃lɔkysjɔ̃] *nf* circumlocution.

circonscription [siʀkɔ̃skʀipsjɔ̃] *nf* district; **~ électorale** (*d'un député*) constituency; **~ militaire** military area.

circonscrire [siʀkɔ̃skʀiʀ] *vt* to define, delimit; (*incendie*) to contain; (*propriété*) to mark out; (*sujet*) to define.

circonspect, e [siʀkɔ̃spɛkt] *adj* circumspect, cautious.

circonspection [siʀkɔ̃spɛksjɔ̃] *nf* circumspection, caution.

circonstance [siʀkɔ̃stɑ̃s] *nf* circumstance; (*occasion*) occasion; **œuvre de ~** occasional work; **air de ~** fitting air; **tête de ~** appropriate demeanour (*BRIT*) *ou* demeanor (*US*); **~s atténuantes** mitigating circumstances.

circonstancié, e [siʀkɔ̃stɑ̃sje] *adj* detailed.

circonstanciel, le [siʀkɔ̃stɑ̃sjɛl] *adj*: **complément/proposition ~(le)** adverbial phrase/clause.

circonvenir [siʀkɔ̃vniʀ] *vt* to circumvent.

circonvolutions [siʀkɔ̃vɔlysjɔ̃] *nfpl* twists, convolutions.

circuit [siʀkɥi] *nm* (*trajet*) tour, (round) trip; (*ÉLEC, TECH*) circuit; **~ automobile** motor circuit; **~ de distribution** distribution network; **~ fermé** closed circuit; **~ intégré** integrated circuit.

circulaire [siʀkylɛʀ] *adj, nf* circular.

circulation [siʀkylɑsjɔ̃] *nf* circulation; (*AUTO*): **la ~** (the) traffic; **bonne/mauvaise ~** good/bad circulation; **mettre en ~** to put into circulation.

circulatoire [siʀkylatwaʀ] *adj*: **avoir des troubles ~s** to have problems with one's circulation.

circuler [siʀkyle] *vi* to drive (along); to walk along; (*train etc*) to run; (*sang, devises*) to circulate; **faire ~** (*nouvelle*) to spread (about), circulate; (*badauds*) to move on.

cire [siʀ] *nf* wax; ~ **à cacheter** sealing wax.

ciré [siʀe] *nm* oilskin.

cirer [siʀe] *vt* to wax, polish.

cireur [siʀœʀ] *nm* shoeshine-boy.

cireuse [siʀøz] *nf* floor polisher.

cireux, euse [siʀø, -øz] *adj* (*fig: teint*) sallow, waxen.

cirque [siʀk(ə)] *nm* circus; (*arène*) amphitheatre (*BRIT*), amphitheater (*US*); (*GÉO*) cirque; (*fig: désordre*) chaos, bedlam; (*: chichis*) carry-on.

cirrhose [siʀoz] *nf*: ~ **du foie** cirrhosis of the liver.

cisailler [sizaje] *vt* to clip.

cisaille(s) [sizaj] *nf(pl)* (gardening) shears *pl*.

ciseau, x [sizo] *nm*: ~ **(à bois)** chisel ♦ *nmpl* (pair of) scissors; **sauter en ~x** to do a scissors jump; ~ **à froid** cold chisel.

ciseler [sizle] *vt* to chisel, carve.

ciselure [sizlyʀ] *nf* engraving; (*bois*) carving.

Cisjordanie [sisʒɔʀdani] *nf*: **la** ~ the West Bank (of Jordan).

citadelle [sitadɛl] *nf* citadel.

citadin, e [sitadɛ̃, -in] *nm/f* city dweller ♦ *adj* town *cpd*, city *cpd*, urban.

citation [sitasjɔ̃] *nf* (*d'auteur*) quotation; (*JUR*) summons *sg*; (*MIL: récompense*) mention.

cité [site] *nf* town; (*plus grande*) city; ~ **ouvrière** (workers') housing estate; ~ **universitaire** students' residences *pl*.

cité-dortoir, *pl* **cités-dortoirs** [sitedɔʀtwaʀ] *nf* dormitory town.

cité-jardin, *pl* **cités-jardins** [siteʒaʀdɛ̃] *nf* garden city.

citer [site] *vt* (*un auteur*) to quote (from); (*nommer*) to name; (*JUR*) to summon; ~ **(en exemple)** (*personne*) to hold up (as an example); **je ne veux** ~ **personne** I don't want to name names.

citerne [sitɛʀn(ə)] *nf* tank.

cithare [sitaʀ] *nf* zither.

citoyen, ne [sitwajɛ̃, -ɛn] *nm/f* citizen.

citoyenneté [sitwajɛnte] *nf* citizenship.

citrique [sitʀik] *adj*: **acide** ~ citric acid.

citron [sitʀɔ̃] *nm* lemon; ~ **pressé** (fresh) lemon juice; ~ **vert** lime.

citronnade [sitʀɔnad] *nf* lemonade.

citronné, e [sitʀɔne] *adj* (*boisson*) lemonflavoured (*BRIT*) ou -flavored (*US*); (*eau de toilette*) lemon-scented.

citronnelle [sitʀɔnɛl] *nf* citronella.

citronnier [sitʀɔnje] *nm* lemon tree.

citrouille [sitʀuj] *nf* pumpkin.

cive(s) [siv] *nf(pl)* (*BOT*) chive(s); (*CULIN*) chives.

civet [sivɛ] *nm* stew; ~ **de lièvre** jugged hare.

civette [sivɛt] *nf* (*BOT*) chives *pl*; (*ZOOL*) civet (cat).

civière [sivjɛʀ] *nf* stretcher.

civil, e [sivil] *adj* (*JUR, ADMIN, poli*) civil; (*non militaire*) civilian ♦ *nm* civilian; **en** ~ in civilian clothes; **dans le** ~ in civilian life.

civilement [sivilmɑ̃] *adv* (*poliment*) civilly; **se marier** ~ to have a civil wedding.

civilisation [sivilizasjɔ̃] *nf* civilization.

civilisé, e [sivilize] *adj* civilized.

civiliser [sivilize] *vt* to civilize.

civilité [sivilite] *nf* civility; **présenter ses** ~**s** to present one's compliments.

civique [sivik] *adj* civic; **instruction** ~ (*SCOL*) civics *sg*.

civisme [sivism(ə)] *nm* public-spiritedness.

cl. *abr* (= *centilitre*) cl.

clafoutis [klafuti] *nm* batter pudding (*containing fruit*).

claie [klɛ] *nf* grid, riddle.

clair, e [klɛʀ] *adj* light; (*chambre*) light, bright; (*eau, son, fig*) clear ♦ *adv*: **voir** ~ to see clearly ♦ *nm*: **mettre au** ~ (*notes etc*) to tidy up; **tirer qch au** ~ to clear sth up, clarify sth; **bleu** ~ light blue; **pour être** ~ so as to make it plain; **y voir** ~ (*comprendre*) to understand, see; **le plus** ~ **de son temps/argent** the better part of his time/money; **en** ~ (*non codé*) in clear; ~ **de lune** moonlight.

claire [klɛʀ] *nf*: **(huître de)** ~ fattened oyster.

clairement [klɛʀmɑ̃] *adv* clearly.

claire-voie [klɛʀvwa]: **à** ~ *adj* letting the light through; openwork *cpd*.

clairière [klɛʀjɛʀ] *nf* clearing.

clair-obscur, *pl* **clairs-obscurs** [klɛʀɔpskyʀ] *nm* half-light; (*fig*) uncertainty.

clairon [klɛʀɔ̃] *nm* bugle.

claironner [klɛʀɔne] *vt* (*fig*) to trumpet, shout from the rooftops.

clairsemé, e [klɛʀsəme] *adj* sparse.

clairvoyance [klɛʀvwajɑ̃s] *nf* clearsightedness.

clairvoyant, e [klɛʀvwajɑ̃, -ɑ̃t] *adj* perceptive, clear-sighted.

clam [klam] *nm* (*ZOOL*) clam.

clamer [klame] *vt* to proclaim.

clameur [klamœʀ] *nf* clamour (*BRIT*), clamor (*US*).

clan [klɑ̃] *nm* clan.

clandestin, e [klɑ̃dɛstɛ̃, -in] *adj* clandestine, covert; (*POL*) underground, clandestine; **passager** ~ stowaway.

clandestinement [klɑ̃dɛstinmɑ̃] *adv* secretly; **s'embarquer** ~ to stow away.

clandestinité [klɑ̃dɛstinite] *nf*: **dans la** ~ (*en secret*) under cover; (*en se cachant: vivre*) underground; **entrer dans la** ~ to go underground.

clapet [klapɛ] *nm* (*TECH*) valve.

clapier [klapje] *nm* (rabbit) hutch.

clapotement [klapɔtmɑ̃] *nm* lap(ping).

clapoter [klapɔte] *vi* to lap.

clapotis [klapɔti] *nm* lap(ping).

claquage [klakaʒ] *nm* pulled *ou* strained muscle.

claque [klak] *nf* (*gifle*) slap; (*THÉÂT*) claque ♦ *nm* (*chapeau*) opera hat.

claquement [klakmɑ̃] *nm* (*de porte: bruit ré-pété*) banging; (: *bruit isolé*) slam.

claquemurer [klakmyʀe]: **se** ~ *vi* to shut o.s. away, closet o.s.

claquer [klake] *vi* (*drapeau*) to flap; (*porte*) to bang, slam; (*coup de feu*) to ring out ♦ *vt* (*porte*) to slam, bang; (*doigts*) to snap; **elle claquait des dents** her teeth were chattering; **se** ~ **un muscle** to pull *ou* strain a muscle.

claquettes [klakɛt] *nfpl* tap-dancing *sg*.

clarification [klaʀifikɑsjɔ̃] *nf* (*fig*) clarification.

clarifier [klaʀifje] *vt* (*fig*) to clarify.

clarinette [klaʀinɛt] *nf* clarinet.

clarinettiste [klaʀinetist(ə)] *nm/f* clarinettist.

clarté [klaʀte] *nf* lightness; brightness; (*d'un son, de l'eau*) clearness; (*d'une explication*) clarity.

classe [klɑs] *nf* class; (*SCOL: local*) class(room); (: *leçon*) class; (: *élèves*) class, form; **1ère/2ème** ~ 1st/2nd class; **un (soldat de) deuxième** ~ (*MIL: armée de terre*) ≈ private (soldier); (: *armée de l'air*) ≈ aircraftman (*BRIT*), ≈ airman basic (*US*); **de** ~ luxury *cpd*; **faire ses** ~**s** (*MIL*) to do one's (recruit's) training; **faire la** ~ (*SCOL*) to be a *ou* the teacher; to teach; **aller en** ~ to go to school; **aller en** ~ **verte/de neige/de mer** to go to the countryside/skiing/to the seaside with the school; ~ **ouvrière** working class; ~ **préparatoire** *class which prepares students for the Grandes Écoles entry exams*; ~ **sociale** social class; ~ **touriste** economy class.

Classes préparatoires *is the term given to the two years of intensive study required to sit the competitive entry examinations to the* grandes écoles. *They are extremely demanding post-*baccalauréat *courses, usually taken in a* lycée. *Schools which provide such classes are more highly regarded than those which do not.*

---

classement [klɑsmɑ̃] *nm* classifying; filing; grading; closing; (*rang: SCOL*) place; (: *SPORT*) placing; (*liste: SCOL*) class list (in order of merit); (: *SPORT*) placings *pl*; **premier au** ~ **général** (*SPORT*) first overall.

classer [klɑse] *vt* (*idées, livres*) to classify; (*papiers*) to file; (*candidat, concurrent*) to grade; (*personne: juger, péj*) to rate; (*JUR: affaire*) to close; **se** ~ **premier/dernier** to come first/last; (*SPORT*) to finish first/last.

classeur [klɑsœʀ] *nm* (*cahier*) file; (*meuble*) filing cabinet; ~ **à feuillets mobiles** ring binder.

classification [klasifikɑsjɔ̃] *nf* classification.

classifier [klasifje] *vt* to classify.

classique [klasik] *adj* classical; (*sobre: coupe etc*) classic(al); (*habituel*) standard, classic ♦ *nm* classic; classical author; **études** ~**s** classical studies, classics.

claudication [klodikɑsjɔ̃] *nf* limp.

clause [kloz] *nf* clause.

claustrer [klostʀe] *vt* to confine.

claustrophobie [klostʀofɔbi] *nf* claustrophobia.

clavecin [klavsɛ̃] *nm* harpsichord.

claveciniste [klavsinist(ə)] *nm/f* harpsichordist.

clavicule [klavikyl] *nf* clavicle, collarbone.

clavier [klavje] *nm* keyboard.

clé *ou* **clef** [kle] *nf* key; (*MUS*) clef; (*de mécanicien*) spanner (*BRIT*), wrench (*US*) ♦ *adj*: **problème/position** ~ key problem/position; **mettre sous** ~ to place under lock and key; **prendre la** ~ **des champs** to run away, make off; **prix** ~**s en main** (*d'une voiture*) on-the-road price; (*d'un appartement*) price with immediate entry; ~ **de sol/de fa/d'ut** treble/bass/alto clef; **livre/film** etc **à** ~ *book/film etc in which real people are depicted under fictitious names*; **à la** ~ (*à la fin*) at the end of it all; ~ **anglaise** = ~ **à molette**; ~ **de contact** ignition key; ~ **à molette** adjustable spanner (*BRIT*) *ou* wrench, monkey wrench; ~ **de voûte** keystone.

clématite [klematit] *nf* clematis.

clémence [klemɑ̃s] *nf* mildness; leniency.

clément, e [klemɑ̃, -ɑ̃t] *adj* (*temps*) mild; (*indulgent*) lenient.

clémentine [klemɑ̃tin] *nf* (*BOT*) clementine.

clenche [klɑ̃ʃ] *nf* latch.

cleptomane [klɛptɔman] *nm/f* = **kleptomane**.

clerc [klɛʀ] *nm*: ~ **de notaire** *ou* **d'avoué** lawyer's clerk.

clergé [klɛʀʒe] *nm* clergy.

clérical, e, aux [kleʀikal, -o] *adj* clerical.

cliché [kliʃe] *nm* (*PHOTO*) negative; print; (*TYPO*) (printing) plate; (*LING*) cliché.

client, e [klijɑ̃, -ɑ̃t] *nm/f* (*acheteur*) customer, client; (*d'hôtel*) guest, patron; (*du docteur*) patient; (*de l'avocat*) client.

clientèle [klijɑ̃tɛl] *nf* (*du magasin*) customers *pl*, clientèle; (*du docteur, de l'avocat*) practice; **accorder sa** ~ **à** to give one's custom to; **retirer sa** ~ **à** to take one's business away from.

cligner [kliɲe] *vi*: ~ **des yeux** to blink (one's eyes); ~ **de l'œil** to wink.

clignotant [kliɲɔtɑ̃] *nm* (*AUTO*) indicator.

clignoter [kliɲɔte] *vi* (*étoiles etc*) to twinkle; (*lumière: à intervalles réguliers*) to flash; (: *vaciller*) to flicker; (*yeux*) to blink.

climat [klima] *nm* climate.

climatique [klimatik] *adj* climatic.

climatisation [klimatizɑsjɔ̃] *nf* air conditioning.

climatisé, e [klimatize] *adj* air-conditioned.

climatiseur [klimatizœʀ] *nm* air conditioner.

clin d'œil [klɛ̃dœj] *nm* wink; **en un** ~ in a flash.

clinique [klinik] *adj* clinical ♦ *nf* nursing home, (private) clinic.

clinquant, e [klɛ̃kɑ̃, -ɑ̃t] *adj* flashy.

clip [klip] *nm* (*pince*) clip; (*vidéo*) pop (*ou* promotional) video.

clique [klik] *nf* (*péj: bande*) clique, set; **prendre ses ~s et ses claques** to pack one's bags.

cliqueter [klikte] *vi* to clash; (*ferraille, clefs, monnaie*) to jangle, jingle; (*verres*) to chink.

cliquetis [klikti] *nm* jangle, jingle; chink.

clitoris [klitɔris] *nm* clitoris.

clivage [klivaʒ] *nm* cleavage; (*fig*) rift, split.

cloaque [klɔak] *nm* (*fig*) cesspit.

clochard, e [klɔʃaʀ, -aʀd(ə)] *nm/f* tramp.

cloche [klɔʃ] *nf* (*d'église*) bell; (*fam*) clot; (*chapeau*) cloche (hat); **~ à fromage** cheese-cover.

cloche-pied [klɔʃpje]: **à ~** *adv* on one leg, hopping (along).

clocher [klɔʃe] *nm* church tower; (*en pointe*) steeple ♦ *vi* (*fam*) to be *ou* go wrong; **de ~** (*péj*) parochial.

clocheton [klɔʃtɔ̃] *nm* pinnacle.

clochette [klɔʃɛt] *nf* bell.

clodo [klɔdo] *nm* (*fam: = clochard*) tramp.

cloison [klwazɔ̃] *nf* partition (wall); **~ étanche** (*fig*) impenetrable barrier, brick wall (*fig*).

cloisonner [klwazɔne] *vt* to partition (off); to divide up; (*fig*) to compartmentalize.

cloître [klwatʀ(ə)] *nm* cloister.

cloîtrer [klwatʀe] *vt*: **se ~** to shut o.s. up *ou* away; (*REL*) to enter a convent *ou* monastery.

clone [klɔn] *nm* clone.

clope [klɔp] *nm ou f* (*fam*) fag (*BRIT*), cigarette.

clopin-clopant [klɔpɛ̃klɔpɑ̃] *adv* hobbling along; (*fig*) so-so.

clopiner [klɔpine] *vi* to hobble along.

cloporte [klɔpɔʀt(ə)] *nm* woodlouse (*pl* -lice).

cloque [klɔk] *nf* blister.

cloqué, e [klɔke] *adj*: **étoffe ~e** seersucker.

cloquer [klɔke] *vi* (*peau, peinture*) to blister.

clore [klɔʀ] *vt* to close; **~ une session** (*INFORM*) to log out.

clos, e [klo, -oz] *pp de* **clore** ♦ *adj voir* **maison, huis, vase** ♦ *nm* (enclosed) field.

clôt [klo] *vb voir* **clore**.

clôture [klotyʀ] *nf* closure, closing; (*barrière*) enclosure, fence.

clôturer [klotyʀe] *vt* (*terrain*) to enclose, close off; (*festival, débats*) to close.

clou [klu] *nm* nail; (*MÉD*) boil; **~s** *nmpl* = **passage clouté; pneus à ~s** studded tyres; **le ~ du spectacle** the highlight of the show; **~ de girofle** clove.

clouer [klue] *vt* to nail down (*ou* up); (*fig*): **~ sur/contre** to pin to/against.

clouté, e [klute] *adj* studded.

clown [klun] *nm* clown; **faire le ~** (*fig*) to clown (about), play the fool.

clownerie [klunʀi] *nf* clowning *no pl*; **faire des ~s** to clown around.

CLT *sigle f* = Compagnie Luxembourgeoise de Télévision.

club [klœb] *nm* club.

CM *sigle f* = **chambre des métiers** ♦ *sigle m* = **conseil municipal;** (*SCOL*) = **cours moyen**.

cm. *abr* (= centimètre) cm.

CNAT *sigle f* (= Commission nationale d'aménagement du territoire) national development agency.

CNC *sigle m* (= Conseil national de la consommation) national consumers' council.

CNCL *sigle f* (= Commission nationale de la communication et des libertés) independent broadcasting authority.

CNDP *sigle m* = Centre national de documentation pédagogique.

CNE *sigle f* (= Caisse nationale d'épargne) national savings bank.

CNEC *sigle m* (= Centre national de l'enseignement par correspondance) ≈ Open University.

CNIL *sigle f* (= Commission nationale de l'informatique et des libertés) board which enforces law on data protection.

CNIT *sigle m* (= Centre national des industries et des techniques) exhibition centre in Paris.

CNJA *sigle m* (= Centre national des jeunes agriculteurs) farmers' union.

CNL *sigle f* (= Confédération nationale du logement) consumer group for housing.

CNP *sigle f* (= Caisse nationale de prévoyance) savings bank.

CNPF *sigle m* (= Conseil national du patronat français) national council of French employers.

CNRS *sigle m* = Centre national de la recherche scientifique.

c/o *abr* (= care of) c/o.

coagulant [kɔagylɑ̃] *nm* (*MÉD*) coagulant.

coaguler [kɔagyle] *vi, vt, se ~ vi* to coagulate.

coaliser [kɔalize]: **se ~** *vi* to unite, join forces.

coalition [kɔalisjɔ̃] *nf* coalition.

coasser [kɔase] *vi* to croak.

coauteur [kɔotœʀ] *nm* co-author.

coaxial, e, aux [kɔaksjal, -o] *adj* coaxial.

cobalt [kɔbalt] *nm* cobalt.

cobaye [kɔbaj] *nm* guinea-pig.

COBOL, Cobol [kɔbɔl] *nm* COBOL, Cobol.

cobra [kɔbʀa] *nm* cobra.

coca [kɔka] *nm ®* Coke ®.

cocagne [kɔkaɲ] *nf*: **pays de ~** land of plenty; **mât de ~** greasy pole (*fig*).

cocaïne [kɔkain] *nf* cocaine.

cocarde [kɔkaʀd(ə)] *nf* rosette.

cocardier, ière [kɔkaʀdje, -jɛʀ] *adj* jingoistic, chauvinistic; militaristic.

cocasse [kɔkas] *adj* comical, funny.

coccinelle [kɔksinɛl] *nf* ladybird (*BRIT*), ladybug (*US*).

coccyx [kɔksis] *nm* coccyx.

cocher [kɔʃe] *nm* coachman ♦ *vt* to tick off; (*entailler*) to notch.

cochère [kɔʃɛʀ]

cochon, ne [kɔʃɔ̃, -ɔn] *nm* pig ♦ *nm/f* (*péj: sale*)

(filthy) pig; (: *méchant*) swine ♦ *adj* (*fam*) dirty, smutty; ~ **d'Inde** guinea-pig; ~ **de lait** (*CULIN*) sucking pig.

cochonnaille [kɔʃɔnaj] *nf* (*péj*: *charcuterie*) (cold) pork.

cochonnerie [kɔʃɔnʀi] *nf* (*fam*: *saleté*) filth; (: *marchandises*) rubbish, trash.

cochonnet [kɔʃɔnɛ] *nm* (*BOULES*) jack.

cocker [kɔkɛʀ] *nm* cocker spaniel.

cocktail [kɔktɛl] *nm* cocktail; (*réception*) cocktail party.

coco [koko] *nm voir* **noix**; (*fam*) bloke (*BRIT*), dude (*US*).

cocon [kɔkɔ̃] *nm* cocoon.

cocorico [kɔkɔʀiko] *excl, nm* cock-a-doodle-do.

cocotier [kɔkɔtje] *nm* coconut palm.

cocotte [kɔkɔt] *nf* (*en fonte*) casserole; **ma** ~ (*fam*) sweetie (pie); ~ **(minute)** ® pressure cooker; ~ **en papier** paper shape.

cocu [kɔky] *nm* cuckold.

code [kɔd] *nm* code; **se mettre en** ~**(s)** to dip (*BRIT*) *ou* dim (*US*) one's (head)lights; ~ **à barres** bar code; ~ **de caractère** (*INFORM*) character code; ~ **civil** Common Law; ~ **machine** machine code; ~ **pénal** penal code; ~ **postal** (*numéro*) postcode (*BRIT*), zip code (*US*); ~ **de la route** highway code; ~ **secret** cipher.

codéine [kɔdein] *nf* codeine.

coder [kɔde] *vt* to (en)code.

codétenu, e [kɔdetny] *nm/f* fellow prisoner *ou* inmate.

codicille [kɔdisil] *nm* codicil.

codifier [kɔdifje] *vt* to codify.

codirecteur, trice [kɔdiʀɛktœʀ, -tʀis] *nm/f* co-director.

coéditeur, trice [kɔeditœʀ, -tʀis] *nm/f* co-publisher; (*rédacteur*) co-editor.

coefficient [kɔefisjɑ̃] *nm* coefficient; ~ **d'erreur** margin of error.

coéquipier, ière [kɔekipje, -jɛʀ] *nm/f* teammate, partner.

coercition [kɔɛʀsisjɔ̃] *nf* coercion.

cœur [kœʀ] *nm* heart; (*CARTES*: *couleur*) hearts *pl*; (: *carte*) heart; (*CULIN*): ~ **de laitue/d'artichaut** lettuce/artichoke heart; (*fig*): ~ **du débat** heart of the debate; ~ **de l'été** height of summer; ~ **de la forêt** depths *pl* of the forest; **affaire de** ~ love affair; **avoir bon** ~ to be kind-hearted; **avoir mal au** ~ to feel sick; **contre** *ou* **sur son** ~ to one's breast; **opérer qn à** ~ **ouvert** to perform open-heart surgery on sb; **recevoir qn à** ~ **ouvert** to welcome sb with open arms; **parler à** ~ **ouvert** to open one's heart; **de tout son** ~ with all one's heart; **avoir le** ~ **gros** *ou* **serré** to have a heavy heart; **en avoir le** ~ **net** to be clear in one's own mind (about it); **par** ~ by heart; **de bon** ~ willingly; **avoir à** ~ **de faire** to be very keen to do; **cela lui tient à** ~ that's (very) close to his heart; **prendre les choses à** ~ to take things to heart; **à** ~ **joie**

to one's heart's content; **être de tout** ~ **avec qn** to be (completely) in accord with sb.

coexistence [kɔɛgzistɑ̃s] *nf* coexistence.

coexister [kɔɛgziste] *vi* to coexist.

coffrage [kɔfʀaʒ] *nm* (*CONSTR*: *dispositif*) form(work).

coffre [kɔfʀ(ə)] *nm* (*meuble*) chest; (*coffre-fort*) safe; (*d'auto*) boot (*BRIT*), trunk (*US*); **avoir du** ~ (*fam*) to have a lot of puff.

coffre-fort, *pl* **coffres-forts** [kɔfʀəfɔʀ] *nm* safe.

coffrer [kɔfʀe] *vt* (*fam*) to put inside, lock up.

coffret [kɔfʀɛ] *nm* casket; ~ **à bijoux** jewel box.

cogérant, e [kɔʒeʀɑ̃, -ɑ̃t] *nm/f* joint manager/manageress.

cogestion [kɔʒɛstjɔ̃] *nf* joint management.

cogiter [kɔʒite] *vi* to cogitate.

cognac [kɔɲak] *nm* brandy, cognac.

cognement [kɔɲmɑ̃] *nm* knocking.

cogner [kɔɲe] *vi* to knock, bang; **se** ~ to bump o.s.

cohabitation [kɔabitasjɔ̃] *nf* living together; (*POL, JUR*) cohabitation.

cohabiter [kɔabite] *vi* to live together.

cohérence [kɔeʀɑ̃s] *nf* coherence.

cohérent, e [kɔeʀɑ̃, -ɑ̃t] *adj* coherent.

cohésion [kɔezjɔ̃] *nf* cohesion.

cohorte [kɔɔʀt(ə)] *nf* troop.

cohue [kɔy] *nf* crowd.

coi, coite [kwa, kwat] *adj*: **rester** ~ to remain silent.

coiffe [kwaf] *nf* headdress.

coiffé, e [kwafe] *adj*: **bien/mal** ~ with tidy/untidy hair; ~ **d'un béret** wearing a beret; ~ **en arrière** with one's hair brushed *ou* combed back; ~ **en brosse** with a crew cut.

coiffer [kwafe] *vt* (*fig*) to cover, top; ~ **qn** to do sb's hair; ~ **qn d'un béret** to put a beret on sb; **se** ~ to do one's hair; to put on a *ou* one's hat.

coiffeur, euse [kwafœʀ, -øz] *nm/f* hairdresser ♦ *nf* (*table*) dressing table.

coiffure [kwafyʀ] *nf* (*cheveux*) hairstyle, hairdo; (*chapeau*) hat, headgear *no pl*; (*art*): **la** ~ hairdressing.

coin [kwɛ̃] *nm* corner; (*pour graver*) die; (*pour coincer*) wedge; (*poinçon*) hallmark; **l'épicerie du** ~ the local grocer; **dans le** ~ (*aux alentours*) in the area, around about; locally; **au** ~ **du feu** by the fireside; **du** ~ **de l'œil** out of the corner of one's eye; **regard en** ~ side(ways) glance; **sourire en** ~ half-smile.

coincé, e [kwɛ̃se] *adj* stuck, jammed; (*fig*: *inhibé*) inhibited, with hang-ups.

coincer [kwɛ̃se] *vt* to jam; (*fam*) to catch (out); to nab; **se** ~ to get stuck *ou* jammed.

coïncidence [kɔɛ̃sidɑ̃s] *nf* coincidence.

coïncider [kɔɛ̃side] *vi*: ~ **(avec)** to coincide (with); (*correspondre*: *témoignage etc*) to correspond *ou* tally (with).

coin-coin [kwɛkwɛ] *nm inv* quack.

coing [kwɛ̃] *nm* quince.

coït [kɔit] *nm* coitus.

coite [kwat] *adj f voir* **coi**.

coke [kɔk] *nm* coke.

col [kɔl] *nm* (*de chemise*) collar; (*encolure, cou*) neck; (*de montagne*) pass; ~ **du fémur** neck of the thighbone; ~ **roulé** polo-neck; ~ **de l'utérus** cervix.

coléoptère [kɔleɔptɛʀ] *nm* beetle.

colère [kɔlɛʀ] *nf* anger; **une** ~ a fit of anger; **être en** ~ (**contre qn**) to be angry (with sb); **mettre qn en** ~ to make sb angry; **se mettre en** ~ to get angry.

coléreux, euse [kɔleʀø, -øz] *adj*, **colérique** [kɔleʀik] *adj* quick-tempered, irascible.

colibacille [kɔlibasil] *nm* colon bacillus.

colibacillose [kɔlibasiloz] *nf* colibacillosis.

colifichet [kɔlifiʃɛ] *nm* trinket.

colimaçon [kɔlimasɔ̃] *nm*: **escalier en** ~ spiral staircase.

colin [kɔlɛ̃] *nm* hake.

colin-maillard [kɔlɛ̃majaʀ] *nm* (*jeu*) blind man's buff.

colique [kɔlik] *nf* diarrhoea (*BRIT*), diarrhea (*US*); (*douleurs*) colic (*pains pl*); (*fam: personne ou chose ennuyeuse*) pain.

colis [kɔli] *nm* parcel; **par** ~ **postal** by parcel post.

colistier, ière [kɔlistje, -jɛʀ] *nm/f* fellow candidate.

colite [kɔlit] *nf* colitis.

coll. *abr* = **collection**; (= *collaborateurs*): **et** ~ **et al.**

collaborateur, trice [kɔlabɔʀatœʀ, -tʀis] *nm/f* (*aussi POL*) collaborator; (*d'une revue*) contributor.

collaboration [kɔlabɔʀɑsjɔ̃] *nf* collaboration.

collaborer [kɔlabɔʀe] *vi* to collaborate; ~ **à** to collaborate on; (*revue*) to contribute to.

collage [kɔlaʒ] *nm* (*ART*) collage.

collagène [kɔlaʒɛn] *nm* collagen.

collant, e [kɔlɑ̃, -ɑ̃t] *adj* sticky; (*robe etc*) clinging, skintight; (*péj*) clinging ♦ *nm* (*bas*) tights *pl*.

collatéral, e, aux [kɔlateʀal, -o] *nm/f* collateral.

collation [kɔlɑsjɔ̃] *nf* light meal.

colle [kɔl] *nf* glue; (*à papiers peints*) (wallpaper) paste; (*devinette*) teaser, riddle; (*SCOL fam*) detention; ~ **forte** superglue ®.

collecte [kɔlɛkt(ə)] *nf* collection; **faire une** ~ to take up a collection.

collecter [kɔlɛkte] *vt* to collect.

collecteur [kɔlɛktœʀ] *nm* (*égout*) main sewer.

collectif, ive [kɔlɛktif, -iv] *adj* collective; (*visite, billet etc*) group *cpd* ♦ *nm*: ~ **budgétaire** mini-budget (*BRIT*), mid-term budget; **immeuble** ~ block of flats.

collection [kɔlɛksjɔ̃] *nf* collection; (*ÉDITION*) series; **pièce de** ~ collector's item; **faire (la)** ~ **de** to collect; (**toute**) **une** ~ **de** ... (*fig*) a

(complete) set of ....

collectionner [kɔlɛksjɔne] *vt* (*tableaux, timbres*) to collect.

collectionneur, euse [kɔlɛksjɔnœʀ, -øz] *nm/f* collector.

collectivement [kɔlɛktivmɑ̃] *adv* collectively.

collectiviser [kɔlɛktivize] *vt* to collectivize.

collectivisme [kɔlɛktivism(ə)] *nm* collectivism.

collectiviste [kɔlɛktivist(ə)] *adj* collectivist.

collectivité [kɔlɛktivite] *nf* group; **la** ~ **the** community, the collectivity; **les** ~**s locales** local authorities.

collège [kɔlɛʒ] *nm* (*école*) (secondary) school; (*assemblée*) body; ~ **électoral** electoral college; ~ **d'enseignement secondaire (CES)** ≈ junior secondary school (*BRIT*), ≈ junior high school (*US*).

> *The* **collège** *is a state secondary school for children aged between eleven and fifteen. Pupils follow a nationally prescribed curriculum consisting of a common core and various options. Schools are free to arrange their own timetable and choose their own teaching methods. Before leaving the* **collège**, *pupils are assessed by examination and course work for their* **brevet des collèges**.

collégial, e, aux [kɔleʒjal, -o] *adj* collegiate.

collégien, ne [kɔleʒjɛ̃, -ɛn] *nm/f* secondary school pupil (*BRIT*), high school student (*US*).

collègue [kɔlɛg] *nm/f* colleague.

coller [kɔle] *vt* (*papier, timbre*) to stick (on); (*affiche*) to stick up; (*appuyer, placer contre*): ~ **son front à la vitre** to press one's face to the window; (*enveloppe*) to stick down; (*morceaux*) to stick *ou* glue together; (*fam: mettre, fourrer*) to stick, shove; (*SCOL fam*) to keep in, give detention to ♦ *vi* (*être collant*) to be sticky; (*adhérer*) to stick; ~ **qch sur** to stick (*ou* paste *ou* glue) sth on(to); ~ **à** to stick to; (*fig*) to cling to.

collerette [kɔlʀɛt] *nf* ruff; (*TECH*) flange.

collet [kɔlɛ] *nm* (*piège*) snare, noose; (*cou*): **prendre qn au** ~ to grab sb by the throat; ~ **monté** *adj inv* straight-laced.

colleter [kɔlte] *vt* (*adversaire*) to collar, grab by the throat; **se** ~ **avec** to wrestle with.

colleur [kɔlœʀ] *nm*: ~ **d'affiches** bill-poster.

collier [kɔlje] *nm* (*bijou*) necklace; (*de chien, TECH*) collar; ~ (**de barbe**), **barbe en** ~ narrow beard along the line of the jaw; ~ **de serrage** choke collar.

collimateur [kɔlimatœʀ] *nm*: **être dans le** ~ (*fig*) to be in the firing line; **avoir qn/qch dans le** ~ (*fig*) to have sb/sth in one's sights.

colline [kɔlin] *nf* hill.

collision [kɔlizjɔ̃] *nf* collision, crash; **entrer en** ~ (**avec**) to collide (with).

colloque [kɔlɔk] *nm* colloquium, symposium.

collusion [kɔlyzjɔ̃] *nf* collusion.
collutoire [kɔlytwaʀ] *nm* (*MÉD*) oral medication; (*en bombe*) throat spray.
collyre [kɔliʀ] *nm* (*MÉD*) eye lotion.
colmater [kɔlmate] *vt* (*fuite*) to seal off; (*brèche*) to plug, fill in.
Cologne [kɔlɔɲ] *n* Cologne.
colombage [kɔlɔ̃baʒ] *nm* half-timbering; **une maison à ~s** a half-timbered house.
colombe [kɔlɔ̃b] *nf* dove.
Colombie [kɔlɔ̃bi] *nf*: **la ~** Colombia.
colombien, ne [kɔlɔ̃bjɛ̃, -ɛn] *adj* Colombian ♦ *nm/f*: **C~, ne** Colombian.
colon [kɔlɔ̃] *nm* settler; (*enfant*) boarder (*in children's holiday camp*).
côlon [kolɔ̃] *nm* colon (*MÉD*).
colonel [kɔlɔnɛl] *nm* colonel; (*armée de l'air*) group captain.
colonial, e, aux [kɔlɔnjal, -o] *adj* colonial.
colonialisme [kɔlɔnjalism(ə)] *nm* colonialism.
colonialiste [kɔlɔnjalist(ə)] *adj, nm/f* colonialist.
colonie [kɔlɔni] *nf* colony; **~ (de vacances)** holiday camp (*for children*).
colonisation [kɔlɔnizasjɔ̃] *nf* colonization.
coloniser [kɔlɔnize] *vt* to colonize.
colonnade [kɔlɔnad] *nf* colonnade.
colonne [kɔlɔn] *nf* column; **se mettre en ~ par deux/quatre** to get into twos/fours; **en ~ par deux** in double file; **~ de secours** rescue party; **~ (vertébrale)** spine, spinal column.
colonnette [kɔlɔnɛt] *nf* small column.
colophane [kɔlɔfan] *nf* rosin.
colorant [kɔlɔʀɑ̃] *nm* colo(u)ring.
coloration [kɔlɔʀasjɔ̃] *nf* colour(ing) (*BRIT*), color(ing) (*US*); **se faire faire une ~** (*chez le coiffeur*) to have one's hair dyed.
coloré, e [kɔlɔʀe] *adj* (*fig*) colo(u)rful.
colorer [kɔlɔʀe] *vt* to colour (*BRIT*), color (*US*); **se ~** *vi* to turn red; to blush.
coloriage [kɔlɔʀjaʒ] *nm* colo(u)ring.
colorier [kɔlɔʀje] *vt* to colo(u)r (in); **album à ~** colouring book.
coloris [kɔlɔʀi] *nm* colo(u)r, shade.
coloriste [kɔlɔʀist(ə)] *nm/f* colo(u)rist.
colossal, e, aux [kɔlɔsal, -o] *adj* colossal, huge.
colosse [kɔlɔs] *nm* giant.
colostrum [kɔlɔstʀɔm] *nm* colostrum.
colporter [kɔlpɔʀte] *vt* to hawk, peddle.
colporteur, euse [kɔlpɔʀtœʀ, -øz] *nm/f* hawker, pedlar.
colt [kɔlt] *nm* revolver, Colt ®.
coltiner [kɔltine] *vt* to lug about.
colza [kɔlza] *nm* rape(seed).
coma [kɔma] *nm* coma; **être dans le ~** to be in a coma.
comateux, euse [kɔmatø, -øz] *adj* comatose.
combat [kɔ̃ba] *vb voir* **combattre** ♦ *nm* fight; fighting *no pl*; **~ de boxe** boxing match; **~ de rues** street fighting *no pl*; **~ singulier** single combat.
combatif, ive [kɔ̃batif, -iv] *adj* with a lot of

fight.
combativité [kɔ̃bativite] *nf* fighting spirit.
combattant [kɔ̃batɑ̃] *vb voir* **combattre** ♦ *nm* combatant; (*d'une rixe*) brawler; **ancien ~** war veteran.
combattre [kɔ̃batʀ(ə)] *vi* to fight ♦ *vt* to fight; (*épidémie, ignorance*) to combat, fight (against).
combien [kɔ̃bjɛ̃] *adv* (*quantité*) how much; (*nombre*) how many; (*exclamatif*) how; **~ de** how much; how many; **~ de temps** how long, how much time; **~ coûte/pèse ceci?** how much does this cost/weigh?; **vous mesurez ~?** what size are you?; **ça fait ~ en largeur?** how wide is that?
combinaison [kɔ̃binɛzɔ̃] *nf* combination; (*astuce*) device, scheme; (*de femme*) slip; (*d'aviateur*) flying suit; (*d'homme-grenouille*) wetsuit; (*bleu de travail*) boilersuit (*BRIT*), coveralls *pl* (*US*).
combine [kɔ̃bin] *nf* trick; (*péj*) scheme, fiddle (*BRIT*).
combiné [kɔ̃bine] *nm* (*aussi*: **~ téléphonique**) receiver; (*SKI*) combination (event); (*vêtement de femme*) corselet.
combiner [kɔ̃bine] *vt* to combine; (*plan, horaire*) to work out, devise.
comble [kɔ̃bl(ə)] *adj* (*salle*) packed (full) ♦ *nm* (*du bonheur, plaisir*) height; **~s** *nmpl* (*CONSTR*) attic *sg*, loft *sg*; **de fond en ~** from top to bottom; **pour ~ de malchance** to cap it all; **c'est le ~!** that beats everything!, that takes the biscuit! (*BRIT*); **sous les ~s** in the attic.
combler [kɔ̃ble] *vt* (*trou*) to fill in; (*besoin, lacune*) to fill; (*déficit*) to make good; (*satisfaire*) to gratify, fulfil (*BRIT*), fulfill (*US*); **~ qn de joie** to fill sb with joy; **~ qn d'honneurs** to shower sb with honours.
combustible [kɔ̃bystibl(ə)] *adj* combustible ♦ *nm* fuel.
combustion [kɔ̃bystjɔ̃] *nf* combustion.
COMECON [kɔmekɔn] *sigle m* Comecon.
comédie [kɔmedi] *nf* comedy; (*fig*) playacting *no pl*; **jouer la ~** (*fig*) to put on an act; **~ musicale** musical.

Founded in 1680 by Louis XIV, the **Comédie française** *is the French national theatre. Subsidized by the state, the company performs mainly in the Palais-Royal in Paris and concentrates on staging classical French plays.*

---

comédien, ne [kɔmedjɛ̃, -ɛn] *nm/f* actor/ actress; (*comique*) comedy actor/actress, comedian/comedienne; (*fig*) sham.
COMES [kɔmes] *sigle m* = Commissariat à l'énergie solaire.
comestible [kɔmɛstibl(ə)] *adj* edible; **~s** *nmpl* foods.
comète [kɔmɛt] *nf* comet.
comice [kɔmis] *nm*: **~ agricole** agricultural show.

comique [kɔmik] *adj* (*drôle*) comical; (*THÉÂT*) comic ♦ *nm* (*artiste*) comic, comedian; **le ~ de qch** the funny *ou* comical side of sth.

comité [kɔmite] *nm* committee; **petit ~** select group; **~ directeur** management committee; **~ d'entreprise (CE)** works council; **~ des fêtes** festival committee.

commandant [kɔmɑ̃dɑ̃] *nm* (*gén*) commander, commandant; (*MIL: grade*) major; (*: armée de l'air*) squadron leader; (*NAVIG*) captain; **~ (de bord)** (*AVIAT*) captain.

commande [kɔmɑ̃d] *nf* (*COMM*) order; (*INFORM*) command; **~s** *nfpl* (*AVIAT etc*) controls; **passer une ~ (de)** to put in an or- der (for); **sur ~** to order; **~ à distance** remote control; **véhicule à double ~** vehicle with dual controls.

commandement [kɔmɑ̃dmɑ̃] *nm* command; (*ordre*) command, order; (*REL*) commandment.

commander [kɔmɑ̃de] *vt* (*COMM*) to order; (*diriger, ordonner*) to command; **~ à** (*MIL*) to command; (*contrôler, maîtriser*) to have control over; **~ à qn de faire** to command *ou* order sb to do.

commanditaire [kɔmɑ̃ditɛʀ] *nm* sleeping (*BRIT*) *ou* silent (*US*) partner.

commandite [kɔmɑ̃dit] *nf*: **(société en) ~** limited partnership.

commanditer [kɔmɑ̃dite] *vt* (*COMM*) to finance, back; to commission.

commando [kɔmɑ̃do] *nm* commando (squad).

========================= *MOT-CLÉ*

comme [kɔm] *prép* **1** (*comparaison*) like; **tout ~ son père** just like his father; **fort ~ un bœuf** as strong as an ox; **joli ~ tout** ever so pretty

2 (*manière*) like; **faites-le ~ ça** do it like this, do it this way; **~ ça** *ou* **cela on n'aura pas d'ennuis** that way we won't have any problems; **~ ci, ~ ça** so-so, middling; **comment ça va? — ~ ça** how are things? — OK; **~ on dit** as they say

3 (*en tant que*) as a; **donner ~ prix** to give as a prize; **travailler ~ secrétaire** to work as a secretary

4: **~ quoi** (*d'où il s'ensuit que*) which shows that; **il a écrit une lettre ~ quoi il ...** he's written a letter saying that ...

5: **~ il faut** *phr adv* properly; *phr adj* (*correct*) proper, correct

♦ *conj* **1** (*ainsi que*) as; **elle écrit ~ elle parle** she writes as she talks; **~ si** as if

2 (*au moment où, alors que*) as; **il est parti ~ j'arrivais** he left as I arrived

3 (*parce que, puisque*) as, since; **~ il était en retard, il ...** as he was late, he ...

♦ *adv*: **~ il est fort/c'est bon!** he's so strong/ it's so good!; **il est malin ~ c'est pas permis** he's as smart as anything.

commémoratif, ive [kɔmemɔʀatif, -iv] *adj* commemorative; **un monument ~** a memorial.

commémoration [kɔmemɔʀasjɔ̃] *nf* commemoration.

commémorer [kɔmemɔʀe] *vt* to commemorate.

commencement [kɔmɑ̃smɑ̃] *nm* beginning, start, commencement; **~s** *nmpl* (*débuts*) beginnings.

commencer [kɔmɑ̃se] *vt* to begin, start, commence; (*être placé au début de*) to begin ♦ *vi* to begin, start, commence; **~ à** *ou* **de faire** to begin *ou* start doing; **~ par qch** to begin with sth; **~ par faire qch** to begin by doing sth.

commensal, e, aux [kɔmɑ̃sal, -o] *nm/f* companion at table.

comment [kɔmɑ̃] *adv* how; **~?** (*que dites-vous*) (I beg your) pardon?; **~!** what! ♦ *nm*: **le ~ et le pourquoi** the whys and wherefores; **et ~!** and how!; **~ donc!** of course!; **~ faire?** how will we do it?; **~ se fait-il que?** how is it that?

commentaire [kɔmɑ̃tɛʀ] *nm* comment; remark; **~ (de texte)** (*SCOL*) commentary; **~ sur image** voice-over.

commentateur, trice [kɔmɑ̃tatœʀ, -tʀis] *nm/f* commentator.

commenter [kɔmɑ̃te] *vt* (*jugement, événement*) to comment (up)on; (*RADIO, TV: match, manifestation*) to cover, give a commentary on.

commérages [kɔmeʀaʒ] *nmpl* gossip *sg*.

commerçant, e [kɔmɛʀsɑ̃, -ɑ̃t] *adj* commercial; trading; (*rue*) shopping *cpd*; (*personne*) commercially shrewd ♦ *nm/f* shopkeeper, trader.

commerce [kɔmɛʀs(ə)] *nm* (*activité*) trade, commerce; (*boutique*) business; **le petit ~** small shopowners *pl*, small traders *pl*; **faire ~ de** to trade in; (*fig: péj*) to trade on; **chambre de ~** Chamber of Commerce; **livres de ~** (account) books; **vendu dans le ~** sold in the shops; **vendu hors-~** sold directly to the public; **~ en** *ou* **de gros/détail** wholesale/retail trade; **~ intérieur/ extérieur** home/foreign trade.

commercer [kɔmɛʀse] *vi*: **~ avec** to trade with.

commercial, e, aux [kɔmɛʀsjal, -o] *adj* commercial, trading; (*péj*) commercial ♦ *nm*: **les commerciaux** the commercial people.

commercialisable [kɔmɛʀsjalizabl(ə)] *adj* marketable.

commercialisation [kɔmɛʀsjalizasjɔ̃] *nf* marketing.

commercialiser [kɔmɛʀsjalize] *vt* to market.

commère [kɔmɛʀ] *nf* gossip.

commettant [kɔmetɑ̃] *vb voir* **commettre** ♦ *nm* (*JUR*) principal.

commettre [kɔmetʀ(ə)] *vt* to commit; **se ~** to compromise one's good name.

commis [kɔmi] *vb voir* **commettre** ♦ *nm* (*de magasin*) (shop) assistant (*BRIT*), sales clerk (*US*); (*de banque*) clerk; ~ **voyageur** commercial traveller (*BRIT*) *ou* traveler (*US*).
commis, e [kɔmi, -iz] *pp de* **commettre**.
commisération [kɔmizeʀɑsjɔ̃] *nf* commiseration.
commissaire [kɔmisɛʀ] *nm* (*de police*) ≈ (police) superintendent (*BRIT*), ≈ (police) captain (*US*); (*de rencontre sportive etc*) steward; ~ **du bord** (*NAVIG*) purser; ~ **aux comptes** (*ADMIN*) auditor.
commissaire-priseur, *pl* **commissaires-priseurs** [kɔmisɛʀpʀizœʀ] *nm* (official) auctioneer.
commissariat [kɔmisaʀja] *nm* police station; (*ADMIN*) commissionership.
commission [kɔmisjɔ̃] *nf* (*comité, pourcentage*) commission; (*message*) message; (*course*) errand; ~**s** *nfpl* (*achats*) shopping *sg*; ~ **d'examen** examining board.
commissionnaire [kɔmisjɔnɛʀ] *nm* delivery boy (*ou* man); messenger; (*TRANSPORTS*) (forwarding) agent.
commissure [kɔmisyʀ] *nf*: **les** ~**s des lèvres** the corners of the mouth.
commode [kɔmɔd] *adj* (*pratique*) convenient, handy; (*facile*) easy; (*air, personne*) easygoing; (*personne*): **pas** ~ awkward (to deal with) ♦ *nf* chest of drawers.
commodité [kɔmɔdite] *nf* convenience.
commotion [kɔmosjɔ̃] *nf*: ~ (**cérébrale**) concussion.
commotionné, e [kɔmosjɔne] *adj* shocked, shaken.
commuer [kɔmɥe] *vt* to commute.
commun, e [kɔmœ̃, -yn] *adj* common; (*pièce*) communal, shared; (*réunion, effort*) joint ♦ *nf* (*ADMIN*) commune, ≈ district; (: *urbaine*) ≈ borough; ~**s** *nmpl* (*bâtiments*) outbuildings; **cela sort du** ~ it's out of the ordinary; **le** ~ **des mortels** the common run of people; **sans** ~**e mesure** incomparable; **être** ~ **à** (*suj: chose*) to be shared by; **en** ~ (*faire*) jointly; **mettre en** ~ to pool, share; **peu** ~ unusual; **d'un** ~ **accord** of one accord; with one accord.
communal, e, aux [kɔmynal, -o] *adj* (*ADMIN*) of the commune, ≈ (district *ou* borough) council *cpd*.
communard, e [kɔmynaʀ, -aʀd(ə)] *nm/f* (*HIST*) Communard; (*péj: communiste*) commie.
communautaire [kɔmynotɛʀ] *adj* community *cpd*.
communauté [kɔmynote] *nf* community; (*JUR*): **régime de la** ~ communal estate settlement.
commune [kɔmyn] *adj f*, *nf voir* **commun**.
communément [kɔmynemɑ̃] *adv* commonly.
Communes [kɔmyn] *nfpl* (*BRIT: parlement*) Commons.
communiant, e [kɔmynjɑ̃, -ɑ̃t] *nm/f* communicant; **premier** ~ child taking his first communion.
communicant, e [kɔmynikɑ̃, -ɑ̃t] *adj* communicating.
communicatif, ive [kɔmynikatif, -iv] *adj* (*personne*) communicative; (*rire*) infectious.
communication [kɔmynikasjɔ̃] *nf* communication; ~ (**téléphonique**) (telephone) call; **avoir la** ~ (**avec**) to get *ou* be through (to); **vous avez la** ~ you're through; **donnez-moi la** ~ **avec** put me through to; **mettre qn en** ~ **avec qn** (*en contact*) to put sb in touch with sb; (*au téléphone*) to connect sb with sb; ~ **interurbaine** long-distance call; ~ **en PCV** reverse charge (*BRIT*) *ou* collect (*US*) call; ~ **avec préavis** personal call.
communier [kɔmynje] *vi* (*REL*) to receive communion; (*fig*) to be united.
communion [kɔmynjɔ̃] *nf* communion.
communiqué [kɔmynike] *nm* communiqué; ~ **de presse** press release.
communiquer [kɔmynike] *vt* (*nouvelle, dossier*) to pass on, convey; (*maladie*) to pass on; (*peur etc*) to communicate; (*chaleur, mouvement*) to transmit ♦ *vi* to communicate; ~ **avec** (*suj: salle*) to communicate with; **se** ~ **à** (*se propager*) to spread to.
communisant, e [kɔmynizɑ̃, -ɑ̃t] *adj* communistic ♦ *nm/f* communist sympathizer.
communisme [kɔmynism(ə)] *nm* communism.
communiste [kɔmynist(ə)] *adj, nm/f* communist.
commutateur [kɔmytatœʀ] *nm* (*ÉLEC*) (change-over) switch, commutator.
commutation [kɔmytasjɔ̃] *nf* (*INFORM*): ~ **de messages** message switching; ~ **de paquets** packet switching.
Comores [kɔmɔʀ] *nfpl*: **les** (**îles**) ~ the Comoros (Islands).
comorien, ne [kɔmɔʀjɛ̃, -ɛn] *adj* of *ou* from the Comoros.
compact, e [kɔ̃pakt] *adj* dense; compact.
compagne [kɔ̃paɲ] *nf* companion.
compagnie [kɔ̃paɲi] *nf* (*firme, MIL*) company; (*groupe*) gathering; (*présence*): **la** ~ **de qn** sb's company; **homme/femme de** ~ escort; **tenir** ~ **à qn** to keep sb company; **fausser** ~ **à qn** to give sb the slip, slip *ou* sneak away from sb; **en** ~ **de** in the company of; **Dupont et** ~, **Dupont et Cie** Dupont and Company, Dupont and Co; ~ **aérienne** airline (company).
compagnon [kɔ̃paɲɔ̃] *nm* companion; (*autrefois: ouvrier*) craftsman; journeyman.
comparable [kɔ̃paʀabl(ə)] *adj*: ~ (**à**) comparable (to).
comparaison [kɔ̃paʀɛzɔ̃] *nf* comparison; (*métaphore*) simile; **en** ~ (**de**) in comparison (with); **par** ~ (**à**) by comparison (with).
comparaître [kɔ̃paʀɛtʀ(ə)] *vi*: ~ (**devant**) to appear (before).
comparatif, ive [kɔ̃paʀatif, -iv] *adj, nm* com-

parative.

comparativement [kɔ̃paʀativmɑ̃] *adv* comparatively; ~ **à** by comparison with.

comparé, e [kɔ̃paʀe] *adj*: **littérature** *etc* ~**e** comparative literature *etc*.

comparer [kɔ̃paʀe] *vt* to compare; ~ **qch/qn à** *ou* **et** (*pour choisir*) to compare sth/sb with *ou* and; (*pour établir une similitude*) to compare sth/sb to *ou* and.

comparse [kɔ̃paʀs(ə)] *nm/f* (*péj*) associate, stooge.

compartiment [kɔ̃paʀtimɑ̃] *nm* compartment.

compartimenté, e [kɔ̃paʀtimɑ̃te] *adj* partitioned; (*fig*) compartmentalized.

comparu, e [kɔ̃paʀy] *pp de* **comparaître**.

comparution [kɔ̃paʀysjɔ̃] *nf* appearance.

compas [kɔ̃pa] *nm* (*GÉOM*) (pair of) compasses *pl*; (*NAVIG*) compass.

compassé, e [kɔ̃pase] *adj* starchy, formal.

compassion [kɔ̃pasjɔ̃] *nf* compassion.

compatibilité [kɔ̃patibilite] *nf* compatibility.

compatible [kɔ̃patibl(ə)] *adj*: ~ (**avec**) compatible (with).

compatir [kɔ̃patiʀ] *vi*: ~ (**à**) to sympathize (with).

compatissant, e [kɔ̃patisɑ̃, -ɑ̃t] *adj* sympathetic.

compatriote [kɔ̃patʀijɔt] *nm/f* compatriot, fellow countryman/woman.

compensateur, trice [kɔ̃pɑ̃satœʀ, -tʀis] *adj* compensatory.

compensation [kɔ̃pɑ̃sɑsjɔ̃] *nf* compensation; (*BANQUE*) clearing; **en** ~ in *ou* as compensation.

compensé, e [kɔ̃pɑ̃se] *adj*: **semelle** ~**e** platform sole.

compenser [kɔ̃pɑ̃se] *vt* to compensate for, make up for.

compère [kɔ̃pɛʀ] *nm* accomplice; fellow musician *ou* comedian *etc*.

compétence [kɔ̃petɑ̃s] *nf* competence.

compétent, e [kɔ̃petɑ̃, -ɑ̃t] *adj* (*apte*) competent, capable; (*JUR*) competent.

compétitif, ive [kɔ̃petitif, -iv] *adj* competitive.

compétition [kɔ̃petisjɔ̃] *nf* (*gén*) competition; (*SPORT*: *épreuve*) event; **la** ~ competitive sport; **être en** ~ **avec** to be competing with; **la** ~ **automobile** motor racing.

compétitivité [kɔ̃petitivite] *nf* competitiveness.

compilateur [kɔ̃pilatœʀ] *nm* (*INFORM*) compiler.

compiler [kɔ̃pile] *vt* to compile.

complainte [kɔ̃plɛ̃t] *nf* lament.

complaire [kɔ̃plɛʀ]: **se** ~ *vi*: **se** ~ **dans/parmi** to take pleasure in/in being among.

complaisais [kɔ̃plɛze] *etc vb voir* **complaire**.

complaisamment [kɔ̃plɛzamɑ̃] *adv* kindly; complacently.

complaisance [kɔ̃plɛzɑ̃s] *nf* kindness; (*péj*) indulgence; (*: fatuité*) complacency; **attestation de** ~ certificate produced to oblige a

patient etc; **pavillon de** ~ flag of convenience.

complaisant, e [kɔ̃plɛzɑ̃, -ɑ̃t] *vb voir* **complaire** ♦ *adj* (*aimable*) kind; obliging; (*péj*) accommodating; (*: fat*) complacent.

complaît [kɔ̃plɛ] *vb voir* **complaire**.

complément [kɔ̃plemɑ̃] *nm* complement; (*reste*) remainder; (*LING*) complement; ~ **d'information** (*ADMIN*) supplementary *ou* further information; ~ **d'agent** agent; ~ (**d'objet**) **direct/indirect** direct/indirect object; ~ (**circonstanciel**) **de lieu/temps** adverbial phrase of place/time; ~ **de nom** possessive phrase.

complémentaire [kɔ̃plemɑ̃tɛʀ] *adj* complementary; (*additionnel*) supplementary.

complet, ète [kɔ̃plɛ, -ɛt] *adj* complete; (*plein*: *hôtel etc*) full ♦ *nm* (*aussi*: ~**-veston**) suit; **au** (**grand**) ~ all together.

complètement [kɔ̃plɛtmɑ̃] *adv* (*en entier*) completely; (*absolument*: *fou, faux etc*) absolutely; (*à fond*: *étudier etc*) fully, in depth.

compléter [kɔ̃plete] *vt* (*porter à la quantité voulue*) to complete; (*augmenter*) to complement, supplement; to add to; **se** ~ (*personnes*) to complement one another; (*collection etc*) to become complete.

complexe [kɔ̃plɛks(ə)] *adj* complex ♦ *nm* (*PSYCH*) complex, hang-up; (*bâtiments*): ~ **hospitalier/industriel** hospital/industrial complex.

complexé, e [kɔ̃plɛkse] *adj* mixed-up, hung-up.

complexité [kɔ̃plɛksite] *nf* complexity.

complication [kɔ̃plikasjɔ̃] *nf* complexity, intricacy; (*difficulté, ennui*) complication; ~**s** *nfpl* (*MÉD*) complications.

complice [kɔ̃plis] *nm* accomplice.

complicité [kɔ̃plisite] *nf* complicity.

compliment [kɔ̃plimɑ̃] *nm* (*louange*) compliment; ~**s** *nmpl* (*félicitations*) congratulations.

complimenter [kɔ̃plimɑ̃te] *vt*: ~ **qn** (**sur** *ou* **de**) to congratulate *ou* compliment sb (on).

compliqué, e [kɔ̃plike] *adj* complicated, complex, intricate; (*personne*) complicated.

compliquer [kɔ̃plike] *vt* to complicate; **se** ~ *vi* (*situation*) to become complicated; **se** ~ **la vie** to make life difficult *ou* complicated for o.s.

complot [kɔ̃plo] *nm* plot.

comploter [kɔ̃plɔte] *vi, vt* to plot.

complu, e [kɔ̃ply] *pp de* **complaire**.

comportement [kɔ̃pɔʀtəmɑ̃] *nm* behaviour (*BRIT*), behavior (*US*); (*TECH*: *d'une pièce, d'un véhicule*) behavio(u)r, performance.

comporter [kɔ̃pɔʀte] *vt* to be composed of, consist of, comprise; (*être équipé de*) to have; (*impliquer*) to entail, involve; **se** ~ *vi* to behave; (*TECH*) to behave, perform.

composant [kɔ̃pozɑ̃] *nm* component, constituent.

composante [kɔ̃pozɑ̃t] *nf* component.

composé, e [kɔ̃poze] *adj* (*visage, air*) studied; (*BIO, CHIMIE, LING*) compound ♦ *nm* (*CHIMIE, LING*) compound; ~ **de** made up of.

composer [kɔ̃poze] *vt* (*musique, texte*) to compose; (*mélange, équipe*) to make up; (*faire partie de*) to make up, form; (*TYPO*) to (type)set ♦ *vi* (*SCOL*) to sit *ou* do a test; (*transiger*) to come to terms; **se** ~ **de** to be composed of, be made up of; ~ **un numéro** (*au téléphone*) to dial a number.

composite [kɔ̃pozit] *adj* heterogeneous.

compositeur, trice [kɔ̃pozitœR, -tRis] *nm/f* (*MUS*) composer; (*TYPO*) compositor, typesetter.

composition [kɔ̃pozisjɔ̃] *nf* composition; (*SCOL*) test; (*TYPO*) (type)setting, composition; **de bonne** ~ (*accommodant*) easy to deal with; **amener qn à** ~ to get sb to come to terms; ~ **française** (*SCOL*) French essay.

compost [kɔ̃pɔst] *nm* compost.

composter [kɔ̃pɔste] *vt* to date-stamp; to punch.

composteur [kɔ̃pɔstœR] *nm* date stamp; punch; (*TYPO*) composing stick.

compote [kɔ̃pɔt] *nf* stewed fruit *no pl*; ~ **de pommes** stewed apples.

compotier [kɔ̃pɔtje] *nm* fruit dish *ou* bowl.

compréhensible [kɔ̃pReɑ̃sibl(ə)] *adj* comprehensible; (*attitude*) understandable.

compréhensif, ive [kɔ̃pReɑ̃sif, -iv] *adj* understanding.

compréhension [kɔ̃pReɑ̃sjɔ̃] *nf* understanding; comprehension.

comprendre [kɔ̃pRɑ̃dR(ə)] *vt* to understand; (*se composer de*) to comprise, consist of; (*inclure*) to include; **se faire** ~ to make o.s. understood; to get one's ideas across; **mal** ~ to misunderstand.

compresse [kɔ̃pRɛs] *nf* compress.

compresser [kɔ̃pRese] *vt* to squash in, crush together.

compresseur [kɔ̃pRɛsœR] *adj m voir* **rouleau.**

compressible [kɔ̃pResibl(ə)] *adj* (*PHYSIQUE*) compressible; (*dépenses*) reducible.

compression [kɔ̃pResjɔ̃] *nf* compression; (*d'un crédit etc*) reduction.

comprimé, e [kɔ̃pRime] *adj*: **air** ~ compressed air ♦ *nm* tablet.

comprimer [kɔ̃pRime] *vt* to compress; (*fig: crédit etc*) to reduce, cut down.

compris, e [kɔ̃pRi, -iz] *pp de* **comprendre** ♦ *adj* (*inclus*) included; ~**?** understood?, is that clear?; ~ **entre** (*situé*) contained between; **la maison** ~**e/non** ~**e, y/non** ~ **la maison** including/excluding the house; **service** ~ service (charge) included; **100 F tout** ~ 100 F all inclusive *ou* all-in.

compromettant, e [kɔ̃pRɔmetɑ̃, -ɑ̃t] *adj* compromising.

compromettre [kɔ̃pRɔmetR(ə)] *vt* to compromise.

compromis [kɔ̃pRɔmi] *vb voir* **compromettre**

♦ *nm* compromise.

compromission [kɔ̃pRɔmisjɔ̃] *nf* compromise, deal.

comptabiliser [kɔ̃tabilize] *vt* (*valeur*) to post; (*fig*) to evaluate.

comptabilité [kɔ̃tabilite] *nf* (*activité, technique*) accounting, accountancy; (*d'une société: comptes*) accounts *pl*, books *pl*; (: *service*) accounts office *ou* department; ~ **à partie double** double-entry book-keeping.

comptable [kɔ̃tabl(ə)] *nm/f* accountant ♦ *adj* accounts *cpd*, accounting.

comptant [kɔ̃tɑ̃] *adv*: **payer** ~ to pay cash; **acheter** ~ to buy for cash.

compte [kɔ̃t] *nm* count, counting; (*total, montant*) count, (right) number; (*bancaire, facture*) account; ~**s** *nmpl* accounts, books; (*fig*) explanation *sg*; **ouvrir un** ~ to open an account; **rendre des** ~**s à qn** (*fig*) to be answerable to sb; **faire le** ~ **de** to count up, make a count of; **tout** ~ **fait** on the whole; **à ce** ~**-là** (*dans ce cas*) in that case; (*à ce train-là*) at that rate; **en fin de** ~ (*fig*) all things considered, weighing it all up; **au bout du** ~ in the final analysis; **à bon** ~ at a favourable price; (*fig*) lightly; **avoir son** ~ (*fig: fam*) to have had it; **pour le** ~ **de** on behalf of; **pour son propre** ~ for one's own benefit; **sur le** ~ **de qn** (*à son sujet*) about sb; **travailler à son** ~ to work for oneself; **mettre qch sur le** ~ **de qn** (*le rendre responsable*) to attribute sth to sb; **prendre qch à son** ~ to take responsibility for sth; **trouver son** ~ **à qch** to do well out of sth; **régler un** ~ (*s'acquitter de qch*) to settle an account; (*se venger*) to get one's own back; **rendre** ~ (**à qn**) **de qch** to give (sb) an account of sth; **tenir** ~ **de qch** to take sth into account; ~ **tenu de** taking into account; ~ **chèque(s)** current account; ~ **chèque postal (CCP)** Post Office account; ~ **client** (*sur bilan*) accounts receivable; ~ **courant (CC)** current account; ~ **de dépôt** deposit account; ~ **d'exploitation** operating ac- count; ~ **fournisseur** (*sur bilan*) accounts payable; ~ **à rebours** countdown; ~ **rendu** account, report; (*de film, livre*) review; *voir aussi* **rendre.**

compte-gouttes [kɔ̃tgut] *nm inv* dropper.

compter [kɔ̃te] *vt* to count; (*facturer*) to charge for; (*avoir à son actif, comporter*) to have; (*prévoir*) to allow, reckon; (*tenir compte de, inclure*) to include; (*penser, espérer*): ~ **réussir/revenir** to expect to succeed/return ♦ *vi* to count; (*être économe*) to economize; (*être non négligeable*) to count, matter; (*valoir*): ~ **pour** to count for; (*figurer*): ~ **parmi** to be *ou* rank among; ~ **sur** to count (up)on; ~ **avec qch/qn** to reckon with *ou* take account of sth/sb; ~ **sans qch/qn** to reckon without sth/sb; **sans** ~ **que** besides which; **à** ~ **du 10 janvier** (*COMM*) (as) from 10th January.

compte-tours [kɔ̃ttuR] *nm inv* rev(olution) counter.

compteur [kɔ̃tœR] *nm* meter; ~ **de vitesse** speedometer.

comptine [kɔ̃tin] *nf* nursery rhyme.

comptoir [kɔ̃twaR] *nm* (*de magasin*) counter; (*de café*) counter, bar; (*colonial*) trading post.

compulser [kɔ̃pylse] *vt* to consult.

comte, comtesse [kɔ̃t, kɔ̃tɛs] *nm/f* count/ countess.

con, ne [kɔ̃, kɔn] *adj* (*fam!*) bloody (*BRIT*) *ou* damned stupid (*!*).

concasser [kɔ̃kase] *vt* (*pierre, sucre*) to crush; (*poivre*) to grind.

concave [kɔ̃kav] *adj* concave.

concéder [kɔ̃sede] *vt* to grant; (*défaite, point*) to concede; ~ **que** to concede that.

concentration [kɔ̃sɑ̃tRasjɔ̃] *nf* concentration.

concentrationnaire [kɔ̃sɑ̃tRasjɔnɛR] *adj* of *ou* in concentration camps.

concentré [kɔ̃sɑ̃tRe] *nm* concentrate; ~ **de tomates** tomato purée.

concentrer [kɔ̃sɑ̃tRe] *vt* to concentrate; **se** ~ to concentrate.

concentrique [kɔ̃sɑ̃tRik] *adj* concentric.

concept [kɔ̃sɛpt] *nm* concept.

concepteur, trice [kɔ̃sɛptœR, -tRis] *nm/f* designer.

conception [kɔ̃sɛpsjɔ̃] *nf* conception; (*d'une machine etc*) design.

concernant [kɔ̃sɛRnɑ̃] *prép* (*se rapportant à*) concerning; (*en ce qui concerne*) as regards.

concerner [kɔ̃sɛRne] *vt* to concern; **en ce qui me concerne** as far as I am concerned; **en ce qui concerne ceci** as far as this is concerned, with regard to this.

concert [kɔ̃sɛR] *nm* concert; **de** ~ *adv* in unison; together.

concertation [kɔ̃sɛRtasjɔ̃] *nf* (*échange de vues*) dialogue; (*rencontre*) meeting.

concerter [kɔ̃sɛRte] *vt* to devise; **se** ~ *vi* (*collaborateurs etc*) to put our (*ou* their *etc*) heads together, consult (each other).

concertiste [kɔ̃sɛRtist(ə)] *nm/f* concert artist.

concerto [kɔ̃sɛRto] *nm* concerto.

concession [kɔ̃sesjɔ̃] *nf* concession.

concessionnaire [kɔ̃sesjɔnɛR] *nm/f* agent, dealer.

concevable [kɔ̃svabl(ə)] *adj* conceivable.

concevoir [kɔ̃svwaR] *vt* (*idée, projet*) to conceive (of); (*méthode, plan d'appartement, décoration etc*) to plan, design; (*enfant*) to conceive; **maison bien/mal conçue** well-/badly-designed *ou* -planned house.

concierge [kɔ̃sjɛRʒ(ə)] *nm/f* caretaker; (*d'hôtel*) head porter.

conciergerie [kɔ̃sjɛRʒəRi] *nf* caretaker's lodge.

concile [kɔ̃sil] *nm* council, synod.

conciliable [kɔ̃siljabl(ə)] *adj* (*opinions etc*) reconcilable.

conciliabules [kɔ̃siljabyl] *nmpl* (private) discussions, confabulations (*BRIT*).

conciliant, e [kɔ̃siljɑ̃, -ɑ̃t] *adj* conciliatory.

conciliateur, trice [kɔ̃siljatœR, -tRis] *nm/f* mediator, go-between.

conciliation [kɔ̃siljasjɔ̃] *nf* conciliation.

concilier [kɔ̃silje] *vt* to reconcile; **se** ~ **qn/ l'appui de qn** to win sb over/sb's support.

concis, e [kɔ̃si, -iz] *adj* concise.

concision [kɔ̃sizjɔ̃] *nf* concision, conciseness.

concitoyen, ne [kɔ̃sitwajɛ̃, -ɛn] *nm/f* fellow citizen.

conclave [kɔ̃klav] *nm* conclave.

concluant, e [kɔ̃klyɑ̃, -ɑ̃t] *vb voir* **conclure** ♦ *adj* conclusive.

conclure [kɔ̃klyR] *vt* to conclude; (*signer: accord, pacte*) to enter into; (*déduire*): ~ **qch de qch** to deduce sth from sth; ~ **à l'acquittement** to decide in favour of an acquittal; ~ **au suicide** to come to the conclusion (*ou* (*JUR*) to pronounce) that it is a case of suicide; ~ **un marché** to clinch a deal; **j'en conclus que** from that I conclude that.

conclusion [kɔ̃klyzjɔ̃] *nf* conclusion; ~**s** *nfpl* (*JUR*) submissions; findings; **en** ~ in conclusion.

concocter [kɔ̃kɔkte] *vt* to concoct.

conçois [kɔ̃swa], **conçoive** [kɔ̃swav] *etc vb voir* **concevoir**.

concombre [kɔ̃kɔ̃bR(ə)] *nm* cucumber.

concomitant, e [kɔ̃kɔmitɑ̃, -ɑ̃t] *adj* concomitant.

concordance [kɔ̃kɔRdɑ̃s] *nf* concordance; **la** ~ **des temps** (*LING*) the sequence of tenses.

concordant, e [kɔ̃kɔRdɑ̃, -ɑ̃t] *adj* (*témoignages, versions*) corroborating.

concorde [kɔ̃kɔRd(ə)] *nf* concord.

concorder [kɔ̃kɔRde] *vi* to tally, agree.

concourir [kɔ̃kuRiR] *vi* (*SPORT*) to compete; ~ **à** *vt* (*effet etc*) to work towards.

concours [kɔ̃kuR] *vb voir* **concourir** ♦ *nm* competition; (*SCOL*) competitive examination; (*assistance*) aid, help; **recrutement par voie de** ~ recruitment by (competitive) examination; **apporter son** ~ **à** to give one's support to; ~ **de circonstances** combination of circumstances; ~ **hippique** horse show; *voir* **hors**.

concret, ète [kɔ̃kRɛ, -ɛt] *adj* concrete.

concrètement [kɔ̃kRɛtmɑ̃] *adv* in concrete terms.

concrétisation [kɔ̃kRetizasjɔ̃] *nf* realization.

concrétiser [kɔ̃kRetize] *vt* to realize; **se** ~ *vi* to materialize.

conçu, e [kɔ̃sy] *pp de* **concevoir**.

concubin, e [kɔ̃kybɛ̃, -in] *nm/f* (*JUR*) cohabitant.

concubinage [kɔ̃kybinaʒ] *nm* (*JUR*) cohabitation.

concupiscence [kɔ̃kypisɑ̃s] *nf* concupiscence.

concurremment [kɔ̃kyRamɑ̃] *adv* concurrently; jointly.

concurrence [kɔ̃kyʀɑ̃s] *nf* competition; **jusqu'à ~ de** up to; **~ déloyale** unfair competition.

concurrencer [kɔ̃kyʀɑ̃se] *vt* to compete with; **ils nous concurrencent dangereusement** they are a serious threat to us.

concurrent, e [kɔ̃kyʀɑ̃, -ɑ̃t] *adj* competing ♦ *nm/f* (*SPORT, ÉCON etc*) competitor; (*SCOL*) candidate.

concurrentiel, le [kɔ̃kyʀɑ̃sjɛl] *adj* competitive.

conçus [kɔ̃sy] *vb voir* **concevoir**.

condamnable [kɔ̃danabl(ə)] *adj* (*action, opinion*) reprehensible.

condamnation [kɔ̃danasjɔ̃] *nf* (*action*) condemnation; sentencing; (*peine*) sentence; conviction; **~ à mort** death sentence.

condamné, e [kɔ̃dane] *nm/f* (*JUR*) convict.

condamner [kɔ̃dane] *vt* (*blâmer*) to condemn; (*JUR*) to sentence; (*porte, ouverture*) to fill in, block up; (*malade*) to give up (hope for); (*obliger*): **~ qn à qch/à faire** to condemn sb to sth/to do; **~ qn à 2 ans de prison** to sentence sb to 2 years' imprisonment; **~ qn à une amende** to impose a fine on sb.

condensateur [kɔ̃dɑ̃satœʀ] *nm* condenser.

condensation [kɔ̃dɑ̃sasjɔ̃] *nf* condensation.

condensé [kɔ̃dɑ̃se] *nm* digest.

condenser [kɔ̃dɑ̃se] *vt*, **se ~** *vi* to condense.

condescendance [kɔ̃desɑ̃dɑ̃s] *nf* condescension.

condescendant, e [kɔ̃desɑ̃dɑ̃, -ɑ̃t] *adj* (*personne, attitude*) condescending.

condescendre [kɔ̃desɑ̃dʀ(ə)] *vi*: **~ à** to condescend to.

condiment [kɔ̃dimɑ̃] *nm* condiment.

condisciple [kɔ̃disipl(ə)] *nm/f* school fellow, fellow student.

condition [kɔ̃disjɔ̃] *nf* condition; **~s** *nfpl* (*tarif, prix*) terms; (*circonstances*) conditions; **sans ~** *adj* unconditional ♦ *adv* unconditionally; **sous ~ que** on condition that; **à ~ de** *ou* **que** provided that; **en bonne ~** in good condition; **mettre en ~** (*SPORT etc*) to get fit; (*PSYCH*) to condition (mentally); **~s de vie** living conditions.

conditionnel, le [kɔ̃disjɔnɛl] *adj* conditional ♦ *nm* conditional (tense).

conditionnement [kɔ̃disjɔnmɑ̃] *nm* (*emballage*) packaging; (*fig*) conditioning.

conditionner [kɔ̃disjɔne] *vt* (*déterminer*) to determine; (*COMM: produit*) to package; (*fig: personne*) to condition; **air conditionné** air conditioning; **réflexe conditionné** conditioned reflex.

condoléances [kɔ̃dɔleɑ̃s] *nfpl* condolences.

conducteur, trice [kɔ̃dyktœʀ, -tʀis] *adj* (*ÉLEC*) conducting ♦ *nm/f* (*AUTO etc*) driver; (*machine*) operator ♦ *nm* (*ÉLEC etc*) conductor.

conduire [kɔ̃dɥiʀ] *vt* (*véhicule, passager*) to drive; (*délégation, troupeau*) to lead; **se ~** *vi* to behave; **~ vers/à** to lead towards/to; **~ qn quelque part** to take sb somewhere; to drive sb somewhere.

conduit, e [kɔ̃dɥi, -it] *pp de* **conduire** ♦ *nm* (*TECH*) conduit, pipe; (*ANAT*) duct, canal.

conduite [kɔ̃dɥit] *nf* (*en auto*) driving; (*comportement*) behaviour (*BRIT*), behavior (*US*); (*d'eau, de gaz*) pipe; **sous la ~ de** led by; **~ forcée** pressure pipe; **~ à gauche** left-hand drive; **~ intérieure** saloon (car).

cône [kon] *nm* cone; **en forme de ~** coneshaped.

conf. *abr* (= *confort*): **tt ~** all mod cons (*BRIT*).

confection [kɔ̃fɛksjɔ̃] *nf* (*fabrication*) making; (*COUTURE*): **la ~** the clothing industry, the rag trade (*fam*); **vêtement de ~** ready-to-wear *ou* off-the-peg garment.

confectionner [kɔ̃fɛksjɔne] *vt* to make.

confédération [kɔ̃federasjɔ̃] *nf* confederation.

conférence [kɔ̃feʀɑ̃s] *nf* (*exposé*) lecture; (*pourparlers*) conference; **~ de presse** press conference; **~ au sommet** summit (conference).

conférencier, ière [kɔ̃feʀɑ̃sje, -jɛʀ] *nm/f* lecturer.

conférer [kɔ̃feʀe] *vt*: **~ à qn** (*titre, grade*) to confer on sb; **~ à qch/qn** (*aspect etc*) to endow sth/sb with, give (to) sth/sb.

confesser [kɔ̃fese] *vt* to confess; **se ~** *vi* (*REL*) to go to confession.

confesseur [kɔ̃fesœʀ] *nm* confessor.

confession [kɔ̃fɛsjɔ̃] *nf* confession; (*culte: catholique etc*) denomination.

confessionnal, aux [kɔ̃fesjɔnal, -o] *nm* confessional.

confessionnel, le [kɔ̃fesjɔnɛl] *adj* denominational.

confetti [kɔ̃feti] *nm* confetti *no pl*.

confiance [kɔ̃fjɑ̃s] *nf* confidence, trust; faith; **avoir ~ en** to have confidence ou faith in, trust; **faire ~ à** to trust; **en toute ~** with complete confidence; **de ~** trustworthy, reliable; **mettre qn en ~** to win sb's trust; **vote de ~** (*POL*) vote of confidence; **inspirer ~ à** to inspire confidence in; **~ en soi** selfconfidence; *voir* **question**.

confiant, e [kɔ̃fjɑ̃, -ɑ̃t] *adj* confident; trusting.

confidence [kɔ̃fidɑ̃s] *nf* confidence.

confident, e [kɔ̃fidɑ̃, -ɑ̃t] *nm/f* confidant/confidante.

confidentiel, le [kɔ̃fidɑ̃sjɛl] *adj* confidential.

confidentiellement [kɔ̃fidɑ̃sjɛlmɑ̃] *adv* in confidence, confidentially.

confier [kɔ̃fje] *vt*: **~ à qn** (*objet en dépôt, travail etc*) to entrust to sb; (*secret, pensée*) to confide to sb; **se ~ à qn** to confide in sb.

configuration [kɔ̃figyʀasjɔ̃] *nf* configuration, layout; (*INFORM*) configuration.

configurer [kɔ̃figyʀe] *vt* to configure.

confiné, e [kɔ̃fine] *adj* enclosed; (*air*) stale.

confiner [kɔ̃fine] *vt*: **~ à** to confine to;

(*toucher*) to border on; **se** ~ **dans** *ou* **à** to confine o.s. to.

confins [kɔ̃fɛ̃] *nmpl*: **aux** ~ **de** on the borders of.

confirmation [kɔ̃fiʀmasjɔ̃] *nf* confirmation.

confirmer [kɔ̃fiʀme] *vt* to confirm; ~ **qn dans une croyance/ses fonctions** to strengthen sb in a belief/his duties.

confiscation [kɔ̃fiskasjɔ̃] *nf* confiscation.

confiserie [kɔ̃fizʀi] *nf* (*magasin*) confectioner's *ou* sweet shop (*BRIT*), candy store (*US*); ~**s** *nfpl* (*bonbons*) confectionery *sg*, sweets, candy *no pl*.

confiseur, euse [kɔ̃fizœʀ, -øz] *nm/f* confectioner.

confisquer [kɔ̃fiske] *vt* to confiscate.

confit, e [kɔ̃fi, -it] *adj*: **fruits** ~**s** crystallized fruits ♦ *nm*: ~ **d'oie** potted goose.

confiture [kɔ̃fityʀ] *nf* jam; ~ **d'oranges** (orange) marmalade.

conflagration [kɔ̃flagʀasjɔ̃] *nf* cataclysm.

conflictuel, le [kɔ̃fliktɥɛl] *adj* full of clashes *ou* conflicts.

conflit [kɔ̃fli] *nm* conflict.

confluent [kɔ̃flyɑ̃] *nm* confluence.

confondre [kɔ̃fɔ̃dʀ(ə)] *vt* (*jumeaux, faits*) to confuse, mix up; (*témoin, menteur*) to confound; **se** ~ *vi* to merge; **se** ~ **en excuses** to offer profuse apologies, apologize profusely; ~ **qch/qn avec qch/qn d'autre** to mistake sth/sb for sth/sb else.

confondu, e [kɔ̃fɔ̃dy] *pp de* **confondre** ♦ *adj* (*stupéfait*) speechless, overcome; **toutes catégories** ~**es** taking all categories together.

conformation [kɔ̃fɔʀmasjɔ̃] *nf* conformation.

conforme [kɔ̃fɔʀm(ə)] *adj*: ~ **à** (*en accord avec*) in accordance with, in keeping with; (*identique à*) true to; **copie certifiée** ~ (*ADMIN*) certified copy; ~ **à la commande** as per order.

conformé, e [kɔ̃fɔʀme] *adj*: **bien** ~ wellformed.

conformément [kɔ̃fɔʀmemɑ̃] *adv*: ~ **à** in accordance with.

conformer [kɔ̃fɔʀme] *vt*: ~ **qch à** to model sth on; **se** ~ **à** to conform to.

conformisme [kɔ̃fɔʀmism(ə)] *nm* conformity.

conformiste [kɔ̃fɔʀmist(ə)] *adj, nm/f* conformist.

conformité [kɔ̃fɔʀmite] *nf* conformity; agreement; **en** ~ **avec** in accordance with.

confort [kɔ̃fɔʀ] *nm* comfort; **tout** ~ (*COMM*) with all mod cons (*BRIT*) *ou* modern conveniences.

confortable [kɔ̃fɔʀtabl(ə)] *adj* comfortable.

confortablement [kɔ̃fɔʀtabləmɑ̃] *adv* comfortably.

conforter [kɔ̃fɔʀte] *vt* to reinforce, strengthen.

confrère [kɔ̃fʀɛʀ] *nm* colleague; fellow member.

confrérie [kɔ̃fʀeʀi] *nf* brotherhood.

confrontation [kɔ̃fʀɔ̃tasjɔ̃] *nf* confrontation.

confronté, e [kɔ̃fʀɔ̃te] *adj*: ~ **à** confronted by, facing.

confronter [kɔ̃fʀɔ̃te] *vt* to confront; (*textes*) to compare, collate.

confus, e [kɔ̃fy, -yz] *adj* (*vague*) confused; (*embarrassé*) embarrassed.

confusément [kɔ̃fyzemɑ̃] *adv* (*distinguer, ressentir*) vaguely; (*parler*) confusedly.

confusion [kɔ̃fyzjɔ̃] *nf* (*voir confus*) confusion; embarrassment; (*voir confondre*) confusion; mixing up; (*erreur*) confusion; ~ **des peines** (*JUR*) concurrency of sentences.

congé [kɔ̃ʒe] *nm* (*vacances*) holiday; (*arrêt de travail*) time off *no pl*; leave *no pl*; (*MIL*) leave *no pl*; (*avis de départ*) notice; **en** ~ on holiday; off (work); on leave; **semaine/jour de** ~ week/day off; **prendre** ~ **de qn** to take one's leave of sb; **donner son** ~ **à** to hand *ou* give in one's notice to; ~ **de maladie** sick leave; ~ **de maternité** maternity leave; ~**s payés** paid holiday *ou* leave.

congédier [kɔ̃ʒedje] *vt* to dismiss.

congélateur [kɔ̃ʒelatœʀ] *nm* freezer, deep freeze.

congélation [kɔ̃ʒelasjɔ̃] *nf* freezing; (*de l'huile*) congealing.

congeler [kɔ̃ʒle] *vt*, **se** ~ *vi* to freeze.

congénère [kɔ̃ʒenɛʀ] *nm/f* fellow (bear *ou* lion *etc*), fellow creature.

congénital, e, aux [kɔ̃ʒenital, -o] *adj* congenital.

congère [kɔ̃ʒɛʀ] *nf* snowdrift.

congestion [kɔ̃ʒɛstjɔ̃] *nf* congestion; ~ **cérébrale** stroke; ~ **pulmonaire** congestion of the lungs.

congestionner [kɔ̃ʒɛstjɔne] *vt* to congest; (*MÉD*) to flush.

conglomérat [kɔ̃glɔmeʀa] *nm* conglomerate.

Congo [kɔ̃go] *nm*: **le** ~ (*pays, fleuve*) the Congo.

congolais, e [kɔ̃gɔlɛ, -ɛz] *adj* Congolese ♦ *nm/f*: **C**~, **e** Congolese.

congratuler [kɔ̃gʀatyle] *vt* to congratulate.

congre [kɔ̃gʀ(ə)] *nm* conger (eel).

congrégation [kɔ̃gʀegasjɔ̃] *nf* (*REL*) congregation; (*gén*) assembly; gathering.

congrès [kɔ̃gʀɛ] *nm* congress.

congressiste [kɔ̃gʀesist(ə)] *nm/f* delegate, participant (at a congress).

congru, e [kɔ̃gʀy] *adj*: **la portion** ~**e** the smallest *ou* meanest share.

conifère [kɔnifɛʀ] *nm* conifer.

conique [kɔnik] *adj* conical.

conjecture [kɔ̃ʒɛktyʀ] *nf* conjecture, speculation *no pl*.

conjecturer [kɔ̃ʒɛktyʀe] *vt, vi* to conjecture.

conjoint, e [kɔ̃ʒwɛ̃, -wɛ̃t] *adj* joint ♦ *nm/f* spouse.

conjointement [kɔ̃ʒwɛ̃tmɑ̃] *adv* jointly.

conjonctif, ive [kɔ̃ʒɔ̃ktif, -iv] *adj*: **tissu** ~ connective tissue.

conjonction [kɔ̃ʒɔ̃ksjɔ̃] *nf* (*LING*) conjunction.

conjonctivite [kɔ̃ʒɔ̃ktivit] *nf* conjunctivitis.

conjoncture [kɔ̃ʒɔ̃ktyʀ] *nf* circumstances *pl*; **la ~ (économique)** the economic climate *ou* situation.

conjoncturel, le [kɔ̃ʒɔ̃ktyʀɛl] *adj*: **variations/ tendances ~les** economic fluctuations/ trends.

conjugaison [kɔ̃ʒygɛzɔ̃] *nf* (*LING*) conjugation.

conjugal, e, aux [kɔ̃ʒygal, -o] *adj* conjugal; married.

conjugué, e [kɔ̃ʒyge] *adj* combined.

conjuguer [kɔ̃ʒyge] *vt* (*LING*) to conjugate; (*efforts etc*) to combine.

conjuration [kɔ̃ʒyʀasjɔ̃] *nf* conspiracy.

conjuré, e [kɔ̃ʒyʀe] *nm/f* conspirator.

conjurer [kɔ̃ʒyʀe] *vt* (*sort, maladie*) to avert; (*implorer*): **~ qn de faire qch** to beseech *ou* entreat sb to do sth.

connais [kɔnɛ], **connaissais** [kɔnɛsɛ] *etc vb voir* **connaître**.

connaissance [kɔnɛsɑ̃s] *nf* (*savoir*) knowledge *no pl*; (*personne connue*) acquaintance; (*conscience, perception*) consciousness; **~s** *nfpl* knowledge *no pl*; **être sans ~** to be unconscious; **perdre/reprendre ~** to lose/regain consciousness; **à ma/sa ~** to (the best of) my/his knowledge; **faire ~ avec qn** *ou* **la ~ de qn** (*rencontrer*) to meet sb; (*apprendre à connaître*) to get to know sb; **avoir ~ de** to be aware of; **prendre ~ de** (*document etc*) to peruse; **en ~ de cause** with full knowledge of the facts; **de ~** (*personne, visage*) familiar.

connaissant [kɔnɛsɑ̃] *etc vb voir* **connaître**.

connaissement [kɔnɛsmɑ̃] *nm* bill of lading.

connaisseur, euse [kɔnɛsœʀ, -øz] *nm/f* connoisseur ♦ *adj* expert.

connaître [kɔnɛtʀ(ə)] *vt* to know; (*éprouver*) to experience; (*avoir*) to have; to enjoy; **~ de nom/vue** to know by name/sight; **se ~** to know each other; (*soi-même*) to know o.s.; **ils se sont connus à Genève** they (first) met in Geneva; **s'y ~ en qch** to know about sth.

connasse [kɔnas] *nf* (*fam!*) stupid bitch (*!*) *ou* cow (*!*).

connecté, e [kɔnɛkte] *adj* (*INFORM*) on line.

connecter [kɔnɛkte] *vt* to connect.

connerie [kɔnʀi] *nf* (*fam*) (bloody) stupid (*BRIT*) *ou* damn-fool (*US*) thing to do *ou* say.

connexe [kɔnɛks(ə)] *adj* closely related.

connexion [kɔnɛksjɔ̃] *nf* connection.

connivence [kɔnivɑ̃s] *nf* connivance.

connotation [kɔnɔtasjɔ̃] *nf* connotation.

connu, e [kɔny] *pp de* **connaître** ♦ *adj* (*célèbre*) well-known.

conque [kɔ̃k] *nf* (*coquille*) conch (shell).

conquérant, e [kɔ̃keʀɑ̃, -ɑ̃t] *nm/f* conqueror.

conquérir [kɔ̃keʀiʀ] *vt* to conquer, win.

conquerrai [kɔ̃kɛʀʀe] *etc vb voir* **conquérir**.

conquête [kɔ̃kɛt] *nf* conquest.

conquière, conquiers [kɔ̃kjɛʀ] *etc vb voir* **conquérir**.

conquis, e [kɔ̃ki, -iz] *pp de* **conquérir**.

consacrer [kɔ̃sakʀe] *vt* (*REL*): **~ qch (à)** to consecrate sth (to); (*fig: usage etc*) to sanction, establish; (*employer*): **~ qch à** to devote *ou* dedicate sth to; **se ~ à qch/faire** to dedicate *ou* devote o.s. to sth/to doing.

consanguin, e [kɔ̃sɑ̃gɛ̃, -in] *adj* between blood relations; **frère ~** half-brother (*on father's side*); **mariage ~** intermarriage.

consciemment [kɔ̃sjamɑ̃] *adv* consciously.

conscience [kɔ̃sjɑ̃s] *nf* conscience; (*perception*) consciousness; **avoir/prendre ~ de** to be/become aware of; **perdre/reprendre ~** to lose/regain consciousness; **avoir bonne/ mauvaise ~** to have a clear/guilty conscience; **en (toute) ~** in all conscience; **~ professionnelle** professional conscience.

consciencieux, euse [kɔ̃sjɑ̃sjø, -øz] *adj* conscientious.

conscient, e [kɔ̃sjɑ̃, -ɑ̃t] *adj* conscious; **~ de** aware *ou* conscious of.

conscription [kɔ̃skʀipsjɔ̃] *nf* conscription.

conscrit [kɔ̃skʀi] *nm* conscript.

consécration [kɔ̃sekʀasjɔ̃] *nf* consecration.

consécutif, ive [kɔ̃sekytif, -iv] *adj* consecutive; **~ à** following upon.

consécutivement [kɔ̃sekytivmɑ̃] *adv* consecutively; **~ à** following on.

conseil [kɔ̃sɛj] *nm* (*avis*) piece of advice, advice *no pl*; (*assemblée*) council; (*expert*): **~ en recrutement** recruitment consultant ♦ *adj*: **ingénieur-~** consulting engineer, engineering consultant; **tenir ~** to hold a meeting; to deliberate; **donner un ~** *ou* **des ~s à qn** to give sb (a piece of) advice; **demander ~ à qn** to ask sb's advice; **prendre ~ (auprès de qn)** to take advice (from sb); **~ d'administration (CA)** board (of directors); **~ de classe** (*SCOL*) meeting of teachers, parents and class representatives to discuss pupils' progress; **~ de discipline** disciplinary committee; **~ général** regional council; **~ de guerre** court-martial; **le ~ des ministres** ≈ the Cabinet; **~ municipal (CM)** town council; **~ régional** regional board of elected representatives; **~ de révision** recruitment *ou* draft (*US*) board.

Each **département** *has an elected body called a* **Conseil général** *made up of* **conseillers généraux** *each of whom represents a* **canton** *and is elected for a six year term. Half of the council's membership is elected every three years. The remit of the Conseil général is to administer matters affecting the département, including personnel, transport infrastructure, housing, school grants and economic development.*

---

conseiller¹ [kɔ̃seje] *vt* (*personne*) to advise; (*méthode, action*) to recommend, advise; **~ qch à qn** to recommend sth to sb; **~ à qn de faire qch** to advise sb to do sth.

conseiller², **ère** [kɔ̃seje, -ɛʀ] *nm/f* adviser; ~ **général** regional councillor; ~ **matrimonial** marriage guidance counsellor; ~ **municipal** town councillor.

consensuel, le [kɔ̃sɑ̃sɥɛl] *adj* consensual.

consensus [kɔ̃sɛ̃sys] *nm* consensus.

consentement [kɔ̃sɑ̃tmɑ̃] *nm* consent.

consentir [kɔ̃sɑ̃tiʀ] *vt:* ~ (**à qch/faire**) to agree *ou* consent (to sth/to doing); ~ **qch à qn** to grant sb sth.

conséquence [kɔ̃sekɑ̃s] *nf* consequence, outcome; ~**s** *nfpl* consequences, repercussions; **en** ~ (*donc*) consequently; (*de façon appropriée*) accordingly; **ne pas tirer à** ~ to be unlikely to have any repercussions; **sans** ~ unimportant; **de** ~ important.

conséquent, e [kɔ̃sekɑ̃, -ɑ̃t] *adj* logical, rational; (*fam: important*) substantial; **par** ~ consequently.

conservateur, trice [kɔ̃sɛʀvatœʀ, -tʀis] *adj* conservative ♦ *nm/f* (*POL*) conservative; (*de musée*) curator.

conservation [kɔ̃sɛʀvasjɔ̃] *nf* retention; keeping; preserving; preservation.

conservatisme [kɔ̃sɛʀvatism(ə)] *nm* conservatism.

conservatoire [kɔ̃sɛʀvatwaʀ] *nm* academy; (*ÉCOLOGIE*) conservation area.

conserve [kɔ̃sɛʀv(ə)] *nf* (*gén pl*) canned *ou* tinned (*BRIT*) food; ~**s de poisson** canned *ou* tinned (*BRIT*) fish; **en** ~ canned, tinned (*BRIT*); **de** ~ (*ensemble*) in concert; (*naviguer*) in convoy.

conservé, e [kɔ̃sɛʀve] *adj:* **bien** ~ (*personne*) well-preserved.

conserver [kɔ̃sɛʀve] *vt* (*faculté*) to retain, keep; (*habitude*) to keep up; (*amis, livres*) to keep; (*préserver, aussi CULIN*) to preserve; **se** ~ *vi* (*aliments*) to keep; **"~ au frais"** "store in a cool place".

conserverie [kɔ̃sɛʀvəʀi] *nf* canning factory.

considérable [kɔ̃sideʀabl(ə)] *adj* considerable, significant, extensive.

considération [kɔ̃sideʀasjɔ̃] *nf* consideration; (*estime*) esteem, respect; ~**s** *nfpl* (*remarques*) reflections; **prendre en** ~ to take into consideration *ou* account; **ceci mérite** ~ this is worth considering; **en** ~ **de** given, because of.

considéré, e [kɔ̃sideʀe] *adj* respected; **tout bien** ~ all things considered.

considérer [kɔ̃sideʀe] *vt* to consider; (*regarder*) to consider, study; ~ **qch comme** to regard sth as.

consigne [kɔ̃siɲ] *nf* (*COMM*) deposit; (*de gare*) left luggage (office) (*BRIT*), checkroom (*US*); (*punition: SCOL*) detention; (: *MIL*) confinement to barracks; (*ordre, instruction*) instructions *pl*; ~ **automatique** left-luggage locker; ~**s de sécurité** safety instructions.

consigné, e [kɔ̃siɲe] *adj* (*COMM: bouteille, emballage*) returnable; **non** ~ non-returnable.

consigner [kɔ̃siɲe] *vt* (*note, pensée*) to record; (*marchandises*) to deposit; (*punir: MIL*) to confine to barracks; (: *élève*) to put in detention; (*COMM*) to put a deposit on.

consistance [kɔ̃sistɑ̃s] *nf* consistency.

consistant, e [kɔ̃sistɑ̃, -ɑ̃t] *adj* thick; solid.

consister [kɔ̃siste] *vi:* ~ **en/dans/à faire** to consist of/in/in doing.

consœur [kɔ̃sœʀ] *nf* (*lady*) colleague; fellow member.

consolation [kɔ̃sɔlasjɔ̃] *nf* consolation *no pl*, comfort *no pl*.

console [kɔ̃sɔl] *nf* console; ~ **graphique** *ou* **de visualisation** (*INFORM*) visual display unit, VDU; ~ **de jeux vidéo** games console.

consoler [kɔ̃sɔle] *vt* to console; **se** ~ (**de qch**) to console o.s. (for sth).

consolider [kɔ̃sɔlide] *vt* to strengthen, reinforce; (*fig*) to consolidate; **bilan consolidé** consolidated balance sheet.

consommateur, trice [kɔ̃sɔmatœʀ, -tʀis] *nm/f* (*ÉCON*) consumer; (*dans un café*) customer.

consommation [kɔ̃sɔmasjɔ̃] *nf* consumption; (*JUR*) consummation; (*boisson*) drink; ~ **aux 100 km** (*AUTO*) (fuel) consumption per 100 km, ≈ miles per gallon (mpg), ≈ gas mileage (*US*); **de** ~ (*biens, société*) consumer *cpd*.

consommé, e [kɔ̃sɔme] *adj* consummate ♦ *nm* consommé.

consommer [kɔ̃sɔme] *vt* (*suj: personne*) to eat *ou* drink, consume; (*suj: voiture, usine, poêle*) to use, consume; (*JUR*) to consummate ♦ *vi* (*dans un café*) to (have a) drink.

consonance [kɔ̃sɔnɑ̃s] *nf* consonance; **nom à** ~ **étrangère** foreign-sounding name.

consonne [kɔ̃sɔn] *nf* consonant.

consortium [kɔ̃sɔʀsjɔm] *nm* consortium.

consorts [kɔ̃sɔʀ] *nmpl:* **et** ~ (*péj*) and company, and his bunch *ou* like.

conspirateur, trice [kɔ̃spiʀatœʀ, -tʀis] *nm/f* conspirator, plotter.

conspiration [kɔ̃spiʀasjɔ̃] *nf* conspiracy.

conspirer [kɔ̃spiʀe] *vi* to conspire, plot; ~ **à** (*tendre à*) to conspire to.

conspuer [kɔ̃spɥe] *vt* to boo, shout down.

constamment [kɔ̃stamɑ̃] *adv* constantly.

constance [kɔ̃stɑ̃s] *nf* permanence, constancy; (*d'une amitié*) steadfastness; **travailler avec** ~ to work steadily; **il faut de la** ~ **pour la supporter** (*fam*) you need a lot of patience to put up with her.

constant, e [kɔ̃stɑ̃, -ɑ̃t] *adj* constant; (*personne*) steadfast ♦ *nf* constant.

Constantinople [kɔ̃stɑ̃tinɔpl(ə)] *n* Constantinople.

constat [kɔ̃sta] *nm* (*d'huissier*) certified report (*by bailiff*); (*de police*) report; (*observation*) (observed) fact, observation; (*affirmation*) statement; ~ (**à l'amiable**) (*jointly agreed*) statement for insurance purposes.

constatation [kɔ̃statasjɔ̃] *nf* noticing; certifying; (*remarque*) observation.

constater [kɔ̃state] *vt* (*remarquer*) to note, notice; (*ADMIN, JUR: attester*) to certify; (*dégâts*) to note; ~ **que** (*dire*) to state that.

constellation [kɔ̃stelasjɔ̃] *nf* constellation.

constellé, e [kɔ̃stele] *adj*: ~ **de** (*étoiles*) studded *ou* spangled with; (*taches*) spotted with.

consternant, e [kɔ̃stɛʀnɑ̃ -ɑ̃t] *adj* (*nouvelle*) dismaying; (*attristant, étonnant: bêtise*) appalling.

consternation [kɔ̃stɛʀnasjɔ̃] *nf* consternation, dismay.

consterner [kɔ̃stɛʀne] *vt* to dismay.

constipation [kɔ̃stipasjɔ̃] *nf* constipation.

constipé, e [kɔ̃stipe] *adj* constipated; (*fig*) stiff.

constituant, e [kɔ̃stitɥɑ̃, -ɑ̃t] *adj* (*élément*) constituent; **assemblée ~e** (*POL*) constituent assembly.

constitué, e [kɔ̃stitɥe] *adj*: ~ **de** made up *ou* composed of; **bien** ~ of sound constitution; well-formed.

constituer [kɔ̃stitɥe] *vt* (*comité, équipe*) to set up, form; (*dossier, collection*) to put together, build up; (*suj: éléments, parties: composer*) to make up, constitute; (*représenter, être*) to constitute; **se** ~ **prisonnier** to give o.s. up; **se** ~ **partie civile** *to bring an independent action for damages*.

constitution [kɔ̃stitysjɔ̃] *nf* setting up; building up; (*composition*) composition, make-up; (*santé, POL*) constitution.

constitutionnel, le [kɔ̃stitysjɔnɛl] *adj* constitutional.

constructeur [kɔ̃stʀyktœʀ] *nm* manufacturer, builder.

constructif, ive [kɔ̃stʀyktif, -iv] *adj* (*positif*) constructive.

construction [kɔ̃stʀyksjɔ̃] *nf* construction, building.

construire [kɔ̃stʀɥiʀ] *vt* to build, construct; **se** ~: **l'immeuble s'est construit très vite** the building went up *ou* was built very quickly.

consul [kɔ̃syl] *nm* consul.

consulaire [kɔ̃sylɛʀ] *adj* consular.

consulat [kɔ̃syla] *nm* consulate.

consultant, e [kɔ̃syltɑ̃, -ɑ̃t] *adj* consultant.

consultatif, ive [kɔ̃syltatif, -iv] *adj* advisory.

consultation [kɔ̃syltasjɔ̃] *nf* consultation; ~**s** *nfpl* (*POL*) talks; **être en** ~ (*délibération*) to be in consultation; (*médecin*) to be consulting; **aller à la** ~ (*MÉD*) to go to the surgery (*BRIT*) *ou* doctor's office (*US*); **heures de** ~ (*MÉD*) surgery (*BRIT*) *ou* office (*US*) hours.

consulter [kɔ̃sylte] *vt* to consult ♦ *vi* (*médecin*) to hold surgery (*BRIT*), be in (the office) (*US*); **se** ~ to confer.

consumer [kɔ̃syme] *vt* to consume; **se** ~ *vi* to burn; **se** ~ **de chagrin/douleur** to be consumed with sorrow/grief.

consumérisme [kɔ̃symeʀism(ə)] *nm* consumerism.

contact [kɔ̃takt] *nm* contact; **au** ~ **de** (*air, peau*) on contact with; (*gens*) through contact with; **mettre/couper le** ~ (*AUTO*) to switch on/off the ignition; **entrer en** ~ (*fils, objets*) to come into contact, make contact; **se mettre en** ~ **avec** (*RADIO*) to make contact with; **prendre** ~ **avec** (*relation d'affaires, connaissance*) to get in touch *ou* contact with.

contacter [kɔ̃takte] *vt* to contact, get in touch with.

contagieux, euse [kɔ̃taʒjø, -øz] *adj* contagious; infectious.

contagion [kɔ̃taʒjɔ̃] *nf* contagion.

container [kɔ̃tɛnɛʀ] *nm* container.

contamination [kɔ̃taminasjɔ̃] *nf* infection; contamination.

contaminer [kɔ̃tamine] *vt* (*par un virus*) to infect; (*par des radiations*) to contaminate.

conte [kɔ̃t] *nm* tale; ~ **de fées** fairy tale.

contemplatif, ive [kɔ̃tɑ̃platif, -iv] *adj* contemplative.

contemplation [kɔ̃tɑ̃plasjɔ̃] *nf* contemplation; (*REL, PHILOSOPHIE*) meditation.

contempler [kɔ̃tɑ̃ple] *vt* to contemplate, gaze at.

contemporain, e [kɔ̃tɑ̃pɔʀɛ̃, -ɛn] *adj, nm/f* contemporary.

contenance [kɔ̃tnɑ̃s] *nf* (*d'un récipient*) capacity; (*attitude*) bearing, attitude; **perdre** ~ to lose one's composure; **se donner une** ~ to give the impression of composure; **faire bonne** ~ (**devant**) to put on a bold front (in the face of).

conteneur [kɔ̃tnœʀ] *nm* container; ~ (**de bouteilles**) bottle bank.

conteneurisation [kɔ̃tnœʀizasjɔ̃] *nf* containerization.

contenir [kɔ̃tniʀ] *vt* to contain; (*avoir une capacité de*) to hold; **se** ~ (*se retenir*) to control o.s. *ou* one's emotions, contain o.s.

content, e [kɔ̃tɑ̃, -ɑ̃t] *adj* pleased, glad; ~ **de** pleased with; **je serais** ~ **que tu** ... I would be pleased if you ....

contentement [kɔ̃tɑ̃tmɑ̃] *nm* contentment, satisfaction.

contenter [kɔ̃tɑ̃te] *vt* to satisfy, please; (*envie*) to satisfy; **se** ~ **de** to content o.s. with.

contentieux [kɔ̃tɑ̃sjø] *nm* (*COMM*) litigation; (: *service*) litigation department; (*POL etc*) contentious issues *pl*.

contenu, e [kɔ̃tny] *pp de* **contenir** ♦ *nm* (*d'un bol*) contents *pl*; (*d'un texte*) content.

conter [kɔ̃te] *vt* to recount, relate; **en** ~ **de belles à qn** to tell tall stories to sb.

contestable [kɔ̃tɛstabl(ə)] *adj* questionable.

contestataire [kɔ̃tɛstatɛʀ] *adj* (*journal, étudiant*) anti-establishment ♦ *nm/f* (anti-establishment) protester.

contestation [kɔ̃tɛstasjɔ̃] *nf* questioning, contesting; (*POL*): **la** ~ anti-establishment activity, protest.

conteste [kɔ̃tɛst(ə)]: **sans** ~ *adv* unquestionably, indisputably.

contesté, e [kɔ̃tɛste] *adj* (*roman, écrivain*) controversial.

contester [kɔ̃tɛste] *vt* to question, contest ♦ *vi* (*POL, gén*) to protest, rebel (against established authority).

conteur, euse [kɔ̃tœʀ, -øz] *nm/f* story-teller.

contexte [kɔ̃tɛkst(ə)] *nm* context.

contiendrai [kɔ̃tjɛ̃dʀe], **contiens** [kɔ̃tjɛ̃] *etc vb voir* **contenir**.

contigu, ë [kɔ̃tigy] *adj*: ~ **(à)** adjacent (to).

continent [kɔ̃tinɑ̃] *nm* continent.

continental, e, aux [kɔ̃tinɑ̃tal, -o] *adj* continental.

contingences [kɔ̃tɛ̃ʒɑ̃s] *nfpl* contingencies.

contingent [kɔ̃tɛ̃ʒɑ̃] *nm* (*MIL*) contingent; (*COMM*) quota.

contingenter [kɔ̃tɛ̃ʒɑ̃te] *vt* (*COMM*) to fix a quota on.

contins [kɔ̃tɛ̃] *etc vb voir* **contenir**.

continu, e [kɔ̃tiny] *adj* continuous; (**courant**) ~ direct current, DC.

continuation [kɔ̃tinɥasjɔ̃] *nf* continuation.

continuel, le [kɔ̃tinɥɛl] *adj* (*qui se répète*) constant, continual; (*continu*) continuous.

continuellement [kɔ̃tinɥɛlmɑ̃] *adv* continually; continuously.

continuer [kɔ̃tinɥe] *vt* (*travail, voyage etc*) to continue (with), carry on (with), go on with; (*prolonger: alignement, rue*) to continue ♦ *vi* (*pluie, vie, bruit*) to continue, go on; (*voyageur*) to go on; **se** ~ *vi* to carry on; ~ **à** *ou* **de faire** to go on *ou* continue doing.

continuité [kɔ̃tinɥite] *nf* continuity; continuation.

contondant, e [kɔ̃tɔ̃dɑ̃, -ɑ̃t] *adj*: **arme** ~**e** blunt instrument.

contorsion [kɔ̃tɔʀsjɔ̃] *nf* contortion.

contorsionner [kɔ̃tɔʀsjɔne]: **se** ~ *vi* to contort o.s., writhe about.

contorsionniste [kɔ̃tɔʀsjɔnist(ə)] *nm/f* contortionist.

contour [kɔ̃tuʀ] *nm* outline, contour; ~**s** *nmpl* (*d'une rivière etc*) windings.

contourner [kɔ̃tuʀne] *vt* to bypass, walk (*ou* drive) round.

contraceptif, ive [kɔ̃tʀasɛptif, -iv] *adj, nm* contraceptive.

contraception [kɔ̃tʀasɛpsjɔ̃] *nf* contraception.

contracté, e [kɔ̃tʀakte] *adj* (*muscle*) tense, contracted; (*personne: tendu*) tense, tensed up; **article** ~ (*LING*) contracted article.

contracter [kɔ̃tʀakte] *vt* (*muscle etc*) to tense, contract; (*maladie, dette, obligation*) to contract; (*assurance*) to take out; **se** ~ *vi* (*métal, muscles*) to contract.

contraction [kɔ̃tʀaksjɔ̃] *nf* contraction.

contractuel, le [kɔ̃tʀaktɥɛl] *adj* contractual ♦ *nm/f* (*agent*) traffic warden; (*employé*) contract employee.

contradiction [kɔ̃tʀadiksjɔ̃] *nf* contradiction.

contradictoire [kɔ̃tʀadiktwaʀ] *adj* contradic-

tory, conflicting; **débat** ~ (open) debate.

contraignant, e [kɔ̃tʀɛɲɑ̃, -ɑ̃t] *vb voir* **contraindre** ♦ *adj* restricting.

contraindre [kɔ̃tʀɛ̃dʀ(ə)] *vt*: ~ **qn à faire** to force *ou* compel sb to do.

contraint, e [kɔ̃tʀɛ̃, -ɛ̃t] *pp de* **contraindre** ♦ *adj* (*mine, air*) constrained, forced ♦ *nf* constraint; **sans** ~**e** unrestrainedly, unconstrainedly.

contraire [kɔ̃tʀɛʀ] *adj, nm* opposite; ~ **à** contrary to; **au** ~ *adv* on the contrary.

contrairement [kɔ̃tʀɛʀmɑ̃] *adv*: ~ **à** contrary to, unlike.

contralto [kɔ̃tʀalto] *nm* contralto.

contrariant, e [kɔ̃tʀaʀjɑ̃, -ɑ̃t] *adj* (*personne*) contrary, perverse; (*incident*) annoying.

contrarier [kɔ̃tʀaʀje] *vt* (*personne*) to annoy, bother; (*fig*) to impede; to thwart, frustrate.

contrariété [kɔ̃tʀaʀjete] *nf* annoyance.

contraste [kɔ̃tʀast(ə)] *nm* contrast.

contraster [kɔ̃tʀaste] *vt, vi* to contrast.

contrat [kɔ̃tʀa] *nm* contract; (*fig: accord, pacte*) agreement; ~ **de travail** employment contract.

contravention [kɔ̃tʀavɑ̃sjɔ̃] *nf* (*infraction*): ~ **à** contravention of; (*amende*) fine; (*PV pour stationnement interdit*) parking ticket; **dresser** ~ **à** (*automobiliste*) to book; to write out a parking ticket for.

contre [kɔ̃tʀ(ə)] *prép* against; (*en échange*) (in exchange) for; **par** ~ on the other hand.

contre-amiral, aux [kɔ̃tʀamiʀal, -o] *nm* rear admiral.

contre-attaque [kɔ̃tʀatak] *nf* counterattack.

contre-attaquer [kɔ̃tʀatake] *vi* to counterattack.

contre-balancer [kɔ̃tʀəbalɑ̃se] *vt* to counterbalance; (*fig*) to offset.

contrebande [kɔ̃tʀəbɑ̃d] *nf* (*trafic*) contraband, smuggling; (*marchandise*) contraband, smuggled goods *pl*; **faire la** ~ **de** to smuggle.

contrebandier, ière [kɔ̃tʀəbɑ̃dje, -jɛʀ] *nm/f* smuggler.

contrebas [kɔ̃tʀəba]: **en** ~ *adv* (down) below.

contrebasse [kɔ̃tʀəbas] *nf* (double) bass.

contrebassiste [kɔ̃tʀəbasist(ə)] *nm/f* (double) bass player.

contre-braquer [kɔ̃tʀəbʀake] *vi* to steer into a skid.

contrecarrer [kɔ̃tʀəkaʀe] *vt* to thwart.

contrechamp [kɔ̃tʀəʃɑ̃] *nm* (*CINÉ*) reverse shot.

contrecœur [kɔ̃tʀəkœʀ]: **à** ~ *adv* (be)grudgingly, reluctantly.

contrecoup [kɔ̃tʀəku] *nm* repercussions *pl*; **par** ~ as an indirect consequence.

contre-courant [kɔ̃tʀəkuʀɑ̃]: **à** ~ *adv* against the current.

contredire [kɔ̃tʀədiʀ] *vt* (*personne*) to contradict; (*témoignage, assertion, faits*) to refute; **se** ~ to contradict o.s.

contredit, e [kɔ̃tʀədi, -it] *pp de* **contredire**

◆ *nm*: **sans** ~ without question.
contrée [kɔ̃tre] *nf* region; land.
contre-écrou [kɔ̃trekru] *nm* lock nut.
contre-enquête [kɔ̃trɑ̃kɛt] *nf* counter-inquiry.
contre-espionnage [kɔ̃trɛspjɔnaʒ] *nm* counter-espionage.
contre-exemple [kɔ̃trɛgzɑ̃pl(ə)] *nf* counter-example.
contre-expertise [kɔ̃trɛkspɛrtiz] *nf* second (expert) assessment.
contrefaçon [kɔ̃trəfasɔ̃] *nf* forgery; ~ **de brevet** patent infringement.
contrefaire [kɔ̃trəfɛr] *vt* (*document, signature*) to forge, counterfeit; (*personne, démarche*) to mimic; (*dénaturer: sa voix etc*) to disguise.
contrefait, e [kɔ̃trəfɛ, -ɛt] *pp de* **contrefaire** ◆ *adj* misshapen, deformed.
contrefasse [kɔ̃trəfas], **contreferai** [kɔ̃trəfre] *etc vb voir* **contrefaire**.
contre-filet [kɔ̃trəfilɛ] *nm* (*CULIN*) sirloin.
contreforts [kɔ̃trəfɔr] *nmpl* foothills.
contre-haut [kɔ̃trəo]: **en** ~ *adv* (up) above.
contre-indication [kɔ̃trɛ̃dikasjɔ̃] *nf* contra-indication.
contre-indiqué, e [kɔ̃trɛ̃dike] *adj* (*MÉD*) contraindicated.
contre-interrogatoire [kɔ̃trɛ̃terɔgatwar] *nm*: **faire subir un** ~ **à qn** to cross-examine sb.
contre-jour [kɔ̃trəʒur]: **à** ~ *adv* against the light.
contremaître [kɔ̃trəmɛtr(ə)] *nm* foreman.
contre-manifestant, e [kɔ̃trəmanifɛstɑ̃, -ɑ̃t] *nm/f* counter-demonstrator.
contre-manifestation [kɔ̃trəmanifɛstasjɔ̃] *nf* counter-demonstration.
contremarque [kɔ̃trəmark(ə)] *nf* (*ticket*) pass-out ticket.
contre-offensive [kɔ̃trɔfɑ̃siv] *nf* counter-offensive.
contre-ordre [kɔ̃trɔrdr(ə)] *nm* = **contrordre**.
contrepartie [kɔ̃trəparti] *nf* compensation; **en** ~ in compensation; in return.
contre-performance [kɔ̃trəpɛrfɔrmɑ̃s] *nf* below-average performance.
contrepèterie [kɔ̃trəpetri] *nf* spoonerism.
contre-pied [kɔ̃trəpje] *nm* (*inverse, opposé*): **le** ~ **de ...** the exact opposite of ...; **prendre le** ~ **de** to take the opposing view of; to take the opposite course to; **prendre qn à** ~ (*SPORT*) to wrong-foot sb.
contre-plaqué [kɔ̃trəplake] *nm* plywood.
contre-plongée [kɔ̃trəplɔ̃ʒe] *nf* low-angle shot.
contrepoids [kɔ̃trəpwa] *nm* counterweight, counterbalance; **faire** ~ to act as a counterbalance.
contrepoil [kɔ̃trəpwal]: **à** ~ *adv* the wrong way.
contrepoint [kɔ̃trəpwɛ̃] *nm* counterpoint.
contrepoison [kɔ̃trəpwazɔ̃] *nm* antidote.
contrer [kɔ̃tre] *vt* to counter.

contre-révolution [kɔ̃trərevɔlysjɔ̃] *nf* counter-revolution.
contre-révolutionnaire [kɔ̃trərevɔlysjɔnɛr] *nm/f* counter-revolutionary.
contresens [kɔ̃trəsɑ̃s] *nm* misinterpretation; (*mauvaise traduction*) mistranslation; (*absurdité*) nonsense no *pl*; **à** ~ *adv* the wrong way.
contresigner [kɔ̃trəsiɲe] *vt* to countersign.
contretemps [kɔ̃trətɑ̃] *nm* hitch, contretemps; **à** ~ *adv* (*MUS*) out of time; (*fig*) at an inopportune moment.
contre-terrorisme [kɔ̃trəterɔrism(ə)] *nm* counter-terrorism.
contre-terroriste [kɔ̃trəterɔrist(ə)] *nm/f* counter-terrorist.
contre-torpilleur [kɔ̃trətɔrpijœr] *nm* destroyer.
contrevenant, e [kɔ̃trəvnɑ̃, -ɑ̃t] *vb voir* **contrevenir** ◆ *nm/f* offender.
contrevenir [kɔ̃trəvnir]: ~ **à** *vt* to contravene.
contre-voie [kɔ̃trəvwa]: **à** ~ *adv* (*en sens inverse*) on the wrong track; (*du mauvais côté*) on the wrong side.
contribuable [kɔ̃tribɥabl(ə)] *nm/f* taxpayer.
contribuer [kɔ̃tribɥe]: ~ **à** *vt* to contribute towards.
contribution [kɔ̃tribɥsjɔ̃] *nf* contribution; **les** ~**s** (*bureaux*) the tax office; **mettre à** ~ to call upon; ~**s directes/indirectes** direct/indirect taxation.
contrit, e [kɔ̃tri, -it] *adj* contrite.
contrôlable [kɔ̃trolabl(ə)] *adj* (*maîtrisable: situation, débit*) controllable; (*alibi, déclarations*) verifiable.
contrôle [kɔ̃trol] *nm* checking no *pl*, check; supervision; monitoring; (*test*) test, examination; **perdre le** ~ **de son véhicule** to lose control of one's vehicle; ~ **des changes** (*COMM*) exchange controls; ~ **continu** (*SCOL*) continuous assessment; ~ **d'identité** identity check; ~ **des naissances** birth control; ~ **des prix** price control.
contrôler [kɔ̃trole] *vt* (*vérifier*) to check; (*surveiller*) to supervise; to monitor, control; (*maîtriser, COMM: firme*) to control; **se** ~ to control o.s.
contrôleur, euse [kɔ̃trolœr, -øz] *nm/f* (*de train*) (ticket) inspector; (*de bus*) (bus) conductor/tress; ~ **de la navigation aérienne**, ~ **aérien** air traffic controller; ~ **financier** financial controller.
contrordre [kɔ̃trɔrdr(ə)] *nm* counter-order, countermand; **sauf** ~ unless otherwise directed.
controverse [kɔ̃trɔvɛrs(ə)] *nf* controversy.
controversé, e [kɔ̃trɔvɛrse] *adj* (*personnage, question*) controversial.
contumace [kɔ̃tymas]: **par** ~ *adv* in absentia.
contusion [kɔ̃tyzjɔ̃] *nf* bruise, contusion.
contusionné, e [kɔ̃tyzjɔne] *adj* bruised.
conurbation [kɔnyrbasjɔ̃] *nf* conurbation.
convaincant, e [kɔ̃vɛ̃kɑ̃, -ɑ̃t] *vb voir* **convaincre**

♦ adj convincing.

convaincre [kɔ̃vɛ̃kʀ(ə)] vt: ~ ~ qn **(de qch)** to convince sb (of sth); ~ qn **(de faire)** to persuade sb (to do); ~ **qn de** (JUR: délit) to convict sb of.

convaincu, e [kɔ̃vɛ̃ky] pp de **convaincre** ♦ adj: **d'un ton** ~ with conviction.

convainquais [kɔ̃vɛ̃kɛ] etc vb voir **convaincre**.

convalescence [kɔ̃valesɑ̃s] nf convalescence; **maison de** ~ convalescent home.

convalescent, e [kɔ̃valesɑ̃, -ɑ̃t] adj, nm/f convalescent.

convenable [kɔ̃vnabl(ə)] adj suitable; (décent) acceptable, proper; (assez bon) decent, acceptable; adequate, passable.

convenablement [kɔ̃vnabləmɑ̃] adv (placé, choisi) suitably; (s'habiller, s'exprimer) properly; (payé, logé) decently.

convenance [kɔ̃vnɑ̃s] nf: **à ma/votre** ~ to my/ your liking; ~**s** nfpl proprieties.

convenir [kɔ̃vniʀ] vt to be suitable; ~ **à** to suit; **il convient de** it is advisable to; (bienséant) it is right ou proper to; ~ **de** (bienfondé de qch) to admit (to), acknowledge; (date, somme etc) to agree upon; ~ **que** (admettre) to admit that, acknowledge the fact that; ~ **de faire qch** to agree to do sth; **il a été convenu que** it has been agreed that; **comme convenu** as agreed.

convention [kɔ̃vɑ̃sjɔ̃] nf convention; ~**s** nfpl (convenances) convention sg, social conventions; **de** ~ conventional; ~ **collective** (ÉCON) collective agreement.

conventionnalisme [kɔ̃vɑ̃sjɔnalism(ə)] nm (des idées) conventionality.

conventionné, e [kɔ̃vɑ̃sjɔne] adj (ADMIN) applying charges laid down by the state.

conventionnel, le [kɔ̃vɑ̃sjɔnɛl] adj conventional.

conventionnellement [kɔ̃vɑ̃sjɔnɛlmɑ̃] adv conventionally.

conventuel, le [kɔ̃vɑ̃tɥɛl] adj monastic; monastery cpd; conventual, convent cpd.

convenu, e [kɔ̃vny] pp de **convenir** ♦ adj agreed.

convergent, e [kɔ̃vɛʀʒɑ̃, -ɑ̃t] adj convergent.

converger [kɔ̃vɛʀʒe] vi to converge; ~ **vers** ou **sur** to converge on.

conversation [kɔ̃vɛʀsasjɔ̃] nf conversation; **avoir de la** ~ to be a good conversationalist.

converser [kɔ̃vɛʀse] vi to converse.

conversion [kɔ̃vɛʀsjɔ̃] nf conversion; (SKI) kick turn.

convertible [kɔ̃vɛʀtibl(ə)] adj (ÉCON) convertible; **(canapé)** ~ sofa bed.

convertir [kɔ̃vɛʀtiʀ] vt: ~ **qn (à)** to convert sb (to); ~ **qch en** to convert sth into; **se** ~ **(à)** to be converted (to).

convertisseur [kɔ̃vɛʀtisœʀ] nm (ÉLEC) converter.

convexe [kɔ̃vɛks(ə)] adj convex.

conviction [kɔ̃viksjɔ̃] nf conviction.

conviendrai [kɔ̃vjɛ̃dʀe], **conviens** [kɔ̃vjɛ̃] etc vb voir **convenir**.

convier [kɔ̃vje] vt: ~ **qn à** (dîner etc) to (cordially) invite sb to; ~ **qn à faire** to urge sb to do.

convint [kɔ̃vɛ̃] etc vb voir **convenir**.

convive [kɔ̃viv] nm/f guest (at table).

convivial, e [kɔ̃vivjal] adj (INFORM) userfriendly.

convocation [kɔ̃vɔkasjɔ̃] nf (voir convoquer) convening, convoking; summoning; invitation; (document) notification to attend; summons sg.

convoi [kɔ̃vwa] nm (de voitures, prisonniers) convoy; (train) train; ~ **(funèbre)** funeral procession.

convoiter [kɔ̃vwate] vt to covet.

convoitise [kɔ̃vwatiz] nf covetousness; (sexuelle) lust, desire.

convoler [kɔ̃vɔle] vi: ~ **(en justes noces)** to be wed.

convoquer [kɔ̃vɔke] vt (assemblée) to convene, convoke; (subordonné, témoin) to summon; (candidat) to ask to attend; ~ **qn (à)** (réunion) to invite sb (to attend).

convoyer [kɔ̃vwaje] vt to escort.

convoyeur [kɔ̃vwajœʀ] nm (NAVIG) escort ship; ~ **de fonds** security guard.

convulsé, e [kɔ̃vylse] adj (visage) distorted.

convulsif, ive [kɔ̃vylsif, -iv] adj convulsive.

convulsions [kɔ̃vylsjɔ̃] nfpl convulsions.

coopérant [kɔɔpeʀɑ̃] nm ≈ person doing Voluntary Service Overseas (BRIT), ≈ member of the Peace Corps (US).

coopératif, ive [kɔɔpeʀatif, -iv] adj, nf cooperative.

coopération [kɔɔpeʀasjɔ̃] nf co-operation; (ADMIN): **la C**~ ≈ Voluntary Service Overseas (BRIT) ou the Peace Corps (US) (done as alternative to military service).

coopérer [kɔɔpeʀe] vi: ~ **(à)** to co-operate (in).

coordination [kɔɔʀdinasjɔ̃] nf coordination.

coordonnateur, trice [kɔɔʀdɔnatœʀ, -tʀis] adj coordinating ♦ nm/f coordinator.

coordonné, e [kɔɔʀdɔne] adj coordinated ♦ nf (LING) coordinate clause; ~**s** nmpl (vêtements) coordinates; ~**es** nfpl (MATH) coordinates; (détails personnels) address, phone number, schedule etc; whereabouts.

coordonner [kɔɔʀdɔne] vt to coordinate.

copain, copine [kɔpɛ̃, kɔpin] nm/f mate (BRIT), pal ♦ adj: **être** ~ **avec** to be pally with.

copeau, x [kɔpo] nm shaving; (de métal) turning.

Copenhague [kɔpənag] n Copenhagen.

copie [kɔpi] nf copy; (SCOL) script, paper; exercise; ~ **certifiée conforme** certified copy; ~ **papier** (INFORM) hard copy.

copier [kɔpje] vt, vi to copy; ~ **sur** to copy from.

copieur [kɔpjœʀ] nm (photo)copier.

copieusement [kɔpjøzmɑ̃] adv copiously.

copieux, euse [kɔpjø, -øz] *adj* copious, hearty.

copilote [kɔpilɔt] *nm* (*AVIAT*) co-pilot; (*AUTO*) co-driver, navigator.

copinage [kɔpinaʒ] *nm*: **obtenir qch par ~** to get sth through contacts.

copine [kɔpin] *nf voir* **copain**.

copiste [kɔpist(ə)] *nm/f* copyist, transcriber.

coproduction [kɔprɔdyksjɔ̃] *nf* coproduction, joint production.

copropriétaire [kɔprɔprijetɛʀ] *nm/f* co-owner.

copropriété [kɔprɔprijete] *nf* co-ownership, joint ownership; **acheter en ~** to buy on a co-ownership basis.

copulation [kɔpylɑsjɔ̃] *nf* copulation.

copyright [kɔpiʀajt] *nm* copyright.

coq [kɔk] *nm* cock, rooster ♦ *adj inv* (*BOXE*): **poids ~** bantamweight; **~ de bruyère** grouse; **~ du village** (*fig: péj*) ladykiller.

coq-à-l'âne [kɔkalɑn] *nm inv* abrupt change of subject.

coque [kɔk] *nf* (*de noix, mollusque*) shell; (*de bateau*) hull; **à la ~** (*CULIN*) (soft-)boiled.

coquelet [kɔklɛ] *nm* (*CULIN*) cockerel.

coquelicot [kɔkliko] *nm* poppy.

coqueluche [kɔklyʃ] *nf* whooping-cough; (*fig*): **être la ~ de qn** to be sb's flavour of the month.

coquet, te [kɔkɛ, -ɛt] *adj* appearance-conscious; (*joli*) pretty.

coquetier [kɔktje] *nm* egg-cup.

coquettement [kɔkɛtmɑ̃] *adv* (*s'habiller*) attractively; (*meubler*) prettily.

coquetterie [kɔkɛtʀi] *nf* appearance-consciousness.

coquillage [kɔkijaʒ] *nm* (*mollusque*) shellfish *inv*; (*coquille*) shell.

coquille [kɔkij] *nf* shell; (*TYPO*) misprint; **~ de beurre** shell of butter; **~ d'œuf** *adj* (*couleur*) eggshell; **~ de noix** nutshell; **~ St Jacques** scallop.

coquillettes [kɔkijɛt] *nfpl* pasta shells.

coquin, e [kɔkɛ̃, -in] *adj* mischievous, roguish; (*polisson*) naughty ♦ *nm/f* (*péj*) rascal.

cor [kɔʀ] *nm* (*MUS*) horn; (*MÉD*): **~ (au pied)** corn; **réclamer à ~ et à cri** to clamour for; **~ anglais** cor anglais; **~ de chasse** hunting horn.

corail, aux [kɔʀaj, -o] *nm* coral *no pl*.

Coran [kɔʀɑ̃] *nm*: **le ~** the Koran.

coraux [kɔʀo] *pl de* **corail**.

corbeau, x [kɔʀbo] *nm* crow.

corbeille [kɔʀbɛj] *nf* basket; (*BOURSE*): **la ~** ≈ the floor (of the Stock Exchange); **~ de mariage** (*fig*) wedding presents *pl*; **~ à ouvrage** work-basket; **~ à pain** breadbasket; **~ à papier** waste paper basket *ou* bin.

corbillard [kɔʀbijaʀ] *nm* hearse.

cordage [kɔʀdaʒ] *nm* rope; **~s** *nmpl* (*de voilure*) rigging *sg*.

corde [kɔʀd(ə)] *nf* rope; (*de violon, raquette, d'arc*) string; (*trame*): **la ~** the thread; (*ATH-*

LÉTISME, AUTO): **la ~** the rails *pl*; **les ~s** (*BOXE*) the ropes; **les (instruments à) ~s** (*MUS*) the strings, the stringed instruments; **semelles de ~** rope soles; **tenir la ~** (*ATH-LÉTISME, AUTO*) to be in the inside lane; **tomber des ~s** to rain cats and dogs; **tirer sur la ~** to go too far; **la ~ sensible** the right chord; **usé jusqu'à la ~** threadbare; **~ à linge** washing *ou* clothes line; **~ lisse** (climbing) rope; **~ à nœuds** knotted climbing rope; **~ raide** tightrope; **~ à sauter** skipping rope; **~s vocales** vocal cords.

cordeau, x [kɔʀdo] *nm* string, line; **tracé au ~** as straight as a die.

cordée [kɔʀde] *nf* (*d'alpinistes*) rope, roped party.

cordelière [kɔʀdəljɛʀ] *nf* cord (belt).

cordial, e, aux [kɔʀdjal, -o] *adj* warm, cordial ♦ *nm* cordial, pick-me-up.

cordialement [kɔʀdjalmɑ̃] *adv* cordially, heartily; (*formule épistolaire*) (kind) regards.

cordialité [kɔʀdjalite] *nf* warmth, cordiality.

cordillère [kɔʀdijɛʀ] *nf*: **la ~ des Andes** the Andes cordillera *ou* range.

cordon [kɔʀdɔ̃] *nm* cord, string; **~ sanitaire/police** sanitary/police cordon; **~ littoral** sandbank, sandbar; **~ ombilical** umbilical cord.

cordon-bleu [kɔʀdɔ̃blø] *adj, nm/f* cordon bleu.

cordonnerie [kɔʀdɔnʀi] *nf* shoe repairer's *ou* mender's (shop).

cordonnier [kɔʀdɔnje] *nm* shoe repairer *ou* mender, cobbler.

cordouan, e [kɔʀduɑ̃, -an] *adj* Cordovan.

Cordoue [kɔʀdu] *n* Cordoba.

Corée [kɔʀe] *nf*: **la ~** Korea; **la ~ du Sud/du Nord** South/North Korea; **la République (démocratique populaire) de ~** the (Democratic People's) Republic of Korea.

coréen, ne [kɔʀeɛ̃, -ɛn] *adj* Korean ♦ *nm* (*LING*) Korean ♦ *nm/f*: **C~, ne** Korean.

coreligionnaire [kɔʀəliʒjɔnɛʀ] *nm/f* fellow Christian/Muslim/Jew *etc*.

Corfou [kɔʀfu] *n* Corfu.

coriace [kɔʀjas] *adj* tough.

coriandre [kɔʀjɑ̃dʀ(ə)] *nf* coriander.

Corinthe [kɔʀɛ̃t] *n* Corinth.

cormoran [kɔʀmɔʀɑ̃] *nm* cormorant.

cornac [kɔʀnak] *nm* elephant driver.

corne [kɔʀn(ə)] *nf* horn; (*de cerf*) antler; (*de la peau*) callus; **~ d'abondance** horn of plenty; **~ de brume** (*NAVIG*) foghorn.

cornée [kɔʀne] *nf* cornea.

corneille [kɔʀnɛj] *nf* crow.

cornélien, ne [kɔʀneljɛ̃, -ɛn] *adj* (*débat etc*) where love and duty conflict.

cornemuse [kɔʀnəmyz] *nf* bagpipes *pl*; **joueur de ~** piper.

corner *nm* [kɔʀnɛʀ] (*FOOTBALL*) corner (kick) ♦ *vb* [kɔʀne] *vt* (*pages*) to make dog-eared ♦ *vi* (*klaxonner*) to blare out.

cornet [kɔʀnɛ] *nm* (*paper*) cone; (*de glace*) cornet, cone; ~ **à pistons** cornet.

cornette [kɔrnɛt] *nf* cornet (*headgear*).

corniaud [kɔrnjo] *nm* (*chien*) mongrel; (*péj*) twit, clot.

corniche [kɔrniʃ] *nf* (*de meuble, neigeuse*) cornice; (*route*) coast road.

cornichon [kɔrniʃɔ̃] *nm* gherkin.

Cornouailles [kɔrnwaj] *nf(pl)* Cornwall.

cornue [kɔrny] *nf* retort.

corollaire [kɔrɔlɛr] *nm* corollary.

corolle [kɔrɔl] *nf* corolla.

coron [kɔrɔ̃] *nm* mining cottage; mining village.

coronaire [kɔrɔnɛr] *adj* coronary.

corporation [kɔrpɔrasjɔ̃] *nf* corporate body; (*au Moyen-Âge*) guild.

corporel, le [kɔrpɔrɛl] *adj* bodily; (*punition*) corporal; **soins** ~**s** care *sg* of the body.

corps [kɔr] *nm* (*gén*) body; (*cadavre*) (dead) body; **à son** ~ **défendant** against one's will; **à** ~ **perdu** headlong; **perdu** ~ **et biens** lost with all hands; **prendre** ~ to take shape; **faire** ~ **avec** to be joined to; to form one body with; ~ **d'armée (CA)** army corps; ~ **de ballet** corps de ballet; ~ **constitués** (*POL*) constitutional bodies; **le** ~ **consulaire (CC)** the consular corps; ~ **à** ~ *adv* hand-to-hand ♦ *nm* clinch; **le** ~ **du délit** (*JUR*) corpus delicti; **le** ~ **diplomatique (CD)** the diplomatic corps; **le** ~ **électoral** the electorate; **le** ~ **enseignant** the teaching profession; ~ **étranger** (*MÉD*) foreign body; ~ **expéditionnaire** task force; ~ **de garde** guardroom; ~ **législatif** legislative body; **le** ~ **médical** the medical profession.

corpulence [kɔrpylãs] *nf* build; (*embonpoint*) stoutness (*BRIT*), corpulence; **de forte** ~ **of** large build.

corpulent, e [kɔrpylã, -ãt] *adj* stout (*BRIT*), corpulent.

corpus [kɔrpys] *nm* (*LING*) corpus.

correct, e [kɔrɛkt] *adj* (*exact*) accurate, correct; (*bienséant, honnête*) correct; (*passable*) adequate.

correctement [kɔrɛktəmã] *adv* accurately; correctly; adequately.

correcteur, trice [kɔrɛktœr, -tris] *nm/f* (*SCOL*) examiner, marker; (*TYPO*) proofreader.

correctif, ive [kɔrɛktif, -iv] *adj* corrective ♦ *nm* (*mise au point*) rider, qualification.

correction [kɔrɛksjɔ̃] *nf* (*voir corriger*) correction; marking; (*voir correct*) correctness; (*rature, surcharge*) correction, emendation; (*coups*) thrashing; ~ **sur écran** (*INFORM*) screen editing; ~ **des épreuves**) proofreading.

correctionnel, le [kɔrɛksjɔnɛl] *adj* (*JUR*): **tribunal** ~ ≈ criminal court.

corrélation [kɔrelasjɔ̃] *nf* correlation.

correspondance [kɔrɛspɔ̃dãs] *nf* correspondence; (*de train, d'avion*) connection; **ce train assure la** ~ **avec l'avion de 10 heures** this

train connects with the 10 o'clock plane; **cours par** ~ correspondence course; **vente par** ~ mail-order business.

correspondancier, ière [kɔrɛspɔ̃dãsje, -jɛr] *nm/f* correspondence clerk.

correspondant, e [kɔrɛspɔ̃dã, -ãt] *nm/f* correspondent; (*TÉL*) person phoning (*ou* being phoned).

correspondre [kɔrɛspɔ̃dr(ə)] *vi* (*données, témoignages*) to correspond, tally; (*chambres*) to communicate; ~ **à** to correspond to; ~ **avec qn** to correspond with sb.

Corrèze [kɔrɛz] *nf*: **la** ~ the Corrèze.

corrézien, ne [kɔrezjɛ̃, -ɛn] *adj* of *ou* from the Corrèze.

corrida [kɔrida] *nf* bullfight.

corridor [kɔridɔr] *nm* corridor, passage.

corrigé [kɔriʒe] *nm* (*SCOL*) correct version; fair copy.

corriger [kɔriʒe] *vt* (*devoir*) to correct, mark; (*texte*) to correct, emend; (*erreur, défaut*) to correct, put right; (*punir*) to thrash; ~ **qn de** (*défaut*) to cure sb of; **se** ~ **de** to cure o.s. of.

corroborer [kɔrɔbɔre] *vt* to corroborate.

corroder [kɔrɔde] *vt* to corrode.

corrompre [kɔrɔ̃pr(ə)] *vt* (*dépraver*) to corrupt; (*acheter: témoin etc*) to bribe.

corrompu, e [kɔrɔ̃py] *adj* corrupt.

corrosif, ive [kɔrɔzif, -iv] *adj* corrosive.

corrosion [kɔrɔziɔ̃] *nf* corrosion.

corruption [kɔrypsjɔ̃] *nf* corruption; bribery.

corsage [kɔrsaʒ] *nm* (*d'une robe*) bodice; (*chemisier*) blouse.

corsaire [kɔrsɛr] *nm* pirate, corsair; privateer.

corse [kɔrs(ə)] *adj* Corsican ♦ *nm/f*: **C**~ Corsican ♦ *nf*: **la C**~ Corsica.

corsé, e [kɔrse] *adj* vigorous; (*café etc*) full-flavoured (*BRIT*) *ou* -flavored (*US*); (*goût*) full; (*fig*) spicy; tricky.

corselet [kɔrsəlɛ] *nm* corselet.

corser [kɔrse] *vt* (*difficulté*) to aggravate; (*intrigue*) to liven up; (*sauce*) to add spice to.

corset [kɔrsɛ] *nm* corset; (*d'une robe*) bodice; ~ **orthopédique** surgical corset.

corso [kɔrso] *nm*: ~ **fleuri** procession of floral floats.

cortège [kɔrtɛʒ] *nm* procession.

cortisone [kɔrtizon] *nf* (*MÉD*) cortisone.

corvée [kɔrve] *nf* chore, drudgery *no pl*; (*MIL*) fatigue (duty).

cosaque [kɔzak] *nm* cossack.

cosignataire [kɔsiɲatɛr] *adj*, *nm/f* co-signatory.

cosinus [kɔsinys] *nm* (*MATH*) cosine.

cosmétique [kɔsmetik] *nm* (*pour les cheveux*) hair-oil; (*produit de beauté*) beauty care product.

cosmétologie [kɔsmetɔlɔʒi] *nf* beauty care.

cosmique [kɔsmik] *adj* cosmic.

cosmonaute [kɔsmɔnot] *nm/f* cosmonaut, astronaut.

cosmopolite [kɔsmɔpɔlit] *adj* cosmopolitan.
cosmos [kɔsmɔs] *nm* outer space; cosmos.
cosse [kɔs] *nf* (*BOT*) pod, hull.
cossu, e [kɔsy] *adj* opulent-looking, well-to-do.
Costa Rica [kɔstaʀika] *nm*: **le ~** Costa Rica.
costaricien, ne [kɔstaʀisjɛ̃, -ɛn] *adj* Costa Rican ♦ *nm/f*: **C~**, **ne** Costa Rican.
costaud, e [kɔsto, -od] *adj* strong, sturdy.
costume [kɔstym] *nm* (*d'homme*) suit; (*de théâtre*) costume.
costumé, e [kɔstyme] *adj* dressed up.
costumier, ière [kɔstymje, -jɛʀ] *nm/f* (*fabricant, loueur*) costumier; (*THÉÂT*) wardrobe master/mistress.
cotangente [kɔtɑ̃ʒɑ̃t] *nf* (*MATH*) cotangent.
cotation [kɔtasjɔ̃] *nf* quoted value.
cote [kɔt] *nf* (*en Bourse etc*) quotation; quoted value; (*d'un cheval*): **la ~ de** the odds *pl* on; (*d'un candidat etc*) rating; (*mesure: sur une carte*) spot height; (: *sur un croquis*) dimension; (*de classement*) (classification) mark; reference number; **avoir la ~** to be very popular; **inscrit à la ~** quoted on the Stock Exchange; **~ d'alerte** danger *ou* flood level; **~ mal taillée** (*fig*) compromise; **~ de popularité** popularity rating.
coté, e [kɔte] *adj*: **être ~** to be listed *ou* quoted; **être ~ en Bourse** to be quoted on the Stock Exchange; **être bien/mal ~** to be highly/poorly rated.
côte [kot] *nf* (*rivage*) coast(line); (*pente*) slope; (: *sur une route*) hill; (*ANAT*) rib; (*d'un tricot, tissu*) rib, ribbing *no pl*; **~ à ~** *adv* side by side; **la C~** (**d'Azur**) the (French) Riviera; **la C~ d'Ivoire** the Ivory Coast.
côté [kote] *nm* (*gén*) side; (*direction*) way, direction; **de chaque ~** (**de**) on each side of; **de tous les ~s** from all directions; **de quel ~ est-il parti?** which way *ou* in which direction did he go?; **de ce/de l'autre ~** this/the other way; **d'un ~ ... de l'autre ~** (*alternative*) on (the) one hand ... on the other (hand); **du ~ de** (*provenance*) from; (*direction*) towards; **du ~ de Lyon** (*proximité*) near Lyons; **du ~ gauche** on the left-hand side; **de ~** *adv* sideways; on one side; to one side; aside; **laisser de ~** to leave on one side; **mettre de ~** to put on one side, put aside; **de mon ~** (*quant à moi*) for my part; **à ~** *adv* (right) nearby; beside; next door; (*d'autre part*) besides; **à ~ de** beside; next to; (*fig*) in comparison to; **à ~** (**de la cible**) off target, wide (of the mark); **être aux ~s de** to be by the side of.
coteau, x [kɔto] *nm* hill.
côtelé, e [kotle] *adj* ribbed; **pantalon en velours ~** corduroy trousers *pl*.
côtelette [kotlɛt] *nf* chop.
coter [kɔte] *vt* (*BOURSE*) to quote.
coterie [kɔtʀi] *nf* set.
côtier, ière [kotje, -jɛʀ] *adj* coastal.
cotisation [kɔtizasjɔ̃] *nf* subscription, dues *pl*;

(*pour une pension*) contributions *pl*.
cotiser [kɔtize] *vi*: **~** (**à**) to pay contributions (to); (*à une association*) to subscribe (to); **se ~** to club together.
coton [kɔtɔ̃] *nm* cotton; **~ hydrophile** cotton wool (*BRIT*), absorbent cotton (*US*).
cotonnade [kɔtɔnad] *nf* cotton (fabric).
Coton-Tige [kɔtɔ̃tiʒ] *nm* ® cotton bud ®.
côtoyer [kotwaje] *vt* to be close to; (*rencontrer*) to rub shoulders with; (*longer*) to run alongside; (*fig: friser*) to be bordering *ou* verging on.
cotte [kɔt] *nf*: **~ de mailles** coat of mail.
cou [ku] *nm* neck.
couac [kwak] *nm* (*fam*) bum note.
couard, e [kwaʀ, -aʀd(ə)] *adj* cowardly.
couchage [kuʃaʒ] *nm voir* **sac**.
couchant [kuʃɑ̃] *adj*: **soleil ~** setting sun.
couche [kuʃ] *nf* (*strate: gén, GÉO*) layer, stratum (*pl* -a); (*de peinture, vernis*) coat; (*de poussière, crème*) layer; (*de bébé*) nappy (*BRIT*), diaper (*US*); **~ d'ozone** ozone layer; **~s** *nfpl* (*MÉD*) confinement *sg*; **~s sociales** social levels *ou* strata.
couché, e [kuʃe] *adj* (*étendu*) lying down; (*au lit*) in bed.
couche-culotte, *pl* **couches-culottes** [kuʃkylɔt] *nf* (plastic-coated) disposable nappy (*BRIT*) *ou* diaper (*US*).
coucher [kuʃe] *nm* (*du soleil*) setting ♦ *vt* (*personne*) to put to bed; (: *loger*) to put up; (*objet*) to lay on its side; (*écrire*) to inscribe, couch ♦ *vi* (*dormir*) to sleep, spend the night; **~ avec qn** to sleep with sb, go to bed with sb; **se ~** *vi* (*pour dormir*) to go to bed; (*pour se reposer*) to lie down; (*soleil*) to set, go down; **à ~ prendre avant le ~** (*MÉD*) take at night *ou* before going to bed; **~ de soleil** sunset.
couchette [kuʃɛt] *nf* couchette; (*de marin*) bunk.
coucheur [kuʃœʀ] *nm*: **mauvais ~** awkward customer.
couci-couça [kusikusa] *adv* (*fam*) so-so.
coucou [kuku] *nm* cuckoo ♦ *excl* peek-a-boo.
coude [kud] *nm* (*ANAT*) elbow; (*de tuyau, de la route*) bend; **~ à ~** *adv* shoulder to shoulder, side by side.
coudée [kude] *nf*: **avoir ses ~s franches** (*fig*) to have a free rein.
cou-de-pied, *pl* **cous-de-pied** [kudpje] *nm* instep.
coudoyer [kudwaje] *vt* to brush past *ou* against; (*fig*) to rub shoulders with.
coudre [kudʀ(ə)] *vt* (*bouton*) to sew on; (*robe*) to sew (up) ♦ *vi* to sew.
couenne [kwan] *nf* (*de lard*) rind.
couette [kwɛt] *nf* duvet, (continental) quilt; **~s** *nfpl* (*cheveux*) bunches.
couffin [kufɛ̃] *nm* Moses basket; (straw) basket.
couilles [kuj] *nfpl* (*fam!*) balls (!).
couiner [kwine] *vi* to squeal.

coulage [kulaʒ] *nm* (*COMM*) loss of stock (*due to theft or negligence*).

coulant, e [kulɑ̃, -ɑ̃t] *adj* (*indulgent*) easy-going; (*fromage etc*) runny.

coulée [kule] *nf* (*de lave, métal en fusion*) flow; ~ **de neige** snowslide.

couler [kule] *vi* to flow, run; (*fuir: stylo, récipient*) to leak; (*sombrer: bateau*) to sink ♦ *vt* (*cloche, sculpture*) to cast; (*bateau*) to sink; (*fig*) to ruin, bring down; (: *passer*): ~ **une vie heureuse** to enjoy a happy life; **se** ~ **dans** (*interstice etc*) to slip into; **faire** ~ (*eau*) to run; **faire** ~ **un bain** to run a bath; **il a coulé une bielle** (*AUTO*) his big end went; ~ **de source** to follow on naturally; ~ **à pic** to sink *ou* go straight to the bottom.

couleur [kulœʀ] *nf* colour (*BRIT*), color (*US*); (*CARTES*) suit; ~**s** *nfpl* (*du teint*) colo(u)r *sg*; **les** ~**s** (*MIL*) the colo(u)rs; **en** ~**s** (*film*) in colo(u)r; **télévision en** ~**s** colo(u)r television; **de** ~ (*homme, femme*) colo(u)red; **sous** ~ **de** on the pretext of.

couleuvre [kulœvʀ(ə)] *nf* grass snake.

coulisse [kulis] *nf* (*TECH*) runner; ~**s** *nfpl* (*THÉÂT*) wings; (*fig*): **dans les** ~**s** behind the scenes; **porte à** ~ sliding door.

coulisser [kulise] *vi* to slide, run.

couloir [kulwaʀ] *nm* corridor, passage; (*d'avion*) aisle; (*de bus*) gangway; (: *sur la route*) bus lane; (*SPORT: de piste*) lane; (*GÉO*) gully; ~ **aérien** air corridor *ou* lane; ~ **de navigation** shipping lane.

coulpe [kulp(ə)] *nf*: **battre sa** ~ to repent openly.

coup [ku] *nm* (*heurt, choc*) knock; (*affectif*) blow, shock; (*agressif*) blow; (*avec arme à feu*) shot; (*de l'horloge*) chime; stroke; (*SPORT*) stroke; shot; blow; (*fam: fois*) time; (*ÉCHECS*) move; ~ **de coude/genou** nudge (with the elbow)/with the knee; **à** ~**s de hache/marteau** (hitting) with an axe/a hammer; ~ **de tonnerre** clap of thunder; ~ **de sonnette** ring of the bell; ~ **de crayon/pinceau** stroke of the pencil/brush; **donner un** ~ **de balai** to sweep up, give the floor a sweep; **donner un** ~ **de chiffon** to go round with the duster; **avoir le** ~ (*fig*) to have the knack; **être dans le/hors du** ~ to be/not to be in on it; **boire un** ~ to have a drink; **d'un seul** ~ (*subitement*) suddenly; (*à la fois*) at one go; in one blow; **du** ~ so (you see); **du premier** ~ first time *ou* go, at the first attempt; **du même** ~ at the same time; **à** ~ **sûr** definitely, without fail; **après** ~ afterwards; ~ **sur** ~ in quick succession; **être sur un** ~ to be on to something; **sur le** ~ outright; **sous le** ~ **de** (*surprise etc*) under the influence of; **tomber sous le** ~ **de la loi** to constitute a statutory offence; **à tous les** ~**s** every time; **il a raté son** ~ he missed his turn; **pour le** ~ for once; ~ **bas** (*fig*): **donner un** ~ **bas à qn** to hit sb below the belt; ~ **de chance** stroke of luck; ~ **de chapeau** (*fig*) pat on the back; ~ **de couteau** stab (of a knife); ~ **dur** hard blow; ~ **d'éclat** (great) feat; ~ **d'envoi** kick-off; ~ **d'essai** first attempt; ~ **d'état** coup d'état; ~ **de feu** shot; ~ **de filet** (*POLICE*) haul; ~ **de foudre** (*fig*) love at first sight; ~ **fourré** stab in the back; ~ **franc** free kick; ~ **de frein** (sharp) braking *no pl*; ~ **de fusil** rifle shot; ~ **de grâce** coup de grâce; ~ **du lapin** (*AUTO*) whiplash; ~ **de main**: **donner un** ~ **de main à qn** to give sb a (helping) hand; ~ **de maître** master stroke; ~ **d'œil** glance; ~ **de pied** kick; ~ **de poing** punch; ~ **de soleil** sunburn *no pl*; ~ **de téléphone** phone call; ~ **de tête** (*fig*) (sudden) impulse; ~ **de théâtre** (*fig*) dramatic turn of events; ~ **de vent** gust of wind; **en** ~ **de vent** (*rapidement*) in a tearing hurry.

coupable [kupabl(ə)] *adj* guilty; (*pensée*) guilty, culpable ♦ *nm/f* (*gén*) culprit; (*JUR*) guilty party; ~ **de** guilty of.

coupant, e [kupɑ̃, -ɑ̃t] *adj* (*lame*) sharp; (*fig: voix, ton*) cutting.

coupe [kup] *nf* (*verre*) goblet; (*à fruits*) dish; (*SPORT*) cup; (*de cheveux, de vêtement*) cut; (*graphique, plan*) (cross) section; **être sous la** ~ **de** to be under the control of; **faire des** ~**s sombres dans** to make drastic cuts in.

coupé, e [kupe] *adj* (*communications, route*) cut, blocked; (*vêtement*): **bien/mal** ~ well/badly cut ♦ *nm* (*AUTO*) coupé.

coupe-circuit [kupsiʀkɥi] *nm inv* cutout, circuit breaker.

coupée [kupe] *nf* (*NAVIG*) gangway.

coupe-feu [kupfø] *nm inv* firebreak.

coupe-gorge [kupgɔʀʒ(ə)] *nm inv* cut-throats' den.

coupe-ongles [kupɔ̃gl(ə)] *nm inv* (*pince*) nail clippers; (*ciseaux*) nail scissors.

coupe-papier [kuppapje] *nm inv* paper knife.

couper [kupe] *vt* to cut; (*retrancher*) to cut (out), take out; (*route, courant*) to cut off; (*appétit*) to take away; (*fièvre*) to take down, reduce; (*vin, cidre*) to blend; (: *à table*) to dilute (with water) ♦ *vi* to cut; (*prendre un raccourci*) to take a short-cut; (*CARTES: diviser le paquet*) to cut; (: *avec l'atout*) to trump; **se** ~ (*se blesser*) to cut o.s.; (*en témoignant etc*) to give o.s. away; ~ **l'appétit à qn** to spoil sb's appetite; ~ **la parole à qn** to cut sb short; ~ **les vivres à qn** to cut off sb's vital supplies; ~ **le contact** *ou* **l'allumage** (*AUTO*) to turn off the ignition; ~ **les ponts avec qn** to break with sb; **se faire** ~ **les cheveux** to have *ou* get one's hair cut.

couperet [kupʀɛ] *nm* cleaver, chopper.

couperosé, e [kupʀoze] *adj* blotchy.

couple [kupl(ə)] *nm* couple; ~ **de torsion** torque.

coupler [kuple] *vt* to couple (together).

couplet [kuplɛ] *nm* verse.

coupleur [kuplœʀ] *nm*: ~ **acoustique** acoustic

coupler.

coupole [kupɔl] *nf* dome; cupola.

coupon [kupɔ̃] *nm* (*ticket*) coupon; (*de tissu*) remnant; roll.

coupon-réponse, *pl* **coupons-réponses** [kupɔ̃repɔ̃s] *nm* reply coupon.

coupure [kupyʀ] *nf* cut; (*billet de banque*) note; (*de journal*) cutting; ~ **de courant** power cut.

cour [kuʀ] *nf* (*de ferme, jardin*) (court)yard; (*d'immeuble*) back yard; (*JUR, royale*) court; **faire la ~ à qn** to court sb; ~ **d'appel** appeal court (*BRIT*), appellate court (*US*); ~ **d'assises** court of assizes, ≈ Crown Court (*BRIT*); ~ **de cassation** final court of appeal; ~ **des comptes** (*ADMIN*) revenue court; ~ **martiale** court-martial; ~ **de récréation** (*SCOL*) schoolyard, playground.

courage [kuʀaʒ] *nm* courage, bravery.

courageusement [kuʀaʒøzmɑ̃] *adv* bravely, courageously.

courageux, euse [kuʀaʒø, -øz] *adj* brave, courageous.

couramment [kuʀamɑ̃] *adv* commonly; (*parler*) fluently.

courant, e [kuʀɑ̃, -ɑ̃t] *adj* (*fréquent*) common; (*COMM, gén: normal*) standard; (*en cours*) current ♦ *nm* current; (*fig*) movement; trend; **être au ~ (de)** (*fait, nouvelle*) to know (about); **mettre qn au ~ (de)** (*fait, nouvelle*) to tell sb (about); (*nouveau travail etc*) to teach sb the basics (of), brief sb (about); **se tenir au ~ (de)** (*techniques etc*) to keep o.s. up-to-date (on); **dans le ~ de** (*pendant*) in the course of; ~ **octobre** *etc* in the course of October *etc*; **le 10 ~** (*COMM*) the 10th inst; ~ **d'air** draught (*BRIT*), draft (*US*); ~ **électrique** (electric) current, power.

courbature [kuʀbatyʀ] *nf* ache.

courbaturé, e [kuʀbatyʀe] *adj* aching.

courbe [kuʀb(ə)] *adj* curved ♦ *nf* curve; ~ **de niveau** contour line.

courber [kuʀbe] *vt* to bend; ~ **la tête** to bow one's head; **se ~** *vi* (*branche etc*) to bend, curve; (*personne*) to bend (down).

courbette [kuʀbet] *nf* low bow.

coure [kuʀ] *etc vb voir* **courir.**

coureur, euse [kuʀœʀ, -øz] *nm/f* (*SPORT*) runner (*ou* driver); (*péj*) womanizer/manhunter; ~ **cycliste/automobile** racing cyclist/driver.

courge [kuʀʒ(ə)] *nf* (*BOT*) gourd; (*CULIN*) marrow.

courgette [kuʀʒet] *nf* courgette (*BRIT*), zucchini (*US*).

courir [kuʀiʀ] *vi* (*gén*) to run; (*se dépêcher*) to rush; (*fig: rumeurs*) to go round; (*COMM: intérêt*) to accrue ♦ *vt* (*SPORT: épreuve*) to compete in; (*risque*) to run; (*danger*) to face; ~ **les cafés/bals** to do the rounds of the cafés/dances; **le bruit court que** the rumour is going round that; **par les temps qui courent** at the present time; ~ **après qn** to run after

sb, chase (after) sb; **laisser ~** to let things alone; **faire ~ qn** to make sb run around (all over the place); **tu peux (toujours) ~!** you've got a hope!

couronne [kuʀɔn] *nf* crown; (*de fleurs*) wreath, circlet; ~ **(funéraire** *ou* **mortuaire)** (funeral) wreath.

couronnement [kuʀɔnmɑ̃] *nm* coronation, crowning; (*fig*) crowning achievement.

couronner [kuʀɔne] *vt* to crown.

courons [kuʀɔ̃], **courrai** [kuʀe] *etc vb voir* **courir.**

courre [kuʀ] *vb voir* **chasse.**

courrier [kuʀje] *nm* mail, post; (*lettres à écrire*) letters *pl*; (*rubrique*) column; **qualité** ~ letter quality; **long/moyen** ~ *adj* (*AVIAT*) long-/medium-haul; ~ **du cœur** problem page; ~ **électronique** electronic mail, E-mail.

courroie [kuʀwa] *nf* strap; (*TECH*) belt; ~ **de transmission/de ventilateur** driving/fan belt.

courrons [kuʀɔ̃] *etc vb voir* **courir.**

courroucé, e [kuʀuse] *adj* wrathful.

cours [kuʀ] *vb voir* **courir** ♦ *nm* (*leçon*) lesson; class; (*série de leçons*) course; (*cheminement*) course; (*écoulement*) flow; (*avenue*) walk; (*COMM*) rate; price; (*BOURSE*) quotation; **donner libre** ~ **à** to give free expression to; **avoir** ~ (*monnaie*) to be legal tender; (*fig*) to be current; (*SCOL*) to have a class *ou* lecture; **en** ~ (*année*) current; (*travaux*) in progress; **en** ~ **de route** on the way; **au** ~ **de** in the course of, during; **le** ~ **du change** the exchange rate; ~ **d'eau** waterway; ~ **élémentaire (CE)** *2nd and 3rd years of primary school*; ~ **moyen (CM)** *4th and 5th years of primary school*; ~ **préparatoire** ≈ infants' class (*BRIT*), ≈ 1st grade (*US*); ~ **du soir** night school.

course [kuʀs(ə)] *nf* running; (*SPORT: épreuve*) race; (*trajet: du soleil*) course; (: *d'un projectile*) flight; (: *d'une pièce mécanique*) travel; (*excursion*) outing; climb; (*d'un taxi, autocar*) journey, trip; (*petite mission*) errand; ~**s** *nfpl* (*achats*) shopping *sg*; (*HIPPISME*) races; **faire les** *ou* **ses** ~**s** to go shopping; **jouer aux** ~**s** to bet on the races; **à bout de** ~ (*épuisé*) exhausted; ~ **automobile** car race; ~ **de côte** (*AUTO*) hill climb; ~ **par étapes** *ou* **d'étapes** race in stages; ~ **d'obstacles** obstacle race; ~ **à pied** walking race; ~ **de vitesse** sprint; ~**s de chevaux** horse racing.

coursier, ière [kuʀsje, -jɛʀ] *nm/f* courier.

court, e [kuʀ, kuʀt(ə)] *adj* short ♦ *adv* short ♦ *nm*: ~ **(de tennis)** (tennis) court; **tourner** ~ to come to a sudden end; **couper** ~ **à** to cut short; **à** ~ **de** short of; **prendre qn de** ~ to catch sb unawares; **pour faire** ~ briefly, to cut a long story short; **ça fait** ~ that's not very long; **tirer à la** ~**e paille** to draw lots; **faire la** ~**e échelle à qn** to give sb a leg up; ~ **métrage** (*CINÉ*) short (film).

court-bouillon, *pl* **courts-bouillons**
[kurbujɔ̃] *nm* court-bouillon.

court-circuit, *pl* **courts-circuits** [kursirkɥi]
nm short-circuit.

court-circuiter [kursirkɥite] *vt* (*fig*) to bypass.

courtier, ière [kurtje, -jɛr] *nm/f* broker.

courtisan [kurtizɑ̃] *nm* courtier.

courtisane [kurtizan] *nf* courtesan.

courtiser [kurtize] *vt* to court, woo.

courtois, e [kurtwa, -waz] *adj* courteous.

courtoisement [kurtwazmɑ̃] *adv* courteously.

courtoisie [kurtwazi] *nf* courtesy.

couru, e [kury] *pp de* **courir ♦** *adj* (*spectacle etc*)
popular; **c'est ~ (d'avance)!** (*fam*) it's a safe
bet!

cousais [kuzɛ] *etc vb voir* **coudre.**

couscous [kuskus] *nm* couscous.

cousin, e [kuzɛ̃, -in] *nm/f* cousin ♦ *nm* (*ZOOL*)
mosquito; **~ germain** first cousin.

cousons [kuzɔ̃] *etc vb voir* **coudre.**

coussin [kusɛ̃] *nm* cushion; **~ d'air** (*TECH*) air
cushion.

cousu, e [kuzy] *pp de* **coudre ♦** *adj:* **~ d'or** rolling in riches.

coût [ku] *nm* cost; **le ~ de la vie** the cost of living.

coûtant [kutɑ̃] *adj m:* **au prix ~** at cost price.

couteau, x [kuto] *nm* knife; **~ à cran d'arrêt**
flick-knife; **~ de cuisine** kitchen knife; **~ à
pain** bread knife; **~ de poche** pocket knife.

couteau-scie, *pl* **couteaux-scies** [kutosi] *nm*
serrated(-edged) knife.

coutelier, ière [kutəlje, -jɛr] *adj:* **l'industrie
~ière** the cutlery industry ♦ *nm/f* cutler.

coutellerie [kutɛlri] *nf* cutlery shop; cutlery.

coûter [kute] *vt* to cost ♦ *vi:* **~ à qn** to cost sb a
lot; **~ cher** to be expensive; **~ cher à qn** (*fig*)
to cost sb dear *ou* dearly; **combien ça
coûte?** how much is it?, what does it cost?;
coûte que coûte at all costs.

coûteux, euse [kutø, -øz] *adj* costly, expensive.

coutume [kutym] *nf* custom; **de ~** usual, customary.

coutumier, ière [kutymje, -jɛr] *adj* customary: **elle est coutumière du fait** that's her
usual trick.

couture [kutyr] *nf* sewing; dress-making;
(*points*) seam.

couturier [kutyrje] *nm* fashion designer, couturier.

couturière [kutyrjɛr] *nf* dressmaker.

couvée [kuve] *nf* brood, clutch.

couvent [kuvɑ̃] *nm* (*de sœurs*) convent; (*de
frères*) monastery; (*établissement scolaire*)
convent (school).

couver [kuve] *vt* to hatch; (*maladie*) to be sickening for ♦ *vi* (*feu*) to smoulder (*BRIT*), smolder (*US*); (*révolte*) to be brewing; **~ qn/qch
des yeux** to look lovingly at sb/sth; (*convoiter*) to look longingly at sb/sth.

couvercle [kuvɛrkl(ə)] *nm* lid; (*de bombe aéro-*

sol etc, qui se visse) cap, top.

couvert, e [kuvɛr, -ɛrt(ə)] *pp de* **couvrir ♦** *adj*
(*ciel*) overcast; (*coiffé d'un chapeau*) wearing
a hat ♦ *nm* place setting; (*place à table*) place;
(*au restaurant*) cover charge; **~s** *nmpl* place
settings; cutlery *sg;* **~ de** covered with *ou*
in; **bien ~** (*habillé*) well wrapped up; **mettre
le ~** to lay the table; **à ~** under cover; **sous
le ~ de** under the shelter of; (*fig*) under cover of.

couverture [kuvɛrtyr] *nf* (*de lit*) blanket; (*de
bâtiment*) roofing; (*de livre, fig: d'un espion etc,
ASSURANCES*) cover; (*PRESSE*) coverage; **de
~** (*lettre etc*) covering; **~ chauffante** electric
blanket.

couveuse [kuvøz] *nf* (*à poules*) sitter, brooder;
(*de maternité*) incubator.

couvre [kuvr(ə)] *etc vb voir* **couvrir.**

couvre-chef [kuvrəʃɛf] *nm* hat.

couvre-feu, x [kuvrəfø] *nm* curfew.

couvre-lit [kuvrəli] *nm* bedspread.

couvre-pieds [kuvrəpje] *nm inv* quilt.

couvreur [kuvrœr] *nm* roofer.

couvrir [kuvrir] *vt* to cover; (*dominer, étouffer:
voix, pas*) to drown out; (*erreur*) to cover up;
(*ZOOL: s'accoupler à*) to cover; **se ~** (*ciel*) to
cloud over; (*s'habiller*) to cover up, wrap up;
(*se coiffer*) to put one's hat on; (*par une assurance*) to cover o.s.; **se ~ de** (*fleurs, boutons*)
to become covered in.

cover-girl [kɔvœrgœrl] *nf* model.

cow-boy [kɔbɔj] *nm* cowboy.

coyote [kɔjɔt] *nm* coyote.

CP *sigle m* = **cours préparatoire.**

CPAM *sigle f* (= *Caisse primaire d'assurances
maladie*) *health insurance office.*

cps *abr* (= *caractères par seconde*) cps.

cpt *abr* = **comptant.**

CQFD *abr* (= *ce qu'il fallait démontrer*) QED (=
quod erat demonstrandum).

CR *sigle m* = **compte rendu.**

crabe [krɑb] *nm* crab.

crachat [kraʃa] *nm* spittle *no pl,* spit *no pl.*

craché, e [kraʃe] *adj:* **son père tout ~** the spitting image of his (*ou* her) father.

cracher [kraʃe] *vi* to spit ♦ *vt* to spit out; (*fig:
lave etc*) to belch (out); **~ du sang** to spit
blood.

crachin [kraʃɛ̃] *nm* drizzle.

crachiner [kraʃine] *vi* to drizzle.

crachoir [kraʃwar] *nm* spittoon; (*de dentiste*)
bowl.

crachotement [kraʃɔtmɑ̃] *nm* crackling *no pl.*

crachoter [kraʃɔte] *vi* (*haut-parleur, radio*) to
crackle.

crack [krak] *nm* (*intellectuel*) whizzkid; (*sportif*)
ace; (*poulain*) hot favourite (*BRIT*) *ou* favorite (*US*).

Cracovie [krakɔvi] *n* Cracow.

cradingue [kradɛ̃g] *adj* (*fam*) disgustingly
dirty, filthy-dirty.

craie [krɛ] *nf* chalk.

craignais [kʀɛɲɛ] *etc vb voir* **craindre.**

craindre [kʀɛ̃dʀ(ə)] *vt* to fear, be afraid of; (*être sensible à: chaleur, froid*) to be easily damaged by; ~ **de/que** to be afraid of/that; **je crains qu'il (ne) vienne** I am afraid he may come.

crainte [kʀɛ̃t] *nf* fear; **de** ~ **de/que** for fear of/that.

craintif, ive [kʀɛ̃tif, -iv] *adj* timid.

craintivement [kʀɛ̃tivmɑ̃] *adv* timidly.

cramer [kʀame] *vi* (*fam*) to burn.

cramoisi, e [kʀamwazi] *adj* crimson.

crampe [kʀɑ̃p] *nf* cramp; ~ **d'estomac** stomach cramp.

crampon [kʀɑ̃pɔ̃] *nm* (*de semelle*) stud; (*ALPINISME*) crampon.

cramponner [kʀɑ̃pɔne]: **se** ~ *vi*: **se** ~ **(à)** to hang *ou* cling on (to).

cran [kʀɑ̃] *nm* (*entaille*) notch; (*de courroie*) hole; (*courage*) guts *pl*; ~ **d'arrêt** safety catch; ~ **de mire** bead; ~ **de sûreté** safety catch.

crâne [kʀɑn] *nm* skull.

crâner [kʀɑne] *vi* (*fam*) to swank, show off.

crânien, ne [kʀɑnjɛ̃, -ɛn] *adj* cranial, skull *cpd*, brain *cpd*.

crapaud [kʀapo] *nm* toad.

crapule [kʀapyl] *nf* villain.

crapuleux, euse [kʀapylø, -øz] *adj*: **crime** ~ villainous crime.

craquelure [kʀaklyʀ] *nf* crack; crackle *no pl*.

craquement [kʀakmɑ̃] *nm* crack, snap; (*du plancher*) creak, creaking *no pl*.

craquer [kʀake] *vi* (*bois, plancher*) to creak; (*fil, branche*) to snap; (*couture*) to come apart, burst; (*fig*) to break down, fall apart; (*: être enthousiasmé*) to go wild ♦ *vt*: ~ **une allumette** to strike a match.

crasse [kʀas] *nf* grime, filth ♦ *adj* (*fig: ignorance*) crass.

crasseux, euse [kʀasø, øz] *adj* filthy.

crassier [kʀasje] *nm* slag heap.

cratère [kʀatɛʀ] *nm* crater.

cravache [kʀavaʃ] *nf* (riding) crop.

cravacher [kʀavaʃe] *vt* to use the crop on.

cravate [kʀavat] *nf* tie.

cravater [kʀavate] *vt* to put a tie on; (*fig*) to grab round the neck.

crawl [kʀol] *nm* crawl.

crawlé, e [kʀole] *adj*: **dos** ~ backstroke.

crayeux, euse [kʀɛjø, -øz] *adj* chalky.

crayon [kʀɛjɔ̃] *nm* pencil; (*de rouge à lèvres etc*) stick, pencil; **écrire au** ~ to write in pencil; ~ **à bille** ball-point pen; ~ **de couleur** crayon; ~ **optique** light pen.

crayon-feutre, *pl* **crayons-feutres** [kʀɛjɔ̃-føtʀ(ə)] *nm* felt(-tip) pen.

crayonner [kʀɛjɔne] *vt* to scribble, sketch.

CRDP *sigle m* (= *Centre régional de documentation pédagogique*) *teachers' resource centre*.

créance [kʀeɑ̃s] *nf* (*COMM*) (financial) claim, (recoverable) debt; **donner** ~ **à qch** to lend credence to sth.

créancier, ière [kʀeɑ̃sje, -jɛʀ] *nm/f* creditor.

créateur, trice [kʀeatœʀ, -tʀis] *adj* creative ♦ *nm/f* creator; **le C**~ (*REL*) the Creator.

créatif, ive [kʀeatif, -iv] *adj* creative.

création [kʀeasjɔ̃] *nf* creation.

créativité [kʀeativite] *nf* creativity.

créature [kʀeatyʀ] *nf* creature.

crécelle [kʀesɛl] *nf* rattle.

crèche [kʀɛʃ] *nf* (*de Noël*) crib; (*garderie*) crèche, day nursery.

---

*In France the Christmas crib (***crèche***) usually contains figurines representing a miller, a wood-cutter and other villagers in addition to the Holy Family and the traditional cow, donkey and shepherds. Figurines representing the magi are added to the nativity scene at Epiphany; see also* **fête des Rois***.*

---

crédence [kʀedɑ̃s] *nf* (small) sideboard.

crédibilité [kʀedibilite] *nf* credibility.

crédible [kʀedibl(ə)] *adj* credible.

CREDIF [kʀedif] *sigle m* (= *Centre de recherche et d'étude pour la diffusion du français*) *official body promoting use of the French language.*

crédit [kʀedi] *nm* (*gén*) credit; ~**s** *nmpl* funds; **payer/acheter à** ~ to pay/buy on credit *ou* on easy terms; **faire** ~ **à qn** to give sb credit; ~ **municipal** pawnshop; ~ **relais** bridging loan.

crédit-bail, *pl* **crédits-bails** [kʀedibaj] *nm* (*ÉCON*) leasing.

créditer [kʀedite] *vt*: ~ **un compte (de)** to credit an account (with).

créditeur, trice [kʀeditœʀ, -tʀis] *adj* in credit, credit *cpd* ♦ *nm/f* customer in credit.

credo [kʀedo] *nm* credo, creed.

crédule [kʀedyl] *adj* credulous, gullible.

crédulité [kʀedylite] *nf* credulity, gullibility.

créer [kʀee] *vt* to create; (*THÉÂT: pièce*) to produce (for the first time); (*: rôle*) to create.

crémaillère [kʀemajɛʀ] *nf* (*RAIL*) rack; (*tige crantée*) trammel; **direction à** ~ (*AUTO*) rack and pinion steering; **pendre la** ~ to have a house-warming party.

crémation [kʀemasjɔ̃] *nf* cremation.

crématoire [kʀematwaʀ] *adj*: **four** ~ crematorium.

crématorium [kʀematɔʀjɔm] *nm* crematorium.

crème [kʀɛm] *nf* cream; (*entremets*) cream dessert ♦ *adj inv* cream; **un (café)** ~ ≈ a white coffee; ~ **chantilly** whipped cream, crème Chantilly; ~ **fouettée** whipped cream; ~ **glacée** ice cream; ~ **à raser** shaving cream.

crémerie [kʀemʀi] *nf* dairy; (*tearoom*) teashop.

crémeux, euse [kʀemø, -øz] *adj* creamy.

crémier, ière [kʀemje, -jɛʀ] *nm/f* dairyman/woman.

créneau, x [kʀeno] *nm* (*de fortification*) crenel(le); (*fig*, *aussi* COMM) gap, slot; (AUTO): **faire un** ~ to reverse into a parking space (*between cars alongside the kerb*).

créole [kʀeɔl] *adj*, *nm/f* Creole.

créosote [kʀeozɔt] *nf* creosote.

crêpe [kʀɛp] *nf* (*galette*) pancake ♦ *nm* (*tissu*) crêpe; (*de deuil*) black mourning crêpe; (*ruban*) black armband (*ou* hatband *ou* ribbon); **semelle (de)** ~ crêpe sole; ~ **de Chine** crêpe de Chine.

crêpé, e [kʀɛpe] *adj* (*cheveux*) backcombed.

crêperie [kʀɛpʀi] *nf* pancake shop *ou* restaurant.

crépi [kʀepi] *nm* roughcast.

crépir [kʀepiʀ] *vt* to roughcast.

crépitement [kʀepitmɑ̃] *nm* (*du feu*) crackling *no pl*; (*d'une arme automatique*) rattle *no pl*.

crépiter [kʀepite] *vi* to sputter, splutter, crackle.

crépon [kʀepɔ̃] *nm* seersucker.

CREPS [kʀɛps] *sigle m* (= *Centre régional d'éducation physique et sportive*) ≈ sports *ou* leisure centre.

crépu, e [kʀepy] *adj* frizzy, fuzzy.

crépuscule [kʀepyskyl] *nm* twilight, dusk.

crescendo [kʀeʃɛndo] *nm*, *adv* (MUS) crescendo; **aller** ~ (*fig*) to rise higher and higher, grow ever greater.

cresson [kʀesɔ̃] *nm* watercress.

Crète [kʀɛt] *nf*: **la** ~ Crete.

crête [kʀɛt] *nf* (*de coq*) comb; (*de vague, montagne*) crest.

crétin, e [kʀetɛ̃, -in] *nm/f* cretin.

crétois, e [kʀetwa, -waz] *adj* Cretan.

cretonne [kʀətɔn] *nf* cretonne.

creuser [kʀøze] *vt* (*trou, tunnel*) to dig; (*sol*) to dig a hole in; (*bois*) to hollow out; (*fig*) to go (deeply) into; **ça creuse** that gives you a real appetite; **se** ~ **(la cervelle)** to rack one's brains.

creuset [kʀøzɛ] *nm* crucible; (*fig*) melting pot; (*severe*) test.

creux, euse [kʀø, -øz] *adj* hollow ♦ *nm* hollow; (*fig: sur graphique etc*) trough; **heures creuses** slack periods; off-peak periods; **le** ~ **de l'estomac** the pit of the stomach.

crevaison [kʀəvɛzɔ̃] *nf* puncture, flat.

crevant, e [kʀəvɑ̃, -ɑ̃t] *adj* (*fam: fatigant*) knackering; (: *très drôle*) priceless.

crevasse [kʀəvas] *nf* (*dans le sol*) crack, fissure; (*de glacier*) crevasse; (*de la peau*) crack.

crevé, e [kʀəve] *adj* (*fam: fatigué*) worn out, dead beat.

crève-cœur [kʀɛvkœʀ] *nm inv* heartbreak.

crever [kʀəve] *vt* (*papier*) to tear, break; (*tambour, ballon*) to burst ♦ *vi* (*pneu*) to burst; (*automobiliste*) to have a puncture (BRIT) *ou* a flat (tire) (US); (*abcès, outre, nuage*) to burst (open); (*fam*) to die; **cela lui a crevé un œil** it blinded him in one eye; ~ **l'écran** to have real screen presence.

crevette [kʀəvɛt] *nf*: ~ **(rose)** prawn; ~ **grise** shrimp.

CRF *sigle f* (= *Croix-Rouge française*) French Red Cross.

cri [kʀi] *nm* cry, shout; (*d'animal: spécifique*) cry, call; **à grands ~s** at the top of one's voice; **c'est le dernier** ~ (*fig*) it's the latest fashion.

criant, e [kʀijɑ̃, -ɑ̃t] *adj* (*injustice*) glaring.

criard, e [kʀijaʀ, -aʀd(ə)] *adj* (*couleur*) garish, loud; (*voix*) yelling.

crible [kʀibl(ə)] *nm* riddle; (*mécanique*) screen, jig; **passer qch au** ~ to put sth through a riddle; (*fig*) to go over sth with a fine-tooth comb.

criblé, e [kʀible] *adj*: ~ **de** riddled with.

cric [kʀik] *nm* (AUTO) jack.

cricket [kʀikɛt] *nm* cricket.

criée [kʀije] *nf*: **(vente à la)** ~ (sale by) auction.

crier [kʀije] *vi* (*pour appeler*) to shout, cry (out); (*de peur, de douleur etc*) to scream, yell; (*fig: grincer*) to squeal, screech ♦ *vt* (*ordre, injure*) to shout (out), yell (out); **sans** ~ **gare** without warning; ~ **grâce** to cry for mercy; ~ **au secours** to shout for help.

crieur, euse [kʀijœʀ, -øz] *nm/f*: ~ **de journaux** newspaper seller.

crime [kʀim] *nm* crime; (*meurtre*) murder.

Crimée [kʀime] *nf*: **la** ~ the Crimea.

criminaliste [kʀiminalist(ə)] *nm/f* specialist in criminal law.

criminalité [kʀiminalite] *nf* criminality, crime.

criminel, le [kʀiminɛl] *adj* criminal ♦ *nm/f* criminal; murderer; ~ **de guerre** war criminal.

criminologie [kʀiminɔlɔʒi] *nf* criminology.

criminologiste [kʀiminɔlɔʒist(ə)] *nm/f* criminologist.

criminologue [kʀiminɔlɔg] *nm/f* criminologist.

crin [kʀɛ̃] *nm* hair *no pl*; (*fibre*) horsehair; **à tous ~s, à tout** ~ diehard, out-and-out.

crinière [kʀinjɛʀ] *nf* mane.

crique [kʀik] *nf* creek, inlet.

criquet [kʀikɛ] *nm* grasshopper.

crise [kʀiz] *nf* crisis (*pl* crises); (MÉD) attack; fit; ~ **cardiaque** heart attack; ~ **de foi** crisis of belief; ~ **de foie** bilious attack; ~ **de nerfs** attack of nerves.

crispant, e [kʀispɑ̃, -ɑ̃t] *adj* annoying, irritating.

crispation [kʀispasjɔ̃] *nf* (*spasme*) twitch; (*contraction*) contraction; tenseness.

crispé, e [kʀispe] *adj* tense, nervous.

crisper [kʀispe] *vt* to tense; (*poings*) to clench; **se** ~ to tense; to clench; (*personne*) to get tense.

crissement [kʀismɑ̃] *nm* crunch; rustle; screech.

crisser [kʀise] *vi* (*neige*) to crunch; (*tissu*) to rustle; (*pneu*) to screech.

cristal, aux [kʀistal, -o] *nm* crystal ♦ *nmpl* (*objets*) crystal(ware) *sg*; ~ **de plomb** (lead)

crystal; ~ **de roche** rock-crystal; **cristaux de soude** washing soda *sg*.

cristallin, e [kʀistalɛ̃, -in] *adj* crystal-clear ♦ *nm* (*ANAT*) crystalline lens.

cristalliser [kʀistalize] *vi*, *vt*, **se** ~ *vi* to crystallize.

critère [kʀitɛʀ] *nm* criterion (*pl* -ia).

critiquable [kʀitikabl(ə)] *adj* open to criticism.

critique [kʀitik] *adj* critical ♦ *nm/f* (*de théâtre, musique*) critic ♦ *nf* criticism; (*THÉÂT etc*: *article*) review; **la** ~ (*activité*) criticism; (*personnes*) the critics *pl*.

critiquer [kʀitike] *vt* (*dénigrer*) to criticize; (*évaluer, juger*) to assess, examine (critically).

croasser [kʀɔase] *vi* to caw.

croate [kʀɔat] *adj* Croatian ♦ *nm* (*LING*) Croat, Croatian.

Croatie [kʀɔasi] *nf*: **la** ~ Croatia.

croc [kʀo] *nm* (*dent*) fang; (*de boucher*) hook.

croc-en-jambe, *pl* **crocs-en-jambe** [kʀɔkɑ̃-ʒɑ̃b] *nm*: **faire un** ~ **à qn** to trip sb up.

croche [kʀɔʃ] *nf* (*MUS*) quaver (*BRIT*), eighth note (*US*); **double** ~ semiquaver (*BRIT*), sixteenth note (*US*).

croche-pied [kʀɔʃpje] *nm* = **croc-en-jambe**.

crochet [kʀɔʃɛ] *nm* hook; (*clef*) picklock; (*détour*) detour; (*BOXE*): ~ **du gauche** left hook; (*TRICOT: aiguille*) crochet hook; (*: technique*) crochet; ~**s** *nmpl* (*TYPO*) square brackets; **vivre aux** ~**s de qn** to live *ou* sponge off sb.

crocheter [kʀɔʃte] *vt* (*serrure*) to pick.

crochu, e [kʀɔʃy] *adj* hooked; claw-like.

crocodile [kʀɔkɔdil] *nm* crocodile.

crocus [kʀɔkys] *nm* crocus.

croire [kʀwaʀ] *vt* to believe; ~ **qn honnête** to believe sb (to be) honest; **se** ~ **fort** to think one is strong; ~ **que** to believe *ou* think that; **vous croyez?** do you think so?; ~ **être/faire** to think one is/does; ~ **à**, ~ **en** to believe in.

croîs [kʀwa] *etc vb voir* **croître**.

croisade [kʀwazad] *nf* crusade.

croisé, e [kʀwaze] *adj* (*veston*) double-breasted ♦ *nm* (*guerrier*) crusader ♦ *nf* (*fenêtre*) window, casement; ~**e d'ogives** intersecting ribs; **à la** ~**e des chemins** at the crossroads.

croisement [kʀwazmɑ̃] *nm* (*carrefour*) crossroads *sg*; (*BIO*) crossing; crossbreed.

croiser [kʀwaze] *vt* (*personne, voiture*) to pass; (*route*) to cross, cut across; (*BIO*) to cross ♦ *vi* (*NAVIG*) to cruise; ~ **les jambes/bras** to cross one's legs/fold one's arms; **se** ~ (*personnes, véhicules*) to pass each other; (*routes*) to cross, intersect; (*lettres*) to cross (in the post); (*regards*) to meet; **se** ~ **les bras** (*fig*) to twiddle one's thumbs.

croiseur [kʀwazœʀ] *nm* cruiser (*warship*).

croisière [kʀwazjɛʀ] *nf* cruise; **vitesse de** ~ (*AUTO etc*) cruising speed.

croisillon [kʀwazijɔ̃] *nm*: **motif/fenêtre à** ~**s** lattice pattern/window.

croissais [kʀwasɛ] *etc vb voir* **croître**.

croissance [kʀwasɑ̃s] *nf* growing, growth; **troubles de la** ~ growing pains; **maladie de** ~ growth disease; ~ **économique** economic growth.

croissant, e [kʀwasɑ̃, -ɑ̃t] *vb voir* **croître** ♦ *adj* growing; rising ♦ *nm* (*à manger*) croissant; (*motif*) crescent; ~ **de lune** crescent moon.

croître [kʀwatʀ(ə)] *vi* to grow; (*lune*) to wax.

croix [kʀwa] *nf* cross; **en** ~ *adj*, *adv* in the form of a cross; **la C**~ **Rouge** the Red Cross.

croquant, e [kʀɔkɑ̃, -ɑ̃t] *adj* crisp, crunchy ♦ *nm/f* (*péj*) yokel, (country) bumpkin.

croque-madame [kʀɔkmadam] *nm inv* toasted cheese sandwich with a fried egg on top.

croque-mitaine [kʀɔkmitɛn] *nm* bog(e)y-man (*pl* -men).

croque-monsieur [kʀɔkməsjø] *nm inv* toasted ham and cheese sandwich.

croque-mort [kʀɔkmɔʀ] *nm* (*péj*) pallbearer.

croquer [kʀɔke] *vt* (*manger*) to crunch; to munch; (*dessiner*) to sketch ♦ *vi* to be crisp *ou* crunchy; **chocolat à** ~ plain dessert chocolate.

croquet [kʀɔkɛ] *nm* croquet.

croquette [kʀɔkɛt] *nf* croquette.

croquis [kʀɔki] *nm* sketch.

cross(-country), *pl* **cross(-countries)** [kʀɔs(kuntʀi)] *nm* cross-country race *ou* run; cross-country racing *ou* running.

crosse [kʀɔs] *nf* (*de fusil*) butt; (*de revolver*) grip; (*d'évêque*) crook, crosier; (*de hockey*) hockey stick.

crotale [kʀɔtal] *nm* rattlesnake.

crotte [kʀɔt] *nf* droppings *pl*; ~! (*fam*) damn!

crotté, e [kʀɔte] *adj* muddy, mucky.

crottin [kʀɔtɛ̃] *nm*: ~ (**de cheval**) (horse) dung *ou* manure.

croulant, e [kʀulɑ̃, -ɑ̃t] *nm/f* (*fam*) old fogey.

crouler [kʀule] *vi* (*s'effondrer*) to collapse; (*être délabré*) to be crumbling.

croupe [kʀup] *nf* croup, rump; **en** ~ pillion.

croupier [kʀupje] *nm* croupier.

croupion [kʀupjɔ̃] *nm* (*d'un oiseau*) rump; (*CULIN*) parson's nose.

croupir [kʀupiʀ] *vi* to stagnate.

CROUS [kʀus] *sigle m* (= *Centre régional des œuvres universitaires et scolaires*) students' representative body.

croustade [kʀustad] *nf* (*CULIN*) croustade.

croustillant, e [kʀustijɑ̃, -ɑ̃t] *adj* crisp; (*fig*) spicy.

croustiller [kʀustije] *vi* to be crisp *ou* crusty.

croûte [kʀut] *nf* crust; (*du fromage*) rind; (*de vol-au-vent*) case; (*MÉD*) scab; **en** ~ (*CULIN*) in pastry, in a pie; ~ **aux champignons** mushrooms on toast; ~ **au fromage** cheese on toast *no pl*; ~ **de pain** (*morceau*) crust (of bread); ~ **terrestre** earth's crust.

croûton [kʀutɔ̃] *nm* (*CULIN*) crouton; (*bout du pain*) crust, heel.

croyable [kʀwajabl(ə)] *adj* believable, credible.

croyais [kʀwajɛ] *etc vb voir* **croire**.

croyance [kʀwajɑ̃s] *nf* belief.

croyant, e [kʀwajɑ̃, -ɑ̃t] *vb voir* **croire** ♦ *adj*: **être/ne pas être** ~ to be/not to be a believer ♦ *nm/f* believer.

Crozet [kʀɔzɛ] *n*: **les îles** ~ the Crozet Islands.

CRS *sigle fpl* (= *Compagnies républicaines de sécurité*) state security police force ♦ *sigle m* member of the CRS.

cru, e [kʀy] *pp de* **croire** ♦ *adj* (*non cuit*) raw; (*lumière, couleur*) harsh; (*description*) crude; (*paroles, langage: franc*) blunt; (: *grossier*) crude ♦ *nm* (*vignoble*) vineyard; (*vin*) wine ♦ *nf* (*d'un cours d'eau*) swelling, rising; **de son (propre)** ~ (*fig*) of his own devising; **monter à** ~ to ride bareback; **du** ~ local; **en ~e** in spate.

crû [kʀy] *pp de* **croître**.

cruauté [kʀyote] *nf* cruelty.

cruche [kʀyʃ] *nf* pitcher, (earthenware) jug.

crucial, e, aux [kʀysjal, -o] *adj* crucial.

crucifier [kʀysifje] *vt* to crucify.

crucifix [kʀysifi] *nm* crucifix.

crucifixion [kʀysifiksjɔ̃] *nf* crucifixion.

cruciforme [kʀysifɔʀm(ə)] *adj* cruciform, cross-shaped.

cruciverbiste [kʀysivɛʀbist(ə)] *nm/f* crossword puzzle enthusiast.

crudité [kʀydite] *nf* crudeness *no pl*; harshness *no pl*; ~**s** *nfpl* (*CULIN*) mixed salads (*as hors d'œuvre*).

crue [kʀy] *nf voir* **cru**.

cruel, le [kʀyɛl] *adj* cruel.

cruellement [kʀyɛlmɑ̃] *adv* cruelly.

crûment [kʀymɑ̃] *adv* (*voir cru*) harshly; bluntly; crudely.

crus, crûs [kʀy] *etc vb voir* **croire; croître**.

crustacés [kʀystase] *nmpl* shellfish.

crypte [kʀipt(ə)] *nf* crypt.

CSA *sigle f* (= *Conseil supérieur de l'audiovisuel*) French broadcasting regulatory body, ≈ IBA (*BRIT*), ≈ FCC (*US*).

CSCE *sigle f* (= *Conférence sur la sécurité et la coopération en Europe*) CSCE.

cse *abr* = **cause**.

CSEN *sigle f* (= *Confédération des syndicats de l'éducation nationale*) group of teachers' unions.

CSG *sigle f* (= *contribution sociale généralisée*) supplementary social security contribution in aid of the underprivileged.

Cte *abr* = **Comtesse**.

CU *sigle f* = **communauté urbaine**.

Cuba [kyba] *nm*: **le** ~ Cuba.

cubage [kybaʒ] *nm* cubage, cubic content.

cubain, e [kybɛ̃, -ɛn] *adj* Cuban ♦ *nm/f*: **C**~, **e** Cuban.

cube [kyb] *nm* cube; (*jouet*) brick, building block; **gros** ~ powerful motorbike; **mètre** ~ cubic metre; **2 au** ~ **= 8** 2 cubed is 8; **élever au** ~ to cube.

cubique [kybik] *adj* cubic.

cubisme [kybism(ə)] *nm* cubism.

cubiste [kybist(ə)] *adj, nm/f* cubist.

cubitus [kybitys] *nm* ulna.

cueillette [kœjɛt] *nf* picking, gathering; harvest *ou* crop (of fruit).

cueillir [kœjiʀ] *vt* (*fruits, fleurs*) to pick, gather; (*fig*) to catch.

cuiller *ou* **cuillère** [kɥijɛʀ] *nf* spoon; ~ **à café** coffee spoon; (*CULIN*) ≈ teaspoonful; ~ **à soupe** soup spoon; (*CULIN*) ≈ tablespoonful.

cuillerée [kɥijʀe] *nf* spoonful; (*CULIN*): ~ **à soupe/café** tablespoonful/teaspoonful.

cuir [kɥiʀ] *nm* leather; (*avant tannage*) hide; ~ **chevelu** scalp.

cuirasse [kɥiʀas] *nf* breastplate.

cuirassé [kɥiʀase] *nm* (*NAVIG*) battleship.

cuire [kɥiʀ] *vt* (*aliments*) to cook; (*au four*) to bake; (*poterie*) to fire ♦ *vi* to cook; (*picoter*) to smart, sting, burn; **bien cuit** (*viande*) well done; **trop cuit** overdone; **pas assez cuit** underdone; **cuit à point** medium done; done to a turn.

cuisant, e [kɥizɑ̃, -ɑ̃t] *vb voir* **cuire** ♦ *adj* (*douleur*) smarting, burning; (*fig: souvenir, échec*) bitter.

cuisine [kɥizin] *nf* (*pièce*) kitchen; (*art culinaire*) cookery, cooking; (*nourriture*) cooking, food; **faire la** ~ to cook.

cuisiné, e [kɥizine] *adj*: **plat** ~ ready-made meal *ou* dish.

cuisiner [kɥizine] *vt* to cook; (*fam*) to grill ♦ *vi* to cook.

cuisinette [kɥizinɛt] *nf* kitchenette.

cuisinier, ière [kɥizinje, -jɛʀ] *nm/f* cook ♦ *nf* (*poêle*) cooker.

cuisis [kɥizi] *etc vb voir* **cuire**.

cuissardes [kɥisaʀd] *nfpl* (*de pêcheur*) waders; (*de femme*) thigh boots.

cuisse [kɥis] *nf* (*ANAT*) thigh; (*CULIN*) leg.

cuisson [kɥisɔ̃] *nf* cooking; (*de poterie*) firing.

cuissot [kɥiso] *nm* haunch.

cuistre [kɥistʀ(ə)] *nm* prig.

cuit, e [kɥi, -it] *pp de* **cuire** ♦ *nf* (*fam*): **prendre une** ~**e** to get plastered *ou* smashed.

cuivre [kɥivʀ(ə)] *nm* copper; **les** ~**s** (*MUS*) the brass; ~ **rouge** copper; ~ **jaune** brass.

cuivré, e [kɥivʀe] *adj* coppery; (*peau*) bronzed.

cul [ky] *nm* (*fam!*) arse (*BRIT !*), ass (*US !*), bum (*BRIT*); ~ **de bouteille** bottom of a bottle.

culasse [kylas] *nf* (*AUTO*) cylinder-head; (*de fusil*) breech.

culbute [kylbyt] *nf* somersault; (*accidentelle*) tumble, fall.

culbuter [kylbyte] *vi* to (take a) tumble, fall (head over heels).

culbuteur [kylbytœʀ] *nm* (*AUTO*) rocker arm.

cul-de-jatte, *pl* **culs-de-jatte** [kydʒat] *nm/f* legless cripple.

cul-de-sac, *pl* **culs-de-sac** [kydsak] *nm* cul-de-sac.

culinaire [kylinɛʀ] *adj* culinary.
culminant, e [kylminã, -ãt] *adj*: **point ~** highest point; (*fig*) height, climax.
culminer [kylmine] *vi* to reach its highest point; to tower.
culot [kylo] *nm* (*d'ampoule*) cap; (*effronterie*) cheek, nerve.
culotte [kylɔt] *nf* (*de femme*) panties *pl*, knickers *pl* (*BRIT*); (*d'homme*) underpants *pl*; (*pantalon*) trousers *pl* (*BRIT*), pants *pl* (*US*); **~ de cheval** riding breeches *pl*.
culotté, e [kylɔte] *adj* (*pipe*) seasoned; (*cuir*) mellowed; (*effronté*) cheeky.
culpabiliser [kylpabilize] *vt*: **~ qn** to make sb feel guilty.
culpabilité [kylpabilite] *nf* guilt.
culte [kylt(ə)] *adj*: **livre/film ~** cult film/book ♦ *nm* (*religion*) religion; (*hommage, vénération*) worship; (*protestant*) service.
cultivable [kyltivabl(ə)] *adj* cultivable.
cultivateur, trice [kyltivatœʀ, -tʀis] *nm/f* farmer.
cultivé, e [kyltive] *adj* (*personne*) cultured, cultivated.
cultiver [kyltive] *vt* to cultivate; (*légumes*) to grow, cultivate.
culture [kyltyʀ] *nf* cultivation; growing; (*connaissances etc*) culture; (**champs de**) **~s** land(s) under cultivation; **~ physique** physical training.
culturel, le [kyltyʀɛl] *adj* cultural.
culturisme [kyltyʀism(ə)] *nm* body-building.
culturiste [kyltyʀist(ə)] *nm/f* body-builder.
cumin [kymɛ̃] *nm* (*CULIN*) caraway seeds *pl*; cumin.
cumul [kymyl] *nm* (*voir cumuler*) holding (*ou* drawing) concurrently; **~ de peines** sentences to run consecutively.
cumulable [kymylabl(ə)] *adj* (*fonctions*) which may be held concurrently.
cumuler [kymyle] *vt* (*emplois, honneurs*) to hold concurrently; (*salaires*) to draw concurrently; (*JUR: droits*) to accumulate.
cupide [kypid] *adj* greedy, grasping.
cupidité [kypidite] *nf* greed.
curable [kyʀabl(ə)] *adj* curable.
Curaçao [kyʀaso] *n* Curaçao ♦ *nm*: **c~** curaçao.
curare [kyʀaʀ] *nm* curare.
curatif, ive [kyʀatif, -iv] *adj* curative.
cure [kyʀ] *nf* (*MÉD*) course of treatment; (*REL*) cure, ≈ living; presbytery, ≈ vicarage; **faire une ~ de fruits** to go on a fruit cure *ou* diet; **faire une ~ thermale** to take the waters; **n'avoir ~ de** to pay no attention to; **~ d'amaigrissement** slimming course; **~ de repos** rest cure; **~ de sommeil** sleep therapy *no pl*.
curé [kyʀe] *nm* parish priest; **M le ~** ≈ Vicar.
cure-dent [kyʀdã] *nm* toothpick.
curée [kyʀe] *nf* (*fig*) scramble for the pickings.
cure-ongles [kyʀɔ̃gl(ə)] *nm inv* nail cleaner.

cure-pipe [kyʀpip] *nm* pipe cleaner.
curer [kyʀe] *vt* to clean out; **se ~ les dents** to pick one's teeth.
curetage [kyʀtaʒ] *nm* (*MÉD*) curettage.
curieusement [kyʀjøzmã] *adv* oddly.
curieux, euse [kyʀjø, -øz] *adj* (*étrange*) strange, curious; (*indiscret*) curious, inquisitive; (*intéressé*) inquiring, curious ♦ *nmpl* (*badauds*) onlookers, bystanders.
curiosité [kyʀjozite] *nf* curiosity, inquisitiveness; (*objet*) curio(sity); (*site*) unusual feature *ou* sight.
curiste [kyʀist(ə)] *nm/f* person taking the waters at a spa.
curriculum vitae (CV) [kyʀikylɔmvite] *nm inv* curriculum vitae (CV).
curry [kyʀi] *nm* curry; **poulet au ~** curried chicken, chicken curry.
curseur [kyʀsœʀ] *nm* (*INFORM*) cursor; (*de règle*) slide; (*de fermeture-éclair*) slider.
cursif, ive [kyʀsif, -iv] *adj*: **écriture cursive** cursive script.
cursus [kyʀsys] *nm* degree course.
curviligne [kyʀviliɲ] *adj* curvilinear.
cutané, e [kytane] *adj* cutaneous, skin *cpd*.
cuti-réaction [kytiʀeaksjɔ̃] *nf* (*MÉD*) skin-test.
cuve [kyv] *nf* vat; (*à mazout etc*) tank.
cuvée [kyve] *nf* vintage.
cuvette [kyvɛt] *nf* (*récipient*) bowl, basin; (*du lavabo*) (wash)basin; (*des w.-c.*) pan; (*GÉO*) basin.
CV *sigle m* (*AUTO*) = **cheval vapeur**; (*ADMIN*) = **curriculum vitae**.
CVS *sigle adj* (= *corrigées des variations saisonnières*) seasonally adjusted.
cx *abr* (= *coefficient de pénétration dans l'air*) drag coefficient.
cyanure [sjanyʀ] *nm* cyanide.
cybernétique [sibɛʀnetik] *nf* cybernetics *sg*.
cyclable [siklabl(ə)] *adj*: **piste ~** cycle track.
cyclamen [siklamɛn] *nm* cyclamen.
cycle [sikl(ə)] *nm* cycle; (*SCOL*): **premier/second ~** ≈ middle/upper school (*BRIT*), ≈ junior/senior high school (*US*).
cyclique [siklik] *adj* cyclic(al).
cyclisme [siklism(ə)] *nm* cycling.
cycliste [siklist(ə)] *nm/f* cyclist ♦ *adj* cycle *cpd*; **coureur ~** racing cyclist.
cyclo-cross [siklokʀos] *nm* (*SPORT*) cyclocross; (*épreuve*) cyclo-cross race.
cyclomoteur [siklomotœʀ] *nm* moped.
cyclomotoriste [siklomotoʀist(ə)] *nm/f* moped rider.
cyclone [siklon] *nm* hurricane.
cyclotourisme [sikloturism(ə)] *nm* (bi)cycle touring.
cygne [siɲ] *nm* swan.
cylindre [silɛ̃dʀ(ə)] *nm* cylinder; **moteur à 4 ~s en ligne** straight-4 engine.
cylindrée [silɛ̃dʀe] *nf* (*AUTO*) (cubic) capacity; **une (voiture de) grosse ~** a big-engined car.
cylindrique [silɛ̃dʀik] *adj* cylindrical.

cymbale [sɛ̃bal] *nf* cymbal.
cynique [sinik] *adj* cynical.
cyniquement [sinikmɑ̃] *adv* cynically.
cynisme [sinism(ə)] *nm* cynicism.
cyprès [siprɛ] *nm* cypress.
cypriote [siprijɔt] *adj* Cypriot ♦ *nm/f*: C~ Cypriot.
cyrillique [sirilik] *adj* Cyrillic.
cystite [sistit] *nf* cystitis.
cytise [sitiz] *nm* laburnum.
cytologie [sitɔlɔʒi] *nf* cytology.

D d

D, d [de] *nm inv* D, d ♦ *abr*: **D** (*MÉTÉO*: = *dépression*) low, depression; **D comme Désiré** D for David (*BRIT*) *ou* Dog (*US*); *voir* **système**.
d' *prép, dét voir* **de**.
Dacca [daka] *n* Dacca.
dactylo [daktilo] *nf* (*aussi*: ~**graphe**) typist; (*aussi*: ~**graphie**) typing, typewriting.
dactylographier [daktilɔgrafje] *vt* to type (out).
dada [dada] *nm* hobby-horse.
dadais [dadɛ] *nm* ninny, lump.
dague [dag] *nf* dagger.
dahlia [dalja] *nm* dahlia.
dahoméen, ne [daɔmeɛ̃, -ɛn] *adj* Dahomean.
Dahomey [daɔme] *nm*: **le** ~ Dahomey.
daigner [deɲe] *vt* to deign.
daim [dɛ̃] *nm* (*fallow*) deer *inv*; (*peau*) buckskin; (*imitation*) suede.
dais [dɛ] *nm* (*tenture*) canopy.
Dakar [dakar] *n* Dakar.
dal. *abr* (= *décalitre*) dal.
dallage [dalaʒ] *nm* paving.
dalle [dal] *nf* slab; (*au sol*) paving stone, flag(stone); **que** ~ nothing at all, damn all (*BRIT*).
daller [dale] *vt* to pave.
dalmate [dalmat] *adj* Dalmatian.
Dalmatie [dalmasi] *nf*: **la** ~ Dalmatia.
dalmatien, ne [dalmasjɛ̃, -ɛn] *nm/f* (*chien*) Dalmatian.
daltonien, ne [daltɔnjɛ̃, -ɛn] *adj* colour-blind (*BRIT*), color-blind (*US*).
daltonisme [daltɔnism(ə)] *nm* colour (*BRIT*) *ou* color (*US*) blindness.
dam [dam] *nm*: **au grand** ~ **de** much to the detriment (*ou* annoyance) of.
Damas [dama] *n* Damascus.
damas [dama] *nm* (*étoffe*) damask.
damassé, e [damase] *adj* damask *cpd*.
dame [dam] *nf* lady; (*CARTES, ÉCHECS*) queen; ~**s** *nfpl* (*jeu*) draughts *sg* (*BRIT*), checkers *sg*

(*US*); **les (toilettes des)** ~**s** the ladies' (toilets); ~ **de charité** benefactress; ~ **de compagnie** lady's companion.
dame-jeanne, *pl* **dames-jeannes** [damʒɑn] *nf* demijohn.
damer [dame] *vt* to ram *ou* pack down; ~ **le pion à** (*fig*) to get the better of.
damier [damje] *nm* draughtboard (*BRIT*), checkerboard (*US*); (*dessin*) check (pattern); **en** ~ check.
damner [dane] *vt* to damn.
dancing [dɑ̃siŋ] *nm* dance hall.
dandiner [dɑ̃dine]: **se** ~ *vi* to sway about; (*en marchant*) to waddle along.
Danemark [danmark] *nm*: **le** ~ Denmark.
danger [dɑ̃ʒe] *nm* danger; **mettre en** ~ to endanger, put in danger; **être en** ~ **de mort** to be in peril of one's life; **être hors de** ~ to be out of danger.
dangereusement [dɑ̃ʒrøzmɑ̃] *adv* dangerously.
dangereux, euse [dɑ̃ʒrø, -øz] *adj* dangerous.
danois, e [danwa, -waz] *adj* Danish ♦ *nm* (*LING*) Danish ♦ *nm/f*: **D~**, e Dane.

════════ *MOT-CLÉ*

dans [dɑ̃] *prép* **1** (*position*) in; (*à l'intérieur de*) inside; **c'est** ~ **le tiroir/le salon** it's in the drawer/lounge; ~ **la boîte** in *ou* inside the box; **marcher** ~ **la ville/la rue** to walk about the town/along the street; **je l'ai lu** ~ **le journal** I read it in the newspaper; **être** ~ **les meilleurs** to be among *ou* one of the best
2 (*direction*) into; **elle a couru** ~ **le salon** she ran into the lounge
3 (*provenance*) out of, from; **je l'ai pris** ~ **le tiroir/salon** I took it out of *ou* from the drawer/lounge; **boire** ~ **un verre** to drink out of *ou* from a glass
4 (*temps*) in; ~ **2 mois** in 2 months, in 2 months' time
5 (*approximation*) about; ~ **les 20 F** about 20 F.

dansant, e [dɑ̃sɑ̃, -ɑ̃t] *adj*: **soirée** ~**e** evening of dancing; (*bal*) dinner dance.
danse [dɑ̃s] *nf*: **la** ~ dancing; (*classique*) (ballet) dancing; **une** ~ a dance; ~ **du ventre** belly dancing.
danser [dɑ̃se] *vi, vt* to dance.
danseur, euse [dɑ̃sœr, -øz] *nm/f* ballet dancer; (*au bal etc*) dancer; (: *cavalier*) partner; ~ **de claquettes** tap-dancer; **en danseuse** (*à vélo*) standing on the pedals.
Danube [danyb] *nm*: **le** ~ the Danube.
DAO *sigle m* (= *dessin assisté par ordinateur*) CAD.
dard [dar] *nm* sting (*organ*).
Dardanelles [dardanɛl] *nfpl*: **les** ~ the Dardanelles.
darder [darde] *vt* to shoot, send forth.
dare-dare [dardar] *adv* in double quick time.

Dar-es-Salaam, Dar-es-Salam [daʀɛsalam] *n* Dar-es-Salaam.

darne [daʀn] *nf* steak (*of fish*).

darse [daʀs(ə)] *nf* sheltered dock (*in a Mediterranean port*).

dartre [daʀtʀ(ə)] *nf* (*MÉD*) sore.

datation [datɑsjɔ̃] *nf* dating.

date [dat] *nf* date; **faire ~** to mark a milestone; **de longue ~** *adj* longstanding; **~ de naissance** date of birth; **~ limite** deadline; (*d'un aliment: aussi:* **~ limite de vente**) sell-by date.

dater [date] *vt, vi* to date; **~ de** to date from, go back to; **à ~ de** (as) from.

dateur [datœʀ] *nm* (*de montre*) date indicator; **timbre ~** date stamp.

datif [datif] *nm* dative.

datte [dat] *nf* date.

dattier [datje] *nm* date palm.

daube [dob] *nf:* **bœuf en ~** beef casserole.

dauphin [dofɛ̃] *nm* (*ZOOL*) dolphin; (*du roi*) dauphin; (*fig*) heir apparent.

Dauphiné [dofine] *nm:* **le ~** the Dauphiné.

dauphinois, e [dofinwa, -waz] *adj* of *ou* from the Dauphiné.

daurade [dɔʀad] *nf* sea bream.

davantage [davɑ̃taʒ] *adv* more; (*plus longtemps*) longer; **~ de** more; **~ que** more than.

DB *sigle f* (*MIL*) = division blindée.

DCA *sigle f* (= *défense contre avions*) anti-aircraft defence.

DCC *sigle f* ® (= *digital compact cassette*) DCC ®.

DCT *sigle m* (= *diphtérie coqueluche tétanos*) DPT.

DDASS [das] *sigle f* (= *Direction départementale d'action sanitaire et sociale*) ≈ DHSS (= *Department of Health and Social Security*) (*BRIT*), ≈ SSA (= *Social Security Administration*) (*US*).

DDT *sigle m* (= *dichloro-diphénol-trichloréthane*) DDT.

=============== *MOT-CLÉ* ===============

de (d') (*de +le = du, de +les = des*) *prép* **1** (*appartenance*) of; **le toit ~ la maison** the roof of the house; **la voiture d'Elisabeth/~ mes parents** Elizabeth's/my parents' car

2 (*provenance*) from; **il vient ~ Londres** he comes from London; **~ Londres à Paris** from London to Paris; **elle est sortie du cinéma** she came out of the cinema

3 (*moyen*) with; **je l'ai fait ~ mes propres mains** I did it with my own two hands

4 (*caractérisation, mesure*): **un mur ~ brique/ bureau d'acajou** a brick wall/mahogany desk; **un billet ~ 50 F** a 50 F note; **une pièce ~ 2 m ~ large** *ou* **large ~ 2 m** a room 2 m wide, a 2m-wide room; **un bébé ~ 10 mois** a 10-month-old baby; **12 mois ~ crédit/travail** 12 months' credit/work; **elle est payée 20 F ~ l'heure** she's paid 20 F an hour *ou* per hour; **augmenter ~ 10 F** to increase by 10 F;

3 jours ~ libres 3 free days, 3 days free; **un verre d'eau** a glass of water; **il mange ~ tout** he'll eat anything

5 (*rapport*) from; **~ 4 à 6** from 4 to 6

6 (*de la part de*): **estimé ~ ses collègues** respected by his colleagues

7 (*cause*): **mourir ~ faim** to die of hunger; **rouge ~ colère** red with fury

8 (*vb +de +infin*) to; **il m'a dit ~ rester** he told me to stay

9 (*en apposition*): **cet imbécile ~ Paul** that idiot Paul; **le terme ~ franglais** the term "franglais"

♦ *dét* **1** (*phrases affirmatives*) some (*souvent omis*); **du vin, ~ l'eau, des pommes** (some) wine, (some) water, (some) apples; **des enfants sont venus** some children came; **pendant des mois** for months

2 (*phrases interrogatives et négatives*) any; **a-t-il du vin?** has he got any wine?; **il n'a pas ~ pommes/d'enfants** he hasn't (got) any apples/children, he has no apples/children.

―――――――――――――――――――――――

dé [de] *nm* (*à jouer*) die *ou* dice (*pl* dice); (*aussi:* **~ à coudre**) thimble; **~s** *nmpl* (*jeu*) (game of) dice; **un coup de ~s** a throw of the dice; **couper en ~s** (*CULIN*) to dice.

DEA *sigle m* (= *Diplôme d'études approfondies*) *post-graduate diploma*.

dealer [dilœʀ] *nm* (*fam*) (drug) pusher.

déambulateur [deãbylatœʀ] *nm* zimmer ®.

déambuler [deãbyle] *vi* to stroll about.

déb. *abr* = **débutant**; (*COMM*) = à débattre.

débâcle [debɑkl(ə)] *nf* rout.

déballage [debalaʒ] *nm* (*de marchandises*) display (*of loose goods*); (*fig: fam*) outpourings *pl*.

déballer [debale] *vt* to unpack.

débandade [debãdad] *nf* scattering; (*déroute*) rout.

débander [debãde] *vt* to unbandage.

débaptiser [debatize] *vt* (*rue*) to rename.

débarbouiller [debaʀbuje] *vt* to wash; **se ~** to wash (one's face).

débarcadère [debaʀkadɛʀ] *nm* landing stage (*BRIT*), wharf.

débardeur [debaʀdœʀ] *nm* docker, stevedore; (*maillot*) slipover, tank top.

débarquement [debaʀkəmã] *nm* unloading, landing; disembarcation; (*MIL*) landing; **le D~** the Normandy landings.

débarquer [debaʀke] *vt* to unload, land ♦ *vi* to disembark; (*fig*) to turn up.

débarras [debaʀa] *nm* lumber room; (*placard*) junk cupboard; (*remise*) outhouse; **bon ~!** good riddance!

débarrasser [debaʀase] *vt* to clear ♦ *vi* (*enlever le couvert*) to clear away; **~ qn de** (*vêtements, paquets*) to relieve sb of; (*habitude, ennemi*) to rid sb of; **~ qch de** (*fouillis etc*) to clear sth of; **se ~ de** *vt* to get rid of; to rid o.s. of.

débat [deba] *vb voir* **débattre** ♦ *nm* discussion,

debate; ~s *nmpl* (*POL*) proceedings, debates.
débattre [debatʀ(ə)] *vt* to discuss, debate; **se ~** *vi* to struggle.

débauchage [deboʃaʒ] *nm* (*licenciement*) laying off (of staff); (*par un concurrent*) poaching.

débauche [deboʃ] *nf* debauchery; **une ~ de** (*fig*) a profusion of; (: *de couleurs*) a riot of.

débauché, e [deboʃe] *adj* debauched ♦ *nm/f* profligate.

débaucher [deboʃe] *vt* (*licencier*) to lay off, dismiss; (*salarié d'une autre entreprise*) to poach; (*entraîner*) to lead astray, debauch; (*inciter à la grève*) to incite.

débile [debil] *adj* weak, feeble; (*fam: idiot*) dim-witted ♦ *nm/f*: **~ mental, e** mental defective.

débilitant, e [debilitɑ̃, -ɑ̃t] *adj* debilitating.

débilité [debilite] *nf* debility; (*fam: idiotie*) stupidity; **~ mentale** mental debility.

débiner [debine]: **se ~** *vi* to do a bunk (*BRIT*), clear out.

débit [debi] *nm* (*d'un liquide, fleuve*) (rate of) flow; (*d'un magasin*) turnover (of goods); (*élocution*) delivery; (*bancaire*) debit; **avoir un ~ de 10 F** to be 10 F in debit; **~ de boissons** drinking establishment; **~ de tabac** tobacconist's (shop) (*BRIT*), tobacco *ou* smoke shop (*US*).

débiter [debite] *vt* (*compte*) to debit; (*liquide, gaz*) to yield, produce, give out; (*couper: bois, viande*) to cut up; (*vendre*) to retail; (*péj: paroles etc*) to come out with, churn out.

débiteur, trice [debitœʀ, -tʀis] *nm/f* debtor ♦ *adj* in debit; (*compte*) debit *cpd*.

déblai [deblɛ] *nm* (*nettoyage*) clearing; **~s** *nmpl* (*terre*) earth; (*décombres*) rubble.

déblaiement [deblɛmɑ̃] *nm* clearing; **travaux de ~** earth moving *sg*.

déblatérer [deblatere] *vi*: **~ contre** to go on about.

déblayer [debleje] *vt* to clear; **~ le terrain** (*fig*) to clear the ground.

déblocage [deblɔkaʒ] *nm* (*des prix, cours*) unfreezing.

débloquer [deblɔke] *vt* (*frein, fonds*) to release; (*prix*) to unfreeze ♦ *vi* (*fam*) to talk rubbish.

débobiner [debɔbine] *vt* to unwind.

déboires [debwaʀ] *nmpl* setbacks.

déboisement [debwazmɑ̃] *nm* deforestation.

déboiser [debwaze] *vt* to clear of trees; (*région*) to deforest; **se ~** *vi* (*colline, montagne*) to become bare of trees.

déboîter [debwate] *vt* (*AUTO*) to pull out; **se ~ le genou** *etc* to dislocate one's knee *etc*.

débonnaire [debɔnɛʀ] *adj* easy-going, good-natured.

débordant, e [debɔʀdɑ̃, -ɑ̃t] *adj* (*joie*) unbounded; (*activité*) exuberant.

débordé, e [debɔʀde] *adj*: **être ~ de** (*travail, demandes*) to be snowed under with.

débordement [debɔʀdəmɑ̃] *nm* overflowing.

déborder [debɔʀde] *vi* to overflow; (*lait etc*) to boil over ♦ *vt* (*MIL, SPORT*) to outflank; **~ (de) qch** (*dépasser*) to extend beyond sth; **~ de** (*joie, zèle*) to be brimming over with *ou* bursting with.

débouché [debuʃe] *nm* (*pour vendre*) outlet; (*perspective d'emploi*) opening; (*sortie*): **au ~ de la vallée** where the valley opens out (onto the plain).

déboucher [debuʃe] *vt* (*évier, tuyau etc*) to unblock; (*bouteille*) to uncork, open ♦ *vi*: **~ de** to emerge from, come out of; **~ sur** to come out onto; to open out onto; (*fig*) to arrive at, lead up to.

débouler [debule] *vi* to go (*ou* come) tumbling down; (*sans tomber*) to come careering down ♦ *vt*: **~ l'escalier** to belt down the stairs.

déboulonner [debulɔne] *vt* to dismantle; (*fig: renvoyer*) to dismiss; (: *détruire le prestige de*) to discredit.

débours [debuʀ] *nmpl* outlay.

débourser [debuʀse] *vt* to pay out, lay out.

déboussoler [debusɔle] *vt* to disorientate, disorient.

debout [dəbu] *adv*: **être ~** (*personne*) to be standing, stand; (: *levé, éveillé*) to be up (and about); (*chose*) to be upright; **être encore ~** (*fig: en état*) to be still going; to be still standing; to be still up; **mettre qn ~** to get sb to his feet; **mettre qch ~** to stand sth up; **se mettre ~** to get up (on one's feet); **se tenir ~** to stand; **~! get up!**; **cette histoire ne tient pas ~** this story doesn't hold water.

débouter [debute] *vt* (*JUR*) to dismiss; **~ qn de sa demande** to dismiss sb's petition.

déboutonner [debutɔne] *vt* to undo, unbutton; **se ~** *vi* to come undone *ou* unbuttoned.

débraillé, e [debʀaje] *adj* slovenly, untidy.

débrancher [debʀɑ̃ʃe] *vt* (*appareil électrique*) to unplug; (*téléphone, courant électrique*) to disconnect, cut off.

débrayage [debʀɛjaʒ] *nm* (*AUTO*) clutch; (: *action*) disengaging the clutch; (*grève*) stoppage; **faire un double ~** to double-declutch.

débrayer [debʀeje] *vi* (*AUTO*) to declutch, disengage the clutch; (*cesser le travail*) to stop work.

débridé, e [debʀide] *adj* unbridled, unrestrained.

débrider [debʀide] *vt* (*cheval*) to unbridle; (*CULIN: volaille*) to untruss.

débris [debʀi] *nm* (*fragment*) fragment ♦ *nmpl* (*déchets*) pieces, debris *sg*; rubbish *sg* (*BRIT*), garbage *sg* (*US*).

débrouillard, e [debʀujaʀ, -aʀd(ə)] *adj* smart, resourceful.

débrouillardise [debʀujaʀdiz] *nf* smartness, resourcefulness.

débrouiller [debʀuje] *vt* to disentangle, untangle; (*fig*) to sort out, unravel; **se ~** *vi* to manage.

débroussailler [debʀusɑje] *vt* to clear (of brushwood).

débusquer [debyske] *vt* to drive out (from cover).

début [deby] *nm* beginning, start; ~**s** *nmpl* beginnings; (*de carrière*) début *sg*; **faire ses** ~**s** to start out; **au** ~ in *ou* at the beginning, at first; **au** ~ **de** at the beginning *ou* start of; **dès le** ~ from the start.

débutant, e [debytɑ̃, -ɑ̃t] *nm/f* beginner, novice.

débuter [debyte] *vi* to begin, start; (*faire ses débuts*) to start out.

deçà [dəsa]: **en** ~ **de** *prép* this side of; **en** ~ *adv* on this side.

décacheter [dekaʃte] *vt* to unseal, open.

décade [dekad] *nf* (*10 jours*) (period of) ten days; (*10 ans*) decade.

décadence [dekadɑ̃s] *nf* decadence; decline.

décadent, e [dekadɑ̃, -ɑ̃t] *adj* decadent.

décaféiné, e [dekafeine] *adj* decaffeinated, caffeine-free.

décalage [dekalaʒ] *nm* move forward *ou* back; shift forward *ou* back; (*écart*) gap; (*désaccord*) discrepancy; ~ **horaire** time difference (between time zones), time-lag.

décalaminer [dekalamine] *vt* to decoke.

décalcification [dekalsifikasjɔ̃] *nf* decalcification.

décalcifier [dekalsifje]: **se** ~ *vr* to decalcify.

décalcomanie [dekalkɔmani] *nf* transfer.

décaler [dekale] *vt* (*dans le temps: avancer*) to bring forward; (: *retarder*) to put back; (*changer de position*) to shift forward *ou* back; ~ **de 10 cm** to move forward *ou* back by 10 cm; ~ **de 2 h** to bring *ou* move forward 2 hours; to put back 2 hours.

décalitre [dekalitʀ(ə)] *nm* decalitre (*BRIT*), decaliter (*US*).

décalogue [dekalɔg] *nm* Decalogue.

décalquer [dekalke] *vt* to trace; (*par pression*) to transfer.

décamètre [dekamɛtʀ(ə)] *nm* decametre (*BRIT*), decameter (*US*).

décamper [dekɑ̃pe] *vi* to clear out *ou* off.

décan [dekɑ̃] *nm* (*ASTROLOGIE*) decan.

décanter [dekɑ̃te] *vt* to (allow to) settle (and decant); **se** ~ *vi* to settle.

décapage [dekapaʒ] *nm* stripping; scouring; sanding.

décapant [dekapɑ̃] *nm* acid solution; scouring agent; paint stripper.

décaper [dekape] *vt* to strip; (*avec abrasif*) to scour; (*avec papier de verre*) to sand.

décapiter [dekapite] *vt* to behead; (*par accident*) to decapitate; (*fig*) to cut the top off; (: *organisation*) to remove the top people from.

décapotable [dekapɔtabl(ə)] *adj* convertible.

décapoter [dekapɔte] *vt* to put down the top of.

décapsuler [dekapsyle] *vt* to take the cap *ou*

top off.

décapsuleur [dekapsylœr] *nm* bottle-opener.

décarcasser [dekaʀkase] *vt*: **se** ~ **pour qn/ pour faire qch** (*fam*) to slog one's guts out for sb/to do sth.

décathlon [dekatlɔ̃] *nm* decathlon.

décati, e [dekati] *adj* faded, aged.

décédé, e [desede] *adj* deceased.

décéder [desede] *vi* to die.

décelable [des(ə)labl(ə)] *adj* discernible.

déceler [desle] *vt* to discover, detect; (*révéler*) to indicate, reveal.

décélération [deseleʀasjɔ̃] *nf* deceleration.

décélérer [deseleʀe] *vi* to decelerate, slow down.

décembre [desɑ̃bʀ(ə)] *nm* December; *voir aussi* **juillet**.

décemment [desamɑ̃] *adv* decently.

décence [desɑ̃s] *nf* decency.

décennal, e, aux [desenal, -o] *adj* (*qui dure dix ans*) having a term of ten years, ten-year; (*qui revient tous les dix ans*) ten-yearly.

décennie [desni] *nf* decade.

décent, e [desɑ̃, -ɑ̃t] *adj* decent.

décentralisation [desɑ̃tʀalizasjɔ̃] *nf* decentralization.

décentraliser [desɑ̃tʀalize] *vt* to decentralize.

décentrer [desɑ̃tʀe] *vt* to decentre; **se** ~ to move off-centre.

déception [desɛpsjɔ̃] *nf* disappointment.

décerner [desɛʀne] *vt* to award.

décès [desɛ] *nm* death, decease; **acte de** ~ death certificate.

décevant, e [desvɑ̃, -ɑ̃t] *adj* disappointing.

décevoir [desvwaʀ] *vt* to disappoint.

déchaîné, e [deʃene] *adj* unbridled, raging.

déchaînement [deʃɛnmɑ̃] *nm* (*de haine, violence*) outbreak, outburst.

déchaîner [deʃene] *vt* (*passions, colère*) to unleash; (*rires etc*) to give rise to, arouse; **se** ~ *vi* to be unleashed; (*rires*) to burst out; (*se mettre en colère*) to fly into a rage; **se** ~ **contre qn** to unleash one's fury on sb.

déchanter [deʃɑ̃te] *vi* to become disillusioned.

décharge [deʃaʀʒ(ə)] *nf* (*dépôt d'ordures*) rubbish tip *ou* dump; (*électrique*) electrical discharge; (*salve*) volley of shots; **à la** ~ **de** in defence of.

déchargement [deʃaʀʒəmɑ̃] *nm* unloading.

décharger [deʃaʀʒe] *vt* (*marchandise, véhicule*) to unload; (*ÉLEC*) to discharge; (*arme: neutraliser*) to unload; (: *faire feu*) to discharge, fire; ~ **qn de** (*responsabilité*) to relieve sb of, release sb from; ~ **sa colère (sur)** to vent one's anger (on); ~ **sa conscience** to unburden one's conscience; **se** ~ **dans** (*se déverser*) to flow into; **se** ~ **d'une affaire sur qn** to hand a matter over to sb.

décharné, e [deʃaʀne] *adj* bony, emaciated, fleshless.

déchaussé, e [deʃose] *adj* (*dent*) loose.

déchausser [deʃose] *vt* (*personne*) to take the shoes off; (*skis*) to take off; **se** ~ to take off one's shoes; (*dent*) to come *ou* work loose.

dèche [dɛʃ] *nf* (*fam*): **être dans la** ~ to be flat broke.

déchéance [deʃeɑ̃s] *nf* (*déclin*) degeneration, decay, decline; (*chute*) fall.

déchet [deʃɛ] *nm* (*de bois, tissu etc*) scrap; (*perte: gén COMM*) wastage, waste; ~**s** *nmpl* (*ordures*) refuse *sg*, rubbish *sg* (*BRIT*), garbage *sg* (*US*); ~**s radioactifs** radioactive waste.

déchiffrage [deʃifraʒ] *nm* sight-reading.

déchiffrer [deʃifre] *vt* to decipher.

déchiqueté, e [deʃikte] *adj* jagged(-edged), ragged.

déchiqueter [deʃikte] *vt* to tear *ou* pull to pieces.

déchirant, e [deʃirɑ̃, -ɑ̃t] *adj* heart-breaking, heart-rending.

déchiré, e [deʃire] *adj* torn; (*fig*) heart-broken.

déchirement [deʃirmɑ̃] *nm* (*chagrin*) wrench, heartbreak; (*gén pl: conflit*) rift, split.

déchirer [deʃire] *vt* to tear, rip; (*mettre en morceaux*) to tear up; (*pour ouvrir*) to tear off; (*arracher*) to tear out; (*fig*) to tear apart; **se** ~ *vi* to tear, rip; **se** ~ **un muscle/tendon** to tear a muscle/tendon.

déchirure [deʃiryr] *nf* (*accroc*) tear, rip; ~ **musculaire** torn muscle.

déchoir [deʃwar] *vi* (*personne*) to lower o.s., demean o.s; ~ **de** to fall from.

déchu, e [deʃy] *pp de* **déchoir** ♦ *adj* fallen; (*roi*) deposed.

décibel [desibɛl] *nm* decibel.

décidé, e [deside] *adj* (*personne, air*) determined; **c'est** ~ it's decided; **être** ~ **à faire** to be determined to do.

décidément [desidemɑ̃] *adv* undoubtedly; really.

décider [deside] *vt:* ~ **qch** to decide on sth; ~ **de faire/que** to decide to do/that; ~ **qn (à faire qch)** to persuade *ou* induce sb (to do sth); ~ **de qch** to decide upon sth; (*suj: chose*) to determine sth; **se** ~ *vi* (*personne*) to decide, make up one's mind; (*problème, affaire*) to be resolved; **se** ~ **à qch** to decide on sth; **se** ~ **à faire** to decide *ou* make up one's mind to do; **se** ~ **pour qch** to decide on *ou* in favour of sth.

décideur [desidœr] *nm* decision-maker.

décilitre [desilitr(ə)] *nm* decilitre (*BRIT*), deciliter (*US*).

décimal, e, aux [desimal, -o] *adj, nf* decimal.

décimalisation [desimalizɑsjɔ̃] *nf* decimalization.

décimaliser [desimalize] *vt* to decimalize.

décimer [desime] *vt* to decimate.

décimètre [desimɛtr(ə)] *nm* decimetre (*BRIT*), decimeter (*US*); **double** ~ (20 cm) ruler.

décisif, ive [desizif, -iv] *adj* decisive; (*qui l'emporte*): **le facteur/l'argument** ~ the de-ciding factor/argument.

décision [desizjɔ̃] *nf* decision; (*fermeté*) decisiveness, decision; **prendre une** ~ to make a decision; **prendre la** ~ **de faire** to take the decision to do; **emporter** *ou* **faire la** ~ to be decisive.

déclamation [deklamɑsjɔ̃] *nf* declamation; (*péj*) ranting, spouting.

déclamatoire [deklamatwar] *adj* declamatory.

déclamer [deklame] *vt* to declaim; (*péj*) to spout ♦ *vi*: ~ **contre** to rail against.

déclarable [deklarabl(ə)] *adj* (*marchandise*) dutiable; (*revenus*) declarable.

déclaration [deklarɑsjɔ̃] *nf* declaration; registration; (*discours: POL etc*) statement; (*compte rendu*) report; **fausse** ~ misrepresentation; ~ **(d'amour)** declaration; ~ **de décès** registration of death; ~ **de guerre** declaration of war; ~ **(d'impôts)** statement of income, tax declaration, ≈ tax return; ~ **(de sinistre)** (insurance) claim; ~ **de revenus** statement of income.

déclaré, e [deklare] *adj* (*juré*) avowed.

déclarer [deklare] *vt* to declare, announce; (*revenus, employés, marchandises*) to declare; (*décès, naissance*) to register; (*vol etc: à la police*) to report; **se** ~ *vi* (*feu, maladie*) to break out; ~ **la guerre** to declare war.

déclassé, e [deklɑse] *adj* relegated, downgraded; (*matériel*) (to be) sold off.

déclassement [deklɑsmɑ̃] *nm* relegation, downgrading; (*RAIL etc*) change of class.

déclasser [deklɑse] *vt* to relegate, downgrade; (*déranger: fiches, livres*) to get out of order.

déclenchement [deklɑ̃ʃmɑ̃] *nm* release; setting off.

déclencher [deklɑ̃ʃe] *vt* (*mécanisme etc*) to release; (*sonnerie*) to set off, activate; (*attaque, grève*) to launch; (*provoquer*) to trigger off; **se** ~ *vi* to release itself; to go off.

déclencheur [deklɑ̃ʃœr] *nm* release mechanism.

déclic [deklik] *nm* trigger mechanism; (*bruit*) click.

déclin [deklɛ̃] *nm* decline.

déclinaison [deklinɛzɔ̃] *nf* declension.

décliner [dekline] *vi* to decline ♦ *vt* (*invitation*) to decline, refuse; (*responsabilité*) to refuse to accept; (*nom, adresse*) to state; (*LING*) to decline; **se** ~ (*LING*) to decline.

déclivité [deklivite] *nf* slope, incline; **en** ~ sloping, on the incline.

décloisonner [deklwazɔne] *vt* to decompartmentalize.

déclouer [deklue] *vt* to unnail.

décocher [dekɔʃe] *vt* to hurl; (*flèche, regard*) to shoot.

décoction [dekɔksjɔ̃] *nf* decoction.

décodage [dekɔdaʒ] *nm* deciphering, decoding.

décoder [dekɔde] *vt* to decipher, decode.

décodeur [dekɔdœr] *nm* decoder.

décoiffé, e [dekwafe] *adj*: **elle est toute ~e** her hair is in a mess.

décoiffer [dekwafe] *vt*: **~ qn** to disarrange *ou* mess up sb's hair; to take sb's hat off; **se ~** to take off one's hat.

décoincer [dekwɛse] *vt* to unjam, loosen.

déçois [deswa] *etc*, **déçoive** [deswav] *etc vb voir* **décevoir**.

décolérer [dekɔleʀe] *vi*: **il ne décolère pas** he's still angry, he hasn't calmed down.

décollage [dekɔlaʒ] *nm* (*AVIAT, ÉCON*) takeoff.

décollé, e [dekɔle] *adj*: **oreilles ~es** sticking-out ears.

décollement [dekɔlmɑ̃] *nm* (*MÉD*): **~ de la rétine** retinal detachment.

décoller [dekɔle] *vt* to unstick ♦ *vi* to take off; (*projet, entreprise*) to take off, get off the ground; **se ~** *vi* to come unstuck.

décolleté, e [dekɔlte] *adj* low-necked, low-cut; (*femme*) wearing a low-cut dress ♦ *nm* low neck(line); (*épaules*) (bare) neck and shoulders; (*plongeant*) cleavage.

décolleter [dekɔlte] *vt* (*vêtement*) to give a low neckline to; (*TECH*) to cut.

décolonisation [dekɔlɔnizasjɔ̃] *nf* decolonization.

décoloniser [dekɔlɔnize] *vt* to decolonize.

décolorant [dekɔlɔʀɑ̃] *nm* decolorant, bleaching agent.

décoloration [dekɔlɔʀasjɔ̃] *nf*: **se faire faire une ~** (*chez le coiffeur*) to have one's hair bleached *ou* lightened.

décoloré, e [dekɔlɔʀe] *adj* (*vêtement*) faded; (*cheveux*) bleached.

décolorer [dekɔlɔʀe] *vt* (*tissu*) to fade; (*cheveux*) to bleach, lighten; **se ~** *vi* to fade.

décombres [dekɔ̃bʀ(ə)] *nmpl* rubble *sg*, debris *sg*.

décommander [dekɔmɑ̃de] *vt* to cancel; (*invités*) to put off; **se ~** to cancel, cry off.

décomposé, e [dekɔ̃poze] *adj* (*pourri*) decomposed; (*visage*) haggard, distorted.

décomposer [dekɔ̃poze] *vt* to break up; (*CHIMIE*) to decompose; (*MATH*) to factorize; **se ~** *vi* to decompose.

décomposition [dekɔ̃pozisjɔ̃] *nf* breaking up; decomposition; factorization; **en ~** (*organisme*) in a state of decay, decomposing.

décompresser [dekɔ̃pʀese] *vi* (*fam: se détendre*) to unwind.

décompresseur [dekɔ̃pʀesœʀ] *nm* decompressor.

décompression [dekɔ̃pʀesjɔ̃] *nf* decompression.

décomprimer [dekɔ̃pʀime] *vt* to decompress.

décompte [dekɔ̃t] *nm* deduction; (*facture*) breakdown (of an account), detailed account.

décompter [dekɔ̃te] *vt* to deduct.

déconcentration [dekɔ̃sɑ̃tʀasjɔ̃] *nf* (*des industries etc*) dispersal; **~ des pouvoirs** devolution.

déconcentré, e [dekɔ̃sɑ̃tʀe] *adj* (*sportif etc*) who has lost (his/her) concentration.

déconcentrer [dekɔ̃sɑ̃tʀe] *vt* (*ADMIN*) to disperse; **se ~** *vi* to lose (one's) concentration.

déconcertant, e [dekɔ̃sɛʀtɑ̃, -ɑ̃t] *adj* disconcerting.

déconcerter [dekɔ̃sɛʀte] *vt* to disconcert, confound.

déconditionner [dekɔ̃disjɔne] *vt*: **~ l'opinion américaine** to change the way the Americans have been forced to think.

déconfit, e [dekɔ̃fi, -it] *adj* crestfallen, downcast.

déconfiture [dekɔ̃fityʀ] *nf* collapse, ruin; (*morale*) defeat.

décongélation [dekɔ̃ʒelasjɔ̃] *nf* defrosting, thawing.

décongeler [dekɔ̃ʒle] *vt* to thaw (out).

décongestionner [dekɔ̃ʒɛstjɔne] *vt* (*MÉD*) to decongest; (*rues*) to relieve congestion in.

déconnecter [dekɔnɛkte] *vt* to disconnect.

déconner [dekɔne] *vi* (*fam!: en parlant*) to talk (a load of) rubbish (*BRIT*) *ou* garbage (*US*); (*: faire des bêtises*) to muck about; **sans ~** no kidding.

déconseiller [dekɔ̃seje] *vt*: **~ qch (à qn)** to advise (sb) against sth; **~ à qn de faire** to advise sb against doing; **c'est déconseillé** it's not advised *ou* advisable.

déconsidérer [dekɔ̃sidere] *vt* to discredit.

décontamination [dekɔ̃taminasjɔ̃] *nf* decontamination.

décontaminer [dekɔ̃tamine] *vt* to decontaminate.

décontenancer [dekɔ̃tnɑ̃se] *vt* to disconcert, discountenance.

décontracté, e [dekɔ̃tʀakte] *adj* relaxed.

décontracter [dekɔ̃tʀakte] *vt*, **se ~** *vi* to relax.

décontraction [dekɔ̃tʀaksjɔ̃] *nf* relaxation.

déconvenue [dekɔ̃vny] *nf* disappointment.

décor [dekɔʀ] *nm* décor; (*paysage*) scenery; **~s** *nmpl* (*THÉÂT*) scenery *sg*, decor *sg*; (*CINÉ*) set *sg*; **changement de ~** (*fig*) change of scene; **entrer dans le ~** (*fig*) to run off the road; **en ~ naturel** (*CINÉ*) on location.

décorateur, trice [dekɔʀatœʀ, -tʀis] *nm/f* (*interior*) decorator; (*CINÉ*) set designer.

décoratif, ive [dekɔʀatif, -iv] *adj* decorative.

décoration [dekɔʀasjɔ̃] *nf* decoration.

décorer [dekɔʀe] *vt* to decorate.

décortiqué, e [dekɔʀtike] *adj* shelled; hulled.

décortiquer [dekɔʀtike] *vt* to shell; (*riz*) to hull; (*fig*) to dissect.

décorum [dekɔʀɔm] *nm* decorum; etiquette.

décote [dekɔt] *nf* tax relief.

découcher [dekuʃe] *vi* to spend the night away.

découdre [dekudʀ(ə)] *vt* (*vêtement, couture*) to unpick, take the stitching out of; (*bouton*) to take off; **se ~** *vi* to come unstitched; (*bouton*) to come off; **en ~** (*fig*) to fight, do battle.

découler – dédommager

découler [dekule] *vi:* ~ **de** to ensue *ou* follow from.

découpage [dekupaʒ] *nm* cutting up; carving; (*image*) cut-out (figure); ~ **électoral** division into constituencies.

découper [dekupe] *vt* (*papier, tissu etc*) to cut up; (*volaille, viande*) to carve; (*détacher: manche, article*) to cut out; **se** ~ **sur** (*ciel, fond*) to stand out against.

découplé, e [dekuple] *adj:* **bien** ~ well-built, well-proportioned.

découpure [dekupyʀ] *nf:* ~**s** (*morceaux*) cut-out bits; (*d'une côte, arête*) indentations, jagged outline *sg*.

décourageant, e [dekuʀaʒɑ̃, ɑ̃t] *adj* discouraging; (*personne, attitude*) discouraging, negative.

découragement [dekuʀaʒmɑ̃] *nm* discouragement, despondency.

décourager [dekuʀaʒe] *vt* to discourage, dishearten; (*dissuader*) to discourage, put off; **se** ~ *vi* to lose heart, become discouraged; ~ **qn de faire/de qch** to discourage sb from doing/from sth, put sb off doing/sth.

décousu, e [dekuzy] *pp de* **découdre** ♦ *adj* unstitched; (*fig*) disjointed, disconnected.

découvert, e [dekuvɛʀ, -ɛʀt(ə)] *pp de* **découvrir** ♦ *adj* (*tête*) bare, uncovered; (*lieu*) open, exposed ♦ *nm* (*bancaire*) overdraft ♦ *nf* discovery; **à** ~ *adv* (*MIL*) exposed, without cover; (*fig*) openly ♦ *adj* (*COMM*) overdrawn; **à visage** ~ openly; **aller à la** ~**e de** to go in search of.

découvrir [dekuvʀiʀ] *vt* to discover; (*apercevoir*) to see; (*enlever ce qui couvre ou protège*) to uncover; (*montrer, dévoiler*) to reveal; **se** ~ to take off one's hat; (*se déshabiller*) to take something off; (*au lit*) to uncover o.s.; (*ciel*) to clear; **se** ~ **des talents** to find hidden talents in o.s.

décrasser [dekʀase] *vt* to clean.

décrêper [dekʀepe] *vt* (*cheveux*) to straighten.

décrépi, e [dekʀepi] *adj* peeling; with roughcast rendering removed.

décrépit, e [dekʀepi, -it] *adj* decrepit.

décrépitude [dekʀepityd] *nf* decrepitude; decay.

decrescendo [dekʀeʃɛndo] *nm* (*MUS*) decrescendo; **aller** ~ (*fig*) to decline, be on the wane.

décret [dekʀɛ] *nm* decree.

décréter [dekʀete] *vt* to decree; (*ordonner*) to order.

décret-loi [dekʀɛlwa] *nm* statutory order.

décrié, e [dekʀije] *adj* disparaged.

décrire [dekʀiʀ] *vt* to describe; (*courbe, cercle*) to follow, describe.

décrisper [dekʀispe] *vt* to defuse.

décrit, e [dekʀi, -it] *pp de* **décrire**.

décrivais [dekʀive] *etc vb voir* **décrire**.

décrochement [dekʀɔʃmɑ̃] *nm* (*d'un mur etc*) recess.

décrocher [dekʀɔʃe] *vt* (*dépendre*) to take down; (*téléphone*) to take off the hook; (*: pour répondre*): ~ (**le téléphone**) to pick up *ou* lift the receiver; (*fig: contrat etc*) to get, land ♦ *vi* to drop out; to switch off; **se** ~ *vi* (*tableau, rideau*) to fall down.

décrois [dekʀwa] *etc vb voir* **décroître**.

décroiser [dekʀwaze] *vt* (*bras*) to unfold; (*jambes*) to uncross.

décroissant, e [dekʀwasɑ̃, -ɑ̃t] *vb voir* **décroître** ♦ *adj* decreasing, declining, diminishing; **par ordre** ~ in descending order.

décroître [dekʀwatʀ(ə)] *vi* to decrease, decline, diminish.

décrotter [dekʀɔte] *vt* (*chaussures*) to clean the mud from; **se** ~ **le nez** to pick one's nose.

décru, e [dekʀy] *pp de* **décroître**.

décrue [dekʀy] *nf* drop in level (of the waters).

décrypter [dekʀipte] *vt* to decipher.

déçu, e [desy] *pp de* **décevoir** ♦ *adj* disappointed.

déculotter [dekylɔte] *vt:* ~ **qn** to take off *ou* down sb's trousers; **se** ~ to take off *ou* down one's trousers.

déculpabiliser [dekylpabilize] *vt* (*personne*) to relieve of guilt; (*chose*) to decriminalize.

décuple [dekypl(ə)] *nm:* **le** ~ **de** ten times; **au** ~ tenfold.

décupler [dekyple] *vt, vi* to increase tenfold.

déçut [desy] *etc vb voir* **décevoir**.

dédaignable [dedɛɲabl(ə)] *adj:* **pas** ~ not to be despised.

dédaigner [dedɛɲe] *vt* to despise, scorn; (*négliger*) to disregard, spurn; ~ **de faire** to consider it beneath one to do, not deign to do.

dédaigneusement [dedɛɲøzmɑ̃] *adv* scornfully, disdainfully.

dédaigneux, euse [dedɛɲø, -øz] *adj* scornful, disdainful.

dédain [dedɛ̃] *nm* scorn, disdain.

dédale [dedal] *nm* maze.

dedans [dədɑ̃] *adv* inside; (*pas en plein air*) indoors, inside ♦ *nm* inside; **au** ~ on the inside; inside; **en** ~ (*vers l'intérieur*) inwards; *voir aussi* **là**.

dédicace [dedikas] *nf* (*imprimée*) dedication; (*manuscrite, sur une photo etc*) inscription.

dédicacer [dedikase] *vt:* ~ (**à qn**) to sign (for sb), autograph (for sb), inscribe (to sb).

dédié, e [dedje] *adj:* **ordinateur** ~ dedicated computer.

dédier [dedje] *vt* to dedicate.

dédire [dediʀ]: **se** ~ *vi* to go back on one's word; (*se rétracter*) to retract, recant.

dédit, e [dedi, -it] *pp de* **dédire** ♦ *nm* (*COMM*) forfeit, penalty.

dédommagement [dedɔmaʒmɑ̃] *nm* compensation.

dédommager [dedɔmaʒe] *vt:* ~ **qn** (**de**) to compensate sb (for); (*fig*) to repay sb (for).

dédouaner – déficit 118 *FRANÇAIS–ANGLAIS*

dédouaner [dedwane] *vt* to clear through customs.

dédoublement [dedubləmɑ̃] *nm* splitting; (*PSYCH*): ~ **de la personnalité** split *ou* dual personality.

dédoubler [deduble] *vt* (*classe, effectifs*) to split (into two); (*couverture etc*) to unfold; (*manteau*) to remove the lining of; ~ **un train/les trains** to run a relief train/ additional trains; **se** ~ *vi* (*PSYCH*) to have a split personality.

dédramatiser [dedʀamatize] *vt* (*situation*) to defuse; (*événement*) to play down.

déductible [dedyktibl(ə)] *adj* deductible.

déduction [dedyksjɔ̃] *nf* (*d'argent*) deduction; (*raisonnement*) deduction, inference.

déduire [deduiʀ] *vt*: ~ **qch (de)** (*ôter*) to deduct sth (from); (*conclure*) to deduce *ou* infer sth (from).

déesse [deɛs] *nf* goddess.

DEFA *sigle m* (= *Diplôme d'État relatif aux fonctions d'animation*) *diploma for senior youth leaders.*

défaillance [defajɑ̃s] *nf* (*syncope*) blackout; (*fatigue*) (sudden) weakness *no pl*; (*technique*) fault, failure; (*morale etc*) weakness; ~ **cardiaque** heart failure.

défaillant, e [defajɑ̃, -ɑ̃t] *adj* defective; (*JUR*: *témoin*) defaulting.

défaillir [defajiʀ] *vi* to faint; to feel faint; (*mémoire etc*) to fail.

défaire [defɛʀ] *vt* (*installation, échafaudage*) to take down, dismantle; (*paquet etc, nœud, vêtement*) to undo; (*bagages*) to unpack; (*ouvrage*) to undo, unpick; (*cheveux*) to take out; **se** ~ *vi* to come undone; **se** ~ **de** *vt* (*se débarrasser de*) to get rid of; (*se séparer de*) to part with; ~ **le lit** (*pour changer les draps*) to strip the bed; (*pour se coucher*) to turn back the bedclothes.

défait, e [defɛ, -ɛt] *pp de* **défaire** ♦ *adj* (*visage*) haggard, ravaged ♦ *nf* defeat.

défaites [defɛt] *vb voir* **défaire**.

défaitisme [defetism(ə)] *nm* defeatism.

défaitiste [defetist(ə)] *adj, nm/f* defeatist.

défalcation [defalkasjɔ̃] *nf* deduction.

défalquer [defalke] *vt* to deduct.

défasse [defas] *etc vb voir* **défaire**.

défausser [defose] *vt* to get rid of; **se** ~ *vi* (*CARTES*) to discard.

défaut [defo] *nm* (*moral*) fault, failing, defect; (*d'étoffe, métal*) fault, flaw, defect; (*manque, carence*): ~ **de** lack of; shortage of; (*INFORM*) bug; ~ **de la cuirasse** (*fig*) chink in the armour (*BRIT*) *ou* armor (*US*); **en** ~ at fault; in the wrong; **faire** ~ (*manquer*) to be lacking; **à** ~ *adv* failing that; **à** ~ **de** for lack *ou* want of; **par** ~ (*JUR*) in his (*ou* her *etc*) absence.

défaveur [defavœʀ] *nf* disfavour (*BRIT*), disfavor (*US*).

défavorable [defavɔʀabl(ə)] *adj* unfavourable (*BRIT*), unfavorable (*US*).

défavoriser [defavɔʀize] *vt* to put at a disadvantage.

défectif, ive [defɛktif, -iv] *adj*: **verbe** ~ defective verb.

défection [defɛksjɔ̃] *nf* defection, failure to give support *ou* assistance; failure to appear; **faire** ~ (*d'un parti etc*) to withdraw one's support, leave.

défectueux, euse [defɛktyø, -øz] *adj* faulty, defective.

défectuosité [defɛktyozite] *nf* defectiveness *no pl*; (*défaut*) defect, fault.

défendable [defɑ̃dabl(ə)] *adj* defensible.

défendeur, eresse [defɑ̃dœʀ, -dʀɛs] *nm/f* (*JUR*) defendant.

défendre [defɑ̃dʀ(ə)] *vt* to defend; (*interdire*) to forbid; ~ **à qn qch/de faire** to forbid sb sth/ to do; **il est défendu de cracher** spitting (is) prohibited *ou* is not allowed; **c'est défendu** it is forbidden; **se** ~ to defend o.s.; **il se défend** (*fig*) he can hold his own; **ça se défend** (*fig*) it holds together; **se** ~ **de/contre** (*se protéger*) to protect o.s. from/against; **se** ~ **de** (*se garder de*) to refrain from; (*nier*): **se** ~ **de vouloir** to deny wanting.

défenestrer [defənɛstʀe] *vt* to throw out of the window.

défense [defɑ̃s] *nf* defence (*BRIT*), defense (*US*); (*d'éléphant etc*) tusk; **ministre de la** ~ Minister of Defence (*BRIT*), Defence Secretary; **la** ~ **nationale** defence, the defence of the realm (*BRIT*); **la** ~ **contre avions** anti-aircraft defence; "~ **de fumer/cracher**" "no smoking/spitting", "smoking/spitting prohibited"; **prendre la** ~ **de qn** to stand up for sb; ~ **des consommateurs** consumerism.

défenseur [defɑ̃sœʀ] *nm* defender; (*JUR*) counsel for the defence.

défensif, ive [defɑ̃sif, -iv] *adj, nf* defensive; **être sur la défensive** to be on the defensive.

déféquer [defeke] *vi* to defecate.

déferai [defʀe] *etc vb voir* **défaire**.

déférence [defeʀɑ̃s] *nf* deference.

déférent, e [defeʀɑ̃, -ɑ̃t] *adj* (*poli*) deferential, deferent.

déférer [defeʀe] *vt* (*JUR*) to refer; ~ **à** *vt* (*requête, décision*) to defer to; ~ **qn à la justice** to hand sb over to justice.

déferlant, e [defɛʀlɑ̃, -ɑ̃t] *adj*: **vague** ~**e** breaker.

déferlement [defɛʀləmɑ̃] *nm* breaking; surge.

déferler [defɛʀle] *vi* (*vagues*) to break; (*fig*) to surge.

défi [defi] *nm* (*provocation*) challenge; (*bravade*) defiance; **mettre qn au** ~ **de faire qch** to challenge sb to do sth; **relever un** ~ to take up *ou* accept a challenge.

défiance [defjɑ̃s] *nf* mistrust, distrust.

déficeler [defisle] *vt* (*paquet*) to undo, untie.

déficience [defisjɑ̃s] *nf* deficiency.

déficient, e [defisjɑ̃, -ɑ̃t] *adj* deficient.

déficit [defisit] *nm* (*COMM*) deficit; (*PSYCH etc*:

manque) defect; ~ **budgétaire** budget deficit; **être en** ~ to be in deficit.

déficitaire [defisitɛʀ] *adj* (*année, récolte*) bad; **entreprise/budget** ~ business/budget in deficit.

défier [defje] *vt* (*provoquer*) to challenge; (*fig*) to defy, brave; **se** ~ **de** (*se méfier de*) to distrust, mistrust; ~ **qn de faire** to challenge *ou* defy sb to do; ~ **qn à** to challenge sb to; ~ **toute comparaison/concurrence** to be incomparable/unbeatable.

défigurer [defigyʀe] *vt* to disfigure; (*suj: boutons etc*) to mar *ou* spoil (the looks of); (*fig: œuvre*) to mutilate, deface.

défilé [defile] *nm* (*GÉO*) (narrow) gorge *ou* pass; (*soldats*) parade; (*manifestants*) procession, march; **un** ~ **de** (*voitures, visiteurs etc*) a stream of.

défiler [defile] *vi* (*troupes*) to march past; (*sportifs*) to parade; (*manifestants*) to march; (*visiteurs*) to pour, stream; **se** ~ *vi* (*se dérober*) to slip away, sneak off; **faire** ~ (*bande, film*) to put on; (*INFORM*) to scroll.

défini, e [defini] *adj* definite.

définir [definiʀ] *vt* to define.

définissable [definisabl(ə)] *adj* definable.

définitif, ive [definitif, -iv] *adj* (*final*) final, definitive; (*pour longtemps*) permanent, definitive; (*sans appel*) final, definite ♦ *nf*: **en définitive** eventually; (*somme toute*) when all is said and done.

définition [definisjɔ̃] *nf* definition; (*de mots croisés*) clue; (*TV*) (picture) resolution.

définitivement [definitivmɑ̃] *adv* definitively; permanently; definitely.

défit [defi] *etc vb voir* **défaire**.

déflagration [deflagʀasjɔ̃] *nf* explosion.

déflation [deflasjɔ̃] *nf* deflation.

déflationniste [deflasjɔnist(ə)] *adj* deflationist, deflationary.

déflecteur [deflɛktœʀ] *nm* (*AUTO*) quarterlight (*BRIT*), deflector (*US*).

déflorer [deflɔʀe] *vt* (*jeune fille*) to deflower; (*fig*) to spoil the charm of.

défoncé, e [defɔ̃se] *adj* smashed in; broken down; (*route*) full of potholes ♦ *nm/f* addict.

défoncer [defɔ̃se] *vt* (*caisse*) to stave in; (*porte*) to smash in *ou* down; (*lit, fauteuil*) to burst (the springs of); (*terrain, route*) to rip *ou* plough up; **se** ~ *vi* (*se donner à fond*) to give it all one's got.

défont [defɔ̃] *vb voir* **défaire**.

déformant, e [defɔʀmɑ̃, -ɑ̃t] *adj*: **glace** ~**e** *ou* **miroir** ~ distorting mirror.

déformation [defɔʀmasjɔ̃] *nf* loss of shape; deformation; distortion; ~ **professionnelle** conditioning by one's job.

déformer [defɔʀme] *vt* to put out of shape; (*corps*) to deform; (*pensée, fait*) to distort; **se** ~ *vi* to lose its shape.

défoulement [defulmɑ̃] *nm* release of tension; unwinding.

défouler [defule]: **se** ~ *vi* (*PSYCH*) to work off one's tensions, release one's pent-up feelings; (*gén*) to unwind, let off steam.

défraîchi, e [defʀeʃi] *adj* faded; (*article à vendre*) shop-soiled.

défraîchir [defʀeʃiʀ]: **se** ~ *vi* to fade; to become shop-soiled.

défrayer [defʀeje] *vt*: ~ **qn** to pay sb's expenses; ~ **la chronique** to be in the news; ~ **la conversation** to be the main topic of conversation.

défrichement [defʀiʃmɑ̃] *nm* clearance.

défricher [defʀiʃe] *vt* to clear (for cultivation).

défriser [defʀize] *vt* (*cheveux*) to straighten; (*fig*) to annoy.

défroisser [defʀwase] *vt* to smooth out.

défroque [defʀɔk] *nf* cast-off.

défroqué [defʀɔke] *nm* former monk (*ou* priest).

défroquer [defʀɔke] *vi* (*aussi:* **se** ~) to give up the cloth, renounce one's vows.

défunt, e [defœ̃, -œ̃t] *adj*: **son** ~ **père** his late father ♦ *nm/f* deceased.

dégagé, e [degaʒe] *adj* clear; (*ton, air*) casual, jaunty.

dégagement [degaʒmɑ̃] *nm* emission; freeing; clearing; (*espace libre*) clearing; passage; clearance; (*FOOTBALL*) clearance; **voie de** ~ slip road; **itinéraire de** ~ alternative route (*to relieve traffic congestion*).

dégager [degaʒe] *vt* (*exhaler*) to give off, emit; (*délivrer*) to free, extricate; (*MIL: troupes*) to relieve; (*désencombrer*) to clear; (*isoler, mettre en valeur*) to bring out; (*crédits*) to release; **se** ~ *vi* (*odeur*) to emanate, be given off; (*passage, ciel*) to clear; ~ **qn de** (*engagement, parole etc*) to release *ou* free sb from; **se** ~ **de** (*fig: engagement etc*) to get out of; (*: promesse*) to go back on.

dégaine [degɛn] *nf* awkward way of walking.

dégainer [degene] *vt* to draw.

dégarni, e [degaʀni] *adj* bald.

dégarnir [degaʀniʀ] *vt* (*vider*) to empty, clear; **se** ~ *vi* to empty; to be cleaned out *ou* cleared; (*tempes, crâne*) to go bald.

dégâts [dega] *nmpl* damage *sg*; **faire des** ~ to damage.

dégauchir [degoʃiʀ] *vt* (*TECH*) to surface.

dégazer [degaze] *vi* (*pétrolier*) to clean its tanks.

dégel [deʒɛl] *nm* thaw; (*fig: des prix etc*) unfreezing.

dégeler [deʒle] *vt* to thaw (out); (*fig*) to unfreeze ♦ *vi* to thaw (out); **se** ~ *vi* (*fig*) to thaw out.

dégénéré, e [deʒeneʀe] *adj, nm/f* degenerate.

dégénérer [deʒeneʀe] *vi* to degenerate; (*empirer*) to go from bad to worse; (*devenir*): ~ **en** to degenerate into.

dégénérescence [deʒeneʀesɑ̃s] *nf* degeneration.

dégingandé, e [deʒɛ̃gɑ̃de] *adj* gangling, lanky.

dégivrage [deʒivraʒ] *nm* defrosting; de-icing.

dégivrer [deʒivʀe] *vt* (*frigo*) to defrost; (*vitres*) to de-ice.

dégivreur [deʒivʀœʀ] *nm* defroster; de-icer.

déglinguer [deglɛ̃ge] *vt* to bust.

déglutir [deglytiʀ] *vt, vi* to swallow.

déglutition [deglytisjɔ̃] *nf* swallowing.

dégonflé, e [degɔ̃fle] *adj* (*pneu*) flat; (*fam*) chicken ♦ *nm/f* (*fam*) chicken.

dégonfler [degɔ̃fle] *vt* (*pneu, ballon*) to let down, deflate ♦ *vi* (*désenfler*) to go down; **se** ~ *vi* (*fam*) to chicken out.

dégorger [degɔʀʒe] *vi* (*CULIN*): **faire** ~ to leave to sweat; (*aussi*: **se** ~: *rivière*): ~ **dans** to flow into ♦ *vt* to disgorge.

dégoter [degɔte] *vt* (*fam*) to dig up, find.

dégouliner [deguline] *vi* to trickle, drip; ~ **de** to be dripping with.

dégoupiller [degupije] *vt* (*grenade*) to take the pin out of.

dégourdi, e [deguʀdi] *adj* smart, resourceful.

dégourdir [deguʀdiʀ] *vt* to warm (up); **se** ~ **(les jambes)** to stretch one's legs.

dégoût [degu] *nm* disgust, distaste.

dégoûtant, e [degutɑ̃, -ɑ̃t] *adj* disgusting.

dégoûté, e [degute] *adj* disgusted; ~ **de** sick of.

dégoûter [degute] *vt* to disgust; **cela me dégoûte** I find this disgusting *ou* revolting; ~ **qn de qch** to put sb off sth; **se** ~ **de** to get *ou* become sick of.

dégoutter [degute] *vi* to drip; ~ **de** to be dripping with.

dégradant, e [degʀadɑ̃, -ɑ̃t] *adj* degrading.

dégradation [degʀadasjɔ̃] *nf* reduction in rank; defacement; degradation, debasement; deterioration; (*aussi*: ~**s**: *dégâts*) damage *no pl*.

dégradé, e [degʀade] *adj* (*couleur*) shaded off; (*teintes*) faded; (*cheveux*) layered ♦ *nm* (*PEINTURE*) gradation.

dégrader [degʀade] *vt* (*MIL*: *officier*) to degrade; (*abîmer*) to damage, deface; (*avilir*) to degrade, debase; **se** ~ *vi* (*relations, situation*) to deteriorate.

dégrafer [degʀafe] *vt* to unclip, unhook, unfasten.

dégraissage [degʀɛsaʒ] *nm* (*ÉCON*) cutbacks *pl*; ~ **et nettoyage à sec** dry cleaning.

dégraissant [degʀɛsɑ̃] *nm* spot remover.

dégraisser [degʀese] *vt* (*soupe*) to skim; (*vêtement*) to take the grease marks out of; (*ÉCON*) to cut back; (*: entreprise*) to slim down.

degré [dagʀe] *nm* degree; (*d'escalier*) step; **brûlure au 1er/2ème** ~ 1st/2nd degree burn; **équation du 1er/2ème** ~ linear/quadratic equation; **le premier** ~ (*SCOL*) primary level; **alcool à 90** ~**s** surgical spirit; **vin de 10** ~**s** 10° wine (*on Gay-Lussac scale*); **par** ~**(s)** *adv* by degrees, gradually.

dégressif, ive [degʀesif, -iv] *adj* on a decreasing scale, degressive; **tarif** ~ decreasing rate of charge.

dégrèvement [degʀɛvmɑ̃] *nm* tax relief.

dégrever [degʀəve] *vt* to grant tax relief to; to reduce the tax burden on.

dégriffé, e [degʀife] *adj* (*vêtement*) sold without the designer's label.

dégringolade [degʀɛ̃gɔlad] *nf* tumble; (*fig*) collapse.

dégringoler [degʀɛ̃gɔle] *vi* to tumble (down); (*fig: prix, monnaie etc*) to collapse.

dégriser [degʀize] *vt* to sober up.

dégrossir [degʀosiʀ] *vt* (*bois*) to trim; (*fig*) to work out roughly; (*: personne*) to knock the rough edges off.

déguenillé, e [dəgnije] *adj* ragged, tattered.

déguerpir [degɛʀpiʀ] *vi* to clear off.

dégueulasse [degœlas] *adj* (*fam*) disgusting.

dégueuler [degœle] *vi* (*fam*) to puke, throw up.

déguisé, e [degize] *adj* disguised; dressed up; ~ **en** disguised (*ou* dressed up) as.

déguisement [degizmɑ̃] *nm* disguise; (*habits: pour s'amuser*) dressing-up clothes; (*: pour tromper*) disguise.

déguiser [degize] *vt* to disguise; **se** ~ **(en)** (*se costumer*) to dress up (as); (*pour tromper*) to disguise o.s. (as).

dégustation [degystasjɔ̃] *nf* tasting; sampling; savouring (*BRIT*), savoring (*US*); (*séance*): ~ **de vin(s)** wine-tasting.

déguster [degyste] *vt* (*vins*) to taste; (*fromages etc*) to sample; (*savourer*) to enjoy, savour (*BRIT*), savor (*US*).

déhancher [deɑ̃ʃe]: **se** ~ *vi* to sway one's hips; to lean (one's weight) on one hip.

dehors [dəɔʀ] *adv* outside; (*en plein air*) outdoors, outside ♦ *nm* outside ♦ *nmpl* (*apparences*) appearances, exterior *sg*; **mettre** *ou* **jeter** ~ to throw out; **au** ~ outside; (*en apparence*) outwardly; **au** ~ **de** outside; **de** ~ from outside; **en** ~ outside; outwards; **en** ~ **de** apart from.

déifier [deifje] *vt* to deify.

déjà [deʒa] *adv* already; (*auparavant*) before, already; **as-tu** ~ **été en France?** have you been to France before?; **c'est** ~ **pas mal** that's not too bad (at all); **c'est** ~ **quelque chose** (at least) it's better than nothing; **quel nom,** ~? what was the name again?

déjanter [deʒɑ̃te]: **se** ~ *vi* (*pneu*) to come off the rim.

déjà-vu [deʒavy] *nm*: **c'est du** ~ there's nothing new in that.

déjeté, e [dɛʒte] *adj* lop-sided, crooked.

déjeuner [deʒœne] *vi* to (have) lunch; (*le matin*) to have breakfast ♦ *nm* lunch; (*petit déjeuner*) breakfast; ~ **d'affaires** business lunch.

déjouer [deʒwe] *vt* to elude; to foil, thwart.

déjuger [deʒyʒe]: **se** ~ *vi* to go back on one's opinion.

delà [dəla] *adv*: **par** ~, **en** ~ **(de)**, **au** ~ **(de)** beyond.

délabré, e [delabʀe] *adj* dilapidated, broken-down.

délabrement [delabʀəmɑ̃] *nm* decay, dilapidation.

délabrer [delabʀe]: **se** ~ *vi* to fall into decay, become dilapidated.

délacer [delase] *vt* to unlace, undo.

délai [delɛ] *nm* (*attente*) waiting period; (*sursis*) extension (of time); (*temps accordé: aussi*: ~**s**) time limit; **sans** ~ without delay; **à bref** ~ shortly, very soon; **at short notice**; **dans les** ~**s** within the time limit; **un** ~ **de 30 jours** a period of 30 days; **comptez un** ~ **de livraison de 10 jours** allow 10 days for delivery.

délaissé, e [delese] *adj* abandoned, deserted; neglected.

délaisser [delese] *vt* (*abandonner*) to abandon, desert; (*négliger*) to neglect.

délassant, e [delasɑ̃, -ɑ̃t] *adj* relaxing.

délassement [delasmɑ̃] *nm* relaxation.

délasser [delase] *vt* (*reposer*) to relax; (*divertir*) to divert, entertain; **se** ~ *vi* to relax.

délateur, trice [delatœʀ, -tʀis] *nm/f* informer.

délation [delasjɔ̃] *nf* denouncement, informing.

délavé, e [delave] *adj* faded.

délayage [delɛjaʒ] *nm* mixing; thinning down.

délayer [deleje] *vt* (*CULIN*) to mix (with water *etc*); (*peinture*) to thin down; (*fig*) to pad out, spin out.

delco [dɛlko] *nm* ® (*AUTO*) distributor; **tête de** ~ distributor cap.

délectation [delɛktasjɔ̃] *nf* delight.

délecter [delɛkte]: **se** ~ *vi*: **se** ~ **de** to revel *ou* delight in.

délégation [delegasjɔ̃] *nf* delegation; ~ **de pouvoir** delegation of power.

délégué, e [delege] *adj* delegated ♦ *nm/f* delegate; representative; **ministre** ~ **à** minister with special responsibility for.

déléguer [delege] *vt* to delegate.

délestage [delɛstaʒ] *nm*: **itinéraire de** ~ alternative route (*to relieve traffic congestion*).

délester [delɛste] *vt* (*navire*) to unballast; ~ **une route** to relieve traffic congestion on a road by diverting traffic.

Delhi [dɛli] *n* Delhi.

délibérant, e [deliberɑ̃, -ɑ̃t] *adj*: **assemblée** ~**e** deliberative assembly.

délibératif, ive [deliberatif, -iv] *adj*: **avoir voix délibérative** to have voting rights.

délibération [deliberasjɔ̃] *nf* deliberation.

délibéré, e [delibere] *adj* (*conscient*) deliberate; (*déterminé*) determined, resolute; **de propos** ~ (*à dessein, exprès*) intentionally.

délibérément [deliberemɑ̃] *adv* deliberately; (*résolument*) resolutely.

délibérer [delibere] *vi* to deliberate.

délicat, e [delika, -at] *adj* delicate; (*plein de tact*) tactful; (*attentionné*) thoughtful; (*exigeant*) fussy, particular; **procédés peu** ~**s** unscrupulous methods.

délicatement [delikatmɑ̃] *adv* delicately; (*avec douceur*) gently.

délicatesse [delikatɛs] *nf* delicacy; tactfulness; thoughtfulness; ~**s** *nfpl* attentions, consideration *sg*.

délice [delis] *nm* delight.

délicieusement [delisjøzmɑ̃] *adv* deliciously; delightfully.

délicieux, euse [delisjø, -øz] *adj* (*au goût*) delicious; (*sensation, impression*) delightful.

délictueux, euse [deliktɥø, -øz] *adj* criminal.

délié, e [delje] *adj* nimble, agile; (*mince*) slender, fine ♦ *nm*: **les** ~**s** the upstrokes (*in handwriting*).

délier [delje] *vt* to untie; ~ **qn de** (*serment etc*) to free *ou* release sb from.

délimitation [delimitasjɔ̃] *nf* delimitation.

délimiter [delimite] *vt* to delimit.

délinquance [delɛ̃kɑ̃s] *nf* criminality; ~ **juvénile** juvenile delinquency.

délinquant, e [delɛ̃kɑ̃, -ɑ̃t] *adj*, *nm/f* delinquent.

déliquescence [delikesɑ̃s] *nf*: **en** ~ in a state of decay.

déliquescent, e [delikesɑ̃, -ɑ̃t] *adj* decaying.

délirant, e [delirɑ̃, -ɑ̃t] *adj* (*MÉD: fièvre*) delirious; (*imagination*) frenzied; (*fam: déraisonnable*) crazy.

délire [delir] *nm* (*fièvre*) delirium; (*fig*) frenzy; (: *folie*) lunacy.

délirer [delire] *vi* to be delirious; (*fig*) to be raving.

délit [deli] *nm* (criminal) offence; ~ **de droit commun** violation of common law; ~ **de fuite** failure to stop after an accident; ~ **d'initiés** insider dealing *ou* trading; ~ **de presse** violation of the press laws.

délivrance [delivrɑ̃s] *nf* freeing, release; (*sentiment*) relief.

délivrer [delivre] *vt* (*prisonnier*) to (set) free, release; (*passeport, certificat*) to issue; ~ **qn de** (*ennemis*) to set sb free from, deliver *ou* free sb from; (*fig*) to rid sb of.

déloger [deloʒe] *vt* (*locataire*) to turn out; (*objet coincé, ennemi*) to dislodge.

déloyal, e, aux [delwajal, -o] *adj* (*personne, conduite*) disloyal; (*procédé*) unfair.

Delphes [dɛlf] *n* Delphi.

delta [dɛlta] *nm* (*GÉO*) delta.

deltaplane [dɛltaplan] *nm* ® hang-glider.

déluge [delyʒ] *nm* (*biblique*) Flood, Deluge; (*grosse pluie*) downpour, deluge; (*grand nombre*): ~ **de** flood of.

déluré, e [delyre] *adj* smart, resourceful; (*péj*) forward, pert.

démagnétiser [demaɲetize] *vt* to demagnetize.

démagogie [demagɔʒi] *nf* demagogy.

démagogique [demagɔʒik] *adj* demagogic, popularity-seeking; (*POL*) vote-catching.

démagogue [demagɔg] *adj* demagogic ♦ *nm* demagogue.

démaillé, e [demaje] *adj* (*bas*) laddered (*BRIT*), with a run (*ou* runs).

demain [dəmɛ̃] *adv* tomorrow; ~ **matin/soir** tomorrow morning/evening; ~ **midi** tomorrow at midday; **à** ~! see you tomorrow!

demande [dəmɑ̃d] *nf* (*requête*) request; (*revendication*) demand; (*ADMIN, formulaire*) application; (*ÉCON*): **la** ~ demand; "~**s d'emploi**" "situations wanted"; **à la** ~ **générale** by popular request; ~ **en mariage** (marriage) proposal; **faire sa** ~ **(en mariage)** to propose (marriage); ~ **de naturalisation** application for naturalization; ~ **de poste** job application.

demandé, e [dəmɑ̃de] *adj* (*article etc*): **très** ~ (very) much in demand.

demander [dəmɑ̃de] *vt* to ask for; (*question: date, heure, chemin*) to ask; (*requérir, nécessiter*) to require, demand; ~ **qch à qn** to ask sb for sth, ask sb sth; **ils demandent 2 secrétaires et un ingénieur** they're looking for 2 secretaries and an engineer; ~ **la main de qn** to ask for sb's hand (in marriage); ~ **pardon à qn** to apologize to sb; ~ **à** *ou* **de voir/faire** to ask to see/ask if one can do; ~ **à qn de faire** to ask sb to do; ~ **que/pourquoi** to ask that/why; **se** ~ **si/pourquoi** *etc* to wonder if/why *etc*; (*sens purement réfléchi*) to ask o.s. if/why *etc*; **on vous demande au téléphone** you're wanted on the phone, there's someone for you on the phone; **il ne demande que ça** that's all he wants; **je ne demande pas mieux** I'm asking nothing more; **il ne demande qu'à faire** all he wants is to do.

demandeur, euse [dəmɑ̃dœʀ, -øz] *nm/f*: ~ **d'emploi** job-seeker.

démangeaison [demɑ̃ʒɛzɔ̃] *nf* itching.

démanger [demɑ̃ʒe] *vi* to itch; **la main me démange** my hand is itching; **l'envie** *ou* **ça me démange de faire** I'm itching to do.

démantèlement [demɑ̃tɛlmɑ̃] *nm* breaking up.

démanteler [demɑ̃tle] *vt* to break up; to demolish.

démaquillant [demakijɑ̃] *nm* make-up remover.

démaquiller [demakije] *vt*: **se** ~ to remove one's make-up.

démarcage [demaʀkaʒ] *nm* = **démarquage**.

démarcation [demaʀkasjɔ̃] *nf* demarcation.

démarchage [demaʀʃaʒ] *nm* (*COMM*) door-to-door selling.

démarche [demaʀʃ(ə)] *nf* (*allure*) gait, walk; (*intervention*) step; approach; (*fig: intellectuelle*) thought processes *pl*; approach; **faire** *ou* **entreprendre des** ~**s** to take action; **faire**

des ~**s auprès de qn** to approach sb.

démarcheur, euse [demaʀʃœʀ, -øz] *nm/f* (*COMM*) door-to-door salesman/woman; (*POL etc*) canvasser.

démarquage [demaʀkaʒ] *nm* marking down.

démarque [demaʀk(ə)] *nf* (*COMM: d'un article*) mark-down.

démarqué, e [demaʀke] *adj* (*FOOTBALL*) unmarked; (*COMM*) reduced; **prix** ~**s** marked-down prices.

démarquer [demaʀke] *vt* (*prix*) to mark down; (*joueur*) to stop marking; **se** ~ *vi* (*SPORT*) to shake off one's marker.

démarrage [demaʀaʒ] *nm* starting *no pl*, start; ~ **en côte** hill start.

démarrer [demaʀe] *vt* to start up ♦ *vi* (*conducteur*) to start (up); (*véhicule*) to move off; (*travaux, affaire*) to get moving; (*coureur: accélérer*) to pull away.

démarreur [demaʀœʀ] *nm* (*AUTO*) starter.

démasquer [demaske] *vt* to unmask; **se** ~ to unmask; (*fig*) to drop one's mask.

démâter [demate] *vt* to dismast ♦ *vi* to be dismasted.

démêlant, e [demelɑ̃, -ɑ̃t] *adj*: **baume** ~, **crème** ~**e** (hair) conditioner.

démêler [demele] *vt* to untangle, disentangle.

démêlés [demele] *nmpl* problems.

démembrement [demɑ̃bʀəmɑ̃] *nm* dismemberment.

démembrer [demɑ̃bʀe] *vt* to dismember.

déménagement [demenaʒmɑ̃] *nm* (*du point de vue du locataire etc*) move; (*: du déménageur*) removal (*BRIT*), moving (*US*); **entreprise/camion de** ~ removal (*BRIT*) *ou* moving (*US*) firm/van.

déménager [demenaʒe] *vt* (*meubles*) to (re)move ♦ *vi* to move (house).

déménageur [demenaʒœʀ] *nm* removal man (*BRIT*), (furniture) mover (*US*); (*entrepreneur*) furniture remover.

démence [demɑ̃s] *nf* madness, insanity; (*MÉD*) dementia.

démener [demne]: **se** ~ *vi* to thrash about; (*fig*) to exert o.s.

dément, e [demɑ̃, -ɑ̃t] *vb voir* **démentir** ♦ *adj* (*fou*) mad (*BRIT*), crazy; (*fam*) brilliant, fantastic.

démenti [demɑ̃ti] *nm* refutation.

démentiel, le [demɑ̃sjɛl] *adj* insane.

démentir [demɑ̃tiʀ] *vt* (*nouvelle, témoin*) to refute; (*suj: faits etc*) to belie, refute; ~ **que** to deny that; **ne pas se** ~ not to fail, keep up.

démerder [demɛʀde]: **se** ~ *vi* (*fam!*) to bloody well manage for o.s.

démériter [demeʀite] *vi*: ~ **auprès de qn** to come down in sb's esteem.

démesure [deməzyʀ] *nf* immoderation, immoderateness.

démesuré, e [deməzyʀe] *adj* immoderate, disproportionate.

démesurément [deməzyʀemɑ̃] *adv* disproportionately.

démettre [demɛtR(ə)] *vt:* ~ **qn de** (*fonction, poste*) to dismiss sb from; **se** ~ **(de ses fonctions)** to resign (from) one's duties; **se** ~ **l'épaule** *etc* to dislocate one's shoulder *etc.*

demeurant [dəmœRɑ̃]: **au** ~ *adv* for all that.

demeure [dəmœR] *nf* residence; **dernière** ~ (*fig*) last resting place; **mettre qn en** ~ **de faire** to enjoin *ou* order sb to do; **à** ~ *adv* permanently.

demeuré, e [dəmœRe] *adj* backward ♦ *nm/f* backward person.

demeurer [dəmœRe] *vi* (*habiter*) to live; (*séjourner*) to stay; (*rester*) to remain; **en** ~ **là** (*suj: personne*) to leave it at that; (*: choses*) to be left at that.

demi, e [dəmi] *adj:* **et** ~: **trois heures/ bouteilles et** ~**e** three and a half hours/ bottles, three hours/bottles and a half ♦ *nm* (*bière:* = *0.25 litre*) ≈ half-pint; (*FOOTBALL*) half-back; **il est 2 heures et** ~**e** it's half past 2; **il est midi et** ~ it's half past 12; ~ **de mêlée/d'ouverture** (*RUGBY*) scrum/fly half; **à** ~ *adv* half-; **ouvrir à** ~ to half-open; **faire les choses à** ~ to do things by halves; **à la** ~**e** (*heure*) on the half-hour.

demi... [dəmi] *préfixe* half-, semi..., demi-.

demi-bas [dəmibɑ] *nm inv* (*chaussette*) knee-sock.

demi-bouteille [dəmibutɛj] *nf* half-bottle.

demi-cercle [dəmisɛRkl(ə)] *nm* semicircle; **en** ~ *adj* semicircular ♦ *adv* in a semicircle.

demi-douzaine [dəmiduzɛn] *nf* half-dozen, half a dozen.

demi-finale [dəmifinal] *nf* semifinal.

demi-finaliste [dəmifinalist(ə)] *nm/f* semifinalist.

demi-fond [dəmifɔ̃] *nm* (*SPORT*) medium-distance running.

demi-frère [dəmifRɛR] *nm* half-brother.

demi-gros [dəmigRo] *nm inv* wholesale trade.

demi-heure [dəmijœR] *nf:* **une** ~ a half-hour, half an hour.

demi-jour [dəmiʒuR] *nm* half-light.

demi-journée [dəmiʒuRne] *nf* half-day, half a day.

démilitariser [demilitaRize] *vt* to demilitarize.

demi-litre [dəmilitR(ə)] *nm* half-litre (*BRIT*), half-liter (*US*), half a litre *ou* liter.

demi-livre [dəmilivR(ə)] *nf* half-pound, half a pound.

demi-longueur [dəmilɔ̃gœR] *nf* (*SPORT*) half-length, half a length.

demi-lune [dəmilyn]: **en** ~ *adj inv* semicircular.

demi-mal [dəmimal] *nm:* **il n'y a que** ~ there's not much harm done.

demi-mesure [dəmimzyR] *nf* half-measure.

demi-mot [dəmimo]: **à** ~ *adv* without having to spell things out.

déminer [demine] *vt* to clear of mines.

démineur [deminœR] *nm* bomb disposal ex-

pert.

demi-pension [dəmipɑ̃sjɔ̃] *nf* half-board; **être en** ~ (*SCOL*) to take school meals.

demi-pensionnaire [dəmipɑ̃sjɔnɛR] *nm/f* (*SCOL*) half-boarder.

demi-place [dəmiplas] *nf* half-price; (*TRANSPORTS*) half-fare.

démis, e [demi, -iz] *pp de* **démettre** ♦ *adj* (*épaule etc*) dislocated.

demi-saison [dəmisɛzɔ̃] *nf:* **vêtements de** ~ spring *ou* autumn clothing.

demi-sel [dəmisɛl] *adj inv* slightly salted.

demi-sœur [dəmisœR] *nf* half-sister.

demi-sommeil [dəmisɔmɛj] *nm* doze.

demi-soupir [dəmisupiR] *nm* (*MUS*) quaver (*BRIT*) *ou* eighth note (*US*) rest.

démission [demisjɔ̃] *nf* resignation; **donner sa** ~ to give *ou* hand in one's notice, hand in one's resignation.

démissionnaire [demisjɔnɛR] *adj* outgoing ♦ *nm/f* person resigning.

démissionner [demisjɔne] *vi* (*de son poste*) to resign, give *ou* hand in one's notice.

demi-tarif [dəmitaRif] *nm* half-price; (*TRANSPORTS*) half-fare.

demi-ton [dəmitɔ̃] *nm* (*MUS*) semitone.

demi-tour [dəmituR] *nm* about-turn; **faire un** ~ (*MIL etc*) to make an about-turn; **faire** ~ to turn (and go) back; (*AUTO*) to do a U-turn.

démobilisation [demɔbilizasjɔ̃] *nf* demobilization; (*fig*) demotivation, demoralization.

démobiliser [demɔbilize] *vt* to demobilize; (*fig*) to demotivate, demoralize.

démocrate [demɔkRat] *adj* democratic ♦ *nm/f* democrat.

démocrate-chrétien, ne [demɔkRatkRetjɛ̃, -ɛn] *nm/f* Christian Democrat.

démocratie [demɔkRasi] *nf* democracy; ~ **populaire/libérale** people's/liberal democracy.

démocratique [demɔkRatik] *adj* democratic.

démocratiquement [demɔkRatikmɑ̃] *adv* democratically.

démocratisation [demɔkRatizasjɔ̃] *nf* democratization.

démocratiser [demɔkRatize] *vt* to democratize.

démodé, e [demɔde] *adj* old-fashioned.

démoder [demɔde]: **se** ~ *vi* to go out of fashion.

démographe [demɔgRaf] *nm/f* demographer.

démographie [demɔgRafi] *nf* demography.

démographique [demɔgRafik] *adj* demographic; **poussée** ~ increase in population.

demoiselle [dəmwazɛl] *nf* (*jeune fille*) young lady; (*célibataire*) single lady, maiden lady; ~ **d'honneur** bridesmaid.

démolir [demɔliR] *vt* to demolish; (*fig: personne*) to do for.

démolisseur [demɔlisœR] *nm* demolition worker.

démolition [demɔlisjɔ̃] *nf* demolition.

démon [demɔ̃] *nm* demon, fiend; evil spirit; (*enfant turbulent*) devil, demon; **le ~ du jeu/ des femmes** a mania for gambling/women; **le D~** the Devil.
démonétiser [demɔnetize] *vt* to demonetize.
démoniaque [demɔnjak] *adj* fiendish.
démonstrateur, trice [demɔ̃stratœr, -tris] *nm/f* demonstrator.
démonstratif, ive [demɔ̃stratif, -iv] *adj, nm* (*aussi* LING) demonstrative.
démonstration [demɔ̃strasjɔ̃] *nf* demonstration; (*aérienne, navale*) display.
démontable [demɔ̃tabl(ə)] *adj* folding.
démontage [demɔ̃taʒ] *nm* dismantling.
démonté, e [demɔ̃te] *adj* (*fig*) raging, wild.
démonte-pneu [demɔ̃təpnø] *nm* tyre lever (*BRIT*), tire iron (*US*).
démonter [demɔ̃te] *vt* (*machine etc*) to take down, dismantle; (*pneu, porte*) to take off; (*cavalier*) to throw, unseat; (*fig: personne*) to disconcert; **se ~** *vi* (*personne*) to lose countenance.
démontrable [demɔ̃trabl(ə)] *adj* demonstrable.
démontrer [demɔ̃tre] *vt* to demonstrate, show.
démoralisant, e [demɔralizɑ̃, -ɑ̃t] *adj* demoralizing.
démoralisateur, trice [demɔralizatœr, -tris] *adj* demoralizing.
démoraliser [demɔralize] *vt* to demoralize.
démordre [demɔrdr(ə)] *vi*: **ne pas ~ de** to refuse to give up, stick to.
démouler [demule] *vt* (*gâteau*) to turn out.
démoustiquer [demustike] *vt* to clear of mosquitoes.
démultiplication [demyltiplikasjɔ̃] *nf* reduction; reduction ratio.
démuni, e [demyni] *adj* (*sans argent*) impoverished; **~ de** without, lacking in.
démunir [demynir] *vt*: **~ qn de** to deprive sb of; **se ~ de** to part with, give up.
démuseler [demyzle] *vt* to unmuzzle.
démystifier [demistifje] *vt* to demystify.
démythifier [demitifje] *vt* to demythologize.
dénatalité [denatalite] *nf* fall in the birth rate.
dénationalisation [denasjɔnalizasjɔ̃] *nf* denationalization.
dénationaliser [denasjɔnalize] *vt* to denationalize.
dénaturé, e [denatyre] *adj* (*alcool*) denatured; (*goûts*) unnatural.
dénaturer [denatyre] *vt* (*goût*) to alter (completely); (*pensée, fait*) to distort, misrepresent.
dénégations [denegasjɔ̃] *nfpl* denials.
déneigement [denɛʒmɑ̃] *nf* snow clearance.
déneiger [deneʒe] *vt* to clear snow from.
déni [deni] *nm*: **~ (de justice)** denial of justice.
déniaiser [denjeze] *vt*: **~ qn** to teach sb about life.
dénicher [deniʃe] *vt* to unearth.

dénicotinisé, e [denikɔtinize] *adj* nicotine-free.
denier [dənje] *nm* (*monnaie*) formerly, a coin of small value; (*de bas*) denier; **~ du culte** contribution to parish upkeep; **~s publics** public money; **de ses (propres) ~s** out of one's own pocket.
dénier [denje] *vt* to deny; **~ qch à qn** to deny sb sth.
dénigrement [denigrəmɑ̃] *nm* denigration; **campagne de ~** smear campaign.
dénigrer [denigre] *vt* to denigrate, run down.
dénivelé, e [denivle] *adj* (*chaussée*) on a lower level ◊ *nm* difference in height.
déniveler [denivle] *vt* to make uneven; to put on a lower level.
dénivellation [denivɛlasjɔ̃] *nf*, **dénivellement** [denivɛlmɑ̃] *nm* difference in level; (*pente*) ramp; (*creux*) dip.
dénombrer [denɔ̃bre] *vt* (*compter*) to count; (*énumérer*) to enumerate, list.
dénominateur [denɔminatœr] *nm* denominator; **~ commun** common denominator.
dénomination [denɔminasjɔ̃] *nf* designation, appellation.
dénommé, e [denɔme] *adj*: **le ~ Dupont** the man by the name of Dupont.
dénommer [denɔme] *vt* to name.
dénoncer [denɔ̃se] *vt* to denounce; **se ~ to** give o.s. up, come forward.
dénonciation [denɔ̃sjasjɔ̃] *nf* denunciation.
dénoter [denɔte] *vt* to denote.
dénouement [denumɑ̃] *nm* outcome, conclusion; (*THÉÂT*) dénouement.
dénouer [denwe] *vt* to unknot, undo.
dénoyauter [denwajote] *vt* to stone; **appareil à ~ stoner.**
dénoyauteur [denwajotœr] *nm* stoner.
denrée [dɑ̃re] *nf* commodity; (*aussi*: **~ alimentaire**) food(stuff).
dense [dɑ̃s] *adj* dense.
densité [dɑ̃site] *nf* denseness; (*PHYSIQUE*) density.
dent [dɑ̃] *nf* tooth (*pl* teeth); **avoir/garder une ~ contre qn** to have/hold a grudge against sb; **se mettre qch sous la ~** to eat sth; **être sur les ~s** to be on one's last legs; **faire ses ~s** to teethe, cut (one's) teeth; **en ~s de scie** serrated; (*irrégulier*) jagged; **avoir les ~s longues** (*fig*) to be ruthlessly ambitious; **~ de lait/sagesse** milk/wisdom tooth.
dentaire [dɑ̃tɛr] *adj* dental; **cabinet ~** dental surgery; **école ~** dental school.
denté, e [dɑ̃te] *adj*: **roue ~e** cog wheel.
dentelé, e [dɑ̃tle] *adj* jagged, indented.
dentelle [dɑ̃tɛl] *nf* lace *no pl*.
dentelure [dɑ̃tlyr] *nf* (*aussi*: **~s**) jagged outline.
dentier [dɑ̃tje] *nm* denture.
dentifrice [dɑ̃tifris] *adj, nm*: (**pâte**) **~** toothpaste; **eau ~** mouthwash.
dentiste [dɑ̃tist(ə)] *nm/f* dentist.

dentition [dɑ̃tisjɔ̃] *nf* teeth *pl*, dentition.
dénucléariser [denykleaʀize] *vt* to make nuclear-free.
dénudé, e [denyde] *adj* bare.
dénuder [denyde] *vt* to bare; **se** ~ (*personne*) to strip.
dénué, e [denɥe] *adj*: ~ **de** lacking in; (*intérêt*) devoid of.
dénuement [denymɑ̃] *nm* destitution.
dénutrition [denytʀisjɔ̃] *nf* undernourishment.
déodorant [deɔdɔʀɑ̃] *nm* deodorant.
déodoriser [deɔdɔʀize] *vt* to deodorize.
déontologie [deɔ̃tɔlɔʒi] *nf* code of ethics; (*professionnelle*) (professional) code of practice.
dép. *abr* (*ADMIN*: = *département*) dept; (= *départ*) dep.
dépannage [depanaʒ] *nm*: **service/camion de** ~ (*AUTO*) breakdown service/truck.
dépanner [depane] *vt* (*voiture, télévision*) to fix, repair; (*fig*) to bail out, help out.
dépanneur [depanœʀ] *nm* (*AUTO*) breakdown mechanic; (*TV*) television engineer.
dépanneuse [depanøz] *nf* breakdown lorry (*BRIT*), tow truck (*US*).
dépareillé, e [depaʀeje] *adj* (*collection, service*) incomplete; (*gant, volume, objet*) odd.
déparer [depaʀe] *vt* to spoil, mar.
départ [depaʀ] *nm* leaving *no pl*, departure; (*SPORT*) start; (*sur un horaire*) departure; **à son** ~ when he left; **au** ~ (*au début*) initially, at the start; **courrier au** ~ outgoing mail.
départager [depaʀtaʒe] *vt* to decide between.
département [depaʀtəmɑ̃] *nm* department.

France is divided into 96 administrative units called **départements**. *These local government divisions are headed by a state-appointed* **préfet**, *and administered by an elected* **Conseil général**. *Départements are usually named after prominent geographical features such as rivers or mountain ranges; see also* **DOM-TOM**.

---

départemental, e, aux [depaʀtəmɑ̃tal, -o] *adj* departmental.
départementaliser [depaʀtəmɑ̃talize] *vt* to devolve authority to.
départir [depaʀtiʀ]: **se** ~ **de** *vt* to abandon, depart from.
dépassé, e [depɑse] *adj* superseded, outmoded; (*fig*) out of one's depth.
dépassement [depɑsmɑ̃] *nm* (*AUTO*) overtaking *no pl*.
dépasser [depɑse] *vt* (*véhicule, concurrent*) to overtake; (*endroit*) to pass, go past; (*somme, limite*) to exceed; (*fig: en beauté etc*) to surpass, outshine; (*être en saillie sur*) to jut out above (*ou* in front of); (*dérouter*): **cela me dépasse** it's beyond me ♦ *vi* (*AUTO*) to overtake; (*jupon*) to show; **se** ~ to excel o.s.
dépassionner [depɑsjɔne] *vt* (*débat etc*) to

take the heat out of.
dépaver [depave] *vt* to remove the cobblestones from.
dépaysé, e [depeize] *adj* disorientated.
dépaysement [depeizmɑ̃] *nm* disorientation; change of scenery.
dépayser [depeize] *vt* (*désorienter*) to disorientate; (*changer agréablement*) to provide with a change of scenery.
dépecer [depəse] *vt* (*suj: boucher*) to joint, cut up; (*suj: animal*) to dismember.
dépêche [depɛʃ] *nf* dispatch; ~ (**télégraphique**) telegram, wire.
dépêcher [depeʃe] *vt* to dispatch; **se** ~ *vi* to hurry; **se** ~ **de faire qch** to hasten to do sth, hurry (in order) to do sth.
dépeindre [depɛ̃dʀ(ə)] *vt* to depict.
dépénalisation [depenalizasjɔ̃] *nf* decriminalization.
dépendance [depɑ̃dɑ̃s] *nf* (*interdépendance*) dependence *no pl*, dependency; (*bâtiment*) outbuilding.
dépendant, e [depɑ̃dɑ̃, -ɑ̃t] *vb voir* **dépendre** ♦ *adj* (*financièrement*) dependent.
dépendre [depɑ̃dʀ(ə)] *vt* (*tableau*) to take down; ~ **de** *vt* to depend on; (*financièrement etc*) to be dependent on; (*appartenir*) to belong to.
dépens [depɑ̃] *nmpl*: **aux** ~ **de** at the expense of.
dépense [depɑ̃s] *nf* spending *no pl*, expense, expenditure *no pl*; (*fig*) consumption; (: *de temps, de forces*) expenditure; **pousser qn à la** ~ to make sb incur an expense; ~ **physique** (physical) exertion; ~ **de temps** investment of time; ~**s de fonctionnement** revenue expenditure; ~**s d'investissement** capital expenditure; ~**s publiques** public expenditure.
dépenser [depɑ̃se] *vt* to spend; (*gaz, eau*) to use; (*fig*) to expend, use up; **se** ~ (*se fatiguer*) to exert o.s.
dépensier, ière [depɑ̃sje, -jɛʀ] *adj*: **il est** ~ he's a spendthrift.
déperdition [depɛʀdisjɔ̃] *nf* loss.
dépérir [depeʀiʀ] *vi* (*personne*) to waste away; (*plante*) to wither.
dépersonnaliser [depɛʀsɔnalize] *vt* to depersonalize.
dépêtrer [depetʀe] *vt*: **se** ~ **de** (*situation*) to extricate o.s. from.
dépeuplé, e [depœple] *adj* depopulated.
dépeuplement [depœpləmɑ̃] *nm* depopulation.
dépeupler [depœple] *vt* to depopulate; **se** ~ to be depopulated.
déphasage [defazaʒ] *nm* (*fig*) being out of touch.
déphasé, e [defaze] *adj* (*ÉLEC*) out of phase; (*fig*) out of touch.
déphaser [defaze] *vt* (*fig*) to put out of touch.
dépilation [depilasjɔ̃] *nf* hair loss; hair re-

moval.

dépilatoire [depilatwaʀ] *adj* depilatory, hair-removing.

dépiler [depile] *vt* (*épiler*) to depilate, remove hair from.

dépistage [depistaʒ] *nm* (*MÉD*) screening.

dépister [depiste] *vt* to detect; (*MÉD*) to screen; (*voleur*) to track down; (*poursuivants*) to throw off the scent.

dépit [depi] *nm* vexation, frustration; **en ~ de** *prép* in spite of; **en ~ du bon sens** contrary to all good sense.

dépité, e [depite] *adj* vexed, frustrated.

dépiter [depite] *vt* to vex, frustrate.

déplacé, e [deplase] *adj* (*propos*) out of place, uncalled-for; **personne ~e** displaced person.

déplacement [deplasmɑ̃] *nm* moving; shifting; transfer; (*voyage*) trip, travelling *no pl* (*BRIT*), traveling *no pl* (*US*); **en ~** away (on a trip); **~ d'air** displacement of air; **~ de vertèbre** slipped disc.

déplacer [deplase] *vt* (*table, voiture*) to move, shift; (*employé*) to transfer, move; **se ~** *vi* (*objet*) to move; (*organe*) to become displaced; (*personne: bouger*) to move, walk; (: *voyager*) to travel ♦ *vt* (*vertèbre etc*) to displace.

déplaire [deplɛʀ] *vi*: **ceci me déplaît** I don't like this, I dislike this; **il cherche à nous ~** he's trying to displease us *ou* be disagreeable to us; **se ~ quelque part** to dislike it *ou* be unhappy somewhere.

déplaisant, e [deplɛzɑ̃, -ɑ̃t] *vb voir* **déplaire** ♦ *adj* disagreeable, unpleasant.

déplaisir [depleziʀ] *nm* displeasure, annoyance.

déplaît [deplɛ] *vb voir* **déplaire**.

dépliant [deplijɑ̃] *nm* leaflet.

déplier [deplije] *vt* to unfold; **se ~** (*parachute*) to open.

déplisser [deplise] *vt* to smooth out.

déploiement [deplwamɑ̃] *nm* (*voir déployer*) deployment; display.

déplomber [deplɔ̃be] *vt* (*caisse, compteur*) to break (open) the seal of.

déplorable [deplɔʀabl(ə)] *adj* deplorable; lamentable.

déplorer [deplɔʀe] *vt* (*regretter*) to deplore; (*pleurer sur*) to lament.

déployer [deplwaje] *vt* to open out, spread; (*MIL*) to deploy; (*montrer*) to display, exhibit.

déplu [deply] *pp de* **déplaire**.

dépointer [depwɛ̃te] *vi* to clock out.

dépoli, e [depɔli] *adj*: **verre ~** frosted glass.

dépolitiser [depɔlitize] *vt* to depoliticize.

dépopulation [depɔpylasjɔ̃] *nf* depopulation.

déportation [depɔʀtasjɔ̃] *nf* deportation.

déporté, e [depɔʀte] *nm/f* deportee; (*1939-45*) concentration camp prisoner.

déporter [depɔʀte] *vt* (*POL*) to deport; (*dévier*) to carry off course; **se ~** *vi* (*voiture*) to

swerve.

déposant, e [depozɑ̃, -ɑ̃t] *nm/f* (*épargnant*) depositor.

dépose [depoz] *nf* taking out; taking down.

déposé, e [depoze] *adj* registered; *voir aussi* **marque**.

déposer [depoze] *vt* (*gén: mettre, poser*) to lay down, put down, set down; (*à la banque, à la consigne*) to deposit; (*caution*) to put down; (*passager*) to drop (off), set down; (*démonter: serrure, moteur*) to take out; (: *rideau*) to take down; (*roi*) to depose; (*ADMIN: faire enregistrer*) to file; to register ♦ *vi* to form a sediment *ou* deposit; (*JUR*): **~ (contre)** to testify *ou* give evidence (against); **se ~** *vi* to settle; **~ son bilan** (*COMM*) to go into (voluntary) liquidation.

dépositaire [depozitɛʀ] *nm/f* (*JUR*) depository; (*COMM*) agent; **~ agréé** authorized agent.

déposition [depozisjɔ̃] *nf* (*JUR*) deposition.

déposséder [deposede] *vt* to dispossess.

dépôt [depo] *nm* (*à la banque, sédiment*) deposit; (*entrepôt, réserve*) warehouse, store; (*gare*) depot; (*prison*) cells *pl*; **~ d'ordures** rubbish (*BRIT*) *ou* garbage (*US*) dump, tip (*BRIT*); **~ de bilan** (voluntary) liquidation; **~ légal** registration of copyright.

dépoter [depɔte] *vt* (*plante*) to take from the pot, transplant.

dépotoir [depɔtwaʀ] *nm* dumping ground, rubbish (*BRIT*) *ou* garbage (*US*) dump; **~ nucléaire** nuclear (waste) dump.

dépouille [depuj] *nf* (*d'animal*) skin, hide; (*humaine*): **~ (mortelle)** mortal remains *pl*.

dépouillé, e [depuje] *adj* (*fig*) bare, bald; **~ de** stripped of; lacking in.

dépouillement [depujmɑ̃] *nm* (*de scrutin*) count, counting *no pl*.

dépouiller [depuje] *vt* (*animal*) to skin; (*spolier*) to deprive of one's possessions; (*documents*) to go through, peruse; **~ qn/qch de** to strip sb/sth of; **~ le scrutin** to count the votes.

dépourvu, e [depuʀvy] *adj*: **~ de** lacking in, without; **au ~** *adv*: **prendre qn au ~** to catch sb unawares.

dépoussiérer [depusjere] *vt* to remove dust from.

dépravation [depʀavasjɔ̃] *nf* depravity.

dépravé, e [depʀave] *adj* depraved.

dépraver [depʀave] *vt* to deprave.

dépréciation [depʀesjasjɔ̃] *nf* depreciation.

déprécier [depʀesje] *vt*, **se ~** *vi* to depreciate.

déprédations [depʀedɑsjɔ̃] *nfpl* damage *sg*.

dépressif, ive [depʀesif, -iv] *adj* depressive.

dépression [depʀesjɔ̃] *nf* depression; **~ (nerveuse)** (nervous) breakdown.

déprimant, e [depʀimɑ̃, -ɑ̃t] *adj* depressing.

déprime [depʀim] *nf* (*fam*): **la ~** depression.

déprimé, e [depʀime] *adj* (*découragé*) depressed.

déprimer [depʀime] *vt* to depress.

déprogrammer [depʀɔgʀame] vt (*supprimer*) to cancel.

DEPS sigle (= *dernier entré premier sorti*) LIFO (= *last in first out*).

dépt abr (= *département*) dept.

dépuceler [depysle] vt (*fam*) to take the virginity of.

====================== *MOT-CLÉ* ======================

depuis [dəpɥi] prép **1** (*point de départ dans le temps*) since; **il habite Paris ~ 1983/l'an dernier** he has been living in Paris since 1983/last year; **~ quand?** since when? **~ quand le connaissez-vous?** how long have you known him?; **~ lors** since then
2 (*temps écoulé*) for; **il habite Paris ~ 5 ans** he has been living in Paris for 5 years; **je le connais ~ 3 ans** I've known him for 3 years; **~ combien de temps êtes-vous ici?** how long have you been here?
3 (*lieu*): **il a plu ~ Metz** it's been raining since Metz; **elle a téléphoné ~ Valence** she rang from Valence
4 (*quantité, rang*) from; **~ les plus petits jusqu'aux plus grands** from the youngest to the oldest
♦ adv (*temps*) since (then); **je ne lui ai pas parlé ~** I haven't spoken to him since (then); **~ que** conj (ever) since; **~ qu'il m'a dit ça** (ever) since he said that to me

==

dépuratif, ive [depyʀatif, -iv] adj depurative, purgative.

députation [depytasjɔ̃] nf deputation; (*fonction*) position of deputy, ≈ parliamentary seat (*BRIT*), ≈ seat in Congress (*US*).

député, e [depyte] nm/f (*POL*) deputy, ≈ Member of Parliament (*BRIT*), ≈ Congressman/woman (*US*).

députer [depyte] vt to delegate; **~ qn auprès de** to send sb (as a representative) to.

déracinement [deʀasinmɑ̃] nm (*gén*) uprooting; (*d'un préjugé*) eradication.

déraciner [deʀasine] vt to uproot.

déraillement [deʀajmɑ̃] nm derailment.

dérailler [deʀaje] vi (*train*) to be derailed, go off ou jump the rails; (*fam*) to be completely off the track; **faire ~** to derail.

dérailleur [deʀajœʀ] nm (*de vélo*) dérailleur gears pl.

déraison [deʀɛzɔ̃] nf unreasonableness.

déraisonnable [deʀɛzɔnabl(ə)] adj unreasonable.

déraisonner [deʀɛzɔne] vi to talk nonsense, rave.

dérangement [deʀɑ̃ʒmɑ̃] nm (*gêne, déplacement*) trouble; (*gastrique etc*) disorder; (*mécanique*) breakdown; **en ~** (*téléphone*) out of order.

déranger [deʀɑ̃ʒe] vt (*personne*) to trouble, bother, disturb; (*projets*) to disrupt, upset; (*objets, vêtements*) to disarrange; **se ~** to put

o.s. out; (*se déplacer*) to (take the trouble to) come (ou go) out; **est-ce que cela vous dérange si ...?** do you mind if ...?; **ça te dérangerait de faire ...?** would you mind doing ...?; **ne vous dérangez pas** don't go to any trouble; don't disturb yourself.

dérapage [deʀapaʒ] nm skid, skidding no pl; going out of control.

déraper [deʀape] vi (*voiture*) to skid; (*personne, semelles, couteau*) to slip; (*fig: économie etc*) to go out of control.

dératé, e [deʀate] nm/f: **courir comme un ~** to run like the clappers.

dératiser [deʀatize] vt to rid of rats.

déréglé, e [deʀegle] adj (*mœurs*) dissolute.

dérèglement [deʀɛgləmɑ̃] nm upsetting no pl, upset.

déréglementation [deʀɛgləmɑ̃tasjɔ̃] nf deregulation.

dérégler [deʀegle] vt (*mécanisme*) to put out of order, cause to break down; (*estomac*) to upset; **se ~** vi to break down, go wrong.

dérider [deʀide] vt, **se ~** vi to brighten ou cheer up.

dérision [deʀizjɔ̃] nf derision; **tourner en ~** to deride; **par ~** in mockery.

dérisoire [deʀizwaʀ] adj derisory.

dérivatif [deʀivatif] nm distraction.

dérivation [deʀivasjɔ̃] nf derivation; diversion.

dérive [deʀiv] nf (*de dériveur*) centre-board; **aller à la ~** (*NAVIG, fig*) to drift; **~ des continents** (*GÉO*) continental drift.

dérivé, e [deʀive] adj derived ♦ nm (*LING*) derivative; (*TECH*) by-product ♦ nf (*MATH*) derivative.

dériver [deʀive] vt (*MATH*) to derive; (*cours d'eau etc*) to divert ♦ vi (*bateau*) to drift; **~ de** to derive from.

dériveur [deʀivœʀ] nm sailing dinghy.

dermatite [dɛʀmatit] nf dermatitis.

dermato [dɛʀmato] nm/f (*fam*: = *dermatologue*) dermatologist.

dermatologie [dɛʀmatɔlɔʒi] nf dermatology.

dermatologue [dɛʀmatɔlɔg] nm/f dermatologist.

dermatose [dɛʀmatoz] nf dermatosis.

dermite [dɛʀmit] nf = **dermatite**.

dernier, ière [dɛʀnje, -jɛʀ] adj (*dans le temps, l'espace*) last; (*le plus récent: gén avant n*) latest, last; (*final, ultime: effort*) final; (*échelon, grade*) top, highest ♦ nm (*étage*) top floor; **lundi/le mois ~** last Monday/month; **du ~ chic** extremely smart; **le ~ cri** the last word (in fashion); **les ~s honneurs** the last tribute; **le ~ soupir: rendre le ~ soupir** to breathe one's last; **en ~** adv last; **ce ~, cette dernière** the latter.

dernièrement [dɛʀnjɛʀmɑ̃] adv recently.

dernier-né, dernière-née [dɛʀnjene, dɛʀnjɛʀne] nm/f (*enfant*) last-born.

dérobade [deʀɔbad] nf side-stepping no pl.

dérobé, e [deʀɔbe] *adj* (*porte*) secret, hidden; **à la ~e** surreptitiously.

dérober [deʀɔbe] *vt* to steal; (*cacher*): **~ qch à (la vue de) qn** to conceal *ou* hide sth from sb('s view); **se ~** *vi* (*s'esquiver*) to slip away; (*fig*) to shy away; **se ~ sous** (*s'effondrer*) to give way beneath; **se ~ à** (*justice, regards*) to hide from; (*obligation*) to shirk.

dérogation [deʀɔgasjɔ̃] *nf* (special) dispensation.

déroger [deʀɔʒe]: **~ à** *vt* to go against, depart from.

dérouiller [deʀuje] *vt*: **se ~ les jambes** to stretch one's legs.

déroulement [deʀulmɑ̃] *nm* (*d'une opération etc*) progress.

dérouler [deʀule] *vt* (*ficelle*) to unwind; (*papier*) to unroll; **se ~** *vi* to unwind; to unroll, come unrolled; (*avoir lieu*) to take place; (*se passer*) to go.

déroutant, e [deʀutɑ̃, -ɑ̃t] *adj* disconcerting.

déroute [deʀut] *nf* (*MIL*) rout; (*fig*) total collapse; **mettre en ~** to rout; **en ~** routed.

dérouter [deʀute] *vt* (*avion, train*) to reroute, divert; (*étonner*) to disconcert, throw (out).

derrick [deʀik] *nm* derrick (*over oil well*).

derrière [dɛʀjɛʀ] *adv, prép* behind ♦ *nm* (*d'une maison*) back; (*postérieur*) behind, bottom; **les pattes de ~** the back legs, the hind legs; **par ~** from behind; (*fig*) in an underhand way, behind one's back.

derviche [dɛʀviʃ] *nm* dervish.

DES *sigle m* (= *diplôme d'études supérieures*) *university post-graduate degree.*

des [de] *dét, prép* + *dét voir* **de**.

dès [dɛ] *prép* from; **~ que** *conj* as soon as; **~ à présent** here and now; **~ son retour** as soon as he was (*ou* is) back; **~ réception** upon receipt; **~ lors** *adv* from then on; **~ lors que** *conj* from the moment (that).

désabusé, e [dezabyze] *adj* disillusioned.

désaccord [dezakɔʀ] *nm* disagreement.

désaccordé, e [dezakɔʀde] *adj* (*MUS*) out of tune.

désacraliser [desakʀalize] *vt* to deconsecrate; (*fig: profession, institution*) to take the mystique out of.

désaffecté, e [dezafɛkte] *adj* disused.

désaffection [dezafɛksjɔ̃] *nf*: **~ pour** estrangement from.

désagréable [dezagʀeable(ə)] *adj* unpleasant, disagreeable.

désagréablement [dezagʀeabləmɑ̃] *adv* disagreeably, unpleasantly.

désagrégation [dezagʀegasjɔ̃] *nf* disintegration.

désagréger [dezagʀeʒe]: **se ~** *vi* to disintegrate, break up.

désagrément [dezagʀemɑ̃] *nm* annoyance, trouble *no pl*.

désaltérant, e [dezalteʀɑ̃, -ɑ̃t] *adj* thirst-quenching.

désaltérer [dezalteʀe] *vt*: **se ~** to quench one's thirst; **ça désaltère** it's thirst-quenching, it quenches your thirst.

désamorcer [dezamɔʀse] *vt* to remove the primer from; (*fig*) to defuse; (: *prévenir*) to forestall.

désappointé, e [dezapwɛ̃te] *adj* disappointed.

désapprobateur, trice [dezapʀɔbatœʀ, -tʀis] *adj* disapproving.

désapprobation [dezapʀɔbasjɔ̃] *nf* disapproval.

désapprouver [dezapʀuve] *vt* to disapprove of.

désarçonner [dezaʀsɔne] *vt* to unseat, throw; (*fig*) to throw, nonplus (*BRIT*), disconcert.

désargenté, e [dezaʀʒɑ̃te] *adj* impoverished.

désarmant, e [dezaʀmɑ̃, -ɑ̃t] *adj* disarming.

désarmé, e [dezaʀme] *adj* (*fig*) disarmed.

désarmement [dezaʀməmɑ̃] *nm* disarmament.

désarmer [dezaʀme] *vt* (*MIL, aussi fig*) to disarm; (*NAVIG*) to lay up; (*fusil*) to unload; (: *mettre le cran de sûreté*) to put the safety catch on ♦ *vi* (*pays*) to disarm; (*haine*) to wane; (*personne*) to give up.

désarrimer [dezaʀime] *vt* to shift.

désarroi [dezaʀwa] *nm* helplessness, disarray.

désarticulé, e [dezaʀtikyle] *adj* (*pantin, corps*) dislocated.

désarticuler [dezaʀtikyle] *vt*: **se ~** to contort (o.s.).

désassorti, e [dezasɔʀti] *adj* unmatching, unmatched; (*magasin, marchand*) sold out.

désastre [dezastʀ(ə)] *nm* disaster.

désastreux, euse [dezastʀø, -øz] *adj* disastrous.

désavantage [dezavɑ̃taʒ] *nm* disadvantage; (*inconvénient*) drawback, disadvantage.

désavantager [dezavɑ̃taʒe] *vt* to put at a disadvantage.

désavantageux, euse [dezavɑ̃taʒø, -øz] *adj* unfavourable, disadvantageous.

désaveu [dezavø] *nm* repudiation; (*déni*) disclaimer.

désavouer [dezavwe] *vt* to disown, repudiate, disclaim.

désaxé, e [dezakse] *adj* (*fig*) unbalanced.

désaxer [dezakse] *vt* (*roue*) to put out of true; (*personne*) to throw off balance.

desceller [desele] *vt* (*pierre*) to pull free.

descendance [desɑ̃dɑ̃s] *nf* (*famille*) descendants *pl*, issue; (*origine*) descent.

descendant, e [desɑ̃dɑ̃, -ɑ̃t] *vb voir* **descendre** ♦ *nm/f* descendant.

descendeur, euse [desɑ̃dœʀ, -øz] *nm/f* (*SPORT*) downhiller.

descendre [desɑ̃dʀ(ə)] *vt* (*escalier, montagne*) to go (*ou* come) down; (*valise, paquet*) to take *ou* get down; (*étagère etc*) to lower; (*fam: abattre*) to shoot down; (: *boire*) to knock back ♦ *vi* to go (*ou* come) down; (*passager: s'arrêter*) to get out, alight; (*niveau, tempéra-*

ture) to go *ou* come down, fall, drop; (*marée*) to go out; ~ **à pied/en voiture** to walk/drive down, go down on foot/by car; ~ **de** (*famille*) to be descended from; ~ **du train** to get out of *ou* off the train; ~ **d'un arbre** to climb down from a tree; ~ **de cheval** to dismount, get off one's horse; ~ **à l'hôtel** to stay at a hotel; ~ **dans la rue** (*manifester*) to take to the streets; ~ **en ville** to go into town, go down town.

descente [desɑ̃t] *nf* descent, going down; (*chemin*) way down; (*SKI*) downhill (race); **au milieu de la** ~ halfway down; **freinez dans les** ~**s** use the brakes going downhill; ~ **de lit** bedside rug; ~ **(de police)** (police) raid.

descriptif, ive [dɛskʀiptif, -iv] *adj* descriptive ♦ *nm* explanatory leaflet.

description [dɛskʀipsjɔ̃] *nf* description.

désembourber [dezɑ̃buʀbe] *vt* to pull out of the mud.

désembourgeoiser [dezɑ̃buʀʒwaze] *vt*: ~ **qn** to get sb out of his (*ou* her) middle-class attitudes.

désembuer [dezɑ̃bɥe] *vt* to demist.

désemparé, e [dezɑ̃paʀe] *adj* bewildered, distraught; (*bateau, avion*) crippled.

désemparer [dezɑ̃paʀe] *vi*: **sans** ~ without stopping.

désemplir [dezɑ̃pliʀ] *vi*: **ne pas** ~ to be always full.

désenchanté, e [dezɑ̃ʃɑ̃te] *adj* disenchanted, disillusioned.

désenchantement [dezɑ̃ʃɑ̃tmɑ̃] *nm* disenchantment, disillusion.

désenclaver [dezɑ̃klave] *vt* to open up.

désencombrer [dezɑ̃kɔ̃bʀe] *vt* to clear.

désenfler [dezɑ̃fle] *vi* to become less swollen.

désengagement [dezɑ̃gaʒmɑ̃] *nm* (*POL*) disengagement.

désensabler [dezɑ̃sable] *vt* to pull out of the sand.

désensibiliser [desɑ̃sibilize] *vt* (*MÉD*) to desensitize.

désenvenimer [dezɑ̃vnime] *vt* (*plaie*) to remove the poison from; (*fig*) to take the sting out of.

désépaissir [dezepesiʀ] *vt* to thin (out).

déséquilibre [dezekilibʀ(ə)] *nm* (*position*): **être en** ~ to be unsteady; (*fig: des forces, du budget*) imbalance; (*PSYCH*) unbalance.

déséquilibré, e [dezekilibʀe] *nm/f* (*PSYCH*) unbalanced person.

déséquilibrer [dezekilibʀe] *vt* to throw off balance.

désert, e [dezɛʀ, -ɛʀt(ə)] *adj* deserted ♦ *nm* desert.

déserter [dezɛʀte] *vi, vt* to desert.

déserteur [dezɛʀtœʀ] *nm* deserter.

désertion [dezɛʀsjɔ̃] *nf* desertion.

désertique [dezɛʀtik] *adj* desert *cpd*; (*inculte*) barren, empty.

désescalade [dezɛskalad] *nf* (*MIL*) de-

escalation.

désespérant, e [dezɛspeʀɑ̃, -ɑ̃t] *adj* hopeless, despairing.

désespéré, e [dezɛspeʀe] *adj* desperate; (*regard*) despairing; **état** ~ (*MÉD*) hopeless condition.

désespérément [dezɛspeʀemɑ̃] *adv* desperately.

désespérer [dezɛspeʀe] *vt* to drive to despair ♦ *vi*, **se** ~ *vi* to despair; ~ **de** to despair of.

désespoir [dezɛspwaʀ] *nm* despair; **être** *ou* **faire le** ~ **de qn** to be the despair of sb; **en** ~ **de cause** in desperation.

déshabillé, e [dezabije] *adj* undressed ♦ *nm* négligée.

déshabiller [dezabije] *vt* to undress; **se** ~ to undress (o.s.).

déshabituer [dezabitɥe] *vt*: **se** ~ **de** to get out of the habit of.

désherbant [dezɛʀbɑ̃] *nm* weed-killer.

désherber [dezɛʀbe] *vt* to weed.

déshérité, e [dezeʀite] *adj* disinherited ♦ *nm/f*: **les** ~**s** (*pauvres*) the underprivileged, the deprived.

déshériter [dezeʀite] *vt* to disinherit.

déshonneur [dezɔnœʀ] *nm* dishonour (*BRIT*), dishonor (*US*), disgrace.

déshonorer [dezɔnɔʀe] *vt* to dishonour (*BRIT*), dishonor (*US*), bring disgrace upon; **se** ~ to bring dishono(u)r on o.s.

déshumaniser [dezymanize] *vt* to dehumanize.

déshydratation [dezidʀatasjɔ̃] *nf* dehydration.

déshydraté, e [dezidʀate] *adj* dehydrated.

déshydrater [dezidʀate] *vt* to dehydrate.

desiderata [dezideʀata] *nmpl* requirements.

design [dizajn] *adj* (*mobilier*) designer *cpd* ♦ *nm* (industrial) design.

désignation [deziɲasjɔ̃] *nf* naming, appointment; (*signe, mot*) name, designation.

designer [dizajnœʀ] *nm* designer.

désigner [deziɲe] *vt* (*montrer*) to point out, indicate; (*dénommer*) to denote, refer to; (*nommer: candidat etc*) to name, appoint.

désillusion [dezilyzjɔ̃] *nf* disillusion(ment).

désillusionner [dezilyzjɔne] *vt* to disillusion.

désincarné, e [dezɛ̃kaʀne] *adj* disembodied.

désinence [dezinɑ̃s] *nf* ending, inflexion.

désinfectant, e [dezɛ̃fɛktɑ̃, -ɑ̃t] *adj, nm* disinfectant.

désinfecter [dezɛ̃fɛkte] *vt* to disinfect.

désinfection [dezɛ̃fɛksjɔ̃] *nf* disinfection.

désinformation [dezɛ̃fɔʀmasjɔ̃] *nf* disinformation.

désintégration [dezɛ̃tegʀasjɔ̃] *nf* disintegration.

désintégrer [dezɛ̃tegʀe] *vt*, **se** ~ *vi* to disintegrate.

désintéressé, e [dezɛ̃teʀese] *adj* (*généreux, bénévole*) disinterested, unselfish.

désintéressement [dezɛ̃teʀesmɑ̃] *nm* (*géné-*

rosité) disinterestedness.

désintéresser [dezɛ̃teʀese] *vt*: **se** ~ **(de)** to lose interest (in).

désintérêt [dezɛ̃teʀɛ] *nm* (*indifférence*) disinterest.

désintoxication [dezɛ̃tɔksikasjɔ̃] *nf* treatment for alcoholism (*ou* drug addiction); **faire une cure de** ~ to have *ou* undergo treatment for alcoholism (*ou* drug addiction).

désintoxiquer [dezɛ̃tɔksike] *vt* to treat for alcoholism (*ou* drug addiction).

désinvolte [dezɛ̃vɔlt(ə)] *adj* casual, off-hand.

désinvolture [dezɛ̃vɔltyʀ] *nf* casualness.

désir [deziʀ] *nm* wish; (*fort, sensuel*) desire.

désirable [deziʀabl(ə)] *adj* desirable.

désirer [deziʀe] *vt* to want, wish for; (*sexuellement*) to desire; **je désire ...** (*formule de politesse*) I would like ...; **il désire que tu l'aides** he would like *ou* he wants you to help him; ~ **faire** to want *ou* wish to do; **ça laisse à** ~ it leaves something to be desired.

désireux, euse [deziʀø, -øz] *adj*: ~ **de faire** anxious to do.

désistement [dezistəmã] *nm* withdrawal.

désister [deziste]: **se** ~ *vi* to stand down, withdraw.

désobéir [dezɔbeiʀ] *vi*: ~ **(à qn/qch)** to disobey (sb/sth).

désobéissance [dezɔbeisãs] *nf* disobedience.

désobéissant, e [dezɔbeisã, -ãt] *adj* disobedient.

désobligeant, e [dezɔbliʒã, -ãt] *adj* disagreeable, unpleasant.

désobliger [dezɔbliʒe] *vt* to offend.

désodorisant [dezɔdɔʀizã] *nm* air freshener, deodorizer.

désodoriser [dezɔdɔʀize] *vt* to deodorize.

désœuvré, e [dezœvʀe] *adj* idle.

désœuvrement [dezœvʀəmã] *nm* idleness.

désolant, e [dezɔlã, -ãt] *adj* distressing.

désolation [dezɔlasjɔ̃] *nf* (*affliction*) distress, grief; (*d'un paysage etc*) desolation, devastation.

désolé, e [dezɔle] *adj* (*paysage*) desolate; **je suis** ~ I'm sorry.

désoler [dezɔle] *vt* to distress, grieve; **se** ~ to be upset.

désolidariser [desɔlidaʀize] *vt*: **se** ~ **de** *ou* **d'avec** to dissociate o.s. from.

désopilant, e [dezɔpilã, -ãt] *adj* screamingly funny, hilarious.

désordonné, e [dezɔʀdɔne] *adj* untidy, disorderly.

désordre [dezɔʀdʀ(ə)] *nm* disorder(liness), untidiness; (*anarchie*) disorder; ~**s** *nmpl* (*POL*) disturbances, disorder *sg*; **en** ~ in a mess, untidy.

désorganiser [dezɔʀganize] *vt* to disorganize.

désorienté, e [dezɔʀjãte] *adj* disorientated; (*fig*) bewildered.

désorienter [dezɔʀjãte] *vt* (*fig*) to confuse.

désormais [dezɔʀmɛ] *adv* in future, from now

on.

désosser [dezɔse] *vt* to bone.

despote [dɛspɔt] *nm* despot; (*fig*) tyrant.

despotique [dɛspɔtik] *adj* despotic.

despotisme [dɛspɔtism(ə)] *nm* despotism.

desquamer [dɛskwame]: **se** ~ *vi* to flake off.

desquels, desquelles [dekɛl] *prép* + *pron voir* **lequel**.

DESS *sigle m* (= *Diplôme d'études supérieures spécialisées*) *post-graduate diploma*.

dessaisir [deseziʀ] *vt*: ~ **un tribunal d'une affaire** to remove a case from a court; **se** ~ **de** *vt* to give up, part with.

dessaler [desale] *vt* (*eau de mer*) to desalinate; (*CULIN: morue etc*) to soak; (*fig fam: délurer*): ~ **qn** to teach sb a thing or two ♦ *vi* (*voilier*) to capsize.

Desse *abr* = **duchesse**.

desséché, e [deseʃe] *adj* dried up.

dessèchement [deseʃmã] *nm* drying out; dryness; hardness.

dessécher [deseʃe] *vt* (*terre, plante*) to dry out, parch; (*peau*) to dry out; (*volontairement: aliments etc*) to dry, dehydrate; (*fig: cœur*) to harden; **se** ~ *vi* to dry out; (*peau, lèvres*) to go dry.

dessein [desɛ̃] *nm* design; **dans le** ~ **de** with the intention of; **à** ~ intentionally, deliberately.

desseller [desele] *vt* to unsaddle.

desserrer [deseʀe] *vt* to loosen; (*frein*) to release; (*poing, dents*) to unclench; (*objets alignés*) to space out; **ne pas** ~ **les dents** not to open one's mouth.

dessert [desɛʀ] *vb voir* **desservir** ♦ *nm* dessert, pudding.

desserte [desɛʀt(ə)] *nf* (*table*) side table; (*transport*): **la** ~ **du village est assurée par autocar** there is a coach service to the village; **chemin** *ou* **voie de** ~ service road.

desservir [desɛʀviʀ] *vt* (*ville, quartier*) to serve; (: *suj: voie de communication*) to lead into; (*suj: vicaire: paroisse*) to serve; (*nuire à: personne*) to do a disservice to; (*débarrasser*): ~ **(la table)** to clear the table.

dessiller [desije] *vt* (*fig*): ~ **les yeux à qn** to open sb's eyes.

dessin [desɛ̃] *nm* (*œuvre, art*) drawing; (*motif*) pattern, design; (*contour*) (out)line; **le** ~ **industriel** draughtsmanship (*BRIT*), draftsmanship (*US*); ~ **animé** cartoon (film); ~ **humoristique** cartoon.

dessinateur, trice [desinatœʀ, -tʀis] *nm/f* drawer; (*de bandes dessinées*) cartoonist; (*industriel*) draughtsman (*BRIT*), draftsman (*US*); **dessinatrice de mode** fashion designer.

dessiner [desine] *vt* to draw; (*concevoir: carrosserie, maison*) to design; (*suj: robe: taille*) to show off; **se** ~ *vi* (*forme*) to be outlined; (*fig: solution*) to emerge.

dessoûler [desule] *vt, vi* to sober up.

dessous [dəsu] *adv* underneath, beneath ♦ *nm* underside; (*étage inférieur*): **les voisins du ~** the downstairs neighbours ♦ *nmpl* (*sous-vêtements*) underwear *sg*; (*fig*) hidden aspects; **en ~** underneath; below; (*fig: en catimini*) slyly, on the sly; **par ~** underneath; below; **de ~ le lit** from under the bed; **au-~** *adv* below; **au-~ de** *prép* below; (*peu digne de*) beneath; **au-~ de tout** the (absolute) limit; **avoir le ~** to get the worst of it.

dessous-de-bouteille [dəsudbutɛj] *nm* bottle mat.

dessous-de-plat [dəsudpla] *nm inv* tablemat.

dessous-de-table [dəsudtabl(ə)] *nm* (*fig*) bribe, under-the-counter payment.

dessus [dəsy] *adv* on top; (*collé, écrit*) on it ♦ *nm* top; (*étage supérieur*): **les voisins/l'appartement du ~** the upstairs neighbours/flat; **en ~** above; **par ~** *adv* over it ♦ *prép* over; **au-~** above; **au-~ de** above; **avoir/prendre le ~** to have/get the upper hand; **reprendre le ~** to get over it; **bras ~ bras dessous** arm in arm; **sens ~ dessous** upside down; *voir* **ci-**; **là-**.

dessus-de-lit [dəsydli] *nm inv* bedspread.

déstabiliser [destabilize] *vt* (*POL*) to destabilize.

destin [dɛstɛ̃] *nm* fate; (*avenir*) destiny.

destinataire [dɛstinatɛʀ] *nm/f* (*POSTES*) addressee; (*d'un colis*) consignee; (*d'un mandat*) payee; **aux risques et périls du ~** at owner's risk.

destination [dɛstinasjɔ̃] *nf* (*lieu*) destination; (*usage*) purpose; **à ~ de** (*avion etc*) bound for; (*voyageur*) bound for, travelling to.

destinée [dɛstine] *nf* fate; (*existence, avenir*) destiny.

destiner [dɛstine] *vt*: **~ qn à** (*poste, sort*) to destine sb for, intend sb to + *verbe*; **~ qn/qch à** (*prédestiner*) to mark sb/sth out for, destine sb/sth to + *verbe*; **~ qch à** (*envisager d'affecter*) to intend to use sth for; **~ qch à qn** (*envisager de donner*) to intend to give sth to sb, intend sb to have sth; (*adresser*) to intend sth for sb; **se ~ à l'enseignement** to intend to become a teacher; **être destiné à** (*sort*) to be destined to + *verbe*; (*usage*) to be intended *ou* meant for; (*suj: sort*) to be in store for.

destituer [dɛstitɥe] *vt* to depose; **~ qn de ses fonctions** to relieve sb of his duties.

destitution [dɛstitysjɔ̃] *nf* deposition.

destructeur, trice [dɛstʀyktœʀ, -tʀis] *adj* destructive.

destructif, ive [dɛstʀyktif, -iv] *adj* destructive.

destruction [dɛstʀyksjɔ̃] *nf* destruction.

déstructuré, e [destʀyktyʀe] *adj*: **vêtements ~s** casual clothes.

déstructurer [destʀyktyʀe] *vt* to break down, take to pieces.

désuet, ète [desɥɛ, -ɛt] *adj* outdated, outmoded.

désuétude [desɥetyd] *nf*: **tomber en ~** to fall into disuse, become obsolete.

désuni, e [dezyni] *adj* divided, disunited.

désunion [dezynjɔ̃] *nf* disunity.

désunir [dezyniʀ] *vt* to disunite; **se ~** *vi* (*athlète*) to get out of one's stride.

détachable [detaʃabl(ə)] *adj* (*coupon etc*) tear-off *cpd*; (*capuche etc*) detachable.

détachant [detaʃɑ̃] *nm* stain remover.

détaché, e [detaʃe] *adj* (*fig*) detached ♦ *nm/f* (*représentant*) person on secondment (*BRIT*) *ou* a posting.

détachement [detaʃmɑ̃] *nm* detachment; (*fonctionnaire, employé*): **être en ~** to be on secondment (*BRIT*) *ou* a posting.

détacher [detaʃe] *vt* (*enlever*) to detach, remove; (*délier*) to untie; (*ADMIN*): **~ qn (auprès de** *ou* **à)** to send sb on secondment (to) (*BRIT*), post sb (to); (*MIL*) to detail; (*vêtement: nettoyer*) to remove the stains from; **se ~** *vi* (*tomber*) to come off; to come out; (*se défaire*) to come undone; (*SPORT*) to pull *ou* break away; (*se délier: chien, prisonnier*) to break loose; **se ~ sur** to stand out against; **se ~ de** (*se désintéresser*) to grow away from.

détail [detaj] *nm* detail; (*COMM*): **le ~** retail; **prix de ~** retail price; **au ~** *adv* (*COMM*) retail; (*: individuellement*) separately; **donner le ~ de** to give a detailed account of; (*compte*) to give a breakdown of; **en ~** in detail.

détaillant, e [detajɑ̃, -ɑ̃t] *nm/f* retailer.

détaillé, e [detaje] *adj* (*récit*) detailed.

détailler [detaje] *vt* (*COMM*) to sell retail; to sell separately; (*expliquer*) to explain in detail; to detail; (*examiner*) to look over, examine.

détaler [detale] *vi* (*lapin*) to scamper off; (*fam: personne*) to make off, scarper (*fam*).

détartrant [detaʀtʀɑ̃] *nm* descaling agent (*BRIT*), scale remover.

détartrer [detaʀtʀe] *vt* to descale; (*dents*) to scale.

détaxe [detaks(ə)] *nf* (*réduction*) reduction in tax; (*suppression*) removal of tax; (*remboursement*) tax refund.

détaxer [detakse] *vt* (*réduire*) to reduce the tax on; (*ôter*) to remove the tax on.

détecter [detɛkte] *vt* to detect.

détecteur [detɛktœʀ] *nm* detector, sensor; **~ de mensonges** lie detector; **~ (de mines)** mine detector.

détection [detɛksjɔ̃] *nf* detection.

détective [detɛktiv] *nm* (*BRIT: policier*) detective; **~ (privé)** private detective *ou* investigator.

déteindre [detɛ̃dʀ(ə)] *vi* to fade; (*fig*): **~ sur** to rub off on.

déteint, e [detɛ̃, -ɛ̃t] *pp de* **déteindre**.

dételer [detle] *vt* to unharness; (*voiture, wagon*) to unhitch ♦ *vi* (*fig: s'arrêter*) to leave off (working).

détendeur [detɑ̃dœʀ] *nm* (*de bouteille à gaz*) regulator.

détendre [detɑ̃dʀ(ə)] *vt* (*fil*) to slacken, loosen; (*relaxer: personne, atmosphère*) to relax; (*: situation*) to relieve; **se** ~ to lose its tension; to relax.

détendu, e [detɑ̃dy] *adj* relaxed.

détenir [detniʀ] *vt* (*fortune, objet, secret*) to be in possession of, have (in one's possession); (*prisonnier*) to detain, hold; (*record*) to hold; ~ **le pouvoir** to be in power.

détente [detɑ̃t] *nf* relaxation; (*POL*) détente; (*d'une arme*) trigger; (*d'un athlète qui saute*) spring.

détenteur, trice [detɑ̃tœʀ, -tʀis] *nm/f* holder.

détention [detɑ̃sjɔ̃] *nf* (*voir détenir*) possession; detention; holding; ~ **préventive** (pretrial) custody.

détenu, e [detny] *pp de* **détenir** ♦ *nm/f* prisoner.

détergent [deteʀʒɑ̃] *nm* detergent.

détérioration [deteʀjɔʀɑsjɔ̃] *nf* damaging; deterioration.

détériorer [deteʀjɔʀe] *vt* to damage; **se** ~ *vi* to deteriorate.

déterminant, e [detɛʀminɑ̃, -ɑ̃t] *adj*: **un facteur** ~ a determining factor ♦ *nm* (*LING*) determiner.

détermination [detɛʀminɑsjɔ̃] *nf* determining; (*résolution*) decision; (*fermeté*) determination.

déterminé, e [detɛʀmine] *adj* (*résolu*) determined; (*précis*) specific, definite.

déterminer [detɛʀmine] *vt* (*fixer*) to determine; (*décider*): ~ **qn à faire** to decide sb to do; **se** ~ **à faire** to make up one's mind to do.

déterminisme [detɛʀminism(ə)] *nm* determinism.

déterré, e [detere] *nm/f*: **avoir une mine de** ~ to look like death warmed up (*BRIT*) *ou* warmed over (*US*).

déterrer [detere] *vt* to dig up.

détersif, ive [detɛʀsif, -iv] *adj, nm* detergent.

détestable [detɛstabl(ə)] *adj* foul, detestable.

détester [detɛste] *vt* to hate, detest.

détiendrai [detjɛ̃dʀe], **détiens** [detjɛ̃] *etc vb voir* **détenir**.

détonant, e [detɔnɑ̃, -ɑ̃t] *adj*: **mélange** ~ explosive mixture.

détonateur [detɔnatœʀ] *nm* detonator.

détonation [detɔnɑsjɔ̃] *nf* detonation, bang, report (of a gun).

détoner [detɔne] *vi* to detonate, explode.

détonner [detɔne] *vi* (*MUS*) to go out of tune; (*fig*) to clash.

détordre [detɔʀdʀ(ə)] *vt* to untwist, unwind.

détour [detuʀ] *nm* detour; (*tournant*) bend, curve; (*fig: subterfuge*) roundabout means; **au** ~ **de chemin** at the bend in the path; **sans** ~ (*fig*) plainly.

détourné, e [detuʀne] *adj* (*sentier, chemin, moyen*) roundabout.

détournement [detuʀnəmɑ̃] *nm* diversion, rerouting; ~ **d'avion** hijacking; ~ (**de fonds**) embezzlement *ou* misappropriation (of funds); ~ **de mineur** corruption of a minor.

détourner [detuʀne] *vt* to divert; (*avion*) to divert, reroute; (*: par la force*) to hijack; (*yeux, tête*) to turn away; (*de l'argent*) to embezzle, misappropriate; **se** ~ to turn away; ~ **la conversation** to change the subject; ~ **qn de son devoir** to divert sb from his duty; ~ **l'attention (de qn)** to distract *ou* divert (sb's) attention.

détracteur, trice [detʀaktœʀ, -tʀis] *nm/f* disparager, critic.

détraqué, e [detʀake] *adj* (*machine, santé*) broken-down ♦ *nm/f* (*fam*): **c'est un** ~ he's unhinged.

détraquer [detʀake] *vt* to put out of order; (*estomac*) to upset; **se** ~ *vi* to go wrong.

détrempe [detʀɑ̃p] *nf* (*ART*) tempera.

détrempé, e [detʀɑ̃pe] *adj* (*sol*) sodden, waterlogged.

détremper [detʀɑ̃pe] *vt* (*peinture*) to water down.

détresse [detʀɛs] *nf* distress; **en** ~ (*avion etc*) in distress; **appel/signal de** ~ distress call/signal.

détriment [detʀimɑ̃] *nm*: **au** ~ **de** to the detriment of.

détritus [detʀitys] *nmpl* rubbish *sg*, refuse *sg*, garbage *sg* (*US*).

détroit [detʀwa] *nm* strait; **le** ~ **de Bering** *ou* **Behring** the Bering Strait; **le** ~ **de Gibraltar** the Straits of Gibraltar; **le** ~ **du Bosphore** the Bosphorus; **le** ~ **de Magellan** the Strait of Magellan, the Magellan Strait.

détromper [detʀɔ̃pe] *vt* to disabuse; **se** ~: **détrompez-vous** don't believe it.

détrôner [detʀone] *vt* to dethrone, depose; (*fig*) to oust, dethrone.

détrousser [detʀuse] *vt* to rob.

détruire [detʀɥiʀ] *vt* to destroy; (*fig: santé, réputation*) to ruin; (*documents*) to shred.

détruit, e [detʀɥi, -it] *pp de* **détruire**.

dette [dɛt] *nf* debt; ~ **publique** *ou* **de l'État** national debt.

DEUG [døg] *sigle m = Diplôme d'études universitaires générales.*

French students sit their **DEUG** *after two years of university study. Students can leave university after the DEUG, which may be awarded with distinction, or proceed to the* **licence**. *The certificate obtained specifies the principal subject area studied.*

---

deuil [dœj] *nm* (*perte*) bereavement; (*période*) mourning; (*chagrin*) grief; **porter le** ~ to wear mourning; **prendre le/être en** ~ to go into/be in mourning.

DEUST [dœst] *sigle m = Diplôme d'études universitaires scientifiques et techniques.*

deux [dø] *num* two; **les** ~ both; **ses** ~ **mains** both his hands, his two hands; **à** ~ **pas** a short distance away; **tous les** ~ **mois** every two months, every other month; ~ **points** colon *sg*.

deuxième [døzjɛm] *num* second.

deuxièmement [døzjɛmmã] *adv* secondly, in the second place.

deux-pièces [døpjɛs] *nm inv* (*tailleur*) two-piece (suit); (*de bain*) two-piece (swimsuit); (*appartement*) two-roomed flat (*BRIT*) *ou* apartment (*US*).

deux-roues [døʀu] *nm* two-wheeled vehicle.

deux-temps [døtã] *adj* two-stroke.

devais [dəvɛ] *etc vb voir* **devoir**.

dévaler [devale] *vt* to hurtle down.

dévaliser [devalize] *vt* to rob, burgle.

dévalorisant, e [devalɔrizã, -ãt] *adj* depreciatory.

dévalorisation [devalɔrizasjɔ̃] *nf* depreciation.

dévaloriser [devalɔrize] *vt*, **se** ~ *vi* to depreciate.

dévaluation [devalɥasjɔ̃] *nf* depreciation; (*ÉCON: mesure*) devaluation.

dévaluer [devalɥe] *vt*, **se** ~ *vi* to devalue.

devancer [dəvãse] *vt* to be ahead of; (*distancer*) to get ahead of; (*arriver avant*) to arrive before; (*prévenir*) to anticipate; ~ **l'appel** (*MIL*) to enlist before call-up.

devancier, ière [dəvãsje, -jɛr] *nm/f* precursor.

devant [dəvã] *vb voir* **devoir** ♦ *adv* in front; (*à distance: en avant*) ahead ♦ *prép* in front of; ahead of; (*avec mouvement: passer*) past; (*fig*) before, in front of; (*: face à*) faced with, in the face of; (*: vu*) in view of ♦ *nm* front; **prendre les** ~**s** to make the first move; **de** ~ (*roue, porte*) front; **les pattes de** ~ the front legs, the forelegs; **par** ~ (*boutonner*) at the front; (*entrer*) the front way; **par-**~ **notaire** in the presence of a notary; **aller au-**~ **de qn** to go out to meet sb; **aller au-**~ **de** (*désirs de qn*) to anticipate; **aller au-**~ **des ennuis** *ou* **difficultés** to be asking for trouble.

devanture [dəvãtyr] *nf* (*façade*) (shop) front; (*étalage*) display; (shop) window.

dévastateur, trice [devastatœr, -tris] *adj* devastating.

dévastation [devastasjɔ̃] *nf* devastation.

dévaster [devaste] *vt* to devastate.

déveine [devɛn] *nf* rotten luck *no pl*.

développement [devlɔpmã] *nm* development.

développer [devlɔpe] *vt*, **se** ~ *vi* to develop.

devenir [dəvnir] *vb avec attribut* to become; ~ **instituteur** to become a teacher; **que sont-ils devenus?** what has become of them?

devenu, e [dəvny] *pp de* **devenir**.

dévergondé, e [devɛrgɔ̃de] *adj* wild, shameless.

dévergonder [devɛrgɔ̃de] *vt*, **se** ~ *vi* to get into bad ways.

déverrouiller [devɛruje] *vt* to unbolt.

devers [dəvɛr] *adv*: **par** ~ **soi** to oneself.

déverser [devɛrse] *vt* (*liquide*) to pour (out); (*ordures*) to tip (out); **se** ~ **dans** (*fleuve, mer*) to flow into.

déversoir [devɛrswar] *nm* overflow.

dévêtir [devetir] *vt*, **se** ~ *vi* to undress.

devez [dəve] *vb voir* **devoir**.

déviation [devjasjɔ̃] *nf* deviation; (*AUTO*) diversion (*BRIT*), detour (*US*); ~ **de la colonne** (**vertébrale**) curvature of the spine.

dévider [devide] *vt* to unwind.

dévidoir [devidwar] *nm* reel.

deviendrai [dəvjɛ̃dre], **deviens** [dəvjɛ̃] *etc vb voir* **devenir**.

dévier [devje] *vt* (*fleuve, circulation*) to divert; (*coup*) to deflect ♦ *vi* to veer (off course); (**faire**) ~ (*projectile*) to deflect; (*véhicule*) to push off course.

devin [dəvɛ̃] *nm* soothsayer, seer.

deviner [dəvine] *vt* to guess; (*prévoir*) to foretell, foresee; (*apercevoir*) to distinguish.

devinette [dəvinɛt] *nf* riddle.

devint [dəvɛ̃] *etc vb voir* **devenir**.

devis [dəvi] *nm* estimate, quotation; ~ **descriptif/estimatif** detailed/preliminary estimate.

dévisager [devizaʒe] *vt* to stare at.

devise [dəviz] *nf* (*formule*) motto, watchword; (*ÉCON: monnaie*) currency; ~**s** *nfpl* (*argent*) currency *sg*.

deviser [dəvize] *vi* to converse.

dévisser [devise] *vt* to unscrew, undo; **se** ~ *vi* to come unscrewed.

de visu [dəvizy] *adv*: **se rendre compte de qch** ~ to see sth for o.s.

dévitaliser [devitalize] *vt* (*dent*) to remove the nerve from.

dévoiler [devwale] *vt* to unveil.

devoir [dəvwar] *nm* duty; (*SCOL*) piece of homework, homework *no pl*; (*: en classe*) exercise ♦ *vt* (*argent, respect*): ~ **qch (à qn)** to owe (sb) sth; (*suivi de l'infinitif: obligation*): **il doit le faire** he has to do it, he must do it; (*: fatalité*): **cela devait arriver un jour** it was bound to happen; (*: intention*): **il doit partir demain** he is (due) to leave tomorrow; (*: probabilité*): **il doit être tard** it must be late; **se faire un** ~ **de faire qch** to make it one's duty to do sth; ~**s de vacances** homework set for the holidays; **se** ~ **de faire qch** to be duty bound to do sth; **je devrais faire** I ought to *ou* should do; **tu n'aurais pas dû** you ought not to have *ou* shouldn't have; **comme il se doit** (*comme il faut*) as is right and proper.

dévolu, e [devɔly] *adj*: ~ **à** allotted to ♦ *nm*: **jeter son** ~ **sur** to fix one's choice on.

devons [dəvɔ̃] *vb voir* **devoir**.

dévorant, e [devɔrã, -ãt] *adj* (*faim, passion*) raging.

dévorer [devɔre] *vt* to devour; (*suj: feu, soucis*) to consume; ~ **qn/qch des yeux** *ou* **du re-**

gard (*fig*) to eye sb/sth intently; (*: convoitise*) to eye sb/sth greedily.

dévot, e [devo, -ɔt] *adj* devout, pious ♦ *nm/f* devout person; **un faux** ~ a falsely pious person.

dévotion [devosjɔ̃] *nf* devoutness; **être à la** ~ **de qn** to be totally devoted to sb; **avoir une** ~ **pour qn** to worship sb.

dévoué, e [devwe] *adj* devoted.

dévouement [devumɑ̃] *nm* devotion, dedication.

dévouer [devwe]: **se** ~ *vi* (*se sacrifier*): **se** ~ **(pour)** to sacrifice o.s. (for); (*se consacrer*): **se** ~ **à** to devote *ou* dedicate o.s. to.

dévoyé, e [devwaje] *adj* delinquent.

dévoyer [devwaje] *vt* to lead astray; **se** ~ *vi* to go off the rails; ~ **l'opinion publique** to influence public opinion.

devrai [dəvʀe] *etc vb voir* **devoir**.

dextérité [dɛksteʀite] *nf* skill, dexterity.

dfc *abr* (= *désire faire connaissance*) *in personal column of newspaper.*

DG *sigle m* = **directeur général**.

dg. *abr* (= *décigramme*) dg.

DGE *sigle f* (= *Dotation globale d'équipement*) *state contribution to local government budget.*

DGSE *sigle f* (= *Direction générale des services extérieurs*) ≈ MI6 (*BRIT*), ≈ CIA (*US*).

DI *sigle f* (*MIL*) = *division d'infanterie.*

dia [dja] *abr* = **diapositive**.

diabète [djabɛt] *nm* diabetes *sg*.

diabétique [djabetik] *nm/f* diabetic.

diable [djabl(ə)] *nm* devil; **une musique du** ~ an unholy racket; **il fait une chaleur du** ~ it's fiendishly hot; **avoir le** ~ **au corps** to be the very devil.

diablement [djabləmɑ̃] *adv* fiendishly.

diableries [djabləʀi] *nfpl* (*d'enfant*) devilment *sg*, mischief *sg*.

diablesse [djablɛs] *nf* (*petite fille*) little devil.

diablotin [djablɔtɛ̃] *nm* imp; (*pétard*) cracker.

diabolique [djabɔlik] *adj* diabolical.

diabolo [djabɔlo] *nm* (*jeu*) diabolo; (*boisson*) lemonade and fruit cordial; ~(**-menthe**) lemonade and mint cordial.

diacre [djakʀ(ə)] *nm* deacon.

diadème [djadɛm] *nm* diadem.

diagnostic [djagnɔstik] *nm* diagnosis *sg*.

diagnostiquer [djagnɔstike] *vt* to diagnose.

diagonal, e, aux [djagɔnal, -o] *adj*, *nf* diagonal; **en** ~**e** diagonally; **lire en** ~**e** (*fig*) to skim through.

diagramme [djagʀam] *nm* chart, graph.

dialecte [djalɛkt(ə)] *nm* dialect.

dialectique [djalɛktik] *adj* dialectic(al).

dialogue [djalɔg] *nm* dialogue; ~ **de sourds** dialogue of the deaf.

dialoguer [djalɔge] *vi* to converse; (*POL*) to have a dialogue.

dialoguiste [djalɔgist(ə)] *nm/f* dialogue writer.

dialyse [djaliz] *nf* dialysis.

diamant [djamɑ̃] *nm* diamond.

diamantaire [djamɑ̃tɛʀ] *nm* diamond dealer.

diamétralement [djametʀalmɑ̃] *adv* diametrically; ~ **opposés** (*opinions*) diametrically opposed.

diamètre [djamɛtʀ(ə)] *nm* diameter.

diapason [djapazɔ̃] *nm* tuning fork; (*fig*): **être/se mettre au** ~ **(de)** to be/get in tune (with).

diaphane [djafan] *adj* diaphanous.

diaphragme [djafʀagm(ə)] *nm* (*ANAT*, *PHOTO*) diaphragm; (*contraceptif*) diaphragm, cap; **ouverture du** ~ (*PHOTO*) aperture.

diapo [djapo], **diapositive** [djapozitiv] *nf* transparency, slide.

diaporama [djapɔʀama] *nm* slide show.

diapré, e [djapʀe] *adj* many-coloured (*BRIT*), many-colored (*US*).

diarrhée [djaʀe] *nf* diarrhoea (*BRIT*), diarrhea (*US*).

diatribe [djatʀib] *nf* diatribe.

dichotomie [dikɔtɔmi] *nf* dichotomy.

dictaphone [diktafɔn] *nm* Dictaphone ®.

dictateur [diktatœʀ] *nm* dictator.

dictatorial, e, aux [diktatɔʀjal, -o] *adj* dictatorial.

dictature [diktatyʀ] *nf* dictatorship.

dictée [dikte] *nf* dictation; **prendre sous** ~ to take down (*sth dictated*).

dicter [dikte] *vt* to dictate.

diction [diksjɔ̃] *nf* diction, delivery; **cours de** ~ speech production lesson(s).

dictionnaire [diksjɔnɛʀ] *nm* dictionary; ~ **géographique** gazetteer.

dicton [diktɔ̃] *nm* saying, dictum.

didacticiel [didaktisjɛl] *nm* educational software.

didactique [didaktik] *adj* didactic.

dièse [djɛz] *nm* (*MUS*) sharp.

diesel [djezɛl] *nm*, *adj inv* diesel.

diète [djɛt] *nf* diet; **être à la** ~ to be on a diet.

diététicien, ne [djetetisjɛ̃, -ɛn] *nm/f* dietician.

diététique [djetetik] *nf* dietetics *sg* ♦ *adj*: **magasin** ~ health food shop (*BRIT*) *ou* store (*US*).

dieu, x [djø] *nm* god; **D**~ God; **le bon D**~ the good Lord; **mon D**~! good heavens!

diffamant, e [difamɑ̃, -ɑ̃t] *adj* slanderous, defamatory; libellous.

diffamation [difamasjɔ̃] *nf* slander; (*écrite*) libel; **attaquer qn en** ~ to sue sb for slander (*ou* libel).

diffamatoire [difamatwaʀ] *adj* slanderous, defamatory; libellous.

diffamer [difame] *vt* to slander, defame; to libel.

différé [difeʀe] *adj* (*INFORM*): **traitement** ~ batch processing; **crédit** ~ deferred credit ♦ *nm* (*TV*): **en** ~ (pre-)recorded.

différemment [difeʀamɑ̃] *adv* differently.

différence [difeʀɑ̃s] *nf* difference; **à la** ~ **de** unlike.

différenciation [difeʀɑ̃sjɑsjɔ̃] *nf* differentiation.

différencier [difeʀɑ̃sje] *vt* to differentiate; **se** ~ *vi* (*organisme*) to become differentiated; **se** ~ **de** to differentiate o.s. from; (*être différent*) to differ from.

différend [difeʀɑ̃] *nm* difference (of opinion), disagreement.

différent, e [difeʀɑ̃, -ɑ̃t] *adj*: ~ **(de)** different (from); ~**s objets** different *ou* various objects; **à** ~**es reprises** on various occasions.

différentiel, le [difeʀɑ̃sjɛl] *adj, nm* differential.

différer [difeʀe] *vt* to postpone, put off ♦ *vi*: ~ **(de)** to differ (from); ~ **de faire** (*tarder*) to delay doing.

difficile [difisil] *adj* difficult; (*exigeant*) hard to please, difficult (to please); **faire le** *ou* **la** ~ to be hard to please, be difficult.

difficilement [difisilmɑ̃] *adv* (*marcher, s'expliquer etc*) with difficulty; ~ **lisible/compréhensible** difficult *ou* hard to read/understand.

difficulté [difikylte] *nf* difficulty; **en** ~ (*bateau, alpiniste*) in trouble *ou* difficulties; **avoir de la** ~ **à faire** to have difficulty (in) doing.

difforme [difɔrm(ə)] *adj* deformed, misshapen.

difformité [difɔrmite] *nf* deformity.

diffracter [difʀakte] *vt* to diffract.

diffus, e [dify, -yz] *adj* diffuse.

diffuser [difyze] *vt* (*chaleur, bruit, lumière*) to diffuse; (*émission, musique*) to broadcast; (*nouvelle, idée*) to circulate; (*COMM: livres, journaux*) to distribute.

diffuseur [difyzœʀ] *nm* diffuser; distributor.

diffusion [difyzjɔ̃] *nf* diffusion; broadcast(ing); circulation; distribution.

digérer [diʒeʀe] *vt* (*suj: personne*) to digest; (*: machine*) to process; (*fig: accepter*) to stomach, put up with.

digeste [diʒɛst(ə)] *adj* easily digestible.

digestible [diʒɛstibl(ə)] *adj* digestible.

digestif, ive [diʒɛstif, -iv] *adj* digestive ♦ *nm* (after-dinner) liqueur.

digestion [diʒɛstjɔ̃] *nf* digestion.

digit [didʒit] *nm*: ~ **binaire** binary digit.

digital, e, aux [diʒital, -o] *adj* digital.

digitale [diʒital] *nf* digitalis, foxglove.

digne [diɲ] *adj* dignified; ~ **de** worthy of; ~ **de foi** trustworthy.

dignitaire [diɲitɛʀ] *nm* dignitary.

dignité [diɲite] *nf* dignity.

digression [digʀesjɔ̃] *nf* digression.

digue [dig] *nf* dike, dyke; (*pour protéger la côte*) sea wall.

dijonnais, e [diʒɔnɛ, -ɛz] *adj* of *ou* from Dijon ♦ *nm/f*: **D~, e** inhabitant *ou* native of Dijon.

diktat [diktat] *nm* diktat.

dilapidation [dilapidɑsjɔ̃] *nf* (*voir vb*) squandering; embezzlement, misappropriation.

dilapider [dilapide] *vt* to squander, waste; (*détourner: biens, fonds publics*) to embezzle, misappropriate.

dilater [dilate] *vt* to dilate; (*gaz, métal*) to cause to expand; (*ballon*) to distend; **se** ~ *vi* to expand.

dilemme [dilɛm] *nm* dilemma.

dilettante [diletɑ̃t] *nm/f* dilettante; **en** ~ in a dilettantish way.

dilettantisme [diletɑ̃tism(ə)] *nm* dilettant(e)ism.

diligence [diliʒɑ̃s] *nf* stagecoach, diligence; (*empressement*) despatch; **faire** ~ to make haste.

diligent, e [diliʒɑ̃, -ɑ̃t] *adj* prompt and efficient; diligent.

diluant [dilɥɑ̃] *nm* thinner(s).

diluer [dilɥe] *vt* to dilute.

dilution [dilysjɔ̃] *nf* dilution.

diluvien, ne [dilyvjɛ̃, -ɛn] *adj*: **pluie** ~**ne** torrential rain.

dimanche [dimɑ̃ʃ] *nm* Sunday; **le** ~ **des Rameaux/de Pâques** Palm/Easter Sunday; *voir aussi* **lundi**.

dîme [dim] *nf* tithe.

dimension [dimɑ̃sjɔ̃] *nf* (*grandeur*) size; (*gén pl: cotes, MATH: de l'espace*) dimension.

diminué, e [diminɥe] *adj* (*personne: physiquement*) run-down; (*: mentalement*) less alert.

diminuer [diminɥe] *vt* to reduce, decrease; (*ardeur etc*) to lessen; (*personne: physiquement*) to undermine; (*dénigrer*) to belittle ♦ *vi* to decrease, diminish.

diminutif [diminytif] *nm* (*LING*) diminutive; (*surnom*) pet name.

diminution [diminysjɔ̃] *nf* decreasing, diminishing.

dînatoire [dinatwaʀ] *adj*: **goûter** ~ ≈ high tea (*BRIT*); **apéritif** ~ ≈ evening buffet.

dinde [dɛ̃d] *nf* turkey; (*femme stupide*) goose.

dindon [dɛ̃dɔ̃] *nm* turkey.

dindonneau, x [dɛ̃dɔno] *nm* turkey poult.

dîner [dine] *nm* dinner ♦ *vi* to have dinner; ~ **d'affaires/de famille** business/family dinner.

dînette [dinɛt] *nf* (*jeu*): **jouer à la** ~ to play at tea parties.

dingue [dɛ̃g] *adj* (*fam*) crazy.

dinosaure [dinozɔʀ] *nm* dinosaur.

diocèse [djɔsɛz] *nm* diocese.

diode [djɔd] *nf* diode.

diphasé, e [difaze] *adj* (*ÉLEC*) two-phase.

diphtérie [difteʀi] *nf* diphtheria.

diphtongue [diftɔ̃g] *nf* diphthong.

diplomate [diplɔmat] *adj* diplomatic ♦ *nm* diplomat; (*fig: personne habile*) diplomatist; (*CULIN: gâteau*) dessert made of sponge cake, candied fruit and custard, ≈ trifle (*BRIT*).

diplomatie [diplɔmasi] *nf* diplomacy.

diplomatique [diplɔmatik] *adj* diplomatic.

diplôme [diplom] *nm* diploma certificate; (*examen*) (diploma) examination.

diplômé, e [diplome] *adj* qualified.

dire [diʀ] *nm:* **au ~ de** according to; **leurs ~s** what they say ♦ *vt* to say; (*secret, mensonge*) to tell; **~ l'heure/la vérité** to tell the time/the truth; **dis pardon/merci** say sorry/thank you; **~ qch à qn** to tell sb sth; **~ à qn qu'il fasse** *ou* **de faire** to tell sb to do; **~ que** to say that; **on dit que** they say that; **comme on dit** as they say; **on dirait qu'il** it looks (*ou* sounds *etc*) as though; **on dirait du vin** you'd *ou* one would think it was wine; **que dites-vous de** (*penser*) what do you think of; **si cela lui dit** if he feels like it, if he fancies it; **cela ne me dit rien** that doesn't appeal to me; **à vrai ~** truth to tell; **pour ainsi ~** so to speak; **cela va sans ~** that goes without saying; **dis donc!, dites donc!** (*pour attirer l'attention*) hey!; (*au fait*) by the way; **et ~ que ...** and to think that ...; **ceci** *ou* **cela dit** that being said; (*à ces mots*) whereupon; **c'est dit, voilà qui est dit** so that's settled; **il n'y a pas à ~** there's no getting away from it; **c'est ~ si ...** that just shows that ...; **c'est beaucoup/peu ~** that's saying a lot/not saying much; **se ~** (*à soi-même*) to say to oneself; (*se prétendre*): **se ~ malade** *etc* to say (that) one is ill *etc*; **ça se dit ... en anglais** that is ... in English; **cela ne se dit pas comme ça** you don't say it like that; **se ~ au revoir** to say goodbye (to each other).

direct, e [diʀɛkt] *adj* direct ♦ *nm* (*train*) through train; **en ~** (*émission*) live; **train/bus ~** express train/bus.

directement [diʀɛktəmã] *adv* directly.

directeur, trice [diʀɛktœʀ, -tʀis] *nm/f* (*d'entreprise*) director; (*de service*) manager/eress; (*d'école*) head(teacher) (*BRIT*), principal (*US*); **comité ~** management *ou* steering committee; **~ général** general manager; **~ de thèse** ≈ PhD supervisor.

direction [diʀɛksjɔ̃] *nf* management; conducting; supervision; (*AUTO*) steering; (*sens*) direction; **sous la ~ de** (*MUS*) conducted by; **en ~ de** (*avion, train, bateau*) for; **"toutes ~s"** (*AUTO*) "all routes".

directive [diʀɛktiv] *nf* directive, instruction.

directorial, e, aux [diʀɛktɔʀjal, -o] *adj* (*bureau*) director's; manager's; head teacher's.

directrice [diʀɛktʀis] *adj f, nf voir* **directeur**.

dirent [diʀ] *vb voir* **dire**.

dirigeable [diʀiʒabl(ə)] *adj, nm:* (**ballon**) **~** dirigible.

dirigeant, e [diʀiʒã, -ãt] *adj* managerial; (*classes*) ruling ♦ *nm/f* (*d'un parti etc*) leader; (*d'entreprise*) manager, member of the management.

diriger [diʀiʒe] *vt* (*entreprise*) to manage, run; (*véhicule*) to steer; (*orchestre*) to conduct; (*recherches, travaux*) to supervise, be in charge of; (*braquer: regard, arme*): **~ sur** to point *ou* level *ou* aim at; (*fig: critiques*): **~ contre** to aim at; **se ~** (*s'orienter*) to find one's way; **se ~ vers** *ou* **sur** to make *ou* head for.

dirigisme [diʀiʒism(ə)] *nm* (*ÉCON*) state intervention, interventionism.

dirigiste [diʀiʒist(ə)] *adj* interventionist.

dis [di], **disais** [dizɛ] *etc vb voir* **dire**.

discal, e, aux [diskal, -o] *adj* (*MÉD*): **hernie ~e** slipped disc.

discernement [disɛʀnəmã] *nm* discernment, judgment.

discerner [disɛʀne] *vt* to discern, make out.

disciple [disipl(ə)] *nm/f* disciple.

disciplinaire [disiplinɛʀ] *adj* disciplinary.

discipline [disiplin] *nf* discipline.

discipliné, e [disipline] *adj* (well-)disciplined.

discipliner [discipline] *vt* to discipline; (*cheveux*) to control.

discobole [diskɔbɔl] *nm/f* discus thrower.

discographie [diskɔgʀafi] *nf* discography.

discontinu, e [diskɔ̃tiny] *adj* intermittent; (*bande: sur la route*) broken.

discontinuer [diskɔ̃tinɥe] *vi:* **sans ~** without stopping, without a break.

disconvenir [diskɔ̃vniʀ] *vi:* **ne pas ~ de qch/que** not to deny sth/that.

discophile [diskɔfil] *nm/f* record enthusiast.

discordance [diskɔʀdãs] *nf* discordance; conflict.

discordant, e [diskɔʀdã, -ãt] *adj* discordant; conflicting.

discorde [diskɔʀd(ə)] *nf* discord, dissension.

discothèque [diskɔtɛk] *nf* (*disques*) record collection; (*: dans une bibliothèque*): **~ (de prêt)** record library; (*boîte de nuit*) disco(thèque).

discourais [diskuʀɛ] *etc vb voir* **discourir**.

discourir [diskuʀiʀ] *vi* to discourse, hold forth.

discours [diskuʀ] *vb voir* **discourir** ♦ *nm* speech; **~ direct/indirect** (*LING*) direct/indirect *ou* reported speech.

discourtois, e [diskuʀtwa, waz] *adj* discourteous.

discrédit [diskʀedi] *nm:* **jeter le ~ sur** to discredit.

discréditer [diskʀedite] *vt* to discredit.

discret, ète [diskʀɛ, -ɛt] *adj* discreet; (*fig: musique, style*) unobtrusive; (*: endroit*) quiet.

discrètement [diskʀɛtmã] *adv* discreetly.

discrétion [diskʀesjɔ̃] *nf* discretion; **à la ~ de qn** at sb's discretion; in sb's hands; **à ~** (*boisson etc*) unlimited, as much as one wants.

discrétionnaire [diskʀesjɔnɛʀ] *adj* discretionary.

discrimination [diskʀiminasjɔ̃] *nf* discrimination; **sans ~** indiscriminately.

discriminatoire [diskʀiminatwaʀ] *adj* discriminatory.

disculper [diskylpe] *vt* to exonerate.

discussion [diskysjɔ̃] *nf* discussion.

discutable [diskytabl(ə)] *adj* (*contestable*) doubtful; (*à débattre*) debatable.

discuté, e [diskyte] *adj* controversial.

discuter [diskyte] *vt* (*contester*) to question, dispute; (*débattre: prix*) to discuss ♦ *vi* to talk; (*ergoter*) to argue; ~ **de** to discuss.

dise [diz] *etc vb voir* **dire.**

disert, e [dizɛʀ, -ɛʀt(ə)] *adj* loquacious.

disette [dizɛt] *nf* food shortage.

diseuse [dizøz] *nf*: ~ **de bonne aventure** fortuneteller.

disgrâce [disɡʀɑs] *nf* disgrace; **être en** ~ to be in disgrace.

disgracié, e [disɡʀasje] *adj* (*en disgrâce*) disgraced.

disgracieux, euse [disɡʀasjø, -øz] *adj* ungainly, awkward.

disjoindre [disʒwɛ̃dʀ(ə)] *vt* to take apart; **se** ~ *vi* to come apart.

disjoint, e [disʒwɛ̃, -wɛ̃t] *pp de* **disjoindre** ♦ *adj* loose.

disjoncteur [disʒɔ̃ktœʀ] *nm* (*ÉLEC*) circuit breaker.

dislocation [dislɔkasjɔ̃] *nf* dislocation.

disloquer [dislɔke] *vt* (*membre*) to dislocate; (*chaise*) to dismantle; (*troupe*) to disperse; **se** ~ *vi* (*parti, empire*) to break up; **se** ~ **l'épaule** to dislocate one's shoulder.

disons [dizɔ̃] *etc vb voir* **dire.**

disparaître [dispaʀɛtʀ(ə)] *vi* to disappear; (*à la vue*) to vanish, disappear; to be hidden *ou* concealed; (*être manquant*) to go missing, disappear; (*se perdre: traditions etc*) to die out; (*personne: mourir*) to die; **faire** ~ (*objet, tache, trace*) to remove; (*personne*) to get rid of.

disparate [dispaʀat] *adj* disparate; (*couleurs*) ill-assorted.

disparité [dispaʀite] *nf* disparity.

disparition [dispaʀisjɔ̃] *nf* disappearance.

disparu, e [dispaʀy] *pp de* **disparaître** ♦ *nm/f* missing person; (*défunt*) departed; **être porté** ~ to be reported missing.

dispendieux, euse [dispɑ̃djø, -øz] *adj* extravagant, expensive.

dispensaire [dispɑ̃sɛʀ] *nm* community clinic.

dispense [dispɑ̃s] *nf* exemption; (*permission*) special permission; ~ **d'âge** special exemption from age limit.

dispenser [dispɑ̃se] *vt* (*donner*) to lavish, bestow; (*exempter*): ~ **qn de** to exempt sb from; **se** ~ **de** *vt* to avoid, get out of.

disperser [dispɛʀse] *vt* to scatter; (*fig: son attention*) to dissipate; **se** ~ *vi* to scatter; (*fig*) to dissipate one's efforts.

dispersion [dispɛʀsjɔ̃] *nf* scattering; (*des efforts*) dissipation.

disponibilité [dispɔnibilite] *nf* availability; (*ADMIN*): **être en** ~ to be on leave of absence; ~**s** *nfpl* (*COMM*) liquid assets.

disponible [dispɔnibl(ə)] *adj* available.

dispos [dispo] *adj m*: (**frais et**) ~ fresh (as a daisy).

disposé, e [dispoze] *adj* (*d'une certaine manière*) arranged, laid-out; **bien/mal** ~ (*hu-*

meur) in a good/bad mood; **bien/mal** ~ **pour** *ou* **envers qn** well/badly disposed towards sb; ~ **à** (*prêt à*) willing *ou* prepared to.

disposer [dispoze] *vt* (*arranger, placer*) to arrange; (*inciter*): ~ **qn à qch/faire qch** to dispose *ou* incline sb towards sth/to do sth ♦ *vi*: **vous pouvez** ~ you may leave; ~ **de** *vt* to have (at one's disposal); **se** ~ **à faire** to prepare to do, be about to do.

dispositif [dispozitif] *nm* device; (*fig*) system, plan of action; set-up; (*d'un texte de loi*) operative part; ~ **de sûreté** safety device.

disposition [dispozisjɔ̃] *nf* (*arrangement*) arrangement, layout; (*humeur*) mood; (*tendance*) tendency; ~**s** *nfpl* (*mesures*) steps, measures; (*préparatifs*) arrangements; (*de loi, testament*) provisions; (*aptitudes*) bent *sg*, aptitude *sg*; **à la** ~ **de qn** at sb's disposal.

disproportion [dispʀɔpɔʀsjɔ̃] *nf* disproportion.

disproportionné, e [dispʀɔpɔʀsjɔne] *adj* disproportionate, out of all proportion.

dispute [dispyt] *nf* quarrel, argument.

disputer [dispyte] *vt* (*match*) to play; (*combat*) to fight; (*course*) to run; **se** ~ *vi* to quarrel, have a quarrel; (*match, combat, course*) to take place; ~ **qch à qn** to fight with sb for *ou* over sth.

disquaire [diskɛʀ] *nm/f* record dealer.

disqualification [diskalifikasjɔ̃] *nf* disqualification.

disqualifier [diskalifje] *vt* to disqualify; **se** ~ *vi* to bring discredit on o.s.

disque [disk(ə)] *nm* (*MUS*) record; (*INFORM*) disk, disc; (*forme, pièce*) disc; (*SPORT*) discus; ~ **compact** compact disc; ~ **compact interactif** CD-I ®; ~ **dur** hard disk; ~ **d'embrayage** (*AUTO*) clutch plate; ~ **laser** compact disc; ~ **de stationnement** parking disc; ~ **système** system disk.

disquette [diskɛt] *nf* diskette, floppy (disk); ~ **(à) simple/double densité** single/double density disk; ~ **une face/double face** single-/double-sided disk.

dissection [disɛksjɔ̃] *nf* dissection.

dissemblable [disɑ̃blabl(ə)] *adj* dissimilar.

dissemblance [disɑ̃blɑ̃s] *nf* dissimilarity, difference.

dissémination [diseminasjɔ̃] *nf* (*voir vb*) scattering; dispersal; (*des armes*) proliferation.

disséminer [disemine] *vt* to scatter; (*troupes: sur un territoire*) to disperse.

dissension [disɑ̃sjɔ̃] *nf* dissension; ~**s** *nfpl* dissension.

disséquer [diseke] *vt* to dissect.

dissertation [disɛʀtasjɔ̃] *nf* (*SCOL*) essay.

disserter [disɛʀte] *vi*: ~ **sur** to discourse upon.

dissidence [disidɑ̃s] *nf* (*concept*) dissidence; **rejoindre la** ~ to join the dissidents.

dissident, e [disidɑ̃, -ɑ̃t] *adj*, *nm/f* dissident.

dissimilitude [disimilityd] *nf* dissimilarity.

dissimulateur, trice [disimyltœʀ, -tʀis] *adj*

dissembling ♦ *nm/f* dissembler.
dissimulation [disimylɑsjɔ̃] *nf* concealing; (*duplicité*) dissimulation; ~ **de bénéfices/de revenus** concealment of profits/income.
dissimulé, e [disimyle] (*personne: secret*) secretive; (*: fourbe, hypocrite*) deceitful.
dissimuler [disimyle] *vt* to conceal; **se ~** to conceal o.s.; to be concealed.
dissipation [disipɑsjɔ̃] *nf* squandering; unruliness; (*débauche*) dissipation.
dissipé, e [disipe] *adj* (*indiscipliné*) unruly.
dissiper [disipe] *vt* to dissipate; (*fortune*) to squander, fritter away; **se ~** *vi* (*brouillard*) to clear, disperse; (*doutes*) to disappear, melt away; (*élève*) to become undisciplined *ou* unruly.
dissociable [disɔsjabl(ə)] *adj* separable.
dissocier [disɔsje] *vt* to dissociate; **se ~** *vi* (*éléments, groupe*) to break up, split up; **se ~ de** (*groupe, point de vue*) to dissociate o.s. from.
dissolu, e [disɔly] *adj* dissolute.
dissoluble [disɔlybl(ə)] *adj* (*POL: assemblée*) dissolvable.
dissolution [disɔlysjɔ̃] *nf* dissolving; (*POL, JUR*) dissolution.
dissolvant, e [disɔlvɑ̃, -ɑ̃t] *vb voir* **dissoudre** ♦ *nm* (*CHIMIE*) solvent; ~ (**gras**) nail polish remover.
dissonant, e [disɔnɑ̃, -ɑ̃t] *adj* discordant.
dissoudre [disudr(ə)] *vt*, **se ~** *vi* to dissolve.
dissous, oute [disu, -ut] *pp de* **dissoudre**.
dissuader [disɥade] *vt*: ~ **qn de faire/de qch** to dissuade sb from doing/from sth.
dissuasif, ive [disɥazif, iv] *adj* dissuasive.
dissuasion [disɥazjɔ̃] *nf* dissuasion; **force de ~** deterrent power.
distance [distɑ̃s] *nf* distance; (*fig: écart*) gap; **à ~** *at ou* from a distance; (*mettre en marche, commander*) by remote control; (**situé**) **à ~** (*INFORM*) remote; **tenir qn à ~** to keep sb at a distance; **se tenir à ~** to keep one's distance; **à une ~ de 10 km, à 10 km de ~** 10 km away, at a distance of 10 km; **à 2 ans de ~** with a gap of 2 years; **prendre ses ~s** to space out; **garder ses ~s** to keep one's distance; **tenir la ~** (*SPORT*) to cover the distance, last the course; ~ **focale** (*PHOTO*) focal length.
distancer [distɑ̃se] *vt* to outdistance, leave behind.
distancier [distɑ̃sje]: **se ~** *vi* to distance o.s.
distant, e [distɑ̃, -ɑ̃t] *adj* (*réservé*) distant, aloof; (*éloigné*) distant, far away; ~ **de** (*lieu*) far away *ou* a long way from; ~ **de 5 km** (**d'un lieu**) 5 km away (from a place).
distendre [distɑ̃dr(ə)] *vt*, **se ~** *vi* to distend.
distillation [distilɑsjɔ̃] *nf* distillation, distilling.
distillé, e [distile] *adj*: **eau ~e** distilled water.
distiller [distile] *vt* to distil; (*fig*) to exude; to elaborate.
distillerie [distilʀi] *nf* distillery.

distinct, e [distɛ̃(kt), distɛ̃kt(ə)] *adj* distinct.
distinctement [distɛ̃ktəmɑ̃] *adv* distinctly.
distinctif, ive [distɛ̃ktif, -iv] *adj* distinctive.
distinction [distɛ̃ksjɔ̃] *nf* distinction.
distingué, e [distɛ̃ge] *adj* distinguished.
distinguer [distɛ̃ge] *vt* to distinguish; **se ~** *vi* (*s'illustrer*) to distinguish o.s.; (*différer*): **se ~ (de)** to distinguish o.s. *ou* be distinguished (from).
distinguo [distɛ̃go] *nm* distinction.
distorsion [distɔʀsjɔ̃] *nf* (*gén*) distorsion; (*fig: déséquilibre*) disparity, imbalance.
distraction [distʀaksjɔ̃] *nf* (*manque d'attention*) absent-mindedness; (*oubli*) lapse (in concentration *ou* attention); (*détente*) diversion, recreation; (*passe-temps*) distraction, entertainment.
distraire [distʀɛʀ] *vt* (*déranger*) to distract; (*divertir*) to entertain, divert; (*détourner: somme d'argent*) to divert, misappropriate; **se ~** to amuse *ou* enjoy o.s.
distrait, e [distʀɛ, -ɛt] *pp de* **distraire** ♦ *adj* absent-minded.
distraitement [distʀɛtmɑ̃] *adv* absent-mindedly.
distrayant, e [distʀɛjɑ̃, -ɑ̃t] *vb voir* **distraire** ♦ *adj* entertaining.
distribanque [distʀibɑ̃k] *nm* cash dispenser.
distribuer [distʀibɥe] *vt* to distribute; to hand out; (*CARTES*) to deal (out); (*courrier*) to deliver.
distributeur [distʀibytœʀ] *nm* (*AUTO, COMM*) distributor; (*automatique*) (vending) machine; ~ **de billets** (*RAIL*) ticket machine; (*BANQUE*) cash dispenser.
distribution [distʀibysjɔ̃] *nf* distribution; (*postale*) delivery; (*choix d'acteurs*) casting; **circuits de ~** (*COMM*) distribution network; ~ **des prix** (*SCOL*) prize giving.
district [distʀik(t)] *nm* district.
dit, e [di, dit] *pp de* **dire** ♦ *adj* (*fixé*): **le jour ~** the arranged day; (*surnommé*): **X, ~ Pierrot** X, known as *ou* called Pierrot.
dites [dit] *vb voir* **dire**.
dithyrambique [ditiʀɑ̃bik] *adj* eulogistic.
DIU *sigle m* (= *dispositif intra-utérin*) IUD.
diurétique [djyʀetik] *adj, nm* diuretic.
diurne [djyʀn(ə)] *adj* diurnal, daytime *cpd*.
divagations [divagɑsjɔ̃] *nfpl* ramblings; ravings.
divaguer [divage] *vi* to ramble; (*malade*) to rave.
divan [divɑ̃] *nm* divan.
divan-lit [divɑ̃li] *nm* divan (bed).
divergence [divɛʀʒɑ̃s] *nf* divergence; **des ~s d'opinion au sein de ...** differences of opinion within ....
divergent, e [divɛʀʒɑ̃, -ɑ̃t] *adj* divergent.
diverger [divɛʀʒe] *vi* to diverge.
divers, e [divɛʀ, -ɛʀs(ə)] *adj* (*varié*) diverse, varied; (*différent*) different, various ♦ *dét* (*plusieurs*) various, several; (**frais**) ~ (*COMM*)

sundries, miscellaneous (expenses); "~" (*rubrique*) "miscellaneous".

diversement [divɛʀsəmɑ̃] *adv* in various *ou* diverse ways.

diversification [divɛʀsifikasjɔ̃] *nf* diversification.

diversifier [divɛʀsifje] *vt*, **se ~** *vi* to diversify.

diversion [divɛʀsjɔ̃] *nf* diversion; **faire ~** to create a diversion.

diversité [divɛʀsite] *nf* diversity, variety.

divertir [divɛʀtiʀ] *vt* to amuse, entertain; **se ~** to amuse *ou* enjoy o.s.

divertissant, e [divɛʀtisɑ̃, -ɑ̃t] *adj* entertaining.

divertissement [divɛʀtismɑ̃] *nm* entertainment; (*MUS*) divertimento, divertissement.

dividende [dividɑ̃d] *nm* (*MATH, COMM*) dividend.

divin, e [divɛ̃, -in] *adj* divine; (*fig: excellent*) heavenly, divine.

divinateur, trice [divinatœʀ, -tʀis] *adj* perspicacious.

divinatoire [divinatwaʀ] *adj* (*art, science*) divinatory; **baguette ~** divining rod.

diviniser [divinize] *vt* to deify.

divinité [divinite] *nf* divinity.

divisé, e [divize] *adj* divided.

diviser [divize] *vt* (*gén, MATH*) to divide; (*morceler, subdiviser*) to divide (up), split (up); **se ~ en** to divide into; **~ par** to divide by.

diviseur [divizœʀ] *nm* (*MATH*) divisor.

divisible [divizibl(ə)] *adj* divisible.

division [divizjɔ̃] *nf* (*gén*) division; **~ du travail** (*ÉCON*) division of labour.

divisionnaire [divizjɔnɛʀ] *adj*: **commissaire ~** ≈ chief superintendent (*BRIT*), ≈ police chief (*US*).

divorce [divɔʀs(ə)] *nm* divorce.

divorcé, e [divɔʀse] *nm/f* divorcee.

divorcer [divɔʀse] *vi* to get a divorce, get divorced; **~ de** *ou* **d'avec qn** to divorce sb.

divulgation [divylɡasjɔ̃] *nf* disclosure.

divulguer [divylɡe] *vt* to divulge, disclose.

dix [di, dis, diz] *num* ten.

dix-huit [dizɥit] *num* eighteen.

dix-huitième [dizɥitjɛm] *num* eighteenth.

dixième [dizjɛm] *num* tenth.

dix-neuf [diznœf] *num* nineteen.

dix-neuvième [diznœvjɛm] *num* nineteenth.

dix-sept [disɛt] *num* seventeen.

dix-septième [disɛtjɛm] *num* seventeenth.

dizaine [dizɛn] *nf* (*10*) ten; (*environ 10*): **une ~ (de)** about ten, ten or so.

Djakarta [dʒakaʀta] *n* Djakarta.

Djibouti [dʒibuti] *n* Djibouti.

dl *abr* (= *décilitre*) dl.

DM *abr* (= *Deutschmark*) DM.

dm. *abr* (= *décimètre*) dm.

do [do] *nm* (*note*) C; (*en chantant la gamme*) do(h).

docile [dɔsil] *adj* docile.

docilement [dɔsilmɑ̃] *adv* docilely.

docilité [dɔsilite] *nf* docility.

dock [dɔk] *nm* dock; (*hangar, bâtiment*) warehouse.

docker [dɔkɛʀ] *nm* docker.

docte [dɔkt(ə)] *adj* (*péj*) learned.

docteur [dɔktœʀ] *nm* doctor; **~ en médecine** doctor of medicine.

doctoral, e, aux [dɔktɔʀal, -o] *adj* pompous, bombastic.

doctorat [dɔktɔʀa] *nm*: **~ (d'Université)** ≈ doctorate; **~ d'État** ≈ PhD; **~ de troisième cycle** ≈ doctorate.

doctoresse [dɔktɔʀɛs] *nf* lady doctor.

doctrinaire [dɔktʀinɛʀ] *adj* doctrinaire; (*sententieux*) pompous, sententious.

doctrinal, e, aux [dɔktʀinal, o] *adj* doctrinal.

doctrine [dɔktʀin] *nf* doctrine.

document [dɔkymɑ̃] *nm* document.

documentaire [dɔkymɑ̃tɛʀ] *adj*, *nm* documentary.

documentaliste [dɔkymɑ̃talist(ə)] *nm/f* archivist; (*PRESSE, TV*) researcher.

documentation [dɔkymɑ̃tasjɔ̃] *nf* documentation, literature; (*PRESSE, TV: service*) research.

documenté, e [dɔkymɑ̃te] *adj* well-informed, well-documented; well-researched.

documenter [dɔkymɑ̃te] *vt*: **se ~ (sur)** to gather information *ou* material (on *ou* about).

Dodécanèse [dɔdekanɛz] *nm* Dodecanese (Islands).

dodeliner [dɔdline] *vi*: **~ de la tête** to nod one's head gently.

dodo [dɔdo] *nm*: **aller faire ~** to go to beddy-byes.

dodu, e [dɔdy] *adj* plump.

dogmatique [dɔɡmatik] *adj* dogmatic.

dogmatisme [dɔɡmatism(ə)] *nm* dogmatism.

dogme [dɔɡm(ə)] *nm* dogma.

dogue [dɔɡ] *nm* mastiff.

doigt [dwa] *nm* finger; **à deux ~s de** within an ace of (*BRIT*) *ou* an inch of; **un ~ de lait/whisky** a drop of milk/whisky; **désigner** *ou* **montrer du ~** to point at; **au ~ et à l'œil** to the letter; **connaître qch sur le bout du ~** to know sth backwards; **mettre le ~ sur la plaie** (*fig*) to find the sensitive spot; **~ de pied** toe.

doigté [dwate] *nm* (*MUS*) fingering; (*fig: habileté*) diplomacy, tact.

doigtier [dwatje] *nm* fingerstall.

dois [dwa] *etc vb voir* **devoir**.

doive [dwav] *etc vb voir* **devoir**.

doléances [dɔleɑ̃s] *nfpl* complaints; (*réclamations*) grievances.

dolent, e [dɔlɑ̃, -ɑ̃t] *adj* doleful, mournful.

dollar [dɔlaʀ] *nm* dollar.

dolmen [dɔlmɛn] *nm* dolmen.

DOM [deɔɛm, dɔm] *sigle m ou mpl* = *Département(s) d'outre-mer*.

France has four overseas départements or **DOMs**: *French Guiana, Guadeloupe, Martinique and Réunion. Since 1982 each of these has also had regional status. France also has five overseas territories or* **TOMs**: *Austral and Antarctic French territories, French Polynesia, Mayotte, New Caledonia and Wallis and Futuna. Citizens of both DOMs and TOMs have French nationality.*

domaine [dɔmɛn] *nm* estate, property; (*fig*) domain, field; **tomber dans le ~ public** (*livre etc*) to be out of copyright; **dans tous les ~s** in all areas.

domanial, e, aux [dɔmanjal, -o] *adj* national, state *cpd*.

dôme [dom] *nm* dome.

domestication [dɔmɛstikɑsjɔ̃] *nf* (*voir domestiquer*) domestication; harnessing.

domesticité [dɔmɛstisite] *nf* (domestic) staff.

domestique [dɔmɛstik] *adj* domestic ♦ *nm/f* servant, domestic.

domestiquer [dɔmɛstike] *vt* to domesticate; (*vent, marées*) to harness.

domicile [dɔmisil] *nm* home, place of residence; **à ~** at home; **élire ~ à** to take up residence in; **sans ~ fixe** of no fixed abode; **~ conjugal** marital home; **~ légal** domicile.

domicilié, e [dɔmisilje] *adj*: **être ~ à** to have one's home in *ou* at.

dominant, e [dɔminɑ̃, -ɑ̃t] *adj* dominant; (*plus important*) predominant ♦ *nf* (*caractéristique*) dominant characteristic; (*couleur*) dominant colour.

dominateur, trice [dɔminatœʀ, -tʀis] *adj* dominating; (*qui aime à dominer*) domineering.

domination [dɔminasjɔ̃] *nf* domination.

dominer [dɔmine] *vt* to dominate; (*passions etc*) to control, master; (*surpasser*) to outclass, surpass; (*surplomber*) to tower above, dominate ♦ *vi* to be in the dominant position; **se ~** to control o.s.

dominicain, e [dɔminikɛ̃, -ɛn] *adj* Dominican.

dominical, e, aux [dɔminikal, -o] *adj* Sunday *cpd*, dominical.

Dominique [dɔminik] *nf*: **la ~** Dominica.

domino [dɔmino] *nm* domino; **~s** *nmpl* (*jeu*) dominoes *sg*.

dommage [dɔmaʒ] *nm* (*préjudice*) harm, injury; (*dégâts, pertes*) damage *no pl*; **c'est ~ de faire/que** it's a shame *ou* pity to do/that; **~s corporels** physical injury.

dommages-intérêts [dɔmaʒ(əz)ɛ̃teʀɛ] *nmpl* damages.

dompter [dɔ̃te] *vt* to tame.

dompteur, euse [dɔ̃tœʀ, -øz] *nm/f* trainer; (*de lion*) liontamer.

DOM-TOM [dɔmtɔm] *sigle m ou mpl* = Département(s) d'outre-mer/Territoire(s) d'outre-mer.

don [dɔ̃] *nm* (*cadeau*) gift; (*charité*) donation; (*aptitude*) gift, talent; **avoir des ~s pour** to have a gift *ou* talent for; **faire ~ de** to make a gift of; **~ en argent** cash donation.

donateur, trice [dɔnatœʀ, -tʀis] *nm/f* donor.

donation [dɔnasjɔ̃] *nf* donation.

donc [dɔ̃k] *conj* therefore, so; (*après une digression*) so, then; (*intensif*): **voilà ~ la solution** so there's the solution; **je disais ~ que** ... as I was saying, ...; **venez ~ dîner à la maison** do come for dinner; **allons ~!** come now!; **faites ~** go ahead.

donjon [dɔ̃ʒɔ̃] *nm* keep.

don Juan [dɔ̃ʒɥɑ̃] *nm* Don Juan.

donnant, e [dɔnɑ̃, -ɑ̃t] *adj*: **~, ~** fair's fair.

donne [dɔn] *nf* (*CARTES*): **il y a mauvaise** *ou* **fausse ~** there's been a misdeal.

donné, e [dɔne] *adj* (*convenu*) given; (*pas cher*) dirt cheap, very cheap ♦ *nf* (*MATH, INFORM, gén*) datum (*pl* data); **c'est ~** it's a gift; **étant ~ ... given ....**

donner [dɔne] *vt* to give; (*vieux habits etc*) to give away; (*spectacle*) to put on; (*film*) to show; **~ qch à qn** to give sb sth, give sth to sb; **~ sur** (*suj: fenêtre, chambre*) to look (out) onto; **~ dans** (*piège etc*) to fall into; **faire ~ l'infanterie** (*MIL*) to send in the infantry; **~ l'heure à qn** to tell sb the time; **~ le ton** (*fig*) to set the tone; **~ à penser/entendre que ...** to make one think/give one to understand that ...; **se ~ à fond (à son travail)** to give one's all (to one's work), devote o.s. heart and soul (to one's work); **se ~ du mal** *ou* **de la peine (pour faire qch)** to go to a lot of trouble (to do sth); **s'en ~ à cœur joie** (*fam*) to have a great time (of it).

donneur, euse [dɔnœʀ, -øz] *nm/f* (*MÉD*) donor; (*CARTES*) dealer; **~ de sang** blood donor.

━━━━━━━━━━━━━━━ *MOT-CLÉ*

dont [dɔ̃] *pron relatif* **1** (*appartenance: objets*) whose, of which; (*: êtres animés*) whose; **la maison ~ le toit est rouge** the house the roof of which is red, the house whose roof is red; **l'homme ~ je connais la sœur** the man whose sister I know

2 (*parmi lesquel(le)s*): **2 livres, ~ l'un est** ... 2 books, one of which is ...; **il y avait plusieurs personnes, ~ Gabrielle** there were several people, among them Gabrielle; **10 blessés, ~ 2 grièvement** 10 injured, 2 of them seriously

3 (*complément d'adjectif, de verbe*): **le fils ~ il est si fier** the son he's so proud of; **ce ~ je parle** what I'm talking about; **la façon ~ il l'a fait** the way (in which) he did it.

donzelle [dɔ̃zɛl] *nf* (*péj*) young madam.

dopage [dɔpaʒ] *nm* doping.

dopant [dɔpɑ̃] *nm* dope.

doper [dɔpe] *vt* to dope; **se ~** to take dope.

doping [dɔpiŋ] *nm* doping; (*excitant*) dope.

dorade [dɔrad] *nf* = **daurade**.

doré, e [dɔre] *adj* golden; (*avec dorure*) gilt,

gilded.

dorénavant [dɔrenavɑ̃] *adv* from now on, henceforth.

dorer [dɔre] *vt* (*cadre*) to gild; (**faire**) ~ (*CULIN*) to brown; (: *gâteau*) to glaze; **se** ~ **au soleil** to sunbathe; ~ **la pilule à qn** to sugar the pill for sb.

dorloter [dɔrlɔte] *vt* to pamper, cosset (*BRIT*); **se faire** ~ to be pampered *ou* cosseted.

dormant, e [dɔrmɑ̃, -ɑ̃t] *adj*: **eau** ~**e** still water.

dorme [dɔrm(ə)] *etc vb voir* **dormir**.

dormeur, euse [dɔrmœr, -øz] *nm/f* sleeper.

dormir [dɔrmir] *vi* to sleep; (*être endormi*) to be asleep; ~ **à poings fermés** to sleep very soundly.

dorsal, e, aux [dɔrsal, -o] *adj* dorsal; *voir* **rouleau**.

dortoir [dɔrtwar] *nm* dormitory.

dorure [dɔryr] *nf* gilding.

doryphore [dɔrifɔr] *nm* Colorado beetle.

dos [do] *nm* back; (*de livre*) spine; "**voir au** ~" "see over"; **robe décolletée dans le** ~ low-backed dress; **de** ~ from the back, from behind; ~ **à** ~ back to back; **sur le** ~ on one's back; **à** ~ **de chameau** riding on a camel; **avoir bon** ~ to be a good excuse; **se mettre qn à** ~ to turn sb against one.

dosage [dozaʒ] *nm* mixture.

dos-d'âne [dodɑn] *nm* humpback; **pont en** ~ humpbacked bridge.

dose [doz] *nf* (*MÉD*) dose; **forcer la** ~ (*fig*) to overstep the mark.

doser [doze] *vt* to measure out; (*mélanger*) to mix in the correct proportions; (*fig*) to expend in the right amounts *ou* proportions; to strike a balance between.

doseur [dozœr] *nm* measure; **bouchon** ~ measuring cap.

dossard [dosar] *nm* number (*worn by competitor*).

dossier [dosje] *nm* (*renseignements, fichier*) file; (*enveloppe*) folder, file; (*de chaise*) back; (*PRESSE*) feature; **le** ~ **social/monétaire** (*fig*) the social/financial question; ~ **suspendu** suspension file.

dot [dɔt] *nf* dowry.

dotation [dɔtasjɔ̃] *nf* block grant; endowment.

doté, e [dɔte] *adj*: ~ **de** equipped with.

doter [dɔte] *vt*: ~ **qn/qch de** to equip sb/sth with.

douairière [dwɛrjɛr] *nf* dowager.

douane [dwan] *nf* (*poste, bureau*) customs *pl*; (*taxes*) (customs) duty; **passer la** ~ to go through customs; **en** ~ (*marchandises, entrepôt*) bonded.

douanier, ière [dwanje, -jɛr] *adj* customs *cpd* ♦ *nm* customs officer.

doublage [dublaʒ] *nm* (*CINÉ*) dubbing.

double [dubl(ə)] *adj, adv* double ♦ *nm* (*2 fois plus*): **le** ~ (**de**) twice as much (*ou* many)

(as), double the amount (*ou* number) (of); (*autre exemplaire*) duplicate, copy; (*sosie*) double; (*TENNIS*) doubles *sg*; **voir** ~ to see double; **en** ~ (**exemplaire**) in duplicate; **faire** ~ **emploi** to be redundant; **à** ~ **sens** with a double meaning; **à** ~ **tranchant** two-edged; ~ **carburateur** twin carburettor; **à** ~**s commandes** dual-control; ~ **messieurs/mixte** men's/mixed doubles *sg*; ~ **toit** (*de tente*) fly sheet; ~ **vue** second sight.

doublé, e [duble] *adj* (*vêtement*): ~ (**de**) lined (with).

doublement [dubləmɑ̃] *nm* doubling; twofold increase ♦ *adv* doubly; (*pour deux raisons*) in two ways, on two counts.

doubler [duble] *vt* (*multiplier par 2*) to double; (*vêtement*) to line; (*dépasser*) to overtake, pass; (*film*) to dub; (*acteur*) to stand in for ♦ *vi* to double, increase twofold; **se** ~ **de** to be coupled with; ~ (**la classe**) (*SCOL*) to repeat a year; ~ **un cap** (*NAVIG*) to round a cape; (*fig*) to get over a hurdle.

doublure [dublyr] *nf* lining; (*CINÉ*) stand-in.

douce [dus] *adj f voir* **doux**.

douceâtre [dusɑtr(ə)] *adj* sickly sweet.

doucement [dusmɑ̃] *adv* gently; (*à voix basse*) softly; (*lentement*) slowly.

doucereux, euse [dusrø, -øz] *adj* (*péj*) sugary.

douceur [dusœr] *nf* softness; sweetness; mildness; gentleness; ~**s** *nfpl* (*friandises*) sweets (*BRIT*), candy *sg* (*US*); **en** ~ gently.

douche [duʃ] *nf* shower; ~**s** *nfpl* shower room *sg*; **prendre une** ~ to have *ou* take a shower; ~ **écossaise** (*fig*), ~ **froide** (*fig*) let-down.

doucher [duʃe] *vt*: ~ **qn** to give sb a shower; (*mouiller*) to drench sb; (*fig*) to give sb a telling-off; **se** ~ to have *ou* take a shower.

doudoune [dudun] *nf* padded jacket; (*fam*) boob.

doué, e [dwe] *adj* gifted, talented; ~ **de** endowed with; **être** ~ **pour** to have a gift for.

douille [duj] *nf* (*ÉLEC*) socket; (*de projectile*) case.

douillet, te [dujɛ, -ɛt] *adj* cosy; (*péj*) soft.

douleur [dulœr] *nf* pain; (*chagrin*) grief, distress; **ressentir des** ~**s** to feel pain; **il a eu la** ~ **de perdre son père** he suffered the grief of losing his father.

douloureux, euse [dulurø, -øz] *adj* painful.

doute [dut] *nm* doubt; **sans** ~ *adv* no doubt; (*probablement*) probably; **sans nul** *ou* **aucun** ~ without (a) doubt; **hors de** ~ beyond doubt; **nul** ~ **que** there's no doubt that; **mettre en** ~ to call into question; **mettre en** ~ **que** to question whether.

douter [dute] *vt* to doubt; ~ **de** *vt* (*allié*) to doubt, have (one's) doubts about; (*résultat*) to be doubtful of; ~ **que** to doubt whether *ou* if; **j'en doute** I have my doubts; **se** ~ **de qch/que** to suspect sth/that; **je m'en doutais** I suspected as much; **il ne se doutait de rien**

he didn't suspect a thing.

douteux, euse [dutø, -øz] *adj* (*incertain*) doubtful; (*discutable*) dubious, questionable; (*péj*) dubious-looking.

douve [duv] *nf* (*de château*) moat; (*de tonneau*) stave.

Douvres [duvʀ(ə)] *n* Dover.

doux, douce [du, dus] *adj* (*lisse, moelleux, pas vif: couleur, non calcaire: eau*) soft; (*sucré, agréable*) sweet; (*peu fort: moutarde etc, clément: climat*) mild; (*pas brusque*) gentle; **en douce** (*partir etc*) on the quiet.

douzaine [duzɛn] *nf* (*12*) dozen; (*environ 12*): **une ~ (de)** a dozen or so, twelve or so.

douze [duz] *num* twelve; **les D~** (*membres de la CEE*) the Twelve.

douzième [duzjɛm] *num* twelfth.

doyen, ne [dwajɛ̃, -ɛn] *nm/f* (*en âge, ancienneté*) most senior member; (*de faculté*) dean.

DPLG *sigle* (= *diplômé par le gouvernement*) *extra certificate for architects, engineers etc*.

Dr *abr* (= *docteur*) Dr.

dr. *abr* (= *droit(e)*) R, r.

draconien, ne [dʀakɔnjɛ̃, -ɛn] *adj* draconian, stringent.

dragage [dʀagaʒ] *nm* dredging.

dragée [dʀaʒe] *nf* sugared almond; (*MÉD*) (sugar-coated) pill.

dragéifié, e [dʀaʒeifje] *adj* (*MÉD*) sugar-coated.

dragon [dʀagɔ̃] *nm* dragon.

drague [dʀag] *nf* (*filet*) dragnet; (*bateau*) dredger.

draguer [dʀage] *vt* (*rivière: pour nettoyer*) to dredge; (*: pour trouver qch*) to drag; (*fam*) to try and pick up, chat up (*BRIT*) ♦ *vi* (*fam*) to try and pick sb up, chat sb up (*BRIT*).

dragueur [dʀagœʀ] *nm* (*aussi:* **~ de mines**) minesweeper; (*fam*): **quel ~!** he's a great one for picking up girls!

drain [dʀɛ̃] *nm* (*MÉD*) drain.

drainage [dʀɛnaʒ] *nm* drainage.

drainer [dʀene] *vt* to drain; (*fig: visiteurs, région*) to drain off.

dramatique [dʀamatik] *adj* dramatic; (*tragique*) tragic ♦ *nf* (*TV*) (television) drama.

dramatisation [dʀamatizɑsjɔ̃] *nf* dramatization.

dramatiser [dʀamatize] *vt* to dramatize.

dramaturge [dʀamatyʀʒ(ə)] *nm* dramatist, playwright.

drame [dʀam] *nm* (*THÉÂT*) drama; (*catastrophe*) drama, tragedy; **~ familial** family drama.

drap [dʀa] *nm* (*de lit*) sheet; (*tissu*) woollen fabric; **~ de plage** beach towel.

drapé [dʀape] *nm* (*d'un vêtement*) hang.

drapeau, x [dʀapo] *nm* flag; **sous les ~x** with the colours (*BRIT*) *ou* colors (*US*), in the army.

draper [dʀape] *vt* to drape; (*robe, jupe*) to arrange.

draperies [dʀapʀi] *nfpl* hangings.

drap-housse, *pl* **draps-housses** [dʀaus] *nm* fitted sheet.

drapier [dʀapje] *nm* (woollen) cloth manufacturer; (*marchand*) clothier.

drastique [dʀastik] *adj* drastic.

dressage [dʀɛsaʒ] *nm* training.

dresser [dʀese] *vt* (*mettre vertical, monter: tente*) to put up, erect; (*fig: liste, bilan, contrat*) to draw up; (*animal*) to train; **se ~** *vi* (*falaise, obstacle*) to stand; (*avec grandeur, menace*) to tower (up); (*personne*) to draw o.s. up; **~ l'oreille** to prick up one's ears; **~ la table** to set *ou* lay the table; **~ qn contre qn d'autre** to set sb against sb else; **~ un procès-verbal** *ou* **une contravention à qn** to book sb.

dresseur, euse [dʀesœʀ, -øz] *nm/f* trainer.

dressoir [dʀeswaʀ] *nm* dresser.

dribbler [dʀible] *vt, vi* (*SPORT*) to dribble.

drille [dʀij] *nm*: **joyeux ~** cheerful sort.

drogue [dʀɔg] *nf* drug; **la ~** drugs *pl*; **~ dure/douce** hard/soft drugs *pl*.

drogué, e [dʀɔge] *nm/f* drug addict.

droguer [dʀɔge] *vt* (*victime*) to drug; (*malade*) to give drugs to; **se ~** (*aux stupéfiants*) to take drugs; (*péj: de médicaments*) to dose o.s. up.

droguerie [dʀɔgʀi] *nf* ≈ hardware shop (*BRIT*) *ou* store (*US*).

droguiste [dʀɔgist(ə)] *nm* ≈ keeper (*ou* owner) of a hardware shop *ou* store.

droit, e [dʀwa, dʀwat] *adj* (*non courbe*) straight; (*vertical*) upright, straight; (*fig: loyal, franc*) upright, straight(forward); (*opposé à gauche*) right, right-hand ♦ *adv* straight ♦ *nm* (*prérogative, BOXE*) right; (*taxe*) duty, tax; (*: d'inscription*) fee; (*lois, branche*): **le ~** law ♦ *nf* (*POL*) right (wing); (*ligne*) straight line; **~ au but** *ou* **au fait/cœur** straight to the point/heart; **avoir le ~ de** to be allowed to; **avoir ~ à** to be entitled to; **être en ~ de** to have a *ou* the right to; **faire ~ à** to grant, accede to; **être dans son ~** to be within one's rights; **à bon ~** (*justement*) with good reason; **de quel ~?** by what right?; **à qui de ~** to whom it may concern; **à ~e** on the right; (*direction*) (to the) right; **à ~e de** to the right of; **de ~e** (*POL*) right-wing; **~ d'auteur** copyright; **avoir ~ de cité (dans)** (*fig*) to belong (to); **~ coutumier** common law; **~ de regard** right of access *ou* inspection; **~ de réponse** right to reply; **~ de visite** (right of) access; **~ de vote** (right to) vote; **~s d'auteur** royalties; **~s de douane** customs duties; **~s de l'homme** human rights; **~s d'inscription** enrolment *ou* registration fees.

droitement [dʀwatmɑ̃] *adv* (*agir*) uprightly.

droitier, ière [dʀwatje, -jɛʀ] *nm/f* right-handed person.

droiture [dʀwatyʀ] *nf* uprightness, straightness.

drôle [dʀol] *adj* (*amusant*) funny, amusing; (*bizarre*) funny, peculiar; **un ~ de ...** (*bizarre*) a strange *ou* funny ...; (*intensif*) an incredible ..., a terrific ....

drôlement [dʀolmɑ̃] *adv* funnily; peculiarly; (*très*) terribly, awfully; **il fait ~ froid** it's awfully cold.

drôlerie [dʀolʀi] *nf* funniness; funny thing.

dromadaire [dʀɔmadɛʀ] *nm* dromedary.

dru, e [dʀy] *adj* (*cheveux*) thick, bushy; (*pluie*) heavy ♦ *adv* (*pousser*) thickly; (*tomber*) heavily.

drugstore [dʀœgstɔʀ] *nm* drugstore.

druide [dʀɥid] *nm* Druid.

ds *abr* = **dans**.

DST *sigle f* (= *Direction de la surveillance du territoire*) *internal security service*, ≈ MI5 (*BRIT*).

DT *sigle m* (= *diphtérie tétanos*) *vaccine*.

DTCP *sigle m* (= *diphtérie tétanos coqueluche polio*) *vaccine*.

DTP *sigle m* (= *diphtérie tétanos polio*) *vaccine*.

DTTAB *sigle m* (= *diphtérie tétanos typhoïde A et B*) *vaccine*.

du [dy] *prép + dét, dét voir* **de**.

dû, due [dy] *pp de* **devoir** ♦ *adj* (*somme*) owing, owed; (*: venant à échéance*) due; (*causé par*): **~ à** due to ♦ *nm* due; (*somme*) dues *pl*.

dualisme [dɥalism(ə)] *nm* dualism.

Dubaï, Dubay [dybaj] *n* Dubai.

dubitatif, ive [dybitatif, -iv] *adj* doubtful, dubious.

Dublin [dyblɛ̃] *n* Dublin.

duc [dyk] *nm* duke.

duché [dyʃe] *nm* dukedom, duchy.

duchesse [dyʃɛs] *nf* duchess.

DUEL [dɥɛl] *sigle m* = *Diplôme universitaire d'études littéraires*.

duel [dɥɛl] *nm* duel.

DUES [dyɛs] *sigle m* = *Diplôme universitaire d'études scientifiques*.

duettiste [dɥetist(ə)] *nm/f* duettist.

duffel-coat [dœfœlkot] *nm* duffelcoat.

dûment [dymɑ̃] *adv* duly.

dumping [dœmpiŋ] *nm* dumping.

dune [dyn] *nf* dune.

Dunkerque [dœ̃kɛʀk] *n* Dunkirk.

duo [dɥo] *nm* (*MUS*) duet; (*fig: couple*) duo, pair.

dupe [dyp] *nf* dupe ♦ *adj*: **(ne pas) être ~ de** (not) to be taken in by.

duper [dype] *vt* to dupe, deceive.

duperie [dypʀi] *nf* deception, dupery.

duplex [dyplɛks] *nm* (*appartement*) split-level apartment, duplex; (*TV*): **émission en ~** link-up.

duplicata [dyplikata] *nm* duplicate.

duplicateur [dyplikatœʀ] *nm* duplicator; **~ à alcool** spirit duplicator.

duplicité [dyplisite] *nf* duplicity.

duquel [dykɛl] *prép + pron voir* **lequel**.

dur, e [dyʀ] *adj* (*pierre, siège, travail, problème*) hard; (*lumière, voix, climat*) harsh; (*sévère*) hard, harsh; (*cruel*) hard(-hearted); (*porte, col*) stiff; (*viande*) tough ♦ *adv* hard ♦ *nf*: **à la ~e** rough; **mener la vie ~e à qn** to give sb a hard time; **~ d'oreille** hard of hearing.

durabilité [dyʀabilite] *nf* durability.

durable [dyʀabl(ə)] *adj* lasting.

durablement [dyʀabləmɑ̃] *adv* for the long term.

durant [dyʀɑ̃] *prép* (*au cours de*) during; (*pendant*) for; **~ des mois, des mois ~** for months.

durcir [dyʀsiʀ] *vt, vi,* **se ~** *vi* to harden.

durcissement [dyʀsismɑ̃] *nm* hardening.

durée [dyʀe] *nf* length; (*d'une pile etc*) life; (*déroulement: des opérations etc*) duration; **pour une ~ illimitée** for an unlimited length of time; **de courte ~** (*séjour, répit*) brief, short-term; **de longue ~** (*effet*) long-term; **pile de longue ~** long-life battery.

durement [dyʀmɑ̃] *adv* harshly.

durent [dyʀ] *vb voir* **devoir**.

durer [dyʀe] *vi* to last.

dureté [dyʀte] *nf* (*voir dur*) hardness; harshness; stiffness; toughness.

durillon [dyʀijɔ̃] *nm* callus.

durit [dyʀit] *nf* ® (car radiator) hose.

DUT *sigle m* = *Diplôme universitaire de technologie*.

dut [dy] *etc vb voir* **devoir**.

duvet [dyvɛ] *nm* down; **(sac de couchage en) ~** down-filled sleeping bag.

duveteux, euse [dyvtø, -øz] *adj* downy.

dynamique [dinamik] *adj* dynamic.

dynamiser [dinamize] *vt* to pep up, enliven; (*équipe, service*) to inject some dynamism into.

dynamisme [dinamism(ə)] *nm* dynamism.

dynamite [dinamit] *nf* dynamite.

dynamiter [dinamite] *vt* to (blow up with) dynamite.

dynamo [dinamo] *nf* dynamo.

dynastie [dinasti] *nf* dynasty.

dysenterie [disɑ̃tʀi] *nf* dysentery.

dyslexie [dislɛksi] *nf* dyslexia, word blindness.

dyslexique [dislɛksik] *adj* dyslexic.

dyspepsie [dispɛpsi] *nf* dyspepsia.

E e

E, e [ə] *nm inv* E, e ♦ *abr* (= *Est*) E; **E comme Eugène** E for Edward (*BRIT*) *ou* Easy (*US*).

EAO *sigle m* (= *enseignement assisté par ordinateur*) CAL (= *computer-aided learning*).

EAU *sigle mpl* (= *Émirats arabes unis*) UAE (= *United Arab Emirates*).

eau, x [o] *nf* water ♦ *nfpl* waters; **prendre l'~** (*chaussure etc*) to leak, let in water; **prendre les ~x** to take the waters; **faire ~** to leak; **tomber à l'~** (*fig*) to fall through; **à l'~ de rose** slushy, sentimental; **~ bénite** holy water; **~ de Cologne** eau de Cologne; **~ courante** running water; **~ distillée** distilled water; **~ douce** fresh water; **~ de Javel** bleach; **~ lourde** heavy water; **~ minérale** mineral water; **~ oxygénée** hydrogen peroxide; **~ plate** still water; **~ de pluie** rainwater; **~ salée** salt water; **~ de toilette** toilet water; **~x ménagères** dirty water (*from washing up etc*); **~x territoriales** territorial waters; **~x usées** liquid waste.

eau-de-vie, *pl* **eaux-de-vie** [odvi] *nf* brandy.

eau-forte, *pl* **eaux-fortes** [ofɔrt(ə)] *nf* etching.

ébahi, e [ebai] *adj* dumbfounded, flabbergasted.

ébahir [ebaiʀ] *vt* to astonish, astound.

ébats [eba] *vb voir* **ébattre** ♦ *nmpl* frolics, gambols.

ébattre [ebatʀ(ə)]: **s'~** *vi* to frolic.

ébauche [ebof] *nf* (rough) outline, sketch.

ébaucher [ebofe] *vt* to sketch out, outline; (*fig*): **~ un sourire/geste** to give a hint of a smile/make a slight gesture; **s'~** *vi* to take shape.

ébène [ebɛn] *nf* ebony.

ébéniste [ebenist(ə)] *nm* cabinetmaker.

ébénisterie [ebenistʀi] *nf* cabinetmaking; (*bâti*) cabinetwork.

éberlué, e [ebɛʀlɥe] *adj* astounded, flabbergasted.

éblouir [ebluiʀ] *vt* to dazzle.

éblouissant, e [ebluisɑ̃, -ɑ̃t] *adj* dazzling.

éblouissement [ebluismɑ̃] *nm* dazzle; (*faiblesse*) dizzy turn.

ébonite [ebɔnit] *nf* vulcanite.

éborgner [ebɔʀɲe] *vt*: **~ qn** to blind sb in one eye.

éboueur [ebwœʀ] *nm* dustman (*BRIT*), garbageman (*US*).

ébouillanter [ebujɑ̃te] *vt* to scald; (*CULIN*) to blanch; **s'~** to scald o.s.

éboulement [ebulmɑ̃] *nm* falling rocks *pl*, rock fall; (*amas*) heap of boulders *etc*.

ébouler [ebule]: **s'~** *vi* to crumble, collapse.

éboulis [ebuli] *nmpl* fallen rocks.

ébouriffé, e [eburife] *adj* tousled, ruffled.

ébouriffer [eburife] *vt* to tousle, ruffle.

ébranlement [ebrɑ̃lmɑ̃] *nm* shaking.

ébranler [ebrɑ̃le] *vt* to shake; (*rendre instable: mur, santé*) to weaken; **s'~** *vi* (*partir*) to move off.

ébrécher [ebreʃe] *vt* to chip.

ébriété [ebrijete] *nf*: **en état d'~** in a state of intoxication.

ébrouer [ebrue]: **s'~** *vi* (*souffler*) to snort; (*s'agiter*) to shake o.s.

ébruiter [ebrɥite] *vt*, **s'~** *vi* to spread.

ébullition [ebylisjɔ̃] *nf* boiling point; **en ~** boiling; (*fig*) in an uproar.

écaille [ekaj] *nf* (de poisson) scale; (de coquillage) shell; (matière) tortoiseshell; (de roc etc) flake.

écaillé, e [ekaje] *adj* (peinture) flaking.

écailler [ekaje] *vt* (poisson) to scale; (huître) to open; **s'~** *vi* to flake *ou* peel (off).

écarlate [ekarlat] *adj* scarlet.

écarquiller [ekarkije] *vt*: **~ les yeux** to stare wide-eyed.

écart [ekar] *nm* gap; (embardée) swerve; (saut) sideways leap; (fig) departure, deviation; **à l'~** *adv* out of the way; **à l'~ de** *prép* away from; (fig) out of; **faire le grand ~** (DANSE, GYMNASTIQUE) to do the splits; **~ de conduite** misdemeanour.

écarté, e [ekarte] *adj* (lieu) out-of-the-way, remote; (ouvert): **les jambes ~es** legs apart; **les bras ~s** arms outstretched.

écarteler [ekartəle] *vt* to quarter; (fig) to tear.

écartement [ekartəmɑ̃] *nm* space, gap; (RAIL) gauge.

écarter [ekarte] *vt* (séparer) to move apart, separate; (éloigner) to push back, move away; (ouvrir: bras, jambes) to spread, open; (: rideau) to draw (back); (éliminer: candidat, possibilité) to dismiss; (CARTES) to discard; **s'~** *vi* to part; (personne) to move away; **s'~ de** to wander from.

ecchymose [ekimoz] *nf* bruise.

ecclésiastique [eklezjastik] *adj* ecclesiastical ♦ *nm* ecclesiastic.

écervelé, e [esɛrvəle] *adj* scatterbrained, featherbrained.

ECG *sigle m* (= *électrocardiogramme*) ECG.

échafaud [eʃafo] *nm* scaffold.

échafaudage [eʃafodaʒ] *nm* scaffolding; (fig) heap, pile.

échafauder [eʃafode] *vt* (plan) to construct.

échalas [eʃala] *nm* stake, pole; (personne) beanpole.

échalote [eʃalɔt] *nf* shallot.

échancré, e [eʃɑ̃kre] *adj* (robe, corsage) lownecked; (côte) indented.

échancrure [eʃɑ̃kryr] *nf* (de robe) scoop neckline; (de côte, arête rocheuse) indentation.

échange [eʃɑ̃ʒ] nm exchange; **en ~** in exchange; **en ~ de** in exchange ou return for; **libre ~** free trade; **~ de lettres/politesses/ vues** exchange of letters/civilities/views; **~s commerciaux** trade; **~s culturels** cultural exchanges.

échangeable [eʃɑ̃ʒabl(ə)] adj exchangeable.

échanger [eʃɑ̃ʒe] vt: **~ qch (contre)** to exchange sth (for).

échangeur [eʃɑ̃ʒœr] nm (AUTO) interchange.

échantillon [eʃɑ̃tijɔ̃] nm sample.

échantillonnage [eʃɑ̃tijɔnaʒ] nm selection of samples.

échappatoire [eʃapatwar] nf way out.

échappée [eʃape] nf (vue) vista; (CYCLISME) breakaway.

échappement [eʃapmɑ̃] nm (AUTO) exhaust; **~ libre** cutout.

échapper [eʃape]: **~ à** vt (gardien) to escape (from); (punition, péril) to escape; **~ à qn** (détail, sens) to escape sb; (objet qu'on tient: aussi: **~ des mains de qn**) to slip out of sb's hands; **laisser ~** to let fall; (cri etc) to let out; **s'~** vi to escape; **l'~ belle** to have a narrow escape.

écharde [eʃard(ə)] nf splinter (of wood).

écharpe [eʃarp(ə)] nf scarf (pl scarves); (de maire) sash; (MÉD) sling; **prendre en ~** (dans une collision) to hit sideways on.

écharper [eʃarpe] vt to tear to pieces.

échasse [eʃɑs] nf stilt.

échassier [eʃɑsje] nm wader.

échauder [eʃode] vt: **se faire ~** (fig) to get one's fingers burnt.

échauffement [eʃofmɑ̃] nm overheating; (SPORT) warm-up.

échauffer [eʃofe] vt (métal, moteur) to overheat; (fig: exciter) to fire, excite; **s'~** vi (SPORT) to warm up; (discussion) to become heated.

échauffourée [eʃofure] nf clash, brawl; (MIL) skirmish.

échéance [eʃeɑ̃s] nf (d'un paiement: date) settlement date; (: somme due) financial commitment(s); (fig) deadline; **à brève/longue ~** adj short-/long-term ♦ adv in the short/long term.

échéancier [eʃeɑ̃sje] nm schedule.

échéant [eʃeɑ̃]: **le cas ~** adv if the case arises.

échec [eʃɛk] nm failure; (ÉCHECS): **~ et mat/au roi** checkmate/check; **~s** nmpl (jeu) chess sg; **mettre en ~** to put in check; **tenir en ~** to hold in check; **faire ~ à** to foil, thwart.

échelle [eʃɛl] nf ladder; (fig, d'une carte) scale; **à l'~ de** on the scale of; **sur une grande/ petite ~** on a large/small scale; **faire la courte ~ à qn** to give sb a leg up; **~ de corde** rope ladder.

échelon [eʃlɔ̃] nm (d'échelle) rung; (ADMIN) grade.

échelonner [eʃlɔne] vt to space out, spread

out; (versement) **échelonné** (payment) by instalments.

écheveau, x [eʃvo] nm skein, hank.

échevelé, e [eʃəvle] adj tousled, dishevelled; (fig) wild, frenzied.

échine [eʃin] nf backbone, spine.

échiner [eʃine]: **s'~** vi (se fatiguer) to work o.s. to the bone.

échiquier [eʃikje] nm chessboard.

écho [eko] nm echo; **~s** nmpl (potins) gossip sg, rumours; (PRESSE: rubrique) "news in brief"; **rester sans ~** (suggestion etc) to come to nothing; **se faire l'~ de** to repeat, spread about.

échographie [ekɔɡrafi] nf ultrasound (scan).

échoir [eʃwar] vi (dette) to fall due; (délais) to expire; **~ à** vt to fall to.

échoppe [eʃɔp] nf stall, booth.

échouer [eʃwe] vi to fail; (débris etc : sur la plage) to be washed up; (aboutir: personne dans un café etc) to arrive ♦ vt (bateau) to ground; **s'~** vi to run aground.

échu, e [eʃy] pp de **échoir** ♦ adj due, mature.

échut [eʃy] etc vb voir **échoir**.

éclabousser [eklabuse] vt to splash; (fig) to tarnish.

éclaboussure [eklabusyr] nf splash; (fig) stain.

éclair [eklɛr] nm (d'orage) flash of lightning, lightning no pl; (PHOTO: de flash) flash; (fig) flash, spark; (gâteau) éclair.

éclairage [eklɛraʒ] nm lighting.

éclairagiste [eklɛraʒist(ə)] nm/f lighting engineer.

éclaircie [eklɛrsi] nf bright ou sunny interval.

éclaircir [eklɛrsir] vt to lighten; (fig) to clear up, clarify; (CULIN) to thin (down); **s'~** vi (ciel) to brighten up, clear; (cheveux) to go thin; (situation etc) to become clearer; **s'~ la voix** to clear one's throat.

éclaircissement [eklɛrsismɑ̃] nm clearing up, clarification.

éclairer [eklɛre] vt (lieu) to light (up); (personne: avec une lampe de poche etc) to light the way for; (fig: instruire) to enlighten; (: rendre compréhensible) to shed light on ♦ vi: **~ mal/bien** to give a poor/good light; **s'~** vi (phare, rue) to light up; (situation etc) to become clearer; **s'~ à la bougie/l'électricité** to use candlelight/have electric lighting.

éclaireur, euse [eklɛrœr, -øz] nm/f (scout) (boy) scout/(girl) guide ♦ nm (MIL) scout; **partir en ~** to go off to reconnoitre.

éclat [ekla] nm (de bombe, de verre) fragment; (du soleil, d'une couleur etc) brightness, brilliance; (d'une cérémonie) splendour; (scandale): **faire un ~** to cause a commotion; **action d'~** outstanding action; **voler en ~s** to shatter; **des ~s de verre** broken glass; flying glass; **~ de rire** burst ou roar of laughter; **~ de voix** shout.

éclatant, e [eklatɑ̃, -ɑ̃t] adj brilliant, bright;

(*succès*) resounding; (*revanche*) devastating.
éclater [eklate] *vi* (*pneu*) to burst; (*bombe*) to explode; (*guerre, épidémie*) to break out; (*groupe, parti*) to break up; ~ **de rire/en sanglots** to burst out laughing/sobbing.
éclectique [eklɛktik] *adj* eclectic.
éclipse [eklips(ə)] *nf* eclipse.
éclipser [eklipse] *vt* to eclipse; **s'**~ *vi* to slip away.
éclopé, e [eklɔpe] *adj* lame.
éclore [eklɔʀ] *vi* (*œuf*) to hatch; (*fleur*) to open (out).
éclosion [eklozjɔ̃] *nf* blossoming.
écluse [eklyz] *nf* lock.
éclusier [eklyzje] *nm* lock keeper.
éco- [eko] *préfixe* eco-.
écœurant, e [ekœʀɑ̃, -ɑ̃t] *adj* sickening; (*gâteau etc*) sickly.
écœurement [ekœʀmɑ̃] *nm* disgust.
écœurer [ekœʀe] *vt*: ~ **qn** to make sb feel sick; (*fig: démoraliser*) to disgust sb.
école [ekɔl] *nf* school; **aller à l'**~ to go to school; **faire** ~ to collect a following; **les grandes** ~**s** *prestige university-level colleges with competitive entrance examinations*; ~ **maternelle** nursery school; ~ **primaire** primary (*BRIT*) *ou* grade (*US*) school; ~ **secondaire** secondary (*BRIT*) *ou* high (*US*) school; ~ **privée/publique/élementaire** private/state/elementary school; ~ **de dessin/danse/musique** art/dancing/music school; ~ **hôtelière** catering college; ~ **normale (d'instituteurs) (ENI)** *primary school teachers' training college*; ~ **normale supérieure (ENS)** *grande école for training secondary school teachers*; ~ **de secrétariat** secretarial college.

Nursery school (**l'école maternelle**) *is publicly funded in France and, though not compulsory, is attended by most children between the ages of two and six. Statutory education begins with primary school* (**l'école primaire**) *from the age of six to ten or eleven; see also* **collège, lycée**.

écolier, ière [ekɔlje, -jɛʀ] *nm/f* schoolboy/girl.
écolo [ekɔlo] *nm/f* (*fam*) ecologist ♦ *adj* ecological.
écologie [ekɔlɔʒi] *nf* ecology; (*sujet scolaire*) environmental studies *pl*.
écologique [ekɔlɔʒik] *adj* ecological; environmental.
écologiste [ekɔlɔʒist(ə)] *nm/f* ecologist; environmentalist.
éconduire [ekɔ̃dɥiʀ] *vt* to dismiss.
économat [ekɔnɔma] *nm* (*fonction*) bursarship (*BRIT*), treasurership (*US*); (*bureau*) bursar's office (*BRIT*), treasury (*US*).
économe [ekɔnɔm] *adj* thrifty ♦ *nm/f* (*de lycée etc*) bursar (*BRIT*), treasurer (*US*).
économétrie [ekɔnɔmetʀi] *nf* econometrics *sg*.
économie [ekɔnɔmi] *nf* (*vertu*) economy,

thrift; (*gain: d'argent, de temps etc*) saving; (*science*) economics *sg*; (*situation économique*) economy; ~**s** *nfpl* (*pécule*) savings; **une** ~ **de temps/d'argent** a saving in time/of money; ~ **dirigée** planned economy; ~ **de marché** market economy.
économique [ekɔnɔmik] *adj* (*avantageux*) economical; (*ÉCON*) economic.
économiquement [ekɔnɔmikmɑ̃] *adv* economically; **les** ~ **faibles** (*ADMIN*) the low-paid, people on low incomes.
économiser [ekɔnɔmize] *vt, vi* to save.
économiste [ekɔnɔmist(ə)] *nm/f* economist.
écoper [ekɔpe] *vi* to bale out; (*fig*) to cop it; ~ (**de**) *vt* to get.
écorce [ekɔʀs(ə)] *nf* bark; (*de fruit*) peel.
écorcer [ekɔʀse] *vt* to bark.
écorché, e [ekɔʀʃe] *adj*: ~ **vif** flayed alive ♦ *nm* cut-away drawing.
écorcher [ekɔʀʃe] *vt* (*animal*) to skin; (*égratigner*) to graze; ~ **une langue** to speak a language brokenly; **s'**~ **le genou** *etc* to scrape *ou* graze one's knee *etc*.
écorchure [ekɔʀʃyʀ] *nf* graze.
écorner [ekɔʀne] *vt* (*taureau*) to dehorn; (*livre*) to make dog-eared.
écossais, e [ekɔsɛ, -ɛz] *adj* (*lacs, tempérament*) Scottish, Scots; (*whisky, confiture*) Scotch; (*écharpe, tissu*) tartan ♦ *nm* (*LING*) Scots; (*: gaélique*) Gaelic; (*tissu*) tartan (cloth) ♦ *nm/f*: É~, e Scot, Scotsman/woman; **les É**~ the Scots.
écosser [ekɔse] *vt* to shell.
écosystème [ekɔsistɛm] *nm* ecosystem.
écot [eko] *nm*: **payer son** ~ to pay one's share.
écoulement [ekulmɑ̃] *nm* (*de faux billets*) circulation; (*de stock*) selling.
écouler [ekule] *vt* to dispose of; **s'**~ *vi* (*eau*) to flow (out); (*foule*) to drift away; (*jours, temps*) to pass (by).
écourter [ekuʀte] *vt* to curtail, cut short.
écoute [ekut] *nf* (*NAVIG: cordage*) sheet; (*RADIO, TV*): **temps/heure d'**~ (listening *ou* viewing) time/ hour; **heure de grande** ~ peak listening *ou* viewing time; **prendre l'**~ to tune in; **rester à l'**~ (**de**) to stay listening (to) *ou* tuned in (to); ~**s téléphoniques** phone tapping *sg*.
écouter [ekute] *vt* to listen to.
écouteur [ekutœʀ] *nm* (*TÉL*) (additional) earpiece; ~**s** *nmpl* (*RADIO*) headphones, headset *sg*.
écoutille [ekutij] *nf* hatch.
écr. *abr* = **écrire**.
écrabouiller [ekʀabuje] *vt* to squash, crush.
écran [ekʀɑ̃] *nm* screen; (*INFORM*) VDU, screen; ~ **de fumée/d'eau** curtain of smoke/water; **porter à l'**~ (*CINÉ*) to adapt for the screen; **le petit** ~ television, the small screen.
écrasant, e [ekʀazɑ̃, -ɑ̃t] *adj* overwhelming.
écraser [ekʀaze] *vt* to crush; (*piéton*) to run

over; (*INFORM*) to overwrite; **se faire ~** to be run over; **écrase(-toi)!** shut up!; **s'~ (au sol)** to crash; **s'~ contre** to crash into.

écrémer [ekʀeme] *vt* to skim.

écrevisse [ekʀəvis] *nf* crayfish *inv*.

écrier [ekʀije]: **s'~** *vi* to exclaim.

écrin [ekʀɛ̃] *nm* case, box.

écrire [ekʀiʀ] *vt, vi* to write ♦ *vi*: **ça s'écrit comment?** how is it spelt?; **~ à qn que** to write and tell sb that; **s'~** to write to one another.

écrit, e [ekʀi, -it] *pp de* **écrire** ♦ *adj*: **bien/mal ~** well/badly written ♦ *nm* document; (*examen*) written paper; **par ~** in writing.

écriteau, x [ekʀito] *nm* notice, sign.

écritoire [ekʀitwaʀ] *nf* writing case.

écriture [ekʀityʀ] *nf* writing; (*COMM*) entry; **~s** *nfpl* (*COMM*) accounts, books; **l'É~ (sainte), les É~s** the Scriptures.

écrivain [ekʀivɛ̃] *nm* writer.

écrivais [ekʀivɛ] *etc vb voir* **écrire**.

écrou [ekʀu] *nm* nut.

écrouer [ekʀue] *vt* to imprison; (*provisoirement*) to remand in custody.

écroulé, e [ekʀule] *adj* (*de fatigue*) exhausted; (*par un malheur*) overwhelmed; **~ (de rire)** in stitches.

écroulement [ekʀulmɑ̃] *nm* collapse.

écrouler [ekʀule]: **s'~** *vi* to collapse.

écru, e [ekʀy] *adj* (*toile*) raw, unbleached; (*couleur*) off-white, écru.

écu [eky] *nm* (*bouclier*) shield; (*monnaie: ancienne*) crown; (*: de la CEE*) ecu.

écueil [ekœj] *nm* reef; (*fig*) pitfall; stumbling block.

écuelle [ekɥɛl] *nf* bowl.

éculé, e [ekyle] *adj* (*chaussure*) down-at-heel; (*fig: péj*) hackneyed.

écume [ekym] *nf* foam; (*CULIN*) scum; **~ de mer** meerschaum.

écumer [ekyme] *vt* (*CULIN*) to skim; (*fig*) to plunder ♦ *vi* (*mer*) to foam; (*fig*) to boil with rage.

écumoire [ekymwaʀ] *nf* skimmer.

écureuil [ekyʀœj] *nm* squirrel.

écurie [ekyʀi] *nf* stable.

écusson [ekysɔ̃] *nm* badge.

écuyer, ère [ekɥije, -ɛʀ] *nm/f* rider.

eczéma [egzema] *nm* eczema.

éd. *abr* = **édition**.

édam [edam] *nm* (*fromage*) edam.

edelweiss [edɛlvajs] *nm inv* edelweiss.

éden [edɛn] *nm* Eden.

édenté, e [edɑ̃te] *adj* toothless.

EDF *sigle f* (= *Électricité de France*) *national electricity company*.

édifiant, e [edifjɑ̃, -ɑ̃t] *adj* edifying.

édification [edifikasjɔ̃] *nf* (*d'un bâtiment*) building, erection.

édifice [edifis] *nm* building, edifice.

édifier [edifje] *vt* to build, erect; (*fig*) to edify.

édiles [edil] *nmpl* city fathers.

Édimbourg [edɛ̃buʀ] *n* Edinburgh.

édit [edi] *nm* edict.

édit. *abr* = **éditeur**.

éditer [edite] *vt* (*publier*) to publish; (*: disque*) to produce; (*préparer: texte, INFORM*) to edit.

éditeur, trice [editœʀ, -tʀis] *nm/f* publisher; editor.

édition [edisjɔ̃] *nf* editing *no pl*; (*série d'exemplaires*) edition; (*industrie du livre*): **l'~** publishing; **~ sur écran** (*INFORM*) screen editing.

édito [edito] *nm* (*fam: éditorial*) editorial, leader.

éditorial, aux [editɔʀjal, -o] *nm* editorial, leader.

éditorialiste [editɔʀjalist(ə)] *nm/f* editorial *ou* leader writer.

édredon [edʀədɔ̃] *nm* eiderdown, comforter (*US*).

éducateur, trice [edykatœʀ, -tʀis] *nm/f* teacher; **~ spécialisé** specialist teacher.

éducatif, ive [edykatif, -iv] *adj* educational.

éducation [edykasjɔ̃] *nf* education; (*familiale*) upbringing; (*manières*) (good) manners *pl*; **bonne/mauvaise ~** good/bad upbringing; **sans ~** bad-mannered, ill-bred; **l'É~ (nationale)** ≈ the Department for Education; **~ permanente** continuing education; **~ physique** physical education.

édulcorer [edylkɔʀe] *vt* to sweeten; (*fig*) to tone down.

éduquer [edyke] *vt* to educate; (*élever*) to bring up; (*faculté*) to train; **bien/mal éduqué** well/badly brought up.

EEG *sigle m* (= *électroencéphalogramme*) EEG.

effacé, e [efase] *adj* (*fig*) retiring, unassuming.

effacer [efase] *vt* to erase, rub out; (*bande magnétique*) to erase; (*INFORM: fichier, fiche*) to delete, erase; **s'~** *vi* (*inscription etc*) to wear off; (*pour laisser passer*) to step aside; **~ le ventre** to pull one's stomach in.

effarant, e [efaʀɑ̃, -ɑ̃t] *adj* alarming.

effaré, e [efaʀe] *adj* alarmed.

effarement [efaʀmɑ̃] *nm* alarm.

effarer [efaʀe] *vt* to alarm.

effarouchement [efaʀuʃmɑ̃] *nm* alarm.

effaroucher [efaʀuʃe] *vt* to frighten *ou* scare away; (*personne*) to alarm.

effectif, ive [efɛktif, -iv] *adj* real; effective ♦ *nm* (*MIL*) strength; (*SCOL*) total number of pupils, size; **~s** numbers, strength *sg*; (*COMM*) manpower *sg*; **réduire l'~ de** to downsize.

effectivement [efɛktivmɑ̃] *adv* effectively; (*réellement*) actually, really; (*en effet*) indeed.

effectuer [efɛktɥe] *vt* (*opération, mission*) to carry out; (*déplacement, trajet*) to make, complete; (*mouvement*) to execute, make; **s'~** to be carried out.

efféminé, e [efemine] *adj* effeminate.

effervescence [efɛʀvesɑ̃s] *nf* (*fig*): **en ~** in a turmoil.

effervescent, e [efɛʀvesɑ̃, -ɑ̃t] *adj* (*cachet, boisson*) effervescent; (*fig*) agitated, in a turmoil.

effet [efɛ] *nm* (*résultat, artifice*) effect; (*impression*) impression; (*COMM*) bill; (*JUR: d'une loi, d'un jugement*): **avec ~ rétroactif** applied retrospectively; **~s** *nmpl* (*vêtements etc*) things; **~ de style/couleur/lumière** stylistic/colour/lighting effect; **~s de voix** dramatic effects with one's voice; **faire de l'~** (*médicament, menace*) to have an effect, be effective; **sous l'~ de** under the effect of; **donner de l'~ à une balle** (*TENNIS*) to put some spin on a ball; **à cet ~** to that end; **en ~** *adv* indeed; **~ (de commerce)** bill of exchange; **~ de serre** greenhouse effect; **~s spéciaux** (*CINÉ*) special effects.

effeuiller [efœje] *vt* to remove the leaves (*ou* petals) from.

efficace [efikas] *adj* (*personne*) efficient; (*action, médicament*) effective.

efficacité [efikasite] *nf* efficiency; effectiveness.

effigie [efiʒi] *nf* effigy; **brûler qn en ~** to burn an effigy of sb.

effilé, e [efile] *adj* slender; (*pointe*) sharp; (*carrosserie*) streamlined.

effiler [efile] *vt* (*cheveux*) to thin (out); (*tissu*) to fray.

effilocher [efilɔʃe]: **s'~** *vi* to fray.

efflanqué, e [eflɑ̃ke] *adj* emaciated.

effleurement [eflœrmɑ̃] *nm*: **touche à ~** touch-sensitive control *ou* key.

effleurer [eflœre] *vt* to brush (against); (*sujet*) to touch upon; (*suj: idée, pensée*): **~ qn** to cross sb's mind.

effluves [eflyv] *nmpl* exhalation(s).

effondré, e [efɔ̃dre] *adj* (*abattu: par un malheur, échec*) overwhelmed.

effondrement [efɔ̃drəmɑ̃] *nm* collapse.

effondrer [efɔ̃dre]: **s'~** *vi* to collapse.

efforcer [efɔrse]: **s'~ de** *vt*: **s'~ de faire** to try hard to do.

effort [efɔr] *nm* effort; **faire un ~** to make an effort; **faire tous ses ~s** to try one's hardest; **faire l'~ de ...** to make the effort to ...; **sans ~** *adj* effortless ♦ *adv* effortlessly; **~ de mémoire** attempt to remember; **~ de volonté** effort of will.

effraction [efraksjɔ̃] *nf* breaking-in; **s'introduire par ~ dans** to break into.

effrangé, e [efrɑ̃ʒe] *adj* fringed; (*effiloché*) frayed.

effrayant, e [efrɛjɑ̃, -ɑ̃t] *adj* frightening, fearsome; (*sens affaibli*) dreadful.

effrayer [efreje] *vt* to frighten, scare; (*rebuter*) to put off; **s'~ (de)** to be frightened *ou* scared (by).

effréné, e [efrene] *adj* wild.

effritement [efritmɑ̃] *nm* crumbling; erosion; slackening off.

effriter [efrite]: **s'~** *vi* to crumble; (*monnaie*) to be eroded; (*valeurs*) to slacken off.

effroi [efrwa] *nm* terror, dread *no pl*.

effronté, e [efrɔ̃te] *adj* insolent.

effrontément [efrɔ̃temɑ̃] *adv* insolently.

effronterie [efrɔ̃tri] *nf* insolence.

effroyable [efrwajabl(ə)] *adj* horrifying, appalling.

effusion [efyzjɔ̃] *nf* effusion; **sans ~ de sang** without bloodshed.

égailler [egaje]: **s'~** *vi* to scatter, disperse.

égal, e, aux [egal, -o] *adj* (*identique, ayant les mêmes droits*) equal; (*plan: surface*) even, level; (*constant: vitesse*) steady; (*équitable*) even ♦ *nm/f* equal; **être ~ à** (*prix, nombre*) to be equal to; **ça lui est ~** it's all the same to him, it doesn't matter to him, he doesn't mind; **c'est ~, ...** all the same, ...; **sans ~** matchless, unequalled; **à l'~ de** (*comme*) just like; **d'~ à ~** as equals.

également [egalmɑ̃] *adv* equally; evenly; steadily; (*aussi*) too, as well.

égaler [egale] *vt* to equal.

égalisateur, trice [egalizatœr, -tris] *adj* (*SPORT*): **but ~** equalizing goal, equalizer.

égalisation [egalizasjɔ̃] *nf* (*SPORT*) equalization.

égaliser [egalize] *vt* (*sol, salaires*) to level (out); (*chances*) to equalize ♦ *vi* (*SPORT*) to equalize.

égalitaire [egaliter] *adj* egalitarian.

égalitarisme [egalitarism(ə)] *nm* egalitarianism.

égalité [egalite] *nf* equality; evenness; steadiness; (*MATH*) identity; **être à ~ (de points)** to be level; **~ de droits** equality of rights; **~ d'humeur** evenness of temper.

égard [egar] *nm*: **~s** *nmpl* consideration *sg*; **à cet ~** in this respect; **à certains ~s/tous ~s** in certain respects/all respects; **eu ~ à** in view of; **par ~ pour** out of consideration for; **sans ~ pour** without regard for; **à l'~ de** *prép* towards; (*en ce qui concerne*) concerning, as regards.

égaré, e [egare] *adj* lost.

égarement [egarmɑ̃] *nm* distraction; aberration.

égarer [egare] *vt* (*objet*) to mislay; (*moralement*) to lead astray; **s'~** *vi* to get lost, lose one's way; (*objet*) to go astray; (*fig: dans une discussion*) to wander.

égayer [egeje] *vt* (*personne*) to amuse; (: *remonter*) to cheer up; (*récit, endroit*) to brighten up, liven up.

Égée [eʒe] *adj*: **la mer ~** the Aegean (Sea).

égéen, ne [eʒeɛ̃, -ɛn] *adj* Aegean.

égérie [eʒeri] *nf*: **l'~ de qn/qch** the brains behind sb/sth.

égide [eʒid] *nf*: **sous l'~ de** under the aegis of.

églantier [eglɑ̃tje] *nm* wild *ou* dog rose(-bush).

églantine [eglɑ̃tin] *nf* wild *ou* dog rose.

églefin [egləfɛ̃] *nm* haddock.

église [egliz] *nf* church.
égocentrique [egɔsɑ̃tʀik] *adj* egocentric, self-centred.
égocentrisme [egɔsɑ̃tʀism(ə)] *nm* egocentricity.
égoïne [egɔin] *nf* handsaw.
égoïsme [egɔism(ə)] *nm* selfishness, egoism.
égoïste [egɔist(ə)] *adj* selfish, egoistic ♦ *nm/f* egoist.
égoïstement [egɔistəmɑ̃] *adv* selfishly.
égorger [egɔʀʒe] *vt* to cut the throat of.
égosiller [egozije]: **s'~** *vi* to shout o.s. hoarse.
égotisme [egɔtism(ə)] *nm* egotism, egoism.
égout [egu] *nm* sewer; **eaux d'~** sewage.
égoutier [egutje] *nm* sewer worker.
égoutter [egute] *vt* (*linge*) to wring out; (*vaisselle, fromage*) to drain ♦ *vi*, **s'~** *vi* to drip.
égouttoir [egutwaʀ] *nm* draining board; (*mobile*) draining rack.
égratigner [egʀatiɲe] *vt* to scratch; **s'~** to scratch o.s.
égratignure [egʀatiɲyʀ] *nf* scratch.
égrener [egʀəne] *vt*: **~ une grappe, ~ des raisins** to pick grapes off a bunch; **s'~** *vi* (*fig: heures etc*) to pass by; (*: notes*) to chime out.
égrillard, e [egʀijaʀ, -aʀd(ə)] *adj* ribald, bawdy.
Égypte [eʒipt] *nf*: **l'~** Egypt.
égyptien, ne [eʒipsjɛ̃, -ɛn] *adj* Egyptian ♦ *nm/f*: **E~, ne** Egyptian.
égyptologue [eʒiptɔlɔg] *nm/f* Egyptologist.
eh [e] *excl* hey!; **~ bien** well.
éhonté, e [eɔ̃te] *adj* shameless, brazen (*BRIT*).
éjaculation [eʒakylasjɔ̃] *nf* ejaculation.
éjaculer [eʒakyle] *vi* to ejaculate.
éjectable [eʒɛktabl(ə)] *adj*: **siège ~** ejector seat.
éjecter [eʒɛkte] *vt* (*TECH*) to eject; (*fam*) to kick *ou* chuck out.
éjection [eʒɛksjɔ̃] *nf* ejection.
élaboration [elabɔʀasjɔ̃] *nf* elaboration.
élaboré, e [elabɔʀe] *adj* (*complexe*) elaborate.
élaborer [elabɔʀe] *vt* to elaborate; (*projet, stratégie*) to work out; (*rapport*) to draft.
élagage [elagaʒ] *nm* pruning.
élaguer [elage] *vt* to prune.
élan [elɑ̃] *nm* (*ZOOL*) elk, moose; (*SPORT: avant le saut*) run up; (*de véhicule ou objet en mouvement*) momentum; (*fig: de tendresse etc*) surge; **prendre son ~/de l'~** to take a run up/gather speed; **perdre son ~** to lose one's momentum.
élancé, e [elɑ̃se] *adj* slender.
élancement [elɑ̃smɑ̃] *nm* shooting pain.
élancer [elɑ̃se]: **s'~** *vi* to dash, hurl o.s.; (*fig: arbre, clocher*) to soar (upwards).
élargir [elaʀʒiʀ] *vt* to widen; (*vêtement*) to let out; (*JUR*) to release; **s'~** *vi* to widen; (*vêtement*) to stretch.
élargissement [elaʀʒismɑ̃] *nm* widening; letting out.
élasticité [elastisite] *nf* (*aussi ÉCON*) elasticity;

~ de l'offre/de la demande flexibility of supply/demand.
élastique [elastik] *adj* elastic ♦ *nm* (*de bureau*) rubber band; (*pour la couture*) elastic *no pl*.
élastomère [elastɔmɛʀ] *nm* elastomer.
Elbe [ɛlb] *nf*: **l'île d'~** (the Island of) Elba; (*fleuve*): **l'~** the Elbe.
eldorado [ɛldɔʀado] *nm* Eldorado.
électeur, trice [elɛktœʀ, -tʀis] *nm/f* elector, voter.
électif, ive [elɛktif, -iv] *adj* elective.
élection [elɛksjɔ̃] *nf* election; **~s** *nfpl* (*POL*) election(s); **sa terre/patrie d'~** one's chosen land/country, the land/country of one's choice; **~ partielle** ≈ by-election; **~s législatives/présidentielles** general/presidential election *sg*.

> **Élections législatives** *are held in France every five years to elect* **députés** *to the* **Assemblée nationale**. *The president is elected in the* **élection présidentielle**, *held every seven years. Elections are by universal direct suffrage and two rounds of voting take place. Elections take place on a Sunday.*

électoral, e, aux [elɛktɔʀal, -o] *adj* electoral, election *cpd*.
électoralisme [elɛktɔʀalism(ə)] *nm* electioneering.
électorat [elɛktɔʀa] *nm* electorate.
électricien, ne [elɛktʀisjɛ̃, -ɛn] *nm/f* electrician.
électricité [elɛktʀisite] *nf* electricity; **allumer/éteindre l'~** to put on/off the light; **~ statique** static electricity.
électrification [elɛktʀifikasjɔ̃] *nf* (*RAIL*) electrification; (*d'un village etc*) laying on of electricity.
électrifier [elɛktʀifje] *vt* (*RAIL*) to electrify.
électrique [elɛktʀik] *adj* electric(al).
électriser [elɛktʀize] *vt* to electrify.
électro... [elɛktʀo] *préfixe* electro....
électro-aimant [elɛktʀoɛmɑ̃] *nm* electromagnet.
électrocardiogramme [elɛktʀokaʀdjɔgʀam] *nm* electrocardiogram.
électrocardiographe [elɛktʀokaʀdjɔgʀaf] *nm* electrocardiograph.
électrochoc [elɛktʀoʃɔk] *nm* electric shock treatment.
électrocuter [elɛktʀokyte] *vt* to electrocute.
électrocution [elɛktʀokysjɔ̃] *nf* electrocution.
électrode [elɛktʀɔd] *nf* electrode.
électro-encéphalogramme [elɛktʀoɑ̃sefalogʀam] *nm* electroencephalogram.
électrogène [elɛktʀoʒɛn] *adj*: **groupe ~** generating set.
électrolyse [elɛktʀoliz] *nf* electrolysis *sg*.
électromagnétique [elɛktʀomaɲetik] *adj* electromagnetic.
électroménager [elɛktʀomenaʒe] *adj*: **appa-**

reils ~s domestic (electrical) appliances ♦ *nm:* l'~ household appliances.
électron [elɛktRɔ̃] *nm* electron.
électronicien, ne [elɛktRɔnisjɛ̃, -ɛn] *nm/f* electronics (*BRIT*) *ou* electrical (*US*) engineer.
électronique [elɛktRɔnik] *adj* electronic ♦ *nf* (*science*) electronics *sg*.
électronucléaire [elɛktRɔnykleɛR] *adj* nuclear power *cpd* ♦ *nm:* l'~ nuclear power.
électrophone [elɛktRɔfɔn] *nm* record player.
électrostatique [elɛktRɔstatik] *adj* electrostatic ♦ *nf* electrostatics *sg*.
élégamment [elegamɑ̃] *adv* elegantly.
élégance [elegɑ̃s] *nf* elegance.
élégant, e [elegɑ̃, -ɑ̃t] *adj* elegant; (*solution*) neat, elegant; (*attitude, procédé*) courteous, civilized.
élément [elemɑ̃] *nm* element; (*pièce*) component, part; ~s *nmpl* (*aussi: rudiments*) elements.
élémentaire [elemɑ̃tɛR] *adj* elementary; (*CHIMIE*) elemental.
éléphant [elefɑ̃] *nm* elephant; ~ **de mer** elephant seal.
éléphanteau, x [elefɑ̃to] *nm* baby elephant.
éléphantesque [elefɑ̃tɛsk(ə)] *adj* elephantine.
élevage [ɛlvaʒ] *nm* breeding; (*de bovins*) cattle breeding *ou* rearing; (*ferme*) cattle farm.
élévateur [elevatœR] *nm* elevator.
élévation [elevasjɔ̃] *nf* (*gén*) elevation; (*voir élever*) raising; (*voir s'élever*) rise.
élevé, e [ɛlve] *adj* (*prix, sommet*) high; (*fig: noble*) elevated; **bien/mal** ~ well-/ill-mannered.
élève [elɛv] *nm/f* pupil; ~ **infirmière** student nurse.
élever [ɛlve] *vt* (*enfant*) to bring up, raise; (*bétail, volaille*) to breed; (*abeilles*) to keep; (*hausser: taux, niveau*) to raise; (*fig: âme, esprit*) to elevate; (*édifier: monument*) to put up, erect; **s'**~ *vi* (*avion, alpiniste*) to go up; (*niveau, température, aussi: cri etc*) to rise; (*survenir: difficultés*) to arise; **s'**~ **à** (*suj: frais, dégâts*) to amount to, add up to; **s'**~ **contre** to rise up against; ~ **une protestation/critique** to raise a protest/make a criticism; ~ **la voix** to raise one's voice; ~ **qn au rang de** to raise *ou* elevate sb to the rank of; ~ **un nombre au carré/au cube** to square/cube a number.
éleveur, euse [ɛlvœR, -øz] *nm/f* stock breeder.
elfe [ɛlf(ə)] *nm* elf.
élidé, e [elide] *adj* elided.
élider [elide] *vt* to elide.
éligibilité [eliʒibilite] *nf* eligibility.
éligible [eliʒibl(ə)] *adj* eligible.
élimé, e [elime] *adj* worn (thin), threadbare.
élimination [eliminasjɔ̃] *nf* elimination.
éliminatoire [eliminatwaR] *adj* eliminatory; (*SPORT*) disqualifying ♦ *nf* (*SPORT*) heat.
éliminer [elimine] *vt* to eliminate.
élire [eliR] *vt* to elect; ~ **domicile à** to take up

residence in *ou* at.
élision [elizjɔ̃] *nf* elision.
élite [elit] *nf* elite; **tireur d'**~ crack rifleman; **chercheur d'**~ top-notch researcher.
élitisme [elitism(ə)] *nm* elitism.
élitiste [elitist(ə)] *adj* elitist.
élixir [eliksiR] *nm* elixir.
elle [ɛl] *pron* (*sujet*) she; (: *chose*) it; (*complément*) her; it; ~**s** (*sujet*) they; (*complément*) them; ~**-même** herself; itself; ~**s-mêmes** themselves; *voir* **il**.
ellipse [elips(ə)] *nf* ellipse; (*LING*) ellipsis *sg*.
elliptique [eliptik] *adj* elliptical.
élocution [elɔkysjɔ̃] *nf* delivery; **défaut d'**~ speech impediment.
éloge [elɔʒ] *nm* praise (*gén no pl*); **faire l'**~ **de** to praise.
élogieusement [elɔʒjøzmɑ̃] *adv* very favourably.
élogieux, euse [elɔʒjø, -øz] *adj* laudatory, full of praise.
éloigné, e [elwaɲe] *adj* distant, far-off.
éloignement [elwaɲmɑ̃] *nm* removal; putting off; estrangement; (*fig: distance*) distance.
éloigner [elwaɲe] *vt* (*objet*): ~ **qch (de)** to move *ou* take sth away (from); (*personne*): ~ **qn (de)** to take sb away *ou* remove sb (from); (*échéance*) to put off, postpone; (*soupçons, danger*) to ward off; **s'**~ **(de)** (*personne*) to go away (from); (*véhicule*) to move away (from); (*affectivement*) to become estranged (from).
élongation [elɔ̃gasjɔ̃] *nf* strained muscle.
éloquence [elɔkɑ̃s] *nf* eloquence.
éloquent, e [elɔkɑ̃, -ɑ̃t] *adj* eloquent.
élu, e [ely] *pp de* **élire** ♦ *nm/f* (*POL*) elected representative.
élucider [elyside] *vt* to elucidate.
élucubrations [elykybRasjɔ̃] *nf/pl* wild imaginings.
éluder [elyde] *vt* to evade.
élus [ely] *etc vb voir* **élire**.
élusif, ive [elyzif, -iv] *adj* elusive.
Élysée [elize] *nm:* (**le palais de**) **l'**~ the Élysée palace; **les Champs** ~**s** the Champs Élysées.

The **palais de l'Élysée**, *situated in the heart of Paris off the Champs-Élysées, is the official residence of the French President. Built in the eighteenth century, it has been used in its present role since 1876.* **L'Élysée** *is frequently used to mean the presidency itself.*

émacié, e [emasje] *adj* emaciated.
émail, aux [emaj, -o] *nm* enamel.
émaillé, e [emaje] *adj* enamelled; (*fig*): ~ **de** dotted with.
émailler [emaje] *vt* to enamel.
émanation [emanasjɔ̃] *nf* emanation; **être l'**~ **de** to emanate from; to proceed from.
émancipation [emɑ̃sipasjɔ̃] *nf* emancipation.
émancipé, e [emɑ̃sipe] *adj* emancipated.

émanciper [emãsipe] vt to emancipate; **s'~** (fig) to become emancipated ou liberated.

émaner [emane]: **~ de** vt to emanate from; (ADMIN) to proceed from.

émarger [emaʀʒe] vt to sign; **~ de 1 000 F à un budget** to receive 1000 F out of a budget.

émasculer [emaskyle] vt to emasculate.

emballage [ãbalaʒ] nm wrapping; packing; (papier) wrapping; (carton) packaging.

emballer [ãbale] vt to wrap (up); (dans un carton) to pack (up); (fig: fam) to thrill (to bits); **s'~** vi (moteur) to race; (cheval) to bolt; (fig: personne) to get carried away.

emballeur, euse [ãbalœʀ, -øz] nm/f packer.

embarcadère [ãbaʀkadɛʀ] nm landing stage (BRIT), pier.

embarcation [ãbaʀkasjɔ̃] nf (small) boat, (small) craft inv.

embardée [ãbaʀde] nf swerve; **faire une ~** to swerve.

embargo [ãbaʀgo] nm embargo; **mettre l'~ sur** to put an embargo on, embargo.

embarquement [ãbaʀkəmã] nm embarkation; loading; boarding.

embarquer [ãbaʀke] vt (personne) to embark; (marchandise) to load; (fam) to cart off; (: arrêter) to nick ♦ vi (passager) to board; (NAVIG) to ship water; **s'~** vi to board; **s'~ dans** (affaire, aventure) to embark upon.

embarras [ãbaʀa] nm (obstacle) hindrance; (confusion) embarrassment; (ennuis): **être dans l'~** to be in a predicament ou an awkward position; (gêne financière) to be in difficulties; **~ gastrique** stomach upset.

embarrassant, e [ãbaʀasã, -ãt] adj cumbersome; embarrassing; awkward.

embarrassé, e [ãbaʀase] adj (encombré) encumbered; (gêné) embarrassed; (explications etc) awkward.

embarrasser [ãbaʀase] vt (encombrer) to clutter (up); (gêner) to hinder, hamper; (fig) to cause embarrassment to; (: put in an awkward position; **s'~ de** to burden o.s. with.

embauche [ãboʃ] nf hiring; **bureau d'~** labour office.

embaucher [ãboʃe] vt to take on, hire; **s'~ comme** to get (o.s.) a job as.

embauchoir [ãboʃwaʀ] nm shoetree.

embaumer [ãbome] vt to embalm; (parfumer) to fill with its fragrance; **~ la lavande** to be fragrant with (the scent of) lavender.

embellie [ãbeli] nf bright spell, brighter period.

embellir [ãbeliʀ] vt to make more attractive; (une histoire) to embellish ♦ vi to grow lovelier ou more attractive.

embellissement [ãbelismã] nm embellishment.

embêtant, e [ãbɛtã, -ãt] adj annoying.

embêtement [ãbɛtmã] nm problem, difficulty; **~s** nmpl trouble sg.

embêter [ãbete] vt to bother; **s'~** vi (s'ennuyer)

to be bored; **il ne s'embête pas!** (ironique) he does all right for himself!

emblée [ãble]: **d'~** adv straightaway.

emblème [ãblɛm] nm emblem.

embobiner [ãbɔbine] vt (enjôler): **~ qn** to get round sb.

emboîtable [ãbwatabl(ə)] adj interlocking.

emboîter [ãbwate] vt to fit together; **s'~ dans** to fit into; **s'~ (l'un dans l'autre)** to fit together; **~ le pas à qn** to follow in sb's footsteps.

embolie [ãbɔli] nf embolism.

embonpoint [ãbɔ̃pwɛ̃] nm stoutness (BRIT), corpulence; **prendre de l'~** to grow stout (BRIT) ou corpulent.

embouché, e [ãbuʃe] adj: **mal ~** foulmouthed.

embouchure [ãbuʃyʀ] nf (GÉO) mouth; (MUS) mouthpiece.

embourber [ãbuʀbe]: **s'~** vi to get stuck in the mud; (fig): **s'~ dans** to sink into.

embourgeoiser [ãbuʀʒwaze]: **s'~** vi to adopt a middle-class outlook.

embout [ãbu] nm (de canne) tip; (de tuyau) nozzle.

embouteillage [ãbutɛjaʒ] nm traffic jam, (traffic) holdup (BRIT).

embouteiller [ãbuteje] vt (suj: véhicules etc) to block.

emboutir [ãbutiʀ] vt (TECH) to stamp; (heurter) to crash into, ram.

embranchement [ãbʀãʃmã] nm (routier) junction; (classification) branch.

embrancher [ãbʀãʃe] vt (tuyaux) to join; **~ qch sur** to join sth to.

embraser [ãbʀaze]: **s'~** vi to flare up.

embrassade [ãbʀasad] nf (gén pl) hugging and kissing no pl.

embrasse [ãbʀas] nf (de rideau) tie-back, loop.

embrasser [ãbʀase] vt to kiss; (sujet, période) to embrace, encompass; (carrière) to embark on; (métier) to go in for, take up; **~ du regard** to take in (with eyes); **s'~** to kiss (each other).

embrasure [ãbʀazyʀ] nf: **dans l'~ de la porte** in the door(way).

embrayage [ãbʀɛjaʒ] nm clutch.

embrayer [ãbʀeje] vi (AUTO) to let in the clutch ♦ vt (fig: affaire) to set in motion; **~ sur qch** to begin on sth.

embrigader [ãbʀigade] vt to recruit.

embrocher [ãbʀɔʃe] vt to (put on a) spit (ou skewer).

embrouillamini [ãbʀujamini] nm (fam) muddle.

embrouillé, e [ãbʀuje] adj (affaire) confused, muddled.

embrouiller [ãbʀuje] vt (fils) to tangle (up); (fiches, idées, personne) to muddle up; **s'~** vi to get in a muddle.

embroussaillé, e [ãbʀusaje] adj overgrown, scrubby; (cheveux) bushy, shaggy.

embruns [ɑ̃bRœ̃] *nmpl* sea spray *sg*.
embryologie [ɑ̃bRijɔlɔʒi] *nf* embryology.
embryon [ɑ̃bRijɔ̃] *nm* embryo.
embryonnaire [ɑ̃bRijɔnɛR] *adj* embryonic.
embûches [ɑ̃byʃ] *nfpl* pitfalls, traps.
embué, e [ɑ̃bɥe] *adj* misted up; **yeux ~s de larmes** eyes misty with tears.
embuscade [ɑ̃byskad] *nf* ambush; **tendre une ~ à** to lay an ambush for.
embusqué, e [ɑ̃byske] *adj* in ambush ♦ *nm* (*péj*) shirker, skiver (*BRIT*).
embusquer [ɑ̃byske] **s'~** *vi* to take up position (for an ambush).
éméché, e [emeʃe] *adj* tipsy, merry.
émeraude [ɛmRod] *nf* emerald ♦ *adj inv* emerald-green.
émergence [emɛRʒɑ̃s] *nf* (*fig*) emergence.
émerger [emɛRʒe] *vi* to emerge; (*faire saillie, aussi fig*) to stand out.
émeri [ɛmRi] *nm*: **toile** *ou* **papier ~** emery paper.
émérite [emeRit] *adj* highly skilled.
émerveillement [emɛRvɛjmɑ̃] *nm* wonderment.
émerveiller [emɛRveje] *vt* to fill with wonder; **s'~ de** to marvel at.
émet [emɛ] *etc vb voir* **émettre**.
émétique [emetik] *nm* emetic.
émetteur, trice [emetœR, -tRis] *adj* transmitting; (*poste*) ~ transmitter.
émetteur-récepteur, *pl* **émetteurs-récepteurs** [emetœRResɛptœR] *nm* transceiver.
émettre [emɛtR(ə)] *vt* (*son, lumière*) to give out, emit; (*message etc: RADIO*) to transmit; (*billet, timbre, emprunt, chèque*) to issue; (*hypothèse, avis*) to voice, put forward; (*vœu*) to express ♦ *vi*: **~ sur ondes courtes** to broadcast on short wave.
émeus [emø] *etc vb voir* **émouvoir**.
émeute [emøt] *nf* riot.
émeutier, ière [emøtje, -jɛR] *nm/f* rioter.
émeuve [emœv] *etc vb voir* **émouvoir**.
émietter [emjete] *vt* (*pain, terre*) to crumble; (*fig*) to split up, disperse; **s'~** *vi* (*pain, terre*) to crumble.
émigrant, e [emigRɑ̃, -ɑ̃t] *nm/f* emigrant.
émigration [emigRɑsjɔ̃] *nf* emigration.
émigré, e [emigRe] *nm/f* expatriate.
émigrer [emigRe] *vi* to emigrate.
émincer [emɛ̃se] *vt* (*CULIN*) to slice thinly.
éminemment [eminamɑ̃] *adv* eminently.
éminence [eminɑ̃s] *nf* distinction; (*colline*) knoll, hill; **Son É~** His Eminence; **~ grise** éminence grise.
éminent, e [eminɑ̃, -ɑ̃t] *adj* distinguished.
émir [emiR] *nm* emir.
émirat [emira] *nm* emirate; **les É~s arabes unis (EAU)** the United Arab Emirates (UAE).
émis, e [emi, -iz] *pp de* **émettre**.
émissaire [emisɛR] *nm* emissary.

émission [emisjɔ̃] *nf* (*voir émettre*) emission; transmission; issue; (*RADIO, TV*) programme, broadcast.
émit [emi] *etc vb voir* **émettre**.
emmagasinage [ɑ̃magazinaʒ] *nm* storage; storing away.
emmagasiner [ɑ̃magazine] *vt* to (put into) store; (*fig*) to store up.
emmailloter [ɑ̃majɔte] *vt* to wrap up.
emmanchure [ɑ̃mɑ̃ʃyR] *nf* armhole.
emmêlement [ɑ̃mɛlmɑ̃] *nm* (*état*) tangle.
emmêler [ɑ̃mele] *vt* to tangle (up); (*fig*) to muddle up; **s'~** to get into a tangle.
emménagement [ɑ̃menaʒmɑ̃] *nm* settling in.
emménager [ɑ̃menaʒe] *vi* to move in; **~ dans** to move into.
emmener [ɑ̃mne] *vt* to take (with one); (*comme otage, capture*) to take away; **~ qn au concert** to take sb to a concert.
emment(h)al [emɛtal] *nm* (*fromage*) Emmenthal.
emmerder [ɑ̃mɛRde] (*fam!*) *vt* to bug, bother; **s'~** *vi* (*s'ennuyer*) to be bored stiff; **je t'emmerde!** to hell with you!
emmitoufler [ɑ̃mitufle] *vt* to wrap up (warmly); **s'~** to wrap (o.s.) up (warmly).
emmurer [ɑ̃myRe] *vt* to wall up, immure.
émoi [emwa] *nm* (*agitation, effervescence*) commotion; (*trouble*) agitation; **en ~** (*sens*) excited, stirred.
émollient, e [emɔljɑ̃, -ɑ̃t] *adj* (*MÉD*) emollient.
émoluments [emɔlymɑ̃] *nmpl* remuneration *sg*, fee *sg*.
émonder [emɔ̃de] *vt* (*arbre etc*) to prune; (*amande etc*) to blanch.
émotif, ive [emɔtif, -iv] *adj* emotional.
émotion [emɔsjɔ̃] *nf* emotion; **avoir des ~s** (*fig*) to get a fright; **donner des ~s à** to give a fright to; **sans ~** without emotion, coldly.
émotionnant, e [emɔsjɔnɑ̃, -ɑ̃t] *adj* upsetting.
émotionnel, le [emɔsjɔnɛl] *adj* emotional.
émotionner [emɔsjɔne] *vt* to upset.
émoulu, e [emuly] *adj*: **frais ~ de** fresh from, just out of.
émoussé, e [emuse] *adj* blunt.
émousser [emuse] *vt* to blunt; (*fig*) to dull.
émoustiller [emustije] *vt* to titillate, arouse.
émouvant, e [emuvɑ̃, -ɑ̃t] *adj* moving.
émouvoir [emuvwaR] *vt* (*troubler*) to stir, affect; (*toucher, attendrir*) to move; (*indigner*) to rouse; (*effrayer*) to disturb, worry; **s'~** *vi* to be affected; to be moved; to be roused; to be disturbed *ou* worried.
empailler [ɑ̃paje] *vt* to stuff.
empailleur, euse [ɑ̃pajœR, -øz] *nm/f* (*d'animaux*) taxidermist.
empaler [ɑ̃pale] *vt* to impale.
empaquetage [ɑ̃paktaʒ] *nm* packing, packaging.
empaqueter [ɑ̃pakte] *vt* to pack up.
emparer [ɑ̃paRe]: **s'~ de** *vt* (*objet*) to seize, grab; (*comme otage, MIL*) to seize; (*suj: peur*

etc) to take hold of.

empâter [ɑ̃pate]: **s'~** *vi* to thicken out.

empattement [ɑ̃patmɑ̃] *nm* (*AUTO*) wheel-base; (*TYPO*) serif.

empêché, e [ɑ̃peʃe] *adj* detained.

empêchement [ɑ̃pɛʃmɑ̃] *nm* (unexpected) obstacle, hitch.

empêcher [ɑ̃peʃe] *vt* to prevent; **~ qn de faire** to prevent *ou* stop sb (from) doing; **~ que qch (n')arrive/qn (ne) fasse** to prevent sth from happening/sb from doing; **il n'empêche que** nevertheless, be that as it may; **il n'a pas pu s'~ de rire** he couldn't help laughing.

empêcheur [ɑ̃peʃœʀ] *nm*: **~ de danser en rond** spoilsport, killjoy (*BRIT*).

empeigne [ɑ̃pɛɲ] *nf* upper (of shoe).

empennage [ɑ̃penaʒ] *nm* (*AVIAT*) tailplane.

empereur [ɑ̃pʀœʀ] *nm* emperor.

empesé, e [ɑ̃pəze] *adj* (*fig*) stiff, starchy.

empeser [ɑ̃pəze] *vt* to starch.

empester [ɑ̃pɛste] *vt* (*lieu*) to stink out ♦ *vi* to stink, reek; **~ le tabac/le vin** to stink *ou* reek of tobacco/wine.

empêtrer [ɑ̃petʀe] *vt*: **s'~ dans** (*fils etc, aussi fig*) to get tangled up in.

emphase [ɑ̃faz] *nf* pomposity, bombast; **avec ~** pompously.

emphatique [ɑ̃fatik] *adj* emphatic.

empiècement [ɑ̃pjɛsmɑ̃] *nm* (*COUTURE*) yoke.

empierrer [ɑ̃pjeʀe] *vt* (*route*) to metal.

empiéter [ɑ̃pjete]: **~ sur** *vt* to encroach upon.

empiffrer [ɑ̃pifʀe]: **s'~** *vi* (*péj*) to stuff o.s.

empiler [ɑ̃pile] *vt* to pile (up), stack (up); **s'~** *vi* to pile up.

empire [ɑ̃piʀ] *nm* empire; (*fig*) influence; **style E~** Empire style; **sous l'~ de** in the grip of.

empirer [ɑ̃piʀe] *vi* to worsen, deteriorate.

empirique [ɑ̃piʀik] *adj* empirical.

empirisme [ɑ̃piʀism(ə)] *nm* empiricism.

emplacement [ɑ̃plasmɑ̃] *nm* site; **sur l'~ de** on the site of.

emplâtre [ɑ̃plɑtʀ(ə)] *nm* plaster; (*fam*) twit.

emplette [ɑ̃plɛt] *nf*: **faire l'~ de** to purchase; **~s** shopping *sg*; **faire des ~s** to go shopping.

emplir [ɑ̃pliʀ] *vt* to fill; **s'~ (de)** to fill (with).

emploi [ɑ̃plwa] *nm* use; (*COMM, ÉCON*): **l'~** employment; (*poste*) job, situation; **d'~ facile** easy to use; **le plein ~** full employment; **~ du temps** timetable, schedule.

emploie [ɑ̃plwa] *etc vb voir* **employer**.

employé, e [ɑ̃plwaje] *nm/f* employee; **~ de bureau/banque** office/bank employee *ou* clerk; **~ de maison** domestic (servant).

employer [ɑ̃plwaje] *vt* (*outil, moyen, méthode, mot*) to use; (*ouvrier, main-d'œuvre*) to employ; **s'~ à qch/à faire** to apply *ou* devote o.s. to sth/to doing.

employeur, euse [ɑ̃plwajœʀ, -øz] *nm/f* employer.

empocher [ɑ̃pɔʃe] *vt* to pocket.

empoignade [ɑ̃pwaɲad] *nf* row, set-to.

empoigne [ɑ̃pwaɲ] *nf*: **foire d'~** free-for-all.

empoigner [ɑ̃pwaɲe] *vt* to grab; **s'~** (*fig*) to have a row *ou* set-to.

empois [ɑ̃pwa] *nm* starch.

empoisonnement [ɑ̃pwazɔnmɑ̃] *nm* poisoning; (*fam: ennui*) annoyance, irritation.

empoisonner [ɑ̃pwazɔne] *vt* to poison; (*empester: air, pièce*) to stink out; (*fam*): **~ qn** to drive sb mad; **s'~** to poison o.s.; **~ l'atmosphère** (*aussi fig*) to poison the atmosphere; **il nous empoisonne l'existence** he's the bane of our life.

empoissonner [ɑ̃pwasɔne] *vt* (*étang, rivière*) to stock with fish.

emporté, e [ɑ̃pɔʀte] *adj* (*personne, caractère*) fiery.

emportement [ɑ̃pɔʀtəmɑ̃] *nm* fit of rage, anger *no pl*.

emporte-pièce [ɑ̃pɔʀtəpjɛs] *nm inv* (*TECH*) punch; **à l'~** *adj* (*fig*) incisive.

emporter [ɑ̃pɔʀte] *vt* to take (with one); (*en dérobant ou enlevant, emmener: blessés, voyageurs*) to take away; (*entraîner*) to carry away *ou* along; (*arracher*) to tear off; (*suj: rivière, vent*) to carry away; (*MIL: position*) to take; (*avantage, approbation*) to win; **s'~** *vi* (*de colère*) to fly into a rage, lose one's temper; **la maladie qui l'a emporté** the illness which caused his death; **l'~** to gain victory; **l'~ (sur)** to get the upper hand (of); (*méthode etc*) to prevail (over); **boissons à ~** take-away drinks.

empoté, e [ɑ̃pɔte] *adj* (*maladroit*) clumsy.

empourpré, e [ɑ̃puʀpʀe] *adj* crimson.

empreint, e [ɑ̃pʀɛ̃, -ɛ̃t] *adj*: **~ de** marked with; tinged with ♦ *nf* (*de pied, main*) print; (*fig*) stamp, mark; **~e (digitale)** fingerprint.

empressé, e [ɑ̃pʀese] *adj* attentive; (*péj*) over-anxious to please, overattentive.

empressement [ɑ̃pʀɛsmɑ̃] *nm* eagerness.

empresser [ɑ̃pʀese]: **s'~** *vi*: **s'~ auprès de qn** to surround sb with attentions; **s'~ de faire** to hasten to do.

emprise [ɑ̃pʀiz] *nf* hold, ascendancy; **sous l'~ de** under the influence of.

emprisonnement [ɑ̃pʀizɔnmɑ̃] *nm* imprisonment.

emprisonner [ɑ̃pʀizɔne] *vt* to imprison, jail.

emprunt [ɑ̃pʀœ̃] *nm* borrowing *no pl*, loan (*from debtor's point of view*); (*LING etc*) borrowing; **nom d'~** assumed name; **~ d'État** government *ou* state loan; **~ public à 5%** 5% public loan.

emprunté, e [ɑ̃pʀœ̃te] *adj* (*fig*) ill-at-ease, awkward.

emprunter [ɑ̃pʀœ̃te] *vt* to borrow; (*itinéraire*) to take, follow; (*style, manière*) to adopt, assume.

emprunteur, euse [ɑ̃pʀœ̃tœʀ, -øz] *nm/f* borrower.

empuantir [ɑ̃pɥɑ̃tiʀ] *vt* to stink out.

EMT *sigle f* (= *éducation manuelle et technique*)

handwork as a school subject.
ému, e [emy] *pp de* **émouvoir** ♦ *adj* excited; touched; moved.
émulation [emylɑsjɔ̃] *nf* emulation.
émule [emyl] *nm/f* imitator.
émulsion [emylsjɔ̃] *nf* emulsion; (*cosmétique*) (water-based) lotion.
émut [emy] *etc vb voir* **émouvoir**.
EN *sigle f* (= *Éducation nationale*) *voir* **éducation**.

=================== MOT-CLÉ ===================

en [ɑ̃] *prép* **1** (*endroit, pays*) in; (*direction*) to; **habiter** ~ **France/ville** to live in France/town; **aller** ~ **France/ville** to go to France/town
2 (*moment, temps*) in; ~ **été/juin** in summer/June; ~ **3 jours/20 ans** in 3 days/20 years
3 (*moyen*) by; ~ **avion/taxi** by plane/taxi
4 (*composition*) made of; **c'est** ~ **verre** it's (made of) glass; **un collier** ~ **argent** a silver necklace; ~ **2 volumes/une pièce** in 2 volumes/one piece
5 (*description, état*): **une femme (habillée)** ~ **rouge** a woman (dressed) in red; **peindre qch** ~ **rouge** to paint sth red; ~ **T/étoile** T-/star-shaped; ~ **chemise/chaussettes** in one's shirt sleeves/socks; ~ **soldat** as a soldier; ~ **civil** in civilian clothes; **cassé** ~ **plusieurs morceaux** broken into several pieces; ~ **réparation** being repaired, under repair; ~ **vacances** on holiday; ~ **bonne santé** healthy, in good health; ~ **deuil** in mourning; **le même** ~ **plus grand** the same but *ou* only bigger
6 (*avec gérondif*) while; on; ~ **dormant** while sleeping, as one sleeps; ~ **sortant** on going out, as he *etc* went out; **sortir** ~ **courant** to run out; ~ **apprenant la nouvelle, il s'est évanoui** he fainted at the news *ou* when he heard the news
7 (*matière*): **fort** ~ **math** good at maths; **expert** ~ **expert** in
8 (*conformité*): ~ **tant que** as; ~ **bon politicien, il ...** good politician that he is, he ..., like a good *ou* true politician, he ...; **je te parle** ~ **ami** I'm talking to you as a friend
♦ *pron* **1** (*indéfini*): **j'**~ **ai/veux** I have/want some; ~ **as-tu?** have you got any?; **je n'**~ **veux pas** I don't want any; **j'**~ **ai 2** I've got 2; **combien y** ~ **a-t-il?** how many (of them) are there?; **j'**~ **ai assez** I've got enough (of it *ou* them); (*j'en ai marre*) I've had enough; **où** ~ **étais-je?** where was I?
2 (*provenance*) from there; **j'**~ **viens** I've come from there
3 (*cause*): **il** ~ **est malade/perd le sommeil** he is ill/can't sleep because of it
4 (*de la part de*): **elle** ~ **est aimée** she is loved by him (*ou* them *etc*)
5 (*complément de nom, d'adjectif, de verbe*): **j'**~ **connais les dangers** I know its *ou* the dangers; **j'**~ **suis fier/ai besoin** I am proud

of it/need it; **il** ~ **est ainsi** *ou* **de même pour moi** it's the same for me, same here.

ENA [ena] *sigle f* (= *École nationale d'administration*) *grande école for training civil servants.*
énarque [enaʀk(ə)] *nm/f* former ENA student.
encablure [ɑ̃kablyʀ] *nf* (*NAVIG*) cable's length.
encadrement [ɑ̃kɑdʀəmɑ̃] *nm* framing; training; (*de porte*) frame; ~ **du crédit** credit restrictions.
encadrer [ɑ̃kɑdʀe] *vt* (*tableau, image*) to frame; (*fig: entourer*) to surround; (*personnel, soldats etc*) to train; (*COMM: crédit*) to restrict.
encadreur [ɑ̃kɑdʀœʀ] *nm* (picture) framer.
encaisse [ɑ̃kɛs] *nf* cash in hand; ~ **or/ métallique** gold/gold and silver reserves.
encaissé, e [ɑ̃kese] *adj* (*vallée*) steep-sided; (*rivière*) with steep banks.
encaisser [ɑ̃kese] *vt* (*chèque*) to cash; (*argent*) to collect; (*fig: coup, défaite*) to take.
encaisseur [ɑ̃kesœʀ] *nm* collector (*of debts etc*).
encan [ɑ̃kɑ̃] : **à l'**~ *adv* by auction.
encanailler [ɑ̃kanaje] : **s'**~ *vi* to become vulgar *ou* common; to mix with the riffraff.
encart [ɑ̃kaʀ] *nm* insert; ~ **publicitaire** publicity insert.
encarter [ɑ̃kaʀte] *vt* to insert.
en-cas [ɑ̃kɑ] *nm inv* snack.
encastrable [ɑ̃kastʀabl(ə)] *adj* (*four, élément*) that can be built in.
encastré, e [ɑ̃kastʀe] *adj* (*four, baignoire*) built-in.
encastrer [ɑ̃kastʀe] *vt*: ~ **qch dans** (*mur*) to embed sth in(to); (*boîtier*) to fit sth into; **s'**~ **dans** to fit into; (*heurter*) to crash into.
encaustiquage [ɑ̃kɔstikaʒ] *nm* polishing, waxing.
encaustique [ɑ̃kɔstik] *nf* polish, wax.
encaustiquer [ɑ̃kɔstike] *vt* to polish, wax.
enceinte [ɑ̃sɛ̃t] *adj f*: ~ **(de 6 mois)** (6 months) pregnant ♦ *nf* (*mur*) wall; (*espace*) enclosure; ~ **(acoustique)** speaker.
encens [ɑ̃sɑ̃] *nm* incense.
encenser [ɑ̃sɑ̃se] *vt* to (in)cense; (*fig*) to praise to the skies.
encensoir [ɑ̃sɑ̃swaʀ] *nm* thurible (*BRIT*), censer.
encéphalogramme [ɑ̃sefalɔgʀam] *nm* encephalogram.
encercler [ɑ̃sɛʀkle] *vt* to surround.
enchaîné [ɑ̃ʃene] *nm* (*CINÉ*) link shot.
enchaînement [ɑ̃ʃɛnmɑ̃] *nm* (*fig*) linking.
enchaîner [ɑ̃ʃene] *vt* to chain up; (*mouvements, séquences*) to link (together) ♦ *vi* to carry on.
enchanté, e [ɑ̃ʃɑ̃te] *adj* (*ravi*) delighted; (*ensorcelé*) enchanted; ~ **(de faire votre connaissance)** pleased to meet you, how do you do?

enchantement [ɑ̃ʃɑ̃tmɑ̃] *nm* delight; (*magie*) enchantment; **comme par** ~ as if by magic.
enchanter [ɑ̃ʃɑ̃te] *vt* to delight.
enchanteur, teresse [ɑ̃ʃɑ̃tœʀ, -tʀɛs] *adj* enchanting.
enchâsser [ɑ̃ʃase] *vt*: ~ **qch (dans)** to set sth (in).
enchère [ɑ̃ʃɛʀ] *nf* bid; **faire une** ~ to (make a) bid; **mettre/vendre aux** ~**s** to put up for (sale by)/sell by auction; **les** ~**s montent** the bids are rising; **faire monter les** ~**s** (*fig*) to raise the bidding.
enchérir [ɑ̃ʃeʀiʀ] *vi*: ~ **sur qn** (*aux enchères, aussi fig*) to outbid sb.
enchérisseur, euse [ɑ̃ʃeʀisœʀ, -øz] *nm/f* bidder.
enchevêtrement [ɑ̃ʃvɛtʀəmɑ̃] *nm* tangle.
enchevêtrer [ɑ̃ʃvetʀe] *vt* to tangle (up).
enclave [ɑ̃klav] *nf* enclave.
enclaver [ɑ̃klave] *vt* to enclose, hem in.
enclencher [ɑ̃klɑ̃ʃe] *vt* (*mécanisme*) to engage; (*fig: affaire*) to set in motion; **s'**~ *vi* to engage.
enclin, e [ɑ̃klɛ̃, -in] *adj*: ~ **à qch/à faire** inclined *ou* prone to sth/to do.
enclore [ɑ̃klɔʀ] *vt* to enclose.
enclos [ɑ̃klo] *nm* enclosure; (*clôture*) fence.
enclume [ɑ̃klym] *nf* anvil.
encoche [ɑ̃kɔʃ] *nf* notch.
encoder [ɑ̃kɔde] *vt* to encode.
encodeur [ɑ̃kɔdœʀ] *nm* encoder.
encoignure [ɑ̃kɔɲyʀ] *nf* corner.
encoller [ɑ̃kɔle] *vt* to paste.
encolure [ɑ̃kɔlyʀ] *nf* (*tour de cou*) collar size; (*col, cou*) neck.
encombrant, e [ɑ̃kɔ̃bʀɑ̃, -ɑ̃t] *adj* cumbersome, bulky.
encombre [ɑ̃kɔ̃bʀ(ə)]: **sans** ~ *adv* without mishap *ou* incident.
encombré, e [ɑ̃kɔ̃bʀe] *adj* (*pièce, passage*) cluttered; (*lignes téléphoniques*) engaged; (*marché*) saturated.
encombrement [ɑ̃kɔ̃bʀəmɑ̃] *nm* (*d'un lieu*) cluttering (up); (*d'un objet: dimensions*) bulk.
encombrer [ɑ̃kɔ̃bʀe] *vt* to clutter (up); (*gêner*) to hamper; **s'**~ **de** (*bagages etc*) to load *ou* burden o.s. with; ~ **le passage** to block *ou* obstruct the way.
encontre [ɑ̃kɔ̃tʀ(ə)]: **à l'**~ **de** *prép* against, counter to.
encorbellement [ɑ̃kɔʀbɛlmɑ̃] *nm*: **fenêtre en** ~ oriel window.
encorder [ɑ̃kɔʀde] *vt*: **s'**~ (*ALPINISME*) to rope up.

================= *MOT-CLÉ* =================

encore [ɑ̃kɔʀ] *adv* **1** (*continuation*) still; **il y travaille** ~ he's still working on it; **pas** ~ not yet
2 (*de nouveau*) again; **j'irai** ~ **demain** I'll go again tomorrow; ~ **une fois** (once) again; ~ **un effort** one last effort; ~ **deux jours** two more days

3 (*intensif*) even, still; ~ **plus fort/mieux** even louder/better, louder/better still; **hier** ~ even yesterday; **non seulement ..., mais** ~ ... not only ..., but also ...; ~**!** (*insatisfaction*) not again!; **quoi** ~**?** what now?
4 (*restriction*) even so *ou* then, only; ~ **pourrais-je le faire si ...** even so, I might be able to do it if ...; **si** ~ if only
encore que *conj* although.

_____

encourageant, e [ɑ̃kuʀaʒɑ̃, -ɑ̃t] *adj* encouraging.
encouragement [ɑ̃kuʀaʒmɑ̃] *nm* encouragement; (*récompense*) incentive.
encourager [ɑ̃kuʀaʒe] *vt* to encourage; ~ **qn à faire qch** to encourage sb to do sth.
encourir [ɑ̃kuʀiʀ] *vt* to incur.
encrasser [ɑ̃kʀase] *vt* to foul up; (*AUTO etc*) to soot up.
encre [ɑ̃kʀ(ə)] *nf* ink; ~ **de Chine** Indian ink; ~ **indélébile** indelible ink; ~ **sympathique** invisible ink.
encrer [ɑ̃kʀe] *vt* to ink.
encreur [ɑ̃kʀœʀ] *adj m*: **rouleau** ~ inking roller.
encrier [ɑ̃kʀije] *nm* inkwell.
encroûter [ɑ̃kʀute]: **s'**~ *vi* (*fig*) to get into a rut, get set in one's ways.
encyclique [ɑ̃siklik] *nf* encyclical.
encyclopédie [ɑ̃siklɔpedi] *nf* encyclopaedia (*BRIT*), encyclopedia (*US*).
encyclopédique [ɑ̃siklɔpedik] *adj* encyclopaedic (*BRIT*), encyclopedic (*US*).
endémique [ɑ̃demik] *adj* endemic.
endetté, e [ɑ̃dete] *adj* in debt; (*fig*): **très** ~ **envers qn** deeply indebted to sb.
endettement [ɑ̃dɛtmɑ̃] *nm* debts *pl*.
endetter [ɑ̃dete] *vt*, **s'**~ *vi* to get into debt.
endeuiller [ɑ̃dœje] *vt* to plunge into mourning; **manifestation endeuillée par** event over which a tragic shadow was cast by.
endiablé, e [ɑ̃djable] *adj* furious; (*enfant*) boisterous.
endiguer [ɑ̃dige] *vt* to dyke (up); (*fig*) to check, hold back.
endimancher [ɑ̃dimɑ̃ʃe] *vt*: **s'**~ to put on one's Sunday best; **avoir l'air endimanché** to be all done up to the nines (*fam*).
endive [ɑ̃div] *nf* chicory *no pl*.
endocrine [ɑ̃dɔkʀin] *adj f*: **glande** ~ endocrine (gland).
endoctrinement [ɑ̃dɔktʀinmɑ̃] *nm* indoctrination.
endoctriner [ɑ̃dɔktʀine] *vt* to indoctrinate.
endolori, e [ɑ̃dɔlɔʀi] *adj* painful.
endommager [ɑ̃dɔmaʒe] *vt* to damage.
endormant, e [ɑ̃dɔʀmɑ̃, -ɑ̃t] *adj* dull, boring.
endormi, e [ɑ̃dɔʀmi] *pp de* **endormir ♦** *adj* (*personne*) asleep; (*fig: indolent, lent*) sluggish; (*engourdi: main, pied*) numb.
endormir [ɑ̃dɔʀmiʀ] *vt* to put to sleep; (*suj: chaleur etc*) to send to sleep; (*MÉD: dent, nerf*)

to anaesthetize; (*fig: soupçons*) to allay; **s'~** *vi* to fall asleep, go to sleep.

endoscope [ɑ̃dɔskɔp] *nm* (*MÉD*) endoscope.

endoscopie [ɑ̃dɔskɔpi] *nf* endoscopy.

endosser [ɑ̃dose] *vt* (*responsabilité*) to take, shoulder; (*chèque*) to endorse; (*uniforme, tenue*) to put on, don.

endroit [ɑ̃dʀwa] *nm* place; (*localité*): **les gens de l'~** the local people; (*opposé à l'envers*) right side; **à cet ~** in this place; **à l'~** right side out; the right way up; (*vêtement*) the right way out; **à l'~ de** *prép* regarding, with regard to; **par ~s** in places.

enduire [ɑ̃dɥiʀ] *vt* to coat; **~ qch de** to coat sth with.

enduit, e [ɑ̃dɥi, -it] *pp de* **enduire** ♦ *nm* coating.

endurance [ɑ̃dyʀɑ̃s] *nf* endurance.

endurant, e [ɑ̃dyʀɑ̃, -ɑ̃t] *adj* tough, hardy.

endurcir [ɑ̃dyʀsiʀ] *vt* (*physiquement*) to toughen; (*moralement*) to harden; **s'~** *vi* to become tougher; to become hardened.

endurer [ɑ̃dyʀe] *vt* to endure, bear.

énergétique [enɛʀʒetik] *adj* (*ressources etc*) energy *cpd*; (*aliment*) energizing.

énergie [enɛʀʒi] *nf* (*PHYSIQUE*) energy; (*TECH*) power; (*fig: physique*) energy; (: *morale*) vigour, spirit; **~ éolienne/solaire** wind/solar power.

énergique [enɛʀʒik] *adj* energetic; vigorous; (*mesures*) drastic, stringent.

énergiquement [enɛʀʒikmɑ̃] *adv* energetically; drastically.

énergisant, e [enɛʀʒizɑ̃, -ɑ̃t] *adj* energizing.

énergumène [enɛʀɡymɛn] *nm* rowdy character *ou* customer.

énervant, e [enɛʀvɑ̃, -ɑ̃t] *adj* irritating.

énervé, e [enɛʀve] *adj* nervy, on edge; (*agacé*) irritated.

énervement [enɛʀvəmɑ̃] *nm* nerviness; irritation.

énerver [enɛʀve] *vt* to irritate, annoy; **s'~** *vi* to get excited, get worked up.

enfance [ɑ̃fɑ̃s] *nf* (*âge*) childhood; (*fig*) infancy; (*enfants*) children *pl*; **c'est l'~ de l'art** it's child's play; **petite ~** infancy; **souvenir/ami d'~** childhood memory/friend; **retomber en ~** to lapse into one's second childhood.

enfant [ɑ̃fɑ̃] *nm/f* child (*pl* children); **~ adoptif/naturel** adopted/natural child; **bon ~** *adj* good-natured, easy-going; **~ de chœur** *nm* (*REL*) altar boy; **~ prodige** child prodigy; **~ unique** only child.

enfanter [ɑ̃fɑ̃te] *vi* to give birth ♦ *vt* to give birth to.

enfantillage [ɑ̃fɑ̃tijaʒ] *nm* (*péj*) childish behaviour *no pl*.

enfantin, e [ɑ̃fɑ̃tɛ̃, -in] *adj* childlike; (*péj*) childish; (*langage*) child *cpd*.

enfer [ɑ̃fɛʀ] *nm* hell; **allure/bruit d'~** horrendous speed/noise.

enfermer [ɑ̃fɛʀme] *vt* to shut up; (*à clef, inter-*

ner) to lock up; **s'~** to shut o.s. away; **s'~ à clé** to lock o.s. in; **s'~ dans la solitude/le mutisme** to retreat into solitude/silence.

enferrer [ɑ̃feʀe]: **s'~** *vi*: **s'~ dans** to tangle o.s. up in.

enfiévré, e [ɑ̃fjevʀe] *adj* (*fig*) feverish.

enfilade [ɑ̃filad] *nf*: **une ~ de** a series *ou* line of; **prendre des rues en ~** to cross directly from one street into the next.

enfiler [ɑ̃file] *vt* (*vêtement*): **~ qch** to slip sth on, slip into sth; (*insérer*): **~ qch dans** to stick sth into; (*rue, couloir*) to take; (*perles*) to string; (*aiguille*) to thread; **s'~ dans** to disappear into.

enfin [ɑ̃fɛ̃] *adv* at last; (*en énumérant*) lastly; (*de restriction, résignation*) still; (*eh bien*) well; (*pour conclure*) in a word.

enflammé, e [ɑ̃flame] *adj* (*torche, allumette*) burning; (*MÉD: plaie*) inflamed; (*fig: nature, discours, déclaration*) fiery.

enflammer [ɑ̃flame] *vt* to set fire to; (*MÉD*) to inflame; **s'~** *vi* to catch fire; to become inflamed.

enflé, e [ɑ̃fle] *adj* swollen; (*péj: style*) bombastic, turgid.

enfler [ɑ̃fle] *vi* to swell (up); **s'~** *vi* to swell.

enflure [ɑ̃flyʀ] *nf* swelling.

enfoncé, e [ɑ̃fɔ̃se] *adj* staved-in, smashed-in; (*yeux*) deep-set.

enfoncement [ɑ̃fɔ̃smɑ̃] *nm* (*recoin*) nook.

enfoncer [ɑ̃fɔ̃se] *vt* (*clou*) to drive in; (*faire pénétrer*): **~ qch dans** to push (*ou* drive) sth into; (*forcer: porte*) to break open; (: *plancher*) to cause to cave in; (*défoncer: côtes etc*) to smash; (*fam: surpasser*) to lick, beat (hollow) ♦ *vi* (*dans la vase etc*) to sink in; (*sol, surface porteuse*) to give way; **s'~** *vi* to sink; **s'~ dans** to sink into; (*forêt, ville*) to disappear into; **~ un chapeau sur la tête** to cram *ou* jam a hat on one's head; **~ qn dans la dette** to drag sb into debt.

enfouir [ɑ̃fwiʀ] *vt* (*dans le sol*) to bury; (*dans un tiroir etc*) to tuck away; **s'~ dans/sous** to bury o.s. in/under.

enfourcher [ɑ̃fuʀʃe] *vt* to mount; **~ son dada** (*fig*) to get on one's hobby-horse.

enfourner [ɑ̃fuʀne] *vt* to put in the oven; (*poterie*) to put in the kiln; **~ qch dans** to shove *ou* stuff sth into; **s'~ dans** (*suj: personne*) to dive into.

enfreignais [ɑ̃fʀɛɲɛ] *etc vb voir* **enfreindre**.

enfreindre [ɑ̃fʀɛ̃dʀ(ə)] *vt* to infringe, break.

enfuir [ɑ̃fɥiʀ]: **s'~** *vi* to run away *ou* off.

enfumer [ɑ̃fyme] *vt* to smoke out.

enfuyais [ɑ̃fɥijɛ] *etc vb voir* **enfuir**.

engagé, e [ɑ̃ɡaʒe] *adj* (*littérature etc*) engagé, committed.

engageant, e [ɑ̃ɡaʒɑ̃, -ɑ̃t] *adj* attractive, appealing.

engagement [ɑ̃ɡaʒmɑ̃] *nm* taking on, engaging; starting; investing; (*promesse*) commitment; (*MIL: combat*) engagement; (: *recrute-*

ment) enlistment; (*SPORT*) entry; **prendre l'~ de faire** to undertake to do; **sans ~** (*COMM*) without obligation.

engager [ɑ̃gaʒe] *vt* (*embaucher*) to take on, engage; (*commencer*) to start; (*lier*) to bind, commit; (*impliquer, entraîner*) to involve; (*investir*) to invest, lay out; (*faire intervenir*) to engage; (*SPORT: concurrents, chevaux*) to enter; (*inciter*): **~ qn à faire** to urge sb to do; (*faire pénétrer*): **~ qch dans** to insert sth into; **~ qn à qch** to urge sth on sb; **s'~** to get taken on; (*MIL*) to enlist; (*promettre, politiquement*) to commit o.s.; (*débuter*) to start (up); **s'~ à faire** to undertake to do; **s'~ dans** (*rue, passage*) to enter, turn into; (*s'emboîter*) to engage *ou* fit into; (*fig: affaire, discussion*) to enter into, embark on.

engazonner [ɑ̃gazɔne] *vt* to turf.

engeance [ɑ̃ʒɑ̃s] *nf* mob.

engelure [ɑ̃ʒlyʁ] *nf* chilblain.

engendrer [ɑ̃ʒɑ̃dʁe] *vt* to father; (*fig*) to create, breed.

engin [ɑ̃ʒɛ̃] *nm* machine; instrument; vehicle; (*péj*) gadget; (*AVIAT: avion*) aircraft *inv*; (: *missile*) missile; **~ blindé** armoured vehicle; **~ (explosif)** (explosive) device; **~s (spéciaux)** missiles.

englober [ɑ̃glɔbe] *vt* to include.

engloutir [ɑ̃glutiʁ] *vt* to swallow up; (*fig: dépenses*) to devour; **s'~** to be engulfed.

englué, e [ɑ̃glye] sticky.

engoncé, e [ɑ̃gɔ̃se] *adj*: **~ dans** cramped in.

engorgement [ɑ̃gɔʁʒəmɑ̃] *nm* blocking; (*MÉD*) engorgement.

engorger [ɑ̃gɔʁʒe] *vt* to obstruct, block; **s'~** *vi* to become blocked.

engouement [ɑ̃gumɑ̃] *nm* (sudden) passion.

engouffrer [ɑ̃gufʁe] *vt* to swallow up, devour; **s'~ dans** to rush into.

engourdi, e [ɑ̃guʁdi] *adj* numb.

engourdir [ɑ̃guʁdiʁ] *vt* to numb; (*fig*) to dull, blunt; **s'~** *vi* to go numb.

engrais [ɑ̃gʁɛ] *nm* manure; **~ (chimique)** (chemical) fertilizer; **~ organique/inorganique** organic/inorganic fertilizer.

engraisser [ɑ̃gʁese] *vt* to fatten (up); (*terre: fertiliser*) to fertilize ♦ *vi* (*péj*) to get fat(ter).

engranger [ɑ̃gʁɑ̃ʒe] *vt* (*foin*) to bring in; (*fig*) to store away.

engrenage [ɑ̃gʁənaʒ] *nm* gears *pl*, gearing; (*fig*) chain.

engueuler [ɑ̃gœle] *vt* (*fam*) to bawl at *ou* out.

enguirlander [ɑ̃giʁlɑ̃de] *vt* (*fam*) to give sb a bawling out, bawl at.

enhardir [ɑ̃aʁdiʁ] **s'~** *vi* to grow bolder.

ENI [eni] *sigle f* = **école normale (d'instituteurs)**.

énième [ɛnjɛm] *adj* = **nième**.

énigmatique [enigmatik] *adj* enigmatic.

énigmatiquement [enigmatikmɑ̃] *adv* enigmatically.

énigme [enigm(ə)] *nf* riddle.

enivrant, e [ɑ̃nivʁɑ̃, -ɑ̃t] *adj* intoxicating.

enivrer [ɑ̃nivʁe] *vt*: **s'~** to get drunk; **s'~ de** (*fig*) to become intoxicated with.

enjambée [ɑ̃ʒɑ̃be] *nf* stride; **d'une ~** with one stride.

enjamber [ɑ̃ʒɑ̃be] *vt* to stride over; (*suj: pont etc*) to span, straddle.

enjeu, x [ɑ̃ʒø] *nm* stakes *pl*.

enjoindre [ɑ̃ʒwɛ̃dʁ(ə)] *vt*: **~ à qn de faire** to enjoin *ou* order sb to do.

enjôler [ɑ̃ʒole] *vt* to coax, wheedle.

enjôleur, euse [ɑ̃ʒolœʁ, -øz] *adj* (*sourire, paroles*) winning.

enjolivement [ɑ̃ʒolivmɑ̃] *nm* embellishment.

enjoliver [ɑ̃ʒolive] *vt* to embellish.

enjoliveur [ɑ̃ʒolivœʁ] *nm* (*AUTO*) hub cap.

enjoué, e [ɑ̃ʒwe] *adj* playful.

enlacer [ɑ̃lase] *vt* (*étreindre*) to embrace, hug; (*suj: lianes*) to wind round, entwine.

enlaidir [ɑ̃lediʁ] *vt* to make ugly ♦ *vi* to become ugly.

enlevé, e [ɑ̃lve] *adj* (*morceau de musique*) played brightly.

enlèvement [ɑ̃lɛvmɑ̃] *nm* removal; (*rapt*) abduction, kidnapping; **l'~ des ordures ménagères** refuse collection.

enlever [ɑ̃lve] *vt* (*ôter: gén*) to remove; (: *vêtement, lunettes*) to take off; (: *MÉD: organe*) to remove; (*emporter: ordures etc*) to collect, take away; (*kidnapper*) to abduct, kidnap; (*obtenir: prix, contrat*) to win; (*MIL: position*) to take; (*morceau de piano etc*) to execute with spirit *ou* brio; (*prendre*): **~ qch à qn** to take sth (away) from sb; **s'~** *vi* (*tache*) to come out *ou* off; **la maladie qui nous l'a enlevé** (*euphémisme*) the illness which took him from us.

enliser [ɑ̃lize]: **s'~** *vi* to sink, get stuck; (*dialogue etc*) to get bogged down.

enluminure [ɑ̃lyminyʁ] *nf* illumination.

ENM *sigle f* (= *École nationale de la magistrature*) *grande école for law students*.

enneigé, e [ɑ̃neʒe] *adj* snowy; (*col*) snowed-up; (*maison*) snowed-in.

enneigement [ɑ̃nɛʒmɑ̃] *nm* depth of snow, snowfall; **bulletin d'~** snow report.

ennemi, e [ɛnmi] *adj* hostile; (*MIL*) enemy *cpd* ♦ *nm/f* enemy; **être ~ de** to be strongly averse *ou* opposed to.

ennième [ɛnjɛm] *adj* = **nième**.

ennoblir [ɑ̃nɔbliʁ] *vt* to ennoble.

ennui [ɑ̃nɥi] *nm* (*lassitude*) boredom; (*difficulté*) trouble *no pl*; **avoir des ~s** to have problems; **s'attirer des ~s** to cause problems for o.s.

ennuie [ɑ̃nɥi] *etc vb voir* **ennuyer**.

ennuyé, e [ɑ̃nɥije] *adj* (*air, personne*) preoccupied, worried.

ennuyer [ɑ̃nɥije] *vt* to bother; (*lasser*) to bore; **s'~** *vi* to be bored; **s'~ de** (*regretter*) to miss; **si cela ne vous ennuie pas** if it's no trouble to you.

ennuyeux, euse [ɑ̃nɥijø, -øz] *adj* boring, tedious; (*agaçant*) annoying.

énoncé [enɔ̃se] *nm* terms *pl*; wording; (*LING*) utterance.

énoncer [enɔ̃se] *vt* to say, express; (*conditions*) to set out, lay down, state.

énonciation [enɔ̃sjasjɔ̃] *nf* statement.

enorgueillir [ɑ̃nɔʀgœjiʀ]: **s'~ de** *vt* to pride o.s. on; to boast.

énorme [enɔʀm(ə)] *adj* enormous, huge.

énormément [enɔʀmemɑ̃] *adv* enormously, tremendously; **~ de neige/gens** an enormous amount of snow/number of people.

énormité [enɔʀmite] *nf* enormity, hugeness; (*propos*) outrageous remark.

en part. *abr* (= en particulier) esp.

enquérir [ɑ̃keʀiʀ]: **s'~ de** *vt* to inquire about.

enquête [ɑ̃kɛt] *nf* (*de journaliste, de police*) investigation; (*judiciaire, administrative*) inquiry; (*sondage d'opinion*) survey.

enquêter [ɑ̃kete] *vi* to investigate; to hold an inquiry; (*faire un sondage*): **~ (sur)** to do a survey (on), carry out an opinion poll (on).

enquêteur, euse *ou* **trice** [ɑ̃kɛtœʀ, -øz, -tʀis] *nm/f* officer in charge of an investigation; person conducting a survey; pollster.

enquiers, enquière [ɑ̃kjɛʀ] *etc* *vb* *voir* **enquérir.**

enquiquiner [ɑ̃kikine] *vt* to rile, irritate.

enquis, e [ɑ̃ki, -iz] *pp de* **enquérir.**

enraciné, e [ɑ̃ʀasine] *adj* deep-rooted.

enragé, e [ɑ̃ʀaʒe] *adj* (*MÉD*) rabid, with rabies; (*furieux*) furiously angry; (*fig*) fanatical; **~ de** wild about.

enrageant, e [ɑ̃ʀaʒɑ̃, -ɑ̃t] *adj* infuriating.

enrager [ɑ̃ʀaʒe] *vi* to be furious, be in a rage; **faire ~ qn** to make sb wild with anger.

enrayer [ɑ̃ʀeje] *vt* to check, stop; **s'~** *vi* (*arme à feu*) to jam.

enrégimenter [ɑ̃ʀeʒimɑ̃te] *vt* (*péj*) to enlist.

enregistrement [ɑ̃ʀʒistʀəmɑ̃] *nm* recording; (*ADMIN*) registration; **~ des bagages** (*à l'aéroport*) baggage check-in; **~ magnétique** tape-recording.

enregistrer [ɑ̃ʀʒistʀe] *vt* (*MUS, INFORM etc*) to record; (*remarquer, noter*) to note, record; (*COMM: commande*) to note, enter; (*fig: mémoriser*) to make a mental note of; (*ADMIN*) to register; (*aussi:* **faire ~**: *bagages: par train*) to register; (*: à l'aéroport*) to check in.

enregistreur, euse [ɑ̃ʀʒistʀœʀ, -øz] *adj* (*machine*) recording *cpd* ♦ *nm* (*appareil*): **~ de vol** (*AVIAT*) flight recorder.

enrhumé, e [ɑ̃ʀyme] *adj*: **il est ~** he has a cold.

enrhumer [ɑ̃ʀyme]: **s'~** *vi* to catch a cold.

enrichir [ɑ̃ʀiʃiʀ] *vt* to make rich(er); (*fig*) to enrich; **s'~** to get rich(er).

enrichissant, e [ɑ̃ʀiʃisɑ̃, -ɑ̃t] *adj* instructive.

enrichissement [ɑ̃ʀiʃismɑ̃] *nm* enrichment.

enrober [ɑ̃ʀɔbe] *vt*: **~ qch de** to coat sth with; (*fig*) to wrap sth up in.

enrôlement [ɑ̃ʀolmɑ̃] *nm* enlistment.

enrôler [ɑ̃ʀole] *vt* to enlist; **s'~ (dans)** to enlist

(in).

enroué, e [ɑ̃ʀwe] *adj* hoarse.

enrouer [ɑ̃ʀwe]: **s'~** *vi* to go hoarse.

enrouler [ɑ̃ʀule] *vt* (*fil, corde*) to wind (up); **s'~** to coil up; **~ qch autour de** to wind sth (a)round.

enrouleur, euse [ɑ̃ʀulœʀ, -øz] *adj* (*TECH*) winding ♦ *nm voir* **ceinture.**

enrubanné, e [ɑ̃ʀybane] *adj* trimmed with ribbon.

ENS *sigle f* = école normale supérieure.

ensabler [ɑ̃sable] *vt* (*port, canal*) to silt up, sand up; (*embarcation*) to strand (on a sandbank); **s'~** *vi* to silt up; to get stranded.

ensacher [ɑ̃saʃe] *vt* to pack into bags.

ENSAM *sigle f* (= École nationale supérieure des arts et métiers) *grande école for engineering students.*

ensanglanté, e [ɑ̃sɑ̃glɑ̃te] *adj* covered with blood.

enseignant, e [ɑ̃sɛɲɑ̃, -ɑ̃t] *adj* teaching ♦ *nm/f* teacher.

enseigne [ɑ̃sɛɲ] *nf* sign ♦ *nm*: **~ de vaisseau** lieutenant; **à telle ~ que** so much so that; **être logés à la même ~** (*fig*) to be in the same boat; **~ lumineuse** neon sign.

enseignement [ɑ̃sɛɲmɑ̃] *nm* teaching; **~ ménager** home economics; **~ primaire** primary (*BRIT*) *ou* grade school (*US*) education; **~ secondaire** secondary (*BRIT*) *ou* high school (*US*) education.

enseigner [ɑ̃seɲe] *vt, vi* to teach; **~ qch à qn/ à qn que** to teach sb sth/sb that.

ensemble [ɑ̃sɑ̃bl(ə)] *adv* together ♦ *nm* (*assemblage, MATH*) set; (*totalité*): **l'~ du/de la** the whole *ou* entire; (*vêtement féminin*) ensemble, suit; (*unité, harmonie*) unity; (*résidentiel*) housing development; **aller ~** to go together; **impression/idée d'~** overall *ou* general impression/idea; **dans l'~** (*en gros*) on the whole; **dans son ~** overall, in general; **~ vocal/musical** vocal/musical ensemble.

ensemblier [ɑ̃sɑ̃blije] *nm* interior designer.

ensemencer [ɑ̃səmɑ̃se] *vt* to sow.

enserrer [ɑ̃seʀe] *vt* to hug (tightly).

ENSET [ɛnsɛt] *sigle f* (= École normale supérieure de l'enseignement technique) *grande école for training technical teachers.*

ensevelir [ɑ̃səvliʀ] *vt* to bury.

ensilage [ɑ̃silaʒ] *nm* (*aliment*) silage.

ensoleillé, e [ɑ̃sɔleje] *adj* sunny.

ensoleillement [ɑ̃sɔlɛjmɑ̃] *nm* period *ou* hours *pl* of sunshine.

ensommeillé, e [ɑ̃sɔmeje] *adj* sleepy, drowsy.

ensorceler [ɑ̃sɔʀsəle] *vt* to enchant, bewitch.

ensuite [ɑ̃sɥit] *adv* then, next; (*plus tard*) afterwards, later; **~ de quoi** after which.

ensuivre [ɑ̃sɥivʀ(ə)]: **s'~** *vi* to follow, ensue; **il s'ensuit que ...** it follows that ...; **et tout ce qui s'ensuit** and all that goes with it.

entaché, e [ɑ̃taʃe] *adj*: **~ de** marred by; **~ de nullité** null and void.

entacher [ɑ̃taʃe] vt to soil.
entaille [ɑ̃taj] nf (encoche) notch; (blessure) cut; **se faire une ~** to cut o.s.
entailler [ɑ̃taje] vt to notch; to cut; **s'~ le doigt** to cut one's finger.
entamer [ɑ̃tame] vt to start; (hostilités, pourparlers) to open; (fig: altérer) to make a dent in; to damage.
entartrer [ɑ̃tartre]: **s'~** vi to fur up; (dents) to become covered with plaque.
entassement [ɑ̃tasmɑ̃] nm (tas) pile, heap.
entasser [ɑ̃tase] vt (empiler) to pile up, heap up; (tenir à l'étroit) to cram together; **s'~** vi to pile up; to cram; **s'~ dans** to cram into.
entendement [ɑ̃tɑ̃dmɑ̃] nm understanding.
entendre [ɑ̃tɑ̃dʀ(ə)] vt to hear; (comprendre) to understand; (vouloir dire) to mean; (vouloir): **~ être obéi/que** to intend ou mean to be obeyed/that; **j'ai entendu dire que** I've heard (it said) that; **je suis heureux de vous l'~ dire** I'm pleased to hear you say it; **~ parler de** to hear of; **laisser ~ que, donner à ~ que** to let it be understood that; **~ raison** to see sense, listen to reason; **qu'est-ce qu'il ne faut pas ~!** whatever next!; **j'ai mal entendu** I didn't catch what was said; **je vous entends très mal** I can hardly hear you; **s'~** vi (sympathiser) to get on; (se mettre d'accord) to agree; **s'~ à qch/à faire** (être compétent) to be good at sth/doing; **ça s'entend** (est audible) it's audible; **je m'entends** I mean; **entendons-nous!** let's be clear what we mean.
entendu, e [ɑ̃tɑ̃dy] pp de **entendre** ♦ adj (réglé) agreed; (au courant: air) knowing; **étant ~ que** since (it's understood ou agreed that); **(c'est) ~** all right, agreed; **c'est ~** (concession) all right, granted; **bien ~** of course.
entente [ɑ̃tɑ̃t] nf (entre amis, pays) understanding, harmony; (accord, traité) agreement, understanding; **à double ~** (sens) with a double meaning.
entériner [ɑ̃teʀine] vt to ratify, confirm.
entérite [ɑ̃teʀit] nf enteritis no pl.
enterrement [ɑ̃tɛʀmɑ̃] nm burying; (cérémonie) funeral, burial; (cortège funèbre) funeral procession.
enterrer [ɑ̃teʀe] vt to bury.
entêtant, e [ɑ̃tɛtɑ̃, -ɑ̃t] adj heady.
entêté, e [ɑ̃tete] adj stubborn.
en-tête [ɑ̃tɛt] nm heading; (de papier à lettres) letterhead; **papier à ~** headed notepaper.
entêtement [ɑ̃tɛtmɑ̃] nm stubbornness.
entêter [ɑ̃tete]: **s'~** vi: **s'~ (à faire)** to persist (in doing).
enthousiasmant, e [ɑ̃tuzjasmɑ̃, -ɑ̃t] adj exciting.
enthousiasme [ɑ̃tuzjasm(ə)] nm enthusiasm; **avec ~** enthusiastically.
enthousiasmé, e [ɑ̃tuzjasme] adj filled with enthusiasm.
enthousiasmer [ɑ̃tuzjasme] vt to fill with en-

thusiasm; **s'~ (pour qch)** to get enthusiastic (about sth).
enthousiaste [ɑ̃tuzjast(ə)] adj enthusiastic.
enticher [ɑ̃tiʃe]: **s'~ de** vt to become infatuated with.
entier, ière [ɑ̃tje, -jɛʀ] adj (non entamé, en totalité) whole; (total, complet) complete; (fig: caractère) unbending, averse to compromise ♦ nm (MATH) whole; **en ~** totally; in its entirety; **se donner tout ~ à qch** to devote o.s. completely to sth; **lait ~** full-cream milk; **pain ~** wholemeal bread; **nombre ~** whole number.
entièrement [ɑ̃tjɛʀmɑ̃] adv entirely, completely, wholly.
entité [ɑ̃tite] nf entity.
entomologie [ɑ̃tɔmɔlɔʒi] nf entomology.
entonner [ɑ̃tɔne] vt (chanson) to strike up.
entonnoir [ɑ̃tɔnwaʀ] nm (ustensile) funnel; (trou) shell-hole, crater.
entorse [ɑ̃tɔʀs(ə)] nf (MÉD) sprain; (fig): **~ à la loi/au règlement** infringement of the law/rule; **se faire une ~ à la cheville/au poignet** to sprain one's ankle/wrist.
entortiller [ɑ̃tɔʀtije] vt (envelopper): **~ qch dans/avec** to wrap sth in/with; (enrouler): **~ qch autour de** to twist ou wind sth (a)round; (fam): **~ qn** to get (a)round sb; (: duper) to hoodwink sb (BRIT), trick sb; **s'~ dans** (draps) to roll o.s. up in; (fig: réponses) to get tangled up in.
entourage [ɑ̃tuʀaʒ] nm circle; family (circle); (d'une vedette etc) entourage; (ce qui enclôt) surround.
entouré, e [ɑ̃tuʀe] adj (recherché, admiré) popular; **~ de** surrounded by.
entourer [ɑ̃tuʀe] vt to surround; (apporter son soutien à) to rally round; **~ de** to surround with; (trait) to encircle with; **s'~ de** to surround o.s. with; **s'~ de précautions** to take all possible precautions.
entourloupette [ɑ̃tuʀlupɛt] nf mean trick.
entournures [ɑ̃tuʀnyʀ] nfpl: **gêné aux ~** in financial difficulties; (fig) a bit awkward.
entracte [ɑ̃tʀakt(ə)] nm interval.
entraide [ɑ̃tʀɛd] nf mutual aid ou assistance.
entraider [ɑ̃tʀede]: **s'~** vi to help each other.
entrailles [ɑ̃tʀaj] nfpl entrails; (humaines) bowels.
entrain [ɑ̃tʀɛ̃] nm spirit; **avec ~** (répondre, travailler) energetically; **faire qch sans ~** to do sth half-heartedly ou without enthusiasm.
entraînant, e [ɑ̃tʀɛnɑ̃, -ɑ̃t] adj (musique) stirring, rousing.
entraînement [ɑ̃tʀɛnmɑ̃] nm training; (TECH): **~ à chaîne/galet** chain/wheel drive; **manquer d'~** to be unfit; **~ par ergots/friction** (INFORM) tractor/friction feed.
entraîner [ɑ̃tʀene] vt (tirer: wagons) to pull; (charrier) to carry ou drag along; (TECH) to drive; (emmener: personne) to take (off); (mener à l'assaut, influencer) to lead; (SPORT)

to train; (*impliquer*) to entail; (*causer*) to lead to, bring about; ~ **qn à faire** (*inciter*) to lead sb to do; **s'~** (*SPORT*) to train; **s'~ à qch/à faire** to train o.s. for sth/to do.

entraîneur [ɑ̃tʀɛnœʀ] *nm* (*SPORT*) coach, trainer; (*HIPPISME*) trainer.

entraîneuse [ɑ̃tʀɛnøz] *nf* (*de bar*) hostess.

entrapercevoir [ɑ̃tʀapɛʀsəvwaʀ] *vt* to catch a glimpse of.

entrave [ɑ̃tʀav] *nf* hindrance.

entraver [ɑ̃tʀave] *vt* (*circulation*) to hold up; (*action, progrès*) to hinder, hamper.

entre [ɑ̃tʀ(ə)] *prép* between; (*parmi*) among(st); **l'un d'~ eux/nous** one of them/us; **le meilleur d'~ eux/nous** the best of them/us; **ils préfèrent rester ~ eux** they prefer to keep to themselves; **~ autres (choses)** among other things; **~ nous, ...** between ourselves ..., between you and me ...; **ils se battent ~ eux** they are fighting among(st) themselves.

entrebâillé, e [ɑ̃tʀəbaje] *adj* half-open, ajar.

entrebâillement [ɑ̃tʀəbajmɑ̃] *nm*: **dans l'~ (de la porte)** in the half-open door.

entrebâiller [ɑ̃tʀəbaje] *vt* to half open.

entrechat [ɑ̃tʀəʃa] *nm* leap.

entrechoquer [ɑ̃tʀəʃɔke]: **s'~** *vi* to knock *ou* bang together.

entrecôte [ɑ̃tʀəkot] *nf* entrecôte *ou* rib steak.

entrecoupé, e [ɑ̃tʀəkupe] *adj* (*paroles, voix*) broken.

entrecouper [ɑ̃tʀəkupe] *vt*: **~ qch de** to intersperse sth with; **~ un récit/voyage de** to interrupt a story/journey with; **s'~** (*traits, lignes*) to cut across each other.

entrecroiser [ɑ̃tʀəkʀwaze] *vt*, **s'~** *vi* to intertwine.

entrée [ɑ̃tʀe] *nf* entrance; (*accès: au cinéma etc*) admission; (*billet*) (admission) ticket; (*CULIN*) first course; (*COMM: de marchandises*) entry; (*INFORM*) entry, input; **~s** *nfpl*: **avoir ses ~s chez** *ou* **auprès de** to be a welcome visitor to; **d'~** *adv* from the outset; **erreur d'~** input error; **"~ interdite"** "no admittance *ou* entry"; **~ des artistes** stage door; **~ en matière** introduction; **~ en scène** entrance; **~ de service** service entrance.

entrefaites [ɑ̃tʀəfɛt]: **sur ces ~** *adv* at this juncture.

entrefilet [ɑ̃tʀəfilɛ] *nm* (*article*) paragraph, short report.

entregent [ɑ̃tʀəʒɑ̃] *nm*: **avoir de l'~** to have an easy manner.

entre-jambes [ɑ̃tʀəʒɑ̃b] *nm inv* crotch.

entrelacement [ɑ̃tʀəlasmɑ̃] *nm*: **un ~ de ...** a network of ....

entrelacer [ɑ̃tʀəlase] *vt*, **s'~** *vi* to intertwine.

entrelarder [ɑ̃tʀəlaʀde] *vt* to lard; (*fig*): **entrelardé de** interspersed with.

entremêler [ɑ̃tʀəmele] *vt*: **~ qch de** to (inter)mingle sth with.

entremets [ɑ̃tʀəmɛ] *nm* (cream) dessert.

entremetteur, euse [ɑ̃tʀəmɛtœʀ, -øz] *nm/f* go-between.

entremettre [ɑ̃tʀəmɛtʀ(ə)]: **s'~** *vi* to intervene.

entremise [ɑ̃tʀəmiz] *nf* intervention; **par l'~ de** through.

entrepont [ɑ̃tʀəpɔ̃] *nm* steerage; **dans l'~** in steerage.

entreposer [ɑ̃tʀəpoze] *vt* to store, put into storage.

entrepôt [ɑ̃tʀəpo] *nm* warehouse.

entreprenant, e [ɑ̃tʀəpʀənɑ̃, -ɑ̃t] *vb voir* **entreprendre** ♦ *adj* (*actif*) enterprising; (*trop galant*) forward.

entreprendre [ɑ̃tʀəpʀɑ̃dʀ(ə)] *vt* (*se lancer dans*) to undertake; (*commencer*) to begin *ou* start (upon); (*personne*) to buttonhole; **~ qn sur un sujet** to tackle sb on a subject; **~ de faire** to undertake to do.

entrepreneur [ɑ̃tʀəpʀənœʀ] *nm*: **~ (en bâtiment)** (building) contractor; **~ de pompes funèbres** funeral director, undertaker.

entreprenne [ɑ̃tʀəpʀɛn] *etc vb voir* **entreprendre**.

entrepris, e [ɑ̃tʀəpʀi, -iz] *pp de* **entreprendre** ♦ *nf* (*société*) firm, business; (*action*) undertaking, venture.

entrer [ɑ̃tʀe] *vi* to go (*ou* come) in, enter ♦ *vt* (*INFORM*) to input, enter; **(faire) ~ qch dans** to get sth into; (*gén*) to enter; (*pièce*) to go (*ou* come) into, enter; (*club*) to join; (*heurter*) to run into; (*partager: vues, craintes de qn*) to share; (*être une composante de*) to go into; (*faire partie de*) to form part of; **~ au couvent** to enter a convent; **~ à l'hôpital** to go into hospital; **~ dans le système** (*INFORM*) to log in; **~ en fureur** to become angry; **~ en ébullition** to start to boil; **~ en scène** to come on stage; **laisser ~ qn/qch** to let sb/sth in; **faire ~** (*visiteur*) to show in.

entresol [ɑ̃tʀəsɔl] *nm* entresol, mezzanine.

entre-temps [ɑ̃tʀətɑ̃] *adv* meanwhile, (in the) meantime.

entretenir [ɑ̃tʀətniʀ] *vt* to maintain; (*amitié*) to keep alive; (*famille, maîtresse*) to support, keep; **~ qn (de)** to speak to sb (about); **s'~ (de)** to converse (about); **~ qn dans l'erreur** to let sb remain in ignorance.

entretenu, e [ɑ̃tʀətny] *pp de* **entretenir** ♦ *adj* (*femme*) kept; **bien/mal ~** (*maison, jardin*) well/badly kept.

entretien [ɑ̃tʀətjɛ̃] *nm* maintenance; (*discussion*) discussion, talk; (*audience*) interview; **frais d'~** maintenance charges.

entretiendrai [ɑ̃tʀətjɛ̃dʀe], **entretiens** [ɑ̃tʀətjɛ̃] *etc vb voir* **entretenir**.

entretuer [ɑ̃tʀətɥe]: **s'~** *vi* to kill one another.

entreverrai [ɑ̃tʀəveʀe], **entrevit** [ɑ̃tʀəvi] *etc vb voir* **entrevoir**.

entrevoir [ɑ̃tʀəvwaʀ] *vt* (*à peine*) to make out; (*brièvement*) to catch a glimpse of.

entrevu, e [ɑ̃tʀəvy] *pp de* **entrevoir** ♦ *nf* meeting; (*audience*) interview.

entrouvert, e [ɑ̃tʀuvɛʀ, -ɛʀt(ə)] *pp de* **entrouvrir** ♦ *adj* half-open.

entrouvrir [ɑ̃tʀuvʀiʀ] *vt*, **s'~** *vi* to half open.

énumération [enymeʀɑsjɔ̃] *nf* enumeration.

énumérer [enymeʀe] *vt* to list, enumerate.

énurésie [enyʀezi] *nf* enuresis.

envahir [ɑ̃vaiʀ] *vt* to invade; (*suj: inquiétude, peur*) to come over.

envahissant, e [ɑ̃vaisɑ̃, -ɑ̃t] *adj* (*péj: personne*) interfering, intrusive.

envahissement [ɑ̃vaismɑ̃] *nm* invasion.

envahisseur [ɑ̃vaisœʀ] *nm* (*MIL*) invader.

envasement [ɑ̃nvazmɑ̃] *nm* silting up.

envaser [ɑ̃vaze]: **s'~** *vi* to get bogged down (in the mud).

enveloppe [ɑ̃vlɔp] *nf* (*de lettre*) envelope; (*TECH*) casing; outer layer; **mettre sous ~** to put in an envelope; **~ autocollante** self-seal envelope; **~ budgétaire** budget; **~ à fenêtre** window envelope.

envelopper [ɑ̃vlɔpe] *vt* to wrap; (*fig*) to envelop, shroud; **s'~ dans un châle/une couverture** to wrap o.s. in a shawl/blanket.

envenimer [ɑ̃vnime] *vt* to aggravate; **s'~** *vi* (*plaie*) to fester; (*situation, relations*) to worsen.

envergure [ɑ̃vɛʀgyʀ] *nf* (*d'un oiseau, avion*) wingspan; (*fig: étendue*) scope; (*: valeur*) calibre.

enverrai [ɑ̃vɛʀe] *etc vb voir* **envoyer**.

envers [ɑ̃vɛʀ] *prép* towards, to ♦ *nm* other side; (*d'une étoffe*) wrong side; **à l'~** upside down; back to front; (*vêtement*) inside out; **~ et contre tous** *ou* **tout** against all opposition.

enviable [ɑ̃vjabl(ə)] *adj* enviable; **peu ~** unenviable.

envie [ɑ̃vi] *nf* (*sentiment*) envy; (*souhait*) desire, wish; (*tache sur la peau*) birthmark; (*filet de peau*) hangnail; **avoir ~ de** to feel like; (*désir plus fort*) to want; **avoir ~ de faire** to feel like doing; to want to do; **avoir ~ que** to wish that; **donner à qn l'~ de faire** to make sb want to do; **ça lui fait ~** he would like that.

envier [ɑ̃vje] *vt* to envy; **~ qch à qn** to envy sb sth; **n'avoir rien à ~ à** to have no cause to be envious of.

envieux, euse [ɑ̃vjø, -øz] *adj* envious.

environ [ɑ̃viʀɔ̃] *adv*: **~ 3 h/2 km, 3 h/2 km ~** (around) about 3 o'clock/2 km, 3 o'clock/2 km or so.

environnant, e [ɑ̃viʀɔnɑ̃, -ɑ̃t] *adj* surrounding.

environnement [ɑ̃viʀɔnmɑ̃] *nm* environment.

environnementaliste [ɑ̃viʀɔnmɑ̃talist(ə)] *nm/f* environmentalist.

environner [ɑ̃viʀɔne] *vt* to surround.

environs [ɑ̃viʀɔ̃] *nmpl* surroundings; **aux ~ de** around.

envisageable [ɑ̃vizaʒabl(ə)] *adj* conceivable.

envisager [ɑ̃vizaʒe] *vt* (*examiner, considérer*) to view, contemplate; (*avoir en vue*) to envisage; **~ de faire** to consider *ou* contemplate doing.

envoi [ɑ̃vwa] *nm* sending; (*paquet*) parcel, consignment; **~ contre remboursement** (*COMM*) cash on delivery.

envoie [ɑ̃vwa] *etc vb voir* **envoyer**.

envol [ɑ̃vɔl] *nm* takeoff.

envolée [ɑ̃vɔle] *nf* (*fig*) flight.

envoler [ɑ̃vɔle]: **s'~** *vi* (*oiseau*) to fly away *ou* off; (*avion*) to take off; (*papier, feuille*) to blow away; (*fig*) to vanish (into thin air).

envoûtant, e [ɑ̃vutɑ̃, -ɑ̃t] *adj* enchanting.

envoûtement [ɑ̃vutmɑ̃] *nm* bewitchment.

envoûter [ɑ̃vute] *vt* to bewitch.

envoyé, e [ɑ̃vwaje] *nm/f* (*POL*) envoy; (*PRESSE*) correspondent ♦ *adj*: **bien ~** (*remarque, réponse*) well-aimed.

envoyer [ɑ̃vwaje] *vt* to send; (*lancer*) to hurl, throw; **~ une gifle/un sourire à qn** to aim a blow/flash a smile at sb; **~ les couleurs** to run up the colours; **~ chercher** to send for; **~ par le fond** (*bateau*) to send to the bottom.

envoyeur, euse [ɑ̃vwajœʀ, -øz] *nm/f* sender.

enzyme [ɑ̃zim] *nf ou m* enzyme.

éolien, ne [eɔljɛ̃, -ɛn] *adj* wind *cpd*; **pompe ~ne** windpump.

EOR *sigle m* (= *élève officier de réserve*) ≈ military cadet.

éosine [eɔzin] *nf* eosin (*antiseptic used in France to treat skin ailments*).

épagneul, e [epaɲœl] *nm/f* spaniel.

épais, se [epɛ, -ɛs] *adj* thick.

épaisseur [epɛsœʀ] *nf* thickness.

épaissir [epesiʀ] *vt*, **s'~** *vi* to thicken.

épaississement [epesismɑ̃] *nm* thickening.

épanchement [epɑ̃ʃmɑ̃] *nm*: **un ~ de sinovie** water on the knee; **~s** *nmpl* (*fig*) (*sentimental*) outpourings.

épancher [epɑ̃ʃe] *vt* to give vent to; **s'~** *vi* to open one's heart; (*liquide*) to pour out.

épandage [epɑ̃daʒ] *nm* manure spreading.

épanoui, e [epanwi] *adj* (*éclos, ouvert, développé*) blooming; (*radieux*) radiant.

épanouir [epanwiʀ]: **s'~** *vi* (*fleur*) to bloom, open out; (*visage*) to light up; (*fig: se développer*) to blossom (out); (*: mentalement*) to open up.

épanouissement [epanwismɑ̃] *nm* blossoming; opening up.

épargnant, e [eparɲɑ̃, -ɑ̃t] *nm/f* saver, investor.

épargne [eparɲ(ə)] *nf* saving; **l'~-logement** property investment.

épargner [eparɲe] *vt* to save; (*ne pas tuer ou endommager*) to spare ♦ *vi* to save; **~ qch à qn** to spare sb sth.

éparpillement [eparpijmɑ̃] *nm* (*de papier*) scattering; (*des efforts*) dissipation.

éparpiller [eparpije] *vt* to scatter; (*pour répartir*) to disperse; (*fig: efforts*) to dissipate; **s'~**

vi to scatter; *(fig)* to dissipate one's efforts.

épars, e [epaʀ, -aʀs(ə)] *adj (maisons)* scattered; *(cheveux)* sparse.

épatant, e [epatɑ̃, -ɑ̃t] *adj (fam)* super, splendid.

épaté, e [epate] *adj:* **nez** ~ flat nose (with wide nostrils).

épater [epate] *vt* to amaze; *(impressionner)* to impress.

épaule [epol] *nf* shoulder.

épaulé-jeté, *pl* **épaulés-jetés** [epoleʒəte] *nm (SPORT)* clean-and-jerk.

épaulement [epolmɑ̃] *nm* escarpment; *(mur)* retaining wall.

épauler [epole] *vt (aider)* to back up, support; *(arme)* to raise (to one's shoulder) ♦ *vi* to (take) aim.

épaulette [epolɛt] *nf (MIL, d'un veston)* epaulette; *(de combinaison)* shoulder strap.

épave [epav] *nf* wreck.

épée [epe] *nf* sword.

épeler [eple] *vt* to spell.

éperdu, e [epɛʀdy] *adj (personne)* overcome; *(sentiment)* passionate; *(fuite)* frantic.

éperdument [epɛʀdymɑ̃] *adv (aimer)* wildly; *(espérer)* fervently.

éperlan [epɛʀlɑ̃] *nm (ZOOL)* smelt.

éperon [epʀɔ̃] *nm* spur.

éperonner [epʀɔne] *vt* to spur (on); *(navire)* to ram.

épervier [epɛʀvje] *nm (ZOOL)* sparrowhawk; *(PÊCHE)* casting net.

éphèbe [efɛb] *nm* beautiful young man.

éphémère [efemɛʀ] *adj* ephemeral, fleeting.

éphéméride [efemeʀid] *nf* block *ou* tear-off calendar.

épi [epi] *nm (de blé, d'orge)* ear; ~ **de cheveux** tuft of hair; **stationnement/se garer en** ~ parking/to park at an angle to the kerb.

épice [epis] *nf* spice.

épicé, e [epise] *adj* highly spiced, spicy; *(fig)* spicy.

épicéa [episea] *nm* spruce.

épicentre [episɑ̃tʀ(ə)] *nm* epicentre.

épicer [epise] *vt* to spice; *(fig)* to add spice to.

épicerie [episʀi] *nf (magasin)* grocer's shop; *(denrées)* groceries *pl;* ~ **fine** delicatessen (shop).

épicier, ière [episje, -jɛʀ] *nm/f* grocer.

épicurien, ne [epikyʀjɛ̃, -ɛn] *adj* epicurean.

épidémie [epidemi] *nf* epidemic.

épidémique [epidemik] *adj* epidemic.

épiderme [epidɛʀm(ə)] *nm* skin, epidermis.

épidermique [epidɛʀmik] *adj* skin *cpd,* epidermic.

épier [epje] *vt* to spy on, watch closely; *(occasion)* to look out for.

épieu, x [epjø] *nm* (hunting-)spear.

épigramme [epigʀam] *nf* epigram.

épigraphe [epigʀaf] *nf* epigraph.

épilation [epilɑsjɔ̃] *nf* removal of unwanted hair.

épilatoire [epilatwaʀ] *adj* depilatory, hair-removing.

épilepsie [epilɛpsi] *nf* epilepsy.

épileptique [epilɛptik] *adj, nm/f* epileptic.

épiler [epile] *vt (jambes)* to remove the hair from; *(sourcils)* to pluck; **s'**~ **les jambes** to remove the hair from one's legs; **s'**~ **les sourcils** to pluck one's eyebrows; **se faire** ~ to get unwanted hair removed; **crème à** ~ hair-removing *ou* depilatory cream; **pince à** ~ eyebrow tweezers.

épilogue [epilɔg] *nm (fig)* conclusion, dénouement.

épiloguer [epilɔge] *vi:* ~ **sur** to hold forth on.

épinard [epinaʀ] *nm (aussi:* ~**s)** spinach *sg.*

épine [epin] *nf* thorn, prickle; *(d'oursin etc)* spine, prickle; ~ **dorsale** backbone.

épineux, euse [epinø, -øz] *adj* thorny, prickly.

épinglage [epɛ̃glaʒ] *nm* pinning.

épingle [epɛ̃gl(ə)] *nf* pin; **tirer son** ~ **du jeu** to play one's game well; **tiré à quatre** ~**s** well turned-out; **monter qch en** ~ to build sth up, make a thing of sth *(fam);* ~ **à chapeau** hat-pin; ~ **à cheveux** hairpin; **virage en** ~ **à cheveux** hairpin bend; ~ **de cravate** tie pin; ~ **de nourrice** *ou* **de sûreté** *ou* **double** safety pin, nappy *(BRIT) ou* diaper *(US)* pin.

épingler [epɛ̃gle] *vt (badge, décoration):* ~ **qch sur** to pin sth on(to); *(COUTURE: tissu, robe)* to pin together; *(fam)* to catch, nick.

épinière [epinjɛʀ] *adj f voir* **moelle.**

Épiphanie [epifani] *nf* Epiphany.

épique [epik] *adj* epic.

épiscopal, e, aux [episkɔpal, -o] *adj* episcopal.

épiscopat [episkɔpa] *nm* bishopric, episcopate.

épisiotomie [epizjɔtomi] *nf (MÉD)* episiotomy.

épisode [epizɔd] *nm* episode; **film/roman à** ~**s** serialized film/novel, serial.

épisodique [epizɔdik] *adj* occasional.

épisodiquement [epizɔdikmɑ̃] *adv* occasionally.

épissure [episyʀ] *nf* splice.

épistémologie [epistemɔlɔʒi] *nf* epistemology.

épistolaire [epistɔlɛʀ] *adj* epistolary; **être en relations** ~**s avec qn** to correspond with sb.

épitaphe [epitaf] *nf* epitaph.

épithète [epitɛt] *nf (nom, surnom)* epithet; **adjectif** ~ attributive adjective.

épître [epitʀ(ə)] *nf* epistle.

éploré, e [eplɔʀe] *adj* in tears, tearful.

épluchage [eplyʃaʒ] *nm* peeling; *(de dossier etc)* careful reading *ou* analysis.

épluche-légumes [eplyʃlegym] *nm inv* potato peeler.

éplucher [eplyʃe] *vt (fruit, légumes)* to peel; *(comptes, dossier)* to go over with a fine-tooth comb.

éplucheur [eplyʃœʀ] *nm* (automatic) peeler.

épluchures [eplyʃyʀ] *nfpl* peelings.

épointer [epwɛ̃te] *vt* to blunt.

éponge [epɔ̃ʒ] *nf* sponge; **passer l'~ (sur)** (*fig*) to let bygones be bygones (with regard to); **jeter l'~** (*fig*) to throw in the towel; **~ métallique** scourer.

éponger [epɔ̃ʒe] *vt* (*liquide*) to mop *ou* sponge up; (*surface*) to sponge; (*fig: déficit*) to soak up, absorb; **s'~ le front** to mop one's brow.

épopée [epɔpe] *nf* epic.

époque [epɔk] *nf* (*de l'histoire*) age, era; (*de l'année, la vie*) time; **d'~** *adj* (*meuble*) period *cpd*; **à cette ~** at this (*ou* that) time *ou* period; **faire ~** to make history.

épouiller [epuje] *vt* to pick lice off; (*avec un produit*) to delouse.

époumoner [epumɔne]: **s'~** *vi* to shout (*ou* sing) o.s. hoarse.

épouse [epuz] *nf* wife (*pl* wives).

épouser [epuze] *vt* to marry; (*fig: idées*) to espouse; (*: forme*) to fit.

époussetage [epustaʒ] *nm* dusting.

épousseter [epuste] *vt* to dust.

époustouflant, e [epustuflɑ̃, -ɑ̃t] *adj* staggering, mind-boggling.

époustoufler [epustufle] *vt* to flabbergast, astound.

épouvantable [epuvɑ̃tabl(ə)] *adj* appalling, dreadful.

épouvantablement [epuvɑ̃tabləmɑ̃] *adj* terribly, dreadfully.

épouvantail [epuvɑ̃taj] *nm* (*à moineaux*) scarecrow; (*fig*) bog(e)y; bugbear.

épouvante [epuvɑ̃t] *nf* terror; **film d'~** horror film.

épouvanter [epuvɑ̃te] *vt* to terrify.

époux [epu] *nm* husband ♦ *nmpl*: **les ~** the (married) couple, the husband and wife.

éprendre [eprɑ̃dʀ(ə)]: **s'~ de** *vt* to fall in love with.

épreuve [eprœv] *nf* (*d'examen*) test; (*malheur, difficulté*) trial, ordeal; (*PHOTO*) print; (*TYPO*) proof; (*SPORT*) event; **à l'~ des balles/du feu** (*vêtement*) bulletproof/fireproof; **à toute ~** unfailing; **mettre à l'~** to put to the test; **~ de force** trial of strength; (*fig*) showdown; **~ de résistance** test of resistance; **~ de sélection** (*SPORT*) heat.

épris, e [epʀi, -iz] *vb voir* **éprendre** ♦ *adj*: **~ de** in love with.

éprouvant, e [epʀuvɑ̃, -ɑ̃t] *adj* trying.

éprouvé, e [epʀuve] *adj* tested, proven.

éprouver [epʀuve] *vt* (*tester*) to test; (*mettre à l'épreuve*) to put to the test; (*marquer, faire souffrir*) to afflict, distress; (*ressentir*) to experience.

éprouvette [epʀuvɛt] *nf* test tube.

EPS *sigle f* (= *Éducation physique et sportive*) ≈ PE.

épuisant, e [epɥizɑ̃, -ɑ̃t] *adj* exhausting.

épuisé, e [epɥize] *adj* exhausted; (*livre*) out of print.

épuisement [epɥizmɑ̃] *nm* exhaustion; **jusqu'à ~ des stocks** while stocks last.

épuiser [epɥize] *vt* (*fatiguer*) to exhaust, wear *ou* tire out; (*stock, sujet*) to exhaust; **s'~** *vi* to wear *ou* tire o.s. out, exhaust o.s.; (*stock*) to run out.

épuisette [epɥizɛt] *nf* landing net; shrimping net.

épuration [epyʀasjɔ̃] *nf* purification; purging; refinement.

épure [epyʀ] *nf* working drawing.

épurer [epyʀe] *vt* (*liquide*) to purify; (*parti, administration*) to purge; (*langue, texte*) to refine.

équarrir [ekaʀiʀ] *vt* (*pierre, arbre*) to square (off); (*animal*) to quarter.

équateur [ekwatœʀ] *nm* equator; **(la république de) l'É~** Ecuador.

équation [ekwasjɔ̃] *nf* equation; **mettre en ~** to equate; **~ du premier/second degré** simple/quadratic equation.

équatorial, e, aux [ekwatɔʀjal, -o] *adj* equatorial.

équatorien, ne [ekwatɔʀjɛ̃, -ɛn] *adj* Ecuadorian ♦ *nm/f*: **É~, ne** Ecuadorian.

équerre [ekɛʀ] *nf* (*à dessin*) (set) square; (*pour fixer*) brace; **en ~** at right angles; **à l'~, d'~** straight; **double ~** T-square.

équestre [ekɛstʀ(ə)] *adj* equestrian.

équeuter [ekøte] *vt* (*CULIN*) to remove the stalk(s) from.

équidé [ekide] *nm* (*ZOOL*) member of the horse family.

équidistance [ekɥidistɑ̃s] *nf*: **à ~ (de)** equidistant (from).

équidistant, e [ekɥidistɑ̃, -ɑ̃t] *adj*: **~ (de)** equidistant (from).

équilatéral, e, aux [ekɥilateʀal, -o] *adj* equilateral.

équilibrage [ekilibʀaʒ] *nm* (*AUTO*): **~ des roues** wheel balancing.

équilibre [ekilibʀ(ə)] *nm* balance; (*d'une balance*) equilibrium; **~ budgétaire** balanced budget; **garder/perdre l'~** to keep/lose one's balance; **être en ~** to be balanced; **mettre en ~** to make steady; **avoir le sens de l'~** to be well-balanced.

équilibré, e [ekilibʀe] *adj* (*fig*) well-balanced, stable.

équilibrer [ekilibʀe] *vt* to balance; **s'~** (*poids*) to balance; (*fig: défauts etc*) to balance each other out.

équilibriste [ekilibʀist(ə)] *nm/f* tightrope walker.

équinoxe [ekinɔks] *nm* equinox.

équipage [ekipaʒ] *nm* crew; **en grand ~** in great array.

équipe [ekip] *nf* team; (*bande: parfois péj*) bunch; **travailler par ~s** to work in shifts; **travailler en ~** to work as a team; **faire ~ avec** to team up with; **~ de chercheurs** research team; **~ de secours** *ou* **de sauvetage** rescue team.

équipé, e [ekipe] *adj* (*cuisine etc*) equipped, fitted(-out) ♦ *nf* escapade.

équipement [ekipmɑ̃] *nm* equipment; **~s** *nmpl* amenities, facilities; installations; **biens/dépenses d'~** capital goods/expenditure; **ministère de l'É~** department of public works; **~s sportifs/collectifs** sports/community facilities *ou* resources.

équiper [ekipe] *vt* to equip; (*voiture, cuisine*) to equip, fit out; **~ qn/qch de** to equip sb/sth with; **s'~** (*sportif*) to equip o.s., kit o.s. out.

équipier, ière [ekipje, -jɛʀ] *nm/f* team member.

équitable [ekitabl(ə)] *adj* fair.

équitablement [ekitabləmɑ̃] *adv* fairly, equitably.

équitation [ekitɑsjɔ̃] *nf* (horse-)riding; **faire de l'~** to go (horse-)riding.

équité [ekite] *nf* equity.

équivaille [ekivaj] *etc vb voir* **équivaloir**.

équivalence [ekivalɑ̃s] *nf* equivalence.

équivalent, e [ekivalɑ̃, -ɑ̃t] *adj, nm* equivalent.

équivaloir [ekivalwaʀ] **~ à** *vt* to be equivalent to; (*représenter*) to amount to.

équivaut [ekivo] *etc vb voir* **équivaloir**.

équivoque [ekivɔk] *adj* equivocal, ambiguous; (*louche*) dubious ♦ *nf* ambiguity.

érable [eʀabl(ə)] *nm* maple.

éradication [eʀadikɑsjɔ̃] *nf* eradication.

éradiquer [eʀadike] *vt* to eradicate.

érafler [eʀafle] *vt* to scratch; **s'~ la main/les jambes** to scrape *ou* scratch one's hand/legs.

éraflure [eʀaflyʀ] *nf* scratch.

éraillé, e [eʀaje] *adj* (*voix*) rasping, hoarse.

ère [ɛʀ] *nf* era; **en l'an 1050 de notre ~** in the year 1050 A.D.

érection [eʀɛksjɔ̃] *nf* erection.

éreintant, e [eʀɛ̃tɑ̃, -ɑ̃t] *adj* exhausting.

éreinté, e [eʀɛ̃te] *adj* exhausted.

éreintement [eʀɛ̃tmɑ̃] *nm* exhaustion.

éreinter [eʀɛ̃te] *vt* to exhaust, wear out; (*fig: critiquer*) to slate; **s'~** (**à faire qch/à qch**) to wear o.s. out (doing sth/with sth).

ergonomie [ɛʀgɔnɔmi] *nf* ergonomics *sg*.

ergonomique [ɛʀgɔnɔmik] *adj* ergonomic.

ergot [ɛʀgo] *nm* (*de coq*) spur; (*TECH*) lug.

ergoter [ɛʀgɔte] *vi* to split hairs, argue over details.

ergoteur, euse [ɛʀgɔtœʀ, -øz] *nm/f* hairsplitter.

ériger [eʀiʒe] *vt* (*monument*) to erect; **~ qch en principe/loi** to make sth a principle/law; **s'~ en critique (de)** to set o.s. up as a critic (of).

ermitage [ɛʀmitaʒ] *nm* retreat.

ermite [ɛʀmit] *nm* hermit.

éroder [eʀɔde] *vt* to erode.

érogène [eʀɔʒɛn] *adj* erogenous.

érosion [eʀozjɔ̃] *nf* erosion.

érotique [eʀɔtik] *adj* erotic.

érotiquement [eʀɔtikmɑ̃] *adv* erotically.

érotisme [eʀɔtism(ə)] *nm* eroticism.

errance [eʀɑ̃s] *nf* wandering.

errant, e [eʀɑ̃, -ɑ̃t] *adj*: **un chien ~** a stray dog.

erratum, a [eʀatɔm, -a] *nm* erratum (*pl* -a).

errements [eʀmɑ̃] *nmpl* misguided ways.

errer [eʀe] *vi* to wander.

erreur [eʀœʀ] *nf* mistake, error; (*INFORM*: *de programme*) bug; (*morale*): **~s** *nfpl* errors; **être dans l'~** to be wrong; **induire qn en ~** to mislead sb; **par ~** by mistake; **sauf ~** unless I'm mistaken; **faire ~** to be mistaken; **~ de date** mistake in the date; **~ de fait** error of fact; **~ d'impression** (*TYPO*) misprint; **~ judiciaire** miscarriage of justice; **~ de jugement** error of judgment; **~ matérielle** *ou* **d'écriture** clerical error; **~ tactique** tactical error.

erroné, e [eʀɔne] *adj* wrong, erroneous.

ersatz [ɛʀzats] *nm* substitute, ersatz; **~ de café** coffee substitute.

éructer [eʀykte] *vi* to belch.

érudit, e [eʀydi, -it] *adj* erudite, learned ♦ *nm/f* scholar.

érudition [eʀydisjɔ̃] *nf* erudition, scholarship.

éruptif, ive [eʀyptif, -iv] *adj* eruptive.

éruption [eʀypsjɔ̃] *nf* eruption; (*cutanée*) outbreak; (: *boutons*) rash; (*fig: de joie, colère, folie*) outburst.

es [ɛ] *vb voir* **être**.

ès [ɛs] *prép*: **licencié ~ lettres/sciences** ≈ Bachelor of Arts/Science; **docteur ~ lettres** ≈ doctor of philosophy, PhD.

E/S *abr* (= *entrée/sortie*) I/O (= *in/out*).

esbroufe [ɛsbʀuf] *nf*: **faire de l'~** to have people on.

escabeau, x [ɛskabo] *nm* (*tabouret*) stool; (*échelle*) stepladder.

escadre [ɛskadʀ(ə)] *nf* (*NAVIG*) squadron; (*AVIAT*) wing.

escadrille [ɛskadʀij] *nf* (*AVIAT*) flight.

escadron [ɛskadʀɔ̃] *nm* squadron.

escalade [ɛskalad] *nf* climbing *no pl*; (*POL etc*) escalation.

escalader [ɛskalade] *vt* to climb, scale.

escalator [ɛskalatɔʀ] *nm* escalator.

escale [ɛskal] *nf* (*NAVIG*) call; (: *port*) port of call; (*AVIAT*) stop(over); **faire ~ à** to put in at, call in at; to stop over at; **~ technique** (*AVIAT*) refuelling stop.

escalier [ɛskalje] *nm* stairs *pl*; **dans l'~** *ou* **les ~s** on the stairs; **descendre l'~** *ou* **les ~s** to go downstairs; **~ mécanique** *ou* **roulant** escalator; **~ de secours** fire escape; **~ de service** backstairs; **~ à vis** *ou* **en colimaçon** spiral staircase.

escalope [ɛskalɔp] *nf* escalope.

escamotable [ɛskamɔtabl(ə)] *adj* (*train d'atterrissage, antenne*) retractable; (*table, lit*) fold-away.

escamoter [ɛskamɔte] *vt* (*esquiver*) to get round, evade; (*faire disparaître*) to conjure away; (*dérober: portefeuille etc*) to snatch; (*train d'atterrissage*) to retract; (*mots*) to miss out.

escapade [ɛskapad] *nf*: **faire une** ~ to go on a jaunt; (*s'enfuir*) to run away *ou* off.

escarbille [ɛskaʀbij] *nf* bit of grit.

escarcelle [ɛskaʀsɛl] *nf*: **faire tomber dans l'**~ (*argent*) to bring in.

escargot [ɛskaʀgo] *nm* snail.

escarmouche [ɛskaʀmuʃ] *nf* (*MIL*) skirmish; (*fig: propos hostiles*) angry exchange.

escarpé, e [ɛskaʀpe] *adj* steep.

escarpement [ɛskaʀpəmɑ̃] *nm* steep slope.

escarpin [ɛskaʀpɛ̃] *nm* flat(-heeled) shoe.

escarre [ɛskaʀ] *nf* bedsore.

Escaut [ɛsko] *nm*: **l'**~ the Scheldt.

escient [ɛsjɑ̃] *nm*: **à bon** ~ advisedly.

esclaffer [ɛsklafe]: **s'**~ *vi* to guffaw.

esclandre [ɛsklɑ̃dʀ(ə)] *nm* scene, fracas.

esclavage [ɛsklavaʒ] *nm* slavery.

esclavagiste [ɛsklavaʒist(ə)] *adj* pro-slavery ♦ *nm/f* supporter of slavery.

esclave [ɛsklav] *nm/f* slave; **être** ~ **de** (*fig*) to be a slave of.

escogriffe [ɛskɔgʀif] *nm* (*péj*) beanpole.

escompte [ɛskɔ̃t] *nm* discount.

escompter [ɛskɔ̃te] *vt* (*COMM*) to discount; (*espérer*) to expect, reckon upon; ~ **que** to reckon *ou* expect that.

escorte [ɛskɔʀt(ə)] *nf* escort; **faire** ~ **à** to escort.

escorter [ɛskɔʀte] *vt* to escort.

escorteur [ɛskɔʀtœʀ] *nm* (*NAVIG*) escort (ship).

escouade [ɛskwad] *nf* squad; (*fig: groupe de personnes*) group.

escrime [ɛskʀim] *nf* fencing; **faire de l'**~ to fence.

escrimer [ɛskʀime]: **s'**~ *vi*: **s'**~ **à faire** to wear o.s. out doing.

escrimeur, euse [ɛskʀimœʀ, -øz] *nm/f* fencer.

escroc [ɛskʀo] *nm* swindler, con-man.

escroquer [ɛskʀɔke] *vt*: ~ **qn (de qch)/qch à qn** to swindle sb (out of sth)/sth out of sb.

escroquerie [ɛskʀɔkʀi] *nf* swindle.

ésotérique [ezɔteʀik] *adj* esoteric.

espace [ɛspas] *nm* space; ~ **publicitaire** advertising space; ~ **vital** living space.

espacé, e [ɛspase] *adj* spaced out.

espacement [ɛspasmɑ̃] *nm*: ~ **proportionnel** proportional spacing (*on printer*).

espacer [ɛspase] *vt* to space out; **s'**~ *vi* (*visites etc*) to become less frequent.

espadon [ɛspadɔ̃] *nm* swordfish *inv*.

espadrille [ɛspadʀij] *nf* rope-soled sandal.

Espagne [ɛspaɲ(ə)] *nf*: **l'**~ Spain.

espagnol, e [ɛspaɲɔl] *adj* Spanish ♦ *nm* (*LING*) Spanish ♦ *nm/f*: **E**~, **e** Spaniard.

espagnolette [ɛspaɲɔlɛt] *nf* (window) catch; **fermé à l'**~ resting on the catch.

espalier [ɛspalje] *nm* (*arbre fruitier*) espalier.

espèce [ɛspɛs] *nf* (*BIO, BOT, ZOOL*) species *inv*; (*gén: sorte*) sort, kind, type; (*péj*): ~ **de maladroit/de brute!** you clumsy oaf/you

brute!; ~**s** *nfpl* (*COMM*) cash *sg*; (*REL*) species; **de toute** ~ of all kinds *ou* sorts; **en l'**~ *adv* in the case in point; **payer en** ~**s** to pay (in) cash; **cas d'**~ individual case; **l'**~ **humaine** humankind.

espérance [ɛspeʀɑ̃s] *nf* hope; ~ **de vie** life expectancy.

espéranto [ɛspeʀɑ̃to] *nm* esperanto.

espérer [ɛspeʀe] *vt* to hope for; **j'espère (bien)** I hope so; ~ **que/faire** to hope that/to do; ~ **en** to trust in.

espiègle [ɛspjɛgl(ə)] *adj* mischievous.

espièglerie [ɛspjɛgləʀi] *nf* mischievousness; (*tour, farce*) piece of mischief, prank.

espion, ne [ɛspjɔ̃, -ɔn] *nm/f* spy; **avion** ~ spy plane.

espionnage [ɛspjɔnaʒ] *nm* espionage, spying; **film/roman d'**~ spy film/novel.

espionner [ɛspjɔne] *vt* to spy (up)on.

espionnite [ɛspjɔnit] *nf* spy mania.

esplanade [ɛsplanad] *nf* esplanade.

espoir [ɛspwaʀ] *nm* hope; **l'**~ **de qch/de faire qch** the hope of sth/of doing sth; **avoir bon** ~ **que ...** to have high hopes that ...; **garder l'**~ **que ...** to remain hopeful that ...; **un** ~ **de la boxe/du ski** one of boxing's/skiing's hopefuls, one of the hopes of boxing/skiing; **sans** ~ *adj* hopeless.

esprit [ɛspʀi] *nm* (*pensée, intellect*) mind; (*humour, ironie*) wit; (*mentalité, d'une loi etc, fantôme etc*) spirit; **l'**~ **d'équipe/de compétition** team/competitive spirit; **faire de l'**~ to try to be witty; **reprendre ses** ~**s** to come to; **perdre l'**~ to lose one's mind; **avoir bon/mauvais** ~ to be of a good/bad disposition; **avoir l'**~ **à faire qch** to have a mind to do sth; **avoir l'**~ **critique** to be critical; ~ **de contradiction** contrariness; ~ **de corps** esprit de corps; ~ **de famille** family loyalty; **l'**~ **malin** (*le diable*) the Evil One; ~**s chagrins** faultfinders.

esquif [ɛskif] *nm* skiff.

esquimau, de, x [ɛskimo, -od] *adj* Eskimo ♦ *nm* (*LING*) Eskimo; (*glace*): **E**~ ® ice lolly (*BRIT*), popsicle (*US*) ♦ *nm/f*: **E**~, **de** Eskimo; **chien** ~ husky.

esquinter [ɛskɛ̃te] *vt* (*fam*) to mess up; **s'**~ *vi*: **s'**~ **à faire qch** to knock o.s. out doing sth.

esquisse [ɛskis] *nf* sketch; **d'un sourire/changement** a hint of a smile/of change.

esquisser [ɛskise] *vt* to sketch; **s'**~ *vi* (*amélioration*) to begin to be detectable; ~ **un sourire** to give a hint of a smile.

esquive [ɛskiv] *nf* (*BOXE*) dodging; (*fig*) side-stepping.

esquiver [ɛskive] *vt* to dodge; **s'**~ *vi* to slip away.

essai [ɛsɛ] *nm* trying; (*tentative*) attempt, try; (*RUGBY*) try; (*LITTÉRATURE*) essay; ~**s** *nmpl* (*AUTO*) trials; **à l'**~ on a trial basis; ~ **gratuit** (*COMM*) free trial.

essaim [ɛsɛ̃] *nm* swarm.

essaimer [eseme] *vi* to swarm; (*fig*) to spread, expand.

essayage [esɛjaʒ] *nm* (*d'un vêtement*) trying on, fitting; **salon d'~** fitting room; **cabine d'~** fitting room (*cubicle*).

essayer [eseje] *vt* (*gén*) to try; (*vêtement, chaussures*) to try (on); (*restaurant, méthode, voiture*) to try (out) ♦ *vi* to try; **~ de faire** to try *ou* attempt to do; **s'~ à faire** to try one's hand at doing; **essayez un peu!** (*menace*) just you try!

essayeur, euse [esɛjœʀ, -øz] *nm/f* (*chez un tailleur etc*) fitter.

essayiste [esejist(ə)] *nm/f* essayist.

ESSEC [esɛk] *sigle f* (= *École supérieure des sciences économiques et sociales*) *grande école for management and business studies.*

essence [esɑ̃s] *nf* (*de voiture*) petrol (*BRIT*), gas(oline) (*US*); (*extrait de plante, PHILOSOPHIE*) essence; (*espèce: d'arbre*) species *inv*; **prendre de l'~** to get (some) petrol *ou* gas; **par ~** (*essentiellement*) essentially; **~ de citron/rose** lemon/rose oil; **~ de térébenthine** turpentine.

essentiel, le [esɑ̃sjɛl] *adj* essential ♦ *nm*: **l'~ d'un discours/d'une œuvre** the essence of a speech/work of art; **emporter l'~** to take the essentials; **c'est l'~** (*ce qui importe*) that's the main thing; **l'~ de** (*la majeure partie*) the main part of.

essentiellement [esɑ̃sjɛlmɑ̃] *adv* essentially.

esseulé, e [esœle] *adj* forlorn.

essieu, x [esjø] *nm* axle.

essor [esɔʀ] *nm* (*de l'économie etc*) rapid expansion; **prendre son ~** (*oiseau*) to fly off.

essorage [esɔʀaʒ] *nm* wringing out; spin-drying; spinning; shaking.

essorer [esɔʀe] *vt* (*en tordant*) to wring (out); (*par la force centrifuge*) to spin-dry; (*salade*) to spin; (: *en secouant*) to shake dry.

essoreuse [esɔʀøz] *nf* mangle, wringer; (*à tambour*) spin-dryer.

essouffler [esufle] *vt* to make breathless; **s'~** *vi* to get out of breath; (*fig: économie*) to run out of steam.

essuie [esɥi] *etc vb voir* **essuyer.**

essuie-glace [esɥiglas] *nm* windscreen (*BRIT*) *ou* windshield (*US*) wiper.

essuie-mains [esɥimɛ̃] *nm inv* hand towel.

essuierai [esɥiʀe] *etc vb voir* **essuyer.**

essuie-tout [esɥitu] *nm inv* kitchen paper.

essuyer [esɥije] *vt* to wipe; (*fig: subir*) to suffer; **s'~** (*après le bain*) to dry o.s.; **~ la vaisselle** to dry up, dry the dishes.

est [ɛ] *vb voir* **être** ♦ *nm* [ɛst]: **l'~** the east ♦ *adj inv* east; (*région*) east(ern); **à l'~** in the east; (*direction*) to the east, east(wards); **à l'~ de** (to the) east of; **les pays de l'E~** the eastern countries.

estafette [ɛstafɛt] *nf* (*MIL*) dispatch rider.

estafilade [ɛstafilad] *nf* gash, slash.

est-allemand, e [ɛstalmɑ̃, -ɑ̃d] *adj* East German.

estaminet [ɛstaminɛ] *nm* tavern.

estampe [ɛstɑ̃p] *nf* print, engraving.

estamper [ɛstɑ̃pe] *vt* (*monnaies etc*) to stamp; (*fam: escroquer*) to swindle.

estampille [ɛstɑ̃pij] *nf* stamp.

est-ce que [ɛskə] *adv*: **~ c'est cher/c'était bon?** is it expensive/was it good?; **quand est-ce qu'il part?** when does he leave?, when is he leaving?; **où est-ce qu'il va?** where's he going?; **qui est-ce qui le connaît/a fait ça?** who knows him/did that?; *voir aussi* **que.**

este [ɛst(ə)] *adj* Estonian ♦ *nm/f*: **E~** Estonian.

esthète [ɛstɛt] *nm/f* aesthete.

esthéticienne [ɛstetisjɛn] *nf* beautician.

esthétique [ɛstetik] *adj* (*sens, jugement*) aesthetic; (*beau*) attractive, aesthetically pleasing ♦ *nf* aesthetics *sg*; **l'~ industrielle** industrial design.

esthétiquement [ɛstetikmɑ̃] *adv* aesthetically.

estimable [ɛstimabl(ə)] *adj* respected.

estimatif, ive [ɛstimatif, -iv] *adj* estimated.

estimation [ɛstimasjɔ̃] *nf* valuation; assessment; **d'après mes ~s** according to my calculations.

estime [ɛstim] *nf* esteem, regard; **avoir de l'~ pour qn** to think highly of sb.

estimer [ɛstime] *vt* (*respecter*) to esteem, hold in high regard; (*expertiser*) to value; (*évaluer*) to assess, estimate; (*penser*): **~ que/être** to consider that/o.s. to be; **s'~ satisfait/heureux** to feel satisfied/happy; **j'estime la distance à 10 km** I reckon the distance to be 10 km.

estival, e, aux [ɛstival, -o] *adj* summer *cpd*; **station ~e** (summer) holiday resort.

estivant, e [ɛstivɑ̃, -ɑ̃t] *nm/f* (summer) holiday-maker.

estoc [ɛstɔk] *nm*: **frapper d'~ et de taille** to cut and thrust.

estocade [ɛstɔkad] *nf* death-blow.

estomac [ɛstɔma] *nm* stomach; **avoir mal à l'~** to have stomach ache; **avoir l'~ creux** to have an empty stomach.

estomaqué, e [ɛstɔmake] *adj* flabbergasted.

estompe [ɛstɔ̃p] *nf* stump; (*dessin*) stump drawing.

estompé, e [ɛstɔ̃pe] *adj* blurred.

estomper [ɛstɔ̃pe] *vt* (*ART*) to shade off; (*fig*) to blur, dim; **s'~** *vi* (*sentiments*) to soften; (*contour*) to become blurred.

Estonie [ɛstɔni] *nf*: **l'~** Estonia.

estonien, ne [ɛstɔnjɛ̃, -ɛn] *adj* Estonian ♦ *nm* (*LING*) Estonian ♦ *nm/f*: **E~, ne** Estonian.

estrade [ɛstʀad] *nf* platform, rostrum.

estragon [ɛstʀagɔ̃] *nm* tarragon.

estropié, e [ɛstʀɔpje] *nm/f* cripple.

estropier [ɛstʀɔpje] *vt* to cripple, maim; (*fig*) to twist, distort.

estuaire [ɛstɥɛʀ] *nm* estuary.

estudiantin, e [ɛstydjɑ̃tɛ̃, -in] *adj* student *cpd*.

esturgeon [ɛstyʀʒɔ̃] *nm* sturgeon.

et [e] *conj* and; ~ **lui?** what about him?; ~ **alors?**, ~ **(puis) après?** so what?; *(ensuite)* and then?

ét. *abr* = **étage**.

ETA [eta] *sigle m (POL)* ETA.

étable [etabl(ə)] *nf* cowshed.

établi, e [etabli] *adj* established ♦ *nm* (work)bench.

établir [etabliʀ] *vt (papiers d'identité, facture)* to make out; *(liste, programme)* to draw up; *(gouvernement, artisan etc: aider à s'installer)* to set up, establish; *(entreprise, atelier, camp)* to set up; *(réputation, usage, fait, culpabilité, relations)* to establish; *(SPORT: record)* to set; **s'~** *vi (se faire: entente etc)* to be established; **s'~ (à son compte)** to set up in business; **s'~ à/près de** to settle in/near.

établissement [etablismɑ̃] *nm* making out; drawing up; setting up, establishing; *(entreprise, institution)* establishment; ~ **de crédit** credit institution; ~ **hospitalier** hospital complex; ~ **industriel** industrial plant, factory; ~ **scolaire** school, educational establishment.

étage [etaʒ] *nm (d'immeuble)* storey *(BRIT)*, story *(US)*, floor; *(de fusée)* stage; *(GÉO: de culture, végétation)* level; **au 2ème** ~ on the 2nd *(BRIT)* ou 3rd *(US)* floor; **à l'**~ upstairs; **maison à deux** ~**s** two-storey *ou* -story house; **de bas** ~ *adj* low-born; *(médiocre)* inferior.

étager [etaʒe] *vt (cultures)* to lay out in tiers; **s'~** *vi (prix)* to range; *(zones, cultures)* to lie on different levels.

étagère [etaʒɛʀ] *nf (rayon)* shelf; *(meuble)* shelves *pl*, set of shelves.

étai [etɛ] *nm* stay, prop.

étain [etɛ̃] *nm* tin; *(ORFÈVRERIE)* pewter *no pl*.

étais [etɛ] *etc vb voir* **être**.

étal [etal] *nm* stall.

étalage [etalaʒ] *nm* display; *(vitrine)* display window; **faire** ~ **de** to show off, parade.

étalagiste [etalaʒist(ə)] *nm/f* window-dresser.

étale [etal] *adj (mer)* slack.

étalement [etalmɑ̃] *nm* spreading; *(échelonnement)* staggering.

étaler [etale] *vt (carte, nappe)* to spread (out); *(peinture, liquide)* to spread; *(échelonner: paiements, dates, vacances)* to spread, stagger; *(exposer: marchandises)* to display; *(richesses, connaissances)* to parade; **s'~** *vi (liquide)* to spread out; *(fam)* to come a cropper *(BRIT)*, fall flat on one's face; **s'~ sur** *(suj: paiements etc)* to be spread over.

étalon [etalɔ̃] *nm (mesure)* standard; *(cheval)* stallion; **l'~-or** the gold standard.

étalonner [etalɔne] *vt* to calibrate.

étamer [etame] *vt (casserole)* to tin(plate); *(glace)* to silver.

étamine [etamin] *nf (BOT)* stamen; *(tissu)* butter muslin.

étanche [etɑ̃ʃ] *adj (récipient; aussi fig)* watertight; *(montre, vêtement)* waterproof; ~ **à l'air** airtight.

étanchéité [etɑ̃ʃeite] *nf* watertightness; airtightness.

étancher [etɑ̃ʃe] *vt (liquide)* to stop (flowing); ~ **sa soif** to quench *ou* slake one's thirst.

étançon [etɑ̃sɔ̃] *nm (TECH)* prop.

étançonner [etɑ̃sɔne] *vt* to prop up.

étang [etɑ̃] *nm* pond.

étant [etɑ̃] *vb voir* **être, donné**.

étape [etap] *nf* stage; *(lieu d'arrivée)* stopping place; *(: CYCLISME)* staging point; **faire** ~ **à** to stop off at; **brûler les** ~**s** *(fig)* to cut corners.

état [eta] *nm (POL, condition)* state; *(d'un article d'occasion etc)* condition, state; *(liste)* inventory, statement; *(condition: professionnelle)* profession, trade; *(: sociale)* status; **en mauvais** ~ in poor condition; **en** ~ **(de marche)** in (working) order; **remettre en** ~ to repair; **hors d'**~ out of order; **être en** ~**/hors d'**~ **de faire** to be in a state/in no fit state to do; **en tout** ~ **de cause** in any event; **être dans tous ses** ~**s** to be in a state; **faire** ~ **de** *(alléguer)* to put forward; **en** ~ **d'arrestation** under arrest; ~ **de grâce** *(REL)* state of grace; *(fig)* honeymoon period; **en** ~ **de grâce** *(fig)* inspired; **en** ~ **d'ivresse** under the influence of drink; ~ **de choses** *(situation)* state of affairs; ~ **civil** civil status; *(bureau)* registry office *(BRIT)*; ~ **d'esprit** frame of mind; ~ **des lieux** inventory of fixtures; ~ **de santé** state of health; ~ **de siège/d'urgence** state of siege/emergency; ~ **de veille** *(PSYCH)* waking state; ~**s d'âme** moods; **les É~s barbaresques** the Barbary States; **les É~s du Golfe** the Gulf States; ~**s de service** service record *sg*.

étatique [etatik] *adj* state *cpd*, State *cpd*.

étatisation [etatizasjɔ̃] *nf* nationalization.

étatiser [etatize] *vt* to bring under state control.

étatisme [etatism(ə)] *nm* state control.

étatiste [etatist(ə)] *adj (doctrine etc)* of state control ♦ *nm/f* partisan of state control.

état-major, *pl* **états-majors** [etamaʒɔʀ] *nm (MIL)* staff; *(d'un parti etc)* top advisers *pl*; *(d'une entreprise)* top management.

État-providence [etapʀɔvidɑ̃s] *nm* welfare state.

États-Unis [etazyni] *nmpl*: **les** ~ **(d'Amérique)** the United States (of America).

étau, x [eto] *nm* vice *(BRIT)*, vise *(US)*.

étayer [eteje] *vt* to prop *ou* shore up; *(fig)* to back up.

et c(a)etera [ɛtseteʀa], **etc.** *adv* et cetera, and so on, etc.

été [ete] *pp de* **être** ♦ *nm* summer; **en** ~ in summer.

éteignais [etɛɲɛ] *etc vb voir* **éteindre**.

éteignoir [etɛɲwaʀ] *nm* (candle) snuffer; *(péj)* killjoy, wet blanket.

éteindre [etɛ̃dʀ(ə)] *vt* (*lampe, lumière, radio, chauffage*) to turn *ou* switch off; (*cigarette, incendie, bougie*) to put out, extinguish; (*JUR: dette*) to extinguish; **s'~** *vi* to go off; to go out; (*mourir*) to pass away.

éteint, e [etɛ̃, -ɛ̃t] *pp de* **éteindre** ♦ *adj* (*fig*) lacklustre, dull; (*volcan*) extinct; **tous feux ~s** (*AUTO: rouler*) without lights.

étendard [etɑ̃daʀ] *nm* standard.

étendre [etɑ̃dʀ(ə)] *vt* (*appliquer: pâte, liquide*) to spread; (*déployer: carte etc*) to spread out; (*sur un fil: lessive, linge*) to hang up *ou* out; (*bras, jambes, par terre: blessé*) to stretch out; (*diluer*) to dilute, thin; (*fig: agrandir*) to extend; (*fam: adversaire*) to floor; **s'~** *vi* (*augmenter, se propager*) to spread; (*terrain, forêt etc*): **s'~ jusqu'à/de ... à** to stretch as far as/ from ... to; **s'~** (**sur**) (*s'allonger*) to stretch out (upon); (*se coucher*) to lie down (on); (*fig: expliquer*) to elaborate *ou* enlarge (upon).

étendu, e [etɑ̃dy] *adj* extensive ♦ *nf* (*d'eau, de sable*) stretch, expanse; (*importance*) extent.

éternel, le [etɛʀnɛl] *adj* eternal; **les neiges ~les** perpetual snow.

éternellement [etɛʀnɛlmɑ̃] *adv* eternally.

éterniser [etɛʀnize]: **s'~** *vi* to last for ages; (*personne*) to stay for ages.

éternité [etɛʀnite] *nf* eternity; **il y a** *ou* **ça fait une ~ que** it's ages since; **de toute ~** from time immemorial.

éternuement [etɛʀnymɑ̃] *nm* sneeze.

éternuer [etɛʀnɥe] *vi* to sneeze.

êtes [ɛt] *vb voir* **être**.

étêter [etete] *vt* (*arbre*) to poll(ard); (*clou, poisson*) to cut the head off.

éther [etɛʀ] *nm* ether.

éthéré, e [etere] *adj* ethereal.

Ethiopie [etjɔpi] *nf*: **l'~** Ethiopia.

éthiopien, ne [etjɔpjɛ̃, -ɛn] *adj* Ethiopian.

éthique [etik] *adj* ethical ♦ *nf* ethics *sg*.

ethnie [ɛtni] *nf* ethnic group.

ethnique [ɛtnik] *adj* ethnic.

ethnographe [ɛtnɔgʀaf] *nm/f* ethnographer.

ethnographie [ɛtnɔgʀafi] *nf* ethnography.

ethnographique [ɛtnɔgʀafik] *adj* ethnographic(al).

ethnologie [ɛtnɔlɔʒi] *nf* ethnology.

ethnologique [ɛtnɔlɔʒik] *adj* ethnological.

ethnologue [ɛtnɔlɔg] *nm/f* ethnologist.

éthylique [etilik] *adj* alcoholic.

éthylisme [etilism(ə)] *nm* alcoholism.

étiage [etjaʒ] *nm* low water.

étiez [etje] *vb voir* **être**.

étincelant, e [etɛ̃slɑ̃, -ɑ̃t] *adj* sparkling.

étinceler [etɛ̃sle] *vi* to sparkle.

étincelle [etɛ̃sɛl] *nf* spark.

étioler [etjɔle]: **s'~** *vi* to wilt.

étions [etjɔ̃] *vb voir* **être**.

étique [etik] *adj* skinny, bony.

étiquetage [etiktaʒ] *nm* labelling.

étiqueter [etikte] *vt* to label.

étiquette [etikɛt] *vb voir* **étiqueter** ♦ *nf* label; (*protocole*): **l'~** etiquette.

étirer [etiʀe] *vt* to stretch; (*ressort*) to stretch out; **s'~** *vi* (*personne*) to stretch; (*convoi, route*): **s'~ sur** to stretch out over.

étoffe [etɔf] *nf* material, fabric; **avoir l'~ d'un chef** *etc* to be cut out to be a leader *etc*; **avoir de l'~** to be a forceful personality.

étoffer [etɔfe] *vt*, **s'~** *vi* to fill out.

étoile [etwal] *nf* star ♦ *adj*: **danseuse** *ou* **danceur ~** leading dancer; **la bonne/mauvaise ~ de qn** sb's lucky/unlucky star; **à la belle ~** (out) in the open; **~ filante** shooting star; **~ de mer** starfish; **~ polaire** pole star.

étoilé, e [etwale] *adj* starry.

étole [etɔl] *nf* stole.

étonnamment [etɔnamɑ̃] *adv* amazingly.

étonnant, e [etɔnɑ̃, -ɑ̃t] *adj* surprising.

étonné, e [etɔne] *adj* surprised.

étonnement [etɔnmɑ̃] *nm* surprise; **à mon grand ~ ...** to my great surprise *ou* amazement ....

étonner [etɔne] *vt* to surprise; **s'~ que/de** be surprised that/at; **cela m'étonnerait (que)** (*j'en doute*) I'd be (very) surprised (if).

étouffant, e [etufɑ̃, -ɑ̃t] *adj* stifling.

étouffé, e [etufe] *adj* (*asphyxié*) suffocated; (*assourdi: cris, rires*) smothered ♦ *nf*: **à l'~** (*CULIN: poisson, légumes*) steamed; (: *viande*) braised.

étouffement [etufmɑ̃] *nm* suffocation.

étouffer [etufe] *vt* to suffocate; (*bruit*) to muffle; (*scandale*) to hush up ♦ *vi* to suffocate; (*avoir trop chaud; aussi fig*) to feel stifled; **s'~** *vi* (*en mangeant etc*) to choke.

étouffoir [etufwaʀ] *nm* (*MUS*) damper.

étourderie [etuʀdəʀi] *nf* heedlessness *no pl*; thoughtless blunder; **faute d'~** careless mistake.

étourdi, e [etuʀdi] *adj* (*distrait*) scatterbrained, heedless.

étourdiment [etuʀdimɑ̃] *adv* rashly.

étourdir [etuʀdiʀ] *vt* (*assommer*) to stun, daze; (*griser*) to make dizzy *ou* giddy.

étourdissant, e [etuʀdisɑ̃, -ɑ̃t] *adj* staggering.

étourdissement [etuʀdismɑ̃] *nm* dizzy spell.

étourneau, x [etuʀno] *nm* starling.

étrange [etʀɑ̃ʒ] *adj* strange.

étrangement [etʀɑ̃ʒmɑ̃] *adv* strangely.

étranger, ère [etʀɑ̃ʒe, -ɛʀ] *adj* foreign; (*pas de la famille, non familier*) strange ♦ *nm/f* foreigner; stranger ♦ *nm*: **l'~** foreign countries; **à l'~** abroad; **de l'~** from abroad; **~ à** (*mal connu*) unfamiliar to; (*sans rapport*) irrelevant to.

étrangeté [etʀɑ̃ʒte] *nf* strangeness.

étranglé, e [etʀɑ̃gle] *adj*: **d'une voix ~e** in a strangled voice.

étranglement [etʀɑ̃gləmɑ̃] *nm* (*d'une vallée etc*) constriction, narrow passage.

étrangler [etʀɑ̃gle] *vt* to strangle; (*fig: presse, libertés*) to stifle; **s'~** *vi* (*en mangeant etc*) to choke; (*se resserrer*) to make a bottleneck.

étrave [etʀav] *nf* stem.

================== MOT-CLÉ ==================

être [ɛtʀ(ə)] *nm* being; ~ **humain** human being
♦ *vb +attrib* **1** (*état, description*) to be; **il est instituteur** he is *ou* he's a teacher; **vous êtes grand/intelligent/fatigué** you are *ou* you're tall/clever/tired
2 (*+à: appartenir*) to be; **le livre est à Paul** the book is Paul's *ou* belongs to Paul; **c'est à moi/eux** it is *ou* it's mine/theirs
3 (*+de: provenance*): **il est de Paris** he is from Paris; (: *appartenance*): **il est des nôtres** he is one of us
4 (*date*): **nous sommes le 10 janvier** it's the 10th of January (today)
♦ *vi* to be; **je ne serai pas ici demain** I won't be here tomorrow
♦ *vb aux* **1** to have; to be; ~ **arrivé/allé** to have arrived/gone; **il est parti** he has left, he has gone
2 (*forme passive*) to be; ~ **fait par** to be made by; **il a été promu** he has been promoted
3 (*+à +inf: obligation, but*): **c'est à réparer** it needs repairing; **c'est à essayer** it should be tried; **il est à espérer que ...** it is *ou* it's to be hoped that ...
♦ *vb impers* **1**: **il est** *+adjectif* it is *+adjective*; **il est impossible de le faire** it's impossible to do it
2 (*heure, date*): **il est 10 heures** it is *ou* it's 10 o'clock
3 (*emphatique*): **c'est moi** it's me; **c'est à lui de le faire** it's up to him to do it; *voir aussi* **est-ce que, n'est-ce pas, c'est-à-dire, ce.**

étreindre [etʀɛ̃dʀ(ə)] *vt* to clutch, grip; (*amoureusement, amicalement*) to embrace; **s'**~ to embrace.
étreinte [etʀɛ̃t] *nf* clutch, grip; embrace; **resserrer son** ~ **autour de** (*fig*) to tighten one's grip on *ou* around.
étrenner [etʀene] *vt* to use (*ou* wear) for the first time.
étrennes [etʀɛn] *nfpl* (*cadeaux*) New Year's present; (*gratifications*) ≈ Christmas box *sg*, ≈ Christmas bonus.
étrier [etʀije] *nm* stirrup.
étriller [etʀije] *vt* (*cheval*) to curry; (*fam: battre*) to slaughter (*fig*).
étriper [etʀipe] *vt* to gut; (*fam*): ~ **qn** to tear sb's guts out.
étriqué, e [etʀike] *adj* skimpy.
étroit, e [etʀwa, -wat] *adj* narrow; (*vêtement*) tight; (*fig: serré*) close, tight; **à l'**~ cramped; ~ **d'esprit** narrow-minded.
étroitement [etʀwatmã] *adv* closely.
étroitesse [etʀwatɛs] *nf* narrowness; ~ **d'esprit** narrow-mindedness.
Étrurie [etʀyʀi] *nf*: **l'**~ Etruria.
étrusque [etʀysk(ə)] *adj* Etruscan.
étude [etyd] *nf* studying; (*ouvrage, rapport,*

MUS) study; (*de notaire: bureau*) office; (*: charge*) practice; (*SCOL: salle de travail*) study room; ~**s** *nfpl* (*SCOL*) studies; **être à l'**~ (*projet etc*) to be under consideration; **faire des** ~**s** (**de droit/médecine**) to study (law/medicine); ~**s secondaires/supérieures** secondary/higher education; ~ **de cas** case study; ~ **de faisabilité** feasibility study; ~ **de marché** (*ÉCON*) market research.
étudiant, e [etydjɑ̃, -ãt] *adj, nm/f* student.
étudié, e [etydje] *adj* (*démarche*) studied; (*système*) carefully designed; (*prix*) keen.
étudier [etydje] *vt, vi* to study.
étui [etɥi] *nm* case.
étuve [etyv] *nf* steamroom; (*appareil*) sterilizer.
étuvée [etyve]: **à l'**~ *adv* braised.
étymologie [etimɔlɔʒi] *nf* etymology.
étymologique [etimɔlɔʒik] *adj* etymological.
eu, eue [y] *pp de* **avoir.**
EU(A) *sigle mpl* (= *États-Unis (d'Amérique)*) US(A).
eucalyptus [økaliptys] *nm* eucalyptus.
Eucharistie [økaʀisti] *nf*: **l'**~ the Eucharist, the Lord's Supper.
eucharistique [økaʀistik] *adj* eucharistic.
euclidien, ne [øklidjɛ̃, -ɛn] *adj* Euclidian.
eugénique [øʒenik] *adj* eugenic ♦ *nf* eugenics *sg*.
eugénisme [øʒenism(ə)] *nm* eugenics *sg*.
euh [ø] *excl* er.
eunuque [ønyk] *nm* eunuch.
euphémique [øfemik] *adj* euphemistic.
euphémisme [øfemism(ə)] *nm* euphemism.
euphonie [øfɔni] *nf* euphony.
euphorbe [øfɔʀb(ə)] *nf* (*BOT*) spurge.
euphorie [øfɔʀi] *nf* euphoria.
euphorique [øfɔʀik] *adj* euphoric.
euphorisant, e [øfɔʀizã, -ãt] *adj* exhilarating.
Euphrate [øfʀat] *nm*: **l'**~ the Euphrates *sg*.
eurafricain, e [øʀafʀikɛ̃, -ɛn] *adj* Eurafrican.
eurasiatique [øʀazjatik] *adj* Eurasiatic.
Eurasie [øʀazi] *nf*: **l'**~ Eurasia.
eurasien, ne [øʀazjɛ̃, -ɛn] *adj* Eurasian.
EURATOM [øʀatɔm] *sigle f* Euratom.
eurent [yʀ(ə)] *vb voir* **avoir.**
euro- [øʀo] *préfixe* Euro-.
eurocrate [øʀɔkʀat] *nm/f* (*péj*) Eurocrat.
eurodevise [øʀodəviz] *nf* Eurocurrency.
eurodollar [øʀodɔlaʀ] *nm* Eurodollar.
euromonnaie [øʀomɔnɛ] *nf* Eurocurrency.
Europe [øʀɔp] *nf*: **l'**~ Europe; **l'**~ **centrale** Central Europe; **l'**~ **verte** European agriculture.
européanisation [øʀɔpeanizasjõ] *nf* Europeanization.
européaniser [øʀɔpeanize] *vt* to Europeanize.
européen, ne [øʀɔpeɛ̃, -ɛn] *adj* European ♦ *nm/f*: **E**~, **ne** European.
eurosceptique [øʀosɛptik] *nm/f* Eurosceptic.
Eurovision [øʀoviʒõ] *nf* Eurovision; **émission en** ~ Eurovision broadcast.

eus [y] *etc vb voir* **avoir**.
euthanasie [øtanazi] *nf* euthanasia.
eux [ø] *pron* (*sujet*) they; (*objet*) them; ~, **ils ont fait ... THEY** did ....
EV *abr* (= *en ville*) *used on mail to be delivered by hand, courier etc within the same town.*
évacuation [evakчasjɔ̃] *nf* evacuation.
évacué, e [evakчe] *nm/f* evacuee.
évacuer [evakчe] *vt* (*salle, région*) to evacuate, clear; (*occupants, population*) to evacuate; (*toxine etc*) to evacuate, discharge.
évadé, e [evade] *adj* escaped ♦ *nm/f* escapee.
évader [evade]: **s'~** *vi* to escape.
évaluation [evalчasjɔ̃] *nf* assessment, evaluation.
évaluer [evalчe] *vt* to assess, evaluate.
évanescent, e [evanesɑ̃, -ɑ̃t] *adj* evanescent.
évangélique [evɑ̃ʒelik] *adj* evangelical.
évangélisation [evɑ̃ʒelizasjɔ̃] *nf* evangelization.
évangéliser [evɑ̃ʒelize] *vt* to evangelize.
évangéliste [evɑ̃ʒelist(ə)] *nm* evangelist.
évangile [evɑ̃ʒil] *nm* gospel; (*texte de la Bible*): **É~** Gospel; **ce n'est pas l'É~** (*fig*) it's not gospel.
évanoui, e [evanwi] *adj* in a faint; **tomber ~** to faint.
évanouir [evanwiʀ]: **s'~** *vi* to faint, pass out; (*disparaître*) to vanish, disappear.
évanouissement [evanwismɑ̃] *nm* (*syncope*) fainting fit; (*MÉD*) loss of consciousness.
évaporation [evapɔʀasjɔ̃] *nf* evaporation.
évaporé, e [evapɔʀe] *adj* giddy, scatterbrained.
évaporer [evapɔʀe]: **s'~** *vi* to evaporate.
évasé, e [evaze] *adj* (*jupe etc*) flared.
évaser [evaze] *vt* (*tuyau*) to widen, open out; (*jupe, pantalon*) to flare; **s'~** *vi* to widen, open out.
évasif, ive [evazif, -iv] *adj* evasive.
évasion [evazjɔ̃] *nf* escape; **littérature d'~** escapist literature; ~ **des capitaux** (*ÉCON*) flight of capital; ~ **fiscale** tax avoidance.
évasivement [evazivmɑ̃] *adv* evasively.
évêché [eveʃe] *nm* (*fonction*) bishopric; (*palais*) bishop's palace.
éveil [evɛj] *nm* awakening; **être en ~** to be alert; **mettre qn en ~, donner l'~ à qn** to arouse sb's suspicions; **activités d'~** earlylearning activities.
éveillé, e [eveje] *adj* awake; (*vif*) alert, sharp.
éveiller [eveje] *vt* to (a)waken; **s'~** *vi* to (a)waken; (*fig*) to be aroused.
événement [evɛnmɑ̃] *nm* event.
éventail [evɑ̃taj] *nm* fan; (*choix*) range; **en ~** fanned out; fan-shaped.
éventaire [evɑ̃tɛʀ] *nm* stall, stand.
éventé, e [evɑ̃te] *adj* (*parfum, vin*) stale.
éventer [evɑ̃te] *vt* (*secret, complot*) to uncover; (*avec un éventail*) to fan; **s'~** *vi* (*parfum, vin*) to go stale.
éventrer [evɑ̃tʀe] *vt* to disembowel; (*fig*) to

tear *ou* rip open.
éventualité [evɑ̃tчalite] *nf* eventuality; possibility; **dans l'~ de** in the event of; **parer à toute ~** to guard against all eventualities.
éventuel, le [evɑ̃tчɛl] *adj* possible.
éventuellement [evɑ̃tчɛlmɑ̃] *adv* possibly.
évêque [evɛk] *nm* bishop.
Everest [evʀɛst] *nm*: (**mont**) ~ (Mount) Everest.
évertuer [evɛʀtчe]: **s'~** *vi*: **s'~ à faire** to try very hard to do.
éviction [eviksjɔ̃] *nf* ousting, supplanting; (*de locataire*) eviction.
évidemment [evidamɑ̃] *adv* obviously.
évidence [evidɑ̃s] *nf* obviousness; (*fait*) obvious fact; **se rendre à l'~** to bow before the evidence; **nier l'~** to deny the evidence; **à l'~** evidently; **de toute ~** quite obviously *ou* evidently; **en ~** conspicuous; **mettre en ~** to bring to the fore.
évident, e [evidɑ̃t, -ɑ̃t] *adj* obvious, evident; **ce n'est pas ~** (*cela pose des problèmes*) it's not (all that) straightforward, it's not as simple as all that.
évider [evide] *vt* to scoop out.
évier [evje] *nm* (kitchen) sink.
évincement [evɛ̃smɑ̃] *nm* ousting.
évincer [evɛ̃se] *vt* to oust, supplant.
évitable [evitabl(ə)] *adj* avoidable.
évitement [evitmɑ̃] *nm*: **place d'~** (*AUTO*) passing place.
éviter [evite] *vt* to avoid; ~ **de faire/que qch ne se passe** to avoid doing/sth happening; ~ **qch à qn** to spare sb sth.
évocateur, trice [evɔkatœʀ, -tʀis] *adj* evocative, suggestive.
évocation [evɔkasjɔ̃] *nf* evocation.
évolué, e [evɔlчe] *adj* advanced; (*personne*) broad-minded.
évoluer [evɔlчe] *vi* (*enfant, maladie*) to develop; (*situation, moralement*) to evolve, develop; (*aller et venir: danseur etc*) to move about, circle.
évolutif, ive [evɔlytif, -iv] *adj* evolving.
évolution [evɔlysjɔ̃] *nf* development; evolution; ~**s** *nfpl* movements.
évolutionnisme [evɔlysjɔnism(ə)] *nm* evolutionism.
évoquer [evɔke] *vt* to call to mind, evoke; (*mentionner*) to mention.
ex. *abr* (= *exemple*) ex.
ex- [ɛks] *préfixe* ex-.
exacerbé, e [ɛgzasɛʀbe] *adj* (*orgueil, sensibilité*) exaggerated.
exacerber [ɛgzasɛʀbe] *vt* to exacerbate.
exact, e [ɛgzakt] *adj* (*précis*) exact, accurate, precise; (*correct*) correct; (*ponctuel*) punctual; **l'heure ~e** the right *ou* exact time.
exactement [ɛgzaktəmɑ̃] *adv* exactly, accurately, precisely; correctly; (*c'est cela même*) exactly.
exaction [ɛgzaksjɔ̃] *nf* (*d'argent*) exaction; (*gén*

pl: actes de violence) abuse(s).

exactitude [ɛgzaktityd] *nf* exactitude, accurateness, precision.

ex aequo [ɛgzeko] *adj* equally placed; **classé 1er** ~ placed equal first.

exagération [ɛgzaʒeʀasjɔ̃] *nf* exaggeration.

exagéré, e [ɛgzaʒeʀe] *adj (prix etc)* excessive.

exagérément [ɛgzaʒeʀemɑ̃] *adv* excessively.

exagérer [ɛgzaʒeʀe] *vt* to exaggerate ♦ *vi (abuser)* to go too far; *(dépasser les bornes)* to overstep the mark; *(déformer les faits)* to exaggerate; **s'~ qch** to exaggerate sth.

exaltant, e [ɛgzaltɑ̃, -ɑ̃t] *adj* exhilarating.

exaltation [ɛgzaltɑsjɔ̃] *nf* exaltation.

exalté, e [ɛgzalte] *adj* (over)excited ♦ *nm/f (péj)* fanatic.

exalter [ɛgzalte] *vt (enthousiasmer)* to excite, elate; *(glorifier)* to exalt.

examen [ɛgzamɛ̃] *nm* examination; *(SCOL)* exam, examination; **à l'~** *(dossier, projet)* under consideration; *(COMM)* on approval; ~ **blanc** mock exam(ination); ~ **de la vue** sight test.

examinateur, trice [ɛgzaminatœʀ, -tʀis] *nm/f* examiner.

examiner [ɛgzamine] *vt* to examine.

exaspérant, e [ɛgzaspeʀɑ̃, -ɑ̃t] *adj* exasperating.

exaspération [ɛgzaspeʀasjɔ̃] *nf* exasperation.

exaspéré, e [egzaspeʀe] *adj* exasperated.

exaspérer [ɛgzaspeʀe] *vt* to exasperate; *(aggraver)* to exacerbate.

exaucer [ɛgzose] *vt (vœu)* to grant, fulfil; ~ **qn** to grant sb's wishes.

ex cathedra [ɛkskatedʀa] *adj, adv* ex cathedra.

excavateur [ɛkskavatœʀ] *nm* excavator, mechanical digger.

excavation [ɛkskavasjɔ̃] *nf* excavation.

excavatrice [ɛkskavatʀis] *nf* = **excavateur**.

excédent [ɛksedɑ̃] *nm* surplus; **en** ~ surplus; **payer 600 F d'~** *(de bagages)* to pay 600 francs excess luggage; ~ **de bagages** excess luggage; ~ **commercial** trade surplus.

excédentaire [ɛksedɑ̃tɛʀ] *adj* surplus, excess.

excéder [ɛksede] *vt (dépasser)* to exceed; *(agacer)* to exasperate; **excédé de fatigue** exhausted; **excédé de travail** worn out with work.

excellence [ɛksɛlɑ̃s] *nf* excellence; *(titre)* Excellency; **par** ~ par excellence.

excellent, e [ɛksɛlɑ̃, -ɑ̃t] *adj* excellent.

exceller [ɛksele] *vi:* ~ **(dans)** to excel (in).

excentricité [ɛksɑ̃tʀisite] *nf* eccentricity.

excentrique [ɛksɑ̃tʀik] *adj* eccentric; *(quartier)* outlying ♦ *nm/f* eccentric.

excentriquement [ɛksɑ̃tʀikmɑ̃] *adv* eccentrically.

excepté, e [ɛksɛpte] *adj, prép:* **les élèves ~s,** ~ **les élèves** except for *ou* apart from the pupils; ~ **si/quand** except if/when; ~ **que** except that.

excepter [ɛksɛpte] *vt* to except.

exception [ɛksɛpsjɔ̃] *nf* exception; **faire** ~ to be an exception; **faire une** ~ to make an exception; **sans** ~ without exception; **à l'~ de** except for, with the exception of; **d'~** *(mesure, loi)* special, exceptional.

exceptionnel, le [ɛksɛpsjɔnɛl] *adj* exceptional; *(prix)* special.

exceptionnellement [ɛksɛpsjɔnɛlmɑ̃] *adv* exceptionally; *(par exception)* by way of an exception, on this occasion.

excès [ɛksɛ] *nm* surplus ♦ *nmpl* excesses; **à l'~** *(méticuleux, généreux)* to excess; **avec** ~ to excess; **sans** ~ in moderation; **tomber dans l'~ inverse** to go to the opposite extreme; ~ **de langage** immoderate language; ~ **de pouvoir** abuse of power; ~ **de vitesse** speeding *no pl*, exceeding the speed limit; ~ **de zèle** overzealousness *no pl*.

excessif, ive [ɛksesif, -iv] *adj* excessive.

excessivement [ɛksesivmɑ̃] *adv (trop: cher)* excessively, inordinately; *(très: riche, laid)* extremely, incredibly; **manger/boire** ~ to eat/drink to excess.

exciper [ɛksipe]: ~ **de** *vt* to plead.

excipient [ɛksipjɑ̃] *nm (MÉD)* inert base, excipient.

exciser [ɛksize] *vt (MÉD)* to excise.

excision [ɛksizjɔ̃] *nf (MÉD)* excision; *(rituelle)* circumcision.

excitant, e [ɛksitɑ̃, -ɑ̃t] *adj* exciting ♦ *nm* stimulant.

excitation [ɛksitasjɔ̃] *nf (état)* excitement.

excité, e [ɛksite] *adj* excited.

exciter [ɛksite] *vt* to excite; *(suj: café etc)* to stimulate; **s'~** *vi* to get excited; ~ **qn à** *(révolte etc)* to incite sb to.

exclamation [ɛksklamasjɔ̃] *nf* exclamation.

exclamer [ɛksklame]: **s'~** *vi* to exclaim.

exclu, e [ɛkskly] *pp de* **exclure** ♦ *adj:* **il est/n'est pas** ~ **que ...** it's out of the question/not impossible that ...; **ce n'est pas exclu** it's not impossible, I don't rule that out.

exclure [ɛksklyʀ] *vt (faire sortir)* to expel; *(ne pas compter)* to exclude, leave out; *(rendre impossible)* to exclude, rule out.

exclusif, ive [ɛksklyzif, -iv] *adj* exclusive; **avec la mission exclusive/dans le but** ~ **de ...** with the sole mission/aim of ...; **agent** ~ sole agent.

exclusion [ɛksklyzjɔ̃] *nf* expulsion; **à l'~ de** with the exclusion *ou* exception of.

exclusivement [ɛksklyzivmɑ̃] *adv* exclusively.

exclusivité [ɛksklyzivite] *nf* exclusiveness; *(COMM)* exclusive rights *pl*; **passer en** ~ *(film)* to go on general release.

excommunier [ɛkskɔmynje] *vt* to excommunicate.

excréments [ɛkskʀemɑ̃] *nmpl* excrement *sg*, faeces.

excréter [ɛkskʀete] *vt* to excrete.

excroissance [ɛkskʀwasɑ̃s] *nf* excrescence, outgrowth.

excursion [ɛkskyʀsjɔ̃] *nf* (*en autocar*) excursion, trip; (*à pied*) walk, hike; **faire une** ~ **to** go on an excursion *ou* a trip; to go on a walk *ou* hike.

excursionniste [ɛkskyʀsjɔnist(ə)] *nm/f* tripper; hiker.

excusable [ɛkskyzabl(ə)] *adj* excusable.

excuse [ɛkskyz] *nf* excuse; ~**s** *nfpl* apology *sg*, apologies; **faire des** ~**s** to apologize; **faire ses** ~**s** to offer one's apologies; **mot d'**~ (*SCOL*) note from one's parent(s) (*to explain absence etc*); **lettre d'**~**s** letter of apology.

excuser [ɛkskyze] *vt* to excuse; ~ **qn de qch** (*dispenser*) to excuse sb from sth; **s'**~ (**de**) to apologize (for); **"excusez-moi"** "I'm sorry"; (*pour attirer l'attention*) "excuse me"; **se faire** ~ to ask to be excused.

exécrable [ɛgzekʀabl(ə)] *adj* atrocious.

exécrer [ɛgzekʀe] *vt* to loathe, abhor.

exécutant, e [ɛgzekytɑ̃, -ɑ̃t] *nm/f* performer.

exécuter [ɛgzekyte] *vt* (*prisonnier*) to execute; (*tâche etc*) to execute, carry out; (*MUS: jouer*) to perform, execute; (*INFORM*) to run; **s'**~ *vi* to comply.

exécuteur, trice [ɛgzekytœʀ, -tʀis] *nm/f* (*testamentaire*) executor ♦ *nm* (*bourreau*) executioner.

exécutif, ive [ɛgzekytif, -iv] *adj, nm* (*POL*) executive.

exécution [ɛgzekysjɔ̃] *nf* execution; carrying out; **mettre à** ~ to carry out.

exécutoire [ɛgzekytwaʀ] *adj* (*JUR*) (legally) binding.

exégèse [ɛgzeʒez] *nf* exegesis.

exégète [ɛgzeʒet] *nm* exegete.

exemplaire [ɛgzɑ̃plɛʀ] *adj* exemplary ♦ *nm* copy.

exemple [ɛgzɑ̃pl(ə)] *nm* example; **par** ~ for instance, for example; (*valeur intensive*) really!; **sans** ~ (*bêtise, gourmandise etc*) unparalleled; **donner l'**~ to set an example; **prendre** ~ **sur** to take as a model; **à l'**~ **de** just like; **pour l'**~ (*punir*) as an example.

exempt, e [ɛgzɑ̃, -ɑ̃t] *adj*: ~ **de** (*dispensé de*) exempt from; (*sans*) free from; ~ **de taxes** tax-free.

exempter [ɛgzɑ̃te] *vt*: ~ **de** to exempt from.

exercé, e [ɛgzɛʀse] *adj* trained.

exercer [ɛgzɛʀse] *vt* (*pratiquer*) to exercise, practise; (*faire usage de: prérogative*) to exercise; (*effectuer: influence, contrôle, pression*) to exert; (*former*) to exercise, train ♦ *vi* (*médecin*) to be in practice; **s'**~ (*sportif, musicien*) to practise; (*se faire sentir: pression etc*): **s'**~ (**sur** *ou* **contre**) to be exerted (on); **s'**~ **à faire qch** to train o.s. to do sth.

exercice [ɛgzɛʀsis] *nm* practice; exercising; (*tâche, travail*) exercise; (*COMM, ADMIN: période*) accounting period; **l'**~ (*sportive etc*) exercise; (*MIL*) drill; **en** ~ (*juge*) in office; (*médecin*) practising; **dans l'**~ **de ses fonctions** in the discharge of his duties; ~**s** in the discharge of his duties; ~**s**

d'assouplissement limbering-up (exercises).

exergue [ɛgzɛʀg(ə)] *nm*: **mettre en** ~ (*inscription*) to inscribe; **porter en** ~ to be inscribed with.

exhalaison [ɛgzalɛzɔ̃] *nf* exhalation.

exhaler [ɛgzale] *vt* (*parfum*) to exhale; (*souffle, son, soupir*) to utter, breathe; **s'**~ *vi* to rise (up).

exhausser [ɛgzose] *vt* to raise (up).

exhausteur [ɛgzostœʀ] *nm* extractor fan.

exhaustif, ive [ɛgzostif, -iv] *adj* exhaustive.

exhiber [ɛgzibe] *vt* (*montrer: papiers, certificat*) to present, produce; (*péj*) to display, flaunt; **s'**~ (*personne*) to parade; (*suj: exhibitionniste*) to expose o.s.

exhibitionnisme [ɛgzibisjɔnism(ə)] *nm* exhibitionism.

exhibitionniste [ɛgzibisjɔnist(ə)] *nm/f* exhibitionist.

exhortation [ɛgzɔʀtasjɔ̃] *nf* exhortation.

exhorter [ɛgzɔʀte] *vt*: ~ **qn à faire** to urge sb to do.

exhumer [ɛgzyme] *vt* to exhume.

exigeant, e [ɛgziʒɑ̃, -ɑ̃t] *adj* demanding; (*péj*) hard to please.

exigence [ɛgziʒɑ̃s] *nf* demand, requirement.

exiger [ɛgziʒe] *vt* to demand, require.

exigible [ɛgziʒibl(ə)] *adj* (*COMM, JUR*) payable.

exigu, ë [ɛgzigy] *adj* cramped, tiny.

exiguïté [ɛgziguite] *nf* (*d'un lieu*) cramped nature.

exil [ɛgzil] *nm* exile; **en** ~ in exile.

exilé, e [ɛgzile] *nm/f* exile.

exiler [ɛgzile] *vt* to exile; **s'**~ to go into exile.

existant, e [ɛgzistɑ̃, -ɑ̃t] *adj* (*actuel, présent*) existing.

existence [ɛgzistɑ̃s] *nf* existence; **dans l'**~ in life.

existentialisme [ɛgzistɑ̃sjalism(ə)] *nm* existentialism.

existentiel, le [ɛgzistɑ̃sjɛl] *adj* existential.

exister [ɛgziste] *vi* to exist; **il existe un/des** there is a/are (some).

exode [ɛgzɔd] *nm* exodus.

exonération [ɛgzɔneʀasjɔ̃] *nf* exemption.

exonéré, e [ɛgzɔneʀe] *adj*: ~ **de TVA** zero-rated (for VAT).

exonérer [ɛgzɔneʀe] *vt*: ~ **de** to exempt from.

exorbitant, e [ɛgzɔʀbitɑ̃, -ɑ̃t] *adj* exorbitant.

exorbité, e [ɛgzɔʀbite] *adj*: **yeux** ~**s** bulging eyes.

exorciser [ɛgzɔʀsize] *vt* to exorcize.

exorde [ɛgzɔʀd(ə)] *nm* introduction.

exotique [ɛgzɔtik] *adj* exotic.

exotisme [ɛgzɔtism(ə)] *nm* exoticism.

expansif, ive [ɛkspɑ̃sif, -iv] *adj* expansive, communicative.

expansion [ɛkspɑ̃sjɔ̃] *nf* expansion.

expansionniste [ɛkspɑ̃sjɔnist(ə)] *adj* expansionist.

expansivité [ɛkspɑ̃sivite] *nf* expansiveness.

expatrié, e [ɛkspatʀije] nm/f expatriate.

expatrier [ɛkspatʀije] vt (argent) to take ou send out of the country; **s'~** to leave one's country.

expectative [ɛkspɛktativ] nf: **être dans l'~** to be waiting to see.

expectorant, e [ɛkspɛktɔʀɑ̃, -ɑ̃t] adj: **sirop ~** expectorant (syrup).

expectorer [ɛkspɛktɔʀe] vi to expectorate.

expédient [ɛkspedjɑ̃] nm (parfois péj) expedient; **vivre d'~s** to live by one's wits.

expédier [ɛkspedje] vt (lettre, paquet) to send; (troupes, renfort) to dispatch; (péj: travail etc) to dispose of, dispatch.

expéditeur, trice [ɛkspeditœʀ, -tʀis] nm/f (POSTES) sender.

expéditif, ive [ɛkspeditif, -iv] adj quick, expeditious.

expédition [ɛkspedisjɔ̃] nf sending; (scientifique, sportive, MIL) expedition; **~ punitive** punitive raid.

expéditionnaire [ɛkspedisjɔnɛʀ] adj: **corps ~** (MIL) task force.

expérience [ɛkspeʀjɑ̃s] nf (de la vie, des choses) experience; (scientifique) experiment; **avoir de l'~** to have experience, be experienced; **avoir l'~ de** to have experience of; **faire l'~ de qch** to experience sth; **~ de chimie/d'électricité** chemical/electrical experiment.

expérimental, e, aux [ɛkspeʀimɑ̃tal, -o] adj experimental.

expérimentalement [ɛkspeʀimɑ̃talmɑ̃] adv experimentally.

expérimenté, e [ɛkspeʀimɑ̃te] adj experienced.

expérimenter [ɛkspeʀimɑ̃te] vt (machine, technique) to test out, experiment with.

expert, e [ɛkspɛʀ, -ɛʀt(ə)] adj: **~ en** expert in ♦ nm (spécialiste) expert; **~ en assurances** insurance valuer.

expert-comptable, pl **experts-comptables** [ɛkspɛʀkɔ̃tabl(ə)] nm ≈ chartered (BRIT) ou certified public (US) accountant.

expertise [ɛkspɛʀtiz] nf valuation; assessment; valuer's (ou assessor's) report; (JUR) (forensic) examination.

expertiser [ɛkspɛʀtize] vt (objet de valeur) to value; (voiture accidentée etc) to assess damage to.

expier [ɛkspje] vt to expiate, atone for.

expiration [ɛkspiʀasjɔ̃] nf expiry (BRIT), expiration; breathing out no pl.

expirer [ɛkspiʀe] vi (prendre fin, littéraire: mourir) to expire; (respirer) to breathe out.

explétif, ive [ɛkspletif, -iv] adj (LING) expletive.

explicable [ɛksplikabl(ə)] adj: **pas ~** inexplicable.

explicatif, ive [ɛksplikatif, -iv] adj (mot, texte, note) explanatory.

explication [ɛksplikasjɔ̃] nf explanation; (dis-

cussion) discussion; **~ de texte** (SCOL) critical analysis (of a text).

explicite [ɛksplisit] adj explicit.

explicitement [ɛksplisitmɑ̃] adv explicitly.

expliciter [ɛksplisite] vt to make explicit.

expliquer [ɛksplike] vt to explain; **~ (à qn) comment/que** to point out ou explain (to sb) how/that; **s'~** (se faire comprendre: personne) to explain o.s.; (discuter) to discuss things; (se disputer) to have it out; (comprendre): **je m'explique son retard/absence** I understand his lateness/absence; **son erreur s'explique** one can understand his mistake.

exploit [ɛksplwa] nm exploit, feat.

exploitable [ɛksplwatabl(ə)] adj (gisement etc) that can be exploited; **~ par une machine** machine-readable.

exploitant [ɛksplwatɑ̃] nm farmer.

exploitation [ɛksplwatasjɔ̃] nf exploitation; running; (entreprise): **~ agricole** farming concern.

exploiter [ɛksplwate] vt to exploit; (entreprise, ferme) to run, operate.

exploiteur, euse [ɛksplwatœʀ, -øz] nm/f (péj) exploiter.

explorateur, trice [ɛksplɔʀatœʀ, -tʀis] nm/f explorer.

exploration [ɛksplɔʀasjɔ̃] nf exploration.

explorer [ɛksplɔʀe] vt to explore.

exploser [ɛksploze] vi to explode, blow up; (engin explosif) to go off; (fig: joie, colère) to burst out, explode; (: personne: de colère) to explode, flare up; **faire ~** (bombe) to explode, detonate; (bâtiment, véhicule) to blow up.

explosif, ive [ɛksplozif, -iv] adj, nm explosive.

explosion [ɛksplozjɔ̃] nf explosion; **~ de joie/colère** outburst of joy/rage; **~ démographique** population explosion.

exponentiel, le [ɛkspɔnɑ̃sjɛl] adj exponential.

exportateur, trice [ɛkspɔʀtatœʀ, -tʀis] adj exporting ♦ nm exporter.

exportation [ɛkspɔʀtasjɔ̃] nf export.

exporter [ɛkspɔʀte] vt to export.

exposant [ɛkspozɑ̃] nm exhibitor; (MATH) exponent.

exposé, e [ɛkspoze] nm (écrit) exposé; (oral) talk ♦ adj: **~ au sud** facing south, with a southern aspect; **bien ~** well situated; **très ~** very exposed.

exposer [ɛkspoze] vt (montrer: marchandise) to display; (: peinture) to exhibit, show; (parler de: problème, situation) to explain, expose, set out; (mettre en danger, orienter: maison etc) to expose; **~ qn/qch à** to expose sb/sth to; **~ sa vie** to risk one's life; **s'~ à** (soleil, danger) to expose o.s. to; (critiques, punition) to lay o.s. open to.

exposition [ɛkspozisjɔ̃] nf (voir exposer) displaying; exhibiting; explanation, exposition; exposure; (voir exposé) aspect, situation; (manifestation) exhibition; (PHOTO) exposure;

(*introduction*) exposition.

exprès [ɛkspʀɛ] *adv* (*délibérément*) on purpose; (*spécialement*) specially; **faire ~ de faire qch** to do sth on purpose.

exprès, esse [ɛkspʀɛs] *adj* (*ordre, défense*) express, formal ♦ *adj inv, adv* (*POSTES*) express; **envoyer qch en ~** to send sth express.

express [ɛkspʀɛs] *adj, nm*: (**café**) ~ espresso; (**train**) ~ fast train.

expressément [ɛkspʀɛsemɑ̃] *adv* expressly, specifically.

expressif, ive [ɛkspʀesif, -iv] *adj* expressive.

expression [ɛkspʀesjɔ̃] *nf* expression; **réduit à sa plus simple** ~ reduced to its simplest terms; **liberté/moyens d'~** freedom/means of expression; ~ **toute faite** set phrase.

expressionnisme [ɛkspʀesjɔnism(ə)] *nm* expressionism.

expressivité [ɛkspʀesivite] *nf* expressiveness.

exprimer [ɛkspʀime] *vt* (*sentiment, idée*) to express; (*faire sortir: jus, liquide*) to press out; **s'~** *vi* (*personne*) to express o.s.

expropriation [ɛkspʀɔpʀijɑsjɔ̃] *nf* expropriation; **frapper d'~** to put a compulsory purchase order on.

exproprier [ɛkspʀɔpʀije] *vt* to buy up (*ou* buy the property of) by compulsory purchase, expropriate.

expulser [ɛkspylse] *vt* (*d'une salle, d'un groupe*) to expel; (*locataire*) to evict; (*FOOTBALL*) to send off.

expulsion [ɛkspylsjɔ̃] *nf* expulsion; eviction; sending off.

expurger [ɛkspyʀʒe] *vt* to expurgate, bowdlerize.

exquis, e [ɛkski, -iz] *adj* (*gâteau, parfum, élégance*) exquisite; (*personne, temps*) delightful.

exsangue [ɛksɑ̃g] *adj* bloodless, drained of blood.

exsuder [ɛksyde] *vt* to exude.

extase [ɛkstɑz] *nf* ecstasy; **être en ~** to be in raptures.

extasier [ɛkstɑzje]: **s'~** *vi*: **s'~ sur** to go into raptures over.

extatique [ɛkstatik] *adj* ecstatic.

extenseur [ɛkstɑ̃sœʀ] *nm* (*SPORT*) chest expander.

extensible [ɛkstɑ̃sibl(ə)] *adj* extensible.

extensif, ive [ɛkstɑ̃sif, -iv] *adj* extensive.

extension [ɛkstɑ̃sjɔ̃] *nf* (*d'un muscle, ressort*) stretching; (*MÉD*): **à l'~** in traction; (*fig*) extension; expansion.

exténuant [ɛkstenɥɑ̃, -ɑ̃t] *adj* exhausting.

exténuer [ɛkstenɥe] *vt* to exhaust.

extérieur, e [ɛksteʀjœʀ] *adj* (*de dehors: porte, mur etc*) outer, outside; (: *commerce, politique*) foreign; (: *influences, pressions*) external; (*au dehors: escalier, w.-c.*) outside; (*apparent: calme, gaieté etc*) outer ♦ *nm* (*d'une maison, d'un récipient etc*) outside, exterior; (*d'une personne: apparence*) exterior; (*d'un* pays, *d'un groupe social*): **l'~** the outside world; **à l'~** (*dehors*) outside; (*fig: à l'étranger*) abroad.

extérieurement [ɛksteʀjœʀmɑ̃] *adv* (*de dehors*) on the outside; (*en apparence*) on the surface.

extérioriser [ɛksteʀjɔʀize] *vt* to exteriorize.

extermination [ɛkstɛʀminɑsjɔ̃] *nf* extermination, wiping out.

exterminer [ɛkstɛʀmine] *vt* to exterminate, wipe out.

externat [ɛkstɛʀna] *nm* day school.

externe [ɛkstɛʀn(ə)] *adj* external, outer ♦ *nm/f* (*MÉD*) non-resident medical student, extern (*US*); (*SCOL*) day pupil.

extincteur [ɛkstɛ̃ktœʀ] *nm* (fire) extinguisher.

extinction [ɛkstɛ̃ksjɔ̃] *nf* extinction; (*JUR: d'une dette*) extinguishment; ~ **de voix** (*MÉD*) loss of voice.

extirper [ɛkstiʀpe] *vt* (*tumeur*) to extirpate; (*plante*) to root out, pull up; (*préjugés*) to eradicate.

extorquer [ɛkstɔʀke] *vt* (*de l'argent, un renseignement*): ~ **qch à qn** to extort sth from sb.

extorsion [ɛkstɔʀsjɔ̃] *nf*: ~ **de fonds** extortion of money.

extra [ɛkstʀa] *adj inv* first-rate; (*marchandises*) top-quality ♦ *nm inv* extra help ♦ *préfixe* extra(-).

extraction [ɛkstʀaksjɔ̃] *nf* extraction.

extrader [ɛkstʀade] *vt* to extradite.

extradition [ɛkstʀadisjɔ̃] *nf* extradition.

extra-fin, e [ɛkstʀafɛ̃, -in] *adj* extra-fine.

extra-fort, e [ɛkstʀafɔʀ] *adj* extra strong.

extraire [ɛkstʀɛʀ] *vt* to extract.

extrait, e [ɛkstʀɛ, -ɛt] *pp de* **extraire** ♦ *nm* (*de plante*) extract; (*de film, livre*) extract, excerpt; ~ **de naissance** birth certificate.

extra-lucide [ɛkstʀalysid] *adj*: **voyante** ~ clairvoyant.

extraordinaire [ɛkstʀaɔʀdinɛʀ] *adj* extraordinary; (*POL, ADMIN*) special; **ambassadeur** ~ ambassador extraordinary; **assemblée** ~ extraordinary meeting; **par** ~ by some unlikely chance.

extraordinairement [ɛkstʀaɔʀdinɛʀmɑ̃] *adv* extraordinarily.

extrapoler [ɛkstʀapɔle] *vt, vi* to extrapolate.

extra-sensoriel, le [ɛkstʀasɑ̃sɔʀjɛl] *adj* extrasensory.

extra-terrestre [ɛkstʀatɛʀɛstʀ(ə)] *nm/f* extraterrestrial.

extra-utérin, e [ɛkstʀayteʀɛ̃, -in] *adj* extrauterine.

extravagance [ɛkstʀavagɑ̃s] *nf* extravagance *no pl*; extravagant behaviour *no pl*.

extravagant, e [ɛkstʀavagɑ̃, -ɑ̃t] *adj* (*personne, attitude*) extravagant; (*idée*) wild.

extraverti, e [ɛkstʀavɛʀti] *adj* extrovert.

extrayais [ɛkstʀɛjɛ] *etc vb voir* **extraire**.

extrême [ɛkstʀɛm] *adj, nm* extreme; (*intensif*): **d'une** ~ **simplicité/brutalité** extremely simple/brutal; **d'un ~ à l'autre** from one extreme to another; **à l'~ in** the extreme; **à l'~ rigueur** in the absolute extreme.

extrêmement [εkstRεmmɑ̃] adv extremely.

extrême-onction, pl **extrêmes-onctions** [εkstRεmɔ̃ksjɔ̃] nf (REL) last rites pl, Extreme Unction.

Extrême-Orient [εkstRεmɔRjɑ̃] nm: **l'~** the Far East.

extrême-oriental, e, aux [εkstRεmɔRjɑtal, -o] adj Far Eastern.

extrémisme [εkstRemism(ə)] nm extremism.

extrémiste [εkstRemist(ə)] adj, nm/f extremist.

extrémité [εkstRemite] nf (bout) end; (situation) straits pl, plight; (geste désespéré) extreme action; **~s** nfpl (pieds et mains) extremities; **à la dernière ~** (à l'agonie) on the point of death.

extroverti, e [εkstRɔvεRti] adj = extraverti.

exubérance [εgzybeRɑ̃s] nf exuberance.

exubérant, e [εgzybeRɑ̃, -ɑ̃t] adj exuberant.

exulter [εgzylte] vi to exult.

exutoire [εgzytwaR] nm outlet, release.

ex-voto [εksvɔto] nm inv ex-voto.

eye-liner [ajlajnœR] nm eyeliner.

F f

F, f [εf] nm inv, nf, f ♦ abr = **féminin**; (= franc) fr.; (= Fahrenheit) F; (= frère) Br(o).; (= femme) W; (appartement): **un F2/F3** a 2-/3-roomed flat (BRIT) ou apartment (US); **F comme François** F for Frederick (BRIT) ou Fox (US).

fa [fɑ] nm inv (MUS) F; (en chantant la gamme) fa.

fable [fabl(ə)] nf fable; (mensonge) story, tale.

fabricant [fabRikɑ̃] nm manufacturer, maker.

fabrication [fabRikasjɔ̃] nf manufacture, making.

fabrique [fabRik] nf factory.

fabriquer [fabRike] vt to make; (industriellement) to manufacture, make; (construire: voiture) to manufacture, build; (: maison) to build; (fig: inventer: histoire, alibi) to make up; (fam): **qu'est-ce qu'il fabrique?** what is he up to?; **~ en série** to mass-produce.

fabulateur, trice [fabylatœR, -tRis] nm/f: **c'est un ~** he fantasizes, he makes up stories.

fabulation [fabylasjɔ̃] nf (PSYCH) fantasizing.

fabuleusement [fabyløzmɑ̃] adv fabulously, fantastically.

fabuleux, euse [fabylø, -øz] adj fabulous, fantastic.

fac [fak] abr f (fam: = faculté) Uni (BRIT fam), ≈ college (US).

façade [fasad] nf front, façade; (fig) façade.

face [fas] nf face; (fig: aspect) side ♦ adj: **le côté ~** heads; **perdre/sauver la ~** to lose/save face; **regarder qn en ~** to look sb in the face; **la maison/le trottoir d'en ~** the house/pavement opposite; **en ~ de** prép opposite; (fig) in front of; **de ~** adv from the front; face on; **~ à** prép facing; (fig) faced with, in the face of; **faire ~ à** to face; **faire ~ à la demande** (COMM) to meet the demand; **~ à ~** adv facing each other ♦ nm inv encounter.

face-à-main, pl **faces-à-main** [fasamɛ̃] nm lorgnette.

facéties [fasesi] nfpl jokes, pranks.

facétieux, euse [fasesjø, -øz] adj mischievous.

facette [fasεt] nf facet.

fâché, e [fɑʃe] adj angry; (désolé) sorry.

fâcher [fɑʃe] vt to anger; **se ~** vi to get angry; **se ~ avec** (se brouiller) to fall out with.

fâcherie [fɑʃRi] nf quarrel.

fâcheusement [fɑʃøzmɑ̃] adv unpleasantly; (impressionné etc) badly; **avoir ~ tendance à** to have an irritating tendency to.

fâcheux, euse [fɑʃø, -øz] adj unfortunate, regrettable.

facho [faʃo] adj, nm/f (fam: = fasciste) fascist.

facial, e, aux [fasjal, -o] adj facial.

faciès [fasjεs] nm (visage) features pl.

facile [fasil] adj easy; (accommodant) easygoing; **~ d'emploi** (INFORM) user-friendly.

facilement [fasilmɑ̃] adv easily.

facilité [fasilite] nf easiness; (disposition, don) aptitude; (moyen, occasion, possibilité): **il a la ~ de rencontrer les gens** he has every opportunity to meet people; **~s** nfpl facilities; (COMM) terms; **~s de crédit** credit terms; **~s de paiement** easy terms.

faciliter [fasilite] vt to make easier.

façon [fasɔ̃] nf (manière) way; (d'une robe etc) making-up; (: main-d'œuvre) labour (BRIT), labor (US); (imitation): **châle ~ cachemire** cashmere-style shawl; **~s** nfpl (péj) fuss sg; **faire des ~s** (péj: être affecté) to be affected; (: faire des histoires) to make a fuss; **de quelle ~?** (in) what way?; **sans ~** adv without fuss ♦ adj unaffected; **d'une autre ~** in another way; **en aucune ~** in no way; **de ~ à so as to; de ~ à ce que, de (telle) ~ que** so that; **de toute ~** anyway, in any case; **(c'est une) ~ de parler** it's a way of putting it; **travail à ~** tailoring.

façonner [fasɔne] vt (fabriquer) to manufacture; (travailler: matière) to shape, fashion; (fig) to mould, shape.

fac-similé [faksimile] nm facsimile.

facteur, trice [faktœR, -tRis] nm/f postman/woman (BRIT), mailman/woman (US) ♦ nm (MATH, gén) factor; **~ d'orgues** organ builder; **~ de pianos** piano maker; **~ rhésus** rhesus factor.

factice [faktis] adj artificial.

faction [faksjɔ̃] *nf* (*groupe*) faction; (*MIL*) guard *ou* sentry (duty); watch; **en ~** on guard; standing watch.

factionnaire [faksjɔnɛʀ] *nm* guard, sentry.

factoriel, le [faktɔʀjɛl] *adj*, *nf* factorial.

factotum [faktɔtɔm] *nm* odd-job man, dogs-body (*BRIT*).

factuel, le [faktɥɛl] *adj* factual.

facturation [faktyʀɑsjɔ̃] *nf* invoicing; (*bureau*) invoicing (office).

facture [faktyʀ] *nf* (*à payer:* gén) bill; (*: COMM*) invoice; (*d'un artisan, artiste*) technique, workmanship.

facturer [faktyʀe] *vt* to invoice.

facturier, ière [faktyʀje, -jɛʀ] *nm/f* invoice clerk.

facultatif, ive [fakyltatif, -iv] *adj* optional; (*arrêt de bus*) request *cpd*.

faculté [fakylte] *nf* (*intellectuelle, d'université*) faculty; (*pouvoir, possibilité*) power.

fadaises [fadɛz] *nfpl* twaddle *sg*.

fade [fad] *adj* insipid.

fading [fadiŋ] *nm* (*RADIO*) fading.

fagot [fago] *nm* (*de bois*) bundle of sticks.

fagoté, e [fagɔte] *adj* (*fam*): **drôlement ~** oddly dressed.

faible [fɛbl(ə)] *adj* weak; (*voix, lumière, vent*) faint; (*élève, copie*) poor; (*rendement, intensité, revenu etc*) low ♦ *nm* weak point; (*pour quelqu'un*) weakness, soft spot; **~ d'esprit** feeble-minded.

faiblement [fɛbləmɑ̃] *adv* weakly; (*peu: éclairer etc*) faintly.

faiblesse [fɛblɛs] *nf* weakness.

faiblir [febliʀ] *vi* to weaken; (*lumière*) to dim; (*vent*) to drop.

faïence [fajɑ̃s] *nf* earthenware *no pl*; (*objet*) piece of earthenware.

faignant, e [fɛɲɑ̃, -ɑ̃t] *nm/f* = **fainéant, e**.

faille [faj] *vb voir* **falloir** ♦ *nf* (*GÉO*) fault; (*fig*) flaw, weakness.

failli, e [faji] *adj*, *nm/f* bankrupt.

faillible [fajibl(ə)] *adj* fallible.

faillir [fajiʀ] *vi*: **j'ai failli tomber/lui dire** I almost *ou* nearly fell/told him; **~ à une promesse/un engagement** to break a promise/an agreement.

faillite [fajit] *nf* bankruptcy; (*échec: d'une politique etc*) collapse; **être en ~** to be bankrupt; **faire ~** to go bankrupt.

faim [fɛ̃] *nf* hunger; (*fig*): **~ d'amour/de richesse** hunger *ou* yearning for love/wealth; **avoir ~** to be hungry; **rester sur sa ~** (*aussi fig*) to be left wanting more.

fainéant, e [fɛneɑ̃, -ɑ̃t] *nm/f* idler, loafer.

fainéantise [fɛneɑ̃tiz] *nf* idleness, laziness.

═══════════════════ *MOT-CLÉ*

faire [fɛʀ] *vt* **1** (*fabriquer, être l'auteur de*) to make; (*produire*) to produce; (*construire: maison, bateau*) to build; **~ du vin/une offre/un film** to make wine/an offer/a film; **~ du bruit**

---

to make a noise

2 (*effectuer: travail, opération*) to do; **que faites-vous?** (*quel métier etc*) what do you do?; (*quelle activité: au moment de la question*) what are you doing?; **que ~?** what are we going to do?, what can be done (about it)?; **~ la lessive/le ménage** to do the washing/the housework

3 (*études*) to do; (*sport, musique*) to play; **~ du droit/du français** to do law/French; **~ du rugby/piano** to play rugby/the piano; **~ du cheval/du ski** to go riding/skiing

4 (*visiter*): **~ les magasins** to go shopping; **~ l'Europe** to tour *ou* do Europe

5 (*simuler*): **~ le malade/l'ignorant** to act the invalid/the fool

6 (*transformer, avoir un effet sur*): **~ de qn un frustré/avocat** to make sb frustrated/a lawyer; **ça ne me fait rien** (*m'est égal*) I don't care *ou* mind; (*me laisse froid*) it has no effect on me; **ça ne fait rien** it doesn't matter; **~ que** (*impliquer*) to mean that

7 (*calculs, prix, mesures*): **2 et 2 font** 4 2 and 2 are *ou* make 4; **ça fait 10 m/15 F** it's 10 m/15 F; **je vous le fais 10 F** I'll let you have it for 10 F

8 (*vb +de*): **qu'a-t-il fait de sa valise/de sa sœur?** what has he done with his case/his sister?

9: **ne ~ que**: **il ne fait que critiquer** (*sans cesse*) all he (ever) does is criticize; (*seulement*) he's only criticizing

10 (*dire*) to say; **vraiment? fit-il** really? he said

11 (*maladie*) to have; **~ du diabète/de la tension** to have diabetes *sg*/high blood pressure

♦ *vi* **1** (*agir, s'y prendre*) to act, do; **il faut ~ vite** we (*ou* you *etc*) must act quickly; **comment a-t-il fait pour?** how did he manage to?; **faites comme chez vous** make yourself at home; **je n'ai pas pu ~ autrement** there was nothing else I could do

2 (*paraître*) to look; **~ vieux/démodé** to look old/old-fashioned; **ça fait bien** it looks good; **tu fais jeune dans cette robe** that dress makes you look young(er)

♦ *vb substitut* to do; **ne le casse pas comme je l'ai fait** don't break it as I did; **je peux le voir? — faites!** can I see it? — please do!; **remets-le en place — je viens de le ~** put it back in its place — I just have (done)

♦ *vb impers* **1**: **il fait beau** *etc* the weather is fine *etc*; *voir aussi* **jour**; **froid** *etc*

2 (*temps écoulé, durée*): **ça fait 2 ans qu'il est parti** it's 2 years since he left; **ça fait 2 ans qu'il y est** he's been there for 2 years

♦ *vb semi-aux* **1**: **~ +infinitif** (*action directe*) to make; **~ tomber/bouger qch** to make sth fall/move; **~ démarrer un moteur/chauffer de l'eau** to start up an engine/heat some water; **cela fait dormir** it makes you sleep; **~**

travailler les enfants to make the children work *ou* get the children to work; **il m'a fait traverser la rue** he helped me to cross the road

2 (*indirectement, par un intermédiaire*): ~ **réparer qch** to get *ou* have sth repaired; ~ **punir les enfants** to have the children punished; **il m'a fait ouvrir la porte** he got me to open the door

se ~ *vi* **1** (*vin, fromage*) to mature

2: **cela se fait beaucoup/ne se fait pas** it's done a lot/not done

3 (+*nom ou pron*): **se** ~ **une jupe** to make o.s. a skirt; **se** ~ **des amis** to make friends; **se** ~ **du souci** to worry; **se** ~ **des illusions** to delude o.s.; **se** ~ **beaucoup d'argent** to make a lot of money; **il ne s'en fait pas** he doesn't worry

4 (+*adj*) (*devenir*): **se** ~ **vieux** to be getting old; (*délibérément*): **se** ~ **beau** to do o.s. up

5: **se** ~ **à** (*s'habituer*) to get used to; **je n'arrive pas à me** ~ **à la nourriture/au climat** I can't get used to the food/climate

6 (+*infinitif*): **se** ~ **examiner la vue/opérer** to have one's eyes tested/have an operation; **se** ~ **couper les cheveux** to get one's hair cut; **il va se** ~ **tuer/punir** he's going to get himself killed/get (himself) punished; **il s'est fait aider** he got somebody to help him; **il s'est fait aider par Simon** he got Simon to help him; **se** ~ **un vêtement** to get a garment made for o.s.

7 (*impersonnel*): **comment se fait-il/faisait-il que?** how is it/was it that?; **il peut se** ~ **que nous utilisions ...** it's possible that we could use ...

faire-part [fɛʀpaʀ] *nm inv* announcement (*of birth, marriage etc*).

fair-play [fɛʀplɛ] *adj inv* fair.

fais [fɛ] *vb voir* **faire**.

faisabilité [fəzabilite] *nf* feasibility.

faisable [fəzabl(ə)] *adj* feasible.

faisais [fəzɛ] *etc vb voir* **faire**.

faisan, e [fəzɑ̃, -an] *nm/f* pheasant.

faisandé, e [fəzɑ̃de] *adj* high (*bad*); (*fig péj*) corrupt, decadent.

faisceau, x [fɛso] *nm* (*de lumière etc*) beam; (*de branches etc*) bundle.

faiseur, euse [fəzœʀ, -øz] *nm/f* (*gén: péj*): ~ **de** maker of ♦ *nm* (*bespoke*) tailor; ~ **d'embarras** fusspot; ~ **de projets** schemer.

faisons [fəzɔ̃] *etc vb voir* **faire**.

faisselle [fɛsɛl] *nf* cheese strainer.

fait [fɛ] *vb voir* **faire** ♦ *nm* (*événement*) event, occurrence; (*réalité, donnée*) fact; **le** ~ **que/de manger** the fact that/of eating; **être le** ~ **de** (*causé par*) to be the work of; **être au** ~ **(de)** to be informed (of); **mettre qn au** ~ to inform sb, put sb in the picture; **au** ~ (*à propos*) by the way; **en venir au** ~ to get to the point; **de** ~ *adj* (*opposé à: de droit*) de facto

♦ *adv* in fact; **du** ~ **de ceci/qu'il a menti** because of *ou* on account of this/his having lied; **de ce** ~ therefore, for this reason; **en** ~ in fact; **en** ~ **de repas** by way of a meal; **prendre** ~ **et cause pour qn** to support sb, side with sb; **prendre qn sur le** ~ to catch sb in the act; **dire à qn son** ~ to give sb a piece of one's mind; **hauts** ~s (*exploits*) exploits; ~ **d'armes** feat of arms; ~ **divers** (short) news item; **les** ~s **et gestes de qn** sb's actions *ou* doings.

fait, e [fɛ, fɛt] *pp de* **faire** ♦ *adj* (*mûr: fromage, melon*) ripe; (*maquillé: yeux*) made-up; (*vernis: ongles*) painted, polished; **un homme** ~ a grown man; **tout(e)** ~(e) (*préparé à l'avance*) ready-made; **c'en est** ~ **de notre tranquillité** that's the end of our peace; **c'est bien** ~ **(pour lui** *ou* **eux etc)** it serves him (*ou* them *etc*) right.

faîte [fɛt] *nm* top; (*fig*) pinnacle, height.

faites [fɛt] *vb voir* **faire**.

faîtière [fɛtjɛʀ] *nf* (*de tente*) ridge pole.

fait-tout *nm inv*, **faitout** *nm* [fɛtu] stewpot.

fakir [fakiʀ] *nm* (*THÉÂT*) wizard.

falaise [falɛz] *nf* cliff.

falbalas [falbala] *nmpl* fripperies, frills.

fallacieux, euse [falasjø, -øz] *adj* (*raisonnement*) fallacious; (*apparences*) deceptive; (*espoir*) illusory.

falloir [falwaʀ] *vb impers*: **il faut faire les lits** we (*ou* you *etc*) must make the beds; **il faut que je fasse les lits** I have to *ou* must make the beds; **il a fallu qu'il parte** he had to leave; **il faudrait qu'elle rentre** she ought to go home; **il va** ~ **100 F** we'll (*ou* I'll *etc*) need 100 F; **il doit** ~ **du temps** that must take time; **il vous faut tourner à gauche après l'église** you have to turn left past the church; **nous avons ce qu'il (nous) faut** we have what we need; **il faut qu'il ait oublié** he must have forgotten; **il a fallu qu'il l'apprenne** he would have to hear about it; **il ne fallait pas** (*pour remercier*) you shouldn't have (done); **faut le faire!** (it) takes some doing! ♦ *vi*: **s'en** ~: **il s'en est fallu de 100 F/5 minutes** we (*ou* they *etc*) were 100 F short/5 minutes late (*ou* early); **il s'en faut de beaucoup qu'il soit ...** he is far from being ...; **il s'en est fallu de peu que cela n'arrive** it very nearly happened; **ou peu s'en faut** or just about, or as good as; **comme il faut** *adj* proper ♦ *adv* properly.

fallu [faly] *pp de* **falloir**.

falot, e [falo, -ɔt] *adj* dreary, colourless (*BRIT*), colorless (*US*) ♦ *nm* lantern.

falsification [falsifikasjɔ̃] *nf* falsification.

falsifier [falsifje] *vt* to falsify.

famé, e [fame] *adj*: **mal** ~ disreputable, of ill repute.

famélique [famelik] *adj* half-starved.

fameux, euse [famø, -øz] *adj* (*illustre: parfois péj*) famous; (*bon: repas, plat etc*) first-rate,

first-class; (*intensif*): **un ~ problème** *etc* a real problem *etc*; **pas ~** not great, not much good.

familial, e, aux [familjal, -o] *adj* family *cpd* ♦ *nf* (*AUTO*) family estate car (*BRIT*), station wagon (*US*).

familiariser [familjaʀize] *vt*: **~ qn avec** to familiarize sb with; **se ~ avec** to familiarize o.s. with.

familiarité [familjaʀite] *nf* familiarity; informality; **~s** *nfpl* familiarities; **~ avec** (*sujet, science*) familiarity with.

familier, ière [familje, -jɛʀ] *adj* (*connu, impertinent*) familiar; (*dénotant une certaine intimité*) informal, friendly; (*LING*) informal, colloquial ♦ *nm* regular (visitor).

familièrement [familjɛʀmɑ̃] *adv* (*sans façon: s'entretenir*) informally; (*cavalièrement*) familiarly.

famille [famij] *nf* family; **il a de la ~ à Paris** he has relatives in Paris.

famine [famin] *nf* famine.

fan [fan] *nm/f* fan.

fana [fana] *adj, nm/f* (*fam*) = **fanatique**.

fanal, aux [fanal, -o] *nm* beacon; lantern.

fanatique [fanatik] *adj*: **~ (de)** fanatical (about) ♦ *nm/f* fanatic.

fanatisme [fanatism(ə)] *nm* fanaticism.

fane [fan] *nf* top.

fané, e [fane] *adj* faded.

faner [fane]: **se ~** *vi* to fade.

faneur, euse [fanœʀ, -øz] *nm/f* haymaker ♦ *nf* (*TECH*) tedder.

fanfare [fɑ̃faʀ] *nf* (*orchestre*) brass band; (*musique*) fanfare; **en ~** (*avec bruit*) noisily.

fanfaron, ne [fɑ̃faʀɔ̃, -ɔn] *nm/f* braggart.

fanfaronnades [fɑ̃faʀɔnad] *nfpl* bragging *no pl*.

fanfreluches [fɑ̃fʀəlyʃ] *nfpl* trimming *no pl*.

fange [fɑ̃ʒ] *nf* mire.

fanion [fanjɔ̃] *nm* pennant.

fanon [fanɔ̃] *nm* (*de baleine*) plate of baleen; (*repli de peau*) dewlap, wattle.

fantaisie [fɑ̃tezi] *nf* (*spontanéité*) fancy, imagination; (*caprice*) whim; extravagance; (*MUS*) fantasia ♦ *adj*: **bijou (de) ~** (piece of) costume jewellery (*BRIT*) *ou* jewelry (*US*); **pain (de) ~** fancy bread.

fantaisiste [fɑ̃tezist(ə)] *adj* (*péj*) unorthodox, eccentric ♦ *nm/f* (*de music-hall*) variety artist *ou* entertainer.

fantasmagorique [fɑ̃tasmagɔʀik] *adj* phantasmagorical.

fantasme [fɑ̃tasm(ə)] *nm* fantasy.

fantasmer [fɑ̃tasme] *vi* to fantasize.

fantasque [fɑ̃task(ə)] *adj* whimsical, capricious; fantastic.

fantassin [fɑ̃tasɛ̃] *nm* infantryman.

fantastique [fɑ̃tastik] *adj* fantastic.

fantoche [fɑ̃tɔʃ] *nm* (*péj*) puppet.

fantomatique [fɑ̃tɔmatik] *adj* ghostly.

fantôme [fɑ̃tom] *nm* ghost, phantom.

FAO *sigle f* (= *Food and Agricultural Organization*) FAO.

faon [fɑ̃] *nm* fawn (*deer*).

faramineux, euse [faʀaminø, -øz] *adj* (*fam*) fantastic.

farandole [faʀɑ̃dɔl] *nf* farandole.

farce [faʀs(ə)] *nf* (*viande*) stuffing; (*blague*) (practical) joke; (*THÉÂT*) farce; **faire une ~ à qn** to play a (practical) joke on sb; **~s et attrapes** jokes and novelties.

farceur, euse [faʀsœʀ, -øz] *nm/f* · practical joker; (*fumiste*) clown.

farci, e [faʀsi] *adj* (*CULIN*) stuffed.

farcir [faʀsiʀ] *vt* (*viande*) to stuff; (*fig*): **~ qch de** to stuff sth with; **se ~** (*fam*): **je me suis farci la vaisselle** I've got stuck *ou* landed with the washing-up.

fard [faʀ] *nm* make-up; **~ à joues** blusher.

fardeau, x [faʀdo] *nm* burden.

farder [faʀde] *vt* to make up; (*vérité*) to disguise; **se ~** to make o.s. up.

farfelu, e [faʀfəly] *adj* wacky (*fam*), harebrained.

farfouiller [faʀfuje] *vi* (*péj*) to rummage around.

fariboles [faʀibɔl] *nfpl* nonsense *no pl*.

farine [faʀin] *nf* flour; **~ de blé** wheatflour; **~ de maïs** cornflour (*BRIT*), cornstarch (*US*); **~ lactée** (*pour bouillie*) gruel.

fariner [faʀine] *vt* to flour.

farineux, euse [faʀinø, -øz] *adj* (*sauce, pomme*) floury ♦ *nmpl* (*aliments*) starchy foods.

farniente [faʀnjɛnte] *nm* idleness.

farouche [faʀuʃ] *adj* shy, timid; (*sauvage*) savage, wild; (*violent*) fierce.

farouchement [faʀuʃmɑ̃] *adv* fiercely.

fart [faʀ(t)] *nm* (ski) wax.

farter [faʀte] *vt* to wax.

fascicule [fasikyl] *nm* volume.

fascinant, e [fasinɑ̃, -ɑ̃t] *adj* fascinating.

fascination [fasinɑsjɔ̃] *nf* fascination.

fasciner [fasine] *vt* to fascinate.

fascisant, e [faʃizɑ̃, -ɑ̃t] *adj* fascistic.

fascisme [faʃism(ə)] *nm* fascism.

fasciste [faʃist(ə)] *adj, nm/f* fascist.

fasse [fas] *etc vb voir* **faire**.

faste [fast(ə)] *nm* splendour (*BRIT*), splendor (*US*) ♦ *adj*: **c'est un jour ~** it's his (*ou* our *etc*) lucky day.

fastidieux, euse [fastidjø, -øz] *adj* tedious, tiresome.

fastueux, euse [fastɥø, -øz] *adj* sumptuous, luxurious.

fat [fa] *adj m* conceited, smug.

fatal, e [fatal] *adj* fatal; (*inévitable*) inevitable.

fatalement [fatalmɑ̃] *adv* inevitably.

fatalisme [fatalism(ə)] *nm* fatalism.

fataliste [fatalist(ə)] *adj* fatalistic.

fatalité [fatalite] *nf* (*destin*) fate; (*coïncidence*) fateful coincidence; (*caractère inévitable*) inevitability.

fatidique [fatidik] *adj* fateful.

fatigant, e [fatigɑ̃, -ɑ̃t] *adj* tiring; (*agaçant*) tiresome.

fatigue [fatig] *nf* tiredness, fatigue; (*détérioration*) fatigue; **les ~s du voyage** the wear and tear of the journey.

fatigué, e [fatige] *adj* tired.

fatiguer [fatige] *vt* to tire, make tired; (*TECH*) to put a strain on, strain; (*fig: importuner*) to wear out ♦ *vi* (*moteur*) to labour (*BRIT*), labor (*US*), strain; **se ~** *vi* to get tired; to tire o.s. (out); **se ~ à faire qch** to tire o.s. out doing sth.

fatras [fatra] *nm* jumble, hotchpotch.

fatuité [fatɥite] *nf* conceitedness, smugness.

faubourg [fobur] *nm* suburb.

faubourien, ne [foburjɛ̃, -ɛn] *adj* (*accent*) working-class.

fauché, e [foʃe] *adj* (*fam*) broke.

faucher [foʃe] *vt* (*herbe*) to cut; (*champs, blés*) to reap; (*fig*) to cut down; to mow down; (*fam: voler*) to pinch, nick.

faucheur, euse [foʃœr, -øz] *nm/f* reaper, mower.

faucille [fosij] *nf* sickle.

faucon [fokɔ̃] *nm* falcon, hawk.

faudra [fodra] *etc vb voir* **falloir**.

faufil [fofil] *nm* (*COUTURE*) tacking thread.

faufilage [fofilaʒ] *nm* (*COUTURE*) tacking.

faufiler [fofile] *vt* to tack, baste; **se ~** *vi*: **se ~ dans** to edge one's way into; **se ~ parmi/entre** to thread one's way among/between.

faune [fon] *nf* (*ZOOL*) wildlife, fauna; (*fig péj*) set, crowd ♦ *nm* faun; **~ marine** marine (animal) life.

faussaire [fosɛr] *nm/f* forger.

fausse [fos] *adj f voir* **faux**.

faussement [fosmɑ̃] *adv* (*accuser*) wrongly, wrongfully; (*croire*) falsely, erroneously.

fausser [fose] *vt* (*objet*) to bend, buckle; (*fig*) to distort; **~ compagnie à qn** to give sb the slip.

fausset [fosɛ] *nm*: **voix de ~** falsetto voice.

fausseté [foste] *nf* wrongness; falseness.

faut [fo] *vb voir* **falloir**.

faute [fot] *nf* (*erreur*) mistake, error; (*péché, manquement*) misdemeanour; (*FOOTBALL etc*) offence; (*TENNIS*) fault; (*responsabilité*): **par la ~ de** through the fault of, because of; **c'est de sa/ma ~** it's his/my fault; **être en ~** to be in the wrong; **prendre qn en ~** to catch sb out; **~ de** (*temps, argent*) for *ou* through lack of; **~ de mieux** for want of anything *ou* something better; **sans ~** *adv* without fail; **~ de frappe** typing error; **~ d'inattention** careless mistake; **~ d'orthographe** spelling mistake; **~ professionnelle** professional misconduct *no pl*.

fauteuil [fotœj] *nm* armchair; **~ à bascule** rocking chair; **~ club** (big) easy chair; **~ d'orchestre** seat in the front stalls (*BRIT*) *ou* the orchestra (*US*); **~ roulant** wheelchair.

fauteur [fotœr] *nm*: **~ de troubles** trouble-

maker.

fautif, ive [fotif, -iv] *adj* (*incorrect*) incorrect, inaccurate; (*responsable*) at fault, in the wrong; (*coupable*) guilty ♦ *nm/f* culprit.

fauve [fov] *nm* wildcat; (*peintre*) Fauve ♦ *adj* (*couleur*) fawn.

fauvette [fovɛt] *nf* warbler.

fauvisme [fovism(ə)] *nm* (*ART*) Fauvism.

faux¹ [fo] *nf* scythe.

faux², fausse [fo, fos] *adj* (*inexact*) wrong; (*piano, voix*) out of tune; (*falsifié*) fake, forged; (*sournois, postiche*) false ♦ *adv* (*MUS*) out of tune ♦ *nm* (*copie*) fake, forgery; (*opposé au vrai*): **le ~** falsehood; **le ~ numéro/la fausse clé** the wrong number/key; **faire fausse route** to go the wrong way; **faire ~ bond à qn** to let sb down; **~ ami** (*LING*) faux ami; **~ col** detachable collar; **~ départ** (*SPORT, fig*) false start; **~ frais** *nmpl* extras, incidental expenses; **~ frère** (*fig péj*) false friend; **~ mouvement** awkward movement; **~ nez** false nose; **~ nom** assumed name; **~ pas** tripping *no pl*; (*fig*) faux pas; **~ témoignage** (*délit*) perjury; **fausse alerte** false alarm; **fausse clé** skeleton key; **fausse couche** (*MÉD*) miscarriage; **fausse joie** vain joy; **fausse note** wrong note.

faux-filet [fofilɛ] *nm* sirloin.

faux-fuyant [fofɥijɑ̃] *nm* equivocation.

faux-monnayeur [fomɔnɛjœr] *nm* counterfeiter, forger.

faux-semblant [fosɑ̃blɑ̃] *nm* pretence (*BRIT*), pretense (*US*).

faux-sens [fosɑ̃s] *nm* mistranslation.

faveur [favœr] *nf* favour (*BRIT*), favor (*US*); **traitement de ~** preferential treatment; **à la ~ de** under cover of; (*grâce à*) thanks to; **en ~ de** in favo(u)r of.

favorable [favɔrabl(ə)] *adj* favo(u)rable.

favori, te [favɔri, -it] *adj*, *nm/f* favo(u)rite.

favoris [favɔri] *nmpl* (*barbe*) sideboards (*BRIT*), sideburns.

favoriser [favɔrize] *vt* to favour (*BRIT*), favor (*US*).

favoritisme [favɔritism(ə)] *nm* (*péj*) favo(u)ritism.

fayot [fajo] *nm* (*fam*) crawler.

FB *abr* (= franc belge) BF, FB.

FBI *sigle m* FBI.

FC *sigle m* (= Football Club) FC.

fébrile [febril] *adj* feverish, febrile; **capitaux ~s** (*ÉCON*) hot money.

fébrilement [febrilmɑ̃] *adv* feverishly.

fécal, e, aux [fekal, -o] *adj voir* **matière**.

FECOM [fekɔm] *sigle m* (= Fonds européen de coopération militaire) EMCF.

fécond, e [fekɔ̃, -ɔ̃d] *adj* fertile.

fécondation [fekɔ̃dasjɔ̃] *nf* fertilization.

féconder [fekɔ̃de] *vt* to fertilize.

fécondité [fekɔ̃dite] *nf* fertility.

fécule [fekyl] *nf* potato flour.

féculent [fekylɑ̃] *nm* starchy food.

fédéral, e, aux [fedeʀal, -o] *adj* federal.
fédéralisme [fedeʀalism(ə)] *nm* federalism.
fédéraliste [fedeʀalist(ə)] *adj* federalist.
fédération [fedeʀasjɔ̃] *nf* federation.
fée [fe] *nf* fairy.
féerie [feʀi] *nf* enchantment.
féerique [feʀik] *adj* magical, fairytale *cpd*.
feignant, e [fɛɲɑ̃, -ɑ̃t] *nm/f* = **fainéant, e.**
feindre [fɛ̃dʀ(ə)] *vt* to feign ♦ *vi* to dissemble; ~ **de faire** to pretend to do.
feint, e [fɛ̃, fɛ̃t] *pp de* **feindre** ♦ *adj* feigned ♦ *nf* (*SPORT: escrime*) feint; (: *football, rugby*) dummy (*BRIT*), fake (*US*): (*fam: ruse*) sham.
feinter [fɛ̃te] *vi* (*SPORT: escrime*) to feint; (: *football, rugby*) to dummy (*BRIT*), fake (*US*) ♦ *vt* (*fam: tromper*) to fool.
fêlé, e [fele] *adj* (*aussi fig*) cracked.
fêler [fele] *vt* to crack.
félicitations [felisitasjɔ̃] *nfpl* congratulations.
félicité [felisite] *nf* bliss.
féliciter [felisite] *vt*: ~ **qn (de)** to congratulate sb (on).
félin, e [felɛ̃, -in] *adj* feline ♦ *nm* (big) cat.
félon, ne [felɔ̃, -ɔn] *adj* perfidious, treacherous.
félonie [feloni] *nf* treachery.
fêlure [felyʀ] *nf* crack.
femelle [fəmɛl] *adj* (*aussi ÉLEC, TECH*) female ♦ *nf* female.
féminin, e [feminɛ̃, -in] *adj* feminine; (*sexe*) female; (*équipe, vêtements etc*) women's; (*parfois péj: homme*) effeminate ♦ *nm* (*LING*) feminine.
féminiser [feminize] *vt* to feminize; (*rendre efféminé*) to make effeminate; **se** ~ *vi*: **cette profession se féminise** this profession is attracting more women.
féminisme [feminism(ə)] *nm* feminism.
féministe [feminist(ə)] *adj, nf* feminist.
féminité [feminite] *nf* femininity.
femme [fam] *nf* woman; (*épouse*) wife (*pl* wives); **être très** ~ to be very much a woman; **devenir** ~ to attain womanhood; ~ **d'affaires** businesswoman; ~ **de chambre** chambermaid; ~ **fatale** femme fatale; ~ **au foyer** housewife; ~ **d'intérieur** (real) homemaker; ~ **de ménage** domestic help, cleaning lady; ~ **du monde** society woman; ~-**objet** sex object; ~ **de tête** determined, intellectual woman.
fémoral, e, aux [femoʀal, -o] *adj* femoral.
fémur [femyʀ] *nm* femur, thighbone.
FEN [fɛn] *sigle f* (= Fédération de l'Éducation nationale) *teachers' trades union.*
fenaison [fənɛzɔ̃] *nf* haymaking.
fendillé, e [fɑ̃dije] *adj* (*terre etc*) crazed.
fendre [fɑ̃dʀ(ə)] *vt* (*couper en deux*) to split; (*fissurer*) to crack; (*fig: traverser*) to cut through; to push one's way through; **se** ~ *vi* to crack.
fendu, e [fɑ̃dy] *adj* (*sol, mur*) cracked; (*jupe*) slit.

fenêtre [fənɛtʀ(ə)] *nf* window; ~ **à guillotine** sash window.
fennec [fenɛk] *nm* fennec.
fenouil [fənuj] *nm* fennel.
fente [fɑ̃t] *nf* slit; (*fissure*) crack.
féodal, e, aux [feodal, -o] *adj* feudal.
féodalisme [feodalism(ə)] *nm* feudalism.
féodalité [feodalite] *nf* feudalism.
fer [fɛʀ] *nm* iron; (*de cheval*) shoe; ~**s** *pl* (*MÉD*) forceps; **mettre aux** ~**s** (*enchaîner*) to put in chains; **au** ~ **rouge** with a red-hot iron; **santé/main de** ~ iron constitution/hand; ~ **à cheval** horseshoe; **en** ~ **à cheval** (*fig*) horseshoe-shaped; ~ **forgé** wrought iron; ~ **à friser** curling tongs; ~ **de lance** spearhead; ~ (**à repasser**) iron; ~ **à souder** soldering iron.
ferai [fəʀe] *etc vb voir* **faire.**
fer-blanc [fɛʀblɑ̃] *nm* tin(plate).
ferblanterie [fɛʀblɑ̃tʀi] *nf* tinplate making; (*produit*) tinware.
ferblantier [fɛʀblɑ̃tje] *nm* tinsmith.
férié, e [feʀje] *adj*: **jour** ~ public holiday.
férir [feʀiʀ]: **sans coup** ~ *adv* without meeting any opposition.
fermage [fɛʀmaʒ] *nm* tenant farming.
ferme [fɛʀm(ə)] *adj* firm ♦ *adv* (*travailler etc*) hard; (*discuter*) ardently ♦ *nf* (*exploitation*) farm; (*maison*) farmhouse; **tenir** ~ to stand firm.
fermé, e [fɛʀme] *adj* closed, shut; (*gaz, eau etc*) off; (*fig: personne*) uncommunicative; (: *milieu*) exclusive.
fermement [fɛʀməmɑ̃] *adv* firmly.
ferment [fɛʀmɑ̃] *nm* ferment.
fermentation [fɛʀmɑ̃tasjɔ̃] *nf* fermentation.
fermenter [fɛʀmɑ̃te] *vi* to ferment.
fermer [fɛʀme] *vt* to close, shut; (*cesser l'exploitation de*) to close down, shut down; (*eau, lumière, électricité, robinet*) to put off, turn off; (*aéroport, route*) to close ♦ *vi* to close, shut; to close down, shut down; **se** ~ *vi* (*yeux*) to close, shut; (*fleur, blessure*) to close up; ~ **à clef** to lock; ~ **au verrou** to bolt; ~ **les yeux (sur qch)** (*fig*) to close one's eyes (to sth); **se** ~ **à** (*pitié, amour*) to close one's heart *ou* mind to.
fermeté [fɛʀməte] *nf* firmness.
fermette [fɛʀmɛt] *nf* farmhouse.
fermeture [fɛʀmətyʀ] *nf* (*voir fermer*) closing; shutting; closing *ou* shutting down; putting *ou* turning off; (*dispositif*) catch; fastening; fastener; **heure de** ~ (*COMM*) closing time; **jour de** ~ (*COMM*) day on which the shop (*etc*) is closed; ~ **éclair** ® *ou* **à glissière** zip (fastener) (*BRIT*), zipper.
fermier, ière [fɛʀmje, -jɛʀ] *nm/f* farmer ♦ *nf* (*femme de fermier*) farmer's wife ♦ *adj*: **beurre/cidre** ~ farm butter/cider.
fermoir [fɛʀmwaʀ] *nm* clasp.
féroce [feʀɔs] *adj* ferocious, fierce.
férocement [feʀɔsmɑ̃] *adv* ferociously.

férocité [feʀɔsite] *nf* ferocity, ferociousness.
ferons [fəʀɔ̃] *etc vb voir* **faire**.
ferraille [feʀaj] *nf* scrap iron; **mettre à la ~** to scrap; **bruit de ~** clanking.
ferrailler [feʀaje] *vi* to clank.
ferrailleur [feʀajœʀ] *nm* scrap merchant.
ferrant [feʀɑ̃] *adj m voir* **maréchal-ferrant**.
ferré, e [feʀe] *adj* (*chaussure*) hobnailed; (*canne*) steel-tipped; **~ sur** (*fam: savant*) well up on.
ferrer [feʀe] *vt* (*cheval*) to shoe; (*chaussure*) to nail; (*canne*) to tip; (*poisson*) to strike.
ferreux, euse [feʀø, -øz] *adj* ferrous.
ferronnerie [feʀɔnʀi] *nf* ironwork; **~ d'art** wrought iron work.
ferronnier [feʀɔnje] *nm* craftsman in wrought iron; (*marchand*) ironware merchant.
ferroviaire [feʀɔvjɛʀ] *adj* rail *cpd*, railway *cpd* (*BRIT*), railroad *cpd* (*US*).
ferrugineux, euse [feʀyʒinø, -øz] *adj* ferruginous.
ferrure [feʀyʀ] *nf* (*ornamental*) hinge.
ferry(-boat) [feʀe(bɔt)] *nm* ferry.
fertile [feʀtil] *adj* fertile; **~ en incidents** eventful, packed with incidents.
fertilisant [feʀtilizɑ̃] *nm* fertilizer.
fertilisation [feʀtilizasjɔ̃] *nf* fertilization.
fertiliser [feʀtilize] *vt* to fertilize.
fertilité [feʀtilite] *nf* fertility.
féru, e [feʀy] *adj*: **~ de** with a keen interest in.
férule [feʀyl] *nf*: **être sous la ~ de qn** to be under sb's (iron) rule.
fervent, e [feʀvɑ̃, -ɑ̃t] *adj* fervent.
ferveur [feʀvœʀ] *nf* fervour (*BRIT*), fervor (*US*).
fesse [fɛs] *nf* buttock; **les ~s** the bottom *sg*, the buttocks.
fessée [fese] *nf* spanking.
fessier [fesje] *nm* (*fam*) behind.
festin [fɛstɛ̃] *nm* feast.
festival [fɛstival] *nm* festival.
festivalier [fɛstivalje] *nm* festival-goer.
festivités [fɛstivite] *nfpl* festivities, merry-making *sg*.
feston [fɛstɔ̃] *nm* (*ARCHIT*) festoon; (*COUTURE*) scallop.
festoyer [fɛstwaje] *vi* to feast.
fêtard [fɛtaʀ] *nm* (*péj*) high liver, merry-maker.
fête [fɛt] *nf* (*religieuse*) feast; (*publique*) holiday; (*en famille etc*) celebration; (*kermesse*) fête, fair, festival; (*du nom*) feast day, name day; **faire la ~** to live it up; **faire ~ à qn** to give sb a warm welcome; **se faire une ~ de** to look forward to; to enjoy; **ça va être sa ~!** (*fam*) he's going to get it!; **jour de ~** holiday; **les ~s (de fin d'année)** the festive season; **la salle/le comité des ~s** the village hall/festival committee; **la ~ des Mères/Pères** Mother's/Father's Day; **~ de charité** charity fair *ou* fête; **~ foraine** (fun)fair; **~ mobile** movable feast (day); **la F~ Nationale** the national holiday.

Fête-Dieu [fɛtdjø] *nf*: **la ~** Corpus Christi.
fêter [fɛte] *vt* to celebrate; (*personne*) to have a celebration for.
fétiche [fetiʃ] *nm* fetish; **animal ~**, **objet ~** mascot.
fétichisme [fetiʃism(ə)] *nm* fetishism.
fétichiste [fetiʃist(ə)] *adj* fetishist.
fétide [fetid] *adj* fetid.
fétu [fety] *nm*: **~ de paille** wisp of straw.
feu¹ [fø] *adj inv*: **~ son père** his late father.
feu², x [fø] *nm* (*gén*) fire; (*signal lumineux*) light; (*de cuisinière*) ring; (*sensation de brûlure*) burning (sensation); **~x** *nmpl* fire *sg*; (*AUTO*) (traffic) lights; **tous ~x éteints** (*NAVIG, AUTO*) without lights; **au ~!** (*incendie*) fire!; **à ~ doux/vif** over a slow/brisk heat; **à petit ~** (*CULIN*) over a gentle heat; (*fig*) slowly; **faire ~** to fire; **ne pas faire long ~** (*fig*) not to last long; **commander le ~** (*MIL*) to give the order to (open) fire; **tué au ~** (*MIL*) killed in action; **mettre à ~** (*fusée*) to fire off; **pris entre deux ~x** caught in the crossfire; **en ~** on fire; **être tout ~ tout flamme (pour)** (*passion*) to be aflame with passion (for); (*enthousiasme*) to be fired with enthusiasm (for); **prendre ~** to catch fire; **mettre le ~ à** to set fire to, set on fire; **faire du ~** to make a fire; **avez-vous du ~?** (*pour cigarette*) have you (got) a light?; **~ rouge/vert/orange** (*AUTO*) red/green/amber (*BRIT*) *ou* yellow (*US*) light; **donner le ~ vert à qch/qn** (*fig*) to give sth/sb the go-ahead *ou* green light; **~ arrière** (*AUTO*) rear light; **~ d'artifice** firework; (*spectacle*) fireworks *pl*; **~ de camp** campfire; **~ de joie** bonfire; **~ de paille** (*fig*) flash in the pan; **~x de brouillard** (*AUTO*) fog lights *ou* lamps; **~x de croisement** (*AUTO*) dipped (*BRIT*) *ou* dimmed (*US*) headlights; **~x de position** (*AUTO*) sidelights; **~x de route** (*AUTO*) headlights (on full (*BRIT*) *ou* high (*US*) beam); **~x de stationnement** parking lights.
feuillage [fœjaʒ] *nm* foliage, leaves *pl*.
feuille [fœj] *nf* (*d'arbre*) leaf (*pl* leaves); **~ (de papier)** sheet (of paper); **rendre ~ blanche** (*SCOL*) to give in a blank paper; **~ d'or/de métal** gold/metal leaf; **~ de chou** (*péj: journal*) rag; **~ d'impôts** tax form; **~ de maladie** medical expenses claim form; **~ morte** dead leaf; **~ de paye** pay slip; **~ de présence** attendance sheet; **~ de température** temperature chart; **~ de vigne** (*BOT*) vine leaf; (*sur statue*) fig leaf; **~ volante** loose sheet.

tional holiday.

feuillet [fœjɛ] *nm* leaf (*pl* leaves), page.

feuilletage [fœjtaʒ] *nm* (*aspect feuilleté*) flakiness.

feuilleté, e [fœjte] *adj* (*CULIN*) flaky; (*verre*) laminated.

feuilleter [fœjte] *vt* (*livre*) to leaf through.

feuilleton [fœjtɔ̃] *nm* serial.

feuillette [fœjɛt] *etc vb voir* **feuilleter**.

feuillu, e [fœjy] *adj* leafy ♦ *nm* broad-leaved tree.

feulement [fœlmɑ̃] *nm* growl.

feutre [føtʀ(ə)] *nm* felt; (*chapeau*) felt hat; (*stylo*) felt-tip(ped pen).

feutré, e [føtʀe] *adj* feltlike; (*pas, voix*) muffled.

feutrer [føtʀe] *vt* to felt; (*fig: bruits*) to muffle ♦ *vi*, **se ~** *vi* (*tissu*) to felt.

feutrine [føtʀin] *nf* (lightweight) felt.

fève [fɛv] *nf* broad bean; (*dans la galette des Rois*) charm (*hidden in cake eaten on Twelfth Night*).

février [fevʀije] *nm* February; *voir aussi* **juillet**.

fez [fɛz] *nm* fez.

FF *abr* (= *franc français*) FF.

FFA *sigle fpl* (= *Forces françaises en Allemagne*) French forces in Germany.

FFI *sigle fpl* = *Forces françaises de l'intérieur (1942-45)* ♦ *sigle m* member of the FFI.

FFL *sigle fpl* (= *Forces françaises libres*) Free French Army.

Fg *abr* = **faubourg**.

FGA *sigle m* (= *Fonds de garantie automobile*) *fund financed through insurance premiums, to compensate victims of uninsured losses.*

FGEN *sigle f* (= *Fédération générale de l'éducation nationale*) *teachers' trade union.*

fi [fi] *excl*: **faire ~ de** to snap one's fingers at.

fiabilité [fjabilite] *nf* reliability.

fiable [fjabl(ə)] *adj* reliable.

fiacre [fjakʀ(ə)] *nm* (hackney) cab *ou* carriage.

fiançailles [fjɑ̃saj] *nfpl* engagement *sg.*

fiancé, e [fjɑ̃se] *nm/f* fiancé/fiancée ♦ *adj*: **être ~ (à)** to be engaged (to).

fiancer [fjɑ̃se]: **se ~** *vi*: **se ~ (avec)** to become engaged (to).

fiasco [fjasko] *nm* fiasco.

fibranne [fibʀan] *nf* bonded fibre *ou* fiber (*US*).

fibre [fibʀ(ə)] *nf* fibre, fiber (*US*); **avoir la ~ paternelle/militaire** to be a born father/soldier; **~ optique** optical fibre *ou* fiber; **~ de verre** fibreglass (*BRIT*), fiberglass (*US*), glass fibre *ou* fiber.

fibreux, euse [fibʀø, -øz] *adj* fibrous; (*viande*) stringy.

fibrome [fibʀom] *nm* (*MÉD*) fibroma.

ficelage [fislaʒ] *nm* tying (up).

ficelé, e [fisle] *adj* (*fam*): **être mal ~** (*habillé*) to be badly got up; **bien/mal ~** (*conçu: roman, projet*) well/badly put together.

ficeler [fisle] *vt* to tie up.

ficelle [fisɛl] *nf* string *no pl*; (*morceau*) piece *ou*

length of string; (*pain*) stick of French bread; **~s** *pl* (*fig*) strings; **tirer sur la ~** (*fig*) to go too far.

fiche [fiʃ] *nf* (*carte*) (index) card; (*INFORM*) record; (*formulaire*) form; (*ÉLEC*) plug; **~ de paye** pay slip; **~ signalétique** (*POLICE*) identification card; **~ technique** data sheet, specification *ou* spec sheet.

ficher [fiʃe] *vt* (*dans un fichier*) to file; (*: POLICE*) to put on file; (*fam*) to do; (*: donner*) to give; (*: mettre*) to stick *ou* shove; (*planter*): **~ qch dans** to stick *ou* drive sth into; **~ qn à la porte** (*fam*) to chuck sb out; **fiche(-moi) le camp** (*fam*) clear off; **fiche-moi la paix** (*fam*) leave me alone; **se ~ dans** (*s'enfoncer*) to get stuck in, embed itself in; **se ~ de** (*fam*) to make fun of; not to care about.

fichier [fiʃje] *nm* (*gén, INFORM*) file; (*à cartes*) card index; **~ actif** *ou* **en cours d'utilisation** (*INFORM*) active file; **~ d'adresses** mailing list; **~ d'archives** (*INFORM*) archive file.

fichu, e [fiʃy] *pp de* **ficher** (*fam*) ♦ *adj* (*fam: fini, inutilisable*) bust, done for; (*: intensif*) wretched, darned ♦ *nm* (*foulard*) (head)scarf (*pl* -scarves); **être ~ de** to be capable of; **mal ~** feeling lousy; **bien ~** great.

fictif, ive [fiktif, -iv] *adj* fictitious.

fiction [fiksjɔ̃] *nf* fiction; (*fait imaginé*) invention.

fictivement [fiktivmɑ̃] *adv* fictitiously.

fidèle [fidɛl] *adj*: **~ (à)** faithful (to) ♦ *nm/f* (*REL*): **les ~s** the faithful; (*à l'église*) the congregation.

fidèlement [fidɛlmɑ̃] *adv* faithfully.

fidélité [fidelite] *nf* faithfulness.

Fidji [fidʒi] *nfpl*: (**les îles**) **~** Fiji.

fiduciaire [fidysjɛʀ] *adj* fiduciary; **héritier ~** heir, trustee; **monnaie ~** flat money.

fief [fjɛf] *nm* fief; (*fig*) preserve; stronghold.

fieffé, e [fjefe] *adj* (*ivrogne, menteur*) arrant, out-and-out.

fiel [fjɛl] *nm* gall.

fiente [fjɑ̃t] *nf* (bird) droppings *pl.*

fier¹ [fje]: **se ~ à** *vt* to trust.

fier², fière [fjɛʀ] *adj* proud; **~ de** proud of; **avoir fière allure** to cut a fine figure.

fièrement [fjɛʀmɑ̃] *adv* proudly.

fierté [fjɛʀte] *nf* pride.

fièvre [fjɛvʀ(ə)] *nf* fever; **avoir de la ~/39 de ~** to have a high temperature/a temperature of 39°C; **~ typhoïde** typhoid fever.

fiévreusement [fjevʀøzmɑ̃] *adv* (*fig*) feverishly.

fiévreux, euse [fjevʀø, -øz] *adj* feverish.

FIFA [fifa] *sigle f* (= *Fédération internationale de Football association*) FIFA.

fifre [fifʀ(ə)] *nm* fife; (*personne*) fife-player.

fig *abr* (= *figure*) fig.

figer [fiʒe] *vt* to congeal; (*fig: personne*) to freeze, root to the spot; **se ~** *vi* to congeal; to freeze; (*institutions etc*) to become set, stop evolving.

fignoler [fiɲɔle] vt to put the finishing touches to.

figue [fig] nf fig.

figuier [figje] nm fig tree.

figurant, e [figyʀɑ̃, -ɑ̃t] nm/f (THÉÂT) walk-on; (CINÉ) extra.

figuratif, ive [figyʀatif, -iv] adj representational, figurative.

figuration [figyʀasjɔ̃] nf walk-on parts pl; extras pl.

figure [figyʀ] nf (visage) face; (image, tracé, forme, personnage) figure; (illustration) picture, diagram; **faire ~ de** to look like; **faire bonne ~** to put up a good show; **faire triste ~** to be a sorry sight; **~ de rhétorique** figure of speech.

figuré, e [figyʀe] adj (sens) figurative.

figurer [figyʀe] vi to appear ♦ vt to represent; **se ~ que** to imagine that; **figurez-vous que ... ** would you believe that ...?

figurine [figyʀin] nf figurine.

fil [fil] nm (brin, fig: d'une histoire) thread; (du téléphone) cable, wire; (textile de lin) linen; (d'un couteau: tranchant) edge; **au ~ des années** with the passing of the years; **au ~ de l'eau** with the stream ou current; **de ~ en aiguille** one thing leading to another; **ne tenir qu'à un ~** (vie, réussite etc) to hang by a thread; **donner du ~ à retordre à qn** to make life difficult for sb; **donner/recevoir un coup de ~** to make/get a phone call; **~ à coudre** (sewing) thread ou yarn; **~ dentaire** dental floss; **~ électrique** electric wire; **~ de fer** wire; **~ de fer barbelé** barbed wire; **~ à pêche** fishing line; **~ à plomb** plumbline; **~ à souder** soldering wire.

filament [filamɑ̃] nm (ÉLEC) filament; (de liquide) trickle, thread.

filandreux, euse [filɑ̃dʀø, -øz] adj stringy.

filant, e [filɑ̃, -ɑ̃t] adj: **étoile ~e** shooting star.

filasse [filas] adj inv white blond.

filature [filatyʀ] nf (fabrique) mill; (policière) shadowing no pl, tailing no pl; **prendre qn en ~** to shadow ou tail sb.

fil-de-fériste [fildəfeʀist(ə)] nm/f high-wire artist.

file [fil] nf line; **~ (d'attente)** queue (BRIT), line (US); **prendre la ~** to join the (end of the) queue ou line; **prendre la ~ de droite** (AUTO) to move into the right-hand lane; **se mettre en ~** to form a line; (AUTO) to get into lane; **stationner en double ~** (AUTO) to double-park; **à la ~** (d'affilée) in succession; (à la suite) one after another; **à la ou en ~ indienne** in single file.

filer [file] vt (tissu, toile, verre) to spin; (dérouler: câble etc) to pay ou let out; (prendre en filature) to shadow, tail; (fam: donner): **~ qch à qn** to slip sb sth ♦ vi (bas, maille, liquide, pâte) to run; (aller vite) to fly past ou by; (fam: partir) to make off; **~ à l'anglaise** to take French leave; **~ doux** to behave o.s., toe the

line; **~ un mauvais coton** to be in a bad way.

filet [filɛ] nm net; (CULIN) fillet; (d'eau, de sang) trickle; **tendre un ~** (suj: police) to set a trap; **~ (à bagages)** (RAIL) luggage rack; **~ (à provisions)** string bag.

filetage [filtaʒ] nm threading; thread.

fileter [filte] vt to thread.

filial, e, aux [filjal, -o] adj filial ♦ nf (COMM) subsidiary; affiliate.

filiation [filjasjɔ̃] nf filiation.

filière [filjɛʀ] nf: **passer par la ~** to go through the (administrative) channels; **suivre la ~** to work one's way up (through the hierarchy).

filiforme [filifɔʀm(ə)] adj spindly; threadlike.

filigrane [filigʀan] nm (d'un billet, timbre) watermark; **en ~** (fig) showing just beneath the surface.

filin [filɛ̃] nm (NAVIG) rope.

fille [fij] nf girl; (opposé à fils) daughter; **vieille ~** old maid; **~ de joie** prostitute; **~ de salle** waitress.

fille-mère, pl **filles-mères** [fijmɛʀ] nf unmarried mother.

fillette [fijɛt] nf (little) girl.

filleul, e [fijœl] nm/f godchild, godson/daughter.

film [film] nm (pour photo) (roll of) film; (œuvre) film, picture, movie; (couche) film; **~ muet/parlant** silent/talking picture ou movie; **~ alimentaire** clingfilm; **~ d'animation** animated film; **~ policier** thriller.

filmer [filme] vt to film.

filon [filɔ̃] nm vein, lode; (fig) lucrative line, moneyspinner.

filou [filu] nm (escroc) swindler.

fils [fis] nm son; **~ de famille** moneyed young man; **~ à papa** (péj) daddy's boy.

filtrage [filtʀaʒ] nm filtering.

filtrant, e [filtʀɑ̃, -ɑ̃t] adj (huile solaire etc) filtering.

filtre [filtʀ(ə)] nm filter; **"~ ou sans ~?"** (cigarettes) "tipped or plain?"; **~ à air** air filter.

filtrer [filtʀe] vt to filter; (fig: candidats, visiteurs) to screen ♦ vi to filter (through).

fin¹ [fɛ̃] nf end; **~s** nfpl (but) ends; **à (la) ~ mai**, **~ mai** at the end of May; **en ~ de semaine** at the end of the week; **prendre ~** to come to an end; **toucher à sa ~** to be drawing to a close; **mettre ~ à** to put an end to; **mener à bonne ~** to bring to a successful conclusion; **à cette ~** to this end; **à toutes ~s utiles** for your information; **à la ~** in the end, eventually; **sans ~** adj endless ♦ adv endlessly; **~ de non-recevoir** (JUR, ADMIN) objection; **~ de section** (de ligne d'autobus) (fare) stage.

fin², e [fɛ̃, fin] adj (papier, couche, fil) thin; (cheveux, poudre, pointe, visage) fine; (taille) neat, slim; (esprit, remarque) subtle; shrewd ♦ adv (moudre, couper) finely ♦ nm: **vouloir jouer au plus ~ (avec qn)** to try to outsmart sb ♦ nf (*alcool*) liqueur brandy; **c'est ~!** (*ironique*) how clever!; **~ prêt/soûl** quite ready/drunk; **un ~ gourmet** a gourmet; **un ~ tireur** a crack shot; **avoir la vue/l'ouïe ~e** to have sharp eyes/ears, have keen eyesight/hearing; **or/linge/vin ~** fine gold/linen/wine; **le ~ fond de** the very depths of; **le ~ mot de** the real story behind; **la ~e fleur de** the flower of; **une ~e mouche** (*fig*) a sharp customer; **~es herbes** mixed herbs.

final, e [final] *adj, nf* final ♦ *nm* (*MUS*) finale; **quarts de ~e** quarter finals; **8èmes/16èmes de ~e** 2nd/1st round (*in 5 round knock-out competition*).

finalement [finalmã] *adv* finally, in the end; (*après tout*) after all.

finaliste [finalist(ə)] *nm/f* finalist.

finalité [finalite] *nf* (*but*) aim, goal; (*fonction*) purpose.

finance [finãs] *nf* finance; **~s** *nfpl* (*situation financière*) finances; (*activités financières*) finance *sg*; **moyennant ~** for a fee *ou* consideration.

financement [finãsmã] *nm* financing.

financer [finãse] *vt* to finance.

financier, ière [finãsje, -jɛR] *adj* financial ♦ *nm* financier.

financièrement [finãsjɛRmã] *adv* financially.

finasser [finase] *vi* (*péj*) to wheel and deal.

finaud, e [fino, -od] *adj* wily.

fine [fin] *adj f, nf voir* **fin, e**.

finement [finmã] *adv* thinly; finely; neatly, slimly; subtly; shrewdly.

finesse [finɛs] *nf* thinness; fineness; neatness, slimness; subtlety; shrewdness; **~s** *nfpl* (*subtilités*) niceties; finer points.

fini, e [fini] *adj* finished; (*MATH*) finite; (*intensif*): **un menteur ~** a liar through and through ♦ *nm* (*d'un objet manufacturé*) finish.

finir [finiR] *vt* to finish ♦ *vi* to finish, end; **~ quelque part** to end *ou* finish up somewhere; **~ de faire** to finish doing; (*cesser*) to stop doing; **~ par faire** to end *ou* finish up doing; **il finit par m'agacer** he's beginning to get on my nerves; **~ en pointe/tragédie** to end in a point/in tragedy; **en ~ avec** to be *ou* have done with; **à n'en plus ~** (*route, discussions*) never-ending; **il va mal ~** he will come to a bad end; **c'est bientôt fini?** (*reproche*) have you quite finished?

finish [finiʃ] *nm* (*SPORT*) finish.

finissage [finisaʒ] *nm* finishing.

finisseur, euse [finisœR, -øz] *nm/f* (*SPORT*) strong finisher.

finition [finisjõ] *nf* finishing; finish.

finlandais, e [fɛ̃ladɛ, -ɛz] *adj* Finnish ♦ *nm/f*: **F~, e** Finn.

Finlande [fɛ̃lãd] *nf*: **la ~** Finland.

finnois, e [finwa, -waz] *adj* Finnish ♦ *nm* (*LING*) Finnish.

fiole [fjɔl] *nf* phial.

fiord [fjɔR(d)] *nm* = **fjord**.

fioriture [fjɔRityR] *nf* embellishment, flourish.

fioul [fjul] *nm* fuel oil.

firent [fiR] *vb voir* **faire**.

firmament [fiRmamã] *nm* firmament, skies *pl*.

firme [fiRm(ə)] *nf* firm.

fis [fi] *vb voir* **faire**.

fisc [fisk] *nm* tax authorities *pl*, ≈ Inland Revenue (*BRIT*), ≈ Internal Revenue Service (*US*).

fiscal, e, aux [fiskal, -o] *adj* tax *cpd*, fiscal.

fiscaliser [fiskalize] *vt* to subject to tax.

fiscaliste [fiskalist(ə)] *nm/f* tax specialist.

fiscalité [fiskalite] *nf* tax system; (*charges*) taxation.

fissible [fisibl(ə)] *adj* fissile.

fission [fisjõ] *nf* fission.

fissure [fisyR] *nf* crack.

fissurer [fisyre] *vt, se ~ vi* to crack.

fiston [fistõ] *nm* (*fam*) son, lad.

fit [fi] *vb voir* **faire**.

FIV *sigle f* (= *fécondation in vitro*) IVF.

fixage [fiksaʒ] *nm* (*PHOTO*) fixing.

fixateur [fiksatœR] *nm* (*PHOTO*) fixer; (*pour cheveux*) hair cream.

fixatif [fiksatif] *nm* fixative.

fixation [fiksasjõ] *nf* fixing; fastening; setting; (*de ski*) binding; (*PSYCH*) fixation.

fixe [fiks(ə)] *adj* fixed; (*emploi*) steady, regular ♦ *nm* (*salaire*) basic salary; **à heure ~** at a set time; **menu à prix ~** set menu.

fixé, e [fikse] *adj* (*heure, jour*) appointed; **être ~ (sur)** to have made up one's mind (about); to know for certain (about).

fixement [fiksəmã] *adv* fixedly, steadily.

fixer [fikse] *vt* (*attacher*): **~ qch (à/sur)** to fix *ou* fasten sth (to/onto); (*déterminer*) to fix, set; (*CHIMIE, PHOTO*) to fix; (*poser son regard sur*) to look hard at, stare at; **se ~** (*s'établir*) to settle down; **~ son choix sur qch** to decide on sth; **se ~ sur** (*suj: attention*) to focus on.

fixité [fiksite] *nf* fixedness.

fjord [fjɔR(d)] *nm* fjord, fiord.

fl. *abr* (= *fleuve*) r, R; (= *florin*) fl.

flacon [flakõ] *nm* bottle.

flagada [flagada] *adj inv* (*fam: fatigué*) shattered.

flagellation [flaʒɛlasjõ] *nf* flogging.

flageller [flaʒele] *vt* to flog, scourge.

flageoler [flaʒɔle] *vi* to have knees like jelly.

flageolet [flaʒɔlɛ] *nm* (*MUS*) flageolet; (*CULIN*) dwarf kidney bean.

flagornerie [flagɔRnəRi] *nf* toadying, fawning.

flagorneur, euse [flagɔRnœR, -øz] *nm/f* toady, fawner.

flagrant, e [flagRã, -ãt] *adj* flagrant, blatant; **en ~ délit** in the act, in flagrante delicto.

flair [flɛR] *nm* sense of smell; (*fig*) intuition.

flairer [flere] *vt* (*humer*) to sniff (at); (*détecter*) to scent.

flamand, e [flamã, -ãd] *adj* Flemish ♦ *nm* (*LING*) Flemish ♦ *nm/f*: **F~, e** Fleming; **les F~s** the Flemish.

flamant [flamɑ̃] *nm* flamingo.

flambant [flɑ̃bɑ̃] *adv*: ~ **neuf** brand new.

flambé, e [flɑ̃be] *adj* (*CULIN*) flambé ♦ *nf* blaze; (*fig*) flaring-up, explosion.

flambeau, x [flɑ̃bo] *nm* (flaming) torch; **se passer le** ~ (*fig*) to hand down the (*ou* a) tradition.

flambée [flɑ̃be] *nf* (*feu*) blaze; (*COMM*): ~ **des prix** (sudden) shooting up of prices.

flamber [flɑ̃be] *vi* to blaze (up) ♦ *vt* (*poulet*) to singe; (*aiguille*) to sterilize.

flambeur, euse [flɑ̃bœr, -øz] *nm/f* big-time gambler.

flamboyant, e [flɑ̃bwajɑ̃, -ɑ̃t] *adj* blazing; flaming.

flamboyer [flɑ̃bwaje] *vi* to blaze (up); (*fig*) to flame.

flamenco [flamɛnko] *nm* flamenco.

flamingant, e [flamɛ̃gɑ̃, -ɑ̃t] *adj* Flemish-speaking ♦ *nm/f*: **F~, e** Flemish speaker; (*POL*) Flemish nationalist.

flamme [flam] *nf* flame; (*fig*) fire, fervour; **en ~s** on fire, ablaze.

flammèche [flamɛʃ] *nf* (flying) spark.

flammerole [flamrɔl] *nf* will-o'-the-wisp.

flan [flɑ̃] *nm* (*CULIN*) custard tart *ou* pie.

flanc [flɑ̃] *nm* side; (*MIL*) flank; **à** ~ **de colline** on the hillside; **prêter le** ~ **à** (*fig*) to lay o.s. open to.

flancher [flɑ̃ʃe] *vi* (*cesser de fonctionner*) to fail, pack up; (*armée*) to quit.

Flandre [flɑ̃dR(ə)] *nf*: **la** ~ (*aussi*: **les ~s**) Flanders.

flanelle [flanɛl] *nf* flannel.

flâner [flɑne] *vi* to stroll.

flânerie [flɑnRi] *nf* stroll.

flâneur, euse [flɑnœr, -øz] *adj* idle ♦ *nm/f* stroller.

flanquer [flɑ̃ke] *vt* to flank; (*fam: jeter*): ~ **par terre/à la porte** to fling to the ground/chuck out; (*: donner*): ~ **la frousse à qn** to put the wind up sb, give sb an awful fright.

flapi, e [flapi] *adj* dog-tired.

flaque [flak] *nf* (*d'eau*) puddle; (*d'huile, de sang etc*) pool.

flash, *pl* **flashes** [flaʃ] *nm* (*PHOTO*) flash; ~ (**d'information**) newsflash.

flasque [flask(ə)] *adj* flabby ♦ *nf* (*flacon*) flask.

flatter [flate] *vt* to flatter; (*caresser*) to stroke; **se** ~ **de qch** to pride o.s. on sth.

flatterie [flatRi] *nf* flattery.

flatteur, euse [flatœr, -øz] *adj* flattering ♦ *nm/f* flatterer.

flatulence [flatylɑ̃s], **flatuosité** [flatɥozite] *nf* (*MÉD*) flatulence, wind.

FLB *abr* (= *franco long du bord*) FAS ♦ *sigle m* (*POL*) = *Front de libération de la Bretagne*.

FLC *sigle m* = *Front de libération de la Corse*.

fléau, x [fleo] *nm* scourge, curse; (*de balance*) beam; (*pour le blé*) flail.

fléchage [fleʃaʒ] *nm* (*d'un itinéraire*) signposting.

flèche [flɛʃ] *nf* arrow; (*de clocher*) spire; (*de grue*) jib; (*trait d'esprit, critique*) shaft; **monter en** ~ (*fig*) to soar, rocket; **partir en** ~ (*fig*) to be off like a shot; **à** ~ **variable** (*avion*) swing-wing *cpd*.

flécher [fleʃe] *vt* to arrow, mark with arrows.

fléchette [fleʃɛt] *nf* dart; **~s** *nfpl* (*jeu*) darts *sg*.

fléchir [fleʃir] *vt* (*corps, genou*) to bend; (*fig*) to sway, weaken ♦ *vi* (*poutre*) to sag, bend; (*fig*) to weaken, flag; (*: baisser: prix*) to fall off.

fléchissement [fleʃismɑ̃] *nm* bending; sagging; flagging; (*de l'économie*) dullness.

flegmatique [flegmatik] *adj* phlegmatic.

flegme [flegm(ə)] *nm* composure.

flemmard, e [flemar, -ard(ə)] *nm/f* lazybones *sg*, loafer.

flemme [flɛm] *nf* (*fam*): **j'ai la** ~ **de faire** I can't be bothered to do.

flétan [fletɑ̃] *nm* (*ZOOL*) halibut.

flétrir [fletrir] *vt* to wither; (*stigmatiser*) to condemn (in the most severe terms); **se** ~ *vi* to wither.

fleur [flœr] *nf* flower; (*d'un arbre*) blossom; **être en** ~ (*arbre*) to be in blossom; **tissu à ~s** flowered *ou* flowery fabric; **la (fine)** ~ **de** (*fig*) the flower of; **être** ~ **bleue** to be soppy *ou* sentimental; **à** ~ **de terre** just above the ground; **faire une** ~ **à qn** to do sb a favour (*BRIT*) *ou* favor (*US*); ~ **de lis** fleur-de-lis.

fleurer [flœre] *vt*: ~ **la lavande** to have the scent of lavender.

fleuret [flœrɛ] *nm* (*arme*) foil; (*sport*) fencing.

fleurette [flœrɛt] *nf*: **conter** ~ **à qn** to whisper sweet nothings to sb.

fleuri, e [flœri] *adj* in flower *ou* bloom; surrounded by flowers; (*fig: style*) flowery; (*: teint*) glowing.

fleurir [flœrir] *vi* (*rose*) to flower; (*arbre*) to blossom; (*fig*) to flourish ♦ *vt* (*tombe*) to put flowers on; (*chambre*) to decorate with flowers.

fleuriste [flœrist(ə)] *nm/f* florist.

fleuron [flœrɔ̃] *nm* jewel (*fig*).

fleuve [flœv] *nm* river; **roman-~** saga; **discours-~** interminable speech.

flexibilité [flɛksibilite] *nf* flexibility.

flexible [flɛksibl(ə)] *adj* flexible.

flexion [flɛksjɔ̃] *nf* flexing, bending; (*LING*) inflection.

flibustier [flibystje] *nm* buccaneer.

flic [flik] *nm* (*fam: péj*) cop.

flingue [flɛ̃g] *nm* (*fam*) shooter.

flipper *nm* [flipœr] pinball (machine) ♦ *vi* [flipe] (*fam: être déprimé*) to feel down, be on a downer; (*: être exalté*) to freak out.

flirt [flœrt] *nm* flirting; (*personne*) boyfriend, girlfriend.

flirter [flœrte] *vi* to flirt.

FLN *sigle m* = *Front de libération nationale* (*during the Algerian war*).

FLNKS *sigle m* (= *Front de libération nationale kanak et socialiste*) *political movement in New*

Caledonia.

flocon [flɔkɔ̃] *nm* flake; (*de laine etc: boulette*) flock; **~s d'avoine** oatflakes, porridge oats.

floconneux, euse [flɔkɔnø, -øz] *adj* fluffy, fleecy.

flonflons [flɔ̃flɔ̃] *nmpl* blare *sg*.

flopée [flɔpe] *nf:* **une ~ de** loads of.

floraison [flɔʀɛzɔ̃] *nf* (*voir fleurir*) flowering; blossoming; flourishing.

floral, e, aux [flɔʀal, -o] *adj* floral, flower *cpd*.

floralies [flɔʀali] *nfpl* flower show *sg*.

flore [flɔʀ] *nf* flora.

Florence [flɔʀɑ̃s] *n* (*ville*) Florence.

florentin, e [flɔʀɑ̃tɛ̃, -in] *adj* Florentine.

floriculture [flɔʀikyltyʀ] *nf* flower-growing.

florissant, e [flɔʀisɑ̃, -ɑ̃t] *vb voir* **fleurir** ♦ *adj* flourishing; (*santé, teint, mine*) blooming.

flot [flo] *nm* flood, stream; (*marée*) flood tide; **~s** *nmpl* (*de la mer*) waves; **être à ~** (*NAVIG*) to be afloat; (*fig*) to be on an even keel; **à ~s** (*couler*) in torrents; **entrer à ~s** to stream *ou* pour in.

flottage [flɔtaʒ] *nm* (*du bois*) floating.

flottaison [flɔtɛzɔ̃] *nf:* **ligne de ~** waterline.

flottant, e [flɔtɑ̃, -ɑ̃t] *adj* (*vêtement*) loose(-fitting); (*cours, barème*) floating.

flotte [flɔt] *nf* (*NAVIG*) fleet; (*fam*) water; rain.

flottement [flɔtmɑ̃] *nm* (*fig*) wavering, hesitation; (*ÉCON*) floating.

flotter [flɔte] *vi* to float; (*nuage, odeur*) to drift; (*drapeau*) to fly; (*vêtements*) to hang loose ♦ *vb impers* (*fam: pleuvoir*): **il flotte** it's raining ♦ *vt* to float; **faire ~** to float.

flotteur [flɔtœʀ] *nm* float.

flottille [flɔtij] *nf* flotilla.

flou, e [flu] *adj* fuzzy, blurred; (*fig*) woolly (*BRIT*), vague; (*non ajusté: robe*) loose(-fitting).

flouer [flue] *vt* to swindle.

FLQ *abr* (= *franco long du quai*) FAQ.

fluctuant, e [flyktɥɑ̃, -ɑ̃t] *adj* (*prix, cours*) fluctuating; (*opinions*) changing.

fluctuation [flyktɥasjɔ̃] *nf* fluctuation.

fluctuer [flyktɥe] *vi* to fluctuate.

fluet, te [flyɛ, -ɛt] *adj* thin, slight; (*voix*) thin.

fluide [flɥid] *adj* fluid; (*circulation etc*) flowing freely ♦ *nm* fluid; (*force*) (mysterious) power.

fluidifier [flyidifje] *vt* to make fluid.

fluidité [flyidite] *nf* fluidity; free flow.

fluor [flyɔʀ] *nm* fluorine.

fluoré, e [flyɔʀe] *adj* fluoridated.

fluorescent, e [flyɔʀesɑ̃, -ɑ̃t] *adj* fluorescent.

flûte [flyt] *nf* (*aussi:* **~ traversière**) flute; (*verre*) flute glass; (*pain*) long loaf (*pl* loaves); **petite ~** piccolo (*pl* -s); **~!** drat it!; **~ (à bec)** recorder; **~ de Pan** panpipes *pl*.

flûtiste [flytist(ə)] *nm/f* flautist, flute player.

fluvial, e, aux [flyvjal, -o] *adj* river *cpd*, fluvial.

flux [fly] *nm* incoming tide; (*écoulement*) flow; **le ~ et le reflux** the ebb and flow.

fluxion [flyksjɔ̃] *nf:* **~ de poitrine** pneumonia.

FM *sigle f* (= *frequency modulation*) FM.

Fme *abr* (= *femme*) W.

FMI *sigle m* (= *Fonds monétaire international*) IMF.

FN *sigle m* (= *Front national*) ≈ NF (= *National Front*).

FNAC [fnak] *sigle f* (= *Fédération nationale des achats des cadres*) chain of discount shops (*hi-fi, photo etc*).

FNAH *sigle m* = *Fonds national d'amélioration de l'habitat*.

FNEF [fnɛf] *sigle f* (= *Fédération nationale des étudiants de France*) student union.

FNSEA *sigle f* (= *Fédération nationale des syndicats d'exploitants agricoles*) farmers' union.

FO *sigle f* (= *Force ouvrière*) trades union.

foc [fɔk] *nm* jib.

focal, e, aux [fɔkal, -o] *adj* focal ♦ *nf* focal length.

focaliser [fɔkalize] *vt* to focus.

foehn [føn] *nm* foehn, föhn.

fœtal, e, aux [fetal, -o] *adj* fetal, foetal (*BRIT*).

fœtus [fetys] *nm* fetus, foetus (*BRIT*).

foi [fwa] *nf* faith; **sous la ~ du serment** under *ou* on oath; **ajouter ~ à** to lend credence to; **faire ~** (*prouver*) to be evidence; **digne de ~** reliable; **sur la ~ de** on the word *ou* strength of; **être de bonne/mauvaise ~** to be in good faith/not to be in good faith; **ma ~!** well!

foie [fwa] *nm* liver; **~ gras** foie gras.

foin [fwɛ̃] *nm* hay; **faire les ~s** to make hay; **faire du ~** (*fam*) to kick up a row.

foire [fwaʀ] *nf* fair; (*fête foraine*) (fun) fair; (*fig: désordre, confusion*) bear garden; **faire la ~** to whoop it up; **~ (exposition)** trade fair.

fois [fwa] *nf* time; **une/deux ~** once/twice; **trois/vingt ~** three/twenty times; **2 ~ 2** 2 times 2; **deux/quatre ~ plus grand (que)** twice/four times as big (as); **une ~** (*passé*) once; (*futur*) sometime; **une (bonne) ~ pour toutes** once and for all; **encore une ~** again, once more; **il était une ~** once upon a time; **une ~ que c'est fait** once it's done; **une ~ parti** once he (*ou* I *etc*) had left; **des ~** (*parfois*) sometimes; **si des ~ ...** (*fam*) if ever ...; **non mais des ~!** (*fam*) (now) look here!; **à la ~ (ensemble)** (all) at once; **à la ~ grand et beau** both tall and handsome.

foison [fwazɔ̃] *nf:* **une ~ de** an abundance of; **à ~** *adv* in plenty.

foisonnant, e [fwazɔnɑ̃, -ɑ̃t] *adj* teeming.

foisonnement [fwazɔnmɑ̃] *nm* profusion, abundance.

foisonner [fwazɔne] *vi* to abound; **~ en** *ou* **de** to abound in.

fol [fɔl] *adj m voir* **fou**.

folâtre [fɔlɑtʀ(ə)] *adj* playful.

folâtrer [fɔlɑtʀe] *vi* to frolic (about).

folichon, ne [fɔliʃɔ̃, -ɔn] *adj:* **ça n'a rien de ~** it's not a lot of fun.

olie [fɔli] *nf* (*d'une décision, d'un acte*) madness, folly; (*état*) madness, insanity; (*acte*) folly; **la ~ des grandeurs** delusions of grandeur; **faire des ~s** (*en dépenses*) to be extravagant.

olklore [fɔlklɔR] *nm* folklore.

olklorique [fɔlklɔRik] *adj* folk *cpd*; (*fam*) weird.

olle [fɔl] *adj f, nf voir* **fou**.

ollement [fɔlmã] *adv* (*très*) madly, wildly.

ollet [fɔlɛ] *adj m*: **feu ~** will-o'-the-wisp.

omentateur, trice [fɔmãtatœR, -tRis] *nm/f* agitator.

omenter [fɔmãte] *vt* to stir up, foment.

oncé, e [fɔ̃se] *adj* dark; **bleu ~** dark blue.

oncer [fɔ̃se] *vt* to make darker; (*CULIN: moule etc*) to line ♦ *vi* to go darker; (*fam: aller vite*) to tear *ou* belt along; **~ sur** to charge at.

onceur, euse [fɔ̃sœR, -øz] *nm/f* whizz kid.

oncier, ière [fɔ̃sje, -jɛR] *adj* (*honnêteté etc*) basic, fundamental; (*malhonnêteté*) deep-rooted; (*COMM*) real estate *cpd*.

oncièrement [fɔ̃sjɛRmã] *adv* basically; (*absolument*) thoroughly.

onction [fɔ̃ksjɔ̃] *nf* (*rôle, MATH, LING*) function; (*emploi, poste*) post, position; **~s** (*professionnelles*) duties; **entrer en ~s** to take up one's post *ou* duties; to take up office; **voiture de ~** company car; **être ~ de** (*dépendre de*) to depend on; **en ~ de** (*par rapport à*) according to; **faire ~ de** to serve as; **la ~ publique** the state *ou* civil (*BRIT*) service.

onctionnaire [fɔ̃ksjɔnɛR] *nm/f* state employee *ou* official; (*dans l'administration*) ≈ civil servant (*BRIT*).

onctionnariser [fɔ̃ksjɔnaRize] *vt* (*ADMIN: personne*) to give the status of a state employee to.

onctionnel, le [fɔ̃ksjɔnɛl] *adj* functional.

onctionnellement [fɔ̃ksjɔnɛlmã] *adv* functionally.

onctionnement [fɔ̃ksjɔnmã] *nm* working; functioning; operation.

onctionner [fɔ̃ksjɔne] *vi* to work, function; (*entreprise*) to operate, function; **faire ~** to work, operate.

ond [fɔ̃] *nm voir aussi* **fonds**; (*d'un récipient, trou*) bottom; (*d'une salle, scène*) back; (*d'un tableau, décor*) background; (*opposé à la forme*) content; (*petite quantité*) **un ~ de verre** a drop; (*SPORT*): **le ~** long distance (running); **course/épreuve de ~** long-distance race/trial; **au ~** at the bottom of; at the back of; **aller au ~ des choses** to get to the root of things; **le ~ de sa pensée** his (*ou* her) true thoughts *ou* feelings; **sans ~** *adj* bottomless; **envoyer par le ~** (*NAVIG: couler*) to sink, scuttle; **à ~** *adv* (*connaître, soutenir*) thoroughly; (*appuyer, visser*) right down *ou* home; **à ~** (*de train*) *adv* (*fam*) full tilt; **dans le ~, au ~** *adv* (*en somme*) basically, really; **de ~ en comble** *adv* from top to bottom; **~**

sonore background noise; background music; **~ de teint** (*make-up*) foundation.

fondamental, e, aux [fɔ̃damãtal, -o] *adj* fundamental.

fondamentalement [fɔ̃damãtalmã] *adv* fundamentally.

fondamentalisme [fɔ̃damãtalism(ə)] *nm* fundamentalism.

fondamentaliste [fɔ̃damãtalist(ə)] *adj, nm/f* fundamentalist.

fondant, e [fɔ̃dã, -ãt] *adj* (*neige*) melting; (*poire*) that melts in the mouth; (*chocolat*) fondant.

fondateur, trice [fɔ̃datœR, -tRis] *nm/f* founder; **membre ~** founder (*BRIT*) *ou* founding (*US*) member.

fondation [fɔ̃dasjɔ̃] *nf* founding; (*établissement*) foundation; **~s** *nfpl* (*d'une maison*) foundations; **travail de ~** foundation works *pl*.

fondé, e [fɔ̃de] *adj* (*accusation etc*) well-founded ♦ *nm*: **~ de pouvoir** authorized representative; **mal ~** unfounded; **être ~ à croire** to have grounds for believing *ou* good reason to believe.

fondement [fɔ̃dmã] *nm* (*derrière*) behind; **~s** *nmpl* foundations; **sans ~** *adj* (*rumeur etc*) groundless, unfounded.

fonder [fɔ̃de] *vt* to found; (*fig*): **~ qch sur** to base sth on; **se ~ sur** (*suj: personne*) to base o.s. on; **~ un foyer** (*se marier*) to set up home.

fonderie [fɔ̃dRi] *nf* smelting works *sg*.

fondeur, euse [fɔ̃dœR, -øz] *nm/f* (*skieur*) long-distance skier ♦ *nm*: (*ouvrier*) **~** caster.

fondre [fɔ̃dR(ə)] *vt* to melt; (*dans l'eau: sucre, sel*) to dissolve; (*fig: mélanger*) to merge, blend ♦ *vi* to melt; (*fig*) to melt away; (*se précipiter*): **~ sur** to swoop down on; **se ~** *vi* (*se combiner, se confondre*) to merge into each other; to dissolve; **~ en larmes** to dissolve into tears.

fondrière [fɔ̃dRijeR] *nf* rut.

fonds [fɔ̃] *nm* (*de bibliothèque*) collection; (*COMM*): **(de commerce)** business; (*fig*): **~ de probité etc** fund of integrity *etc* ♦ *nmpl* (*argent*) funds; **à ~ perdus** *adv* with little or no hope of getting the money back; **être en ~** to be in funds; **mise de ~** investment, (*capital*) outlay; **F~ monétaire international (FMI)** International Monetary Fund (IMF); **~ de roulement** *nm* float.

fondu, e [fɔ̃dy] *adj* (*beurre, neige*) melted; (*métal*) molten ♦ *nm* (*CINÉ*): **~ (enchaîné)** dissolve ♦ *nf* (*CULIN*) fondue.

fongicide [fɔ̃ʒisid] *nm* fungicide.

font [fɔ̃] *vb voir* **faire**.

fontaine [fɔ̃tɛn] *nf* fountain; (*source*) spring.

fontanelle [fɔ̃tanɛl] *nf* fontanelle.

fonte [fɔ̃t] *nf* melting; (*métal*) cast iron; **la ~ des neiges** the (spring) thaw.

fonts baptismaux [fɔ̃batismo] *nmpl* (*baptis-*

mal) font *sg.*

foot(ball) [fut(bol)] *nm* football, soccer.

footballeur, euse [futbolœR, -øz] *nm/f* footballer (*BRIT*), football *ou* soccer player.

footing [futiŋ] *nm* jogging; **faire du** ~ to go jogging.

for [fɔR] *nm*: **dans** *ou* **en son** ~ **intérieur** in one's heart of hearts.

forage [fɔRaʒ] *nm* drilling, boring.

forain, e [fɔRɛ̃, -ɛn] *adj* fairground *cpd* ♦ *nm* (*marchand*) stallholder; (*acteur etc*) fairground entertainer.

forban [fɔRbɑ̃] *nm* (*pirate*) pirate; (*escroc*) crook.

forçat [fɔRsa] *nm* convict.

force [fɔRs(ə)] *nf* strength; (*puissance: surnaturelle etc*) power; (*PHYSIQUE, MÉCANIQUE*) force; ~**s** *nfpl* (*physiques*) strength *sg*; (*MIL*) forces; (*effectifs*): **d'importantes** ~**s de police** large contingents of police; **avoir de la** ~ to be strong; **être à bout de** ~ to have no strength left; **à la** ~ **du poignet** (*fig*) by the sweat of one's brow; **à** ~ **de faire** by dint of doing; **arriver en** ~ (*nombreux*) to arrive in force; **cas de** ~ **majeure** case of absolute necessity; (*ASSURANCES*) act of God; ~ **de la nature** natural force; **de** ~ *adv* forcibly, by force; **de toutes mes/ses** ~**s** with all my/his strength; **par la** ~ using force; **par la** ~ **des choses/d'habitude** by force of circumstances/habit; **à toute** ~ (*absolument*) at all costs; **faire** ~ **de rames/voiles** to ply the oars/cram on sail; **être de** ~ **à faire** to be up to doing; **de première** ~ first class; **la** ~ **armée** (*les troupes*) the army; ~ **d'âme** fortitude; ~ **de frappe** strike force; ~ **d'inertie** force of inertia; **la** ~ **publique** the authorities responsible for public order; ~**s d'intervention** (*MIL, POLICE*) peace-keeping force *sg*; **les** ~**s de l'ordre** the police.

forcé, e [fɔRse] *adj* forced; (*bain*) unintended; (*inévitable*): **c'est** ~**!** it's inevitable!, it HAS to be!

forcément [fɔRsemɑ̃] *adv* necessarily; inevitably; (*bien sûr*) of course.

forcené, e [fɔRsəne] *adj* frenzied ♦ *nm/f* maniac.

forceps [fɔRsɛps] *nm* forceps *pl*.

forcer [fɔRse] *vt* (*contraindre*): ~ **qn à faire** to force sb to do; (*porte, serrure, plante*) to force; (*moteur, voix*) to strain ♦ *vi* (*SPORT*) to overtax o.s.; **se** ~ **à faire qch** to force o.s. to do sth; ~ **la dose/l'allure** to overdo it/ increase the pace; ~ **l'attention/le respect** to command attention/respect; ~ **la consigne** to bypass orders.

forcing [fɔRsiŋ] *nm* (*SPORT*): **faire le** ~ to pile on the pressure.

forcir [fɔRsiR] *vi* (*grossir*) to broaden out; (*vent*) to freshen.

forclore [fɔRklɔR] *vt* (*JUR: personne*) to debar.

forclusion [fɔRklyzjɔ̃] *nf* (*JUR*) debarment.

forer [fɔRe] *vt* to drill, bore.

forestier, ière [fɔRɛstje, -jɛR] *adj* forest *cpd*.

foret [fɔRɛ] *nm* drill.

forêt [fɔRɛ] *nf* forest; **Office National des F**~**s** (*ADMIN*) ≈ Forestry Commission (*BRIT*), ≈ National Forest Service (*US*); **la F**~ **Noire** the Black Forest.

foreuse [fɔRøz] *nf* (electric) drill.

forfait [fɔRfɛ] *nm* (*COMM*) fixed *ou* set price; all-in deal *ou* price; (*crime*) infamy; **déclarer** ~ to withdraw; **gagner par** ~ to win by a walkover; **travailler à** ~ to work for a lump sum.

forfaitaire [fɔRfɛtɛR] *adj* set; inclusive.

forfait-vacances, *pl* **forfaits-vacances** [fɔRfɛvakɑ̃s] *nm* package holiday.

forfanterie [fɔRfɑ̃tRi] *nf* boastfulness *no pl.*

forge [fɔRʒ(ə)] *nf* forge, smithy.

forgé, e [fɔRʒe] *adj*: ~ **de toutes pièces** (*histoire*) completely fabricated.

forger [fɔRʒe] *vt* to forge; (*fig: personnalité*) to form; (*: prétexte*) to contrive, make up.

forgeron [fɔRʒəRɔ̃] *nm* (black)smith.

formaliser [fɔRmalize]: **se** ~ *vi*: **se** ~ **(de)** to take offence (at).

formalisme [fɔRmalism(ə)] *nm* formality.

formalité [fɔRmalite] *nf* formality.

format [fɔRma] *nm* size; **petit** ~ small size; (*PHOTO*) 35 mm (film).

formater [fɔRmate] *vt* (*disque*) to format; **non formaté** unformatted.

formateur, trice [fɔRmatœR, -tRis] *adj* formative.

formation [fɔRmasjɔ̃] *nf* forming; (*éducation*) training; (*MUS*) group; (*MIL, AVIAT, GÉO*) formation; **la** ~ **permanente** *ou* **continue** continuing education; **la** ~ **professionnelle** vocational training.

forme [fɔRm(ə)] *nf* (*gén*) form; (*d'un objet*) shape, form; ~**s** *nfpl* (*bonnes manières*) proprieties; (*d'une femme*) figure *sg*; **en** ~ **de poire** pear-shaped, in the shape of a pear; **sous** ~ **de** in the form of; in the guise of; **sous** ~ **de cachets** in the form of tablets; **être en (bonne** *ou* **pleine)** ~, **avoir la** ~ (*SPORT etc*) to be on form; **en bonne et due** ~ in due form; **pour la** ~ for the sake of form; **sans autre** ~ **de procès** (*fig*) without further ado; **prendre** ~ to take shape.

formel, le [fɔRmɛl] *adj* (*preuve, décision*) definite, positive; (*logique*) formal.

formellement [fɔRmɛlmɑ̃] *adv* (*interdit*) strictly.

former [fɔRme] *vt* (*gén*) to form; (*éduquer: soldat, ingénieur etc*) to train; **se** ~ to form; to train.

formidable [fɔRmidabl(ə)] *adj* tremendous.

formidablement [fɔRmidabləmɑ̃] *adv* tremendously.

formol [fɔRmɔl] *nm* formalin, formol.

formosan, e [fɔRmɔzɑ̃, -an] *adj* Formosan.

Formose [fɔRmoz] *nm* Formosa.

ormulaire [fɔʀmylɛʀ] *nm* form.

ormulation [fɔʀmylɑsjɔ̃] *nf* (*voir vb*) formulation; expression.

ormule [fɔʀmyl] *nf* (*gén*) formula; (*formulaire*) form; **selon la ~ consacrée** as one says; **~ de politesse** polite phrase; (*en fin de lettre*) letter ending.

ormuler [fɔʀmyle] *vt* (*émettre: réponse, vœux*) to formulate; (*expliciter: sa pensée*) to express.

orniquer [fɔʀnike] *vi* to fornicate.

ORPRONU [fɔʀpʀɔny] *sigle f* (= Force de protection des Nations unies) UNPROFOR.

ort, e [fɔʀ, fɔʀt(ə)] *adj* strong; (*intensité, rendement*) high, great; (*corpulent*) large; (*doué*): **être ~ (en)** to be good (at) ♦ *adv* (*serrer, frapper*) hard; (*sonner*) loud(ly); (*beaucoup*) greatly, very much; (*très*) very ♦ *nm* (*édifice*) fort; (*point fort*) strong point, forte; (*gén pl: personne, pays*): **le ~, les ~s** the strong; **c'est un peu ~!** it's a bit much!; **à plus ~e raison** even more so, all the more reason; **avoir ~ à faire avec qn** to have a hard job with sb; **se faire ~ de faire** to claim one can do; **~ bien/peu** very well/few; **au plus ~ de** (*au milieu de*) in the thick of, at the height of; **~e tête** rebel.

ortement [fɔʀtəmɑ̃] *adv* strongly; (*s'intéresser*) deeply.

orteresse [fɔʀtəʀɛs] *nf* fortress.

ortifiant [fɔʀtifjɑ̃] *nm* tonic.

ortifications [fɔʀtifikɑsjɔ̃] *nfpl* fortifications.

ortifier [fɔʀtifje] *vt* to strengthen, fortify; (*MIL*) to fortify; **se ~** *vi* (*personne, santé*) to grow stronger.

ortin [fɔʀtɛ̃] *nm* (small) fort.

ortiori [fɔʀtjɔʀi]: **à ~** *adv* all the more so.

ORTRAN [fɔʀtʀɑ̃] *nm* FORTRAN.

ortuit, e [fɔʀtɥi, -it] *adj* fortuitous, chance *cpd*.

ortuitement [fɔʀtɥitmɑ̃] *adv* fortuitously.

ortune [fɔʀtyn] *nf* fortune; **faire ~** to make one's fortune; **de ~** *adj* makeshift; (*compagnon*) chance *cpd*.

ortuné, e [fɔʀtyne] *adj* wealthy, well-off.

orum [fɔʀɔm] *nm* forum.

osse [fos] *nf* (*grand trou*) pit; (*tombe*) grave; **la ~ aux lions/ours** the lions' den/bear pit; **~ commune** common *ou* communal grave; **~ (d'orchestre)** (*orchestra*) pit; **~ à purin** cesspit; **~ septique** septic tank; **~s nasales** nasal fossae.

ossé [fose] *nm* ditch; (*fig*) gulf, gap.

ossette [fosɛt] *nf* dimple.

ossile [fosil] *nm* fossil ♦ *adj* fossilized, fossil *cpd*.

ossilisé, e [fosilize] *adj* fossilized.

ossoyeur [foswajœʀ] *nm* gravedigger.

ou (fol), folle [fu, fɔl] *adj* mad, crazy; (*déréglé etc*) wild, erratic; (*mèche*) stray; (*herbe*) wild; (*fam: extrême, très grand*) terrific, tremendous ♦ *nm/f* madman/woman ♦ *nm* (*du roi*) jester, fool; (*ÉCHECS*) bishop; **~ à lier, ~ furieux (folle furieuse)** raving mad; **être ~ de** to be mad *ou* crazy about; (*chagrin, joie, colère*) to be wild with; **faire le ~** to play *ou* act the fool; **avoir le ~ rire** to have the giggles.

foucade [fukad] *nf* caprice.

foudre [fudʀ(ə)] *nf* lightning; **~s** *nfpl* (*fig: colère*) wrath *sg*.

foudroyant, e [fudʀwajɑ̃, -ɑ̃t] *adj* devastating; (*maladie, poison*) violent.

foudroyer [fudʀwaje] *vt* to strike down; **~ qn du regard** to look daggers at sb; **il a été foudroyé** he was struck by lightning.

fouet [fwɛ] *nm* whip; (*CULIN*) whisk; **de plein ~** *adv* head on.

fouettement [fwɛtmɑ̃] *nm* lashing *no pl*.

fouetter [fwete] *vt* to whip; to whisk.

fougasse [fugas] *nf* type of flat pastry.

fougère [fuʒɛʀ] *nf* fern.

fougue [fug] *nf* ardour (*BRIT*), ardor (*US*), spirit.

fougueusement [fugøzmɑ̃] *adv* ardently.

fougueux, euse [fugø, -øz] *adj* fiery, ardent.

fouille [fuj] *nf* search; **~s** *nfpl* (*archéologiques*) excavations; **passer à la ~** to be searched.

fouillé, e [fuje] *adj* detailed.

fouiller [fuje] *vt* to search; (*creuser*) to dig; (*: suj: archéologue*) to excavate; (*approfondir: étude etc*) to go into ♦ *vi* (*archéologue*) to excavate; **~ dans/parmi** to rummage in/among.

fouillis [fuji] *nm* jumble, muddle.

fouine [fwin] *nf* stone marten.

fouiner [fwine] *vi* (*péj*): **~ dans** to nose around *ou* about in.

fouineur, euse [fwinœʀ, -øz] *adj* nosey ♦ *nm/f* nosey parker, snooper.

fouir [fwiʀ] *vt* to dig.

fouisseur, euse [fwisœʀ, -øz] *adj* burrowing.

foulage [fulaʒ] *nm* pressing.

foulante [fulɑ̃t] *adj f*: **pompe ~** force pump.

foulard [fulaʀ] *nm* scarf (*pl* scarves).

foule [ful] *nf* crowd; **une ~ de** masses of; **venir en ~** to come in droves.

foulée [fule] *nf* stride; **dans la ~ de** on the heels of.

fouler [fule] *vt* to press; (*sol*) to tread upon; **se ~** *vi* (*fam*) to overexert o.s.; **se ~ la cheville** to sprain one's ankle; **~ aux pieds** to trample underfoot.

foulure [fulyʀ] *nf* sprain.

four [fuʀ] *nm* oven; (*de potier*) kiln; (*THÉÂT: échec*) flop; **allant au ~** ovenproof.

fourbe [fuʀb(ə)] *adj* deceitful.

fourberie [fuʀbəʀi] *nf* deceit.

fourbi [fuʀbi] *nm* (*fam*) gear, junk.

fourbir [fuʀbiʀ] *vt*: **~ ses armes** (*fig*) to get ready for the fray.

fourbu, e [fuʀby] *adj* exhausted.

fourche [fuʀʃ(ə)] *nf* pitchfork; (*de bicyclette*) fork.

fourcher [fuʀʃe] *vi*: **ma langue a fourché** it

was a slip of the tongue.

fourchette [fuʀʃɛt] *nf* fork; (*STATISTIQUE*) bracket, margin.

fourchu, e [fuʀʃy] *adj* split; (*arbre etc*) forked.

fourgon [fuʀgɔ̃] *nm* van; (*RAIL*) wag(g)on; ~ **mortuaire** hearse.

fourgonnette [fuʀgɔnɛt] *nf* (delivery) van.

fourmi [fuʀmi] *nf* ant; **avoir des** ~**s** (*fig*) to have pins and needles.

fourmilière [fuʀmiljɛʀ] *nf* ant-hill; (*fig*) hive of activity.

fourmillement [fuʀmijmɑ̃] *nm* (*démangeaison*) pins and needles *pl*; (*grouillement*) swarming *no pl*.

fourmiller [fuʀmije] *vi* to swarm; ~ **de** to be teeming with, be swarming with.

fournaise [fuʀnɛz] *nf* blaze; (*fig*) furnace, oven.

fourneau, x [fuʀno] *nm* stove.

fournée [fuʀne] *nf* batch.

fourni, e [fuʀni] *adj* (*barbe, cheveux*) thick; (*magasin*): **bien** ~ (**en**) well stocked (with).

fournil [fuʀni] *nm* bakehouse.

fournir [fuʀniʀ] *vt* to supply; (*preuve, exemple*) to provide, supply; (*effort*) to put in; ~ **qch à qn** to supply sth to sb, supply *ou* provide sb with sth; ~ **qn en** (*COMM*) to supply sb with; **se** ~ **chez** to shop at.

fournisseur, euse [fuʀnisœʀ, -øz] *nm/f* supplier.

fourniture [fuʀnityʀ] *nf* supply(ing); ~**s** *nfpl* supplies; ~**s de bureau** office supplies, stationery; ~**s scolaires** school stationery.

fourrage [fuʀaʒ] *nm* fodder.

fourrager [fuʀaʒe] *vi*: ~ **dans/parmi** to rummage through/among.

fourrager, ère [fuʀaʒe, -ɛʀ] *adj* fodder *cpd* ♦ *nf* (*MIL*) fourragère.

fourré, e [fuʀe] *adj* (*bonbon, chocolat*) filled; (*manteau, botte*) fur-lined ♦ *nm* thicket.

fourreau, x [fuʀo] *nm* sheath; (*de parapluie*) cover; **robe/jupe** ~ figure-hugging dress/skirt.

fourrer [fuʀe] *vt* (*fam*): ~ **qch dans** to stick *ou* shove sth into; **se** ~ **dans/sous** to get into/under; **se** ~ **dans** (*une mauvaise situation*) to land o.s. in.

fourre-tout [fuʀtu] *nm inv* (*sac*) holdall; (*péj*) junk room (*ou* cupboard); (*fig*) rag-bag.

fourreur [fuʀœʀ] *nm* furrier.

fourrière [fuʀjɛʀ] *nf* pound.

fourrure [fuʀyʀ] *nf* fur; (*sur l'animal*) coat; **manteau/col de** ~ fur coat/collar.

fourvoyer [fuʀvwaje]: **se** ~ *vi* to go astray, stray; **se** ~ **dans** to stray into.

foutre [futʀ(ə)] *vt* (*fam!*) = **ficher** (*fam*).

foutu, e [futy] *adj* (*fam!*) = **fichu**.

foyer [fwaje] *nm* (*de cheminée*) hearth; (*fig*) seat, centre; (*famille*) family; (*domicile*) home; (*local de réunion*) (social) club; (*résidence*) hostel; (*salon*) foyer; (*OPTIQUE, PHOTO*) focus; **lunettes à double** ~ bi-focal glasses.

FP *sigle f* (= *franchise postale*) exemption from postage.

FPA *sigle f* (= *Formation professionnelle pour adultes*) adult education.

FPLP *sigle m* (= *Front populaire de la libération de la Palestine*) PFLP (= *Popular Front for the Liberation of Palestine*).

FR3 [ɛfɛʀtʀwa] *sigle f* (= *France Régions 3*) TV channel.

fracas [fʀaka] *nm* din; crash.

fracassant, e [fʀakasɑ̃, -ɑ̃t] *adj* sensational, staggering.

fracasser [fʀakase] *vt* to smash; **se** ~ **contre** *ou* **sur** to crash against.

fraction [fʀaksjɔ̃] *nf* fraction.

fractionnement [fʀaksjɔnmɑ̃] *nm* division.

fractionner [fʀaksjɔne] *vt* to divide (up), split (up).

fracture [fʀaktyʀ] *nf* fracture; ~ **du crâne** fractured skull; ~ **de la jambe** broken leg.

fracturer [fʀaktyʀe] *vt* (*coffre, serrure*) to break open; (*os, membre*) to fracture.

fragile [fʀaʒil] *adj* fragile, delicate; (*fig*) frail.

fragiliser [fʀaʒilize] *vt* to weaken, make fragile.

fragilité [fʀaʒilite] *nf* fragility.

fragment [fʀagmɑ̃] *nm* (*d'un objet*) fragment, piece; (*d'un texte*) passage, extract.

fragmentaire [fʀagmɑ̃tɛʀ] *adj* sketchy.

fragmenter [fʀagmɑ̃te] *vt* to split up.

frai [fʀɛ] *nm* spawn; (*ponte*) spawning.

fraîche [fʀɛʃ] *adj f voir* **frais**.

fraîchement [fʀɛʃmɑ̃] *adv* (*sans enthousiasme*) coolly; (*récemment*) freshly, newly.

fraîcheur [fʀɛʃœʀ] *nf* (*voir frais*) coolness; freshness.

fraîchir [fʀɛʃiʀ] *vi* to get cooler; (*vent*) to freshen.

frais, fraîche [fʀɛ, fʀɛʃ] *adj* (*air, eau, accueil*) cool; (*petit pois, œufs, nouvelles, couleur troupes*) fresh; **le voilà** ~! he's in a (right) mess! ♦ *adv* (*récemment*) newly, fresh(ly); **il fait** ~ it's cool; **servir** ~ chill before serving, serve chilled ♦ *nm*: **mettre au** ~ to put in a cool place; **prendre le** ~ to take a breath of cool air ♦ *nmpl* (*débours*) expenses; (*COMM*) costs; charges; **faire des** ~ to spend; to go to a lot of expense; **faire les** ~ **de** to bear the brunt of; **faire les** ~ **de la conversation** (*parler*) to do most of the talking; (*en être le sujet*) to be the topic of conversation; **il en a été pour ses** ~ he could have spared himself the trouble; **rentrer dans ses** ~ to recover one's expenses; ~ **de déplacement** travel(ling) expenses; ~ **d'entretien** upkeep; ~ **généraux** overheads; ~ **de scolarité** school fees, tuition (*US*).

fraise [fʀɛz] *nf* strawberry; (*TECH*) countersink (bit); (*de dentiste*) drill; ~ **des bois** wild strawberry.

fraiser [fʀeze] *vt* to countersink; (*CULIN: pâte*)

to knead.

fraiseuse [fʀɛzøz] *nf* (*TECH*) milling machine.

fraisier [fʀɛzje] *nm* strawberry plant.

framboise [fʀɑ̃bwaz] *nf* raspberry.

framboisier [fʀɑ̃bwazje] *nm* raspberry bush.

franc, franche [fʀɑ̃, fʀɑ̃ʃ] *adj* (*personne*) frank, straightforward; (*visage*) open; (*net: refus, couleur*) clear; (*: coupure*) clean; (*intensif*) downright; (*exempt*): ~ **de port** post free, postage paid; (*zone, port*) free; (*boutique*) duty-free ♦ *adv*: **parler** ~ to be frank *ou* candid ♦ *nm* franc.

français, e [fʀɑ̃sɛ, -ɛz] *adj* French ♦ *nm* (*LING*) French ♦ *nm/f*: **F~, e** Frenchman/woman; **les F~** the French.

franc-comtois, e, *mpl* **francs-comtois** [fʀɑ̃kɔ̃twa, -waz] *adj* of *ou* from (the) Franche-Comté.

France [fʀɑ̃s] *nf*: **la** ~ France; **en** ~ in France.

Francfort [fʀɑ̃kfɔʀ] *n* Frankfurt.

franche [fʀɑ̃ʃ] *adj f voir* **franc**.

Franche-Comté [fʀɑ̃ʃkɔ̃te] *nf* Franche-Comté.

franchement [fʀɑ̃ʃmɑ̃] *adv* (*voir franc*) frankly; clearly; (*tout à fait*) downright ♦ *excl* well, really!

franchir [fʀɑ̃ʃiʀ] *vt* (*obstacle*) to clear, get over; (*seuil, ligne, rivière*) to cross; (*distance*) to cover.

franchisage [fʀɑ̃ʃizaʒ] *nm* (*COMM*) franchising.

franchise [fʀɑ̃ʃiz] *nf* frankness; (*douanière, d'impôt*) exemption; (*ASSURANCES*) excess; (*COMM*) franchise; ~ **de bagages** baggage allowance.

franchissable [fʀɑ̃ʃisabl(ə)] *adj* (*obstacle*) surmountable.

francilien, ne [fʀɑ̃siljɛ̃, -ɛn] *adj* of *ou* from the Île-de-France region ♦ *nm/f*: **F~, ne** person from the Île-de-France region.

franciscain, e [fʀɑ̃siskɛ̃, -ɛn] *adj* Franciscan.

franciser [fʀɑ̃size] *vt* to gallicize, Frenchify.

franc-jeu [fʀɑ̃ʒø] *nm*: **jouer** ~ to play fair.

franc-maçon, *pl* **francs-maçons** [fʀɑ̃masɔ̃] *nm* Freemason.

franc-maçonnerie [fʀɑ̃masɔnʀi] *nf* Freemasonry.

franco [fʀɑ̃ko] *adv* (*COMM*): ~ **(de port)** postage paid.

franco... [fʀɑ̃ko] *préfixe* franco-.

franco-canadien [fʀɑ̃kɔkanadjɛ̃] *nm* (*LING*) Canadian French.

francophile [fʀɑ̃kɔfil] *adj* Francophile.

francophobe [fʀɑ̃kɔfɔb] *adj* Francophobe.

francophone [fʀɑ̃kɔfɔn] *adj* French-speaking ♦ *nm/f* French speaker.

francophonie [fʀɑ̃kɔfɔni] *nf* French-speaking communities *pl*.

franco-québécois [fʀɑ̃kɔkebekwa] *nm* (*LING*) Quebec French.

franc-parler [fʀɑ̃paʀle] *nm inv* outspokenness.

franc-tireur [fʀɑ̃tiʀœʀ] *nm* (*MIL*) irregular; (*fig*) freelance.

frange [fʀɑ̃ʒ] *nf* fringe; (*cheveux*) fringe (*BRIT*), bangs (*US*).

frangé, e [fʀɑ̃ʒe] *adj* (*tapis, nappe*): ~ **de** trimmed with.

frangin [fʀɑ̃ʒɛ̃] *nm* (*fam*) brother.

frangine [fʀɑ̃ʒin] *nf* (*fam*) sis, sister.

frangipane [fʀɑ̃ʒipan] *nf* almond paste.

franglais [fʀɑ̃glɛ] *nm* Franglais.

franquette [fʀɑ̃kɛt]: **à la bonne** ~ *adv* without any fuss.

frappant, e [fʀapɑ̃, -ɑ̃t] *adj* striking.

frappe [fʀap] *nf* (*d'une dactylo, pianiste, machine à écrire*) touch; (*BOXE*) punch; (*péj*) hood, thug.

frappé, e [fʀape] *adj* (*CULIN*) iced; ~ **de panique** panic-stricken; ~ **de stupeur** thunderstruck, dumbfounded.

frapper [fʀape] *vt* to hit, strike; (*étonner*) to strike; (*monnaie*) to strike, stamp; **se** ~ *vi* (*s'inquiéter*) to get worked up; ~ **à la porte** to knock at the door; ~ **dans ses mains** to clap one's hands; ~ **du poing sur** to bang one's fist on; ~ **un grand coup** (*fig*) to strike a blow.

frasques [fʀask(ə)] *nfpl* escapades; **faire des** ~**s** to get up to mischief.

fraternel, le [fʀatɛʀnɛl] *adj* brotherly, fraternal.

fraternellement [fʀatɛʀnɛlmɑ̃] *adv* in a brotherly way.

fraterniser [fʀatɛʀnize] *vi* to fraternize.

fraternité [fʀatɛʀnite] *nf* brotherhood.

fratricide [fʀatʀisid] *adj* fratricidal.

fraude [fʀod] *nf* fraud; (*SCOL*) cheating; **passer qch en** ~ to smuggle sth in (*ou* out); ~ **fiscale** tax evasion.

frauder [fʀode] *vi, vt* to cheat; ~ **le fisc** to evade paying tax(es).

fraudeur, euse [fʀodœʀ, -øz] *nm/f* person guilty of fraud; (*candidat*) candidate who cheats; (*au fisc*) tax evader.

frauduleux, euse [fʀodylø, -øz] *adj* fraudulent.

frauduleusement [fʀodyløzmɑ̃] *adv* fraudulently.

frayer [fʀeje] *vt* to open up, clear ♦ *vi* to spawn; (*fréquenter*): ~ **avec** to mix *ou* associate with; **se** ~ **un passage dans** to clear o.s. a path through, force one's way through.

frayeur [fʀejœʀ] *nf* fright.

fredaines [fʀədɛn] *nfpl* mischief *sg*, escapades.

fredonner [fʀədɔne] *vt* to hum.

freezer [fʀizœʀ] *nm* freezing compartment.

frégate [fʀegat] *nf* frigate.

frein [fʀɛ̃] *nm* brake; **mettre un** ~ **à** (*fig*) to put a brake on, check; **sans** ~ (*sans limites*) unchecked; ~ **à main** handbrake; ~ **moteur** engine braking; ~**s à disques** disc brakes; ~**s à tambour** drum brakes.

freinage [fʀenaʒ] *nm* braking; **distance de** ~ braking distance; **traces de** ~ tyre (*BRIT*) *ou* tire (*US*) marks.

freiner [fʀene] *vi* to brake ♦ *vt* (*progrès etc*) to check.

frelaté, e [fʀəlate] *adj* adulterated; (*fig*) tainted.

frêle [fʀɛl] *adj* frail, fragile.

frelon [fʀəlɔ̃] *nm* hornet.

freluquet [fʀəlykɛ] *nm* (*péj*) whippersnapper.

frémir [fʀemiʀ] *vi* (*de froid, de peur*) to tremble, shiver; (*de joie*) to quiver; (*eau*) to (begin to) bubble.

frémissement [fʀemismɑ̃] *nm* shiver; quiver; bubbling *no pl*.

frêne [fʀɛn] *nm* ash (tree).

frénésie [fʀenezi] *nf* frenzy.

frénétique [fʀenetik] *adj* frenzied, frenetic.

frénétiquement [fʀenetikmɑ̃] *adv* frenetically.

fréon [fʀeɔ̃] *nm* ® Freon ®.

fréquemment [fʀekamɑ̃] *adv* frequently.

fréquence [fʀekɑ̃s] *nf* frequency.

fréquent, e [fʀekɑ̃, -ɑ̃t] *adj* frequent.

fréquentable [fʀekɑ̃tabl(ə)] *adj*: **il est peu ~** he's not the type one can associate oneself with.

fréquentation [fʀekɑ̃tasjɔ̃] *nf* frequenting; seeing; **~s** *nfpl* company *sg*.

fréquenté, e [fʀekɑ̃te] *adj*: **très ~** (very) busy; **mal ~** patronized by disreputable elements.

fréquenter [fʀekɑ̃te] *vt* (*lieu*) to frequent; (*personne*) to see; **se ~** to see a lot of each other.

frère [fʀɛʀ] *nm* brother ♦ *adj*: **partis/pays ~s** sister parties/countries.

fresque [fʀɛsk(ə)] *nf* (*ART*) fresco.

fret [fʀɛ] *nm* freight.

fréter [fʀete] *vt* to charter.

frétiller [fʀetije] *vi* to wriggle; to quiver; **~ de la queue** to wag its tail.

fretin [fʀətɛ̃] *nm*: **le menu ~** the small fry.

freudien, ne [fʀødjɛ̃, -ɛn] *adj* Freudian.

freux [fʀø] *nm* (*ZOOL*) rook.

friable [fʀijabl(ə)] *adj* crumbly.

friand, e [fʀijɑ̃, -ɑ̃d] *adj*: **~ de** very fond of ♦ *nm* (*CULIN*) small minced-meat (*BRIT*) *ou* ground-meat (*US*) pie; (*: sucré*) small almond cake.

friandise [fʀijɑ̃diz] *nf* sweet.

fric [fʀik] *nm* (*fam*) cash, bread.

fricassée [fʀikase] *nf* fricassee.

fric-frac [fʀikfʀak] *nm* break-in.

friche [fʀiʃ] *nm*: **en ~** *adj, adv* (lying) fallow.

friction [fʀiksjɔ̃] *nf* (*massage*) rub, rub-down; (*chez le coiffeur*) scalp massage; (*TECH, fig*) friction.

frictionner [fʀiksjɔne] *vt* to rub (down); to massage.

frigidaire [fʀiʒidɛʀ] *nm* ® refrigerator.

frigide [fʀiʒid] *adj* frigid.

frigidité [fʀiʒidite] *nf* frigidity.

frigo [fʀigo] *nm* (= *frigidaire*) fridge.

frigorifier [fʀigɔʀifje] *vt* to refrigerate; (*fig: personne*) to freeze.

frigorifique [fʀigɔʀifik] *adj* refrigerating.

frileusement [fʀiløzmɑ̃] *adv* with a shiver.

frileux, euse [fʀilø, -øz] *adj* sensitive to (the) cold; (*fig*) overcautious.

frimas [fʀima] *nmpl* wintry weather *sg*.

frime [fʀim] *nf* (*fam*): **c'est de la ~** it's all put on; **pour la ~** just for show.

frimer [fʀime] *vi* to put on an act.

frimeur, euse [fʀimœʀ, -øz] *nm/f* poser.

frimousse [fʀimus] *nf* (sweet) little face.

fringale [fʀɛ̃gal] *nf*: **avoir la ~** to be ravenous.

fringant, e [fʀɛ̃gɑ̃, -ɑ̃t] *adj* dashing.

fringues [fʀɛ̃g] *nfpl* (*fam*) clothes, gear *no pl*.

fripé, e [fʀipe] *adj* crumpled.

friperie [fʀipʀi] *nf* (*commerce*) secondhand clothes shop; (*vêtements*) secondhand clothes.

fripes [fʀip] *nfpl* secondhand clothes.

fripier, ière [fʀipje, -jɛʀ] *nm/f* secondhand clothes dealer.

fripon, ne [fʀipɔ̃, -ɔn] *adj* roguish, mischievous ♦ *nm/f* rascal, rogue.

fripouille [fʀipuj] *nf* scoundrel.

frire [fʀiʀ] *vt* (*aussi*: **faire ~**), *vi* to fry.

Frisbee [fʀizbi] *nm* ® Frisbee ®.

frise [fʀiz] *nf* frieze.

frisé, e [fʀize] *adj* curly, curly-haired ♦ *nf*: (**chicorée**) **~e** curly endive.

friser [fʀize] *vt* to curl; (*fig: surface*) to skim, graze; (*: mort*) to come within a hair's breadth of; (*: hérésie*) to verge on ♦ *vi* (*cheveux*) to curl; (*personne*) to have curly hair; **se faire ~** to have one's hair curled.

frisette [fʀizɛt] *nf* little curl.

frisotter [fʀizɔte] *vi* (*cheveux*) to curl tightly.

frisquet [fʀiskɛ] *adj m* chilly.

frisson [fʀisɔ̃], **frissonnement** [fʀisɔnmɑ̃] *nm* shudder, shiver; quiver.

frissonner [fʀisɔne] *vi* (*personne*) to shudder, shiver; (*feuilles*) to quiver.

frit, e [fʀi, fʀit] *pp de* **frire** ♦ *adj* fried ♦ *nf*: (**pommes**) **~es** chips (*BRIT*), French fries.

friterie [fʀitʀi] *nf* ≈ chip shop (*BRIT*), ≈ hamburger stand (*US*).

friteuse [fʀitøz] *nf* chip pan (*BRIT*), deep (fat) fryer.

friture [fʀityʀ] *nf* (*huile*) (deep) fat; (*plat*): **~ (de poissons)** fried fish; (*RADIO*) crackle, crackling *no pl*; **~s** *nfpl* (*aliments frits*) fried food *sg*.

frivole [fʀivɔl] *adj* frivolous.

frivolité [fʀivɔlite] *nf* frivolity.

froc [fʀɔk] *nm* (*REL*) habit; (*fam: pantalon*) trousers *pl*, pants *pl*.

froid, e [fʀwa, fʀwad] *adj* cold ♦ *nm* cold; (*absence de sympathie*) coolness *no pl*; **il fait ~** it's cold; **avoir ~** to be cold; **prendre ~** to catch a chill *ou* cold; **à ~** *adv* (*démarrer*) (from) cold; (**pendant**) **les grands ~s** (in) the depths of winter, (during) the cold season; **jeter un ~** (*fig*) to cast a chill; **être en ~ avec** to be on bad terms with; **battre ~ à qn** to give sb the cold shoulder.

froidement [fʀwadmɑ̃] adv (accueillir) coldly; (décider) coolly.

froideur [fʀwadœʀ] nf coolness no pl.

froisser [fʀwase] vt to crumple (up), crease; (fig) to hurt, offend; **se ~** vi to crumple, crease; to take offence (BRIT) ou offense (US); **se ~ un muscle** to strain a muscle.

frôlement [fʀolmɑ̃] nm (contact) light touch.

frôler [fʀole] vt to brush against; (suj: projectile) to skim past; (fig) to come within a hair's breadth of, come very close to.

fromage [fʀɔmaʒ] nm cheese; **~ blanc** soft white cheese; **~ de tête** pork brawn.

fromager, ère [fʀɔmaʒe, -ɛʀ] nm/f cheese merchant ♦ adj (industrie) cheese cpd.

fromagerie [fʀɔmaʒʀi] nf cheese dairy.

froment [fʀɔmɑ̃] nm wheat.

fronce [fʀɔ̃s] nf (de tissu) gather.

froncement [fʀɔ̃smɑ̃] nm: **~ de sourcils** frown.

froncer [fʀɔ̃se] vt to gather; **~ les sourcils** to frown.

frondaison [fʀɔ̃dɛzɔ̃] nf foliage.

fronde [fʀɔ̃d] nf sling; (fig) rebellion, rebelliousness.

frondeur, euse [fʀɔ̃dœʀ, -øz] adj rebellious.

front [fʀɔ̃] nm forehead, brow; (MIL, MÉTÉOROLOGIE, POL) front; **avoir le ~ de faire** to have the effrontery ou front to do; **de ~** adv (se heurter) head-on; (rouler) together (i.e. 2 or 3 abreast); (simultanément) at once; **faire ~ à** to face up to; **~ de mer** (sea) front.

frontal, e, aux [fʀɔ̃tal, -o] adj frontal.

frontalier, ière [fʀɔ̃talje, -jɛʀ] adj border cpd, frontier cpd ♦ nm/f: **(travailleurs) ~s** workers who cross the border to go to work, commuters from across the border.

frontière [fʀɔ̃tjɛʀ] nf (GÉO, POL) frontier, border; (fig) frontier, boundary.

frontispice [fʀɔ̃tispis] nm frontispiece.

fronton [fʀɔ̃tɔ̃] nm pediment; (de pelote basque) (front) wall.

frottement [fʀɔtmɑ̃] nm rubbing, scraping; **~s** nmpl (fig: difficultés) friction sg.

frotter [fʀɔte] vi to rub, scrape ♦ vt to rub; (pour nettoyer) to rub (up); (: avec une brosse) to scrub; **~ une allumette** to strike a match; **se ~ à qn** to cross swords with sb; **se ~ à qch** to come up against sth; **se ~ les mains** (fig) to rub one's hands (gleefully).

frottis [fʀɔti] nm (MÉD) smear.

frottoir [fʀɔtwaʀ] nm (d'allumettes) friction strip; (pour encaustiquer) (long-handled) brush.

frou-frou, pl **frous-frous** [fʀufʀu] nm rustle.

frousse [fʀus] nf (fam: peur): **avoir la ~** to be in a blue funk.

fructifier [fʀyktifje] vi to yield a profit; **faire ~** to turn to good account.

fructueux, euse [fʀyktɥø, -øz] adj fruitful; profitable.

frugal, e, aux [fʀygal, -o] adj frugal.

frugalement [fʀygalmɑ̃] adv frugally.

frugalité [fʀygalite] nf frugality.

fruit [fʀɥi] nm fruit gén no pl; **~s de mer** (CULIN) seafood(s); **~s secs** dried fruit sg.

fruité, e [fʀɥite] adj (vin) fruity.

fruiterie [fʀɥitʀi] nf (boutique) greengrocer's (BRIT), fruit (and vegetable) store (US).

fruitier, ière [fʀɥitje, -jɛʀ] adj: **arbre ~** fruit tree ♦ nm/f fruiterer (BRIT), fruit merchant (US).

fruste [fʀyst(ə)] adj unpolished, uncultivated.

frustrant, e [fʀystʀɑ̃, -ɑ̃t] adj frustrating.

frustration [fʀystʀasjɔ̃] nf frustration.

frustré, e [fʀystʀe] adj frustrated.

frustrer [fʀystʀe] vt to frustrate; (priver): **~ qn de qch** to deprive sb of sth.

FS abr (= franc suisse) FS, SF.

FSE sigle m (= foyer socio-éducatif) community home.

FTP sigle mpl (= Francs-tireurs et partisans) Communist Resistance in 1940-45.

fuchsia [fyʃja] nm fuchsia.

fuel(-oil) [fjul(ɔjl)] nm fuel oil; (pour chauffer) heating oil.

fugace [fygas] adj fleeting.

fugitif, ive [fyʒitif, -iv] adj (lueur, amour) fleeting; (prisonnier etc) runaway ♦ nm/f fugitive, runaway.

fugue [fyg] nf (d'un enfant) running away no pl; (MUS) fugue; **faire une ~** to run away, abscond.

fuir [fɥiʀ] vt to flee from; (éviter) to shun ♦ vi to run away; (gaz, robinet) to leak.

fuite [fɥit] nf flight; (écoulement) leak, leakage; (divulgation) leak; **être en ~** to be on the run; **mettre en ~** to put to flight; **prendre la ~** to take flight.

fulgurant, e [fylgyʀɑ̃, -ɑ̃t] adj lightning cpd, dazzling.

fulminant, e [fylminɑ̃, -ɑ̃t] adj (lettre, regard) furious; **~ de colère** raging with anger.

fulminer [fylmine] vi: **~ (contre)** to thunder forth (against).

fumant, e [fymɑ̃, -ɑ̃t] adj smoking; (liquide) steaming; **un coup ~** (fam) a master stroke.

fumé, e [fyme] adj (CULIN) smoked; (verre) tinted ♦ nf smoke; **partir en ~e** to go up in smoke.

fume-cigarette [fymsigaʀɛt] nm inv cigarette holder.

fumer [fyme] vi to smoke; (liquide) to steam ♦ vt to smoke; (terre, champ) to manure.

fumerie [fymʀi] nf: **~ d'opium** opium den.

fumerolles [fymʀɔl] nfpl gas and smoke (from volcano).

fûmes [fym] vb voir être.

fumet [fymɛ] nm aroma.

fumeur, euse [fymœʀ, -øz] nm/f smoker; **(compartiment) ~s** smoking compartment.

fumeux, euse [fymø, -øz] adj (péj) woolly (BRIT), hazy.

fumier [fymje] nm manure.

fumigation [fymigasjɔ̃] nf fumigation.

fumigène [fymiʒɛn] *adj* smoke *cpd*.
fumiste [fymist(ə)] *nm* (*ramoneur*) chimney sweep ♦ *nmf* (*péj: paresseux*) shirker; (*charlatan*) phoney.
fumisterie [fymistəʀi] *nf* (*péj*) fraud, con.
fumoir [fymwaʀ] *nm* smoking room.
funambule [fynɑ̃byl] *nm* tightrope walker.
funèbre [fynɛbʀ(ə)] *adj* funeral *cpd*; (*fig*) doleful; funereal.
funérailles [fyneʀaj] *nfpl* funeral *sg*.
funéraire [fyneʀɛʀ] *adj* funeral *cpd*, funerary.
funeste [fynɛst(ə)] *adj* disastrous; deathly.
funiculaire [fynikylɛʀ] *nm* funicular (railway).
FUNU [fyny] *sigle f* (= *Force d'urgence des Nations unies*) UNEF (= *United Nations Emergency Forces*).
fur [fyʀ]: **au ~ et à mesure** *adv* as one goes along; **au ~ et à mesure que** as; **au ~ et à mesure de leur progression** as they advance (*ou* advanced).
furax [fyʀaks] *adj inv* (*fam*) livid.
furent [fyʀ] *vb voir* **être**.
furet [fyʀɛ] *nm* ferret.
fureter [fyʀte] *vi* (*péj*) to nose about.
fureur [fyʀœʀ] *nf* fury; (*passion*): **~ de** passion for; **faire ~** to be all the rage.
furibard, e [fyʀibaʀ, -aʀd(ə)] *adj* (*fam*) livid, absolutely furious.
furibond, e [fyʀibɔ̃, -ɔ̃d] *adj* livid, absolutely furious.
furie [fyʀi] *nf* fury; (*femme*) shrew, vixen; **en ~** (*mer*) raging.
furieusement [fyʀjøzmɑ̃] *adv* furiously.
furieux, euse [fyʀjø, -øz] *adj* furious.
furoncle [fyʀɔ̃kl(ə)] *nm* boil.
furtif, ive [fyʀtif, -iv] *adj* furtive.
furtivement [fyʀtivmɑ̃] *adv* furtively.
fus [fy] *vb voir* **être**.
fusain [fyzɛ̃] *nm* (*BOT*) spindle-tree; (*ART*) charcoal.
fuseau, x [fyzo] *nm* (*pantalon*) (ski-)pants *pl*; (*pour filer*) spindle; **en ~** (*jambes*) tapering; (*colonne*) bulging; **~ horaire** time zone.
fusée [fyze] *nf* rocket; **~ éclairante** flare.
fuselage [fyzlaʒ] *nm* fuselage.
fuselé, e [fyzle] *adj* slender; (*galbé*) tapering.
fuser [fyze] *vi* (*rires etc*) to burst forth.
fusible [fyzibl(ə)] *nm* (*ÉLEC: fil*) fuse wire; (*: fiche*) fuse.
fusil [fyzi] *nm* (*de guerre, à canon rayé*) rifle, gun; (*de chasse, à canon lisse*) shotgun, gun; **~ à deux coups** double-barrelled rifle *ou* shotgun; **~ sous-marin** spear-gun.
fusilier [fyzilje] *nm* (*MIL*) rifleman.
fusillade [fyzijad] *nf* gunfire *no pl*, shooting *no pl*; (*combat*) gun battle.
fusiller [fyzije] *vt* to shoot; **~ qn du regard** to look daggers at sb.
fusil-mitrailleur, *pl* **fusils-mitrailleurs** [fyzimitʀajœʀ] *nm* machine gun.
fusion [fyzjɔ̃] *nf* fusion, melting; (*fig*) merging; (*COMM*) merger; **en ~** (*métal, roches*)

molten.
fusionnement [fyzjɔnmɑ̃] *nm* merger.
fusionner [fyzjɔne] *vi* to merge.
fustiger [fystiʒe] *vt* to denounce.
fut [fy] *vb voir* **être**.
fût [fy] *vb voir* **être** ♦ *nm* (*tonneau*) barrel, cask; (*de canon*) stock; (*d'arbre*) bole, trunk; (*de colonne*) shaft.
futaie [fytɛ] *nf* forest, plantation.
futé, e [fyte] *adj* crafty.
fûtes [fyt] *vb voir* **être**.
futile [fytil] *adj* (*inutile*) futile; (*frivole*) frivolous.
futilement [fytilmɑ̃] *adv* frivolously.
futilité [fytilite] *nf* futility; frivolousness; (*chose futile*) futile pursuit (*ou* thing *etc*).
futon [fytɔ̃] *nm* futon.
futur, e [fytyʀ] *adj, nm* future; **son ~ époux** her husband-to-be; **au ~** (*LING*) in the future.
futuriste [fytyʀist(ə)] *adj* futuristic.
futurologie [fytyʀɔlɔʒi] *nf* futurology.
fuyant, e [fɥijɑ̃, -ɑ̃t] *vb voir* **fuir** ♦ *adj* (*regard etc*) evasive; (*lignes etc*) receding; (*perspective*) vanishing.
fuyard, e [fɥijaʀ, -aʀd(ə)] *nmf* runaway.
fuyons [fɥijɔ̃] *etc vb voir* **fuir**.

G g

G, g [ʒe] *nm inv* G, g ♦ *abr* (= *gramme*) g; (= *gauche*) L, l; **G comme Gaston** G for George; **le G7** (*POL*) the G7 nations, the Group of Seven.
gabardine [gabaʀdin] *nf* gabardine.
gabarit [gabaʀi] *nm* (*fig: dimension, taille*) size; (*: valeur*) calibre; (*TECH*) template; **du même ~** (*fig*) of the same type, of that ilk.
gabegie [gabʒi] *nf* (*péj*) chaos.
Gabon [gabɔ̃] *nm*: **le ~** Gabon.
gabonais, e [gabɔnɛ, -ɛz] *adj* Gabonese.
gâcher [gaʃe] *vt* (*gâter*) to spoil, ruin; (*gaspiller*) to waste; (*plâtre*) to temper; (*mortier*) to mix.
gâchette [gaʃɛt] *nf* trigger.
gâchis [gaʃi] *nm* (*désordre*) mess; (*gaspillage*) waste *no pl*.
gadget [gadʒɛt] *nm* thingumajig; (*nouveauté*) gimmick.
gadin [gadɛ̃] *nm* (*fam*): **prendre un ~** to come a cropper (*BRIT*).
gadoue [gadu] *nf* sludge.
gaélique [gaelik] *adj* Gaelic ♦ *nm* (*LING*) Gaelic.
gaffe [gaf] *nf* (*instrument*) boat hook; (*fam: er-*

reur) blunder; **faire ~** *(fam)* to watch out.
gaffer [gafe] *vi* to blunder.
gaffeur, euse [gafœʀ, -øz] *nm/f* blunderer.
gag [gag] *nm* gag.
gaga [gaga] *adj (fam)* gaga.
gage [gaʒ] *nm (dans un jeu)* forfeit; *(fig: de fidé-lité)* token; **~s** *nmpl (salaire)* wages; *(garantie)* guarantee *sg*; **mettre en ~** to pawn; **laisser en ~** to leave as security.
gager [gaʒe] *vt*: **~ que** to bet *ou* wager that.
gageure [gaʒyʀ] *nf*: **c'est une ~** it's attempting the impossible.
gagnant, e [gaɲɑ̃, -ɑ̃t] *adj*: **billet/numéro ~** winning ticket/number ♦ *adv*: **jouer ~** *(aux courses)* to be bound to win ♦ *nm/f* winner.
gagne-pain [gaɲpɛ̃] *nm inv* job.
gagne-petit [gaɲpəti] *nm inv* low wage earner.
gagner [gaɲe] *vt (concours, procès, pari)* to win; *(somme d'argent, revenu)* to earn; *(aller vers, atteindre)* to reach; *(s'emparer de)* to overcome; *(envahir)* to spread to; *(se conci-lier)*: **~ qn** to win sb over ♦ *vi* to win; *(fig)* to gain; **~ du temps/de la place** to gain time/save space; **~ sa vie** to earn one's living; **~ du terrain** *(aussi fig)* to gain ground; **~ qn de vitesse** *(aussi fig)* to outstrip sb; **~ à faire** *(s'en trouver bien)* to be better off doing; **il y gagne** it's in his interest, it's to his advantage.
gagneur [gaɲœʀ] *nm* winner.
gai, e [ge] *adj* cheerful; *(livre, pièce de théâtre)* light-hearted; *(un peu ivre)* merry.
gaiement [gemɑ̃] *adv* cheerfully.
gaieté [gete] *nf* cheerfulness; **~s** *nfpl (souvent ironique)* delights; **de ~ de cœur** with a light heart.
gaillard, e [gajaʀ, -aʀd(ə)] *adj (robuste)* sprightly; *(grivois)* bawdy, ribald ♦ *nm/f (strapping)* fellow/wench.
gaillardement [gajaʀdəmɑ̃] *adv* cheerfully.
gain [gɛ̃] *nm (revenu)* earnings *pl*; *(bénéfice: gén pl)* profits *pl*; *(au jeu: gén pl)* winnings *pl*; *(fig: de temps, place)* saving; *(: avantage)* benefit; *(: lucre)* gain; **avoir ~ de cause** to win the case; *(fig)* to be proved right; **obte-nir ~ de cause** *(fig)* to win out.
gaine [gɛn] *nf (corset)* girdle; *(fourreau)* sheath; *(de fil électrique etc)* outer covering.
gaine-culotte, *pl* **gaines-culottes** [gɛnkylɔt] *nf* pantie girdle.
gainer [gene] *vt* to cover.
gala [gala] *nm* official reception; **soirée de ~** gala evening.
galamment [galamɑ̃] *adv* courteously.
galant, e [galɑ̃, -ɑ̃t] *adj (courtois)* courteous, gentlemanly; *(entreprenant)* flirtatious, gal-lant; *(aventure, poésie)* amorous; **en ~e com-pagnie** *(homme)* with a lady friend; *(femme)* with a gentleman friend.
galanterie [galɑ̃tʀi] *nf* gallantry.
galantine [galɑ̃tin] *nf* galantine.
Galapagos [galapagɔs] *nfpl*: **les (îles) ~** the Ga-

lapagos Islands.
galaxie [galaksi] *nf* galaxy.
galbe [galb(ə)] *nm* curve(s); shapeliness.
galbé, e [galbe] *adj (jambes)* (well-)rounded; **bien ~** shapely.
gale [gal] *nf (MÉD)* scabies *sg*; *(de chien)* mange.
galéjade [galeʒad] *nf* tall story.
galère [galɛʀ] *nf* galley.
galérer [galeʀe] *vi (fam)* to work hard, slave (away).
galerie [galʀi] *nf* gallery; *(THÉÂT)* circle; *(de voiture)* roof rack; *(fig: spectateurs)* audience; **~ marchande** shopping mall; **~ de peinture** (private) art gallery.
galérien [galeʀjɛ̃] *nm* galley slave.
galet [galɛ] *nm* pebble; *(TECH)* wheel; **~s** *nmpl* pebbles, shingle *sg*.
galette [galɛt] *nf (gâteau)* flat pastry cake; *(crêpe)* savoury pancake; **la ~ des Rois** *cake traditionally eaten on Twelfth Night.*
galeux, euse [galø, -øz] *adj*: **un chien ~** a mangy dog.
Galice [galis] *nf*: **la ~** Galicia *(in Spain).*
Galicie [galisi] *nf*: **la ~** Galicia *(in Central Europe).*
galiléen, ne [galileɛ̃, -ɛn] *adj* Galilean.
galimatias [galimatja] *nm (péj)* gibberish.
galipette [galipɛt] *nf*: **faire des ~s** to turn som-ersaults.
Galles [gal] *nfpl*: **le pays de ~** Wales.
gallicisme [galisism(ə)] *nm* French idiom; *(tournure fautive)* gallicism.
gallois, e [galwa, -waz] *adj* Welsh ♦ *nm (LING)* Welsh ♦ *nm/f*: **G~, e** Welshman/woman.
gallo-romain, e [galoʀɔmɛ̃, -ɛn] *adj* Gallo-Roman.
galoche [galɔʃ] *nf* clog.
galon [galɔ̃] *nm (MIL)* stripe; *(décoratif)* piece of braid; **prendre du ~** to be promoted.
galop [galo] *nm* gallop; **au ~** at a gallop; **~ d'essai** *(fig)* trial run.
galopade [galɔpad] *nf* stampede.
galopant, e [galɔpɑ̃, -ɑ̃t] *adj*: **inflation ~e** gal-loping inflation; **démographie ~e** exploding population.
galoper [galɔpe] *vi* to gallop.
galopin [galɔpɛ̃] *nm* urchin, ragamuffin.
galvaniser [galvanize] *vt* to galvanize.
galvaudé, e [galvode] *adj (expression)* hack-neyed; *(mot)* clichéd.
galvauder [galvode] *vt* to debase.
gambade [gɑ̃bad] *nf*: **faire des ~s** to skip *ou* frisk about.
gambader [gɑ̃bade] *vi* to skip *ou* frisk about.
gamberger [gɑ̃bɛʀʒe] *(fam) vi* to (have a) think ♦ *vt* to dream up.
Gambie [gɑ̃bi] *nf*: **la ~** *(pays)* Gambia; *(fleuve)* the Gambia.
gamelle [gamɛl] *nf* mess tin; billy can; *(fam)*: **ramasser une ~** to fall flat on one's face.
gamin, e [gamɛ̃, -in] *nm/f* kid ♦ *adj* mischie-

vous, playful.

gaminerie [gaminʀi] *nf* mischievousness, playfulness.

gamme [gam] *nf* (*MUS*) scale; (*fig*) range.

gammé, e [game] *adj*: **croix ~e** swastika.

Gand [gɑ̃] *n* Ghent.

gang [gɑ̃g] *nm* gang.

Gange [gɑ̃ʒ] *nm*: **le ~** the Ganges.

ganglion [gɑ̃glijɔ̃] *nm* ganglion; (*lymphatique*) gland; **avoir des ~s** to have swollen glands.

gangrène [gɑ̃gʀɛn] *nf* gangrene; (*fig*) corruption; corrupting influence.

gangster [gɑ̃gstɛʀ] *nm* gangster.

gangstérisme [gɑ̃gsteʀism(ə)] *nm* gangsterism.

gangue [gɑ̃g] *nf* coating.

ganse [gɑ̃s] *nf* braid.

gant [gɑ̃] *nm* glove; **prendre des ~s** (*fig*) to handle the situation with kid gloves; **relever le ~** (*fig*) to take up the gauntlet; **~ de crin** massage glove; **~ de toilette** (face) flannel (*BRIT*), face cloth; **~s de boxe** boxing gloves; **~s de caoutchouc** rubber gloves.

ganté, e [gɑ̃te] *adj*: **~ de blanc** wearing white gloves.

ganterie [gɑ̃tʀi] *nf* glove trade; (*magasin*) glove shop.

garage [gaʀaʒ] *nm* garage; **~ à vélos** bicycle shed.

garagiste [gaʀaʒist(ə)] *nm/f* (*propriétaire*) garage owner; (*mécanicien*) garage mechanic.

garant, e [gaʀɑ̃, -ɑ̃t] *nm/f* guarantor ♦ *nm* guarantee; **se porter ~ de** to vouch for; to be answerable for.

garantie [gaʀɑ̃ti] *nf* guarantee, warranty; (*gage*) security, surety; (**bon de**) **~** guarantee *ou* warranty slip; **~ de bonne exécution** performance bond.

garantir [gaʀɑ̃tiʀ] *vt* to guarantee; (*protéger*): **~ de** to protect from; **je vous garantis que** I can assure you that; **garanti pure laine/2 ans** guaranteed pure wool/for 2 years.

garce [gaʀs(ə)] *nf* (*péj*) bitch.

garçon [gaʀsɔ̃] *nm* boy; (*célibataire*) bachelor; (*jeune homme*) boy, lad; (*aussi*: **~ de café**) waiter; **~ boucher/coiffeur** butcher's/hairdresser's assistant; **~ de courses** messenger; **~ d'écurie** stable lad; **~ manqué** tomboy.

garçonnet [gaʀsɔnɛ] *nm* small boy.

garçonnière [gaʀsɔnjɛʀ] *nf* bachelor flat.

garde [gaʀd(ə)] *nm* (*de prisonnier*) guard; (*de domaine etc*) warden; (*soldat, sentinelle*) guardsman ♦ *nf* guarding; looking after; (*soldats, BOXE, ESCRIME*) guard; (*faction*) watch; (*d'une arme*) hilt; (*TYPO: aussi*: **page** *ou* **feuille de ~**) flyleaf; (: *collée*) endpaper; **de ~** *adj, adv* on duty; **monter la ~** to stand guard; **être sur ses ~s** to be on one's guard; **mettre en ~** to warn; **mise en ~** warning; **prendre ~ (à)** to be careful (of); **avoir la ~ des enfants** (*après divorce*) to have custody

of the children; **~ champêtre** *nm* rural policeman; **~ du corps** *nm* bodyguard; **~ d'enfants** *nf* child minder; **~ forestier** *nm* forest warden; **~ mobile** *nm, nf* mobile guard; **des Sceaux** *nm* ≈ Lord Chancellor (*BRIT*), Attorney General (*US*); **~ à vue** *nf* (*JUR*) ≈ police custody.

garde-à-vous [gaʀdavu] *nm inv*: **être/se mettre au ~** to be at/stand to attention; **~ (fixe)!** (*MIL*) attention!

garde-barrière, *pl* **gardes-barrière(s)** [gaʀdəbaʀjɛʀ] *nm/f* level-crossing keeper.

garde-boue [gaʀdəbu] *nm inv* mudguard.

garde-chasse, *pl* **gardes-chasse(s)** [gaʀdəʃas] *nm* gamekeeper.

garde-côte [gaʀdəkot] *nm* (*vaisseau*) coastguard boat.

garde-feu [gaʀdəfø] *nm inv* fender.

garde-fou [gaʀdəfu] *nm* railing, parapet.

garde-malade, *pl* **gardes-malade(s)** [gaʀdəmalad] *nf* home nurse.

garde-manger [gaʀdəmɑ̃ʒe] *nm inv* (*boîte*) meat safe; (*placard*) pantry, larder.

garde-meuble [gaʀdəmœbl(ə)] *nm* furniture depository.

garde-pêche [gaʀdəpɛʃ] *nm inv* (*personne*) water bailiff; (*navire*) fisheries protection ship.

garder [gaʀde] *vt* (*conserver*) to keep; (: *sur soi: vêtement, chapeau*) to keep on; (*surveiller: enfants*) to look after; (: *immeuble, lieu, prisonnier*) to guard; **se ~** *vi* (*aliment: se conserver*) to keep; **se ~ de faire** to be careful not to do; **~ le lit/la chambre** to stay in bed/indoors; **~ le silence** to keep silent *ou* quiet; **~ la ligne** to keep one's figure; **~ à vue** to keep in custody; **pêche/chasse gardée** private fishing/hunting (ground).

garderie [gaʀdəʀi] *nf* day nursery, crèche.

garde-robe [gaʀdəʀɔb] *nf* wardrobe.

gardeur, euse [gaʀdœʀ, -øz] *nm/f* (*de vaches*) cowherd; (*de chèvres*) goatherd.

gardian [gaʀdjɑ̃] *nm* cowboy (*in the Camargue*).

gardien, ne [gaʀdjɛ̃, -ɛn] *nm/f* (*garde*) guard; (*de prison*) warder; (*de domaine, réserve*) warden; (*de musée etc*) attendant; (*de phare, cimetière*) keeper; (*d'immeuble*) caretaker; (*fig*) guardian; **~ de but** goalkeeper; **~ de nuit** night watchman; **~ de la paix** policeman.

gardiennage [gaʀdjenaʒ] *nm* (*emploi*) caretaking; **société de ~** security firm.

gardon [gaʀdɔ̃] *nm* roach.

gare [gaʀ] *nf* (railway) station, train station (*US*) ♦ *excl*: **~ à ...** mind ...!, watch out for ...!; **~ à ne pas ...** mind you don't ...; **~ à toi!** watch out!; **sans crier ~** without warning; **~ maritime** harbour station; **~ routière** coach (*BRIT*) *ou* bus station; (*camions*) haulage (*BRIT*) *ou* trucking (*US*) depot; **~ de triage** marshalling yard.

garenne [gaʀɛn] *nf voir* lapin.

garer [gaʀe] *vt* to park; **se ~** to park; (*pour lais-*

ser passer) to draw into the side.

gargantuesque [gaʀgɑ̃tyɛsk(ə)] *adj* gargantuan.

gargariser [gaʀgaʀize]: **se** ~ *vi* to gargle; **se** ~ **de** (*fig*) to revel in.

gargarisme [gaʀgaʀism(ə)] *nm* gargling *no pl*; (*produit*) gargle.

gargote [gaʀgɔt] *nf* cheap restaurant, greasy spoon (*fam*).

gargouille [gaʀguj] *nf* gargoyle.

gargouillement [gaʀgujmɑ̃] *nm* = **gargouillis**.

gargouiller [gaʀguje] *vi* (*estomac*) to rumble; (*eau*) to gurgle.

gargouillis [gaʀguji] *nm* (*gén pl: voir vb*) rumbling; gurgling.

garnement [gaʀnəmɑ̃] *nm* rascal, scallywag.

garni, e [gaʀni] *adj* (*plat*) served with vegetables (*and chips or pasta or rice*) ♦ *nm* (*appartement*) furnished accommodation *no pl* (*BRIT*) *ou* accommodations *pl* (*US*).

garnir [gaʀniʀ] *vt* to decorate; (*remplir*) to fill; (*recouvrir*) to cover; **se** ~ *vi* (*pièce, salle*) to fill up; ~ **qch de** (*orner*) to decorate sth with; to trim sth with; (*approvisionner*) to fill *ou* stock sth with; (*protéger*) to fit sth with; (*CULIN*) to garnish sth with.

garnison [gaʀnizɔ̃] *nf* garrison.

garniture [gaʀnityʀ] *nf* (*CULIN: légumes*) vegetables *pl*; (*: persil etc*) garnish; (*: farce*) filling; (*décoration*) trimming; (*protection*) fittings *pl*; ~ **de cheminée** mantelpiece ornaments *pl*; ~ **de frein** (*AUTO*) brake lining; ~ **intérieure** (*AUTO*) interior trim; ~ **périodique** sanitary towel (*BRIT*) *ou* napkin (*US*).

garrigue [gaʀig] *nf* scrubland.

garrot [gaʀo] *nm* (*MÉD*) tourniquet; (*torture*) garrotte.

garrotter [gaʀɔte] *vt* to tie up; (*fig*) to muzzle.

gars [ga] *nm* lad; (*type*) guy.

Gascogne [gaskɔɲ] *nf*: **la** ~ Gascony.

gascon, ne [gaskɔ̃, -ɔn] *adj* Gascon ♦ *nm*: **G~** (*hâbleur*) braggart.

gas-oil [gazɔjl] *nm* diesel oil.

gaspillage [gaspijaʒ] *nm* waste.

gaspiller [gaspije] *vt* to waste.

gaspilleur, euse [gaspijœʀ, -øz] *adj* wasteful.

gastrique [gastʀik] *adj* gastric, stomach *cpd*.

gastro-entérite [gastʀoɑ̃teʀit] *nf* (*MÉD*) gastro-enteritis.

gastro-intestinal, e, aux [gastʀoɛ̃testinal, -o] *adj* gastrointestinal.

gastronome [gastʀɔnɔm] *nm/f* gourmet.

gastronomie [gastʀɔnɔmi] *nf* gastronomy.

gastronomique [gastʀɔnɔmik] *adj*: **menu** ~ gourmet menu.

gâteau, x [gato] *nm* cake ♦ *adj inv* (*fam: trop indulgent*): **papa-/maman-**~ doting father/mother; ~ **d'anniversaire** birthday cake; ~ **de riz** ≈ rice pudding; ~ **sec** biscuit.

gâter [gate] *vt* to spoil; **se** ~ *vi* (*dent, fruit*) to go bad; (*temps, situation*) to change for the worse.

gâterie [gatʀi] *nf* little treat.

gâteux, euse [gatø, -øz] *adj* senile.

gâtisme [gatism(ə)] *nm* senility.

GATT [gat] *sigle m* (= *General Agreement on Tariffs and Trade*) GATT.

gauche [goʃ] *adj* left, left-hand; (*maladroit*) awkward, clumsy ♦ *nf* (*POL*) left (wing); (*BOXE*) left; **à** ~ on the left; (*direction*) (to the) left; **à** ~ **de** (on *ou* to the) left of; **à la** ~ **de** to the left of; **de** ~ (*POL*) left-wing.

gauchement [goʃmɑ̃] *adv* awkwardly, clumsily.

gaucher, ère [goʃe, -ɛʀ] *adj* left-handed.

gaucherie [goʃʀi] *nf* awkwardness, clumsiness.

gauchir [goʃiʀ] *vt* (*planche, objet*) to warp; (*fig: fait, idée*) to distort.

gauchisant, e [goʃizɑ̃, -ɑ̃t] *adj* with left-wing tendencies.

gauchisme [goʃism(ə)] *nm* leftism.

gauchiste [goʃist(ə)] *adj, nm/f* leftist.

gaufre [gofʀ(ə)] *nf* (*pâtisserie*) waffle; (*de cire*) honeycomb.

gaufrer [gofʀe] *vt* (*papier*) to emboss; (*tissu*) to goffer.

gaufrette [gofʀɛt] *nf* wafer.

gaufrier [gofʀije] *nm* (*moule*) waffle iron.

Gaule [gol] *nf*: **la** ~ Gaul.

gaule [gol] *nf* (*perche*) (long) pole; (*canne à pêche*) fishing rod.

gauler [gole] *vt* (*arbre*) to beat (*using a long pole to bring down fruit etc*); (*fruits*) to beat down (*with a pole*).

gaullisme [golism(ə)] *nm* Gaullism.

gaulliste [golist(ə)] *adj, nm/f* Gaullist.

gaulois, e [golwa, -waz] *adj* Gallic; (*grivois*) bawdy ♦ *nm/f*: **G~, e** Gaul.

gauloiserie [golwazʀi] *nf* bawdiness.

gausser [gose]: **se** ~ **de** *vt* to deride.

gaver [gave] *vt* to force-feed; (*fig*): ~ **de** to cram with, fill up with; (*personne*): **se** ~ **de** to stuff o.s. with.

gay [gɛ] *adj, nm* (*fam*) gay.

gaz [gaz] *nm inv* gas; **mettre les** ~ (*AUTO*) to put one's foot down; **chambre/masque à** ~ gas chamber/mask; ~ **butane** Calor gas ® (*BRIT*), butane gas; ~ **carbonique** carbon dioxide; ~ **hilarant** laughing gas; ~ **lacrymogène** tear gas; ~ **naturel** natural gas; ~ **de ville** town gas (*BRIT*), manufactured domestic gas.

gaze [gaz] *nf* gauze.

gazéifié, e [gazeifje] *adj* carbonated, aerated.

gazelle [gazɛl] *nf* gazelle.

gazer [gaze] *vt* to gas ♦ *vi* (*fam*) to be going *ou* working well.

gazette [gazɛt] *nf* news sheet.

gazeux, euse [gazø, -øz] *adj* gaseous; (*eau*) sparkling; (*boisson*) fizzy.

gazoduc [gazodyk] *nm* gas pipeline.

gazole [gazɔl] *nm* = **gas-oil**.

gazomètre [gazɔmɛtʀ(ə)] *nm* gasometer.

gazon [gɑzɔ̃] *nm* (*herbe*) turf, grass; (*pelouse*) lawn.

gazonner [gɑzɔne] *vt* (*terrain*) to grass over.

gazouillement [gazujmɑ̃] *nm* (*voir vb*) chirping; babbling.

gazouiller [gazuje] *vi* (*oiseau*) to chirp; (*enfant*) to babble.

gazouillis [gazuji] *nmpl* chirp *sg*.

GB *sigle f* (= *Grande Bretagne*) GB.

gd *abr* (= *grand*) L.

GDF *sigle m* (= *Gaz de France*) national gas company.

geai [ʒɛ] *nm* jay.

géant, e [ʒeɑ̃, -ɑ̃t] *adj* gigantic, giant; (*COMM*) giant-size ♦ *nm/f* giant.

geignement [ʒɛɲmɑ̃] *nm* groaning, moaning.

geindre [ʒɛ̃dʀ(ə)] *vi* to groan, moan.

gel [ʒɛl] *nm* frost; (*de l'eau*) freezing; (*fig: des salaires, prix*) freeze; freezing; (*produit de beauté*) gel.

gélatine [ʒelatin] *nf* gelatine.

gélatineux, euse [ʒelatinø, -øz] *adj* jelly-like, gelatinous.

gelé, e [ʒəle] *adj* frozen ♦ *nf* jelly; (*gel*) frost; ~ **blanche** hoarfrost, white frost.

geler [ʒəle] *vt*, *vi* to freeze; **il gèle** it's freezing.

gélule [ʒelyl] *nf* capsule.

gelures [ʒəlyʀ] *nfpl* frostbite *sg*.

Gémeaux [ʒemo] *nmpl*: **les ~** Gemini, the Twins; **être des ~** to be Gemini.

gémir [ʒemiʀ] *vi* to groan, moan.

gémissement [ʒemismɑ̃] *nm* groan, moan.

gemme [ʒɛm] *nf* gem(stone).

gémonies [ʒemɔni] *nfpl*: **vouer qn aux ~** to subject sb to public scorn.

gén. *abr* (= *généralement*) gen.

gênant, e [ʒɛnɑ̃, -ɑ̃t] *adj* (*objet*) awkward, in the way; (*histoire, personne*) embarrassing.

gencive [ʒɑ̃siv] *nf* gum.

gendarme [ʒɑ̃daʀm(ə)] *nm* gendarme.

gendarmer [ʒɑ̃daʀme]: **se ~** *vi* to kick up a fuss.

gendarmerie [ʒɑ̃daʀməʀi] *nf military police force in countryside and small towns; their police station or barracks.*

gendre [ʒɑ̃dʀ(ə)] *nm* son-in-law.

gène [ʒɛn] *nm* (*BIO*) gene.

gêne [ʒɛn] *nf* (*à respirer, bouger*) discomfort, difficulty; (*dérangement*) bother, trouble; (*manque d'argent*) financial difficulties *pl ou* straits *pl*; (*confusion*) embarrassment; **sans ~** *adj* inconsiderate.

gêné, e [ʒene] *adj* embarrassed; (*dépourvu d'argent*) short (of money).

généalogie [ʒenealɔʒi] *nf* genealogy.

généalogique [ʒenealɔʒik] *adj* genealogical.

gêner [ʒene] *vt* (*incommoder*) to bother; (*encombrer*) to hamper; (*bloquer le passage*) to be in the way of; (*déranger*) to bother; (*embarrasser*): ~ **qn** to make sb feel ill-at-ease; **se ~** to put o.s. out; **ne vous gênez pas!** (*ironique*) go right ahead!, don't mind me!; **je**

vais me ~! (*ironique*) why should I care?

général, e, aux [ʒeneʀal, -o] *adj*, *nm* general ♦ *nf*: (**répétition**) ~**e** final dress rehearsal; **en ~** usually, in general; **à la satisfaction** ~**e** to everyone's satisfaction.

généralement [ʒeneʀalmɑ̃] *adv* generally.

généralisable [ʒeneʀalizabl(ə)] *adj* generally applicable.

généralisation [ʒeneʀalizasjɔ̃] *nf* generalization.

généraliser [ʒeneʀalize] *vt*, *vi* to generalize; **se ~** *vi* to become widespread.

généraliste [ʒeneʀalist(ə)] *nm/f* (*MÉD*) general practitioner, GP.

généralité [ʒeneʀalite] *nf*: **la ~ des ...** the majority of ...; ~**s** *nfpl* generalities; (*introduction*) general points.

générateur, trice [ʒeneʀatœʀ, -tʀis] *adj*: ~ **de** which causes *ou* brings about ♦ *nf* (*ÉLEC*) generator.

génération [ʒeneʀasjɔ̃] *nf* (*aussi INFORM*) generation.

généreusement [ʒeneʀøzmɑ̃] *adv* generously.

généreux, euse [ʒeneʀø, -øz] *adj* generous.

générique [ʒeneʀik] *adj* generic ♦ *nm* (*CINÉ*, *TV*) credits *pl*, credit titles *pl*.

générosité [ʒeneʀozite] *nf* generosity.

Gênes [ʒɛn] *n* Genoa.

genèse [ʒənɛz] *nf* genesis.

genêt [ʒənɛ] *nm* (*BOT*) broom *no pl*.

généticien, ne [ʒenetisjɛ̃, -ɛn] *nm/f* geneticist.

génétique [ʒenetik] *adj* genetic ♦ *nf* genetics *sg*.

génétiquement [ʒenetikmɑ̃] *adv* genetically.

gêneur, euse [ʒɛnœʀ, -øz] *nm/f* (*personne qui gêne*) obstacle; (*importun*) intruder.

Genève [ʒənɛv] Geneva.

genevois, e [ʒənəvwa, -waz] *adj* Genevan.

genévrier [ʒənevʀije] *nm* juniper.

génial, e, aux [ʒenjal, -o] *adj* of genius; (*fam*) fantastic, brilliant.

génie [ʒeni] *nm* genius; (*MIL*): **le ~** ≈ the Engineers *pl*; **avoir du ~** to have genius; ~ **civil** civil engineering; ~ **génétique** genetic engineering.

genièvre [ʒənjɛvʀ(ə)] *nm* (*BOT*) juniper (tree); (*boisson*) geneva; **grain de ~** juniper berry.

génisse [ʒenis] *nf* heifer; **foie de ~** ox liver.

génital, e, aux [ʒenital, -o] *adj* genital.

génitif [ʒenitif] *nm* genitive.

génocide [ʒenɔsid] *nm* genocide.

génois, e [ʒenwa, -waz] *adj* Genoese ♦ *nf* (*gâteau*) ≈ sponge cake.

genou, x [ʒnu] *nm* knee; **à ~x** on one's knees; **se mettre à ~x** to kneel down.

genouillère [ʒənujɛʀ] *nf* (*SPORT*) kneepad.

genre [ʒɑ̃ʀ] *nm* (*espèce, sorte*) kind, type, sort; (*allure*) manner; (*LING*) gender; (*ART*) genre; (*ZOOL etc*) genus; **se donner du ~** to give o.s. airs; **avoir bon ~** to have style; **avoir mauvais ~** to be ill-mannered.

gens [ʒɑ̃] *nmpl* (*f in some phrases*) people *pl*; **les**

~ **d'Église** the clergy; **les** ~ **du monde** society people; ~ **de maison** domestics.

gentiane [ʒɑ̃sjan] *nf* gentian.

gentil, le [ʒɑ̃ti, -ij] *adj* kind; (*enfant: sage*) good; (*sympa: endroit etc*) nice; **c'est très** ~ **à vous** it's very kind *ou* good *ou* nice of you.

gentilhommière [ʒɑ̃tijɔmjɛʀ] *nf* (small) manor house *ou* country seat.

gentillesse [ʒɑ̃tijɛs] *nf* kindness.

gentillet, te [ʒɑ̃tijɛ, -ɛt] *adj* nice little.

gentiment [ʒɑ̃timɑ̃] *adv* kindly.

génuflexion [ʒenyflɛksjɔ̃] *nf* genuflexion.

géodésique [ʒeodezik] *adj* geodesic.

géographe [ʒeɔgraf] *nm/f* geographer.

géographie [ʒeɔgrafi] *nf* geography.

géographique [ʒeɔgrafik] *adj* geographical.

geôlier [ʒolje] *nm* jailer.

géologie [ʒeɔlɔʒi] *nf* geology.

géologique [ʒeɔlɔʒik] *adj* geological.

géologiquement [ʒeɔlɔʒikmɑ̃] *adv* geologically.

géologue [ʒeɔlɔg] *nm/f* geologist.

géomètre [ʒeɔmɛtʀ(ə)] *nm*: **(arpenteur-)**~ (land) surveyor.

géométrie [ʒeɔmetʀi] *nf* geometry; **à** ~ **variable** (*AVIAT*) swing-wing.

géométrique [ʒeɔmetʀik] *adj* geometric.

géophysique [ʒeofizik] *nf* geophysics *sg*.

géopolitique [ʒeɔpɔlitik] *nf* geopolitics *sg*.

Géorgie [ʒeɔʀʒi] *nf*: **la** ~ (*URSS, USA*) Georgia; **la** ~ **du Sud** South Georgia.

géorgien, ne [ʒeɔʀʒjɛ̃, -ɛn] *adj* Georgian.

géostationnaire [ʒeɔstasjɔnɛʀ] *adj* geostationary.

géothermique [ʒeɔtɛʀmik] *adj*: **énergie** ~ geothermal energy.

gérance [ʒeʀɑ̃s] *nf* management; **mettre en** ~ to appoint a manager for; **prendre en** ~ to take over (the management of).

géranium [ʒeʀanjɔm] *nm* geranium.

gérant, e [ʒeʀɑ̃, -ɑ̃t] *nm/f* manager/manageress; ~ **d'immeuble** managing agent.

gerbe [ʒɛʀb(ə)] *nf* (*de fleurs, d'eau*) spray; (*de blé*) sheaf (*pl* sheaves); (*fig*) shower, burst.

gercé, e [ʒɛʀse] *adj* chapped.

gercer [ʒɛʀse] *vi*, **se** ~ *vi* to chap.

gerçure [ʒɛʀsyʀ] *nf* crack.

gérer [ʒeʀe] *vt* to manage.

gériatrie [ʒeʀjatʀi] *nf* geriatrics *sg*.

gériatrique [ʒeʀjatʀik] *adj* geriatric.

germain, e [ʒɛʀmɛ̃, -ɛn] *adj*: **cousin** ~ first cousin.

germanique [ʒɛʀmanik] *adj* Germanic.

germaniste [ʒɛʀmanist(ə)] *nm/f* German scholar.

germe [ʒɛʀm(ə)] *nm* germ.

germer [ʒɛʀme] *vi* to sprout; (*semence, aussi fig*) to germinate.

gérondif [ʒeʀɔ̃dif] *nm* gerund; (*en latin*) gerundive.

gérontologie [ʒeʀɔ̃tɔlɔʒi] *nf* gerontology.

gérontologue [ʒeʀɔ̃tɔlɔg] *nm/f* gerontologist.

gésier [ʒezje] *nm* gizzard.

gésir [ʒeziʀ] *vi* to be lying (down); *voir aussi* **ci-gît**.

gestation [ʒɛstasjɔ̃] *nf* gestation.

geste [ʒɛst(ə)] *nm* gesture; move; motion; **il fit un** ~ **de la main pour m'appeler** he signed to me to come over, he waved me over; **ne faites pas un** ~ (*ne bougez pas*) don't move.

gesticuler [ʒɛstikyle] *vi* to gesticulate.

gestion [ʒɛstjɔ̃] *nf* management; ~ **des disques** (*INFORM*) housekeeping; ~ **de fichier(s)** (*INFORM*) file management.

gestionnaire [ʒɛstjɔnɛʀ] *nm/f* administrator; ~ **de fichier** (*INFORM*) file manager.

geyser [ʒezɛʀ] *nm* geyser.

Ghana [gana] *nm*: **le** ~ Ghana.

ghanéen, ne [ganeɛ̃, -ɛn] *adj* Ghanaian.

ghetto [gɛto] *nm* ghetto.

gibecière [ʒibsjɛʀ] *nf* (*de chasseur*) gamebag; (*sac en bandoulière*) shoulder bag.

gibelotte [ʒiblɔt] *nf* rabbit fricassee in white wine.

gibet [ʒibɛ] *nm* gallows *pl*.

gibier [ʒibje] *nm* (*animaux*) game; (*fig*) prey.

giboulée [ʒibule] *nf* sudden shower.

giboyeux, euse [ʒibwajø, -øz] *adj* well-stocked with game.

Gibraltar [ʒibraltaʀ] *nm* Gibraltar.

gibus [ʒibys] *nm* opera hat.

giclée [ʒikle] *nf* spurt, squirt.

gicler [ʒikle] *vi* to spurt, squirt.

gicleur [ʒiklœʀ] *nm* (*AUTO*) jet.

GIE *sigle m* = groupement d'intérêt économique.

gifle [ʒifl(ə)] *nf* slap (in the face).

gifler [ʒifle] *vt* to slap (in the face).

gigantesque [ʒigɑ̃tɛsk(ə)] *adj* gigantic.

gigantisme [ʒigɑ̃tism(ə)] *nm* (*MÉD*) gigantism; (*des mégalopoles*) vastness.

gigaoctet [ʒigaɔktɛ] *nm* gigabyte.

GIGN *sigle m* (= *Groupe d'intervention de la gendarmerie nationale*) *special crack force of the gendarmerie*, ≈ SAS (*BRIT*).

gigogne [ʒigɔɲ] *adj*: **lits** ~**s** truckle (*BRIT*) *ou* trundle (*US*) beds; **tables/poupées** ~**s** nest of tables/dolls.

gigolo [ʒigɔlo] *nm* gigolo.

gigot [ʒigo] *nm* leg (of mutton *ou* lamb).

gigoter [ʒigɔte] *vi* to wriggle (about).

gilet [ʒilɛ] *nm* waistcoat; (*pull*) cardigan; (*de corps*) vest; ~ **pare-balles** bulletproof jacket; ~ **de sauvetage** life jacket.

gin [dʒin] *nm* gin.

gingembre [ʒɛ̃ʒɑ̃bʀ(ə)] *nm* ginger.

gingivite [ʒɛ̃ʒivit] *nf* inflammation of the gums, gingivitis.

ginseng [ʒinsɛŋ] *nm* ginseng.

girafe [ʒiʀaf] *nf* giraffe.

giratoire [ʒiʀatwaʀ] *adj*: **sens** ~ roundabout.

girofle [ʒiʀɔfl(ə)] *nm*: **clou de** ~ clove.

giroflée [ʒiʀɔfle] *nf* wallflower.

girolle [ʒiʀɔl] *nf* chanterelle.

giron [ʒiʀɔ̃] *nm* (*genoux*) lap; (*fig: sein*) bosom.

Gironde [ʒiʀɔ̃d] *nf*: **la** ~ the Gironde.

girophare [ʒiʀɔfaʀ] *nm* revolving (flashing) light.

girouette [ʒiʀwɛt] *nf* weather vane *ou* cock.

gis [ʒi], **gisais** [ʒizɛ] *etc vb voir* **gésir**.

gisement [ʒizmɑ̃] *nm* deposit.

gît [ʒi] *vb voir* **gésir**.

gitan, e [ʒitɑ̃, -an] *nm/f* gipsy.

gîte [ʒit] *nm* home; shelter; (*du lièvre*) form; ~ **(rural)** (country) holiday cottage *ou* apartment.

gîter [ʒite] *vi* (*NAVIG*) to list.

givrage [ʒivʀaʒ] *nm* icing.

givrant, e [ʒivʀɑ̃, -ɑ̃t] *adj*: **brouillard** ~ freezing fog.

givre [ʒivʀ(ə)] *nm* (hoar)frost.

givré, e [ʒivʀe] *adj*: **citron** ~/**orange** ~**e** lemon/orange sorbet (*served in fruit skin*).

glabre [glabʀ(ə)] *adj* hairless; (*menton*) clean-shaven.

glaçage [glasaʒ] *nm* (*au sucre*) icing; (*au blanc d'œuf, de la viande*) glazing.

glace [glas] *nf* ice; (*crème glacée*) ice cream; (*verre*) sheet of glass; (*miroir*) mirror; (*de voiture*) window; ~**s** *nfpl* (*GÉO*) ice sheets, ice *sg*; **de** ~ (*fig: accueil, visage*) frosty, icy; **rester de** ~ to remain unmoved.

glacé, e [glase] *adj* icy; (*boisson*) iced.

glacer [glase] *vt* to freeze; (*boisson*) to chill, ice; (*gâteau*) to ice (*BRIT*), frost (*US*); (*papier, tissu*) to glaze; (*fig*): ~ **qn** to chill sb; (*fig*) to make sb's blood run cold.

glaciaire [glasjɛʀ] *adj* (*période*) ice *cpd*; (*relief*) glacial.

glacial, e [glasjal] *adj* icy.

glacier [glasje] *nm* (*GÉO*) glacier; (*marchand*) ice-cream maker.

glacière [glasjɛʀ] *nf* icebox.

glaçon [glasɔ̃] *nm* icicle; (*pour boisson*) ice cube.

gladiateur [gladjatœʀ] *nm* gladiator.

glaïeul [glajœl] *nm* gladiola.

glaire [glɛʀ] *nf* (*MÉD*) phlegm *no pl*.

glaise [glɛz] *nf* clay.

glaive [glɛv] *nm* two-edged sword.

gland [glɑ̃] *nm* (*de chêne*) acorn; (*décoration*) tassel; (*ANAT*) glans.

glande [glɑ̃d] *nf* gland.

glander [glɑ̃de] *vi* (*fam*) to fart around (*BRIT !*), screw around (*US !*).

glaner [glane] *vt, vi* to glean.

glapir [glapiʀ] *vi* to yelp.

glapissement [glapismɑ̃] *nm* yelping.

glas [glɑ] *nm* knell, toll.

glauque [glok] *adj* dull blue-green.

glissade [glisad] *nf* (*par jeu*) slide; (*chute*) slip; (*dérapage*) skid; **faire des** ~**s** to slide.

glissant, e [glisɑ̃, -ɑ̃t] *adj* slippery.

glisse [glis] *nf*: **sports de** ~ *sports involving sliding or gliding (eg skiing, surfing, wind-surfing)*.

glissement [glismɑ̃] *nm* sliding; (*fig*) shift; ~ **de terrain** landslide.

glisser [glise] *vi* (*avancer*) to glide *ou* slide along; (*coulisser, tomber*) to slide; (*déraper*) to slip; (*être glissant*) to be slippery ♦ *vt*: ~ **qch sous/dans/à** to slip sth under/into/to; ~ **sur** (*fig: détail etc*) to skate over; **se** ~ **dans/entre** to slip into/between.

glissière [glisjɛʀ] *nf* slide channel; **à** ~ (*porte, fenêtre*) sliding; ~ **de sécurité** (*AUTO*) crash barrier.

glissoire [gliswaʀ] *nf* slide.

global, e, aux [glɔbal, -o] *adj* overall.

globalement [glɔbalmɑ̃] *adv* taken as a whole.

globe [glɔb] *nm* globe; **sous** ~ under glass; ~ **oculaire** eyeball; **le** ~ **terrestre** the globe.

globe-trotter [glɔbtʀɔtœʀ] *nm* globe-trotter.

globule [glɔbyl] *nm* (*du sang*): ~ **blanc/rouge** white/red corpuscle.

globuleux, euse [glɔbylø, -øz] *adj*: **yeux** ~ protruding eyes.

gloire [glwaʀ] *nf* glory; (*mérite*) distinction, credit; (*personne*) celebrity.

glorieux, euse [glɔʀjø, -øz] *adj* glorious.

glorifier [glɔʀifje] *vt* to glorify, extol; **se** ~ **de** to glory in.

gloriole [glɔʀjɔl] *nf* vainglory.

glose [gloz] *nf* gloss.

glossaire [glɔsɛʀ] *nm* glossary.

glotte [glɔt] *nf* (*ANAT*) glottis.

glouglouter [gluglute] *vi* to gurgle.

gloussement [glusmɑ̃] *nm* (*de poule*) cluck; (*rire*) chuckle.

glousser [gluse] *vi* to cluck; (*rire*) to chuckle.

glouton, ne [glutɔ̃, -ɔn] *adj* gluttonous, greedy.

gloutonnerie [glutɔnʀi] *nf* gluttony.

glu [gly] *nf* birdlime.

gluant, e [glyɑ̃, -ɑ̃t] *adj* sticky, gummy.

glucide [glysid] *nm* carbohydrate.

glucose [glykoz] *nm* glucose.

gluten [glytɛn] *nm* gluten.

glycérine [gliseʀin] *nf* glycerine.

glycine [glisin] *nf* wisteria.

GMT *sigle adj* (= *Greenwich Mean Time*) GMT.

gnangnan [ɲɑ̃ɲɑ̃] *adj inv* (*fam: livre, film*) soppy.

GNL *sigle m* (= *gaz naturel liquéfié*) LNG (= *liquefied natural gas*).

gnôle [njol] *nf* (*fam*) booze *no pl*; **un petit verre de** ~ a drop of the hard stuff.

gnome [gnom] *nm* gnome.

gnon [nɔ̃] *nm* (*fam: coup de poing*) bash; (: *marque*) dent.

GO *sigle fpl* (= *grandes ondes*) LW ♦ *sigle m* (= *gentil organisateur*) title given to leaders on Club Méditerranée holidays; extended to refer to easy-going leader of any group.

go [go]: **tout de** ~ *adv* straight out.

goal [gol] *nm* goalkeeper.

gobelet [gɔblɛ] *nm* (*en métal*) tumbler; (*en*

plastique) beaker; *(à dés)* cup.
gober [gɔbe] *vt* to swallow.
goberger [gɔbɛʀʒe]: **se ~** *vi* to cosset o.s.
Gobi [gɔbi] *n*: **désert de ~** Gobi Desert.
godasse [gɔdas] *nf (fam)* shoe.
godet [gɔdɛ] *nm* pot; *(COUTURE)* unpressed pleat.
godiller [gɔdije] *vi (NAVIG)* to scull; *(SKI)* to wedeln.
goéland [gɔelɑ̃] *nm* (sea)gull.
goélette [gɔelɛt] *nf* schooner.
goémon [gɔemɔ̃] *nm* wrack.
gogo [gɔgo] *nm (péj)* mug, sucker; **à ~** *adv* galore.
goguenard, e [gɔgnaʀ, -aʀd(ə)] *adj* mocking.
goguette [gɔgɛt] *nf*: **en ~** on the binge.
goinfre [gwɛ̃fʀ(ə)] *nm* glutton.
goinfrer [gwɛ̃fʀe]: **se ~** *vi* to make a pig of o.s.; **se ~ de** to guzzle.
goitre [gwatʀ(ə)] *nm* goitre.
golf [gɔlf] *nm (jeu)* golf; *(terrain)* golf course; **~ miniature** crazy *ou* miniature golf.
golfe [gɔlf(ə)] *nm* gulf; bay; **le ~ d'Aden** the Gulf of Aden; **le ~ de Gascogne** the Bay of Biscay; **le ~ du Lion** the Gulf of Lions; **le ~ Persique** the Persian Gulf.
golfeur, euse [gɔlfœʀ, -øz] *nm/f* golfer.
gominé, e [gɔmine] *adj* slicked down.
gomme [gɔm] *nf (à effacer)* rubber *(BRIT)*, eraser; *(résine)* gum; **boule** *ou* **pastille de ~** throat pastille.
gommé, e [gɔme] *adj*: **papier ~** gummed paper.
gommer [gɔme] *vt (effacer)* to rub out *(BRIT)*, erase; *(enduire de gomme)* to gum.
gond [gɔ̃] *nm* hinge; **sortir de ses ~s** *(fig)* to fly off the handle.
gondole [gɔ̃dɔl] *nf* gondola; *(pour l'étalage)* shelves *pl*, gondola.
gondoler [gɔ̃dɔle]: **se ~** *vi* to warp, buckle; *(fam: rire)* to hoot with laughter; to be in stitches.
gondolier [gɔ̃dɔlje] *nm* gondolier.
gonflable [gɔ̃flabl(ə)] *adj* inflatable.
gonflage [gɔ̃flaʒ] *nm* inflating, blowing up.
gonflé, e [gɔ̃fle] *adj* swollen; *(ventre)* bloated; *(fam: culotté)*: **être ~** to have a nerve.
gonflement [gɔ̃fləmɑ̃] *nm* inflation; *(MÉD)* swelling.
gonfler [gɔ̃fle] *vt (pneu, ballon)* to inflate, blow up; *(nombre, importance)* to inflate ♦ *vi (pied etc)* to swell (up); *(CULIN: pâte)* to rise.
gonfleur [gɔ̃flœʀ] *nm* air pump.
gong [gɔ̃g] *nm* gong.
gonzesse [gɔ̃zɛs] *nf (fam)* chick, bird *(BRIT)*.
goret [gɔʀɛ] *nm* piglet.
gorge [gɔʀʒ(ə)] *nf (ANAT)* throat; *(poitrine)* breast; *(GÉO)* gorge; *(rainure)* groove; **avoir mal à la ~** to have a sore throat; **avoir la ~ serrée** to have a lump in one's throat.
gorgé, e [gɔʀʒe] *adj*: **~ de** filled with; *(eau)* saturated with ♦ *nf* mouthful; sip; gulp;

boire à petites/grandes ~es to take little sips/big gulps.
gorille [gɔʀij] *nm* gorilla; *(fam)* bodyguard.
gosier [gozje] *nm* throat.
gosse [gɔs] *nm/f* kid.
gothique [gɔtik] *adj* gothic.
gouache [gwaʃ] *nf* gouache.
gouaille [gwaj] *nf* street wit, cocky humour *(BRIT)* *ou* humor *(US)*.
goudron [gudʀɔ̃] *nm (asphalte)* tar(mac) *(BRIT)*, asphalt; *(du tabac)* tar.
goudronner [gudʀɔne] *vt* to tar(mac) *(BRIT)*, asphalt.
gouffre [gufʀ(ə)] *nm* abyss, gulf.
goujat [guʒa] *nm* boor.
goujon [guʒɔ̃] *nm* gudgeon.
goulée [gule] *nf* gulp.
goulet [gulɛ] *nm* bottleneck.
goulot [gulo] *nm* neck; **boire au ~** to drink from the bottle.
goulu, e [guly] *adj* greedy.
goulûment [gulymɑ̃] *adv* greedily.
goupille [gupij] *nf* (metal) pin.
goupiller [gupije] *vt* to pin (together).
goupillon [gupijɔ̃] *nm (REL)* sprinkler; *(brosse)* bottle brush; **le ~** *(fig)* the cloth, the clergy.
gourd, e [guʀ, guʀd(ə)] *adj* numb (with cold); *(fam)* oafish.
gourde [guʀd(ə)] *nf (récipient)* flask; *(fam)* (clumsy) clot *ou* oaf.
gourdin [guʀdɛ̃] *nm* club, bludgeon.
gourmand, e [guʀmɑ̃, -ɑ̃d] *adj* greedy.
gourmandise [guʀmɑ̃diz] *nf* greed; *(bonbon)* sweet *(BRIT)*, piece of candy *(US)*.
gourmet [guʀmɛ] *nm* epicure.
gourmette [guʀmɛt] *nf* chain bracelet.
gourou [guʀu] *nm* guru.
gousse [gus] *nf (de vanille etc)* pod; **~ d'ail** clove of garlic.
gousset [gusɛ] *nm (de gilet)* fob.
goût [gu] *nm* taste; *(fig: appréciation)* taste, liking; **le (bon) ~** good taste; **de bon ~** in good taste, tasteful; **de mauvais ~** in bad taste, tasteless; **avoir bon/mauvais ~** *(aliment)* to taste nice/nasty; *(personne)* to have good/bad taste; **avoir du/manquer de ~** to have/lack taste; **avoir du ~ pour** to have a liking for; **prendre ~ à** to develop a taste *ou* a liking for.
goûter [gute] *vt (essayer)* to taste; *(apprécier)* to enjoy ♦ *vi* to have (afternoon) tea ♦ *nm* (afternoon) tea; **~ à** to taste, sample; **~ de** to have a taste of; **~ d'enfants/ d'anniversaire** children's tea/birthday party.
goutte [gut] *nf* drop; *(MÉD)* gout; *(alcool)* nip *(BRIT)*, tot *(BRIT)*, drop *(US)*; **~s** *nfpl (MÉD)* drops; **~ à ~** *adv* a drop at a time; **tomber ~ à ~** to drip.
goutte-à-goutte [gutagut] *nm inv (MÉD)* drip; **alimenter au ~** to drip-feed.
gouttelette [gutlɛt] *nf* droplet.
goutter [gute] *vi* to drip.

gouttière [gutjɛʀ] *nf* gutter.
gouvernail [guvɛʀnaj] *nm* rudder; (*barre*) helm, tiller.
gouvernant, e [guvɛʀnɑ̃, -ɑ̃t] *adj* ruling *cpd* ♦ *nf* housekeeper; (*d'un enfant*) governess.
gouverne [guvɛʀn(ə)] *nf*: **pour sa** ~ for his guidance.
gouvernement [guvɛʀnəmɑ̃] *nm* government.
gouvernemental, e, aux [guvɛʀnəmɑ̃tal, -o] *adj* (*politique*) government *cpd*; (*journal, parti*) pro-government.
gouverner [guvɛʀne] *vt* to govern; (*diriger*) to steer; (*fig*) to control.
gouverneur [guvɛʀnœʀ] *nm* governor; (*MIL*) commanding officer.
goyave [gɔjav] *nf* guava.
GPL *sigle m* (= *gaz de pétrole liquéfié*) LPG (= *liquefied petroleum gas*).
GQG *sigle m* (= *grand quartier général*) GHQ.
grabataire [gʀabatɛʀ] *adj* bedridden ♦ *nm/f* bedridden invalid.
grâce [gʀɑs] *nf* grace; (*faveur*) favour; (*JUR*) pardon; ~**s** *nfpl* (*REL*) grace *sg*; **de bonne/ mauvaise** ~ with (a) good/bad grace; **dans les bonnes** ~**s de qn** in favour with sb; **faire** ~ **à qn de qch** to spare sb sth; **rendre** ~**(s) à** to give thanks to; **demander** ~ to beg for mercy; **droit de** ~ right of reprieve; **recours en** ~ plea for pardon; ~ **à** *prép* thanks to.
gracier [gʀasje] *vt* to pardon.
gracieusement [gʀasjøzmɑ̃] *adv* graciously, kindly; (*gratuitement*) freely; (*avec grâce*) gracefully.
gracieux, euse [gʀasjø, -øz] *adj* (*charmant, élégant*) graceful; (*aimable*) gracious, kind; **à titre** ~ free of charge.
gracile [gʀasil] *adj* slender.
gradation [gʀadɑsjɔ̃] *nf* gradation.
grade [gʀad] *nm* (*MIL*) rank; (*SCOL*) degree; **monter en** ~ to be promoted.
gradé [gʀade] *nm* (*MIL*) officer.
gradin [gʀadɛ̃] *nm* (*dans un théâtre*) tier; (*de stade*) step; ~**s** *nmpl* (*de stade*) terracing *no pl* (*BRIT*), standing area; **en** ~**s** terraced.
graduation [gʀadɥɑsjɔ̃] *nf* graduation.
gradué, e [gʀadɥe] *adj* (*exercices*) graded (for difficulty); (*thermomètre, verre*) graduated.
graduel, le [gʀadɥɛl] *adj* gradual; progressive.
graduer [gʀadɥe] *vt* (*effort etc*) to increase gradually; (*règle, verre*) to graduate; (*exercices*) to increase in difficulty.
graffiti [gʀafiti] *nmpl* graffiti.
grain [gʀɛ̃] *nm* (*gén*) grain; (*de chapelet*) bead; (*NAVIG*) squall; (*averse*) heavy shower; (*fig: petite quantité*): **un** ~ **de** a touch of; ~ **de beauté** beauty spot; ~ **de café** coffee bean; ~ **de poivre** peppercorn; ~ **de poussière** speck of dust; ~ **de raisin** grape.
graine [gʀɛn] *nf* seed; **mauvaise** ~ (*mauvais sujet*) bad lot; **une** ~ **de voyou** a hooligan in the making.

graineterie [gʀɛntʀi] *nf* seed merchant's (shop).
grainetier, -ière [gʀɛntje, -jɛʀ] *nm/f* seed merchant.
graissage [gʀɛsaʒ] *nm* lubrication, greasing.
graisse [gʀɛs] *nf* fat; (*lubrifiant*) grease; ~ **saturée** saturated fat.
graisser [gʀɛse] *vt* to lubricate, grease; (*tacher*) to make greasy.
graisseux, euse [gʀɛsø, -øz] *adj* greasy; (*ANAT*) fatty.
grammaire [gʀamɛʀ] *nf* grammar.
grammatical, e, aux [gʀamatikal, -o] *adj* grammatical.
gramme [gʀam] *nm* gramme.
grand, e [gʀɑ̃, gʀɑ̃d] *adj* (*haut*) tall; (*gros, vaste, large*) big, large; (*long*) long; (*sens abstraits*) great ♦ *adv*: ~ **ouvert** wide open; **un** ~ **buveur** a heavy drinker; **un** ~ **homme** a great man; **son** ~ **frère** his big *ou* older brother; **avoir** ~ **besoin de** to be in dire *ou* desperate need of; **il est** ~ **temps de** it's high time to; **il est assez** ~ **pour** he's big *ou* old enough to; **voir** ~ to think big; **en** ~ on a large scale; **au** ~ **air** in the open (air); **les** ~**s blessés/brûlés** the severely injured/burned; **de** ~ **matin** at the crack of dawn; ~ **écart** splits *pl*; ~ **ensemble** housing scheme; ~ **jour** broad daylight; ~ **livre** (*COMM*) ledger; ~ **magasin** department store; ~ **malade** very sick person; ~ **public** general public; ~**e personne** grown-up; ~**e surface** hypermarket, superstore; ~**es écoles** *prestige university-level colleges with competitive entrance examinations*; ~**es lignes** (*RAIL*) main lines; ~**es vacances** summer holidays.

*The **grandes écoles** are prestigious French establishments of tertiary education preparing students for specific careers. Students who have undertaken two years study after the **baccalauréat** in the **classes préparatoires** are recruited by competitive entry examination. The grandes écoles have a strong corporate identity and provide the intellectual, administrative and political elite of the country.*

grand-angle, *pl* **grands-angles** [gʀɑ̃tɑ̃gl(ə)] *nm* (*PHOTO*) wide-angle lens.
grand-angulaire, *pl* **grands-angulaires** [gʀɑ̃tɑ̃gylɛʀ] *nm* (*PHOTO*) wide-angle lens.
grand-chose [gʀɑ̃ʃoz] *nm/f inv*: **pas** ~ not much.
Grande-Bretagne [gʀɑ̃dbʀətaɲ] *nf*: **la** ~ (Great) Britain; **en** ~ in (Great) Britain.
grandement [gʀɑ̃dmɑ̃] *adv* (*tout à fait*) greatly; (*largement*) easily; (*généreusement*) lavishly.
grandeur [gʀɑ̃dœʀ] *nf* (*dimension*) size; (*fig: ampleur, importance*) magnitude; (*: gloire, puissance*) greatness; ~ **nature** *adj* life-size.
grand-guignolesque [gʀɑ̃giɲɔlɛsk(ə)] *adj* gruesome.

grandiloquent, e [gʀɑ̃dilɔkɑ̃, -ɑ̃t] *adj* bombastic, grandiloquent.

grandiose [gʀɑ̃djoz] *adj* (*paysage, spectacle*) imposing.

grandir [gʀɑ̃diʀ] *vi* (*enfant, arbre*) to grow; (*bruit, hostilité*) to increase, grow ♦ *vt:* ~ **qn** (*suj: vêtement, chaussure*) to make sb look taller; (*fig*) to make sb grow in stature.

grandissant, e [gʀɑ̃disɑ̃, -ɑ̃t] growing.

grand-mère, *pl* **grand(s)-mères** [gʀɑ̃mɛʀ] *nf* grandmother.

grand-messe [gʀɑ̃mɛs] *nf* high mass.

grand-oncle, *pl* **grands-oncles** [gʀɑ̃tɔ̃kl(ə), gʀɑ̃zɔ̃kl(ə)] *nm* great-uncle.

grand-peine [gʀɑ̃pɛn]: **à** ~ *adv* with (great) difficulty.

grand-père, *pl* **grands-pères** [gʀɑ̃pɛʀ] *nm* grandfather.

grand-route [gʀɑ̃ʀut] *nf* main road.

grand-rue [gʀɑ̃ʀy] *nf* high street.

grands-parents [gʀɑ̃paʀɑ̃] *nmpl* grandparents.

grand-tante, *pl* **grand(s)-tantes** [gʀɑ̃tɑ̃t] *nf* great-aunt.

grand-voile [gʀɑ̃vwal] *nf* mainsail.

grange [gʀɑ̃ʒ] *nf* barn.

granit(e) [gʀanit] *nm* granite.

granitique [gʀanitik] *adj* granite; (*terrain*) granitic.

granule [gʀanyl] *nm* small pill.

granulé [gʀanyle] *nm* granule.

granuleux, euse [gʀanylø, -øz] *adj* granular.

graphe [gʀaf] *nm* graph.

graphie [gʀafi] *nf* written form.

graphique [gʀafik] *adj* graphic ♦ *nm* graph.

graphisme [gʀafism(ə)] *nm* graphic arts *pl*; graphics *sg*; (*écriture*) handwriting.

graphiste [gʀafist(ə)] *nm/f* graphic designer.

graphologie [gʀafɔlɔʒi] *nf* graphology.

graphologue [gʀafɔlɔg] *nm/f* graphologist.

grappe [gʀap] *nf* cluster; ~ **de raisin** bunch of grapes.

grappiller [gʀapije] *vt* to glean.

grappin [gʀapɛ̃] *nm* grapnel; **mettre le** ~ **sur** (*fig*) to get one's claws on.

gras, se [gʀɑ, gʀɑs] *adj* (*viande, soupe*) fatty; (*personne*) fat; (*surface, main, cheveux*) greasy; (*terre*) sticky; (*toux*) loose, phlegmy; (*rire*) throaty; (*plaisanterie*) coarse; (*crayon*) soft-lead; (*TYPO*) bold ♦ *nm* (*CULIN*) fat; **faire la** ~**se matinée** to have a lie-in (*BRIT*), sleep late; **matière** ~**se** fat (content).

gras-double [gʀadubl(ə)] *nm* (*CULIN*) tripe.

grassement [gʀasmɑ̃] *adv* (*généreusement*): ~ **payé** handsomely paid; (*grossièrement: rire*) coarsely.

grassouillet, te [gʀasujɛ, -ɛt] *adj* podgy, plump.

gratifiant, e [gʀatifjɑ̃, -ɑ̃t] *adj* gratifying, rewarding.

gratification [gʀatifikasjɔ̃] *nf* bonus.

gratifier [gʀatifje] *vt:* ~ **qn de** to favour (*BRIT*)

ou favor (*US*) sb with; to reward sb with; (*sourire etc*) to favo(u)r sb with.

gratin [gʀatɛ̃] *nm* (*CULIN*) cheese- (*ou* crumb-) topped dish; (: *croûte*) topping; **au** ~ au gratin; **tout le** ~ **parisien** all the best people of Paris.

gratiné, e [gʀatine] *adj* (*CULIN*) au gratin; (*fam*) hellish ♦ *nf* (*soupe*) onion soup au gratin.

gratis [gʀatis] *adv, adj* free.

gratitude [gʀatityd] *nf* gratitude.

gratte-ciel [gʀatsjɛl] *nm inv* skyscraper.

grattement [gʀatmɑ̃] *nm* (*bruit*) scratching (noise).

gratte-papier [gʀatpapje] *nm inv* (*péj*) penpusher.

gratter [gʀate] *vt* (*frotter*) to scrape; (*enlever*) to scrape off; (*bras, bouton*) to scratch; **se** ~ to scratch o.s.

grattoir [gʀatwaʀ] *nm* scraper.

gratuit, e [gʀatɥi, -ɥit] *adj* (*entrée*) free; (*billet*) free, complimentary; (*fig*) gratuitous.

gratuité [gʀatɥite] *nf* being free (of charge); gratuitousness.

gratuitement [gʀatɥitmɑ̃] *adv* (*sans payer*) free; (*sans preuve, motif*) gratuitously.

gravats [gʀava] *nmpl* rubble *sg*.

grave [gʀav] *adj* (*dangereux: maladie, accident*) serious, bad; (*sérieux: sujet, problème*) serious, grave; (*personne, air*) grave, solemn; (*voix, son*) deep, low-pitched ♦ *nm* (*MUS*) low register; **ce n'est pas** ~! it's all right, don't worry; **blessé** ~ seriously injured person.

graveleux, euse [gʀavlø, -øz] *adj* (*terre*) gravelly; (*fruit*) gritty; (*contes, propos*) smutty.

gravement [gʀavmɑ̃] *adv* seriously; badly; gravely.

graver [gʀave] *vt* (*plaque, nom*) to engrave; (*fig*): ~ **qch dans son esprit/sa mémoire** to etch sth in one's mind/memory.

graveur [gʀavœʀ] *nm* engraver.

gravier [gʀavje] *nm* (loose) gravel *no pl*.

gravillons [gʀavijɔ̃] *nmpl* gravel *sg*, loose chippings *ou* gravel.

gravir [gʀaviʀ] *vt* to climb (up).

gravitation [gʀavitasjɔ̃] *nf* gravitation.

gravité [gʀavite] *nf* (*voir grave*) seriousness; gravity; (*PHYSIQUE*) gravity.

graviter [gʀavite] *vi:* ~ **autour de** to revolve around.

gravure [gʀavyʀ] *nf* engraving; (*reproduction*) print; plate.

GRE *sigle f* (= garantie contre les risques à l'exportation) ≈ service provided by ECGD (= Export Credit Guarantees Department).

gré [gʀe] *nm:* **à son** ~ *adj* to his liking ♦ *adv* as he pleases; **au** ~ **de** according to, following; **contre le** ~ **de qn** against sb's will; **de son (plein)** ~ of one's own free will; **de** ~ **ou de force** whether one likes it or not; **de bon** ~ willingly; **bon** ~ **mal** ~ like it or not; willy-nilly; **de** ~ **à** ~ (*COMM*) by mutual agreement; **savoir (bien)** ~ **à qn de qch** to be (most) grateful to sb for sth.

grec, grecque [gʀɛk] *adj* Greek; (*classique: vase etc*) Grecian ♦ *nm* (*LING*) Greek ♦ *nm/f*: **G~, Grecque** Greek.

Grèce [gʀɛs] *nf*: **la** ~ Greece.

gredin, e [gʀədɛ̃, -in] *nm/f* rogue, rascal.

gréement [gʀemɑ̃] *nm* rigging.

greffe [gʀɛf] *nf* graft; transplant ♦ *nm* (*JUR*) office.

greffer [gʀefe] *vt* (*BOT, MÉD: tissu*) to graft; (*MÉD: organe*) to transplant.

greffier [gʀefje] *nm* clerk of the court.

grégaire [gʀegɛʀ] *adj* gregarious.

grège [gʀɛʒ] *adj*: **soie** ~ raw silk.

grêle [gʀɛl] *adj* (*very*) thin ♦ *nf* hail.

grêlé, e [gʀele] *adj* pockmarked.

grêler [gʀele] *vb impers*: **il grêle** it's hailing ♦ *vt*: **la région a été grêlée** the region was damaged by hail.

grêlon [gʀelɔ̃] *nm* hailstone.

grelot [gʀəlo] *nm* little bell.

grelottant, e [gʀəlɔtɑ̃, -ɑ̃t] *adj* shivering, shivery.

grelotter [gʀəlɔte] *vi* (*trembler*) to shiver.

Grenade [gʀənad] *n* Granada ♦ *nf* (*île*) Grenada.

grenade [gʀənad] *nf* (*explosive*) grenade; (*BOT*) pomegranate; ~ **lacrymogène** teargas grenade.

grenadier [gʀənadje] *nm* (*MIL*) grenadier; (*BOT*) pomegranate tree.

grenadine [gʀənadin] *nf* grenadine.

grenat [gʀəna] *adj inv* dark red.

grenier [gʀənje] *nm* (*de maison*) attic; (*de ferme*) loft.

grenouille [gʀənuj] *nf* frog.

grenouillère [gʀənujɛʀ] *nf* (*de bébé*) leggings; (*: combinaison*) sleepsuit.

grenu, e [gʀəny] *adj* grainy, grained.

grès [gʀɛ] *nm* (*roche*) sandstone; (*poterie*) stoneware.

grésil [gʀezi] *nm* (fine) hail.

grésillement [gʀezijmɑ̃] *nm* sizzling; crackling.

grésiller [gʀezije] *vi* to sizzle; (*RADIO*) to crackle.

grève [gʀɛv] *nf* (*d'ouvriers*) strike; (*plage*) shore; **se mettre en/faire** ~ to go on/be on strike; ~ **bouchon** partial strike (*in key areas of a company*); ~ **de la faim** hunger strike; ~ **perlée** go-slow (*BRIT*), slowdown (*US*); ~ **sauvage** wildcat strike; ~ **de solidarité** sympathy strike; ~ **surprise** lightning strike; ~ **sur le tas** sit down strike; ~ **tournante** strike by rota; ~ **du zèle** work-to-rule (*BRIT*), slowdown (*US*).

grever [gʀəve] *vt* (*budget, économie*) to put a strain on; **grevé d'impôts** crippled by taxes; **grevé d'hypothèques** heavily mortgaged.

gréviste [gʀevist(ə)] *nm/f* striker.

gribouillage [gʀibujaʒ] *nm* scribble, scrawl.

gribouiller [gʀibuje] *vt* to scribble, scrawl ♦ *vi* to doodle.

gribouillis [gʀibuji] *nm* (*dessin*) doodle; (*action*) doodling no pl; (*écriture*) scribble.

grief [gʀijɛf] *nm* grievance; **faire** ~ **à qn de** to reproach sb for.

grièvement [gʀijɛvmɑ̃] *adv* seriously.

griffe [gʀif] *nf* claw; (*fig*) signature; (*: d'un couturier, parfumeur*) label, signature.

griffé, e [gʀife] *adj* designer(-label) *cpd*.

griffer [gʀife] *vt* to scratch.

griffon [gʀifɔ̃] *nm* (*chien*) griffon.

griffonnage [gʀifɔnaʒ] *nm* scribble.

griffonner [gʀifɔne] *vt* to scribble.

griffure [gʀifyʀ] *nf* scratch.

grignoter [gʀiɲɔte] *vt*, *vi* to nibble.

gril [gʀil] *nm* steak *ou* grill pan.

grillade [gʀijad] *nf* grill.

grillage [gʀijaʒ] *nm* (*treillis*) wire netting; (*clôture*) wire fencing.

grillager [gʀijaʒe] *vt* (*objet*) to put wire netting on; (*périmètre, jardin*) to put wire fencing around.

grille [gʀij] *nf* (*portail*) (metal) gate; (*clôture*) railings *pl*; (*d'égout*) (metal) grate; (*fig*) grid.

grille-pain [gʀijpɛ̃] *nm inv* toaster.

griller [gʀije] *vt* (*aussi*: **faire** ~: *pain*) to toast; (*: viande*) to grill (*BRIT*), broil (*US*); (*: café*) to roast; (*fig: ampoule etc*) to burn out, blow; ~ **un feu rouge** to jump the lights (*BRIT*), run a stoplight (*US*) ♦ *vi* (*brûler*) to be roasting.

grillon [gʀijɔ̃] *nm* (*ZOOL*) cricket.

grimace [gʀimas] *nf* grimace; (*pour faire rire*): **faire des** ~**s** to pull *ou* make faces.

grimacer [gʀimase] *vi* to grimace.

grimacier, ière [gʀimasje, -jɛʀ] *adj*: **c'est un enfant** ~ that child is always pulling faces.

grimer [gʀime] *vt* to make up.

grimoire [gʀimwaʀ] *nm* (*illisible*) unreadable scribble; (*livre de magie*) book of magic spells.

grimpant, e [gʀɛ̃pɑ̃, -ɑ̃t] *adj*: **plante** ~**e** climbing plant, climber.

grimper [gʀɛ̃pe] *vi*, *vt* to climb ♦ *nm*: **le** ~ (*SPORT*) rope-climbing; ~ **à/sur** to climb (up)/climb onto.

grimpeur, euse [gʀɛ̃pœʀ, -øz] *nm/f* climber.

grinçant, e [gʀɛ̃sɑ̃, -ɑ̃t] *adj* grating.

grincement [gʀɛ̃smɑ̃] *nm* grating (noise); creaking (noise).

grincer [gʀɛ̃se] *vi* (*porte, roue*) to grate; (*plancher*) to creak; ~ **des dents** to grind one's teeth.

grincheux, euse [gʀɛ̃ʃø, -øz] *adj* grumpy.

gringalet [gʀɛ̃galɛ] *adj m* puny ♦ *nm* weakling.

griotte [gʀijɔt] *nf* Morello cherry.

grippal, e, aux [gʀipal, -o] *adj* (*état*) flu-like.

grippe [gʀip] *nf* flu, influenza; **avoir la** ~ to have (the) flu; **prendre qn/qch en** ~ (*fig*) to take a sudden dislike to sb/sth.

grippé, e [gʀipe] *adj*: **être** ~ to have (the) flu; (*moteur*) to have seized up (*BRIT*) *ou*

jammed.
gripper [gʀipe] *vt, vi* to jam.
grippe-sou [gʀipsu] *nmf* penny pincher.
gris, e [gʀi, gʀiz] *adj* grey (*BRIT*), gray (*US*); (*ivre*) tipsy ♦ *nm* (*couleur*) grey (*BRIT*), gray (*US*); **il fait ~** it's a dull *ou* grey day; **faire ~e mine** to look miserable *ou* morose; **faire ~e mine à qn** to give sb a cool reception.
grisaille [gʀizaj] *nf* greyness (*BRIT*), grayness (*US*), dullness.
grisant, e [gʀizɑ̃, -ɑ̃t] *adj* intoxicating, exhilarating.
grisâtre [gʀizɑtʀ(ə)] *adj* greyish (*BRIT*), grayish (*US*).
griser [gʀize] *vt* to intoxicate; **se ~ de** (*fig*) to become intoxicated with.
griserie [gʀizʀi] *nf* intoxication.
grisonnant, e [gʀizɔnɑ̃, -ɑ̃t] *adj* greying (*BRIT*), graying (*US*).
grisonner [gʀizɔne] *vi* to be going grey (*BRIT*) *ou* gray (*US*).
Grisons [gʀizɔ̃] *nmpl*: **les ~** Graubünden.
grisou [gʀizu] *nm* firedamp.
gris-vert [gʀivɛʀ] *adj* grey-green.
grive [gʀiv] *nf* (*ZOOL*) thrush.
grivois, e [gʀivwa, -waz] *adj* saucy.
grivoiserie [gʀivwazʀi] *nf* sauciness.
Groenland [gʀɔɛnlɑ̃d] *nm*: **le ~** Greenland.
groenlandais, e [gʀɔɛnlɑ̃dɛ, -ɛz] *adj* of *ou* from Greenland ♦ *nm/f*: **G~, e** Greenlander.
grog [gʀɔg] *nm* grog.
groggy [gʀɔgi] *adj inv* dazed.
grogne [gʀɔɲ] *nf* grumble.
grognement [gʀɔɲmɑ̃] *nm* grunt; growl.
grogner [gʀɔɲe] *vi* to growl; (*fig*) to grumble.
grognon, ne [gʀɔɲɔ̃, -ɔn] *adj* grumpy, grouchy.
groin [gʀwɛ̃] *nm* snout.
grommeler [gʀɔmle] *vi* to mutter to o.s.
grondement [gʀɔ̃dmɑ̃] *nm* rumble; growl.
gronder [gʀɔ̃de] *vi* (*canon, moteur, tonnerre*) to rumble; (*animal*) to growl; (*fig: révolte*) to be brewing ♦ *vt* to scold.
groom [gʀum] *nm* page, bellhop (*US*).
gros, se [gʀo, gʀos] *adj* big, large; (*obèse*) fat; (*problème, quantité*) great; (*travaux, dégâts*) extensive; (*large: trait, fil*) thick, heavy ♦ *adv*: **risquer/gagner ~** to risk/win a lot ♦ *nm* (*COMM*): **le ~** the wholesale business; **écrire ~** to write in big letters; **prix de ~** wholesale price; **par ~ temps/~se mer** in rough weather/heavy seas; **le ~ de** the main body of; (*du travail etc*) the bulk of; **en avoir ~ sur le cœur** to be upset; **en ~** roughly; (*COMM*) wholesale; **~ intestin** large intestine; **~ lot** jackpot; **~ mot** coarse word, vulgarity; **~ œuvre** shell (of building); **~ plan** (*PHOTO*) close-up; **~ porteur** wide-bodied aircraft, jumbo (jet); **~ sel** cooking salt; **~ titre** headline; **~se caisse** big drum.
groseille [gʀozɛj] *nf*: **~ (rouge)/(blanche)** red/white currant; **~ à maquereau** gooseberry.

groseillier [gʀozeje] *nm* red *ou* white currant bush; gooseberry bush.
grosse [gʀos] *adj f voir* **gros** ♦ *nf* (*COMM*) gross.
grossesse [gʀosɛs] *nf* pregnancy; **~ nerveuse** phantom pregnancy.
grosseur [gʀosœʀ] *nf* size; fatness; (*tumeur*) lump.
grossier, ière [gʀosje, -jɛʀ] *adj* coarse; (*travail*) rough; crude; (*évident: erreur*) gross.
grossièrement [gʀosjɛʀmɑ̃] *adv* coarsely; roughly; crudely; (*en gros*) roughly.
grossièreté [gʀosjɛʀte] *nf* coarseness; rudeness.
grossir [gʀosiʀ] *vi* (*personne*) to put on weight; (*fig*) to grow, get bigger; (*rivière*) to swell ♦ *vt* to increase; (*exagérer*) to exaggerate; (*au microscope*) to magnify, enlarge; (*suj: vêtement*): **~ qn** to make sb look fatter.
grossissant, e [gʀosisɑ̃, -ɑ̃t] *adj* magnifying, enlarging.
grossissement [gʀosismɑ̃] *nm* (*optique*) magnification.
grossiste [gʀosist(ə)] *nmf* wholesaler.
grosso modo [gʀosomɔdo] *adv* roughly.
grotesque [gʀɔtɛsk(ə)] *adj* grotesque.
grotte [gʀɔt] *nf* cave.
grouiller [gʀuje] *vi* (*foule*) to mill about; (*fourmis*) to swarm about; **~ de** to be swarming with.
groupe [gʀup] *nm* group; **cabinet de ~** group practice; **médecine de ~** group practice; **~ électrogène** generator; **~ de pression** pressure group; **~ sanguin** blood group; **~ scolaire** school complex.
groupement [gʀupmɑ̃] *nm* grouping; (*groupe*) group; **~ d'intérêt économique (GIE)** ≈ trade association.
grouper [gʀupe] *vt* to group; (*ressources, moyens*) to pool; **se ~** to get together.
groupuscule [gʀupyskyl] *nm* clique.
gruau [gʀyo] *nm*: **pain de ~** wheaten bread.
grue [gʀy] *nf* crane; **faire le pied de ~** (*fam*) to hang around (waiting), kick one's heels (*BRIT*).
gruger [gʀyʒe] *vt* to cheat, dupe.
grumeaux [gʀymo] *nmpl* (*CULIN*) lumps.
grumeleux, euse [gʀymlø, -øz] *adj* (*sauce etc*) lumpy; (*peau etc*) bumpy.
grutier [gʀytje] *nm* crane driver.
gruyère [gʀyjɛʀ] *nm* gruyère (*BRIT*) *ou* Swiss cheese.
Guadeloupe [gwadlup] *nf*: **la ~** Guadeloupe.
guadeloupéen, ne [gwadlupeɛ̃, -ɛn] *adj* Guadelupian.
Guatémala [gwatemala] *nm*: **le ~** Guatemala.
guatémalien, ne [gwatemaljɛ̃, -ɛn] *adj* Guatemalan.
guatémaltèque [gwatemaltɛk] *adj* Guatemalan.
GUD [gyd] *sigle m* (= *Groupe Union Défense*) student union.
gué [ge] *nm* ford; **passer à ~** to ford.

guenilles [gənij] *nfpl* rags.

guenon [gənɔ̃] *nf* female monkey.

guépard [gepaʀ] *nm* cheetah.

guêpe [gɛp] *nf* wasp.

guêpier [gepje] *nm* (*fig*) trap.

guère [gɛʀ] *adv* (*avec adjectif, adverbe*): **ne ... ~** hardly; (*avec verbe*): **ne ... ~** *tournure négative +* much; hardly ever; *tournure négative +* (very) long; **il n'y a ~ que/de** there's hardly anybody (*ou* anything) but/hardly any.

guéridon [geʀidɔ̃] *nm* pedestal table.

guérilla [geʀija] *nf* guerrilla warfare.

guérillero [geʀijeʀo] *nm* guerrilla.

guérir [geʀiʀ] *vt* (*personne, maladie*) to cure; (*membre, plaie*) to heal ♦ *vi* (*personne*) to recover, be cured; (*plaie, chagrin*) to heal; **~ de** to be cured of, recover from; **~ qn de** to cure sb of.

guérison [geʀizɔ̃] *nf* curing; healing; recovery.

guérissable [geʀisabl(ə)] *adj* curable.

guérisseur, euse [geʀisœʀ, -øz] *nm/f* healer.

guérite [geʀit] *nf* (*MIL*) sentry box; (*sur un chantier*) (workman's) hut.

Guernesey [gɛʀnəzɛ] *nf* Guernsey.

guernesiais, e [gɛʀnəzjɛ, -ɛz] *adj* of *ou* from Guernsey.

guerre [gɛʀ] *nf* war; (*méthode*): **~ atomique/de tranchées** atomic/trench warfare *no pl*; **en ~** at war; **faire la ~ à** to wage war against; **de ~ lasse** (*fig*) tired of fighting *ou* resisting; **de bonne ~** fair and square; **~ civile/mondiale** civil/world war; **~ froide/sainte** cold/holy war; **~ d'usure** war of attrition.

guerrier, ière [gɛʀje, -jɛʀ] *adj* warlike ♦ *nm/f* warrior.

guerroyer [gɛʀwaje] *vi* to wage war.

guet [gɛ] *nm*: **faire le ~** to be on the watch *ou* look-out.

guet-apens, *pl* **guets-apens** [gɛtapɑ̃] *nm* ambush.

guêtre [gɛtʀ(ə)] *nf* gaiter.

guetter [gete] *vt* (*épier*) to watch (intently); (*attendre*) to watch (out) for; (: *pour surprendre*) to be lying in wait for.

guetteur [getœʀ] *nm* look-out.

gueule [gœl] *nf* mouth; (*fam: visage*) mug; (: *bouche*) gob (!), mouth; **ta ~!** (*fam*) shut up!; **~ de bois** (*fam*) hangover.

gueule-de-loup, *pl* **gueules-de-loup** [gœldə-lu] *nf* snapdragon.

gueuler [gœle] *vi* (*fam*) to bawl.

gueuleton [gœltɔ̃] *nm* (*fam*) blowout (*BRIT*), big meal.

gueux [gø] *nm* beggar; (*coquin*) rogue.

gui [gi] *nm* mistletoe.

guibole [gibɔl] *nf* (*fam*) leg.

guichet [giʃɛ] *nm* (*de bureau, banque*) counter, window; (*d'une porte*) wicket, hatch; **les ~s** (*à la gare, au théâtre*) the ticket office; **jouer à ~s fermés** to play to a full house.

guichetier, ière [giʃtje, -jɛʀ] *nm/f* counter clerk.

guide [gid] *nm* guide; (*livre*) guide(book) ♦ *nf* (*fille scout*) (girl) guide (*BRIT*), girl scout (*US*); **~s** *nfpl* (*d'un cheval*) reins.

guider [gide] *vt* to guide.

guidon [gidɔ̃] *nm* handlebars *pl*.

guigne [giɲ] *nf* (*fam*): **avoir la ~** to be jinxed.

guignol [giɲɔl] *nm* ≈ Punch and Judy show; (*fig*) clown.

guillemets [gijmɛ] *nmpl*: **entre ~** in inverted commas *ou* quotation marks; **~ de répétition** ditto marks.

guilleret, te [gijʀɛ, -ɛt] *adj* perky, bright.

guillotine [gijɔtin] *nf* guillotine.

guillotiner [gijɔtine] *vt* to guillotine.

guimauve [gimov] *nf* (*BOT*) marshmallow; (*fig*) sentimentality, sloppiness.

guimbarde [gɛ̃baʀd(ə)] *nf* old banger (*BRIT*), jalopy.

guindé, e [gɛ̃de] *adj* stiff, starchy.

Guinée [gine] *nf*: **la (République de) ~** (the Republic of) Guinea; **la ~ équatoriale** Equatorial Guinea.

Guinée-Bissau [ginebiso] *nf*: **la ~** Guinea-Bissau.

guinéen, ne [gineɛ̃, -ɛn] *adj* Guinean.

guingois [gɛ̃gwa]: **de ~** *adv* askew.

guinguette [gɛ̃gɛt] *nf* open-air café or dance hall.

guirlande [giʀlɑ̃d] *nf* garland; (*de papier*) paper chain; **~ lumineuse** (fairy (*BRIT*)) lights *pl*; **~ de Noël** tinsel *no pl*.

guise [giz] *nf*: **à votre ~** as you wish *ou* please; **en ~ de** by way of.

guitare [gitaʀ] *nf* guitar.

guitariste [gitaʀist(ə)] *nm/f* guitarist, guitar player.

gustatif, ive [gystatif, -iv] *adj* gustatory; *voir* **papille**.

guttural, e, aux [gytyʀal, -o] *adj* guttural.

guyanais, e [gɥijanɛ, -ɛz] *adj* Guyanese, Guyanan; (*français*) Guianese, Guianan.

Guyane [gɥijan] *nf*: **la ~** Guyana; **la ~ (française)** (French) Guiana.

gvt *abr* (= *gouvernement*) govt.

gymkhana [ʒimkana] *nm* rally; **~ motocycliste** (motorbike) scramble (*BRIT*), motocross.

gymnase [ʒimnaz] *nm* gym(nasium).

gymnaste [ʒimnast(ə)] *nm/f* gymnast.

gymnastique [ʒimnastik] *nf* gymnastics *sg*; (*au réveil etc*) keep-fit exercises *pl*; **~ corrective** remedial gymnastics.

gynécologie [ʒinekɔlɔʒi] *nf* gynaecology (*BRIT*), gynecology (*US*).

gynécologique [ʒinekɔlɔʒik] *adj* gynaecological (*BRIT*), gynecological (*US*).

gynécologue [ʒinekɔlɔg] *nm/f* gynaecologist (*BRIT*), gynecologist (*US*).

gypse [ʒips(ə)] *nm* gypsum.

gyrophare [ʒiʀofaʀ] *nm* (*sur une voiture*) revolving (flashing) light.

H h

H, h [aʃ] nm inv H, h ♦ abr (= homme) M; (= hydrogène) H; (= heure): **à l'heure** ~ at zero hour; **bombe** ~ H bomb; **H comme Henri** H for Harry (BRIT) ou How (US).

ha. abr (= hectare) ha.

hab. abr = **habitant**.

habile [abil] adj skilful; (malin) clever.

habilement [abilmã] adv skilfully; cleverly.

habileté [abilte] nf skill, skilfulness; cleverness.

habilité, e [abilite] adj: ~ **à faire** entitled to do, empowered to do.

habiliter [abilite] vt empower, entitle.

habillage [abijaʒ] nm dressing.

habillé, e [abije] adj dressed; (chic) dressy; (TECH): ~ **de** covered with; encased in.

habillement [abijmã] nm clothes pl; (profession) clothing industry.

habiller [abije] vt to dress; (fournir en vêtements) to clothe; **s'** ~ to dress (o.s.); (se déguiser, mettre des vêtements chic) to dress up; **s'** ~ **de/en** to dress in/dress up as; **s'** ~ **chez/à** to buy one's clothes from/at.

habilleuse [abijøz] nf (CINÉ, THÉÂT) dresser.

habit [abi] nm outfit; ~**s** nmpl (vêtements) clothes; ~ **(de soirée)** tails pl; evening dress; **prendre l'** ~ (REL: entrer en religion) to enter (holy) orders.

habitable [abitabl(ə)] adj (in)habitable.

habitacle [abitakl(ə)] nm cockpit; (AUTO) passenger cell.

habitant, e [abitã, -ãt] nm/f inhabitant; (d'une maison) occupant, occupier; **loger chez l'** ~ to stay with the locals.

habitat [abita] nm housing conditions pl; (BOT, ZOOL) habitat.

habitation [abitasjɔ̃] nf living; (demeure) residence, home; (maison) house; ~**s à loyer modéré (HLM)** low-rent, state-owned housing, ≈ council housing sg (BRIT), ≈ public housing units (US).

habité, e [abite] adj inhabited; lived in.

habiter [abite] vt to live in; (suj: sentiment) to dwell in ♦ vi: ~ **à/dans** to live in ou at/in; ~ **chez** ou **avec qn** to live with sb; ~ **16 rue Montmartre** to live at number 16 rue Montmartre; ~ **rue Montmartre** to live in rue Montmartre.

habitude [abityd] nf habit; **avoir l'** ~ **de faire** to be in the habit of doing; **avoir l'** ~ **des enfants** to be used to children; **prendre l'** ~ **de faire qch** to get into the habit of doing sth;

perdre une ~ to get out of a habit; **d'** ~ usually; **comme d'** ~ as usual; **par** ~ out of habit.

habitué, e [abitye] adj: **être** ~ **à** to be used ou accustomed to ♦ nm/f regular visitor; (client) regular (customer).

habituel, le [abituɛl] adj usual.

habituellement [abituɛlmã] adv usually.

habituer [abitye] vt: ~ **qn à** to get sb used to; **s'** ~ **à** to get used to.

'hâbleur, euse ['ablœʀ, -øz] adj boastful.

'hache ['aʃ] nf axe.

'haché, e ['aʃe] adj minced (BRIT), ground (US); (persil) chopped; (fig) jerky.

'hache-légumes ['aʃlegym] nm inv vegetable chopper.

'hacher ['aʃe] vt (viande) to mince (BRIT), grind (US); (persil) to chop; ~ **menu** to mince ou grind finely; to chop finely.

'hachette ['aʃɛt] nf hatchet.

'hache-viande ['aʃvjãd] nm inv (meat) mincer (BRIT) ou grinder (US); (couteau) (meat) cleaver.

'hachis ['aʃi] nm mince no pl (BRIT), hamburger meat (US); ~ **de viande** minced (BRIT) ou ground (US) meat.

'hachisch ['aʃiʃ] nm hashish.

'hachoir ['aʃwaʀ] nm chopper; (meat) mincer (BRIT) ou grinder (US); (planche) chopping board.

'hachurer ['aʃyʀe] vt to hatch.

'hachures ['aʃyʀ] nfpl hatching sg.

'hagard, e ['agaʀ, -aʀd(ə)] adj wild, distraught.

'haie ['ɛ] nf hedge; (SPORT) hurdle; (fig: rang) line, row; **200 m** ~ **s** 200 m hurdles; ~ **d'honneur** guard of honour.

'haillons ['ajɔ̃] nmpl rags.

'haine ['ɛn] nf hatred.

'haineux, euse ['ɛnø, -øz] adj full of hatred.

'haïr ['aiʀ] vt to detest, hate; **se** ~ to hate each other.

'hais ['ɛ], **'haïs** ['ai] etc vb voir **haïr**.

'haïssable ['aisabl(ə)] adj detestable.

Haïti [aiti] n Haiti.

haïtien, ne [aisjɛ̃, -ɛn] adj Haitian.

'halage ['alaʒ] nm: **chemin de** ~ towpath.

'hâle ['al] nm (sun)tan.

'hâlé, e ['ale] adj (sun)tanned, sunburnt.

haleine [alɛn] nf breath; **perdre** ~ to get out of breath; **à perdre** ~ until one is gasping for breath; **avoir mauvaise** ~ to have bad breath; **reprendre** ~ to get one's breath back; **hors d'** ~ out of breath; **tenir en** ~ to hold spellbound; (en attente) to keep in suspense; **de longue** ~ adj long-term.

'haler ['ale] vt to haul in; (remorquer) to tow.

'haleter ['alte] vi to pant.

'hall ['ol] nm hall.

'hallali [alali] nm kill.

'halle ['al] nf (covered) market; ~**s** nfpl central food market sg.

'hallebarde ['albaʀd] nf halberd; **il pleut des**

~s (*fam*) it's bucketing down.
hallucinant, e [alysinɑ̃, -ɑ̃t] *adj* staggering.
hallucination [alysinasjɔ̃] *nf* hallucination.
hallucinatoire [alysinatwaʀ] *adj* hallucinatory.
halluciné, e [alysine] *nm/f* person suffering from hallucinations; (*fou*) (raving) lunatic.
hallucinogène [a(l)lysinɔʒɛn] *adj* hallucinogenic ♦ *nm* hallucinogen.
'**halo** ['alo] *nm* halo.
halogène [alɔʒɛn] *nm*: **lampe (à)** ~ halogen lamp.
'**halte** ['alt(ə)] *nf* stop, break; (*escale*) stopping place; (*RAIL*) halt ♦ *excl* stop!; **faire** ~ to stop.
'**halte-garderie,** *pl* '**haltes-garderies** ['altgaʀdəʀi] *nf* crèche.
haltère [altɛʀ] *nm* (*à boules, disques*) dumbbell, barbell; (**poids et**) ~s weightlifting.
haltérophile [alteʀɔfil] *nm/f* weightlifter.
haltérophilie [alteʀɔfili] *nf* weightlifting.
'**hamac** ['amak] *nm* hammock.
'**Hambourg** ['ɑ̃buʀ] *n* Hamburg.
'**hamburger** ['ɑ̃buʀgœʀ] *nm* hamburger.
'**hameau, x** ['amo] *nm* hamlet.
hameçon [amsɔ̃] *nm* (fish) hook.
'**hampe** ['ɑ̃p] *nf* (*de drapeau etc*) pole; (*de lance*) shaft.
'**hamster** ['amstɛʀ] *nm* hamster.
'**hanche** ['ɑ̃ʃ] *nf* hip.
'**hand-ball** ['ɑ̃dbal] *nm* handball.
'**handballeur, euse** ['ɑ̃dbalœʀ, -øz] *nm/f* handball player.
'**handicap** ['ɑ̃dikap] *nm* handicap.
'**handicapé, e** ['ɑ̃dikape] *adj* handicapped ♦ *nm/f* physically (*ou* mentally) handicapped person; ~ **moteur** spastic.
'**handicaper** ['ɑ̃dikape] *vt* to handicap.
'**hangar** ['ɑ̃gaʀ] *nm* shed; (*AVIAT*) hangar.
'**hanneton** ['antɔ̃] *nm* cockchafer.
'**Hanovre** ['anɔvʀ(ə)] *n* Hanover.
'**hanovrien, ne** ['anɔvʀjɛ̃, -ɛn] *adj* Hanoverian.
'**hanter** ['ɑ̃te] *vt* to haunt.
'**hantise** ['ɑ̃tiz] *nf* obsessive fear.
'**happer** ['ape] *vt* to snatch; (*suj: train etc*) to hit.
'**harangue** ['aʀɑ̃g] *nf* harangue.
'**haranguer** ['aʀɑ̃ge] *vt* to harangue.
'**haras** ['aʀɑ] *nm* stud farm.
'**harassant, e** ['aʀasɑ̃, -ɑ̃t] *adj* exhausting.
'**harcèlement** ['aʀsɛlmɑ̃] *nm* harassment; ~ **sexuel** sexual harassment.
'**harceler** ['aʀsəle] *vt* (*MIL, CHASSE*) to harass, harry; (*importuner*) to plague.
'**hardes** ['aʀd(ə)] *nfpl* rags.
'**hardi, e** ['aʀdi] *adj* bold, daring.
'**hardiesse** ['aʀdjɛs] *nf* audacity; **avoir la** ~ **de** to have the audacity *ou* effrontery to.
'**harem** ['aʀɛm] *nm* harem.
'**hareng** ['aʀɑ̃] *nm* herring.
'**hargne** ['aʀɲ(ə)] *nf* aggressivity, aggressiveness.

'**hargneusement** ['aʀɲøzmɑ̃] *adv* belligerently, aggressively.
'**hargneux, -euse** ['aʀɲ ø, -øz] *adj* (*propos, personne*) belligerent, aggressive; (*chien*) fierce.
'**haricot** ['aʀiko] *nm* bean; ~ **blanc/rouge** haricot/kidney bean; ~ **vert** French (*BRIT*) *ou* green bean.
harmonica [aʀmɔnika] *nm* mouth organ.
harmonie [aʀmɔni] *nf* harmony.
harmonieux, euse [aʀmɔnjø, -øz] *adj* harmonious.
harmonique [aʀmɔnik] *adj, nm ou nf* harmonic.
harmoniser [aʀmɔnize] *vt* to harmonize; **s'**~ (*couleurs, teintes*) to go well together.
harmonium [aʀmɔnjɔm] *nm* harmonium.
'**harnaché, e** ['aʀnaʃe] *adj* (*fig*) rigged out.
'**harnachement** ['aʀnaʃmɑ̃] *nm* (*habillement*) rig-out; (*équipement*) harness, equipment.
'**harnacher** ['aʀnaʃe] *vt* to harness.
'**harnais** ['aʀnɛ] *nm* harness.
'**haro** ['aʀo] *nm*: **crier** ~ **sur qn/qch** to inveigh against sb/sth.
'**harpe** ['aʀp(ə)] *nf* harp.
'**harpie** ['aʀpi] *nf* harpy.
'**harpiste** ['aʀpist(ə)] *nm/f* harpist.
'**harpon** ['aʀpɔ̃] *nm* harpoon.
'**harponner** ['aʀpɔne] *vt* to harpoon; (*fam*) to collar.
'**hasard** ['azaʀ] *nm*: **le** ~ chance, fate; **un** ~ a coincidence; (*aubaine, chance*) a stroke of luck; **au** ~ (*sans but*) aimlessly; (*à l'aveuglette*) at random, haphazardly; **par** ~ by chance; **comme par** ~ as if by chance; **à tout** ~ on the off chance; (*en cas de besoin*) just in case.
'**hasarder** ['azaʀde] *vt* (*mot*) to venture; (*fortune*) to risk; **se** ~ **à faire** to risk doing, venture to do.
'**hasardeux, euse** ['azaʀdø, -øz] *adj* hazardous, risky; (*hypothèse*) rash.
'**haschisch** ['aʃiʃ] *nm* hashish.
'**hâte** ['ɑt] *nf* haste; **à la** ~ hurriedly, hastily; **en** ~ posthaste, with all possible speed; **avoir** ~ **de** to be eager *ou* anxious to.
'**hâter** ['ɑte] *vt* to hasten; **se** ~ to hurry; **se** ~ **de** to hurry *ou* hasten to.
'**hâtif, ive** ['ɑtif, -iv] *adj* (*travail*) hurried; (*décision*) hasty; (*légume*) early.
'**hâtivement** ['ɑtivmɑ̃] *adv* hurriedly; hastily.
'**hauban** ['obɑ̃] *nm* (*NAVIG*) shroud.
'**hausse** ['os] *nf* rise, increase; (*de fusil*) backsight adjuster; **à la** ~ upwards; **en** ~ rising.
'**hausser** ['ose] *vt* to raise; ~ **les épaules** to shrug (one's shoulders); **se** ~ **sur la pointe des pieds** to stand (up) on tiptoe *ou* tippytoe (*US*).
'**haut, e** ['o, 'ot] *adj* high; (*grand*) tall; (*son, voix*) high(-pitched) ♦ *adv* high ♦ *nm* top (part); **de 3 m de** ~, ~ **de 3 m** 3 m high, 3 m in height; **en** ~e **montagne** high up in the mountains; **en** ~ **lieu** in high places; **à** ~e

voix, (tout) ~ aloud, out loud; **des ~s et des bas** ups and downs; **du ~ de** from the top of; **tomber de** ~ to fall from a height; *(fig)* to have one's hopes dashed; **dire qch bien** ~ to say sth plainly; **prendre qch de (très)** ~ to react haughtily to sth; **traiter qn de** ~ to treat sb with disdain; **de** ~ **en bas** from top to bottom; downwards; **en couleur** *(chose)* highly coloured; *(personne)*: **un personnage** ~ **en couleur** a colourful character; **plus** ~ higher up, further up; *(dans un texte)* above; *(parler)* louder; **en** ~ up above; at *(ou* to) the top; *(dans une maison)* upstairs; **en** ~ **de** at the top of; ~ **les mains!** hands up!, stick 'em up!; **la** ~**e couture/coiffure** haute couture/coiffure; ~**e fidélité** hi-fi, high fidelity; **la** ~**e finance** high finance; ~**e trahison** high treason.

'**hautain, e** ['otɛ̃, -ɛn] *adj (personne, regard)* haughty.

'**hautbois** ['obwa] *nm* oboe.

'**hautboïste** ['oboist(ə)] *nm/f* oboist.

'**haut-de-forme,** *pl* '**hauts-de-forme** ['odfɔʀm(ə)] *nm* top hat.

'**haute-contre,** *pl* '**hautes-contre** ['otkɔ̃tʀ(ə)] *nf* counter-tenor.

'**hautement** ['otmɑ̃] *adv (ouvertement)* openly; *(supérieurement)*: ~ **qualifié** highly qualified.

'**hauteur** ['otœʀ] *nf* height; *(GÉO)* height, hill; *(fig)* loftiness; haughtiness; **à** ~ **de** up to (the level of); **à** ~ **des yeux** at eye level; **à la** ~ **de** *(sur la même ligne)* level with; by; *(fig)* equal to; **à la** ~ *(fig)* up to it, equal to the task.

'**Haute-Volta** ['otvɔlta] *nf*: **la** ~ Upper Volta.

'**haut-fond,** *pl* '**hauts-fonds** ['ofɔ̃] *nm* shallow.

'**haut-fourneau,** *pl* '**hauts-fourneaux** ['ofuʀno] *nm* blast *ou* smelting furnace.

'**haut-le-cœur** ['olkœʀ] *nm inv* retch, heave.

'**haut-le-corps** ['olkɔʀ] *nm inv* start, jump.

'**haut-parleur,** *pl* '**haut-parleurs** ['opaʀlœʀ] *nm* (loud)speaker.

'**hauturier, ière** ['otyʀje, -jɛʀ] *adj (NAVIG)* deep-sea.

'**havanais, e** ['avanɛ, -ɛz] *adj* of *ou* from Havana.

'**Havane** ['avan] *nf*: **la** ~ Havana ♦ *nm*: '**h**~ *(cigare)* Havana.

'**hâve** ['av] *adj* gaunt.

'**havrais, e** ['avʀɛ, -ɛz] *adj* of *ou* from Le Havre.

'**havre** ['avʀ(ə)] *nm* haven.

'**havresac** ['avʀəsak] *nm* haversack.

Hawaï [awai] *n* Hawaii; **les îles** ~ the Hawaiian Islands.

hawaïen, ne [awajɛ̃, -ɛn] *adj* Hawaiian ♦ *nm (LING)* Hawaiian.

'**Haye** ['ɛ] *n*: **la** ~ the Hague.

'**hayon** ['ɛjɔ̃] *nm* tailgate.

HCR *sigle m* (= *Haut-Commissariat des Nations unies pour les réfugiés)* UNHCR.

hdb. *abr* (= *heures de bureau)* o.h. (= *office hours)*.

'**hé** ['e] *excl* hey!

hebdo [ɛbdo] *nm (fam)* weekly.

hebdomadaire [ɛbdɔmadɛʀ] *adj, nm* weekly.

hébergement [ebɛʀʒəmɑ̃] *nm* accommodation, lodging; taking in.

héberger [ebɛʀʒe] *vt* to accommodate, lodge; *(réfugiés)* to take in.

hébété, e [ebete] *adj* dazed.

hébétude [ebetyd] *nf* stupor.

hébraïque [ebʀaik] *adj* Hebrew, Hebraic.

hébreu, x [ebʀø] *adj m, nm* Hebrew.

Hébrides [ebʀid] *nf*: **les** ~ the Hebrides.

HEC *sigle fpl* (= *École des hautes études commerciales) grande école for management and business studies.*

hécatombe [ekatɔ̃b] *nf* slaughter.

hectare [ɛktaʀ] *nm* hectare, 10,000 square metres.

hecto... [ɛkto] *préfixe* hecto....

hectolitre [ɛktɔlitʀ(ə)] *nm* hectolitre.

hédoniste [edɔnist(ə)] *adj* hedonistic.

hégémonie [eʒemɔni] *nf* hegemony.

'**hein** ['ɛ̃] *excl* eh?; *(sollicitant l'approbation)*: **tu m'approuves,** ~? so I did the right thing then?; **Paul est venu,** ~? Paul came, did he?; **que fais-tu,** ~? hey! what are you doing?

'**hélas** ['elas] *excl* alas! ♦ *adv* unfortunately.

'**héler** ['ele] *vt* to hail.

hélice [elis] *nf* propeller.

hélicoïdal, e, aux [elikɔidal, -o] *adj* helical; helicoid.

hélicoptère [elikɔptɛʀ] *nm* helicopter.

hélio(gravure) [eljɔgʀavyʀ] *nf* heliogravure.

héliomarin, e [eljɔmaʀɛ̃, -in] *adj*: **centre** ~ centre offering sea and sun therapy.

héliotrope [eljɔtʀɔp] *nm (BOT)* heliotrope.

héliport [elipɔʀ] *nm* heliport.

héliporté, e [elipɔʀte] *adj* transported by helicopter.

hélium [eljɔm] *nm* helium.

hellénique [elenik] *adj* Hellenic.

hellénisant, e [elenizɑ̃, -ɑ̃t], **helléniste** [elenist(ə)] *nm/f* hellenist.

Helsinki [ɛlzinki] *n* Helsinki.

helvète [ɛlvɛt] *adj* Helvetian ♦ *nm/f*: **H**~ Helvetian.

Helvétie [ɛlvesi] *nf*: **la** ~ Helvetia.

helvétique [ɛlvetik] *adj* Swiss.

hématologie [ematɔlɔʒi] *nf (MÉD)* haematology.

hématome [ematom] *nm* haematoma.

hémicycle [emisikl(ə)] *nm* semicircle; *(POL)*: **l'**~ the benches *(in French parliament)*.

hémiplégie [emipleʒi] *nf* paralysis of one side, hemiplegia.

hémisphère [emisfɛʀ] *nf*: ~ **nord/sud** northern/southern hemisphere.

hémisphérique [emisfeʀik] *adj* hemispherical.

hémoglobine [emɔglɔbin] *nf* haemoglobin

(*BRIT*), hemoglobin (*US*).
hémophile [emɔfil] *adj* haemophiliac (*BRIT*), hemophiliac (*US*).
hémophilie [emɔfili] *nf* haemophilia (*BRIT*), hemophilia (*US*).
hémorragie [emɔʀaʒi] *nf* bleeding *no pl*, haemorrhage (*BRIT*), hemorrhage (*US*); ~ **cérébrale** cerebral haemorrhage; ~ **interne** internal bleeding *ou* haemorrhage.
hémorroïdes [emɔʀɔid] *nfpl* piles, haemorrhoids (*BRIT*), hemorrhoids (*US*).
hémostatique [emɔstatik] *adj* haemostatic (*BRIT*), hemostatic (*US*).
'henné ['ene] *nm* henna.
'hennir ['eniʀ] *vi* to neigh, whinny.
'hennissement ['enismɑ̃] *nm* neighing, whinnying.
'hep ['ɛp] *excl* hey!
hépatite [epatit] *nf* hepatitis, liver infection.
héraldique [eʀaldik] *adj* heraldry.
herbacé, e [ɛʀbase] *adj* herbaceous.
herbage [ɛʀbaʒ] *nm* pasture.
herbe [ɛʀb(ə)] *nf* grass; (*CULIN, MÉD*) herb; **en** ~ unripe; (*fig*) budding; **touffe/brin d'**~ clump/blade of grass.
herbeux, euse [ɛʀbø, -øz] *adj* grassy.
herbicide [ɛʀbisid] *nm* weed-killer.
herbier [ɛʀbje] *nm* herbarium.
herbivore [ɛʀbivɔʀ] *nm* herbivore.
herboriser [ɛʀbɔʀize] *vi* to collect plants.
herboriste [ɛʀbɔʀist(ə)] *nm/f* herbalist.
herboristerie [ɛʀbɔʀistʀi] *nf* (*magasin*) herbalist's shop; (*commerce*) herb trade.
herculéen, ne [ɛʀkyleɛ̃, -ɛn] *adj* (*fig*) herculean.
'hère ['ɛʀ] *nm*: **pauvre** ~ poor wretch.
héréditaire [eʀeditɛʀ] *adj* hereditary.
hérédité [eʀedite] *nf* heredity.
hérésie [eʀezi] *nf* heresy.
hérétique [eʀetik] *nm/f* heretic.
'hérissé, e ['eʀise] *adj* bristling; ~ **de** spiked with; (*fig*) bristling with.
'hérisser ['eʀise] *vt*: ~ **qn** (*fig*) to ruffle sb; **se** ~ *vi* to bristle, bristle up.
'hérisson ['eʀisɔ̃] *nm* hedgehog.
héritage [eʀitaʒ] *nm* inheritance; (*fig*) heritage; (*: legs*) legacy; **faire un (petit)** ~ to come into (a little) money.
hériter [eʀite] *vi*: ~ **de qch (de qn)** to inherit sth (from sb); ~ **de qn** to inherit sb's property.
héritier, ière [eʀitje, -jɛʀ] *nm/f* heir/heiress.
hermaphrodite [ɛʀmafʀɔdit] *adj* (*BOT, ZOOL*) hermaphrodite.
hermétique [ɛʀmetik] *adj* (*à l'air*) airtight; (*à l'eau*) watertight; (*fig: écrivain, style*) abstruse; (*: visage*) impenetrable.
hermétiquement [ɛʀmetikmɑ̃] *adv* hermetically.
hermine [ɛʀmin] *nf* ermine.
'hernie ['ɛʀni] *nf* hernia.
héroïne [eʀɔin] *nf* heroine; (*drogue*) heroin.

héroïnomane [eʀɔinɔman] *nm/f* heroin addict.
héroïque [eʀɔik] *adj* heroic.
héroïquement [eʀɔikmɑ̃] *adv* heroically.
héroïsme [eʀɔism(ə)] *nm* heroism.
'héron ['eʀɔ̃] *nm* heron.
'héros ['eʀo] *nm* hero.
herpès [ɛʀpɛs] *nm* herpes.
'herse ['ɛʀs(ə)] *nf* harrow; (*de château*) portcullis.
hertz [ɛʀts] *nm* (*ÉLEC*) hertz.
hertzien, ne [ɛʀtsjɛ̃, -ɛn] *adj* (*ÉLEC*) Hertzian.
hésitant, e [ezitɑ̃, -ɑ̃t] *adj* hesitant.
hésitation [ezitɑsjɔ̃] *nf* hesitation.
hésiter [ezite] *vi*: ~ **(à faire)** to hesitate (to do); ~ **sur qch** to hesitate over sth.
hétéro [eteʀo] *adj inv* (= *hétérosexuel(le)*) hetero.
hétéroclite [eteʀɔklit] *adj* heterogeneous; (*objets*) sundry.
hétérogène [eteʀɔʒɛn] *adj* heterogeneous.
hétérosexuel, le [eteʀɔsɛkɥɛl] *adj* heterosexual.
'hêtre ['ɛtʀ(ə)] *nm* beech.
heure [œʀ] *nf* hour; (*SCOL*) period; (*moment, moment fixé*) time; **c'est l'**~ it's time; **pourriez-vous me donner l'**~, **s'il vous plaît?** could you tell me the time, please?; **quelle** ~ **est-il?** what time is it?; **2** ~**s (du matin)** 2 o'clock (in the morning); **à la bonne** ~! (*parfois ironique*) splendid!; **être à l'**~ to be on time; (*montre*) to be right; **le bus passe à l'**~ the bus runs on the hour; **mettre à l'**~ to set right; **100 km à l'**~ ≈ 60 miles an *ou* per hour; **à toute** ~ at any time; **24** ~**s sur 24** round the clock, 24 hours a day; **à l'**~ **qu'il est** at this time (of day); (*fig*) now; **à l'**~ **actuelle** at the present time; **sur l'**~ at once; **pour l'**~ for the time being; **d'**~ **en** ~ from one hour to the next; (*régulièrement*) hourly; **d'une** ~ **à l'autre** from hour to hour; **de bonne** ~ early; **2** ~**s de marche/travail** 2 hours' walking/work; **une** ~ **d'arrêt** an hour's break *ou* stop; ~ **d'été** summer time (*BRIT*), daylight saving time (*US*); ~ **de pointe** rush hour; ~**s de bureau** office hours; ~**s supplémentaires** overtime *sg*.
heureusement [œʀøzmɑ̃] *adv* (*par bonheur*) fortunately, luckily; ~ **que** ... it's a good job that ..., fortunately ....
heureux, euse [œʀø, -øz] *adj* happy; (*chanceux*) lucky, fortunate; (*judicieux*) felicitous, fortunate; **être** ~ **de qch** to be pleased *ou* happy about sth; **être** ~ **de faire/que** to be pleased *ou* happy to do/that; **s'estimer** ~ **de qch/que** to consider o.s. fortunate with/that; **encore** ~ **que** ... just as well that ....
'heurt ['œʀ] *nm* (*choc*) collision; ~**s** *nmpl* (*fig*) clashes.
'heurté, e ['œʀte] *adj* (*fig*) jerky, uneven; (*: couleurs*) clashing.
'heurter ['œʀte] *vt* (*mur*) to strike, hit; (*personne*) to collide with; (*fig*) to go against, up-

set; **se** ~ (*couleurs, tons*) to clash; **se** ~ **à** to collide with; (*fig*) to come up against; ~ **qn de front** to clash head-on with sb.

'**heurtoir** ['œʀtwaʀ] *nm* door knocker.

'**hévéa** [evea] *nm* rubber tree.

hexagonal, e, aux [ɛgzagɔnal, -o] *adj* hexagonal; (*français*) French (*see note at hexagone*).

'**hexagone** [ɛgzagɔn] *nm* hexagon; (*la France*) France (*because of its roughly hexagonal shape*).

HF *sigle f* (= *haute fréquence*) HF.

'**hiatus** [jatys] *nm* hiatus.

hibernation [ibɛʀnasjɔ̃] *nf* hibernation.

hiberner [ibɛʀne] *vi* to hibernate.

hibiscus [ibiskys] *nm* hibiscus.

'**hibou, x** ['ibu] *nm* owl.

'**hic** ['ik] *nm* (*fam*) snag.

'**hideusement** ['idøzmɑ̃] *adv* hideously.

'**hideux, euse** ['idø, -øz] *adj* hideous.

'**hier** [jɛʀ] *adv* yesterday; ~ **matin/soir/midi** yesterday morning/evening/at midday; **toute la journée d'**~ all day yesterday; **toute la matinée d'**~ all yesterday morning.

'**hiérarchie** ['jeʀaʀʃi] *nf* hierarchy.

'**hiérarchique** ['jeʀaʀʃik] *adj* hierarchic.

'**hiérarchiquement** ['jeʀaʀʃikmɑ̃] *adv* hierarchically.

'**hiérarchiser** ['jeʀaʀʃize] *vt* to organize into a hierarchy.

'**hiéroglyphe** ['jeʀɔglif] *nm* hieroglyphic.

'**hiéroglyphique** ['jeʀɔglifik] *adj* hieroglyphic.

'**hi-fi** ['ifi] *nf inv* hi-fi.

hilarant, e [ilaʀɑ̃, -ɑ̃t] *adj* hilarious.

hilare [ilaʀ] *adj* mirthful.

hilarité [ilaʀite] *nf* hilarity, mirth.

Himalaya [imalaja] *nm*: **l'**~ the Himalayas *pl*.

himalayen, ne [imalajɛ̃, -ɛn] *adj* Himalayan.

hindou, e [ɛ̃du] *adj, nm/f* Hindu; (*Indien*) Indian.

hindouisme [ɛ̃duism(ə)] *nm* Hinduism.

Hindoustan [ɛ̃dustɑ̃] *nm*: **l'**~ Hindustan.

'**hippie** ['ipi] *nm/f* hippy.

hippique [ipik] *adj* equestrian, horse *cpd*.

hippisme [ipism(ə)] *nm* (horse-)riding.

hippocampe [ipɔkɑ̃p] *nm* sea horse.

hippodrome [ipɔdʀom] *nm* racecourse.

hippophagique [ipɔfaʒik] *adj*: **boucherie** ~ horse butcher's.

hippopotame [ipɔpɔtam] *nm* hippopotamus.

hirondelle [iʀɔ̃dɛl] *nf* swallow.

hirsute [iʀsyt] *adj* (*personne*) hairy; (*barbe*) shaggy; (*tête*) tousled.

hispanique [ispanik] *adj* Hispanic.

hispanisant, e [ispanizɑ̃, -ɑ̃t] *adj*, **hispaniste** [ispanist(ə)] *nm/f* Hispanist.

hispano-américain, e [ispanɔameʀikɛ̃, -ɛn] *adj* Spanish-American.

hispano-arabe [ispanɔaʀab] *adj* Hispano-Moresque.

'**hisser** ['ise] *vt* to hoist, haul up; **se** ~ **sur** to haul o.s. up onto.

histoire [istwaʀ] *nf* (*science, événements*) his-

tory; (*anecdote, récit, mensonge*) story; (*affaire*) business *no pl*; (*chichis: gén pl*) fuss *no pl*; ~**s** *nfpl* (*ennuis*) trouble *sg*; **l'**~ **de France** French history, the history of France; **l'**~ **sainte** biblical history; **une** ~ **de** (*fig*) a question of.

histologie [istɔlɔʒi] *nf* histology.

historien, ne [istɔʀjɛ̃, -ɛn] *nm/f* historian.

historique [istɔʀik] *adj* historical; (*important*) historic ♦ *nm* (*exposé, récit*): **faire l'**~ **de** to give the background to.

historiquement [istɔʀikmɑ̃] *adv* historically.

'**hit-parade** ['itpaʀad] *nm*: **le** ~ the charts.

HIV *sigle m* (= *human immunodeficiency virus*) HIV.

hiver [ivɛʀ] *nm* winter; **en** ~ in winter.

hivernal, e, aux [ivɛʀnal, -o] *adj* (*de l'hiver*) winter *cpd*; (*comme en hiver*) wintry.

hivernant, e [ivɛʀnɑ̃, -ɑ̃t] *n* winter holiday-maker.

hiverner [ivɛʀne] *vi* to winter.

HLM *sigle m ou f* (= *habitations à loyer modéré*) low-rent, state-owned housing; **un(e)** ~ ≈ a council flat (*ou* house) (*BRIT*), ≈ a public housing unit (*US*).

Hme *abr* (= *homme*) M.

HO *abr* (= *hors œuvre*) labour not included (*on invoices*).

'**hobby** ['ɔbi] *nm* hobby.

'**hochement** ['ɔʃmɑ̃] *nm*: ~ **de tête** nod; shake of the head.

'**hocher** ['ɔʃe] *vt*: ~ **la tête** to nod; (*signe négatif ou dubitatif*) to shake one's head.

'**hochet** ['ɔʃɛ] *nm* rattle.

'**hockey** ['ɔkɛ] *nm*: ~ **(sur glace/gazon)** (ice/field) hockey.

'**hockeyeur, euse** ['ɔkejœʀ, -øz] *nm/f* hockey player.

'**holà** ['ɔla] *nm*: **mettre le** ~ **à qch** to put a stop to sth.

'**holding** ['ɔldiŋ] *nm* holding company.

'**hold-up** ['ɔldœp] *nm inv* hold-up.

'**hollandais, e** ['ɔlɑ̃dɛ, -ɛz] *adj* Dutch ♦ *nm* (*LING*) Dutch ♦ *nm/f*: **H**~, **e** Dutchman/woman; **les H**~ the Dutch.

'**Hollande** ['ɔlɑ̃d] *nf*: **la** ~ Holland ♦ *nm*: **h**~ (*fromage*) Dutch cheese.

holocauste [ɔlɔkost(ə)] *nm* holocaust.

hologramme [ɔlɔgʀam] *nm* hologram.

'**homard** ['ɔmaʀ] *nm* lobster.

homéopathe [ɔmeɔpat] *n* homoeopath.

homéopathie [ɔmeɔpati] *nf* homoeopathy.

homéopathique [ɔmeɔpatik] *adj* homoeopathic.

homérique [ɔmeʀik] *adj* Homeric.

homicide [ɔmisid] *nm* murder ♦ *nm/f* murderer/eress; ~ **involontaire** manslaughter.

hommage [ɔmaʒ] *nm* tribute; ~**s** *nmpl*: **présenter ses** ~**s** to pay one's respects; **rendre** ~ **à** to pay tribute *ou* homage to; **en** ~ **de** as a token of; **faire** ~ **de qch à qn** to present sb with sth.

homme [ɔm] *nm* man; (*espèce humaine*): **l'~** man, mankind; **~ d'affaires** businessman; **~ des cavernes** caveman; **~ d'Église** churchman, clergyman; **~ d'État** statesman; **~ de loi** lawyer; **~ de main** hired man; **~ de paille** stooge; **l'~ de la rue** the man in the street; **~ à tout faire** odd-job man.

homme-grenouille, *pl* **hommesgrenouilles** [ɔmɡrɔnuj] *nm* frogman.

homme-orchestre, *pl* **hommes-orchestres** [ɔmɔrkɛstr(ə)] *nm* one-man band.

homme-sandwich, *pl* **hommes-sandwichs** [ɔmsɑ̃dwitʃ] *nm* sandwich (board) man.

homo [ɔmo] *adj, nm/f* = **homosexuel.**

homogène [ɔmɔʒɛn] *adj* homogeneous.

homogénéisé, e [ɔmɔʒeneize] *adj:* **lait ~** homogenized milk.

homogénéité [ɔmɔʒeneite] *nf* homogeneity.

homologation [ɔmɔlɔɡasjɔ̃] *nf* ratification; official recognition.

homologue [ɔmɔlɔɡ] *nm/f* counterpart, opposite number.

homologué, e [ɔmɔlɔɡe] *adj* (*SPORT*) officially recognized, ratified; (*tarif*) authorized.

homologuer [ɔmɔlɔɡe] *vt* (*JUR*) to ratify; (*SPORT*) to recognize officially, ratify.

homonyme [ɔmɔnim] *nm* (*LING*) homonym; (*d'une personne*) namesake.

homosexualité [ɔmɔsɛksyalite] *nf* homosexuality.

homosexuel, le [ɔmɔsɛksyɛl] *adj* homosexual.

'Honduras ['ɔ̃dyras] *nm:* **le ~** Honduras.

'hondurien, ne ['ɔ̃dyrjɛ̃, -ɛn] *adj* Honduran.

'Hong-Kong ['ɔ̃ɡkɔ̃ɡ] *n* Hong Kong.

'hongre ['ɔ̃ɡr(ə)] *adj* (*cheval*) gelded ♦ *nm* gelding.

'Hongrie ['ɔ̃ɡri] *nf:* **la ~** Hungary.

'hongrois, e ['ɔ̃ɡrwa, -waz] *adj* Hungarian ♦ *nm* (*LING*) Hungarian ♦ *nm/f:* **'H~, e** Hungarian.

honnête [ɔnɛt] *adj* (*intègre*) honest; (*juste, satisfaisant*) fair.

honnêtement [ɔnɛtmɑ̃] *adv* honestly.

honnêteté [ɔnɛtte] *nf* honesty.

honneur [ɔnœr] *nm* honour; (*mérite*): **l'~ lui revient** the credit is his; **à qui ai-je l'~?** to whom have I the pleasure of speaking?; **"j'ai l'~ de ..."** "I have the honour of ..."; **en l'~ de** (*personne*) in honour of; (*événement*) on the occasion of; **faire ~ à** (*engagements*) to honour; (*famille, professeur*) to be a credit to; (*fig: repas etc*) to do justice to; **être à l'~** to be in the place of honour; **être en ~** to be in favour; **membre d'~** honorary member; **table d'~** top table.

Honolulu [ɔnɔlyly] *n* Honolulu.

honorable [ɔnɔrabl(ə)] *adj* worthy, honourable; (*suffisant*) decent.

honorablement [ɔnɔrabləmɑ̃] *adv* honourably; decently.

honoraire [ɔnɔrɛr] *adj* honorary; **~s** *nmpl*

fees; **professeur ~** professor emeritus.

honorer [ɔnɔre] *vt* to honour; (*estimer*) to hold in high regard; (*faire honneur à*) to do credit to; **~ qn de** to honour sb with; **s'~ de** to pride o.s. upon.

honorifique [ɔnɔrifik] *adj* honorary.

'honte ['ɔ̃t] *nf* shame; **avoir ~ de** to be ashamed of; **faire ~ à qn** to make sb (feel) ashamed.

'honteusement ['ɔ̃tøzmɑ̃] *adv* ashamedly; shamefully.

'honteux, euse ['ɔ̃tø, -øz] *adj* ashamed; (*conduite, acte*) shameful, disgraceful.

hôpital, aux [ɔpital, -o] *nm* hospital.

'hoquet ['ɔkɛ] *nm* hiccough; **avoir le ~** to have (the) hiccoughs.

'hoqueter ['ɔkte] *vi* to hiccough.

horaire [ɔrɛr] *adj* hourly ♦ *nm* timetable, schedule; **~s** *nmpl* (*heures de travail*) hours; **~ flexible** *ou* **mobile** *ou* **à la carte** *ou* **souple** flex(i)time.

'horde ['ɔrd(ə)] *nf* horde.

'horions ['ɔrjɔ̃] *nmpl* blows.

horizon [ɔrizɔ̃] *nm* horizon; (*paysage*) landscape, view; **sur l'~** on the skyline *ou* horizon.

horizontal, e, aux [ɔrizɔ̃tal, -o] *adj* horizontal ♦ *nf:* **à l'~e** on the horizontal.

horizontalement [ɔrizɔ̃talmɑ̃] *adv* horizontally.

horloge [ɔrlɔʒ] *nf* clock; **l'~ parlante** the speaking clock; **~ normande** grandfather clock; **~ physiologique** biological clock.

horloger, ère [ɔrlɔʒe, -ɛr] *nm/f* watchmaker; clockmaker.

horlogerie [ɔrlɔʒri] *nf* watchmaking; watchmaker's (shop); clockmaker's (shop); **pièces d'~** watch parts *ou* components.

'hormis ['ɔrmi] *prép* save.

hormonal, e, aux [ɔrmɔnal, -o] *adj* hormonal.

hormone [ɔrmɔn] *nf* hormone.

horodaté, e [ɔrɔdate] *adj* (*ticket*) time- and date-stamped; (*stationnement*) pay and display.

horodateur, trice [ɔrɔdatœr, -tris] *adj* (*appareil*) for stamping the time and date ♦ *nm/f* (parking) ticket machine.

horoscope [ɔrɔskɔp] *nm* horoscope.

horreur [ɔrœr] *nf* horror; **avoir ~ de** to loathe, detest; **quelle ~!** how awful!; **cela me fait ~** I find that awful.

horrible [ɔribl(ə)] *adj* horrible.

horriblement [ɔribləmɑ̃] *adv* horribly.

horrifiant, e [ɔrifjɑ̃, -ɑ̃t] *adj* horrifying.

horrifier [ɔrifje] *vt* to horrify.

horrifique [ɔrifik] *adj* horrific.

horripilant, e [ɔripilɑ̃, -ɑ̃t] *adj* exasperating.

horripiler [ɔripile] *vt* to exasperate.

'hors ['ɔr] *prép* except (for); **~ de** out of; **~ ligne, ~ pair** outstanding; **~ de propos** inopportune; **~ série** (*sur mesure*) made-to-order; (*exceptionnel*) exceptional; **~ service (HS), ~**

d'usage out of service; **être ~ de soi** to be beside o.s.

hors-bord ['ɔRbɔR] *nm inv* outboard motor; (*canot*) speedboat (with outboard motor).

hors-concours ['ɔRkɔ̃kuR] *adj inv* ineligible to compete; (*fig*) in a class of one's own.

hors-d'œuvre ['ɔRdœvR(ə)] *nm inv* hors d'œuvre.

hors-jeu ['ɔRʒø] *nm inv* being offside *no pl*.

hors-la-loi ['ɔRlalwa] *nm inv* outlaw.

hors-piste(s) ['ɔRpist] *nm inv* (*SKI*) cross-country.

hors-taxe [ɔRtaks] *adj* (*sur une facture, prix*) excluding VAT; (*boutique, marchandises*) duty-free.

hors-texte ['ɔRtɛkst(ə)] *nm inv* plate.

hortensia [ɔRtɑ̃sja] *nm* hydrangea.

horticole [ɔRtikɔl] *adj* horticultural.

horticulteur, trice [ɔRtikyltœR, -tRis] *nm/f* horticulturalist (*BRIT*), horticulturist (*US*).

horticulture [ɔRtikyltyR] *nf* horticulture.

hospice [ɔspis] *nm* (*de vieillards*) home; (*asile*) hospice.

hospitalier, ière [ɔspitalje, -jɛR] *adj* (*accueillant*) hospitable; (*MÉD: service, centre*) hospital *cpd*.

hospitalisation [ɔspitalizɑsjɔ̃] *nf* hospitalization.

hospitaliser [ɔspitalize] *vt* to take (*ou* send) to hospital, hospitalize.

hospitalité [ɔspitalite] *nf* hospitality.

hospitalo-universitaire [ɔspitaloynivɛRsitɛR] *adj*: **centre ~ (CHU)** ≈ (teaching) hospital.

hostie [ɔsti] *nf* host (*REL*).

hostile [ɔstil] *adj* hostile.

hostilité [ɔstilite] *nf* hostility; **~s** *nfpl* hostilities.

hôte [ot] *nm* (*maître de maison*) host; (*client*) patron; (*fig*) inhabitant, occupant ♦ *nm/f* (*invité*) guest; **~ payant** paying guest.

hôtel [otɛl] *nm* hotel; **aller à l'~** to stay in a hotel; **~ (particulier)** (private) mansion; **~ de ville** town hall.

hôtelier, ière [otəlje, -jɛR] *adj* hotel *cpd* ♦ *nm/f* hotelier, hotel-keeper.

hôtellerie [otɛlRi] *nf* (*profession*) hotel business; (*auberge*) inn.

hôtesse [otɛs] *nf* hostess; **~ de l'air** air hostess (*BRIT*) *ou* stewardess; **~ (d'accueil)** receptionist.

hotte ['ɔt] *nf* (*panier*) basket (*carried on the back*); (*de cheminée*) hood; **~ aspirante** cooker hood.

houblon ['ublɔ̃] *nm* (*BOT*) hop; (*pour la bière*) hops *pl*.

houe ['u] *nf* hoe.

houille ['uj] *nf* coal; **~ blanche** hydroelectric power.

houiller, ère ['uje, -ɛR] *adj* coal *cpd*; (*terrain*) coal-bearing ♦ *nf* coal mine.

houle ['ul] *nf* swell.

houlette ['ulɛt] *nf*: **sous la ~ de** under the

guidance of.

houleux, euse ['ulø, -øz] *adj* heavy, swelling; (*fig*) stormy, turbulent.

houppe ['up] *nf*, **houppette** ['upɛt] *nf* powder puff; (*cheveux*) tuft.

hourra ['uRa] *nm* cheer ♦ *excl* hurrah!

houspiller ['uspije] *vt* to scold.

housse ['us] *nf* cover; (*pour protéger provisoirement*) dust cover; (*pour recouvrir à neuf*) loose *ou* stretch cover; **~ (penderie)** hanging wardrobe.

houx ['u] *nm* holly.

HS *abr* = **hors service**.

HT *abr* = **hors taxe**.

hublot ['yblo] *nm* porthole.

huche ['yʃ] *nf*: **~ à pain** bread bin.

huées ['ɥe] *nfpl* boos.

huer ['ɥe] *vt* to boo; (*hibou, chouette*) to hoot.

huile [ɥil] *nf* oil; (*ART*) oil painting; (*fam*) bigwig; **mer d'~** (*très calme*) glassy sea, sea of glass; **faire tache d'~** (*fig*) to spread; **~ d'arachide** groundnut oil; **~ essentielle** essential oil; **~ de foie de morue** cod-liver oil; **~ de ricin** castor oil; **~ solaire** suntan oil; **~ de table** salad oil.

huiler [ɥile] *vt* to oil.

huilerie [ɥilRi] *nf* (*usine*) oil-works.

huileux, euse [ɥilø, -øz] *adj* oily.

huilier [ɥilje] *nm* (oil and vinegar) cruet.

huis [ɥi] *nm*: **à ~ clos** in camera.

huissier [ɥisje] *nm* usher; (*JUR*) ≈ bailiff.

huit ['ɥi(t)] *num* eight; **samedi en ~** a week on Saturday; **dans ~ jours** in a week('s time).

huitaine ['ɥitɛn] *nf*: **une ~ de** about eight, eight or so; **une ~ de jours** a week or so.

huitante ['ɥitɑ̃t] *num* (*Suisse*) eighty.

huitième ['ɥitjɛm] *num* eighth.

huître [ɥitR(ə)] *nf* oyster.

hululement ['ylylmɑ̃] *nm* hooting.

hululer ['ylyle] *vi* to hoot.

humain, e [ymɛ̃, -ɛn] *adj* human; (*compatissant*) humane ♦ *nm* human (being).

humainement [ymɛnmɑ̃] *adv* humanly, humanely.

humanisation [ymanizɑsjɔ̃] *nf* humanization.

humaniser [ymanize] *vt* to humanize.

humaniste [ymanist(ə)] *nm/f* (*LING*) classicist; humanist.

humanitaire [ymanitɛR] *adj* humanitarian.

humanitarisme [ymanitaRism(ə)] *nm* humanitarianism.

humanité [ymanite] *nf* humanity.

humanoïde [ymanɔid] *nm/f* humanoid.

humble [œ̃bl(ə)] *adj* humble.

humblement [œ̃bləmɑ̃] *adv* humbly.

humecter [ymɛkte] *vt* to dampen; **s'~ les lèvres** to moisten one's lips.

humer ['yme] *vt* to inhale; (*pour sentir*) to smell.

humérus [ymeRys] *nm* (*ANAT*) humerus.

humeur [ymœR] *nf* mood; (*tempérament*) temper; (*irritation*) bad temper; **de bonne/**

mauvaise ~ in a good/bad mood; **être d'~ à faire qch** to be in the mood for doing sth.
humide [ymid] *adj* (*linge*) damp; (*main, yeux*) moist; (*climat, chaleur*) humid; (*saison, route*) wet.
humidificateur [ymidifikatœR] *nm* humidifier.
humidifier [ymidifje] *vt* to humidify.
humidité [ymidite] *nf* humidity; dampness; **traces d'~** traces of moisture *ou* damp.
humiliant, e [ymiljɑ̃, -ɑ̃t] *adj* humiliating.
humiliation [ymiljasjɔ̃] *nf* humiliation.
humilier [ymilje] *vt* to humiliate; **s'~ devant qn** to humble o.s. before sb.
humilité [ymilite] *nf* humility.
humoriste [ymɔRist(ə)] *nm/f* humorist.
humoristique [ymɔRistik] *adj* humorous; humoristic.
humour [ymuR] *nm* humour; **avoir de l'~** to have a sense of humour; ~ **noir** sick humour.
humus [ymys] *nm* humus.
'huppé, e ['ype] *adj* crested; (*fam*) posh.
'hurlement ['yRləmɑ̃] *nm* howling *no pl*, howl; yelling *no pl*, yell.
'hurler ['yRle] *vi* to howl, yell; (*fig: vent*) to howl; (: *couleurs etc*) to clash; ~ **à la mort** (*suj: chien*) to bay at the moon.
hurluberlu [yRlybeRly] *nm* (*péj*) crank ♦ *adj* cranky.
'hutte ['yt] *nf* hut.
hybride [ibRid] *adj* hybrid.
hydratant, e [idratɑ̃, -ɑ̃t] *adj* (*crème*) moisturizing.
hydrate [idrat] *nm*: ~**s de carbone** carbohydrates.
hydrater [idrate] *vt* to hydrate.
hydraulique [idRolik] *adj* hydraulic.
hydravion [idRavjɔ̃] *nm* seaplane, hydroplane.
hydro... [idRo] *préfixe* hydro....
hydrocarbure [idRokaRbyR] *nm* hydrocarbon.
hydrocution [idRokysjɔ̃] *nf* immersion syncope.
hydro-électrique [idRoelɛktRik] *adj* hydroelectric.
hydrogène [idRoʒɛn] *nm* hydrogen.
hydroglisseur [idRoglisœR] *nm* hydroplane.
hydrographie [idRoɡRafi] *nf* (*fleuves*) hydrography.
hydrophile [idRofil] *adj voir* **coton**.
hyène [jɛn] *nf* hyena.
hygiène [iʒjɛn] *nf* hygiene; ~ **intime** personal hygiene.
hygiénique [iʒenik] *adj* hygienic.
hymne [imn(ə)] *nm* hymn; ~ **national** national anthem.
hyper... [ipeR] *préfixe* hyper....
hypermarché [ipeRmaRʃe] *nm* hypermarket.
hypermétrope [ipeRmetRɔp] *adj* long-sighted.
hypernerveux, euse [ipeRnɛRvø, -øz] *adj* highly-strung.
hypersensible [ipeRsɑ̃sibl(ə)] *adj* hypersensitive.

hypertendu, e [ipeRtɑ̃dy] *adj* having high blood pressure, hypertensive.
hypertension [ipeRtɑ̃sjɔ̃] *nf* high blood pressure, hypertension.
hypertrophié, e [ipeRtRɔfje] *adj* hypertrophic.
hypnose [ipnoz] *nf* hypnosis.
hypnotique [ipnɔtik] *adj* hypnotic.
hypnotiser [ipnɔtize] *vt* to hypnotize.
hypnotiseur [ipnɔtizœR] *nm* hypnotist.
hypnotisme [ipnɔtism(ə)] *nm* hypnotism.
hypocondriaque [ipɔkɔ̃dRijak] *adj* hypochondriac.
hypocrisie [ipɔkRizi] *nf* hypocrisy.
hypocrite [ipɔkRit] *adj* hypocritical ♦ *nm/f* hypocrite.
hypocritement [ipɔkRitmɑ̃] *adv* hypocritically.
hypotendu, e [ipɔtɑ̃dy] *adj* having low blood pressure, hypotensive.
hypotension [ipɔtɑ̃sjɔ̃] *nf* low blood pressure, hypotension.
hypoténuse [ipɔtenyz] *nf* hypotenuse.
hypothécaire [ipɔtekeR] *adj* hypothecary **garantie/prêt** ~ mortgage security/loan.
hypothèque [ipɔtɛk] *nf* mortgage.
hypothéquer [ipɔteke] *vt* to mortgage.
hypothermie [ipɔtɛRmi] *nf* hypothermia.
hypothèse [ipɔtɛz] *nf* hypothesis; **dans l'~ où** assuming that.
hypothétique [ipɔtetik] *adj* hypothetical.
hypothétiquement [ipɔtetikmɑ̃] *adv* hypothetically.
hystérectomie [isteRɛktɔmi] *nf* hysterectomy.
hystérie [isteRi] *nf* hysteria; ~ **collective** mass hysteria.
hystérique [isteRik] *adj* hysterical.
Hz *abr* (= *Hertz*) Hz.

I i

I, i [i] *nm inv* I, i; **I comme Irma** I for Isaac (*BRIT*) *ou* Item (*US*).
IAC *sigle f* (= *insémination artificielle entre conjoints*) AIH.
IAD *sigle f* (= *insémination artificielle par donneur extérieur*) AID.
ibère [ibeR] *adj* Iberian ♦ *nmf*: **I~** Iberian.
ibérique [ibeRik] *adj*: **la péninsule** ~ the Iberian peninsula.
ibid. [ibid] *abr* (= *ibidem*) ibid., ib.
iceberg [isbɛRg] *nm* iceberg.
ici [isi] *adv* here; **jusqu'~** as far as this; (*temporel*) until now; **d'~ là** by then; (*en attendant*)

dant) in the meantime; **d'~ peu** before long.
icône [ikon] *nf* (*aussi INFORM*) icon.
iconoclaste [ikɔnɔklast(ə)] *nm/f* iconoclast.
iconographie [ikɔnɔgrafi] *nf* iconography; (*illustrations*) (collection of) illustrations.
id. [id] *abr* (= *idem*) id.
idéal, e, aux [ideal, -o] *adj* ideal ♦ *nm* ideal; (*système de valeurs*) ideals *pl*.
idéalement [idealmɑ̃] *adv* ideally.
idéalisation [idealizasjɔ̃] *nf* idealization.
idéaliser [idealize] *vt* to idealize.
idéalisme [idealism(ə)] *nm* idealism.
idéaliste [idealist(ə)] *adj* idealistic ♦ *nm/f* idealist.
idée [ide] *nf* idea; (*illusion*): **se faire des ~s** to imagine things, get ideas into one's head; **avoir dans l'~ que** to have an idea that; **mon ~, c'est que** ... I suggest that ..., I think that ...; **à l'~ de/que** at the idea of/that, at the thought of/that; **je n'ai pas la moindre ~** I haven't the faintest idea; **avoir ~ que** to have an idea that; **avoir des ~s larges/étroites** to be broad-/narrow-minded; **venir à l'~ de qn** to occur to sb; **en voilà des ~s!** the very idea!; **~ fixe** idée fixe, obsession; **~s noires** black *ou* dark thoughts; **~s reçues** accepted ideas *ou* wisdom.
identifiable [idɑ̃tifjabl(ə)] *adj* identifiable.
identification [idɑ̃tifikasjɔ̃] *nf* identification.
identifier [idɑ̃tifje] *vt* to identify; **~ qch/qn à** to identify sth/sb with; **s'~ avec** *ou* **à qn/qch** (*héros etc*) to identify with sb/sth.
identique [idɑ̃tik] *adj*: **~ (à)** identical (to).
identité [idɑ̃tite] *nf* identity; **~ judiciaire** (*POLICE*) ≈ Criminal Records Office.
idéogramme [ideɔgram] *nm* ideogram.
idéologie [ideɔlɔʒi] *nf* ideology.
idéologique [ideɔlɔʒik] *adj* ideological.
idiomatique [idjɔmatik] *adj*: **expression ~** idiom, idiomatic expression.
idiome [idjom] *nm* (*LING*) idiom.
idiot, e [idjo, idjɔt] *adj* idiotic ♦ *nm/f* idiot.
idiotie [idjɔsi] *nf* idiocy; (*propos*) idiotic remark *etc*.
idiotisme [idjɔtism(ə)] *nm* idiom, idiomatic phrase.
idoine [idwan] *adj* fitting.
idolâtrer [idɔlɑtre] *vt* to idolize.
idolâtrie [idɔlɑtri] *nf* idolatry.
idole [idɔl] *nf* idol.
IDS *sigle f* (= *Initiative de défense stratégique*) SDI.
idylle [idil] *nf* idyll.
idyllique [idilik] *adj* idyllic.
if [if] *nm* yew.
IFOP [ifɔp] *sigle m* (= *Institut français d'opinion publique*) French market research institute.
IGF *sigle m* (= *impôt sur les grandes fortunes*) *wealth tax*.
IGH *sigle m* = *immeuble de grande hauteur*.
igloo [iglu] *nm* igloo.
IGN *sigle m* = *Institut géographique national*.

ignare [iɲar] *adj* ignorant.
ignifuge [ignifyʒ] *adj* fireproofing ♦ *nm* fireproofing (substance).
ignifuger [ignifyʒe] *vt* to fireproof.
ignoble [iɲɔbl(ə)] *adj* vile.
ignominie [iɲɔmini] *nf* ignominy; (*acte*) ignominious *ou* base act.
ignominieux, euse [iɲɔminjø, øz] *adj* ignominious.
ignorance [iɲɔrɑ̃s] *nf* ignorance; **dans l'~ de** in ignorance of, ignorant of.
ignorant, e [iɲɔrɑ̃, -ɑ̃t] *adj* ignorant ♦ *nm/f*: **faire l'~** to pretend one doesn't know; **~ de** ignorant of, not aware of; **~ en** ignorant of, knowing nothing of.
ignoré, e [iɲɔre] *adj* unknown.
ignorer [iɲɔre] *vt* (*ne pas connaître*) not to know, be unaware *ou* ignorant of; (*être sans expérience de: plaisir, guerre etc*) not to know about, have no experience of; (*bouder: personne*) to ignore; **j'ignore comment/si** I do not know how/if; **~ que** to be unaware that, not to know that; **je n'ignore pas que** ... I'm not forgetting that ..., I'm not unaware that ...; **je l'ignore** I don't know.
IGPN *sigle f* (= *Inspection générale de la police nationale*) *police disciplinary body*.
IGS *sigle f* (= *Inspection générale des services*) *police disciplinary body for Paris*.
iguane [igwan] *nm* iguana.
il [il] *pron* he; (*animal, chose, en tournure impersonnelle*) it; *NB: en anglais les navires et les pays sont en général assimilés aux femelles, et les bébés aux choses, si le sexe n'est pas spécifié*; **~s** they; **~ neige** it's snowing; *voir aussi* **avoir**.
île [il] *nf* island; **les Î~s** the West Indies; **l'~ de Beauté** Corsica; **l'~ Maurice** Mauritius; **les ~s anglo- normandes** the Channel Islands; **les ~s Britanniques** the British Isles; **les ~s Cocos** *ou* **Keeling** the Cocos *ou* Keeling Islands; **les ~s Cook** the Cook Islands; **les ~s Scilly** the Scilly Isles, the Scillies; **les ~s Shetland** the Shetland Islands, Shetland; **les ~s Sorlingues = les ~s Scilly**; **les ~s Vierges** the Virgin Islands.
iliaque [iljak] *adj* (*ANAT*): **os/artère ~** iliac bone/artery.
illégal, e, aux [ilegal, -o] *adj* illegal, unlawful (*ADMIN*).
illégalement [ilegalmɑ̃] *adv* illegally.
illégalité [ilegalite] *nf* illegality; unlawfulness; **être dans l'~** to be outside the law.
illégitime [ileʒitim] *adj* illegitimate; (*optimisme, sévérité*) unjustified, unwarranted.
illégitimement [ileʒitimmɑ̃] *adv* illegitimately.
illégitimité [ileʒitimite] *nf* illegitimacy; **gouverner dans l'~** to rule illegally.
illettré, e [iletre] *adj, nm/f* illiterate.
illicite [ilisit] *adj* illicit.
illicitement [ilisitmɑ̃] *adv* illicitly.

illico [iliko] *adv* (*fam*) pronto.
illimité, e [ilimite] *adj* (*immense*) boundless, unlimited; (*congé, durée*) indefinite, unlimited.
illisible [ilizibl(ə)] *adj* illegible; (*roman*) unreadable.
illisiblement [ilizibləmɑ̃] *adv* illegibly.
illogique [ilɔʒik] *adj* illogical.
illogisme [ilɔʒism(ə)] *nm* illogicality.
illumination [ilyminasjɔ̃] *nf* illumination, floodlighting; (*inspiration*) flash of inspiration; ~s *nfpl* illuminations, lights.
illuminé, e [ilymine] *adj* lit up; illuminated, floodlit ♦ *nm/f* (*fig: péj*) crank.
illuminer [ilymine] *vt* to light up; (*monument, rue: pour une fête*) to illuminate, floodlight; **s'~** *vi* to light up.
illusion [ilyzjɔ̃] *nf* illusion; **se faire des ~s** to delude o.s.; **faire ~** to delude *ou* fool people; **~ d'optique** optical illusion.
illusionner [ilyzjɔne] *vt* to delude; **s'~** (**sur qn/qch**) to delude o.s. (about sb/sth).
illusionnisme [ilyzjɔnism(ə)] *nm* conjuring.
illusionniste [ilyzjɔnist(ə)] *nm/f* conjuror.
illusoire [ilyzwaʀ] *adj* illusory, illusive.
illustrateur [ilystʀatœʀ] *nm* illustrator.
illustratif, ive [ilystʀatif, -iv] *adj* illustrative.
illustration [ilystʀasjɔ̃] *nf* illustration; (*d'un ouvrage: photos*) illustrations *pl*.
illustre [ilystʀ(ə)] *adj* illustrious, renowned.
illustré, e [ilystʀe] *adj* illustrated ♦ *nm* illustrated magazine; (*pour enfants*) comic.
illustrer [ilystʀe] *vt* to illustrate; **s'~** to become famous, win fame.
îlot [ilo] *nm* small island, islet; (*de maisons*) block; (*petite zone*): **un ~ de verdure** an island of greenery, a patch of green.
ils [il] *pron voir* **il**.
image [imaʒ] *nf* (*gén*) picture; (*comparaison, ressemblance, OPTIQUE*) image; **~ de** picture *ou* image of; **~ d'Épinal** (*social*) stereotype; **~ de marque** brand image; (*d'une personne*) (public) image; (*d'une entreprise*) corporate image; **~ pieuse** holy picture.
imagé, e [imaʒe] *adj* full of imagery.
imaginable [imaʒinabl(ə)] *adj* imaginable; **difficilement ~** hard to imagine.
imaginaire [imaʒinɛʀ] *adj* imaginary.
imaginatif, ive [imaʒinatif, -iv] *adj* imaginative.
imagination [imaʒinasjɔ̃] *nf* imagination; (*chimère*) fancy, imagining; **avoir de l'~** to be imaginative, have a good imagination.
imaginer [imaʒine] *vt* to imagine; (*croire*): **qu'allez-vous ~ là?** what on earth are you thinking of?; (*inventer: expédient, mesure*) to devise, think up; **s'~** *vt* (*se figurer: scène etc*) to imagine, picture; **s'~ à 60 ans** to picture *ou* imagine o.s. at 60; **s'~ que** to imagine that; **s'~ pouvoir faire qch** to think one can do sth; **j'imagine qu'il a voulu plaisanter** I suppose he was joking; **~ de faire** (*se mettre*

dans l'idée de) to dream up the idea of doing.
imbattable [ɛ̃batabl(ə)] *adj* unbeatable.
imbécile [ɛ̃besil] *adj* idiotic ♦ *nm/f* idiot; (*MÉD*) imbecile.
imbécillité [ɛ̃besilite] *nf* idiocy; imbecility; idiotic action (*ou* remark *etc*).
imberbe [ɛ̃bɛʀb(ə)] *adj* beardless.
imbiber [ɛ̃bibe] *vt*: **~ qch de** to moisten *ou* wet sth with; **s'~ de** to become saturated with; **imbibé(e) d'eau** (*chaussures, étoffe*) saturated; (*terre*) waterlogged.
imbriqué, e [ɛ̃bʀike] *adj* overlapping.
imbriquer [ɛ̃bʀike]: **s'~** *vi* to overlap (each other); (*fig*) to become interlinked *ou* interwoven.
imbroglio [ɛ̃bʀɔljo] *nm* imbroglio.
imbu, e [ɛ̃by] *adj*: **~ de** full of; **~ de soi-même/sa supériorité** full of oneself/one's superiority.
imbuvable [ɛ̃byvabl(ə)] *adj* undrinkable.
imitable [imitabl(ə)] *adj* imitable; **facilement ~** easily imitated.
imitateur, trice [imitatœʀ, -tʀis] *nm/f* (*gén*) imitator; (*MUSIC-HALL: d'une personnalité*) impersonator.
imitation [imitasjɔ̃] *nf* imitation; impersonation; **sac ~ cuir** bag in imitation *ou* simulated leather; **à l'~ de** in imitation of.
imiter [imite] *vt* to imitate; (*personne*) to imitate, impersonate; (*contrefaire: signature, document*) to forge, copy; (*ressembler à*) to look like; **il se leva et je l'imitai** he got up and I did likewise.
imm. *abr* = **immeuble**.
immaculé, e [imakyle] *adj* spotless, immaculate; **l'I~e Conception** (*REL*) the Immaculate Conception.
immanent, e [imanɑ̃, -ɑ̃t] *adj* immanent.
immangeable [ɛ̃mɑ̃ʒabl(ə)] *adj* inedible, uneatable.
immanquable [ɛ̃mɑ̃kabl(ə)] *adj* (*cible*) impossible to miss; (*fatal, inévitable*) bound to happen, inevitable.
immanquablement [ɛ̃mɑ̃kabləmɑ̃] *adv* inevitably.
immatériel, le [imateʀjɛl] *adj* ethereal; (*PHILOSOPHIE*) immaterial.
immatriculation [imatʀikylasjɔ̃] *nf* registration.
immatriculer [imatʀikyle] *vt* to register; **faire/se faire ~** to register; **voiture immatriculée dans la Seine** car with a Seine registration (number).
immature [imatyʀ] *adj* immature.
immaturité [imatyʀite] *nf* immaturity.
immédiat, e [imedja, -at] *adj* immediate ♦ *nm*: **dans l'~** for the time being; **dans le voisinage ~ de** in the immediate vicinity of.
immédiatement [imedjatmɑ̃] *adv* immediately.
immémorial, e, aux [imemɔʀjal, -o] *adj* ancient, age-old.

immense [imᾶs] *adj* immense.
immensément [imᾶsemᾶ] *adv* immensely.
immensité [imᾶsite] *nf* immensity.
immerger [imɛʀʒe] *vt* to immerse, submerge; (*câble etc*) to lay under water; (*déchets*) to dump at sea; **s'~** *vi* (*sous-marin*) to dive, submerge.
immérité, e [imeʀite] *adj* undeserved.
immersion [imɛʀsjɔ̃] *nf* immersion.
immettable [ɛ̃metabl(ə)] *adj* unwearable.
immeuble [imœbl(ə)] *nm* building ♦ *adj* (*JUR*) immovable, real; **~ locatif** block of rented flats (*BRIT*), rental building (*US*); **~ de rapport** investment property.
immigrant, e [imigʀᾶ, -ᾶt] *nm/f* immigrant.
immigration [imigʀasjɔ̃] *nf* immigration.
immigré, e [imigʀe] *nm/f* immigrant.
immigrer [imigʀe] *vi* to immigrate.
imminence [iminᾶs] *nf* imminence.
imminent, e [iminᾶ, -ᾶt] *adj* imminent, impending.
immiscer [imise]: **s'~** *vi*: **s'~ dans** to interfere in *ou* with.
immixtion [imiksjɔ̃] *nf* interference.
immobile [imɔbil] *adj* still, motionless; (*pièce de machine*) fixed; (*fig*) unchanging; **rester/ se tenir ~** to stay/keep still.
immobilier, ière [imɔbilje, -jɛʀ] *adj* property *cpd*, in real property ♦ *nm*: **l'~** the property *ou* the real estate business.
immobilisation [imɔbilizasjɔ̃] *nf* immobilization; **~s** *nfpl* (*JUR*) fixed assets.
immobiliser [imɔbilize] *vt* (*gén*) to immobilize; (*circulation, véhicule, affaires*) to bring to a standstill; **s'~** (*personne*) to stand still; (*machine, véhicule*) to come to a halt *ou* a standstill.
immobilisme [imɔbilism(ə)] *nm* strong resistance *ou* opposition to change.
immobilité [imɔbilite] *nf* immobility.
immodéré, e [imɔdeʀe] *adj* immoderate, inordinate.
immodérément [imɔdeʀemᾶ] *adv* immoderately.
immoler [imɔle] *vt* to sacrifice.
immonde [imɔ̃d] *adj* foul; (*sale: ruelle, taudis*) squalid.
immondices [imɔ̃dis] *nfpl* (*ordures*) refuse *sg*; (*saletés*) filth *sg*.
immoral, e, aux [imɔʀal, -o] *adj* immoral.
immoralisme [imɔʀalism(ə)] *nm* immoralism.
immoralité [imɔʀalite] *nf* immorality.
immortaliser [imɔʀtalize] *vt* to immortalize.
immortel, le [imɔʀtɛl] *adj* immortal ♦ *nf* (*BOT*) everlasting (flower).
immuable [imɥabl(ə)] *adj* (*inébranlable*) immutable; (*qui ne change pas*) unchanging; (*personne*): **~ dans ses convictions** immoveable (in one's convictions).
immunisation [imynizasjɔ̃] *nf* immunization.
immuniser [imynize] *vt* (*MÉD*) to immunize; **~ qn contre** to immunize sb against; (*fig*) to

make sb immune to.
immunitaire [imynitɛʀ] *adj* immune.
immunité [imynite] *nf* immunity; **~ diplomatique** diplomatic immunity; **~ parlementaire** parliamentary privilege.
immunologie [imynɔlɔʒi] *nf* immunology.
immutabilité [imytabilite] *nf* immutability.
impact [ɛ̃pakt] *nm* impact; **point d'~** point of impact.
impair, e [ɛ̃pɛʀ] *adj* odd ♦ *nm* faux pas, blunder; **numéros ~s** odd numbers.
impalpable [ɛ̃palpabl(ə)] *adj* impalpable.
impaludation [ɛ̃palydasjɔ̃] *nf* inoculation against malaria.
imparable [ɛ̃paʀabl(ə)] *adj* unstoppable.
impardonnable [ɛ̃paʀdɔnabl(ə)] *adj* unpardonable, unforgivable; **vous êtes ~ d'avoir fait cela** it's unforgivable of you to have done that.
imparfait, e [ɛ̃paʀfɛ, -ɛt] *adj* imperfect ♦ *nm* (*LING*) imperfect (tense).
imparfaitement [ɛ̃paʀfɛtmᾶ] *adv* imperfectly.
impartial, e, aux [ɛ̃paʀsjal, -o] *adj* impartial, unbiased.
impartialité [ɛ̃paʀsjalite] *nf* impartiality.
impartir [ɛ̃paʀtir] *vt*: **~ qch à qn** to assign sth to sb; (*dons*) to bestow sth upon sb; **dans les délais impartis** in the time allowed.
impasse [ɛ̃pas] *nf* dead-end, cul-de-sac; (*fig*) deadlock; **être dans l'~** (*négociations*) to have reached deadlock; **~ budgétaire** budget deficit.
impassibilité [ɛ̃pasibilite] *nf* impassiveness.
impassible [ɛ̃pasibl(ə)] *adj* impassive.
impassiblement [ɛ̃pasiblᾶmᾶ] *adv* impassively.
impatiemment [ɛ̃pasjamᾶ] *adv* impatiently.
impatience [ɛ̃pasjᾶs] *nf* impatience.
impatient, e [ɛ̃pasjᾶ, -ᾶt] *adj* impatient; **~ de faire qch** keen *ou* impatient to do sth.
impatienter [ɛ̃pasjᾶte] *vt* to irritate, annoy; **s'~** *vi* to get impatient; **s'~ de/contre** to lose patience at/with, grow impatient at/with.
impayable [ɛ̃pɛjabl(ə)] *adj* (*drôle*) priceless.
impayé, e [ɛ̃pɛje] *adj* unpaid, outstanding.
impeccable [ɛ̃pekabl(ə)] *adj* faultless, impeccable; (*propre*) spotlessly clean; (*chic*) impeccably dressed; (*fam*) smashing.
impeccablement [ɛ̃pekablᾶmᾶ] *adv* impeccably.
impénétrable [ɛ̃penetʀabl(ə)] *adj* impenetrable.
impénitent, e [ɛ̃penitᾶ, -ᾶt] *adj* unrepentant.
impensable [ɛ̃pᾶsabl(ə)] *adj* unthinkable, unbelievable.
imper [ɛ̃pɛʀ] *nm* (= *imperméable*) mac.
impératif, ive [ɛ̃peʀatif, -iv] *adj* imperative; (*JUR*) mandatory ♦ *nm* (*LING*) imperative; **~s** *nmpl* requirements; demands.
impérativement [ɛ̃peʀativmᾶ] *adv* imperatively.
impératrice [ɛ̃peʀatʀis] *nf* empress.

imperceptible [ɛpɛʀsɛptibl(ə)] *adj* imperceptible.

imperceptiblement [ɛpɛʀsɛptibləmɑ̃] *adv* imperceptibly.

imperdable [ɛpɛʀdabl(ə)] *adj* that cannot be lost.

imperfectible [ɛpɛʀfɛktibl(ə)] *adj* which cannot be perfected.

imperfection [ɛpɛʀfɛksjɔ̃] *nf* imperfection.

impérial, e, aux [ɛpeʀjal, -o] *adj* imperial ♦ *nf* upper deck; **autobus à ~e** double-decker bus.

impérialisme [ɛpeʀjalism(ə)] *nm* imperialism.

impérialiste [ɛpeʀjalist(ə)] *adj* imperialist.

impérieusement [ɛpeʀjøzmɑ̃] *adv*: **avoir ~ besoin de qch** to have urgent need of sth.

impérieux, euse [ɛpeʀjø, -øz] *adj* (*caractère, ton*) imperious; (*obligation, besoin*) pressing, urgent.

impérissable [ɛpeʀisabl(ə)] *adj* undying, imperishable.

imperméabilisation [ɛpɛʀmeabilizɑsjɔ̃] *nf* waterproofing.

imperméabiliser [ɛpɛʀmeabilize] *vt* to waterproof.

imperméable [ɛpɛʀmeabl(ə)] *adj* waterproof; (*GÉO*) impermeable; (*fig*): **~ à** impervious to ♦ *nm* raincoat; **~ à l'air** airtight.

impersonnel, le [ɛpɛʀsɔnɛl] *adj* impersonal.

impertinemment [ɛpɛʀtinamɑ̃] *adv* impertinently.

impertinence [ɛpɛʀtinɑ̃s] *nf* impertinence.

impertinent, e [ɛpɛʀtinɑ̃, -ɑ̃t] *adj* impertinent.

imperturbable [ɛpɛʀtyʀbabl(ə)] *adj* (*personne*) imperturbable; (*sang-froid*) unshakeable; **rester ~** to remain unruffled.

imperturbablement [ɛpɛʀtyʀbabləmɑ̃] *adv* imperturbably; unshakeably.

impétrant, e [ɛpetʀɑ̃, -ɑ̃t] *nm/f* (*JUR*) applicant.

impétueux, euse [ɛpetɥø, -øz] *adj* fiery.

impétuosité [ɛpetɥozite] *nf* fieriness.

impie [ɛpi] *adj* impious, ungodly.

impiété [ɛpjete] *nf* impiety.

impitoyable [ɛpitwajabl(ə)] *adj* pitiless, merciless.

impitoyablement [ɛpitwajabləmɑ̃] *adv* mercilessly.

implacable [ɛplakabl(ə)] *adj* implacable.

implacablement [ɛplakabləmɑ̃] *adv* implacably.

implant [ɛplɑ̃] *nm* (*MÉD*) implant.

implantation [ɛplɑ̃tɑsjɔ̃] *nf* establishment; settling; implantation.

implanter [ɛplɑ̃te] *vt* (*usine, industrie, usage*) to establish; (*colons etc*) to settle; (*idée, préjugé*) to implant; **s'~ dans** to be established in; to settle in; to become implanted in.

implémenter [ɛplemɑ̃te] *vt* to implement.

implication [ɛplikɑsjɔ̃] *nf* implication.

implicite [ɛplisit] *adj* implicit.

implicitement [ɛplisitmɑ̃] *adv* implicitly.

impliquer [ɛplike] *vt* to imply; **~ qn (dans)** to implicate sb (in).

implorant, e [ɛplɔʀɑ̃, -ɑ̃t] *adj* imploring.

implorer [ɛplɔʀe] *vt* to implore.

imploser [ɛploze] *vi* to implode.

implosion [ɛplozjɔ̃] *nf* implosion.

impoli, e [ɛpɔli] *adj* impolite, rude.

impoliment [ɛpɔlimɑ̃] *adv* impolitely.

impolitesse [ɛpɔlites] *nf* impoliteness, rudeness; (*propos*) impolite *ou* rude remark.

impondérable [ɛpɔ̃deʀabl(ə)] *nm* imponderable.

impopulaire [ɛpɔpylɛʀ] *adj* unpopular.

impopularité [ɛpɔpylaʀite] *nf* unpopularity.

importable [ɛpɔʀtabl(ə)] *adj* (*COMM: marchandise*) importable; (*vêtement: immettable*) unwearable.

importance [ɛpɔʀtɑ̃s] *nf* importance; **avoir de l'~** to be important; **sans ~** unimportant; **d'~** important, considerable; **quelle ~?** what does it matter?

important, e [ɛpɔʀtɑ̃, -ɑ̃t] *adj* important; (*en quantité*) considerable, sizeable; (*: gamme, dégâts*) extensive; (*péj: airs, ton*) self-important ♦ *nm*: **l'~** the important thing.

importateur, trice [ɛpɔʀtatœʀ, -tʀis] *adj* importing ♦ *nm/f* importer; **pays ~ de blé** wheat-importing country.

importation [ɛpɔʀtɑsjɔ̃] *nf* import; introduction; (*produit*) import.

importer [ɛpɔʀte] *vt* (*COMM*) to import; (*maladies, plantes*) to introduce ♦ *vi* (*être important*) to matter; **~ à qn** to matter to sb; **il importe de** it is important to; **il importe qu'il fasse** he must do, it is important that he should do; **peu m'importe** I don't mind, I don't care; **peu importe** it doesn't matter; **peu importe (que)** it doesn't matter (if); **peu importe le prix** never mind the price; *voir aussi* **n'importe**.

import-export [ɛpɔʀɛkspɔʀ] *nm* import-export business.

importun, e [ɛpɔʀtœ̃, -yn] *adj* irksome, importunate; (*arrivée, visite*) inopportune, ill-timed ♦ *nm* intruder.

importuner [ɛpɔʀtyne] *vt* to bother.

imposable [ɛpozabl(ə)] *adj* taxable.

imposant, e [ɛpozɑ̃, -ɑ̃t] *adj* imposing.

imposé, e [ɛpoze] *adj* (*soumis à l'impôt*) taxed; (*GYM etc: figures*) set.

imposer [ɛpoze] *vt* (*taxer*) to tax; (*REL*): **~ les mains** to lay on hands; **~ qch à qn** to impose sth on sb; **s'~** (*être nécessaire*) to be imperative; (*montrer sa proéminence*) to stand out, emerge; (*artiste: se faire connaître*) to win recognition, come to the fore; **en ~** to be imposing; **en ~ à** to impress; **ça s'impose** it's essential, it's vital.

imposition [ɛpozisjɔ̃] *nf* (*ADMIN*) taxation.

impossibilité [ɛpɔsibilite] *nf* impossibility; **être dans l'~ de faire** to be unable to do, find it impossible to do.

impossible [ɛpɔsibl(ə)] *adj* impossible ♦ *nm*: l'~ the impossible; ~ à faire impossible to do; il m'est ~ de le faire it is impossible for me to do it, I can't possibly do it; faire l'~ (pour que) to do one's utmost (so that); si, par ~ ... if, by some miracle ....

imposteur [ɛpɔstœʀ] *nm* impostor.

imposture [ɛpɔstyʀ] *nf* imposture, deception.

impôt [ɛpo] *nm* tax; (*taxes*) taxation, taxes *pl*; ~s *nmpl* (*contributions*) (income) tax *sg*; payer 1 000 F d'~s to pay 1,000 F in tax; ~ direct/indirect direct/indirect tax; ~ sur le chiffre d'affaires tax on turnover; ~ foncier land tax; ~ sur la fortune wealth tax; ~ sur les plus-values capital gains tax; ~ sur le revenu income tax; ~ sur le RPP personal income tax; ~ sur les sociétés tax on companies; ~s locaux rates, local taxes (*US*), ≈ council tax (*BRIT*).

impotence [ɛpɔtɑ̃s] *nf* disability.

impotent, e [ɛpɔtɑ̃, -ɑ̃t] *adj* disabled.

impraticable [ɛpʀatikabl(ə)] *adj* (*projet*) impracticable, unworkable; (*piste*) impassable.

imprécation [ɛpʀekasjɔ̃] *nf* imprecation.

imprécis, e [ɛpʀesi, -iz] *adj* (*contours, souvenir*) imprecise, vague; (*tir*) inaccurate, imprecise.

imprécision [ɛpʀesizjɔ̃] *nf* imprecision.

imprégner [ɛpʀeɲe] *vt* (*tissu, tampon*): ~ (de) to soak *ou* impregnate (with); (*lieu, air*): ~ (de) to fill (with); (*suj: amertume, ironie*) to pervade; s'~ de to become impregnated with; to be filled with; (*fig*) to absorb.

imprenable [ɛpʀənabl(ə)] *adj* (*forteresse*) impregnable; vue ~ unimpeded outlook.

impresario [ɛpʀesaʀjo] *nm* manager, impresario.

impression [ɛpʀesjɔ̃] *nf* impression; (*d'un ouvrage, tissu*) printing; (*PHOTO*) exposure; faire bonne ~ to make a good impression; donner une ~ de/l'~ que to give the impression of/that; avoir l'~ de/que to have the impression of/that; faire ~ to make an impression; ~s de voyage impressions of one's journey.

impressionnable [ɛpʀesjɔnabl(ə)] *adj* impressionable.

impressionnant, e [ɛpʀesjɔnɑ̃, -ɑ̃t] *adj* impressive; upsetting.

impressionner [ɛpʀesjɔne] *vt* (*frapper*) to impress; (*troubler*) to upset; (*PHOTO*) to expose.

impressionnisme [ɛpʀesjɔnism(ə)] *nm* impressionism.

impressionniste [ɛpʀesjɔnist(ə)] *adj, nm/f* impressionist.

imprévisible [ɛpʀevizibl(ə)] *adj* unforeseeable; (*réaction, personne*) unpredictable.

imprévoyance [ɛpʀevwajɑ̃s] *nf* lack of foresight.

imprévoyant, e [ɛpʀevwajɑ̃, -ɑ̃t] *adj* lacking in foresight; (*en matière d'argent*) improvident.

imprévu, e [ɛpʀevy] *adj* unforeseen, unexpected ♦ *nm* unexpected incident; l'~ the unexpected; en cas d'~ if anything unexpected happens; sauf ~ barring anything unexpected.

imprimante [ɛpʀimɑ̃t] *nf* (*INFORM*) printer; ~ à bulle d'encre bubblejet printer; ~ à jet d'encre ink-jet printer; ~ à laser laser printer; ~ (ligne par) ligne line printer; ~ à marguerite daisy-wheel printer; ~ matricielle dot-matrix printer; ~ thermique thermal printer.

imprimé [ɛpʀime] *nm* (*formulaire*) printed form; (*POSTES*) printed matter *no pl*; (*tissu*) printed fabric; un ~ à fleurs/pois (*tissu*) a floral/polka-dot print.

imprimer [ɛpʀime] *vt* to print; (*INFORM*) to print (out); (*apposer: visa, cachet*) to stamp; (*empreinte etc*) to imprint; (*publier*) to publish; (*communiquer: mouvement, impulsion*) to impart, transmit.

imprimerie [ɛpʀimʀi] *nf* printing; (*établissement*) printing works *sg*; (*atelier*) printing house, printery.

imprimeur [ɛpʀimœʀ] *nm* printer; imprimeur-éditeur/-libraire printer and publisher/bookseller.

improbable [ɛpʀɔbabl(ə)] *adj* unlikely, improbable.

improductif, ive [ɛpʀɔdyktif, -iv] *adj* unproductive.

impromptu, e [ɛpʀɔ̃pty] *adj* impromptu; (*départ*) sudden.

imprononçable [ɛpʀɔnɔ̃sabl(ə)] *adj* unpronounceable.

impropre [ɛpʀɔpʀ(ə)] *adj* inappropriate; ~ à unsuitable for.

improprement [ɛpʀɔpʀəmɑ̃] *adv* improperly.

impropriété [ɛpʀɔpʀijete] *nf*: ~ (de langage) incorrect usage *no pl*.

improvisation [ɛpʀɔvizasjɔ̃] *nf* improvization.

improvisé, e [ɛpʀɔvize] *adj* makeshift, improvized; (*jeu etc*) scratch, improvized; avec des moyens ~s using whatever comes to hand.

improviser [ɛpʀɔvize] *vt, vi* to improvize; s'~ (*secours, réunion*) to be improvized; s'~ cuisinier to (decide to) act as cook; ~ qn cuisinier to get sb to act as cook.

improviste [ɛpʀɔvist(ə)]: à l'~ *adv* unexpectedly, without warning.

imprudemment [ɛpʀydamɑ̃] *adv* carelessly; unwisely, imprudently.

imprudence [ɛpʀydɑ̃s] *nf* carelessness *no pl*; imprudence *no pl*; act of carelessness; foolish *ou* unwise action.

imprudent, e [ɛpʀydɑ̃, -ɑ̃t] *adj* (*conducteur, geste, action*) careless; (*remarque*) unwise, imprudent; (*projet*) foolhardy.

impubère [ɛpybɛʀ] *adj* below the age of puberty.

impubliable [ɛpyblijabl(ə)] *adj* unpublishable.

impudemment [ɛ̃pydamɑ̃] *adv* impudently.
impudence [ɛ̃pydɑ̃s] *nf* impudence.
impudent, e [ɛ̃pydɑ̃, -ɑ̃t] *adj* impudent.
impudeur [ɛ̃pydœʀ] *nf* shamelessness.
impudique [ɛ̃pydik] *adj* shameless.
impuissance [ɛ̃pɥisɑ̃s] *nf* helplessness; ineffectualness; impotence.
impuissant, e [ɛ̃pɥisɑ̃, -ɑ̃t] *adj* helpless; (*sans effet*) ineffectual; (*sexuellement*) impotent ♦ *nm* impotent man; ~ **à faire qch** powerless to do sth.
impulsif, ive [ɛ̃pylsif, -iv] *adj* impulsive.
impulsion [ɛ̃pylsjɔ̃] *nf* (*ÉLEC, instinct*) impulse; (*élan, influence*) impetus.
impulsivement [ɛ̃pylsivmɑ̃] *adv* impulsively.
impulsivité [ɛ̃pylsivite] *nf* impulsiveness.
impunément [ɛ̃pynemɑ̃] *adv* with impunity.
impuni, e [ɛ̃pyni] *adj* unpunished.
impunité [ɛ̃pynite] *nf* impunity.
impur, e [ɛ̃pyʀ] *adj* impure.
impureté [ɛ̃pyʀte] *nf* impurity.
imputable [ɛ̃pytabl(ə)] *adj* (*attribuable*): ~ **à** imputable to, ascribable to; (*COMM: somme*): ~ **sur** chargeable to.
imputation [ɛ̃pytasjɔ̃] *nf* imputation, charge.
imputer [ɛ̃pyte] *vt* (*attribuer*): ~ **qch à** to ascribe *ou* impute sth to; (*COMM*): ~ **qch à** *ou* **sur** to charge sth to.
imputrescible [ɛ̃pytʀesibl(ə)] *adj* rotproof.
in [in] *adj inv* in, trendy.
INA [ina] *sigle m* (= *Institut national de l'audiovisuel*) *library of television archives*.
inabordable [inabɔʀdabl(ə)] *adj* (*lieu*) inaccessible; (*cher*) prohibitive.
inaccentué, e [inaksɑ̃tɥe] *adj* (*LING*) unstressed.
inacceptable [inakseptabl(ə)] *adj* unacceptable.
inaccessible [inaksesibl(ə)] *adj* inaccessible; (*objectif*) unattainable; (*insensible*): ~ **à** impervious to.
inaccoutumé, e [inakutyme] *adj* unaccustomed.
inachevé, e [inaʃve] *adj* unfinished.
inactif, ive [inaktif, -iv] *adj* inactive, idle.
inaction [inaksjɔ̃] *nf* inactivity.
inactivité [inaktivite] *nf* (*ADMIN*): **en** ~ out of active service.
inadaptation [inadaptasjɔ̃] *nf* (*PSYCH*) maladjustment.
inadapté, e [inadapte] *adj* (*PSYCH: adulte, enfant*) maladjusted ♦ *nm/f* (*péj: adulte: asocial*) misfit; ~ **à** not adapted to, unsuited to.
inadéquat, e [inadekwa, wat] *adj* inadequate.
inadéquation [inadekwasjɔ̃] *nf* inadequacy.
inadmissible [inadmisibl(ə)] *adj* inadmissible.
inadvertance [inadvɛʀtɑ̃s]: **par** ~ *adv* inadvertently.
inaliénable [inaljenabl(ə)] *adj* inalienable.
inaltérable [inalteʀabl(ə)] *adj* (*matière*) stable; (*fig*) unchanging; ~ **à** unaffected by; **couleur** ~ **(au lavage/à la lumière)** fast colour/ fade-resistant colour.
inamovible [inamɔvibl(ə)] *adj* fixed; (*JUR*) irremovable.
inanimé, e [inanime] *adj* (*matière*) inanimate; (*évanoui*) unconscious; (*sans vie*) lifeless.
inanité [inanite] *nf* futility.
inanition [inanisjɔ̃] *nf*: **tomber d'**~ to faint with hunger (and exhaustion).
inaperçu, e [inapɛʀsy] *adj*: **passer** ~ to go unnoticed.
inappétence [inapetɑ̃s] *nf* lack of appetite.
inapplicable [inaplikabl(ə)] *adj* inapplicable.
inapplication [inaplikasjɔ̃] *nf* lack of application.
inappliqué, e [inaplike] *adj* lacking in application.
inappréciable [inapʀesjabl(ə)] *adj* (*service*) invaluable; (*différence, nuance*) inappreciable.
inapte [inapt(ə)] *adj*: ~ **à** incapable of; (*MIL*) unfit for.
inaptitude [inaptityd] *nf* inaptitude; unfitness.
inarticulé, e [inaʀtikyle] *adj* inarticulate.
inassimilable [inasimilabl(ə)] *adj* that cannot be assimilated.
inassouvi, e [inasuvi] *adj* unsatisfied, unfulfilled.
inattaquable [inatakabl(ə)] *adj* (*MIL*) unassailable; (*texte, preuve*) irrefutable.
inattendu, e [inatɑ̃dy] *adj* unexpected ♦ *nm*: **l'**~ the unexpected.
inattentif, ive [inatɑ̃tif, -iv] *adj* inattentive; ~ **à** (*dangers, détails*) heedless of.
inattention [inatɑ̃sjɔ̃] *nf* inattention; (*inadvertance*): **une minute d'**~ a minute of inattention, a minute's carelessness; **par** ~ inadvertently; **faute d'**~ careless mistake.
inaudible [inodibl(ə)] *adj* inaudible.
inaugural, e, aux [inɔgyʀal, -o] *adj* (*cérémonie*) inaugural, opening; (*vol, voyage*) maiden.
inauguration [inɔgyʀasjɔ̃] *nf* unveiling; opening; **discours/cérémonie d'**~ inaugural speech/ceremony.
inaugurer [inɔgyʀe] *vt* (*monument*) to unveil; (*exposition, usine*) to open; (*fig*) to inaugurate.
inauthenticité [inɔtɑ̃tisite] *nf* inauthenticity.
inavouable [inavwabl(ə)] *adj* undisclosable; (*honteux*) shameful.
inavoué, e [inavwe] *adj* unavowed.
INC *sigle m* (= *Institut national de la consommation*) *consumer research organization*.
inca [ɛ̃ka] *adj inv* Inca ♦ *nm/f*: **l'**~ Inca.
incalculable [ɛ̃kalkylabl(ə)] *adj* incalculable; **un nombre** ~ **de** countless numbers of.
incandescence [ɛ̃kɑ̃desɑ̃s] *nf* incandescence; **en** ~ incandescent, white-hot; **porter à** ~ to heat white-hot; **lampe/manchon à** ~ incandescent lamp/(gas) mantle.
incandescent, e [ɛ̃kɑ̃desɑ̃, -ɑ̃t] *adj* incandescent, white-hot.
incantation [ɛ̃kɑ̃tasjɔ̃] *nf* incantation.

incantatoire [ɛ̃kɑ̃tatwaʀ] *adj*: **formule ~** incantation.

incapable [ɛ̃kapabl(ə)] *adj* incapable; **~ de faire** incapable of doing; (*empêché*) unable to do.

incapacitant, e [ɛ̃kapasitɑ̃, -ɑ̃t] *adj* (*MIL*) incapacitating.

incapacité [ɛ̃kapasite] *nf* incapability; (*JUR*) incapacity; **être dans l'~ de faire** to be unable to do; **~ permanente/de travail** permanent/industrial disablement; **~ électorale** ineligibility to vote.

incarcération [ɛ̃kaʀseʀasjɔ̃] *nf* incarceration.

incarcérer [ɛ̃kaʀseʀe] *vt* to incarcerate.

incarnat, e [ɛ̃kaʀna, -at] *adj* (*rosy*) pink.

incarnation [ɛ̃kaʀnɑsjɔ̃] *nf* incarnation.

incarné, e [ɛ̃kaʀne] *adj* incarnate; (*ongle*) ingrown.

incarner [ɛ̃kaʀne] *vt* to embody, personify; (*THÉÂT*) to play; (*REL*) to incarnate; **s'~ dans** (*REL*) to be incarnate in.

incartade [ɛ̃kaʀtad] *nf* prank, escapade.

incassable [ɛ̃kasabl(ə)] *adj* unbreakable.

incendiaire [ɛ̃sɑ̃djɛʀ] *adj* incendiary; (*fig: discours*) inflammatory ♦ *nm/f* fire-raiser, arsonist.

incendie [ɛ̃sɑ̃di] *nm* fire; **~ criminel** arson *no pl*; **~ de forêt** forest fire.

incendier [ɛ̃sɑ̃dje] *vt* (*mettre le feu à*) to set fire to, set alight; (*brûler complètement*) to burn down.

incertain, e [ɛ̃sɛʀtɛ̃, -ɛn] *adj* uncertain; (*temps*) uncertain, unsettled; (*imprécis: contours*) indistinct, blurred.

incertitude [ɛ̃sɛʀtityd] *nf* uncertainty.

incessamment [ɛ̃sɛsamɑ̃] *adv* very shortly.

incessant, e [ɛ̃sɛsɑ̃, -ɑ̃t] *adj* incessant, unceasing.

incessible [ɛ̃sesibl(ə)] *adj* (*JUR*) nontransferable.

inceste [ɛ̃sɛst(ə)] *nm* incest.

incestueux, euse [ɛ̃sɛstɥø, -øz] *adj* incestuous.

inchangé, e [ɛ̃ʃɑ̃ʒe] *adj* unchanged, unaltered.

inchantable [ɛ̃ʃɑ̃tabl(ə)] *adj* unsingable.

inchauffable [ɛ̃ʃofabl(ə)] *adj* impossible to heat.

incidemment [ɛ̃sidamɑ̃] *adv* in passing.

incidence [ɛ̃sidɑ̃s] *nf* (*effet, influence*) effect; (*PHYSIQUE*) incidence.

incident [ɛ̃sidɑ̃] *nm* incident; **~ de frontière** border incident; **~ de parcours** minor hitch *ou* setback; **~ technique** technical difficulties *pl*, technical hitch.

incinérateur [ɛ̃sineʀatœʀ] *nm* incinerator.

incinération [ɛ̃sineʀasjɔ̃] *nf* (*d'ordures*) incineration; (*crémation*) cremation.

incinérer [ɛ̃sineʀe] *vt* (*ordures*) to incinerate; (*mort*) to cremate.

incise [ɛ̃siz] *nf* (*LING*) interpolated clause.

inciser [ɛ̃size] *vt* to make an incision in; (*abcès*) to lance.

incisif, ive [ɛ̃sizif, -iv] *adj* incisive, cutting ♦ *nf* incisor.

incision [ɛ̃sizjɔ̃] *nf* incision; (*d'un abcès*) lancing.

incitation [ɛ̃sitasjɔ̃] *nf* (*encouragement*) incentive; (*provocation*) incitement.

inciter [ɛ̃site] *vt*: **~ qn à (faire) qch** to prompt *ou* encourage sb to do sth; (*à la révolte etc*) to incite sb to do sth.

incivil, e [ɛ̃sivil] *adj* uncivil.

incivilité [ɛ̃sivilite] *nf* incivility.

inclinable [ɛ̃klinabl(ə)] *adj* (*dossier etc*) tilting; **siège à dossier ~** reclining seat.

inclinaison [ɛ̃klinɛzɔ̃] *nf* (*déclivité: d'une route etc*) incline; (*: d'un toit*) slope; (*état penché: d'un mur*) lean; (*: de la tête*) tilt; (*: d'un navire*) list.

inclination [ɛ̃klinɑsjɔ̃] *nf* (*penchant*) inclination, tendency; **montrer de l'~ pour les sciences** *etc* to show an inclination for the sciences *etc*; **~s égoïstes/altruistes** egoistic/altruistic tendencies; **~ de (la) tête** nod (of the head); **~ (de buste)** bow.

incliner [ɛ̃kline] *vt* (*bouteille*) to tilt; (*tête*) to incline; (*inciter*): **~ qn à qch/à faire** to encourage sb towards sth/to do ♦ *vi*: **~ à qch/à faire** (*tendre à, pencher pour*) to incline towards sth/doing, tend towards sth/to do; **s'~** (*route*) to slope; (*toit*) to be sloping; **s'~ (devant)** to bow to (before).

inclure [ɛ̃klyʀ] *vt* to include; (*joindre à un envoi*) to enclose; **jusqu'au 10 mars inclus** until 10th March inclusive.

inclus, e [ɛ̃kly, -yz] *pp de* **inclure** ♦ *adj* (*joint à un envoi*) enclosed; (*compris: frais, dépense*) included; (*MATH: ensemble*): **~ dans** included in; **jusqu'au troisième chapitre ~** up to and including the third chapter.

inclusion [ɛ̃klyzjɔ̃] *nf* (*voir inclure*) inclusion; enclosing.

inclusivement [ɛ̃klyzivmɑ̃] *adv* inclusively.

inclut [ɛ̃kly] *vb voir* **inclure**.

incoercible [ɛ̃kɔɛʀsibl(ə)] *adj* uncontrollable.

incognito [ɛ̃kɔɲito] *adv* incognito ♦ *nm*: **garder l'~** to remain incognito.

incohérence [ɛ̃kɔeʀɑ̃s] *nf* inconsistency; incoherence.

incohérent, e [ɛ̃kɔeʀɑ̃, -ɑ̃t] *adj* inconsistent; incoherent.

incollable [ɛ̃kɔlabl(ə)] *adj* (*riz*) that does not stick; (*fam: personne*): **il est ~** he's got all the answers.

incolore [ɛ̃kɔlɔʀ] *adj* colourless.

incomber [ɛ̃kɔ̃be]: **~ à** *vt* (*suj: devoirs, responsabilité*) to rest *ou* be incumbent upon; (*: frais, travail*) to be the responsibility of.

incombustible [ɛ̃kɔ̃bystibl(ə)] *adj* incombustible.

incommensurable [ɛ̃kɔmɑ̃syʀabl(ə)] *adj* immeasurable.

incommodant, e [ɛ̃kɔmɔdɑ̃, -ɑ̃t] *adj* (*bruit*) an-

noying; (*chaleur*) uncomfortable.
incommode [ɛkɔmɔd] *adj* inconvenient; (*posture, siège*) uncomfortable.
incommodément [ɛkɔmɔdemã] *adv* (*installé, assis*) uncomfortably; (*logé, situé*) inconveniently.
incommoder [ɛkɔmɔde] *vt*: ~ qn to bother *ou* inconvenience sb; (*embarrasser*) to make sb feel uncomfortable *ou* ill at ease.
incommodité [ɛkɔmɔdite] *nf* inconvenience.
incommunicable [ɛkɔmynikabl(ə)] *adj* (*JUR*: *droits, privilèges*) non-transferable; (*pensée*) incommunicable.
incomparable [ɛkɔparabl(ə)] *adj* not comparable; (*inégalable*) incomparable, matchless.
incomparablement [ɛkɔparabləmã] *adv* incomparably.
incompatibilité [ɛkɔpatibilite] *nf* incompatibility; ~ d'humeur (mutual) incompatibility.
incompatible [ɛkɔpatibl(ə)] *adj* incompatible.
incompétence [ɛkɔpetãs] *nf* lack of expertise; incompetence.
incompétent, e [ɛkɔpetã, -ãt] *adj* (*ignorant*) inexpert; (*incapable*) incompetent, not competent.
incomplet, ète [ɛkɔplɛ, -ɛt] *adj* incomplete.
incomplètement [ɛkɔplɛtmã] *adv* not completely, incompletely.
incompréhensible [ɛkɔpreãsibl(ə)] *adj* incomprehensible.
incompréhensif, ive [ɛkɔpreãsif, -iv] *adj* lacking in understanding, unsympathetic.
incompréhension [ɛkɔpreãsjɔ] *nf* lack of understanding.
incompressible [ɛkɔpresibl(ə)] *adj* (*PHYSIQUE*) incompressible; (*fig: dépenses*) that cannot be reduced; (*JUR: peine*) irreducible.
incompris, e [ɛkɔpri, -iz] *adj* misunderstood.
inconcevable [ɛkɔsvabl(ə)] *adj* (*conduite etc*) inconceivable; (*mystère*) incredible.
inconciliable [ɛkɔsiljabl(ə)] *adj* irreconcilable.
inconditionnel, le [ɛkɔdisjɔnɛl] *adj* unconditional; (*partisan*) unquestioning ♦ *nm/f* (*partisan*) unquestioning supporter.
inconditionnellement [ɛkɔdisjɔnɛlmã] *adv* unconditionally.
inconduite [ɛkɔdɥit] *nf* bad *ou* unsuitable behaviour *no pl*.
inconfort [ɛkɔfɔʀ] *nm* lack of comfort, discomfort.
inconfortable [ɛkɔfɔʀtabl(ə)] *adj* uncomfortable.
inconfortablement [ɛkɔfɔʀtabləmã] *adv* uncomfortably.
incongru, e [ɛkɔgʀy] *adj* unseemly; (*remarque*) ill-chosen, incongruous.
incongruité [ɛkɔgʀyite] *nf* unseemliness; incongruity; (*parole incongrue*) ill-chosen remark.
inconnu, e [ɛkɔny] *adj* unknown, (*sentiment, plaisir*) new, strange ♦ *nm/f* stranger; un-

known person (*ou* artist etc) ♦ *nm*: l'~ the unknown ♦ *nf* (*MATH*) unknown; (*fig*) unknown factor.
inconsciemment [ɛkɔsjamã] *adv* unconsciously.
inconscience [ɛkɔsjãs] *nf* unconsciousness; recklessness.
inconscient, e [ɛkɔsjã, -ãt] *adj* unconscious; (*irréfléchi*) reckless ♦ *nm* (*PSYCH*): l'~ the subconscious, the unconscious; ~ de unaware of.
inconséquence [ɛkɔsekãs] *nf* inconsistency; thoughtlessness; (*action, parole*) thoughtless thing to do (*ou* say).
inconséquent, e [ɛkɔsekã, -ãt] *adj* (*illogique*) inconsistent; (*irréfléchi*) thoughtless.
inconsidéré, e [ɛkɔsideʀe] *adj* ill-considered.
inconsidérément [ɛkɔsideʀemã] *adv* thoughtlessly.
inconsistant, e [ɛkɔsistã, -ãt] *adj* flimsy, weak; (*crème etc*) runny.
inconsolable [ɛkɔsɔlabl(ə)] *adj* inconsolable.
inconstance [ɛkɔstãs] *nf* inconstancy, fickleness.
inconstant, e [ɛkɔstã, -ãt] *adj* inconstant, fickle.
inconstitutionnel, le [ɛkɔstitysjɔnɛl] *adj* unconstitutional.
incontestable [ɛkɔtɛstabl(ə)] *adj* unquestionable, indisputable.
incontestablement [ɛkɔtɛstabləmã] *adv* unquestionably, indisputably.
incontesté, e [ɛkɔtɛste] *adj* undisputed.
incontinence [ɛkɔtinãs] *nf* (*MÉD*) incontinence.
incontinent, e [ɛkɔtinã, -ãt] *adj* (*MÉD*) incontinent ♦ *adv* (*tout de suite*) forthwith.
incontournable [ɛkɔtuʀnabl(ə)] *adj* unavoidable.
incontrôlable [ɛkɔtʀolabl(ə)] *adj* unverifiable.
incontrôlé, e [ɛkɔtʀole] *adj* uncontrolled.
inconvenance [ɛkɔvnãs] *nf* (*parole, action*) impropriety.
inconvenant, e [ɛkɔvnã, -ãt] *adj* unseemly, improper.
inconvénient [ɛkɔvenjã] *nm* (*d'une situation, d'un projet*) disadvantage, drawback; (*d'un remède, changement etc*) risk, inconvenience; **si vous n'y voyez pas d'**~ if you have no objections; **y a-t-il un** ~ **à ...?** (*risque*) isn't there a risk in ...?; (*objection*) is there any objection to ...?
inconvertible [ɛkɔvɛʀtibl(ə)] *adj* inconvertible.
incorporation [ɛkɔʀpɔʀasjɔ] *nf* (*MIL*) call-up.
incorporé, e [ɛkɔʀpɔʀe] *adj* (*micro etc*) built-in.
incorporel, le [ɛkɔʀpɔʀɛl] *adj* (*JUR*): **biens** ~**s** intangible property.
incorporer [ɛkɔʀpɔʀe] *vt*: ~ **(à)** to mix in (with); (*paragraphe etc*): ~ **(dans)** to incorporate (in); (*territoire, immigrants*): ~ **(dans)**

to incorporate (into); (*MIL: appeler*) to recruit, call up; (*: affecter*): ~ **qn dans** to enlist sb into.

incorrect, e [ɛkɔʀɛkt] *adj* (*impropre, inconvenant*) improper; (*défectueux*) faulty; (*inexact*) incorrect; (*impoli*) impolite; (*déloyal*) underhand.

incorrectement [ɛkɔʀɛktəmɑ̃] *adv* improperly; faultily; incorrectly; impolitely; in an underhand way.

incorrection [ɛkɔʀɛksjɔ̃] *nf* impropriety; incorrectness; underhand nature; (*terme impropre*) impropriety; (*action, remarque*) improper behaviour (*ou* remark).

incorrigible [ɛkɔʀiʒibl(ə)] *adj* incorrigible.

incorruptible [ɛkɔʀyptibl(ə)] *adj* incorruptible.

incrédibilité [ɛkʀedibilite] *nf* incredibility.

incrédule [ɛkʀedyl] *adj* incredulous; (*REL*) unbelieving.

incrédulité [ɛkʀedylite] *nf* incredulity; **avec** ~ incredulously.

increvable [ɛkʀəvabl(ə)] *adj* (*pneu*) punctureproof; (*fam*) tireless.

incriminer [ɛkʀimine] *vt* (*personne*) to incriminate; (*action, conduite*) to bring under attack; (*bonne foi, honnêteté*) to call into question; **livre/article incriminé** offending book/article.

incrochetable [ɛkʀɔʃtabl(ə)] *adj* (*serrure*) that can't be picked, burglarproof.

incroyable [ɛkʀwajabl(ə)] *adj* incredible, unbelievable.

incroyablement [ɛkʀwajabləmɑ̃] *adv* incredibly, unbelievably.

incroyant, e [ɛkʀwajɑ̃, -ɑ̃t] *nm/f* non-believer.

incrustation [ɛkʀystɑsjɔ̃] *nf* inlaying *no pl*; inlay; (*dans une chaudière etc*) fur *no pl*, scale *no pl*.

incruster [ɛkʀyste] *vt* (*ART*): ~ **qch dans/qch de** to inlay sth into/sth with; (*radiateur etc*) to coat with scale *ou* fur; **s'**~ *vi* (*invité*) to take root; (*radiateur etc*) to become coated with fur *ou* scale; **s'**~ **dans** (*suj: corps étranger, caillou*) to become embedded in.

incubateur [ɛkybatœʀ] *nm* incubator.

incubation [ɛkybɑsjɔ̃] *nf* incubation.

inculpation [ɛkylpɑsjɔ̃] *nf* charging *no pl*; charge; **sous l'**~ **de** on a charge of.

inculpé, e [ɛkylpe] *nm/f* accused.

inculper [ɛkylpe] *vt*: ~ **(de)** to charge (with).

inculquer [ɛkylke] *vt*: ~ **qch à** to inculcate sth in, instil sth into.

inculte [ɛkylt(ə)] *adj* uncultivated; (*esprit, peuple*) uncultured; (*barbe*) unkempt.

incultivable [ɛkyltivabl(ə)] *adj* (*terrain*) unworkable.

inculture [ɛkyltyʀ] *nf* lack of education.

incurable [ɛkyʀabl(ə)] *adj* incurable.

incurie [ɛkyʀi] *nf* carelessness.

incursion [ɛkyʀsjɔ̃] *nf* incursion, foray.

incurvé, e [ɛkyʀve] *adj* curved.

incurver [ɛkyʀve] *vt* (*barre de fer*) to bend into a curve; **s'**~ *vi* (*planche, route*) to bend.

Inde [ɛ̃d] *nf*: **l'**~ India.

indécemment [ɛ̃desamɑ̃] *adv* indecently.

indécence [ɛ̃desɑ̃s] *nf* indecency; (*propos, acte*) indecent remark (*ou* act *etc*).

indécent, e [ɛ̃desɑ̃, -ɑ̃t] *adj* indecent.

indéchiffrable [ɛ̃deʃifʀabl(ə)] *adj* indecipherable.

indéchirable [ɛ̃deʃiʀabl(ə)] *adj* tearproof.

indécis, e [ɛ̃desi, -iz] *adj* indecisive; (*perplexe*) undecided.

indécision [ɛ̃desizjɔ̃] *nf* indecision, indecisiveness.

indéclinable [ɛ̃deklinabl(ə)] *adj* (*LING: mot*) indeclinable.

indécomposable [ɛ̃dekɔ̃pozabl(ə)] *adj* that cannot be broken down.

indécrottable [ɛ̃dekʀɔtabl(ə)] *adj* (*fam*) hopeless.

indéfectible [ɛ̃defɛktibl(ə)] *adj* (*attachement*) indestructible.

indéfendable [ɛ̃defɑ̃dabl(ə)] *adj* indefensible.

indéfini, e [ɛ̃defini] *adj* (*imprécis, incertain*) undefined; (*illimité, LING*) indefinite.

indéfiniment [ɛ̃definimɑ̃] *adv* indefinitely.

indéfinissable [ɛ̃definisabl(ə)] *adj* indefinable.

indéformable [ɛ̃defɔʀmabl(ə)] *adj* that keeps its shape.

indélébile [ɛ̃delebil] *adj* indelible.

indélicat, e [ɛ̃delika, -at] *adj* tactless; (*malhonnête*) dishonest.

indélicatesse [ɛ̃delikatɛs] *nf* tactlessness; dishonesty.

indémaillable [ɛ̃demajabl(ə)] *adj* run-resist.

indemne [ɛ̃dɛmn(ə)] *adj* unharmed.

indemnisable [ɛ̃dɛmnizabl(ə)] *adj* entitled to compensation.

indemnisation [ɛ̃dɛmnizɑsjɔ̃] *nf* (*somme*) indemnity, compensation.

indemniser [ɛ̃dɛmnize] *vt*: ~ **qn (de)** to compensate sb (for); **se faire** ~ to get compensation.

indemnité [ɛ̃dɛmnite] *nf* (*dédommagement*) compensation *no pl*; (*allocation*) allowance; ~ **de licenciement** redundancy payment; ~ **de logement** housing allowance; ~ **parlementaire** ≈ M.P.'s (*BRIT*) *ou* Congressman's (*US*) salary.

indémontable [ɛ̃demɔ̃tabl(ə)] *adj* (*meuble etc*) that cannot be dismantled, in one piece.

indéniable [ɛ̃denjabl(ə)] *adj* undeniable, indisputable.

indéniablement [ɛ̃denjabləmɑ̃] *adv* undeniably.

indépendamment [ɛ̃depɑ̃damɑ̃] *adv* independently; ~ **de** independently of; (*abstraction faite de*) irrespective of; (*en plus de*) over and above.

indépendance [ɛ̃depɑ̃dɑ̃s] *nf* independence; ~ **matérielle** financial independence.

indépendant, e [ɛ̃depɑ̃dɑ̃, -ɑ̃t] *adj* independent; ~ **de** independent of; **chambre** ~**e** room with private entrance; **travailleur** ~ self-employed worker.

indépendantiste [ɛ̃depãdãtist(ə)] *adj, nm/f* separatist.

indéracinable [ɛ̃deʀasinabl(ə)] *adj* (*fig: croyance etc*) ineradicable.

indéréglable [ɛ̃deʀeglabl(ə)] *adj* which will not break down.

indescriptible [ɛ̃dɛskʀiptibl(ə)] *adj* indescribable.

indésirable [ɛ̃deziʀabl(ə)] *adj* undesirable.

indestructible [ɛ̃dɛstʀyktibl(ə)] *adj* indestructible; (*marque, impression*) indelible.

indéterminable [ɛ̃detɛʀminabl(ə)] *adj* indeterminable.

indétermination [ɛ̃detɛʀminasjɔ̃] *nf* indecision, indecisiveness.

indéterminé, e [ɛ̃detɛʀmine] *adj* unspecified; indeterminate; indeterminable.

index [ɛ̃dɛks] *nm* (*doigt*) index finger; (*d'un livre etc*) index; **mettre à l'**~ to blacklist.

indexation [ɛ̃dɛksasjɔ̃] *nf* indexing.

indexé, e [ɛ̃dɛkse] *adj* (*ÉCON*): ~ **(sur)** index-linked (to).

indexer [ɛ̃dɛkse] *vt* (*salaire, emprunt*): ~ **(sur)** to index (on).

indicateur [ɛ̃dikatœʀ] *nm* (*POLICE*) informer; (*livre*) guide; (*: liste*) directory; (*TECH*) gauge; indicator; (*ÉCON*) indicator ♦ *adj*: **poteau** ~ signpost; **tableau** ~ indicator (board); ~ **des chemins de fer** railway timetable; ~ **de direction** (*AUTO*) indicator; ~ **immobilier** property gazette; ~ **de niveau** level, gauge; ~ **de pression** pressure gauge; ~ **de rues** street directory; ~ **de vitesse** speedometer.

indicatif, ive [ɛ̃dikatif, -iv] *adj*: **à titre** ~ for (your) information ♦ *nm* (*LING*) indicative; (*d'une émission*) theme *ou* signature tune; (*TÉL*) dialling code; ~ **d'appel** (*RADIO*) call sign.

indication [ɛ̃dikasjɔ̃] *nf* indication; (*renseignement*) information *no pl*; ~**s** *nfpl* (*directives*) instructions; ~ **d'origine** (*COMM*) place of origin.

indice [ɛ̃dis] *nm* (*marque, signe*) indication, sign; (*POLICE: lors d'une enquête*) clue; (*JUR: présomption*) piece of evidence; (*SCIENCE, ÉCON, TECH*) index; (*ADMIN*) grading; rating; ~ **du coût de la vie** cost-of-living index; ~ **inférieur** subscript; ~ **d'octane** octane rating; ~ **des prix** price index; ~ **de traitement** salary grading.

indicible [ɛ̃disibl(ə)] *adj* inexpressible.

indien, ne [ɛ̃djɛ̃, -ɛn] *adj* Indian ♦ *nm/f*: **I**~, **ne** (*d'Amérique*) (American *ou* Red) Indian; (*d'Inde*) Indian.

indifféremment [ɛ̃diferamã] *adv* (*sans distinction*) equally; indiscriminately.

indifférence [ɛ̃diferãs] *nf* indifference.

indifférencié, e [ɛ̃diferãsje] *adj* undifferentiated.

indifférent, e [ɛ̃diferã, -ãt] *adj* (*peu intéressé*) indifferent; ~ **à** (*insensible à*) indifferent to, unconcerned about; (*peu intéressant pour*) indifferent to; immaterial to; **ça m'est** ~ (**que** ...) it doesn't matter to me (whether ...).

indifférer [ɛ̃difeʀe] *vt*: **cela m'indiffère** I'm indifferent about it.

indigence [ɛ̃diʒãs] *nf* poverty; **être dans l'**~ to be destitute.

indigène [ɛ̃diʒɛn] *adj* native, indigenous; (*de la région*) local ♦ *nm/f* native.

indigent, e [ɛ̃diʒã, -ãt] *adj* destitute, poverty-stricken; (*fig*) poor.

indigeste [ɛ̃diʒɛst(ə)] *adj* indigestible.

indigestion [ɛ̃diʒɛstjɔ̃] *nf* indigestion *no pl*; **avoir une** ~ to have indigestion.

indignation [ɛ̃diɲasjɔ̃] *nf* indignation; **avec** ~ indignantly.

indigne [ɛ̃diɲ] *adj*: ~ **(de)** unworthy (of).

indigné, e [ɛ̃diɲe] *adj* indignant.

indignement [ɛ̃diɲmã] *adv* shamefully.

indigner [ɛ̃diɲe] *vt* to make indignant; **s'**~ **(de/contre)** to be (*ou* become) indignant (at).

indignité [ɛ̃diɲite] *nf* unworthiness *no pl*; (*acte*) shameful act.

indigo [ɛ̃digo] *nm* indigo.

indiqué, e [ɛ̃dike] *adj* (*date, lieu*) given, appointed; (*adéquat*) appropriate, suitable; (*conseillé*) advisable; (*remède, traitement*) appropriate.

indiquer [ɛ̃dike] *vt* (*désigner*): ~ **qch/qn à qn** to point sth/sb out to sb; (*suj: pendule, aiguille*) to show; (*suj: étiquette, plan*) to show, indicate; (*faire connaître: médecin, restaurant*): ~ **qch/qn à qn** to tell sb of sth/sb; (*renseigner sur*) to point out, tell; (*déterminer: date, lieu*) to give, state; (*dénoter*) to indicate, point to; ~ **du doigt** to point out; ~ **de la main** to indicate with one's hand; ~ **du regard** to glance towards *ou* in the direction of; **pourriez-vous m'**~ **les toilettes/l'heure?** could you direct me to the toilets/tell me the time?

indirect, e [ɛ̃diʀɛkt] *adj* indirect.

indirectement [ɛ̃diʀɛktəmã] *adv* indirectly; (*apprendre*) in a roundabout way.

indiscernable [ɛ̃disɛʀnabl(ə)] *adj* indiscernible.

indiscipline [ɛ̃disiplin] *nf* lack of discipline.

indiscipliné, e [ɛ̃disipline] *adj* undisciplined; (*fig*) unmanageable.

indiscret, ète [ɛ̃diskʀɛ, -ɛt] *adj* indiscreet.

indiscrétion [ɛ̃diskʀesjɔ̃] *nf* indiscretion; **sans** ~, ... without wishing to be indiscreet, ...

indiscutable [ɛ̃diskytabl(ə)] *adj* indisputable.

indiscutablement [ɛ̃diskytabləmã] *adv* indisputably.

indiscuté, e [ɛ̃diskyte] *adj* (*incontesté: droit, chef*) undisputed.

indispensable [ɛ̃dispãsabl(ə)] *adj* indispensable, essential; ~ **à qn/pour faire qch** essential for sb/to do sth.

indisponibilité [ɛ̃dispɔnibilite] *nf* unavailability.

indisponible [ɛ̃dispɔnibl(ə)] *adj* unavailable.

indisposé, e [ɛ̃dispoze] *adj* indisposed, unwell.

indisposer [ɛ̃dispoze] *vt* (*incommoder*) to upset; (*déplaire à*) to antagonize.

indisposition [ɛ̃dispozisjɔ̃] *nf* (slight) illness, indisposition.

indissociable [ɛ̃disɔsjabl(ə)] *adj* indissociable.

indissoluble [ɛ̃disɔlybl(ə)] *adj* indissoluble.

indissolublement [ɛ̃disɔlyblǝmɑ̃] *adv* indissolubly.

indistinct, e [ɛ̃distɛ̃, -ɛkt(ə)] *adj* indistinct.

indistinctement [ɛ̃distɛ̃ktǝmɑ̃] *adv* (*voir, pronocer*) indistinctly; (*sans distinction*) without distinction, indiscriminately.

individu [ɛ̃dividy] *nm* individual.

individualiser [ɛ̃dividɥalize] *vt* to individualize; (*personnaliser*) to tailor to individual requirements; **s'~** to develop one's own identity.

individualisme [ɛ̃dividɥalism(ə)] *nm* individualism.

individualiste [ɛ̃dividɥalist(ə)] *nmf* individualist.

individualité [ɛ̃dividɥalite] *nf* individuality.

individuel, le [ɛ̃dividɥɛl] *adj* (*gén*) individual; (*opinion, livret, contrôle, avantages*) personal; **chambre ~le** single room; **maison ~le** detached house; **propriété ~le** personal *ou* private property.

individuellement [ɛ̃dividɥɛlmɑ̃] *adv* individually.

indivis, e [ɛ̃divi, -iz] *adj* (*JUR: bien, propriété, succession*) indivisible; (*: cohéritiers, propriétaires*) joint.

indivisible [ɛ̃divizibl(ə)] *adj* indivisible.

Indochine [ɛ̃dɔʃin] *nf*: **l'~** Indochina.

indochinois, e [ɛ̃dɔʃinwa, -waz] *adj* Indochinese.

indocile [ɛ̃dɔsil] *adj* unruly.

indo-européen, ne [ɛ̃dɔøʀɔpeɛ̃, -ɛn] *adj* Indo-European ♦ *nm* (*LING*) Indo-European.

indolence [ɛ̃dɔlɑ̃s] *nf* indolence.

indolent, e [ɛ̃dɔlɑ̃, -ɑ̃t] *adj* indolent.

indolore [ɛ̃dɔlɔʀ] *adj* painless.

indomptable [ɛ̃dɔ̃tabl(ə)] *adj* untameable; (*fig*) invincible, indomitable.

indompté, e [ɛ̃dɔ̃te] *adj* (*cheval*) unbroken.

Indonésie [ɛ̃dɔnezi] *nf*: **l'~** Indonesia.

indonésien, ne [ɛ̃dɔnezjɛ̃, -ɛn] *adj* Indonesian ♦ *nm/f*: **l'~, ne** Indonesian.

indu, e [ɛ̃dy] *adj*: **à des heures ~es** at an ungodly hour.

indubitable [ɛ̃dybitabl(ə)] *adj* indubitable.

indubitablement [ɛ̃dybitablǝmɑ̃] *adv* indubitably.

induction [ɛ̃dyksjɔ̃] *nf* induction.

induire [ɛ̃dɥiʀ] *vt*: **~ qch de** to induce sth from; **~ qn en erreur** to lead sb astray, mis-

lead sb.

indulgence [ɛ̃dylʒɑ̃s] *nf* indulgence; leniency; **avec ~** indulgently; leniently.

indulgent, e [ɛ̃dylʒɑ̃, -ɑ̃t] *adj* (*parent, regard*) indulgent; (*juge, examinateur*) lenient.

indûment [ɛ̃dymɑ̃] *adv* without due cause; (*illégitimement*) wrongfully.

industrialisation [ɛ̃dystʀijalizɑsjɔ̃] *nf* industrialization.

industrialiser [ɛ̃dystʀijalize] *vt* to industrialize; **s'~** to become industrialized.

industrie [ɛ̃dystʀi] *nf* industry; **~ automobile/textile** car/textile industry; **~ du spectacle** entertainment business.

industriel, le [ɛ̃dystʀijɛl] *adj* industrial; (*produit industriellement: pain etc*) mass-produced, factory-produced ♦ *nm* industrialist; (*fabricant*) manufacturer.

industriellement [ɛ̃dystʀijɛlmɑ̃] *adv* industrially.

industrieux, euse [ɛ̃dystʀijø, -øz] *adj* industrious.

inébranlable [inebʀɑ̃labl(ə)] *adj* (*masse, colonne*) solid; (*personne, certitude, foi*) steadfast, unwavering.

inédit, e [inedi, -it] *adj* (*correspondance etc*) (hitherto) unpublished; (*spectacle, moyen*) novel, original.

ineffable [inefabl(ə)] *adj* inexpressible, ineffable.

ineffaçable [inefasabl(ə)] *adj* indelible.

inefficace [inefikas] *adj* (*remède, moyen*) ineffective; (*machine, employé*) inefficient.

inefficacité [inefikasite] *nf* ineffectiveness; inefficiency.

inégal, e, aux [inegal, -o] *adj* unequal; (*irrégulier*) uneven.

inégalable [inegalabl(e)] *adj* matchless.

inégalé, e [inegale] *adj* unmatched, unequalled.

inégalement [inegalmɑ̃] *adv* unequally.

inégalité [inegalite] *nf* inequality; unevenness *no pl*; **~ de 2 hauteurs** difference *ou* disparity between 2 heights; **~s de terrain** uneven ground.

inélégance [inelegɑ̃s] *nf* inelegance.

inélégant, e [inelegɑ̃, -ɑ̃t] *adj* inelegant; (*indélicat*) discourteous.

inéligible [ineliʒibl(ə)] *adj* ineligible.

inéluctable [inelyktabl(ə)] *adj* inescapable.

inéluctablement [inelyktablǝmɑ̃] *adv* inescapably.

inemployable [inɑ̃plwajabl(ə)] *adj* unusable.

inemployé, e [inɑ̃plwaje] *adj* unused.

inénarrable [inenaʀabl(ə)] *adj* hilarious.

inepte [inɛpt(ə)] *adj* inept.

ineptie [inɛpsi] *nf* ineptitude; (*propos*) nonsense *no pl*.

inépuisable [inepɥizabl(ə)] *adj* inexhaustible.

inéquitable [inekitabl(ə)] *adj* inequitable.

inerte [inɛʀt(ə)] *adj* lifeless; (*apathique*) passive, inert; (*PHYSIQUE, CHIMIE*) inert.

inertie [inɛʀsi] *nf* inertia.
inescompté, e [inɛskɔ̃te] *adj* unexpected, unhoped-for.
inespéré, e [inɛspeʀe] *adj* unhoped-for, unexpected.
inesthétique [inɛstetik] *adj* unsightly.
inestimable [inɛstimabl(e)] *adj* priceless; (*fig: bienfait*) invaluable.
inévitable [inevitabl(e)] *adj* unavoidable; (*fatal, habituel*) inevitable.
inévitablement [inevitabləmɑ̃] *adv* inevitably.
inexact, e [inɛgzakt] *adj* inaccurate, inexact; (*non ponctuel*) unpunctual.
inexactement [inɛgzaktəmɑ̃] *adv* inaccurately.
inexactitude [inɛgzaktityd] *nf* inaccuracy.
inexcusable [inɛkskyzabl(e)] *adj* inexcusable, unforgivable.
inexécutable [inɛgzekytabl(e)] *adj* impracticable, unworkable; (*MUS*) unplayable.
inexistant, e [inɛgzistɑ̃, -ɑ̃t] *adj* non-existent.
inexorable [inɛgzɔʀabl(e)] *adj* inexorable; (*personne: dur*): ~ **(à)** unmoved (by).
inexorablement [inɛgzɔʀabləmɑ̃] *adv* inexorably.
inexpérience [inɛkspeʀjɑ̃s] *nf* inexperience, lack of experience.
inexpérimenté, e [inɛkspeʀimɑ̃te] *adj* inexperienced; (*arme, procédé*) untested.
inexplicable [inɛksplikabl(e)] *adj* inexplicable.
inexplicablement [inɛksplikabləmɑ̃] *adv* inexplicably.
inexpliqué, e [inɛksplike] *adj* unexplained.
inexploitable [inɛksplwatabl(e)] *adj* (*gisement, richesse*) unexploitable; (*données, renseignements*) unusable.
inexploité, e [inɛksplwate] *adj* unexploited, untapped.
inexploré, e [inɛksplɔʀe] *adj* unexplored.
inexpressif, ive [inɛkspʀesif, -iv] *adj* inexpressive; (*regard etc*) expressionless.
inexpressivité [inɛkspʀesivite] *nf* expressionlessness.
inexprimable [inɛkspʀimabl(e)] *adj* inexpressible.
inexprimé, e [inɛkspʀime] *adj* unspoken, unexpressed.
inexpugnable [inɛkspygnabl(e)] *adj* impregnable.
inextensible [inɛkstɑ̃sibl(e)] *adj* (*tissu*) non-stretch.
in extenso [inɛkstɛ̃so] *adv* in full.
inextinguible [inɛkstɛ̃gibl(e)] *adj* (*soif*) unquenchable; (*rire*) uncontrollable.
in extremis [inɛkstʀemis] *adv* at the last minute ♦ *adj* last-minute; (*testament*) death bed *cpd*.
inextricable [inɛkstʀikabl(e)] *adj* inextricable.
inextricablement [inɛkstʀikabləmɑ̃] *adv* inextricably.
infaillibilité [ɛ̃fajibilite] *nf* infallibility.
infaillible [ɛ̃fajibl(e)] *adj* infallible; (*instinct*) in-

fallible, unerring.
infailliblement [ɛ̃fajibləmɑ̃] *adv* (*certainement*) without fail.
infaisable [ɛ̃fəzabl(e)] *adj* (*travail etc*) impossible, impractical.
infamant, e [ɛ̃famɑ̃, -ɑ̃t] *adj* libellous, defamatory.
infâme [ɛ̃fɑm] *adj* vile.
infamie [ɛ̃fami] *nf* infamy.
infanterie [ɛ̃fɑ̃tʀi] *nf* infantry.
infanticide [ɛ̃fɑ̃tisid] *nm/f* child-murderer/eress ♦ *nm* (*meurtre*) infanticide.
infantile [ɛ̃fɑ̃til] *adj* (*MÉD*) infantile, child *cpd*; (*péj: ton, réaction*) infantile, childish.
infantilisme [ɛ̃fɑ̃tilism(e)] *nm* infantilism.
infarctus [ɛ̃faʀktys] *nm*: ~ **(du myocarde)** coronary (thrombosis).
infatigable [ɛ̃fatigabl(e)] *adj* tireless, indefatigable.
infatigablement [ɛ̃fatigabləmɑ̃] *adv* tirelessly, indefatigably.
infatué, e [ɛ̃fatɥe] *adj* conceited; ~ **de** full of.
infécond, e [ɛ̃fekɔ̃, -ɔ̃d] *adj* infertile, barren.
infect, e [ɛ̃fɛkt] *adj* vile, foul; (*repas, vin*) revolting, foul.
infecter [ɛ̃fɛkte] *vt* (*atmosphère, eau*) to contaminate; (*MÉD*) to infect; **s'~** to become infected *ou* septic.
infectieux, euse [ɛ̃fɛksjø, -øz] *adj* infectious.
infection [ɛ̃fɛksjɔ̃] *nf* infection.
inféoder [ɛ̃feɔde] *vt*: **s'~ à** to pledge allegiance to.
inférer [ɛ̃feʀe] *vt*: ~ **qch de** to infer sth from.
inférieur, e [ɛ̃feʀjœʀ] *adj* lower; (*en qualité, intelligence*) inferior ♦ *nm/f* inferior; ~ **à** (*somme, quantité*) less *ou* smaller than; (*moins bon que*) inferior to; (*tâche: pas à la hauteur de*) unequal to.
infériorité [ɛ̃feʀjɔʀite] *nf* inferiority; ~ **en nombre** inferiority in numbers.
infernal, e, aux [ɛ̃fɛʀnal, -o] *adj* (*chaleur, rythme*) infernal; (*méchanceté, complot*) diabolical.
infester [ɛ̃fɛste] *vt* to infest; **infesté de moustiques** infested with mosquitoes, mosquito-ridden.
infidèle [ɛ̃fidɛl] *adj* unfaithful; (*REL*) infidel.
infidélité [ɛ̃fidelite] *nf* unfaithfulness *no pl*.
infiltration [ɛ̃filtʀasjɔ̃] *nf* infiltration.
infiltrer [ɛ̃filtʀe]: **s'~** *vi*: **s'~ dans** to penetrate into; (*liquide*) to seep into; (*fig: noyauter*) to infiltrate.
infime [ɛ̃fim] *adj* minute, tiny; (*inférieur*) lowly.
infini, e [ɛ̃fini] *adj* infinite ♦ *nm* infinity; **à l'~** (*MATH*) to infinity; (*discourir*) ad infinitum, endlessly; (*agrandir, varier*) infinitely; (*à perte de vue*) endlessly (into the distance).
infiniment [ɛ̃finimɑ̃] *adv* infinitely; ~ **grand/petit** (*MATH*) infinitely great/infinitessimal.
infinité [ɛ̃finite] *nf*: **une ~ de** an infinite number of.

infinitésimal, e, aux [ɛ̃finitezimal, -o] adj infinitessimal.

infinitif, ive [ɛ̃finitif, -iv] adj, nm infinitive.

infirme [ɛ̃fiʀm(ə)] adj disabled ♦ nm/f disabled person; ~ **mental** mentally-handicapped person; ~ **moteur** spastic; ~ **de guerre** war cripple; ~ **du travail** industrially disabled person.

infirmer [ɛ̃fiʀme] vt to invalidate.

infirmerie [ɛ̃fiʀməʀi] nf sick bay.

infirmier, ière [ɛ̃fiʀmje, -jɛʀ] nm/f nurse ♦ adj: **élève** ~ student nurse; **infirmière chef** sister; **infirmière diplômée** registered nurse; **infirmière visiteuse** visiting nurse, ≈ district nurse (BRIT).

infirmité [ɛ̃fiʀmite] nf disability.

inflammable [ɛ̃flamabl(ə)] adj (in)flammable.

inflammation [ɛ̃flamɑsjɔ̃] nf inflammation.

inflammatoire [ɛ̃flamatwaʀ] adj (MÉD) inflammatory.

inflation [ɛ̃flɑsjɔ̃] nf inflation; ~ **rampante/galopante** creeping/galloping inflation.

inflationniste [ɛ̃flɑsjɔnist(ə)] adj inflationist.

infléchir [ɛ̃fleʃiʀ] vt (fig: politique) to reorientate, redirect; **s'**~ vi (poutre, tringle) to bend, sag.

inflexibilité [ɛ̃flɛksibilite] nf inflexibility.

inflexible [ɛ̃flɛksibl(ə)] adj inflexible.

inflexion [ɛ̃flɛksjɔ̃] nf inflexion; ~ **de la tête** slight nod (of the head).

infliger [ɛ̃fliʒe] vt: ~ **qch (à qn)** to inflict sth (on sb); (amende, sanction) to impose sth (on sb).

influençable [ɛ̃flyɑ̃sabl(ə)] adj easily influenced.

influence [ɛ̃flyɑ̃s] nf influence; (d'un médicament) effect.

influencer [ɛ̃flyɑ̃se] vt to influence.

influent, e [ɛ̃flyɑ̃, -ɑ̃t] adj influential.

influer [ɛ̃flye]: ~ **sur** vt to have an influence upon.

influx [ɛ̃fly] nm: ~ **nerveux** (nervous) impulse.

infographie [ɛ̃fɔgʀafi] nf computer graphics sg.

informateur, trice [ɛ̃fɔʀmatœʀ, -tʀis] nm/f informant.

informaticien, ne [ɛ̃fɔʀmatisjɛ̃, -ɛn] nm/f computer scientist.

informatif, ive [ɛ̃fɔʀmatif, -iv] adj informative.

information [ɛ̃fɔʀmɑsjɔ̃] nf (renseignement) piece of information; (PRESSE, TV: nouvelle) item of news; (diffusion de renseignements, INFORM) inquiry, news, investigation; ~**s** nfpl (TV) news sg; **voyage d'**~ fact-finding trip; **agence d'**~ news agency; **journal d'**~ quality (BRIT) ou serious newspaper.

informatique [ɛ̃fɔʀmatik] nf (technique) data processing; (science) computer science ♦ adj computer cpd.

informatisation [ɛ̃fɔʀmatizɑsjɔ̃] nf computerization.

informatiser [ɛ̃fɔʀmatize] vt to computerize.

informe [ɛ̃fɔʀm(ə)] adj shapeless.

informé, e [ɛ̃fɔʀme] adj: **jusqu'à plus ample** ~ until further information is available.

informel, le [ɛ̃fɔʀmɛl] adj informal.

informer [ɛ̃fɔʀme] vt: ~ **qn (de)** to inform sb (of) ♦ vi (JUR): ~ **contre qn/sur qch** to initiate inquiries about sb/sth; **s'**~ **(sur)** to inform o.s. (about); **s'**~ **(de qch/si)** to inquire ou find out (about sth/whether ou if).

informulé, e [ɛ̃fɔʀmyle] adj unformulated.

infortune [ɛ̃fɔʀtyn] nf misfortune.

infos [ɛ̃fo] nfpl (= informations) news.

infraction [ɛ̃fʀaksjɔ̃] nf offence; ~ **à** violation ou breach of; **être en** ~ to be in breach of the law.

infranchissable [ɛ̃fʀɑ̃ʃisabl(ə)] adj impassable; (fig) insuperable.

infrarouge [ɛ̃fʀaʀuʒ] adj, nm infrared.

infrason [ɛ̃fʀasɔ̃] nm infrasonic vibration.

infrastructure [ɛ̃fʀastʀyktyʀ] nf (d'une route etc) substructure; (AVIAT, MIL) ground installations pl; (touristique etc) facilities.

infréquentable [ɛ̃fʀekɑ̃tabl(ə)] adj not to be associated with.

infroissable [ɛ̃fʀwasabl(ə)] adj crease-resistant.

infructueux, euse [ɛ̃fʀyktɥø, -øz] adj fruitless, unfruitful.

infus, e [ɛ̃fy, -yz] adj: **avoir la science** ~e to have innate knowledge.

infuser [ɛ̃fyze] vt (aussi: **faire** ~: thé) to brew; (: tisane) to infuse ♦ vi to brew; to infuse; **laisser** ~ (to leave) to brew.

infusion [ɛ̃fyzjɔ̃] nf (tisane) infusion, herb tea.

ingambe [ɛ̃gɑ̃b] adj spry, nimble.

ingénier [ɛ̃ʒenje]: **s'**~ vi: **s'**~ **à faire** to strive to do.

ingénierie [ɛ̃ʒeniʀi] nf engineering.

ingénieur [ɛ̃ʒenjœʀ] nm engineer; ~ **agronome/chimiste** agricultural/chemical engineer; ~ **conseil** consulting engineer; ~ **du son** sound engineer.

ingénieusement [ɛ̃ʒenjøzmɑ̃] adv ingeniously.

ingénieux, euse [ɛ̃ʒenjø, -øz] adj ingenious, clever.

ingéniosité [ɛ̃ʒenjozite] nf ingenuity.

ingénu, e [ɛ̃ʒeny] adj ingenuous, artless ♦ nf (THÉÂT) ingénue.

ingénuité [ɛ̃ʒenɥite] nf ingenuousness.

ingénument [ɛ̃ʒenymɑ̃] adv ingenuously.

ingérence [ɛ̃ʒeʀɑ̃s] nf interference.

ingérer [ɛ̃ʒeʀe]: **s'**~ vi: **s'**~ **dans** to interfere in.

ingouvernable [ɛ̃guvɛʀnabl(ə)] adj ungovernable.

ingrat, e [ɛ̃gʀa, -at] adj (personne) ungrateful; (sol) poor; (travail, sujet) arid, thankless; (visage) unprepossessing.

ingratitude [ɛ̃gʀatityd] nf ingratitude.

ingrédient [ɛ̃gʀedjɑ̃] *nm* ingredient.
inguérissable [ɛ̃geʀisabl(ə)] *adj* incurable.
ingurgiter [ɛ̃gyʀʒite] *vt* to swallow; **faire ~ qch à qn** to make sb swallow sth; (*fig:* connaissances) to force sth into sb.
inhabile [inabil] *adj* clumsy; (*fig*) inept.
inhabitable [inabitabl(ə)] *adj* uninhabitable.
inhabité, e [inabite] *adj* (*régions*) uninhabited; (*maison*) unoccupied.
inhabituel, le [inabitɥɛl] *adj* unusual.
inhalateur [inalatœʀ] *nm* inhaler; **~ d'oxygène** oxygen mask.
inhalation [inalɑsjɔ̃] *nf* (*MÉD*) inhalation; **faire des ~s** to use an inhalation bath.
inhaler [inale] *vt* to inhale.
inhérent, e [ineʀɑ̃, -ɑ̃t] *adj:* **~ à** inherent in.
inhiber [inibe] *vt* to inhibit.
inhibition [inibisjɔ̃] *nf* inhibition.
inhospitalier, ière [inɔspitalje, -jɛʀ] *adj* inhospitable.
inhumain, e [inymɛ̃, -ɛn] *adj* inhuman.
inhumation [inymɑsjɔ̃] *nf* interment, burial.
inhumer [inyme] *vt* to inter, bury.
inimaginable [inimaʒinabl(ə)] *adj* unimaginable.
inimitable [inimitabl(ə)] *adj* inimitable.
inimitié [inimitje] *nf* enmity.
ininflammable [inɛ̃flamabl(ə)] *adj* nonflammable.
inintelligent, e [inɛ̃teliʒɑ̃, -ɑ̃t] *adj* unintelligent.
inintelligible [inɛ̃teliʒibl(ə)] *adj* unintelligible.
inintelligiblement [inɛ̃teliʒibləmɑ̃] *adv* unintelligibly.
inintéressant, e [inɛ̃teʀesɑ̃, -ɑ̃t] *adj* uninteresting.
ininterrompu, e [inɛ̃teʀɔ̃py] *adj* (*file, série*) unbroken; (*flot, vacarme*) uninterrupted, nonstop; (*effort*) unremitting, continuous.
iniquité [inikite] *nf* iniquity.
initial, e, aux [inisjal, -o] *adj*, *nf* initial; **~es** *nfpl* initials.
initialement [inisjalmɑ̃] *adv* initially.
initialiser [inisjalize] *vt* to initialize.
initiateur, trice [inisjatœʀ, -tʀis] *nm/f* initiator; (*d'une mode, technique*) innovator, pioneer.
initiation [inisjɑsjɔ̃] *nf* initiation.
initiatique [inisjatik] *adj* (*rites, épreuves*) initiatory.
initiative [inisjativ] *nf* initiative; **prendre l'~ de qch/de faire** to take the initiative for sth/of doing; **avoir de l'~** to have initiative, show enterprise; **esprit/qualités d'~** spirit/ qualities of initiative; **à** *ou* **sur l'~ de qn** on sb's initiative; **de sa propre ~** on one's own initiative.
initié, e [inisje] *adj* initiated ♦ *nm/f* initiate.
initier [inisje] *vt* to initiate; **~ qn à** to initiate sb into; (*faire découvrir: art, jeu*) to introduce sb to; **s'~ à** (*métier, profession, technique*) to become initiated into.
injectable [ɛ̃ʒɛktabl(ə)] *adj* injectable.

injecté, e [ɛ̃ʒɛkte] *adj:* **yeux ~s de sang** bloodshot eyes.
injecter [ɛ̃ʒɛkte] *vt* to inject.
injection [ɛ̃ʒɛksjɔ̃] *nf* injection; **à ~** (*AUTO*) fuel injection *cpd*.
injonction [ɛ̃ʒɔ̃ksjɔ̃] *nf* injunction, order; **~ de payer** (*JUR*) order to pay.
injouable [ɛ̃ʒwabl(ə)] *adj* unplayable.
injure [ɛ̃ʒyʀ] *nf* insult, abuse *no pl*.
injurier [ɛ̃ʒyʀje] *vt* to insult, abuse.
injurieux, euse [ɛ̃ʒyʀjø, -øz] *adj* abusive, insulting.
injuste [ɛ̃ʒyst(ə)] *adj* unjust, unfair.
injustement [ɛ̃ʒystəmɑ̃] *adv* unjustly, unfairly.
injustice [ɛ̃ʒystis] *nf* injustice.
injustifiable [ɛ̃ʒystifjabl(ə)] *adj* unjustifiable.
injustifié, e [ɛ̃ʒystifje] *adj* unjustified, unwarranted.
inlassable [ɛ̃lɑsabl(ə)] *adj* tireless, indefatigable.
inlassablement [ɛ̃lɑsabləmɑ̃] *adv* tirelessly.
inné, e [ine] *adj* innate, inborn.
innocemment [inɔsamɑ̃] *adv* innocently.
innocence [inɔsɑ̃s] *nf* innocence.
innocent, e [inɔsɑ̃, -ɑ̃t] *adj* innocent ♦ *nm/f* innocent person; **faire l'~** to play *ou* come the innocent.
innocenter [inɔsɑ̃te] *vt* to clear, prove innocent.
innocuité [inɔkɥite] *nf* innocuousness.
innombrable [inɔ̃bʀabl(ə)] *adj* innumerable.
innommable [inɔmabl(ə)] *adj* unspeakable.
innovateur, trice [inɔvatœʀ, -tʀis] *adj* innovatory.
innovation [inɔvasjɔ̃] *nf* innovation.
innover [inɔve] *vi:* **~ en matière d'art** to break new ground in the field of art.
inobservance [inɔpsɛʀvɑ̃s] *nf* nonobservance.
inobservation [inɔpsɛʀvasjɔ̃] *nf* nonobservation, inobservance.
inoccupé, e [inɔkype] *adj* unoccupied.
inoculer [inɔkyle] *vt:* **~ qch à qn** (*volontairement*) to inoculate sb with sth; (*accidentellement*) to infect sb with sth; **~ qn contre** to inoculate sb against.
inodore [inɔdɔʀ] *adj* (*gaz*) odourless; (*fleur*) scentless.
inoffensif, ive [inɔfɑ̃sif, -iv] *adj* harmless, innocuous.
inondable [inɔ̃dabl(ə)] *adj* (*zone etc*) liable to flooding.
inondation [inɔ̃dasjɔ̃] *nf* flooding *no pl*; (*torrent, eau*) flood.
inonder [inɔ̃de] *vt* to flood; (*fig*) to inundate, overrun; **~ de** (*fig*) to flood *ou* swamp with.
inopérable [inɔpeʀabl(ə)] *adj* inoperable.
inopérant, e [inɔpeʀɑ̃, -ɑ̃t] *adj* inoperative, ineffective.
inopiné, e [inɔpine] *adj* unexpected, sudden.
inopinément [inɔpinemɑ̃] *adv* unexpectedly.

inopportun, e [inɔpɔʀtœ̃, -yn] *adj* ill-timed, untimely; inappropriate; *(moment)* inopportune.

inorganisation [inɔʀɡanizɑsjɔ̃] *nf* lack of organization.

inorganisé, e [inɔʀɡanize] *adj (travailleurs)* non-organized.

inoubliable [inublijabl(ə)] *adj* unforgettable.

inouï, e [inwi] *adj* unheard-of, extraordinary.

inox [inɔks] *adj, nm* (= *inoxydable*) stainless (steel).

inoxydable [inɔksidabl(ə)] *adj* stainless; *(couverts)* stainless steel *cpd*.

inqualifiable [ɛ̃kalifjabl(ə)] *adj* unspeakable.

inquiet, ète [ɛ̃kjɛ, -ɛt] *adj (par nature)* anxious; *(momentanément)* worried; ~ **de qch/au sujet de qn** worried about sth/sb.

inquiétant, e [ɛ̃kjetɑ̃, -ɑ̃t] *adj* worrying, disturbing.

inquiéter [ɛ̃kjete] *vt* to worry, disturb; *(harceler)* to harass; **s'~** to worry, become anxious; **s'~ de** to worry about; *(s'enquérir de)* to inquire about.

inquiétude [ɛ̃kjetyd] *nf* anxiety; **donner de l'~** *ou* **des ~s à** to worry; **avoir de l'~** *ou* **des ~s au sujet de** to feel anxious *ou* worried about.

inquisiteur, trice [ɛ̃kizitœʀ, -tʀis] *adj (regards, questions)* inquisitive, prying.

inquisition [ɛ̃kizisjɔ̃] *nf* inquisition.

INR *sigle m* = *Institut national (belge) de radiodiffusion.*

INRA [inʀa] *sigle m* = *Institut national de la recherche agronomique.*

inracontable [ɛ̃ʀakɔ̃tabl(ə)] *adj (trop osé)* unrepeatable; *(trop compliqué)*: **l'histoire est** ~ the story is too complicated to relate.

insaisissable [ɛ̃sezizabl(ə)] *adj* elusive.

insalubre [ɛ̃salybʀ(ə)] *adj* unhealthy, insalubrious.

insalubrité [ɛ̃salybʀite] *nf* unhealthiness, insalubrity.

insanité [ɛ̃sanite] *nf* madness *no pl*, insanity *no pl*.

insatiable [ɛ̃sasjabl(ə)] *adj* insatiable.

insatisfaction [ɛ̃satisfaksjɔ̃] *nf* dissatisfaction.

insatisfait, e [ɛ̃satisfɛ, -ɛt] *adj (non comblé)* unsatisfied; *(: passion, envie)* unfulfilled; *(mécontent)* dissatisfied.

inscription [ɛ̃skʀipsjɔ̃] *nf (sur un mur, écriteau etc)* inscription; *(à une institution: voir s'inscrire)* enrolment; registration.

inscrire [ɛ̃skʀiʀ] *vt (marquer: sur son calepin etc)* to note *ou* write down; *(: sur un mur, une affiche etc)* to write; *(: dans la pierre, le métal)* to inscribe; *(mettre: sur une liste, un budget etc)* to put down; *(enrôler: soldat)* to enlist; ~ **qn à** *(club, école etc)* to enrol sb at; **s'~** *(pour une excursion etc)* to put one's name down; **s'~ (à)** *(club, parti)* to join; *(université)* to register *ou* enrol (at); *(examen, concours)* to register *ou* enter (for); **s'~ dans** *(se situer: négociations etc)* to come within the scope of; **s'~ en faux contre** to deny (strongly); *(JUR)* to challenge.

inscrit, e [ɛ̃skʀi, it] *pp de* **inscrire** ♦ *adj (étudiant, électeur etc)* registered.

insécable [ɛ̃sekabl(ə)] *adj (INFORM)* indivisible.

insecte [ɛ̃sɛkt(ə)] *nm* insect.

insecticide [ɛ̃sɛktisid] *nm* insecticide.

insécurité [ɛ̃sekyʀite] *nf* insecurity, lack of security.

INSEE [inse] *sigle m* (= *Institut national de la statistique et des études économiques*) national institute of statistical and economic information.

insémination [ɛ̃seminasjɔ̃] *nf* insemination.

insensé, e [ɛ̃sɑ̃se] *adj* insane, mad.

insensibiliser [ɛ̃sɑ̃sibilize] *vt* to anaesthetize; *(à une allergie)* to desensitize; ~ **à qch** *(fig)* to cause to become insensitive to sth.

insensibilité [ɛ̃sɑ̃sibilite] *nf* insensitivity.

insensible [ɛ̃sɑ̃sibl(ə)] *adj (nerf, membre)* numb; *(dur, indifférent)* insensitive; *(imperceptible)* imperceptible.

insensiblement [ɛ̃sɑ̃sibləmɑ̃] *adv (doucement, peu à peu)* imperceptibly.

inséparable [ɛ̃sepaʀabl(ə)] *adj*: ~ **(de)** inseparable (from) ♦ *nmpl*: ~**s** *(oiseaux)* lovebirds.

insérer [ɛ̃seʀe] *vt* to insert; **s'~ dans** to fit into; *(fig)* to come within.

INSERM [ɛ̃sɛʀm] *sigle m* (= *Institut national de la santé et de la recherche médicale*) national institute for medical research.

insert [ɛ̃sɛʀ] *nm* enclosed fireplace burning solid fuel.

insertion [ɛ̃sɛʀsjɔ̃] *nf (d'une personne)* integration.

insidieusement [ɛ̃sidjøzmɑ̃] *adv* insidiously.

insidieux, euse [ɛ̃sidjø, -øz] *adj* insidious.

insigne [ɛ̃siɲ] *nm (d'un parti, club)* badge ♦ *adj* distinguished; ~**s** *nmpl (d'une fonction)* insignia *pl*.

insignifiant, e [ɛ̃siɲifjɑ̃, -ɑ̃t] *adj* insignificant; *(somme, affaire, détail)* trivial, insignificant.

insinuant, e [ɛ̃sinɥɑ̃, -ɑ̃t] *adj* ingratiating.

insinuation [ɛ̃sinɥasjɔ̃] *nf* innuendo, insinuation.

insinuer [ɛ̃sinɥe] *vt* to insinuate, imply; **s'~ dans** to seep into; *(fig)* to worm one's way into, creep into.

insipide [ɛ̃sipid] *adj* insipid.

insistance [ɛ̃sistɑ̃s] *nf* insistence; **avec ~** insistently.

insistant, e [ɛ̃sistɑ̃, -ɑ̃t] *adj* insistent.

insister [ɛ̃siste] *vi* to insist; *(s'obstiner)* to keep on; ~ **sur** *(détail, note)* to stress; ~ **pour qch/pour faire qch** to be insistent about sth/about doing sth.

insociable [ɛ̃sɔsjabl(ə)] *adj* unsociable.

insolation [ɛ̃sɔlasjɔ̃] *nf (MÉD)* sunstroke *no pl*; *(ensoleillement)* period of sunshine.

insolence [ɛ̃sɔlɑ̃s] *nf* insolence *no pl*; **avec ~ in-**

solently.

insolent, e [ɛ̃sɔlɑ̃, -ɑ̃t] *adj* insolent.

insolite [ɛ̃sɔlit] *adj* strange, unusual.

insoluble [ɛ̃sɔlybl(ə)] *adj* insoluble.

insolvable [ɛ̃sɔlvabl(ə)] *adj* insolvent.

insomniaque [ɛ̃sɔmnjak] *adj, nm/f* insomniac.

insomnie [ɛ̃sɔmni] *nf* insomnia *no pl,* sleeplessness *no pl;* **avoir des ~s** to suffer from insomnia.

insondable [ɛ̃sɔ̃dabl(ə)] *adj* unfathomable.

insonore [ɛ̃sɔnɔʀ] *adj* soundproof.

insonorisation [ɛ̃sɔnɔʀizɑsjɔ̃] *nf* soundproofing.

insonoriser [ɛ̃sɔnɔʀize] *vt* to soundproof.

insouciance [ɛ̃susjɑ̃s] *nf* carefree attitude; heedless attitude.

insouciant, e [ɛ̃susjɑ̃, -ɑ̃t] *adj* carefree; (*imprévoyant*) heedless.

insoumis, e [ɛ̃sumi, -iz] *adj* (*caractère, enfant*) rebellious, refractory; (*contrée, tribu*) unsubdued; (*MIL: soldat*) absent without leave ♦ *nm* (*MIL: soldat*) absentee.

insoumission [ɛ̃sumisjɔ̃] *nf* rebelliousness; (*MIL*) absence without leave.

insoupçonnable [ɛ̃supsɔnabl(ə)] *adj* above suspicion.

insoupçonné, e [ɛ̃supsɔne] *adj* unsuspected.

insoutenable [ɛ̃sutnabl(ə)] *adj* (*argument*) untenable; (*chaleur*) unbearable.

inspecter [ɛ̃spɛkte] *vt* to inspect.

inspecteur, trice [ɛ̃spɛktœʀ, -tʀis] *nm/f* inspector; (*des assurances*) assessor; ~ **d'Académie** (regional) director of education; ~ **(de l'enseignement) primaire** primary school inspector; ~ **des finances** ≈ tax inspector (*BRIT*), ≈ Internal Revenue Service agent (*US*); ~ **(de police)** (police) inspector.

inspection [ɛ̃spɛksjɔ̃] *nf* inspection.

inspirateur, trice [ɛ̃spiʀatœʀ, -tʀis] *nm/f* (*instigateur*) instigator; (*animateur*) inspirer.

inspiration [ɛ̃spiʀɑsjɔ̃] *nf* inspiration; breathing in *no pl;* (*idée*) flash of inspiration, brainwave; **sous l'~ de** prompted by.

inspiré, e [ɛ̃spiʀe] *adj:* **être bien/mal ~ de faire qch** to be well-advised/ill-advised to do sth.

inspirer [ɛ̃spiʀe] *vt* (*gén*) to inspire ♦ *vi* (*aspirer*) to breathe in; **s'~ de** (*suj: artiste*) to draw one's inspiration from; (*suj: tableau*) to be inspired by; ~ **qch à qn** (*œuvre, project, action*) to inspire sb with sth; (*dégoût, crainte, horreur*) to fill sb with sth; **ça ne m'inspire pas** I'm not keen on the idea.

instabilité [ɛ̃stabilite] *nf* instability.

instable [ɛ̃stabl(ə)] *adj* (*meuble, équilibre*) unsteady; (*population, temps*) unsettled; (*paix, régime, caractère*) unstable.

installateur [ɛ̃stalatœʀ] *nm* fitter.

installation [ɛ̃stalɑsjɔ̃] *nf* installation; putting in *ou* up; fitting out; settling in; (*appareils etc*) fittings *pl,* installations *pl;* **~s** *nfpl* installations; (*industrielles*) plant *sg;* (*de loisirs*) fa-

cilities.

installé, e [ɛ̃stale] *adj:* **bien/mal ~** well/poorly equipped; (*personne*) well/not very well set up *ou* organized.

installer [ɛ̃stale] *vt* (*loger*): ~ **qn** to get sb settled, install sb; (*asseoir, coucher*) to settle (down); (*placer*) to put, place; (*meuble*) to put in; (*rideau, étagère, tente*) to put up; (*gaz, électricité etc*) to put in, install; (*appartement*) to fit out; (*aménager*): ~ **une salle de bains dans une pièce** to fit out a room with a bathroom suite; **s'~** (*s'établir: artisan, dentiste etc*) to set o.s. up; (*se loger*): **s'~ à l'hôtel/chez qn** to move into a hotel/in with sb; (*emménager*) to settle in; (*sur un siège, à un emplacement*) to settle (down); (*fig: maladie, grève*) to take a firm hold *ou* grip.

instamment [ɛ̃stamɑ̃] *adv* urgently.

instance [ɛ̃stɑ̃s] *nf* (*JUR: procédure*) (legal) proceedings *pl;* (*ADMIN: autorité*) authority; **~s** *nfpl* (*prières*) entreaties; **affaire en ~** matter pending; **courrier en ~** mail ready for posting; **être en ~ de divorce** to be awaiting a divorce; **train en ~ de départ** train on the point of departure; **tribunal de première ~** court of first instance; **en seconde ~** on appeal.

instant [ɛ̃stɑ̃] *nm* moment, instant; **dans un ~** in a moment; **à l'~** this instant; **je l'ai vu à l'~** I've just this minute seen him, I saw him a moment ago; **à l'~ (même)** at the (very) moment that *ou* when, (just) as; **à chaque ~, à tout ~** at any moment; constantly; **pour l'~** for the moment, for the time being; **par ~s** at times; **de tous les ~s** perpetual; **dès l'~ où *ou* que ...** from the moment when ..., since that moment when ....

instantané, e [ɛ̃stɑ̃tane] *adj* (*lait, café*) instant; (*explosion, mort*) instantaneous ♦ *nm* snapshot.

instantanément [ɛ̃stɑ̃tanemɑ̃] *adv* instantaneously.

instar [ɛ̃staʀ]: **à l'~ de** *prép* following the example of, like.

instaurer [ɛ̃stɔʀe] *vt* to institute; **s'~** *vi* to set o.s. up; (*collaboration etc*) to be established.

instigateur, trice [ɛ̃stigatœʀ, -tʀis] *nm/f* instigator.

instigation [ɛ̃stigɑsjɔ̃] *nf:* **à l'~ de qn** at sb's instigation.

instiller [ɛ̃stile] *vt* to instil, apply.

instinct [ɛ̃stɛ̃] *nm* instinct; **d'~** (*spontanément*) instinctively; ~ **grégaire** herd instinct; ~ **de conservation** instinct of self-preservation.

instinctif, ive [ɛ̃stɛ̃ktif, -iv] *adj* instinctive.

instinctivement [ɛ̃stɛ̃ktivmɑ̃] *adv* instinctively.

instituer [ɛ̃stitɥe] *vt* to institute, set up; **s'~ défenseur d'une cause** to set o.s up as defender of a cause.

institut [ɛ̃stity] *nm* institute; ~ **de beauté** beauty salon; ~ **médico-légal** mortuary; **I~**

universitaire de technologie (IUT) technical college.

instituteur, trice [ɛ̃stitytœʀ, -tʀis] nm/f (primary (BRIT) ou grade (US)) school) teacher.

institution [ɛ̃stitysjɔ̃] nf institution; (collège) private school.

institutionnaliser [ɛ̃stitysjɔnalize] vt to institutionalize.

instructeur, trice [ɛ̃stʀyktœʀ, -tʀis] adj (MIL): **sergent** ~ drill sergeant; (JUR): **juge** ~ examining (BRIT) ou committing (US) magistrate ♦ nm/f instructor.

instructif, ive [ɛ̃stʀyktif, -iv] adj instructive.

instruction [ɛ̃stʀyksjɔ̃] nf (enseignement, savoir) education; (JUR) (preliminary) investigation and hearing; (directive) instruction; (ADMIN: document) directive; ~s nfpl instructions; (mode d'emploi) directions, instructions; ~ **civique** civics sg; ~ **primaire/publique** primary/public education; ~ **religieuse** religious instruction; ~ **professionnelle** vocational training.

instruire [ɛ̃stʀɥiʀ] vt (élèves) to teach; (recrues) to train; (JUR: affaire) to conduct the investigation for; **s'~** to educate o.s.; **s'~ auprès de qn de qch** (s'informer) to find sth out from sb; ~ **qn de qch** (informer) to inform ou advise sb of sth; ~ **contre qn** (JUR) to investigate sb.

instruit, e [ɛ̃stʀɥi, -it] pp de **instruire** ♦ adj educated.

instrument [ɛ̃stʀymɑ̃] nm instrument; ~ **à cordes/vent** stringed/wind instrument; ~ **de mesure** measuring instrument; ~ **de musique** musical instrument; ~ **de travail** (working) tool.

instrumental, e, aux [ɛ̃stʀymɑ̃tal, -o] adj instrumental.

instrumentation [ɛ̃stʀymɑ̃tasjɔ̃] nf instrumentation.

instrumentiste [ɛ̃stʀymɑ̃tist(ə)] nm/f instrumentalist.

insu [ɛ̃sy] nm: **à l'~ de qn** without sb knowing.

insubmersible [ɛ̃sybmɛʀsibl(ə)] adj unsinkable.

insubordination [ɛ̃sybɔʀdinasjɔ̃] nf rebelliousness; (MIL) insubordination.

insubordonné, e [ɛ̃sybɔʀdɔne] adj insubordinate.

insuccès [ɛ̃syksɛ] nm failure.

insuffisamment [ɛ̃syfizamɑ̃] adv insufficiently.

insuffisance [ɛ̃syfizɑ̃s] nf insufficiency; inadequacy; ~s nfpl (lacunes) inadequacies; ~ **cardiaque** cardiac insufficiency no pl; ~ **hépatique** liver deficiency.

insuffisant, e [ɛ̃syfizɑ̃, -ɑ̃t] adj insufficient; (élève, travail) inadequate.

insuffler [ɛ̃syfle] vt: ~ **qch dans** to blow sth into; ~ **qch à qn** to inspire sb with sth.

insulaire [ɛ̃sylɛʀ] adj island cpd; (attitude) insular.

insularité [ɛ̃sylaʀite] nf insularity.

insuline [ɛ̃sylin] nf insulin.

insultant, e [ɛ̃syltɑ̃, -ɑ̃t] adj insulting.

insulte [ɛ̃sylt(ə)] nf insult.

insulter [ɛ̃sylte] vt to insult.

insupportable [ɛ̃sypɔʀtabl(ə)] adj unbearable.

insurgé, e [ɛ̃syʀʒe] adj, nm/f insurgent, rebel.

insurger [ɛ̃syʀʒe]: **s'~** vi: **s'~ (contre)** to rise up ou rebel (against).

insurmontable [ɛ̃syʀmɔ̃tabl(ə)] adj (difficulté) insuperable; (aversion) unconquerable.

insurpassable [ɛ̃syʀpasabl(ə)] adj unsurpassable, unsurpassed.

insurrection [ɛ̃syʀɛksjɔ̃] nf insurrection, revolt.

insurrectionnel, le [ɛ̃syʀɛksjɔnɛl] adj insurrectionary.

intact, e [ɛ̃takt] adj intact.

intangible [ɛ̃tɑ̃ʒibl(ə)] adj intangible; (principe) inviolable.

intarissable [ɛ̃taʀisabl(ə)] adj inexhaustible.

intégral, e, aux [ɛ̃tegʀal, -o] adj complete ♦ nf (MATH) integral; (œuvres complètes) complete works.

intégralement [ɛ̃tegʀalmɑ̃] adv in full, fully.

intégralité [ɛ̃tegʀalite] nf (d'une somme, d'un revenu) whole (ou full) amount; **dans son ~** in its entirety.

intégrant, e [ɛ̃tegʀɑ̃, -ɑ̃t] adj: **faire partie ~e de** to be an integral part of, be part and parcel of.

intégration [ɛ̃tegʀasjɔ̃] nf integration.

intégrationniste [ɛ̃tegʀasjɔnist(ə)] adj, nm/f integrationist.

intègre [ɛ̃tɛgʀ(ə)] adj perfectly honest, upright.

intégré, e [ɛ̃tegʀe] adj: **circuit** ~ integrated circuit.

intégrer [ɛ̃tegʀe] vt: ~ **qch à** ou **dans** to integrate sth into; **s'~ à** ou **dans** to become integrated into.

intégrisme [ɛ̃tegʀism(ə)] nm fundamentalism.

intégriste [ɛ̃tegʀist(ə)] adj, nm/f fundamentalist.

intégrité [ɛ̃tegʀite] nf integrity.

intellect [ɛ̃telɛkt] nm intellect.

intellectualisme [ɛ̃telɛkt̨ualism(ə)] nm intellectualism.

intellectuel, le [ɛ̃telɛkt̨uɛl] adj, nm/f intellectual; (péj) highbrow.

intellectuellement [ɛ̃telɛkt̨uɛlmɑ̃] adv intellectually.

intelligemment [ɛ̃teliʒamɑ̃] adv intelligently.

intelligence [ɛ̃teliʒɑ̃s] nf intelligence; (compréhension): **l'~ de** the understanding of; (complicité): **regard d'~** glance of complicity, meaningful ou knowing look; (accord): **vivre en bonne ~ avec qn** to be on good terms with sb; ~s nfpl (MIL, fig) secret contacts; **être d'~** to have an understanding; ~ **artificielle** artificial intelligence (A.I.).

intelligent, e [ɛ̃teliʒɑ̃, -ɑ̃t] adj intelligent; (ca-

pable): ~ **en affaires** competent in business.

intelligentsia [ɛ̃telidʒɛnsja] *nf* intelligentsia.

intelligible [ɛ̃teliʒibl(ə)] *adj* intelligible.

intello [ɛ̃telo] *adj, nm/f* (*fam*) highbrow.

intempérance [ɛ̃tɑ̃peRɑ̃s] *nf* overindulgence *no pl*; intemperance *no pl*.

intempérant, e [ɛ̃tɑ̃peRɑ̃, -ɑ̃t] *adj* overindulgent; (*moralement*) intemperate.

intempéries [ɛ̃tɑ̃peRi] *nfpl* bad weather *sg*.

intempestif, ive [ɛ̃tɑ̃pɛstif, -iv] *adj* untimely.

intenable [ɛ̃tnabl(ə)] *adj* unbearable.

intendance [ɛ̃tɑ̃dɑ̃s] *nf* (*MIL*) supply corps; (: *bureau*) supplies office; (*SCOL*) bursar's office.

intendant, e [ɛ̃tɑ̃dɑ̃, -ɑ̃t] *nm/f* (*MIL*) quartermaster; (*SCOL*) bursar; (*d'une propriété*) steward.

intense [ɛ̃tɑ̃s] *adj* intense.

intensément [ɛ̃tɑ̃semɑ̃] *adv* intensely.

intensif, ive [ɛ̃tɑ̃sif, -iv] *adj* intensive; **cours** ~ crash course; ~ **en main-d'œuvre** labour-intensive; ~ **en capital** capital-intensive.

intensification [ɛ̃tɑ̃sifikasjɔ̃] *nf* intensification.

intensifier [ɛ̃tɑ̃sifje] *vt*, **s'**~ *vi* to intensify.

intensité [ɛ̃tɑ̃site] *nf* intensity.

intensivement [ɛ̃tɑ̃sivmɑ̃] *adv* intensively.

intenter [ɛ̃tɑ̃te] *vt*: ~ **un procès contre** *ou* **à qn** to start proceedings against sb.

intention [ɛ̃tɑ̃sjɔ̃] *nf* intention; (*JUR*) intent; **avoir l'**~ **de faire** to intend to do, have the intention of doing; **dans l'**~ **de faire qch** with a view to doing sth; **à l'**~ **de** *prép* for; (*renseignement*) for the benefit *ou* information of; (*film, ouvrage*) aimed at; **à cette** ~ with this aim in view; **sans** ~ unintentionally; **faire qch sans mauvaise** ~ to do sth without ill intent; **agir dans une bonne** ~ to act with good intentions.

intentionné, e [ɛ̃tɑ̃sjɔne] *adj*: **bien** ~ well-meaning *ou* -intentioned; **mal** ~ ill-intentioned.

intentionnel, le [ɛ̃tɑ̃sjɔnɛl] *adj* intentional, deliberate.

intentionnellement [ɛ̃tɑ̃sjɔnɛlmɑ̃] *adv* intentionally, deliberately.

inter [ɛ̃tɛR] *nm* (*TÉL*: = *interurbain*) long-distance call service; (*SPORT*): ~ **gauche/droit** inside-left/-right.

interactif, ive [ɛ̃tɛRaktif, -iv] *adj* (*aussi IN-FORM*) interactive.

interaction [ɛ̃tɛRaksjɔ̃] *nf* interaction.

interarmées [ɛ̃tɛRaRme] *adj inv* inter-army, combined.

interbancaire [ɛ̃tɛRbɑ̃kɛR] *adj* interbank.

intercalaire [ɛ̃tɛRkalɛR] *adj, nm*: (**feuillet**) ~ insert; (**fiche**) ~ divider.

intercaler [ɛ̃tɛRkale] *vt* to insert; **s'**~ **entre** to come in between; to slip in between.

intercéder [ɛ̃tɛRsede] *vi*: ~ (**pour qn**) to intercede (on behalf of sb).

intercepter [ɛ̃tɛRsɛpte] *vt* to intercept; (*lu-*

mière, chaleur) to cut off.

intercepteur [ɛ̃tɛRsɛptœR] *nm* (*AVIAT*) interceptor.

interception [ɛ̃tɛRsɛpsjɔ̃] *nf* interception; **avion d'**~ interceptor.

intercession [ɛ̃tɛRsesjɔ̃] *nf* intercession.

interchangeable [ɛ̃tɛRʃɑ̃ʒabl(ə)] *adj* interchangeable.

interclasse [ɛ̃tɛRklɑs] *nm* (*SCOL*) break (between classes).

interclubs [ɛ̃tɛRklœb] *adj inv* interclub.

intercommunal, e, aux [ɛ̃tɛRkɔmynal, -o] *adj* intervillage, intercommunity.

intercommunautaire [ɛ̃tɛRkɔmynotɛR] *adj* intercommunity.

interconnexion [ɛ̃tɛRkɔnɛksjɔ̃] *nf* (*INFORM*) networking.

intercontinental, e, aux [ɛ̃tɛRkɔ̃tinɑ̃tal, -o] *adj* intercontinental.

intercostal, e, aux [ɛ̃tɛRkɔstal, -o] *adj* intercostal, between the ribs.

interdépartemental, e, aux [ɛ̃tɛRdepaRtəmɑ̃tal, -o] *adj* interdepartmental.

interdépendance [ɛ̃tɛRdepɑ̃dɑ̃s] *nf* interdependence.

interdépendant, e [ɛ̃tɛRdepɑ̃dɑ̃, -ɑ̃t] *adj* interdependent.

interdiction [ɛ̃tɛRdiksjɔ̃] *nf* ban; ~ **de faire qch** ban on doing sth; ~ **de séjour** (*JUR*) *order banning ex-prisoner from frequenting specified places*.

interdire [ɛ̃tɛRdiR] *vt* to forbid; (*ADMIN: stationnement, meeting, passage*) to ban, prohibit; (: *journal, livre*) to ban; ~ **qch à qn** to forbid sb sth; ~ **à qn de faire** to forbid sb to do, prohibit sb from doing; (*suj: empêchement*) to prevent *ou* preclude sb from doing; **s'**~ **qch** (*éviter*) to refrain *ou* abstain from sth; (*se refuser*): **il s'interdit d'y penser** he doesn't allow himself to think about it.

interdisciplinaire [ɛ̃tɛRdisiplinɛR] *adj* interdisciplinary.

interdit, e [ɛ̃tɛRdi, -it] *pp de* **interdire** ♦ *adj* (*stupéfait*) taken aback; (*défendu*) forbidden, prohibited ♦ *nm* interdict, prohibition; **film** ~ **aux moins de 18/13 ans** ≈ 18-/PG-rated film; **sens** ~ one way; **stationnement** ~ no parking; ~ **de chéquier** having cheque book facilities suspended; ~ **de séjour** subject to an *interdiction de séjour*.

intéressant, e [ɛ̃teRɛsɑ̃, -ɑ̃t] *adj* interesting; **faire l'**~ to draw attention to o.s.

intéressé, e [ɛ̃teRese] *adj* (*parties*) involved, concerned; (*amitié, motifs*) self-interested ♦ *nm*: **l'**~ the interested party; **les** ~**s** those concerned *ou* involved.

intéressement [ɛ̃teRɛsmɑ̃] *nm* (*COMM*) profit-sharing.

intéresser [ɛ̃teRese] *vt* to interest; (*toucher*) to be of interest *ou* concern to; (*ADMIN: concerner*) to affect, concern; (*COMM: travailleur*) to give a share in the profits to; (: *partenaire*) to interest (in the business); **s'~ à** to take an interest in, be interested in; **~ qn à qch** to get sb interested in sth.

intérêt [ɛ̃teʀɛ] nm (aussi COMM) interest; (égoïsme) self-interest; **porter de l'~ à qn** to take an interest in sb; **agir par ~** to act out of self-interest; **avoir des ~s dans** (COMM) to have a financial interest ou a stake in; **avoir ~ à faire** to do well to do; **il y a un ~ à ... il** would be a good thing to ...; **~ composé** compound interest.

interface [ɛ̃teʀfas] nf (INFORM) interface.

interférence [ɛ̃teʀfeʀɑ̃s] nf interference.

interférer [ɛ̃teʀfeʀe] vi: **~ (avec)** to interfere (with).

intergouvernemental, e, aux [ɛ̃teʀguvɛʀnəmɑ̃tal, -o] adj intergovernmental.

intérieur, e [ɛ̃teʀjœʀ] adj (mur, escalier, poche) inside; (commerce, politique) domestic; (cour, calme, vie) inner; (navigation) inland ♦ nm (d'une maison, d'un récipient etc) inside; (d'un pays, aussi: décor, mobilier) interior; (POL): **l'I~** (the Department of) the Interior, ≈ the Home Office (BRIT); **à l'~ (de)** inside; (fig) within; **de l'~** (fig) from the inside; **en ~** (CINÉ) in the studio; **vêtement d'~** indoor garment.

intérieurement [ɛ̃teʀjœʀmɑ̃] adv inwardly.

intérim [ɛ̃teʀim] nm interim period; **assurer l'~ (de)** to deputize (for); **par ~** adj interim ♦ adv in a temporary capacity.

intérimaire [ɛ̃teʀimɛʀ] adj temporary, interim ♦ nm/f (secrétaire etc) temporary, temp (BRIT); (suppléant) deputy.

intérioriser [ɛ̃teʀjɔʀize] vt to internalize.

interjection [ɛ̃teʀʒɛksjɔ̃] nf interjection.

interjeter [ɛ̃teʀʒəte] vt (JUR): **~ appel** to lodge an appeal.

interligne [ɛ̃teʀliɲ] nm inter-line space ♦ nf (TYPO) lead, leading; **simple/double ~** single/double spacing.

interlocuteur, trice [ɛ̃teʀlɔkytœʀ, -tʀis] nm/f speaker; (POL): **~ valable** valid representative; **son ~** the person he ou she was speaking to.

interlope [ɛ̃teʀlɔp] adj illicit; (milieu, bar) shady.

interloquer [ɛ̃teʀlɔke] vt to take aback.

interlude [ɛ̃teʀlyd] nm interlude.

intermède [ɛ̃teʀmɛd] nm interlude.

intermédiaire [ɛ̃teʀmedjɛʀ] adj intermediate; middle; half-way ♦ nm/f intermediary; (COMM) middleman; **sans ~** directly; **par l'~ de** through.

interminable [ɛ̃teʀminabl(ə)] adj never-ending.

interminablement [ɛ̃teʀminabləmɑ̃] adv interminably.

interministériel, le [ɛ̃teʀministeʀjɛl] adj: **comité ~** interdepartmental committee.

intermittence [ɛ̃teʀmitɑ̃s] nf: **par ~** intermittently, sporadically.

intermittent, e [ɛ̃teʀmitɑ̃, -ɑ̃t] adj intermittent, sporadic.

internat [ɛ̃teʀna] nm (SCOL) boarding school.

international, e, aux [ɛ̃teʀnasjɔnal, -o] adj, nm/f international.

internationalisation [ɛ̃teʀnasjɔnalizasjɔ̃] nf internationalization.

internationaliser [ɛ̃teʀnasjɔnalize] vt to internationalize.

internationalisme [ɛ̃teʀnasjɔnalism(ə)] nm internationalism.

interne [ɛ̃teʀn(ə)] adj internal ♦ nm/f (SCOL) boarder; (MÉD) houseman (BRIT), intern (US).

internement [ɛ̃teʀnəmɑ̃] nm (POL) internment; (MÉD) confinement.

interner [ɛ̃teʀne] vt (POL) to intern; (MÉD) to confine to a mental institution.

interparlementaire [ɛ̃teʀpaʀləmɑ̃tɛʀ] adj interparliamentary.

interpellation [ɛ̃teʀpelasjɔ̃] nf interpellation; (POL) question.

interpeller [ɛ̃teʀpele] vt (appeler) to call out to; (apostropher) to shout at; (POLICE) to take in for questioning; (POL) to question; **s'~** to exchange insults.

interphone [ɛ̃teʀfɔn] nm intercom.

interplanétaire [ɛ̃teʀplanetɛʀ] adj interplanetary.

Interpol [ɛ̃teʀpɔl] sigle m Interpol.

interpoler [ɛ̃teʀpɔle] vt to interpolate.

interposer [ɛ̃teʀpoze] vt to interpose; **s'~** vi to intervene; **par personnes interposées** through a third party.

interprétariat [ɛ̃teʀpʀetaʀja] nm interpreting.

interprétation [ɛ̃teʀpʀetasjɔ̃] nf interpretation.

interprète [ɛ̃teʀpʀɛt] nm/f interpreter; (porte-parole) spokesman.

interpréter [ɛ̃teʀpʀete] vt to interpret.

interprofessionnel, le [ɛ̃teʀpʀɔfesjɔnɛl] adj interprofessional.

interrogateur, trice [ɛ̃teʀɔgatœʀ, -tʀis] adj questioning, inquiring ♦ nm/f (SCOL) (oral) examiner.

interrogatif, ive [ɛ̃teʀɔgatif, -iv] adj (LING) interrogative.

interrogation [ɛ̃teʀɔgasjɔ̃] nf question; (SCOL) (written ou oral) test.

interrogatoire [ɛ̃teʀɔgatwaʀ] nm (POLICE) questioning no pl; (JUR) cross-examination, interrogation.

interroger [ɛ̃teʀɔʒe] vt to question; (INFORM) to interrogate; (SCOL: candidat) to test; **~ qn (sur qch)** to question sb (about sth); **~ qn du regard** to look questioningly at sb, give sb a questioning look; **s'~ sur qch** to ask o.s. about sth, ponder (about) sth.

interrompre [ɛ̃teʀɔ̃pʀ(ə)] vt (gén) to interrupt; (travail, voyage) to break off, interrupt; **s'~** to break off.

interrupteur [ɛ̃teʀyptœʀ] nm switch; **~ à bas-**

cule (*INFORM*) toggle switch.

interruption [ɛ̃terypsjɔ̃] *nf* interruption; **sans** ~ without a break; ~ **de grossesse** termination of pregnancy; ~ **volontaire de grossesse** voluntary termination of pregnancy, abortion.

interscolaire [ɛ̃tɛrskɔlɛr] *adj* interschool(s).

intersection [ɛ̃tɛrsɛksjɔ̃] *nf* intersection.

intersidéral, e, aux [ɛ̃tɛrsideral, -o] *adj* intersidereal, interstellar.

interstice [ɛ̃tɛrstis] *nm* crack, slit.

intersyndical, e, aux [ɛ̃tɛrsɛ̃dikal, -o] *adj* interunion.

interurbain [ɛ̃tɛryrbɛ̃] (*TÉL*) *nm* long-distance call service ♦ *adj* long-distance.

intervalle [ɛ̃tɛrval] *nm* (*espace*) space; (*de temps*) interval; **dans l'**~ in the meantime; **à 2 mois d'**~ after a space of 2 months; **à** ~**s rapprochés** at close intervals; **par** ~**s** at intervals.

intervenant, e [ɛ̃tɛrvənɑ̃, -ɑ̃t] *vb voir* **intervenir** ♦ *nm/f* speaker (*at conference*).

intervenir [ɛ̃tɛrvənir] *vi* (*gén*) to intervene; (*survenir*) to take place; (*faire une conférence*) to give a talk *ou* lecture; ~ **auprès de/en faveur de qn** to intervene with/on behalf of sb; **la police a dû** ~ police had to step in *ou* intervene; **les médecins ont dû** ~ the doctors had to operate.

intervention [ɛ̃tɛrvɑ̃sjɔ̃] *nf* intervention; (*conférence*) talk, paper; ~ **(chirurgicale)** operation.

interventionnisme [ɛ̃tɛrvɑ̃sjɔnism(ə)] *nm* interventionism.

interventionniste [ɛ̃tɛrvɑ̃sjɔnist(ə)] *adj* interventionist.

intervenu, e [ɛ̃tɛrv(ə)ny] *pp de* **intervenir**.

intervertible [ɛ̃tɛrvɛrtibl(ə)] *adj* interchangeable.

intervertir [ɛ̃tɛrvɛrtir] *vt* to invert (the order of), reverse.

interviendrai [ɛ̃tɛrvjɛ̃dre], **interviens** [ɛ̃tɛrvjɛ̃] *etc vb voir* **intervenir**.

interview [ɛ̃tɛrvju] *nf* interview.

interviewer [ɛ̃tɛrvjuve] *vt* to interview ♦ *nm* [ɛ̃tɛrvjuvœr] (*journaliste*) interviewer.

intervins [ɛ̃tɛrvɛ̃] *etc vb voir* **intervenir**.

intestat [ɛ̃tɛsta] *adj* (*JUR*): **décéder** ~ to die intestate.

intestin, e [ɛ̃tɛstɛ̃, -in] *adj* internal ♦ *nm* intestine; ~ **grêle** small intestine.

intestinal, e, aux [ɛ̃tɛstinal, -o] *adj* intestinal.

intime [ɛ̃tim] *adj* intimate; (*vie, journal*) private; (*convictions*) inmost; (*dîner, cérémonie*) held among friends, quiet ♦ *nm/f* close friend.

intimement [ɛ̃timmɑ̃] *adv* (*profondément*) deeply, firmly; (*étroitement*) intimately.

intimer [ɛ̃time] *vt* (*JUR*) to notify; ~ **à qn l'ordre de faire** to order sb to do.

intimidant, e [ɛ̃timidɑ̃, -ɑ̃t] *adj* intimidating.

intimidation [ɛ̃timidasjɔ̃] intimidation; **ma-**

nœuvres d'~ (*action*) acts of intimidation; (*stratégie*) intimidatory tactics.

intimider [ɛ̃timide] *vt* to intimidate.

intimité [ɛ̃timite] *nf* intimacy; (*vie privée*) privacy; private life; **dans l'**~ in private; (*sans formalités*) with only a few friends, quietly.

intitulé [ɛ̃tityle] *nm* title.

intituler [ɛ̃tityle] *vt*: **comment a-t-il intitulé son livre?** what title did he give his book?; **s'**~ to be entitled; (*personne*) to call o.s.

intolérable [ɛ̃tɔlerabl(ə)] *adj* intolerable.

intolérance [ɛ̃tɔlerɑ̃s] *nf* intolerance; ~ **aux antibiotiques** intolerance to antibiotics.

intolérant, e [ɛ̃tɔlerɑ̃, -ɑ̃t] *adj* intolerant.

intonation [ɛ̃tɔnasjɔ̃] *nf* intonation.

intouchable [ɛ̃tuʃabl(ə)] *adj* (*fig*) above the law, sacrosanct; (*REL*) untouchable.

intoxication [ɛ̃tɔksikasjɔ̃] *nf* poisoning *no pl*; (*toxicomanie*) drug addiction; (*fig*) brainwashing; ~ **alimentaire** food poisoning.

intoxiqué, e [ɛ̃tɔksike] *nm/f* addict.

intoxiquer [ɛ̃tɔksike] *vt* to poison; (*fig*) to brainwash; **s'**~ to poison o.s.

intradermique [ɛ̃tradɛrmik] *adj*, *nf*: **(injection)** ~ intradermal *ou* intracutaneous injection.

intraduisible [ɛ̃traduizibl(ə)] *adj* untranslatable; (*fig*) inexpressible.

intraitable [ɛ̃trɛtabl(ə)] *adj* inflexible, uncompromising.

intramusculaire [ɛ̃tramyskylɛr] *adj*, *nf*: **(injection)** ~ intramuscular injection.

intransigeance [ɛ̃trɑ̃ziʒɑ̃s] *nf* intransigence.

intransigeant, e [ɛ̃trɑ̃ziʒɑ̃, -ɑ̃t] *adj* intransigent; (*morale, passion*) uncompromising.

intransitif, ive [ɛ̃trɑ̃zitif, -iv] *adj* (*LING*) intransitive.

intransportable [ɛ̃trɑ̃spɔrtabl(ə)] *adj* (*blessé*) unable to travel.

intraveineux, euse [ɛ̃travɛnø, -øz] *adj* intravenous.

intrépide [ɛ̃trepid] *adj* dauntless, intrepid.

intrépidité [ɛ̃trepidite] *nf* dauntlessness.

intrigant, e [ɛ̃trigɑ̃, -ɑ̃t] *nm/f* schemer.

intrigue [ɛ̃trig] *nf* intrigue; (*scénario*) plot.

intriguer [ɛ̃trige] *vi* to scheme ♦ *vt* to puzzle, intrigue.

intrinsèque [ɛ̃trɛ̃sɛk] *adj* intrinsic.

introductif, ive [ɛ̃trɔdyktif, -iv] *adj* introductory.

introduction [ɛ̃trɔdyksjɔ̃] *nf* introduction; **paroles/chapitre d'**~ introductory words/chapter; **lettre/mot d'**~ letter/note of introduction.

introduire [ɛ̃trɔduir] *vt* to introduce; (*visiteur*) to show in; (*aiguille, clef*): ~ **qch dans** to insert *ou* introduce sth into; (*personne*): ~ **à qch** to introduce to sth; (: *présenter*): ~ **qn à qn/dans un club** to introduce sb to sb/to a club; (*INFORM*) to input, enter; **s'**~ (*techniques, usages*) to be introduced; **s'**~, **dans** to gain entry into; to get o.s. accepted into; (*eau, fumée*) to get into; ~ **au clavier** to key in.

introduit, e [ɛ̃tʀɔdɥi, -it] *pp de* **introduire ♦** *adj*: **bien** ~ (*personne*) well-received.

introniser [ɛ̃tʀɔnize] *vt* to enthrone.

introspection [ɛ̃tʀɔspɛksjɔ̃] *nf* introspection.

introuvable [ɛ̃tʀuvabl(ə)] *adj* which cannot be found; (*COMM*) unobtainable.

introverti, e [ɛ̃tʀɔvɛʀti] *nm/f* introvert.

intrus, e [ɛ̃tʀy, -yz] *nm/f* intruder.

intrusion [ɛ̃tʀyzjɔ̃] *nf* intrusion; (*ingérence*) interference.

intuitif, ive [ɛ̃tɥitif, -iv] *adj* intuitive.

intuition [ɛ̃tɥisjɔ̃] *nf* intuition; **avoir une** ~ to have a feeling; **avoir l'**~ **de qch** to have an intuition of sth; **avoir de l'**~ to have intuition.

intuitivement [ɛ̃tɥitivmɑ̃] *adv* intuitively.

inusable [inyzabl(ə)] *adj* hard-wearing.

inusité, e [inyzite] *adj* rarely used.

inutile [inytil] *adj* useless; (*superflu*) unnecessary.

inutilement [inytilmɑ̃] *adv* needlessly.

inutilisable [inytilizabl(ə)] *adj* unusable.

inutilisé, e [inytilize] *adj* unused.

inutilité [inytilite] *nf* uselessness.

invaincu, e [ɛ̃vɛ̃ky] *adj* unbeaten; (*armée, peuple*) unconquered.

invalide [ɛ̃valid] *adj* disabled **♦** *nm/f*: ~ **de guerre** disabled ex-serviceman; ~ **du travail** industrially disabled person.

invalider [ɛ̃valide] *vt* to invalidate.

invalidité [ɛ̃validite] *nf* disability.

invariable [ɛ̃vaʀjabl(ə)] *adj* invariable.

invariablement [ɛ̃vaʀjabləmɑ̃] *adv* invariably.

invasion [ɛ̃vazjɔ̃] *nf* invasion.

invective [ɛ̃vɛktiv] *nf* invective.

invectiver [ɛ̃vɛktive] *vt* to hurl abuse at **♦** *vi*: ~ **contre** to rail against.

invendable [ɛ̃vɑ̃dabl(ə)] *adj* unsaleable, unmarketable.

invendu, e [ɛ̃vɑ̃dy] *adj* unsold **♦** *nm* return; ~**s** *nmpl* unsold goods.

inventaire [ɛ̃vɑ̃tɛʀ] *nm* inventory; (*COMM: liste*) stocklist; (: *opération*) stocktaking *no pl*; (*fig*) survey; **faire un** ~ to make an inventory; (*COMM*) to take stock; **faire** *ou* **procéder à l'**~ to take stock.

inventer [ɛ̃vɑ̃te] *vt* to invent; (*subterfuge*) to devise, invent; (*histoire, excuse*) to make up, invent; ~ **de faire** to hit on the idea of doing.

inventeur, trice [ɛ̃vɑ̃tœʀ, -tʀis] *nm/f* inventor.

inventif, ive [ɛ̃vɑ̃tif, -iv] *adj* inventive.

invention [ɛ̃vɑ̃sjɔ̃] *nf* invention; (*imagination, inspiration*) inventiveness.

inventivité [ɛ̃vɑ̃tivite] *nf* inventiveness.

inventorier [ɛ̃vɑ̃tɔʀje] *vt* to make an inventory of.

invérifiable [ɛ̃veʀifjabl(ə)] *adj* unverifiable.

inverse [ɛ̃vɛʀs(ə)] *adj* (*ordre*) reverse; (*sens*) opposite; (*rapport*) inverse **♦** *nm* reverse; inverse; **en proportion** ~ in inverse proportion; **dans le sens** ~ **des aiguilles d'une mon-**

tre anti-clockwise; **en sens** ~ in (*ou* from) the opposite direction; **à l'**~ conversely.

inversement [ɛ̃vɛʀsəmɑ̃] *adv* conversely.

inverser [ɛ̃vɛʀse] *vt* to reverse, invert; (*ÉLEC*) to reverse.

inversion [ɛ̃vɛʀsjɔ̃] *nf* reversal; inversion.

invertébré, e [ɛ̃vɛʀtebʀe] *adj*, *nm* invertebrate.

inverti, e [ɛ̃vɛʀti] *nm/f* homosexual.

investigation [ɛ̃vɛstigɑsjɔ̃] *nf* investigation, inquiry.

investir [ɛ̃vɛstiʀ] *vt* to invest; **s'**~ *vi* (*PSYCH*) to involve o.s.; ~ **qn de** to vest *ou* invest sb with.

investissement [ɛ̃vɛstismɑ̃] *nm* investment; (*PSYCH*) involvement.

investisseur [ɛ̃vɛstisœʀ] *nm* investor.

investiture [ɛ̃vɛstityʀ] *nf* investiture; (*à une élection*) nomination.

invétéré, e [ɛ̃veteʀe] *adj* (*habitude*) ingrained; (*bavard, buveur*) inveterate.

invincible [ɛ̃vɛ̃sibl(ə)] *adj* invincible, unconquerable.

invinciblement [ɛ̃vɛ̃sibləmɑ̃] *adv* (*fig*) invincibly.

inviolabilité [ɛ̃vjɔlabilite] *nf*: ~ **parlementaire** parliamentary immunity.

inviolable [ɛ̃vjɔlabl(ə)] *adj* inviolable.

invisible [ɛ̃vizibl(ə)] *adj* invisible; (*fig: personne*) not available.

invitation [ɛ̃vitɑsjɔ̃] *nf* invitation; **à/sur l'**~ **de qn** at/on sb's invitation; **carte/lettre d'**~ invitation card/letter.

invite [ɛ̃vit] *nf* invitation.

invité, e [ɛ̃vite] *nm/f* guest.

inviter [ɛ̃vite] *vt* to invite; ~ **qn à faire qch** to invite sb to do sth; (*suj: chose*) to induce *ou* tempt sb to do sth.

invivable [ɛ̃vivabl(ə)] *adj* unbearable, impossible.

involontaire [ɛ̃vɔlɔ̃tɛʀ] *adj* (*mouvement*) involuntary; (*insulte*) unintentional; (*complice*) unwitting.

involontairement [ɛ̃vɔlɔ̃tɛʀmɑ̃] *adv* involuntarily.

invoquer [ɛ̃vɔke] *vt* (*Dieu, muse*) to call upon, invoke; (*prétexte*) to put forward (as an excuse); (*témoignage*) to call upon; (*loi, texte*) to refer to; ~ **la clémence de qn** to beg sb *ou* appeal to sb for clemency.

invraisemblable [ɛ̃vʀɛsɑ̃blabl(ə)] *adj* unlikely, improbable; (*bizarre*) incredible.

invraisemblance [ɛ̃vʀɛsɑ̃blɑ̃s] *nf* unlikelihood *no pl*, improbability.

invulnérable [ɛ̃vylneʀabl(ə)] *adj* invulnerable.

iode [jɔd] *nm* iodine.

iodé, e [jɔde] *adj* iodized.

ion [jɔ̃] *nm* ion.

ionique [jɔnik] *adj* (*ARCHIT*) Ionic; (*SCIENCE*) ionic.

ioniseur [jɔnizœʀ] *nm* ionizer.

iota [jɔta] *nm*: **sans changer un** ~ without

changing one iota *ou* the tiniest bit.

IPC *sigle m* (= *Indice des prix à la consommation*) CPI.

IR. *abr* = **infrarouge.**

IRA *sigle f* (= *Irish Republican Army*) IRA.

irai [iʀe] *etc vb voir* **aller.**

Irak [iʀɑk] *nm:* **l'~** Iraq *ou* Irak.

irakien, ne [iʀakjɛ̃, -ɛn] *adj* Iraqi ♦ *nm/f:* **I~, ne** Iraqi.

Iran [iʀɑ̃] *nm:* **l'~** Iran.

iranien, ne [iʀanjɛ̃, -ɛn] *adj* Iranian ♦ *nm* (*LING*) Iranian ♦ *nm/f:* **I~, ne** Iranian.

Iraq [iʀɑk] = **Irak.**

iraquien, ne [iʀakjɛ̃, -ɛn] = **irakien, ne.**

irascible [iʀasibl(ə)] *adj* short-tempered, irascible.

irions [iʀjɔ̃] *etc vb voir* **aller.**

iris [iʀis] *nm* iris.

irisé, e [iʀize] *adj* iridescent.

irlandais, e [iʀlɑ̃dɛ, -ɛz] *adj, nm* (*LING*) Irish ♦ *nm/f:* **I~, e** Irishman/woman; **les I~** the Irish.

Irlande [iʀlɑ̃d] *nf:* **l'~** (*pays*) Ireland; (*état*) the Irish Republic, the Republic of Ireland, Eire; **~ du Nord** Northern Ireland, Ulster; **~ du Sud** Southern Ireland, Irish Republic, Eire; **la mer d'~** the Irish Sea.

ironie [iʀɔni] *nf* irony.

ironique [iʀɔnik] *adj* ironical.

ironiquement [iʀɔnikmɑ̃] *adv* ironically.

ironiser [iʀɔnize] *vi* to be ironical.

irons [iʀɔ̃] *etc vb voir* **aller.**

IRPP *sigle m* (= *impôt sur le revenu des personnes physiques*) income tax.

irradiation [iʀadjɑsjɔ̃] *nf* irradiation.

irradier [iʀadje] *vi* to radiate ♦ *vt* to irradiate.

irraisonné, e [iʀezɔne] *adj* irrational, unreasoned.

irrationnel, le [iʀasjɔnɛl] *adj* irrational.

irrattrapable [iʀatʀapabl(ə)] *adj* (*retard*) that cannot be made up; (*bévue*) that cannot be made good.

irréalisable [iʀealizabl(ə)] *adj* unrealizable; (*projet*) impracticable.

irréalisme [iʀealism(ə)] *nm* lack of realism.

irréaliste [iʀealist(ə)] *adj* unrealistic.

irréalité [iʀealite] *nf* unreality.

irrecevable [iʀsəvabl(ə)] *adj* unacceptable.

irréconciliable [iʀekɔ̃siljabl(ə)] *adj* irreconcilable.

irrécouvrable [iʀekuvʀabl(ə)] *adj* irrecoverable.

irrécupérable [iʀekypeʀabl(ə)] *adj* unreclaimable, beyond repair; (*personne*) beyond redemption *ou* recall.

irrécusable [iʀekyzabl(ə)] *adj* (*témoignage*) unimpeachable; (*preuve*) incontestable, indisputable.

irréductible [iʀedyktibl(ə)] *adj* indomitable, implacable; (*MATH: fraction, équation*) irreducible.

irréductiblement [iʀedyktibləmɑ̃] *adv* implacably.

irréel, le [iʀeɛl] *adj* unreal.

irréfléchi, e [iʀefleʃi] *adj* thoughtless.

irréfutable [iʀefytabl(ə)] *adj* irrefutable.

irréfutablement [iʀefytabləmɑ̃] *adv* irrefutably.

irrégularité [iʀegylaʀite] *nf* irregularity; unevenness *no pl.*

irrégulier, ière [iʀegylje, -jɛʀ] *adj* irregular; (*surface, rythme, écriture*) uneven, irregular; (*élève, athlète*) erratic.

irrégulièrement [iʀegyljɛʀmɑ̃] *adv* irregularly.

irrémédiable [iʀemedjabl(ə)] *adj* irreparable.

irrémédiablement [iʀemedjabləmɑ̃] *adv* irreparably.

irremplaçable [iʀɑ̃plasabl(ə)] *adj* irreplaceable.

irréparable [iʀepaʀabl(ə)] *adj* beyond repair, irreparable; (*fig*) irreparable.

irrépréhensible [iʀepʀeɑ̃sibl(ə)] *adj* irreprehensible.

irrépressible [iʀepʀesibl(ə)] *adj* irrepressible.

irréprochable [iʀepʀɔʃabl(ə)] *adj* irreproachable, beyond reproach; (*tenue, toilette*) impeccable.

irrésistible [iʀezistibl(ə)] *adj* irresistible; (*preuve, logique*) compelling.

irrésistiblement [iʀezistibləmɑ̃] *adv* irresistibly.

irrésolu, e [iʀezɔly] *adj* irresolute.

irrésolution [iʀezɔlysjɔ̃] *nf* irresoluteness.

irrespectueux, euse [iʀɛspɛktɥø, -øz] *adj* disrespectful.

irrespirable [iʀɛspiʀabl(ə)] *adj* unbreathable; (*fig*) oppressive, stifling.

irresponsabilité [iʀɛspɔ̃sabilite] *nf* irresponsibility.

irresponsable [iʀɛspɔ̃sabl(ə)] *adj* irresponsible.

irrévérencieux, euse [iʀeveʀɑ̃sjø, -øz] *adj* irreverent.

irréversible [iʀevɛʀsibl(ə)] *adj* irreversible.

irréversiblement [iʀevɛʀsibləmɑ̃] *adv* irreversibly.

irrévocable [iʀevɔkabl(ə)] *adj* irrevocable.

irrévocablement [iʀevɔkabləmɑ̃] *adv* irrevocably.

irrigation [iʀigɑsjɔ̃] *nf* irrigation.

irriguer [iʀige] *vt* to irrigate.

irritabilité [iʀitabilite] *nf* irritability.

irritable [iʀitabl(ə)] *adj* irritable.

irritant, e [iʀitɑ̃, -ɑ̃t] *adj* irritating; (*MÉD*) irritant.

irritation [iʀitɑsjɔ̃] *nf* irritation.

irrité, e [iʀite] *adj* irritated.

irriter [iʀite] *vt* (*agacer*) to irritate, annoy; (*MÉD: enflammer*) to irritate; **s'~ contre qn/ de qch** to get annoyed *ou* irritated with sb/ at sth.

irruption [iʀypsjɔ̃] *nf* irruption *no pl;* **faire ~ dans** to burst into.

ISBN *sigle m* (= *International Standard Book*

Number) ISBN.

Islam [islam] *nm* Islam.

islamique [islamik] *adj* Islamic.

islamiste [islamist(ə)] *adj*, *nm/f* Islamic.

islandais, e [islɑ̃dɛ, -ɛz] *adj* Icelandic ♦ *nm* (*LING*) Icelandic ♦ *nm/f*: I~, e Icelander.

Islande [islɑ̃d] *nf*: l'~ Iceland.

ISMH *sigle m* (= *Inventaire supplémentaire des monuments historiques*): **monument inscrit à l'~** ≈ listed building.

isocèle [izɔsɛl] *adj* isoceles.

isolant, e [izɔlɑ̃, -ɑ̃t] *adj* insulating; (*insonorisant*) soundproofing ♦ *nm* insulator.

isolateur [izɔlatœR] *nm* (*ÉLEC*) insulator.

isolation [izɔlasjɔ̃] *nf* insulation; ~ **acoustique/thermique** sound/thermal insulation.

isolationnisme [izɔlasjɔnism(ə)] *nm* isolationism.

isolé, e [izɔle] *adj* isolated; (*ÉLEC*) insulated.

isolement [izɔlmɑ̃] *nm* isolation; solitary confinement.

isolément [izɔlemɑ̃] *adv* in isolation.

isoler [izɔle] *vt* to isolate; (*prisonnier*) to put in solitary confinement; (*ville*) to cut off, isolate; (*ÉLEC*) to insulate.

isoloir [izɔlwaR] *nm* polling booth.

isorel [izɔRɛl] *nm* ® hardboard.

isotherme [izɔtɛRm(ə)] *adj* (*camion*) refrigerated.

Israël [israɛl] *nm*: l'~ Israel.

israélien, ne [israeljɛ̃, -ɛn] *adj* Israeli ♦ *nm/f*: I~, ne Israeli.

israélite [israelit] *adj* Jewish; (*dans l'Ancien Testament*) Israelite ♦ *nm/f*: I~ Jew/Jewess; Israelite.

issu, e [isy] *adj*: ~ **de** descended from; (*fig*) stemming from ♦ *nf* (*ouverture, sortie*) exit; (*solution*) way out, solution; (*dénouement*) outcome; **à l'~e de** at the conclusion *ou* close of; **rue sans ~e** dead end, no through road (*BRIT*), no outlet (*US*); ~**e de secours** emergency exit.

Istamboul *ou* **Istanbul** [istɑ̃bul] *n* Istanbul.

isthme [ism(ə)] *nm* isthmus.

Italie [itali] *nf*: l'~ Italy.

italien, ne [italjɛ̃, -ɛn] *adj* Italian ♦ *nm* (*LING*) Italian ♦ *nm/f*: I~, ne Italian.

italique [italik] *nm*: **en ~(s)** in italics.

item [itɛm] *nm* item; (*question*) question, test.

itinéraire [itineRɛR] *nm* itinerary, route.

itinérant, e [itineRɑ̃, -ɑ̃t] *adj* itinerant, travelling.

ITP *sigle m* (= *ingénieur des travaux publics*) civil engineer.

IUT *sigle m* = **Institut universitaire de technologie**.

IVG *sigle f* (= *interruption volontaire de grossesse*) abortion.

ivoire [ivwaR] *nm* ivory.

ivoirien, ne [ivwaRjɛ̃, -ɛn] *adj* of *ou* from the Ivory Coast.

ivraie [ivRɛ] *nf*: **séparer le bon grain de l'~** (*fig*) to separate the wheat from the chaff.

ivre [ivR(ə)] *adj* drunk; ~ **de** (*colère*) wild with; (*bonheur*) drunk *ou* intoxicated with; ~ **mort** dead drunk.

ivresse [ivRɛs] *nf* drunkenness; (*euphorie*) intoxication.

ivrogne [ivRɔɲ] *nm/f* drunkard.

J j

J, j [ʒi] *nm inv* J, j ♦ *abr* (= *jour*): **jour ~** D-day; (= *Joule*) J; **J comme Joseph** J for Jack (*BRIT*) *ou* Jig (*US*).

j' [ʒ] *pron voir* **je**.

jabot [ʒabo] *nm* (*ZOOL*) crop; (*de vêtement*) jabot.

JAC [ʒak] *sigle f* (= *Jeunesse agricole catholique*) *youth organization*.

jacasser [ʒakase] *vi* to chatter.

jachère [ʒaʃɛR] *nf*: **(être) en ~** (to lie) fallow.

jacinthe [ʒasɛ̃t] *nf* hyacinth; ~ **des bois** bluebell.

jack [dʒak] *nm* jack plug.

jacquard [ʒakaR] *adj inv* Fair Isle.

jacquerie [ʒakRi] *nf* riot.

jade [ʒad] *nm* jade.

jadis [ʒadis] *adv* in times past, formerly.

jaguar [ʒagwaR] *nm* (*ZOOL*) jaguar.

jaillir [ʒajiR] *vi* (*liquide*) to spurt out, gush out; (*lumière*) to flood out; (*fig*) to rear up; to burst out.

jaillissement [ʒajismɑ̃] *nm* spurt, gush.

jais [ʒɛ] *nm* jet; (**d'un noir**) **de ~** jet-black.

jalon [ʒalɔ̃] *nm* range pole; (*fig*) milestone; **poser des ~s** (*fig*) to pave the way.

jalonner [ʒalɔne] *vt* to mark out; (*fig*) to mark, punctuate.

jalousement [ʒaluzmɑ̃] *adv* jealously.

jalouser [ʒaluze] *vt* to be jealous of.

jalousie [ʒaluzi] *nf* jealousy; (*store*) (venetian) blind.

jaloux, ouse [ʒalu, -uz] *adj* jealous; **être ~ de qn/qch** to be jealous of sb/sth.

jamaïquain, e [ʒamaikɛ̃, -ɛn] *adj* Jamaican.

Jamaïque [ʒamaik] *nf*: **la ~** Jamaica.

jamais [ʒamɛ] *adv* never; (*sans négation*) ever; **ne ... ~** never; ~ **de la vie!** never!; **si ~ ...** if ever ...; **à (tout) ~**, **pour ~** for ever, for ever and ever.

jambage [ʒɑ̃baʒ] *nm* (*de lettre*) downstroke; (*de porte*) jamb.

jambe [ʒɑ̃b] *nf* leg; **à toutes ~s** as fast as one's legs can carry one.

jambières [ʒɑ̃bjɛR] *nfpl* legwarmers; (*SPORT*)

shin pads.

jambon [ʒɑ̃bɔ̃] nm ham.

jambonneau, x [ʒɑ̃bɔno] nm knuckle of ham.

jante [ʒɑ̃t] nf (wheel) rim.

janvier [ʒɑ̃vje] nm January; voir aussi **juillet**.

Japon [ʒapɔ̃] nm: **le ~** Japan.

japonais, e [ʒapɔnɛ, -ɛz] adj Japanese ♦ nm (LING) Japanese ♦ nm/f: **J~, e** Japanese.

japonaiserie [ʒapɔnɛzʀi] nf (bibelot) Japanese curio.

jappement [ʒapmɑ̃] nm yap, yelp.

japper [ʒape] vi to yap, yelp.

jaquette [ʒakɛt] nf (de cérémonie) morning coat; (de femme) jacket; (de livre) dust cover, (dust) jacket.

jardin [ʒaʀdɛ̃] nm garden; **~ d'acclimatation** zoological gardens pl; **~ botanique** botanical gardens pl; **~ d'enfants** nursery school; **~ potager** vegetable garden; **~ public** (public) park, public gardens pl; **~s suspendus** hanging gardens.

jardinage [ʒaʀdinaʒ] nm gardening.

jardiner [ʒaʀdine] vi to garden, do some gardening.

jardinet [ʒaʀdinɛ] nm little garden.

jardinier, ière [ʒaʀdinje, -jɛʀ] nm/f gardener ♦ nf (de fenêtre) window box; **jardinière d'enfants** nursery school teacher; **jardinière (de légumes)** (CULIN) mixed vegetables.

jargon [ʒaʀgɔ̃] nm (charabia) gibberish; (publicitaire, scientifique etc) jargon.

jarre [ʒaʀ] nf (earthenware) jar.

jarret [ʒaʀɛ] nm back of knee; (CULIN) knuckle, shin.

jarretelle [ʒaʀtɛl] nf suspender (BRIT), garter (US).

jarretière [ʒaʀtjɛʀ] nf garter.

jars [ʒaʀ] nm (ZOOL) gander.

jaser [ʒaze] vi to chatter, prattle; (indiscrètement) to gossip.

jasmin [ʒasmɛ̃] nm jasmin.

jaspe [ʒasp(ə)] nm jasper.

jaspé, e [ʒaspe] adj marbled, mottled.

jatte [ʒat] nf basin, bowl.

jauge [ʒoʒ] nf (capacité) capacity, tonnage; (instrument) gauge; **~ (de niveau) d'huile** dipstick.

jauger [ʒoʒe] vt to gauge the capacity of; (fig) to size up; **~ 3 000 tonneaux** to measure 3,000 tons.

jaunâtre [ʒonɑtʀ(ə)] adj (couleur, teint) yellowish.

jaune [ʒon] adj, nm yellow ♦ nm/f Asiatic; (briseur de grève) blackleg ♦ adv (fam): **rire ~** to laugh on the other side of one's face; **~ d'œuf** (egg) yolk.

jaunir [ʒoniʀ] vi, vt to turn yellow.

jaunisse [ʒonis] nf jaundice.

Java [ʒava] nf Java.

java [ʒava] nf (fam): **faire la ~** to live it up, have a real party.

javanais, e [ʒavanɛ, -ɛz] adj Javanese.

Javel [ʒavɛl] nf voir **eau**.

javelliser [ʒavelize] vt (eau) to chlorinate.

javelot [ʒavlo] nm javelin; (SPORT): **faire du ~** to throw the javelin.

jazz [dʒaz] nm jazz.

J.-C. abr = **Jésus-Christ**.

JCR sigle f (= Jeunesse communiste révolutionnaire) communist youth movement.

je, j' [ʒ(ə)] pron I.

jean [dʒin] nm jeans pl.

jeannette [ʒanɛt] nf (planchette) sleeveboard; (petite fille scout) Brownie.

JEC [ʒɛk] sigle f (= Jeunesse étudiante chrétienne) youth organization.

jeep [(d)ʒip] nf® (AUTO) jeep®.

jérémiades [ʒeʀemjad] nfpl moaning sg.

jerrycan [ʒeʀikan] nm jerrycan.

Jersey [ʒɛʀzɛ] nf Jersey.

jersey [ʒɛʀzɛ] nm jersey; (TRICOT): **pointe de ~** stocking stitch.

jersiais, e [ʒɛʀzjɛ, -ɛz] adj Jersey cpd, of ou from Jersey.

Jérusalem [ʒeʀyzalɛm] n Jerusalem.

jésuite [ʒezɥit] nm Jesuit.

Jésus-Christ [ʒezykʀi(st)] n Jesus Christ; **600 avant/après ~** ou **J.-C.** 600 B.C./A.D.

jet[1] [ʒɛ] nm (lancer) throwing no pl, throw; (jaillissement) jet; spurt; (de tuyau) nozzle; (fig): **premier ~** (ébauche) rough outline; **arroser au ~** to hose; **d'un (seul) ~** (d'un seul coup) at (ou in) one go; **du premier ~** at the first attempt ou shot; **~ d'eau** spray; (fontaine) fountain.

jet[2] [dʒɛt] nm (avion) jet.

jetable [ʒətabl(ə)] adj disposable.

jeté [ʒəte] nm (TRICOT): **un ~** make one; **~ de table** (table) runner; **~ de lit** bedspread.

jetée [ʒəte] nf jetty; pier.

jeter [ʒəte] vt (gén) to throw; (se défaire de) to throw away ou out; (son, lueur etc) to give out; **~ qch à qn** to throw sth to sb; (de façon agressive) to throw sth at sb; (NAVIG): **~ l'ancre** to cast anchor; **~ un coup d'œil (à)** to take a look (at); **~ les bras en avant/la tête en arrière** to throw one's arms forward/one's head back(ward); **~ l'effroi parmi** to spread fear among; **~ un sort à qn** to cast a spell on sb; **~ qn dans la misère** to reduce sb to poverty; **~ qn dehors/en prison** to throw sb out/into prison; **~ l'éponge** (fig) to throw in the towel; **~ des fleurs à qn** (fig) to say lovely things to sb; **~ la pierre à qn** (accuser, blâmer) to accuse sb; **se ~ sur** to throw o.s. onto; **se ~ dans** (suj: fleuve) to flow into; **se ~ par la fenêtre** to throw o.s. out of the window; **se ~ à l'eau** (fig) to take the plunge.

jeton [ʒətɔ̃] nm (au jeu) counter; (de téléphone) token; **~s de présence** (director's) fees.

jette [ʒɛt] etc vb voir **jeter**.

jeu, x [ʒø] nm (divertissement, TECH: d'une pièce) play; (défini par des règles, TENNIS: partie,

FOOTBALL etc: façon de jouer) game; (THÉÂT etc) acting; (fonctionnement) working, interplay; (série d'objets, jouet) set; (CARTES) hand; (au casino): le ~ gambling; **cacher son** ~ (fig) to keep one's cards hidden, conceal one's hand; **c'est un** ~ **d'enfant!** (fig) it's child's play!; **en** ~ at stake; at work; (FOOTBALL) in play; **remettre en** ~ to throw in; **entrer/mettre en** ~ to come/bring into play; **par** ~ (pour s'amuser) for fun; **d'entrée de** ~ (tout de suite, dès le début) from the outset; **entrer dans le** ~**/le** ~ **de qn** (fig) to play the game/sb's game; **jouer gros** ~ to play for high stakes; **se piquer/se prendre au** ~ to get excited over/get caught up in ou involved in the game; ~ **de boules** game of bowls; (endroit) bowling pitch; (boules) set of bowls; ~ **de cartes** card game; (paquet) pack of cards; ~ **de construction** building set; ~ **d'échecs** chess set; ~ **d'écritures** (COMM) paper transaction; ~ **de hasard** game of chance; ~ **de mots** pun; **le** ~ **de l'oie** snakes and ladders sg; ~ **d'orgue(s)** organ stop; ~ **de patience** puzzle; ~ **de physionomie** facial expressions pl; ~ **de société** parlour game; ~ **vidéo** computer game; ~**x de lumière** lighting effects; **J~x olympiques** (JO) Olympic Games.

jeu-concours, pl **jeux-concours** [ʒøkɔ̃kuʀ] nm competition.

jeudi [ʒødi] nm Thursday; ~ **saint** Maundy Thursday; voir aussi **lundi**.

jeun [ʒœ̃n]: **à** ~ adv on an empty stomach.

jeune [ʒœn] adj young ♦ adv: **faire/s'habiller** ~ to look/dress young; **les** ~**s** young people, the young; ~ **fille** nf girl; ~ **homme** nm young man; ~ **loup** nm (POL, ÉCON) young go-getter; ~ **premier** leading man; ~**s gens** nmpl young people; ~**s mariés** nmpl newly weds.

jeûne [ʒøn] nm fast.

jeûner [ʒøne] vt to fast, go without food.

jeunesse [ʒœnɛs] nf youth; (aspect) youthfulness; (jeunes) young people pl, youth.

jf sigle f = **jeune fille**.

jh sigle m = **jeune homme**.

JI sigle m = **juge d'instruction**.

jiu-jitsu [ʒyʒitsy] nm inv (SPORT) jujitsu.

JMF sigle f (= Jeunesses musicales de France) association to promote music among the young.

JO sigle m = **Journal officiel** ♦ sigle mpl = **Jeux olympiques**.

joaillerie [ʒɔɑjʀi] nf jewel trade; jewellery (BRIT), jewelry (US).

joaillier, ière [ʒɔɑje, -jɛʀ] nm/f jeweller (BRIT), jeweler (US).

job [dʒɔb] nm job.

jobard [ʒɔbaʀ] nm (péj) sucker, mug.

JOC [ʒɔk] sigle f (= Jeunesse ouvrière chrétienne) youth organization.

jockey [ʒɔkɛ] nm jockey.

jodler [ʒɔdle] vi to yodel.

jogging [dʒɔgiŋ] nm tracksuit (BRIT), sweatsuit (US); **faire du** ~ to jog, go jogging.

joie [ʒwa] nf joy.

joignais [ʒwɛɲɛ] etc vb voir **joindre**.

joindre [ʒwɛ̃dʀ(ə)] vt to join; (à une lettre): ~ **qch à** to enclose sth with; (contacter) to contact, get in touch with; ~ **les mains/talons** to put one's hands/heels together; ~ **les deux bouts** (fig: du mois) to make ends meet; **se** ~ (mains etc) to come together; **se** ~ **à qn** to join sb; **se** ~ **à qch** to join in sth.

joint, e [ʒwɛ̃, -ɛ̃t] pp de **joindre** ♦ adj: ~ **(à)** (lettre, paquet) attached (to), enclosed (with); **pièce** ~**e** enclosure ♦ nm joint; (ligne) join; (de ciment etc) pointing no pl; **chercher/trouver le** ~ (fig) to look for/come up with the answer; ~ **de cardan** cardan joint; ~ **de culasse** cylinder head gasket; ~ **de robinet** washer; ~ **universel** universal joint.

jointure [ʒwɛ̃tyʀ] nf (ANAT: articulation) joint; (TECH: assemblage) joint; (: ligne) join.

joker [ʒɔkɛʀ] nm (CARTES) joker.

joli, e [ʒɔli] adj pretty, attractive; **une** ~**e somme/situation** a nice little sum/situation; **un** ~ **gâchis** etc a nice mess etc; **c'est du** ~! that's very nice!; **tout ça, c'est bien** ~ **mais** ... that's all very well but ....

joliment [ʒɔlimɑ̃] adv prettily, attractively; (fam: très) pretty.

jonc [ʒɔ̃] nm (bul)rush; (bague, bracelet) band.

joncher [ʒɔ̃ʃe] vt (suj: choses) to be strewed on; **jonché de** strewn with.

jonction [ʒɔ̃ksjɔ̃] nf joining; **(point de)** ~ (de routes) junction; (de fleuves) confluence; **opérer une** ~ (MIL etc) to rendez-vous.

jongler [ʒɔ̃gle] vi to juggle; (fig): ~ **avec** to juggle with, play with.

jongleur, euse [ʒɔ̃glœʀ, -øz] nm/f juggler.

jonquille [ʒɔ̃kij] nf daffodil.

Jordanie [ʒɔʀdani] nf: **la** ~ Jordan.

jordanien, ne [ʒɔʀdanjɛ̃, -ɛn] adj Jordanian ♦ nm/f: **J~, ne** Jordanian.

jouable [ʒwabl(ə)] adj playable.

joue [ʒu] nf cheek; **mettre en** ~ to take aim at.

jouer [ʒwe] vt (partie, carte, coup, MUS: morceau) to play; (somme d'argent, réputation) to stake, wager; (pièce, rôle) to perform; (film) to show; (simuler: sentiment) to affect, feign ♦ vi to play; (THÉÂT, CINÉ) to act, perform; (bois, porte: se voiler) to warp; (clef, pièce: avoir du jeu) to be loose; (entrer ou être en jeu) to come into play, come into it; ~ **sur** (miser) to gamble on; ~ **de** (MUS) to play; ~ **du couteau/des coudes** to use knives/one's elbows; ~ **à** (jeu, sport, roulette) to play; ~ **au héros** to act ou play the hero; ~ **avec** (risquer) to gamble with; **se** ~ **de** (difficultés) to make light of; **se** ~ **de qn** to deceive ou dupe sb; ~ **un tour à qn** to play a trick on sb; ~ **la comédie** (fig) to put on an act, put it on; ~ **aux courses** to back horses, bet on horses; ~ **à la baisse/hausse** (BOURSE) to play for a fall/rise; ~ **serré** to play a close game; ~ **de malchance** to be dogged with ill-luck; ~ **sur les mots** to play with words; **à toi/nous de** ~ it's your/our go *ou* turn.

jouet [ʒwɛ] *nm* toy; **être le** ~ **de** (*illusion etc*) to be the victim of.

joueur, euse [ʒwœʀ, -øz] *nm/f* player ♦ *adj* (*enfant, chat*) playful; **être beau/mauvais** ~ to be a good/bad loser.

joufflu, e [ʒufly] *adj* chubby(-cheeked).

joug [ʒu] *nm* yoke.

jouir [ʒwiʀ]: ~ **de** *vt* to enjoy.

jouissance [ʒwisɑ̃s] *nf* pleasure; (*JUR*) use.

jouisseur, euse [ʒwisœʀ, -øz] *nm/f* sensualist.

joujou [ʒuʒu] *nm* (*fam*) toy.

jour [ʒuʀ] *nm* day; (*opposé à la nuit*) day, daytime; (*clarté*) daylight; (*fig: aspect*): **sous un** ~ **favourable/nouveau** in a favourable/new light; (*ouverture*) opening; (*COUTURE*) openwork *no pl*; **au** ~ **le** ~ from day to day; **de nos** ~s these days, nowadays; **tous les** ~s every day; **de** ~ **en** ~ day by day; **d'un** ~ **à l'autre** from one day to the next; **du** ~ **au lendemain** overnight; **il fait** ~ it's daylight; **en plein** ~ in broad daylight; **au** ~ in daylight; **au petit** ~ at daybreak; **au grand** ~ (*fig*) in the open; **mettre au** ~ to uncover, disclose; **être à** ~ to be up to date; **mettre à** ~ to bring up to date, update; **mise à** ~ updating; **donner le** ~ **à** to give birth to; **voir le** ~ to be born; **se faire** ~ (*fig*) to become clear; ~ **férié** public holiday; **le** ~ **J** D-day.

Jourdain [ʒuʀdɛ̃] *nm*: **le** ~ the (River) Jordan.

journal, aux [ʒuʀnal, -o] *nm* (news)paper; (*personnel*) journal, diary; ~ **de bord** log; ~ **de mode** fashion magazine; **le J~ officiel (de la République française) (JO)** *bulletin giving details of laws and official announcements*; ~ **parlé/télévisé** radio/television news *sg*.

journalier, ière [ʒuʀnalje, -jɛʀ] *adj* daily; (*banal*) everyday ♦ *nm* day labourer.

journalisme [ʒuʀnalism(ə)] *nm* journalism.

journaliste [ʒuʀnalist(ə)] *nm/f* journalist.

journalistique [ʒuʀnalistik] *adj* journalistic.

journée [ʒuʀne] *nf* day; **la** ~ **continue** the 9 to 5 working day (*with shorter lunch break*).

journellement [ʒuʀnɛlmɑ̃] *adv* (*tous les jours*) daily; (*souvent*) every day.

joute [ʒut] *nf* (*tournoi*) duel; (*verbale*) duel, battle of words.

jouvence [ʒuvɑ̃s] *nf*: **bain de** ~ rejuvenating experience.

jouxter [ʒukste] *vt* to adjoin.

jovial [ʒɔvjal] *adj* jovial, jolly.

jovialité [ʒɔvjalite] *nf* joviality.

joyau, x [ʒwajo] *nm* gem, jewel.

joyeusement [ʒwajøzmɑ̃] *adv* joyfully, gladly.

joyeux, euse [ʒwajø, -øz] *adj* joyful, merry; ~ **Noël!** merry *ou* happy Christmas!; ~ **anniversaire!** many happy returns!

JT *sigle m* = **journal télévisé**.

jubilation [ʒybilɑsjɔ̃] *nf* jubilation.

jubilé [ʒybile] *nm* jubilee.

jubiler [ʒybile] *vi* to be jubilant, exult.

jucher [ʒyʃe] *vt*: ~ **qch sur** to perch sth (up)on ♦ *vi* (*oiseau*): ~ **sur** to perch (up)on; **se** ~ **sur** to perch o.s. (up)on.

judaïque [ʒydaik] *adj* (*loi*) Judaic; (*religion*) Jewish.

judaïsme [ʒydaism(ə)] *nm* Judaism.

judas [ʒyda] *nm* (*trou*) spy-hole.

Judée [ʒyde] *nf*: **la** ~ Jud(a)ea.

judéo- [ʒydeo] *préfixe* Judeo-.

judéo-allemand, e [ʒydeoalmɑ̃, -ɑ̃d] *adj, nm* Yiddish.

judéo-chrétien, ne [ʒydeokʀetjɛ̃, -ɛn] *adj* Judeo-Christian.

judiciaire [ʒydisjɛʀ] *adj* judicial.

judicieusement [ʒydisjøzmɑ̃] *adv* judiciously.

judicieux, euse [ʒydisjø, -øz] *adj* judicious.

judo [ʒydo] *nm* judo.

judoka [ʒydɔka] *nm/f* judoka.

juge [ʒyʒ] *nm* judge; ~ **des enfants** children's judge, ≈ juvenile magistrate; ~ **d'instruction** examining (*BRIT*) *ou* committing (*US*) magistrate; ~ **de paix** justice of the peace; ~ **de touche** linesman.

jugé [ʒyʒe]: **au** ~ *adv* by guesswork.

jugement [ʒyʒmɑ̃] *nm* judgment; (*JUR: au pénal*) sentence; (*: au civil*) decision; ~ **de valeur** value judgment.

jugeote [ʒyʒɔt] *nf* (*fam*) gumption.

juger [ʒyʒe] *vt* to judge ♦ *nm*: **au** ~ by guesswork; ~ **qn/qch satisfaisant** to consider sb/sth (to be) satisfactory; ~ **que** to think *ou* consider that; ~ **bon de faire** to consider it a good idea to do, see fit to do; ~ **de** *vt* to judge; **jugez de ma surprise** imagine my surprise.

jugulaire [ʒygylɛʀ] *adj* jugular ♦ *nf* (*MIL*) chinstrap.

juguler [ʒygyle] *vt* (*maladie*) to halt; (*révolte*) to suppress, put down; (*inflation etc*) to control, curb.

juif, ive [ʒɥif, -iv] *adj* Jewish ♦ *nm/f*: **J~, ive** Jew/Jewess *ou* Jewish woman.

juillet [ʒɥijɛ] *nm* July; **le premier** ~ the first of July (*BRIT*), July first (*US*); **le deux/onze** ~ the second/eleventh of July, July second/eleventh; **il est venu le 5** ~ he came on 5th July *ou* July 5th; **en** ~ in July; **début/fin** ~ at the beginning/end of July.

In France, le 14 juillet is a national holiday commemorating the storming of the Bastille during the French Revolution. Throughout the country there are celebrations, parades, music, dancing and firework displays. In Paris, there is a military parade, along the Champs-Élysées, attended by the President.

---

juin [ʒɥɛ̃] *nm* June; *voir aussi* **juillet**.

juive [ʒɥiv] *voir* **juif**.

jumeau, elle, x [ʒymo, -ɛl] *adj, nm/f* twin; **maisons jumelles** semidetached houses.

jumelage [ʒymlaʒ] *nm* twinning.

jumeler [ʒymle] *vt* to twin; **roues jumelées** double wheels; **billets de loterie jumelés** double series lottery tickets; **pari jumelé** double bet.

jumelle [ʒymɛl] *adj f, nf voir* **jumeau** ♦ *vb voir* **jumeler.**

jumelles [ʒymɛl] *nfpl* binoculars.

jument [ʒymɑ̃] *nf* mare.

jungle [ʒɔ̃gl(ə)] *nf* jungle.

junior [ʒynjɔʀ] *adj* junior.

junte [ʒœ̃t] *nf* junta.

jupe [ʒyp] *nf* skirt.

jupe-culotte, *pl* **jupes-culottes** [ʒypkylɔt] *nf* divided skirt, culotte(s).

jupette [ʒypɛt] *nf* short skirt.

jupon [ʒypɔ̃] *nm* waist slip *ou* petticoat.

Jura [ʒyʀa] *nm:* **le ~** the Jura (Mountains).

jurassien, ne [ʒyʀasjɛ̃, -ɛn] *adj of ou* from the Jura Mountains.

juré, e [ʒyʀe] *nm/f* juror ♦ *adj:* **ennemi ~** sworn *ou* avowed enemy.

jurer [ʒyʀe] *vt* (*obéissance etc*) to swear, vow ♦ *vi* (*dire des jurons*) to swear, curse; (*dissoner*): **~ (avec)** to clash (with); (*s'engager*): **~ de faire/que** to swear *ou* vow to do/that; (*affirmer*): **~ que** to swear *ou* vouch that; **~ de qch** (*s'en porter garant*) to swear to sth; **ils ne jurent que par lui** they swear by him; **je vous jure!** honestly!

juridiction [ʒyʀidiksjɔ̃] *nf* jurisdiction; (*tribunal, tribunaux*) court(s) of law.

juridique [ʒyʀidik] *adj* legal. •

juridiquement [ʒyʀidikmɑ̃] *adv* (*devant la justice*) juridically; (*du point de vue du droit*) legally.

jurisconsulte [ʒyʀikɔ̃sylt(ə)] *nm* jurisconsult.

jurisprudence [ʒyʀispʀydɑ̃s] *nf* (*JUR: décisions*) (legal) precedents; (*principes juridiques*) jurisprudence; **faire ~** (*faire autorité*) to set a precedent.

juriste [ʒyʀist(ə)] *nm/f* jurist; lawyer.

juron [ʒyʀɔ̃] *nm* curse, swearword.

jury [ʒyʀi] *nm* (*JUR*) jury; (*SCOL*) board (of examiners), jury.

jus [ʒy] *nm* juice; (*de viande*) gravy, (meat) juice; **~ de fruits** fruit juice; **~ de raisin/ tomates** grape/tomato juice.

jusant [ʒyzɑ̃] *nm* ebb (tide).

jusqu'au-boutiste [ʒyskobutist(ə)] *nm/f* extremist, hardliner.

jusque [ʒysk(ə)]: **jusqu'à** *prép* (*endroit*) as far as, (up) to; (*moment*) until, till; (*limite*) up to; **~ sur/dans** up to, as far as; (*y compris*) even on/in; **jusque vers** until about; **jusqu'à ce que** *conj* until; **jusque-là** (*temps*) until then; (*espace*) up to there; **jusqu'ici** (*temps*) until now; (*espace*) up to here; **jusqu'à présent** until now, so far.

justaucorps [ʒystokɔʀ] *nm inv* (*DANSE, SPORT*) leotard.

juste [ʒyst(ə)] *adj* (*équitable*) just, fair; (*légitime*) just, justified; (*exact, vrai*) right; (*étroit, insuffisant*) tight ♦ *adv* right; tight; (*chanter*) in tune; (*seulement*) just; **~ assez/au-dessus** just enough/above; **pouvoir tout ~ faire** to be only just able to do; **au ~** exactly, actually; **comme de ~** of course, naturally; **le ~ milieu** the happy medium; **à ~ titre** rightfully.

justement [ʒystəmɑ̃] *adv* rightly; justly; (*précisément*): **c'est ~ ce qu'il fallait faire** that's just *ou* precisely what needed doing.

justesse [ʒystɛs] *nf* (*précision*) accuracy; (*d'une remarque*) aptness; (*d'une opinion*) soundness; **de ~** just, by a narrow margin.

justice [ʒystis] *nf* (*équité*) fairness, justice; (*ADMIN*) justice; **rendre la ~** to dispense justice; **traduire en ~** to bring before the courts; **obtenir ~** to obtain justice; **rendre ~ à qn** to do sb justice; **se faire ~** to take the law into one's own hands; (*se suicider*) to take one's life.

justiciable [ʒystisjabl(ə)] *adj:* **~ de** (*JUR*) answerable to.

justicier, ière [ʒystisje, -jɛʀ] *nm/f* judge, righter of wrongs.

justifiable [ʒystifjabl(ə)] *adj* justifiable.

justificatif, ive [ʒystifikatif, -iv] *adj* (*document etc*) supporting ♦ *nm* supporting proof.

justification [ʒystifikasjɔ̃] *nf* justification.

justifier [ʒystifje] *vt* to justify; **~ de** *vt* to prove; **non justifié** unjustified; **justifié à droite/gauche** ranged right/left.

jute [ʒyt] *nm* jute.

juteux, euse [ʒytø, -øz] *adj* juicy.

juvénile [ʒyvenil] *adj* young, youthful.

juxtaposer [ʒykstapoze] *vt* to juxtapose.

juxtaposition [ʒykstapozisjɔ̃] *nf* juxtaposition.

K k

K, k [ka] *nm inv* K, k ♦ *abr* (= *kilo*) kg; (= *kilooctet*) K; **K comme Kléber** K for King.

Kaboul, Kabul [kabul] *n* Kabul.

kabyle [kabil] *adj* Kabyle ♦ *nm* (*LING*) Kabyle ♦ *nm/f:* **K~** Kabyle.

Kabylie [kabili] *nf:* **la ~** Kabylia.

kafkaïen, ne [kafkajɛ̃, -ɛn] *adj* Kafkaesque.

kaki [kaki] *adj inv* khaki.

Kalahari [kalaaʀi] *n:* **désert de ~** Kalahari Desert.

kaléidoscope [kaleidɔskɔp] *nm* kaleidoscope.

Kampala [kɑ̃pala] *n* Kampala.

Kampuchéa [kɑ̃putʃea] *nm:* **le ~ (démocrati-**

que) (the People's Republic of) Kampuchea.
kangourou [kãguʀu] *nm* kangaroo.
kaolin [kaɔlɛ̃] *nm* kaolin.
kapok [kapɔk] *nm* kapok.
karaoke [kaʀaɔke] *nm* karaoke.
karaté [kaʀate] *nm* karate.
kart [kaʀt] *nm* go-cart.
karting [kaʀtiŋ] *nm* go-carting, karting.
kascher [kaʃɛʀ] *adj inv* kosher.
kayac, kayak [kajak] *nm* kayak.
Kazakhstan [kaʒakstɑ̃] *nm* Kazakhstan.
Kenya [kenja] *nm:* **le** ~ Kenya.
kenyan, e [kenjɑ̃, -an] *adj* Kenyan ♦ *nm/f:* **K~, ne** Kenyan.
képi [kepi] *nm* kepi.
Kerguelen [kɛʀgelɛn]: **les (îles)** ~ Kerguelen.
kermesse [kɛʀmɛs] *nf* bazaar, (charity) fête; village fair.
kérosène [keʀozɛn] *nm* jet fuel; rocket fuel.
kg *abr* (= *kilogramme*) kg.
KGB *sigle m* KGB.
khmer, ère [kmɛʀ] *adj* Khmer ♦ *nm* (*LING*) Khmer.
khôl [kol] *nm* khol.
kibboutz [kibuts] *nm* kibbutz.
kidnapper [kidnape] *vt* to kidnap.
kidnappeur, euse [kidnapœʀ, -øz] *nm/f* kidnapper.
kidnapping [kidnapiŋ] *nm* kidnapping.
Kilimandjaro [kilimɑ̃dʒaʀo] *nm:* **le** ~ Mount Kilimanjaro.
kilo [kilo] *nm* kilo.
kilogramme [kilɔgʀam] *nm* kilogramme (*BRIT*), kilogram (*US*).
kilométrage [kilɔmetʀaʒ] *nm* number of kilometres travelled, ≈ mileage.
kilomètre [kilɔmetʀ(ə)] *nm* kilometre (*BRIT*), kilometer (*US*); ~**s-heure** kilometres per hour.
kilométrique [kilɔmetʀik] *adj* (*distance*) in kilometres; **compteur** ~ ≈ mileage indicator.
kilooctet [kilɔɔktɛ] *nm* kilobyte.
kilowatt [kilɔwat] *nm* kilowatt.
kinésithérapeute [kineziteʀapøt] *nm/f* physiotherapist.
kinésithérapie [kineziteʀapi] *nf* physiotherapy.
kiosque [kjɔsk(ə)] *nm* kiosk, stall; (*TÉL etc*) *telephone and/or videotext information service.*
Kirghizistan [kiʀgizistɑ̃] *nm* Kirghizia.
kirsch [kiʀʃ] *nm* kirsch.
kitchenette [kitʃ(ə)nɛt] *nf* kitchenette.
kiwi [kiwi] *nm* (*ZOOL*) kiwi; (*BOT*) kiwi (fruit).
klaxon [klaksɔn] *nm* horn.
klaxonner [klaksɔne] *vi, vt* to hoot (*BRIT*), honk (one's horn) (*US*).
kleptomane [klɛptɔman] *nm/f* kleptomaniac.
km *abr* (= *kilomètre*) km.
km/h *abr* (= *kilomètres/heure*) km/h.
knock-out [nɔkawt] *nm* knock-out.
Ko *abr* (*INFORM*: = *kilooctet*) K.

K.-O. [kao] *adj inv* (knocked) out, out for the count.
koala [kɔala] *nm* koala (bear).
kolkhoze [kɔlkoz] *nm* kolkhoz.
Koweit ou Kuweit [kɔwɛt] *nm:* **le** ~ Kuwait, Koweit.
koweitien, ne [kɔwɛtjɛ̃, -ɛn] *adj* Kuwaiti ♦ *nm/f:* **K~, ne** Kuwaiti.
krach [kʀak] *nm* (*ÉCON*) crash.
kraft [kʀaft] *nm* brown *ou* kraft paper.
Kremlin [kʀɛmlɛ̃] *nm:* **le** ~ the Kremlin.
Kuala Lumpur [kwalalympuʀ] *n* Kuala Lumpur.
kurde [kyʀd(ə)] *adj* Kurdish ♦ *nm* (*LING*) Kurdish ♦ *nm/f:* **K~** Kurd.
Kurdistan [kyʀdistɑ̃] *nm:* **le** ~ Kurdistan.
Kuweit [kɔwɛt] = **Koweit.**
kW *abr* (= *kilowatt*) kW.
kW/h *abr* (= *kilowatt/heure*) kW/h.
kyrielle [kiʀjɛl] *nf:* **une** ~ **de** a stream of.
kyste [kist(ə)] *nm* cyst.

L l

L, l [ɛl] *nm inv* L, l ♦ *abr* (= *litre*) l; (*SCOL*): **L ès L = Licence ès Lettres; L en D = Licence en Droit; L comme Louis** L for Lucy (*BRIT*) *ou* Love (*US*).
l' [l] *art déf voir* **le.**
la [la] *art déf, pron voir* **le** ♦ *nm* (*MUS*) A; (*en chantant la gamme*) la.
là [la] *adv* (*voir aussi* **-ci, celui**) there; (*ici*) here; (*dans le temps*) then; **est-ce que Catherine est** ~**?** is Catherine there (*ou* here)?; **c'est** ~ **que** this is where; ~ **où** where; **de** ~ (*fig*) hence; **par** ~ (*fig*) by that; **tout est** ~ (*fig*) that's what it's all about.
là-bas [labɑ] *adv* there.
label [label] *nm* stamp, seal.
labeur [labœʀ] *nm* toil *no pl*, toiling *no pl.*
labo [labo] *nm* (= *laboratoire*) lab.
laborantin, e [labɔʀɑ̃tɛ̃, -in] *nm/f* laboratory assistant.
laboratoire [labɔʀatwaʀ] *nm* laboratory; ~ **de langues/d'analyses** language/(medical) analysis laboratory.
laborieux, euse [labɔʀjø, -øz] *adj* (*tâche*) laborious; **classes** ~**euses** working classes.
laborieusement [labɔʀjøzmɑ̃] *adv* laboriously.
labour [labuʀ] *nm* ploughing *no pl* (*BRIT*), plowing *no pl* (*US*); ~**s** *nmpl* (*champs*) ploughed fields; **cheval de** ~ plough- *ou* cart-horse; **bœuf de** ~ ox (*pl* oxen).
labourage [labuʀaʒ] *nm* ploughing (*BRIT*),

plowing (US).

labourer [labuʀe] vt to plough (BRIT), plow (US); (fig) to make deep gashes ou furrows in.

laboureur [labuʀœʀ] nm ploughman (BRIT), plowman (US).

labrador [labʀadɔʀ] nm (chien) labrador; (GÉO): **le L~** Labrador.

labyrinthe [labiʀɛ̃t] nm labyrinth, maze.

lac [lak] nm lake; **le ~ Léman** Lake Geneva; **les Grands L~s** the Great Lakes; voir aussi **lacs**.

lacer [lase] vt to lace ou do up.

lacérer [laseʀe] vt to tear to shreds.

lacet [lasɛ] nm (de chaussure) lace; (de route) sharp bend; (piège) snare; **chaussures à ~s** lace-up ou lacing shoes.

lâche [lɑʃ] adj (poltron) cowardly; (desserré) loose, slack; (morale, mœurs) lax ♦ nm/f coward.

lâchement [lɑʃmɑ̃] adv (par peur) like a coward; (par bassesse) despicably.

lâcher [lɑʃe] nm (de ballons, oiseaux) release ♦ vt to let go of; (ce qui tombe, abandonner) to drop; (oiseau, animal: libérer) to release, set free; (fig: mot, remarque) to let slip, come out with; (SPORT: distancer) to leave behind ♦ vi (fil, amarres) to break, give way; (freins) to fail; **les amarres** (NAVIG) to cast off (the moorings); **~ prise** to let go.

lâcheté [lɑʃte] nf cowardice; (bassesse) lowness.

lacis [lasi] nm (de ruelles) maze.

laconique [lakɔnik] adj laconic.

laconiquement [lakɔnikmɑ̃] adv laconically.

lacrymal, e, aux [lakʀimal, -o] adj (canal, glande) tear cpd.

lacrymogène [lakʀimɔʒɛn] adj: **grenade/gaz ~** tear gas grenade/tear gas.

lacs [lɑ] nm (piège) snare.

lactation [laktɑsjɔ̃] nf lactation.

lacté, e [lakte] adj milk cpd.

lactique [laktik] adj: **acide/ferment ~** lactic acid/ferment.

lactose [laktoz] nm lactose, milk sugar.

lacune [lakyn] nf gap.

lacustre [lakystʀ(ə)] adj lake cpd, lakeside cpd.

lad [lad] nm stable-lad.

là-dedans [ladədɑ̃] adv inside (there), in it; (fig) in that.

là-dehors [ladəɔʀ] adv out there.

là-derrière [ladɛʀjɛʀ] adv behind there; (fig) behind that.

là-dessous [ladsu] adv underneath, under there; (fig) behind that.

là-dessus [ladsy] adv on there; (fig) at that point; (: à ce sujet) about that.

là-devant [ladvɑ̃] adv there (in front).

ladite [ladit] dét voir **ledit**.

ladre [ladʀ(ə)] adj miserly.

lagon [lagɔ̃] nm lagoon.

Lagos [lagɔs] n Lagos.

lagune [lagyn] nf lagoon.

là-haut [lao] adv up there.

laïc [laik] adj, nm/f = **laïque**.

laïciser [laisize] vt to secularize.

laïcité [laisite] nf secularity, secularism.

laid, e [lɛ, lɛd] adj ugly; (fig: acte) mean, cheap.

laideron [lɛdʀɔ̃] nm ugly girl.

laideur [lɛdœʀ] nf ugliness no pl; meanness no pl.

laie [lɛ] nf wild sow.

lainage [lɛnaʒ] nm woollen garment; (étoffe) woollen material.

laine [lɛn] nf wool; **~ peignée** worsted (wool); **~ à tricoter** knitting wool; **~ de verre** glass wool; **~ vierge** new wool.

laineux, euse [lɛnø, -øz] adj woolly.

lainier, ière [lɛnje, -jɛʀ] adj (industrie etc) woollen.

laïque [laik] adj lay, civil; (SCOL) state cpd (as opposed to private and Roman Catholic) ♦ nm/f layman/woman.

laisse [lɛs] nf (de chien) lead, leash; **tenir en ~** to keep on a lead ou leash.

laissé-pour-compte, laissée-, laissés- [lesepuʀkɔ̃t] adj (COMM) unsold; (: refusé) returned ♦ nm/f (fig) reject; **les laissés-pour-compte de la reprise économique** those who are left out of the economic upturn.

laisser [lese] vt to leave ♦ vb aux: **~ qn faire** to let sb do; **se ~ exploiter** to let o.s. be exploited; **se ~ aller** to let o.s. go; **~ qn tranquille** to leave sb alone; **laisse-toi faire** let me (ou him) do it; **rien ne laisse penser que ...** there is no reason to think that ...; **cela ne laisse pas de surprendre** nonetheless it is surprising.

laisser-aller [leseale] nm carelessness, slovenliness.

laisser-faire [lesefɛʀ] nm laissez-faire.

laissez-passer [lesepase] nm inv pass.

lait [lɛ] nm milk; **frère/sœur de ~** foster brother/sister; **~ écrémé/concentré/condensé** skimmed/condensed/evaporated milk; **~ en poudre** powdered milk, milk powder; **~ de chèvre/vache** goat's/cow's milk; **~ maternel** mother's milk; **~ démaquillant/de beauté** cleansing/beauty lotion.

laitage [lɛtaʒ] nm milk product.

laiterie [lɛtʀi] nf dairy.

laiteux, euse [lɛtø, -øz] adj milky.

laitier, ière [letje, -jɛʀ] adj dairy ♦ nm/f milkman/dairywoman.

laiton [lɛtɔ̃] nm brass.

laitue [lety] nf lettuce.

laïus [lajys] nm (péj) spiel.

lama [lama] nm llama.

lambeau, x [lɑ̃bo] nm scrap; **en ~x** in tatters, tattered.

lambin, e [lɑ̃bɛ̃, -in] adj (péj) slow.

lambiner [lɑ̃bine] vi (péj) to dawdle.

lambris [lɑ̃bʀi] nm panelling no pl.

lambrissé, e [lɑ̃bʀise] adj panelled.

lame [lam] *nf* blade; (*vague*) wave; (*lamelle*) strip; ~ **de fond** ground swell *no pl*; ~ **de rasoir** razor blade.

lamé [lame] *nm* lamé.

lamelle [lamɛl] *nf* (*lame*) small blade; (*morceau*) sliver; (*de champignon*) gill; **couper en** ~**s** to slice thinly.

lamentable [lamɑ̃tabl(ə)] *adj* (*déplorable*) appalling; (*pitoyable*) pitiful.

lamentablement [lamɑ̃tabləmɑ̃] *adv* (*échouer*) miserably; (*se conduire*) appallingly.

lamentation [lamɑ̃tɑsjɔ̃] *nf* wailing *no pl*, lamentation; moaning *no pl*.

lamenter [lamɑ̃te]: **se** ~ *vi*: **se** ~ (**sur**) to moan (over).

laminage [laminaʒ] *nm* lamination.

laminer [lamine] *vt* to laminate; (*fig: écraser*) to wipe out.

laminoir [laminwaʀ] *nm* rolling mill; **passer au** ~ (*fig*) to go (*ou* put) through the mill.

lampadaire [lɑ̃padɛʀ] *nm* (*de salon*) standard lamp; (*dans la rue*) street lamp.

lampe [lɑ̃p(ə)] *nf* lamp; (*TECH*) valve; ~ **à alcool** spirit lamp; ~ **à bronzer** sunlamp; ~ **de poche** torch (*BRIT*), flashlight (*US*); ~ **à souder** blowlamp; ~ **témoin** warning light.

lampée [lɑ̃pe] *nf* gulp, swig.

lampe-tempête, *pl* **lampes-tempête** [lɑ̃ptɑ̃pɛt] *nf* storm lantern.

lampion [lɑ̃pjɔ̃] *nm* Chinese lantern.

lampiste [lɑ̃pist(ə)] *nm* light (maintenance) man; (*fig*) underling.

lamproie [lɑ̃pʀwa] *nf* lamprey.

lance [lɑ̃s] *nf* spear; ~ **d'arrosage** garden hose; ~ **à eau** water hose; ~ **d'incendie** fire hose.

lancée [lɑ̃se] *nf*: **être/continuer sur sa** ~ to be under way/keep going.

lance-flammes [lɑ̃sflam] *nm inv* flamethrower.

lance-fusées [lɑ̃sfyze] *nm inv* rocket launcher.

lance-grenades [lɑ̃sgʀənad] *nm inv* grenade launcher.

lancement [lɑ̃smɑ̃] *nm* launching *no pl*, launch; **offre de** ~ introductory offer.

lance-missiles [lɑ̃smisil] *nm inv* missile launcher.

lance-pierres [lɑ̃spjɛʀ] *nm inv* catapult.

lancer [lɑ̃se] *nm* (*SPORT*) throwing *no pl*, throw; (*PÊCHE*) rod and reel fishing ♦ *vt* to throw; (*émettre, projeter*) to throw out, send out; (*produit, fusée, bateau, artiste*) to launch; (*injure*) to hurl, fling; (*proclamation, mandat d'arrêt*) to issue; (*emprunt*) to float; (*moteur*) to send roaring away; ~ **qch à qn** to throw sth to sb; (*de façon agressive*) to throw sth at sb; ~ **un cri** *ou* **un appel** to shout *ou* call out; **se** ~ *vi* (*prendre de l'élan*) to build up speed; (*se précipiter*): **se** ~ **sur** *ou* **contre** to rush at; **se** ~ **dans** (*discussion*) to launch into; (*aventure*) to embark on; (*les affaires, la politique*) to go into; ~ **du poids** *nm* putting the shot.

lance-roquettes [lɑ̃sʀɔkɛt] *nm inv* rocket launcher.

lance-torpilles [lɑ̃stɔʀpij] *nm inv* torpedo tube.

lanceur, euse [lɑ̃sœʀ, -øz] *nm/f* bowler; (*BASE-BALL*) pitcher ♦ *nm* (*ESPACE*) launcher.

lancinant, e [lɑ̃sinɑ̃, -ɑ̃t] *adj* (*regrets etc*) haunting; (*douleur*) shooting.

lanciner [lɑ̃sine] *vi* to throb; (*fig*) to nag.

landais, e [lɑ̃dɛ, -ɛz] *adj* of *ou* from the Landes.

landau [lɑ̃do] *nm* pram (*BRIT*), baby carriage (*US*).

lande [lɑ̃d] *nf* moor.

Landes [lɑ̃d] *nfpl*: **les** ~ the Landes.

langage [lɑ̃gaʒ] *nm* language; ~ **d'assemblage** (*INFORM*) assembly language; ~ **du corps** body language; ~ **évolué/machine** (*INFORM*) high-level/machine language; ~ **de programmation** (*INFORM*) programming language.

lange [lɑ̃ʒ] *nm* flannel blanket; ~**s** *nmpl* swaddling clothes.

langer [lɑ̃ʒe] *vt* to change (the nappy (*BRIT*) *ou* diaper (*US*) of); **table à** ~ changing table.

langoureux, euse [lɑ̃guʀø, -øz] *adj* languorous.

langoureusement [lɑ̃guʀøzmɑ̃] *adv* languorously.

langouste [lɑ̃gust(ə)] *nf* crayfish *inv*.

langoustine [lɑ̃gustin] *nf* Dublin Bay prawn.

langue [lɑ̃g] *nf* (*ANAT, CULIN*) tongue; (*LING*) language; (*bande*): ~ **de terre** spit of land; **tirer la** ~ (**à**) to stick out one's tongue (at); **donner sa** ~ **au chat** to give up, give in; **de** ~ **française** French-speaking; ~ **de bois** officialese; ~ **maternelle** native language, mother tongue; ~ **verte** slang; ~ **vivante** modern language.

langue-de-chat [lɑ̃gdəʃa] *nf* finger biscuit.

languedocien, ne [lɑ̃gdɔsjɛ̃, -ɛn] *adj* of *ou* from the Languedoc.

languette [lɑ̃gɛt] *nf* tongue.

langueur [lɑ̃gœʀ] *nf* languidness.

languir [lɑ̃giʀ] *vi* to languish; (*conversation*) to flag; **se** ~ *vi* to be languishing; **faire** ~ **qn** to keep sb waiting.

languissant, e [lɑ̃gisɑ̃, -ɑ̃t] *adj* languid.

lanière [lanjɛʀ] *nf* (*de fouet*) lash; (*de valise, bretelle*) strap.

lanoline [lanɔlin] *nf* lanolin.

lanterne [lɑ̃tɛʀn(ə)] *nf* (*portable*) lantern; (*électrique*) light, lamp; (*de voiture*) (side)light; ~ **rouge** (*fig*) tail-ender; ~ **vénitienne** Chinese lantern.

lanterneau, x [lɑ̃tɛʀno] *nm* skylight.

lanterner [lɑ̃tɛʀne] *vi*: **faire** ~ **qn** to keep sb hanging around.

Laos [laɔs] *nm*: **le** ~ Laos.

laotien, ne [laɔsjɛ̃, -ɛn] *adj* Laotian.

lapalissade [lapalisad] *nf* statement of the obvious.

La Paz [lapaz] *n* La Paz.

laper [lape] *vt* to lap up.

lapereau, x [lapʀo] *nm* young rabbit.
lapidaire [lapidɛʀ] *adj* stone *cpd*; (*fig*) terse.
lapider [lapide] *vt* to stone.
lapin [lapɛ̃] *nm* rabbit; (*fourrure*) cony; **coup du**
~ rabbit punch; **poser un** ~ **à qn** to stand sb
up; ~ **de garenne** wild rabbit.
lapis(-lazuli) [lapis(lazyli)] *nm inv* lapis lazuli.
lapon, e [lapɔ̃, -ɔn] *adj* Lapp, Lappish ♦ *nm*
(*LING*) Lapp, Lappish ♦ *nm/f*: **L~, e** Lapp, Lap-
lander.
Laponie [lapɔni] *nf*: **la** ~ Lapland.
laps [laps] *nm*: ~ **de temps** space of time, time
no pl.
lapsus [lapsys] *nm* slip.
laquais [lakɛ] *nm* lackey.
laque [lak] *nf* lacquer; (*brute*) shellac; (*pour
cheveux*) hair spray ♦ *nm* lacquer; piece of
lacquer ware.
laqué, e [lake] *adj* lacquered.
laquelle [lakɛl] *pron voir* **lequel**.
larbin [laʀbɛ̃] *nm* (*péj*) flunkey.
larcin [laʀsɛ̃] *nm* theft.
lard [laʀ] *nm* (*graisse*) fat; (*bacon*) (streaky) bacon.
larder [laʀde] *vt* (*CULIN*) to lard.
lardon [laʀdɔ̃] *nm* (*CULIN*) piece of chopped
bacon; (*fam: enfant*) kid.
large [laʀʒ(ə)] *adj* wide; broad; (*fig*) generous
♦ *adv*: **calculer/voir** ~ to allow extra/think
big ♦ *nm* (*largeur*): **5 m de** ~ 5 m wide *ou* in
width; (*mer*): **le** ~ the open sea; **en** ~ *adv*
sideways; **au** ~ **de** off; ~ **d'esprit** broad-
minded; **ne pas en mener** ~ to have one's
heart in one's boots.
largement [laʀʒəmã] *adv* widely; (*de loin*)
greatly; (*amplement, au minimum*) easily;
(*sans compter: donner etc*) generously.
largesse [laʀʒɛs] *nf* generosity; ~**s** *nfpl* liberal-
ities.
largeur [laʀʒœʀ] *nf* (*qu'on mesure*) width; (*impression visuelle*) wideness, width; breadth;
broadness.
larguer [laʀge] *vt* to drop; (*fam: se débarrasser
de*) to get rid of; ~ **les amarres** to cast off
(the moorings).
larme [laʀm(ə)] *nf* tear; (*fig*): **une** ~ **de** a drop
of; **en** ~**s** in tears; **pleurer à chaudes** ~**s** to
cry one's eyes out, cry bitterly.
larmoyant, e [laʀmwajã, -ãt] *adj* tearful.
larmoyer [laʀmwaje] *vi* (*yeux*) to water; (*se
plaindre*) to whimper.
larron [laʀɔ̃] *nm* thief (*pl* thieves).
larve [laʀv(ə)] *nf* (*ZOOL*) larva (*pl* -ae); (*fig*)
worm.
larvé, e [laʀve] *adj* (*fig*) latent.
laryngite [laʀɛ̃ʒit] *nf* laryngitis.
laryngologiste [laʀɛ̃gɔlɔʒist(ə)] *nm/f* throat
specialist.
larynx [laʀɛ̃ks] *nm* larynx.
las, lasse [lɑ, lɑs] *adj* weary.
lasagne [lazaɲ] *nf* lasagne.
lascar [laskaʀ] *nm* character; (*malin*) rogue.

lascif, ive [lasif, -iv] *adj* lascivious.
laser [lazɛʀ] *nm*: (**rayon**) ~ laser (beam);
chaîne *ou* **platine** ~ compact disc (player);
disque ~ compact disc.
lassant, e [lɑsã, -ãt] *adj* tiresome, wearisome.
lasse [lɑs] *adj f voir* **las**.
lasser [lɑse] *vt* to weary, tire; **se** ~ **de** to grow
weary *ou* tired of.
lassitude [lɑsityd] *nf* lassitude, weariness.
lasso [laso] *nm* lasso; **prendre au** ~ to lasso.
latent, e [latã, -ãt] *adj* latent.
latéral, e, aux [lateʀal, -o] *adj* side *cpd*, lateral.
latéralement [lateʀalmã] *adv* edgeways; (*arriver, souffler*) from the side.
latex [latɛks] *nm inv* latex.
latin, e [latɛ̃, -in] *adj* Latin ♦ *nm* (*LING*) Latin
♦ *nm/f*: **L~, e** Latin; **j'y perds mon** ~ it's all
Greek to me.
latiniste [latinist(ə)] *nm/f* Latin scholar (*ou* student).
latino-américain, e [latinɔameʀikɛ̃, -ɛn] *adj*
Latin-American.
latitude [latityd] *nf* latitude; (*fig*): **avoir la** ~ **de
faire** to be left free *ou* at liberty to do; **à
48° de** ~ **Nord** at latitude 48° North; **sous
toutes les** ~**s** (*fig*) world-wide, throughout
the world.
latrines [latʀin] *nfpl* latrines.
latte [lat] *nf* lath, slat; (*de plancher*) board.
lattis [lati] *nm* lathwork.
laudanum [lodanɔm] *nm* laudanum.
laudatif, ive [lodatif, -iv] *adj* laudatory.
lauréat, e [loʀea, -at] *nm/f* winner.
laurier [loʀje] *nm* (*BOT*) laurel; (*CULIN*) bay
leaves *pl*; ~**s** *nmpl* (*fig*) laurels.
laurier-rose, *pl* **lauriers-roses** [loʀjeʀoz] *nm*
oleander.
laurier-tin, *pl* **lauriers-tins** [loʀjetɛ̃] *nm* lau-
rustinus.
lavable [lavabl(ə)] *adj* washable.
lavabo [lavabo] *nm* washbasin; ~**s** *nmpl* toilet
sg.
lavage [lavaʒ] *nm* washing *no pl*, wash; ~
d'estomac/d'intestin stomach/intestinal
wash; ~ **de cerveau** brainwashing *no pl*.
lavande [lavãd] *nf* lavender.
lavandière [lavãdjɛʀ] *nf* washerwoman.
lave [lav] *nf* lava *no pl*.
lave-glace [lavglas] *nm* (*AUTO*) windscreen
(*BRIT*) *ou* windshield (*US*) washer.
lave-linge [lavlɛ̃ʒ] *nm inv* washing machine.
lavement [lavmã] *nm* (*MÉD*) enema.
laver [lave] *vt* to wash; (*tache*) to wash off; (*fig:
affront*) to avenge; **se** ~ to have a wash,
wash; **se** ~ **les mains/dents** to wash one's
hands/clean one's teeth; ~ **la vaisselle/le
linge** to wash the dishes/clothes; ~ **qn de**
(*accusation*) to clear sb of.
laverie [lavʀi] *nf*: ~ (**automatique**) launderette.
lavette [lavɛt] *nf* (*chiffon*) dish cloth; (*brosse*)
dish mop; (*fam: homme*) wimp, drip.

laveur, euse [lavœʀ, -øz] *nm/f* cleaner.
lave-vaisselle [lavvɛsɛl] *nm inv* dishwasher.
lavis [lavi] *nm* (*technique*) washing; (*dessin*) wash drawing.
lavoir [lavwaʀ] *nm* wash house; (*bac*) washtub.
laxatif, ive [laksatif, -iv] *adj, nm* laxative.
laxisme [laksism(ə)] *nm* laxity.
laxiste [laksist(ə)] *adj* lax.
layette [lɛjɛt] *nf* layette.
layon [lɛjɔ̃] *nm* trail.
lazaret [lazaʀɛ] *nm* quarantine area.
lazzi [ladzi] *nm* gibe.
LCR *sigle f* (= *Ligue communiste révolutionnaire*) political party.

=================== MOT-CLÉ ===================

le (l'), la [l(ə)] (*pl* **les**) *art déf* **1** the; ~ **livre/la pomme/l'arbre** the book/the apple/the tree; **les étudiants** the students
2 (*noms abstraits*): ~ **courage/l'amour/la jeunesse** courage/love/youth
3 (*indiquant la possession*): **se casser la jambe** *etc* to break one's leg *etc*; **levez la main** put your hand up; **avoir les yeux gris/** ~ **nez rouge** to have grey eyes/a red nose
4 (*temps*): **le matin/soir** in the morning/evening; **mornings/evenings;** ~ **jeudi** *etc* (*d'habitude*) on Thursdays *etc*; (*ce jeudi-là etc*) on (the) Thursday; **nous venons** ~ **3 décembre** (*parlé*) we're coming on the 3rd of December *ou* on December the 3rd; (*écrit*) we're coming (on) 3rd *ou* 3 December
5 (*distribution, évaluation*) a, an; **10 F** ~ **mètre/kilo** 10 F a *ou* per metre/kilo; ~ **tiers/quart de** a third/quarter of
♦ *pron* **1** (*personne: mâle*) him; (*: femelle*) her; (*: pluriel*) them; **je** ~**/la/les vois** I can see him/her/them
2 (*animal, chose: singulier*) it; (*: pluriel*) them; **je** ~ (*ou* **la**) **vois** I can see it; **je les vois** I can see them
3 (*remplaçant une phrase*): **je ne** ~ **savais pas** I didn't know (about it); **il était riche et ne l'est plus** he was once rich but no longer is.

lé [le] *nm* (*de tissu*) width; (*de papier peint*) strip, length.
leader [lidœʀ] *nm* leader.
leadership [lidœʀʃip] *nm* (*POL*) leadership.
leasing [liziŋ] *nm* leasing.
lèche-bottes [lɛʃbɔt] *nm inv* bootlicker.
lèchefrite [lɛʃfʀit] *nf* dripping pan *ou* tray.
lécher [leʃe] *vt* to lick; (*laper: lait, eau*) to lick *ou* lap up; (*finir, polir*) to over-refine; ~ **les vitrines** to go window-shopping; **se** ~ **les doigts/lèvres** to lick one's fingers/lips.
lèche-vitrines [lɛʃvitʀin] *nm inv*: **faire du** ~ to go window-shopping.
leçon [ləsɔ̃] *nf* lesson; **faire la** ~ to teach; **faire la** ~ **à** (*fig*) to give a lecture to; ~**s de conduite** driving lessons; ~**s particulières** private lessons *ou* tuition *sg* (*BRIT*).

lecteur, trice [lɛktœʀ, -tʀis] *nm/f* reader; (*d'université*) (foreign language) assistant (*BRIT*), (foreign) teaching assistant (*US*) ♦ *nm* (*TECH*): ~ **de cassettes** cassette player; (*INFORM*): ~ **de disquette(s)** *ou* **de disque** disk drive; ~ **compact-disc** *ou* **CD** compact disc (player).
lectorat [lɛktɔʀa] *nm* (foreign language *ou* teaching) assistantship.
lecture [lɛktyʀ] *nf* reading.
LED [lɛd] *sigle f* (= *light emitting diode*) LED; **affichage** ~ LED display.
ledit [lədi], **ladite** [ladit], *mpl* **lesdits** [ledi], *fpl* **lesdites** [ledit] *dét* the aforesaid.
légal, e, aux [legal, -o] *adj* legal.
légalement [legalmɑ̃] *adv* legally.
légalisation [legalizasjɔ̃] *nf* legalization.
légaliser [legalize] *vt* to legalize.
légalité [legalite] *nf* legality, lawfulness; **être dans/sortir de la** ~ to be within/step outside the law.
légat [lega] *nm* (*REL*) legate.
légataire [legatɛʀ] *nm* legatee.
légendaire [leʒɑ̃dɛʀ] *adj* legendary.
légende [leʒɑ̃d] *nf* (*mythe*) legend; (*de carte, plan*) key, legend; (*de dessin*) caption, legend.
léger, ère [leʒe, -ɛʀ] *adj* light; (*bruit, retard*) slight; (*boisson, parfum*) weak; (*couche, étoffe*) thin; (*superficiel*) thoughtless; (*volage*) free and easy; (*peu sérieux*) light-weight; **blessé** ~ slightly injured person; **à la légère** *adv* (*parler, agir*) rashly, thoughtlessly.
légèrement [leʒɛʀmɑ̃] *adv* lightly; thoughtlessly, rashly; ~ **plus grand** slightly bigger.
légèreté [leʒɛʀte] *nf* lightness; thoughtlessness.
légiférer [leʒifeʀe] *vi* to legislate.
légion [leʒjɔ̃] *nf* legion; **la L**~ **étrangère** the Foreign Legion; **la L**~ **d'honneur** the Legion of Honour.

┌───┐
Created by Napoleon in 1802 to reward service to the state, **la Légion d'honneur** *is a prestigious French order headed by the President of the Republic, the Grand Maître. Members receive a nominal tax-free payment each year.*
└───┘

légionnaire [leʒjɔnɛʀ] *nm* (*MIL*) legionnaire; (*de la Légion d'honneur*) holder of the Legion of Honour.
législateur [leʒislatœʀ] *nm* legislator, lawmaker.
législatif, ive [leʒislatif, -iv] *adj* legislative; **législatives** *nfpl* general election *sg*.
législation [leʒislasjɔ̃] *nf* legislation.
législature [leʒislatyʀ] *nf* legislature; (*période*) term (of office).
légiste [leʒist(ə)] *nm* jurist ♦ *adj*: **médecin** ~ forensic scientist (*BRIT*), medical examiner (*US*).

légitime [leʒitim] *adj* (*JUR*) lawful, legitimate; (*enfant*) legitimate; (*fig*) rightful, legitimate; **en état de ~ défense** in self-defence.

légitimement [leʒitimmɑ̃] *adv* lawfully; legitimately; rightfully.

légitimer [leʒitime] *vt* (*enfant*) to legitimize; (*justifier: conduite etc*) to justify.

légitimité [leʒitimite] *nf* (*JUR*) legitimacy.

legs [leg] *nm* legacy.

léguer [lege] *vt*: **~ qch à qn** (*JUR*) to bequeath sth to sb; (*fig*) to hand sth down *ou* pass sth on to sb.

légume [legym] *nm* vegetable; **~s verts** green vegetables; **~s secs** pulses.

légumier [legymje] *nm* vegetable dish.

leitmotiv [lejtmɔtiv] *nm* leitmotiv, leitmotif.

Léman [lemɑ̃] *nm voir* **lac**.

lendemain [lɑ̃dmɛ̃] *nm*: **le ~** the next *ou* following day; **le ~ matin/soir** the next *ou* following morning/evening; **le ~ de** the day after; **au ~ de** in the days following; in the wake of; **penser au ~** to think of the future; **sans ~** short-lived; **de beaux ~s** bright prospects; **des ~s qui chantent** a rosy future.

lénifiant, e [lenifjɑ̃, -ɑ̃t] *adj* soothing.

léniniste [leninist(ə)] *adj*, *nm/f* Leninist.

lent, e [lɑ̃, lɑ̃t] *adj* slow.

lente [lɑ̃t] *nf* nit.

lentement [lɑ̃tmɑ̃] *adv* slowly.

lenteur [lɑ̃tœʀ] *nf* slowness *no pl*; **~s** *nfpl* (*actions, décisions lentes*) slowness *sg*.

lentille [lɑ̃tij] *nf* (*OPTIQUE*) lens *sg*; (*BOT*) lentil; **~ d'eau** duckweed; **~s de contact** contact lenses.

léonin, e [leɔnɛ̃, -in] *adj* (*fig: contrat etc*) one-sided.

léopard [leɔpaʀ] *nm* leopard.

LEP [lɛp] *sigle m* (= *lycée d'enseignement professionnel*) secondary school for vocational training, pre-1986.

lèpre [lɛpʀ(ə)] *nf* leprosy.

lépreux, euse [lepʀø, -øz] *nm/f* leper ♦ *adj* (*fig*) flaking, peeling.

=========== *MOT-CLÉ* ===========

lequel, laquelle [ləkɛl, lakɛl] (*mpl* **lesquels**, *fpl* **lesquelles**; *à* + *lequel* = **auquel**, *de* + *lequel* = **duquel**) *pron* **1** (*interrogatif*) which, which one **2** (*relatif: personne: sujet*) who; (*: objet, après préposition*) whom; (*: sujet: possessif*) whose; (*: chose*) which; **je l'ai proposé au directeur, ~ est d'accord** I suggested it to the director, who agrees; **la femme à laquelle j'ai acheté mon chien** the woman from whom I bought my dog; **le pont sur ~ nous sommes passés** the bridge (over) which we crossed; **un homme sur la compétence duquel on peut compter** a man whose competence one can count on
♦ *adj*: **auquel cas** in which case.

les [le] *voir* **le**.

lesbienne [lɛsbjɛn] *nf* lesbian.

lesdits [ledi], **lesdites** [ledit] *dét voir* **ledit**.

lèse-majesté [lɛzmaʒɛste] *nf inv*: **crime de ~** crime of lese-majesty.

léser [leze] *vt* to wrong; (*MÉD*) to injure.

lésiner [lezine] *vt*: **~ (sur)** to skimp (on).

lésion [lezjɔ̃] *nf* lesion, damage *no pl*; **~s cérébrales** brain damage.

Lesotho [lezoto] *nm*: **le ~** Lesotho.

lesquels, lesquelles [lekɛl] *pron voir* **lequel**.

lessivable [lesivabl(ə)] *adj* washable.

lessive [lesiv] *nf* (*poudre*) washing powder; (*linge*) washing *no pl*, wash; (*opération*) washing *no pl*; **faire la ~** to do the washing.

lessivé, e [lesive] *adj* (*fam*) washed out.

lessiver [lesive] *vt* to wash.

lessiveuse [lesivøz] *nf* (*récipient*) washtub.

lessiviel [lesivjɛl] *adj* detergent.

lest [lɛst] *nm* ballast; **jeter** *ou* **lâcher du ~** (*fig*) to make concessions.

leste [lɛst(ə)] *adj* (*personne, mouvement*) sprightly, nimble; (*désinvolte: manières*) offhand; (*osé: plaisanterie*) risqué.

lestement [lɛstəmɑ̃] *adv* nimbly.

lester [lɛste] *vt* to ballast.

letchi [letʃi] *nm* = **litchi**.

léthargie [letaʀʒi] *nf* lethargy.

léthargique [letaʀʒik] *adj* lethargic.

letton, ne [letɔ̃, -ɔn] *adj* Latvian, Lett.

Lettonie [letɔni] *nf*: **la ~** Latvia.

lettre [lɛtʀ(ə)] *nf* letter; **~s** *nfpl* (*étude, culture*) literature *sg*; (*SCOL*) arts (subjects); **à la ~** (*au sens propre*) literally; (*ponctuellement*) to the letter; **en ~s majuscules** *ou* **capitales** in capital letters, in capitals; **en toutes ~s** in words, in full; **~ de change** bill of exchange; **~ piégée** letter bomb; **~ de voiture (aérienne)** (air) waybill, (air) bill of lading; **~s de noblesse** pedigree.

lettré, e [letʀe] *adj* well-read, scholarly.

lettre-transfert, *pl* **lettres-transferts** [lɛtʀɔtʀɑ̃sfɛʀ] *nf* (*pressure*) transfer.

leu [lø] *voir* **queue**.

leucémie [løsemi] *nf* leukaemia.

=========== *MOT-CLÉ* ===========

leur [lœʀ] *adj possessif* their; **~ maison** their house; **~s amis** their friends; **à ~ approche** as they came near; **à ~ vue** at the sight of them
♦ *pron* **1** (*objet indirect*) (to) them; **je ~ ai dit la vérité** I told them the truth; **je le ~ ai donné** I gave it to them, I gave it them
2 (*possessif*): **le(la) ~**, **les ~s** theirs.

leurre [lœʀ] *nm* (*appât*) lure; (*fig*) delusion; (*: piège*) snare.

leurrer [lœʀe] *vt* to delude, deceive.

levain [ləvɛ̃] *nm* leaven; **sans ~** unleavened.

levant, e [ləvɑ̃, -ɑ̃t] *adj*: **soleil ~** rising sun
♦*nm*: **le L~** the Levant; **au soleil ~** at sunrise.

levantin, e [ləvɑ̃tɛ̃, -in] *adj* Levantine ♦ *nm/f*:

L~, e Levantine.

levé, e [ləve] *adj*: **être ~** to be up ♦ *nm*: **~ de terrain** land survey; **à mains ~es** (*vote*) by a show of hands; **au pied ~** at a moment's notice.

levée [ləve] *nf* (*POSTES*) collection; (*CARTES*) trick; **~ de boucliers** general outcry; **~ du corps** *collection of the body from house of the deceased, before funeral*; **~ d'écrou** release from custody; **~ de terre** levee; **~ de troupes** levy.

lever [ləve] *vt* (*vitre, bras etc*) to raise; (*soulever de terre, supprimer: interdiction, siège*) to lift; (*: difficulté*) to remove; (*séance*) to close; (*impôts, armée*) to levy; (*CHASSE: lièvre*) to start; (*: perdrix*) to flush; (*fam: fille*) to pick up ♦ *vi* (*CULIN*) to rise ♦ *nm*: **au ~** on getting up; **se ~** *vi* to get up; (*soleil*) to rise; (*jour*) to break; (*brouillard*) to lift; **ça va se ~** the weather will clear; **~ du jour** daybreak; **~ du rideau** (*THÉÂT*) curtain; **~ de rideau** (*pièce*) curtain raiser; **~ de soleil** sunrise.

lève-tard [lɛvtaʀ] *nm/f inv* late riser.

lève-tôt [lɛvto] *nm/f inv* early riser, early bird.

levier [ləvje] *nm* lever; **faire ~ sur** to lever up (*ou* off); **~ de changement de vitesse** gear lever.

lévitation [levitɑsjɔ̃] *nf* levitation.

levraut [ləvʀo] *nm* (*ZOOL*) leveret.

lèvre [lɛvʀ(ə)] *nf* lip; **~s** *nfpl* (*d'une plaie*) edges; **petites/grandes ~s** labia minora/majora; **du bout des ~s** half-heartedly.

lévrier [levʀije] *nm* greyhound.

levure [ləvyʀ] *nf* yeast; **~ chimique** baking powder.

lexical, e, aux [lɛksikal, -o] *adj* lexical.

lexicographe [lɛksikɔgʀaf] *nm/f* lexicographer.

lexicographie [lɛksikɔgʀafi] *nf* lexicography, dictionary writing.

lexicologie [lɛksikɔlɔʒi] *nf* lexicology.

lexique [lɛksik] *nm* vocabulary, lexicon; (*glossaire*) vocabulary.

lézard [lezaʀ] *nm* lizard; (*peau*) lizardskin.

lézarde [lezaʀd(ə)] *nf* crack.

lézarder [lezaʀde]: **se ~** *vi* to crack.

liaison [ljɛzɔ̃] *nf* (*rapport*) connection, link; (*RAIL, AVIAT etc*) link; (*relation: d'amitié*) friendship; (*: d'affaires*) relationship; (*: amoureuse*) affair; (*CULIN, PHONÉTIQUE*) liaison; **entrer/être en ~ avec** to get/be in contact with; **~ radio** radio contact; **~ (de transmission de données)** (*INFORM*) data link.

liane [ljan] *nf* creeper.

liant, e [ljɑ̃, -ɑ̃t] *adj* sociable.

liasse [ljas] *nf* wad, bundle.

Liban [libɑ̃] *nm*: **le ~** (the) Lebanon.

libanais, e [libanɛ, -ɛz] *adj* Lebanese ♦ *nm/f*: **L~, e** Lebanese.

libations [libasjɔ̃] *nfpl* libations.

libelle [libɛl] *nm* lampoon.

libellé [libele] *nm* wording.

libeller [libele] *vt* (*chèque, mandat*): **~ (au nom de)** to make out (to); (*lettre*) to word.

libellule [libelyl] *nf* dragonfly.

libéral, e, aux [libeʀal, -o] *adj, nm/f* liberal; **les professions ~es** the professions.

libéralement [libeʀalmɑ̃] *adv* liberally.

libéralisation [libeʀalizɑsjɔ̃] *nf* liberalization; **~ du commerce** easing of trade restrictions.

libéraliser [libeʀalize] *vt* to liberalize.

libéralisme [libeʀalism(ə)] *nm* liberalism.

libéralité [libeʀalite] *nf* liberality *no pl*, generosity *no pl*.

libérateur, trice [libeʀatœʀ, -tʀis] *adj* liberating ♦ *nm/f* liberator.

libération [libeʀasjɔ̃] *nf* liberation, freeing; release; discharge; **~ conditionnelle** release on parole.

libéré, e [libeʀe] *adj* liberated; **~ de** freed from; **être ~ sous caution/sur parole** to be released on bail/on parole.

libérer [libeʀe] *vt* (*délivrer*) to free, liberate; (*: moralement, PSYCH*) to liberate; (*relâcher: prisonnier*) to release; (*: soldat*) to discharge; (*dégager: gaz, cran d'arrêt*) to release; (*ÉCON: échanges commerciaux*) to ease restrictions on; **se ~** (*de rendez-vous*) to try and be free, get out of previous engagements; **~ qn de** (*liens, dette*) to free sb from; (*promesse*) to release sb from.

Libéria [libeʀja] *nm*: **le ~** Liberia.

libérien, ne [libeʀjɛ̃, -ɛn] *adj* Liberian ♦ *nm/f*: **L~, ne** Liberian.

libéro [libeʀo] *nm* (*FOOTBALL*) sweeper.

libertaire [libeʀtɛʀ] *adj* libertarian.

liberté [libeʀte] *nf* freedom; (*loisir*) free time; **~s** *nfpl* (*privautés*) liberties; **mettre/être en ~** to set/be free; **en ~ provisoire/surveillée/conditionnelle** on bail/probation/parole; **~ d'association** right of association; **~ de conscience** freedom of conscience; **~ du culte** freedom of worship; **~ d'esprit** independence of mind; **~ d'opinion** freedom of thought; **~ de la presse** freedom of the press; **~ de réunion** right to hold meetings; **~ syndicale** union rights *pl*; **~s individuelles** personal freedom *sg*; **~s publiques** civil rights.

libertin, e [libeʀtɛ̃, -in] *adj* libertine, licentious.

libertinage [libeʀtinaʒ] *nm* licentiousness.

libidineux, euse [libidinø, -øz] *adj* libidinous, lustful.

libido [libido] *nf* libido.

libraire [libʀɛʀ] *nm/f* bookseller.

libraire-éditeur, *pl* **libraires-éditeurs** [libʀɛʀeditœʀ] *nm* publisher and bookseller.

librairie [libʀeʀi] *nf* bookshop.

librairie-papeterie, *pl* **librairies-papeteries** [libʀɛʀipapetʀi] bookseller's and stationer's.

libre [libʀ(ə)] *adj* free; (*route*) clear; (*place etc*) vacant, free; (*fig: propos, manières*) open;

(SCOL) private and Roman Catholic (as opposed to "laïque"); **de ~** (place) free; **~ de qch/de faire** free from sth/to do; **vente ~** (COMM) unrestricted sale; **~ arbitre** free will; **~ concurrence** free-market economy; **~ entreprise** free enterprise.

libre-échange [librəʃɑ̃ʒ] nm free trade.

librement [librəmɑ̃] adv freely.

libre-penseur, euse [librəpɑ̃sœr, -øz] nm/f free thinker.

libre-service [librəsɛrvis] nm inv (magasin) self-service store; (restaurant) self-service restaurant.

librettiste [libretist(ə)] nm/f librettist.

Libye [libi] nf: **la ~** Libya.

libyen, ne [libjɛ̃, -ɛn] adj Libyan ♦ nm/f: **L~, ne** Libyan.

lice [lis] nf: **entrer en ~** (fig) to enter the lists.

licence [lisɑ̃s] nf (permis) permit; (diplôme) (first) degree; (liberté) liberty; (poétique, orthographique) licence (BRIT), license (US); (des mœurs) licentiousness; **~ ès lettres/en droit** arts/law degree.

> After gaining their **DEUG**, French university students take their **licence** after a third year of study. It is roughly equivalent to a Bachelor's Degree in Britain.

licencié, e [lisɑ̃sje] nm/f (SCOL): **~ ès lettres/en droit** ≈ Bachelor of Arts/Law, arts/law graduate; (SPORT) permit-holder.

licenciement [lisɑ̃simɑ̃] nm dismissal; redundancy; laying off no pl.

licencier [lisɑ̃sje] vt (renvoyer) to dismiss; (débaucher) to make redundant; to lay off.

licencieux, euse [lisɑ̃sjø, -øz] adj licentious.

lichen [likɛn] nm lichen.

licite [lisit] adj lawful.

licorne [likɔrn(ə)] nf unicorn.

licou [liku] nm halter.

lie [li] nf dregs pl, sediment.

lié, e [lje] adj: **très ~ avec** (fig) very friendly with ou close to; **~ par** (serment, promesse) bound by; **avoir partie ~e (avec qn)** to be involved (with sb).

Liechtenstein [liʃtɛnʃtajn] nm: **le ~** Liechtenstein.

lie-de-vin [lidvɛ̃] adj inv wine(-coloured).

liège [ljɛʒ] nm cork.

liégeois, e [ljeʒwa, -waz] adj of ou from Liège ♦ nm/f: **L~, e** inhabitant ou native of Liège; **café/chocolat ~** coffee/chocolate ice cream topped with whipped cream.

lien [ljɛ̃] nm (corde, fig: affectif, culturel) bond; (rapport) link, connection; (analogie) link; **~ de parenté** family tie.

lier [lje] vt (attacher) to tie up; (joindre) to link up; (fig: unir, engager) to bind; (CULIN) to thicken; **~ qch à** (attacher) to tie sth to; (associer) to link sth to; **~ amitié/ conversation (avec)** to strike up a friendship/

conversation (with); **se ~ avec** to make friends with.

lierre [ljɛr] nm ivy.

liesse [ljɛs] nf: **être en ~** to be jubilant.

lieu, x [ljø] nm place; **~x** nmpl (locaux) premises; (endroit: d'un accident etc) scene sg; **en ~ sûr** in a safe place; **en haut ~** in high places; **vider ou quitter les ~x** to leave the premises; **arriver/être sur les ~x** to arrive/be on the scene; **en premier ~** in the first place; **en dernier ~** lastly; **avoir ~** to take place; **avoir ~ de faire** to have grounds ou good reason for doing; **tenir ~ de** to take the place of; (servir de) to serve as; **donner ~ à** to give rise to, give cause for; **au ~ de** instead of; **au ~ qu'il y aille** instead of him going; **~ commun** commonplace; **~ géométrique** locus; **~ de naissance** place of birth; **~ de rendez-vous** venue, meeting place.

lieu-dit, pl **lieux-dits** [ljødi] nm locality.

lieue [ljø] nf league.

lieutenant [ljøtnɑ̃] nm lieutenant; **~ de vaisseau** (NAVIG) lieutenant.

lieutenant-colonel, pl **lieutenants-colonels** [ljøtnɑ̃kɔlɔnɛl] nm (armée de terre) lieutenant colonel; (armée de l'air) wing commander (BRIT), lieutenant colonel (US).

lièvre [ljɛvr(ə)] nm hare; (coureur) pacemaker; **lever un ~** (fig) to bring up a prickly subject.

liftier, ière [liftje, -jɛr] lift (BRIT) ou elevator (US) attendant.

lifting [liftiŋ] nm face lift.

ligament [ligamɑ̃] nm ligament.

ligature [ligatyr] nf ligature.

lige [liʒ] adj: **homme ~** (péj) henchman.

ligne [liɲ] nf (gén) line; (TRANSPORTS: liaison) service; (: trajet) route; (silhouette): **garder la ~** to keep one's figure; **en ~** (INFORM) on line; **en ~ droite** as the crow flies; **"à la ~"** "new paragraph"; **entrer en ~ de compte** to be taken into account; to come into it; **~ de but/médiane** goal/halfway line; **~ d'arrivée/ de départ** finishing/starting line; **~ de conduite** course of action; **~ directrice** guiding line; **~ d'horizon** skyline; **~ de mire** line of sight; **~ de touche** touchline.

ligné, e [liɲe] adj: **papier ~** ruled paper ♦ nf (race, famille) line, lineage; (postérité) descendants pl.

ligneux, euse [liɲø, -øz] adj ligneous, woody.

lignite [liɲit] nm lignite.

ligoter [ligɔte] vt to tie up.

ligue [lig] nf league.

liguer [lige]: **se ~** vi to form a league; **se ~ contre** (fig) to combine against.

lilas [lila] nm lilac.

lillois, e [lilwa, -waz] adj of ou from Lille.

Lima [lima] n Lima.

limace [limas] nf slug.

limaille [limaj] nf: **~ de fer** iron filings pl.

limande [limɑ̃d] nf dab.

limande-sole [limɑ̃dsɔl] *nf* lemon sole.

limbes [lɛ̃b] *nmpl* limbo *sg*; **être dans les ~** (*fig: projet etc*) to be up in the air.

lime [lim] *nf* (*TECH*) file; (*BOT*) lime; **~ à ongles** nail file.

limer [lime] *vt* (*bois, métal*) to file (down); (*ongles*) to file; (*fig: prix*) to pare down.

limier [limje] *nm* (*ZOOL*) bloodhound; (*détective*) sleuth.

liminaire [liminɛʀ] *adj* (*propos*) introductory.

limitatif, ive [limitatif, -iv] *adj* restrictive.

limitation [limitasjɔ̃] *nf* limitation, restriction; **sans ~ de temps** with no time limit; **~ des naissances** birth control; **~ de vitesse** speed limit.

limite [limit] *nf* (*de terrain*) boundary; (*partie ou point extrême*) limit; **dans la ~ de** within the limits of; **à la ~** (*au pire*) if the worst comes (*ou* came) to the worst; **sans ~s** (*bêtise, richesse, pouvoir*) limitless, boundless; **vitesse/charge ~** maximum speed/load; **cas ~** borderline case; **date ~** deadline; **date ~ de vente/consommation** sell-by/best-before date; **prix ~** upper price limit; **~ d'âge** maximum age, age limit.

limiter [limite] *vt* (*restreindre*) to limit, restrict; (*délimiter*) to border, form the boundary of; **se ~** (*à qch/à faire*) (*personne*) to limit *ou* confine o.s. (to sth/to doing sth); **se ~ à** (*chose*) to be limited to.

limitrophe [limitʀɔf] *adj* border *cpd*; **~ de** bordering on.

limogeage [limɔʒaʒ] *nm* dismissal.

limoger [limɔʒe] *vt* to dismiss.

limon [limɔ̃] *nm* silt.

limonade [limɔnad] *nf* lemonade (*BRIT*), (lemon) soda (*US*).

limonadier, ière [limɔnadje, -jɛʀ] *nm/f* (*commerçant*) café owner; (*fabricant de limonade*) soft drinks manufacturer.

limoneux, euse [limɔnø, -øz] *adj* muddy.

limousin, e [limuzɛ̃, -in] *adj* of *ou* from Limousin ♦ *nm* (*région*): **le L~** the Limousin ♦ *nf* limousine.

limpide [lɛ̃pid] *adj* limpid.

lin [lɛ̃] *nm* (*BOT*) flax; (*tissu, toile*) linen.

linceul [lɛ̃sœl] *nm* shroud.

linéaire [lineɛʀ] *adj* linear ♦ *nm*: **~ (de vente)** shelves *pl*.

linéament [lineamɑ̃] *nm* outline.

linge [lɛ̃ʒ] *nm* (*serviettes etc*) linen; (*pièce de tissu*) cloth; (*aussi: ~ de corps*) underwear; (*aussi: ~ de toilette*) towel; (*lessive*) washing; **~ sale** dirty linen.

lingère [lɛ̃ʒɛʀ] *nf* linen maid.

lingerie [lɛ̃ʒʀi] *nf* lingerie, underwear.

lingot [lɛ̃go] *nm* ingot.

linguiste [lɛ̃gɥist(ə)] *nm/f* linguist.

linguistique [lɛ̃gɥistik] *adj* linguistic ♦ *nf* linguistics *sg*.

lino(léum) [linɔ(leɔm)] *nm* lino(leum).

linotte [linɔt] *nf*: **tête de ~** bird brain.

linteau, x [lɛ̃to] *nm* lintel.

lion, ne [ljɔ̃, ljɔn] *nm/f* lion/lioness; (*signe*): **le L~** Leo, the Lion; **être du L~** to be Leo; **~ de mer** sealion.

lionceau, x [ljɔ̃so] *nm* lion cub.

liposuccion [liposyksjɔ̃] *nf* liposuction.

lippu, e [lipy] *adj* thick-lipped.

liquéfier [likefje] *vt* to liquefy; **se ~** *vi* (*gaz etc*) to liquefy; (*fig: personne*) to succumb.

liqueur [likœʀ] *nf* liqueur.

liquidateur, trice [likidatœʀ, -tʀis] *nm/f* (*JUR*) receiver; **~ judiciaire** official liquidator.

liquidation [likidasjɔ̃] *nf* liquidation; (*COMM*) clearance (sale); **~ judiciaire** compulsory liquidation.

liquide [likid] *adj* liquid ♦ *nm* liquid; (*COMM*): **en ~** in ready money *ou* cash.

liquider [likide] *vt* (*société, biens, témoin gênant*) to liquidate; (*compte, problème*) to settle; (*COMM: articles*) to clear, sell off.

liquidités [likidite] *nfpl* (*COMM*) liquid assets.

liquoreux, euse [likɔʀø, -øz] *adj* syrupy.

lire [liʀ] *nf* (*monnaie*) lira ♦ *vt, vi* to read; **~ qch à qn** to read sth (out) to sb.

lis *vb* [li] *voir* **lire** ♦ *nm* [lis] = **lys**.

lisais [lizɛ] *etc vb voir* **lire**.

Lisbonne [lizbɔn] *n* Lisbon.

lise [liz] *etc vb voir* **lire**.

liseré [lizʀe] *nm* border, edging.

liseron [lizʀɔ̃] *nm* bindweed.

liseuse [lizøz] *nf* book-cover; (*veste*) bedjacket.

lisible [lizibl(ə)] *adj* legible; (*digne d'être lu*) readable.

lisiblement [lizibləmɑ̃] *adv* legibly.

lisière [lizjɛʀ] *nf* (*de forêt*) edge; (*de tissu*) selvage.

lisons [lizɔ̃] *vb voir* **lire**.

lisse [lis] *adj* smooth.

lisser [lise] *vt* to smooth.

listage [listaʒ] *nm* (*INFORM*) listing.

liste [list(ə)] *nf* list; (*INFORM*) listing; **faire la ~ de** to list, make out a list of; **~ d'attente** waiting list; **~ civile** civil list; **~ électorale** electoral roll; **~ de mariage** wedding (present) list; **~ noire** hit list.

lister [liste] *vt* (*aussi INFORM*) to list; **~ la mémoire** to dump.

listéria [listeʀja] *nf* listeria.

listing [listiŋ] *nm* (*INFORM*) listing; **qualité ~** draft quality.

lit [li] *nm* (*gén*) bed; **faire son ~** to make one's bed; **aller/se mettre au ~** to go to/get into bed; **prendre le ~** to take to one's bed; **d'un premier ~** (*JUR*) of a first marriage; **~ de camp** campbed (*BRIT*), cot (*US*); **~ d'enfant** cot (*BRIT*), crib (*US*).

litanie [litani] *nf* litany.

lit-cage, *pl* **lits-cages** [likaʒ] *nm* folding bed.

litchi [litʃi] *nm* lychee.

literie [litʀi] *nf* bedding; (*linge*) bedding, bedclothes *pl*.

litho [lito], **lithographie** [litɔgʀafi] *nf*

litho(graphy); (*épreuve*) litho(graph).
litière [litjɛʀ] *nf* litter.
litige [litiʒ] *nm* dispute; **en ~** in contention.
litigieux, euse [litiʒjø, -øz] *adj* litigious, contentious.
litote [litɔt] *nf* understatement.
litre [litʀ(ə)] *nm* litre; (*récipient*) litre measure.
littéraire [liteʀɛʀ] *adj* literary.
littéral, e, aux [liteʀal, -o] *adj* literal.
littéralement [liteʀalmã] *adv* literally.
littérature [liteʀatyʀ] *nf* literature.
littoral, e, aux [litɔʀal, -o] *adj* coastal ♦ *nm* coast.
Lituanie [lityani] *nf*: **la ~** Lithuania.
lituanien, ne [lityanjɛ̃, -ɛn] *adj* Lithuanian ♦ *nm* (*LING*) Lithuanian ♦ *nm/f*: **L~, ne** Lithuanian.
liturgie [lityʀʒi] *nf* liturgy.
liturgique [lityʀʒik] *adj* liturgical.
livide [livid] *adj* livid, pallid.
living(-room) [liviŋ(ʀum)] *nm* living room.
livrable [livʀabl(ə)] *adj* (*COMM*) that can be delivered.
livraison [livʀɛzɔ̃] *nf* delivery; **~ à domicile** home delivery (service).
livre [livʀ(ə)] *nm* book; (*imprimerie etc*): **le ~** the book industry ♦ *nf* (*poids, monnaie*) pound; **traduire qch à ~ ouvert** to translate sth off the cuff *ou* at sight; **~ blanc** official report (*prepared by independent body, following war, natural disaster etc*); **~ de bord** (*NAVIG*) logbook; **~ de comptes** account(s) book; **~ de cuisine** cookery book (*BRIT*), cookbook; **~ de messe** mass *ou* prayer book; **~ d'or** visitors' book; **~ de poche** paperback (*cheap and pocket size*); **~ verte** green pound.
livré, e [livʀe] *nf* livery ♦ *adj*: **~ à** (*l'anarchie etc*) given over to; **~ à soi-même** left to oneself *ou* one's own devices.
livrer [livʀe] *vt* (*COMM*) to deliver; (*otage, coupable*) to hand over; (*secret, information*) to give away; **se ~ à** (*se confier*) to confide in; (*se rendre*) to give o.s. up to; (*s'abandonner à: débauche etc*) to give o.s. up *ou* over to; (*faire: pratiques, actes*) to indulge in; (*travail*) to be engaged in, engage in; (*: sport*) to practise; (*: enquête*) to carry out; **~ bataille** to give battle.
livresque [livʀɛsk(ə)] *adj* (*péj*) bookish.
livret [livʀɛ] *nm* booklet; (*d'opéra*) libretto (*pl* -s); **~ de caisse d'épargne** (savings) bankbook; **~ de famille** (official) family record book; **~ scolaire** (school) report book.
livreur, euse [livʀœʀ, -øz] *nm/f* delivery boy *ou* man/girl *ou* woman.
LO *sigle f* (= *Lutte ouvrière*) *political party*.
lob [lɔb] *nm* lob.
lobe [lɔb] *nm*: **~ de l'oreille** ear lobe.
lobé, e [lɔbe] *adj* (*ARCHIT*) foiled.
lober [lɔbe] *vt* to lob.
local, e, aux [lɔkal, -o] *adj* local ♦ *nm* (*salle*) premises *pl* ♦ *nmpl* premises.

localement [lɔkalmã] *adv* locally.
localisé, e [lɔkalize] *adj* localized.
localiser [lɔkalize] *vt* (*repérer*) to locate, place; (*limiter*) to localize, confine.
localité [lɔkalite] *nf* locality.
locataire [lɔkatɛʀ] *nm/f* tenant; (*de chambre*) lodger.
locatif, ive [lɔkatif, -iv] *adj* (*charges, réparations*) incumbent upon the tenant; (*valeur*) rental; (*immeuble*) with rented flats, used as a letting *ou* rental (*US*) concern.
location [lɔkasjɔ̃] *nf* (*par le locataire*) renting; (*par l'usager: de voiture etc*) hiring (*BRIT*), renting (*US*); (*par le propriétaire*) renting out, letting; hiring out (*BRIT*); (*de billets, places*) booking; (*bureau*) booking office; "**~ de voitures**" "car hire (*BRIT*) *ou* rental (*US*)".
location-vente [lɔkasjɔ̃vãt] *nf* form of hire purchase (*BRIT*) *ou* instalment plan (*US*).
lock-out [lɔkawt] *nm inv* lockout.
locomoteur, trice [lɔkɔmɔtœʀ, -tʀis] *adj, nf* locomotive.
locomotion [lɔkɔmosjɔ̃] *nf* locomotion.
locomotive [lɔkɔmɔtiv] *nf* locomotive, engine; (*fig*) pacesetter, pacemaker.
locuteur, trice [lɔkytœʀ, -tʀis] *nm/f* (*LING*) speaker.
locution [lɔkysjɔ̃] *nf* phrase.
loden [lɔdɛn] *nm* loden.
lofer [lɔfe] *vi* (*NAVIG*) to luff.
logarithme [lɔgaʀitm(ə)] *nm* logarithm.
loge [lɔʒ] *nf* (*THÉÂT: d'artiste*) dressing room; (*: de spectateurs*) box; (*de concierge, franc-maçon*) lodge.
logeable [lɔʒabl(ə)] *adj* habitable; (*spacieux*) roomy.
logement [lɔʒmã] *nm* flat (*BRIT*), apartment (*US*); accommodation *no pl* (*BRIT*), accommodations *pl* (*US*); **le ~** housing; **chercher un ~** to look for a flat *ou* apartment, look for accommodation(s); **construire des ~s bon marché** to build cheap housing *sg*; **crise du ~** housing shortage; **~ de fonction** (*ADMIN*) company flat *ou* apartment, accommodation(s) provided with one's job.
loger [lɔʒe] *vt* to accommodate ♦ *vi* to live; **se ~: trouver à se ~** to find accommodation; **se ~ dans** (*suj: balle, flèche*) to lodge itself in.
logeur, euse [lɔʒœʀ, -øz] *nm/f* landlord/landlady.
loggia [lɔdʒja] *nf* loggia.
logiciel [lɔʒisjɛl] *nm* software.
logicien, ne [lɔʒisjɛ̃, -ɛn] *nm/f* logician.
logique [lɔʒik] *adj* logical ♦ *nf* logic; **c'est ~** it stands to reason.
logiquement [lɔʒikmã] *adv* logically.
logis [lɔʒi] *nm* home; abode, dwelling.
logisticien, ne [lɔʒistisjɛ̃, -ɛn] *nm/f* logistician.
logistique [lɔʒistik] *nf* logistics *sg* ♦ *adj* logistic.
logo [lɔgo], **logotype** [lɔgɔtip] *nm* logo.
loi [lwa] *nf* law; **faire la ~** to lay down the law;

les ~s de la mode (fig) the dictates of fashion; **proposition de** ~ (private member's) bill; **projet de** ~ (government) bill.

loi-cadre, pl **lois-cadres** [lwakadʀ(ə)] nf (POL) blueprint law.

loin [lwɛ̃] adv far; (dans le temps: futur) a long way off; (: passé) a long time ago; **plus** ~ further; **moins** ~ **(que)** not as far (as); ~ **de** far from; **pas** ~ **de 1 000 F** not far off 1000 F; **au** ~ far off; **de** ~ adv from a distance; (fig: de beaucoup) by far; **il vient de** ~ he's come a long way; he comes from a long way away; **de** ~ **en** ~ here and there; (de temps en temps) (every) now and then; ~ **de là** (au contraire) far from it.

lointain, e [lwɛ̃tɛ̃, -ɛn] adj faraway, distant; (dans le futur, passé) distant, far-off; (cause, parent) remote, distant ♦ nm: **dans le** ~ in the distance.

loi-programme, pl **lois-programmes** [lwapʀɔgʀam] nf (POL) act providing framework for government programme.

loir [lwaʀ] nm dormouse (pl -mice).

Loire [lwaʀ] nf: **la** ~ the Loire.

loisible [lwazibl(ə)] adj: **il vous est** ~ **de ...** you are free to ....

loisir [lwaziʀ] nm: **heures de** ~ spare time; ~**s** nmpl leisure sg; (activités) leisure activities; **avoir le** ~ **de faire** to have the time ou opportunity to do; **(tout) à** ~ (en prenant son temps) at leisure; (autant qu'on le désire) at one's pleasure.

lombaire [lɔ̃bɛʀ] adj lumbar.

lombalgie [lɔ̃balʒi] nf back pain.

lombard, e [lɔ̃baʀ, -aʀd(ə)] adj Lombard.

Lombardie [lɔ̃baʀdi] nf: **la** ~ Lombardy.

londonien, ne [lɔ̃dɔnjɛ̃, -ɛn] adj London cpd, of London ♦ nm/f: **L**~, **ne** Londoner.

Londres [lɔ̃dʀ(ə)] n London.

long, longue [lɔ̃, lɔ̃g] adj long ♦ adv: **en savoir** ~ to know a great deal ♦ nm: **de 3 m de** ~ 3 m long, 3 m in length ♦ nf: **à la longue** in the end; **faire** ~ **feu** to fizzle out; **ne pas faire** ~ **feu** not to last long; **au** ~ **cours** (NAVIG) ocean cpd, ocean-going; **de longue date** adj long-standing; **longue durée** adj long-term; **de longue haleine** adj long-term; **être** ~ **à faire** to take a long time to do; **en** ~ adv lengthwise, lengthways; **(tout) le** ~ **de** (all) along; **tout au** ~ **de** (année, vie) throughout; **de** ~ **en large** (marcher) to and fro, up and down; **en** ~ **et en large** (fig) in every detail.

longanimité [lɔ̃ganimite] nf forbearance.

long-courrier [lɔ̃kuʀje] nm (AVIAT) long-haul aircraft.

longe [lɔ̃ʒ] nf (corde: pour attacher) tether; (pour mener) lead; (CULIN) loin.

longer [lɔ̃ʒe] vt to go (ou walk ou drive) along(side); (suj: mur, route) to border.

longévité [lɔ̃ʒevite] nf longevity.

longiligne [lɔ̃ʒiliɲ] adj long-limbed.

longitude [lɔ̃ʒityd] nf longitude; **à 45° de** ~ **ouest** at 45° longitude west.

longitudinal, e, aux [lɔ̃ʒitydinal, -o] adj longitudinal, lengthways; (entaille, vallée) running lengthways.

longtemps [lɔ̃tɑ̃] adv (for) a long time, (for) long; **ça ne va pas durer** ~ it won't last long; **avant** ~ before long; **pour/pendant** ~ for a long time; **je n'en ai pas pour** ~ I shan't be long; **mettre** ~ **à faire** to take a long time to do; **il en a pour** ~ he'll be a long time; **il y a** ~ **que je travaille** I have been working (for) a long time; **il n'y a pas** ~ **que je l'ai rencontré** it's not long since I met him.

longue [lɔ̃g] adj f voir **long**.

longuement [lɔ̃gmɑ̃] adv (longtemps: parler, regarder) for a long time; (en détail: expliquer, raconter) at length.

longueur [lɔ̃gœʀ] nf length; ~**s** nfpl (fig: d'un film etc) tedious parts; **sur une** ~ **de 10 km** for ou over 10 km; **en** ~ adv lengthwise, lengthways; **tirer en** ~ to drag on; **à** ~ **de journée** all day long; **d'une** ~ (gagner) by a length; ~ **d'onde** wavelength.

longue-vue [lɔ̃gvy] nf telescope.

looping [lupiŋ] nm (AVIAT): **faire des** ~**s** to loop the loop.

lopin [lɔpɛ̃] nm: ~ **de terre** patch of land.

loquace [lɔkas] adj talkative, loquacious.

loque [lɔk] nf (personne) wreck; ~**s** nfpl (habits) rags; **être** ou **tomber en** ~**s** to be in rags.

loquet [lɔkɛ] nm latch.

lorgner [lɔʀɲe] vt to eye; (convoiter) to have one's eye on.

lorgnette [lɔʀɲɛt] nf opera glasses pl.

lorgnon [lɔʀɲɔ̃] nm (face-à-main) lorgnette; (pince-nez) pince-nez.

loriot [lɔʀjo] nm (golden) oriole.

lorrain, e [lɔʀɛ̃, -ɛn] adj of ou from Lorraine; **quiche** ~**e** quiche lorraine.

lors [lɔʀ]: ~ **de** prép (au moment de) at the time of; (pendant) during; ~ **même que** even though.

lorsque [lɔʀsk(ə)] conj when, as.

losange [lɔzɑ̃ʒ] nm diamond; (GÉOM) lozenge; **en** ~ diamond-shaped.

lot [lo] nm (part) share; (de loterie) prize; (fig: destin) fate, lot; (COMM, INFORM) batch; ~ **de consolation** consolation prize.

loterie [lɔtʀi] nf lottery; (tombola) raffle; **L**~ **nationale** (formerly) French national lottery.

loti, e [lɔti] adj: **bien/mal** ~ well-/badly off, lucky/unlucky.

lotion [losjɔ̃] nf lotion; ~ **après rasage** aftershave (lotion); ~ **capillaire** hair lotion.

lotir [lɔtiʀ] vt (terrain: diviser) to divide into plots; (: vendre) to sell by lots.

lotissement [lɔtismɑ̃] nm (groupe de maisons, d'immeubles) housing development; (parcelle) (building) plot, lot.

loto [lɔto] nm lotto.

lotte – luisant

Le Loto *is a state-run national lottery with large cash prizes. Participants select 7 numbers out of 49. There is a sliding scale of winnings: all 7 numbers correct wins the top prize, 6 correct wins a smaller sum and so on. The draw is televised twice weekly.*

lotte [lɔt] *nf* (*ZOOL: de rivière*) burbot; (*: de mer*) monkfish.

louable [lwabl(ə)] *adj* (*appartement, garage*) rentable; (*action, personne*) praiseworthy, commendable.

louage [lwaʒ] *nm*: **voiture de ~** hired (*BRIT*) *ou* rented (*US*) car; (*à louer*) hire (*BRIT*) *ou* rental (*US*) car.

louange [lwãʒ] *nf*: **à la ~ de** in praise of; **~s** *nfpl* praise *sg*.

loubar(d) [lubaʀ] *nm* (*fam*) lout.

louche [luʃ] *adj* shady, fishy, dubious ♦ *nf* ladle.

loucher [luʃe] *vi* to squint; (*fig*): **~ sur** to have one's (beady) eye on.

louer [lwe] *vt* (*maison: suj: propriétaire*) to let, rent (out); (*: locataire*) to rent; (*voiture etc*) to hire out (*BRIT*), rent (out); to hire (*BRIT*), rent; (*réserver*) to book; (*faire l'éloge de*) to praise; **"à ~"** "to let" (*BRIT*), "for rent" (*US*); **~ qn de** to praise sb for; **se ~ de** to congratulate o.s. on.

loufoque [lufɔk] *adj* (*fam*) crazy, zany.

loukoum [lukum] *nm* Turkish delight.

loulou [lulu] *nm* (*chien*) spitz; **~ de Poméranie** Pomeranian (dog).

loup [lu] *nm* wolf (*pl* wolves); (*poisson*) bass; (*masque*) (eye) mask; **jeune ~** young go-getter; **~ de mer** (*marin*) old seadog.

loupe [lup] *nf* magnifying glass; **~ de noyer** burr walnut; **à la ~** (*fig*) in minute detail.

louper [lupe] *vt* (*fam: manquer*) to miss; (*: gâcher*) to mess up, bungle.

lourd, e [luʀ, luʀd(ə)] *adj* heavy; (*chaleur, temps*) sultry; (*fig: personne, style*) heavy-handed ♦ *adv*: **peser ~** to be heavy; **~ de** (*menaces*) charged with; (*conséquences*) fraught with; **artillerie/industrie ~e** heavy artillery/industry.

lourdaud, e [luʀdo, -od] *adj* oafish.

lourdement [luʀdəmã] *adv* heavily; **se tromper ~** to make a big mistake.

lourdeur [luʀdœʀ] *nf* heaviness; **~ d'estomac** indigestion *no pl*.

loustic [lustik] *nm* (*fam péj*) joker.

loutre [lutʀ(ə)] *nf* otter; (*fourrure*) otter skin.

louve [luv] *nf* she-wolf.

louveteau, x [luvto] *nm* (*ZOOL*) wolf-cub; (*scout*) cub (scout).

louvoyer [luvwaje] *vi* (*NAVIG*) to tack; (*fig*) to hedge, evade the issue.

lover [lɔve]: **se ~** *vi* to coil up.

loyal, e, aux [lwajal, -o] *adj* (*fidèle*) loyal, faithful; (*fair-play*) fair.

loyalement [lwajalmã] *adv* loyally, faithfully; fairly.

loyalisme [lwajalism(ə)] *nm* loyalty.

loyauté [lwajote] *nf* loyalty, faithfulness; fairness.

loyer [lwaje] *nm* rent; **~ de l'argent** interest rate.

LP *sigle m* (= *lycée professionnel*) secondary school for vocational training.

LPO *sigle f* (= *Ligue pour la protection des oiseaux*) bird protection society.

LSD *sigle m* (= *Lyserg Säure Diäthylamid*) LSD.

lu, e [ly] *pp de* **lire**.

lubie [lybi] *nf* whim, craze.

lubricité [lybʀisite] *nf* lust.

lubrifiant [lybʀifjã] *nm* lubricant.

lubrifier [lybʀifje] *vt* to lubricate.

lubrique [lybʀik] *adj* lecherous.

lucarne [lykaʀn(ə)] *nf* skylight.

lucide [lysid] *adj* (*conscient*) lucid, conscious; (*perspicace*) clear-headed.

lucidité [lysidite] *nf* lucidity.

luciole [lysjɔl] *nf* firefly.

lucratif, ive [lykʀatif, -iv] *adj* lucrative, profitable; **à but non ~** non profit-making.

ludique [lydik] *adj* play *cpd*, playing.

ludothèque [lydɔtɛk] *nf* toy library.

luette [lɥɛt] *nf* uvula.

lueur [lɥœʀ] *nf* (*chatoyante*) glimmer *no pl*; (*métallique, mouillée*) gleam *no pl*; (*rougeoyante, chaude*) glow *no pl*; (*pâle*) (faint) light; (*fig*) spark; (*: d'espérance*) glimmer, gleam.

luge [lyʒ] *nf* sledge (*BRIT*), sled (*US*); **faire de la ~** to sledge (*BRIT*), sled (*US*), toboggan.

lugubre [lygybʀ(ə)] *adj* gloomy; dismal.

═══════════════════ *MOT-CLÉ*

lui [lɥi] *pp de* **luire**
♦ *pron* **1** (*objet indirect: mâle*) (to) him; (*: femelle*) (to) her; (*: chose, animal*) (to) it; **je ~ ai parlé** I have spoken to him (*ou* her); **il ~ a offert un cadeau** he gave him (*ou* her) a present; **je le ~ ai donné** I gave it to him (*ou* her)
2 (*après préposition, comparatif: personne*) him; (*: chose, animal*) it; **elle est contente de ~** she is pleased with him; **je la connais mieux que ~** I know her better than he does; I know her better than him; **cette voiture est à ~** this car belongs to him, this is HIS car
3 (*sujet, forme emphatique*) he; **~, il est à Paris** HE is in Paris; **c'est ~ qui l'a fait** HE did it.

lui-même [lɥimɛm] *pron* (*personne*) himself; (*chose*) itself.

luire [lɥiʀ] *vi* (*gén*) to shine, gleam; (*surface mouillée*) to glisten; (*reflets chauds, cuivrés*) to glow.

luisant, e [lɥizã, -ãt] *vb voir* **luire** ♦ *adj* shining, gleaming.

lumbago [lɔ̃bago] *nm* lumbago.

lumière [lymjɛʀ] *nf* light; **~s** *nfpl* (*d'une personne*) knowledge *sg*, wisdom *sg*; **à la ~ de** by the light of; (*fig: événements*) in the light of; **fais de la ~** let's have some light, give us some light; **faire (toute) la ~ sur** (*fig*) to clarify (completely); **mettre en ~** (*fig*) to highlight; **~ du jour/soleil** day/sunlight.

luminaire [lyminɛʀ] *nm* lamp, light.

lumineux, euse [lyminø, -øz] *adj* (*émettant de la lumière*) luminous; (*éclairé*) illuminated; (*ciel, journée, couleur*) bright; (*relatif à la lumière: rayon etc*) of light, light *cpd*; (*fig: regard*) radiant.

luminosité [lyminozite] *nf* (*TECH*) luminosity.

lump [lœp] *nm*: **œufs de ~** lump-fish roe.

lunaire [lynɛʀ] *adj* lunar, moon *cpd*.

lunatique [lynatik] *adj* whimsical, temperamental.

lunch [lœntʃ] *nm* (*réception*) buffet lunch.

lundi [lœdi] *nm* Monday; **on est ~** it's Monday; **le ~ 20 août** Monday 20th August; **il est venu ~** he came on Monday; **le(s) ~(s)** on Mondays; **à ~!** see you (on) Monday!; **~ de Pâques** Easter Monday; **~ de Pentecôte** Whit Monday (*BRIT*).

lune [lyn] *nf* moon; **pleine/nouvelle ~** full/new moon; **être dans la ~** (*distrait*) to have one's head in the clouds; **~ de miel** honeymoon.

luné, e [lyne] *adj*: **bien/mal ~** in a good/bad mood.

lunette [lynɛt] *nf*: **~s** *nfpl* glasses, spectacles; (*protectrices*) goggles; **~ d'approche** telescope; **~ arrière** (*AUTO*) rear window; **~s noires** dark glasses; **~s de soleil** sunglasses.

lurent [lyʀ] *vb voir* **lire**.

lurette [lyʀɛt] *nf*: **il y a belle ~** ages ago.

luron, ne [lyʀɔ̃, -ɔn] *nm/f* lad/lass; **joyeux** *ou* **gai ~** gay dog.

lus [ly] *etc vb voir* **lire**.

lustre [lystʀ(ə)] *nm* (*de plafond*) chandelier; (*fig: éclat*) lustre.

lustrer [lystʀe] *vt*: **~ qch** (*faire briller*) to make sth shine; (*user*) to make sth shiny.

lut [ly] *vb voir* **lire**.

luth [lyt] *nm* lute.

luthier [lytje] *nm* (stringed-)instrument maker.

lutin [lytɛ̃] *nm* imp, goblin.

lutrin [lytʀɛ̃] *nm* lectern.

lutte [lyt] *nf* (*conflit*) struggle; (*SPORT*): **la ~** wrestling; **de haute ~** after a hard-fought struggle; **~ des classes** class struggle; **~ libre** (*SPORT*) all-in wrestling.

lutter [lyte] *vi* to fight, struggle; (*SPORT*) to wrestle.

lutteur, euse [lytœʀ, -øz] *nm/f* (*SPORT*) wrestler; (*fig*) battler, fighter.

luxation [lyksasjɔ̃] *nf* dislocation.

luxe [lyks(ə)] *nm* luxury; **un ~ de** (*détails, précautions*) a wealth of; **de ~** *adj* luxury *cpd*.

Luxembourg [lyksɑ̃buʀ] *nm*: **le ~** Luxembourg.

luxembourgeois, e [lyksɑ̃buʀʒwa, -waz] *adj* of *ou* from Luxembourg ♦ *nm/f*: **L~, e** inhabitant *ou* native of Luxembourg.

luxer [lykse] *vt*: **se ~ l'épaule** to dislocate one's shoulder.

luxueusement [lyksyøzmɑ̃] *adv* luxuriously.

luxueux, euse [lyksyø, -øz] *adj* luxurious.

luxure [lyksyʀ] *nf* lust.

luxuriant, e [lyksyʀjɑ̃, -ɑ̃t] *adj* luxuriant, lush.

luzerne [lyzɛʀn(ə)] *nf* lucerne, alfalfa.

lycée [lise] *nm* (*state*) secondary (*BRIT*) *ou* high (*US*) school; **~ technique** technical secondary *ou* high school.

French pupils spend the last three years of their secondary education at a **lycée**, where they sit their **baccalauréat** before leaving school or going on to higher education. There are various types of lycée, including the "lycées d'enseignement technologique" providing technical courses and the "lycées d'enseignement professionnel" providing vocational courses. Some lycées, particularly those with a wide catchment area or those providing specialist courses, have boarding facilities; *see also* **école maternelle/primaire, collège**.

lycéen, ne [liseɛ̃, -ɛn] *nm/f* secondary school pupil.

Lycra [likra] *nm* ® Lycra ®.

lymphatique [lɛ̃fatik] *adj* (*fig*) lethargic, sluggish.

lymphe [lɛ̃f] *nf* lymph.

lyncher [lɛ̃ʃe] *vt* to lynch.

lynx [lɛ̃ks] *nm* lynx.

Lyon [ljɔ̃] *n* Lyons.

lyonnais, e [ljɔnɛ, -ɛz] *adj* of *ou* from Lyons; (*CULIN*) Lyonnaise.

lyophilisé, e [ljɔfilize] *adj* freeze-dried.

lyre [liʀ] *nf* lyre.

lyrique [liʀik] *adj* lyrical; (*OPÉRA*) lyric; **artiste ~** opera singer; **comédie ~** comic opera; **théâtre ~** opera house (*for light opera*).

lyrisme [liʀism(ə)] *nm* lyricism.

lys [lis] *nm* lily.

M m

M, m [ɛm] *nm inv* M, m ♦ *abr* = **majeur, masculin, mètre, Monsieur**; (= *million*) M; **M comme Marcel** M for Mike.

m' [m] *pron voir* **me.**

MA *sigle m* = **maître auxiliaire.**

ma [ma] *adj possessif voir* **mon.**

maboul, e [mabul] *adj (fam)* loony.

macabre [makɑbʀ(ə)] *adj* macabre, gruesome.

macadam [makadam] *nm* tarmac (*BRIT*), asphalt.

Macao [makao] *nf* Macao.

macaron [makaʀɔ̃] *nm (gâteau)* macaroon; (*insigne*) (round) badge.

macaroni(s) [makaʀɔni] *nm(pl)* macaroni *sg*; ~ **au fromage** *ou* **au gratin** macaroni cheese (*BRIT*), macaroni and cheese (*US*).

Macédoine [masedwan] *nf* Macedonia.

macédoine [masedwan] *nf*: ~ **de fruits** fruit salad; ~ **de légumes** mixed vegetables *pl*.

macédonien, ne [masedɔnjɛ̃, -ɛn] *adj* Macedonian ♦ *nm/f*: **M~, ne** Macedonian.

macérer [maseʀe] *vi, vt* to macerate; (*dans du vinaigre*) to pickle.

mâchefer [mɑʃfɛʀ] *nm* clinker, cinders *pl*.

mâcher [mɑʃe] *vt* to chew; **ne pas** ~ **ses mots** not to mince one's words; ~ **le travail à qn** (*fig*) to spoonfeed sb, do half sb's work for him.

machiavélique [makjavelik] *adj* Machiavellian.

machin [maʃɛ̃] *nm (fam)* thingamajig, thing; (*personne*): **M~** what's-his(*ou*-her)-name.

machinal, e, aux [maʃinal, -o] *adj* mechanical, automatic.

machination [maʃinɑsjɔ̃] *nf* scheming, frame-up.

machine [maʃin] *nf* machine; (*locomotive; de navire etc*) engine; (*fig: rouages*) machinery; (*fam: personne*): **M~** what's-her-name; **faire** ~ **arrière** (*NAVIG*) to go astern; (*fig*) to backpedal; ~ **à laver/coudre/tricoter** washing/sewing/knitting machine; ~ **à écrire** typewriter; ~ **à sous** fruit machine; ~ **à vapeur** steam engine.

machine-outil, *pl* **machines-outils** [maʃinuti] *nf* machine tool.

machinerie [maʃinʀi] *nf* machinery, plant; (*d'un navire*) engine room.

machinisme [maʃinism(ə)] *nm* mechanization.

machiniste [maʃinist(ə)] *nm (THÉÂT)* scene shifter; (*de bus, métro*) driver.

mâchoire [mɑʃwaʀ] *nf* jaw; ~ **de frein** brake shoe.

mâchonner [mɑʃɔne] *vt* to chew (at).

mâcon [makɔ̃] *nm* Mâcon wine.

maçon [masɔ̃] *nm* bricklayer; (*constructeur*) builder.

maçonner [masɔne] *vt (revêtir)* to face, render (with cement); (*boucher*) to brick up.

maçonnerie [masɔnʀi] *nf (murs: de brique)* brickwork; (: *de pierre*) masonry, stonework; (*activité*) bricklaying; building; ~ **de béton** concrete.

maçonnique [masɔnik] *adj* masonic.

macramé [makʀame] *nm* macramé.

macrobiotique [makʀɔbjɔtik] *adj* macrobiotic.

macrocosme [makʀɔkɔsm(ə)] *nm* macrocosm.

macro-économie [makʀɔekɔnɔmi] *nf* macroeconomics *sg*.

macrophotographie [makʀɔfɔtɔgʀafi] *nf* macrophotography.

maculer [makyle] *vt* to stain; (*TYPO*) to mackle.

Madagascar [madagaskaʀ] *nf* Madagascar.

Madame [madam], *pl* **Mesdames** [medam] *nf*: ~ **X** Mrs X ['mɪsɪz]; **occupez-vous de** ~/ **Monsieur/Mademoiselle** please serve this lady/gentleman/(young) lady; **bonjour** ~/ **Monsieur/Mademoiselle** good morning; (*ton déférent*) good morning Madam/Sir/Madam; (*le nom est connu*) good morning Mrs X/Mr X/Miss X; ~/**Monsieur/Mademoiselle!** (*pour appeler*) excuse me!; (*ton déférent*) Madam/ Sir/Miss!; ~/**Monsieur/Mademoiselle** (*sur lettre*) Dear Madam/Sir/Madam; **chère** ~/ **cher Monsieur/chère Mademoiselle** Dear Mrs X/Mr X/Miss X; ~ **la Directrice** the director; the manageress; the headteacher; **Mesdames** Ladies.

Madeleine [madlɛn]: **îles de la** ~ *nfpl* Magdalen Islands.

madeleine [madlɛn] *nf* madeleine, ≈ sponge finger cake.

Madelinot, e [madlino, -ɔt] *nm/f* inhabitant *ou* native of the Magdalen Islands.

Mademoiselle [madmwazɛl], *pl* **Mesdemoiselles** [medmwazɛl] *nf* Miss; *voir aussi* **Madame.**

Madère [madɛʀ] *nf* Madeira ♦ *nm*: **m~** Madeira (wine).

madone [madɔn] *nf* madonna.

madré, e [madʀe] *adj* crafty, wily.

Madrid [madʀid] *n* Madrid.

madrier [madʀije] *nm* beam.

madrigal, aux [madʀigal, -o] *nm* madrigal.

madrilène [madʀilɛn] *adj* of *ou* from Madrid.

maestria [maɛstʀija] *nf* (masterly) skill.

maestro [maɛstʀo] *nm* maestro.

maf(f)ia [mafja] *nf* Maf(f)ia.

magasin [magazɛ̃] *nm (boutique)* shop; (*entrepôt*) warehouse; (*d'arme, appareil-photo*) magazine; **en** ~ (*COMM*) in stock; **faire les** ~s to go (a)round the shops, do the shops; ~

d'alimentation grocer's shop (*BRIT*), grocery store (*US*).

magasinier [magazinje] *nm* warehouseman.

magazine [magazin] *nm* magazine.

mage [maʒ] *nm*: **les Rois M~s** the Magi, the (Three) Wise Men.

Maghreb [magʀɛb] *nm*: **le** ~ the Maghreb, North(-West) Africa.

maghrébin, e [magʀebɛ̃, -in] *adj* of *ou* from the Maghreb ♦ *nm/f*: **M~, e** North African, Maghrebi.

magicien, ne [maʒisjɛ̃, -ɛn] *nm/f* magician.

magie [maʒi] *nf* magic; ~ **noire** black magic.

magique [maʒik] *adj* (*occulte*) magic; (*fig*) magical.

magistral, e, aux [maʒistʀal, -o] *adj* (*œuvre, adresse*) masterly; (*ton*) authoritative; (*gifle etc*) sound, resounding; (*ex cathedra*): **enseignement** ~ lecturing, lectures *pl*; **cours** ~ lecture.

magistrat [maʒistʀa] *nm* magistrate.

magistrature [maʒistʀatyʀ] *nf* magistracy, magistrature; ~ **assise** judges *pl*, bench; ~ **debout** state prosecutors *pl*.

magma [magma] *nm* (*GÉO*) magma; (*fig*) jumble.

magnanerie [maɲanʀi] *nf* silk farm.

magnanime [maɲanim] *adj* magnanimous.

magnanimité [maɲanimite] *nf* magnanimity.

magnat [magna] *nm* tycoon, magnate; ~ **de la presse** press baron.

magner [maɲe]: **se** ~ *vi* (*fam*) to get a move on.

magnésie [maɲezi] *nf* magnesia.

magnésium [maɲezjɔm] *nm* magnesium.

magnétique [maɲetik] *adj* magnetic.

magnétiser [maɲetize] *vt* to magnetize; (*fig*) to mesmerize, hypnotize.

magnétiseur, euse [maɲetizœʀ, -øz] *nm/f* hypnotist.

magnétisme [maɲetism(ə)] *nm* magnetism.

magnéto [maɲeto] *nm* (= *magnétocassette*) cassette deck; (= *magnétophone*) tape recorder.

magnétocassette [maɲetokasɛt] *nm* cassette deck.

magnétophone [maɲetɔfɔn] *nm* tape recorder; ~ **à cassettes** cassette recorder.

magnétoscope [maɲetɔskɔp] *nm*: ~ **(à cassette)** video (recorder).

magnificence [maɲifisɑ̃s] *nf* (*faste*) magnificence, splendour (*BRIT*), splendor (*US*); (*générosité, prodigalité*) munificence, lavishness.

magnifier [maɲifje] *vt* (*glorifier*) to glorify; (*idéaliser*) to idealize.

magnifique [maɲifik] *adj* magnificent.

magnifiquement [maɲifikmɑ̃] *adv* magnificently.

magnolia [maɲɔlja] *nm* magnolia.

magnum [magnɔm] *nm* magnum.

magot [mago] *nm* (*argent*) pile (of money); (*économies*) nest egg.

magouille [maguj] *nf* (*fam*) scheming.

mahométan, e [maɔmetɑ̃, -an] *adj* Mohammedan, Mahometan.

mai [mɛ] *nm* May; *voir aussi* **juillet**.

Le premier mai is *a public holiday in France commemorating demonstrations by the unions in the United States in 1886 to secure the eight-hour working day. It is traditional in France to exchange sprigs of lily of the valley.*
Le 8 mai is *a public holiday in France commemorating the surrender of the German army to Eisenhower on May 7, 1945. There are parades of ex-servicemen in most towns.*
The social upheavals of May and June 1968, marked by student demonstrations, workers' strikes and general rioting, are generally referred to as "les événements de **mai 68**". *De Gaulle's government survived the onslaught, but reforms in education and a move towards decentralization ensued.*

---

maigre [mɛgʀ(ə)] *adj* (very) thin, skinny; (*viande*) lean; (*fromage*) low-fat; (*végétation*) thin, sparse; (*fig*) poor, meagre, skimpy ♦ *adv*: **faire** ~ not to eat meat; **jours** ~s days of abstinence, fish days.

maigrelet, te [mɛgʀəlɛ, -ɛt] *adj* skinny, scrawny.

maigreur [mɛgʀœʀ] *nf* thinness.

maigrichon, ne [megʀiʃɔ̃, -ɔn] *adj* = **maigrelet, te**.

maigrir [megʀiʀ] *vi* to get thinner, lose weight ♦ *vt*: ~ **qn** (*suj: vêtement*) to make sb look slim(mer).

mailing [mɛliŋ] *nm* direct mail *no pl*; **un** ~ a mailshot.

maille [maj] *nf* (*boucle*) stitch; (*ouverture*) hole (in the mesh); **avoir** ~ **à partir avec qn** to have a brush with sb; ~ **à l'endroit/à l'envers** knit one/purl one; (*boucle*) plain/purl stitch.

maillechort [majʃɔʀ] *nm* nickel silver.

maillet [majɛ] *nm* mallet.

maillon [majɔ̃] *nm* link.

maillot [majo] *nm* (*aussi*: ~ **de corps**) vest; (*de danseur*) leotard; (*de sportif*) jersey; ~ **de bain** bathing costume (*BRIT*), swimsuit; (*d'homme*) bathing trunks *pl*; ~ **une pièce** one-piece swimsuit; ~ **deux pièces** two-piece swimsuit, bikini.

main [mɛ̃] *nf* hand; **la** ~ **dans la** ~ hand in hand; **à deux** ~s with both hands; **à une** ~ with one hand; **à la** ~ (*tenir, avoir*) in one's hand; (*faire, tricoter etc*) by hand; **se donner la** ~ to hold hands; **donner** *ou* **tendre la** ~ **à qn** to hold out one's hand to sb; **se serrer la** ~ to shake hands; **serrer la** ~ **à qn** to shake hands with sb; **sous la** ~ to *ou* at hand; **haut les** ~s! hands up!; **à** ~ **levée** (*ART*) freehand;

à ~s **levées** (*voter*) with a show of hands; **attaque à ~ armée** armed attack; **à ~ droite/gauche** to the right/left; **à remettre en ~s propres** to be delivered personally; **de première ~** (*renseignement*) first-hand; (*COMM: voiture etc*) with only one previous owner; **faire ~ basse sur** to help o.s. to; **mettre la dernière ~ à** to put the finishing touches to; **mettre la ~ à la pâte** (*fig*) to lend a hand; **prendre qch en ~** (*fig*) to take sth in hand; **avoir/passer la ~** (*CARTES*) to lead/hand over the lead; **s'en laver les ~s** (*fig*) to wash one's hands of it; **se faire/perdre la ~** to get one's hand in/lose one's touch; **avoir qch bien en ~** to have got the hang of sth; **en un tour de ~** (*fig*) in the twinkling of an eye; **~ courante** handrail.

mainate [mɛnat] *nm* myna(h) bird.

main-d'œuvre [mɛ̃dœvʀ(ə)] *nf* manpower, labour (*BRIT*), labor (*US*).

main-forte [mɛ̃fɔʀt(ə)] *nf*: **prêter ~ à qn** to come to sb's assistance.

mainmise [mɛ̃miz] *nf* seizure; (*fig*): **avoir la ~ sur** to have a complete hold on.

maint, e [mɛ̃, mɛ̃t] *adj* many a; **~s** many; **à ~es reprises** time and (time) again.

maintenance [mɛ̃tnɑ̃s] *nf* maintenance.

maintenant [mɛ̃tnɑ̃] *adv* now; (*actuellement*) nowadays.

maintenir [mɛ̃tniʀ] *vt* (*retenir, soutenir*) to support; (*contenir: foule etc*) to keep in check, hold back; (*conserver*) to maintain, uphold; (*affirmer*) to maintain; **se ~** *vi* (*paix, temps*) to hold; (*préjugé*) to persist; (*malade*) to remain stable.

maintien [mɛ̃tjɛ̃] *nm* maintaining, upholding; (*attitude*) bearing; **~ de l'ordre** maintenance of law and order.

maintiendrai [mɛ̃tjɛ̃dʀe], **maintiens** [mɛ̃tjɛ̃] *etc vb voir* **maintenir**.

maire [mɛʀ] *nm* mayor.

mairie [meʀi] *nf* (*endroit*) town hall; (*administration*) town council.

mais [mɛ] *conj* but; **~ non!** of course not!; **~ enfin** but after all; (*indignation*) look here!; **~ encore?** is that all?

maïs [mais] *nm* maize (*BRIT*), corn (*US*).

maison [mɛzɔ̃] *nf* (*bâtiment*) house; (*chez-soi*) home; (*COMM*) firm; (*famille*): **ami de la ~** friend of the family ♦ *adj inv* (*CULIN*) home-made; (: *au restaurant*) made by the chef; (*COMM*) in-house, own; (*fam*) first-rate; **à la ~** at home; (*direction*) home; **~ d'arrêt** (short-stay) prison; **~ de campagne** country cottage; **~ centrale** prison; **~ close** brothel; **~ de correction** ≈ remand home (*BRIT*), ≈ reformatory (*US*); **~ de la culture** ≈ arts centre; **~ des jeunes** ≈ youth club; **~ mère** parent company; **~ de passe** = **~ close**; **~ de repos** convalescent home; **~ de retraite** old people's home; **~ de santé** mental home.

Maisons des jeunes et de la culture *are centres for young people which combine the functions of youth club and community arts centre. They organize a wide range of sporting and cultural activities (theatre, music, exhibitions), and are also engaged in welfare work. The centres are, in part, publicly financed.*

Maison-Blanche [mɛzɔ̃blɑ̃ʃ] *nf*: **la ~** the White House.

maisonnée [mɛzɔne] *nf* household, family.

maisonnette [mɛzɔnɛt] *nf* small house, cottage.

maître, esse [mɛtʀ(ə), mɛtʀɛs] *nm/f* master/mistress; (*SCOL*) teacher, schoolmaster/mistress ♦ *nm* (*peintre etc*) master; (*titre*): **M~ (Me)** Maître, *term of address for lawyers etc* ♦ *nf* (*amante*) mistress ♦ *adj* (*principal, essentiel*) main; **maison de ~** family seat; **être ~ de** (*soi-même, situation*) to be in control of; **se rendre ~ de** (*pays, ville*) to gain control of; (*situation, incendie*) to bring under control; **être passé ~ dans l'art de** to be a (past) master in the art of; **une maîtresse femme** a forceful woman; **~ d'armes** fencing master; **~ auxiliaire (MA)** (*SCOL*) temporary teacher; **~ chanteur** blackmailer; **~ de chapelle** choirmaster; **~ de conférences** ≈ senior lecturer (*BRIT*), ≈ assistant professor (*US*); **~/maîtresse d'école** teacher, schoolmaster/mistress; **~ d'hôtel** (*domestique*) butler; (*d'hôtel*) head waiter; **~ de maison** host; **~ nageur** lifeguard; **~ d'œuvre** (*CONSTR*) project manager; **~ d'ouvrage** (*CONSTR*) client; **~ à penser** intellectual leader; **~ queux** chef; **maîtresse de maison** hostess; (*ménagère*) housewife (*pl* -wives).

maître-assistant, e, *pl* **maîtres-assistants, es** [mɛtʀasistɑ̃, -ɑ̃t] *nm/f* ≈ lecturer.

maître-autel, *pl* **maîtres-autels** [mɛtʀotɛl] *nm* high altar.

maîtrise [metʀiz] *nf* (*aussi*: **~ de soi**) self-control, self-possession; (*habileté*) skill, mastery; (*suprématie*) mastery, command; (*diplôme*) ≈ master's degree; (*chefs d'équipe*) supervisory staff.

The **maîtrise** *is a French university degree awarded following two years successful study after the* **DEUG.** *Students wishing to undertake research and prepare a doctorate must hold a maîtrise.*

maîtriser [metʀize] *vt* (*cheval, incendie*) to (bring under) control; (*sujet*) to master; (*émotion*) to control; **se ~** to control o.s.

majesté [maʒɛste] *nf* majesty.

majestueux, euse [maʒɛstɥø, -øz] *adj* majestic.

majeur, e [maʒœʀ] *adj* (*important*) major; (*JUR*) of age; (*fig*) adult ♦ *nm/f* (*JUR*) person who has come of age *ou* attained his (*ou* her) majority ♦ *nm* (*doigt*) middle finger; **en** ~**e partie** for the most part; **la** ~**e partie de** the major part of.

major [maʒɔʀ] *nm* adjutant; (*SCOL*): ~ **de la promotion** first in one's year.

majoration [maʒɔʀɑsjɔ̃] *nf* increase.

majordome [maʒɔʀdɔm] *nm* major-domo.

majorer [maʒɔʀe] *vt* to increase.

majorette [maʒɔʀɛt] *nf* majorette.

majoritaire [maʒɔʀitɛʀ] *adj* majority *cpd*; **système/scrutin** ~ majority system/ballot.

majorité [maʒɔʀite] *nf* (*gén*) majority; (*parti*) party in power; **en** ~ (*composé etc*) mainly.

Majorque [maʒɔʀk(ə)] *nf* Majorca.

majorquin, e [maʒɔʀkɛ̃, -in] *adj* Majorcan ♦ *nm/f*: **M**~, **e** Majorcan.

majuscule [maʒyskyl] *adj*, *nf*: (**lettre**) ~ capital (letter).

MAL [mal] *sigle f* (= *Maison d'animation et des loisirs*) cultural centre.

mal, maux [mal, mo] *nm* (*opposé au bien*) evil; (*tort, dommage*) harm; (*douleur physique*) pain, ache; (*maladie*) illness, sickness *no pl*; (*difficulté, peine*) trouble; (*souffrance morale*) pain ♦ *adv* badly ♦ *adj*: **c'est** ~ (**de faire**) it's bad *ou* wrong (to do); **être** ~ to be uncomfortable; **être** ~ **avec qn** to be on bad terms with sb; **être au plus** ~ (*malade*) to be very bad; (*brouillé*) to be at daggers drawn; **il comprend** ~ he has difficulty in understanding; **il a** ~ **compris** he misunderstood; ~ **tourner** to go wrong; **dire/penser du** ~ **de** to speak/think ill of; **ne vouloir de** ~ **à personne** to wish nobody any ill; **il n'a rien fait de** ~ he has done nothing wrong; **avoir du** ~ **à faire qch** to have trouble doing sth; **se donner du** ~ **pour faire qch** to go to a lot of trouble to do sth; **ne voir aucun** ~ **à** to see no harm in, see nothing wrong in; **craignant** ~ **faire** fearing he *etc* was doing the wrong thing; **sans penser** *ou* **songer à** ~ without meaning any harm; **faire du** ~ **à qn** to hurt sb; **to harm sb; se faire** ~ to hurt o.s.; **se faire** ~ **au pied** to hurt one's foot; **ça fait** ~ it hurts; **j'ai** ~ (**ici**) it hurts (here); **j'ai** ~ **au dos** my back aches, I've got a pain in my back; **avoir** ~ **à la tête/à la gorge/aux dents** to have a headache/a sore throat/toothache; **avoir le** ~ **de l'air** to be airsick; **avoir le** ~ **du pays** to be homesick; ~ **de mer** seasickness; ~ **de la route** carsickness; ~ **en point** *adj inv* in a bad state; **maux de ventre** stomach ache *sg; voir* **cœur.**

Malabar [malabaʀ] *nm*: **le** ~, **la côte de** ~ the Malabar (Coast).

malabar [malabaʀ] *nm* (*fam*) muscle man.

malade [malad] *adj* ill, sick; (*poitrine, jambe*) bad; (*plante*) diseased; (*fig: entreprise, monde*) ailing ♦ *nm/f* invalid, sick person; (*à l'hôpital etc*) patient; **tomber** ~ to fall ill; **être** ~ **du cœur** to have heart trouble *ou* a bad heart;

grand ~ seriously ill person; ~ **mental** mentally sick *ou* ill person.

maladie [maladi] *nf* (*spécifique*) disease, illness; (*mauvaise santé*) illness, sickness; (*fig: manie*) mania; **être rongé par la** ~ to be wasting away (through illness); ~ **d'Alzheimer** Alzheimer's disease; ~ **de peau** skin disease.

maladif, ive [maladif, -iv] *adj* sickly; (*curiosité, besoin*) pathological.

maladresse [maladʀɛs] *nf* clumsiness *no pl*; (*gaffe*) blunder.

maladroit, e [maladʀwa, -wat] *adj* clumsy.

maladroitement [maladʀwatmɑ̃] *adv* clumsily.

mal-aimé, e [maleme] *nm/f* unpopular person; (*de la scène politique, de la société*) persona non grata; **le** ~ **du bureau** the unpopular one in the office.

malais, e [malɛ, -ɛz] *adj* Malay, Malayan ♦ *nm* (*LING*) Malay ♦ *nm/f*: **M**~, **e** Malay, Malayan.

malaise [malɛz] *nm* (*MÉD*) feeling of faintness; feeling of discomfort; (*fig*) uneasiness, malaise; **avoir un** ~ to feel faint *ou* dizzy.

malaisé, e [maleze] *adj* difficult.

Malaisie [malɛzi] *nf*: **la** ~ Malaya, West Malaysia; **la péninsule de** ~ the Malay Peninsula.

malappris, e [malapʀi, -iz] *nm/f* ill-mannered *ou* boorish person.

malaria [malaʀja] *nf* malaria.

malavisé, e [malavize] *adj* ill-advised, unwise.

Malawi [malawi] *nm*: **le** ~ Malawi.

malaxer [malakse] *vt* (*pétrir*) to knead; (*mêler*) to mix.

Malaysia [malɛzja] *nf*: **la** ~ Malaysia.

malchance [malʃɑ̃s] *nf* misfortune, ill luck *no pl*; **par** ~ unfortunately; **quelle** ~! what bad luck!

malchanceux, euse [malʃɑ̃sø, -øz] *adj* unlucky.

malcommode [malkɔmɔd] *adj* impractical, inconvenient.

Maldives [maldiv] *nfpl*: **les** ~ the Maldive Islands.

maldonne [maldɔn] *nf* (*CARTES*) misdeal; **il y a** ~ (*fig*) there's been a misunderstanding.

mâle [mɑl] *adj* (*aussi ÉLEC, TECH*) male; (*viril: voix, traits*) manly ♦ *nm* male.

malédiction [malediksjɔ̃] *nf* curse.

maléfice [malefis] *nm* evil spell.

maléfique [malefik] *adj* evil, baleful.

malencontreusement [malɑ̃kɔ̃tʀøzmɑ̃] *adv* (*arriver*) at the wrong moment; (*rappeler, mentionner*) inopportunely.

malencontreux, euse [malɑ̃kɔ̃tʀø, -øz] *adj* unfortunate, untoward.

malentendant, e [malɑ̃tɑ̃dɑ̃, -ɑ̃t] *nm/f*: **les** ~**s** the hard of hearing.

malentendu [malɑ̃tɑ̃dy] *nm* misunderstanding.

malfaçon [malfasɔ̃] *nf* fault.

malfaisant, e [malfəzɑ̃, -ɑ̃t] *adj* evil, harmful.
malfaiteur [malfɛtœʀ] *nm* lawbreaker, criminal; (*voleur*) thief (*pl* thieves).
malfamé, e [malfame] *adj* disreputable, of ill repute.
malfrat [malfʀɑ] *nm* villain, crook.
malgache [malgaʃ] *adj* Malagasy, Madagascan ♦ *nm* (*LING*) Malagasy ♦ *nm/f*: **M~** Malagasy, Madagascan.
malgré [malgʀe] *prép* in spite of, despite; **~ tout** *adv* in spite of everything.
malhabile [malabil] *adj* clumsy.
malheur [malœʀ] *nm* (*situation*) adversity, misfortune; (*événement*) misfortune; (*: plus fort*) disaster, tragedy; **par ~** unfortunately; **quel ~!** what a shame *ou* pity!; **faire un ~** (*fam: un éclat*) to do something desperate; (*: avoir du succès*) to be a smash hit.
malheureusement [malœʀøzmɑ̃] *adv* unfortunately.
malheureux, euse [malœʀø, -øz] *adj* (*triste*) unhappy, miserable; (*infortuné, regrettable*) unfortunate; (*malchanceux*) unlucky; (*insignifiant*) wretched ♦ *nm/f* (*infortuné, misérable*) poor soul; (*indigent, miséreux*) unfortunate creature; **les ~** the destitute; **avoir la main malheureuse** (*au jeu*) to be unlucky; (*tout casser*) to be ham-fisted.
malhonnête [malɔnɛt] *adj* dishonest; (*impoli*) rude.
malhonnêtement [malɔnɛtmɑ̃] *adv* dishonestly.
malhonnêteté [malɔnɛtte] *nf* dishonesty; rudeness *no pl*.
Mali [mali] *nm*: **le ~** Mali.
malice [malis] *nf* mischievousness; (*méchanceté*): **par ~** out of malice *ou* spite; **sans ~** guileless.
malicieusement [malisjøzmɑ̃] *adv* mischievously.
malicieux, euse [malisjø, -øz] *adj* mischievous.
malien, ne [maljɛ̃, -ɛn] *adj* Malian.
malignité [maliɲite] *nf* (*d'une tumeur, d'un mal*) malignancy.
malin, igne [malɛ̃, -iɲ] *adj* (*futé: f gén: maline*) smart, shrewd; (*: sourire*) knowing; (*MED, influence*) malignant; **faire le ~** to show off; **éprouver un ~ plaisir à** to take malicious pleasure in.
malingre [malɛ̃gʀ(ə)] *adj* puny.
malintentionné, e [malɛ̃tɑ̃sjɔne] *adj* ill-intentioned, malicious.
malle [mal] *nf* trunk; (*AUTO*): **~ (arrière)** boot (*BRIT*), trunk (*US*).
malléable [maleabl(ə)] *adj* malleable.
malle-poste, *pl* **malles-poste** [malpɔst(ə)] *nf* mail coach.
mallette [malɛt] *nf* (*valise*) (small) suitcase; (*aussi: ~ de voyage*) overnight case; (*pour documents*) attaché case.
malmener [malməne] *vt* to manhandle; (*fig*) to

give a rough ride to.
malnutrition [malnytʀisjɔ̃] *nf* malnutrition.
malodorant, e [malɔdɔʀɑ̃, -ɑ̃t] *adj* foul-smelling.
malotru [malɔtʀy] *nm* lout, boor.
malouin, e [malwɛ̃, -in] *adj* of *ou* from Saint Malo.
Malouines [malwin] *nfpl*: **les ~** the Falklands, the Falkland Islands.
malpoli, e [malpɔli] *nm/f* rude individual.
malpropre [malpʀɔpʀ(ə)] *adj* (*personne, vêtement*) dirty; (*travail*) slovenly; (*histoire, plaisanterie*) unsavoury (*BRIT*), unsavory (*US*), smutty; (*malhonnête*) dishonest.
malpropreté [malpʀɔpʀəte] *nf* dirtiness.
malsain, e [malsɛ̃, -ɛn] *adj* unhealthy.
malséant, e [malseɑ̃, -ɑ̃t] *adj* unseemly, unbecoming.
malsonnant, e [malsɔnɑ̃, -ɑ̃t] *adj* offensive.
malt [malt] *nm* malt; **pur ~** (*whisky*) malt (whisky).
maltais, e [maltɛ, -ɛz] *adj* Maltese.
Malte [malt(ə)] *nf* Malta.
malté, e [malte] *adj* (*lait etc*) malted.
maltraiter [maltʀɛte] *vt* (*brutaliser*) to manhandle, ill-treat; (*critiquer, éreinter*) to slate (*BRIT*), roast.
malus [malys] *nm* (*ASSURANCES*) car insurance weighting, penalty.
malveillance [malvɛjɑ̃s] *nf* (*animosité*) ill will; (*intention de nuire*) malevolence; (*JUR*) malicious intent *no pl*.
malveillant, e [malvɛjɑ̃, -ɑ̃t] *adj* malevolent, malicious.
malvenu, e [malvəny] *adj*: **être ~ de** *ou* **à faire qch** not to be in a position to do sth.
malversation [malvɛʀsasjɔ̃] *nf* embezzlement, misappropriation (of funds).
maman [mamɑ̃] *nf* mum(my) (*BRIT*), mom (*US*).
mamelle [mamɛl] *nf* teat.
mamelon [mamlɔ̃] *nm* (*ANAT*) nipple; (*colline*) knoll, hillock.
mamie [mami] *nf* (*fam*) granny.
mammifère [mamifɛʀ] *nm* mammal.
mammouth [mamut] *nm* mammoth.
manager [manadʒɛʀ] *nm* (*SPORT*) manager; (*COMM*): **~ commercial** commercial director.
manceau, elle, x [mɑ̃so, -ɛl] *adj* of *ou* from Le Mans.
manche [mɑ̃ʃ] *nf* (*de vêtement*) sleeve; (*d'un jeu, tournoi*) round; (*GÉO*): **la M~** the (English) Channel ♦ *nm* (*d'outil, casserole*) handle; (*de pelle, pioche etc*) shaft; (*de violon, guitare*) neck; (*fam*) clumsy oaf; **faire la ~** to pass the hat; **~ à air** *nf* (*AVIAT*) wind-sock; **~ à balai** *nm* broomstick; (*AVIAT, INFORM*) joystick.
manchette [mɑ̃ʃɛt] *nf* (*de chemise*) cuff; (*coup*) forearm blow; (*titre*) headline.
manchon [mɑ̃ʃɔ̃] *nm* (*de fourrure*) muff; **~ à incandescence** incandescent (gas) mantle.

manchot [mɑ̃ʃo] *nm* one-armed man; armless man; (*ZOOL*) penguin.

mandarine [mɑ̃daʀin] *nf* mandarin (orange), tangerine.

mandat [mɑ̃da] *nm* (*postal*) postal *ou* money order; (*d'un député etc*) mandate; (*procuration*) power of attorney, proxy; (*POLICE*) warrant; ~ **d'amener** summons *sg*; ~ **d'arrêt** warrant for arrest; ~ **de dépôt** committal order; ~ **de perquisition** (*POLICE*) search warrant.

mandataire [mɑ̃datɛʀ] *nm/f* (*représentant, délégué*) representative; (*JUR*) proxy.

mandat-carte, *pl* **mandats-cartes** [mɑ̃dakaʀt(ə)] *nm* money order (*in postcard form*).

mandater [mɑ̃date] *vt* (*personne*) to appoint; (*POL: député*) to elect.

mandat-lettre, *pl* **mandats-lettres** [mɑ̃dalɛtʀ(ə)] *nm* money order (*with space for correspondence*).

mandchou, e [mɑ̃tʃu] *adj* Manchu, Manchurian ♦ *nm* (*LING*) Manchu ♦ *nm/f:* **M~, e** Manchu.

Mandchourie [mɑ̃tʃuʀi] *nf:* **la** ~ Manchuria.

mander [mɑ̃de] *vt* to summon.

mandibule [mɑ̃dibyl] *nf* mandible.

mandoline [mɑ̃dɔlin] *nf* mandolin(e).

manège [manɛʒ] *nm* riding school; (*à la foire*) roundabout (*BRIT*), merry-go-round; (*fig*) game, ploy; **faire un tour de** ~ to go for a ride on a *ou* the roundabout *etc*; ~ (**de chevaux de bois**) roundabout (*BRIT*), merry-go-round.

manette [manɛt] *nf* lever, tap; ~ **de jeu** (*INFORM*) joystick.

manganèse [mɑ̃ganɛz] *nm* manganese.

mangeable [mɑ̃ʒabl(ə)] *adj* edible, eatable.

mangeaille [mɑ̃ʒaj] *nf* (*péj*) grub.

mangeoire [mɑ̃ʒwaʀ] *nf* trough, manger.

manger [mɑ̃ʒe] *vt* to eat; (*ronger: suj: rouille etc*) to eat into *ou* away; (*utiliser, consommer*) to eat up ♦ *vi* to eat.

mange-tout [mɑ̃ʒtu] *nm inv* mange-tout.

mangeur, euse [mɑ̃ʒœʀ, -øz] *nm/f* eater.

mangouste [mɑ̃gust(ə)] *nf* mongoose.

mangue [mɑ̃g] *nf* mango.

maniabilité [manjabilite] *nf* (*d'un outil*) handiness; (*d'un véhicule, voilier*) manoeuvrability.

maniable [manjabl(ə)] *adj* (*outil*) handy; (*voiture, voilier*) easy to handle, manoeuvrable (*BRIT*), maneuverable (*US*); (*fig: personne*) easily influenced, manipulable.

maniaque [manjak] *adj* (*pointilleux, méticuleux*) finicky, fussy; (*atteint de manie*) suffering from a mania ♦ *nm/f* maniac.

manie [mani] *nf* mania; (*tic*) odd habit.

maniement [manimɑ̃] *nm* handling; ~ **d'armes** arms drill.

manier [manje] *vt* to handle; **se** ~ *vi* (*fam*) to get a move on.

manière [manjɛʀ] *nf* (*façon*) way, manner; (*genre, style*) style; ~**s** *nfpl* (*attitude*) manners; (*chichis*) fuss *sg*; **de** ~ **à** so as to; **de telle** ~ **que** in such a way that; **de cette** ~ in this way *ou* manner; **d'une** ~ **générale** generally speaking, as a general rule; **de toute** ~ in any case; **d'une certaine** ~ in a (certain) way; **faire des** ~**s** to put on airs; **employer la** ~ **forte** to use strong-arm tactics; **adverbe de** ~ adverb of manner.

maniéré, e [manjeʀe] *adj* affected.

manif [manif] *nf* (= *manifestation*) demo (*pl* -s).

manifestant, e [manifɛstɑ̃, -ɑ̃t] *nm/f* demonstrator.

manifestation [manifɛstasjɔ̃] *nf* (*de joie, mécontentement*) expression, demonstration; (*symptôme*) outward sign; (*fête etc*) event; (*POL*) demonstration.

manifeste [manifɛst(ə)] *adj* obvious, evident ♦ *nm* manifesto (*pl* -s).

manifestement [manifɛstəmɑ̃] *adv* obviously.

manifester [manifɛste] *vt* (*volonté, intentions*) to show, indicate; (*joie, peur*) to express, show ♦ *vi* (*POL*) to demonstrate; **se** ~ *vi* (*émotion*) to show *ou* express itself; (*difficultés*) to arise; (*symptômes*) to appear; (*témoin etc*) to come forward.

manigance [manigɑ̃s] *nf* scheme.

manigancer [manigɑ̃se] *vt* to plot, devise.

Manille [manij] *n* Manila.

manioc [manjɔk] *nm* cassava, manioc.

manipulateur, trice [manipylatœʀ, -tʀis] *adj* (*technicien*) technician, operator; (*prestidigitateur*) conjurer; (*péj*) manipulator.

manipulation [manipylasjɔ̃] *nf* handling; manipulation.

manipuler [manipyle] *vt* to handle; (*fig*) to manipulate.

manivelle [manivɛl] *nf* crank.

manne [man] *nf* (*REL*) manna; (*fig*) godsend.

mannequin [mankɛ̃] *nm* (*COUTURE*) dummy; (*MODE*) model.

manœuvrable [manœvʀabl(ə)] *adj* (*bateau, véhicule*) manoeuvrable (*BRIT*), maneuverable (*US*).

manœuvre [manœvʀ(ə)] *nf* (*gén*) manoeuvre (*BRIT*), maneuver (*US*) ♦ *nm* (*ouvrier*) labourer (*BRIT*), laborer (*US*).

manœuvrer [manœvʀe] *vt* to manoeuvre (*BRIT*), maneuver (*US*); (*levier, machine*) to operate; (*personne*) to manipulate ♦ *vi* to manoeuvre *ou* maneuver.

manoir [manwaʀ] *nm* manor *ou* country house.

manomètre [manɔmɛtʀ(ə)] *nm* gauge, manometer.

manquant, e [mɑ̃kɑ̃, -ɑ̃t] *adj* missing.

manque [mɑ̃k] *nm* (*insuffisance*): ~ **de** lack of; (*vide*) emptiness, gap; (*MÉD*) withdrawal; ~**s** *nmpl* (*lacunes*) faults, defects; **par** ~ **de** for want of; ~ **à gagner** loss of profit *ou* earnings.

manqué, e [mɑ̃ke] *adj* failed; **garçon** ~ tomboy.

manquement [mɑ̃kmɑ̃] *nm*: ~ **à** (*discipline, règle*) breach of.

manquer [mɑ̃ke] *vi* (*faire défaut*) to be lacking; (*être absent*) to be missing; (*échouer*) to fail ♦ *vt* to miss ♦ *vb impers*: **il (nous) manque encore 100 F** we are still 100 F short; **il manque des pages (au livre)** there are some pages missing *ou* some pages are missing (from the book); **l'argent qui leur manque** the money they need *ou* are short of; **le pied/la voix lui manqua** he missed his footing/his voice failed him; ~ **à qn** (*absent etc*): **il/cela me manque** I miss him/that; ~ **à** *vt* (*règles etc*) to be in breach of, fail to observe; ~ **de** *vt* to lack; (*COMM*) to be out of (stock of); **ne pas** ~ **de faire: il n'a pas manqué de le dire** he certainly said it; ~ **(de) faire: il a manqué (de) se tuer** he very nearly got killed; **il ne manquerait plus qu'il fasse** all we need now is for him to do; **je n'y manquerai pas** leave it to me, I'll definitely do it.

mansarde [mɑ̃saʀd(ə)] *nf* attic.

mansardé, e [mɑ̃saʀde] *adj* attic *cpd*.

mansuétude [mɑ̃sɥetyd] *nf* leniency.

mante [mɑ̃t] *nf*: ~ **religieuse** praying mantis.

manteau, x [mɑ̃to] *nm* coat; ~ **de cheminée** mantelpiece; **sous le** ~ (*fig*) under cover.

mantille [mɑ̃tij] *nf* mantilla.

Mantoue [mɑ̃tu] *n* Mantua.

manucure [manykyʀ] *nf* manicurist.

manuel, le [manɥɛl] *adj* manual ♦ *nm/f* manually gifted pupil *etc* (*as opposed to intellectually gifted*) ♦ *nm* (*ouvrage*) manual, handbook.

manuellement [manɥɛlmɑ̃] *adv* manually.

manufacture [manyfaktyʀ] *nf* (*établissement*) factory; (*fabrication*) manufacture.

manufacturé, e [manyfaktyʀe] *adj* manufactured.

manufacturier, ière [manyfaktyʀje, -jɛʀ] *nm/f* factory owner.

manuscrit, e [manyskʀi, -it] *adj* handwritten ♦ *nm* manuscript.

manutention [manytɑ̃sjɔ̃] *nf* (*COMM*) handling; (*local*) storehouse.

manutentionnaire [manytɑ̃sjɔnɛʀ] *nm/f* warehouseman/woman, packer.

manutentionner [manytɑ̃sjɔne] *vt* to handle.

MAP *sigle f* (*PHOTO: = mise au point*) focusing.

mappemonde [mapmɔ̃d] *nf* (*plane*) map of the world; (*sphère*) globe.

maquereau, x [makʀo] *nm* mackerel *inv*; (*fam: proxénète*) pimp.

maquerelle [makʀɛl] *nf* (*fam*) madam.

maquette [makɛt] *nf* (*d'un décor, bâtiment, véhicule*) (scale) model; (*TYPO*) mockup; (*: d'une page illustrée, affiche*) paste-up; (*: prêt à la réproduction*) artwork.

maquignon [makiɲɔ̃] *nm* horse-dealer.

maquillage [makijaʒ] *nm* making up; faking; (*produits*) make-up.

maquiller [makije] *vt* (*personne, visage*) to make up; (*truquer: passeport, statistique*) to fake; (*: voiture volée*) to do over (*respray etc*); **se** ~ to make o.s. up.

maquilleur, euse [makijœʀ, -øz] *nm/f* makeup artist.

maquis [maki] *nm* (*GÉO*) scrub; (*fig*) tangle; (*MIL*) maquis, underground fighting *no pl*.

maquisard, e [makizaʀ, -aʀd(ə)] *nm/f* maquis, member of the Resistance.

marabout [maʀabu] *nm* (*ZOOL*) marabou(t).

maraîcher, ère [maʀeʃe, maʀɛʃɛʀ] *adj*: **cultures maraîchères** market gardening *sg* ♦ *nm/f* market gardener.

marais [maʀɛ] *nm* marsh, swamp; ~ **salant** saltworks.

marasme [maʀasm(ə)] *nm* (*POL, ÉCON*) stagnation, sluggishness; (*accablement*) dejection, depression.

marathon [maʀatɔ̃] *nm* marathon.

marâtre [maʀɑtʀ(ə)] *nf* cruel mother.

maraude [maʀod] *nf* pilfering, thieving (*of poultry, crops*); (*dans un verger*) scrumping; (*vagabondage*) prowling; **en** ~ on the prowl; (*taxi*) cruising.

maraudeur, euse [maʀodœʀ, -øz] *nm/f* marauder; prowler.

marbre [maʀbʀ(ə)] *nm* (*pierre, statue*) marble; (*d'une table, commode*) marble top; (*TYPO*) stone, bed; **rester de** ~ to remain stonily indifferent.

marbrer [maʀbʀe] *vt* to mottle, blotch; (*TECH: papier*) to marble.

marbrerie [maʀbʀəʀi] *nf* (*atelier*) marble mason's workshop; (*industrie*) marble industry.

marbrier [maʀbʀije] *nm* monumental mason.

marbrière [maʀbʀijɛʀ] *nf* marble quarry.

marbrures [maʀbʀyʀ] *nfpl* blotches *pl*; (*TECH*) marbling *sg*.

marc [maʀ] *nm* (*de raisin, pommes*) marc; ~ **de café** coffee grounds *pl ou* dregs *pl*.

marcassin [maʀkasɛ̃] *nm* young wild boar.

marchand, e [maʀʃɑ̃, -ɑ̃d] *nm/f* shopkeeper, tradesman/woman; (*au marché*) stallholder; (*spécifique*): ~ **de cycles/tapis** bicycle/carpet dealer; ~ **de charbon/vins** coal/wine merchant ♦ *adj*: **prix/valeur** ~**(e)** market price/value; **qualité** ~**e** standard quality; ~ **en gros/au détail** wholesaler/retailer; ~ **de biens** real estate agent; ~ **de canons** (*péj*) arms dealer; ~ **de couleurs** ironmonger (*BRIT*), hardware dealer (*US*); ~**/e de fruits** fruiterer (*BRIT*), fruit seller (*US*); ~ **de journaux** newsagent (*BRIT*), newsdealer (*US*); ~**/e de légumes** greengrocer (*BRIT*), produce dealer (*US*); ~**/e de poisson** fishmonger (*BRIT*), fish seller (*US*); ~**/e de(s) quatre-saisons** costermonger (*BRIT*), street vendor (selling fresh fruit and vegetables); ~ **de sable** (*fig*) sandman; ~ **de tableaux** art dealer.

marchandage [maʀʃɑ̃daʒ] *nm* bargaining; (*péj: électoral*) bargaining, manoeuvring.

marchander [maʀʃɑ̃de] *vt* (*article*) to bargain *ou* haggle over; (*éloges*) to be sparing with ♦ *vi* to bargain, haggle.

marchandisage [maʀʃɑ̃dizaʒ] *nm* merchandizing.

marchandise [maʀʃɑ̃diz] *nf* goods *pl*, merchandise *no pl*.

marche [maʀʃ(ə)] *nf* (*d'escalier*) step; (*activité*) walking; (*promenade, trajet, allure*) walk; (*démarche*) walk, gait; (*MIL etc, MUS*) march; (*fonctionnement*) running; (*progression*) progress; course; **à une heure de** ~ an hour's walk (away); **ouvrir/fermer la** ~ to lead the way/bring up the rear; **dans le sens de la** ~ (*RAIL*) facing the engine; **en** ~ (*monter etc*) while the vehicle is moving *ou* in motion; **mettre en** ~ to start; **remettre qch en** ~ to set *ou* start sth going again; **se mettre en** ~ (*personne*) to get moving; (*machine*) to start; ~ **arrière** (*AUTO*) reverse (gear); **faire** ~ **arrière** (*AUTO*) to reverse; (*fig*) to backtrack, back-pedal; ~ **à suivre** (*correct*) procedure; (*sur notice*) (step by step) instructions *pl*.

marché [maʀʃe] *nm* (*lieu, COMM, ÉCON*) market; (*ville*) trading centre; (*transaction*) bargain, deal; **par-dessus le** ~ into the bargain; **faire son** ~ to do one's shopping; **mettre le** ~ **en main à qn** to tell sb to take it or leave it; ~ **au comptant** (*BOURSE*) spot market; **M~ commun** Common Market; ~ **aux fleurs** flower market; ~ **noir** black market; **faire du** ~ **noir** to buy and sell on the black market; ~ **aux puces** flea market; ~ **à terme** (*BOURSE*) forward market; ~ **du travail** labour market.

marchepied [maʀʃəpje] *nm* (*RAIL*) step; (*AUTO*) running board; (*fig*) stepping stone.

marcher [maʀʃe] *vi* to walk; (*MIL*) to march; (*aller: voiture, train, affaires*) to go; (*prospérer*) to go well; (*fonctionner*) to work, run; (*fam*) to go along, agree; (: *croire naïvement*) to be taken in; ~ **sur** to walk on; (*mettre le pied sur*) to step on *ou* in; (*MIL*) to march upon; ~ **dans** (*herbe etc*) to walk in *ou* on; (*flaque*) to step in; **faire** ~ **qn** (*pour rire*) to pull sb's leg; (*pour tromper*) to lead sb up the garden path.

marcheur, euse [maʀʃœʀ, -øz] *nm/f* walker.

marcotter [maʀkɔte] *vt* to layer.

mardi [maʀdi] *nm* Tuesday; **M~ gras** Shrove Tuesday; *voir aussi* **lundi**.

mare [maʀ] *nf* pond; ~ **de sang** pool of blood.

marécage [maʀekaʒ] *nm* marsh, swamp.

marécageux, euse [maʀekaʒø, -øz] *adj* marshy, swampy.

maréchal, aux [maʀeʃal, -o] *nm* marshal; ~ **des logis** (*MIL*) sergeant.

maréchal-ferrant, *pl* **maréchaux-ferrants** [maʀeʃalfeʀɑ̃, maʀeʃo-] *nm* blacksmith, farrier (*BRIT*).

maréchaussée [maʀeʃose] *nf* (*humoristique*): *gendarmes*) constabulary (*BRIT*), police.

marée [maʀe] *nf* tide; (*poissons*) fresh (sea) fish; ~ **haute/basse** high/low tide; ~ **montante/descendante** rising/ebb tide; ~ **noire** oil slick.

marelle [maʀɛl] *nf*: (**jouer à**) **la** ~ (to play) hopscotch.

marémotrice [maʀemɔtʀis] *adj f* tidal.

mareyeur, euse [maʀejœʀ, -øz] *nm/f* wholesale (sea) fish merchant.

margarine [maʀgaʀin] *nf* margarine.

marge [maʀʒ(ə)] *nf* margin; **en** ~ in the margin; **en** ~ **de** (*fig*) on the fringe of; (*en dehors de*) cut off from; (*qui se rapporte à*) connected with; ~ **bénéficiaire** profit margin, mark-up; ~ **de sécurité** safety margin.

margelle [maʀʒɛl] *nf* coping.

margeur [maʀʒœʀ] *nm* margin stop.

marginal, e, aux [maʀʒinal, -o] *adj* marginal ♦ *nm/f* dropout.

marguerite [maʀgəʀit] *nf* marguerite, (oxeye) daisy; (*INFORM*) daisy wheel.

marguillier [maʀgije] *nm* churchwarden.

mari [maʀi] *nm* husband.

mariage [maʀjaʒ] *nm* (*union, état, fig*) marriage; (*noce*) wedding; ~ **civil/religieux** registry office (*BRIT*) *ou* civil/church wedding; **un** ~ **de raison/d'amour** a marriage of convenience/a love match; ~ **blanc** unconsummated marriage; ~ **en blanc** white wedding.

marié, e [maʀje] *adj* married ♦ *nm/f* (bride)groom/bride; **les** ~**s** the bride and groom; **les** (**jeunes**) ~**s** the newly-weds.

marier [maʀje] *vt* to marry; (*fig*) to blend; **se** ~ (**avec**) to marry, get married (to); (*fig*) to blend (with).

marijuana [maʀiʒwana] *nf* marijuana.

marin, e [maʀɛ̃, -in] *adj* sea *cpd*, marine ♦ *nm* sailor ♦ *nf* navy; (*ART*) seascape; (*couleur*) navy (blue); **avoir le pied** ~ to be a good sailor; (*garder son équilibre*) to have one's sea legs; ~**e de guerre** navy; ~**e marchande** merchant navy; ~**e à voiles** sailing ships *pl*.

marina [maʀina] *nf* marina.

marinade [maʀinad] *nf* marinade.

marine [maʀin] *adj f, nf voir* **marin** ♦ *adj inv* navy (blue) ♦ *nm* (*MIL*) marine.

mariner [maʀine] *vi, vt* to marinate, marinade.

marinier [maʀinje] *nm* bargee.

marinière [maʀinjɛʀ] *nf* (*blouse*) smock ♦ *adj inv*: **moules** ~ (*CULIN*) mussels in white wine.

marionnette [maʀjɔnɛt] *nf* puppet.

marital, e, aux [maʀital, -o] *adj*: **autorisation** ~**e** husband's permission.

maritalement [maʀitalmɑ̃] *adv*: **vivre** ~ to live together (as husband and wife).

maritime [maʀitim] *adj* sea *cpd*, maritime; (*ville*) coastal, seaside; (*droit*) shipping, maritime.

marjolaine [maʀʒɔlɛn] *nf* marjoram.

mark [maʀk] *nm* (*monnaie*) mark.
marketing [maʀkətiŋ] *nm* (*COMM*) marketing.
marmaille [maʀmɑj] *nf* (*péj*) (gang of) brats *pl*.
marmelade [maʀməlad] *nf* (*compote*) stewed fruit, compote; ~ **d'oranges** (orange) marmalade; **en** ~ (*fig*) crushed (to a pulp).
marmite [maʀmit] *nf* (cooking-)pot.
marmiton [maʀmitɔ̃] *nm* kitchen boy.
marmonner [maʀmɔne] *vt, vi* to mumble, mutter.
marmot [maʀmo] *nm* (*fam*) brat.
marmotte [maʀmɔt] *nf* marmot.
marmotter [maʀmɔte] *vt* (*prière*) to mumble, mutter.
marne [maʀn(ə)] *nf* (*GÉO*) marl.
Maroc [maʀɔk] *nm*: **le** ~ Morocco.
marocain, e [maʀɔkɛ̃, -ɛn] *adj* Moroccan ♦ *nm/ f*: **M~**, e Moroccan.
maroquin [maʀɔkɛ̃] *nm* (*peau*) morocco (leather); (*fig*) (minister's) portfolio.
maroquinerie [maʀɔkinʀi] *nf* (*industrie*) leather craft; (*commerce*) leather shop; (*articles*) fine leather goods *pl*.
maroquinier [maʀɔkinje] *nm* (*fabricant*) leather craftsman; (*marchand*) leather dealer.
marotte [maʀɔt] *nf* fad.
marquant, e [maʀkɑ̃, -ɑ̃t] *adj* outstanding.
marque [maʀk(ə)] *nf* mark; (*SPORT, JEU*: *décompte des points*) score; (*COMM*: *de produits*) brand, make; (: *de disques*) label; (*insigne: d'une fonction*) badge; (*fig*): ~ **d'affection** token of affection; ~ **de joie** sign of joy; **à vos ~s!** (*SPORT*) on your marks!; **de** ~ *adj* (*COMM*) brand-name *cpd*; proprietary; (*fig*) high-class; (: *personnage, hôte*) distinguished; **produit de** ~ (*COMM*) quality product; ~ **déposée** registered trademark; ~ **de fabrique** trademark.
marqué, e [maʀke] *adj* marked.
marquer [maʀke] *vt* to mark; (*inscrire*) to write down; (*bétail*) to brand; (*SPORT: but etc*) to score; (: *joueur*) to mark; (*accentuer: taille etc*) to emphasize; (*manifester: refus, intérêt*) to show ♦ *vi* (*événement, personnalité*) to stand out, be outstanding; (*SPORT*) to score; ~ **qn de son influence/empreinte** to have an influence/leave its impression on sb; ~ **un temps d'arrêt** to pause momentarily; ~ **le pas** (*fig*) to mark time; **il a marqué ce jour-là d'une pierre blanche** that was a red-letter day for him; ~ **les points** (*tenir la marque*) to keep the score.
marqueté, e [maʀkəte] *adj* inlaid.
marqueterie [maʀkətʀi] *nf* inlaid work, marquetry.
marqueur, euse [maʀkœʀ, -øz] *nm/f* (*SPORT: de but*) scorer ♦ *nm* (*crayon feutre*) marker pen.
marquis, e [maʀki, -iz] *nm/f* marquis *ou* marquess/marchioness ♦ *nf* (*auvent*) glass

canopy *ou* awning.
Marquises [maʀkiz] *nfpl*: **les (îles)** ~ the Marquesas Islands.
marraine [maʀɛn] *nf* godmother; (*d'un navire, d'une rose etc*) namer.
Marrakech [maʀakɛʃ] *n* Marrakech *ou* Marrakesh.
marrant, e [maʀɑ̃, -ɑ̃t] *adj* (*fam*) funny.
marre [maʀ] *adv* (*fam*): **en avoir** ~ **de** to be fed up with.
marrer [maʀe]: **se** ~ *vi* (*fam*) to have a (good) laugh.
marron, ne [maʀɔ̃, -ɔn] *nm* (*fruit*) chestnut ♦ *adj inv* brown ♦ *adj* (*péj*) crooked; (: *faux*) bogus; ~**s glacés** marrons glacés.
marronnier [maʀɔnje] *nm* chestnut (tree).
Mars [maʀs] *nm ou f* Mars.
mars [maʀs] *nm* March; *voir aussi* **juillet**.
marseillais, e [maʀsɛjɛ, -ɛz] *adj* of *ou* from Marseilles ♦ *nf*: **la M~e** the French national anthem.

La Marseillaise has been France's national anthem since 1879. The words of the "Chant de guerre de l'armée du Rhin", as the song was originally called, were written to an anonymous tune by the army captain Rouget de Lisle in 1792. Adopted as a marching song by the battalion of Marseille, it was finally popularized as the Marseillaise.

Marseille [maʀsɛj] *n* Marseilles.
marsouin [maʀswɛ̃] *nm* porpoise.
marsupiaux [maʀsypjo] *nmpl* marsupials.
marteau, x [maʀto] *nm* hammer; (*de porte*) knocker; ~ **pneumatique** pneumatic drill.
marteau-pilon, *pl* **marteaux-pilons** [maʀtopilɔ̃] *nm* power hammer.
marteau-piqueur, *pl* **marteaux-piqueurs** [maʀtopikœʀ] *nm* pneumatic drill.
martel [maʀtɛl] *nm*: **se mettre** ~ **en tête** to worry o.s.
martèlement [maʀtɛlmɑ̃] *nm* hammering.
marteler [maʀtəle] *vt* to hammer; (*mots, phrases*) to rap out.
martial, e, aux [maʀsjal, -o] *adj* martial; **cour ~e** court-martial.
martien, ne [maʀsjɛ̃, -ɛn] *adj* Martian, of *ou* from Mars.
martinet [maʀtinɛ] *nm* (*fouet*) small whip; (*ZOOL*) swift.
martingale [maʀtɛ̃gal] *nf* (*COUTURE*) half-belt; (*JEU*) winning formula.
martiniquais, e [maʀtinikɛ, -ɛz] *adj* of *ou* from Martinique.
Martinique [maʀtinik] *nf*: **la** ~ Martinique.
martin-pêcheur, *pl* **martins-pêcheurs** [maʀtɛ̃pɛʃœʀ] *nm* kingfisher.
martre [maʀtʀ(ə)] *nf* marten; ~ **zibeline** sable.
martyr, e [maʀtiʀ] *nm/f* martyr ♦ *adj* martyred; **enfants** ~**s** battered children.
martyre [maʀtiʀ] *nm* martyrdom; (*fig: sens af-*

faibli) agony, torture; **souffrir le** ~ to suffer agonies.

martyriser [maʀtiʀize] *vt* (*REL*) to martyr; (*fig*) to bully; (*: enfant*) to batter.

marxisme [maʀksism(ə)] *nm* Marxism.

marxiste [maʀksist(ə)] *adj, nm/f* Marxist.

mas [mɑ(s)] *nm traditional house or farm in Provence.*

mascara [maskaʀa] *nm* mascara.

mascarade [maskaʀad] *nf* masquerade.

mascotte [maskɔt] *nf* mascot.

masculin, e [maskylɛ̃, -in] *adj* masculine; (*sexe, population*) male; (*équipe, vêtements*) men's; (*viril*) manly ♦ *nm* masculine.

masochisme [mazɔʃism(ə)] *nm* masochism.

masochiste [mazɔʃist(ə)] *adj* masochistic ♦ *nm/f* masochist.

masque [mask(ə)] *nm* mask; ~ **de beauté** face pack; ~ **à gaz** gas mask; ~ **de plongée** diving mask.

masqué, e [maske] *adj* masked.

masquer [maske] *vt* (*cacher: porte, goût*) to hide, conceal; (*dissimuler: vérité, projet*) to mask, obscure.

massacrant, e [masakʀɑ̃, -ɑ̃t] *adj*: **humeur** ~**e** foul temper.

massacre [masakʀ(ə)] *nm* massacre, slaughter; **jeu de** ~ (*fig*) wholesale slaughter.

massacrer [masakʀe] *vt* to massacre, slaughter; (*fig: adversaire*) to slaughter; (*: texte etc*) to murder.

massage [masaʒ] *nm* massage.

masse [mas] *nf* mass; (*péj*): **la** ~ the masses *pl*; (*ÉLEC*) earth; (*maillet*) sledgehammer; ~**s** *nfpl* masses; **une** ~ **de, des** ~**s de** (*fam*) masses *ou* loads of; **en** ~ *adv* (*en bloc*) in bulk; (*en foule*) en masse ♦ *adj* (*exécutions, production*) mass *cpd*; ~ **monétaire** (*ÉCON*) money supply; ~ **salariale** (*COMM*) wage(s) bill.

massepain [maspɛ̃] *nm* marzipan.

masser [mase] *vt* (*assembler*) to gather; (*pétrir*) to massage; **se** ~ *vi* to gather.

masseur, euse [masœʀ, -øz] *nm/f* (*personne*) masseur/masseuse ♦ *nm* (*appareil*) massager.

massicot [masiko] *nm* (*TYPO*) guillotine.

massif, ive [masif, -iv] *adj* (*porte*) solid, massive; (*visage*) heavy, large; (*bois, or*) solid; (*dose*) massive; (*déportations etc*) mass *cpd* ♦ *nm* (*montagneux*) massif; (*de fleurs*) clump, bank.

massivement [masivmɑ̃] *adv* (*répondre*) en masse; (*administrer, injecter*) in massive doses.

mass media [masmedja] *nmpl* mass media.

massue [masy] *nf* club, bludgeon ♦ *adj inv*: **argument** ~ sledgehammer argument.

mastectomie [mastɛktɔmi] *nf* mastectomy.

mastic [mastik] *nm* (*pour vitres*) putty; (*pour fentes*) filler.

masticage [mastikaʒ] *nm* (*d'une fente*) filling; (*d'une vitre*) puttying.

mastication [mastikasjɔ̃] *nf* chewing, masti-

cation.

mastiquer [mastike] *vt* (*aliment*) to chew, masticate; (*fente*) to fill; (*vitre*) to putty.

mastoc [mastɔk] *adj inv* hefty.

mastodonte [mastɔdɔ̃t] *nm* monster (*fig*).

masturbation [mastyʀbasjɔ̃] *nf* masturbation.

masturber [mastyʀbe] *vt*: **se** ~ to masturbate.

m'as-tu-vu [matyvy] *nm/f inv* show-off.

masure [mazyʀ] *nf* tumbledown cottage.

mat, e [mat] *adj* (*couleur, métal*) mat(t); (*bruit, son*) dull ♦ *adj inv* (*ÉCHECS*): **être** ~ to be checkmate.

mât [mɑ] *nm* (*NAVIG*) mast; (*poteau*) pole, post.

matamore [matamɔʀ] *nm* braggart, blusterer.

match [matʃ] *nm* match; ~ **nul** draw, tie (*US*); **faire** ~ **nul** to draw (*BRIT*), tie (*US*); ~ **aller** first leg; ~ **retour** second leg, return match.

matelas [matla] *nm* mattress; ~ **pneumatique** air bed *ou* mattress; ~ **à ressorts** spring *ou* interior-sprung mattress.

matelasser [matlase] *vt* to pad.

matelot [matlo] *nm* sailor, seaman.

mater [mate] *vt* (*personne*) to bring to heel, subdue; (*révolte*) to put down; (*fam*) to watch, look at.

matérialisation [mateʀjalizasjɔ̃] *nf* materialization.

matérialiser [mateʀjalize]: **se** ~ *vi* to materialize.

matérialisme [mateʀjalism(ə)] *nm* materialism.

matérialiste [mateʀjalist(ə)] *adj* materialistic ♦ *nm/f* materialist.

matériau, x [mateʀjo] *nm* material; ~**x** *nmpl* material(s); ~**x de construction** building materials.

matériel, le [mateʀjɛl] *adj* material; (*organisation, aide, obstacle*) practical; (*fig: péj: personne*) materialistic ♦ *nm* equipment *no pl*; (*de camping etc*) gear *no pl*; **il n'a pas le temps** ~ **de le faire** he doesn't have the time (needed) to do it; ~ **d'exploitation** (*COMM*) plant; ~ **roulant** rolling stock.

matériellement [mateʀjɛlmɑ̃] *adv* (*financièrement*) materially; ~ **à l'aise** comfortably off; **je n'en ai** ~ **pas le temps** I simply do not have the time.

maternel, le [mateʀnɛl] *adj* (*amour, geste*) motherly, maternal; (*grand-père, oncle*) maternal ♦ *nf* (*aussi*: **école** ~**le**) (state) nursery school.

materner [mateʀne] *vt* (*personne*) to mother.

maternisé, e [mateʀnize] *adj*: **lait** ~ (infant) formula.

maternité [mateʀnite] *nf* (*établissement*) maternity hospital; (*état de mère*) motherhood, maternity; (*grossesse*) pregnancy.

math [mat] *nfpl* maths (*BRIT*), math (*US*).

mathématicien, ne [matematisjɛ̃, -ɛn] *nm/f* mathematician.

mathématique [matematik] *adj* mathematical.

mathématiques [matematik] *nfpl* mathematics *sg*.

matheux, euse [matø, -øz] *nm/f* (*fam*) maths (*BRIT*) *ou* math (*US*) student; (*fort en math*) mathematical genius.

maths [mat] *nfpl* maths (*BRIT*), math (*US*).

matière [matjɛʀ] *nf* (*PHYSIQUE*) matter; (*COMM, TECH*) material, matter *no pl*; (*fig: d'un livre etc*) subject matter; (*SCOL*) subject; **en ~ de** as regards; **donner ~ à** to give cause to; **~ grise** grey matter; **~ plastique** plastic; **~s fécales** faeces; **~s grasses** fat (content) *sg*; **~s premières** raw materials.

MATIF [matif] *sigle m* (= *Marché à terme des instruments financiers*) *body which regulates the activities of the French Stock Exchange*.

L'hôtel Matignon is the Paris office and residence of the French Prime Minister. By extension, the term "Matignon" is often used to refer to the Prime Minister or his staff.

matin [matɛ̃] *nm, adv* morning; **le ~** (*pendant le ~*) in the morning; **demain ~** tomorrow morning; **le lendemain ~** (the) next morning; **du ~ au soir** from morning till night; **une heure du ~** one o'clock in the morning; **de grand** *ou* **bon ~** early in the morning.

matinal, e, aux [matinal, -o] *adj* (*toilette, gymnastique*) morning *cpd*; (*de bonne heure*) early; **être ~** (*personne*) to be up early; (*: habituellement*) to be an early riser.

mâtiné, e [matine] *adj* crossbred, mixed race *cpd*.

matinée [matine] *nf* morning; (*spectacle*) matinée, afternoon performance.

matois, e [matwa, -waz] *adj* wily.

matou [matu] *nm* tom(cat).

matraquage [matrakaʒ] *nm* beating up; **~ publicitaire** plug, plugging.

matraque [matrak] *nf* (*de malfaiteur*) cosh (*BRIT*), club; (*de policier*) truncheon (*BRIT*), billy (*US*).

matraquer [matrake] *vt* to beat up (with a truncheon *ou* billy); to cosh (*BRIT*), club; (*fig: touristes etc*) to rip off; (*: disque*) to plug.

matriarcal, e, aux [matrijarkal, -o] *adj* matriarchal.

matrice [matris] *nf* (*ANAT*) womb; (*TECH*) mould; (*MATH etc*) matrix.

matricule [matrikyl] *nf* (*aussi*: **registre ~**) roll, register ♦ *nm* (*aussi*: **numéro ~**: *MIL*) regimental number; (*: ADMIN*) reference number.

matrimonial, e, aux [matrimɔnjal, -o] *adj* marital, marriage *cpd*.

matrone [matrɔn] *nf* matron.

mâture [matyʀ] *nf* masts *pl*.

maturité [matyʀite] *nf* maturity; (*d'un fruit*) ripeness, maturity.

maudire [modiʀ] *vt* to curse.

maudit, e [modi, -it] *adj* (*fam: satané*) blasted, confounded.

maugréer [mogʀee] *vi* to grumble.

mauresque [mɔʀɛsk(ə)] *adj* Moorish.

Maurice [mɔʀis] *nf*: **(l'île) ~** Mauritius.

mauricien, ne [mɔʀisjɛ̃, -ɛn] *adj* Mauritian.

Mauritanie [mɔʀitani] *nf*: **la ~** Mauritania.

mauritanien, ne [mɔʀitanjɛ̃, -ɛn] *adj* Mauritanian.

mausolée [mozɔle] *nm* mausoleum.

maussade [mosad] *adj* (*air, personne*) sullen; (*ciel, temps*) dismal.

mauvais, e [mɔvɛ, -ɛz] *adj* bad; (*faux*): **le ~ numéro/moment** the wrong number/moment; (*méchant, malveillant*) malicious, spiteful ♦ *nm*: **le ~** the bad side ♦ *adv*: **il fait ~** the weather is bad; **sentir ~** to have a nasty smell, smell bad *ou* nasty; **la mer est ~e** the sea is rough; **~ coucheur** awkward customer; **~ coup** (*fig*) criminal venture; **~ garçon** tough; **~ pas** tight spot; **~ plaisant** hoaxer; **~ traitements** ill treatment *sg*; **~e herbe** weed; **~e langue** gossip, scandalmonger (*BRIT*); **~e passe** difficult situation; (*période*) bad patch; **~e tête** rebellious *ou* headstrong customer.

mauve [mov] *adj* (*couleur*) mauve ♦ *nf* (*BOT*) mallow.

mauviette [movjɛt] *nf* (*péj*) weakling.

maux [mo] *nmpl voir* **mal**.

max. *abr* (= *maximum*) max.

maximal, e, aux [maksimal, -o] *adj* maximal.

maxime [maksim] *nf* maxim.

maximum [maksimɔm] *adj, nm* maximum; **atteindre un/son ~** to reach a/his peak; **au ~** *adv* (*le plus possible*) to the full; as much as one can; (*tout au plus*) at the (very) most *ou* maximum.

Mayence [majɑ̃s] *n* Mainz.

mayonnaise [majɔnɛz] *nf* mayonnaise.

Mayotte [majɔt] *nf* Mayotte.

mazout [mazut] *nm* (fuel) oil; **chaudière/poêle à ~** oil-fired boiler/stove.

mazouté, e [mazute] *adj* oil-polluted.

MDM *sigle mpl* (= *Médecins du Monde*) *medical association for aid to Third World countries*.

Me *abr* = **Maître**.

me, m' [m(ə)] *pron* me; (*réfléchi*) myself.

méandres [meɑ̃dʀ(ə)] *nmpl* meanderings.

mec [mɛk] *nm* (*fam*) guy, bloke (*BRIT*).

mécanicien, ne [mekanisjɛ̃, -ɛn] *nm/f* mechanic; (*RAIL*) (train *ou* engine) driver; **~ navigant** *ou* **de bord** (*AVIAT*) flight engineer.

mécanicien-dentiste [mekanisjɛ̃dɑ̃tist(ə)], **mécanicienne-dentiste** [mekanisjɛn-] (*pl* **~s-~s**) *nm/f* dental technician.

mécanique [mekanik] *adj* mechanical ♦ *nf* (*science*) mechanics *sg*; (*technologie*) mechanical engineering; (*mécanisme*) mechanism; engineering; works *pl*; **ennui ~** engine trouble *no pl*; **s'y connaître en ~** to be mechanically minded; ~ **hydraulique** hydraulics *sg*; ~ **ondulataire** wave mechanics *sg*.

mécaniquement [mekanikmɑ̃] *adv* mechanically.

mécanisation [mekanizɑsjɔ̃] *nf* mechanization.

mécaniser [mekanize] *vt* to mechanize.

mécanisme [mekanism(ə)] *nm* mechanism; ~ **des taux de change** exchange rate mechanism.

mécano [mekano] *nm* (*fam*) mechanic.

mécanographie [mekanɔgʀafi] *nf* (mechanical) data processing.

mécène [mesɛn] *nm* patron.

méchamment [meʃamɑ̃] *adv* nastily, maliciously, spitefully; viciously.

méchanceté [meʃɑ̃ste] *nf* (*d'une personne, d'une parole*) nastiness, maliciousness, spitefulness; (*parole, action*) nasty *ou* spiteful *ou* malicious remark (*ou* action).

méchant, e [meʃɑ̃, -ɑ̃t] *adj* nasty, malicious, spiteful; (*enfant: pas sage*) naughty; (*animal*) vicious; (*avant le nom: valeur péjorative*) nasty; miserable; (*: intensive*) terrific.

mèche [mɛʃ] *nf* (*de lampe, bougie*) wick; (*d'un explosif*) fuse; (*MÉD*) pack, dressing; (*de vilebrequin, perceuse*) bit; (*de dentiste*) drill; (*de fouet*) lash; (*de cheveux*) lock; **se faire faire des ~s** (*chez le coiffeur*) to have one's hair streaked, have highlights put in one's hair; **vendre la ~** to give the game away; **de ~ avec** in league with.

méchoui [meʃwi] *nm* whole sheep barbecue.

mécompte [mekɔ̃t] *nm* (*erreur*) miscalculation; (*déception*) disappointment.

méconnais [mekɔnɛ] *etc vb voir* **méconnaître**.

méconnaissable [mekɔnɛsabl(ə)] *adj* unrecognizable.

méconnaissais [mekɔnɛsɛ] *etc vb voir* **méconnaître**.

méconnaissance [mekɔnɛsɑ̃s] *nf* ignorance.

méconnaître [mekɔnɛtʀ(ə)] *vt* (*ignorer*) to be unaware of; (*mésestimer*) to misjudge.

méconnu, e [mekɔny] *pp de* **méconnaître ♦** *adj* (*génie etc*) unrecognized.

mécontent, e [mekɔ̃tɑ̃, -ɑ̃t] *adj*: ~ **(de)** (*insatisfait*) discontented *ou* dissatisfied *ou* displeased (with); (*contrarié*) annoyed (at) **♦** *nm/f* malcontent, dissatisfied person.

mécontentement [mekɔ̃tɑ̃tmɑ̃] *nm* dissatisfaction, discontent, displeasure; annoyance.

mécontenter [mekɔ̃tɑ̃te] *vt* to displease.

Mecque [mɛk] *nf*: **la ~** Mecca.

mécréant, e [mekʀeɑ̃, -ɑ̃t] *adj* (*peuple*) infidel; (*personne*) atheistic.

méd. *abr* = **médecin**.

médaille [medaj] *nf* medal.

médaillé, e [medaje] *nm/f* (*SPORT*) medalholder.

médaillon [medajɔ̃] *nm* (*portrait*) medallion; (*bijou*) locket; (*CULIN*) médaillon; **en ~** *adj* (*carte etc*) inset.

médecin [medsɛ̃] *nm* doctor; ~ **du bord** (*NAVIG*) ship's doctor; ~ **généraliste** general practitioner, GP; ~ **légiste** forensic scientist (*BRIT*), medical examiner (*US*); ~ **traitant** family doctor, GP.

médecine [medsin] *nf* medicine; ~ **générale** general medicine; ~ **infantile** paediatrics *sg* (*BRIT*), pediatrics *sg* (*US*); ~ **légale** forensic medicine; ~ **préventive** preventive medicine; ~ **du travail** occupational *ou* industrial medicine; ~**s parallèles** *ou* **douces** alternative medicine.

médian, e [medjɑ̃, -an] *adj* median.

médias [medja] *nmpl*: **les ~** the media.

médiateur, trice [medjatœʀ, -tʀis] *nm/f* (*voir médiation*) mediator; arbitrator.

médiathèque [medjatɛk] *nf* media library.

médiation [medjɑsjɔ̃] *nf* mediation; (*dans conflit social etc*) arbitration.

médiatique [medjatik] *adj* media *cpd*.

médiatisé, e [medjatize] *adj* reported in the media; **ce procès a été très ~** (*péj*) this trial was turned into a media event.

médiator [medjatɔʀ] *nm* plectrum.

médical, e, aux [medikal, -o] *adj* medical; **visiteur** *ou* **délégué ~** medical rep *ou* representative.

médicalement [medikalmɑ̃] *adv* medically.

médicament [medikamɑ̃] *nm* medicine, drug.

médicamenteux, euse [medikamɑ̃tø, -øz] *adj* medicinal.

médication [medikɑsjɔ̃] *nf* medication.

médicinal, e, aux [medisinal, -o] *adj* medicinal.

médico-légal, e, aux [medikɔlegal, -o] *adj* forensic.

médico-social, e, aux [medikɔsɔsjal, -o] *adj*: **assistance ~e** medical and social assistance.

médiéval, e, aux [medjeval, -o] *adj* medieval.

médiocre [medjɔkʀ(ə)] *adj* mediocre, poor.

médiocrité [medjɔkʀite] *nf* mediocrity.

médire [mediʀ] *vi*: ~ **de** to speak ill of.

médisance [medizɑ̃s] *nf* scandalmongering *no pl* (*BRIT*), mud-slinging *no pl*; (*propos*) piece of scandal *ou* malicious gossip.

médisant, e [medizɑ̃, -ɑ̃t] *vb voir* **médire ♦** *adj* slanderous, malicious.

médit, e [medi, -it] *pp de* **médire**.

méditatif, ive [meditatif, -iv] *adj* thoughtful.

méditation [meditɑsjɔ̃] *nf* meditation.

méditer [medite] *vt* (*approfondir*) to meditate on, ponder (over); (*combiner*) to meditate **♦** *vi* to meditate; ~ **de faire** to contemplate doing, plan to do.

Méditerranée [meditɛʀane] *nf*: **la (mer) ~** the Mediterranean (Sea).

méditerranéen, ne [meditɛʀaneɛ̃, -ɛn] *adj* Mediterranean **♦** *nm/f*: **M~, ne** Mediterranean.

médium [medjɔm] *nm* medium (*spiritualist*).

médius [medjys] *nm* middle finger.

méduse [medyz] *nf* jellyfish.
méduser [medyze] *vt* to dumbfound.
meeting [mitiŋ] *nm* (*POL, SPORT*) rally, meeting; ~ **d'aviation** air show.
méfait [mefɛ] *nm* (*faute*) misdemeanour, wrongdoing; ~**s** *nmpl* (*ravages*) ravages.
méfiance [mefjãs] *nf* mistrust, distrust.
méfiant, e [mefjã, -ãt] *adj* mistrustful, distrustful.
méfier [mefje]: **se** ~ *vi* to be wary; (*faire attention*) to be careful; **se** ~ **de** *vt* to mistrust, distrust, be wary of; to be careful about.
mégalomane [megalɔman] *adj* megalomaniac.
mégalomanie [megalɔmani] *nf* megalomania.
mégalopole [megalɔpɔl] *nf* megalopolis.
méga-octet [megaɔktɛ] *nm* megabyte.
mégarde [megaʀd(ə)] *nf*: **par** ~ accidentally; (*par erreur*) by mistake.
mégatonne [megatɔn] *nf* megaton.
mégère [meʒɛʀ] *nf* (*péj: femme*) shrew.
mégot [mego] *nm* cigarette end *ou* butt.
mégoter [megɔte] *vi* to nitpick.
meilleur, e [mɛjœʀ] *adj, adv* better; (*valeur superlative*) best ♦ *nm*: **le** ~ (*celui qui ...*) the best (one); (*ce qui ...*) the best ♦ *nf*: **la** ~**e** the best (one); **le** ~ **des deux** the better of the two; **de** ~**e heure** earlier; ~ **marché** cheaper.
méjuger [meʒyʒe] *vt* to misjudge.
mélancolie [melãkɔli] *nf* melancholy, gloom.
mélancolique [melãkɔlik] *adj* melancholy, gloomy.
Mélanésie [melanezi] *nf*: **la** ~ Melanesia.
mélange [melãʒ] *nm* (*opération*) mixing; blending; (*résultat*) mixture; blend; **sans** ~ unadulterated.
mélanger [melãʒe] *vt* (*substances*) to mix; (*vins, couleurs*) to blend; (*mettre en désordre, confondre*) to mix up, muddle (up); **se** ~ (*liquides, couleurs*) to blend, mix.
mélanine [melanin] *nf* melanin.
mélasse [melas] *nf* treacle, molasses *sg*.
mêlée [mele] *nf* (*bataille, cohue*) mêlée, scramble; (*lutte, conflit*) tussle, scuffle; (*RUGBY*) scrum(mage).
mêler [mele] *vt* (*substances, odeurs, races*) to mix; (*embrouiller*) to muddle (up), mix up; **se** ~ to mix; (*se joindre, s'allier*) to mingle; **se** ~ **à** (*suj: personne*) to join; to mix with; (: *odeurs etc*) to mingle with; **se** ~ **de** (*suj: personne*) to meddle with, interfere in; **mêle-toi de tes affaires!** mind your own business!; ~ **à** *ou* **avec** *ou* **de** to mix with; to mingle with; ~ **qn à** (*affaire*) to get sb mixed up *ou* involved in.
mélo [melo] *nm, adj* = **mélodrame, mélodramatique**.
mélodie [melɔdi] *nf* melody.
mélodieux, euse [melɔdjø, -øz] *adj* melodious, tuneful.
mélodique [melɔdik] *adj* melodic.
mélodramatique [melɔdʀamatik] *adj* melodramatic.
mélodrame [melɔdʀam] *nm* melodrama.
mélomane [melɔman] *nm/f* music lover.
melon [məlɔ̃] *nm* (*BOT*) (honeydew) melon; (*aussi*: **chapeau** ~) bowler (hat); ~ **d'eau** watermelon.
mélopée [melɔpe] *nf* monotonous chant.
membrane [mãbʀan] *nf* membrane.
membre [mãbʀ(ə)] *nm* (*ANAT*) limb; (*personne, pays, élément*) member ♦ *adj* member; **être** ~ **de** to be a member of; ~ (**viril**) (male) organ.
mémé [meme] *nf* (*fam*) granny; (: *vieille femme*) old dear.

━━━━━━━━━━━━━━━━━━━ *MOT-CLÉ*

même [mɛm] *adj* **1** (*avant le nom*) same; **en** ~ **temps** at the same time; **ils ont les** ~**s goûts** they have the same *ou* similar tastes
2 (*après le nom: renforcement*): **il est la loyauté** ~ he is loyalty itself; **ce sont ses paroles/celles-là** ~ they are his very words/the very ones
♦ *pron*: **le(la)** ~ the same one
♦ *adv* **1** (*renforcement*): **il n'a** ~ **pas pleuré** he didn't even cry; ~ **lui l'a dit** even HE said it; **ici** ~ at this very place; ~ **si** even if
2: **à** ~: **à** ~ **la bouteille** straight from the bottle; **à** ~ **la peau** next to the skin; **être à** ~ **de faire** to be in a position to do, be able to do; **mettre qn à** ~ **de faire** to enable sb to do
3: **de** ~ likewise; **faire de** ~ to do likewise *ou* the same; **lui de** ~ so does (*ou* did *ou* is) he; **de** ~ **que** just as; **il en va de** ~ **pour** the same goes for.

━━━━━━━━━━━━━━━━━━━

mémento [memɛ̃to] *nm* (*agenda*) appointments diary; (*ouvrage*) summary.
mémoire [memwaʀ] *nf* memory ♦ *nm* (*ADMIN, JUR*) memorandum (*pl* -a); (*SCOL*) dissertation, paper; **avoir la** ~ **des visages/chiffres** to have a (good) memory for faces/figures; **n'avoir aucune** ~ to have a terrible memory; **avoir de la** ~ to have a good memory; **à la** ~ **de** to the *ou* in memory of; **pour** ~ *adv* for the record; **de** ~ *adv* from memory; **de** ~ **d'homme** in living memory; **mettre en** ~ (*INFORM*) to store; ~ **morte** ROM; ~ **rémanente** *ou* **non volatile** non-volatile memory; ~ **vive** RAM.
mémoires [memwaʀ] *nmpl* memoirs.
mémorable [memɔʀabl(ə)] *adj* memorable.
mémorandum [memɔʀãdɔm] *nm* memorandum (*pl* -a); (*carnet*) notebook.
mémorial, aux [memɔʀjal, -o] *nm* memorial.
mémoriser [memɔʀize] *vt* to memorize; (*INFORM*) to store.
menaçant, e [mənasã, -ãt] *adj* threatening, menacing.
menace [mənas] *nf* threat; ~ **en l'air** empty threat.
menacer [mənase] *vt* to threaten; ~ **qn de qch/de faire qch** to threaten sb with sth/to

do sth.

ménage [menaʒ] *nm* (*travail*) housekeeping, housework; (*couple*) (married) couple; (*famille*, ADMIN) household; **faire le ~** to do the housework; **faire des ~s** to work as a cleaner (*in people's homes*); **monter son ~** to set up house; **se mettre en ~ (avec)** to set up house (with); **heureux en ~** happily married; **faire bon ~ avec** to get on well with; **~ de poupée** doll's kitchen set; **~ à trois** love triangle.

ménagement [menaʒmɑ̃] *nm* care and attention; **~s** *nmpl* (*égards*) consideration *sg*, attention *sg*.

ménager [menaʒe] *vt* (*traiter avec mesure*) to handle with tact; to treat considerately; (*utiliser*) to use with care; (: *avec économie*) to use sparingly; (*prendre soin de*) to take (great) care of, look after; (*organiser*) to arrange; (*installer*) to put in; to make; **se ~** to look after o.s.; **~ qch à qn** (*réserver*) to have sth in store for sb.

ménager, ère [menaʒe, -ɛʀ] *adj* household *cpd*, domestic ♦ *nf* (*femme*) housewife (*pl* -wives); (*couverts*) canteen (of cutlery).

ménagerie [menaʒʀi] *nf* menagerie.

mendiant, e [mɑ̃djɑ̃, -ɑ̃t] *nm/f* beggar.

mendicité [mɑ̃disite] *nf* begging.

mendier [mɑ̃dje] *vi* to beg ♦ *vt* to beg (for); (*fig: éloges, compliments*) to fish for.

menées [məne] *nfpl* intrigues, manœuvres (BRIT), maneuvers (US); (COMM) activities.

mener [məne] *vt* to lead; (*enquête*) to conduct; (*affaires*) to manage, conduct, run ♦ *vi*: **~ (à la marque)** to lead, be in the lead; **~ à/dans** (*emmener*) to take to/into; **~ qch à bonne fin** *ou* **à terme** *ou* **à bien** to see sth through (to a successful conclusion), complete sth successfully.

meneur, euse [mənœʀ, -øz] *nm/f* leader; (*péj: agitateur*) ringleader; **~ d'hommes** born leader; **~ de jeu** host, quizmaster (BRIT).

menhir [meniʀ] *nm* standing stone.

méningite [menɛ̃ʒit] *nf* meningitis *no pl*.

ménisque [menisk] *nm* (ANAT) meniscus.

ménopause [menɔpoz] *nf* menopause.

menotte [mənɔt] *nf* (*langage enfantin*) handie; **~s** *nfpl* handcuffs; **passer les ~s à** to handcuff.

mens [mɑ̃] *vb voir* **mentir**.

mensonge [mɑ̃sɔ̃ʒ] *nm*: **le ~** lying *no pl*; **un ~** a lie.

mensonger, ère [mɑ̃sɔ̃ʒe, -ɛʀ] *adj* false.

menstruation [mɑ̃stʀyasjɔ̃] *nf* menstruation.

menstruel, le [mɑ̃stʀyɛl] *adj* menstrual.

mensualiser [mɑ̃syalize] *vt* to pay monthly.

mensualité [mɑ̃syalite] *nf* (*somme payée*) monthly payment; (*somme perçue*) monthly salary.

mensuel, le [mɑ̃syɛl] *adj* monthly ♦ *nm/f* (*employé*) employee paid monthly ♦ *nm* (PRESSE) monthly.

mensuellement [mɑ̃syɛlmɑ̃] *adv* monthly.

mensurations [mɑ̃syʀɑsjɔ̃] *nfpl* measurements.

mentais [mɑ̃tɛ] *etc vb voir* **mentir**.

mental, e, aux [mɑ̃tal, -o] *adj* mental.

mentalement [mɑ̃talmɑ̃] *adv* in one's head, mentally.

mentalité [mɑ̃talite] *nf* mentality.

menteur, euse [mɑ̃tœʀ, -øz] *nm/f* liar.

menthe [mɑ̃t] *nf* mint; **~ (à l'eau)** peppermint cordial.

mentholé, e [mɑ̃tɔle] *adj* menthol *cpd*, mentholated.

mention [mɑ̃sjɔ̃] *nf* (*note*) note, comment; (SCOL): **~ (très) bien/passable** (*very*) *good/satisfactory pass*; **faire ~ de** to mention; **"rayer la ~ inutile"** "delete as appropriate".

mentionner [mɑ̃sjɔne] *vt* to mention.

mentir [mɑ̃tiʀ] *vi* to lie.

menton [mɑ̃tɔ̃] *nm* chin.

mentonnière [mɑ̃tɔnjɛʀ] *nf* chin strap.

menu, e [məny] *adj* (*mince*) thin; (*petit*) tiny; (*frais, difficulté*) minor ♦ *adv* (*couper, hacher*) very fine ♦ *nm* menu; **par le ~** (*raconter*) in minute detail; **~ touristique** popular *ou* tourist menu; **~e monnaie** small change.

menuet [mənyɛ] *nm* minuet.

menuiserie [mənyizʀi] *nf* (*travail*) joinery, carpentry; (*d'amateur*) woodwork; (*local*) joiner's workshop; (*ouvrages*) woodwork *no pl*.

menuisier [mənyizje] *nm* joiner, carpenter.

méprendre [mepʀɑ̃dʀ(ə)]: **se ~** *vi*: **se ~ sur** to be mistaken about.

mépris, e [mepʀi, -iz] *pp de* **méprendre** ♦ *nm* (*dédain*) contempt, scorn; (*indifférence*): **le ~ de** contempt *ou* disregard for; **au ~ de** regardless of, in defiance of.

méprisable [mepʀizabl(ə)] *adj* contemptible, despicable.

méprisant, e [mepʀizɑ̃, -ɑ̃t] *adj* contemptuous, scornful.

méprise [mepʀiz] *nf* mistake, error; (*malentendu*) misunderstanding.

mépriser [mepʀize] *vt* to scorn, despise; (*gloire, danger*) to scorn, spurn.

mer [mɛʀ] *nf* sea; (*marée*) tide; **~ fermée** inland sea; **en ~** at sea; **prendre la ~** to put out to sea; **en haute** *ou* **pleine ~** off shore, on the open sea; **la ~ Adriatique** the Adriatic (Sea); **la ~ des Antilles** *ou* **des Caraïbes** the Caribbean (Sea); **la ~ Baltique** the Baltic (Sea); **la ~ Caspienne** the Caspian Sea; **la ~ de Corail** the Coral Sea; **la ~ Égée** the Aegean (Sea); **la ~ Ionienne** the Ionian Sea; **la ~ Morte** the Dead Sea; **la ~ Noire** the Black Sea; **la ~ du Nord** the North Sea; **la ~ Rouge** the Red Sea; **la ~ des Sargasses** the Sargasso Sea, the Sargasso Sea; **les ~s du Sud** the South Seas; **la ~ Tyrrhénienne** the Tyrrhenian Sea.

mercantile [mɛʀkɑ̃til] *adj* (*péj*) mercenary.

mercantilisme [mɛʀkɑ̃tilism(ə)] *nm* (*esprit*

mercantile) mercenary attitude.

mercenaire [mɛRsənɛR] *nm* mercenary.

mercerie [mɛRsəRi] *nf* (*COUTURE*) haberdashery (*BRIT*), notions *pl* (*US*); (*boutique*) haberdasher's shop (*BRIT*), notions store (*US*).

merci [mɛRsi] *excl* thank you ♦ *nf*: **à la ~ de qn/qch** at sb's mercy/the mercy of sth; **~ beaucoup** thank you very much; **~ de** *ou* **pour** thank you for; **sans ~** *adj* merciless ♦ *adv* mercilessly.

mercier, ière [mɛRsje, -jɛR] *nm/f* haberdasher.

mercredi [mɛRkRədi] *nm* Wednesday; **~ des Cendres** Ash Wednesday; *voir aussi* **lundi**.

mercure [mɛRkyR] *nm* mercury.

merde [mɛRd(ə)] (*fam!*) *nf* shit (*!*) ♦ *excl* (bloody) hell (*!*).

merdeux, euse [mɛRdø, -øz] *nm/f* (*fam!*) little bugger (*BRIT !*), little devil.

mère [mɛR] *nf* mother ♦ *adj inv* mother *cpd*; **~ célibataire** single parent, unmarried mother.

merguez [mɛRgɛz] *nf* spicy North African sausage.

méridien [meRidjɛ̃] *nm* meridian.

méridional, e, aux [meRidjɔnal, -o] *adj* southern; (*du midi de la France*) Southern (French) ♦ *nm/f* Southerner.

meringue [məRɛ̃g] *nf* meringue.

mérinos [meRinos] *nm* merino.

merisier [məRizje] *nm* wild cherry (tree).

méritant, e [meRitɑ̃, -ɑ̃t] *adj* deserving.

mérite [meRit] *nm* merit; **le ~ (de ceci) lui revient** the credit (for this) is his.

mériter [meRite] *vt* to deserve; **~ de réussir** to deserve to succeed; **il mérite qu'on fasse ...** he deserves people to do ....

méritocratie [meRitɔkRasi] *nf* meritocracy.

méritoire [meRitwaR] *adj* praiseworthy, commendable.

merlan [mɛRlɑ̃] *nm* whiting.

merle [mɛRl(ə)] *nm* blackbird.

mérou [meRu] *nm* grouper (*fish*).

merveille [mɛRvɛj] *nf* marvel, wonder; **faire ~** *ou* **des ~s** to work wonders; **à ~** perfectly, wonderfully.

merveilleux, euse [mɛRvɛjø, -øz] *adj* marvellous, wonderful.

mes [me] *adj possessif voir* **mon.**

mésalliance [mezaljɑ̃s] *nf* misalliance, mismatch.

mésallier [mezalje]: **se ~** *vi* to marry beneath (*ou* above) o.s.

mésange [mezɑ̃ʒ] *nf* tit(mouse) (*pl* -mice); **~ bleue** bluetit.

mésaventure [mezavɑ̃tyR] *nf* misadventure, misfortune.

Mesdames [medam] *nfpl voir* **Madame.**

Mesdemoiselles [medmwazɛl] *nfpl voir* **Mademoiselle.**

mésentente [mezɑ̃tɑ̃t] *nf* dissension, disagreement.

mésestimer [mezɛstime] *vt* to underestimate,

underrate.

Mésopotamie [mezɔpɔtami] *nf*: **la ~** Mesopotamia.

mésopotamien, ne [mezɔpɔtamjɛ̃, -ɛn] *adj* Mesopotamian.

mesquin, e [mɛskɛ̃, -in] *adj* mean, petty.

mesquinerie [mɛskinRi] *nf* meanness *no pl*, pettiness *no pl*.

mess [mɛs] *nm* mess.

message [mesaʒ] *nm* message; **~ d'erreur** (*INFORM*) error message; **~ (de guidage)** (*INFORM*) prompt; **~ publicitaire** ad, advertisement; **~ téléphoné** telegram dictated by telephone.

messager, ère [mesaʒe, -ɛR] *nm/f* messenger.

messagerie [mesaʒRi] *nf*: **~ (électronique)** (electronic) bulletin board; **~ rose** *lonely hearts and contact service on videotext*; **~s aériennes/ maritimes** air freight/shipping service *sg*; **~s de presse** press distribution service.

messe [mɛs] *nf* mass; **aller à la ~** to go to mass; **~ de minuit** midnight mass; **faire des ~s basses** (*fig, péj*) to mutter.

messie [mesi] *nm*: **le M~** the Messiah.

Messieurs [mesjø] *nmpl voir* **Monsieur.**

mesure [məzyR] *nf* (*évaluation, dimension*) measurement; (*étalon, récipient, contenu*) measure; (*MUS*: *cadence*) time, tempo; (*: division*) bar; (*retenue*) moderation; (*disposition*) measure, step; **unité/système de ~** unit/ system of measurement; **sur ~** (*costume*) made-to-measure; (*fig*) personally adapted; **à la ~ de** (*fig: personne*) worthy of; (*chambre etc*) on the same scale as; **dans la ~ où** insofar as, inasmuch as; **dans une certaine ~** to some *ou* a certain extent; **à ~ que** as; **en ~** (*MUS*) in time *ou* tempo; **être en ~ de** to be in a position to; **dépasser la ~** (*fig*) to overstep the mark.

mesuré, e [məzyRe] *adj* (*ton, effort*) measured; (*personne*) restrained.

mesurer [məzyRe] *vt* to measure; (*juger*) to weigh up, assess; (*limiter*) to limit, ration; (*modérer*) to moderate; (*proportionner*): **~ qch à** to match sth to, gear sth to; **se ~ avec** to have a confrontation with; to tackle; **il mesure 1 m 80** he's 1 m 80 tall.

met [mɛ] *vb voir* **mettre.**

métabolisme [metabɔlism(ə)] *nm* metabolism.

métairie [meteRi] *nf* smallholding.

métal, aux [metal, -o] *nm* metal.

métalangage [metalɑ̃gaʒ] *nm* metalanguage.

métallique [metalik] *adj* metallic.

métallisé, e [metalize] *adj* metallic.

métallurgie [metalyRʒi] *nf* metallurgy.

métallurgique [metalyRʒik] *adj* steel *cpd*, metal *cpd*.

métallurgiste [metalyRʒist(ə)] *nm/f* (*ouvrier*) steel *ou* metal worker; (*industriel*) metallurgist.

métamorphose [metamɔRfoz] *nf* metamorphosis (*pl* -oses).

métamorphoser [metamɔʀfoze] *vt* to transform.

métaphore [metafɔʀ] *nf* metaphor.

métaphorique [metafɔʀik] *adj* metaphorical, figurative.

métaphoriquement [metafɔʀikmɑ̃] *adv* metaphorically.

métaphysique [metafizik] *nf* metaphysics *sg* ♦ *adj* metaphysical.

métapsychique [metapsiʃik] *adj* psychic, parapsychological.

métayer, ère [meteje, metɛjɛʀ] *nm/f* (tenant) farmer.

météo [meteo] *nf* (*bulletin*) (weather) forecast; (*service*) ≈ Met Office (*BRIT*), ≈ National Weather Service (*US*).

météore [meteɔʀ] *nm* meteor.

météorite [meteɔʀit] *nm ou f* meteorite.

météorologie [meteɔʀɔlɔʒi] *nf* (*étude*) meteorology; (*service*) ≈ Meteorological Office (*BRIT*), ≈ National Weather Service (*US*).

météorologique [meteɔʀɔlɔʒik] *adj* meteorological, weather *cpd*.

météorologue [meteɔʀɔlɔg] *nm/f*, **météorologiste** [meteɔʀɔlɔʒist(ə)] *nm/f* meteorologist, weather forecaster.

métèque [metɛk] *nm* (*péj*) wop (!).

méthane [metan] *nm* methane.

méthanier [metanje] *nm* (*bateau*) (liquefied) gas carrier *ou* tanker.

méthode [metɔd] *nf* method; (*livre, ouvrage*) manual, tutor.

méthodique [metɔdik] *adj* methodical.

méthodiquement [metɔdikmɑ̃] *adv* methodically.

méthodiste [metɔdist(ə)] *adj, nm/f* (*REL*) Methodist.

méthylène [metilɛn] *nm*: **bleu de ~** *nm* methylene blue.

méticuleux, euse [metikylø, -øz] *adj* meticulous.

métier [metje] *nm* (*profession: gén*) job; (*: manuel*) trade; (*: artisanal*) craft; (*technique, expérience*) (acquired) skill *ou* technique; (*aussi: ~ à tisser*) (weaving) loom; **être du ~** to be in the trade *ou* profession.

métis, se [metis] *adj, nm/f* half-caste, half-breed.

métisser [metise] *vt* to cross(breed).

métrage [metraʒ] *nm* (*de tissu*) length; (*CINÉ*) footage, length; **long/moyen/court ~** feature *ou* full-length/medium-length/short film.

mètre [mɛtʀ(ə)] *nm* metre (*BRIT*), meter (*US*); (*règle*) (metre *ou* meter) rule; (*ruban*) tape measure; **~ carré/cube** square/cubic metre *ou* meter.

métrer [metʀe] *vt* (*TECH*) to measure (in metres *ou* meters); (*CONSTR*) to survey.

métreur, euse [metʀœʀ, -øz] *nm/f*: **~ (vérificateur)**, **métreuse (vérificatrice)** (quantity)

surveyor.

métrique [metʀik] *adj* metric ♦ *nf* metrics *sg*.

métro [metʀo] *nm* underground (*BRIT*), subway (*US*).

métronome [metʀɔnɔm] *nm* metronome.

métropole [metʀɔpɔl] *nf* (*capitale*) metropolis; (*pays*) home country.

métropolitain, e [metʀɔpɔlitɛ̃, -ɛn] *adj* metropolitan.

mets [mɛ] *nm* dish ♦ *vb voir* **mettre**.

mettable [metabl(ə)] *adj* fit to be worn, decent.

metteur [metœʀ] *nm*: **~ en scène** (*THÉÂT*) producer; (*CINÉ*) director; **~ en ondes** (*RADIO*) producer.

═══════════════════════════ *MOT-CLÉ*

mettre [mɛtʀ(ə)] *vt* **1** (*placer*) to put; **~ en bouteille/en sac** to bottle/put in bags *ou* sacks; **~ qch à la poste** to post sth (*BRIT*), mail sth; **~ en examen (pour)** to charge (with) (*BRIT*), indict (for) (*US*); **~ une note gaie/amusante** to inject a cheerful/an amusing note; **~ qn debout/assis** to help sb up *ou* to their feet/help sb to sit down

2 (*vêtements: revêtir*) to put on; (*: porter*) to wear; **mets ton gilet** put your cardigan on; **je ne mets plus mon manteau** I no longer wear my coat

3 (*faire fonctionner: chauffage, électricité*) to put on; (*: reveil, minuteur*) to set; (*installer: gaz, eau*) to put in, lay on; **~ en marche** to start up

4 (*consacrer*): **~ du temps/2 heures à faire qch** to take time/2 hours to do sth *ou* over sth; **y ~ du sien** to pull one's weight

5 (*noter, écrire*) to say, put (down); **qu'est-ce qu'il a mis sur la carte?** what did he say *ou* write on the card?; **mettez au pluriel** ... put ... into the plural

6 (*supposer*): **mettons que** ... let's suppose *ou* say that ...

7 (*faire +vb*): **faire ~ le gaz/l'électricité** to have gas/electricity put in *ou* installed

se ~ *vi* **1** (*se placer*): **vous pouvez vous ~ là** you can sit (*ou* stand) there; **où ça se met?** where does it go?; **se ~ au lit** to get into bed; **se ~ au piano** to sit down at the piano; **se ~ à l'eau** to get into the water; **se ~ de l'encre sur les doigts** to get ink on one's fingers

2 (*s'habiller*): **se ~ en maillot de bain** to get into *ou* put on a swimsuit; **n'avoir rien à se ~** to have nothing to wear

3 (*dans rapports*): **se ~ bien/mal avec qn** to get on the right/wrong side of sb; **se ~ qn à dos** to get on sb's bad side; **se ~ avec qn** (*prendre parti*) to side with sb; (*faire équipe*) to team up with sb; (*en ménage*) to move in with sb

4: **se ~ à** to begin, start; **se ~ à faire** to begin *ou* start doing *ou* to do; **se ~ au piano** to start learning the piano; **se ~ au régime** to go on a diet; **se ~ au travail/à l'étude** to get down to work/one's studies; **il est temps de s'y ~** it's time we got down to it *ou* got on with it.

meublant, e [mœblã, -ãt] *adj* (*tissus etc*) effective (in the room).

meuble [mœbl(ə)] *nm* (*objet*) piece of furniture; (*ameublement*) furniture *no pl* ♦ *adj* (*terre*) loose, friable; (*JUR*): **biens ~s** movables.

meublé [mœble] *nm* (*pièce*) furnished room; (*appartement*) furnished flat (*BRIT*) *ou* apartment (*US*).

meubler [mœble] *vt* to furnish; (*fig*): **~ qch (de)** to fill sth (with); **se ~** to furnish one's house.

meugler [møgle] *vi* to low, moo.

meule [møl] *nf* (*à broyer*) millstone; (*à aiguiser*) grindstone; (*à polir*) buffwheel; (*de foin, blé*) stack; (*de fromage*) round.

meunerie [mønʀi] *nf* (*industrie*) flour trade; (*métier*) milling.

meunier, ière [mønje, -jɛʀ] *nm* miller ♦ *nf* miller's wife ♦ *adj f* (*CULIN*) meunière.

meurs [mœʀ] *etc vb voir* **mourir**.

meurtre [mœʀtʀ(ə)] *nm* murder.

meurtrier, ière [mœʀtʀije, -jɛʀ] *adj* (*arme, épidémie, combat*) deadly; (*accident*) fatal; (*carrefour, route*) lethal; (*fureur, instincts*) murderous ♦ *nm/f* murderer/murderess ♦ *nf* (*ouverture*) loophole.

meurtrir [mœʀtʀiʀ] *vt* to bruise; (*fig*) to wound.

meurtrissure [mœʀtʀisyʀ] *nf* bruise; (*fig*) scar.

meus [mœ] *etc vb voir* **mouvoir**.

Meuse [mœz] *nf*: **la ~** the Meuse.

meute [møt] *nf* pack.

meuve [mœv] *etc vb voir* **mouvoir**.

mévente [mevãt] *nf* slump (in sales).

mexicain, e [mɛksikɛ̃, -ɛn] *adj* Mexican ♦ *nm/f*: **M~, e** Mexican.

Mexico [mɛksiko] *n* Mexico City.

Mexique [mɛksik] *nm*: **le ~** Mexico.

mezzanine [mɛdzanin] *nf* mezzanine (floor).

MF *sigle mpl* = **millions de francs** ♦ *sigle f* (*RADIO*: = *modulation de fréquence*) FM.

Mgr *abr* = **Monseigneur**.

mi [mi] *nm* (*MUS*) E; (*en chantant la gamme*) mi.

mi... [mi] *préfixe* half(-); mid-; **à la ~-janvier** in mid-January; **~-bureau, ~-chambre** half office, half bedroom; **à ~-jambes/-corps** (up *ou* down) to the knees/waist; **à ~-hauteur/-pente** halfway up (*ou* down)/up (*ou* down) the hill.

miaou [mjau] *nm* miaow.

miaulement [mjolmã] *nm* (*cri*) miaow; (*continu*) miaowing *no pl*.

miauler [mjole] *vi* to miaow.

mi-bas [miba] *nm inv* knee-length sock.

mica [mika] *nm* mica.

mi-carême [mikaʀɛm] *nf*: **la ~** the third Thursday in Lent.

miche [miʃ] *nf* round *ou* cob loaf.

mi-chemin [miʃmɛ̃]: **à ~** *adv* halfway, midway.

mi-clos, e [miklo, -kloz] *adj* half-closed.

micmac [mikmak] *nm* (*péj*) carry-on.

mi-côte [mikot]: **à ~** *adv* halfway up (*ou* down) the hill.

mi-course [mikuʀs]: **à ~** *adv* halfway through the race.

micro [mikʀo] *nm* mike, microphone; (*INFORM*) micro; **~ cravate** lapel mike.

microbe [mikʀɔb] *nm* germ, microbe.

microbiologie [mikʀɔbjɔlɔʒi] *nf* microbiology.

microchirurgie [mikʀoʃiʀyʀʒi] *nf* microsurgery.

microclimat [mikʀoklima] *nm* microclimate.

microcosme [mikʀɔkɔsm(ə)] *nm* microcosm.

micro-édition [mikʀoedisjɔ̃] *nf* desk-top publishing.

micro-électronique [mikʀoelɛktʀonik] *nf* microelectronics *sg*.

microfiche [mikʀɔfiʃ] *nf* microfiche.

microfilm [mikʀofilm] *nm* microfilm.

micro-onde [mikʀoɔ̃d] *nf*: **four à ~s** microwave oven.

micro-ordinateur [mikʀoɔʀdinatœʀ] *nm* microcomputer.

micro-organisme [mikʀoɔʀganism(ə)] *nm* micro-organism.

microphone [mikʀofɔn] *nm* microphone.

microplaquette [mikʀoplakɛt] *nf* microchip.

microprocesseur [mikʀopʀosɛsœʀ] *nm* microprocessor.

microscope [mikʀoskɔp] *nm* microscope; **au ~** under *ou* through the microscope.

microscopique [mikʀoskɔpik] *adj* microscopic.

microsillon [mikʀosijɔ̃] *nm* long-playing record.

MIDEM [midɛm] *sigle m* (= *Marché international du disque et de l'édition musicale*) *music industry trade fair*.

midi [midi] *nm* (*milieu du jour*) midday, noon; (*moment du déjeuner*) lunchtime; (*sud*) south; (: *de la France*): **le M~** the South (of France), the Midi; **à ~** at 12 (o'clock) *ou* midday *ou* noon; **tous les ~s** every lunchtime; **le repas de ~** lunch; **en plein ~** (right) in the middle of the day; (*sud*) facing south.

midinette [midinɛt] *nf* silly young townie.

mie [mi] *nf* inside (of the loaf).

miel [mjɛl] *nm* honey; **être tout ~** (*fig*) to be all sweetness and light.

mielleux, euse [mjɛlø, -øz] *adj* (*péj*) sugary, honeyed.

mien, ne [mjɛ̃, mjɛn] *adj, pron*: **le (la) ~(ne), les ~s** mine; **les ~s** (*ma famille*) my family.

miette [mjɛt] *nf* (*de pain, gâteau*) crumb; (*fig*: *de la conversation etc*) scrap; **en ~s** (*fig*) in pieces *ou* bits.

═══════════════════ *MOT-CLÉ*

mieux [mjø] *adv* **1** (*d'une meilleure façon*): ~ **(que)** better (than); **elle travaille/mange** ~ she works/eats better; **aimer** ~ to prefer; **j'attendais** ~ **de vous** I expected better of you; **elle va** ~ she is better; **de** ~ **en** ~ better and better

2 (*de la meilleure façon*) best; **ce que je sais le** ~ what I know best; **les livres les** ~ **faits** the best made books

3 (*intensif*): **vous feriez** ~ **de faire** ... you would be better to do ...; **crier à qui** ~ ~ to try to shout each other down

♦ *adj* **1** (*plus à l'aise, en meilleure forme*) better; **se sentir** ~ to feel better

2 (*plus satisfaisant*) better; **c'est** ~ **ainsi** it's better like this; **c'est le** ~ **des deux** it's the better of the two; **le(la)** ~, **les** ~ the best; **demandez-lui, c'est le** ~ ask him, it's the best thing

3 (*plus joli*) better-looking; (*plus gentil*) nicer; **il est** ~ **que son frère** (*plus beau*) he's better-looking than his brother; (*plus gentil*) he's nicer than his brother; **il est** ~ **sans moustache** he looks better without a moustache

4: **au** ~ at best; **au** ~ **avec** on the best of terms with; **pour le** ~ for the best; **qui** ~ **est** even better, better still

♦ *nm* **1** (*progrès*) improvement

2: **de mon/ton** ~ as best I/you can (*ou* could); **faire de son** ~ to do one's best; **du** ~ **qu'il peut** the best he can; **faute de** ~ for want of anything better, failing anything better.

─────────────────────────

mieux-être [mjøzɛtʀ(ə)] *nm* greater well-being; (*financier*) improved standard of living.
mièvre [mjɛvʀ(ə)] *adj* sickly sentimental.
mignon, ne [miɲɔ̃, -ɔn] *adj* sweet, cute.
migraine [migʀɛn] *nf* headache; migraine.
migrant, e [migʀɑ̃, -ɑ̃t] *adj, nm/f* migrant.
migrateur, trice [migʀatœʀ, -tʀis] *adj* migratory.
migration [migʀasjɔ̃] *nf* migration.
mijaurée [miʒɔʀe] *nf* pretentious (young) madam.
mijoter [miʒɔte] *vt* to simmer; (*préparer avec soin*) to cook lovingly; (*affaire, projet*) to plot, cook up ♦ *vi* to simmer.
mil [mil] *num* = **mille**.
Milan [milɑ̃] *n* Milan.
milanais, e [milanɛ, -ɛz] *adj* Milanese.
mildiou [mildju] *nm* mildew.
milice [milis] *nf* militia.
milicien, ne [milisjɛ̃, -ɛn] *nm/f* militiaman/woman.
milieu, x [miljø] *nm* (*centre*) middle; (*fig*) middle course *ou* way; (*aussi: juste* ~) happy medium; (*BIO, GÉO*) environment; (*entourage social*) milieu; (*familial*) background; circle; (*pègre*): **le** ~ the underworld; **au** ~ **de** in the middle of; **au beau** *ou* **en plein** ~ **(de)** right in the middle (of); ~ **de terrain** (*FOOTBALL: joueur*) midfield player; (: *joueurs*) midfield.
militaire [militɛʀ] *adj* military ♦ *nm* serviceman; **service** ~ military service.
militant, e [militɑ̃, -ɑ̃t] *adj, nm/f* militant.
militantisme [militɑ̃tism(ə)] *nm* militancy.
militariser [militaʀize] *vt* to militarize.
militarisme [militaʀism(ə)] *nm* (*péj*) militarism.
militer [milite] *vi* to be a militant; ~ **pour/contre** to militate in favour of/against.
milk-shake [milkʃɛk] *nm* milk shake.
mille [mil] *num* a *ou* one thousand ♦ *nm* (*mesure*): ~ **(marin)** nautical mile; **mettre dans le** ~ to hit the bull's-eye; (*fig*) to be bang on (target).
millefeuille [milfœj] *nm* cream *ou* vanilla slice.
millénaire [milenɛʀ] *nm* millennium ♦ *adj* thousand-year-old; (*fig*) ancient.
mille-pattes [milpat] *nm inv* centipede.
millésime [milezim] *nm* year.
millésimé, e [milezime] *adj* vintage *cpd*.
millet [mijɛ] *nm* millet.
milliard [miljaʀ] *nm* milliard, thousand million (*BRIT*), billion (*US*).
milliardaire [miljaʀdɛʀ] *nm/f* multimillionaire (*BRIT*), billionaire (*US*).
millième [miljɛm] *num* thousandth.
millier [milje] *nm* thousand; **un** ~ **(de)** a thousand or so, about a thousand; **par** ~**s** in (their) thousands, by the thousand.
milligramme [miligʀam] *nm* milligramme (*BRIT*), milligram (*US*).
millimètre [milimɛtʀ(ə)] *nm* millimetre (*BRIT*), millimeter (*US*).
millimétré, e [milimetʀe] *adj*: **papier** ~ graph paper.
million [miljɔ̃] *nm* million; **deux** ~**s de** two million; **riche à** ~**s** worth millions.
millionième [miljɔnjɛm] *num* millionth.
millionnaire [miljɔnɛʀ] *nm/f* millionaire.
mi-lourd [miluʀ] *adj m, nm* light heavyweight.
mime [mim] *nm/f* (*acteur*) mime(r); (*imitateur*) mimic ♦ *nm* (*art*) mime, miming.
mimer [mime] *vt* to mime; (*singer*) to mimic, take off.
mimétisme [mimetism(ə)] *nm* (*BIO*) mimicry.
mimique [mimik] *nf* (*funny*) face; (*signes*) gesticulations *pl*, sign language *no pl*.
mimosa [mimoza] *nm* mimosa.
mi-moyen [mimwajɛ̃] *adj m, nm* welterweight.
MIN *sigle m* (= *Marché d'intérêt national*) wholesale market for fruit, vegetables and agricultural produce.
min. *abr* (= *minimum*) min.
minable [minabl(ə)] *adj* (*personne*) shabby(-looking); (*travail*) pathetic.

minaret [minaʀɛ] *nm* minaret.
minauder [minode] *vi* to mince, simper.
minauderies [minodʀi] *nfpl* simperings.
mince [mɛ̃s] *adj* thin; (*personne, taille*) slim, slender; (*fig: profit, connaissances*) slight, small; (*: prétexte*) weak ♦ *excl:* ~ **(alors)**! darn it!
minceur [mɛ̃sœʀ] *nf* thinness; slimness, slenderness.
mincir [mɛ̃siʀ] *vi* to get slimmer *ou* thinner.
mine [min] *nf* (*physionomie*) expression, look; (*extérieur*) exterior, appearance; (*de crayon*) lead; (*gisement, exploitation, explosif*) mine; ~**s** *nfpl* (*péj*) simpering airs; **les M~s** (*ADMIN*) *the national mining and geological service; the government vehicle testing department;* **avoir bonne** ~ (*personne*) to look well; (*ironique*) to look an utter idiot; **avoir mauvaise** ~ to look unwell *ou* poorly; **faire** ~ **de faire** to make a pretence of doing; to make as if to do; **ne pas payer de** ~ to be not much to look at; ~ **de rien** *adv* with a casual air; although you wouldn't think so; ~ **de charbon** coalmine; ~ **à ciel ouvert** opencast (*BRIT*) *ou* open-air (*US*) mine.
miner [mine] *vt* (*saper*) to undermine, erode; (*MIL*) to mine.
minerai [minʀɛ] *nm* ore.
minéral, e, aux [mineʀal, -o] *adj* mineral; (*CHIMIE*) inorganic ♦ *nm* mineral.
minéralier [mineʀalje] *nm* (*bateau*) ore tanker.
minéralisé, e [mineʀalize] *adj* mineralized.
minéralogie [mineʀalɔʒi] *nf* mineralogy.
minéralogique [mineʀalɔʒik] *adj* mineralogical; **plaque** ~ **number** (*BRIT*) *ou* license (*US*) plate; **numéro** ~ **registration** (*BRIT*) *ou* license (*US*) number.
minet, te [minɛ, -ɛt] *nm/f* (*chat*) pussy-cat; (*péj*) young trendy.
mineur, e [minœʀ] *adj* minor ♦ *nm/f* (*JUR*) minor ♦ *nm* (*travailleur*) miner; (*MIL*) sapper; ~ **de fond** face worker.
miniature [minjatyʀ] *adj, nf* miniature.
miniaturisation [minjatyʀizasjɔ̃] *nf* miniaturization.
miniaturiser [minjatyʀize] *vt* to miniaturize.
minibus [minibys] *nm* minibus.
mini-cassette [minikasɛt] *nf* cassette (recorder).
minichaîne [miniʃɛn] *nf* mini system.
minier, ière [minje, -jɛʀ] *adj* mining.
mini-jupe [miniʒyp] *nf* mini-skirt.
minimal, e, aux [minimal, -o] *adj* minimum.
minimaliste [minimalist(ə)] *adj* (*ART*) minimalist.
minime [minim] *adj* minor, minimal ♦ *nm/f* (*SPORT*) junior.
minimiser [minimize] *vt* to minimize; (*fig*) to play down.
minimum [minimɔm] *adj, nm* minimum; **au** ~ at the very least; ~ **vital** (*salaire*) living wage; (*niveau de vie*) subsistance level.

mini-ordinateur [miniɔʀdinatœʀ] *nm* minicomputer.
ministère [ministɛʀ] *nm* (*cabinet*) government; (*département*) ministry (*BRIT*), department; (*REL*) ministry; ~ **public** (*JUR*) Prosecution, State Prosecutor.
ministériel, le [ministeʀjɛl] *adj* government *cpd*; ministerial, departmental; (*partisan*) pro-government.
ministrable [ministʀabl(ə)] *adj* (*POL*): **il est** ~ he's a potential minister.
ministre [ministʀ(ə)] *nm* minister (*BRIT*), secretary; (*REL*) minister; ~ **d'État** senior minister *ou* secretary.
Minitel [minitɛl] *nm* ® videotext terminal and service.

> **Minitel** *is a personal computer terminal supplied by France-Télécom to telephone subscribers. It serves as a computerized telephone directory as well as giving access to a wide variety of services, including information on train timetables, the stock market and situations vacant. Services are accessed by dialling the relevant number on the telephone, and services used are included in the subscriber's phone bill.*

minium [minjɔm] *nm* red lead paint.
minois [minwa] *nm* little face.
minorer [minɔʀe] *vt* to cut, reduce.
minoritaire [minɔʀitɛʀ] *adj* minority *cpd*.
minorité [minɔʀite] *nf* minority; **être en** ~ to be in the *ou* a minority; **mettre en** ~ (*POL*) to defeat.
Minorque [minɔʀk] *nf* Minorca.
minorquin, e [minɔʀkɛ̃, -in] *adj* Minorcan.
minoterie [minɔtʀi] *nf* flour-mill.
minuit [minɥi] *nm* midnight.
minuscule [minyskyl] *adj* minute, tiny ♦ *nf:* **(lettre)** ~ small letter.
minutage [minytaʒ] *nm* timing.
minute [minyt] *nf* minute; (*JUR: original*) minute, draft ♦ *excl* just a minute!, hang on!; **à la** ~ (*présent*) (just) this instant; (*passé*) there and then; **entrecôte** *ou* **steak** ~ minute steak.
minuter [minyte] *vt* to time.
minuterie [minytʀi] *nf* time switch.
minuteur [minytœʀ] *nm* timer.
minutie [minysi] *nf* meticulousness; minute detail; **avec** ~ meticulously; in minute detail.
minutieusement [minysjøzmɑ̃] *adv* (*organiser, travailler*) meticulously; (*examiner*) minutely.
minutieux, euse [minysjø, -øz] *adj* (*personne*) meticulous; (*inspection*) minutely detailed; (*travail*) requiring painstaking attention to detail.
mioche [mjɔʃ] *nm* (*fam*) nipper, brat.
mirabelle [miʀabɛl] *nf* (*fruit*) (cherry) plum; (*eau-de-vie*) plum brandy.

miracle [miʀakl(ə)] *nm* miracle.
miraculé, e [miʀakyle] *adj* who has been miraculously cured (*ou* rescued).
miraculeux, euse [miʀakylø, -øz] *adj* miraculous.
mirador [miʀadɔʀ] *nm* (*MIL*) watchtower.
mirage [miʀaʒ] *nm* mirage.
mire [miʀ] *nf* (*d'un fusil*) sight; (*TV*) test card; **point de** ~ target; (*fig*) focal point; **ligne de** ~ line of sight.
mirent [miʀ] *vb voir* **mettre**.
mirer [miʀe] *vt* (*œufs*) to candle; **se** ~ *vi*: **se** ~ **dans** (*suj: personne*) to gaze at one's reflection in; (*: chose*) to be mirrored in.
mirifique [miʀifik] *adj* wonderful.
mirobolant, e [miʀɔbɔlɑ̃, -ɑ̃t] *adj* fantastic.
miroir [miʀwaʀ] *nm* mirror.
miroiter [miʀwate] *vi* to sparkle, shimmer; **faire** ~ **qch à qn** to paint sth in glowing colours for sb, dangle sth in front of sb's eyes.
miroiterie [miʀwatʀi] *nf* (*usine*) mirror factory; (*magasin*) mirror dealer's (shop).
Mis *abr* = **marquis**.
mis, e [mi, miz] *pp de* **mettre** ♦ *adj* (*couvert, table*) set, laid; (*personne*): **bien** ~ well dressed ♦ *nf* (*argent: au jeu*) stake; (*tenue*) clothing; attire; **être de** ~**e** to be acceptable *ou* in season; ~**e en bouteilles** bottling; ~**e en examen** charging, indictment; ~**e à feu** blast-off; ~**e de fonds** capital outlay; ~**e à jour** updating; ~**e à mort** kill; ~**e à pied** (*d'un employé*) suspension; lay-off; ~**e sur pied** (*d'une affaire, entreprise*) setting up; ~**e en plis** set; ~**e au point** (*PHOTO*) focusing; (*fig*) clarification; ~**e à prix** reserve (*BRIT*) *ou* upset price; ~**e en scène** production.
misaine [mizɛn] *nf*: **mât de** ~ foremast.
misanthrope [mizɑ̃tʀɔp] *nm/f* misanthropist.
Mise *abr* = **marquise**.
mise [miz] *adj f, nf voir* **mis**.
miser [mize] *vt* (*enjeu*) to stake, bet; ~ **sur** *vt* (*cheval, numéro*) to bet on; (*fig*) to bank *ou* count on.
misérable [mizeʀabl(ə)] *adj* (*lamentable, malheureux*) pitiful, wretched; (*pauvre*) poverty-stricken; (*insignifiant, mesquin*) miserable ♦ *nm/f* wretch; (*miséreux*) poor wretch.
misère [mizɛʀ] *nf* (*pauvreté*) (extreme) poverty, destitution; ~**s** *nfpl* (*malheurs*) woes, miseries; (*ennuis*) little troubles; **être dans la** ~ to be destitute *ou* poverty-stricken; **salaire de** ~ starvation wage; **faire des** ~**s à qn** to torment sb; ~ **noire** utter destitution, abject poverty.
miséreux, euse [mizeʀø, -øz] *adj* poverty-stricken ♦ *nm/f* down-and-out.
miséricorde [mizeʀikɔʀd(ə)] *nf* mercy, forgiveness.
miséricordieux, euse [mizeʀikɔʀdjø, -øz] *adj* merciful, forgiving.

misogyne [mizɔʒin] *adj* misogynous ♦ *nm/f* misogynist.
missel [misɛl] *nm* missal.
missile [misil] *nm* missile.
mission [misjɔ̃] *nf* mission; **partir en** ~ (*ADMIN, POL*) to go on an assignment.
missionnaire [misjɔnɛʀ] *nm/f* missionary.
missive [misiv] *nf* missive.
mistral [mistʀal] *nm* mistral (wind).
mit [mi] *vb voir* **mettre**.
mitaine [mitɛn] *nf* mitt(en).
mite [mit] *nf* clothes moth.
mité, e [mite] *adj* moth-eaten.
mi-temps [mitɑ̃] *nf inv* (*SPORT: période*) half (*pl* halves); (*: pause*) half-time; **à** ~ *adj, adv* part-time.
miteux, euse [mitø, -øz] *adj* seedy, shabby.
mitigé, e [mitiʒe] *adj* (*conviction, ardeur*) lukewarm; (*sentiments*) mixed.
mitonner [mitɔne] *vt* (*préparer*) to cook with loving care; (*fig*) to cook up quietly.
mitoyen, ne [mitwajɛ̃, -ɛn] *adj* common, party *cpd*; **maisons** ~**nes** semi-detached houses; (*plus de deux*) terraced (*BRIT*) *ou* row (*US*) houses.
mitraille [mitʀaj] *nf* (*balles de fonte*) grapeshot; (*décharge d'obus*) shellfire.
mitrailler [mitʀaje] *vt* to machine-gun; (*fig: photographier*) to snap away at; ~ **qn de** to pelt *ou* bombard sb with.
mitraillette [mitʀajɛt] *nf* submachine gun.
mitrailleur [mitʀajœʀ] *nm* machine gunner ♦ *adj m*: **fusil** ~ machine gun.
mitrailleuse [mitʀajøz] *nf* machine gun.
mitre [mitʀ(ə)] *nf* mitre.
mitron [mitʀɔ̃] *nm* baker's boy.
mi-voix [mivwa]: **à** ~ *adv* in a low *ou* hushed voice.
mixage [miksaʒ] *nm* (*CINÉ*) (sound) mixing.
mixer, mixeur [miksœʀ] *nm* (*CULIN*) (food) mixer.
mixité [miksite] *nf* (*SCOL*) coeducation.
mixte [mikst(ə)] *adj* (*gén*) mixed; (*SCOL*) mixed, coeducational; **à usage** ~ dual-purpose; **cuisinière** ~ combined gas and electric cooker; **équipe** ~ combined team.
mixture [mikstyʀ] *nf* mixture; (*fig*) concoction.
MJC *sigle f* (= *maison des jeunes et de la culture*) community arts centre and youth club.
ml *abr* (= *millilitre*) ml.
MLF *sigle m* (= *Mouvement de libération de la femme*) Women's Movement.
Mlle, *pl* **Mlles** *abr* = **Mademoiselle**.
MM *abr* = **Messieurs**; *voir* **Monsieur**.
Mme, *pl* **Mmes** *abr* = **Madame**.
mn. *abr* (= *minute*) min.
mnémotechnique [mnemɔtɛknik] *adj* mnemonic.
MNS *sigle m* (= *maître nageur sauveteur*) ≈ lifeguard.
MO *sigle f* (= *main-d'œuvre*) *labour costs* (*on in-*

voices).

Mo _abr_ = **méga-octet, métro.**

mobile [mɔbil] _adj_ mobile; (_amovible_) loose, removable; (_pièce de machine_) moving; (_élément de meuble etc_) movable ♦ _nm_ (_motif_) motive; (_œuvre d'art_) mobile; (_PHYSIQUE_) moving object _ou_ body.

mobilier, ière [mɔbilje, -jɛʀ] _adj_ (_JUR_) personal ♦ _nm_ (_meubles_) furniture; **valeurs mobilières** transferable securities; **vente mobilière** sale of personal property _ou_ chattels.

mobilisation [mɔbilizasjɔ̃] _nf_ mobilization.

mobiliser [mɔbilize] _vt_ (_MIL, gén_) to mobilize.

mobilité [mɔbilite] _nf_ mobility.

mobylette [mɔbilɛt] _nf_ ® moped.

mocassin [mɔkasɛ̃] _nm_ moccasin.

moche [mɔʃ] _adj_ (_fam: laid_) ugly; (: _mauvais, méprisable_) rotten.

modalité [mɔdalite] _nf_ form, mode; ~**s** _nfpl_ (_d'un accord etc_) clauses, terms; ~**s de paiement** methods of payment.

mode [mɔd] _nf_ fashion; (_commerce_) fashion trade _ou_ industry ♦ _nm_ (_manière_) form, mode, method; (_LING_) mood; (_INFORM, MUS_) mode; **travailler dans la** ~ to be in the fashion business; **à la** ~ fashionable, in fashion; ~ **dialogué** (_INFORM_) interactive _ou_ conversational mode; ~ **d'emploi** directions _pl_ (for use); ~ **de vie** way of life.

modelage [mɔdlaʒ] _nm_ modelling.

modelé [mɔdle] _nm_ (_GÉO_) relief; (_du corps etc_) contours _pl_.

modèle [mɔdɛl] _adj_ model ♦ _nm_ model; (_qui pose: de peintre_) sitter; (_type_) type; (_gabarit, patron_) pattern; ~ **courant** _ou_ **de série** (_COMM_) production model; ~ **déposé** registered design; ~ **réduit** small-scale model.

modeler [mɔdle] _vt_ (_ART_) to model, mould; (_suj: vêtement, érosion_) to mould, shape; ~ **qch sur/d'après** to model sth on.

modélisation [mɔdelizasjɔ̃] _nf_ (_MATH_) modelling.

modéliste [mɔdelist(ə)] _nm/f_ (_COUTURE_) designer; (_de modèles réduits_) model maker.

modem [mɔdɛm] _nm_ modem.

Modène [mɔdɛn] _n_ Modena.

modérateur, trice [mɔdeʀatœʀ, -tʀis] _adj_ moderating ♦ _nm/f_ moderator.

modération [mɔdeʀasjɔ̃] _nf_ moderation; ~ **de peine** reduction of sentence.

modéré, e [mɔdeʀe] _adj, nm/f_ moderate.

modérément [mɔdeʀemɑ̃] _adv_ moderately, in moderation.

modérer [mɔdeʀe] _vt_ to moderate; **se** ~ _vi_ to restrain o.s.

moderne [mɔdɛʀn(ə)] _adj_ modern ♦ _nm_ (_ART_) modern style; (_ameublement_) modern furniture.

modernisation [mɔdɛʀnizasjɔ̃] _nf_ modernization.

moderniser [mɔdɛʀnize] _vt_ to modernize.

modernisme [mɔdɛʀnism(ə)] _nm_ modernism.

modernité [mɔdɛʀnite] _nf_ modernity.

modeste [mɔdɛst(ə)] _adj_ modest; (_origine_) humble, lowly.

modestement [mɔdɛstəmɑ̃] _adv_ modestly.

modestie [mɔdɛsti] _nf_ modesty; **fausse** ~ false modesty.

modicité [mɔdisite] _nf_: **la** ~ **des prix** _etc_ the low prices _etc_.

modificatif, ive [mɔdifikatif, -iv] _adj_ modifying.

modification [mɔdifikasjɔ̃] _nf_ modification.

modifier [mɔdifje] _vt_ to modify, alter; (_LING_) to modify; **se** ~ _vi_ to alter.

modique [mɔdik] _adj_ (_salaire, somme_) modest.

modiste [mɔdist(ə)] _nf_ milliner.

modulaire [mɔdylɛʀ] _adj_ modular.

modulation [mɔdylasjɔ̃] _nf_ modulation; ~ **de fréquence (FM** _ou_ **MF)** frequency modulation (FM).

module [mɔdyl] _nm_ module.

moduler [mɔdyle] _vt_ to modulate; (_air_) to warble.

moelle [mwal] _nf_ marrow; (_fig_) pith, core; ~ **épinière** spinal chord.

moelleux, euse [mwalø, -øz] _adj_ soft; (_au goût, à l'ouïe_) mellow; (_gracieux, souple_) smooth.

moellon [mwalɔ̃] _nm_ rubble stone.

mœurs [mœʀ] _nfpl_ (_conduite_) morals; (_manières_) manners; (_pratiques sociales_) habits; (_mode de vie_) life style _sg_; (_d'une espèce animale_) behaviour _sg_ (_BRIT_), behavior _sg_ (_US_); **femme de mauvaises** ~ loose woman; **passer dans les** ~ to become the custom; **contraire aux bonnes** ~ contrary to proprieties.

mohair [mɔɛʀ] _nm_ mohair.

moi [mwa] _pron_ me; (_emphatique_): ~**, je** ... for my part, I ..., I myself ... ♦ _nm inv_ (_PSYCH_) ego, self; **à** ~! (_à l'aide_) help (me)!

moignon [mwaɲɔ̃] _nm_ stump.

moi-même [mwamɛm] _pron_ myself; (_emphatique_) I myself.

moindre [mwɛ̃dʀ(ə)] _adj_ lesser; lower; **le(la)** ~, **les** ~**s** the least; the slightest; **le(la)** ~ **de** the least of; **c'est la** ~ **des choses** it's nothing at all.

moindrement [mwɛ̃dʀəmɑ̃] _adv_: **pas le** ~ not in the least.

moine [mwan] _nm_ monk, friar.

moineau, x [mwano] _nm_ sparrow.

================================ _MOT-CLÉ_

moins [mwɛ̃] _adv_ **1** (_comparatif_): ~ **(que)** less (than); ~ **grand que** less tall than, not as tall as; **il a 3 ans de** ~ **que moi** he's 3 years younger than me; **il est** ~ **intelligent que moi** he's not as clever as me, he's less clever than me; ~ **je travaille, mieux je me porte** the less I work, the better I feel
2 (_superlatif_): **le** ~ (the) least; **c'est ce que j'aime le** ~ it's what I like (the) least; **le(la)** ~ **doué(e)** the least gifted; **au** ~, **du** ~ at least; **pour le** ~ at the very least

3: ~ **de** (*quantité*) less (than); (*nombre*) fewer (than); ~ **de sable/d'eau** less sand/water; ~ **de livres/gens** fewer books/people; ~ **de 2 ans** less than 2 years; ~ **de midi** not yet midday

4: **de** ~, **en** ~: **100 F/3 jours de** ~ 100 F/3 days less; **3 livres en** ~ 3 books fewer; **3 books too few**; **de l'argent en** ~ less money; **le soleil en** ~ but for the sun, minus the sun; **de** ~ **en** ~ less and less; **en** ~ **de deux** in a flash *ou* a trice

5: **à** ~ **de, à** ~ **que** unless; **à** ~ **de faire** unless we do (*ou* he does *etc*); **à** ~ **que tu ne fasses** unless you do; **à** ~ **d'un accident** barring any accident

♦ *prép*: **4** ~ **2** 4 minus 2; **10 heures** ~ **5** 5 to 10; **il fait** ~ **5** it's 5 (degrees) below (freezing), it's minus 5; **il est** ~ **5** it's 5 to

♦ *nm* (*signe*) minus sign.

moins-value [mwɛ̃valy] *nf* (*ÉCON*, *COMM*) depreciation.

moire [mwar] *nf* moiré.

moiré, e [mware] *adj* (*tissu, papier*) moiré, watered; (*reflets*) shimmering.

mois [mwa] *nm* month; (*salaire, somme dû*) (monthly) pay *ou* salary; **treizième** ~, **double** ~ extra month's salary.

moïse [mɔiz] *nm* Moses basket.

moisi, e [mwazi] *adj* mouldy (*BRIT*), moldy (*US*), mildewed ♦ *nm* mould, mold, mildew; **odeur de** ~ musty smell.

moisir [mwazir] *vi* to go mouldy (*BRIT*) *ou* moldy (*US*); (*fig*) to rot; (*personne*) to hang about ♦ *vt* to make mouldy *ou* moldy.

moisissure [mwazisyr] *nf* mould *no pl* (*BRIT*), mold *no pl* (*US*).

moisson [mwasɔ̃] *nf* harvest; (*époque*) harvest (time); (*fig*): **faire une** ~ **de** to gather a wealth of.

moissonner [mwasɔne] *vt* to harvest, reap; (*fig*) to collect.

moissonneur, euse [mwasɔnœr, -øz] *nm/f* harvester, reaper ♦ *nf* (*machine*) harvester.

moissonneuse-batteuse, *pl* **moissonneuses-batteuses** [mwasɔnøzbatøz] *nf* combine harvester.

moite [mwat] *adj* (*peau, mains*) sweaty, sticky; (*atmosphère*) muggy.

moitié [mwatje] *nf* half (*pl* halves); (*épouse*) **sa** ~ his better half; **la** ~ half; **la** ~ **de** half (of), half the amount (*ou* number) of; **la** ~ **du temps/des gens** half the time/the people; **à la** ~ halfway through; ~ **moins grand** half as tall; ~ **plus long** half as long again, longer by half; **à** ~ half (*avant le verbe*), half- (*avant l'adjectif*); **à** ~ **prix** (at) half price, half-price; **de** ~ by half; ~ ~ half-and-half.

moka [mɔka] *nm* (*café*) mocha coffee; (*gâteau*) mocha cake.

mol [mɔl] *adj m voir* **mou**.

molaire [mɔlɛr] *nf* molar.

moldave [mɔldav] *adj* Moldavian.

Moldavie [mɔldavi] *nf*: **la** ~ Moldavia.

môle [mol] *nm* jetty.

moléculaire [mɔlekylɛr] *adj* molecular.

molécule [mɔlekyl] *nf* molecule.

moleskine [mɔlɛskin] *nf* imitation leather.

molester [mɔlɛste] *vt* to manhandle, maul (about).

molette [mɔlɛt] *nf* toothed *ou* cutting wheel.

mollasse [mɔlas] *adj* (*péj: sans énergie*) sluggish; (: *flasque*) flabby.

molle [mɔl] *adj f voir* **mou**.

mollement [mɔlmɑ̃] *adv* softly; (*péj*) sluggishly; (*protester*) feebly.

mollesse [mɔlɛs] *nf* (*voir mou*) softness; flabbiness; limpness; sluggishness; feebleness.

mollet [mɔlɛ] *nm* calf (*pl* calves) ♦ *adj m*: **œuf** ~ soft-boiled egg.

molletière [mɔltjɛr] *adj f*: **bande** ~ puttee.

molleton [mɔltɔ̃] *nm* (*TEXTILES*) felt.

molletonné, e [mɔltɔne] *adj* (*gants etc*) fleece-lined.

mollir [mɔlir] *vi* (*jambes*) to give way; (*NAVIG: vent*) to drop, die down; (*fig: personne*) to relent; (: *courage*) to fail, flag.

mollusque [mɔlysk(ə)] *nm* (*ZOOL*) mollusc; (*fig: personne*) lazy lump.

molosse [mɔlɔs] *nm* big ferocious dog.

môme [mom] *nm/f* (*fam: enfant*) brat; (: *fille*) bird (*BRIT*), chick.

moment [mɔmɑ̃] *nm* moment; (*occasion*): **profiter du** ~ to take (advantage of) the opportunity; **ce n'est pas le** ~ this is not the right time; **à un certain** ~ at some point; **à un** ~ **donné** at a certain point; **à quel** ~? when exactly?; **au même** ~ at the same time; (*instant*) at the same moment; **pour un bon** ~ for a good while; **pour le** ~ for the moment, for the time being; **au** ~ **de** at the time of; **au** ~ **où** as; at a time when; **à tout** ~ at any time *ou* moment; (*continuellement*) constantly, continually; **en ce** ~ at the moment; (*aujourd'hui*) at present; **sur le** ~ at the time; **par** ~**s** now and then, at times; **d'un** ~ **à l'autre** any time (now); **du** ~ **où** *ou* **que** seeing that, since; **n'avoir pas un** ~ **à soi** not to have a minute to oneself.

momentané, e [mɔmɑ̃tane] *adj* temporary, momentary.

momentanément [mɔmɑ̃tanemɑ̃] *adv* for a moment, for a while.

momie [mɔmi] *nf* mummy.

mon [mɔ̃], **ma** [ma], *pl* **mes** [me] *adj possessif* my.

monacal, e, aux [mɔnakal, -o] *adj* monastic.

Monaco [mɔnako] *nm*: **le** ~ Monaco.

monarchie [mɔnarʃi] *nf* monarchy.

monarchiste [mɔnarʃist(ə)] *adj*, *nm/f* monarchist.

monarque [mɔnark(ə)] *nm* monarch.

monastère [mɔnastɛr] *nm* monastery.

monastique [mɔnastik] *adj* monastic.

monceau, x [mɔ̃so] nm heap.

mondain, e [mɔ̃dɛ̃, -ɛn] adj (soirée, vie) society cpd; (obligations) social; (peintre, écrivain) fashionable; (personne) society cpd ♦ nm/f: society man/woman, socialite ♦ nf: **la M~e, la police** ~e ≈ the vice squad.

mondanités [mɔ̃danite] nfpl (vie mondaine) society life sg; (paroles) (society) small talk sg; (PRESSE) (society) gossip column sg.

monde [mɔ̃d] nm world; (personnes mondaines): **le** ~ (high) society; (milieu): **être du même** ~ to move in the same circles; (gens): **il y a du** ~ (beaucoup de gens) there are a lot of people; (quelques personnes) there are some people; **y a-t-il du** ~ **dans le salon?** is there anybody in the lounge?; **beaucoup/peu de** ~ many/few people; **le meilleur** etc **du** ~ the best etc in the world ou on earth; **mettre au** ~ to bring into the world; **pas le moins du** ~ not in the least; **se faire un** ~ **de qch** to make a great deal of fuss about sth; **tour du** ~ round-the-world trip; **homme/femme du** ~ society man/woman.

mondial, e, aux [mɔ̃djal, -o] adj (population) world cpd; (influence) world-wide.

mondialement [mɔ̃djalmɑ̃] adv throughout the world.

mondialisation [mɔ̃djalizasjɔ̃] nf (d'une technique) global application; (d'un conflit) global spread.

mondovision [mɔ̃dovizjɔ̃] nf (world coverage by) satellite television.

monégasque [monegask(ə)] adj Monegasque, of ou from Monaco ♦ nm/f: **M~** Monegasque.

monétaire [monetɛʀ] adj monetary.

monétarisme [monetaʀism(ə)] nm monetarism.

monétique [monetik] nf electronic money.

mongol, e [mɔ̃gɔl] adj Mongol, Mongolian ♦ nm (LING) Mongolian ♦ nm/f: **M~, e** (de la Mongolie) Mongolian.

Mongolie [mɔ̃gɔli] nf: **la** ~ Mongolia.

mongolien, ne [mɔ̃gɔljɛ̃, -ɛn] adj, nm/f mongol.

mongolisme [mɔ̃gɔlism(ə)] nm mongolism, Down's syndrome.

moniteur, trice [monitœʀ, -tʀis] nm/f (SPORT) instructor/instructress; (de colonie de vacances) supervisor ♦ nm (écran) monitor; ~ **cardiaque** cardiac monitor; ~ **d'auto-école** driving instructor.

monitorage [monitɔʀaʒ] nm monitoring.

monitorat [monitɔʀa] nm (formation) instructor's training (course); (fonction) instructorship.

monnaie [monɛ] nf (pièce) coin; (ÉCON, gén: moyen d'échange) currency; (petites pièces): **avoir de la** ~ to have (some) change; **faire de la** ~ to get (some) change; **avoir/faire la** ~ **de 20 F** to have change of/get change for 20 F; **faire** ou **donner à qn la** ~ **de 20 F** to give sb change for 20 F, change 20 F for sb;

rendre à qn la ~ (**sur 20 F**) to give sb the change (from ou out of 20 F); **servir de** ~ **d'échange** (fig) to be used as a bargaining counter ou as bargaining counters; **payer en** ~ **de singe** to fob (sb) off with empty promises; **c'est** ~ **courante** it's a common occurrence; ~ **légale** legal tender.

monnayable [monɛjabl(ə)] adj (vendable) convertible into cash; **mes services sont** ~s my services are worth money.

monnayer [monɛje] vt to convert into cash; (talent) to capitalize on.

monnayeur [monɛjœʀ] nm voir **faux**.

mono [mono] nf (= monophonie) mono ♦ nm (= monoski) monoski.

monochrome [monokʀom] adj monochrome.

monocle [monokl(ə)] nm monocle, eyeglass.

monocoque [monokɔk] adj (voiture) monocoque ♦ nm (voilier) monohull.

monocorde [monokɔʀd(ə)] adj monotonous.

monoculture [monokyltyʀ] nf single-crop farming, monoculture.

monogamie [monogami] nf monogamy.

monogramme [monogʀam] nm monogram.

monokini [monokini] nm one-piece bikini, bikini pants pl.

monolingue [monolɛ̃g] adj monolingual.

monolithique [monolitik] adj (lit, fig) monolithic.

monologue [monolog] nm monologue, soliloquy; ~ **intérieur** stream of consciousness.

monologuer [monologe] vi to soliloquize.

monôme [monom] nm (MATH) monomial; (d'étudiants) students' rag procession.

monoparental, e, aux [monopaʀɑ̃tal, -o] adj: **famille** ~e single-parent ou one-parent family.

monophasé, e [monofaze] adj single-phase cpd.

monophonie [monofoni] nf monophony.

monoplace [monoplas] adj, nm, nf single-seater, one-seater.

monoplan [monoplɑ̃] nm monoplane.

monopole [monopol] nm monopoly.

monopolisation [monopolizasjɔ̃] nf monopolization.

monopoliser [monopolize] vt to monopolize.

monorail [monoʀaj] nm monorail; monorail train.

monoski [monoski] nm monoski.

monosyllabe [monosilab] nm monosyllable, word of one syllable.

monosyllabique [monosilabik] adj monosyllabic.

monotone [monoton] adj monotonous.

monotonie [monotoni] nf monotony.

monseigneur [mɔ̃sɛɲœʀ] nm (archevêque, évêque) Your (ou His) Grace; (cardinal) Your (ou His) Eminence; **Mgr Thomas** Bishop Thomas; Cardinal Thomas.

Monsieur [məsjø] pl **Messieurs** [mesjø] titre Mr ['mɪstə*] ♦ nm (homme quelconque): **un/le**

m~ a/the gentleman; *voir aussi* **Madame**.

monstre [mɔ̃stʀ(ə)] *nm* monster ♦ *adj* (*fam: effet, publicité*) massive; **un travail** ~ a fantastic amount of work; an enormous job; ~ **sacré** superstar.

monstrueux, euse [mɔ̃stʀyø, -øz] *adj* monstrous.

monstruosité [mɔ̃stʀyozite] *nf* monstrosity.

mont [mɔ̃] *nm:* **par** ~**s et par vaux** up hill and down dale; **le M**~ **Blanc** Mont Blanc; ~ **de Vénus** mons veneris.

montage [mɔ̃taʒ] *nm* putting up; (*d'un bijou*) mounting, setting; (*d'une machine etc*) assembly; (*PHOTO*) photomontage; (*CINÉ*) editing; ~ **sonore** sound editing.

montagnard, e [mɔ̃taɲaʀ, -aʀd(ə)] *adj* mountain *cpd* ♦ *nm/f* mountain-dweller.

montagne [mɔ̃taɲ] *nf* (*cime*) mountain; (*région*): **la** ~ the mountains *pl*; **la haute** ~ the high mountains; **les** ~**s Rocheuses** the Rocky Mountains, the Rockies; ~**s russes** big dipper *sg*, switchback *sg*.

montagneux, euse [mɔ̃taɲø, -øz] *adj* mountainous; hilly.

montant, e [mɔ̃tɑ̃, -ɑ̃t] *adj* (*mouvement, marée*) rising; (*chemin*) uphill; (*robe, corsage*) highnecked ♦ *nm* (*somme, total*) (sum) total, (total) amount; (*de fenêtre*) upright; (*de lit*) post.

mont-de-piété, *pl* **monts-de-piété** [mɔ̃dpjete] *nm* pawnshop.

monte [mɔ̃t] *nf* (*accouplement*): **la** ~ stud; (*d'un jockey*) seat.

monté, e [mɔ̃te] *adj:* **être** ~ **contre qn** to be angry with sb; (*fourni, équipé*): ~ **en** equipped with.

monte-charge [mɔ̃tʃaʀʒ(ə)] *nm inv* goods lift, hoist.

montée [mɔ̃te] *nf* rising, rise; (*escalade*) ascent, climb; (*chemin*) way up; (*côte*) hill; **au milieu de la** ~ halfway up; **le moteur chauffe dans les** ~**s** the engine overheats going uphill.

monte-plats [mɔ̃tpla] *nm inv* service lift.

monter [mɔ̃te] *vt* (*escalier, côte*) to go (*ou* come) up; (*valise, paquet*) to take (*ou* bring) up; (*cheval*) to mount; (*femelle*) to cover, serve; (*tente, échafaudage*) to put up; (*machine*) to assemble; (*bijou*) to mount, set; (*COUTURE*) to sew on; (*: manche*) to set in; (*CINÉ*) to edit; (*THÉÂT*) to put on, stage; (*société, coup etc*) to set up; (*fournir, équiper*) to equip ♦ *vi* to go (*ou* come) up; (*avion, voiture*) to climb, go up; (*chemin, niveau, température, voix, prix*) to go up, rise; (*brouillard, bruit*) to rise, come up; (*passager*) to get on; (*à cheval*): ~ **bien/mal** to ride well/badly; ~ **à cheval/bicyclette** to get on *ou* mount a horse/bicycle; (*faire du cheval etc*) to ride (a horse); to (ride a) bicycle; ~ **à pied/en voiture** to walk/drive up, go up on foot/by car; ~ **dans le train/l'avion** to get into the train/plane, board the train/plane; ~ **sur** to climb

up onto; ~ **sur** *ou* **à un arbre/une échelle** to climb (up) a tree/ladder; ~ **à bord** to (get on) board; ~ **à la tête de qn** to go to sb's head; ~ **sur les planches** to go on the stage; ~ **en grade** to be promoted; **se** ~ (*s'équiper*) to equip o.s., get kitted out (*BRIT*); **se** ~ **à** (*frais etc*) to add up to, come to; ~ **qn contre qn** to set sb against sb; ~ **la tête à qn** to give sb ideas.

monteur, euse [mɔ̃tœʀ, -øz] *nm/f* (*TECH*) fitter; (*CINÉ*) (film) editor.

monticule [mɔ̃tikyl] *nm* mound.

montmartrois, e [mɔ̃maʀtʀwa, -waz] *adj* of *ou* from Montmartre.

montre [mɔ̃tʀ(ə)] *nf* watch; (*ostentation*): **pour la** ~ for show; ~ **en main** exactly, to the minute; **faire** ~ **de** to show, display; **contre la** ~ (*SPORT*) against the clock; ~ **de plongée** diver's watch.

Montréal [mɔ̃ʀeal] *n* Montreal.

montréalais, e [mɔ̃ʀeale, -ez] *adj* of *ou* from Montreal ♦ *nm/f:* **M**~**, e** Montrealer.

montre-bracelet, *pl* **montres-bracelets** [mɔ̃tʀəbʀaslɛ] *nf* wrist watch.

montrer [mɔ̃tʀe] *vt* to show; **se** ~ to appear; ~ **qch à qn** to show sb sth; ~ **qch du doigt** to point to sth, point one's finger at sth; **se** ~ **intelligent** to prove (to be) intelligent.

montreur, euse [mɔ̃tʀœʀ, -øz] *nm/f:* ~ **de marionnettes** puppeteer.

monture [mɔ̃tyʀ] *nf* (*bête*) mount; (*d'une bague*) setting; (*de lunettes*) frame.

monument [mɔnymɑ̃] *nm* monument; ~ **aux morts** war memorial.

monumental, e, aux [mɔnymɑ̃tal, -o] *adj* monumental.

moquer [mɔke]: **se** ~ **de** *vt* to make fun of, laugh at; (*fam: se désintéresser de*) not to care about; (*tromper*): **se** ~ **de qn** to take sb for a ride.

moquerie [mɔkʀi] *nf* mockery *no pl*.

moquette [mɔkɛt] *nf* fitted carpet, wall-to-wall carpeting *no pl*.

moquetter [mɔkete] *vt* to carpet.

moqueur, euse [mɔkœʀ, -øz] *adj* mocking.

moral, e, aux [mɔʀal, -o] *adj* moral ♦ *nm* morale ♦ *nf* (*conduite*) morals *pl*; (*règles*) moral code, ethic; (*valeurs*) moral standards *pl*, morality; (*science*) ethics *sg*, moral philosophy; (*conclusion: d'une fable etc*) moral; **au** ~, **sur le plan** ~ morally; **avoir le** ~ **à zéro** to be really down; **faire la** ~**e à** to lecture, preach at.

moralement [mɔʀalmɑ̃] *adv* morally.

moralisateur, trice [mɔʀalizatœʀ, -tʀis] *adj* moralizing, sanctimonious ♦ *nm/f* moralizer.

moraliser [mɔʀalize] *vt* (*sermonner*) to lecture, preach at.

moraliste [mɔʀalist(ə)] *nm/f* moralist ♦ *adj* moralistic.

moralité [mɔʀalite] *nf* (*d'une action, attitude*) morality; (*conduite*) morals *pl*; (*conclusion,* *enseignement*) moral.

moratoire [mɔʀatwaʀ] *adj m*: **intérêts ~s** (*ÉCON*) interest on arrears.

morave [mɔʀav] *adj* Moravian.

Moravie [mɔʀavi] *nf*: **la ~** Moravia.

morbide [mɔʀbid] *adj* morbid.

morceau, x [mɔʀso] *nm* piece, bit; (*d'une œuvre*) passage, extract; (*MUS*) piece; (*CULIN: de viande*) cut; **mettre en ~x** to pull to pieces *ou* bits.

morceler [mɔʀsəle] *vt* to break up, divide up.

morcellement [mɔʀsɛlmɑ̃] *nm* breaking up.

mordant, e [mɔʀdɑ̃, -ɑ̃t] *adj* scathing, cutting; (*froid*) biting ♦ *nm* (*dynamisme, énergie*) spirit; (*fougue*) bite, punch.

mordicus [mɔʀdikys] *adv* (*fam*) obstinately, stubbornly.

mordiller [mɔʀdije] *vt* to nibble at, chew at.

mordoré, e [mɔʀdɔʀe] *adj* lustrous bronze.

mordre [mɔʀdʀ(ə)] *vt* to bite; (*suj: lime, vis*) to bite into ♦ *vi* (*poisson*) to bite; **~ dans** to bite into; **~ sur** (*fig*) to go over into, overlap into; **~ à qch** (*comprendre, aimer*) to take to; **~ à l'hameçon** to bite, rise to the bait.

mordu, e [mɔʀdy] *pp de* **mordre** ♦ *adj* (*amoureux*) smitten ♦ *nm/f*: **un ~ du jazz/de la voile** a jazz/sailing fanatic *ou* buff.

morfondre [mɔʀfɔ̃dʀ(ə)]: **se ~** *vi* to mope.

morgue [mɔʀg(ə)] *nf* (*arrogance*) haughtiness; (*lieu: de la police*) morgue; (*: à l'hôpital*) mortuary.

moribond, e [mɔʀibɔ̃, -ɔ̃d] *adj* dying, moribund.

morille [mɔʀij] *nf* morel (*mushroom*).

mormon, e [mɔʀmɔ̃, -ɔn] *adj, nm/f* Mormon.

morne [mɔʀn(ə)] *adj* (*personne, visage*) glum, gloomy; (*temps, vie*) dismal, dreary.

morose [mɔʀoz] *adj* sullen, morose; (*marché*) sluggish.

morphine [mɔʀfin] *nf* morphine.

morphinomane [mɔʀfinɔman] *nm/f* morphine addict.

morphologie [mɔʀfɔlɔʒi] *nf* morphology.

morphologique [mɔʀfɔlɔʒik] *adj* morphological.

mors [mɔʀ] *nm* bit.

morse [mɔʀs(ə)] *nm* (*ZOOL*) walrus; (*TÉL*) Morse (code).

morsure [mɔʀsyʀ] *nf* bite.

mort¹ [mɔʀ] *nf* death; **se donner la ~** to take one's own life; **de ~** (*silence, pâleur*) deathly; **blessé à ~** fatally wounded *ou* injured; **à la vie, à la ~** for better, for worse; **~ clinique** brain death; **~ subite du nourrisson, ~ au berceau** cot death.

mort², e [mɔʀ, mɔʀt(ə)] *pp de* **mourir** ♦ *adj* dead ♦ *nm/f* (*défunt*) dead man/woman; (*victime*): **il y a eu plusieurs ~s** several people were killed, there were several killed ♦ *nm* (*CARTES*) dummy; **~ ou vif** dead or alive; **~ de peur/fatigue** frightened to death/dead tired; **~s et blessés** casualties; **faire le ~** to

play dead; (*fig*) to lie low.

mortadelle [mɔʀtadɛl] *nf* mortadella (*type of luncheon meat*).

mortalité [mɔʀtalite] *nf* mortality, death rate.

mort-aux-rats [mɔʀtɔʀa] *nf inv* rat poison.

mortel, le [mɔʀtɛl] *adj* (*poison etc*) deadly, lethal; (*accident, blessure*) fatal; (*REL, danger, frayeur*) mortal; (*fig: froid*) deathly; (*: ennui, soirée*) deadly (boring) ♦ *nm/f* mortal.

mortellement [mɔʀtɛlmɑ̃] *adv* (*blessé etc*) fatally, mortally; (*pâle etc*) deathly; (*fig: ennuyeux etc*) deadly.

morte-saison, pl mortes-saisons [mɔʀtəsɛzɔ̃] *nf* slack *ou* off season.

mortier [mɔʀtje] *nm* (*gén*) mortar.

mortifier [mɔʀtifje] *vt* to mortify.

mort-né, e [mɔʀne] *adj* (*enfant*) stillborn; (*fig*) abortive.

mortuaire [mɔʀtɥɛʀ] *adj* funeral *cpd*; **avis ~s** death announcements, intimations; **chapelle ~** mortuary chapel; **couronne ~** (*funeral*) wreath; **domicile ~** house of the deceased; **drap ~** pall.

morue [mɔʀy] *nf* (*ZOOL*) cod *inv*; (*CULIN: salée*) salt-cod.

morutier [mɔʀytje] *nm* (*pêcheur*) cod fisherman; (*bateau*) cod fishing boat.

morvandeau, elle, x [mɔʀvɑ̃do, -ɛl] *adj* of *ou* from the Morvan region.

morveux, euse [mɔʀvø, -øz] *adj* (*fam*) snotty-nosed.

mosaïque [mɔzaik] *nf* (*ART*) mosaic; (*fig*) patchwork.

Moscou [mɔsku] *n* Moscow.

moscovite [mɔskɔvit] *adj* of *ou* from Moscow, Moscow *cpd* ♦ *nm/f*: **M~** Muscovite.

mosquée [mɔske] *nf* mosque.

mot [mo] *nm* word; (*message*) line, note; (*bon mot etc*) saying; **le ~ de la fin** the last word; **~ à ~** *adj, adv* word for word; **~ pour ~** word for word, verbatim; **sur ou à ces ~s** with these words; **en un ~** in a word; **à ~s couverts** in veiled terms; **prendre qn au ~** to take sb at his word; **se donner le ~** to send the word round; **avoir son ~ à dire** to have a say; **~ d'ordre** watchword; **~ de passe** password; **~s croisés** crossword (puzzle) *sg*.

motard [mɔtaʀ] *nm* biker; (*policier*) motorcycle cop.

motel [mɔtɛl] *nm* motel.

moteur, trice [mɔtœʀ, -tʀis] *adj* (*ANAT, PHYSIOL*) motor; (*TECH*) driving; (*AUTO*): **à 4 roues motrices** 4-wheel drive ♦ *nm* engine, motor; (*fig*) mover, mainspring; **à ~** power-driven, motor *cpd*; **~ à deux temps** two-stroke engine; **~ à explosion** internal combustion engine; **~ à réaction** jet engine; **~ thermique** heat engine.

motif [mɔtif] *nm* (*cause*) motive; (*décoratif*) design, pattern, motif; (*d'un tableau*) subject, motif; (*MUS*) figure, motif; **~s** *nmpl* (*JUR*) grounds *pl*; **sans ~** *adj* groundless.

motion [mosjɔ̃] *nf* motion; ~ **de censure** motion of censure, vote of no confidence.

motivation [mɔtivasjɔ̃] *nf* motivation.

motivé, e [mɔtive] *adj* (*acte*) justified; (*personne*) motivated.

motiver [mɔtive] *vt* (*justifier*) to justify, account for; (*ADMIN, JUR, PSYCH*) to motivate.

moto [mɔto] *nf* (motor)bike; ~ **verte** *ou* **de trial** trail (*BRIT*) *ou* dirt (*US*) bike.

moto-cross [mɔtɔkrɔs] *nm* motocross.

motoculteur [mɔtɔkyltœr] *nm* (motorized) cultivator.

motocyclette [mɔtɔsiklɛt] *nf* motorbike, motorcycle.

motocyclisme [mɔtɔsiklism(ə)] *nm* motorcycle racing.

motocycliste [mɔtɔsiklist(ə)] *nm/f* motorcyclist.

motoneige [mɔtɔnɛʒ] *nf* snow bike.

motorisé, e [mɔtɔrize] *adj* (*troupe*) motorized; (*personne*) having one's own transport.

motrice [mɔtris] *adj f voir* **moteur**.

motte [mɔt] *nf*: ~ **de terre** lump of earth, clod (of earth); ~ **de gazon** turf, sod; ~ **de beurre** lump of butter.

motus [mɔtys] *excl*: ~ **(et bouche cousue)!** mum's the word!

mou (mol), molle [mu, mɔl] *adj* soft; (*péj: visage, traits*) flabby; (*: geste*) limp; (*: personne*) sluggish; (*: résistance, protestations*) feeble ♦ *nm* (*homme mou*) wimp; (*abats*) lights *pl*, lungs *pl*; (*de la corde*): **avoir du** ~ to be slack; **donner du** ~ to slacken, loosen; **avoir les jambes molles** to be weak at the knees.

mouchard, e [muʃar, -ard(ə)] *nm/f* (*péj: SCOL*) sneak; (*: POLICE*) stool pigeon, grass (*BRIT*) ♦ *nm* (*appareil*) control device; (*: de camion*) tachograph.

mouche [muʃ] *nf* fly; (*ESCRIME*) button; (*de taffetas*) patch; **prendre la** ~ to go into a huff; **faire** ~ to score a bull's-eye.

moucher [muʃe] *vt* (*enfant*) to blow the nose of; (*chandelle*) to snuff (out); **se** ~ to blow one's nose.

moucheron [muʃrɔ̃] *nm* midge.

moucheté, e [muʃte] *adj* (*cheval*) dappled; (*laine*) flecked; (*ESCRIME*) buttoned.

mouchoir [muʃwar] *nm* handkerchief, hanky; ~ **en papier** tissue, paper hanky.

moudre [mudr(ə)] *vt* to grind.

moue [mu] *nf* pout; **faire la** ~ to pout; (*fig*) to pull a face.

mouette [mwɛt] *nf* (sea)gull.

mouf(f)ette [mufɛt] *nf* skunk.

moufle [mufl(ə)] *nf* (*gant*) mitt(en); (*TECH*) pulley block.

mouflon [muflɔ̃] *nm* mouf(f)lon.

mouillage [mujaʒ] *nm* (*NAVIG: lieu*) anchorage, moorings *pl*.

mouillé, e [muje] *adj* wet.

mouiller [muje] *vt* (*humecter*) to wet, moisten; (*tremper*): ~ **qn/qch** to make sb/sth wet; (*CU-*

LIN: ragoût) to add stock *ou* wine to; (*couper, diluer*) to water down; (*mine etc*) to lay ♦ *vi* (*NAVIG*) to lie *ou* be at anchor; **se** ~ to get wet; (*fam*) to commit o.s.; to get (o.s.) involved; ~ **l'ancre** to drop *ou* cast anchor.

mouillette [mujɛt] *nf* (bread) finger.

mouillure [mujyr] *nf* wet *no pl*; (*tache*) wet patch.

moulage [mulaʒ] *nm* moulding (*BRIT*), molding (*US*); casting; (*objet*) cast.

moulais [mulɛ] *etc vb voir* **moudre**.

moulant, e [mulɑ̃, -ɑ̃t] *adj* figure-hugging.

moule [mul] *vb voir* **moudre** ♦ *nf* (*mollusque*) mussel ♦ *nm* (*creux, CULIN*) mould (*BRIT*), mold (*US*); (*modèle plein*) cast; ~ **à gâteau** cake tin (*BRIT*) *ou* pan (*US*); ~ **à gaufre** *nm* waffle iron; ~ **à tarte** *nm* pie *ou* flan dish.

moulent [mul] *vb voir* **moudre, mouler**.

mouler [mule] *vt* (*brique*) to mould (*BRIT*), mold (*US*); (*statue*) to cast; (*visage, bas-relief*) to make a cast of; (*lettre*) to shape with care; (*suj: vêtement*) to hug, fit closely round; ~ **qch sur** (*fig*) to model sth on.

moulin [mulɛ̃] *nm* mill; (*fam*) engine; ~ **à café** coffee mill; ~ **à eau** watermill; ~ **à légumes** (vegetable) shredder; ~ **à paroles** (*fig*) chatterbox; ~ **à poivre** pepper mill; ~ **à prières** prayer wheel; ~ **à vent** windmill.

mouliner [muline] *vt* to shred.

moulinet [mulinɛ] *nm* (*de treuil*) winch; (*de canne à pêche*) reel; (*mouvement*): **faire des** ~**s avec qch** to whirl sth around.

moulinette [mulinɛt] *nf* ® (vegetable) shredder.

moulons [mulɔ̃] *etc vb voir* **moudre**.

moulu, e [muly] *pp de* **moudre** ♦ *adj* (*café*) ground.

moulure [mulyr] *nf* (*ornement*) moulding (*BRIT*), molding (*US*).

mourant, e [murɑ̃, -ɑ̃t] *vb voir* **mourir** ♦ *adj* dying ♦ *nm/f* dying man/woman.

mourir [murir] *vi* to die; (*civilisation*) to die out; ~ **assassiné** to be murdered; ~ **de froid/faim/vieillesse** to die of exposure/hunger/old age; ~ **de faim/d'ennui** (*fig*) to be starving/be bored to death; ~ **d'envie de faire** to be dying to do; **s'ennuyer à** ~ to be bored to death.

mousquetaire [muskətɛr] *nm* musketeer.

mousqueton [muskɔtɔ̃] *nm* (*fusil*) carbine; (*anneau*) snap-link, karabiner.

moussant, e [musɑ̃, -ɑ̃t] *adj* foaming; **bain** ~ foam *ou* bubble bath, bath foam.

mousse [mus] *nf* (*BOT*) moss; (*écume: sur eau, bière*) froth, foam; (*: shampooing*) lather; (*de champagne*) bubbles *pl*; (*CULIN*) mousse; (*en caoutchouc etc*) foam ♦ *nm* (*NAVIG*) ship's boy; **bain de** ~ bubble bath; **bas** ~ stretch stockings; **balle** ~ rubber ball; ~ **carbonique** (fire-fighting) foam; ~ **de nylon** nylon foam; (*tissu*) stretch nylon; ~ **à raser** shaving foam.

mousseline [muslin] *nf* (*TEXTILES*) muslin; chiffon; **pommes** ~ (*CULIN*) creamed potatoes.

mousser [muse] *vi* to foam; to lather.

mousseux, euse [musø, -øz] *adj* (*chocolat*) frothy; (*eau*) foamy, frothy; (*vin*) sparkling ♦ *nm*: (**vin**) ~ sparkling wine.

mousson [musɔ̃] *nf* monsoon.

moussu, e [musy] *adj* mossy.

moustache [mustaʃ] *nf* moustache; ~**s** *nfpl* (*d'animal*) whiskers *pl*.

moustachu, e [mustaʃy] *adj* wearing a moustache.

moustiquaire [mustikɛʀ] *nf* (*rideau*) mosquito net; (*chassis*) mosquito screen.

moustique [mustik] *nm* mosquito.

moutarde [mutaʀd(ə)] *nf* mustard ♦ *adj inv* mustard(-coloured).

moutardier [mutaʀdje] *nm* mustard jar.

mouton [mutɔ̃] *nm* (*ZOOL, péj*) sheep *inv*; (*peau*) sheepskin; (*CULIN*) mutton.

mouture [mutyʀ] *nf* grinding; (*péj*) rehash.

mouvant, e [muvɑ̃, -ɑ̃t] *adj* unsettled; changing; shifting.

mouvement [muvmɑ̃] *nm* (*gén, aussi: mécanisme*) movement; (*ligne courbe*) contours *pl*; (*fig: tumulte, agitation*) activity, bustle; (: *impulsion*) impulse; reaction; (*geste*) gesture; (*MUS: rythme*) tempo (*pl* -s *ou* tempi); **en** ~ in motion; on the move; **mettre qch en** ~ to set sth in motion, set sth going; ~ **d'humeur** fit *ou* burst of temper; ~ **d'opinion** trend of (public) opinion; **le** ~ **perpétuel** perpetual motion.

mouvementé, e [muvmɑ̃te] *adj* (*vie, poursuite*) eventful; (*réunion*) turbulent.

mouvoir [muvwaʀ] *vt* (*levier, membre*) to move; (*machine*) to drive; **se** ~ to move.

moyen, ne [mwajɛ̃, -ɛn] *adj* average; (*tailles, prix*) medium; (*de grandeur moyenne*) medium-sized ♦ *nm* (*façon*) means *sg*, way ♦ *nf* average; (*STATISTIQUE*) mean; (*SCOL: à l'examen*) pass mark; (*AUTO*) average speed; ~**s** *nmpl* (*capacités*) means; **au** ~ **de** by means of; **y a-t-il** ~ **de** ...? is it possible to ...?, can one ...?; **par quel** ~? how?, which way?, by which means?; **par tous les** ~**s** by every possible means, every possible way; **avec les** ~**s du bord** (*fig*) with what's available *ou* what comes to hand; **employer les grands** ~**s** to resort to drastic measures; **par ses propres** ~**s** all by oneself; **en** ~**ne** on (an) average; **faire la** ~**ne** to work out the average; ~ **de locomotion/d'expression** means of transport/expression; ~ **âge** Middle Ages; ~ **de transport** means of transport; ~**ne d'âge** average age; ~**ne entreprise** (*COMM*) medium-sized firm.

moyenâgeux, euse [mwajɛnaʒø, -øz] *adj* medieval.

moyen-courrier [mwajɛ̃kuʀje] *nm* (*AVIAT*) medium-haul aircraft.

moyennant [mwajɛnɑ̃] *prép* (*somme*) for; (*service, conditions*) in return for; (*travail, effort*) with.

moyennement [mwajɛnmɑ̃] *adv* fairly, moderately; (*faire qch*) fairly *ou* moderately well.

Moyen-Orient [mwajɛnɔʀjɑ̃] *nm*: **le** ~ the Middle East.

moyeu, x [mwajø] *nm* hub.

mozambicain, e [mɔzɑ̃bikɛ̃, -ɛn] *adj* Mozambican.

Mozambique [mɔzɑ̃bik] *nm*: **le** ~ Mozambique.

MRAP *sigle m* = *Mouvement contre le racisme, l'antisémitisme et pour la paix.*

MRG *sigle m* (= *Mouvement des radicaux de gauche*) *political party.*

MRP *sigle m* (= *Mouvement républicain populaire*) *political party.*

ms *abr* (= *manuscrit*) MS., ms.

MST *sigle f* (= *maladie sexuellement transmissible*) STD (= *sexually transmitted disease*).

mû, mue [my] *pp de* **mouvoir**.

mucosité [mykozite] *nf* mucus *no pl.*

mucus [mykys] *nm* mucus *no pl.*

mue [my] *pp de* **mouvoir** ♦ *nf* moulting (*BRIT*), molting (*US*); sloughing; breaking of the voice.

muer [mɥe] *vi* (*oiseau, mammifère*) to moult (*BRIT*), molt (*US*); (*serpent*) to slough; (*jeune garçon*): **il mue** his voice is breaking; **se** ~ **en** to transform into.

muet, te [mɥɛ, -ɛt] *adj* dumb; (*fig*): ~ **d'admiration** *etc* speechless with admiration *etc*; (*joie, douleur, CINÉ*) silent; (*LING: lettre*) silent, mute; (*carte*) blank ♦ *nm/f* mute ♦ *nm*: **le** ~ (*CINÉ*) the silent cinema *ou* movies (*esp US*).

mufle [myfl(ə)] *nm* muzzle; (*goujat*) boor ♦ *adj* boorish.

mugir [myʒiʀ] *vi* (*bœuf*) to bellow; (*vache*) to low, moo; (*fig*) to howl.

mugissement [myʒismɑ̃] *nm* (*voir mugir*) bellowing; lowing, mooing; howling.

muguet [mygɛ] *nm* (*BOT*) lily of the valley; (*MÉD*) thrush.

mulâtre, tresse [mylɑtʀ(ə), -tʀɛs] *nm/f* mulatto.

mule [myl] *nf* (*ZOOL*) (she-)mule.

mules [myl] *nfpl* (*pantoufles*) mules.

mulet [mylɛ] *nm* (*ZOOL*) (he-)mule; (*poisson*) mullet.

muletier, ière [myltje, -jɛʀ] *adj*: **sentier** *ou* **chemin** ~ mule track.

mulot [mylo] *nm* fieldmouse (*pl* -mice).

multicolore [myltikɔlɔʀ] *adj* multicoloured (*BRIT*), multicolored (*US*).

multicoque [myltikɔk] *nm* multihull.

multidisciplinaire [myltidisiplinɛʀ] *adj* multidisciplinary.

multiforme [myltifɔʀm(ə)] *adj* many-sided.

multilatéral, e, aux [myltilateʀal, -o] *adj*

multilateral.
multimilliardaire [myltimiljaʀdɛʀ], **multimillionnaire** [myltimiljɔnɛʀ] *adj, nm/f* multimillionaire.
multinational, e, aux [myltinasjɔnal, -o] *adj, nf* multinational.
multiple [myltipl(ə)] *adj* multiple, numerous; (*varié*) many, manifold ♦ *nm* (*MATH*) multiple.
multiplex [myltiplɛks] *nm* (*RADIO*) live link-up.
multiplicateur [myltiplikatœʀ] *nm* multiplier.
multiplication [myltiplikasjɔ̃] *nf* multiplication.
multiplicité [myltiplisite] *nf* multiplicity.
multiplier [myltiplije] *vt* to multiply; **se ~** *vi* to multiply; (*fig: personne*) to be everywhere at once.
multiprogrammation [myltipʀɔgʀamasjɔ̃] *nf* (*INFORM*) multiprogramming.
multipropriété [myltipʀɔpʀijete] *nf* time-sharing *no pl.*
multirisque [myltiʀisk] *adj:* **assurance ~** multiple-risk insurance.
multisalles [myltisal] *adj:* (**cinéma**) **~** multiplex (cinema).
multitraitement [myltitʀɛtmɑ̃] *nm* (*INFORM*) multiprocessing.
multitude [myltityd] *nf* multitude; mass; **une ~ de** a vast number of, a multitude of.
Munich [mynik] *n* Munich.
munichois, e [mynikwa, -waz] *adj* of *ou* from Munich.
municipal, e, aux [mynisipal, -o] *adj* municipal; town *cpd.*
municipalité [mynisipalite] *nf* (*corps municipal*) town council, corporation; (*commune*) town, municipality.
munificence [mynifisɑ̃s] *nf* munificence.
munir [myniʀ] *vt:* **~ qn/qch de** to equip sb/sth with; **se ~ de** to provide o.s. with.
munitions [mynisjɔ̃] *nfpl* ammunition *sg.*
muqueuse [mykøz] *nf* mucous membrane.
mur [myʀ] *nm* wall; (*fig*) stone *ou* brick wall; **faire le ~** (*interne, soldat*) to jump the wall; **~ du son** sound barrier.
mûr, e [myʀ] *adj* ripe; (*personne*) mature ♦ *nf* (*de la ronce*) blackberry; (*du mûrier*) mulberry.
muraille [myʀaj] *nf* (high) wall.
mural, e, aux [myʀal, -o] *adj* wall *cpd* ♦ *nm* (*ART*) mural.
mûre [myʀ] *nf voir* **mûr.**
mûrement [myʀmɑ̃] *adv:* **ayant ~ réfléchi** having given the matter much thought.
murène [myʀɛn] *nf* moray (eel).
murer [myʀe] *vt* (*enclos*) to wall (in); (*porte, issue*) to wall up; (*personne*) to wall up *ou* in.
muret [myʀɛ] *nm* low wall.
mûrier [myʀje] *nm* mulberry tree; (*ronce*) blackberry bush.
mûrir [myʀiʀ] *vi* (*fruit, blé*) to ripen; (*abcès, furoncle*) to come to a head; (*fig: idée, personne*)

to mature; (*projet*) to develop ♦ *vt* (*fruit, blé*) to ripen; (*personne*) to (make) mature; (*pensée, projet*) to nurture.
murmure [myʀmyʀ] *nm* murmur; **~s** *nmpl* (*plaintes*) murmurings, mutterings.
murmurer [myʀmyʀe] *vi* to murmur; (*se plaindre*) to mutter, grumble.
mus [my] *etc vb voir* **mouvoir.**
musaraigne [myzaʀɛɲ] *nf* shrew.
musarder [myzaʀde] *vi* to idle (about); (*en marchant*) to dawdle (along).
musc [mysk] *nm* musk.
muscade [myskad] *nf* (*aussi:* **noix ~**) nutmeg.
muscat [myska] *nm* (*raisin*) muscat grape; (*vin*) muscatel (wine).
muscle [myskl(ə)] *nm* muscle.
musclé, e [myskle] *adj* (*personne, corps*) muscular; (*fig: politique, régime etc*) strong-arm *cpd.*
muscler [myskle] *vt* to develop the muscles of.
musculaire [myskylɛʀ] *adj* muscular.
musculation [myskylasjɔ̃] *nf:* **exercices de ~** muscle-developing exercises.
musculature [myskylatyʀ] *nf* muscle structure, muscles *pl,* musculature.
muse [myz] *nf* muse.
museau, x [myzo] *nm* muzzle.
musée [myze] *nm* museum; (*de peinture*) art gallery.
museler [myzle] *vt* to muzzle.
muselière [myzəljɛʀ] *nf* muzzle.
musette [myzɛt] *nf* (*sac*) lunchbag ♦ *adj inv* (*orchestre etc*) accordion *cpd.*
muséum [myzeɔm] *nm* museum.
musical, e, aux [myzikal, -o] *adj* musical.
music-hall [myzikol] *nm* variety theatre; (*genre*) variety.
musicien, ne [myzisjɛ̃, -ɛn] *adj* musical ♦ *nm/f* musician.
musique [myzik] *nf* music; (*fanfare*) band; **faire de la ~** to make music; (*jouer d'un instrument*) to play an instrument; **~ de chambre** chamber music; **~ de fond** background music.
musqué, e [myske] *adj* musky.
must [mœst] *nm* must.
musulman, e [myzylmɑ̃, -an] *adj, nm/f* Moslem, Muslim.
mutant, e [mytɑ̃, -ɑ̃t] *nm/f* mutant.
mutation [mytasjɔ̃] *nf* (*ADMIN*) transfer; (*BIO*) mutation.
muter [myte] *vt* (*ADMIN*) to transfer.
mutilation [mytilasjɔ̃] *nf* mutilation.
mutilé, e [mytile] *nm/f* disabled person (*through loss of limbs*); **~ de guerre** disabled ex-serviceman; **grand ~** severely disabled person.
mutiler [mytile] *vt* to mutilate, maim; (*fig*) to mutilate, deface.
mutin, e [mytɛ̃, -in] *adj* (*enfant, air, ton*) mischievous, impish ♦ *nm/f* (*MIL, NAVIG*) muti-

neer.
mutiner [mytine]: **se ~** *vi* to mutiny.
mutinerie [mytinʀi] *nf* mutiny.
mutisme [mytism(ə)] *nm* silence.
mutualiste [mytɥalist(ə)] *adj*: **société ~** mutual benefit society, ≈ Friendly Society.
mutualité [mytɥalite] *nf* (*assurance*) mutual (benefit) insurance scheme.
mutuel, le [mytɥɛl] *adj* mutual ♦ *nf* mutual benefit society.
mutuellement [mytɥɛlmɑ̃] *adv* each other, one another.
Myanmar [mjanmaʀ] *nm* Myanmar.
myocarde [mjɔkaʀd(ə)] *nm voir* **infarctus**.
myope [mjɔp] *adj* short-sighted.
myopie [mjɔpi] *nf* short-sightedness, myopia.
myosotis [mjɔzɔtis] *nm* forget-me-not.
myriade [miʀjad] *nf* myriad.
myrtille [miʀtij] *nf* bilberry (*BRIT*), blueberry (*US*), whortleberry.
mystère [mistɛʀ] *nm* mystery.
mystérieusement [misteʀjøzmɑ̃] *adv* mysteriously.
mystérieux, euse [misteʀjø, -øz] *adj* mysterious.
mysticisme [mistisism(ə)] *nm* mysticism.
mystificateur, trice [mistifikatœʀ, -tʀis] *nm/f* hoaxer, practical joker.
mystification [mistifikasjɔ̃] *nf* (*tromperie, mensonge*) hoax; (*mythe*) mystification.
mystifier [mistifje] *vt* to fool, take in; (*tromper*) to mystify.
mystique [mistik] *adj* mystic, mystical ♦ *nm/f* mystic.
mythe [mit] *nm* myth.
mythifier [mitifje] *vt* to turn into a myth, mythologize.
mythique [mitik] *adj* mythical.
mythologie [mitɔlɔʒi] *nf* mythology.
mythologique [mitɔlɔʒik] *adj* mythological.
mythomane [mitɔman] *adj, nm/f* mythomaniac.

N n

N, n [ɛn] *nm inv* N, n ♦ *abr* (= *nord*) N; **N comme Nicolas** N for Nelly (*BRIT*) *ou* Nan (*US*).
n' [n] *adv voir* **ne**.
nabot [nabo] *nm* dwarf.
nacelle [nasɛl] *nf* (*de ballon*) basket.
nacre [nakʀ(ə)] *nf* mother-of-pearl.
nacré, e [nakʀe] *adj* pearly.
nage [naʒ] *nf* swimming; (*manière*) style of swimming, stroke; **traverser/s'éloigner à la ~** to swim across/away; **en ~** bathed in perspiration; **~ indienne** sidestroke; **~ libre** freestyle; **~ papillon** butterfly.
nageoire [naʒwaʀ] *nf* fin.
nager [naʒe] *vi* to swim; (*fig: ne rien comprendre*) to be all at sea; **~ dans** to be swimming in; (*vêtements*) to be lost in; **~ dans le bonheur** to be overjoyed.
nageur, euse [naʒœʀ, -øz] *nm/f* swimmer.
naguère [nagɛʀ] *adv* (*il y a peu de temps*) not long ago; (*autrefois*) formerly.
naïf, ïve [naif, naiv] *adj* naïve.
nain, e [nɛ̃, nɛn] *adj, nm/f* dwarf.
Nairobi [naiʀɔbi] *n* Nairobi.
nais [nɛ], **naissais** [nɛsɛ] *etc vb voir* **naître**.
naissance [nɛsɑ̃s] *nf* birth; **donner ~ à** to give birth to; (*fig*) to give rise to; **prendre ~** to originate; **aveugle de ~** born blind; **Français de ~** French by birth; **à la ~ des cheveux** at the roots of the hair; **lieu de ~** place of birth.
naissant, e [nɛsɑ̃, -ɑ̃t] *vb voir* **naître** ♦ *adj* budding, incipient; (*jour*) dawning.
naît [nɛ] *vb voir* **naître**.
naître [nɛtʀ(ə)] *vi* to be born; (*conflit, complications*): **~ de** to arise from, be born out of; **~ à** (*amour, poésie*) to awaken to; **il est né en 1960** he was born in 1960; **il naît plus de filles que de garçons** there are more girls born than boys; **faire ~** (*fig*) to give rise to, arouse.
naïvement [naivmɑ̃] *adv* naïvely.
naïveté [naivte] *nf* naïvety.
Namibie [namibi] *nf*: **la ~** Namibia.
nana [nana] *nf* (*fam: fille*) bird (*BRIT*), chick.
nancéien, ne [nɑ̃sejɛ̃, -ɛn] *adj* of *ou* from Nancy.
nantais, e [nɑ̃tɛ, -ɛz] *adj* of *ou* from Nantes.
nantir [nɑ̃tiʀ] *vt*: **~ qn de** to provide sb with; **les nantis** (*péj*) the well-to-do.
NAP *sigle a* (= *Neuilly Auteuil Passy*) ≈ preppy, ≈ Sloane Ranger *cpd* (*BRIT*).
napalm [napalm] *nm* napalm.
naphtaline [naftalin] *nf*: **boules de ~** mothballs.
Naples [napl(ə)] *n* Naples.
napolitain, e [napɔlitɛ̃, -ɛn] *adj* Neapolitan; **tranche ~e** Neapolitan ice cream.
nappe [nap] *nf* tablecloth; (*fig*) sheet; layer; **~ de mazout** oil slick; **~ (phréatique)** water table.
napper [nape] *vt*: **~ qch de** to coat sth with.
napperon [napʀɔ̃] *nm* table-mat; **~ individuel** place mat.
naquis [naki] *etc vb voir* **naître**.
narcisse [naʀsis] *nm* narcissus.
narcissique [naʀsisik] *adj* narcissistic.
narcissisme [naʀsisism(ə)] *nm* narcissism.
narcodollars [naʀkodɔlaʀ] *nmpl* drug money *no pl*.
narcotique [naʀkɔtik] *adj, nm* narcotic.
narguer [naʀge] *vt* to taunt.
narine [naʀin] *nf* nostril.

narquois, e [naʀkwa, -waz] *adj* derisive, mocking.

narrateur, trice [naʀatœʀ, -tʀis] *nm/f* narrator.

narration [naʀɑsjɔ̃] *nf* narration, narrative; (*SCOL*) essay.

narrer [naʀe] *vt* to tell the story of, recount.

NASA [naza] *sigle f* (= *National Aeronautics and Space Administration*) NASA.

nasal, e, aux [nazal, -o] *adj* nasal.

naseau, x [nazo] *nm* nostril.

nasillard, e [nazijaʀ, -aʀd(ə)] *adj* nasal.

nasiller [nazije] *vi* to speak with a (nasal) twang.

Nassau [naso] *n* Nassau.

nasse [nas] *nf* fish-trap.

natal, e [natal] *adj* native.

nataliste [natalist(ə)] *adj* supporting a rising birth rate.

natalité [natalite] *nf* birth rate.

natation [natasjɔ̃] *nf* swimming; **faire de la ~** to go swimming (*regularly*); **~ synchronisée** synchronized swimming.

natif, ive [natif, -iv] *adj* native.

nation [nɑsjɔ̃] *nf* nation; **les N~s unies (NU)** the United Nations (UN).

national, e, aux [nasjɔnal, -o] *adj* national ♦ *nf*: **(route) ~e** ≈ A road (*BRIT*), ≈ state highway (*US*); **obsèques ~es** state funeral.

nationalisation [nasjɔnalizasjɔ̃] *nf* nationalization.

nationaliser [nasjɔnalize] *vt* to nationalize.

nationalisme [nasjɔnalism(ə)] *nm* nationalism.

nationaliste [nasjɔnalist(ə)] *adj, nm/f* nationalist.

nationalité [nasjɔnalite] *nf* nationality; **de ~ française** of French nationality.

natte [nat] *nf* (*tapis*) mat; (*cheveux*) plait.

natter [nate] *vt* (*cheveux*) to plait.

naturalisation [natyʀalizasjɔ̃] *nf* naturalization.

naturaliser [natyʀalize] *vt* to naturalize; (*empailler*) to stuff.

naturaliste [natyʀalist(ə)] *nm/f* naturalist; (*empailleur*) taxidermist.

nature [natyʀ] *nf* nature ♦ *adj, adv* (*CULIN*) plain, without seasoning or sweetening; (*café, thé: sans lait*) black; (*: sans sucre*) without sugar; **payer en ~** to pay in kind; **peint d'après ~** painted from life; **être de ~ à faire qch** (*propre à*) to be the sort of thing (*ou* person) to do sth; **~ morte** still-life.

naturel, le [natyʀɛl] *adj* (*gén, aussi: enfant*) natural ♦ *nm* naturalness; (*caractère*) disposition, nature; (*autochtone*) native; **au ~** (*CULIN*) in water; in its own juices.

naturellement [natyʀɛlmɑ̃] *adv* naturally; (*bien sûr*) of course.

naturisme [natyʀism(ə)] *nm* naturism.

naturiste [natyʀist(ə)] *nm/f* naturist.

naufrage [nofʀaʒ] *nm* (ship)wreck; (*fig*) wreck; **faire ~** to be shipwrecked.

naufragé, e [nofʀaʒe] *nm/f* shipwreck victim, castaway.

Nauru [noʀy] *nm* Nauru.

nauséabond, e [nozeabɔ̃, -ɔ̃d] *adj* foul, nauseous.

nausée [noze] *nf* nausea; **avoir la ~** to feel sick; **avoir des ~s** to have waves of nausea, feel nauseous *ou* sick.

nautique [notik] *adj* nautical, water *cpd*; **sports ~s** water sports.

nautisme [notism(ə)] *nm* water sports *pl*.

naval, e [naval] *adj* naval.

navarrais, e [navaʀɛ, -ɛz] *adj* Navarrian.

navet [navɛ] *nm* turnip; (*péj*) third-rate film.

navette [navɛt] *nf* shuttle; (*en car etc*) shuttle (service); **faire la ~ (entre)** to go to and fro (between), shuttle (between); **~ spatiale** space shuttle.

navigabilité [navigabilite] *nf* (*d'un navire*) seaworthiness; (*d'un avion*) airworthiness.

navigable [navigabl(ə)] *adj* navigable.

navigant, e [navigɑ̃, -ɑ̃t] *adj* (*AVIAT: personnel*) flying ♦ *nm/f*: **les ~s** the flying staff *ou* personnel.

navigateur [navigatœʀ] *nm* (*NAVIG*) seafarer, sailor; (*AVIAT*) navigator.

navigation [navigasjɔ̃] *nf* navigation, sailing; (*COMM*) shipping; **compagnie de ~** shipping company; **~ spatiale** space navigation.

naviguer [navige] *vi* to navigate, sail.

navire [naviʀ] *nm* ship; **~ de guerre** warship; **~ marchand** merchantman.

navire-citerne, *pl* **navires-citernes** [naviʀsitɛʀn(ə)] *nm* tanker.

navire-hôpital, *pl* **navires-hôpitaux** [naviʀopital, -to] *nm* hospital ship.

navrant, e [navʀɑ̃, -ɑ̃t] *adj* (*affligeant*) upsetting; (*consternant*) annoying.

navrer [navʀe] *vt* to upset, distress; **je suis navré (de/de faire/que)** I'm so sorry (for/for doing/that).

nazaréen, ne [nazaʀeɛ̃, -ɛn] *adj* Nazarene.

Nazareth [nazaʀɛt] *n* Nazareth.

NB *abr* (= *nota bene*) NB.

nbr. *abr* = **nombreux**.

nbses *abr* = **nombreuses**.

n.c. *abr* = *non communiqué, non coté*.

ND *sigle f* = *Notre Dame*.

n.d. *abr* = *non daté, non disponible*.

NDA *sigle f* = *note de l'auteur*.

NDE *sigle f* = *note de l'éditeur*.

NDLR *sigle f* = *note de la rédaction*.

ne, n' [n(ə)] *adv voir* **pas, plus, jamais** *etc*; (*explétif*) *non traduit*.

né, e [ne] *pp de* **naître**; **~ en 1960** born in 1960; **~e Scott** née Scott; **~(e) de ... et de ... son/daughter of ... and of ...; **~ d'une mère française** having a French mother; **~ pour commander** born to lead ♦ *adj*: **un comédien ~** a born comedian.

néanmoins [neɑ̃mwɛ̃] *adv* nevertheless, yet.

néant [neɑ̃] *nm* nothingness; **réduire à ~** to bring to nought; (*espoir*) to dash.

nébuleux, euse [nebylø, -øz] *adj* (*ciel*) cloudy; (*fig*) nebulous ♦ *nf* (*ASTRONOMIE*) nebula.
nébuliser [nebylize] *vt* (*liquide*) to spray.
nébulosité [nebylozite] *nf* cloud cover; ~ **variable** cloudy in places.
nécessaire [neseseʀ] *adj* necessary ♦ *nm* necessary; (*sac*) kit; **faire le** ~ to do the necessary; **n'emporter que le strict** ~ to take only what is strictly necessary; ~ **de couture** sewing kit; ~ **de toilette** toilet bag; ~ **de voyage** overnight bag.
nécessairement [neseseʀmɑ̃] *adv* necessarily.
nécessité [nesesite] *nf* necessity; **se trouver dans la** ~ **de faire qch** to find it necessary to do sth; **par** ~ out of necessity.
nécessiter [nesesite] *vt* to require.
nécessiteux, euse [nesesitø, -øz] *adj* needy.
nec plus ultra [nekplysyltʀa] *nm*: **le** ~ **de** the last word in.
nécrologie [nekʀɔlɔʒi] *nf* obituary.
nécrologique [nekʀɔlɔʒik] *adj*: **article** ~ obituary; **rubrique** ~ obituary column.
nécromancie [nekʀɔmɑ̃si] *nf* necromancy.
nécromancien, ne [nekʀɔmɑ̃sjɛ̃, -ɛn] *nm/f* necromancer.
nécrose [nekʀoz] *nf* necrosis.
nectar [nektaʀ] *nm* nectar.
nectarine [nɛktaʀin] *nf* nectarine.
néerlandais, e [neeʀlɑ̃dɛ, -ɛz] *adj* Dutch, of the Netherlands ♦ *nm* (*LING*) Dutch ♦ *nm/f*: **N~, e** Dutchman/woman; **les N~** the Dutch.
nef [nɛf] *nf* (*d'église*) nave.
néfaste [nefast(ə)] *adj* baneful; ill-fated.
négatif, ive [negatif, iv] *adj* negative ♦ *nm* (*PHOTO*) negative.
négation [negasjɔ̃] *nf* denial; (*LING*) negation.
négativement [negativmɑ̃] *adv*: **répondre** ~ to give a negative response.
négligé, e [negliʒe] *adj* (*en désordre*) slovenly ♦ *nm* (*tenue*) negligee.
négligeable [negliʒabl(ə)] *adj* insignificant, negligible.
négligemment [negliʒamɑ̃] *adv* carelessly.
négligence [negliʒɑ̃s] *nf* carelessness *no pl*; (*faute*) careless omission.
négligent, e [negliʒɑ̃, -ɑ̃t] *adj* careless; (*JUR etc*) negligent.
négliger [negliʒe] *vt* (*épouse, jardin*) to neglect; (*tenue*) to be careless about; (*avis, précautions*) to disregard, overlook; ~ **de faire** to fail to do, not bother to do; **se** ~ to neglect o.s.
négoce [negɔs] *nm* trade.
négociable [negɔsjabl(ə)] *adj* negotiable.
négociant [negɔsjɑ̃] *nm* merchant.
négociateur [negɔsjatœʀ] *nm* negotiator.
négociation [negɔsjasjɔ̃] *nf* negotiation; ~**s collectives** collective bargaining *sg*.
négocier [negɔsje] *vi, vt* to negotiate.
nègre [nɛgʀ(ə)] *nm* (*péj*) Negro; (*péj: écrivain*) ghost writer ♦ *adj* Negro.
négresse [negʀɛs] *nf* (*péj*) Negress.

négrier [negʀije] *nm* (*fig*) slave driver.
négroïde [negʀɔid] *adj* negroid.
neige [nɛʒ] *nf* snow; **battre les œufs en** ~ (*CULIN*) to whip *ou* beat the egg whites until stiff; ~ **carbonique** dry ice; ~ **fondue** (*par terre*) slush; (*qui tombe*) sleet; ~ **poudreuse** powder snow.
neiger [neʒe] *vi* to snow.
neigeux, euse [nɛʒø, -øz] *adj* snowy, snow-covered.
nénuphar [nenyfaʀ] *nm* water-lily.
néo-calédonien, ne [neɔkaledɔnjɛ̃, -ɛn] *adj* New Caledonian ♦ *nm/f*: **N~, ne** native of New Caledonia.
néocapitalisme [neokapitalism(ə)] *nm* neocapitalism.
néo-colonialisme [neokɔlɔnjalism(ə)] *nm* neocolonialism.
néologisme [neɔlɔʒism(ə)] *nm* neologism.
néon [neɔ̃] *nm* neon.
néo-natal, e [neɔnatal] *adj* neonatal.
néophyte [neɔfit] *nm/f* novice.
néo-zélandais, e [neɔzelɑ̃dɛ, -ɛz] *adj* New Zealand *cpd* ♦ *nm/f*: **N~, e** New Zealander.
Népal [nepal] *nm*: **le** ~ Nepal.
népalais, e [nepalɛ, -ɛz] *adj* Nepalese, Nepali ♦ *nm* (*LING*) Nepalese, Nepali ♦ *nm/f*: **N~, e** Nepalese, Nepali.
néphrétique [nefʀetik] *adj* (*MÉD: colique*) nephritic.
néphrite [nefʀit] *nf* (*MÉD*) nephritis.
népotisme [nepɔtism(ə)] *nm* nepotism.
nerf [nɛʀ] *nm* nerve; (*fig*) spirit; (*: forces*) stamina; ~**s** *nmpl* nerves; **être** *ou* **vivre sur les** ~**s** to live on one's nerves; **être à bout de** ~**s** to be at the end of one's tether; **passer ses** ~**s sur qn** to take it out on sb.
nerveusement [nɛʀvøzmɑ̃] *adv* nervously.
nerveux, euse [nɛʀvø, -øz] *adj* nervous; (*cheval*) highly-strung; (*voiture*) nippy, responsive; (*tendineux*) sinewy.
nervosité [nɛʀvozite] *nf* nervousness; (*émotivité*) excitability.
nervure [nɛʀvyʀ] *nf* (*de feuille*) vein; (*ARCHIT, TECH*) rib.
n'est-ce pas [nɛspa] *adv* isn't it?, won't you? *etc, selon le verbe qui précède*; **c'est bon,** ~**?** it's good, isn't it?; **il a peur,** ~**?** he's afraid, isn't he?; ~ **que c'est bon?** don't you think it's good?; **lui,** ~, **il peut se le permettre** he, of course, can afford to do that, can't he?
net, nette [nɛt] *adj* (*sans équivoque, distinct*) clear; (*photo*) sharp; (*évident*) definite; (*propre*) neat, clean; (*COMM: prix, salaire, poids*) net ♦ *adv* (*refuser*) flatly ♦ *nm*: **mettre au** ~ to copy out; **s'arrêter** ~ to stop dead; **la lame a cassé** ~ the blade snapped clean through; **faire place nette** to make a clean sweep; ~ **d'impôt** tax free.
nettement [nɛtmɑ̃] *adv* (*distinctement*) clearly; (*évidemment*) definitely; (*avec comparatif, superlatif*): ~ **mieux** definitely *ou* clearly bet-

ter.

netteté [nɛtte] *nf* clearness.

nettoie [nɛtwa] *etc vb voir* **nettoyer**.

nettoiement [netwamɑ̃] *nm (ADMIN)* cleaning; **service du ~** refuse collection.

nettoierai [nɛtwaʀe] *etc vb voir* **nettoyer**.

nettoyage [nɛtwajaʒ] *nm* cleaning; **~ à sec** dry cleaning.

nettoyant [nɛtwajɑ̃] *nm (produit)* cleaning agent.

nettoyer [nɛtwaje] *vt* to clean; *(fig)* to clean out.

neuf [nœf] *num* nine.

neuf, neuve [nœf, nœv] *adj* new ♦ *nm*: **repeindre à ~** to redecorate; **remettre à ~** to do up (as good as new), refurbish; **n'acheter que du ~** to buy everything new; **quoi de ~?** what's new?

neurasthénique [nøʀastenik] *adj* neurasthenic.

neurochirurgie [nøʀoʃiʀyʀʒi] *nf* neurosurgery.

neurochirurgien [nøʀoʃiʀyʀʒjɛ̃] *nm* neurosurgeon.

neuroleptique [nøʀolɛptik] *adj* neuroleptic.

neurologie [nøʀolɔʒi] *nf* neurology.

neurologique [nøʀolɔʒik] *adj* neurological.

neurologue [nøʀolɔg] *nm/f* neurologist.

neurone [nøʀon] *nm* neuron(e).

neuropsychiatre [nøʀopsikjatʀ(ə)] *nm/f* neuropsychiatrist.

neutralisation [nøtʀalizasjɔ̃] *nf* neutralization.

neutraliser [nøtʀalize] *vt* to neutralize.

neutralisme [nøtʀalism(ə)] *nm* neutralism.

neutraliste [nøtʀalist(ə)] *adj* neutralist.

neutralité [nøtʀalite] *nf* neutrality.

neutre [nøtʀ(ə)] *adj*, *nm (aussi LING)* neutral.

neutron [nøtʀɔ̃] *nm* neutron.

neuve [nœv] *adj f voir* **neuf**.

neuvième [nœvjɛm] *num* ninth.

névé [neve] *nm* permanent snowpatch.

neveu, x [nəvø] *nm* nephew.

névralgie [nevʀalʒi] *nf* neuralgia.

névralgique [nevʀalʒik] *adj (fig: sensible)* sensitive; **centre ~** nerve centre.

névrite [nevʀit] *nf* neuritis.

névrose [nevʀoz] *nf* neurosis.

névrosé, e [nevʀoze] *adj*, *nm/f* neurotic.

névrotique [nevʀotik] *adj* neurotic.

New York [njujɔʀk] *n* New York.

new-yorkais, e [njujɔʀkɛ, -ɛz] *adj* of *ou* from New York, New York *cpd* ♦ *nm/f*: **New-Yorkais, e** New Yorker.

nez [ne] *nm* nose; **rire au ~ de qn** to laugh in sb's face; **avoir du ~** to have flair; **avoir le fin ~** to have foresight; **~ à ~ avec** face to face with; **à vue de ~** roughly.

NF *sigle mpl = nouveaux francs* ♦ *sigle f (INDUSTRIE: = norme française)* industrial standard.

ni [ni] *conj*: **~ l'un ~ l'autre ne sont** *ou* **n'est** neither one nor the other is; **il n'a rien dit ~**

fait he hasn't said or done anything.

Niagara [njagaʀa] *nm*: **les chutes du ~** the Niagara Falls.

niais, e [njɛ, -ɛz] *adj* silly, thick.

niaiserie [njɛzʀi] *nf* gullibility; *(action, propos, futilité)* silliness.

Nicaragua [nikaʀagwa] *nm*: **le ~** Nicaragua.

nicaraguayen, ne [nikaʀagwajɛ̃, -ɛn] *adj* Nicaraguan ♦ *nm/f*: **N~, ne** Nicaraguan.

Nice [nis] *n* Nice.

niche [niʃ] *nf (du chien)* kennel; *(de mur)* recess, niche; *(farce)* trick.

nichée [niʃe] *nf* brood, nest.

nicher [niʃe] *vi* to nest; **se ~ dans** *(personne: se blottir)* to snuggle into; *(: se cacher)* to hide in; *(objet)* to lodge itself in.

nichon [niʃɔ̃] *nm (fam)* boob, tit.

nickel [nikɛl] *nm* nickel.

niçois, e [niswa, -waz] *adj* of *ou* from Nice; *(CULIN)* Nicoise.

Nicosie [nikɔsi] *n* Nicosia.

nicotine [nikɔtin] *nf* nicotine.

nid [ni] *nm* nest; *(fig: repaire etc)* den, lair; **~ d'abeilles** *(COUTURE, TEXTILE)* honeycomb stitch; **~ de poule** pothole.

nièce [njɛs] *nf* niece.

nième [ɛnjɛm] *adj*: **la ~ fois** the nth *ou* umpteenth time.

nier [nje] *vt* to deny.

nigaud, e [nigo, -od] *nm/f* booby, fool.

Niger [niʒɛʀ] *nm*: **le ~** Niger; *(fleuve)* the Niger.

Nigéria [niʒeʀja] *nm ou nf* Nigeria.

nigérian, e [niʒeʀjɑ̃, -an] *adj* Nigerian ♦ *nm/f*: **N~, e** Nigerian.

nigérien, ne [niʒeʀjɛ̃, -ɛn] *adj* of *ou* from Niger.

night-club [najtklœb] *nm* nightclub.

nihilisme [niilism(ə)] *nm* nihilism.

nihiliste [niilist(ə)] *adj* nihilist, nihilistic.

Nil [nil] *nm*: **le ~** the Nile.

n'importe [nɛ̃pɔʀt(ə)] *adv*: **~!** no matter!; **~ qui/quoi/où** anybody/anything/anywhere; **~ quoi!** *(fam: désapprobation)* what rubbish!; **~ quand** any time; **~ quel/quelle** any; **~ lequel/laquelle** any (one); **~ comment** *(sans soin)* carelessly; **~ comment, il part ce soir** he's leaving tonight in any case.

nippes [nip] *nfpl (fam)* togs.

nippon, e *ou* **ne** [nipɔ̃, -ɔn] *adj* Japanese.

nique [nik] *nf*: **faire la ~ à** to thumb one's nose at *(fig)*.

nitouche [nituʃ] *nf (péj)*: **c'est une sainte ~** she looks as if butter wouldn't melt in her mouth.

nitrate [nitʀat] *nm* nitrate.

nitrique [nitʀik] *adj*: **acide ~** nitric acid.

nitroglycérine [nitʀoɡliseʀin] *nf* nitroglycerin(e).

niveau, x [nivo] *nm* level; *(des élèves, études)* standard; **au ~ de** at the level of; *(personne)* on a level with; **de ~ (avec)** level (with); **le**

~ **de la mer** sea level; ~ **(à bulle)** spirit level; ~ **(d'eau)** water level; ~ **de vie** standard of living.

niveler [nivle] *vt* to level.

niveleuse [nivløz] *nf* (*TECH*) grader.

nivellement [nivɛlmɑ̃] *nm* levelling.

nivernais, e [nivɛʀnɛ, -ɛz] *adj* of *ou* from Nevers (and region) ♦ *nm/f*: **N~, e** inhabitant *ou* native of Nevers (and region).

NL *sigle f* = *nouvelle lune*.

NN *abr* (= *nouvelle norme*) revised standard of hotel classification.

n° *abr* (= *numéro*) no.

nobiliaire [nɔbiljɛʀ] *adj f voir* **particule**.

noble [nɔbl(ə)] *adj* noble; (*de qualité: métal etc*) precious ♦ *nm/f* noble(man/woman).

noblesse [nɔblɛs] *nf* (*classe sociale*) nobility; (*d'une action etc*) nobleness.

noce [nɔs] *nf* wedding; (*gens*) wedding party (*ou* guests *pl*); **il l'a épousée en secondes ~s** she was his second wife; **faire la ~** (*fam*) to go on a binge; ~**s d'or/d'argent/de diamant** golden/silver/diamond wedding.

noceur [nɔsœʀ] *nm* (*fam*): **c'est un sacré ~** he's a real party animal.

nocif, ive [nɔsif, -iv] *adj* harmful, noxious.

noctambule [nɔktɑ̃byl] *nm* night-bird.

nocturne [nɔktyʀn(ə)] *adj* nocturnal ♦ *nf* (*SPORT*) floodlit fixture; (*d'un magasin*) late opening.

Noël [nɔɛl] *nm* Christmas; **la (fête de) ~** Christmas time.

nœud [nø] *nm* (*de corde, du bois, NAVIG*) knot; (*ruban*) bow; (*fig: liens*) bond, tie; (: *d'une question*) crux; (*THÉÂT etc*): **le ~ de l'action** the web of events; ~ **coulant** noose; ~ **gordien** Gordian knot; ~ **papillon** bow tie.

noie [nwa] *etc vb voir* **noyer**.

noir, e [nwaʀ] *adj* black; (*obscur, sombre*) dark ♦ *nm/f* black man/woman, Negro/Negro woman ♦ *nm*: **dans le ~** in the dark ♦ *nf* (*MUS*) crotchet (*BRIT*), quarter note (*US*); **il fait ~** it is dark; **au ~** *adv* (*acheter, vendre*) on the black market; **travail au ~** moonlighting.

noirâtre [nwaʀɑtʀ(ə)] *adj* (*teinte*) blackish.

noirceur [nwaʀsœʀ] *nf* blackness; darkness.

noircir [nwaʀsiʀ] *vt, vi* to blacken.

noise [nwaz] *nf*: **chercher ~ à** to try and pick a quarrel with.

noisetier [nwaztje] *nm* hazel (tree).

noisette [nwazɛt] *nf* hazelnut; (*morceau: de beurre etc*) small knob ♦ *adj* (*yeux*) hazel.

noix [nwa] *nf* walnut; (*fam*) twit; (*CULIN*): **une ~ de beurre** a knob of butter; **à la ~** (*fam*) worthless; ~ **de cajou** cashew nut; ~ **de coco** coconut; ~ **muscade** nutmeg; ~ **de veau** (*CULIN*) round fillet of veal.

nom [nɔ̃] *nm* name; (*LING*) noun; **connaître qn de ~** to know sb by name; **au ~ de** in the name of; ~ **d'une pipe** *ou* **d'un chien!** (*fam*) for goodness' sake!; ~ **de Dieu!** (*fam!*) bloody hell! (*BRIT*), my God!; ~ **commun/**

propre common/proper noun; ~ **composé** (*LING*) compound noun; ~ **déposé** trade name; ~ **d'emprunt** assumed name; ~ **de famille** surname; ~ **de fichier** file name; ~ **de jeune fille** maiden name.

nomade [nɔmad] *adj* nomadic ♦ *nm/f* nomad.

nombre [nɔ̃bʀ(ə)] *nm* number; **venir en ~** to come in large numbers; **depuis ~ d'années** for many years; **ils sont au ~ de 3** there are 3 of them; **au ~ de mes amis** among my friends; **sans ~** countless; **(bon) ~ de** (*beaucoup, plusieurs*) a (large) number of; ~ **premier/entier** prime/whole number.

nombreux, euse [nɔ̃bʀø, -øz] *adj* many, numerous; (*avec nom sg: foule etc*) large; **peu ~** few; small; **de ~ cas** many cases.

nombril [nɔ̃bʀi] *nm* navel.

nomenclature [nɔmɑ̃klatyʀ] *nf* wordlist; list of items.

nominal, e, aux [nɔminal, -o] *adj* nominal; (*appel, liste*) of names.

nominatif, ive [nɔminatif, -iv] *nm* (*LING*) nominative ♦ *adj*: **liste ~ive** list of names; **carte ~ive** calling card; **titre ~** registered name.

nomination [nɔminasjɔ̃] *nf* nomination.

nommément [nɔmemɑ̃] *adv* (*désigner*) by name.

nommer [nɔme] *vt* (*baptiser*) to name, give a name to; (*qualifier*) to call; (*mentionner*) to name, give the name of; (*élire*) to appoint, nominate; **se ~**: **il se nomme Pascal** his name's Pascal, he's called Pascal.

non [nɔ̃] *adv* (*réponse*) no; (*suivi d'un adjectif, adverbe*) not; **Paul est venu, ~?** Paul came, didn't he?; **répondre** *ou* **dire que ~** to say no; ~ **pas que** not that; ~ **plus: moi ~ plus** neither do I, I don't either; **je préférerais que ~** I would prefer not; **il se trouve que ~** perhaps not; **je pense que ~** I don't think so; ~ **mais!** well really!; ~ **mais des fois!** you must be joking!; ~ **alcoolisé** non-alcoholic; ~ **loin/seulement** not far/only.

nonagénaire [nɔnaʒenɛʀ] *nm/f* nonagenarian.

non-agression [nɔnagʀesjɔ̃] *nf*: **pacte de ~** non-aggression pact.

non aligné, e [nɔnaliɲe] *adj* (*POL*) non-aligned.

nonante [nɔnɑ̃t] *num* (*Belgique, Suisse*) ninety.

non-assistance [nɔnasistɑ̃s] *nf* (*JUR*): ~ **à personne en danger** *failure to render assistance to a person in danger*.

nonce [nɔ̃s] *nm* (*REL*) nuncio.

nonchalamment [nɔ̃ʃalamɑ̃] *adv* nonchalantly.

nonchalance [nɔ̃ʃalɑ̃s] *nf* nonchalance, casualness.

nonchalant, e [nɔ̃ʃalɑ̃, -ɑ̃t] *adj* nonchalant, casual.

non-conformisme [nɔ̃kɔ̃fɔʀmism(ə)] *nm* nonconformism.

non-conformiste [nɔ̃kɔ̃fɔʀmist(ə)] *adj, nm/f* non-conformist.

non-conformité [nɔ̃kɔ̃fɔʀmite] *nf* nonconformity.

non-croyant, e [nɔ̃kʀwajɑ̃, -ɑ̃t] *nm/f* (*REL*) non-believer.

non(-)engagé, e [nɔ̃nɑ̃gaʒe] *adj* non-aligned.

non-fumeur [nɔ̃fymœʀ] *nm* non-smoker.

non-ingérence [nɔ̃nɛ̃ʒeʀɑ̃s] *nf* non-interference.

non-initié, e [nɔ̃ninisje] *nm/f* lay person; **les ~s** the uninitiated.

non-inscrit, e [nɔ̃nɛ̃skʀi, -it] *nm/f* (*POL: député*) independent.

non-intervention [nɔ̃nɛ̃tɛʀvɑ̃sjɔ̃] *nf* non-intervention.

non-lieu [nɔ̃ljø] *nm:* **il y a eu ~** the case was dismissed.

nonne [nɔn] *nf* nun.

nonobstant [nɔnɔpstɑ̃] *prép* notwithstanding.

non-paiement [nɔ̃pɛmɑ̃] *nm* non-payment.

non-prolifération [nɔ̃pʀɔlifeʀasjɔ̃] *nf* non-proliferation.

non-résident [nɔ̃ʀezidɑ̃] *nm* (*ÉCON*) non-resident.

non-retour [nɔ̃ʀətuʀ] *nm:* **point de ~** point of no return.

non-sens [nɔ̃sɑ̃s] *nm* absurdity.

non-spécialiste [nɔ̃spesjalist(ə)] *nm/f* non-specialist.

non-stop [nɔnstɔp] *adj inv* nonstop.

non-syndiqué, e [nɔ̃sɛ̃dike] *nm/f* non-union member.

non-violence [nɔ̃vjɔlɑ̃s] *nf* nonviolence.

non-violent, e [nɔ̃vjɔlɑ̃, -ɑ̃t] *adj* non-violent.

nord [nɔʀ] *nm* North ♦ *adj* northern; north; **au ~** (*situation*) in the north; (*direction*) to the north; **au ~ de** north of, to the north of; **perdre le ~** to lose the place (*fig*).

nord-africain, e [nɔʀafʀikɛ̃, -ɛn] *adj* North-African ♦ *nm/f:* **Nord-Africain, e** North African.

nord-américain, e [nɔʀameʀikɛ̃, -ɛn] *adj* North American ♦ *nm/f:* **Nord-Américain, e** North American.

nord-coréen, ne [nɔʀkɔʀeɛ̃, -ɛn] *adj* North Korean ♦ *nm/f:* **Nord-Coréen, ne** North Korean.

nord-est [nɔʀɛst] *nm* North-East.

nordique [nɔʀdik] *adj* (*pays, race*) Nordic; (*langues*) Scandinavian, Nordic ♦ *nm/f:* **N~** Scandinavian.

nord-ouest [nɔʀwɛst] *nm* North-West.

nord-vietnamien, ne [nɔʀvjɛtnamjɛ̃, -ɛn] *adj* North Vietnamese ♦ *nm/f:* **Nord-Vietnamien, ne** North Vietnamese.

normal, e, aux [nɔʀmal, -o] *adj* normal ♦ *nf:* **la ~e** the norm, the average.

normalement [nɔʀmalmɑ̃] *adv* (*en général*) normally; (*comme prévu*): **~, il le fera demain** he should be doing it tomorrow, he's supposed to do it tomorrow.

normalien, ne [nɔʀmaljɛ̃, -ɛn] *nm/f* student of École normale supérieure.

normalisation [nɔʀmalizasjɔ̃] *nf* standardization; normalization.

normaliser [nɔʀmalize] *vt* (*COMM, TECH*) to standardize; (*POL*) to normalize.

normand, e [nɔʀmɑ̃, -ɑ̃d] *adj* (*de Normandie*) Norman ♦ *nm/f:* **N~, e** (*de Normandie*) Norman.

Normandie [nɔʀmɑ̃di] *nf:* **la ~** Normandy.

norme [nɔʀm(ə)] *nf* norm; (*TECH*) standard.

Norvège [nɔʀvɛʒ] *nf:* **la ~** Norway.

norvégien, ne [nɔʀveʒjɛ̃, -ɛn] *adj* Norwegian ♦ *nm* (*LING*) Norwegian ♦ *nm/f:* **N~, ne** Norwegian.

nos [no] *adj possessif voir* **notre.**

nostalgie [nɔstalʒi] *nf* nostalgia.

nostalgique [nɔstalʒik] *adj* nostalgic.

notabilité [nɔtabilite] *nf* notability.

notable [nɔtabl(ə)] *adj* notable, noteworthy; (*marqué*) noticeable, marked ♦ *nm* prominent citizen.

notablement [nɔtabləmɑ̃] *adv* notably; (*sensiblement*) noticeably.

notaire [nɔtɛʀ] *nm* notary; solicitor.

notamment [nɔtamɑ̃] *adv* in particular, among others.

notariat [nɔtaʀja] *nm* profession of notary (*ou* solicitor).

notarié, e [nɔtaʀje] *adj:* **acte ~** deed drawn up by a notary (*ou* solicitor).

notation [nɔtasjɔ̃] *nf* notation.

note [nɔt] *nf* (*écrite, MUS*) note; (*SCOL*) mark (*BRIT*), grade; (*facture*) bill; **prendre des ~s** to take notes; **prendre ~ de** to note; (*par écrit*) to note, write down; **dans la ~** exactly right; **forcer la ~** to exaggerate; **une ~ de tristesse/de gaieté** a sad/happy note; **~ de service** memorandum.

noté, e [nɔte] *adj:* **être bien/mal ~** (*employé etc*) to have a good/bad record.

noter [nɔte] *vt* (*écrire*) to write down, note; (*remarquer*) to note, notice; (*SCOL, ADMIN: donner une appréciation*) to mark, give a grade to; **notez bien que ...** (please) note that ....

notice [nɔtis] *nf* summary, short article; (*brochure*): **~ explicative** explanatory leaflet, instruction booklet.

notification [nɔtifikasjɔ̃] *nf* notification.

notifier [nɔtifje] *vt:* **~ qch à qn** to notify sb of sth, notify sth to sb.

notion [nɔsjɔ̃] *nf* notion, idea; **~s** *nfpl* (*rudiments*) rudiments.

notoire [nɔtwaʀ] *adj* widely known; (*en mal*) notorious; **le fait est ~** the fact is common knowledge.

notoriété [nɔtɔʀjete] *nf:* **c'est de ~ publique** it's common knowledge.

notre, nos [nɔtʀ(ə), no] *adj possessif* our.

nôtre [notʀ(ə)] *adj* ours ♦ *pron:* **le/la ~** ours; **les ~s** ours; (*alliés etc*) our own people; **soyez des ~s** join us.

nouba [nuba] *nf* (*fam*): **faire la ~** to live it up.

nouer [nwe] *vt* to tie, knot; (*fig: alliance etc*) to strike up; **~ la conversation** to start a conversation; **se ~** *vi*: **c'est là où l'intrigue se noue** it's at that point that the strands of the plot come together; **ma gorge se noua** a lump came to my throat.

noueux, euse [nwø, -øz] *adj* gnarled.

nougat [nuga] *nm* nougat.

nougatine [nugatin] *nf* kind of nougat.

nouille [nuj] *nf* (*pâtes*): **~s** noodles; pasta *sg*; (*fam*) noodle (*BRIT*), fathead.

nounou [nunu] *nf* nanny.

nounours [nunuʀs] *nm* teddy (bear).

nourri, e [nuʀi] *adj* (*feu etc*) sustained.

nourrice [nuʀis] *nf* ≈ baby-minder; (*autrefois*) wet-nurse.

nourrir [nuʀiʀ] *vt* to feed; (*fig: espoir*) to harbour, nurse; **logé nourri** with board and lodging; **~ au sein** to breast-feed; **se ~ de légumes/rêves** to live on vegetables/dreams.

nourrissant, e [nuʀisɑ̃, -ɑ̃t] *adj* nourishing, nutritious.

nourrisson [nuʀisɔ̃] *nm* (unweaned) infant.

nourriture [nuʀityʀ] *nf* food.

nous [nu] *pron* (*sujet*) we; (*objet*) us.

nous-mêmes [numɛm] *pron* ourselves.

nouveau (nouvel), elle, x [nuvo, -ɛl] *adj* new; (*original*) novel ♦ *nm/f* new pupil (*ou* employee) ♦ *nm*: **il y a du ~** there's something new ♦ *nf* (piece of) news *sg*; (*LITTÉRATURE*) short story; **nouvelles** *nfpl* (*PRESSE, TV*) news; **de ~, à ~** again; **je suis sans nouvelles de lui** I haven't heard from him; **Nouvel An** New Year; **~ riche** nouveau riche; **~ venu, nouvelle venue** newcomer; **~x mariés** newlyweds; **nouvelle vague** new wave.

nouveau-né, e [nuvone] *nm/f* newborn (baby).

nouveauté [nuvote] *nf* novelty; (*chose nouvelle*) innovation, something new; (*COMM*) new film (*ou* book *ou* creation *etc*).

nouvel *adj m*, **nouvelle** *adj f*, *nf* [nuvɛl] *voir* **nouveau**.

Nouvelle-Angleterre [nuvɛlɑ̃glətɛʀ] *nf*: **la ~** New England.

Nouvelle-Calédonie [nuvɛlkaledɔni] *nf*: **la ~** New Caledonia.

Nouvelle-Écosse [nuvɛlekɔs] *nf*: **la ~** Nova Scotia.

Nouvelle-Galles du Sud [nuvɛlgaldysyd] *nf*: **la ~** New South Wales.

Nouvelle-Guinée [nuvɛlgine] *nf*: **la ~** New Guinea.

nouvellement [nuvɛlmɑ̃] *adv* (*arrivé etc*) recently, newly.

Nouvelle-Orléans [nuvɛlɔʀleɑ̃] *nf*: **la ~** New Orleans.

Nouvelles-Hébrides [nuvɛlsebʀid] *nfpl*: **les ~** the New Hebrides.

Nouvelle-Zélande [nuvɛlzelɑ̃d] *nf*: **la ~** New Zealand.

nouvelliste [nuvelist(ə)] *nm/f* editor *ou* writer of short stories.

novateur, trice [nɔvatœʀ, -tʀis] *adj* innovative

♦ *nm/f* innovator.

novembre [nɔvɑ̃bʀ(ə)] *nm* November; *voir aussi* **juillet**.

Le 11 novembre *is a public holiday in France commemorating the signing of the armistice, near Compiègne, at the end of World War I.*

---

novice [nɔvis] *adj* inexperienced ♦ *nm/f* novice.

noviciat [nɔvisja] *nm* (*REL*) noviciate.

noyade [nwajad] *nf* drowning *no pl*.

noyau, x [nwajo] *nm* (*de fruit*) stone; (*BIO, PHYSIQUE*) nucleus; (*ÉLEC, GÉO, fig: centre*) core; (*fig: d'artistes etc*) group; (*: de résistants etc*) cell.

noyautage [nwajotaʒ] *nm* (*POL*) infiltration.

noyauter [nwajote] *vt* (*POL*) to infiltrate.

noyé, e [nwaje] *nm/f* drowning (*ou* drowned) man/woman ♦ *adj* (*fig: dépassé*) out of one's depth.

noyer [nwaje] *nm* walnut (tree); (*bois*) walnut ♦ *vt* to drown; (*fig*) to flood; to submerge; (*AUTO: moteur*) to flood; **se ~** to be drowned, drown; (*suicide*) to drown o.s; **~ son chagrin** to drown one's sorrows; **~ le poisson** to duck the issue.

NSP *sigle m* (*REL*) = *Notre Saint Père*; (*dans les sondages*: = *ne sais pas*) don't know.

NT *sigle m* (= *Nouveau Testament*) NT.

NU *sigle fpl* (= *Nations unies*) UN.

nu, e [ny] *adj* naked; (*membres*) naked, bare; (*chambre, fil, plaine*) bare ♦ *nm* (*ART*) nude; **~ intégral** total nudity; **à mains ~es** with one's bare hands; **se mettre ~** to strip; **mettre à ~** to bare.

nuage [nɥaʒ] *nm* cloud; **être dans les ~s** (*distrait*) to have one's head in the clouds; **~ de lait** drop of milk.

nuageux, euse [nɥaʒø, -øz] *adj* cloudy.

nuance [nɥɑ̃s] *nf* (*de couleur, sens*) shade; **il y a une ~ (entre)** there's a slight difference (between); **une ~ de tristesse** a tinge of sadness.

nuancé, e [nɥɑ̃se] *adj* (*opinion*) finely-shaded, subtly differing; **être ~ dans ses opinions** to have finely-shaded opinions.

nuancer [nɥɑ̃se] *vt* (*pensée, opinion*) to qualify.

nubile [nybil] *adj* nubile.

nucléaire [nykleɛʀ] *adj* nuclear ♦ *nm* nuclear power.

nudisme [nydism(ə)] *nm* nudism.

nudiste [nydist(ə)] *adj, nm/f* nudist.

nudité [nydite] *nf* (*voir* **nu**) nudity, nakedness; bareness.

nuée [nɥe] *nf*: **une ~ de** a cloud *ou* host *ou* swarm of.

nues [ny] *nfpl*: **tomber des ~** to be taken aback; **porter qn aux ~** to praise sb to the skies.

nui [nɥi] *pp de* **nuire**.

nuire [nɥiʀ] *vi* to be harmful; **~ à** to harm, do damage to.

nuisance [nɥizɑ̃s] *nf* nuisance; **~s** *nfpl* pollution *sg*.

nuisible [nɥizibl(ə)] *adj* harmful; **(animal)** ~ pest.

nuisis [nɥizi] *etc vb voir* **nuire**.

nuit [nɥi] *nf* night; **payer sa** ~ to pay for one's overnight accommodation; **il fait** ~ it's dark; **cette** ~ *(hier)* last night; *(aujourd'hui)* tonight; **de** ~ *(vol, service)* night *cpd*; ~ **blanche** sleepless night; ~ **de noces** wedding night; ~ **de Noël** Christmas Eve.

nuitamment [nɥitamɑ̃] *adv* by night.

nuitées [nɥite] *nfpl* overnight stays, beds occupied *(in statistics)*.

nul, nulle [nyl] *adj (aucun)* no; *(minime)* nil, non-existent; *(non valable)* null; *(péj)* useless, hopeless ♦ *pron* none, no one; **résultat** ~, **match** ~ draw; **nulle part** *adv* nowhere.

nullement [nylmɑ̃] *adv* by no means.

nullité [nylite] *nf* nullity; *(péj)* hopelessness; *(: personne)* hopeless individual, nonentity.

numéraire [nymeʀɛʀ] *nm* cash; metal currency.

numéral, e, aux [nymeʀal, -o] *adj* numeral.

numérateur [nymeʀatœʀ] *nm* numerator.

numération [nymeʀasjɔ̃] *nf*: ~ **décimale/ binaire** decimal/binary notation; ~ **globulaire** blood count.

numérique [nymeʀik] *adj* numerical; *(INFORM)* digital.

numériquement [nymeʀikmɑ̃] *adv* numerically.

numériser [nymeʀize] *vt (INFORM)* to digitize.

numéro [nymeʀo] *nm* number; *(spectacle)* act, turn; **faire** *ou* **composer un** ~ to dial a number; ~ **d'identification personnel** personal identification number (PIN); ~ **d'immatriculation** *ou* **minéralogique** *ou* **de police** registration *(BRIT)* *ou* license *(US)* number; ~ **de téléphone** (tele)phone number; ~ **vert** ≈ Freefone ® number *(BRIT)*, ≈ toll-free number *(US)*.

numérotage [nymeʀotaʒ] *nm* numbering.

numérotation [nymeʀotasjɔ̃] *nf* numeration.

numéroter [nymeʀote] *vt* to number.

numerus clausus [nymeʀysklozys] *nm inv* restriction *ou* limitation of numbers.

numismate [nymismat] *nm/f* numismatist, coin collector.

nu-pieds [nypje] *nm inv* sandal ♦ *adj inv* barefoot.

nuptial, e, aux [nypsjal, -o] *adj* nuptial; wedding *cpd*.

nuptialité [nypsjalite] *nf*: **taux de** ~ marriage rate.

nuque [nyk] *nf* nape of the neck.

nu-tête [nytɛt] *adj inv* bareheaded.

nutritif, ive [nytʀitif, -iv] *adj* nutritional; *(aliment)* nutritious, nourishing.

nutrition [nytʀisjɔ̃] *nf* nutrition.

nutritionnel, le [nytʀisjɔnɛl] *adj* nutritional.

nutritionniste [nytʀisjɔnist(ə)] *nm/f* nutritionist.

nylon [nilɔ̃] *nm* nylon.

nymphomane [nɛ̃fɔman] *adj, nf* nymphomaniac.

O o

O, o [o] *nm inv* O, o ♦ *abr (= ouest)* W; **O comme Oscar** ≈ O for Oliver *(BRIT)* *ou* Oboe *(US)*.

OAS *sigle f (= Organisation de l'armée secrète)* organization opposed to Algerian independence *(1961-63)*.

oasis [ɔazis] *nf ou m* oasis *(pl* oases).

obédience [ɔbedjɑ̃s] *nf* allegiance.

obéir [ɔbeiʀ] *vi* to obey; ~ **à** to obey; *(suj: moteur, véhicule)* to respond to.

obéissance [ɔbeisɑ̃s] *nf* obedience.

obéissant, e [ɔbeisɑ̃, -ɑ̃t] *adj* obedient.

obélisque [ɔbelisk(ə)] *nm* obelisk.

obèse [ɔbɛz] *adj* obese.

obésité [ɔbezite] *nf* obesity.

objecter [ɔbʒɛkte] *vt (prétexter)* to plead, put forward as an excuse; ~ **qch à** *(argument)* to put forward sth against; ~ **(à qn) que** to object (to sb) that.

objecteur [ɔbʒɛktœʀ] *nm*: ~ **de conscience** conscientious objector.

objectif, ive [ɔbʒɛktif, -iv] *adj* objective ♦ *nm (OPTIQUE, PHOTO)* lens *sg*; *(MIL, fig)* objective; ~ **grand angulaire/à focale variable** wide-angle/zoom lens.

objection [ɔbʒɛksjɔ̃] *nf* objection; ~ **de conscience** conscientious objection.

objectivement [ɔbʒɛktivmɑ̃] *adv* objectively.

objectivité [ɔbʒɛktivite] *nf* objectivity.

objet [ɔbʒɛ] *nm (chose)* object; *(d'une discussion, recherche)* subject; **être** *ou* **faire l'~ de** *(discussion)* to be the subject of; *(soins)* to be given *ou* shown; **sans** ~ *adj* purposeless; *(sans fondement)* groundless; ~ **d'art** objet d'art; **~s personnels** personal items; **~s de toilette** toiletries; **~s trouvés** lost property *sg (BRIT)*, lost-and-found *sg (US)*.

objurgations [ɔbʒyʀɡasjɔ̃] *nfpl* objurgations; *(prières)* entreaties.

obligataire [ɔbliɡatɛʀ] *adj* bond *cpd* ♦ *nm/f* bondholder, debenture holder.

obligation [ɔbliɡasjɔ̃] *nf* obligation; *(gén pl: devoir)* duty; *(COMM)* bond, debenture; **sans** ~ **d'achat** with no obligation (to buy); **être dans l'~ de faire** to be obliged to do; **avoir l'~ de faire** to be under an obligation to do; **~s familiales** family obligations *ou* responsibilities; **~s militaires** military obligations *ou* duties.

obligatoire [ɔbligatwaʀ] *adj* compulsory, obligatory.

obligatoirement [ɔbligatwaʀmɑ̃] *adv* compulsorily; (*fatalement*) necessarily.

obligé, e [ɔbliʒe] *adj* (*redevable*): **être très ~ à qn** to be most obliged to sb; (*contraint*): **je suis (bien) ~ (de le faire)** I have to (do it); (*nécessaire: conséquence*) necessary; **c'est ~!** it's inevitable!

obligeamment [ɔbliʒamɑ̃] *adv* obligingly.

obligeance [ɔbliʒɑ̃s] *nf*: **avoir l'~ de** to be kind *ou* good enough to.

obligeant, e [ɔbliʒɑ̃, -ɑ̃t] *adj* obliging; kind.

obliger [ɔbliʒe] *vt* (*contraindre*): **~ qn à faire** to force *ou* oblige sb to do; (*JUR: engager*) to bind; (*rendre service à*) to oblige.

oblique [ɔblik] *adj* oblique; **regard ~** sidelong glance; **en ~** *adv* diagonally.

obliquer [ɔblike] *vi*: **~ vers** to turn off towards.

oblitération [ɔbliteʀasjɔ̃] *nf* cancelling *no pl*, cancellation; obstruction.

oblitérer [ɔblitere] *vt* (*timbre-poste*) to cancel; (*MÉD: canal, vaisseau*) to obstruct.

oblong, oblongue [ɔblɔ̃, ɔblɔ̃g] *adj* oblong.

obnubiler [ɔbnybile] *vt* to obsess.

obole [ɔbɔl] *nf* offering.

obscène [ɔpsɛn] *adj* obscene.

obscénité [ɔpsenite] *nf* obscenity.

obscur, e [ɔpskyʀ] *adj* (*sombre*) dark; (*fig: raisons*) obscure; (*: sentiment, malaise*) vague; (*: personne, vie*) humble, lowly.

obscurcir [ɔpskyʀsiʀ] *vt* to darken; (*fig*) to obscure; **s'~** *vi* to grow dark.

obscurité [ɔpskyʀite] *nf* darkness; **dans l'~** in the dark, in darkness; (*anonymat, médiocrité*) in obscurity.

obsédant, e [ɔpsedɑ̃, -ɑ̃t] *adj* obsessive.

obsédé, e [ɔpsede] *nm/f* fanatic; **~(e) sexuel(le)** sex maniac.

obséder [ɔpsede] *vt* to obsess, haunt.

obsèques [ɔpsɛk] *nfpl* funeral *sg*.

obséquieux, euse [ɔpsekjø, -øz] *adj* obsequious.

observance [ɔpsɛʀvɑ̃s] *nf* observance.

observateur, trice [ɔpsɛʀvatœʀ, -tʀis] *adj* observant, perceptive ♦ *nm/f* observer.

observation [ɔpsɛʀvasjɔ̃] *nf* observation; (*d'un règlement etc*) observance; (*commentaire*) observation, remark; (*reproche*) reproof; **en ~** (*MÉD*) under observation.

observatoire [ɔpsɛʀvatwaʀ] *nm* observatory; (*lieu élevé*) observation post, vantage point.

observer [ɔpsɛʀve] *vt* (*regarder*) to observe, watch; (*examiner*) to examine; (*scientifiquement, aussi: règlement, jeûne etc*) to observe; (*surveiller*) to watch; (*remarquer*) to observe, notice; **faire ~ qch à qn** (*dire*) to point out sth to sb; **s'~** (*se surveiller*) to keep a check on o.s.

obsession [ɔpsesjɔ̃] *nf* obsession; **avoir l'~ de** to have an obsession with.

obsessionnel, le [ɔpsesjɔnɛl] *adj* obsessive.

obsolescent, e [ɔpsɔlesɑ̃, -ɑ̃t] *adj* obsolescent.

obstacle [ɔpstakl(ə)] *nm* obstacle; (*ÉQUITATION*) jump, hurdle; **faire ~ à** (*lumière*) to block out; (*projet*) to hinder, put obstacles in the path of; **~s antichars** tank defences.

obstétricien, ne [ɔpstetʀisjɛ̃, -ɛn] *nm/f* obstetrician.

obstétrique [ɔpstetʀik] *nf* obstetrics *sg*.

obstination [ɔpstinasjɔ̃] *nf* obstinacy.

obstiné, e [ɔpstine] *adj* obstinate.

obstinément [ɔpstinemɑ̃] *adv* obstinately.

obstiner [ɔpstine]: **s'~** *vi* to insist, dig one's heels in; **s'~ à faire** to persist (obstinately) in doing; **s'~ sur qch** to keep working at sth, labour away at sth.

obstruction [ɔpstʀyksjɔ̃] *nf* obstruction, blockage; (*SPORT*) obstruction; **faire de l'~** (*fig*) to be obstructive.

obstruer [ɔpstʀye] *vt* to block, obstruct; **s'~** *vi* to become blocked.

obtempérer [ɔptɑ̃peʀe] *vi* to obey; **~ à** to obey, comply with.

obtenir [ɔptəniʀ] *vt* to obtain, get; (*total*) to arrive at, reach; (*résultat*) to achieve, obtain; **~ de pouvoir faire** to obtain permission to do; **~ qch à qn** to obtain sth for sb; **~ de qn qu'il fasse** to get sb to agree to do(ing).

obtention [ɔptɑ̃sjɔ̃] *nf* obtaining.

obtenu, e [ɔpt(ə)ny] *pp de* obtenir.

obtiendrai [ɔptjɛ̃dʀe], **obtiens** [ɔptjɛ̃], **obtint** [ɔptɛ̃] *etc vb voir* obtenir.

obturateur [ɔptyʀatœʀ] *nm* (*PHOTO*) shutter; **~ à rideau** focal plane shutter.

obturation [ɔptyʀasjɔ̃] *nf* closing (up); **~ (dentaire)** filling; **vitesse d'~** (*PHOTO*) shutter speed.

obturer [ɔptyʀe] *vt* to close (up); (*dent*) to fill.

obtus, e [ɔpty, -yz] *adj* obtuse.

obus [ɔby] *nm* shell; **~ explosif** high-explosive shell; **~ incendiaire** incendiary device, fire bomb.

obvier [ɔbvje]: **~ à** *vt* to obviate.

OC *sigle fpl* (= *ondes courtes*) SW.

occasion [ɔkazjɔ̃] *nf* (*aubaine, possibilité*) opportunity; (*circonstance*) occasion; (*COMM: article non neuf*) secondhand buy; (*: acquisition avantageuse*) bargain; **à plusieurs ~s** on several occasions; **à la première ~** at the first *ou* earliest opportunity; **avoir l'~ de faire** to have the opportunity to do; **être l'~ de** to occasion, give rise to; **à l'~** *adv* sometimes, on occasions; (*un jour*) some time; **à l'~ de** on the occasion of; **d'~** *adj, adv* secondhand.

occasionnel, le [ɔkazjɔnɛl] *adj* (*fortuit*) chance *cpd*; (*non régulier*) occasional; (*: travail*) casual.

occasionner [ɔkazjɔne] *vt* to cause, bring about; **~ qch à qn** to cause sb sth.

occident [ɔksidɑ̃] *nm*: **l'O~** the West.

occidental, e, aux [ɔksidɑ̃tal, -o] *adj* western;

(*POL*) Western ♦ *nm/f* Westerner.

occidentaliser [ɔksidɑ̃talize] *vt* (*coutumes, mœurs*) to westernize.

occiput [ɔksipyt] *nm* back of the head, occiput.

occire [ɔksiʀ] *vt* to slay.

occitan, e [ɔksitɑ̃, -an] *adj* of the langue d'oc, of Provençal French.

occlusion [ɔklyzjɔ̃] *nf*: ~ **intestinale** obstruction of the bowel.

occulte [ɔkylt(ə)] *adj* occult, supernatural.

occulter [ɔkylte] *vt* (*fig*) to overshadow.

occupant, e [ɔkypɑ̃, -ɑ̃t] *adj* occupying ♦ *nm/f* (*d'un appartement*) occupier, occupant; (*d'un véhicule*) occupant ♦ *nm* (*MIL*) occupying forces *pl*; (*POL: d'usine etc*) occupier.

occupation [ɔkypasjɔ̃] *nf* occupation; **l'O~** the Occupation (of France).

occupationnel, le [ɔkypasjɔnɛl] *adj*: **thérapie ~le** occupational therapy.

occupé, e [ɔkype] *adj* (*MIL, POL*) occupied; (*personne: affairé, pris*) busy; (*esprit: absorbé*) occupied; (*place, sièges*) taken; (*toilettes, ligne*) engaged.

occuper [ɔkype] *vt* to occupy; (*poste, fonction*) to hold; (*main-d'œuvre*) to employ; **s'~** (*à qch*) to occupy o.s. *ou* keep o.s. busy (with sth); **s'~ de** (*être responsable de*) to be in charge of; (*se charger de: affaire*) to take charge of, deal with; (*: clients etc*) to attend to; (*s'intéresser à, pratiquer: politique etc*) to be involved in; **ça occupe trop de place** it takes up too much room.

occurrence [ɔkyʀɑ̃s] *nf*: **en l'~** in this case.

OCDE *sigle f* (= *Organisation de coopération et de développement économique*) OECD.

océan [ɔseɑ̃] *nm* ocean; **l'~ Indien** the Indian Ocean.

Océanie [ɔseani] *nf*: **l'~** Oceania, South Sea Islands.

océanique [ɔseanik] *adj* oceanic.

océanographe [ɔseanɔgʀaf] *nm/f* oceanographer.

océanographie [ɔseanɔgʀafi] *nf* oceanography.

océanologie [ɔseanɔlɔʒi] *nf* oceanology.

ocelot [ɔslo] *nm* (*ZOOL*) ocelot; (*fourrure*) ocelot fur.

ocre [ɔkʀ(ə)] *adj inv* ochre.

octane [ɔktan] *nm* octane.

octante [ɔktɑ̃t] *num* (*Belgique, Suisse*) eighty.

octave [ɔktav] *nf* octave.

octet [ɔktɛ] *nm* byte.

octobre [ɔktɔbʀ(ə)] *nm* October; *voir aussi* **juillet**.

octogénaire [ɔktɔʒenɛʀ] *adj, nm/f* octogenarian.

octogonal, e, aux [ɔktɔgɔnal, -o] *adj* octagonal.

octogone [ɔktɔgɔn] *nm* octagon.

octroi [ɔktʀwa] *nm* granting.

octroyer [ɔktʀwaje] *vt*: ~ **qch à qn** to grant

sth to sb, grant sb sth.

oculaire [ɔkylɛʀ] *adj* ocular, eye *cpd* ♦ *nm* (*de microscope*) eyepiece.

oculiste [ɔkylist(ə)] *nm/f* eye specialist, oculist.

ode [ɔd] *nf* ode.

odeur [ɔdœʀ] *nf* smell.

odieusement [ɔdjøzmɑ̃] *adv* odiously.

odieux, euse [ɔdjø, -øz] *adj* odious, hateful.

odontologie [ɔdɔ̃tɔlɔʒi] *nf* odontology.

odorant, e [ɔdɔʀɑ̃, -ɑ̃t] *adj* sweet-smelling, fragrant.

odorat [ɔdɔʀa] *nm* (sense of) smell; **avoir l'~ fin** to have a keen sense of smell.

odoriférant, e [ɔdɔʀifeʀɑ̃, -ɑ̃t] *adj* sweet-smelling, fragrant.

odyssée [ɔdise] *nf* odyssey.

OEA *sigle f* (= *Organisation des États américains*) OAS.

œcuménique [ekymenik] *adj* ecumenical.

œdème [edɛm] *nm* oedema (*BRIT*), edema (*US*).

œil [œj], *pl* **yeux** [jø] *nm* eye; **avoir un ~ poché** *ou* **au beurre noir** to have a black eye; **à l'~** (*fam*) for free; **à l'~ nu** with the naked eye; **tenir qn à l'~** to keep an eye *ou* a watch on sb; **avoir l'~ à** to keep an eye on; **faire de l'~ à qn** to make eyes at sb; **voir qch d'un bon/mauvais ~** to view sth in a favourable/an unfavourable light; **à l'~ vif** with a lively expression; **à mes/ses yeux** in my/his eyes; **de ses propres yeux** with his own eyes; **fermer les yeux (sur)** (*fig*) to turn a blind eye (to); **les yeux fermés** (*aussi fig*) with one's eyes shut; **fermer l'~** to get a moment's sleep; **~ pour ~, dent pour dent** an eye for an eye, a tooth for a tooth; **pour les beaux yeux de qn** (*fig*) for love of sb; **~ de verre** glass eye.

œil-de-bœuf, *pl* **œils-de-bœuf** [œjdəbœf] *nm* bull's-eye (window).

œillade [œjad] *nf*: **lancer une ~ à qn** to wink at sb, give sb a wink; **faire des ~s à** to make eyes at.

œillères [œjɛʀ] *nfpl* blinkers (*BRIT*), blinders (*US*); **avoir des ~** (*fig*) to be blinkered, wear blinders.

œillet [œjɛ] *nm* (*BOT*) carnation; (*trou*) eyelet.

œnologue [enɔlɔg] *nm/f* wine expert.

œsophage [ezɔfaʒ] *nm* oesophagus (*BRIT*), esophagus (*US*).

œstrogène [ɛstʀɔʒɛn] *adj* oestrogen (*BRIT*), estrogen (*US*).

œuf [œf, *pl* ø] *nm* egg; **étouffer dans l'~** to nip in the bud; **~ à la coque/dur/mollet** boiled/hard-boiled/soft-boiled egg; **~ au plat/poché** fried/poached egg; **~s brouillés** scrambled eggs; **~ de Pâques** Easter egg; **~ à repriser** darning egg.

œuvre [œvʀ(ə)] *nf* (*tâche*) task, undertaking; (*ouvrage achevé, livre, tableau etc*) work; (*ensemble de la production artistique*) works *pl*;

(*organisation charitable*) charity ♦ *nm* (*d'un artiste*) works *pl*; (*CONSTR*): **le gros** ~ the shell; **~s** *nfpl* (*actes*) deeds, works; **être/se mettre à l'**~ to be at/get (down) to work; **mettre en** ~ (*moyens*) to make use of; (*plan, loi, projet etc*) to implement; ~ **d'art** work of art; **bonnes ~s** good works *ou* deeds; **~s de bienfaisance** charitable works.

OFCE *sigle m* (= *Observatoire français des conjonctures économiques*) *economic research institute*.

offensant, e [ɔfɑ̃sɑ̃, -ɑ̃t] *adj* offensive, insulting.

offense [ɔfɑ̃s] *nf* (*affront*) insult; (*REL*: *péché*) transgression, trespass.

offenser [ɔfɑ̃se] *vt* to offend, hurt; (*principes, Dieu*) to offend against; **s'**~ **de** to take offence (*BRIT*) *ou* offense (*US*) at.

offensif, ive [ɔfɑ̃sif, -iv] *adj* (*armes, guerre*) offensive ♦ *nf* offensive; (*fig: du froid, de l'hiver*) onslaught; **passer à l'offensive** to go into the attack *ou* offensive.

offert, e [ɔfɛʁ, -ɛʁt(ə)] *pp de* **offrir**.

offertoire [ɔfɛʁtwaʁ] *nm* offertory.

office [ɔfis] *nm* (*charge*) office; (*agence*) bureau, agency; (*REL*) service ♦ *nm ou nf* (*pièce*) pantry; **faire** ~ **de** to act as; to do duty as; **d'**~ *adv* automatically; **bons ~s** (*POL*) good offices; ~ **du tourisme** tourist bureau.

officialiser [ɔfisjalize] *vt* to make official.

officiel, le [ɔfisjɛl] *adj, nm/f* official.

officiellement [ɔfisjɛlmɑ̃] *adv* officially.

officier [ɔfisje] *nm* officer ♦ *vi* (*REL*) to officiate; ~ **de l'état-civil** registrar; ~ **ministériel** member of the legal profession; ~ **de police** ≈ police officer.

officieusement [ɔfisjøzmɑ̃] *adv* unofficially.

officieux, euse [ɔfisjø, -øz] *adj* unofficial.

officinal, e, aux [ɔfisinal, -o] *adj*: **plantes ~es** medicinal plants.

officine [ɔfisin] *nf* (*de pharmacie*) dispensary; (*ADMIN*: *pharmacie*) pharmacy; (*gén péj*: *bureau*) agency, office.

offrais [ɔfʁɛ] *etc vb voir* **offrir**.

offrande [ɔfʁɑ̃d] *nf* offering.

offrant [ɔfʁɑ̃] *nm*: **au plus** ~ to the highest bidder.

offre [ɔfʁ(ə)] *vb voir* **offrir** ♦ *nf* offer; (*aux enchères*) bid; (*ADMIN*: *soumission*) tender; (*ÉCON*): ~ **d'emploi** job advertised; **"~s d'emploi"** "situations vacant"; ~ **publique d'achat (OPA)** takeover bid; **~s de service** offer of service.

offrir [ɔfʁiʁ] *vt*: ~ **(à qn)** to offer (to sb); (*faire cadeau*) to give to (sb); **s'**~ *vi* (*se présenter: occasion, paysage*) to present itself ♦ *vt* (*se payer: vacances, voiture*) to treat o.s. to; ~ **(à qn) de faire qch** to offer to do sth (for sb); ~ **à boire à qn** to offer sb a drink; **s'**~ **à faire qch** to offer *ou* volunteer to do sth; **s'**~ **comme guide/en otage** to offer one's services as (a) guide/offer o.s. as (a) hostage;

s'~ **aux regards** (*suj: personne*) to expose o.s. to the public gaze.

offset [ɔfsɛt] *nm* offset (printing).

offusquer [ɔfyske] *vt* to offend; **s'**~ **de** to take offence (*BRIT*) *ou* offense (*US*) at, be offended by.

ogive [ɔʒiv] *nf* (*ARCHIT*) diagonal rib; (*d'obus, de missile*) nose cone; **voûte en** ~ rib vault; **arc en** ~ lancet arch; ~ **nucléaire** nuclear warhead.

ogre [ɔgʁ(ə)] *nm* ogre.

oh [o] *excl* oh!; ~ **la la!** oh (dear)!; **pousser des** ~! **et des ah!** to gasp with admiration.

oie [wa] *nf* (*ZOOL*) goose (*pl* geese); ~ **blanche** (*fig*) young innocent.

oignon [ɔɲɔ̃] *nm* (*CULIN*) onion; (*de tulipe etc*: *bulbe*) bulb; (*MÉD*) bunion; **ce ne sont pas tes ~s** (*fam*) that's none of your business.

oindre [wɛ̃dʁ(ə)] *vt* to anoint.

oiseau, x [wazo] *nm* bird; ~ **de proie** bird of prey.

oiseau-mouche, *pl* **oiseaux-mouches** [wazomuʃ] *nm* hummingbird.

oiseleur [wazlœʁ] *nm* bird-catcher.

oiselier, ière [wazəlje, -jɛʁ] *nm/f* bird-seller.

oisellerie [wazɛlʁi] *nf* bird shop.

oiseux, euse [wazø, -øz] *adj* pointless, idle; (*sans valeur, importance*) trivial.

oisif, ive [wazif, -iv] *adj* idle ♦ *nm/f* (*péj*) man/lady of leisure.

oisillon [wazijɔ̃] *nm* little *ou* baby bird.

oisiveté [wazivte] *nf* idleness.

OIT *sigle f* (= *Organisation internationale du travail*) ILO.

OK [ɔke] *excl* OK!, all right!

OL *sigle fpl* (= *ondes longues*) LW.

oléagineux, euse [ɔleaʒinø, -øz] *adj* oleaginous, oil-producing.

oléiculture [ɔleikyltyʁ] *nm* olive growing.

oléoduc [ɔleɔdyk] *nm* (oil) pipeline.

olfactif, ive [ɔlfaktif, -iv] *adj* olfactory.

olibrius [ɔlibʁijys] *nm* oddball.

oligarchie [ɔligaʁʃi] *nf* oligarchy.

oligo-élément [ɔligɔelemɑ̃] *nm* trace element.

oligopole [ɔligɔpɔl] *nm* oligopoly.

olivâtre [ɔlivɑtʁ(ə)] *adj* olive-greenish; (*teint*) sallow.

olive [ɔliv] *nf* (*BOT*) olive ♦ *adj inv* olive(-green).

oliveraie [ɔlivʁɛ] *nf* olive grove.

olivier [ɔlivje] *nm* olive (tree); (*bois*) olive (wood).

olographe [ɔlɔgʁaf] *adj*: **testament** ~ *will* written, dated and signed by the testator.

OLP *sigle f* (= *Organisation de libération de la Palestine*) PLO.

olympiade [ɔlɛ̃pjad] *nf* (*période*) Olympiad; **les ~s** (*jeux*) the Olympiad *sg*.

olympien, ne [ɔlɛ̃pjɛ̃, -ɛn] *adj* Olympian, Olympian aloofness.

olympique [ɔlɛ̃pik] *adj* Olympic.

OM *sigle fpl* (= *ondes moyennes*) MW.

Oman [ɔman] *nm*: l'~, **le sultanat d'~** (the Sultanate of) Oman.

ombilical, e, aux [ɔ̃bilikal, -o] *adj* umbilical.

ombrage [ɔ̃braʒ] *nm* (*ombre*) (leafy) shade; (*fig*): **prendre ~ de** to take umbrage at; **faire** *ou* **porter ~ à qn** to offend sb.

ombragé, e [ɔ̃braʒe] *adj* shaded, shady.

ombrageux, euse [ɔ̃braʒø, -øz] *adj* (*cheval*) skittish, nervous; (*personne*) touchy, easily offended.

ombre [ɔ̃br(ə)] *nf* (*espace non ensoleillé*) shade; (*ombre portée, tache*) shadow; **à l'~** in the shade; (*fam: en prison*) behind bars; **à l'~ de** in the shade of; (*tout près de, fig*) in the shadow of; **tu me fais de l'~** you're in my light; **ça nous donne de l'~** it gives us (some) shade; **il n'y a pas l'~ d'un doute** there's not the shadow of a doubt; **dans l'~** in the shade; **vivre dans l'~** (*fig*) to live in obscurity; **laisser dans l'~** (*fig*) to leave in the dark; **~ à paupières** eyeshadow; **~ portée** shadow; **~s chinoises** (*spectacle*) shadow show *sg*.

ombrelle [ɔ̃brɛl] *nf* parasol, sunshade.

ombrer [ɔ̃bre] *vt* to shade.

omelette [ɔmlɛt] *nf* omelette; **~ baveuse** runny omelette; **~ au fromage/au jambon** cheese/ham omelette; **~ aux herbes** omelette with herbs; **~ norvégienne** baked Alaska.

omettre [ɔmɛtr(ə)] *vt* to omit, leave out; **~ de faire** to fail *ou* omit to do.

omis, e [ɔmi, -iz] *pp de* **omettre**.

omission [ɔmisjɔ̃] *nf* omission.

omnibus [ɔmnibys] *nm* slow *ou* stopping train.

omnipotent, e [ɔmnipɔtɑ̃, -ɑ̃t] *adj* omnipotent.

omnipraticien, ne [ɔmnipratisjɛ̃, -ɛn] *nm/f* (*MÉD*) general practitioner.

omniprésent, e [ɔmniprezɑ̃, -ɑ̃t] *adj* omnipresent.

omniscient, e [ɔmnisjɑ̃, -ɑ̃t] *adj* omniscient.

omnisports [ɔmnispɔr] *adj inv* (*club*) general sports *cpd*; (*salle*) multi-purpose *cpd*; (*terrain*) all-purpose *cpd*.

omnium [ɔmnjɔm] *nm* (*COMM*) corporation; (*CYCLISME*) omnium, tache; (*COURSES*) open handicap.

omnivore [ɔmnivɔr] *adj* omnivorous.

omoplate [ɔmɔplat] *nf* shoulder blade.

OMS *sigle f* (= *Organisation mondiale de la santé*) WHO.

══════════════ *MOT-CLÉ*

on [ɔ̃] *pron* **1** (*indéterminé*) you, one; **~ peut le faire ainsi** you *ou* one can do it like this, it can be done like this; **~ dit que ...** they say that ..., it is said that ...

2 (*quelqu'un*): **~ les a attaqués** they were attacked; **~ vous demande au téléphone** there's a phone call for you, you're wanted on the phone; **~ frappe à la porte** someone's knocking at the door

3 (*nous*) we; **~ va y aller demain** we're going tomorrow

4 (*les gens*) they; **autrefois, ~ croyait ...** they used to believe ...

5: **~ ne peut plus** *adv*: **~ ne peut plus stupide** as stupid as can be.

once [ɔ̃s] *nf*: **une ~ de** an ounce of.

oncle [ɔ̃kl(ə)] *nm* uncle.

onction [ɔ̃ksjɔ̃] *nf voir* **extrême-onction**.

onctueux, euse [ɔ̃ktɥø, -øz] *adj* creamy, smooth; (*fig*) smooth, unctuous.

onde [ɔ̃d] *nf* (*PHYSIQUE*) wave; **sur l'~** on the waters; **sur les ~s** on the radio; **mettre en ~s** to produce for the radio; **~ de choc** shock wave; **~s courtes (OC)** short wave *sg*; **petites ~s (PO)**, **~s moyennes (OM)** medium wave *sg*; **grandes ~s (GO)**, **~s longues (OL)** long wave *sg*; **~s sonores** sound waves.

ondée [ɔ̃de] *nf* shower.

on-dit [ɔ̃di] *nm inv* rumour.

ondoyer [ɔ̃dwaje] *vi* to ripple, wave ♦ *vt* (*REL*) to baptize (*in an emergency*).

ondulant, e [ɔ̃dylɑ̃, -ɑ̃t] *adj* (*démarche*) swaying; (*ligne*) undulating.

ondulation [ɔ̃dylasjɔ̃] *nf* undulation; wave.

ondulé, e [ɔ̃dyle] *adj* undulating; wavy.

onduler [ɔ̃dyle] *vi* to undulate; (*cheveux*) to wave.

onéreux, euse [ɔnerø, -øz] *adj* costly; **à titre ~** in return for payment.

ONF *sigle m* (= *Office national des forêts*) ≈ Forestry Commission (*BRIT*), ≈ National Forest Service (*US*).

ongle [ɔ̃gl(ə)] *nm* (*ANAT*) nail; **manger** *ou* **ronger ses ~s** to bite one's nails; **se faire les ~s** to do one's nails.

onglet [ɔ̃glɛ] *nm* (*rainure*) (thumbnail) groove; (*bande de papier*) tab.

onguent [ɔ̃gɑ̃] *nm* ointment.

onirique [ɔnirik] *adj* dreamlike, dream *cpd*.

onirisme [ɔnirism(ə)] *nm* dreams *pl*.

onomatopée [ɔnɔmatɔpe] *nf* onomatopoeia.

ont [ɔ̃] *vb voir* **avoir**.

ontarien, ne [ɔ̃tarjɛ̃, -ɛn] *adj* Ontarian.

ONU [ɔny] *sigle f* (= *Organisation des Nations unies*) UN(O).

onusien, ne [ɔnyzjɛ̃, -ɛn] *adj* of the UN(O), of the United Nations (Organization).

onyx [ɔniks] *nm* onyx.

onze [ɔ̃z] *num* eleven.

onzième [ɔ̃zjɛm] *num* eleventh.

op [ɔp] *nf* (= *opération*): **salle d'~** (operating) theatre.

OPA *sigle f* = **offre publique d'achat**.

opacité [ɔpasite] *nf* opaqueness.

opale [ɔpal] *nf* opal.

opalescent, e [ɔpalesɑ̃, -ɑ̃t] *adj* opalescent.

opalin, e [ɔpalɛ̃, -in] *adj*, *nf* opaline.

opaque [ɔpak] *adj* (*vitre, verre*) opaque; (*brouillard, nuit*) impenetrable.

OPE *sigle f* (= *offre publique d'échange*) take-

over bid where bidder offers shares in his company in exchange for shares in target company.

OPEP [ɔpɛp] *sigle f* (= *Organisation des pays exportateurs de pétrole*) OPEC.

opéra [ɔpeʀa] *nm* opera; (*édifice*) opera house.

opérable [ɔpeʀabl(ə)] *adj* operable.

opéra-comique, *pl* **opéras-comiques** [ɔpeʀakɔmik] *nm* light opera, opéra comique.

opérant, e [ɔpeʀɑ̃, -ɑ̃t] *adj* (*mesure*) effective.

opérateur, trice [ɔpeʀatœʀ, -tʀis] *nm/f* operator; ~ **(de prise de vues)** cameraman.

opération [ɔpeʀasjɔ̃] *nf* operation; (*COMM*) dealing; **salle/table d'**~ operating theatre/ table; ~ **de sauvetage** rescue operation; ~ **à cœur ouvert** open-heart surgery *no pl*.

opérationnel, le [ɔpeʀasjɔnel] *adj* operational.

opératoire [ɔpeʀatwaʀ] *adj* (*manœuvre, méthode*) operating; (*choc etc*) post-operative.

opéré, e [ɔpeʀe] *nm/f* post-operative patient.

opérer [ɔpeʀe] *vt* (*MÉD*) to operate on; (*faire, exécuter*) to carry out, make ♦ *vi* (*remède: faire effet*) to act, work; (*procéder*) to proceed; (*MÉD*) to operate; **s'**~ *vi* (*avoir lieu*) to occur, take place; **se faire** ~ to have an operation; **se faire** ~ **des amygdales/du cœur** to have one's tonsils out/have a heart operation.

opérette [ɔpeʀet] *nf* operetta, light opera.

ophtalmique [ɔftalmik] *adj* ophthalmic.

ophtalmologie [ɔftalmɔlɔʒi] *nf* ophthalmology.

ophtalmologue [ɔftalmɔlɔg] *nm/f* ophthalmologist.

opiacé, e [ɔpjase] *adj* opiate.

opiner [ɔpine] *vi*: ~ **de la tête** to nod assent ♦ *vt*: ~ **à** to consent to.

opiniâtre [ɔpinjɑtʀ(ə)] *adj* stubborn.

opiniâtreté [ɔpinjɑtʀəte] *nf* stubbornness.

opinion [ɔpinjɔ̃] *nf* opinion; **l'**~ **(publique)** public opinion; **avoir bonne/mauvaise** ~ **de** to have a high/low opinion of.

opiomane [ɔpjɔman] *nm/f* opium addict.

opium [ɔpjɔm] *nm* opium.

OPJ *sigle m* (= *officier de police judiciaire*) ≈ DC (= *Detective Constable*).

opportun, e [ɔpɔʀtœ̃, -yn] *adj* timely, opportune; **en temps** ~ at the appropriate time.

opportunément [ɔpɔʀtynemɑ̃] *adv* opportunely.

opportunisme [ɔpɔʀtynism(ə)] *nm* opportunism.

opportuniste [ɔpɔʀtynist(ə)] *adj*, *nm/f* opportunist.

opportunité [ɔpɔʀtynite] *nf* timeliness, opportuneness.

opposant, e [ɔpozɑ̃, -ɑ̃t] *adj* opposing ♦ *nm/f* opponent.

opposé, e [ɔpoze] *adj* (*direction, rive*) opposite; (*faction*) opposing; (*couleurs*) contrasting; (*opinions, intérêts*) conflicting; (*contre*): ~ **à** opposed to, against ♦ *nm*: **l'**~ the other *ou* opposite side (*ou* direction); (*contraire*) the opposite; **être** ~ **à** to be opposed to; **à l'**~ (*fig*) on the other hand; **à l'**~ **de** on the other *ou* opposite side from; (*fig*) contrary to, unlike.

opposer [ɔpoze] *vt* (*meubles, objets*) to place opposite each other; (*personnes, armées, équipes*) to oppose; (*couleurs, termes, tons*) to contrast; (*comparer: livres, avantages*) to contrast; ~ **qch à** (*comme obstacle, défense*) to set sth against; (*comme objection*) to put sth forward against; (*en contraste*) to set sth opposite; to match sth with; **s'**~ (*sens réciproque*) to conflict; to clash; to face each other; to contrast; **s'**~ **à** (*interdire, empêcher*) to oppose; (*tenir tête à*) to rebel against; **sa religion s'y oppose** it's against his religion; **s'**~ **à ce que qn fasse** to be opposed to sb's doing.

opposition [ɔpozisjɔ̃] *nf* opposition; **par** ~ in contrast; **par** ~ **à** as opposed to, in contrast with; **entrer en** ~ **avec** to come into conflict with; **être en** ~ **avec** (*idées, conduite*) to be at variance with; **faire** ~ **à un chèque** to stop a cheque.

oppressant, e [ɔpʀesɑ̃, -ɑ̃t] *adj* oppressive.

oppresser [ɔpʀese] *vt* to oppress; **se sentir oppressé** to feel breathless.

oppresseur [ɔpʀesœʀ] *nm* oppressor.

oppressif, ive [ɔpʀesif, -iv] *adj* oppressive.

oppression [ɔpʀesjɔ̃] *nf* oppression; (*malaise*) feeling of suffocation.

opprimer [ɔpʀime] *vt* (*asservir: peuple, faibles*) to oppress; (*étouffer: liberté, opinion*) to suppress, stifle; (*suj: chaleur etc*) to suffocate, oppress.

opprobre [ɔpʀɔbʀ(ə)] *nm* disgrace.

opter [ɔpte] *vi*: ~ **pour** to opt for; ~ **entre** to choose between.

opticien, ne [ɔptisjɛ̃, -ɛn] *nm/f* optician.

optimal, e, aux [ɔptimal, -o] *adj* optimal.

optimisation [ɔptimizasjɔ̃] *nf* optimization.

optimiser [ɔptimize] *vt* to optimize.

optimisme [ɔptimism(ə)] *nm* optimism.

optimiste [ɔptimist(ə)] *adj* optimistic ♦ *nm/f* optimist.

optimum [ɔptimɔm] *adj*, *nm* optimum.

option [ɔpsjɔ̃] *nf* option; (*AUTO: supplément*) optional extra; **matière à** ~ (*SCOL*) optional subject (*BRIT*), elective (*US*); **prendre une** ~ **sur** to take (out) an option on; ~ **par défaut** (*INFORM*) default (option).

optionnel, le [ɔpsjɔnel] *adj* optional.

optique [ɔptik] *adj* (*nerf*) optic; (*verres*) optical ♦ *nf* (*PHOTO: lentilles etc*) optics *pl*; (*science, industrie*) optics *sg*; (*fig: manière de voir*) perspective.

opulence [ɔpylɑ̃s] *nf* wealth, opulence.

opulent, e [ɔpylɑ̃, -ɑ̃t] *adj* wealthy, opulent; (*formes, poitrine*) ample, generous.

OPV *sigle f* (= *offre publique de vente*) public offer of sale.

or [ɔʀ] *nm* gold ◊ *conj* now, but; **d'~** (*fig*) golden; **en ~** gold *cpd*; (*occasion*) golden; **un mari/enfant en ~** a treasure; **une affaire en ~** (*achat*) a real bargain; (*commerce*) a gold mine; **plaqué ~** gold-plated; **~ noir** black gold.

oracle [ɔʀɑkl(ə)] *nm* oracle.

orage [ɔʀaʒ] *nm* (thunder)storm.

orageux, euse [ɔʀaʒø, -øz] *adj* stormy.

oraison [ɔʀɛzɔ̃] *nf* orison, prayer; **~ funèbre** funeral oration.

oral, e, aux [ɔʀal, -o] *adj* (*déposition, promesse*) oral, verbal; (*MÉD*): **par voie ~e** by mouth, orally ◊ *nm* (*SCOL*) oral.

oralement [ɔʀalmɑ̃] *adv* orally.

orange [ɔʀɑ̃ʒ] *adj inv, nf* orange; **~ sanguine** blood orange; **~ pressée** freshly-squeezed orange juice.

orangé, e [ɔʀɑ̃ʒe] *adj* orangey, orange-coloured.

orangeade [ɔʀɑ̃ʒad] *nf* orangeade.

oranger [ɔʀɑ̃ʒe] *nm* orange tree.

orangeraie [ɔʀɑ̃ʒʀɛ] *nf* orange grove.

orangerie [ɔʀɑ̃ʒʀi] *nf* orangery.

orang-outan(g) [ɔʀɑ̃utɑ̃] *nm* orangutan.

orateur [ɔʀatœʀ] *nm* speaker; orator.

oratoire [ɔʀatwaʀ] *nm* (*lieu, chapelle*) oratory; (*au bord du chemin*) wayside shrine ◊ *adj* oratorical.

oratorio [ɔʀatɔʀjo] *nm* oratorio.

orbital, e, aux [ɔʀbital, -o] *adj* orbital; **station ~e** space station.

orbite [ɔʀbit] *nf* (*ANAT*) (eye-)socket; (*PHYSIQUE*) orbit; **mettre sur ~** to put into orbit; (*fig*) to launch; **dans l'~ de** (*fig*) within the sphere of influence of.

Orcades [ɔʀkad] *nfpl*: **les ~** the Orkneys, the Orkney Islands.

orchestral, e, aux [ɔʀkɛstʀal, -o] *adj* orchestral.

orchestrateur, trice [ɔʀkɛstʀatœʀ, -tʀis] *nm/f* orchestrator.

orchestration [ɔʀkɛstʀasjɔ̃] *nf* orchestration.

orchestre [ɔʀkɛstʀ(ə)] *nm* orchestra; (*de jazz, danse*) band; (*places*) stalls *pl* (*BRIT*), orchestra (*US*).

orchestrer [ɔʀkɛstʀe] *vt* (*MUS*) to orchestrate; (*fig*) to mount, stage-manage.

orchidée [ɔʀkide] *nf* orchid.

ordinaire [ɔʀdinɛʀ] *adj* ordinary; (*coutumier: maladresse etc*) usual; (*de tous les jours*) everyday; (*modèle, qualité*) standard ◊ *nm* ordinary; (*menus*) everyday fare ◊ *nf* (*essence*) ≈ two-star (petrol) (*BRIT*), ≈ regular (gas) (*US*); **d'~** usually, normally; **à l'~** usually, ordinarily.

ordinairement [ɔʀdinɛʀmɑ̃] *adv* ordinarily, usually.

ordinal, e, aux [ɔʀdinal, -o] *adj* ordinal.

ordinateur [ɔʀdinatœʀ] *nm* computer; **mettre**

sur ~ to computerize, put on computer; **~ de bureau** desktop computer; **~ domestique** home computer; **~ individuel** *ou* **personnel** personal computer; **~ portatif** laptop (computer).

ordination [ɔʀdinasjɔ̃] *nf* ordination.

ordonnance [ɔʀdɔnɑ̃s] *nf* organization; (*groupement, disposition*) layout; (*MÉD*) prescription; (*JUR*) order; (*MIL*) orderly, batman (*BRIT*); **d'~** (*MIL*) regulation *cpd*; **officier d'~** aide-de-camp.

ordonnateur, trice [ɔʀdɔnatœʀ, -tʀis] *nm/f* (*d'une cérémonie, fête*) organizer; **~ des pompes funèbres** funeral director.

ordonné, e [ɔʀdɔne] *adj* tidy, orderly; (*MATH*) ordered ◊ *nf* (*MATH*) Y-axis, ordinate.

ordonner [ɔʀdɔne] *vt* (*agencer*) to organize, arrange; (*: meubles, appartement*) to lay out, arrange; (*donner un ordre*): **~ à qn de faire** to order sb to do; (*MATH*) to (arrange in) order; (*REL*) to ordain; (*MÉD*) to prescribe; (*JUR*) to order; **s'~** (*faits*) to organize themselves.

ordre [ɔʀdʀ(ə)] *nm* (*gén*) order; (*propreté et soin*) orderliness, tidiness; (*association professionnelle, honorifique*) association; (*COMM*): **à l'~ de** payable to; (*nature*): **d'~ pratique** of a practical nature; **~s** *nmpl* (*REL*) holy orders; **avoir de l'~** to be tidy *ou* orderly; **mettre en ~** to tidy (up), put in order; **mettre bon ~ à** to put to rights, sort out; **procéder par ~** to take things one at a time; **être aux ~s de qn/sous les ~s de qn** to be at sb's disposal/under sb's command; **rappeler qn à l'~** to call sb to order; **jusqu'à nouvel ~** until further notice; **dans le même ~ d'idées** in this connection; **par ~ d'entrée en scène** in order of appearance; **un ~ de grandeur** some idea of the size (*ou* amount); **de premier ~** first-rate; **de grève** strike call; **~ du jour** (*d'une réunion*) agenda; (*MIL*) order of the day; **à l'~ du jour** on the agenda; (*fig*) topical; (*MIL*: citer) in dispatches; **~ de mission** (*MIL*) orders *pl*; **~ public** law and order; **~ de route** marching orders *pl*.

ordure [ɔʀdyʀ] *nf* filth *no pl*; (*propos, écrit*) obscenity, (piece of) filth; **~s** *nfpl* (*balayures, déchets*) rubbish *sg*, refuse *sg*; **~s ménagères** household refuse.

ordurier, ière [ɔʀdyʀje, -jɛʀ] *adj* lewd, filthy.

oreille [ɔʀɛj] *nf* (*ANAT*) ear; (*de marmite, tasse*) handle; (*TECH: d'un écrou*) wing; **avoir de l'~** to have a good ear (for music); **avoir l'~ fine** to have good *ou* sharp ears; **l'~ basse** crestfallen, dejected; **se faire tirer l'~** to take a lot of persuading; **dire qch à l'~ de qn** to have a word in sb's ear (about sth).

oreiller [ɔʀeje] *nm* pillow.

oreillette [ɔʀɛjɛt] *nf* (*ANAT*) auricle.

oreillons [ɔʀɛjɔ̃] *nmpl* mumps *sg*.

ores [ɔʀ]: **d'~ et déjà** *adv* already.

orfèvre [ɔʀfɛvʀ(ə)] *nm* goldsmith; silversmith.

orfèvrerie [ɔʀfɛvʀəʀi] *nf* (*art, métier*) goldsmith's (ou silversmith's) trade; (ouvrage) (silver ou gold) plate.

orfraie [ɔʀfʀɛ] nm white-tailed eagle; **pousser des cris d'~** to yell at the top of one's voice.

organe [ɔʀgan] nm organ; (véhicule, instrument) instrument; (voix) voice; (porte-parole) representative, mouthpiece; **~s de commande** (TECH) controls; **~s de transmission** (TECH) transmission system sg.

organigramme [ɔʀganigʀam] nm (hiérarchique, structurel) organization chart; (des opérations) flow chart.

organique [ɔʀganik] adj organic.

organisateur, trice [ɔʀganizatœʀ, -tʀis] nm/f organizer.

organisation [ɔʀganizasjɔ̃] nf organization; **O~ des Nations unies (ONU)** United Nations (Organization) (UN, UNO); **O~ mondiale de la santé (OMS)** World Health Organization (WHO); **O~ du traité de l'Atlantique Nord (OTAN)** North Atlantic Treaty Organization (NATO).

organisationnel, le [ɔʀganizasjɔnɛl] adj organizational.

organiser [ɔʀganize] vt to organize; (mettre sur pied: service etc) to set up; **s'~** to get organized.

organisme [ɔʀganism(ə)] nm (BIO) organism; (corps humain) body; (ADMIN, POL etc) body, organism.

organiste [ɔʀganist(ə)] nm/f organist.

orgasme [ɔʀgasm(ə)] nm orgasm, climax.

orge [ɔʀʒ(ə)] nf barley.

orgeat [ɔʀʒa] nm: **sirop d'~** barley water.

orgelet [ɔʀʒəlɛ] nm sty(e).

orgie [ɔʀʒi] nf orgy.

orgue [ɔʀg(ə)] nm organ; **~s** nfpl organ sg; **~ de Barbarie** barrel ou street organ.

orgueil [ɔʀgœj] nm pride.

orgueilleux, euse [ɔʀgœjø, -øz] adj proud.

Orient [ɔʀjɑ̃] nm: **l'~** the East, the Orient.

orientable [ɔʀjɑ̃tabl(ə)] adj (phare, lampe etc) adjustable.

oriental, e, aux [ɔʀjɑ̃tal, -o] adj oriental, eastern; (frontière) eastern ♦ nm/f: **O~, e** Oriental.

orientation [ɔʀjɑ̃tasjɔ̃] nf positioning; adjustment; orientation; direction; (d'une maison etc) aspect; (d'un journal) leanings pl; **avoir le sens de l'~** to have a (good) sense of direction; **course d'~** orienteering exercise; **~ professionnelle** careers advice ou guidance; (service) careers advisory service.

orienté, e [ɔʀjɑ̃te] adj (fig: article, journal) slanted; **bien/mal ~** (appartement) well/badly positioned; **~ au sud** facing south, with a southern aspect.

orienter [ɔʀjɑ̃te] vt (situer) to position; (placer, disposer: pièce mobile) to adjust, position; (tourner) to direct, turn; (voyageur, touriste, recherches) to direct; (fig: élève) to orientate; **s'~** (se repérer) to find one's bearings; **s'~ vers** (fig) to turn towards.

orienteur, euse [ɔʀjɑ̃tœʀ, -øz] nm/f (SCOL) careers adviser.

orifice [ɔʀifis] nm opening, orifice.

oriflamme [ɔʀiflam] nf banner, standard.

origan [ɔʀigɑ̃] nm oregano.

originaire [ɔʀiʒinɛʀ] adj original; **être ~ de** (pays, lieu) to be a native of; (provenir de) to originate from; to be native to.

original, e, aux [ɔʀiʒinal, -o] adj original; (bizarre) eccentric ♦ nm/f (fam: excentrique) eccentric; (: fantaisiste) joker ♦ nm (document etc, ART) original; (dactylographie) top copy.

originalité [ɔʀiʒinalite] nf (d'un nouveau modèle) originality no pl; (excentricité, bizarrerie) eccentricity.

origine [ɔʀiʒin] nf origin; (d'un message, appel téléphonique) source; (d'une révolution, réussite) root; **~s** nfpl (d'une personne) origins; **d'~** of origin; (pneus etc) original; (bureau postal) dispatching; **d'~ française** of French origin; **dès l'~** at ou from the outset; **à l'~** originally; **avoir son ~ dans** to have its origins in, originate in.

originel, le [ɔʀiʒinɛl] adj original.

originellement [ɔʀiʒinɛlmɑ̃] adv (à l'origine) originally; (dès l'origine) from the beginning.

oripeaux [ɔʀipo] nmpl rags.

ORL sigle f (= oto-rhino-laryngologie) ENT ♦ sigle m/f (= oto-rhino-laryngologiste) ENT specialist; **être en ~** (malade) to be in the ENT hospital ou department.

orme [ɔʀm(ə)] nm elm.

orné, e [ɔʀne] adj ornate; **~ de** adorned ou decorated with.

ornement [ɔʀnəmɑ̃] nm ornament; (fig) embellishment, adornment; **~s sacerdotaux** vestments.

ornemental, e, aux [ɔʀnəmɑ̃tal, -o] adj ornamental.

ornementer [ɔʀnəmɑ̃te] vt to ornament.

orner [ɔʀne] vt to decorate, adorn; **~ qch de** to decorate sth with.

ornière [ɔʀnjɛʀ] nf rut; (fig): **sortir de l'~** (routine) to get out of the rut; (impasse) to get out of a spot.

ornithologie [ɔʀnitɔlɔʒi] nf ornithology.

ornithologue [ɔʀnitɔlɔg] nm/f ornithologist; **~ amateur** birdwatcher.

orphelin, e [ɔʀfəlɛ̃, -in] adj orphan(ed) ♦ nm/f orphan; **~ de père/mère** fatherless/motherless.

orphelinat [ɔʀfəlina] nm orphanage.

ORSEC [ɔʀsɛk] sigle f (= Organisation des secours): **le plan ~** disaster contingency plan.

ORSECRAD [ɔʀsɛkʀad] sigle m = ORSEC en cas d'accident nucléaire.

orteil [ɔʀtɛj] nm toe; **gros ~** big toe.

ORTF sigle m (= Office de radio-diffusion télévision française) (former) French broadcasting corporation.

orthodontiste [ɔʀtɔdɔ̃tist(ə)] nm/f orthodontist.

orthodoxe [ɔʀtɔdɔks(ə)] *adj* orthodox.

orthodoxie [ɔʀtɔdɔksi] *nf* orthodoxy.

orthogénie [ɔʀtɔʒeni] *nf* family planning.

orthographe [ɔʀtɔgʀaf] *nf* spelling.

orthographier [ɔʀtɔgʀafje] *vt* to spell; **mal orthographié** misspelt.

orthopédie [ɔʀtɔpedi] *nf* orthopaedics *sg* (*BRIT*), orthopedics *sg* (*US*).

orthopédique [ɔʀtɔpedik] *adj* orthopaedic (*BRIT*), orthopedic (*US*).

orthopédiste [ɔʀtɔpedist(ə)] *nm/f* orthopaedic (*BRIT*) *ou* orthopedic (*US*) specialist.

orthophonie [ɔʀtɔfɔni] *nf* (*MÉD*) speech therapy; (*LING*) correct pronunciation.

orthophoniste [ɔʀtɔfɔnist(ə)] *nm/f* speech therapist.

ortie [ɔʀti] *nf* (stinging) nettle; ~ **blanche** white dead-nettle.

OS *sigle m* = **ouvrier spécialisé.**

os [ɔs, *pl* o] *nm* bone; **sans** ~ (*BOUCHERIE*) off the bone, boned; ~ **à moelle** marrowbone.

oscillation [ɔsilɑsjɔ̃] *nf* oscillation; ~**s** *nfpl* (*fig*) fluctuations.

osciller [ɔsile] *vi* (*pendule*) to swing; (*au vent etc*) to rock; (*TECH*) to oscillate; (*fig*): ~ **entre** to waver *ou* fluctuate between.

osé, e [oze] *adj* daring, bold.

oseille [ozɛj] *nf* sorrel.

oser [oze] *vi*, *vt* to dare; ~ **faire** to dare (to) do.

osier [ozje] *nm* (*BOT*) willow; **d'**~, **en** ~ wicker(work) *cpd*.

Oslo [ɔslo] *n* Oslo.

osmose [ɔsmoz] *nf* osmosis.

ossature [ɔsatyʀ] *nf* (*ANAT*: *squelette*) frame, skeletal structure; (: *du visage*) bone structure; (*fig*) framework.

osselet [ɔslɛ] *nm* (*ANAT*) ossicle; **jouer aux** ~**s** to play jacks.

ossements [ɔsmɑ̃] *nmpl* bones.

osseux, euse [ɔsø, -øz] *adj* bony; (*tissu, maladie, greffe*) bone *cpd*.

ossifier [ɔsifje]: **s'**~ *vi* to ossify.

ossuaire [ɔsɥɛʀ] *nm* ossuary.

Ostende [ɔstɑ̃d] *n* Ostend.

ostensible [ɔstɑ̃sibl(ə)] *adj* conspicuous.

ostensiblement [ɔstɑ̃siblǝmɑ̃] *adv* conspicuously.

ostensoir [ɔstɑ̃swaʀ] *nm* monstrance.

ostentation [ɔstɑ̃tɑsjɔ̃] *nf* ostentation; **faire** ~ **de** to parade, make a display of.

ostentatoir [ɔstɑ̃tatwaʀ] *adj* ostentatious.

ostracisme [ɔstʀasism(ə)] *nm* ostracism; **frapper d'**~ to ostracize.

ostréicole [ɔstʀeikɔl] *adj* oyster *cpd*.

ostréiculture [ɔstʀeikyltyʀ] *nf* oyster-farming.

otage [ɔtaʒ] *nm* hostage; **prendre qn comme** ~ to take sb hostage.

OTAN [ɔtɑ̃] *sigle f* (= *Organisation du traité de l'Atlantique Nord*) NATO.

otarie [ɔtaʀi] *nf* sea-lion.

OTASE [ɔtaz] *sigle f* (= *Organisation du traité de l'Asie du Sud-Est*) SEATO (= *Southeast Asia Treaty Organization*).

ôter [ote] *vt* to remove; (*soustraire*) to take away; ~ **qch à qn** to take sth (away) from sb; ~ **qch de** to remove sth from; **6 ôté de 10 égale 4** 6 from 10 equals *ou* is 4.

otite [ɔtit] *nf* ear infection.

oto-rhino(-laryngologiste) [ɔtɔʀinɔ(-laʀɛ̃gɔlɔʒist(ə))] *nm/f* ear, nose and throat specialist.

ottomane [ɔtɔman] *nf* ottoman.

ou [u] *conj* or; ~ ... ~ either ... or; ~ **bien** or (else).

════════════ *MOT-CLÉ*

où [u] *pron relatif* **1** (*position, situation*) where, that (*souvent omis*); **la chambre** ~ **il était** the room (that) he was in, the room where he was; **la ville** ~ **je l'ai rencontré** the town where I met him; **la pièce d'**~ **il est sorti** the room he came out of; **le village d'**~ **je viens** the village I come from; **les villes par** ~ **il est passé** the towns he went through

2 (*temps, état*) that (*souvent omis*); **le jour** ~ **il est parti** the day (that) he left; **au prix** ~ **c'est** at the price it is

♦ *adv* **1** (*interrogation*) where?; ~ **est-il/va-t-il?** where is he/is he going?; **par** ~**?** which way?; **d'**~ **vient que ...?** how come ...?

2 (*position*) where; **je sais** ~ **il est** I know where he is; ~ **que l'on aille** wherever you go.
└───────────────────────────

OUA *sigle f* (= *Organisation de l'unité africaine*) OAU (= *Organization of African Unity*).

ouais [wɛ] *excl* yeah.

ouate [wat] *nf* cotton wool (*BRIT*), cotton (*US*); (*bourre*) padding, wadding; ~ **(hydrophile)** cotton wool (*BRIT*), (absorbent) cotton (*US*).

ouaté, e [wate] *adj* cotton-wool; (*doublé*) padded; (*fig*: *atmosphère*) cocoon-like; (: *pas, bruit*) muffled.

oubli [ubli] *nm* (*acte*): **l'**~ **de** forgetting; (*étourderie*) forgetfulness *no pl*; (*négligence*) omission, oversight; (*absence de souvenirs*) oblivion; ~ **de soi** self-effacement, self-negation.

oublier [ublije] *vt* (*gén*) to forget; (*ne pas voir: erreurs etc*) to miss; (*ne pas mettre: virgule, nom*) to leave out, forget; (*laisser quelque part: chapeau etc*) to leave behind; **s'**~ to forget o.s.; (*enfant, animal*) to have an accident (*euphemism*); ~ **l'heure** to forget (about) the time.

oubliettes [ublijɛt] *nfpl* dungeon *sg*; **(jeter) aux** ~ (*fig*) (to put) completely out of mind.

oublieux, euse [ublijø, -øz] *adj* forgetful.

oued [wed] *nm* wadi.

ouest [wɛst] *nm* west ♦ *adj inv* west; (*région*) western; **à l'**~ in the west; (to the) west, westwards; **à l'**~ **de** (to the) west of; **vent d'**~ westerly wind.

ouest-allemand, e [wɛstalmɑ̃, -ɑ̃d] *adj* West German.

ouf [uf] *excl* phew!

Ouganda [ugɑ̃da] *nm*: l'~ Uganda.

ougandais, e [ugɑ̃dɛ, -ɛz] *adj* Ugandan.

oui [wi] *adv* yes; **répondre (par)** ~ to answer yes; **mais ~, bien sûr** yes, of course; **je pense que** ~ I think so; **pour un** ~ **ou pour un non** for no apparent reason.

ouï-dire [widiʀ]: **par** ~ *adv* by hearsay.

ouïe [wi] *nf* hearing; **~s** *nfpl* (*de poisson*) gills; (*de violon*) sound-hole *sg.*

ouïr [wiʀ] *vt* to hear; **avoir ouï dire que** to have heard it said that.

ouistiti [wistiti] *nm* marmoset.

ouragan [uʀagɑ̃] *nm* hurricane; (*fig*) storm.

Oural [uʀal] *nm*: l'~ (*fleuve*) the Ural; (*aussi*: **les monts** ~) the Urals, the Ural Mountains.

ouralo-altaïque [uʀaloaltaik] *adj*, *nm* Ural-Altaic.

ourdir [uʀdiʀ] *vt* (*complot*) to hatch.

ourdou [uʀdu] *adj inv* Urdu ♦ *nm* (*LING*) Urdu.

ourlé, e [uʀle] *adj* hemmed; (*fig*) rimmed.

ourler [uʀle] *vt* to hem.

ourlet [uʀlɛ] *nm* hem; (*de l'oreille*) rim; **faire un** ~ **à** to hem.

ours [uʀs] *nm* bear; ~ **brun/blanc** brown/polar bear; ~ **marin** fur seal; ~ **mal léché** uncouth fellow; ~ **(en peluche)** teddy (bear).

ourse [uʀs(ə)] *nf* (*ZOOL*) she-bear; **la Grande/ Petite O**~ the Great/Little Bear, Ursa Major/Minor.

oursin [uʀsɛ̃] *nm* sea urchin.

ourson [uʀsɔ̃] *nm* (bear-)cub.

ouste [ust(ə)] *excl* hop it!

outil [uti] *nm* tool.

outillage [utijaʒ] *nm* set of tools; (*d'atelier*) equipment *no pl.*

outiller [utije] *vt* (*ouvrier, usine*) to equip.

outrage [utʀaʒ] *nm* insult; **faire subir les derniers ~s à** (*femme*) to ravish; ~ **aux bonnes mœurs** (*JUR*) outrage to public decency; ~ **à magistrat** (*JUR*) contempt of court; ~ **à la pudeur** (*JUR*) indecent behaviour *no pl.*

outragé, e [utʀaʒe] *adj* offended; outraged.

outrageant, e [utʀaʒɑ̃, -ɑ̃t] *adj* offensive.

outrager [utʀaʒe] *vt* to offend gravely; (*fig: contrevenir à*) to outrage, insult.

outrageusement [utʀaʒøzmɑ̃] *adv* outrageously.

outrance [utʀɑ̃s] *nf* excessiveness *no pl*, excess; **à** ~ *adv* excessively, to excess.

outrancier, ière [utʀɑ̃sje, -jɛʀ] *adj* extreme.

outre [utʀ(ə)] *nf* goatskin, water skin ♦ *prép* besides ♦ *adv*: **passer** ~ to carry on regardless; **passer** ~ **à** to disregard, take no notice of; **en** ~ besides, moreover; ~ **que** apart from the fact that; ~ **mesure** immoderately; unduly.

outré, e [utʀe] *adj* (*flatterie, éloge*) excessive, exaggerated; (*indigné, scandalisé*) outraged.

outre-Atlantique [utʀatlɑ̃tik] *adv* across the Atlantic.

outrecuidance [utʀəkɥidɑ̃s] *nf* presumptuousness *no pl.*

outre-Manche [utʀəmɑ̃ʃ] *adv* across the Channel.

outremer [utʀəmɛʀ] *adj inv* ultramarine.

outre-mer [utʀəmɛʀ] *adv* overseas; **d'**~ overseas.

outrepasser [utʀəpase] *vt* to go beyond, exceed.

outrer [utʀe] *vt* (*pensée, attitude*) to exaggerate; (*indigner: personne*) to outrage.

outre-Rhin [utʀəʀɛ̃] *adv* across the Rhine, in Germany.

outsider [awtsajdœʀ] *nm* outsider.

ouvert, e [uvɛʀ, -ɛʀt(ə)] *pp de* **ouvrir** ♦ *adj* open; (*robinet, gaz etc*) on; **à bras** ~**s** with open arms.

ouvertement [uvɛʀtəmɑ̃] *adv* openly.

ouverture [uvɛʀtyʀ] *nf* opening; (*MUS*) overture; (*POL*): l'~ the widening of the political spectrum; (*PHOTO*): ~ **(du diaphragme)** aperture; ~**s** *nfpl* (*propositions*) overtures; ~ **d'esprit** open-mindedness; **heures d'**~ (*COMM*) opening hours; **jours d'**~ (*COMM*) days of opening.

ouvrable [uvʀabl(ə)] *adj*: **jour** ~ working day, weekday; **heures** ~**s** business hours.

ouvrage [uvʀaʒ] *nm* (*tâche, de tricot etc, MIL*) work *no pl*; (*objet: COUTURE, ART*) (piece of) work; (*texte, livre*) work; **panier** *ou* **corbeille à** ~ work basket; ~ **d'art** (*GÉNIE CIVIL*) bridge or tunnel etc.

ouvragé, e [uvʀaʒe] *adj* finely embroidered (*ou* worked *ou* carved).

ouvrant, e [uvʀɑ̃, -ɑ̃t] *vb voir* **ouvrir** ♦ *adj*: **toit** ~ sunroof.

ouvré, e [uvʀe] *adj* finely-worked; **jour** ~ working day.

ouvre-boîte(s) [uvʀəbwat] *nm inv* tin (*BRIT*) *ou* can opener.

ouvre-bouteille(s) [uvʀəbutɛj] *nm inv* bottle-opener.

ouvreuse [uvʀøz] *nf* usherette.

ouvrier, ière [uvʀije, -jɛʀ] *nm/f* worker ♦ *nf* (*ZOOL*) worker (bee) ♦ *adj* working-class; (*problèmes, conflit*) industrial, labour *cpd* (*BRIT*), labor *cpd* (*US*); (*revendications*) workers'; **classe ouvrière** working class; ~ **agricole** farmworker; ~ **qualifié** skilled worker; ~ **spécialisé (OS)** semiskilled worker; ~ **d'usine** factory worker.

ouvrir [uvʀiʀ] *vt* (*gén*) to open; (*brèche, passage*) to open up; (*commencer l'exploitation de, créer*) to open (up); (*eau, électricité, chauffage, robinet*) to turn on; (*MÉD: abcès*) to open up, cut open ♦ *vi* to open; to open up; (*CARTES*): **à trèfle** to open in clubs; **s'**~ to open; **s'**~ **à** (*art etc*) to open one's mind to; **s'**~ **à qn (de qch)** to open one's heart to sb (about sth); **s'**~ **les veines** to slash *ou* cut one's wrists; ~ **sur** to open onto; ~ **l'appétit**

à qn to whet sb's appetite; ~ **des horizons** to open up new horizons; ~ **l'esprit** to broaden one's horizons; ~ **une session** (_INFORM_) to log in.

ouvroir [uvʀwaʀ] _nm_ workroom, sewing room.

ovaire [ɔvɛʀ] _nm_ ovary.

ovale [ɔval] _adj_ oval.

ovation [ɔvasjɔ̃] _nf_ ovation.

ovationner [ɔvasjɔne] _vt:_ ~ **qn** to give sb an ovation.

ovin, e [ɔvɛ̃, -in] _adj_ ovine.

OVNI [ɔvni] _sigle m_ (= _objet volant non identifié_) UFO.

ovoïde [ɔvɔid] _adj_ egg-shaped.

ovulation [ɔvylasjɔ̃] _nf_ (_PHYSIOL_) ovulation.

ovule [ɔvyl] _nm_ (_PHYSIOL_) ovum (_pl_ ova); (_MÉD_) pessary.

oxfordien, ne [ɔksfɔʀdjɛ̃, -ɛn] _adj_ Oxonian ♦ _nm/f:_ **O~, ne** Oxonian.

oxydable [ɔksidabl(ə)] _adj_ liable to rust.

oxyde [ɔksid] _nm_ oxide; ~ **de carbone** carbon monoxide.

oxyder [ɔkside]: **s'~** _vi_ to become oxidized.

oxygène [ɔksiʒɛn] _nm_ oxygen; (_fig_): **cure d'~** fresh air cure.

oxygéné, e [ɔksiʒene] _adj:_ **eau ~e** hydrogen peroxide; **cheveux ~s** bleached hair.

ozone [ozɔn] _nm_ ozone; **trou dans la couche d'~** ozone hole.

_P p_

P, p [pe] _nm inv_ P, p ♦ _abr_ (= _Père_) Fr; (= _page_) p; **P comme Pierre** P for Peter.

PA _sigle fpl_ = **petites annonces**.

PAC _sigle f_ (= _Politique agricole commune_) CAP.

pacage [pakaʒ] _nm_ grazing, pasture.

pace-maker [pɛsmekœʀ] _nm_ pacemaker.

pachyderme [paʃidɛʀm(ə)] _nm_ pachyderm; elephant.

pacificateur, trice [pasifikatœʀ, -tʀis] _adj_ pacificatory.

pacification [pasifikasjɔ̃] _nf_ pacification.

pacifier [pasifje] _vt_ to pacify.

pacifique [pasifik] _adj_ (_personne_) peaceable; (_intentions, coexistence_) peaceful ♦ _nm:_ **le P~, l'océan P~** the Pacific (Ocean).

pacifiquement [pasifikmɑ̃] _adv_ peaceably; peacefully.

pacifisme [pasifism(ə)] _nm_ pacifism.

pacifiste [pasifist(ə)] _nm/f_ pacifist.

pack [pak] _nm_ pack.

pacotille [pakɔtij] _nf_ (_péj_) cheap goods _pl_; **de ~** cheap.

pacte [pakt(ə)] _nm_ pact, treaty.

pactiser [paktize] _vi:_ ~ **avec** to come to terms with.

pactole [paktɔl] _nm_ gold mine (_fig_).

paddock [padɔk] _nm_ paddock.

Padoue [padu] _n_ Padua.

PAF _sigle f_ (= _Police de l'air et des frontières_) police authority responsible for civil aviation, border control _etc_ ♦ _sigle m_ (= _paysage audio-visuel français_) French broadcasting scene.

pagaie [pagɛ] _nf_ paddle.

pagaille [pagaj] _nf_ mess, shambles _sg_; **il y en a en ~** there are loads _ou_ heaps of them.

paganisme [paganism(ə)] _nm_ paganism.

pagayer [pageje] _vi_ to paddle.

page [paʒ] _nf_ page; (_passage: d'un roman_) passage ♦ _nm_ page (boy); **mettre en ~s** to make up (into pages); **mise en ~** layout; **à la ~** (_fig_) up-to-date; ~ **blanche** blank page; ~ **de garde** endpaper.

page-écran, _pl_ **pages-écrans** [paʒekʀɑ̃] _nf_ (_INFORM_) screen page.

pagination [paʒinasjɔ̃] _nf_ pagination.

paginer [paʒine] _vt_ to paginate.

pagne [paɲ] _nm_ loincloth.

pagode [pagɔd] _nf_ pagoda.

paie [pɛ] _nf_ = **paye**.

paiement [pɛmɑ̃] _nm_ = **payement**.

païen, ne [pajɛ̃, -ɛn] _adj, nm/f_ pagan, heathen.

paillard, e [pajaʀ, -aʀd(ə)] _adj_ bawdy.

paillasse [pajas] _nf_ (_matelas_) straw mattress; (_d'un évier_) draining board.

paillasson [pajasɔ̃] _nm_ doormat.

paille [paj] _nf_ straw; (_défaut_) flaw; **être sur la ~** to be ruined; ~ **de fer** steel wool.

paillé, e [paje] _adj_ with a straw seat.

pailleté, e [pajte] _adj_ sequined.

paillette [pajɛt] _nf_ speck, flake; **~s** _nfpl_ (_dé-coratives_) sequins, spangles; **lessive en ~s** soapflakes _pl_.

pain [pɛ̃] _nm_ (_substance_) bread; (_unité_) loaf (_pl_ loaves) (of bread); (_morceau_): ~ **de cire** _etc_ bar of wax _etc_; (_CULIN_): ~ **de poisson/légumes** fish/vegetable loaf; **petit ~** (bread) roll; ~ **bis/complet** brown/wholemeal (_BRIT_) _ou_ wholewheat (_US_) bread; ~ **de campagne** farmhouse bread; ~ **d'épice** ≈ gingerbread; ~ **grillé** toast; ~ **de mie** sandwich loaf; ~ **perdu** French toast; ~ **de seigle** rye bread; ~ **de sucre** sugar loaf.

pair, e [pɛʀ] _adj_ (_nombre_) even ♦ _nm_ peer; **aller de ~ (avec)** to go hand in hand _ou_ together (with); **au ~** (_FINANCE_) at par; **valeur au ~** par value; **jeune fille au ~** au pair.

paire [pɛʀ] _nf_ pair; **une ~ de lunettes/tenailles** a pair of glasses/pincers; **faire la ~**: **les deux font la ~** they are two of a kind.

pais [pɛ] _vb voir_ **paître**.

paisible [pezibl(ə)] _adj_ peaceful, quiet.

paisiblement [peziblɑ̃] _adv_ peacefully, quietly.

paître [pɛtʀ(ə)] _vi_ to graze.

paix [pɛ] *nf* peace; *(fig)* peacefulness, peace; **faire la ~ avec** to make peace with; **avoir la ~** to have peace (and quiet).

Pakistan [pakistɑ̃] *nm*: **le ~** Pakistan.

pakistanais, e [pakistanɛ, -ɛz] *adj* Pakistani.

PAL *sigle m* (= *Phase Alternation Line*) PAL.

palabrer [palabʀe] *vi* to argue endlessly.

palabres [palabʀ(ə)] *nfpl ou mpl* endless discussions.

palace [palas] *nm* luxury hotel.

palais [palɛ] *nm* palace; (*ANAT*) palate; **le P~ Bourbon** the seat of the French National Assembly; **le P~ de l'Élysée** the Élysée Palace; **~ des expositions** exhibition centre; **le P~ de Justice** the Law Courts *pl*.

palan [palɑ̃] *nm* hoist.

Palatin [palatɛ̃]: **le (mont) ~** the Palatine (Hill).

pale [pal] *nf* (*d'hélice, de rame*) blade; *(de roue)* paddle.

pâle [pɑl] *adj* pale; *(fig)*: **une ~ imitation** a pale imitation; **bleu ~** pale blue; **~ de colère** white *ou* pale with anger.

palefrenier [palfʀənje] *nm* groom (*for horses*).

paléontologie [paleɔ̃tɔlɔʒi] *nf* paleontology.

paléontologiste [paleɔ̃tɔlɔʒist(ə)], **paléontologue** [paleɔ̃tɔlɔg] *nm/f* paleontologist.

Palerme [palɛʀm] *n* Palermo.

Palestine [palestin] *nf*: **la ~** Palestine.

palestinien, ne [palestinjɛ̃, -ɛn] *adj* Palestinian ♦ *nm/f*: **P~, ne** Palestinian.

palet [palɛ] *nm* disc; (*HOCKEY*) puck.

paletot [palto] *nm* (short) coat.

palette [palɛt] *nf* palette; *(produits)* range.

palétuvier [paletyvje] *nm* mangrove.

pâleur [pɑlœʀ] *nf* paleness.

palier [palje] *nm* (*d'escalier*) landing; *(fig)* level, plateau; (: *phase stable*) levelling (*BRIT*) *ou* leveling (*US*) off, new level; (*TECH*) bearing; **nos voisins de ~** our neighbo(u)rs across the landing (*BRIT*) *ou* the hall (*US*); **en ~** *adv* level; **par ~s** in stages.

palière [paljɛʀ] *adj f* landing *cpd*.

pâlir [pɑliʀ] *vi* to turn *ou* go pale; *(couleur)* to fade; **faire ~ qn** *(de jalousie)* to make sb green (with envy).

palissade [palisad] *nf* fence.

palissandre [palisɑ̃dʀ(ə)] *nm* rosewood.

palliatif [paljatif] *nm* palliative; *(expédient)* stopgap measure.

pallier [palje] *vt*, **~ à** *vt* to offset, make up for.

palmarès [palmaʀɛs] *nm* record (of achievements); *(SCOL)* prize list; *(SPORT)* list of winners.

palme [palm(ə)] *nf* (*BOT*) palm leaf (*pl* leaves); *(symbole)* palm; *(de plongeur)* flipper; **~s (académiques)** *decoration for services to education*.

palmé, e [palme] *adj (pattes)* webbed.

palmeraie [palməʀɛ] *nf* palm grove.

palmier [palmje] *nm* palm tree.

palmipède [palmipɛd] *nm* palmiped, web-footed bird.

palois, e [palwa, -waz] *adj* of *ou* from Pau ♦ *nm/f*: **P~, e** inhabitant *ou* native of Pau.

palombe [palɔ̃b] *nf* woodpigeon, ringdove.

pâlot, te [palo, -ɔt] *adj* pale, peaky.

palourde [paluʀd(ə)] *nf* clam.

palpable [palpabl(ə)] *adj* tangible, palpable.

palper [palpe] *vt* to feel, finger.

palpitant, e [palpitɑ̃, -ɑ̃t] *adj* thrilling, gripping.

palpitation [palpitasjɔ̃] *nf* palpitation.

palpiter [palpite] *vi (cœur, pouls)* to beat; (: *plus fort*) to pound, throb; *(narines, chair)* to quiver.

paludisme [palydism(ə)] *nm* malaria.

palustre [palystʀ(ə)] *adj (coquillage etc)* marsh *cpd*; *(fièvre)* malarial.

pâmer [pame] : **se ~** *vi* to swoon; *(fig)*: **se ~ devant** to go into raptures over.

pâmoison [pamwazɔ̃] *nf*: **tomber en ~** to swoon.

pampa [pɑ̃pa] *nf* pampas *pl*.

pamphlet [pɑ̃flɛ] *nm* lampoon, satirical tract.

pamphlétaire [pɑ̃fletɛʀ] *nm/f* lampoonist.

pamplemousse [pɑ̃pləmus] *nm* grapefruit.

pan [pɑ̃] *nm* section, piece; (*côté: d'un prisme, d'une tour*) side, face ♦ *excl* bang!; **~ de chemise** shirt tail; **~ de mur** section of wall.

panacée [panase] *nf* panacea.

panachage [panaʃaʒ] *nm* blend, mix; (*POL*) *voting for candidates from different parties instead of for the set list of one party*.

panache [panaʃ] *nm* plume; *(fig)* spirit, panache.

panaché, e [panaʃe] *adj*: **œillet ~** variegated carnation; **glace ~e** mixed ice cream; **salade ~e** mixed salad; **bière ~e** shandy.

panais [panɛ] *nm* parsnip.

Panama [panama] *nm*: **le ~** Panama.

panaméen, ne [panameɛ̃, -ɛn] *adj* Panamanian ♦ *nm/f*: **P~, ne** Panamanian.

panaris [panaʀi] *nm* whitlow.

pancarte [pɑ̃kaʀt(ə)] *nf* sign, notice; *(dans un défilé)* placard.

pancréas [pɑ̃kʀeas] *nm* pancreas.

panda [pɑ̃da] *nm* panda.

pané, e [pane] *adj* fried in breadcrumbs.

panégyrique [paneʒiʀik] *nm*: **faire le ~ de qn** to extol sb's merits *ou* virtues.

panier [panje] *nm* basket; (*à diapositives*) magazine; **mettre au ~** to chuck away; **~ de crabes: c'est un ~ de crabes** *(fig)* they're constantly at one another's throats; **~ percé** *(fig)* spendthrift; **~ à provisions** shopping basket; **~ à salade** (*CULIN*) salad shaker; (*POLICE*) paddy wagon, police van.

panier-repas, *pl* **paniers-repas** [panjɛʀ(ə)pa] *nm* packed lunch.

panification [panifikasjɔ̃] *nf* bread-making.

panique [panik] *adj* panicky ♦ *nf* panic.

paniquer [panike] *vi* to panic.

panne [pan] *nf* (*d'un mécanisme, moteur*)

breakdown; **être/tomber en** ~ to have broken down/break down; **être en** ~ **d'essence** *ou* **en** ~ **sèche** to have run out of petrol (*BRIT*) *ou* gas (*US*); **mettre en** ~ (*NAVIG*) to bring to; ~ **d'électricité** *ou* **de courant** power *ou* electrical failure.

panneau, x [pano] *nm* (*écriteau*) sign, notice; (*de boiserie, de tapisserie etc*) panel; **tomber dans le** ~ (*fig*) to walk into the trap; ~ **d'affichage** notice (*BRIT*) *ou* bulletin (*US*) board; ~ **électoral** board for election poster; ~ **indicateur** signpost; ~ **publicitaire** hoarding (*BRIT*), billboard (*US*); ~ **de signalisation** roadsign; ~ **solaire** solar panel.

panneau-réclame, *pl* **panneaux-réclame** [panoʀeklam] *nm* hoarding (*BRIT*), billboard (*US*).

panonceau, x [panɔso] *nm* (*de magasin etc*) sign; (*de médecin etc*) plaque.

panoplie [panɔpli] *nf* (*jouet*) outfit; (*d'armes*) display; (*fig*) array.

panorama [panɔʀama] *nm* (*vue*) all-round view, panorama; (*peinture*) panorama; (*fig: étude complète*) complete overview.

panoramique [panɔʀamik] *adj* panoramic; (*carrosserie*) with panoramic windows ♦ *nm* (*CINÉ, TV*) panoramic shot.

panse [pɑ̃s] *nf* paunch.

pansement [pɑ̃smɑ̃] *nm* dressing, bandage; ~ **adhésif** sticking plaster (*BRIT*), bandaid ® (*US*).

panser [pɑ̃se] *vt* (*plaie*) to dress, bandage; (*bras*) to put a dressing on, bandage; (*cheval*) to groom.

pantalon [pɑ̃talɔ̃] *nm* (*aussi:* ~**s, paire de** ~**s**) trousers *pl* (*BRIT*), pants *pl* (*US*), pair of trousers *ou* pants; ~ **de ski** ski pants *pl*.

pantalonnade [pɑ̃talɔnad] *nf* slapstick (comedy).

pantelant, e [pɑ̃tlɑ̃, -ɑ̃t] *adj* gasping for breath, panting.

panthère [pɑ̃tɛʀ] *nf* panther.

pantin [pɑ̃tɛ̃] *nm* (*jouet*) jumping jack; (*péj: personne*) puppet.

pantois [pɑ̃twa] *adj m*: **rester** ~ to be flabbergasted.

pantomime [pɑ̃tɔmim] *nf* mime; (*pièce*) mime show; (*péj*) fuss, carry-on.

pantouflard, e [pɑ̃tuflaʀ, -aʀd(ə)] *adj* (*péj*) stay-at-home.

pantoufle [pɑ̃tufl(ə)] *nf* slipper.

panure [panyʀ] *nf* breadcrumbs *pl*.

PAO *sigle f* (= *publication assistée par ordinateur*) desk-top publishing.

paon [pɑ̃] *nm* peacock.

papa [papa] *nm* dad(dy).

papauté [papote] *nf* papacy.

papaye [papaj] *nf* pawpaw.

pape [pap] *nm* pope.

paperasse [papʀas] *nf* (*péj*) bumf *no pl*, papers *pl*; forms *pl*.

paperasserie [papʀasʀi] *nf* (*péj*) red tape *no pl*;

paperwork *no pl*.

papeterie [papetʀi] *nf* (*fabrication du papier*) paper-making (industry); (*usine*) paper mill; (*magasin*) stationer's (shop (*BRIT*)); (*articles*) stationery.

papetier, ière [paptje, -jɛʀ] *nm/f* paper-maker; stationer.

papetier-libraire, *pl* **papetiers-libraires** [paptjelibʀɛʀ] *nm* bookseller and stationer.

papier [papje] *nm* paper; (*feuille*) sheet *ou* piece of paper; (*article*) article; (*écrit officiel*) document; ~**s** *nmpl* (*aussi:* ~**s d'identité**) (identity) papers; **sur le** ~ (*théoriquement*) on paper; **noircir du** ~ to write page after page; ~ **couché/glacé** art/glazed paper; ~ **(d')aluminium** aluminium (*BRIT*) *ou* aluminum (*US*) foil, tinfoil; ~ **d'Arménie** incense paper; ~ **bible** India *ou* bible paper; ~ **de brouillon** rough *ou* scrap paper; ~ **bulle** manil(l)a paper; ~ **buvard** blotting paper; ~ **calque** tracing paper; ~ **carbone** carbon paper; ~ **collant** Sellotape ® (*BRIT*), Scotch ® (*US*) *ou* sticky tape; ~ **en continu** continuous stationery; ~ **à dessin** drawing paper; ~ **d'emballage** wrapping paper; ~ **gommé** gummed paper; ~ **hygiénique** toilet paper; ~ **journal** newsprint; (*pour emballer*) newspaper; ~ **à lettres** writing paper, notepaper; ~ **mâché** papier-mâché; ~ **machine** typing paper; ~ **peint** wallpaper; ~ **pelure** India paper; ~ **à pliage accordéon** fanfold paper; ~ **de soie** tissue paper; ~ **thermique** thermal paper; ~ **de tournesol** litmus paper; ~ **de verre** sandpaper.

papier-filtre, *pl* **papiers-filtres** [papjefiltʀ(ə)] *nm* filter paper.

papier-monnaie, *pl* **papiers-monnaies** [papjemɔnɛ] *nm* paper money.

papille [papij] *nf*: ~**s gustatives** taste buds.

papillon [papijɔ̃] *nm* butterfly; (*fam: contravention*) (parking) ticket; (*TECH: écrou*) wing *ou* butterfly nut; ~ **de nuit** moth.

papillonner [papijɔne] *vi* to flit from one thing (*ou* person) to another.

papillote [papijɔt] *nf* (*pour cheveux*) curlpaper; (*de gigot*) (paper) frill.

papilloter [papijɔte] *vi* (*yeux*) to blink; (*paupières*) to flutter; (*lumière*) to flicker.

papotage [papɔtaʒ] *nm* chitchat.

papoter [papɔte] *vi* to chatter.

papou, e [papu] *adj* Papuan.

Papouasie-Nouvelle-Guinée [papwazinuvɛlgine] *nf*: **la** ~ Papua-New-Guinea.

paprika [papʀika] *nm* paprika.

papyrus [papiʀys] *nm* papyrus.

pâque [pɑk] *nf*: **la** ~ Passover; *voir aussi* **Pâques**.

paquebot [pakbo] *nm* liner.

pâquerette [pakʀɛt] *nf* daisy.

Pâques [pɑk] *nm*, *nfpl* Easter; **faire ses** ~ to do one's Easter duties; **l'île de** ~ Easter Island.

paquet [pakɛ] *nm* packet; (*colis*) parcel; (*bal-*

lot) bundle; (*dans négociations*) package (deal); (*fig: tas*): ~ **de** pile *ou* heap of; **~s** *nmpl* (*bagages*) bags; **mettre le** ~ (*fam*) to give one's all; ~ **de mer** big wave.

paquetage [pakta3] *nm* (*MIL*) kit, pack.

paquet-cadeau,   *pl*   **paquets-cadeaux** [pakɛkado] *nm* gift-wrapped parcel.

par [paʀ] *prép* by; **finir** *etc* ~ to end *etc* with; ~ **amour** out of love; **passer** ~ **Lyon/la côte** to go via *ou* through Lyons/along by the coast; ~ **la fenêtre** (*jeter, regarder*) out of the window; **3** ~ **jour/personne** 3 a *ou* per day/head; **deux** ~ **deux** two at a time; (*marcher etc*) in twos; ~ **où?** which way?; ~ **ici** this way; (*dans le coin*) round here; **~-ci, ~-là** here and there.

para [paʀa] *nm* (= *parachutiste*) para.

parabole [paʀabɔl] *nf* (*REL*) parable; (*GÉOM*) parabola.

parabolique [paʀabɔlik] *adj* parabolic; **antenne** ~ satellite dish.

parachever [paʀaʃve] *vt* to perfect.

parachutage [paʀaʃyta3] *nm* (*de soldats, vivres*) parachuting-in; **nous sommes contre le** ~ **d'un candidat parisien dans notre circonscription** (*POL, fig*) we are against a Parisian candidate being landed on us.

parachute [paʀaʃyt] *nm* parachute.

parachuter [paʀaʃyte] *vt* (*soldat etc*) to parachute; (*fig*) to pitchfork; **il a été parachuté à la tête de l'entreprise** he was brought in from outside as head of the company.

parachutisme [paʀaʃytism(ə)] *nm* parachuting.

parachutiste [paʀaʃytist(ə)] *nm/f* parachutist; (*MIL*) paratrooper.

parade [paʀad] *nf* (*spectacle, défilé*) parade; (*ESCRIME, BOXE*) parry; (*ostentation*): **faire** ~ **de** to display, show off; (*défense, riposte*): **trouver la** ~ **à une attaque** to find the answer to an attack; **de** ~ *adj* ceremonial; (*superficiel*) superficial, outward.

parader [paʀade] *vi* to swagger (around), show off.

paradis [paʀadi] *nm* heaven, paradise; **P~ terrestre** (*REL*) Garden of Eden; (*fig*) heaven on earth.

paradisiaque [paʀadizjak] *adj* heavenly, divine.

paradoxal, e, aux [paʀadɔksal, -o] *adj* paradoxical.

paradoxalement [paʀadɔksalmɑ̃] *adv* paradoxically.

paradoxe [paʀadɔks(ə)] *nm* paradox.

parafe [paʀaf] *nm*, **parafer** [paʀafe] *vt* = **paraphe, parapher**.

paraffine [paʀafin] *nf* paraffin; paraffin wax.

paraffiné, e [paʀafine] *adj*: **papier** ~ wax(ed) paper.

parafoudre [paʀafudʀ(ə)] *nm* (*ÉLEC*) lightning conductor.

parages [paʀa3] *nmpl* (*NAVIG*) waters; **dans les**

~ **(de)** in the area *ou* vicinity (of).

paragraphe [paʀagʀaf] *nm* paragraph.

Paraguay [paʀagwɛ] *nm*: **le** ~ Paraguay.

paraguayen, ne [paʀagwajɛ̃, -ɛn] *adj* Paraguayan ♦ *nm/f*: **P~, ne** Paraguayan.

paraître [paʀɛtʀ(ə)] *vb avec attribut* to seem, look, appear ♦ *vi* to appear; (*être visible*) to show; (*PRESSE, ÉDITION*) to be published, come out, appear; (*briller*) to show off; **laisser** ~ **qch** to let (sth) show ♦ *vb impers*: **il paraît que** it seems *ou* appears that; **il me paraît que** it seems to me that; **il paraît absurde de** it seems absurd to; **il ne paraît pas son âge** he doesn't look his age; ~ **en justice** to appear before the court(s); ~ **en scène/en public/à l'écran** to appear on stage/in public/on the screen.

parallèle [paʀalɛl] *adj* parallel; (*police, marché*) unofficial; (*société, énergie*) alternative ♦ *nm* (*comparaison*): **faire un** ~ **entre** to draw a parallel between; (*GÉO*) parallel ♦ *nf* parallel (line); **en** ~ in parallel; **mettre en** ~ (*choses opposées*) to compare; (*choses semblables*) to parallel.

parallèlement [paʀalɛlmɑ̃] *adv* in parallel; (*fig: en même temps*) at the same time.

parallélépipède [paʀalelepipɛd] *nm* parallelepiped.

parallélisme [paʀalelism(ə)] *nm* parallelism; (*AUTO*) wheel alignment.

parallélogramme [paʀalelɔgʀam] *nm* parallelogram.

paralyser [paʀalize] *vt* to paralyze.

paralysie [paʀalizi] *nf* paralysis.

paralytique [paʀalitik] *adj*, *nm/f* paralytic.

paramédical, e, aux [paʀamedikal, -o] *adj* paramedical.

paramètre [paʀamɛtʀ(ə)] *nm* parameter.

paramilitaire [paʀamilitɛʀ] *adj* paramilitary.

paranoïa [paʀanɔja] *nf* paranoia.

paranoïaque [paʀanɔjak] *nm/f* paranoiac.

paranormal, e, aux [paʀanɔʀmal, -o] *adj* paranormal.

parapet [paʀapɛ] *nm* parapet.

paraphe [paʀaf] *nm* (*trait*) flourish; (*signature*) initials *pl*; signature.

parapher [paʀafe] *vt* to initial; to sign.

paraphrase [paʀafʀaz] *nf* paraphrase.

paraphraser [paʀafʀaze] *vt* to paraphrase.

paraplégie [paʀaple3i] *nf* paraplegia.

paraplégique [paʀaple3ik] *adj*, *nm/f* paraplegic.

parapluie [paʀaplɥi] *nm* umbrella; ~ **atomique** *ou* **nucléaire** nuclear umbrella; ~ **pliant** telescopic umbrella.

parapsychique [paʀapsiʃik] *adj* parapsychological.

parapsychologie [paʀapsikɔlɔ3i] *nf* parapsychology.

parapublic, ique [paʀapyblik] *adj* *partly state-controlled*.

parascolaire [paʀaskɔlɛʀ] *adj* extracurricular.

parasitaire [paʀazitɛʀ] *adj* parasitic(al).
parasite [paʀazit] *nm* parasite ♦ *adj* (*BOT*, *BIO*) parasitic(al); ~**s** *nmpl* (*TÉL*) interference *sg*.
parasitisme [paʀazitism(ə)] *nm* parasitism.
parasol [paʀasɔl] *nm* parasol, sunshade.
paratonnerre [paʀatɔnɛʀ] *nm* lightning conductor.
paravent [paʀavɑ̃] *nm* folding screen; (*fig*) screen.
parc [paʀk] *nm* (*public*) park, gardens *pl*; (*de château etc*) grounds *pl*; (*pour le bétail*) pen, enclosure; (*d'enfant*) playpen; (*MIL*: *entrepôt*) depot; (*ensemble d'unités*) stock; (*de voitures etc*) fleet; ~ **d'attractions** amusement park; ~ **automobile** (*d'un pays*) number of cars on the roads; ~ **à huîtres** oyster bed; ~ **à thème** theme park; ~ **national** national park; ~ **naturel** nature reserve; ~ **de stationnement** car park; ~ **zoologique** zoological gardens *pl*.
parcelle [paʀsɛl] *nf* fragment, scrap; (*de terrain*) plot, parcel.
parcelliser [paʀselize] *vt* to divide *ou* split up.
parce que [paʀsk(ə)] *conj* because.
parchemin [paʀʃəmɛ̃] *nm* parchment.
parcheminé, e [paʀʃəmine] *adj* wrinkled; (*papier*) with a parchment finish.
parcimonie [paʀsimɔni] *nf* parsimony, parsimoniousness.
parcimonieux, euse [paʀsimɔnjø, -øz] *adj* parsimonious, miserly.
parc(o)mètre [paʀk(ɔ)mɛtʀ(ə)] *nm* parking meter.
parcotrain [paʀkɔtʀɛ̃] *nm* station car park (*BRIT*) *ou* parking lot (*US*), park-and-ride car park (*BRIT*).
parcourir [paʀkuʀiʀ] *vt* (*trajet, distance*) to cover; (*article, livre*) to skim *ou* glance through; (*lieu*) to go all over, travel up and down; (*suj: frisson, vibration*) to run through; ~ **des yeux** to run one's eye over.
parcours [paʀkuʀ] *vb voir* **parcourir** ♦ *nm* (*trajet*) journey, (*itinéraire*) route; (*SPORT: terrain*) course; (*: tour*) round; run; lap; ~ **du combattant** assault course.
parcouru, e [paʀkuʀy] *pp de* **parcourir**.
par-delà [paʀdəla] *prép* beyond.
par-dessous [paʀdəsu] *prép, adv* under(neath).
pardessus [paʀdəsy] *nm* overcoat.
par-dessus [paʀdəsy] *prép* over (the top of) ♦ *adv* over (the top); ~ **le marché** on top of it all.
par-devant [paʀdəvɑ̃] *prép* in the presence of, before ♦ *adv* at the front; round the front.
pardon [paʀdɔ̃] *nm* forgiveness *no pl* ♦ *excl* (*excuses*) (I'm) sorry; (*pour interpeller etc*) excuse me; (*demander de répéter*) (I beg your) pardon? (*BRIT*), pardon me? (*US*).
pardonnable [paʀdɔnabl(ə)] *adj* forgivable, excusable.
pardonner [paʀdɔne] *vt* to forgive; ~ **qch à qn** to forgive sb for sth; **qui ne pardonne**

pas (*maladie, erreur*) fatal.
paré, e [paʀe] *adj* ready, prepared.
pare-balles [paʀbal] *adj inv* bulletproof.
pare-boue [paʀbu] *nm inv* mudflap.
pare-brise [paʀbʀiz] *nm inv* windscreen (*BRIT*), windshield (*US*).
pare-chocs [paʀʃɔk] *nm inv* bumper (*BRIT*), fender (*US*).
pare-étincelles [paʀetɛ̃sɛl] *nm inv* fireguard.
pare-feu [paʀfø] *nm inv* firebreak ♦ *adj inv*: **portes** ~ fire (resistant) doors.
pareil, le [paʀɛj] *adj* (*identique*) the same, alike; (*similaire*) similar; (*tel*): **un courage/ livre** ~ such courage/a book, courage/a book like this; **de** ~**s livres** such books ♦ *adv*: **habillés** ~ dressed the same (way), dressed alike; **faire** ~ to do the same (thing); **j'en veux un** ~ I'd like one just like it; **rien de** ~ no (*ou* any) such thing, nothing (*ou* anything) like it; **ses** ~**s** one's fellow men; one's peers; **ne pas avoir son (sa)** ~**(le)** to be second to none; ~ **à** the same as; similar to; **sans** ~ unparalleled, unequalled; **c'est du** ~ **au même** it comes to the same thing, it's six (of one) and half-a-dozen (of the other); **en** ~ **cas** in such a case; **rendre la** ~**le à qn** to pay sb back in his own coin.
pareillement [paʀɛjmɑ̃] *adv* the same, alike; in such a way; (*également*) likewise.
parement [paʀmɑ̃] *nm* (*CONSTR, revers d'un col, d'une manche*) facing; (*REL*): ~ **d'autel** antependium.
parent, e [paʀɑ̃, -ɑ̃t] *nm/f*: **un/une** ~**/e** a relative *ou* relation ♦ *adj*: **être** ~ **de** to be related to; ~**s** *nmpl* (*père et mère*) parents; (*famille, proches*) relatives, relations; ~ **unique** lone parent; ~**s par alliance** relatives *ou* relations by marriage; ~**s en ligne directe** blood relations.
parental, e, aux [paʀɑ̃tal, -o] *adj* parental.
parenté [paʀɑ̃te] *nf* (*lien*) relationship; (*personnes*) relatives *pl*, relations *pl*.
parenthèse [paʀɑ̃tɛz] *nf* (*ponctuation*) bracket, parenthesis; (*MATH*) bracket; (*digression*) parenthesis, digression; **ouvrir/fermer la** ~ to open/close the brackets; **entre** ~**s** in brackets; (*fig*) incidentally.
parer [paʀe] *vt* to adorn; (*CULIN*) to dress, trim; (*éviter*) to ward off; ~ **à** (*danger*) to ward off; (*inconvénient*) to deal with; **se** ~ **de** (*fig: qualité, titre*) to assume; ~ **à toute éventualité** to be ready for every eventuality; ~ **au plus pressé** to attend to what's most urgent.
pare-soleil [paʀsɔlɛj] *nm inv* sun visor.
paresse [paʀɛs] *nf* laziness.
paresser [paʀese] *vi* to laze around.
paresseusement [paʀɛsøzmɑ̃] *adv* lazily; sluggishly.
paresseux, euse [paʀɛsø, -øz] *adj* lazy; (*fig*) slow, sluggish ♦ *nm* (*ZOOL*) sloth.
parfaire [paʀfɛʀ] *vt* to perfect, complete.

parfait, e [parfɛ, -ɛt] *pp de* **parfaire** ♦ *adj* perfect ♦ *nm* (*LING*) perfect (tense); (*CULIN*) parfait ♦ *excl* fine, excellent.

parfaitement [parfɛtmɑ̃] *adv* perfectly ♦ *excl* (*most*) certainly.

parfaites [parfɛt], **parfasse** [parfas], **parferai** [parfre] *etc vb voir* **parfaire**.

parfois [parfwa] *adv* sometimes.

parfum [parfœ̃] *nm* (*produit*) perfume, scent; (*odeur: de fleur*) scent, fragrance; (*: de tabac, vin*) aroma; (*goût: de glace, milk-shake*) flavour (*BRIT*), flavor (*US*).

parfumé, e [parfyme] *adj* (*fleur, fruit*) fragrant; (*papier à lettres etc*) scented; (*femme*) wearing perfume *ou* scent, perfumed; (*aromatisé*): ~ **au café** coffee-flavoured (*BRIT*) *ou* -flavored (*US*).

parfumer [parfyme] *vt* (*suj: odeur, bouquet*) to perfume; (*mouchoir*) to put scent *ou* perfume on; (*crème, gâteau*) to flavour (*BRIT*), flavor (*US*); **se** ~ to put on (some) perfume *ou* scent; (*d'habitude*) to use perfume *ou* scent.

parfumerie [parfymri] *nf* (*commerce*) perfumery; (*produits*) perfumes *pl*; (*boutique*) perfume shop (*BRIT*) *ou* store (*US*).

pari [pari] *nm* bet, wager; (*SPORT*) bet; ~ **mutuel urbain (PMU)** *system of betting on horses*.

paria [parja] *nm* outcast.

parier [parje] *vt* to bet; **j'aurais parié que si/ non** I'd have said he (*ou* you *etc*) would/ wouldn't.

parieur [parjœr] *nm* (*turfiste etc*) punter.

Paris [pari] *n* Paris.

parisien, ne [parizjɛ̃, -ɛn] *adj* Parisian; (*GÉO, ADMIN*) Paris *cpd* ♦ *nm/f*: **P~, ne** Parisian.

paritaire [pariter] *adj*: **commission** ~ joint commission.

parité [parite] *nf* parity; ~ **de change** (*ÉCON*) exchange parity.

parjure [parʒyr] *nm* (*faux serment*) false oath, perjury; (*violation de serment*) breach of oath, perjury ♦ *nm/f* perjurer.

parjurer [parʒyre]: **se** ~ *vi* to perjure o.s.

parka [parka] *nf* parka.

parking [parkiŋ] *nm* (*lieu*) car park (*BRIT*), parking lot (*US*).

parlant, e [parlɑ̃, -ɑ̃t] *adj* (*fig*) graphic, vivid; (*: comparaison, preuve*) eloquent; (*CINÉ*) talking ♦ *adv*: **généralement** ~ generally speaking.

parlé, e [parle] *adj*: **langue** ~**e** spoken language.

parlement [parləmɑ̃] *nm* parliament; **le P~ européen** the European Parliament.

parlementaire [parləmɑ̃tɛr] *adj* parliamentary ♦ *nm/f* (*député*) ≈ Member of Parliament (*BRIT*) *ou* Congress (*US*); parliamentarian; (*négociateur*) negotiator, mediator.

parlementarisme [parləmɑ̃tarism(ə)] *nm* parliamentary government.

parlementer [parləmɑ̃te] *vi* (*ennemis*) to negotiate, parley; (*s'entretenir, discuter*) to argue at length, have lengthy talks.

parler [parle] *nm* speech; dialect ♦ *vi* to speak, talk; (*avouer*) to talk; ~ (**à qn**) **de** to talk *ou* speak (to sb) about; ~ **pour qn** (*intercéder*) to speak for sb; ~ **en l'air** to say the first thing that comes into one's head; ~ **le/en français** to speak French/in French; ~ **affaires** to talk business; ~ **en dormant/du nez** to talk in one's sleep/through one's nose; **sans** ~ **de** (*fig*) not to mention, to say nothing of; **tu parles!** you must be joking!; **n'en parlons plus!** let's forget it!

parleur [parlœr] *nm*: **beau** ~ fine talker.

parloir [parlwar] *nm* (*d'une prison, d'un hôpital*) visiting room; (*REL*) parlour (*BRIT*), parlor (*US*).

parlote [parlɔt] *nf* chitchat.

Parme [parm(ə)] *n* Parma.

parme [parm(ə)] *adj* violet (blue).

parmesan [parməzɑ̃] *nm* Parmesan (cheese).

parmi [parmi] *prép* among(st).

parodie [parɔdi] *nf* parody.

parodier [parɔdje] *vt* (*œuvre, auteur*) to parody.

paroi [parwa] *nf* wall; (*cloison*) partition; ~ **rocheuse** rock face.

paroisse [parwas] *nf* parish.

paroissial, e, aux [parwasjal, -o] *adj* parish *cpd*.

paroissien, ne [parwasjɛ̃, -ɛn] *nm/f* parishioner ♦ *nm* prayer book.

parole [parɔl] *nf* (*faculté*): **la** ~ speech; (*mot, promesse*) word; (*REL*): **la bonne** ~ the word of God; ~**s** *nfpl* (*MUS*) words, lyrics; **tenir** ~ to keep one's word; **avoir la** ~ to have the floor; **n'avoir qu'une** ~ to be true to one's word; **donner la** ~ **à qn** to hand over to sb; **prendre la** ~ to speak; **demander la** ~ to ask for permission to speak; **perdre la** ~ to lose the power of speech; (*fig*) to lose one's tongue; **je le crois sur** ~ I'll take his word for it, I'll take him at his word; **temps de** ~ (*TV, RADIO etc*) discussion time; **ma** ~! my word!, good heavens!; ~ **d'honneur** word of honour (*BRIT*) *ou* honor (*US*).

parolier, ière [parɔlje, -jɛr] *nm/f* lyricist; (*OPÉRA*) librettist.

paroxysme [parɔksism(ə)] *nm* height, paroxysm.

parpaing [parpɛ̃] *nm* bond-stone, parpen.

parquer [parke] *vt* (*voiture, matériel*) to park; (*bestiaux*) to pen (in *ou* up); (*prisonniers*) to pack in.

parquet [parkɛ] *nm* (*parquet*) floor; (*JUR: bureau*) public prosecutor's office; **le** ~ (**général**) (*magistrats*) ≈ the Bench.

parqueter [parkəte] *vt* to lay a parquet floor in.

parrain [parɛ̃] *nm* godfather; (*d'un navire*) namer; (*d'un nouvel adhérent*) sponsor, proposer.

parrainage [paʀɛnaʒ] *nm* sponsorship.

parrainer [paʀene] *vt* (*nouvel adhérent*) to sponsor, propose; (*entreprise*) to promote, sponsor.

parricide [paʀisid] *nm, nf* parricide.

pars [paʀ] *vb voir* **partir**.

parsemer [paʀsəme] *vt* (*suj: feuilles, papiers*) to be scattered over; ~ **qch de** to scatter sth with.

parsi, e [paʀsi] *adj* Parsee.

part [paʀ] *vb voir* **partir** ♦ *nf* (*qui revient à qn*) share; (*fraction, partie*) part; (*de gâteau, fromage*) portion; (*FINANCE*) (non-voting) share; **prendre ~ à** (*débat etc*) to take part in; (*soucis, douleur de qn*) to share in; **faire ~ de qch à qn** to announce sth to sb, inform sb of sth; **pour ma ~** as for me, as far as I'm concerned; **à ~ entière** *adj* full; **de la ~ de** (*au nom de*) on behalf of; (*donné par*) from; **c'est de la ~ de qui?** (*au téléphone*) who's calling *ou* speaking (please)?; **de toute(s) ~(s)** from all sides *ou* quarters; **de ~ et d'autre** on both sides, on either side; **de ~ en ~** right through; **d'une ~ ... d'autre ~** on the one hand ... on the other hand; **nulle/autre/quelque ~** nowhere/elsewhere/somewhere; **à ~** *adv* separately; (*de côté*) aside ♦ *prép* apart from, except for ♦ *adj* exceptional, special; **pour une large** *ou* **bonne ~** to a great extent; **prendre qch en bonne/mauvaise ~** to take sth well/badly; **faire la ~ des choses** to make allowances; **faire la ~ du feu** (*fig*) to cut one's losses; **faire la ~ (trop) belle à qn** to give sb more than his (*ou* her) share.

part. *abr =* **particulier**.

partage [paʀtaʒ] *nm* (*voir partager*) sharing (out) *no pl*, share-out; sharing; dividing up; (*POL: de suffrages*) share; **recevoir qch en ~** to receive sth as one's share (*ou* lot); **sans ~** undivided.

partagé, e [paʀtaʒe] *adj* (*opinions etc*) divided; (*amour*) shared; **temps ~** (*INFORM*) time sharing; **être ~ entre** to be shared between; **être ~ sur** to be divided about.

partager [paʀtaʒe] *vt* to share; (*distribuer, répartir*) to share (out); (*morceler, diviser*) to divide (up); **se ~** *vt* (*héritage etc*) to share between themselves (*ou* ourselves *etc*).

partance [paʀtɑ̃s]: **en ~** *adv* outbound, due to leave; **en ~ pour** (bound) for.

partant, e [paʀtɑ̃, -ɑ̃t] *vb voir* **partir** ♦ *adj:* **être ~ pour qch** (*d'accord pour*) to be quite ready for sth ♦ *nm* (*SPORT*) starter; (*HIPPISME*) runner.

partenaire [paʀtənɛʀ] *nm/f* partner; **~s sociaux** management and workforce.

parterre [paʀtɛʀ] *nm* (*de fleurs*) (flower) bed, border; (*THÉÂT*) stalls *pl*.

parti [paʀti] *nm* (*POL*) party; (*décision*) course of action; (*personne à marier*) match; **tirer ~**

de to take advantage of, turn to good account; **prendre le ~ de faire** to make up one's mind to do, resolve to do; **prendre le ~ de qn** to stand up for sb, side with sb; **prendre ~ (pour/contre)** to take sides *ou* a stand (for/against); **prendre son ~ de** to come to terms with; **~ pris** bias.

partial, e, aux [paʀsjal, -o] *adj* biased, partial.

partialement [paʀsjalmɑ̃] *adv* in a biased way.

partialité [paʀsjalite] *nf* bias, partiality.

participant, e [paʀtisipɑ̃, -ɑ̃t] *nm/f* participant; (*à un concours*) entrant; (*d'une société*) member.

participation [paʀtisipɑsjɔ̃] *nf* participation; sharing; (*COMM*) interest; **la ~ aux bénéfices** profit-sharing; **la ~ ouvrière** worker participation; "**avec la ~ de ...**" "featuring ...".

participe [paʀtisip] *nm* participle; **~ passé/présent** past/present participle.

participer [paʀtisipe]: **~ à** *vt* (*course, réunion*) to take part in; (*profits etc*) to share in; (*frais etc*) to contribute to; (*entreprise: financièrement*) to cooperate in; (*chagrin, succès de qn*) to share (in); **~ de** *vt* to partake of.

particulariser [paʀtikylaʀize] *vt:* **se ~** to mark o.s. (*ou* itself) out.

particularisme [paʀtikylaʀism(ə)] *nm* sense of identity.

particularité [paʀtikylaʀite] *nf* particularity; (*distinctive*) characteristic, feature.

particule [paʀtikyl] *nf* particle; **~ (nobiliaire)** nobiliary particle.

particulier, ière [paʀtikylje, -jɛʀ] *adj* (*personnel, privé*) private; (*spécial*) special, particular; (*caractéristique*) characteristic, distinctive; (*spécifique*) particular ♦ *nm* (*individu: ADMIN*) private individual; "**~ vend ...**" (*COMM*) "for sale privately ...", "for sale by owner ..." (*US*); **~ à** peculiar to; **en ~** *adv* (*surtout*) in particular, particularly; (*à part*) separately; (*en privé*) in private.

particulièrement [paʀtikyljɛʀmɑ̃] *adv* particularly.

partie [paʀti] *nf* (*gén*) part; (*profession, spécialité*) field, subject; (*JUR etc: protagonistes*) party; (*de cartes, tennis etc*) game; (*fig: lutte, combat*) struggle, fight; **une ~ de campagne/de pêche** an outing in the country/a fishing party *ou* trip; **en ~** *adv* partly, in part; **faire ~ de** to belong to; (*suj: chose*) to be part of; **prendre qn à ~** to take sb to task; (*malmener*) to set on sb; **en grande ~** largely, in the main; **ce n'est que ~ remise** it will be for another time *ou* the next time; **avoir ~ liée avec qn** to be in league with sb; **~ civile** (*JUR*) party claiming damages in a criminal case.

partiel, le [paʀsjɛl] *adj* partial ♦ *nm* (*SCOL*) class exam.

partiellement [paʀsjɛlmɑ̃] *adv* partially, partly.

partir [paʀtiʀ] *vi* (*gén*) to go; (*quitter*) to go,

leave; (s'éloigner) to go (ou drive etc) away ou off; (moteur) to start; (pétard) to go off; (bouchon) to come out; (bouton) to come off; ~ **de** (lieu: quitter) to leave; (: commencer à) to start from; (date) to run ou start from; ~ **pour/à** (lieu, pays etc) to leave for/go off to; **à ~ de** from.

partisan, e [paʀtizɑ̃, -an] nm/f partisan; (d'un parti, régime etc) supporter ♦ adj (lutte, querelle) partisan, one-sided; **être ~ de qch/faire** to be in favour (BRIT) ou favor (US) of sth/doing.

partitif, ive [paʀtitif, -iv] adj: **article ~** partitive article.

partition [paʀtisjɔ̃] nf (MUS) score; (POL) partition.

partout [paʀtu] adv everywhere; ~ **où il allait** everywhere ou wherever he went; **trente ~** (TENNIS) thirty all.

paru [paʀy] pp de **paraître**.

parure [paʀyʀ] nf (bijoux etc) finery no pl; jewellery no pl (BRIT), jewelry no pl (US); (assortiment) set.

parus [paʀy] etc vb voir **paraître**.

parution [paʀysjɔ̃] nf publication, appearance.

parvenir [paʀvəniʀ]: ~ **à** vt (atteindre) to reach; (obtenir, arriver à) to attain; (réussir): ~ **à faire** to manage to do, succeed in doing; **faire ~ qch à qn** to have sth sent to sb.

parvenu, e [paʀvəny] pp de **parvenir** ♦ nm/f (péj) parvenu, upstart.

parviendrai [paʀvjɛ̃dʀe], **parviens** [paʀvjɛ̃] etc voir **parvenir**.

parvis [paʀvi] nm square (in front of a church).

============== MOT-CLÉ ==============

pas¹ [pa] adv 1 (en corrélation avec ne, non etc) not; **il ne pleure ~** (habituellement) he does not ou doesn't cry; (maintenant) he's not ou isn't crying; **je ne mange ~ de viande** I don't ou do not eat meat; **il n'a ~ pleuré/ne pleurera ~** he did not ou didn't/will not ou won't cry; **ils n'ont ~ de voiture/d'enfants** they haven't got a car/any children, they have no car/children; **il m'a dit de ne ~ le faire** he told me not to do it; **non ~ que ...** not that ...

2 (employé sans ne etc): ~ **moi** not me, not I, I don't ou (can't etc); **elle travaille, (mais) lui ~ ou ~ lui** she works but he doesn't ou does not; **une pomme ~ mûre** an apple which isn't ripe; ~ **plus tard qu'hier** only yesterday; ~ **du tout** not at all; ~ **de sucre, merci** no sugar, thanks; **ceci est à vous ou ~?** is this yours or not?, is this yours or isn't it?

3: ~ **mal** (joli: personne, maison) not bad; ~ **mal fait** not badly done ou made; **comment ça va? — ~ mal** how are things? — not bad; ~ **mal de** quite a lot of.

pas² [pa] nm (allure, mesure) pace; (démarche)

tread; (enjambée, DANSE, fig: étape) step; (bruit) (foot)step; (trace) footprint; (allure) pace; (d'un cheval) walk; (mesure) pace; (TECH: de vis, d'écrou) thread; ~ **à ~** step by step; **au ~** at walking pace; **de ce ~** (à l'instant même) straightaway, at once; **marcher à grands ~** to stride along; **mettre qn au ~** to bring sb to heel; **au ~ de gymnastique/de course** at a jog trot/at a run; **à ~ de loup** stealthily; **faire les cent ~** to pace up and down; **faire les premiers ~** to make the first move; **retourner** ou **revenir sur ses ~** to retrace one's steps; **se tirer d'un mauvais ~** to get o.s. out of a tight spot; **sur le ~ de la porte** on the doorstep; **le ~ de Calais** (détroit) the Straits pl of Dover; ~ **de porte** (fig) key money.

pascal, e, aux [paskal, -o] adj Easter cpd.

passable [pɑsabl(ə)] adj passable, tolerable.

passablement [pɑsabləmɑ̃] adv (pas trop mal) reasonably well; (beaucoup) quite a lot.

passade [pɑsad] nf passing fancy, whim.

passage [pɑsaʒ] nm (fait de passer) voir **passer**; (lieu, prix de la traversée, extrait de livre etc) passage; (chemin) way; (itinéraire): **sur le ~ du cortège** along the route of the procession; **"laissez/n'obstruez pas le ~"** "keep clear/do not obstruct"; **au ~** (en passant) as I (ou he etc) went by; **de ~** (touristes) passing through; (amants etc) casual; ~ **clouté** pedestrian crossing; **"~ interdit"** "no entry"; ~ **à niveau** level (BRIT) ou grade (US) crossing; **"~ protégé"** right of way over secondary road(s) on your right; ~ **souterrain** subway (BRIT), underpass; ~ **à tabac** beating-up; ~ **à vide** (fig) bad patch.

passager, ère [pɑsaʒe, -ɛʀ] adj passing; (hôte) short-stay cpd; (oiseau) migratory ♦ nm/f passenger; ~ **clandestin** stowaway.

passagèrement [pɑsaʒɛʀmɑ̃] adv temporarily, for a short time.

passant, e [pɑsɑ̃, -ɑ̃t] adj (rue, endroit) busy ♦ nm/f passer-by ♦ nm (pour ceinture etc) loop; **en ~: remarquer qch en ~** to notice sth in passing.

passation [pɑsasjɔ̃] nf (JUR: d'un acte) signing; ~ **des pouvoirs** transfer ou handover of power.

passe [pas] nf (SPORT, magnétique) pass; (NAVIG) channel ♦ nm (passe-partout) master ou skeleton key; **être en ~ de faire** to be on the way to doing; **être dans une bonne/mauvaise ~** (fig) to be going through a good/bad patch; ~ **d'armes** (fig) heated exchange.

passé, e [pɑse] adj (événement, temps) past; (couleur, tapisserie) faded; (précédent): **dimanche ~** last Sunday ♦ prép after ♦ nm past; (LING) past (tense); **il est ~ midi** ou **midi ~** it's gone (BRIT) ou past twelve; ~ **de mode** out of fashion; ~ **composé** perfect (tense); ~ **simple** past historic.

passe-droit [pɑsdʀwa] *nm* special privilege.
passéiste [pɑseist(ə)] *adj* backward-looking.
passementerie [pɑsmɑ̃tʀi] *nf* trimmings *pl*.
passe-montagne [pɑsmɔ̃taɲ] *nm* balaclava.
passe-partout [pɑspaʀtu] *nm inv* master *ou* skeleton key ♦ *adj inv* all-purpose.
passe-passe [pɑspas] *nm*: **tour de** ~ trick, sleight of hand *no pl*.
passe-plat [pɑspla] *nm* serving hatch.
passeport [pɑspɔʀ] *nm* passport.

passer [pɑse] *vi* (*se rendre, aller*) to go; (*voiture, piétons: défiler*) to pass (by), go by; (*faire une halte rapide: facteur, laitier etc*) to come, call; (*: pour rendre visite*) to call *ou* drop in; (*courant, air, lumière, franchir un obstacle etc*) to get through; (*accusé, projet de loi*): ~ **devant** to come before; (*film, émission*) to be on; (*temps, jours*) to pass, go by; (*liquide, café*) to go through; (*être digéré, avalé*) to go down; (*couleur, papier*) to fade; (*mode*) to die out; (*douleur*) to pass, go away; (*CARTES*) to pass; (*SCOL*) to go up (to the next class); (*devenir*): ~ **président** to be appointed *ou* become president ♦ *vt* (*frontière, rivière etc*) to cross; (*douane*) to go through; (*examen*) to sit, take; (*visite médicale etc*) to have; (*journée, temps*) to spend; (*donner*): ~ **qch à qn** to pass sth to sb; to give sth to sb; (*transmettre*): ~ **qch à qn** to pass sth on to sb; (*enfiler: vêtement*) to slip on; (*faire entrer, mettre*): (*faire*) ~ **qch dans/par** to get sth into/through; (*café*) to pour the water on; (*thé, soupe*) to strain; (*film, pièce*) to show, put on; (*disque*) to play, put on; (*marché, accord*) to agree on; (*tolérer*): ~ **qch à qn** to let sb get away with sth; **se** ~ *vi* (*avoir lieu: scène, action*) to take place; (*se dérouler: entretien etc*) to go; (*arriver*): **que s'est-il passé?** what happened?; (*s'écouler: semaine etc*) to pass, go by; **se** ~ **de** *vt* to go *ou* do without; **se** ~ **les mains sous l'eau/de l'eau sur le visage** to put one's hands under the tap/run water over one's face; **en passant** in passing; ~ **par** to go through; **passez devant/par ici** go in front/this way; ~ **sur** *vt* (*faute, détail inutile*) to pass over; ~ **dans les mœurs/l'usage** to become the custom/normal usage; ~ **avant qch/qn** (*fig*) to come before sth/sb; **laisser** ~ (*air, lumière, personne*) to let through; (*occasion*) to let slip, miss; (*erreur*) to overlook; **faire** ~ (*message*) to get over *ou* across; **faire** ~ **à qn le goût de qch** to cure sb of his (*ou* her) taste for sth; ~ **à la radio/ fouille** to be X-rayed/searched; ~ **à la radio/télévision** to be on the radio/on television; ~ **à table** to sit down to eat; ~ **au salon** to go into the sitting room; ~ **à l'opposition** to go over to the opposition; ~ **aux aveux** to confess, make a confession; ~ **à l'action** to go into action; ~ **pour riche** to be taken for a rich man; **il passait pour avoir** he was said to have; **faire** ~ **qn/qch pour** to make sb/sth out to be; **passe encore de le**

penser, mais de le dire! it's one thing to think it, but to say it!; **passons!** let's say no more (about it); **et j'en passe!** and that's not all!; ~ **en seconde**, ~ **la seconde** (*AUTO*) to change into second; ~ **qch en fraude** to smuggle sth in (*ou* out); ~ **la main par la portière** to stick one's hand out of the door; ~ **le balai/l'aspirateur** to sweep up/hoover; ~ **commande/la parole à qn** to hand over to sb; **je vous passe M X** (*je vous mets en communication avec lui*) I'm putting you through to Mr X; (*je lui passe l'appareil*) here is Mr X, I'll hand you over to Mr X; ~ **prendre** to (come and) collect.

passereau, x [pɑsʀo] *nm* sparrow.
passerelle [pɑsʀɛl] *nf* footbridge; (*de navire, avion*) gangway; (*NAVIG*): ~ (**de commandement**) bridge.
passe-temps [pɑstɑ̃] *nm inv* pastime.
passette [pɑsɛt] *nf* (tea-)strainer.
passeur, euse [pɑsœʀ, -øz] *nm/f* smuggler.
passible [pɑsibl(ə)] *adj*: ~ **de** liable to.
passif, ive [pasif, -iv] *adj* passive ♦ *nm* (*LING*) passive; (*COMM*) liabilities *pl*.
passion [pɑsjɔ̃] *nf* passion; **avoir la** ~ **de** to have a passion for; **fruit de la** ~ passion fruit.
passionnant, e [pɑsjɔnɑ̃, -ɑ̃t] *adj* fascinating.
passionné, e [pɑsjɔne] *adj* (*personne, tempérament*) passionate; (*description*) impassioned ♦ *nm/f*: **c'est un** ~ **d'échecs** he's a chess fanatic; **être** ~ **de** *ou* **pour qch** to have a passion for sth.
passionnel, le [pɑsjɔnɛl] *adj* of passion.
passionnément [pɑsjɔnemɑ̃] *adv* passionately.
passionner [pɑsjɔne] *vt* (*personne*) to fascinate, grip; (*débat, discussion*) to inflame; **se** ~ **pour** to take an avid interest in; to have a passion for.
passivement [pasivmɑ̃] *adv* passively.
passivité [pasivite] *nf* passivity, passiveness.
passoire [pɑswaʀ] *nf* sieve; (*à légumes*) colander; (*à thé*) strainer.
pastel [pastɛl] *nm, adj inv* (*ART*) pastel.
pastèque [pastɛk] *nf* watermelon.
pasteur [pastœʀ] *nm* (*protestant*) minister, pastor.
pasteurisation [pastœʀizasjɔ̃] *nf* pasteurization.
pasteuriser [pastœʀize] *vt* to pasteurize.
pastiche [pastiʃ] *nm* pastiche.
pastille [pastij] *nf* (*à sucer*) lozenge, pastille; (*de papier etc*) (small) disc; ~**s pour la toux** cough drops *ou* lozenges.
pastis [pastis] *nm* anise-flavoured alcoholic drink.
pastoral, e, aux [pastɔʀal, -o] *adj* pastoral.
patagon, ne [patagɔ̃, -ɔn] *adj* Patagonian.
Patagonie [patagɔni] *nf*: **la** ~ Patagonia.
patate [patat] *nf* spud; ~ **douce** sweet potato.
pataud, e [pato, -od] *adj* lumbering.

patauger [patɔʒe] *vi* (*pour s'amuser*) to splash about; (*avec effort*) to wade about; (*fig*) to flounder; ~ **dans** (*en marchant*) to wade through.

patch [patʃ] *nm* nicotine patch.

patchouli [patʃuli] *nm* patchouli.

patchwork [patʃwœrk] *nm* patchwork.

pâte [pat] *nf* (*à tarte*) pastry; (*à pain*) dough; (*à frire*) batter; (*substance molle*) paste; cream; ~**s** *nfpl* (*macaroni etc*) pasta *sg*; **fromage à ~ dure/molle** hard/soft cheese; ~ **d'amandes** almond paste; ~ **brisée** shortcrust (*BRIT*) *ou* pie crust (*US*) pastry; ~ **à choux/feuilletée** choux/puff *ou* flaky (*BRIT*) pastry; ~ **de fruits** crystallized fruit *no pl*; ~ **à modeler** modelling clay, Plasticine ® (*BRIT*); ~ **à papier** paper pulp.

pâté [pate] *nm* (*charcuterie: terrine*) pâté; (*tache*) ink blot; (*de sable*) sandpie; ~ **(en croûte)** ≈ meat pie; ~ **de foie** liver pâté; ~ **de maisons** block (of houses).

pâtée [pate] *nf* mash, feed.

patelin [patlɛ̃] *nm* little place.

patente [patɑ̃t] *nf* (*COMM*) trading licence (*BRIT*) *ou* license (*US*).

patenté, e [patɑ̃te] *adj* (*COMM*) licensed; (*fig: attitré*) registered, (*officially*) recognized.

patère [patɛʀ] *nf* (coat-)peg.

paternalisme [patɛʀnalism(ə)] *nm* paternalism.

paternaliste [patɛʀnalist(ə)] *adj* paternalistic.

paternel, le [patɛʀnɛl] *adj* (*amour, soins*) fatherly; (*ligne, autorité*) paternal.

paternité [patɛʀnite] *nf* paternity, fatherhood.

pâteux, euse [patø, -øz] *adj* thick; pasty; **avoir la bouche** *ou* **langue pâteuse** to have a furred (*BRIT*) *ou* coated tongue.

pathétique [patetik] *adj* pathetic, moving.

pathologie [patɔlɔʒi] *nf* pathology.

pathologique [patɔlɔʒik] *adj* pathological.

patibulaire [patibylɛʀ] *adj* sinister.

patiemment [pasjamɑ̃] *adv* patiently.

patience [pasjɑ̃s] *nf* patience; **être à bout de** ~ to have run out of patience; **perdre/prendre** ~ to lose (one's)/have patience.

patient, e [pasjɑ̃, -ɑ̃t] *adj*, *nm/f* patient.

patienter [pasjɑ̃te] *vi* to wait.

patin [patɛ̃] *nm* skate; (*sport*) skating; (*de traîneau, luge*) runner; (*pièce de tissu*) cloth pad (*used as slippers to protect polished floor*); ~ **(de frein)** brake block; ~**s (à glace)** (ice) skates; ~**s à roulettes** roller skates.

patinage [patinaʒ] *nm* skating; ~ **artistique/de vitesse** figure/speed skating.

patine [patin] *nf* sheen.

patiner [patine] *vi* to skate; (*embrayage*) to slip; (*roue, voiture*) to spin; **se** ~ *vi* (*meuble, cuir*) to acquire a sheen, become polished.

patineur, euse [patinœʀ, -øz] *nm/f* skater.

patinoire [patinwaʀ] *nf* skating rink, (ice) rink.

patio [patjo] *nm* patio.

pâtir [patiʀ]: ~ **de** *vt* to suffer because of.

pâtisserie [patisʀi] *nf* (*boutique*) cake shop; (*métier*) confectionery; (*à la maison*) pastry-*ou* cake-making, baking; ~**s** *nfpl* (*gâteaux*) pastries, cakes.

pâtissier, ière [patisje, -jɛʀ] *nm/f* pastrycook; confectioner.

patois [patwa] *nm* dialect, patois.

patriarche [patʀijaʀʃ(ə)] *nm* patriarch.

patrie [patʀi] *nf* homeland.

patrimoine [patʀimwan] *nm* inheritance, patrimony; (*culture*) heritage; ~ **génétique** *ou* **héréditaire** genetic inheritance.

patriote [patʀijɔt] *adj* patriotic ♦ *nm/f* patriot.

patriotique [patʀijɔtik] *adj* patriotic.

patriotisme [patʀijɔtism(ə)] *nm* patriotism.

patron, ne [patʀɔ̃, -ɔn] *nm/f* (*chef*) boss, manager/eress; (*propriétaire*) owner, proprietor/tress; (*employeur*) employer; (*MÉD*) ≈ senior consultant; (*REL*) patron saint ♦ *nm* (*COUTURE*) pattern; ~ **de thèse** supervisor (of postgraduate thesis).

patronage [patʀɔnaʒ] *nm* patronage; (*organisation, club*) (parish) youth club; (parish) children's club.

patronal, e, aux [patʀɔnal, -o] *adj* (*syndicat, intérêts*) employers'.

patronat [patʀɔna] *nm* employers *pl*.

patronner [patʀɔne] *vt* to sponsor, support.

patronnesse [patʀɔnɛs] *adj f*: **dame** ~ patroness.

patronyme [patʀɔnim] *nm* name.

patronymique [patʀɔnimik] *adj*: **nom** ~ patronymic (name).

patrouille [patʀuj] *nf* patrol.

patrouiller [patʀuje] *vi* to patrol, be on patrol.

patrouilleur [patʀujœʀ] *nm* (*AVIAT*) scout (plane); (*NAVIG*) patrol boat.

patte [pat] *nf* (*jambe*) leg; (*pied: de chien, chat*) paw; (*: d'oiseau*) foot; (*languette*) strap; (*: de poche*) flap; (*favoris*): ~**s (de lapin)** (short) sideburns; **à** ~**s d'éléphant** *adj* (*pantalon*) flared; ~**s de mouche** (*fig*) spidery scrawl *sg*; ~**s d'oie** (*fig*) crow's feet.

pattemouille [patmuj] *nf* damp cloth (*for ironing*).

pâturage [patyʀaʒ] *nm* pasture.

pâture [patyʀ] *nf* food.

paume [pom] *nf* palm.

paumé, e [pome] *nm/f* (*fam*) drop-out.

paumer [pome] *vt* (*fam*) to lose.

paupérisation [popeʀizasjɔ̃] *nf* pauperization.

paupérisme [popeʀism(ə)] *nm* pauperism.

paupière [popjɛʀ] *nf* eyelid.

paupiette [popjɛt] *nf*: ~**s de veau** veal olives.

pause [poz] *nf* (*arrêt*) break; (*en parlant, MUS*) pause.

pause-café, *pl* **pauses-café** [pozkafe] *nf* coffee-break.

pauvre [povʀ(ə)] *adj* poor ♦ *nm/f* poor man/woman; **les** ~**s** the poor; ~ **en calcium** low in calcium.

pauvrement [povʀəmɑ̃] *adv* poorly.
pauvreté [povʀəte] *nf* (*état*) poverty.
pavage [pavaʒ] *nm* paving; cobbles *pl.*
pavaner [pavane]: **se ~** *vi* to strut about.
pavé, e [pave] *adj* (*cour*) paved; (*rue*) cobbled ♦ *nm* (*bloc*) paving stone; cobblestone; (*pavage*) paving; (*bifteck*) slab of steak; (*fam: livre*) hefty tome; **être sur le ~** (*sans domicile*) to be on the streets; (*sans emploi*) to be out of a job; **~ numérique** (*INFORM*) keypad.
pavillon [pavijɔ̃] *nm* (*de banlieue*) small (detached) house; (*kiosque*) lodge; pavilion; (*d'hôpital*) ward; (*MUS: de cor etc*) bell; (*ANAT: de l'oreille*) pavilion, pinna; (*NAVIG*) flag; **~ de complaisance** flag of convenience.
pavoiser [pavwaze] *vt* to deck with flags ♦ *vi* to put out flags; (*fig*) to rejoice, exult.
pavot [pavo] *nm* poppy.
payable [pɛjabl(ə)] *adj* payable.
payant, e [pɛjɑ̃, -ɑ̃t] *adj* (*spectateurs etc*) paying; (*billet*) that you pay for, to be paid for; (*fig: entreprise*) profitable; **c'est ~** you have to pay, there is a charge.
paye [pɛj] *nf* pay, wages *pl.*
payement [pɛjmɑ̃] *nm* payment.
payer [peje] *vt* (*créancier, employé, loyer*) to pay; (*achat, réparations, fig: faute*) to pay for ♦ *vi* to pay; (*métier*) to pay, be well-paid; (*effort, tactique etc*) to pay off; **il me l'a fait ~ 10 F** he charged me 10 F for it; **~ qn de** (*ses efforts, peines*) to reward sb for; **~ qch à qn** to buy sth for sb, buy sb sth; **ils nous ont payé le voyage** they paid for our trip; **~ de sa personne** to give of oneself; **~ d'audace** to act with great daring; **~ cher qch** to pay dear(ly) for sth; **cela ne paie pas de mine** it doesn't look much; **se ~ qch** to buy o.s. sth; **se ~ de mots** to shoot one's mouth off; **se ~ la tête de qn** to take the mickey out of sb (*BRIT*), make a fool of sb; (*duper*) to take sb for a ride.
payeur, euse [pɛjœʀ, -øz] *adj* (*organisme, bureau*) payments *cpd* ♦ *nm/f* payer.
pays [pei] *nm* (*territoire, habitants*) country, land; (*région*) region; (*village*) village; **du ~** *adj* local; **le ~ de Galles** Wales.
paysage [peizaʒ] *nm* landscape.
paysager, ère [peizaʒe, -ɛʀ] *adj* (*jardin, parc*) landscaped.
paysagiste [peizaʒist(ə)] *nm/f* (*de jardin*) landscape gardener; (*ART*) landscapist, landscape painter.
paysan, ne [peizɑ̃, -an] *nm/f* countryman/woman; farmer; (*péj*) peasant ♦ *adj* country *cpd*, farming; farmers'.
paysannat [peizana] *nm* peasantry.
Pays-Bas [peiba] *nmpl*: **les ~** the Netherlands.
PC *sigle m* (*POL*) = **parti communiste**; (*INFORM*: = *personal computer*) PC; (= *prêt conventionné*) *type of loan for house purchase*; (*CONSTR*) = **permis de construire**; (*MIL*) = **poste de commandement**.

pcc *abr* (= *pour copie conforme*) c.c.
Pce *abr* = **prince**.
Pcesse *abr* = **princesse**.
PCV *abr* (= *percevoir*) *voir* **communication**.
p de p *abr* = **pas de porte**.
PDG *sigle m* = **président directeur général**.
p.ê. *abr* = **peut-être**.
PEA *sigle m* (= *plan d'épargne en actions*) *building society savings plan.*
péage [peaʒ] *nm* toll; (*endroit*) tollgate; **pont à ~** toll bridge.
peau, x [po] *nf* skin; (*cuir*): **gants de ~** leather gloves; **être bien/mal dans sa ~** to be at ease/odds with oneself; **se mettre dans la ~ de qn** to put o.s. in sb's place *ou* shoes; **faire ~ neuve** (*se renouveler*) to change one's image; **~ de chamois** (*chiffon*) chamois leather, shammy; **~ d'orange** orange peel.
peaufiner [pofine] *vt* to polish (up).
Peau-Rouge [poʀuʒ] *nm/f* Red Indian, red skin.
peccadille [pekadij] *nf* trifle, peccadillo.
péché [peʃe] *nm* sin; **~ mignon** weakness.
pêche [pɛʃ] *nf* (*sport, activité*) fishing; (*poissons pêchés*) catch; (*fruit*) peach; **aller à la ~** to go fishing; **avoir la ~** (*fam*) to be on (top) form; **~ à la ligne** (*en rivière*) angling; **~ sous-marine** deep-sea fishing.
pêche-abricot, *pl* **pêches-abricots** [pɛʃabʀiko] *nf* yellow peach.
pécher [peʃe] *vi* (*REL*) to sin; (*fig: personne*) to err; (: *chose*) to be flawed; **~ contre la bienséance** to break the rules of good behaviour.
pêcher [peʃe] *nm* peach tree ♦ *vi* to go fishing; (*en rivière*) to go angling ♦ *vt* (*attraper*) to catch, land; (*chercher*) to fish for; **~ au chalut** to trawl.
pécheur, eresse [peʃœʀ, peʃʀɛs] *nm/f* sinner.
pêcheur [peʃœʀ] *nm* (*voir pêcher*) fisherman; angler; **~ de perles** pearl diver.
pectine [pɛktin] *nf* pectin.
pectoral, e, aux [pɛktɔʀal, -o] *adj* (*ANAT*) pectoral; (*sirop*) throat *cpd*, cough *cpd* ♦ *nmpl* pectoral muscles.
pécule [pekyl] *nm* savings *pl*, nest egg; (*d'un détenu*) earnings *pl* (*paid on release*).
pécuniaire [pekynjɛʀ] *adj* financial.
pédagogie [pedagɔʒi] *nf* educational methods *pl*, pedagogy.
pédagogique [pedagɔʒik] *adj* educational; **formation ~** teacher training.
pédagogue [pedagɔg] *nm/f* teacher; education(al)ist.
pédale [pedal] *nf* pedal; **mettre la ~ douce** to soft-pedal.
pédaler [pedale] *vi* to pedal.
pédalier [pedalje] *nm* pedal and gear mechanism.
pédalo [pedalo] *nm* pedalo, pedal-boat.
pédant, e [pedɑ̃, -ɑ̃t] *adj* (*péj*) pedantic ♦ *nm/f* pedant.

pédantisme [pedɑ̃tism(ə)] *nm* pedantry.
pédéraste [pederast(ə)] *nm* homosexual, pederast.
pédérastie [pederasti] *nf* homosexuality, pederasty.
pédestre [pedɛstʀ(ə)] *adj*: **tourisme** ~ hiking; **randonnée** ~ (*activité*) rambling; (*excursion*) ramble.
pédiatre [pedjatʀ(ə)] *nm/f* paediatrician (*BRIT*), pediatrician *ou* pediatrist (*US*), child specialist.
pédiatrie [pedjatʀi] *nf* paediatrics *sg* (*BRIT*), pediatrics *sg* (*US*).
pédicure [pedikyʀ] *nm/f* chiropodist.
pedigree [pedigʀe] *nm* pedigree.
peeling [piliŋ] *nm* exfoliation treatment.
PEEP *sigle f* = *Fédération des parents d'élèves de l'enseignement public.*
pègre [pɛgʀ(ə)] *nf* underworld.
peignais [pɛɲɛ] *etc vb voir* **peindre**.
peigne [pɛɲ] *vb voir* **peindre, peigner** ♦ *nm* comb.
peigné, e [peɲe] *adj*: **laine** ~**e** wool worsted; combed wool.
peigner [peɲe] *vt* to comb (the hair of); **se** ~ to comb one's hair.
peignez [pɛɲe] *etc vb voir* **peindre**.
peignoir [pɛɲwaʀ] *nm* dressing gown; ~ **de bain** bathrobe; ~ **de plage** beach robe.
peignons [pɛɲɔ̃] *vb voir* **peindre**.
peinard, e [penaʀ, -aʀd(ə)] *adj* (*emploi*) cushy (*BRIT*), easy; (*personne*): **on est** ~ **ici** we're left in peace here.
peindre [pɛ̃dʀ(ə)] *vt* to paint; (*fig*) to portray, depict.
peine [pɛn] *nf* (*affliction*) sorrow, sadness *no pl*; (*mal, effort*) trouble *no pl*, effort; (*difficulté*) difficulty; (*punition, châtiment*) punishment; (*JUR*) sentence; **faire de la** ~ **à qn** to distress *ou* upset sb; **prendre la** ~ **de faire** to go to the trouble of doing; **se donner de la** ~ to make an effort; **ce n'est pas la** ~ **de faire** there's no point in doing, it's not worth doing; **ce n'est pas la** ~ **que vous fassiez** there's no point (in) you doing; **avoir de la** ~ **à faire** to have difficulty doing; **donnez-vous** *ou* **veuillez-vous donner la** ~ **d'entrer** please do come in; **c'est** ~ **perdue** it's a waste of time (and effort); **à** ~ *adv* scarcely, hardly, barely; **à** ~ ... **que** hardly ... than; **c'est à** ~ **si** ... it's (*ou* it was) a job to ...; **sous** ~: **sous** ~ **d'être puni** for fear of being punished; **défense d'afficher sous** ~ **d'amende** billposters will be fined; ~ **capitale** capital punishment; ~ **de mort** death sentence *ou* penalty.
peiner [pene] *vi* to work hard; to struggle; (*moteur, voiture*) to labour (*BRIT*), labor (*US*) ♦ *vt* to grieve, sadden.
peint, e [pɛ̃, pɛ̃t] *pp de* **peindre**.
peintre [pɛ̃tʀ(ə)] *nm* painter; ~ **en bâtiment** house painter, painter and decorator; ~ **d'enseignes** signwriter.

peinture [pɛ̃tyʀ] *nf* painting; (*couche de couleur, couleur*) paint; (*surfaces peintes: aussi:* ~**s**) paintwork; **je ne peux pas le voir en** ~ I can't stand the sight of him; ~ **mate/ brillante** matt/gloss paint; "~ **fraîche**" "wet paint".
péjoratif, ive [peʒɔʀatif, -iv] *adj* pejorative, derogatory.
Pékin [pekɛ̃] *n* Peking.
pékinois, e [pekinwa, -waz] *adj* Pekin(g)ese ♦ *nm* (*chien*) peke, pekin(g)ese; (*LING*) Mandarin, Pekin(g)ese ♦ *nm/f*: **P**~, **e** Pekin(g)ese.
PEL *sigle m* (= *plan d'épargne logement*) *savings scheme providing lower-interest mortgages.*
pelade [pəlad] *nf* alopecia.
pelage [pəlaʒ] *nm* coat, fur.
pelé, e [pəle] *adj* (*chien*) hairless; (*vêtement*) threadbare; (*terrain*) bare.
pêle-mêle [pɛlmɛl] *adv* higgledy-piggledy.
peler [pəle] *vt*, *vi* to peel.
pèlerin [pɛlʀɛ̃] *nm* pilgrim.
pèlerinage [pɛlʀinaʒ] *nm* (*voyage*) pilgrimage; (*lieu*) place of pilgrimage, shrine.
pèlerine [pɛlʀin] *nf* cape.
pélican [pelikɑ̃] *nm* pelican.
pelisse [pəlis] *nf* fur-lined cloak.
pelle [pɛl] *nf* shovel; (*d'enfant, de terrassier*) spade; ~ **à gâteau** cake slice; ~ **mécanique** mechanical digger.
pelletée [pɛlte] *nf* shovelful; spadeful.
pelleter [pɛlte] *vt* to shovel (up).
pelleteuse [pɛltøz] *nf* mechanical digger, excavator.
pelletier [pɛltje] *nm* furrier.
pellicule [pelikyl] *nf* film; ~**s** *nfpl* (*MÉD*) dandruff *sg*.
Péloponnèse [pelɔpɔnɛz] *nm*: **le** ~ the Peloponnese.
pelote [pəlɔt] *nf* (*de fil, laine*) ball; (*d'épingles*) pin cushion; ~ **basque** pelota.
peloter [pəlɔte] *vt* (*fam*) to feel (up); **se** ~ to pet.
peloton [pəlɔtɔ̃] *nm* (*groupe: personnes*) group; (*: pompiers, gendarmes*) squad; (*: SPORT*) pack; (*de laine*) ball; ~ **d'exécution** firing squad.
pelotonner [pəlɔtɔne]: **se** ~ *vi* to curl (o.s.) up.
pelouse [pəluz] *nf* lawn; (*HIPPISME*) *spectating area inside racetrack.*
peluche [pəlyʃ] *nf* (bit of) fluff; **animal en** ~ soft toy, fluffy animal.
pelucher [p(ə)lyʃe] *vi* to become fluffy, fluff up.
pelucheux, euse [p(ə)lyʃø, -øz] *adj* fluffy.
pelure [pəlyʀ] *nf* peeling, peel *no pl*; ~ **d'oignon** onion skin.
pénal, e, aux [penal, -o] *adj* penal.
pénalisation [penalizasjɔ̃] *nf* (*SPORT*) sanction, penalty.
pénaliser [penalize] *vt* to penalize.
pénalité [penalite] *nf* penalty.

penalty, ies [penalti, -z] *nm* (*SPORT*) penalty (kick).

pénard, e [penaʀ, -aʀd(ə)] *adj* = **peinard**.

pénates [penat] *nmpl*: **regagner ses ~** to return to the bosom of one's family.

penaud, e [pəno, -od] *adj* sheepish, contrite.

penchant [pɑ̃ʃɑ̃] *nm*: **un ~ à faire/à qch** a tendency to do/to sth; **un ~ pour qch** a liking *ou* fondness for sth.

penché, e [pɑ̃ʃe] *adj* slanting.

pencher [pɑ̃ʃe] *vi* to tilt, lean over ♦ *vt* to tilt; **se ~** *vi* to lean over; (*se baisser*) to bend down; **se ~ sur** to bend over; (*fig: problème*) to look into; **se ~ au dehors** to lean out; **~ pour** to be inclined to favour (*BRIT*) *ou* favor (*US*).

pendable [pɑ̃dabl(ə)] *adj*: **tour ~** rotten trick; **c'est un cas ~!** he (*ou* she) deserves to be shot!

pendaison [pɑ̃dɛzɔ̃] *nf* hanging.

pendant, e [pɑ̃dɑ̃, -ɑ̃t] *adj* hanging (out); (*ADMIN, JUR*) pending ♦ *nm* counterpart; matching piece ♦ *prép* during; **faire ~ à** to match; to be the counterpart of; **~ que** while; **~s d'oreilles** drop *ou* pendant earrings.

pendeloque [pɑ̃dlɔk] *nf* pendant.

pendentif [pɑ̃dɑ̃tif] *nm* pendant.

penderie [pɑ̃dʀi] *nf* wardrobe; (*placard*) walk-in cupboard.

pendiller [pɑ̃dije] *vi* to flap (about).

pendre [pɑ̃dʀ(ə)] *vt, vi* to hang; **se ~ (à)** (*se suicider*) to hang o.s. (on); **se ~ à** (*se suspendre*) to hang from; **~ à** to hang (down) from; **~ qch à** (*mur*) to hang sth (up) on; (*plafond*) to hang sth (up) from.

pendu, e [pɑ̃dy] *pp de* **pendre** ♦ *nm/f* hanged man (*ou* woman).

pendulaire [pɑ̃dylɛʀ] *adj* pendular, of a pendulum.

pendule [pɑ̃dyl] *nf* clock ♦ *nm* pendulum.

pendulette [pɑ̃dylɛt] *nf* small clock.

pêne [pɛn] *nm* bolt.

pénétrant, e [penetʀɑ̃, -ɑ̃t] *adj* (*air, froid*) biting; (*pluie*) that soaks right through you; (*fig: odeur*) noticeable; (*œil, regard*) piercing; (*clairvoyant, perspicace*) perceptive ♦ *nf* (*route*) expressway.

pénétration [penetʀasjɔ̃] *nf* (*fig: d'idées etc*) penetration; (*perspicacité*) perception.

pénétré, e [penetʀe] *adj* (*air, ton*) earnest; **être ~ de soi-même/son importance** to be full of oneself/one's own importance.

pénétrer [penetʀe] *vi* to come *ou* get in ♦ *vt* to penetrate; **~ dans** to enter; (*suj: froid, projectile*) to penetrate; (: *air, eau*) to come into, get into; (*mystère, secret*) to fathom; **se ~ de qch** to get sth firmly set in one's mind.

pénible [penibl(ə)] *adj* (*astreignant*) hard; (*affligeant*) painful; (*personne, caractère*) tiresome; **il m'est ~ de ...** I'm sorry to ....

péniblement [peniblǝmɑ̃] *adv* with difficulty.

péniche [peniʃ] *nf* barge; **~ de débarquement** landing craft *inv*.

pénicilline [penisilin] *nf* penicillin.

péninsulaire [penɛ̃sylɛʀ] *adj* peninsular.

péninsule [penɛ̃syl] *nf* peninsula.

pénis [penis] *nm* penis.

pénitence [penitɑ̃s] *nf* (*repentir*) penitence; (*peine*) penance; (*punition, châtiment*) punishment; **mettre un enfant en ~ ≈** to make a child stand in the corner; **faire ~** to do a penance.

pénitencier [penitɑ̃sje] *nm* prison, penitentiary (*US*).

pénitent, e [penitɑ̃, -ɑ̃t] *adj* penitent.

pénitentiaire [penitɑ̃sjɛʀ] *adj* prison *cpd*, penitentiary (*US*).

pénombre [penɔ̃bʀ(ə)] *nf* half-light.

pensable [pɑ̃sabl(ə)] *adj*: **ce n'est pas ~** it's unthinkable.

pensant, e [pɑ̃sɑ̃, -ɑ̃t] *adj*: **bien ~** right-thinking.

pense-bête [pɑ̃sbɛt] *nm* aide-mémoire, mnemonic device.

pensée [pɑ̃se] *nf* thought; (*démarche, doctrine*) thinking *no pl*; (*BOT*) pansy; **se représenter qch par la ~** to conjure up a mental picture of sth; **en ~** in one's mind.

penser [pɑ̃se] *vi* to think ♦ *vt* to think; (*concevoir: problème, machine*) to think out; **~ à** to think of; (*songer à: ami, vacances*) to think of *ou* about; (*réfléchir à: problème, offre*): **~ à qch** to think about sth, think sth over; **~ à faire qch** to think of doing sth; **~ faire qch** to think of doing sth, intend to do sth; **faire ~ à** to remind one of; **n'y pensons plus** let's forget it; **vous n'y pensez pas!** don't let it bother you!; **sans ~ à mal** without meaning any harm; **je le pense aussi** I think so too; **je pense que oui/non** I think so/don't think so.

penseur [pɑ̃sœʀ] *nm* thinker; **libre ~** free-thinker.

pensif, ive [pɑ̃sif, -iv] *adj* pensive, thoughtful.

pension [pɑ̃sjɔ̃] *nf* (*allocation*) pension; (*prix du logement*) board and lodging, bed and board; (*maison particulière*) boarding house; (*hôtel*) guesthouse, hotel; (*école*) boarding school; **prendre ~ chez** to take board and lodging at; **prendre qn en ~** to take sb (in) as a lodger; **mettre en ~** to send to boarding school; **~ alimentaire** (*d'étudiant*) living allowance; (*de divorcée*) maintenance allowance; alimony; **~ complète** full board; **~ de famille** boarding house, guesthouse; **~ de guerre/d'invalidité** war/disablement pension.

pensionnaire [pɑ̃sjɔnɛʀ] *nm/f* boarder; guest.

pensionnat [pɑ̃sjɔna] *nm* boarding school.

pensionné, e [pɑ̃sjɔne] *nm/f* pensioner.

pensivement [pɑ̃sivmɑ̃] *adv* pensively, thoughtfully.

pensum [pɛ̃sɔm] *nm* (*SCOL*) punishment exercise; (*fig*) chore.

pentagone [pɛ̃tagɔn] *nm* pentagon; **le P~** the

pentathlon – perforé

Pentagon.
pentathlon [pɛ̃tatlɔ̃] *nm* pentathlon.
pente [pɑ̃t] *nf* slope; **en** ~ *adj* sloping.
Pentecôte [pɑ̃tkot] *nf*: **la** ~ Whitsun (*BRIT*), Pentecost; (*dimanche*) Whitsunday (*BRIT*); **lundi de** ~ Whit Monday (*BRIT*).
pénurie [penyʀi] *nf* shortage; ~ **de main-d'œuvre** undermanning.
PEP [pɛp] *sigle m* (= *plan d'épargne populaire*) individual savings plan.
pépé [pepe] *nm* (*fam*) grandad.
pépère [pepɛʀ] *adj* (*fam*) cushy (*fam*), quiet ♦ *nm* (*fam*) grandad.
pépier [pepje] *vi* to chirp, tweet.
pépin [pepɛ̃] *nm* (*BOT: graine*) pip; (*fam: ennui*) snag, hitch; (*: parapluie*) brolly (*BRIT*), umbrella.
pépinière [pepinjɛʀ] *nf* nursery; (*fig*) nest, breeding-ground.
pépiniériste [pepinjeʀist(ə)] *nm* nurseryman.
pépite [pepit] *nf* nugget.
PEPS *abr* (= *premier entré premier sorti*) first in first out.
PER [pɛʀ] *sigle m* (= *plan d'épargne retraite*) type of personal pension plan.
perçant, e [pɛʀsɑ̃, -ɑ̃t] *adj* (*vue, regard, yeux*) sharp, keen; (*cri, voix*) piercing, shrill.
percée [pɛʀse] *nf* (*trouée*) opening; (*MIL, COMM, fig*) breakthrough; (*SPORT*) break.
perce-neige [pɛʀsənɛʒ] *nm ou f inv* snowdrop.
perce-oreille [pɛʀsɔʀɛj] *nm* earwig.
percepteur [pɛʀsɛptœʀ] *nm* tax collector.
perceptible [pɛʀsɛptibl(ə)] *adj* (*son, différence*) perceptible; (*impôt*) payable, collectable.
perception [pɛʀsɛpsjɔ̃] *nf* perception; (*d'impôts etc*) collection; (*bureau*) tax (collector's) office.
percer [pɛʀse] *vt* to pierce; (*ouverture etc*) to make; (*mystère, énigme*) to penetrate ♦ *vi* to come through; (*réussir*) to break through; ~ **une dent** to cut a tooth.
perceuse [pɛʀsøz] *nf* drill; ~ **à percussion** hammer drill.
percevable [pɛʀsəvabl(ə)] *adj* collectable, payable.
percevoir [pɛʀsəvwaʀ] *vt* (*distinguer*) to perceive, detect; (*taxe, impôt*) to collect; (*revenu, indemnité*) to receive.
perche [pɛʀʃ(ə)] *nf* (*ZOOL*) perch; (*bâton*) pole; ~ **à son** (sound) boom.
percher [pɛʀʃe] *vt*: ~ **qch sur** to perch sth on ♦ *vi*, **se** ~ *vi* (*oiseau*) to perch.
perchiste [pɛʀʃist(ə)] *nm/f* (*SPORT*) pole vaulter; (*TV etc*) boom operator.
perchoir [pɛʀʃwaʀ] *nm* perch; (*fig*) *presidency of the French National Assembly*.
perclus, e [pɛʀkly, -yz] *adj*: ~ **de** (*rhumatismes*) crippled with.
perçois [pɛʀswa] *etc vb voir* **percevoir**.
percolateur [pɛʀkɔlatœʀ] *nm* percolator.
perçu, e [pɛʀsy] *pp de* **percevoir**.
percussion [pɛʀkysjɔ̃] *nf* percussion.

percussionniste [pɛʀkysjɔnist(ə)] *nm/f* percussionist.
percutant, e [pɛʀkytɑ̃, -ɑ̃t] *adj* (*article etc*) resounding, forceful.
percuter [pɛʀkyte] *vt* to strike; (*suj: véhicule*) to crash into ♦ *vi*: ~ **contre** to crash into.
percuteur [pɛʀkytœʀ] *nm* firing pin, hammer.
perdant, e [pɛʀdɑ̃, -ɑ̃t] *nm/f* loser ♦ *adj* losing.
perdition [pɛʀdisjɔ̃] *nf* (*morale*) ruin; **en** ~ (*NAVIG*) in distress; **lieu de** ~ den of vice.
perdre [pɛʀdʀ(ə)] *vt* to lose; (*gaspiller: temps, argent*) to waste; (*: occasion*) to waste, miss; (*personne: moralement etc*) to ruin ♦ *vi* to lose; (*sur une vente etc*) to lose out; (*récipient*) to leak; **se** ~ *vi* (*s'égarer*) to get lost, lose one's way; (*fig: se gâter*) to go to waste; (*disparaître*) to disappear, vanish; **il ne perd rien pour attendre** it can wait, it'll keep.
perdreau, x [pɛʀdʀo] *nm* (young) partridge.
perdrix [pɛʀdʀi] *nf* partridge.
perdu, e [pɛʀdy] *pp de* **perdre** ♦ *adj* (*enfant, cause, objet*) lost; (*isolé*) out-of-the-way; (*COMM: emballage*) non-returnable; (*récolte etc*) ruined; (*malade*): **il est** ~ there's no hope left for him; **à vos moments** ~**s** in your spare time.
père [pɛʀ] *nm* father; ~**s** *nmpl* (*ancêtres*) forefathers; **de** ~ **en fils** from father to son; ~ **de famille** father; family man; **mon** ~ (*REL*) Father; **le** ~ **Noël** Father Christmas.
pérégrinations [peʀegʀinasjɔ̃] *nfpl* travels.
péremption [peʀɑ̃psjɔ̃] *nf*: **date de** ~ expiry date.
péremptoire [peʀɑ̃ptwaʀ] *adj* peremptory.
pérennité [peʀenite] *nf* durability, lasting quality.
péréquation [peʀekwasjɔ̃] *nf* (*des salaires*) realignment; (*des prix, impôts*) equalization.
perfectible [pɛʀfɛktibl(ə)] *adj* perfectible.
perfection [pɛʀfɛksjɔ̃] *nf* perfection; **à la** ~ *adv* to perfection.
perfectionné, e [pɛʀfɛksjɔne] *adj* sophisticated.
perfectionnement [pɛʀfɛksjɔnmɑ̃] *nm* improvement.
perfectionner [pɛʀfɛksjɔne] *vt* to improve, perfect; **se** ~ **en anglais** to improve one's English.
perfectionniste [pɛʀfɛksjɔnist(ə)] *nm/f* perfectionist.
perfide [pɛʀfid] *adj* perfidious, treacherous.
perfidie [pɛʀfidi] *nf* treachery.
perforant, e [pɛʀfɔʀɑ̃, -ɑ̃t] *adj* (*balle*) armour-piercing (*BRIT*), armor-piercing (*US*).
perforateur, trice [pɛʀfɔʀatœʀ, -tʀis] *nm/f* punch-card operator ♦ *nm* (*perceuse*) borer; drill ♦ *nf* (*perceuse*) borer; drill; (*pour cartes*) card-punch; (*de bureau*) punch.
perforation [pɛʀfɔʀasjɔ̃] *nf* perforation; punching; (*trou*) hole.
perforatrice [pɛʀfɔʀatʀis] *nf voir* **perforateur**.
perforé, e [pɛʀfɔʀe] *adj*: **bande** ~ punched

tape; **carte** ~ punch card.
perforer [pɛʀfɔʀe] *vt* to perforate, punch a hole (*ou* holes) in; (*ticket, bande, carte*) to punch.
perforeuse [pɛʀfɔʀøz] *nf* (*machine*) (card) punch; (*personne*) card punch operator.
performance [pɛʀfɔʀmɑ̃s] *nf* performance.
performant, e [pɛʀfɔʀmɑ̃, -ɑ̃t] *adj* (*ÉCON: produit, entreprise*) high-return *cpd*; (*TECH: appareil, machine*) high-performance *cpd*.
perfusion [pɛʀfyzjɔ̃] *nf* perfusion; **faire une** ~ **à qn** to put sb on a drip.
péricliter [peʀiklite] *vi* to go downhill.
péridurale [peʀidyʀal] *nf* epidural.
périgourdin, e [peʀiguʀdɛ̃, -in] *adj* of *ou* from the Perigord.
péril [peʀil] *nm* peril; **au** ~ **de sa vie** at the risk of his life; **à ses risques et** ~**s** at his (*ou* her) own risk.
périlleux, euse [peʀijø, -øz] *adj* perilous.
périmé, e [peʀime] *adj* (out)dated; (*ADMIN*) out-of-date, expired.
périmètre [peʀimɛtʀ(ə)] *nm* perimeter.
périnatal, e [peʀinatal] *adj* perinatal.
période [peʀjɔd] *nf* period.
périodique [peʀjɔdik] *adj* (*phases*) periodic; (*publication*) periodical; (*MATH: fraction*) recurring ♦ *nm* periodical; **garniture** *ou* **serviette** ~ sanitary towel (*BRIT*) *ou* napkin (*US*).
périodiquement [peʀjɔdikmɑ̃] *adv* periodically.
péripéties [peʀipesi] *nfpl* events, episodes.
périphérie [peʀifeʀi] *nf* periphery; (*d'une ville*) outskirts *pl*.
périphérique [peʀifeʀik] *adj* (*quartiers*) outlying; (*ANAT, TECH*) peripheral; (*station de radio*) operating from a neighbouring country ♦ *nm* (*INFORM*) peripheral; (*AUTO*): (**boulevard**) ~ ring road (*BRIT*), circular route (*US*).
périphrase [peʀifʀaz] *nf* circumlocution.
périple [peʀipl(ə)] *nm* journey.
périr [peʀiʀ] *vi* to die, perish.
périscolaire [peʀiskɔlɛʀ] *adj* extracurricular.
périscope [peʀiskɔp] *nm* periscope.
périssable [peʀisabl(ə)] *adj* perishable.
péristyle [peʀistil] *nm* peristyle.
péritonite [peʀitɔnit] *nf* peritonitis.
perle [pɛʀl(ə)] *nf* pearl; (*de plastique, métal, sueur*) bead; (*personne, chose*) gem, treasure; (*erreur*) gem, howler.
perlé, e [pɛʀle] *adj* (*rire*) rippling, ⋅tinkling; (*travail*) exquisite; (*orge*) pearl *cpd*; **grève** ~**e** go-slow, selective strike (action).
perler [pɛʀle] *vi* to form in droplets.
perlier, ière [pɛʀlje, -jɛʀ] *adj* pearl *cpd*.
permanence [pɛʀmanɑ̃s] *nf* permanence; (*local*) (duty) office; strike headquarters; (*service des urgences*) emergency service; (*SCOL*) study room; **assurer une** ~ (*service public, bureaux*) to operate *ou* maintain a basic service; **être de** ~ to be on call *ou* duty;

en ~ *adv* (*toujours*) permanently; (*continûment*) continuously.
permanent, e [pɛʀmanɑ̃, -ɑ̃t] *adj* permanent; (*spectacle*) continuous; (*armée, comité*) standing ♦ *nf* perm ♦ *nm/f* (*d'un syndicat, parti*) paid official.
perméable [pɛʀmeabl(ə)] *adj* (*terrain*) permeable; ~ **à** (*fig*) receptive *ou* open to.
permettre [pɛʀmɛtʀ(ə)] *vt* to allow, permit; ~ **à qn de faire/qch** to allow sb to do/sth; **se** ~ **de faire qch** to take the liberty of doing sth; **permettez!** excuse me!
permis, e [pɛʀmi, -iz] *pp de* **permettre** ♦ *nm* permit, licence (*BRIT*), license (*US*); ~ **de chasse** hunting permit; ~ (**de conduire**) (driving) licence (*BRIT*), (driver's) license (*US*); ~ **de construire** planning permission (*BRIT*), building permit (*US*); ~ **d'inhumer** burial certificate; ~ **poids lourds** ≈ HGV (driving) licence (*BRIT*), ≈ class E (driver's) license (*US*); ~ **de séjour** residence permit; ~ **de travail** work permit.
permissif, ive [pɛʀmisif, -iv] *adj* permissive.
permission [pɛʀmisjɔ̃] *nf* permission; (*MIL*) leave; (*: papier*) pass; **en** ~ on leave; **avoir la** ~ **de faire** to have permission to do, be allowed to do.
permissionnaire [pɛʀmisjɔnɛʀ] *nm* soldier on leave.
permutable [pɛʀmytabl(ə)] *adj* which can be changed *ou* switched around.
permuter [pɛʀmyte] *vt* to change around, permutate ♦ *vi* to change, swap.
pernicieux, euse [pɛʀnisjø, -øz] *adj* pernicious.
péroné [peʀɔne] *nm* fibula.
pérorer [peʀɔʀe] *vi* to hold forth.
Pérou [peʀu] *nm:* **le** ~ Peru.
perpendiculaire [pɛʀpɑ̃dikylɛʀ] *adj, nf* perpendicular.
perpendiculairement [pɛʀpɑ̃dikylɛʀmɑ̃] *adv* perpendicularly.
perpète [pɛʀpɛt] *nf:* **à** ~ (*fam: loin*) miles away; (*: longtemps*) forever.
perpétrer [pɛʀpetʀe] *vt* to perpetrate.
perpétuel, le [pɛʀpetɥɛl] *adj* perpetual; (*ADMIN etc*) permanent; for life.
perpétuellement [pɛʀpetɥɛlmɑ̃] *adv* perpetually, constantly.
perpétuer [pɛʀpetɥe] *vt* to perpetuate; **se** ~ (*usage, injustice*) to be perpetuated; (*espèces*) to survive.
perpétuité [pɛʀpetɥite] *nf:* **à** ~ *adj, adv* for life; **être condamné à** ~ to be sentenced to life imprisonment, receive a life sentence.
perplexe [pɛʀplɛks(ə)] *adj* perplexed, puzzled.
perplexité [pɛʀplɛksite] *nf* perplexity.
perquisition [pɛʀkizisjɔ̃] *nf* (police) search.
perquisitionner [pɛʀkizisjɔne] *vi* to carry out a search.
perron [pɛʀɔ̃] *nm* steps *pl* (*in front of mansion etc*).

perroquet [pɛʀɔkɛ] nm parrot.
perruche [peʀyʃ] nf budgerigar (BRIT), budgie (BRIT), parakeet (US).
perruque [peʀyk] nf wig.
persan, e [pɛʀsɑ̃, -an] adj Persian ♦ nm (LING) Persian.
perse [pɛʀs(ə)] adj Persian ♦ nm (LING) Persian ♦ nm/f: P~ Persian ♦ nf: la P~ Persia.
persécuter [pɛʀsekyte] vt to persecute.
persécution [pɛʀsekysjɔ̃] nf persecution.
persévérance [pɛʀseveʀɑ̃s] nf perseverance.
persévérant, e [pɛʀseveʀɑ̃, -ɑ̃t] adj persevering.
persévérer [pɛʀseveʀe] vi to persevere; ~ à croire que to continue to believe that.
persiennes [pɛʀsjɛn] nfpl (slatted) shutters.
persiflage [pɛʀsiflaʒ] nm mockery no pl.
persifleur, euse [pɛʀsiflœʀ, -øz] adj mocking.
persil [pɛʀsi] nm parsley.
persillé, e [pɛʀsije] adj (sprinkled) with parsley; (fromage) veined; (viande) marbled, with fat running through.
Persique [pɛʀsik] adj: le golfe ~ the (Persian) Gulf.
persistance [pɛʀsistɑ̃s] nf persistence.
persistant, e [pɛʀsistɑ̃, -ɑ̃t] adj persistent; (feuilles) evergreen; à feuillage ~ evergreen.
persister [pɛʀsiste] vi to persist; ~ à faire qch to persist in doing sth.
personnage [pɛʀsɔnaʒ] nm (notable) personality; figure; (individu) character, individual; (THÉÂT) character; (PEINTURE) figure.
personnaliser [pɛʀsɔnalize] vt to personalize; (appartement) to give a personal touch to.
personnalité [pɛʀsɔnalite] nf personality; (personnage) prominent figure.
personne [pɛʀsɔn] nf person ♦ pron nobody, no one; (quelqu'un) anybody, anyone; ~s nfpl people pl; il n'y a ~ there's nobody in ou there, there isn't anybody in ou there; 10 F par ~ 10 F per person ou a head; en ~ personally, in person; ~ âgée elderly person; ~ à charge (JUR) dependent; ~ morale ou civile (JUR) legal entity.
personnel, le [pɛʀsɔnɛl] adj personal; (égoïste: personne) selfish, self-centred; (idée, opinion): j'ai des idées ~les à ce sujet I have my own ideas about that ♦ nm personnel, staff; service du ~ personnel department.
personnellement [pɛʀsɔnɛlmɑ̃] adv personally.
personnification [pɛʀsɔnifikasjɔ̃] nf personification; c'est la ~ de la cruauté he's cruelty personified.
personnifier [pɛʀsɔnifje] vt to personify; to typify; c'est l'honnêteté personnifiée he (ou she etc) is honesty personified.
perspective [pɛʀspɛktiv] nf (ART) perspective; (vue, coup d'œil) view; (point de vue) viewpoint, angle; (chose escomptée, envisagée) prospect; en ~ in prospect.

perspicace [pɛʀspikas] adj clear-sighted, gifted with (ou showing) insight.
perspicacité [pɛʀspikasite] nf insight, perspicacity.
persuader [pɛʀsɥade] vt: ~ qn (de/de faire) to persuade sb (of/to do); j'en suis persuadé I'm quite sure ou convinced (of it).
persuasif, ive [pɛʀsɥazif, -iv] adj persuasive.
persuasion [pɛʀsɥazjɔ̃] nf persuasion.
perte [pɛʀt(ə)] nf loss; (de temps) waste; (fig: morale) ruin; ~s nfpl losses; à ~ (COMM) at a loss; à ~ de vue as far as the eye can (ou could) see; (fig) interminably; en pure ~ for absolutely nothing; courir à sa ~ to be on the road to ruin; être en ~ de vitesse (fig) to be losing momentum; avec ~ et fracas forcibly; ~ de chaleur heat loss; ~ sèche dead loss; ~s blanches (vaginal) discharge sg.
pertinemment [pɛʀtinamɑ̃] adv to the point; (savoir) perfectly well, full well.
pertinence [pɛʀtinɑ̃s] nf pertinence, relevance; discernment.
pertinent, e [pɛʀtinɑ̃, -ɑ̃t] adj (remarque) apt, pertinent, relevant; (analyse) discerning, judicious.
perturbateur, trice [pɛʀtyʀbatœʀ, -tʀis] adj disruptive.
perturbation [pɛʀtyʀbasjɔ̃] nf (dans un service public) disruption; (agitation, trouble) perturbation; ~ (atmosphérique) atmospheric disturbance.
perturber [pɛʀtyʀbe] vt to disrupt; (PSYCH) to perturb, disturb.
péruvien, ne [peʀyvjɛ̃, -ɛn] adj Peruvian ♦ nm/f: P~, ne Peruvian.
pervenche [pɛʀvɑ̃ʃ] nf periwinkle; (fam) traffic warden (BRIT), meter maid (US).
pervers, e [pɛʀvɛʀ, -ɛʀs(ə)] adj perverted, depraved; (malfaisant) perverse.
perversion [pɛʀvɛʀsjɔ̃] nf perversion.
perversité [pɛʀvɛʀsite] nf depravity; perversity.
perverti, e [pɛʀvɛʀti] nm/f pervert.
pervertir [pɛʀvɛʀtiʀ] vt to pervert.
pesage [pəzaʒ] nm weighing; (HIPPISME: action) weigh-in; (: salle) weighing room; (: enceinte) enclosure.
pesamment [pəzamɑ̃] adv heavily.
pesant, e [pəzɑ̃, -ɑ̃t] adj heavy; (fig) burdensome ♦ nm: valoir son ~ de to be worth one's weight in.
pesanteur [pəzɑ̃tœʀ] nf gravity.
pèse-bébé [pɛzbebe] nm (baby) scales pl.
pesée [pəze] nf weighing; (BOXE) weigh-in; (pression) pressure.
pèse-lettre [pɛzlɛtʀ(ə)] nm letter scales pl.
pèse-personne [pɛzpɛʀsɔn] nm (bathroom) scales pl.
peser [pəze] vt, vb avec attribut to weigh; (considérer, comparer) to weigh up ♦ vi to be heavy; (fig) to carry weight; ~ sur (levier, bouton) to press, push; (fig: accabler) to lie heavy on;

(*: influencer*) to influence; ~ **à qn** to weigh heavy on sb.

pessaire [pɛsɛʀ] *nm* pessary.

pessimisme [pesimism(ə)] *nm* pessimism.

pessimiste [pesimist(ə)] *adj* pessimistic ♦ *nm/f* pessimist.

peste [pɛst(ə)] *nf* plague; (*fig*) pest, nuisance.

pester [pɛste] *vi*: ~ **contre** to curse.

pesticide [pɛstisid] *nm* pesticide.

pestiféré, e [pɛstifeʀe] *nm/f* plague victim.

pestilentiel, le [pɛstilɑ̃sjɛl] *adj* foul.

pet [pɛ] *nm* (*fam!*) fart (*!*).

pétale [petal] *nm* petal.

pétanque [petɑ̃k] *nf* type of bowls.

Pétanque *is a version of the game of* **boules***, played on a variety of hard surfaces. Standing with their feet together, players throw steel bowls towards a wooden jack. Pétanque originated in the south of France and is still very much associated with that area.*

---

pétarade [petaʀad] *nf* backfiring *no pl*.

pétarader [petaʀade] *vi* to backfire.

pétard [petaʀ] *nm* (*feu d'artifice*) banger (*BRIT*), firecracker; (*de cotillon*) cracker; (*RAIL*) detonator.

pet-de-nonne, *pl* **pets-de-nonne** [pɛdnɔn] *nm* ≈ choux bun.

péter [pete] *vi* (*fam: casser, sauter*) to burst; to bust; (*fam!*) to fart (*!*).

pète-sec [pɛtsɛk] *adj inv* abrupt, sharp(-tongued).

pétillant, e [petijɑ̃, -ɑ̃t] *adj* sparkling.

pétiller [petije] *vi* (*flamme, bois*) to crackle; (*mousse, champagne*) to bubble; (*pierre, métal*) to glisten; (*yeux*) to sparkle; (*fig*): ~ **d'esprit** to sparkle with wit.

petit, e [pəti, -it] *adj* (*gén*) small; (*main, objet, colline, en âge: enfant*) small, little; (*mince, fin: personne, taille, pluie*) slight; (*voyage*) short, little; (*bruit etc*) faint, slight; (*mesquin*) mean; (*peu important*) minor ♦ *nm/f* (*petit enfant*) little one, child ♦ *nmpl* (*d'un animal*) young *pl*; **faire des** ~**s** to have kittens (*ou* puppies *etc*); **en** ~ in miniature; **mon** ~ son; little one; **ma** ~**e** dear; little one; **pauvre** ~ poor little thing; **la classe des** ~**s** the infant class; **pour** ~**s et grands** for children and adults; **les tout-**~**s** the little ones, the tiny tots; ~ **à** ~ bit by bit, gradually; ~**(e) ami/e** boyfriend/girlfriend; **les** ~**es annonces** the small ads; ~ **déjeuner** breakfast; ~ **doigt** little finger; **le** ~ **écran** the small screen; ~ **four** petit four; ~ **pain** (bread) roll; ~**e monnaie** small change; ~**e vérole** smallpox; ~**s pois** petit pois *pl*, garden peas; ~**es gens** people of modest means.

petit-beurre, *pl* **petits-beurre** [pətibœʀ] *nm* sweet butter biscuit (*BRIT*) *ou* cookie (*US*).

petit(e)-bourgeois(e), *pl* **petit(e)s-bourgeois(es)** [pəti(t)buʀʒwa(z)] *adj* (*péj*) petit-bourgeois, middle-class.

petite-fille, *pl* **petites-filles** [pətitfij] *nf* granddaughter.

petitement [pətitmɑ̃] *adv* poorly; meanly; **être logé** ~ to be in cramped accommodation.

petitesse [pətitɛs] *nf* smallness; (*d'un salaire, de revenus*) modestness; (*mesquinerie*) meanness.

petit-fils, *pl* **petits-fils** [pətifis] *nm* grandson.

pétition [petisjɔ̃] *nf* petition; **faire signer une** ~ to get up a petition.

pétitionnaire [petisjɔnɛʀ] *nm/f* petitioner.

pétitionner [petisjɔne] *vi* to petition.

petit-lait, *pl* **petits-laits** [pətilɛ] *nm* whey *no pl*.

petit-nègre [pətinɛgʀ(ə)] *nm* (*péj*) pidgin French.

petits-enfants [pətizɑ̃fɑ̃] *nmpl* grandchildren.

petit-suisse, *pl* **petits-suisses** [pətisɥis] *nm* small individual pot of cream cheese.

pétoche [petɔʃ] *nf* (*fam*): **avoir la** ~ to be scared out of one's wits.

pétri, e [petʀi] *adj*: ~ **d'orgueil** filled with pride.

pétrifier [petʀifje] *vt* to petrify; (*fig*) to paralyze, transfix.

pétrin [petʀɛ̃] *nm* kneading-trough; (*fig*): **dans le** ~ in a jam *ou* fix.

pétrir [petʀiʀ] *vt* to knead.

pétrochimie [petʀoʃimi] *nf* petrochemistry.

pétrochimique [petʀoʃimik] *adj* petrochemical.

pétrodollar [petʀodɔlaʀ] *nm* petrodollar.

pétrole [petʀɔl] *nm* oil; (*aussi*: ~ **lampant**) paraffin (*BRIT*), kerosene (*US*).

pétrolier, ière [petʀɔlje, -jɛʀ] *adj* oil *cpd*; (*pays*) oil-producing ♦ *nm* (*navire*) oil tanker; (*financier*) oilman; (*technicien*) petroleum engineer.

pétrolifère [petʀɔlifɛʀ] *adj* oil(-bearing).

P et T *sigle fpl* = *postes et télécommunications*.

pétulant, e [petylɑ̃, -ɑ̃t] *adj* exuberant.

pétunia [petynja] *nm* petunia.

═══════════════ *MOT-CLÉ*

peu [pø] *adv* **1** (*modifiant verbe, adjectif, adverbe*): **il boit** ~ he doesn't drink (very) much; **il est** ~ **bavard** he's not very talkative; ~ **avant/après** shortly before/afterwards; **pour** ~ **qu'il fasse** if he should do, if by any chance he does

2 (*modifiant nom*): ~ **de:** ~ **de gens/d'arbres** few *ou* not (very) many people/trees; **il a** ~ **d'espoir** he hasn't (got) much hope, he has little hope; **pour** ~ **de temps** for (only) a short while; **à** ~ **de frais** for very little cost

3: ~ **à** ~ little by little; **à** ~ **près** just about, more or less; **à** ~ **près 10 kg/10 F** approximately 10 kg/10 F

♦ *nm* **1**: **le** ~ **de gens qui** the few people who; **le** ~ **de sable qui** what little sand, the little sand which

2: **un** ~ a little; **un petit** ~ a little bit; **un** ~

d'espoir a little hope; **elle est un ~ bavarde** she's rather talkative; **un ~ plus/moins de** slightly more/less (*ou* fewer) than; **pour un ~ il ..., un ~ plus et il ...** he very nearly *ou* all but ...; **essayez un ~!** have a go!, just try it!

♦ *pron*: **~ le savent** few know (it); **avant** *ou* **sous ~** shortly, before long; **depuis ~** for a short *ou* little while; (*au passé*) a short *ou* little while ago; **de ~** (only) just; **c'est ~ de chose** it's nothing; **il est de ~ mon cadet** he's just a little *ou* bit younger than me.

peuplade [pœplad] *nf* (*horde, tribu*) tribe, people.

peuple [pœpl(ə)] *nm* people; (*masse indifférenciée*): **un ~ de vacanciers** a crowd of holiday-makers; **il y a du ~** there are a lot of people.

peuplé, e [pœple] *adj*: **très/peu ~** densely/sparsely populated.

peupler [pœple] *vt* (*pays, région*) to populate; (*étang*) to stock; (*suj: hommes, poissons*) to inhabit; (*fig: imagination, rêves*) to fill; **se ~** *vi* (*ville, région*) to become populated; (*fig: s'animer*) to fill (up), be filled.

peuplier [pøplije] *nm* poplar (tree).

peur [pœʀ] *nf* fear; **avoir ~ (de/de faire/que)** to be frightened *ou* afraid (of/of doing/that); **prendre ~** to take fright; **faire ~ à** to frighten; **de ~ de/que** for fear of/that; **j'ai ~ qu'il ne soit trop tard** I'm afraid it might be too late; **j'ai ~ qu'il (ne) vienne (pas)** I'm afraid he may (not) come.

peureux, euse [pœʀø, -øz] *adj* fearful, timorous.

peut [pø] *vb voir* **pouvoir.**

peut-être [pøtɛtʀ(ə)] *adv* perhaps, maybe; **~ que** perhaps, maybe; **~ bien qu'il fera/est** he may well do/be.

peuvent [pœv], **peux** [pø] *etc vb voir* **pouvoir.**

p. ex. *abr* (= *par exemple*) e.g.

phalange [falɑ̃ʒ] *nf* (*ANAT*) phalanx (*pl* phalanges); (*MIL, fig*) phalanx (*pl* -es).

phallique [falik] *adj* phallic.

phallocrate [falɔkʀat] *nm* male chauvinist.

phallocratie [falɔkʀasi] *nf* male chauvinism.

phallus [falys] *nm* phallus.

pharaon [faʀaɔ̃] *nm* Pharaoh.

phare [faʀ] *nm* (*en mer*) lighthouse; (*d'aéroport*) beacon; (*de véhicule*) headlight, headlamp (*BRIT*) ♦ *adj*: **produit ~** leading product; **se mettre en ~s,** **mettre ses ~s** to put on one's headlights; **~s de recul** reversing (*BRIT*) *ou* back-up (*US*) lights.

pharmaceutique [faʀmasøtik] *adj* pharmaceutic(al).

pharmacie [faʀmasi] *nf* (*science*) pharmacology; (*magasin*) chemist's (*BRIT*), pharmacy; (*officine*) dispensary; (*produits*) pharmaceuticals *pl*; (*armoire*) medicine chest *ou* cupboard, first-aid cupboard.

pharmacien, ne [faʀmasjɛ̃, -ɛn] *nm/f* pharmacist, chemist (*BRIT*).

pharmacologie [faʀmakɔlɔʒi] *nf* pharmacology.

pharyngite [faʀɛ̃ʒit] *nf* pharyngitis *no pl.*

pharynx [faʀɛ̃ks] *nm* pharynx.

phase [faz] *nf* phase.

phénoménal, e, aux [fenɔmenal, -o] phenomenal.

phénomène [fenɔmɛn] *nm* phenomenon (*pl* -a); (*monstre*) freak.

philanthrope [filɑ̃tʀɔp] *nm/f* philanthropist.

philanthropie [filɑ̃tʀɔpi] *nf* philanthropy.

philanthropique [filɑ̃tʀɔpik] *adj* philanthropic.

philatélie [filateli] *nf* philately, stamp collecting.

philatélique [filatelik] *adj* philatelic.

philatéliste [filatelist(ə)] *nm/f* philatelist, stamp collector.

philharmonique [filaʀmɔnik] *adj* philharmonic.

philippin, e [filipɛ̃, -in] *adj* Filipino.

Philippines [filipin] *nfpl*: **les ~** the Philippines.

philistin [filistɛ̃] *nm* philistine.

philo [filo] *nf* (*fam*: = *philosophie*) philosophy.

philosophe [filozɔf] *nm/f* philosopher ♦ *adj* philosophical.

philosopher [filozɔfe] *vi* to philosophize.

philosophie [filozɔfi] *nf* philosophy.

philosophique [filozɔfik] *adj* philosophical.

philosophiquement [filozɔfikmɑ̃] *adv* philosophically.

philtre [filtʀ(ə)] *nm* philtre, love potion.

phlébite [flebit] *nf* phlebitis.

phlébologue [flebɔlɔg] *nm/f* vein specialist.

phobie [fɔbi] *nf* phobia.

phonétique [fɔnetik] *adj* phonetic ♦ *nf* phonetics *sg.*

phonétiquement [fɔnetikmɑ̃] *adv* phonetically.

phonographe [fɔnɔgʀaf] *nm* (wind-up) gramophone.

phoque [fɔk] *nm* seal; (*fourrure*) sealskin.

phosphate [fɔsfat] *nm* phosphate.

phosphaté, e [fɔsfate] *adj* phosphate-enriched.

phosphore [fɔsfɔʀ] *nm* phosphorus.

phosphoré, e [fɔsfɔʀe] *adj* phosphorous.

phosphorescent, e [fɔsfɔʀesɑ̃, -ɑ̃t] *adj* luminous.

phosphorique [fɔsfɔʀik] *adj*: **acide ~** phosphoric acid.

photo [fɔto] *nf* (= *photographie*) photo ♦ *adj*: **appareil/pellicule ~** camera/film; **en ~** in *ou* on a photo; **prendre en ~** to take a photo of; **aimer la/faire de la ~** to like taking/take photos; **~ en couleurs** colour photo; **~ d'identité** passport photo.

photo... [fɔtɔ] *préfixe* photo....

photocopie [fɔtɔkɔpi] *nf* (*procédé*) photocopying; (*document*) photocopy.

photocopier [fɔtɔkɔpje] *vt* to photocopy.
photocopieur [fɔtɔkɔpjœʀ] *nm*, **photocopieuse** [fɔtɔkɔpjøz] *nf* (photo)copier.
photo-électrique [fɔtɔelɛktʀik] *adj* photoelectric.
photo-finish, *pl* **photos-finish** [fɔtɔfiniʃ] *nf* (*appareil*) photo finish camera; (*photo*) photo finish picture; **il y a eu ~ pour la troisième place** there was a photo finish for third place.
photogénique [fɔtɔʒenik] *adj* photogenic.
photographe [fɔtɔgʀaf] *nm/f* photographer.
photographie [fɔtɔgʀafi] *nf* (*procédé, technique*) photography; (*cliché*) photograph; **faire de la ~** to have photography as a hobby; (*comme métier*) to be a photographer.
photographier [fɔtɔgʀafje] *vt* to photograph, take.
photographique [fɔtɔgʀafik] *adj* photographic.
photogravure [fɔtɔgʀavyʀ] *nf* photoengraving.
photomaton [fɔtɔmatɔ̃] *nm* photo-booth, photomat.
photomontage [fɔtɔmɔ̃taʒ] *nm* photomontage.
photo-robot [fɔtɔʀɔbo] *nf* Identikit ® (picture).
photosensible [fɔtɔsɑ̃sibl(ə)] *adj* photosensitive.
photostat [fɔtɔsta] *nm* photostat.
phrase [fʀɑz] *nf* (*LING*) sentence; (*propos, MUS*) phrase; **~s** *nfpl* (*péj*) flowery language *sg*.
phraséologie [fʀazeɔlɔʒi] *nf* phraseology; (*rhétorique*) flowery language.
phraseur, euse [fʀazœʀ, -øz] *nm/f*: **c'est un ~** he uses such flowery language.
phrygien, ne [fʀiʒjɛ̃, -ɛn] *adj*: **bonnet ~** Phrygian cap.
phtisie [ftizi] *nf* consumption.
phylloxéra [filɔkseʀa] *nm* phylloxera.
physicien, ne [fizisjɛ̃, -ɛn] *nm/f* physicist.
physiologie [fizjɔlɔʒi] *nf* physiology.
physiologique [fizjɔlɔʒik] *adj* physiological.
physiologiquement [fizjɔlɔʒikmɑ̃] *adv* physiologically.
physionomie [fizjɔnɔmi] *nf* face; (*d'un paysage etc*) physiognomy.
physionomiste [fizjɔnɔmist(ə)] *nm/f* good judge of faces; person who has a good memory for faces.
physiothérapie [fizjɔteʀapi] *nf* natural medicine, alternative medicine.
physique [fizik] *adj* physical ♦ *nm* physique ♦ *nf* physics *sg*; **au ~** physically.
physiquement [fizikmɑ̃] *adv* physically.
phytothérapie [fitɔteʀapi] *nf* herbal medicine.
p.i. *abr* = **par intérim;** *voir* **intérim.**
piaffer [pjafe] *vi* to stamp.
piaillement [pjajmɑ̃] *nm* squawking *no pl*.

piailler [pjaje] *vi* to squawk.
pianiste [pjanist(ə)] *nm/f* pianist.
piano [pjano] *nm* piano; **~ à queue** grand piano.
pianoter [pjanɔte] *vi* to tinkle away (at the piano); (*tapoter*): **~ sur** to drum one's fingers on.
piaule [pjol] *nf* (*fam*) pad.
piauler [pjole] *vi* (*enfant*) to whimper; (*oiseau*) to cheep.
PIB *sigle m* (= *produit intérieur brut*) GDP.
pic [pik] *nm* (*instrument*) pick(axe); (*montagne*) peak; (*ZOOL*) woodpecker; **à ~** *adv* vertically; (*fig*) just at the right time; **couler à ~** (*bateau*) to go straight down; **~ à glace** ice pick.
picard, e [pikaʀ, -aʀd(ə)] *adj* of *ou* from Picardy.
Picardie [pikaʀdi] *nf*: **la ~** Picardy.
picaresque [pikaʀɛsk(ə)] *adj* picaresque.
piccolo [pikɔlo] *nm* piccolo.
pichenette [piʃnɛt] *nf* flick.
pichet [piʃɛ] *nm* jug.
pickpocket [pikpɔkɛt] *nm* pickpocket.
pick-up [pikœp] *nm inv* record player.
picorer [pikɔʀe] *vt* to peck.
picot [piko] *nm* sprocket; **entraînement par roue à ~s** sprocket feed.
picotement [pikɔtmɑ̃] *nm* smarting *no pl*, prickling *no pl*.
picoter [pikɔte] *vt* (*suj: oiseau*) to peck ♦ *vi* (*irriter*) to smart, prickle.
pictural, e, aux [piktyʀal, -o] *adj* pictorial.
pie [pi] *nf* magpie; (*fig*) chatterbox ♦ *adj inv*: **cheval ~** piebald; **vache ~** black and white cow.
pièce [pjɛs] *nf* (*d'un logement*) room; (*THÉÂT*) play; (*de mécanisme, machine*) part; (*de monnaie*) coin; (*COUTURE*) patch; (*document*) document; (*de drap, fragment, d'une collection*) piece; (*de bétail*) head; **mettre en ~s** to smash to pieces; **dix francs ~** ten francs each; **vendre à la ~** to sell separately *ou* individually; **travailler/payer à la ~** to do piecework/pay piece rate; **de toutes ~s:** **c'est inventé de toutes ~s** it's a complete fabrication; **un maillot une ~** a one-piece swimsuit; **un deux-~s cuisine** a two-room(ed) flat (*BRIT*) *ou* apartment (*US*) with kitchen; **tout d'une ~** (*personne: franc*) blunt; (*: sans souplesse*) inflexible; **~ à conviction** exhibit; **~ d'eau** ornamental lake *ou* pond; **~ d'identité: avez-vous une ~ d'identité?** have you got any (means of) identification?; **~ montée** tiered cake; **~ de rechange** spare (part); **~ de résistance** pièce de résistance; (*plat*) main dish; **~s détachées** spares, (spare) parts; **en ~s détachées** (*à monter*) in kit form; **~s justificatives** supporting documents.
pied [pje] *nm* foot (*pl* feet); (*de verre*) stem; (*de table*) leg; (*de lampe*) base; (*plante*) plant; **~s**

nus barefoot; **à ~ on** foot; **à ~ sec** without getting one's feet wet; **à ~ d'œuvre** ready to start (work); **au ~ de la lettre** literally; **au ~ levé** at a moment's notice; **de ~ en cap** from head to foot; **en ~** (*portrait*) full-length; **avoir ~ to** be able to touch the bottom, not to be out of one's depth; **avoir le ~ marin** to be a good sailor; **perdre ~ to** lose one's footing; (*fig*) to get out of one's depth; **sur ~** (*AGR*) on the stalk, uncut; (*debout, rétabli*) up and about; **mettre sur ~** (*entreprise*) to set up; **mettre à ~ to** suspend; to lay off; **mettre qn au ~ du mur** to get sb with his (*ou* her) back to the wall; **sur le ~ de guerre** ready for action; **sur un ~ d'égalité** on an equal footing; **sur ~ d'intervention** on stand-by; **faire du ~ à qn** (*prévenir*) to give sb a (warning) kick; (*galamment*) to play footsie with sb; **mettre les ~s quelque part** to set foot somewhere; **faire des ~s et des mains** (*fig*) to move heaven and earth, pull out all the stops; **c'est le ~!** (*fam*) it's terrific!; **se lever du bon ~/du ~ gauche** to get out of bed on the right/ wrong side; **~ de lit** footboard; **~ de nez: faire un ~ de nez à** to thumb one's nose at; **~ de vigne** vine.

pied-à-terre [pjetatɛʀ] *nm inv* pied-à-terre.

pied-bot, *pl* **pieds-bots** [pjebo] *nm* person with a club foot.

pied-de-biche, *pl* **pieds-de-biche** [pjedbiʃ] *nm* claw; (*COUTURE*) presser foot.

pied-de-poule [pjedpul] *adj inv* hound's-tooth.

piédestal, aux [pjedɛstal, -o] *nm* pedestal.

pied-noir, *pl* **pieds-noirs** [pjenwaʀ] *nm* Algerian-born Frenchman.

piège [pjɛʒ] *nm* trap; **prendre au ~ to** trap.

piéger [pjeʒe] *vt* (*animal, fig*) to trap; (*avec une bombe*) to booby-trap; **lettre/voiture piégée** letter-/car-bomb.

pierraille [pjɛʀaj] *nf* loose stones *pl*.

pierre [pjɛʀ] *nf* stone; **première ~** (*d'un édifice*) foundation stone; **mur de ~s sèches** dry-stone wall; **faire d'une ~ deux coups** to kill two birds with one stone; **~ à briquet** flint; **~ fine** semiprecious stone; **~ ponce** pumice stone; **~ de taille** freestone *no pl*; **~ tombale** tombstone, gravestone; **~ de touche** touchstone.

pierreries [pjɛʀʀi] *nfpl* gems, precious stones.

pierreux, euse [pjɛʀø, -øz] *adj* stony.

piété [pjete] *nf* piety.

piétinement [pjetinmɑ̃] *nm* stamping *no pl*.

piétiner [pjetine] *vi* (*trépigner*) to stamp (one's foot); (*marquer le pas*) to stand about; (*fig*) to be at a standstill ♦ *vt* to trample on.

piéton, ne [pjetɔ̃, -ɔn] *nm/f* pedestrian ♦ *adj* pedestrian *cpd*.

piétonnier, ière [pjetɔnje, -jɛʀ] *adj* pedestrian *cpd*.

piètre [pjɛtʀ(ə)] *adj* poor, mediocre.

pieu, x [pjø] *nm* (*piquet*) post; (*pointu*) stake; (*fam: lit*) bed.

pieusement [pjøzmɑ̃] *adv* piously.

pieuvre [pjœvʀ(ə)] *nf* octopus.

pieux, euse [pjø, -øz] *adj* pious.

pif [pif] *nm* (*fam*) conk (*BRIT*), beak; **au ~ = au pifomètre**.

piffer [pife] *vt* (*fam*): **je ne peux pas le ~** I can't stand him.

pifomètre [pifɔmɛtʀ(ə)] *nm* (*fam*): **choisir** *etc* **au ~** to follow one's nose when choosing *etc*.

pige [piʒ] *nf* piecework rate.

pigeon [piʒɔ̃] *nm* pigeon; **~ voyageur** homing pigeon.

pigeonnant, e [piʒɔnɑ̃, -ɑ̃t] *adj* full, well-developed.

pigeonneau, x [piʒɔno] *nm* young pigeon.

pigeonnier [piʒɔnje] *nm* pigeon loft, dove-cot(e).

piger [piʒe] *vi* (*fam*) to get it ♦ *vt* (*fam*) to get, understand.

pigiste [piʒist(ə)] *nm/f* (*typographe*) typesetter on piecework; (*journaliste*) freelance journalist (*paid by the line*).

pigment [pigmɑ̃] *nm* pigment.

pignon [piɲɔ̃] *nm* (*de mur*) gable; (*d'engrenage*) cog(wheel), gearwheel; (*graine*) pine kernel; **avoir ~ sur rue** (*fig*) to have a prosperous business.

pile [pil] *nf* (*tas, pilier*) pile; (*ÉLEC*) battery ♦ *adj*: **le côté ~** tails ♦ *adv* (*net, brusquement*) dead; (*à temps, à point nommé*) just at the right time; **à deux heures ~** at two on the dot; **jouer à ~ ou face** to toss up (for it); **~ ou face?** heads or tails?

piler [pile] *vt* to crush, pound.

pileux, euse [pilø, -øz] *adj*: **système ~** (body) hair.

pilier [pilje] *nm* (*colonne, support*) pillar; (*personne*) mainstay; (*RUGBY*) prop (forward).

pillage [pijaʒ] *nm* pillaging, plundering, looting.

pillard, e [pijaʀ, -aʀd(ə)] *nm/f* looter; plunderer.

piller [pije] *vt* to pillage, plunder, loot.

pilleur, euse [pijœʀ, -øz] *nm/f* looter.

pilon [pilɔ̃] *nm* (*instrument*) pestle; (*de volaille*) drumstick; **mettre un livre au ~** to pulp a book.

pilonner [pilɔne] *vt* to pound.

pilori [pilɔʀi] *nm*: **mettre** *ou* **clouer au ~** to pillory.

pilotage [pilɔtaʒ] *nm* piloting; flying; **~ automatique** automatic piloting; **~ sans visibilité** blind flying.

pilote [pilɔt] *nm* pilot; (*de char, voiture*) driver ♦ *adj* pilot *cpd*; **usine/ferme ~** experimental factory/farm; **~ de chasse/d'essai/de ligne** fighter/test/airline pilot; **~ de course** racing driver.

piloter [pilɔte] *vt* (*navire*) to pilot; (*avion*) to fly; (*automobile*) to drive; (*fig*): **~ qn** to guide sb round; **piloté par menu** (*INFORM*) menu-driven.

pilotis [piloti] *nm* pile; stilt.

pilule [pilyl] *nf* pill; **prendre la ~** to be on the pill; **~ du lendemain** morning-after pill.

pimbêche [pɛ̃bɛʃ] *nf (péj)* stuck-up girl.

piment [pimɑ̃] *nm (BOT)* pepper, capsicum; *(fig)* spice, piquancy; **~ rouge** *(CULIN)* chilli.

pimenté, e [pimɑ̃te] *adj* hot and spicy.

pimenter [pimɑ̃te] *vt (plat)* to season (with peppers *ou* chillis); *(fig)* to add *ou* give spice to.

pimpant, e [pɛ̃pɑ̃, -ɑ̃t] *adj* spruce.

pin [pɛ̃] *nm* pine (tree); *(bois)* pine(wood).

pinacle [pinakl(ə)] *nm*: **porter qn au ~** *(fig)* to praise sb to the skies.

pinard [pinaʀ] *nm (fam)* (cheap) wine, plonk *(BRIT)*.

pince [pɛ̃s] *nf (outil)* pliers *pl*; *(de homard, crabe)* pincer, claw; *(COUTURE: pli)* dart; **~ à sucre/glace** sugar/ice tongs *pl*; **~ à épiler** tweezers *pl*; **~ à linge** clothes peg *(BRIT)* ou pin *(US)*; **~ universelle** (universal) pliers *pl*; **~s de cycliste** bicycle clips.

pincé, e [pɛ̃se] *adj (air)* stiff; *(mince: bouche)* pinched ♦ *nf*: **une ~e de** a pinch of.

pinceau, x [pɛ̃so] *nm* (paint)brush.

pincement [pɛ̃smɑ̃] *nm*: **~ au cœur** twinge of regret.

pince-monseigneur, *pl* **pinces-monseigneur** [pɛ̃smɔ̃sɛɲœʀ] *nf* crowbar.

pince-nez [pɛ̃sne] *nm inv* pince-nez.

pincer [pɛ̃se] *vt* to pinch; *(MUS: cordes)* to pluck; *(COUTURE)* to dart, put darts in; *(fam)* to nab; **se ~ le doigt** to squeeze *ou* nip one's finger; **se ~ le nez** to hold one's nose.

pince-sans-rire [pɛ̃ssɑ̃ʀiʀ] *adj inv* deadpan.

pincettes [pɛ̃sɛt] *nfpl* tweezers; *(pour le feu)* (fire) tongs.

pinçon [pɛ̃sɔ̃] *nm* pinch mark.

pinède [pined] *nf* pinewood, pine forest.

pingouin [pɛ̃gwɛ̃] *nm* penguin.

ping-pong [piŋpɔ̃g] *nm* table tennis.

pingre [pɛ̃gʀ(ə)] *adj* niggardly.

pinson [pɛ̃sɔ̃] *nm* chaffinch.

pintade [pɛ̃tad] *nf* guinea-fowl.

pin up [pinœp] *nf inv* pin-up (girl).

pioche [pjɔʃ] *nf* pickaxe.

piocher [pjɔʃe] *vt* to dig up (with a pickaxe); *(fam)* to swot *(BRIT)* ou grind *(US)* at; **~ dans** to dig into.

piolet [pjɔlɛ] *nm* ice axe.

pion, ne [pjɔ̃, pjɔn] *nm/f (SCOL: péj)* student *paid to supervise schoolchildren* ♦ *nm (ÉCHECS)* pawn; *(DAMES)* piece, draught *(BRIT)*, checker *(US)*.

pionnier [pjɔnje] *nm* pioneer.

pipe [pip] *nf* pipe; **fumer la** *ou* **une ~** to smoke a pipe; **~ de bruyère** briar pipe.

pipeau, x [pipo] *nm* (reed-)pipe.

pipe-line [piplin] *nm* pipeline.

piper [pipe] *vt (dé)* to load; *(carte)* to mark; **sans ~ mot** *(fam)* without a squeak; **les dés**

sont pipés *(fig)* the dice are loaded.

pipette [pipɛt] *nf* pipette.

pipi [pipi] *nm (fam)*: **faire ~** to have a wee.

piquant, e [pikɑ̃, -ɑ̃t] *adj (barbe, rosier etc)* prickly; *(saveur, sauce)* hot, pungent; *(fig: description, style)* racy; *(: mordant, caustique)* biting ♦ *nm (épine)* thorn, prickle; *(de hérisson)* quill, spine; *(fig)* spiciness, spice.

pique [pik] *nf (arme)* pike; *(fig)*: **envoyer** *ou* **lancer des ~s à qn** to make cutting remarks to sb ♦ *nm (CARTES: couleur)* spades *pl*; *(: carte)* spade.

piqué, e [pike] *adj (COUTURE)* (machine-) stitched; quilted; *(livre, glace)* mildewed; *(vin)* sour; *(MUS: note)* staccato; *(fam: personne)* nuts ♦ *nm (AVIAT)* dive; *(TEXTILE)* piqué.

pique-assiette [pikasjɛt] *nm/f inv (péj)* scrounger, sponger.

pique-fleurs [pikflœʀ] *nm inv* flower holder.

pique-nique [piknik] *nm* picnic.

pique-niquer [piknike] *vi* to (have a) picnic.

pique-niqueur, euse [piknikœʀ, -øz] *nm/f* picnicker.

piquer [pike] *vt (percer)* to prick; *(planter)*: **~ qch dans** to stick sth into; *(fixer)*: **~ qch à** *ou* **sur** to pin sth onto; *(MÉD)* to give an injection to; *(: animal blessé etc)* to put to sleep; *(suj: insecte, fumée, ortie)* to sting; *(: poivre)* to burn; *(: froid)* to bite; *(COUTURE)* to machine (stitch); *(intérêt etc)* to arouse; *(fam: prendre)* to pick up; *(: voler)* to pinch; *(: arrêter)* to nab ♦ *vi (oiseau, avion)* to go into a dive; *(saveur)* to be pungent; to be sour; **se ~** *(avec une aiguille)* to prick o.s.; *(se faire une piqûre)* to inject o.s.; *(se vexer)* to get annoyed; **se ~ de faire** to pride o.s. on doing; **~ sur** to swoop down on; to head straight for; **~ du nez** *(avion)* to go into a nose-dive; **~ une tête** *(plonger)* to dive headfirst; **~ un galop/un cent mètres** to break into a gallop/put on a sprint; **~ une crise** to throw a fit; **~ au vif** *(fig)* to sting.

piquet [pikɛ] *nm (pieu)* post, stake; *(de tente)* peg; **mettre un élève au ~** to make a pupil stand in the corner; **~ de grève** (strike) picket; **~ d'incendie** fire-fighting squad.

piqueté, e [pikte] *adj*: **~ de** dotted with.

piquette [pikɛt] *nf (fam)* cheap wine, plonk *(BRIT)*.

piqûre [pikyʀ] *nf (d'épingle)* prick; *(d'ortie)* sting; *(de moustique)* bite; *(MÉD)* injection, shot *(US)*; *(COUTURE)* (straight) stitch; straight stitching; *(de ver)* hole; *(tache)* (spot of) mildew; **faire une ~ à qn** to give sb an injection.

piranha [piʀana] *nm* piranha.

piratage [piʀataʒ] *nm* piracy.

pirate [piʀat] *adj* pirate *cpd* ♦ *nm* pirate; *(fig: escroc)* crook, shark; **~ de l'air** hijacker.

pirater [piʀate] *vt* to pirate.

piraterie [piʀatʀi] *nf* (act of) piracy; **~**

aérienne hijacking.

pire [piʀ] *adj* (*comparatif*) worse; (*superlatif*): **le (la)** ~ ... the worst ... ♦ *nm*: **le** ~ **(de)** the worst (of).

Pirée [piʀe] *n* Piraeus.

pirogue [piʀɔg] *nf* dugout (canoe).

pirouette [piʀwɛt] *nf* pirouette; (*fig: volte-face*) about-turn.

pis [pi] *nm* (*de vache*) udder; (*pire*): **le** ~ **the worst** ♦ *adj, adv* worse; **qui** ~ **est** what is worse; **au** ~ **aller** if the worst comes to the worst, at worst.

pis-aller [pizale] *nm inv* stopgap.

pisciculture [pisikyltyʀ] *nf* fish farming.

piscine [pisin] *nf* (swimming) pool; ~ **couverte** indoor (swimming) pool.

Pise [piz] *n* Pisa.

pissenlit [pisɑ̃li] *nm* dandelion.

pisser [pise] *vi* (*fam!*) to pee.

pissotière [pisɔtjɛʀ] *nf* (*fam*) public urinal.

pistache [pistaʃ] *nf* pistachio (nut).

pistard [pistaʀ] *nm* (*CYCLISME*) track cyclist.

piste [pist(ə)] *nf* (*d'un animal, sentier*) track, trail; (*indice*) lead; (*de stade, de magnétophone, INFORM*) track; (*de cirque*) ring; (*de danse*) floor; (*de patinage*) rink; (*de ski*) run; (*AVIAT*) runway; ~ **cavalière** bridle path; ~ **cyclable** cycle track, bikeway (*US*); ~ **sonore** sound track.

pister [piste] *vt* to track, trail.

pisteur [pistœʀ] *nm* (*SKI*) member of the ski patrol.

pistil [pistil] *nm* pistil.

pistolet [pistɔlɛ] *nm* (*arme*) pistol, gun; (*à peinture*) spray gun; ~ **à bouchon/air comprimé** popgun/airgun; ~ **à eau** water pistol.

pistolet-mitrailleur, *pl* **pistolets-mitrailleurs** [pistɔlɛmitʀajœʀ] *nm* submachine gun.

piston [pistɔ̃] *nm* (*TECH*) piston; (*MUS*) valve; (*fig: appui*) string-pulling.

pistonner [pistɔne] *vt* (*candidat*) to pull strings for.

pitance [pitɑ̃s] *nf* (*péj*) (means of) sustenance.

piteusement [pitøzmɑ̃] *adv* (*échouer*) miserably.

piteux, euse [pitø, -øz] *adj* pitiful, sorry (*avant le nom*); **en** ~ **état** in a sorry state.

pitié [pitje] *nf* pity; **sans** ~ *adj* pitiless, merciless; **faire** ~ to inspire pity; **il me fait** ~ **I** pity him, I feel sorry for him; **avoir** ~ **de** (*compassion*) to pity, feel sorry for; (*merci*) to have pity *ou* mercy on; **par** ~**!** for pity's sake!

piton [pitɔ̃] *nm* (*clou*) peg, bolt; ~ **rocheux** rocky outcrop.

pitoyable [pitwajabl(ə)] *adj* pitiful.

pitre [pitʀ(ə)] *nm* clown.

pitrerie [pitʀəʀi] *nf* tomfoolery *no pl*.

pittoresque [pitɔʀɛsk(ə)] *adj* picturesque; (*expression, détail*) colourful (*BRIT*), colorful (*US*).

pivert [pivɛʀ] *nm* green woodpecker.

pivoine [pivwan] *nf* peony.

pivot [pivo] *nm* pivot; (*d'une dent*) post.

pivoter [pivɔte] *vi* (*fauteuil*) to swivel; (*porte*) to revolve; ~ **sur ses talons** to swing round.

pixel [piksɛl] *nm* pixel.

pizza [pidza] *nf* pizza.

PJ *sigle f* = **police judiciaire** ♦ *sigle fpl* (= *pièces jointes*) encl.

PL *sigle m* (*AUTO*) = **poids lourd**.

Pl. *abr* = **place**.

placage [plakaʒ] *nm* (*bois*) veneer.

placard [plakaʀ] *nm* (*armoire*) cupboard; (*affiche*) poster, notice; (*TYPO*) galley; ~ **publicitaire** display advertisement.

placarder [plakaʀde] *vt* (*affiche*) to put up; (*mur*) to stick posters on.

place [plas] *nf* (*emplacement, situation, classement*) place; (*de ville, village*) square; (*ÉCON*): ~ **financière/boursière** money/stock market; (*espace libre*) room, space; (*de parking*) space; (*siège: de train, cinéma, voiture*) seat; (*prix: au cinéma etc*) price; (: *dans un bus, taxi*) fare; (*emploi*) job; **en** ~ (*mettre*) in its place; **de** ~ **en** ~, **par** ~**s** here and there, in places; **sur** ~ on the spot; **faire** ~ **à** to give way to; **faire de la** ~ **à** to make room for; **ça prend de la** ~ it takes up a lot of room *ou* space; **prendre** ~ to take one's place; **remettre qn à sa** ~ to put sb in his (*ou* her) place; **ne pas rester** *ou* **tenir en** ~ to be always on the go; **à la** ~ **de** in place of, instead of; **une quatre** ~**s** (*AUTO*) a four-seater; **il y a 20** ~**s assises/debout** there are 20 seats/there is standing room for 20; ~ **forte** fortified town; ~ **d'honneur** place (*ou* seat) of honour (*BRIT*) *ou* honor (*US*).

placé, e [plase] *adj* (*HIPPISME*) placed; **haut** ~ (*fig*) high-ranking; **être bien/mal** ~ to be well/badly placed; (*spectateur*) to have a good/bad seat; **être bien/mal** ~ **pour faire** to be in/not to be in a position to do.

placebo [plasebo] *nm* placebo.

placement [plasmɑ̃] *nm* placing; (*FINANCE*) investment; **agence** *ou* **bureau de** ~ employment agency.

placenta [plasɛ̃ta] *nm* placenta.

placer [plase] *vt* to place, put; (*convive, spectateur*) to seat; (*capital, argent*) to place, invest; (*dans la conversation*) to put *ou* get in; ~ **qn chez** to get sb a job at (*ou* with); **se** ~ **au premier rang** to go and stand (*ou* sit) in the first row.

placide [plasid] *adj* placid.

placidité [plasidite] *nf* placidity.

placier, ière [plasje, -jɛʀ] *nm/f* commercial rep(resentative), salesman/woman.

Placoplâtre [plakɔplɑtʀ] *nm* ® plasterboard.

plafond [plafɔ̃] *nm* ceiling.

plafonner [plafɔne] *vt* (*pièce*) to put a ceiling (up) in ♦ *vi* to reach one's (*ou* a) ceiling.

plafonnier [plafɔnje] *nm* ceiling light; (*AUTO*)

interior light.

plage [plaʒ] *nf* beach; (*station*) (*seaside*) resort; (*fig*) band, bracket; (*de disque*) track, band; ~ **arrière** (*AUTO*) parcel *ou* back shelf.

plagiaire [plaʒjɛʀ] *nm/f* plagiarist.

plagiat [plaʒja] *nm* plagiarism.

plagier [plaʒje] *vt* to plagiarize.

plagiste [plaʒist(ə)] *nm/f* beach attendant.

plaid [plɛd] *nm* (tartan) car rug, lap robe (*US*).

plaidant, e [plɛdɑ̃, -ɑ̃t] *adj* litigant.

plaider [plede] *vi* (*avocat*) to plead; (*plaignant*) to go to court, litigate ♦ *vt* to plead; ~ **pour** (*fig*) to speak for.

plaideur, euse [plɛdœʀ, -øz] *nm/f* litigant.

plaidoirie [plɛdwaʀi] *nf* (*JUR*) speech for the defence (*BRIT*) *ou* defense (*US*).

plaidoyer [plɛdwaje] *nm* (*JUR*) speech for the defence (*BRIT*) *ou* defense (*US*); (*fig*) plea.

plaie [plɛ] *nf* wound.

plaignant, e [plɛɲɑ̃, -ɑ̃t] *vb voir* **plaindre** ♦ *nm/f* plaintiff.

plaindre [plɛ̃dʀ(ə)] *vt* to pity, feel sorry for; **se** ~ *vi* (*gémir*) to moan; (*protester, rouspéter*) to ~ **(à qn) (de)** to complain (to sb) (about); (*souffrir*): **se** ~ **de** to complain of.

plaine [plɛn] *nf* plain.

plain-pied [plɛ̃pje]: **de** ~ *adv* at street-level; (*fig*) straight; **de** ~ **(avec)** on the same level (as).

plaint, e [plɛ̃, -ɛ̃t] *pp de* **plaindre** ♦ *nf* (*gémissement*) moan, groan; (*doléance*) complaint; **porter** ~**e** to lodge a complaint.

plaintif, ive [plɛ̃tif, -iv] *adj* plaintive.

plaire [plɛʀ] *vi* to be a success, be successful; to please; ~ **à:** **cela me plaît** I like it; **essayer de** ~ **à qn** (*en étant serviable etc*) to try and please sb; **elle plaît aux hommes** she's a success with men, men like her; **se** ~ **quelque part** to like being somewhere, like it somewhere; **se** ~ **à faire** to take pleasure in doing; **ce qu'il vous plaira** what(ever) you like *ou* wish; **s'il vous plaît** please.

plaisamment [plɛzamɑ̃] *adv* pleasantly.

plaisance [plɛzɑ̃s] *nf* (*aussi:* **navigation de** ~) (pleasure) sailing, yachting.

plaisancier [plɛzɑ̃sje] *nm* amateur sailor, yachting enthusiast.

plaisant, e [plɛzɑ̃, -ɑ̃t] *adj* pleasant; (*histoire, anecdote*) amusing.

plaisanter [plɛzɑ̃te] *vi* to joke ♦ *vt* (*personne*) to tease, make fun of; **pour** ~ for a joke; **on ne plaisante pas avec cela** that's no joking matter; **tu plaisantes!** you're joking *ou* kidding!

plaisanterie [plɛzɑ̃tʀi] *nf* joke; joking *no pl*.

plaisantin [plɛzɑ̃tɛ̃] *nm* joker; (*fumiste*) fly-by-night.

plaise [plɛz] *etc vb voir* **plaire**.

plaisir [plɛziʀ] *nm* pleasure; **faire** ~ **à qn** (*délibérément*) to be nice to sb, please sb; (*suj: cadeau, nouvelle etc*): **ceci me fait** ~ I'm delighted *ou* very pleased with this; **prendre** ~

à/à faire to take pleasure in/in doing; **j'ai le** ~ **de ...** it is with great pleasure that I ...; **M. et Mme X ont le** ~ **de vous faire part de ...** M. and Mme X are pleased to announce ...; **se faire un** ~ **de faire qch** to be (only too) pleased to do sth; **faites-moi le** ~ **de ...** would you mind ..., would you be kind enough to ...; **à** ~: freely; for the sake of it; **au** ~ **(de vous revoir)** (I hope to) see you again; **pour le** *ou* **pour son** *ou* **par** ~ for pleasure.

plaît [plɛ] *vb voir* **plaire**.

plan, e [plɑ̃, -an] *adj* flat ♦ *nm* plan; (*GÉOM*) plane; (*fig*) level, plane; (*CINÉ*) shot; **au premier/second** ~ in the foreground/middle distance; **à l'arrière** ~ in the background; **mettre qch au premier** ~ (*fig*) to consider sth to be of primary importance; **sur le** ~ **sexuel** sexually, as far as sex is concerned; **laisser/rester en** ~ to abandon/be abandoned; ~ **d'action** plan of action; ~ **directeur** (*ÉCON*) master plan; ~ **d'eau** lake; pond; ~ **de travail** work-top, work surface; ~ **de vol** (*AVIAT*) flight plan.

planche [plɑ̃ʃ] *nf* (*pièce de bois*) plank, (wooden) board; (*illustration*) plate; (*de salades, radis, poireaux*) bed; (*d'un plongeoir*) (diving) board; **les** ~**s** (*THÉÂT*) the boards; **en** ~**s** wooden; **faire la** ~ (*dans l'eau*) to float on one's back; **avoir du pain sur la** ~ to have one's work cut out; ~ **à découper** chopping board; ~ **à dessin** drawing board; ~ **à pain** breadboard; ~ **à repasser** ironing board; ~ **(à roulettes)** (*planche*) skateboard; (*sport*) skateboarding; ~ **de salut** (*fig*) sheet anchor; ~ **à voile** (*planche*) windsurfer, sailboard; (*sport*) windsurfing.

plancher [plɑ̃ʃe] *nm* floor; (*planches*) floorboards *pl*; (*fig*) minimum level ♦ *vi* to work hard.

planchiste [plɑ̃ʃist(ə)] *nm/f* windsurfer.

plancton [plɑ̃ktɔ̃] *nm* plankton.

planer [plane] *vi* (*oiseau, avion*) to glide; (*fumée, vapeur*) to float, hover; (*drogué*) to be (on a) high; ~ **sur** (*fig*) to hang over; to hover above.

planétaire [planetɛʀ] *adj* planetary.

planétarium [planetaʀjɔm] *nm* planetarium.

planète [planɛt] *nf* planet.

planeur [planœʀ] *nm* glider.

planification [planifikasjɔ̃] *nf* (economic) planning.

planifier [planifje] *vt* to plan.

planisphère [planisfɛʀ] *nm* planisphere.

planning [planiŋ] *nm* programme (*BRIT*), program (*US*), schedule; ~ **familial** family planning.

planque [plɑ̃k] *nf* (*fam: combine, filon*) cushy (*BRIT*) *ou* easy number; (: *cachette*) hideout.

planquer [plɑ̃ke] *vt* (*fam*) to hide (away), stash away; **se** ~ to hide.

plant [plɑ̃] *nm* seedling, young plant.

plantaire [plɑ̃tɛʀ] *adj voir* **voûte**.

plantation [plɑ̃tasjɔ̃] nf planting; (de fleurs, légumes) bed; (exploitation) plantation.

plante [plɑ̃t] nf plant; ~ **d'appartement** house ou pot plant; ~ **du pied** sole (of the foot); ~ **verte** house plant.

planter [plɑ̃te] vt (plante) to plant; (enfoncer) to hammer ou drive in; (tente) to put up, pitch; (drapeau, échelle, décors) to put up; (fam: mettre) to dump; (: abandonner): ~ **là** to ditch; **se** ~ vi (fam: se tromper) to get it wrong; ~ **qch dans** to hammer ou drive sth into; to stick sth into; **se** ~ **dans** to sink into; to get stuck in; **se** ~ **devant** to plant o.s. in front of.

planteur [plɑ̃tœʀ] nm planter.

planton [plɑ̃tɔ̃] nm orderly.

plantureux, euse [plɑ̃tyʀø, -øz] adj (repas) copious, lavish; (femme) buxom.

plaquage [plakaʒ] nm (RUGBY) tackle.

plaque [plak] nf plate; (de verre) sheet; (de verglas, d'eczéma) patch; (dentaire) plaque; (avec inscription) plaque; ~ **(minéralogique ou de police ou d'immatriculation)** number (BRIT) ou license (US) plate; ~ **de beurre** slab of butter; ~ **chauffante** hotplate; ~ **de chocolat** bar of chocolate; ~ **de cuisson** hob; ~ **d'identité** identity disc; ~ **tournante** (fig) centre (BRIT), center (US).

plaqué, e [plake] adj: ~ **or/argent** gold-/silver-plated ♦ nm: ~ **or/argent** gold/silver plate; ~ **acajou** with a mahogany veneer.

plaquer [plake] vt (bijou) to plate; (bois) to veneer; (aplatir): ~ **qch sur/contre** to make sth stick ou cling to; (RUGBY) to bring down; (fam: laisser tomber) to drop, ditch; **se** ~ **contre** to flatten o.s. against; ~ **qn contre** to pin sb to.

plaquette [plakɛt] nf tablet; (de chocolat) bar; (de beurre) slab, packet; (livre) small volume; (MÉD: de pilules, gélules) pack, packet; (INFORM) circuit board; ~ **de frein** (AUTO) brake pad.

plasma [plasma] nm plasma.

plastic [plastik] nm plastic explosive.

plastifié, e [plastifje] adj plastic-coated.

plastifier [plastifje] vt (document, photo) to laminate.

plastiquage [plastikaʒ] nm bombing, bomb attack.

plastique [plastik] adj plastic ♦ nm plastic ♦ nf plastic arts pl; (d'une statue) modelling.

plastiquer [plastike] vt to blow up.

plastiqueur [plastikœʀ] nm terrorist (planting a plastic bomb).

plastron [plastʀɔ̃] nm shirt front.

plastronner [plastʀɔne] vi to swagger.

plat, e [pla, -at] adj flat; (fade: vin) flat-tasting, insipid; (personne, livre) dull ♦ nm (récipient, CULIN) dish; (d'un repas): **le premier** ~ the first course; (partie plate): **le** ~ **de la main** the flat of the hand; (: d'une route) flat (part); **à** ~ **ventre** adv face down; (tomber) flat on one's

face; **à** ~ adj (pneu, batterie) flat; (fam: fatigué) dead beat, tired out; ~ **cuisiné** pre-cooked meal (ou dish); ~ **du jour** dish of the day; ~ **de résistance** main course; ~**s préparés** convenience food(s).

platane [platan] nm plane tree.

plateau, x [plato] nm (support) tray; (d'une table) top; (d'une balance) pan; (GÉO) plateau; (de tourne-disques) turntable; (CINÉ) set; (TV): **nous avons 2 journalistes sur le** ~ **ce soir** we have 2 journalists with us tonight; ~ **à fromages** cheeseboard.

plateau-repas, pl **plateaux-repas** [platoʀəpa] nm tray meal, TV dinner (US).

plate-bande, pl **plates-bandes** [platbɑ̃d] nf flower bed.

platée [plate] nf dish(ful).

plate-forme, pl **plates-formes** [platfɔʀm(ə)] nf platform; ~ **de forage/pétrolière** drilling/oil rig.

platine [platin] nm platinum ♦ nf (d'un tourne-disque) turntable; ~ **disque/cassette** record/cassette deck; ~ **laser** ou **compact-disc** compact disc (player).

platitude [platityd] nf platitude.

platonique [platɔnik] adj platonic.

plâtras [platʀa] nm rubble no pl.

plâtre [platʀ(ə)] nm (matériau) plaster; (statue) plaster statue; (MÉD) (plaster) cast; ~**s** nmpl plasterwork sg; **avoir un bras dans le** ~ to have an arm in plaster.

plâtrer [platʀe] vt to plaster; (MÉD) to set ou put in a (plaster) cast.

plâtrier [platʀije] nm plasterer.

plausible [plozibl(ə)] adj plausible.

play-back [plɛbak] nm miming.

play-boy [plɛbɔj] nm playboy.

plébiscite [plebisit] nm plebiscite.

plébisciter [plebisite] vt (approuver) to give overwhelming support to; (élire) to elect by an overwhelming majority.

plectre [plɛktʀ(ə)] nm plectrum.

plein, e [plɛ̃, -ɛn] adj full; (porte, roue) solid; (chienne, jument) big (with young) ♦ nm: **faire le** ~ **(d'essence)** to fill up (with petrol (BRIT) ou gas (US)) ♦ prép: **avoir de l'argent** ~ **les poches** to have loads of money; ~ **de** full of; **avoir les mains** ~**es** to have one's hands full; **à** ~**es mains** (ramasser) in handfuls; (empoigner) firmly; **à** ~ **régime** at maximum revs; (fig) at full speed; **à** ~ **temps** full-time; **en** ~ **air** in the open air; **jeux en** ~ **air** outdoor games; **en** ~**e mer** on the open sea; **en** ~ **soleil** in direct sunlight; **en** ~**e nuit/rue** in the middle of the night/street; **en** ~ **milieu** right in the middle; **en** ~ **jour** in broad daylight; **les** ~**s** the downstrokes (in handwriting); **faire le** ~ **des voix** to get the maximum number of votes possible; **en** ~ **sur** right on; **en avoir** ~ **le dos** (fam) to have had it up to here.

pleinement [plɛnmɑ̃] adv fully; to the full.

plein-emploi [plɛnɑ̃plwa] *nm* full employment.

plénière [plenjɛʀ] *adj f:* **assemblée ~** plenary assembly.

plénipotentiaire [plenipɔtɑ̃sjɛʀ] *nm* plenipotentiary.

plénitude [plenityd] *nf* fullness.

pléthore [pletɔʀ] *nf:* **~ de** overabundance *ou* plethora of.

pléthorique [pletɔʀik] *adj* (*classes*) overcrowded; (*documentation*) excessive.

pleurer [plœʀe] *vi* to cry; (*yeux*) to water ♦ *vt* to mourn (for); **~ sur** *vt* to lament (over), bemoan; **~ de rire** to laugh till one cries.

pleurésie [plœʀezi] *nf* pleurisy.

pleureuse [plœʀøz] *nf* professional mourner.

pleurnicher [plœʀniʃe] *vi* to snivel, whine.

pleurs [plœʀ] *nmpl:* **en ~** in tears.

pleut [plø] *vb voir* **pleuvoir**.

pleutre [pløtʀ(ə)] *adj* cowardly.

pleuvait [pløvɛ] *etc vb voir* **pleuvoir**.

pleuviner [pløvine] *vb impers* to drizzle.

pleuvoir [pløvwaʀ] *vb impers* to rain ♦ *vi* (*fig*): **~ (sur)** to shower down (upon), be showered upon; **il pleut** it's raining; **il pleut des cordes** *ou* **à verse** *ou* **à torrents** it's pouring (down), it's raining cats and dogs.

pleuvra [pløvʀa] *etc vb voir* **pleuvoir**.

Plexiglas [plɛksiglas] *nm* ® Plexiglas ® (*US*).

pli [pli] *nm* fold; (*de jupe*) pleat; (*de pantalon*) crease; (*aussi:* **faux ~**) crease; (*enveloppe*) envelope; (*lettre*) letter; (*CARTES*) trick; **prendre le ~ de faire** to get into the habit of doing; **ça ne fait pas un ~!** don't you worry!; **~ d'aisance** inverted pleat.

pliable [plijabl(ə)] *adj* pliable, flexible.

pliage [plijaʒ] *nm* folding; (*ART*) origami.

pliant, e [plijɑ̃, -ɑ̃t] *adj* folding ♦ *nm* folding stool, campstool.

plier [plije] *vt* to fold; (*pour ranger*) to fold up; (*table pliante*) to fold down; (*genou, bras*) to bend ♦ *vi* to bend; (*fig*) to yield; **se ~ à** to submit to; **~ bagages** (*fig*) to pack up (and go).

plinthe [plɛ̃t] *nf* skirting board.

plissé, e [plise] *adj* (*jupe, robe*) pleated; (*peau*) wrinkled; (*GÉO*) folded ♦ *nm* (*COUTURE*) pleats *pl*.

plissement [plismɑ̃] *nm* (*GÉO*) fold.

plisser [plise] *vt* (*chiffonner: papier, étoffe*) to crease; (*rider: front*) to furrow, wrinkle; (*: bouche*) to pucker; (*jupe*) to put pleats in; **se ~** *vi* (*vêtement, étoffe*) to crease.

pliure [plijyʀ] *nf* (*du bras, genou*) bend; (*d'un ourlet*) fold.

plomb [plɔ̃] *nm* (*métal*) lead; (*d'une cartouche*) (lead) shot; (*PÊCHE*) sinker; (*sceau*) (lead) seal; (*ÉLEC*) fuse; **de ~** (*soleil*) blazing; **sommeil de ~** heavy *ou* very deep sleep; **mettre à ~** to plumb.

plombage [plɔ̃baʒ] *nm* (*de dent*) filling.

plomber [plɔ̃be] *vt* (*canne, ligne*) to weight (with lead); (*colis, wagon*) to put a lead seal on; (*TECH: mur*) to plumb; (*dent*) to fill (*BRIT*), stop (*US*); (*INFORM*) to protect.

plomberie [plɔ̃bʀi] *nf* plumbing.

plombier [plɔ̃bje] *nm* plumber.

plonge [plɔ̃ʒ] *nf:* **faire la ~** to be a washer-up (*BRIT*) *ou* dishwasher (*person*).

plongeant, e [plɔ̃ʒɑ̃, -ɑ̃t] *adj* (*vue*) from above; (*tir, décolleté*) plunging.

plongée [plɔ̃ʒe] *nf* (*SPORT*) diving *no pl*; (*: sans scaphandre*) skin diving; (*de sous-marin*) submersion, dive; **en ~** (*sous-marin*) submerged; (*prise de vue*) high angle.

plongeoir [plɔ̃ʒwaʀ] *nm* diving board.

plongeon [plɔ̃ʒɔ̃] *nm* dive.

plonger [plɔ̃ʒe] *vi* to dive ♦ *vt:* **~ qch dans** to plunge sth into; **~ dans un sommeil profond** to sink straight into a deep sleep; **~ qn dans l'embarras** to throw sb into a state of confusion.

plongeur, euse [plɔ̃ʒœʀ, -øz] *nm/f* diver; (*de café*) washer-up (*BRIT*), dishwasher (*person*).

plot [plo] *nm* (*ÉLEC*) contact.

ploutocratie [plutɔkʀasi] *nf* plutocracy.

ploutocratique [plutɔkʀatik] *adj* plutocratic.

ployer [plwaje] *vt* to bend ♦ *vi* to bend; (*plancher*) to sag.

plu [ply] *pp de* **plaire, pleuvoir**.

pluie [plɥi] *nf* rain; (*averse, ondée*): **une ~ brève** a shower; (*fig*): **~ de** shower of; **une ~ fine** fine rain; **retomber en ~** to shower down; **sous la ~** in the rain.

plumage [plymaʒ] *nm* plumage *no pl*, feathers *pl*.

plume [plym] *nf* feather; (*pour écrire*) (pen) nib; (*fig*) pen; **dessin à la ~** pen and ink drawing.

plumeau, x [plymo] *nm* feather duster.

plumer [plyme] *vt* to pluck.

plumet [plymɛ] *nm* plume.

plumier [plymje] *nm* pencil box.

plupart [plypaʀ]: **la ~** *pron* the majority, most (of them); **la ~ des** most, the majority of; **la ~ du temps/d'entre nous** most of the time/of us; **pour la ~** *adv* for the most part, mostly.

pluralisme [plyʀalism(ə)] *nm* pluralism.

pluralité [plyʀalite] *nf* plurality.

pluridisciplinaire [plyʀidisiplinɛʀ] *adj* multidisciplinary.

pluriel [plyʀjɛl] *nm* plural; **au ~** in the plural.

plus[1] [ply] *vb voir* **plaire**.

===================================== *MOT-CLÉ*

plus[2] [ply] *adv* **1** (*forme négative*): **ne ... ~** no more, no longer; **je n'ai ~ d'argent** I've got no more money *ou* no money left; **il ne travaille ~** he's no longer working, he doesn't work any more

2 [ply, plyz +*voyelle*] (*comparatif*) more, ...+er; (*superlatif*): **le ~** the most, the ...+est; **~ grand/intelligent (que)** bigger/more intelligent (than); **le ~ grand/intelligent** the biggest/most intelligent; **tout au ~** at the very most

3 [plys] (*davantage*) more; **il travaille ~ (que)** he works more (than); **~ il travaille, ~ il est heureux** the more he works, the happier he is; **~ de pain** more bread; **~ de 10 personnes/3 heures/4 kilos** more than *ou* over 10 people/3 hours/4 kilos; **3 heures de ~ que** 3 hours more than; **~ de minuit** after *ou* past midnight; **de ~** what's more, moreover; **il a 3 ans de ~ que moi** he's 3 years older than me; **3 kilos en ~** 3 kilos more; **en ~ de** in addition to; **de ~ en ~** more and more; **en ~ de cela ...** what is more ...; **~ ou moins** more or less; **ni ~ ni moins** no more, no less; **sans ~** (but) no more than that, (but) that's all; **qui ~ est** what is more ♦ *prép* [plys]: **4 ~ 2** 4 plus 2.

plusieurs [plyzjœʀ] *dét, pron* several; **ils sont ~** there are several of them.

plus-que-parfait [plyskəpaʀfɛ] *nm* pluperfect, past perfect.

plus-value [plyvaly] *nf* (*d'un bien*) appreciation; (*bénéfice*) capital gain; (*budgétaire*) surplus.

plut [ply] *vb voir* **plaire, pleuvoir**.

plutonium [plytɔnjɔm] *nm* plutonium.

plutôt [plyto] *adv* rather; **je ferais ~ ceci** I'd rather *ou* sooner do this; **fais ~ comme ça** try this way instead, you'd better try this way; **~ que (de) faire** rather than *ou* instead of doing.

pluvial, e, aux [plyvjal, -o] *adj* (*eaux*) rain *cpd*.

pluvieux, euse [plyvjø, -øz] *adj* rainy, wet.

pluviosité [plyvjozite] *nf* rainfall.

PM *sigle f = Police militaire*.

p.m. *abr* (= *pour mémoire*) for the record.

PME *sigle fpl = petites et moyennes entreprises*.

PMI *sigle fpl = petites et moyennes industries* ♦ *sigle f =* **protection maternelle et infantile**.

PMU *sigle m = pari mutuel urbain*; (*café*) betting agency.

> *The **PMU** is a government-regulated network of horse-race betting counters run from bars displaying the PMU sign. Punters buy fixed-price tickets predicting winners or finishing positions. The traditional bet is the **tiercé**, a triple forecast, although other multiple forecasts (**quarté** etc) are becoming increasingly popular.*

PNB *sigle m* (= *produit national brut*) GNP.

pneu [pnø] *nm* (*de roue*) tyre (*BRIT*), tire (*US*); (*message*) letter sent by pneumatic tube.

pneumatique [pnømatik] *adj* pneumatic; (*gonflable*) inflatable ♦ *nm* tyre (*BRIT*), tire (*US*).

pneumonie [pnømɔni] *nf* pneumonia.

PO *sigle fpl* (= *petites ondes*) MW.

po [po] *abr voir* **science**.

Pô [po] *nm*: **le ~** the Po.

p.o. *abr* (= *par ordre*) p.p. (*on letters etc*).

poche [pɔʃ] *nf* pocket; (*déformation*): **faire une/des ~(s)** to bag; (*sous les yeux*) bag, pouch; (*ZOOL*) pouch ♦ *nm* (= *livre de ~*) (pocket-size) paperback; **de ~** pocket *cpd*; **en être de sa ~** to be out of pocket; **c'est dans la ~** it's in the bag.

poché, e [pɔʃe] *adj*: **œuf ~** poached egg; **œil ~** black eye.

pocher [pɔʃe] *vt* (*CULIN*) to poach; (*ART*) to sketch ♦ *vi* (*vêtement*) to bag.

poche-revolver, *pl* **poches-revolver** [pɔʃʀəvɔlvɛʀ] *nf* hip pocket.

pochette [pɔʃɛt] *nf* (*de timbres*) wallet, envelope; (*d'aiguilles etc*) case; (*sac: de femme*) clutch bag, purse; (: *d'homme*) bag; (*sur veston*) breast pocket; (*mouchoir*) breast pocket handkerchief; **~ d'allumettes** book of matches; **~ de disque** record sleeve; **~ surprise** lucky bag.

pochoir [pɔʃwaʀ] *nm* (*ART: cache*) stencil; (: *tampon*) transfer.

podium [pɔdjɔm] *nm* podium (*pl* -ia).

poêle [pwal] *nm* stove ♦ *nf*: **~ (à frire)** frying pan.

poêlon [pwalɔ̃] *nm* casserole.

poème [pɔɛm] *nm* poem.

poésie [pɔezi] *nf* (*poème*) poem; (*art*): **la ~** poetry.

poète [pɔɛt] *nm* poet; (*fig*) dreamer ♦ *adj* poetic.

poétique [pɔetik] *adj* poetic.

pognon [pɔɲɔ̃] *nm* (*fam: argent*) dough.

poids [pwa] *nm* weight; (*SPORT*) shot; **vendre au ~** to sell by weight; **de ~** *adj* (*argument etc*) weighty; **prendre du ~** to put on weight; **faire le ~** (*fig*) to measure up; **plume/ mouche/coq/moyen** (*BOXE*) feather/fly/ bantam/ middleweight; **~ et haltères** *nmpl* weight lifting *sg*; **~ lourd** (*BOXE*) heavyweight; (*camion: aussi*: **PL**) (big) lorry (*BRIT*), truck (*US*); (: *ADMIN*) large goods vehicle (*BRIT*), truck (*US*); **~ mort** dead weight; **~ utile** net weight.

poignant, e [pwaɲɑ̃, -ɑ̃t] *adj* poignant, harrowing.

poignard [pwaɲaʀ] *nm* dagger.

poignarder [pwaɲaʀde] *vt* to stab, knife.

poigne [pwaɲ] *nf* grip; (*fig*) firm-handedness; **à ~** firm-handed.

poignée [pwaɲe] *nf* (*de sel etc, fig*) handful; (*de couvercle, porte*) handle; **~ de main** handshake.

poignet [pwaɲɛ] *nm* (*ANAT*) wrist; (*de chemise*) cuff.

poil [pwal] *nm* (*ANAT*) hair; (*de pinceau, brosse*) bristle; (*de tapis, tissu*) strand; (*pelage*) coat; (*ensemble des poils*): **avoir du ~ sur la poitrine** to have hair(s) on one's chest, have a hairy chest; **à ~** *adj* (*fam*) starkers; **au ~** *adj* (*fam*) hunky-dory; **de tout** ~ of all kinds; **être de bon/mauvais** ~ to be in a good/bad mood; ~ **à gratter** itching powder.

poilu, e [pwaly] *adj* hairy.

poinçon [pwɛ̃sɔ̃] *nm* awl; bodkin; (*marque*) hallmark.

poinçonner [pwɛ̃sɔne] *vt* (*marchandise*) to stamp; (*bijou etc*) to hallmark; (*billet, ticket*) to clip, punch.

poinçonneuse [pwɛ̃sɔnøz] *nf* (*outil*) punch.

poindre [pwɛ̃dʀ(ə)] *vi* (*fleur*) to come up; (*aube*) to break; (*jour*) to dawn.

poing [pwɛ̃] *nm* fist; **dormir à** ~**s fermés** to sleep soundly.

point [pwɛ̃] *vb voir* **poindre** ♦ *nm* (*marque, signe*) dot; (: *de ponctuation*) full stop, period (*US*); (*moment, de score etc, fig: question*) point; (*endroit*) spot; (*COUTURE, TRICOT*) stitch ♦ *adv* = **pas; ne ...** ~ not (at all); **faire le** ~ (*NAVIG*) to take a bearing; (*fig*) to take stock of the situation); **faire le** ~ **sur** to review; **en tout** ~ in every respect; **sur le** ~ **de faire** (just) about to do; **au** ~ **que, à tel** ~ **que** so much so that; **mettre au** ~ (*mécanisme, procédé*) to develop; (*appareil-photo*) to focus; (*affaire*) to settle; **à** ~ (*CULIN*) just right; (: *viande*) medium; **à** ~ (*nommé*) just at the right time; ~ **de croix/tige/chaînette** (*COUTURE*) cross/stem/chain stitch; ~ **mousse/jersey** (*TRICOT*) garter/stocking stitch; ~ **de départ/d'arrivée/d'arrêt** departure/arrival/stopping point; ~ **chaud** (*MIL, POL*) hot spot; ~ **de chute** landing place; (*fig*) stopping-off point; ~ (**de côté**) stitch (*pain*); ~ **culminant** summit; (*fig*) height, climax; ~ **d'eau** spring; water point; ~ **d'exclamation** exclamation mark; ~ **faible** weak spot; ~ **final** full stop, period (*US*); ~ **d'interrogation** question mark; ~ **mort** (*FINANCE*) break-even point; **au** ~ **mort** (*AUTO*) in neutral; (*affaire, entreprise*) at a standstill; ~ **noir** (*sur le visage*) blackhead; (*AUTO*) accident black spot; ~ **de non-retour** point of no return; ~ **de repère** landmark; (*dans le temps*) point of reference; ~ **de vente** retail outlet; ~ **de vue** viewpoint; (*fig: opinion*) point of view; **du** ~ **de vue de** from the point of view of; ~**s cardinaux** points of the compass, cardinal points; ~**s de suspension** suspension points.

pointage [pwɛ̃taʒ] *nm* ticking off; checking in.

pointe [pwɛ̃t] *nf* point; (*de la côte*) headland; (*allusion*) dig; sally; (*fig*): **une** ~ **d'ail/d'accent** a touch *ou* hint of garlic/of an accent; ~**s** *nfpl* (*DANSE*) points, point shoes; **être à la** ~ **de** (*fig*) to be in the forefront of; **faire** *ou* **pousser une** ~ **jusqu'à** ... to press on as far as ...; **sur la** ~ **des pieds** on tiptoe; **en** ~ *adv* (*tailler*) into a point ♦ *adj* pointed, tapered; **de** ~ *adj* (*technique etc*) leading; (*vitesse*) maximum, top; **heures/jours de** ~ peak hours/days; **faire du 180 en** ~ (*AUTO*) to

have a top *ou* maximum speed of 180; **faire des** ~**s** (*DANSE*) to dance on points; ~ **d'asperge** asparagus tip; ~ **de courant** surge (of current); ~ **de tension** (*INFORM*) spike; ~ **de vitesse** burst of speed.

pointer [pwɛ̃te] *vt* (*cocher*) to tick off; (*employés etc*) to check in; (*diriger: canon, longue-vue, doigt*): ~ **vers qch** to point at sth; (*MUS: note*) to dot ♦ *vi* (*employé*) to clock in; (*pousses*) to come through; (*jour*) to break; ~ **les oreilles** (*chien*) to prick up its ears.

pointeur, euse [pwɛ̃tœʀ, -øz] *nm/f* timekeeper ♦ *nf* timeclock.

pointillé [pwɛ̃tije] *nm* (*trait*) dotted line; (*ART*) stippling *no pl*.

pointilleux, euse [pwɛ̃tijø, -øz] *adj* particular, pernickety.

pointu, e [pwɛ̃ty] *adj* pointed; (*clou*) sharp; (*voix*) shrill; (*analyse*) precise.

pointure [pwɛ̃tyʀ] *nf* size.

point-virgule, *pl* **points-virgules** [pwɛ̃viʀgyl] *nm* semi-colon.

poire [pwaʀ] *nf* pear; (*fam: péj*) mug; ~ **électrique** (*pear-shaped*) switch; ~ **à injections** syringe.

poireau, x [pwaʀo] *nm* leek.

poireauter [pwaʀote] *vi* (*fam*) to hang about (waiting).

poirier [pwaʀje] *nm* pear tree; (*GYMNASTIQUE*) **faire le** ~ to do a headstand.

pois [pwa] *nm* (*BOT*) pea; (*sur une étoffe*) dot, spot; **à** ~ (*cravate etc*) spotted, polka-dot *cpd*; ~ **chiche** chickpea; ~ **de senteur** sweet pea; ~ **cassés** split peas.

poison [pwazɔ̃] *nm* poison.

poisse [pwas] *nf* rotten luck.

poisser [pwase] *vt* to make sticky.

poisseux, euse [pwasø, -øz] *adj* sticky.

poisson [pwasɔ̃] *nm* fish *gén inv*; **les P**~**s** (*signe*) Pisces, the Fish; **être des P**~**s** to be Pisces; **pêcher** *ou* **prendre du** ~ *ou* **des** ~**s** to fish; ~ **d'avril** April fool!; (*blague*) April fool's day trick; ~ **rouge** goldfish.

The traditional prank in France on April 1 involves placing a cut-out paper fish, known as a **poisson d'avril,** *on the back of one's victim, without being caught.*

---

poisson-chat, *pl* **poissons-chats** [pwasɔ̃ʃa] *nm* catfish.

poissonnerie [pwasɔnʀi] *nf* fishmonger's (*BRIT*), fish store (*US*).

poissonneux, euse [pwasɔnø, -øz] *adj* abounding in fish.

poissonnier, ière [pwasɔnje, -jɛʀ] *nm/f* fishmonger (*BRIT*), fish merchant (*US*) ♦ *nf* (*ustensile*) fish kettle.

poisson-scie, *pl* **poissons-scies** [pwasɔ̃si] *nm* sawfish.

poitevin, e [pwatvɛ̃, -in] *adj* (*région*) of *ou* from Poitou; (*ville*) of *ou* from Poitiers.

poitrail [pwatʀaj] *nm* (*d'un cheval etc*) breast.

poitrine [pwatʀin] *nf* (*ANAT*) chest; (*seins*) bust, bosom; (*CULIN*) breast; ~ **de bœuf** brisket.

poivre [pwavʀ(ə)] *nm* pepper; ~ **en grains/moulu** whole/ground pepper; ~ **de cayenne** cayenne (pepper); ~ **et sel** *adj* (*cheveux*) pepper-and-salt.

poivré, e [pwavʀe] *adj* peppery.

poivrer [pwavʀe] *vt* to pepper.

poivrier [pwavʀije] *nm* (*BOT*) pepper plant.

poivrière [pwavʀijɛʀ] *nf* pepperpot, pepper shaker (*US*).

poivron [pwavʀɔ̃] *nm* pepper, capsicum; ~ **vert/rouge** green/red pepper.

poix [pwa] *nf* pitch (*tar*).

poker [pɔkɛʀ] *nm*: **le** ~ poker; **partie de** ~ (*fig*) gamble; ~ **d'as** four aces.

polaire [pɔlɛʀ] *adj* polar.

polarisation [pɔlaʀizasjɔ̃] *nf* (*PHYSIQUE, ÉLEC*) polarization; (*fig*) focusing.

polariser [pɔlaʀize] *vt* to polarize; (*fig: attirer*) to attract; (*: réunir, concentrer*) to focus; **être polarisé sur** (*personne*) to be completely bound up with *ou* absorbed by.

pôle [pol] *nm* (*GÉO, ÉLEC*) pole; **le** ~ **Nord/Sud** the North/South Pole; ~ **d'attraction** (*fig*) centre of attraction.

polémique [pɔlemik] *adj* controversial, polemic(al) ♦ *nf* controversy.

polémiquer [pɔlemike] *vi* to be involved in controversy.

polémiste [pɔlemist(ə)] *nm/f* polemist, polemicist.

poli, e [pɔli] *adj* polite; (*lisse*) smooth; polished.

police [pɔlis] *nf* police; (*discipline*): **assurer la** ~ **de** *ou* **dans** to keep order in; **peine de simple** ~ *sentence given by a magistrates' or police court*; ~ (**d'assurance**) (insurance) policy; ~ (**de caractères**) (*TYPO, INFORM*) typeface; ~ **judiciaire (PJ)** ≈ Criminal Investigation Department (CID) (*BRIT*), ≈ Federal Bureau of Investigation (FBI) (*US*); ~ **des mœurs** ≈ vice squad; ~ **secours** ≈ emergency services *pl*.

polichinelle [pɔliʃinɛl] *nm* Punch; (*péj*) buffoon; **secret de** ~ open secret.

policier, ière [pɔlisje, -jɛʀ] *adj* police *cpd* ♦ *nm* policeman; (*aussi: roman* ~) detective novel.

policlinique [pɔliklinik] *nf* ≈ outpatients *sg* (clinic).

poliment [pɔlimɑ̃] *adv* politely.

polio(myélite) [pɔljɔ(mjelit)] *nf* polio(myelitis).

polio(myélitique) [pɔljɔ(mjelitik)] *nm/f* polio patient *ou* case.

polir [pɔliʀ] *vt* to polish.

polisson, ne [pɔlisɔ̃, -ɔn] *adj* naughty.

politesse [pɔlites] *nf* politeness; ~**s** *nfpl* (exchange of) courtesies; **rendre une** ~ **à qn** to

return sb's favour (*BRIT*) *ou* favor (*US*).

politicard [pɔlitikaʀ] *nm* (*péj*) politico, political schemer.

politicien, ne [pɔlitisjɛ̃, -ɛn] *adj* political ♦ *nm/f* politician.

politique [pɔlitik] *adj* political ♦ *nf* (*science, activité*) politics *sg*; (*principes, tactique*) policy, policies *pl* ♦ *nm* (*politicien*) politician; ~ **étrangère/intérieure** foreign/domestic policy.

politique-fiction [pɔlitikfiksjɔ̃] *nf* political fiction.

politiquement [pɔlitikmɑ̃] *adv* politically.

politisation [pɔlitizasjɔ̃] *nf* politicization.

politiser [pɔlitize] *vt* to politicize; ~ **qn** to make sb politically aware.

pollen [pɔlɛn] *nm* pollen.

polluant, e [pɔlɥɑ̃, -ɑ̃t] *adj* polluting ♦ *nm* polluting agent, pollutant.

polluer [pɔlɥe] *vt* to pollute.

pollueur, euse [pɔlɥœʀ, -øz] *nm/f* polluter.

pollution [pɔlysjɔ̃] *nf* pollution.

polo [pɔlo] *nm* (*sport*) polo; (*tricot*) polo shirt.

Pologne [pɔlɔɲ] *nf*: **la** ~ Poland.

polonais, e [pɔlɔnɛ, -ɛz] *adj* Polish ♦ *nm* (*LING*) Polish ♦ *nm/f*: **P~, e** Pole.

poltron, ne [pɔltʀɔ̃, -ɔn] *adj* cowardly.

poly... [pɔli] *préfixe* poly....

polyamide [pɔliamid] *nf* polyamide.

polychrome [pɔlikʀom] *adj* polychrome, polychromatic.

polyclinique [pɔliklinik] *nf* (private) clinic (*treating different illnesses*).

polycopie [pɔlikɔpi] *nf* (*procédé*) duplicating; (*reproduction*) duplicated copy.

polycopié, e [pɔlikɔpje] *adj* duplicated ♦ *nm* handout, duplicated notes *pl*.

polycopier [pɔlikɔpje] *vt* to duplicate.

polyculture [pɔlikyltyʀ] *nf* mixed farming.

polyester [pɔliɛstɛʀ] *nm* polyester.

polyéthylène [pɔlietilɛn] *nm* polyethylene.

polygame [pɔligam] *adj* polygamous.

polygamie [pɔligami] *nf* polygamy.

polyglotte [pɔliglɔt] *adj* polyglot.

polygone [pɔligɔn] *nm* polygon.

Polynésie [pɔlinezi] *nf*: **la** ~ Polynesia; **la** ~ **française** French Polynesia.

polynésien, ne [pɔlinezjɛ̃, -ɛn] *adj* Polynesian.

polynôme [pɔlinom] *nm* polynomial.

polype [pɔlip] *nm* polyp.

polystyrène [pɔlistiʀɛn] *nm* polystyrene.

polytechnicien, ne [pɔliteknisjɛ̃, -ɛn] *nm/f* student or former student of the École polytechnique.

Polytechnique [pɔliteknik] *nf*: (**École**) **p**~ prestigious military academy producing high-ranking officers and engineers.

polyvalent, e [pɔlivalɑ̃, -ɑ̃t] *adj* (*vaccin*) polyvalent; (*personne*) versatile; (*salle*) multipurpose ♦ *nm* ≈ tax inspector.

pomélo [pomelo] *nm* pomelo, grapefruit.

Poméranie [pomeʀani] *nf*: **la** ~ Pomerania.

pommade [pɔmad] *nf* ointment, cream.

pomme [pɔm] *nf* (*BOT*) apple; (*boule décorative*) knob; (*pomme de terre*): **steak ~s (frites)** steak and chips (*BRIT*) *ou* (French) fries (*US*); **tomber dans les ~s** (*fam*) to pass out; **~ d'Adam** Adam's apple; **~s allumettes** French fries (*thin-cut*); **~ d'arrosoir** (sprinkler) rose; **~ de pin** pine *ou* fir cone; **~ de terre** potato; **~s vapeur** boiled potatoes.

pommé, e [pɔme] *adj* (*chou etc*) firm, with a firm heart.

pommeau, x [pɔmo] *nm* (*boule*) knob; (*de selle*) pommel.

pommelé, e [pɔmle] *adj*: **gris ~** dapple grey.

pommette [pɔmɛt] *nf* cheekbone.

pommier [pɔmje] *nm* apple tree.

pompe [pɔ̃p] *nf* pump; (*faste*) pomp (and ceremony); **~ de bicyclette** bicycle pump; **~ à eau/essence** water/petrol pump; **~ à huile** oil pump; **~ à incendie** fire engine (*apparatus*); **~s funèbres** undertaker's *sg*, funeral parlour *sg* (*BRIT*), mortician's *sg* (*US*).

Pompéi [pɔ̃pei] *n* Pompeii.

pompéien, ne [pɔ̃pejɛ̃, -ɛn] *adj* Pompeiian.

pomper [pɔ̃pe] *vt* to pump; (*évacuer*) to pump out; (*aspirer*) to pump up; (*absorber*) to soak up ♦ *vi* to pump.

pompeusement [pɔ̃pøzmɑ̃] *adv* pompously.

pompeux, euse [pɔ̃pø, -øz] *adj* pompous.

pompier [pɔ̃pje] *nm* fireman ♦ *adj m* (*style*) pretentious, pompous.

pompiste [pɔ̃pist(ə)] *nm/f* petrol (*BRIT*) *ou* gas (*US*) pump attendant.

pompon [pɔ̃pɔ̃] *nm* pompom, bobble.

pomponner [pɔ̃pɔne] *vt* to titivate (*BRIT*), dress up.

ponce [pɔ̃s] *nf*: **pierre ~** pumice stone.

poncer [pɔ̃se] *vt* to sand (down).

ponceuse [pɔ̃søz] *nf* sander.

poncif [pɔ̃sif] *nm* cliché.

ponction [pɔ̃ksjɔ̃] *nf* (*d'argent etc*) withdrawal; **~ lombaire** lumbar puncture.

ponctualité [pɔ̃ktɥalite] *nf* punctuality.

ponctuation [pɔ̃ktɥasjɔ̃] *nf* punctuation.

ponctuel, le [pɔ̃ktɥɛl] *adj* (*à l'heure, aussi TECH*) punctual; (*fig: opération etc*) one-off, single; (*scrupuleux*) punctilious, meticulous.

ponctuellement [pɔ̃ktɥɛlmɑ̃] *adv* punctually; punctiliously, meticulously.

ponctuer [pɔ̃ktɥe] *vt* to punctuate; (*MUS*) to phrase.

pondéré, e [pɔ̃deʀe] *adj* level-headed, composed.

pondérer [pɔ̃deʀe] *vt* to balance.

pondeuse [pɔ̃døz] *nf* layer, laying hen.

pondre [pɔ̃dʀ(ə)] *vt* to lay; (*fig*) to produce ♦ *vi* to lay.

poney [pɔnɛ] *nm* pony.

pongiste [pɔ̃ʒist(ə)] *nm/f* table tennis player.

pont [pɔ̃] *nm* bridge; (*AUTO*): **~ arrière/avant** rear/front axle; (*NAVIG*) deck; **faire le ~** to take the extra day off; **faire un ~ d'or à qn**

to offer sb a fortune to take a job; **~ aérien** airlift; **~ basculant** bascule bridge; **~ d'envol** flight deck; **~ élévateur** hydraulic ramp; **~ de graissage** ramp (*in garage*); **~ à péage** tollbridge; **~ roulant** travelling crane; **~ suspendu** suspension bridge; **~ tournant** swing bridge; **P~s et Chaussées** highways department.

---

*The expression "**faire le pont**" refers to the practice of taking a Monday or Friday off to make a long weekend if a public holiday falls on a Tuesday or Thursday. The French commonly take an extra day off to give four consecutive days holiday at* **l'Ascension, le 14 juillet** *and* **le 15 août**.

---

ponte [pɔ̃t] *nf* laying; (*œufs pondus*) clutch ♦ *nm* (*fam*) big shot.

pontife [pɔ̃tif] *nm* pontiff.

pontifier [pɔ̃tifje] *vi* to pontificate.

pont-levis, *pl* **ponts-levis** [pɔ̃lvi] *nm* drawbridge.

ponton [pɔ̃tɔ̃] *nm* pontoon (*on water*).

pop [pɔp] *adj inv* pop ♦ *nm*: **le ~** pop (music).

pop-corn [pɔpkɔʀn] *nm* popcorn.

popeline [pɔplin] *nf* poplin.

populace [pɔpylas] *nf* (*péj*) rabble.

populaire [pɔpylɛʀ] *adj* popular; (*manifestation*) mass *cpd*, of the people; (*milieux, clientèle*) working-class; (*LING: mot etc*) used by the lower classes (of society).

populariser [pɔpylaʀize] *vt* to popularize.

popularité [pɔpylaʀite] *nf* popularity.

population [pɔpylasjɔ̃] *nf* population; **~ active/agricole** working/farming population.

populeux, euse [pɔpylø, -øz] *adj* densely populated.

porc [pɔʀ] *nm* (*ZOOL*) pig; (*CULIN*) pork; (*peau*) pigskin.

porcelaine [pɔʀsəlɛn] *nf* (*substance*) porcelain, china; (*objet*) piece of china(ware).

porcelet [pɔʀsəlɛ] *nm* piglet.

porc-épic, *pl* **porcs-épics** [pɔʀkepik] *nm* porcupine.

porche [pɔʀʃ(ə)] *nm* porch.

porcher, ère [pɔʀʃe, -ɛʀ] *nm/f* pig-keeper.

porcherie [pɔʀʃəʀi] *nf* pigsty.

porcin, e [pɔʀsɛ̃, -in] *adj* (*race*) porcine; (*élevage*) pig *cpd*; (*fig*) piglike.

pore [pɔʀ] *nm* pore.

poreux, euse [pɔʀø, -øz] *adj* porous.

porno [pɔʀno] *adj* porno ♦ *nm* porn.

pornographie [pɔʀnɔgʀafi] *nf* pornography.

pornographique [pɔʀnɔgʀafik] *adj* pornographic.

port [pɔʀ] *nm* (*NAVIG*) harbour (*BRIT*), harbor (*US*), port; (*ville, aussi INFORM*) port; (*de l'uniforme etc*) wearing; (*pour lettre*) postage; (*pour colis, aussi: posture*) carriage; **~ de commerce/de pêche** commercial/fishing port; **arriver à bon ~** to arrive safe and sound; ~ **d'arme** (*JUR*) carrying of a firearm; ~ **d'attache** (*NAVIG*) port of registry; (*fig*) home base; ~ **d'escale** port of call; ~ **franc** free port.

portable [pɔʀtabl(ə)] *adj* (*vêtement*) wearable; (*portatif*) transportable.

portail [pɔʀtaj] *nm* gate; (*de cathédrale*) portal.

portant, e [pɔʀtã, -ãt] *adj* (*murs*) structural, supporting; (*roues*) running; **bien/mal** ~ **in** good/poor health.

portatif, ive [pɔʀtatif, -iv] *adj* portable.

porte [pɔʀt(ə)] *nf* door; (*de ville, forteresse, SKI*) gate; **mettre à la** ~ to throw out; **prendre la** ~ to leave, go away; **à ma/sa** ~ (*tout près*) on my/his (*ou* her) doorstep; ~ (**d'embarquement**) (*AVIAT*) (departure) gate; ~ **d'entrée** front door; ~ **à** ~ *nm* door-to-door selling; ~ **de secours** emergency exit; ~ **de service** service entrance.

porté, e [pɔʀte] *adj*: **être** ~ **à faire qch** to be apt to do sth, tend to do sth; **être** ~ **sur qch** to be partial to sth.

porte-à-faux [pɔʀtafo] *nm*: **en** ~ cantilevered; (*fig*) in an awkward position.

porte-aiguilles [pɔʀteguij] *nm inv* needle case.

porte-avions [pɔʀtavjɔ̃] *nm inv* aircraft carrier.

porte-bagages [pɔʀtbagaʒ] *nm inv* luggage rack (*ou* basket *etc*).

porte-bébé [pɔʀtbebe] *nm* baby sling *ou* carrier.

porte-bonheur [pɔʀtbɔnœʀ] *nm inv* lucky charm.

porte-bouteilles [pɔʀtbutεj] *nm inv* bottle carrier; (*à casiers*) wine rack.

porte-cartes [pɔʀtəkaʀt(ə)] *nm inv* (*de cartes d'identité*) card holder; (*de cartes géographiques*) map wallet.

porte-cigarettes [pɔʀtsigaʀεt] *nm inv* cigarette case.

porte-clefs [pɔʀtəkle] *nm inv* key ring.

porte-conteneurs [pɔʀtəkɔ̃tnœʀ] *nm inv* container ship.

porte-couteau, x [pɔʀtkuto] *nm* knife rest.

porte-crayon [pɔʀtkʀεjɔ̃] *nm* pencil holder.

porte-documents [pɔʀtdɔkymã] *nm inv* attaché *ou* document case.

porte-drapeau, x [pɔʀtdʀapo] *nm* standard bearer.

portée [pɔʀte] *nf* (*d'une arme*) range; (*fig: importance*) impact, import; (*: capacités*) scope, capability; (*de chatte etc*) litter; (*MUS*) stave, staff (*pl* staves); **à/hors de** ~ (**de**) within/out of reach (of); **à** ~ **de** (**la**) **main** within (arm's) reach; **à** ~ **de voix** within earshot; **à la** ~ **de qn** (*fig*) at sb's level, within sb's capabilities; **à la** ~ **de toutes les bourses** to suit every pocket, within everyone's means.

portefaix [pɔʀtəfε] *nm inv* porter.

porte-fenêtre, *pl* **portes-fenêtres** [pɔʀtfənε-tʀ(ə)] *nf* French window.

portefeuille [pɔʀtəfœj] *nm* wallet; (*POL, BOURSE*) portfolio; **faire un lit en** ~ to make an apple-pie bed.

porte-jarretelles [pɔʀtʒaʀtεl] *nm inv* suspender belt (*BRIT*), garter belt (*US*).

porte-jupe [pɔʀtəʒyp] *nm* skirt hanger.

portemanteau, x [pɔʀtmãto] *nm* coat rack.

porte-mine [pɔʀtəmin] *nm* propelling (*BRIT*) *ou* mechanical (*US*) pencil.

porte-monnaie [pɔʀtmɔnε] *nm inv* purse.

porte-parapluies [pɔʀtpaʀaplɥi] *nm inv* umbrella stand.

porte-parole [pɔʀtpaʀɔl] *nm inv* spokesperson.

porte-plume [pɔʀtəplym] *nm inv* penholder.

porter [pɔʀte] *vt* (*charge ou sac etc, aussi: fœtus*) to carry; (*sur soi: vêtement, barbe, bague*) to wear; (*fig: responsabilité etc*) to bear, carry; (*inscription, marque, titre, patronyme, suj: arbre: fruits, fleurs*) to bear; (*jugement*) to pass; (*apporter*): ~ **qch quelque part/à qn** to take sth somewhere/to sb; (*inscrire*): ~ **qch sur** to put sth down on; to enter sth in ♦ *vi* (*voix, regard, canon*) to carry; (*coup, argument*) to hit home; **se** ~ *vi* (*se sentir*): **se** ~ **bien/mal** to be well/unwell; (*aller*): **se** ~ **vers** to go towards; ~ **sur** (*peser*) to rest on; (*accent*) to fall on; (*conférence etc*) to concern; (*heurter*) to strike; **être porté à faire** to be apt *ou* inclined to do; **elle portait le nom de Rosalie** she was called Rosalie; ~ **qn au pouvoir** to bring sb to power; ~ **bonheur à qn** to bring sb luck; ~ **qn à croire** to lead sb to believe; ~ **son âge** to look one's age; ~ **un toast** to drink a toast; ~ **de l'argent au crédit d'un compte** to credit an account with some money; **se** ~ **partie civile** to associate in a court action with the public prosecutor; **se** ~ **garant de qch** to guarantee sth, vouch for sth; **se** ~ **candidat à la députation** to stand for Parliament (*BRIT*), ≈ run for Congress (*US*); **se faire** ~ **malade** to report sick; ~ **la main à son chapeau** to raise one's hand to one's hat; ~ **son effort sur** to direct one's efforts towards; ~ **un fait à la connaissance de qn** to bring a fact to sb's attention *ou* notice.

porte-savon [pɔʀtsavɔ̃] *nm* soap dish.

porte-serviettes [pɔʀtsεʀvjεt] *nm inv* towel rail.

portes-ouvertes [pɔʀtuvεʀt(ə)] *adj inv*: **journée** ~ open day.

porteur, euse [pɔʀtœʀ, -øz] *adj* (*COMM*) strong, promising; (*nouvelle, chèque etc*): **être** ~ **de** to be the bearer of ♦ *nm/f* (*de messages*) bearer ♦ *nm* (*de bagages*) porter; (*COMM: de chèque*) bearer; (*: d'actions*) holder; (**avion**) **gros** ~ wide-bodied aircraft, jumbo (jet).

porte-voix [pɔʀtvwa] *nm inv* megaphone, loudhailer (*BRIT*).

portier [pɔʀtje] *nm* doorman, commissionaire (*BRIT*).

portière [pɔʀtjɛʀ] *nf* door.

portillon [pɔʀtijɔ̃] *nm* gate.

portion [pɔʀsjɔ̃] *nf* (*part*) portion, share; (*partie*) portion, section.

portique [pɔʀtik] *nm* (*GYMNASTIQUE*) crossbar; (*ARCHIT*) portico; (*RAIL*) gantry.

porto [pɔʀto] *nm* port (wine).

portoricain, e [pɔʀtɔʀikɛ̃, -ɛn] *adj* Puerto Rican.

Porto Rico [pɔʀtɔʀiko] *nf* Puerto Rico.

portrait [pɔʀtʀɛ] *nm* portrait; (*photographie*) photograph; (*fig*): **elle est le ~ de sa mère** she's the image of her mother.

portraitiste [pɔʀtʀetist(ə)] *nm/f* portrait painter.

portrait-robot [pɔʀtʀeʀɔbo] *nm* Identikit ® *ou* Photo-fit ® (*BRIT*) picture.

portuaire [pɔʀtɥɛʀ] *adj* port *cpd*, harbour *cpd* (*BRIT*), harbor *cpd* (*US*).

portugais, e [pɔʀtɥgɛ, -ɛz] *adj* Portuguese ♦ *nm* (*LING*) Portuguese ♦ *nm/f*: **P~, e** Portuguese.

Portugal [pɔʀtɥgal] *nm*: **le ~** Portugal.

POS *sigle m* (= *plan d'occupation des sols*) zoning ordinances *ou* regulations.

pose [poz] *nf* (*de moquette*) laying; (*de rideaux, papier peint*) hanging; (*attitude, d'un modèle*) pose; (*PHOTO*) exposure.

posé, e [poze] *adj* calm, unruffled.

posément [pozemɑ̃] *adv* calmly.

posemètre [pozmɛtʀ(ə)] *nm* exposure meter.

poser [poze] *vt* (*déposer*): **~ qch (sur)/qn à** to put sth down (on)/drop sb at; (*placer*): **~ qch sur/quelque part** to put sth on/somewhere; (*installer: moquette, carrelage*) to lay; (*rideaux, papier peint*) to hang; (*MATH: chiffre*) to put (down); (*question*) to ask; (*principe, conditions*) to lay *ou* set down; (*problème*) to formulate; (*difficulté*) to pose; (*personne: mettre en valeur*) to give standing to ♦ *vi* (*modèle*) to pose; to sit; **se ~** (*oiseau, avion*) to land; (*question*) to arise; **se ~ en** to pass o.s. off as, pose as; **~ son** *ou* **un regard sur qn/qch** to turn one's gaze on sb/sth; **~ sa candidature** to apply; (*POL*) to put o.s. up for election.

poseur, euse [pozœʀ, -øz] *nm/f* (*péj*) show-off, poseur; **~ de parquets/carrelages** floor/tile layer.

positif, ive [pozitif, -iv] *adj* positive.

position [pozisjɔ̃] *nf* position; **prendre ~** (*fig*) to take a stand.

positionner [pozisjone] *vt* to position; (*compte en banque*) to calculate the balance of.

positivement [pozitivmɑ̃] *adv* positively.

posologie [pozɔlɔʒi] *nf* directions *pl* for use, dosage.

possédant, e [pɔsedɑ̃, -ɑ̃t] *adj* (*classe*) wealthy ♦ *nm/f*: **les ~s** the haves, the wealthy.

possédé, e [pɔsede] *nm/f* person possessed.

posséder [pɔsede] *vt* to own, possess; (*qualité, talent*) to have, possess; (*bien connaître: mé-*

tier, langue) to have mastered, have a thorough knowledge of; (*sexuellement, aussi: suj: colère etc*) to possess; (*fam: duper*) to take in.

possesseur [pɔsesœʀ] *nm* owner.

possessif, ive [pɔsesif, -iv] *adj, nm* (*aussi LING*) possessive.

possession [pɔsesjɔ̃] *nf* ownership *no pl*; possession; **être/entrer en ~ de qch** to be in/ take possession of sth.

possibilité [pɔsibilite] *nf* possibility; **~s** *nfpl* (*moyens*) means; (*potentiel*) potential *sg*; **avoir la ~ de faire** to be in a position to do; to have the opportunity to do.

possible [pɔsibl(ə)] *adj* possible; (*projet, entreprise*) feasible ♦ *nm*: **faire son ~** to do all one can, do one's utmost; **(ce n'est) pas ~!** impossible!; **le plus/moins de livres ~** as many/few books as possible; **dès que ~** as soon as possible; **gentil** *etc* **au ~** as nice *etc* as it is possible to be.

postal, e, aux [pɔstal, -o] *adj* postal, post office *cpd*; **sac ~** mailbag, postbag.

postdater [pɔstdate] *vt* to postdate.

poste [pɔst(ə)] *nf* (*service*) post, postal service; (*administration, bureau*) post office ♦ *nm* (*fonction, MIL*) post; (*TÉL*) extension; (*de radio etc*) set; (*de budget*) item; **~s** *nfpl* post office *sg*; **P~s télécommunications et télédiffusion (PTT)** *postal and telecommunications service*; **agent** *ou* **employé des ~s** post office worker; **mettre à la ~** to post; **~ de commandement (PC)** *nm* (*MIL etc*) headquarters; **~ de contrôle** *nm* checkpoint; **~ de douane** *nm* customs post; **~ émetteur** *nm* transmitting set; **~ d'essence** *nm* filling station; **~ d'incendie** *nm* fire point; **~ de péage** *nm* tollgate; **~ de pilotage** *nm* cockpit; **~ (de police)** *nm* police station; **~ de radio** *nm* radio set; **~ restante (PR)** *nf* poste restante (*BRIT*), general delivery (*US*); **~ de secours** *nm* first-aid post; **~ de télévision** *nm* television set; **~ de travail** *nm* work station.

poster *vt* [pɔste] to post ♦ *nm* [pɔstɛʀ] poster; **se ~** to position o.s.

postérieur, e [pɔsteʀjœʀ] *adj* (*date*) later; (*partie*) back ♦ *nm* (*fam*) behind.

postérieurement [pɔsteʀjœʀmɑ̃] *adv* later, subsequently; **~ à** after.

posteriori [pɔsteʀjɔʀi]: **a ~** *adv* with hindsight, a posteriori.

postérité [pɔsteʀite] *nf* posterity.

postface [pɔstfas] *nf* appendix.

posthume [pɔstym] *adj* posthumous.

postiche [pɔstiʃ] *adj* false ♦ *nm* hairpiece.

postier, ière [pɔstje, -jɛʀ] *nm/f* post office worker.

postillon [pɔstijɔ̃] *nm*: **envoyer des ~s** to splutter.

postillonner [pɔstijone] *vi* to splutter.

post-natal, e [pɔstnatal] *adj* postnatal.

postopératoire [pɔstɔpeʀatwaʀ] *adj* postoperative.

postscolaire [pɔstskɔlɛʀ] *adj* further, continuing.

post-scriptum [pɔstskʀiptɔm] *nm inv* postscript.

postsynchronisation [pɔstsɛ̃kʀɔnizɑsjɔ̃] *nf* dubbing.

postsynchroniser [pɔstsɛ̃kʀɔnize] *vt* to dub.

postulant, e [pɔstylɑ̃, -ɑ̃t] *nm/f* (*candidat*) applicant; (*REL*) postulant.

postulat [pɔstyla] *nm* postulate.

postuler [pɔstyle] *vt* (*emploi*) to apply for, put in for.

posture [pɔstyʀ] *nf* posture, position; (*fig*) position.

pot [po] *nm* jar, pot; (*en plastique, carton*) carton; (*en métal*) tin; (*fam*): **avoir du ~** to be lucky; **boire** *ou* **prendre un ~** (*fam*) to have a drink; **découvrir le ~ aux roses** to find out what's been going on; **~ catalytique** catalytic converter; **~ (de chambre)** (chamber)pot; **~ d'échappement** exhaust pipe; **~ de fleurs** plant pot, flowerpot; (*plante*) pot plant; **~ à tabac** tobacco jar.

potable [pɔtabl(ə)] *adj* (*fig: boisson*) drinkable; (: *travail, devoir*) decent; **eau (non) ~** (not) drinking water.

potache [pɔtaʃ] *nm* schoolboy.

potage [pɔtaʒ] *nm* soup.

potager, ère [pɔtaʒe, -ɛʀ] *adj* (*plante*) edible, vegetable *cpd*; (**jardin) ~** kitchen *ou* vegetable garden.

potasse [pɔtas] *nf* potassium hydroxide; (*engrais*) potash.

potasser [pɔtase] *vt* (*fam*) to swot up (*BRIT*), cram.

potassium [pɔtasjɔm] *nm* potassium.

pot-au-feu [pɔtofø] *nm inv* (beef) stew; (*viande*) stewing beef ♦ *adj* (*fam: personne*) stay-at-home.

pot-de-vin, *pl* **pots-de-vin** [podvɛ̃] *nm* bribe.

pote [pɔt] *nm* (*fam*) mate (*BRIT*), pal.

poteau, x [pɔto] *nm* post; **~ de départ/arrivée** starting/finishing post; **~ (d'exécution)** execution post, stake; **~ indicateur** signpost; **~ télégraphique** telegraph pole; **~x (de but)** goal-posts.

potée [pɔte] *nf* hotpot (*of pork and cabbage*).

potelé, e [pɔtle] *adj* plump, chubby.

potence [pɔtɑ̃s] *nf* gallows *sg*; **en ~** T-shaped.

potentat [pɔtɑ̃ta] *nm* potentate; (*fig: péj*) despot.

potentiel, le [pɔtɑ̃sjɛl] *adj, nm* potential.

potentiellement [pɔtɑ̃sjɛlmɑ̃] *adv* potentially.

poterie [pɔtʀi] *nf* (*fabrication*) pottery; (*objet*) piece of pottery.

potiche [pɔtiʃ] *nf* large vase.

potier [pɔtje] *nm* potter.

potins [pɔtɛ̃] *nmpl* gossip *sg*.

potion [posjɔ̃] *nf* potion.

potiron [pɔtiʀɔ̃] *nm* pumpkin.

pot-pourri, *pl* **pots-pourris** [popuʀi] *nm* (*MUS*) potpourri, medley.

pou, x [pu] *nm* louse (*pl* lice).

pouah [pwa] *excl* ugh!, yuk!

poubelle [pubɛl] *nf* (dust)bin.

pouce [pus] *nm* thumb; **se tourner** *ou* **se rouler les ~s** (*fig*) to twiddle one's thumbs; **manger sur le ~** to eat on the run, snatch something to eat.

poudre [pudʀ(ə)] *nf* powder; (*fard*) (face) powder; (*explosif*) gunpowder; **en ~: café en ~** instant coffee; **savon en ~** soap powder; **lait en ~** dried *ou* powdered milk; **~ à canon** gunpowder; **~ à éternuer** sneezing powder; **~ à récurer** scouring powder; **~ de riz** face powder.

poudrer [pudʀe] *vt* to powder.

poudrerie [pudʀəʀi] *nf* gunpowder factory.

poudreux, euse [pudʀø, -øz] *adj* dusty; (*neige*) powdery, powder *cpd*.

poudrier [pudʀije] *nm* (powder) compact.

poudrière [pudʀijɛʀ] *nf* powder magazine; (*fig*) powder keg.

poudroyer [pudʀwaje] *vi* to rise in clouds *ou* a flurry.

pouf [puf] *nm* pouffe.

pouffer [pufe] *vi*: **~ (de rire)** to snigger; to giggle.

pouffiasse [pufjas] *nf* (*fam*) fat cow; (*prostituée*) tart.

pouilleux, euse [pujø, -øz] *adj* flea-ridden; (*fig*) seedy.

poulailler [pulaje] *nm* henhouse; (*THÉÂT*): **le ~** the gods *sg*.

poulain [pulɛ̃] *nm* foal; (*fig*) protégé.

poularde [pulaʀd(ə)] *nf* fatted chicken.

poule [pul] *nf* (*ZOOL*) hen; (*CULIN*) (boiling) fowl; (*SPORT*) (round-robin) tournament; (*RUGBY*) group; (*fam*) bird (*BRIT*), chick, broad (*US*); (*prostituée*) tart; **~ d'eau** moorhen; **~ mouillée** coward; **~ pondeuse** laying hen, layer; **~ au riz** chicken and rice.

poulet [pulɛ] *nm* chicken; (*fam*) cop.

poulette [pulɛt] *nf* (*jeune poule*) pullet.

pouliche [puliʃ] *nf* filly.

poulie [puli] *nf* pulley.

poulpe [pulp(ə)] *nm* octopus.

pouls [pu] *nm* pulse (*ANAT*); **prendre le ~ de qn** to feel sb's pulse.

poumon [pumɔ̃] *nm* lung; **~ d'acier** *ou* **artificiel** iron *ou* artificial lung.

poupe [pup] *nf* stern; **en ~** astern.

poupée [pupe] *nf* doll; **jouer à la ~** to play with one's doll (*ou* dolls); **de ~** (*très petit*): **jardin de ~** doll's garden, pocket-handkerchief-sized garden.

poupin, e [pupɛ̃, -in] *adj* chubby.

poupon [pupɔ̃] *nm* babe-in-arms.

pouponner [pupɔne] *vi* to fuss (around).

pouponnière [pupɔnjɛʀ] *nf* crèche, day nursery.

pour [puʀ] *prép* for ♦ *nm*: **le ~ et le contre** the pros and cons; **~ faire** (so as) to do, in order to do; **~ avoir fait** for having done; **~ que** so that, in order that; ~ **moi** (*à mon avis, pour ma part*) for my part, personally; ~ **riche qu'il soit** rich though he may be; ~ **100 francs d'essence** 100 francs' worth of petrol; ~ **cent** per cent; ~ **ce qui est de** as for; **y être ~ quelque chose** to have something to do with it.

pourboire [puʀbwaʀ] *nm* tip.

pourcentage [puʀsɑ̃taʒ] *nm* percentage; **travailler au ~** to work on commission.

pourchasser [puʀʃase] *vt* to pursue.

pourfendeur [puʀfɑ̃dœʀ] *nm* sworn opponent.

pourfendre [puʀfɑ̃dʀ(ə)] *vt* to assail.

pourlécher [puʀleʃe]: **se ~** *vi* to lick one's lips.

pourparlers [puʀpaʀle] *nmpl* talks, negotiations; **être en ~ avec** to be having talks with.

pourpre [puʀpʀ(ə)] *adj* crimson.

pourquoi [puʀkwa] *adv, conj* why ♦ *nm inv*: **le ~ (de)** the reason (for).

pourrai [puʀe] *etc vb voir* **pouvoir**.

pourri, e [puʀi] *adj* rotten; (*roche, pierre*) crumbling; (*temps, climat*) filthy, foul ♦ *nm*: **sentir le ~** to smell rotten.

pourrir [puʀiʀ] *vi* to rot; (*fruit*) to go rotten *ou* bad; (*fig: situation*) to deteriorate ♦ *vt* to rot; (*fig: corrompre: personne*) to corrupt; (*: gâter: enfant*) to spoil thoroughly.

pourrissement [puʀismɑ̃] *nm* deterioration.

pourriture [puʀityʀ] *nf* rot.

pourrons [puʀɔ̃] *etc vb voir* **pouvoir**.

poursuis [puʀsɥi] *etc vb voir* **poursuivre**.

poursuite [puʀsɥit] *nf* pursuit, chase; **~s** *nfpl* (*JUR*) legal proceedings; (**course**) **~ track race**; (*fig*) chase.

poursuivant, e [puʀsɥivɑ̃, -ɑ̃t] *vb voir* **poursuivre** ♦ *nm/f* pursuer; (*JUR*) plaintiff.

poursuivre [puʀsɥivʀ(ə)] *vt* to pursue, chase (after); (*relancer*) to hound, harry; (*obséder*) to haunt; (*JUR*) to bring proceedings against, prosecute; (*: au civil*) to sue; (*but*) to strive towards; (*voyage, études*) to carry on with, continue ♦ *vi* to carry on, go on; **se ~** *vi* to go on, continue.

pourtant [puʀtɑ̃] *adv* yet; **mais ~** but nevertheless, but even so; **c'est ~ facile** (and) yet it's easy.

pourtour [puʀtuʀ] *nm* perimeter.

pourvoi [puʀvwa] *nm* appeal.

pourvoir [puʀvwaʀ] *nm* (*COMM*) supply ♦ *vt*: **~ qch/qn de** to equip sth/sb with ♦ *vi*: **~ à** to provide for; (*emploi*) to fill; **se ~** (*JUR*): **se ~ en cassation** to take one's case to the Court of Appeal.

pourvoyeur, euse [puʀvwajœʀ, -øz] *nm/f* supplier.

pourvu, e [puʀvy] *pp de* **pourvoir** ♦ *adj*: **~ de** equipped with; **~ que** *conj* (*si*) provided that, so long as; (*espérons que*) let's hope (that).

pousse [pus] *nf* growth; (*bourgeon*) shoot.

poussé, e [puse] *adj* sophisticated, advanced; (*moteur*) souped-up.

pousse-café [puskafe] *nm inv* (after-dinner) liqueur.

poussée [puse] *nf* thrust; (*coup*) push; (*MÉD*) eruption; (*fig*) upsurge.

pousse-pousse [puspus] *nm inv* rickshaw.

pousser [puse] *vt* to push; (*inciter*): **~ qn à** to urge *ou* press sb to + *infinitif*; (*acculer*): **~ qn à** to drive sb to; (*moteur, voiture*) to drive hard; (*émettre: cri etc*) to give; (*stimuler*) to urge on; to drive hard; (*poursuivre*) to carry on ♦ *vi* to push; (*croître*) to grow; (*aller*): **~ plus loin** to push on a bit further; **se ~** *vi* to move over; **faire ~** (*plante*) to grow; **~ le dévouement** *etc* **jusqu'à ...** to take devotion *etc* as far as ....

poussette [puset] *nf* (*voiture d'enfant*) pushchair (*BRIT*), stroller (*US*).

poussette-canne, *pl* **poussettes-cannes** [pusetkan] *nf* baby buggy (*BRIT*), (folding) stroller (*US*).

poussier [pusje] *nm* coaldust.

poussière [pusjɛʀ] *nf* dust; (*grain*) speck of dust; **et des ~s** (*fig*) and a bit; **~ de charbon** coaldust.

poussiéreux, euse [pusjeʀø, -øz] *adj* dusty.

poussif, ive [pusif, -iv] *adj* wheezy, wheezing.

poussin [pusɛ̃] *nm* chick.

poussoir [puswaʀ] *nm* button.

poutre [putʀ(ə)] *nf* beam; (*en fer, ciment armé*) girder; **~s apparentes** exposed beams.

poutrelle [putʀɛl] *nf* (*petite poutre*) small beam; (*barre d'acier*) girder.

══════════════════════ *MOT-CLÉ*

pouvoir [puvwaʀ] *nm* power; (*POL: dirigeants*): **le ~** those in power; **les ~s publics** the authorities; **avoir ~ de faire** (*autorisation*) to have (the) authority to do; (*droit*) to have the right to do; **~ absolu** absolute power; **~ absorbant** absorbency; **~ d'achat** purchasing power; **~ calorifique** calorific value

♦ *vb semi-aux* **1** (*être en état de*) can, be able to; **je ne peux pas le réparer** I can't *ou* I am not able to repair it; **déçu de ne pas ~ le faire** disappointed not to be able to do it

2 (*avoir la permission*) can, may, be allowed to; **vous pouvez aller au cinéma** you can *ou* may go to the pictures

3 (*probabilité, hypothèse*) may, might, could; **il a pu avoir un accident** he may *ou* might *ou* could have had an accident; **il aurait pu le dire!** he might *ou* could have said (so)!

4 (*expressions*): **tu ne peux pas savoir!** you have no idea!; **tu peux le dire!** you can say that again!

♦ *vb impers* may, might, could; **il peut arriver que** it may *ou* might *ou* could happen that; **il pourrait pleuvoir** it might rain

♦ *vt* can, be able to; **j'ai fait tout ce que j'ai pu** I did all I could; **je n'en peux plus** (*épuisé*) I'm exhausted; (*à bout*) I can't take

any more
2 (*vb +adj ou adv comparatif*): **je me porte on ne peut mieux** I'm absolutely fine, I couldn't be better; **elle est on ne peut plus gentille** she couldn't be nicer, she's as nice as can be
se ~ *vi*: **il se peut que** it may *ou* might be that; **cela se pourrait** that's quite possible.

PP *sigle f* (= *préventive de la pellagre: vitamine*) niacin ♦ *abr* (= *pages*) pp.

p.p. *abr* (= *par procuration*) p.p.

p.p.c.m. *sigle m* (*MATH*: = *plus petit commun multiple*) LCM (= *lowest common multiple*).

PQ *sigle f* (*Canada*: = *province de Québec*) PQ.

PR *sigle m* = *parti républicain* ♦ *sigle f* = **poste restante.**

pr *abr* = **pour.**

pragmatique [pʀagmatik] *adj* pragmatic.

pragmatisme [pʀagmatism(ə)] *nm* pragmatism.

Prague [pʀag] *n* Prague.

prairie [pʀeʀi] *nf* meadow.

praline [pʀalin] *nf* (*bonbon*) sugared almond; (*au chocolat*) praline.

praliné, e [pʀaline] *adj* (*amande*) sugared; (*chocolat, glace*) praline *cpd*.

praticable [pʀatikabl(ə)] *adj* (*route etc*) passable, practicable; (*projet*) practicable.

praticien, ne [pʀatisjɛ̃, -ɛn] *nm/f* practitioner.

pratiquant, e [pʀatikɑ̃, -ɑ̃t] *adj* practising (*BRIT*), practicing (*US*).

pratique [pʀatik] *nf* practice ♦ *adj* practical; (*commode: horaire etc*) convenient; (*: outil*) handy, useful; **dans la ~** in (actual) practice; **mettre en ~** to put into practice.

pratiquement [pʀatikmɑ̃] *adv* (*dans la pratique*) in practice; (*pour ainsi dire*) practically, virtually.

pratiquer [pʀatike] *vt* to practise (*BRIT*), practice (*US*); (*SPORT etc*) to go in for, play; (*appliquer: méthode, théorie*) to apply; (*intervention, opération*) to carry out; (*ouverture, abri*) to make ♦ *vi* (*REL*) to be a churchgoer.

pré [pʀe] *nm* meadow.

préalable [pʀealabl(ə)] *adj* preliminary; **condition ~** (**de**) precondition (for), prerequisite (for); **sans avis ~** without prior *ou* previous notice; **au ~** first, beforehand.

préalablement [pʀealabləmɑ̃] *adv* first, beforehand.

Préalpes [pʀealp(ə)] *nfpl*: **les ~** the Pre-Alps.

préalpin, e [pʀealpɛ̃, -in] *adj* of the Pre-Alps.

préambule [pʀeɑ̃byl] *nm* preamble; (*fig*) prelude; **sans ~** straight away.

préau, x [pʀeo] *nm* (*d'une cour d'école*) covered playground; (*d'un monastère, d'une prison*) inner courtyard.

préavis [pʀeavi] *nm* notice; **~ de congé** notice; **communication avec ~** (*TÉL*) personal *ou* person-to-person call.

prébende [pʀebɑ̃d] *nf* (*péj*) remuneration.

précaire [pʀekɛʀ] *adj* precarious.

précaution [pʀekosjɔ̃] *nf* precaution; **avec ~** cautiously; **prendre des** *ou* **ses ~s** to take precautions; **par ~** as a precaution; **pour plus de ~** to be on the safe side; **~s oratoires** carefully phrased remarks.

précautionneux, euse [pʀekosjɔnø, -øz] *adj* cautious, careful.

précédemment [pʀesedamɑ̃] *adv* before, previously.

précédent, e [pʀesedɑ̃, -ɑ̃t] *adj* previous ♦ *nm* precedent; **sans ~** unprecedented; **le jour ~** the day before, the previous day.

précéder [pʀesede] *vt* to precede; (*marcher ou rouler devant*) to be in front of; (*arriver avant*) to get ahead of.

précepte [pʀesɛpt(ə)] *nm* precept.

précepteur, trice [pʀesɛptœʀ, -tʀis] *nm/f* (private) tutor.

préchauffer [pʀeʃofe] *vt* to preheat.

prêcher [pʀeʃe] *vt, vi* to preach.

prêcheur, euse [pʀeʃœʀ, -øz] *adj* moralizing ♦ *nm/f* (*REL*) preacher; (*fig*) moralizer.

précieusement [pʀesjøzmɑ̃] *adv* (*avec soin*) carefully; (*avec préciosité*) preciously.

précieux, euse [pʀesjø, -øz] *adj* precious; (*collaborateur, conseils*) invaluable; (*style, écrivain*) précieux, precious.

préciosité [pʀesjozite] *nf* preciosity, preciousness.

précipice [pʀesipis] *nm* drop, chasm; (*fig*) abyss; **au bord du ~** at the edge of the precipice.

précipitamment [pʀesipitamɑ̃] *adv* hurriedly, hastily.

précipitation [pʀesipitasjɔ̃] *nf* (*hâte*) haste; **~s (atmosphériques)** *nfpl* precipitation *sg*.

précipité, e [pʀesipite] *adj* (*respiration*) fast; (*pas*) hurried; (*départ*) hasty.

précipiter [pʀesipite] *vt* (*faire tomber*): **~ qn/ qch du haut de** to throw *ou* hurl sb/sth off *ou* from; (*hâter: marche*) to quicken; (*: départ*) to hasten; **se ~** *vi* (*événements*) to move faster; (*respiration*) to speed up; **se ~ sur/ vers** to rush at/towards; **se ~ au-devant de qn** to throw o.s. before sb.

précis, e [pʀesi, -iz] *adj* precise; (*tir, mesures*) accurate, precise ♦ *nm* handbook.

précisément [pʀesizemɑ̃] *adv* precisely; **ma vie n'est pas ~ distrayante** my life is not exactly entertaining.

préciser [pʀesize] *vt* (*expliquer*) to be more specific about, clarify; (*spécifier*) to state, specify; **se ~** *vi* to become clear(er).

précision [pʀesizjɔ̃] *nf* precision; accuracy; (*détail*) point *ou* detail (*made clear or to be clarified*); **~s** *nfpl* further details.

précoce [pʀekɔs] *adj* early; (*enfant*) precocious; (*calvitie*) premature.

précocité [pʀekɔsite] *nf* earliness; precociousness.

préconçu, e [pʀekɔ̃sy] *adj* preconceived.

préconiser [pʀekɔnize] *vt* to advocate.

précontraint, e [pʀekɔ̃tʀɛ̃, -ɛt] *adj*: **béton** ~ prestressed concrete.

précuit, e [pʀekɥi, -it] *adj* precooked.

précurseur [pʀekyʀsœʀ] *adj m* precursory ♦ *nm* forerunner, precursor.

prédateur [pʀedatœʀ] *nm* predator.

prédécesseur [pʀedesesœʀ] *nm* predecessor.

prédécoupé, e [pʀedekupe] *adj* pre-cut.

prédestiner [pʀedɛstine] *vt*: ~ **qn à qch/à faire** to predestine sb for sth/to do.

prédicateur [pʀedikatœʀ] *nm* preacher.

prédiction [pʀediksjɔ̃] *nf* prediction.

prédilection [pʀedilɛksjɔ̃] *nf*: **avoir une** ~ **pour** to be partial to; **de** ~ favourite (*BRIT*), favorite (*US*).

prédire [pʀediʀ] *vt* to predict.

prédisposer [pʀedispoze] *vt*: ~ **qn à qch/à faire** to predispose sb to sth/to do.

prédisposition [pʀedispozisjɔ̃] *nf* predisposition.

prédit, e [pʀedi, -it] *pp de* **prédire**.

prédominance [pʀedɔminɑ̃s] *nf* predominance.

prédominant, e [pʀedɔminɑ̃, -ɑ̃t] *adj* predominant; prevailing.

prédominer [pʀedɔmine] *vi* to predominate; (*avis*) to prevail.

pré-électoral, e, aux [pʀeelɛktɔʀal, -o] *adj* pre-election *cpd*.

pré-emballé, e [pʀeɑ̃bale] *adj* pre-packed.

prééminent, e [pʀeeminɑ̃, -ɑ̃t] *adj* pre-eminent.

préemption [pʀeɑ̃psjɔ̃] *nf*: **droit de** ~ (*JUR*) pre-emptive right.

pré-encollé, e [pʀeɑ̃kɔle] *adj* pre-pasted.

préétabli, e [pʀeetabli] *adj* pre-established.

préexistant, e [pʀeɛgzistɑ̃, -ɑ̃t] *adj* pre-existing.

préfabriqué, e [pʀefabʀike] *adj* prefabricated; (*péj: sourire*) artificial ♦ *nm* prefabricated material.

préface [pʀefas] *nf* preface.

préfacer [pʀefase] *vt* to write a preface for.

préfectoral, e, aux [pʀefɛktɔʀal, -o] *adj* prefectorial.

préfecture [pʀefɛktyʀ] *nf* prefecture; ~ **de police** police headquarters *pl*.

---

*The **préfecture** is the administrative headquarters of the **département**. The **préfet**, a senior civil servant appointed by the government, is responsible for executing government decisions. France's 22 regions, each comprising a number of départements, also have a préfet, the préfet de région.*

---

préférable [pʀefeʀabl(ə)] *adj* preferable.

préféré, e [pʀefeʀe] *adj, nm/f* favourite (*BRIT*), favorite (*US*).

préférence [pʀefeʀɑ̃s] *nf* preference; **de** ~ preferably; **de** *ou* **par** ~ **à** in preference to, rather than; **donner la** ~ **à qn** to give preference to sb; **par ordre de** ~ in order of preference; **obtenir la** ~ **sur** to have preference over.

préférentiel, le [pʀefeʀɑ̃sjɛl] *adj* preferential.

préférer [pʀefeʀe] *vt*: ~ **qn/qch (à)** to prefer sb/sth (to), like sb/sth better (than); ~ **faire** to prefer to do; **je préférerais du thé** I would rather have tea, I'd prefer tea.

préfet [pʀefɛ] *nm* prefect; ~ **de police** ≈ Chief Constable (*BRIT*), ≈ Police Commissioner (*US*).

préfigurer [pʀefigyʀe] *vt* to prefigure.

préfixe [pʀefiks(ə)] *nm* prefix.

préhistoire [pʀeistwaʀ] *nf* prehistory.

préhistorique [pʀeistɔʀik] *adj* prehistoric.

préjudice [pʀeʒydis] *nm* (*matériel*) loss; (*moral*) harm *no pl*; **porter** ~ **à** to harm, be detrimental to; **au** ~ **de** at the expense of.

préjudiciable [pʀeʒydisjabl(ə)] *adj*: ~ **à** prejudicial *ou* harmful to.

préjugé [pʀeʒyʒe] *nm* prejudice; **avoir un** ~ **contre** to be prejudiced *ou* biased against; **bénéficier d'un** ~ **favorable** to be viewed favourably.

préjuger [pʀeʒyʒe] ~ **de** *vt* to prejudge.

prélasser [pʀelase] **se** ~ *vi* to lounge.

prélat [pʀela] *nm* prelate.

prélavage [pʀelavaʒ] *nm* pre-wash.

prélèvement [pʀelɛvmɑ̃] *nm* deduction; withdrawal; **faire un** ~ **de sang** to take a blood sample.

prélever [pʀelve] *vt* (*échantillon*) to take; (*argent*): ~ **(sur)** to deduct (from); (*: sur son compte*): ~ **(sur)** to withdraw (from).

préliminaire [pʀeliminɛʀ] *adj* preliminary; ~**s** *nmpl* preliminaries; (*négociations*) preliminary talks.

prélude [pʀelyd] *nm* prelude; (*avant le concert*) warm-up.

prématuré, e [pʀematyʀe] *adj* premature; (*retraite*) early ♦ *nm* premature baby.

prématurément [pʀematyʀemɑ̃] *adv* prematurely.

préméditation [pʀemeditasjɔ̃] *nf*: **avec** ~ *adj* premeditated ♦ *adv* with intent.

préméditer [pʀemedite] *vt* to premeditate, plan.

prémices [pʀemis] *nfpl* beginnings.

premier, ière [pʀəmje, -jɛʀ] *adj* first; (*branche, marche, grade*) bottom; (*fig: fondamental*) basic; prime; (*en importance*) first, foremost ♦ *nm* (~ *étage*) first (*BRIT*) *ou* second (*US*) floor ♦ *nf* (*AUTO*) first (gear); (*RAIL, AVIAT etc*) first class; (*SCOL: classe*) penultimate school year (*age 16-17*); (*THÉÂT*) first night; (*CINÉ*) première; (*exploit*) first; **au** ~ **abord** at first sight; **au** ~ **ou du** ~ **coup** at the first attempt *ou* go; **de** ~ **ordre** first-class, first-rate; **de première qualité, de** ~ **choix** best *ou* top quality; **de première importance** of the highest importance; **de première nécessité** absolutely essential; **le** ~ **venu** the first person to come along; **jeune** ~ leading man; **le** ~ **de l'an** New Year's Day; **enfant du** ~ **lit** child of a first marriage; **en** ~ **lieu** in the first place; ~ **âge** (*d'un enfant*) the first 3 months (of life); **P**~ **Ministre** Prime Minister.

premièrement [pʀəmjɛʀmɑ̃] *adv* firstly.

première-née, *pl* **premières-nées** [pʀəmjɛʀne] *nf* first-born.

premier-né, *pl* **premiers-nés** [pʀəmjene] *nm* first-born.

prémisse [pʀemis] *nf* premise.

prémolaire [pʀemɔlɛʀ] *nf* premolar.

prémonition [pʀemɔnisjɔ̃] *nf* premonition.

prémonitoire [pʀemɔnitwaʀ] *adj* premonitory.

prémunir [pʀemyniʀ]: **se** ~ *vi*: **se** ~ **contre** to protect o.s. from, guard against.

prenant, e [pʀənɑ̃, -ɑ̃t] *vb voir* **prendre** ♦ *adj* absorbing, engrossing.

prénatal, e [pʀenatal] *adj* (*MÉD*) antenatal; (*allocation*) maternity *cpd*.

prendre [pʀɑ̃dʀ(ə)] *vt* to take; (*ôter*): ~ **qch à** to take sth from; (*aller chercher*) to get, fetch; (*se procurer*) to get; (*réserver: place*) to book; (*acquérir: du poids, de la valeur*) to put on, gain; (*malfaiteur, poisson*) to catch; (*passager*) to pick up; (*personnel, aussi: couleur, goût*) to take on; (*locataire*) to take in; (*traiter: enfant, problème*) to handle; (*voix, ton*) to put on; (*prélever: pourcentage, argent*) to take off; (*coincer*): **se** ~ **les doigts dans** to get one's fingers caught in ♦ *vi* (*liquide, ciment*) to set; (*greffe, vaccin*) to take; (*mensonge*) to be successful; (*feu: foyer*) to go; (: *incendie*) to start; (*allumette*) to light; (*se diriger*): ~ **à gauche** to turn (to the) left; ~ **son origine** *ou* **sa source** (*mot, rivière*) to have its source; ~ **qn pour** to take sb for; **se** ~ **pour** to think one is; ~ **sur soi de faire qch** to take it upon o.s. to do sth; ~ **qn en sympathie/horreur** to get to like/loathe sb; **à tout** ~ all things considered; **s'en** ~ **à** (*agresser*) to set about; (*passer sa colère sur*) to take it out on; (*critiquer*) to attack; (*remettre en question*) to challenge; **se** ~ **d'amitié/d'affection pour** to befriend/become fond of; **s'y** ~ (*procéder*) to set about it; **s'y** ~ **à l'avance** to see to it in advance; **s'y** ~ **à deux fois** to try twice, make two attempts.

preneur [pʀənœʀ] *nm*: **être** ~ to be willing to buy; **trouver** ~ to find a buyer.

prénom [pʀenɔ̃] *nm* first name.

prénommer [pʀenɔme] *vt*: **elle se prénomme Claude** her (first) name is Claude.

prénuptial, e, aux [pʀenypsjal, -o] *adj* premarital.

préoccupant, e [pʀeɔkypɑ̃, -ɑ̃t] *adj* worrying.

préoccupation [pʀeɔkypasjɔ̃] *nf* (*souci*) concern; (*idée fixe*) preoccupation.

préoccupé, e [pʀeɔkype] *adj* concerned; preoccupied.

préoccuper [pʀeɔkype] *vt* (*tourmenter, tracas-*

ser) to concern; (*absorber, obséder*) to preoccupy; **se** ~ **de qch** to be concerned about sth; to show concern about sth.

préparateur, trice [pʀepaʀatœʀ, -tʀis] *nm/f* assistant.

préparatifs [pʀepaʀatif] *nmpl* preparations.

préparation [pʀepaʀasjɔ̃] *nf* preparation; (*SCOL*) piece of homework.

préparatoire [pʀepaʀatwaʀ] *adj* preparatory.

préparer [pʀepaʀe] *vt* to prepare; (*café, repas*) to make; (*examen*) to prepare for; (*voyage, entreprise*) to plan; **se** ~ *vi* (*orage, tragédie*) to brew, be in the air; **se** ~ (**à qch/à faire**) to prepare (o.s.) *ou* get ready (for sth/to do); ~ **qch à qn** (*surprise etc*) to have sth in store for sb; ~ **qn à qch** (*nouvelle etc*) to prepare sb for sth.

prépondérance [pʀepɔ̃deʀɑ̃s] *nf*: ~ (**sur**) predominance (over).

prépondérant, e [pʀepɔ̃deʀɑ̃, -ɑ̃t] *adj* major, dominating; **voix** ~**e** casting vote.

préposé, e [pʀepoze] *adj*: ~ **à** in charge of ♦ *nm/f* (*gén: employé*) employee; (*ADMIN: facteur*) postman/woman (*BRIT*), mailman/woman (*US*); (*de la douane etc*) official; (*de vestiaire*) attendant.

préposer [pʀepoze] *vt*: ~ **qn à qch** to appoint sb to sth.

préposition [pʀepozisjɔ̃] *nf* preposition.

prérentrée [pʀeʀɑ̃tʀe] *nf* in-service training period before start of school term.

préretraite [pʀeʀətʀɛt] *nf* early retirement.

prérogative [pʀeʀɔgativ] *nf* prerogative.

près [pʀɛ] *adv* near, close; ~ **de** *prép* near (to), close to; (*environ*) nearly, almost; **de** ~ *adv* closely; **à 5 kg** ~ to within about 5 kg; **à cela** ~ **que** apart from the fact that; **je ne suis pas** ~ **de lui pardonner** I'm nowhere near ready to forgive him; **on n'est pas à un jour** ~ one day (either way) won't make any difference, we're not going to quibble over the odd day.

présage [pʀezaʒ] *nm* omen.

présager [pʀezaʒe] *vt* (*prévoir*) to foresee; (*annoncer*) to portend.

pré-salé, *pl* **prés-salés** [pʀesale] *nm* (*CULIN*) salt-meadow lamb.

presbyte [pʀɛsbit] *adj* long-sighted (*BRIT*), far-sighted (*US*).

presbytère [pʀɛsbitɛʀ] *nm* presbytery.

presbytérien, ne [pʀɛsbiteʀjɛ̃, -ɛn] *adj, nm/f* Presbyterian.

presbytie [pʀɛsbisi] *nf* long-sightedness (*BRIT*), far-sightedness (*US*).

prescience [pʀesjɑ̃s] *nf* prescience, foresight.

préscolaire [pʀeskɔlɛʀ] *adj* preschool *cpd*.

prescription [pʀɛskʀipsjɔ̃] *nf* (*instruction*) order, instruction; (*MÉD, JUR*) prescription.

prescrire [pʀɛskʀiʀ] *vt* to prescribe; **se** ~ *vi* (*JUR*) to lapse.

prescrit, e [pʀɛskʀi, -it] *pp de* **prescrire** ♦ *adj* (*date etc*) stipulated.

préséance [pʀeseɑ̃s] *nf* precedence *no pl.*

présélection [pʀeselɛksjɔ̃] *nf* (*de candidats*) short-listing; **effectuer une** ~ to draw up a shortlist.

présélectionner [pʀeselɛksjɔne] *vt* to preselect; (*dispositif*) to preset; (*candidats*) to make an initial selection from among, short-list (*BRIT*).

présence [pʀezɑ̃s] *nf* presence; (*au bureau etc*) attendance; **en** ~ face to face; **en** ~ **de** in (the) presence of; (*fig*) in the face of; **faire acte de** ~ to put in a token appearance; ~ **d'esprit** presence of mind.

présent, e [pʀezɑ̃, -ɑ̃t] *adj, nm* present; (*ADMIN, COMM*): **la** ~**e lettre/loi** this letter/law ♦ *nm/f*: **les** ~**s** (*personnes*) those present ♦ *nf* (*COMM*: *lettre*): **la** ~**e** this letter; **à** ~ now, at present; **dès à** ~ here and now; **jusqu'à** ~ up till now, until now; **à** ~ **que** now that.

présentable [pʀezɑ̃tabl(ə)] *adj* presentable.

présentateur, trice [pʀezɑ̃tatœʀ, -tʀis] *nm/f* presenter.

présentation [pʀezɑ̃tasjɔ̃] *nf* presentation; introduction; (*allure*) appearance.

présenter [pʀezɑ̃te] *vt* to present; (*invité, candidat*) to introduce; (*félicitations, condoléances*) to offer; (*montrer: billet, pièce d'identité*) to show, produce; (*faire inscrire: candidat*) to put forward; (*soumettre*) to submit ♦ *vi*: ~ **mal/bien** to have an unattractive/a pleasing appearance; **se** ~ *vi* (*sur convocation*) to report, come; (*se faire connaître*) to come forward; (*à une élection*) to stand; (*occasion*) to arise; **se** ~ **à un examen** to sit an exam; **se** ~ **bien/mal** to look good/not too good.

présentoir [pʀezɑ̃twaʀ] *nm* (*étagère*) display shelf (*pl* shelves); (*vitrine*) showcase; (*étal*) display stand.

préservatif [pʀezɛʀvatif] *nm* condom, sheath.

préservation [pʀezɛʀvasjɔ̃] *nf* protection, preservation.

préserver [pʀezɛʀve] *vt*: ~ **de** (*protéger*) to protect from; (*sauver*) to save from.

présidence [pʀezidɑ̃s] *nf* presidency; chairmanship.

président [pʀezidɑ̃] *nm* (*POL*) president; (*d'une assemblée, COMM*) chairman; ~ **directeur général (PDG)** chairman and managing director (*BRIT*), chairman and president (*US*); ~ **du jury** (*JUR*) foreman of the jury; (*d'examen*) chief examiner.

présidente [pʀezidɑ̃t] *nf* president; (*femme du président*) president's wife; (*d'une réunion*) chairwoman.

présidentiable [pʀezidɑ̃sjabl(ə)] *adj, nm/f* potential president.

présidentiel, le [pʀezidɑ̃sjɛl] *adj* presidential; ~**les** *nfpl* presidential election(s).

présider [pʀezide] *vt* to preside over; (*dîner*) to be the guest of honour (*BRIT*) *ou* honor (*US*) at; ~ **à** *vt* to direct; to govern.

présomption [pʀezɔ̃psjɔ̃] *nf* presumption.

présomptueux, euse [pʀezɔ̃ptɥø, -øz] *adj* presumptuous.

presque [pʀɛsk(ə)] *adv* almost, nearly; ~ **rien** hardly anything; ~ **pas** hardly (at all); ~ **pas de** hardly any; **personne, ou** ~ next to nobody, hardly anyone; **la** ~ **totalité (de)** almost *ou* nearly all.

presqu'île [pʀɛskil] *nf* peninsula.

pressant, e [pʀɛsɑ̃, -ɑ̃t] *adj* urgent; (*personne*) insistent; **se faire** ~ to become insistent.

presse [pʀɛs] *nf* press; (*affluence*): **heures de** ~ busy times; **sous** ~ gone to press; **mettre sous** ~ to send to press; **avoir une bonne/ mauvaise** ~ to have a good/bad press; ~ **féminine** women's magazines *pl*; ~ **d'information** quality newspapers *pl*.

pressé, e [pʀese] *adj* in a hurry; (*air*) hurried; (*besogne*) urgent ♦ *nm*: **aller au plus** ~ to see to first things first; **être** ~ **de faire qch** to be in a hurry to do sth; **orange** ~**e** freshly squeezed orange juice.

presse-citron [pʀɛsitʀɔ̃] *nm inv* lemon squeezer.

presse-fruits [pʀɛsfʀɥi] *nm inv* lemon squeezer.

pressentiment [pʀesɑ̃timɑ̃] *nm* foreboding, premonition.

pressentir [pʀesɑ̃tiʀ] *vt* to sense; (*prendre contact avec*) to approach.

presse-papiers [pʀɛspapje] *nm inv* paperweight.

presse-purée [pʀɛspyʀe] *nm inv* potato masher.

presser [pʀese] *vt* (*fruit, éponge*) to squeeze; (*interrupteur, bouton*) to press, push; (*allure, affaire*) to speed up; (*débiteur etc*) to press; (*inciter*): ~ **qn de faire** to urge *ou* press sb to do ♦ *vi* to be urgent; **se** ~ (*se hâter*) to hurry (up); (*se grouper*) to crowd; **rien ne presse** there's no hurry; **se** ~ **contre qn** to squeeze up against sb; ~ **le pas** to quicken one's step; ~ **qn entre ses bras** to squeeze sb tight.

pressing [pʀesiŋ] *nm* (*repassage*) steampressing; (*magasin*) dry-cleaner's.

pression [pʀesjɔ̃] *nf* pressure; (*bouton*) press stud (*BRIT*), snap fastener; **faire** ~ **sur** to put pressure on; **sous** ~ pressurized, under pressure; (*fig*) keyed up; ~ **artérielle** blood pressure.

pressoir [pʀeswaʀ] *nm* (*wine ou oil etc*) press.

pressurer [pʀesyʀe] *vt* (*fig*) to squeeze.

pressurisé, e [pʀesyʀize] *adj* pressurized.

prestance [pʀɛstɑ̃s] *nf* presence, imposing bearing.

prestataire [pʀɛstatɛʀ] *nm/f* person receiving benefits; (*COMM*): ~ **de services** provider of services.

prestation [pʀɛstasjɔ̃] *nf* (*allocation*) benefit; (*d'une assurance*) cover *no pl*; (*d'une entreprise*) service provided; (*d'un joueur, artiste*) performance; ~ **de serment** taking the oath; ~ **de service** provision of a service; ~**s familiales** ≈ child benefit.

preste [pʀɛst(ə)] adj nimble.

prestement [pʀɛstəmɑ̃] adv nimbly.

prestidigitateur, trice [pʀɛstidiʒitatœʀ, -tʀis] nm/f conjurer.

prestidigitation [pʀɛstidiʒitasjɔ̃] nf conjuring.

prestige [pʀɛstiʒ] nm prestige.

prestigieux, euse [pʀɛstiʒjø, -øz] adj prestigious.

présumer [pʀezyme] vt: ~ **que** to presume ou assume that; ~ **de** to overrate; ~ **qn coupable** to presume sb guilty.

présupposé [pʀesypoze] nm presupposition.

présupposer [pʀesypoze] vt to presuppose.

présupposition [pʀesypozisjɔ̃] nf presupposition.

présure [pʀezyʀ] nf rennet.

prêt, e [pʀɛ, pʀɛt] adj ready ♦ nm lending no pl; (somme prêtée) loan; ~ **à faire** ready to do; ~ **à tout** ready for anything; ~ **sur gages** pawnbroking no pl.

prêt-à-porter, pl **prêts-à-porter** [pʀɛtapɔʀte] nm ready-to-wear ou off-the-peg (BRIT) clothes pl.

prétendant [pʀetɑ̃dɑ̃] nm pretender; (d'une femme) suitor.

prétendre [pʀetɑ̃dʀ(ə)] vt (affirmer): ~ **que** to claim that; (avoir l'intention de): ~ **faire qch** to mean ou intend to do sth; ~ **à** vt (droit, titre) to lay claim to.

prétendu, e [pʀetɑ̃dy] adj (supposé) so-called.

prétendument [pʀetɑ̃dymɑ̃] adv allegedly.

prête-nom [pʀɛtnɔ̃] nm (péj) figurehead; (COMM etc) dummy.

prétentieux, euse [pʀetɑ̃sjø, -øz] adj pretentious.

prétention [pʀetɑ̃sjɔ̃] nf pretentiousness; (exigence, ambition) claim; **sans** ~ unpretentious.

prêter [pʀete] vt (livres, argent): ~ **qch (à)** to lend sth (to); (supposer): ~ **à** qn (caractère, propos) to attribute to sb ♦ vi (aussi: **se** ~: tissu, cuir) to give; ~ **à** (commentaires etc) to be open to, give rise to; **se** ~ **à** to lend o.s. (ou itself) to; (manigances etc) to go along with; ~ **assistance à** to give help to; ~ **attention à** to pay attention to; ~ **serment** to take the oath; ~ **l'oreille** to listen.

prêteur, euse [pʀetœʀ, -øz] nm/f moneylender; ~ **sur gages** pawnbroker.

prétexte [pʀetɛkst(ə)] nm pretext, excuse; **sous aucun** ~ on no account; **sous (le)** ~ **que/de** on the pretext that/of.

prétexter [pʀetɛkste] vt to give as a pretext ou an excuse.

prêtre [pʀetʀ(ə)] nm priest.

prêtre-ouvrier, pl **prêtres-ouvriers** [pʀetʀuvʀije] nm worker-priest.

prêtrise [pʀetʀiz] nf priesthood.

preuve [pʀœv] nf proof; (indice) proof, evi-

dence no pl; **jusqu'à** ~ **du contraire** until proved otherwise; **faire** ~ **de** to show; **faire ses** ~**s** to prove o.s. (ou itself); ~ **matérielle** material evidence.

prévaloir [pʀevalwaʀ] vi to prevail; **se** ~ **de** vt to take advantage of; (tirer vanité de) to pride o.s. on.

prévarication [pʀevaʀikasjɔ̃] nf maladministration.

prévaut [pʀevo] etc vb voir **prévaloir**.

prévenances [pʀevnɑ̃s] nfpl thoughtfulness sg, kindness sg.

prévenant, e [pʀevnɑ̃, -ɑ̃t] adj thoughtful, kind.

prévenir [pʀevniʀ] vt (avertir): ~ **qn (de)** to warn sb (about); (informer): ~ **qn (de)** to tell ou inform sb (about); (éviter) to avoid, prevent; (anticiper) to anticipate; (influencer): ~ **qn contre** to prejudice sb against.

préventif, ive [pʀevɑ̃tif, -iv] adj preventive.

prévention [pʀevɑ̃sjɔ̃] nf prevention; (préjugé) prejudice; (JUR) custody, detention; ~ **routière** road safety.

prévenu, e [pʀevny] nm/f (JUR) defendant, accused.

prévisible [pʀevizibl(ə)] adj foreseeable.

prévision [pʀevizjɔ̃] nf: ~**s** predictions; (météorologiques, économiques) forecast sg; **en** ~ **de** in anticipation of; ~**s météorologiques** ou **du temps** weather forecast sg.

prévisionnel, le [pʀevizjɔnɛl] adj concerned with future requirements.

prévit [pʀevi] etc vb voir **prévoir**.

prévoir [pʀevwaʀ] vt (deviner) to foresee; (s'attendre à) to expect, reckon on; (prévenir) to anticipate; (organiser) to plan; (préparer, réserver) to allow; **prévu pour 4 personnes** designed for 4 people; **prévu pour 10 h** scheduled for 10 o'clock.

prévoyance [pʀevwajɑ̃s] nf foresight; **société/caisse de** ~ provident society/contingency fund.

prévoyant, e [pʀevwajɑ̃, -ɑ̃t] vb voir **prévoir** ♦ adj gifted with (ou showing) foresight, far-sighted.

prévu, e [pʀevy] pp de **prévoir**.

prier [pʀije] vi to pray ♦ vt (Dieu) to pray to; (implorer) to beg; (demander): ~ **qn de faire** to ask sb to do; (inviter): ~ **qn à dîner** to invite sb to dinner; **se faire** ~ to need coaxing ou persuading; **je vous en prie** (allez-y) please do; (de rien) don't mention it; **je vous prie de faire** please (would you) do.

prière [pʀijɛʀ] nf prayer; (demande instante) plea, entreaty; "~ **de faire** ..." "please do ...".

primaire [pʀimɛʀ] adj primary; (péj: personne) simple-minded; (: idées) simplistic ♦ nm (SCOL) primary education.

primauté [pʀimote] nf (fig) primacy.

prime [pʀim] nf (bonification) bonus; (subside) allowance; (COMM: cadeau) free gift; (ASSU-

RANCES, BOURSE) premium ♦ adj: **de ~ abord**
at first glance; **~ de risque** danger money *no
pl*; **~ de transport** travel allowance.

primer [pRime] *vt* (*l'emporter sur*) to prevail
over; (*récompenser*) to award a prize to ♦ *vi*
to dominate, prevail.

primesautier, ière [pRimsotje, -jɛR] *adj* impulsive.

primeur [pRimœR] *nf*: **avoir la ~ de** to be the
first to hear (*ou* see *etc*); **~s** *nfpl* (*fruits, légumes*) early fruits and vegetables; **mar-
chand de ~** greengrocer (*BRIT*), produce
dealer (*US*).

primevère [pRimvɛR] *nf* primrose.

primitif, ive [pRimitif, -iv] *adj* primitive; (*originel*) original ♦ *nm/f* primitive.

primo [pRimo] *adv* first (of all), firstly.

primordial, e, aux [pRimɔRdjal, -o] *adj* essential, primordial.

prince [pRɛ̃s] *nm* prince; **~ charmant** Prince
Charming; **~ de Galles** *nm inv* (*tissu*) check
cloth; **~ héritier** crown prince.

princesse [pRɛ̃sɛs] *nf* princess.

princier, ière [pRɛ̃sje, -jɛR] *adj* princely.

principal, e, aux [pRɛ̃sipal, -o] *adj* principal,
main ♦ *nm* (*SCOL*) head(teacher) (*BRIT*), principal (*US*); (*essentiel*) main thing ♦ *nf* (*LING*):
(**proposition**) **~e** main clause.

principalement [pRɛ̃sipalmɑ̃] *adv* principally,
mainly.

principauté [pRɛ̃sipote] *nf* principality.

principe [pRɛ̃sip] *nm* principle; **partir du ~ que**
to work on the principle *ou* assumption
that; **pour le ~** on principle, for the sake of
it; **de ~** *adj* (*hostilité*) automatic; (*accord*) in
principle; **par ~** on principle; **en ~** (*habituellement*) as a rule; (*théoriquement*) in principle.

printanier, ière [pRɛ̃tanje, -jɛR] *adj* spring *cpd*;
spring-like.

printemps [pRɛ̃tɑ̃] *nm* spring; **au ~** in spring.

priori [pRijɔRi]: **a ~** *adv* at first glance; initially; a priori.

prioritaire [pRijɔRitɛR] *adj* having priority;
(*AUTO*) having right of way; (*INFORM*) foreground.

priorité [pRijɔRite] *nf* (*AUTO*): **avoir la ~ (sur)**
to have right of way (over); **~ à droite**
right of way to vehicles coming from the
right; **en ~** as a (matter of) priority.

pris, e [pRi, pRiz] *pp de* **prendre** ♦ *adj* (*place*)
taken; (*billets*) sold; (*journée, mains*) full;
(*personne*) busy; (*crème, ciment*) set; (*MÉD:
enflammé*): **avoir le nez/la gorge ~(e)** to have
a stuffy nose/a bad throat; (*saisi*): **être ~ de
peur/de fatigue** to be stricken with fear/
overcome with fatigue.

prise [pRiz] *nf* (*d'une ville*) capture; (*PÊCHE,
CHASSE*) catch; (*de judo ou catch, point d'appui
ou pour empoigner*) hold; (*ÉLEC: fiche*) plug;
(: *femelle*) socket; (: *au mur*) point; **en ~**
(*AUTO*) in gear; **être aux ~s avec** to be grap-

pling with; to be battling with; **lâcher ~** to
let go; **donner ~ à** (*fig*) to give rise to; **avoir
~ sur qn** to have a hold over sb; **~ en charge**
(*taxe*) pick-up charge; (*par la sécurité sociale*)
undertaking to reimburse costs; **~ de contact** initial meeting, first contact; **~ de courant** power point; **~ d'eau** water (supply)
point; tap; **~ multiple** adaptor; **~ d'otages**
hostage-taking; **~ à partie** (*JUR*) action
against a judge; **~ de sang** blood test; **~ de
son** sound recording; **~ de tabac** pinch of
snuff; **~ de terre** earth; **~ de vue** (*photo*)
shot; (*action*): **~ de vue(s)** filming, shooting.

priser [pRize] *vt* (*tabac, héroïne*) to take; (*estimer*) to prize, value ♦ *vi* to take snuff.

prisme [pRism(ə)] *nm* prism.

prison [pRizɔ̃] *nf* prison; **aller/être en ~** to go
to/be in prison *ou* jail; **faire de la ~** to serve
time; **être condamné à 5 ans de ~** to be sentenced to 5 years' imprisonment *ou* 5 years
in prison.

prisonnier, ière [pRizɔnje, -jɛR] *nm/f* prisoner
♦ *adj* captive; **faire qn ~** to take sb prisoner.

prit [pRi] *vb voir* **prendre**.

privatif, ive [pRivatif, -iv] *adj* (*jardin etc*) private; (*peine*) which deprives one of one's
liberties.

privations [pRivɑsjɔ̃] *nfpl* privations, hard-
ships.

privatisation [pRivatizasjɔ̃] *nf* privatization.

privatiser [pRivatize] *vt* to privatize.

privautés [pRivote] *nfpl* liberties.

privé, e [pRive] *adj* private; (*dépourvu*): **~ de**
without, lacking; **en ~, dans le ~** in private.

priver [pRive] *vt*: **~ qn de** to deprive sb of; **se
~ de** to go *ou* do without; **ne pas se ~ de
faire** not to refrain from doing.

privilège [pRivilɛʒ] *nm* privilege.

privilégié, e [pRivileʒje] *adj* privileged.

privilégier [pRivileʒje] *vt* to favour (*BRIT*), favor (*US*).

prix [pRi] *nm* (*valeur*) price; (*récompense, SCOL*)
prize; **mettre à ~** to set a reserve (*BRIT*) *ou*
an upset (*US*) price on; **au ~ fort** at a very
high price; **acheter qch à ~ d'or** to pay a
(small) fortune for sth; **hors de ~** exorbitantly priced; **à aucun ~** not at any price; **à
tout ~** at all costs; **grand ~** (*SPORT*) Grand
Prix; **~ d'achat/de vente/de revient**
purchasing/selling/cost price; **~ conseillé**
manufacturer's recommended price
(MRP).

pro [pRo] *nm* (= *professionnel*) pro.

probabilité [pRobabilite] *nf* probability; **selon
toute ~** in all probability.

probable [pRobabl(ə)] *adj* likely, probable.

probablement [pRobabləmɑ̃] *adv* probably.

probant, e [pRobɑ̃, -ɑ̃t] *adj* convincing.

probatoire [pRobatwaR] *adj* (*examen, test*) preliminary; (*stage*) probationary, trial *cpd*.

probité [pRobite] *nf* integrity, probity.

problématique [pRoblematik] *adj* problematic(al) ♦ *nf* problematics *sg*; (*problème*) problem.

problème [pʀɔblɛm] *nm* problem.

procédé [pʀɔsede] *nm* (*méthode*) process; (*comportement*) behaviour *no pl* (*BRIT*), behavior *no pl* (*US*).

procéder [pʀɔsede] *vi* to proceed; to behave; ~ **à** *vt* to carry out.

procédure [pʀɔsedyʀ] *nf* (*ADMIN, JUR*) procedure.

procès [pʀɔsɛ] *nm* (*JUR*) trial; (: *poursuites*) proceedings *pl*; **être en** ~ **avec** to be involved in a lawsuit with; **faire le** ~ **de qn/qch** (*fig*) to put sb/sth on trial; **sans autre forme de** ~ without further ado.

processeur [pʀɔsesœʀ] *nm* processor.

procession [pʀɔsesjɔ̃] *nf* procession.

processus [pʀɔsesys] *nm* process.

procès-verbal, aux [pʀɔsɛvɛʀbal, -o] *nm* (*constat*) statement; (*aussi*: **PV**): **avoir un** ~ to get a parking ticket; to be booked; (*de réunion*) minutes *pl*.

prochain, e [pʀɔʃɛ̃, -ɛn] *adj* next; (*proche*) impending; near ♦ *nm* fellow man; **la** ~**e fois/semaine** ~**e** next time/week; **à la** ~**e!** (*fam*), **à la** ~**e fois** see you!, till the next time!; **un** ~ **jour** (some day) soon.

prochainement [pʀɔʃɛnmɑ̃] *adv* soon, shortly.

proche [pʀɔʃ] *adj* nearby; (*dans le temps*) imminent; close at hand; (*parent, ami*) close; ~**s** *nmpl* (*parents*) close relatives, next of kin; (*amis*): **l'un de ses** ~**s** one of those close to him (*ou* her); **être** ~ (**de**) to be near, be close (to); **de** ~ **en** ~ gradually.

Proche-Orient [pʀɔʃɔʀjɑ̃] *nm*: **le** ~ the Near East.

proclamation [pʀɔklamɑsjɔ̃] *nf* proclamation.

proclamer [pʀɔklame] *vt* to proclaim; (*résultat d'un examen*) to announce.

procréer [pʀɔkʀee] *vt* to procreate.

procuration [pʀɔkyʀɑsjɔ̃] *nf* proxy; power of attorney; **voter par** ~ to vote by proxy.

procurer [pʀɔkyʀe] *vt* (*fournir*): ~ **qch à qn** to get *ou* obtain sth for sb; (*causer: plaisir etc*): ~ **qch à qn** to bring *ou* give sb sth; **se** ~ *vt* to get.

procureur [pʀɔkyʀœʀ] *nm* public prosecutor; ~ **général** public prosecutor (*in appeal court*).

prodigalité [pʀɔdigalite] *nf* (*générosité*) generosity; (*extravagance*) extravagance, wastefulness.

prodige [pʀɔdiʒ] *nm* (*miracle, merveille*) marvel, wonder; (*personne*) prodigy.

prodigieusement [pʀɔdiʒjøzmɑ̃] *adv* tremendously.

prodigieux, euse [pʀɔdiʒjø, -øz] *adj* prodigious; phenomenal.

prodigue [pʀɔdig] *adj* (*généreux*) generous; (*dépensier*) extravagant, wasteful; **fils** ~ prodigal son.

prodiguer [pʀɔdige] *vt* (*argent, biens*) to be lavish with; (*soins, attentions*): ~ **qch à qn** to lavish sth on sb.

producteur, trice [pʀɔdyktœʀ, -tʀis] *adj*: ~ **de blé** wheat-producing; (*CINÉ*): **société productrice** film *ou* movie company ♦ *nm/f* producer.

productif, ive [pʀɔdyktif, -iv] *adj* productive.

production [pʀɔdyksjɔ̃] *nf* (*gén*) production; (*rendement*) output; (*produits*) products *pl*, goods *pl*; (*œuvres*): **la** ~ **dramatique du XVIIe siècle** the plays of the 17th century.

productivité [pʀɔdyktivite] *nf* productivity.

produire [pʀɔdɥiʀ] *vt, vi* to produce; **se** ~ *vi* (*acteur*) to perform, appear; (*événement*) to happen, occur.

produit, e [pʀɔdɥi, -it] *pp de* **produire** ♦ *nm* (*gén*) product; ~ **d'entretien** cleaning product; ~ **national brut (PNB)** gross national product (GNP); ~ **net** net profit; ~ **pour la vaisselle** washing-up (*BRIT*) *ou* dish-washing (*US*) liquid; ~ **des ventes** income from sales; ~**s agricoles** farm produce *sg*; ~**s alimentaires** foodstuffs; ~**s de beauté** beauty products, cosmetics.

proéminent, e [pʀɔeminɑ̃, -ɑ̃t] *adj* prominent.

prof [pʀɔf] *nm* (*fam*: = *professeur*) teacher; professor; lecturer.

prof. [pʀɔf] *abr* = **professeur, professionnel**.

profane [pʀɔfan] *adj* (*REL*) secular; (*ignorant, non initié*) uninitiated ♦ *nm/f* layman.

profaner [pʀɔfane] *vt* to desecrate; (*fig: sentiment*) to defile; (: *talent*) to debase.

proférer [pʀɔfeʀe] *vt* to utter.

professer [pʀɔfese] *vt* to profess.

professeur [pʀɔfesœʀ] *nm* teacher; (*titulaire d'une chaire*) professor; ~ **(de faculté)** (university) lecturer.

profession [pʀɔfesjɔ̃] *nf* (*libérale*) profession; (*gén*) occupation; **faire** ~ **de** (*opinion, religion*) to profess; **de** ~ by profession; "**sans** ~" "unemployed"; (*femme mariée*) "housewife".

professionnel, le [pʀɔfesjɔnɛl] *adj* professional ♦ *nm/f* professional; (*ouvrier qualifié*) skilled worker.

professoral, e, aux [pʀɔfesɔʀal, -o] *adj* professorial; **le corps** ~ the teaching profession.

professorat [pʀɔfesɔʀa] *nm*: **le** ~ the teaching profession.

profil [pʀɔfil] *nm* profile; (*d'une voiture*) line, contour; **de** ~ in profile.

profilé, e [pʀɔfile] *adj* shaped; (*aile etc*) streamlined.

profiler [pʀɔfile] *vt* to streamline; **se** ~ *vi* (*arbre, tour*) to stand out, be silhouetted.

profit [pʀɔfi] *nm* (*avantage*) benefit, advantage; (*COMM, FINANCE*) profit; **au** ~ **de** in aid of; **tirer** *ou* **retirer** ~ **de** to profit from; **mettre à** ~ to take advantage of; to turn to good account; ~**s et pertes** (*COMM*) profit and loss(es).

profitable [pʀɔfitabl(ə)] *adj* beneficial; profitable.

profiter [pʀɔfite] *vi*: ~ **de** to take advantage of; to make the most of; ~ **de ce que** ... to take advantage of the fact that ...; ~ **à** to be of benefit to, benefit; to be profitable to.

profiteur, euse [pʀɔfitœʀ, -øz] *nm/f (péj)* profiteer.

profond, e [pʀɔfɔ̃, -ɔ̃d] *adj* deep; *(méditation, mépris)* profound; **au plus** ~ **de** in the depths of, at the (very) bottom of; **la France** ~**e** the heartlands of France.

profondément [pʀɔfɔ̃demɑ̃] *adv* deeply; profoundly.

profondeur [pʀɔfɔ̃dœʀ] *nf* depth.

profusément [pʀɔfyzemɑ̃] *adv* profusely.

profusion [pʀɔfyzjɔ̃] *nf* profusion; **à** ~ in plenty.

progéniture [pʀɔʒenityʀ] *nf* offspring *inv*.

progiciel [pʀɔʒisjɛl] *nm (INFORM)* (software) package; ~ **d'application** applications package, applications software *no pl*.

progouvernemental, e, aux [pʀɔguvɛʀnəmɑ̃tal, -o] *adj* pro-government *cpd*.

programmable [pʀɔgʀamabl(ə)] *adj* programmable.

programmateur, trice [pʀɔgʀamatœʀ, -tʀis] *nm/f (CINÉ, TV)* programme *(BRIT) ou* program *(US)* planner ♦ *nm (de machine à laver etc)* timer.

programmation [pʀɔgʀamasjɔ̃] *nf* programming.

programme [pʀɔgʀam] *nm* programme *(BRIT)*, program *(US)*; *(TV, RADIO)* program(me)s *pl*; *(SCOL)* syllabus, curriculum; *(INFORM)* program; **au** ~ **de ce soir** *(TV)* among tonight's program(me)s.

programmé, e [pʀɔgʀame] *adj*: **enseignement** ~ programmed learning.

programmer [pʀɔgʀame] *vt (TV, RADIO)* to put on, show; *(organiser, prévoir)* to schedule; *(INFORM)* to program.

programmeur, euse [pʀɔgʀamœʀ, -øz] *nm/f* (computer) programmer.

progrès [pʀɔgʀɛ] *nm* progress *no pl*; **faire des/être en** ~ to make/be making progress.

progresser [pʀɔgʀese] *vi* to progress; *(troupes etc)* to make headway *ou* progress.

progressif, ive [pʀɔgʀesif, -iv] *adj* progressive.

progression [pʀɔgʀesjɔ̃] *nf* progression; *(d'une troupe etc)* advance, progress.

progressiste [pʀɔgʀesist(ə)] *adj* progressive.

progressivement [pʀɔgʀesivmɑ̃] *adv* progressively.

prohiber [pʀɔibe] *vt* to prohibit, ban.

prohibitif, ive [pʀɔibitif, -iv] *adj* prohibitive.

prohibition [pʀɔibisjɔ̃] *nf* ban, prohibition; *(HIST)* Prohibition.

proie [pʀwa] *nf* prey *no pl*; **être la** ~ **de** to fall prey to; **être en** ~ **à** *(doutes, sentiment)* to be

prey to; *(douleur, mal)* to be suffering.

projecteur [pʀɔʒɛktœʀ] *nm* projector; *(de théâtre, cirque)* spotlight.

projectile [pʀɔʒɛktil] *nm* missile; *(d'arme)* projectile, bullet *(ou* shell *etc)*.

projection [pʀɔʒɛksjɔ̃] *nf* projection; showing; **conférence avec** ~**s** lecture with slides *(ou* a film*)*.

projectionniste [pʀɔʒɛksjɔnist(ə)] *nm/f (CINÉ)* projectionist.

projet [pʀɔʒɛ] *nm* plan; *(ébauche)* draft; **faire des** ~**s** to make plans; ~ **de loi** bill.

projeter [pʀɔʒte] *vt (envisager)* to plan; *(film, photos)* to project; *(passer)* to show; *(ombre, lueur)* to throw, cast, project; *(jeter)* to throw up *(ou* off *ou* out); ~ **de faire qch** to plan to do sth.

prolétaire [pʀɔletɛʀ] *adj, nm/f* proletarian.

prolétariat [pʀɔletaʀja] *nm* proletariat.

prolétarien, -ne [pʀɔletaʀjɛ̃, -ɛn] *adj* proletarian.

prolifération [pʀɔlifeʀasjɔ̃] *nf* proliferation.

proliférer [pʀɔlifeʀe] *vi* to proliferate.

prolifique [pʀɔlifik] *adj* prolific.

prolixe [pʀɔliks(ə)] *adj* verbose.

prolo [pʀɔlo] *nm/f (fam: = prolétaire)* prole *(péj)*.

prologue [pʀɔlɔg] *nm* prologue.

prolongateur [pʀɔlɔ̃gatœʀ] *nm (ÉLEC)* extension cable.

prolongation [pʀɔlɔ̃gasjɔ̃] *nf* prolongation; extension; ~**s** *nfpl (FOOTBALL)* extra time *sg*.

prolongement [pʀɔlɔ̃ʒmɑ̃] *nm* extension; ~**s** *nmpl (fig)* repercussions, effects; **dans le** ~ **de** running on from.

prolonger [pʀɔlɔ̃ʒe] *vt (débat, séjour)* to prolong; *(délai, billet, rue)* to extend; *(suj: chose)* to be a continuation *ou* an extension of; **se** ~ *vi* to go on.

promenade [pʀɔmnad] *nf* walk *(ou* drive *ou* ride); **faire une** ~ to go for a walk; **une** ~ **(à pied)/en voiture/à vélo** a walk/drive/(bicycle) ride.

promener [pʀɔmne] *vt (personne, chien)* to take out for a walk; *(fig)* to carry around; to trail round; *(doigts, regard)*: ~ **qch sur** to run sth over; **se** ~ *vi (à pied)* to go for *(ou* be out for) a walk; *(en voiture)* to go for *(ou* be out for) a drive; *(fig)*: **se** ~ **sur** to wander over.

promeneur, euse [pʀɔmnœʀ, -øz] *nm/f* walker, stroller.

promenoir [pʀɔmənwaʀ] *nm* gallery, (covered) walkway.

promesse [pʀɔmɛs] *nf* promise; ~ **d'achat** commitment to buy.

prometteur, euse [pʀɔmɛtœʀ, -øz] *adj* promising.

promettre [pʀɔmɛtʀ(ə)] *vt* to promise ♦ *vi (récolte, arbre)* to look promising; *(enfant, musicien)* to be promising; **se** ~ **de faire** to resolve *ou* mean to do; ~ **à qn de faire** to promise sb that one will do.

promeus [pʀɔmø] *etc vb voir* **promouvoir**.

promis, e [pʀɔmi, -iz] *pp de* **promettre** ♦ *adj*: **être ~ à qch** (*destiné*) to be destined for sth.

promiscuité [pʀɔmiskɥite] *nf* crowding; lack of privacy.

promit [pʀɔmi] *vb voir* **promettre**.

promontoire [pʀɔmɔ̃twaʀ] *nm* headland.

promoteur, trice [pʀɔmɔtœʀ, -tʀis] *nm/f* (*instigateur*) instigator, promoter; ~ **immobilier** property developer (*BRIT*), real estate promoter (*US*).

promotion [pʀɔmɔsjɔ̃] *nf* (*avancement*) promotion; (*SCOL*) year (*BRIT*), class; **en ~** (*COMM*) on promotion, on (special) offer.

promotionnel, le [pʀɔmɔsjɔnɛl] *adj* (*article*) on promotion, on (special) offer; (*vente*) promotional.

promouvoir [pʀɔmuvwaʀ] *vt* to promote.

prompt, e [pʀɔ̃, pʀɔ̃t] *adj* swift, rapid; (*intervention, changement*) sudden; ~ **à faire qch** quick to do sth.

promptement [pʀɔ̃ptəmã] *adv* swiftly.

prompteur [pʀɔ̃tœʀ] *nm* ® Autocue ® (*BRIT*), Teleprompter ® (*US*).

promptitude [pʀɔ̃tityd] *nf* swiftness, rapidity.

promu, e [pʀɔmy] *pp de* **promouvoir**.

promulguer [pʀɔmylɡe] *vt* to promulgate.

prôner [pʀone] *vt* (*louer*) to laud, extol; (*préconiser*) to advocate, commend.

pronom [pʀɔnɔ̃] *nm* pronoun.

pronominal, e, aux [pʀɔnɔminal, -o] *adj* pronominal; (*verbe*) reflexive, pronominal.

prononcé, e [pʀɔnɔ̃se] *adj* pronounced, marked.

prononcer [pʀɔnɔ̃se] *vt* (*son, mot, jugement*) to pronounce; (*dire*) to utter; (*allocution*) to deliver ♦ *vi* (*JUR*) to deliver *ou* give a verdict; ~ **bien/mal** to have a good/poor pronunciation; **se ~** *vi* to reach a decision, give a verdict; **se ~ sur** to give an opinion on; **se ~ contre** to come down against; **ça se prononce comment?** how do you pronounce this?

prononciation [pʀɔnɔ̃sjasjɔ̃] *nf* pronunciation.

pronostic [pʀɔnɔstik] *nm* (*MÉD*) prognosis (*pl* -oses); (*fig: aussi*: **~s**) forecast.

pronostiquer [pʀɔnɔstike] *vt* (*MÉD*) to prognosticate; (*annoncer, prévoir*) to forecast, foretell.

pronostiqueur, euse [pʀɔnɔstikœʀ, -øz] *nm/f* forecaster.

propagande [pʀɔpagɑ̃d] *nf* propaganda; **faire de la ~ pour qch** to plug *ou* push sth.

propagandiste [pʀɔpagɑ̃dist(ə)] *nm/f* propagandist.

propagation [pʀɔpagasjɔ̃] *nf* propagation.

propager [pʀɔpaʒe] *vt* to spread; **se ~** *vi* to spread; (*PHYSIQUE*) to be propagated.

propane [pʀɔpan] *nm* propane.

propension [pʀɔpɑ̃sjɔ̃] *nf*: ~ **à (faire) qch** propensity to (do) sth.

prophète [pʀɔfɛt], **prophétesse** [pʀɔfetɛs] *nm/f* prophet(ess).

prophétie [pʀɔfesi] *nf* prophecy.

prophétique [pʀɔfetik] *adj* prophetic.

prophétiser [pʀɔfetize] *vt* to prophesy.

prophylactique [pʀɔfilaktik] *adj* prophylactic.

propice [pʀɔpis] *adj* favourable (*BRIT*), favorable (*US*).

proportion [pʀɔpɔʀsjɔ̃] *nf* proportion; **il n'y a aucune ~ entre le prix demandé et le prix réel** the asking price bears no relation to the real price; **à ~ de** proportionally to, in proportion to; **en ~ (de)** in proportion (to); **hors de ~** out of proportion; **toute(s) ~(s) gardée(s)** making due allowance(s).

proportionné, e [pʀɔpɔʀsjɔne] *adj*: **bien ~** well-proportioned; ~ **à** proportionate to.

proportionnel, le [pʀɔpɔʀsjɔnɛl] *adj* proportional; ~ **à** proportional to ♦ *nf* proportional representation.

proportionnellement [pʀɔpɔʀsjɔnɛlmã] *adv* proportionally, proportionately.

proportionner [pʀɔpɔʀsjɔne] *vt*: ~ **qch à** to proportion *ou* adjust sth to.

propos [pʀɔpo] *nm* (*paroles*) talk *no pl*, remark; (*intention, but*) intention, aim; (*sujet*): **à quel ~?** what about?; **à ~ de** about, regarding; **à tout ~** for no reason at all; **à ce ~** on that subject, in this connection; **à ~** *adv* by the way; (*opportunément*) (just) at the right moment; **hors de ~, mal à ~** *adv* at the wrong moment.

proposer [pʀɔpoze] *vt* (*suggérer*): ~ **qch (à qn)/de faire** to suggest sth (to sb)/doing, propose sth (to sb)/to do; (*offrir*): ~ **qch à qn/de faire** to offer sb sth/to do; (*candidat*) to nominate, put forward; (*loi, motion*) to propose; **se ~ (pour faire)** to offer one's services (to do); **se ~ de faire** to intend *ou* propose to do.

proposition [pʀɔpozisjɔ̃] *nf* suggestion; proposal; offer; (*LING*) clause; **sur la ~ de** at the suggestion of; ~ **de loi** private bill.

propre [pʀɔpʀ(ə)] *adj* clean; (*net*) neat, tidy; (*qui ne salit pas: chien, chat*) house-trained; (*: enfant*) toilet-trained; (*fig: honnête*) honest; (*possessif*) own; (*sens*) literal; (*particulier*): ~ **à** peculiar to, characteristic of; (*approprié*): ~ **à** suitable *ou* appropriate for; (*de nature à*): ~ **à faire** likely to do, that will do ♦ *nm*: **recopier au ~** to make a fair copy of; (*particularité*): **le ~ de** the peculiarity of, the distinctive feature of; **au ~** (*LING*) literally; **appartenir à qn en ~** to belong to sb (exclusively); ~ **à rien** *nm/f* (*péj*) good-for-nothing.

proprement [pʀɔpʀəmã] *adv* cleanly; neatly, tidily; **à ~ parler** strictly speaking; **le village ~ dit** the actual village, the village itself.

propret, te [pʀɔpʀɛ, -ɛt] *adj* neat and tidy, spick-and-span.

propreté [pʀɔpʀəte] *nf* cleanliness, cleanness; neatness, tidiness.

propriétaire [prɔprijetɛr] *nm/f* owner; (*d'hôtel etc*) proprietor/tress, owner; (*pour le locataire*) landlord/lady; ~ **(immobilier)** householder; householder; ~ **récoltant** grower; ~ **(terrien)** landowner.

propriété [prɔprijete] *nf* (*droit*) ownership; (*objet, immeuble etc*) property *gén no pl*; (*villa*) residence, property; (*terres*) property *gén no pl*, land *gén no pl*; (*qualité, CHIMIE, MATH*) property; (*correction*) appropriateness, suitability; ~ **artistique et littéraire** artistic and literary copyright; ~ **industrielle** patent rights *pl*.

propulser [prɔpylse] *vt* (*missile*) to propel; (*projeter*) to hurl, fling.

propulsion [prɔpylsjɔ̃] *nf* propulsion.

prorata [prɔrata] *nm inv*: **au ~ de** in proportion to, on the basis of.

prorogation [prɔrɔgasjɔ̃] *nf* deferment; extension; adjournment.

proroger [prɔrɔʒe] *vt* to put back, defer; (*prolonger*) to extend; (*assemblée*) to adjourn, prorogue.

prosaïque [prɔzaik] *adj* mundane, prosaic.

proscription [prɔskripsjɔ̃] *nf* banishment; (*interdiction*) banning; prohibition.

proscrire [prɔskrir] *vt* (*bannir*) to banish; (*interdire*) to ban, prohibit.

prose [proz] *nf* prose (*style*).

prosélyte [prɔzelit] *nm/f* proselyte, convert.

prospecter [prɔspɛkte] *vt* to prospect; (*COMM*) to canvass.

prospecteur-placier, *pl* **prospecteurs-placiers** [prɔspɛktœrplasje] *nm* placement officer.

prospectif, ive [prɔspɛktif, -iv] *adj* prospective.

prospectus [prɔspɛktys] *nm* (*feuille*) leaflet; (*dépliant*) brochure, leaflet.

prospère [prɔspɛr] *adj* prosperous; (*santé, entreprise*) thriving, flourishing.

prospérer [prɔspere] *vi* to thrive.

prospérité [prɔsperite] *nf* prosperity.

prostate [prɔstat] *nf* prostate (gland).

prosterner [prɔstɛrne]: **se ~** *vi* to bow low, prostrate o.s.

prostituée [prɔstitɥe] *nf* prostitute.

prostitution [prɔstitysjɔ̃] *nf* prostitution.

prostré, e [prɔstre] *adj* prostrate.

protagoniste [prɔtagɔnist(ə)] *nm* protagonist.

protecteur, trice [prɔtɛktœr, -tris] *adj* protective; (*air, ton: péj*) patronizing ♦ *nm/f* (*défenseur*) protector; (*des arts*) patron.

protection [prɔtɛksjɔ̃] *nf* protection; (*d'un personnage influent: aide*) patronage; **écran de ~** protective screen; ~ **civile** *state-financed civilian rescue service*; ~ **maternelle et infantile (PMI)** *social service concerned with child welfare*.

protectionnisme [prɔtɛksjɔnism(ə)] *nm* protectionism.

protectionniste [prɔtɛksjɔnist(ə)] *adj* protec-

tionist.

protégé, e [prɔteʒe] *nm/f* protégé/e.

protège-cahier [prɔtɛʒkaje] *nm* exercise book cover.

protéger [prɔteʒe] *vt* to protect; (*aider, patronner: personne, arts*) to be a patron of; (*: carrière*) to further; **se ~ de/contre** to protect o.s. from.

protéine [prɔtein] *nf* protein.

protestant, e [prɔtɛstɑ̃, -ɑ̃t] *adj*, *nm/f* Protestant.

protestantisme [prɔtɛstɑ̃tism(ə)] *nm* Protestantism.

protestataire [prɔtɛstatɛr] *nm/f* protestor.

protestation [prɔtɛstasjɔ̃] *nf* (*plainte*) protest; (*déclaration*) protestation, profession.

protester [prɔtɛste] *vi*: ~ **(contre)** to protest (against *ou* about); ~ **de** (*son innocence, sa loyauté*) to protest.

prothèse [prɔtɛz] *nf* artificial limb, prosthesis (*pl* -ses); ~ **dentaire** (*appareil*) denture; (*science*) dental engineering.

protocolaire [prɔtɔkɔlɛr] *adj* formal; (*questions, règles*) of protocol.

protocole [prɔtɔkɔl] *nm* protocol; (*fig*) etiquette; ~ **d'accord** draft treaty; ~ **opératoire** (*MÉD*) operating procedure.

prototype [prɔtɔtip] *nm* prototype.

protubérance [prɔtyberɑ̃s] *nf* bulge, protuberance.

protubérant, e [prɔtyberɑ̃, -ɑ̃t] *adj* protruding, bulging, protuberant.

proue [pru] *nf* bow(s *pl*), prow.

prouesse [prues] *nf* feat.

prouver [pruve] *vt* to prove.

provenance [prɔvnɑ̃s] *nf* origin; (*de mot, coutume*) source; **avion en ~ de** plane (arriving) from.

provençal, e, aux [prɔvɑ̃sal, -o] *adj* Provençal ♦ *nm* (*LING*) Provençal.

Provence [prɔvɑ̃s] *nf*: **la ~** Provence.

provenir [prɔvnir]: ~ **de** *vt* to come from; (*résulter de*) to be due to, be the result of.

proverbe [prɔvɛrb(ə)] *nm* proverb.

proverbial, e, aux [prɔvɛrbjal, -o] *adj* proverbial.

providence [prɔvidɑ̃s] *nf*: **la ~** providence.

providentiel, le [prɔvidɑ̃sjɛl] *adj* providential.

province [prɔvɛ̃s] *nf* province.

provincial, e, aux [prɔvɛ̃sjal, -o] *adj*, *nm/f* provincial.

proviseur [prɔvizœr] *nm* ≈ head(teacher) (*BRIT*), ≈ principal (*US*).

provision [prɔvizjɔ̃] *nf* (*réserve*) stock, supply; (*avance: à un avocat, avoué*) retainer, retaining fee; (*COMM*) funds *pl* (in account); reserve; ~**s** *nfpl* (*vivres*) provisions, food *no pl*; **faire ~ de** to stock up with; **placard** *ou* **armoire à ~s** food cupboard.

provisoire [prɔvizwar] *adj* temporary; (*JUR*) provisional; **mise en liberté ~** release on bail.

provisoirement [pʀɔvizwaʀmɑ̃] *adv* temporarily, for the time being.
provocant, e [pʀɔvɔkɑ̃, -ɑ̃t] *adj* provocative.
provocateur, trice [pʀɔvɔkatœʀ, -tʀis] *adj* provocative ♦ *nm* (*meneur*) agitator.
provocation [pʀɔvɔkasjɔ̃] *nf* provocation.
provoquer [pʀɔvɔke] *vt* (*défier*) to provoke; (*causer*) to cause, bring about; (*: curiosité*) to arouse, give rise to; (*: aveux*) to prompt, elicit; (*inciter*): ~ qn à to incite sb to.
prox. *abr* = proximité.
proxénète [pʀɔksenɛt] *nm* procurer.
proxénétisme [pʀɔksenetism(ə)] *nm* procuring.
proximité [pʀɔksimite] *nf* nearness, closeness, proximity; (*dans le temps*) imminence, closeness; à ~ near *ou* close by; à ~ de near (to), close to.
prude [pʀyd] *adj* prudish.
prudemment [pʀydamɑ̃] *adv* (*voir prudent*) carefully; cautiously; prudently; wisely, sensibly.
prudence [pʀydɑ̃s] *nf* carefulness; caution; prudence; **avec** ~ carefully; cautiously; wisely; **par (mesure de)** ~ as a precaution.
prudent, e [pʀydɑ̃, -ɑ̃t] *adj* (*pas téméraire*) careful, cautious, prudent; (*: en général*) safety-conscious; (*sage, conseillé*) wise, sensible; (*réservé*) cautious; **ce n'est pas** ~ it's risky; it's not sensible; **soyez** ~ take care, be careful.
prune [pʀyn] *nf* plum.
pruneau, x [pʀyno] *nm* prune.
prunelle [pʀynɛl] *nf* pupil; (*œil*) eye; (*BOT*) sloe; (*eau de vie*) sloe gin.
prunier [pʀynje] *nm* plum tree.
Prusse [pʀys] *nf*: **la** ~ Prussia.
PS *sigle m* = parti socialiste; (= post-scriptum) PS.
psalmodier [psalmɔdje] *vt* to chant; (*fig*) to drone out.
psaume [psom] *nm* psalm.
pseudonyme [psødɔnim] *nm* (*gén*) fictitious name; (*d'écrivain*) pseudonym, pen name; (*de comédien*) stage name.
PSIG *sigle m* (= Peloton de surveillance et d'intervention de gendarmerie) type of police commando squad.
PSU *sigle m* = parti socialiste unifié.
psy [psi] *nm/f* (*fam, péj*: = psychiatre, psychologue*) shrink.
psychanalyse [psikanaliz] *nf* psychoanalysis.
psychanalyser [psikanalize] *vt* to psychoanalyze; **se faire** ~ to undergo (psycho-) analysis.
psychanalyste [psikanalist(ə)] *nm/f* psychoanalyst.
psychanalytique [psikanalitik] *adj* psychoanalytical.
psychédélique [psikedelik] *adj* psychedelic.
psychiatre [psikjatʀ(ə)] *nm/f* psychiatrist.
psychiatrie [psikjatʀi] *nf* psychiatry.
psychiatrique [psikjatʀik] *adj* psychiatric;

(*hôpital*) mental, psychiatric.
psychique [psiʃik] *adj* psychological.
psychisme [psiʃism(ə)] *nm* psyche.
psychologie [psikɔlɔʒi] *nf* psychology.
psychologique [psikɔlɔʒik] *adj* psychological.
psychologiquement [psikɔlɔʒikmɑ̃] *adv* psychologically.
psychologue [psikɔlɔg] *nm/f* psychologist; **être** ~ (*fig*) to be a good psychologist.
psychomoteur, trice [psikɔmɔtœʀ, -tʀis] *adj* psychomotor.
psychopathe [psikɔpat] *nm/f* psychopath.
psychopédagogie [psikɔpedagɔʒi] *nf* educational psychology.
psychose [psikoz] *nf* (*MÉD*) psychosis (*pl* -ses); (*obsession, idée fixe*) obsessive fear.
psychosomatique [psikɔsɔmatik] *adj* psychosomatic.
psychothérapie [psikɔteʀapi] *nf* psychotherapy.
psychotique [psikɔtik] *adj* psychotic.
PTCA *sigle m* = poids total en charge autorisé.
Pte *abr* = **Porte**.
pte *abr* (= pointe) pt.
PTMA *sigle m* (= poids total maximum autorisé) maximum loaded weight.
PTT *sigle fpl voir* poste.
pu [py] *pp de* pouvoir.
puanteur [pɥɑ̃tœʀ] *nf* stink, stench.
pub [pyb] *nf* (*fam*: = publicité): **la** ~ advertising.
pubère [pybɛʀ] *adj* pubescent.
puberté [pybɛʀte] *nf* puberty.
pubis [pybis] *nm* (*bas-ventre*) pubes *pl*; (*os*) pubis.
public, ique [pyblik] *adj* public; (*école, instruction*) state *cpd*; (*scrutin*) open ♦ *nm* public; (*assistance*) audience; **en** ~ in public; **le grand** ~ the general public.
publication [pyblikasjɔ̃] *nf* publication.
publiciste [pyblisist(ə)] *nm/f* adman.
publicitaire [pyblisitɛʀ] *adj* advertising *cpd*; (*film, voiture*) publicity *cpd*; (*vente*) promotional ♦ *nm* adman; **rédacteur** ~ copywriter.
publicité [pyblisite] *nf* (*méthode, profession*) advertising; (*annonce*) advertisement; (*révélations*) publicity.
publier [pyblije] *vt* to publish; (*nouvelle*) to publicize, make public.
publipostage [pyblipostaʒ] *nm* mailshot, (mass) mailing.
publique [pyblik] *adj f voir* public.
publiquement [pyblikmɑ̃] *adv* publicly.
puce [pys] *nf* flea; (*INFORM*) chip; (**marché aux**) ~**s** flea market *sg*; **mettre la** ~ **à l'oreille de qn** to give sb something to think about.
puceau, x [pyso] *adj m*: **être** ~ to be a virgin.
pucelle [pysɛl] *adj f*: **être** ~ to be a virgin.
puceron [pysʀɔ̃] *nm* aphid.
pudeur [pydœʀ] *nf* modesty.
pudibond, e [pydibɔ̃, -ɔ̃d] *adj* prudish.
pudique [pydik] *adj* (*chaste*) modest; (*discret*)

discreet.

pudiquement [pydikmɑ̃] *adv* modestly.

puer [pɥe] (*péj*) *vi* to stink ♦ *vt* to stink of, reek of.

puéricultrice [pɥerikyltʀis] *nf* ≈ nursery nurse.

puériculture [pɥerikyltyʀ] *nf* infant care.

puéril, e [pɥeʀil] *adj* childish.

puérilement [pɥeʀilmɑ̃] *adv* childishly.

puérilité [pɥeʀilite] *nf* childishness; (*acte, idée*) childish thing.

pugilat [pyʒila] *nm* (fist) fight.

puis [pɥi] *vb voir* **pouvoir** ♦ *adv* (*ensuite*) then; (*dans une énumération*) next; (*en outre*): **et** ~ and (then); **et** ~ (**après** *ou* **quoi**)? so (what)?

puisard [pɥizaʀ] *nm* (*égout*) cesspool.

puiser [pɥize] *vt*: ~ (**dans**) to draw (from); ~ **dans qch** to dip into sth.

puisque [pɥisk(ə)] *conj* since; (*valeur intensive*): ~ **je te le dis!** I'm telling you!

puissamment [pɥisamɑ̃] *adv* powerfully.

puissance [pɥisɑ̃s] *nf* power; **en** ~ *adj* potential; **2 (à la)** ~ **5** 2 to the power (of) 5.

puissant, e [pɥisɑ̃, -ɑ̃t] *adj* powerful.

puisse [pɥis] *etc vb voir* **pouvoir**.

puits [pɥi] *nm* well; ~ **artésien** artesian well; ~ **de mine** mine shaft; ~ **de science** fount of knowledge.

pull(-over) [pyl(ɔvœʀ)] *nm* sweater, jumper (*BRIT*).

pulluler [pylyle] *vi* to swarm; (*fig: erreurs*) to abound, proliferate.

pulmonaire [pylmɔnɛʀ] *adj* lung *cpd*; (*artère*) pulmonary.

pulpe [pylp(ə)] *nf* pulp.

pulsation [pylsɑsjɔ̃] *nf* (*MÉD*) beat.

pulsé [pylse] *adj m*: **chauffage à air** ~ warm air heating.

pulsion [pylsjɔ̃] *nf* (*PSYCH*) drive, urge.

pulvérisateur [pylveʀizatœʀ] *nm* spray.

pulvérisation [pylveʀizɑsjɔ̃] *nf* spraying.

pulvériser [pylveʀize] *vt* (*solide*) to pulverize; (*liquide*) to spray; (*fig: anéantir: adversaire*) to pulverize; (*: record*) to smash, shatter; (*: argument*) to demolish.

puma [pyma] *nm* puma, cougar.

punaise [pynɛz] *nf* (*ZOOL*) bug; (*clou*) drawing pin (*BRIT*), thumb tack (*US*).

punch [pɔ̃ʃ] *nm* (*boisson*) punch; [pœnʃ] (*BOXE*) punching ability; (*fig*) punch.

punching-ball [pœnʃiŋbol] *nm* punchball.

punir [pyniʀ] *vt* to punish; ~ **qn de qch** to punish sb for sth.

punitif, ive [pynitif, -iv] *adj* punitive.

punition [pynisjɔ̃] *nf* punishment.

pupille [pypij] *nf* (*ANAT*) pupil ♦ *nm/f* (*enfant*) ward; ~ **de l'État** child in care; ~ **de la Nation** war orphan.

pupitre [pypitʀ(ə)] *nm* (*SCOL*) desk; (*REL*) lectern; (*de chef d'orchestre*) rostrum; (*INFORM*) console; ~ **de commande** control panel.

pupitreur, euse [pypitʀœʀ, -øz] *nm/f* (*INFORM*)

(computer) operator, keyboarder.

pur, e [pyʀ] *adj* pure; (*vin*) undiluted; (*whisky*) neat; (*intentions*) honourable (*BRIT*), honorable (*US*) ♦ *nm* (*personne*) hard-liner; **en** ~**e perte** fruitlessly, to no avail.

purée [pyʀe] *nf*: ~ (**de pommes de terre**) ≈ mashed potatoes *pl*; ~ **de marrons** chestnut purée; ~ **de pois** (*fig*) peasoup(er).

purement [pyʀmɑ̃] *adv* purely.

pureté [pyʀte] *nf* purity.

purgatif [pyʀgatif] *nm* purgative, purge.

purgatoire [pyʀgatwaʀ] *nm* purgatory.

purge [pyʀʒ(ə)] *nf* (*POL*) purge; (*MÉD*) purging *no pl*; purge.

purger [pyʀʒe] *vt* (*radiateur*) to flush (out), drain; (*circuit hydraulique*) to bleed; (*MÉD, POL*) to purge; (*JUR: peine*) to serve.

purification [pyʀifikɑsjɔ̃] *nf* (*de l'eau*) purification; ~ **ethnique** ethnic cleansing.

purifier [pyʀifje] *vt* to purify; (*TECH: métal*) to refine.

purin [pyʀɛ̃] *nm* liquid manure.

puriste [pyʀist(ə)] *nm/f* purist.

puritain, e [pyʀitɛ̃, -ɛn] *adj, nm/f* Puritan.

puritanisme [pyʀitanism(ə)] *nm* Puritanism.

pur-sang [pyʀsɑ̃] *nm inv* thoroughbred, purebred.

purulent, e [pyʀylɑ̃, -ɑ̃t] *adj* purulent.

pus [py] *vb voir* **pouvoir** ♦ *nm* pus.

pusillanime [pyzilanim] *adj* fainthearted.

pustule [pystyl] *nf* pustule.

putain [pytɛ̃] *nf* (*fam!*) whore (*!*); **ce/cette** ~ **de ...** this bloody (*BRIT*) *ou* goddamn (*US*) ... (*!*).

putois [pytwa] *nm* polecat; **crier comme un** ~ to yell one's head off.

putréfaction [pytʀefaksjɔ̃] *nf* putrefaction.

putréfier [pytʀefje] *vt*, **se** ~ *vi* to putrefy, rot.

putride [pytʀid] *adj* putrid.

putsch [putʃ] *nm* (*POL*) putsch.

puzzle [pœzl(ə)] *nm* jigsaw (puzzle).

PV *sigle m* = **procès-verbal**.

PVC *sigle f* (= *polychlorure de vinyle*) PVC.

PVD *sigle mpl* (= *pays en voie de développement*) developing countries.

Px *abr* = **prix**.

pygmée [pigme] *nm* pygmy.

pyjama [piʒama] *nm* pyjamas *pl*, pair of pyjamas.

pylône [pilon] *nm* pylon.

pyramide [piʀamid] *nf* pyramid.

pyrénéen, ne [piʀeneɛ̃, -ɛn] *adj* Pyrenean.

Pyrénées [piʀene] *nfpl*: **les** ~ the Pyrenees.

pyrex [piʀɛks] *nm* ® Pyrex ®.

pyrogravure [piʀɔgʀavyʀ] *nf* poker-work.

pyromane [piʀɔman] *nm/f* arsonist.

python [pitɔ̃] *nm* python.

Q q

Q, q [ky] *nm inv* Q, q ♦ *abr* (= *quintal*) q; **Q comme Quintal** Q for Queen.

Qatar [katar] *nm*: **le ~** Qatar.

qcm *sigle m* (= *questionnaire à choix multiple*) multiple choice question paper.

QG *sigle m* (= *quartier général*) HQ.

QHS *sigle m* (= *quartier de haute sécurité*) high-security wing *ou* prison.

QI *sigle m* (= *quotient intellectuel*) IQ.

qqch. *abr* (= *quelque chose*) sth.

qqe(s) *abr* = **quelque(s)**.

qqn *abr* (= *quelqu'un*) sb, s.o.

quadragénaire [kadraʒenɛr] *nm/f* (*de quarante ans*) forty-year-old; (*de quarante à cinquante ans*) man/woman in his/her forties.

quadrangulaire [kwadrɑ̃gylɛr] *adj* quadrangular.

quadrature [kwadratyr] *nf*: **c'est la ~ du cercle** it's like trying to square the circle.

quadrichromie [kwadrikromi] *nf* four-colour (*BRIT*) *ou* -color (*US*) printing.

quadrilatère [k(w)adrilatɛr] *nm* (*GÉOM, MIL*) quadrilateral; (*terrain*) four-sided area.

quadrillage [kadrijaʒ] *nm* (*lignes etc*) square pattern, criss-cross pattern.

quadrillé, e [kadrije] *adj* (*papier*) squared.

quadriller [kadrije] *vt* (*papier*) to mark out in squares; (*POLICE: ville, région etc*) to keep under tight control, be positioned throughout.

quadrimoteur [k(w)adrimɔtœr] *nm* four-engined plane.

quadripartite [kwadripartit] *adj* (*entre pays*) four-power; (*entre partis*) four-party.

quadriphonie [kadrifɔni] *nf* quadraphony.

quadriréacteur [k(w)adrireaktœr] *nm* four-engined jet.

quadrupède [k(w)adrypɛd] *nm* quadruped.

quadruple [k(w)adrypl(ə)] *nm*: **le ~ de** four times as much as.

quadrupler [k(w)adryple] *vt, vi* to quadruple, increase fourfold.

quadruplés, ées [k(w)adryple] *nm/fpl* quadruplets, quads.

quai [ke] *nm* (*de port*) quay; (*de gare*) platform; (*de cours d'eau, canal*) embankment; **être à ~** (*navire*) to be alongside; (*train*) to be in the station; **le Q~ d'Orsay** offices of the French Ministry for Foreign Affairs; **le Q~ des Orfèvres** central police headquarters.

qualifiable [kalifjabl(ə)] *adj*: **ce n'est pas ~** it defies description.

qualificatif, ive [kalifikatif, -iv] *adj* (*LING*) quali-fying ♦ *nm* (*terme*) term; (*LING*) qualifier.

qualification [kalifikɑsjɔ̃] *nf* qualification.

qualifier [kalifje] *vt* to qualify; (*appeler*): **~ qch/qn de** to describe sth/sb as; **se ~** *vi* (*SPORT*) to qualify; **être qualifié pour** to be qualified for.

qualitatif, ive [kalitatif, -iv] *adj* qualitative.

qualité [kalite] *nf* quality; (*titre, fonction*) position; **en ~ de** in one's capacity as; **ès ~s** in an official capacity; **avoir ~ pour** to have authority to; **de ~** *adj* quality *cpd*; **rapport ~-prix** value (for money).

quand [kɑ̃] *conj, adv* when; **~ je serai riche** when I'm rich; **~ même** (*cependant, pourtant*) nevertheless; (*tout de même*) all the same; really; **~ bien même** even though.

quant [kɑ̃]: **~ à** *prép* (*pour ce qui est de*) as for, as to; (*au sujet de*) regarding.

quant-à-soi [kɑ̃taswa] *nm*: **rester sur son ~** to remain aloof.

quantième [kɑ̃tjɛm] *nm* date, day (of the month).

quantifiable [kɑ̃tifjabl(ə)] *adj* quantifiable.

quantifier [kɑ̃tifje] *vt* to quantify.

quantitatif, ive [kɑ̃titatif, -iv] *adj* quantita-tive.

quantitativement [kɑ̃titativmɑ̃] *adv* quantita-tively.

quantité [kɑ̃tite] *nf* quantity, amount; (*SCIENCE*) quantity; (*grand nombre*): **une ~ ou des ~(s) de** a great deal of; a lot of; **en grande ~** in large quantities; **en ~s indus-trielles** in vast amounts; **du travail en ~** a great deal of work; **~ de** many.

quarantaine [karɑ̃tɛn] *nf* (*isolement*) quaran-tine; (*âge*): **avoir la ~** to be around forty; (*nombre*): **une ~ (de)** forty or so, about for-ty; **mettre en ~** to put into quarantine; (*fig*) to send to Coventry (*BRIT*), ostracize.

quarante [karɑ̃t] *num* forty.

quarantième [karɑ̃tjɛm] *num* fortieth.

quark [kwark] *nm* quark.

quart [kar] *nm* (*fraction*) quarter; (*surveillance*) watch; (*partie*): **un ~ de poulet/fromage** a chicken quarter/a quarter of a cheese; **un ~ de beurre** a quarter kilo of butter; **≈ a half pound of butter; un ~ de vin** a quarter litre of wine; **une livre un ~** *ou* **et ~** one and a quarter pounds; **le ~ de** a quarter of; (*heure*): **d'heure** quarter of an hour; **2 h et** *ou* **un ~** (a) quarter past 2, (a) quarter after 2 (*US*); **il est le ~** it's (a) quarter past *ou* after (*US*); **une heure moins le ~** (a) quarter to one, (a) quarter of one (*US*); **il est moins le ~** it's (a) quarter to; **être de/prendre le ~** to keep/take the watch; **~ de tour** quarter turn; **au ~ de tour** (*fig*) straight off; **~s de finale** (*SPORT*) quarter finals.

quarté [karte] *nm* (*COURSES*) system of fore-cast betting giving first four horses.

quarteron [kartərɔ̃] *nm* (*péj*) small bunch, handful.

quartette [kwartɛt] *nm* quartet(te).

quartier [kartje] *nm* (*de ville*) district, area; (*de bœuf, de la lune*) quarter; (*de fruit, fromage*) piece; ~s *nmpl* (*MIL, BLASON*) quarters; **cinéma/salle de** ~ local cinema/hall; **avoir** ~ **libre** to be free; (*MIL*) to have leave from barracks; **ne pas faire de** ~ to spare no one, give no quarter; ~ **commerçant/résidentiel** shopping/residential area; ~ **général (QG)** headquarters (HQ).

quartier-maître [kartjemɛtr(ə)] *nm* ≈ leading seaman.

quasi [kazi] *adv* almost, nearly ♦ *préfixe:* ~-**certitude** near certainty.

quasiment [kazimɑ̃] *adv* almost, very nearly.

quaternaire [kwatɛrnɛr] *adj* (*GÉO*) Quaternary.

quatorze [katɔrz(ə)] *num* fourteen.

quatorzième [katɔrzjɛm] *num* fourteenth.

quatrain [katrɛ̃] *nm* quatrain.

quatre [katr(ə)] *num* four; **à** ~ **pattes** on all fours; **tiré à** ~ **épingles** dressed up to the nines; **faire les** ~ **cent coups** to be a bit wild; **se mettre en** ~ **pour qn** to go out of one's way for sb; ~ **à** ~ (*monter, descendre*) four at a time; **à** ~ **mains** (*jouer*) four-handed.

quatre-vingt-dix [katrəvɛ̃dis] *num* ninety.

quatre-vingts [katrəvɛ̃] *num* eighty.

quatrième [katrijɛm] *num* fourth.

quatuor [kwatɥɔr] *nm* quartet(te).

════════════════ *MOT-CLÉ*

que [kə] *conj* **1** (*introduisant complétive*) that; **il sait** ~ **tu es là** he knows (that) you're here; **je veux** ~ **tu acceptes** I want you to accept; **il a dit** ~ **oui** he said he would (*ou* it was *etc*)
2 (*reprise d'autres conjonctions*): **quand il rentrera et qu'il aura mangé** when he gets back and (when) he has eaten; **si vous y allez ou** ~ **vous ...** if you go there or if you ...
3 (*en tête de phrase: hypothèse, souhait etc*): **qu'il le veuille ou non** whether he likes it or not; **qu'il fasse ce qu'il voudra!** let him do as he pleases!
4 (*but*): **tenez-le qu'il ne tombe pas** hold it so (that) it doesn't fall
5 (*après comparatif*) than; as; *voir aussi* **plus**; **aussi; autant** *etc*
6 (*seulement*): **ne ...** ~ only; **il ne boit** ~ **de l'eau** he only drinks water
7 (*temps*): **elle venait à peine de sortir qu'il se mit à pleuvoir** she had just gone out when it started to rain, no sooner had she gone out than it started to rain; **il y a 4 ans qu'il est parti** it is 4 years since he left, he left 4 years ago
♦ *adv* (*exclamation*): **qu'il** *ou* **qu'est-ce qu'il est bête/court vite!** he's so silly!/he runs so fast!; ~ **de livres!** what a lot of books!
♦ *pron* **1** (*relatif: personne*) whom; (*: chose*) that, which; **l'homme** ~ **je vois** the man (whom) I see; **le livre** ~ **tu vois** the book

(that *ou* which) you see; **un jour** ~ **j'étais ...** a day when I was ...
2 (*interrogatif*) what; ~ **fais-tu?, qu'est-ce** ~ **tu fais?** what are you doing?; **qu'est-ce** ~ **c'est?** what is it?, what's that?; ~ **faire?** what can one do?; ~ **préfères-tu, celui-ci ou celui-là?** which (one) do you prefer, this one or that one?

Québec [kebɛk] *n* (*ville*) Quebec ♦ *nm:* **le** ~ Quebec (Province).

québécois, e [kebekwa, -waz] *adj* Quebec *cpd* ♦ *nm* (*LING*) Quebec French ♦ *nm/f:* **Q~, e** Quebecois, Quebec(k)er.

════════════════ *MOT-CLÉ*

quel, quelle [kɛl] *adj* **1** (*interrogatif: personne*) who; (*: chose*) what; which; ~ **est cet homme?** who is this man?; ~ **est ce livre?** what is this book?; ~ **livre/homme?** what book/man?; (*parmi un certain choix*) which book/man?; ~s **acteurs préférez-vous?** which actors do you prefer?; **dans** ~s **pays êtes-vous allé?** which *ou* what countries did you go to?
2 (*exclamatif*): **quelle surprise/coïncidence!** what a surprise/coincidence!
3: ~ **que soit le coupable** whoever is guilty; ~ **que soit votre avis** whatever your opinion (may be).

quelconque [kɛlkɔ̃k] *adj* (*médiocre*) indifferent, poor; (*sans attrait*) ordinary, plain; (*indéfini*): **un ami/prétexte** ~ some friend/pretext or other; **un livre** ~ **suffira** any book will do; **pour une raison** ~ for some reason (or other).

════════════════ *MOT-CLÉ*

quelque [kɛlkə] *adj* **1** some; a few; (*tournure interrogative*) any; ~ **espoir** some hope; **il a** ~s **amis** he has a few *ou* some friends; **a-t-il** ~s **amis?** has he any friends?; **les** ~s **livres qui** the few books which; **20 kg et** ~(s) a bit over 20 kg; **il habite à** ~ **distance d'ici** he lives some distance *ou* way (away) from here
2: ~ **... que** whatever, whichever; ~ **livre qu'il choisisse** whatever (*ou* whichever) book he chooses; **par** ~ **temps qu'il fasse** whatever the weather
3: ~ **chose** something; (*tournure interrogative*) anything; ~ **chose d'autre** something else; anything else; **y être pour** ~ **chose** to have something to do with it; **faire** ~ **chose à qn** to have an effect on sb, do something to sb; ~ **part** somewhere; anywhere; **en** ~ **sorte** as it were
♦ *adv* **1** (*environ*): ~ **100 mètres** some 100 metres
2: ~ **peu** rather, somewhat.

quelquefois [kɛlkəfwa] *adv* sometimes.

quelques-uns, -unes [kɛlkəzœ̃, -yn] *pron* some, a few; ~ **des lecteurs** some of the readers.

quelqu'un [kɛlkœ̃] *pron* someone, somebody, *tournure interrogative ou négative* + anyone *ou* anybody; ~ **d'autre** someone *ou* somebody else; anybody else.

quémander [kemɑ̃de] *vt* to beg for.

qu'en dira-t-on [kɑ̃diʀatɔ̃] *nm inv*: **le** ~ gossip, what people say.

quenelle [kənɛl] *nf* quenelle.

quenouille [kənuj] *nf* distaff.

querelle [kəʀɛl] *nf* quarrel; **chercher** ~ **à qn** to pick a quarrel with sb.

quereller [kəʀele]: **se** ~ *vi* to quarrel.

querelleur, euse [kəʀɛlœʀ, -øz] *adj* quarrelsome.

qu'est-ce que (ou qui) [kɛskə(ki)] *voir* **que, qui.**

question [kɛstjɔ̃] *nf* (*gén*) question; (*fig*) matter; issue; **il a été** ~ **de** we (*ou* they) spoke about; **il est** ~ **de les emprisonner** there's talk of them being jailed; **c'est une** ~ **de temps** it's a matter *ou* question of time; **de quoi est-il** ~? what is it about?; **il n'en est pas** ~ there's no question of it; **en** ~ in question; **hors de** ~ out of the question; **je ne me suis jamais posé la** ~ I've never thought about it; **(re)mettre en** ~ (*autorité, science*) to question; **poser la** ~ **de confiance** (*POL*) to ask for a vote of confidence; ~ **piège** (*d'apparence facile*) trick question; (*pour nuire*) loaded question; ~ **subsidiaire** tiebreaker.

questionnaire [kɛstjɔnɛʀ] *nm* questionnaire.

questionner [kɛstjɔne] *vt* to question.

quête [kɛt] *nf* (*collecte*) collection; (*recherche*) quest, search; **faire la** ~ (*à l'église*) to take the collection; (*artiste*) to pass the hat round; **se mettre en** ~ **de qch** to go in search of sth.

quêter [kete] *vi* (*à l'église*) to take the collection; (*dans la rue*) to collect money (for charity) ♦ *vt* to seek.

quetsche [kwɛtʃ(ə)] *nf* damson.

queue [kø] *nf* tail; (*fig: du classement*) bottom; (: *de poêle*) handle; (: *de fruit, feuille*) stalk; (: *de train, colonne, file*) rear; (*file: de personnes*) queue (*BRIT*), line (*US*); **en** ~ (**de train**) at the rear (of the train); **faire la** ~ to queue (up) (*BRIT*), line up (*US*); **se mettre à la** ~ to join the queue *ou* line; **histoire sans** ~ **ni tête** cock and bull story; **à la** ~ **leu leu** in single file; (*fig*) one after the other; ~ **de cheval** ponytail; ~ **de poisson: faire une** ~ **de poisson à qn** (*AUTO*) to cut in front of sb; **finir en** ~ **de poisson** (*film*) to come to an abrupt end.

queue-de-pie, *pl* **queues-de-pie** [kødpi] *nf* (*habit*) tails *pl*, tail coat.

queux [kø] *adj m voir* **maître.**

qui [ki] *pron* (*personne*) who, *prép* + whom; (*chose, animal*) which, that; (*interrogatif indirect: sujet*): **je me demande** ~ **est là?** I wonder who is there?; (: *objet*): **elle ne sait à** ~ **se plaindre** she doesn't know who to complain to *ou* to whom to complain; **qu'est-ce** ~ **est sur la table?** what is on the table?; **à** ~ **est ce sac?** whose bag is this?; **à** ~ **parlais-tu?** who were you talking to?, to whom were you talking?; **chez** ~ **allez-vous?** whose house are you going to?; **amenez** ~ **vous voulez** bring who(ever) you like; ~ **est-ce** ~ **...?** who?; ~ **est-ce que ...?** who?; whom?; ~ **que ce soit** whoever it may be.

quiche [kiʃ] *nf* quiche; ~ **lorraine** quiche Lorraine.

quiconque [kikɔ̃k] *pron* (*celui qui*) whoever, anyone who; (*n'importe qui, personne*) anyone, anybody.

quidam [kɥidam] *nm* (*hum*) fellow.

quiétude [kjetyd] *nf* (*d'un lieu*) quiet, tranquillity; (*d'une personne*) peace (of mind), serenity; **en toute** ~ in complete peace; (*mentale*) with complete peace of mind.

quignon [kiɲɔ̃] *nm*: ~ **de pain** (*croûton*) crust of bread; (*morceau*) hunk of bread.

quille [kij] *nf* ninepin, skittle (*BRIT*); (*NAVIG: d'un bateau*) keel; (**jeu de**) ~**s** ninepins *sg*, skittles *sg* (*BRIT*).

quincaillerie [kɛ̃kajʀi] *nf* (*ustensiles, métier*) hardware, ironmongery (*BRIT*); (*magasin*) hardware shop *ou* store (*US*), ironmonger's (*BRIT*).

quincaillier, ière [kɛ̃kaje, -jɛʀ] *nm/f* hardware dealer, ironmonger (*BRIT*).

quinconce [kɛ̃kɔ̃s] *nm*: **en** ~ in staggered rows.

quinine [kinin] *nf* quinine.

quinquagénaire [kɛ̃kaʒenɛʀ] *nm/f* (*de cinquante ans*) fifty-year old; (*de cinquante à soixante ans*) man/woman in his/her fifties.

quinquennal, e, aux [kɛ̃kenal, -o] *adj* five-year, quinquennial.

quintal, aux [kɛ̃tal, -o] *nm* quintal (*100 kg*).

quinte [kɛ̃t] *nf*: ~ (**de toux**) coughing fit.

quintessence [kɛ̃tesɑ̃s] *nf* quintessence, very essence.

quintette [kɛ̃tɛt] *nm* quintet(te).

quintuple [kɛ̃typl(ə)] *nm*: **le** ~ **de** five times as much as.

quintupler [kɛ̃typle] *vt, vi* to increase fivefold.

quintuplés, ées [kɛ̃typle] *nm/fpl* quintuplets, quins.

quinzaine [kɛ̃zɛn] *nf*: **une** ~ (**de**) about fifteen, fifteen or so; **une** ~ (**de jours**) (*deux semaines*) a fortnight (*BRIT*), two weeks; ~ **publicitaire** *ou* **commerciale** (two-week) sale.

quinze [kɛ̃z] *num* fifteen; **demain en** ~ a fortnight (*BRIT*) *ou* two weeks tomorrow; **dans** ~ **jours** in a fortnight('s time) (*BRIT*), in two weeks(' time).

quinzième [kɛ̃zjɛm] *num* fifteenth.

quiproquo [kiprɔko] *nm* (*méprise sur une personne*) mistake; (*malentendu sur un sujet*) misunderstanding; (*THÉÂT*) (case of) mistaken identity.

Quito [kito] *n* Quito.

quittance [kitɑ̃s] *nf* (*reçu*) receipt; (*facture*) bill.

quitte [kit] *adj*: **être ~ envers qn** to be no longer in sb's debt; (*fig*) to be quits with sb; **être ~ de** (*obligation*) to be clear of; **en être ~ à bon compte** to have got off lightly; **~ à faire** even if it means doing; **~ ou double** (*jeu*) double or quits; (*fig*): **c'est du ~ ou double** it's a big risk.

quitter [kite] *vt* to leave; (*espoir, illusion*) to give up; (*vêtement*) to take off; **se ~** (*couples, interlocuteurs*) to part; **ne quittez pas** (*au téléphone*) hold the line; **ne pas ~ qn d'une semelle** to stick to sb like glue.

quitus [kitys] *nm* final discharge; **donner ~ à** to discharge.

qui-vive [kiviv] *nm inv*: **être sur le ~** to be on the alert.

quoi [kwa] *pron* (*interrogatif*) what; **~ de neuf** *ou* **de nouveau?** what's new *ou* the news?; **as-tu de ~ écrire?** have you anything to write with?; **il n'a pas de ~ se l'acheter** he can't afford it, he hasn't got the money to buy it; **il y a de ~ être fier** that's something to be proud of; **"il n'y a pas de ~"** "(please) don't mention it", "not at all"; **~ qu'il arrive** whatever happens; **~ qu'il en soit** be that as it may; **~ que ce soit** anything at all; **en ~ puis-je vous aider?** how can I help you?; **à ~ bon?** what's the use *ou* point?; **et puis ~ encore!** what(ever) next!; **~ faire?** what's to be done?; **sans ~** (*ou sinon*) otherwise.

quoique [kwak(ə)] *conj* (al)though.

quolibet [kɔlibɛ] *nm* gibe, jeer.

quorum [kɔrɔm] *nm* quorum.

quota [kwɔta] *nm* quota.

quote-part [kɔtpar] *nf* share.

quotidien, ne [kɔtidjɛ̃, -ɛn] *adj* (*journalier*) daily; (*banal*) ordinary, everyday ♦ *nm* (*journal*) daily (paper); (*vie quotidienne*) daily life, day-to-day existence; **les grands ~s** the big (national) dailies.

quotidiennement [kɔtidjɛnmɑ̃] *adv* daily, every day.

quotient [kɔsjɑ̃] *nm* (*MATH*) quotient; **~ intellectuel (QI)** intelligence quotient (IQ).

quotité [kɔtite] *nf* (*FINANCE*) quota.

R r

R, r [ɛr] *nm inv* R, r ♦ *abr* = **route, rue; R comme Raoul** R for Robert (*BRIT*) *ou* Roger (*US*).

rab [rab] (*fam*), **rabiot** [rabjo] *nm* extra, more.

rabâcher [rabɑʃe] *vi* to harp on ♦ *vt* keep on repeating.

rabais [rabɛ] *nm* reduction, discount; **au ~** at a reduction *ou* discount.

rabaisser [rabese] *vt* (*rabattre*) to reduce; (*dénigrer*) to belittle.

rabane [raban] *nf* raffia (matting).

Rabat [raba(t)] *n* Rabat.

rabat [raba] *vb voir* **rabattre** ♦ *nm* flap.

rabat-joie [rabaʒwa] *nm/f inv* killjoy (*BRIT*), spoilsport.

rabatteur, euse [rabatœr, -øz] *nm/f* (*de gibier*) beater; (*péj*) tout.

rabattre [rabatr(ə)] *vt* (*couvercle, siège*) to pull down; (*col*) to turn down; (*couture*) to stitch down; (*gibier*) to drive; (*somme d'un prix*) to deduct, take off; (*orgueil, prétentions*) to humble; (*TRICOT*) to decrease; **se ~** *vi* (*bords, couvercle*) to fall shut; (*véhicule, coureur*) to cut in; **se ~ sur** (*accepter*) to fall back on.

rabattu, e [rabaty] *pp de* **rabattre** ♦ *adj* turned down.

rabbin [rabɛ̃] *nm* rabbi.

rabique [rabik] *adj* rabies *cpd*.

râble [rɑbl(ə)] *nm* back; (*CULIN*) saddle.

râblé, e [rɑble] *adj* broad-backed, stocky.

rabot [rabo] *nm* plane.

raboter [rabɔte] *vt* to plane (down).

raboteux, euse [rabɔtø, -øz] *adj* uneven, rough.

rabougri, e [rabugri] *adj* stunted.

rabrouer [rabrue] *vt* to snub, rebuff.

racaille [rakɑj] *nf* (*péj*) rabble, riffraff.

raccommodage [rakɔmɔdaʒ] *nm* mending *ou* pl, repairing *no pl*; darning *no pl*.

raccommoder [rakɔmɔde] *vt* to mend, repair; (*chaussette etc*) to darn; (*fam: réconcilier: amis, ménage*) to bring together again; **se ~ (avec)** (*fam*) to patch it up (with).

raccompagner [rakɔ̃paɲe] *vt* to take *ou* see back.

raccord [rakɔr] *nm* link; **~ de maçonnerie** pointing *no pl*; **~ de peinture** join; touch-up.

raccordement [rakɔrdəmɑ̃] *nm* joining up; connection.

raccorder [rakɔrde] *vt* to join (up), link up; (*suj: pont etc*) to connect, link; **se ~ à** to join up with; (*fig: se rattacher à*) to tie in with; **~ au réseau du téléphone** to connect to the telephone service.

raccourci [rakursi] *nm* short cut; **en ~** in brief.

raccourcir [rakursir] *vt* to shorten ♦ *vi* (*vêtement*) to shrink.

raccroc [rakro]: **par ~** *adv* by chance.

raccrocher [rakrɔʃe] *vt* (*tableau, vêtement*) to hang back up; (*récepteur*) to put down; (*fig: affaire*) to save ♦ *vi* (*TÉL*) to hang up, ring off; **se ~ à** *vt* to cling to, hang on to; **ne raccrochez pas** (*TÉL*) hold on, don't hang up.

race [ras] *nf* race; (*d'animaux, fig: espèce*) breed; (*ascendance, origine*) stock, race; **de ~** *adj* purebred, pedigree.

racé, e [rase] *adj* thoroughbred.

rachat [raʃa] *nm* buying; buying back; redemption; atonement.

racheter [raʃte] *vt* (*article perdu*) to buy another; (*davantage*): **~ du lait/3 œufs** to buy more milk/another 3 eggs *ou* 3 more eggs; (*après avoir vendu*) to buy back; (*d'occasion*) to buy; (*COMM: part, firme*) to buy up; (*: pension, rente*) to redeem; (*REL: pécheur*) to redeem; (*: péché*) to atone for, expiate; (*mauvaise conduite, oubli, défaut*) to make up for; **se ~** (*REL*) to redeem o.s.; (*gén*) to make amends, make up for it.

rachidien, ne [raʃidjɛ̃, -ɛn] *adj* rachidian, of the spine.

rachitique [raʃitik] *adj* suffering from rickets; (*fig*) scraggy, scrawny.

rachitisme [raʃitism(ə)] *nm* rickets *sg*.

racial, e, aux [rasjal, -o] *adj* racial.

racine [rasin] *nf* root; (*fig: attache*) roots *pl*; **~ carrée/cubique** square/cube root; **prendre ~** (*fig*) to take root; to put down roots.

racisme [rasism(ə)] *nm* racism, racialism.

raciste [rasist(ə)] *adj, nm/f* racist, racialist.

racket [rakɛt] *nm* racketeering *no pl*.

racketteur [rakɛtœr] *nm* racketeer.

raclée [rakle] *nf* (*fam*) hiding, thrashing.

raclement [rakləmɑ̃] *nm* (*bruit*) scraping (noise).

racler [rakle] *vt* (*os, plat*) to scrape; (*tache, boue*) to scrape off; (*fig: instrument*) to scrape on; (*suj: chose: frotter contre*) to scrape (against).

raclette [raklɛt] *nf* (*CULIN*) raclette (*Swiss cheese dish*).

racloir [raklwar] *nm* (*outil*) scraper.

racolage [rakɔlaʒ] *nm* soliciting; touting.

racoler [rakɔle] *vt* (*attirer: suj: prostituée*) to solicit; (*: parti, marchand*) to tout for; (*attraper*) to pick up.

racoleur, euse [rakɔlœr, -øz] *adj* (*péj: publicité*) cheap and alluring ♦ *nm* (*péj: de clients etc*) tout ♦ *nf* streetwalker.

racontars [rakɔ̃tar] *nmpl* stories, gossip *sg*.

raconter [rakɔ̃te] *vt*: **~ (à qn)** (*décrire*) to relate (to sb), tell (sb) about; (*dire*) to tell (sb).

racorni, e [rakɔrni] *adj* hard(ened).

racornir [rakɔrnir] *vt* to harden.

radar [radar] *nm* radar; **système ~** radar system; **écran ~** radar screen.

rade [rad] *nf* (*natural*) harbour; **en ~ de Toulon** in Toulon harbour; **rester en ~** (*fig*) to be left stranded.

radeau, x [rado] *nm* raft; **~ de sauvetage** life raft.

radial, e, aux [radjal, -o] *adj* radial; **pneu à carcasse ~e** radial tyre.

radiant, e [radjɑ̃, -ɑ̃t] *adj* radiant.

radiateur [radjatœr] *nm* radiator, heater; (*AUTO*) radiator; **~ électrique/à gaz** electric/gas heater *ou* fire.

radiation [radjasjɔ̃] *nf* (*d'un nom etc*) striking off *no pl*; (*PHYSIQUE*) radiation.

radical, e, aux [radikal, -o] *adj* radical ♦ *nm* (*LING*) stem; (*MATH*) root sign; (*POL*) radical.

radicalement [radikalmɑ̃] *adv* radically, completely.

radicaliser [radikalize] *vt* (*durcir: opinions etc*) to harden; **se ~** *vi* (*mouvement etc*) to become more radical.

radicalisme [radikalism(ə)] *nm* (*POL*) radicalism.

radier [radje] *vt* to strike off.

radiesthésie [radjɛstezi] *nf* divination (by radiation).

radiesthésiste [radjɛstezist(ə)] *nm/f* diviner.

radieux, euse [radjø, -øz] *adj* (*visage, personne*) radiant; (*journée, soleil*) brilliant, glorious.

radin, e [radɛ̃, -in] *adj* (*fam*) stingy.

radio [radjo] *nf* radio; (*MÉD*) X-ray ♦ *nm* (*personne*) radio operator; **à la ~** on the radio; **avoir la ~** to have a radio; **passer à la ~** to be on the radio; **se faire faire une ~/une ~ des poumons** to have an X-ray/a chest X-ray.

radio... [radjo] *préfixe* radio....

radioactif, ive [radjɔaktif, -iv] *adj* radioactive.

radioactivité [radjɔaktivite] *nf* radioactivity.

radioamateur [radjɔamatœr] *nm* (radio) ham.

radiobalise [radjɔbaliz] *nf* radio beacon.

radiocassette [radjɔkasɛt] *nf* cassette radio.

radiodiffuser [radjɔdifyze] *vt* to broadcast.

radiodiffusion [radjɔdifyzjɔ̃] *nf* (radio) broadcasting.

radioélectrique [radjɔelɛktrik] *adj* radio *cpd*.

radiogoniomètre [radjɔgɔnjɔmɛtr(ə)] *nm* direction finder, radiogoniometer.

radiographie [radjɔgrafi] *nf* radiography; (*photo*) X-ray photograph, radiograph.

radiographier [radjɔgrafje] *vt* to X-ray; **se faire ~** to have an X-ray.

radioguidage [radjɔgidaʒ] *nm* (*NAVIG, AVIAT*) radio control; (*AUTO*) (broadcast of) traffic information.

radioguider [radjɔgide] *vt* (*NAVIG, AVIAT*) to guide by radio, control by radio.

radiologie [radjɔlɔʒi] *nf* radiology.

radiologique [radjɔlɔʒik] *adj* radiological.

radiologue [radjɔlɔg] *nm/f* radiologist.

radionavigant [ʀadjɔnavigɑ̃] *nm* radio officer.

radiophare [ʀadjɔfaʀ] *nm* radio beacon.

radiophonique [ʀadjɔfɔnik] *adj*: **programme/ émission/jeu** ~ radio programme/ broadcast/game.

radioreportage [ʀadjɔʀəpɔʀtaʒ] *nm* radio report.

radio(-)réveil [ʀadjɔʀevɛj] *nm* clock radio.

radioscopie [ʀadjɔskɔpi] *nf* radioscopy.

radio-taxi [ʀadjɔtaksi] *nm* radiotaxi.

radiotélégraphie [ʀadjɔtelegʀafi] *nf* radiotelegraphy.

radiotéléphone [ʀadjɔtelefɔn] *nm* radiotelephone.

radiotélescope [ʀadjɔteleskɔp] *nm* radiotelescope.

radiotélévisé, e [ʀadjɔtelevize] *adj* broadcast on radio and television.

radiothérapie [ʀadjɔteʀapi] *nf* radiotherapy.

radis [ʀadi] *nm* radish; ~ **noir** horseradish *no pl.*

radium [ʀadjɔm] *nm* radium.

radoter [ʀadɔte] *vi* to ramble on.

radoub [ʀadu] *nm*: **bassin** *ou* **cale de** ~ dry dock.

radouber [ʀadube] *vt* to repair, refit.

radoucir [ʀadusiʀ]: **se** ~ *vi* (*se réchauffer*) to become milder; (*se calmer*) to calm down; to soften.

radoucissement [ʀadusismɑ̃] *nm* milder period, better weather.

rafale [ʀafal] *nf* (*vent*) gust (of wind); (*de balles, d'applaudissements*) burst; ~ **de mitrailleuse** burst of machine-gun fire.

raffermir [ʀafɛʀmiʀ] *vt*, **se** ~ *vi* (*tissus, muscle*) to firm up; (*fig*) to strengthen.

raffermissement [ʀafɛʀmismɑ̃] *nm* (*fig*) strengthening.

raffinage [ʀafinaʒ] *nm* refining.

raffiné, e [ʀafine] *adj* refined.

raffinement [ʀafinmɑ̃] *nm* refinement.

raffiner [ʀafine] *vt* to refine.

raffinerie [ʀafinʀi] *nf* refinery.

raffoler [ʀafɔle]: ~ **de** *vt* to be very keen on.

raffut [ʀafy] *nm* (*fam*) row, racket.

rafiot [ʀafjo] *nm* tub.

rafistoler [ʀafistɔle] *vt* (*fam*) to patch up.

rafle [ʀafl(ə)] *nf* (*de police*) roundup, raid.

rafler [ʀafle] *vt* (*fam*) to swipe, nick.

rafraîchir [ʀafʀeʃiʀ] *vt* (*atmosphère, température*) to cool (down); (*aussi*: **mettre à** ~) to chill; (*suj*: *air, eau*) to freshen up; (: *boisson*) to refresh; (*fig: rénover*) to brighten up ♦ *vi*: **mettre du vin/une boisson à** ~ to chill wine/a drink; **se** ~ to grow cooler; to freshen up; (*personne: en buvant etc*) to refresh o.s.; ~ **la mémoire** *ou* **les idées à qn** to refresh sb's memory.

rafraîchissant, e [ʀafʀeʃisɑ̃, -ɑ̃t] *adj* refreshing.

rafraîchissement [ʀafʀeʃismɑ̃] *nm* cooling; (*boisson*) cool drink; ~**s** *nmpl* (*boissons, fruits etc*) refreshments.

ragaillardir [ʀagajaʀdiʀ] *vt* (*fam*) to perk *ou* buck up.

rage [ʀaʒ] *nf* (*MÉD*): **la** ~ rabies; (*fureur*) rage, fury; **faire** ~ to rage; ~ **de dents** (raging) toothache.

rager [ʀaʒe] *vi* to fume (with rage); **faire** ~ **qn** to enrage sb, get sb mad.

rageur, euse [ʀaʒœʀ, -øz] *adj* snarling; ill-tempered.

raglan [ʀaglɑ̃] *adj inv* raglan.

ragot [ʀago] *nm* (*fam*) malicious gossip *no pl.*

ragoût [ʀagu] *nm* (*plat*) stew.

ragoûtant, e [ʀagutɑ̃, -ɑ̃t] *adj*: **peu** ~ unpalatable.

rai [ʀɛ] *nm*: **un** ~ **de soleil/lumière** a shaft of sunshine/light.

raid [ʀɛd] *nm* (*MIL*) raid; (*attaque aérienne*) air raid; (*SPORT*) long-distance trek.

raide [ʀɛd] *adj* (*tendu*) taut, tight; (*escarpé*) steep; (*droit: cheveux*) straight; (*ankylosé, dur, guindé*) stiff; (*fam: cher*) steep, stiff; (: *sans argent*) flat broke; (*osé, licencieux*) daring ♦ *adv* (*en pente*) steeply; ~ **mort** stone dead.

raideur [ʀɛdœʀ] *nf* steepness; stiffness.

raidir [ʀediʀ] *vt* (*muscles*) to stiffen; (*câble*) to pull taut, tighten; **se** ~ *vi* to stiffen; to become taut; (*personne: se crisper*) to tense up; (: *devenir intransigeant*) to harden.

raidissement [ʀedismɑ̃] *nm* stiffening; tightening; hardening.

raie [ʀɛ] *nf* (*ZOOL*) skate, ray; (*rayure*) stripe; (*des cheveux*) parting.

raifort [ʀɛfɔʀ] *nm* horseradish.

rail [ʀaj] *nm* (*barre d'acier*) rail; (*chemins de fer*) railways *pl* (*BRIT*), railroads *pl* (*US*); **les** ~**s** (*la voie ferrée*) the rails, the track *sg*; **par** ~ by rail; ~ **conducteur** live *ou* conductor rail.

railler [ʀaje] *vt* to scoff at, jeer at.

raillerie [ʀɑjʀi] *nf* mockery.

railleur, euse [ʀɑjœʀ, -øz] *adj* mocking.

rail-route [ʀɑjʀut] *nm* road-rail.

rainurage [ʀɛnyʀaʒ] *nm* (*AUTO*) uneven road surface.

rainure [ʀɛnyʀ] *nf* groove; slot.

rais [ʀɛ] *nm inv* = **rai.**

raisin [ʀɛzɛ̃] *nm* (*aussi*: ~**s**) grapes *pl*; (*variété*): ~ **blanc/noir** white (*ou* green)/black grape; ~ **muscat** muscat grape; ~**s secs** raisins.

raison [ʀɛzɔ̃] *nf* reason; **avoir** ~ to be right; **donner** ~ **à qn** (*personne*) to agree with sb; (*fait*) to prove sb right; **avoir** ~ **de qn/qch** to get the better of sb/sth; **se faire une** ~ to learn to live with it; **perdre la** ~ to become insane; (*fig*) to take leave of one's senses; **recouvrer la** ~ to come to one's senses; **ramener qn à la** ~ to make sb see sense; **demander** ~ **à qn de** (*affront etc*) to demand satisfaction from sb for; **entendre** ~ to listen to reason, see reason; **plus que de** ~ too much, more than is reasonable; ~ **de plus** all the more reason; **à plus forte** ~ all the more so; **en ~ de** (*à cause de*) because of; (*à proportion de*) in proportion to; **à ~ de** at the rate of; **~ d'État** reason of state; **~ d'être** raison d'être; **~ sociale** corporate name.

raisonnable [ʀɛzɔnabl(ə)] *adj* reasonable, sensible.

raisonnablement [ʀɛzɔnabləmɑ̃] *adv* reasonably.

raisonné, e [ʀɛzɔne] *adj* reasoned.

raisonnement [ʀɛzɔnmɑ̃] *nm* reasoning; arguing; argument.

raisonner [ʀɛzɔne] *vi* (*penser*) to reason; (*argumenter, discuter*) to argue ♦ *vt* (*personne*) to reason with; (*attitude: justifier*) to reason out; **se ~** to reason with oneself.

raisonneur, euse [ʀɛzɔnœʀ, -øz] *adj* (*péj*) quibbling.

rajeunir [ʀaʒœniʀ] *vt* (*suj: coiffure, robe*): **~ qn** to make sb look younger; (*suj: cure etc*) to rejuvenate; (*fig: rafraîchir*) to brighten up; (*: moderniser*) to give a new look to; (*: en recrutant*) to inject new blood into ♦ *vi* (*personne*) to become (*ou* look) younger; (*entreprise, quartier*) to be modernized.

rajout [ʀaʒu] *nm* addition.

rajouter [ʀaʒute] *vt* (*commentaire*) to add; **~ du sel/un œuf** to add some more salt/another egg; **~ que** to add that; **en ~** to lay it on thick.

rajustement [ʀaʒystəmɑ̃] *nm* adjustment.

rajuster [ʀaʒyste] *vt* (*vêtement*) to straighten, tidy; (*salaires*) to adjust; (*machine*) to readjust; **se ~** to tidy *ou* straighten o.s. up.

râle [ʀɑl] *nm* groan; **~ d'agonie** death rattle.

ralenti [ʀalɑ̃ti] *nm*: **au ~** (*CINÉ*) in slow motion; (*fig*) at a slower pace; **tourner au ~** (*AUTO*) to tick over, idle.

ralentir [ʀalɑ̃tiʀ] *vt, vi, se ~ vi* to slow down.

ralentissement [ʀalɑ̃tismɑ̃] *nm* slowing down.

râler [ʀɑle] *vi* to groan; (*fam*) to grouse, moan (and groan).

ralliement [ʀalimɑ̃] *nm* (*rassemblement*) rallying; (*adhésion: à une cause, une opinion*) winning over; **point/signe de ~** rallying point/sign.

rallier [ʀalje] *vt* (*rassembler*) to rally; (*rejoindre*) to rejoin; (*gagner à sa cause*) to win over; **se ~ à** (*avis*) to come over *ou* round to.

rallonge [ʀalɔ̃ʒ] *nf* (*de table*) (extra) leaf (*pl* leaves); (*argent etc*) extra *no pl*; (*ÉLEC*) extension (cable *ou* flex); (*fig: de crédit etc*) extension.

rallonger [ʀalɔ̃ʒe] *vt* to lengthen.

rallumer [ʀalyme] *vt* to light up again, relight; (*fig*) to revive; **se ~** *vi* (*lumière*) to come on again.

rallye [ʀali] *nm* rally; (*POL*) march.

ramages [ʀamaʒ] *nmpl* (*dessin*) leaf pattern *sg*; (*chants*) songs.

ramassage [ʀamasaʒ] *nm*: **~ scolaire** school bus service.

ramassé, e [ʀamase] *adj* (*trapu*) squat, stocky; (*concis: expression etc*) compact.

ramasse-miettes [ʀamasmjɛt] *nm inv* tabletidy.

ramasse-monnaie [ʀamasmɔnɛ] *nm inv* change-tray.

ramasser [ʀamase] *vt* (*objet tombé ou par terre, fam*) to pick up; (*recueillir*) to collect; (*récolter*) to gather; (*: pommes de terre*) to lift; **se ~** *vi* (*sur soi-même*) to huddle up; to crouch.

ramasseur, euse [ʀamasœʀ, -øz] *nm/f*: **~ de balles** ballboy/girl.

ramassis [ʀamasi] *nm* (*péj: de gens*) bunch; (*: de choses*) jumble.

rambarde [ʀɑ̃baʀd(ə)] *nf* guardrail.

rame [ʀam] *nf* (*aviron*) oar; (*de métro*) train; (*de papier*) ream; **~ de haricots** bean support; **faire force de ~s** to row hard.

rameau, x [ʀamo] *nm* (small) branch; (*fig*) branch; **les R~x** (*REL*) Palm Sunday *sg*.

ramener [ʀamne] *vt* to bring back; (*reconduire*) to take back; (*rabattre: couverture, visière*): **~ qch sur** to pull sth back over; **~ qch à** (*réduire à, aussi MATH*) to reduce sth to; **~ qn à la vie/raison** to bring sb back to life/bring sb to his (*ou* her) senses; **se ~** *vi* (*fam*) to roll *ou* turn up; **se ~ à** (*se réduire à*) to come *ou* boil down to.

ramequin [ʀamkɛ̃] *nm* ramekin.

ramer [ʀame] *vi* to row.

rameur, euse [ʀamœʀ, -øz] *nm/f* rower.

rameuter [ʀamøte] *vt* to gather together.

ramier [ʀamje] *nm*: **(pigeon) ~** woodpigeon.

ramification [ʀamifikasjɔ̃] *nf* ramification.

ramifier [ʀamifje]: **se ~** *vi* (*tige, secte, réseau*): **se ~ (en)** to branch out (into); (*veines, nerfs*) to ramify.

ramolli, e [ʀamɔli] *adj* soft.

ramollir [ʀamɔliʀ] *vt* to soften; **se ~** *vi* (*os, tissus*) to get (*ou* go) soft; (*beurre, asphalte*) to soften.

ramonage [ʀamɔnaʒ] *nm* (chimney-) sweeping.

ramoner [ʀamɔne] *vt* (*cheminée*) to sweep; (*pipe*) to clean.

ramoneur [ʀamɔnœʀ] *nm* (chimney) sweep.

rampe [ʀɑ̃p] *nf* (*d'escalier*) banister(s *pl*); (*dans un garage, d'un terrain*) ramp; (*THÉÂT*): **la ~** the footlights *pl*; (*lampes: lumineuse, de balisage*) floodlights *pl*; **passer la ~** (*toucher le public*) to get across to the audience; **~ de lancement** launching pad.

ramper [ʀɑ̃pe] *vi* (*reptile, animal*) to crawl; (*plante*) to creep.

rancard [ʀɑ̃kaʀ] *nm* (*fam*) date; tip.

rancart [ʀɑ̃kaʀ] *nm*: **mettre au ~** (*article, projet*) to scrap; (*personne*) to put on the scrapheap.

rance [ʀɑ̃s] *adj* rancid.

rancir [ʀɑ̃siʀ] *vi* to go off, go rancid.

rancœur [ʀɑ̃kœʀ] *nf* rancour (*BRIT*), rancor (*US*), resentment.

rançon [ʀɑ̃sɔ̃] *nf* ransom; (*fig*): **la ~ du succès**

etc the price of success *etc*.

rançonner [ʀɑ̃sɔne] *vt* to hold to ransom.

rancune [ʀɑ̃kyn] *nf* grudge, rancour (*BRIT*), rancor (*US*); **garder** ~ **à qn** (**de qch**) to bear sb a grudge (for sth); **sans** ~! no hard feelings!

rancunier, ière [ʀɑ̃kynje, -jɛʀ] *adj* vindictive, spiteful.

randonnée [ʀɑ̃dɔne] *nf* ride; (*à pied*) walk, ramble; hike, hiking *no pl*.

randonneur, euse [ʀɑ̃dɔnœʀ, -øz] *nm/f* hiker.

rang [ʀɑ̃] *nm* (*rangée*) row; (*de perles*) row, string, rope; (*grade, condition sociale, classement*) rank; ~s *nmpl* (*MIL*) ranks; **se mettre en** ~**s/sur un** ~ to get into *ou* form rows/a line; **sur 3** ~**s** (lined up) 3 deep; **se mettre en** ~**s par 4** to form fours *ou* rows of 4; **se mettre sur les** ~**s** (*fig*) to get into the running; **au premier** ~ in the first row; (*fig*) ranking first; **rentrer dans le** ~ to get into line; **au** ~ **de** (*au nombre de*) among (the ranks of); **avoir** ~ **de** to hold the rank of.

rangé, e [ʀɑ̃ʒe] *adj* (*sérieux*) orderly, steady.

rangée [ʀɑ̃ʒe] *nf* row.

rangement [ʀɑ̃ʒmɑ̃] *nm* tidying-up, putting-away; **faire des** ~**s** to tidy up.

ranger [ʀɑ̃ʒe] *vt* (*classer, grouper*) to order, arrange; (*mettre à sa place*) to put away; (*voiture dans la rue*) to park; (*mettre de l'ordre dans*) to tidy up; (*arranger, disposer: en cercle etc*) to arrange; (*fig: classer*): ~ **qn/qch parmi** to rank sb/sth among; **se** ~ *vi* (*se placer, se disposer: autour d'une table etc*) to take one's place, sit round; (*véhicule, conducteur: s'écarter*) to pull over; (: *s'arrêter*) to pull in; (*piéton*) to step aside; (*s'assagir*) to settle down; **se** ~ **à** (*avis*) to come round to, fall in with.

ranimer [ʀanime] *vt* (*personne évanouie*) to bring round; (*revigorer: forces, courage*) to restore; (*réconforter: troupes etc*) to kindle new life in; (*douleur, souvenir*) to revive; (*feu*) to rekindle.

rapace [ʀapas] *nm* bird of prey ♦ *adj* (*péj*) rapacious, grasping; ~ **diurne/nocturne** diurnal/nocturnal bird of prey.

rapatrié, e [ʀapatʀije] *nm/f* repatriate (*esp French North African settler*).

rapatriement [ʀapatʀimɑ̃] *nm* repatriation.

rapatrier [ʀapatʀije] *vt* to repatriate; (*capitaux*) to bring (back) into the country.

râpe [ʀɑp] *nf* (*CULIN*) grater; (*à bois*) rasp.

râpé, e [ʀɑpe] *adj* (*tissu*) threadbare; (*CULIN*) grated.

râper [ʀɑpe] *vt* (*CULIN*) to grate; (*gratter, râcler*) to rasp.

rapetasser [ʀaptase] *vt* (*fam*) to patch up.

rapetisser [ʀaptise] *vt*: ~ **qch** to shorten sth; to make sth look smaller ♦ *vi*, **se** ~ *vi* to shrink.

râpeux, euse [ʀɑpø, -øz] *adj* rough.

raphia [ʀafja] *nm* raffia.

rapide [ʀapid] *adj* fast; (*prompt*) quick; (*intelligence*) quick ♦ *nm* express (train); (*de cours d'eau*) rapid.

rapidement [ʀapidmɑ̃] *adv* fast; quickly.

rapidité [ʀapidite] *nf* speed; quickness.

rapiécer [ʀapjese] *vt* to patch.

rappel [ʀapɛl] *nm* (*d'un ambassadeur, MIL*) recall; (*THÉÂT*) curtain call; (*MÉD: vaccination*) booster; (*ADMIN: de salaire*) back pay *no pl*; (*d'une aventure, d'un nom*) reminder; (*de limitation de vitesse: sur écriteau*) speed limit sign (*reminder*); (*TECH*) return; (*NAVIG*) sitting out; (*ALPINISME: aussi*: ~ **de corde**) abseiling *no pl*, roping down *no pl*; abseil; ~ **à l'ordre** call to order.

rappeler [ʀaple] *vt* (*pour faire revenir, retéléphoner*) to call back; (*ambassadeur, MIL, INFORM*) to recall; (*acteur*) to call back (onto the stage); (*faire se souvenir*): ~ **qch à qn** to remind sb of sth; **se** ~ *vt* (*se souvenir de*) to remember, recall; ~ **qn à la vie** to bring sb back to life; ~ **qn à la décence** to recall sb to a sense of decency; **ça rappelle la Provence** it's reminiscent of Provence, it reminds you of Provence; **se** ~ **que...** to remember that....

rappelle [ʀapɛl] *etc vb voir* **rappeler**.

rappliquer [ʀaplike] *vi* (*fam*) to turn up.

rapport [ʀapɔʀ] *nm* (*compte rendu*) report; (*profit*) yield, return; revenue; (*lien, analogie*) relationship; (*corrélation*) connection; (*proportion: MATH, TECH*) ratio (*pl* -s); ~**s** *nmpl* (*entre personnes, pays*) relations; **avoir** ~ **à** to have something to do with, concern; **être en** ~ **avec** (*idée de corrélation*) to be related to; **être/se mettre en** ~ **avec qn** to be/get in touch with sb; **par** ~ **à** (*comparé à*) in relation to; (*à propos de*) with regard to; **sous le** ~ **de** from the point of view of; **sous tous (les)** ~**s** in all respects; ~**s (sexuels)** (sexual) intercourse *sg*; ~ **qualité-prix** value (for money).

rapporté, e [ʀapɔʀte] *adj*: **pièce** ~**e** (*COUTURE*) patch.

rapporter [ʀapɔʀte] *vt* (*rendre, ramener*) to bring back; (*apporter davantage*) to bring more; (*COUTURE*) to sew on; (*suj: investissement*) to yield; (: *activité*) to bring in; (*relater*) to report; (*JUR: annuler*) to revoke ♦ *vi* (*investissement*) to give a good return *ou* yield; (*activité*) to be very profitable; (*péj: moucharder*) to tell; ~ **qch à** (*fig: rattacher*) to relate sth to; **se** ~ **à** (*correspondre à*) to relate to; **s'en** ~ **à** to rely on.

rapporteur, euse [ʀapɔʀtœʀ, -øz] *nm/f* (*de procès, commission*) reporter; (*péj*) telltale ♦ *nm* (*GÉOM*) protractor.

rapproché, e [ʀapʀɔʃe] *adj* (*proche*) near, close at hand; ~**s** (*l'un de l'autre*) at close intervals.

rapprochement [ʀapʀɔʃmɑ̃] *nm* (*réconciliation: de nations, familles*) reconciliation; (*analogie,* *rapport*) parallel.

rapprocher [ʀapʀɔʃe] *vt* (*chaise d'une table*): ~ **qch (de)** to bring sth closer (to); (*deux objets*) to bring closer together; (*réunir*) to bring together; (*comparer*) to establish a parallel between; **se** ~ *vi* to draw closer *ou* nearer; (*fig: familles, pays*) to come together; to come closer together; **se** ~ **de** to come closer to; (*présenter une analogie avec*) to be close to.

rapt [ʀapt] *nm* abduction.

raquette [ʀakɛt] *nf* (*de tennis*) racket; (*de ping-pong*) bat; (*à neige*) snowshoe.

rare [ʀaʀ] *adj* rare; (*main-d'œuvre, denrées*) scarce; (*cheveux, herbe*) sparse; **il est** ~ **que** it's rare that, it's unusual that; **se faire** ~ to become scarce; (*fig: personne*) to make oneself scarce.

raréfaction [ʀaʀefaksjɔ̃] *nf* scarcity; (*de l'air*) rarefaction.

raréfier [ʀaʀefje]: **se** ~ *vi* to grow scarce; (*air*) to rarefy.

rarement [ʀaʀmɑ̃] *adv* rarely, seldom.

rareté [ʀaʀte] *nf* (*voir rare*) rarity; scarcity.

rarissime [ʀaʀisim] *adj* extremely rare.

RAS *abr* = *rien à signaler*.

ras, e [ʀa, ʀaz] *adj* (*tête, cheveux*) close-cropped; (*poil, herbe*) short; (*mesure, cuillère*) level ♦ *adv* short; **faire table ~e** to make a clean sweep; **en ~e campagne** in open country; **à** ~ **bords** to the brim; **au** ~ **de** level with; **en avoir** ~ **le bol** (*fam*) to be fed up; ~ **du cou** *adj* (*pull, robe*) crew-neck.

rasade [ʀazad] *nf* glassful.

rasant, e [ʀazɑ̃, ɑ̃t] *adj* (*MIL: balle, tir*) grazing; (*fam*) boring.

rascasse [ʀaskas] *nf* (*ZOOL*) scorpion fish.

rasé, e [ʀaze] *adj*: ~ **de frais** freshly shaven; ~ **de près** close-shaven.

rase-mottes [ʀazmɔt] *nm inv*: **faire du** ~ to hedgehop; **vol en** ~ hedgehopping.

raser [ʀaze] *vt* (*barbe, cheveux*) to shave off; (*menton, personne*) to shave; (*fam: ennuyer*) to bore; (*démolir*) to raze (to the ground); (*frôler*) to graze, skim; **se** ~ to shave; (*fam*) to be bored (to tears).

rasoir [ʀazwaʀ] *nm* razor; ~ **électrique** electric shaver *ou* razor; ~ **mécanique** *ou* **de sûreté** safety razor.

rassasier [ʀazazje] *vt* to satisfy; **être rassasié** (*dégoûté*) to be sated; to have had more than enough.

rassemblement [ʀasɑ̃bləmɑ̃] *nm* (*groupe*) gathering; (*POL*) union; association; (*MIL*): **le** ~ **parade**.

rassembler [ʀasɑ̃ble] *vt* (*réunir*) to assemble, gather; (*regrouper, amasser*) to gather together, collect; **se** ~ *vi* to gather; ~ **ses idées/ses esprits/son courage** to collect one's thoughts/gather one's wits/screw up one's courage.

rasseoir [ʀaswaʀ]: **se** ~ *vi* to sit down again.

rasséréner [ʀaseʀene] *vt*: **se** ~ *vi* to recover one's serenity.

rassir [ʀasiʀ] *vi* to go stale.

rassis, e [ʀasi, -iz] *adj* (*pain*) stale.

rassurant, e [ʀasyʀɑ̃, -ɑ̃t] *adj* (*nouvelles etc*) reassuring.

rassuré, e [ʀasyʀe] *adj*: **ne pas être très** ~ to be rather ill at ease.

rassurer [ʀasyʀe] *vt* to reassure; **se** ~ to be reassured; **rassure-toi** don't worry.

rat [ʀa] *nm* rat; ~ **d'hôtel** hotel thief (*pl* thieves); ~ **musqué** muskrat.

ratatiné, e [ʀatatine] *adj* shrivelled (up), wrinkled.

ratatiner [ʀatatine] *vt* to shrivel; (*peau*) to wrinkle; **se** ~ *vi* to shrivel; to become wrinkled.

ratatouille [ʀatatuj] *nf* (*CULIN*) ratatouille.

rate [ʀat] *nf* female rat; (*ANAT*) spleen.

raté, e [ʀate] *adj* (*tentative*) unsuccessful, failed ♦ *nm/f* failure ♦ *nm* misfiring *no pl*.

râteau, x [ʀato] *nm* rake.

râtelier [ʀatəlje] *nm* rack; (*fam*) false teeth *pl*.

rater [ʀate] *vi* (*ne pas partir: coup de feu*) to fail to go off; (*affaire, projet etc*) to go wrong, fail ♦ *vt* (*cible, train, occasion*) to miss; (*démonstration, plat*) to spoil; (*examen*) to fail; ~ **son coup** to fail, not to bring it off.

raticide [ʀatisid] *nm* rat poison.

ratification [ʀatifikasjɔ̃] *nf* ratification.

ratifier [ʀatifje] *vt* to ratify.

ratio [ʀasjo] *nm* ratio (*pl* -s).

ration [ʀasjɔ̃] *nf* ration; (*fig*) share; ~ **alimentaire** food intake.

rationalisation [ʀasjɔnalizasjɔ̃] *nf* rationalization.

rationaliser [ʀasjɔnalize] *vt* to rationalize.

rationnel, le [ʀasjɔnɛl] *adj* rational.

rationnellement [ʀasjɔnɛlmɑ̃] *adv* rationally.

rationnement [ʀasjɔnmɑ̃] *nm* rationing; **ticket de** ~ ration coupon.

rationner [ʀasjɔne] *vt* to ration; (*personne*) to put on rations; **se** ~ to ration o.s.

ratisser [ʀatise] *vt* (*allée*) to rake; (*feuilles*) to rake up; (*suj: armée, police*) to comb; ~ **large** to cast one's nets wide.

raton [ʀatɔ̃] *nm*: ~ **laveur** raccoon.

RATP *sigle f* (= *Régie autonome des transports parisiens*) *Paris transport authority*.

rattacher [ʀataʃe] *vt* (*animal, cheveux*) to tie up again; (*incorporer: ADMIN etc*): ~ **qch à** to join sth to, unite sth with; (*fig: relier*): ~ **qch à** to link sth with, relate sth to; (*: lier*): ~ **qn à** to bind *ou* tie sb to; **se** ~ **à** (*fig: avoir un lien avec*) to be linked *ou* connected with.

rattrapage [ʀatʀapaʒ] *nm* (*SCOL*) remedial classes *pl*; (*ÉCON*) catching up.

rattraper [ʀatʀape] *vt* (*fugitif*) to recapture; (*retenir, empêcher de tomber*) to catch (hold of); (*atteindre, rejoindre*) to catch up with; (*réparer: imprudence, erreur*) to make up for; **se** ~ *vi* (*regagner: du temps*) to make up for lost time; (: *de l'argent etc*) to make good one's losses; (*réparer une gaffe etc*) to make up for it; **se ~ (à)** (*se raccrocher*) to stop o.s. falling (by catching hold of); **~ son retard/le temps perdu** to make up (for) lost time.

rature [ʀatyʀ] *nf* deletion, erasure.

raturer [ʀatyʀe] *vt* to cross out, delete, erase.

rauque [ʀok] *adj* raucous; hoarse.

ravagé, e [ʀavaʒe] *adj* (*visage*) harrowed.

ravager [ʀavaʒe] *vt* to devastate, ravage.

ravages [ʀavaʒ] *nmpl* ravages; **faire des ~** to wreak havoc; (*fig: séducteur*) to break hearts.

ravalement [ʀavalmã] *nm* restoration.

ravaler [ʀavale] *vt* (*mur, façade*) to restore; (*déprécier*) to lower; (*avaler de nouveau*) to swallow again; **~ sa colère/son dégoût** to stifle one's anger/distaste.

ravaudage [ʀavodaʒ] *nm* repairing, mending.

ravauder [ʀavode] *vt* to repair, mend.

rave [ʀav] *nf* (*BOT*) rape.

R avec AR *abr* (= *recommandé avec accusé de réception*) recorded delivery.

ravi, e [ʀavi] *adj* delighted; **être ~ de/que** to be delighted with/that.

ravier [ʀavje] *nm* hors d'œuvre dish.

ravigote [ʀavigɔt] *adj:* **sauce ~** oil and vinegar dressing with shallots.

ravigoter [ʀavigɔte] *vt* (*fam*) to buck up.

ravin [ʀavɛ̃] *nm* gully, ravine.

raviner [ʀavine] *vt* to furrow, gully.

ravioli [ʀavjɔli] *nmpl* ravioli *sg.*

ravir [ʀaviʀ] *vt* (*enchanter*) to delight; (*enlever*): **~ qch à qn** to rob sb of sth; **à ~** *adv* delightfully, beautifully; **être beau à ~** to be ravishingly beautiful.

raviser [ʀavize]: **se ~** *vi* to change one's mind.

ravissant, e [ʀavisã, -ãt] *adj* delightful.

ravissement [ʀavismã] *nm* (*enchantement, délice*) rapture.

ravisseur, euse [ʀavisœʀ, -øz] *nm/f* abductor, kidnapper.

ravitaillement [ʀavitajmã] *nm* resupplying; refuelling; (*provisions*) supplies *pl*; **aller au ~** to go for fresh supplies; **~ en vol** (*AVIAT*) in-flight refuelling.

ravitailler [ʀavitaje] *vt* to resupply; (*véhicule*) to refuel; **se ~** *vi* to get fresh supplies.

raviver [ʀavive] *vt* (*feu, douleur*) to revive; (*couleurs*) to brighten up.

ravoir [ʀavwaʀ] *vt* to get back.

rayé, e [ʀeje] *adj* (*à rayures*) striped; (*éraflé*) scratched.

rayer [ʀeje] *vt* (*érafler*) to scratch; (*barrer*) to cross *ou* score out; (*d'une liste: radier*) to cross *ou* strike off.

rayon [ʀɛjɔ̃] *nm* (*de soleil etc*) ray; (*GÉOM*) radius; (*de roue*) spoke; (*étagère*) shelf (*pl* shelves); (*de grand magasin*) department; (*fig: domaine*) responsibility, concern; (*de ruche*) (honey)comb; **dans un ~ de** within a radius of; **~s** *nmpl* (*radiothérapie*) radiation;

~ d'action range; **~ de braquage** (*AUTO*) turning circle; **~ laser** laser beam; **~ de soleil** sunbeam, ray of sunshine; **~s X** X-rays.

rayonnage [ʀɛjɔnaʒ] *nm* set of shelves.

rayonnant, e [ʀɛjɔnã, -ãt] *adj* radiant.

rayonne [ʀɛjɔn] *nf* rayon.

rayonnement [ʀɛjɔnmã] *nm* radiation; (*fig: éclat*) radiance; (: *influence*) influence.

rayonner [ʀɛjɔne] *vi* (*chaleur, énergie*) to radiate; (*fig: émotion*) to shine forth; (: *visage*) to be radiant; (*avenues, axes etc*) to radiate; (*touriste*) to go touring (*from one base*).

rayure [ʀejyʀ] *nf* (*motif*) stripe; (*éraflure*) scratch; (*rainure, d'un fusil*) groove; **à ~s** striped.

raz-de-marée [ʀɑdmaʀe] *nm inv* tidal wave.

razzia [ʀazja] *nf* raid, foray.

RBE *sigle m* (= *revenu brut d'exploitation*) gross profit (*of a farm*).

R-D *sigle f* (= *Recherche-Développement*) R & D.

RDA *sigle f* (= *République démocratique allemande*) GDR.

RDB *sigle m* (*STATISTIQUES:* = *revenu disponible brut*) total income (*of a family etc*).

rdc *abr* = **rez-de-chaussée.**

ré [ʀe] *nm* (*MUS*) D; (*en chantant la gamme*) re.

réabonnement [ʀeabɔnmã] *nm* renewal of subscription.

réabonner [ʀeabɔne] *vt:* **~ qn à** to renew sb's subscription to; **se ~ (à)** to renew one's subscription (to).

réac [ʀeak] *adj, nm/f* (*fam:* = *réactionnaire*) reactionary.

réacteur [ʀeaktœʀ] *nm* jet engine; **~ nucléaire** nuclear reactor.

réactif [ʀeaktif] *nm* reagent.

réaction [ʀeaksjɔ̃] *nf* reaction; **par ~** jet-propelled; **avion/moteur à ~** jet (plane)/jet engine; **~ en chaîne** chain reaction.

réactionnaire [ʀeaksjɔnɛʀ] *adj, nm/f* reactionary.

réactualiser [ʀeaktyalize] *vt* to update, bring up to date.

réadaptation [ʀeadaptasjɔ̃] *nf* readjustment; rehabilitation.

réadapter [ʀeadapte] *vt* to readjust; (*MÉD*) to rehabilitate; **se ~ (à)** to readjust (to).

réaffirmer [ʀeafiʀme] *vt* to reaffirm, reassert.

réagir [ʀeaʒiʀ] *vi* to react.

réajuster [ʀeaʒyste] *vt* = **rajuster.**

réalisable [ʀealizabl(ə)] *adj* (*projet, plan*) feasible; (*COMM: valeur*) realizable.

réalisateur, trice [ʀealizatœʀ, -tʀis] *nm/f* (*TV, CINÉ*) director.

réalisation [ʀealizasjɔ̃] *nf* carrying out; realization; fulfilment; achievement; production; (*œuvre*) production, work; (*création*) creation.

réaliser [ʀealize] *vt* (*projet, opération*) to carry out, realize; (*rêve, souhait*) to realize, fulfil; (*exploit*) to achieve; (*achat, vente*) to make; (*film*) to produce; (*se rendre compte de,*

COMM: bien, capital) to realize; **se** ~ *vi* to be realized.

réalisme [realism(ə)] *nm* realism.

réaliste [realist(ə)] *adj* realistic; *(peintre, roman)* realist ♦ *nm/f* realist.

réalité [realite] *nf* reality; **en** ~ in (actual) fact; **dans la** ~ in reality; ~ **virtuelle** virtual reality.

réanimation [reanimɑsjɔ̃] *nf* resuscitation; **service de** ~ intensive care unit.

réanimer [reanime] *vt (MÉD)* to resuscitate.

réapparaître [reaparɛtr(ə)] *vi* to reappear.

réapparition [reaparisjɔ̃] *nf* reappearance.

réapprovisionner [reaprɔvizjɔne] *vt (magasin)* to restock; **se** ~ **(en)** to restock (with).

réarmement [rearməmɑ̃] *nm* rearmament.

réarmer [rearme] *vt (arme)* to reload ♦ *vi (état)* to rearm.

réassortiment [reasɔrtimɑ̃] *nm (COMM)* restocking.

réassortir [reasɔrtir] *vt* to match up.

réassurance [reasyrɑ̃s] *nf* reinsurance.

réassurer [reasyre] *vt* to reinsure.

réassureur [reasyre] *nm* reinsurer.

rebaptiser [rəbatize] *vt (rue)* to rename.

rébarbatif, ive [rebarbatif, -iv] *adj* forbidding; *(style)* off-putting *(BRIT)*, crabbed.

rebattre [rəbatr(ə)] *vt:* ~ **les oreilles à qn de qch** to keep harping on to sb about sth.

rebattu, e [rəbaty] *pp de* **rebattre** ♦ *adj* hackneyed.

rebelle [rəbɛl] *nm/f* rebel ♦ *adj (troupes)* rebel; *(enfant)* rebellious; *(mèche etc)* unruly; ~ **à qch** unamenable to sth; ~ **à faire** unwilling to do.

rebeller [rəbele]: **se** ~ *vi* to rebel.

rébellion [rebeljɔ̃] *nf* rebellion; *(rebelles)* rebel forces *pl*.

rebiffer [rəbife]: **se** ~ *vr* to fight back.

reboisement [rəbwazmɑ̃] *nm* reafforestation.

reboiser [rəbwaze] *vt* to replant with trees, reafforest.

rebond [rəbɔ̃] *nm (voir rebondir)* bounce; rebound.

rebondi, e [rəbɔ̃di] *adj (ventre)* rounded; *(joues)* chubby, well-rounded.

rebondir [rəbɔ̃dir] *vi (ballon: au sol)* to bounce; *(: contre un mur)* to rebound; *(fig: procès, action, conversation)* to get moving again, be suddenly revived.

rebondissement [rəbɔ̃dismɑ̃] *nm* new development.

rebord [rəbɔr] *nm* edge.

reboucher [rəbuʃe] *vt (flacon)* to put the stopper *(ou* top) back on, recork; *(trou)* to stop up.

rebours [rəbur]: **à** ~ *adv* the wrong way.

rebouteux, euse [rəbutø, -øz] *nm/f (péj)* bonesetter.

reboutonner [rəbutɔne] *vt (vêtement)* to button up (again).

rebrousse-poil [rəbruspwal]: **à** ~ *adv* the

wrong way.

rebrousser [rəbruse] *vt (cheveux, poils)* to brush back, brush up; ~ **chemin** to turn back.

rebuffade [rəbyfad] *nf* rebuff.

rébus [rebys] *nm inv (jeu d'esprit)* rebus; *(fig)* puzzle.

rebut [rəby] *nm:* **mettre au** ~ to scrap, discard.

rebutant, e [rəbytɑ̃, -ɑ̃t] *adj (travail, démarche)* off-putting, disagreeable.

rebuter [rəbyte] *vt* to put off.

récalcitrant, e [rekalsitrɑ̃, -ɑ̃t] *adj* refractory, recalcitrant.

recaler [rəkale] *vt (SCOL)* to fail.

récapitulatif, ive [rekapitylatif, -iv] *adj (liste, tableau)* summary *cpd*, that sums up.

récapituler [rekapityle] *vt* to recapitulate; *(résumer)* to sum up.

recel [rəsɛl] *nm* receiving (stolen goods).

receler [rəsəle] *vt (produit d'un vol)* to receive; *(malfaiteur)* to harbour; *(fig)* to conceal.

receleur, euse [rəsəlœr, -øz] *nm/f* receiver.

récemment [resamɑ̃] *adv* recently.

recensement [rəsɑ̃smɑ̃] *nm* census; inventory.

recenser [rəsɑ̃se] *vt (population)* to take a census of; *(inventorier)* to make an inventory of; *(dénombrer)* to list.

récent, e [resɑ̃, -ɑ̃t] *adj* recent.

recentrer [rəsɑ̃tre] *vt (POL)* to move towards the centre.

récépissé [resepise] *nm* receipt.

réceptacle [resɛptakl(ə)] *nm (où les choses aboutissent)* recipient; *(où les choses sont stockées)* repository; *(BOT)* receptacle.

récepteur, trice [resɛptœr, -tris] *adj* receiving ♦ *nm* receiver; ~ **(de papier)** *(INFORM)* stacker; ~ **(de radio)** radio set *ou* receiver.

réceptif, ive [resɛptif, -iv] *adj:* ~ **(à)** receptive (to).

réception [resɛpsjɔ̃] *nf* receiving *no pl*; *(d'une marchandise, commande)* receipt; *(accueil)* reception, welcome; *(bureau)* reception (desk); *(réunion mondaine)* reception, party; *(pièces)* reception rooms *pl*; *(SPORT: après un saut)* landing; *(du ballon)* catching *no pl*; **jour/heures de** ~ day/hours for receiving visitors *(ou* students *etc).*

réceptionnaire [resɛpsjɔnɛr] *nm/f* receiving clerk.

réceptionner [resɛpsjɔne] *vt (COMM)* to take delivery of; *(SPORT: ballon)* to catch (and control).

réceptionniste [resɛpsjɔnist(ə)] *nm/f* receptionist.

réceptivité [resɛptivite] *nf (à une influence)* receptiveness; *(à une maladie)* susceptibility.

récessif, ive [resesif, -iv] *adj (BIOL)* recessive.

récession [resesjɔ̃] *nf* recession.

recette [rəsɛt] *nf (CULIN)* recipe; *(fig)* formula, recipe; *(COMM)* takings *pl*; *(ADMIN: bureau)* tax *ou* revenue office; **~s** *nfpl* (*COMM*: *rentrées*) receipts; **faire ~** (*spectacle, exposition*) to be a winner.

receveur, euse [RəsvœR, -øz] *nm/f* (*des contributions*) tax collector; (*des postes*) postmaster/mistress; (*d'autobus*) conductor/conductress; (*MÉD*: *de sang, organe*) recipient.

recevoir [RəsvwaR] *vt* to receive; (*lettre, prime*) to receive, get; (*client, patient, représentant*) to see; (*jour, soleil: suj: pièce*) to get; (*SCOL*: *candidat*) to pass ♦ *vi* to receive visitors; to give parties; to see patients *etc*; **se ~** *vi* (*athlète*) to land; **~ qn à dîner** to invite sb to dinner; **il reçoit de 8 à 10** he's at home from 8 to 10, he will see visitors from 8 to 10; (*docteur, dentiste etc*) he sees patients from 8 to 10; **être reçu** (*à un examen*) to pass; **être bien/mal reçu** to be well/badly received.

rechange [Rəʃɑ̃ʒ]: **de ~** *adj* (*pièces, roue*) spare; (*fig: solution*) alternative; **des vêtements de ~** a change of clothes.

rechaper [Rəʃape] *vt* to remould (*BRIT*), remold (*US*), retread.

réchapper [Reʃape]: **~ de ou à** *vt* (*accident, maladie*) to come through; **va-t-il en ~?** is he going to get over it?, is he going to come through (it)?

recharge [RəʃaRʒ(ə)] *nf* refill.

rechargeable [RəʃaRʒabl(ə)] *adj* refillable; rechargeable.

recharger [RəʃaRʒe] *vt* (*camion, fusil, appareilphoto*) to reload; (*briquet, stylo*) to refill; (*batterie*) to recharge.

réchaud [Reʃo] *nm* (portable) stove; platewarmer.

réchauffé [Reʃofe] *nm* (*nourriture*) reheated food; (*fig*) stale news (*ou* joke *etc*).

réchauffement [Reʃofmɑ̃] *nm* warming (up); **le ~ de la planète** global warming.

réchauffer [Reʃofe] *vt* (*plat*) to reheat; (*mains, personne*) to warm; **se ~** *vi* to get warmer; **se ~ les doigts** to warm (up) one's fingers.

rêche [Rɛʃ] *adj* rough.

recherche [RəʃɛRʃ(ə)] *nf* (*action*): **la ~ de** the search for; (*raffinement*) affectedness, studied elegance; (*scientifique etc*): **la ~** research; **~s** *nfpl* (*de la police*) investigations; (*scientifiques*) research *sg*; **être/se mettre à la ~ de** to be/go in search of.

recherché, e [RəʃɛRʃe] *adj* (*rare, demandé*) much sought-after; (*entouré: acteur, femme*) in demand; (*raffiné*) studied, affected.

rechercher [RəʃɛRʃe] *vt* (*objet égaré, personne*) to look for, search for; (*témoins, coupable, main-d'œuvre*) to look for; (*causes d'un phénomène, nouveau procédé*) to try to find; (*bonheur etc, l'amitié de qn*) to seek; **"~ et remplacer"** (*INFORM*) "search and replace".

rechigner [Rəʃiɲe] *vi*: **~ (à)** to balk (at).

rechute [Rəʃyt] *nf* (*MÉD*) relapse; (*dans le péché, le vice*) lapse; **faire une ~** to have a relapse.

rechuter [Rəʃyte] *vi* (*MÉD*) to relapse.

récidive [Residiv] *nf* (*JUR*) second (*ou* subsequent) offence; (*fig*) repetition; (*MÉD*) recurrence.

récidiver [Residive] *vi* to commit a second (*ou* subsequent) offence; (*fig*) to do it again.

récidiviste [Residivist(ə)] *nm/f* second (*ou* habitual) offender, recidivist.

récif [Resif] *nm* reef.

récipiendaire [Resipjɑ̃dɛR] *nm* recipient (*of diploma etc*); (*d'une societé*) newly elected member.

récipient [Resipjɑ̃] *nm* container.

réciproque [ResipRɔk] *adj* reciprocal ♦ *nf*: **la ~** (*l'inverse*) the converse.

réciproquement [ResipRɔkmɑ̃] *adv* reciprocally; **et ~** and vice versa.

récit [Resi] *nm* (*action de narrer*) telling; (*conte, histoire*) story.

récital [Resital] *nm* recital.

récitant, e [Resitɑ̃, -ɑ̃t] *nm/f* narrator.

récitation [Resitasjɔ̃] *nf* recitation.

réciter [Resite] *vt* to recite.

réclamation [Reklamasjɔ̃] *nf* complaint; **~s** *nfpl* (*bureau*) complaints department *sg*.

réclame [Reklam] *nf*: **la ~** advertising; **une ~** an ad(vertisement), an advert (*BRIT*); **faire de la ~ (pour qch/qn)** to advertise (sth/sb); **article en ~** special offer.

réclamer [Reklame] *vt* (*aide, nourriture etc*) to ask for; (*revendiquer: dû, part, indemnité*) to claim, demand; (*nécessiter*) to demand, require ♦ *vi* to complain; **se ~ de** to give as one's authority; to claim filiation with.

reclassement [Rəklasmɑ̃] *nm* reclassifying; regrading; rehabilitation.

reclasser [Rəklase] *vt* (*fiches, dossiers*) to reclassify; (*fig: fonctionnaire etc*) to regrade; (*: ouvrier licencié*) to place, rehabilitate.

reclus, e [Rəkly, -yz] *nm/f* recluse.

réclusion [Reklyzjɔ̃] *nf* imprisonment; **~ à perpétuité** life imprisonment.

recoiffer [Rəkwafe] *vt*: **~ un enfant** to do a child's hair again; **se ~** to do one's hair again.

recoin [Rəkwɛ̃] *nm* nook, corner; (*fig*) hidden recess.

reçois [Rəswa] *etc vb voir* **recevoir**.

reçoive [Rəswav] *etc vb voir* **recevoir**.

recoller [Rəkɔle] *vt* (*enveloppe*) to stick back down.

récolte [Rekɔlt(ə)] *nf* harvesting, gathering; (*produits*) harvest, crop; (*fig*) crop, collection; (*: d'observations*) findings.

récolter [Rekɔlte] *vt* to harvest, gather (in); (*fig*) to get.

recommandable [Rəkɔmɑ̃dabl(ə)] *adj* commendable; **peu ~** not very commendable.

recommandation [Rəkɔmɑ̃dasjɔ̃] *nf* recommendation.

recommandé [Rəkɔmɑ̃de] *nm* (*méthode etc*)

recommended; (*POSTES*): **en** ~ by registered mail.

recommander [ʀəkɔmɑ̃de] *vt* to recommend; (*suj: qualités etc*) to commend; (*POSTES*) to register; ~ **qch à qn** to recommend sth to sb; ~ **à qn de faire** to recommend sb to do; ~ **qn auprès de qn** *ou* **à qn** to recommend sb to sb; **il est recommandé de faire ...** it is recommended that one does ...; **se** ~ **à** to commend o.s. to sb; **se** ~ **de qn** to give sb's name as a reference.

recommencer [ʀəkɔmɑ̃se] *vt* (*reprendre: lutte, séance*) to resume, start again; (*refaire: travail, explications*) to start afresh, start (over) again; (*récidiver: erreur*) to make again ♦ *vi* to start again; (*récidiver*) to do it again; ~ **à faire** to start doing again; **ne recommence pas!** don't do that again!

récompense [ʀekɔ̃pɑ̃s] *nf* reward; (*prix*) award; **recevoir qch en** ~ to get sth as a reward, be rewarded with sth.

récompenser [ʀekɔ̃pɑ̃se] *vt*: ~ **qn (de** *ou* **pour)** to reward sb (for).

réconciliation [ʀekɔ̃siljasjɔ̃] *nf* reconciliation.

réconcilier [ʀekɔ̃silje] *vt* to reconcile; ~ **qn avec qn** to reconcile sb with sb; ~ **qn avec qch** to reconcile sb to sth; **se** ~ **(avec)** to be reconciled (with).

reconductible [ʀəkɔ̃dyktibl(ə)] *adj* (*JUR: contrat, bail*) renewable.

reconduction [ʀəkɔ̃dyksjɔ̃] *nf* renewal; (*POL: d'une politique*) continuation.

reconduire [ʀəkɔ̃dɥiʀ] *vt* (*raccompagner*) to take *ou* see back; (*: à la porte*) to show out; (*: à son domicile*) to see home, take home; (*JUR, POL: renouveler*) to renew.

réconfort [ʀekɔ̃fɔʀ] *nm* comfort.

réconfortant, e [ʀekɔ̃fɔʀtɑ̃, -ɑ̃t] *adj* (*idée, paroles*) comforting; (*boisson*) fortifying.

réconforter [ʀekɔ̃fɔʀte] *vt* (*consoler*) to comfort; (*revigorer*) to fortify.

reconnais [ʀ(ə)kɔnɛ] *etc vb voir* **reconnaître**.

reconnaissable [ʀ(ə)kɔnɛsabl(ə)] *adj* recognizable.

reconnaissais [ʀ(ə)kɔnɛsɛ] *etc vb voir* **reconnaître**.

reconnaissance [ʀəkɔnɛsɑ̃s] *nf* recognition; acknowledgement; (*gratitude*) gratitude, gratefulness; (*MIL*) reconnaissance, recce; **en** ~ (*MIL*) on reconnaissance; ~ **de dette** acknowledgement of a debt, IOU.

reconnaissant, e [ʀəkɔnɛsɑ̃, -ɑ̃t] *vb voir* **reconnaître** ♦ *adj* grateful; **je vous serais** ~ **de bien vouloir** I should be most grateful if you would (kindly).

reconnaître [ʀəkɔnɛtʀ(ə)] *vt* to recognize; (*MIL: lieu*) to reconnoitre; (*JUR: enfant, dette, droit*) to acknowledge; ~ **que** to admit *ou* acknowledge that; ~ **qn/qch à** (*l'identifier grâce à*) to recognize sb/sth by; ~ **à qn:** **je lui reconnais certaines qualités** I recognize certain qualities in him; **se** ~ **quelque part** (*s'y*

retrouver*) to find one's way around (a place).

reconnu, e [ʀ(ə)kɔny] *pp de* **reconnaître** ♦ *adj* (*indiscuté, connu*) recognized.

reconquérir [ʀəkɔ̃keʀiʀ] *vt* (*aussi fig*) to reconquer, recapture; (*sa dignité etc*) to recover.

reconquête [ʀəkɔ̃kɛt] *nf* recapture; recovery.

reconsidérer [ʀəkɔ̃sideʀe] *vt* to reconsider.

reconstituant, e [ʀəkɔ̃stitɥɑ̃, -ɑ̃t] *adj* (*régime*) strength-building ♦ *nm* tonic, pick-me-up.

reconstituer [ʀəkɔ̃stitɥe] *vt* (*monument ancien*) to recreate, build a replica of; (*fresque, vase brisé*) to piece together, reconstitute; (*événement, accident*) to reconstruct; (*fortune, patrimoine*) to rebuild; (*BIO: tissus etc*) to regenerate.

reconstitution [ʀəkɔ̃stitysjɔ̃] *nf* (*d'un accident etc*) reconstruction.

reconstruction [ʀəkɔ̃stʀyksjɔ̃] *nf* rebuilding, reconstruction.

reconstruire [ʀəkɔ̃stʀɥiʀ] *vt* to rebuild, reconstruct.

reconversion [ʀəkɔ̃vɛʀsjɔ̃] *nf* (*du personnel*) redeployment.

reconvertir [ʀəkɔ̃vɛʀtiʀ] *vt* (*usine*) to reconvert; (*personnel, troupes etc*) to redeploy; **se** ~ **dans** (*un métier, une branche*) to move into, be redeployed into.

recopier [ʀəkɔpje] *vt* (*transcrire*) to copy out again, write out again; (*mettre au propre: devoir*) to make a clean *ou* fair copy of.

record [ʀəkɔʀ] *nm, adj* record; ~ **du monde** world record.

recoucher [ʀəkuʃe] *vt* (*enfant*) to put back to bed.

recoudre [ʀəkudʀ(ə)] *vt* (*bouton*) to sew back on; (*plaie, incision*) to sew (back) up, stitch up.

recoupement [ʀəkupmɑ̃] *nm*: **faire un** ~ *ou* **des** ~s to cross-check; **par** ~ by cross-checking.

recouper [ʀəkupe] *vt* (*tranche*) to cut again; (*vêtement*) to recut ♦ *vi* (*CARTES*) to cut again; **se** ~ *vi* (*témoignages*) to tie *ou* match up.

recourais [ʀəkuʀɛ] *etc vb voir* **recourir**.

recourbé, e [ʀəkuʀbe] *adj* curved; hooked; bent.

recourber [ʀəkuʀbe] *vt* (*branche, tige de métal*) to bend.

recourir [ʀəkuʀiʀ] *vi* (*courir de nouveau*) to run again; (*refaire une course*) to race again; ~ **à** *vt* (*ami, agence*) to turn *ou* appeal to; (*force, ruse, emprunt*) to resort to, have recourse to.

recours [ʀəkuʀ] *vb voir* **recourir** ♦ *nm* (*JUR*) appeal; **avoir** ~ **à** = **recourir à; en dernier** ~ as a last resort; **sans** ~ final; with no way out; ~ **en grâce** plea for clemency (*ou* pardon).

recouru, e [ʀəkuʀy] *pp de* **recourir**.

recousu, e [ʀəkuzy] *pp de* **recoudre**.

recouvert, e [ʀəkuvɛʀ, -ɛʀt(ə)] *pp de* **recouvrir**.

recouvrable [ʀəkuvʀabl(ə)] *adj* (*somme*) recoverable.

recouvrais [ʀəkuvʀɛ] *etc vb voir* **recouvrer, recouvrir.**

recouvrement [ʀəkuvʀəmɑ̃] *nm* recovery.

recouvrer [ʀəkuvʀe] *vt* (*vue, santé etc*) to recover, regain; (*impôts*) to collect; (*créance*) to recover.

recouvrir [ʀəkuvʀiʀ] *vt* (*couvrir à nouveau*) to re-cover; (*couvrir entièrement, aussi fig*) to cover; (*cacher, masquer*) to conceal, hide; **se ~** (*se superposer*) to overlap.

recracher [ʀəkʀaʃe] *vt* to spit out.

récréatif, ive [ʀekʀeatif, -iv] *adj* of entertainment; recreational.

récréation [ʀekʀeasjɔ̃] *nf* recreation, entertainment; (*SCOL*) break.

recréer [ʀəkʀee] *vt* to recreate.

récrier [ʀekʀije]: **se ~** *vi* to exclaim.

récriminations [ʀekʀiminasjɔ̃] *nfpl* remonstrations, complaints.

récriminer [ʀekʀimine] *vi*: **~ contre qn/qch** to remonstrate against sb/sth.

recroqueviller [ʀəkʀɔkvije]: **se ~** *vi* (*feuilles*) to curl *ou* shrivel up; (*personne*) to huddle up.

recru, e [ʀəkʀy] *adj*: **~ de fatigue** exhausted ♦ *nf* recruit.

recrudescence [ʀəkʀydesɑ̃s] *nf* fresh outbreak.

recrutement [ʀəkʀytmɑ̃] *nm* recruiting, recruitment.

recruter [ʀəkʀyte] *vt* to recruit.

rectal, e, aux [ʀɛktal, -o] *adj*: **par voie ~e** rectally.

rectangle [ʀɛktɑ̃gl(ə)] *nm* rectangle; **~ blanc** (*TV*) "adults only" symbol.

rectangulaire [ʀɛktɑ̃gylɛʀ] *adj* rectangular.

recteur [ʀɛktœʀ] *nm* ≈ (regional) director of education (*BRIT*), ≈ state superintendent of education (*US*).

rectificatif, ive [ʀɛktifikatif, -iv] *adj* corrected ♦ *nm* correction.

rectification [ʀɛktifikasjɔ̃] *nf* correction.

rectifier [ʀɛktifje] *vt* (*tracé, virage*) to straighten; (*calcul, adresse*) to correct; (*erreur, faute*) to rectify, put right.

rectiligne [ʀɛktiliɲ] *adj* straight; (*GÉOM*) rectilinear.

rectitude [ʀɛktityd] *nf* rectitude, uprightness.

recto [ʀɛkto] *nm* front (*of a sheet of paper*).

rectorat [ʀɛktɔʀa] *nm* (*fonction*) position of *recteur*; (*bureau*) *recteur's office; see also* **recteur.**

rectum [ʀɛktɔm] *nm* rectum.

reçu, e [ʀəsy] *pp de* **recevoir** ♦ *adj* (*admis, consacré*) accepted ♦ *nm* (*COMM*) receipt.

recueil [ʀəkœj] *nm* collection.

recueillement [ʀəkœjmɑ̃] *nm* meditation, contemplation.

recueilli, e [ʀəkœji] *adj* contemplative.

recueillir [ʀəkœjiʀ] *vt* to collect; (*voix, suffrages*) to win; (*accueillir: réfugiés, chat*) to take in; **se ~** *vi* to gather one's thoughts; to

meditate.

recuire [ʀəkɥiʀ] *vi*: **faire ~** to recook.

recul [ʀəkyl] *nm* retreat; recession; decline; (*d'arme à feu*) recoil, kick; **avoir un mouvement de ~** to recoil, start back; **prendre du ~** to stand back; **avec le ~** with the passing of time, in retrospect.

reculade [ʀəkylad] *nf* (*péj*) climb-down.

reculé, e [ʀəkyle] *adj* remote.

reculer [ʀəkyle] *vi* to move back, back away; (*AUTO*) to reverse, back (up); (*fig: civilisation, épidémie*) to (be on the) decline; (*: se dérober*) to shrink back ♦ *vt* to move back; to reverse, back (up); (*fig: possibilités, limites*) to extend; (*: date, décision*) to postpone; **~ devant** (*danger, difficulté*) to shrink from; **~ pour mieux sauter** (*fig*) to postpone the evil day.

reculons [ʀəkylɔ̃]: **à ~** *adv* backwards.

récupérable [ʀekypeʀabl(ə)] *adj* (*créance*) recoverable; (*heures*) which can be made up; (*ferraille*) salvageable.

récupération [ʀekypeʀasjɔ̃] *nf* (*de vieux métaux etc*) salvage, reprocessing; (*POL*) bringing into line.

récupérer [ʀekypeʀe] *vt* (*rentrer en possession de*) to recover, get back; (*: forces*) to recover; (*déchets etc*) to salvage (for reprocessing); (*remplacer: journée, heures de travail*) to make up; (*délinquant etc*) to rehabilitate; (*POL*) to bring into line ♦ *vi* to recover.

récurer [ʀekyʀe] *vt* to scour; **poudre à ~** scouring powder.

reçus [ʀəsy] *etc vb voir* **recevoir.**

récusable [ʀekyzabl(ə)] *adj* (*témoin*) challengeable; (*témoignage*) impugnable.

récuser [ʀekyze] *vt* to challenge; **se ~** to decline to give an opinion.

recyclage [ʀəsiklaʒ] *nm* reorientation; retraining; recycling; **cours de ~** retraining course.

recycler [ʀəsikle] *vt* (*SCOL*) to reorientate; (*employés*) to retrain; (*matériau*) to recycle; **se ~** to retrain; to go on a retraining course.

rédacteur, trice [ʀedaktœʀ, -tʀis] *nm/f* (*journaliste*) writer; subeditor; (*d'ouvrage de référence*) editor, compiler; **~ en chef** chief editor; **~ publicitaire** copywriter.

rédaction [ʀedaksjɔ̃] *nf* writing; (*rédacteurs*) editorial staff; (*bureau*) editorial office(s); (*SCOL: devoir*) essay, composition.

reddition [ʀedisjɔ̃] *nf* surrender.

redéfinir [ʀədefiniʀ] *vt* to redefine.

redemander [ʀədmɑ̃de] *vt* (*renseignement*) to ask again for; (*nourriture*): **~ de** to ask for more (*ou* another); (*objet prêté*): **~ qch** to ask for sth back.

redémarrer [ʀədemaʀe] *vi* (*véhicule*) to start again, get going again; (*fig: industrie etc*) to get going again.

rédemption [ʀedɑ̃psjɔ̃] *nf* redemption.

redéploiement [ʀədeplwamɑ̃] *nm* redeployment.

redescendre [ʀədesɑ̃dʀ(ə)] *vi* (*à nouveau*) to go back down; (*après la montée*) to go down (again) ♦ *vt* (*pente etc*) to go down.

redevable [ʀədvabl(ə)] *adj*: **être** ~ **de qch à qn** (*somme*) to owe sb sth; (*fig*) to be indebted to sb for sth.

redevance [ʀədvɑ̃s] *nf* (*TÉL*) rental charge; (*TV*) licence (*BRIT*) *ou* license (*US*) fee.

redevenir [ʀədvəniʀ] *vi* to become again.

rédhibitoire [ʀedibitwaʀ] *adj*: **vice** ~ (*JUR*) *latent defect in merchandise that renders the sales contract void*; (*fig*: *défaut*) crippling.

rediffuser [ʀədifyze] *vt* (*RADIO*, *TV*) to repeat, broadcast again.

rediffusion [ʀədifyzjɔ̃] *nf* repeat (programme).

rédiger [ʀediʒe] *vt* to write; (*contrat*) to draw up.

redire [ʀədiʀ] *vt* to repeat; **trouver à** ~ **à** to find fault with.

redistribuer [ʀədistʀibɥe] *vt* (*cartes etc*) to deal again; (*richesses, tâches, revenus*) to redistribute.

redite [ʀədit] *nf* (*needless*) repetition.

redondance [ʀədɔ̃dɑ̃s] *nf* redundancy.

redonner [ʀədɔne] *vt* (*restituer*) to give back, return; (*du courage, des forces*) to restore.

redoublé, e [ʀəduble] *adj*: **à coups** ~**s** even harder, twice as hard.

redoubler [ʀəduble] *vi* (*tempête, violence*) to intensify, get even stronger *ou* fiercer *etc*; (*SCOL*) to repeat a year ♦ *vt* (*SCOL*: *classe*) to repeat; (*LING*: *lettre*) to double; ~ **de** *vt* to be twice as + *adjectif*; **le vent redouble de violence** the wind is blowing twice as hard.

redoutable [ʀədutabl(ə)] *adj* formidable, fearsome.

redouter [ʀədute] *vt* to fear; (*appréhender*) to dread; ~ **de faire** to dread doing.

redoux [ʀədu] *nm* milder spell.

redressement [ʀədʀɛsmɑ̃] *nm* (*de l'économie etc*) putting right; **maison de** ~ reformatory; ~ **fiscal** repayment of back taxes.

redresser [ʀədʀese] *vt* (*arbre, mât*) to set upright, right; (*pièce tordue*) to straighten out; (*AVIAT*, *AUTO*) to straighten up; (*situation, économie*) to put right; **se** ~ *vi* (*objet penché*) to right itself; (*personne*) to straighten up; to sit (*ou* stand) up; to sit (*ou* stand) up straight; (*fig*: *pays, situation*) to recover; ~ (**les roues**) (*AUTO*) to straighten up.

redresseur [ʀədʀesœʀ] *nm*: ~ **de torts** righter of wrongs.

réducteur, trice [ʀedyktœʀ, -tʀis] *adj* simplistic.

réduction [ʀedyksjɔ̃] *nf* reduction; **en** ~ *adv* in miniature, scaled-down.

réduire [ʀedɥiʀ] *vt* (*gén, aussi CULIN, MATH*) to reduce; (*prix, dépenses*) to cut, reduce; (*carte*) to scale down, reduce; (*MÉD*: *fracture*)

to set; ~ **qn/qch à** to reduce sb/sth to; **se** ~ **à** (*revenir à*) to boil down to; **se** ~ **en** (*se transformer en*) to be reduced to; **en être réduit à** to be reduced to.

réduit, e [ʀedɥi, -it] *pp de* **réduire** ♦ *adj* (*prix, tarif, échelle*) reduced; (*mécanisme*) scaled-down; (*vitesse*) reduced ♦ *nm* tiny room; recess.

rééchelonner [ʀeeʃlɔne] *vt* to reschedule.

rééditer [ʀeedite] *vt* to republish.

réédition [ʀeedisjɔ̃] *nf* new edition.

rééducation [ʀeedykasjɔ̃] *nf* (*d'un membre*) re-education; (*de délinquants, d'un blessé*) rehabilitation; ~ **de la parole** speech therapy; **centre de** ~ physiotherapy *ou* physical therapy (*US*) centre.

rééduquer [ʀeedyke] *vt* to reeducate; to rehabilitate.

réel, le [ʀeɛl] *adj* real ♦ *nm*: **le** ~ reality.

réélection [ʀeelɛksjɔ̃] *nf* re-election.

rééligible [ʀeeliʒibl(ə)] *adj* re-eligible.

réélire [ʀeeliʀ] *vt* to re-elect.

réellement [ʀeɛlmɑ̃] *adv* really.

réembaucher [ʀeɑ̃boʃe] *vt* to take on again.

réemploi [ʀeɑ̃plwa] *nm* = **remploi**.

réemployer [ʀeɑ̃plwaje] *vt* (*méthode, produit*) to re-use; (*argent*) to reinvest; (*personnel, employé*) to re-employ.

rééquilibrer [ʀeekilibʀe] *vt* (*budget*) to balance (again).

réescompte [ʀeɛskɔ̃t] *nm* rediscount.

réessayer [ʀeeseje] *vt* to try on again.

réévaluation [ʀeevalɥasjɔ̃] *nf* revaluation.

réévaluer [ʀeevalɥe] *vt* to revalue.

réexaminer [ʀeɛgzamine] *vt* to re-examine.

réexpédier [ʀeɛkspedje] *vt* (*à l'envoyeur*) to return, send back; (*au destinataire*) to send on, forward.

réexporter [ʀeɛkspɔʀte] *vt* to re-export.

réf. *abr* (= *référence(s)*): **V/**~ Your ref.

refaire [ʀəfɛʀ] *vt* (*faire de nouveau, recommencer*) to do again; (*réparer, restaurer*) to do up; **se** ~ *vi* (*en argent*) to make up one's losses; **se** ~ **une santé** to recuperate; **se** ~ **à qch** (*se réhabituer à*) to get used to sth again.

refasse [ʀəfas] *etc vb voir* **refaire**.

réfection [ʀefɛksjɔ̃] *nf* repair; **en** ~ under repair.

réfectoire [ʀefɛktwaʀ] *nm* refectory.

referai [ʀ(ə)fʀe] *etc vb voir* **refaire**.

référé [ʀefeʀe] *nm* (*JUR*) emergency interim proceedings *ou* ruling.

référence [ʀefeʀɑ̃s] *nf* reference; ~**s** *nfpl* (*recommandations*) reference *sg*; **faire** ~ **à** to refer to; **ouvrage de** ~ reference work; **ce n'est pas une** ~ (*fig*) that's no recommendation.

référendum [ʀefeʀɑ̃dɔm] *nm* referendum.

référer [ʀefeʀe]: **se** ~ **à** *vt* to refer to; **en** ~ **à qn** to refer the matter to sb.

refermer [ʀəfɛʀme] *vt* to close again, shut again.

refiler [Rəfile] *vt* (*fam*): ~ **qch à qn** to palm (*BRIT*) *ou* fob sth off on sb; to pass sth on to sb.

refit [Rəfi] *etc vb voir* **refaire**.

réfléchi, e [Reflefi] *adj* (*caractère*) thoughtful; (*action*) well-thought-out; (*LING*) reflexive.

réfléchir [Reflefir] *vt* to reflect ♦ *vi* to think; ~ **à** *ou* **sur** to think about; **c'est tout réfléchi** my mind's made up.

réflecteur [Reflɛktœr] *nm* (*AUTO*) reflector.

reflet [Rəflɛ] *nm* reflection; (*sur l'eau etc*) sheen *no pl*, glint; ~**s** *nmpl* gleam *sg*.

refléter [Rəflete] *vt* to reflect; **se** ~ *vi* to be reflected.

réflex [Reflɛks] *adj inv* (*PHOTO*) reflex.

réflexe [Reflɛks(ə)] *adj*, *nm* reflex; ~ **conditionné** conditioned reflex.

réflexion [Reflɛksjɔ̃] *nf* (*de la lumière etc, pensée*) reflection; (*fait de penser*) thought; (*remarque*) remark; ~**s** *nfpl* (*méditations*) thought *sg*, reflection *sg*; **sans** ~ without thinking; ~ **faite, à la** ~, **après** ~ on reflection; **délai de** ~ cooling-off period; **groupe de** ~ think tank.

refluer [Rəflye] *vi* to flow back; (*foule*) to surge back.

reflux [Rəfly] *nm* (*de la mer*) ebb; (*fig*) backward surge.

refondre [Rəfɔ̃dR(ə)] *vt* (*texte*) to recast.

refont [R(ə)fɔ̃] *vb voir* **refaire**.

reformater [Rəfɔrmate] *vt* to reformat.

réformateur, trice [Reformatœr, -tris] *nm/f* reformer ♦ *adj* (*mesures*) reforming.

Réformation [Reformasjɔ̃] *nf*: **la** ~ the Reformation.

réforme [Reform(ə)] *nf* reform; (*MIL*) declaration of unfitness for service; discharge (*on health grounds*); (*REL*): **la R**~ the Reformation.

réformé, e [Reforme] *adj*, *nm/f* (*REL*) Protestant.

reformer [Rəfɔrme] *vt*, **se** ~ *vi* to reform; ~ **les rangs** (*MIL*) to fall in again.

réformer [Reforme] *vt* to reform; (*MIL: recrue*) to declare unfit for service; (*: soldat*) to discharge, invalid out; (*matériel*) to scrap.

réformisme [Reformism(ə)] *nm* reformism, policy of reform.

réformiste [Reformist(ə)] *adj*, *nm/f* (*POL*) reformist.

refoulé, e [Rəfule] *adj* (*PSYCH*) repressed.

refoulement [Rəfulmɑ̃] *nm* (*d'une armée*) driving back; (*PSYCH*) repression.

refouler [Rəfule] *vt* (*envahisseurs*) to drive back, repulse; (*liquide*) to force back; (*fig*) to suppress; (*PSYCH*) to repress.

réfractaire [Refraktɛr] *adj* (*minerai*) refractory; (*brique*) fire *cpd*; (*maladie*) which is resistant to treatment; (*prêtre*) non-juring; **soldat** ~ draft evader; **être** ~ **à** to resist.

réfracter [Refrakte] *vt* to refract.

réfraction [Refraksjɔ̃] *nf* refraction.

refrain [Rəfrɛ̃] *nm* (*MUS*) refrain, chorus; (*air, fig*) tune.

refréner, réfréner [Rəfrene, Refrene] *vt* to curb, check.

réfrigérant, e [Refriʒerɑ̃, -ɑ̃t] *adj* refrigerant, cooling.

réfrigérateur [Refriʒeratœr] *nm* refrigerator; ~**-congélateur** fridge-freezer.

réfrigération [Refriʒerɑsjɔ̃] *nf* refrigeration.

réfrigéré, e [Refriʒere] *adj* (*camion, wagon*) refrigerated.

réfrigérer [Refriʒere] *vt* to refrigerate; (*fam: glacer, aussi fig*) to cool.

refroidir [Rəfrwadir] *vt* to cool; (*fig*) to have a cooling effect on ♦ *vi* to cool (down); **se** ~ *vi* (*prendre froid*) to catch a chill; (*temps*) to get cooler *ou* colder; (*fig*) to cool (off).

refroidissement [Rəfrwadismɑ̃] *nm* cooling; (*grippe etc*) chill.

refuge [Rəfyʒ] *nm* refuge; (*pour piétons*) (traffic) island; **demander** ~ **à qn** to ask sb for refuge.

réfugié, e [Refyʒje] *adj*, *nm/f* refugee.

réfugier [Refyʒje]: **se** ~ *vi* to take refuge.

refus [Rəfy] *nm* refusal; **ce n'est pas de** ~ I won't say no, it's very welcome.

refuser [Rəfyze] *vt* to refuse; (*SCOL: candidat*) to fail ♦ *vi* to refuse; ~ **qch à qn/de faire** to refuse sb sth/to do; ~ **du monde** to have to turn people away; **se** ~ **à qch** *ou* **à faire qch** to refuse to do sth; **il ne se refuse rien** he doesn't stint himself; **se** ~ **à qn** to refuse sb.

réfutable [Refytabl(ə)] *adj* refutable.

réfuter [Refyte] *vt* to refute.

regagner [Rəgaɲe] *vt* (*argent, faveur*) to win back; (*lieu*) to get back to; ~ **le temps perdu** to make up (for) lost time; ~ **du terrain** to regain ground.

regain [Rəgɛ̃] *nm* (*herbe*) second crop of hay; (*renouveau*): **un** ~ **de** renewed + *nom*.

régal [Regal] *nm* treat; **un** ~ **pour les yeux** a pleasure *ou* delight to look at.

régalade [Regalad] *adv*: **à la** ~ from the bottle (held away from the lips).

régaler [Regale] *vt*: ~ **qn** to treat sb to a delicious meal; ~ **qn de** to treat sb to; **se** ~ *vi* to have a delicious meal; (*fig*) to enjoy o.s.

regard [Rəgar] *nm* (*coup d'œil*) look, glance; (*expression*) look (in one's eye); **parcourir/menacer du** ~ to cast an eye over/look at threateningly at; **au** ~ **de** (*loi, morale*) from the point of view of; **en** ~ (*vis à vis*) opposite; **en** ~ **de** in comparison with.

regardant, e [Rəgardɑ̃, -ɑ̃t] *adj*: **très/peu** ~ (**sur**) quite fussy/very free (about); (*économe*) very tight-fisted/quite generous (with).

regarder [Rəgarde] *vt* (*examiner, observer, lire*) to look at; (*film, télévision, match*) to watch; (*envisager: situation, avenir*) to view; (*considérer: son intérêt etc*) to be concerned with; (*être orienté vers*): ~ (**vers**) to face; (*concer-*

ner) to concern ♦ *vi* to look; ~ **à** *vt* (*dépense, qualité, détails*) to be fussy with *ou* over; ~ **à faire** to hesitate to do; **dépenser sans** ~ to spend freely; ~ **qn/qch comme** to regard sb/sth as; ~ **(qch) dans le dictionnaire/ l'annuaire** to look (sth up) in the dictionary/ directory; ~ **par la fenêtre** to look out of the window; **cela me regarde** it concerns me, it's my business.

régate(s) [ʀegat] *nf(pl)* regatta.

régénérer [ʀeʒeneʀe] *vt* to regenerate; (*fig*) to revive.

régent [ʀeʒɑ̃] *nm* regent.

régenter [ʀeʒɑ̃te] *vt* to rule over; to dictate to.

régie [ʀeʒi] *nf* (*COMM, INDUSTRIE*) state-owned company; (*THÉÂT, CINÉ*) production; (*RADIO, TV*) control room; **la ~ de l'État** state control.

regimber [ʀəʒɛ̃be] *vi* to balk, jib.

régime [ʀeʒim] *nm* (*POL, GÉO*) régime; (*ADMIN: carcéral, fiscal etc*) system; (*MÉD*) diet; (*TECH*) (engine) speed; (*fig*) rate, pace; (*de bananes, dattes*) bunch; **se mettre au/suivre un** ~ to go on/be on a diet; ~ **sans sel** salt-free diet; **à bas/haut** ~ (*AUTO*) at low/high revs; **à plein** ~ flat out, at full speed; ~ **matrimonial** marriage settlement.

régiment [ʀeʒimɑ̃] *nm* (*MIL: unité*) regiment; (*fig: fam*): **un** ~ **de** an army of; **un copain de** ~ a pal from military service *ou* (one's) army days.

région [ʀeʒjɔ̃] *nf* region; **la** ~ **parisienne** the Paris area.

régional, e, aux [ʀeʒjɔnal, -o] *adj* regional.

régionalisation [ʀeʒjɔnalizasjɔ̃] *nf* regionalization.

régionalisme [ʀeʒjɔnalism(ə)] *nm* regionalism.

régir [ʀeʒiʀ] *vt* to govern.

régisseur [ʀeʒisœʀ] *nm* (*d'un domaine*) steward; (*CINÉ, TV*) assistant director; (*THÉÂT*) stage manager.

registre [ʀəʒistʀ(ə)] *nm* (*livre*) register; logbook; ledger; (*MUS, LING*) register; (*d'orgue*) stop; ~ **de comptabilité** ledger; ~ **de l'état civil** register of births, marriages and deaths.

réglable [ʀeglabl(ə)] *adj* (*siège, flamme etc*) adjustable; (*achat*) payable.

réglage [ʀeglaʒ] *nm* (*d'une machine*) adjustment; (*d'un moteur*) tuning.

règle [ʀegl(ə)] *nf* (*instrument*) ruler; (*loi, prescription*) rule; ~**s** *nfpl* (*PHYSIOL*) period *sg*; **avoir pour** ~ **de** to make it a rule that *ou* to; **en** ~ (*papiers d'identité*) in order; **être/se mettre en** ~ to be/put o.s. straight with the authorities; **en** ~ **générale** as a (general) rule; **être la** ~ to be the rule; **être de** ~ to be usual; ~ **à calcul** slide rule; ~ **de trois** (*MATH*) rule of three.

réglé, e [ʀegle] *adj* well-ordered; stable, steady; (*papier*) ruled; (*arrangé*) settled; (*fem-*

me): **bien ~e** whose periods are regular.

règlement [ʀɛgləmɑ̃] *nm* settling; (*paiement*) settlement; (*arrêté*) regulation; (*règles, statuts*) regulations *pl*, rules *pl*; ~ **à la commande** cash with order; ~ **de compte(s)** settling of scores; ~ **en espèces/par chèque** payment in cash/by cheque; ~ **intérieur** (*SCOL*) school rules *pl*; (*ADMIN*) by-laws *pl*; ~ **judiciaire** compulsory liquidation.

réglementaire [ʀɛgləmɑ̃tɛʀ] *adj* conforming to the regulations; (*tenue, uniforme*) regulation *cpd*.

réglementation [ʀɛgləmɑ̃tasjɔ̃] *nf* regulation, control; (*règlements*) regulations *pl*.

réglementer [ʀɛgləmɑ̃te] *vt* to regulate, control.

régler [ʀegle] *vt* (*mécanisme, machine*) to regulate, adjust; (*moteur*) to tune; (*thermostat etc*) to set, adjust; (*emploi du temps etc*) to organize, plan; (*question, conflit, facture, dette*) to settle; (*fournisseur*) to settle up with, pay; (*papier*) to rule; ~ **qch sur** to model sth on; ~ **son compte à qn** to sort sb out, settle sb; ~ **un compte avec qn** to settle a score with sb.

réglisse [ʀeglis] *nf ou m* liquorice; **bâton de** ~ liquorice stick.

règne [ʀɛɲ] *nm* (*d'un roi etc, fig*) reign; (*BIO*): **le** ~ **végétal/animal** the vegetable/animal kingdom.

régner [ʀeɲe] *vi* (*roi*) to rule, reign; (*fig*) to reign.

regonfler [ʀ(ə)gɔ̃fle] *vt* (*ballon, pneu*) to reinflate, blow up again.

regorger [ʀəgɔʀʒe] *vi* to overflow; ~ **de** to overflow with, be bursting with.

régresser [ʀegʀese] *vi* (*phénomène*) to decline; (*enfant, malade*) to regress.

régressif, ive [ʀegʀesif, -iv] *adj* regressive.

régression [ʀegʀesjɔ̃] *nf* decline; regression; **être en** ~ to be on the decline.

regret [ʀəgʀɛ] *nm* regret; **à** ~ with regret; **avec** ~ regretfully; **être au** ~ **de devoir/ne pas pouvoir faire** to regret to have to/that one is unable to do; **j'ai le** ~ **de vous informer que ...** I regret to inform you that ....

regrettable [ʀəgʀɛtabl(ə)] *adj* regrettable.

regretter [ʀəgʀete] *vt* to regret; (*personne*) to miss; ~ **d'avoir fait** to regret doing; ~ **que** to regret that, be sorry that; **non, je regrette** no, I'm sorry.

regroupement [ʀ(ə)gʀupmɑ̃] *nm* grouping together; (*groupe*) group.

regrouper [ʀəgʀupe] *vt* (*grouper*) to group together; (*contenir*) to include, comprise; **se** ~ *vi* to gather (together).

régularisation [ʀegylaʀizasjɔ̃] *nf* (*de papiers, passeport*) putting in order; (*de sa situation: par le mariage*) regularization; (*d'un mécanisme*) regulation.

régulariser [ʀegylaʀize] *vt* (*fonctionnement, trafic*) to regulate; (*passeport, papiers*) to put in order; (*sa situation*) to straighten out, regularize.

régularité [ʀegylaʀite] *nf* regularity.

régulateur, trice [ʀegylatœʀ, -tʀis] *adj* regulating ♦ *nm* (*TECH*): ~ **de vitesse/de température** speed/temperature regulator.

régulation [ʀegylɑsjɔ̃] *nf* (*du trafic*) regulation; ~ **des naissances** birth control.

régulier, ière [ʀegylje, -jɛʀ] *adj* (*gén*) regular; (*vitesse, qualité*) steady; (*répartition, pression, paysage*) even; (*TRANSPORTS: ligne, service*) scheduled, regular; (*légal, réglementaire*) lawful, in order; (*fam: correct*) straight, on the level.

régulièrement [ʀegyljɛʀmɑ̃] *adv* regularly; steadily; evenly; normally.

régurgiter [ʀegyʀʒite] *vt* to regurgitate.

réhabiliter [ʀeabilite] *vt* to rehabilitate; (*fig*) to restore to favour (*BRIT*) *ou* favor (*US*).

réhabituer [ʀeabitɥe] *vt*: **se ~ à qch/à faire qch** to get used to sth again/to doing sth again.

rehausser [ʀəose] *vt* to heighten, raise; (*fig*) to set off, enhance.

réimporter [ʀeɛ̃pɔʀte] *vt* to reimport.

réimposer [ʀeɛ̃poze] *vt* (*FINANCE*) to reimpose; to tax again.

réimpression [ʀeɛ̃pʀesjɔ̃] *nf* reprinting; (*ouvrage*) reprint.

réimprimer [ʀeɛ̃pʀime] *vt* to reprint.

Reims [ʀɛ̃s] *n* Rheims.

rein [ʀɛ̃] *nm* kidney; ~**s** *nmpl* (*dos*) back *sg*; **avoir mal aux ~s** to have backache; ~ **artificiel** kidney machine.

réincarnation [ʀeɛ̃kaʀnɑsjɔ̃] *nf* reincarnation.

réincarner [ʀeɛ̃kaʀne]: **se ~** *vr* to be reincarnated.

reine [ʀɛn] *nf* queen.

reine-claude [ʀɛnklod] *nf* greengage.

reinette [ʀɛnɛt] *nf* rennet, pippin.

réinitialisation [ʀeinisjalizɑsjɔ̃] *nf* (*INFORM*) reset.

réinsérer [ʀeɛ̃seʀe] *vt* (*délinquant, handicapé etc*) to rehabilitate.

réinsertion [ʀeɛ̃sɛʀsjɔ̃] *nf* rehabilitation.

réintégrer [ʀeɛ̃tegʀe] *vt* (*lieu*) to return to; (*fonctionnaire*) to reinstate.

réitérer [ʀeiteʀe] *vt* to repeat, reiterate.

rejaillir [ʀəʒajiʀ] *vi* to splash up; ~ **sur** to splash up onto; (*fig*) to rebound on; to fall upon.

rejet [ʀəʒɛ] *nm* (*action, aussi MÉD*) rejection; (*POÉSIE*) enjambement, rejet; (*BOT*) shoot.

rejeter [ʀəʒte] *vt* (*relancer*) to throw back; (*vomir*) to bring *ou* throw up; (*écarter*) to reject; (*déverser*) to throw out, discharge; (*reporter*): ~ **un mot à la fin d'une phrase** to transpose a word to the end of a sentence; **se ~ sur qch** (*accepter faute de mieux*) to fall back on sth; ~ **la tête/les épaules en arrière** to throw one's head/pull one's shoulders back; ~ **la responsabilité de qch sur qn** to lay the responsibility for sth at sb's door.

rejeton [ʀəʒtɔ̃] *nm* offspring.

rejette [ʀ(ə)ʒɛt] *etc vb voir* **rejeter**.

rejoignais [ʀ(ə)ʒwaɲɛ] *etc vb voir* **rejoindre**.

rejoindre [ʀəʒwɛ̃dʀ(ə)] *vt* (*famille, régiment*) to rejoin, return to; (*lieu*) to get (back) to; (*suj: route etc*) to meet, join; (*rattraper*) to catch up (with); **se ~** *vi* to meet; **je te rejoins au café** I'll see *ou* meet you at the café.

réjoui, e [ʀeʒwi] *adj* joyous.

réjouir [ʀeʒwiʀ] *vt* to delight; **se ~** *vi* to be delighted; **se ~ de qch/de faire** to be delighted about sth/to do; **se ~ que** to be delighted that.

réjouissances [ʀeʒwisɑ̃s] *nfpl* (*joie*) rejoicing *sg*; (*fête*) festivities, merry-making *sg*.

réjouissant, e [ʀeʒwisɑ̃, -ɑ̃t] *adj* heartening, delightful.

relâche [ʀəlɑʃ]: **faire ~** *vi* (*navire*) to put into port; (*CINÉ*) to be closed; **c'est le jour de ~** (*CINÉ*) it's closed today; **sans ~** *adv* without respite *ou* a break.

relâché, e [ʀəlɑʃe] *adj* loose, lax.

relâchement [ʀəlɑʃmɑ̃] *nm* (*d'un prisonnier*) release; (*de la discipline, musculaire*) relaxation.

relâcher [ʀəlɑʃe] *vt* (*ressort, prisonnier*) to release; (*étreinte, cordes*) to loosen; (*discipline*) to relax ♦ *vi* (*NAVIG*) to put into port; **se ~** *vi* to loosen; (*discipline*) to become slack *ou* lax; (*élève etc*) to slacken off.

relais [ʀəlɛ] *nm* (*SPORT*): (**course de**) ~ relay (race); (*RADIO, TV*) relay; (*intermédiaire*) go-between; **équipe de ~** shift team; (*SPORT*) relay team; **prendre le ~ (de)** to take over (from); ~ **de poste** post house, coaching inn; ~ **routier** ≈ transport café (*BRIT*), ≈ truck stop (*US*).

relance [ʀəlɑ̃s] *nf* boosting, revival; (*ÉCON*) reflation.

relancer [ʀəlɑ̃se] *vt* (*balle*) to throw back (again); (*moteur*) to restart; (*fig*) to boost, revive; (*personne*): ~ **qn** to pester sb; to get on to sb again.

relater [ʀəlate] *vt* to relate, recount.

relatif, ive [ʀəlatif, -iv] *adj* relative.

relation [ʀəlɑsjɔ̃] *nf* (*récit*) account, report; (*rapport*) relation(ship); ~**s** *nfpl* (*rapports*) relations; relationship; (*connaissances*) connections; **être/entrer en ~(s) avec** to be in contact *ou* be dealing/get in contact with; **mettre qn en ~(s) avec** to put sb in touch with; ~**s internationales** international relations; ~**s publiques (RP)** public relations (PR); ~**s (sexuelles)** sexual relations, (sexual) intercourse *sg*.

relativement [ʀəlativmɑ̃] *adv* relatively; ~ **à** in relation to.

relativiser [ʀəlativize] *vt* to see in relation to; to put into context.

relativité [ʀəlativite] *nf* relativity.

relax [ʀəlaks] *adj inv*, **relaxe** [ʀəlaks(ə)] *adj* relaxed, informal, casual; easy-going;

(fauteuil-)~ *nm* reclining chair.
relaxant, e [Rəlaksɑ̃, -ɑ̃t] *adj* (*cure, médicament*) relaxant; (*ambiance*) relaxing.
relaxation [R(ə)laksɑsjɔ̃] *nf* relaxation.
relaxer [Rəlakse] *vt* to relax; (*JUR*) to discharge; **se** ~ *vi* to relax.
relayer [Rəleje] *vt* (*collaborateur, coureur etc*) to relieve, take over from; (*RADIO, TV*) to relay; **se** ~ (*dans une activité*) to take it in turns.
relecture [R(ə)lɛktyR] *nf* rereading.
relégation [Rəlegɑsjɔ̃] *nf* (*SPORT*) relegation.
reléguer [Rəlege] *vt* to relegate; ~ **au second plan** to push into the background.
relent(s) [Rəlɑ̃] *nm(pl)* stench *sg.*
relevé, e [Rəlve] *adj* (*bord de chapeau*) turned-up; (*manches*) rolled-up; (*fig: style*) elevated; (: *sauce*) highly-seasoned ♦ *nm* (*lecture*) reading; (*de cotes*) plotting; (*liste*) statement; list; (*facture*) account; ~ **de compte** bank statement; ~ **d'identité bancaire (RIB)** (bank) account number.
relève [Rəlɛv] *nf* relief; (*équipe*) relief team (*ou* troops *pl*); **prendre la** ~ to take over.
relèvement [Rəlɛvmɑ̃] *nm* (*d'un taux, niveau*) raising.
relever [Rəlve] *vt* (*statue, meuble*) to stand up again; (*personne tombée*) to help up; (*vitre, plafond, niveau de vie*) to raise; (*pays, économie, entreprise*) to put back on its feet; (*col*) to turn up; (*style, conversation*) to elevate; (*plat, sauce*) to season; (*sentinelle, équipe*) to relieve; (*souligner: fautes, points*) to pick out; (*constater: traces etc*) to find, pick up; (*répliquer à: remarque*) to react to, reply to; (: *défi*) to accept, take up; (*noter: adresse etc*) to take down, note; (: *plan*) to sketch; (: *cotes etc*) to plot; (*compteur*) to read; (*ramasser: cahiers, copies*) to collect, take in ♦ *vi* (*jupe, bord*) to ride up; ~ **de** *vt* (*maladie*) to be recovering from; (*être du ressort de*) to be a matter for; (*ADMIN: dépendre de*) to come under; (*fig*) to pertain to; **se** ~ *vi* (*se remettre debout*) to get up; (*fig*): **se** ~ **(de)** to recover (from); ~ **qn de** (*vœux*) to release sb from; (*fonctions*) to relieve sb of; ~ **la tête** to look up; to hold up one's head.
relief [Rəljɛf] *nm* relief; (*de pneu*) tread pattern; ~**s** *nmpl* (*restes*) remains; **en** ~ in relief; (*photographie*) three-dimensional; **mettre en** ~ (*fig*) to bring out, highlight.
relier [Rəlje] *vt* to link up; (*livre*) to bind; ~ **qch à** to link sth to; **livre relié cuir** leather-bound book.
relieur, euse [RəljœR, -øz] *nm/f* (book)binder.
religieusement [R(ə)liʒjøzmɑ̃] *adv* religiously; (*enterré, mariés*) in church; **vivre** ~ to lead a religious life.
religieux, euse [Rəliʒjø, -øz] *adj* religious ♦ *nm* monk ♦ *nf* nun; (*gâteau*) cream bun.
religion [Rəliʒjɔ̃] *nf* religion; (*piété, dévotion*) faith; **entrer en** ~ to take one's vows.
reliquaire [RəlikɛR] *nm* reliquary.

reliquat [Rəlika] *nm* (*d'une somme*) balance; (*JUR: de succession*) residue.
relique [Rəlik] *nf* relic.
relire [RəliR] *vt* (*à nouveau*) to reread, read again; (*vérifier*) to read over; **se** ~ to read through what one has written.
reliure [RəljyR] *nf* binding; (*art, métier*): **la** ~ book-binding.
reloger [R(ə)lɔʒe] *vt* (*locataires, sinistrés*) to rehouse.
relu, e [Rəly] *pp de* **relire**.
reluire [RəlyiR] *vi* to gleam.
reluisant, e [RəlyizÃ, -Ãt] *vb voir* **reluire** ♦ *adj* gleaming; **peu** ~ (*fig*) unattractive; unsavoury (*BRIT*), unsavory (*US*).
reluquer [R(ə)lyke] *vt* (*fam*) to eye (up), ogle.
remâcher [Rəmɑʃe] *vt* to chew *ou* ruminate over.
remailler [Rəmaje] *vt* (*tricot*) to darn; (*filet*) to mend.
remaniement [Rəmanimɑ̃] *nm*: ~ **ministériel** Cabinet reshuffle.
remanier [Rəmanje] *vt* to reshape, recast; (*POL*) to reshuffle.
remarier [R(ə)marje]: **se** ~ *vi* to remarry, get married again.
remarquable [RəmaRkabl(ə)] *adj* remarkable.
remarquablement [R(ə)maRkabləmɑ̃] *adv* remarkably.
remarque [RəmaRk(ə)] *nf* remark; (*écrite*) note.
remarquer [Rəmarke] *vt* (*voir*) to notice; (*dire*): ~ **que** to remark that; **se** ~ to be noticeable; **se faire** ~ to draw attention to o.s.; **faire** ~ (**à qn**) **que** to point out (to sb) that; **faire** ~ **qch (à qn)** to point sth out (to sb); **remarquez, ...** mark you, ..., mind you, ...
remballer [Rɑ̃bale] *vt* to wrap up (again); (*dans un carton*) to pack up (again).
rembarrer [Rɑ̃baRe] *vt*: ~ **qn** (*repousser*) to rebuff sb; (*remettre à sa place*) to put sb in his (*ou* her) place.
remblai [Rɑ̃blɛ] *nm* embankment.
remblayer [Rɑ̃bleje] *vt* to bank up; (*fossé*) to fill in.
rembobiner [Rɑ̃bɔbine] *vt* to rewind.
rembourrage [Rɑ̃buRaʒ] *nm* stuffing; padding.
rembourré, e [Rɑ̃buRe] *adj* padded.
rembourrer [Rɑ̃buRe] *vt* to stuff; (*dossier, vêtement, souliers*) to pad.
remboursable [Rɑ̃buRsabl(ə)] *adj* repayable.
remboursement [Rɑ̃buRsəmɑ̃] *nm* repayment; **envoi contre** ~ cash on delivery.
rembourser [Rɑ̃buRse] *vt* to pay back, repay.
rembrunir [Rɑ̃bRyniR]: **se** ~ *vi* to grow sombre (*BRIT*) *ou* somber (*US*).
remède [Rəmɛd] *nm* (*médicament*) medicine; (*traitement, fig*) remedy, cure; **trouver un** ~ **à** (*MÉD, fig*) to find a cure for.
remédier [Rəmedje]: ~ **à** *vt* to remedy.
remembrement [Rəmɑ̃bRəmɑ̃] *nm* (*AGR*) regrouping of lands.
remémorer [Rəmemɔre]: **se** ~ *vt* to recall,

recollect.

remerciements [RǝmɛRsimɑ̃] *nmpl* thanks; **(avec) tous mes ~** (with) grateful *ou* many thanks.

remercier [RǝmɛRsje] *vt* to thank; (*congédier*) to dismiss; **~ qn de/d'avoir fait** to thank sb for/for having done; **non, je vous remercie** no thank you.

remettre [RǝmɛtR(ǝ)] *vt* (*vêtement*): **~ qch** to put sth back on, put sth on again; (*replacer*): **~ qch quelque part** to put sth back somewhere; (*ajouter*): **~ du sel/un sucre** to add more salt/another lump of sugar; (*rétablir: personne*): **~ qn** to set sb back on his (*ou* her) feet; (*rendre, restituer*): **~ qch à qn** to give sth back to sb, return sth to sb; (*donner, confier: paquet, argent*): **~ qch à qn** to hand sth over to sb, deliver sth to sb; (*prix, décoration*): **~ qch à qn** to present sb with sth; (*ajourner*): **~ qch (à)** to postpone sth *ou* put sth off (until); **se ~** *vi* to get better, recover; **se ~ de** to recover from, get over; **s'en ~ à** to leave it (up) to; **se ~ à faire/qch** to start doing/sth again; **~ une pendule à l'heure** to put a clock right; **~ un moteur/une machine en marche** to get an engine/a machine going again; **~ en état/en ordre** to repair/sort out; **~ en cause/question** to challenge/question again; **~ sa démission** to hand in one's notice; **~ qch à neuf** to make sth as good as new; **~ qn à sa place** (*fig*) to put sb in his (*ou* her) place.

réminiscence [Reminisɑ̃s] *nf* reminiscence.

remis, e [Rǝmi, -iz] *pp de* **remettre** ♦ *nf* delivery; presentation; (*rabais*) discount; (*local*) shed; **~ en marche/en ordre** starting up again/sorting out; **~ en cause/question** calling into question/challenging; **~ de fonds** remittance; **~ en jeu** (*FOOTBALL*) throw-in; **~ à neuf** restoration; **~ de peine** remission of sentence.

remiser [Rǝmize] *vt* to put away.

rémission [Remisjɔ̃] *nf*: **sans ~** *adj* irremediable ♦ *adv* unremittingly.

remodeler [Rǝmɔdle] *vt* to remodel; (*fig: restructurer*) to restructure.

rémois, e [Remwa, -waz] *adj* of *ou* from Rheims ♦ *nm/f*: **R~, e** inhabitant *ou* native of Rheims.

remontant [Rǝmɔ̃tɑ̃] *nm* tonic, pick-me-up.

remontée [Rǝmɔ̃te] *nf* rising; ascent; **~s mécaniques** (*SKI*) ski lifts, ski tows.

remonte-pente [Rǝmɔ̃tpɑ̃t] *nm* ski lift, (ski) tow.

remonter [Rǝmɔ̃te] *vi* (*à nouveau*) to go back up; (*sur un cheval*) to remount; (*après une descente*) to go up (again); (*dans une voiture*) to get back in; (*jupe*) to ride up ♦ *vt* (*pente*) to go up; (*fleuve*) to sail (*ou* swim *etc*) up; (*manches, pantalon*) to roll up; (*col*) to turn up; (*niveau, limite*) to raise; (*fig: personne*) to buck up; (*moteur, meuble*) to put back to-

gether, reassemble; (*garde-robe etc*) to renew, replenish; (*montre, mécanisme*) to wind up; **~ le moral à qn** to raise sb's spirits; **~ à** (*dater de*) to date *ou* go back to; **~ en voiture** to get back into the car.

remontoir [Rǝmɔ̃twaR] *nm* winding mechanism, winder.

remontrance [Rǝmɔ̃tRɑ̃s] *nf* reproof, reprimand.

remontrer [Rǝmɔ̃tRe] *vt* (*montrer de nouveau*): **~ qch (à qn)** to show sth again (to sb); (*fig*): **en ~ à** to prove one's superiority over.

remords [RǝmɔR] *nm* remorse *no pl*; **avoir des ~** to feel remorse, be conscience-stricken.

remorque [RǝmɔRk(ǝ)] *nf* trailer; **prendre/être en ~** to tow/be on tow; **être à la ~** (*fig*) to tag along (behind).

remorquer [RǝmɔRke] *vt* to tow.

remorqueur [RǝmɔRkœR] *nm* tug(boat).

rémoulade [Remulad] *nf* dressing with mustard and herbs.

rémouleur [RemulœR] *nm* (knife- *ou* scissor-) grinder.

remous [Rǝmu] *nm* (*d'un navire*) (back)wash *no pl*; (*de rivière*) swirl, eddy ♦ *nmpl* (*fig*) stir *sg*.

rempailler [Rɑ̃pɑje] *vt* to reseat (*with straw*).

rempart [Rɑ̃paR] *nm* rampart; **faire à qn un ~ de son corps** to shield sb with one's (own) body.

rempiler [Rɑ̃pile] *vt* (*dossiers, livres etc*) to pile up again ♦ *vi* (*MIL: fam*) to join up again.

remplaçant, e [Rɑ̃plasɑ̃, -ɑ̃t] *nm/f* replacement, substitute, stand-in; (*THÉÂT*) understudy; (*SCOL*) supply (*BRIT*) *ou* substitute (*US*) teacher.

remplacement [Rɑ̃plasmɑ̃] *nm* replacement; (*job*) replacement work *no pl*; (*suppléance: SCOL*) supply (*BRIT*) *ou* substitute (*US*) teacher; **assurer le ~ de qn** (*suj: remplaçant*) to stand in *ou* substitute for sb; **faire des ~s** (*professeur*) to do supply *ou* substitute teaching; (*médecin*) to do locum work.

remplacer [Rɑ̃plase] *vt* to replace; (*prendre temporairement la place de*) to stand in for; (*tenir lieu de*) to take the place of, act as a substitute for; **~ qch/qn par** to replace sth/ sb with.

rempli, e [Rɑ̃pli] *adj* (*emploi du temps*) full, busy; **~ de** full of, filled with.

remplir [Rɑ̃pliR] *vt* to fill (up); (*questionnaire*) to fill out *ou* up; (*obligations, fonction, condition*) to fulfil; **se ~** *vi* to fill up; **~ qch de** to fill sth with.

remplissage [Rɑ̃plisaʒ] *nm* (*fig: péj*) padding.

remploi [Rɑ̃plwa] *nm* re-use.

rempocher [Rɑ̃pɔʃe] *vt* to put back into one's pocket.

remporter [Rɑ̃pɔRte] *vt* (*marchandise*) to take away; (*fig*) to win, achieve.

rempoter [Rɑ̃pɔte] *vt* to repot.

remuant, e [Rǝmɥɑ̃, -ɑ̃t] *adj* restless.

remue-ménage [Rǝmymenaʒ] *nm inv* commo-

tion.
remuer [ʀəmɥe] *vt* to move; (*café, sauce*) to stir ♦ *vi* to move; (*fig: opposants*) to show signs of unrest; **se ~** *vi* to move; (*se démener*) to stir o.s.; (*fam*) to get a move on.
rémunérateur, trice [ʀemyneʀatœʀ, -tʀis] *adj* remunerative, lucrative.
rémunération [ʀemyneʀasjɔ̃] *nf* remuneration.
rémunérer [ʀemyneʀe] *vt* to remunerate, pay.
renâcler [ʀənɑkle] *vi* to snort; (*fig*) to grumble, balk.
renaissance [ʀənɛsɑ̃s] *nf* rebirth, revival; **la R~** the Renaissance.
renaître [ʀənɛtʀ(ə)] *vi* to be revived; **~ à la vie** to take on a new lease of life; **~ à l'espoir** to find fresh hope.
rénal, e, aux [ʀenal, -o] *adj* renal, kidney *cpd*.
renard [ʀənaʀ] *nm* fox.
renardeau [ʀənaʀdo] *nm* fox cub.
rencard [ʀɑkaʀ] *nm* = **rancard**.
rencart [ʀɑkaʀ] *nm* = **rancart**.
renchérir [ʀɑ̃ʃeʀiʀ] *vi* to become more expensive; (*fig*): **~ (sur)** to add something (to).
renchérissement [ʀɑ̃ʃeʀismɑ̃] *nm* increase (in the cost *ou* price of).
rencontre [ʀɑ̃kɔ̃tʀ(ə)] *nf* (*de cours d'eau*) confluence; (*véhicules*) collision; (*entrevue, congrès, match etc*) meeting; (*imprévue*) encounter; **faire la ~ de qn** to meet sb; **aller à la ~ de qn** to go and meet sb; **amours de ~** casual love affairs.
rencontrer [ʀɑ̃kɔ̃tʀe] *vt* to meet; (*mot, expression*) to come across; (*difficultés*) to meet with; **se ~** to meet; (*véhicules*) to collide.
rendement [ʀɑ̃dmɑ̃] *nm* (*d'un travailleur, d'une machine*) output; (*d'une culture*) yield; (*d'un investissement*) return; **à plein ~** at full capacity.
rendez-vous [ʀɑ̃devu] *nm* (*rencontre*) appointment; (: *d'amoureux*) date; (*lieu*) meeting place; **donner ~ à qn** to arrange to meet sb; **recevoir sur ~** to have an appointment system; **fixer un ~ à qn** to give sb an appointment; **avoir/prendre ~ (avec)** to have/make an appointment (with); **prendre ~ chez le médecin** to make an appointment with the doctor; **~ spatial** *ou* **orbital** docking (in space).
rendormir [ʀɑ̃dɔʀmiʀ]: **se ~** *vr* to go back to sleep.
rendre [ʀɑ̃dʀ(ə)] *vt* (*livre, argent etc*) to give back, return; (*otages, politesse, JUR: verdict*) to return; (*honneurs*) to pay; (*sang, aliments*) to bring up; (*sons: suj: instrument*) to produce, make; (*exprimer, traduire*) to render; (*jugement*) to pronounce, render; (*faire devenir*): **~ qn célèbre/qch possible** to make sb famous/sth possible; **se ~** *vi* (*capituler*) to surrender, give o.s. up; (*aller*): **se ~ quelque part** to go somewhere; **se ~ à** (*arguments etc*) to bow to; (*ordres*) to comply with; **se ~**

compte de qch to realize sth; **~ la vue/la santé à qn** to restore sb's sight/health; **~ la liberté à qn** to set sb free; **~ la monnaie** to give change; **se ~ insupportable/malade** to become unbearable/make o.s. ill.
rendu, e [ʀɑ̃dy] *pp de* **rendre** ♦ *adj* (*fatigué*) exhausted.
renégat, e [ʀənega, -at] *nm/f* renegade.
renégocier [ʀənegɔsje] *vt* to renegociate.
rênes [ʀɛn] *nfpl* reins.
renfermé, e [ʀɑ̃fɛʀme] *adj* (*fig*) withdrawn ♦ *nm*: **sentir le ~** to smell stuffy.
renfermer [ʀɑ̃fɛʀme] *vt* to contain; **se ~ (sur soi-même)** to withdraw into o.s.
renfiler [ʀɑ̃file] *vt* (*collier*) to rethread; (*pull*) to slip on.
renflé, e [ʀɑ̃fle] *adj* bulging, bulbous.
renflement [ʀɑ̃fləmɑ̃] *nm* bulge.
renflouer [ʀɑ̃flue] *vt* to refloat; (*fig*) to set back on its (*ou* his/her *etc*) feet (again).
renfoncement [ʀɑ̃fɔ̃smɑ̃] *nm* recess.
renforcer [ʀɑ̃fɔʀse] *vt* to reinforce; **~ qn dans ses opinions** to confirm sb's opinion.
renfort [ʀɑ̃fɔʀ]: **~s** *nmpl* reinforcements; **en ~** as a back-up; **à grand ~ de** with a great deal of.
renfrogné, e [ʀɑ̃fʀɔɲe] *adj* sullen, scowling.
renfrogner [ʀɑ̃fʀɔɲe]: **se ~** *vi* to scowl.
rengager [ʀɑ̃gaʒe] *vt* (*personnel*) to take on again; **se ~** (*MIL*) to re-enlist.
rengaine [ʀɑ̃gɛn] *nf* (*péj*) old tune.
rengainer [ʀɑ̃gɛne] *vt* (*revolver*) to put back in its holster; (*épée*) to sheathe; (*fam: compliment, discours*) to save, withhold.
rengorger [ʀɑ̃gɔʀʒe]: **se ~** *vi* (*fig*) to puff o.s. up.
renier [ʀənje] *vt* (*parents*) to disown, repudiate; (*engagements*) to go back on; (*foi*) to renounce.
renifler [ʀənifle] *vi* to sniff ♦ *vt* (*tabac*) to sniff up; (*odeur*) to sniff.
rennais, e [ʀɛnɛ, -ɛz] *adj* of *ou* from Rennes ♦ *nm/f*: **R~, e** inhabitant *ou* native of Rennes.
renne [ʀɛn] *nm* reindeer *inv*.
renom [ʀənɔ̃] *nm* reputation; (*célébrité*) renown; **vin de grand ~** celebrated *ou* highly renowned wine.
renommé, e [ʀ(ə)nɔme] *adj* celebrated, renowned ♦ *nf* fame.
renoncement [ʀənɔ̃smɑ̃] *nm* abnegation, renunciation.
renoncer [ʀənɔ̃se] *vi*: **~ à** *vt* to give up; **~ à faire** to give up the idea of doing; **j'y renonce!** I give up!
renouer [ʀənwe] *vt* (*cravate etc*) to retie; (*fig: conversation, liaison*) to renew, resume; **~ avec** (*tradition*) to revive; (*habitude*) to take up again; **~ avec qn** to take up with sb again.
renouveau, x [ʀənuvo] *nm* revival; **~ de succès** renewed success.
renouvelable [ʀ(ə)nuvlabl(ə)] *adj* (*contrat, bail*)

renewable; (*expérience*) which can be renewed.

renouveler [ʀənuvle] *vt* to renew; (*exploit, méfait*) to repeat; **se** ~ *vi* (*incident*) to recur, happen again, be repeated; (*cellules etc*) to be renewed *ou* replaced; (*artiste, écrivain*) to try something new.

renouvellement [ʀ(ə)nuvɛlmɑ̃] *nm* renewal; recurrence.

rénovation [ʀenɔvɑsjɔ̃] *nf* renovation; restoration; reform(ing); redevelopment.

rénover [ʀenɔve] *vt* (*immeuble*) to renovate, do up; (*meuble*) to restore; (*enseignement*) to reform; (*quartier*) to redevelop.

renseignement [ʀɑ̃sɛɲmɑ̃] *nm* information *no pl*, piece of information; (*MIL*) intelligence *no pl*; **prendre des ~s sur** to make inquiries about, ask for information about; **(guichet des)** ~**s** information desk; **(service des)** ~**s** (*TÉL*) directory inquiries (*BRIT*), information (*US*); **service/agent de** ~**s** (*MIL*) intelligence service/agent; **les** ~**s généraux** ≈ the secret police.

renseigner [ʀɑ̃sɛɲe] *vt*: ~ **qn (sur)** to give information to sb (about); **se** ~ *vi* to ask for information, make inquiries.

rentabiliser [ʀɑ̃tabilize] *vt* (*capitaux, production*) to make profitable.

rentabilité [ʀɑ̃tabilite] *nf* profitability; cost-effectiveness; (*d'un investissement*) return; **seuil de** ~ break-even point.

rentable [ʀɑ̃tabl(ə)] *adj* profitable; cost-effective.

rente [ʀɑ̃t] *nf* income; (*pension*) pension; (*titre*) government stock *ou* bond; ~ **viagère** life annuity.

rentier, ière [ʀɑ̃tje, -jɛʀ] *nm/f* person of private *ou* independent means.

rentrée [ʀɑ̃tʀe] *nf*: ~ **(d'argent)** cash *no pl* coming in; **la** ~ **(des classes)** the start of the new school year; **la** ~ **(parlementaire)** the reopening *ou* reassembly of parliament; **faire sa** ~ (*artiste, acteur*) to make a comeback.

La rentrée (des classes) *in September each year is more than going back to school for children and teachers. It is also the time when political and social life begin again after the long summer break, and it thus marks an important point in the French year.*

---

rentrer [ʀɑ̃tʀe] *vi* (*entrer de nouveau*) to go (*ou* come) back in; (*entrer*) to go (*ou* come) in; (*revenir chez soi*) to go (*ou* come) (back) home; (*air, clou: pénétrer*) to go in; (*revenu, argent*) to come in ♦ *vt* (*foins*) to bring in; (*véhicule*) to put away; (*chemise dans pantalon etc*) to tuck in; (*griffes*) to draw in; (*train d'atterrissage*) to raise; (*fig: larmes, colère etc*) to hold back; ~ **le ventre** to pull in one's stomach; ~ **dans** to go (*ou* come) back into; to go (*ou* come) into; (*famille, patrie*) to go

back *ou* return to; (*heurter*) to crash into; (*appartenir à*) to be included in; (*: catégorie etc*) to fall into; ~ **dans l'ordre** to get back to normal; ~ **dans ses frais** to recover one's expenses (*ou* initial outlay).

renverrai [ʀɑ̃vʀe] *etc vb voir* **renvoyer.**

renversant, e [ʀɑ̃vɛʀsɑ̃, -ɑ̃t] *adj* amazing, astounding.

renverse [ʀɑ̃vɛʀs(ə)]: **à la** ~ *adv* backwards.

renversé, e [ʀɑ̃vɛʀse] *adj* (*écriture*) backhand; (*image*) reversed; (*stupéfait*) staggered.

renversement [ʀɑ̃vɛʀsəmɑ̃] *nm* (*d'un régime, des traditions*) overthrow; ~ **de la situation** reversal of the situation.

renverser [ʀɑ̃vɛʀse] *vt* (*faire tomber: chaise, verre*) to knock over, overturn; (*piéton*) to knock down; (*liquide, contenu*) to spill, upset; (*retourner: verre, image*) to turn upside down, invert; (*: ordre des mots etc*) to reverse; (*fig: gouvernement etc*) to overthrow; (*stupéfier*) to bowl over, stagger; **se** ~ *vi* to fall over; to overturn; to spill; **se** ~ **(en arrière)** to lean back; ~ **la tête/le corps (en arrière)** to tip one's head back/throw oneself back; ~ **la vapeur** (*fig*) to change course.

renvoi [ʀɑ̃vwa] *nm* dismissal; return; reflection; postponement; (*référence*) cross-reference; (*éructation*) belch.

renvoyer [ʀɑ̃vwaje] *vt* to send back; (*congédier*) to dismiss; (*TENNIS*) to return; (*lumière*) to reflect; (*son*) to echo; (*ajourner*): ~ **qch (à)** to put sth off *ou* postpone sth (until); ~ **qch à qn** (*rendre*) to return sth to sb; ~ **qn à** (*fig*) to refer sb to.

réorganisation [ʀeɔʀganizɑsjɔ̃] *nf* reorganization.

réorganiser [ʀeɔʀganize] *vt* to reorganize.

réorienter [ʀeɔʀjɑ̃te] *vt* to reorient(ate), redirect.

réouverture [ʀeuvɛʀtyʀ] *nf* reopening.

repaire [ʀəpɛʀ] *nm* den.

repaître [ʀəpɛtʀ(ə)] *vt* to feast; to feed; **se** ~ **de** *vt* (*animal*) to feed on; (*fig*) to wallow *ou* revel in.

répandre [ʀepɑ̃dʀ(ə)] *vt* (*renverser*) to spill; (*étaler, diffuser*) to spread; (*lumière*) to shed; (*chaleur, odeur*) to give off; **se** ~ *vi* to spill; to spread; **se** ~ **en** (*injures etc*) to pour out.

répandu, e [ʀepɑ̃dy] *pp de* **répandre** ♦ *adj* (*opinion, usage*) widespread.

réparable [ʀepaʀabl(ə)] *adj* (*montre etc*) repairable; (*perte etc*) which can be made up for.

reparaître [ʀəpaʀɛtʀ(ə)] *vi* to reappear.

réparateur, trice [ʀepaʀatœʀ, -tʀis] *nm/f* repairer.

réparation [ʀepaʀɑsjɔ̃] *nf* repairing *no pl*, repair; **en** ~ (*machine etc*) under repair; **demander à qn** ~ **de** (*offense etc*) to ask sb to make amends for.

réparer [ʀepaʀe] *vt* to repair; (*fig: offense*) to make up for, atone for; (*: oubli, erreur*) to put right.

reparler [ʁəpaʁle] vi: ~ **de** qn/qch to talk about sb/sth again; ~ **à** qn to speak to sb again.

repars [ʁəpaʁ] etc vb voir **repartir**.

repartie [ʁəpaʁti] nf retort; **avoir de la** ~ to be quick at repartee.

repartir [ʁəpaʁtiʁ] vi to set off again; to leave again; (fig) to get going again, pick up again; ~ **à zéro** to start from scratch (again).

répartir [ʁepaʁtiʁ] vt (pour attribuer) to share out; (pour disperser, disposer) to divide up; (poids, chaleur) to distribute; (étaler: dans le temps): ~ **sur** to spread over; (classer, diviser): ~ **en** to divide into, split up into; **se** ~ vt (travail, rôles) to share out between themselves.

répartition [ʁepaʁtisjɔ̃] nf sharing out; dividing up; distribution.

repas [ʁəpa] nm meal; **à l'heure des** ~ at mealtimes.

repassage [ʁəpasaʒ] nm ironing.

repasser [ʁəpase] vi to come (ou go) back ♦ vt (vêtement, tissu) to iron; (examen) to retake, resit; (film) to show again; (lame) to sharpen; (leçon, rôle: revoir) to go over (again); (plat, pain): ~ qch à qn to pass sth back to sb.

repasseuse [ʁəpasøz] nf (machine) ironing machine.

repayer [ʁəpeje] vt to pay again.

repêchage [ʁəpɛʃaʒ] nm (SCOL): **question de** ~ question to give candidates a second chance.

repêcher [ʁəpeʃe] vt (noyé) to recover the body of, fish out; (fam: candidat) to pass (by inflating marks); to give a second chance to.

repeindre [ʁəpɛ̃dʁ(ə)] vt to repaint.

repentir [ʁəpɑ̃tiʁ] nm repentance; **se** ~ vi: **se** ~ **(de)** to repent (of).

répercussions [ʁepɛʁkysjɔ̃] nfpl repercussions.

répercuter [ʁepɛʁkyte] vt (réfléchir, renvoyer: son, voix) to reflect; (faire transmettre: consignes, charges etc) to pass on; **se** ~ vi (bruit) to reverberate; (fig): **se** ~ **sur** to have repercussions on.

repère [ʁəpɛʁ] nm mark; (monument etc) landmark; **(point de)** ~ point of reference.

repérer [ʁəpeʁe] vt (erreur, connaissance) to spot; (abri, ennemi) to locate; **se** ~ vi to get one's bearings; **se faire** ~ to be spotted.

répertoire [ʁepɛʁtwaʁ] nm (liste) (alphabetical) list; (carnet) index notebook; (INFORM) directory; (de carnet) thumb index; (indicateur) directory, index; (d'un théâtre, artiste) repertoire.

répertorier [ʁepɛʁtɔʁje] vt to itemize, list.

répéter [ʁepete] vt to repeat; (préparer: leçon; aussi vi) to learn, go over; (THÉÂT) to rehearse; **se** ~ (redire) to repeat o.s.; (se reproduire) to be repeated, recur.

répéteur [ʁepetœʁ] nm (TÉL) repeater.

répétitif, ive [ʁepetitif, -iv] adj repetitive.

répétition [ʁepetisjɔ̃] nf repetition; (THÉÂT) rehearsal; **~s** nfpl (leçons) private coaching sg; **armes à** ~ repeater weapons; ~ **générale** final dress rehearsal.

repeupler [ʁəpœple] vt to repopulate; (forêt, rivière) to restock.

repiquage [ʁəpikaʒ] nm pricking out, planting out; re-recording.

repiquer [ʁəpike] vt (plants) to prick out, plant out; (enregistrement) to re-record.

répit [ʁepi] nm respite; **sans** ~ without letting up.

replacer [ʁəplase] vt to replace, put back.

replanter [ʁəplɑ̃te] vt to replant.

replat [ʁəpla] nm ledge.

replâtrer [ʁəplɑtʁe] vt (mur) to replaster; (fig) to patch up.

replet, ète [ʁəplɛ, -ɛt] adj chubby, fat.

repli [ʁəpli] nm (d'une étoffe) fold; (MIL, fig) withdrawal.

replier [ʁəplije] vt (rabattre) to fold down ou over; **se** ~ vi (troupes, armée) to withdraw, fall back; **se** ~ **sur soi-même** to withdraw into oneself.

réplique [ʁeplik] nf (repartie, fig) reply; (objection) retort; (THÉÂT) line; (copie) replica; **donner la** ~ **à** to play opposite; **sans** ~ adj no-nonsense; irrefutable.

répliquer [ʁeplike] vi to reply; (avec impertinence) to answer back; (riposter) to retaliate.

replonger [ʁəplɔ̃ʒe] vt: ~ qch **dans** to plunge sth back into; **se** ~ **dans** (journal etc) to immerse o.s. in again.

répondant, e [ʁepɔ̃dɑ̃, -ɑ̃t] nm/f (garant) guarantor, surety.

répondeur [ʁepɔ̃dœʁ] nm: ~ **(automatique)** (TÉL) (telephone) answering machine.

répondre [ʁepɔ̃dʁ(ə)] vi to answer, reply; (freins, mécanisme) to respond; ~ **à** vt to reply to, answer; (avec impertinence): ~ **à** qn to answer sb back; (invitation, convocation) to reply to; (affection, salut) to return; (provocation, suj: mécanisme etc) to respond to; (correspondre à: besoin) to answer; (: conditions) to meet; (: description) to match; ~ **que** to answer ou reply that; ~ **de** to answer for.

réponse [ʁepɔ̃s] nf answer, reply; **avec** ~ **payée** (POSTES) reply-paid, post-paid (US); **avoir** ~ **à tout** to have an answer for everything; **en** ~ **à** in reply to; **carte-/bulletin-**~ reply card/slip.

report [ʁəpɔʁ] nm postponement; transfer; ~ **d'incorporation** (MIL) deferment.

reportage [ʁəpɔʁtaʒ] nm (bref) report; (écrit: documentaire) story; article; (en direct) commentary; (genre, activité): **le** ~ reporting.

reporter nm [ʁəpɔʁtɛʁ] reporter ♦ vt [ʁəpɔʁte] (total): ~ qch **sur** to carry sth forward ou over to; (ajourner): ~ qch **(à)** to postpone sth (until); (transférer): ~ qch **sur** to transfer sth to; **se ~ à** (*époque*) to think back to; (*document*) to refer to.

repos [Rəpo] *nm* rest; (*fig*) peace (and quiet); (*mental*) peace of mind; (*MIL*): ~! (stand) at ease!; **en ~** at rest; **au ~** at rest; (*soldat*) at ease; **de tout ~** safe.

reposant, e [R(ə)pozɑ̃, -ɑ̃t] *adj* restful; (*sommeil*) refreshing.

repose [Rəpoz] *nf* refitting.

reposé, e [Rəpoze] *adj* fresh, rested; **à tête ~e** in a leisurely way, taking time to think.

repose-pied [Rəpozpje] *nm inv* footrest.

reposer [Rəpoze] *vt* (*verre, livre*) to put down; (*rideaux, carreaux*) to put back; (*délasser*) to rest; (*problème*) to reformulate ♦ *vi* (*liquide, pâte*) to settle, rest; (*personne*): **ici repose ...** here lies ...; **~ sur** to be built on; (*fig*) to rest on; **se ~** *vi* to rest; **se ~ sur qn** to rely on sb.

repoussant, e [Rəpusɑ̃, -ɑ̃t] *adj* repulsive.

repoussé, e [Rəpuse] *adj* (*cuir*) embossed (by hand).

repousser [Rəpuse] *vi* to grow again ♦ *vt* to repel, repulse; (*offre*) to turn down, reject; (*tiroir, personne*) to push back; (*différer*) to put back.

répréhensible [Repreɑ̃sibl(ə)] *adj* reprehensible.

reprendre [Rəprɑ̃dr(ə)] *vt* (*prisonnier, ville*) to recapture; (*objet prêté, donné*) to take back; (*chercher*): **je viendrai te ~ à 4 h** I'll come and fetch you *ou* I'll come back for you at 4; (*se resservir de*): **~ du pain/un œuf** to take (*ou* eat) more bread/another egg; (*COMM: article usagé*) to take back; to take in part exchange; (*firme, entreprise*) to take over; (*travail, promenade*) to resume; (*emprunter: argument, idée*) to take up, use; (*refaire: article etc*) to go over again; (*jupe etc*) to alter; (*émission, pièce*) to put on again; (*réprimander*) to tell off; (*corriger*) to correct ♦ *vi* (*classes, pluie*) to start (up) again; (*activités, travaux, combats*) to resume, start (up) again; (*affaires, industrie*) to pick up; (*dire*): **reprit-il** he went on; **se ~** (*se ressaisir*) to recover, pull o.s. together; **s'y ~** to make another attempt; **~ des forces** to recover one's strength; **~ courage** to take new heart; **~ ses habitudes/sa liberté** to get back into one's old habits/regain one's freedom; **~ la route** to resume one's journey, set off again; **~ connaissance** to come to, regain consciousness; **~ haleine** *ou* **son souffle** to get one's breath back; **~ la parole** to speak again.

repreneur [Rəprənœr] *nm* company fixer *ou* doctor.

reprenne [Rəprɛn] *etc vb voir* **reprendre**.

représailles [Rəprezaj] *nfpl* reprisals, retaliation *sg*.

représentant, e [Rəprezɑ̃tɑ̃, -ɑ̃t] *nm/f* representative.

représentatif, ive [Rəprezɑ̃tatif, -iv] *adj* representative.

représentation [Rəprezɑ̃tasjɔ̃] *nf* representation; performing; (*symbole, image*) representation; (*spectacle*) performance; (*COMM*): **la ~** commercial travelling; sales representation; **frais de ~** (*d'un diplomate*) entertainment allowance.

représenter [Rəprezɑ̃te] *vt* to represent; (*donner: pièce, opéra*) to perform; **se ~** *vt* (*se figurer*) to imagine; to visualize ♦ *vi*: **se ~ à** (*POL*) to stand *ou* run again at; (*SCOL*) to resit.

répressif, ive [Represif, -iv] *adj* repressive.

répression [Represjɔ̃] *nf* (*voir réprimer*) suppression; repression; (*POL*): **la ~** repression; **mesures de ~** repressive measures.

réprimande [Reprimɑ̃d] *nf* reprimand, rebuke.

réprimander [Reprimɑ̃de] *vt* to reprimand, rebuke.

réprimer [Reprime] *vt* (*émotions*) to suppress; (*peuple etc*) repress.

repris, e [Rəpri, -iz] *pp de* **reprendre** ♦ *nm*: **~ de justice** ex-prisoner, ex-convict.

reprise [Rəpriz] *nf* (*recommencement*) resumption; (*économique*) recovery; (*TV*) repeat; (*CINÉ*) rerun; (*BOXE etc*) round; (*AUTO*) acceleration *no pl*; (*COMM*) trade-in, part exchange; (*de location*) sum asked for any extras or improvements made to the property; (*raccommodage*) darn; mend; **la ~ des hostilités** the resumption of hostilities; **à plusieurs ~s** on several occasions, several times.

repriser [Rəprize] *vt* to darn; to mend; **aiguille/coton à ~** darning needle/thread.

réprobateur, trice [Reprobatœr, -tris] *adj* reproving.

réprobation [Reprobasjɔ̃] *nf* reprobation.

reproche [Rəprɔʃ] *nm* (*remontrance*) reproach; **ton/air de ~** reproachful tone/look; **faire des ~s à qn** to reproach sb; **faire ~ à qn de qch** to reproach sb for sth; **sans ~(s)** beyond *ou* above reproach.

reprocher [Rəprɔʃe] *vt*: **~ qch à qn** to reproach *ou* blame sb for sth; **~ qch à** (*machine, théorie*) to have sth against; **se ~ qch/d'avoir fait qch** to blame o.s. for sth/for doing sth.

reproducteur, trice [Rəprodyktœr, -tris] *adj* reproductive.

reproduction [Rəprodyksjɔ̃] *nf* reproduction; **~ interdite** all rights (of reproduction) reserved.

reproduire [Rəprodɥir] *vt* to reproduce; **se ~** *vi* (*BIO*) to reproduce; (*recommencer*) to recur, re-occur.

reprographie [Rəprɔgrafi] *nf* (photo)copying.

réprouvé, e [Repruve] *nm/f* reprobate.

réprouver [Repruve] *vt* to reprove.

reptation [Rɛptasjɔ̃] *nf* crawling.

reptile [Rɛptil] *nm* reptile.

repu, e [Rəpy] *pp de* **repaître** ♦ *adj* satisfied,

sated.

républicain, e [Repyblikɛ̃, -ɛn] *adj, nm/f* republican.

république [Repyblik] *nf* republic; **R~ arabe du Yémen** Yemen Arab Republic; **R~ Centrafricaine** Central African Republic; **R~ de Corée** South Korea; **R~ démocratique allemande (RDA)** German Democratic Republic (GDR); **R~ dominicaine** Dominican Republic; **R~ fédérale d'Allemagne (RFA)** Federal Republic of Germany (FRG); **R~ d'Irlande** Irish Republic, Eire; **R~ populaire de Chine** People's Republic of China; **R~ populaire démocratique de Corée** Democratic People's Republic of Korea; **R~ populaire du Yémen** People's Democratic Republic of Yemen.

répudier [Repydje] *vt* (*femme*) to repudiate; (*doctrine*) to renounce.

répugnance [Repyɲɑ̃s] *nf* repugnance, loathing; **avoir** *ou* **éprouver de la ~ pour** (*médicament, comportement, travail etc*) to have an aversion to; **avoir** *ou* **éprouver de la ~ à faire qch** to be reluctant to do sth.

répugnant, e [Repyɲɑ̃, -ɑ̃t] *adj* repulsive, loathsome.

répugner [Repyɲe]: **~ à** *vi*: **~ à qn** to repel *ou* disgust sb; **~ à faire** to be loath *ou* reluctant to do.

répulsion [Repylsjɔ̃] *nf* repulsion.

réputation [Repytɑsjɔ̃] *nf* reputation; **avoir la ~ d'être ...** to have a reputation for being ...; **connaître qn/qch de ~** to know sb/sth by repute; **de ~ mondiale** world-renowned.

réputé, e [Repyte] *adj* renowned; **être ~ pour** to have a reputation for, be renowned for.

requérir [RəkeRiR] *vt* (*nécessiter*) to require, call for; (*au nom de la loi*) to call upon; (*JUR: peine*) to call for, demand.

requête [Rəkɛt] *nf* request, petition; (*JUR*) petition.

requiem [Rekɥijɛm] *nm* requiem.

requiers [RəkjɛR] *etc vb voir* **requérir.**

requin [Rəkɛ̃] *nm* shark.

requinquer [Rəkɛ̃ke] *vt* to set up, pep up.

requis, e [Rəki, -iz] *pp de* **requérir** ♦ *adj* required.

réquisition [Rekizisjɔ̃] *nf* requisition.

réquisitionner [Rekizisjɔne] *vt* to requisition.

réquisitoire [RekizitwaR] *nm* (*JUR*) closing speech for the prosecution; (*fig*): **~ contre** indictment of.

RER *sigle m* (= *Réseau express régional*) Greater Paris high speed train service.

rescapé, e [Rɛskape] *nm/f* survivor.

rescousse [Rɛskus] *nf*: **aller à la ~ de qn** to go to sb's aid *ou* rescue; **appeler qn à la ~** to call on sb for help.

réseau, x [Rezo] *nm* network.

réséda [Rezeda] *nm* (*BOT*) reseda, mignonette.

réservation [RezɛRvɑsjɔ̃] *nf* reservation; booking.

réserve [RezɛRv(ə)] *nf* (*retenue*) reserve; (*entrepôt*) storeroom; (*restriction, aussi: d'Indiens*) reservation; (*de pêche, chasse*) preserve; (*restrictions*): **faire des ~s** to have reservations; **officier de ~** reserve officer; **sous toutes ~s** with all reserve; (*dire*) with reservations; **sous ~ de** subject to; **sans ~** *adv* unreservedly; **en ~** in reserve; **de ~** (*provisions etc*) in reserve.

réservé, e [RezɛRve] *adj* (*discret*) reserved; (*chasse, pêche*) private; **~ à** *ou* **pour** reserved for.

réserver [RezɛRve] *vt* (*gén*) to reserve; (*chambre, billet etc*) to book, reserve; (*mettre de côté, garder*): **~ qch pour** *ou* **à** to keep *ou* save sth for; **~ qch à qn** to reserve (*ou* book) sth for sb; (*fig: destiner*) to have sth in store for sb; **se ~ le droit de faire** to reserve the right to do.

réserviste [RezɛRvist(ə)] *nm* reservist.

réservoir [RezɛRvwaR] *nm* tank.

résidence [Rezidɑ̃s] *nf* residence; **~ principale/secondaire** main/second home; **~ universitaire** hall of residence; **(en) ~ surveillée** (under) house arrest.

résident, e [Rezidɑ̃, -ɑ̃t] *nm/f* (*ressortissant*) foreign resident; (*d'un immeuble*) resident ♦ *adj* (*INFORM*) resident.

résidentiel, le [Rezidɑ̃sjɛl] *adj* residential.

résider [Rezide] *vi*: **~ à** *ou* **dans** *ou* **en** to reside in; **~ dans** (*fig*) to lie in.

résidu [Rezidy] *nm* residue *no pl*.

résiduel, le [Rezidɥɛl] *adj* residual.

résignation [Reziɲɑsjɔ̃] *nf* resignation.

résigné, e [Reziɲe] *adj* resigned.

résigner [Reziɲe] *vt* to relinquish, resign; **se ~** *vi*: **se ~ (à qch/à faire)** to resign o.s. (to sth/to doing).

résiliable [Reziljabl(ə)] *adj* which can be terminated.

résilier [Rezilje] *vt* to terminate.

résille [Rezij] *nf* (hair)net.

résine [Rezin] *nf* resin.

résiné, e [Rezine] *adj*: **vin ~** retsina.

résineux, euse [Rezinø, -øz] *adj* resinous ♦ *nm* coniferous tree.

résistance [Rezistɑ̃s] *nf* resistance; (*de réchaud, bouilloire: fil*) element.

résistant, e [Rezistɑ̃, -ɑ̃t] *adj* (*personne*) robust, tough; (*matériau*) strong, hard-wearing ♦ *nm/f* (*patriote*) Resistance worker *ou* fighter.

résister [Reziste] *vi* to resist; **~ à** *vt* (*assaut, tentation*) to resist; (*effort, souffrance*) to withstand; (*suj: matériau, plante*) to stand up to, withstand; (*personne: désobéir à*) to stand up to, oppose.

résolu, e [Rezɔly] *pp de* **résoudre** ♦ *adj* (*ferme*) resolute; **être ~ à qch/faire** to be set upon sth/doing.

résolument [Rezɔlymɑ̃] *adv* resolutely, steadfastly; **~ contre qch** firmly against sth.

résolution [Rezɔlysjɔ̃] *nf* solving; (*fermeté, décision,* INFORM) resolution; **prendre la ~ de** to make a resolution to.

résolvais [Rezɔlvɛ] *etc vb voir* **résoudre**.

résonance [Rezɔnɑ̃s] *nf* resonance.

résonner [Rezɔne] *vi* (*cloche, pas*) to reverberate, resound; (*salle*) to be resonant; **~ de** to resound with.

résorber [RezɔRbe]: **se ~** *vi* (MÉD) to be resorbed; (*fig*) to be absorbed.

résoudre [RezudR(ə)] *vt* to solve; **~ qn à faire qch** to get sb to make up his (*ou* her) mind to do sth; **~ de faire** to resolve to do; **se ~ à faire** to bring o.s. to do.

respect [Rɛspɛ] *nm* respect; **tenir en ~** to keep at bay.

respectabilité [Rɛspɛktabilite] *nf* respectability.

respectable [Rɛspɛktabl(ə)] *adj* respectable.

respecter [Rɛspɛkte] *vt* to respect; **faire ~** to enforce; **le lexicographe qui se respecte** (*fig*) any self-respecting lexicographer.

respectif, ive [Rɛspɛktif, -iv] *adj* respective.

respectivement [Rɛspɛktivmɑ̃] *adv* respectively.

respectueusement [Rɛspɛktɥøzmɑ̃] *adv* respectfully.

respectueux, euse [Rɛspɛktɥø, -øz] *adj* respectful; **~ de** respectful of.

respirable [RɛspiRabl(ə)] *adj*: **peu ~** unbreathable.

respiration [RɛspiRasjɔ̃] *nf* breathing *no pl*; **faire une ~ complète** to breathe in and out; **retenir sa ~** to hold one's breath; **~ artificielle** artificial respiration.

respiratoire [RɛspiRatwaR] *adj* respiratory.

respirer [RɛspiRe] *vi* to breathe; (*fig: se reposer*) to get one's breath, have a break; (: *être soulagé*) to breathe again ♦ *vt* to breathe (in), inhale; (*manifester: santé, calme etc*) to exude.

resplendir [Rɛsplɑ̃diR] *vi* to shine; (*fig*): **~ (de)** to be radiant (with).

resplendissant, e [Rɛsplɑ̃disɑ̃, -ɑ̃t] *adj* radiant.

responsabilité [Rɛspɔ̃sabilite] *nf* responsibility; (*légale*) liability; **refuser la ~ de** to deny responsibility (*ou* liability) for; **prendre ses ~s** to assume responsibility for one's actions; **~ civile** civil liability; **~ pénale/morale/collective** criminal/moral/collective responsibility.

responsable [Rɛspɔ̃sabl(ə)] *adj* responsible ♦ *nm/f* (*du ravitaillement etc*) person in charge; (*de parti, syndicat*) official; **~ de** responsible for; (*légalement: de dégâts etc*) liable for; (*chargé de*) in charge of, responsible for.

resquiller [Rɛskije] *vi* (*au cinéma, au stade*) to get in on the sly; (*dans le train*) to fiddle a free ride.

resquilleur, euse [RɛskijœR, -øz] *nm/f* (*qui n'est pas invité*) gatecrasher; (*qui ne paie pas*) fare dodger.

ressac [Rəsak] *nm* backwash.

ressaisir [RəseziR]: **se ~** *vi* to regain one's self-control; (*équipe sportive*) to rally.

ressasser [Rəsase] *vt* (*remâcher*) to keep turning over; (*redire*) to keep trotting out.

ressemblance [Rəsɑ̃blɑ̃s] *nf* (*visuelle*) resemblance, similarity, likeness; (: ART) likeness; (*analogie, trait commun*) similarity.

ressemblant, e [Rəsɑ̃blɑ̃, -ɑ̃t] *adj* (*portrait*) lifelike, true to life.

ressembler [Rəsɑ̃ble]: **~ à** *vt* to be like, resemble; (*visuellement*) to look like; **se ~** to be (*ou* look) alike.

ressemeler [Rəsəmle] *vt* to (re)sole.

ressens [R(ə)sɑ̃] *etc vb voir* **ressentir**.

ressentiment [Rəsɑ̃timɑ̃] *nm* resentment.

ressentir [Rəsɑ̃tiR] *vt* to feel; **se ~ de** to feel (*ou* show) the effects of.

resserre [RəseR] *nf* shed.

resserrement [R(ə)seRmɑ̃] *nm* narrowing; strengthening; (*goulet*) narrow part.

resserrer [Rəsere] *vt* (*pores*) to close; (*nœud, boulon*) to tighten (up); (*fig: liens*) to strengthen; **se ~** *vi* (*route, vallée*) to narrow; (*liens*) to strengthen; **se ~ (autour de)** to draw closer (around); to close in (on).

ressers [R(ə)seR] *etc vb voir* **resservir**.

resservir [RəseRviR] *vi* to do *ou* serve again ♦ *vt*: **~ qch (à qn)** to serve sth up again (to sb); **~ qch (à qn)** to give (sb) a second helping of sth; **~ qn (d'un plat)** to give sb a second helping (of a dish); **se ~ de** (*plat*) to take a second helping of; (*outil etc*) to use again.

ressort [RəsɔR] *vb voir* **ressortir** ♦ *nm* (*pièce*) spring; (*force morale*) spirit; (*recours*): **en dernier ~** as a last resort; (*compétence*): **être du ~ de** to fall within the competence of.

ressortir [RəsɔRtiR] *vi* to go (*ou* come) out (again); (*contraster*) to stand out; **~ de** (*résulter de*): **il ressort de ceci que** it emerges from this that; **~ à** (JUR) to come under the jurisdiction of; (ADMIN) to be the concern of; **faire ~** (*fig: souligner*) to bring out.

ressortissant, e [RəsɔRtisɑ̃, -ɑ̃t] *nm/f* national.

ressouder [Rəsude] *vt* to solder together again.

ressource [RəsuRs(ə)] *nf*: **avoir la ~ de** to have the possibility of; **~s** *nfpl* resources; (*fig*) possibilities; **leur seule ~ était de** the only course open to them was to; **~s d'énergie** energy resources.

ressusciter [Resysite] *vt* to resuscitate, restore to life; (*fig*) to revive, bring back ♦ *vi* to rise (from the dead); (*fig: pays*) to come back to life.

restant, e [Rɛstɑ̃, -ɑ̃t] *adj* remaining ♦ *nm*: **le ~ (de)** the remainder (of); **un ~ de** (*de trop*) some leftover; (*fig: vestige*) a remnant *ou* last trace of.

restaurant [RɛstɔRɑ̃] *nm* restaurant; **manger au ~** to eat out; **~ d'entreprise** staff canteen *ou* cafeteria *(US)*; ~ **universitaire (RU)** university refectory *ou* cafeteria *(US)*.

restaurateur, trice [ʀɛstɔʀatœʀ, -tʀis] *nm/f* restaurant owner, restaurateur; *(de tableaux)* restorer.

restauration [ʀɛstɔʀasjɔ̃] *nf* restoration; *(hôtellerie)* catering; ~ **rapide** fast food.

restaurer [ʀɛstɔʀe] *vt* to restore; **se ~** *vi* to have something to eat.

restauroute [ʀɛstɔʀut] *nm* = **restoroute**.

reste [ʀɛst(ə)] *nm (restant)*: **le ~ (de)** the rest (of); *(de trop)*: **un ~ (de)** some leftover; *(vestige)*: **un ~ de** a remnant *ou* last trace of; *(MATH)* remainder; **~s** *nmpl* leftovers; *(d'une cité etc, dépouille mortelle)* remains; **avoir du temps de ~** to have time to spare; **ne voulant pas être en ~** not wishing to be outdone; **partir sans attendre** *ou* **demander son ~** *(fig)* to leave without waiting to hear more; **du ~, au ~** *adv* besides, moreover; **pour le reste, quant au ~** *adv* as for the rest.

rester [ʀɛste] *vi (dans un lieu, un état, une position)* to stay, remain; *(subsister)* to remain, be left; *(durer)* to last, live on ♦ *vb impers*: **il reste du pain/2 œufs** there's some bread/ there are 2 eggs left (over); **il reste du temps/10 minutes** there's some time/there are 10 minutes left; **il me reste assez de temps** I have enough time left; **voilà tout ce qui (me) reste** that's all I've got left; **ce qui reste à faire** what remains to be done; **ce qui me reste à faire** what remains for me to do; **(il) reste à savoir/établir si ...** it remains to be seen/established if *ou* whether ...; **il n'en reste pas moins que ...** the fact remains that ..., it's nevertheless a fact that ...; **en ~ à** *(stade, menaces)* to go no further than, only go as far as; **restons-en là** let's leave it at that; ~ **sur une impression** to retain an impression; **y ~**: **il a failli y ~** he nearly met his end.

restituer [ʀɛstitɥe] *vt (objet, somme)*: ~ **qch (à qn)** to return *ou* restore sth (to sb); *(énergie)* to release; *(son)* to reproduce.

restitution [ʀɛstitysjɔ̃] *nf* restoration.

restoroute [ʀɛstɔʀut] *nm* motorway *(BRIT)* ou highway *(US)* restaurant.

restreindre [ʀɛstʀɛ̃dʀ(ə)] *vt* to restrict, limit; **se ~** *(dans ses dépenses etc)* to cut down; *(champ de recherches)* to narrow.

restreint, e [ʀɛstʀɛ̃, -ɛ̃t] *pp de* **restreindre** ♦ *adj* restricted, limited.

restrictif, ive [ʀɛstʀiktif, -iv] *adj* restrictive, limiting.

restriction [ʀɛstʀiksjɔ̃] *nf* restriction; *(condition)* qualification; **~s** *nfpl (mentales)* reservations; **sans ~** *adv* unreservedly.

restructuration [ʀəstʀyktyʀasjɔ̃] *nf* restructuring.

restructurer [ʀəstʀyktyʀe] *vt* to restructure.

résultante [ʀezyltɑ̃t] *nf (conséquence)* result, consequence.

résultat [ʀezylta] *nm* result; *(conséquence)* outcome *no pl*, result; *(d'élection etc)* results *pl*; **~s** *nmpl (d'une enquête)* findings; **~s sportifs** sports results.

résulter [ʀezylte]: ~ **de** *vt* to result from, be the result of; **il résulte de ceci que ...** the result of this is that ....

résumé [ʀezyme] *nm* summary, résumé; **faire le ~ de** to summarize; **en ~** *adv* in brief; *(pour conclure)* to sum up.

résumer [ʀezyme] *vt (texte)* to summarize; *(récapituler)* to sum up; *(fig)* to epitomize, typify; **se ~** *vi (personne)* to sum up (one's ideas); **se ~ à** to come down to.

resurgir [ʀəsyʀʒiʀ] *vi* to reappear, re-emerge.

résurrection [ʀezyʀɛksjɔ̃] *nf* resurrection; *(fig)* revival.

rétablir [ʀetabliʀ] *vt* to restore, re-establish; *(personne: suj: traitement)*: ~ **qn** to restore sb to health, help sb recover; *(ADMIN)*: ~ **qn dans son emploi/ses droits** to reinstate sb in his post/restore sb's rights; **se ~** *vi (guérir)* to recover; *(silence, calme)* to return, be restored; *(GYM etc)*: **se ~ (sur)** to pull o.s. up (onto).

rétablissement [ʀetablismɑ̃] *nm* restoring; recovery; pull-up.

rétamer [ʀetame] *vt* to re-coat, re-tin.

rétameur [ʀetamœʀ] *nm* tinker.

retaper [ʀətape] *vt (maison, voiture etc)* to do up; *(fam: revigorer)* to buck up; *(redactylographier)* to retype.

retard [ʀətaʀ] *nm (d'une personne attendue)* lateness *no pl*; *(sur l'horaire, un programme, une échéance)* delay; *(fig: scolaire, mental etc)* backwardness; **être ~ (de)** *(pays)* to be backward; *(dans paiement, travail)* to be behind; **en ~ (de 2 heures)** (2 hours) late; **avoir un ~ de 2 km** *(SPORT)* to be 2 km behind; **rattraper son ~** to catch up; **avoir du ~** to be late; *(sur un programme)* to be behind (schedule); **prendre du ~** *(train, avion)* to be delayed; *(montre)* to lose (time); **sans ~** *adv* without delay; ~ **à l'allumage** *(AUTO)* retarded spark; ~ **scolaire** backwardness at school.

retardataire [ʀətaʀdatɛʀ] *adj* late; *(enfant, idées)* backward ♦ *nm/f* latecomer; backward child.

retardé, e [ʀətaʀde] *adj* backward.

retardement [ʀətaʀdəmɑ̃]: **à ~** *adj* delayed action *cpd*; **bombe à ~** time bomb.

retarder [ʀətaʀde] *vt (sur un horaire)*: ~ **qn (d'une heure)** to delay sb (an hour); *(sur un programme)*: ~ **qn (de 3 mois)** to set sb back *ou* delay sb (3 months); *(départ, date)*: ~ **qch (de 2 jours)** to put sth back (2 days), delay sth (for *ou* by 2 days); *(horloge)* to put back ♦ *vi (montre)* to be slow; *(: habituellement)* to lose (time); **je retarde (d'une heure)** I'm (an hour) slow.

retendre [ʀətɑ̃dʀ(ə)] *vt (câble etc)* to stretch again; *(MUS: cordes)* to retighten.

retenir [ʀətniʀ] *vt* (*garder, retarder*) to keep, detain; (*maintenir: objet qui glisse, fig: colère, larmes, rire*) to hold back; (: *objet suspendu*) to hold; (: *chaleur, odeur*) to retain; (*fig: empêcher d'agir*): ~ **qn (de faire)** to hold sb back (from doing); (*se rappeler*) to retain; (*réserver*) to reserve; (*accepter*) to accept; (*prélever*): ~ **qch (sur)** to deduct sth (from); **se** ~ (*euphémisme*) to hold on; (*se raccrocher*): **se** ~ **à** to hold onto; (*se contenir*): **se** ~ **de faire** to restrain o.s. from doing; ~ **son souffle** *ou* **haleine** to hold one's breath; ~ **qn à dîner** to ask sb to stay for dinner; **je pose 3 et je retiens 2** put down 3 and carry 2.

rétention [ʀetɑ̃sjɔ̃] *nf*: ~ **d'urine** urine retention.

retentir [ʀətɑ̃tiʀ] *vi* to ring out; (*salle*): ~ **de** to ring *ou* resound with; ~ **sur** *vt* (*fig*) to have an effect upon.

retentissant, e [ʀətɑ̃tisɑ̃, -ɑ̃t] *adj* resounding; (*fig*) impact-making.

retentissement [ʀətɑ̃tismɑ̃] *nm* (*retombées*) repercussions *pl*; effect, impact.

retenu, e [ʀətny] *pp de* **retenir** ♦ *adj* (*place*) reserved; (*personne: empêché*) held up; (*propos: contenu, discret*) restrained ♦ *nf* (*prélèvement*) deduction; (*MATH*) number to carry over; (*SCOL*) detention; (*modération*) (self-)restraint; (*réserve*) reserve, reticence; (*AUTO*) tailback.

réticence [ʀetisɑ̃s] *nf* reticence *no pl*, reluctance *no pl*; **sans** ~ without hesitation.

réticent, e [ʀetisɑ̃, -ɑ̃t] *adj* reticent, reluctant.

retiendrai [ʀətjɛ̃dʀe], **retiens** [ʀətjɛ̃] *etc vb voir* **retenir**.

rétif, ive [ʀetif, -iv] *adj* restive.

rétine [ʀetin] *nf* retina.

retint [ʀətɛ̃] *etc vb voir* **retenir**.

retiré, e [ʀətiʀe] *adj* (*solitaire*) secluded; (*éloigné*) remote.

retirer [ʀətiʀe] *vt* to withdraw; (*vêtement, lunettes*) to take off, remove; (*enlever*): ~ **qch à qn** to take sth from sb; (*extraire*): ~ **qn/qch de** to take sb away from/sth out of, remove sb/sth from; (*reprendre: bagages, billets*) to collect, pick up; ~ **des avantages de** to derive advantages from; **se** ~ *vi* (*partir, reculer*) to withdraw; (*prendre sa retraite*) to retire; **se** ~ **de** to withdraw from; to retire from.

retombées [ʀətɔ̃be] *nfpl* (*radioactives*) fallout *sg*; (*fig*) fallout; spin-offs.

retomber [ʀətɔ̃be] *vi* (*à nouveau*) to fall again; (*rechuter*): ~ **malade/dans l'erreur** to fall ill again/fall back into error; (*atterrir: après un saut etc*) to land; (*tomber, redescendre*) to fall back; (*pendre*) to fall, hang (down); (*échoir*): ~ **sur qn** to fall on sb.

retordre [ʀətɔʀdʀ(ə)] *vt*: **donner du fil à** ~ **à qn** to make life difficult for sb.

rétorquer [ʀetɔʀke] *vt*: ~ **(à qn) que** to retort (to sb) that.

retors, e [ʀətɔʀ, -ɔʀs(ə)] *adj* wily.

rétorsion [ʀetɔʀsjɔ̃] *nf*: **mesures de** ~ reprisals.

retouche [ʀətuʃ] *nf* touching up *no pl*; alteration; **faire une** ~ *ou* **des** ~**s à** to touch up.

retoucher [ʀətuʃe] *vt* (*photographie, tableau*) to touch up; (*texte, vêtement*) to alter.

retour [ʀətuʀ] *nm* return; **au** ~ (*en arrivant*) when we (*ou* they *etc*) get (*ou* got) back; (*en route*) on the way back; **pendant le** ~ on the way *ou* journey back; **à mon/ton** ~ on my/your return; **au** ~ **de** on the return of; **être de** ~ **(de)** to be back (from); **de** ~ **à .../chez moi** back at .../back home; **en** ~ *adv* in return; **par** ~ **du courrier** by return of post; **par un juste** ~ **des choses** by a favourable twist of fate; **match** ~ return match; ~ **en arrière** (*CINÉ*) flashback; (*mesure*) backward step; ~ **de bâton** kickback; ~ **de chariot** carriage return; ~ **à l'envoyeur** (*POSTES*) return to sender; ~ **de flamme** backfire; ~ **(automatique) à la ligne** (*INFORM*) wordwrap; ~ **de manivelle** (*fig*) backfire; ~ **offensif** renewed attack; ~ **aux sources** (*fig*) return to basics.

retournement [ʀətuʀnəmɑ̃] *nm* (*d'une personne: revirement*) turning (round); ~ **de la situation** reversal of the situation.

retourner [ʀətuʀne] *vt* (*dans l'autre sens: matelas, crêpe*) to turn (over); (: *caisse*) to turn upside down; (: *sac, vêtement*) to turn inside out; (*fig: argument*) to turn back; (*en remuant: terre, sol, foin*) to turn over; (*émouvoir: personne*) to shake; (*renvoyer, restituer*): ~ **qch à qn** to return sth to sb ♦ *vi* (*aller, revenir*): ~ **quelque part/à** to go back *ou* return somewhere/to; ~ **à** (*état, activité*) to return to, go back to; **se** ~ *vi* to turn over; (*tourner la tête*) to turn round; **s'en** ~ to go back; **se** ~ **contre** (*fig*) to turn against; **savoir de quoi il retourne** to know what it is all about; ~ **sa veste** (*fig*) to turn one's coat; ~ **en arrière** *ou* **sur ses pas** to turn back, retrace one's steps; ~ **aux sources** to go back to basics.

retracer [ʀətʀase] *vt* to relate, recount.

rétracter [ʀetʀakte] *vt*, **se** ~ *vi* to retract.

retraduire [ʀətʀadɥiʀ] *vt* to translate again; (*dans la langue de départ*) to translate back.

retrait [ʀətʀɛ] *nm* (*voir retirer*) withdrawal; collection; (*voir se retirer*) withdrawal; (*rétrécissement*) shrinkage; **en** ~ *adj* set back; **écrire en** ~ to indent; ~ **du permis (de conduire)** disqualification from driving (*BRIT*), revocation of driver's license (*US*).

retraite [ʀətʀɛt] *nf* (*d'une armée, REL, refuge*) retreat; (*d'un employé*) retirement; (*revenu*) (retirement) pension; **être/mettre à la** ~ to be retired/pension off *ou* retire; **prendre sa** ~ to retire; ~ **anticipée** early retirement; ~ **aux flambeaux** torchlight tattoo.

retraité, e [ʀətʀete] *adj* retired ♦ *nm/f* (old age) pensioner.

retraitement [ʀətʀɛtmɑ̃] *nm* reprocessing.

retraiter [ʀətʀɛte] vt to reprocess.

retranchement [ʀətʀɑ̃ʃmɑ̃] nm entrenchment; **poursuivre qn dans ses derniers ~s** to drive sb into a corner.

retrancher [ʀətʀɑ̃ʃe] vt (passage, détails) to take out, remove; (nombre, somme): **~ qch de** to take ou deduct sth from; (couper) to cut off; **se ~ derrière/dans** to entrench o.s. behind/in; (fig) to take refuge behind/in.

retranscrire [ʀətʀɑ̃skʀiʀ] vt to retranscribe.

retransmettre [ʀətʀɑ̃smɛtʀ(ə)] vt (RADIO) to broadcast, relay; (TV) to show.

retransmission [ʀətʀɑ̃smisjɔ̃] nf broadcast; showing.

retravailler [ʀətʀavaje] vi to start work again ♦ vt to work on again.

retraverser [ʀətʀavɛʀse] vt (dans l'autre sens) to cross back over.

rétréci, e [ʀetʀesi] adj (idées, esprit) narrow.

rétrécir [ʀetʀesiʀ] vt (vêtement) to take in ♦ vi to shrink; **se ~** vi to narrow.

rétrécissement [ʀetʀesismɑ̃] nm narrowing.

retremper [ʀətʀɑ̃pe] vt: **se ~ dans** (fig) to re-immerse o.s. in.

rétribuer [ʀetʀibɥe] vt (travail) to pay for; (personne) to pay.

rétribution [ʀetʀibysjɔ̃] nf payment.

rétro [ʀetʀo] adj inv old-style ♦ nm (= rétroviseur) (rear-view) mirror; **la mode ~** the nostalgia vogue.

rétroactif, ive [ʀetʀoaktif, -iv] adj retroactive.

rétrocéder [ʀetʀosede] vt to retrocede.

rétrocession [ʀetʀosesjɔ̃] nf retrocession.

rétrofusée [ʀetʀofyze] nf retrorocket.

rétrograde [ʀetʀogʀad] adj reactionary, backward-looking.

rétrograder [ʀetʀogʀade] vi (élève) to fall back; (économie) to regress; (AUTO) to change down.

rétroprojecteur [ʀetʀopʀoʒɛktœʀ] nm overhead projector.

rétrospectif, ive [ʀetʀospɛktif, -iv] adj, nf retrospective.

rétrospectivement [ʀetʀospɛktivmɑ̃] adv in retrospect.

retroussé, e [ʀətʀuse] adj: **nez ~** turned-up nose.

retrousser [ʀətʀuse] vt to roll up; (fig: nez) to wrinkle; (: lèvres) to curl up.

retrouvailles [ʀətʀuvaj] nfpl reunion sg.

retrouver [ʀətʀuve] vt (fugitif, objet perdu) to find; (occasion) to find again; (calme, santé) to regain; (reconnaître: expression, style) to recognize; (revoir) to see again; (rejoindre) to meet (again), join; **se ~** vi to meet; (s'orienter) to find one's way; **se ~ quelque part** to find o.s. somewhere; to end up somewhere; **se ~ seul/sans argent** to find o.s. alone/with no money; **se ~ dans** (calculs, dossiers, désordre) to make sense of; **s'y ~** (rentrer dans ses frais) to break even.

rétroviseur [ʀetʀovizœʀ] nm (rear-view) mirror.

réunifier [ʀeynifje] vt to reunify.

Réunion [ʀeynjɔ̃] nf: **la ~, l'île de la ~** Réunion.

réunion [ʀeynjɔ̃] nf bringing together; joining; (séance) meeting.

réunionnais, e [ʀeynjonɛ, -ɛz] adj of ou from Réunion.

réunir [ʀeyniʀ] vt (convoquer) to call together; (rassembler) to gather together; (cumuler) to combine; (rapprocher) to bring together (again), reunite; (rattacher) to join (together); **se ~** vi (se rencontrer) to meet; (s'allier) to unite.

réussi, e [ʀeysi] adj successful.

réussir [ʀeysiʀ] vi to succeed, be successful; (à un examen) to pass; (plante, culture) to thrive, do well ♦ vt to make a success of; to bring off; **~ à faire** to succeed in doing; **~ à qn** to go right for sb; (aliment) to agree with sb; **le travail/le mariage lui réussit** work/married life agrees with him.

réussite [ʀeysit] nf success; (CARTES) patience.

réutiliser [ʀeytilize] vt to re-use.

revaloir [ʀəvalwaʀ] vt: **je vous revaudrai cela** I'll repay you some day; (en mal) I'll pay you back for this.

revalorisation [ʀəvaloʀizasjɔ̃] nf revaluation; raising.

revaloriser [ʀəvaloʀize] vt (monnaie) to revalue; (salaires, pensions) to raise the level of; (institution, tradition) to reassert the value of.

revanche [ʀəvɑ̃ʃ] nf revenge; **prendre sa ~ (sur)** to take one's revenge (on); **en ~** (par contre) on the other hand; (en compensation) in return.

rêvasser [ʀɛvase] vi to daydream.

rêve [ʀɛv] nm dream; (activité psychique): **le ~** dreaming; **paysage/silence de ~** dreamlike landscape/silence; **~ éveillé** daydreaming no pl, daydream.

rêvé, e [ʀeve] adj (endroit, mari etc) ideal.

revêche [ʀəvɛʃ] adj surly, sour-tempered.

réveil [ʀevɛj] nm (d'un dormeur) waking up no pl; (fig) awakening; (pendule) alarm (clock); **au ~** when I (ou you etc) wake (ou woke) up, on waking (up); **sonner le ~** (MIL) to sound the reveille.

réveille-matin [ʀevɛjmatɛ̃] nm inv alarm clock.

réveiller [ʀeveje] vt (personne) to wake up; (fig) to awaken, revive; **se ~** vi to wake up; (fig) to be revived, reawaken.

réveillon [ʀevɛjɔ̃] nm Christmas Eve; (de la Saint-Sylvestre) New Year's Eve; Christmas Eve (ou New Year's Eve) party ou dinner.

réveillonner [ʀevɛjone] vi to celebrate Christmas Eve (ou New Year's Eve).

révélateur, trice [ʀevelatœʀ, -tʀis] adj: **~ (de qch)** revealing (sth) ♦ nm (PHOTO) developer.

révélation [ʀevelasjɔ̃] nf revelation.

révéler [Revele] *vt* (*gén*) to reveal; (*divulguer*) to disclose, reveal; (*dénoter*) to reveal, show; (*faire connaître au public*): ~ **qn/qch** to make sb/sth widely known, bring sb/sth to the public's notice; **se** ~ *vi* to be revealed, reveal itself ♦ *vb avec attribut*: **se** ~ **facile/faux** to prove (to be) easy/false; **se** ~ **cruel/un allié sûr** to show o.s. to be cruel/a trustworthy ally.

revenant, e [Rəvɑ̃nɑ̃, -ɑ̃t] *nm/f* ghost.

revendeur, euse [Rəvɑ̃dœR, -øz] *nm/f* (*détaillant*) retailer; (*d'occasions*) secondhand dealer.

revendicatif, ive [Rəvɑ̃dikatif, -iv] *adj* (*mouvement*) of protest.

revendication [Rəvɑ̃dikasjɔ̃] *nf* claim, demand; **journée de** ~ day of action (in support of one's claims).

revendiquer [Rəvɑ̃dike] *vt* to claim, demand; (*responsabilité*) to claim ♦ *vi* to agitate in favour of one's claims.

revendre [Rəvɑ̃dR(ə)] *vt* (*d'occasion*) to resell; (*détailler*) to sell; (*vendre davantage de*): ~ **du sucre/un foulard/deux bagues** to sell more sugar/another scarf/another two rings; **à** ~ *adv* (*en abondance*) to spare.

revenir [RəvniR] *vi* to come back; (*CULIN*): **faire** ~ to brown; (*coûter*): ~ **cher/à 100 F (à qn)** to cost (sb) a lot/100 F; ~ **à** (*études, projet*) to return to, go back to; (*équivaloir à*) to amount to; ~ **à qn** (*rumeur, nouvelle*) to get back to sb, reach sb's ears; (*part, honneur*) to go to sb, be sb's; (*souvenir, nom*) to come back to sb; ~ **de** (*fig: maladie, étonnement*) to recover from; ~ **sur** (*question, sujet*) to go back over; (*engagement*) to go back on; ~ **à la charge** to return to the attack; ~ **à soi** to come round; **n'en pas** ~: **je n'en reviens pas** I can't get over it; ~ **sur ses pas** to retrace one's steps; **cela revient à dire que/au même** it amounts to saying that/to the same thing; ~ **de loin** (*fig*) to have been at death's door.

revente [Rəvɑ̃t] *nf* resale.

revenu, e [Rəvny] *pp de* **revenir** ♦ *nm* income; (*de l'État*) revenue; (*d'un capital*) yield; ~**s** *nmpl* income *sg*; ~ **national brut** gross national income.

rêver [Reve] *vi, vt* to dream; (*rêvasser*) to (day)dream; ~ **de** (*voir en rêve*) to dream of *ou* about; ~ **de qch/de faire** to dream of sth/of doing; ~ **à** to dream of.

réverbération [RevERberɑsjɔ̃] *nf* reflection.

réverbère [RevERbɛR] *nm* street lamp *ou* light.

réverbérer [RevERbere] *vt* to reflect.

reverdir [RəvERdiR] *vi* (*arbre etc*) to turn green again.

révérence [Reverɑ̃s] *nf* (*vénération*) reverence; (*salut: d'homme*) bow; (*: de femme*) curtsey.

révérencieux, euse [Reverɑ̃sjø, -øz] *adj* reverent.

révérend, e [Reverɑ̃, -ɑ̃d] *adj*: **le** ~ **père Pascal** the Reverend Father Pascal.

révérer [Revere] *vt* to revere.

rêverie [RevRi] *nf* daydreaming *no pl*, daydream.

reverrai [RəvERe] *etc vb voir* **revoir**.

revers [RəvɛR] *nm* (*de feuille, main*) back; (*d'étoffe*) wrong side; (*de pièce, médaille*) back, reverse; (*TENNIS, PING-PONG*) backhand; (*de veston*) lapel; (*de pantalon*) turn-up; (*fig: échec*) setback; ~ **de fortune** reverse of fortune; **d'un** ~ **de main** with the back of one's hand; **le** ~ **de la médaille** (*fig*) the other side of the coin; **prendre à** ~ (*MIL*) to take from the rear.

reverser [RəvERse] *vt* (*reporter: somme etc*): ~ **sur** to put back into; (*liquide*): ~ **(dans)** to pour some more (into).

réversible [RevERsibl(ə)] *adj* reversible.

revêtement [Rəvɛtmɑ̃] *nm* (*de paroi*) facing; (*des sols*) flooring; (*de chaussée*) surface; (*de tuyau etc: enduit*) coating.

revêtir [RəvetiR] *vt* (*habit*) to don, put on; (*fig*) to take on; ~ **qn de** to dress sb in; (*fig*) to endow *ou* invest sb with; ~ **qch de** to cover sth with; (*fig*) to cloak sth in; ~ **d'un visa** to append a visa to.

rêveur, euse [RevœR, -øz] *adj* dreamy ♦ *nm/f* dreamer.

reviendrai [Rəvjɛ̃dRe] *etc vb voir* **revenir**.

revienne [Rəvjɛn] *etc vb voir* **revenir**.

revient [Rəvjɛ̃] *vb voir* **revenir** ♦ *nm*: **prix de** ~ cost price.

revigorer [RəvigɔRe] *vt* to invigorate, revive, buck up.

revint [Rəvɛ̃] *etc vb voir* **revenir**.

revirement [RəviRmɑ̃] *nm* change of mind; (*d'une situation*) reversal.

revis [Rəvi] *etc vb voir* **revoir**.

révisable [Revizabl(ə)] *adj* (*procès, taux etc*) reviewable, subject to review.

réviser [Revize] *vt* (*texte, SCOL: matière*) to revise; (*comptes*) to audit; (*machine, installation, moteur*) to overhaul, service; (*JUR: procès*) to review.

révision [Revizjɔ̃] *nf* revision; auditing *no pl*; overhaul, servicing *no pl*; review; **conseil de** ~ (*MIL*) recruiting board; **faire ses** ~**s** (*SCOL*) to do one's revision (*BRIT*), revise (*BRIT*), review (*US*); **la** ~ **des 10 000 km** (*AUTO*) the 10,000 km service.

révisionnisme [Revizjɔnism(ə)] *nm* revisionism.

revisser [Rəvise] *vt* to screw back again.

revit [Rəvi] *vb voir* **revoir**.

revitaliser [Rəvitalize] *vt* to revitalize.

revivifier [Rəvivifje] *vt* to revitalize.

revivre [RəvivR(ə)] *vi* (*reprendre des forces*) to come alive again; (*traditions*) to be revived ♦ *vt* (*épreuve, moment*) to relive; **faire** ~ (*mode, institution, usage*) to bring back to life.

révocable [Revɔkabl(ə)] *adj* (*délégué*) dismissible; (*contrat*) revocable.

révocation [Revɔkɑsjɔ̃] *nf* dismissal; revocation.

revoir [Rəvwar] *vt* to see again; (*réviser*) to revise (*BRIT*), review (*US*) ♦ *nm*: **au ~ goodbye**; **dire au ~ à qn** to say goodbye to sb; **se ~** (*amis*) to meet (again), see each other again.

révoltant, e [Revɔltɑ̃, -ɑ̃t] *adj* revolting.

révolte [Revɔlt(ə)] *nf* rebellion, revolt.

révolter [Revɔlte] *vt* to revolt, outrage; **se ~** *vi*: **se ~ (contre)** to rebel (against); **se ~ (à)** to be outraged (by).

révolu, e [Revɔly] *adj* past; (*ADMIN*): **âgé de 18 ans ~s** over 18 years of age; **après 3 ans ~s** when 3 full years have passed.

révolution [Revɔlysjɔ̃] *nf* revolution; **être en ~** (*pays etc*) to be in revolt; **la ~ industrielle** the industrial revolution.

révolutionnaire [RevɔlysjɔnɛR] *adj, nm/f* revolutionary.

révolutionner [Revɔlysjɔne] *vt* to revolutionize; (*fig*) to stir up.

revolver [RevɔlvɛR] *nm* gun; (*à barillet*) revolver.

révoquer [Revɔke] *vt* (*fonctionnaire*) to dismiss, remove from office; (*arrêt, contrat*) to revoke.

revoyais [Rəvwaje] *etc vb voir* **revoir**.

revu, e [Rəvy] *pp de* **revoir** ♦ *nf* (*inventaire, examen*) review; (*MIL*: *défilé*) review, march past; (*: inspection*) inspection, review; (*périodique*) review, magazine; (*pièce satirique*) revue; (*de music-hall*) variety show; **passer en ~** to review, inspect; (*fig*) to review; **~ de (la) presse** press review.

révulsé, e [Revylse] *adj* (*yeux*) rolled upwards; (*visage*) contorted.

Reykjavik [Rekjavik] *n* Reykjavik.

rez-de-chaussée [Redʃose] *nm inv* ground floor.

rez-de-jardin [RedʒaRdɛ̃] *nm inv* garden level.

RF *sigle f* = *République française*.

RFA *sigle f* (= *République fédérale d'Allemagne*) FRG.

RFO *sigle f* (= *Radio-Télévision Française d'Outre-mer*) French overseas broadcasting service.

RG *sigle mpl* (= *renseignements généraux*) security section of the police force.

rhabiller [Rabije] *vt*: **se ~** to get dressed again, put one's clothes on again.

rhapsodie [Rapsɔdi] *nf* rhapsody.

rhénan, e [Renɑ̃, -an] *adj* Rhine *cpd*, of the Rhine.

Rhénanie [Renani] *nf*: **la ~** the Rhineland.

rhéostat [Reɔsta] *nm* rheostat.

rhésus [Rezys] *adj, nm* rhesus; **~ positif/ négatif** rhesus positive/negative.

rhétorique [RetɔRik] *nf* rhetoric ♦ *adj* rhetorical.

rhéto-roman, e [RetɔRɔmɑ̃, -an] *adj* Rhaeto-Romanic.

Rhin [Rɛ̃] *nm*: **le ~** the Rhine.

rhinite [Rinit] *nf* rhinitis.

rhinocéros [RinɔseRɔs] *nm* rhinoceros.

rhinopharyngite [RinɔfaRɛ̃ʒit] *nf* throat infection.

rhodanien, ne [Rɔdanjɛ̃, -ɛn] *adj* Rhône *cpd*, of the Rhône.

Rhodes [Rɔd] *n*: **(l'île de) ~** (the island of) Rhodes.

Rhodésie [Rɔdezi] *nf*: **la ~** Rhodesia.

rhodésien, ne [Rɔdezjɛ̃, -ɛn] *adj* Rhodesian.

rhododendron [Rɔdɔdɛ̃dRɔ̃] *nm* rhododendron.

Rhône [Ron] *nm*: **le ~** the Rhone.

rhubarbe [RybaRb(ə)] *nf* rhubarb.

rhum [Rɔm] *nm* rum.

rhumatisant, e [Rymatizɑ̃, -ɑ̃t] *adj, nm/f* rheumatic.

rhumatismal, e, aux [Rymatismal, -o] *adj* rheumatic.

rhumatisme [Rymatism(ə)] *nm* rheumatism *no pl*.

rhumatologie [Rymatɔlɔʒi] *nf* rheumatology.

rhumatologue [Rymatɔlɔg] *nm/f* rheumatologist.

rhume [Rym] *nm* cold; **~ de cerveau** head cold; **le ~ des foins** hay fever.

rhumerie [RɔmRi] *nf* (*distillerie*) rum distillery.

RI *sigle m* (*MIL*) = *régiment d'infanterie* ♦ *sigle mpl* (= *Républicains indépendants*) *political party*.

ri [Ri] *pp de* **rire**.

riant, e [Rjɑ̃, -ɑ̃t] *vb voir* **rire** ♦ *adj* smiling, cheerful; (*campagne, paysage*) pleasant.

RIB *sigle m* = **relevé d'identité bancaire**.

ribambelle [Ribɑ̃bɛl] *nf*: **une ~ de** a herd *ou* swarm of.

ricain, e [Rikɛ̃, -ɛn] *adj* (*fam*) Yank, Yankee.

ricanement [Rikanmɑ̃] *nm* snigger; giggle.

ricaner [Rikane] *vi* (*avec méchanceté*) to snigger; (*bêtement, avec gêne*) to giggle.

riche [Riʃ] *adj* (*gén*) rich; (*personne, pays*) rich, wealthy; **~ en** rich in; **~ de** full of; rich in.

richement [Riʃmɑ̃] *adv* richly.

richesse [Riʃɛs] *nf* wealth; (*fig*) richness; **~s** *nfpl* wealth *sg*; treasures; **~ en vitamines** high vitamin content.

richissime [Riʃisim] *adj* extremely rich *ou* wealthy.

ricin [Risɛ̃] *nm*: **huile de ~** castor oil.

ricocher [Rikɔʃe] *vi*: **~ (sur)** to rebound (off); (*sur l'eau*) to bounce (on *ou* off); **faire ~** (*galet*) to skim.

ricochet [Rikɔʃɛ] *nm* rebound; bounce; **faire ~** to rebound, bounce; (*fig*) to rebound; **faire des ~s** to skip stones; **par ~** *adv* on the rebound; (*fig*) as an indirect result.

rictus [Riktys] *nm* grin; (*snarling*) grimace.

ride [Rid] *nf* wrinkle; (*fig*) ripple.

ridé, e [Ride] *adj* wrinkled.

rideau, x [Rido] *nm* curtain; **tirer/ouvrir les ~x** to draw/open the curtains; **~ de fer** metal shutter; (*POL*): **le ~ de fer** the Iron Curtain.

ridelle [Ridɛl] *nf* slatted side (*of truck*).

rider [Ride] *vt* to wrinkle; (*fig*) to ripple, ruffle

the surface of; **se** ~ *vi* to become wrinkled.
ridicule [Ridikyl] *adj* ridiculous ♦ *nm* ridiculousness *no pl*; **le** ~ ridicule; (*travers: gén pl*) absurdities *pl*; **tourner en** ~ to ridicule.
ridiculement [Ridikylmã] *adv* ridiculously.
ridiculiser [Ridikylize] *vt* to ridicule; **se** ~ to make a fool of o.s.
ridule [Ridyl] *nf* (*euph: ride*) little wrinkle.
rie [Ri] *etc vb voir* **rire**.

=== *MOT-CLÉ*

rien [Rjɛ̃] *pron* **1**: **(ne)** ... ~ nothing; *tournure negative* + anything; **qu'est-ce que vous avez?** - ~ what have you got? — nothing; **il n'a** ~ **dit/fait** he said/did nothing; he hasn't said/done anything; **il n'a** ~ (*n'est pas blessé*) he's all right; **ça ne fait** ~ it doesn't matter; **il n'y est pour** ~ he's got nothing to do with it
2 (*quelque chose*): **a-t-il jamais** ~ **fait pour nous?** has he ever done anything for us?
3: ~ **de**: ~ **d'intéressant** nothing interesting; ~ **d'autre** nothing else; ~ **du tout** nothing at all; **il n'a** ~ **d'un champion** he's no champion, there's nothing of the champion about him
4: ~ **que** just, only; nothing but; ~ **que pour lui faire plaisir** only *ou* just to please him; ~ **que la vérité** nothing but the truth; ~ **que cela** that alone
♦ *excl*: **de** ~**!** not at all!, don't mention it!; **il n'en est** ~**!** nothing of the sort!; ~ **à faire!** it's no good!, it's no use!
♦ *nm*: **un petit** ~ (*cadeau*) a little something; **des** ~**s** trivia *pl*; **un** ~ **de** a hint of; **en un** ~ **de temps** in no time at all; **avoir peur d'un** ~ to be frightened of the slightest thing.

rieur, euse [RjœR, -øz] *adj* cheerful.
rigide [Riʒid] *adj* stiff; (*fig*) rigid; (*moralement*) strict.
rigidité [Riʒidite] *nf* stiffness; **la** ~ **cadavérique** rigor mortis.
rigolade [Rigɔlad] *nf*: **la** ~ fun; (*fig*): **c'est de la** ~ it's a big farce; (*c'est facile*) it's a cinch.
rigole [Rigɔl] *nf* (*conduit*) channel; (*filet d'eau*) rivulet.
rigoler [Rigɔle] *vi* (*rire*) to laugh; (*s'amuser*) to have (some) fun; (*plaisanter*) to be joking *ou* kidding.
rigolo, ote [Rigɔlo, -ɔt] *adj* (*fam*) funny ♦ *nm/f* comic; (*péj*) fraud, phoney.
rigorisme [Rigɔrism(ə)] *nm* (moral) rigorism.
rigoriste [Rigɔrist(ə)] *adj* rigorist.
rigoureusement [Rigurøzmã] *adv* rigorously; ~ **vrai/interdit** strictly true/forbidden.
rigoureux, euse [Riguʀø, -øz] *adj* (*morale*) rigorous, strict; (*personne*) stern, strict; (*climat, châtiment*) rigorous, harsh, severe; (*interdiction, neutralité*) strict; (*preuves, analyse, méthode*) rigorous.
rigueur [RigœR] *nf* rigour (*BRIT*), rigor (*US*); strictness; harshness; **"tenue de soirée de**

~**"** "evening dress (to be worn)"; **être de** ~ to be the usual thing, be the rule; **à la** ~ at a pinch; possibly; **tenir** ~ **à qn de qch** to hold sth against sb.
riions [Rijɔ̃] *etc vb voir* **rire**.
rillettes [Rijet] *nfpl* ≈ potted meat *sg*.
rime [Rim] *nf* rhyme; **n'avoir ni** ~ **ni raison** to have neither rhyme nor reason.
rimer [Rime] *vi*: ~ (**avec**) to rhyme (with); **ne** ~ **à rien** not to make sense.
Rimmel [Rimɛl] *nm* ® mascara.
rinçage [Rɛ̃saʒ] *nm* rinsing (out); (*opération*) rinse.
rince-doigts [Rɛ̃sdwa] *nm inv* finger-bowl.
rincer [Rɛ̃se] *vt* to rinse; (*récipient*) to rinse out; **se** ~ **la bouche** to rinse out one's mouth.
ring [Riŋ] *nm* (boxing) ring; **monter sur le** ~ (*aussi fig*) to enter the ring; (*: faire carrière de boxeur*) to take up boxing.
ringard, e [Rɛ̃gaR, -aRd(ə)] *adj* (*péj*) old-fashioned.
Rio de Janeiro [RiodʒaneR(o)] *n* Rio de Janeiro.
rions [Rijɔ̃] *vb voir* **rire**.
ripaille [Ripaj] *nf*: **faire** ~ to feast.
riper [Ripe] *vi* to slip, slide.
ripoliné, e [Ripɔline] *adj* enamel-painted.
riposte [Ripɔst(ə)] *nf* retort, riposte; (*fig*) counter-attack, reprisal.
riposter [Ripɔste] *vi* to retaliate ♦ *vt*: ~ **que** to retort that; ~ **à** *vt* to counter; to reply to.
rire [RiR] *vi* to laugh; (*se divertir*) to have fun; (*plaisanter*) to joke ♦ *nm* laugh; **le** ~ laughter; ~ **de** *vt* to laugh at; **se** ~ **de** to make light of; **tu veux** ~**!** you must be joking!; ~ **aux éclats/aux larmes** to roar with laughter/laugh until one cries; ~ **jaune** to force oneself to laugh; ~ **sous cape** to laugh up one's sleeve; ~ **au nez de qn** to laugh in sb's face; **pour** ~ (*pas sérieusement*) for a joke *ou* a laugh.
ris [Ri] *vb voir* **rire** ♦ *nm*: ~ **de veau** (calf) sweetbread.
risée [Rize] *nf*: **être la** ~ **de** to be the laughing stock of.
risette [Rizɛt] *nf*: **faire** ~ (**à**) to give a nice little smile (to).
risible [Rizibl(ə)] *adj* laughable, ridiculous.
risque [Risk(ə)] *nm* risk; **l'attrait du** ~ the lure of danger; **prendre des** ~**s** to take risks; **à ses** ~**s et périls** at his own risk; **au** ~ **de** at the risk of; ~ **d'incendie** fire risk; ~ **calculé** calculated risk.
risqué, e [Riske] *adj* risky; (*plaisanterie*) risqué, daring.
risquer [Riske] *vt* to risk; (*allusion, question*) to venture, hazard; **tu risques qu'on te renvoie** you risk being dismissed; **ça ne risque rien** it's quite safe; ~ **de**: **il risque de se tuer** he could get *ou* risks getting himself killed; **il a risqué de se tuer** he almost got himself

killed; **ce qui risque de se produire** what might *ou* could well happen; **il ne risque pas de recommencer** there's no chance of him doing that again; **se ~ dans** (*s'aventurer*) to venture into; **se ~ à faire** (*tenter*) to venture *ou* dare to do; **~ le tout pour le tout** to risk the lot.

risque-tout [Riskətu] *nm/f inv* daredevil.

rissoler [Risɔle] *vi*, *vt*: **(faire) ~** to brown.

ristourne [Risturn(ə)] *nf* rebate; discount.

rit [Ri] *etc vb voir* **rire**.

rite [Rit] *nm* rite; (*fig*) ritual; **~s d'initiation** initiation rites.

ritournelle [Riturnɛl] *nf* (*fig*) tune; **c'est toujours la même ~** (*fam*) it's always the same old story.

rituel, le [Rituɛl] *adj, nm* ritual.

rituellement [Rituɛlmɑ̃] *adv* religiously.

riv. *abr* (= *rivière*) R.

rivage [Rivaʒ] *nm* shore.

rival, e, aux [Rival, -o] *adj, nm/f* rival; **sans ~** *adj* unrivalled.

rivaliser [Rivalize] *vi*: **~ avec** to rival, vie with; (*être comparable*) to hold its own against, compare with; **~ avec qn de** (*élégance etc*) to vie with *ou* rival sb in.

rivalité [Rivalite] *nf* rivalry.

rive [Riv] *nf* shore; (*de fleuve*) bank.

river [Rive] *vt* (*clou, pointe*) to clinch; (*plaques*) to rivet together; **être rivé sur/à** to be riveted on/to.

riverain, e [Rivʀɛ̃, -ɛn] *adj* riverside *cpd*; lakeside *cpd*; roadside *cpd* ♦ *nm/f* riverside (*ou* lakeside) resident; local *ou* roadside resident.

rivet [Rivɛ] *nm* rivet.

riveter [Rivte] *vt* to rivet (together).

Riviera [Rivjɛʀa] *nf*: **la ~** (**italienne**) the Italian Riviera.

rivière [Rivjɛʀ] *nf* river; **~ de diamants** diamond rivière.

rixe [Riks(ə)] *nf* brawl, scuffle.

riz [Ri] *nm* rice; **~ au lait** rice pudding.

rizière [Rizjɛʀ] *nf* paddy field.

RMC *sigle f* = *Radio Monte Carlo*.

RMI *sigle m* (= *revenu minimum d'insertion*) ≈ income support (*BRIT*), ≈ welfare (*US*).

RN *sigle f* = *route nationale*.

robe [Rɔb] *nf* dress; (*de juge, d'ecclésiastique*) robe; (*de professeur*) gown; (*pelage*) coat; **~ de soirée/de mariée** evening/wedding dress; **~ de baptême** christening robe; **~ de chambre** dressing gown; **~ de grossesse** maternity dress.

robinet [Rɔbinɛ] *nm* tap, faucet (*US*); **~ du gaz** gas tap; **~ mélangeur** mixer tap.

robinetterie [Rɔbinɛtʀi] *nf* taps *pl*, plumbing.

roboratif, ive [Rɔbɔratif, -iv] *adj* bracing, invigorating.

robot [Rɔbo] *nm* robot; **~ de cuisine** food processor.

robotique [Rɔbɔtik] *nf* robotics *sg*.

robotiser [Rɔbɔtize] *vt* (*personne, travailleur*) to turn into a robot; (*monde, vie*) to automate.

robuste [Rɔbyst(ə)] *adj* robust, sturdy.

robustesse [Rɔbystɛs] *nf* robustness, sturdiness.

roc [Rɔk] *nm* rock.

rocade [Rɔkad] *nf* (*AUTO*) bypass.

rocaille [Rɔkaj] *nf* (*pierres*) loose stones *pl*; (*terrain*) rocky *ou* stony ground; (*jardin*) rockery, rock garden ♦ *adj* (*style*) rocaille.

rocailleux, euse [Rɔkajø, -øz] *adj* rocky, stony; (*voix*) harsh.

rocambolesque [Rɔkɑ̃bɔlɛsk(ə)] *adj* fantastic, incredible.

roche [Rɔʃ] *nf* rock.

rocher [Rɔʃe] *nm* rock; (*ANAT*) petrosal bone.

rochet [Rɔʃɛ] *nm*: **roue à ~** ratchet wheel.

rocheux, euse [Rɔʃø, -øz] *adj* rocky; **les (montagnes) Rocheuses** the Rockies, the Rocky Mountains.

rock (and roll) [Rɔk(ɛnRɔl)] *nm* (*musique*) rock(-'n'-roll); (*danse*) rock.

rocker [Rɔkœr] *nm* (*chanteur*) rock musician; (*adepte*) rock fan.

rocking-chair [Rɔkiŋ(t)ʃɛʀ] *nm* rocking chair.

rodage [Rɔdaʒ] *nm* running in (*BRIT*), breaking in (*US*); **en ~** (*AUTO*) running *ou* breaking in.

rodé, e [Rɔde] *adj* run in (*BRIT*), broken in (*US*); (*personne*): **~ à qch** having got the hang of sth.

rodéo [Rɔdeo] *nm* rodeo (*pl* -s).

roder [Rɔde] *vt* (*moteur, voiture*) to run in (*BRIT*), break in (*US*); **~ un spectacle/service** to iron out the initial problems of a show/service.

rôder [Rode] *vi* to roam *ou* wander about; (*de façon suspecte*) to lurk (about *ou* around).

rôdeur, euse [Rodœr, -øz] *nm/f* prowler.

rodomontades [Rɔdɔmɔ̃tad] *nfpl* bragging *sg*; sabre rattling *sg*.

rogatoire [Rɔgatwaʀ] *adj*: **commission ~** letters rogatory.

rogne [Rɔɲ] *nf*: **être en ~** to be mad *ou* in a temper; **se mettre en ~** to get mad *ou* in a temper.

rogner [Rɔɲe] *vt* to trim; (*fig*) to whittle down; **~ sur** (*fig*) to cut down *ou* back on.

rognons [Rɔɲɔ̃] *nmpl* kidneys.

rognures [Rɔɲyʀ] *nfpl* trimmings.

rogue [Rɔg] *adj* arrogant.

roi [Rwa] *nm* king; **les R~s mages** the Three Wise Men, the Magi; **le jour** *ou* **la fête des R~s, les R~s** Twelfth Night.

La fête des Rois *is celebrated on January 6. Figurines representing the magi are traditionally added to the Christmas crib and people eat* **la galette des Rois,** *a plain, flat cake in which a porcelain charm* (**la fève**) *is hidden. Whoever finds the charm is king or queen for the day and chooses a partner.*

roitelet [ʀwatlɛ] *nm* wren; (*péj*) kinglet.
rôle [ʀol] *nm* role; (*contribution*) part.
rollmops [ʀɔlmɔps] *nm* rollmop.
romain, e [ʀɔmɛ̃, -ɛn] *adj* Roman ♦ *nm/f*: **R~, e** Roman ♦ *nf* (*CULIN*) cos (lettuce).
roman, e [ʀɔmɑ̃, -an] *adj* (*ARCHIT*) Romanesque; (*LING*) Romance *cpd*, Romanic ♦ *nm* novel; ~ **policier** detective novel; ~ **d'espionnage** spy novel *ou* story; ~ **noir** thriller.
romance [ʀɔmɑ̃s] *nf* ballad.
romancer [ʀɔmɑ̃se] *vt* to romanticize.
romanche [ʀɔmɑ̃ʃ] *adj, nm* Romansh.
romancier, ière [ʀɔmɑ̃sje, -jɛʀ] *nm/f* novelist.
romand, e [ʀɔmɑ̃, -ɑ̃d] *adj* of *ou* from French-speaking Switzerland ♦ *nm/f*: **R~, e** French-speaking Swiss.
romanesque [ʀɔmanɛsk(ə)] *adj* (*fantastique*) fantastic; storybook *cpd*; (*sentimental*) romantic; (*LITTÉRATURE*) novelistic.
roman-feuilleton, *pl* **romans-feuilletons** [ʀɔmɑ̃fœjtɔ̃] *nm* serialized novel.
roman-fleuve, *pl* **romans-fleuves** [ʀɔmɑ̃flœv] *nm* saga, roman-fleuve.
romanichel, le [ʀɔmaniʃɛl] *nm/f* gipsy.
roman-photo, *pl* **romans-photos** [ʀɔmɑ̃fɔto] *nm* (*romantic*) picture story.
romantique [ʀɔmɑ̃tik] *adj* romantic.
romantisme [ʀɔmɑ̃tism(ə)] *nm* romanticism.
romarin [ʀɔmaʀɛ̃] *nm* rosemary.
rombière [ʀɔ̃bjɛʀ] *nf* (*péj*) old bag.
Rome [ʀɔm] *n* Rome.
rompre [ʀɔ̃pʀ(ə)] *vt* to break; (*entretien, fiançailles*) to break off ♦ *vi* (*fiancés*) to break it off; **se** ~ *vi* to break; (*MÉD*) to burst, rupture; **se** ~ **les os** *ou* **le cou** to break one's neck; ~ **avec** to break with; **à tout** ~ *adv* wildly; **applaudir à tout** ~ to bring down the house, applaud wildly; ~ **la glace** (*fig*) to break the ice; **rompez (les rangs)!** (*MIL*) dismiss!, fall out!
rompu, e [ʀɔ̃py] *pp de* **rompre** ♦ *adj* (*fourbu*) exhausted, worn out; ~ **à** with wide experience of; inured to.
romsteck [ʀɔ̃mstɛk] *nm* rump steak *no pl*.
ronce [ʀɔ̃s] *nf* (*BOT*) bramble branch; (*MENUISERIE*): ~ **de noyer** burr walnut; ~**s** *nfpl* brambles, thorns.
ronchonner [ʀɔ̃ʃɔne] *vi* (*fam*) to grouse, grouch.
rond, e [ʀɔ̃, ʀɔ̃d] *adj* round; (*joues, mollets*) well-rounded; (*fam: ivre*) tight; (*sincère, décidé*): **être** ~ **en affaires** to be on the level in business, do an honest deal ♦ *nm* (*cercle*) ring; (*fam: sou*): **je n'ai plus un** ~ I haven't a penny left ♦ *nf* (*gén: de surveillance*) rounds *pl*, patrol; (*danse*) round (dance); (*MUS*) semibreve (*BRIT*), whole note (*US*) ♦ *adv*: **tourner** ~ (*moteur*) to run smoothly; **ça ne tourne pas** ~ (*fig*) there's something not quite right about it; **pour faire un compte** ~ to make (it) a round figure, to round (it) off;

avoir le dos ~ to be round-shouldered; **en** ~ (*s'asseoir, danser*) in a ring; **à la** ~**e** (*alentour*): **à 10 km à la** ~**e** for 10 km round; (*à chacun son tour*): **passer qch à la** ~**e** to pass sth (a)round; **faire des** ~**s de jambe** to bow and scrape; ~ **de serviette** napkin ring.
rond-de-cuir, *pl* **ronds-de-cuir** [ʀɔ̃dkɥiʀ] *nm* (*péj*) penpusher.
rondelet, te [ʀɔ̃dlɛ, -ɛt] *adj* plump; (*fig: somme*) tidy; (*: bourse*) well-lined, fat.
rondelle [ʀɔ̃dɛl] *nf* (*TECH*) washer; (*tranche*) slice, round.
rondement [ʀɔ̃dmɑ̃] *adv* (*avec décision*) briskly; (*loyalement*) frankly.
rondeur [ʀɔ̃dœʀ] *nf* (*d'un bras, des formes*) plumpness; (*bonhomie*) friendly straightforwardness; ~**s** *nfpl* (*d'une femme*) curves.
rondin [ʀɔ̃dɛ̃] *nm* log.
rond-point, *pl* **ronds-points** [ʀɔ̃pwɛ̃] *nm* roundabout (*BRIT*), traffic circle (*US*).
ronéotyper [ʀɔneɔtipe] *vt* to duplicate, roneo.
ronflant, e [ʀɔ̃flɑ̃, -ɑ̃t] *adj* (*péj*) high-flown, grand.
ronflement [ʀɔ̃fləmɑ̃] *nm* snoring, snoring *no pl*.
ronfler [ʀɔ̃fle] *vi* to snore; (*moteur, poêle*) to hum; (*: plus fort*) to roar.
ronger [ʀɔ̃ʒe] *vt* to gnaw (at); (*suj: vers, rouille*) to eat into; ~ **son frein** to champ (at) the bit (*fig*); **se** ~ **de souci, se** ~ **les sangs** to worry o.s. sick, fret; **se** ~ **les ongles** to bite one's nails.
rongeur, euse [ʀɔ̃ʒœʀ, -øz] *nm/f* rodent.
ronronnement [ʀɔ̃ʀɔnmɑ̃] *nm* purring; (*bruit*) purr.
ronronner [ʀɔ̃ʀɔne] *vi* to purr.
roque [ʀɔk] *nm* (*ÉCHECS*) castling.
roquefort [ʀɔkfɔʀ] *nm* Roquefort.
roquer [ʀɔke] *vi* to castle.
roquet [ʀɔkɛ] *nm* nasty little lap-dog.
roquette [ʀɔkɛt] *nf* rocket; ~ **antichar** anti-tank rocket.
rosace [ʀozas] *nf* (*vitrail*) rose window, rosace; (*motif: de plafond etc*) rose.
rosaire [ʀozɛʀ] *nm* rosary.
rosbif [ʀɔsbif] *nm*: **du** ~ roasting beef; (*cuit*) roast beef; **un** ~ a joint of (roasting) beef.
rose [ʀoz] *nf* rose; (*vitrail*) rose window ♦ *adj* pink; ~ **bonbon** *adj inv* candy pink; ~ **des vents** compass card.
rosé, e [ʀoze] *adj* pinkish; (*vin*) ~ rosé (wine).
roseau, x [ʀozo] *nm* reed.
rosée [ʀoze] *adj f voir* **rosé** ♦ *nf*: **goutte de** ~ dewdrop.
roseraie [ʀozʀɛ] *nf* rose garden; (*plantation*) rose nursery.
rosette [ʀozɛt] *nf* rosette (*gen of the Légion d'honneur*).
rosier [ʀozje] *nm* rosebush, rose tree.
rosir [ʀoziʀ] *vi* to go pink.
rosse [ʀɔs] *nf* (*péj: cheval*) nag ♦ *adj* nasty, vicious.

rosser [ʀɔse] *vt* (*fam*) to thrash.
rossignol [ʀɔsiɲɔl] *nm* (*ZOOL*) nightingale; (*crochet*) picklock.
rot [ʀo] *nm* belch; (*de bébé*) burp.
rotatif, ive [ʀɔtatif, -iv] *adj* rotary ♦ *nf* rotary press.
rotation [ʀɔtasjɔ̃] *nf* rotation; (*fig*) rotation, swap-around; (*renouvellement*) turnover; **par ~ on a rota** (*BRIT*) *ou* rotation (*US*) basis; **~ des cultures** rotation of crops; **~ des stocks** stock turnover.
rotatoire [ʀɔtatwaʀ] *adj*: **mouvement ~** rotary movement.
roter [ʀɔte] *vi* (*fam*) to burp, belch.
rôti [ʀoti] *nm*: **du ~** roasting meat; (*cuit*) roast meat; **un ~ de bœuf/porc** a joint of (roasting) beef/pork.
rotin [ʀɔtɛ̃] *nm* rattan (cane); **fauteuil en ~** cane (arm)chair.
rôtir [ʀotiʀ] *vt* (*aussi*: **faire ~**) to roast ♦ *vi* to roast; **se ~ au soleil** to bask in the sun.
rôtisserie [ʀotisʀi] *nf* (*restaurant*) steakhouse; (*comptoir, magasin*) roast meat counter (*ou* shop).
rôtissoire [ʀotiswaʀ] *nf* (roasting) spit.
rotonde [ʀɔtɔ̃d] *nf* (*ARCHIT*) rotunda; (*RAIL*) engine shed.
rotondité [ʀɔtɔ̃dite] *nf* roundness.
rotor [ʀɔtɔʀ] *nm* rotor.
Rotterdam [ʀɔtɛʀdam] *n* Rotterdam.
rotule [ʀɔtyl] *nf* kneecap, patella.
roturier, ière [ʀɔtyʀje, -jɛʀ] *nm/f* commoner.
rouage [ʀwaʒ] *nm* cog(wheel), gearwheel; (*de montre*) part; (*fig*) cog; **~s** *nmpl* (*fig*) internal structure *sg*.
Rouanda [ʀwɑ̃da] *nm*: **le ~** Rwanda.
roubaisien, ne [ʀubezjɛ̃, -ɛn] *adj* of *ou* from Roubaix.
roublard, e [ʀublaʀ, -aʀd(ə)] *adj* (*péj*) crafty, wily.
rouble [ʀubl(ə)] *nm* rouble.
roucoulement [ʀukulmɑ̃] *nm* (*de pigeons, fig*) coo, cooing.
roucouler [ʀukule] *vi* to coo; (*fig: péj*) to warble; (*: amoureux*) to bill and coo.
roue [ʀu] *nf* wheel; **faire la ~** (*paon*) to spread *ou* fan its tail; (*GYM*) to do a cartwheel; **descendre en ~ libre** to freewheel *ou* coast down; **pousser à la ~** to put one's shoulder to the wheel; **grande ~** (*à la foire*) big wheel; **~ à aubes** paddle wheel; **~ dentée** cogwheel; **~ de secours** spare wheel.
roué, e [ʀwe] *adj* wily.
rouennais, e [ʀwanɛ, -ɛz] *adj* of *ou* from Rouen.
rouer [ʀwe] *vt*: **~ qn de coups** to give sb a thrashing.
rouet [ʀwe] *nm* spinning wheel.
rouge [ʀuʒ] *adj, nm/f* red ♦ *nm* red; (*fard*) rouge; (**vin**) **~** red wine; **passer au ~** (*signal*) to go red; (*automobiliste*) to go through a red light; **porter au ~** (*métal*) to bring to red

heat; **sur la liste ~** (*TÉL*) ex-directory (*BRIT*), unlisted (*US*); **~ de honte/colère** red with shame/anger; **se fâcher tout/voir ~** to blow one's top/see red; **~ (à lèvres)** lipstick.
rougeâtre [ʀuʒɑtʀ(ə)] *adj* reddish.
rougeaud, e [ʀuʒo, -od] *adj* (*teint*) red; (*personne*) red-faced.
rouge-gorge [ʀuʒɡɔʀʒ(ə)] *nm* robin (redbreast).
rougeoiement [ʀuʒwamɑ̃] *nm* reddish glow.
rougeole [ʀuʒɔl] *nf* measles *sg*.
rougeoyant, e [ʀuʒwajɑ̃, -ɑ̃t] *adj* (*ciel, braises*) glowing; (*aube, reflets*) glowing red.
rougeoyer [ʀuʒwaje] *vi* to glow red.
rouget [ʀuʒɛ] *nm* mullet.
rougeur [ʀuʒœʀ] *nf* redness; (*du visage*) red face; **~s** *nfpl* (*MÉD*) red blotches.
rougir [ʀuʒiʀ] *vi* (*de honte, timidité*) to blush, flush; (*de plaisir, colère*) to flush; (*fraise, tomate*) to go *ou* turn red; (*ciel*) to redden.
rouille [ʀuj] *adj inv* rust-coloured, rusty ♦ *nf* rust; (*CULIN*) spicy (Provençal) sauce served with fish dishes.
rouillé, e [ʀuje] *adj* rusty.
rouiller [ʀuje] *vt* to rust ♦ *vi* to rust, go rusty; **se ~** *vi* to rust; (*fig: mentalement*) to become rusty; (*: physiquement*) to grow stiff.
roulade [ʀulad] *nf* (*GYM*) roll; (*CULIN*) rolled meat *no pl*; (*MUS*) roulade, run.
roulage [ʀulaʒ] *nm* (*transport*) haulage.
roulant, e [ʀulɑ̃, -ɑ̃t] *adj* (*meuble*) on wheels; (*surface, trottoir*) moving; **matériel ~** (*RAIL*) rolling stock; **personnel ~** (*RAIL*) train crews *pl*.
roulé, e [ʀule] *adj*: **bien ~e** (*fam: femme*) shapely, curvy.
rouleau, x [ʀulo] *nm* (*de papier, tissu, pièces de monnaie, SPORT*) roll; (*de machine à écrire*) roller, platen; (*à mise en plis, à peinture, vague*) roller; **être au bout du ~** (*fig*) to be at the end of the line; **~ compresseur** steamroller; **~ à pâtisserie** rolling pin; **~ de pellicule** roll of film.
roulé-boulé, *pl* **roulés-boulés** [ʀulebule] (*SPORT*) roll.
roulement [ʀulmɑ̃] *nm* (*bruit*) rumbling *no pl*, rumble; (*rotation*) rotation; turnover; (*: de capitaux*) circulation; **par ~** on a rota (*BRIT*) *ou* rotation (*US*) basis; **~ (à billes)** ball bearings *pl*; **~ de tambour** drum roll; **~ d'yeux** roll(ing) of the eyes.
rouler [ʀule] *vt* to roll; (*papier, tapis*) to roll up; (*CULIN: pâte*) to roll out; (*fam*) to do, con ♦ *vi* (*bille, boule*) to roll; (*voiture, train*) to go, run; (*automobiliste*) to drive; (*cycliste*) to ride; (*bateau*) to roll; (*tonnerre*) to rumble, roll; (*dégringoler*): **~ en bas de** to roll down; **~ sur** (*suj: conversation*) to turn on; **se ~ dans** (*boue*) to roll in; (*couverture*) to roll o.s. (up) in; **~ dans la farine** (*fam*) to con; **~ les épaules/hanches** to sway one's shoulders/wiggle one's hips; **~ les "r"** to roll one's r's;

~ **sur l'or** to be rolling in money, be rolling in it; ~ **(sa bosse)** to go places.

roulette [Rulɛt] *nf* (*de table, fauteuil*) castor; (*de pâtissier*) pastry wheel; (*jeu*): **la** ~ roulette; **à** ~**s** on castors; **la** ~ **russe** Russian roulette.

roulis [Ruli] *nm* roll(ing).

roulotte [Rulɔt] *nf* caravan.

roumain, e [Rumɛ̃, -ɛn] *adj* Rumanian, Romanian ♦ *nm* (*LING*) Rumanian, Romanian ♦ *nm/f*: R~, e Rumanian, Romanian.

Roumanie [Rumani] *nf*: **la** ~ Rumania, Romania.

roupiller [Rupije] *vi* (*fam*) to sleep.

rouquin, e [Rukɛ̃, -in] *nm/f* (*péj*) redhead.

rouspéter [Ruspete] *vi* (*fam*) to moan, grouse.

rousse [Rus] *adj f voir* **roux.**

rousseur [RusœR] *nf*: **tache de** ~ freckle.

roussi [Rusi] *nm*: **ça sent le** ~ there's a smell of burning; (*fig*) I can smell trouble.

roussir [Rusir] *vt* to scorch ♦ *vi* (*feuilles*) to go *ou* turn brown; (*CULIN*): **faire** ~ to brown.

routage [Rutaʒ] *nm* (collective) mailing.

routard, e [Rutar, -ard(ə)] *nm/f* traveller.

route [Rut] *nf* road; (*fig: chemin*) way; (*itinéraire, parcours*) route; (*fig: voie*) road, path; **par (la)** ~ by road; **il y a 3 heures de** ~ it's a 3-hour ride *ou* journey; **en** ~ *adv* on the way; **en** ~! let's go!; **en cours de** ~ en route; **mettre en** ~ to start up; **se mettre en** ~ to set off; **faire** ~ **vers** to head towards; **faire fausse** ~ (*fig*) to be on the wrong track; ~ **nationale (RN)** ≈ A-road (*BRIT*), ≈ state highway (*US*).

routier, ière [Rutje, -jɛR] *adj* road *cpd* ♦ *nm* (*camionneur*) (long-distance) lorry (*BRIT*) *ou* truck driver; (*restaurant*) ≈ transport café (*BRIT*), ≈ truck stop (*US*); (*scout*) ≈ rover; (*cycliste*) road racer ♦ *nf* (*voiture*) touring car; **vieux** ~ old stager; **carte routière** road map.

routine [Rutin] *nf* routine; **visite/contrôle de** ~ routine visit/check.

routinier, ière [Rutinje, -jɛR] *adj* (*péj: travail*) humdrum, routine; (*: personne*) addicted to routine.

rouvert, e [RuvɛR, -ɛRt(ə)] *pp de* **rouvrir.**

rouvrir [RuvRiR] *vt, vi* to reopen, open again; **se** ~ *vi* (*blessure*) to open up again.

roux, rousse [Ru, Rus] *adj* red; (*personne*) red-haired ♦ *nm/f* redhead ♦ *nm* (*CULIN*) roux.

royal, e, aux [Rwajal, -o] *adj* royal; (*fig*) fit for a king, princely; blissful; thorough.

royalement [Rwajalmɑ̃] *adv* royally.

royaliste [Rwajalist(ə)] *adj, nm/f* royalist.

royaume [Rwajom] *nm* kingdom; (*fig*) realm; **le** ~ **des cieux** the kingdom of heaven.

Royaume-Uni [Rwajomyni] *nm*: **le** ~ the United Kingdom.

royauté [Rwajote] *nf* (*dignité*) kingship; (*régime*) monarchy.

RP *sigle f* (= *recette principale*) ≈ main post office; = *région parisienne* ♦ *sigle fpl* (= *relations*

publiques) PR.

RPR *sigle m* (= *Rassemblement pour la République*) *political party.*

R.S.V.P. *abr* (= *répondez s'il vous plaît*) R.S.V.P.

RTB *sigle f* = *Radio-Télévision belge.*

Rte *abr* = **route.**

RTL *sigle f* = *Radio-Télévision Luxembourg.*

RTVE *sigle f* = *Radio-Télévision espagnole.*

RU [Ry] *sigle m* = **restaurant universitaire.**

ruade [Ryad] *nf* kick.

Ruanda [Rwɑ̃da] *nm*: **le** ~ Rwanda.

ruban [Rybɑ̃] *nm* (*gén*) ribbon; (*pour ourlet, couture*) binding; (*de téléscripteur etc*) tape; (*d'acier*) strip; ~ **adhésif** adhesive tape; ~ **carbone** carbon ribbon.

rubéole [Rybeɔl] *nf* German measles *sg*, rubella.

rubicond, e [Rybikɔ̃, -ɔd] *adj* rubicund, ruddy.

rubis [Rybi] *nm* ruby; (*HORLOGERIE*) jewel; **payer** ~ **sur l'ongle** to pay cash on the nail.

rubrique [RybRik] *nf* (*titre, catégorie*) heading, rubric; (*PRESSE: article*) column.

ruche [Ryʃ] *nf* hive.

rucher [Ryʃe] *nm* apiary.

rude [Ryd] *adj* (*barbe, toile*) rough; (*métier, tâche*) hard, tough; (*climat*) severe, harsh; (*bourru*) harsh, rough; (*fruste*) rugged, tough; (*fam*) jolly good; **être mis à** ~ **épreuve** to be put through the mill.

rudement [Rydmɑ̃] *adv* (*tomber, frapper*) hard; (*traiter, reprocher*) harshly; (*fam: très*) terribly; (*: beaucoup*) terribly hard.

rudesse [Rydɛs] *nf* roughness; toughness; severity; harshness.

rudimentaire [Rydimɑ̃tɛR] *adj* rudimentary, basic.

rudiments [Rydimɑ̃] *nmpl* rudiments; basic knowledge *sg*; basic principles.

rudoyer [Rydwaje] *vt* to treat harshly.

rue [Ry] *nf* street; **être/jeter qn à la** ~ to be on the streets/throw sb out onto the street.

ruée [Rɥe] *nf* rush; **la** ~ **vers l'or** the gold rush.

ruelle [Rɥɛl] *nf* alley(way).

ruer [Rɥe] *vi* (*cheval*) to kick out; **se** ~ *vi*: **se** ~ **sur** to pounce on; **se** ~ **vers/dans/hors de** to rush *ou* dash towards/into/out of; ~ **dans les brancards** to become rebellious.

rugby [Rygbi] *nm* rugby (football); ~ **à treize/quinze** rugby league/union.

rugir [RyʒiR] *vi* to roar.

rugissement [Ryʒismɑ̃] *nm* roar, roaring *no pl.*

rugosité [Rygozite] *nf* roughness; (*aspérité*) rough patch.

rugueux, euse [Rygø, -øz] *adj* rough.

ruine [Rɥin] *nf* ruin; ~**s** *nfpl* ruins; **tomber en** ~ to fall into ruin(s).

ruiner [Rɥine] *vt* to ruin.

ruineux, euse [Rɥinø, -øz] *adj* terribly expensive to buy (*ou* run), ruinous; extravagant.

ruisseau, x [Rɥiso] *nm* stream, brook; (*caniveau*) gutter; (*fig*): ~**x de larmes/sang** floods of tears/streams of blood.

ruisselant, e [ʀɥislɑ̃, -ɑ̃t] adj streaming.
ruisseler [ʀɥisle] vi to stream; ~ **(d'eau)** to be streaming (with water); ~ **de lumière** to stream with light.
ruissellement [ʀɥisɛlmɑ̃] nm streaming; ~ **de lumière** stream of light.
rumeur [ʀymœʀ] nf (bruit confus) rumbling; hubbub no pl; (protestation) murmur(ing); (nouvelle) rumour (BRIT), rumor (US).
ruminer [ʀymine] vt (herbe) to ruminate; (fig) to ruminate on ou over, chew over ♦ vi (vache) to chew the cud, ruminate.
rumsteck [ʀɔ̃mstɛk] nm = **romsteck**.
rupestre [ʀypɛstʀ(ə)] adj (plante) rock cpd; (art) wall cpd.
rupture [ʀyptyʀ] nf (de câble, digue) breaking; (de tendon) rupture, tearing; (de négociations etc) breakdown; (de contrat) breach; (séparation, désunion) break-up, split; **en** ~ **de ban** at odds with authority; **en** ~ **de stock** (COMM) out of stock.
rural, e, aux [ʀyʀal, -o] adj rural, country cpd ♦ nmpl: **les ruraux** country people.
ruse [ʀyz] nf: **la** ~ cunning, craftiness; trickery; **une** ~ a trick, a ruse; **par** ~ by trickery.
rusé, e [ʀyze] adj cunning, crafty.
russe [ʀys] adj Russian ♦ nm (LING) Russian ♦ nm/f: **R**~ Russian.
Russie [ʀysi] nf: **la** ~ Russia; **la** ~ **blanche** White Russia; **la** ~ **soviétique** Soviet Russia.
rustine [ʀystin] nf repair patch (for bicycle inner tube).
rustique [ʀystik] adj rustic; (plante) hardy.
rustre [ʀystʀ(ə)] nm boor.
rut [ʀyt] nm: **être en** ~ (animal domestique) to be in ou on heat; (animal sauvage) to be rutting.
rutabaga [ʀytabaga] nm swede.
rutilant, e [ʀytilɑ̃, -ɑ̃t] adj gleaming.
RV sigle m = **rendez-vous**.
Rwanda [ʀwɑ̃da] nm: **le** ~ Rwanda.
rythme [ʀitm(ə)] nm rhythm; (vitesse) rate; (: de la vie) pace, tempo; **au** ~ **de 10 par jour** at the rate of 10 a day.
rythmé, e [ʀitme] adj rhythmic(al).
rythmer [ʀitme] vt to give rhythm to.
rythmique [ʀitmik] adj rhythmic(al) ♦ nf rhythmics sg.

S s

S, s [ɛs] nm inv S, s ♦ abr (= sud) S; (= seconde) sec; (= siècle) c., century; **S comme Suzanne** S for Sugar.
s' [s] pron voir **se**.
s/ abr = **sur**.
SA sigle f = **société anonyme**; (= Son Altesse) HH.
sa [sa] adj possessif voir **son**.
sabbatique [sabatik] adj: **année** ~ sabbatical year.
sable [sɑbl(ə)] nm sand; ~**s mouvants** quicksand(s).
sablé [sɑble] adj (allée) sandy ♦ nm shortbread biscuit; **pâte** ~**e** (CULIN) shortbread dough.
sabler [sɑble] vt to sand; (contre le verglas) to grit; ~ **le champagne** to drink champagne.
sableux, euse [sɑblø, -øz] adj sandy.
sablier [sɑblije] nm hourglass; (de cuisine) egg timer.
sablière [sɑblijɛʀ] nf sand quarry.
sablonneux, euse [sɑblɔnø, -øz] adj sandy.
saborder [sabɔʀde] vt (navire) to scuttle; (fig) to wind up, shut down.
sabot [sabo] nm clog; (de cheval, bœuf) hoof; ~ **(de Denver)** (wheel) clamp; ~ **de frein** brake shoe.
sabotage [sabɔtaʒ] nm sabotage.
saboter [sabɔte] vt (travail, morceau de musique) to botch, make a mess of; (machine, installation, négociation etc) to sabotage.
saboteur, euse [sabɔtœʀ, -øz] nm/f saboteur.
sabre [sɑbʀ(ə)] nm sabre; **le** ~ (fig) the sword, the army.
sabrer [sɑbʀe] vt to cut down.
SAC [sɑk] sigle m (= Service d'action civique) former Gaullist parapolice.
sac [sak] nm bag; (à charbon etc) sack; (pillage) sack(ing); **mettre à** ~ to sack; ~ **à provisions/de voyage** shopping/travelling bag; ~ **de couchage** sleeping bag; ~ **à dos** rucksack; ~ **à main** handbag; ~ **de plage** beach bag.
saccade [sakad] nf jerk; **par** ~**s** jerkily; haltingly.
saccadé, e [sakade] adj jerky.
saccage [sakaʒ] nm havoc.
saccager [sakaʒe] vt (piller) to sack, lay waste; (dévaster) to create havoc in, wreck.
saccharine [sakaʀin] nf saccharin(e).
saccharose [sakaʀoz] nm sucrose.
SACEM [sasɛm] sigle f (= Société des auteurs, compositeurs et éditeurs de musique) body re-

sponsible for collecting and distributing royalties.

sacerdoce [sasɛRdɔs] nm priesthood; (fig) calling, vocation.

sacerdotal, e, aux [sasɛRdɔtal, -o] adj priestly, sacerdotal.

sachant [saʃɑ̃] etc vb voir **savoir**.

sache [saʃ] etc vb voir **savoir**.

sachet [saʃɛ] nm (small) bag; (de lavande, poudre, shampooing) sachet; **thé en ~s** tea bags; ~ **de thé** tea bag.

sacoche [sakɔʃ] nf (gén) bag; (de bicyclette) saddlebag; (du facteur) (post-)bag; (d'outils) toolbag.

sacquer [sake] vt (fam: candidat, employé) to sack; (: réprimander, mal noter) to plough.

sacraliser [sakRalize] vt to make sacred.

sacre [sakR(ə)] nm coronation; consecration.

sacré, e [sakRe] adj sacred; (fam: satané) blasted; (: fameux): **un ~ ... a heck of a ...**; (ANAT) sacral.

sacrement [sakRəmɑ̃] nm sacrament; **les derniers ~s** the last rites.

sacrer [sakRe] vt (roi) to crown; (évêque) to consecrate ♦ vi to curse, swear.

sacrifice [sakRifis] nm sacrifice; **faire le ~ de** to sacrifice.

sacrificiel, le [sakRifisjɛl] adj sacrificial.

sacrifier [sakRifje] vt to sacrifice; ~ **à** vt to conform to; **se ~** to sacrifice o.s.; **articles sacrifiés** (COMM) items sold at rock-bottom ou give-away prices.

sacrilège [sakRilɛʒ] nm sacrilege ♦ adj sacrilegious.

sacristain [sakRistɛ̃] nm sexton; sacristan.

sacristie [sakRisti] nf sacristy; (culte protestant) vestry.

sacro-saint, e [sakRɔsɛ̃, -ɛ̃t] adj sacrosanct.

sadique [sadik] adj sadistic ♦ nm/f sadist.

sadisme [sadism(ə)] nm sadism.

sadomasochisme [sadɔmazɔʃism(ə)] nm sadomasochism.

sadomasochiste [sadɔmazɔʃist(ə)] nm/f sadomasochist.

safari [safaRi] nm safari; **faire un ~** to go on safari.

safari-photo [safaRifɔto] nm photographic safari.

SAFER [safɛR] sigle f (= Société d'aménagement foncier et d'établissement rural) organization with the right to buy land in order to retain it for agricultural use.

safran [safRɑ̃] nm saffron.

saga [saga] nf saga.

sagace [sagas] adj sagacious, shrewd.

sagacité [sagasite] nf sagacity, shrewdness.

sagaie [sagɛ] nf assegai.

sage [saʒ] adj wise; (enfant) good ♦ nm wise man; sage.

sage-femme [saʒfam] nf midwife (pl -wives).

sagement [saʒmɑ̃] adv (raisonnablement) wisely, sensibly; (tranquillement) quietly.

sagesse [saʒɛs] nf wisdom.

Sagittaire [saʒitɛR] nm: **le ~** Sagittarius, the Archer; **être du ~** to be Sagittarius.

Sahara [saaRa] nm: **le ~** the Sahara (Desert); **le ~ occidental** (pays) Western Sahara.

saharien, ne [saaRjɛ̃, -ɛn] adj Saharan ♦ nf safari jacket.

Sahel [saɛl] nm: **le ~** the Sahel.

sahélien, ne [saeljɛ̃, -ɛn] adj Sahelian.

saignant, e [sɛɲɑ̃, -ɑ̃t] adj (viande) rare; (blessure, plaie) bleeding.

saignée [seɲe] nf (MÉD) bleeding no pl, bloodletting no pl; (ANAT): **la ~ du bras** the bend of the arm; (fig: MIL) heavy losses pl; (: prélèvement) savage cut.

saignement [sɛɲmɑ̃] nm bleeding; ~ **de nez** nosebleed.

saigner [seɲe] vi to bleed ♦ vt to bleed; (animal) to bleed to death; ~ **qn à blanc** (fig) to bleed sb white; ~ **du nez** to have a nosebleed.

Saigon [sajgɔ̃] n Saigon.

saillant, e [sajɑ̃, -ɑ̃t] adj (pommettes, menton) prominent; (corniche etc) projecting; (fig) salient, outstanding.

saillie [saji] nf (sur un mur etc) projection; (trait d'esprit) witticism; (accouplement) covering, serving; **faire ~** to project, stick out; **en ~, formant ~** projecting, overhanging.

saillir [sajiR] vi to project, stick out; (veine, muscle) to bulge ♦ vt (ÉLEVAGE) to cover, serve.

sain, e [sɛ̃, sɛn] adj healthy; (dents, constitution) healthy, sound; (lectures) wholesome; ~ **et sauf** safe and sound, unharmed; ~ **d'esprit** sound in mind, sane.

saindoux [sɛ̃du] nm lard.

sainement [sɛnmɑ̃] adv (vivre) healthily; (raisonner) soundly.

saint, e [sɛ̃, sɛ̃t] adj holy; (fig) saintly ♦ nm/f saint; **la S~e Vierge** the Blessed Virgin.

saint-bernard [sɛ̃bɛRnaR] nm inv (chien) St Bernard.

Sainte-Hélène [sɛ̃telɛn] nf St Helena.

Sainte-Lucie [sɛ̃tlysi] nf Saint Lucia.

Saint-Esprit [sɛ̃tɛspRi] nm: **le ~** the Holy Spirit ou Ghost.

sainteté [sɛ̃te] nf holiness; saintliness.

Saint-Laurent [sɛ̃lɔRɑ̃] nm: **le ~** the St Lawrence.

Saint-Marin [sɛ̃maRɛ̃] nm: **le ~** San Marino.

Saint-Père [sɛ̃pɛR] nm: **le ~** the Holy Father, the Pontiff.

Saint-Pierre [sɛ̃pjɛR] nm Saint Peter; (église) Saint Peter's.

Saint-Pierre-et-Miquelon [sɛ̃pjɛRemiklɔ̃] nm Saint Pierre and Miquelon.

Saint-Siège [sɛ̃sjɛʒ] nm: **le ~** the Holy See.

Saint-Sylvestre [sɛ̃silvɛstR(ə)] nf: **la ~** New Year's Eve.

Saint-Thomas [sɛ̃tɔma] nf Saint Thomas.

Saint-Vincent et les Grenadines

[sɛ̃vɛ̃sɑ̃elegʀənadin] *nm* St Vincent and the Grenadines.

sais [sɛ] *etc vb voir* **savoir**.

saisie [sezi] *nf* seizure; **à la** ~ (*texte*) being keyed; ~ **(de données)** (data) capture.

saisine [sezin] *nf (JUR) submission of a case to the court.*

saisir [seziʀ] *vt* to take hold of, grab; (*fig: occasion*) to seize; (*comprendre*) to grasp; (*entendre*) to get, catch; (*suj: émotions*) to take hold of, come over; (*INFORM*) to capture, keyboard; (*CULIN*) to fry quickly; (*JUR: biens, publication*) to seize; (: *juridiction*): ~ **un tribunal d'une affaire** to submit *ou* refer a case to a court; **se** ~ **de** *vt* to seize; **être saisi** (*frappé de*) to be overcome.

saisissant, e [sezisɑ̃, -ɑ̃t] *adj* startling, striking; (*froid*) biting.

saisissement [sezismɑ̃] *nm*: **muet/figé de** ~ speechless/frozen with emotion.

saison [sɛzɔ̃] *nf* season; **la belle/mauvaise** ~ the summer/winter months; **être de** ~ to be in season; **en/hors** ~ in/out of season; **haute/basse/morte** ~ high/low/slack season; **la** ~ **des pluies/des amours** the rainy/mating season.

saisonnier, ière [sɛzɔnje, -jɛʀ] *adj* seasonal ♦ *nm* (*travailleur*) seasonal worker; (*vacancier*) seasonal holidaymaker.

sait [sɛ] *vb voir* **savoir**.

salace [salas] *adj* salacious.

salade [salad] *nf* (*BOT*) lettuce *etc* (*generic term*); (*CULIN*) (green) salad; (*fam*) tangle, muddle; ~**s** *nfpl* (*fam*): **raconter des** ~**s** to tell tales (*fam*); **haricots en** ~ bean salad; ~ **de concombres** cucumber salad; ~ **de fruits** fruit salad; ~ **niçoise** salade niçoise; ~ **russe** Russian salad.

saladier [saladje] *nm* (salad) bowl.

salaire [salɛʀ] *nm* (*annuel, mensuel*) salary; (*hebdomadaire, journalier*) pay, wages *pl*; (*fig*) reward; ~ **de base** basic salary (*ou* wage); ~ **de misère** starvation wage; ~ **minimum interprofessionnel de croissance (SMIC)** *index-linked guaranteed minimum wage*.

salaison [salɛzɔ̃] *nf* salting; ~**s** *nfpl* salt meat *sg*.

salamandre [salamɑ̃dʀ(ə)] *nf* salamander.

salami [salami] *nm* salami *no pl*, salami sausage.

salant [salɑ̃] *adj m*: **marais** ~ salt pan.

salarial, e, aux [salaʀjal, -o] *adj* salary *cpd*, wage(s) *cpd*.

salariat [salaʀja] *nm* salaried staff.

salarié, e [salaʀje] *adj* salaried; wage-earning ♦ *nm/f* salaried employee; wage-earner.

salaud [salo] *nm* (*fam!*) sod (*!*), bastard (*!*).

sale [sal] *adj* dirty; (*fig: avant le nom*) nasty.

salé, e [sale] *adj* (*liquide, saveur*) salty; (*CULIN*) salted, salt *cpd*; (*fig*) spicy, juicy; (: *note, facture*) steep, stiff ♦ *nm* (*porc salé*) salt pork; **petit** ~ ≈ boiling bacon.

salement [salmɑ̃] *adv* (*manger etc*) dirtily, messily.

saler [sale] *vt* to salt.

saleté [salte] *nf* (*état*) dirtiness; (*crasse*) dirt, filth; (*tache etc*) dirt *no pl*, something dirty, dirty mark; (*fig: tour*) filthy trick; (: *chose sans valeur*) rubbish *no pl*; (: *obscénité*) filth *no pl*; (: *microbe etc*) bug; **vivre dans la** ~ to live in squalor.

salière [saljɛʀ] *nf* saltcellar.

saligaud [saligo] *nm* (*fam!*) bastard (*!*), sod (*!*).

salin, e [salɛ̃, -in] *adj* saline ♦ *nf* saltworks *sg*.

salinité [salinite] *nf* salinity, salt-content.

salir [saliʀ] *vt* to (make) dirty; (*fig*) to soil the reputation of; **se** ~ to get dirty.

salissant, e [salisɑ̃, -ɑ̃t] *adj* (*tissu*) which shows the dirt; (*métier*) dirty, messy.

salissure [salisyʀ] *nf* dirt *no pl*; (*tache*) dirty mark.

salive [saliv] *nf* saliva.

saliver [salive] *vi* to salivate.

salle [sal] *nf* room; (*d'hôpital*) ward; (*de restaurant*) dining room; (*d'un cinéma*) auditorium; (: *public*) audience; **faire** ~ **comble** to have a full house; ~ **d'armes** (*pour l'escrime*) arms room; ~ **d'attente** waiting room; ~ **de bain(s)** bathroom; ~ **de bal** ballroom; ~ **de cinéma** cinema; ~ **de classe** classroom; ~ **commune** (*d'hôpital*) ward; ~ **de concert** concert hall; ~ **de consultation** consulting room (*BRIT*), office (*US*); ~ **de danse** dance hall; ~ **de douches** shower-room; ~ **d'eau** shower-room; ~ **d'embarquement** (*à l'aéroport*) departure lounge; ~ **d'exposition** showroom; ~ **de jeux** games room; playroom; ~ **des machines** engine room; ~ **à manger** dining room; (*mobilier*) dining room suite; ~ **obscure** cinema (*BRIT*), movie theater (*US*); ~ **d'opération** (*d'hôpital*) operating theatre; ~ **de projection** film theatre; ~ **de séjour** living room; ~ **de spectacle** theatre; cinema; ~ **des ventes** saleroom.

salmonellose [salmɔneloz] *nf* (*MÉD*) salmonella poisoning.

Salomon [salɔmɔ̃]: **les îles** ~ the Solomon Islands.

salon [salɔ̃] *nm* lounge, sitting room; (*mobilier*) lounge suite; (*exposition*) exhibition, show; (*mondain, littéraire*) salon; ~ **de coiffure** hairdressing salon; ~ **de thé** tearoom.

salopard [salɔpaʀ] *nm* (*fam!*) bastard (*!*).

salope [salɔp] *nf* (*fam!*) bitch (*!*).

saloper [salɔpe] *vt* (*fam!*) to muck up, mess up.

saloperie [salɔpʀi] *nf* (*fam!*) filth *no pl*; dirty trick; rubbish *no pl*.

salopette [salɔpɛt] *nf* dungarees *pl*; (*d'ouvrier*) overall(s).

salpêtre [salpɛtʀ(ə)] *nm* saltpetre.

salsifis [salsifi] *nm* salsify, oyster plant.

SALT [salt] *sigle* (= *Strategic Arms Limitation Talks ou Treaty*) SALT.

saltimbanque [saltɛ̃bɑ̃k] *nm/f* (travelling) acrobat.

salubre [salybʀ(ə)] *adj* healthy, salubrious.

salubrité [salybʀite] *nf* healthiness, salubrity; ~ **publique** public health.

saluer [salɥe] *vt* (*pour dire bonjour, fig*) to greet; (*pour dire au revoir*) to take one's leave; (*MIL*) to salute.

salut [saly] *nm* (*sauvegarde*) safety; (*REL*) salvation; (*geste*) wave; (*parole*) greeting; (*MIL*) salute ♦ *excl* (*fam: pour dire bonjour*) hi (there); (*: pour dire au revoir*) see you!, bye!; (*style relevé*) (all) hail.

salutaire [salytɛʀ] *adj* (*remède*) beneficial; (*conseils*) salutary.

salutations [salytɑsjɔ̃] *nfpl* greetings; **recevez mes ~ distinguées** *ou* **respectueuses** yours faithfully.

salutiste [salytist(ə)] *nm/f* Salvationist.

Salvador [salvadɔʀ] *nm*: **le ~** El Salvador.

salve [salv(ə)] *nf* salvo; volley of shots; ~ **d'applaudissements** burst of applause.

Samarie [samaʀi] *nf*: **la ~** Samaria.

samaritain [samaʀitɛ̃] *nm*: **le bon S~** the Good Samaritan.

samedi [samdi] *nm* Saturday; *voir aussi* **lundi**.

Samoa [samɔa] *nfpl*: **les (îles) ~** Samoa, the Samoa Islands.

SAMU [samy] *sigle m* (= *service d'assistance médicale d'urgence*) ≈ ambulance (service) (*BRIT*), ≈ paramedics (*US*).

sanatorium [sanatɔʀjɔm] *nm* sanatorium (*pl* -a).

sanctifier [sɑ̃ktifje] *vt* to sanctify.

sanction [sɑ̃ksjɔ̃] *nf* sanction; (*fig*) penalty; **prendre des ~s contre** to impose sanctions on.

sanctionner [sɑ̃ksjɔne] *vt* (*loi, usage*) to sanction; (*punir*) to punish.

sanctuaire [sɑ̃ktɥɛʀ] *nm* sanctuary.

sandale [sɑ̃dal] *nf* sandal.

sandalette [sɑ̃dalɛt] *nf* sandal.

sandow [sɑ̃do] *nm* ® luggage elastic.

sandwich [sɑ̃dwitʃ] *nm* sandwich; **pris en ~** sandwiched.

sang [sɑ̃] *nm* blood; **en ~** covered in blood; **jusqu'au ~** (*mordre, pincer*) till the blood comes; **se faire du mauvais ~** to fret, get in a state.

sang-froid [sɑ̃fʀwa] *nm* calm, sangfroid; **garder/perdre/reprendre son ~** to keep/lose/regain one's cool; **de ~** in cold blood.

sanglant, e [sɑ̃glɑ̃, -ɑ̃t] *adj* bloody, covered in blood; (*combat*) bloody; (*fig: reproche, affront*) cruel.

sangle [sɑ̃gl(ə)] *nf* strap; **~s** *nfpl* (*pour lit etc*) webbing *sg*.

sangler [sɑ̃gle] *vt* to strap up; (*animal*) to girth.

sanglier [sɑ̃glije] *nm* (wild) boar.

sanglot [sɑ̃glo] *nm* sob.

sangloter [sɑ̃glɔte] *vi* to sob.

sangsue [sɑ̃sy] *nf* leech.

sanguin, e [sɑ̃gɛ̃, -in] *adj* blood *cpd*; (*fig*) fiery ♦ *nf* blood orange; (*ART*) red pencil drawing.

sanguinaire [sɑ̃ginɛʀ] *adj* (*animal, personne*) bloodthirsty; (*lutte*) bloody.

sanguinolent, e [sɑ̃ginɔlɑ̃, -ɑ̃t] *adj* streaked with blood.

Sanisette [sanizɛt] *nf* ® coin-operated public lavatory.

sanitaire [sanitɛʀ] *adj* health *cpd*; **~s** *nmpl* (*salle de bain et w.-c.*) bathroom *sg*; **installation/appareil ~** bathroom plumbing/appliance.

sans [sɑ̃] *prép* without; ~ **qu'il s'en aperçoive** without him *ou* his noticing; ~ **scrupules** unscrupulous; ~ **manches** sleeveless.

sans-abri [sɑ̃zabʀi] *nmpl* homeless.

sans-emploi [sɑ̃zɑ̃plwa] *nmpl* jobless.

sans-façon [sɑ̃fasɔ̃] *adj inv* fuss-free; free and easy.

sans-gêne [sɑ̃ʒɛn] *adj inv* inconsiderate ♦ *nm inv* (*attitude*) lack of consideration.

sans-logis [sɑ̃lɔʒi] *nmpl* homeless.

sans-souci [sɑ̃susi] *adj inv* carefree.

sans-travail [sɑ̃tʀavaj] *nmpl* unemployed, jobless.

santal [sɑ̃tal] *nm* sandal(wood).

santé [sɑ̃te] *nf* health; **avoir une ~ de fer** to be bursting with health; **être en bonne ~** to be in good health, be healthy; **boire à la ~ qn** to drink (to) sb's health; **"à la ~ de"** "here's to"; **à ta** *ou* **votre ~!** cheers!; **service de ~** (*dans un port etc*) quarantine service; **la ~ publique** public health.

Santiago (du Chili) [sɑ̃tjago(dyʃili)] *n* Santiago (de Chile).

santon [sɑ̃tɔ̃] *nm* ornamental figure at a Christmas crib.

saoudien, ne [saudjɛ̃, -ɛn] *adj* Saudi (Arabian) ♦ *nm/f*: **S~, ne** Saudi (Arabian).

saoul, e [su, sul] *adj* = **soûl, e**.

sape [sap] *nf*: **travail de ~** (*MIL*) sap; (*fig*) insidious undermining process *ou* work; **~s** *nfpl* (*fam*) gear *sg*, togs.

saper [sape] *vt* to undermine, sap; **se ~** *vi* (*fam*) to dress.

sapeur [sapœʀ] *nm* sapper.

sapeur-pompier [sapœʀpɔ̃pje] *nm* fireman.

saphir [safiʀ] *nm* sapphire; (*d'électrophone*) needle, sapphire.

sapin [sapɛ̃] *nm* fir (tree); (*bois*) fir; ~ **de Noël** Christmas tree.

sapinière [sapinjɛʀ] *nf* fir plantation *ou* forest.

SAR *sigle f* (= *Son Altesse Royale*) HRH.

sarabande [saʀabɑ̃d] *nf* saraband; (*fig*) hullabaloo; whirl.

sarbacane [saʀbakan] *nf* blowpipe, blowgun; (*jouet*) peashooter.

sarcasme [saʀkasm(ə)] *nm* sarcasm *no pl*; (*propos*) piece of sarcasm.

sarcastique [saʀkastik] *adj* sarcastic.

sarcastiquement [saʀkastikmɑ̃] *adv* sarcastically.

sarclage [saʀklaʒ] *nm* weeding.
sarcler [saʀkle] *vt* to weed.
sarcloir [saʀklwaʀ] *nm* (weeding) hoe, spud.
sarcophage [saʀkɔfaʒ] *nm* sarcophagus (*pl* -i).
Sardaigne [saʀdɛɲ] *nf*: **la** ~ Sardinia.
sarde [saʀd(ə)] *adj* Sardinian.
sardine [saʀdin] *nf* sardine; ~**s à l'huile** sardines in oil.
sardinerie [saʀdinʀi] *nf* sardine cannery.
sardinier, ière [saʀdinje, -jɛʀ] *adj* (*pêche, industrie*) sardine *cpd* ♦ *nm* (*bateau*) sardine boat.
sardonique [saʀdɔnik] *adj* sardonic.
sari [saʀi] *nm* sari.
SARL [saʀl] *sigle f* = **société à responsabilité limitée.**
sarment [saʀmɑ̃] *nm*: ~ **(de vigne)** vine shoot.
sarrasin [saʀazɛ̃] *nm* buckwheat.
sarrau [saʀo] *nm* smock.
Sarre [saʀ] *nf*: **la** ~ the Saar.
sarriette [saʀjɛt] *nf* savory.
sarrois, e [saʀwa, -waz] *adj* Saar *cpd* ♦ *nm/f*: **S~, e** inhabitant *ou* native of the Saar.
sas [sas] *nm* (*de sous-marin, d'engin spatial*) airlock; (*d'écluse*) lock.
satané, e [satane] *adj* (*fam*) confounded.
satanique [satanik] *adj* satanic, fiendish.
satelliser [satelize] *vt* (*fusée*) to put into orbit; (*fig: pays*) to make into a satellite.
satellite [satelit] *nm* satellite; **pays** ~ satellite country.
satellite-espion, *pl* **satellites-espions** [satelitɛspjɔ̃] *nm* spy satellite.
satellite-observatoire, *pl* **satellites-observatoires** [satelitɔpsɛʀvatwaʀ] *nm* observation satellite.
satellite-relais, *pl* **satellites-relais** [satelitʀəlɛ] *nm* (*TV*) relay satellite.
satiété [sasjete] **à** ~ *adv* to satiety *ou* satiation; (*répéter*) ad nauseam.
satin [satɛ̃] *nm* satin.
satiné, e [satine] *adj* satiny; (*peau*) satin-smooth.
satinette [satinɛt] *nf* satinet, sateen.
satire [satiʀ] *nf* satire; **faire la** ~ to satirize.
satirique [satiʀik] *adj* satirical.
satiriser [satiʀize] *vt* to satirize.
satiriste [satiʀist(ə)] *nm/f* satirist.
satisfaction [satisfaksjɔ̃] *nf* satisfaction; **à ma grande** ~ to my great satisfaction; **obtenir** ~ to obtain *ou* get satisfaction; **donner** ~ **(à)** to give satisfaction (to).
satisfaire [satisfɛʀ] *vt* to satisfy; **se** ~ **de** to be satisfied *ou* content with; ~ **à** *vt* (*engagement*) to fulfil; (*revendications, conditions*) to satisfy, meet.
satisfaisant, e [satisfəzɑ̃, -ɑ̃t] *vb voir* **satisfaire** ♦ *adj* satisfactory; (*qui fait plaisir*) satisfying.
satisfait, e [satisfɛ, -ɛt] *pp de* **satisfaire** ♦ *adj* satisfied; ~ **de** happy *ou* satisfied with.
satisfasse [satisfas], **satisferai** [satisfʀe] *etc vb voir* **satisfaire.**
saturation [satyʀasjɔ̃] *nf* saturation; **arriver à**

~ to reach saturation point.
saturer [satyʀe] *vt* to saturate; ~ **qn/qch de** to saturate sb/sth with.
saturnisme [satyʀnism(ə)] *nm* (*MÉD*) lead poisoning.
satyre [satiʀ] *nm* satyr; (*péj*) lecher.
sauce [sos] *nf* sauce; (*avec un rôti*) gravy; **en** ~ in a sauce; ~ **blanche** white sauce; ~ **chasseur** sauce chasseur; ~ **tomate** tomato sauce.
saucer [sose] *vt* (*assiette*) to soak up the sauce from.
saucière [sosjɛʀ] *nf* sauceboat; gravy boat.
saucisse [sosis] *nf* sausage.
saucisson [sosisɔ̃] *nm* (slicing) sausage; ~ **à l'ail** garlic sausage.
saucissonner [sosisɔne] *vt* to cut up, slice ♦ *vi* to picnic.
sauf [sof] *prép* except; ~ **si** (*à moins que*) unless; ~ **avis contraire** unless you hear to the contrary; ~ **empêchement** barring (any) problems; ~ **erreur** if I'm not mistaken; ~ **imprévu** unless anything unforeseen arises, barring accidents.
sauf, sauve [sof, sov] *adj* unharmed, unhurt; (*fig: honneur*) intact, saved; **laisser la vie sauve à qn** to spare sb's life.
sauf-conduit [sofkɔ̃dɥi] *nm* safe-conduct.
sauge [soʒ] *nf* sage.
saugrenu, e [sogʀəny] *adj* preposterous, ludicrous.
saule [sol] *nm* willow (tree); ~ **pleureur** weeping willow.
saumâtre [somɑtʀ(ə)] *adj* briny; (*désagréable: plaisanterie*) unsavoury (*BRIT*), unsavory (*US*).
saumon [somɔ̃] *nm* salmon *inv* ♦ *adj inv* salmon (pink).
saumoné, e [somɔne] *adj*: **truite** ~**e** salmon trout.
saumure [somyʀ] *nf* brine.
sauna [sona] *nm* sauna.
saupoudrer [sopudʀe] *vt*: ~ **qch de** to sprinkle sth with.
saupoudreuse [sopudʀøz] *nf* dredger.
saur [sɔʀ] *adj m*: **hareng** ~ smoked *ou* red herring, kipper.
saurai [sɔʀe] *etc vb voir* **savoir.**
saut [so] *nm* jump; (*discipline sportive*) jumping; **faire un** ~ to (make a) jump *ou* leap; **faire un** ~ **chez qn** to pop over to sb's (place); **au** ~ **du lit** on getting out of bed; ~ **en hauteur/longueur** high/long jump; ~ **à la corde** skipping; ~ **de page** (*INFORM*) page break; ~ **en parachute** parachuting *no pl*; ~ **à la perche** pole vaulting; ~ **à l'élastique** bungee jumping; ~ **périlleux** somersault.
saute [sot] *nf*: ~ **de vent/température** sudden change of wind direction/in the temperature; **avoir des** ~**s d'humeur** to have sudden changes of mood.
sauté, e [sote] *adj* (*CULIN*) sauté ♦ *nm*: ~ **de**

veau sauté of veal.

saute-mouton [sotmutɔ̃] *nm*: **jouer à ~** to play leapfrog.

sauter [sote] *vi* to jump, leap; (*exploser*) to blow up, explode; (: *fusibles*) to blow; (*se rompre*) to snap, burst; (*se détacher*) to pop out (*ou* off) ♦ *vt* to jump (over), leap (over); (*fig: omettre*) to skip, miss (out); **faire ~** to blow up; to burst open; (*CULIN*) to sauté; **~ à pieds joints/à cloche-pied** to make a standing jump/to hop; **~ en parachute** to make a parachute jump; **~ à la corde** to skip; **~ de joie** to jump for joy; **~ de colère** to be hopping with rage *ou* hopping mad; **~ au cou de qn** to fly into sb's arms; **~ aux yeux** to be quite obvious; **~ au plafond** (*fig*) to hit the roof.

sauterelle [sotʀɛl] *nf* grasshopper.

sauterie [sotʀi] *nf* party, hop.

sauteur, euse [sotœʀ, -øz] *nm/f* (*athlète*) jumper ♦ *nf* (*casserole*) shallow pan, frying pan; **~ à la perche** pole vaulter; **~ à skis** skijumper.

sautillement [sotijmɑ̃] *nm* hopping; skipping.

sautiller [sotije] *vi* to hop; to skip.

sautoir [sotwaʀ] *nm* chain; (*SPORT: emplacement*) jumping pit; **~ (de perles)** string of pearls.

sauvage [sovaʒ] *adj* (*gén*) wild; (*peuplade*) savage; (*farouche*) unsociable; (*barbare*) wild, savage; (*non officiel*) unauthorized, unofficial ♦ *nm/f* savage; (*timide*) unsociable type, recluse.

sauvagement [sovaʒmɑ̃] *adv* savagely.

sauvageon, ne [sovaʒɔ̃, -ɔn] *nm/f* little savage.

sauvagerie [sovaʒʀi] *nf* wildness; savagery; unsociability.

sauve [sov] *adj f voir* **sauf**.

sauvegarde [sovgaʀd(ə)] *nf* safeguard; **sous la ~ de** under the protection of; **disquette/ fichier de ~** (*INFORM*) backup disk/file.

sauvegarder [sovgaʀde] *vt* to safeguard; (*IN-FORM: enregistrer*) to save; (: *copier*) to back up.

sauve-qui-peut [sovkipø] *nm inv* stampede, mad rush ♦ *excl* run for your life!

sauver [sove] *vt* to save; (*porter secours à*) to rescue; (*récupérer*) to salvage, rescue; **se ~** *vi* (*s'enfuir*) to run away; (*fam: partir*) to be off; **~ qn de** to save sb from; **~ la vie à qn** to save sb's life; **~ les apparences** to keep up appearances.

sauvetage [sovtaʒ] *nm* rescue; **~ en montagne** mountain rescue; **ceinture de ~** lifebelt (*BRIT*), life preserver (*US*); **brassière** *ou* **gilet de ~** lifejacket (*BRIT*), life preserver (*US*).

sauveteur [sovtœʀ] *nm* rescuer.

sauvette [sovɛt]: **à la ~** *adv* (*vendre*) without authorization; (*se marier etc*) hastily, hurriedly; **vente à la ~** (unauthorized) street

trading, (street) peddling.

sauveur [sovœʀ] *nm* saviour (*BRIT*), savior (*US*).

SAV *sigle m* = **service après-vente**.

savais [save] *etc vb voir* **savoir**.

savamment [savamɑ̃] *adv* (*avec érudition*) learnedly; (*habilement*) skilfully, cleverly.

savane [savan] *nf* savannah.

savant, e [savɑ̃, -ɑ̃t] *adj* scholarly, learned; (*calé*) clever ♦ *nm* scientist; **animal ~** performing animal.

savate [savat] *nf* worn-out shoe; (*SPORT*) French boxing.

saveur [savœʀ] *nf* flavour (*BRIT*), flavor (*US*); (*fig*) savour (*BRIT*), savor (*US*).

Savoie [savwa] *nf*: **la ~** Savoy.

savoir [savwaʀ] *vt* to know; (*être capable de*): **il sait nager** he knows how to swim, he can swim ♦ *nm* knowledge; **se ~** (*être connu*) to be known; **se ~ malade/incurable** to know that one is ill/incurably ill; **il est petit: tu ne peux pas ~!** you won't believe how small he is!; **vous n'êtes pas sans ~ que** you are not *ou* will not be unaware of the fact that; **je crois ~ que ...** I believe that ..., I think I know that ...; **je n'en sais rien** I (really) don't know; **à ~ (que)** that is, namely; **faire ~ qch à qn** to inform sb about sth, let sb know sth; **pas que je sache** not as far as I know; **sans le ~** *adv* unknowingly, unwittingly; **en long** to know a lot.

savoir-faire [savwaʀfɛʀ] *nm inv* savoir-faire, know-how.

savoir-vivre [savwaʀvivʀ(ə)] *nm inv*: **le ~** savoir-faire, good manners *pl*.

savon [savɔ̃] *nm* (*produit*) soap; (*morceau*) bar *ou* tablet of soap; (*fam*): **passer un ~ à qn** to give sb a good dressing-down.

savonner [savɔne] *vt* to soap.

savonnerie [savɔnʀi] *nf* soap factory.

savonnette [savɔnɛt] *nf* bar *ou* tablet of soap.

savonneux, euse [savɔnø, -øz] *adj* soapy.

savons [savɔ̃] *vb voir* **savoir**.

savourer [savuʀe] *vt* to savour (*BRIT*), savor (*US*).

savoureux, euse [savuʀø, -øz] *adj* tasty; (*fig*) spicy, juicy.

savoyard, e [savwajaʀ, -aʀd(ə)] *adj* Savoyard.

Saxe [saks(ə)] *nf*: **la ~** Saxony.

saxo(phone) [saksɔ(fɔn)] *nm* sax(ophone).

saxophoniste [saksɔfɔnist(ə)] *nm/f* saxophonist, sax(ophone) player.

saynète [sɛnɛt] *nf* playlet.

SBB *sigle f* (= *Schweizerische Bundesbahn*) Swiss federal railways.

sbire [sbiʀ] *nm* (*péj*) henchman.

sc. *abr* = **scène**.

s/c *abr* (= *sous couvert de*) ≈ c/o.

scabreux, euse [skabʀø, -øz] *adj* risky; (*indécent*) improper, shocking.

scalpel [skalpɛl] *nm* scalpel.

scalper [skalpe] *vt* to scalp.

scampi [skãpi] *nmpl* scampi.

scandale [skãdal] *nm* scandal; (*tapage*): **faire du ~** to make a scene, create a disturbance; **faire ~** to scandalize people; **au grand ~ de ...** to the great indignation of ....

scandaleusement [skãdaløzmã] *adv* scandalously, outrageously.

scandaleux, euse [skãdalø, -øz] *adj* scandalous, outrageous.

scandaliser [skãdalize] *vt* to scandalize; **se ~ (de)** to be scandalized (by).

scander [skãde] *vt* (*vers*) to scan; (*mots, syllabes*) to stress separately; (*slogans*) to chant.

scandinave [skãdinav] *adj* Scandinavian ♦ *nm/f*: **S~** Scandinavian.

Scandinavie [skãdinavi] *nf*: **la ~** Scandinavia.

scanner [skanɛʀ] *nm* (*MÉD*) scanner.

scanographie [skanɔgʀafi] *nf* (*MÉD*) scanning; (*image*) scan.

scaphandre [skafãdʀ(ə)] *nm* (*de plongeur*) diving suit; (*de cosmonaute*) space-suit; **~ autonome** aqualung.

scaphandrier [skafãdʀije] *nm* diver.

scarabée [skaʀabe] *nm* beetle.

scarlatine [skaʀlatin] *nf* scarlet fever.

scarole [skaʀɔl] *nf* endive.

scatologique [skatɔlɔʒik] *adj* scatological, lavatorial.

sceau, x [so] *nm* seal; (*fig*) stamp, mark; **sous le ~ du secret** under the seal of secrecy.

scélérat, e [selera, -at] *nm/f* villain, blackguard ♦ *adj* villainous, blackguardly.

sceller [sele] *vt* to seal.

scellés [sele] *nmpl* seals.

scénario [senaʀjo] *nm* (*CINÉ*) screenplay, script; (*: idée, plan*) scenario; (*fig*) pattern; scenario.

scénariste [senaʀist(ə)] *nm/f* scriptwriter.

scène [sɛn] *nf* (*gén*) scene; (*estrade, fig: théâtre*) stage; **entrer en ~** to come on stage; **mettre en ~** (*THÉÂT*) to stage; (*CINÉ*) to direct; (*fig*) to present, introduce; **sur le devant de la ~** (*en pleine actualité*) in the forefront; **porter à la ~** to adapt for the stage; **faire une ~** (à **qn**) to make a scene (with sb); **~ de ménage** domestic fight *ou* scene.

scénique [senik] *adj* (*effets*) theatrical; (*art*) scenic.

scepticisme [sɛptisism(ə)] *nm* scepticism.

sceptique [sɛptik] *adj* sceptical ♦ *nm/f* sceptic.

sceptre [sɛptʀ(ə)] *nm* sceptre.

schéma [ʃema] *nm* (*diagramme*) diagram, sketch; (*fig*) outline.

schématique [ʃematik] *adj* diagrammatic(al), schematic; (*fig*) oversimplified.

schématiquement [ʃematikmã] *adv* schematically, diagrammatically.

schématisation [ʃematizasjɔ̃] *nf* schematization; oversimplification.

schématiser [ʃematize] *vt* to schematize; to (over)simplify.

schismatique [ʃismatik] *adj* schismatic.

schisme [ʃism(ə)] *nm* schism; rift, split.

schiste [ʃist(ə)] *nm* schist.

schizophrène [skizɔfʀɛn] *nm/f* schizophrenic.

schizophrénie [skizɔfʀeni] *nf* schizophrenia.

sciatique [sjatik] *adj*: **nerf ~** sciatic nerve ♦ *nf* sciatica.

scie [si] *nf* saw; (*fam: rengaine*) catch-tune; (*: personne*) bore; **~ à bois** wood saw; **~ circulaire** circular saw; **~ à découper** fretsaw; **~ à métaux** hacksaw; **~ sauteuse** jigsaw.

sciemment [sjamã] *adv* knowingly, wittingly.

science [sjãs] *nf* science; (*savoir*) knowledge; (*savoir-faire*) art, skill; **~s humaines/sociales** social sciences; **~s naturelles** natural science *sg*, biology *sg*; **~s po** political studies.

science-fiction [sjãsfiksjɔ̃] *nf* science fiction.

scientifique [sjãtifik] *adj* scientific ♦ *nm/f* (*savant*) scientist; (*étudiant*) science student.

scientifiquement [sjãtifikmã] *adv* scientifically.

scier [sje] *vt* to saw; (*retrancher*) to saw off.

scierie [siʀi] *nf* sawmill.

scieur [sjœʀ] *nm*: **~ de long** pit sawyer.

Scilly [sili]: **les îles ~** the Scilly Isles, the Scillies, the Isles of Scilly.

scinder [sɛ̃de] *vt, se ~ vi* to split (up).

scintillant, e [sɛ̃tijã, -ãt] *adj* sparkling.

scintillement [sɛ̃tijmã] *nm* sparkling *no pl*.

scintiller [sɛ̃tije] *vi* to sparkle.

scission [sisjɔ̃] *nf* split.

sciure [sjyʀ] *nf*: **~ (de bois)** sawdust.

sclérose [skleʀoz] *nf* sclerosis; (*fig*) ossification; **~ en plaques (SEP)** multiple sclerosis (MS).

sclérosé, e [skleʀoze] *adj* sclerosed, sclerotic; ossified.

scléroser [skleʀoze]: **se ~ vi** to become sclerosed; (*fig*) to become ossified.

scolaire [skɔlɛʀ] *adj* school *cpd*; (*péj*) schoolish; **l'année ~** the school year; (*à l'université*) the academic year; **en âge ~** of school age.

scolarisation [skɔlaʀizasjɔ̃] *nf* (*d'un enfant*) schooling; **la ~ d'une région** the provision of schooling in a region; **le taux de ~** the proportion of children in full-time education.

scolariser [skɔlaʀize] *vt* to provide with schooling (*ou* schools).

scolarité [skɔlaʀite] *nf* schooling; **frais de ~** school fees (*BRIT*), tuition (*US*).

scolastique [skɔlastik] *adj* (*péj*) scholastic.

scoliose [skɔljoz] *nf* curvature of the spine, scoliosis.

scoop [skup] *nm* (*PRESSE*) scoop, exclusive.

scooter [skutœʀ] *nm* (motor) scooter.

scorbut [skɔʀbyt] *nm* scurvy.

score [skɔʀ] *nm* score; (*électoral etc*) result.

scories [skɔʀi] *nfpl* scoria *pl*.

scorpion [skɔʀpjɔ̃] *nm* (*signe*): **le S~** Scorpio, the Scorpion; **être du S~** to be Scorpio.

scotch [skɔtʃ] *nm* (*whisky*) scotch, whisky; (*ad-*

hésif) Sellotape ® (*BRIT*), Scotch tape ® (*US*).

scotcher [skɔtʃe] *vt* to sellotape ® (*BRIT*), scotchtape ® (*US*).

scout, e [skut] *adj, nm* scout.

scoutisme [skutism(ə)] *nm* (boy) scout movement; (*activités*) scouting.

scribe [skʀib] *nm* scribe; (*péj*) penpusher.

scribouillard [skʀibujaʀ] *nm* penpusher.

script [skʀipt(ə)] *nm* printing; (*CINÉ*) (shooting) script.

scripte [skʀipt(ə)] *nf* continuity girl.

script-girl [skʀiptgœʀl] *nf* continuity girl.

scriptural, e, aux [skʀiptyʀal, -o] *adj*: **monnaie** ~e bank money.

scrupule [skʀypyl] *nm* scruple; **être sans** ~s to be unscrupulous; **se faire un** ~ **de qch** to have scruples *ou* qualms about doing sth.

scrupuleusement [skʀypyløzmɑ̃] *adv* scrupulously.

scrupuleux, euse [skʀypylø, -øz] *adj* scrupulous.

scrutateur, trice [skʀytatœʀ, -tʀis] *adj* searching ♦ *nm/f* scrutineer.

scruter [skʀyte] *vt* to search, scrutinize; (*l'obscurité*) to peer into; (*motifs, comportement*) to examine, scrutinize.

scrutin [skʀytɛ̃] *nm* (*vote*) ballot; (*ensemble des opérations*) poll; ~ **proportionnel/majoritaire** election on a proportional/majority basis; ~ **à deux tours** poll with two ballots *ou* rounds; ~ **de liste** list system.

sculpter [skylte] *vt* to sculpt; (*suj: érosion*) to carve.

sculpteur [skyltœʀ] *nm* sculptor.

sculptural, e, aux [skyltyʀal, -o] *adj* sculptural; (*fig*) statuesque.

sculpture [skyltyʀ] *nf* sculpture; ~ **sur bois** wood carving.

sdb. *abr* = **salle de bain**.

S.D.F. *sigle m* (= *sans domicile fixe*) homeless person; **les** ~ the homeless.

SDN *sigle f* (= *Société des Nations*) League of Nations.

SE *sigle f* (= *Son Excellence*) HE.

═══════════════════════ *MOT-CLÉ*

se (s') [s(ə)] *pron* **1** (*emploi réfléchi*) oneself; (: *masc*) himself; (: *fém*) herself; (: *sujet non humain*) itself; (: *pl*) themselves; **se voir comme l'on est** to see o.s. as one is

2 (*réciproque*) one another, each other; **ils s'aiment** they love one another *ou* each other

3 (*passif*): **cela se répare facilement** it is easily repaired

4 (*possessif*): **se casser la jambe/laver les mains** to break one's leg/wash one's hands.

────────────────────────────

séance [seɑ̃s] *nf* (*d'assemblée, récréative*) meeting, session; (*de tribunal*) sitting, session; (*musicale, CINÉ, THÉÂT*) performance; **ouvrir/lever la** ~ to open/close the meeting; ~ **te-**

nante forthwith.

séant, e [seɑ̃, -ɑ̃t] *adj* seemly, fitting ♦ *nm* posterior.

seau, x [so] *nm* bucket, pail; ~ **à glace** ice bucket.

sébum [sebɔm] *nm* sebum.

sec, sèche [sɛk, sɛʃ] *adj* dry; (*raisins, figues*) dried; (*cœur, personne: insensible*) hard, cold; (*maigre, décharné*) spare, lean; (*réponse, ton*) sharp, curt; (*démarrage*) sharp, sudden ♦ *nm*: **tenir au** ~ to keep in a dry place ♦ *adv* hard; (*démarrer*) sharply; **boire** ~ to be a heavy drinker; **je le bois** ~ I drink it straight *ou* neat; **à pied** ~ without getting one's feet wet; **à** ~ *adj* dried up; (*à court d'argent*) broke.

SECAM [sekam] *sigle m* (= *procédé séquentiel à mémoire*) SECAM.

sécante [sekɑ̃t] *nf* secant.

sécateur [sekatœʀ] *nm* secateurs *pl* (*BRIT*), shears *pl*, pair of secateurs *ou* shears.

sécession [sesesjɔ̃] *nf*: **faire** ~ to secede; **la guerre de S**~ the American Civil War.

séchage [seʃaʒ] *nm* drying; (*de bois*) seasoning.

sèche [sɛʃ] *adj f voir* **sec** ♦ *nf* (*fam*) cigarette, fag (*BRIT*).

sèche-cheveux [sɛʃʃəvø] *nm inv* hair-drier.

sèche-linge [sɛʃlɛ̃ʒ] *nm inv* drying cabinet.

sèche-mains [sɛʃmɛ̃] *nm inv* hand drier.

sèchement [sɛʃmɑ̃] *adv* (*frapper etc*) sharply; (*répliquer etc*) drily, sharply.

sécher [seʃe] *vt* to dry; (*dessécher: peau, blé*) to dry (out); (: *étang*) to dry up; (*bois*) to season; (*fam: classe, cours*) to skip, miss ♦ *vi* to dry; to dry out; to dry up; (*fam: candidat*) to be stumped; **se** ~ (*après le bain*) to dry o.s.

sécheresse [seʃʀɛs] *nf* dryness; (*absence de pluie*) drought.

séchoir [seʃwaʀ] *nm* drier.

second, e [s(ə)gɔ̃, -ɔ̃d] *adj* second ♦ *nm* (*assistant*) second in command; (*étage*) second floor (*BRIT*), third floor (*US*); (*NAVIG*) first mate ♦ *nf* second; (*SCOL*) ≈ fifth form (*BRIT*), ≈ tenth grade (*US*); **en** ~ (*en second rang*) in second place; **voyager en** ~e to travel second-class; **doué de** ~**e vue** having (the gift of) second sight; **trouver son** ~ **souffle** (*SPORT, fig*) to get one's second wind; **être dans un état** ~ to be in a daze (*ou* trance); **de** ~**e main** second-hand.

secondaire [s(ə)gɔ̃dɛʀ] *adj* secondary.

seconder [s(ə)gɔ̃de] *vt* to assist; (*favoriser*) to back.

secouer [s(ə)kwe] *vt* to shake; (*passagers*) to rock; (*traumatiser*) to shake (up); **se** ~ (*chien*) to shake itself; (*fam: se démener*) to shake o.s. up; ~ **la poussière d'un tapis** to shake the dust off a carpet; ~ **la tête** to shake one's head.

secourable [s(ə)kuʀabl(ə)] *adj* helpful.

secourir [s(ə)kuʀiʀ] *vt* (*aller sauver*) to (go and)

rescue; (*prodiguer des soins à*) to help, assist; (*venir en aide à*) to assist, aid.

secourisme [səkuʀism(ə)] *nm* (*premiers soins*) first aid; (*sauvetage*) life saving.

secouriste [səkuʀist(ə)] *nm/f* first-aid worker.

secourons [səkuʀɔ̃] *etc vb voir* **secourir**.

secours [səkuʀ] *vb voir* **secourir** ♦ *nm* help, aid, assistance ♦ *nmpl* aid *sg*; **cela lui a été d'un grand** ~ this was a great help to him; **au** ~! help!; **appeler au** ~ to shout *ou* call for help; **appeler qn à** **son** ~ to call sb to one's assistance; **porter** ~ **à qn** to give sb assistance, help sb; **les premiers** ~ first aid *sg*; **le** ~ **en montagne** mountain rescue.

secouru, e [səkuʀy] *pp de* **secourir**.

secousse [səkus] *nf* jolt, bump; (*électrique*) shock; (*fig: psychologique*) jolt, shock; ~ **sismique** *ou* **tellurique** earth tremor.

secret, ète [səkʀɛ, -ɛt] *adj* secret; (*fig: renfermé*) reticent, reserved ♦ *nm* secret; (*discrétion absolue*): **le** ~ secrecy; **en** ~ in secret, secretly; **au** ~ in solitary confinement; ~ **de fabrication** trade secret; ~ **professionnel** professional secrecy.

secrétaire [səkʀetɛʀ] *nm/f* secretary ♦ *nm* (*meuble*) writing desk, secretaire; ~ **d'ambassade** embassy secretary; ~ **de direction** private *ou* personal secretary; ~ **d'État** ≈ junior minister; ~ **général (SG)** Secretary-General; (*COMM*) company secretary; ~ **de mairie** town clerk; ~ **médicale** medical secretary; ~ **de rédaction** sub-editor.

secrétariat [s(ə)kʀetaʀja] *nm* (*profession*) secretarial work; (*bureau: d'entreprise, d'école*) (secretary's) office; (*: d'organisation internationale*) secretariat; (*POL etc: fonction*) secretaryship, office of Secretary.

secrètement [səkʀɛtmɑ̃] *adv* secretly.

sécréter [sekʀete] *vt* to secrete.

sécrétion [sekʀesjɔ̃] *nf* secretion.

sectaire [sɛktɛʀ] *adj* sectarian, bigoted.

sectarisme [sɛktaʀism(ə)] *nm* sectarianism.

secte [sɛkt(ə)] *nf* sect.

secteur [sɛktœʀ] *nm* sector; (*ADMIN*) district; (*ÉLEC*): **branché sur le** ~ plugged into the mains (supply); **fonctionne sur pile et** ~ battery or mains operated; **le** ~ **privé/public** (*ÉCON*) the private/public sector; **le** ~ **primaire/tertiaire** the primary/tertiary sector.

section [sɛksjɔ̃] *nf* section; (*de parcours d'autobus*) fare stage; (*MIL: unité*) platoon; ~ **rythmique** rhythm section.

sectionner [sɛksjɔne] *vt* to sever; **se** ~ *vi* to be severed.

sectionneur [sɛksjɔnœʀ] *nm* (*ÉLEC*) isolation switch.

sectoriel, le [sɛktɔʀjɛl] *adj* sector-based.

sectorisation [sɛktɔʀizasjɔ̃] *nf* division into sectors.

sectoriser [sɛktɔʀize] *vt* to divide into sec-

tors.

sécu [seky] *nf* (*fam*: = *sécurité sociale*) ≈ dole (*BRIT*), ≈ Welfare (*US*).

séculaire [sekylɛʀ] *adj* secular; (*très vieux*) age-old.

séculariser [sekylaʀize] *vt* to secularize.

séculier, ière [sekylje, -jɛʀ] *adj* secular.

sécurisant, e [sekyʀizɑ̃, -ɑ̃t] *adj* secure, giving a sense of security.

sécuriser [sekyʀize] *vt* to give a sense of security to.

sécurité [sekyʀite] *nf* security; (*absence de danger*) safety; **impression de** ~ sense of security; **la** ~ **internationale** international security; **système de** ~ security (*ou* safety) system; **être en** ~ to be safe; **la** ~ **de l'emploi** job security; **la** ~ **routière** road safety; **la** ~ **sociale** ≈ (the) Social Security (*BRIT*), ≈ (the) Welfare (*US*).

sédatif, ive [sedatif, -iv] *adj, nm* sedative.

sédentaire [sedɑ̃tɛʀ] *adj* sedentary.

sédiment [sedimɑ̃] *nm* sediment; ~**s** *nmpl* (*alluvions*) sediment *sg*.

sédimentaire [sedimɑ̃tɛʀ] *adj* sedimentary.

sédimentation [sedimɑ̃tasjɔ̃] *nf* sedimentation.

séditieux, euse [sedisjø, -øz] *adj* insurgent; seditious.

sédition [sedisjɔ̃] *nf* insurrection; sedition.

séducteur, trice [sedyktœʀ, -tʀis] *adj* seductive ♦ *nm/f* seducer/seductress.

séduction [sedyksjɔ̃] *nf* seduction; (*charme, attrait*) appeal, charm.

séduire [sedɥiʀ] *vt* to charm; (*femme: abuser de*) to seduce; (*suj: chose*) to appeal to.

séduisant, e [sedɥizɑ̃, -ɑ̃t] *vb voir* **séduire** ♦ *adj* (*femme*) seductive; (*homme, offre*) very attractive.

séduit, e [sedɥi, -it] *pp de* **séduire**.

segment [sɛgmɑ̃] *nm* segment; (*AUTO*): ~ (**de piston**) piston ring; ~ **de frein** brake shoe.

segmenter [sɛgmɑ̃te] *vt, se* ~ *vi* to segment.

ségrégation [segʀegasjɔ̃] *nf* segregation.

ségrégationnisme [segʀegasjɔnism(ə)] *nm* segregationism.

ségrégationniste [segʀegasjɔnist(ə)] *adj* segregationist.

seiche [sɛʃ] *nf* cuttlefish.

séide [seid] *nm* (*péj*) henchman.

seigle [sɛgl(ə)] *nm* rye.

seigneur [sɛɲœʀ] *nm* lord; **le S**~ the Lord.

seigneurial, e, aux [sɛɲœʀjal, -o] *adj* lordly, stately.

sein [sɛ̃] *nm* breast; (*entrailles*) womb; **au** ~ **de** *prép* (*équipe, institution*) within; (*flots, bonheur*) in the midst of; **donner le** ~ **à** (*bébé*) to feed (at the breast); to breast-feed; **nourrir au** ~ to breast-feed.

Seine [sɛn] *nf*: **la** ~ the Seine.

séisme [seism(ə)] *nm* earthquake.

séismique *etc* [seismik] *voir* **sismique** *etc*.

SEITA [seita] *sigle f* = *Société d'exploitation indus-*

trielle des tabacs et allumettes.
seize [sɛz] *num* sixteen.
seizième [sɛzjɛm] *num* sixteenth.
séjour [seʒuR] *nm* stay; (*pièce*) living room.
séjourner [seʒuRne] *vi* to stay.
sel [sɛl] *nm* salt; (*fig*) wit; spice; ~ **de cuisine/ de table** cooking/table salt; ~ **gemme** rock salt; ~**s de bain** bathsalts.
sélect, e [selɛkt] *adj* select.
sélectif, ive [selɛktif, -iv] *adj* selective.
sélection [selɛksjɔ̃] *nf* selection; **faire/opérer une** ~ **parmi** to make a selection from among; **épreuve de** ~ (*SPORT*) trial (for selection); ~ **naturelle** natural selection; ~ **professionnelle** professional recruitment.
sélectionné, e [selɛksjɔne] *adj* (*joueur*) selected; (*produit*) specially selected.
sélectionner [selɛksjɔne] *vt* to select.
sélectionneur, euse [selɛksjɔnœR, -øz] *nm/f* selector.
sélectivement [selɛktivmɑ̃] *adv* selectively.
sélectivité [selɛktivite] *nf* selectivity.
sélénologie [selenɔlɔʒi] *nf* study of the moon, selenology.
self [sɛlf] *nm* (*fam*) self-service.
self-service [sɛlfsɛRvis] *adj* self-service ♦ *nm* self-service (restaurant); (*magasin*) self-service shop.
selle [sɛl] *nf* saddle; ~**s** *nfpl* (*MÉD*) stools; **aller à la** ~ (*MÉD*) to have a bowel movement; **se mettre en** ~ to mount, get into the saddle.
seller [sele] *vt* to saddle.
sellette [selɛt] *nf*: **être sur la** ~ to be on the carpet (*fig*).
sellier [selje] *nm* saddler.
selon [səlɔ̃] *prép* according to; (*en se conformant à*) in accordance with; ~ **moi** as I see it; ~ **que** according to, depending on whether.
SEm *sigle f* (= Son Éminence) HE.
semailles [səmɑj] *nfpl* sowing *sg*.
semaine [səmɛn] *nf* week; (*salaire*) week's wages *ou* pay, weekly wages *ou* pay; **en** ~ during the week, on weekdays; **à la petite** ~ from day to day; **la** ~ **sainte** Holy Week.
semainier [səmenje] *nm* (*bracelet*) bracelet made up of seven bands; (*calendrier*) desk diary; (*meuble*) chest of (seven) drawers.
sémantique [semɑ̃tik] *adj* semantic ♦ *nf* semantics *sg*.
sémaphore [semafɔR] *nm* (*RAIL*) semaphore signal.
semblable [sɑ̃blabl(ə)] *adj* similar; (*de ce genre*): **de** ~**s mésaventures** such mishaps ♦ *nm* fellow creature *ou* man; ~ **à** similar to, like.
semblant [sɑ̃blɑ̃] *nm*: **un** ~ **de vérité** a semblance of truth; **faire** ~ **(de faire)** to pretend (to do).
sembler [sɑ̃ble] *vb avec attribut* to seem ♦ *vb impers*: **il semble (bien) que/inutile de** it (really) seems *ou* appears that/useless to; **il me**

semble (bien) que it (really) seems to me that, I (really) think (that); **il me semble le connaître** I think *ou* I've a feeling I know him; ~ **être** to seem to be; **comme bon lui semble** as he sees fit; **me semble-t-il, à ce qu'il me semble** it seems to me, to my mind.
semelle [səmɛl] *nf* sole; (*intérieure*) insole, inner sole; **battre la** ~ to stamp one's feet (to keep them warm); (*fig*) to hang around (waiting); ~**s compensées** platform soles.
semence [səmɑ̃s] *nf* (*graine*) seed; (*clou*) tack.
semer [səme] *vt* to sow; (*fig: éparpiller*) to scatter; (*confusion*) to spread; (: *poursui- vants*) to lose, shake off; ~ **la discorde/terreur parmi** to sow discord/terror among; **semé de** (*difficultés*) riddled with.
semestre [səmɛstR(ə)] *nm* half-year; (*SCOL*) semester.
semestriel, le [səmɛstRijɛl] *adj* half-yearly; semestral.
semeur, euse [səmœR, -øz] *nm/f* sower.
semi-automatique [səmiɔtɔmatik] *adj* semi-automatic.
semiconducteur [səmikɔ̃dyktœR] *nm* (*INFORM*) semiconductor.
semi-conserve [səmikɔ̃sɛRv(ə)] *nf* semi-perishable foodstuff.
semi-fini [səmifini] *adj m* (*produit*) semi-finished.
semi-liberté [səmilibɛRte] *nf* (*JUR*) partial release from prison (*in order to follow a profession or undergo medical treatment*).
sémillant, e [semijɑ̃, -ɑ̃t] *adj* vivacious; dashing.
séminaire [seminɛR] *nm* seminar; (*REL*) seminary.
séminariste [seminaRist(ə)] *nm* seminarist.
sémiologie [semjɔlɔʒi] *nf* semiology.
semi-public, ique [səmipyblik] *adj* (*JUR*) semi-public.
semi-remorque [səmiRəmɔRk(ə)] *nf* trailer ♦ *nm* articulated lorry (*BRIT*), semi(trailer) (*US*).
semis [səmi] *nm* (*terrain*) seedbed, seed plot; (*plante*) seedling.
sémite [semit] *adj* Semitic.
sémitique [semitik] *adj* Semitic.
semoir [səmwaR] *nm* seed-bag; seeder.
semonce [səmɔ̃s] *nf*: **un coup de** ~ a shot across the bows.
semoule [səmul] *nf* semolina; ~ **de riz** ground rice.
sempiternel, le [sɛ̃pitɛRnɛl] *adj* eternal, never-ending.
sénat [sena] *nm* senate.

The **Sénat** *is the upper house of the French parliament, sitting in the Palais du Luxembourg in Paris. One third of* **sénateurs** *are elected for a nine-year term every three years by an electoral college consisting of* **députés** *and other elected representatives. The Sénat has a wide* *range of powers but is overidden by the* **Assemblée nationale** *in cases of disagreement.*

sénateur [senatœʀ] *nm* senator.

sénatorial, e, aux [senatɔʀjal, -o] *adj* senatorial, Senate *cpd.*

Sénégal [senegal] *nm:* **le ~** Senegal.

sénégalais, e [senegalɛ, -ɛz] *adj* Senegalese.

sénevé [sɛnve] *nm* (*BOT*) mustard; (*graine*) mustard seed.

sénile [senil] *adj* senile.

sénilité [senilite] *nf* senility.

senior [senjɔʀ] *nm/f* (*SPORT*) senior.

sens [sã] *vb voir* sentir ♦ *nm* [sãs] (*PHYSIOL, instinct*) sense; (*signification*) meaning, sense; (*direction*) direction, way ♦ *nmpl* (*sensualité*) senses; **reprendre ses ~** to regain consciousness; **avoir le ~ des affaires/de la mesure** to have business sense/a sense of moderation; **ça n'a pas de ~** that doesn't make (any) sense; **en dépit du bon ~** contrary to all good sense; **tomber sous le ~** to stand to reason, be perfectly obvious; **en un ~, dans un ~** in a way; **en ce ~ que** in the sense that; **à mon ~** to my mind; **dans le ~ des aiguilles d'une montre** clockwise; **dans le ~ de la longueur/largeur** lengthways/ widthways; **dans le mauvais ~** the wrong way; in the wrong direction; **bon ~** good sense; **~ commun** common sense; **~ dessus dessous** upside down; **~ interdit, ~ unique** one-way street.

sensass [sãsas] *adj* (*fam*) fantastic.

sensation [sãsasjɔ̃] *nf* sensation; **faire ~** to cause a sensation, create a stir; **à ~** (*péj*) sensational.

sensationnel, le [sãsasjɔnɛl] *adj* sensational.

sensé, e [sãse] *adj* sensible.

sensibilisation [sãsibilizasjɔ̃] *nf* consciousness-raising: **une campagne de ~ de l'opinion** a campaign to raise public awareness.

sensibiliser [sãsibilize] *vt* to sensitize; **~ qn (à)** to make sb sensitive to.

sensibilité [sãsibilite] *nf* sensitivity; (*affectivité, émotivité*) sensitivity, sensibility.

sensible [sãsibl(ə)] *adj* sensitive; (*aux sens*) perceptible; (*appréciable: différence, progrès*) appreciable, noticeable; **~ à** sensitive to.

sensiblement [sãsibləmã] *adv* (*notablement*) appreciably, noticeably; (*à peu près*): **ils ont ~ le même poids** they weigh approximately the same.

sensiblerie [sãsibləʀi] *nf* sentimentality; squeamishness.

sensitif, ive [sãsitif, -iv] *adj* (*nerf*) sensory; (*personne*) oversensitive.

sensoriel, le [sãsɔʀjɛl] *adj* sensory, sensorial.

sensualité [sãsyalite] *nf* sensuality, sensuousness.

sensuel, le [sãsyɛl] *adj* sensual; sensuous.

sent [sã] *vb voir* **sentir.**

sente [sãt] *nf* path.

sentence [sãtãs] *nf* (*jugement*) sentence; (*adage*) maxim.

sentencieusement [sãtãsjøzmã] *adv* sententiously.

sentencieux, euse [sãtãsjø, -øz] *adj* sententious.

senteur [sãtœʀ] *nf* scent, perfume.

senti, e [sãti] *adj:* **bien ~** (*mots etc*) well-chosen.

sentier [sãtje] *nm* path.

sentiment [sãtimã] *nm* feeling; (*conscience, impression*): **avoir le ~ de/que** to be aware of/have the feeling that; **recevez mes ~s respectueux** yours faithfully; **faire du ~** (*péj*) to be sentimental; **si vous me prenez par les ~s** if you appeal to my feelings.

sentimental, e, aux [sãtimãtal, -o] *adj* sentimental; (*vie, aventure*) love *cpd.*

sentimentalisme [sãtimãtalism(ə)] *nm* sentimentalism.

sentimentalité [sãtimãtalite] *nf* sentimentality.

sentinelle [sãtinɛl] *nf* sentry; **en ~** standing guard; (*soldat: en faction*) on sentry duty.

sentir [sãtiʀ] *vt* (*par l'odorat*) to smell; (*par le goût*) to taste; (*au toucher, fig*) to feel; (*répandre une odeur de*) to smell of; (: *ressemblance*) to smell like; (*avoir la saveur de*) to taste of; to taste like; (*fig: dénoter, annoncer*) to be indicative of; to smack of; to foreshadow ♦ *vi* to smell; **~ mauvais** to smell bad; **se ~ bien** to feel good; **se ~ mal** (*être indisposé*) to feel unwell *ou* ill; **se ~ le courage/la force de faire** to feel brave/ strong enough to do; **ne plus se ~ de joie** to be beside o.s. with joy; **il ne peut pas le ~** (*fam*) he can't stand him.

seoir [swaʀ]: **~ à** *vt* to become, befit; **comme il (leur) sied** as it is fitting (to them).

Seoul [seul] *n* Seoul.

SEP *sigle f* (= *sclérose en plaques*) MS.

séparation [separasjɔ̃] *nf* separation; (*cloison*) division, partition; **~ de biens** division of property (*in marriage settlement*); **~ de corps** legal separation.

séparatisme [separatism(ə)] *nm* separatism.

séparatiste [separatist(ə)] *adj, nm/f* (*POL*) separatist.

séparé, e [separe] *adj* (*appartements, pouvoirs*) separate; (*époux*) separated; **~ de** separate from; separated from.

séparément [separemã] *adv* separately.

séparer [separe] *vt* (*gén*) to separate; (*suj: divergences etc*) to divide; to drive apart; (: *différences, obstacles*) to stand between; (*détacher*): **~ qch de** to pull sth (off) from; (*dissocier*) to distinguish between; (*diviser*): **~ qch par** to divide sth (up) with; **~ une pièce en deux** to divide a room into two; **se ~** (*époux*) to separate, part; (*prendre congé: amis etc*) to part, leave each other; (*adversaires*) to separate; (*se diviser: route, tige etc*) to divide; (*se détacher*): **se ~ (de)** to split off (from); to come off; **se ~ de** (*époux*) to separate *ou* part from; (*employé, objet personnel*) to part with.

sépia [sepja] *nf* sepia.

sept [sɛt] *num* seven.

septante [sɛptɑ̃t] *num* (*Belgique, Suisse*) seventy.

septembre [sɛptɑ̃bʀ(ə)] *nm* September; *voir aussi* **juillet**.

septennal, e, aux [sɛptenal, -o] *adj* seven-year; (*festival*) seven-year, septennial.

septennat [sɛptena] *nm* seven-year term (of office); seven-year reign.

septentrional, e, aux [sɛptɑ̃tʀijɔnal, -o] *adj* northern.

septicémie [sɛptisemi] *nf* blood poisoning, septicaemia.

septième [sɛtjɛm] *num* seventh; **être au ~ ciel** to be on cloud nine.

septique [sɛptik] *adj*: **fosse ~** septic tank.

septuagénaire [sɛptɥaʒenɛʀ] *adj, nm/f* septuagenarian.

sépulcral, e, aux [sepylkʀal, -o] *adj* (*voix*) sepulchral.

sépulcre [sepylkʀ(ə)] *nm* sepulchre.

sépulture [sepyltyʀ] *nf* burial; (*tombeau*) burial place, grave.

séquelles [sekɛl] *nfpl* after-effects; (*fig*) aftermath *sg*; consequences.

séquence [sekɑ̃s] *nf* sequence.

séquentiel, le [sekɑ̃sjɛl] *adj* sequential.

séquestration [sekɛstʀasjɔ̃] *nf* illegal confinement; impounding.

séquestre [sekɛstʀ(ə)] *nm* impoundment; **mettre sous ~** to impound.

séquestrer [sekɛstʀe] *vt* (*personne*) to confine illegally; (*biens*) to impound.

serai [səʀe] *etc vb voir* **être**.

sérail [seʀaj] *nm* seraglio; harem; **rentrer au ~** to return to the fold.

serbe [sɛʀb(ə)] *adj* Serbian ♦ *nm* (*LING*) Serbian ♦ *nm/f*: **S~** Serb.

Serbie [sɛʀbi] *nf*: **la ~** Serbia.

serbo-croate [sɛʀbɔkʀɔat] *adj* Serbo-Croat, Serbo-Croatian ♦ *nm* (*LING*) Serbo-Croat.

serein, e [səʀɛ̃, -ɛn] *adj* serene; (*jugement*) dispassionate.

sereinement [səʀɛnmɑ̃] *adv* serenely.

sérénade [seʀenad] *nf* serenade; (*fam*) hullabaloo.

sérénité [seʀenite] *nf* serenity.

serez [səʀe] *vb voir* **être**.

serf, serve [sɛʀ, sɛʀv(ə)] *nm/f* serf.

serfouette [sɛʀfwɛt] *nf* weeding hoe.

serge [sɛʀʒ(ə)] *nf* serge.

sergent [sɛʀʒɑ̃] *nm* sergeant.

sergent-chef [sɛʀʒɑ̃ʃɛf] *nm* staff sergeant.

sergent-major [sɛʀʒɑ̃maʒɔʀ] *nm* ≈ quartermaster sergeant.

sériciculture [seʀisikyltyʀ] *nf* silkworm breeding, sericulture.

série [seʀi] *nf* (*de questions, d'accidents, TV*) series *inv*; (*de clés, casseroles, outils*) set; (*catégorie: SPORT*) rank; class; **en ~** in quick succession; (*COMM*) mass *cpd*; **de ~** *adj* standard; **hors ~** (*COMM*) custom-built; (*fig*) outstanding; **imprimante ~** (*INFORM*) serial printer; **soldes de fin de ~s** end of line special offers; **~ noire** *nm* (*crime*) thriller ♦ *nf* (*suite de malheurs*) run of bad luck.

sérier [seʀje] *vt* to classify, sort out.

sérieusement [seʀjøzmɑ̃] *adv* seriously; reliably; responsibly; **il parle ~** he's serious, he means it; **~?** are you serious?, do you mean it?

sérieux, euse [seʀjø, -øz] *adj* serious; (*élève, employé*) reliable, responsible; (*client, maison*) reliable, dependable; (*offre, proposition*) genuine, serious; (*grave, sévère*) serious, solemn; (*maladie, situation*) serious, grave; (*important*) considerable ♦ *nm* seriousness; reliability; **ce n'est pas ~** (*raisonnable*) that's not on; **garder son ~** to keep a straight face; **manquer de ~** not to be very responsible (*ou* reliable); **prendre qch/qn au ~** to take sth/sb seriously.

sérigraphie [seʀigʀafi] *nf* silk screen printing.

serin [səʀɛ̃] *nm* canary.

seriner [səʀine] *vt*: **~ qch à qn** to drum sth into sb.

seringue [səʀɛ̃g] *nf* syringe.

serions [səʀjɔ̃] *etc vb voir* **être**.

serment [sɛʀmɑ̃] *nm* (*juré*) oath; (*promesse*) pledge, vow; **prêter ~** to take the *ou* an oath; **faire le ~ de** to take a vow to, swear to; **sous ~** on *ou* under oath.

sermon [sɛʀmɔ̃] *nm* sermon; (*péj*) sermon, lecture.

sermonner [sɛʀmɔne] *vt* to lecture.

SERNAM [sɛʀnam] *sigle m* (= *Service national de messageries*) *rail delivery service.*

sérologie [seʀɔlɔʒi] *nf* serology.

séronégatif, ive [seʀonegatif, -iv] *adj* HIV negative.

séropositif, ive [seʀopozitif, -iv] *adj* HIV positive.

serpe [sɛʀp(ə)] *nf* billhook.

serpent [sɛʀpɑ̃] *nm* snake; **~ à sonnettes** rattlesnake; **~ monétaire (européen)** (European) monetary snake.

serpenter [sɛʀpɑ̃te] *vi* to wind.

serpentin [sɛʀpɑ̃tɛ̃] *nm* (*tube*) coil; (*ruban*) streamer.

serpillière [sɛʀpijɛʀ] *nf* floorcloth.

serrage [seʀaʒ] *nm* tightening; **collier de ~** clamp.

serre [sɛʀ] *nf* (*AGR*) greenhouse; **~ chaude** hothouse; **~ froide** unheated greenhouse.

serré, e [seʀe] *adj* (*tissu*) closely woven; (*réseau*) dense; (*écriture*) close; (*habits*) tight; (*fig: lutte, match*) tight, close-fought; (*passagers etc*) (tightly) packed; (*café*) strong ♦ *adv*: **jouer ~** to play it close, play a close game;

écrire ~ to write a cramped hand; **avoir la gorge** ~**e** to have a lump in one's throat.

serre-livres [sɛʀlivʀ(ə)] nm inv book ends pl.

serrement [sɛʀmɑ̃] nm: ~ **de main** handshake; ~ **de cœur** pang of anguish.

serrer [seʀe] vt (tenir) to grip ou hold tight; (comprimer, coincer) to squeeze; (poings, mâchoires) to clench; (suj: vêtement) to be too tight for; to fit tightly; (rapprocher) to close up, move closer together; (ceinture, nœud, frein, vis) to tighten ♦ vi: ~ **à droite** to keep to the right; to move into the right-hand lane; **se** ~ (se rapprocher) to squeeze up; **se** ~ **contre qn** to huddle up to sb; **se** ~ **les coudes** to stick together, back one another up; **se** ~ **la ceinture** to tighten one's belt; ~ **la main à qn** to shake sb's hand; ~ **qn dans ses bras** to hug sb, clasp sb in one's arms; ~ **la gorge à qn** (suj: chagrin) to bring a lump to sb's throat; ~ **les dents** to clench ou grit one's teeth; ~ **qn de près** to follow close behind sb; ~ **le trottoir** to hug the kerb; ~ **sa droite** to keep well to the right; ~ **la vis à qn** to crack down harder on sb; ~ **les rangs** to close ranks.

serres [sɛʀ] nfpl (griffes) claws, talons.

serre-tête [sɛʀtɛt] nm inv (bandeau) headband; (bonnet) skullcap.

serrure [seʀyʀ] nf lock.

serrurerie [seʀyʀʀi] nf (métier) locksmith's trade; (ferronnerie) ironwork; ~ **d'art** ornamental ironwork.

serrurier [seʀyʀje] nm locksmith.

sers, sert [sɛʀ] vb voir **servir**.

sertir [sɛʀtiʀ] vt (pierre) to set; (pièces métalliques) to crimp.

sérum [seʀɔm] nm serum; ~ **antivenimeux** snakebite serum; ~ **sanguin** (blood) serum; ~ **de vérité** truth drug.

servage [sɛʀvaʒ] nm serfdom.

servant [sɛʀvɑ̃] nm server.

servante [sɛʀvɑ̃t] nf (maid)servant.

serve [sɛʀv] nf voir **serf** ♦ vb voir **servir**.

serveur, euse [sɛʀvœʀ, -øz] nm/f waiter/waitress ♦ adj: **centre** ~ (INFORM) service centre.

servi, e [sɛʀvi] adj: **être bien** ~ to get a large helping (ou helpings); **vous êtes** ~? are you being served?

serviable [sɛʀvjabl(ə)] adj obliging, willing to help.

service [sɛʀvis] nm (gén) service; (série de repas): **premier** ~ first sitting; (pourboire) service (charge); (assortiment de vaisselle) set; service; (linge de table) set; (bureau: de la vente etc) department, section; (travail): **pendant le** ~ on duty; ~**s** nmpl (travail, ÉCON) services, inclusive/exclusive of services; **faire le** ~ to serve; **être en** ~ **chez qn** (domestique) to be in sb's service; **être au** ~ **de** (patron, patrie) to be in the service of; **être au** ~ **de qn** (collaborateur, voiture) to be at sb's ser-

vice; **porte de** ~ tradesman's entrance; **rendre** ~ **à** to help; **il aime rendre** ~ he likes to help; **rendre un** ~ **à qn** to do sb a favour; **heures de** ~ hours of duty; **être de** ~ to be on duty; **reprendre du** ~ to get back into action; **avoir 25 ans de** ~ to have completed 25 years' service; **être/mettre en** ~ to be in/put into service ou action; **hors** ~ not in use; out of order; ~ **à thé/café** tea/ coffee set ou service; ~ **après-vente (SAV)** after-sales service; **en** ~ **commandé** on an official assignment; ~ **funèbre** funeral service; ~ **militaire** military service; ~ **d'ordre** police (ou stewards) in charge of maintaining order; ~**s publics** public services, (public) utilities; ~**s secrets** secret service sg; ~**s sociaux** social services.

> French men over eighteen years of age are required to do ten months' **service militaire** if passed fit. The call-up can be delayed if the conscript is a full-time student in higher education. Conscientious objectors are required to do two years' public service. Since 1970, women have been able to do military service, though few do.

serviette [sɛʀvjɛt] nf (de table) (table) napkin, serviette; (de toilette) towel; (porte-documents) briefcase; ~ **éponge** terry towel; ~ **hygiénique** sanitary towel.

servile [sɛʀvil] adj servile.

servir [sɛʀviʀ] vt (gén) to serve; (dîneur: au restaurant) to wait on; (client: au magasin) to serve, attend to; (fig: aider): ~ **qn** to aid sb; to serve sb's interests; to stand sb in good stead; (COMM: rente) to pay ♦ vi (TENNIS) to serve; (CARTES) to deal; (être militaire) to serve; ~ **qch à qn** to serve sb with sth, help sb to sth; **qu'est-ce que je vous sers?** what can I get you?; **se** ~ (prendre d'un plat) to help o.s.; (s'approvisionner): **se** ~ **chez** to shop at; **se** ~ **de** (plat) to help o.s. to; (voiture, outil, relations) to use; ~ **à qn** (diplôme, livre) to be of use to sb; **ça m'a servi pour faire** it was useful to me when I did; I used it to do; ~ **à qch/à faire** (outil etc) to be used for sth/for doing; **ça peut** ~ it may come in handy; **ça peut encore** ~ it can still be used (ou of use); **à quoi cela sert-il (de faire)?** what's the use (of doing)?; **cela ne sert à rien** it's no use; ~ **(à qn) de ...** to serve as ... (for sb); ~ **à dîner (à qn)** to serve dinner (to sb).

serviteur [sɛʀvitœʀ] nm servant.

servitude [sɛʀvityd] nf servitude; (fig) constraint; (JUR) easement.

servofrein [sɛʀvɔfʀɛ̃] nm servo(-assisted) brake.

servomécanisme [sɛʀvɔmekanism(ə)] nm servo system.

ses [se] adj possessif voir **son**.

sésame [sezam] *nm* (*BOT*) sesame; (*graine*) sesame seed.
session [sesjɔ̃] *nf* session.
set [sɛt] *nm* set; (*napperon*) placemat; ~ **de table** set of placemats.
seuil [sœj] *nm* doorstep; (*fig*) threshold; **sur le** ~ **de sa maison** in the doorway of his house, on his doorstep; **au** ~ **de** (*fig*) on the threshold *ou* brink *ou* edge of; ~ **de rentabilité** (*COMM*) breakeven point.
seul, e [sœl] *adj* (*sans compagnie*) alone; (*avec nuance affective: isolé*) lonely; (*unique*): **un** ~ **livre** only one book, a single book; **le** ~ **livre** the only book; ~ **ce livre, ce livre** ~ this book alone, only this book; **d'un** ~ **coup** (*soudainement*) all at once; (*à la fois*) at one blow ♦ *adv* (*vivre*) alone, on one's own; **parler tout** ~ to talk to oneself; **faire qch (tout)** ~ to do sth (all) on one's own *ou* (all) by oneself ♦ *nm, nf*: **il en reste un(e)** ~**(e)** there's only one left; **pas un(e)** ~**(e)** not a single; **à lui (tout)** ~ single-handed, on his own; ~ **à** ~ in private.
seulement [sœlmɑ̃] *adv* (*pas davantage*): ~ **5, 5** ~ only 5; (*exclusivement*): ~ **eux** only them, them alone; (*pas avant*): ~ **hier/à 10h** only yesterday/at 10 o'clock; (*mais, toutefois*): **il consent,** ~ **il demande des garanties** he agrees, only he wants guarantees; **non** ~ ... **mais aussi** *ou* **encore** not only ... but also.
sève [sɛv] *nf* sap.
sévère [sevɛʀ] *adj* severe.
sévèrement [sevɛʀmɑ̃] *adv* severely.
sévérité [severite] *nf* severity.
sévices [sevis] *nmpl* (*physical*) cruelty *sg*, ill treatment *sg*.
Séville [sevil] *n* Seville.
sévir [seviʀ] *vi* (*punir*) to use harsh measures, crack down; (*suj: fléau*) to rage, be rampant; ~ **contre** (*abus*) to deal ruthlessly with, crack down on.
sevrage [səvʀaʒ] *nm* weaning; deprivation; (*d'un toxicomane*) withdrawal.
sevrer [səvʀe] *vt* to wean; (*fig*): ~ **qn de** to deprive sb of.
sexagénaire [sɛgzaʒenɛʀ] *adj, nm/f* sexagenarian.
SExc *sigle f* (= *Son Excellence*) HE.
sexe [sɛks(ə)] *nm* sex; (*organe mâle*) member.
sexisme [sɛksism(ə)] *nm* sexism.
sexiste [sɛksist(ə)] *adj, nm* sexist.
sexologie [sɛksɔlɔʒi] *nf* sexology.
sexologue [sɛksɔlɔg] *nm/f* sexologist, sex specialist.
sextant [sɛkstɑ̃] *nm* sextant.
sexualité [sɛksɥalite] *nf* sexuality.
sexué, e [sɛksɥe] *adj* sexual.
sexuel, le [sɛksɥɛl] *adj* sexual; **acte** ~ sex act.
sexuellement [sɛksɥɛlmɑ̃] *adv* sexually.
seyait [sejɛ] *vb voir* **seoir**.
seyant, e [sɛjɑ̃, -ɑ̃t] *vb voir* **seoir** ♦ *adj* becoming.
Seychelles [seʃɛl] *nfpl*: **les** ~ the Seychelles.

SFIO *sigle f* (= *Section française de l'internationale ouvrière*) *former name of French Socialist Party*.
SG *sigle m* = **secrétaire général**.
SGEN *sigle m* (= *Syndicat général de l'éducation nationale*) *trades union*.
shaker [ʃɛkœʀ] *nm* (*cocktail*) shaker.
shampooiner [ʃɑ̃pwine] *vt* to shampoo.
shampooineur, euse [ʃɑ̃pwinœʀ, -øz] *nm/f* (*personne*) junior (*who does the shampooing*).
shampooing [ʃɑ̃pwɛ̃] *nm* shampoo; **se faire un** ~ to shampoo one's hair; ~ **colorant** (*colour*) rinse; ~ **traitant** medicated shampoo.
Shetland [ʃɛtlɑ̃d] *n*: **les îles** ~ the Shetland Islands, Shetland.
shoot [ʃut] *nm* (*FOOTBALL*) shot.
shooter [ʃute] *vi* (*FOOTBALL*) to shoot; **se** ~ (*drogué*) to mainline.
shopping [ʃɔpiŋ] *nm*: **faire du** ~ to go shopping.
short [ʃɔʀt] *nm* (pair of) shorts *pl*.
SI *sigle m* = **syndicat d'initiative**.

═══════════════════════════ *MOT-CLÉ*

si [si] *nm* (*MUS*) B; (*en chantant la gamme*) ti
♦ *adv* **1** (*oui*) yes; **"Paul n'est pas venu"** — **"**~**!"** "Paul hasn't come" — "Yes he has!"; **je vous assure que** ~ I assure you he did/she is *etc*
2 (*tellement*) so; ~ **gentil/rapidement** so kind/fast; (*tant et*) ~ **bien que** so much so that; ~ **rapide qu'il soit** however fast he may be
♦ *conj* if; ~ **tu veux** if you want; **je me demande** ~ I wonder if *ou* whether; ~ **j'étais toi** if I were you; ~ **seulement** if only; ~ **ce n'est que** apart from; **une des plus belles,** ~ **ce n'est la plus belle** one of the most beautiful, if not THE most beautiful; **s'il est aimable, eux par contre** ... while *ou* whereas he's nice, they (on the other hand) ...

siamois, e [sjamwa, -waz] *adj* Siamese; **frères/sœurs** ~**(es)** Siamese twins.
Sibérie [sibeʀi] *nf*: **la** ~ Siberia.
sibérien, ne [sibeʀjɛ̃, -ɛn] *adj* Siberian ♦ *nm/f*: **S**~, **ne** Siberian.
sibyllin, e [sibilɛ̃, -in] *adj* sibylline.
SICAV [sikav] *sigle f* (= *société d'investissement à capital variable*) open-ended investment trust; share in such a trust.
Sicile [sisil] *nf*: **la** ~ Sicily.
sicilien, ne [sisiljɛ̃, -ɛn] *adj* Sicilian.
SIDA, sida [sida] *nm* (= *syndrome immuno-déficitaire acquis*) AIDS *sg*.
sidéral, e, aux [sideʀal, -o] *adj* sideral.
sidérant, e [sideʀɑ̃, -ɑ̃t] *adj* staggering.
sidéré, e [sideʀe] *adj* staggered.
sidérurgie [sideʀyʀʒi] *nf* steel industry.
sidérurgique [sideʀyʀʒik] *adj* steel *cpd*.
sidérurgiste [sideʀyʀʒist(ə)] *nm/f* steel work-

er.

siècle [sjɛkl(ə)] *nm* century; (*époque*): **le ~ des lumières/de l'atome** the age of enlightenment/atomic age; (*REL*): **le ~** the world.

sied [sje] *vb voir* **seoir.**

siège [sjɛʒ] *nm* seat; (*d'entreprise*) head office; (*d'organisation*) headquarters *pl*; (*MIL*) siege; **lever le ~** to raise the siege; **mettre le ~ devant** to besiege; **présentation par le ~** (*MÉD*) breech presentation; **~ avant/arrière** (*AUTO*) front/back seat; **~ baquet** bucket seat; **~ social** registered office.

siéger [sjeʒe] *vi* (*assemblée, tribunal*) to sit; (*résider, se trouver*) to lie, be located.

sien, ne [sjɛ̃, sjɛn] *pron*: **le(la) ~(ne), les ~s(~nes)** *m* his; *f* hers; *non humain* its; **y mettre du ~** to pull one's weight; **faire des ~nes** (*fam*) to be up to one's (usual) tricks; **les ~s** (*sa famille*) one's family.

siérait [sjɛʀɛ] *etc vb voir* **seoir.**

Sierra Leone [sjɛʀaleɔne] *nf*: **la ~** Sierra Leone.

sieste [sjɛst(ə)] *nf* (afternoon) snooze *ou* nap, siesta; **faire la ~** to have a snooze *ou* nap.

sieur [sjœʀ] *nm*: **le ~ Thomas** Mr Thomas; (*en plaisantant*) Master Thomas.

sifflant, e [siflɑ̃, -ɑ̃t] *adj* (*bruit*) whistling; (*toux*) wheezing; **(consonne)** ~e sibilant.

sifflement [sifləmɑ̃] *nm* whistle, whistling *no pl*; wheezing *no pl*; hissing *no pl*.

siffler [sifle] *vi* (*gén*) to whistle; (*avec un sifflet*) to blow (on) one's whistle; (*en respirant*) to wheeze; (*serpent, vapeur*) to hiss ♦ *vt* (*chanson*) to whistle; (*chien etc*) to whistle for; (*fille*) to whistle at; (*pièce, orateur*) to hiss, boo; (*faute*) to blow one's whistle at; (*fin du match, départ*) to blow one's whistle for; (*fam: verre, bouteille*) to guzzle, knock back (*BRIT*).

sifflet [siflɛ] *nm* whistle; **~s** *nmpl* (*de mécontentement*) whistles, boos; **coup de ~** whistle.

siffloter [siflɔte] *vi, vt* to whistle.

sigle [sigl(ə)] *nm* acronym, (set of) initials *pl*.

signal, aux [siɲal, -o] *nm* (*signe convenu, appareil*) signal; (*indice, écriteau*) sign; **donner le ~ de** to give the signal for; **~ d'alarme** alarm signal; **~ d'alerte/de détresse** warning/distress signal; **~ horaire** time signal; **~ optique/sonore** warning light/sound; visual/acoustic signal; **signaux (lumineux)** (*AUTO*) traffic signals; **signaux routiers** road signs; (*lumineux*) traffic lights.

signalement [siɲalmɑ̃] *nm* description, particulars *pl*.

signaler [siɲale] *vt* to indicate; to announce; to report; (*être l'indice de*) to indicate; (*faire remarquer*): **~ qch à qn/à qn que** to point out sth to sb/to sb that; (*appeler l'attention sur*): **~ qn à la police** to bring sb to the notice of the police; **se ~ par** to distinguish o.s. by; **se ~ à l'attention de qn** to attract sb's attention.

signalétique [siɲaletik] *adj*: **fiche ~** identifica-

tion sheet.

signalisation [siɲalizasjɔ̃] *nf* signalling, signposting; signals *pl*; roadsigns *pl*; **panneau de ~** roadsign.

signaliser [siɲalize] *vt* to put up roadsigns on; to put signals on.

signataire [siɲatɛʀ] *nm/f* signatory.

signature [siɲatyʀ] *nf* signature; (*action*) signing.

signe [siɲ] *nm* sign; (*TYPO*) mark; **ne pas donner ~ de vie** to give no sign of life; **c'est bon ~** it's a good sign; **c'est que** it's a sign that; **faire un ~ de la main/tête** to give a sign with one's hand/shake one's head; **faire ~ à qn** (*fig*) to get in touch with sb; **faire ~ à qn d'entrer** to motion (to) sb to come in; **en ~ de** as a sign *ou* mark of; **le ~ de la croix** the sign of the Cross; **~ de ponctuation** punctuation mark; **~ du zodiaque** sign of the zodiac; **~s particuliers** distinguishing marks.

signer [siɲe] *vt* to sign; **se ~** *vi* to cross o.s.

signet [siɲɛ] *nm* bookmark.

significatif, ive [siɲifikatif, -iv] *adj* significant.

signification [siɲifikasjɔ̃] *nf* meaning.

signifier [siɲifje] *vt* (*vouloir dire*) to mean, signify; (*faire connaître*): **~ qch (à qn)** to make sth known (to sb); (*JUR*): **~ qch à qn** to serve notice of sth on sb.

silence [silɑ̃s] *nm* silence; (*MUS*) rest; **garder le ~ (sur qch)** to keep silent (about sth), say nothing (about sth); **passer sous ~** to pass over (in silence); **réduire au ~** to silence.

silencieusement [silɑ̃sjøzmɑ̃] *adv* silently.

silencieux, euse [silɑ̃sjø, -øz] *adj* quiet, silent ♦ *nm* silencer (*BRIT*), muffler (*US*).

silex [silɛks] *nm* flint.

silhouette [silwɛt] *nf* outline, silhouette; (*lignes, contour*) outline; (*figure*) figure.

silice [silis] *nf* silica.

siliceux, euse [silisø, -øz] *adj* (*terrain*) chalky.

silicium [silisjɔm] *nm* silicon; **plaquette de ~** silicon chip.

silicone [silikon] *nf* silicone.

silicose [silikoz] *nf* silicosis, dust disease.

sillage [sijaʒ] *nm* wake; (*fig*) trail; **dans le ~ de** (*fig*) in the wake of.

sillon [sijɔ̃] *nm* (*d'un champ*) furrow; (*de disque*) groove.

sillonner [sijɔne] *vt* (*creuser*) to furrow; (*traverser*) to cross, criss-cross.

silo [silo] *nm* silo.

simagrées [simagʀe] *nfpl* fuss *sg*; airs and graces.

simiesque [simjɛsk(ə)] *adj* monkey-like, ape-like.

similaire [similɛʀ] *adj* similar.

similarité [similaʀite] *nf* similarity.

simili [simili] *nm* imitation; (*TYPO*) half-tone ♦ *nf* half-tone engraving.

simili... [simili] *préfixe* imitation *cpd*, artificial.

similicuir [similikɥiʀ] *nm* imitation leather.

similigravure [similigʀavyʀ] *nf* half-tone engraving.

similitude [similityd] *nf* similarity.

simple [sɛ̃pl(ə)] *adj* (*gén*) simple; (*non multiple*) single; **~s** *nmpl* (*MÉD*) medicinal plants; ~ **messieurs** *nm* (*TENNIS*) men's singles *sg*; **un** ~ **particulier** an ordinary citizen; **une** ~ **formalité** a mere formality; **cela varie du** ~ **au double** it can double, it can double the price *etc*; **dans le plus** ~ **appareil** in one's birthday suit; ~ **course** *adj* single; ~ **d'esprit** *nm/f* simpleton; ~ **soldat** private.

simplement [sɛ̃pləmɑ̃] *adv* simply.

simplet, te [sɛ̃plɛ, -ɛt] *adj* (*personne*) simple-minded.

simplicité [sɛ̃plisite] *nf* simplicity; **en toute** ~ quite simply.

simplification [sɛ̃plifikɑsjɔ̃] *nf* simplification.

simplifier [sɛ̃plifje] *vt* to simplify.

simpliste [sɛ̃plist(ə)] *adj* simplistic.

simulacre [simylakʀ(ə)] *nm* enactment; (*péj*): **un** ~ **de** a pretence of, a sham.

simulateur, trice [simylatœʀ, -tʀis] *nm/f* shammer, pretender; (*qui se prétend malade*) malingerer **♦** *nm*: ~ **de vol** flight simulator.

simulation [simylɑsjɔ̃] *nf* shamming, simulation; malingering.

simuler [simyle] *vt* to sham, simulate.

simultané, e [simyltane] *adj* simultaneous.

simultanéité [simyltaneite] *nf* simultaneity.

simultanément [simyltanemɑ̃] *adv* simultaneously.

Sinaï [sinai] *nm*: **le** ~ Sinai.

sinapisme [sinapism(ə)] *nm* (*MÉD*) mustard poultice.

sincère [sɛ̃sɛʀ] *adj* sincere; genuine; heartfelt; **mes** **~s** **condoléances** my deepest sympathy.

sincèrement [sɛ̃sɛʀmɑ̃] *adv* sincerely; genuinely.

sincérité [sɛ̃seʀite] *nf* sincerity; **en toute** ~ in all sincerity.

sinécure [sinekyʀ] *nf* sinecure.

sine die [sinedje] *adv* sine die, indefinitely.

sine qua non [sinekwanɔn] *adj*: **condition** ~ indispensable condition.

Singapour [sɛ̃gapuʀ] *nm*: **le** ~ Singapore.

singe [sɛ̃ʒ] *nm* monkey; (*de grande taille*) ape.

singer [sɛ̃ʒe] *vt* to ape, mimic.

singeries [sɛ̃ʒʀi] *nfpl* antics; (*simagrées*) airs and graces.

singulariser [sɛ̃gylaʀize] *vt* to mark out; **se** ~ to call attention to o.s.

singularité [sɛ̃gylaʀite] *nf* peculiarity.

singulier, ière [sɛ̃gylje, -jɛʀ] *adj* remarkable, singular; (*LING*) singular **♦** *nm* singular.

singulièrement [sɛ̃gyljɛʀmɑ̃] *adv* singularly, remarkably.

sinistre [sinistʀ(ə)] *adj* sinister; (*intensif*): **un** ~ **imbécile** an incredible idiot **♦** *nm* (*incendie*) blaze; (*catastrophe*) disaster; (*ASSURANCES*) damage (*giving rise to a claim*).

sinistré, e [sinistʀe] *adj* disaster-stricken **♦** *nm/f* disaster victim.

sinistrose [sinistʀoz] *nf* pessimism.

sino... [sino] *préfixe*: **~-indien** Sino-Indian, Chinese-Indian.

sinon [sinɔ̃] *conj* (*autrement, sans quoi*) otherwise, or else; (*sauf*) except, other than; (*si ce n'est*) if not.

sinueux, euse [sinɥø, -øz] *adj* winding; (*fig*) tortuous.

sinuosités [sinɥozite] *nfpl* winding *sg*, curves.

sinus [sinys] *nm* (*ANAT*) sinus; (*GÉOM*) sine.

sinusite [sinyzit] *nf* sinusitis, sinus infection.

sinusoïdal, e, aux [sinyzoidal, -o] *adj* sinusoidal.

sinusoïde [sinyzoid] *nf* sinusoid.

sionisme [sjɔnism(ə)] *nm* Zionism.

sioniste [sjɔnist(ə)] *adj*, *nm/f* Zionist.

siphon [sifɔ̃] *nm* (*tube, d'eau gazeuse*) siphon; (*d'évier etc*) U-bend.

siphonner [sifɔne] *vt* to siphon.

sire [siʀ] *nm* (*titre*): **S~** Sire; **un triste** ~ an unsavoury individual.

sirène [siʀɛn] *nf* siren; ~ **d'alarme** fire alarm; (*pendant la guerre*) air-raid siren.

sirop [siʀo] *nm* (*à diluer: de fruit etc*) syrup, cordial (*BRIT*); (*boisson*) fruit drink; (*pharmaceutique*) syrup, mixture; ~ **de menthe** mint syrup *ou* cordial; ~ **contre la toux** cough syrup *ou* mixture.

siroter [siʀote] *vt* to sip.

sirupeux, euse [siʀypø, -øz] *adj* syrupy.

sis, e [si, siz] *adj*: ~ **rue de la Paix** located in the rue de la Paix.

sisal [sizal] *nm* (*BOT*) sisal.

sismique [sismik] *adj* seismic.

sismographe [sismɔgʀaf] *nm* seismograph.

sismologie [sismɔlɔʒi] *nf* seismology.

site [sit] *nm* (*paysage, environnement*) setting; (*d'une ville: emplacement*) site; ~ (**pittoresque**) beauty spot; **~s touristiques** places of interest; **~s naturels/historiques** natural/historic sites.

sitôt [sito] *adv*: ~ **parti** as soon as he *etc* had left; ~ **après** straight after; **pas de** ~ not for a long time; ~ (**après**) **que** as soon as.

situation [sitɥɑsjɔ̃] *nf* (*gén*) situation; (*d'un édifice, d'une ville*) situation, position; (*emplacement*) location; **être en** ~ **de faire qch** to be in a position to do sth; ~ **de famille** marital status.

situé, e [sitɥe] *adj*: **bien** ~ well situated, in a good location; ~ **à/près de** situated at/near.

situer [sitɥe] *vt* to site, situate; (*en pensée*) to set, place; **se** ~ *vi*: **se** ~ **à/près de** to be situated at/near.

SIVOM [sivɔm] *sigle m* (= *Syndicat intercommunal à vocation multiple*) *association of "communes"*.

six [sis] *num* six.

sixième [sizjɛm] *num* sixth.

skaï [skaj] *nm* ® ≈ Leatherette ®.

skate(-board) [sket(bɔRd)] *nm* (*sport*) skate-boarding; (*planche*) skateboard.
sketch [skɛtʃ] *nm* (variety) sketch.
ski [ski] *nm* (*objet*) ski; (*sport*) skiing; **faire du** ~ to ski; ~ **alpin** Alpine skiing; ~ **court** short ski; ~ **évolutif** short ski method; ~ **de fond** cross-country skiing; ~ **nautique** water-skiing; ~ **de piste** downhill skiing; ~ **de randonnée** cross-country skiing.
ski-bob [skibɔb] *nm* skibob.
skier [skje] *vi* to ski.
skieur, euse [skjœR, -øz] *nm/f* skier.
skif(f) [skif] *nm* skiff.
slalom [slalɔm] *nm* slalom; **faire du** ~ **entre** to slalom between; ~ **géant/spécial** giant/special slalom.
slalomer [slalɔme] *vi* (*entre des obstacles*) to weave in and out; (*SKI*) to slalom.
slalomeur, euse [slalɔmœR, -øz] *nm/f* (*SKI*) slalom skier.
slave [slav] *adj* Slav(onic), Slavic ♦ *nm* (*LING*) Slavonic ♦ *nm/f*: **S**~ Slav.
slip [slip] *nm* (*sous-vêtement*) underpants *pl*, pants *pl* (*BRIT*), briefs *pl*; (*de bain: d'homme*) (bathing *ou* swimming) trunks *pl*; (*: du bikini*) (bikini) briefs *pl ou* bottoms *pl*.
slogan [slɔgã] *nm* slogan.
slovaque [slɔvak] *adj* Slovak ♦ *nm* (*LING*) Slovak ♦ *nm/f*: **S**~ Slovak.
Slovaquie [slɔvaki] *nf*: **la** ~ Slovakia.
slovène [slɔvɛn] *adj* Slovene ♦ *nm* (*LING*) Slovene ♦ *nm/f*: **S**~ Slovene.
Slovénie [slɔveni] *nf*: **la** ~ Slovenia.
slow [slo] *nm* (*danse*) slow number.
SM *sigle f* (= *Sa Majesté*) HM.
SMAG [smag] *sigle m* = *salaire minimum agricole garanti*.
smasher [smaʃe] *vi* to smash the ball ♦ *vt* (*balle*) to smash.
SME *sigle m* (= *Système monétaire européen*) EMS.
SMIC [smik] *sigle m* = *salaire minimum interprofessionnel de croissance*.

> *In France, the **SMIC** is the minimum hourly rate below which it is illegal to pay workers over the age of eighteen. The SMIC is index-linked and is raised each time the cost of living rises by 2%.*

smicard, e [smikaR, -aRd(ə)] *nm/f* minimum wage earner.
smocks [smɔk] *nmpl* (*COUTURE*) smocking *no pl*.
smoking [smɔkiŋ] *nm* dinner *ou* evening suit.
SMUR [smyR] *sigle m* (= *service médical d'urgence et de réanimation*) specialist mobile emergency unit.
snack [snak] *nm* snack bar.
SNC *abr* = *service non compris*.
SNCB *sigle f* (= *Société nationale des chemins de fer belges*) Belgian railways.

SNCF *sigle f* (= *Société nationale des chemins de fer français*) French railways.
SNES [snɛs] *sigle m* (= *Syndicat national de l'enseignement secondaire*) secondary teachers' union.
SNE-sup [ɛsɛnəsyp] *sigle m* (= *Syndicat national de l'enseignement supérieur*) university teachers' union.
SNI *sigle m* (= *Syndicat national des instituteurs*) primary teachers' union.
SNJ *sigle m* (= *Syndicat national des journalistes*) journalists' union.
snob [snɔb] *adj* snobbish ♦ *nm/f* snob.
snober [snɔbe] *vt*: ~ **qn** to give sb the cold shoulder, treat sb with disdain.
snobinard, e [snɔbinaR, -aRd(ə)] *nm/f* snooty *ou* stuck-up person.
snobisme [snɔbism(ə)] *nm* snobbery.
SNSM *sigle f* (= *Société nationale de sauvetage en mer*) national sea-rescue association.
s.o. *abr* (= *sans objet*) no longer applicable.
sobre [sɔbR(ə)] *adj* temperate, abstemious; (*élégance, style*) restrained, sober; ~ **de** (*gestes, compliments*) sparing of.
sobrement [sɔbRəmã] *adv* in moderation, abstemiously; soberly.
sobriété [sɔbRijete] *nf* temperance, abstemiousness; sobriety.
sobriquet [sɔbRikɛ] *nm* nickname.
soc [sɔk] *nm* ploughshare.
sociabilité [sɔsjabilite] *nf* sociability.
sociable [sɔsjabl(ə)] *adj* sociable.
social, e, aux [sɔsjal, -o] *adj* social.
socialement [sɔsjalmã] *adv* socially.
socialisant, e [sɔsjalizã, -ãt] *adj* with socialist tendencies.
socialisation [sɔsjalizasjõ] *nf* socialisation.
socialiser [sɔsjalize] *vt* to socialize.
socialisme [sɔsjalism(ə)] *nm* socialism.
socialiste [sɔsjalist(ə)] *adj, nm/f* socialist.
sociétaire [sɔsjetɛR] *nm/f* member.
société [sɔsjete] *nf* society; (*d'abeilles, de fourmis*) colony; (*sportive*) club; (*COMM*) company; **la bonne** ~ polite society; **se plaire dans la** ~ **de** to enjoy the society of; **l'archipel de la S**~ the Society Islands; **la** ~ **d'abondance/de consommation** the affluent/consumer society; ~ **par actions** joint stock company; ~ **anonyme (SA)** ≈ limited company (Ltd) (*BRIT*), ≈ incorporated company (Inc.) (*US*); ~ **d'investissement à capital variable (SICAV)** ≈ investment trust (*BRIT*), ≈ mutual fund (*US*); ~ **à responsabilité limitée (SARL)** *type of limited liability company (with non-negotiable shares)*; ~ **savante** learned society; ~ **de services** service company.
socioculturel, le [sɔsjokyltyRɛl] *adj* sociocultural.
socio-économique [sɔsjoekɔnɔmik] *adj* socioeconomic.
socio-éducatif, -ive [sɔsjoedykatif, -iv] *adj* so-

cioeducational.

sociolinguistique [sɔsjolɛ̃gɥistik] *adj* sociolinguistic.

sociologie [sɔsjɔlɔʒi] *nf* sociology.

sociologique [sɔsjɔlɔʒik] *adj* sociological.

sociologue [sɔsjɔlɔg] *nm/f* sociologist.

socio-professionnel, le [sɔsjopRɔfɛsjɔnɛl] *adj* socioprofessional.

socle [sɔkl(ə)] *nm* (*de colonne, statue*) plinth, pedestal; (*de lampe*) base.

socquette [sɔkɛt] *nf* ankle sock.

soda [sɔda] *nm* (*boisson*) fizzy drink, soda (*US*).

sodium [sɔdjɔm] *nm* sodium.

sodomie [sɔdɔmi] *nf* sodomy; buggery.

sodomiser [sɔdɔmize] *vt* to sodomize; to bugger.

sœur [sœR] *nf* sister; (*religieuse*) nun, sister; ~ **Élisabeth** (*REL*) Sister Elizabeth; ~ **de lait** foster sister.

sofa [sɔfa] *nm* sofa.

Sofia [sɔfja] *n* Sofia.

SOFRES [sɔfRɛs] *sigle f* (= *Société française d'enquête par sondage*) *company which conducts opinion polls.*

soi [swa] *pron* oneself; **cela va de** ~ that *ou* it goes without saying, it stands to reason.

soi-disant [swadizɑ̃] *adj inv* so-called ♦ *adv* supposedly.

soie [swa] *nf* silk; (*de porc, sanglier: poil*) bristle.

soient [swa] *vb voir* **être**.

soierie [swaRi] *nf* (*industrie*) silk trade; (*tissu*) silk.

soif [swaf] *nf* thirst; (*fig*): ~ **de** thirst *ou* craving for; **avoir** ~ to be thirsty; **donner** ~ **à qn** to make sb thirsty.

soigné, e [swaɲe] *adj* (*tenue*) well-groomed, neat; (*travail*) careful, meticulous; (*fam*) whopping; stiff.

soigner [swaɲe] *vt* (*malade, maladie: suj: docteur*) to treat; (: *suj: infirmière, mère*) to nurse, look after; (*blessé*) to tend; (*travail, détails*) to take care over; (*jardin, chevelure, invités*) to look after.

soigneur [swaɲœR] *nm* (*CYCLISME, FOOTBALL'.*) trainer; (*BOXE*) second.

soigneusement [swaɲøzmɑ̃] *adv* carefully.

soigneux, euse [swaɲø, -øz] *adj* (*propre*) tidy, neat; (*méticuleux*) painstaking, careful; ~ **de** careful with.

soi-même [swamɛm] *pron* oneself.

soin [swɛ̃] *nm* (*application*) care; (*propreté, ordre*) tidiness, neatness; (*responsabilité*): **le** ~ **de qch** the care of sth; ~**s** *nmpl* (*à un malade, blessé*) treatment *sg*, medical attention *sg*; (*attentions, prévenance*) care and attention *sg*; (*hygiène*) care *sg*; ~**s de la chevelure/de beauté** hair/beauty care; ~**s du corps/ménage** care of one's body/the home; **avoir** *ou* **prendre** ~ **de** to take care of, look after; **avoir** *ou* **prendre** ~ **de faire** to take care to

do; **sans** ~ *adj* careless; untidy; **les premiers** ~**s** first aid *sg*; **aux bons** ~**s de** c/o, care of; **être aux petits** ~**s pour qn** to wait on sb hand and foot, see to sb's every need; **confier qn aux** ~**s de qn** to hand sb over to sb's care.

soir [swaR] *nm, adv* evening; **le** ~ in the evening(s); **ce** ~ this evening, tonight; **à ce** ~! see you this evening (*ou* tonight)!; **la veille au** ~ the previous evening; **sept/dix heures du** ~ seven in the evening/ten at night; **le repas/journal du** ~ the evening meal/ newspaper: **dimanche** ~ Sunday evening; **hier** ~ yesterday evening; **demain** ~ tomorrow evening, tomorrow night.

soirée [swaRe] *nf* evening; (*réception*) party; **donner en** ~ (*film, pièce*) to give an evening performance of.

soit [swa] *vb voir* **être** ♦ *conj* (*à savoir*) namely, to wit; (*ou*): ~ ... ~ either ... or ♦ *adv* so be it, very well; ~ **un triangle ABC** let ABC be a triangle; ~ **que** ... ~ **que** *ou* **ou que** whether ... or whether.

soixantaine [swasɑ̃tɛn] *nf*: **une** ~ (**de**) sixty or so, about sixty; **avoir la** ~ to be around sixty.

soixante [swasɑ̃t] *num* sixty.

soixante-dix [swasɑ̃tdis] *num* seventy.

soixante-dixième [swasɑ̃tdizjɛm] *num* seventieth.

soixante-huitard, e [swazɑ̃tɥitaR, -aRd(ə)] *adj* relating to the demonstrations of May 1968 ♦ *nm/f* participant in the demonstrations of May 1968.

soixantième [swasɑ̃tjɛm] *num* sixtieth.

soja [sɔʒa] *nm* soya; (*graines*) soya beans *pl*; **germes de** ~ beansprouts.

sol [sɔl] *nm* ground; (*de logement*) floor; (*revêtement*) flooring *no pl*; (*territoire, AGR, GÉO*) soil; (*MUS*) G; (: *en chantant la gamme*) so(h).

solaire [sɔlɛR] *adj* solar, sun *cpd*.

solarium [sɔlaRjɔm] *nm* solarium.

soldat [sɔlda] *nm* soldier; **S**~ **inconnu** Unknown Warrior *ou* Soldier; ~ **de plomb** tin *ou* toy soldier.

solde [sɔld(ə)] *nf* pay ♦ *nm* (*COMM*) balance; ~**s** *nmpl ou nfpl* (*COMM*) sales; (*articles*) sale goods; **à la** ~ **de qn** (*péj*) in sb's pay; ~ **créditeur/débiteur** credit/debit balance; ~ **à payer** balance outstanding; **en** ~ at sale price; **aux** ~**s** at the sales.

solder [sɔlde] *vt* (*compte*) to settle; (*marchandise*) to sell at sale price, sell off; **se** ~ **par** (*fig*) to end in; **article soldé (à) 10 F** item reduced to 10 F.

soldeur, euse [sɔldœR, -øz] *nm/f* (*COMM*) discounter.

sole [sɔl] *nf* sole *inv* (*fish*).

soleil [sɔlɛj] *nm* sun; (*lumière*) sun(light); (*temps ensoleillé*) sun(shine); (*feu d'artifice*) Catherine wheel; (*ACROBATIE*) grand circle; (*BOT*) sunflower; **il y a** *ou* **il fait du** ~ it's sun-

ny; **au** ~ in the sun; **en plein** ~ in full sun; **le**
~ **levant/couchant** the rising/setting sun; **le**
~ **de minuit** the midnight sun.

solennel, le [sɔlanɛl] *adj* solemn; ceremonial.

solennellement [sɔlanɛlmɑ̃] *adv* solemnly.

solenniser [sɔlanize] *vt* to solemnize.

solennité [sɔlanite] *nf* (*d'une fête*) solemnity;
~**s** *nfpl* (*formalités*) formalities.

solénoïde [sɔlenɔid] *nm* (*ÉLEC*) solenoid.

solfège [sɔlfɛʒ] *nm* rudiments *pl* of music;
(*exercices*) ear training *no pl.*

solfier [sɔlfje] *vt*: ~ **un morceau** to sing a
piece using the sol-fa.

soli [sɔli] *pl de* **solo.**

solidaire [sɔlidɛʀ] *adj* (*personnes*) who stand
together, who show solidarity; (*pièces mécaniques*) interdependent; (*JUR: engagement*)
binding on all parties; (*: débiteurs*) jointly
liable; **être** ~ **de** (*collègues*) to stand by; (*mécanisme*) to be bound up with, be dependent
on.

solidairement [sɔlidɛʀmɑ̃] *adv* jointly.

solidariser [sɔlidaʀize]: **se** ~ **avec** *vt* to show
solidarity with.

solidarité [sɔlidaʀite] *nf* (*entre personnes*) solidarity; (*de mécanisme, phénomènes*) interdependence; **par** ~ (**avec**) (*cesser le travail etc*)
in sympathy (with).

solide [sɔlid] *adj* solid; (*mur, maison, meuble*)
solid, sturdy; (*connaissances, argument*)
sound; (*personne*) robust, sturdy; (*estomac*)
strong ♦ *nm* solid; **avoir les reins** ~**s** (*fig*) to
be in a good financial position; to have
sound financial backing.

solidement [sɔlidmɑ̃] *adv* solidly; (*fermement*)
firmly.

solidifier [sɔlidifje] *vt*, **se** ~ *vi* to solidify.

solidité [sɔlidite] *nf* solidity; sturdiness.

soliloque [sɔlilɔk] *nm* soliloquy.

soliste [sɔlist(ə)] *nm/f* soloist.

solitaire [sɔlitɛʀ] *adj* (*sans compagnie*) solitary, lonely; (*isolé*) solitary, isolated, lone;
(*lieu*) lonely ♦ *nm/f* recluse; loner ♦ *nm* (*diamant, jeu*) solitaire.

solitude [sɔlityd] *nf* loneliness; (*paix*) solitude.

solive [sɔliv] *nf* joist.

sollicitations [sɔlisitasjɔ̃] *nfpl* (*requêtes*) entreaties, appeals; (*attractions*) enticements;
(*TECH*) stress *sg.*

solliciter [sɔlisite] *vt* (*personne*) to appeal to;
(*emploi, faveur*) to seek; (*moteur*) to prompt;
(*suj: occupations, attractions etc*): ~ **qn** to appeal to sb's curiosity *etc*; to entice sb; to
make demands on sb's time; ~ **qn de faire** to
appeal to sb *ou* request sb to do.

sollicitude [sɔlisityd] *nf* concern.

solo [sɔlo] *nm*, *pl* **soli** [sɔli] (*MUS*) solo (*pl* -s *ou*
soli).

sol-sol [sɔlsɔl] *adj inv* surface-to-surface.

solstice [sɔlstis] *nm* solstice; ~ **d'hiver/d'été**
winter/summer solstice.

solubilisé, e [sɔlybilize] *adj* soluble.

solubilité [sɔlybilite] *nf* solubility.

soluble [sɔlybl(ə)] *adj* (*sucre, cachet*) soluble;
(*problème etc*) soluble, solvable.

soluté [sɔlyte] *nm* solution.

solution [sɔlysjɔ̃] *nf* solution; ~ **de continuité**
gap, break; ~ **de facilité** easy way out.

solutionner [sɔlysjɔne] *vt* to solve, find a solution for.

solvabilité [sɔlvabilite] *nf* solvency.

solvable [sɔlvabl(ə)] *adj* solvent.

solvant [sɔlvɑ̃] *nm* solvent.

Somalie [sɔmali] *nf*: **la** ~ Somalia.

somalien, ne [sɔmaljɛ̃, -ɛn] *adj* Somalian.

Somaliland [sɔmalilɑ̃d] *nm* Somaliland.

somatique [sɔmatik] *adj* somatic.

sombre [sɔ̃bʀ(ə)] *adj* dark; (*fig*) sombre,
gloomy; (*sinistre*) awful, dreadful.

sombrer [sɔ̃bʀe] *vi* (*bateau*) to sink, go down;
~ **corps et biens** to go down with all hands;
~ **dans** (*misère, désespoir*) to sink into.

sommaire [sɔmɛʀ] *adj* (*simple*) basic; (*expéditif*) summary ♦ *nm* summary; **faire le** ~ **de** to
make a summary of, summarize; **exécution**
~ summary execution.

sommairement [sɔmɛʀmɑ̃] *adv* basically;
summarily.

sommation [sɔmasjɔ̃] *nf* (*JUR*) summons *sg*;
(*avant de faire feu*) warning.

somme [sɔm] *nf* (*MATH*) sum; (*fig*) amount;
(*argent*) sum, amount ♦ *nm*: **faire un** ~ **to**
have a (short) nap; **faire la** ~ **de** to add up;
en ~, ~ **toute** *adv* all in all.

sommeil [sɔmɛj] *nm* sleep; **avoir** ~ to be
sleepy; **avoir le** ~ **léger** to be a light sleeper;
en ~ (*fig*) dormant.

sommeiller [sɔmeje] *vi* to doze; (*fig*) to lie
dormant.

sommelier [sɔmalje] *nm* wine waiter.

sommer [sɔme] *vt*: ~ **qn de faire** to command
ou order sb to do; (*JUR*) to summon sb to do.

sommes [sɔm] *vb voir* **être**; *voir aussi* **somme.**

sommet [sɔmɛ] *nm* top; (*d'une montagne*) summit, top; (*fig: de la perfection, gloire*) height;
(*GÉOM: d'angle*) vertex (*pl* vertices); (*conférence*) summit (conference).

sommier [sɔmje] *nm* bed base, bedspring
(*US*); (*ADMIN: registre*) register; ~ **à ressorts**
(interior sprung) divan base (*BRIT*), box
spring (*US*); ~ **à lattes** slatted bed base.

sommité [sɔmite] *nf* prominent person, leading light.

somnambule [sɔmnɑbyl] *nm/f* sleepwalker.

somnambulisme [sɔmnɑbylism(ə)] *nm* sleep-
walking.

somnifère [sɔmnifɛʀ] *nm* sleeping drug; (*comprimé*) sleeping pill *ou* tablet.

somnolence [sɔmnɔlɑ̃s] *nf* drowsiness.

somnolent, e [sɔmnɔlɑ̃, -ɑ̃t] *adj* sleepy,
drowsy.

somnoler [sɔmnɔle] *vi* to doze.

somptuaire [sɔ̃ptɥɛʀ] *adj*: **lois** ~**s** sumptuary
laws; **dépenses** ~**s** extravagant expenditure

sg.

somptueusement [sɔ̃ptɥøzmɑ̃] *adv* sumptuously.

sompueux, euse [sɔ̃ptɥø, -øz] *adj* sumptuous; (*cadeau*) lavish.

somptuosité [sɔ̃ptɥozite] *nf* sumptuousness; (*d'un cadeau*) lavishness.

son [sɔ̃], **sa** [sa], *pl* **ses** [se] *adj possessif* (*antécédent humain mâle*) his; (*: femelle*) her; (*: valeur indéfinie*) one's, his/her; (*: non humain*) its; *voir note sous* **il**.

son [sɔ̃] *nm* sound; (*de blé etc*) bran; ~ **et lumière** *adj inv* son et lumière.

sonar [sɔnaʀ] *nm* (*NAVIG*) sonar.

sonate [sɔnat] *nf* sonata.

sondage [sɔ̃daʒ] *nm* (*de terrain*) boring, drilling; (*mer, atmosphère*) sounding; probe; (*enquête*) survey, sounding out of opinion; ~ **(d'opinion)** (opinion) poll.

sonde [sɔ̃d] *nf* (*NAVIG*) lead *ou* sounding line; (*MÉTÉOROLOGIE*) sonde; (*MÉD*) probe; catheter; (*d'alimentation*) feeding tube; (*TECH*) borer, driller; (*de forage, sondage*) drill; (*pour fouiller etc*) probe; ~ **à avalanche** pole (*for probing snow and locating victims*); ~ **spatiale** probe.

sonder [sɔ̃de] *vt* (*NAVIG*) to sound; (*atmosphère, plaie, bagages etc*) to probe; (*TECH*) to bore, drill; (*fig: personne*) to sound out; (*: opinion*) to probe; ~ **le terrain** (*fig*) to see how the land lies.

songe [sɔ̃ʒ] *nm* dream.

songer [sɔ̃ʒe] *vi* to dream; ~ **à** (*rêver à*) to muse over, think over; (*penser à*) to think of; (*envisager*) to contemplate, think of, consider; ~ **que** to consider that; to think that.

songerie [sɔ̃ʒʀi] *nf* reverie.

songeur, euse [sɔ̃ʒœʀ, -øz] *adj* pensive; **ça me laisse** ~ that makes me wonder.

sonnailles [sɔnɑj] *nfpl* jingle of bells.

sonnant, e [sɔnɑ̃, -ɑ̃t] *adj*: **en espèces** ~**es et trébuchantes** in coin of the realm; **à 8 heures** ~**es** on the stroke of 8.

sonné, e [sɔne] *adj* (*fam*) cracked; (*passé*): **il est midi** ~ it's gone twelve; **il a quarante ans bien** ~**s** he's well into his forties.

sonner [sɔne] *vi* (*retentir*) to ring; (*donner une impression*) to sound ♦ *vt* (*cloche*) to ring; (*glas, tocsin*) to sound; (*portier, infirmière*) to ring for; (*messe*) to ring the bell for; (*fam: suj: choc, coup*) to knock out; ~ **du clairon** to sound the bugle; ~ **bien/mal/creux** to sound good/bad/hollow; ~ **faux** (*instrument*) to sound out of tune; (*rire*) to ring false; ~ **les heures** to strike the hours; **minuit vient de** ~ midnight has just struck; ~ **chez qn** to ring sb's doorbell, ring at sb's door.

sonnerie [sɔnʀi] *nf* (*son*) ringing; (*sonnette*) bell; (*mécanisme d'horloge*) striking mechanism; ~ **d'alarme** alarm bell; ~ **de clairon** bugle call.

sonnet [sɔnɛ] *nm* sonnet.

sonnette [sɔnɛt] *nf* bell; ~ **d'alarme** alarm bell; ~ **de nuit** night-bell.

sono [sɔno] *nf* (= *sonorisation*) PA (system); (*d'une discothèque*) sound system.

sonore [sɔnɔʀ] *adj* (*voix*) sonorous, ringing; (*salle, métal*) resonant; (*ondes, film, signal*) sound *cpd*; (*LING*) voiced; **effets** ~**s** sound effects.

sonorisation [sɔnɔʀizasjɔ̃] *nf* (*installations*) public address system; (*d'une discothèque*) sound system.

sonoriser [sɔnɔʀize] *vt* (*film, spectacle*) to add the sound track to; (*salle*) to fit with a public address system.

sonorité [sɔnɔʀite] *nf* (*de piano, violon*) tone; (*de voix, mot*) sonority; (*d'une salle*) resonance; acoustics *pl*.

sonothèque [sɔnɔtɛk] *nf* sound library.

sont [sɔ̃] *vb voir* **être**.

sophisme [sɔfism(ə)] *nm* sophism.

sophiste [sɔfist(ə)] *nm/f* sophist.

sophistication [sɔfistikasjɔ̃] *nf* sophistication.

sophistiqué, e [sɔfistike] *adj* sophisticated.

soporifique [sɔpɔʀifik] *adj* soporific.

soprano [sɔpʀano] *nm/f* soprano (*pl* -s).

sorbet [sɔʀbɛ] *nm* water ice, sorbet.

sorbetière [sɔʀbətjɛʀ] *nf* ice-cream maker.

sorbier [sɔʀbje] *nm* service tree.

sorcellerie [sɔʀsɛlʀi] *nf* witchcraft *no pl*, sorcery *no pl*.

sorcier, ière [sɔʀsje, -jɛʀ] *nm/f* sorcerer/witch *ou* sorceress ♦ *adj*: **ce n'est pas** ~ (*fam*) it's as easy as pie.

sordide [sɔʀdid] *adj* sordid; squalid.

Sorlingues [sɔʀlɛ̃g] *nfpl*: **les (îles)** ~ the Scilly Isles, the Isles of Scilly, the Scillies.

sornettes [sɔʀnɛt] *nfpl* twaddle *sg*.

sort [sɔʀ] *vb voir* **sortir** ♦ *nm* (*fortune, destinée*) fate; (*condition, situation*) lot; (*magique*): **jeter un** ~ to cast a spell; **un coup du** ~ a blow dealt by fate; **le** ~ **en est jeté** the die is cast; **tirer au** ~ to draw lots; **tirer qch au** ~ to draw lots for sth.

sortable [sɔʀtabl(ə)] *adj*: **il n'est pas** ~ you can't take him anywhere.

sortant, e [sɔʀtɑ̃, -ɑ̃t] *vb voir* **sortir** ♦ *adj* (*numéro*) which comes up (*in a draw etc*); (*député, président*) outgoing.

sorte [sɔʀt(ə)] *vb voir* **sortir** ♦ *nf* sort, kind; **de la** ~ *adv* in that way; **en quelque** ~ in a way; **de** ~ **à** so as to, in order to; **de (telle)** ~ **que, en** ~ **que** (*de manière que*) so that; (*si bien que*) so much so that; **faire en** ~ **que** to see to it that.

sortie [sɔʀti] *nf* (*issue*) way out, exit; (*MIL*) sortie; (*fig: verbale*) outburst; sally; (*: parole incongrue*) odd remark; (*d'un gaz, de l'eau*) outlet; (*promenade*) outing; (*le soir: au restaurant etc*) night out; (*de produits*) export; (*de capitaux*) outflow; (*COMM: somme*): ~**s** items of expenditure; outgoings *sans sg*; (*INFORM*) output; (*d'imprimante*) printout; **à sa** ~ as he went out *ou* left; **à la ~ de l'école/l'usine** (*moment*) after school/work; when school/ the factory comes out; (*lieu*) at the school/ factory gates; **à la ~ de ce nouveau modèle** when this new model comes (*ou* came) out, when they bring (*ou* brought) out this new model; **~ de bain** (*vêtement*) bathrobe; **"~ de camions"** "vehicle exit"; **~ papier** hard copy; **~ de secours** emergency exit.

sortilège [sɔʀtilɛʒ] *nm* (magic) spell.

sortir [sɔʀtiʀ] *vi* (*gén*) to come out; (*partir, se promener, aller au spectacle etc*) to go out; (*bourgeon, plante, numéro gagnant*) to come up ♦ *vt* (*gén*) to take out; (*produit, ouvrage, modèle*) to bring out; (*boniments, incongruités*) to come out with; (*INFORM*) to output; (*: sur papier*) to print out; (*fam: expulser*) to throw out ♦ *nm*: **au ~ de l'hiver/l'enfance** as winter/childhood nears its end; **~ qch de** to take sth out of; **~ qn d'embarras** to get sb out of trouble; **~ de** (*gén*) to leave; (*endroit*) to go (*ou* come) out of, leave; (*rainure etc*) to come out of; (*maladie*) to get over; (*époque*) to get through; (*cadre, compétence*) to be outside; (*provenir de: famille etc*) to come from; **~ de table** to leave the table; **~ du système** (*INFORM*) to log out; **~ de ses gonds** (*fig*) to fly off the handle; **se ~ de** (*affaire, situation*) to get out of; **s'en ~** (*malade*) to pull through; (*d'une difficulté etc*) to come through all right; to get through, be able to manage.

SOS *sigle m* mayday, SOS.

sosie [sɔzi] *nm* double.

sot, sotte [so, sɔt] *adj* silly, foolish ♦ *nm/f* fool.

sottement [sɔtmɑ̃] *adv* foolishly.

sottise [sɔtiz] *nf* silliness *no pl*, foolishness *no pl*; (*propos, acte*) silly *ou* foolish thing (to do *ou* say).

sou [su] *nm*: **près de ses ~s** tight-fisted; **sans le ~** penniless; **~ à ~** penny by penny; **pas un ~ de bon sens** not a scrap *ou* an ounce of good sense; **de quatre ~s** worthless.

souahéli, e [swaeli] *adj* Swahili ♦ *nm* (*LING*) Swahili.

soubassement [subɑsmɑ̃] *nm* base.

soubresaut [subʀəso] *nm* (*de peur etc*) start; (*cahot: d'un véhicule*) jolt.

soubrette [subʀɛt] *nf* soubrette, maidservant.

souche [suʃ] *nf* (*d'arbre*) stump; (*de carnet*) counterfoil (*BRIT*), stub; **dormir comme une ~** to sleep like a log; **de vieille ~** of old stock.

souci [susi] *nm* (*inquiétude*) worry; (*préoccupation*) concern; (*BOT*) marigold; **se faire du ~** to worry; **avoir (le) ~ de** to have concern for; **par ~ de** for the sake of, out of concern for.

soucier [susje]: **se ~ de** *vt* to care about.

soucieux, euse [susjø, -øz] *adj* concerned, worried; **~ de** concerned about; **peu ~ de/ que** caring little about/whether.

soucoupe [sukup] *nf* saucer; **~ volante** flying saucer.

soudain, e [sudɛ̃, -ɛn] *adj* (*douleur, mort*) sudden ♦ *adv* suddenly, all of a sudden.

soudainement [sudɛnmɑ̃] *adv* suddenly.

soudaineté [sudɛnte] *nf* suddenness.

Soudan [sudɑ̃] *nm*: **le ~** the Sudan.

soudanais, e [sudanɛ, -ɛz] *adj* Sudanese.

soude [sud] *nf* soda.

soudé, e [sude] *adj* (*fig: pétales, organes*) joined (together).

souder [sude] *vt* (*avec fil à souder*) to solder; (*par soudure autogène*) to weld; (*fig*) to bind *ou* knit together; to fuse (together); **se ~** *vi* (*os*) to knit (together).

soudeur, euse [sudœʀ, -øz] *nm/f* (*ouvrier*) welder.

soudoyer [sudwaje] *vt* (*péj*) to bribe, buy over.

soudure [sudyʀ] *nf* soldering; welding; (*joint*) soldered joint; weld; **faire la ~** (*COMM*) to fill a gap; (*fig: assurer une transition*) to bridge the gap.

souffert, e [sufɛʀ, -ɛʀt(ə)] *pp de* **souffrir**.

soufflage [suflaʒ] *nm* (*du verre*) glass-blowing.

souffle [sufl(ə)] *nm* (*en expirant*) breath; (*en soufflant*) puff, blow; (*respiration*) breathing; (*d'explosion, de ventilateur*) blast; (*du vent*) blowing; (*fig*) inspiration; **retenir son ~** to hold one's breath; **avoir du/manquer de ~** to have a lot of puff/be short of breath; **être à bout de ~** to be out of breath; **avoir le ~ court** to be short-winded; **un ~ d'air** *ou* **de vent** a breath of air, a puff of wind; **~ au cœur** (*MÉD*) heart murmur.

soufflé, e [sufle] *adj* (*CULIN*) soufflé; (*fam: ahuri, stupéfié*) staggered ♦ *nm* (*CULIN*) soufflé.

souffler [sufle] *vi* (*gén*) to blow; (*haleter*) to puff (and blow) ♦ *vt* (*feu, bougie*) to blow out; (*chasser: poussière etc*) to blow away; (*TECH: verre*) to blow; (*suj: explosion*) to destroy (with its blast); (*dire*): **~ qch à qn** to whisper sth to sb; (*fam: voler*): **~ qch à qn** to pinch sth from sb; **~ son rôle à qn** to prompt sb; **ne pas ~ mot** not to breathe a word; **laisser ~ qn** (*fig*) to give sb a breather.

soufflet [suflɛ] *nm* (*instrument*) bellows *pl*; (*entre wagons*) vestibule; (*COUTURE*) gusset; (*gifle*) slap (in the face).

souffleur, euse [suflœʀ, -øz] *nm/f* (*THÉÂT*) prompter; (*TECH*) glass-blower.

souffrance [sufʀɑ̃s] *nf* suffering; **en ~** (*marchandise*) awaiting delivery; (*affaire*) pending.

souffrant, e [sufʀɑ̃, -ɑ̃t] *adj* unwell.

souffre-douleur [sufʀədulœʀ] *nm inv* whipping boy (*BRIT*), butt, underdog.

souffreteux, euse [sufʀətø, -øz] *adj* sickly.

souffrir [sufʀiʀ] *vi* to suffer; (*éprouver des douleurs*) to be in pain ♦ *vt* to suffer, endure; (*supporter*) to bear, stand; (*admettre: excep-*

tion etc) to allow ou admit of; ~ **de** (maladie, froid) to suffer from; ~ **des dents** to have trouble with one's teeth; **ne pas pouvoir** ~ **qch/que** ... not to be able to endure ou bear sth/that ...; **faire** ~ **qn** (suj: personne) to make sb suffer; (: dents, blessure etc) to hurt sb.

soufre [sufʀ(ə)] nm sulphur (BRIT), sulfur (US).

soufrer [sufʀe] vt (vignes) to treat with sulphur ou sulfur.

souhait [swɛ] nm wish; **tous nos** ~**s de** good wishes ou our best wishes for; **riche** etc **à** ~ as rich etc as one could wish; **à vos** ~**s!** bless you!

souhaitable [swɛtabl(ə)] adj desirable.

souhaiter [swete] vt to wish for; ~ **le bonjour à qn** to bid sb good day; ~ **la bonne année à qn** to wish sb a happy New Year; **il est à** ~ **que** it is to be hoped that.

souiller [suje] vt to dirty, soil; (fig) to sully, tarnish.

souillure [sujyʀ] nf stain.

soûl, e [su, sul] adj drunk; (fig): ~ **de musique/plaisirs** drunk with music/pleasure ♦ nm: **tout son** ~ to one's heart's content.

soulagement [sulaʒmã] nm relief.

soulager [sulaʒe] vt to relieve; ~ **qn de** to relieve sb of.

soûler [sule] vt: ~ **qn** to get sb drunk; (suj: boisson) to make sb drunk; (fig) to make sb's head spin ou reel; **se** ~ to get drunk; **se** ~ **de** (fig) to intoxicate o.s. with.

soûlerie [sulʀi] nf (péj) drunken binge.

soulèvement [sulɛvmã] nm uprising; (GÉO) upthrust.

soulever [sulve] vt to lift; (vagues, poussière) to send up; (peuple) to stir up (to revolt); (enthousiasme) to arouse; (question, débat, protestations, difficultés) to raise; **se** ~ vi (peuple) to rise up; (personne couchée) to lift o.s. up; (couvercle etc) to lift; **cela me soulève le cœur** it makes me feel sick.

soulier [sulje] nm shoe; ~**s bas** low-heeled shoes; ~**s plats/à talons** flat/heeled shoes.

souligner [suliɲe] vt to underline; (fig) to emphasize, stress.

soumettre [sumɛtʀ(ə)] vt (pays) to subject, subjugate; (rebelles) to put down, subdue; ~ **qn/qch à** to subject sb/sth to; ~ **qch à qn** (projet etc) to submit sth to sb; **se** ~ (**à**) (se rendre, obéir) to submit (to); **se** ~ **à** (formalités etc) to submit to; (régime etc) to submit o.s. to.

soumis, e [sumi, -iz] pp de **soumettre** ♦ adj submissive; **revenus** ~ **à l'impôt** taxable income.

soumission [sumisjɔ̃] nf (voir se soumettre) submission; (docilité) submissiveness; (COMM) tender.

soumissionner [sumisjɔne] vt (COMM: travaux) to bid for, tender for.

soupape [supap] nf valve; ~ **de sûreté** safety valve.

soupçon [supsɔ̃] nm suspicion; (petite quantité): **un** ~ **de** a hint ou touch of; **avoir** ~ to suspect; **au dessus de tout** ~ above (all) suspicion.

soupçonner [supsɔne] vt to suspect; ~ **qn de qch/d'être** to suspect sb of sth/of being.

soupçonneux, euse [supsɔnø, -øz] adj suspicious.

soupe [sup] nf soup; ~ **au lait** adj inv quick-tempered; ~ **à l'oignon/de poisson** onion/fish soup; ~ **populaire** soup kitchen.

soupente [supãt] nf (mansarde) attic; (placard) cupboard (BRIT) ou closet (US) under the stairs.

souper [supe] vi to have supper ♦ nm supper; **avoir soupé de** (fam) to be sick and tired of.

soupeser [supəze] vt to weigh in one's hand(s), feel the weight of; (fig) to weigh up.

soupière [supjɛʀ] nf (soup) tureen.

soupir [supiʀ] nm sigh; (MUS) crotchet rest (BRIT), quarter note rest (US); **rendre le dernier** ~ to breathe one's last.

soupirail, aux [supiʀaj, -o] nm (small) basement window.

soupirant [supiʀã] nm (péj) suitor, wooer.

soupirer [supiʀe] vi to sigh; ~ **après qch** to yearn for sth.

souple [supl(ə)] adj supple; (col) soft; (fig: règlement, caractère) flexible; (: démarche, taille) lithe, supple; **disque(tte)** ~ (INFORM) floppy disk, diskette.

souplesse [suplɛs] nf suppleness; flexibility.

source [suʀs(ə)] nf (point d'eau) spring; (d'un cours d'eau, fig) source; **prendre sa** ~ **à/dans** (suj: cours d'eau) to have its source at/in; **tenir qch de bonne** ~/**de** ~ **sûre** to have sth on good authority/from a reliable source; ~ **thermale/d'eau minérale** hot ou thermal/mineral spring.

sourcier, ière [suʀsje, -jɛʀ] nm water diviner.

sourcil [suʀsij] nm (eye)brow.

sourcilière [suʀsiljɛʀ] adj f voir **arcade**.

sourciller [suʀsije] vi: **sans** ~ without turning a hair ou batting an eyelid.

sourcilleux, euse [suʀsijø, -øz] adj (hautain, sévère) haughty, supercilious; (pointilleux) finicky, pernickety.

sourd, e [suʀ, suʀd(ə)] adj deaf; (bruit, voix) muffled; (couleur) muted; (douleur) dull; (lutte) silent, hidden; (LING) voiceless ♦ nm/f deaf person; **être** ~ **à** to be deaf to.

sourdement [suʀdəmã] adv (avec un bruit sourd) dully; (secrètement) silently.

sourdine [suʀdin] nf (MUS) mute; **en** ~ adv softly, quietly; **mettre une** ~ **à** (fig) to tone down.

sourd-muet, sourde-muette [suʀmyɛ, suʀdmyɛt] adj deaf-and-dumb ♦ nm/f deaf-mute.

sourdre [suʀdʀ(ə)] vi (eau) to spring up; (fig) to rise.

souriant, e [suʀjɑ̃, -ɑ̃t] *vb voir* **sourire** ♦ *adj* cheerful.

souricière [suʀisjɛʀ] *nf* mousetrap; (*fig*) trap.

sourie [suʀi] *etc vb voir* **sourire**.

sourire [suʀiʀ] *nm* smile ♦ *vi* to smile; ~ **à qn** to smile at sb; (*fig*) to appeal to sb; (*: chance*) to smile on sb; **faire un** ~ **à qn** to give sb a smile; **garder le** ~ to keep smiling.

souris [suʀi] *nf* mouse (*pl* mice); (*INFORM*) mouse.

sournois, e [suʀnwa, -waz] *adj* deceitful, underhand.

sournoisement [suʀnwazmɑ̃] *adv* deceitfully.

sournoiserie [suʀnwazʀi] *nf* deceitfulness, underhandedness.

sous [su] *prép* (*gén*) under; ~ **la pluie/le soleil** in the rain/sunshine; ~ **mes yeux** before my eyes; ~ **terre** *adj, adv* underground; ~ **vide** *adj, adv* vacuum-packed; ~ **l'influence/ l'action de** under the influence of/by the action of; ~ **antibiotiques/perfusion** on antibiotics/a drip; ~ **cet angle/ce rapport** from this angle/in this respect; ~ **peu** *adv* shortly, before long.

sous... [su, suz + *vowel*] *préfixe* sub-; under....

sous-alimentation [suzalimɑ̃tɑsjɔ̃] *nf* undernourishment.

sous-alimenté, e [suzalimɑ̃te] *adj* undernourished.

sous-bois [subwa] *nm inv* undergrowth.

sous-catégorie [sukategɔʀi] *nf* subcategory.

sous-chef [suʃɛf] *nm* deputy chief, second in command; ~ **de bureau** deputy head clerk.

sous-comité [sukɔmite] *nm* subcommittee.

sous-commission [sukɔmisjɔ̃] *nf* subcommittee.

sous-continent [sukɔ̃tinɑ̃] *nm* subcontinent.

sous-couche [sukuʃ] *nf* (*de peinture*) undercoat.

souscripteur, trice [suskʀiptœʀ, -tʀis] *nm/f* subscriber.

souscription [suskʀipsjɔ̃] *nf* subscription; **offert en** ~ available on subscription.

souscrire [suskʀiʀ]: ~ **à** *vt* to subscribe to.

sous-cutané, e [sukytane] *adj* subcutaneous.

sous-développé, e [sudevlɔpe] *adj* underdeveloped.

sous-développement [sudevlɔpmɑ̃] *nm* underdevelopment.

sous-directeur, trice [sudiʀɛktœʀ, -tʀis] *nm/f* assistant manager/manageress, submanager/manageress.

sous-emploi [suzɑ̃plwa] *nm* underemployment.

sous-employé, e [suzɑ̃plwaje] *adj* underemployed.

sous-ensemble [suzɑ̃sɑ̃bl(ə)] *nm* subset.

sous-entendre [suzɑ̃tɑ̃dʀ(ə)] *vt* to imply, infer.

sous-entendu, e [suzɑ̃tɑ̃dy] *adj* implied; (*LING*) understood ♦ *nm* innuendo, insinuation.

sous-équipé, e [suzekipe] *adj* under-equipped; ~ **en infrastructures industrielles** (*ÉCON: pays, région*) with an insufficient industrial infrastructure.

sous-estimer [suzɛstime] *vt* to underestimate.

sous-exploiter [suzɛksplwate] *vt* to underexploit.

sous-exposer [suzɛkspoze] *vt* to underexpose.

sous-fifre [sufifʀ(ə)] *nm* (*péj*) underling.

sous-groupe [sugʀup] *nm* subgroup.

sous-homme [suzɔm] *nm* sub-human.

sous-jacent, e [suʒasɑ̃, -ɑ̃t] *adj* underlying.

sous-lieutenant [suljøtnɑ̃] *nm* sub-lieutenant.

sous-locataire [sulɔkatɛʀ] *nm/f* subtenant.

sous-location [sulɔkasjɔ̃] *nf* subletting.

sous-louer [sulwe] *vt* to sublet.

sous-main [sumɛ̃] *nm inv* desk blotter; **en** ~ *adv* secretly.

sous-marin, e [sumaʀɛ̃, -in] *adj* (*flore, volcan*) submarine; (*navigation, pêche, explosif*) underwater ♦ *nm* submarine.

sous-médicalisé, e [sumedikalize] *adj* lacking adequate medical care.

sous-nappe [sunap] *nf* undercloth.

sous-officier [suzɔfisje] *nm* ≈ non-commissioned officer (NCO).

sous-ordre [suzɔʀdʀ(ə)] *nm* subordinate; **créancier en** ~ creditor's creditor.

sous-payé, e [supeje] *adj* underpaid.

sous-préfecture [supʀefɛktyʀ] *nf* sub-prefecture.

sous-préfet [supʀefɛ] *nm* sub-prefect.

sous-production [supʀɔdyksjɔ̃] *nf* underproduction.

sous-produit [supʀɔdɥi] *nm* by-product; (*fig: péj*) pale imitation.

sous-programme [supʀɔgʀam] *nm* (*INFORM*) subroutine.

sous-pull [supul] *nm* thin poloneck sweater.

sous-secrétaire [susəkʀetɛʀ] *nm*: ~ **d'État** Under-Secretary of State.

soussigné, e [susiɲe] *adj*: **je** ~ I the undersigned.

sous-sol [susɔl] *nm* basement; (*GÉO*) subsoil.

sous-tasse [sutas] *nf* saucer.

sous-tendre [sutɑ̃dʀ(ə)] *vt* to underlie.

sous-titre [sutitʀ(ə)] *nm* subtitle.

sous-titré, e [sutitʀe] *adj* with subtitles.

soustraction [sustʀaksjɔ̃] *nf* subtraction.

soustraire [sustʀɛʀ] *vt* to subtract, take away; (*dérober*): ~ **qch à qn** to remove sth from sb; ~ **qn à** (*danger*) to shield sb from; **se** ~ **à** (*autorité, obligation, devoir*) to elude, escape from.

sous-traitance [sutʀɛtɑ̃s(ə)] *nf* subcontracting.

sous-traitant [sutʀɛtɑ̃] *nm* subcontractor.

sous-traiter [sutʀɛte] *vt, vi* to subcontract.

soustrayais [sustʀɛjɛ] *etc vb voir* **soustraire**.

sous-verre [suvɛʀ] *nm inv* glass mount.

sous-vêtement [suvɛtmɑ̃] *nm* undergarment, item of underwear; ~**s** *nmpl* underwear *sg*.

soutane [sutan] *nf* cassock, soutane.

soute [sut] *nf* hold; ~ **à bagages** baggage hold.

soutenable [sutnabl(ə)] *adj* (*opinion*) tenable, defensible.

soutenance [sutnɑ̃s] *nf*: ~ **de thèse** ≈ viva (*voce*).

soutènement [sutɛnmɑ̃] *nm*: **mur de** ~ retaining wall.

souteneur [sutnœʀ] *nm* procurer.

soutenir [sutniʀ] *vt* to support; (*assaut, choc, regard*) to stand up to, withstand; (*intérêt, effort*) to keep up; (*assurer*): ~ **que** to maintain that; **se** ~ (*dans l'eau etc*) to hold o.s. up; (*être soutenable: point de vue*) to be tenable; (*s'aider mutuellement*) to stand by each other; ~ **la comparaison avec** to bear *ou* stand comparison with; ~ **le regard de qn** to be able to look sb in the face.

soutenu, e [sutny] *pp de* **soutenir** ♦ *adj* (*efforts*) sustained, unflagging; (*style*) elevated; (*couleur*) strong.

souterrain, e [sutɛʀɛ̃, -ɛn] *adj* underground; (*fig*) subterranean ♦ *nm* underground passage.

soutien [sutjɛ̃] *nm* support; **apporter son** ~ **à** to lend one's support to; ~ **de famille** breadwinner.

soutiendrai [sutjɛ̃dʀe] *etc vb voir* **soutenir**.

soutien-gorge, *pl* **soutiens-gorge** [sutjɛ̃gɔʀʒ(ə)] *nm* bra; (*de maillot de bain*) top.

soutiens [sutjɛ̃], **soutint** [sutɛ̃] *etc vb voir* **soutenir**.

soutirer [sutiʀe] *vt*: ~ **qch à qn** to squeeze *ou* get sth out of sb.

souvenance [suvnɑ̃s] *nf*: **avoir** ~ **de** to recollect.

souvenir [suvniʀ] *nm* (*réminiscence*) memory; (*cadeau*) souvenir, keepsake; (*de voyage*) souvenir ♦ *vb*: **se** ~ **de** *vt* to remember; **se** ~ **que** to remember that; **garder le** ~ **de** to retain the memory of; **en** ~ **de** in memory *ou* remembrance of; **avec mes affectueux/ meilleurs** ~**s**, ... with love from, .../ regards, ...

souvent [suvɑ̃] *adv* often; **peu** ~ seldom, infrequently; **le plus** ~ more often than not, most often.

souvenu, e [suvəny] *pp de* **se souvenir**.

souverain, e [suvʀɛ̃, -ɛn] *adj* sovereign; (*fig: mépris*) supreme ♦ *nm/f* sovereign, monarch.

souverainement [suvʀɛnmɑ̃] *adv* (*sans appel*) with sovereign power; (*extrêmement*) supremely, intensely.

souveraineté [suvʀɛnte] *nf* sovereignty.

souviendrai [suvjɛ̃dʀe], **souviens** [suvjɛ̃], **souvint** [suvɛ̃] *etc vb voir* **se souvenir**.

soviétique [sɔvjetik] *adj* Soviet ♦ *nm/f*: **S**~ Soviet citizen.

soviétiser [sɔvjetize] *vt* to sovietize.

soviétologue [sɔvjetɔlɔg] *nm/f* Kremlinologist.

soyeux, euse [swajø, -øz] *adj* silky.

soyez [swaje] *etc vb voir* **être**.

SPA *sigle f* (= *Société protectrice des animaux*) ≈ RSPCA (*BRIT*), ≈ SPCA (*US*).

spacieux, euse [spasjø, -øz] *adj* spacious, roomy.

spaciosité [spasjɔzite] *nf* spaciousness.

spaghettis [spageti] *nmpl* spaghetti *sg*.

sparadrap [spaʀadʀa] *nm* adhesive *ou* sticking (*BRIT*) plaster, bandaid ® (*US*).

Sparte [spaʀt(ə)] *nf* Sparta.

spartiate [spaʀsjat] *adj* Spartan; ~**s** *nfpl* (*sandales*) Roman sandals.

spasme [spasm(ə)] *nm* spasm.

spasmodique [spazmɔdik] *adj* spasmodic.

spatial, e, aux [spasjal, -o] *adj* (*AVIAT*) space *cpd*; (*PSYCH*) spatial.

spatule [spatyl] *nf* (*ustensile*) slice; spatula; (*bout*) tip.

speaker, ine [spikœʀ, -kʀin] *nm/f* announcer.

spécial, e, aux [spesjal, -o] *adj* special; (*bizarre*) peculiar.

spécialement [spesjalmɑ̃] *adv* especially, particularly; (*tout exprès*) specially; **pas** ~ not particularly.

spécialisation [spesjalizɑsjɔ̃] *nf* specialization.

spécialisé, e [spesjalize] *adj* specialised; **ordinateur** ~ dedicated computer.

spécialiser [spesjalize]: **se** ~ *vi* to specialize.

spécialiste [spesjalist(ə)] *nm/f* specialist.

spécialité [spesjalite] *nf* speciality; (*SCOL*) special field; ~ **pharmaceutique** patent medicine.

spécieux, euse [spesjø, -øz] *adj* specious.

spécification [spesifikɑsjɔ̃] *nf* specification.

spécificité [spesifisite] *nf* specificity.

spécifier [spesifje] *vt* to specify, state.

spécifique [spesifik] *adj* specific.

spécifiquement [spesifikmɑ̃] *adv* (*typiquement*) typically; (*tout exprès*) specifically.

spécimen [spesimen] *nm* specimen; (*revue etc*) specimen *ou* sample copy.

spectacle [spɛktakl(ə)] *nm* (*tableau, scène*) sight; (*représentation*) show; (*industrie*) show business, entertainment; **se donner en** ~ (*péj*) to make a spectacle *ou* an exhibition of o.s; **pièce/revue à grand** ~ spectacular (play/revue); **au** ~ **de** ... at the sight of ....

spectaculaire [spɛktakylɛʀ] *adj* spectacular.

spectateur, trice [spɛktatœʀ, -tʀis] *nm/f* (*CINÉ etc*) member of the audience; (*SPORT*) spectator; (*d'un événement*) onlooker, witness.

spectre [spɛktʀ(ə)] *nm* (*fantôme, fig*) spectre; (*PHYSIQUE*) spectrum (*pl* -a); ~ **solaire** solar spectrum.

spéculateur, trice [spekylatœʀ, -tʀis] *nm/f* speculator.

spéculatif, ive [spekylatif, -iv] *adj* speculative.

spéculation [spekylɑsjɔ̃] *nf* speculation.

spéculer [spekyle] *vi* to speculate; ~ **sur** (*COMM*) to speculate in; (*réfléchir*) to speculate on; (*tabler sur*) to bank ou rely on.

spéléologie [speleɔlɔʒi] *nf* (*étude*) speleology; (*activité*) potholing.

spéléologue [speleɔlɔg] *nm/f* speleologist; potholer.

spermatozoïde [spɛrmatozɔid] *nm* sperm, spermatozoon (*pl* -zoa).

sperme [spɛrm(ə)] *nm* semen, sperm.

spermicide [spɛrmisid] *adj*, *nm* spermicide.

sphère [sfɛr] *nf* sphere.

sphérique [sferik] *adj* spherical.

sphincter [sfɛ̃ktɛr] *nm* sphincter.

sphinx [sfɛ̃ks] *nm inv* sphinx; (*ZOOL*) hawkmoth.

spiral, aux [spiral, -o] *nm* hairspring.

spirale [spiral] *nf* spiral; **en** ~ in a spiral.

spire [spir] *nf* (*d'une spirale*) turn; (*d'une coquille*) whorl.

spiritisme [spiritism(ə)] *nm* spiritualism, spiritism.

spirituel, le [spiritɥɛl] *adj* spiritual; (*fin, piquant*) witty; **musique** ~**le** sacred music; **concert** ~ concert of sacred music.

spirituellement [spiritɥɛlmã] *adv* spiritually; wittily.

spiritueux [spiritɥø] *nm* spirit.

splendeur [splãdœr] *nf* splendour (*BRIT*), splendor (*US*).

splendide [splãdid] *adj* splendid, magnificent.

spolier [spɔlje] *vt*: ~ **qn (de)** to despoil sb (of).

spongieux, euse [spɔ̃ʒjø, -øz] *adj* spongy.

sponsor [spɔ̃sɔr] *nm* sponsor.

sponsoriser [spɔ̃sɔrize] *vt* to sponsor.

spontané, e [spɔ̃tane] *adj* spontaneous.

spontanéité [spɔ̃taneite] *nf* spontaneity.

spontanément [spɔ̃tanemã] *adv* spontaneously.

sporadique [spɔradik] *adj* sporadic.

sporadiquement [spɔradikmã] *adv* sporadically.

sport [spɔr] *nm* sport ♦ *adj inv* (*vêtement*) casual; (*fair-play*) sporting; **faire du** ~ to do sport; ~ **individuel/d'équipe** individual/team sport; ~ **de combat** combative sport; ~**s d'hiver** winter sports.

sportif, ive [spɔrtif, -iv] *adj* (*journal, association, épreuve*) sports *cpd*; (*allure, démarche*) athletic; (*attitude, esprit*) sporting; **les résultats** ~**s** the sports results.

sportivement [spɔrtivmã] *adv* sportingly.

sportivité [spɔrtivite] *nf* sportsmanship.

spot [spɔt] *nm* (*lampe*) spot(light); (*annonce*): ~ **(publicitaire)** commercial (break).

spray [sprɛ] *nm* spray, aerosol.

sprint [sprint] *nm* sprint; **piquer un** ~ to put on a (final) spurt.

sprinter *nm* [sprintœr] sprinter ♦ *vi* [sprinte] to sprint.

squale [skwal] *nm* (*type of*) shark.

square [skwar] *nm* public garden(s).

squash [skwaʃ] *nm* squash.

squat [skwat] *nm* (*lieu*) squat.

squatter *nm* [skwatœr] squatter ♦ *vt* [skwate] to squat.

squelette [skəlɛt] *nm* skeleton.

squelettique [skəletik] *adj* scrawny; (*fig*) skimpy.

Sri Lanka [sriláka] *nm* Sri Lanka.

sri-lankais, e [srilákɛ, -ɛz] *adj* Sri-Lankan.

SS *sigle f* = **sécurité sociale**; (= *Sa Sainteté*) HH.

ss *abr* = **sous**.

S/S *sigle m* (= *steamship*) SS.

SSR *sigle f* (= *Société suisse romande*) the Swiss French-language broadcasting company.

stabilisateur, trice [stabilizatœr, -tris] *adj* stabilizing ♦ *nm* stabilizer; (*véhicule*) antiroll device; (*avion*) tailplane.

stabiliser [stabilize] *vt* to stabilize; (*terrain*) to consolidate.

stabilité [stabilite] *nf* stability.

stable [stabl(ə)] *adj* stable, steady.

stade [stad] *nm* (*SPORT*) stadium; (*phase, niveau*) stage.

stage [staʒ] *nm* training period; training course; (*d'avocat stagiaire*) articles *pl*.

stagiaire [staʒjɛr] *nm/f*, *adj* trainee (*cpd*).

stagnant, e [stagnã, -ãt] *adj* stagnant.

stagnation [stagnɑsjɔ̃] *nf* stagnation.

stagner [stagne] *vi* to stagnate.

stalactite [stalaktit] *nf* stalactite.

stalagmite [stalagmit] *nf* stalagmite.

stalle [stal] *nf* stall, box.

stand [stãd] *nm* (*d'exposition*) stand; (*de foire*) stall; ~ **de tir** (*à la foire, SPORT*) shooting range; ~ **de ravitaillement** pit.

standard [stãdar] *adj inv* standard ♦ *nm* (*type, norme*) standard; (*téléphonique*) switchboard.

standardisation [stãdardizɑsjɔ̃] *nf* standardization.

standardiser [stãdardize] *vt* to standardize.

standardiste [stãdardist(ə)] *nm/f* switchboard operator.

standing [stãdiŋ] *nm* standing; **immeuble de grand** ~ block of luxury flats (*BRIT*), condo(minium) (*US*).

star [star] *nf* star.

starlette [starlɛt] *nf* starlet.

starter [startɛr] *nm* (*AUTO*) choke; (*SPORT: personne*) starter; **mettre le** ~ to pull out the choke.

station [stɑsjɔ̃] *nf* station; (*de bus*) stop; (*de villégiature*) resort; (*posture*): **la** ~ **debout** standing, an upright posture; ~ **balnéaire** seaside resort; ~ **de graissage** lubrication bay; ~ **de lavage** carwash; ~ **de ski** ski resort; ~ **de sports d'hiver** winter sports resort; ~ **de taxis** taxi rank (*BRIT*) *ou* stand (*US*); ~ **thermale** thermal spa; ~ **de travail** workstation.

stationnaire [stɑsjɔnɛr] *adj* stationary.

stationnement [stasjɔnmɑ̃] *nm* parking; **zone de ~ interdit** no parking area; **~ alterné** parking on alternate sides.

stationner [stasjɔne] *vi* to park.

station-service [stasjɔ̃sɛʀvis] *nf* service station.

statique [statik] *adj* static.

statisticien, ne [statistisjɛ̃, -ɛn] *nm/f* statistician.

statistique [statistik] *nf* (*science*) statistics *sg*; (*rapport, étude*) statistic ♦ *adj* statistical; **~s** *nfpl* (*données*) statistics *pl*.

statistiquement [statistikmɑ̃] *adv* statistically.

statue [staty] *nf* statue.

statuer [statɥe] *vi*: **~ sur** to rule on, give a ruling on.

statuette [statɥɛt] *nf* statuette.

statu quo [statykwo] *nm* status quo.

stature [statyʀ] *nf* stature; **de haute ~** of great stature.

statut [staty] *nm* status; **~s** *nmpl* (*JUR, ADMIN*) statutes.

statutaire [statytɛʀ] *adj* statutory.

St(e) *abr* (= *Saint(e)*) St.

Sté *abr* (= *société*) soc.

steak [stɛk] *nm* steak.

stèle [stɛl] *nf* stela, stele.

stellaire [stelɛʀ] *adj* stellar.

stencil [stɛnsil] *nm* stencil.

sténodactylo [stenɔdaktilo] *nm/f* shorthand typist (*BRIT*), stenographer (*US*).

sténodactylographie [stenɔdaktilɔgʀafi] *nf* shorthand typing (*BRIT*), stenography (*US*).

sténo(graphe) [stenɔ(gʀaf)] *nm/f* shorthand typist (*BRIT*), stenographer (*US*).

sténo(graphie) [stenɔ(gʀafi)] *nf* shorthand; **prendre en ~** to take down in shorthand.

sténographier [stenɔgʀafje] *vt* to take down in shorthand.

sténographique [stenɔgʀafik] *adj* shorthand *cpd*.

stentor [stɑ̃tɔʀ] *nm*: **voix de ~** stentorian voice.

step [stɛp] *nm* ® step aerobics *sg* ®, step Reebok ®.

stéphanois, e [stefanwa, -waz] *adj* of *ou* from Saint-Étienne.

steppe [stɛp] *nf* steppe.

stère [stɛʀ] *nm* stere.

stéréo(phonie) [steʀeɔ(fɔni)] *nf* stereo(phony); **émission en ~** stereo broadcast.

stéréo(phonique) [steʀeɔ(fɔnik)] *adj* stereo(phonic).

stéréoscope [steʀeɔskɔp] *nm* stereoscope.

stéréoscopique [steʀeɔskɔpik] *adj* stereoscopic.

stéréotype [steʀeɔtip] *nm* stereotype.

stéréotypé, e [steʀeɔtipe] *adj* stereotyped.

stérile [steʀil] *adj* sterile; (*terre*) barren; (*fig*) fruitless, futile.

stérilement [steʀilmɑ̃] *adv* fruitlessly.

stérilet [steʀilɛ] *nm* coil, loop.

stérilisateur [steʀilizatœʀ] *nm* sterilizer.

stérilisation [steʀilizasjɔ̃] *nf* sterilization.

stériliser [steʀilize] *vt* to sterilize.

stérilité [steʀilite] *nf* sterility.

sternum [stɛʀnɔm] *nm* breastbone, sternum.

stéthoscope [stetɔskɔp] *nm* stethoscope.

stick [stik] *nm* stick.

stigmates [stigmat] *nmpl* scars, marks; (*REL*) stigmata *pl*.

stigmatiser [stigmatize] *vt* to denounce, stigmatize.

stimulant, e [stimylɑ̃, -ɑ̃t] *adj* stimulating ♦ *nm* (*MÉD*) stimulant; (*fig*) stimulus (*pl* -i), incentive.

stimulateur [stimylatœʀ] *nm*: **~ cardiaque** pacemaker.

stimulation [stimylasjɔ̃] *nf* stimulation.

stimuler [stimyle] *vt* to stimulate.

stimulus, i [stimylys, -i] *nm* stimulus (*pl* -i).

stipulation [stipylasjɔ̃] *nf* stipulation.

stipuler [stipyle] *vt* to stipulate, specify.

stock [stɔk] *nm* stock; **en ~** in stock.

stockage [stɔkaʒ] *nm* stocking; storage.

stocker [stɔke] *vt* to stock; (*déchets*) to store.

Stockholm [stɔkɔlm] *n* Stockholm.

stockiste [stɔkist(ə)] *nm* stockist.

stoïcisme [stɔisism(ə)] *nm* stoicism.

stoïque [stɔik] *adj* stoic, stoical.

stoïquement [stɔikmɑ̃] *adv* stoically.

stomacal, e, aux [stɔmakal, -o] *adj* gastric, stomach *cpd*.

stomatologie [stɔmatɔlɔʒi] *nf* stomatology.

stomatologue [stɔmatɔlɔg] *nm/f* stomatologist.

stop [stɔp] *nm* (*AUTO: écriteau*) stop sign; (*: signal*) brake-light; (*dans un télégramme*) stop ♦ *excl* stop!

stoppage [stɔpaʒ] *nm* invisible mending.

stopper [stɔpe] *vt* to stop, halt; (*COUTURE*) to mend ♦ *vi* to stop, halt.

store [stɔʀ] *nm* blind; (*de magasin*) shade, awning.

strabisme [stʀabism(ə)] *nm* squint(ing).

strangulation [stʀɑ̃gylasjɔ̃] *nf* strangulation.

strapontin [stʀapɔ̃tɛ̃] *nm* jump *ou* foldaway seat.

Strasbourg [stʀazbuʀ] *n* Strasbourg.

strass [stʀas] *nm* paste, strass.

stratagème [stʀataʒɛm] *nm* stratagem.

strate [stʀat] *nf* (*GÉO*) stratum, layer.

stratège [stʀatɛʒ] *nm* strategist.

stratégie [stʀateʒi] *nf* strategy.

stratégique [stʀateʒik] *adj* strategic.

stratégiquement [stʀateʒikmɑ̃] *adv* strategically.

stratifié, e [stʀatifje] *adj* (*GÉO*) stratified; (*TECH*) laminated.

stratosphère [stʀatɔsfɛʀ] *nf* stratosphere.

stress [stʀɛs] *nm inv* stress.

stressant, e [stʀɛsɑ̃, -ɑ̃t] *adj* stressful.

stresser [stʀɛse] *vt* to stress, cause stress in.

strict, e [stʀikt(ə)] *adj* strict; (*tenue, décor*) severe, plain; **son droit le plus** ~ his most basic right; **dans la plus** ~**e intimité** strictly in private; **le** ~ **nécessaire/minimum** the bare essentials/minimum.

strictement [stʀiktəmɑ̃] *adv* strictly; plainly.

strident, e [stʀidɑ̃, -ɑ̃t] *adj* shrill, strident.

stridulations [stʀidylɑsjɔ̃] *nfpl* stridulations, chirrings.

strie [stʀi] *nf* streak; (*ANAT, GÉO*) stria (*pl* -ae).

strier [stʀije] *vt* to streak; to striate.

strip-tease [stʀiptiz] *nm* striptease.

strip-teaseuse [stʀiptizøz] *nf* stripper, striptease artist.

striures [stʀijyʀ] *nfpl* streaking *sg*.

stroboscope [stʀɔbɔskɔp] *nm* strobe (light).

strophe [stʀɔf] *nf* verse, stanza.

structure [stʀyktyʀ] *nf* structure; ~**s d'accueil/touristiques** reception/tourist facilities.

structurer [stʀyktyʀe] *vt* to structure.

strychnine [stʀiknin] *nf* strychnine.

stuc [styk] *nm* stucco.

studieusement [stydjøzmɑ̃] *adv* studiously.

studieux, euse [stydjø, -øz] *adj* (*élève*) studious; (*vacances*) study *cpd*.

studio [stydjo] *nm* (*logement*) studio flat (*BRIT*) *ou* apartment (*US*); (*d'artiste, TV etc*) studio (*pl* -s).

stupéfaction [stypefaksjɔ̃] *nf* stupefaction, astonishment.

stupéfait, e [stypefɛ, -ɛt] *adj* astonished.

stupéfiant, e [stypefjɑ̃, -ɑ̃t] *adj* stunning, astonishing ♦ *nm* (*MÉD*) drug, narcotic.

stupéfier [stypefje] *vt* to stupefy; (*étonner*) to stun, astonish.

stupeur [stypœʀ] *nf* (*inertie, insensibilité*) stupor; (*étonnement*) astonishment, amazement.

stupide [stypid] *adj* stupid; (*hébété*) stunned.

stupidement [stypidmɑ̃] *adv* stupidly.

stupidité [stypidite] *nf* stupidity *no pl*; (*propos, action*) stupid thing (to say *ou* do).

stups [styp] *nmpl* (= *stupéfiants*): **brigade des** ~ narcotics bureau *ou* squad.

style [stil] *nm* style; **meuble/robe de** ~ piece of period furniture/period dress; ~ **de vie** lifestyle.

stylé, e [stile] *adj* well-trained.

stylet [stilɛ] *nm* (*poignard*) stiletto; (*CHIRURGIE*) stylet.

stylisé, e [stilize] *adj* stylized.

styliste [stilist(ə)] *nm/f* designer; stylist.

stylistique [stilistik] *nf* stylistics *sg* ♦ *adj* stylistic.

stylo [stilo] *nm*: ~ (**à encre**) (fountain) pen; ~ (**à**) **bille** ballpoint pen.

stylo-feutre [stiloføtʀ(ə)] *nm* felt-tip pen.

su, e [sy] *pp de* **savoir** ♦ *nm*: **au** ~ **de** with the knowledge of.

suaire [sɥɛʀ] *nm* shroud.

suant, e [sɥɑ̃, -ɑ̃t] *adj* sweaty.

suave [sɥav] *adj* (*odeur*) sweet; (*voix*) suave, smooth; (*coloris*) soft, mellow.

subalterne [sybaltɛʀn(ə)] *adj* (*employé, officier*) junior; (*rôle*) subordinate, subsidiary ♦ *nm/f* subordinate, inferior.

subconscient [sypkɔ̃sjɑ̃] *nm* subconscious.

subdiviser [sybdivize] *vt* to subdivide.

subdivision [sybdivizjɔ̃] *nf* subdivision.

subir [sybiʀ] *vt* (*affront, dégâts, mauvais traitements*) to suffer; (*influence, charme*) to be under, be subjected to; (*traitement, opération, châtiment*) to undergo; (*personne*) to suffer, be subjected to.

subit, e [sybi, -it] *adj* sudden.

subitement [sybitmɑ̃] *adv* suddenly, all of a sudden.

subjectif, ive [sybʒɛktif, -iv] *adj* subjective.

subjectivement [sybʒɛktivmɑ̃] *adv* subjectively.

subjectivité [sybʒɛktivite] *nf* subjectivity.

subjonctif [sybʒɔ̃ktif] *nm* subjunctive.

subjuguer [sybʒyge] *vt* to subjugate.

sublime [syblim] *adj* sublime.

sublimer [syblime] *vt* to sublimate.

submergé, e [sybmɛʀʒe] *adj* submerged; (*fig*): ~ **de** snowed under with; overwhelmed with.

submerger [sybmɛʀʒe] *vt* to submerge; (*suj: foule*) to engulf; (*fig*) to overwhelm.

submersible [sybmɛʀsibl(ə)] *nm* submarine.

subordination [sybɔʀdinɑsjɔ̃] *nf* subordination.

subordonné, e [sybɔʀdɔne] *adj, nm/f* subordinate; ~ **à** (*personne*) subordinate to; (*résultats etc*) subject to, depending on.

subordonner [sybɔʀdɔne] *vt*: ~ **qn/qch à** to subordinate sb/sth to.

subornation [sybɔʀnɑsjɔ̃] *nf* bribing.

suborner [sybɔʀne] *vt* to bribe.

subrepticement [sybʀɛptismɑ̃] *adv* surreptitiously.

subroger [sybʀɔʒe] *vt* (*JUR*) to subrogate.

subside [sypsid] *nm* grant.

subsidiaire [sypsidjɛʀ] *adj* subsidiary; **question** ~ deciding question.

subsistance [sybzistɑ̃s] *nf* subsistence; **pourvoir à la** ~ **de qn** to keep sb, provide for sb's subsistence *ou* keep.

subsister [sybziste] *vi* (*rester*) to remain, subsist; (*vivre*) to live; (*survivre*) to live on.

subsonique [sybsɔnik] *adj* subsonic.

substance [sypstɑ̃s] *nf* substance; **en** ~ in substance.

substantiel, le [sypstɑ̃sjɛl] *adj* substantial.

substantif [sypstɑ̃tif] *nm* noun, substantive.

substantiver [sypstɑ̃tive] *vt* to nominalize.

substituer [sypstitɥe] *vt*: ~ **qn/qch à** to substitute sb/sth for; **se** ~ **à qn** (*représenter*) to substitute for sb; (*évincer*) to substitute o.s. for sb.

substitut [sypstity] *nm* (*JUR*) deputy public

prosecutor; (*succédané*) substitute.
substitution [sypstitysjɔ̃] *nf* substitution.
subterfuge [syptɛʁfyʒ] *nm* subterfuge.
subtil, e [syptil] *adj* subtle.
subtilement [syptilmɑ̃] *adv* subtly.
subtiliser [syptilize] *vt*: ~ **qch (à qn)** to spirit sth away (from sb).
subtilité [syptilite] *nf* subtlety.
subtropical, e, aux [sybtʁɔpikal, -o] *adj* subtropical.
suburbain, e [sybyʁbɛ̃, -ɛn] *adj* suburban.
subvenir [sybvəniʁ]: ~ **à** *vt* to meet.
subvention [sybvɑ̃sjɔ̃] *nf* subsidy, grant.
subventionner [sybvɑ̃sjɔne] *vt* to subsidize.
subversif, ive [sybvɛʁsif, -iv] *adj* subversive.
subversion [sybvɛʁsjɔ̃] *nf* subversion.
suc [syk] *nm* (*BOT*) sap; (*de viande, fruit*) juice; **~s gastriques** gastric juices.
succédané [syksedane] *nm* substitute.
succéder [syksede]: ~ **à** *vt* (*directeur, roi etc*) to succeed; (*venir après: dans une série*) to follow, succeed; **se** ~ *vi* (*accidents, années*) to follow one another.
succès [syksɛ] *nm* success; **avec** ~ successfully; **sans** ~ unsuccessfully; **avoir du** ~ to be a success, be successful; **à** ~ successful; **livre à** ~ bestseller; ~ **de librairie** bestseller; ~ (**féminins**) conquests.
successeur [syksesœʁ] *nm* successor.
successif, ive [syksesif, -iv] *adj* successive.
succession [syksesjɔ̃] *nf* (*série, POL*) succession; (*JUR: patrimoine*) estate, inheritance; **prendre la** ~ **de** (*directeur*) to succeed, take over from; (*entreprise*) to take over.
successivement [syksesivmɑ̃] *adv* successively.
succinct, e [syksɛ̃, -ɛ̃t] *adj* succinct.
succinctement [syksɛ̃tmɑ̃] *adv* succinctly.
succion [syksjɔ̃] *nf*: **bruit de** ~ sucking noise.
succomber [sykɔ̃be] *vi* to die, succumb; (*fig*): ~ **à** to give way to, succumb to.
succulent, e [sykylɑ̃, -ɑ̃t] *adj* succulent.
succursale [sykyʁsal] *nf* branch; **magasin à ~s multiples** chain *ou* multiple store.
sucer [syse] *vt* to suck.
sucette [sysɛt] *nf* (*bonbon*) lollipop; (*de bébé*) dummy (*BRIT*), comforter, pacifier (*US*).
suçoter [sysɔte] *vt* to suck.
sucre [sykʁ(ə)] *nm* (*substance*) sugar; (*morceau*) lump of sugar, sugar lump *ou* cube; ~ **de canne/betterave** cane/beet sugar; ~ **en morceaux/cristallisé/en poudre** lump *ou* cube/granulated/caster sugar; ~ **glace** icing sugar; ~ **d'orge** barley sugar.
sucré, e [sykʁe] *adj* (*produit alimentaire*) sweetened; (*au goût*) sweet; (*péj*) sugary, honeyed.
sucrer [sykʁe] *vt* (*thé, café*) to sweeten, put sugar in; ~ **qn** to put sugar in sb's tea (*ou* coffee *etc*); **se** ~ to help o.s. to sugar, have some sugar; (*fam*) to line one's pocket(s).
sucrerie [sykʁəʁi] *nf* (*usine*) sugar refinery; **~s** *nfpl* (*bonbons*) sweets, sweet things.

sucrier, ière [sykʁije, -jɛʁ] *adj* (*industrie*) sugar *cpd*; (*région*) sugar-producing ♦ *nm* (*fabricant*) sugar producer; (*récipient*) sugar bowl *ou* basin.
sud [syd] *nm*: **le** ~ the south ♦ *adj inv* south; (*côte*) south, southern; **au** ~ (*situation*) in the south; (*direction*) to the south; **au** ~ **de** (to the) south of.
sud-africain, e [sydafʁikɛ̃, -ɛn] *adj* South African ♦ *nm/f*: **Sud-Africain, e** South African.
sud-américain, e [sydameʁikɛ̃, -ɛn] *adj* South American ♦ *nm/f*: **Sud-Américain, e** South American.
sudation [sydasjɔ̃] *nf* sweating, sudation.
sud-coréen, ne [sydkɔʁeɛ̃, -ɛn] *adj* South Korean ♦ *nm/f*: **Sud-Coréen, ne** South Korean.
sud-est [sydɛst] *nm, adj inv* south-east.
sud-ouest [sydwɛst] *nm, adj inv* south-west.
sud-vietnamien, ne [sydvjɛtnamjɛ̃, -ɛn] *adj* South Vietnamese ♦ *nm/f*: **Sud-Vietnamien, ne** South Vietnamese.
Suède [sɥɛd] *nf*: **la** ~ Sweden.
suédois, e [sɥedwa, -waz] *adj* Swedish ♦ *nm* (*LING*) Swedish ♦ *nm/f*: **S~, e** Swede.
suer [sɥe] *vi* to sweat; (*suinter*) to ooze ♦ *vt* (*fig*) to exude; ~ **à grosses gouttes** to sweat profusely.
sueur [sɥœʁ] *nf* sweat; **en** ~ sweating, in a sweat; **avoir des ~s froides** to be in a cold sweat.
suffire [syfiʁ] *vi* (*être assez*): ~ (**là qn/pour qch/pour faire**) to be enough *ou* sufficient (for sb/for sth/to do); (*satisfaire*): **cela lui suffit** he's content with this, this is enough for him; **se** ~ *vi* to be self-sufficient; **cela suffit pour les irriter/qu'ils se fâchent** it's enough to annoy them/for them to get angry; **il suffit d'une négligence/qu'on oublie pour que ...** it only takes one act of carelessness/one only needs to forget for ...; **ça suffit!** that's enough!, that'll do!
suffisamment [syfizamɑ̃] *adv* sufficiently, enough; ~ **de** sufficient, enough.
suffisance [syfizɑ̃s] *nf* (*vanité*) self-importance, bumptiousness; (*quantité*): **en** ~ in plenty.
suffisant, e [syfizɑ̃, -ɑ̃t] *adj* (*temps, ressources*) sufficient; (*résultats*) satisfactory; (*vaniteux*) self-important, bumptious.
suffisons [syfizɔ̃] *etc vb voir* **suffire**.
suffixe [syfiks(ə)] *nm* suffix.
suffocant, e [syfɔkɑ̃, -ɑ̃t] *adj* (*étouffant*) suffocating; (*stupéfiant*) staggering.
suffocation [syfɔkasjɔ̃] *nf* suffocation.
suffoquer [syfɔke] *vt* to choke, suffocate; (*stupéfier*) to stagger, astound ♦ *vi* to choke, suffocate; ~ **de colère/d'indignation** to choke with anger/indignation.
suffrage [syfʁaʒ] *nm* (*POL: voix*) vote; (: *méthode*): ~ **universel/direct/indirect** universal/direct/indirect suffrage; (*du public etc*) approval *no pl*; **~s exprimés** valid

votes.

suggérer [sygʒeʀe] vt to suggest; ~ **que/de faire** to suggest that/doing.

suggestif, ive [sygʒɛstif, -iv] adj suggestive.

suggestion [sygʒɛstjɔ̃] nf suggestion.

suggestivité [sygʒɛstivite] nf suggestiveness, suggestive nature.

suicidaire [sɥisidɛʀ] adj suicidal.

suicide [sɥisid] nm suicide ♦ adj: **opération** ~ suicide mission.

suicidé, e [sɥiside] nm/f suicide.

suicider [sɥiside]: **se** ~ vi to commit suicide.

suie [sɥi] nf soot.

suif [sɥif] nm tallow.

suinter [sɥɛ̃te] vi to ooze.

suis [sɥi] vb voir **être, suivre.**

suisse [sɥis] adj Swiss ♦ nm (bedeau) ≈ verger ♦ nm/f: **S~** Swiss pl inv ♦ nf: **la S~** Switzerland; **la S~ romande/allemande** French-speaking/German-speaking Switzerland; ~ **romand** Swiss French.

suisse-allemand, e [sɥisalmɑ̃, -ɑ̃d] adj, nm/f Swiss German.

Suissesse [sɥisɛs] nf Swiss (woman ou girl).

suit [sɥi] vb voir **suivre.**

suite [sɥit] nf (continuation: d'énumération etc) rest, remainder; (: de feuilleton) continuation; (: second film etc sur le même thème) sequel; (série: de maisons, succès): **une** ~ **de** a series ou succession of; (MATH) series sg; (conséquence) result; (ordre, liaison logique) coherence; (appartement, MUS) suite; (escorte) retinue, suite; **~s** nfpl (d'une maladie etc) effects; **prendre la** ~ **de** (directeur etc) to succeed, take over from; **donner** ~ **à** (requête, projet) to follow up; **faire** ~ **à** to follow; **(faisant)** ~ **à votre lettre du** further to your letter of the; **sans** ~ adj incoherent, disjointed ♦ adv incoherently, disjointedly; **de** ~ adv (d'affilée) in succession; (immédiatement) at once; **par la** ~ afterwards, subsequently; **à la** ~ adv one after the other; **à la** ~ **de** (derrière) behind; (en conséquence de) following; **par** ~ **de** owing to, as a result of; **avoir de la** ~ **dans les idées** to show great singleness of purpose; **attendre la** ~ **des événements** to (wait and see) what happens.

suivant, e [sɥivɑ̃, -ɑ̃t] vb voir **suivre** ♦ adj next, following; (ci-après): **l'exercice** ~ the following exercise ♦ prép (selon) according to; ~ **que** according to whether; **au** ~! next!

suive [sɥiv] etc vb voir **suivre.**

suiveur [sɥivœʀ] nm (CYCLISME) (official) follower; (péj) (camp) follower.

suivi, e [sɥivi] pp de **suivre** ♦ adj (régulier) regular; (COMM: article) in general production; (cohérent) consistent; coherent ♦ nm follow-up; **très/peu** ~ (cours) well-/poorly-attended; (mode) widely/not widely adopted; (feuilleton etc) widely/not widely followed.

suivre [sɥivʀ(ə)] vt (gén) to follow; (SCOL:

cours) to attend; (: leçon) to follow, attend to; (: programme) to keep up with; (COMM: article) to continue to stock ♦ vi to follow; (élève: écouter) to attend, pay attention; (: assimiler le programme) to keep up, follow; **se** ~ (accidents, personnes, voitures etc) to follow one after the other; (raisonnement) to be coherent; ~ **des yeux** to follow with one's eyes; **faire** ~ (lettre) to forward; ~ **son cours** (suj: enquête etc) to run ou take its course; **"à** ~**"** "to be continued".

sujet, te [syʒɛ, -ɛt] adj: **être** ~ **à** (accidents) to be prone to; (vertige etc) to be liable ou subject to ♦ nm/f (d'un souverain) subject ♦ nm subject; **un** ~ **de dispute/discorde/mécontentement** a cause for argument/dissension/dissatisfaction; **c'est à quel** ~? what is it about?; **avoir** ~ **de se plaindre** to have cause for complaint; **au** ~ **de** prép about; ~ **à caution** adj questionable; ~ **de conversation** topic ou subject of conversation; ~ **d'examen** (SCOL) examination question; examination paper; ~ **d'expérience** (BIO etc) experimental subject.

sujétion [syʒesjɔ̃] nf subjection; (fig) constraint.

sulfater [sylfate] vt to spray with copper sulphate.

sulfureux, euse [sylfyʀø, -øz] adj sulphurous (BRIT), sulfurous (US).

sulfurique [sylfyʀik] adj: **acide** ~ sulphuric (BRIT) ou sulfuric (US) acid.

sulfurisé, e [sylfyʀize] adj: **papier** ~ greaseproof (BRIT) ou wax (US) paper.

Sumatra [symatʀa] nf Sumatra.

summum [sɔmɔm] nm: **le** ~ **de** the height of.

sumo [symo] nm inv sumo (wrestling).

super [sypɛʀ] adj inv great, fantastic ♦ nm (= supercarburant) ≈ 4-star (BRIT), ≈ premium (US).

superbe [sypɛʀb(ə)] adj magnificent, superb ♦ nf arrogance.

superbement [sypɛʀbəmɑ̃] adv superbly.

supercarburant [sypɛʀkaʀbyʀɑ̃] nm ≈ 4-star petrol (BRIT), ≈ premium gas (US).

supercherie [sypɛʀʃəʀi] nf trick, trickery no pl; (fraude) fraud.

supérette [sypeʀɛt] nf minimarket.

superfétatoire [sypɛʀfetatwaʀ] adj superfluous.

superficie [sypɛʀfisi] nf (surface) area; (fig) surface.

superficiel, le [sypɛʀfisjɛl] adj superficial.

superficiellement [sypɛʀfisjɛlmɑ̃] adv superficially.

superflu, e [sypɛʀfly] adj superfluous ♦ nm: **le** ~ the superfluous.

superforme [sypɛʀfɔʀm(ə)] nf (fam) top form, excellent shape.

super-grand [sypɛʀgʀɑ̃] nm superpower.

super-huit [sypɛʀɥit] adj: **camera/film** ~ super-eight camera/film.

supérieur, e [syperjœr] *adj* (*lèvre, étages, classes*) upper; (*plus élevé: température, niveau*): ~ **(à)** higher (than); (*meilleur: qualité, produit*): ~ **(à)** superior (to); (*excellent, hautain*) superior ♦ *nm/f* superior; **Mère** ~**e** Mother Superior; **à l'étage** ~ on the next floor up; ~ **en nombre** superior in number.

supérieurement [syperjœrmɑ̃] *adv* exceptionally well, exceptionally + *adj*.

supériorité [syperjɔrite] *nf* superiority.

superlatif [syperlatif] *nm* superlative.

supermarché [sypermarʃe] *nm* supermarket.

supernova [sypernɔva] *nf* supernova.

superposable [syperpozabl(ə)] *adj* (*figures*) that may be superimposed; (*lits*) stackable.

superposer [syperpoze] *vt* to superpose; (*meubles, caisses*) to stack; (*faire chevaucher*) to superimpose; **se** ~ (*images, souvenirs*) to be superimposed; **lits superposés** bunk beds.

superposition [syperpozisjɔ̃] *nf* superposition; superimposition.

superpréfet [syperprefɛ] *nm* *prefect in charge of a region.*

superproduction [syperprɔdyksjɔ̃] *nf* (*film*) spectacular.

superpuissance [syperpɥisɑ̃s] *nf* superpower.

supersonique [sypersɔnik] *adj* supersonic.

superstitieux, euse [syperstisjø, -øz] *adj* superstitious.

superstition [syperstisjɔ̃] *nf* superstition.

superstructure [syperstryktyr] *nf* superstructure.

supertanker [sypertɑ̃kœr] *nm* supertanker.

superviser [sypervize] *vt* to supervise.

supervision [sypervizjɔ̃] *nf* supervision.

suppl. *abr* = **supplément**.

supplanter [syplɑ̃te] *vt* to supplant.

suppléance [sypleɑ̃s] *nf* (*poste*) supply post (*BRIT*), substitute teacher's post (*US*).

suppléant, e [sypleɑ̃, -ɑ̃t] *adj* (*juge, fonctionnaire*) deputy *cpd*; (*professeur*) supply *cpd* (*BRIT*), substitute *cpd* (*US*) ♦ *nm/f* deputy; supply *ou* substitute teacher; **médecin** ~ locum.

suppléer [syplee] *vt* (*ajouter: mot manquant etc*) to supply, provide; (*compenser: lacune*) to fill in; (*: défaut*) to make up for; (*remplacer: professeur*) to stand in for; (*: juge*) to deputize for; ~ **à** *vt* to make up for; to substitute for.

supplément [syplemɑ̃] *nm* supplement; **un** ~ **de travail** extra *ou* additional work; **un** ~ **de frites** *etc* an extra portion of chips *etc*; **un** ~ **de 100 F** a supplement of 100 F, an extra *ou* additional 100 F; **ceci est en** ~ (*au menu etc*) this is extra, there is an extra charge for this; ~ **d'information** additional information.

supplémentaire [syplemɑ̃tɛr] *adj* additional, further; (*train, bus*) relief *cpd*, extra.

supplétif, ive [sypletif, -iv] *adj* (*MIL*) auxiliary.

suppliant, e [syplijɑ̃, -ɑ̃t] *adj* imploring.

supplication [syplikasjɔ̃] *nf* (*REL*) supplication; ~**s** *nfpl* (*adjurations*) pleas, entreaties.

supplice [syplis] *nm* (*peine corporelle*) torture *no pl*; form of torture; (*douleur physique, morale*) torture, agony; **être au** ~ to be in agony.

supplier [syplije] *vt* to implore, beseech.

supplique [syplik] *nf* petition.

support [sypɔr] *nm* support; (*pour livre, outils*) stand; ~ **audio-visuel** audio-visual aid; ~ **publicitaire** advertising medium.

supportable [sypɔrtabl(ə)] *adj* (*douleur, température*) bearable; (*procédé, conduite*) tolerable.

supporter *nm* [sypɔrtɛr] supporter, fan ♦ *vt* [sypɔrte] (*poids, poussée, SPORT: concurrent, équipe*) to support; (*conséquences, épreuve*) to bear, endure; (*défauts, personne*) to tolerate, put up with; (*suj: chose: chaleur etc*) to withstand; (*suj: personne: chaleur, vin*) to take.

supposé, e [sypoze] *adj* (*nombre*) estimated; (*auteur*) supposed.

supposer [sypoze] *vt* to suppose; (*impliquer*) to presuppose; **en supposant** *ou* **à** ~ **que** supposing (that).

supposition [sypozisjɔ̃] *nf* supposition.

suppositoire [sypozitwar] *nm* suppository.

suppôt [sypo] *nm* (*péj*) henchman.

suppression [sypresjɔ̃] *nf* (*voir supprimer*) removal; deletion; cancellation; suppression.

supprimer [syprime] *vt* (*cloison, cause, anxiété*) to remove; (*clause, mot*) to delete; (*congés, service d'autobus etc*) to cancel; (*publication, article*) to suppress; (*emplois, privilèges, témoin gênant*) to do away with; ~ **qch à qn** to deprive sb of sth.

suppurer [sypyre] *vi* to suppurate.

supputations [sypytasjɔ̃] *nfpl* calculations, reckonings.

supputer [sypyte] *vt* to calculate, reckon.

supranational, e, aux [sypranasjɔnal, -o] *adj* supranational.

suprématie [sypremasi] *nf* supremacy.

suprême [syprɛm] *adj* supreme.

suprêmement [sypremmɑ̃] *adv* supremely.

═══════════════════ *MOT-CLÉ*

sur [syr] *prép* **1** (*position*) on; (*pardessus*) over; (*au-dessus*) above; **pose-le** ~ **la table** put it on the table; **je n'ai pas d'argent** ~ **moi** I haven't any money on me

2 (*direction*) towards; **en allant** ~ **Paris** going towards Paris; ~ **votre droite** on *ou* to your right

3 (*à propos de*) on, about; **un livre/une conférence** ~ **Balzac** a book/lecture on *ou* about Balzac

4 (*proportion, mesures*) out of; by; **un** ~ **10** one in 10; (*SCOL*) one out of 10; ~ **20, 2 sont venus** out of 20, 2 came; **4 m** ~ **2** 4 m by 2; **avoir accident** ~ **accident** to have one accident after another

5 (cause): ~ **sa recommandation** on ou at his recommendation; ~ **son invitation** at his invitation
sur ce adv whereupon; ~ **ce, il faut que je vous quitte** and now I must leave you.

sur, e [syʀ] adj sour.

sûr, e [syʀ] adj sure, certain; (digne de confiance) reliable; (sans danger) safe; **peu** ~ unreliable; ~ **de qch** sure ou certain of sth; **être** ~ **de qn** to be sure of sb; ~ **et certain** absolutely certain; ~ **de soi** self-assured, self-confident; **le plus** ~ **est de** the safest thing is to.

surabondance [syʀabɔ̃dɑ̃s] nf overabundance.

surabondant, e [syʀabɔ̃dɑ̃, -ɑ̃t] adj overabundant.

surabonder [syʀabɔ̃de] vi to be overabundant; ~ **de** to abound with, have an overabundance of.

suractivité [syʀaktivite] nf hyperactivity.

suraigu, ë [syʀegy] adj very shrill.

surajouter [syʀaʒute] vt: ~ **qch à** to add sth to.

suralimentation [syʀalimɑ̃tɑsjɔ̃] nf overfeeding; (TECH: d'un moteur) supercharging.

suralimenté, e [syʀalimɑ̃te] adj (personne) overfed; (moteur) supercharged.

suranné, e [syʀane] adj outdated, outmoded.

surarmement [syʀaʀməmɑ̃] nm (excess) stockpiling of arms (ou weapons).

surbaissé, e [syʀbese] adj lowered, low.

surcapacité [syʀkapasite] nf overcapacity.

surcharge [syʀʃaʀʒ(ə)] nf (de passagers, marchandises) excess load; (de détails, d'ornements) overabundance, excess; (correction) alteration; (POSTES) surcharge; **prendre des passagers en** ~ to take on excess ou extra passengers; ~ **de bagages** excess luggage; ~ **de travail** extra work.

surchargé, e [syʀʃaʀʒe] adj (décoration, style) over-elaborate, overfussy; (voiture, emploi du temps) overloaded.

surcharger [syʀʃaʀʒe] vt to overload; (timbre-poste) to surcharge; (décoration) to overdo.

surchauffe [syʀʃof] nf overheating.

surchauffé, e [syʀʃofe] adj overheated; (fig: imagination) overactive.

surchoix [syʀʃwa] adj inv top-quality.

surclasser [syʀklɑse] vt to outclass.

surconsommation [syʀkɔ̃sɔmɑsjɔ̃] nf (ÉCON) overconsumption.

surcoté, e [syʀkɔte] adj overpriced.

surcouper [syʀkupe] vt to overtrump.

surcroît [syʀkʀwa] nm: **un** ~ **de** additional + nom; **par** ou **de** ~ moreover; **en** ~ in addition.

surdi-mutité [syʀdimytite] nf: **atteint de** ~ deaf and dumb.

surdité [syʀdite] nf deafness; **atteint de** ~ **totale** profoundly deaf.

surdoué, e [syʀdwe] adj gifted.

sureau, x [syʀo] nm elder (tree).

sureffectif [syʀefɛktif] nm overmanning.

surélever [syʀɛlve] vt to raise, heighten.

sûrement [syʀmɑ̃] adv reliably; safely, securely; (certainement) certainly; ~ **pas** certainly not.

suremploi [syʀɑ̃plwa] nm (ÉCON) overemployment.

surenchère [syʀɑ̃ʃɛʀ] nf (aux enchères) higher bid; (sur prix fixe) overbid; (fig) overstatement; outbidding tactics pl; ~ **de violence** build-up of violence; ~ **électorale** political (ou electoral) one-upmanship.

surenchérir [syʀɑ̃ʃeʀiʀ] vi to bid higher; to raise one's bid; (fig) to try and outbid each other.

surendettement [syʀɑ̃dɛtmɑ̃] nm excessive debt.

surent [syʀ] vb voir **savoir**.

surentraîné, e [syʀɑ̃tʀene] adj overtrained.

suréquipé, e [syʀekipe] adj overequipped.

surestimer [syʀɛstime] vt (tableau) to overvalue; (possibilité, personne) to overestimate.

sûreté [syʀte] nf (voir sûr) reliability; safety; (JUR) guaranty; surety; **mettre en** ~ to put in a safe place; **pour plus de** ~ as an extra precaution; **to be on the safe side; la** ~ **de l'État** State security; **la S~ (nationale)** division of the Ministère de l'Intérieur heading all police forces except the gendarmerie and the Paris préfecture de police.

surexcité, e [syʀɛksite] adj overexcited.

surexciter [syʀɛksite] vt (personne) to overexcite; **cela surexcite ma curiosité** it really rouses my curiosity.

surexploiter [syʀɛksplwate] vt to overexploit.

surexposer [syʀɛkspoze] vt to overexpose.

surf [sœʀf] nm surfing; **faire du** ~ to go surfing.

surface [syʀfas] nf surface; (superficie) surface area; **faire** ~ to surface; **en** ~ adv near the surface; (fig) superficially; **la pièce fait 100 m² de** ~ the room has a surface area of 100m²; ~ **de réparation** (SPORT) penalty area; ~ **porteuse** ou **de sustentation** (AVIAT) aerofoil.

surfait, e [syʀfɛ, -ɛt] adj overrated.

surfeur, euse [sœʀfœʀ, -øz] nm/f surfer.

surfiler [syʀfile] vt (COUTURE) to oversew.

surfin, e [syʀfɛ̃, -in] adj superfine.

surgélateur [syʀʒelatœʀ] nm deep freeze.

surgélation [syʀʒelɑsjɔ̃] nf deep-freezing.

surgelé, e [syʀʒəle] adj (deep-)frozen.

surgeler [syʀʒəle] vt to (deep-)freeze.

surgir [syʀʒiʀ] vi (personne, véhicule) to appear suddenly; (jaillir) to shoot up; (montagne etc) to rise up, loom up; (fig: problème, conflit) to arise.

surhomme [syʀɔm] nm superman.

surhumain, e [syʀymɛ̃, -ɛn] adj superhuman.

surimposer [syʀɛ̃poze] vt to overtax.

surimpression [syʀɛpʀesjɔ̃] *nf* (*PHOTO*) double exposure; **en** ~ superimposed.

surimprimer [syʀɛpʀime] *vt* to overstrike, overprint.

Surinam [syʀinam] *nm*: **le** ~ Surinam.

surinfection [syʀɛ̃fɛksjɔ̃] *nf* (*MÉD*) secondary infection.

surjet [syʀʒɛ] *nm* (*COUTURE*) overcast seam.

sur-le-champ [syʀləʃɑ̃] *adv* immediately.

surlendemain [syʀlɑ̃dmɛ̃] *nm*: **le** ~ (**soir**) two days later (in the evening); **le** ~ **de** two days after.

surligneur [syʀliɲœʀ] *nm* (*feutre*) highlighter (pen).

surmenage [syʀmənaʒ] *nm* overwork; **le** ~ **intellectuel** mental fatigue.

surmené, e [syʀmene] *adj* overworked.

surmener [syʀməne] *vt*, **se** ~ *vi* to overwork.

surmonter [syʀmɔ̃te] *vt* (*suj: coupole etc*) to surmount, top; (*vaincre*) to overcome, surmount.

surmultiplié, e [syʀmyltiplije] *adj*, *nf*: (**vitesse**) ~**e** overdrive.

surnager [syʀnaʒe] *vi* to float.

surnaturel, le [syʀnatyʀɛl] *adj*, *nm* supernatural.

surnom [syʀnɔ̃] *nm* nickname.

surnombre [syʀnɔ̃bʀ(ə)] *nm*: **être en** ~ to be too many (*ou* one too many).

surnommer [syʀnɔme] *vt* to nickname.

surnuméraire [syʀnymeʀɛʀ] *nm/f* supernumerary.

suroît [syʀwa] *nm* sou'wester.

surpasser [syʀpase] *vt* to surpass; **se** ~ to surpass o.s., excel o.s.

surpayer [syʀpeje] *vt* (*personne*) to overpay; (*article etc*) to pay too much for.

surpeuplé, e [syʀpœple] *adj* overpopulated.

surpeuplement [syʀpœpləmɑ̃] *nm* overpopulation.

surpiquer [syʀpike] *vt* (*COUTURE*) to overstitch.

surpiqûre [syʀpikyʀ] *nf* (*COUTURE*) overstitching.

surplace [syʀplas] *nm*: **faire du** ~ to mark time.

surplis [syʀpli] *nm* surplice.

surplomb [syʀplɔ̃] *nm* overhang; **en** ~ overhanging.

surplomber [syʀplɔ̃be] *vi* to be overhanging ♦ *vt* to overhang; (*dominer*) to tower above.

surplus [syʀply] *nm* (*COMM*) surplus; (*reste*): ~ **de bois** wood left over; **au** ~ moreover; ~ **américains** American army surplus *sg*.

surpopulation [syʀpɔpylasjɔ̃] *nf* overpopulation.

surprenant, e [syʀpʀənɑ̃, -ɑ̃t] *vb voir* **surprendre** ♦ *adj* amazing.

surprendre [syʀpʀɑ̃dʀ(ə)] *vt* (*étonner, prendre à l'improviste*) to amaze, surprise; (*secret*) to discover; (*tomber sur: intrus etc*) to catch; (*fig*) to detect; to chance *ou* happen upon;

(*clin d'œil*) to intercept; (*conversation*) to overhear; (*suj: orage, nuit etc*) to catch out, take by surprise; ~ **la vigilance/bonne foi de qn** to catch sb out/betray sb's good faith; **se** ~ **à faire** to catch o.s. doing.

surprime [syʀpʀim] *nf* additional premium.

surpris, e [syʀpʀi, -iz] *pp de* **surprendre** ♦ *adj*: ~ (**de/que**) amazed *ou* surprised (at/that).

surprise [syʀpʀiz] *nf* surprise; **faire une** ~. **à qn** to give sb a surprise; **voyage sans** ~**s** uneventful journey; **par** ~ *adv* by surprise.

surprise-partie [syʀpʀizpaʀti] *nf* party.

surprit [syʀpʀi] *vb voir* **surprendre**.

surproduction [syʀpʀɔdyksjɔ̃] *nf* overproduction.

surréaliste [syʀʀealist(ə)] *adj*, *nm/f* surrealist.

sursaut [syʀso] *nm* start, jump; ~ **de** (*énergie, indignation*) sudden fit *ou* burst of; **en** ~ *adv* with a start.

sursauter [syʀsote] *vi* to (give a) start, jump.

surseoir [syʀswaʀ]: ~ **à** *vt* to defer; (*JUR*) to stay.

sursis [syʀsi] *nm* (*JUR: gén*) suspended sentence; (*à l'exécution capitale, aussi fig*) reprieve; (*MIL*): ~ (**d'appel** *ou* **d'incorporation**) deferment; **condamné à 5 mois (de prison) avec** ~ given a 5-month suspended (prison) sentence.

sursitaire [syʀsitɛʀ] *nm* (*MIL*) deferred conscript.

sursois [syʀswa], **sursoyais** [syʀswaje] *etc vb voir* **surseoir**.

surtaxe [syʀtaks(ə)] *nf* surcharge.

surtension [syʀtɑ̃sjɔ̃] *nf* (*ÉLEC*) overvoltage.

surtout [syʀtu] *adv* (*avant tout, d'abord*) above all; (*spécialement, particulièrement*) especially; **il aime le sport,** ~ **le football** he likes sport, especially football; **cet été, il a** ~ **fait de la pêche** this summer he went fishing more than anything (else); ~ **pas d'histoires!** no fuss now!; ~, **ne dites rien!** whatever you do - don't say anything!; ~ **pas!** certainly *ou* definitely not!; ~ **que** ... especially as ....

survécu, e [syʀveky] *pp de* **survivre**.

surveillance [syʀvejɑ̃s] *nf* watch; (*POLICE, MIL*) surveillance; **sous** ~ **médicale** under medical supervision; **la** ~ **du territoire** internal security; *voir aussi* **DST**.

surveillant, e [syʀvejɑ̃, -ɑ̃t] *nm/f* (*de prison*) warder; (*SCOL*) monitor; (*de travaux*) supervisor, overseer.

surveiller [syʀveje] *vt* (*enfant, élèves, bagages*) to watch, keep an eye on; (*malade*) to watch over; (*prisonnier, suspect*) to keep (a) watch on; (*territoire, bâtiment*) to (keep) watch over; (*travaux, cuisson*) to supervise; (*SCOL: examen*) to invigilate; **se** ~ to keep a check *ou* watch on o.s.; ~ **son langage/sa ligne** to watch one's language/figure.

survenir [syʀvəniʀ] *vi* (*incident, retards*) to occur, arise; (*événement*) to take place; (*per-*

sonne) to appear, arrive.
survenu, e [syʀv(ə)ny] *pp de* **survenir**.
survêt(ement) [syʀvɛt(mɑ̃)] *nm* tracksuit (*BRIT*), sweat suit (*US*).
survie [syʀvi] *nf* survival; (*REL*) afterlife; **équipement de** ~ survival equipment; **une** ~ **de quelques mois** a few more months of life.
surviens [syʀvjɛ̃], **survint** [syʀvɛ̃] *etc vb voir* **survenir**.
survit [suʀvi] *etc vb voir* **survivre**.
survitrage [syʀvitʀaʒ] *nm* double-glazing.
survivance [syʀvivɑ̃s] *nf* relic.
survivant, e [syʀvivɑ̃, -ɑ̃t] *vb voir* **survivre** ♦ *nm/f* survivor.
survivre [syʀvivʀ(ə)] *vi* to survive; ~ **à** *vt* (*accident etc*) to survive; (*personne*) to outlive; **la victime a peu de chance de** ~ the victim has little hope of survival.
survol [syʀvɔl] *nm* flying over.
survoler [syʀvɔle] *vt* to fly over; (*fig: livre*) to skim through; (*: question, problèmes*) to skim over.
survolté, e [syʀvɔlte] *adj* (*ÉLEC*) stepped up, boosted; (*fig*) worked up.
sus [sy(s)]: **en** ~ **de** *prép* in addition to, over and above; **en** ~ *adv* in addition; ~ **à** *excl*: ~ **au tyran!** at the tyrant! ♦ *vb* [sy] *voir* **savoir**.
susceptibilité [syseptibilite] *nf* sensitivity *no pl*.
susceptible [syseptibl(ə)] *adj* touchy, sensitive; ~ **d'amélioration** *ou* **d'être amélioré** that can be improved, open to improvement; ~ **de faire** (*capacité*) able to do; (*probabilité*) liable to do.
susciter [sysite] *vt* (*admiration*) to arouse; (*obstacles, ennuis*): ~ **(à qn)** to create (for sb).
susdit, e [sysdi, -dit] *adj* foresaid.
susmentionné, e [sysmɑ̃sjɔne] *adj* above-mentioned.
susnommé, e [sysnɔme] *adj* above-named.
suspect, e [syspɛ(kt), -ɛkt(ə)] *adj* suspicious; (*témoignage, opinions, vin etc*) suspect ♦ *nm/f* suspect; **peu** ~ **de** most unlikely to be suspected of.
suspecter [syspɛkte] *vt* to suspect; (*honnêteté de qn*) to question, have one's suspicions about; ~ **qn d'être/d'avoir fait qch** to suspect sb of being/having done sth.
suspendre [syspɑ̃dʀ(ə)] *vt* (*accrocher: vêtement*): ~ **qch (à)** to hang sth up (on); (*fixer: lustre etc*): ~ **qch à** to hang sth from; (*interrompre, démettre*) to suspend; (*remettre*) to defer; **se** ~ **à** to hang from.
suspendu, e [syspɑ̃dy] *pp de* **suspendre** ♦ *adj* (*accroché*): ~ **à** hanging on (*ou* from); (*perché*): ~ **au-dessus de** suspended over; (*AUTO*): **bien/mal** ~ with good/poor suspension; (*fig*): **être** ~ **aux lèvres de qn** to hang upon sb's every word.
suspens [syspɑ̃]: **en** ~ *adv* (*affaire*) in abeyance; **tenir en** ~ to keep in suspense.

suspense [syspɑ̃s] *nm* suspense.
suspension [syspɑ̃sjɔ̃] *nf* suspension; deferment; (*AUTO*) suspension; (*lustre*) pendant light fitting; **en** ~ in suspension, suspended; ~ **d'audience** adjournment.
suspicieux, euse [syspisjø, -øz] *adj* suspicious.
suspicion [syspisjɔ̃] *nf* suspicion.
sustentation [systɑ̃tasjɔ̃] *nf* (*AVIAT*) lift; **base** *ou* **polygone de** ~ support polygon.
sustenter [systɑ̃te]: **se** ~ *vi* to take sustenance.
susurrer [sysyʀe] *vt* to whisper.
sut [sy] *vb voir* **savoir**.
suture [sytyʀ] *nf*: **point de** ~ stitch.
suturer [sytyʀe] *vt* to stitch up, suture.
suzeraineté [syzʀɛnte] *nf* suzerainty.
svelte [svɛlt(ə)] *adj* slender, svelte.
SVP *sigle* (= *s'il vous plaît*) please.
Swaziland [swazilɑ̃d] *nm*: **le** ~ Swaziland.
syllabe [silab] *nf* syllable.
sylphide [silfid] *nf* (*fig*): **sa taille de** ~ her sylph-like figure.
sylvestre [silvɛstʀ(ə)] *adj*: **pin** ~ Scots pine, Scotch fir.
sylvicole [silvikɔl] *adj* forestry *cpd*.
sylviculteur [silvikyltœʀ] *nm* forester.
sylviculture [silvikyltyʀ] *nf* forestry, sylviculture.
symbole [sɛ̃bɔl] *nm* symbol; ~ **graphique** (*INFORM*) icon.
symbolique [sɛ̃bɔlik] *adj* symbolic; (*geste, offrande*) token *cpd*; (*salaire, dommages-intérêts*) nominal.
symboliquement [sɛ̃bɔlikmɑ̃] *adv* symbolically.
symboliser [sɛ̃bɔlize] *vt* to symbolize.
symétrie [simetʀi] *nf* symmetry.
symétrique [simetʀik] *adj* symmetrical.
symétriquement [simetʀikmɑ̃] *adv* symmetrically.
sympa [sɛ̃pa] *adj inv* (= *sympathique*) nice; friendly; good.
sympathie [sɛ̃pati] *nf* (*inclination*) liking; (*affinité*) fellow feeling; (*condoléances*) sympathy; **accueillir avec** ~ (*projet*) to receive favourably; **avoir de la** ~ **pour qn** to like sb, have a liking for sb; **témoignages de** ~ expressions of sympathy; **croyez à toute ma** ~ you have my deepest sympathy.
sympathique [sɛ̃patik] *adj* (*personne, figure*) nice, friendly, likeable; (*geste*) friendly; (*livre*) good; (*déjeuner*) nice; (*réunion, endroit*) pleasant, nice.
sympathisant, e [sɛ̃patizɑ̃, -ɑ̃t] *nm/f* sympathizer.
sympathiser [sɛ̃patize] *vi* (*voisins etc: s'entendre*) to get on (*BRIT*) *ou* along (*US*) (well); (*: se fréquenter*) to socialize, see each other; ~ **avec** to get on *ou* along (well) with; to see, socialize with.
symphonie [sɛ̃fɔni] *nf* symphony.

symphonique [sɛ̃fɔnik] *adj* (*orchestre, concert*) symphony *cpd*; (*musique*) symphonic.

symposium [sɛ̃pozjɔm] *nm* symposium.

symptomatique [sɛ̃ptɔmatik] *adj* symptomatic.

symptôme [sɛ̃ptom] *nm* symptom.

synagogue [sinagɔg] *nf* synagogue.

synchrone [sɛ̃kʀɔn] *adj* synchronous.

synchronique [sɛ̃kʀɔnik] *adj*: **tableau** ~ synchronic table of events.

synchronisation [sɛ̃kʀɔnizasjɔ̃] *nf* synchronization; (*AUTO*) ~ **des vitesses** synchromesh.

synchronisé, e [sɛ̃kʀɔnize] *adj* synchronized.

synchroniser [sɛ̃kʀɔnize] *vt* to synchronize.

syncope [sɛ̃kɔp] *nf* (*MÉD*) blackout; (*MUS*) syncopation; **tomber en** ~ to faint, pass out.

syncopé, e [sɛ̃kɔpe] *adj* syncopated.

syndic [sɛ̃dik] *nm* managing agent.

syndical, e, aux [sɛ̃dikal, -o] *adj* (trade-)union *cpd*; **centrale** ~**e** group of affiliated trade unions.

syndicalisme [sɛ̃dikalism(ə)] *nm* (*mouvement*) trade unionism; (*activités*) union(ist) activities *pl*.

syndicaliste [sɛ̃dikalist(ə)] *nm/f* trade unionist.

syndicat [sɛ̃dika] *nm* (*d'ouvriers, employés*) (trade(s)) union; (*autre association d'intérêts*) union, association; ~ **d'initiative (SI)** tourist office *ou* bureau; ~ **patronal** employers' syndicate, federation of employers; ~ **de propriétaires** association of property owners.

syndiqué, e [sɛ̃dike] *adj* belonging to a (trade) union; **non** ~ non-union.

syndiquer [sɛ̃dike]: **se** ~ *vi* to form a trade union; (*adhérer*) to join a trade union.

syndrome [sɛ̃dʀom] *nm* syndrome; ~ **prémenstruel** premenstrual syndrome (PMS).

synergie [sinɛʀʒi] *nf* synergy.

synode [sinɔd] *nm* synod.

synonyme [sinɔnim] *adj* synonymous ♦ *nm* synonym; ~ **de** synonymous with.

synopsis [sinɔpsis] *nm ou nf* synopsis.

synoptique [sinɔptik] *adj*: **tableau** ~ synoptic table.

synovie [sinɔvi] *nf* synovia; **épanchement de** ~ water on the knee.

syntaxe [sɛ̃taks(ə)] *nf* syntax.

synthèse [sɛ̃tɛz] *nf* synthesis (*pl* -es); **faire la** ~ **de** to synthesize.

synthétique [sɛ̃tetik] *adj* synthetic.

synthétiser [sɛ̃tetize] *vt* to synthesize.

synthétiseur [sɛ̃tetizœʀ] *nm* (*MUS*) synthesizer.

syphilis [sifilis] *nf* syphilis.

Syrie [siʀi] *nf*: **la** ~ Syria.

syrien, ne [siʀjɛ̃, -ɛn] *adj* Syrian ♦ *nm/f*: **S**~, **ne** Syrian.

systématique [sistematik] *adj* systematic.

systématiquement [sistematikmɑ̃] *adv* systematically.

systématiser [sistematize] *vt* to systematize.

système [sistɛm] *nm* system; **le** ~ **D** resourcefulness; ~ **décimal** decimal system; ~ **expert** expert system; ~ **d'exploitation à disques** (*INFORM*) disk operating system; ~ **immunitaire** immune system; ~ **métrique** metric system; ~ **solaire** solar system.

T t

T, t [te] *nm inv* T, t ♦ *abr* (= *tonne*) t; **T comme Thérèse** T for Tommy.

t' [t(ə)] *pron voir* **te**.

ta [ta] *adj possessif voir* **ton**.

tabac [taba] *nm* tobacco; (*aussi*: **débit** *ou* **bureau de** ~) tobacconist's (shop) ♦ *adj inv*: (**couleur**) ~ buff, tobacco *cpd*; **passer qn à** ~ to beat sb up; **faire un** ~ (*fam*) to be a big hit; ~ **blond/brun** light/dark tobacco; ~ **gris** shag; ~ **à priser** snuff.

tabagie [tabaʒi] *nf* smoke den.

tabagisme [tabaʒism(ə)] *nm* nicotine addiction; ~ **passif** passive smoking.

tabasser [tabase] *vt* to beat up.

tabatière [tabatjɛʀ] *nf* snuffbox.

tabernacle [tabɛʀnakl(ə)] *nm* tabernacle.

table [tabl(ə)] *nf* table; **avoir une bonne** ~ to keep a good table; **à** ~**!** dinner *etc* is ready!; **se mettre à** ~ to sit down to eat; (*fig: fam*) to come clean; **mettre** *ou* **dresser/desservir la** ~ to lay *ou* set/clear the table; **faire** ~ **rase de** to make a clean sweep of; ~ **basse** coffee table; ~ **de cuisson** (*à l'électricité*) hotplate; (*au gas*) gas ring; ~ **d'écoute** wiretapping set; ~ **d'harmonie** sounding board; ~ **d'hôte** set menu; ~ **de lecture** turntable; ~ **des matières** (table of) contents *pl*; ~ **de multiplication** multiplication table; ~ **des négociations** negotiating table; ~ **de nuit** *ou* **de chevet** bedside table; ~ **ronde** (*débat*) round table; ~ **roulante** (tea) trolley; ~ **de toilette** washstand; ~ **traçante** (*INFORM*) plotter.

tableau, x [tablo] *nm* (*ART*) painting; (*reproduction, fig*) picture; (*panneau*) board; (*schéma*) table, chart; ~ **d'affichage** notice board; ~ **de bord** dashboard; (*AVIAT*) instrument panel; ~ **de chasse** tally; ~ **de contrôle** console, control panel; ~ **de maître** masterpiece; ~ **noir** blackboard.

tablée [table] *nf* (*personnes*) table.

tabler [table] *vi*: ~ **sur** to count *ou* bank on.

tablette [tablɛt] *nf* (*planche*) shelf (*pl* shelves); ~ **de chocolat** bar of chocolate.

tableur [tablœʀ] *nm* (*INFORM*) spreadsheet.

tablier [tablije] *nm* apron; (*de pont*) roadway;

(*de cheminée*) (flue-)shutter.
tabou, e [tabu] *adj, nm* taboo.
tabouret [taburɛ] *nm* stool.
tabulateur [tabylatœr] *nm* (*TECH*) tabulator.
TAC *sigle m* (= *train autos-couchettes*) car-sleeper train, ≈ Motorail ® (*BRIT*).
tac [tak] *nm*: **du ~ au ~** tit for tat.
tache [taʃ] *nf* (*saleté*) stain, mark; (*ART, de couleur, lumière*) spot; splash, patch; **faire ~ d'huile** to spread, gain ground; **~ de rousseur** *ou* **de son** freckle; **~ de vin** (*sur la peau*) strawberry mark.
tâche [taʃ] *nf* task; **travailler à la ~** to do piecework.
tacher [taʃe] *vt* to stain, mark; (*fig*) to sully, stain; **se ~** *vi* (*fruits*) to become marked.
tâcher [taʃe] *vi*: **~ de faire** to try to do, endeavour (*BRIT*) *ou* endeavor (*US*) to do.
tâcheron [taʃRɔ̃] *nm* (*fig*) drudge.
tacheté, e [taʃte] *adj*: **~ de** speckled *ou* spotted with.
tachisme [taʃism(ə)] *nm* (*PEINTURE*) tachisme.
tachygraphe [takigraf] *nm* tachograph.
tachymètre [takimɛtr(ə)] *nm* tachometer.
tacite [tasit] *adj* tacit.
tacitement [tasitmɑ̃] *adv* tacitly.
taciturne [tasityrn(ə)] *adj* taciturn.
tacot [tako] *nm* (*péj: voiture*) banger (*BRIT*), clunker (*US*).
tact [takt] *nm* tact; **avoir du ~** to be tactful, have tact.
tacticien, ne [taktisjɛ̃, -ɛn] *nm/f* tactician.
tactile [taktil] *adj* tactile.
tactique [taktik] *adj* tactical ♦ *nf* (*technique*) tactics *sg*; (*plan*) tactic.
Tadjikistan [tadʒikistɑ̃] *nm* Tajikistan.
taffetas [tafta] *nm* taffeta.
Tage [taʒ] *nm*: **le ~** the (river) Tagus.
Tahiti [taiti] *nf* Tahiti.
tahitien, ne [taisjɛ̃, -ɛn] *adj* Tahitian.
taie [tɛ] *nf*: **~ (d'oreiller)** pillowslip, pillowcase.
taillader [tajade] *vt* to gash.
taille [taj] *nf* cutting; pruning; (*milieu du corps*) waist; (*hauteur*) height; (*grandeur*) size; **de ~ à faire** capable of doing; **de ~** *adj* sizeable; **quelle ~ faites- vous?** what size are you?
taillé, e [taje] *adj* (*moustache, ongles, arbre*) trimmed; **~ pour** (*fait pour, apte à*) cut out for; **tailor-made for**; **~ en pointe** sharpened to a point.
taille-crayon(s) [tajkrɛjɔ̃] *nm inv* pencil sharpener.
tailler [taje] *vt* (*pierre, diamant*) to cut; (*arbre, plante*) to prune; (*vêtement*) to cut out; (*crayon*) to sharpen; **se ~** *vt* (*ongles, barbe*) to trim, cut; (*fig: réputation*) to gain, win ♦ *vi* (*fam: s'enfuir*) to beat it; **~ dans** (*chair, bois*) to cut into; **~ grand/petit** to be on the large/small side.
tailleur [tajœr] *nm* (*couturier*) tailor;

(*vêtement*) suit, costume; **en ~** (*assis*) cross-legged; **~ de diamants** diamond-cutter.
tailleur-pantalon [tajœrpɑ̃talɔ̃] *nm* trouser (*BRIT*) *ou* pant(s) suit.
taillis [taji] *nm* copse.
tain [tɛ̃] *nm* silvering; **glace sans ~** two-way mirror.
taire [tɛr] *vt* to keep to o.s., conceal ♦ *vi*: **faire ~ qn** to make sb be quiet; (*fig*) to silence sb; **se ~** *vi* (*s'arrêter de parler*) to fall silent, stop talking; (*ne pas parler*) to be silent *ou* quiet; (*s'abstenir de s'exprimer*) to keep quiet; (*bruit, voix*) to disappear; **tais-toi!, taisez-vous!** be quiet!
Taiwan [tajwan] *nf* Taiwan.
talc [talk] *nm* talc, talcum powder.
talé, e [tale] *adj* (*fruit*) bruised.
talent [talɑ̃] *nm* talent; **avoir du ~** to be talented, have talent.
talentueux, euse [talɑ̃tɥø, -øz] *adj* talented.
talion [taljɔ̃] *nm*: **la loi du ~** an eye for an eye.
talisman [talismɑ̃] *nm* talisman.
talkie-walkie [tɔkiwɔki] *nm* walkie-talkie.
taloche [talɔʃ] *nf* (*fam: claque*) slap; (*TECH*) plaster float.
talon [talɔ̃] *nm* heel; (*de chèque, billet*) stub, counterfoil (*BRIT*); **~s plats/aiguilles** flat/stiletto heels; **être sur les ~s de qn** to be on sb's heels; **tourner les ~s** to turn on one's heel; **montrer les ~s** (*fig*) to show a clean pair of heels.
talonner [talɔne] *vt* to follow hard behind; (*fig*) to hound; (*RUGBY*) to heel.
talonnette [talɔnɛt] *nf* (*de chaussure*) heel-piece; (*de pantalon*) stirrup.
talquer [talke] *vt* to put talc(um powder) on.
talus [taly] *nm* embankment; **~ de remblai/déblai** embankment/excavation slope.
tamarin [tamarɛ̃] *nm* (*BOT*) tamarind.
tambour [tɑ̃bur] *nm* (*MUS, aussi TECH*) drum; (*musicien*) drummer; (*porte*) revolving door(s *pl*); **sans ~ ni trompette** unobtrusively.
tambourin [tɑ̃burɛ̃] *nm* tambourine.
tambouriner [tɑ̃burine] *vi*: **~ contre** to drum against *ou* on.
tambour-major, *pl* **tambours-majors** [tɑ̃burmaʒɔr] *nm* drum major.
tamis [tami] *nm* sieve.
Tamise [tamiz] *nf*: **la ~** the Thames.
tamisé, e [tamize] *adj* (*fig*) subdued, soft.
tamiser [tamize] *vt* to sieve, sift.
tampon [tɑ̃pɔ̃] *nm* (*de coton, d'ouate*) pad; (*aussi:* **~ hygiénique** *ou* **périodique**) tampon; (*amortisseur, INFORM: aussi:* **mémoire ~**) buffer; (*bouchon*) plug, stopper; (*cachet, timbre*) stamp; (*CHIMIE*) buffer; **~ buvard** blotter; **~ encreur** inking pad; **~ (à récurer)** scouring pad.
tamponné, e [tɑ̃pɔne] *adj*: **solution ~e** buffer solution.
tamponner [tɑ̃pɔne] *vt* (*timbres*) to stamp;

(*heurter*) to crash *ou* ram into; (*essuyer*) to mop up; **se** ~ (*voitures*) to crash (into each other).

tamponneuse [tɑ̃pɔnøz] *adj f*: autos ~s dodgems, bumper cars.

tam-tam [tamtam] *nm* tomtom.

tancer [tɑ̃se] *vt* to scold.

tanche [tɑ̃ʃ] *nf* tench.

tandem [tɑ̃dɛm] *nm* tandem; (*fig*) duo, pair.

tandis [tɑ̃di]: ~ **que** *conj* while.

tangage [tɑ̃gaʒ] *nm* pitching (and tossing).

tangent, e [tɑ̃ʒɑ̃, -ɑ̃t] *adj* (*MATH*): ~ **à** tangential to; (*fam*: *de justesse*) close ♦ *nf* (*MATH*) tangent.

Tanger [tɑ̃ʒe] *n* Tangier.

tangible [tɑ̃ʒibl(ə)] *adj* tangible, concrete.

tango [tɑ̃go] *nm* (*MUS*) tango ♦ *adj inv* (*couleur*) dark orange.

tanguer [tɑ̃ge] *vi* to pitch (and toss).

tanière [tanjɛʀ] *nf* lair, den.

tanin [tanɛ̃] *nm* tannin.

tank [tɑ̃k] *nm* tank.

tanker [tɑ̃kɛʀ] *nm* tanker.

tanné, e [tane] *adj* weather-beaten.

tanner [tane] *vt* to tan.

tannerie [tanʀi] *nf* tannery.

tanneur [tanœʀ] *nm* tanner.

tant [tɑ̃] *adv* so much; ~ **de** (*sable, eau*) so much; (*gens, livres*) so many; ~ **que** *conj* as long as; ~ **que** (*comparatif*) as much as; ~ **mieux** that's great; so much the better; ~ **mieux pour lui** good for him; ~ **pis** too bad; **un** ~ **soit peu** (*un peu*) a little bit; (*même un peu*) (even) remotely; ~ **bien que mal** as well as can be expected; ~ **s'en faut** far from it, not by a long way.

tante [tɑ̃t] *nf* aunt.

tantinet [tɑ̃tinɛ]: **un** ~ *adv* a tiny bit.

tantôt [tɑ̃to] *adv* (*parfois*): ~ ... ~ now ... now; (*cet après-midi*) this afternoon.

Tanzanie [tɑ̃zani] *nf*: **la** ~ Tanzania.

tanzanien, ne [tɑ̃zanjɛ̃, -ɛn] *adj* Tanzanian.

TAO *sigle f* (= *traduction assistée par ordinateur*) MAT (= *machine-aided translation*).

taon [tɑ̃] *nm* horsefly, gadfly.

tapage [tapaʒ] *nm* uproar, din; (*fig*) fuss, row; ~ **nocturne** (*JUR*) disturbance of the peace (*at night*).

tapageur, euse [tapaʒœʀ, -øz] *adj* (*bruyant*: *enfants etc*) noisy; (*toilette*) loud, flashy; (*publicité*) obtrusive.

tape [tap] *nf* slap.

tape-à-l'œil [tapalœj] *adj inv* flashy, showy.

taper [tape] *vt* (*personne*) to clout; (*porte*) to bang, slam; (*dactylographier*) to type (out); (*INFORM*) to key(board); (*fam*: *emprunter*): ~ **qn de 10 F** to touch sb for 10 F, cadge 10 F off sb ♦ *vi* (*soleil*) to beat down; **se** ~ *vt* (*fam*: *travail*) to get landed with; (: *boire, manger*) to down; ~ **sur qn** to thump sb; (*fig*) to run sb down; ~ **sur qch** (*clou etc*) to hit sth; (*table etc*) to bang on sth; ~ **à** (*porte etc*) to knock

on; ~ **dans** (*se servir*) to dig into; ~ **des mains/pieds** to clap one's hands/stamp one's feet; ~ (**à la machine**) to type.

tapi, e [tapi] *adj*: ~ **dans/derrière** (*blotti*) crouching *ou* cowering in/behind; (*caché*) hidden away in/behind.

tapinois [tapinwa]: **en** ~ *adv* stealthily.

tapioca [tapjɔka] *nm* tapioca.

tapir [tapiʀ]: **se** ~ *vi* to hide away.

tapis [tapi] *nm* carpet; (*de table*) cloth; **mettre sur le** ~ (*fig*) to bring up for discussion; **aller au** ~ (*BOXE*) to go down; **envoyer au** ~ (*BOXE*) to floor; ~ **roulant** conveyor belt; ~ **de sol** (*de tente*) groundsheet.

tapis-brosse [tapibʀɔs] *nm* doormat.

tapisser [tapise] *vt* (*avec du papier peint*) to paper; (*recouvrir*): ~ **qch** (**de**) to cover sth (with).

tapisserie [tapisʀi] *nf* (*tenture, broderie*) tapestry; (: *travail*) tapestry-making; (: *ouvrage*) tapestry work; (*papier peint*) wallpaper; (*fig*): **faire** ~ to sit out, be a wallflower.

tapissier, ière [tapisje, -jɛʀ] *nm/f*: ~-(**décorateur**) upholsterer (and decorator).

tapoter [tapɔte] *vt* to pat, tap.

taquet [takɛ] *nm* (*cale*) wedge; (*cheville*) peg.

taquin, e [takɛ̃, -in] *adj* teasing.

taquiner [takine] *vt* to tease.

taquinerie [takinʀi] *nf* teasing *no pl*.

tarabiscoté, e [taʀabiskɔte] *adj* over-ornate, fussy.

tarabuster [taʀabyste] *vt* to bother, worry.

tarama [taʀama] *nm* (*CULIN*) taramasalata.

tarauder [taʀode] *vt* (*TECH*) to tap; to thread; (*fig*) to pierce.

tard [taʀ] *adv* late; **au plus** ~ at the latest; **plus** ~ later (on) ♦ *nm*: **sur le** ~ (*à une heure avancée*) late in the day; (*vers la fin de la vie*) late in life.

tarder [taʀde] *vi* (*chose*) to be a long time coming; (*personne*): ~ **à faire** to delay doing; **il me tarde d'être** I am longing to be; **sans** (**plus**) ~ without (further) delay.

tardif, ive [taʀdif, -iv] *adj* (*heure, repas, fruit*) late; (*talent, goût*) late in developing.

tardivement [taʀdivmɑ̃] *adv* late.

tare [taʀ] *nf* (*COMM*) tare; (*fig*) defect; taint, blemish.

targette [taʀʒɛt] *nf* (*verrou*) bolt.

targuer [taʀge]: **se** ~ **de** *vt* to boast about.

tarif [taʀif] *nm* (*liste*) price list, tariff (*BRIT*); (*barème*) rate, rates *pl*, tariff (*BRIT*); (: *de taxis etc*) fares *pl*; **voyager à plein** ~/**à** ~ **réduit** to travel at full/reduced fare.

tarifaire [taʀifɛʀ] *adj* (*voir tarif*) relating to price lists *etc*.

tarifé, e [taʀife] *adj*: ~ **10 F** priced at 10 F.

tarifer [taʀife] *vt* to fix the price *ou* rate for.

tarification [taʀifikasjɔ̃] *nf* fixing of a price scale.

tarir [taʀiʀ] *vi* to dry up, run dry ♦ *vt* to dry up.

tarot(s) [taʀo] *nm(pl)* tarot cards.
tartare [taʀtaʀ] *adj* (*CULIN*) tartar(e).
tarte [taʀt(ə)] *nf* tart; ~ **aux pommes/à la crème** apple/custard tart.
tartelette [taʀtəlɛt] *nf* tartlet.
tartine [taʀtin] *nf* slice of bread (and butter (*ou* jam)); ~ **de miel** slice of bread and honey; ~ **beurrée** slice of bread and butter.
tartiner [taʀtine] *vt* to spread; **fromage à ~** cheese spread.
tartre [taʀtʀ(ə)] *nm* (*des dents*) tartar; (*de chaudière*) fur, scale.
tas [ta] *nm* heap, pile; (*fig*): **un ~ de** heaps of, lots of; **en ~** in a heap *ou* pile; **dans le ~** (*fig*) in the crowd; among them; **formé sur le ~** trained on the job.
Tasmanie [tasmani] *nf*: **la ~** Tasmania.
tasmanien, ne [tasmanjɛ̃, -ɛn] *adj* Tasmanian.
tasse [tas] *nf* cup; **boire la ~** (*en se baignant*) to swallow a mouthful; ~ **à café/thé** coffee/teacup.
tassé, e [tase] *adj*: **bien ~** (*café etc*) strong.
tasseau, x [taso] *nm* length of wood.
tassement [tasmɑ̃] *nm* (*de vertèbres*) compression; (*ÉCON*, *POL*: *ralentissement*) fall-off, slowdown; (*BOURSE*) dullness.
tasser [tase] *vt* (*terre, neige*) to pack down; (*entasser*): ~ **qch dans** to cram sth into; (*INFORM*) to pack; **se ~** *vi* (*terrain*) to settle; (*personne: avec l'âge*) to shrink; (*fig*) to sort itself out, settle down.
tâter [tate] *vt* to feel; (*fig*) to sound out; ~ **de** (*prison etc*) to have a taste of; **se ~** (*hésiter*) to be in two minds; ~ **le terrain** (*fig*) to test the ground.
tatillon, ne [tatijɔ̃, -ɔn] *adj* pernickety.
tâtonnement [tatɔnmɑ̃] *nm*: **par ~s** (*fig*) by trial and error.
tâtonner [tatɔne] *vi* to grope one's way along; (*fig*) to grope around (in the dark).
tâtons [tatɔ̃]: **à ~** *adv*: **chercher/avancer à ~** to grope around for/grope one's way forward.
tatouage [tatwaʒ] *nm* tattooing; (*dessin*) tattoo.
tatouer [tatwe] *vt* to tattoo.
taudis [todi] *nm* hovel, slum.
taule [tol] *nf* (*fam*) nick (*BRIT*), jail.
taupe [top] *nf* mole; (*peau*) moleskin.
taupinière [topinjɛʀ] *nf* molehill.
taureau, x [tɔʀo] *nm* bull; (*signe*): **le T~** Taurus, the Bull; **être du T~** to be Taurus.
taurillon [tɔʀijɔ̃] *nm* bull-calf.
tauromachie [tɔʀomaʃi] *nf* bullfighting.
taux [to] *nm* rate; (*d'alcool*) level; ~ **d'escompte** discount rate; ~ **d'intérêt** interest rate; ~ **de mortalité** mortality rate.
tavelé, e [tavle] *adj* marked.
taverne [tavɛʀn(ə)] *nf* inn, tavern.
taxable [taksabl(ə)] *adj* taxable.
taxation [taksasjɔ̃] *nf* taxation; (*TÉL*) charges *pl*.

taxe [taks(ə)] *nf* tax; (*douanière*) duty; **toutes ~s comprises (TTC)** inclusive of tax; ~ **de base** (*TÉL*) unit charge; ~ **de séjour** tourist tax; ~ **à** *ou* **sur la valeur ajoutée (TVA)** value added tax (VAT) (*BRIT*).
taxer [takse] *vt* (*personne*) to tax; (*produit*) to put a tax on, tax; (*fig*): ~ **qn de** (*qualifier de*) to call sb + *attribut*; (*accuser de*) to accuse sb of, tax sb with.
taxi [taksi] *nm* taxi.
taxidermie [taksidɛʀmi] *nf* taxidermy.
taxidermiste [taksidɛʀmist(ə)] *nm/f* taxidermist.
taximètre [taksimɛtʀ(ə)] *nm* (taxi)meter.
taxiphone [taksifɔn] *nm* pay phone.
TB *abr* = *très bien, très bon*.
tbe *abr* (= *très bon état*) VGC, vgc.
TCA *sigle f* (= *taxe sur le chiffre d'affaires*) tax on turnover.
TCF *sigle m* (= *Touring Club de France*) ≈ AA *ou* RAC (*BRIT*), ≈ AAA (*US*).
Tchad [tʃad] *nm*: **le ~** Chad.
tchadien, ne [tʃadjɛ̃, -ɛn] *adj* Chad(ian), of *ou* from Chad.
tchao [tʃao] *excl* (*fam*) bye(-bye)!
tchécoslovaque [tʃekɔslɔvak] *adj* Czechoslovak(ian) ♦ *nm/f*: **T~** Czechoslovak(ian).
Tchécoslovaquie [tʃekɔslɔvaki] *nf*: **la ~** Czechoslovakia.
tchèque [tʃɛk] *adj* Czech ♦ *nm* (*LING*) Czech ♦ *nm/f*: **T~** Czech.
TCS *sigle m* (= *Touring Club de Suisse*) ≈ AA *ou* RAC (*BRIT*), ≈ AAA (*US*).
TD *sigle mpl* = **travaux dirigés**.
TDF *sigle f* (= *Télévision de France*) French broadcasting authority.
te, t' [t(ə)] *pron* you; (*réfléchi*) yourself.
té [te] *nm* T-square.
technicien, ne [tɛknisjɛ̃, -ɛn] *nm/f* technician.
technicité [tɛknisite] *nf* technical nature.
technico-commercial, e, aux [tɛknikokɔmɛʀsjal, -o] *adj*: **agent ~** sales technician.
technique [tɛknik] *adj* technical ♦ *nf* technique.
techniquement [tɛknikmɑ̃] *adv* technically.
techno [tɛkno] *nf* (*MUS*) techno.
technocrate [tɛknɔkʀat] *nm/f* technocrat.
technocratie [tɛknɔkʀasi] *nf* technocracy.
technologie [tɛknɔlɔʒi] *nf* technology.
technologique [tɛknɔlɔʒik] *adj* technological.
technologue [tɛknɔlɔg] *nm/f* technologist.
teck [tɛk] *nm* teak.
teckel [tekɛl] *nm* dachshund.
TEE *sigle m* = *Trans-Europ-Express*.
tee-shirt [tiʃœʀt] *nm* T-shirt, tee-shirt.
Téhéran [teeʀɑ̃] *n* Teheran.
teigne [tɛɲ] *vb voir* **teindre** ♦ *nf* (*ZOOL*) moth; (*MÉD*) ringworm.
teigneux, euse [tɛɲø, -øz] *adj* (*péj*) nasty, scabby.
teindre [tɛ̃dʀ(ə)] *vt* to dye; **se ~ (les cheveux)**

to dye one's hair.

teint, e [tɛ̃, tɛ̃t] *pp de* **teindre** ♦ *adj* dyed ♦ *nm* (*du visage: permanent*) complexion, colouring (*BRIT*), coloring (*US*); (*momentané*) colour (*BRIT*), color (*US*) ♦ *nf* shade, colour, color; (*fig: petite dose*): **une ~e de** a hint of; **grand ~** *adj inv* colourfast; **bon ~** *adj inv* (*couleur*) fast; (*tissu*) colourfast; (*personne*) staunch, firm.

teinté, e [tɛ̃te] *adj* (*verres*) tinted; (*bois*) stained; **~ acajou** mahogany-stained; **~ de** (*fig*) tinged with.

teinter [tɛ̃te] *vt* to tint; (*bois*) to stain; (*fig: d'ironie etc*) to tinge.

teinture [tɛ̃tyʀ] *nf* dyeing; (*substance*) dye; (*MÉD*): **~ d'iode** tincture of iodine.

teinturerie [tɛ̃tyʀʀi] *nf* dry cleaner's.

teinturier, ière [tɛ̃tyʀje, -jɛʀ] *nm/f* dry cleaner.

tel, telle [tɛl] *adj* (*pareil*) such; (*comme*): **~ un/des ...** like a/like ...; (*indéfini*) such-and-such a, a given; (*intensif*): **un ~/de ~s ...** such (a)/such ...; **rien de ~** nothing like it, no such thing; **~ que** *conj* like, such as; **~ quel** as it is *ou* stands (*ou* was *etc*).

tél. *abr = téléphone*.

Tel Aviv [tɛlaviv] *n* Tel Aviv.

télé [tele] *nf* (*= télévision*) TV, telly (*BRIT*); **à la ~** on TV *ou* telly.

télébenne [telebɛn] *nm, nf* telecabine, gondola.

télécabine [telekabin] *nm, nf* telecabine, gondola.

télécarte [telekaʀt(ə)] *nf* phonecard.

télécharger [teleʃaʀʒe] *vt* (*INFORM*) to download.

TELECOM [telekɔm] *abr* (*= Télécommunications*) ≈ Telecom.

télécommande [telekɔmɑ̃d] *nf* remote control.

télécommander [telekɔmɑ̃de] *vt* to operate by remote control, radio-control.

télécommunications [telekɔmynikasjɔ̃] *nfpl* telecommunications.

télécopie [telekɔpi] *nf* fax, telefax.

télécopieur [telekɔpjœʀ] *nm* fax (machine).

télédétection [teledetɛksjɔ̃] *nf* remote sensing.

télédiffuser [teledifyze] *vt* to broadcast (on television).

télédiffusion [teledifyzjɔ̃] *nf* television broadcasting.

télédistribution [teledistʀibysjɔ̃] *nf* cable TV.

téléenseignement [teleɑ̃sɛɲmɑ̃] *nm* distance teaching (*ou* learning).

téléférique [telefeʀik] *nm = téléphérique*.

téléfilm [telefilm] *nm* film made for TV, TV film.

télégramme [telegʀam] *nm* telegram.

télégraphe [telegʀaf] *nm* telegraph.

télégraphie [telegʀafi] *nf* telegraphy.

télégraphier [telegʀafje] *vt* to telegraph, cable.

télégraphique [telegʀafik] *adj* telegraph *cpd*, telegraphic; (*fig*) telegraphic.

télégraphiste [telegʀafist(ə)] *nm/f* telegraphist.

téléguider [telegide] *vt* to operate by remote control, radio-control.

téléinformatique [teleɛ̃fɔʀmatik] *nf* remote access computing.

téléjournal, aux [teleʒuʀnal, -o] *nm* television news magazine programme.

télématique [telematik] *nf* telematics *sg* ♦ *adj* telematic.

téléobjectif [teleɔbʒɛktif] *nm* telephoto lens *sg*.

télépathie [telepati] *nf* telepathy.

téléphérique [telefeʀik] *nm* cable-car.

téléphone [telefɔn] *nm* telephone; **avoir le ~** to be on the (tele)phone; **au ~** on the phone; **les T~s** the (tele)phone service *sg*; **~ arabe** bush telegraph; **~ à carte (magnétique)** cardphone; **~ cellulaire** cellphone, cellular phone; **~ manuel** manually-operated telephone system; **~ rouge** hotline.

téléphoner [telefɔne] *vt* to telephone ♦ *vi* to telephone; to make a phone call; **~ à** to phone up, ring up, call up.

téléphonie [telefɔni] *nf* telephony.

téléphonique [telefɔnik] *adj* telephone *cpd*, phone *cpd*; **cabine ~** call box (*BRIT*), (tele)phone box (*BRIT*) *ou* booth; **conversation/appel ~** (tele)phone conversation/call.

téléphoniste [telefɔnist(ə)] *nm/f* telephonist, telephone operator; (*d'entreprise*) switchboard operator.

téléport [telepɔʀ] *nm* teleport.

téléprospection [telepʀɔspɛksjɔ̃] *nf* telephone selling.

télescopage [telɛskɔpaʒ] *nm* crash.

télescope [telɛskɔp] *nm* telescope.

télescoper [telɛskɔpe] *vt* to smash up; **se ~** (*véhicules*) to collide, crash into each other.

télescopique [telɛskɔpik] *adj* telescopic.

téléscripteur [teleskʀiptœʀ] *nm* teleprinter.

télésiège [telesjɛʒ] *nm* chairlift.

téléski [teleski] *nm* ski-tow; **~ à archets** T-bar tow; **~ à perche** button lift.

téléspectateur, trice [telespɛktatœʀ, -tʀis] *nm/f* (television) viewer.

télétexte [teletɛkst] *nm* ® Teletext ®.

téléthon [teletɔ̃] *nm* telethon.

télétraitement [teletʀɛtmɑ̃] *nm* remote processing.

télétransmission [teletʀɑ̃smisjɔ̃] *nf* remote transmission.

télétype [teletip] *nm* teleprinter.

télévente [televɑ̃t] *nf* telesales.

téléviser [televize] *vt* to televise.

téléviseur [televizœʀ] *nm* television set.

télévision [televizjɔ̃] *nf* television; (**poste de**) **~** television (set); **avoir la ~** to have a television; **à la** ~ on television; ~ **par câble/ satellite** cable/satellite television.

télex [telɛks] *nm* telex.

télexer [telɛkse] *vt* to telex.

télexiste [telɛksist(ə)] *nm/f* telex operator.

telle [tɛl] *adj f voir* **tel.**

tellement [tɛlmɑ̃] *adv* (*tant*) so much; (*si*) so; ~ **plus grand (que)** so much bigger (than); ~ **de** (*sable, eau*) so much; (*gens, livres*) so many; **il s'est endormi** ~ **il était fatigué** he was so tired (that) he fell asleep; **pas** ~ not really; **pas** ~ **fort/lentement** not (all) that strong/slowly; **il ne mange pas** ~ he doesn't eat (all that) much.

tellurique [telyʀik] *adj:* **secousse** ~ earth tremor.

téméraire [temeʀɛʀ] *adj* reckless, rash.

témérité [temeʀite] *nf* recklessness, rashness.

témoignage [temwaɲaʒ] *nm* (*JUR: déclaration*) testimony *no pl*, evidence *no pl*; (: *faits*) evidence *no pl*; (*gén: rapport, récit*) account; (*fig: d'affection etc*) token, mark; expression.

témoigner [temwaɲe] *vt* (*manifester: intérêt, gratitude*) to show ♦ *vi* (*JUR*) to testify, give evidence; ~ **que** to testify that; (*fig: démontrer*) to reveal that, testify to the fact that; ~ **de** *vt* (*confirmer*) to bear witness to, testify to.

témoin [temwɛ̃] *nm* witness; (*fig*) testimony; (*SPORT*) baton; (*CONSTR*) telltale ♦ *adj* control *cpd*, test *cpd*; ~ **le fait que** ... (as) witness the fact that ...; **appartement-**~ show flat (*BRIT*), model apartment (*US*); **être** ~ **de** (*voir*) to witness; **prendre à** ~ to call to witness; ~ **à charge** witness for the prosecution; **T**~ **de Jehovah** Jehovah's Witness; ~ **de moralité** character reference; ~ **oculaire** eyewitness.

tempe [tɑ̃p] *nf* (*ANAT*) temple.

tempérament [tɑ̃peʀamɑ̃] *nm* temperament, disposition; (*santé*) constitution; **à** ~ (*vente*) on deferred (payment) terms; (*achat*) by instalments, hire purchase *cpd*; **avoir du** ~ to be hot-blooded.

tempérance [tɑ̃peʀɑ̃s] *nf* temperance; **société de** ~ temperance society.

tempérant, e [tɑ̃peʀɑ̃, -ɑ̃t] *adj* temperate.

température [tɑ̃peʀatyʀ] *nf* temperature; **prendre la** ~ **de** to take the temperature of; (*fig*) to gauge the feeling of; **avoir** *ou* **faire de la** ~ to be running *ou* have a temperature.

tempéré, e [tɑ̃peʀe] *adj* temperate.

tempérer [tɑ̃peʀe] *vt* to temper.

tempête [tɑ̃pɛt] *nf* storm; ~ **de sable/neige** sand/snowstorm; **vent de** ~ gale.

tempêter [tɑ̃pete] *vi* to rant and rave.

temple [tɑ̃pl(ə)] *nm* temple; (*protestant*) church.

tempo [tɛmpo] *nm* tempo (*pl* -s).

temporaire [tɑ̃pɔʀɛʀ] *adj* temporary.

temporairement [tɑ̃pɔʀɛʀmɑ̃] *adv* temporarily.

temporel, le [tɑ̃pɔʀɛl] *adj* temporal.

temporisateur, trice [tɑ̃pɔʀizatœʀ, -tʀis] *adj* temporizing, delaying.

temporisation [tɑ̃pɔʀizasjɔ̃] *nf* temporizing, playing for time.

temporiser [tɑ̃pɔʀize] *vi* to temporize, play for time.

temps [tɑ̃] *nm* (*atmosphérique*) weather; (*durée*) time; (*époque*) time, times *pl*; (*LING*) tense; (*MUS*) beat; (*TECH*) stroke; **les** ~ **changent/sont durs** times are changing/ hard; **il fait beau/mauvais** ~ the weather is fine/bad; **avoir le** ~/**tout le** ~/**juste le** ~ to have time/plenty of time/just enough time; **avoir fait son** ~ (*fig*) to have had its (*ou* his *etc*) day; **en** ~ **de paix/guerre** in peacetime/ wartime; **en** ~ **utile** *ou* **voulu** in due time *ou* course; **de** ~ **en** ~, **de** ~ **à autre** from time to time, now and again; **en même** ~ at the same time; **à** ~ (*partir, arriver*) in time; **à plein/mi-**~ *adv, adj* full-/part-time; **à** ~ **partiel** *adv, adj* part-time; **dans le** ~ at one time; **de tout** ~ always; **du** ~ **que** at the time when, in the days when; **dans le** *ou* **du** *ou* **au** ~ **où** at the time when; **pendant ce** ~ in the meantime; ~ **d'accès** (*INFORM*) access time; ~ **d'arrêt** pause, halt; ~ **mort** (*SPORT*) stoppage (time); (*COMM*) slack period; ~ **partagé** (*INFORM*) time-sharing; ~ **réel** (*INFORM*) real time.

tenable [tənabl(ə)] *adj* bearable.

tenace [tənas] *adj* tenacious, persistent.

ténacité [tenasite] *nf* tenacity, persistence.

tenailler [tənaje] *vt* (*fig*) to torment, torture.

tenailles [tənaj] *nfpl* pincers.

tenais [t(ə)nɛ] *etc vb voir* **tenir.**

tenancier, ière [tənɑ̃sje, -jɛʀ] *nm/f* (*d'hôtel, de bistro*) manager/manageress.

tenant, e [tənɑ̃, -ɑ̃t] *adj f voir* **séance** ♦ *nm/f* (*SPORT*): ~ **du titre** title-holder ♦ *nm:* **d'un seul** ~ in one piece; **les** ~**s et les aboutissants** (*fig*) the ins and outs.

tendance [tɑ̃dɑ̃s] *nf* (*opinions*) leanings *pl*, sympathies *pl*; (*inclination*) tendency; (*évolution*) trend; ~ **à la hausse/baisse** upward/ downward trend; **avoir** ~ **à** to have a tendency to, tend to.

tendancieux, euse [tɑ̃dɑ̃sjø, -øz] *adj* tendentious.

tendeur [tɑ̃dœʀ] *nm* (*de vélo*) chain-adjuster; (*de câble*) wire-strainer; (*de tente*) runner; (*attache*) elastic strap.

tendinite [tɑ̃dinit] *nf* tendinitis, tendonitis.

tendon [tɑ̃dɔ̃] *nm* tendon, sinew; ~ **d'Achille** Achilles' tendon.

tendre [tɑ̃dʀ(ə)] *adj* (*viande, légumes*) tender; (*bois, roche, couleur*) soft; (*affectueux*) tender, loving ♦ *vt* (*élastique, peau*) to stretch, draw tight; (*muscle*) to tense; (*donner*): ~ **qch à qn** to hold sth out to sb; to offer sb sth; (*fig: piège*) to set, lay; (*tapisserie*): **tendu de soie** hung with silk, with silk hangings; **se** ~ *vi* (*corde*) to tighten; (*relations*) to become strained; ~ **à qch/à faire** to tend towards sth/to do; ~ **l'oreille** to prick up one's ears; ~ **la main/le bras** to hold out one's hand/ stretch out one's arm; ~ **la perche à qn** (*fig*) to throw sb a line.

tendrement [tɑ̃dʀəmɑ̃] *adv* tenderly, lovingly.

tendresse [tɑ̃dʀɛs] *nf* tenderness; ~**s** *nfpl* (*caresses etc*) tenderness *no pl*, caresses.

tendu, e [tɑ̃dy] *pp de* **tendre** ♦ *adj* tight; tensed; strained.

ténèbres [tenɛbʀ(ə)] *nfpl* darkness *sg*.

ténébreux, euse [tenebʀø, -øz] *adj* obscure, mysterious; (*personne*) saturnine.

Ténérife [teneʀif] *nf* Tenerife.

teneur [tənœʀ] *nf* content, substance; (*d'une lettre*) terms *pl*, content; ~ **en cuivre** copper content.

ténia [tenja] *nm* tapeworm.

tenir [təniʀ] *vt* to hold; (*magasin, hôtel*) to run; (*promesse*) to keep ♦ *vi* to hold; (*neige, gel*) to last; (*survivre*) to survive; **se** ~ *vi* (*avoir lieu*) to be held, take place; (*être: personne*) to stand; **se** ~ **droit** to stand up (*ou* sit up) straight; **bien se** ~ to behave well; **se** ~ **à qch** to hold on to sth; **s'en** ~ **à qch** to confine o.s. to sth; to stick to sth; ~ **à** *vt* to be attached to, care about (*ou* for); (*avoir pour cause*) to be due to, stem from; ~ **à faire** to want to do, be keen to do; ~ **à ce que qn fasse qch** to be anxious that sb should do sth; ~ **de** *vt* to partake of; (*ressembler à*) to take after; **ça ne tient qu'à lui** it is entirely up to him; ~ **qn pour** to take sb for; ~ **qch de qn** (*histoire*) to have heard *ou* learnt sth from sb; (*qualité, défaut*) to have inherited *ou* got sth from sb; ~ **les comptes** to keep the books; ~ **un rôle** to play a part; ~ **de la place** to take up space *ou* room; ~ **l'alcool** to be able to hold a drink; ~ **le coup** to hold out; ~ **bon** to stand *ou* hold fast; ~ **3 jours/2 mois** (*résister*) to hold out *ou* last 3 days/2 months; ~ **au chaud/à l'abri** to keep hot/ under shelter *ou* cover; ~ **prêt** to have ready; ~ **sa langue** (*fig*) to hold one's tongue; **tiens** (*ou* **tenez**)**, voilà le stylo** there's the pen!; **tiens, Alain!** look, here's Alain!; **tiens?** (*surprise*) really?; **tiens-toi bien!** (*pour informer*) brace yourself!, take a deep breath!

tennis [tenis] *nm* tennis; (*aussi:* **court de** ~) tennis court ♦ *nmpl ou fpl* (*aussi:* **chaussures de** ~) tennis *ou* gym shoes; ~ **de table** table tennis.

tennisman [tenisman] *nm* tennis player.

ténor [tenɔʀ] *nm* tenor.

tension [tɑ̃sjɔ̃] *nf* tension; (*fig: des relations, de la situation*) tension; (*: concentration, effort*) strain; (*MÉD*) blood pressure; **faire** *ou* **avoir de la** ~ to have high blood pressure; ~ **nerveuse/raciale** nervous/racial tension.

tentaculaire [tɑ̃takylɛʀ] *adj* (*fig*) sprawling.

tentacule [tɑ̃takyl] *nm* tentacle.

tentant, e [tɑ̃tɑ̃, -ɑ̃t] *adj* tempting.

tentateur, trice [tɑ̃tatœʀ, -tʀis] *adj* tempting ♦ *nm* (*REL*) tempter.

tentation [tɑ̃tasjɔ̃] *nf* temptation.

tentative [tɑ̃tativ] *nf* attempt, bid; ~ **d'évasion** escape bid; ~ **de suicide** suicide attempt.

tente [tɑ̃t] *nf* tent; ~ **à oxygène** oxygen tent.

tenter [tɑ̃te] *vt* (*éprouver, attirer*) to tempt; (*essayer*): ~ **qch/de faire** to attempt *ou* try sth/ to do; **être tenté de** to be tempted to; ~ **sa chance** to try one's luck.

tenture [tɑ̃tyʀ] *nf* hanging.

tenu, e [təny] *pp de* **tenir** ♦ *adj* (*maison, comptes*): **bien** ~ well-kept; (*obligé*): ~ **de faire** under an obligation to do ♦ *nf* (*action de tenir*) running; keeping; holding; (*vêtements*) clothes *pl*, gear; (*allure*) dress *no pl*, appearance; (*comportement*) manners *pl*, behaviour (*BRIT*), behavior (*US*); **être en** ~**e** to be dressed (up); **se mettre en** ~**e** to dress (up); **en grande** ~**e** in full dress; **en petite** ~**e** scantily dressed *ou* clad; **avoir de la** ~**e** to have good manners; (*journal*) to have a high standard; ~**e de combat** combat gear *ou* dress; ~**e de pompier** fireman's uniform; ~**e de route** (*AUTO*) road-holding; ~**e de soirée** evening dress; ~**e de sport/voyage** sports/ travelling clothes *pl ou* gear *no pl*.

ténu, e [təny] *adj* (*indice, nuance*) tenuous, subtle; (*fil, objet*) fine; (*voix*) thin.

ter [tɛʀ] *adj*: **16** ~ 16b *ou* B.

térébenthine [teʀebɑ̃tin] *nf*: (**essence de**) ~ (oil of) turpentine.

tergal [tɛʀgal] *nm* ® Terylene ®.

tergiversations [tɛʀʒivɛʀsasjɔ̃] *nfpl* shilly-shallying *no pl*.

tergiverser [tɛʀʒivɛʀse] *vi* to shilly-shally.

terme [tɛʀm(ə)] *nm* term; (*fin*) end; **être en bons/mauvais** ~**s avec qn** to be on good/bad terms with sb; **vente/achat à** ~ (*COMM*) forward sale/purchase; **au** ~ **de** at the end of; **en d'autres** ~**s** in other words; **moyen** ~ (*solution intermédiare*) middle course; **à court/ long** ~ *adj* short-/long-term *ou* -range ♦ *adv* in the short/long term; **à** ~ *adj* (*MÉD*) fullterm ♦ *adv* sooner or later, eventually; (*MÉD*) at term; **avant** ~ (*MÉD*) *adj* premature ♦ *adv* prematurely; **mettre un** ~ **à** to put an end *ou* a stop to; **toucher à son** ~ to be nearing its end.

terminaison [tɛʀminɛzɔ̃] *nf* (*LING*) ending.

terminal, e, aux [tɛʀminal, -o] *adj* (*partie, phase*) final; (*MÉD*) terminal ♦ *nm* terminal ♦ *nf* (*SCOL*) ≈ sixth form *ou* year (*BRIT*), ≈ twelfth grade (*US*).

terminer [tɛʀmine] *vt* to end; (*travail, repas*) to finish; **se** ~ *vi* to end; **se** ~ **par** to end with.

terminologie [tɛʀminɔlɔʒi] *nf* terminology.

terminus [tɛʀminys] *nm* terminus (*pl* -i); ~! all change!

termite [tɛʀmit] *nm* termite, white ant.

termitière [tɛʀmitjɛʀ] nf ant-hill.
ternaire [tɛʀnɛʀ] adj compound.
terne [tɛʀn(ə)] adj dull.
ternir [tɛʀniʀ] vt to dull; (fig) to sully, tarnish; **se ~** vi to become dull.
terrain [tɛʀɛ̃] nm (sol, fig) ground; (COMM) land no pl, plot (of land); (: à bâtir) site; **sur le ~** (fig) on the field; **~ de football/rugby** football/rugby pitch (BRIT) ou field (US); **~ d'atterrissage** landing strip; **~ d'aviation** airfield; **~ de camping** campsite; **un ~ d'entente** an area of agreement; **~ de golf** golf course; **~ de jeu** playground; (SPORT) games field; **~ de sport** sports ground; **~ vague** waste ground no pl.
terrasse [tɛʀas] nf terrace; (de café) pavement area, terrasse; **à la ~** (café) outside.
terrassement [tɛʀasmɑ̃] nm earth-moving, earthworks pl; embankment.
terrasser [tɛʀase] vt (adversaire) to floor, bring down; (suj: maladie etc) to lay low.
terrassier [tɛʀasje] nm navvy, roadworker.
terre [tɛʀ] nf (gén, aussi ÉLEC) earth; (substance) soil, earth; (opposé à mer) land no pl; (contrée) land; **~s** nfpl (terrains) lands, land sg; **travail de la ~** work on the land; **en ~** (pipe, poterie) clay cpd; **mettre en ~** (plante etc) to plant; (personne: enterrer) to bury; **à** ou **par ~** (mettre, être) on the ground (ou floor); (jeter, tomber) to the ground, down; **~ à ~** adj inv down-to-earth, matter-of-fact; **la T~ Adélie** Adélie Coast ou Land; **~ de bruyère** (heath-) peat; **~ cuite** earthenware; terracotta; **la ~ ferme** dry land, terra firma; **la T~ de Feu** Tierra del Fuego; **~ glaise** clay; **la T~ promise** the Promised Land; **la T~ Sainte** the Holy Land.
terreau [tɛʀo] nm compost.
Terre-Neuve [tɛʀnœv] nf: **la ~** (aussi: **l'île de ~**) Newfoundland.
terre-plein [tɛʀplɛ̃] nm platform.
terrer [tɛʀe]: **se ~** vi to hide away; to go to ground.
terrestre [tɛʀɛstʀ(ə)] adj (surface) earth's, of the earth; (BOT, ZOOL, MIL) land cpd; (REL) earthly, worldly.
terreur [tɛʀœʀ] nf terror no pl, fear.
terreux, euse [tɛʀø, -øz] adj muddy; (goût) earthy.
terrible [tɛʀibl(ə)] adj terrible, dreadful; (fam: fantastique) terrific.
terriblement [tɛʀibləmɑ̃] adv (très) terribly, awfully.
terrien, ne [tɛʀjɛ̃, -ɛn] adj: **propriétaire ~** landowner ♦ nm/f countryman/woman, man/woman of the soil; (non martien etc) earthling; (non marin) landsman.
terrier [tɛʀje] nm burrow, hole; (chien) terrier.
terrifiant, e [tɛʀifjɑ̃, -ɑ̃t] adj (effrayant) terrifying; (extraordinaire) terrible, awful.
terrifier [tɛʀifje] vt to terrify.
terril [tɛʀil] nm slag heap.

terrine [tɛʀin] nf (récipient) terrine; (CULIN) pâté.
territoire [tɛʀitwaʀ] nm territory; **T~ des Afars et des Issas** French Territory of Afars and Issas.
territorial, e, aux [tɛʀitɔʀjal, -o] adj territorial; **eaux ~es** territorial waters; **armée ~e** regional defence force, ≈ Territorial Army (BRIT); **collectivités ~es** local and regional authorities.
terroir [tɛʀwaʀ] nm (AGR) soil; (région) region; **accent du ~** country ou rural accent.
terroriser [tɛʀɔʀize] vt to terrorize.
terrorisme [tɛʀɔʀism(ə)] nm terrorism.
terroriste [tɛʀɔʀist(ə)] nm/f terrorist.
tertiaire [tɛʀsjɛʀ] adj tertiary ♦ nm (ÉCON) tertiary sector, service industries pl.
tertiarisation [tɛʀsjaʀizasjɔ̃] nf expansion or development of the service sector.
tertre [tɛʀtʀ(ə)] nm hillock, mound.
tes [te] adj possessif voir **ton**.
tesson [tesɔ̃] nm: **~ de bouteille** piece of broken bottle.
test [tɛst] nm test; **~ de grossesse** pregnancy test.
testament [tɛstamɑ̃] nm (JUR) will; (fig) legacy; (REL): **T~** Testament; **faire son ~** to make one's will.
testamentaire [tɛstamɑ̃tɛʀ] adj of a will.
tester [tɛste] vt to test.
testicule [tɛstikyl] nm testicle.
tétanie [tetani] nf tetany.
tétanos [tetanos] nm tetanus.
têtard [tɛtaʀ] nm tadpole.
tête [tɛt] nf head; (cheveux) hair no pl; (visage) face; (longueur): **gagner d'une (courte) ~** to win by a (short) head; (FOOTBALL) header; **de ~** adj (wagon etc) front cpd; (concurrent) leading ♦ adv (calculer) in one's head, mentally; **par ~** (par personne) per head; **se mettre en ~ que** to get it into one's head that; **se mettre en ~ de faire** to take it into one's head to do; **prendre la ~ de qch** to take the lead in sth; **perdre la ~** (fig: s'affoler) to lose one's head; (: devenir fou) to go off one's head; **ça ne va pas, la ~?** (fam) are you crazy?; **tenir ~ à qn** to stand up to ou defy sb; **la ~ en bas** with one's head down; **la ~ la première** (tomber) headfirst; **la ~ basse** hanging one's head; **avoir la ~ dure** (fig) to be thickheaded; **faire une ~** (FOOTBALL) to head the ball; **faire la ~** (fig) to sulk; **en ~** (SPORT) in the lead; at the front ou head; **de la ~ aux pieds** from head to toe; **~ d'affiche** (THÉÂT etc) top of the bill; **~ de bétail** head inv of cattle; **~ brûlée** desperado; **~ chercheuse** homing device; **~ d'enregistrement** recording head; **~ d'impression** printhead; **~ de lecture** (play-back) head; **~ de ligne** (TRANSPORTS) start of the line; **~ de liste** (POL) chief candidate; **~ de mort** skull and crossbones; **~ de pont**

(*MIL*) bridge- *ou* beachhead; ~ **de série** (*TEN-NIS*) seeded player, seed; ~ **de Turc** (*fig*) whipping boy (*BRIT*), butt; ~ **de veau** (*CULIN*) calf's head.

tête-à-queue [tɛtakø] *nm inv*: **faire un** ~ to spin round.

tête-à-tête [tɛtatɛt] *nm inv* tête-à-tête; (*service*) breakfast set for two; **en** ~ in private, alone together.

tête-bêche [tɛtbɛʃ] *adv* head to tail.

tétée [tete] *nf* (*action*) sucking; (*repas*) feed.

téter [tete] *vt*: ~ (**sa mère**) to suck at one's mother's breast, feed.

tétine [tetin] *nf* teat; (*sucette*) dummy (*BRIT*), pacifier (*US*).

téton [tetɔ̃] *nm* breast.

têtu, e [tety] *adj* stubborn, pigheaded.

texte [tɛkst(ə)] *nm* text; (*SCOL: d'un devoir*) subject, topic; **apprendre son** ~ (*THÉÂT*) to learn one's lines; **un** ~ **de loi** the wording of a law.

textile [tɛkstil] *adj* textile *cpd* ♦ *nm* textile; (*industrie*) textile industry.

textuel, le [tɛkstɥɛl] *adj* literal, word for word.

textuellement [tɛkstɥɛlmɑ̃] *adv* literally.

texture [tɛkstyʀ] *nf* texture; (*fig: d'un texte, livre*) feel.

TF1 *sigle f* (= *Télévision française 1*) *TV channel*.

TG *sigle f* = **Trésorerie générale**.

TGI *sigle m* = **tribunal de grande instance**.

TGV *sigle m* = **train à grande vitesse**.

thaï, e [taj] *adj* Thai ♦ *nm* (*LING*) Thai.

thaïlandais, e [tailɑ̃dɛ, -ɛz] *adj* Thai.

Thaïlande [tailɑ̃d] *nf*: **la** ~ Thailand.

thalassothérapie [talasɔteʀapi] *nf* sea-water therapy.

thé [te] *nm* tea; (*réunion*) tea party; **prendre le** ~ to have tea; ~ **au lait/citron** tea with milk/lemon.

théâtral, e, aux [teatʀal, -o] *adj* theatrical.

théâtre [teatʀ(ə)] *nm* theatre; (*techniques, genre*) drama, theatre; (*activité*) stage, theatre; (*œuvres*) plays *pl*, dramatic works *pl*; (*fig: lieu*): **le** ~ **de** the scene of; (*péj*) histrionics *pl*, playacting; **faire du** ~ (*en professionnel*) to be on the stage; (*en amateur*) to do some acting; ~ **filmé** filmed stage productions *pl*.

thébain, e [tebɛ̃, -ɛn] *adj* Theban.

Thèbes [tɛb] *n* Thebes.

théière [tejɛʀ] *nf* teapot.

théine [tein] *nf* theine.

théisme [teism(ə)] *nm* theism.

thématique [tematik] *adj* thematic.

thème [tɛm] *nm* theme; (*SCOL: traduction*) prose (composition); ~ **astral** birth chart.

théocratie [teɔkʀasi] *nf* theocracy.

théologie [teɔlɔʒi] *nf* theology.

théologien, ne [teɔlɔʒjɛ̃, -ɛn] *nm* theologian.

théologique [teɔlɔʒik] *adj* theological.

théorème [teɔʀɛm] *nm* theorem.

théoricien, ne [teɔʀisjɛ̃, -ɛn] *nm/f* theoretician, theorist.

théorie [teɔʀi] *nf* theory; **en** ~ in theory.

théorique [teɔʀik] *adj* theoretical.

théoriquement [teɔʀikmɑ̃] *adv* theoretically.

théoriser [teɔʀize] *vi* to theorize.

thérapeutique [teʀapøtik] *adj* therapeutic ♦ *nf* (*MÉD: branche*) therapeutics *sg*; (: *traitement*) therapy.

thérapie [teʀapi] *nf* therapy; ~ **de groupe** group therapy.

thermal, e, aux [tɛʀmal, -o] *adj* thermal; **station** ~**e** spa; **cure** ~**e** water cure.

thermes [tɛʀm(ə)] *nmpl* thermal baths; (*romains*) thermae *pl*.

thermique [tɛʀmik] *adj* (*énergie*) thermic; (*unité*) thermal.

thermodynamique [tɛʀmɔdinamik] *nf* thermodynamics *sg*.

thermoélectrique [tɛʀmoelɛktʀik] *adj* thermoelectric.

thermomètre [tɛʀmɔmɛtʀ(ə)] *nm* thermometer.

thermonucléaire [tɛʀmɔnykleɛʀ] *adj* thermonuclear.

thermos [tɛʀmos] *nm ou nf* ®: (**bouteille**) ~ vacuum *ou* Thermos ® flask (*BRIT*) *ou* bottle (*US*).

thermostat [tɛʀmɔsta] *nm* thermostat.

thésauriser [tezɔʀize] *vi* to hoard money.

thèse [tɛz] *nf* thesis (*pl* theses).

Thessalie [tesali] *nf*: **la** ~ Thessaly.

thessalien, ne [tesaljɛ̃, -ɛn] *adj* Thessalian.

thibaude [tibod] *nf* carpet underlay.

thon [tɔ̃] *nm* tuna (fish).

thonier [tɔnje] *nm* tuna boat.

thoracique [tɔʀasik] *adj* thoracic.

thorax [tɔʀaks] *nm* thorax.

thrombose [tʀɔ̃boz] *nf* thrombosis.

thym [tɛ̃] *nm* thyme.

thyroïde [tiʀɔid] *nf* thyroid (gland).

TI *sigle m* = **tribunal d'instance**.

tiare [tjaʀ] *nf* tiara.

Tibet [tibɛ] *nm*: **le** ~ Tibet.

tibétain, e [tibetɛ̃, -ɛn] *adj* Tibetan.

tibia [tibja] *nm* shin; (*os*) shinbone, tibia.

Tibre [tibʀ(ə)] *nm*: **le** ~ the Tiber.

tic [tik] *nm* tic, (nervous) twitch; (*de langage etc*) mannerism.

ticket [tikɛ] *nm* ticket; ~ **de caisse** till receipt; ~ **modérateur** *patient's contribution towards medical costs*; ~ **de quai** platform ticket; ~ **repas** luncheon voucher.

tic-tac [tiktak] *nm inv* tick-tock.

tictaquer [tiktake] *vi* to tick (away).

tiède [tjɛd] *adj* (*bière etc*) lukewarm; (*thé, café etc*) tepid; (*bain, accueil, sentiment*) lukewarm; (*vent, air*) mild, warm ♦ *adv*: **boire** ~ to drink things lukewarm.

tièdement [tjɛdmɑ̃] *adv* coolly, half-heartedly.

tiédeur [tjedœʀ] *nf* lukewarmness; (*du vent, de*

l'air) mildness.

tiédir [tjediʀ] *vi* (*se réchauffer*) to grow warmer; (*refroidir*) to cool.

tien, tienne [tjɛ̃, tjɛn] *pron:* **le ~ (la tienne), les ~s (tiennes)** yours; **à la tienne!** cheers!

tiendrai [tjɛ̃dʀe] *etc vb voir* **tenir**.

tienne [tjɛn] *vb voir* **tenir** ♦ *pron voir* **tien**.

tiens [tjɛ̃] *vb, excl voir* **tenir**.

tierce [tjɛʀs(ə)] *adj f, nf voir* **tiers**.

tiercé [tjɛʀse] *nm system of forecast betting giving first three horses.*

tiers, tierce [tjɛʀ, tjɛʀs(ə)] *adj* third ♦ *nm* (*JUR*) third party; (*fraction*) third ♦ *nf* (*MUS*) third; (*CARTES*) tierce; **une tierce personne** a third party; **assurance au ~** third-party insurance; **le ~ monde** the third world; **~ payant** *direct payment by insurers of medical expenses*; **~ provisionnel** *interim payment of tax.*

tiersmondisme [tjɛʀmɔ̃dism(ə)] *nm* support for the Third World.

TIG *sigle m* = **travail d'intérêt général**.

tige [tiʒ] *nf* stem; (*baguette*) rod.

tignasse [tiɲas] *nf* (*péj*) shock *ou* mop of hair.

Tigre [tigʀ(ə)] *nm:* **le ~** the Tigris.

tigre [tigʀ(ə)] *nm* tiger.

tigré, e [tigʀe] *adj* (*rayé*) striped; (*tacheté*) spotted.

tigresse [tigʀɛs] *nf* tigress.

tilleul [tijœl] *nm* lime (tree), linden (tree); (*boisson*) lime(-blossom) tea.

tilt [tilt(ə)] *nm:* **faire ~** (*fig: échouer*) to miss the target; (: *inspirer*) to ring a bell.

timbale [tɛ̃bal] *nf* (metal) tumbler; **~s** *nfpl* (*MUS*) timpani, kettledrums.

timbrage [tɛ̃bʀaʒ] *nm:* **dispensé de ~** post(age) paid.

timbre [tɛ̃bʀ(ə)] *nm* (*tampon*) stamp; (*aussi:* **~poste**) (postage) stamp; (*cachet de la poste*) postmark; (*sonnette*) bell; (*MUS: de voix, instrument*) timbre, tone; **~ anti-tabac** nicotine patch; **~ dateur** date stamp.

timbré, e [tɛ̃bʀe] *adj* (*enveloppe*) stamped; (*voix*) resonant; (*fam: fou*) cracked, nuts.

timbrer [tɛ̃bʀe] *vt* to stamp.

timide [timid] *adj* (*emprunté*) shy, timid; (*timoré*) timid, timorous.

timidement [timidmɑ̃] *adv* shyly; timidly.

timidité [timidite] *nf* shyness; timidity.

timonerie [timɔnʀi] *nf* wheelhouse.

timonier [timɔnje] *nm* helmsman.

timoré, e [timɔʀe] *adj* timorous.

tint [tɛ̃] *etc vb voir* **tenir**.

tintamarre [tɛ̃tamaʀ] *nm* din, uproar.

tintement [tɛ̃tmɑ̃] *nm* ringing, chiming; **~s d'oreilles** ringing in the ears.

tinter [tɛ̃te] *vi* to ring, chime; (*argent, clefs*) to jingle.

Tipp-Ex [tipɛks] *nm* ® Tipp-Ex ®.

tique [tik] *nf* tick (*insect*).

tiquer [tike] *vi* (*personne*) to make a face.

TIR *sigle mpl* (= *Transports internationaux rou-*

tiers) TIR.

tir [tiʀ] *nm* (*sport*) shooting; (*fait ou manière de tirer*) firing *no pl*; (*FOOTBALL*) shot; (*stand*) shooting gallery; **~ d'obus/de mitraillette** shell/machine gun fire; **~ à l'arc** archery; **~ de barrage** barrage fire; **~ au fusil** (rifle) shooting; **~ au pigeon** (*d'argile*) clay pigeon shooting.

tirade [tiʀad] *nf* tirade.

tirage [tiʀaʒ] *nm* (*action*) printing; (*PHOTO*) print; (*INFORM*) printout; (*de journal*) circulation; (*de livre*) (print-)run; edition; (*de cheminée*) draught (*BRIT*), draft (*US*); (*de loterie*) draw; (*fig: désaccord*) friction; **~ au sort** drawing lots.

tiraillement [tiʀajmɑ̃] *nm* (*douleur*) sharp pain; (*fig: doutes*) agony *no pl* of indecision; (*conflits*) friction *no pl*.

tirailler [tiʀaje] *vt* to pull at, tug at; (*fig*) to gnaw at ♦ *vi* to fire at random.

tirailleur [tiʀajœʀ] *nm* skirmisher.

tirant [tiʀɑ̃] *nm:* **~ d'eau** draught (*BRIT*), draft (*US*).

tire [tiʀ] *nf:* **vol à la ~** pickpocketing.

tiré [tiʀe] *adj* (*visage, traits*) drawn ♦ *nm* (*COMM*) drawee; **~ par les cheveux** far-fetched; **~ à part** off-print.

tire-au-flanc [tiʀoflɑ̃] *nm inv* (*péj*) skiver.

tire-bouchon [tiʀbuʃɔ̃] *nm* corkscrew.

tire-bouchonner [tiʀbuʃɔne] *vt* to twirl.

tire-d'aile [tiʀdɛl]: **à ~** *adv* swiftly.

tire-fesses [tiʀfɛs] *nm inv* ski-tow.

tire-lait [tiʀlɛ] *nm inv* breast-pump.

tire-larigot [tiʀlaʀigo]: **à ~** *adv* as much as one likes, to one's heart's content.

tirelire [tiʀliʀ] *nf* moneybox.

tirer [tiʀe] *vt* (*gén*) to pull; (*extraire*): **~ qch de** to take *ou* pull sth out of; to get sth out of; to extract sth from; (*tracer: ligne, trait*) to draw, trace; (*fermer: volet, porte, trappe*) to pull to, close; (: *rideau*) to draw; (*choisir: carte, conclusion, aussi COMM: chèque*) to draw; (*en faisant feu: balle, coup*) to fire; (: *animal*) to shoot; (*journal, livre, photo*) to print; (*FOOTBALL: corner etc*) to take ♦ *vi* (*faire feu*) to fire; (*faire du tir, FOOTBALL*) to shoot; (*cheminée*) to draw; **se ~** *vi* (*fam*) to push off; **s'en ~** to pull through; **~ sur** (*corde, poignée*) to pull on *ou* at; (*faire feu sur*) to shoot *ou* fire at; (*pipe*) to draw on; (*fig: avoisiner*) to verge *ou* border on; **~ 6 mètres** (*NAVIG*) to draw 6 metres of water; **~ son nom de** to take *ou* get its name from; **~ la langue** to stick out one's tongue; **~ qn de** (*embarras etc*) to help *ou* get sb out of; **~ à l'arc/la carabine** to shoot with a bow and arrow/with a rifle; **~ en longueur** to drag on; **~ à sa fin** to be drawing to an end; **~ les cartes** to read *ou* tell the cards.

tiret [tiʀɛ] *nm* dash; (*en fin de ligne*) hyphen.

tireur [tiʀœʀ] *nm* gunman; (*COMM*) drawer; **bon ~** good shot; **~ d'élite** marksman; **~ de**

cartes fortuneteller.
tiroir [tiʀwaʀ] *nm* drawer.
tiroir-caisse [tiʀwaʀkɛs] *nm* till.
tisane [tizan] *nf* herb tea.
tison [tizɔ̃] *nm* brand.
tisonner [tizɔne] *vt* to poke.
tisonnier [tizɔnje] *nm* poker.
tissage [tisaʒ] *nm* weaving *no pl*.
tisser [tise] *vt* to weave.
tisserand, e [tisʀɑ̃, -ɑ̃d] *nm/f* weaver.
tissu [tisy] *nm* fabric, material, cloth *no pl*; (*fig*) fabric; (*ANAT, BIO*) tissue; ~ **de mensonges** web of lies.
tissu, e [tisy] *adj*: ~ **de** woven through with.
tissu-éponge [tisyepɔ̃ʒ] *nm* (terry) towelling *no pl*.
titane [titan] *nm* titanium.
titanesque [titanɛsk(ə)] *adj* titanic.
titiller [titile] *vt* to titillate.
titrage [titʀaʒ] *nm* (*d'un film*) titling; (*d'un alcool*) determination of alcohol content.
titre [titʀ(ə)] *nm* (*gén*) title; (*de journal*) headline; (*diplôme*) qualification; (*COMM*) security; (*CHIMIE*) titre; **en** ~ (*champion, responsable*) official, recognized; **à juste** ~ with just cause, rightly; **à quel** ~? on what grounds?; **à aucun** ~ on no account; **au même** ~ **(que)** in the same way (as); **au** ~ **de la coopération** *etc* in the name of cooperation *etc*; **à** ~ **d'exemple** as an *ou* by way of an example; **à** ~ **exceptionnel** exceptionally; **à** ~ **d'information** for (your) information; **à** ~ **gracieux** free of charge; **à** ~ **d'essai** on a trial basis; **à** ~ **privé** in a private capacity; ~ **courant** running head; ~ **de propriété** title deed; ~ **de transport** ticket.
titré, e [titʀe] *adj* (*livre, film*) entitled; (*personne*) titled.
titrer [titʀe] *vt* (*CHIMIE*) to titrate; to assay; (*PRESSE*) to run as a headline; (*suj: vin*): ~ **10°** to be 10° proof.
titubant, e [titybɑ̃, -ɑ̃t] *adj* staggering, reeling.
tituber [titybe] *vi* to stagger *ou* reel (along).
titulaire [titylɛʀ] *adj* (*ADMIN*) appointed, with tenure ♦ *nm* (*ADMIN*) incumbent; **être** ~ **de** to hold.
titularisation [titylaʀizasjɔ̃] *nf* granting of tenure.
titulariser [titylaʀize] *vt* to give tenure to.
TNP *sigle m* = *Théâtre national populaire*.
TNT *sigle m* (= *Trinitrotoluène*) TNT.
toast [tost] *nm* slice *ou* piece of toast; (*de bienvenue*) (welcoming) toast; **porter un** ~ **à qn** to propose *ou* drink a toast to sb.
toboggan [tɔbɔgɑ̃] *nm* toboggan; (*jeu*) slide; (*AUTO*) temporary flyover (*BRIT*) *ou* overpass (*US*); ~ **de secours** (*AVIAT*) escape chute.
toc [tɔk] *nm*: **en** ~ imitation *cpd*.
tocsin [tɔksɛ̃] *nm* alarm (bell).
toge [tɔʒ] *nf* toga; (*de juge*) gown.

Togo [tɔgo] *nm*: **le** ~ Togo.
togolais, e [tɔgɔlɛ, -ɛz] *adj* Togolese.
tohu-bohu [tɔybɔy] *nm* (*désordre*) confusion; (*tumulte*) commotion.
toi [twa] *pron* you; ~, **tu l'as fait?** did YOU do it?
toile [twal] *nf* (*matériau*) cloth *no pl*; (*bâche*) piece of canvas; (*tableau*) canvas; **grosse** ~ canvas; **tisser sa** ~ (*araignée*) to spin its web; ~ **d'araignée** spider's web; (*au plafond etc: à enlever*) cobweb; ~ **cirée** oilcloth; ~ **émeri** emery cloth; ~ **de fond** (*fig*) backdrop; ~ **de jute** hessian; ~ **de lin** linen; ~ **de tente** canvas.
toilettage [twalɛtaʒ] *nm* grooming *no pl*; (*d'un texte*) tidying up.
toilette [twalɛt] *nf* wash; (*s'habiller et se préparer*) getting ready, washing and dressing; (*habits*) outfit; dress *no pl*; ~**s** *nfpl* toilet *sg*; **les** ~**s des dames/messieurs** the ladies'/gents' (toilets) (*BRIT*), the ladies'/mens' (rest)room (*US*); **faire sa** ~ to have a wash, get washed; **faire la** ~ **de** (*animal*) to groom; (*voiture etc*) to clean, wash; (*texte*) to tidy up; **articles de** ~ toiletries; ~ **intime** personal hygiene.
toi-même [twamɛm] *pron* yourself.
toise [twaz] *nf*: **passer à la** ~ to have one's height measured.
toiser [twaze] *vt* to eye up and down.
toison [twazɔ̃] *nf* (*de mouton*) fleece; (*cheveux*) mane.
toit [twa] *nm* roof; ~ **ouvrant** sun roof.
toiture [twatyʀ] *nf* roof.
Tokyo [tɔkjo] *n* Tokyo.
tôle [tol] *nf* sheet metal *no pl*; (*plaque*) steel (*ou* iron) sheet; ~**s** *nfpl* (*carrosserie*) bodywork *sg* (*BRIT*), body *sg*; panels; ~ **d'acier** sheet steel *no pl*; ~ **ondulée** corrugated iron.
Tolède [tɔlɛd] *n* Toledo.
tolérable [tɔleʀabl(ə)] *adj* tolerable, bearable.
tolérance [tɔleʀɑ̃s] *nf* tolerance; (*hors taxe*) allowance.
tolérant, e [tɔleʀɑ̃, -ɑ̃t] *adj* tolerant.
tolérer [tɔleʀe] *vt* to tolerate; (*ADMIN: hors taxe etc*) to allow.
tôlerie [tolʀi] *nf* sheet metal manufacture; (*atelier*) sheet metal workshop; (*ensemble des tôles*) panels *pl*.
tollé [tɔle] *nm*: **un** ~ **(de protestations)** a general outcry.
TOM [*parfois*: tɔm] *sigle m(pl)* = *territoire(s) d'outre-mer*.
tomate [tɔmat] *nf* tomato.
tombal, e [tɔ̃bal] *adj*: **pierre** ~**e** tombstone, gravestone.
tombant, e [tɔ̃bɑ̃, -ɑ̃t] *adj* (*fig*) drooping, sloping.
tombe [tɔ̃b] *nf* (*sépulture*) grave; (*avec monument*) tomb.
tombeau, x [tɔ̃bo] *nm* tomb; **à** ~ **ouvert** at breakneck speed.
tombée [tɔ̃be] *nf*: **à la** ~ **du jour** *ou* **de la nuit**

at the close of day, at nightfall.

tomber [tɔbe] *vi* to fall ♦ *vt*: ~ **la veste** to slip off one's jacket; **laisser** ~ to drop; ~ **sur** *vt* (*rencontrer*) to come across; (*attaquer*) to set about; ~ **de fatigue/sommeil** to drop from exhaustion/be falling asleep on one's feet; ~ **à l'eau** (*fig: projet etc*) to fall through; ~ **en panne** to break down; ~ **juste** (*opération, calcul*) to come out right; ~ **en ruine** to fall into ruins; **ça tombe bien/mal** (*fig*) that's come at the right/wrong time; **il est bien/mal tombé** (*fig*) he's been lucky/unlucky.

tombereau, x [tɔbʀo] *nm* tipcart.

tombeur [tɔbœʀ] *nm* (*péj*) Casanova.

tombola [tɔbɔla] *nf* tombola.

Tombouctou [tɔbuktu] *n* Timbuktu.

tome [tɔm] *nm* volume.

tommette [tɔmɛt] *nf* hexagonal floor tile.

ton, ta, *pl* **tes** [tɔ̃, ta, te] *adj possessif* your.

ton [tɔ̃] *nm* (*gén*) tone; (*couleur*) shade, tone; (*de la voix: hauteur*) pitch; **donner le** ~ to set the tone; **élever** *ou* **hausser le** ~ to raise one's voice; **de bon** ~ in good taste; **si vous le prenez sur ce** ~ if you're going to take it like that; ~ **sur** ~ in matching shades.

tonal, e [tɔnal] *adj* tonal.

tonalité [tɔnalite] *nf* (*au téléphone*) dialling tone; (*MUS*) tonality; (*: ton*) key; (*fig*) tone.

tondeuse [tɔ̃døz] *nf* (*à gazon*) (lawn)mower; (*du coiffeur*) clippers *pl*; (*pour la tonte*) shears *pl*.

tondre [tɔ̃dʀ(ə)] *vt* (*pelouse, herbe*) to mow; (*haie*) to cut, clip; (*mouton, toison*) to shear; (*cheveux*) to crop.

tondu, e [tɔ̃dy] *pp de* **tondre** ♦ *adj* (*cheveux*) cropped; (*mouton, crâne*) shorn.

Tonga [tɔ̃ga]: **les îles** ~ Tonga.

tonicité [tɔnisite] *nf* (*MÉD: des tissus*) tone; (*fig: de l'air, la mer*) bracing effect.

tonifiant, e [tɔnifjɑ̃, -ɑ̃t] *adj* invigorating, revivifying.

tonifier [tɔnifje] *vt* (*air, eau*) to invigorate; (*peau, organisme*) to tone up.

tonique [tɔnik] *adj* fortifying; (*personne*) dynamic ♦ *nm, nf* tonic.

tonitruant, e [tɔnitʀyɑ̃, -ɑ̃t] *adj*: **voix** ~**e** thundering voice.

Tonkin [tɔ̃kɛ̃] *nm*: **le** ~ Tonkin, Tongking.

tonkinois, e [tɔ̃kinwa, -waz] *adj* Tonkinese.

tonnage [tɔnaʒ] *nm* tonnage.

tonnant, e [tɔnɑ̃, -ɑ̃t] *adj* thunderous.

tonne [tɔn] *nf* metric ton, tonne.

tonneau, x [tɔno] *nm* (*à vin, cidre*) barrel; (*NAVIG*) ton; **faire des** ~**x** (*voiture, avion*) to roll over.

tonnelet [tɔnlɛ] *nm* keg.

tonnelier [tɔnəlje] *nm* cooper.

tonnelle [tɔnɛl] *nf* bower, arbour (*BRIT*), arbor (*US*).

tonner [tɔne] *vi* to thunder; (*parler avec véhémence*): ~ **contre qn/qch** to inveigh against

sb/sth; **il tonne** it is thundering, there's some thunder.

tonnerre [tɔnɛʀ] *nm* thunder; **coup de** ~ (*fig*) thunderbolt, bolt from the blue; **un** ~ **d'applaudissements** thunderous applause; **du** ~ *adj* (*fam*) terrific.

tonsure [tɔ̃syʀ] *nf* bald patch; (*de moine*) tonsure.

tonte [tɔ̃t] *nf* shearing.

tonus [tɔnys] *nm* (*des muscles*) tone; (*d'une personne*) dynamism.

top [tɔp] *nm*: **au 3ème** ~ at the 3rd stroke ♦ *adj*: ~ **secret** top secret ♦ *excl* go!

topaze [tɔpaz] *nf* topaz.

toper [tɔpe] *vi*: **tope-/topez-là** it's a deal!, you're on!

topinambour [tɔpinɑ̃buʀ] *nm* Jerusalem artichoke.

topo [tɔpo] *nm* (*discours, exposé*) talk; (*fam*) spiel.

topographie [tɔpɔgʀafi] *nf* topography.

topographique [tɔpɔgʀafik] *adj* topographical.

toponymie [tɔpɔnimi] *nf* study of place names, toponymy.

toquade [tɔkad] *nf* fad, craze.

toque [tɔk] *nf* (*de fourrure*) fur hat; ~ **de jockey/juge** jockey's/judge's cap; ~ **de cuisinier** chef's hat.

toqué, e [tɔke] *adj* (*fam*) touched, cracked.

torche [tɔʀʃ(ə)] *nf* torch; **se mettre en** ~ (*parachute*) to candle.

torcher [tɔʀʃe] *vt* (*fam*) to wipe.

torchère [tɔʀʃɛʀ] *nf* flare.

torchon [tɔʀʃɔ̃] *nm* cloth, duster; (*à vaisselle*) tea towel *ou* cloth.

tordre [tɔʀdʀ(ə)] *vt* (*chiffon*) to wring; (*barre, fig: visage*) to twist; **se** ~ *vi* (*barre*) to bend; (*roue*) to twist, buckle; (*ver, serpent*) to writhe; **se** ~ **le pied/bras** to twist one's foot/arm; **se** ~ **de douleur/rire** to writhe in pain/be doubled up with laughter.

tordu, e [tɔʀdy] *pp de* **tordre** ♦ *adj* (*fig*) warped, twisted.

torero [tɔʀeʀo] *nm* bullfighter.

tornade [tɔʀnad] *nf* tornado.

toron [tɔʀɔ̃] *nm* strand (of rope).

Toronto [tɔʀɔ̃to] *n* Toronto.

torontois, e [tɔʀɔ̃twa, -waz] *adj* Torontonian ♦ *nm/f*: **T~**, e Torontonian.

torpeur [tɔʀpœʀ] *nf* torpor, drowsiness.

torpille [tɔʀpij] *nf* torpedo.

torpiller [tɔʀpije] *vt* to torpedo.

torpilleur [tɔʀpijœʀ] *nm* torpedo boat.

torréfaction [tɔʀefaksjɔ̃] *nf* roasting.

torréfier [tɔʀefje] *vt* to roast.

torrent [tɔʀɑ̃] *nm* torrent, mountain stream; (*fig*): **un** ~ **de** a torrent *ou* flood of; **il pleut à** ~**s** the rain is lashing down.

torrentiel, le [tɔʀɑ̃sjɛl] *adj* torrential.

torride [tɔʀid] *adj* torrid.

tors, torse *ou* **torte** [tɔʀ, tɔʀs(ə) *ou* tɔʀt(ə)]

adj twisted.

torsade [tɔʀsad] *nf* twist; (*ARCHIT*) cable moulding (*BRIT*) *ou* molding (*US*).

torsader [tɔʀsade] *vt* to twist.

torse [tɔʀs(ə)] *nm* torso; (*poitrine*) chest.

torsion [tɔʀsjɔ̃] *nf* (*action*) twisting; (*TECH*, *PHYSIQUE*) torsion.

tort [tɔʀ] *nm* (*défaut*) fault; (*préjudice*) wrong *no pl*; ~**s** *nmpl* (*JUR*) fault *sg*; **avoir** ~ to be wrong; **être dans son** ~ to be in the wrong; **donner** ~ **à qn** to lay the blame on sb; (*fig*) to prove sb wrong; **causer du** ~ **à** to harm; to be harmful *ou* detrimental to; **en** ~ in the wrong, at fault; **à** ~ wrongly; **à** ~ **ou à raison** rightly or wrongly; **à** ~ **et à travers** wildly.

torte [tɔʀt(ə)] *adj f voir* **tors**.

torticolis [tɔʀtikɔli] *nm* stiff neck.

tortiller [tɔʀtije] *vt* (*corde, mouchoir*) to twist; (*doigts*) to twiddle; **se** ~ *vi* to wriggle, squirm.

tortionnaire [tɔʀsjɔnɛʀ] *nm* torturer.

tortue [tɔʀty] *nf* tortoise; (*fig*) slowcoach (*BRIT*), slowpoke (*US*).

tortueux, euse [tɔʀtɥø, -øz] *adj* (*rue*) twisting; (*fig*) tortuous.

torture [tɔʀtyʀ] *nf* torture.

torturer [tɔʀtyʀe] *vt* to torture; (*fig*) to torment.

torve [tɔʀv(ə)] *adj*: **regard** ~ menacing *ou* grim look.

toscan, e [tɔskɑ̃, -an] *adj* Tuscan.

Toscane [tɔskan] *nf*: **la** ~ Tuscany.

tôt [to] *adv* early; ~ **ou tard** sooner or later; **si** ~ so early; (*déjà*) so soon; **au plus** ~ at the earliest; **as soon as possible; plus** ~ earlier; **il eut** ~ **fait de faire** ... he soon did ....

total, e, aux [tɔtal, -o] *adj, nm* total; **au** ~ in total *ou* all; (*fig*) all in all; **faire le** ~ to work out the total.

totalement [tɔtalmɑ̃] *adv* totally, completely.

totalisateur [tɔtalizatœʀ] *nm* adding machine.

totaliser [tɔtalize] *vt* to total (up).

totalitaire [tɔtalitɛʀ] *adj* totalitarian.

totalitarisme [tɔtalitaʀism(ə)] *nm* totalitarianism.

totalité [tɔtalite] *nf*: **la** ~ **de:** **la** ~ **des élèves** all (of) the pupils; **la** ~ **de la population/classe** the whole population/class; **en** ~ entirely.

totem [tɔtɛm] *nm* totem.

toubib [tubib] *nm* (*fam*) doctor.

touchant, e [tuʃɑ̃, -ɑ̃t] *adj* touching.

touche [tuʃ] *nf* (*de piano, de machine à écrire*) key; (*de violon*) fingerboard; (*de télécommande etc*) key, button; (*PEINTURE etc*) stroke, touch; (*fig: de couleur, nostalgie*) touch, hint; (*RUGBY*) line-out; (*FOOTBALL: aussi:* **remise en** ~) throw-in; (*aussi:* **ligne de** ~) touch-line; (*ESCRIME*) hit; **en** ~ in (*ou* into) touch; **avoir une drôle de** ~ to look a sight; ~ **de commande/de fonction/de retour** (*IN-*

FORM) control/function/return key; ~ **à effleurement** *ou* **sensitive** touch-sensitive control *ou* key.

touche-à-tout [tuʃatu] *nm inv* (*péj: gén: enfant*) meddler; (: *fig: inventeur etc*) dabbler.

toucher [tuʃe] *nm* touch ♦ *vt* to touch; (*palper*) to feel; (*atteindre: d'un coup de feu etc*) to hit; (*affecter*) to touch, affect; (*concerner*) to concern, affect; (*contacter*) to reach, contact; (*recevoir: récompense*) to receive, get; (*: salaire*) to draw, get; (*chèque*) to cash; (*aborder: problème, sujet*) to touch on; **au** ~ to the touch; **by the feel;** **se** ~ (*être en contact*) to touch; ~ **à** to touch; (*modifier*) to touch, tamper *ou* meddle with; (*traiter de, concerner*) to have to do with, concern; **je vais lui en** ~ **un mot** I'll have a word with him about it; ~ **au but** (*fig*) to near one's goal; ~ **à sa fin** to be drawing to a close.

touffe [tuf] *nf* tuft.

touffu, e [tufy] *adj* thick, dense; (*fig*) complex, involved.

toujours [tuʒuʀ] *adv* always; (*encore*) still; (*constamment*) forever; **depuis** ~ always; **essaie** ~ (you can) try anyway; **pour** ~ forever; ~ **est-il que** the fact remains that; ~ **plus** more and more.

toulonnais, e [tulɔnɛ, -ɛz] *adj* of *ou* from Toulon.

toulousain, e [tuluzɛ̃, -ɛn] *adj* of *ou* from Toulouse.

toupet [tupɛ] *nm* quiff (*BRIT*), tuft; (*fam*) nerve, cheek (*BRIT*).

toupie [tupi] *nf* (spinning) top.

tour [tuʀ] *nf* tower; (*immeuble*) high-rise block (*BRIT*) *ou* building (*US*), tower block (*BRIT*); (*ÉCHECS*) castle, rook ♦ *nm* (*excursion: à pied*) stroll, walk; (: *en voiture etc*) run, ride; (: *plus long*) trip; (*SPORT: aussi:* ~ **de piste**) lap; (*d'être servi ou de jouer etc, tournure, de vis ou clef*) turn; (*de roue etc*) revolution; (*circonférence*): **de 3 m de** ~ 3 m round, with a circumference *ou* girth of 3 m; (*POL: aussi:* ~ **de scrutin**) ballot; (*ruse, de prestidigitation, de cartes*) trick; (*de potier*) wheel; (*à bois, métaux*) lathe; **faire le** ~ **de** to go (a)round; (*à pied*) to walk (a)round; (*fig*) to review; **faire le** ~ **de l'Europe** to tour Europe; **faire un** ~ to go for a walk; (*en voiture etc*) to go for a ride; **faire 2** ~**s** to go (a)round twice; (*hélice etc*) to turn *ou* revolve twice; **fermer à double** ~ *vi* to double-lock the door; **c'est au** ~ **de Renée** it's Renée's turn; **à** ~ **de rôle**, **à** ~ ~ in turn; **à** ~ **de bras** with all one's strength; (*fig*) non-stop, relentlessly; ~ **de taille/tête** waist/head measurement; ~ **de chant** song recital; ~ **de contrôle** *nf* control tower; ~ **de garde** spell of duty; ~ **d'horizon** (*fig*) general survey; ~ **de lit** valance; ~ **de main** dexterity, knack; **en un** ~ **de main** (as) quick as a flash; ~ **de passe-passe** trick, sleight of hand; ~ **de reins** sprained back.

*The **Tour de France** is an annual road race for professional cyclists taking about three weeks to complete in daily stages or "étapes" of approximately 110 miles over terrain of varying difficulty. The leading cyclist wears a yellow jersey, the **maillot jaune**. There are a number of time trials. The route varies and is not usually confined only to France, but the race always ends in Paris.*

tourangeau, elle, x [tuRɑ̃ʒo, -ɛl] *adj* (*de la région*) of *ou* from Touraine; (*de la ville*) of *ou* from Tours.

tourbe [tuRb(ə)] *nf* peat.

tourbière [tuRbjɛR] *nf* peat-bog.

tourbillon [tuRbijɔ̃] *nm* whirlwind; (*d'eau*) whirlpool; (*fig*) whirl, swirl.

tourbillonner [tuRbijɔne] *vi* to whirl, swirl; (*objet, personne*) to whirl *ou* twirl round.

tourelle [tuRɛl] *nf* turret.

tourisme [tuRism(ə)] *nm* tourism; **agence de ~** tourist agency; **avion/voiture de ~** private plane/car; **faire du ~** to do some sightseeing, go touring.

touriste [tuRist(ə)] *nm/f* tourist.

touristique [tuRistik] *adj* tourist *cpd*; (*région*) touristic (*péj*), with tourist appeal.

tourment [tuRmɑ̃] *nm* torment.

tourmente [tuRmɑ̃t] *nf* storm.

tourmenté, e [tuRmɑ̃te] *adj* tormented, tortured; (*mer, période*) turbulent, tempestuous.

tourmenter [tuRmɑ̃te] *vt* to torment; **se ~** *vi* to fret, worry o.s.

tournage [tuRnaʒ] *nm* (*d'un film*) shooting.

tournant, e [tuRnɑ̃, -ɑ̃t] *adj* (*feu, scène*) revolving; (*chemin*) winding; (*escalier*) spiral *cpd*; (*mouvement*) circling ♦ *nm* (*de route*) bend (*BRIT*), curve (*US*); (*fig*) turning point; *voir* **plaque, grève.**

tourné, e [tuRne] *adj* (*lait, vin*) sour, off; (*MENUISERIE: bois*) turned; (*fig: compliment*) well-phrased; **bien ~** (*personne*) shapely; **mal ~** (*lettre*) badly expressed; **avoir l'esprit mal ~** to have a dirty mind.

tournebroche [tuRnəbRɔʃ] *nm* roasting spit.

tourne-disque [tuRnədisk(ə)] *nm* record player.

tournedos [tuRnədo] *nm* tournedos.

tournée [tuRne] *nf* (*du facteur etc*) round; (*d'artiste, politicien*) tour; (*au café*) round (of drinks); **~ électorale/musicale** election/concert tour; **faire la ~ de** to go (a)round.

tournemain [tuRnəmɛ̃]: **en un ~** *adv* in a flash.

tourner [tuRne] *vt* to turn; (*sauce, mélange*) to stir; (*contourner*) to get (a)round; (*CINÉ*) to shoot; to make ♦ *vi* to turn; (*moteur*) to run; (*compteur*) to tick away; (*lait etc*) to turn (sour); (*fig: chance, vie*) to turn out; **se ~** *vi* to turn (a)round; **se ~ vers** to turn to; to turn towards; **bien ~** to turn out well; **~ autour**

de to go (a)round; (*planète*) to revolve (a)round; (*péj*) to hang (a)round; **~ autour du pot** (*fig*) to go (a)round in circles; **~ à/en** to turn into; **~ à la pluie/au rouge** to turn rainy/red; **~ en ridicule** to ridicule; **~ le dos à** (*mouvement*) to turn one's back on; (*position*) to have one's back to; **~ court** to come to a sudden end; **se ~ les pouces** to twiddle one's thumbs; **~ la tête** to look away; **~ la tête à qn** (*fig*) to go to sb's head; **~ de l'œil** to pass out; **~ la page** (*fig*) to turn the page.

tournesol [tuRnəsɔl] *nm* sunflower.

tourneur [tuRnœR] *nm* turner; lathe-operator.

tournevis [tuRnəvis] *nm* screwdriver.

tourniquer [tuRnike] *vi* to go (a)round in circles.

tourniquet [tuRnikɛ] *nm* (*pour arroser*) sprinkler; (*portillon*) turnstile; (*présentoir*) revolving stand, spinner; (*CHIRURGIE*) tourniquet.

tournis [tuRni] *nm*: **avoir/donner le ~** to feel/make dizzy.

tournoi [tuRnwa] *nm* tournament.

tournoyer [tuRnwaje] *vi* (*oiseau*) to wheel (a)round; (*fumée*) to swirl (a)round.

tournure [tuRnyR] *nf* (*LING: syntaxe*) turn of phrase; form; (: *d'une phrase*) phrasing; (*évolution*): **la ~ de qch** the way sth is developing; (*aspect*): **la ~ de** the look of; **la ~ des événements** the turn of events; **prendre ~** to take shape; **~ d'esprit** turn *ou* cast of mind.

tour-opérateur [tuRɔpeRatœR] *nm* tour operator.

tourte [tuRt(ə)] *nf* pie.

tourteau, x [tuRto] *nm* (*AGR*) oilcake, cattle-cake; (*ZOOL*) edible crab.

tourtereaux [tuRtəRo] *nmpl* lovebirds.

tourterelle [tuRtəRɛl] *nf* turtledove.

tourtière [tuRtjɛR] *nf* pie dish *ou* plate.

tous *dét* [tu] , *pron* [tus] *voir* **tout.**

Toussaint [tusɛ̃] *nf*: **la ~** All Saints' Day.

*La **Toussaint**, November 1, is a public holiday in France. People traditionally visit the graves of friends and relatives and decorate them with chrysanthemums.*

tousser [tuse] *vi* to cough.

toussoter [tusɔte] *vi* to have a slight cough; to cough a little; (*pour avertir*) to give a slight cough.

========= *MOT-CLÉ*

tout, e [tu, tut] (*mpl* **tous**, *fpl* **toutes**) *adj* **1** (*avec article singulier*) all; **~ le lait** all the milk; **~e la nuit** all night, the whole night; **~ le livre** the whole book; **~ un pain** a whole loaf; **~ le temps** all the time, the whole time; **c'est ~ le contraire** it's quite the opposite; **c'est ~e une affaire** *ou* **histoire** it's quite a business, it's a whole rigmarole

2 (*avec article pluriel*) every; all; **tous les**

livres all the books; ~**es les nuits** every night; ~**es les fois** every time; ~**es les trois/deux semaines** every third/other *ou* second week, every three/two weeks; **tous les deux** both *ou* each of us (*ou* them *ou* you); ~**es les trois** all three of us (*ou* them *ou* you)

3 (*sans article*): **à ~ âge** at any age; **pour ~e nourriture, il avait** ... his only food was ...; **de tous côtés, de ~es parts** from everywhere, from every side

♦ *pron* everything, all; **il a ~ fait** he's done everything; **je les vois tous** I can see them all *ou* all of them; **nous y sommes tous allés** all of us went, we all went; **c'est ~** that's all; **en ~ in all; en ~ et pour ~** all in all; **~ qu'il sait** all he knows; **c'était ~ ce qu'il y a de chic** it was the last word *ou* the ultimate in chic

♦ *nm* whole; **le ~** all of it (*ou* them); **le ~ est de** ... the main thing is to ...; **pas du ~** not at all; **elle a ~ d'une mère/d'une intrigante** she's a real *ou* true mother/schemer; **du ~ au ~** utterly

♦ *adv* **1** (*très, complètement*) very; **~ près** *ou* **à côté** very near; **le ~ premier** the very first; **~ seul** all alone; **il était ~ rouge** he was really *ou* all red; **parler ~ bas** to speak very quietly; **le livre ~ entier** the whole book; **~ en haut** right at the top; **~ droit** straight ahead

2: **~ en** while; **~ en travaillant** while working, as he *etc* works

3: **~ d'abord** first of all; **~ à coup** suddenly; **~ à fait** absolutely; **~ a fait!** exactly!; **~ à l'heure** a short while ago; (*futur*) in a short while, shortly; **à ~ à l'heure!** see you later!; **il répondit ~ court que non** he just answered no (and that was all); **~ de même** all the same; **~ le monde** everybody; **~ ou rien** all or nothing; **~ simplement** quite simply; **~ de suite** immediately, straight away

tout-à-l'égout [tutalegu] *nm inv* mains drainage.
toutefois [tutfwa] *adv* however.
toutou [tutu] *nm* (*fam*) doggie.
tout-petit [tup(ə)ti] *nm* toddler.
tout-puissant, toute-puissante [tupɥisɑ̃, tutpɥisɑ̃t] *adj* all-powerful, omnipotent.
tout-venant [tuvnɑ̃] *nm*: **le ~** everyday stuff.
toux [tu] *nf* cough.
toxémie [tɔksemi] *nf* toxaemia (*BRIT*), toxemia (*US*).
toxicité [tɔksisite] *nf* toxicity.
toxicologie [tɔksikɔlɔʒi] *nf* toxicology.
toxicomane [tɔksikɔman] *nm/f* drug addict.
toxicomanie [tɔksikɔmani] *nf* drug addiction.
toxine [tɔksin] *nf* toxin.
toxique [tɔksik] *adj* toxic, poisonous.
toxoplasmose [tɔksɔplasmoz] *nf* toxoplasmosis.

TP *sigle mpl* = **travaux pratiques, travaux publics** ♦ *sigle m* = **trésor public**.
TPG *sigle m* = **Trésorier-payeur général**.
tps *abr* = **temps**.
trac [tʀak] *nm* nerves *pl*; (*THÉÂT*) stage fright; **avoir le ~** to get an attack of nerves; to have stage fright; **tout à ~** all of a sudden.
traçant, e [tʀasɑ̃, -ɑ̃t] *adj*: **table ~e** (*INFORM*) (graph) plotter.
tracas [tʀaka] *nm* bother *no pl*, worry *no pl*.
tracasser [tʀakase] *vt* to worry, bother; (*harceler*) to harass; **se ~** *vi* to worry o.s., fret.
tracasserie [tʀakasʀi] *nf* annoyance *no pl*; harassment *no pl*.
tracassier, ière [tʀakasje, -jɛʀ] *adj* irksome.
trace [tʀas] *nf* (*empreintes*) tracks *pl*; (*marques, aussi fig*) mark; (*restes, vestige*) trace; (*indice*) sign; **suivre à la ~** to track; **~s de pas** footprints.
tracé [tʀase] *nm* (*contour*) line; (*plan*) layout.
tracer [tʀase] *vt* to draw; (*mot*) to trace; (*piste*) to open up; (*fig: chemin*) to show.
traceur [tʀasœʀ] *nm* (*INFORM*) plotter.
trachée(-artère) [tʀaʃe(aʀtɛʀ)] *nf* windpipe, trachea.
trachéite [tʀakeit] *nf* tracheitis.
tract [tʀakt] *nm* tract, pamphlet; (*publicitaire*) handout.
tractations [tʀaktasjɔ̃] *nfpl* dealings, bargaining *sg*.
tracter [tʀakte] *vt* to tow.
tracteur [tʀaktœʀ] *nm* tractor.
traction [tʀaksjɔ̃] *nf* traction; (*GYM*) pull-up; **~ avant/arrière** front-wheel/rear-wheel drive; **~ électrique** electric(al) traction *ou* haulage.
trad. *abr* (= *traduit*) translated; (= *traduction*) translation; (= *traducteur*) translator.
tradition [tʀadisjɔ̃] *nf* tradition.
traditionalisme [tʀadisjɔnalism(ə)] *nm* traditionalism.
traditionaliste [tʀadisjɔnalist(ə)] *adj, nm/f* traditionalist.
traditionnel, le [tʀadisjɔnɛl] *adj* traditional.
traditionnellement [tʀadisjɔnɛlmɑ̃] *adv* traditionally.
traducteur, trice [tʀadyktœʀ, -tʀis] *nm/f* translator.
traduction [tʀadyksjɔ̃] *nf* translation.
traduire [tʀadɥiʀ] *vt* to translate; (*exprimer*) to render, convey; **se ~ par** to find expression in; **~ en français** to translate into French; **~ en justice** to bring before the courts.
traduis [tʀadɥi] *etc vb voir* **traduire**.
traduisible [tʀadɥizibl(ə)] *adj* translatable.
traduit, e [tʀadɥi, -it] *pp de* **traduire**.
trafic [tʀafik] *nm* traffic; **~ d'armes** arms dealing; **~ de drogue** drug peddling.
trafiquant, e [tʀafikɑ̃, -ɑ̃t] *nm/f* trafficker; dealer.
trafiquer [tʀafike] *vt* (*péj*) to doctor, tamper with ♦ *vi* to traffic, be engaged in traffick-

ing.

tragédie [tʀaʒedi] *nf* tragedy.

tragédien, ne [tʀaʒedjɛ̃, -ɛn] *nm/f* tragedian/ tragedienne.

tragi-comique [tʀaʒikɔmik] *adj* tragi-comic.

tragique [tʀaʒik] *adj* tragic ♦ *nm*: **prendre qch au ~** to make a tragedy out of sth.

tragiquement [tʀaʒikmɑ̃] *adv* tragically.

trahir [tʀaiʀ] *vt* to betray; (*fig*) to give away, reveal; **se ~** to betray o.s., give o.s. away.

trahison [tʀaizɔ̃] *nf* betrayal; (*JUR*) treason.

traie [tʀɛ] *etc vb voir* **traire**.

train [tʀɛ̃] *nm* (*RAIL*) train; (*allure*) pace; (*fig: ensemble*) set; **être en ~ de faire qch** to be doing sth; **mettre qch en ~** to get sth under way; **mettre qn en ~** to put sb in good spirits; **se mettre en ~** (*commencer*) to get started; (*faire de la gymnastique*) to warm up; **se sentir en ~** to feel in good form; **aller bon ~** to make good progress; **~ avant/arrière** front-wheel/rear-wheel axle unit; **~ à grande vitesse (TGV)** high-speed train; **~ d'atterrissage** undercarriage; **~ autos-couchettes** car-sleeper train; **~ électrique** (*jouet*) (electric) train set; **~ de pneus** set of tyres *ou* tires; **~ de vie** style of living.

traînailler [tʀenɑje] *vi* = **traînasser**.

traînant, e [tʀenɑ̃, -ɑ̃t] *adj* (*voix, ton*) drawling.

traînard, e [tʀenaʀ, -aʀd(ə)] *nm/f* (*péj*) slow-coach (*BRIT*), slowpoke (*US*).

traînasser [tʀenase] *vi* to dawdle.

traîne [tʀɛn] *nf* (*de robe*) train; **être à la ~** to be in tow; (*en arrière*) to lag behind; (*en désordre*) to be lying around.

traîneau, x [tʀeno] *nm* sleigh, sledge.

traînée [tʀene] *nf* streak, trail; (*péj*) slut.

traîner [tʀene] *vt* (*remorque*) to pull; (*enfant, chien*) to drag *ou* trail along; (*maladie*): **il traîne un rhume depuis l'hiver** he has a cold which has been dragging on since winter ♦ *vi* (*être en désordre*) to lie around; (*marcher lentement*) to dawdle (along); (*vagabonder*) to hang about; (*agir lentement*) to idle about; (*durer*) to drag on; **se ~** *vi* (*ramper*) to crawl along; (*marcher avec difficulté*) to drag o.s. along; (*durer*) to drag on; **se ~ par terre** to crawl (on the ground); **~ qn au cinéma** to drag sb to the cinema; **~ les pieds** to drag one's feet; **~ par terre** to trail on the ground; **~ en longueur** to drag out.

training [tʀeniŋ] *nm* (*pull*) tracksuit top; (*chaussure*) trainer (*BRIT*), sneaker (*US*).

train-train [tʀɛ̃tʀɛ̃] *nm* humdrum routine.

traire [tʀɛʀ] *vt* to milk.

trait, e [tʀɛ, -ɛt] *pp de* **traire** ♦ *nm* (*ligne*) line; (*de dessin*) stroke; (*caractéristique*) feature, trait; (*flèche*) dart, arrow; shaft; **~s** *nmpl* (*du visage*) features; **d'un ~** (*boire*) in one gulp; **de ~** *adj* (*animal*) draught (*BRIT*), draft (*US*); **avoir ~ à** to concern; **~ pour ~** line for line; **~ de caractère** characteristic, trait; **~ d'esprit** flash of wit; **~ de génie** brainwave;

~ d'union hyphen; (*fig*) link.

traitable [tʀɛtabl(ə)] *adj* (*personne*) accommodating; (*sujet*) manageable.

traitant, e [tʀɛtɑ̃, -ɑ̃t] *adj*: **votre médecin ~** your usual *ou* family doctor; **shampooing ~** medicated shampoo; **crème ~e** conditioning cream, conditioner.

traite [tʀɛt] *nf* (*COMM*) draft; (*AGR*) milking; (*trajet*) stretch; **d'une (seule) ~** without stopping (once); **la ~ des noirs** the slave trade; **la ~ des blanches** the white slave trade.

traité [tʀete] *nm* treaty.

traitement [tʀɛtmɑ̃] *nm* treatment; processing; (*salaire*) salary; **suivre un ~** to undergo treatment; **mauvais ~** ill-treatment; **~ de données** *ou* **de l'information** (*INFORM*) data processing; **~ hormono-supplétif** hormone replacement therapy; **~ par lots** (*INFORM*) batch processing; **~ de texte** (*INFORM*) word processing.

traiter [tʀete] *vt* (*gén*) to treat; (*TECH: matériaux*) to process, treat; (*INFORM*) to process; (*affaire*) to deal with, handle; (*qualifier*): **~ qn d'idiot** to call sb a fool ♦ *vi* to deal; **~ de** *vt* to deal with; **bien/mal ~** to treat well/ill-treat.

traiteur [tʀɛtœʀ] *nm* caterer.

traître, esse [tʀɛtʀ(ə), -tʀɛs] *adj* (*dangereux*) treacherous ♦ *nm* traitor; **prendre qn en ~** to take sb off-guard.

traîtrise [tʀetʀiz] *nf* treachery.

trajectoire [tʀaʒɛktwaʀ] *nf* trajectory, path.

trajet [tʀaʒɛ] *nm* journey; (*itinéraire*) route; (*fig*) path, course.

tralala [tʀalala] *nm* (*péj*) fuss.

tram [tʀam] *nm* tram (*BRIT*), streetcar (*US*).

trame [tʀam] *nf* (*de tissu*) weft; (*fig*) framework; texture; (*TYPO*) screen.

tramer [tʀame] *vt* to plot, hatch.

trampoline [tʀɑ̃pɔlin], **trampolino** [tʀɑ̃pɔlino] *nm* trampoline; (*SPORT*) trampolining.

tramway [tʀamwɛ] *nm* tram(way); (*voiture*) tram(car) (*BRIT*), streetcar (*US*).

tranchant, e [tʀɑ̃ʃɑ̃, -ɑ̃t] *adj* sharp; (*fig: personne*) peremptory; (: *couleurs*) striking ♦ *nm* (*d'un couteau*) cutting edge; (*de la main*) edge; **à double ~** (*argument, procédé*) double-edged.

tranche [tʀɑ̃ʃ] *nf* (*morceau*) slice; (*arête*) edge; (*partie*) section; (*série*) block; (*d'impôts, revenus etc*) bracket; (*loterie*) issue; **~ d'âge** age bracket; **~ (de silicium)** wafer.

tranché, e [tʀɑ̃ʃe] *adj* (*couleurs*) distinct, sharply contrasted; (*opinions*) clear-cut, definite ♦ *nf* trench.

trancher [tʀɑ̃ʃe] *vt* to cut, sever; (*fig: résoudre*) to settle ♦ *vi* to be decisive; (*entre deux choses*) to settle the argument; **~ avec** to contrast sharply with.

tranchet [tʀɑ̃ʃɛ] *nm* knife.

tranchoir [tʀɑ̃ʃwaʀ] *nm* chopper.

tranquille [tʀɑ̃kil] *adj* calm, quiet; (*enfant,*

élève) quiet; (*rassuré*) easy in one's mind, with one's mind at rest; **se tenir** ~ (*enfant*) to be quiet; **avoir la conscience** ~ to have an easy conscience; **laisse-moi/laisse-ça** ~ leave me/it alone.

tranquillement [tʀɑ̃kilmɑ̃] *adv* calmly.

tranquillisant, e [tʀɑ̃kilizɑ̃, -ɑ̃t] *adj* (*nouvelle*) reassuring ♦ *nm* tranquillizer.

tranquilliser [tʀɑ̃kilize] *vt* to reassure; **se** ~ to calm (o.s.) down.

tranquillité [tʀɑ̃kilite] *nf* quietness; peace (and quiet); **en toute** ~ with complete peace of mind; ~ **d'esprit** peace of mind.

transaction [tʀɑ̃zaksjɔ̃] *nf* (*COMM*) transaction, deal.

transafricain, e [tʀɑ̃safʀikɛ̃, -ɛn] *adj* transafrican.

transalpin, e [tʀɑ̃zalpɛ̃, -in] *adj* transalpine.

transaméricain, e [tʀɑ̃zameʀikɛ̃, -ɛn] *adj* transamerican.

transat [tʀɑ̃zat] *nm* deckchair ♦ *nf* = *course transatlantique*.

transatlantique [tʀɑ̃zatlɑ̃tik] *adj* transatlantic ♦ *nm* transatlantic liner.

transborder [tʀɑ̃sbɔʀde] *vt* to tran(s)ship.

transcendant, e [tʀɑ̃sɑ̃dɑ̃, -ɑ̃t] *adj* (*PHILOSO-PHIE, MATH*) transcendental; (*supérieur*) transcendent.

transcodeur [tʀɑ̃skɔdœʀ] *nm* compiler.

transcontinental, e, aux [tʀɑ̃skɔ̃tinɑ̃tal, -o] *adj* transcontinental.

transcription [tʀɑ̃skʀipsjɔ̃] *nf* transcription.

transcrire [tʀɑ̃skʀiʀ] *vt* to transcribe.

transe [tʀɑ̃s] *nf*: **entrer en** ~ to go into a trance; ~**s** *nfpl* agony *sg*.

transférable [tʀɑ̃sfeʀabl(ə)] *adj* transferable.

transfèrement [tʀɑ̃sfɛʀmɑ̃] *nm* transfer.

transférer [tʀɑ̃sfeʀe] *vt* to transfer.

transfert [tʀɑ̃sfɛʀ] *nm* transfer.

transfiguration [tʀɑ̃sfigyʀasjɔ̃] *nf* transformation, transfiguration.

transfigurer [tʀɑ̃sfigyʀe] *vt* to transform.

transfo [tʀɑ̃sfo] *nm* (= *transformateur*) transformer.

transformable [tʀɑ̃sfɔʀmabl(ə)] *adj* convertible.

transformateur [tʀɑ̃sfɔʀmatœʀ] *nm* transformer.

transformation [tʀɑ̃sfɔʀmasjɔ̃] *nf* transformation; (*RUGBY*) conversion; **industries de** ~ processing industries.

transformer [tʀɑ̃sfɔʀme] *vt* to transform, alter (*"alter" implique un changement moins radical*); (*matière première, appartement, RUGBY*) to convert; ~ **en** to transform into; to turn into; to convert into; **se** ~ *vi* to be transformed; to alter.

transfuge [tʀɑ̃sfyʒ] *nm* renegade.

transfuser [tʀɑ̃sfyze] *vt* to transfuse.

transfusion [tʀɑ̃sfyzjɔ̃] *nf*: ~ **sanguine** blood transfusion.

transgresser [tʀɑ̃sgʀese] *vt* to contravene, disobey.

transhumance [tʀɑ̃zymɑ̃s] *nf* transhumance, seasonal move to new pastures.

transi, e [tʀɑ̃zi] *adj* numb (with cold), chilled to the bone.

transiger [tʀɑ̃ziʒe] *vi* to compromise, come to an agreement; ~ **sur** *ou* **avec qch** to compromise on sth.

transistor [tʀɑ̃zistɔʀ] *nm* transistor.

transistorisé, e [tʀɑ̃zistɔʀize] *adj* transistorized.

transit [tʀɑ̃zit] *nm* transit; **de** ~ transit *cpd*; **en** ~ in transit.

transitaire [tʀɑ̃zitɛʀ] *nm/f* forwarding agent.

transiter [tʀɑ̃zite] *vi* to pass in transit.

transitif, ive [tʀɑ̃zitif, -iv] *adj* transitive.

transition [tʀɑ̃zisjɔ̃] *nf* transition; **de** ~ transitional.

transitoire [tʀɑ̃zitwaʀ] *adj* (*mesure, gouvernement*) transitional, provisional; (*fugitif*) transient.

translucide [tʀɑ̃slysid] *adj* translucent.

transmet [tʀɑ̃smɛ] *etc vb voir* **transmettre**.

transmettais [tʀɑ̃smɛtɛ] *etc vb voir* **transmettre**.

transmetteur [tʀɑ̃smɛtœʀ] *nm* transmitter.

transmettre [tʀɑ̃smɛtʀ(ə)] *vt* (*passer*): ~ **qch à qn** to pass sth on to sb; (*TECH, TÉL, MÉD*) to transmit; (*TV, RADIO: retransmettre*) to broadcast.

transmis, e [tʀɑ̃smi, -iz] *pp de* **transmettre**.

transmissible [tʀɑ̃smisibl(ə)] *adj* transmissible.

transmission [tʀɑ̃smisjɔ̃] *nf* transmission, passing on; (*AUTO*) transmission; ~**s** *nfpl* (*MIL*) ≈ signals corps *sg*; ~ **de données** (*IN-FORM*) data transmission; ~ **de pensée** thought transmission.

transocéanien, ne [tʀɑ̃zɔseanjɛ̃, -ɛn] *adj*, **transocéanique** [tʀɑ̃zɔseanik] *adj* transoceanic.

transparaître [tʀɑ̃spaʀɛtʀ(ə)] *vi* to show (through).

transparence [tʀɑ̃spaʀɑ̃s] *nf* transparence; **par** ~ (*regarder*) against the light; (*voir*) showing through.

transparent, e [tʀɑ̃spaʀɑ̃, -ɑ̃t] *adj* transparent.

transpercer [tʀɑ̃spɛʀse] *vt* to go through, pierce.

transpiration [tʀɑ̃spiʀasjɔ̃] *nf* perspiration.

transpirer [tʀɑ̃spiʀe] *vi* to perspire; (*information, nouvelle*) to come to light.

transplant [tʀɑ̃splɑ̃] *nm* transplant.

transplantation [tʀɑ̃splɑ̃tasjɔ̃] *nf* transplant.

transplanter [tʀɑ̃splɑ̃te] *vt* (*MÉD, BOT*) to transplant; (*personne*) to uproot, move.

transport [tʀɑ̃spɔʀ] *nm* transport; (*émotions*): ~ **de colère** fit of rage; ~ **de joie** transport of delight; ~ **de voyageurs/marchandises** passenger/goods transportation; ~**s en commun** public transport *sg*; ~**s routiers**

haulage (*BRIT*), trucking (*US*).

transportable [tʀɑ̃spɔʀtabl(ə)] *adj* (*marchandises*) transportable; (*malade*) fit (enough) to be moved.

transporter [tʀɑ̃spɔʀte] *vt* to carry, move; (*COMM*) to transport, convey; (*fig*): ~ **qn (de joie)** to send sb into raptures; **se ~ quelque part** (*fig*) to let one's imagination carry one away (somewhere); ~ **qn à l'hôpital** to take sb to hospital.

transporteur [tʀɑ̃spɔʀtœʀ] *nm* haulage contractor (*BRIT*), trucker (*US*).

transposer [tʀɑ̃spoze] *vt* to transpose.

transposition [tʀɑ̃spozisjɔ̃] *nf* transposition.

transrhénan, e [tʀɑ̃sʀenɑ̃, -an] *adj* transrhenane.

transsaharien, ne [tʀɑ̃ssaaʀjɛ̃, -ɛn] *adj* trans-Saharan.

transsexuel, le [tʀɑ̃ssɛksɥɛl] *adj*, *nm/f* transsexual.

transsibérien, ne [tʀɑ̃ssibeʀjɛ̃, -ɛn] *adj* trans-Siberian.

transvaser [tʀɑ̃svaze] *vt* to decant.

transversal, e, aux [tʀɑ̃svɛʀsal, -o] *adj* transverse, cross(-); (*route etc*) cross-country; (*mur, chemin, rue*) running at right angles; (*AUTO*): **axe** ~ main cross-country road (*BRIT*) *ou* highway (*US*).

transversalement [tʀɑ̃svɛʀsalmɑ̃] *adv* crosswise.

trapèze [tʀapɛz] *nm* (*GÉOM*) trapezium; (*au cirque*) trapeze.

trapéziste [tʀapezist(ə)] *nm/f* trapeze artist.

trappe [tʀap] *nf* (*de cave, grenier*) trap door; (*piège*) trap.

trappeur [tʀapœʀ] *nm* trapper, fur trader.

trapu, e [tʀapy] *adj* squat, stocky.

traquenard [tʀaknaʀ] *nm* trap.

traquer [tʀake] *vt* to track down; (*harceler*) to hound.

traumatisant, e [tʀomatizɑ̃, -ɑ̃t] *adj* traumatic.

traumatiser [tʀomatize] *vt* to traumatize.

traumatisme [tʀomatism(ə)] *nm* traumatism; ~ **crânien** cranial traumatism.

traumatologie [tʀomatɔlɔʒi] *nf* branch of medicine concerned with accidents.

travail, aux [tʀavaj, -o] *nm* (*gén*) work; (*tâche, métier*) work *no pl*, job; (*ÉCON, MÉD*) labour (*BRIT*), labor (*US*); (*INFORM*) job ♦ *nmpl* (*de réparation, agricoles etc*) work *sg*; (*sur route*) roadworks; (*de construction*) building (work) *sg*; **être/entrer en** ~ (*MÉD*) to be in/go into labour; **être sans** ~ (*employé*) to be out of work, be unemployed; ~ **d'intérêt général (TIG)** ≈ community service; ~ **(au) noir** moonlighting; ~ **posté** shiftwork; **travaux des champs** farmwork *sg*; **travaux dirigés (TD)** (*SCOL*) supervised practical work *sg*; **travaux forcés** hard labour *sg*; **travaux manuels** (*SCOL*) handicrafts; **travaux ménagers** housework *sg*; **travaux pratiques (TP)** (*gén*) practical work; (*en laboratoire*) lab work

(*BRIT*), lab (*US*); **travaux publics (TP)** ≈ public works *sg*.

travaillé, e [tʀavaje] *adj* (*style*) polished.

travailler [tʀavaje] *vi* to work; (*bois*) to warp ♦ *vt* (*bois, métal*) to work; (*pâte*) to knead; (*objet d'art, discipline, fig: influencer*) to work on; **cela le travaille** it is on his mind; ~ **la terre** to work the land; ~ **son piano** to do one's piano practice; ~ **à** to work on; (*fig: contribuer à*) to work towards; ~ **à faire** to endeavour (*BRIT*) *ou* endeavor (*US*) to do.

travailleur, euse [tʀavajœʀ, -øz] *adj* hardworking ♦ *nm/f* worker; ~ **de force** labourer (*BRIT*), laborer (*US*); ~ **intellectuel** nonmanual worker; ~ **social** social worker; **travailleuse familiale** home help.

travailliste [tʀavajist(ə)] *adj* ≈ Labour *cpd* ♦ *nm/f* member of the Labour party.

travée [tʀave] *nf* row; (*ARCHIT*) bay; span.

traveller's (chèque) [tʀavlœʀs(ʃɛk)] *nm* traveller's cheque.

travelling [tʀavliŋ] *nm* (*chariot*) dolly; (*technique*) tracking; ~ **optique** zoom shots *pl*.

travelo [tʀavlo] *nm* (*fam*) (drag) queen.

travers [tʀavɛʀ] *nm* fault, failing; **en** ~ **(de)** across; **au** ~ **(de)** through; **de** ~ *adj* askew ♦ *adv* sideways; (*fig*) the wrong way; **à** ~ through; **regarder de** ~ (*fig*) to look askance at.

traverse [tʀavɛʀs(ə)] *nf* (*de voie ferrée*) sleeper; **chemin de** ~ shortcut.

traversée [tʀavɛʀse] *nf* crossing.

traverser [tʀavɛʀse] *vt* (*gén*) to cross; (*ville, tunnel, aussi: percer, fig*) to go through; (*suj: ligne, trait*) to run across.

traversin [tʀavɛʀsɛ̃] *nm* bolster.

travesti [tʀavesti] *nm* (*costume*) fancy dress; (*artiste de cabaret*) female impersonator, drag artist; (*pervers*) transvestite.

travestir [tʀavestiʀ] *vt* (*vérité*) to misrepresent; **se** ~ (*se costumer*) to dress up; (*artiste*) to put on drag; (*PSYCH*) to dress as a woman.

trayais [tʀɛjɛ] *etc vb voir* **traire**.

trayeuse [tʀɛjøz] *nf* milking machine.

trébucher [tʀebyʃe] *vi*: ~ **(sur)** to stumble (over), trip (over).

trèfle [tʀɛfl(ə)] *nm* (*BOT*) clover; (*CARTES: couleur*) clubs *pl*; (*: carte*) club; **à quatre feuilles** four-leaf clover.

treillage [tʀɛjaʒ] *nm* lattice work.

treille [tʀɛj] *nf* (*tonnelle*) vine arbour (*BRIT*) *ou* arbor (*US*); (*vigne*) climbing vine.

treillis [tʀɛji] *nm* (*métallique*) wire-mesh; (*toile*) canvas; (*uniforme*) battle-dress.

treize [tʀɛz] *num* thirteen.

treizième [tʀɛzjɛm] *num* thirteenth.

Le treizième mois *is an end-of-year bonus corresponding roughly to one month's salary. For many employees it is a standard part of their salary package.*

tréma [tʁema] *nm* diaeresis.
tremblant, e [tʁɑ̃blɑ̃, -ɑ̃t] *adj* trembling, shaking.
tremble [tʁɑ̃bl(ə)] *nm* (*BOT*) aspen.
tremblé, e [tʁɑ̃ble] *adj* shaky.
tremblement [tʁɑ̃bləmɑ̃] *nm* trembling *no pl*, shaking *no pl*, shivering *no pl*; ~ **de terre** earthquake.
trembler [tʁɑ̃ble] *vi* to tremble, shake; ~ **de** (*froid, fièvre*) to shiver *ou* tremble with; (*peur*) to shake *ou* tremble with; ~ **pour qn** to fear for sb.
tremblotant, e [tʁɑ̃blɔtɑ̃, -ɑ̃t] *adj* trembling.
trembloter [tʁɑ̃blɔte] *vi* to tremble *ou* shake slightly.
trémolo [tʁemɔlo] *nm* (*d'un instrument*) tremolo; (*de la voix*) quaver.
trémousser [tʁemuse]: **se** ~ *vi* to jig about, wriggle about.
trempe [tʁɑ̃p] *nf* (*fig*): **de cette/sa** ~ of this/his calibre (*BRIT*) *ou* caliber (*US*).
trempé, e [tʁɑ̃pe] *adj* soaking (wet), drenched; (*TECH*): **acier** ~ tempered steel.
tremper [tʁɑ̃pe] *vt* to soak, drench; (*aussi*: **faire** ~, **mettre à** ~) to soak; (*plonger*): ~ **qch dans** to dip sth in(to) ♦ *vi* to soak; (*fig*): ~ **dans** to be involved *ou* have a hand in; **se** ~ *vi* to have a quick dip; **se faire** ~ to get soaked *ou* drenched.
trempette [tʁɑ̃pet] *nf*: **faire** ~ to go paddling.
tremplin [tʁɑ̃plɛ̃] *nm* springboard; (*SKI*) ski jump.
trentaine [tʁɑ̃tɛn] *nf* (*âge*): **avoir la** ~ to be around thirty; **une** ~ **(de)** thirty or so, about thirty.
trente [tʁɑ̃t] *num* thirty; **voir** ~-**six chandelles** (*fig*) to see stars; **être/se mettre sur son** ~ **et un** to be/get dressed to kill; ~-**trois tours** *nm* long-playing record, LP.
trentième [tʁɑ̃tjɛm] *num* thirtieth.
trépanation [tʁepanasjɔ̃] *nf* trepan.
trépaner [tʁepane] *vt* to trepan, trephine.
trépasser [tʁepase] *vi* to pass away.
trépidant, e [tʁepidɑ̃, -ɑ̃t] *adj* (*fig: rythme*) pulsating; (*: vie*) hectic.
trépidation [tʁepidasjɔ̃] *nf* (*d'une machine, d'un moteur*) vibration; (*fig: de la vie*) whirl.
trépider [tʁepide] *vi* to vibrate.
trépied [tʁepje] *nm* (*d'appareil*) tripod; (*meuble*) trivet.
trépignement [tʁepiɲmɑ̃] *nm* stamping (of feet).
trépigner [tʁepiɲe] *vi* to stamp (one's feet).
très [tʁɛ] *adv* very; much + *pp*, highly + *pp*; ~ **beau/bien** very beautiful/well; ~ **critiqué** much criticized; ~ **industrialisé** highly industrialized; **j'ai** ~ **faim** I'm very hungry.
trésor [tʁezɔʁ] *nm* treasure; (*ADMIN*) finances *pl*; (*d'un organisation*) funds *pl*; ~ **(public) (TP)** public revenue; (*service*) public revenue office.
trésorerie [tʁezɔʁʁi] *nf* (*fonds*) funds *pl*; (*gestion*) accounts *pl*; (*bureaux*) accounts department; (*poste*) treasurership; **difficultés de** ~ cash problems, shortage of cash *ou* funds; ~ **générale (TG)** *local government finance office*.
trésorier, ière [tʁezɔʁje, -jɛʁ] *nm/f* treasurer.
Trésorier-payeur [tʁezɔʁjepɛjœʁ] *nm*: ~ **général (TPG)** paymaster.
tressaillement [tʁesajmɑ̃] *nm* shiver, shudder; quiver.
tressaillir [tʁesajiʁ] *vi* (*de peur etc*) to shiver, shudder; (*de joie*) to quiver.
tressauter [tʁesote] *vi* to start, jump.
tresse [tʁɛs] *nf* (*de cheveux*) braid, plait; (*cordon, galon*) braid.
tresser [tʁese] *vt* (*cheveux*) to braid, plait; (*fil, jonc*) to plait; (*corbeille*) to weave; (*corde*) to twist.
tréteau, x [tʁeto] *nm* trestle; **les** ~**x** (*fig: THÉÂT*) the boards.
treuil [tʁœj] *nm* winch.
trêve [tʁɛv] *nf* (*MIL, POL*) truce; (*fig*) respite; **sans** ~ unremittingly; ~ **de** ... enough of this ...; **les États de la T**~ the Trucial States.
tri [tʁi] *nm* (*voir trier*) sorting (out) *no pl*; selection; screening; (*INFORM*) sort; (*POSTES: action*) sorting; (*: bureau*) sorting office.
triage [tʁijaʒ] *nm* (*RAIL*) shunting; (*gare*) marshalling yard.
trial [tʁijal] *nm* (*SPORT*) scrambling.
triangle [tʁijɑ̃gl(ə)] *nm* triangle; ~ **isocèle/équilatéral** isosceles/equilateral triangle; ~ **rectangle** right-angled triangle.
triangulaire [tʁijɑ̃gylɛʁ] *adj* triangular.
triathlon [tʁi(j)atlɔ̃] *nm* triathlon.
tribal, e, aux [tʁibal, -o] *adj* tribal.
tribord [tʁibɔʁ] *nm*: **à** ~ to starboard, on the starboard side.
tribu [tʁiby] *nf* tribe.
tribulations [tʁibylasjɔ̃] *nfpl* tribulations, trials.
tribunal, aux [tʁibynal, -o] *nm* (*JUR*) court; (*MIL*) tribunal; ~ **de police/pour enfants** police/juvenile court; ~ **d'instance (TI)** ≈ magistrates' court (*BRIT*), ≈ district court (*US*); ~ **de grande instance (TGI)** ≈ High Court (*BRIT*), ≈ Supreme Court (*US*).
tribune [tʁibyn] *nf* (*estrade*) platform, rostrum; (*débat*) forum; (*d'église, de tribunal*) gallery; (*de stade*) stand; ~ **libre** (*PRESSE*) opinion column.
tribut [tʁiby] *nm* tribute.
tributaire [tʁibytɛʁ] *adj*: **être** ~ **de** to be dependent on; (*GÉO*) to be a tributary of.
tricentenaire [tʁisɑ̃tnɛʁ] *nm* tercentenary, tricentennial.
tricher [tʁiʃe] *vi* to cheat.
tricherie [tʁiʃʁi] *nf* cheating *no pl*.
tricheur, euse [tʁiʃœʁ, -øz] *nm/f* cheat.
trichromie [tʁikʁɔmi] *nf* three-colour (*BRIT*) -color (*US*) printing.
tricolore [tʁikɔlɔʁ] *adj* three-coloured (*BRIT*),

three-colored (US); (français: drapeau) red, white and blue; (: équipe etc) French.

tricot [tʀiko] nm (technique, ouvrage) knitting no pl; (tissu) knitted fabric; (vêtement) jersey, sweater; ~ **de corps** vest (BRIT), undershirt (US).

tricoter [tʀikɔte] vt to knit; **machine/aiguille à** ~ knitting machine/needle (BRIT) ou pin (US).

trictrac [tʀiktʀak] nm backgammon.

tricycle [tʀisikl(ə)] nm tricycle.

tridimensionnel, le [tʀidimãsjɔnɛl] adj three-dimensional.

triennal, e, aux [tʀiɛnal, -o] adj (prix, foire, élection) three-yearly; (charge, mandat, plan) three-year.

trier [tʀije] vt (classer) to sort (out); (choisir) to select; (visiteurs) to screen; (POSTES, INFORM) to sort.

trieur, euse [tʀijœʀ, -øz] nm/f sorter.

trigonométrie [tʀigɔnɔmetʀi] nf trigonometry.

trigonométrique [tʀigɔnɔmetʀik] adj trigonometric.

trilingue [tʀilɛ̃g] adj trilingual.

trilogie [tʀilɔʒi] nf trilogy.

trimaran [tʀimaʀɑ̃] nm trimaran.

trimbaler [tʀɛ̃bale] vt to cart around, trail along.

trimer [tʀime] vi to slave away.

trimestre [tʀimɛstʀ(ə)] nm (SCOL) term; (COMM) quarter.

trimestriel, le [tʀimɛstʀijɛl] adj quarterly; (SCOL) end-of-term.

trimoteur [tʀimɔtœʀ] nm three-engined aircraft.

tringle [tʀɛ̃gl(ə)] nf rod.

Trinité [tʀinite] nf Trinity.

Trinité et Tobago [tʀiniteetɔbago] nf Trinidad and Tobago.

trinquer [tʀɛ̃ke] vi to clink glasses; (fam) to cop it; ~ **à qch/la santé de qn** to drink to sth/sb.

trio [tʀijo] nm trio.

triolet [tʀijɔlɛ] nm (MUS) triplet.

triomphal, e, aux [tʀijɔ̃fal, -o] adj triumphant, triumphal.

triomphalement [tʀijɔ̃falmã] adv triumphantly.

triomphant, e [tʀijɔ̃fɑ̃, -ɑ̃t] adj triumphant.

triomphateur, trice [tʀijɔ̃fatœʀ, -tʀis] nm/f (triumphant) victor.

triomphe [tʀijɔ̃f] nm triumph; **être reçu/porté en** ~ to be given a triumphant welcome/be carried shoulder-high in triumph.

triompher [tʀijɔ̃fe] vi to triumph; ~ **de** to triumph over, overcome.

triparti, e [tʀipaʀti] adj (aussi: **tripartite**: réunion, assemblée) tripartite, three-party.

triperie [tʀipʀi] nf tripe shop.

tripes [tʀip] nfpl (CULIN) tripe sg; (fam) guts.

triplace [tʀiplas] adj three-seater cpd.

triple [tʀipl(ə)] adj (à trois élements) triple; (trois fois plus grand) treble ♦ nm: **le** ~ **(de)** (comparaison) three times as much (as); **en** ~ **exemplaire** in triplicate; ~ **saut** (SPORT) triple jump.

triplé [tʀiple] nm hat-trick (BRIT), triple success.

triplement [tʀipləmã] adv (à un degré triple) three times over; (de trois façons) in three ways; (pour trois raisons) on three counts ♦ nm trebling, threefold increase.

tripler [tʀiple] vi, vt to triple, treble, increase threefold.

triplés, ées [tʀiple] nm/fpl triplets.

Tripoli [tʀipoli] n Tripoli.

triporteur [tʀipɔʀtœʀ] nm delivery tricycle.

tripot [tʀipo] nm (péj) dive.

tripotage [tʀipotaʒ] nm (péj) jiggery-pokery.

tripoter [tʀipote] vt to fiddle with, finger ♦ vi (fam) to rummage about.

trique [tʀik] nf cudgel.

trisannuel, le [tʀizanɥɛl] adj triennial.

trisomie [tʀizomi] nf Down's syndrome.

triste [tʀist(ə)] adj sad; (péj): ~ **personnage/ affaire** sorry individual/affair; **c'est pas** ~! (fam) it's something else!

tristement [tʀistəmã] adv sadly.

tristesse [tʀistɛs] nf sadness.

triton [tʀitɔ̃] nm triton.

triturer [tʀityʀe] vt (pâte) to knead; (objets) to manipulate.

trivial, e, aux [tʀivjal, -o] adj coarse, crude; (commun) mundane.

trivialité [tʀivjalite] nf coarseness, crudeness; mundaneness.

troc [tʀɔk] nm (ÉCON) barter; (transaction) exchange, swap.

troène [tʀɔɛn] nm privet.

troglodyte [tʀɔglɔdit] nm/f cave dweller, troglodyte.

trognon [tʀɔɲɔ̃] nm (de fruit) core; (de légume) stalk.

trois [tʀwa] num three.

trois-huit [tʀwaɥit] nmpl: **faire les** ~ to work eight-hour shifts (round the clock).

troisième [tʀwazjɛm] num third; **le** ~ **âge** the years of retirement.

troisièmement [tʀwazjɛmmã] adv thirdly.

trois quarts [tʀwakaʀ] nmpl: **les** ~ **de** three-quarters of.

trolleybus [tʀɔlɛbys] nm trolley bus.

trombe [tʀɔ̃b] nf waterspout; **des** ~**s d'eau** a downpour; **en** ~ (arriver, passer) like a whirlwind.

trombone [tʀɔ̃bɔn] nm (MUS) trombone; (de bureau) paper clip; ~ **à coulisse** slide trombone.

tromboniste [tʀɔ̃bonist(ə)] nm/f trombonist.

trompe [tʀɔ̃p] nf (d'éléphant) trunk; (MUS) trumpet, horn; ~ **d'Eustache** Eustachian tube; ~**s utérines** Fallopian tubes.

trompe-l'œil [tʀɔ̃plœj] nm: **en** ~ in trompe-l'œil style.

tromper [tʀɔ̃pe] *vt* to deceive; (*fig: espoir, attente*) to disappoint; (*vigilance, poursuivants*) to elude; **se ~** *vi* to make a mistake, be mistaken; **se ~ de voiture/jour** to take the wrong car/get the day wrong; **se ~ de 3 cm/20 F** to be out by 3 cm/20 F.

tromperie [tʀɔ̃pʀi] *nf* deception, trickery *no pl*.

trompette [tʀɔ̃pɛt] *nf* trumpet; **en ~** (*nez*) turned-up.

trompettiste [tʀɔ̃petist(ə)] *nm/f* trumpet player.

trompeur, euse [tʀɔ̃pœʀ, -øz] *adj* deceptive, misleading.

tronc [tʀɔ̃] *nm* (*BOT, ANAT*) trunk; (*d'église*) collection box; **~ d'arbre** tree trunk; **~ commun** (*SCOL*) common-core syllabus; **~ de cône** truncated cone.

tronche [tʀɔ̃ʃ] *nf* (*fam*) mug, face.

tronçon [tʀɔ̃sɔ̃] *nm* section.

tronçonner [tʀɔ̃sɔne] *vt* (*arbre*) to saw up; (*pierre*) to cut up.

tronçonneuse [tʀɔ̃sɔnøz] *nf* chain saw.

trône [tʀon] *nm* throne; **monter sur le ~** to ascend the throne.

trôner [tʀone] *vi* (*fig*) to have (*ou* take) pride of place (*BRIT*), have the place of honour (*BRIT*) *ou* honor (*US*).

tronquer [tʀɔ̃ke] *vt* to truncate; (*fig*) to curtail.

trop [tʀo] *adv vb +* too much; too + *adjectif, adverbe*; **~ (nombreux)** too many; **~ peu (nombreux)** too few; **~ (souvent)** too often; **~ (longtemps)** (for) too long; **~ de** (*nombre*) too many; (*quantité*) too much; **de ~, en ~**: **des livres en ~** a few books too many, a few extra books; **du lait en ~** too much milk; **3 livres/5 F de ~** 3 books too many/5 F too much.

trophée [tʀɔfe] *nm* trophy.

tropical, e, aux [tʀɔpikal, -o] *adj* tropical.

tropique [tʀɔpik] *nm* tropic; **~s** *nmpl* tropics; **~ du Cancer/Capricorne** Tropic of Cancer/Capricorn.

trop-plein [tʀoplɛ̃] *nm* (*tuyau*) overflow *ou* outlet (pipe); (*liquide*) overflow.

troquer [tʀɔke] *vt*: **~ qch contre** to barter *ou* trade sth for; (*fig*) to swap sth for.

trot [tʀo] *nm* trot; **aller au ~** to trot along; **partir au ~** to set off at a trot.

trotter [tʀɔte] *vi* to trot; (*fig*) to scamper along (*ou* about).

trotteuse [tʀɔtøz] *nf* (*de montre*) second hand.

trottiner [tʀɔtine] *vi* (*fig*) to scamper along (*ou* about).

trottinette [tʀɔtinɛt] *nf* (child's) scooter.

trottoir [tʀɔtwaʀ] *nm* pavement (*BRIT*), sidewalk (*US*); **faire le ~** (*péj*) to walk the streets; **~ roulant** moving pavement (*BRIT*) *ou* walkway.

trou [tʀu] *nm* hole; (*fig*) gap; (*COMM*) deficit; **~ d'aération** (air) vent; **~ d'air** air pocket; **~**

de mémoire blank, lapse of memory; **~ noir** black hole; **~ de la serrure** keyhole.

troublant, e [tʀublɑ̃, -ɑ̃t] *adj* disturbing.

trouble [tʀubl(ə)] *adj* (*liquide*) cloudy; (*image, mémoire*) indistinct, hazy; (*affaire*) shady, murky ♦ *adv* indistinctly ♦ *nm* (*désarroi*) distress, agitation; (*émoi sensuel*) turmoil, agitation; (*embarras*) confusion; (*zizanie*) unrest, discord; **~s** *nmpl* (*POL*) disturbances, troubles, unrest *sg*; (*MÉD*) trouble *sg*, disorders; **~s de la personnalité** personality problems; **~s de la vision** eye trouble.

trouble-fête [tʀubləfɛt] *nm/f inv* spoilsport.

troubler [tʀuble] *vt* (*embarrasser*) to confuse, disconcert; (*émouvoir*) to agitate; to disturb; to perturb; (*perturber: ordre etc*) to disrupt, disturb; (*liquide*) to make cloudy; **se ~** *vi* (*personne*) to become flustered *ou* confused; **~ l'ordre public** to cause a breach of the peace.

troué, e [tʀue] *adj* with a hole (*ou* holes) in it ♦ *nf* gap; (*MIL*) breach.

trouer [tʀue] *vt* to make a hole (*ou* holes) in; (*fig*) to pierce.

trouille [tʀuj] *nf* (*fam*): **avoir la ~** to be scared stiff, be scared out of one's wits.

troupe [tʀup] *nf* (*MIL*) troop; (*groupe*) troop, group; **la ~** (*MIL: l'armée*) the army; (: *les simples soldats*) the troops *pl*; **~ (de théâtre)** (theatrical) company; **~s de choc** shock troops.

troupeau, x [tʀupo] *nm* (*de moutons*) flock; (*de vaches*) herd.

trousse [tʀus] *nf* case, kit; (*d'écolier*) pencil case; (*de docteur*) instrument case; **aux ~s de** (*fig*) on the heels *ou* tail of; **~ à outils** toolkit; **~ de toilette** toilet *ou* sponge (*BRIT*) bag.

trousseau, x [tʀuso] *nm* (*de mariée*) trousseau; **~ de clefs** bunch of keys.

trouvaille [tʀuvaj] *nf* find; (*fig: idée, expression etc*) brainwave.

trouvé, e [tʀuve] *adj*: **tout ~** ready-made.

trouver [tʀuve] *vt* to find; (*rendre visite*): **aller/venir ~ qn** to go/come and see sb; **je trouve que** I find *ou* think that; **~ à boire/critiquer** to find something to drink/criticize; **~ asile/refuge** to find refuge/shelter; **se ~** *vi* (*être*) to be; (*être soudain*) to find o.s.; **se ~ être/avoir** to happen to be/have; **il se trouve que** it happens that, it turns out that; **se ~ bien** to feel well; **se ~ mal** to pass out.

truand [tʀyɑ̃] *nm* villain, crook.

truander [tʀyɑ̃de] *vi* (*fam*) to cheat, do.

trublion [tʀyblijɔ̃] *nm* troublemaker.

truc [tʀyk] *nm* (*astuce*) way, device; (*de cinéma, prestidigitateur*) trick effect; (*chose*) thing; (*machin*) thingumajig, whatsit (*BRIT*); **avoir le ~** to have the knack; **c'est pas son** (*ou* **mon** *etc*) **~** (*fam*) it's not really his (*ou* my *etc*) thing.

truchement [tʀyʃmɑ̃] *nm*: **par le ~ de qn**

through (the intervention of) sb.

trucider [tʀyside] *vt (fam)* to do in, bump off.

truculence [tʀykylɑ̃s] *nf* colourfulness (*BRIT*), colorfulness (*US*).

truculent, e [tʀykylɑ̃, -ɑ̃t] *adj* colourful (*BRIT*), colorful (*US*).

truelle [tʀyɛl] *nf* trowel.

truffe [tʀyf] *nf* truffle; (*nez*) nose.

truffer [tʀyfe] *vt (CULIN)* to garnish with truffles; **truffé de** (*fig: citations*) peppered with; (*: pièges*) bristling with.

truie [tʀɥi] *nf* sow.

truite [tʀɥit] *nf* trout *inv*.

truquage [tʀykaʒ] *nm* fixing; (*CINÉ*) special effects *pl*.

truquer [tʀyke] *vt (élections, serrure, dés)* to fix; (*CINÉ*) to use special effects in.

trust [tʀœst] *nm (COMM)* trust.

truster [tʀœste] *vt (COMM)* to monopolize.

ts *abr* = **tous**.

tsar [dzaʀ] *nm* tsar.

tsé-tsé [tsetse] *nf*: **mouche ~** tsetse fly.

TSF *sigle f* (= *télégraphie sans fil*) wireless.

tsigane [tsigan] *adj, nm/f* = **tzigane**.

TSVP *abr* (= *tournez s'il vous plaît*) PTO.

tt *abr* = **tout**.

TT(A) *sigle m* (= *transit temporaire (autorisé)*) vehicle registration for cars etc bought in France for export tax-free by non-residents.

TTC *abr* = **toutes taxes comprises**.

ttes *abr* = **toutes**.

TU *sigle m* = *temps universel*.

tu [ty] *pron* you ♦ *nm*: **employer le ~** to use the "tu" form.

tu, e [ty] *pp de* **taire**.

tuant, e [tɥɑ̃, -ɑ̃t] *adj (épuisant)* killing; (*énervant*) infuriating.

tuba [tyba] *nm (MUS)* tuba; (*SPORT*) snorkel.

tubage [tybaʒ] *nm (MÉD)* intubation.

tube [tyb] *nm* tube; (*de canalisation, métallique etc*) pipe; (*chanson, disque*) hit song *ou* record; **~ digestif** alimentary canal, digestive tract; **~ à essai** test tube.

tuberculeux, euse [tybɛʀkylø, -øz] *adj* tubercular ♦ *nm/f* tuberculosis *ou* TB patient.

tuberculose [tybɛʀkyloz] *nf* tuberculosis, TB.

tubulaire [tybylɛʀ] *adj* tubular.

tubulure [tybylyʀ] *nf* pipe; piping *no pl*; (*AUTO*): **~ d'échappement/d'admission** exhaust/inlet manifold.

TUC [tyk] *sigle m* (= *travail d'utilité collective*) community work scheme for the young unemployed.

tuciste [tysist(ə)] *nm/f young person on a community work scheme*.

tué, e [tɥe] *nm/f*: **5 ~s** 5 killed *ou* dead.

tue-mouche [tymuʃ] *adj*: **papier ~(s)** flypaper.

tuer [tɥe] *vt* to kill; **se ~** (*se suicider*) to kill o.s.; (*dans un accident*) to be killed; **se ~ au travail** (*fig*) to work o.s. to death.

tuerie [tyʀi] *nf* slaughter *no pl*, massacre.

tue-tête [tytɛt]: **à ~** *adv* at the top of one's voice.

tueur [tɥœʀ] *nm* killer; **~ à gages** hired killer.

tuile [tɥil] *nf* tile; (*fam*) spot of bad luck, blow.

tulipe [tylip] *nf* tulip.

tulle [tyl] *nm* tulle.

tuméfié, e [tymefje] *adj* puffy, swollen.

tumeur [tymœʀ] *nf* growth, tumour (*BRIT*), tumor (*US*).

tumulte [tymylt(ə)] *nm* commotion, hubbub.

tumultueux, euse [tymyltɥø, -øz] *adj* stormy, turbulent.

tuner [tynɛʀ] *nm* tuner.

tungstène [tœ̃kstɛn] *nm* tungsten.

tunique [tynik] *nf* tunic; (*de femme*) smock, tunic.

Tunis [tynis] *n* Tunis.

Tunisie [tynizi] *nf*: **la ~** Tunisia.

tunisien, ne [tynizjɛ̃, -ɛn] *adj* Tunisian ♦ *nm/f*: **T~, ne** Tunisian.

tunisois, e [tynizwa, -waz] *adj* of *ou* from Tunis.

tunnel [tynɛl] *nm* tunnel; **le ~ sous la Manche** the Channel Tunnel, the Chunnel.

TUP *sigle m* (= *titre universel de paiement*) ≈ payment slip.

turban [tyʀbɑ̃] *nm* turban.

turbin [tyʀbɛ̃] *nm (fam)* work *no pl*.

turbine [tyʀbin] *nf* turbine.

turbo [tyʀbo] *nm* turbo; **un moteur ~** a turbo(-charged)engine.

turbomoteur [tyʀbomɔtœʀ] *nm* turbo(-boosted) engine.

turbopropulseur [tyʀbopʀopylsœʀ] *nm* turboprop.

turboréacteur [tyʀboʀeaktœʀ] *nm* turbojet.

turbot [tyʀbo] *nm* turbot.

turbotrain [tyʀbotʀɛ̃] *nm* turbotrain.

turbulences [tyʀbylɑ̃s] *nfpl (AVIAT)* turbulence *sg*.

turbulent, e [tyʀbylɑ̃, -ɑ̃t] *adj* boisterous, unruly.

turc, turque [tyʀk(ə)] *adj* Turkish; (*w.-c.*) seatless ♦ *nm (LING)* Turkish ♦ *nm/f*: **T~, Turque** Turk/Turkish woman; **à la turque** *adv (assis)* cross-legged.

turf [tyʀf] *nm* racing.

turfiste [tyʀfist(ə)] *nm/f* racegoer.

Turks et Caïques *ou* **Caicos** [tyʀkekaik(ɔs)] *nfpl* Turks and Caicos Islands.

turpitude [tyʀpityd] *nf* base act, baseness *no pl*.

turque [tyʀk(ə)] *adj f, nf voir* **turc**.

Turquie [tyʀki] *nf*: **la ~** Turkey.

turquoise [tyʀkwaz] *nf, adj inv* turquoise.

tut [ty] *etc vb voir* **taire**.

tutelle [tytɛl] *nf (JUR)* guardianship; (*POL*) trusteeship; **sous la ~ de** (*fig*) under the supervision of.

tuteur, trice [tytœʀ, -tʀis] *nm/f (JUR)* guardian; (*de plante*) stake, support.

tutoiement [tytwamɑ̃] *nm* use of familiar "tu" form.

tutoyer [tytwaje] _vt_: ~ **qn** to address sb as "tu".

tutti quanti [tutikwɑ̃ti] _nmpl_: **et** ~ and all the rest (of them).

tutu [tyty] _nm_ (_DANSE_) tutu.

Tuvalu [tyvaly] _nm_: **le** ~ Tuvalu.

tuyau, x [tɥijo] _nm_ pipe; (_flexible_) tube; (_fam: conseil_) tip; (: _mise au courant_) gen _no pl_; ~ **d'arrosage** hosepipe; ~ **d'échappement** exhaust pipe; ~ **d'incendie** fire hose.

tuyauté, e [tɥijote] _adj_ fluted.

tuyauterie [tɥijotʀi] _nf_ piping _no pl_.

tuyère [tɥijɛʀ] _nf_ nozzle.

TV [teve] _nf_ TV, telly (_BRIT_).

TVA _sigle f_ = **taxe à** _ou_ **sur la valeur ajoutée**.

tweed [twid] _nm_ tweed.

tympan [tɛ̃pɑ̃] _nm_ (_ANAT_) eardrum.

type [tip] _nm_ type; (_personne, chose: représentant_) classic example, epitome; (_fam_) chap, guy ♦ _adj_ typical, standard; **avoir le** ~ **nordique** to be Nordic-looking.

typé, e [tipe] _adj_ ethnic (_euph_).

typhoïde [tifɔid] _nf_ typhoid (fever).

typhon [tifɔ̃] _nm_ typhoon.

typhus [tifys] _nm_ typhus (fever).

typique [tipik] _adj_ typical.

typiquement [tipikmɑ̃] _adv_ typically.

typographe [tipɔɡʀaf] _nm/f_ typographer.

typographie [tipɔɡʀafi] _nf_ typography; (_procédé_) letterpress (printing).

typographique [tipɔɡʀafik] _adj_ typographical; letterpress _cpd_.

typologie [tipɔlɔʒi] _nf_ typology.

tyran [tiʀɑ̃] _nm_ tyrant.

tyrannie [tiʀani] _nf_ tyranny.

tyrannique [tiʀanik] _adj_ tyrannical.

tyranniser [tiʀanize] _vt_ to tyrannize.

Tyrol [tiʀɔl] _nm_: **le** ~ the Tyrol.

tyrolien, ne [tiʀɔljɛ̃, -ɛn] _adj_ Tyrolean.

tzar [dzaʀ] _nm_ = **tsar**.

tzigane [dzigan] _adj_ gipsy, tzigane ♦ _nm/f_ (Hungarian) gipsy, Tzigane.

U u

U, u [y] _nm inv_ U, u ♦ _abr_ (= _unité_) 10,000 _francs_; **maison à vendre 50 U** house for sale: 500,000 francs; **U comme Ursule** U for Uncle.

ubiquité [ybikɥite] _nf_: **avoir le don d'**~ to be everywhere at once, be ubiquitous.

UDF _sigle f_ (= _Union pour la démocratie française_) political party.

UE _sigle f_ (= _Union européenne_) EU.

UEFA [yefa] _sigle f_ (= _Union of European Football_ _Associations_) UEFA.

UEM _sigle f_ (= _Union économique et monétaire_) EMU.

UER _sigle f_ (= _unité d'enseignement et de recherche_) old title of UFR; (= _Union européenne de radiodiffusion_) EBU (= _European Broadcasting Union_).

UFC _sigle f_ (= _Union fédérale des consommateurs_) national consumer group.

UFR _sigle f_ (= _unité de formation et de recherche_) ≈ university department.

UHF _sigle f_ (= _ultra-haute fréquence_) UHF.

UHT _sigle_ (= _ultra-haute température_) UHT.

UIT _sigle f_ (= _Union internationale des télécommunications_) ITU (= _International Telecommunications Union_).

UJP _sigle f_ (= _Union des jeunes pour le progrès_) _political party_.

Ukraine [ykʀɛn] _nf_: **l'**~ the Ukraine.

ukrainien, ne [ykʀɛnjɛ̃, -ɛn] _adj_ Ukrainian ♦ _nm_ (_LING_) Ukrainian ♦ _nm/f_: **U**~, **ne** Ukrainian.

ulcère [ylsɛʀ] _nm_ ulcer; ~ **à l'estomac** stomach ulcer.

ulcérer [ylseʀe] _vt_ (_MÉD_) to ulcerate; (_fig_) to sicken, appal.

ulcéreux, euse [ylseʀø, -øz] _adj_ (_plaie, lésion_) ulcerous; (_membre_) ulcerated.

ULM _sigle m_ (= _ultra léger motorisé_) microlight.

ultérieur, e [ylteʀjœʀ] _adj_ later, subsequent; **remis à une date** ~**e** postponed to a later date.

ultérieurement [ylteʀjœʀmɑ̃] _adv_ later.

ultimatum [yltimatɔm] _nm_ ultimatum.

ultime [yltim] _adj_ final.

ultra... [yltʀa] _préfixe_ ultra....

ultramoderne [yltʀamɔdɛʀn(ə)] _adj_ ultramodern.

ultra-rapide [yltʀaʀapid] _adj_ ultra-fast.

ultra-sensible [yltʀasɑ̃sibl(ə)] _adj_ (_PHOTO_) high-speed.

ultra(-)son [yltʀasɔ̃] _nm_ ultrasound _no pl_; ~**s** _nmpl_ ultrasonics.

ultra(-)violet, te [yltʀavjɔlɛ, -ɛt] _adj_ ultraviolet ♦ _nm_: **les** ~**s** ultraviolet rays.

ululer [ylyle] _vi_ = **hululer**.

UME _sigle f_ (= _Union monétaire européenne_) EMU.

═══════════ _MOT-CLÉ_

un, une [œ̃, yn] _art indéf_ a; (_devant voyelle_) an; ~ **garçon/vieillard** a boy/an old man; **une fille** a girl

♦ _pron_ one; **l'**~ **des meilleurs** one of the best; **l'**~ **...**, **l'autre** (the) one ..., the other; **les** ~**s ...**, **les autres** some ..., others; **l'**~ **et l'autre** both (of them); **l'**~ **ou l'autre** either (of them); **l'**~ **l'autre, les** ~**s les autres** each other, one another; **pas** ~ **seul** not a single one; ~ **par** ~ one by one

♦ _num_ one; **une pomme seulement** one apple

only
♦ *nf*: **la une** (*PRESSE*) the front page.

unanime [ynanim] *adj* unanimous; **ils sont ~s (à penser que)** they are unanimous (in thinking that).

unanimement [ynanimmɑ̃] *adv* (*par tous*) unanimously; (*d'un commun accord*) with one accord.

unanimité [ynanimite] *nf* unanimity; **à l'~** unanimously; **faire l'~** to be approved unanimously.

UNEF [ynɛf] *sigle f = Union nationale des étudiants de France.*

UNESCO [ynɛsko] *sigle f* (= *United Nations Educational, Scientific and Cultural Organization*) UNESCO.

Unetelle [yntɛl] *nf voir* **Untel.**

UNI *sigle f = Union nationale interuniversitaire.*

uni, e [yni] *adj* (*ton, tissu*) plain; (*surface*) smooth, even; (*famille*) close(-knit); (*pays*) united.

UNICEF [ynisɛf] *sigle m ou f* (= *United Nations International Children's Emergency Fund*) UNICEF.

unidirectionnel, le [ynidirɛksjɔnɛl] *adj* unidirectional, one-way.

unième [ynjɛm] *num*: **vingt/trente et ~** twenty-/thirty-first; **cent ~** (one) hundred and first.

unificateur, trice [ynifikatœr, -tris] *adj* unifying.

unification [ynifikasjɔ̃] *nf* uniting; unification; standardization.

unifier [ynifje] *vt* to unite, unify; (*systèmes*) to standardize, unify; **s'~** to become united.

uniforme [ynifɔrm(ə)] *adj* (*mouvement*) regular, uniform; (*surface, ton*) even; (*objets, maisons*) uniform; (*fig: vie, conduite*) unchanging ♦ *nm* uniform; **être sous l'~** (*MIL*) to be serving.

uniformément [ynifɔrmemɑ̃] *adv* uniformly.

uniformisation [ynifɔrmizasjɔ̃] *nf* standardization.

uniformiser [ynifɔrmize] *vt* to make uniform; (*systèmes*) to standardize.

uniformité [ynifɔrmite] *nf* regularity; uniformity; evenness.

unijambiste [yniʒɑ̃bist(ə)] *nm/f* one-legged man/woman.

unilatéral, e, aux [ynilateral, -o] *adj* unilateral; **stationnement ~** parking on one side only.

unilatéralement [ynilateralmɑ̃] *adv* unilaterally.

uninominal, e, aux [yninɔminal, -o] *adj* uncontested.

union [ynjɔ̃] *nf* union; **~ conjugale** union of marriage; **~ de consommateurs** consumers' association; **~ libre** free love; **l'U~ des Républiques socialistes soviétiques (URSS)** the Union of Soviet Socialist Republics (USSR);

l'U~ soviétique the Soviet Union.

unique [ynik] *adj* (*seul*) only; (*le même*): **un prix/système ~** a single price/system; (*exceptionnel*) unique; **ménage à salaire ~** one-salary family; **route à voie ~** single-lane road; **fils/fille ~** only son/daughter, only child; **~ en France** the only one of its kind in France.

uniquement [ynikmɑ̃] *adv* only, solely; (*juste*) only, merely.

unir [ynir] *vt* (*nations*) to unite; (*éléments, couleurs*) to combine; (*en mariage*) to unite, join together; **~ qch à** to unite sth with; to combine sth with; **s'~** to unite; (*en mariage*) to be joined together; **s'~ à** *ou* **avec** to unite with.

unisexe [ynisɛks] *adj* unisex.

unisson [ynisɔ̃] **: à l'~** *adv* in unison.

unitaire [ynitɛr] *adj* unitary; (*POL*) unitarian; **prix ~** unit price.

unité [ynite] *nf* (*harmonie, cohésion*) unity; (*COMM, MIL, de mesure, MATH*) unit; **~ centrale (de traitement)** central processing unit; **~ de valeur** (university) course, credit.

univers [ynivɛr] *nm* universe.

universalisation [ynivɛrsalizasjɔ̃] *nf* universalization.

universaliser [ynivɛrsalize] *vt* to universalize.

universalité [ynivɛrsalite] *nf* universality.

universel, le [ynivɛrsɛl] *adj* universal; (*esprit*) all-embracing.

universellement [ynivɛrsɛlmɑ̃] *adv* universally.

universitaire [ynivɛrsitɛr] *adj* university *cpd*; (*diplôme, études*) academic, university *cpd* ♦ *nm/f* academic.

université [ynivɛrsite] *nf* university.

univoque [ynivɔk] *adj* unambiguous; (*MATH*) one-to-one.

UNR *sigle f* (= *Union pour la nouvelle république*) *former political party.*

UNSS *sigle f = Union nationale de sport scolaire.*

Untel, Unetelle [œ̃tɛl, yntɛl] *nm/f*: **Monsieur ~** Mr so-and-so.

uranium [yranjɔm] *nm* uranium.

urbain, e [yrbɛ̃, -ɛn] *adj* urban, city *cpd*, town *cpd*; (*poli*) urbane.

urbanisation [yrbanizasjɔ̃] *nf* urbanization.

urbaniser [yrbanize] *vt* to urbanize.

urbanisme [yrbanism(ə)] *nm* town planning.

urbaniste [yrbanist(ə)] *nm/f* town planner.

urbanité [yrbanite] *nf* urbanity.

urée [yre] *nf* urea.

urémie [yremi] *nf* uraemia (*BRIT*), uremia (*US*).

urgence [yrʒɑ̃s] *nf* urgency; (*MÉD etc*) emergency; **d'~** *adj* emergency *cpd* ♦ *adv* as a matter of urgency; **en cas d'~** in case of emergency; **service des ~s** emergency service.

urgent, e [yrʒɑ̃, -ɑ̃t] *adj* urgent.

urinaire [yrinɛr] *adj* urinary.

urinal, aux [yrinal, -o] *nm* (bed) urinal.

urine [yʀin] nf urine.

uriner [yʀine] vi to urinate.

urinoir [yʀinwaʀ] nm (public) urinal.

urne [yʀn(ə)] nf (électorale) ballot box; (vase) urn; **aller aux ~s** (voter) to go to the polls.

urologie [yʀɔlɔʒi] nf urology.

URSS [parfois: yʀs] sigle f (= Union des Républiques Socialistes Soviétiques) USSR.

URSSAF [yʀsaf] sigle f (= Union pour le recouvrement de la sécurité sociale et des allocations familiales) administrative body responsible for social security funds and payments.

urticaire [yʀtikɛʀ] nf nettle rash, urticaria.

Uruguay [yʀygwɛ] nm: l'~ Uruguay.

uruguayen, ne [yʀygwajɛ̃, -ɛn] adj Uruguayan ♦ nm/f: U~, ne Uruguayan.

us [ys] nmpl: ~ **et coutumes** (habits and) customs.

US(A) sigle mpl (= United States (of America)) US(A).

usage [yzaʒ] nm (emploi, utilisation) use; (coutume) custom; (éducation) (good) manners pl, (good) breeding; (LING): l'~ usage; **faire ~ de** (pouvoir, droit) to exercise; **avoir l'~ de** to have the use of; **à l'~** adv with use; **à l'~ de** (pour) for (use of); **en ~** in use; **hors d'~** out of service; **à ~ interne** to be taken; **à ~ externe** for external use only.

usagé, e [yzaʒe] adj (usé) worn; (d'occasion) used.

usager, ère [yzaʒe, -ɛʀ] nm/f user.

usé, e [yze] adj worn (down ou out ou away); ruined; (banal) hackneyed.

user [yze] vt (outil) to wear down; (vêtement) to wear out; (matière) to wear away; (consommer: charbon etc) to use; (fig: santé) to ruin; (: personne) to wear out; **s'~** vi to wear; to wear out; (fig) to decline; **s'~ à la tâche** to wear o.s. out with work; **~ de** vt (moyen, procédé) to use, employ; (droit) to exercise.

usine [yzin] nf factory; **~ atomique** nuclear power plant; **~ à gaz** gasworks sg; **~ marémotrice** tidal power station.

usiner [yzine] vt (TECH) to machine; (fabriquer) to manufacture.

usité, e [yzite] adj in common use, common; **peu ~** rarely used.

ustensile [ystɑ̃sil] nm implement; **~ de cuisine** kitchen utensil.

usuel, le [yzɥɛl] adj everyday, common.

usufruit [yzyfʀɥi] nm usufruct.

usuraire [yzyʀɛʀ] adj usurious.

usure [yzyʀ] nf wear; worn state; (de l'usurier) usury; **avoir qn à l'~** to wear sb down; **~ normale** fair wear and tear.

usurier, ière [yzyʀje, -jɛʀ] nm/f usurer.

usurpateur, trice [yzyʀpatœʀ, -tʀis] nm/f usurper.

usurpation [yzyʀpasjɔ̃] nf usurpation.

usurper [yzyʀpe] vt to usurp.

ut [yt] nm (MUS) C.

UTA sigle f = Union des transporteurs aériens.

utérin, e [yteʀɛ̃, -in] adj uterine.

utérus [yteʀys] nm uterus, womb.

utile [ytil] adj useful; **~ à qn/qch** of use to sb/ sth.

utilement [ytilmɑ̃] adv usefully.

utilisable [ytilizabl(ə)] adj usable.

utilisateur, trice [ytilizatœʀ, -tʀis] nm/f user.

utilisation [ytilizasjɔ̃] nf use.

utiliser [ytilize] vt to use.

utilitaire [ytilitɛʀ] adj utilitarian; (objets) practical ♦ nm (INFORM) utility.

utilité [ytilite] nf usefulness no pl; use; **jouer les ~s** (THÉÂT) to play bit parts; **reconnu d'~ publique** state-approved; **c'est d'une grande ~** it's extremely useful; **il n'y a aucune ~ à ... there's no use in ....**

utopie [ytɔpi] nf (idée, conception) utopian idea ou view; (société etc idéale) utopia.

utopique [ytɔpik] adj utopian.

utopiste [ytɔpist(ə)] nm/f utopian.

UV sigle f (SCOL) = **unité de valeur.**

uvule [yvyl] nf uvula.

V v

V, v [ve] nm inv V, v ♦ abr (= voir, verset) v.; (= vers: de poésie) l.; (: en direction de) toward(s); **V comme Victor** V for Victor; **en ~** V-shaped; **encolure en ~** V-neck; **décolleté en ~** plunging neckline.

va [va] vb voir **aller.**

vacance [vakɑ̃s] nf (ADMIN) vacancy; **~s** pl (ADMIN) holiday(s) (BRIT), vacation sg (US); **les grandes ~s** the summer holidays ou vacation; **prendre des/ses ~s** to take a holiday ou vacation/one's holiday(s) ou vacation; **aller en ~s** to go on holiday ou vacation.

vacancier, ière [vakɑ̃sje, -jɛʀ] nm/f holiday-maker (BRIT), vacationer (US).

vacant, e [vakɑ̃, -ɑ̃t] adj vacant.

vacarme [vakaʀm(ə)] nm row, din.

vacataire [vakatɛʀ] nm/f temporary (employee); (enseignement) supply (BRIT) ou substitute (US) teacher; (UNIVERSITÉ) part-time temporary lecturer.

vaccin [vaksɛ̃] nm vaccine; (opération) vaccination.

vaccination [vaksinasjɔ̃] nf vaccination.

vacciner [vaksine] vt to vaccinate; (fig) to make immune; **être vacciné** (fig) to be immune.

vache [vaʃ] nf (ZOOL) cow; (cuir) cowhide ♦ adj (fam) rotten, mean; **~ à eau** (canvas) water bag; **(manger de la) ~ enragée** (to go through) hard times; **~ à lait** (péj) mug, sucker; ~ **laitière** dairy cow; **période des ~s maigres** lean times pl, lean period.

vachement [vaʃmɑ̃] adv (fam) damned, fantastically.

vacher, ère [vaʃe, -ɛʀ] nm/f cowherd.

vacherie [vaʃʀi] nf (fam) meanness no pl; (action) dirty trick; (propos) nasty remark.

vacherin [vaʃʀɛ̃] nm (fromage) vacherin cheese; (gâteau): ~ **glacé** vacherin (type of cream gâteau).

vachette [vaʃɛt] nf calfskin.

vacillant, e [vasijɑ̃, -ɑ̃t] adj wobbly; flickering; failing, faltering.

vaciller [vasije] vi to sway, wobble; (bougie, lumière) to flicker; (fig) to be failing, falter; ~ **dans ses réponses** to falter in one's replies; ~ **dans ses résolutions** to waver in one's resolutions.

vacuité [vakɥite] nf emptiness, vacuity.

vade-mecum [vademekɔm] nm inv pocketbook.

vadrouille [vadʀuj] nf: **être/partir en** ~ to be on/go for a wander.

vadrouiller [vadʀuje] vi to wander around ou about.

va-et-vient [vaevjɛ̃] nm inv (de pièce mobile) to and fro (ou up and down) movement; (de personnes, véhicules) comings and goings pl, to-ings and fro-ings pl; (ÉLEC) two-way switch.

vagabond, e [vagabɔ̃, -ɔ̃d] adj wandering; (imagination) roaming, roving ♦ nm (rôdeur) tramp, vagrant; (voyageur) wanderer.

vagabondage [vagabɔ̃daʒ] nm roaming, wandering; (JUR) vagrancy.

vagabonder [vagabɔ̃de] vi to roam, wander.

vagin [vaʒɛ̃] nm vagina.

vaginal, e, aux [vaʒinal, -o] adj vaginal.

vagissement [vaʒismɑ̃] nm cry (of newborn baby).

vague [vag] nf wave ♦ adj vague; (regard) faraway; (manteau, robe) loose(-fitting); (quelconque): **un** ~ **bureau/cousin** some office/cousin or other ♦ nm: **être dans le** ~ to be rather in the dark; **rester dans le** ~ to keep things rather vague; **regarder dans le** ~ to gaze into space; ~ **à l'âme** nm vague melancholy; ~ **d'assaut** nf (MIL) wave of assault; ~ **de chaleur** nf heatwave; ~ **de fond** nf ground swell; ~ **de froid** nf cold spell.

vaguelette [vaglɛt] nf ripple.

vaguement [vagmɑ̃] adv vaguely.

vaillamment [vajamɑ̃] adv bravely, gallantly.

vaillant, e [vajɑ̃, -ɑ̃t] adj (courageux) brave, gallant; (robuste) vigorous, hale and hearty; **n'avoir plus un sou** ~ to be penniless.

vaille [vaj] vb voir **valoir**.

vain, e [vɛ̃, vɛn] adj vain; **en** ~ adv in vain.

vaincre [vɛ̃kʀ(ə)] vt to defeat; (fig) to conquer, overcome.

vaincu, e [vɛ̃ky] pp de **vaincre** ♦ nm/f defeated party.

vainement [vɛnmɑ̃] adv vainly.

vainquais [vɛ̃kɛ] etc vb voir **vaincre**.

vainqueur [vɛ̃kœʀ] nm victor; (SPORT) winner ♦ adj m victorious.

vais [vɛ] vb voir **aller**.

vaisseau, x [vɛso] nm (ANAT) vessel; (NAVIG) ship, vessel; ~ **spatial** spaceship.

vaisselier [vɛsəlje] nm dresser.

vaisselle [vɛsɛl] nf (service) crockery; (plats etc à laver) (dirty) dishes pl; **faire la** ~ to do the washing-up (BRIT) ou the dishes.

val, vaux ou **vals** [val, vo] nm valley.

valable [valabl(ə)] adj valid; (acceptable) decent, worthwhile.

valablement [valabləmɑ̃] adv legitimately; (de façon satisfaisante) satisfactorily.

Valence [valɑ̃s] n (en Espagne) Valencia; (en France) Valence.

valent [val] etc vb voir **valoir**.

valet [valɛ] nm valet; (péj) lackey; (CARTES) jack, knave (BRIT); ~ **de chambre** manservant, valet; ~ **de ferme** farmhand; ~ **de pied** footman.

valeur [valœʀ] nf (gén) value; (mérite) worth, merit; (COMM: titre) security; **mettre en** ~ (bien) to exploit; (terrain, région) to develop; (fig) to highlight; to show off to advantage; **avoir de la** ~ to be valuable; **prendre de la** ~ to go up ou gain in value; **sans** ~ worthless; ~ **absolue** absolute value; ~ **d'échange** exchange value; ~ **nominale** face value; ~**s mobilières** transferable securities.

valeureux, euse [valœʀø, -øz] adj valorous.

validation [validasjɔ̃] nf validation.

valide [valid] adj (en bonne santé) fit, well; (indemne) able-bodied, fit; (valable) valid.

valider [valide] vt to validate.

validité [validite] nf validity.

valions [valjɔ̃] etc vb voir **valoir**.

valise [valiz] nf (suit)case; **faire sa** ~ to pack one's (suit)case; **la** ~ **(diplomatique)** the diplomatic bag.

vallée [vale] nf valley.

vallon [valɔ̃] nm small valley.

vallonné, e [valɔne] adj undulating.

vallonnement [valɔnmɑ̃] nm undulation.

valoir [valwaʀ] vi (être valable) to hold, apply ♦ vt (prix, valeur, effort) to be worth; (causer): ~ **qch à qn** to earn sb sth; **se** ~ to be of equal merit; (péj) to be two of a kind; **faire** ~ (droits, prérogatives) to assert; (domaine, capitaux) to exploit; **faire** ~ **que** to point out that; **se faire** ~ to make the most of o.s.; **à** ~ **sur** on account; **à** ~ **sur** to be deducted from; **vaille que vaille** somehow or other; **cela ne me dit rien qui vaille** I don't like the look of it at all; **ce climat ne me vaut rien** this climate doesn't suit me; ~ **la peine** to be worth the trouble, be worth it; ~ **mieux: il vaut mieux se taire** it's better to say nothing; **il vaut mieux que je fasse/comme ceci** it's better if

I do/like this; **ça ne vaut rien** it's worthless; **que vaut ce candidat?** how good is this applicant?

valorisation [valɔʀizasjɔ̃] *nf* (economic) development; increased standing.

valoriser [valɔʀize] *vt* (*ÉCON*) to develop (the economy of); (*produit*) to increase the value of; (*PSYCH*) to increase the standing of; (*fig*) to highlight, bring out.

valse [vals(ə)] *nf* waltz; **c'est la ~ des étiquettes** the prices don't stay the same from one moment to the next.

valser [valse] *vi* to waltz; (*fig*): **aller ~** to go flying.

valu, e [valy] *pp de* **valoir**.

valve [valv(ə)] *nf* valve.

vamp [vãp] *nf* vamp.

vampire [vãpiʀ] *nm* vampire.

van [vã] *nm* horse box (*BRIT*) *ou* trailer (*US*).

vandale [vãdal] *nm/f* vandal.

vandalisme [vãdalism(ə)] *nm* vandalism.

vanille [vanij] *nf* vanilla; **glace à la ~** vanilla ice cream.

vanillé, e [vanije] *adj* vanilla *cpd*.

vanité [vanite] *nf* vanity.

vaniteux, euse [vanitø, -øz] *adj* vain, conceited.

vanity-case [vaniti(e)kɛz] *nm* vanity case.

vanne [van] *nf* gate; (*fam: remarque*) dig, (nasty) crack; **lancer une ~ à qn** to have a go at sb (*BRIT*), knock sb.

vanneau, x [vano] *nm* lapwing.

vanner [vane] *vt* to winnow.

vannerie [vanʀi] *nf* basketwork.

vantail, aux [vãtaj, -o] *nm* door, leaf (*pl* leaves).

vantard, e [vãtaʀ, -aʀd(ə)] *adj* boastful.

vantardise [vãtaʀdiz] *nf* boastfulness *no pl*; boast.

vanter [vãte] *vt* to speak highly of, vaunt; **se ~** *vi* to boast, brag; **se ~ de** to pride o.s. on; (*péj*) to boast of.

Vanuatu [vanwatu] *nm*: **le ~** Vanuatu.

va-nu-pieds [vanypje] *nm/f inv* tramp, beggar.

vapeur [vapœʀ] *nf* steam; (*émanation*) vapour (*BRIT*), vapor (*US*), fumes *pl*; (*brouillard, buée*) haze; **~s** *nfpl* (*bouffées*) vapours, vapors; **à ~** steam-powered, steam *cpd*; **à toute ~** full steam ahead; (*fig*) at full tilt; **renverser la ~** to reverse engines; (*fig*) to backtrack, backpedal; **cuit à la ~** steamed.

vapocuiseur [vapɔkɥizœʀ] *nm* pressure cooker.

vaporeux, euse [vapɔʀø, -øz] *adj* (*flou*) hazy, misty; (*léger*) filmy, gossamer *cpd*.

vaporisateur [vapɔʀizatœʀ] *nm* spray.

vaporiser [vapɔʀize] *vt* (*CHIMIE*) to vaporize; (*parfum etc*) to spray.

vaquer [vake] *vi* (*ADMIN*) to be on vacation; **~ à ses occupations** to attend to one's affairs, go about one's business.

varappe [vaʀap] *nf* rock climbing.

varappeur, euse [vaʀapœʀ, -øz] *nm/f* (rock) climber.

varech [vaʀɛk] *nm* wrack, varec.

vareuse [vaʀøz] *nf* (*blouson*) pea jacket; (*d'uniforme*) tunic.

variable [vaʀjabl(ə)] *adj* variable; (*temps, humeur*) changeable; (*TECH: à plusieurs positions etc*) adaptable; (*LING*) inflectional; (*divers: résultats*) varied, various ♦ *nf* (*INFORM, MATH*) variable.

variante [vaʀjãt] *nf* variant.

variation [vaʀjasjɔ̃] *nf* variation; changing *no pl*, change; (*MUS*) variation.

varice [vaʀis] *nf* varicose vein.

varicelle [vaʀisɛl] *nf* chickenpox.

varié, e [vaʀje] *adj* varied; (*divers*) various; **hors-d'œuvre ~s** selection of hors d'œuvres.

varier [vaʀje] *vi* to vary; (*temps, humeur*) to change ♦ *vt* to vary.

variété [vaʀjete] *nf* variety; **spectacle de ~s** variety show.

variole [vaʀjɔl] *nf* smallpox.

variqueux, euse [vaʀikø, -øz] *adj* varicose.

Varsovie [vaʀsɔvi] *n* Warsaw.

vas [va] *vb voir* **aller**; **~-y!** [vazi] go on!

vasculaire [vaskylɛʀ] *adj* vascular.

vase [vɑz] *nm* vase ♦ *nf* silt, mud; **en ~ clos** in isolation; **~ de nuit** chamberpot; **~s communicants** communicating vessels.

vasectomie [vazɛktɔmi] *nf* vasectomy.

vaseline [vazlin] *nf* Vaseline ®.

vaseux, euse [vazø, -øz] *adj* silty, muddy; (*fig: confus*) woolly, hazy; (*: fatigué*) peaky; (*: étourdi*) woozy.

vasistas [vazistas] *nm* fanlight.

vasque [vask(ə)] *nf* (*bassin*) basin; (*coupe*) bowl.

vassal, e, aux [vasal, -o] *nm/f* vassal.

vaste [vast(ə)] *adj* vast, immense.

Vatican [vatikã] *nm*: **le ~** the Vatican.

vaticiner [vatisine] *vi* (*péj*) to make pompous predictions.

va-tout [vatu] *nm*: **jouer son ~** to stake one's all.

vaudeville [vodvil] *nm* vaudeville, light comedy.

vaudrai [vodʀe] *etc vb voir* **valoir**.

vau-l'eau [volo]: **à ~** *adv* with the current; **s'en aller à ~** (*fig: projets*) to be adrift.

vaurien, ne [voʀjɛ̃, -ɛn] *nm/f* good-for-nothing, guttersnipe.

vaut [vo] *vb voir* **valoir**.

vautour [votuʀ] *nm* vulture.

vautrer [votʀe]: **se ~** *vi*: **se ~ dans** to wallow in; **se ~ sur** to sprawl on.

vaux [vo] *pl de* **val** ♦ *vb voir* **valoir**.

va-vite [vavit]: **à la ~** *adv* in a rush.

vd *abr = vend*.

VDQS *abr* (= *vin délimité de qualité supérieure*) *label guaranteeing quality of wine*.

VDQS, *on a bottle of French wine, indicates that it contains high-quality wine from an approved regional vineyard. It is the second highest French wine classification after* **AOC** *and is followed by* **vin de pays**. *Unlike the previous categories,* **vin de table** *or* **vin ordinaire** *is table wine of unspecified origin, often blended.*

vds *abr =* **vends**.

veau, x [vo] *nm* (*ZOOL*) calf (*pl* calves); (*CULIN*) veal; (*peau*) calfskin; **tuer le ~ gras** to kill the fatted calf.

vecteur [vɛktœʀ] *nm* vector; (*MIL*, *BIO*) carrier.

vécu, e [veky] *pp de* **vivre** ♦ *adj* (*aventure*) real(-life).

vedettariat [vədɛtaʀja] *nm* stardom; (*attitude*) acting like a star.

vedette [vədɛt] *nf* (*artiste etc*) star; (*canot*) patrol boat; launch; **avoir la ~** to top the bill, get star billing; **mettre qn en ~** (*CINÉ etc*) to give sb the starring role; (*fig*) to push sb into the limelight; **voler la ~ à qn** to steal the show from sb.

végétal, e, aux [veʒetal, -o] *adj* vegetable ♦ *nm* vegetable, plant.

végétalien, ne [veʒetaljɛ̃, -ɛn] *adj*, *nm/f* vegan.

végétalisme [veʒetalism(ə)] *nm* veganism.

végétarien, ne [veʒetaʀjɛ̃, -ɛn] *nm/f* vegetarian.

végétarisme [veʒetaʀism(ə)] *nm* vegetarianism.

végétatif, ive [veʒetatif, -iv] *adj*: **une vie ~ive** a vegetable existence.

végétation [veʒetasjɔ̃] *nf* vegetation; **~s** *nfpl* (*MÉD*) adenoids.

végéter [veʒete] *vi* (*fig*) to vegetate; to stagnate.

véhémence [veemɑ̃s] *nf* vehemence.

véhément, e [veemɑ̃, -ɑ̃t] *adj* vehement.

véhicule [veikyl] *nm* vehicle; **~ utilitaire** commercial vehicle.

véhiculer [veikyle] *vt* (*personnes, marchandises*) to transport, convey; (*fig*: *idées, substances*) to convey, serve as a vehicle for.

veille [vɛj] *nf* (*garde*) watch; (*PSYCH*) wakefulness; (*jour*): **la ~** the day before, the previous day; **la ~ au soir** the previous evening; **la ~ de** the day before; **à la ~ de** on the eve of; **l'état de ~** the waking state.

veillée [veje] *nf* (*soirée*) evening; (*réunion*) evening gathering; **~ d'armes** night before combat; (*fig*) vigil; **~ (mortuaire)** watch.

veiller [veje] *vi* (*rester debout*) to stay ou sit up; (*ne pas dormir*) to be awake; (*être de garde*) to be on watch; (*être vigilant*) to be watchful ♦ *vt* (*malade, mort*) to watch over, sit up with; **~ à** *vt* to attend to, see to; **~ à ce que** to make sure that, see to it that; **~ sur** *vt* to keep a watch ou an eye on.

veilleur [vɛjœʀ] *nm*: **~ de nuit** night watchman.

veilleuse [vɛjøz] *nf* (*lampe*) night light; (*AUTO*) sidelight; (*flamme*) pilot light; **en ~** *adj* (*lampe*) dimmed; (*fig*: *affaire*) shelved, set aside.

veinard, e [vɛnaʀ, -aʀd(ə)] *nm/f* (*fam*) lucky devil.

veine [vɛn] *nf* (*ANAT, du bois etc*) vein; (*filon*) vein, seam; (*fam*: *chance*): **avoir de la ~** to be lucky; (*inspiration*) inspiration.

veiné, e [vene] *adj* veined; (*bois*) grained.

veineux, euse [venø, -øz] *adj* venous.

Velcro [vɛlkʀo] *nm* ® Velcro ®.

vêler [vele] *vi* to calve.

vélin [velɛ̃] *nm*: **(papier) ~** vellum (paper).

véliplanchiste [veliplɑ̃ʃist(ə)] *nm/f* windsurfer.

velléitaire [veleitɛʀ] *adj* irresolute, indecisive.

velléités [veleite] *nfpl* vague impulses.

vélo [velo] *nm* bike, cycle; **faire du ~** to go cycling.

véloce [velɔs] *adj* swift.

vélocité [velɔsite] *nf* (*MUS*) nimbleness, swiftness; (*vitesse*) velocity.

vélodrome [velɔdʀom] *nm* velodrome.

vélomoteur [velɔmɔtœʀ] *nm* moped.

véloski [veloski] *nm* skibob.

velours [vəluʀ] *nm* velvet; **~ côtelé** corduroy.

velouté, e [vəlute] *adj* (*au toucher*) velvety; (*à la vue*) soft, mellow; (*au goût*) smooth, mellow ♦ *nm*: **~ d'asperges/de tomates** cream of asparagus/tomato soup.

velouteux, euse [vəlutø, -øz] *adj* velvety.

velu, e [vəly] *adj* hairy.

venais [vənɛ] *etc vb voir* **venir**.

venaison [vənɛzɔ̃] *nf* venison.

vénal, e, aux [venal, -o] *adj* venal.

vénalité [venalite] *nf* venality.

venant [vənɑ̃]: **à tout ~** *adv* to all and sundry.

vendable [vɑ̃dabl(ə)] *adj* saleable, marketable.

vendange [vɑ̃dɑ̃ʒ] *nf* (*opération, période*: *aussi*: **~s**) grape harvest; (*raisins*) grape crop, grapes *pl*.

vendanger [vɑ̃dɑ̃ʒe] *vi* to harvest the grapes.

vendangeur, euse [vɑ̃dɑ̃ʒœʀ, -øz] *nm/f* grape-picker.

vendéen, ne [vɑ̃deɛ̃, -ɛn] *adj* of ou from the Vendée.

vendeur, euse [vɑ̃dœʀ, -øz] *nm/f* (*de magasin*) shop ou sales assistant (*BRIT*), sales clerk (*US*); (*COMM*) salesman/woman ♦ *nm* (*JUR*) vendor, seller; **~ de journaux** newspaper seller.

vendre [vɑ̃dʀ(ə)] *vt* to sell; **~ qch à qn** to sell sb sth; **cela se vend à la douzaine** these are sold by the dozen; **cela se vend bien** it's selling well; **"à ~"** "for sale".

vendredi [vɑ̃dʀədi] *nm* Friday; **V~ saint** Good Friday; *voir aussi* **lundi**.

vendu, e [vɑ̃dy] *pp de* **vendre** ♦ *adj* (*péj*) corrupt.

venelle [vənɛl] *nf* alley.

vénéneux, euse [venenø, -øz] *adj* poisonous.

vénérable [veneʀabl(ə)] *adj* venerable.

vénération [venerɑsjɔ̃] _nf_ veneration.

vénérer [venere] _vt_ to venerate.

vénerie [vɛnʀi] _nf_ hunting.

vénérien, ne [venerjɛ̃, -ɛn] _adj_ venereal.

Venezuela [venezɥela] _nm:_ **le** ~ Venezuela.

vénézuélien, ne [venezɥeljɛ̃, -ɛn] _adj_ Venezuelan ♦ _nm/f:_ **V~, ne** Venezuelan.

vengeance [vɑ̃ʒɑ̃s] _nf_ vengeance _no pl_, revenge _no pl_; (_acte_) act of vengeance _ou_ revenge.

venger [vɑ̃ʒe] _vt_ to avenge; **se** ~ _vi_ to avenge o.s.; (_par rancune_) to take revenge; **se** ~ **de qch** to avenge o.s. for sth; to take one's revenge for sth; **se** ~ **de qn** to take revenge on sb; **se** ~ **sur** to wreak vengeance upon; to take revenge on _ou_ through; to take it out on.

vengeur, eresse [vɑ̃ʒœʀ, -ʒʀɛs] _adj_ vengeful ♦ _nm/f_ avenger.

véniel, le [venjɛl] _adj_ venial.

venimeux, euse [vənimø, -øz] _adj_ poisonous, venomous; (_fig: haineux_) venomous, vicious.

venin [vənɛ̃] _nm_ venom, poison; (_fig_) venom.

venir [vəniʀ] _vi_ to come; ~ **de** to come from; ~ **de faire: je viens d'y aller/de le voir** I've just been there/seen him; **s'il vient à pleuvoir** if it should rain, if it happens to rain; **en** ~ **à faire: j'en viens à croire que** I am coming to believe that; **où veux-tu en** ~**?** what are you getting at?; **il en est venu à mendier** he has been reduced to begging; **en** ~ **aux mains** to come to blows; **les années/générations à** ~ the years/generations to come; **il me vient une idée** an idea has just occurred to me; **il me vient des soupçons** I'm beginning to be suspicious; **je te vois** ~ I know what you're after; **faire** ~ (_docteur, plombier_) to call (out); **d'où vient que ...?** how is it that ...?; ~ **au monde** to come into the world.

Venise [vəniz] _n_ Venice.

vénitien, ne [venisjɛ̃, -ɛn] _adj_ Venetian.

vent [vɑ̃] _nm_ wind; **il y a du** ~ it's windy; **c'est du** ~ (_fam_) it's all hot air; **au** ~ to windward; **sous le** ~ to leeward; **avoir le** ~ **debout/arrière** to head into the wind/have the wind astern; **dans le** ~ (_fam_) trendy; **prendre le** ~ (_fig_) to see which way the wind blows; **avoir** ~ **de** to get wind of; **contre** ~**s et marées** come hell or high water.

vente [vɑ̃t] _nf_ sale; **la** ~ (_activité_) selling; (_secteur_) sales _pl_; **mettre en** ~ to put on sale; (_objets personnels_) to put up for sale; ~ **de charité** jumble (_BRIT_) _ou_ rummage (_US_) sale; ~ **par correspondance (VPC)** mail-order selling; ~ **aux enchères** auction sale.

venté, e [vɑ̃te] _adj_ windswept, windy.

venter [vɑ̃te] _vb impers:_ **il vente** the wind is blowing.

venteux, euse [vɑ̃tø, -øz] _adj_ windswept, windy.

ventilateur [vɑ̃tilatœʀ] _nm_ fan.

ventilation [vɑ̃tilasjɔ̃] _nf_ ventilation.

ventiler [vɑ̃tile] _vt_ to ventilate; (_total, statistiques_) to break down.

ventouse [vɑ̃tuz] _nf_ (_ampoule_) cupping glass; (_de caoutchouc_) suction pad; (_ZOOL_) sucker.

ventre [vɑ̃tʀ(ə)] _nm_ (_ANAT_) stomach; (_fig_) belly; **prendre du** ~ to be getting a paunch; **avoir mal au** ~ to have (a) stomach ache.

ventricule [vɑ̃tʀikyl] _nm_ ventricle.

ventriloque [vɑ̃tʀilɔk] _nm/f_ ventriloquist.

ventripotent, e [vɑ̃tʀipɔtɑ̃, -ɑ̃t] _adj_ potbellied.

ventru, e [vɑ̃tʀy] _adj_ potbellied.

venu, e [vəny] _pp de_ **venir** ♦ _adj:_ **être mal** ~ **à** _ou_ **de faire** to have no grounds for doing, be in no position to do; **mal** ~ ill-timed, unwelcome; **bien** ~ timely, welcome ♦ _nf_ coming.

vêpres [vɛpʀ(ə)] _nfpl_ vespers.

ver [vɛʀ] _nm voir aussi_ **vers**; worm; (_des fruits etc_) maggot; (_du bois_) woodworm _no pl_; ~ **blanc** May beetle grub; ~ **luisant** glowworm; ~ **à soie** silkworm; ~ **solitaire** tapeworm; ~ **de terre** earthworm.

véracité [verasite] _nf_ veracity.

véranda [verɑ̃da] _nf_ veranda(h).

verbal, e, aux [vɛʀbal, -o] _adj_ verbal.

verbalement [vɛʀbalmɑ̃] _adv_ verbally.

verbaliser [vɛʀbalize] _vi_ (_POLICE_) to book _ou_ report an offender; (_PSYCH_) to verbalize.

verbe [vɛʀb(ə)] _nm_ (_LING_) verb; (_voix_): **avoir le** ~ **sonore** to have a sonorous tone (of voice); (_expression_): **la magie du** ~ the magic of language _ou_ the word; (_REL_): **le V~** the Word.

verbeux, euse [vɛʀbø, -øz] _adj_ verbose, wordy.

verbiage [vɛʀbjaʒ] _nm_ verbiage.

verbosité [vɛʀbozite] _nf_ verbosity.

verdâtre [vɛʀdɑtʀ(ə)] _adj_ greenish.

verdeur [vɛʀdœʀ] _nf_ (_vigueur_) vigour (_BRIT_), vigor (_US_), vitality; (_crudité_) forthrightness; (_défaut de maturité_) tartness, sharpness.

verdict [vɛʀdik(t)] _nm_ verdict.

verdir [vɛʀdiʀ] _vi, vt_ to turn green.

verdoyant, e [vɛʀdwajɑ̃, -ɑ̃t] _adj_ green, verdant.

verdure [vɛʀdyʀ] _nf_ (_arbres, feuillages_) greenery; (_légumes verts_) green vegetables _pl_, greens _pl_.

véreux, euse [verø, -øz] _adj_ worm-eaten; (_malhonnête_) shady, corrupt.

verge [vɛʀʒ(ə)] _nf_ (_ANAT_) penis; (_baguette_) stick, cane.

verger [vɛʀʒe] _nm_ orchard.

vergeture [vɛʀʒətyʀ] _nf gén pl_ stretch mark.

verglacé, e [vɛʀglase] _adj_ icy, iced-over.

verglas [vɛʀgla] _nm_ (black) ice.

vergogne [vɛʀgɔɲ]: **sans** ~ _adv_ shamelessly.

véridique [veridik] _adj_ truthful.

verificateur, trice [verifikatœʀ, -tʀis] _nm/f_ controller, checker ♦ _nf_ (_machine_) verifier; ~ **des comptes** (_FINANCE_) auditor.

vérification [verifikasjɔ̃] _nf_ checking _no pl_, check; ~ **d'identité** identity check.

vérifier [verifje] _vt_ to check; (_corroborer_) to

confirm, bear out; (*INFORM*) to verify; **se** ~ *vi* to be confirmed *ou* verified.

vérin [veʀɛ̃] *nm* jack.

véritable [veʀitabl(ə)] *adj* real; (*ami, amour*) true; **un** ~ **désastre** an absolute disaster; **que le** ~ **X sorte du rang!** ≈ will the real X (please) stand up!

véritablement [veʀitabləmɑ̃] *adv* (*effectivement*) really; (*absolument*) absolutely.

vérité [veʀite] *nf* truth; (*d'un portrait*) lifelikeness; (*sincérité*) truthfulness, sincerity; **en** ~, **à la** ~ to tell the truth.

verlan [veʀlɑ̃] *nm* (back) slang.

Verlan is a form of slang popularized in the fifties by Auguste Le Breton. It consists in inverting the syllables of words, verlan itself coming from l'envers (à l'envers = back to front). Typical examples are féca (café), ripou (pourri), meuf (femme), beur (Arabe).

---

vermeil, le [veʀmɛj] *adj* bright red, ruby red ♦ *nm* (*substance*) vermeil.

vermicelles [veʀmisɛl] *nmpl* vermicelli *sg*.

vermifuge [veʀmifyʒ] *nm*: **poudre** ~ worm powder.

vermillon [veʀmijɔ̃] *adj inv* vermilion, scarlet.

vermine [veʀmin] *nf* vermin *pl*.

vermoulu, e [veʀmuly] *adj* worm-eaten, with woodworm.

vermout(h) [veʀmut] *nm* vermouth.

verni, e [veʀni] *adj* varnished; glazed; (*fam*) lucky; **cuir** ~ patent leather; **souliers** ~**s** patent (leather) shoes.

vernir [veʀniʀ] *vt* (*bois, tableau, ongles*) to varnish; (*poterie*) to glaze.

vernis [veʀni] *nm* (*enduit*) varnish; glaze; (*fig*) veneer; ~ **à ongles** nail varnish (*BRIT*) *ou* polish.

vernissage [veʀnisaʒ] *nm* varnishing; glazing; (*d'une exposition*) preview.

vernisser [veʀnise] *vt* to glaze.

vérole [veʀɔl] *nf* (*variole*) smallpox; (*fam: syphilis*) pox.

Vérone [veʀɔn] *n* Verona.

verrai [veʀe] *etc vb voir* **voir**.

verre [veʀ] *nm* glass; (*de lunettes*) lens *sg*; ~**s** *nmpl* (*lunettes*) glasses; **boire** *ou* **prendre un** ~ to have a drink; ~ **à vin/à liqueur** wine/liqueur glass; ~ **à dents** tooth mug; ~ **dépoli** frosted glass; ~ **de lampe** lamp glass *ou* chimney; ~ **de montre** watch glass; ~ **à pied** stemmed glass; ~**s de contact** contact lenses; ~**s fumés** tinted glasses.

verrerie [veʀʀi] *nf* (*fabrique*) glassworks *sg*; (*activité*) glass-making, glass-working; (*objets*) glassware.

verrier [veʀje] *nm* glass-blower.

verrière [veʀjɛʀ] *nf* (*grand vitrage*) window; (*toit vitré*) glass roof.

verrons [veʀɔ̃] *etc vb voir* **voir**.

verroterie [veʀɔtʀi] *nf* glass beads *pl*, glass

jewellery (*BRIT*) *ou* jewelry (*US*).

verrou [veʀu] *nm* (*targette*) bolt; (*fig*) constriction; **mettre le** ~ to bolt the door; **mettre qn sous les** ~**s** to put sb behind bars.

verrouillage [veʀujaʒ] *nm* (*dispositif*) locking mechanism; (*AUTO*): ~ **central** *ou* **centralisé** central locking.

verrouiller [veʀuje] *vt* to bolt; to lock; (*MIL*: *brèche*) to close.

verrue [veʀy] *nf* wart; (*plantaire*) verruca; (*fig*) eyesore.

vers [veʀ] *nm* line ♦ *nmpl* (*poésie*) verse *sg* ♦ *prép* (*en direction de*) toward(s); (*près de*) around (about); (*temporel*) about, around.

versant [veʀsɑ̃] *nm* slopes *pl*, side.

versatile [veʀsatil] *adj* fickle, changeable.

verse [veʀs(ə)]: **à** ~ *adv*: **il pleut à** ~ it's pouring (with rain).

versé, e [veʀse] *adj*: **être** ~ **dans** (*science*) to be (well-)versed in.

Verseau [veʀso] *nm*: **le** ~ Aquarius, the water-carrier; **être du** ~ to be Aquarius.

versement [veʀsəmɑ̃] *nm* payment; (*sur un compte*) deposit, remittance; **en 3** ~**s** in 3 instalments.

verser [veʀse] *vt* (*liquide, grains*) to pour; (*larmes, sang*) to shed; (*argent*) to pay; (*soldat: affecter*): ~ **qn dans** to assign sb to ♦ *vi* (*véhicule*) to overturn; (*fig*): ~ **dans** to lapse into; ~ **à un compte** to pay into an account.

verset [veʀsɛ] *nm* verse; versicle.

verseur [veʀsœʀ] *adj m voir* **bec, bouchon**.

versification [veʀsifikasjɔ̃] *nf* versification.

versifier [veʀsifje] *vt* to put into verse ♦ *vi* to versify, write verse.

version [veʀsjɔ̃] *nf* version; (*SCOL*) translation (*into the mother tongue*); **film en** ~ **originale** film in the original language.

verso [veʀso] *nm* back; **voir au** ~ see over(leaf).

vert, e [veʀ, veʀt(ə)] *adj* green; (*vin*) young; (*vigoureux*) sprightly; (*cru*) forthright ♦ *nm* green; **dire des** ~**es** (**et des pas mûres**) to say some pretty spicy things; **il en a vu des** ~**es** he's seen a thing or two; ~ **bouteille** *adj inv* bottle-green; ~ **d'eau** *adj inv* sea-green; ~ **pomme** *adj inv* apple-green.

vert-de-gris [veʀdəgʀi] *nm* verdigris ♦ *adj inv* grey(ish)-green.

vertébral, e, aux [veʀtebʀal, -o] *adj* back *cpd*; *voir* **colonne**.

vertèbre [veʀtɛbʀ(ə)] *nf* vertebra (*pl* -ae).

vertébré, e [veʀtebʀe] *adj, nm* vertebrate.

vertement [veʀtəmɑ̃] *adv* (*réprimander*) sharply.

vertical, e, aux [veʀtikal, -o] *adj, nf* vertical; **à la** ~**e** *adv* vertically.

verticalement [veʀtikalmɑ̃] *adv* vertically.

verticalité [veʀtikalite] *nf* verticalness, verticality.

vertige [veʀtiʒ] *nm* (*peur du vide*) vertigo; (*étourdissement*) dizzy spell; (*fig*) fever; **ça**

me donne le ~ it makes me dizzy; *(fig)* it makes my head spin *ou* reel.

vertigineux, euse [vɛʀtiʒinø, -øz] *adj (hausse, vitesse)* breathtaking; *(altitude, gorge)* breathtakingly high *(ou* deep).

vertu [vɛʀty] *nf* virtue; **une** ~ a saint, a paragon of virtue; **avoir la** ~ **de faire** to have the virtue of doing; **en** ~ **de** *prép* in accordance with.

vertueusement [vɛʀtɥøzmɑ̃] *adv* virtuously.

vertueux, euse [vɛʀtɥø, -øz] *adj* virtuous.

verve [vɛʀv(ə)] *nf* witty eloquence; **être en** ~ to be in brilliant form.

verveine [vɛʀvɛn] *nf (BOT)* verbena, vervain; *(infusion)* verbena tea.

vésicule [vezikyl] *nf* vesicle; ~ **biliaire** gallbladder.

vespasienne [vɛspazjɛn] *nf* urinal.

vespéral, e, aux [vɛspeʀal, -o] *adj* vespertine, evening *cpd.*

vessie [vesi] *nf* bladder.

veste [vɛst(ə)] *nf* jacket; ~ **droite/croisée** single-/double-breasted jacket; **retourner sa** ~ *(fig)* to change one's colours.

vestiaire [vɛstjɛʀ] *nm (au théâtre etc)* cloakroom; *(de stade etc)* changing-room *(BRIT),* locker-room *(US); (métallique):* **(armoire)** ~ locker.

vestibule [vɛstibyl] *nm* hall.

vestige [vɛstiʒ] *nm (objet)* relic; *(fragment)* trace; *(fig)* remnant, vestige; ~**s** *nmpl (d'une ville)* remains; *(d'une civilisation, du passé)* remnants, relics.

vestimentaire [vɛstimɑ̃tɛʀ] *adj (dépenses)* clothing; *(détail)* of dress; *(élégance)* sartorial.

veston [vɛstɔ̃] *nm* jacket.

Vésuve [vezyv] *nm:* **le** ~ Vesuvius.

vêtais [vɛtɛ] *etc vb voir* **vêtir.**

vêtement [vɛtmɑ̃] *nm* garment, item of clothing; *(COMM):* **le** ~ the clothing industry; ~**s** *nmpl* clothes; ~**s de sport** sportswear *sg,* sports clothes.

vétéran [veteʀɑ̃] *nm* veteran.

vétérinaire [veteʀinɛʀ] *adj* veterinary ♦ *nm/f* vet, veterinary surgeon *(BRIT),* veterinarian *(US).*

vétille [vetij] *nf* trifle, triviality.

vétilleux, euse [vetijø, -øz] *adj* punctilious.

vêtir [vetiʀ] *vt* to clothe, dress; **se** ~ to dress (o.s.).

vêtit [veti] *etc vb voir* **vêtir.**

vétiver [vetivɛʀ] *nm (BOT)* vetiver.

veto [veto] *nm* veto; **droit de** ~ right of veto; **mettre** *ou* **opposer un** ~ to veto.

vêtu, e [vɛty] *pp de* **vêtir** ♦ *adj:* ~ **de** dressed in, wearing; **chaudement** ~ warmly dressed.

vétuste [vetyst(ə)] *adj* ancient, timeworn.

vétusté [vetyste] *nf* age, delapidation.

veuf, veuve [vœf, vœv] *adj* widowed ♦ *nm* widower ♦ *nf* widow.

veuille [vœj], **veuillez** [vœje] *etc vb voir* **vou-**

loir.

veule [vøl] *adj* spineless.

veulent [vœl] *etc vb voir* **vouloir.**

veulerie [vølʀi] *nf* spinelessness.

veut [vø] *vb voir* **vouloir.**

veuvage [vœvaʒ] *nm* widowhood.

veuve [vœv] *adj f, nf voir* **veuf.**

veux [vø] *vb voir* **vouloir.**

vexant, e [vɛksɑ̃, -ɑ̃t] *adj (contrariant)* annoying; *(blessant)* upsetting.

vexations [vɛksasjɔ̃] *nfpl* humiliations.

vexatoire [vɛksatwaʀ] *adj:* **mesures** ~**s** harassment *sg.*

vexer [vɛkse] *vt* to hurt, upset; **se** ~ *vi* to be hurt, get upset.

VF *sigle f (CINÉ)* = version française.

VHF *sigle f (= Very High Frequency)* VHF.

via [vja] *prép* via.

viabiliser [vjabilize] *vt* to provide with services *(water etc).*

viabilité [vjabilite] *nf* viability; *(d'un chemin)* practicability.

viable [vjabl(ə)] *adj* viable.

viaduc [vjadyk] *nm* viaduct.

viager, ère [vjaʒe, -ɛʀ] *adj:* **rente** ~**ère** life annuity ♦ *nm:* **mettre en** ~ to sell in return for a life annuity.

viande [vjɑ̃d] *nf* meat.

viatique [vjatik] *nm (REL)* viaticum; *(fig)* provisions *pl ou* money for the journey.

vibrant, e [vibʀɑ̃, -ɑ̃t] *adj* vibrating; *(voix)* vibrant; *(émouvant)* emotive.

vibraphone [vibʀafɔn] *nm* vibraphone, vibes *pl.*

vibraphoniste [vibʀafɔnist(ə)] *nm/f* vibraphone player.

vibration [vibʀɑsjɔ̃] *nf* vibration.

vibratoire [vibʀatwaʀ] *adj* vibratory.

vibrer [vibʀe] *vi* to vibrate; *(son, voix)* to be vibrant; *(fig)* to be stirred; **faire** ~ to (cause to) vibrate; to stir, thrill.

vibromasseur [vibʀomasœʀ] *nm* vibrator.

vicaire [vikɛʀ] *nm* curate.

vice... [vis] *préfixe* vice-.

vice [vis] *nm* vice; *(défaut)* fault; ~ **caché** *(COMM)* latent *ou* inherent defect; ~ **de forme** legal flaw *ou* irregularity.

vice-consul [viskɔ̃syl] *nm* vice-consul.

vice-présidence [vispʀezidɑ̃s] *nf (d'un pays)* vice-presidency; *(d'une société)* vice-presidency, vice-chairmanship *(BRIT).*

vice-président, e [vispʀezidɑ̃, -ɑ̃t] *nm/f* vice-president; vice-chairman.

vice-roi [visʀwa] *nm* viceroy.

vice-versa [visevɛʀsa] *adv* vice versa.

vichy [viʃi] *nm (toile)* gingham; *(eau)* Vichy water; **carottes V**~**s** boiled carrots.

vichyssois, e [viʃiswa, -waz] *adj of ou* from Vichy, Vichy *cpd* ♦ *nf (soupe)* vichyssoise (soup), *cream of leek and potato soup* ♦ *nm/f:* **V**~, **e** native *ou* inhabitant of Vichy.

vicié, e [visje] *adj (air)* polluted, tainted; *(JUR)*

invalidated.

vicier [visje] *vt* (*JUR*) to invalidate.

vicieux, euse [visjø, -øz] *adj* (*pervers*) dirty(-minded); (*méchant*) nasty; (*fautif*) incorrect, wrong.

vicinal, e, aux [visinal, -o] *adj*: **chemin ~** by-road, byway.

vicissitudes [visisityd] *nfpl* (trials and) tribulations.

vicomte [vikɔ̃t] *nm* viscount.

vicomtesse [vikɔ̃tɛs] *nf* viscountess.

victime [viktim] *nf* victim; (*d'accident*) casualty; **être (la) ~ de** to be the victim of; **être ~ d'une attaque/d'un accident** to suffer a stroke/be involved in an accident.

victoire [viktwar] *nf* victory.

victorieusement [viktɔrjøzmɑ̃] *adv* triumphantly, victoriously.

victorieux, euse [viktɔrjø, -øz] *adj* victorious; (*sourire, attitude*) triumphant.

victuailles [viktɥaj] *nfpl* provisions.

vidange [vidɑ̃ʒ] *nf* (*d'un fossé, réservoir*) emptying; (*AUTO*) oil change; (*de lavabo: bonde*) waste outlet; **~s** *nfpl* (*matières*) sewage *sg*; **faire la ~** (*AUTO*) to change the oil, do an oil change; **tuyau de ~** drainage pipe.

vidanger [vidɑ̃ʒe] *vt* to empty; **faire ~ la voiture** to have the oil changed in one's car.

vide [vid] *adj* empty ♦ *nm* (*PHYSIQUE*) vacuum; (*espace*) (empty) space, gap; (*sous soi: dans une falaise etc*) drop; (*futilité, néant*) void; **~ de** empty of; (*de sens etc*) devoid of; **sous ~** *adv* in a vacuum; **emballé sous ~** vacuum-packed; **regarder dans le ~** to stare into space; **avoir peur du ~** to be afraid of heights; **parler dans le ~** to waste one's breath; **faire le ~** (*dans son esprit*) to make one's mind go blank; **faire le ~ autour de qn** to isolate sb; **à ~** *adv* (*sans occupants*) empty; (*sans charge*) unladen; (*TECH*) without gripping *ou* being in gear.

vidé, e [vide] *adj* (*épuisé*) done in, all in.

vidéo [video] *nf, adj inv* video; **~ inverse** reverse video.

vidéocassette [videokasɛt] *nf* video cassette.

vidéoclub [videoklœb] *nm* video club.

vidéodisque [videodisk] *nm* videodisc.

vide-ordures [vidɔrdyr] *nm inv* (rubbish) chute.

vidéotex [videotɛks] *nm* ® teletext.

vide-poches [vidpɔʃ] *nm inv* tidy; (*AUTO*) glove compartment.

vide-pomme [vidpɔm] *nm inv* apple-corer.

vider [vide] *vt* to empty; (*CULIN: volaille, poisson*) to gut, clean out; (*régler: querelle*) to settle; (*fatiguer*) to wear out; (*fam: expulser*) to throw out, chuck out; **se ~** *vi* to empty; **~ les lieux** to quit *ou* vacate the premises.

videur [vidœr] *nm* (*de boîte de nuit*) bouncer.

vie [vi] *nf* life (*pl* lives); **être en ~** to be alive; **sans ~** lifeless; **à ~** for life; **membre à ~** life member; **dans la ~ courante** in every-day life; **avoir la ~ dure** to have nine lives; to die hard; **mener la ~ dure à qn** to make life a misery for sb.

vieil [vjɛj] *adj m voir* **vieux**.

vieillard [vjɛjar] *nm* old man; **les ~s** old people, the elderly.

vieille [vjɛj] *adj f, nf voir* **vieux**.

vieilleries [vjɛjri] *nfpl* old things *ou* stuff *sg*.

vieillesse [vjɛjɛs] *nf* old age; (*vieillards*): **la ~** the old *pl*, the elderly *pl*.

vieilli, e [vjeji] *adj* (*marqué par l'âge*) aged; (*suranné*) dated.

vieillir [vjejir] *vi* (*prendre de l'âge*) to grow old; (*population, vin*) to age; (*doctrine, auteur*) to become dated ♦ *vt* to age; **il a beaucoup vieilli** he has aged a lot; **se ~** to make o.s. older.

vieillissement [vjejismɑ̃] *nm* growing old; ageing.

vieillot, te [vjɛjo, -ɔt] *adj* antiquated, quaint.

vielle [vjɛl] *nf* hurdy-gurdy.

viendrai [vjɛ̃dre] *etc vb voir* **venir**.

Vienne [vjɛn] *n* (*en Autriche*) Vienna.

vienne [vjɛn], **viens** [vjɛ̃] *etc vb voir* **venir**.

viennois, e [vjɛnwa, -waz] *adj* Viennese.

vierge [vjɛrʒ(ə)] *adj* virgin; (*film*) blank; (*page*) clean, blank; (*jeune fille*): **être ~** to be a virgin ♦ *nf* virgin; (*signe*): **la V~** Virgo, the Virgin; **être de la V~** to be Virgo; **~ de** (*sans*) free from, unsullied by.

Viêt-nam, Vietnam [vjɛtnam] *nm*: **le ~** Vietnam; **le ~ du Nord/du Sud** North/South Vietnam.

vietnamien, ne [vjɛtnamjɛ̃, -ɛn] *adj* Vietnamese ♦ *nm* (*LING*) Vietnamese ♦ *nm/f*: **V~, ne** Vietnamese; **V~, ne du Nord/Sud** North/South Vietnamese.

vieux (vieil), vieille [vjø, vjɛj] *adj* old ♦ *nm/f* old man/woman ♦ *nmpl*: **les ~** the old, old people; (*fam: parents*) the old folk *ou* ones; **un petit ~** a little old man; **mon ~/ma vieille** (*fam*) old man/girl; **pauvre ~** poor old soul; **prendre un coup de ~** to put years on; **se faire ~** to make o.s. look older; **un ~ de la vieille** one of the old brigade; **~ garçon** *nm* bachelor; **~ jeu** *adj inv* old-fashioned; **~ rose** *adj inv* old rose; **vieil or** *adj inv* old gold; **vieille fille** *nf* spinster.

vif, vive [vif, viv] *adj* (*animé*) lively; (*alerte*) sharp, quick; (*brusque*) sharp, brusque; (*aigu*) sharp; (*lumière, couleur*) brilliant; (*air*) crisp; (*vent, émotion*) keen; (*froid*) bitter; (*fort: regret, déception*) great, deep; (*vivant*): **brûlé ~** burnt alive; **eau vive** running water; **de vive voix** personally; **piquer qn au ~** to cut sb to the quick; **tailler dans le ~** to cut into the living flesh; **à ~** (*plaie*) open; **avoir les nerfs à ~** to be on edge; **sur le ~** (*ART*) from life; **entrer dans le ~ du sujet** to get to the very heart of the matter.

vif-argent [vifarʒɑ̃] *nm inv* quicksilver.

vigie [viʒi] *nf* (*matelot*) look-out; (*poste*) look-out post, crow's nest.

vigilance [viʒilɑ̃s] *nf* vigilance.
vigilant, e [viʒilɑ̃, -ɑ̃t] *adj* vigilant.
vigile [viʒil] *nm* (*veilleur de nuit*) (night) watchman; (*police privée*) vigilante.
vigne [viɲ] *nf* (*plante*) vine; (*plantation*) vineyard; ~ **vierge** Virginia creeper.
vigneron [viɲRɔ̃] *nm* wine grower.
vignette [viɲɛt] *nf* (*motif*) vignette; (*de marque*) manufacturer's label *ou* seal; (*petite illustration*) (small) illustration; (*ADMIN*) ≈ (road) tax disc (*BRIT*), ≈ license plate sticker (*US*); (*: sur médicament*) price label (*on medicines for reimbursement by Social Security*).
vignoble [viɲɔbl(ə)] *nm* (*plantation*) vineyard; (*vignes d'une région*) vineyards *pl*.
vigoureusement [viguRøzmɑ̃] *adv* vigorously.
vigoureux, euse [viguRø, -øz] *adj* vigorous, robust.
vigueur [vigœR] *nf* vigour (*BRIT*), vigor (*US*); **être/entrer en** ~ to be in/come into force; **en** ~ current.
vil, e [vil] *adj* vile, base; **à** ~ **prix** at a very low price.
vilain, e [vilɛ̃, -ɛn] *adj* (*laid*) ugly; (*affaire, blessure*) nasty; (*pas sage: enfant*) naughty ♦ *nm* (*paysan*) villein, villain; **ça va tourner au** ~ things are going to turn nasty; ~ **mot** bad word.
vilainement [vilɛnmɑ̃] *adv* badly.
vilebrequin [vilbRəkɛ̃] *nm* (*outil*) (bit-)brace; (*AUTO*) crankshaft.
vilenie [vilni] *nf* vileness *no pl*, baseness *no pl*.
vilipender [vilipɑ̃de] *vt* to revile, vilify.
villa [vila] *nf* (detached) house.
village [vilaʒ] *nm* village; ~ **de toile** tent village; ~ **de vacances** holiday village.
villageois, e [vilaʒwa, -waz] *adj* village *cpd* ♦ *nm/f* villager.
ville [vil] *nf* town; (*importante*) city; (*administration*): **la** ~ ≈ the Corporation; ≈ the (town) council; **aller en** ~ to go to town; **habiter en** ~ to live in town; ~ **nouvelle** new town.
ville-champignon, *pl* **villes-champignons** [vilʃɑ̃piɲɔ̃] *nf* boom town.
ville-dortoir, *pl* **villes-dortoirs** [vildɔRtwaR] *nf* dormitory town.
villégiature [vileʒjatyR] *nf* (*séjour*) holiday; (*lieu*) (holiday) resort.
vin [vɛ̃] *nm* wine; **avoir le** ~ **gai/triste** to get happy/miserable after a few drinks; ~ **blanc/rosé/rouge** white/rosé/red wine; ~ **d'honneur** reception (*with wine and snacks*); ~ **de messe** altar wine; ~ **ordinaire** *ou* **de table** table wine; ~ **de pays** local wine; *voir aussi* **AOC; VDQS.**
vinaigre [vinɛgR(ə)] *nm* vinegar; **tourner au** ~ (*fig*) to turn sour; ~ **de vin/d'alcool** wine/spirit vinegar.
vinaigrette [vinegRɛt] *nf* vinaigrette, French dressing.
vinaigrier [vinɛgRije] *nm* (*fabricant*) vinegar-

maker; (*flacon*) vinegar cruet *ou* bottle.
vinasse [vinas] *nf* (*péj*) cheap wine, plonk (*BRIT*).
vindicatif, ive [vɛ̃dikatif, -iv] *adj* vindictive.
vindicte [vɛ̃dikt(ə)] *nf*: **désigner qn à la** ~ **publique** to expose sb to public condemnation.
vineux, euse [vinø, -øz] *adj* win(e)y.
vingt [vɛ̃, vɛ̃t + *vowel and in* 22, 23 *etc*] *num* twenty; ~**-quatre heures sur** ~**-quatre** twenty-four hours a day, round the clock.
vingtaine [vɛ̃tɛn] *nf*: **une** ~ **(de)** around twenty, twenty or so.
vingtième [vɛ̃tjɛm] *num* twentieth.
vinicole [vinikɔl] *adj* (*production*) wine *cpd*; (*région*) wine-growing.
vinification [vinifikasjɔ̃] *nf* wine-making, wine production; (*des sucres*) vinification.
vinyle [vinil] *nm* vinyl.
viol [vjɔl] *nm* (*d'une femme*) rape; (*d'un lieu sacré*) violation.
violacé, e [vjɔlase] *adj* purplish, mauvish.
violation [vjɔlasjɔ̃] *nf* desecration; violation; (*d'un droit*) breach.
violemment [vjɔlamɑ̃] *adv* violently.
violence [vjɔlɑ̃s] *nf* violence; ~**s** *nfpl* acts of violence; **faire** ~ **à qn** to do violence to sb; **se faire** ~ to force o.s.
violent, e [vjɔlɑ̃, -ɑ̃t] *adj* violent; (*remède*) drastic; (*besoin, désir*) intense, urgent.
violenter [vjɔlɑ̃te] *vt* to assault (sexually).
violer [vjɔle] *vt* (*femme*) to rape; (*sépulture*) to desecrate, violate; (*loi, traité*) to violate.
violet, te [vjɔlɛ, -ɛt] *adj*, *nm* purple, mauve ♦ *nf* (*fleur*) violet.
violeur [vjɔlœR] *nm* rapist.
violine [vjɔlin] *nf* deep purple.
violon [vjɔlɔ̃] *nm* violin; (*dans la musique folklorique etc*) fiddle; (*fam: prison*) lock-up; **premier** ~ first violin; ~ **d'Ingres** (artistic) hobby.
violoncelle [vjɔlɔ̃sɛl] *nm* cello.
violoncelliste [vjɔlɔ̃selist(ə)] *nm/f* cellist.
violoniste [vjɔlɔnist(ə)] *nm/f* violinist, violin-player; (*folklorique etc*) fiddler.
VIP *sigle m* (= *Very Important Person*) VIP.
vipère [vipɛR] *nf* viper, adder.
virage [viRaʒ] *nm* (*d'un véhicule*) turn; (*d'une route, piste*) bend; (*CHIMIE*) change in colour (*BRIT*) *ou* color (*US*); (*de cuti-réaction*) positive reaction; (*PHOTO*) toning; (*fig: POL*) about-turn; **prendre un** ~ to go into a bend, take a bend; ~ **sans visibilité** blind bend.
viral, e, aux [viRal, -o] *adj* viral.
virée [viRe] *nf* (*courte*) run; (*: à pied*) walk; (*longue*) trip; hike, walking tour.
virement [viRmɑ̃] *nm* (*COMM*) transfer; ~ **bancaire** (bank) credit transfer, ≈ (bank) giro transfer (*BRIT*); ~ **postal** Post office credit transfer, ≈ Girobank ® transfer (*BRIT*).
virent [viR] *vb voir* **voir.**
virer [viRe] *vt* (*COMM*): ~ **qch (sur)** to transfer sth (into); (*PHOTO*) to tone; (*fam: renvoyer*) to

sack, boot out ♦ *vi* to turn; (*CHIMIE*) to change colour (*BRIT*) *ou* color (*US*); (*cuti-réaction*) to come up positive; (*PHOTO*) to tone; ~ **au bleu** to turn blue; ~ **de bord** to tack; (*fig*) to change tack; ~ **sur l'aile** to bank.

virevolte [viʀvɔlt(ə)] *nf* twirl; (*d'avis, d'opinion*) about-turn.

virevolter [viʀvɔlte] *vi* to twirl around.

virginal, e, aux [viʀʒinal, -o] *adj* virginal.

virginité [viʀʒinite] *nf* virginity; (*fig*) purity.

virgule [viʀgyl] *nf* comma; (*MATH*) point; **4 ~ 2** 4 point 2; ~ **flottante** floating decimal.

viril, e [viʀil] *adj* (*propre à l'homme*) masculine; (*énergique, courageux*) manly, virile.

viriliser [viʀilize] *vt* to make (more) manly *ou* masculine.

virilité [viʀilite] *nf* (*attributs masculins*) masculinity; (*fermeté, courage*) manliness; (*sexuelle*) virility.

virologie [viʀɔlɔʒi] *nf* virology.

virtualité [viʀtɥalite] *nf* virtuality; potentiality.

virtuel, le [viʀtɥɛl] *adj* potential; (*théorique*) virtual.

virtuellement [viʀtɥɛlmɑ̃] *adj* potentially; (*presque*) virtually.

virtuose [viʀtɥoz] *nm/f* (*MUS*) virtuoso; (*gén*) master.

virtuosité [viʀtɥozite] *nf* virtuosity; masterliness, masterful skills *pl*.

virulence [viʀylɑ̃s] *nf* virulence.

virulent, e [viʀylɑ̃, -ɑ̃t] *adj* virulent.

virus [viʀys] *nm* virus.

vis *vb* [vi] *voir* **voir, vivre** ♦ *nf* [vis] screw; ~ **à tête plate/ronde** flat-headed/round-headed screw; ~ **platinées** (*AUTO*) (contact) points; ~ **sans fin** worm, endless screw.

visa [viza] *nm* (*sceau*) stamp; (*validation de passeport*) visa; ~ **de censure** (censor's) certificate.

visage [vizaʒ] *nm* face; **à ~ découvert** (*franchement*) openly.

visagiste [vizaʒist(ə)] *nm/f* beautician.

vis-à-vis [vizavi] *adv* face to face ♦ *nm* person opposite; house *etc* opposite; ~ **de** *prép* opposite; (*fig*) towards, vis-à-vis; **en ~** facing *ou* opposite each other; **sans ~** (*immeuble*) with an open outlook.

viscéral, e, aux [viseʀal, -o] *adj* (*fig*) deep-seated, deep-rooted.

viscères [viseʀ] *nmpl* intestines, entrails.

viscose [viskoz] *nf* viscose.

viscosité [viskozite] *nf* viscosity.

visée [vize] *nf* (*avec une arme*) aiming; (*ARPENTAGE*) sighting; ~**s** *nfpl* (*intentions*) designs; **avoir des ~s sur qn/qch** to have designs on sb/sth.

viser [vize] *vi* to aim ♦ *vt* to aim at; (*concerner*) to be aimed *ou* directed at; (*apposer un visa sur*) to stamp, visa; ~ **à qch/faire** to aim at sth/at doing *ou* to do.

viseur [vizœʀ] *nm* (*d'arme*) sights *pl*; (*PHOTO*) viewfinder.

visibilité [vizibilite] *nf* visibility; **sans ~** (*pilotage, virage*) blind *cpd*.

visible [vizibl(ə)] *adj* visible; (*disponible*): **est-il ~?** can he see me?, will he see visitors?

visiblement [vizibləmɑ̃] *adv* visibly, obviously.

visière [vizjɛʀ] *nf* (*de casquette*) peak; (*qui s'attache*) eyeshade.

vision [vizjɔ̃] *nf* vision; (*sens*) (eye)sight, vision; (*fait de voir*): **la ~ de** the sight of; **première ~** (*CINÉ*) first showing.

visionnaire [vizjɔnɛʀ] *adj, nm/f* visionary.

visionner [vizjɔne] *vt* to view.

visionneuse [vizjɔnøz] *nf* viewer.

visiophone [vizjɔfɔn] *nm* videophone.

visite [vizit] *nf* visit; (*visiteur*) visitor; (*touristique: d'un musée etc*) tour; (*COMM: de représentant*) call; (*expertise, d'inspection*) inspection; (*médicale, à domicile*) visit, call; **la ~** (*MÉD*) medical examination; (*MIL: d'entrée*) medicals *pl*; (: *quotidienne*) sick parade; **faire une ~ à qn** to call on sb, pay sb a visit; **rendre ~ à qn** to visit sb, pay sb a visit; **être en ~ (chez qn)** to be visiting (sb); **heures de ~** (*hôpital, prison*) visiting hours; **le droit de ~** (*JUR: aux enfants*) right of access, access; ~ **de douane** customs inspection *ou* examination.

visiter [vizite] *vt* to visit; (*musée, ville*) to visit, go round.

visiteur, euse [vizitœʀ, -øz] *nm/f* visitor; ~ **des douanes** customs inspector; ~ **médical** medical rep(resentative); ~ **de prison** prison visitor.

vison [vizɔ̃] *nm* mink.

visqueux, euse [viskø, -øz] *adj* viscous; (*péj*) gooey; (: *manières*) slimy.

visser [vise] *vt*: ~ **qch** (*fixer, serrer*) to screw sth on.

visu [vizy]: **de ~** *adv* with one's own eyes.

visualisation [vizɥalizasjɔ̃] *nf* (*INFORM*) display; **écran de ~** visual display unit (VDU).

visualiser [vizɥalize] *vt* to visualize; (*INFORM*) to display, bring up on screen.

visuel, le [vizɥɛl] *adj* visual ♦ *nm* (visual) display; (*INFORM*) visual display unit (VDU).

visuellement [vizɥɛlmɑ̃] *adv* visually.

vit [vi] *vb voir* **vivre, voir.**

vital, e, aux [vital, -o] *adj* vital.

vitalité [vitalite] *nf* vitality.

vitamine [vitamin] *nf* vitamin.

vitaminé, e [vitamine] *adj* with (added) vitamins.

vitaminique [vitaminik] *adj* vitamin *cpd*.

vite [vit] *adv* (*rapidement*) quickly, fast; (*sans délai*) quickly; soon; **faire ~** (*agir rapidement*) to act fast; (*se dépêcher*) to be quick; **ce sera ~ fini** this will soon be finished; **viens ~** come quick(ly).

vitesse [vitɛs] *nf* speed; (*AUTO: dispositif*) gear;

faire de la ~ to drive fast *ou* at speed; **prendre qn de** ~ to outstrip sb, get ahead of sb; **prendre de la** ~ to pick up *ou* gather speed; **à toute** ~ at full *ou* top speed; **en perte de** ~ *(avion)* losing lift; *(fig)* losing momentum; **changer de** ~ *(AUTO)* to change gear; ~ **acquise** momentum; ~ **de croisière** cruising speed; ~ **de pointe** top speed; ~ **du son** speed of sound.

viticole [vitikɔl] *adj (industrie)* wine *cpd*; *(région)* wine-growing.

viticulteur [vitikyltœʀ] *nm* wine grower.

viticulture [vitikyltyʀ] *nf* wine growing.

vitrage [vitʀaʒ] *nm (cloison)* glass partition; *(toit)* glass roof; *(rideau)* net curtain.

vitrail, aux [vitʀaj, -o] *nm* stained-glass window.

vitre [vitʀ(ə)] *nf* (window) pane; *(de portière, voiture)* window.

vitré, e [vitʀe] *adj* glass *cpd*.

vitrer [vitʀe] *vt* to glaze.

vitreux, euse [vitʀø, -øz] *adj* vitreous; *(terne)* glassy.

vitrier [vitʀije] *nm* glazier.

vitrifier [vitʀifje] *vt* to vitrify; *(parquet)* to glaze.

vitrine [vitʀin] *nf (devanture)* (shop) window; *(étalage)* display; *(petite armoire)* display cabinet; **en** ~ in the window, on display; ~ **publicitaire** display case, showcase.

vitriol [vitʀijɔl] *nm* vitriol; ~ *(fig)* vitriolic.

vitupérations [vityperasjɔ̃] *nfpl* invective *sg*.

vitupérer [vitypeʀe] *vi* to rant and rave; ~ **contre** to rail against.

vivable [vivabl(ə)] *adj (personne)* livable-with; *(endroit)* fit to live in.

vivace *adj* [vivas] *(arbre, plante)* hardy; *(fig)* enduring ♦ *adv* [vivatʃe] *(MUS)* vivace.

vivacité [vivasite] *nf (voir vif)* liveliness, vivacity; sharpness; brilliance.

vivant, e [vivɑ̃, -ɑ̃t] *vb voir* **vivre** ♦ *adj (qui vit)* living, alive; *(animé)* lively; *(preuve, exemple)* living; *(langue)* modern ♦ *nm*: **du** ~ **de qn** in sb's lifetime; **les** ~**s et les morts** the living and the dead.

vivarium [vivaʀjɔm] *nm* vivarium.

vivats [viva] *nmpl* cheers.

vive [viv] *adj f voir* **vif** ♦ *vb voir* **vivre** ♦ *excl*: ~ **le roi!** long live the king!; ~ **les vacances!** hurrah for the holidays!

vivement [vivmɑ̃] *adv* vivaciously; sharply ♦ *excl*: ~ **les vacances!** I can't wait for the holidays!, roll on the holidays!

viveur [vivœʀ] *nm (péj)* high liver, pleasure-seeker.

vivier [vivje] *nm (au restaurant etc)* fish tank; *(étang)* fishpond.

vivifiant, e [vivifjɑ̃, -ɑ̃t] *adj* invigorating.

vivifier [vivifje] *vt* to invigorate; *(fig: souvenirs, sentiments)* to liven up, enliven.

vivipare [vivipaʀ] *adj* viviparous.

vivisection [viviseksjɔ̃] *nf* vivisection.

vivoter [vivɔte] *vi (personne)* to scrape a living, get by; *(fig: affaire etc)* to struggle along.

vivre [vivʀ(ə)] *vi, vt* to live ♦ *nm*: **le** ~ **et le logement** board and lodging ♦ ~**s** *nmpl* provisions, food supplies; **il vit encore** he is still alive; **se laisser** ~ to take life as it comes; **ne plus** ~ *(être anxieux)* to live on one's nerves; **il a vécu** *(eu une vie aventureuse)* he has seen life; **ce régime a vécu** this regime has had its day; **être facile à** ~ to be easy to get on with; **faire** ~ **qn** *(pourvoir à sa subsistance)* to provide (a living) for sb; ~ **mal** *(chichement)* to have a meagre existence; ~ **de** *(salaire etc)* to live on.

vivrier, ière [vivʀije, -jɛʀ] *adj* food-producing *cpd*.

vlan [vlɑ̃] *excl* wham!, bang!

VO *sigle f (CINÉ: = version originale)*: **voir un film en** ~ to see a film in its original language.

vº *abr* = **verso**.

vocable [vɔkabl(ə)] *nm* term.

vocabulaire [vɔkabylɛʀ] *nm* vocabulary.

vocal, e, aux [vɔkal, -o] *adj* vocal.

vocalique [vɔkalik] *adj* vocalic, vowel *cpd*.

vocalise [vɔkaliz] *nf* singing exercise.

vocaliser [vɔkalize] *vi (LING)* to vocalize; *(MUS)* to do one's singing exercises.

vocation [vɔkasjɔ̃] *nf* vocation, calling; **avoir la** ~ to have a vocation.

vociférations [vɔsiferasjɔ̃] *nfpl* cries of rage, screams.

vociférer [vɔsifeʀe] *vi, vt* to scream.

vodka [vɔdka] *nf* vodka.

vœu, x [vø] *nm* wish; *(à Dieu)* vow; **faire** ~ **de** to take a vow of; **avec tous nos** ~**x** with every good wish *ou* our best wishes; ~**x de bonheur** best wishes for your future happiness; ~**x de bonne année** best wishes for the New Year.

vogue [vɔg] *nf* fashion, vogue; **en** ~ in fashion, in vogue.

voguer [vɔge] *vi* to sail.

voici [vwasi] *prép (pour introduire, désigner)* here is + *sg*, here are + *pl*; **et** ~ **que ...** and now it *(ou* he) ...; **il est parti** ~ **3 ans** he left 3 years ago; ~ **une semaine que je l'ai vue** it's a week since I've seen her; **me** ~ here I am; *voir aussi* **voilà**.

voie [vwa] *vb voir* **voir** ♦ *nf* way; *(RAIL)* track, line; *(AUTO)* lane; **par** ~ **buccale** *ou* **orale** orally; **par** ~ **rectale** rectally; **suivre la** ~ **hiérarchique** to go through official channels; **ouvrir/montrer la** ~ to open up/show the way; **être en bonne** ~ to be shaping *ou* going well; **mettre qn sur la** ~ to put sb on the right track; **être en** ~ **d'achèvement/de rénovation** to be nearing completion/in the process of renovation; **à** ~ **étroite** narrow-gauge; **à** ~ **unique** single-track; **route à 2/3** ~**s** 2-/3-lane road; **par la** ~ **aérienne/ maritime** by air/sea; ~ **d'eau** *(NAVIG)* leak; ~ **express** expressway; ~ **de fait** *(JUR)* assault (and battery); ~ **ferrée** track; railway line (*BRIT*), railroad (*US*); **par ~ ferrée** by rail, by railroad; ~ **de garage** (*RAIL*) siding; **la ~ lactée** the Milky Way; ~ **navigable** waterway; ~ **prioritaire** (*AUTO*) road with right of way; ~ **privée** private road; **la ~ publique** the public highway.

voilà [vwala] *prép* (*en désignant*) there is + *sg*, there are + *pl*; **les ~** *ou* **voici** here *ou* there they are; **en ~** *ou* **voici un** here's one, there's one; ~ *ou* **voici deux ans** two years ago; ~ *ou* **voici deux ans que** it's two years since; **et ~!** there we are!; ~ **tout** that's all; "~ *ou* **voici**" (*en offrant etc*) "there *ou* here you are".

voilage [vwalaʒ] *nm* (*rideau*) net curtain; (*tissu*) net.

voile [vwal] *nm* veil; (*tissu léger*) net ♦ *nf* sail; (*sport*) sailing; **prendre le ~** to take the veil; **mettre à la ~** to make way under sail; ~ **du palais** *nm* soft palate, velum; ~ **au poumon** *nm* shadow on the lung.

voiler [vwale] *vt* to veil; (*PHOTO*) to fog; (*fausser: roue*) to buckle; (*: bois*) to warp; **se ~** *vi* (*lune, regard*) to mist over; (*ciel*) to grow hazy; (*voix*) to become husky; (*roue, disque*) to buckle; (*planche*) to warp; **se ~ la face** to hide one's face.

voilette [vwalɛt] *nf* (*hat*) veil.

voilier [vwalje] *nm* sailing ship; (*de plaisance*) sailing boat.

voilure [vwalyʀ] *nf* (*de voilier*) sails *pl*; (*d'avion*) aerofoils *pl* (*BRIT*), airfoils *pl* (*US*); (*de parachute*) canopy.

voir [vwaʀ] *vi, vt* to see; **se ~**: **se ~ critiquer/transformer** to be criticized/transformed; **cela se voit** (*cela arrive*) it happens; (*c'est visible*) that's obvious, it shows; ~ **à faire qch** to see to it that sth is done; ~ **loin** (*fig*) to be far-sighted; ~ **venir** (*fig*) to wait and see; **faire ~ qch à qn** to show sb sth; **en faire ~ à qn** (*fig*) to give sb a hard time; **ne pas pouvoir ~ qn** (*fig*) not to be able to stand sb; **regardez** ~ just look; **montrez** ~ show (me); **dites** ~ tell me; **voyons!** let's see now; (*indignation etc*) come (along) now!; **c'est à ~!** we'll see!; **c'est ce qu'on va ~!** we'll see about that!; **avoir quelque chose à ~ avec** to have something to do with; **ça n'a rien à ~ avec lui** that has nothing to do with him.

voire [vwaʀ] *adv* indeed; nay; or even.

voirie [vwaʀi] *nf* highway maintenance; (*administration*) highways department; (*enlèvement des ordures*) refuse (*BRIT*) *ou* garbage (*US*) collection.

vois [vwa] *vb voir* **voir**.

voisin, e [vwazɛ̃, -in] *adj* (*proche*) neighbouring (*BRIT*), neighboring (*US*); (*contigu*) next; (*ressemblant*) connected ♦ *nm/f* neighbo(u)r; (*de table, de dortoir etc*) person next to me (*ou* him *etc*); ~ **de palier** neighbo(u)r across the landing (*BRIT*) *ou* hall (*US*).

voisinage [vwazinaʒ] *nm* (*proximité*) proximity; (*environs*) vicinity; (*quartier, voisins*) neighbourhood (*BRIT*), neighborhood (*US*); **relations de bon ~** neighbo(u)rly terms.

voisiner [vwazine] *vi*: ~ **avec** to be side by side with.

voit [vwa] *vb voir* **voir**.

voiture [vwatyʀ] *nf* car; (*wagon*) coach, carriage; **en ~!** all aboard!; ~ **à bras** handcart; ~ **d'enfant** pram (*BRIT*), baby carriage (*US*); ~ **d'infirme** invalid carriage; ~ **de sport** sports car.

voiture-lit, *pl* **voitures-lits** [vwatyʀli] *nf* sleeper.

voiture-restaurant, *pl* **voitures-restaurants** [vwatyʀʀɛstɔʀɑ̃] *nf* dining car.

voix [vwa] *nf* voice; (*POL*) vote; **la ~ de la conscience/raison** the voice of conscience/reason; **à haute ~** aloud; **à ~ basse** in a low voice; **faire la grosse ~** to speak gruffly; **avoir de la ~** to have a good voice; **rester sans ~** to be speechless; ~ **de basse/ténor** *etc* bass/tenor *etc* voice; **à 2/4 ~** (*MUS*) in 2/4 parts; **avoir ~ au chapitre** to have a say in the matter; **mettre aux ~** to put to the vote; ~ **off** voice-over.

vol [vɔl] *nm* (*mode de locomotion*) flying; (*trajet, voyage, groupe d'oiseaux*) flight; (*mode d'appropriation*) theft, stealing; (*larcin*) theft; **à ~ d'oiseau** as the crow flies; **au ~**: **attraper qch au ~** to catch sth as it flies past; **saisir une remarque au ~** to pick up a passing remark; **prendre son ~** to take flight; **de haut ~** (*fig*) of the highest order; **en ~** in flight; ~ **avec effraction** breaking and entering *no pl*, break-in; ~ **à l'étalage** shoplifting *no pl*; ~ **libre** hang-gliding; ~ **à main armée** armed robbery; ~ **de nuit** night flight; ~ **plané** (*AVIAT*) glide, gliding *no pl*; ~ **à la tire** pickpocketing *no pl*; ~ **à voile** gliding.

vol. *abr* (= *volume*) vol.

volage [vɔlaʒ] *adj* fickle.

volaille [vɔlaj] *nf* (*oiseaux*) poultry *pl*; (*viande*) poultry *no pl*; (*oiseau*) fowl.

volailler [vɔlaje] *nm* poulterer.

volant, e [vɔlɑ̃, -ɑ̃t] *adj voir* **feuille** *etc* ♦ *nm* (*d'automobile*) (steering) wheel; (*de commande*) wheel; (*objet lancé*) shuttlecock; (*jeu*) battledore and shuttlecock; (*bande de tissu*) flounce; (*feuillet détachable*) tear-off portion; **le personnel ~, les ~s** (*AVIAT*) the flight staff; ~ **de sécurité** (*fig*) reserve, margin, safeguard.

volatil, e [vɔlatil] *adj* volatile.

volatile [vɔlatil] *nm* (*volaille*) bird; (*tout oiseau*) winged creature.

volatiliser [vɔlatilize]: **se ~** *vi* (*CHIMIE*) to volatilize; (*fig*) to vanish into thin air.

vol-au-vent [vɔlovɑ̃] *nm inv* vol-au-vent.

volcan [vɔlkɑ̃] *nm* volcano; (*fig: personne*) hothead.

volcanique [vɔlkanik] *adj* volcanic; (*fig: tem-*

pérament) volatile.

volcanologie [vɔlkanɔlɔʒi] *nf* vulcanology.

volcanologue [vɔlkanɔlɔg] *nm/f* vulcanologist.

volée [vɔle] *nf* (*groupe d'oiseaux*) flight, flock; (*TENNIS*) volley; ~ **de coups/de flèches** volley of blows/arrows; **à la ~: rattraper à la ~** to catch in midair; **lancer à la ~** to fling about; **semer à la ~** to (sow) broadcast; **à toute ~** (*sonner les cloches*) vigorously; (*lancer un projectile*) with full force; **de haute ~** (*fig*) of the highest order.

voler [vɔle] *vi* (*avion, oiseau, fig*) to fly; (*voleur*) to steal ♦ *vt* (*objet*) to steal; (*personne*) to rob; ~ **en éclats** to smash to smithereens; ~ **de ses propres ailes** (*fig*) to stand on one's own two feet; ~ **au vent** to fly in the wind; ~ **qch à qn** to steal sth from sb.

volet [vɔlɛ] *nm* (*de fenêtre*) shutter; (*AVIAT*) flap; (*de feuillet, document*) section; (*fig: d'un plan*) facet; **trié sur le ~** hand-picked.

voleter [vɔlte] *vi* to flutter (about).

voleur, euse [vɔlœʀ, -øz] *nm/f* thief (*pl* thieves) ♦ *adj* thieving.

volière [vɔljɛʀ] *nf* aviary.

volley(-ball) [vɔlɛ(bɔl)] *nm* volleyball.

volleyeur, euse [vɔlɛjœʀ, -øz] *nm/f* volleyball player.

volontaire [vɔlɔ̃tɛʀ] *adj* (*acte, activité*) voluntary; (*délibéré*) deliberate; (*caractère, personne: décidé*) self-willed ♦ *nm/f* volunteer.

volontairement [vɔlɔ̃tɛʀmɑ̃] *adv* voluntarily; deliberately.

volontariat [vɔlɔ̃taʀja] *nm* voluntary service.

volontarisme [vɔlɔ̃taʀism(ə)] *nm* voluntarism.

volontariste [vɔlɔ̃taʀist(ə)] *adj, nm/f* voluntarist.

volonté [vɔlɔ̃te] *nf* (*faculté de vouloir*) will; (*énergie, fermeté*) will(power); (*souhait, désir*) wish; **se servir/boire à ~** to take/drink as much as one likes; **bonne ~** goodwill, willingness; **mauvaise ~** lack of goodwill, unwillingness.

volontiers [vɔlɔ̃tje] *adv* (*de bonne grâce*) willingly; (*avec plaisir*) willingly, gladly; (*habituellement, souvent*) readily, willingly; "~" "with pleasure", "I'd be glad to".

volt [vɔlt] *nm* volt.

voltage [vɔltaʒ] *nm* voltage.

volte-face [vɔltəfas] *nf inv* about-turn; (*fig*) about-turn, U-turn; **faire ~** to do an about-turn; to do a U-turn.

voltige [vɔltiʒ] *nf* (*ÉQUITATION*) trick riding; (*au cirque*) acrobatics *sg*; (*AVIAT*) (aerial) acrobatics *sg*; **numéro de haute ~** acrobatic act.

voltiger [vɔltiʒe] *vi* to flutter (about).

voltigeur [vɔltiʒœʀ] *nm* (*au cirque*) acrobat; (*MIL*) light infantryman.

voltmètre [vɔltmɛtʀ(ə)] *nm* voltmeter.

volubile [vɔlybil] *adj* voluble.

volubilis [vɔlybilis] *nm* convolvulus.

volume [vɔlym] *nm* volume; (*GÉOM: solide*) solid.

volumineux, euse [vɔlyminø, -øz] *adj* voluminous, bulky.

volupté [vɔlypte] *nf* sensual delight *ou* pleasure.

voluptueusement [vɔlyptɥøzmɑ̃] *adv* voluptuously.

voluptueux, euse [vɔlyptɥø, -øz] *adj* voluptuous.

volute [vɔlyt] *nf* (*ARCHIT*) volute; ~ **de fumée** curl of smoke.

vomi [vɔmi] *nm* vomit.

vomir [vɔmiʀ] *vi* to vomit, be sick ♦ *vt* to vomit, bring up; (*fig*) to belch out, spew out; (*exécrer*) to loathe, abhor.

vomissement [vɔmismɑ̃] *nm* (*action*) vomiting *no pl*; **des ~s** vomit *sg*.

vomissure [vɔmisyʀ] *nf* vomit *no pl*.

vomitif [vɔmitif] *nm* emetic.

vont [vɔ̃] *vb voir* **aller**.

vorace [vɔʀas] *adj* voracious.

voracement [vɔʀasmɑ̃] *adv* voraciously.

voracité [vɔʀasite] *nf* voracity.

vos [vo] *adj possessif voir* **votre**.

Vosges [voʒ] *nfpl*: **les ~** the Vosges.

vosgien, ne [voʒjɛ̃, -ɛn] *adj* of *ou* from the Vosges ♦ *nm/f* inhabitant *ou* native of the Vosges.

VOST *sigle f* (*CINÉ: = version originale sous-titrée*) sub-titled version.

votant, e [vɔtɑ̃, -ɑ̃t] *nm/f* voter.

vote [vɔt] *nm* vote; ~ **par correspondance/ procuration** postal/proxy vote; ~ **à main levée** vote by show of hands; ~ **secret**, ~ **à bulletins secrets** secret ballot.

voter [vɔte] *vi* to vote ♦ *vt* (*loi, décision*) to vote for.

votre [vɔtʀ(ə)], *pl* **vos** [vo] *adj possessif* your.

vôtre [votʀ(ə)] *pron*: **le ~**, **la ~**, **les ~s** yours; **les ~s** (*fig*) your family *ou* folks; **à la ~** (*toast*) your (good) health!

voudrai [vudʀe] *etc vb voir* **vouloir**.

voué, e [vwe] *adj*: ~ **à** doomed to, destined for.

vouer [vwe] *vt*: ~ **qch à** (*Dieu/un saint*) to dedicate sth to; ~ **sa vie/son temps à** (*étude, cause etc*) to devote one's life/time to; ~ **une haine/amitié éternelle à qn** to vow undying hatred/friendship to sb.

═══════════════════════════════════ *MOT-CLÉ*

vouloir [vulwaʀ] *nm*: **le bon ~ de qn** sb's goodwill; sb's pleasure

♦ *vt* **1** (*exiger, désirer*) to want; ~ **faire/que qn fasse** to want to do/sb to do; **voulez-vous du thé?** would you like *ou* do you want some tea?; ~ **qch à qn** to wish sth for sb; **que me veut-il?** what does he want with me?; **que veux-tu que je te dise?** what do you want me to say?; **sans le ~** (*involontairement*) without meaning to, unintentionally; **je voudrais ceci/faire** I would *ou* I'd like this/to do; **le**

hasard a voulu que ... as fate would have it, ...; **la tradition veut que** ... tradition demands that ...; ... **qui se veut moderne** ... which purports to be modern
2 (*consentir*): **je veux bien** (*bonne volonté*) I'll be happy to; (*concession*) fair enough, that's fine; **oui, si on veut** (*en quelque sorte*) yes, if you like; **comme tu veux** as you wish; (*en quelque sorte*) if you like; **veuillez attendre** please wait; **veuillez agréer** ... (*formule épistolaire*) yours faithfully
3: **en** ~ (*être ambitieux*) to be out to win; **en** ~ **à qn** to bear sb a grudge; **je lui en veux d'avoir fait ça** I resent his having done that; **s'en** ~ (**de**) to be annoyed with o.s. (for); **il en veut à mon argent** he's after my money
4: ~ **de** to want; **la compagnie ne veut plus de lui** the firm doesn't want him any more; **elle ne veut pas de son aide** she doesn't want his help
5: ~ **dire** to mean.

voulu, e [vuly] *pp de* **vouloir** ♦ *adj* (*requis*) required, requisite; (*délibéré*) deliberate, intentional.
voulus [vuly] *etc vb voir* **vouloir**.
vous [vu] *pron* you; (*objet indirect*) (to) you; (*réfléchi*) yourself (*pl* yourselves); (*réciproque*) each other ♦ *nm*: **employer le** ~ (*vouvoyer*) to use the "vous" form; ~-**même** yourself; ~-**mêmes** yourselves.
voûte [vut] *nf* vault; **la** ~ **céleste** the vault of heaven; ~ **du palais** (*ANAT*) roof of the mouth; ~ **plantaire** arch (of the foot).
voûté, e [vute] *adj* vaulted, arched; (*dos, personne*) stooped, bent.
voûter [vute] *vt* (*ARCHIT*) to arch, vault; **se** ~ *vi* (*dos, personne*) to become stooped.
vouvoiement [vuvwamɑ̃] *nm* use of formal "vous" form.
vouvoyer [vuvwaje] *vt*: ~ **qn** to address sb as "vous".
voyage [vwajaʒ] *nm* journey, trip; (*fait de voyager*): **le** ~ travel(ling); **partir/être en** ~ to go off/be away on a journey *ou* trip; **faire un** ~ to go on *ou* make a trip *ou* journey; **faire bon** ~ to have a good journey; **les gens du** ~ travelling people; ~ **d'agrément/d'affaires** pleasure/business trip; ~ **de noces** honeymoon; ~ **organisé** package tour.
voyager [vwajaʒe] *vi* to travel.
voyageur, euse [vwajaʒœʀ, -øz] *nm/f* traveller; (*passager*) passenger ♦ *adj* (*tempérament*) nomadic, wayfaring; ~ **(de commerce)** commercial traveller.
voyagiste [vwajaʒist(ə)] *nm* tour operator.
voyais [vwajɛ] *etc vb voir* **voir**.
voyance [vwajɑ̃s] *nf* clairvoyance.
voyant, e [vwajɑ̃, -ɑ̃t] *adj* (*couleur*) loud, gaudy ♦ *nm/f* (*personne qui voit*) sighted person ♦ *nm* (*signal*) (warning) light ♦ *nf* clairvoyant.
voyelle [vwajɛl] *nf* vowel.

voyeur, euse [vwajœʀ, -øz] *nm/f* voyeur; peeping Tom.
voyeurisme [vwajœʀism(ə)] *nm* voyeurism.
voyons [vwajɔ̃] *etc vb voir* **voir**.
voyou [vwaju] *nm* lout, hoodlum; (*enfant*) guttersnipe.
VPC *sigle f* (= *vente par correspondance*) mail order selling.
vrac [vʀak]: **en** ~ *adv* higgledy-piggledy; (*COMM*) in bulk.
vrai, e [vʀɛ] *adj* (*véridique: récit, faits*) true; (*non factice, authentique*) real ♦ *nm*: **le** ~ the truth; **à** ~ **dire** to tell the truth; **il est** ~ **que** it is true that; **être dans le** ~ to be right.
vraiment [vʀɛmɑ̃] *adv* really.
vraisemblable [vʀɛsɑ̃blabl(ə)] *adj* (*plausible*) likely, plausible; (*probable*) likely, probable.
vraisemblablement [vʀɛsɑ̃blabləmɑ̃] *adv* in all likelihood, very likely.
vraisemblance [vʀɛsɑ̃blɑ̃s] *nf* likelihood, plausibility; (*romanesque*) verisimilitude; **selon toute** ~ in all likelihood.
vraquier [vʀakje] *nm* freighter.
vrille [vʀij] *nf* (*de plante*) tendril; (*outil*) gimlet; (*spirale*) spiral; (*AVIAT*) spin.
vriller [vʀije] *vt* to bore into, pierce.
vrombir [vʀɔ̃biʀ] *vi* to hum.
vrombissant, e [vʀɔ̃bisɑ̃, -ɑ̃t] *adj* humming.
vrombissement [vʀɔ̃bismɑ̃] *nm* hum(ming).
VRP *sigle m* (= *voyageur, représentant, placier*) (sales) rep.
VTT *sigle m* (= *vélo tout-terrain*) mountain bike.
vu [vy] *prép* (*en raison de*) in view of; ~ **que** in view of the fact that.
vu, e [vy] *pp de* **voir** ♦ *adj*: **bien/mal** ~ (*personne*) well/poorly thought of; (*conduite*) good/bad form ♦ *nm*: **au** ~ **et au su de tous** openly and publicly; **ni** ~ **ni connu** what the eye doesn't see ...!, no one will be any the wiser; **c'est tout** ~ it's a foregone conclusion.
vue [vy] *nf* (*fait de voir*): **la** ~ **de** the sight of; (*sens, faculté*) (eye)sight; (*panorama, image, photo*) view; (*spectacle*) sight; ~**s** *nfpl* (*idées*) views; (*dessein*) designs; **perdre la** ~ to lose one's (eye)sight; **perdre de** ~ to lose sight of; **à la** ~ **de tous** in full view of everybody; **hors de** ~ out of sight; **à première** ~ at first sight; **connaître de** ~ to know by sight; **à** ~ (*COMM*) at sight; **tirer à** ~ to shoot on sight; **à** ~ **d'œil** *adv* visibly; (*à première vue*) at a quick glance; **avoir** ~ **sur** to have a view of; **en** ~ (*visible*) in sight; (*COMM*) in the public eye; **avoir qch en** ~ (*intentions*) to have one's sights on sth; **en** ~ **de faire** with the intention of doing, with a view to doing; ~ **d'ensemble** overall view; ~ **de l'esprit** theoretical view.
vulcanisation [vylkanizasjɔ̃] *nf* vulcanization.
vulcaniser [vylkanize] *vt* to vulcanize.
vulcanologie [vylkanɔlɔʒi] *nf* = **volcanologie**.
vulcanologue [vylkanɔlɔg] *nm/f* = **volcanolo-**

gue.

vulgaire [vylgɛʀ] *adj* (*grossier*) vulgar, coarse; (*trivial*) commonplace, mundane; (*péj*: *quelconque*): **de ~s touristes/chaises de cuisine** common tourists/kitchen chairs; (*BOT, ZOOL*: *non latin*) common.

vulgairement [vylgɛʀmã] *adv* vulgarly, coarsely; (*communément*) commonly.

vulgarisation [vylgaʀizɑsjɔ̃] *nf*: **ouvrage de ~** popularizing work, popularization.

vulgariser [vylgaʀize] *vt* to popularize.

vulgarité [vylgaʀite] *nf* vulgarity, coarseness.

vulnérabilité [vylneʀabilite] *nf* vulnerability.

vulnérable [vylneʀabl(ə)] *adj* vulnerable.

vulve [vylv(ə)] *nf* vulva.

vumètre [vymɛtʀ(ə)] *nm* recording level gauge.

Vve *abr* = **veuve**.

VVF *sigle m* (= *village vacances famille*) *state-subsidized holiday village*.

vx *abr* = **vieux**.

W w

W, w [dubləve] *nm inv* W, w ♦ *abr* (= *watt*) W; **W comme William** W for William.

wagon [vagɔ̃] *nm* (*de voyageurs*) carriage; (*de marchandises*) truck, wagon.

wagon-citerne, *pl* **wagons-citernes** [vagɔ̃sitɛʀn(ə)] *nm* tanker.

wagon-lit, *pl* **wagons-lits** [vagɔ̃li] *nm* sleeper, sleeping car.

wagonnet [vagɔnɛ] *nm* small truck.

wagon-poste, *pl* **wagons-postes** [vagɔ̃pɔst(ə)] *nm* mail van.

wagon-restaurant, *pl* **wagons-restaurants** [vagɔ̃ʀɛstɔʀã] *nm* restaurant *ou* dining car.

Walkman [wɔkman] *nm* ® Walkman ®, personal stereo.

Wallis et Futuna [walisefytyna]: **les îles ~** the Wallis and Futuna Islands.

wallon, ne [walɔ̃, -ɔn] *adj* Walloon ♦ *nm* (*LING*) Walloon ♦ *nm/f*: **W~, ne** Walloon.

Wallonie [walɔni] *nf*: **la ~** French-speaking (part of) Belgium.

water-polo [watɛʀpɔlo] *nm* water polo.

waters [watɛʀ] *nmpl* toilet *sg*, loo *sg* (*BRIT*).

watt [wat] *nm* watt.

w.-c. [vese] *nmpl* toilet *sg*, lavatory *sg*.

week-end [wikɛnd] *nm* weekend.

western [wɛstɛʀn] *nm* western.

Westphalie [vɛsfali] *nf*: **la ~** Westphalia.

whisky, *pl* **whiskies** [wiski] *nm* whisky.

white-spirit [wajtspiʀit] *nm* white spirit.

Winchester [wintʃɛstɛʀ]: **disque ~** Winchester disk.

wok [wɔk] *nm* wok.

X x

X, x [iks] *nm inv* X, x ♦ *sigle m* = (**École**) **polytechnique; plainte contre X** (*JUR*) action against person or persons unknown; **X comme Xavier** X for Xmas.

xénophobe [gzenɔfɔb] *adj* xenophobic ♦ *nm/f* xenophobe.

xénophobie [gzenɔfɔbi] *nf* xenophobia.

xérès [gzeʀɛs] *nm* sherry.

xylographie [ksilɔgʀafi] *nf* xylography; (*image*) xylograph.

xylophone [ksilɔfɔn] *nm* xylophone.

Y y

Y, y [igʀɛk] *nm inv* Y, y; **Y comme Yvonne** Y for Yellow (*BRIT*) *ou* Yoke (*US*).

y [i] *adv* (*à cet endroit*) there; (*dessus*) on it (*ou* them); (*dedans*) in it (*ou* them) ♦ *pron* (*about ou* on *ou* of) it : *vérifier la syntaxe du verbe employé*; **j'~ pense** I'm thinking about it; *voir aussi* **aller, avoir**.

yacht [jɔt] *nm* yacht.

yaourt [jauʀt] *nm* yoghurt.

yaourtière [jauʀtjɛʀ] *nf* yoghurt-maker.

Yémen [jemɛn] *nm*: **le ~** Yemen.

yéménite [jemenit] *adj* Yemeni.

yeux [jø] *pl de* **œil**.

yoga [jɔga] *nm* yoga.

yoghourt [jɔguʀt] *nm* = **yaourt**.

yole [jɔl] *nf* skiff.

yougoslave [jugɔslav] *adj* Yugoslav(ian) ♦ *nm/f*: **Y~** Yugoslav(ian).

Yougoslavie [jugɔslavi] *nf*: **la ~** Yugoslavia.

youyou [juju] *nm* dinghy.

yo-yo [jojo] *nm inv* yo-yo.

yucca [juka] *nm* yucca (tree *ou* plant).

Z z

Z, z [zɛd] *nm inv* Z, z; **Z comme Zoé** Z for Zebra.

ZAC [zak] *sigle f* (= *zone d'aménagement concerté*) urban development zone.

ZAD [zad] *sigle f* (= *zone d'aménagement différé*) future development zone.

Zaïre [zɑː'ɪə*] *nm*: **le** ~ Zaïre.

zaïrois, e [zaiʀwa, -waz] *adj* Zaïrese.

Zambèze [zɑ̃bɛz] *nm*: **le** ~ the Zambezi.

Zambie [zɑ̃bi] *nf*: **la** ~ Zambia.

zambien, ne [zɑ̃bjɛ̃, -ɛn] *adj* Zambian.

zapping [zapiŋ] *nm*: **faire du** ~ to flick through the channels.

zèbre [zɛbʀ(ə)] *nm* (*ZOOL*) zebra.

zébré, e [zebʀe] *adj* striped, streaked.

zébrure [zebʀyʀ] *nf* stripe, streak.

zélateur, trice [zelatœʀ, -tʀis] *nm/f* partisan, zealot.

zèle [zɛl] *nm* diligence, assiduousness; **faire du** ~ (*péj*) to be over-zealous.

zélé, e [zele] *adj* zealous.

zénith [zenit] *nm* zenith.

ZEP [zɛp] *sigle f* (= *zone d'éducation prioritaire*) area targeted for special help in education.

zéro [zeʀo] *nm* zero, nought (*BRIT*); **au-dessous de** ~ below zero (Centigrade), below freezing; **partir de** ~ to start from scratch; **réduire à** ~ to reduce to nothing; **trois (buts) à** ~ 3 (goals to) nil.

zeste [zɛst(ə)] *nm* peel, zest; **un** ~ **de citron** a piece of lemon peel.

zézaiement [zezɛmɑ̃] *nm* lisp.

zézayer [zezeje] *vi* to have a lisp.

ZI *sigle f* = **zone industrielle**.

zibeline [ziblin] *nf* sable.

ZIF [zif] *sigle f* (= *zone d'intervention foncière*) intervention zone.

zigouiller [ziguje] *vt* (*fam*) to do in.

zigzag [zigzag] *nm* zigzag.

zigzaguer [zigzage] *vi* to zigzag (along).

Zimbabwe [zimbabwe] *nm*: **le** ~ Zimbabwe.

zimbabwéen, ne [zimbabweɛ̃, -ɛn] *adj* Zimbabwean.

zinc [zɛ̃g] *nm* (*CHIMIE*) zinc; (*comptoir*) bar, counter.

zinguer [zɛ̃ge] *vt* to cover with zinc.

zircon [ziʀkɔ̃] *nm* zircon.

zizanie [zizani] *nf*: **semer la** ~ to stir up ill-feeling.

zizi [zizi] *nm* (*fam*) willy (*BRIT*), peter (*US*).

zodiacal, e, aux [zɔdjakal, -o] *adj* (*signe*) of the zodiac.

zodiaque [zɔdjak] *nm* zodiac.

zona [zona] *nm* shingles *sg*.

zonage [zonaʒ] *nm* (*ADMIN*) zoning.

zonard, e [zonaʀ, -aʀd] *nm/f* (*fam*) (young) hooligan *ou* thug.

zone [zon] *nf* zone, area; (*INFORM*) field; (*quartiers*): **la** ~ the slum belt; **de seconde** ~ (*fig*) second-rate; ~ **d'action** (*MIL*) sphere of activity; ~ **bleue** ≈ restricted parking area; ~ **d'extension** *ou* **d'urbanisation** urban development area; ~ **franche** free zone; ~ **industrielle (ZI)** industrial estate; ~ **résidentielle** residential area; ~ **tampon** buffer zone.

zoner [zone] *vi* (*fam*) to hang around.

zoo [zoo] *nm* zoo.

zoologie [zɔɔlɔʒi] *nf* zoology.

zoologique [zɔɔlɔʒik] *adj* zoological.

zoologiste [zɔɔlɔʒist(ə)] *nm/f* zoologist.

zoom [zum] *nm* (*PHOTO*) zoom (lens).

ZUP [zyp] *sigle f* (= *zone à urbaniser en priorité*) = ZAC.

Zurich [zyʀik] *n* Zürich.

zut [zyt] *excl* dash (it)! (*BRIT*), nuts! (*US*).

Aa

A, a [eɪ] *n* (*letter*) A, a *m*; (*SCOL: mark*) A; (*MUS*): **A** la *m*; **A for Andrew**, (*US*) **A for Able** A comme Anatole; **A road** *n* (*BRIT AUT*) route nationale; **A shares** *npl* (*BRIT STOCK EXCHANGE*) actions *fpl* prioritaires.

————————————— *KEYWORD*

a [eɪ, ə] (*before vowel or silent h: an*) *indef art* **1** un(e); ~ **book** un livre; **an apple** une pomme; **she's** ~ **doctor** elle est médecin
2 (*instead of the number "one"*) un(e); ~ **year ago** il y a un an; ~ **hundred/thousand** *etc* **pounds** cent/mille *etc* livres
3 (*in expressing ratios, prices etc*): **3** ~ **day/week** 3 par jour/semaine; **10 km an hour** 10 km à l'heure; **30p** ~ **kilo** 30p le kilo.

a. *abbr* = **acre**.

AA *n abbr* (*BRIT*: = *Automobile Association*) ≈ ACF *m*; (*US*: = *Associate in/of Arts*) diplôme universitaire; (= *Alcoholics Anonymous*) AA; (= *anti-aircraft*) AA.

AAA *n abbr* (= *American Automobile Association*) ≈ ACF *m*; (*BRIT*) = *Amateur Athletics Association*.

A & R *n abbr* (*MUS*: = *artists and repertoire*): ~ **man** découvreur *m* de talent.

AAUP *n abbr* (= *American Association of University Professors*) *syndicat universitaire*.

AB *abbr* (*BRIT*) = **able-bodied seaman**; (*Canada*) = *Alberta*.

aback [ə'bæk] *adv*: **to be taken** ~ être décontenancé(e).

abacus, *pl* **abaci** ['æbəkəs, -saɪ] *n* boulier *m*.

abandon [ə'bændən] *vt* abandonner ♦ *n* abandon *m*; **to** ~ **ship** évacuer le navire.

abandoned [ə'bændənd] *adj* (*child, house etc*) abandonné(e); (*unrestrained*) sans retenue.

abase [ə'beɪs] *vt*: **to** ~ **o.s.** (**so far as to do**) s'abaisser (à faire).

abashed [ə'bæʃt] *adj* confus(e), embarrassé(e).

abate [ə'beɪt] *vi* s'apaiser, se calmer.

abatement [ə'beɪtmənt] *n*: **noise** ~ lutte *f* contre le bruit.

abattoir ['æbətwɑː*] *n* (*BRIT*) abattoir *m*.

abbey ['æbɪ] *n* abbaye *f*.

abbot ['æbət] *n* père supérieur.

abbreviate [ə'briːvɪeɪt] *vt* abréger.

abbreviation [əbriːvɪ'eɪʃən] *n* abréviation *f*.

ABC *n abbr* (= *American Broadcasting Company*) chaîne de télévision.

abdicate ['æbdɪkeɪt] *vt*, *vi* abdiquer.

abdication [æbdɪ'keɪʃən] *n* abdication *f*.

abdomen ['æbdəmən] *n* abdomen *m*.

abdominal [æb'dɔmɪnl] *adj* abdominal(e).

abduct [æb'dʌkt] *vt* enlever.

abduction [æb'dʌkʃən] *n* enlèvement *m*.

Aberdonian [æbə'dəʊnɪən] *adj* d'Aberdeen ♦ *n* habitant/e d'Aberdeen; natif/ive d'Aberdeen.

aberration [æbə'reɪʃən] *n* anomalie *f*; **in a moment of mental** ~ dans un moment d'égarement.

abet [ə'bet] *vt see* **aid**.

abeyance [ə'beɪəns] *n*: **in** ~ (*law*) en désuétude; (*matter*) en suspens.

abhor [əb'hɔː*] *vt* abhorrer, exécrer.

abhorrent [əb'hɔrənt] *adj* odieux(euse), exécrable.

abide [ə'baɪd] *vt* souffrir, supporter.
►**abide by** *vt fus* observer, respecter.

abiding [ə'baɪdɪŋ] *adj* (*memory etc*) durable.

ability [ə'bɪlɪtɪ] *n* compétence *f*; capacité *f*; (*skill*) talent *m*; **to the best of my** ~ de mon mieux.

abject ['æbdʒekt] *adj* (*poverty*) sordide; (*coward*) méprisable; **an** ~ **apology** les excuses les plus plates.

ablaze [ə'bleɪz] *adj* en feu, en flammes; ~ **with light** resplendissant de lumière.

able ['eɪbl] *adj* compétent(e); **to be** ~ **to do sth** pouvoir faire qch, être capable de faire qch.

able-bodied ['eɪbl'bɒdɪd] *adj* robuste; ~ **sea-man** (*BRIT*) matelot breveté.

ably ['eɪblɪ] *adv* avec compétence *or* talent, habilement.

ABM *n abbr* = anti-ballistic missile.

abnormal [æb'nɔːməl] *adj* anormal(e).

abnormality [æbnɔː'mælɪtɪ] *n* (*condition*) caractère anormal; (*instance*) anomalie *f*.

aboard [ə'bɔːd] *adv* à bord ♦ *prep* à bord de; (*train*) dans.

abode [ə'bəʊd] *n* (*old*) demeure *f*; (*LAW*): **of no fixed** ~ sans domicile fixe.

abolish [ə'bɒlɪʃ] *vt* abolir.

abolition [æbə'lɪʃən] *n* abolition *f*.

abominable [ə'bɒmɪnəbl] *adj* abominable.

aborigine [æbə'rɪdʒɪnɪ] *n* aborigène *m/f*.

abort [ə'bɔːt] *vt* (*MED, fig*) faire avorter; (*COMPUT*) abandonner.

abortion [ə'bɔːʃən] *n* avortement *m*; **to have an** ~ se faire avorter.

abortionist [ə'bɔːʃənɪst] *n* avorteur/euse.

abortive [ə'bɔːtɪv] *adj* manqué(e).

abound [ə'baʊnd] *vi* abonder; **to** ~ **in** abonder en, regorger de.

================= *KEYWORD*

about [ə'baʊt] *adv* **1** (*approximately*) environ, à peu près; ~ **a hundred/thousand** *etc* environ cent/mille *etc*, une centaine (de)/un millier (de) *etc*; **it takes** ~ **10 hours** ça prend environ *or* à peu près 10 heures; **at** ~ **2 o'clock** vers 2 heures; **I've just** ~ **finished** j'ai presque fini

2 (*referring to place*) çà et là, deci delà; **to run** ~ courir çà et là; **to walk** ~ se promener, aller et venir; **is Paul** ~? (*BRIT*) est-ce que Paul est là?; **it's** ~ **here** c'est par ici, c'est dans les parages; **they left all their things lying** ~ ils ont laissé traîner toutes leurs affaires

3: **to be** ~ **to do sth** être sur le point de faire qch; **I'm not** ~ **to do all that for nothing** (*col*) je ne vais quand même pas faire tout ça pour rien

4 (*opposite*): **it's the other way** ~ (*BRIT*) c'est l'inverse

♦ *prep* **1** (*relating to*) au sujet de, à propos de; **a book** ~ **London** un livre sur Londres; **what is it** ~? de quoi s'agit-il?; **we talked** ~ **it** nous en avons parlé; **do something** ~ **it!** faites quelque chose!; **what** *or* **how** ~ **doing this?** et si nous faisions ceci?

2 (*referring to place*) dans; **to walk** ~ **the town** se promener dans la ville.

about face, about turn *n* (*MIL*) demi-tour *m*; (*fig*) volte-face *f*.

above [ə'bʌv] *adv* au-dessus ♦ *prep* au-dessus de; **mentioned** ~ mentionné ci-dessus; **costing** ~ **£10** coûtant plus de 10 livres; ~ **all** par-dessus tout, surtout.

aboveboard [ə'bʌv'bɔːd] *adj* franc(franche),

loyal(e); honnête.

abrasion [ə'breɪʒən] *n* frottement *m*; (*on skin*) écorchure *f*.

abrasive [ə'breɪzɪv] *adj* abrasif(ive); (*fig*) caustique, agressif(ive).

abreast [ə'brɛst] *adv* de front; **to keep** ~ **of** se tenir au courant de.

abridge [ə'brɪdʒ] *vt* abréger.

abroad [ə'brɔːd] *adv* à l'étranger; **there is a rumour** ~ **that** ... (*fig*) le bruit court que ....

abrupt [ə'brʌpt] *adj* (*steep, blunt*) abrupt(e); (*sudden, gruff*) brusque.

abscess ['æbsɪs] *n* abcès *m*.

abscond [əb'skɒnd] *vi* disparaître, s'enfuir.

absence ['æbsəns] *n* absence *f*; **in the** ~ **of** (*person*) en l'absence de; (*thing*) faute de.

absent ['æbsənt] *adj* absent(e); ~ **without leave (AWOL)** (*MIL*) en absence irrégulière.

absentee [æbsən'tiː] *n* absent/e.

absenteeism [æbsən'tiːɪzəm] *n* absentéisme *m*.

absent-minded ['æbsənt'maɪndɪd] *adj* distrait(e).

absent-mindedness ['æbsənt'maɪndɪdnɪs] *n* distraction *f*.

absolute ['æbsəluːt] *adj* absolu(e).

absolutely [æbsə'luːtlɪ] *adv* absolument.

absolve [əb'zɒlv] *vt*: **to** ~ **sb (from)** (*sin etc*) absoudre qn (de); **to** ~ **sb from** (*oath*) délier qn de.

absorb [əb'zɔːb] *vt* absorber; **to be** ~**ed in a book** être plongé(e) dans un livre.

absorbent [əb'zɔːbənt] *adj* absorbant(e).

absorbent cotton *n* (*US*) coton *m* hydrophile.

absorbing [əb'zɔːbɪŋ] *adj* absorbant(e); (*book, film etc*) captivant(e).

absorption [əb'sɔːpʃən] *n* absorption *f*.

abstain [əb'steɪn] *vi*: **to** ~ **(from)** s'abstenir (de).

abstemious [əb'stiːmɪəs] *adj* sobre, frugal(e).

abstention [əb'stɛnʃən] *n* abstention *f*.

abstinence ['æbstɪnəns] *n* abstinence *f*.

abstract *adj, n* ['æbstrækt] *adj* abstrait(e) ♦ *n* (*summary*) résumé *m* ♦ *vt* [æb'strækt] extraire.

absurd [əb'sɜːd] *adj* absurde.

absurdity [əb'sɜːdɪtɪ] *n* absurdité *f*.

ABTA ['æbtə] *n abbr* = Association of British Travel Agents.

Abu Dhabi ['æbuː'dɑːbɪ] *n* Ab(o)u Dhabî *m*.

abundance [ə'bʌndəns] *n* abondance *f*.

abundant [ə'bʌndənt] *adj* abondant(e).

abuse *n* [ə'bjuːs] insultes *fpl*, injures *fpl*; (*of power etc*) abus *m* ♦ *vt* [ə'bjuːz] abuser de; **to be open to** ~ se prêter à des abus.

abusive [ə'bjuːsɪv] *adj* grossier(ière), injurieux(euse).

abysmal [ə'bɪzməl] *adj* exécrable; (*ignorance etc*) sans bornes.

abyss [ə'bɪs] *n* abîme *m*, gouffre *m*.

AC *n abbr* (*US*) = athletic club.

a/c *abbr* (*BANKING etc*) = account, account cur-

rent.

academic [ækə'dɛmɪk] *adj* universitaire; (*pej: issue*) oiseux(euse), purement théorique ♦ *n* universitaire *m/f*; ~ **freedom** liberté *f* académique.

academic year *n* année *f* universitaire.

academy [ə'kædəmɪ] *n* (*learned body*) académie *f*; (*school*) collège *m*; **military/naval** ~ école militaire/navale; ~ **of music** conservatoire *m*.

ACAS ['eɪkæs] *n abbr* (*BRIT*: = *Advisory, Conciliation and Arbitration Service*) *organisme de conciliation et d'arbitrage des conflits du travail.*

accede [æk'siːd] *vi*: **to** ~ **to** (*request, throne*) accéder à.

accelerate [æk'sɛləreɪt] *vt, vi* accélérer.

acceleration [æksɛlə'reɪʃən] *n* accélération *f*.

accelerator [æk'sɛləreɪtə*] *n* accélérateur *m*.

accent ['æksɛnt] *n* accent *m*.

accentuate [æk'sɛntjueɪt] *vt* (*syllable*) accentuer; (*need, difference etc*) souligner.

accept [ək'sɛpt] *vt* accepter.

acceptable [ək'sɛptəbl] *adj* acceptable.

acceptance [ək'sɛptəns] *n* acceptation *f*; **to meet with general** ~ être favorablement accueilli par tous.

access ['æksɛs] *n* accès *m* ♦ *vt* (*COMPUT*) accéder à; **to have** ~ **to** (*information, library etc*) avoir accès à, pouvoir utiliser *or* consulter; (*person*) avoir accès auprès de; **the burglars gained** ~ **through a window** les cambrioleurs sont entrés par une fenêtre.

accessible [æk'sɛsəbl] *adj* accessible.

accession [æk'sɛʃən] *n* accession *f*; (*of king*) avènement *m*; (*to library*) acquisition *f*.

accessory [æk'sɛsərɪ] *n* accessoire *m*; **toilet accessories** (*BRIT*) articles *mpl* de toilette.

access road *n* voie *f* d'accès; (*to motorway*) bretelle *f* de raccordement.

access time *n* (*COMPUT*) temps *m* d'accès.

accident ['æksɪdənt] *n* accident *m*; (*chance*) hasard *m*; **to meet with** *or* **to have an** ~ avoir un accident; ~**s at work** accidents du travail; **by** ~ par hasard; (*not deliberately*) accidentellement.

accidental [æksɪ'dɛntl] *adj* accidentel(le).

accidentally [æksɪ'dɛntəlɪ] *adv* accidentellement.

accident insurance *n* assurance *f* accident.

accident-prone ['æksɪdənt'prəun] *adj* sujet(te) aux accidents.

acclaim [ə'kleɪm] *vt* acclamer ♦ *n* acclamation *f*.

acclamation [æklə'meɪʃən] *n* (*approval*) acclamation *f*; (*applause*) ovation *f*.

acclimatize [ə'klaɪmətaɪz], (*US*) **acclimate** [ə'klaɪmət] *vt*: **to become** ~**d** s'acclimater.

accolade ['ækəleɪd] *n* accolade *f*; (*fig*) marque *f* d'honneur.

accommodate [ə'kɔmədeɪt] *vt* loger, recevoir; (*oblige, help*) obliger; (*adapt*): **to** ~

one's plans to adapter ses projets à; **this car** ~**s 4 people comfortably** on tient confortablement à 4 dans cette voiture.

accommodating [ə'kɔmədeɪtɪŋ] *adj* obligeant(e), arrangeant(e).

accommodation, (*US*) **accommodations** [əkɔmə'deɪʃən(z)] *n(pl)* logement *m*; **he's found** ~ il a trouvé à se loger; "~ **to let**" (*BRIT*) "appartement (*or* studio *etc*) à louer"; **they have** ~ **for 500** ils peuvent recevoir 500 personnes, il y a de la place pour 500 personnes; **the hall has seating** ~ **for 600** (*BRIT*) la salle contient 600 places assises.

accompaniment [ə'kʌmpənɪmənt] *n* accompagnement *m*.

accompanist [ə'kʌmpənɪst] *n* accompagnateur/trice.

accompany [ə'kʌmpənɪ] *vt* accompagner.

accomplice [ə'kʌmplɪs] *n* complice *m/f*.

accomplish [ə'kʌmplɪʃ] *vt* accomplir.

accomplished [ə'kʌmplɪʃt] *adj* accompli(e).

accomplishment [ə'kʌmplɪʃmənt] *n* accomplissement *m*; (*achievement*) réussite *f*; ~**s** *npl* (*skills*) talents *mpl*.

accord [ə'kɔːd] *n* accord *m* ♦ *vt* accorder; **of his own** ~ de son plein gré; **with one** ~ d'un commun accord.

accordance [ə'kɔːdəns] *n*: **in** ~ **with** conformément à.

according [ə'kɔːdɪŋ]: ~ **to** *prep* selon; ~ **to plan** comme prévu.

accordingly [ə'kɔːdɪŋlɪ] *adv* en conséquence.

accordion [ə'kɔːdɪən] *n* accordéon *m*.

accost [ə'kɔst] *vt* accoster, aborder.

account [ə'kaunt] *n* (*COMM*) compte *m*; (*report*) compte rendu, récit *m*; ~**s** *npl* (*BOOK-KEEPING*) comptabilité *f*, comptes; "~ **payee only**" (*BRIT*) "chèque non endossable"; **to keep an** ~ **of** noter; **to bring sb to** ~ **for sth/for having done sth** amener qn à rendre compte de qch/d'avoir fait qch; **by all** ~**s** au dire de tous; **of little** ~ de peu d'importance; **to pay £5 on** ~ verser un acompte de 5 livres; **to buy sth on** ~ acheter qch à crédit; **on no** ~ en aucun cas; **on** ~ **of** à cause de; **to take into** ~, **take** ~ **of** tenir compte de.

▶**account for** *vt fus* expliquer, rendre compte de; **all the children were** ~**ed for** aucun enfant ne manquait; **4 people are still not** ~**ed for** on n'a toujours pas retrouvé 4 personnes.

accountability [əkauntə'bɪlɪtɪ] *n* responsabilité *f*; (*financial, political*) transparence *f*.

accountable [ə'kauntəbl] *adj*: ~ **(for)** responsable (de).

accountancy [ə'kauntənsɪ] *n* comptabilité *f*.

accountant [ə'kauntənt] *n* comptable *m/f*.

accounting [ə'kauntɪŋ] *n* comptabilité *f*.

accounting period *n* exercice financier, période *f* comptable.

account number *n* numéro *m* de compte.

account payable *n* compte *m* fournisseurs.

account receivable _n_ compte _m_ clients.

accredited [ə'krɛdɪtɪd] _adj_ (_person_) accrédité(e).

accretion [ə'kriːʃən] _n_ accroissement _m_.

accrue [ə'kruː] _vi_ s'accroître; (_mount up_) s'accumuler; **to ~ to** s'ajouter à; **~d interest** intérêt couru.

accumulate [ə'kjuːmjuleɪt] _vt_ accumuler, amasser ♦ _vi_ s'accumuler, s'amasser.

accumulation [əkjuːmjuˈleɪʃən] _n_ accumulation _f_.

accuracy ['ækjurəsɪ] _n_ exactitude _f_, précision _f_.

accurate ['ækjurɪt] _adj_ exact(e), précis(e).

accurately ['ækjurɪtlɪ] _adv_ avec précision.

accusation [ækjuˈzeɪʃən] _n_ accusation _f_.

accusative [ə'kjuːzətɪv] _n_ (_LING_) accusatif _m_.

accuse [ə'kjuːz] _vt_ accuser.

accused [ə'kjuːzd] _n_ accusé/e.

accuser [ə'kjuːzə*] _n_ accusateur/trice.

accustom [ə'kʌstəm] _vt_ accoutumer, habituer; **to ~ o.s. to sth** s'habituer à qch.

accustomed [ə'kʌstəmd] _adj_ (_usual_) habituel(le); **~ to** habitué(e) _or_ accoutumé(e) à.

AC/DC _abbr_ = **alternating current/direct current**.

ACE [eɪs] _n abbr_ = _American Council on Education_.

ace [eɪs] _n_ as _m_; **within an ~ of** (_BRIT_) à deux doigts _or_ un cheveu de.

acerbic [ə'sɔːbɪk] _adj_ (_also fig_) acerbe.

acetate ['æsɪteɪt] _n_ acétate _m_.

ache [eɪk] _n_ mal _m_, douleur _f_ ♦ _vi_ (_be sore_) faire mal, être douloureux(euse); (_yearn_): **to ~ to do sth** mourir d'envie de faire qch; **I've got stomach ~** _or_ (_US_) **a stomach ~** j'ai mal à l'estomac; **my head ~s** j'ai mal à la tête; **I'm aching all over** j'ai mal partout.

achieve [ə'tʃiːv] _vt_ (_aim_) atteindre; (_victory, success_) remporter, obtenir; (_task_) accomplir.

achievement [ə'tʃiːvmənt] _n_ exploit _m_, réussite _f_; (_of aims_) réalisation _f_.

Achilles heel [ə'kɪliːz-] _n_ talon _m_ d'Achille.

acid ['æsɪd] _adj_, _n_ acide (_m_).

acidity [ə'sɪdɪtɪ] _n_ acidité _f_.

acid rain _n_ pluies _fpl_ acides.

acid test _n_ (_fig_) épreuve décisive.

acknowledge [ək'nɔlɪdʒ] _vt_ (_also:_ **~ receipt of**) accuser réception de; (_fact_) reconnaître.

acknowledgement [ək'nɔlɪdʒmənt] _n_ accusé _m_ de réception; **~s** (_in book_) remerciements _mpl_.

ACLU _n abbr_ (= _American Civil Liberties Union_) ligue des droits de l'homme.

acme ['ækmɪ] _n_ point culminant.

acne ['æknɪ] _n_ acné _m_.

acorn ['eɪkɔːn] _n_ gland _m_.

acoustic [ə'kuːstɪk] _adj_ acoustique.

acoustic coupler _n_ (_COMPUT_) coupleur _m_ acoustique.

acoustics [ə'kuːstɪks] _n_, _npl_ acoustique _f_.

acquaint [ə'kweɪnt] _vt_: **to ~ sb with sth** mettre qn au courant de qch; **to be ~ed with** (_person_) connaître; (_fact_) savoir.

acquaintance [ə'kweɪntəns] _n_ connaissance _f_; **to make sb's ~** faire la connaissance de qn.

acquiesce [ækwɪ'ɛs] _vi_ (_agree_): **to ~ (in)** acquiescer (à).

acquire [ə'kwaɪə*] _vt_ acquérir.

acquired [ə'kwaɪəd] _adj_ acquis(e); **an ~ taste** un goût acquis.

acquisition [ækwɪ'zɪʃən] _n_ acquisition _f_.

acquisitive [ə'kwɪzɪtɪv] _adj_ qui a l'instinct de possession _or_ le goût de la propriété.

acquit [ə'kwɪt] _vt_ acquitter; **to ~ o.s. well** s'en tirer très honorablement.

acquittal [ə'kwɪtl] _n_ acquittement _m_.

acre ['eɪkə*] _n_ acre _f_ (= 4047 _m²_).

acreage ['eɪkərɪdʒ] _n_ superficie _f_.

acrid ['ækrɪd] _adj_ (_smell_) âcre; (_fig_) mordant(e).

acrimonious [ækrɪ'məunɪəs] _adj_ acrimonieux(euse), aigre.

acrobat ['ækrəbæt] _n_ acrobate _m/f_.

acrobatic [ækrə'bætɪk] _adj_ acrobatique.

acrobatics [ækrə'bætɪks] _n_, _npl_ acrobatie _f_.

Acropolis [ə'krɔpəlɪs] _n_: **the ~** l'Acropole _f_.

across [ə'krɔs] _prep_ (_on the other side_) de l'autre côté de; (_crosswise_) en travers de ♦ _adv_ de l'autre côté; en travers; **to walk ~ (the road)** traverser (la route); **to take sb ~ the road** faire traverser la route à qn; **a road ~ the wood** une route qui traverse le bois; **the lake is 12 km ~** le lac fait 12 km de large; **~ from** en face de; **to get sth ~ (to sb)** faire comprendre qch (à qn).

acrylic [ə'krɪlɪk] _adj_, _n_ acrylique (_m_).

ACT _n abbr_ (= _American College Test_) _examen de fin d'études secondaires_.

act [ækt] _n_ acte _m_, action _f_; (_THEAT: part of play_) acte; (_: of performer_) numéro _m_; (_LAW_) loi _f_ ♦ _vi_ agir; (_THEAT_) jouer; (_pretend_) jouer la comédie ♦ _vt_ (_role_) jouer, tenir; **~ of God** (_LAW_) catastrophe naturelle; **to catch sb in the ~** prendre qn sur le fait _or_ en flagrant délit; **it's only an ~** c'est du cinéma; **to ~ Hamlet** (_BRIT_) tenir _or_ jouer le rôle d'Hamlet; **to ~ the fool** (_BRIT_) faire l'idiot; **to ~ as** servir de; **it ~s as a deterrent** cela a un effet dissuasif; **~ing in my capacity as chairman, I ...** en ma qualité de président, je ....

▶**act on** _vt_: **to ~ on sth** agir sur la base de qch.

▶**act out** _vt_ (_event_) raconter en mimant; (_fantasies_) réaliser.

acting ['æktɪŋ] _adj_ suppléant(e), par intérim ♦ _n_ (_of actor_) jeu _m_; (_activity_): **to do some ~** faire du théâtre (_or_ du cinéma); **he is the ~ manager** il remplace (provisoirement) le directeur.

action ['ækʃən] _n_ action _f_; (_MIL_) combat(s) _m(pl)_; (_LAW_) procès _m_, action en justice; **to bring an ~ against sb** (_LAW_) poursuivre qn

en justice, intenter un procès contre qn;
killed in ~ (*MIL*) tué au champ d'honneur;
out of ~ hors de combat; (*machine etc*) hors
d'usage; **to take** ~ agir, prendre des mesures; **to put a plan into** ~ mettre un projet
à exécution.

action replay *n* (*BRIT TV*) retour *m* sur une séquence.

activate ['æktɪveɪt] *vt* (*mechanism*) actionner,
faire fonctionner; (*CHEM, PHYSICS*) activer.

active ['æktɪv] *adj* actif(ive); (*volcano*) en activité; **to play an** ~ **part in** jouer un rôle actif
dans.

active duty (AD) *n* (*US MIL*) campagne *f*.

actively ['æktɪvlɪ] *adv* activement.

active partner *n* (*COMM*) associé/e.

active service *n* (*BRIT MIL*) campagne *f*.

activist ['æktɪvɪst] *n* activiste *m/f*.

activity [æk'tɪvɪtɪ] *n* activité *f*.

actor ['æktə*] *n* acteur *m*.

actress ['æktrɪs] *n* actrice *f*.

actual ['æktjuəl] *adj* réel(le), véritable.

actually ['æktjuəlɪ] *adv* réellement, véritablement; (*in fact*) en fait.

actuary ['æktjuərɪ] *n* actuaire *m*.

actuate ['æktjueɪt] *vt* déclencher, actionner.

acuity [ə'kjuːɪtɪ] *n* acuité *f*.

acumen ['ækjumən] *n* perspicacité *f*; **business**
~ sens *m* des affaires.

acupuncture ['ækjupʌŋktʃə*] *n* acuponcture *f*.

acute [ə'kjuːt] *adj* aigu(ë); (*mind, observer*) pé-
nétrant(e).

AD *adv abbr* (= *Anno Domini*) ap. J.-C. ♦ *n abbr*
(*US MIL*) = **active duty**.

ad [æd] *n abbr* = **advertisement**.

adamant ['ædəmənt] *adj* inflexible.

Adam's apple ['ædəmz-] *n* pomme *f* d'Adam.

adapt [ə'dæpt] *vt* adapter ♦ *vi*: **to** ~ **(to)**
s'adapter (à).

adaptability [ədæptə'bɪlɪtɪ] *n* faculté *f*
d'adaptation.

adaptable [ə'dæptəbl] *adj* (*device*) adaptable;
(*person*) qui s'adapte facilement.

adaptation [ædæp'teɪʃən] *n* adaptation *f*.

adapter [ə'dæptə*] *n* (*ELEC*) adapteur *m*.

ADC *n abbr* (*MIL*) = **aide-de-camp**; (*US*: = *Aid to
Dependent Children*) *aide pour enfants as-
sistés*.

add [æd] *vt* ajouter; (*figures*) additionner ♦ *vi*:
to ~ **to** (*increase*) ajouter à, accroître.

▶**add on** *vt* ajouter.

▶**add up** *vt* (*figures*) additionner ♦ *vi* (*fig*): **it
doesn't** ~ **up** cela ne rime à rien; **it doesn't**
~ **up to much** ça n'est pas grand'chose.

adder ['ædə*] *n* vipère *f*.

addict ['ædɪkt] *n* toxicomane *m/f*; (*fig*) fanatique *m/f*; **heroin** ~ héroïnomane *m/f*; **drug** ~
drogué/e *m/f*.

addicted [ə'dɪktɪd] *adj*: **to be** ~ **to** (*drink etc*)
être adonné(e) à; (*fig: football etc*) être un(e)
fanatique de.

addiction [ə'dɪkʃən] *n* (*MED*) dépendance *f*.

adding machine ['ædɪŋ-] *n* machine *f* à calculer.

Addis Ababa ['ædɪs'æbəbə] *n* Addis Abeba,
Addis Ababa.

addition [ə'dɪʃən] *n* addition *f*; **in** ~ de plus, de
surcroît; **in** ~ **to** en plus de.

additional [ə'dɪʃənl] *adj* supplémentaire.

additive ['ædɪtɪv] *n* additif *m*.

addled ['ædld] *adj* (*BRIT: egg*) pourri(e).

address [ə'drɛs] *n* adresse *f*; (*talk*) discours *m*,
allocution *f* ♦ *vt* adresser; (*speak to*)
s'adresser à; **form of** ~ titre *m*; **what form of**
~ **do you use for ...?** comment s'adresse-t-
on à ...?; **to** ~ **(o.s. to) sth** (*problem, issue*)
aborder qch; **absolute/relative** ~ (*COMPUT*)
adresse absolue/relative.

address book *n* carnet *m* d'adresses.

addressee [ædrɛ'siː] *n* destinataire *m/f*.

Aden ['eɪdən] *n*: **Gulf of** ~ Golfe *m* d'Aden.

adenoids ['ædɪnɔɪdz] *npl* végétations *fpl*.

adept ['ædɛpt] *adj*: ~ **at** expert(e) à or en.

adequate ['ædɪkwɪt] *adj* (*enough*) suffisant(e);
to feel ~ **to the task** se sentir à la hauteur
de la tâche.

adequately ['ædɪkwɪtlɪ] *adv* de façon adé-
quate.

adhere [əd'hɪə*] *vi*: **to** ~ **to** adhérer à; (*fig:
rule, decision*) se tenir à.

adhesion [əd'hiːʒən] *n* adhésion *f*.

adhesive [əd'hiːzɪv] *adj* adhésif(ive) ♦ *n* adhésif *m*; ~ **tape** (*BRIT*) ruban adhésif; (*US*)
sparadrap(e).

ad hoc [æd'hɔk] *adj* (*decision*) de circonstance;
(*committee*) ad hoc.

ad infinitum ['ædɪnfɪ'naɪtəm] *adv* à l'infini.

adjacent [ə'dʒeɪsənt] *adj* adjacent(e), conti-
gu(ë); ~ **to** adjacent à.

adjective ['ædʒɛktɪv] *n* adjectif *m*.

adjoin [ə'dʒɔɪn] *vt* jouxter.

adjoining [ə'dʒɔɪnɪŋ] *adj* voisin(e), adja-
cent(e), attenant(e) ♦ *prep* voisin de, adjacent à.

adjourn [ə'dʒəːn] *vt* ajourner ♦ *vi* suspendre la
séance; lever la séance; clore la session;
(*go*) se retirer; **to** ~ **a meeting till the following week** reporter une réunion à la semaine suivante; **they** ~**ed to the pub** (*BRIT
col*) ils ont filé au pub.

adjournment [ə'dʒəːnmənt] *n* (*period*) ajournement *m*.

Adjt *abbr* (*MIL*: = *adjutant*) Adj.

adjudicate [ə'dʒuːdɪkeɪt] *vt* (*contest*) juger;
(*claim*) statuer (sur) ♦ *vi* se prononcer.

adjudication [ədʒuːdɪ'keɪʃən] *n* (*LAW*) jugement *m*.

adjust [ə'dʒʌst] *vt* ajuster, régler; rajuster
♦ *vi*: **to** ~ **(to)** s'adapter (à).

adjustable [ə'dʒʌstəbl] *adj* réglable.

adjuster [ə'dʒʌstə*] *n see* **loss**.

adjustment [ə'dʒʌstmənt] *n* ajustage *m*, réglage *m*; (*of prices, wages*) rajustement *m*; (*of
person*) adaptation *f*.

adjutant ['ædʒətənt] *n* adjudant *m*.

ad-lib [æd'lɪb] *vt*, *vi* improviser ♦ *n* improvisation *f* ♦ *adv*: **ad lib** à volonté, à discrétion.

adman ['ædmæn] *n* (*col*) publicitaire *m*.

admin ['ædmɪn] *n abbr* (*col*) = **administration**.

administer [əd'mɪnɪstə*] *vt* administrer; (*justice*) rendre.

administration [ədmɪnɪs'treɪʃən] *n* administration *f*; **the A**~ (*US*) le gouvernement.

administrative [əd'mɪnɪstrətɪv] *adj* administratif(ive).

administrator [əd'mɪnɪstreɪtə*] *n* administrateur/trice.

admirable ['ædmərəbl] *adj* admirable.

admiral ['ædmərəl] *n* amiral *m*.

Admiralty ['ædmərəltɪ] *n* (*BRIT*: *also*: ~ **Board**) ministère *m* de la Marine.

admiration [ædmə'reɪʃən] *n* admiration *f*.

admire [əd'maɪə*] *vt* admirer.

admirer [əd'maɪərə*] *n* admirateur/trice.

admiring [əd'maɪərɪŋ] *adj* admiratif(ive).

admissible [əd'mɪsəbl] *adj* acceptable, admissible; (*evidence*) recevable.

admission [əd'mɪʃən] *n* admission *f*; (*to exhibition, night club etc*) entrée *f*; (*confession*) aveu *m*; "~ **free**", "**free** ~" "entrée libre"; **by his own** ~ de son propre aveu.

admit [əd'mɪt] *vt* laisser entrer; admettre; (*agree*) reconnaître, admettre; "**children not** ~**ted**" "entrée interdite aux enfants"; **this ticket** ~**s two** ce billet est valable pour deux personnes; **I must** ~ **that** ... je dois admettre *or* reconnaître que ....

▶**admit of** *vt fus* admettre, permettre.

▶**admit to** *vt fus* reconnaître, avouer.

admittance [əd'mɪtəns] *n* admission *f*, (droit *m* d')entrée *f*; "**no** ~" "défense d'entrer"

admittedly [əd'mɪtɪdlɪ] *adv* il faut en convenir.

admonish [əd'mɒnɪʃ] *vt* donner un avertissement à; réprimander.

ad nauseam [æd'nɔːsɪæm] *adv* à satiété.

ado [ə'duː] *n*: **without (any) more** ~ sans plus de cérémonies.

adolescence [ædəu'lɛsns] *n* adolescence *f*.

adolescent [ædəu'lɛsnt] *adj*, *n* adolescent(e).

adopt [ə'dɒpt] *vt* adopter.

adopted [ə'dɒptɪd] *adj* adoptif(ive), adopté(e).

adoption [ə'dɒpʃən] *n* adoption *f*.

adore [ə'dɔː*] *vt* adorer.

adoring [ə'dɔːrɪŋ] *adj*: **his** ~ **wife** sa femme qui est en adoration devant lui.

adoringly [ə'dɔːrɪŋlɪ] *adv* avec adoration.

adorn [ə'dɔːn] *vt* orner.

adornment [ə'dɔːnmənt] *n* ornement *m*.

ADP *n abbr* = **automatic data processing**.

adrenalin [ə'drɛnəlɪn] *n* adrénaline *f*; **to get the** ~ **going** faire monter le taux d'adrénaline.

Adriatic (Sea) [eɪdrɪ'ætɪk-] *n* Adriatique *f*.

adrift [ə'drɪft] *adv* à la dérive; **to come** ~ (*boat*) aller à la dérive; (*wire, rope, fastening*

etc) se défaire.

adroit [ə'drɔɪt] *adj* adroit(e), habile.

ADT *abbr* (*US*: = *Atlantic Daylight Time*) *heure d'été de New York*.

adult ['ædʌlt] *n* adulte *m/f*.

adult education *n* éducation *f* des adultes.

adulterate [ə'dʌltəreɪt] *vt* frelater, falsifier.

adulterer [ə'dʌltərə*] *n* homme *m* adultère.

adulteress [ə'dʌltərɪs] *n* femme *f* adultère.

adultery [ə'dʌltərɪ] *n* adultère *m*.

adulthood ['ædʌlthud] *n* âge *m* adulte.

advance [əd'vɑːns] *n* avance *f* ♦ *vt* avancer ♦ *vi* s'avancer; **in** ~ en avance, d'avance; **to make** ~**s to sb** (*gen*) faire des propositions à qn; (*amorously*) faire des avances à qn.

advanced [əd'vɑːnst] *adj* avancé(e); (*SCOL: studies*) supérieur(e); ~ **in years** d'un âge avancé.

advancement [əd'vɑːnsmənt] *n* avancement *m*.

advance notice *n* préavis *m*.

advantage [əd'vɑːntɪdʒ] *n* (*also TENNIS*) avantage *m*; **to take** ~ **of** profiter de; **it's to our** ~ c'est notre intérêt; **it's to our** ~ **to** ... nous avons intérêt à ....

advantageous [ædvən'teɪdʒəs] *adj* avantageux(euse).

advent ['ædvənt] *n* avènement *m*, venue *f*; **A**~ (*REL*) avent *m*.

Advent calendar *n* calendrier *m* de l'avent.

adventure [əd'vɛntʃə*] *n* aventure *f*.

adventure playground *n* aire *f* de jeux.

adventurous [əd'vɛntʃərəs] *adj* aventureux(euse).

adverb ['ædvɜːb] *n* adverbe *m*.

adversary ['ædvəsərɪ] *n* adversaire *m/f*.

adverse ['ædvɜːs] *adj* contraire, adverse; ~ **to** hostile à; **in** ~ **circumstances** dans l'adversité.

adversity [əd'vɜːsɪtɪ] *n* adversité *f*.

advert ['ædvɜːt] *n abbr* (*BRIT*) = **advertisement**.

advertise ['ædvətaɪz] *vi*(*vt*) faire de la publicité *or* de la réclame (pour); (*in classified ads etc*) mettre une annonce (pour vendre); **to** ~ **for** (*staff*) recruter par (voie d')annonce.

advertisement [əd'vɜːtɪsmənt] *n* (*COMM*) réclame *f*, publicité *f*; (*in classified ads etc*) annonce *f*.

advertiser ['ædvətaɪzə*] *n* annonceur *m*.

advertising ['ædvətaɪzɪŋ] *n* publicité *f*.

advertising agency *n* agence *f* de publicité.

advertising campaign *n* campagne *f* de publicité.

advice [əd'vaɪs] *n* conseils *mpl*; (*notification*) avis *m*; **piece of** ~ conseil; **to ask (sb) for** ~ demander conseil (à qn); **to take legal** ~ consulter un avocat.

advice note *n* (*BRIT*) avis *m* d'expédition.

advisable [əd'vaɪzəbl] *adj* recommandable, indiqué(e).

advise [əd'vaɪz] *vt* conseiller; **to** ~ **sb of sth** aviser *or* informer qn de qch; **to** ~ **sb**

against sth déconseiller qch à qn; **to ~ sb against doing sth** conseiller à qn de ne pas faire qch; **you would be well/ill ~d to go** vous feriez mieux d'y aller/de ne pas y aller, vous auriez intérêt à y aller/à ne pas y aller.

advisedly [əd'vaɪzɪdlɪ] *adv* (*deliberately*) délibérément.

adviser, advisor [əd'vaɪzə*] *n* conseiller/ère.

advisory [əd'vaɪzərɪ] *adj* consultatif(ive); **in an ~ capacity** à titre consultatif.

advocate *n* ['ædvəkɪt] (*upholder*) défenseur *m*, avocat/e ♦ *vt* ['ædvəkeɪt] recommander, prôner; **to be an ~ of** être partisan/e de.

advt. *abbr* = **advertisement**.

AEA *n abbr* (*BRIT*: = *Atomic Energy Authority*) ≈ AEN *f* (= *Agence pour l'énergie nucléaire*).

AEC *n abbr* (*US*: = *Atomic Energy Commission*) CEA *m* (= *Commissariat à l'énergie atomique*).

AEEU *n abbr* (*BRIT*: = *Amalgamated Engineering and Electrical Union*) syndicat de techniciens et d'électriciens.

Aegean (Sea) [iːˈdʒiːən-] *n* mer *f* Égée.

aegis [ˈiːdʒɪs] *n*: **under the ~ of** sous l'égide de.

aeon [ˈiːən] *n* éternité *f*.

aerial [ˈɛərɪəl] *n* antenne *f* ♦ *adj* aérien(ne).

aerie [ˈɛərɪ] *n* (*US*) aire *f*.

aerobatics [ˈɛərəʊˈbætɪks] *npl* acrobaties aériennes.

aerobics [ɛəˈrəʊbɪks] *n* aérobic *m*.

aerodrome [ˈɛərədrəʊm] *n* (*BRIT*) aérodrome *m*.

aerodynamic [ˈɛərəʊdaɪˈnæmɪk] *adj* aérodynamique.

aeronautics [ɛərəˈnɔːtɪks] *n* aéronautique *f*.

aeroplane [ˈɛərəpleɪn] *n* (*BRIT*) avion *m*.

aerosol [ˈɛərəsɔl] *n* aérosol *m*.

aerospace industry [ˈɛərəʊspeɪs-] *n* (industrie) aérospatiale *f*.

aesthetic [ɪsˈθɛtɪk] *adj* esthétique.

afar [əˈfɑː*] *adv*: **from ~** de loin.

AFB *n abbr* (*US*) = *Air Force Base*.

AFDC *n abbr* (*US*: = *Aid to Families with Dependent Children*) aide pour enfants assistés.

affable [ˈæfəbl] *adj* affable.

affair [əˈfɛə*] *n* affaire *f*; (*also*: **love ~**) liaison *f*; aventure *f*; **~s** (*business*) affaires *f*.

affect [əˈfɛkt] *vt* affecter.

affectation [æfɛkˈteɪʃən] *n* affectation *f*.

affected [əˈfɛktɪd] *adj* affecté(e).

affection [əˈfɛkʃən] *n* affection *f*.

affectionate [əˈfɛkʃənɪt] *adj* affectueux(euse).

affectionately [əˈfɛkʃənɪtlɪ] *adv* affectueusement.

affidavit [æfɪˈdeɪvɪt] *n* (*LAW*) déclaration écrite sous serment.

affiliated [əˈfɪlɪeɪtɪd] *adj* affilié(e); **~ company** filiale *f*.

affinity [əˈfɪnɪtɪ] *n* affinité *f*.

affirm [əˈfəːm] *vt* affirmer.

affirmation [æfəˈmeɪʃən] *n* affirmation *f*, assertion *f*.

affirmative [əˈfəːmətɪv] *adj* affirmatif(ive) ♦ *n*: **in the ~** dans *or* par l'affirmative.

affix [əˈfɪks] *vt* apposer, ajouter.

afflict [əˈflɪkt] *vt* affliger.

affliction [əˈflɪkʃən] *n* affliction *f*.

affluence [ˈæfluəns] *n* aisance *f*, opulence *f*.

affluent [ˈæfluənt] *adj* opulent(e); (*person*) dans l'aisance, riche; **the ~ society** la société d'abondance.

afford [əˈfɔːd] *vt* (*goods etc*) avoir les moyens d'acheter *or* d'entretenir; (*behaviour*) se permettre; (*provide*) fournir, procurer; **can we ~ a car?** avons-nous de quoi acheter *or* les moyens d'acheter une voiture?; **I can't ~ the time** je n'ai vraiment pas le temps.

affordable [əˈfɔːdəbl] *adj* abordable.

affray [əˈfreɪ] *n* (*BRIT LAW*) échauffourée *f*, rixe *f*.

affront [əˈfrʌnt] *n* affront *m*.

affronted [əˈfrʌntɪd] *adj* insulté(e).

Afghan [ˈæfgæn] *adj* afghan(e) ♦ *n* Afghan/e.

Afghanistan [æfˈgænɪstæn] *n* Afghanistan *m*.

afield [əˈfiːld] *adv*: **far ~** loin.

AFL-CIO *n abbr* (= *American Federation of Labor and Congress of Industrial Organizations*) confédération syndicale.

afloat [əˈfləʊt] *adj* à flot ♦ *adv*: **to stay ~** surnager; **to keep/get a business ~** maintenir à flot/lancer une affaire.

afoot [əˈfut] *adv*: **there is something ~** il se prépare quelque chose.

aforementioned [əˈfɔːmɛnʃənd] *adj*, **aforesaid** [əˈfɔːsɛd] *adj* susdit(e), susmentionné(e).

afraid [əˈfreɪd] *adj* effrayé(e); **to be ~ of** *or* **to** avoir peur de; **I am ~ that** je crains que + *sub*; **I'm ~ so/not** oui/non, malheureusement.

afresh [əˈfrɛʃ] *adv* de nouveau.

Africa [ˈæfrɪkə] *n* Afrique *f*.

African [ˈæfrɪkən] *adj* africain(e) ♦ *n* Africain/e.

Afrikaans [æfrɪˈkɑːns] *n* afrikaans *m*.

Afrikaner [æfrɪˈkɑːnə*] *n* Afrikaner *m/f*.

Afro-American [ˈæfrəʊəˈmɛrɪkən] *adj* afro-américain(e).

AFT *n abbr* (= *American Federation of Teachers*) syndicat enseignant.

aft [ɑːft] *adv* à l'arrière, vers l'arrière.

after [ˈɑːftə*] *prep*, *adv* ♦ *conj* après que, après avoir *or* être + *pp*; **~ dinner** après (le) dîner; **the day ~ tomorrow** après demain; **quarter ~ two** (*US*) deux heures et quart; **what/who are you ~?** que/qui cherchez-vous?; **the police are ~ him** la police est à ses trousses; **~ you!** après vous!; **~ all** après tout.

afterbirth [ˈɑːftəbəːθ] *n* placenta *m*.

aftercare [ˈɑːftəkɛə*] *n* (*BRIT MED*) post-cure *f*.

after-effects [ˈɑːftərɪfɛkts] *npl* répercussions *fpl*; (*of illness*) séquelles *fpl*, suites *fpl*.

afterlife [ˈɑːftəlaɪf] *n* vie future.

aftermath ['ɑːftəmɑːθ] *n* conséquences *fpl*; **in the ~ of** dans les mois *or* années *etc* qui suivirent, au lendemain de.

afternoon ['ɑːftə'nuːn] *n* après-midi *m or f*; **good ~!** bonjour!; (*goodbye*) au revoir!

afters ['ɑːftəz] *n* (*BRIT col: dessert*) dessert *m*.

after-sales service [ɑːftə'seɪlz-] *n* service *m* après-vente, SAV *m*.

after-shave (lotion) ['ɑːftəʃeɪv-] *n* lotion *f* après-rasage.

aftershock ['ɑːftəʃɔk] *n* réplique *f* (sismique).

aftertaste ['ɑːftəteɪst] *n* arrière-goût *m*.

afterthought ['ɑːftəθɔːt] *n*: **I had an ~** il m'est venu une idée après coup.

afterwards ['ɑːftəwədz] *adv* après.

again [ə'gɛn] *adv* de nouveau, encore une fois; **to begin/see ~** recommencer/revoir; **not ... ~** ne ... plus; **~ and ~** à plusieurs reprises; **he's opened it ~** il l'a rouvert, il l'a de nouveau *or* l'a encore ouvert; **now and ~** de temps à autre.

against [ə'gɛnst] *prep* contre; **~ a blue background** sur un fond bleu; **(as) ~** (*BRIT*) contre.

age [eɪdʒ] *n* âge *m* ♦ *vt, vi* vieillir; **what ~ is he?** quel âge a-t-il?; **he is 20 years of ~** il a 20 ans; **under ~** mineur(e); **to come of ~** atteindre sa majorité; **it's been ~s since** ça fait une éternité que ... ne.

aged ['eɪdʒd] *adj* âgé(e); **~ 10** âgé de 10 ans; **the ~** ['eɪdʒɪd] *npl* les personnes âgées.

age group *n* tranche *f* d'âge; **the 40 to 50 ~** la tranche d'âge des 40 à 50 ans.

ageing ['eɪdʒɪŋ] *adj* vieillissant(e).

ageless ['eɪdʒlɪs] *adj* sans âge.

age limit *n* limite *f* d'âge.

agency ['eɪdʒənsɪ] *n* agence *f*; **through** *or* **by the ~ of** par l'entremise *or* l'action de.

agenda [ə'dʒɛndə] *n* ordre *m* du jour; **on the ~** à l'ordre du jour.

agent ['eɪdʒənt] *n* agent *m*.

aggravate ['ægrəveɪt] *vt* aggraver; (*annoy*) exaspérer, agacer.

aggravation [ægrə'veɪʃən] *n* agacements *mpl*.

aggregate ['ægrɪgɪt] *n* ensemble *m*, total *m*; **on ~** (*SPORT*) au total des points.

aggression [ə'grɛʃən] *n* agression *f*.

aggressive [ə'grɛsɪv] *adj* agressif(ive).

aggressiveness [ə'grɛsɪvnɪs] *n* agressivité *f*.

aggressor [ə'grɛsə*] *n* agresseur *m*.

aggrieved [ə'griːvd] *adj* chagriné(e), affligé(e).

aggro ['ægrəu] *n* (*col: physical*) grabuge *m*; (*: hassle*) embêtements *mpl*.

aghast [ə'gɑːst] *adj* consterné(e), atterré(e).

agile ['ædʒaɪl] *adj* agile.

agility [ə'dʒɪlɪtɪ] *n* agilité *f*, souplesse *f*.

agitate ['ædʒɪteɪt] *vt* rendre inquiet(ète) *or* agité(e) ♦ *vi* faire de l'agitation (politique); **to ~ for** faire campagne pour.

agitator ['ædʒɪteɪtə*] *n* agitateur/trice (politique).

AGM *n abbr* = **annual general meeting**.

ago [ə'gəu] *adv*: **2 days ~** il y a 2 jours; **not long ~** il n'y a pas longtemps; **as long ~ as 1960** déjà en 1960; **how long ~?** il y a combien de temps (de cela)?

agog [ə'gɔg] *adj*: **(all) ~** en émoi.

agonize ['ægənaɪz] *vi*: **he ~d over the problem** ce problème lui a causé bien du tourment.

agonizing ['ægənaɪzɪŋ] *adj* angoissant(e); (*cry*) déchirant(e).

agony ['ægənɪ] *n* grande souffrance *or* angoisse; **to be in ~** souffrir le martyre.

agony aunt *n* (*BRIT col*) journaliste qui tient *la rubrique du courrier du cœur*.

agony column *n* courrier *m* du cœur.

agree [ə'griː] *vt* (*price*) convenir de ♦ *vi*: **to ~ (with)** (*person*) être d'accord (avec); (*statements etc*) concorder (avec); (*LING*) s'accorder (avec); **to ~ to do** accepter de *or* consentir à faire; **to ~ to sth** consentir à qch; **to ~ that** (*admit*) convenir *or* reconnaître que; **it was ~d that ...** il a été convenu que ...; **they ~ on this** ils sont d'accord sur ce point; **they ~d on going/a price** ils se mirent d'accord pour y aller/sur un prix; **garlic doesn't ~ with me** je ne supporte pas l'ail.

agreeable [ə'griːəbl] *adj* (*pleasant*) agréable; (*willing*) consentant(e), d'accord; **are you ~ to this?** est-ce que vous êtes d'accord?

agreed [ə'griːd] *adj* (*time, place*) convenu(e); **to be ~** être d'accord.

agreement [ə'griːmənt] *n* accord *m*; **in ~** d'accord; **by mutual ~** d'un commun accord.

agricultural [ægrɪ'kʌltʃərəl] *adj* agricole.

agriculture ['ægrɪkʌltʃə*] *n* agriculture *f*.

aground [ə'graund] *adv*: **to run ~** s'échouer.

ahead [ə'hɛd] *adv* en avant; devant; **go right** *or* **straight ~** allez tout droit; **go ~!** (*fig*) allezy!; **~ of** devant; (*fig: schedule etc*) en avance sur; **~ of time** en avance; **they were (right) ~ of us** ils nous précédaient (de peu), ils étaient (juste) devant nous.

AI *n abbr* = **Amnesty International**; (*COMPUT*) = **artificial intelligence**.

AIB *n abbr* (*BRIT*: = *Accident Investigation Bureau*) *commission d'enquête sur les accidents*.

AID *n abbr* (= *artificial insemination by donor*) IAD *f*; (*US*: = *Agency for International Development*) *agence pour le développement international*.

aid [eɪd] *n* aide *f* ♦ *vt* aider; **with the ~ of** avec l'aide de; **in ~ of** en faveur de; **to ~ and abet** (*LAW*) se faire le complice de.

aide [eɪd] *n* (*person*) assistant/e.

AIDS [eɪdz] *n abbr* (= *acquired immune* (*or* *immuno-*)*deficiency syndrome*) SIDA *m*.

AIH *n abbr* (= *artificial insemination by husband*) IAC *f*.

ailment ['eɪlmənt] *n* affection *f*.

aim [eɪm] *n* but *m* ♦ *vt*: **to ~ sth at** (*gun,*

camera) braquer *or* pointer qch sur, diriger qch contre; (*missile*) pointer qch vers *or* sur; (*remark, blow*) destiner *or* adresser qch à ♦ *vi* (*also*: **to take** ~) viser; **to** ~ **at** viser; (*fig*) viser (à); avoir pour but *or* ambition; **to** ~ **to do** avoir l'intention de faire.

aimless ['eɪmlɪs] *adj* sans but.

aimlessly ['eɪmlɪslɪ] *adv* sans but.

ain't [eɪnt] (*col*) = **am not, aren't, isn't.**

air [ɛə*] *n* air *m* ♦ *vt* aérer; (*idea, grievance, views*) mettre sur le tapis; (*knowledge*) faire étalage de ♦ *cpd* (*currents, attack etc*) aérien(ne); **by** ~ par avion; **to be on the** ~ (*RADIO, TV: programme*) être diffusé(e); (: *station*) émettre.

air bag *n* airbag *m*.

air base *n* base aérienne.

airbed ['ɛəbɛd] *n* (*BRIT*) matelas *m* pneumatique.

airborne ['ɛəbɔːn] *adj* (*plane*) en vol; (*troops*) aéroporté(e); (*particles*) dans l'air; **as soon as the plane was** ~ dès que l'avion eut décollé.

air cargo *n* fret aérien.

air-conditioned ['ɛəkənˈdɪʃənd] *adj* climatisé(e), à air conditionné.

air conditioning [-kənˈdɪʃnɪŋ] *n* climatisation *f*.

air-cooled ['ɛəkuːld] *adj* à refroidissement à air.

aircraft ['ɛəkrɑːft] *n* (*pl inv*) avion *m*.

aircraft carrier *n* porte-avions *m inv*.

air cushion *n* coussin *m* d'air.

airdrome ['ɛədrəum] *n* (*US*) aérodrome *m*.

airfield ['ɛəfiːld] *n* terrain *m* d'aviation.

Air Force *n* Armée *f* de l'air.

air freight *n* fret aérien.

airgun ['ɛəgʌn] *n* fusil *m* à air comprimé.

air hostess *n* (*BRIT*) hôtesse *f* de l'air.

airily ['ɛərɪlɪ] *adv* d'un air dégagé.

airing ['ɛərɪŋ] *n*: **to give an** ~ **to** aérer; (*fig: ideas, views etc*) mettre sur le tapis.

air letter *n* (*BRIT*) aérogramme *m*.

airlift ['ɛəlɪft] *n* pont aérien.

airline ['ɛəlaɪn] *n* ligne aérienne, compagnie aérienne.

airliner ['ɛəlaɪnə*] *n* avion *m* de ligne.

airlock ['ɛəlɔk] *n* sas *m*.

airmail ['ɛəmeɪl] *n*: **by** ~ par avion.

air mattress *n* matelas *m* pneumatique.

airplane ['ɛəpleɪn] *n* (*US*) avion *m*.

air pocket *n* trou *m* d'air.

airport ['ɛəpɔːt] *n* aéroport *m*.

air raid *n* attaque aérienne.

air rifle *n* carabine *f* à air comprimé.

airsick ['ɛəsɪk] *adj*: **to be** ~ avoir le mal de l'air.

airspeed ['ɛəspiːd] *n* vitesse relative.

airstrip ['ɛəstrɪp] *n* terrain *m* d'atterrissage.

air terminal *n* aérogare *f*.

airtight ['ɛətaɪt] *adj* hermétique.

air time *n* (*RADIO, TV*) temps *m* d'antenne.

air traffic control *n* contrôle *m* de la navigation aérienne.

air traffic controller *n* aiguilleur *m* du ciel.

airway ['ɛəweɪ] *n* (*AVIAT*) voie aérienne; ~**s** (*ANAT*) voies aériennes.

airy ['ɛərɪ] *adj* bien aéré(e); (*manners*) dégagé(e).

aisle [aɪl] *n* (*of church*) allée centrale; nef latérale; (*in theatre*) allée *f*; (*on plane*) couloir *m*.

ajar [əˈdʒɑː*] *adj* entrouvert(e).

AK *abbr* (*US*) = *Alaska.*

aka *abbr* (= *also known as*) alias.

akin [əˈkɪn] *adj*: ~ **to** semblable à, du même ordre que.

AL *abbr* (*US*) = *Alabama.*

ALA *n abbr* = *American Library Association.*

Ala. *abbr* (*US*) = *Alabama.*

alacrity [əˈlækrɪtɪ] *n*: **with** ~ avec empressement, promptement.

alarm [əˈlɑːm] *n* alarme *f* ♦ *vt* alarmer.

alarm clock *n* réveille-matin *m inv*, réveil *m*.

alarmed [əˈlɑːmd] *adj* (*frightened*) alarmé(e); (*protected by an alarm*) protégé(e) par un système d'alarme; **to become** ~ prendre peur.

alarming [əˈlɑːmɪŋ] *adj* alarmant(e).

alarmingly [əˈlɑːmɪŋlɪ] *adv* d'une manière alarmante; ~ **close** dangereusement proche; ~ **quickly** à une vitesse inquiétante.

alarmist [əˈlɑːmɪst] *n* alarmiste *m/f*.

alas [əˈlæs] *excl* hélas.

Alas. *abbr* (*US*) = *Alaska.*

Alaska [əˈlæskə] *n* Alaska *m*.

Albania [ælˈbeɪnɪə] *n* Albanie *f*.

Albanian [ælˈbeɪnɪən] *adj* albanais(e) ♦ *n* Albanais/e; (*LING*) albanais *m*.

albatross ['ælbətrɔs] *n* albatros *m*.

albeit [ɔːlˈbiːɪt] *conj* bien que + *sub*, encore que + *sub*.

album ['ælbəm] *n* album *m*.

albumen ['ælbjumɪn] *n* albumine *f*; (*of egg*) albumen *m*.

alchemy ['ælkɪmɪ] *n* alchimie *f*.

alcohol ['ælkəhɔl] *n* alcool *m*.

alcohol-free ['ælkəhɔlfriː] *adj* sans alcool.

alcoholic [ælkəˈhɔlɪk] *adj, n* alcoolique (*m/f*).

alcoholism ['ælkəhɔlɪzəm] *n* alcoolisme *m*.

alcove ['ælkəuv] *n* alcôve *f*.

Ald. *abbr* = **alderman.**

alderman ['ɔːldəmən] *n* conseiller municipal (*en Angleterre*).

ale [eɪl] *n* bière *f*.

alert [əˈləːt] *adj* alerte, vif(vive); (*watchful*) vigilant(e) ♦ *n* alerte *f* ♦ *vt*: **to** ~ **sb** (**to sth**) attirer l'attention de qn (sur qch); **to** ~ **sb to the dangers of sth** avertir qn des dangers de qch; **on the** ~ sur le qui-vive; (*MIL*) en état d'alerte.

Aleutian Islands [əˈluːʃən-] *npl* îles Aléoutiennes.

A levels *npl* ≈ baccalauréat *msg*.

Alexandria [ælɪg'zɑːndrɪə] *n* Alexandrie.
alfresco [æl'frɛskəu] *adj, adv* en plein air.
algebra ['ældʒɪbrə] *n* algèbre *m*.
Algeria [æl'dʒɪərɪə] *n* Algérie *f*.
Algerian [æl'dʒɪərɪən] *adj* algérien(ne) ♦ *n* Algérien/ne.
Algiers [æl'dʒɪəz] *n* Alger.
algorithm ['ælgərɪðm] *n* algorithme *m*.
alias ['eɪlɪəs] *adv* alias ♦ *n* faux nom, nom d'emprunt.
alibi ['ælɪbaɪ] *n* alibi *m*.
alien ['eɪlɪən] *n* étranger/ère ♦ *adj*: ~ (to) étranger(ère) (à).
alienate ['eɪlɪəneɪt] *vt* aliéner; (*subj: person*) s'aliéner.
alienation [eɪlɪə'neɪʃən] *n* aliénation *f*.
alight [ə'laɪt] *adj, adv* en feu ♦ *vi* mettre pied à terre; (*passenger*) descendre; (*bird*) se poser.
align [ə'laɪn] *vt* aligner.
alignment [ə'laɪnmənt] *n* alignement *m*; **it's out of ~ (with)** ce n'est pas aligné (avec).
alike [ə'laɪk] *adj* semblable, pareil(le) ♦ *adv* de même; **to look ~** se ressembler.
alimony ['ælɪmənɪ] *n* (*payment*) pension *f* alimentaire.
alive [ə'laɪv] *adj* vivant(e); (*active*) plein(e) de vie; ~ **with** grouillant(e) de; ~ **to** sensible à.
alkali ['ælkəlaɪ] *n* alcali *m*.

═══════════ *KEYWORD*

all [ɔːl] *adj* (*singular*) tout(e); (*plural*) tous(toutes); ~ **day** toute la journée; ~ **night** toute la nuit; ~ **men** tous les hommes; ~ **five** tous les cinq; ~ **the food** toute la nourriture; ~ **the books** tous les livres; ~ **the time** tout le temps; ~ **his life** toute sa vie
♦ *pron* **1** tout; **I ate it ~, I ate ~ of it** j'ai tout mangé; ~ **of us went** nous y sommes tous allés; ~ **of the boys went** tous les garçons y sont allés; **is that ~?** c'est tout?; (*in shop*) ce sera tout?
2 (*in phrases*): **above ~** surtout, par-dessus tout; **after ~** après tout; **at ~**: **not at ~** (*in answer to question*) pas du tout; (*in answer to thanks*) je vous en prie!; **I'm not at ~ tired** je ne suis pas du tout fatigué(e); **anything at ~ will do** n'importe quoi fera l'affaire; ~ **in ~** tout bien considéré, en fin de compte
♦ *adv*: ~ **alone** tout(e) seul(e); **it's not as hard as ~ that** ce n'est pas si difficile que ça; ~ **the more/the better** d'autant plus/mieux; ~ **but** presque, pratiquement; **to be ~ in** (*BRIT col*) être complètement à plat; ~ **out** *adv* à fond; **the score is 2 ~** le score est de 2 partout.

all-around [ɔːlə'raund] *adj* (*US*) = **all-round**.
allay [ə'leɪ] *vt* (*fears*) apaiser, calmer.
all clear *n* (*also fig*) fin *f* d'alerte.
allegation [ælɪ'geɪʃən] *n* allégation *f*.
allege [ə'lɛdʒ] *vt* alléguer, prétendre; **he is ~d to have said** il aurait dit.

alleged [ə'lɛdʒd] *adj* prétendu(e).
allegedly [ə'lɛdʒɪdlɪ] *adv* à ce que l'on prétend, paraît-il.
allegiance [ə'liːdʒəns] *n* fidélité *f*, obéissance *f*.
allegory ['ælɪgərɪ] *n* allégorie *f*.
all-embracing ['ɔːlɪm'breɪsɪŋ] *adj* universel(le).
allergic [ə'lɜːdʒɪk] *adj*: ~ **to** allergique à.
allergy ['ælədʒɪ] *n* allergie *f*.
alleviate [ə'liːvɪeɪt] *vt* soulager, adoucir.
alley ['ælɪ] *n* ruelle *f*; (*in garden*) allée *f*.
alleyway ['ælɪweɪ] *n* ruelle *f*.
alliance [ə'laɪəns] *n* alliance *f*.
allied ['ælaɪd] *adj* allié(e).
alligator ['ælɪgeɪtə*] *n* alligator *m*.
all-important ['ɔːlɪm'pɔːtənt] *adj* capital(e), crucial(e).
all-in ['ɔːlɪn] *adj, adv* (*BRIT: charge*) tout compris.
all-in wrestling *n* (*BRIT*) catch *m*.
alliteration [əlɪtə'reɪʃən] *n* allitération *f*.
all-night ['ɔːl'naɪt] *adj* ouvert(e) *or* qui dure toute la nuit.
allocate ['æləkeɪt] *vt* (*share out*) répartir, distribuer; (*duties*): **to** ~ **sth to** assigner *or* attribuer qch à; (*sum, time*): **to** ~ **sth to** allouer qch à; **to** ~ **sth for** affecter qch à.
allocation [æləu'keɪʃən] *n* (*see vb*) répartition *f*; attribution *f*; allocation *f*; affectation *f*; (*money*) crédit(s) *m(pl)*, somme(s) allouée(s).
allot [ə'lɔt] *vt* (*share out*) répartir, distribuer; (*time*): **to** ~ **sth to** allouer qch à; (*duties*): **to** ~ **sth to** assigner qch à; **in the ~ted time** dans le temps imparti.
allotment [ə'lɔtmənt] *n* (*share*) part *f*; (*garden*) lopin *m* de terre (*loué à la municipalité*).
all-out ['ɔːlaut] *adj* (*effort etc*) total(e).
allow [ə'lau] *vt* (*practice, behaviour*) permettre, autoriser; (*sum to spend etc*) accorder, allouer; (*sum, time estimated*) compter, prévoir; (*concede*): **to** ~ **that** convenir que; **to** ~ **sb to do** permettre à qn de faire, autoriser qn à faire; **he is ~ed to ...** on lui permet de ...; **smoking is not ~ed** il est interdit de fumer; **we must ~ 3 days for the journey** il faut compter 3 jours pour le voyage.
▶**allow for** *vt fus* tenir compte de.
allowance [ə'lauəns] *n* (*money received*) allocation *f*; (: *from parent etc*) subside *m*; (: *for expenses*) indemnité *f*; (*TAX*) somme *f* déductible du revenu imposable, abattement *m*; **to make ~s for** tenir compte de.
alloy ['ælɔɪ] *n* alliage *m*.
all right *adv* (*feel, work*) bien; (*as answer*) d'accord.
all-round ['ɔːl'raund] *adj* compétent(e) dans tous les domaines; (*athlete etc*) complet(ète).
all-rounder [ɔːl'raundə*] *n* (*BRIT*): **to be a good ~** être doué(e) en tout.
allspice ['ɔːlspaɪs] *n* poivre *m* de la Jamaïque.
all-time ['ɔːl'taɪm] *adj* (*record*) sans précédent, absolu(e).
allude [ə'luːd] *vi*: **to** ~ **to** faire allusion à.

alluring [ə'ljuərɪŋ] *adj* séduisant(e), alléchant(e).

allusion [ə'luːʒən] *n* allusion *f*.

alluvium [ə'luːvɪəm] *n* alluvions *fpl*.

ally *n* ['ælaɪ] allié *m* ♦ *vt* [ə'laɪ]: **to ~ o.s. with** s'allier avec.

almighty [ɔːl'maɪtɪ] *adj* tout-puissant.

almond ['ɑːmənd] *n* amande *f*.

almost ['ɔːlməust] *adv* presque; **he ~ fell** il a failli tomber.

alms [ɑːmz] *n* aumône(s) *f(pl)*.

aloft [ə'lɔft] *adv* en haut, en l'air; (*NAUT*) dans la mâture.

alone [ə'ləun] *adj*, *adv* seul(e); **to leave sb ~** laisser qn tranquille; **to leave sth ~** ne pas toucher à qch; **let ~ ...** sans parler de ...; encore moins ....

along [ə'lɔŋ] *prep* le long de ♦ *adv*: **is he coming ~?** vient-il avec nous?; **he was hopping/limping ~** il venait *or* avançait en sautillant/boitant; **~ with** avec, en plus de; (*person*) en compagnie de.

alongside [ə'lɔŋ'saɪd] *prep* le long de; au côté de ♦ *adv* bord à bord; côte à côte; **we brought our boat ~** (*of a pier, shore etc*) nous avons accosté.

aloof [ə'luːf] *adj*, *adv* à distance, à l'écart; **to stand ~** se tenir à l'écart *or* à distance.

aloofness [ə'luːfnɪs] *n* réserve (hautaine), attitude distante.

aloud [ə'laud] *adv* à haute voix.

alphabet ['ælfəbɛt] *n* alphabet *m*.

alphabetical [ælfə'bɛtɪkl] *adj* alphabétique; **in ~ order** par ordre alphabétique.

alphanumeric [ælfənjuː'mɛrɪk] *adj* alphanumérique.

alpine ['ælpaɪn] *adj* alpin(e), alpestre; **~ hut** cabane *f* or refuge *m* de montagne; **~ pasture** pâturage *m* (de montagne); **~ skiing** ski alpin.

Alps [ælps] *npl*: **the ~** les Alpes *fpl*.

already [ɔːl'rɛdɪ] *adv* déjà.

alright ['ɔːl'raɪt] *adv* (*BRIT*) = **all right**.

Alsace [æl'sæs] *n* Alsace *f*.

Alsatian [æl'seɪʃən] *adj* alsacien(ne), d'Alsace ♦ *n* Alsacien/ne; (*BRIT: dog*) berger allemand.

also ['ɔːlsəu] *adv* aussi.

Alta. *abbr* (*Canada*) = Alberta.

altar ['ɔltə*] *n* autel *m*.

alter ['ɔltə*] *vt*, *vi* changer, modifier.

alteration [ɔltə'reɪʃən] *n* changement *m*, modification *f*; **~s** (*SEWING*) retouches *fpl*; (*ARCHIT*) modifications *fpl*; **timetable subject to ~** horaires sujets à modifications.

altercation [ɔltə'keɪʃən] *n* altercation *f*.

alternate *adj* [ɔl'tɜːnɪt] alterné(e), alternant(e), alternatif(ive) ♦ *vi* ['ɔltɜːneɪt] alterner; **on ~ days** un jour sur deux, tous les deux jours.

alternately [ɔl'tɜːnɪtlɪ] *adv* alternativement, en alternant.

alternating ['ɔltɜːneɪtɪŋ] *adj* (*current*) alternatif(ive).

alternative [ɔl'tɜːnətɪv] *adj* (*solutions*) interchangeable, possible; (*solution*) autre, de remplacement; (*energy*) doux(douce); (*society*) parallèle ♦ *n* (*choice*) alternative *f*; (*other possibility*) autre possibilité *f*.

alternatively [ɔl'tɜːnətɪvlɪ] *adv*: **~ one could** une autre *or* l'autre solution serait de.

alternative medicine *n* médecines *fpl* parallèles *or* douces.

alternator ['ɔltɜːneɪtə*] *n* (*AUT*) alternateur *m*.

although [ɔːl'ðəu] *conj* bien que + *sub*.

altitude ['æltɪtjuːd] *n* altitude *f*.

alto ['æltəu] *n* (*female*) contralto *m*; (*male*) haute-contre *f*.

altogether [ɔːltə'gɛðə*] *adv* entièrement, tout à fait; (*on the whole*) tout compte fait; (*in all*) en tout; **how much is that ~?** ça fait combien en tout?

altruism ['æltruɪzəm] *n* altruisme *m*.

altruistic [æltru'ɪstɪk] *adj* altruiste.

aluminium [ælju'mɪnɪəm], (*US*) **aluminum** [ə'luːmɪnəm] *n* aluminium *m*.

alumna, *pl* **alumnae** [ə'lʌmnə, -niː] *n* (*US: SCOL*) ancienne élève; (: *UNIVERSITY*) ancienne étudiante.

alumnus, *pl* **alumni** [ə'lʌmnəs, -naɪ] *n* (*US: SCOL*) ancien élève; (:*UNIVERSITY*) ancien étudiant.

always ['ɔːlweɪz] *adv* toujours.

Alzheimer's disease ['æltshaɪməz-] *n* maladie *f* d'Alzheimer.

AM *abbr* = amplitude modulation.

am [æm] *vb see* **be**.

a.m. *adv abbr* (= ante meridiem) du matin.

AMA *n abbr* = American Medical Association.

amalgam [ə'mælgəm] *n* amalgame *m*.

amalgamate [ə'mælgəmeɪt] *vt*, *vi* fusionner.

amalgamation [əmælgə'meɪʃən] *n* fusion *f*; (*COMM*) fusionnement *m*.

amass [ə'mæs] *vt* amasser.

amateur ['æmətə*] *n* amateur *m* ♦ *adj* (*SPORT*) amateur *inv*; **~ dramatics** le théâtre amateur.

amateurish ['æmətərɪʃ] *adj* (*pej*) d'amateur, un peu amateur.

amaze [ə'meɪz] *vt* surprendre, étonner; **to be ~d (at)** être surpris *or* étonné (de).

amazement [ə'meɪzmənt] *n* surprise *f*, étonnement *m*.

amazing [ə'meɪzɪŋ] *adj* étonnant(e), incroyable; (*bargain, offer*) exceptionnel(le).

amazingly [ə'meɪzɪŋlɪ] *adv* incroyablement.

Amazon ['æməzən] *n* (*GEO, MYTHOLOGY*) Amazone *f* ♦ *cpd* amazonien(ne), de l'Amazone; **the ~ basin** le bassin de l'Amazone; **the ~ jungle** la forêt amazonienne.

Amazonian [æmə'zəunɪən] *adj* amazonien(ne).

ambassador [æm'bæsədə*] *n* ambassadeur *m*.

amber ['æmbə*] *n* ambre *m*; **at ~** (*BRIT AUT*) à l'orange.

ambidextrous [æmbɪ'dɛkstrəs] *adj* ambi

dextre.
ambience ['æmbɪəns] n ambiance f.
ambiguity [æmbɪ'ɡjuɪtɪ] n ambiguïté f.
ambiguous [æm'bɪɡjuəs] adj ambigu(ë).
ambition [æm'bɪʃən] n ambition f.
ambitious [æm'bɪʃəs] adj ambitieux(euse).
ambivalent [æm'bɪvələnt] adj (attitude) ambivalent(e).
amble ['æmbl] vi (also: **to** ~ **along**) aller d'un pas tranquille.
ambulance ['æmbjuləns] n ambulance f.
ambush ['æmbuʃ] n embuscade f ♦ vt tendre une embuscade à.
ameba [ə'miːbə] n (US) = amoeba.
ameliorate [ə'miːlɪəreɪt] vt améliorer.
amen ['ɑː'mɛn] excl amen.
amenable [ə'miːnəbl] adj: ~ **to** (advice etc) disposé(e) à écouter or suivre; ~ **to the law** responsable devant la loi.
amend [ə'mɛnd] vt (law) amender; (text) corriger; (habits) réformer ♦ vi s'amender, se corriger; **to make** ~s réparer ses torts, faire amende honorable.
amendment [ə'mɛndmənt] n (to law) amendement m; (to text) correction f.
amenities [ə'miːnɪtɪz] npl aménagements mpl, équipements mpl.
amenity [ə'miːnɪtɪ] n charme m, agrément m.
America [ə'mɛrɪkə] n Amérique f.
American [ə'mɛrɪkən] adj américain(e) ♦ n Américain/e.
americanize [ə'mɛrɪkənaɪz] vt américaniser.
amethyst ['æmɪθɪst] n améthyste f.
Amex ['æmɛks] n abbr = American Stock Exchange.
amiable ['eɪmɪəbl] adj aimable, affable.
amicable ['æmɪkəbl] adj amical(e).
amicably ['æmɪkəblɪ] adv amicalement.
amid(st) [ə'mɪd(st)] prep parmi, au milieu de.
amiss [ə'mɪs] adj, adv: **there's something** ~ il y a quelque chose qui ne va pas or qui cloche; **to take sth** ~ prendre qch mal or de travers.
ammo ['æməu] n abbr (col) = ammunition.
ammonia [ə'məunɪə] n (gas) ammoniac m; (liquid) ammoniaque f.
ammunition [æmju'nɪʃən] n munitions fpl; (fig) arguments mpl.
ammunition dump n dépôt m de munitions.
amnesia [æm'niːzɪə] n amnésie f.
amnesty ['æmnɪstɪ] n amnistie f; **to grant an** ~ **to** accorder une amnistie à.
Amnesty International n Amnesty International.
amoeba, (US) **ameba** [ə'miːbə] n amibe f.
amok [ə'mɔk] adv: **to run** ~ être pris(e) d'un accès de folie furieuse.
among(st) [ə'mʌŋ(st)] prep parmi, entre.
amoral [æ'mɔrəl] adj amoral(e).
amorous ['æmərəs] adj amoureux(euse).
amorphous [ə'mɔːfəs] adj amorphe.
amortization [əmɔːtaɪ'zeɪʃən] n (COMM) amor-

tissement m.
amount [ə'maunt] n (sum of money) somme f; (total) montant m; (quantity) quantité f, nombre m ♦ vi: **to** ~ **to** (total) s'élever à; (be same as) équivaloir à, revenir à; **this** ~s **to a refusal** cela équivaut à un refus; **the total** ~ (of money) le montant total.
amp(ere) ['æmp(ɛə*)] n ampère m; **a 13 amp plug** une fiche de 13 A.
ampersand ['æmpəsænd] n signe &, "et" commercial.
amphetamine [æm'fɛtəmiːn] n amphétamine f.
amphibian [æm'fɪbɪən] n batracien m.
amphibious [æm'fɪbɪəs] adj amphibie.
amphitheatre, (US) **amphitheater** ['æmfɪθɪətə*] n amphithéâtre m.
ample ['æmpl] adj ample; spacieux(euse); (enough): **this is** ~ c'est largement suffisant; **to have** ~ **time/room** avoir bien assez de temps/place, avoir largement le temps/la place.
amplifier ['æmplɪfaɪə*] n amplificateur m.
amplify ['æmplɪfaɪ] vt amplifier.
amply ['æmplɪ] adv amplement, largement.
ampoule, (US) **ampule** ['æmpuːl] n (MED) ampoule f.
amputate ['æmpjuteɪt] vt amputer.
amputee [æmpju'tiː] n amputé/e.
Amsterdam ['æmstədæm] n Amsterdam.
amt abbr = amount.
amuck [ə'mʌk] adv = amok.
amuse [ə'mjuːz] vt amuser; **to** ~ **o.s. with sth/by doing sth** se divertir avec qch/à faire qch; **to be** ~**d at** être amusé par; **he was not** ~**d** il n'a pas apprécié.
amusement [ə'mjuːzmənt] n amusement m.
amusement arcade n salle f de jeu.
amusement park n parc m d'attractions.
amusing [ə'mjuːzɪŋ] adj amusant(e), divertissant(e).
an [æn, ən, n] indef art see **a**.
ANA n abbr = American Newspaper Association; American Nurses Association.
anachronism [ə'nækrənɪzəm] n anachronisme m.
anaemia [ə'niːmɪə] n anémie f.
anaemic [ə'niːmɪk] adj anémique.
anaesthetic [ænɪs'θɛtɪk] adj, n anesthésique (m); **under the** ~ sous anesthésie; **local/general** ~ anesthésie locale/générale.
anaesthetist [æ'niːsθɪtɪst] n anesthésiste m/f.
anagram ['ænəɡræm] n anagramme m.
anal ['eɪnl] adj anal(e).
analgesic [ænæl'dʒiːsɪk] adj, n analgésique (m).
analogous [ə'næləɡəs] adj: ~ **(to** or **with)** analogue (à).
analog(ue) ['ænəlɔɡ] adj (watch, computer) analogique.
analogy [ə'nælədʒɪ] n analogie f; **to draw an** ~ **between** établir une analogie entre.
analyse ['ænəlaɪz] vt (BRIT) analyser.

analysis, pl **analyses** [ə'næləsıs, -siːz] n analyse f; **in the last** ~ en dernière analyse.

analyst ['ænəlıst] n (political ~ etc) analyste m/f; (US) psychanalyste m/f.

analytic(al) [ænə'lıtık(əl)] adj analytique.

analyze ['ænəlaız] vt (US) = analyse.

anarchic [æ'nɑːkık] adj anarchique.

anarchist ['ænəkıst] adj, n anarchiste (m/f).

anarchy ['ænəkı] n anarchie f.

anathema [ə'næθımə] n: **it is ~ to him** il a cela en abomination.

anatomical [ænə'tɔmıkəl] adj anatomique.

anatomy [ə'nætəmı] n anatomie f.

ANC n abbr (= African National Congress) ANC m.

ancestor ['ænsıstə*] n ancêtre m, aïeul m.

ancestral [æn'sɛstrəl] adj ancestral(e).

ancestry ['ænsıstrı] n ancêtres mpl; ascendance f.

anchor ['æŋkə*] n ancre f ♦ vi (also: **to drop** ~) jeter l'ancre, mouiller ♦ vt mettre à l'ancre.

anchorage ['æŋkərıdʒ] n mouillage m, ancrage m.

anchor man, anchor woman n (TV, RADIO) présentateur/trice.

anchovy ['æntʃəvı] n anchois m.

ancient ['eınʃənt] adj ancien(ne), antique; (fig) d'un âge vénérable, antique; ~ **monument** monument m historique.

ancillary [æn'sılərı] adj auxiliaire.

and [ænd] conj et; ~ **so on** et ainsi de suite; **try ~ come** tâchez de venir; **come ~ sit here** venez vous asseoir ici; **better ~ better** de mieux en mieux; **more ~ more** de plus en plus.

Andes ['ændiːz] npl: **the** ~ les Andes fpl.

anecdote ['ænıkdəut] n anecdote f.

anemia [ə'niːmıə] n = **anaemia.**

anemic [ə'niːmık] adj = **anaemic.**

anemone [ə'nɛmənı] n (BOT) anémone f; **sea** ~ anémone de mer.

anesthesiologist [ænısθiːzı'ɔlədʒıst] n (US) anesthésiste m/f.

anesthetic [ænıs'θɛtık] adj, n = **anaesthetic.**

anesthetist [æ'niːsθıtıst] n = **anaesthetist.**

anew [ə'njuː] adv à nouveau.

angel ['eındʒəl] n ange m.

angel dust n poussière f d'ange.

anger ['æŋgə*] n colère f ♦ vt mettre en colère, irriter.

angina [æn'dʒaınə] n angine f de poitrine.

angle ['æŋgl] n angle m ♦ vi: **to ~ for** (trout) pêcher; (compliments) chercher, quêter; **from their ~** on leur point de vue.

angler ['æŋglə*] n pêcheur/euse à la ligne.

Anglican ['æŋglıkən] adj, n anglican(e).

anglicize ['æŋglısaız] vt angliciser.

angling ['æŋglıŋ] n pêche f à la ligne.

Anglo- ['æŋgləu] prefix anglo(-).

Anglo-French ['æŋgləu'frɛntʃ] adj anglo-français(e).

Anglo-Saxon ['æŋgləu'sæksən] adj, n anglo-saxon(ne).

Angola [æŋ'gəulə] n Angola m.

Angolan [æŋ'gəulən] adj angolais(e) ♦ n Angolais/e.

angrily ['æŋgrılı] adv avec colère.

angry ['æŋgrı] adj en colère, furieux(euse); **to be ~ with sb/at sth** être furieux contre qn/de qch; **to get ~** se fâcher, se mettre en colère; **to make sb ~** mettre qn en colère.

anguish ['æŋgwıʃ] n angoisse f.

anguished ['æŋgwıʃt] adj (mentally) angoissé(e); (physically) plein(e) de souffrance.

angular ['æŋgjulə*] adj anguleux(euse).

animal ['ænıməl] n animal m ♦ adj animal(e).

animal rights npl droits mpl de l'animal.

animate vt ['ænımeıt] animer ♦ adj ['ænımıt] animé(e), vivant(e).

animated ['ænımeıtıd] adj animé(e).

animation [ænı'meıʃən] n (of person) entrain m; (of street, CINE) animation f.

animosity [ænı'mɔsıtı] n animosité f.

aniseed ['ænısiːd] n anis m.

Ankara ['æŋkərə] n Ankara.

ankle ['æŋkl] n cheville f.

ankle socks npl socquettes fpl.

annex n ['ænɛks] (also: BRIT: **annexe**) annexe f ♦ vt [ə'nɛks] annexer.

annexation [ænɛks'eıʃən] n annexion f.

annihilate [ə'naıəleıt] vt annihiler, anéantir.

annihilation [ənaıə'leıʃən] n anéantissement m.

anniversary [ænı'vəːsərı] n anniversaire m.

anniversary dinner n dîner commémoratif or anniversaire.

annotate ['ænəuteıt] vt annoter.

announce [ə'nauns] vt annoncer; (birth, death) faire part de; **he ~d that he wasn't going** il a déclaré qu'il n'irait pas.

announcement [ə'naunsmənt] n annonce f; (for births etc: in newspaper) avis m de faire-part; (: letter, card) faire-part m; **I'd like to make an ~** j'ai une communication à faire.

announcer [ə'naunsə*] n (RADIO, TV: between programmes) speaker/ine; (: in a programme) présentateur/trice.

annoy [ə'nɔı] vt agacer, ennuyer, contrarier; **to be ~ed (at sth/with sb)** être en colère or irrité (contre qch/qn); **don't get ~ed!** ne vous fâchez pas!

annoyance [ə'nɔıəns] n mécontentement m, contrariété f.

annoying [ə'nɔııŋ] adj ennuyeux(euse), agaçant(e), contrariant(e).

annual ['ænjuəl] adj annuel(le) ♦ n (BOT) plante annuelle; (book) album m.

annual general meeting (AGM) n (BRIT) assemblée générale annuelle (AGA).

annually ['ænjuəlı] adv annuellement.

annual report n rapport annuel.

annuity [ə'njuːıtı] n rente f; **life ~** rente viagère.

annul [ə'nʌl] vt annuler; (law) abroger.

annulment [ə'nʌlmənt] *n* (*see vb*) annulation *f*; abrogation *f*.
annum ['ænəm] *n see* **per annum**.
Annunciation [ənʌnsɪ'eɪʃən] *n* Annonciation *f*.
anode ['ænəud] *n* anode *f*.
anoint [ə'nɔɪnt] *vt* oindre.
anomalous [ə'nɔmələs] *adj* anormal(e).
anomaly [ə'nɔməlɪ] *n* anomalie *f*.
anon. [ə'nɔn] *abbr* = **anonymous**.
anonymity [ænə'nɪmɪtɪ] *n* anonymat *m*.
anonymous [ə'nɔnɪməs] *adj* anonyme; **to remain** ~ garder l'anonymat.
anorak ['ænəræk] *n* anorak *m*.
anorexia [ænə'rɛksɪə] *n* (*also*: ~ **nervosa**) anorexie *f*.
anorexic [ænə'rɛksɪk] *adj, n* anorexique (*m/f*).
another [ə'nʌðə*] *adj*: ~ **book** (*one more*) un autre livre, encore un livre, un livre de plus; (*a different one*) un autre livre; ~ **drink?** encore un verre?; **in** ~ **5 years** dans 5 ans ♦ *pron* un(e) autre, encore un(e), un(e) de plus; *see also* **one**.
ANSI ['ænsɪ] *n abbr* (= *American National Standards Institution*) ANSI *m* (*Institut américain de normalisation*).
answer ['ɑːnsə*] *n* réponse *f*; (*to problem*) solution *f* ♦ *vi* répondre ♦ *vt* (*reply to*) répondre à; (*problem*) résoudre; (*prayer*) exaucer; **to** ~ **the phone** répondre (au téléphone); **in** ~ **to your letter** suite à *or* en réponse à votre lettre; **to** ~ **the bell** *or* **the door** aller *or* venir ouvrir (la porte).
►**answer back** *vi* répondre, répliquer.
►**answer for** *vt fus* répondre de, se porter garant de; (*crime, one's actions*) répondre de.
►**answer to** *vt fus* (*description*) répondre *or* correspondre à.
answerable ['ɑːnsərəbl] *adj*: ~ **(to sb/for sth)** responsable (devant qn/de qch); **I am** ~ **to no-one** je n'ai de comptes à rendre à personne.
answering machine ['ɑːnsərɪŋ-] *n* répondeur *m*.
ant [ænt] *n* fourmi *f*.
ANTA *n abbr* = *American National Theater and Academy*.
antagonism [æn'tægənɪzəm] *n* antagonisme *m*.
antagonist [æn'tægənɪst] *n* antagoniste *m/f*, adversaire *m/f*.
antagonistic [æntægə'nɪstɪk] *adj* (*attitude, feelings*) hostile.
antagonize [æn'tægənaɪz] *vt* éveiller l'hostilité de, contrarier.
Antarctic [ænt'ɑːktɪk] *adj* antarctique, austral(e) ♦ *n*: **the** ~ l'Antarctique *m*.
Antarctica [ænt'ɑːktɪkə] *n* Antarctique *m*, Terres Australes.
Antarctic Circle *n* cercle *m* Antarctique.
Antarctic Ocean *n* océan *m* Antarctique *or* Austral.
ante ['æntɪ] *n*: **to up the** ~ faire monter les enjeux.

ante... ['æntɪ] *prefix* anté..., anti..., pré....
anteater ['ænti:tə*] *n* fourmilier *m*, tamanoir *m*.
antecedent [æntɪ'si:dənt] *n* antécédent *m*.
antechamber ['æntɪtʃeɪmbə*] *n* antichambre *f*.
antelope ['æntɪləup] *n* antilope *f*.
antenatal ['æntɪ'neɪtl] *adj* prénatal(e).
antenatal clinic *n* service *m* de consultation prénatale.
antenna, *pl* ~**e** [æn'tɛnə, -ni:] *n* antenne *f*.
anthem ['ænθəm] *n* motet *m*; **national** ~ hymne national.
ant-hill ['ænthɪl] *n* fourmilière *f*.
anthology [æn'θɔlədʒɪ] *n* anthologie *f*.
anthropologist [ænθrə'pɔlədʒɪst] *n* anthropologue *m/f*.
anthropology [ænθrə'pɔlədʒɪ] *n* anthropologie *f*.
anti- ['æntɪ] *prefix* anti-.
anti-aircraft ['æntɪ'ɛəkrɑːft] *adj* anti-aérien(ne).
anti-aircraft defence *n* défense *f* contre avions, DCA *f*.
antiballistic ['æntɪbə'lɪstɪk] *adj* antibalistique.
antibiotic ['æntɪbaɪ'ɔtɪk] *adj, n* antibiotique (*m*).
antibody ['æntɪbɔdɪ] *n* anticorps *m*.
anticipate [æn'tɪsɪpeɪt] *vt* s'attendre à, prévoir; (*wishes, request*) aller au devant de, devancer; **this is worse than I** ~**d** c'est pire que je ne pensais; **as** ~**d** comme prévu.
anticipation [æntɪsɪ'peɪʃən] *n* attente *f*; **thanking you in** ~ en vous remerciant d'avance, avec mes remerciements anticipés.
anticlimax ['æntɪ'klaɪmæks] *n* réalisation décevante d'un événement que l'on escomptait important, intéressant etc.
anticlockwise ['æntɪ'klɔkwaɪz] *adj* dans le sens inverse des aiguilles d'une montre.
antics ['æntɪks] *npl* singeries *fpl*.
anticyclone ['æntɪ'saɪkləun] *n* anticyclone *m*.
antidote ['æntɪdəut] *n* antidote *m*, contrepoison *m*.
antifreeze ['æntɪfri:z] *n* antigel *m*.
antihistamine [æntɪ'hɪstəmɪn] *n* antihistaminique *m*.
Antilles [æn'tɪli:z] *npl*: **the** ~ les Antilles *fpl*.
antipathy [æn'tɪpəθɪ] *n* antipathie *f*.
antiperspirant [æntɪ'pə:spɪrənt] *n* déodorant *m* anti-transpiration.
Antipodean [æntɪpə'di:ən] *adj* australien(ne) et néozélandais(e), d'Australie et de Nouvelle-Zélande.
Antipodes [æn'tɪpədi:z] *npl*: **the** ~ l'Australie *f* et la Nouvelle-Zélande.
antiquarian [æntɪ'kwɛərɪən] *adj*: ~ **bookshop** librairie *f* d'ouvrages anciens ♦ *n* expert *m* en objets *or* livres anciens; amateur *m* d'antiquités.
antiquated ['æntɪkweɪtɪd] *adj* vieilli(e), suran-

né(e), vieillot(te).

antique [æn'tiːk] n objet m d'art ancien, meuble ancien or d'époque, antiquité f ♦ adj ancien(ne); (pre-mediaeval) antique.

antique dealer n antiquaire m/f.

antique shop n magasin m d'antiquités.

antiquity [æn'tɪkwɪtɪ] n antiquité f.

anti-Semitic ['æntɪsɪ'mɪtɪk] adj antisémite.

anti-Semitism ['æntɪ'sɛmɪtɪzəm] n antisémitisme m.

antiseptic [æntɪ'sɛptɪk] adj, n antiseptique (m).

antisocial ['æntɪ'səʊʃəl] adj peu liant(e), sauvage, insociable; (against society) antisocial(e).

antitank [æntɪ'tæŋk] adj antichar.

antithesis, pl **antitheses** [æn'tɪθɪsɪs, -siːz] n antithèse f.

antitrust [æntɪ'trʌst] adj: ~ **legislation** loi f anti-trust.

antlers ['æntləz] npl bois mpl, ramure f.

Antwerp ['æntwəːp] n Anvers m.

anus ['eɪnəs] n anus m.

anvil ['ænvɪl] n enclume f.

anxiety [æŋ'zaɪətɪ] n anxiété f; (keenness): ~ **to do** grand désir or impatience f de faire.

anxious ['æŋkʃəs] adj anxieux(euse), (très) inquiet(ète); (keen): ~ **to do/that** qui tient beaucoup à faire/è ce que; impatient(e) de faire/que; **I'm very** ~ **about you** je me fais beaucoup de souci pour toi.

anxiously ['æŋkʃəslɪ] adv anxieusement.

═══════════════════════ KEYWORD

any ['ɛnɪ] adj **1** (in questions etc: singular) du, de l', de la; (in questions etc: plural) des; **have you** ~ **butter/children/ink?** avez-vous du beurre/des enfants/de l'encre?
2 (with negative) de, d'; **I haven't** ~ **money/books** je n'ai pas d'argent/de livres; **without** ~ **difficulty** sans la moindre difficulté
3 (no matter which) n'importe quel(le), quelconque; (each and every) tout(e), chaque; **choose** ~ **book you like** vous pouvez choisir n'importe quel livre
4 (in phrases): **in** ~ **case** de toute façon; ~ **day now** d'un jour à l'autre; **at** ~ **moment** à tout moment, d'un instant à l'autre; **at** ~ **rate** en tout cas
♦ pron **1** (in questions etc) en; **have you got** ~? est-ce que vous en avez?; **can** ~ **of you sing?** est-ce que parmi vous il y en a qui savent chanter?
2 (with negative) en; **I haven't** ~ **(of them)** je n'en ai pas, je n'en ai aucun
3 (no matter which one(s)) n'importe lequel (or laquelle); (anybody) n'importe qui; **take** ~ **of those books (you like)** vous pouvez prendre n'importe lequel de ces livres
♦ adv **1** (in questions etc): **do you want** ~ **more soup/sandwiches?** voulez-vous encore de la soupe/des sandwichs?; **are you feeling** ~ **better?** est-ce que vous vous sentez

mieux?
2 (with negative): **I can't hear him** ~ **more** je ne l'entends plus; **don't wait** ~ **longer** n'attendez pas plus longtemps.

anybody ['ɛnɪbɔdɪ] pron n'importe qui; (in interrogative sentences) quelqu'un; (in negative sentences): **I don't see** ~ je ne vois personne.

anyhow ['ɛnɪhaʊ] adv quoi qu'il en soit; (haphazardly) n'importe comment; **I shall go** ~ j'irai de toute façon.

anyone ['ɛnɪwʌn] = **anybody**.

anyplace ['ɛnɪpleɪs] adv (US) = **anywhere**.

anything ['ɛnɪθɪŋ] pron n'importe quoi; (in interrogative sentences) quelque chose; (in negative sentences): **I don't want** ~ je ne veux rien; ~ **else?** (in shop) et avec ça?; **it can cost** ~ **between £15 and £20** (BRIT) ça peut coûter dans les 15 à 20 livres.

anytime ['ɛnɪtaɪm] adv n'importe quand.

anyway ['ɛnɪweɪ] adv de toute façon.

anywhere ['ɛnɪwɛə*] adv n'importe où; (in interrogative sentences) quelque part; (in negative sentences): **I don't see him** ~ je ne le vois nulle part; ~ **in the world** n'importe où dans le monde.

Anzac ['ænzæk] n abbr (= Australia-New Zealand Army Corps) soldat du corps ANZAC.

┌───┐
Anzac Day est le 25 avril, jour férié en Australie et en Nouvelle-Zélande commémorant le débarquement des soldats du corps **ANZAC** à Gallipoli en 1915, pendant la Première Guerre mondiale. Ce fut la plus célèbre des campagnes du corps **ANZAC**.
└───┘

apart [ə'pɑːt] adv (to one side) à part; de côté; à l'écart; (separately) séparément; **10 miles/a long way** ~ à 10 milles/très éloignés l'un de l'autre; **they are living** ~ ils sont séparés; ~ **from** prep à part, excepté.

apartheid [ə'pɑːteɪt] n apartheid m.

apartment [ə'pɑːtmənt] n (US) appartement m, logement m.

apartment building n (US) immeuble m; maison divisée en appartements.

apathetic [æpə'θɛtɪk] adj apathique, indifférent(e).

apathy ['æpəθɪ] n apathie f, indifférence f.

APB n abbr (US: = all points bulletin) expression de la police signifiant "découvrir et appréhender le suspect".

ape [eɪp] n (grand) singe ♦ vt singer.

Apennines ['æpənaɪnz] npl: **the** ~ les Apennins mpl.

apéritif [ə'pɛrɪtiːf] n apéritif m.

aperture ['æpətʃʊə*] n orifice m, ouverture f; (PHOT) ouverture (du diaphragme).

APEX ['eɪpɛks] n abbr (AVIAT: = advance purchase excursion) APEX m.

apex ['eɪpɛks] n sommet m.

aphid ['eɪfɪd] n puceron m.

aphrodisiac [æfrəu'dızıæk] *adj, n* aphrodisiaque *(m)*.

API *n abbr = American Press Institute*.

apiece [ə'piːs] *adv (for each person)* chacun(e), par tête; *(for each item)* chacun(e), (la) pièce.

aplomb [ə'plɔm] *n* sang-froid *m*, assurance *f*.

APO *n abbr (US: = Army Post Office) service postal de l'armée*.

apocalypse [ə'pɔkəlıps] *n* apocalypse *f*.

apolitical [eɪpə'lıtıkl] *adj* apolitique.

apologetic [əpɔlə'dʒetık] *adj (tone, letter)* d'excuse; **to be very ~ about** s'excuser vivement de.

apologetically [əpɔlə'dʒetıkəlı] *adv (say)* en s'excusant.

apologize [ə'pɔlədʒaız] *vi*: **to ~ (for sth to sb)** s'excuser (de qch auprès de qn), présenter des excuses (à qn pour qch).

apology [ə'pɔlədʒı] *n* excuses *fpl*; **to send one's apologies** envoyer une lettre *or* un mot d'excuse, s'excuser (de ne pas pouvoir venir); **please accept my apologies** vous voudrez bien m'excuser.

apoplectic [æpə'plektık] *adj (MED)* apoplectique; *(col)*: **~ with rage** fou(folle) de rage.

apoplexy ['æpəpleksı] *n* apoplexie *f*.

apostle [ə'pɔsl] *n* apôtre *m*.

apostrophe [ə'pɔstrəfı] *n* apostrophe *f*.

appal [ə'pɔːl] *vt* consterner, atterrer; horrifier.

Appalachian Mountains [æpə'leıʃən-] *npl*: **the ~** les (monts *mpl*) Appalaches *mpl*.

appalling [ə'pɔːlıŋ] *adj* épouvantable; *(stupidity)* consternant(e); **she's an ~ cook** c'est une très mauvaise cuisinière.

apparatus [æpə'reıtəs] *n* appareil *m*, dispositif *m*; *(in gymnasium)* agrès *mpl*.

apparel [ə'pærl] *n (US)* habillement *m*, confection *f*.

apparent [ə'pærənt] *adj* apparent(e); **it is ~ that** il est évident que.

apparently [ə'pærəntlı] *adv* apparemment.

apparition [æpə'rıʃən] *n* apparition *f*.

appeal [ə'piːl] *vi (LAW)* faire *or* interjeter appel ♦ *n (LAW)* appel *m*; *(request)* appel; prière *f*; *(charm)* attrait *m*, charme *m*; **to ~ for** demander (instamment); implorer; **to ~ to** *(subj: person)* faire appel à; *(subj: thing)* plaire à; **to ~ to sb for mercy** implorer la pitié de qn, prier *or* adjurer qn d'avoir pitié; **it doesn't ~ to me** cela ne m'attire pas; **right of ~** droit *m* de recours.

appealing [ə'piːlıŋ] *adj (nice)* attrayant(e); *(touching)* attendrissant(e).

appear [ə'pıə*] *vi* apparaître, se montrer; *(LAW)* comparaître; *(publication)* paraître, sortir, être publié(e); *(seem)* paraître, sembler; **it would ~ that** il semble que; **to ~ in Hamlet** jouer dans Hamlet; **to ~ on TV** passer à la télé.

appearance [ə'pıərəns] *n* apparition *f*; paru-

tion *f*; *(look, aspect)* apparence *f*, aspect *m*; **to put in** *or* **make an ~** faire acte de présence; *(THEAT)*: **by order of ~** par ordre d'entrée en scène; **to keep up ~s** sauver les apparences; **to all ~s** selon toute apparence.

appease [ə'piːz] *vt* apaiser, calmer.

appeasement [ə'piːzmənt] *n (POL)* apaisement *m*.

appellate court [ə'pelıt-] *n (US)* cour *f* d'appel.

append [ə'pend] *vt (COMPUT)* ajouter (à la fin d'un fichier).

appendage [ə'pendıdʒ] *n* appendice *m*.

appendicitis [əpendı'saıtıs] *n* appendicite *f*.

appendix, *pl* **appendices** [ə'pendıks, -siːz] *n* appendice *m*; **to have one's ~ out** se faire opérer de l'appendicite.

appetite ['æpıtaıt] *n* appétit *m*; **that walk has given me an ~** cette promenade m'a ouvert l'appétit.

appetizer ['æpıtaızə*] *n (food)* amuse-gueule *m*; *(drink)* apéritif *m*.

appetizing ['æpıtaızıŋ] *adj* appétissant(e).

applaud [ə'plɔːd] *vt, vi* applaudir.

applause [ə'plɔːz] *n* applaudissements *mpl*.

apple ['æpl] *n* pomme *f*; *(also:* **~ tree)** pommier *m*; **it's the ~ of my eye** j'y tiens comme à la prunelle de mes yeux.

apple turnover *n* chausson *m* aux pommes.

appliance [ə'plaıəns] *n* appareil *m*; **electrical ~s** l'électroménager *m*.

applicable [ə'plıkəbl] *adj* applicable; **the law is ~ from January** la loi entre en vigueur au mois de janvier; **to be ~ to** valoir pour.

applicant ['æplıkənt] *n*: **~ (for)** *(ADMIN: for benefit etc)* demandeur/euse (de); *(for post)* candidat/e (à).

application [æplı'keıʃən] *n* application *f*; *(for a job, a grant etc)* demande *f*; candidature *f*; **on ~** sur demande.

application form *n* formulaire *m* de demande.

application program *n (COMPUT)* programme *m* d'application.

applications package *n (COMPUT)* progiciel *m* d'application.

applied [ə'plaıd] *adj* appliqué(e); **~ arts** *npl* arts décoratifs.

apply [ə'plaı] *vt*: **to ~ (to)** *(paint, ointment)* appliquer (sur); *(theory, technique)* appliquer (à) ♦ *vi*: **to ~ to** *(ask)* s'adresser à; *(be suitable for, relevant to)* s'appliquer à, être valable pour; **to ~ (for)** *(permit, grant)* faire une demande (en vue d'obtenir); *(job)* poser sa candidature (pour), faire une demande d'emploi (concernant); **to ~ the brakes** actionner les freins, freiner; **to ~ o.s. to** s'appliquer à.

appoint [ə'pɔınt] *vt* nommer, engager; *(date, place)* fixer, désigner.

appointee [əpɔın'tiː] *n* personne nommée; candidat retenu.

appointment [ə'pɔɪntmənt] *n* (*to post*) nomination *f*; (*arrangement to meet*) rendez-vous *m*; **to make an ~ (with)** prendre rendez-vous (avec); **"~s (vacant)"** (*PRESS*) "offres d'emploi"; **by ~** sur rendez-vous.

apportion [ə'pɔ:ʃən] *vt* (*share out*) répartir, distribuer; **to ~ sth to sb** attribuer *or* assigner *or* allouer qch à qn.

appraisal [ə'preɪzl] *n* évaluation *f*.

appraise [ə'preɪz] *vt* (*value*) estimer; (*situation etc*) évaluer.

appreciable [ə'pri:ʃəbl] *adj* appréciable.

appreciably [ə'pri:ʃəblɪ] *adv* sensiblement, de façon appréciable.

appreciate [ə'pri:ʃɪeɪt] *vt* (*like*) apprécier, faire cas de; (*be grateful for*) être reconnaissant(e) de; (*assess*) évaluer; (*be aware of*) comprendre, se rendre compte de ♦ *vi* (*FINANCE*) prendre de la valeur; **I ~ your help** je vous remercie pour votre aide.

appreciation [əpri:ʃɪ'eɪʃən] *n* appréciation *f*; (*gratitude*) reconnaissance *f*; (*FINANCE*) hausse *f*, valorisation *f*.

appreciative [ə'pri:ʃɪətɪv] *adj* (*person*) sensible; (*comment*) élogieux(euse).

apprehend [æprɪ'hend] *vt* appréhender, arrêter; (*understand*) comprendre.

apprehension [æprɪ'henʃən] *n* appréhension *f*, inquiétude *f*.

apprehensive [æprɪ'hensɪv] *adj* inquiet(ète), appréhensif(ive).

apprentice [ə'prentɪs] *n* apprenti *m* ♦ *vt*: **to be ~d to** être en apprentissage chez.

apprenticeship [ə'prentɪsʃɪp] *n* apprentissage *m*; **to serve one's ~** faire son apprentissage.

appro. ['æprəʊ] *abbr* (*BRIT COMM: col*) = **approval**.

approach [ə'prəʊtʃ] *vi* approcher ♦ *vt* (*come near*) approcher de; (*ask, apply to*) s'adresser à; (*subject, passer-by*) aborder ♦ *n* approche *f*; accès *m*, abord *m*; démarche *f* (*auprès de qn*); démarche (*intellectuelle*); **to ~ sb about sth** aller *or* venir voir qn pour qch.

approachable [ə'prəʊtʃəbl] *adj* accessible.

approach road *n* voie *f* d'accès.

approbation [æprə'beɪʃən] *n* approbation *f*.

appropriate *vt* [ə'prəʊprɪeɪt] (*take*) s'approprier; (*allot*): **to ~ sth for** affecter qch à ♦ *adj* [ə'prəʊprɪt] qui convient, approprié(e); (*timely*) opportun(e); **~ for** *or* **to** approprié à; **it would not be ~ for me to comment** il ne me serait pas approprié de commenter.

appropriately [ə'prəʊprɪtlɪ] *adv* pertinemment, avec à-propos.

appropriation [əprəʊprɪ'eɪʃən] *n* dotation *f*, affectation *f*.

approval [ə'pru:vəl] *n* approbation *f*; **to meet with sb's ~** (*proposal etc*) recueillir l'assentiment de qn; **on ~** (*COMM*) à l'examen.

approve [ə'pru:v] *vt* approuver.

▶**approve of** *vt fus* approuver.

approved school [ə'pru:vd-] *n* (*BRIT*) centre *m* d'éducation surveillée.

approvingly [ə'pru:vɪŋlɪ] *adv* d'un air approbateur.

approx. *abbr* (= *approximately*) env.

approximate *adj* [ə'prɒksɪmɪt] approximatif(ive) ♦ *vt* [ə'prɒksɪmeɪt] se rapprocher de; être proche de.

approximation [əprɒksɪ'meɪʃən] *n* approximation *f*.

Apr. *abbr* = **April**.

apr *n abbr* (= *annual percentage rate*) taux (d'intérêt) annuel.

apricot ['eɪprɪkɒt] *n* abricot *m*.

April ['eɪprəl] *n* avril *m*; **~ fool!** poisson d'avril!; *for phrases see also* **July**.

April Fool's Day *n* le premier avril.

April Fool's Day est le *1er* avril, à l'occasion duquel on fait des farces de toutes sortes. Les victimes de ces farces sont les "April fools". Les médias britanniques se prennent aussi au jeu, diffusant de fausses nouvelles, comme la découverte d'îles de la taille de l'Irlande, ou faisant des reportages bidon, montrant par exemple la culture d'arbres à spaghettis en Italie.

---

apron ['eɪprən] *n* tablier *m*; (*AVIAT*) aire *f* de stationnement.

apse [æps] *n* (*ARCHIT*) abside *f*.

APT *n abbr* (*BRIT*: = *advanced passenger train*) ≈ TGV *m*.

Apt. *abbr* (= *apartment*) appt.

apt [æpt] *adj* (*suitable*) approprié(e); (*able*): **~ (at)** doué(e) (pour); apte (à); (*likely*): **~ to do** susceptible de faire; ayant tendance à faire.

aptitude ['æptɪtju:d] *n* aptitude *f*.

aptitude test *n* test *m* d'aptitude.

aptly ['æptlɪ] *adv* (fort) à propos.

aqualung ['ækwəlʌŋ] *n* scaphandre *m* autonome.

aquarium [ə'kwɛərɪəm] *n* aquarium *m*.

Aquarius [ə'kwɛərɪəs] *n* le Verseau; **to be ~** être du Verseau.

aquatic [ə'kwætɪk] *adj* aquatique; (*sport*) nautique.

aqueduct ['ækwɪdʌkt] *n* aqueduc *m*.

AR *abbr* (*US*) = *Arkansas*.

ARA *n abbr* (*BRIT*) = *Associate of the Royal Academy*.

Arab ['ærəb] *n* Arabe *m/f* ♦ *adj* arabe.

Arabia [ə'reɪbɪə] *n* Arabie *f*.

Arabian [ə'reɪbɪən] *adj* arabe.

Arabian Desert *n* désert *m* d'Arabie.

Arabian Sea *n* mer *f* d'Arabie.

Arabic ['ærəbɪk] *adj*, *n* arabe (*m*).

Arabic numerals *npl* chiffres *mpl* arabes.

arable ['ærəbl] *adj* arable.

ARAM *n abbr* (*BRIT*) = *Associate of the Royal Academy of Music*.

arbiter ['ɑːbɪtə*] *n* arbitre *m*.
arbitrary ['ɑːbɪtrərɪ] *adj* arbitraire.
arbitrate ['ɑːbɪtreɪt] *vi* arbitrer; trancher.
arbitration [ɑːbɪ'treɪʃən] *n* arbitrage *m*; **the dispute went to** ~ le litige a été soumis à arbitrage.
arbitrator ['ɑːbɪtreɪtə*] *n* arbitre *m*, médiateur/trice.
ARC *n abbr* = *American Red Cross*.
arc [ɑːk] *n* arc *m*.
arcade [ɑː'keɪd] *n* arcade *f*; (*passage with shops*) passage *m*, galerie *f*.
arch [ɑːtʃ] *n* arche *f*; (*of foot*) cambrure *f*, voûte *f* plantaire ♦ *vt* arquer, cambrer ♦ *adj* malicieux(euse) ♦ *prefix:* ~(-) achevé(e); par excellence; **pointed** ~ ogive *f*.
archaeological [ɑːkɪə'lɔdʒɪkl] *adj* archéologique.
archaeologist [ɑːkɪ'ɔlədʒɪst] *n* archéologue *m/f*.
archaeology [ɑːkɪ'ɔlədʒɪ] *n* archéologie *f*.
archaic [ɑː'keɪɪk] *adj* archaïque.
archangel ['ɑːkeɪndʒəl] *n* archange *m*.
archbishop [ɑːtʃ'bɪʃəp] *n* archevêque *m*.
archenemy ['ɑːtʃ'enɪmɪ] *n* ennemi *m* de toujours *or* par excellence.
archeology [ɑːkɪ'ɔlədʒɪ] *etc* (*US*) = **archaeology** *etc*.
archer ['ɑːtʃə*] *n* archer *m*.
archery ['ɑːtʃərɪ] *n* tir *m* à l'arc.
archetypal ['ɑːkɪtaɪpəl] *adj* archétype.
archetype ['ɑːkɪtaɪp] *n* prototype *m*, archétype *m*.
archipelago [ɑːkɪ'pelɪgəu] *n* archipel *m*.
architect ['ɑːkɪtekt] *n* architecte *m*.
architectural [ɑːkɪ'tektʃərəl] *adj* architectural(e).
architecture ['ɑːkɪtektʃə*] *n* architecture *f*.
archive ['ɑːkaɪv] *n* (*often pl*) archives *fpl*.
archive file *n* (*COMPUT*) fichier *m* d'archives.
archives ['ɑːkaɪvz] *npl* archives *fpl*.
archivist ['ɑːkɪvɪst] *n* archiviste *m/f*.
archway ['ɑːtʃweɪ] *n* voûte *f*, porche voûté *or* cintré.
ARCM *n abbr* (*BRIT*) = *Associate of the Royal Colllege of Music*.
Arctic ['ɑːktɪk] *adj* arctique ♦ *n*: **the** ~ l'Arctique *m*.
Arctic Circle *n* cercle *m* Arctique.
Arctic Ocean *n* océan *m* Arctique.
ARD *n abbr* (*US MED*) = *acute respiratory disease*.
ardent ['ɑːdənt] *adj* fervent(e).
ardour, (*US*) **ardor** ['ɑːdə*] *n* ardeur *f*.
arduous ['ɑːdjuəs] *adj* ardu(e).
are [ɑː*] *vb see* **be**.
area ['ɛərɪə] *n* (*GEOM*) superficie *f*; (*zone*) région *f*; (*: smaller*) secteur *m*; **dining** ~ coin *m* salle à manger; **the London** ~ la région Londonienne.
area code *n* (*TEL*) indicatif *m* (téléphonique).
arena [ə'riːnə] *n* arène *f*.
aren't [ɑːnt] = **are not**.

Argentina [ɑːdʒən'tiːnə] *n* Argentine *f*.
Argentinian [ɑːdʒən'tɪnɪən] *adj* argentin(e) ♦ *n* Argentin/e.
arguable ['ɑːgjuəbl] *adj* discutable, contestable; **it is** ~ **whether** on peut se demander si.
arguably ['ɑːgjuəblɪ] *adv*: **it is** ~ ... on peut soutenir que c'est ....
argue ['ɑːgjuː] *vi* (*quarrel*) se disputer; (*reason*) argumenter ♦ *vt* (*debate: case, matter*) débattre; **to** ~ **about sth (with sb)** se disputer (avec qn) au sujet de qch; **to** ~ **that** objecter *or* alléguer que, donner comme argument que.
argument ['ɑːgjumənt] *n* (*reasons*) argument *m*; (*quarrel*) dispute *f*, discussion *f*; (*debate*) discussion, controverse *f*; ~ **for/against** argument pour/contre.
argumentative [ɑːgju'mentətɪv] *adj* ergoteur(euse), raisonneur(euse).
aria ['ɑːrɪə] *n* aria *f*.
ARIBA [ə'riːbə] *n abbr* (*BRIT*) = *Associate of the Royal Institute of British Architects*.
arid ['ærɪd] *adj* aride.
aridity [ə'rɪdɪtɪ] *n* aridité *f*.
Aries ['ɛərɪz] *n* le Bélier; **to be** ~ être du Bélier.
arise, *pt* **arose,** *pp* **arisen** [ə'raɪz, ə'rəuz, ə'rɪzn] *vi* survenir, se présenter; **to** ~ **from** résulter de; **should the need** ~ en cas de besoin.
aristocracy [ærɪs'tɔkrəsɪ] *n* aristocratie *f*.
aristocrat ['ærɪstəkræt] *n* aristocrate *m/f*.
aristocratic [ærɪstə'krætɪk] *adj* aristocratique.
arithmetic [ə'rɪθmətɪk] *n* arithmétique *f*.
arithmetical [ærɪθ'metɪkl] *adj* arithmétique.
Ariz. *abbr* (*US*) = *Arizona*.
ark [ɑːk] *n*: **Noah's A**~ l'Arche *f* de Noé.
Ark. *abbr* (*US*) = *Arkansas*.
arm [ɑːm] *n* bras *m* ♦ *vt* armer; ~ **in** ~ bras dessus bras dessous.
armaments ['ɑːməmənts] *npl* (*weapons*) armement *m*.
armband ['ɑːmbænd] *n* brassard *m*.
armchair ['ɑːmtʃɛə*] *n* fauteuil *m*.
armed [ɑːmd] *adj* armé(e); **the** ~ **forces** les forces armées.
armed robbery *n* vol *m* à main armée.
Armenia [ɑː'miːnɪə] *n* Arménie *f*.
Armenian [ɑː'miːnɪən] *adj* arménien(ne) ♦ *n* Arménien/ne; (*LING*) arménien *m*.
armful ['ɑːmful] *n* brassée *f*.
armistice ['ɑːmɪstɪs] *n* armistice *m*.
armour, (*US*) **armor** ['ɑːmə*] *n* armure *f*; (*also*: ~-**plating**) blindage *m*; (*MIL: tanks*) blindés *mpl*.
armo(u)red car ['ɑːməd-] *n* véhicule blindé.
armo(u)ry ['ɑːmərɪ] *n* arsenal *m*.
armpit ['ɑːmpɪt] *n* aisselle *f*.
armrest ['ɑːmrest] *n* accoudoir *m*.
arms [ɑːmz] *npl* (*weapons, HERALDRY*) armes *fpl*.

arms control n contrôle m des armements.
arms race n course f aux armements.
army ['ɑːmɪ] n armée f.
aroma [ə'rəumə] n arôme m.
aromatherapy [ərəumə'θerəpɪ] n aromathérapie f.
aromatic [ærə'mætɪk] adj aromatique.
arose [ə'rəuz] pt of **arise**.
around [ə'raund] adv (tout) autour; (nearby) dans les parages ♦ prep autour de; (fig: about) environ; vers; **is he ~?** est-il dans les parages or là?
arousal [ə'rauzəl] n (sexual) excitation sexuelle, éveil m.
arouse [ə'rauz] vt (sleeper) éveiller; (curiosity, passions) éveiller, susciter; exciter.
arpeggio [ɑː'pedʒɪəu] n arpège m.
arrange [ə'reɪndʒ] vt arranger; (programme) arrêter, convenir de ♦ vi: **we have ~d for a car to pick you up** nous avons prévu qu'une voiture vienne vous prendre; **it was ~d that** ... il a été convenu que ..., il a été décidé que ...; **to ~ to do sth** prévoir de faire qch.
arrangement [ə'reɪndʒmənt] n arrangement m; (plans etc): **~s** dispositions fpl; **to come to an ~ (with sb)** se mettre d'accord (avec qn); **home deliveries by ~** livraison à domicile sur demande; **I'll make ~s for you to be met** je vous enverrai chercher.
arrant ['ærənt] adj: **he's talking ~ nonsense** il raconte vraiment n'importe quoi.
array [ə'reɪ] n (of objects) déploiement m, étalage m; (MATH, COMPUT) tableau m.
arrears [ə'rɪəz] npl arriéré m; **to be in ~ with one's rent** devoir un arriéré de loyer, être en retard pour le paiement de son loyer.
arrest [ə'rest] vt arrêter; (sb's attention) retenir, attirer ♦ n arrestation f; **under ~** en état d'arrestation.
arresting [ə'restɪŋ] adj (fig: beauty) saisissant(e); (: charm, candour) désarmant(e).
arrival [ə'raɪvl] n arrivée f; (COMM) arrivage m; (person) arrivant/e; **new ~** nouveau venu/nouvelle venue.
arrive [ə'raɪv] vi arriver.
▶**arrive at** vt fus (fig) parvenir à.
arrogance ['ærəgəns] n arrogance f.
arrogant ['ærəgənt] adj arrogant(e).
arrow ['ærəu] n flèche f.
arse [ɑːs] n (BRIT col!) cul m (!).
arsenal ['ɑːsɪnl] n arsenal m.
arsenic ['ɑːsnɪk] n arsenic m.
arson ['ɑːsn] n incendie criminel.
art [ɑːt] n art m; (craft) métier m; **work of ~** œuvre f d'art.
artefact ['ɑːtɪfækt] n objet fabriqué.
arterial [ɑː'tɪərɪəl] adj (ANAT) artériel(le); (road etc) à grande circulation.
artery ['ɑːtərɪ] n artère f.
artful ['ɑːtful] adj rusé(e).
art gallery n musée m d'art; (small and private) galerie f de peinture.

arthritis [ɑː'θraɪtɪs] n arthrite f.
artichoke ['ɑːtɪtʃəuk] n artichaut m; **Jerusalem ~** topinambour m.
article ['ɑːtɪkl] n article m; (BRIT LAW: training): **~s** npl ≈ stage m; **~s of clothing** vêtements mpl.
articles of association npl (COMM) statuts mpl d'une société.
articulate adj [ɑː'tɪkjulɪt] (person) qui s'exprime clairement et aisément; (speech) bien articulé(e), prononcé(e) clairement ♦ vi [ɑː'tɪkjuleɪt] articuler, parler distinctement.
articulated lorry [ɑː'tɪkjuleɪtɪd-] n (BRIT) (camion m) semi-remorque m.
artifact ['ɑːtɪfækt] n (US) objet fabriqué.
artifice ['ɑːtɪfɪs] n ruse f.
artificial [ɑːtɪ'fɪʃəl] adj artificiel(le).
artificial insemination [-ɪnsemɪ'neɪʃən] n insémination artificielle.
artificial intelligence (A.I.) n intelligence artificielle (IA).
artificial respiration n respiration artificielle.
artillery [ɑː'tɪlərɪ] n artillerie f.
artisan ['ɑːtɪzæn] n artisan/e.
artist ['ɑːtɪst] n artiste m/f.
artistic [ɑː'tɪstɪk] adj artistique.
artistry ['ɑːtɪstrɪ] n art m, talent m.
artless ['ɑːtlɪs] adj naïf(naïve), simple, ingénu(e).
arts [ɑːts] npl (SCOL) lettres fpl.
art school n ≈ école f des beaux-arts.
artwork ['ɑːtwɜːk] n maquette f (prête pour la photogravure).
ARV n abbr (= American Revised Version) traduction américaine de la Bible.
AS n abbr (US SCOL: = Associate in/of Science) diplôme universitaire ♦ abbr (US) = American Samoa.

=========================== KEYWORD

as [æz] conj **1** (time: moment) comme, alors que; à mesure que; (: duration) tandis que; **he came in ~ I was leaving** il est arrivé comme je partais; **~ the years went by** à mesure que les années passaient; **~ from tomorrow** à partir de demain
2 (in comparisons): **~ big ~** aussi grand que; **twice ~ big ~** deux fois plus grand que; **big ~ it is** si grand que ce soit; **much ~ I like them, I ...** je les aime bien, mais je ...; **~ much or many ~** autant que; **~ much money/many books** autant d'argent/de livres que; **~ soon ~** dès que
3 (since, because) comme, puisque; **~ he had to be home by 10 ...** comme il or puisqu'il devait être de retour avant 10 h ...
4 (referring to manner, way) comme; **do ~ you wish** faites comme vous voudrez
5 (concerning): **~ for or to that** quant à cela, pour ce qui est de cela

6: ~ **if** or **though** comme si; **he looked** ~ **if he was ill** il avait l'air d'être malade; see also **long; such; well**
♦ prep (in the capacity of) en tant que, en qualité de; **he works** ~ **a driver** il travaille comme chauffeur; ~ **chairman of the company, he** ... en tant que président de la société, il ...; **dressed up** ~ **a cowboy** déguisé en cowboy; **he gave me it** ~ **a present** il me l'a offert, il m'en a fait cadeau.

ASA n abbr (= American Standards Association) association de normalisation.

a.s.a.p. abbr = **as soon as possible.**

asbestos [æz'bestəs] n asbeste m, amiante m.

ascend [ə'send] vt gravir.

ascendancy [ə'sendənsɪ] n ascendant m.

ascendant [ə'sendənt] n: **to be in the** ~ monter.

ascension [ə'senʃən] n: **the A~** (REL) l'Ascension f.

Ascension Island n île f de l'Ascension.

ascent [ə'sent] n ascension f.

ascertain [æsə'teɪn] vt s'assurer de, vérifier; établir.

ascetic [ə'setɪk] adj ascétique.

asceticism [ə'setɪsɪzəm] n ascétisme m.

ASCII ['æskiː] n abbr (= American Standard Code for Information Interchange) ASCII.

ascribe [ə'skraɪb] vt: **to** ~ **sth to** attribuer qch à; (blame) imputer qch à.

ASCU n abbr (US) = Association of State Colleges and Universities.

ASE n abbr = American Stock Exchange.

ASH [æʃ] n abbr (BRIT: = Action on Smoking and Health) ligue anti-tabac.

ash [æʃ] n (dust) cendre f; (also: ~ **tree**) frêne m.

ashamed [ə'ʃeɪmd] adj honteux(euse), confus(e); **to be** ~ **of** avoir honte de; **to be** ~ **(of o.s.) for having done** avoir honte d'avoir fait.

ashen ['æʃən] adj (pale) cendreux(euse), blême.

ashore [ə'ʃɔː*] adv à terre; **to go** ~ aller à terre, débarquer.

ashtray ['æʃtreɪ] n cendrier m.

Ash Wednesday n mercredi m des Cendres.

Asia ['eɪʃə] n Asie f.

Asia Minor n Asie Mineure.

Asian ['eɪʃən] n Asiatique m/f ♦ adj asiatique.

Asiatic [eɪsɪ'ætɪk] adj asiatique.

aside [ə'saɪd] adv de côté; à l'écart ♦ n aparté m; ~ **from** prep à part, excepté.

ask [ɑːsk] vt demander; (invite) inviter; **to** ~ **sb sth/to do sth** demander à qn qch/de faire qch; **to** ~ **sb the time** demander l'heure à qn; **to** ~ **sb about sth** questionner qn au sujet de qch; se renseigner auprès de qn au sujet de qch; **to** ~ **about the price** s'informer du prix, se renseigner au sujet du prix; **to** ~ **(sb) a question** poser une question (à qn); **to** ~ **sb out to dinner** inviter qn au restaurant.

▶**ask after** vt fus demander des nouvelles de.

▶**ask for** vt fus demander; **it's just** ~**ing for trouble** or **for it** ce serait chercher des ennuis.

askance [ə'skɑːns] adv: **to look** ~ **at sb** regarder qn de travers or d'un œil désapprobateur.

askew [ə'skjuː] adv de travers, de guinguois.

asking price ['ɑːskɪŋ-] n prix demandé.

asleep [ə'sliːp] adj endormi(e); **to be** ~ dormir, être endormi; **to fall** ~ s'endormir.

ASLEF ['æzlef] n abbr (BRIT: = Associated Society of Locomotive Engineers and Firemen) syndicat de cheminots.

asp [æsp] n aspic m.

asparagus [əs'pærəgəs] n asperges fpl.

asparagus tips npl pointes fpl d'asperges.

ASPCA n abbr (= American Society for the Prevention of Cruelty to Animals) ≈ SPA f.

aspect ['æspekt] n aspect m; (direction in which a building etc faces) orientation f, exposition f.

aspersions [əs'pɜːʃənz] npl: **to cast** ~ **on** dénigrer.

asphalt ['æsfælt] n asphalte m.

asphyxiate [æs'fɪksɪeɪt] vt asphyxier.

asphyxiation [æsfɪksɪ'eɪʃən] n asphyxie f.

aspirate vt ['æspəreɪt] aspirer ♦ adj ['æspərɪt] aspiré(e).

aspiration [æspə'reɪʃən] n aspiration f.

aspire [əs'paɪə*] vi: **to** ~ **to** aspirer à.

aspirin ['æsprɪn] n aspirine f.

aspiring [əs'paɪərɪŋ] adj (artist, writer) en herbe; (manager) potentiel(le).

ass [æs] n âne m; (col) imbécile m/f; (US col!) cul m (!).

assail [ə'seɪl] vt assaillir.

assailant [ə'seɪlənt] n agresseur m; assaillant m.

assassin [ə'sæsɪn] n assassin m.

assassinate [ə'sæsɪneɪt] vt assassiner.

assassination [əsæsɪ'neɪʃən] n assassinat m.

assault [ə'sɔːlt] n (MIL) assaut m; (gen: attack) agression f; (LAW): ~ **(and battery)** voies fpl de fait, coups mpl et blessures fpl ♦ vt attaquer; (sexually) violenter.

assemble [ə'sembl] vt assembler ♦ vi s'assembler, se rassembler.

assembly [ə'semblɪ] n (meeting) rassemblement m; (construction) assemblage m.

assembly language n (COMPUT) langage m d'assemblage.

assembly line n chaîne f de montage.

assent [ə'sent] n assentiment m, consentement m ♦ vi: **to** ~ **(to sth)** donner son assentiment (à qch), consentir (à qch).

assert [ə'sɜːt] vt affirmer, déclarer; établir; **to** ~ **o.s.** s'imposer.

assertion [ə'sɜːʃən] n assertion f, affirmation f.

assertive [ə'sə:tɪv] *adj* assuré(e); péremptoire.

assess [ə'sɛs] *vt* évaluer, estimer; (*tax, damages*) établir *or* fixer le montant de; (*property etc: for tax*) calculer la valeur imposable de.

assessment [ə'sɛsmənt] *n* évaluation *f*, estimation *f*; (*judgment*): ~ (**of**) jugement *m or* opinion *f* (sur).

assessor [ə'sɛsə*] *n* expert *m* (*en matière d'impôt et d'assurance*).

asset ['æsɛt] *n* avantage *m*, atout *m*; (*person*) atout; **~s** *npl* (*COMM*) capital *m*; avoir(s) *m(pl)*; actif *m*.

asset-stripping ['æsɛt'strɪpɪŋ] *n* (*COMM*) récupération *f* (et démantèlement *m*) d'une entreprise en difficulté.

assiduous [ə'sɪdjuəs] *adj* assidu(e).

assign [ə'saɪn] *vt* (*date*) fixer, arrêter; (*task*): **to ~ sth to** assigner qch à; (*resources*): **to ~ sth to** affecter qch à; (*cause, meaning*): **to ~ sth to** attribuer qch à.

assignment [ə'saɪnmənt] *n* tâche *f*, mission *f*.

assimilate [ə'sɪmɪleɪt] *vt* assimiler.

assimilation [əsɪmɪ'leɪʃən] *n* assimilation *f*.

assist [ə'sɪst] *vt* aider, assister; (*injured person etc*) secourir.

assistance [ə'sɪstəns] *n* aide *f*, assistance *f*; secours *mpl*.

assistant [ə'sɪstənt] *n* assistant/e, adjoint/e; (*BRIT: also:* **shop ~**) vendeur/euse.

assistant manager *n* sous-directeur *m*.

assizes [ə'saɪzɪz] *npl* assises *fpl*.

associate *adj, n* [ə'səuʃiɪt] associé(e) ♦ *vb* [ə'səuʃieɪt] *vt* associer ♦ *vi*: **to ~ with sb** fréquenter qn; **~ director** directeur adjoint; **~d company** société affiliée.

association [əsəusɪ'eɪʃən] *n* association *f*; **in ~ with** en collaboration avec.

association football *n* (*BRIT*) football *m*.

assorted [ə'sɔːtɪd] *adj* assorti(e); **in ~ sizes** en plusieurs tailles.

assortment [ə'sɔːtmənt] *n* assortiment *m*.

Asst. *abbr* = **assistant**.

assuage [ə'sweɪdʒ] *vt* (*grief, pain*) soulager; (*thirst, appetite*) assouvir.

assume [ə'sjuːm] *vt* supposer; (*responsibilities etc*) assumer; (*attitude, name*) prendre, adopter.

assumed name [ə'sjuːmd-] *n* nom *m* d'emprunt.

assumption [ə'sʌmpʃən] *n* supposition *f*, hypothèse *f*; **on the ~ that** dans l'hypothèse où; (*on condition that*) à condition que.

assurance [ə'ʃuərəns] *n* assurance *f*; **I can give you no ~s** je ne peux rien vous garantir.

assure [ə'ʃuə*] *vt* assurer.

assured [ə'ʃuəd] *adj* assuré(e).

AST *abbr* (*US: = Atlantic Standard Time*) heure d'hiver de New York.

asterisk ['æstərɪsk] *n* astérisque *m*.

astern [ə'stə:n] *adv* à l'arrière.

asteroid ['æstərɔɪd] *n* astéroïde *m*.

asthma ['æsmə] *n* asthme *m*.

asthmatic [æs'mætɪk] *adj, n* asthmatique *(m/f)*.

astigmatism [ə'stɪgmətɪzəm] *n* astigmatisme *m*.

astir [ə'stə:*] *adv* en émoi.

astonish [ə'stɔnɪʃ] *vt* étonner, stupéfier.

astonishing [ə'stɔnɪʃɪŋ] *adj* étonnant(e), stupéfiant(e); **I find it ~ that** ... je trouve incroyable que ....

astonishingly [ə'stɔnɪʃɪŋlɪ] *adv* incroyablement.

astonishment [ə'stɔnɪʃmənt] *n* (grand) étonnement, stupéfaction *f*.

astound [ə'staund] *vt* stupéfier, sidérer.

astray [ə'streɪ] *adv*: **to go ~** s'égarer; (*fig*) quitter le droit chemin; **to go ~ in one's calculations** faire fausse route dans ses calculs.

astride [ə'straɪd] *adv* à cheval ♦ *prep* à cheval sur.

astringent [əs'trɪndʒənt] *adj* astringent(e) ♦ *n* astringent *m*.

astrologer [əs'trɔlədʒə*] *n* astrologue *m*.

astrology [əs'trɔlədʒɪ] *n* astrologie *f*.

astronaut ['æstrənɔːt] *n* astronaute *m/f*.

astronomer [əs'trɔnəmə*] *n* astronome *m*.

astronomical [æstrə'nɔmɪkl] *adj* astronomique.

astronomy [əs'trɔnəmɪ] *n* astronomie *f*.

astrophysics ['æstrəu'fɪzɪks] *n* astrophysique *f*.

astute [əs'tjuːt] *adj* astucieux(euse), malin(igne).

asunder [ə'sʌndə*] *adv*: **to tear ~** déchirer.

ASV *n abbr* (= *American Standard Version*) traduction de la Bible.

asylum [ə'saɪləm] *n* asile *m*; **to seek political ~** demander l'asile politique.

asymmetric(al) [eɪsɪ'mɛtrɪk(l)] *adj* asymétrique.

═══════════════════════════ *KEYWORD*

at [æt] *prep* **1** (*referring to position, direction*) à; ~ **the top** au sommet; ~ **home/school** à la maison *or* chez soi/à l'école; ~ **the baker's** à la boulangerie, chez le boulanger; **to look ~ sth** regarder qch

2 (*referring to time*): ~ **4 o'clock** à 4 heures; ~ **Christmas** à Noël; ~ **night** la nuit; ~ **times** par moments, parfois

3 (*referring to rates, speed etc*) à; ~ **£1 a kilo** une livre le kilo; **two ~ a time** deux à la fois; ~ **50 km/h** à 50 km/h; ~ **full speed** à toute vitesse

4 (*referring to manner*): ~ **a stroke** d'un seul coup; ~ **peace** en paix

5 (*referring to activity*): **to be ~ work** être au travail, travailler; **to play ~ cowboys** jouer aux cowboys; **to be good ~ sth** être bon en qch

6 (*referring to cause*): **shocked/surprised/annoyed ~ sth** choqué par/étonné de/agacé par qch; **I went ~ his suggestion** j'y suis allé sur son conseil.

ate [eɪt] *pt of* **eat**.

atheism ['eɪθɪɪzəm] *n* athéisme *m*.

atheist ['eɪθɪɪst] *n* athée *m/f*.

Athenian [ə'θiːnɪən] *adj* athénien(ne) ♦ *n* Athénien/ne.

Athens ['æθɪnz] *n* Athènes *f*.

athlete ['æθliːt] *n* athlète *m/f*.

athletic [æθ'lɛtɪk] *adj* athlétique.

athletics [æθ'lɛtɪks] *n* athlétisme *m*.

Atlantic [ət'læntɪk] *adj* atlantique ♦ *n*: **the ~ (Ocean)** l'Atlantique *m*, l'océan *m* Atlantique.

atlas ['ætləs] *n* atlas *m*.

Atlas Mountains *npl*: **the ~** les monts *mpl* de l'Atlas, l'Atlas *m*.

ATM *abbr* (= *Automated Telling Machine*) guichet *m* automatique.

atmosphere ['ætməsfɪə*] *n* atmosphère *f*; (*air*) air *m*.

atmospheric [ætməs'fɛrɪk] *adj* atmosphérique.

atmospherics [ætməs'fɛrɪks] *n* (*RADIO*) parasites *mpl*.

atoll ['ætɒl] *n* atoll *m*.

atom ['ætəm] *n* atome *m*.

atomic [ə'tɒmɪk] *adj* atomique.

atom(ic) bomb *n* bombe *f* atomique.

atomizer ['ætəmaɪzə*] *n* atomiseur *m*.

atone [ə'təun] *vi*: **to ~ for** expier, racheter.

atonement [ə'təunmənt] *n* expiation *f*.

A to Z *n* ® guide *m* A à Z; (*map*) plan *m* des rues.

ATP *n abbr* (= *Association of Tennis Professionals*) ATP *f* (= *Association des tennismen professionnels*).

atrocious [ə'trəuʃəs] *adj* (*very bad*) atroce, exécrable.

atrocity [ə'trɒsɪtɪ] *n* atrocité *f*.

atrophy ['ætrəfɪ] *n* atrophie *f* ♦ *vt* atrophier ♦ *vi* s'atrophier.

attach [ə'tætʃ] *vt* (*gen*) attacher; (*document, letter*) joindre; (*employee, troops*) affecter; **to be ~ed to sb/sth** (*to like*) être attaché à qn/qch; **the ~ed letter** la lettre ci-jointe.

attaché [ə'tæʃeɪ] *n* attaché *m*.

attaché case *n* mallette *f*, attaché-case *m*.

attachment [ə'tætʃmənt] *n* (*tool*) accessoire *m*; (*love*): **~ (to)** affection *f* (pour), attachement *m* (à).

attack [ə'tæk] *vt* attaquer; (*task etc*) s'attaquer à ♦ *n* attaque *f*; (*also*: **heart ~**) crise *f* cardiaque.

attacker [ə'tækə*] *n* attaquant *m*; agresseur *m*.

attain [ə'teɪn] *vt* (*also*: **to ~ to**) parvenir à, atteindre; acquérir.

attainments [ə'teɪnmənts] *npl* connaissances *fpl*, résultats *mpl*.

attempt [ə'tɛmpt] *n* tentative *f* ♦ *vt* essayer, tenter; **~ed theft** *etc* (*LAW*) tentative de vol

etc; **to make an ~ on sb's life** attenter à la vie de qn; **he made no ~ to help** il n'a rien fait pour m'aider (*or* l'aider *etc*).

attend [ə'tɛnd] *vt* (*course*) suivre; (*meeting, talk*) assister à; (*school, church*) aller à, fréquenter; (*patient*) soigner, s'occuper de; **to ~ (up)on** servir; être au service de.

►**attend to** *vt fus* (*needs, affairs etc*) s'occuper de; (*customer*) s'occuper de, servir.

attendance [ə'tɛndəns] *n* (*being present*) présence *f*; (*people present*) assistance *f*.

attendant [ə'tɛndənt] *n* employé/e; gardien/ne ♦ *adj* concomitant(e), qui accompagne *or* s'ensuit.

attention [ə'tɛnʃən] *n* attention *f*; **~s** attentions *fpl*, prévenances *fpl*; **~!** (*MIL*) garde-à-vous!; **at ~** (*MIL*) au garde-à-vous; **for the ~ of** (*ADMIN*) à l'attention de; **it has come to my ~ that ...** je constate que ....

attentive [ə'tɛntɪv] *adj* attentif(ive); (*kind*) prévenant(e).

attentively [ə'tɛntɪvlɪ] *adv* attentivement, avec attention.

attenuate [ə'tɛnjueɪt] *vt* atténuer ♦ *vi* s'atténuer.

attest [ə'tɛst] *vi*: **to ~ to** témoigner de, attester (de).

attic ['ætɪk] *n* grenier *m*, combles *mpl*.

attire [ə'taɪə*] *n* habit *m*, atours *mpl*.

attitude ['ætɪtjuːd] *n* (*behaviour*) attitude *f*, manière *f*; (*posture*) pose *f*, attitude; (*view*): **~ (to)** attitude (envers).

attorney [ə'tɜːnɪ] *n* (*US: lawyer*) avocat *m*; (*having proxy*) mandataire *m*; **power of ~** procuration *f*.

Attorney General *n* (*BRIT*) ≈ procureur général; (*US*) ≈ garde *m* des Sceaux, ministre *m* de la Justice.

attract [ə'trækt] *vt* attirer.

attraction [ə'trækʃən] *n* (*gen pl: pleasant things*) attraction *f*, attrait *m*; (*PHYSICS*) attraction; (*fig: towards sth*) attirance *f*.

attractive [ə'træktɪv] *adj* séduisant(e), attrayant(e).

attribute *n* ['ætrɪbjuːt] attribut *m* ♦ *vt* [ə'trɪbjuːt]: **to ~ sth to** attribuer qch à.

attrition [ə'trɪʃən] *n*: **war of ~** guerre *f* d'usure.

Atty. Gen. *abbr* = **Attorney General**.

ATV *n abbr* (= *all terrain vehicle*) véhicule *m* tout-terrain.

atypical [eɪ'tɪpɪkl] *adj* atypique.

aubergine ['əubəʒiːn] *n* aubergine *f*.

auburn ['ɔːbən] *adj* auburn *inv*, châtain roux *inv*.

auction ['ɔːkʃən] *n* (*also*: **sale by ~**) vente *f* aux enchères ♦ *vt* (*also*: **to sell by ~**) vendre aux enchères; (*also*: **to put up for ~**) mettre aux enchères.

auctioneer [ɔːkʃə'nɪə*] *n* commissaire-priseur *m*.

auction room *n* salle *f* des ventes.

audacious [ɔːˈdeɪʃəs] *adj* impudent(e); auda-
cieux(euse), intrépide.
audacity [ɔːˈdæsɪtɪ] *n* impudence *f*; audace *f*.
audible [ˈɔːdɪbl] *adj* audible.
audience [ˈɔːdɪəns] *n* (*people*) assistance *f*, auditoire *m*; auditeurs *mpl*; spectateurs *mpl*; (*interview*) audience *f*.
audiotypist [ˈɔːdɪəʊtaɪpɪst] *n* audiotypiste *m/f*.
audiovisual [ɔːdɪəʊˈvɪzjuəl] *adj* audio-
visuel(le); ~ **aids** supports *or* moyens audio-
visuels.
audit [ˈɔːdɪt] *n* vérification *f* des comptes,
apurement *m* ♦ *vt* vérifier, apurer.
audition [ɔːˈdɪʃən] *n* audition *f* ♦ *vi* auditionner.
auditor [ˈɔːdɪtə*] *n* vérificateur *m* des
comptes.
auditorium [ɔːdɪˈtɔːrɪəm] *n* auditorium *m*, salle *f* de concert *or* de spectacle.
Aug. *abbr* = **August.**
augment [ɔːgˈmɛnt] *vt*, *vi* augmenter.
augur [ˈɔːɡə*] *vt* (*be a sign of*) présager, annoncer ♦ *vi*: **it ~s well** c'est bon signe *or* de
bon augure, cela s'annonce bien.
August [ˈɔːɡəst] *n* août *m*; *for phrases see also*
July.
august [ɔːˈɡʌst] *adj* majestueux(euse), impo-
sant(e).
aunt [ɑːnt] *n* tante *f*.
auntie, aunty [ˈɑːntɪ] *n diminutive of* **aunt.**
au pair [ˈəʊˈpɛə*] *n* (*also*: ~ **girl**) jeune fille *f* au
pair.
aura [ˈɔːrə] *n* atmosphère *f*.
auspices [ˈɔːspɪsɪz] *npl*: **under the ~ of** sous
les auspices de.
auspicious [ɔːsˈpɪʃəs] *adj* de bon augure, propice.
austere [ɔsˈtɪə*] *adj* austère.
austerity [ɔsˈtɛrɪtɪ] *n* austérité *f*.
Australasia [ɔːstrəˈleɪzɪə] *n* Australasie *f*.
Australia [ɔsˈtreɪlɪə] *n* Australie *f*.
Australian [ɔsˈtreɪlɪən] *adj* australien(ne) ♦ *n*
Australien/ne.
Austria [ˈɔstrɪə] *n* Autriche *f*.
Austrian [ˈɔstrɪən] *adj* autrichien(ne) ♦ *n*
Autrichien/ne.
AUT *n abbr* (*BRIT*: = *Association of University
Teachers*) *syndicat universitaire.*
authentic [ɔːˈθɛntɪk] *adj* authentique.
authenticate [ɔːˈθɛntɪkeɪt] *vt* établir
l'authenticité de.
authenticity [ɔːθɛnˈtɪsɪtɪ] *n* authenticité *f*.
author [ˈɔːθə*] *n* auteur *m*.
authoritarian [ɔːθɔrɪˈtɛərɪən] *adj* autoritaire.
authoritative [ɔːˈθɔrɪtətɪv] *adj* (*account*) digne
de foi; (*study, treatise*) qui fait autorité;
(*manner*) autoritaire.
authority [ɔːˈθɔrɪtɪ] *n* autorité *f*; (*permission*)
autorisation (formelle); **the authorities** les
autorités, l'administration *f*; **to have ~ to do
sth** être habilité à faire qch.
authorization [ɔːθəraɪˈzeɪʃən] *n* autorisation *f*.

authorize [ˈɔːθəraɪz] *vt* autoriser.
authorized capital [ˈɔːθəraɪzd-] *n* (*COMM*) capital social.
authorship [ˈɔːθəʃɪp] *n* paternité *f* (*littéraire
etc*).
autistic [ɔːˈtɪstɪk] *adj* autistique.
auto [ˈɔːtəʊ] *n* (*US*) auto *f*, voiture *f*.
autobiography [ɔːtəbaɪˈɔɡrəfɪ] *n* autobiographie *f*.
autocratic [ɔːtəˈkrætɪk] *adj* autocratique.
Autocue [ˈɔːtəʊkjuː] *n* ® (télé)prompteur *m*.
autograph [ˈɔːtəɡrɑːf] *n* autographe *m* ♦ *vt*
signer, dédicacer.
autoimmune [ɔːtəʊɪˈmjuːn] *adj* auto-immune.
automat [ˈɔːtəmæt] *n* (*vending machine*) distributeur *m* (automatique); (*US: place*) caféte-
ria *f* avec distributeurs automatiques.
automated [ˈɔːtəmeɪtɪd] *adj* automatisé(e).
automatic [ɔːtəˈmætɪk] *adj* automatique ♦ *n*
(*gun*) automatique *m*; (*washing machine*)
lave-linge *m* automatique; (*BRIT AUT*) voiture
f à transmission automatique.
automatically [ɔːtəˈmætɪklɪ] *adv* automatiquement.
automatic data processing (ADP) *n* traitement *m* automatique des données.
automation [ɔːtəˈmeɪʃən] *n* automatisation *f*.
automaton, *pl* **automata** [ɔːˈtɔmətən, -tə] *n*
automate *m*.
automobile [ˈɔːtəməbiːl] *n* (*US*) automobile *f*.
autonomous [ɔːˈtɔnəməs] *adj* autonome.
autonomy [ɔːˈtɔnəmɪ] *n* autonomie *f*.
autopsy [ˈɔːtɔpsɪ] *n* autopsie *f*.
autumn [ˈɔːtəm] *n* automne *m*.
auxiliary [ɔːɡˈzɪlɪərɪ] *adj*, *n* auxiliaire (*m/f*).
AV *n abbr* (= *Authorized Version*) *traduction anglaise de la Bible* ♦ *abbr* = **audiovisual.**
Av. *abbr* (= *avenue*) Av.
avail [əˈveɪl] *vt*: **to ~ o.s. of** user de; profiter
de ♦ *n*: **to no ~** sans résultat, en vain, en
pure perte.
availability [əveɪləˈbɪlɪtɪ] *n* disponibilité *f*.
available [əˈveɪləbl] *adj* disponible; **every ~
means** tous les moyens possibles *or* à sa (*or*
notre *etc*) disposition; **is the manager ~?**
est-ce que le directeur peut (me) recevoir?;
(*on phone*) pourrais-je parler au directeur?;
to make sth ~ to sb mettre qch à la disposition de qn.
avalanche [ˈævəlɑːnʃ] *n* avalanche *f*.
avant-garde [ˈævɑ̃ˈɡɑːd] *adj* d'avant-garde.
avaricious [ævəˈrɪʃəs] *adj* âpre au gain.
avdp. *abbr* = *avoirdupois*.
Ave. *abbr* (= *avenue*) Av.
avenge [əˈvɛndʒ] *vt* venger.
avenue [ˈævənjuː] *n* avenue *f*.
average [ˈævərɪdʒ] *n* moyenne *f* ♦ *adj*
moyen(ne) ♦ *vt* (*a certain figure*) atteindre *or*
faire *etc* en moyenne; **on ~** en moyenne;
above/below (the) ~ au-dessus/en-dessous
de la moyenne.
►**average out** *vi*: **to ~ out at** représenter en

moyenne, donner une moyenne de.

averse [ə'vəːs] *adj*: **to be ~ to sth/doing** éprouver une forte répugnance envers qch/à faire; **I wouldn't be ~ to a drink** un petit verre ne serait pas de refus, je ne dirais pas non à un petit verre.

aversion [ə'vəːʃən] *n* aversion *f*, répugnance *f*.

avert [ə'vəːt] *vt* prévenir, écarter; (*one's eyes*) détourner.

aviary ['eɪvɪərɪ] *n* volière *f*.

aviation [eɪvɪ'eɪʃən] *n* aviation *f*.

avid ['ævɪd] *adj* avide.

avidly ['ævɪdlɪ] *adv* avidement, avec avidité.

avocado [ævə'kɑːdəʊ] *n* (*also*: *BRIT*: ~ **pear**) avocat *m*.

avoid [ə'vɔɪd] *vt* éviter.

avoidable [ə'vɔɪdəbl] *adj* évitable.

avoidance [ə'vɔɪdəns] *n le fait d'éviter.*

avowed [ə'vaud] *adj* déclaré(e).

AVP *n abbr* (*US*) = *assistant vice-president.*

AWACS ['eɪwæks] *n abbr* (= *airborne warning and control system*) AWACS (*système aéroporté d'alerte et de contrôle*).

await [ə'weɪt] *vt* attendre; **~ing attention/delivery** (*COMM*) en souffrance; **long ~ed** tant attendu(e).

awake [ə'weɪk] *adj* éveillé(e); (*fig*) en éveil ♦ *vb* (*pt* **awoke** [ə'wəuk], *pp* **awoken** [ə'wəukən], **awaked**) *vt* éveiller ♦ *vi* s'éveiller; **~ to** conscient de; **he was still ~** il ne dormait pas encore.

awakening [ə'weɪknɪŋ] *n* réveil *m*.

award [ə'wɔːd] *n* récompense *f*, prix *m* ♦ *vt* (*prize*) décerner; (*LAW*: *damages*) accorder.

aware [ə'wɛə*] *adj*: **~ of** (*conscious*) conscient(e) de; (*informed*) au courant de; **to become ~ of** avoir conscience de, prendre conscience de; se rendre compte de; **politically/socially ~** sensibilisé(e) aux *or* ayant pris conscience des problèmes politiques/sociaux; **I am fully ~ that** je me rends parfaitement compte que.

awareness [ə'wɛənɪs] *n* conscience *f*, connaissance *f*; **to develop people's ~ (of)** sensibiliser le public (à).

awash [ə'wɔʃ] *adj* recouvert(e) (d'eau); **~ with** inondé(e) de.

away [ə'weɪ] *adj*, *adv* (au) loin; absent(e); **two kilometres ~** à (une distance de) deux kilomètres, à deux kilomètres de distance; **two hours ~ by car** à deux heures de voiture *or* de route; **the holiday was two weeks ~** il restait deux semaines jusqu'aux vacances; **~ from** loin de; **he's ~ for a week** il est parti (pour) une semaine; **he's ~ in Milan** il est (parti) à Milan; **to take ~** *vt* emporter; **to pedal/work/laugh** *etc* ~ *la particule indique la constance et l'énergie de l'action*: il pédalait *etc* tant qu'il pouvait; **to fade/wither** *etc* ~ *la particule renforce l'idée de la disparition,* *l'éloignement.*

away game *n* (*SPORT*) match *m* à l'extérieur.

awe [ɔː] *n* respect mêlé de crainte, effroi mêlé d'admiration.

awe-inspiring ['ɔːɪnspaɪərɪŋ], **awesome** ['ɔːsəm] *adj* impressionnant(e).

awestruck ['ɔːstrʌk] *adj* frappé(e) d'effroi.

awful ['ɔːfəl] *adj* affreux(euse); **an ~ lot of** énormément de.

awfully ['ɔːfəlɪ] *adv* (*very*) terriblement, vraiment.

awhile [ə'waɪl] *adv* un moment, quelque temps.

awkward ['ɔːkwəd] *adj* (*clumsy*) gauche, maladroit(e); (*inconvenient*) malaisé(e), d'emploi malaisé, peu pratique; (*embarrassing*) gênant(e).

awkwardness ['ɔːkwədnɪs] *n* (*embarrassment*) gêne *f*.

awl [ɔːl] *n* alêne *f*.

awning ['ɔːnɪŋ] *n* (*of tent*) auvent *m*; (*of shop*) store *m*; (*of hotel etc*) marquise *f* (de toile).

awoke [ə'wəuk] *pt of* **awake**.

awoken [ə'wəukən] *pp of* **awake**.

AWOL ['eɪwɔl] *abbr* (*MIL*) = **absent without leave**.

awry [ə'raɪ] *adv*, *adj* de travers; **to go ~** mal tourner.

axe, (*US*) **ax** [æks] *n* hache *f* ♦ *vt* (*employee*) renvoyer; (*project etc*) abandonner; (*jobs*) supprimer; **to have an ~ to grind** (*fig*) prêcher pour son saint.

axes ['æksiːz] *npl of* **axis**.

axiom ['æksɪəm] *n* axiome *m*.

axiomatic [æksɪəu'mætɪk] *adj* axiomatique.

axis, *pl* **axes** ['æksɪs, -siːz] *n* axe *m*.

axle ['æksl] *n* (*also*: **~-tree**) essieu *m*.

ay(e) [aɪ] *excl* (*yes*) oui ♦ *n*: **the ~s** les oui.

AYH *n abbr* = *American Youth Hostels.*

AZ *abbr* (*US*) = *Arizona.*

azalea [ə'zeɪlɪə] *n* azalée *f*.

Azerbaijan [æzəbaɪ'dʒɑːn] *n* Azerbaïdjan *m*.

Azerbaijani, Azeri [æzəbaɪ'dʒɑːnɪ, ə'zɛərɪ] *adj* azerbaïdjanais(e) ♦ *n* Azerbaïdjanais/e.

Azores [ə'zɔːz] *npl*: **the ~** les Açores *fpl*.

AZT *n abbr* (= *azidothymidine*) AZT *f*.

Aztec ['æztɛk] *adj* aztèque ♦ *n* Aztèque *m/f*.

azure ['eɪʒə*] *adj* azuré(e).

B b

B, b [biː] n (letter) B, b m; (SCOL: mark) B; (MUS): **B** si m; **B for Benjamin**, (US) **B for Baker** B comme Berthe; **B road** n (BRIT AUT) route départementale.

b. abbr = **born**.

BA n abbr = British Academy; (SCOL) = **Bachelor of Arts**.

babble ['bæbl] vi babiller ♦ n babillage m.

baboon [bə'buːn] n babouin m.

baby ['beɪbɪ] n bébé m.

baby carriage n (US) voiture f d'enfant.

baby grand n (also: ~ **piano**) (piano m) demi-queue m.

babyhood ['beɪbɪhud] n petite enfance.

babyish ['beɪbɪɪʃ] adj enfantin(e), de bébé.

baby-minder ['beɪbɪmaɪndə*] n (BRIT) gardienne f (d'enfants).

baby-sit ['beɪbɪsɪt] vi garder les enfants.

baby-sitter ['beɪbɪsɪtə*] n baby-sitter m/f.

bachelor ['bætʃələ*] n célibataire m; **B~ of Arts/Science (BA/BSc)** ≈ licencié/e ès or en lettres/sciences; **B~ of Arts/Science degree (BA/BSc)** n ≈ licence f ès or en lettres/sciences.

Un **Bachelor's degree** est un diplôme accordé après trois ou quatre années d'université. Les Bachelor's degrees les plus courants sont le **BA** (Bachelor of Arts), le **BSc** (Bachelor of Science), le **BEd** (Bachelor of Education) et le **LLB** (Bachelor of Laws).

---

bachelorhood ['bætʃələhud] n célibat m.

bachelor party n (US) enterrement m de vie de garçon.

back [bæk] n (of person, horse) dos m; (of hand) dos, revers m; (of house) derrière m; (of car, train) arrière m; (of chair) dossier m; (of page) verso m; (SPORT) arrière m; **to have one's ~ to the wall** (fig) être au pied du mur; **to break the ~ of a job** (BRIT) faire le gros d'un travail; **~ to front** à l'envers ♦ vt (financially) soutenir (financièrement); (candidate: also: ~ **up**) soutenir, appuyer; (horse: at races) parier or miser sur; (car) (faire) reculer ♦ vi reculer; (car etc) faire marche arrière ♦ adj (in compounds) de derrière, à l'arrière; ~ **seats/wheels** (AUT) sièges mpl/roues fpl arrière; ~ **payments/rent** arriéré m de paiements/loyer; ~ **garden/room** jardin/pièce sur l'arrière; **to take a ~ seat** (fig) se contenter d'un second rôle, être relégué(e) au second plan ♦ adv (not forward) en arrière;

(returned): **he's** ~ il est rentré, il est de retour; **when will you be** ~? quand seras-tu de retour?; **he ran** ~ il est revenu en courant; (restitution): **throw the ball** ~ renvoie la balle; **can I have it** ~? puis-je le ravoir?, peux-tu me le rendre?; (again): **he called** ~ il a rappelé.

backbench ['bæk'bentʃ] n (BRIT) banc des députés sans portefeuille.

▶**back down** vi rabattre de ses prétentions.

▶**back on to** vt fus: **the house** ~s **on to the golf course** la maison donne derrière sur le terrain de golf.

▶**back out** vi (of promise) se dédire.

▶**back up** vt (COMPUT) faire une copie de sauvegarde de.

backache ['bækeɪk] n maux mpl de reins.

Le terme **back benches** désigne les bancs les plus éloignés de l'allée centrale de la Chambre des communes. Les députés qui occupent ces bancs sont les "backbenchers" et ils n'ont pas de portefeuille ministériel.

---

backbiting ['bækbaɪtɪŋ] n médisance(s) f(pl).

backbone ['bækbəʊn] n colonne vertébrale, épine dorsale; **he's the ~ of the organization** c'est sur lui que repose l'organisation.

backchat ['bæktʃæt] n (BRIT col) impertinences fpl.

back-cloth ['bækklɔθ] n (BRIT) toile f de fond.

backcomb ['bækkəʊm] vt (BRIT) crêper.

backdate [bæk'deɪt] vt (letter) antidater; ~**d pay rise** augmentation f avec effet rétroactif.

backdrop ['bækdrɔp] n = **backcloth**.

backer ['bækə*] n partisan m; (COMM) commanditaire m.

backfire [bæk'faɪə*] vi (AUT) pétarader; (plans) mal tourner.

backgammon ['bækgæmən] n trictrac m.

background ['bækgraʊnd] n arrière-plan m; (of events) situation f, conjoncture f; (basic knowledge) éléments mpl de base; (experience) formation f ♦ cpd (noise, music) de fond; ~ **reading** lecture(s) générale(s) (sur un sujet); **family** ~ milieu familial.

backhand ['bækhænd] n (TENNIS: also: ~ **stroke**) revers m.

backhanded ['bæk'hændɪd] adj (fig) déloyal(e); équivoque.

backhander ['bæk'hændə*] n (BRIT: bribe) pot-de-vin m.

backing ['bækɪŋ] n (fig) soutien m, appui m; (COMM) soutien (financier); (MUS) accompagnement m.

backlash ['bæklæʃ] n contre-coup m, répercussion f.

backlog ['bæklɔg] n: ~ **of work** travail m en retard.

back number n (of magazine etc) vieux numéro.

backpack ['bækpæk] *n* sac *m* à dos.
backpacker ['bækpækə*] *n* randonneur/euse.
back pay *n* rappel *m* de salaire.
backpedal ['bækpɛdl] *vi (fig)* faire marche arrière.
backseat driver ['bæksiːt-] *n passager qui donne des conseils au conducteur.*
backside ['bæksaɪd] *n (col)* derrière *m*, postérieur *m*.
backslash ['bækslæʃ] *n* barre oblique inversée.
backslide ['bækslaɪd] *vi* retomber dans l'erreur.
backspace ['bækspeɪs] *vi (in typing)* appuyer sur la touche retour.
backstage [bæk'steɪdʒ] *adv* dans les coulisses.
back-street ['bækstriːt] *adj (abortion)* clandestin(e); ~ **abortionist** avorteur/euse *(clandestin).*
backstroke ['bækstrəuk] *n* dos crawlé.
backtrack ['bæktræk] *vi (fig)* = **backpedal.**
backup ['bækʌp] *adj (train, plane)* supplémentaire, de réserve; *(COMPUT)* de sauvegarde ♦ *n (support)* appui *m*, soutien *m*; *(COMPUT: also:* ~ **file)** sauvegarde *f.*
backward ['bækwəd] *adj (movement)* en arrière; *(measure)* rétrograde; *(person, country)* arriéré(e); attardé(e); *(shy)* hésitant(e); ~ **and forward movement** mouvement de va-et-vient.
backwards ['bækwədz] *adv (move, go)* en arrière; *(read a list)* à l'envers, à rebours; *(fall)* à la renverse; *(walk)* à reculons; *(in time)* en arrière, vers le passé; **to know sth** ~ *or (US)* ~ **and forwards** *(col)* connaître qch sur le bout des doigts.
backwater ['bækwɔːtə*] *n (fig)* coin reculé; bled perdu.
back yard *n* arrière-cour *f.*
bacon ['beɪkən] *n* bacon *m*, lard *m.*
bacteria [bæk'tɪərɪə] *npl* bactéries *fpl.*
bacteriology [bæktɪərɪ'ɔlədʒɪ] *n* bactériologie *f.*
bad [bæd] *adj* mauvais(e); *(child)* vilain(e); *(meat, food)* gâté(e), avarié(e); **his** ~ **leg** sa jambe malade; **to go** ~ *(meat, food)* se gâter; *(milk)* tourner; **to have a** ~ **time of it** traverser une mauvaise passe; **I feel** ~ **about it** *(guilty)* j'ai un peu mauvaise conscience; ~ **debt** créance douteuse; **in** ~ **faith** de mauvaise foi.
baddie, baddy ['bædɪ] *n (col: CINE etc)* méchant *m.*
bade [bæd] *pt of* **bid.**
badge [bædʒ] *n* insigne *m*; *(of policeman)* plaque *f*; *(stick-on, sew-on)* badge *m.*
badger ['bædʒə*] *n* blaireau *m* ♦ *vt* harceler.
badly ['bædlɪ] *adv (work, dress etc)* mal; ~ **wounded** grièvement blessé; **he needs it** ~ il en a absolument besoin; **things are going** ~ les choses vont mal; ~ **off** *adj, adv* dans la gêne.

bad-mannered ['bæd'mænəd] *adj* mal élevé(e).
badminton ['bædmɪntən] *n* badminton *m.*
bad-mouth ['bæd'mauθ] *vt (US col)* débiner.
bad-tempered ['bæd'tɛmpəd] *adj (by nature)* ayant mauvais caractère; *(on one occasion)* de mauvaise humeur.
baffle ['bæfl] *vt (puzzle)* déconcerter.
baffling ['bæflɪŋ] *adj* déroutant(e), déconcertant(e).
bag [bæg] *n* sac *m*; *(of hunter)* gibecière *f*, chasse *f* ♦ *vt (col: take)* empocher; s'approprier; *(TECH)* mettre en sacs; ~**s of** *(col: lots of)* des masses de; **to pack one's** ~**s** faire ses valises *or* bagages; ~**s under the eyes** poches *fpl* sous les yeux.
bagful ['bægful] *n* plein sac.
baggage ['bægɪdʒ] *n* bagages *mpl.*
baggage claim *n (at airport)* livraison *f* des bagages.
baggy ['bægɪ] *adj* avachi(e), qui fait des poches.
Baghdad [bæg'dæd] *n* Baghdâd, Bagdad.
bag lady *n (col)* clocharde *f.*
bagpipes ['bægpaɪps] *npl* cornemuse *f.*
bag-snatcher ['bægsnætʃə*] *n (BRIT)* voleur *m* à l'arraché.
bag-snatching ['bægsnætʃɪŋ] *n (BRIT)* vol *m* à l'arraché.
Bahamas [bə'hɑːməz] *npl*: **the** ~ les Bahamas *fpl.*
Bahrain [bɑː'reɪn] *n* Bahreïn *m.*
bail [beɪl] *n* caution *f* ♦ *vt (prisoner: also:* **grant** ~ **to)** mettre en liberté sous caution; *(boat: also:* ~ **out)** écoper; **to be released on** ~ être libéré(e) sous caution; *see* **bale.**
▶**bail out** *vt (prisoner)* payer la caution de.
bailiff ['beɪlɪf] *n* huissier *m.*
bait [beɪt] *n* appât *m* ♦ *vt* appâter; *(fig)* tourmenter.
bake [beɪk] *vt* (faire) cuire au four ♦ *vi (bread etc)* cuire (au four); *(make cakes etc)* faire de la pâtisserie.
baked beans [beɪkt-] *npl* haricots blancs à la sauce tomate.
baker ['beɪkə*] *n* boulanger *m.*
bakery ['beɪkərɪ] *n* boulangerie *f*; boulangerie industrielle.
baking ['beɪkɪŋ] *n* cuisson *f.*
baking powder *n* levure *f* (chimique).
baking tin *n (for cake)* moule *m* à gâteaux; *(for meat)* plat *m* pour le four.
baking tray *n* plaque *f* à gâteaux.
balaclava [bælə'klɑːvə] *n (also:* ~ **helmet)** passe-montagne *m.*
balance ['bæləns] *n* équilibre *m*; *(COMM: sum)* solde *m*; *(scales)* balance *f* ♦ *vt* mettre or faire tenir en équilibre; *(pros and cons)* peser; *(budget)* équilibrer; *(account)* balancer; *(compensate)* compenser, contrebalancer; ~ **of trade/payments** balance commerciale/des comptes *or* paiements; ~ **carried for-**

ward solde *m* à reporter; ~ **brought forward** solde reporté; **to** ~ **the books** arrêter les comptes, dresser le bilan.

balanced ['bælənst] *adj* (*personality, diet*) équilibré(e).

balance sheet *n* bilan *m*.

balcony ['bælkənɪ] *n* balcon *m*.

bald [bɔːld] *adj* chauve; (*tyre*) lisse.

baldness ['bɔːldnɪs] *n* calvitie *f*.

bale [beɪl] *n* balle *f*, ballot *m*.

▶**bale out** *vi* (*of a plane*) sauter en parachute ♦ *vt* (*NAUT: water, boat*) écoper.

Balearic Islands [bælɪ'ærɪk-] *npl*: **the** ~ **les** (îles *fpl*) Baléares *fpl*.

baleful ['beɪlful] *adj* funeste, maléfique.

balk [bɔːk] *vi*: **to** ~ **(at)** (*person*) regimber (contre); (*horse*) se dérober (devant).

Balkan ['bɔːlkən] *adj* balkanique ♦ *n*: **the** ~**s** les Balkans *mpl*.

ball [bɔːl] *n* boule *f*; (*football*) ballon *m*; (*for tennis, golf*) balle *f*; (*dance*) bal *m*; **to play** ~ **(with sb)** jouer au ballon (*or* à la balle) (avec qn); (*fig*) coopérer (avec qn); **to be on the** ~ (*fig: competent*) être à la hauteur; (*: alert*) être éveillé(e), être vif(vive); **to start the** ~ **rolling** (*fig*) commencer; **the** ~ **is in their court** (*fig*) la balle est dans leur camp.

ballad ['bæləd] *n* ballade *f*.

ballast ['bæləst] *n* lest *m*.

ball bearing *n* roulement *m* à billes.

ball cock *n* robinet *m* à flotteur.

ballerina [bælə'riːnə] *n* ballerine *f*.

ballet ['bæleɪ] *n* ballet *m*; (*art*) danse *f* (classique).

ballet dancer *n* danseur/euse de ballet.

ballistic [bə'lɪstɪk] *adj* balistique.

ballistics [bə'lɪstɪks] *n* balistique *f*.

balloon [bə'luːn] *n* ballon *m*; (*in comic strip*) bulle *f* ♦ *vi* gonfler.

balloonist [bə'luːnɪst] *n* aéronaute *m/f*.

ballot ['bælət] *n* scrutin *m*.

ballot box *n* urne (électorale).

ballot paper *n* bulletin *m* de vote.

ballpark ['bɔːlpɑːk] *n* (*US*) stade *m* de baseball.

ballpark figure *n* (*col*) chiffre approximatif.

ball-point pen ['bɔːlpɔɪnt-] *n* stylo *m* à bille.

ballroom ['bɔːlrum] *n* salle *f* de bal.

balls [bɔːlz] *npl* (*col!*) couilles *fpl* (*!*).

balm [bɑːm] *n* baume *m*.

balmy ['bɑːmɪ] *adj* (*breeze, air*) doux(douce); (*BRIT col*) = **barmy**.

BALPA ['bælpə] *n abbr* (= *British Airline Pilots' Association*) *syndicat des pilotes de ligne*.

balsam ['bɔːlsəm] *n* baume *m*.

balsa (wood) ['bɔːlsə-] *n* balsa *m*.

Baltic [bɔːltɪk] *adj, n*: **the** ~ **(Sea)** la (mer) Baltique.

balustrade [bæləs'treɪd] *n* balustrade *f*.

bamboo [bæm'buː] *n* bambou *m*.

bamboozle [bæm'buːzl] *vt* (*col*) embobiner.

ban [bæn] *n* interdiction *f* ♦ *vt* interdire; **he was** ~**ned from driving** (*BRIT*) on lui a retiré le permis (de conduire).

banal [bə'nɑːl] *adj* banal(e).

banana [bə'nɑːnə] *n* banane *f*.

band [bænd] *n* bande *f*; (*at a dance*) orchestre *m*; (*MIL*) musique *f*, fanfare *f*.

▶**band together** *vi* se liguer.

B & B *n abbr* = **bed and breakfast**.

bandage ['bændɪdʒ] *n* bandage *m*, pansement *m* ♦ *vt* (*wound, leg*) mettre un pansement *or* un bandage sur; (*person*) mettre un pansement *or* un bandage à.

Band-Aid ['bændeɪd] *n* ® (*US*) pansement adhésif.

bandit ['bændɪt] *n* bandit *m*.

bandstand ['bændstænd] *n* kiosque *m* (à musique).

bandwagon ['bændwægən] *n*: **to jump on the** ~ (*fig*) monter dans *or* prendre le train en marche.

bandy ['bændɪ] *vt* (*jokes, insults*) échanger.

▶**bandy about** *vt* employer à tout bout de champ *or* à tort et à travers.

bandy-legged ['bændɪ'lɛgɪd] *adj* aux jambes arquées.

bane [beɪn] *n*: **it** (*or* **he** *etc*) **is the** ~ **of my life** c'est (*or* il est *etc*) le drame de ma vie.

bang [bæŋ] *n* détonation *f*; (*of door*) claquement *m*; (*blow*) coup (violent) ♦ *vt* frapper (violemment); (*door*) claquer ♦ *vi* détoner; claquer ♦ *adv*: **to be** ~ **on time** (*BRIT col*) être à l'heure pile; **to** ~ **at the door** cogner à la porte; **to** ~ **into sth** se cogner contre qch.

banger ['bæŋə*] *n* (*BRIT: car: also*: **old** ~) (vieux) tacot; (*BRIT col: sausage*) saucisse *f*; (*firework*) pétard *m*.

Bangkok [bæŋ'kɔk] *n* Bangkok.

Bangladesh [bæŋglə'dɛʃ] *n* Bangladesh *m*.

bangle ['bæŋgl] *n* bracelet *m*.

bangs [bæŋz] *npl* (*US: fringe*) frange *f*.

banish ['bænɪʃ] *vt* bannir.

banister(s) ['bænɪstə(z)] *n(pl)* rampe *f* (d'escalier).

banjo, ~**es** *or* ~**s** ['bændʒəu] *n* banjo *m*.

bank [bæŋk] *n* banque *f*; (*of river, lake*) bord *m*, rive *f*; (*of earth*) talus *m*, remblai *m* ♦ *vi* (*AVIAT*) virer sur l'aile; (*COMM*): **they** ~ **with Pitt's** leur banque *or* banquier est Pitt's.

▶**bank on** *vt fus* miser *or* tabler sur.

bank account *n* compte *m* en banque.

bank balance *n* solde *m* bancaire.

bank card *n* = **banker's card**.

bank charges *npl* (*BRIT*) frais *mpl* de banque.

bank draft *n* traite *f* bancaire.

banker ['bæŋkə*] *n* banquier *m*; ~**'s card** (*BRIT*) carte *f* d'identité bancaire; ~**'s order** (*BRIT*) ordre *m* de virement.

bank giro *n* paiement *m* par virement.

bank holiday *n* (*BRIT*) jour férié (*où les banques sont fermées*).

Un **bank holiday** *en Grande-Bretagne est un lundi férié et donc l'occasion d'un week-end prolongé. La circulation sur les routes et le trafic dans les gares et les aéroports augmentent considérablement à ces périodes. Les principaux bank holidays, à part Pâques et Noël, se situent au mois de mai et fin août.*

banking ['bæŋkɪŋ] *n* opérations *fpl* bancaires; profession *f* de banquier.
banking hours *npl* heures *fpl* d'ouverture des banques.
bank loan *n* prêt *m* bancaire.
bank manager *n* directeur *m* d'agence (bancaire).
banknote ['bæŋknəut] *n* billet *m* de banque.
bank rate *n* taux *m* de l'escompte.
bankrupt ['bæŋkrʌpt] *n* failli/e ♦ *adj* en faillite; **to go** ~ faire faillite.
bankruptcy ['bæŋkrʌptsɪ] *n* faillite *f*.
bank statement *n* relevé *m* de compte.
banner ['bænə*] *n* bannière *f*.
bannister(s) ['bænɪstə(z)] *n(pl)* = **banister(s)**.
banns [bænz] *npl* bans *mpl* (de mariage).
banquet ['bæŋkwɪt] *n* banquet *m*, festin *m*.
bantam-weight ['bæntəmweɪt] *n* poids *m* coq *inv*.
banter ['bæntə*] *n* badinage *m*.
BAOR *n abbr* (= *British Army of the Rhine*) forces britanniques en Allemagne.
baptism ['bæptɪzəm] *n* baptême *m*.
Baptist ['bæptɪst] *n* baptiste *m/f*.
baptize [bæp'taɪz] *vt* baptiser.
bar [bɑː*] *n* barre *f*; (*of window etc*) barreau *m*; (*of chocolate*) tablette *f*, plaque *f*; (*fig*) obstacle *m*; mesure *f* d'exclusion; (*pub*) bar *m*; (*counter: in pub*) comptoir *m*, bar *m*; (*MUS*) mesure *f* ♦ *vt* (*road*) barrer; (*window*) munir de barreaux; (*person*) exclure; (*activity*) interdire; ~ **of soap** savonnette *f*; **behind** ~**s** (*prisoner*) derrière les barreaux; **the B**~ (*LAW*) le barreau; ~ **none** sans exception.
Barbados [bɑː'beɪdɔs] *n* Barbade *f*.
barbaric [bɑː'bærɪk] *adj* barbare.
barbarous ['bɑːbərəs] *adj* barbare, cruel(le).
barbecue ['bɑːbɪkjuː] *n* barbecue *m*.
barbed wire ['bɑːbd-] *n* fil *m* de fer barbelé.
barber ['bɑːbə*] *n* coiffeur *m* (pour hommes).
barbiturate [bɑː'bɪtjurɪt] *n* barbiturique *m*.
Barcelona [bɑːsə'ləunə] *n* Barcelone *f*.
bar chart *n* diagramme *m* en bâtons.
bar code *n* code *m* à barres.
bare [bɛə*] *adj* nu(e) ♦ *vt* mettre à nu, dénuder; (*teeth*) montrer; **the** ~ **essentials** le strict nécessaire.
bareback ['bɛəbæk] *adv* à cru, sans selle.
barefaced ['bɛəfeɪst] *adj* impudent(e), effronté(e).
barefoot ['bɛəfut] *adj*, *adv* nu-pieds, (les) pieds nus.
bareheaded [bɛə'hɛdɪd] *adj*, *adv* nu-tête, (la)

tête nue.
barely ['bɛəlɪ] *adv* à peine.
Barents Sea ['bærənts-] *n*: **the** ~ la mer de Barents.
bargain ['bɑːgɪn] *n* (*transaction*) marché *m*; (*good buy*) affaire *f*, occasion *f* ♦ *vi* (*haggle*) marchander; (*trade*) négocier, traiter; **into the** ~ par-dessus le marché.
►**bargain for** *vi* (*col*): **he got more than he** ~**ed for!** il en a eu pour son argent!
bargaining ['bɑːgənɪŋ] *n* marchandage *m*; négociations *fpl*.
bargaining position *n*: **to be in a weak/ strong** ~ être en mauvaise/bonne position pour négocier.
barge [bɑːdʒ] *n* péniche *f*.
►**barge in** *vi* (*walk in*) faire irruption; (*interrupt talk*) intervenir mal à propos.
►**barge into** *vt fus* rentrer dans.
baritone ['bærɪtəun] *n* baryton *m*.
barium meal ['bɛərɪəm-] *n* (bouillie *f* de) sulfate *m* de baryum.
bark [bɑːk] *n* (*of tree*) écorce *f*; (*of dog*) aboiement *m* ♦ *vi* aboyer.
barley ['bɑːlɪ] *n* orge *f*.
barley sugar *n* sucre *m* d'orge.
barmaid ['bɑːmeɪd] *n* serveuse *f* (de bar), barmaid *f*.
barman ['bɑːmən] *n* serveur *m* (de bar), barman *m*.
barmy ['bɑːmɪ] *adj* (*BRIT col*) timbré(e), cinglé(e).
barn [bɑːn] *n* grange *f*.
barnacle ['bɑːnəkl] *n* anatife *m*, bernache *f*.
barn owl *n* chouette-effraie *f*, chat-huant *m*.
barometer [bə'rɒmɪtə*] *n* baromètre *m*.
baron ['bærən] *n* baron *m*; **the press/oil** ~**s** les magnats *mpl or* barons *mpl* de la presse/du pétrole.
baroness ['bærənɪs] *n* baronne *f*.
barrack ['bærək] *vt* (*BRIT*) chahuter.
barracking ['bærəkɪŋ] *n* (*BRIT*): **to give sb a** ~ chahuter qn.
barracks ['bærəks] *npl* caserne *f*.
barrage ['bærɑːʒ] *n* (*MIL*) tir *m* de barrage; (*dam*) barrage *m*; **a** ~ **of questions** un feu roulant de questions.
barrel ['bærəl] *n* tonneau *m*; (*of gun*) canon *m*.
barrel organ *n* orgue *m* de Barbarie.
barren ['bærən] *adj* stérile; (*hills*) aride.
barricade [bærɪ'keɪd] *n* barricade *f* ♦ *vt* barricader.
barrier ['bærɪə*] *n* barrière *f*; (*BRIT: also*: **crash** ~) rail *m* de sécurité.
barrier cream *n* (*BRIT*) crème protectrice.
barring ['bɑːrɪŋ] *prep* sauf.
barrister ['bærɪstə*] *n* (*BRIT*) avocat (plaidant).

En Angleterre, un **barrister**, *que l'on appelle également "barrister-at-law", est un avocat qui représente ses clients devant la cour et plaide pour eux. Le client doit d'abord passer* *par l'intermédiaire d'un* **solicitor**. *On obtient le diplôme de barrister après avoir fait des études dans l'une des Inns of Court, les quatre écoles de droit londoniennes.*

barrow ['bærəʊ] *n* (*cart*) charrette *f* à bras.
barstool ['bɑːstuːl] *n* tabouret *m* de bar.
Bart. *abbr* (*BRIT*) = **baronet**.
bartender ['bɑːtɛndə*] *n* (*US*) serveur *m* (*de bar*), barman *m*.
barter ['bɑːtə*] *n* échange *m*, troc *m* ♦ *vt*: **to ~ sth for** échanger qch contre.
base [beɪs] *n* base *f* ♦ *vt* (*troops*): **to be ~d at** être basé(e) à; (*opinion, belief*): **to ~ sth on** baser *or* fonder qch sur ♦ *adj* vil(e), bas(se); **coffee-~d** à base de café; **a Paris-~d firm** une maison opérant de Paris *or* dont le siège est à Paris; **I'm ~d in London** je suis basé(e) à Londres.
baseball ['beɪsbɔːl] *n* base-ball *m*.
baseboard ['beɪsbɔːd] *n* (*US*) plinthe *f*.
base camp *n* camp *m* de base.
Basel [bɑːl] *n* = **Basle**.
baseline ['beɪslaɪn] *n* (*TENNIS*) ligne *f* de fond.
basement ['beɪsmənt] *n* sous-sol *m*.
base rate *n* taux *m* de base.
bases ['beɪsɪz] *npl of* **basis**; ['beɪsɪz] *npl of* **base**.
bash [bæʃ] *vt* (*col*) frapper, cogner ♦ *n*: **I'll have a ~ (at it)** (*BRIT col*) je vais essayer un coup; **~ed in** *adj* enfoncé(e), défoncé(e).
▶**bash up** *vt* (*col: car*) bousiller; (: *BRIT: person*) tabasser.
bashful ['bæʃful] *adj* timide; modeste.
bashing ['bæʃɪŋ] *n* (*col*) raclée *f*; **Paki-~≈** ratonnade *f*; **queer-~** chasse *f* aux pédés.
BASIC ['beɪsɪk] *n* (*COMPUT*) BASIC *m*.
basic ['beɪsɪk] *adj* (*precautions, rules*) élémentaire; (*principles, research*) fondamental(e); (*vocabulary, salary*) de base; réduit(e) au minimum, rudimentaire.
basically ['beɪsɪklɪ] *adv* (*really*) en fait; (*essentially*) fondamentalement.
basic rate *n* (*of tax*) première tranche d'imposition.
basil ['bæzl] *n* basilic *m*.
basin ['beɪsn] *n* (*vessel, also GEO*) cuvette *f*, bassin *m*; (*BRIT: for food*) bol *m*; (: *bigger*) saladier *m*; (*also:* **wash~**) lavabo *m*.
basis, pl bases ['beɪsɪs, -siːz] *n* base *f*; **on the ~ of what you've said** d'après *or* compte tenu de ce que vous dites.
bask [bɑːsk] *vi*: **to ~ in the sun** se chauffer au soleil.
basket ['bɑːskɪt] *n* corbeille *f*; (*with handle*) panier *m*.
basketball ['bɑːskɪtbɔːl] *n* basket-ball *m*.
basketball player *n* basketteur/euse.
Basle [bɑːl] *n* Bâle.
basmati rice [bəz'mætɪ-] *n* riz *m* basmati.
Basque [bæsk] *adj* basque ♦ *n* Basque *m/f*.
bass [beɪs] *n* (*MUS*) basse *f*.
bass clef *n* clé *f* de fa.

bassoon [bə'suːn] *n* basson *m*.
bastard ['bɑːstəd] *n* enfant naturel(le), bâtard/e; (*col!*) salaud *m* (!).
baste [beɪst] *vt* (*CULIN*) arroser; (*SEWING*) bâtir, faufiler.
bastion ['bæstɪən] *n* bastion *m*.
bat [bæt] *n* chauve-souris *f*; (*for baseball etc*) batte *f*; (*BRIT: for table tennis*) raquette *f* ♦ *vt*: **he didn't ~ an eyelid** il n'a pas sourcillé *or* bronché; **off one's own ~** de sa propre initiative.
batch [bætʃ] *n* (*of bread*) fournée *f*; (*of papers*) liasse *f*; (*of applicants, letters*) paquet *m*; (*of work*) monceau *m*; (*of goods*) lot *m*.
batch processing *n* (*COMPUT*) traitement *m* par lot.
bated ['beɪtɪd] *adj*: **with ~ breath** en retenant son souffle.
bath [bɑːθ, *pl* bɑːðz] *n* bain *m*; (*bathtub*) baignoire *f* ♦ *vt* baigner, donner un bain à; **to have a ~** prendre un bain; *see also* **baths**.
Bath chair *n* (*BRIT*) fauteuil roulant.
bathe [beɪð] *vi* se baigner ♦ *vt* baigner; (*wound etc*) laver.
bather ['beɪðə*] *n* baigneur/euse.
bathing ['beɪðɪŋ] *n* baignade *f*.
bathing cap *n* bonnet *m* de bain.
bathing costume, (*US*) **bathing suit** *n* maillot *m* (de bain).
bathmat ['bɑːθmæt] *n* tapis *m* de bain.
bathrobe ['bɑːθrəʊb] *n* peignoir *m* de bain.
bathroom ['bɑːθrum] *n* salle *f* de bains.
baths [bɑːðz] *npl* établissement *m* de bains (-douches).
bath towel *n* serviette *f* de bain.
bathtub ['bɑːθtʌb] *n* baignoire *f*.
batman ['bætmən] *n* (*BRIT MIL*) ordonnance *f*.
baton ['bætən] *n* bâton *m*; (*MUS*) baguette *f*; (*club*) matraque *f*.
battalion [bə'tælɪən] *n* bataillon *m*.
batten ['bætn] *n* (*CARPENTRY*) latte *f*; (*NAUT: on sail*) latte de voile.
▶**batten down** *vt* (*NAUT*): **to ~ down the hatches** fermer les écoutilles.
batter ['bætə*] *vt* battre ♦ *n* pâte *f* à frire.
battered ['bætəd] *adj* (*hat, pan*) cabossé(e); **~ wife/child** épouse/enfant maltraité(e) *or* martyr(e).
battering ram ['bætərɪŋ-] *n* bélier *m* (*fig*).
battery ['bætərɪ] *n* batterie *f*; (*of torch*) pile *f*.
battery charger *n* chargeur *m*.
battery farming *n* élevage *m* en batterie.
battle ['bætl] *n* bataille *f*, combat *m* ♦ *vi* se battre, lutter; **that's half the ~** (*fig*) c'est déjà bien; **it's a** *or* **we're fighting a losing ~** (*fig*) c'est perdu d'avance, c'est peine perdue.
battle dress *n* tenue *f* de campagne *or* d'assaut.
battlefield ['bætlfiːld] *n* champ *m* de bataille.
battlements ['bætlmənts] *npl* remparts *mpl*.
battleship ['bætlʃɪp] *n* cuirassé *m*.

batty ['bætɪ] *adj (col*: *person)* toqué(e); (: *idea, behaviour)* loufoque.
bauble ['bɔːbl] *n* babiole *f*.
baud [bɔːd] *n* (*COMPUT*) baud *m*.
baud rate *n* (*COMPUT*) vitesse *f* de transmission.
baulk [bɔːlk] *vi* = **balk**.
bauxite ['bɔːksaɪt] *n* bauxite *f*.
Bavaria [bə'vɛərɪə] *n* Bavière *f*.
Bavarian [bə'vɛərɪən] *adj* bavarois(e) ♦ *n* Bavarois/e.
bawdy ['bɔːdɪ] *adj* paillard(e).
bawl [bɔːl] *vi* hurler, brailler.
bay [beɪ] *n (of sea)* baie *f*; (*BRIT*: *for parking)* place *f* de stationnement; (: *for loading)* aire *f* de chargement; (*horse)* bai/e *m/f*; **to hold sb at ~** tenir qn à distance *or* en échec.
bay leaf *n* laurier *m*.
bayonet ['beɪənɪt] *n* baïonnette *f*.
bay tree *n* laurier *m*.
bay window *n* baie vitrée.
bazaar [bə'zɑː*] *n* bazar *m*; vente *f* de charité.
bazooka [bə'zuːkə] *n* bazooka *m*.
BB *n abbr* (*BRIT*: = *Boys' Brigade)* mouvement de garçons.
BBB *n abbr* (*US*: = *Better Business Bureau)* organisme *m* de défense du consommateur.
BBC *n abbr* (= *British Broadcasting Corporation)* office de la radiodiffusion et télévision britannique.

La **BBC** est un organisme centralisé dont les membres, nommés par l'État, gèrent les chaînes de télévision publiques (BBC1, qui présente des émissions d'intérêt général, et BBC2, qui est plutôt orientée vers les émissions plus culturelles) et les stations de radio publiques (5 au niveau national, et 37 à l'échelle locale). Bien que non contrôlée par l'État, la BBC est responsable devant le **Parliament** quant au contenu des émissions qu'elle diffuse. Par ailleurs, la BBC offre un service mondial de diffusion d'émissions, en anglais et dans 35 autres langues, appelé BBC World Service. La BBC est financée par la redevance télévision et par l'exportation d'émissions.

BC *adv abbr* (= *before Christ)* av. J.-C. ♦ *abbr* (*Canada*) = *British Columbia*.
BCG *n abbr* (= *Bacillus Calmette-Guérin)* BCG *m*.
BD *n abbr* (= *Bachelor of Divinity)* diplôme universitaire.
B/D *abbr* = **bank draft**.
BDS *n abbr* (= *Bachelor of Dental Surgery)* diplôme universitaire.

================= *KEYWORD*

be [biː] (*pt* **was, were**, *pp* **been**) *aux vb* **1** (*with present participle*: *forming continuous tenses*): **what are you doing?** que faites-vous?; **they're coming tomorrow** ils viennent demain; **I've been waiting for you for 2 hours** je t'attends depuis 2 heures
2 (*with pp*: *forming passives*) être; **to ~ killed** être tué(e); **he was nowhere to ~ seen** on ne le voyait nulle part
3 (*in tag questions*): **it was fun, wasn't it?** c'était drôle, n'est-ce pas?; **she's back, is she?** elle est rentrée, n'est-ce pas *or* alors?
4 (*+to +infinitive*): **the house is to ~ sold** la maison doit être vendue; **he's not to open it** il ne doit pas l'ouvrir; **am I to understand that ...?** dois-je comprendre que ...?; **he was to have come yesterday** il devait venir hier
5 (*possibility, supposition*): **if I were you, I ...** à votre place, je ..., si j'étais vous, je ...
♦ *vb + complement* **1** (*gen*) être; **I'm English** je suis anglais(e); **I'm tired** je suis fatigué(e); **I'm hot/cold** j'ai chaud/froid; **he's a doctor** il est médecin; **2 and 2 are 4** 2 et 2 font 4
2 (*of health*) aller; **how are you?** comment allez-vous?; **he's fine now** il va bien maintenant; **he's very ill** il est très malade
3 (*of age*) avoir; **how old are you?** quel âge avez-vous?; **I'm sixteen (years old)** j'ai seize ans
4 (*cost*) coûter; **how much was the meal?** combien a coûté le repas?; **that'll ~ £5, please** ça fera 5 livres, s'il vous plaît
♦ *vi* **1** (*exist, occur etc*) être, exister; **the prettiest girl that ever was** la fille la plus jolie qui ait jamais existé; **~ that as it may** quoi qu'il en soit; **so ~ it** soit
2 (*referring to place*) être, se trouver; **I won't ~ here tomorrow** je ne serai pas là demain; **Edinburgh is in Scotland** Édimbourg est *or* se trouve en Écosse
3 (*referring to movement*) aller; **where have you been?** où êtes-vous allé(s)?
♦ *impers vb* **1** (*referring to time, distance*) être; **it's 5 o'clock** il est 5 heures; **it's the 28th of April** c'est le 28 avril; **it's 10 km to the village** le village est à 10 km
2 (*referring to the weather*) faire; **it's too hot/cold** il fait trop chaud/froid; **it's windy** il y a du vent
3 (*emphatic*): **it's me/the postman** c'est moi/le facteur.

B/E *abbr* = **bill of exchange**.
beach [biːtʃ] *n* plage *f* ♦ *vt* échouer.
beachcomber ['biːtʃkəumə*] *n* ramasseur *m* d'épaves; (*fig*) glandeur *m*.
beachwear ['biːtʃwɛə*] *n* tenues *fpl* de plage.
beacon ['biːkən] *n* (*lighthouse*) fanal *m*; (*marker*) balise *f*; (*also*: **radio ~**) radiophare *m*.
bead [biːd] *n* perle *f*; (*of dew, sweat*) goutte *f*; **~s** (*necklace*) collier *m*.
beady ['biːdɪ] *adj*: **~ eyes** yeux *mpl* de fouine.
beagle ['biːgl] *n* beagle *m*.
beak [biːk] *n* bec *m*.
beaker ['biːkə*] *n* gobelet *m*.
beam [biːm] *n* poutre *f*; (*of light*) rayon *m*; (*RADIO*) faisceau *m* radio ♦ *vi* rayonner; **to**

drive on full or **main** or (US) **high** ~ rouler en pleins phares.

beaming ['biːmɪŋ] adj (sun, smile) radieux(euse).

bean [biːn] n haricot m; (of coffee) grain m.

beanpole ['biːnpəul] n (col) perche f.

bean sprouts npl pousses fpl (de soja).

bear [bɛə*] n ours m; (STOCK EXCHANGE) baissier m ♦ vb (pt **bore**, pp **borne** [bɔː*, bɔːn]) vt porter; (endure) supporter; (traces, signs) porter; (COMM: interest) rapporter ♦ vi: **to ~ right/left** obliquer à droite/gauche, se diriger vers la droite/gauche; **to ~ the responsibility of** assumer la responsabilité de; **to ~ comparison with** soutenir la comparaison avec; **I can't ~ him** je ne peux pas le supporter or souffrir; **to bring pressure to ~ on sb** faire pression sur qn.

▶**bear out** vt (theory, suspicion) confirmer.

▶**bear up** vi supporter, tenir le coup; **he bore up well** il a tenu le coup.

▶**bear with** vt fus (sb's moods, temper) supporter; **~ with me a minute** un moment, s'il vous plaît.

bearable ['bɛərəbl] adj supportable.

beard [bɪəd] n barbe f.

bearded ['bɪədɪd] adj barbu(e).

bearer ['bɛərə*] n porteur m; (of passport etc) titulaire m/f.

bearing ['bɛərɪŋ] n maintien m, allure f; (connection) rapport m; (TECH): (ball) ~s npl roulement m (à billes); **to take a ~** faire le point; **to find one's ~s** s'orienter.

beast [biːst] n bête f; (col): **he's a ~** c'est une brute.

beastly ['biːstlɪ] adj infect(e).

beat [biːt] n battement m; (MUS) temps m, mesure f; (of policeman) ronde f ♦ vt (pt **beat**, pp **beaten**) battre; **off the ~en track** hors des chemins or sentiers battus; **to ~ about the bush** tourner autour du pot; **to ~ time** battre la mesure; **that ~s everything!** c'est le comble!

▶**beat down** vt (door) enfoncer; (price) faire baisser; (seller) faire descendre ♦ vi (rain) tambouriner; (sun) taper.

▶**beat off** vt repousser.

▶**beat up** vt (eggs) battre; (col: person) tabasser.

beater ['biːtə*] n (for eggs, cream) fouet m, batteur m.

beating ['biːtɪŋ] n raclée f.

beat-up ['biːtʌp] adj (col) déglingué(e).

beautician [bjuːˈtɪʃən] n esthéticien/ne.

beautiful ['bjuːtɪful] adj beau(belle).

beautifully ['bjuːtɪflɪ] adv admirablement.

beautify ['bjuːtɪfaɪ] vt embellir.

beauty ['bjuːtɪ] n beauté f; **the ~ of it is that ...** le plus beau, c'est que ....

beauty contest n concours m de beauté.

beauty queen n reine f de beauté.

beauty salon n institut m de beauté.

beauty sleep n: **I'm going to bed, I need my ~** je vais me coucher, j'ai besoin de faire un gros dodo.

beauty spot n grain m de beauté; (BRIT TOURISM) site m naturel (d'une grande beauté).

beaver ['biːvə*] n castor m.

becalmed [bɪˈkɑːmd] adj immobilisé(e) par le calme plat.

became [bɪˈkeɪm] pt of **become**.

because [bɪˈkɔz] conj parce que; **~ of** prep à cause de.

beck [bɛk] n: **to be at sb's ~ and call** être à l'entière disposition de qn.

beckon ['bɛkən] vt (also: ~ **to**) faire signe (de venir) à.

become [bɪˈkʌm] vi (irreg: like **come**) devenir; **to ~ fat/thin** grossir/maigrir; **to ~ angry** se mettre en colère; **it became known that** on apprit que; **what has ~ of him?** qu'est-il devenu?

becoming [bɪˈkʌmɪŋ] adj (behaviour) convenable, bienséant(e); (clothes) seyant(e).

BECTU ['bɛktu] n abbr (BRIT) = Broadcasting, Entertainment, Cinematographic and Theatre Union.

BEd n abbr (= Bachelor of Education) diplôme d'aptitude à l'enseignement.

bed [bɛd] n lit m; (of flowers) parterre m; (of coal, clay) couche f; (of sea, lake) fond m; **to go to ~** aller se coucher.

▶**bed down** vi se coucher.

bed and breakfast (B & B) n (terms) chambre et petit déjeuner; (place) ≈ chambre f d'hôte.

> Un **bed and breakfast** est une petite pension dans une maison particulière ou une ferme où l'on peut louer une chambre avec petit déjeuner compris pour un prix modique par rapport à ce que l'on paierait dans un hôtel. Ces établissements sont communément appelés B & B, et sont signalés par une pancarte dans le jardin ou au-dessus de la porte.

bedbug ['bɛdbʌg] n punaise f.

bedclothes ['bɛdkləuðz] npl couvertures fpl et draps mpl.

bedcover ['bɛdkʌvə*] n couvre-lit m, dessus-de-lit m.

bedding ['bɛdɪŋ] n literie f.

bedevil [bɪˈdɛvl] vt (harass) harceler; **to be ~led by** être victime de.

bedfellow ['bɛdfɛləu] n: **they are strange ~s** (fig) ça fait un drôle de mélange.

bedlam ['bɛdləm] n chahut m, cirque m.

bedpan ['bɛdpæn] n bassin m (hygiénique).

bedpost ['bɛdpəust] n colonne f de lit.

bedraggled [bɪˈdrægld] adj dépenaillé(e), les vêtements en désordre.

bedridden ['bɛdrɪdn] adj cloué(e) au lit.

bedrock ['bɛdrɔk] n (fig) principes essentiels or de base, essentiel m; (GEO) roche f en place, socle *m*.

bedroom ['bɛdrum] *n* chambre *f* (à coucher).

Beds *abbr* (*BRIT*) = *Bedfordshire*.

bed settee *n* canapé-lit *m*.

bedside ['bɛdsaɪd] *n*: **at sb's** ~ au chevet de qn ♦ *cpd* (*book, lamp*) de chevet.

bedsit(ter) ['bɛdsɪt(ə*)] *n* (*BRIT*) chambre meublée, studio *m*.

bedspread ['bɛdsprɛd] *n* couvre-lit *m*, dessus-de-lit *m*.

bedtime ['bɛdtaɪm] *n*: **it's** ~ c'est l'heure de se coucher.

bee [biː] *n* abeille *f*; **to have a** ~ **in one's bonnet (about sth)** être obnubilé(e) (par qch).

beech [biːtʃ] *n* hêtre *m*.

beef [biːf] *n* bœuf *m*.

▶**beef up** *vt* (*col: support*) renforcer; (*: essay*) étoffer.

beefburger ['biːfbəːgə*] *n* hamburger *m*.

beefeater ['biːfiːtə*] *n* hallebardier *m* (de la tour de Londres).

beehive ['biːhaɪv] *n* ruche *f*.

bee-keeping ['biːkiːpɪŋ] *n* apiculture *f*.

beeline ['biːlaɪn] *n*: **to make a** ~ **for** se diriger tout droit vers.

been [biːn] *pp of* **be**.

beep [biːp] *n* bip *m*.

beeper ['biːpə*] *n* (*pager*) bip *m*.

beer [bɪə*] *n* bière *f*.

beer belly *n* (*col*) bedaine *f* (*de buveur de bière*).

beer can *n* canette *f* de bière.

beetle ['biːtl] *n* scarabée *m*, coléoptère *m*.

beetroot ['biːtruːt] *n* (*BRIT*) betterave *f*.

befall [bɪ'fɔːl] *vt* (*irreg: like* **fall**) advenir (à).

befit [bɪ'fɪt] *vt* seoir à.

before [bɪ'fɔː*] *prep* (*of time*) avant; (*of space*) devant ♦ *conj* avant que + *sub*; avant de ♦ *adv* avant; ~ **going** avant de partir; ~ **she goes** avant qu'elle (ne) parte; **the week** ~ la semaine précédente *or* d'avant; **I've seen it** ~ je l'ai déjà vu; **I've never seen it** ~ c'est la première fois que je le vois.

beforehand [bɪ'fɔːhænd] *adv* au préalable, à l'avance.

befriend [bɪ'frɛnd] *vt* venir en aide à; traiter en ami.

befuddled [bɪ'fʌdld] *adj*: **to be** ~ avoir les idées brouillées.

beg [bɛg] *vi* mendier ♦ *vt* mendier; (*favour*) quémander, solliciter; (*entreat*) supplier; **I** ~ **your pardon** (*apologising*) excusez-moi; (*: not hearing*) pardon?; **that** ~**s the question of** ... cela soulève la question de ..., cela suppose réglée la question de ....

began [bɪ'gæn] *pt of* **begin**.

beggar ['bɛgə*] *n* (*also:* ~**man**, ~**woman**) mendiant/e.

begin, *pt* **began**, *pp* **begun** [bɪ'gɪn, -'gæn, -'gʌn] *vt, vi* commencer; **to** ~ **doing** *or* **to do sth** commencer à faire qch; ~**ning (from)** **Monday** à partir de lundi; **I can't** ~ **to thank**

you je ne saurais vous remercier; **to** ~ **with** d'abord, pour commencer.

beginner [bɪ'gɪnə*] *n* débutant/e.

beginning [bɪ'gɪnɪŋ] *n* commencement *m*, début *m*; **right from the** ~ dès le début.

begrudge [bɪ'grʌdʒ] *vt*: **to** ~ **sb sth** envier qch à qn; donner qch à contrecœur *or* à regret à qn.

beguile [bɪ'gaɪl] *vt* (*enchant*) enjôler.

beguiling [bɪ'gaɪlɪŋ] *adj* (*charming*) séduisant(e), enchanteur(eresse).

begun [bɪ'gʌn] *pp of* **begin**.

behalf [bɪ'hɑːf] *n*: **on** ~ **of**, (*US*) **in** ~ **of** de la part de; au nom de; pour le compte de.

behave [bɪ'heɪv] *vi* se conduire, se comporter; (*well: also:* ~ **o.s.**) se conduire bien *or* comme il faut.

behaviour, (*US*) **behavior** [bɪ'heɪvjə*] *n* comportement *m*, conduite *f*.

behead [bɪ'hɛd] *vt* décapiter.

beheld [bɪ'hɛld] *pt, pp of* **behold**.

behind [bɪ'haɪnd] *prep* derrière; (*time*) en retard sur ♦ *adv* derrière; en retard ♦ *n* derrière *m*; ~ **the scenes** dans les coulisses; **to leave sth** ~ (*forget*) oublier de prendre qch; **to be** ~ **(schedule) with sth** être en retard dans qch.

behold [bɪ'həuld] *vt* (*irreg: like* **hold**) apercevoir, voir.

beige [beɪʒ] *adj* beige.

being ['biːɪŋ] *n* être *m*; **to come into** ~ prendre naissance.

Beirut [beɪ'ruːt] *n* Beyrouth.

Belarus [bɛlə'rus] *n* Bélarus *f*.

Belarussian [bɛlə'rʌʃən] *adj* biélorusse ♦ *n* Biélorusse *m/f*, (*LING*) biélorusse *m*.

belated [bɪ'leɪtɪd] *adj* tardif(ive).

belch [bɛltʃ] *vi* avoir un renvoi, roter ♦ *vt* (*also:* ~ **out:** *smoke etc*) vomir, cracher.

beleaguered [bɪ'liːgɪd] *adj* (*city*) assiégé(e); (*army*) cerné(e); (*fig*) sollicité(e) de toutes parts.

Belfast ['bɛlfɑːst] *n* Belfast.

belfry ['bɛlfrɪ] *n* beffroi *m*.

Belgian ['bɛldʒən] *adj* belge, de Belgique ♦ *n* Belge *m/f*.

Belgium ['bɛldʒəm] *n* Belgique *f*.

Belgrade [bɛl'greɪd] *n* Belgrade.

belie [bɪ'laɪ] *vt* démentir; (*give false impression of*) occulter.

belief [bɪ'liːf] *n* (*opinion*) conviction *f*; (*trust, faith*) foi *f*; (*acceptance as true*) croyance *f*; **it's beyond** ~ c'est incroyable; **in the** ~ **that** dans l'idée que.

believable [bɪ'liːvəbl] *adj* croyable.

believe [bɪ'liːv] *vt, vi* croire, estimer; **to** ~ **in** (*God*) croire en; (*ghosts, method*) croire à; **I don't** ~ **in corporal punishment** je ne suis pas partisan des châtiments corporels; **he is** ~**d to be abroad** il serait à l'étranger.

believer [bɪ'liːvə*] *n* (*in idea, activity*): ~ **in** partisan/e de; (*REL*) croyant/e.

belittle [bɪ'lɪtl] vt déprécier, rabaisser.
Belize [bɛ'liːz] n Bélize m.
bell [bɛl] n cloche f; (small) clochette f, grelot m; (on door) sonnette f; (electric) sonnerie f; **that rings a ~** (fig) cela me rappelle qch.
bell-bottoms ['bɛlbɒtəmz] npl pantalon m à pattes d'éléphant.
bellboy ['bɛlbɔɪ], (US) **bellhop** ['bɛlhɒp] n groom m, chasseur m.
belligerent [bɪ'lɪdʒərənt] adj (at war) belligérant(e); (fig) agressif(ive).
bellow ['bɛləʊ] vi mugir; beugler ♦ vt (orders) hurler.
bellows ['bɛləʊz] npl soufflet m.
bell push n (BRIT) bouton m de sonnette.
belly ['bɛlɪ] n ventre m.
bellyache ['bɛlɪeɪk] (col) n colique f ♦ vi ronchonner.
bellybutton ['bɛlɪbʌtn] n nombril m.
bellyful ['bɛlɪfʊl] n (col): **I've had a ~** j'en ai ras le bol.
belong [bɪ'lɒŋ] vi: **to ~ to** appartenir à; (club etc) faire partie de; **this book ~s here** ce livre va ici, la place de ce livre est ici.
belongings [bɪ'lɒŋɪŋz] npl affaires fpl, possessions fpl; **personal ~** effets personnels.
Belorussia [bɛlə'rʌʃə] n Biélorussie f.
Belorussian [bɛlə'rʌʃən] adj, n = **Belarussian**.
beloved [bɪ'lʌvɪd] adj (bien-)aimé(e), chéri(e) ♦ n bien-aimé/e.
below [bɪ'ləʊ] prep sous, au-dessous de ♦ adv en dessous; en contre-bas; **see ~** voir plus bas or plus loin or ci-dessous; **temperatures ~ normal** températures inférieures à la normale.
belt [bɛlt] n ceinture f; (TECH) courroie f ♦ vt (thrash) donner une raclée à ♦ vi (BRIT col) filer à (toutes jambes); **industrial ~** zone industrielle.
►**belt out** vt (song) chanter à tue-tête or à pleins poumons.
►**belt up** vi (BRIT col) la boucler.
beltway ['bɛltweɪ] n (US AUT) route f de ceinture; (: motorway) périphérique m.
bemoan [bɪ'məʊn] vt se lamenter sur.
bemused [bɪ'mjuːzd] adj médusé(e).
bench [bɛntʃ] n banc m; (in workshop) établi m; **the B~** (LAW) la magistrature, la Cour.
bench mark n repère m.
bend [bɛnd] vb (pt, pp **bent** [bɛnt]) vt courber; (leg, arm) plier ♦ vi se courber ♦ n (BRIT: in road) virage m, tournant m; (in pipe, river) coude m.
►**bend down** vi se baisser.
►**bend over** vi se pencher.
bends [bɛndz] npl (MED) maladie f des caissons.
beneath [bɪ'niːθ] prep sous, au-dessous de; (unworthy of) indigne de ♦ adv dessous, au-dessous, en bas.
benefactor ['bɛnɪfæktə*] n bienfaiteur m.
benefactress ['bɛnɪfæktrɪs] n bienfaitrice f.

beneficial [bɛnɪ'fɪʃəl] adj: **~ (to)** salutaire (pour), bénéfique (à).
beneficiary [bɛnɪ'fɪʃərɪ] n (LAW) bénéficiaire m/f.
benefit ['bɛnɪfɪt] n avantage m, profit m; (allowance of money) allocation f ♦ vt faire du bien à, profiter à ♦ vi: **he'll ~ from it** cela lui fera du bien, il y gagnera or s'en trouvera bien.
benefit performance n représentation f or gala m de bienfaisance.
Benelux ['bɛnɪlʌks] n Bénélux m.
benevolent [bɪ'nɛvələnt] adj bienveillant(e).
BEng n abbr (= Bachelor of Engineering) diplôme universitaire.
benign [bɪ'naɪn] adj (person, smile) bienveillant(e), affable; (MED) bénin(igne).
bent [bɛnt] pt, pp of **bend** ♦ n inclination f, penchant m ♦ adj (wire, pipe) coudé(e); (col: dishonest) véreux(euse); **to be ~ on** être résolu(e) à.
bequeath [bɪ'kwiːð] vt léguer.
bequest [bɪ'kwɛst] n legs m.
bereaved [bɪ'riːvd] n: **the ~** la famille du disparu ♦ adj endeuillé(e).
bereavement [bɪ'riːvmənt] n deuil m.
beret ['bɛreɪ] n béret m.
Bering Sea ['beɪrɪŋ-] n: **the ~** la mer de Béring.
berk [bɜːk] n (BRIT col) andouille m/f.
Berks abbr (BRIT) = Berkshire.
Berlin [bɜː'lɪn] n Berlin; **East/West ~** Berlin Est/Ouest.
berm [bɜːm] n (US AUT) accotement m.
Bermuda [bɜː'mjuːdə] n Bermudes fpl.
Bermuda shorts npl bermuda m.
Bern [bɜːn] n Berne.
berry ['bɛrɪ] n baie f.
berserk [bə'sɜːk] adj: **to go ~** être pris(e) d'une rage incontrôlable; se déchaîner.
berth [bɜːθ] n (bed) couchette f; (for ship) poste m d'amarrage, mouillage m ♦ vi (in harbour) venir à quai; (at anchor) mouiller; **to give sb a wide ~** (fig) éviter qn.
beseech, pt, pp **besought** [bɪ'siːtʃ, -'sɔːt] vt implorer, supplier.
beset, pt, pp **beset** [bɪ'sɛt] vt assaillir ♦ adj: **~ with** semé(e) de.
besetting [bɪ'sɛtɪŋ] adj: **his ~ sin** son vice, son gros défaut.
beside [bɪ'saɪd] prep à côté de; (compared with) par rapport à; **that's ~ the point** ça n'a rien à voir; **to be ~ o.s. (with anger)** être hors de soi.
besides [bɪ'saɪdz] adv en outre, de plus ♦ prep en plus de; (except) excepté.
besiege [bɪ'siːdʒ] vt (town) assiéger; (fig) assaillir.
besotted [bɪ'sɒtɪd] adj (BRIT): **~ with** entiché(e) de.
besought [bɪ'sɔːt] pt, pp of **beseech**.
bespectacled [bɪ'spɛktɪkld] adj à lunettes.

bespoke [bɪ'spəuk] *adj* (*BRIT*: *garment*) fait(e) sur mesure; ~ **tailor** tailleur *m* à façon.

best [bɛst] *adj* meilleur(e) ♦ *adv* le mieux; **the ~ part of** (*quantity*) le plus clair de, la plus grande partie de; **at ~** au mieux; **to make the ~ of sth** s'accommoder de qch (du mieux que l'on peut); **to do one's ~** faire de son mieux; **to the ~ of my knowledge** pour autant que je sache; **to the ~ of my ability** du mieux que je pourrai; **he's not exactly patient at the ~ of times** il n'est jamais spécialement patient; **the ~ thing to do is** ... le mieux, c'est de ....

best man *n* garçon *m* d'honneur.

bestow [bɪ'stəu] *vt* accorder; (*title*) conférer.

bestseller ['bɛst'sɛlə*] *n* bestseller *m*, succès *m* de librairie.

bet [bɛt] *n* pari *m* ♦ *vt*, *vi* (*pt*, *pp* **bet** *or* **betted**) parier; **it's a safe ~** (*fig*) il y a de fortes chances.

Bethlehem ['bɛθlɪhɛm] *n* Bethléem.

betray [bɪ'treɪ] *vt* trahir.

betrayal [bɪ'treɪəl] *n* trahison *f*.

better ['bɛtə*] *adj* meilleur(e) ♦ *adv* mieux ♦ *vt* améliorer ♦ *n*: **to get the ~ of** triompher de, l'emporter sur; **a change for the ~** une amélioration; **I had ~ go** il faut que je m'en aille; **you had ~ do it** vous feriez mieux de le faire; **he thought ~ of it** il s'est ravisé; **to get ~** aller mieux; s'améliorer; **that's ~!** c'est mieux!; ~ **off** *adj* plus à l'aise financièrement; (*fig*): **you'd be ~ off this way** vous vous en trouveriez mieux ainsi, ce serait mieux *or* plus pratique ainsi.

betting ['bɛtɪŋ] *n* paris *mpl*.

betting shop *n* (*BRIT*) bureau *m* de paris.

between [bɪ'twiːn] *prep* entre ♦ *adv* au milieu, dans l'intervalle; **the road ~ here and London** la route d'ici à Londres; **we only had 5 ~ us** nous n'en avions que 5 en tout.

bevel ['bɛvəl] *n* (*also*: ~ **edge**) biseau *m*.

beverage ['bɛvərɪdʒ] *n* boisson *f* (*gén sans alcool*).

bevy ['bɛvɪ] *n*: **a ~ of** un essaim *or* une volée de.

bewail [bɪ'weɪl] *vt* se lamenter sur.

beware [bɪ'wɛə*] *vt*, *vi*: **to ~ (of)** prendre garde (à).

bewildered [bɪ'wɪldəd] *adj* dérouté(e), ahuri(e).

bewildering [bɪ'wɪldrɪŋ] *adj* déroutant(e), ahurissant(e).

bewitching [bɪ'wɪtʃɪŋ] *adj* enchanteur(teresse).

beyond [bɪ'jɒnd] *prep* (*in space*) au-delà de; (*exceeding*) au-dessus de ♦ *adv* au-delà; ~ **doubt** hors de doute; ~ **repair** irréparable.

b/f *abbr* = brought forward.

BFPO *n abbr* (= British Forces Post Office) service postal de l'armée.

bhp *n abbr* (*AUT*: = brake horsepower) puissance *f* aux freins.

bi... [baɪ] *prefix* bi....

biannual [baɪ'ænjuəl] *adj* semestriel(le).

bias ['baɪəs] *n* (*prejudice*) préjugé *m*, parti pris; (*preference*) prévention *f*.

bias(s)ed ['baɪəst] *adj* partial(e), montrant un parti pris; **to be ~ against** avoir un préjugé contre.

biathlon [baɪ'æθlən] *n* biathlon *m*.

bib [bɪb] *n* bavoir *m*, bavette *f*.

Bible ['baɪbl] *n* Bible *f*.

Bible Belt *n* (*US*): **the ~** les États du Sud profondément protestants.

bibliography [bɪblɪ'ɒgrəfɪ] *n* bibliographie *f*.

bicarbonate of soda [baɪ'kɑːbənɪt-] *n* bicarbonate *m* de soude.

bicentenary [baɪsɛn'tiːnərɪ] *n*, **bicentennial** [baɪsɛn'tɛnɪəl] *n* bicentenaire *m*.

biceps ['baɪsɛps] *n* biceps *m*.

bicker ['bɪkə*] *vi* se chamailler.

bicycle ['baɪsɪkl] *n* bicyclette *f*.

bicycle path *n*, **bicycle track** *n* piste *f* cyclable.

bicycle pump *n* pompe *f* à vélo.

bid [bɪd] *n* offre *f*; (*at auction*) enchère *f*; (*attempt*) tentative *f* ♦ *vb* (*pt* **bid** *or* **bade** [bæd], *pp* **bid** *or* **bidden** ['bɪdn]) *vi* faire une enchère *or* offre ♦ *vt* faire une enchère *or* offre de; **to ~ sb good day** souhaiter le bonjour à qn.

bidder ['bɪdə*] *n*: **the highest ~** le plus offrant.

bidding ['bɪdɪŋ] *n* enchères *fpl*.

bide [baɪd] *vt*: **to ~ one's time** attendre son heure.

bidet ['biːdeɪ] *n* bidet *m*.

bidirectional ['baɪdɪ'rɛkʃənl] *adj* bidirectionnel(le).

biennial [baɪ'ɛnɪəl] *adj* biennal(e), bisannuel(le) ♦ *n* biennale *f*; (*plant*) plante bisannuelle.

bier [bɪə*] *n* bière *f* (*cercueil*).

bifocals [baɪ'fəuklz] *npl* lunettes *fpl* à double foyer.

big [bɪg] *adj* (*in height: person, building, tree*) grand(e); (*in bulk, amount: person, parcel, book*) gros(se); **to do things in a ~ way** faire les choses en grand.

bigamy ['bɪgəmɪ] *n* bigamie *f*.

big dipper [-'dɪpə*] *n* montagnes *fpl* russes.

big end *n* (*AUT*) tête *f* de bielle.

biggish ['bɪgɪʃ] *adj* (*see big*) assez grand(e); assez gros(se).

bigheaded ['bɪg'hɛdɪd] *adj* prétentieux(euse).

big-hearted ['bɪg'hɑːtɪd] *adj* au grand cœur.

bigot ['bɪgət] *n* fanatique *m/f*, sectaire *m/f*.

bigoted ['bɪgətɪd] *adj* fanatique, sectaire.

bigotry ['bɪgətrɪ] *n* fanatisme *m*, sectarisme *m*.

big toe *n* gros orteil.

big top *n* grand chapiteau.

big wheel *n* (*at fair*) grande roue.

bigwig ['bɪgwɪg] *n* (*col*) grosse légume, huile *f*.

bike [baɪk] n vélo m, bécane f.

bikini [bɪ'kiːnɪ] n bikini m.

bilateral [baɪ'lætərl] adj bilatéral(e).

bile [baɪl] n bile f.

bilingual [baɪ'lɪŋgwəl] adj bilingue.

bilious ['bɪlɪəs] adj bilieux(euse); (fig) maussade, irritable.

bill [bɪl] n note f, facture f; (POL) projet m de loi; (US: banknote) billet m (de banque); (in restaurant) addition f, note f; (notice) affiche f; (THEAT): **on the ~** à l'affiche; (of bird) bec m ♦ vt (item) facturer; (customer) remettre la facture à; **may I have the ~ please?** (est-ce que je peux avoir) l'addition, s'il vous plaît?; **"stick or post no ~s"** "défense d'afficher"; **to fit** or **fill the ~** (fig) faire l'affaire; **~ of exchange** lettre f de change; **~ of lading** connaissement m; **~ of sale** contrat m de vente.

billboard ['bɪlbɔːd] n panneau m d'affichage.

billet ['bɪlɪt] n cantonnement m (chez l'habitant) ♦ vt (troops) cantonner.

billfold ['bɪlfəʊld] n (US) portefeuille m.

billiards ['bɪljədz] n (jeu m de) billard m.

billion ['bɪljən] n (BRIT) billion m (million de millions); (US) milliard m.

billow ['bɪləʊ] n nuage m ♦ vi (smoke) s'élever en nuage; (sail) se gonfler.

billy goat ['bɪlɪgəʊt] n bouc m.

bimbo ['bɪmbəʊ] n (col) ravissante idiote f.

bin [bɪn] n boîte f; (BRIT: also: dust~, litter~) poubelle f; (for coal) coffre m.

binary ['baɪnərɪ] adj binaire.

bind, pt, pp bound [baɪnd, baʊnd] vt attacher; (book) relier; (oblige) obliger, contraindre.

▶**bind over** vt (LAW) mettre en liberté conditionnelle.

▶**bind up** vt (wound) panser; **to be bound up in** (work, research etc) être complètement absorbé par, être accroché par; **to be bound up with** (person) être accroché à.

binder ['baɪndə*] n (file) classeur m.

binding ['baɪndɪŋ] n (of book) reliure f ♦ adj (contract) qui constitue une obligation.

binge [bɪndʒ] n (col): **to go on a ~** faire la bringue.

bingo ['bɪŋgəʊ] n sorte de jeu de loto pratiqué dans des établissements publics.

bin liner n sac m poubelle.

binoculars [bɪ'nɔkjuləz] npl jumelles fpl.

biochemistry [baɪə'kemɪstrɪ] n biochimie f.

biodegradable ['baɪəʊdɪ'greɪdəbl] adj biodégradable.

biodiversity ['baɪəʊdaɪ'vɜːsɪtɪ] n biodiversité f.

biofuel ['baɪəʊfjuəl] n combustible m organique.

biographer [baɪ'ɔgrəfə*] n biographe m/f.

biographic(al) [baɪə'græfɪk(l)] adj biographique.

biography [baɪ'ɔgrəfɪ] n biographie f.

biological [baɪə'lɔdʒɪkl] adj biologique.

biological clock n horloge f physiologique.

biologist [baɪ'ɔlədʒɪst] n biologiste m/f.

biology [baɪ'ɔlədʒɪ] n biologie f.

biophysics ['baɪəʊ'fɪzɪks] n biophysique f.

biopic ['baɪəʊpɪk] n film m biographique.

biopsy ['baɪɒpsɪ] n biopsie f.

biosphere ['baɪəsfɪə*] n biosphère f.

biotechnology ['baɪəʊtek'nɔlədʒɪ] n biotechnologie f.

birch [bɜːtʃ] n bouleau m.

bird [bɜːd] n oiseau m; (BRIT col: girl) nana f.

bird of prey n oiseau m de proie.

bird's-eye view ['bɜːdzaɪ-] n vue f à vol d'oiseau; (fig) vue d'ensemble or générale.

bird watcher [-wɔtʃə*] n ornithologue m/f amateur.

Biro ['baɪərəʊ] n ® stylo m à bille.

birth [bɜːθ] n naissance f; **to give ~ to** donner naissance à, mettre au monde; (animal) mettre bas.

birth certificate n acte m de naissance.

birth control n limitation f des naissances; méthode(s) contraceptive(s).

birthday ['bɜːθdeɪ] n anniversaire m.

birthmark ['bɜːθmɑːk] n envie f, tache f de vin.

birthplace ['bɜːθpleɪs] n lieu m de naissance.

birth rate n (taux m de) natalité f.

Biscay ['bɪskeɪ] n: **the Bay of ~** le golfe de Gascogne.

biscuit ['bɪskɪt] n (BRIT) biscuit m; (US) petit pain au lait.

bisect [baɪ'sekt] vt couper or diviser en deux.

bisexual ['baɪ'seksjuəl] adj, n bisexuel(le).

bishop ['bɪʃəp] n évêque m; (CHESS) fou m.

bistro ['biːstrəʊ] n petit restaurant m, bistrot m.

bit [bɪt] pt of **bite** ♦ n morceau m; (of tool) mèche f; (of horse) mors m; (COMPUT) bit m, élément m binaire; **a ~ of** un peu de; **a ~ mad/dangerous** un peu fou/risqué; **~ by ~** petit à petit; **to come to ~s** (break) tomber en morceaux, se déglinguer; **bring all your ~s and pieces** apporte toutes tes affaires; **to do one's ~** y mettre du sien.

bitch [bɪtʃ] n (dog) chienne f; (col!) salope f (!), garce f.

bite [baɪt] vt, vi (pt **bit** [bɪt], pp **bitten** ['bɪtn]) mordre ♦ n morsure f; (insect ~) piqûre f; (mouthful) bouchée f; **let's have a ~ (to eat)** mangeons un morceau; **to ~ one's nails** se ronger les ongles.

biting ['baɪtɪŋ] adj mordant(e).

bit part n (THEAT) petit rôle m.

bitten ['bɪtn] pp of **bite**.

bitter ['bɪtə*] adj amer(ère); (criticism) cinglant(e); (icy: weather, wind) glacial(e) ♦ n (BRIT: beer) bière f (à forte teneur en houblon); **to the ~ end** jusqu'au bout.

bitterly ['bɪtəlɪ] adv (complain, weep) amèrement; (oppose, criticise) durement, âprement; (jealous, disappointed) horriblement; **it's ~ cold** il fait un froid de loup.

bitterness ['bɪtənɪs] n amertume f; goût amer.
bittersweet ['bɪtəswiːt] adj aigre-doux(douce).
bitty ['bɪtɪ] adj (BRIT col) décousu(e).
bitumen ['bɪtjumɪn] n bitume m.
bivouac ['bɪvuæk] n bivouac m.
bizarre [bɪ'zɑː*] adj bizarre.
bk abbr = bank, book.
BL n abbr (= Bachelor of Law(s), Bachelor of Letters) diplôme universitaire; (US: = Bachelor of Literature) diplôme universitaire.
bl abbr = bill of lading.
blab [blæb] vi jaser, trop parler ♦ vt (also: ~ out) laisser échapper, aller raconter.
black [blæk] adj noir(e) ♦ n (colour) noir m; (person): B~ noir/e ♦ vt (shoes) cirer; (BRIT INDUSTRY) boycotter; **to give sb a ~ eye** pocher l'œil à qn, faire un œil au beurre noir à qn; ~ **coffee** café noir; **there it is in ~ and white** (fig) c'est écrit noir sur blanc; **to be in the ~** (in credit) avoir un compte créditeur; ~ **and blue** adj couvert(e) de bleus.
▶**black out** vi (faint) s'évanouir.
black belt n (JUDO etc) ceinture noire; **he's a ~** il est ceinture noire.
blackberry ['blækbərɪ] n mûre f.
blackbird ['blækbəːd] n merle m.
blackboard ['blækbɔːd] n tableau noir.
black box n (AVIAT) boîte noire.
Black Country n (BRIT): **the ~** le Pays Noir (dans les Midlands).
blackcurrant ['blæk'kʌrənt] n cassis m.
black economy n (BRIT) travail m (au) noir.
blacken ['blækn] vt noircir.
Black Forest n: **the ~** la Forêt Noire.
blackhead ['blækhɛd] n point noir.
black hole n (ASTRONOMY) trou noir.
black ice n verglas m.
blackjack ['blækdʒæk] n (CARDS) vingt-et-un m; (US: truncheon) matraque f.
blackleg ['blæklɛg] n (BRIT) briseur m de grève, jaune m.
blacklist ['blæklɪst] n liste noire ♦ vt mettre sur la liste noire.
blackmail ['blækmeɪl] n chantage m ♦ vt faire chanter, soumettre au chantage.
blackmailer ['blækmeɪlə*] n maître-chanteur m.
black market n marché noir.
blackout ['blækaut] n panne f d'électricité; (in wartime) black-out m; (TV) interruption f d'émission; (fainting) syncope f.
black pepper n poivre noir.
Black Sea n: **the ~** la mer Noire.
black sheep n brebis galeuse.
blacksmith ['blæksmɪθ] n forgeron m.
black spot n (AUT) point noir.
bladder ['blædə*] n vessie f.
blade [bleɪd] n lame f; (of oar) plat m; ~ **of grass** brin m d'herbe.
blame [bleɪm] n faute f, blâme m ♦ vt: **to ~ sb/ sth for sth** attribuer à qn/qch la responsabi-

lité de qch; reprocher qch à qn/qch; **who's to ~?** qui est le fautif or coupable or responsable?; **I'm not to ~** ce n'est pas ma faute.
blameless ['bleɪmlɪs] adj irréprochable.
blanch [blɑːntʃ] vi (person, face) blêmir ♦ vt (CULIN) blanchir.
bland [blænd] adj affable; (taste) doux(douce).
blank [blæŋk] adj blanc(blanche); (look) sans expression, dénué(e) d'expression ♦ n espace m vide, blanc m; (cartridge) cartouche f à blanc; **we drew a ~** (fig) nous n'avons abouti à rien.
blank cheque, (US) **blank check** n chèque m en blanc; **to give sb a ~ to do ...** (fig) donner carte blanche à qn pour faire ...
blanket ['blæŋkɪt] n couverture f ♦ adj (statement, agreement) global(e), de portée générale; **to give ~ cover** (subj: insurance policy) couvrir tous les risques.
blare [blɛə*] vi (brass band, horns, radio) beugler.
blarney ['blɑːnɪ] n boniment m.
blasé ['blɑːzeɪ] adj blasé(e).
blasphemous ['blæsfɪməs] adj (words) blasphématoire; (person) blasphémateur(trice).
blasphemy ['blæsfɪmɪ] n blasphème m.
blast [blɑːst] n explosion f; (shock wave) souffle m; (of air, steam) bouffée f ♦ vt faire sauter or exploser ♦ excl (BRIT col) zut!; **(at) full ~** (play music etc) à plein volume.
▶**blast off** vi (SPACE) décoller.
blast-off ['blɑːstɔf] n (SPACE) lancement m.
blatant ['bleɪtənt] adj flagrant(e), criant(e).
blatantly ['bleɪtəntlɪ] adv (lie) ouvertement; **it's ~ obvious** c'est l'évidence même.
blaze [bleɪz] n (fire) incendie m; (flames: of fire, sun etc) embrasement m; (: in hearth) flamme f, flambée f; (fig) flamboiement m ♦ vi (fire) flamber; (fig) flamboyer, resplendir ♦ vt: **to ~ a trail** (fig) montrer la voie; **in a ~ of publicity** à grand renfort de publicité.
blazer ['bleɪzə*] n blazer m.
bleach [bliːtʃ] n (also: **household ~**) eau f de Javel ♦ vt (linen) blanchir.
bleached [bliːtʃt] adj (hair) oxygéné(e), décoloré(e).
bleachers ['bliːtʃəz] npl (US SPORT) gradins mpl (en plein soleil).
bleak [bliːk] adj morne, désolé(e); (weather) triste, maussade; (smile) lugubre; (prospect, future) morose.
bleary-eyed ['blɪərɪ'aɪd] adj aux yeux pleins de sommeil.
bleat [bliːt] n bêlement m ♦ vi bêler.
bleed, pt, pp **bled** [bliːd, blɛd] vt saigner; (brakes, radiator) purger ♦ vi saigner; **my nose is ~ing** je saigne du nez.
bleep [bliːp] n (RADIO, TV) top m; (of pocket device) bip m ♦ vi émettre des signaux ♦ vt (doctor etc) appeler (au moyen d'un bip).

bleeper ['bli:pə*] n (of doctor etc) bip m.
blemish ['blɛmɪʃ] n défaut m; (on reputation) tache f.
blend [blɛnd] n mélange m ♦ vt mélanger ♦ vi (colours etc) se mélanger, se fondre, s'allier.
blender ['blɛndə*] n (CULIN) mixeur m.
bless, pt, pp **blessed** or **blest** [blɛs, blɛst] vt bénir; **to be ~ed with** avoir le bonheur de jouir de or d'avoir.
blessed ['blɛsɪd] adj (REL: holy) béni(e); (happy) bienheureux(euse); **it rains every ~ day** il ne se passe pas de jour sans qu'il ne pleuve.
blessing ['blɛsɪŋ] n bénédiction f; bienfait m; **to count one's ~s** s'estimer heureux; **it was a ~ in disguise** c'est un bien pour un mal.
blew [blu:] pt of **blow**.
blight [blaɪt] n (of plants) rouille f ♦ vt (hopes etc) anéantir, briser.
blimey ['blaɪmɪ] excl (BRIT col) mince alors!
blind [blaɪnd] adj aveugle ♦ n (for window) store m ♦ vt aveugler; **to turn a ~ eye (on or to)** fermer les yeux (sur).
blind alley n impasse f.
blind corner n (BRIT) virage m sans visibilité.
blind date n rendez-vous galant (avec un(e) inconnu(e)).
blindfold ['blaɪndfəʊld] n bandeau m ♦ adj, adv les yeux bandés ♦ vt bander les yeux à.
blindly ['blaɪndlɪ] adv aveuglément.
blindness ['blaɪndnɪs] n cécité f; (fig) aveuglement m.
blind spot n (AUT etc) angle m aveugle; (fig) angle mort.
blink [blɪŋk] vi cligner des yeux; (light) clignoter ♦ n: **the TV's on the ~** (col) la télé ne va pas tarder à nous lâcher.
blinkers ['blɪŋkəz] npl œillères fpl.
blinking ['blɪŋkɪŋ] adj (BRIT col): **this ~ ...** ce fichu or sacré ....
blip [blɪp] n (on radar etc) spot m; (on graph) petite aberration; (fig) petite anomalie (passagère).
bliss [blɪs] n félicité f, bonheur m sans mélange.
blissful ['blɪsful] adj (event, day) merveilleux(euse); (smile) de bonheur; **a ~ sigh** un soupir d'aise; **in ~ ignorance** dans une ignorance béate.
blissfully ['blɪsfulɪ] adv (smile) béatement; (happy) merveilleusement.
blister ['blɪstə*] n (on skin) ampoule f, cloque f; (on paintwork) boursouflure f ♦ vi (paint) se boursoufler, se cloquer.
blithely ['blaɪðlɪ] adv (unconcernedly) tranquillement; (joyfully) gaiement.
blithering ['blɪðərɪŋ] adj (col): **this ~ idiot** cet espèce d'idiot.
BLit(t) n abbr (= Bachelor of Literature) diplôme universitaire.
blitz [blɪts] n bombardement (aérien); **to have a ~ on sth** (fig) s'attaquer à qch.

blizzard ['blɪzəd] n blizzard m, tempête f de neige.
BLM n abbr (US: = Bureau of Land Management) ≈ les domaines.
bloated ['bləʊtɪd] adj (face) bouffi(e); (stomach) gonflé(e).
blob [blɔb] n (drop) goutte f; (stain, spot) tache f.
bloc [blɔk] n (POL) bloc m.
block [blɔk] n bloc m; (in pipes) obstruction f; (toy) cube m; (of buildings) pâté m (de maisons) ♦ vt bloquer; (COMPUT) grouper; **~ of flats** (BRIT) immeuble (locatif); **3 ~s from here** à trois rues d'ici; **mental ~** blocage m; **~ and tackle** (TECH) palan m.
▶**block up** vt boucher.
blockade [blɔ'keɪd] n blocus m ♦ vt faire le blocus de.
blockage ['blɔkɪdʒ] n obstruction f.
block booking n réservation f en bloc.
blockbuster ['blɔkbʌstə*] n (film, book) grand succès.
block capitals npl majuscules fpl d'imprimerie.
blockhead ['blɔkhɛd] n imbécile m/f.
block letters npl majuscules fpl.
block release n (BRIT) congé m de formation.
block vote n (BRIT) vote m de délégation.
bloke [bləʊk] n (BRIT col) type m.
blonde [blɔnd] adj, n blond(e).
blood [blʌd] n sang m.
blood bank n banque f du sang.
blood count n numération f globulaire.
bloodcurdling ['blʌdkə:dlɪŋ] adj à vous glacer le sang.
blood donor n donneur/euse de sang.
blood group n groupe sanguin.
bloodhound ['blʌdhaund] n limier m.
bloodless ['blʌdlɪs] adj (victory) sans effusion de sang; (pale) anémié(e).
bloodletting ['blʌdlɛtɪŋ] n (MED) saignée f; (fig) effusion f de sang, représailles fpl.
blood poisoning n empoisonnement m du sang.
blood pressure n tension (artérielle); **to have high/low ~** faire de l'hypertension/l'hypotension.
bloodshed ['blʌdʃɛd] n effusion f de sang, carnage m.
bloodshot ['blʌdʃɔt] adj: **~ eyes** yeux injectés de sang.
bloodstained ['blʌdsteɪnd] adj taché(e) de sang.
bloodstream ['blʌdstri:m] n sang m, système sanguin.
blood test n analyse f de sang.
bloodthirsty ['blʌdθə:stɪ] adj sanguinaire.
blood transfusion n transfusion f de sang.
blood type n groupe sanguin.
blood vessel n vaisseau sanguin.
bloody ['blʌdɪ] adj sanglant(e); (BRIT col!): **this ~ ...** ce foutu ..., ce putain de ... (!); **~**

strong/good (*col!*) vachement *or* sacrément fort/bon.

bloody-minded ['blʌdɪ'maɪndɪd] *adj* (*BRIT col*) contrariant(e), obstiné(e).

bloom [bluːm] *n* fleur *f*; (*fig*) épanouissement *m* ♦ *vi* être en fleur; (*fig*) s'épanouir; être florissant(e).

blooming ['bluːmɪŋ] *adj* (*col*): **this** ~ ... ce fichu *or* sacré ....

blossom ['blɔsəm] *n* fleur(s) *f(pl)* ♦ *vi* être en fleurs; (*fig*) s'épanouir; **to** ~ **into** (*fig*) devenir.

blot [blɔt] *n* tache *f* ♦ *vt* tacher; (*ink*) sécher; **to be a** ~ **on the landscape** gâcher le paysage; **to** ~ **one's copy book** (*fig*) faire un impair.

▶**blot out** *vt* (*memories*) effacer; (*view*) cacher, masquer; (*nation, city*) annihiler.

blotchy ['blɔtʃɪ] *adj* (*complexion*) couvert(e) de marbrures.

blotter ['blɔtə*] *n*, **blotting paper** ['blɔtɪŋ-] *n* buvard *m*.

blotto ['blɔtəu] *adj* (*col*) bourré(e).

blouse [blauz] *n* (*feminine garment*) chemisier *m*, corsage *m*.

blow [bləu] *n* coup *m* ♦ *vb* (*pt* **blew**, *pp* **blown** [bluː, bləun]) *vi* souffler ♦ *vt* (*glass*) souffler; (*fuse*) faire sauter; **to** ~ **one's nose** se moucher; **to** ~ **a whistle** siffler; **to come to** ~**s** en venir aux coups.

▶**blow away** *vi* s'envoler ♦ *vt* chasser, faire s'envoler.

▶**blow down** *vt* faire tomber, renverser.

▶**blow off** *vi* s'envoler ♦ *vt* (*hat*) emporter; (*ship*): **to** ~ **off course** faire dévier.

▶**blow out** *vi* (*tyre*) éclater; (*fuse*) sauter.

▶**blow over** *vi* s'apaiser.

▶**blow up** *vi* exploser, sauter ♦ *vt* faire sauter; (*tyre*) gonfler; (*PHOT*) agrandir.

blow-dry ['bləudraɪ] *n* (*hairstyle*) brushing *m* ♦ *vt* faire un brushing à.

blowlamp ['bləulæmp] *n* (*BRIT*) chalumeau *m*.

blow-out ['bləuaut] *n* (*of tyre*) éclatement *m*; (*BRIT col: big meal*) gueuleton *m*.

blowtorch ['bləutɔːtʃ] *n* chalumeau *m*.

blowzy ['blauzɪ] *adj* (*BRIT*) peu soigné(e).

BLS *n abbr* (*US*) = *Bureau of Labor Statistics*.

blubber ['blʌbə*] *n* blanc *m* de baleine ♦ *vi* (*pej*) pleurer comme un veau.

bludgeon ['blʌdʒən] *n* gourdin *m*, trique *f*.

blue [bluː] *adj* bleu(e); ~ **film/joke** film *m*/ histoire *f* pornographique; (**only**) **once in a** ~ **moon** tous les trente-six du mois; **out of the** ~ (*fig*) à l'improviste, sans qu'on si attende.

blue baby *n* enfant bleu(e).

bluebell ['bluːbɛl] *n* jacinthe *f* des bois.

blueberry ['bluːbərɪ] *n* myrtille *f*, airelle *f*.

bluebottle ['bluːbɔtl] *n* mouche *f* à viande.

blue cheese *n* (*fromage*) bleu *m*.

blue-chip ['bluːtʃɪp] *adj*: ~ **investment** investissement *m* de premier ordre.

blue-collar worker ['bluːkɔlə*-] *n* ouvrier/ ère, col bleu.

blue jeans *npl* blue-jeans *mpl*.

blueprint ['bluːprɪnt] *n* bleu *m*; (*fig*) projet *m*, plan directeur.

blues [bluːz] *npl*: **the** ~ (*MUS*) le blues; **to have the** ~ (*col: feeling*) avoir le cafard.

bluff [blʌf] *vi* bluffer ♦ *n* bluff *m*; (*cliff*) promontoire *m*, falaise *f* ♦ *adj* (*person*) bourru(e), brusque; **to call sb's** ~ mettre qn au défi d'exécuter ses menaces.

blunder ['blʌndə*] *n* gaffe *f*, bévue *f* ♦ *vi* faire une gaffe *or* une bévue; **to** ~ **into sb/sth** buter contre qn/qch.

blunt [blʌnt] *adj* émoussé(e), peu tranchant(e); (*pencil*) mal taillé(e); (*person*) brusque, ne mâchant pas ses mots ♦ *vt* émousser; ~ **instrument** (*LAW*) instrument contondant.

bluntly ['blʌntlɪ] *adv* carrément, sans prendre de gants.

bluntness ['blʌntnɪs] *n* (*of person*) brusquerie *f*, franchise brutale.

blur [bləː*] *n* tache *or* masse floue *or* confuse ♦ *vt* brouiller, rendre flou(e).

blurb [bləːb] *n* (*for book*) texte *m* de présentation; (*pej*) baratin *m*.

blurred [bləːd] *adj* flou(e).

blurt [bləːt]: **to** ~ **out** *vt* (*reveal*) lâcher; (*say*) balbutier, dire d'une voix entrecoupée.

blush [blʌʃ] *vi* rougir ♦ *n* rougeur *f*.

blusher ['blʌʃə*] *n* rouge *m* à joues.

bluster ['blʌstə*] *n* paroles *fpl* en l'air; (*boasting*) fanfaronnades *fpl*; (*threats*) menaces *fpl* en l'air ♦ *vi* parler en l'air; fanfaronner.

blustering ['blʌstərɪŋ] *adj* fanfaron(ne).

blustery ['blʌstərɪ] *adj* (*weather*) à bourrasques.

Blvd *abbr* (= *boulevard*) Bd.

BM *n abbr* = *British Museum*; (*SCOL*: = *Bachelor of Medicine*) diplôme universitaire.

BMA *n abbr* = *British Medical Association*.

BMJ *n abbr* = *British Medical Journal*.

BMus *n abbr* (= *Bachelor of Music*) diplôme universitaire.

BMX *n abbr* (= *bicycle motocross*) BMX *m*.

BO *n abbr* (*col*: = *body odour*) odeurs corporelles; (*US*) = *box office*.

boar [bɔː*] *n* sanglier *m*.

board [bɔːd] *n* planche *f*; (*on wall*) panneau *m*; (*for chess etc*) plateau *m*; (*committee*) conseil *m*, comité *m*; (*in firm*) conseil d'administration; (*NAUT, AVIAT*): **on** ~ à bord ♦ *vt* (*ship*) monter à bord de; (*train*) monter dans; **full** ~ (*BRIT*) pension complète; **half** ~ (*BRIT*) demi-pension *f*; ~ **and lodging** *n* chambre *f* avec pension; **with** ~ **and lodging** logé nourri; **above** ~ (*fig*) régulier(ère); **across the** ~ (*fig: ad*) systématiquement; (: *a*) de portée générale; **to go by the** ~ être abandonné(e); (*be unimportant*) compter pour rien, n'avoir aucune importance.

▶**board up** *vt* (*door*) condamner (*au moyen de planches, de tôle*).

boarder ['bɔːdə*] n pensionnaire m/f; (SCOL) interne m/f, pensionnaire.
board game n jeu m de société.
boarding card ['bɔːdɪŋ-] n (AVIAT, NAUT) carte f d'embarquement.
boarding house ['bɔːdɪŋ-] n pension f.
boarding party ['bɔːdɪŋ-] n section f d'abordage.
boarding pass ['bɔːdɪŋ-] n (BRIT) = **boarding card**.
boarding school ['bɔːdɪŋ-] n internat m, pensionnat m.
board meeting n réunion f du conseil d'administration.
board room n salle f du conseil d'administration.
boardwalk ['bɔːdwɔːk] n (US) cheminement m en planches.
boast [bəust] vi: to ~ (about or of) se vanter (de) ♦ vt s'enorgueillir de ♦ n vantardise f; sujet m d'orgueil or de fierté.
boastful ['bəustful] adj vantard(e).
boastfulness ['bəustfulnɪs] n vantardise f.
boat [bəut] n bateau m; (small) canot m; barque f; to go by ~ aller en bateau; to be in the same ~ (fig) être logé à la même enseigne.
boater ['bəutə*] n (hat) canotier m.
boating ['bəutɪŋ] n canotage m.
boat people npl boat people mpl.
boatswain ['bəusn] n maître m d'équipage.
bob [bɔb] vi (boat, cork on water: also: ~ up and down) danser, se balancer ♦ n (BRIT col) = **shilling**.
►**bob up** vi surgir or apparaître brusquement.
bobbin ['bɔbɪn] n bobine f; (of sewing machine) navette f.
bobby ['bɔbɪ] n (BRIT col) ≈ agent m (de police).
bobby pin n (US) pince f à cheveux.
bobsleigh ['bɔbsleɪ] n bob m.
bode [bəud] vi: to ~ well/ill (for) être de bon/ mauvais augure (pour).
bodice ['bɔdɪs] n corsage m.
bodily ['bɔdɪlɪ] adj corporel(le); (pain, comfort) physique; (needs) matériel(le) ♦ adv (carry, lift) dans ses bras.
body ['bɔdɪ] n corps m; (of car) carrosserie f; (of plane) fuselage m; (also: ~ **stocking**) body m, justaucorps m; (fig: society) organe m, organisme m; (: quantity) ensemble m, masse f; (of wine) corps m; **ruling** ~ organe directeur; **in a** ~ en masse, ensemble; (speak) comme un seul et même homme.
body blow n (fig) coup dur, choc m.
body-building ['bɔdɪbɪldɪŋ] n body-building m, culturisme m.
bodyguard ['bɔdɪgɑːd] n garde m du corps.
body language n langage m du corps.
body repairs npl travaux mpl de carrosserie.
body search n fouille f (corporelle); to carry

out a ~ on sb fouiller qn; to submit to or undergo a ~ se faire fouiller.
bodywork ['bɔdɪwɔːk] n carrosserie f.
boffin ['bɔfɪn] n (BRIT) savant m.
bog [bɔg] n tourbière f ♦ vt: to get ~ged down (in) (fig) s'enliser (dans).
boggle ['bɔgl] vi: the mind ~s c'est incroyable, on en reste sidéré.
bogie ['bəugɪ] n bogie m.
Bogotá [bəugə'tɑː] n Bogotá.
bogus ['bəugəs] adj bidon inv; fantôme.
Bohemia [bəu'hiːmɪə] n Bohême f.
Bohemian [bəu'hiːmɪən] adj bohémien(ne) ♦ n Bohémien/ne; (gipsy: also: **b~**) bohémien/ne.
boil [bɔɪl] vt (faire) bouillir ♦ vi bouillir ♦ n (MED) furoncle m; to come to the or (US) a ~ bouillir; to bring to the or (US) a ~ porter à ébullition; ~ed egg œuf m à la coque; ~ed potatoes pommes fpl à l'anglaise or à l'eau.
►**boil down** vi (fig): to ~ down to se réduire or ramener à.
►**boil over** vi déborder.
boiler ['bɔɪlə*] n chaudière f.
boiler suit n (BRIT) bleu m de travail, combinaison f.
boiling ['bɔɪlɪŋ] adj: I'm ~ (hot) (col) je crève de chaud.
boiling point n point m d'ébullition.
boil-in-the-bag [bɔɪlɪnðə'bæg] adj (rice etc) en sachet cuisson.
boisterous ['bɔɪstərəs] adj bruyant(e), tapageur(euse).
bold [bəuld] adj hardi(e), audacieux(euse); (pej) effronté(e); (outline, colour) franc(franche), tranché(e), marqué(e).
boldness ['bəuldnɪs] n hardiesse f, audace f; aplomb m, effronterie f.
bold type n (TYP) caractères mpl gras.
Bolivia [bə'lɪvɪə] n Bolivie f.
Bolivian [bə'lɪvɪən] adj bolivien(ne) ♦ n Bolivien/ne.
bollard ['bɔləd] n (NAUT) bitte f d'amarrage; (BRIT AUT) borne lumineuse or de signalisation.
bolshy ['bɔlʃɪ] adj râleur(euse); to be in a ~ mood être peu coopératif(ive).
bolster ['bəulstə*] n traversin m.
►**bolster up** vt soutenir.
bolt [bəult] n verrou m; (with nut) boulon m ♦ adv: ~ upright droit(e) comme un piquet ♦ vt verrouiller; (food) engloutir ♦ vi se sauver, filer (comme une flèche); a ~ from the blue (fig) un coup de tonnerre dans un ciel bleu.
bomb [bɔm] n bombe f ♦ vt bombarder.
bombard [bɔm'bɑːd] vt bombarder.
bombardment [bɔm'bɑːdmənt] n bombardement m.
bombastic [bɔm'bæstɪk] adj grandiloquent(e), pompeux(euse).
bomb disposal n: ~ **unit** section f de déminage; ~ **expert** artificier m.

bomber ['bɔmə*] n caporal m d'artillerie; (*AVIAT*) bombardier m; (*terrorist*) poseur m de bombes.

bombing ['bɔmɪŋ] n bombardement m.

bomb scare n alerte f à la bombe.

bombshell ['bɔmʃɛl] n obus m; (*fig*) bombe f.

bomb site n zone f de bombardement.

bona fide ['bəunə'faɪdɪ] adj de bonne foi; (*offer*) sérieux(euse).

bonanza [bə'nænzə] n filon m.

bond [bɔnd] n lien m; (*binding promise*) engagement m, obligation f; (*FINANCE*) obligation; **in ~** (*of goods*) en entrepôt.

bondage ['bɔndɪdʒ] n esclavage m.

bonded warehouse ['bɔndɪd-] n entrepôt m sous douanes.

bone [bəun] n os m; (*of fish*) arête f ♦ vt désosser; ôter les arêtes de.

bone china n porcelaine f tendre.

bone-dry ['bəun'draɪ] adj absolument sec(sèche).

bone idle adj fainéant(e).

bone marrow n moelle osseuse.

boner ['bəunə*] n (*US*) gaffe f, bourde f.

bonfire ['bɔnfaɪə*] n feu m (de joie); (*for rubbish*) feu.

bonk [bɔŋk] (*col!*) vt s'envoyer (!), sauter (!) ♦ vi s'envoyer en l'air (!).

bonkers ['bɔŋkəz] adj (*BRIT col*) cinglé(e), dingue.

Bonn [bɔn] n Bonn.

bonnet ['bɔnɪt] n bonnet m; (*BRIT: of car*) capot m.

bonny [bɔnɪ] adj (*Scottish*) joli(e).

bonus ['bəunəs] n prime f, gratification f; (*on wages*) prime.

bony ['bəunɪ] adj (*arm, face, MED: tissue*) osseux(euse); (*thin: person*) squelettique; (*meat*) plein(e) d'os; (*fish*) plein d'arêtes.

boo [bu:] excl hou!, peuh! ♦ vt huer ♦ n huée f.

boob [bu:b] n (*col: breast*) nichon m; (: *BRIT: mistake*) gaffe f.

booby prize ['bu:bɪ-] n timbale f (ironique).

booby trap ['bu:bɪ-] n guet-apens m.

booby-trapped ['bu:bɪtræpt] adj piégé(e).

book [buk] n livre m; (*of stamps etc*) carnet m; (*COMM*): **~s** comptes mpl, comptabilité f ♦ vt (*ticket*) prendre; (*seat, room, table*) réserver; (*driver*) dresser un procès-verbal à; (*football player*) prendre le nom de, donner un carton à; **to keep the ~s** tenir la comptabilité; **by the ~** à la lettre, selon les règles; **to throw the ~ at sb** passer un savon à qn.

▶**book in** vi (*BRIT: at hotel*) prendre sa chambre.

▶**book up** vt réserver; **all seats are ~ed up** tout est pris, c'est complet; **the hotel is ~ed up** l'hôtel est complet.

bookable ['bukəbl] adj: **seats are ~** on peut réserver ses places.

bookcase ['bukkeɪs] n bibliothèque f (meuble).

book ends npl serre-livres m inv.

booking ['bukɪŋ] n (*BRIT*) réservation f.

booking office n (*BRIT*) bureau m de location.

book-keeping ['buk'ki:pɪŋ] n comptabilité f.

booklet ['buklɪt] n brochure f.

bookmaker ['bukmeɪkə*] n bookmaker m.

bookseller ['buksɛlə*] n libraire m/f.

bookshelf ['bukʃɛlf] n (*single*) étagère f (à livres); **bookshelves** rayons mpl (de bibliothèque).

bookshop ['bukʃɔp] n librairie f.

bookstall ['bukstɔ:l] n kiosque m à journaux.

book token n bon-cadeau m (pour un livre).

book value n valeur f comptable.

bookworm ['bukwə:m] n dévoreur/euse de livres.

boom [bu:m] n (*noise*) grondement m; (*busy period*) boom m, vague f de prospérité ♦ vi gronder; prospérer.

boomerang ['bu:məræŋ] n boomerang m.

boom town n ville f en plein essor.

boon [bu:n] n bénédiction f, grand avantage.

boorish ['buərɪʃ] adj grossier(ère), rustre.

boost [bu:st] n stimulant m, remontant m ♦ vt stimuler; **to give a ~ to sb's spirits** or **to sb** remonter le moral à qn.

booster ['bu:stə*] n (*TV*) amplificateur m (de signal); (*ELEC*) survolteur m; (*also: ~ rocket*) booster m; (*MED: vaccine*) rappel m.

booster seat n (*AUT: for children*) siège m rehausseur.

boot [bu:t] n botte f; (*for hiking*) chaussure f (de marche); (*for football etc*) soulier m; (*ankle ~*) bottine f; (*BRIT: of car*) coffre m ♦ vt (*COMPUT*) lancer, mettre en route; **to ~** (*in addition*) par-dessus le marché, en plus; **to give sb the ~** (*col*) flanquer qn dehors, virer qn.

booth [bu:ð] n (*at fair*) baraque (foraine); (*of cinema, telephone etc*) cabine f; (*also: voting ~*) isoloir m.

bootleg ['bu:tlɛg] adj de contrebande; **~ record** enregistrement m pirate.

booty ['bu:tɪ] n butin m.

booze [bu:z] (*col*) n boissons fpl alcooliques, alcool m ♦ vi boire, picoler.

boozer ['bu:zə*] n (*col: person*): **he's a ~** il picole pas mal; (*BRIT col: pub*) pub m.

border ['bɔ:də*] n bordure f; bord m; (*of a country*) frontière f; **the B~** la frontière entre l'Écosse et l'Angleterre; **the B~s** la région frontière entre l'Écosse et l'Angleterre.

▶**border on** vt fus être voisin(e) de, toucher à.

borderline ['bɔ:dəlaɪn] n (*fig*) ligne f de démarcation ♦ adj: **~ case** cas m limite.

bore [bɔ:*] pt of **bear** ♦ vt (*hole*) percer; (*person*) ennuyer, raser ♦ n (*person*) raseur/euse; (*of gun*) calibre m; **he's ~d to tears** or **~d to death** or **~d stiff** il s'ennuie à mourir.

boredom ['bɔ:dəm] n ennui m.

boring ['bɔ:rɪŋ] adj ennuyeux(euse).

born [bɔ:n] adj: **to be ~** naître; **I was ~ in 1960** je suis né en 1960; **~ blind** aveugle de nais-

sance; **a ~ comedian** un comédien-né.
born-again [bɔːnə'gɛn] *adj*: **~ Christian** ≈ évangeliste *m/f*.
borne [bɔːn] *pp of* **bear**.
Borneo ['bɔːnɪəu] *n* Bornéo *f*.
borough ['bʌrə] *n* municipalité *f*.
borrow ['bɔrəu] *vt*: **to ~ sth (from sb)** emprunter qch (à qn); **may I ~ your car?** est-ce que je peux vous emprunter votre voiture?
borrower ['bɔrəuə*] *n* emprunteur/euse.
borrowing ['bɔrəuɪŋ] *n* emprunt(s) *m(pl)*.
borstal ['bɔːstl] *n* (BRIT) ≈ maison *f* de correction.
Bosnia ['bɔznɪə] *n* Bosnie *f*.
Bosnia-Herzegovina ['bɔznɪəhɜːtsəgəu'viːnə] *n* (*also*: **Bosnia-Hercegovina**) Bosnie-Herzégovine *f*.
Bosnian ['bɔznɪən] *adj* bosniaque, bosnien(ne) ♦ *n* Bosniaque *m/f*, Bosnien/ne.
bosom ['buzəm] *n* poitrine *f*; (*fig*) sein *m*.
bosom friend *n* ami/e intime.
boss [bɔs] *n* patron/ne ♦ *vt* (*also*: **~ about**, **~ around**) mener à la baguette.
bossy ['bɔsɪ] *adj* autoritaire.
bosun ['bəusn] *n* maître *m* d'équipage.
botanical [bə'tænɪkl] *adj* botanique.
botanist ['bɔtənɪst] *n* botaniste *m/f*.
botany ['bɔtənɪ] *n* botanique *f*.
botch [bɔtʃ] *vt* (*also*: **~ up**) saboter, bâcler.
both [bəuθ] *adj* les deux, l'un(e) et l'autre ♦ *pron*: **~ (of them)** les deux, tous(toutes) (les) deux, l'un(e) et l'autre; **~ of us went**, **we ~ went** nous y sommes allés tous les deux ♦ *adv*: **they sell ~ the fabric and the finished curtains** ils vendent (et) le tissu et les rideaux (finis), ils vendent à la fois le tissu et les rideaux (finis).
bother ['bɔðə*] *vt* (*worry*) tracasser; (*needle, bait*) importuner, ennuyer; (*disturb*) déranger ♦ *vi* (*also*: **~ o.s.**) se tracasser, se faire du souci ♦ *n*: **it is a ~ to have to do** c'est vraiment ennuyeux d'avoir à faire ♦ *excl* zut!; **to ~ doing** prendre la peine de faire; **I'm sorry to ~ you** excusez-moi de vous déranger; **please don't ~** ne vous dérangez pas; **don't ~** ce n'est pas la peine; **it's no ~** aucun problème.
Botswana [bɔt'swɑːnə] *n* Botswana *m*.
bottle ['bɔtl] *n* bouteille *f*; (*baby's*) biberon *m*; (*of perfume, medicine*) flacon *m* ♦ *vt* mettre en bouteille(s); **~ of wine/milk** bouteille de vin/lait; **wine/milk ~** bouteille à vin/lait.
▶**bottle up** *vt* refouler, contenir.
bottle bank *n* conteneur *m* (de bouteilles).
bottleneck ['bɔtlnɛk] *n* (*in traffic*) bouchon *m*; (*in production*) goulet *m* d'étranglement.
bottle-opener ['bɔtləupnə*] *n* ouvre-bouteille *m*.
bottom ['bɔtəm] *n* (*of container, sea etc*) fond *m*; (*buttocks*) derrière *m*; (*of page, list*) bas *m*; (*of chair*) siège *m*; (*of mountain, tree, hill*) pied *m* ♦ *adj* du fond; du bas; **to get to the ~ of sth**

(*fig*) découvrir le fin fond de qch.
bottomless ['bɔtəmlɪs] *adj* sans fond, insondable.
bottom line *n*: **the ~ is that ...** l'essentiel, c'est que ....
botulism ['bɔtjulɪzəm] *n* botulisme *m*.
bough [bau] *n* branche *f*, rameau *m*.
bought [bɔːt] *pt, pp of* **buy**.
boulder ['bəuldə*] *n* gros rocher (*gén lisse, arrondi*).
bounce [bauns] *vi* (*ball*) rebondir; (*cheque*) être refusé (*étant sans provision*); (*also*: **to ~ forward/out** *etc*) bondir, s'élancer ♦ *vt* faire rebondir ♦ *n* (*rebound*) rebond *m*; **he's got plenty of ~** (*fig*) il est plein d'entrain *or* d'allant.
bouncer ['baunsə*] *n* (*col*) videur *m*.
bouncy castle ['baunsɪ-] *n* ® château *m* gonflable.
bound [baund] *pt, pp of* **bind** ♦ *n* (*gen pl*) limite *f*; (*leap*) bond *m* ♦ *vt* (*leap*) bondir; (*limit*) borner ♦ *adj*: **to be ~ to do sth** (*obliged*) être obligé(e) *or* avoir obligation de faire qch; **he's ~ to fail** (*likely*) il est sûr d'échouer, son échec est inévitable *or* assuré; **~ for** à destination de; **out of ~s** dont l'accès est interdit.
boundary ['baundrɪ] *n* frontière *f*.
boundless ['baundlɪs] *adj* illimité(e), sans bornes.
bountiful ['bauntɪful] *adj* (*person*) généreux(euse); (*God*) bienfaiteur(trice); (*supply*) ample.
bounty ['bauntɪ] *n* (*generosity*) générosité *f*.
bouquet ['bukeɪ] *n* bouquet *m*.
bourbon ['buəbən] *n* (*US: also*: **~ whiskey**) bourbon *m*.
bourgeois ['buəʒwɑː] *adj, n* bourgeois(e).
bout [baut] *n* période *f*; (*of malaria etc*) accès *m*, crise *f*, attaque *f*; (BOXING *etc*) combat *m*, match *m*.
boutique [buː'tiːk] *n* boutique *f*.
bow[1] [bəu] *n* nœud *m*; (*weapon*) arc *m*; (MUS) archet *m*.
bow[2] [bau] *n* (*with body*) révérence *f*, inclination *f* (du buste *or* corps); (NAUT: *also*: **~s**) proue *f* ♦ *vi* faire une révérence, s'incliner; (*yield*): **to ~ to** *or* **before** s'incliner devant, se soumettre à; **to ~ to the inevitable** accepter l'inévitable *or* l'inéluctable.
bowels [bauəlz] *npl* intestins *mpl*; (*fig*) entrailles *fpl*.
bowl [bəul] *n* (*for eating*) bol *m*; (*for washing*) cuvette *f*; (*ball*) boule *f*; (*of pipe*) fourneau *m* ♦ *vi* (CRICKET) lancer (la balle).
▶**bowl over** *vt* (*fig*) renverser.
bow-legged ['bəu'lɛgɪd] *adj* aux jambes arquées.
bowler ['bəulə*] *n* joueur *m* de boules; (CRICKET) lanceur *m* (de la balle); (BRIT: *also*: **~ hat**) (chapeau *m*) melon *m*.
bowling ['bəulɪŋ] *n* (*game*) jeu *m* de boules;

jeu de quilles.
bowling alley *n* bowling *m*.
bowling green *n* terrain *m* de boules (*gazonné et carré*).
bowls [bəʊlz] *n* (jeu *m* de) boules *fpl*.
bow tie [bəʊ-] *n* nœud *m* papillon.
box [bɔks] *n* boîte *f*; (*also*: **cardboard ~**) carton *m*; (*crate*) caisse *f*; (*THEAT*) loge *f*; (*BRIT AUT*) intersection *f* (*matérialisée par des marques au sol*) ♦ *vt* mettre en boîte; (*SPORT*) boxer avec ♦ *vi* boxer, faire de la boxe.
boxcar [ˈbɔkskɑ:*] *n* (*US RAIL*) wagon *m* (de marchandises) couvert.
boxer [ˈbɔksə*] *n* (*person*) boxeur *m*; (*dog*) boxer *m*.
boxing [ˈbɔksɪŋ] *n* (*sport*) boxe *f*.
Boxing Day *n* (*BRIT*) le lendemain de Noël.

Boxing Day *est le lendemain de Noël, férié en Grande-Bretagne. Si Noël tombe un samedi, le jour férié est reculé jusqu'au lundi suivant. Ce nom vient d'une coutume du XIXe siècle qui consistait à donner des cadeaux de Noël (dans des boîtes) à ses employés etc le 26 décembre.*

---

boxing gloves *npl* gants *mpl* de boxe.
boxing ring *n* ring *m*.
box number *n* (*for advertisements*) numéro *m* d'annonce.
box office *n* bureau *m* de location.
box room *n* débarras *m*; chambrette *f*.
boy [bɔɪ] *n* garçon *m*.
boycott [ˈbɔɪkɔt] *n* boycottage *m* ♦ *vt* boycotter.
boyfriend [ˈbɔɪfrɛnd] *n* (petit) ami.
boyish [ˈbɔɪɪʃ] *adj* d'enfant, de garçon; **to look ~** (*man: appear youthful*) faire jeune.
Bp *abbr* = **bishop**.
BR *abbr* = **British Rail**.
Br. *abbr* (*REL*) = **brother**.
bra [brɑ:] *n* soutien-gorge *m*.
brace [breɪs] *n* attache *f*, agrafe *f*; (*on teeth*) appareil *m* (dentaire); (*tool*) vilbrequin *m*; (*TYP*: *also*: **~ bracket**) accolade *f* ♦ *vt* consolider, soutenir; **to ~ o.s.** (*fig*) se préparer mentalement.
bracelet [ˈbreɪslɪt] *n* bracelet *m*.
braces [ˈbreɪsɪz] *npl* (*BRIT*) bretelles *fpl*.
bracing [ˈbreɪsɪŋ] *adj* tonifiant(e), tonique.
bracken [ˈbrækən] *n* fougère *f*.
bracket [ˈbrækɪt] *n* (*TECH*) tasseau *m*, support *m*; (*group*) classe *f*, tranche *f*; (*also*: **brace ~**) accolade *f*; (*also*: **round ~**) parenthèse *f*; (*also*: **square ~**) crochet *m* ♦ *vt* mettre entre parenthèses; (*fig*: *also*: **~ together**) regrouper; **income ~** tranche *f* des revenus; **in ~s** entre parenthèses (*or* crochets).
brackish [ˈbrækɪʃ] *adj* (*water*) saumâtre.
brag [bræg] *vi* se vanter.
braid [breɪd] *n* (*trimming*) galon *m*; (*of hair*) tresse *f*, natte *f*.
Braille [breɪl] *n* braille *m*.

brain [breɪn] *n* cerveau *m*; **~s** *npl* cervelle *f*; **he's got ~s** il est intelligent.
brainchild [ˈbreɪntʃaɪld] *n* trouvaille (personnelle), invention *f*.
braindead [ˈbreɪndɛd] *adj* (*MED*) dans un coma dépassé; (*col*) demeuré(e).
brainless [ˈbreɪnlɪs] *adj* sans cervelle, stupide.
brainstorm [ˈbreɪnstɔ:m] *n* (*fig*) moment *m* d'égarement; (*US*: **brainwave**) idée *f* de génie.
brainwash [ˈbreɪnwɔʃ] *vt* faire subir un lavage de cerveau à.
brainwave [ˈbreɪnweɪv] *n* idée *f* de génie.
brainy [ˈbreɪnɪ] *adj* intelligent(e), doué(e).
braise [breɪz] *vt* braiser.
brake [breɪk] *n* (*on vehicle*) frein *m* ♦ *vt*, *vi* freiner.
brake light *n* feu *m* de stop.
brake pedal *n* pédale *f* de frein.
bramble [ˈbræmbl] *n* ronces *fpl*; (*fruit*) mûre *f*.
bran [bræn] *n* son *m*.
branch [brɑ:ntʃ] *n* branche *f*; (*COMM*) succursale *f*; (: *bank*) agence *f*; (*of association*) section locale ♦ *vi* bifurquer.
▶**branch out** *vi* diversifier ses activités; **to ~ out into** étendre ses activités à.
branch line *n* (*RAIL*) bifurcation *f*, embranchement *m*.
branch manager *n* directeur/trice de succursale (*or* d'agence).
brand [brænd] *n* marque (commerciale) ♦ *vt* (*cattle*) marquer (au fer rouge); (*fig*: *pej*): **to ~ sb a communist** *etc* traiter *or* qualifier qn de communiste *etc*.
brandish [ˈbrændɪʃ] *vt* brandir.
brand name *n* nom *m* de marque.
brand-new [ˈbrænd'nju:] *adj* tout(e) neuf(neuve), flambant neuf(neuve).
brandy [ˈbrændɪ] *n* cognac *m*, fine *f*.
brash [bræʃ] *adj* effronté(e).
Brasilia [brəˈzɪlɪə] *n* Brasilia.
brass [brɑ:s] *n* cuivre *m* (jaune), laiton *m*; **the ~** (*MUS*) les cuivres.
brass band *n* fanfare *f*.
brassiere [ˈbræsɪə*] *n* soutien-gorge *m*.
brass tacks *npl*: **to get down to ~** en venir au fait.
brat [bræt] *n* (*pej*) mioche *m/f*, môme *m/f*.
bravado [brəˈvɑ:dəʊ] *n* bravade *f*.
brave [breɪv] *adj* courageux(euse), brave ♦ *n* guerrier indien ♦ *vt* braver, affronter.
bravery [ˈbreɪvərɪ] *n* bravoure *f*, courage *m*.
bravo [brɑ:ˈvəʊ] *excl* bravo!
brawl [brɔ:l] *n* rixe *f*, bagarre *f* ♦ *vi* se bagarrer.
brawn [brɔ:n] *n* muscle *m*; (*meat*) fromage *m* de tête.
brawny [ˈbrɔ:nɪ] *adj* musclé(e), costaud(e).
bray [breɪ] *n* braiement *m* ♦ *vi* braire.
brazen [ˈbreɪzn] *adj* impudent(e), effronté(e) ♦ *vt*: **to ~ it out** payer d'effronterie, crâner.
brazier [ˈbreɪzɪə*] *n* brasero *m*.
Brazil [brəˈzɪl] *n* Brésil *m*.

Brazilian [brə'zıljən] *adj* brésilien(ne) ♦ *n* Brésilien/ne.

Brazil nut *n* noix *f* du Brésil.

breach [bri:tʃ] *vt* ouvrir une brèche dans ♦ *n* (*gap*) brèche *f*; (*estrangement*) brouille *f*; (*breaking*): ~ **of contract** rupture *f* de contrat; ~ **of the peace** attentat *m* à l'ordre public; ~ **of trust** abus *m* de confiance.

bread [brɛd] *n* pain *m*; (*col: money*) fric *m*; ~ **and butter** *n* tartines (beurrées); (*fig*) subsistance *f*; **to earn one's daily** ~ gagner son pain; **to know which side one's** ~ **is buttered (on)** savoir où est son avantage *or* intérêt.

breadbin ['brɛdbın] *n* (*BRIT*) boîte *f or* huche *f* à pain.

breadboard ['brɛdbɔːd] *n* planche *f* à pain; (*COMPUT*) montage expérimental.

breadbox ['brɛdbɔks] *n* (*US*) boîte *f or* huche *f* à pain.

breadcrumbs ['brɛdkrʌmz] *npl* miettes *fpl* de pain; (*CULIN*) chapelure *f*, panure *f*.

breadline ['brɛdlaın] *n*: **to be on the** ~ être sans le sou *or* dans l'indigence.

breadth [brɛtθ] *n* largeur *f*.

breadwinner ['brɛdwınə*] *n* soutien *m* de famille.

break [breık] *vb* (*pt* **broke** [brəuk], *pp* **broken** ['brəukən]) *vt* casser, briser; (*promise*) rompre; (*law*) violer ♦ *vi* (se) casser, se briser; (*weather*) tourner ♦ *n* (*gap*) brèche *f*; (*fracture*) cassure *f*; (*rest*) interruption *f*, arrêt *m*; (: *short*) pause *f*; (: *at school*) récréation *f*; (*chance*) chance *f*, occasion *f* favorable; **to** ~ **one's leg** *etc* se casser la jambe *etc*; **to** ~ **a record** battre un record; **to** ~ **the news to sb** annoncer la nouvelle à qn; **to** ~ **with sb** rompre avec qn; **to** ~ **even** *vi* rentrer dans ses frais; **to** ~ **free** *or* **loose** *vi* se dégager, s'échapper; **to take a** ~ (*few minutes*) faire une pause, s'arrêter cinq minutes; (*holiday*) prendre un peu de repos; **without a** ~ sans interruption, sans arrêt.

►**break down** *vt* (*door etc*) enfoncer; (*resistance*) venir à bout de; (*figures, data*) décomposer, analyser ♦ *vi* s'effondrer; (*MED*) faire une dépression (nerveuse); (*AUT*) tomber en panne.

►**break in** *vt* (*horse etc*) dresser ♦ *vi* (*burglar*) entrer par effraction.

►**break into** *vt fus* (*house*) s'introduire *or* pénétrer par effraction dans.

►**break off** *vi* (*speaker*) s'interrompre; (*branch*) se rompre ♦ *vt* (*talks, engagement*) rompre.

►**break open** *vt* (*door etc*) forcer, fracturer.

►**break out** *vi* éclater, se déclarer; **to** ~ **out in spots** se couvrir de boutons.

►**break through** *vi*: **the sun broke through** le soleil a fait son apparition ♦ *vt fus* (*defences, barrier*) franchir; (*crowd*) se frayer un passage à travers.

►**break up** *vi* (*partnership*) cesser, prendre

fin; (*marriage*) se briser; (*friends*) se séparer ♦ *vt* fracasser, casser; (*fight etc*) interrompre, faire cesser; (*marriage*) désunir.

breakable ['breıkəbl] *adj* cassable, fragile ♦ *n*: ~**s** objets *mpl* fragiles.

breakage ['breıkıdʒ] *n* casse *f*; **to pay for** ~**s** payer la casse.

breakaway ['breıkəweı] *adj* (*group etc*) dissident(e).

breakdown ['breıkdaun] *n* (*AUT*) panne *f*; (*in communications*) rupture *f*; (*MED: also:* **nervous** ~) dépression (nerveuse); (*of figures*) ventilation *f*, répartition *f*.

breakdown service *n* (*BRIT*) service *m* de dépannage.

breakdown van *n* (*BRIT*) dépanneuse *f*.

breaker ['breıkə*] *n* brisant *m*.

breakeven ['breık'i:vn] *cpd*: ~ **chart** graphique *m* de rentabilité; ~ **point** seuil *m* de rentabilité.

breakfast ['brɛkfəst] *n* petit déjeuner *m*.

breakfast cereal *n* céréales *fpl*.

break-in ['breıkın] *n* cambriolage *m*.

breaking point ['breıkıŋ-] *n* limites *fpl*.

breakthrough ['breıkθru:] *n* percée *f*.

break-up ['breıkʌp] *n* (*of partnership, marriage*) rupture *f*.

break-up value *n* (*COMM*) valeur *f* de liquidation.

breakwater ['breıkwɔːtə*] *n* brise-lames *m inv*, digue *f*.

breast [brɛst] *n* (*of woman*) sein *m*; (*chest*) poitrine *f*.

breast-feed ['brɛstfi:d] *vt*, *vi* (*irreg: like* **feed**) allaiter.

breast pocket *n* poche *f* (de) poitrine.

breaststroke ['brɛststrəuk] *n* brasse *f*.

breath [brɛθ] *n* haleine *f*, souffle *m*; **to go out for a** ~ **of air** sortir prendre l'air; **out of** ~ à bout de souffle, essoufflé(e).

breathalyse ['brɛeəlaız] *vt* faire subir l'alcootest à.

Breathalyser ['brɛeəlaızə*] *n* ® alcootest *m*.

breathe [bri:ð] *vt*, *vi* respirer; **I won't** ~ **a word about it** je n'en soufflerai pas mot, je n'en dirai rien à personne.

►**breathe in** *vi* inspirer ♦ *vt* aspirer.

►**breathe out** *vt*, *vi* expirer.

breather ['bri:ðə*] *n* moment *m* de repos *or* de répit.

breathing ['bri:ðıŋ] *n* respiration *f*.

breathing space *n* (*fig*) (moment *m* de) répit *m*.

breathless ['brɛθlıs] *adj* essoufflé(e), haletant(e); oppressé(e); ~ **with excitement** le souffle coupé par l'émotion.

breath-taking ['brɛθteıkıŋ] *adj* stupéfiant(e), à vous couper le souffle.

breath test *n* alcootest *m*.

-bred [brɛd] *suffix*: **well/ill**~ bien/mal élevé(e).

breed [bri:d] (*pt*, *pp* **bred** [brɛd]) *vt* élever, faire l'élevage de; (*fig: hate, suspicion*) engendrer ♦ *vi* se reproduire ♦ *n* race *f*, variété *f*.

breeder ['bri:də*] *n* (*person*) éleveur *m*; (*PHYSICS: also*: ~ **reactor**) (réacteur *m*) surrégénérateur *m*.

breeding ['bri:dɪŋ] *n* reproduction *f*; élevage *m*; (*upbringing*) éducation *f*.

breeze [bri:z] *n* brise *f*.

breezeblock ['bri:zblɔk] *n* (*BRIT*) parpaing *m* (*de laitier*).

breezy ['bri:zɪ] *adj* frais(fraîche); aéré(e); désinvolte, jovial(e).

Breton ['brɛtən] *adj* breton(ne) ♦ *n* Breton/ne; (*LING*) breton *m*.

brevity ['brɛvɪtɪ] *n* brièveté *f*.

brew [bru:] *vt* (*tea*) faire infuser; (*beer*) brasser; (*plot*) tramer, préparer ♦ *vi* (*tea*) infuser; (*beer*) fermenter; (*fig*) se préparer, couver.

brewer ['bru:ə*] *n* brasseur *m*.

brewery ['bru:ərɪ] *n* brasserie *f* (*fabrique*).

briar ['braɪə*] *n* (*thorny bush*) ronces *fpl*; (*wild rose*) églantine *f*.

bribe [braɪb] *n* pot-de-vin *m* ♦ *vt* acheter; soudoyer; **to** ~ **sb to do sth** soudoyer qn pour qu'il fasse qch.

bribery ['braɪbərɪ] *n* corruption *f*.

bric-a-brac ['brɪkəbræk] *n* bric-à-brac *m*.

brick [brɪk] *n* brique *f*.

bricklayer ['brɪkleɪə*] *n* maçon *m*.

brickwork ['brɪkwə:k] *n* briquetage *m*, maçonnerie *f*.

brickworks ['brɪkwə:ks] *n* briqueterie *f*.

bridal ['braɪdl] *adj* nuptial(e); ~ **party** noce *f*.

bride [braɪd] *n* mariée *f*, épouse *f*.

bridegroom ['braɪdgru:m] *n* marié *m*, époux *m*.

bridesmaid ['braɪdzmeɪd] *n* demoiselle *f* d'honneur.

bridge [brɪdʒ] *n* pont *m*; (*NAUT*) passerelle *f* (de commandement); (*of nose*) arête *f*; (*CARDS, DENTISTRY*) bridge *m* ♦ *vt* (*river*) construire un pont sur; (*gap*) combler.

bridging loan ['brɪdʒɪŋ-] *n* (*BRIT*) prêt *m* relais.

bridle ['braɪdl] *n* bride *f* ♦ *vt* refréner, mettre la bride à; (*horse*) brider.

bridle path *n* piste *or* allée cavalière.

brief [bri:f] *adj* bref(brève) ♦ *n* (*LAW*) dossier *m*, cause *f* ♦ *vt* (*MIL etc*) donner des instructions à; **in** ~ ... (en) bref ...; **to** ~ **sb** (**about sth**) mettre qn au courant (de qch).

briefcase ['bri:fkeɪs] *n* serviette *f*; porte-documents *m inv*.

briefing ['bri:fɪŋ] *n* instructions *fpl*.

briefly ['bri:flɪ] *adv* brièvement; (*visit*) en coup de vent; **to glimpse** ~ entrevoir.

briefness ['bri:fnɪs] *n* brièveté *f*.

briefs [bri:fs] *npl* slip *m*.

Brig. *abbr* = **brigadier**.

brigade [brɪ'geɪd] *n* (*MIL*) brigade *f*.

brigadier [brɪgə'dɪə*] *n* brigadier général.

bright [braɪt] *adj* brillant(e); (*room, weather*) clair(e); (*person*) intelligent(e), doué(e); (*colour*) vif(vive); **to look on the** ~ **side** regarder le bon côté des choses.

brighten ['braɪtn] (*also*: ~ **up**) *vt* (*room*) éclaircir; égayer ♦ *vi* s'éclaircir; (*person*) retrouver un peu de sa gaieté.

brightly ['braɪtlɪ] *adv* brillamment.

brill [brɪl] *adj* (*BRIT col*) super *inv*.

brilliance ['brɪljəns] *n* éclat *m*; (*fig: of person*) brio *m*.

brilliant ['brɪljənt] *adj* brillant(e).

brim [brɪm] *n* bord *m*.

brimful ['brɪm'ful] *adj* plein(e) à ras bord; (*fig*) débordant(e).

brine [braɪn] *n* eau salée; (*CULIN*) saumure *f*.

bring [brɪŋ], *pt, pp* **brought** [brɔ:t] *vt* (*thing*) apporter; (*person*) amener; **to** ~ **sth to an end** mettre fin à qch; **I can't** ~ **myself to fire him** je ne peux me résoudre à le mettre à la porte.

▶**bring about** *vt* provoquer, entraîner.

▶**bring back** *vt* rapporter; (*person*) ramener.

▶**bring down** *vt* (*lower*) abaisser; (*shoot down*) abattre; (*government*) faire s'effondrer.

▶**bring forward** *vt* avancer; (*BOOK-KEEPING*) reporter.

▶**bring in** *vt* (*person*) faire entrer; (*object*) rentrer; (*POL: legislation*) introduire; (*LAW: verdict*) rendre; (*produce: income*) rapporter.

▶**bring off** *vt* (*task, plan*) réussir, mener à bien; (*deal*) mener à bien.

▶**bring out** *vt* (*meaning*) faire ressortir, mettre en relief; (*new product, book*) sortir.

▶**bring round**, **bring to** *vt* (*unconscious person*) ranimer.

▶**bring up** *vt* élever; (*question*) soulever; (*food: vomit*) vomir, rendre.

brink [brɪŋk] *n* bord *m*; **on the** ~ **of doing** sur le point de faire, à deux doigts de faire; **she was on the** ~ **of tears** elle était au bord des larmes.

brisk [brɪsk] *adj* vif(vive); (*abrupt*) brusque; (*trade etc*) actif(ive); **to go for a** ~ **walk** se promener d'un bon pas; **business is** ~ les affaires marchent (bien).

bristle ['brɪsl] *n* poil *m* ♦ *vi* se hérisser; **bristling with** hérissé(e) de.

bristly ['brɪslɪ] *adj* (*beard, hair*) hérissé(e); **your chin's all** ~ ton menton gratte.

Brit [brɪt] *n abbr* (*col*: = *British person*) Britannique *m/f*.

Britain ['brɪtən] *n* (*also*: **Great** ~) la Grande Bretagne; **in** ~ en Grande-Bretagne.

British ['brɪtɪʃ] *adj* britannique; **the** ~ *npl* les Britanniques *mpl*; **the** ~ **Isles** les îles *fpl* Britanniques.

British Rail (BR) *n* compagnie ferroviaire britannique, ≈ SNCF *f*.

British Summer Time *n* heure *f* d'été britannique.

Briton ['brɪtən] n Britannique m/f.
Brittany ['brɪtənɪ] n Bretagne f.
brittle ['brɪtl] adj cassant(e), fragile.
Bro. abbr (REL) = **brother**.
broach [brəutʃ] vt (subject) aborder.
broad [brɔːd] adj large; (distinction) général(e); (accent) prononcé(e) ♦ n (US col) nana f; ~ **hint** allusion transparente; **in ~ daylight** en plein jour; **the ~ outlines** les grandes lignes.
broad bean n fève f.
broadcast ['brɔːdkɑːst] n émission f ♦ vb (pt, pp **broadcast**) vt radiodiffuser; téléviser ♦ vi émettre.
broadcaster ['brɔːdkɑːstə*] n personnalité f de la radio or de la télévision.
broadcasting ['brɔːdkɑːstɪŋ] n radiodiffusion f; télévision f.
broadcasting station n station f de radio (or de télévision).
broaden ['brɔːdn] vt élargir ♦ vi s'élargir.
broadly ['brɔːdlɪ] adv en gros, généralement.
broad-minded ['brɔːd'maɪndɪd] adj large d'esprit.
broadsheet ['brɔːdʃiːt] n (BRIT) journal m grand format.
broccoli ['brɔkəlɪ] n brocoli m.
brochure ['brəuʃjuə*] n prospectus m, dépliant m.
brogue ['brəug] n (accent) accent régional; (shoe) (sorte de) chaussure basse de cuir épais.
broil [brɔɪl] vt rôtir.
broiler ['brɔɪlə*] n (fowl) poulet m (à rôtir).
broke [brəuk] pt of **break** ♦ adj (col) fauché(e); **to go ~** (business) faire faillite.
broken ['brəukn] pp of **break** ♦ adj (stick, leg etc) cassé(e); (promise, vow) rompu(e); **a ~ marriage** un couple dissocié; **a ~ home** un foyer désuni; **in ~ French/English** dans un français/anglais approximatif or hésitant.
broken-down ['brəukn'daun] adj (car) en panne; (machine) fichu(e); (house) en ruines.
broken-hearted ['brəukn'hɑːtɪd] adj (ayant) le cœur brisé.
broker ['brəukə*] n courtier m.
brokerage ['brəukrɪdʒ] n courtage m.
brolly ['brɔlɪ] n (BRIT col) pépin m, parapluie m.
bronchitis [brɔŋ'kaɪtɪs] n bronchite f.
bronze [brɔnz] n bronze m.
bronzed ['brɔnzd] adj bronzé(e), hâlé(e).
brooch [brəutʃ] n broche f.
brood [bruːd] n couvée f ♦ vi (hen, storm) couver; (person) méditer (sombrement), ruminer.
broody ['bruːdɪ] adj (fig) taciturne, mélancolique.
brook [bruk] n ruisseau m.
broom [brum] n balai m.
broomstick ['brumstɪk] n manche m à balai.
Bros. abbr (COMM: = brothers) Frères.
broth [brɔθ] n bouillon m de viande et de légumes.
brothel ['brɔθl] n maison close, bordel m.
brother ['brʌðə*] n frère m.
brotherhood ['brʌðəhud] n fraternité f.
brother-in-law ['brʌðərɪn'lɔː*] n beau-frère m.
brotherly ['brʌðəlɪ] adj fraternel(le).
brought [brɔːt] pt, pp of **bring**.
brow [brau] n front m; (rare: gen: eye~) sourcil m; (of hill) sommet m.
browbeat ['braubiːt] vt intimider, brusquer.
brown [braun] adj brun(e), marron inv; (hair) châtain inv; (rice, bread, flour) complet(ète) ♦ n (colour) brun m, marron m ♦ vt brunir; (CULIN) faire dorer, faire roussir; **to go ~** (person) bronzer; (leaves) jaunir.
brownie ['braunɪ] n jeannette f, éclaireuse (cadette).
brown paper n papier m d'emballage, papier kraft.
brown sugar n cassonade f.
browse [brauz] vi (among books) bouquiner, feuilleter les livres; (animal) paître; **to ~ through a book** feuilleter un livre.
bruise [bruːz] n bleu m, ecchymose f, contusion f ♦ vt contusionner, meurtrir ♦ vi (fruit) se taler, se meurtrir; **to ~ one's arm** se faire un bleu au bras.
Brum [brʌm] n abbr, **Brummagem** ['brʌmədʒəm] n (col) = Birmingham.
Brummie ['brʌmɪ] n (col) habitant/e de Birmingham; natif/ive de Birmingham.
brunch [brʌntʃ] n brunch m.
brunette [bruː'nɛt] n (femme) brune.
brunt [brʌnt] n: **the ~ of** (attack, criticism etc) le plus gros de.
brush [brʌʃ] n brosse f; (quarrel) accrochage m, prise f de bec ♦ vt brosser; (also: ~ past, ~ against) effleurer, frôler; **to have a ~ with sb** s'accrocher avec qn; **to have a ~ with the police** avoir maille à partir avec la police.
▶**brush aside** vt écarter, balayer.
▶**brush up** vt (knowledge) rafraîchir, réviser.
brushed [brʌʃt] adj (TECH: steel, chrome etc) brossé(e); (nylon, denim etc) gratté(e).
brush-off ['brʌʃɔf] n (col): **to give sb the ~** envoyer qn promener.
brushwood ['brʌʃwud] n broussailles fpl, taillis m.
brusque [bruːsk] adj (person, manner) brusque, cassant(e); (tone) sec(sèche), cassant(e).
Brussels ['brʌslz] n Bruxelles.
Brussels sprout n chou m de Bruxelles.
brutal ['bruːtl] adj brutal(e).
brutality [bruː'tælɪtɪ] n brutalité f.
brutalize ['bruːtəlaɪz] vt (harden) rendre brutal(e); (ill-treat) brutaliser.
brute [bruːt] n brute f ♦ adj: **by ~ force** par la force.
brutish ['bruːtɪʃ] adj grossier(ère), brutal(e).
BS n abbr (US: = Bachelor of Science) diplôme universitaire.

bs *abbr* = **bill of sale**.
BSA *n abbr* = *Boy Scouts of America*.
BSc *n abbr* = **Bachelor of Science**.
BSE *n abbr* (= *bovine spongiform encephalopathy*) ESB *f*, BSE *f*.
BSI *n abbr* (= *British Standards Institution*) association de normalisation.
BST *abbr* (= *British Summer Time*) heure *f* d'été.
Bt. *abbr* (*BRIT*) = baronet.
btu *n abbr* (= *British thermal unit*) btu (= 1054,2 joules).
bubble ['bʌbl] *n* bulle *f* ♦ *vi* bouillonner, faire des bulles; (*sparkle, fig*) pétiller.
bubble bath *n* bain moussant.
bubblejet printer ['bʌbldʒet-] *n* imprimante *f* à bulle d'encre.
bubbly ['bʌblɪ] *adj* (*drink*) pétillant(e); (*person*) plein(e) de vitalité ♦ *n* (*col*) champ *m*.
Bucharest [buːkəˈrɛst] *n* Bucarest.
buck [bʌk] *n* mâle *m* (*d'un lapin, lièvre, daim etc*); (*US col*) dollar *m* ♦ *vi* ruer, lancer une ruade; **to pass the ~ (to sb)** se décharger de la responsabilité (sur qn).
▶**buck up** *vi* (*cheer up*) reprendre du poil de la bête, se remonter ♦ *vt*: **to ~ one's ideas up** se reprendre.
bucket ['bʌkɪt] *n* seau *m* ♦ *vi* (*BRIT col*): **the rain is ~ing (down)** il pleut à verse.

Buckingham Palace *est la résidence officielle londonienne du souverain britannique depuis 1762. Construit en 1703, il fut à l'origine le palais du duc de Buckingham. Il a été partiellement reconstruit au début du siècle.*

buckle ['bʌkl] *n* boucle *f* ♦ *vt* boucler, attacher; (*warp*) tordre, gauchir; (*: wheel*) voiler.
▶**buckle down** *vi* s'y mettre.
Bucks [bʌks] *abbr* (*BRIT*) = Buckinghamshire.
bud [bʌd] *n* bourgeon *m*; (*of flower*) bouton *m* ♦ *vi* bourgeonner; (*flower*) éclore.
Budapest [bjuːdəˈpɛst] *n* Budapest.
Buddha ['budə] *n* Bouddha *m*.
Buddhism ['budɪzəm] *n* bouddhisme m.
Buddhist ['budɪst] *adj* bouddhiste ♦ *n* Bouddhiste *m/f*.
budding ['bʌdɪŋ] *adj* (*flower*) en bouton; (*poet etc*) en herbe; (*passion etc*) naissant(e).
buddy ['bʌdɪ] *n* (*US*) copain *m*.
budge [bʌdʒ] *vt* faire bouger ♦ *vi* bouger.
budgerigar ['bʌdʒərɪgaː*] *n* perruche *f*.
budget ['bʌdʒɪt] *n* budget *m* ♦ *vi*: **to ~ for sth** inscrire qch au budget; **I'm on a tight ~** je dois faire attention à mon budget.
budgie ['bʌdʒɪ] *n* = budgerigar.
Buenos Aires ['bweinɔsˈaɪrɪz] *n* Buenos Aires.
buff [bʌf] *adj* (couleur *f*) chamois *m* ♦ *n* (*enthusiast*) mordu/e.
buffalo, *pl* **~** *or* **~es** ['bʌfələu] *n* buffle *m*; (*US*) bison *m*.
buffer ['bʌfə*] *n* tampon *m*; (*COMPUT*) mémoire *f* tampon.

buffering ['bʌfərɪŋ] *n* (*COMPUT*) mise *f* en mémoire tampon.
buffer state *n* état *m* tampon.
buffer zone *n* zone *f* tampon.
buffet *n* ['bufei] (*food, BRIT: bar*) buffet *m* ♦ *vt* ['bʌfɪt] gifler, frapper; secouer, ébranler.
buffet car *n* (*BRIT RAIL*) voiture-bar *f*.
buffet lunch *n* lunch *m*.
buffoon [bəˈfuːn] *n* buffon *m*, pitre *m*.
bug [bʌg] *n* (*insect*) punaise *f*; (*: gen*) insecte *m*, bestiole *f*; (*fig: germ*) virus *m*, microbe *m*; (*spy device*) dispositif *m* d'écoute (électronique), micro clandestin; (*COMPUT: of program*) erreur *f*; (*: of equipment*) défaut *m* ♦ *vt* (*room*) poser des micros dans; (*col: annoy*) embêter; **I've got the travel ~** (*fig*) j'ai le virus du voyage.
bugbear ['bʌgbeə*] *n* cauchemar *m*, bête noire.
bugger ['bʌgə*] (*col!*) *n* salaud *m* (*!*); connard *m* (*!*) ♦ *vb*: **~ off!** tire-toi! (*!*); **~ (it)!** merde! (*!*).
bugle ['bjuːgl] *n* clairon *m*.
build [bɪld] *n* (*of person*) carrure *f*, charpente *f* ♦ *vt* (*pt, pp* **built** [bɪlt]) construire, bâtir.
▶**build on** *vt fus* (*fig*) tirer parti de, partir de.
▶**build up** *vt* accumuler, amasser; (*business*) développer; (*reputation*) bâtir; (*increase: production*) développer, accroître.
builder ['bɪldə*] *n* entrepreneur *m*.
building ['bɪldɪŋ] *n* construction *f*; (*structure*) bâtiment *m*, construction; (*: residential, offices*) immeuble *m*.
building contractor *n* entrepreneur *m* (en bâtiment).
building industry *n* (industrie *f* du) bâtiment *m*.
building site *n* chantier *m* (de construction).
building society *n* (*BRIT*) société *f* de crédit immobilier.

Une **building society** *est une mutuelle dont les épargnants et emprunteurs sont les propriétaires. Ces mutuelles offrent deux services principaux: on peut y avoir un compte d'épargne duquel on peut retirer son argent sur demande ou moyennant un court préavis; et on peut également y faire des emprunts à long terme, par exemple pour acheter une maison. Les building societies ont eu jusqu'en 1985 le quasi-monopole des comptes d'épargne et des prêts immobiliers, mais les banques ont maintenant une part importante de ce marché.*

building trade *n* = **building industry**.
build-up ['bɪldʌp] *n* (*of gas etc*) accumulation *f*; (*publicity*): **to give sb/sth a good ~** faire de la pub pour qn/qch.
built [bɪlt] *pt, pp of* **build**.
built-in ['bɪltˈɪn] *adj* (*cupboard*) encastré(e); (*device*) incorporé(e); intégré(e).
built-up area ['bɪltʌp-] *n* agglomération (ur-

baine); zone urbanisée.

bulb [bʌlb] n (BOT) bulbe m, oignon m; (ELEC) ampoule f.

bulbous ['bʌlbəs] adj bulbeux(euse).

Bulgaria [bʌl'gɛərɪə] n Bulgarie f.

Bulgarian [bʌl'gɛərɪən] adj bulgare ♦ n Bulgare m/f; (LING) bulgare m.

bulge [bʌldʒ] n renflement m, gonflement m; (in birth rate, sales) brusque augmentation f ♦ vi faire saillie; présenter un renflement; **to be bulging with** être plein(e) à craquer de.

bulimia [bə'lɪmɪə] n boulimie f.

bulk [bʌlk] n masse f, volume m; **in ~** (COMM) en gros, en vrac; **the ~ of** la plus grande or grosse partie de.

bulk buying [-'baɪɪŋ] n achat m en gros.

bulk carrier n cargo m.

bulkhead ['bʌlkhɛd] n cloison f (étanche).

bulky ['bʌlkɪ] adj volumineux(euse), encombrant(e).

bull [bul] n taureau m; (STOCK EXCHANGE) haussier m; (REL) bulle f.

bulldog ['buldɔg] n bouledogue m.

bulldoze ['buldəuz] vt passer or raser au bulldozer; **I was ~d into doing it** (fig: col) on m'a forcé la main.

bulldozer ['buldəuzə*] n bulldozer m.

bullet ['bulɪt] n balle f (de fusil etc).

bulletin ['bulɪtɪn] n bulletin m, communiqué m.

bulletin board n (COMPUT) messagerie f (électronique).

bulletproof ['bulɪtpruːf] adj à l'épreuve des balles; **~ vest** gilet m pare-balles.

bullfight ['bulfaɪt] n corrida f, course f de taureaux.

bullfighter ['bulfaɪtə*] n torero m.

bullfighting ['bulfaɪtɪŋ] n tauromachie f.

bullion ['buljən] n or m or argent m en lingots.

bullock ['bulək] n bœuf m.

bullring ['bulrɪŋ] n arène f.

bull's-eye ['bulzaɪ] n centre m (de la cible).

bullshit ['bulʃɪt] (col!) n connerie(s) f(pl) (!) ♦ vt raconter des conneries à (!) ♦ vi déconner (!).

bully ['bulɪ] n brute f, tyran m ♦ vt tyranniser, rudoyer; (frighten) intimider.

bullying ['bulɪŋ] n brimades fpl.

bum [bʌm] n (col: backside) derrière m; (: tramp) vagabond/e, traîne-savates m/f inv; (: idler) glandeur m.

►**bum around** vi (col) vagabonder.

bumblebee ['bʌmblbiː] n bourdon m.

bumf [bʌmf] n (col: forms etc) paperasses fpl.

bump [bʌmp] n (blow) coup m, choc m; (jolt) cahot m; (on road etc, on head) bosse f ♦ vt heurter, cogner; (car) emboutir.

►**bump along** vi avancer en cahotant.

►**bump into** vt fus rentrer dans; (col: meet) tomber sur.

bumper ['bʌmpə*] n pare-chocs m inv ♦ adj: **~ crop/harvest** récolte/moisson exception-

nelle.

bumper cars npl (US) autos tamponneuses.

bumph [bʌmf] n = **bumf**.

bumptious ['bʌmpʃəs] adj suffisant(e), prétentieux(euse).

bumpy ['bʌmpɪ] adj cahoteux(euse); **it was a ~ flight/ride** on a été secoués dans l'avion/la voiture.

bun [bʌn] n petit pain au lait; (of hair) chignon m.

bunch [bʌntʃ] n (of flowers) bouquet m; (of keys) trousseau m; (of bananas) régime m; (of people) groupe m; **~ of grapes** grappe f de raisin.

bundle ['bʌndl] n paquet m ♦ vt (also: ~ up) faire un paquet de; (put): **to ~ sth/sb into** fourrer or enfourner qch/qn dans.

►**bundle off** vt (person) faire sortir (en toute hâte); expédier.

►**bundle out** vt éjecter, sortir (sans ménagements).

bun fight n (BRIT col) réception f; (tea party) thé m.

bung [bʌŋ] n bonde f, bouchon m ♦ vt (BRIT: throw: also: ~ into) flanquer; (also: ~ up: pipe, hole) boucher; **my nose is ~ed up** j'ai le nez bouché.

bungalow ['bʌŋgələu] n bungalow m.

bungee jumping ['bʌndʒiː'dʒʌmpɪŋ] n saut m à l'élastique.

bungle ['bʌŋgl] vt bâcler, gâcher.

bunion ['bʌnjən] n oignon m (au pied).

bunk [bʌŋk] n couchette f; (BRIT col): **to do a ~** mettre les bouts or les voiles.

►**bunk off** vi (BRIT col: SCOL) sécher (les cours); **I'll ~ off at 3 o'clock this afternoon** je vais mettre les bouts or les voiles à 3 heures cet après-midi.

bunk beds npl lits superposés.

bunker ['bʌŋkə*] n (coal store) soute f à charbon; (MIL, GOLF) bunker m.

bunny ['bʌnɪ] n (also: ~ rabbit) Jeannot m lapin.

bunny girl n (BRIT) hôtesse de cabaret.

bunny hill n (US SKI) piste f pour débutants.

bunting ['bʌntɪŋ] n pavoisement m, drapeaux mpl.

buoy [bɔɪ] n bouée f.

►**buoy up** vt faire flotter; (fig) soutenir, épauler.

buoyancy ['bɔɪənsɪ] n (of ship) flottabilité f.

buoyant ['bɔɪənt] adj (ship) flottable; (carefree) gai(e), plein(e) d'entrain; (COMM: market) actif(ive); (: prices, currency) soutenu(e).

burden ['bəːdn] n fardeau m, charge f ♦ vt charger; (oppress) accabler, surcharger; **to be a ~ to sb** être un fardeau pour qn.

bureau, pl **~x** ['bjuərəu, -z] n (BRIT: writing desk) bureau m, secrétaire m; (US: chest of drawers) commode f; (office) bureau, office m.

bureaucracy [bjuə'rɔkrəsɪ] n bureaucratie f.

bureaucrat ['bjuərəkræt] *n* bureaucrate *m/f*, rond-de-cuir *m*.

bureaucratic [bjuərə'krætɪk] *adj* bureaucratique.

burgeon ['bə:dʒən] *vi* (*fig*) être en expansion rapide.

burger ['bə:gə*] *n* hamburger *m*.

burglar ['bə:glə*] *n* cambrioleur *m*.

burglar alarm *n* sonnerie *f* d'alarme.

burglarize ['bə:gləraɪz] *vt* (*US*) cambrioler.

burglary ['bə:glərɪ] *n* cambriolage *m*.

burgle ['bə:gl] *vt* cambrioler.

Burgundy ['bə:gəndɪ] *n* Bourgogne *f*.

burial ['berɪəl] *n* enterrement *m*.

burial ground *n* cimetière *m*.

burlesque [bə:'lesk] *n* caricature *f*, parodie *f*.

burly ['bə:lɪ] *adj* de forte carrure, costaud(e).

Burma ['bə:mə] *n* Birmanie *f*; *see also* **Myanmar**.

Burmese [bə:'mi:z] *adj* birman(e), de Birmanie ♦ *n* (*pl inv*) Birman/e; (*LING*) birman *m*.

burn [bə:n] *vt, vi* (*pt, pp* **burned** *or* **burnt** [bə:nt]) brûler ♦ *n* brûlure *f*; **the cigarette ~t a hole in her dress** la cigarette a fait un trou dans sa robe; **I've ~t myself!** je me suis brûlé(e)!

▶**burn down** *vt* incendier, détruire par le feu.

▶**burn out** *vt* (*subj: writer etc*): **to ~ o.s. out** s'user (à force de travailler).

burner ['bə:nə*] *n* brûleur *m*.

burning ['bə:nɪŋ] *adj* (*building, forest*) en flammes; (*issue, question*) brûlant(e).

burnish ['bə:nɪʃ] *vt* polir.

Burns Night *est une fête qui a lieu le 25 janvier, à la mémoire du poète écossais Robert Burns (1759-1796), à l'occasion de laquelle les Écossais partout dans le monde organisent un souper, en général arrosé de whisky. Le plat principal est toujours le haggis, servi avec de la purée de pommes de terre et de la purée de rutabagas. On apporte le haggis au son des cornemuses et au cours du repas on lit des poèmes de Burns et on chante ses chansons.*

burnt [bə:nt] *pt, pp of* **burn**.

burnt sugar *n* (*BRIT*) caramel *m*.

burp [bə:p] (*col*) *n* rot *m* ♦ *vi* roter.

burrow ['bʌrəu] *n* terrier *m* ♦ *vt* creuser.

bursar ['bə:sə*] *n* économe *m/f*; (*BRIT: student*) boursier/ère.

bursary ['bə:sərɪ] *n* (*BRIT*) bourse *f* (d'études).

burst [bə:st] *vb* (*pt, pp* **burst**) *vt* faire éclater ♦ *vi* éclater ♦ *n* explosion *f*; (*also: ~* **pipe**) fuite *f* (*due à une rupture*); *~* **of energy** déploiement soudain d'énergie, activité soudaine; *~* **of laughter** éclat *m* de rire; **a** *~* **of applause** une salve d'applaudissement; **a** *~* **of speed** une pointe de vitesse; *~* **blood vessel** rupture *f* de vaisseau sanguin; **the river has** *~* **its banks** le cours d'eau est sorti de son lit; **to** *~* **into flames** s'enflammer soudainement; **to** *~* **out laughing** éclater de rire; **to** *~* **into tears** fondre en larmes; **to** *~* **open** *vi* s'ouvrir violemment *or* soudainement; **to be** *~***ing with** être plein(e) (à craquer) de; regorger de.

▶**burst into** *vt fus* (*room etc*) faire irruption dans.

▶**burst out of** *vt fus* sortir précipitamment de.

bury ['berɪ] *vt* enterrer; **to** *~* **one's face in one's hands** se couvrir le visage de ses mains; **to** *~* **one's head in the sand** (*fig*) pratiquer la politique de l'autruche; **to** *~* **the hatchet** (*fig*) enterrer la hache de guerre.

bus, *~***es** [bʌs, 'bʌsɪz] *n* autobus *m*.

busboy ['bʌsbɔɪ] *n* (*US*) aide-serveur *m*.

bush [buʃ] *n* buisson *m*; (*scrub land*) brousse *f*.

bushed [buʃt] *adj* (*col*) crevé(e), claqué(e).

bushel ['buʃl] *n* boisseau *m*.

bushfire ['buʃfaɪə*] *n* feu *m* de brousse.

bushy ['buʃɪ] *adj* broussailleux(euse), touffu(e).

busily ['bɪzɪlɪ] *adv*: **to be** *~* **doing sth** s'affairer à faire qch.

business ['bɪznɪs] *n* (*matter, firm*) affaire *f*; (*trading*) affaires *fpl*; (*job, duty*) travail *m*; **to be away on** *~* être en déplacement d'affaires; **I'm here on** *~* je suis là pour affaires; **he's in the insurance/transport** *~* il est dans les assurances/les transports; **to do** *~* **with sb** traiter avec qn; **it's none of my** *~* cela ne me regarde pas, ce ne sont pas mes affaires; **he means** *~* il ne plaisante pas, il est sérieux.

business address *n* adresse professionnelle *or* au bureau.

business card *n* carte *f* de visite (professionnelle).

businesslike ['bɪznɪslaɪk] *adj* sérieux(euse), efficace.

businessman ['bɪznɪsmən] *n* homme *m* d'affaires.

business trip *n* voyage *m* d'affaires.

businesswoman ['bɪznɪswumən] *n* femme *f* d'affaires.

busker ['bʌskə*] *n* (*BRIT*) artiste ambulant(e).

bus lane *n* (*BRIT*) voie réservée aux autobus.

bus shelter *n* abribus *m*.

bus station *n* gare routière.

bus stop *n* arrêt *m* d'autobus.

bust [bʌst] *n* buste *m* ♦ *adj* (*col: broken*) fichu(e), fini(e) ♦ *vt* (*col: POLICE: arrest*) pincer; **to go** *~* faire faillite.

bustle ['bʌsl] *n* remue-ménage *m*, affairement *m* ♦ *vi* s'affairer, se démener.

bustling ['bʌslɪŋ] *adj* (*person*) affairé(e); (*town*) très animé(e).

bust-up ['bʌstʌp] *n* (*BRIT col*) engueulade *f*.

busty ['bʌstɪ] *adj* (*col*) à la poitrine plantureuse.

busy ['bɪzɪ] *adj* occupé(e); (*shop, street*) très fréquenté(e); (*US: telephone, line*) occupé

♦ *vt*: **to ~ o.s.** s'occuper; **he's a ~ man** (*normally*) c'est un homme très pris; (*temporarily*) il est très pris.

busybody ['bɪzɪbɔdɪ] *n* mouche *f* du coche, âme *f* charitable.

busy signal *n* (*US*) tonalité *f* occupé.

═══════════════════ KEYWORD

but [bʌt] *conj* mais; **I'd love to come, ~ I'm busy** j'aimerais venir mais je suis occupé
♦ *prep* (*apart from, except*) sauf, excepté; **nothing ~** rien d'autre que; **we've had nothing ~ trouble** nous n'avons eu que des ennuis; **no-one ~ him can do it** lui seul peut le faire; **~ for you/your help** sans toi/ton aide; **anything ~ that** tout sauf *or* excepté ça, tout mais pas ça; **the last ~ one** (*BRIT*) l'avant-dernier(ère)
♦ *adv* (*just, only*) ne ... que; **she's ~ a child** elle n'est qu'une enfant; **had I ~ known** si seulement j'avais su; **all ~ finished** pratiquement terminé; **anything ~ finished** tout sauf fini, très loin d'être fini.

butane ['bju:teɪn] *n* (*also: ~ gas*) butane *m*.

butch [butʃ] *adj* (*col: man*) costaud, viril; (*: woman*) costaude, masculine.

butcher ['butʃə*] *n* boucher *m* ♦ *vt* massacrer; (*cattle etc for meat*) tuer; **~'s (shop)** boucherie *f*.

butler ['bʌtlə*] *n* maître *m* d'hôtel.

butt [bʌt] *n* (*cask*) gros tonneau; (*thick end*) (gros) bout; (*of gun*) crosse *f*; (*of cigarette*) mégot *m*; (*BRIT fig: target*) cible *f* ♦ *vt* donner un coup de tête à.

▶**butt in** *vi* (*interrupt*) interrompre.

butter ['bʌtə*] *n* beurre *m* ♦ *vt* beurrer.

buttercup ['bʌtəkʌp] *n* bouton *m* d'or.

butter dish *n* beurrier *m*.

butterfingers ['bʌtəfɪŋgəz] *n* (*col*) maladroit/e.

butterfly ['bʌtəflaɪ] *n* papillon *m*; (*SWIMMING: also: ~ stroke*) brasse *f* papillon.

buttocks ['bʌtəks] *npl* fesses *fpl*.

button ['bʌtn] *n* bouton *m* ♦ *vt* (*also: ~ up*) boutonner ♦ *vi* se boutonner.

buttonhole ['bʌtnhəul] *n* boutonnière *f* ♦ *vt* accrocher, arrêter, retenir.

buttress ['bʌtrɪs] *n* contrefort *m*.

buxom ['bʌksəm] *adj* aux formes avantageuses *or* épanouies, bien galbé(e).

buy [baɪ] *vb* (*pt, pp* **bought** [bɔ:t]) *vt* acheter; (*COMM: company*) (r)acheter ♦ *n*: **that was a good/bad ~** c'était un bon/mauvais achat; **to ~ sb sth/sth from sb** acheter qch à qn; **to ~ sb a drink** offrir un verre *or* à boire à qn.

▶**buy back** *vt* racheter.

▶**buy in** *vt* (*BRIT: goods*) acheter, faire venir.

▶**buy into** *vt fus* (*BRIT COMM*) acheter des actions de.

▶**buy off** *vt* (*bribe*) acheter.

▶**buy out** *vt* (*partner*) désintéresser; (*busi-*

ness*) racheter.

▶**buy up** *vt* acheter en bloc, rafler.

buyer ['baɪə*] *n* acheteur/euse; **~'s market** marché *m* favorable aux acheteurs.

buy-out ['baɪaut] *n* (*COMM*) rachat *m* (*d'entreprise*).

buzz [bʌz] *n* bourdonnement *m*; (*col: phone call*) coup *m* de fil ♦ *vi* bourdonner ♦ *vt* (*call on intercom*) appeler; (*with buzzer*) sonner; (*AVIAT: plane, building*) raser; **my head is ~ing** j'ai la tête qui bourdonne.

▶**buzz off** *vi* (*col*) s'en aller, ficher le camp.

buzzard ['bʌzəd] *n* buse *f*.

buzzer ['bʌzə*] *n* timbre *m* électrique.

buzz word *n* (*col*) mot *m* à la mode *or* dans le vent.

═══════════════════ KEYWORD

by [baɪ] *prep* **1** (*referring to cause, agent*) par, de; **killed ~ lightning** tué par la foudre; **surrounded ~ a fence** entouré d'une barrière; **a painting ~ Picasso** un tableau de Picasso
2 (*referring to method, manner, means*): **~ bus/car** en autobus/voiture; **~ train** par le *or* en train; **to pay ~ cheque** payer par chèque; **~ saving hard, he ...** à force d'économiser, il ...
3 (*via, through*) par; **we came ~ Dover** nous sommes venus par Douvres
4 (*close to, past*) à côté de; **the house ~ the school** la maison à côté de l'école; **a holiday ~ the sea** des vacances au bord de la mer; **she sat ~ his bed** elle était assise à son chevet; **she went ~ me** elle est passée à côté de moi; **I go ~ the post office every day** je passe devant la poste tous les jours
5 (*with time: not later than*) avant; (*: during*): **~ daylight** à la lumière du jour; **~ night** la nuit, de nuit; **~ 4 o'clock** avant 4 heures; **~ this time tomorrow** d'ici demain à la même heure; **~ the time I got here it was too late** lorsque je suis arrivé il était déjà trop tard
6 (*amount*) à; **the kilo/metre** au kilo/au mètre; **paid ~ the hour** payé à l'heure; **to increase** *etc* **~ the hour** augmenter *etc* d'heure en heure
7 (*MATH, measure*): **to divide/multiply ~ 3** diviser/multiplier par 3; **a room 3 metres ~ 4** une pièce de 3 mètres sur 4; **it's broader ~ a metre** c'est plus large d'un mètre; **the bullet missed him ~ inches** la balle est passée à quelques centimètres de lui; **one ~ one** un à un; **little ~ little** petit à petit, peu à peu
8 (*according to*) d'après, selon; **it's 3 o'clock ~ my watch** il est 3 heures à ma montre; **it's all right ~ me** je n'ai rien contre
9: (*all*) **~ oneself** *etc* tout(e) seul(e)
10: **~ the way** au fait, à propos
♦ *adv* **1** *see* **go; pass** *etc*
2: **~ and ~** un peu plus tard, bientôt; **~ and large** dans l'ensemble.

bye(-bye) ['baɪ('baɪ)] excl au revoir!, salut!
by(e)-law ['baɪlɔː] n arrêté municipal.
by-election ['baɪɪlekʃən] n (BRIT) élection (législative) partielle.
Byelorussia [bjɛləu'rʌʃə] n Biélorussie f.
Byelorussian [bjɛləu'rʌʃən] adj, n = **Belorussian**.
bygone ['baɪgɔn] adj passé(e) ♦ n: **let ~s be ~s** passons l'éponge, oublions le passé.
bypass ['baɪpɑːs] n (route f de) contournement m; (MED) pontage m ♦ vt éviter.
by-product ['baɪprɔdʌkt] n sous-produit m, dérivé m; (fig) conséquence f secondaire, retombée f.
byre ['baɪə*] n (BRIT) étable f (à vaches).
bystander ['baɪstændə*] n spectateur/trice, badaud/e.
byte [baɪt] n (COMPUT) octet m.
byway ['baɪweɪ] n chemin détourné.
byword ['baɪwəːd] n: **to be a ~ for** être synonyme de (fig).
by-your-leave ['baɪjɔː'liːv] n: **without so much as a ~** sans même demander la permission.

C c

C, c [siː] n (letter) C, c m; (SCOL: mark) C; (MUS): **C do** m; **C for Charlie** C comme Célestin.
C abbr (= Celsius, centigrade) C.
c abbr (= century) s.; (= circa) v.; (US etc) = **cent(s)**.
CA n abbr = **Central America**; (BRIT) = **chartered accountant** ♦ abbr (US) = **California**.
ca. abbr (= circa) v.
c/a abbr = **capital account, credit account, current account**.
CAA n abbr (BRIT: = Civil Aviation Authority, US: = Civil Aeronautics Authority) direction de l'aviation civile.
CAB n abbr (BRIT) = **Citizens' Advice Bureau**.
cab [kæb] n taxi m; (of train, truck) cabine f; (horse-drawn) fiacre m.
cabaret ['kæbəreɪ] n attractions fpl, spectacle m de cabaret.
cabbage ['kæbɪdʒ] n chou m.
cabbie, cabby ['kæbɪ] n (col), **cab driver** n taxi m, chauffeur m de taxi.
cabin ['kæbɪn] n cabane f, hutte f; (on ship) cabine f.
cabin cruiser n yacht m (à moteur).
cabinet ['kæbɪnɪt] n (POL) cabinet m; (furniture) petit meuble à tiroirs et rayons; (also: **display ~**) vitrine f, petite armoire vitrée.
cabinet-maker ['kæbɪnɪt'meɪkə*] n ébéniste

m.
cabinet minister n ministre m (membre du cabinet).
cable ['keɪbl] n câble m ♦ vt câbler, télégraphier.
cable-car ['keɪblkɑː*] n téléphérique m.
cablegram ['keɪblgræm] n câblogramme m.
cable railway n (BRIT) funiculaire m.
cable television n télévision f par câble.
cache [kæʃ] n cachette f; **a ~ of food** etc un dépôt secret de provisions etc, une cachette contenant des provisions etc.
cackle ['kækl] vi caqueter.
cactus, pl **cacti** ['kæktəs, -taɪ] n cactus m.
CAD n abbr (= computer-aided design) CAO f.
caddie ['kædɪ] n caddie ® m.
cadet [kə'dɛt] n (MIL) élève m officier; **police ~** élève agent de police.
cadge [kædʒ] vt (col) se faire donner; **to ~ a meal (off sb)** se faire inviter à manger (par qn).
cadger ['kædʒə*] n pique-assiette m/f inv, tapeur/euse.
cadre ['kædrɪ] n cadre m.
Caesarean, (US) **Cesarean** [siː'zɛərɪən] adj: **~ (section)** césarienne f.
CAF abbr (BRIT: = cost and freight) C et F.
café ['kæfeɪ] n ≈ café(-restaurant) m (sans alcool).
cafeteria [kæfɪ'tɪərɪə] n cafeteria f.
caffein(e) ['kæfiːn] n caféine f.
cage [keɪdʒ] n cage f ♦ vt mettre en cage.
cagey ['keɪdʒɪ] adj (col) réticent(e); méfiant(e).
cagoule [kə'guːl] n K-way m ®.
cahoots [kə'huːts] n: **to be in ~ (with)** être de mèche (avec).
CAI n abbr (= computer-aided instruction) EAO m.
Cairo ['kaɪərəu] n le Caire.
cajole [kə'dʒəul] vt couvrir de flatteries or de gentillesses.
cake [keɪk] n gâteau m; **~ of soap** savonnette f; **it's a piece of ~** (col) c'est un jeu d'enfant; **he wants to have his ~ and eat it (too)** (fig) il veut tout avoir.
caked [keɪkt] adj: **~ with** raidi(e) par, couvert(e) d'une croûte de.
cake shop n pâtisserie f.
Cal. abbr (US) = California.
calamitous [kə'læmɪtəs] adj catastrophique, désastreux(euse).
calamity [kə'læmɪtɪ] n calamité f, désastre m.
calcium ['kælsɪəm] n calcium m.
calculate ['kælkjuleɪt] vt calculer; (estimate: chances, effect) évaluer.
► **calculate on** vt fus: **to ~ on sth/on doing sth** compter sur qch/faire qch.
calculated ['kælkjuleɪtɪd] adj (insult, action) délibéré(e); **a ~ risk** un risque pris en toute connaissance de cause.

calculating ['kælkjuleɪtɪŋ] adj calculateur(trice).
calculation [kælkju'leɪʃən] n calcul m.
calculator ['kælkjuleɪtə*] n machine f à calculer, calculatrice f.
calculus ['kælkjuləs] n analyse f (mathématique), calcul infinitésimal; **integral/differential** ~ calcul intégral/différentiel.
calendar ['kæləndə*] n calendrier m.
calendar month n mois m (de calendrier).
calendar year n année civile.
calf, pl **calves** [kɑːf, kɑːvz] n (of cow) veau m; (of other animals) petit m; (also: ~skin) veau m, vachette f; (ANAT) mollet m.
caliber ['kælɪbə*] n (US) = **calibre**.
calibrate ['kælɪbreɪt] vt (gun etc) calibrer; (scale of measuring instrument) étalonner.
calibre, (US) **caliber** ['kælɪbə*] n calibre m.
calico ['kælɪkəʊ] n (BRIT) calicot m; (US) indienne f.
Calif. abbr (US) = California.
California [kælɪ'fɔːnɪə] n Californie f.
calipers ['kælɪpəz] npl (US) = **callipers**.
call [kɔːl] vt (gen, also TEL) appeler; (announce: flight) annoncer; (meeting) convoquer; (strike) lancer ♦ vi appeler; (visit: also: ~ **in,** ~ **round**): **to** ~ **(for)** passer (prendre) ♦ n (shout) appel m, cri m; (summons: for flight etc, fig: lure) appel m; (visit) visite f; (also: **telephone** ~) coup m de téléphone; communication f; **to be on** ~ être de permanence; **she's** ~**ed Suzanne** elle s'appelle Suzanne; **who is** ~**ing?** (TEL) qui est à l'appareil?; **London** ~**ing** (RADIO) ici Londres; **please give me a** ~ **at 7** appelez-moi à 7 heures; **to make a** ~ téléphoner, passer un coup de fil; **to pay a** ~ **on sb** rendre visite à qn, passer voir qn; **there's not much** ~ **for these items** ces articles ne sont pas très demandés.
▶**call at** vt fus (subj: ship) faire escale à; (: train) s'arrêter à.
▶**call back** vi (return) repasser; (TEL) rappeler ♦ vt (TEL) rappeler.
▶**call for** vt fus demander.
▶**call in** vt (doctor, expert, police) appeler, faire venir.
▶**call off** vt annuler; **the strike was** ~**ed off** l'ordre de grève a été rapporté.
▶**call on** vt fus (visit) rendre visite à, passer voir; (request): **to** ~ **on sb to do** inviter qn à faire.
▶**call out** vi pousser un cri or des cris ♦ vt (doctor, police, troops) appeler.
▶**call up** vt (MIL) appeler, mobiliser.
Callanetics [kælə'netɪks] n ® stretching m.
callbox ['kɔːlbɔks] n (BRIT) cabine f téléphonique.
caller ['kɔːlə*] n personne f qui appelle; visiteur m; **hold the line,** ~**!** (TEL) ne quittez pas, Monsieur (or Madame)!
call girl n call-girl f.

call-in ['kɔːlɪn] n (US RADIO, TV) programme m à ligne ouverte.
calling ['kɔːlɪŋ] n vocation f; (trade, occupation) état m.
calling card n (US) carte f de visite.
callipers, (US) **calipers** ['kælɪpəz] npl (MATH) compas m; (MED) appareil m orthopédique; gouttière f; étrier m.
callous ['kæləs] adj dur(e), insensible.
callousness ['kæləsnɪs] n dureté f, manque m de cœur, insensibilité f.
callow ['kæləʊ] adj sans expérience (de la vie).
calm [kɑːm] adj calme ♦ n calme m ♦ vt calmer, apaiser.
▶**calm down** vi se calmer, s'apaiser ♦ vt calmer, apaiser.
calmly ['kɑːmlɪ] adv calmement, avec calme.
calmness ['kɑːmnɪs] n calme m.
Calor gas ['kælə*-] n ® (BRIT) butane m, butagaz m ®.
calorie ['kælərɪ] n calorie f; **low** ~ **product** produit m pauvre en calories.
calve [kɑːv] vi vêler, mettre bas.
calves [kɑːvz] npl of **calf.**
CAM n abbr (= computer-aided manufacturing) FAO f.
camber ['kæmbə*] n (of road) bombement m.
Cambodia [kæm'bəʊdjə] n Cambodge m.
Cambodian [kæm'bəʊdɪən] adj cambodgien(ne) ♦ n Cambodgien/ne.
Cambs abbr (BRIT) = Cambridgeshire.
camcorder ['kæmkɔːdə*] n caméscope m.
came [keɪm] pt of **come.**
camel ['kæməl] n chameau m.
cameo ['kæmɪəʊ] n camée m.
camera ['kæmərə] n appareil m photo; (CINE, TV) caméra f; **35mm** ~ appareil 24 x 36 or petit format; **in** ~ à huis clos, en privé.
cameraman ['kæmərəmæn] n caméraman m.
Cameroon, Cameroun [kæmə'ruːn] n Cameroun m.
camouflage ['kæməflɑːʒ] n camouflage m ♦ vt camoufler.
camp [kæmp] n camp m ♦ vi camper; **to go** ~**ing** faire du camping.
campaign [kæm'peɪn] n (MIL, POL etc) campagne f ♦ vi (also fig) faire campagne; **to** ~ **for/against** militer pour/contre.
campaigner [kæm'peɪnə*] n: ~ **for** partisan/e de; ~ **against** opposant/e à.
campbed ['kæmp'bed] n (BRIT) lit m de camp.
camper ['kæmpə*] n campeur/euse.
camping ['kæmpɪŋ] n camping m.
camp(ing) site n (terrain m de) camping m.
campus ['kæmpəs] n campus m.
camshaft ['kæmʃɑːft] n arbre m à came.
can¹ [kæn] aux vb see keyword ♦ n (of milk, oil, water) bidon m; (tin) boîte f (de conserve) ♦ vt mettre en conserve; **a** ~ **of beer** une canette de bière; **he had to carry the** ~ (BRIT col) on lui a fait porter le chapeau.

=============================== *KEYWORD*

can² [kæn] (*negative* **cannot, can't**; *conditional and pt* **could**) *aux vb* **1** (*be able to*) pouvoir; **you ~ do it if you try** vous pouvez le faire si vous essayez; **I ~'t hear you** je ne t'entends pas
2 (*know how to*) savoir; **I ~ swim/play tennis/drive** je sais nager/jouer au tennis/conduire; **~ you speak French?** parlez-vous français?
3 (*may*) pouvoir; **~ I use your phone?** puis-je me servir de votre téléphone?
4 (*expressing disbelief, puzzlement etc*): **it ~'t be true!** ce n'est pas possible!; **what CAN he want?** qu'est-ce qu'il peut bien vouloir?
5 (*expressing possibility, suggestion etc*): **he could be in the library** il est peut-être dans la bibliothèque; **she could have been delayed** il se peut qu'elle ait été retardée; **they could have forgotten** ils ont pu oublier.

Canada ['kænədə] *n* Canada *m*.
Canadian [kə'neɪdɪən] *adj* canadien(ne) ♦ *n* Canadien/ne.
canal [kə'næl] *n* canal *m*.
canary [kə'nɛərɪ] *n* canari *m*, serin *m*.
Canary Islands, Canaries [kə'nɛərɪz] *npl*: **the ~** les (îles *fpl*) Canaries *fpl*.
Canberra ['kænbərə] *n* Canberra.
cancel ['kænsəl] *vt* annuler; (*train*) supprimer; (*party, appointment*) décommander; (*cross out*) barrer, rayer; (*stamp*) oblitérer; (*cheque*) faire opposition à.
▶**cancel out** *vt* annuler; **they ~ each other out** ils s'annulent.
cancellation [kænsə'leɪʃən] *n* annulation *f*; suppression *f*; oblitération *f*; (*TOURISM*) réservation annulée, client *etc* qui s'est décommandé.
cancer ['kænsə*] *n* cancer *m*; **C~** (*sign*) le Cancer; **to be C~** être du Cancer.
cancerous ['kænsrəs] *adj* cancéreux(euse).
cancer patient *n* cancéreux/euse.
cancer research *n* recherche *f* contre le cancer.
C and F *abbr* (*BRIT*: = *cost and freight*) C et F.
candid ['kændɪd] *adj* (très) franc(franche), sincère.
candidacy ['kændɪdəsɪ] *n* candidature *f*.
candidate ['kændɪdeɪt] *n* candidat/e.
candidature ['kændɪdətʃə*] *n* (*BRIT*) = **candidacy**.
candied ['kændɪd] *adj* confit(e); **~ apple** (*US*) pomme caramélisée.
candle ['kændl] *n* bougie *f*, (*of tallow*) chandelle *f*, (*in church*) cierge *m*.
candlelight ['kændllaɪt] *n*: **by ~** à la lumière d'une bougie; (*dinner*) aux chandelles.
candlestick ['kændlstɪk] *n* (*also*: **candle holder**) bougeoir *m*; (*bigger, ornate*) chandelier *m*.
candour, (*US*) **candor** ['kændə*] *n* (grande)

franchise *or* sincérité.
C & W *n abbr* = **country and western** (music).
candy ['kændɪ] *n* sucre candi; (*US*) bonbon *m*.
candy-floss ['kændɪflɒs] *n* (*BRIT*) barbe *f* à papa.
candy store *n* (*US*) confiserie *f*.
cane [keɪn] *n* canne *f*; (*for baskets, chairs etc*) rotin *m* ♦ *vt* (*BRIT SCOL*) administrer des coups de bâton à.
canine ['keɪnaɪn] *adj* canin(e).
canister ['kænɪstə*] *n* boîte *f* (*gén en métal*).
cannabis ['kænəbɪs] *n* (*drug*) cannabis *m*; (*also*: **~ plant**) chanvre indien.
canned ['kænd] *adj* (*food*) en boîte, en conserve; (*col: music*) enregistré(e); (*BRIT col: drunk*) bourré(e); (*US col: worker*) mis(e) à la porte.
cannibal ['kænɪbəl] *n* cannibale *m/f*, anthropophage *m/f*.
cannibalism ['kænɪbəlɪzəm] *n* cannibalisme *m*, anthropophagie *f*.
cannon, *pl* **~** *or* **~s** ['kænən] *n* (*gun*) canon *m*.
cannonball ['kænənbɔːl] *n* boulet *m* de canon.
cannon fodder *n* chair *f* à canon.
cannot ['kænɒt] = **can not**.
canny ['kænɪ] *adj* madré(e), finaud(e).
canoe [kə'nuː] *n* pirogue *f*; (*SPORT*) canoë *m*.
canoeing [kə'nuːɪŋ] *n* (*sport*) canoë *m*.
canoeist [kə'nuːɪst] *n* canoéiste *m/f*.
canon ['kænən] *n* (*clergyman*) chanoine *m*; (*standard*) canon *m*.
canonize ['kænənaɪz] *vt* canoniser.
can opener [-'əupnə*] *n* ouvre-boîte *m*.
canopy ['kænəpɪ] *n* baldaquin *m*; dais *m*.
cant [kænt] *n* jargon *m* ♦ *vt, vi* pencher.
can't [kænt] = **can not**.
Cantab. *abbr* (*BRIT*: = *cantabrigiensis*) *of* Cambridge.
cantankerous [kæn'tæŋkərəs] *adj* querelleur(euse), acariâtre.
canteen [kæn'tiːn] *n* cantine *f*, (*BRIT*: *of cutlery*) ménagère *f*.
canter ['kæntə*] *n* petit galop ♦ *vi* aller au petit galop.
cantilever ['kæntɪliːvə*] *n* porte-à-faux *m inv*.
canvas ['kænvəs] *n* (*gen*) toile *f*; **under ~** (*camping*) sous la tente; (*NAUT*) toutes voiles dehors.
canvass ['kænvəs] *vt* (*POL: district*) faire la tournée électorale dans; (: *person*) solliciter le suffrage de; (*COMM: district*) prospecter; (*citizens, opinions*) sonder.
canvasser ['kænvəsə*] *n* (*POL*) agent électoral; (*COMM*) démarcheur *m*.
canvassing ['kænvəsɪŋ] *n* (*POL*) prospection électorale, démarchage électoral; (*COMM*) démarchage, prospection.
canyon ['kænjən] *n* cañon *m*, gorge *f* (profonde).
CAP *n abbr* (= *Common Agricultural Policy*) PAC *f*.
cap [kæp] *n* casquette *f*; (*for swimming*) bonnet

m de bain; (*of pen*) capuchon *m*; (*of bottle*) capsule *f*; (*BRIT: contraceptive: also*: **Dutch ~**) diaphragme *m*; (: *FOOTBALL*) sélection *f* pour l'équipe nationale ♦ *vt* capsuler; (*outdo*) surpasser; **~ped with** coiffé(e) de; **and to ~ it all, he** ... (*BRIT*) pour couronner le tout, il ....

capability [keɪpə'bɪlɪtɪ] *n* aptitude *f*, capacité *f*.

capable ['keɪpəbl] *adj* capable; **~ of** (*interpretation etc*) susceptible de.

capacious [kə'peɪʃəs] *adj* vaste.

capacity [kə'pæsɪtɪ] *n* (*of container*) capacité *f*, contenance *f*; (*ability*) aptitude *f*; **filled to ~** plein(e); **in his ~ as** en sa qualité de; **this work is beyond my ~** ce travail dépasse mes capacités; **in an advisory ~** à titre consultatif; **to work at full ~** travailler à plein rendement.

cape [keɪp] *n* (*garment*) cape *f*; (*GEO*) cap *m*.

Cape of Good Hope *n* cap *m* de Bonne Espérance.

caper ['keɪpə*] *n* (*CULIN: also*: **~s**) câpre *f*.

Cape Town *n* Le Cap.

capita ['kæpɪtə] *see* **per capita**.

capital ['kæpɪtl] *n* (*also*: **~ city**) capitale *f*; (*money*) capital *m*; (*also*: **~ letter**) majuscule *f*.

capital account *n* balance *f* des capitaux; (*of country*) compte capital.

capital allowance *n* provision *f* pour amortissement.

capital assets *npl* immobilisations *fpl*.

capital expenditure *n* dépenses *fpl* d'équipement.

capital gains tax *n* impôt *m* sur les plus-values.

capital goods *n* biens *mpl* d'équipement.

capital-intensive ['kæpɪtlɪn'tɛnsɪv] *adj* à forte proportion de capitaux.

capitalism ['kæpɪtəlɪzəm] *n* capitalisme *m*.

capitalist ['kæpɪtəlɪst] *adj*, *n* capitaliste (*m/f*).

capitalize ['kæpɪtəlaɪz] *vt* (*provide with capital*) financer.

► **capitalize on** *vt fus* (*fig*) profiter de.

capital punishment *n* peine capitale.

capital transfer tax *n* (*BRIT*) impôt *m* sur le transfert de propriété.

Capitol ['kæpɪtl] *n*: **the ~** le Capitole.

Le **Capitol** *est le siège du* **Congress**, *à Washington. Il est situé sur Capitol Hill.*

---

capitulate [kə'pɪtjuleɪt] *vi* capituler.

capitulation [kəpɪtju'leɪʃən] *n* capitulation *f*.

capricious [kə'prɪʃəs] *adj* capricieux(euse), fantasque.

Capricorn ['kæprɪkɔːn] *n* le Capricorne; **to be ~** être du Capricorne.

caps [kæps] *abbr* = **capital letters**.

capsize [kæp'saɪz] *vt* faire chavirer ♦ *vi* chavirer.

capstan ['kæpstən] *n* cabestan *m*.

capsule ['kæpsjuːl] *n* capsule *f*.

Capt. *abbr* (= *captain*) Cne.

captain ['kæptɪn] *n* capitaine *m* ♦ *vt* commander, être le capitaine de.

caption ['kæpʃən] *n* légende *f*.

captivate ['kæptɪveɪt] *vt* captiver, fasciner.

captive ['kæptɪv] *adj*, *n* captif(ive).

captivity [kæp'tɪvɪtɪ] *n* captivité *f*.

captor ['kæptə*] *n* (*unlawful*) ravisseur *m*; (*lawful*): **his ~s** les gens (*or* ceux *etc*) qui l'ont arrêté.

capture ['kæptʃə*] *vt* capturer, prendre; (*attention*) capter ♦ *n* capture *f*.

car [kɑː*] *n* voiture *f*, auto *f*; (*US RAIL*) wagon *m*, voiture; **by ~** en voiture.

Caracas [kə'rækəs] *n* Caracas.

carafe [kə'ræf] *n* carafe *f*.

carafe wine *n* (*in restaurant*) ≈ vin ouvert.

caramel ['kærəməl] *n* caramel *m*.

carat ['kærət] *n* carat *m*; **18 ~ gold** or *m* à 18 carats.

caravan ['kærəvæn] *n* caravane *f*.

caravan site *n* (*BRIT*) camping *m* pour caravanes.

caraway ['kærəweɪ] *n*: **~ seed** graine *f* de cumin, cumin *m*.

carbohydrates [kɑːbəu'haɪdreɪts] *npl* (*foods*) aliments *mpl* riches en hydrate de carbone.

carbolic acid [kɑː'bɔlɪk-] *n* phénol *m*.

car bomb *n* voiture piégée.

carbon ['kɑːbən] *n* carbone *m*.

carbonated ['kɑːbəneɪtɪd] *adj* (*drink*) gazeux(euse).

carbon copy *n* carbone *m*.

carbon dioxide *n* gas *m* carbonique, dioxyde *m* de carbone.

carbon paper *n* papier *m* carbone.

carbon ribbon *n* ruban *m* carbone.

car boot sale *n* *marché aux puces où des particuliers vendent des objets entreposés dans le coffre de leur voiture.*

carburettor, (*US*) **carburetor** [kɑːbju'rɛtə*] *n* carburateur *m*.

carcass ['kɑːkəs] *n* carcasse *f*.

carcinogenic [kɑːsɪnə'dʒɛnɪk] *adj* cancérigène.

card [kɑːd] *n* carte *f*; (*membership ~*) carte d'adhérent; **to play ~s** jouer aux cartes.

cardamom ['kɑːdəməm] *n* cardamome *f*.

cardboard ['kɑːdbɔːd] *n* carton *m*.

cardboard box *n* (boîte *f* en) carton *m*.

cardboard city *n* endroit de la ville où dorment les SDF dans des boîtes en carton.

card-carrying member ['kɑːdkærɪɪŋ-] *n* membre actif.

card game *n* jeu *m* de cartes.

cardiac ['kɑːdɪæk] *adj* cardiaque.

cardigan ['kɑːdɪgən] *n* cardigan *m*.

cardinal ['kɑːdɪnl] *adj* cardinal(e) ♦ *n* cardinal *m*.

card index *n* fichier *m* (alphabétique).

cardphone ['kɑːdfəun] *n* téléphone *m* à carte (magnétique).

cardsharp ['kɑːdʃɑːp] n tricheur/euse professionnel(le).

card vote n (BRIT) vote m de délégués.

CARE [kɛə*] n abbr (= Cooperative for American Relief Everywhere) association charitable.

care [kɛə*] n soin m, attention f; (worry) souci m ♦ vi: to ~ **about** se soucier de, s'intéresser à; **in sb's** ~ à la garde de qn, confié à qn; ~ **of** (c/o) (on letter) aux bons soins de; "**with** ~" "fragile"; **to take** ~ **(to do)** faire attention (à faire); **to take** ~ **of** vt s'occuper de, prendre soin de; (details, arrangements) s'occuper de; **the child has been taken into** ~ l'enfant a été placé en institution; **would you** ~ **to/for ...?** voulez-vous ...?; **I wouldn't** ~ **to do it** je n'aimerais pas le faire; **I don't** ~ ça m'est bien égal, peu m'importe; **I couldn't** ~ **less** cela m'est complètement égal, je m'en fiche complètement.
▶**care for** vt fus s'occuper de; (like) aimer.

careen [kə'riːn] vi (ship) donner de la bande ♦ vt caréner, mettre en carène.

career [kə'rɪə*] n carrière f ♦ vi (also: ~ **along**) aller à toute allure.

career girl n jeune fille f (or femme f) qui veut faire carrière.

careers officer n conseiller/ère d'orientation (professionnelle).

carefree ['kɛəfriː] adj sans souci, insouciant(e).

careful ['kɛəful] adj soigneux(euse); (cautious) prudent(e); **(be)** ~! (fais) attention!; **to be** ~ **with one's money** regarder à la dépense.

carefully ['kɛəfəlɪ] adv avec soin, soigneusement; prudemment.

careless ['kɛəlɪs] adj négligent(e); (heedless) insouciant(e).

carelessly ['kɛəlɪslɪ] adv négligemment; avec insouciance.

carelessness ['kɛəlɪsnɪs] n manque m de soin, négligence f; insouciance f.

carer ['kɛərə*] n personne qui s'occupe d'un proche qui est malade.

caress [kə'rɛs] n caresse f ♦ vt caresser.

caretaker ['kɛəteɪkə*] n gardien/ne, concierge m/f.

caretaker government n (BRIT) gouvernement m intérimaire.

car-ferry ['kɑːfɛrɪ] n (on sea) ferry(-boat) m; (on river) bac m.

cargo, pl ~**es** ['kɑːgəu] n cargaison f, chargement m.

cargo boat n cargo m.

cargo plane n avion-cargo m.

car hire n (BRIT) location f de voitures.

Caribbean [kærɪ'biːən] adj des Caraïbes; **the** ~ **(Sea)** la mer des Antilles or des Caraïbes.

caricature ['kærɪkətjuə*] n caricature f.

caring ['kɛərɪŋ] adj (person) bienveillant(e); (society, organization) humanitaire.

carnage ['kɑːnɪdʒ] n carnage m.

carnal ['kɑːnl] adj charnel(le).

carnation [kɑː'neɪʃən] n œillet m.

carnival ['kɑːnɪvl] n (public celebration) carnaval m; (US: funfair) fête foraine.

carnivorous [kɑː'nɪvərəs] adj carnivore, carnassier(ière).

carol ['kærəl] n: **(Christmas)** ~ chant m de Noël.

carouse [kə'rauz] vi faire la bringue.

carousel [kærə'sɛl] n (US) manège m.

carp [kɑːp] n (fish) carpe f.
▶**carp at** vt fus critiquer.

car park n parking m, parc m de stationnement.

carpenter ['kɑːpɪntə*] n charpentier m.

carpentry ['kɑːpɪntrɪ] n charpenterie f, métier m de charpentier; (woodwork: at school etc) menuiserie f.

carpet ['kɑːpɪt] n tapis m ♦ vt recouvrir (d'un tapis); **fitted** ~ (BRIT) moquette f.

carpet bombing n bombardement intensif.

carpet slippers npl pantoufles fpl.

carpet sweeper [-'swiːpə*] n balai m mécanique.

car phone n téléphone m de voiture.

car rental n (US) location f de voitures.

carriage ['kærɪdʒ] n voiture f; (of goods) transport m; (: cost) port m; (of typewriter) chariot m; (bearing) maintien m, port m; ~ **forward** port dû; ~ **free** franco de port; ~ **paid** (en) port payé.

carriage return n retour m à la ligne.

carriageway ['kærɪdʒweɪ] n (BRIT: part of road) chaussée f.

carrier ['kærɪə*] n transporteur m, camionneur m; (MED) porteur/euse; (NAUT) porte-avions m inv.

carrier bag n (BRIT) sac m en papier or en plastique.

carrier pigeon n pigeon voyageur.

carrion ['kærɪən] n charogne f.

carrot ['kærət] n carotte f.

carry ['kærɪ] vt (subj: person) porter; (: vehicle) transporter; (a motion, bill) voter, adopter; (MATH: figure) retenir; (COMM: interest) rapporter; (involve: responsibilities etc) comporter, impliquer ♦ vi (sound) porter; **to be carried away** (fig) s'emballer, s'enthousiasmer; **this loan carries 10% interest** ce prêt est à 10% (d'intérêt).
▶**carry forward** vt (gen, BOOK-KEEPING) reporter.
▶**carry on** vi (continue): **to** ~ **on with sth/doing** continuer qch/à faire; (col: make a fuss) faire des histoires ♦ vt entretenir, poursuivre.
▶**carry out** vt (orders) exécuter; (investigation) effectuer; (idea, threat) mettre à exécution.

carrycot ['kærɪkɔt] n (BRIT) porte-bébé m.

carry-on ['kærɪ'ɔn] n (col: fuss) histoires fpl; (: annoying behaviour) cirque m, cinéma m.

cart [kɑːt] n charrette f ♦ vt transporter.

carte blanche ['kɑːt'blɒnʃ] n: **to give sb** ~

donner carte blanche à qn.

cartel [kɑː'tɛl] n (COMM) cartel m.

cartilage ['kɑːtɪlɪdʒ] n cartilage m.

cartographer [kɑː'tɔgrəfə*] n cartographe m/f.

cartography [kɑː'tɔgrəfɪ] n cartographie f.

carton ['kɑːtən] n (box) carton m; (of yogurt) pot m (en carton); (of cigarettes) cartouche f.

cartoon [kɑː'tuːn] n (PRESS) dessin m (humoristique); (satirical) caricature f; (comic strip) bande dessinée; (CINE) dessin animé.

cartoonist [kɑː'tuːnɪst] n dessinateur/trice humoristique; caricaturiste m/f; auteur m de dessins animés; auteur de bandes dessinées.

cartridge ['kɑːtrɪdʒ] n (for gun, pen) cartouche f; (for camera) chargeur m; (music tape) cassette f; (of record player) cellule f.

cartwheel ['kɑːtwiːl] n roue f; to turn a ~ faire la roue.

carve [kɑːv] vt (meat: also: ~ up) découper; (wood, stone) tailler, sculpter.

carving ['kɑːvɪŋ] n (in wood etc) sculpture f.

carving knife n couteau m à découper.

car wash n station f de lavage (de voitures).

Casablanca [kæsə'blæŋkə] n Casablanca.

cascade [kæs'keɪd] n cascade f ♦ vi tomber en cascade.

case [keɪs] n cas m; (LAW) affaire f, procès m; (box) caisse f, boîte f, étui m; (BRIT: also: suit~) valise f; (TYP): **lower/upper** ~ minuscule f/majuscule f; **to have a good** ~ avoir de bons arguments; **there's a strong** ~ **for reform** il y aurait lieu d'engager une réforme; **in** ~ **of** en cas de; **in** ~ **he** au cas où il; **just in** ~ à tout hasard.

case history n (MED) dossier médical, antécédents médicaux.

case study n étude f de cas.

cash [kæʃ] n argent m; (COMM) argent liquide, numéraire m; liquidités fpl; (: in payment) argent comptant, espèces fpl ♦ vt encaisser; **to pay (in)** ~ payer (en argent) comptant or en espèces; ~ **with order/on delivery** (COMM) payable or paiement à la commande/livraison; **to be short of** ~ être à court d'argent.

▶**cash in** vt (insurance policy etc) toucher.

▶**cash in on** vt fus profiter de.

cash account n compte m caisse.

cash and carry n libre-service m de gros, cash and carry m inv.

cashbook ['kæʃbuk] n livre m de caisse.

cash box n caisse f.

cash card n carte de retrait or accréditive.

cash desk n (BRIT) caisse f.

cash discount n escompte m de caisse (pour paiement au comptant), remise f au comptant.

cash dispenser n distributeur m automatique de billets.

cashew [kæ'ʃuː] n (also: ~ nut) noix f de cajou.

cash flow n cash-flow m, marge brute d'autofinancement.

cashier [kæ'ʃɪə*] n caissier/ère ♦ vt (MIL) destituer, casser.

cashmere ['kæʃmɪə*] n cachemire m.

cash payment n paiement comptant, versement m en espèces.

cash price n prix comptant.

cash register n caisse enregistreuse.

cash sale n vente f au comptant.

casing ['keɪsɪŋ] n revêtement (protecteur), enveloppe (protectrice).

casino [kə'siːnəu] n casino m.

cask [kɑːsk] n tonneau m.

casket ['kɑːskɪt] n coffret m; (US: coffin) cercueil m.

Caspian Sea ['kæspɪən-] n: **the** ~ la mer Caspienne.

casserole ['kæsərəul] n cocotte f; (food) ragoût m (en cocotte).

cassette [kæ'sɛt] n cassette f, musicassette f.

cassette deck n platine f cassette.

cassette player n lecteur m de cassettes.

cassette recorder n magnétophone m à cassettes.

cast [kɑːst] vb (pt, pp **cast**) vt (throw) jeter; (shed) perdre; se dépouiller de; (metal) couler, fondre; (THEAT): **to** ~ **sb as Hamlet** attribuer à qn le rôle d'Hamlet ♦ n (THEAT) distribution f; (mould) moule m; (also: **plaster** ~) plâtre m; **to** ~ **one's vote** voter, exprimer son suffrage.

▶**cast aside** vt (reject) rejeter.

▶**cast off** vi (NAUT) larguer les amarres; (KNITTING) arrêter les mailles ♦ vt (KNITTING) arrêter.

▶**cast on** (KNITTING) vt monter ♦ vi monter les mailles.

castanets [kæstə'nɛts] npl castagnettes fpl.

castaway ['kɑːstəweɪ] n naufragé/e.

caste [kɑːst] n caste f, classe sociale.

caster sugar ['kɑːstə-] n (BRIT) sucre m semoule.

casting vote ['kɑːstɪŋ-] n (BRIT) voix prépondérante (pour départager).

cast iron n fonte f ♦ adj: **cast-iron** (fig: will) de fer; (: alibi) inébranlable.

castle ['kɑːsl] n château-fort m; (manor) château m.

cast-offs ['kɑːstɔfs] npl vêtements mpl dont on ne veut plus.

castor ['kɑːstə*] n (wheel) roulette f.

castor oil n huile f de ricin.

castrate [kæs'treɪt] vt châtrer.

casual ['kæʒjul] adj (by chance) de hasard, fait(e) au hasard, fortuit(e); (irregular: work etc) temporaire; (unconcerned) désinvolte; ~ **wear** vêtements mpl sport inv.

casual labour n main-d'œuvre f temporaire.

casually ['kæʒjulɪ] adv avec désinvolture, négligemment; (by chance) fortuitement.

casualty ['kæʒjultɪ] n accidenté/e, blessé/e;

(*dead*) victime *f*, mort/e; **heavy casualties** lourdes pertes.

casualty ward *n* (*BRIT*) service *m* des urgences.

cat [kæt] *n* chat *m*.

catacombs ['kætəku:mz] *npl* catacombes *fpl*.

catalogue, (*US*) **catalog** ['kætəlɔg] *n* catalogue *m* ♦ *vt* cataloguer.

catalyst ['kætəlɪst] *n* catalyseur *m*.

catalytic converter [kætə'lɪtɪkkən'vɔːtə*] *n* pot *m* catalytique.

catapult ['kætəpʌlt] *n* lance-pierres *m inv*, fronde *m*; (*HISTORY*) catapulte *f*.

cataract ['kætərækt] *n* (*also MED*) cataracte *f*.

catarrh [kə'tɑː*] *n* rhume *m* chronique, catarrhe *f*.

catastrophe [kə'tæstrəfɪ] *n* catastrophe *f*.

catastrophic [kætə'strɔfɪk] *adj* catastrophique.

catcall ['kætkɔːl] *n* (*at meeting etc*) sifflet *m*.

catch [kætʃ] *vb* (*pt, pp* **caught** [kɔːt]) *vt* (*ball, train, thief, cold*) attraper; (*person: by surprise*) prendre, surprendre; (*understand*) saisir; (*get entangled*) accrocher ♦ *vi* (*fire*) prendre; (*get entangled*) s'accrocher ♦ *n* (*fish etc caught*) prise *f*; (*thief etc caught*) capture *f*; (*trick*) attrape *f*; (*TECH*) loquet *m*; cliquet *m*; **to ~ sb's attention** *or* **eye** attirer l'attention de qn; **to ~ fire** prendre feu; **to ~ sight of** apercevoir.

▶**catch on** *vi* (*become popular*) prendre; (*understand*): **to ~ on (to sth)** saisir (qch).

▶**catch out** *vt* (*BRIT fig: with trick question*) prendre en défaut.

▶**catch up** *vi* se rattraper, combler son retard ♦ *vt* (*also: ~ up with*) rattraper.

catching ['kætʃɪŋ] *adj* (*MED*) contagieux(euse).

catchment area ['kætʃmənt-] *n* (*BRIT SCOL*) aire *f* de recrutement; (*GEO*) bassin *m* hydrographique.

catch phrase *n* slogan *m*; expression toute faite.

catch-22 ['kætʃtwentɪ'tuː] *n*: **it's a ~ situation** c'est (une situation) sans issue.

catchy ['kætʃɪ] *adj* (*tune*) facile à retenir.

catechism ['kætɪkɪzəm] *n* catéchisme *m*.

categoric(al) [kætɪ'gɔrɪk(l)] *adj* catégorique.

categorize ['kætɪgəraɪz] *vt* classer par catégories.

category ['kætɪgərɪ] *n* catégorie *f*.

cater ['keɪtə*] *vi* (*provide food*): **to ~ (for)** préparer des repas (pour), se charger de la restauration (pour).

▶**cater for** *vt fus* (*BRIT: needs*) satisfaire, pourvoir à; (*: readers, consumers*) s'adresser à, pourvoir aux besoins de.

caterer ['keɪtərə*] *n* traiteur *m*; fournisseur *m*.

catering ['keɪtərɪŋ] *n* restauration *f*; approvisionnement *m*, ravitaillement *m*.

caterpillar ['kætəpɪlə*] *n* chenille *f* ♦ *cpd* (*vehicle*) à chenille; **~ track** *n* chenille *f*.

cat flap *n* chatière *f*.

cathedral [kə'θiːdrəl] *n* cathédrale *f*.

cathode ['kæθəud] *n* cathode *f*.

cathode ray tube *n* tube *m* cathodique.

catholic ['kæθəlɪk] *adj* éclectique; universel(le); libéral(e); **C~** *adj, n* (*REL*) catholique (*m/f*).

cat's-eye ['kæts'aɪ] *n* (*BRIT AUT*) (*clou m à*) catadioptre *m*.

catsup ['kætsəp] *n* (*US*) ketchup *m*.

cattle ['kætl] *npl* bétail *m*, bestiaux *mpl*.

catty ['kætɪ] *adj* méchant(e).

catwalk ['kætwɔːk] *n* passerelle *f*; (*for models*) podium *m* (*de défilé de mode*).

Caucasian [kɔː'keɪzɪən] *adj, n* caucasien(ne).

Caucasus ['kɔːkəsəs] *n* Caucase *m*.

caucus ['kɔːkəs] *n* (*US POL*) comité électoral (*pour désigner des candidats*); (*BRIT POL: group*) comité local (*d'un parti politique*).

> Un **caucus** aux États-Unis est une réunion restreinte des principaux dirigeants d'un parti politique, précédant souvent une assemblée générale, dans le but de choisir des candidats ou de définir une ligne d'action. Par extension, ce terme désigne également l'état-major d'un parti politique.

caught [kɔːt] *pt, pp of* **catch**.

cauliflower ['kɔlɪflauə*] *n* chou-fleur *m*.

cause [kɔːz] *n* cause *f* ♦ *vt* causer; **there is no ~ for concern** il n'y a pas lieu de s'inquiéter; **to ~ sth to be done** faire faire qch; **to ~ sb to do sth** faire faire qch à qn.

causeway ['kɔːzweɪ] *n* chaussée (surélevée).

caustic ['kɔːstɪk] *adj* caustique.

caution ['kɔːʃən] *n* prudence *f*, (*warning*) avertissement *m* ♦ *vt* avertir, donner un avertissement à.

cautious ['kɔːʃəs] *adj* prudent(e).

cautiously ['kɔːʃəslɪ] *adv* prudemment, avec prudence.

cautiousness ['kɔːʃəsnɪs] *n* prudence *f*.

cavalier [kævə'lɪə*] *adj* cavalier(ère), désinvolte ♦ *n* (*knight*) cavalier *m*.

cavalry ['kævəlrɪ] *n* cavalerie *f*.

cave [keɪv] *n* caverne *f*, grotte *f* ♦ *vi*: **to go caving** faire de la spéléo(logie).

▶**cave in** *vi* (*roof etc*) s'effondrer.

caveman ['keɪvmæn] *n* homme *m* des cavernes.

cavern ['kævən] *n* caverne *f*.

caviar(e) ['kævɪɑː*] *n* caviar *m*.

cavity ['kævɪtɪ] *n* cavité *f*.

cavity wall insulation *n* isolation *f* des murs creux.

cavort [kə'vɔːt] *vi* cabrioler, faire des cabrioles.

cayenne [keɪ'ɛn] *n* (*also: ~ pepper*) poivre *m* de cayenne.

CB *n abbr* (= *Citizens' Band (Radio)*) CB *f*; (*BRIT: = Companion of (the Order of) the Bath*) titre honorifique.

CBC *n abbr* (= *Canadian Broadcasting Corporation*) organisme de radiodiffusion.

CBE *n abbr* (= *Companion of (the Order of) the British Empire*) titre honorifique.

CBI *n abbr* (= *Confederation of British Industry*) ≈ CNPF *m* (= *Conseil national du patronat français*).

CBS *n abbr* (US: = *Columbia Broadcasting System*) chaîne de télévision.

CC *abbr* (BRIT) = *county council*.

cc *abbr* (= *cubic centimetre*) cm³; (*on letter etc*) = **carbon copy**.

CCA *n abbr* (US: = *Circuit Court of Appeals*) cour d'appel itinérante.

CCU *n abbr* (US: = *coronary care unit*) unité *f* de soins cardiologiques.

CD *n abbr* (= *compact disc*) CD *m*; (MIL) = *Civil Defence (Corps)* (BRIT), *Civil Defense* (US) ♦ *abbr* (BRIT: = *Corps Diplomatique*) CD.

CDC *n abbr* (US) = *center for disease control*.

CD-I *n abbr* ® (= *Compact Disc Interactive*) CD-I *m*, disque compact interactif.

CD player *n* platine *f* laser.

Cdr. *abbr* (= *commander*) Cdt.

CD-ROM [siːdiːˈrɔm] *n abbr* (= *compact disc read-only memory*) CD-ROM *m inv*.

CDT *abbr* (US: = *Central Daylight Time*) heure d'été du centre.

CDW *n abbr* = **collision damage waiver**.

cease [siːs] *vt*, *vi* cesser.

ceasefire [ˈsiːsfaɪə*] *n* cessez-le-feu *m*.

ceaseless [ˈsiːslɪs] *adj* incessant(e), continuel(le).

CED *n abbr* (US) = *Committee for Economic Development*.

cedar [ˈsiːdə*] *n* cèdre *m*.

cede [siːd] *vt* céder.

cedilla [sɪˈdɪlə] *n* cédille *f*.

CEEB *n abbr* (US: = *College Entrance Examination Board*) commission d'admission dans l'enseignement supérieur.

ceilidh [ˈkeɪlɪ] *n* bal *m* folklorique écossais *or* irlandais.

ceiling [ˈsiːlɪŋ] *n* (*also fig*) plafond *m*.

celebrate [ˈselɪbreɪt] *vt*, *vi* célébrer.

celebrated [ˈselɪbreɪtɪd] *adj* célèbre.

celebration [selɪˈbreɪʃən] *n* célébration *f*.

celebrity [sɪˈlebrɪtɪ] *n* célébrité *f*.

celeriac [səˈlerɪæk] *n* céleri(-rave) *m*.

celery [ˈselərɪ] *n* céleri *m* (en branches).

celestial [sɪˈlestɪəl] *adj* céleste.

celibacy [ˈselɪbəsɪ] *n* célibat *m*.

cell [sel] *n* (*gen*) cellule *f*; (ELEC) élément *m* (*de pile*).

cellar [ˈselə*] *n* cave *f*.

'cellist [ˈtʃelɪst] *n* violoncelliste *m/f*.

'cello [ˈtʃeləʊ] *n* violoncelle *m*.

cellophane [ˈseləfeɪn] *n* ® cellophane *f* ®.

cellphone [ˈselfəʊn] *n* téléphone *m* cellulaire.

cellular [ˈseljʊlə*] *adj* cellulaire.

Celluloid [ˈseljʊlɔɪd] *n* ® celluloïd *m* ®.

cellulose [ˈseljʊləʊs] *n* cellulose *f*.

Celsius [ˈselsɪəs] *adj* Celsius *inv*.

Celt [kelt, selt] *n* Celte *m/f*.

Celtic [ˈkeltɪk, ˈseltɪk] *adj* celte, celtique ♦ *n* (LING) celtique *m*.

cement [səˈment] *n* ciment *m* ♦ *vt* cimenter.

cement mixer *n* bétonnière *f*.

cemetery [ˈsemɪtrɪ] *n* cimetière *m*.

cenotaph [ˈsenətɑːf] *n* cénotaphe *m*.

censor [ˈsensə*] *n* censeur *m* ♦ *vt* censurer.

censorship [ˈsensəʃɪp] *n* censure *f*.

censure [ˈsenʃə*] *vt* blâmer, critiquer.

census [ˈsensəs] *n* recensement *m*.

cent [sent] *n* (US: *coin*) cent *m* (= 1:100 *du dollar*); *see also* **per**.

centenary [senˈtiːnərɪ], **centennial** [senˈtenɪəl] *n* centenaire *m*.

center [ˈsentə*] *n*, *vt* (US) = **centre**.

centigrade [ˈsentɪgreɪd] *adj* centigrade.

centilitre, (US) **centiliter** [ˈsentiliːtə*] *n* centilitre *m*.

centimetre, (US) **centimeter** [ˈsentimiːtə*] *n* centimètre *m*.

centipede [ˈsentɪpiːd] *n* mille-pattes *m inv*.

central [ˈsentrəl] *adj* central(e).

Central African Republic *n* République Centrafricaine.

Central America *n* Amérique centrale.

central heating *n* chauffage central.

centralize [ˈsentrəlaɪz] *vt* centraliser.

central processing unit (CPU) *n* (COMPUT) unité centrale (de traitement).

central reservation *n* (BRIT AUT) terre-plein central.

centre, (US) **center** [ˈsentə*] *n* centre *m* ♦ *vt* centrer; (PHOT) cadrer; (*concentrate*): **to ~ (on)** centrer (sur).

centrefold, (US) **centerfold** [ˈsentəfəʊld] *n* (PRESS) pages centrales détachables (*avec photo de pin up*).

centre-forward [ˈsentəˈfɔːwəd] *n* (SPORT) avant-centre *m*.

centre-half [ˈsentəˈhɑːf] *n* (SPORT) demi-centre *m*.

centrepiece, (US) **centerpiece** [ˈsentəpiːs] *n* milieu *m* de table; (*fig*) pièce maîtresse.

centre spread *n* (BRIT) publicité *f* en double page.

centre-stage [sentəˈsteɪdʒ] *n*: **to take ~** occuper le centre de la scène.

centrifugal [senˈtrɪfjugl] *adj* centrifuge.

centrifuge [ˈsentrɪfjuːʒ] *n* centrifugeuse *f*.

century [ˈsentjʊrɪ] *n* siècle *m*; **in the twentieth ~** au vingtième siècle.

CEO *n abbr* (US) = **chief executive officer**.

ceramic [sɪˈræmɪk] *adj* céramique.

cereal [ˈsiːrɪəl] *n* céréale *f*.

cerebral [ˈserɪbrəl] *adj* cérébral(e).

ceremonial [serɪˈməʊnɪəl] *n* cérémonial *m*; (*rite*) rituel *m*.

ceremony [ˈserɪmənɪ] *n* cérémonie *f*; **to stand on ~** faire des façons.

cert [səːt] *n* (BRIT *col*): **it's a dead ~** ça ne fait

pas un pli.
certain ['sɜːtən] *adj* certain(e); **to make ~ of** s'assurer de; **for ~** certainement, sûrement.
certainly ['sɜːtənlɪ] *adv* certainement.
certainty ['sɜːtəntɪ] *n* certitude *f*.
certificate [sə'tɪfɪkɪt] *n* certificat *m*.
certified letter ['sɜːtɪfaɪd-] *n* (*US*) lettre recommandée.
certified public accountant (CPA) ['sɜːtɪfaɪd-] *n* (*US*) expert-comptable *m*.
certify ['sɜːtɪfaɪ] *vt* certifier ♦ *vi*: **to ~ to** attester.
cervical ['sɜːvɪkl] *adj*: **~ cancer** cancer *m* du col de l'utérus; **~ smear** frottis vaginal.
cervix ['sɜːvɪks] *n* col *m* de l'utérus.
Cesarean [siː'zɛərɪən] *adj*, *n* (*US*) = **Caesarean**.
cessation [sə'seɪʃən] *n* cessation *f*, arrêt *m*.
cesspit ['sespɪt] *n* fosse *f* d'aisance.
CET *abbr* (= *Central European Time*) heure d'Europe centrale.
Ceylon [sɪ'lɒn] *n* Ceylan *m*.
cf. *abbr* (= *compare*) cf., voir.
c/f *abbr* (*COMM*) = carried forward.
CFC *n abbr* (= *chlorofluorocarbon*) CFC *m*.
CG *n abbr* (*US*) = **coastguard**.
cg *abbr* (= *centigram*) cg.
CH *n abbr* (*BRIT*: = *Companion of Honour*) titre honorifique.
ch *abbr* (*BRIT*: = *central heating*) c.c.
ch. *abbr* (= *chapter*) chap.
Chad [tʃæd] *n* Tchad *m*.
chafe [tʃeɪf] *vt* irriter, frotter contre ♦ *vi* (*fig*): **to ~ against** se rebiffer contre, regimber contre.
chaffinch ['tʃæfɪntʃ] *n* pinson *m*.
chagrin ['ʃægrɪn] *n* contrariété *f*, déception *f*.
chain [tʃeɪn] *n* (*gen*) chaîne *f* ♦ *vt* (*also*: **~ up**) enchaîner, attacher (avec une chaîne).
chain reaction *n* réaction *f* en chaîne.
chain-smoke ['tʃeɪnsməuk] *vi* fumer cigarette sur cigarette.
chain store *n* magasin *m* à succursales multiples.
chair [tʃɛə*] *n* chaise *f*; (*armchair*) fauteuil *m*; (*of university*) chaire *f* ♦ *vt* (*meeting*) présider; **the ~** (*US*: *electric ~*) la chaise électrique.
chairlift ['tʃɛəlɪft] *n* télésiège *m*.
chairman ['tʃɛəmən] *n* président *m*.
chairperson ['tʃɛəpɜːsn] *n* président/e.
chairwoman ['tʃɛəwumən] *n* présidente *f*.
chalet ['ʃæleɪ] *n* chalet *m*.
chalice ['tʃælɪs] *n* calice *m*.
chalk [tʃɔːk] *n* craie *f*.
▶**chalk up** *vt* écrire à la craie; (*fig: success etc*) remporter.
challenge ['tʃælɪndʒ] *n* défi *m* ♦ *vt* défier; (*statement, right*) mettre en question, contester; **to ~ sb to a fight/game** inviter qn à se battre/à jouer (*sous forme d'un défi*); **to ~ sb to do** mettre qn au défi de faire.
challenger ['tʃælɪndʒə*] *n* (*SPORT*) challenger *m*.

challenging ['tʃælɪndʒɪŋ] *adj* de défi, provocateur(trice).
chamber ['tʃeɪmbə*] *n* chambre *f*; **~ of commerce** chambre de commerce.
chambermaid ['tʃeɪmbəmeɪd] *n* femme *f* de chambre.
chamber music *n* musique *f* de chambre.
chamberpot ['tʃeɪmbəpɒt] *n* pot *m* de chambre.
chameleon [kə'miːlɪən] *n* caméléon *m*.
chamois ['ʃæmwɑː] *n* chamois *m*.
chamois leather ['ʃæmɪ-] *n* peau *f* de chamois.
champagne [ʃæm'peɪn] *n* champagne *m*.
champers ['ʃæmpəz] *n* (*col*) champ *m*.
champion ['tʃæmpɪən] *n* (*also of cause*) champion/ne ♦ *vt* défendre.
championship ['tʃæmpɪənʃɪp] *n* championnat *m*.
chance [tʃɑːns] *n* hasard *m*; (*opportunity*) occasion *f*, possibilité *f*; (*hope, likelihood*) chance *f* ♦ *vt* (*risk*): **to ~ it** risquer (le coup), essayer; (*happen*): **to ~ to do** faire par hasard ♦ *adj* fortuit(e), de hasard; **there is little ~ of his coming** il est peu probable *or* il y a peu de chances qu'il vienne; **to take a ~** prendre un risque; **it's the ~ of a lifetime** c'est une occasion unique; **by ~** par hasard.
▶**chance (up)on** *vt fus* (*person*) tomber sur, rencontrer par hasard; (*thing*) trouver par hasard.
chancel ['tʃɑːnsəl] *n* chœur *m*.
chancellor ['tʃɑːnsələ*] *n* chancelier *m*; **C~ of the Exchequer** (*BRIT*) chancelier de l'Échiquier.
chandelier [ʃændə'lɪə*] *n* lustre *m*.
change [tʃeɪndʒ] *vt* (*alter, replace, COMM: money*) changer; (*switch, substitute: gear, hands, trains, clothes, one's name etc*) changer de; (*transform*): **to ~ sb into** changer *or* transformer qn en ♦ *vi* (*gen*) changer; (*change clothes*) se changer; (*be transformed*): **to ~ into** se changer *or* transformer en ♦ *n* changement *m*; (*money*) monnaie *f*; **to ~ one's mind** changer d'avis; **she ~d into an old skirt** elle (s'est changée et) a enfilé une vieille jupe; **a ~ of clothes** des vêtements de rechange; **for a ~** pour changer; **small ~** petite monnaie; **to give sb ~ for** *or* **of £10** faire à qn la monnaie de 10 livres.
changeable ['tʃeɪndʒəbl] *adj* (*weather*) variable; (*person*) d'humeur changeante.
change machine *n* distributeur *m* de monnaie.
changeover ['tʃeɪndʒəuvə*] *n* (*to new system*) changement *m*, passage *m*.
changing ['tʃeɪndʒɪŋ] *adj* changeant(e).
changing room *n* (*BRIT*: *in shop*) salon *m* d'essayage; (: *SPORT*) vestiaire *m*.
channel ['tʃænl] *n* (*TV*) chaîne *f*; (*waveband, groove, fig: medium*) canal *m*; (*of river, sea*) chenal *m* ♦ *vt* canaliser; (*fig: interest, ener-*

gies): **to ~ into** diriger vers; **through the usual ~s** en suivant la filière habituelle; **green/red ~** (*CUSTOMS*) couloir *m or* sortie *f* "rien à déclarer"/"marchandises à déclarer"; **the (English) C~** la Manche.

Channel Islands *npl*: **the ~** les îles de la Manche, les îles anglo-normandes.

Channel Tunnel *n*: **the ~** le tunnel sous la Manche.

chant [tʃɑːnt] *n* chant *m*; mélopée *f*; psalmodie *f* ♦ *vt* chanter, scander; psalmodier.

chaos ['keɪɔs] *n* chaos *m*.

chaos theory *n* théorie *f* du chaos.

chaotic [keɪ'ɔtɪk] *adj* chaotique.

chap [tʃæp] *n* (*BRIT col*: *man*) type *m*; (*term of address*): **old ~** mon vieux ♦ *vt* (*skin*) gercer, crevasser.

chapel ['tʃæpl] *n* chapelle *f*.

chaperon ['ʃæpərəun] *n* chaperon *m* ♦ *vt* chaperonner.

chaplain ['tʃæplɪn] *n* aumônier *m*.

chapter ['tʃæptə*] *n* chapitre *m*.

char [tʃɑː*] *vt* (*burn*) carboniser ♦ *vi* (*BRIT*: *cleaner*) faire des ménages ♦ *n* (*BRIT*) = **charlady**.

character ['kærɪktə*] *n* caractère *m*; (*in novel, film*) personnage *m*; (*eccentric*) numéro *m*, phénomène *m*; **a person of good ~** une personne bien.

character code *n* (*COMPUT*) code *m* de caractère.

characteristic ['kærɪktə'rɪstɪk] *adj*, *n* caractéristique (*f*).

characterize ['kærɪktəraɪz] *vt* caractériser; **to ~ (as)** définir (comme).

charade [ʃə'rɑːd] *n* charade *f*.

charcoal ['tʃɑːkəul] *n* charbon *m* de bois.

charge [tʃɑːdʒ] *n* accusation *f*; (*LAW*) inculpation *f*; (*cost*) prix (demandé); (*of gun, battery, MIL*: *attack*) charge *f* ♦ *vt* (*LAW*): **to ~ sb (with)** inculper qn (de); (*gun, battery, MIL*: *enemy*) charger; (*customer, sum*) faire payer ♦ *vi* (*gen with*: *up, along etc*) foncer; **~s** *npl*: **bank/labour ~s** frais *mpl* de banque/main-d'œuvre; **to ~ in/out** entrer/sortir en trombe; **to ~ down/up** dévaler/grimper à toute allure; **is there a ~?** doit-on payer?; **there's no ~** c'est gratuit, on ne fait pas payer; **extra ~** supplément *m*; **to take ~ of** se charger de; **to be in ~ of** être responsable de, s'occuper de; **to have ~ of sb** avoir la charge de qn; **they ~d us £10 for the meal** ils nous ont fait payer le repas 10 livres, ils nous ont compté 10 livres pour le repas; **how much do you ~ for this repair?** combien demandez-vous pour cette réparation?; **to ~ an expense (up) to sb** mettre une dépense sur le compte de qn; **~ it to my account** facturez-le sur mon compte.

charge account *n* compte *m* client.

charge card *n* carte *f* de client (*émise par un grand magasin*).

chargehand ['tʃɑːdʒhænd] *n* (*BRIT*) chef *m* d'équipe.

charger ['tʃɑːdʒə*] *n* (*also*: **battery ~**) chargeur *m*; (*old*: *warhorse*) cheval *m* de bataille.

charitable ['tʃærɪtəbl] *adj* charitable.

charity ['tʃærɪtɪ] *n* charité *f*; (*organization*) institution *f* charitable *or* de bienfaisance, œuvre *f* (de charité).

charlady ['tʃɑːleɪdɪ] *n* (*BRIT*) femme *f* de ménage.

charm [tʃɑːm] *n* charme *m* ♦ *vt* charmer, enchanter.

charm bracelet *n* bracelet *m* à breloques.

charming ['tʃɑːmɪŋ] *adj* charmant(e).

chart [tʃɑːt] *n* tableau *m*, diagramme *m*; graphique *m*; (*map*) carte marine; (*weather ~*) carte *f* du temps ♦ *vt* dresser *or* établir la carte de; (*sales, progress*) établir la courbe de; **to be in the ~s** (*record, pop group*) figurer au hit-parade.

charter ['tʃɑːtə*] *vt* (*plane*) affréter ♦ *n* (*document*) charte *f*; **on ~** (*plane*) affrété(e).

chartered accountant (CA) ['tʃɑːtəd-] *n* (*BRIT*) expert-comptable *m*.

charter flight *n* charter *m*.

charwoman ['tʃɑːwumən] *n* = **charlady**.

chase [tʃeɪs] *vt* poursuivre, pourchasser ♦ *n* poursuite *f*, chasse *f*.

▶**chase down** *vt* (*US*) = **chase up**.

▶**chase up** *vt* (*BRIT*: *person*) relancer; (*: information*) rechercher.

chasm ['kæzəm] *n* gouffre *m*, abîme *m*.

chassis ['ʃæsɪ] *n* châssis *m*.

chastened ['tʃeɪsnd] *adj* assagi(e), rappelé(e) à la raison.

chastening ['tʃeɪsnɪŋ] *adj* qui fait réfléchir.

chastise [tʃæs'taɪz] *vt* punir, châtier; corriger.

chastity ['tʃæstɪtɪ] *n* chasteté *f*.

chat [tʃæt] *vi* (*also*: **have a ~**) bavarder, causer ♦ *n* conversation *f*.

▶**chat up** *vt* (*BRIT col*: *girl*) baratiner.

chatline ['tʃætlaɪn] *n* numéro téléphonique qui permet de bavarder avec plusieurs personnes en même temps.

chat show *n* (*BRIT*) entretien télévisé.

chattel ['tʃætl] *see* **goods**.

chatter ['tʃætə*] *vi* (*person*) bavarder, papoter ♦ *n* bavardage *m*, papotage *m*; **my teeth are ~ing** je claque des dents.

chatterbox ['tʃætəbɔks] *n* moulin *m* à paroles, babillard/e.

chattering classes ['tʃætərɪŋ-] *npl*: **the ~** (*col, pej*) les intellos *mpl*.

chatty ['tʃætɪ] *adj* (*style*) familier(ière); (*person*) enclin(e) à bavarder *or* au papotage.

chauffeur ['ʃəufə*] *n* chauffeur *m* (de maître).

chauvinism ['ʃəuvɪnɪzəm] *n* (*also*: **male ~**) phallocratie *f*, machisme *m*; (*nationalism*) chauvinisme *m*.

chauvinist ['ʃəuvɪnɪst] *n* (*also*: **male ~**) phallocrate *m*, macho *m*; (*nationalist*) chauvin/e.

ChE *abbr* = **chemical engineer**.

cheap [tʃiːp] adj bon marché inv, pas cher(chère); (reduced: ticket) à prix réduit; (: fare) réduit(e); (joke) facile, d'un goût douteux; (poor quality) à bon marché, de qualité médiocre ♦ adv à bon marché, pour pas cher; ~er adj moins cher(chère).

cheapen ['tʃiːpn] vt rabaisser, déprécier.

cheaply ['tʃiːplɪ] adv à bon marché, à bon compte.

cheat [tʃiːt] vi tricher; (in exam) copier ♦ vt tromper, duper; (rob) escroquer ♦ n tricheur/euse; escroc m; (trick) duperie f, tromperie f; **to ~ on sb** (col: husband, wife etc) tromper qn.

cheating ['tʃiːtɪŋ] n tricherie f.

check [tʃɛk] vt vérifier; (passport, ticket) contrôler; (halt) enrayer; (restrain) maîtriser ♦ vi (official etc) se renseigner ♦ n vérification f; contrôle m; (curb) frein m; (bill) addition f; (pattern: gen pl) carreaux mpl; (US) = **cheque** ♦ adj (also: ~ed: pattern, cloth) à carreaux; **to ~ with sb** demander à qn; **to keep a ~ on sb/sth** surveiller qn/qch.

▶**check in** vi (in hotel) remplir sa fiche (d'hôtel); (at airport) se présenter à l'enregistrement ♦ vt (luggage) (faire) enregistrer.

▶**check off** vt cocher.

▶**check out** vi (in hotel) régler sa note ♦ vt (luggage) retirer; (investigate: story) vérifier; (person) prendre des renseignements sur.

▶**check up** vi: **to ~ up (on sth)** vérifier (qch); **to ~ up on sb** se renseigner sur le compte de qn.

checkered ['tʃɛkəd] adj (US) = **chequered**.

checkers ['tʃɛkəz] n (US) jeu m de dames.

check guarantee card n (US) carte f (d'identité) bancaire.

check-in ['tʃɛkin] n (also: ~ **desk**: at airport) enregistrement m.

checking account ['tʃɛkɪŋ-] n (US) compte courant.

checklist ['tʃɛklɪst] n liste f de contrôle.

checkmate ['tʃɛkmeɪt] n échec et mat m.

checkout ['tʃɛkaut] n (in supermarket) caisse f.

checkpoint ['tʃɛkpɔint] n contrôle m.

checkup ['tʃɛkʌp] n (MED) examen médical, check-up m.

cheek [tʃiːk] n joue f; (impudence) toupet m, culot m.

cheekbone ['tʃiːkbəun] n pommette f.

cheeky ['tʃiːkɪ] adj effronté(e), culotté(e).

cheep [tʃiːp] n (of bird) piaulement m ♦ vi piauler.

cheer [tʃɪə*] vt acclamer, applaudir; (gladden) réjouir, réconforter ♦ vi applaudir ♦ n (gen pl) acclamations fpl, applaudissements mpl; bravos mpl, hourras mpl; ~**s!** (à votre) santé!

▶**cheer on** vt encourager (par des cris etc).

▶**cheer up** vi se dérider, reprendre courage ♦ vt remonter le moral à or de, dérider, égayer.

cheerful ['tʃɪəful] adj gai(e), joyeux(euse).

cheerfulness ['tʃɪəfulnɪs] n gaieté f, bonne humeur.

cheerio [tʃɪərɪ'əu] excl (BRIT) salut!, au revoir!

cheerleader ['tʃɪəliːdə*] n membre d'un groupe de majorettes qui chantent et dansent pour soutenir leur équipe pendant les matchs de football américain.

cheerless ['tʃɪəlɪs] adj sombre, triste.

cheese [tʃiːz] n fromage m.

cheeseboard ['tʃiːzbɔːd] n plateau m à fromages; (with cheese on it) plateau m de fromages.

cheeseburger ['tʃiːzbəːgə*] n cheeseburger m.

cheesecake ['tʃiːzkeɪk] n tarte f au fromage.

cheetah ['tʃiːtə] n guépard m.

chef [ʃɛf] n chef (cuisinier).

chemical ['kɛmɪkl] adj chimique ♦ n produit m chimique.

chemist ['kɛmɪst] n (BRIT: pharmacist) pharmacien/ne; (scientist) chimiste m/f; ~'**s (shop)** n (BRIT) pharmacie f.

chemistry ['kɛmɪstrɪ] n chimie f.

chemotherapy [kiːməu'θɛrəpɪ] n chimiothérapie f.

cheque, (US) check [tʃɛk] n chèque m; **to pay by ~** payer par chèque.

chequebook, (US) checkbook ['tʃɛkbuk] n chéquier m, carnet m de chèques.

cheque card n (BRIT) carte f (d'identité) bancaire.

chequered, (US) checkered ['tʃɛkəd] adj (fig) varié(e).

cherish ['tʃɛrɪʃ] vt chérir; (hope etc) entretenir.

cheroot [ʃə'ruːt] n cigare m de Manille.

cherry ['tʃɛrɪ] n cerise f.

Ches abbr (BRIT) = Cheshire.

chess [tʃɛs] n échecs mpl.

chessboard ['tʃɛsbɔːd] n échiquier m.

chessman ['tʃɛsmən] n pièce f (de jeu d'échecs).

chessplayer ['tʃɛspleɪə*] n joueur/euse d'échecs.

chest [tʃɛst] n poitrine f; (box) coffre m, caisse f; **to get sth off one's ~** (col) vider son sac; ~ **of drawers** n commode f.

chest measurement n tour m de poitrine.

chestnut ['tʃɛsnʌt] n châtaigne f; (also: ~ **tree**) châtaignier m; (colour) châtain m ♦ adj (hair) châtain inv; (horse) alezan.

chesty ['tʃɛstɪ] adj (cough) de poitrine.

chew [tʃuː] vt mâcher.

chewing gum ['tʃuːɪŋ-] n chewing-gum m.

chic [ʃiːk] adj chic inv, élégant(e).

chick [tʃɪk] n poussin m; (US col) pépée f.

chicken ['tʃɪkɪn] n poulet m; (col: coward) poule mouillée.

▶**chicken out** vi (col) se dégonfler.

chicken feed n (fig) broutilles fpl, bagatelle f.

chickenpox ['tʃɪkɪnpɔks] n varicelle f.

chickpea ['tʃɪkpiː] n pois m chiche.
chicory ['tʃɪkərɪ] n (*for coffee*) chicorée f; (*salad*) endive f.
chide [tʃaɪd] vt réprimander, gronder.
chief [tʃiːf] n chef m ♦ adj principal(e); **C~ of Staff** (*MIL*) chef d'État-major.
chief constable n (*BRIT*) ≈ préfet m de police.
chief executive, (*US*) **chief executive officer** n directeur général.
chiefly ['tʃiːflɪ] adv principalement, surtout.
chiffon ['ʃɪfɔn] n mousseline f de soie.
chilblain ['tʃɪlbleɪn] n engelure f.
child, pl ~**ren** [tʃaɪld, 'tʃɪldrən] n enfant m/f.
child benefit n (*BRIT*) ≈ allocations familiales.
childbirth ['tʃaɪldbəːθ] n accouchement m.
childhood ['tʃaɪldhud] n enfance f.
childish ['tʃaɪldɪʃ] adj puéril(e), enfantin(e).
childless ['tʃaɪldlɪs] adj sans enfants.
childlike ['tʃaɪldlaɪk] adj innocent(e), pur(e).
child minder n (*BRIT*) garde f d'enfants.
child prodigy n enfant m/f prodige.
children ['tʃɪldrən] npl of **child**.
children's home ['tʃɪldrənz-] n ≈ foyer m d'accueil (*pour enfants*).
Chile ['tʃɪlɪ] n Chili m.
Chilean ['tʃɪlɪən] adj chilien(ne) ♦ n Chilien/ne.
chill [tʃɪl] n froid m; (*MED*) refroidissement m, coup m de froid ♦ adj froid(e), glacial(e) ♦ vt faire frissonner; refroidir; (*CULIN*) mettre au frais, rafraîchir; **"serve ~ed"** "à servir frais".
►**chill out** vi (*col: esp US*) se relaxer.
chilli, (*US*) **chili** ['tʃɪlɪ] n piment m (*rouge*).
chilling ['tʃɪlɪŋ] adj (*wind*) frais(fraîche), froid(e); (*look, smile*) glacé(e); (*thought*) qui donne le frisson.
chilly ['tʃɪlɪ] adj froid(e), glacé(e); (*sensitive to cold*) frileux(euse); **to feel ~** avoir froid.
chime [tʃaɪm] n carillon m ♦ vi carillonner, sonner.
chimney ['tʃɪmnɪ] n cheminée f.
chimney sweep n ramoneur m.
chimpanzee [tʃɪmpæn'ziː] n chimpanzé m.
chin [tʃɪn] n menton m.
China ['tʃaɪnə] n Chine f.
china ['tʃaɪnə] n porcelaine f; (*vaisselle* f en) porcelaine.
Chinese [tʃaɪ'niːz] adj chinois(e) ♦ n (*pl inv*) Chinois/e; (*LING*) chinois m.
chink [tʃɪŋk] n (*opening*) fente f, fissure f; (*noise*) tintement m.
chinwag ['tʃɪnwæg] n (*BRIT col*): **to have a ~** tailler une bavette.
chip [tʃɪp] n (*gen pl: CULIN*) frite f; (: *US: also:* **potato ~**) chip m; (*of wood*) copeau m; (*of glass, stone*) éclat m; (*also:* **micro~**) puce f; (*in gambling*) fiche f ♦ vt (*cup, plate*) ébrécher; **when the ~s are down** (*fig*) au moment critique.
►**chip in** vi (*col*) mettre son grain de sel.

chipboard ['tʃɪpbɔːd] n aggloméré m, panneau m de particules.
chipmunk ['tʃɪpmʌŋk] n suisse m (*animal*).
chippings ['tʃɪpɪŋz] npl: **loose ~** gravillons mpl.
chip shop n (*BRIT*) friterie f.

Un **chip shop**, que l'on appelle également un "fish-and-chip shop", est un magasin où l'on vend des plats à emporter. Les chip shops sont d'ailleurs à l'origine des **takeaways**. On y achète en particulier du poisson frit et des frites, mais on y trouve également des plats traditionnels britanniques (steak pies, saucisses, etc). Tous les plats étaient à l'origine emballés dans du papier journal. Dans certains de ces magasins, on peut s'asseoir pour consommer sur place.

---

chiropodist [kɪ'rɔpədɪst] n (*BRIT*) pédicure m/f.
chiropody [kɪ'rɔpədɪ] n (*BRIT*) pédicurie f.
chirp [tʃəːp] n pépiement m, gazouillis m; (*of crickets*) stridulation f ♦ vi pépier, gazouiller; chanter, striduler.
chirpy ['tʃəːpɪ] adj (*col*) plein(e) d'entrain, tout guilleret(te).
chisel ['tʃɪzl] n ciseau m.
chit [tʃɪt] n mot m, note f.
chitchat ['tʃɪttʃæt] n bavardage m, papotage m.
chivalrous ['ʃɪvəlrəs] adj chevaleresque.
chivalry ['ʃɪvəlrɪ] n chevalerie f; esprit m chevaleresque.
chives [tʃaɪvz] npl ciboulette f, civette f.
chloride ['klɔːraɪd] n chlorure m.
chlorinate ['klɔrɪneɪt] vt chlorer.
chlorine ['klɔːriːn] n chlore m.
chock [tʃɔk] n cale f.
chock-a-block ['tʃɔkə'blɔk], **chock-full** [tʃɔk'ful] adj plein(e) à craquer.
chocolate ['tʃɔklɪt] n chocolat m.
choice [tʃɔɪs] n choix m ♦ adj de choix; **by** or **from ~** par choix; **a wide ~** un grand choix.
choir ['kwaɪə*] n chœur m, chorale f.
choirboy ['kwaɪəbɔɪ] n jeune choriste m, petit chanteur m.
choke [tʃəuk] vi étouffer ♦ vt étrangler; étouffer; (*block*) boucher, obstruer ♦ n (*AUT*) starter m.
cholera ['kɔlərə] n choléra m.
cholesterol [kə'lɛstərɔl] n cholestérol m.
choose, pt **chose,** pp **chosen** [tʃuːz, tʃəuz, 'tʃəuzn] vt choisir ♦ vi: **to ~ between** choisir entre; **to ~ from** choisir parmi; **to ~ to do** décider de faire, juger bon de faire.
choosy ['tʃuːzɪ] adj: **(to be) ~** (faire le) difficile.
chop [tʃɔp] vt (*wood*) couper (à la hache); (*CULIN: also:* **~ up**) couper (fin), émincer, hacher (en morceaux) ♦ n coup m (*de hache, du tranchant de la main*); (*CULIN*) côtelette f; **to get the ~** (*BRIT col: project*) tomber à l'eau;

(*: person: be sacked*) se faire renvoyer.

▶**chop down** *vt* (*tree*) abattre.

chopper ['tʃɔpə*] *n* (*helicopter*) hélicoptère *m*, hélico *m*.

choppy ['tʃɔpɪ] *adj* (*sea*) un peu agité(e).

chops [tʃɔps] *npl* (*jaws*) mâchoires *fpl*; babines *fpl*.

chopsticks ['tʃɔpstɪks] *npl* baguettes *fpl*.

choral ['kɔːrəl] *adj* choral(e), chanté(e) en chœur.

chord [kɔːd] *n* (*MUS*) accord *m*.

chore [tʃɔː*] *n* travail *m* de routine; **household ~s** travaux *mpl* du ménage.

choreographer [kɔrɪ'ɔgrəfə*] *n* chorégraphe *m/f*.

choreography [kɔrɪ'ɔgrəfɪ] *n* chorégraphie *f*.

chorister ['kɔrɪstə*] *n* choriste *m/f*.

chortle ['tʃɔːtl] *vi* glousser.

chorus ['kɔːrəs] *n* chœur *m*; (*repeated part of song, also fig*) refrain *m*.

chose [tʃəuz] *pt of* **choose**.

chosen ['tʃəuzn] *pp of* **choose**.

chow [tʃau] *n* (*dog*) chow-chow *m*.

chowder ['tʃaudə*] *n* soupe *f* de poisson.

Christ [kraɪst] *n* Christ *m*.

christen ['krɪsn] *vt* baptiser.

christening ['krɪsnɪŋ] *n* baptême *m*.

Christian ['krɪstɪən] *adj*, *n* chrétien(ne).

Christianity [krɪstɪ'ænɪtɪ] *n* christianisme *m*.

Christian name *n* prénom *m*.

Christmas ['krɪsməs] *n* Noël *m or f*; **happy or merry ~!** joyeux Noël!

Christmas card *n* carte *f* de Noël.

Christmas Day *n* le jour de Noël.

Christmas Eve *n* la veille de Noël; la nuit de Noël.

Christmas Island *n* île *f* Christmas.

Christmas tree *n* arbre *m* de Noël.

chrome [krəum] *n* = **chromium**.

chromium ['krəumɪəm] *n* chrome *m*; (*also: ~ plating*) chromage *m*.

chromosome ['krəuməsəum] *n* chromosome *m*.

chronic ['krɔnɪk] *adj* chronique; (*fig: liar, smoker*) invétéré(e).

chronicle ['krɔnɪkl] *n* chronique *f*.

chronological [krɔnə'lɔdʒɪkl] *adj* chronologique.

chrysanthemum [krɪ'sænθəməm] *n* chrysanthème *m*.

chubby ['tʃʌbɪ] *adj* potelé(e), rondelet(te).

chuck [tʃʌk] *vt* lancer, jeter; **to ~** (**up or in**) *vt* (*BRIT: job*) lâcher; (*: person*) plaquer.

▶**chuck out** *vt* flanquer dehors *or* à la porte.

chuckle ['tʃʌkl] *vi* glousser.

chuffed [tʃʌft] *adj* (*BRIT col*): **to be ~ about sth** être content(e) de qch.

chug [tʃʌg] *vi* faire teuf-teuf, souffler.

chum [tʃʌm] *n* copain/copine.

chump ['tʃʌmp] *n* (*col*) imbécile *m/f*, crétin/e.

chunk [tʃʌŋk] *n* gros morceau; (*of bread*) quignon *m*.

chunky ['tʃʌŋkɪ] *adj* (*furniture etc*) massif(ive); (*person*) trapu(e); (*knitwear*) en grosse laine.

Chunnel ['tʃʌnəl] *n* = **Channel Tunnel**.

church [tʃɜːtʃ] *n* église *f*; **the C~ of England** l'Église anglicane.

churchyard ['tʃɜːtʃjɑːd] *n* cimetière *m*.

churlish ['tʃɜːlɪʃ] *adj* grossier(ère); hargneux(euse).

churn [tʃɜːn] *n* (*for butter*) baratte *f*; (*for transport: also:* **milk ~**) (grand) bidon à lait.

▶**churn out** *vt* débiter.

chute [ʃuːt] *n* glissoire *f*; (*also:* **rubbish ~**) vide-ordures *m inv*; (*BRIT: children's slide*) toboggan *m*.

chutney ['tʃʌtnɪ] *n* chutney *m*.

CIA *n abbr* (*US:* = *Central Intelligence Agency*) CIA *f*.

CID *n abbr* (*BRIT:* = *Criminal Investigation Department*) ≈ P.J. *f* (= *police judiciaire*).

cider ['saɪdə*] *n* cidre *m*.

CIF *abbr* (= *cost, insurance and freight*) CAF.

cigar [sɪ'gɑː*] *n* cigare *m*.

cigarette [sɪgə'rɛt] *n* cigarette *f*.

cigarette case *n* étui *m* à cigarettes.

cigarette end *n* mégot *m*.

cigarette holder *n* fume-cigarettes *m inv*.

C-in-C *abbr* = **commander-in-chief**.

cinch [sɪntʃ] *n* (*col*): **it's a ~** c'est du gâteau, c'est l'enfance de l'art.

cinder ['sɪndə*] *n* cendre *f*.

Cinderella [sɪndə'rɛlə] *n* Cendrillon.

cine-camera ['sɪnɪ'kæmərə] *n* (*BRIT*) caméra *f*.

cine-film ['sɪnɪfɪlm] *n* (*BRIT*) film *m*.

cinema ['sɪnəmə] *n* cinéma *m*.

cine-projector ['sɪnɪprə'dʒɛktə*] *n* (*BRIT*) projecteur *m* de cinéma.

cinnamon ['sɪnəmən] *n* cannelle *f*.

cipher ['saɪfə*] *n* code secret; (*fig: faceless employee etc*) numéro *m*; **in ~** codé(e).

circa ['sɜːkə] *prep* circa, environ.

circle ['sɜːkl] *n* cercle *m*; (*in cinema*) balcon *m* ♦ *vi* faire *or* décrire des cercles ♦ *vt* (*surround*) entourer, encercler; (*move round*) faire le tour de, tourner autour de.

circuit ['sɜːkɪt] *n* circuit *m*.

circuit board *n* plaquette *f*.

circuitous [sɜː'kjuɪtəs] *adj* indirect(e), qui fait un détour.

circular ['sɜːkjulə*] *adj* circulaire ♦ *n* circulaire *f*; (*as advertisement*) prospectus *m*.

circulate ['sɜːkjuleɪt] *vi* circuler ♦ *vt* faire circuler.

circulation [sɜːkju'leɪʃən] *n* circulation *f*; (*of newspaper*) tirage *m*.

circumcise ['sɜːkəmsaɪz] *vt* circoncire.

circumference [sə'kʌmfərəns] *n* circonférence *f*.

circumflex ['sɜːkəmflɛks] *n* (*also:* **~ accent**) accent *m* circonflexe.

circumscribe ['sɜːkəmskraɪb] *vt* circonscrire.

circumspect ['sɜːkəmspɛkt] *adj* circonspect(e).

circumstances ['sɔːkəmstənsɪz] *npl* circonstances *fpl*; (*financial condition*) moyens *mpl*, situation financière; **in the** ~ dans ces conditions; **under no** ~ en aucun cas, sous aucun prétexte.

circumstantial [sɔːkəm'stænʃl] *adj* (*report, statement*) circonstancié(e); ~ **evidence** preuve indirecte.

circumvent [sɔːkəm'vɛnt] *vt* (*rule etc*) tourner.

circus ['sɔːkəs] *n* cirque *m*; (*also*: **C**~: *in place names*) place *f*.

cirrhosis [sɪ'rəusɪs] *n* (*also*: ~ **of the liver**) cirrhose *f* (du foie).

CIS *n abbr* (= *Commonwealth of Independent States*) CEI *f*.

cissy ['sɪsɪ] *n* = **sissy**.

cistern ['sɪstən] *n* réservoir *m* (d'eau); (*in toilet*) réservoir de la chasse d'eau.

citation [saɪ'teɪʃən] *n* citation *f*; (*US*) P.-V. *m*.

cite [saɪt] *vt* citer.

citizen ['sɪtɪzn] *n* (*POL*) citoyen/ne; (*resident*): **the** ~**s of this town** les habitants de cette ville.

Citizens' Advice Bureau ['sɪtɪznz-] *n* (*BRIT*) ≈ Bureau *m* d'aide sociale.

citizenship ['sɪtɪznʃɪp] *n* citoyenneté *f*.

citric ['sɪtrɪk] *adj*: ~ **acid** acide *m* citrique.

citrus fruit ['sɪtrəs-] *n* agrume *m*.

city ['sɪtɪ] *n* ville *f*, cité *f*; **the C**~ la Cité de Londres (*centre des affaires*).

city centre *n* centre-ville *m*.

City Hall *n* (*US*) ≈ hôtel *m* de ville.

City Technology College *n* (*BRIT*) établissement *m* d'enseignement technologique (*situé dans un quartier défavorisé*).

civic ['sɪvɪk] *adj* civique.

civic centre *n* (*BRIT*) centre administratif (municipal).

civil ['sɪvɪl] *adj* civil(e); (*polite*) poli(e), civil(e).

civil disobedience *n* désobéissance civile.

civil engineer *n* ingénieur civil.

civil engineering *n* génie civil, travaux publics.

civilian [sɪ'vɪlɪən] *adj*, *n* civil(e).

civilization [sɪvɪlaɪ'zeɪʃən] *n* civilisation *f*.

civilized ['sɪvɪlaɪzd] *adj* civilisé(e); (*fig*) où règnent les bonnes manières, empreint(e) d'une courtoisie de bon ton.

civil law *n* code civil; (*study*) droit civil.

civil liberties *npl* libertés *fpl* civiques.

civil rights *npl* droits *mpl* civiques.

civil servant *n* fonctionnaire *m/f*.

Civil Service *n* fonction publique, administration *f*.

civil war *n* guerre civile.

civvies ['sɪvɪz] *npl*: **in** ~ (*col*) en civil.

cl *abbr* (= *centilitre*) cl.

clad [klæd] *adj*: ~ **(in)** habillé(e) de, vêtu(e) de.

claim [kleɪm] *vt* (*rights etc*) revendiquer; (*compensation*) réclamer; **to** ~ **that/to be** prétendre que/être ♦ *vi* (*for insurance*) faire une déclaration de sinistre ♦ *n* revendication *f*;

prétention *f*; (*right*) droit *m*; (*for expenses*) note *f* de frais; (**insurance**) ~ demande *f* d'indemnisation, déclaration *f* de sinistre; **to put in a** ~ **for** (*pay rise etc*) demander.

claimant ['kleɪmənt] *n* (*ADMIN, LAW*) requérant/e.

claim form *n* (*gen*) formulaire *m* de demande.

clairvoyant [klɛə'vɔɪənt] *n* voyant/e, extralucide *m/f*.

clam [klæm] *n* palourde *f*.

▶**clam up** *vi* (*col*) la boucler.

clamber ['klæmbə*] *vi* grimper, se hisser.

clammy ['klæmɪ] *adj* humide et froid(e) (au toucher), moite.

clamour, (*US*) **clamor** ['klæmə*] *n* (*noise*) clameurs *fpl*; (*protest*) protestations bruyantes ♦ *vi*: **to** ~ **for sth** réclamer qch à grands cris.

clamp [klæmp] *n* étau *m* à main; agrafe *f*, crampon *m* ♦ *vt* serrer; cramponner.

▶**clamp down on** *vt fus* sévir contre, prendre des mesures draconiennes à l'égard de.

clampdown ['klæmpdaun] *n*: **there has been a** ~ **on** ... des mesures énergiques ont été prises contre ....

clan [klæn] *n* clan *m*.

clandestine [klæn'dɛstɪn] *adj* clandestin(e).

clang [klæŋ] *n* bruit *m* or fracas *m* métallique ♦ *vi* émettre un bruit or fracas métallique.

clanger ['klæŋə*] *n*: **to drop a** ~ (*BRIT col*) faire une boulette.

clansman ['klænzmən] *n* membre *m* d'un clan (écossais).

clap [klæp] *vi* applaudir ♦ *vt*: **to** ~ (**one's hands**) battre des mains ♦ *n* claquement *m*; tape *f*; **a** ~ **of thunder** un coup de tonnerre.

clapping ['klæpɪŋ] *n* applaudissements *mpl*.

claptrap ['klæptræp] *n* (*col*) baratin *m*.

claret ['klærət] *n* (*vin m de*) bordeaux *m* (rouge).

clarification [klærɪfɪ'keɪʃən] *n* (*fig*) clarification *f*, éclaircissement *m*.

clarify ['klærɪfaɪ] *vt* clarifier.

clarinet [klærɪ'nɛt] *n* clarinette *f*.

clarity ['klærɪtɪ] *n* clarté *f*.

clash [klæʃ] *n* (*sound*) choc *m*, fracas *m*; (*with police*) affrontement *m*; (*fig*) conflit *m* ♦ *vi* se heurter; être or entrer en conflit; (*dates, events*) tomber en même temps.

clasp [klɑːsp] *n* fermoir *m* ♦ *vt* serrer, étreindre.

class [klɑːs] *n* (*gen*) classe *f*; (*group, category*) catégorie *f* ♦ *vt* classer, classifier.

class-conscious ['klɑːs'kɒnʃəs] *adj* conscient(e) de son appartenance sociale.

class consciousness *n* conscience *f* de classe.

classic ['klæsɪk] *adj* classique ♦ *n* (*author*) classique *m*; (*race etc*) classique *f*.

classical ['klæsɪkl] *adj* classique.

classics ['klæsɪks] *npl* (*SCOL*) lettres *fpl* classiques.

classification [klæsɪfɪ'keɪʃən] *n* classification *f*.

classified ['klæsɪfaɪd] *adj* (*information*) secret(ète); ~ **ads** petites annonces.

classify ['klæsɪfaɪ] *vt* classifier, classer.

classless society ['klɑːslɪs-] *n* société *f* sans classes.

classmate ['klɑːsmeɪt] *n* camarade *m/f* de classe.

classroom ['klɑːsrum] *n* (salle *f* de) classe *f*.

clatter ['klætə*] *n* cliquetis *m* ♦ *vi* cliqueter.

clause [klɔːz] *n* clause *f*; (*LING*) proposition *f*.

claustrophobia [klɔːstrə'fəubɪə] *n* claustrophobie *f*.

claustrophobic [klɔːstrə'fəubɪk] *adj* (*person*) claustrophobe; (*place*) claustrophobique.

claw [klɔː] *n* griffe *f*; (*of bird of prey*) serre *f*; (*of lobster*) pince *f* ♦ *vt* griffer; déchirer.

clay [kleɪ] *n* argile *f*.

clean [kliːn] *adj* propre; (*clear, smooth*) net(te) ♦ *vt* nettoyer ♦ *adv*: **he ~ forgot** il a complètement oublié; **to come ~** (*col: admit guilt*) se mettre à table; **to ~ one's teeth** (*BRIT*) se laver les dents; ~ **driving licence** *or* (*US*) **record** permis *où n'est portée aucune indication de contravention*.

►**clean off** *vt* enlever.

►**clean out** *vt* nettoyer (à fond).

►**clean up** *vt* nettoyer; (*fig*) remettre de l'ordre dans ♦ *vi* (*fig: make profit*): **to ~ up on** faire son beurre avec.

clean-cut ['kliːn'kʌt] *adj* (*man*) soigné; (*situation etc*) bien délimité(e), net(te), clair(e).

cleaner ['kliːnə*] *n* (*person*) nettoyeur/euse, femme *f* de ménage; (*also:* **dry ~er**) teinturier/ière; (*product*) détachant *m*.

cleaning ['kliːnɪŋ] *n* nettoyage *m*.

cleaning lady *n* femme *f* de ménage.

cleanliness ['klɛnlɪnɪs] *n* propreté *f*.

cleanly ['kliːnlɪ] *adv* proprement; nettement.

cleanse [klɛnz] *vt* nettoyer; purifier.

cleanser ['klɛnzə*] *n* détergent *m*; (*for face*) démaquillant *m*.

clean-shaven ['kliːn'ʃeɪvn] *adj* rasé(e) de près.

cleansing department ['klɛnzɪŋ-] *n* (*BRIT*) service *m* de voirie.

clean sweep *n*: **to make a ~** (*SPORT*) rafler tous les prix.

clean-up ['kliːnʌp] *n* nettoyage *m*.

clear [klɪə*] *adj* clair(e); (*road, way*) libre, dégagé(e); (*profit, majority*) net(te) ♦ *vt* dégager, déblayer, débarrasser; (*room etc: of people*) faire évacuer; (*woodland*) défricher; (*cheque*) compenser; (*COMM: goods*) liquider; (*LAW: suspect*) innocenter; (*obstacle*) franchir *or* sauter sans heurter ♦ *vi* (*weather*) s'éclaircir; (*fog*) se dissiper ♦ *adv*: ~ **of** à distance de, à l'écart de ♦ *n*: **to be in the ~** (*out of debt*) être dégagé(e) de toute dette; (*out of suspicion*) être lavé(e) de tout soup-

çon; (*out of danger*) être hors de danger; **to ~ the table** débarrasser la table, desservir; **to ~ one's throat** s'éclaircir la gorge; **to ~ a profit** faire un bénéfice net; **to make o.s. ~** se faire bien comprendre; **to make it ~ to sb that** ... bien faire comprendre à qn que ...; **I have a ~ day tomorrow** (*BRIT*) je n'ai rien de prévu demain; **to keep ~ of sb/sth** éviter qn/qch.

►**clear off** *vi* (*col: leave*) dégager.

►**clear up** *vi* s'éclaircir, se dissiper ♦ *vt* ranger, mettre en ordre; (*mystery*) éclaircir, résoudre.

clearance ['klɪərəns] *n* (*removal*) déblayage *m*; (*free space*) dégagement *m*; (*permission*) autorisation *f*.

clearance sale *n* (*COMM*) liquidation *f*.

clear-cut ['klɪə'kʌt] *adj* précis(e), nettement défini(e).

clearing ['klɪərɪŋ] *n* (*in forest*) clairière *f*; (*BRIT BANKING*) compensation *f*, clearing *m*.

clearing bank *n* (*BRIT*) banque *f* qui appartient à une chambre de compensation.

clearly ['klɪəlɪ] *adv* clairement; (*obviously*) de toute évidence.

clearway ['klɪəweɪ] *n* (*BRIT*) route *f* à stationnement interdit.

cleavage ['kliːvɪdʒ] *n* (*of dress*) décolleté *m*.

cleaver ['kliːvə*] *n* fendoir *m*, couperet *m*.

clef [klɛf] *n* (*MUS*) clé *f*.

cleft [klɛft] *n* (*in rock*) crevasse *f*, fissure *f*.

clemency ['klɛmənsɪ] *n* clémence *f*.

clement ['klɛmənt] *adj* (*weather*) clément(e).

clench [klɛntʃ] *vt* serrer.

clergy ['klɜːdʒɪ] *n* clergé *m*.

clergyman ['klɜːdʒɪmən] *n* ecclésiastique *m*.

clerical ['klɛrɪkl] *adj* de bureau, d'employé de bureau; (*REL*) clérical(e), du clergé.

clerk [klɑːk, (*US*) klɜːrk] *n* employé/e de bureau; (*US: salesman/woman*) vendeur/euse; **C~ of Court** (*LAW*) greffier *m* (du tribunal).

clever ['klɛvə*] *adj* (*mentally*) intelligent(e); (*deft, crafty*) habile, adroit(e); (*device, arrangement*) ingénieux(euse), astucieux(euse).

cleverly ['klɛvəlɪ] *adv* (*skilfully*) habilement; (*craftily*) astucieusement.

clew [kluː] *n* (*US*) = **clue**.

cliché ['kliːʃeɪ] *n* cliché *m*.

click [klɪk] *vi* faire un bruit sec *or* un déclic ♦ *vt*: **to ~ one's tongue** faire claquer sa langue; **to ~ one's heels** claquer des talons.

client ['klaɪənt] *n* client/e.

clientele [kliːɑːn'tɛl] *n* clientèle *f*.

cliff [klɪf] *n* falaise *f*.

cliffhanger ['klɪfhæŋə*] *n* (*TV*, *fig*) histoire pleine de suspense.

climactic [klaɪ'mæktɪk] *adj* à son point culminant, culminant(e).

climate ['klaɪmɪt] *n* climat *m*.

climax ['klaɪmæks] *n* apogée *m*, point culminant; (*sexual*) orgasme *m*.

climb [klaɪm] *vi* grimper, monter; (*plane*)

prendre de l'altitude ♦ vt gravir, escalader, monter sur ♦ n montée f, escalade f; **to ~ over a wall** passer par dessus un mur.

▶**climb down** vi (re)descendre; (BRIT fig) rabattre de ses prétentions.

climbdown ['klaɪmdaʊn] n (BRIT) reculade f.

climber ['klaɪmə*] n (also: **rock ~**) grimpeur/euse, varappeur/euse.

climbing ['klaɪmɪŋ] n (also: **rock ~**) escalade f, varappe f.

clinch [klɪntʃ] vt (deal) conclure, sceller.

clincher ['klɪntʃə*] n: **that was the ~** c'est ce qui a fait pencher la balance.

cling, pt, pp **clung** [klɪŋ, klʌŋ] vi: **to ~ (to)** se cramponner (à), s'accrocher (à); (of clothes) coller (à).

clingfilm ['klɪŋfɪlm] n film m alimentaire.

clinic ['klɪnɪk] n clinique f; centre médical; (session: MED) consultation(s) f(pl), séance(s) f(pl); (: SPORT) séance(s) de perfectionnement.

clinical ['klɪnɪkl] adj clinique; (fig) froid(e).

clink [klɪŋk] vi tinter, cliqueter.

clip [klɪp] n (for hair) barrette f; (also: **paper ~**) trombone m; (BRIT: also: **bulldog ~**) pince f de bureau; (holding hose etc) collier m or bague f (métallique) de serrage ♦ vt (also: **~ together**: papers) attacher; (hair, nails) couper; (hedge) tailler.

clippers ['klɪpəz] npl tondeuse f; (also: **nail ~**) coupe-ongles m inv.

clipping ['klɪpɪŋ] n (from newspaper) coupure f de journal.

clique [kliːk] n clique f, coterie f.

cloak [kləʊk] n grande cape.

cloakroom ['kləʊkrʊm] n (for coats etc) vestiaire m; (BRIT: W.C.) toilettes fpl.

clock [klɔk] n (large) horloge f; (small) pendule f; **round the ~** (work etc) vingt-quatre heures sur vingt-quatre; **to sleep round the ~** or **the ~ round** faire le tour du cadran; **30,000 on the ~** (BRIT AUT) 30 000 milles au compteur; **to work against the ~** faire la course contre la montre.

▶**clock in, clock on** vi (BRIT) pointer (en arrivant).

▶**clock off, clock out** vi (BRIT) pointer (en partant).

▶**clock up** vt (miles, hours etc) faire.

clockwise ['klɔkwaɪz] adv dans le sens des aiguilles d'une montre.

clockwork ['klɔkwɜːk] n mouvement m (d'horlogerie); rouages mpl, mécanisme m ♦ adj (toy, train) mécanique.

clog [klɔg] n sabot m ♦ vt boucher, encrasser ♦ vi se boucher, s'encrasser.

cloister ['klɔɪstə*] n cloître m.

clone [kləʊn] n clone m.

close adj, adv and derivatives [kləʊs] adj (near): **~ (to)** près (de), proche (de); (writing, texture) serré(e); (watch) étroit(e), strict(e); (examination) attentif(ive), minutieux(euse);

(weather) lourd(e), étouffant(e); (room) mal aéré(e) ♦ adv près, à proximité; **~ to** prep près de; **~ by, ~ at hand** adj, adv tout(e) près; **how ~ is Edinburgh to Glasgow?** combien de kilomètres y-a-t-il entre Édimbourg et Glasgow?; **a ~ friend** un ami intime; **to have a ~ shave** (fig) l'échapper belle; **at ~ quarters** tout près, à côté ♦ vb and derivatives [kləʊz] vt fermer; (bargain, deal) conclure ♦ vi (shop etc) fermer; (lid, door etc) se fermer; (end) se terminer, se conclure ♦ n (end) conclusion f; **to bring sth to a ~** mettre fin à qch.

▶**close down** vt, vi fermer (définitivement).

▶**close in** vi (hunters) approcher; (night, fog) tomber; **the days are closing in** les jours raccourcissent; **to ~ in on sb** cerner qn.

▶**close off** vt (area) boucler.

closed [kləʊzd] adj (shop etc) fermé(e); (road) fermé à la circulation.

closed-circuit ['kləʊzd'sɜːkɪt] adj: **~ television** télévision f en circuit fermé.

closed shop n organisation f qui n'admet que des travailleurs syndiqués.

close-knit ['kləʊs'nɪt] adj (family, community) très uni(e).

closely ['kləʊslɪ] adv (examine, watch) de près; **we are ~ related** nous sommes proches parents; **a ~ guarded secret** un secret bien gardé.

close season [kləʊs-] n (BRIT: HUNTING) fermeture f de la chasse/pêche; (: FOOTBALL) trêve f.

closet ['klɔzɪt] n (cupboard) placard m, réduit m.

close-up ['kləʊsʌp] n gros plan m.

closing ['kləʊzɪŋ] adj (stages, remarks) final(e); **~ price** (STOCK EXCHANGE) cours m de clôture; **~ time** heure f de fermeture.

closure ['kləʊʒə*] n fermeture f.

clot [klɔt] n (gen: blood ~) caillot m; (col: person) ballot m ♦ vi (blood) former des caillots; (: external bleeding) se coaguler.

cloth [klɔθ] n (material) tissu m, étoffe f; (BRIT: also: **tea~**) torchon m; lavette f; (also: **table~**) nappe f.

clothe [kləʊð] vt habiller, vêtir.

clothes [kləʊðz] npl vêtements mpl, habits mpl; **to put one's ~ on** s'habiller; **to take one's ~ off** enlever ses vêtements.

clothes brush n brosse f à habits.

clothes line n corde f (à linge).

clothes peg, (US) **clothes pin** n pince f à linge.

clothing ['kləʊðɪŋ] n = **clothes.**

clotted cream ['klɔtɪd-] n (BRIT) crème caillée.

cloud [klaʊd] n nuage m ♦ vt (liquid) troubler; **to ~ the issue** brouiller les cartes; **every ~ has a silver lining** (proverb) à quelque chose malheur est bon (proverbe).

▶**cloud over** vi se couvrir; (fig) s'assombrir.

cloudburst ['klaudbəːst] *n* violente averse.
cloud-cuckoo-land ['klaud'kukuː'lænd] *n* (*BRIT*) monde *m* imaginaire.
cloudy ['klaudɪ] *adj* nuageux(euse), couvert(e); (*liquid*) trouble.
clout [klaut] *n* (*blow*) taloche *f*; (*fig*) pouvoir *m*
♦ *vt* flanquer une taloche à.
clove [kləuv] *n* clou *m* de girofle; ~ **of garlic** gousse *f* d'ail.
clover ['kləuvə*] *n* trèfle *m*.
cloverleaf ['kləuvəliːf] *n* feuille *f* de trèfle; (*AUT*) croisement *m* en trèfle.
clown [klaun]·*n* clown *m* ♦ *vi* (*also*: ~ **about**, ~ **around**) faire le clown.
cloying ['klɔɪɪŋ] *adj* (*taste, smell*) écœurant(e).
club [klʌb] *n* (*society*) club *m*; (*weapon*) massue *f*, matraque *f*; (*also*: **golf** ~) club ♦ *vt* matraquer ♦ *vi*: **to** ~ **together** s'associer; ~**s** *npl* (*CARDS*) trèfle *m*.
club car *n* (*US RAIL*) wagon-restaurant *m*.
club class *n* (*AVIAT*) classe *f* club.
clubhouse ['klʌbhaus] *n* pavillon *m*.
club soda *n* (*US*) eau *f* de seltz.
cluck [klʌk] *vi* glousser.
clue [kluː] *n* indice *m*; (*in crosswords*) définition *f*; **I haven't a** ~ je n'en ai pas la moindre idée.
clued up, (*US*) **clued in** [kluːd-] *adj* (*col*) (vachement) calé(e).
clump [klʌmp] *n*: ~ **of trees** bouquet *m* d'arbres.
clumsy ['klʌmzɪ] *adj* (*person*) gauche, maladroit(e); (*object*) malcommode, peu maniable.
clung [klʌŋ] *pt, pp of* **cling**.
cluster ['klʌstə*] *n* (petit) groupe ♦ *vi* se rassembler.
clutch [klʌtʃ] *n* (*grip, grasp*) étreinte *f*, prise *f*; (*AUT*) embrayage *m* ♦ *vt* agripper, serrer fort; **to** ~ **at** se cramponner à.
clutter ['klʌtə*] *vt* (*also*: ~ **up**) encombrer ♦ *n* désordre *m*, fouillis *m*.
CM *abbr* (*US POST*) = *North Mariana Islands*.
cm *abbr* (= *centimetre*) cm.
CNAA *n abbr* (*BRIT*: = *Council for National Academic Awards*) *organisme non universitaire délivrant des diplômes*.
CND *n abbr* = *Campaign for Nuclear Disarmament*.
CO *n abbr* (= *commanding officer*) Cdt; (*BRIT*) = *Commonwealth Office* ♦ *abbr* (*US*) = *Colorado*.
Co. *abbr* = **company, county**.
c/o *abbr* (= *care of*) c/o, aux bons soins de.
coach [kəutʃ] *n* (*bus*) autocar *m*; (*horse-drawn*) diligence *f*; (*of train*) voiture *f*, wagon *m*; (*SPORT*: *trainer*) entraîneur/euse; (*school*: *tutor*) répétiteur/trice ♦ *vt* entraîner; donner des leçons particulières à.
coach trip *n* excursion *f* en car.
coagulate [kəu'ægjuleɪt] *vt* coaguler ♦ *vi* se coaguler.
coal [kəul] *n* charbon *m*.

coal face *n* front *m* de taille.
coalfield ['kəulfiːld] *n* bassin houiller.
coalition [kəuə'lɪʃən] *n* coalition *f*.
coalman ['kəulmən] *n* charbonnier *m*, marchand *m* de charbon.
coal mine *n* mine *f* de charbon.
coal miner *n* mineur *m*.
coal mining *n* extraction *f* du charbon.
coarse [kɔːs] *adj* grossier(ère), rude; (*vulgar*) vulgaire.
coast [kəust] *n* côte *f* ♦ *vi* (*with cycle etc*) descendre en roue libre.
coastal ['kəustl] *adj* côtier(ère).
coaster ['kəustə*] *n* (*NAUT*) caboteur *m*; (*for glass*) dessous *m* de verre.
coastguard ['kəustgɑːd] *n* garde-côte *m*.
coastline ['kəustlaɪn] *n* côte *f*, littoral *m*.
coat [kəut] *n* manteau *m*; (*of animal*) pelage *m*, poil *m*; (*of paint*) couche *f* ♦ *vt* couvrir, enduire; ~ **of arms** blason *m*, armoiries *fpl*.
coat hanger *n* cintre *m*.
coating ['kəutɪŋ] *n* couche *f*, enduit *m*.
co-author ['kəu'ɔːθə*] *n* co-auteur *m*.
coax [kəuks] *vt* persuader par des cajoleries.
cob [kɔb] *n see* **corn**.
cobbler ['kɔblə*] *n* cordonnier *m*.
cobbles, cobblestones ['kɔblz, 'kɔblstəunz] *npl* pavés (ronds).
COBOL ['kəubɔl] *n* COBOL *m*.
cobra ['kəubrə] *n* cobra *m*.
cobweb ['kɔbweb] *n* toile *f* d'araignée.
cocaine [kə'keɪn] *n* cocaïne *f*.
cock [kɔk] *n* (*rooster*) coq *m*; (*male bird*) mâle *m* ♦ *vt* (*gun*) armer; **to** ~ **one's ears** (*fig*) dresser l'oreille.
cock-a-hoop [kɔkə'huːp] *adj* jubilant(e).
cockerel ['kɔkərl] *n* jeune coq *m*.
cock-eyed ['kɔkaɪd] *adj* (*fig*) de travers; qui louche; qui ne tient pas debout (*fig*).
cockle ['kɔkl] *n* coque *f*.
cockney ['kɔknɪ] *n* cockney *m/f* (*habitant des quartiers populaires de l'East End de Londres*), ≈ faubourien/ne.
cockpit ['kɔkpɪt] *n* (*in aircraft*) poste *m* de pilotage, cockpit *m*.
cockroach ['kɔkrəutʃ] *n* cafard *m*, cancrelat *m*.
cocktail ['kɔkteɪl] *n* cocktail *m*; **prawn** ~, (*US*) **shrimp** ~ cocktail de crevettes.
cocktail cabinet *n* (*meuble-*)bar *m*.
cocktail party *n* cocktail *m*.
cocktail shaker [-'ʃeɪkə*] *n* shaker *m*.
cocky ['kɔkɪ] *adj* trop sûr(e) de soi.
cocoa ['kəukəu] *n* cacao *m*.
coconut ['kəukənʌt] *n* noix *f* de coco.
cocoon [kə'kuːn] *n* cocon *m*.
COD *abbr* = **cash on delivery, collect on delivery** (*US*).
cod [kɔd] *n* morue (fraîche), cabillaud *m*.
code [kəud] *n* code *m*; ~ **of behaviour** règles *fpl* de conduite; ~ **of practice** déontologie *f*.
codeine ['kəudiːn] *n* codéine *f*.

codger ['kɔdʒə*] n: **an old** ~ (BRIT col) un drôle de vieux bonhomme.

codicil ['kɔdɪsɪl] n codicille m.

codify ['kəudɪfaɪ] vt codifier.

cod-liver oil ['kɔdlɪvər-] n huile f de foie de morue.

co-driver ['kəu'draɪvə*] n (in race) copilote m; (of lorry) deuxième chauffeur m.

co-ed ['kəu'ɛd] adj abbr = **coeducational ♦** n abbr (US: female student) étudiante d'une université mixte; (BRIT: school) école f mixte.

coeducational ['kəuɛdju'keɪʃənl] adj mixte.

coerce [kəu'əːs] vt contraindre.

coercion [kəu'əːʃən] n contrainte f.

coexistence ['kəuɪg'zɪstəns] n coexistence f.

C. of C. n abbr = **chamber of commerce**.

C of E abbr = **Church of England**.

coffee ['kɔfɪ] n café m; **white** ~, (US) ~ **with cream** (café-)crème m.

coffee bar n (BRIT) café m.

coffee bean n grain m de café.

coffee break n pause-café f.

coffeecake ['kɔfɪkeɪk] n (US) ≈ petit pain aux raisins.

coffee cup n tasse f à café.

coffeepot ['kɔfɪpɔt] n cafetière f.

coffee table n (petite) table basse.

coffin ['kɔfɪn] n cercueil m.

C of I abbr = **Church of Ireland**.

C of S abbr = **Church of Scotland**.

cog [kɔg] n dent f (d'engrenage).

cogent ['kəudʒənt] adj puissant(e), convaincant(e).

cognac ['kɔnjæk] n cognac m.

cogwheel ['kɔgwiːl] n roue dentée.

cohabit [kəu'hæbɪt] vi (formal): **to** ~ **(with sb)** cohabiter (avec qn).

coherent [kəu'hɪərənt] adj cohérent(e).

cohesion [kəu'hiːʒən] n cohésion f.

cohesive [kəu'hiːsɪv] adj (fig) cohésif(ive).

COI n abbr (BRIT: = Central Office of Information) service d'information gouvernemental.

coil [kɔɪl] n rouleau m, bobine f; (one loop) anneau m, spire f; (of smoke) volute f; (contraceptive) stérilet m ♦ vt enrouler.

coin [kɔɪn] n pièce f de monnaie ♦ vt (word) inventer.

coinage ['kɔɪnɪdʒ] n monnaie f, système m monétaire.

coin-box ['kɔɪnbɔks] n (BRIT) cabine f téléphonique.

coincide [kəuɪn'saɪd] vi coïncider.

coincidence [kəu'ɪnsɪdəns] n coïncidence f.

coin-operated ['kɔɪn'ɔpəreɪtɪd] adj (machine, launderette) automatique.

Coke [kəuk] n ® coca m.

coke [kəuk] n coke m.

Col. abbr (= colonel) Col; (US) = Colorado.

COLA n abbr (US: = cost-of-living adjustment) réajustement (des salaires, indemnités etc) en fonction du coût de la vie.

colander ['kɔləndə*] n passoire f (à légumes).

cold [kəuld] adj froid(e) ♦ n froid m; (MED) rhume m; **it's** ~ il fait froid; **to be** ~ avoir froid; **to catch** ~ prendre or attraper froid; **to catch a** ~ s'enrhumer, attraper un rhume; **in** ~ **blood** de sang-froid; **to have** ~ **feet** avoir froid aux pieds; (fig) avoir la frousse or la trouille; **to give sb the** ~ **shoulder** battre froid à qn.

cold-blooded ['kəuld'blʌdɪd] adj (ZOOL) à sang froid.

cold cream n crème f de soins.

coldly ['kəuldlɪ] adv froidement.

cold sore n bouton m de fièvre.

cold sweat n: **to be in a** ~ **(about sth)** avoir des sueurs froides (au sujet de qch).

cold turkey n (col) manque m; **to go** ~ être en manque.

Cold War n: **the** ~ la guerre froide.

coleslaw ['kəulslɔː] n sorte de salade de chou cru.

colic ['kɔlɪk] n colique(s) f(pl).

colicky ['kɔlɪkɪ] adj qui souffre de coliques.

collaborate [kə'læbəreɪt] vi collaborer.

collaboration [kəlæbə'reɪʃən] n collaboration f.

collaborator [kə'læbəreɪtə*] n collaborateur/trice.

collage [kɔ'lɑːʒ] n (ART) collage m.

collagen ['kɔlədʒən] n collagène m.

collapse [kə'læps] vi s'effondrer, s'écrouler ♦ n effondrement m, écroulement m; (of government) chute f.

collapsible [kə'læpsəbl] adj pliant(e); télescopique.

collar ['kɔlə*] n (of coat, shirt) col m; (for dog) collier m; (TECH) collier m, bague f ♦ vt (col: person) pincer.

collarbone ['kɔləbəun] n clavicule f.

collate [kɔ'leɪt] vt collationner.

collateral [kə'lætərl] n nantissement m.

collation [kə'leɪʃən] n collation f.

colleague ['kɔliːg] n collègue m/f.

collect [kə'lɛkt] vt rassembler; (pick up) ramasser; (as a hobby) collectionner; (BRIT: call for) (passer) prendre; (mail) faire la levée de, ramasser; (money owed) encaisser; (donations, subscriptions) recueillir ♦ vi (people) se rassembler; (dust, dirt) s'amasser; **to** ~ **one's thoughts** réfléchir, réunir ses idées; ~ **on delivery (COD)** (US COMM) payable or paiement à la livraison; **to call** ~ (US TEL) téléphoner en PCV.

collected [kə'lɛktɪd] adj: ~ **works** œuvres complètes.

collection [kə'lɛkʃən] n collection f; (of mail) levée f; (for money) collecte f, quête f.

collective [kə'lɛktɪv] adj collectif(ive) ♦ n collectif m.

collective bargaining n convention collective.

collector [kə'lɛktə*] n collectionneur m; (of taxes) percepteur m; (of rent, cash) encaisseur _m_; ~'s **item** _or_ **piece** pièce _f_ de collection.

college ['kɔlɪdʒ] _n_ collège _m_; (_of technology, agriculture etc_) institut _m_; **to go to** ~ faire des études supérieures; ~ **of education** ≈ école normale.

collide [kə'laɪd] _vi_: **to** ~ **(with)** entrer en collision (avec).

collie ['kɔlɪ] _n_ (_dog_) colley _m_.

colliery ['kɔlɪərɪ] _n_ (_BRIT_) mine _f_ de charbon, houillère _f_.

collision [kə'lɪʒən] _n_ collision _f_, heurt _m_; **to be on a** ~ **course** aller droit à la collision; (_fig_) aller vers l'affrontement.

collision damage waiver _n_ (_INSURANCE_) rachat _m_ de franchise.

colloquial [kə'ləukwɪəl] _adj_ familier(ère).

collusion [kə'luːʒən] _n_ collusion _f_; **in** ~ **with** en complicité avec.

Colo. _abbr_ (_US_) = Colorado.

cologne [kə'ləun] _n_ (_also_: **eau de** ~) eau _f_ de cologne.

Colombia [kə'lɔmbɪə] _n_ Colombie _f_.

Colombian [kə'lɔmbɪən] _adj_ colombien(ne) ♦ _n_ Colombien/ne.

colon ['kəulən] _n_ (_sign_) deux-points _mpl_; (_MED_) côlon _m_.

colonel ['kɔːnl] _n_ colonel _m_.

colonial [kə'ləunɪəl] _adj_ colonial(e).

colonize ['kɔlənaɪz] _vt_ coloniser.

colony ['kɔlənɪ] _n_ colonie _f_.

color _etc_ ['kʌlə*] (_US_) = **colour** _etc_.

Colorado beetle [kɔlə'rɑːdəu-] _n_ doryphore _m_.

colossal [kə'lɔsl] _adj_ colossal(e).

colour, (_US_) **color** ['kʌlə*] _n_ couleur _f_ ♦ _vt_ colorer; peindre; (_with crayons_) colorier; (_news_) fausser, exagérer ♦ _vi_ rougir ♦ _cpd_ (_film, photograph, television_) en couleur; ~**s** _npl_ (_of party, club_) couleurs _fpl_.

colo(u)r bar _n_ discrimination raciale (_dans un établissement etc_).

colo(u)r-blind ['kʌləblaɪnd] _adj_ daltonien(ne).

colo(u)red ['kʌləd] _adj_ coloré(e); (_photo_) en couleur.

colo(u)rful ['kʌləful] _adj_ coloré(e), vif(vive); (_personality_) pittoresque, haut(e) en couleurs.

colo(u)ring ['kʌlərɪŋ] _n_ colorant _m_; (_complexion_) teint _m_.

colo(u)r scheme _n_ combinaison _f_ de(s) couleur(s).

colour supplement _n_ (_BRIT PRESS_) supplément _m_ magazine.

colt [kəult] _n_ poulain _m_.

column ['kɔləm] _n_ colonne _f_; (_fashion/sports ~ etc_) rubrique _f_; **the editorial** ~ l'éditorial _m_.

columnist ['kɔləmnɪst] _n_ rédacteur/trice d'une rubrique.

coma ['kəumə] _n_ coma _m_.

comb [kəum] _n_ peigne _m_ ♦ _vt_ (_hair_) peigner; (_area_) ratisser, passer au peigne fin.

combat ['kɔmbæt] _n_ combat _m_ ♦ _vt_ combattre, lutter contre.

combination [kɔmbɪ'neɪʃən] _n_ (_gen_) combinaison _f_.

combination lock _n_ serrure _f_ à combinaison.

combine _vb_ [kəm'baɪn] _vt_ combiner; (_one quality with another_): **to** ~ **sth with sth** joindre qch à qch, allier qch à qch ♦ _vi_ s'associer; (_CHEM_) se combiner ♦ _n_ ['kɔmbaɪn] association _f_; (_ECON_) trust _m_; **a** ~**d effort** un effort conjugué.

combine (harvester) _n_ moissonneuse-batteuse(-lieuse) _f_.

combo ['kɔmbəu] _n_ (_JAZZ etc_) groupe _m_ de musiciens.

combustible [kəm'bʌstɪbl] _adj_ combustible.

combustion [kəm'bʌstʃən] _n_ combustion _f_.

come, _pt_ **came,** _pp_ **come** [kʌm, keɪm] _vi_ venir; (_col: sexually_) jouir; ~ **with me** suivez-moi; **we've just** ... **from Paris** nous arrivons de Paris; ... **what might** ... **of it** ... ce qui pourrait en résulter, ... ce qui pourrait advenir _or_ se produire; **to** ~ **into sight** _or_ **view** apparaître; **to** ~ **to** (_decision etc_) parvenir _or_ arriver à; **to** ~ **undone/loose** se défaire/desserrer; **coming!** j'arrive!; **if it** ~**s to it** s'il le faut, dans le pire des cas.

▶**come about** _vi_ se produire, arriver.

▶**come across** _vt fus_ rencontrer par hasard, tomber sur ♦ _vi_: **to** ~ **across well/badly** faire une bonne/mauvaise impression.

▶**come along** _vi_ (_pupil, work_) faire des progrès, avancer; ~ **along!** viens!; allons!, allez!; **if you** ~ **along on Thursday** ... si vous venez jeudi ...

▶**come apart** _vi_ s'en aller en morceaux; se détacher.

▶**come away** _vi_ partir, s'en aller; (_become detached_) se détacher.

▶**come back** _vi_ revenir; (_reply_): **can I** ~ **back to you on that one?** est-ce qu'on peut revenir là-dessus plus tard?

▶**come by** _vt fus_ (_acquire_) obtenir, se procurer.

▶**come down** _vi_ descendre; (_prices_) baisser; (_buildings_) s'écrouler; (: _be demolished_) être démoli(e).

▶**come forward** _vi_ s'avancer; (_make o.s. known_) se présenter, s'annoncer.

▶**come from** _vt fus_ venir de; (_place_) venir de, être originaire de.

▶**come in** _vi_ entrer.

▶**come in for** _vt fus_ (_criticism etc_) être l'objet de.

▶**come into** _vt fus_ (_money_) hériter de.

▶**come off** _vi_ (_button_) se détacher; (_stain_) s'enlever; (_attempt_) réussir.

▶**come on** _vi_ (_lights, electricity_) s'allumer; (_central heating_) se mettre en marche; (_pupil, work, project_) faire des progrès, avancer; ~ **on!** viens!; allons!, allez!

▶**come out** _vi_ sortir; (_book_) paraître; (_strike_)

cesser le travail, se mettre en grève.

▶**come over** *vt fus*: **I don't know what's ~ over him!** je ne sais pas ce qui lui a pris!

▶**come round** *vi* (*after faint, operation*) revenir à soi, reprendre connaissance.

▶**come through** *vi* (*survive*) s'en sortir; (*telephone call*): **the call came through** l'appel est bien parvenu.

▶**come to** *vi* revenir à soi ♦ *vt* (*add up to: amount*): **how much does it ~ to?** ça fait combien?

▶**come under** *vt fus* (*heading*) se trouver sous; (*influence*) subir.

▶**come up** *vi* monter.

▶**come up against** *vt fus* (*resistance, difficulties*) rencontrer.

▶**come up to** *vt fus* arriver à; **the film didn't ~ up to our expectations** le film nous a déçu.

▶**come up with** *vt fus*: **he came up with an idea** il a eu une idée, il a proposé quelque chose.

▶**come upon** *vt fus* tomber sur.

comeback ['kʌmbæk] *n* (*reaction*) réaction *f*; (*response*) réponse *f*; (*THEAT etc*) rentrée *f*.

Comecon ['kɔmɪkɔn] *n abbr* (= *Council for Mutual Economic Aid*) COMECON *m*.

comedian [kə'miːdɪən] *n* (*in music hall etc*) comique *m*; (*THEAT*) comédien *m*.

comedienne [kəmiːdɪ'ɛn] *n* comique *f*.

comedown ['kʌmdaun] *n* déchéance *f*.

comedy ['kɔmɪdɪ] *n* comédie *f*.

comet ['kɔmɪt] *n* comète *f*.

comeuppance [kʌm'ʌpəns] *n*: **to get one's ~** recevoir ce qu'on mérite.

comfort ['kʌmfət] *n* confort *m*, bien-être *m*; (*solace*) consolation *f*, réconfort *m* ♦ *vt* consoler, réconforter.

comfortable ['kʌmfətəbl] *adj* confortable; **I don't feel very ~ about it** cela m'inquiète un peu.

comfortably ['kʌmfətəblɪ] *adv* (*sit*) confortablement; (*live*) à l'aise.

comforter ['kʌmfətə*] *n* (*US*) édredon *m*.

comforts ['kʌmfəts] *npl* aises *fpl*.

comfort station *n* (*US*) toilettes *fpl*.

comic ['kɔmɪk] *adj* comique ♦ *n* comique *m*; (*magazine*) illustré *m*.

comical ['kɔmɪkl] *adj* amusant(e).

comic strip *n* bande dessinée.

coming ['kʌmɪŋ] *n* arrivée *f* ♦ *adj* (*next*) prochain(e); (*future*) à venir; **in the ~ weeks** dans les prochaines semaines.

coming(s) and going(s) *n(pl)* va-et-vient *m inv*.

Comintern ['kɔmɪntəːn] *n* Comintern *m*.

comma ['kɔmə] *n* virgule *f*.

command [kə'mɑːnd] *n* ordre *m*, commandement *m*; (*MIL: authority*) commandement; (*mastery*) maîtrise *f*; (*COMPUT*) commande *f* ♦ *vt* (*troops*) commander; (*be able to get*) (pouvoir) disposer de, avoir à sa disposi-

tion; (*deserve*) avoir droit à; **to ~ sb to do** donner l'ordre *or* commander à qn de faire; **to have/take ~ of** avoir/prendre le commandement de; **to have at one's ~** (*money, resources etc*) disposer de.

command economy *n* économie planifiée.

commandeer [kɔmən'dɪə*] *vt* réquisitionner (par la force).

commander [kə'mɑːndə*] *n* chef *m*; (*MIL*) commandant *m*.

commander-in-chief [kə'mɑːndərɪn'tʃiːf] *n* (*MIL*) commandant *m* en chef.

commanding [kə'mɑːndɪŋ] *adj* (*appearance*) imposant(e); (*voice, tone*) autoritaire; (*lead, position*) dominant(e).

commanding officer *n* commandant *m*.

commandment [kə'mɑːndmənt] *n* (*REL*) commandement *m*.

command module *n* (*SPACE*) module *m* de commande.

commando [kə'mɑːndəu] *n* commando *m*; membre *m* d'un commando.

commemorate [kə'mɛməreɪt] *vt* commémorer.

commemoration [kəmɛmə'reɪʃən] *n* commémoration *f*.

commemorative [kə'mɛmərətɪv] *adj* commémoratif(ive).

commence [kə'mɛns] *vt*, *vi* commencer.

commend [kə'mɛnd] *vt* louer; recommander.

commendable [kə'mɛndəbl] *adj* louable.

commendation [kɔmɛn'deɪʃən] *n* éloge *m*; recommandation *f*.

commensurate [kə'mɛnʃərɪt] *adj*: **~ with/to** en rapport avec/selon.

comment ['kɔmɛnt] *n* commentaire *m* ♦ *vi* faire des remarques *or* commentaires; **to ~ on** faire des remarques sur; **to ~ that** faire remarquer que; **"no ~"** "je n'ai rien à déclarer".

commentary ['kɔməntərɪ] *n* commentaire *m*; (*SPORT*) reportage *m* (en direct).

commentator ['kɔmənteɪtə*] *n* commentateur *m*; (*SPORT*) reporter *m*.

commerce ['kɔməːs] *n* commerce *m*.

commercial [kə'məːʃəl] *adj* commercial(e) ♦ *n* (*RADIO, TV*) annonce *f* publicitaire, spot *m* (publicitaire).

commercial bank *n* banque *f* d'affaires.

commercial break *n* (*RADIO, TV*) spot *m* (publicitaire).

commercial college *n* école *f* de commerce.

commercialism [kə'məːʃəlɪzəm] *n* mercantilisme *m*.

commercial television *n* publicité *f* à la télévision; chaînes privées (financées par la publicité).

commercial traveller *n* voyageur *m* de commerce.

commercial vehicle *n* véhicule *m* utilitaire.

commiserate [kə'mɪzəreɪt] *vi*: **to ~ with sb** témoigner de la sympathie pour qn.

commission [kə'mɪʃən] n (*committee; fee: also for salesman*) commission f; (*order for work of art etc*) commande f ♦ vt (*MIL*) nommer (à un commandement); (*work of art*) commander, charger un artiste de l'exécution de; **out of ~** (*NAUT*) hors de service; (*machine*) hors service; **I get 10% ~** je reçois une commission de 10%; **~ of inquiry** (*BRIT*) commission d'enquête.

commissionaire [kəmɪʃə'nɛə*] n (*BRIT: at shop, cinema etc*) portier m (en uniforme).

commissioner [kə'mɪʃənə*] n membre m d'une commission; (*POLICE*) préfet m (de police).

commit [kə'mɪt] vt (*act*) commettre; (*to sb's care*) confier (à); **to ~ o.s. (to do)** s'engager (à faire); **to ~ suicide** se suicider; **to ~ to writing** coucher par écrit; **to ~ sb for trial** traduire qn en justice.

commitment [kə'mɪtmənt] n engagement m; (*obligation*) responsabilité(s) f(pl).

committed [kə'mɪtɪd] adj (*writer, politician etc*) engagé(e).

committee [kə'mɪtɪ] n comité m; commission f; **to be on a ~** siéger dans un comité (*or* une commission).

committee meeting n réunion f de comité *or* commission.

commodity [kə'mɔdɪtɪ] n produit m, marchandise f, article m; (*food*) denrée f.

commodity exchange n bourse f de marchandises.

common ['kɔmən] adj (*gen, also pej*) commun(e); (*usual*) courant(e) ♦ n terrain communal; **in ~** en commun; **in ~ use** d'un usage courant; **it's ~ knowledge that** il est bien connu *or* notoire que; **to the ~ good** pour le bien de tous, dans l'intérêt général.

common cold n: **the ~** le rhume.

common denominator n dénominateur commun.

commoner ['kɔmənə*] n roturier/ière.

common ground n (*fig*) terrain m d'entente.

common land n terrain communal.

common law n droit coutumier.

common-law ['kɔmənlɔ:] adj: **~ wife** épouse f de facto.

commonly ['kɔmənlɪ] adv communément, généralement; couramment.

Common Market n Marché commun.

commonplace ['kɔmənpleɪs] adj banal(e), ordinaire.

commonroom ['kɔmənrum] n salle commune; (*SCOL*) salle des professeurs.

Commons ['kɔmənz] npl (*BRIT POL*): **the (House of) ~** la chambre des Communes.

common sense n bon sens.

Commonwealth ['kɔmənwɛlθ] n: **the ~** le Commonwealth.

Le **Commonwealth** regroupe 50 États indépendants et plusieurs territoires qui reconnaissent tous le souverain britannique comme chef de cette association.

---

commotion [kə'məʊʃən] n désordre m, tumulte m.

communal ['kɔmju:nl] adj (*life*) communautaire; (*for common use*) commun(e).

commune n ['kɔmju:n] (*group*) communauté f ♦ vi [kə'mju:n]: **to ~ with** converser intimement avec; communier avec.

communicate [kə'mju:nɪkeɪt] vt communiquer, transmettre ♦ vi: **to ~ (with)** communiquer (avec).

communication [kəmju:nɪ'keɪʃən] n communication f.

communication cord n (*BRIT*) sonnette f d'alarme.

communications network n réseau m de communications.

communications satellite n satellite m de télécommunications.

communicative [kə'mju:nɪkətɪv] adj communicatif(ive).

communion [kə'mju:nɪən] n (*also*: **Holy C~**) communion f.

communiqué [kə'mju:nɪkeɪ] n communiqué m.

communism ['kɔmjunɪzəm] n communisme m.

communist ['kɔmjunɪst] adj, n communiste (m/f).

community [kə'mju:nɪtɪ] n communauté f.

community centre n foyer socio-éducatif, centre m de loisirs.

community chest n (*US*) fonds commun.

community health centre n centre médico-social.

community service n ≈ travail m d'intérêt général, TIG m.

community spirit n solidarité f.

commutation ticket [kɔmju'teɪʃən-] n (*US*) carte f d'abonnement.

commute [kə'mju:t] vi faire le trajet journalier (de son domicile à un lieu de travail assez éloigné) ♦ vt (*LAW*) commuer; (*MATH: terms etc*) opérer la commutation de.

commuter [kə'mju:tə*] n banlieusard/e (qui ... *see vi*).

compact adj [kəm'pækt] compact(e) ♦ n ['kɔmpækt] contrat m, entente f; (*also*: **powder ~**) poudrier m.

compact disc n disque compact.

compact disc player n lecteur m de disques compacts.

companion [kəm'pænjən] n compagnon/compagne.

companionship [kəm'pænjənʃɪp] n camaraderie f.

companionway [kəm'pænjənweɪ] n (*NAUT*)

escalier *m* des cabines.

company ['kʌmpənɪ] *n* (*also COMM, MIL, THEAT*) compagnie *f*; **he's good** ~ il est d'une compagnie agréable; **we have** ~ nous avons de la visite; **to keep sb** ~ tenir compagnie à qn; **to part** ~ **with** se séparer de; **Smith and C**~ Smith et Compagnie.

company car *n* voiture *f* de fonction.

company director *n* administrateur/trice.

company secretary *n* (*BRIT COMM*) secrétaire général (*d'une société*).

comparable ['kɔmpərəbl] *adj* comparable.

comparative [kəm'pærətɪv] *adj* comparatif(ive); (*relative*) relatif(ive).

comparatively [kəm'pærətɪvlɪ] *adv* (*relatively*) relativement.

compare [kəm'pɛə*] *vt*: **to** ~ **sth/sb with/to** comparer qch/qn avec *or* et/à ♦ *vi*: **to** ~ **(with)** se comparer (à); être comparable (à); **how do the prices** ~? comment sont les prix?, est-ce que les prix sont comparables?; ~**d with** *or* **to** par rapport à.

comparison [kəm'pærɪsn] *n* comparaison *f*; **in** ~ **(with)** en comparaison (de).

compartment [kəm'pɑːtmənt] *n* (*also RAIL*) compartiment *m*.

compass ['kʌmpəs] *n* boussole *f*; **within the** ~ **of** dans les limites de.

compasses ['kʌmpəsɪz] *npl* compas *m*.

compassion [kəm'pæʃən] *n* compassion *f*, humanité *f*.

compassionate [kəm'pæʃənɪt] *adj* accessible à la compassion, au cœur charitable et bienveillant; **on** ~ **grounds** pour raisons personnelles *or* de famille.

compassionate leave *n* congé exceptionnel (*pour raisons de famille*).

compatibility [kəmpætɪ'bɪlɪtɪ] *n* compatibilité *f*.

compatible [kəm'pætɪbl] *adj* compatible.

compel [kəm'pɛl] *vt* contraindre, obliger.

compelling [kəm'pɛlɪŋ] *adj* (*fig: argument*) irrésistible.

compendium [kəm'pɛndɪəm] *n* (*summary*) abrégé *m*.

compensate ['kɔmpənseɪt] *vt* indemniser, dédommager ♦ *vi*: **to** ~ **for** compenser.

compensation [kɔmpən'seɪʃən] *n* compensation *f*, (*money*) dédommagement *m*, indemnité *f*.

compere ['kɔmpɛə*] *n* présentateur/trice, animateur/trice.

compete [kəm'piːt] *vi* (*take part*) concourir; (*vie*): **to** ~ **(with)** rivaliser (avec), faire concurrence (à).

competence ['kɔmpɪtəns] *n* compétence *f*, aptitude *f*.

competent ['kɔmpɪtənt] *adj* compétent(e), capable.

competing [kəm'piːtɪŋ] *adj* (*ideas, theories*) opposé(e); (*companies*) concurrent(e).

competition [kɔmpɪ'tɪʃən] *n* compétition *f*,

concours *m*; (*ECON*) concurrence *f*; **in** ~ **with** en concurrence avec.

competitive [kəm'pɛtɪtɪv] *adj* (*ECON*) concurrentiel(le); (*sports*) de compétition.

competitive examination *n* concours *m*.

competitor [kəm'pɛtɪtə*] *n* concurrent/e.

compile [kəm'paɪl] *vt* compiler.

complacency [kəm'pleɪsnsɪ] *n* contentement *m* de soi, autosatisfaction *f*.

complacent [kəm'pleɪsnt] *adj* (trop) content(e) de soi.

complain [kəm'pleɪn] *vi*: **to** ~ **(about)** se plaindre (de); (*in shop etc*) réclamer (au sujet de).

▸**complain of** *vt fus* (*MED*) se plaindre de.

complaint [kəm'pleɪnt] *n* plainte *f*; (*in shop etc*) réclamation *f*; (*MED*) affection *f*.

complement ['kɔmplɪmənt] *n* complément *m*; (*esp of ship's crew etc*) effectif complet ♦ *vt* compléter.

complementary [kɔmplɪ'mɛntərɪ] *adj* complémentaire.

complete [kəm'pliːt] *adj* complet(ète) ♦ *vt* achever, parachever; (*a form*) remplir.

completely [kəm'pliːtlɪ] *adv* complètement.

completion [kəm'pliːʃən] *n* achèvement *m*; **to be nearing** ~ être presque terminé; **on** ~ **of contract** dès signature du contrat.

complex ['kɔmplɛks] *adj* complexe ♦ *n* (*PSYCH, buildings etc*) complexe *m*.

complexion [kəm'plɛkʃən] *n* (*of face*) teint *m*; (*of event etc*) aspect *m*, caractère *m*.

complexity [kəm'plɛksɪtɪ] *n* complexité *f*.

compliance [kəm'plaɪəns] *n* (*submission*) docilité *f*; (*agreement*): ~ **with** le fait de se conformer à; **in** ~ **with** en conformité avec, conformément à.

compliant [kəm'plaɪənt] *adj* docile, très accommodant(e).

complicate ['kɔmplɪkeɪt] *vt* compliquer.

complicated ['kɔmplɪkeɪtɪd] *adj* compliqué(e).

complication [kɔmplɪ'keɪʃən] *n* complication *f*.

complicity [kəm'plɪsɪtɪ] *n* complicité *f*.

compliment *n* ['kɔmplɪmənt] compliment *m* ♦ *vt* ['kɔmplɪmɛnt] complimenter; ~**s** *npl* compliments *mpl*, hommages *mpl*; vœux *mpl*; **to pay sb a** ~ faire *or* adresser un compliment à qn; **to** ~ **sb (on sth/on doing sth)** féliciter qn (pour qch/de faire qch).

complimentary [kɔmplɪ'mɛntərɪ] *adj* flatteur(euse); (*free*) à titre gracieux.

complimentary ticket *n* billet *m* de faveur.

compliments slip *n* fiche *f* de transmission.

comply [kəm'plaɪ] *vi*: **to** ~ **with** se soumettre à, se conformer à.

component [kəm'pəunənt] *adj* composant(e), constituant(e) ♦ *n* composant *m*, élément *m*.

compose [kəm'pəuz] *vt* composer; **to** ~ **o.s.** se calmer, se maîtriser; prendre une contenance.

composed [kəm'pəuzd] *adj* calme, posé(e).

composer [kəm'pəuzə*] *n* (*MUS*) compositeur *m*.

composite ['kɔmpəzɪt] *adj* composite; (*BOT*, *MATH*) composé(e).

composition [kɔmpə'zɪʃən] *n* composition *f*.

compost ['kɔmpɔst] *n* compost *m*.

composure [kəm'pəuʒə*] *n* calme *m*, maîtrise *f* de soi.

compound ['kɔmpaund] *n* (*CHEM*, *LING*) composé *m*; (*enclosure*) enclos *m*, enceinte *f* ♦ *adj* composé(e) ♦ *vt* [kəm'paund] (*fig: problem etc*) aggraver.

compound fracture *n* fracture compliquée.

compound interest *n* intérêt composé.

comprehend [kɔmprɪ'hɛnd] *vt* comprendre.

comprehension [kɔmprɪ'hɛnʃən] *n* compréhension *f*.

comprehensive [kɔmprɪ'hɛnsɪv] *adj* (très) complet(ète).

comprehensive insurance policy *n* assurance *f* tous risques.

comprehensive (school) *n* (*BRIT*) école secondaire non sélective avec libre circulation d'une section à l'autre, ≈ CES *m*.

compress *vt* [kəm'prɛs] comprimer ♦ *n* ['kɔmprɛs] (*MED*) compresse *f*.

compression [kəm'prɛʃən] *n* compression *f*.

comprise [kəm'praɪz] *vt* (*also:* be ~d of) comprendre.

compromise ['kɔmprəmaɪz] *n* compromis *m* ♦ *vt* compromettre ♦ *vi* transiger, accepter un compromis ♦ *cpd* (*decision, solution*) de compromis.

compulsion [kəm'pʌlʃən] *n* contrainte *f*, force *f*; **under** ~ sous la contrainte.

compulsive [kəm'pʌlsɪv] *adj* (*PSYCH*) compulsif(ive); **he's a ~ smoker** c'est un fumeur invétéré.

compulsory [kəm'pʌlsərɪ] *adj* obligatoire.

compulsory purchase *n* expropriation *f*.

compunction [kəm'pʌŋkʃən] *n* scrupule *m*; **to have no ~ about doing sth** n'avoir aucun scrupule à faire qch.

computer [kəm'pju:tə*] *n* ordinateur *m*; (*mechanical*) calculatrice *f*.

computer game *n* jeu *m* vidéo.

computerize [kəm'pju:təraɪz] *vt* traiter *or* automatiser par ordinateur.

computer language *n* langage *m* machine *or* informatique.

computer literate *adj* initié(e) à l'informatique.

computer peripheral *n* périphérique *m*.

computer program *n* programme *m* informatique.

computer programmer *n* programmeur/euse.

computer programming *n* programmation *f*.

computer science *n* informatique *f*.

computer scientist *n* informaticien/ne.

computing [kəm'pju:tɪŋ] *n* informatique *f*.

comrade ['kɔmrɪd] *n* camarade *m/f*.

comradeship ['kɔmrɪdʃɪp] *n* camaraderie *f*.

comsat ['kɔmsæt] *n abbr* = **communications satellite**.

con [kɔn] *vt* duper; escroquer ♦ *n* escroquerie *f*; **to ~ sb into doing sth** tromper qn pour lui faire faire qch.

concave ['kɔn'keɪv] *adj* concave.

conceal [kən'si:l] *vt* cacher, dissimuler.

concede [kən'si:d] *vt* concéder ♦ *vi* céder.

conceit [kən'si:t] *n* vanité *f*, suffisance *f*, prétention *f*.

conceited [kən'si:tɪd] *adj* vaniteux(euse), suffisant(e).

conceivable [kən'si:vəbl] *adj* concevable, imaginable; **it is ~ that** il est concevable que.

conceivably [kən'si:vəblɪ] *adv*: **he may ~ be right** il n'est pas impossible qu'il ait raison.

conceive [kən'si:v] *vt* concevoir ♦ *vi*: **to ~ of sth/of doing sth** imaginer qch/de faire qch.

concentrate ['kɔnsəntreɪt] *vi* se concentrer ♦ *vt* concentrer.

concentration [kɔnsən'treɪʃən] *n* concentration *f*.

concentration camp *n* camp *m* de concentration.

concentric [kɔn'sɛntrɪk] *adj* concentrique.

concept ['kɔnsɛpt] *n* concept *m*.

conception [kən'sɛpʃən] *n* conception *f*; (*idea*) idée *f*.

concern [kən'sə:n] *n* affaire *f*; (*COMM*) entreprise *f*, firme *f*; (*anxiety*) inquiétude *f*, souci *m* ♦ *vt* concerner; **to be ~ed (about)** s'inquiéter (de), être inquiet(ète) (au sujet de); **"to whom it may ~"** "à qui de droit"; **as far as I am ~ed** en ce qui me concerne; **to be ~ed with** (*person: involved with*) s'occuper de; **the department ~ed** (*under discussion*) le service en question; (*involved*) le service concerné.

concerning [kən'sə:nɪŋ] *prep* en ce qui concerne, à propos de.

concert ['kɔnsət] *n* concert *m*; **in ~** à l'unisson, en chœur; ensemble.

concerted [kən'sə:tɪd] *adj* concerté(e).

concert hall *n* salle *f* de concert.

concertina [kɔnsə'ti:nə] *n* concertina *m* ♦ *vi* se télescoper, se caramboler.

concerto [kən't∫ə:təu] *n* concerto *m*.

concession [kən'sɛʃən] *n* concession *f*.

concessionaire [kənsɛʃə'nɛə*] *n* concessionnaire *m/f*.

concessionary [kən'sɛʃənrɪ] *adj* (*ticket, fare*) à tarif réduit.

conciliation [kənsɪlɪ'eɪʃən] *n* conciliation *f*, apaisement *m*.

conciliatory [kən'sɪlɪətrɪ] *adj* conciliateur(trice); conciliant(e).

concise [kən'saɪs] *adj* concis(e).

conclave ['kɔnkleɪv] *n* assemblée secrète; (*REL*) conclave *m*.

conclude [kən'klu:d] *vt* conclure ♦ *vi* (*speaker*)

conclure; (*events*): **to ~ (with)** se terminer (par).

concluding [kən'kluːdɪŋ] *adj* (*remarks etc*) final(e).

conclusion [kən'kluːʒən] *n* conclusion *f*; **to come to the ~ that** (en) conclure que.

conclusive [kən'kluːsɪv] *adj* concluant(e), définitif(ive).

concoct [kən'kɔkt] *vt* confectionner, composer.

concoction [kən'kɔkʃən] *n* (*food, drink*) mélange *m*.

concord ['kɔŋkɔːd] *n* (*harmony*) harmonie *f*; (*treaty*) accord *m*.

concourse ['kɔŋkɔːs] *n* (*hall*) hall *m*, salle *f* des pas perdus; (*crowd*) affluence *f*, multitude *f*.

concrete ['kɔŋkriːt] *n* béton *m* ♦ *adj* concret(ète); (*CONSTR*) en béton.

concrete mixer *n* bétonnière *f*.

concur [kən'kəː*] *vi* être d'accord.

concurrently [kən'kʌrntlɪ] *adv* simultanément.

concussion [kən'kʌʃən] *n* (*MED*) commotion (cérébrale).

condemn [kən'dɛm] *vt* condamner.

condemnation [kɔndɛm'neɪʃən] *n* condamnation *f*.

condensation [kɔndɛn'seɪʃən] *n* condensation *f*.

condense [kən'dɛns] *vi* se condenser ♦ *vt* condenser.

condensed milk [kən'dɛnst-] *n* lait concentré (sucré).

condescend [kɔndɪ'sɛnd] *vi* condescendre, s'abaisser; **to ~ to do sth** daigner faire qch.

condescending [kɔndɪ'sɛndɪŋ] *adj* condescendant(e).

condition [kən'dɪʃən] *n* condition *f*; (*disease*) maladie *f* ♦ *vt* déterminer, conditionner; **in good/poor ~** en bon/mauvais état; **a heart ~** une maladie cardiaque; **weather ~s** conditions *fpl* météorologiques; **on ~ that** à condition que + *sub*, à condition de.

conditional [kən'dɪʃənl] *adj* conditionnel(le); **to be ~ upon** dépendre de.

conditioner [kən'dɪʃənə*] *n* (*for hair*) baume démêlant.

condo ['kɔndəu] *n abbr* (*US col*) = **condominium**.

condolences [kən'dəulənsɪz] *npl* condoléances *fpl*.

condom ['kɔndəm] *n* préservatif *m*.

condominium [kɔndə'mɪnɪəm] *n* (*US: building*) immeuble *m* (en copropriété); (*: rooms*) appartement *m* (dans un immeuble en copropriété).

condone [kən'dəun] *vt* fermer les yeux sur, approuver (tacitement).

conducive [kən'djuːsɪv] *adj*: **~ to** favorable à, qui contribue à.

conduct *n* ['kɔndʌkt] conduite *f* ♦ *vt* [kən'dʌkt] conduire; (*manage*) mener, diriger; (*MUS*) diriger; **to ~ o.s.** se conduire, se comporter.

conducted tour [kən'dʌktɪd-] *n* voyage organisé; (*of building*) visite guidée.

conductor [kən'dʌktə*] *n* (*of orchestra*) chef *m* d'orchestre; (*on bus*) receveur *m*; (*US: on train*) chef *m* de train; (*ELEC*) conducteur *m*.

conductress [kən'dʌktrɪs] *n* (*on bus*) receveuse *f*.

conduit ['kɔndɪt] *n* conduit *m*, tuyau *m*; tube *m*.

cone [kəun] *n* cône *m*; (*for ice-cream*) cornet *m*; (*BOT*) pomme *f* de pin, cône.

confectioner [kən'fɛkʃənə*] *n* (*of cakes*) pâtissier/ière; (*of sweets*) confiseur/euse; **~'s (shop)** confiserie(-pâtisserie) *f*.

confectionery [kən'fɛkʃənrɪ] *n* (*cakes*) pâtisserie *f*; (*sweets*) confiserie *f*.

confederate [kən'fɛdrɪt] *adj* confédéré(e) ♦ *n* (*pej*) acolyte *m*; (*US HISTORY*) confédéré/e.

confederation [kənfɛdə'reɪʃən] *n* confédération *f*.

confer [kən'fəː*] *vt*: **to ~ sth on** conférer qch à ♦ *vi* conférer, s'entretenir; **to ~ (with sb about sth)** s'entretenir (de qch avec qn).

conference ['kɔnfərns] *n* conférence *f*; **to be in ~** être en réunion *or* en conférence.

conference room *n* salle *f* de conférence.

confess [kən'fɛs] *vt* confesser, avouer ♦ *vi* se confesser.

confession [kən'fɛʃən] *n* confession *f*.

confessional [kən'fɛʃənl] *n* confessional *m*.

confessor [kən'fɛsə*] *n* confesseur *m*.

confetti [kən'fɛtɪ] *n* confettis *mpl*.

confide [kən'faɪd] *vi*: **to ~ in** s'ouvrir à, se confier à.

confidence ['kɔnfɪdns] *n* confiance *f*; (*also: self-~*) assurance *f*, confiance en soi; (*secret*) confidence *f*; **to have (every) ~ that** être certain que; **motion of no ~** motion *f* de censure; **to tell sb sth in strict ~** dire qch à qn en toute confidence.

confidence trick *n* escroquerie *f*.

confident ['kɔnfɪdənt] *adj* sûr(e), assuré(e).

confidential [kɔnfɪ'dɛnʃəl] *adj* confidentiel(le); (*secretary*) particulier(ère).

confidentiality ['kɔnfɪdɛnʃɪ'ælɪtɪ] *n* confidentialité *f*.

configuration [kən'fɪgju'reɪʃən] *n* (*also COMPUT*) configuration *f*.

confine [kən'faɪn] *vt* limiter, borner; (*shut up*) confiner, enfermer; **to ~ o.s. to doing sth/to sth** se contenter de faire qch/se limiter à qch.

confined [kən'faɪnd] *adj* (*space*) restreint(e), réduit(e).

confinement [kən'faɪnmənt] *n* emprisonnement *m*, détention *f*; (*MIL*) consigne *f* (au quartier); (*MED*) accouchement *m*.

confines ['kɔnfaɪnz] *npl* confins *mpl*, bornes *fpl*.

confirm [kən'fəːm] *vt* (*report, REL*) confirmer; (*appointment*) ratifier.

confirmation [kɔnfə'meɪʃən] *n* confirmation *f*; ratification *f*.

confirmed [kən'fɜːmd] *adj* invétéré(e), incorrigible.
confiscate ['kɒnfɪskeɪt] *vt* confisquer.
confiscation [kɒnfɪs'keɪʃən] *n* confiscation *f*.
conflagration [kɒnflə'greɪʃən] *n* incendie *m*; (*fig*) conflagration *f*.
conflict *n* ['kɒnflɪkt] conflit *m*, lutte *f* ♦ *vi* [kən'flɪkt] être *or* entrer en conflit; (*opinions*) s'opposer, se heurter.
conflicting [kən'flɪktɪŋ] *adj* contradictoire.
conform [kən'fɔːm] *vi*: **to ~ (to)** se conformer (à).
conformist [kən'fɔːmɪst] *n* conformiste *m/f*.
confound [kən'faʊnd] *vt* confondre; (*amaze*) rendre perplexe.
confounded [kən'faʊndɪd] *adj* maudit(e), sacré(e).
confront [kən'frʌnt] *vt* confronter, mettre en présence; (*enemy, danger*) affronter, faire face à.
confrontation [kɒnfrən'teɪʃən] *n* confrontation *f*.
confrontational [kɒnfrən'teɪʃənl] *adj* conflictuel(le).
confuse [kən'fjuːz] *vt* embrouiller; (*one thing with another*) confondre.
confused [kən'fjuːzd] *adj* (*person*) dérouté(e), désorienté(e); (*situation*) embrouillé(e).
confusing [kən'fjuːzɪŋ] *adj* peu clair(e), déroutant(e).
confusion [kən'fjuːʒən] *n* confusion *f*.
congeal [kən'dʒiːl] *vi* (*oil*) se figer; (*blood*) se coaguler.
congenial [kən'dʒiːnɪəl] *adj* sympathique, agréable.
congenital [kən'dʒenɪtl] *adj* congénital(e).
conger eel ['kɒŋgər-] *n* congre *m*.
congested [kən'dʒestɪd] *adj* (*MED*) congestionné(e); (*fig*) surpeuplé(e); congestionné(e); bloqué(e); (*telephone lines*) encombré(e).
congestion [kən'dʒestʃən] *n* congestion *f*; (*fig*) encombrement *m*.
conglomerate [kən'glɒmərɪt] *n* (*COMM*) conglomérat *m*.
conglomeration [kənglɒmə'reɪʃən] *n* groupement *m*; agglomération *f*.
Congo ['kɒŋgəʊ] *n* (*state*) (république *f* du) Congo.
congratulate [kən'grætjʊleɪt] *vt*: **to ~ sb (on)** féliciter qn (de).
congratulations [kəngrætjʊ'leɪʃənz] *npl*: **~ (on)** félicitations *fpl* (pour) ♦ *excl*: **~!** (toutes mes) félicitations!
congregate ['kɒŋgrɪgeɪt] *vi* se rassembler, se réunir.
congregation [kɒŋgrɪ'geɪʃən] *n* assemblée *f* (des fidèles).
congress ['kɒŋgres] *n* congrès *m*.

Le **Congress** *est le parlement des États-Unis. Il comprend la* **House of Representatives** *et le Senate. Représentants et sénateurs sont élus au*

suffrage universel direct. Le Congrès se réunit au **Capitol***, à Washington.*

congressman ['kɒŋgresmən], **congresswoman** ['kɒŋgreswʊmən] *n* (*US*) membre *m* du Congrès.
conical ['kɒnɪkl] *adj* (*de forme*) conique.
conifer ['kɒnɪfə*] *n* conifère *m*.
coniferous [kə'nɪfərəs] *adj* (*forest*) de conifères.
conjecture [kən'dʒektʃə*] *n* conjecture *f* ♦ *vt*, *vi* conjecturer.
conjugal ['kɒndʒʊgl] *adj* conjugal(e).
conjugate ['kɒndʒʊgeɪt] *vt* conjuguer.
conjugation [kɒndʒə'geɪʃən] *n* conjugaison *f*.
conjunction [kən'dʒʌŋkʃən] *n* conjonction *f*; **in ~ with** (conjointement) avec.
conjunctivitis [kəndʒʌŋktɪ'vaɪtɪs] *n* conjonctivite *f*.
conjure ['kʌndʒə*] *vt* faire apparaître (par la prestidigitation); [kən'dʒʊə*] conjurer, supplier ♦ *vi* faire des tours de passe-passe.
►**conjure up** *vt* (*ghost, spirit*) faire apparaître; (*memories*) évoquer.
conjurer ['kʌndʒərə*] *n* prestidigitateur *m*, illusionniste *m/f*.
conjuring trick ['kʌndʒərɪŋ-] *n* tour *m* de prestidigitation.
conker ['kɒŋkə*] *n* (*BRIT*) marron *m* (d'Inde).
conk out [kɒŋk-] *vi* (*col*) tomber *or* rester en panne.
conman ['kɒnmæn] *n* escroc *m*.
Conn. *abbr* (*US*) = Connecticut.
connect [kə'nekt] *vt* joindre, relier; (*ELEC*) connecter; (*fig*) établir un rapport entre, faire un rapprochement entre ♦ *vi* (*train*): **to ~ with** assurer la correspondance avec; **to be ~ed with** avoir un rapport avec; (*have dealings with*) avoir des rapports avec, être en relation avec; **I am trying to ~ you** (*TEL*) j'essaie d'obtenir votre communication.
connection [kə'nekʃən] *n* relation *f*, lien *m*; (*ELEC*) connexion *f*; (*TEL*) communication *f*; (*train etc*) correspondance *f*; **in ~ with** à propos de; **what is the ~ between them?** quel est le lien entre eux?; **business ~s** relations d'affaires; **to miss/get one's ~** (*train etc*) rater/avoir sa correspondance.
connexion [kə'nekʃən] *n* (*BRIT*) = **connection**.
conning tower ['kɒnɪŋ-] *n* kiosque *m* (*de sous-marin*).
connive [kə'naɪv] *vi*: **to ~ at** se faire le complice de.
connoisseur [kɒnɪ'sɜː*] *n* connaisseur *m*.
connotation [kɒnə'teɪʃən] *n* connotation *f*, implication *f*.
connubial [kə'njuːbɪəl] *adj* conjugal(e).
conquer ['kɒŋkə*] *vt* conquérir; (*feelings*) vaincre, surmonter.
conqueror ['kɒŋkərə*] *n* conquérant *m*, vainqueur *m*.
conquest ['kɒŋkwest] *n* conquête *f*.

cons [kɒnz] *npl see* **pro, convenience.**
conscience ['kɒnʃəns] *n* conscience *f*; **in all ~** en conscience.
conscientious [kɒnʃɪ'ɛnʃəs] *adj* consciencieux(euse); (*scruple, objection*) de conscience.
conscientious objector *n* objecteur *m* de conscience.
conscious ['kɒnʃəs] *adj* conscient(e); (*deliberate: insult, error*) délibéré(e); **to become ~ of sth/that** prendre conscience de qch/que.
consciousness ['kɒnʃəsnɪs] *n* conscience *f*; (*MED*) connaissance *f*; **to lose/regain ~** perdre/reprendre connaissance.
conscript ['kɒnskrɪpt] *n* conscrit *m*.
conscription [kən'skrɪpʃən] *n* conscription *f*.
consecrate ['kɒnsɪkreɪt] *vt* consacrer.
consecutive [kən'sɛkjʊtɪv] *adj* consécutif(ive); **on three ~ occasions** trois fois de suite.
consensus [kən'sɛnsəs] *n* consensus *m*; **the ~ (of opinion)** le consensus (d'opinion).
consent [kən'sɛnt] *n* consentement *m* ♦ *vi*: **to ~ (to)** consentir (à); **age of ~** âge nubile (légal); **by common ~** d'un commun accord.
consenting adults [kən'sɛntɪŋ-] *npl* personnes consentantes.
consequence ['kɒnsɪkwəns] *n* suites *fpl*, conséquence *f*; importance *f*; **in ~** en conséquence, par conséquent.
consequently ['kɒnsɪkwəntlɪ] *adv* par conséquent, donc.
conservation [kɒnsə'veɪʃən] *n* préservation *f*, protection *f*; (*also: nature ~*) défense *f* de l'environnement; **energy ~** économies *fpl* d'énergie.
conservationist [kɒnsə'veɪʃnɪst] *n* protecteur/trice de la nature.
conservative [kən'sɜːvətɪv] *adj* conservateur(trice); (*cautious*) prudent(e); **C~** *adj*, *n* (*BRIT POL*) conservateur(trice); **the C~ Party** le parti conservateur.
conservatory [kən'sɜːvətrɪ] *n* (*greenhouse*) serre *f*.
conserve [kən'sɜːv] *vt* conserver, préserver; (*supplies, energy*) économiser ♦ *n* confiture *f*, conserve *f* (de fruits).
consider [kən'sɪdə*] *vt* considérer, réfléchir à; (*take into account*) penser à, prendre en considération; (*regard, judge*) considérer, estimer; **to ~ doing sth** envisager de faire qch; **~ yourself lucky** estimez-vous heureux; **all things ~ed** (toute) réflexion faite.
considerable [kən'sɪdərəbl] *adj* considérable.
considerably [kən'sɪdərəblɪ] *adv* nettement.
considerate [kən'sɪdərɪt] *adj* prévenant(e), plein(e) d'égards.
consideration [kənsɪdə'reɪʃən] *n* considération *f*; (*reward*) rétribution *f*, rémunération *f*; **out of ~ for** par égard pour; **under ~** à l'étude; **my first ~ is my family** ma famille passe avant tout le reste.

considered [kən'sɪdəd] *adj*: **it is my ~ opinion that ...** après avoir mûrement réfléchi, je pense que ....
considering [kən'sɪdərɪŋ] *prep*: **~ (that)** étant donné (que).
consign [kən'saɪn] *vt* expédier, livrer.
consignee [kɒnsaɪ'niː] *n* destinataire *m/f*.
consignment [kən'saɪnmənt] *n* arrivage *m*, envoi *m*.
consignment note *n* (*COMM*) bordereau *m* d'expédition.
consignor [kən'saɪnə*] *n* expéditeur/trice.
consist [kən'sɪst] *vi*: **to ~ of** consister en, se composer de.
consistency [kən'sɪstənsɪ] *n* consistance *f*; (*fig*) cohérence *f*.
consistent [kən'sɪstənt] *adj* logique, cohérent(e); **~ with** compatible avec, en accord avec.
consolation [kɒnsə'leɪʃən] *n* consolation *f*.
console *vt* [kən'səul] consoler ♦ *n* ['kɒnsəul] console *f*.
consolidate [kən'sɒlɪdeɪt] *vt* consolider.
consols ['kɒnsɒlz] *npl* (*BRIT STOCK EXCHANGE*) rente *f* d'État.
consommé [kən'sɒmeɪ] *n* consommé *m*.
consonant ['kɒnsənənt] *n* consonne *f*.
consort *n* ['kɒnsɔːt] époux/épouse; **prince ~** prince *m* consort ♦ *vi* [kən'sɔːt] (*often pej*): **to ~ with sb** frayer avec qn.
consortium [kən'sɔːtɪəm] *n* consortium *m*, comptoir *m*.
conspicuous [kən'spɪkjuəs] *adj* voyant(e), qui attire la vue *or* l'attention; **to make o.s. ~** se faire remarquer.
conspiracy [kən'spɪrəsɪ] *n* conspiration *f*, complot *m*.
conspiratorial [kən'spɪrə'tɔːrɪəl] *adj* (*behaviour*) de conspirateur; (*glance*) conspirateur(trice).
conspire [kən'spaɪə*] *vi* conspirer, comploter.
constable ['kʌnstəbl] *n* (*BRIT*) ≈ agent *m* de police, gendarme *m*.
constabulary [kən'stæbjulərɪ] *n* ≈ police *f*, gendarmerie *f*.
constant ['kɒnstənt] *adj* constant(e); incessant(e).
constantly ['kɒnstəntlɪ] *adv* constamment, sans cesse.
constellation [kɒnstə'leɪʃən] *n* constellation *f*.
consternation [kɒnstə'neɪʃən] *n* consternation *f*.
constipated ['kɒnstɪpeɪtɪd] *adj* constipé(e).
constipation [kɒnstɪ'peɪʃən] *n* constipation *f*.
constituency [kən'stɪtjuənsɪ] *n* circonscription électorale; (*people*) électorat *m*.

Une constituency est à la fois une région qui élit un député au parlement et l'ensemble des électeurs dans cette région. En Grande-Bretagne, les députés font régulièrement des "permanences" dans leur circonscription élec-

torale lors desquelles les électeurs peuvent venir les voir pour parler de leurs problèmes de logement etc.

constituency party _n_ section locale (d'un parti).

constituent [kən'stɪtjuənt] _n_ électeur/trice; (_part_) élément constitutif, composant _m_.

constitute ['kɔnstɪtjuːt] _vt_ constituer.

constitution [kɔnstɪ'tjuːʃən] _n_ constitution _f_.

constitutional [kɔnstɪ'tjuːʃənl] _adj_ constitutionnel(le).

constitutional monarchy _n_ monarchie constitutionnelle.

constrain [kən'streɪn] _vt_ contraindre, forcer.

constrained [kən'streɪnd] _adj_ contraint(e), gêné(e).

constraint [kən'streɪnt] _n_ contrainte _f_; (_embarrassment_) gêne _f_.

constrict [kən'strɪkt] _vt_ rétrécir, resserrer; gêner, limiter.

construct [kən'strʌkt] _vt_ construire.

construction [kən'strʌkʃən] _n_ construction _f_; (_fig: interpretation_) interprétation _f_; **under** ~ (_building etc_) en construction.

construction industry _n_ (industrie _f_ du) bâtiment.

constructive [kən'strʌktɪv] _adj_ constructif(ive).

construe [kən'struː] _vt_ analyser, expliquer.

consul ['kɔnsl] _n_ consul _m_.

consulate ['kɔnsjulɪt] _n_ consulat _m_.

consult [kən'sʌlt] _vt_ consulter; **to ~ sb (about sth)** consulter qn (à propos de qch).

consultancy [kən'sʌltənsɪ] _n_ service _m_ de conseils.

consultancy fee _n_ honoraires _mpl_ d'expert.

consultant [kən'sʌltənt] _n_ (_MED_) médecin consultant; (_other specialist_) consultant _m_, (expert-)conseil _m_ ♦ _cpd_: ~ **engineer** _n_ ingénieur-conseil _m_; ~ **paediatrician** _n_ pédiatre _m_; **legal/management** ~ conseiller _m_ juridique/en gestion.

consultation [kɔnsəl'teɪʃən] _n_ consultation _f_; **in ~ with** en consultation avec.

consultative [kən'sʌltətɪv] _adj_ consultatif(ive).

consulting room [kən'sʌltɪŋ-] _n_ (_BRIT_) cabinet _m_ de consultation.

consume [kən'sjuːm] _vt_ consommer.

consumer [kən'sjuːmə*] _n_ consommateur/trice; (_of electricity, gas etc_) usager _m_.

consumer credit _n_ crédit _m_ aux consommateurs.

consumer durables _npl_ biens _mpl_ de consommation durables.

consumer goods _npl_ biens _mpl_ de consommation.

consumerism [kən'sjuːmərɪzəm] _n_ (_consumer protection_) défense _f_ du consommateur; (_ECON_) consumérisme _m_.

consumer society _n_ société _f_ de consomma-

tion.

consumer watchdog _n_ organisme _m_ pour la défense des consommateurs.

consummate ['kɔnsʌmeɪt] _vt_ consommer.

consumption [kən'sʌmpʃən] _n_ consommation _f_; (_MED_) consomption _f_ (pulmonaire); **not fit for human** ~ non comestible.

cont. _abbr_ = **continued**.

contact ['kɔntækt] _n_ contact _m_; (_person_) connaissance _f_, relation _f_ ♦ _vt_ se mettre en contact _or_ en rapport avec; **to be in ~ with sb/sth** être en contact avec qn/qch; **business** ~**s** relations _fpl_ d'affaires, contacts _mpl_.

contact lenses _npl_ verres _mpl_ de contact.

contagious [kən'teɪdʒəs] _adj_ contagieux(euse).

contain [kən'teɪn] _vt_ contenir; **to ~ o.s.** se contenir, se maîtriser.

container [kən'teɪnə*] _n_ récipient _m_; (_for shipping etc_) conteneur _m_.

containerize [kən'teɪnəraɪz] _vt_ conteneuriser.

container ship _n_ porte-conteneurs _m inv_.

contaminate [kən'tæmɪneɪt] _vt_ contaminer.

contamination [kəntæmɪ'neɪʃən] _n_ contamination _f_.

cont'd _abbr_ = **continued**.

contemplate ['kɔntəmpleɪt] _vt_ contempler; (_consider_) envisager.

contemplation [kɔntəm'pleɪʃən] _n_ contemplation _f_.

contemporary [kən'tɛmpərərɪ] _adj_ contemporain(e); (_design, wallpaper_) moderne ♦ _n_ contemporain/e.

contempt [kən'tɛmpt] _n_ mépris _m_, dédain _m_; ~ **of court** (_LAW_) outrage _m_ à l'autorité de la justice.

contemptible [kən'tɛmptəbl] _adj_ méprisable, vil(e).

contemptuous [kən'tɛmptjuəs] _adj_ dédaigneux(euse), méprisant(e).

contend [kən'tɛnd] _vt_: **to ~ that** soutenir _or_ prétendre que ♦ _vi_: **to ~ with** (_compete_) lutter avec; **to have to ~ with** (_be faced with_) avoir affaire à, être aux prises avec.

contender [kən'tɛndə*] _n_ prétendant/e; candidat/e.

content [kən'tɛnt] _adj_ content(e), satisfait(e) ♦ _vt_ contenter, satisfaire ♦ _n_ ['kɔntɛnt] contenu _m_; teneur _f_; ~**s** _npl_ contenu _m_; (**table of**) ~**s** table _f_ des matières; **to be ~ with** se contenter de; **to ~ o.s. with sth/with doing sth** se contenter de qch/de faire qch.

contented [kən'tɛntɪd] _adj_ content(e), satisfait(e).

contentedly [kən'tɛntɪdlɪ] _adv_ avec un sentiment de (profonde) satisfaction.

contention [kən'tɛnʃən] _n_ dispute _f_, contestation _f_; (_argument_) assertion _f_, affirmation _f_; **bone of** ~ sujet _m_ de discorde.

contentious [kən'tɛnʃəs] _adj_ querelleur(euse); litigieux(euse).

contentment [kən'tɛntmənt] _n_ contentement

m, satisfaction *f*.

contest *n* ['kɔntɛst] combat *m*, lutte *f*; (*competition*) concours *m* ♦ *vt* [kən'tɛst] contester, discuter; (*compete for*) disputer; (*LAW*) attaquer.

contestant [kən'tɛstənt] *n* concurrent/e; (*in fight*) adversaire *m/f*.

context ['kɔntɛkst] *n* contexte *m*; **in/out of** ~ dans le/hors contexte.

continent ['kɔntɪnənt] *n* continent *m*; **the C~** (*BRIT*) l'Europe continentale; **on the C~** en Europe (continentale).

continental [kɔntɪ'nɛntl] *adj* continental(e) ♦ *n* (*BRIT*) Européen/ne (continental(e)).

continental breakfast *n* café (*or* thé) complet.

continental quilt *n* (*BRIT*) couette *f*.

contingency [kən'tɪndʒənsɪ] *n* éventualité *f*, événement imprévu.

contingency plan *n* plan *m* d'urgence.

contingent [kən'tɪndʒənt] *adj* contingent(e) ♦ *n* contingent *m*; **to be** ~ **upon** dépendre de.

continual [kən'tɪnjuəl] *adj* continuel(le).

continually [kən'tɪnjuəlɪ] *adv* continuellement, sans cesse.

continuation [kəntɪnju'eɪʃən] *n* continuation *f*; (*after interruption*) reprise *f*; (*of story*) suite *f*.

continue [kən'tɪnjuː] *vi* continuer ♦ *vt* continuer; (*start again*) reprendre; **to be** ~**d** (*story*) à suivre; ~**d on page 10** suite page 10.

continuing education [kən'tɪnjuɪŋ-] *n* formation permanente *or* continue.

continuity [kɔntɪ'njuːɪtɪ] *n* continuité *f*; (*CINE*) script *m*.

continuity girl *n* (*CINE*) script-girl *f*.

continuous [kən'tɪnjuəs] *adj* continu(e), permanent(e); ~ **performance** (*CINE*) séance permanente; ~ **stationery** (*COMPUT*) papier *m* en continu.

continuously [kən'tɪnjuəslɪ] *adv* (*repeatedly*) continuellement; (*uninterruptedly*) sans interruption.

contort [kən'tɔːt] *vt* tordre, crisper.

contortion [kən'tɔːʃən] *n* crispation *f*, torsion *f*; (*of acrobat*) contorsion *f*.

contortionist [kən'tɔːʃənɪst] *n* contorsionniste *m/f*.

contour ['kɔntuə*] *n* contour *m*, profil *m*; (*also*: ~ **line**) courbe *f* de niveau.

contraband ['kɔntrəbænd] *n* contrebande *f* ♦ *adj* de contrebande.

contraception [kɔntrə'sɛpʃən] *n* contraception *f*.

contraceptive [kɔntrə'sɛptɪv] *adj* contraceptif(ive), anticonceptionnel(le) ♦ *n* contraceptif *m*.

contract *n* ['kɔntrækt] contrat *m* ♦ *cpd* ['kɔntrækt] (*price, date*) contractuel(le); (*work*) à forfait ♦ *vb* [kən'trækt] *vi* (*become smaller*) se contracter, se resserrer; (*COMM*): **to** ~ **to do sth** s'engager (par con-

trat) à faire qch ♦ *vt* contracter; ~ **of employment/service** contrat de travail/de service.

▶**contract in** *vi* s'engager (par contrat); (*BRIT ADMIN*) s'affilier au régime de retraite complémentaire.

▶**contract out** *vi* se dégager; (*BRIT ADMIN*) opter pour la non-affiliation au régime de retraite complémentaire.

contraction [kən'trækʃən] *n* contraction *f*; (*LING*) forme contractée.

contractor [kən'træktə*] *n* entrepreneur *m*.

contractual [kən'træktʃuəl] *adj* contractuel(le).

contradict [kɔntrə'dɪkt] *vt* contredire; (*be contrary to*) démentir, être en contradiction avec.

contradiction [kɔntrə'dɪkʃən] *n* contradiction *f*; **to be in** ~ **with** contredire, être en contradiction avec.

contradictory [kɔntrə'dɪktərɪ] *adj* contradictoire.

contralto [kən'træltəu] *n* contralto *m*.

contraption [kən'træpʃən] *n* (*pej*) machin *m*, truc *m*.

contrary[1] ['kɔntrərɪ] *adj* contraire, opposé(e) ♦ *n* contraire *m*; **on the** ~ au contraire; **unless you hear to the** ~ sauf avis contraire; ~ **to what we thought** contrairement à ce que nous pensions.

contrary[2] [kən'trɛərɪ] *adj* (*perverse*) contrariant(e), entêté(e).

contrast *n* ['kɔntrɑːst] contraste *m* ♦ *vt* [kən'trɑːst] mettre en contraste, contraster; **in** ~ **to** *or* **with** contrairement à, par opposition à.

contrasting [kən'trɑːstɪŋ] *adj* opposé(e), contrasté(e).

contravene [kɔntrə'viːn] *vt* enfreindre, violer, contrevenir à.

contravention [kɔntrə'vɛnʃən] *n*: ~ (**of**) infraction *f* (à).

contribute [kən'trɪbjuːt] *vi* contribuer ♦ *vt*: **to** ~ **£10/an article to** donner 10 livres/un article à; **to** ~ **to** (*gen*) contribuer à; (*newspaper*) collaborer à; (*discussion*) prendre part à.

contribution [kɔntrɪ'bjuːʃən] *n* contribution *f*.

contributor [kən'trɪbjutə*] *n* (*to newspaper*) collaborateur/trice.

contributory [kən'trɪbjutərɪ] *adj* (*cause*) annexe; **it was a** ~ **factor in ...** ce facteur a contribué à ....

contributory pension scheme *n* (*BRIT*) régime *m* de retraite salariale.

contrite ['kɔntraɪt] *adj* contrit(e).

contrivance [kən'traɪvəns] *n* (*scheme*) machination *f*, combinaison *f*; (*device*) appareil *m*, dispositif *m*.

contrive [kən'traɪv] *vt* combiner, inventer ♦ *vi*: **to** ~ **to do** s'arranger pour faire, trouver le moyen de faire.

control [kən'trəul] vt maîtriser; (*check*) contrôler ♦ n maîtrise f; ~**s** npl commandes fpl; **to take ~ of** se rendre maître de; (*COMM*) acquérir une participation majoritaire dans; **to be in ~ of** être maître de, maîtriser; (*in charge of*) être responsable de; **to ~ o.s.** se contrôler; **everything is under ~** j'ai (*or* il a *etc*) la situation en main; **the car went out of ~** j'ai (*or* il a *etc*) perdu le contrôle du véhicule; **beyond our ~** indépendant(e) de notre volonté.

control key n (*COMPUT*) touche f de commande.

controller [kən'trəulə*] n contrôleur m.

controlling interest [kən'trəuliŋ-] n (*COMM*) participation f majoritaire.

control panel n (*on aircraft, ship, TV etc*) tableau m de commandes.

control point n (poste m de) contrôle m.

control room n (*NAUT, MIL*) salle f des commandes; (*RADIO, TV*) régie f.

control tower n (*AVIAT*) tour f de contrôle.

control unit n (*COMPUT*) unité f de contrôle.

controversial [kɔntrə'vəːʃl] adj discutable, controversé(e).

controversy ['kɔntrəvəːsɪ] n controverse f, polémique f.

conurbation [kɔnə'beɪʃən] n conurbation f.

convalesce [kɔnvə'lɛs] vi relever de maladie, se remettre (d'une maladie).

convalescence [kɔnvə'lɛsns] n convalescence f.

convalescent [kɔnvə'lɛsnt] adj, n convalescent(e).

convector [kən'vɛktə*] n radiateur m à convection, appareil m de chauffage par convection.

convene [kən'viːn] vt convoquer, assembler ♦ vi se réunir, s'assembler.

convener [kən'viːnə*] n organisateur m.

convenience [kən'viːnɪəns] n commodité f; **at your ~** quand or comme cela vous convient; **at your earliest ~** (*COMM*) dans les meilleurs délais, le plus tôt possible; **all modern ~s**, (*BRIT*) **all mod cons** avec tout le confort moderne, tout confort.

convenience foods npl plats cuisinés.

convenient [kən'viːnɪənt] adj commode; **if it is ~ to you** si cela vous convient, si cela ne vous dérange pas.

conveniently [kən'viːnɪəntlɪ] adv (*happen*) à pic; (*situated*) commodément.

convent ['kɔnvənt] n couvent m.

convention [kən'vɛnʃən] n convention f.

conventional [kən'vɛnʃənl] adj conventionnel(le).

convent school n couvent m.

converge [kən'vəːdʒ] vi converger.

conversant [kən'vəːsnt] adj: **to be ~ with** s'y connaître en; être au courant de.

conversation [kɔnvə'seɪʃən] n conversation f.

conversational [kɔnvə'seɪʃənl] adj de la conversation; (*COMPUT*) conversationnel(le).

conversationalist [kɔnvə'seɪʃnəlɪst] n brillant(e) causeur/euse.

converse n ['kɔnvəːs] contraire m, inverse m ♦ vi [kən'vəːs]: **to ~ (with sb about sth)** s'entretenir (avec qn de qch).

conversely [kɔn'vəːslɪ] adv inversement, réciproquement.

conversion [kən'vəːʃən] n conversion f; (*BRIT: of house*) transformation f, aménagement m.

conversion table n table f de conversion.

convert vt [kən'vəːt] (*REL, COMM*) convertir; (*alter*) transformer, aménager; (*RUGBY*) transformer ♦ n ['kɔnvəːt] converti/e.

convertible [kən'vəːtəbl] adj convertible ♦ n (voiture f) décapotable f.

convex ['kɔn'vɛks] adj convexe.

convey [kən'veɪ] vt transporter; (*thanks*) transmettre; (*idea*) communiquer.

conveyance [kən'veɪəns] n (*of goods*) transport m de marchandises; (*vehicle*) moyen m de transport.

conveyancing [kən'veɪənsɪŋ] n (*LAW*) rédaction f des actes de cession de propriété.

conveyor belt [kən'veɪə*-] n convoyeur m, tapis roulant.

convict vt [kən'vɪkt] déclarer (or reconnaître) coupable ♦ n ['kɔnvɪkt] forçat m, convict m.

conviction [kən'vɪkʃən] n condamnation f; (*belief*) conviction f.

convince [kən'vɪns] vt convaincre, persuader; **to ~ sb (of sth/that)** persuader qn (de qch/que).

convincing [kən'vɪnsɪŋ] adj persuasif(ive), convaincant(e).

convincingly [kən'vɪnsɪŋlɪ] adv de façon convaincante.

convivial [kən'vɪvɪəl] adj joyeux(euse), plein(e) d'entrain.

convoluted ['kɔnvəluːtɪd] adj (*shape*) tarabiscoté(e); (*argument*) compliqué(e).

convoy ['kɔnvɔɪ] n convoi m.

convulse [kən'vʌls] vt ébranler; **to be ~d with laughter** se tordre de rire.

convulsion [kən'vʌlʃən] n convulsion f.

coo [kuː] vi roucouler.

cook [kuk] vt (faire) cuire ♦ vi cuire; (*person*) faire la cuisine ♦ n cuisinier/ière.

▶**cook up** vt (*col: excuse, story*) inventer.

cookbook ['kukbuk] n livre m de cuisine.

cooker ['kukə*] n cuisinière f.

cookery ['kukərɪ] n cuisine f.

cookery book n (*BRIT*) = **cookbook**.

cookie ['kukɪ] n (*US*) biscuit m, petit gâteau sec.

cooking ['kukɪŋ] n cuisine f ♦ cpd (*apples, chocolate*) à cuire; (*utensils, salt*) de cuisine.

cookout ['kukaut] n (*US*) barbecue m.

cool [kuːl] adj frais(fraîche); (*not afraid*) calme; (*unfriendly*) froid(e); (*impertinent*) effronté(e) ♦ vt, vi rafraîchir, refroidir; **it's ~** (*weather*) il fait frais; **to keep sth ~** or **in a ~**

place garder or conserver qch au frais.
►**cool down** vi refroidir; (fig: person, situation) se calmer.
coolant ['ku:lənt] n liquide m de refroidissement.
cool box, (US) **cooler** ['ku:lə*] n boîte f isotherme.
cooling ['ku:lɪŋ] adj (breeze) rafraîchissant(e).
cooling tower n refroidisseur m.
coolly ['ku:lɪ] adv (calmly) calmement; (audaciously) sans se gêner; (unenthusiastically) froidement.
coolness ['ku:lnɪs] n fraîcheur f; sang-froid m, calme m; froideur f.
coop [ku:p] n poulailler m ♦ vt: **to ~ up** (fig) cloîtrer, enfermer.
co-op ['kəuɔp] n abbr (= cooperative (society)) coop f.
cooperate [kəu'ɔpəreɪt] vi coopérer, collaborer.
cooperation [kəuɔpə'reɪʃən] n coopération f, collaboration f.
cooperative [kəu'ɔpərətɪv] adj coopératif(ive) ♦ n coopérative f.
coopt [kəu'ɔpt] vt: **to ~ sb onto a committee** coopter qn pour faire partie d'un comité.
coordinate vt [kəu'ɔːdɪneɪt] coordonner ♦ n [kəu'ɔdɪnət] (MATH) coordonnée f; **~s** npl (clothes) ensemble m, coordonnés mpl.
coordination [kəuɔːdɪ'neɪʃən] n coordination f.
coot [ku:t] n foulque f.
co-ownership ['kəu'əunəʃɪp] n copropriété f.
cop [kɔp] n (col) flic m.
cope [kəup] vi s'en sortir, tenir le coup; **to ~ with** faire face à; (take care of) s'occuper de.
Copenhagen ['kəupn'heɪgən] n Copenhague.
copier ['kɔpɪə*] n (also: photo~) copieur m.
co-pilot ['kəu'paɪlət] n copilote m.
copious ['kəupɪəs] adj copieux(euse), abondant(e).
copper ['kɔpə*] n cuivre m; (col: policeman) flic m; **~s** npl petite monnaie f.
coppice ['kɔpɪs], **copse** [kɔps] n taillis m.
copulate ['kɔpjuleɪt] vi copuler.
copy ['kɔpɪ] n copie f; (book etc) exemplaire m; (material: for printing) copie ♦ vt copier; (imitate) imiter; **rough ~** (gen) premier jet; (SCOL) brouillon m; **fair ~** version définitive; propre m; **to make good ~** (PRESS) faire un bon sujet d'article.
►**copy out** vt copier.
copycat ['kɔpɪkæt] n (pej) copieur/euse.
copyright ['kɔpɪraɪt] n droit m d'auteur, copyright m; **~ reserved** tous droits (de reproduction) réservés.
copy typist n dactylo m/f.
copywriter ['kɔpɪraɪtə*] n rédacteur/trice publicitaire.
coral ['kɔrəl] n corail m.
coral reef n récif m de corail.
Coral Sea n: **the ~** la mer de Corail.

cord [kɔːd] n corde f; (fabric) velours côtelé; whipcord m; corde f; (ELEC) cordon m (d'alimentation), fil m (électrique); **~s** npl (trousers) pantalon m de velours côtelé.
cordial ['kɔːdɪəl] adj cordial(e), chaleureux(euse) ♦ n sirop m; cordial m.
cordless ['kɔːdlɪs] adj sans fil.
cordon ['kɔːdn] n cordon m.
►**cordon off** vt (area) interdire l'accès à; (crowd) tenir à l'écart.
corduroy ['kɔːdərɔɪ] n velours côtelé.
CORE [kɔː*] n abbr (US) = Congress of Racial Equality.
core [kɔː*] n (of fruit) trognon m, cœur m; (TECH: also of earth) noyau m; (of nuclear reactor, fig: of problem etc) cœur ♦ vt enlever le trognon or le cœur de; **rotten to the ~** complètement pourri.
Corfu [kɔː'fuː] n Corfou.
coriander [kɔrɪ'ændə*] n coriandre f.
cork [kɔːk] n liège m; (of bottle) bouchon m.
corkage ['kɔːkɪdʒ] n droit payé par le client qui apporte sa propre bouteille de vin.
corked [kɔːkt], (US) **corky** ['kɔːkɪ] adj (wine) qui sent le bouchon.
corkscrew ['kɔːkskruː] n tire-bouchon m.
cormorant ['kɔːmərnt] n cormoran m.
Corn abbr (BRIT) = Cornwall.
corn [kɔːn] n (BRIT: wheat) blé m; (US: maize) maïs m; (on foot) cor m; **~ on the cob** (CULIN) épi m de maïs au naturel.
cornea ['kɔːnɪə] n cornée f.
corned beef ['kɔːnd-] n corned-beef m.
corner ['kɔːnə*] n coin m; (AUT) tournant m, virage m; (FOOTBALL: also: ~ **kick**) corner m ♦ vt acculer, mettre au pied du mur; coincer; (COMM: market) accaparer ♦ vi prendre un virage; **to cut ~s** (fig) prendre des raccourcis.
corner flag n (FOOTBALL) piquet m de coin.
corner kick n (FOOTBALL) corner m.
cornerstone ['kɔːnəstəun] n pierre f angulaire.
cornet ['kɔːnɪt] n (MUS) cornet m à pistons; (BRIT: of ice-cream) cornet (de glace).
cornflakes ['kɔːnfleɪks] npl cornflakes mpl.
cornflour ['kɔːnflauə*] n (BRIT) farine f de maïs, maïzena f®.
cornice ['kɔːnɪs] n corniche f.
Cornish ['kɔːnɪʃ] adj de Cornouailles, cornouaillais(e).
corn oil n huile f de maïs.
cornstarch ['kɔːnstaːtʃ] n (US) farine f de maïs, maïzena f®.
cornucopia [kɔːnju'kəupɪə] n corne f d'abondance.
Cornwall ['kɔːnwəl] n Cornouailles f.
corny ['kɔːnɪ] adj (col) rebattu(e), galvaudé(e).
corollary [kə'rɔlərɪ] n corollaire m.
coronary ['kɔrənərɪ] n: **~ (thrombosis)** infarctus m (du myocarde), thrombose f coronaire.

coronation [kɔrə'neɪʃən] n couronnement m.
coroner ['kɔrənə*] n coroner m.
coronet ['kɔrənɪt] n couronne f.
Corp. abbr = corporation.
corporal ['kɔːpərl] n caporal m, brigadier m ♦ adj: ~ **punishment** châtiment corporel.
corporate ['kɔːpərɪt] adj en commun; (COMM) constitué(e) (en corporation).
corporate hospitality n arrangement selon lequel une entreprise offre des places de théâtre, concert etc à ses clients.
corporate identity, corporate image n (of organization) image f de l'entreprise.
corporation [kɔːpə'reɪʃən] n (of town) municipalité f, conseil municipal; (COMM) société f.
corporation tax n ≈ impôt m sur les bénéfices.
corps [kɔː*], pl **corps** [kɔːz] n corps m; **the press** ~ la presse.
corpse [kɔːps] n cadavre m.
corpuscle ['kɔːpʌsl] n corpuscule m.
corral [kə'raːl] n corral m.
correct [kə'rɛkt] adj (accurate) correct(e), exact(e); (proper) correct, convenable ♦ vt corriger; **you are** ~ vous avez raison.
correction [kə'rɛkʃən] n correction f.
correlate ['kɔrɪleɪt] vt mettre en corrélation ♦ vi: **to** ~ **with** correspondre à.
correlation [kɔrɪ'leɪʃən] n corrélation f.
correspond [kɔrɪs'pɔnd] vi correspondre.
correspondence [kɔrɪs'pɔndəns] n correspondance f.
correspondence course n cours m par correspondance.
correspondent [kɔrɪs'pɔndənt] n correspondant/e.
corridor ['kɔrɪdɔː*] n couloir m, corridor m.
corroborate [kə'rɔbəreɪt] vt corroborer, confirmer.
corrode [kə'rəud] vt corroder, ronger ♦ vi se corroder.
corrosion [kə'rəuʒən] n corrosion f.
corrosive [kə'rəuzɪv] adj corrosif(ive).
corrugated ['kɔrəgeɪtɪd] adj plissé(e); ondulé(e).
corrugated iron n tôle ondulée.
corrupt [kə'rʌpt] adj corrompu(e) ♦ vt corrompre; (data) altérer; ~ **practices** (dishonesty, bribery) malversation f.
corruption [kə'rʌpʃən] n corruption f; altération f (de données).
corset ['kɔːsɪt] n corset m.
Corsica ['kɔːsɪkə] n Corse f.
Corsican ['kɔːsɪkən] adj corse ♦ n Corse m/f.
cortège [kɔː'teɪʒ] n cortège m (gén funèbre).
cortisone ['kɔːtɪzəun] n cortisone f.
coruscating ['kɔrəskeɪtɪŋ] adj scintillant(e).
c.o.s. abbr (= cash on shipment) paiement m à l'expédition.
cosh [kɔʃ] n (BRIT) matraque f.
cosignatory ['kəu'sɪgnətərɪ] n cosignataire m/f.

cosiness ['kəuzɪnɪs] n atmosphère douillette, confort m.
cos lettuce ['kɔs-] n (laitue f) romaine f.
cosmetic [kɔz'mɛtɪk] n produit m de beauté, cosmétique m ♦ adj (preparation) cosmétique; (surgery) esthétique; (fig: reforms) symbolique, superficiel(le).
cosmic ['kɔzmɪk] adj cosmique.
cosmonaut ['kɔzmənɔːt] n cosmonaute m/f.
cosmopolitan [kɔzmə'pɔlɪtn] adj cosmopolite.
cosmos ['kɔzmɔs] n cosmos m.
cosset ['kɔsɪt] vt choyer, dorloter.
cost [kɔst] n coût m ♦ vb (pt, pp **cost**) vi coûter ♦ vt établir or calculer le prix de revient de; ~**s** npl (LAW) dépens mpl; **how much does it** ~? combien ça coûte?; **it** ~**s £5/too much** cela coûte 5 livres/trop cher; **what will it** ~ **to have it repaired?** combien cela coûtera de le faire réparer?; **it** ~ **him his life/job** ça lui a coûté la vie/son emploi; **the** ~ **of living** le coût de la vie; **at all** ~**s** coûte que coûte, à tout prix.
cost accountant n analyste m/f de coûts.
co-star ['kəustɑː*] n partenaire m/f.
Costa Rica ['kɔstə'riːkə] n Costa Rica m.
cost centre n centre m de coût.
cost control n contrôle m des coûts.
cost-effective ['kɔstɪ'fɛktɪv] adj rentable.
cost-effectiveness ['kɔstɪ'fɛktɪvnɪs] n rentabilité f.
costing ['kɔstɪŋ] n calcul m du prix de revient.
costly ['kɔstlɪ] adj coûteux(euse).
cost-of-living ['kɔstəv'lɪvɪŋ] adj: ~ **allowance** indemnité f de vie chère; ~ **index** indice m du coût de la vie.
cost price n (BRIT) prix coûtant or de revient.
costume ['kɔstjuːm] n costume m; (lady's suit) tailleur m; (BRIT: also: swimming ~) maillot m (de bain).
costume jewellery n bijoux mpl de fantaisie.
cosy, (US) **cozy** ['kəuzɪ] adj (bed) douillet(te); (scarf, gloves) bien chaud(e); (atmosphere) chaleureux(euse); (room) mignon(ne).
cot [kɔt] n (BRIT: child's) lit m d'enfant, petit lit; (US: campbed) lit de camp.
cot death n mort subite du nourrisson.
Cotswolds ['kɔtswəuldz] npl: **the** ~ région de collines du Gloucestershire.
cottage ['kɔtɪdʒ] n petite maison (à la campagne), cottage m.
cottage cheese n fromage blanc (maigre).
cottage industry n industrie familiale or artisanale.
cottage pie n ≈ hachis m Parmentier.
cotton ['kɔtn] n coton m; ~ **dress** etc robe etc en or de coton.
▶**cotton on** vi (col): **to** ~ **on (to sth)** piger (qch).
cotton wool n (BRIT) ouate f, coton m hydrophile.
couch [kautʃ] n canapé m; divan m; (doctor's)

table *f* d'examen; (*psychiatrist's*) divan ♦ *vt* formuler, exprimer.

couchette [kuːʃɛt] *n* couchette *f*.

couch potato *n* (*col*) mollasson/ne (*qui passe son temps devant la télé*).

cough [kɔf] *vi* tousser ♦ *n* toux *f*.

cough drop *n* pastille *f* pour *or* contre la toux.

cough mixture, cough syrup *n* sirop *m* pour la toux.

could [kud] *pt of* **can**.

couldn't ['kudnt] = **could not**.

council ['kaunsl] *n* conseil *m*; **city** *or* **town** ~ conseil municipal; **C~ of Europe** Conseil de l'Europe.

council estate *n* (*BRIT*) (quartier *m or* zone *f* de) logements loués à/par la municipalité.

council house *n* (*BRIT*) maison *f* (à loyer modéré) louée par la municipalité.

councillor ['kaunslə*] *n* conseiller/ère.

council tax *n* (*BRIT*) impôts locaux.

counsel ['kaunsl] *n* consultation *f*, délibération *f*; (*person*) avocat/e ♦ *vt*: **to ~ sth/sb to do sth** conseiller qch/à qn de faire qch; ~ **for the defence/the prosecution** (avocat de la) défense/avocat du ministère public.

counsellor, (*US*) **counselor** ['kaunslə*] *n* conseiller/ère; (*US LAW*) avocat *m*.

count [kaunt] *vt, vi* compter ♦ *n* compte *m*; (*nobleman*) comte *m*; **to ~ (up) to 10** compter jusqu'à 10; **to keep ~ of sth** tenir le compte de qch; **not ~ing the children** sans compter les enfants; **10 ~ing him** 10 avec lui, 10 en le comptant; **to ~ the cost of** établir le coût de; **it ~s for very little** cela n'a pas beaucoup d'importance; ~ **yourself lucky** estimez-vous heureux.

▶**count on** *vt fus* compter sur; **to ~ on doing sth** compter faire qch.

▶**count up** *vt* compter, additionner.

countdown ['kauntdaun] *n* compte *m* à rebours.

countenance ['kauntɪnəns] *n* expression *f* ♦ *vt* approuver.

counter ['kauntə*] *n* comptoir *m*; (*in post office, bank*) guichet *m*; (*in game*) jeton *m* ♦ *vt* aller à l'encontre de, opposer; (*blow*) parer ♦ *adv*: ~ **to** à l'encontre de; contrairement à; **to buy under the** ~ (*fig*) acheter sous le manteau *or* en sous-main; **to** ~ **sth with sth/by doing sth** contrer *or* riposter à qch par qch/en faisant qch.

counteract ['kauntər'ækt] *vt* neutraliser, contrebalancer.

counterattack ['kauntərə'tæk] *n* contreattaque *f* ♦ *vi* contre-attaquer.

counterbalance ['kauntə'bæləns] *vt* contrebalancer, faire contrepoids à.

counter-clockwise ['kauntə'klɔkwaɪz] *adv* en sens inverse des aiguilles d'une montre.

counter-espionage ['kauntər'ɛspɪənɑːʒ] *n* contre-espionnage *m*.

counterfeit ['kauntəfɪt] *n* faux *m*, contrefaçon *f* ♦ *vt* contrefaire ♦ *adj* faux(fausse).

counterfoil ['kauntəfɔɪl] *n* talon *m*, souche *f*.

counterintelligence ['kauntərɪn'tɛlɪdʒəns] *n* contre-espionnage *m*.

countermand ['kauntəmɑːnd] *vt* annuler.

countermeasure ['kauntəmɛʒə*] *n* contremesure *f*.

counteroffensive ['kauntərə'fɛnsɪv] *n* contreoffensive *f*.

counterpane ['kauntəpeɪn] *n* dessus-de-lit *m*.

counterpart ['kauntəpɑːt] *n* (*of document etc*) double *m*; (*of person*) homologue *m/f*.

counterproductive ['kauntəprə'dʌktɪv] *adj* contre-productif(ive).

counterproposal ['kauntəprə'pəuzl] *n* contreproposition *f*.

countersign ['kauntəsaɪn] *vt* contresigner.

countersink ['kauntəsɪŋk] *vt* (*hole*) fraiser.

countess ['kauntɪs] *n* comtesse *f*.

countless ['kauntlɪs] *adj* innombrable.

countrified ['kʌntrɪfaɪd] *adj* rustique, à l'air campagnard.

country ['kʌntrɪ] *n* pays *m*; (*native land*) patrie *f*; (*as opposed to town*) campagne *f*; (*region*) région *f*, pays; **in the** ~ à la campagne; **mountainous** ~ pays de montagne, région montagneuse.

country and western (music) *n* musique *f* country.

country dancing *n* (*BRIT*) danse *f* folklorique.

country house *n* manoir *m*, (petit) château.

countryman ['kʌntrɪmən] *n* (*national*) compatriote *m*; (*rural*) habitant *m* de la campagne, campagnard *m*.

countryside ['kʌntrɪsaɪd] *n* campagne *f*.

countrywide ['kʌntrɪ'waɪd] *adj* s'étendant à l'ensemble du pays; (*problem*) à l'échelle nationale ♦ *adv* à travers *or* dans tout le pays.

county ['kauntɪ] *n* comté *m*.

county council *n* (*BRIT*) ≈ conseil régional.

county town *n* (*BRIT*) chef-lieu *m*.

coup, ~**s** [kuː, -z] *n* beau coup; (*also:* ~ **d'état**) coup d'État.

coupé [kuː'peɪ] *n* (*AUT*) coupé *m*.

couple ['kʌpl] *n* couple *m* ♦ *vt* (*carriages*) atteler; (*TECH*) coupler; (*ideas, names*) associer; **a ~ of** deux; (*a few*) deux ou trois.

couplet ['kʌplɪt] *n* distique *m*.

coupling ['kʌplɪŋ] *n* (*RAIL*) attelage *m*.

coupon ['kuːpɔn] *n* (*voucher*) bon-prime *m*, bon-réclame *m*; (*detachable form*) coupon *m* détachable, coupon-réponse *m*; (*FINANCE*) coupon.

courage ['kʌrɪdʒ] *n* courage *m*.

courageous [kə'reɪdʒəs] *adj* courageux(euse).

courgette [kuə'ʒɛt] *n* (*BRIT*) courgette *f*.

courier ['kurɪə*] *n* messager *m*, courrier *m*; (*for tourists*) accompagnateur/trice.

course [kɔːs] *n* cours *m*; (*of ship*) route *f*; (*for golf*) terrain *m*; (*part of meal*) plat *m*; **first** ~ entrée *f*; **of** ~ *adv* bien sûr; **(no) of** ~ **not!**

bien sûr que non!, évidemment que non!; **in the ~ of the next few days** au cours des prochains jours; **in due ~** en temps utile *or* voulu; **~ (of action)** parti *m*, ligne *f* de conduite; **the best ~ would be to** ... le mieux serait de ...; **we have no other ~ but to** ... nous n'avons pas d'autre solution que de ...; **~ of lectures** série *f* de conférences; **~ of treatment** (*MED*) traitement *m*.

court [kɔːt] *n* cour *f*, (*LAW*) cour, tribunal *m*; (*TENNIS*) court *m* ♦ *vt* (*woman*) courtiser, faire la cour à; (*fig: favour, popularity*) rechercher; (*: death, disaster*) courir après, flirter avec; **out of ~** (*LAW: settle*) à l'amiable; **to take to ~** actionner *or* poursuivre en justice; **~ of appeal** cour d'appel.

courteous ['kɔːtɪəs] *adj* courtois(e), poli(e).

courtesan [kɔːtɪ'zæn] *n* courtisane *f*.

courtesy ['kɔːtəsɪ] *n* courtoisie *f*, politesse *f*; **by ~ of** avec l'aimable autorisation de.

courtesy light *n* (*AUT*) plafonnier *m*.

court-house ['kɔːthaus] *n* (*US*) palais *m* de justice.

courtier ['kɔːtɪə*] *n* courtisan *m*, dame *f* de cour.

court martial, *pl* **courts martial** *n* cour martiale, conseil *m* de guerre.

courtroom ['kɔːtrum] *n* salle *f* de tribunal.

court shoe *n* escarpin *m*.

courtyard ['kɔːtjɑːd] *n* cour *f*.

cousin ['kʌzn] *n* cousin/e.

cove [kəuv] *n* petite baie, anse *f*.

covenant ['kʌvənənt] *n* contrat *m*, engagement *m* ♦ *vt*: **to ~ £200 per year to a charity** s'engager à verser 200 livres par an à une œuvre de bienfaisance.

Coventry ['kɔvəntrɪ] *n*: **to send sb to ~** (*fig*) mettre qn en quarantaine.

cover ['kʌvə*] *vt* couvrir; (*PRESS: report on*) faire un reportage sur ♦ *n* (*for bed, of book, COMM*) couverture *f*; (*of pan*) couvercle *m*; (*over furniture*) housse *f*; (*shelter*) abri *m*; **to take ~** se mettre à l'abri; **under ~** à l'abri; **under ~ of darkness** à la faveur de la nuit; **under separate ~** (*COMM*) sous pli séparé; **£10 will ~ everything** 10 livres suffiront (pour tout payer).

▶**cover up** *vt* (*person, object*): **to ~ up (with)** couvrir (de); (*fig: truth, facts*) occulter; **to ~ up for sb** (*fig*) couvrir qn.

coverage ['kʌvərɪdʒ] *n* (*in media*) reportage *m*; (*INSURANCE*) couverture *f*.

cover charge *n* couvert *m* (*supplément à payer*).

covering ['kʌvərɪŋ] *n* couverture *f*, enveloppe *f*.

covering letter, (*US*) **cover letter** *n* lettre explicative.

cover note *n* (*INSURANCE*) police *f* provisoire.

cover price *n* prix *m* de l'exemplaire.

covert ['kʌvət] *adj* (*threat*) voilé(e), caché(e); (*attack*) indirect(e); (*glance*) furtif(ive).

cover-up ['kʌvərʌp] *n* tentative *f* pour étouffer une affaire.

covet ['kʌvɪt] *vt* convoiter.

cow [kau] *n* vache *f* ♦ *cpd* femelle ♦ *vt* effrayer, intimider.

coward ['kauəd] *n* lâche *m/f*.

cowardice ['kauədɪs] *n* lâcheté *f*.

cowardly ['kauədlɪ] *adj* lâche.

cowboy ['kaubɔɪ] *n* cow-boy *m*.

cower ['kauə*] *vi* se recroqueviller; trembler.

cowshed ['kauʃɛd] *n* étable *f*.

cowslip ['kauslɪp] *n* (*BOT*) (fleur *f* de) coucou *m*.

coxswain ['kɔksn] *n* (*abbr:* **cox**) barreur *m*; (*of ship*) patron *m*.

coy [kɔɪ] *adj* faussement effarouché(e) *or* timide.

coyote [kɔɪ'əutɪ] *n* coyote *m*.

cozy ['kəuzɪ] *adj* (*US*) = **cosy**.

CP *n abbr* (= *Communist Party*) PC *m*.

cp. *abbr* (= *compare*) cf.

c/p *abbr* (*BRIT*) = **carriage paid**.

CPA *n abbr* (*US*) = **certified public accountant**.

CPI *n abbr* (= *Consumer Price Index*) IPC *m*.

Cpl. *abbr* (= *corporal*) C/C.

CP/M *n abbr* (= *Central Program for Microprocessors*) CP/M *m*.

c.p.s. *abbr* (= *characters per second*) caractères/seconde.

CPSA *n abbr* (*BRIT*) = *Civil and Public Services Association*) syndicat de la fonction publique.

CPU *n abbr* = **central processing unit**.

cr. *abbr* = **credit; creditor**.

crab [kræb] *n* crabe *m*.

crab apple *n* pomme *f* sauvage.

crack [kræk] *n* fente *f*, fissure *f*; (*in bone, dish, glass*) fêlure *f*; (*in wall*) lézarde *f*; (*noise*) craquement *m*, coup (sec); (*joke*) plaisanterie *f*; (*col: attempt*): **to have a ~ (at sth)** essayer (qch); (*DRUGS*) crack *m* ♦ *vt* fendre, fissurer; fêler; lézarder; (*whip*) faire claquer; (*nut*) casser; (*solve*) résoudre, trouver la clef de; déchiffrer ♦ *cpd* (*athlete*) de première classe, d'élite; **to ~ jokes** (*col*) raconter des blagues; **to get ~ing** (*col*) s'y mettre, se magner.

▶**crack down on** *vt fus* (*crime*) sévir contre, réprimer; (*spending*) mettre un frein à.

▶**crack up** *vi* être au bout de son rouleau, flancher.

crackdown ['krækdaun] *n*: **~ (on)** (*on crime*) répression *f* (de); (*on spending*) restrictions *fpl* (de).

cracked [krækt] *adj* (*col*) toqué(e), timbré(e).

cracker ['krækə*] *n* pétard *m*; (*biscuit*) biscuit (salé), craquelin *m*; **a ~ of a** ... (*BRIT col*) un(e) ... formidable; **he's ~s** (*BRIT col*) il est cinglé.

crackle ['krækl] *vi* crépiter, grésiller.

crackling ['kræklɪŋ] *n* crépitement *m*, grésillement *m*; (*on radio, telephone*) grésillement, friture *f*; (*of pork*) couenne *f*.

crackpot ['krækpɔt] n (col) tordu/e.
cradle ['kreɪdl] n berceau m ♦ vt (child) bercer; (object) tenir dans ses bras.
craft [krɑ:ft] n métier (artisanal); (cunning) ruse f, astuce f; (boat) embarcation f, barque f.
craftsman ['krɑ:ftsmən] n artisan m, ouvrier (qualifié).
craftsmanship ['krɑ:ftsmənʃɪp] n métier m, habileté f.
crafty ['krɑ:ftɪ] adj rusé(e), malin(igne), astucieux(euse).
crag [kræg] n rocher escarpé.
craggy ['krægɪ] adj escarpé(e), rocheux(euse).
cram [kræm] vt (fill): **to ~ sth with** bourrer qch de; (put): **to ~ sth into** fourrer qch dans.
cramming ['kræmɪŋ] n (for exams) bachotage m.
cramp [kræmp] n crampe f ♦ vt gêner, entraver.
cramped [kræmpt] adj à l'étroit, très serré(e).
crampon ['kræmpən] n crampon m.
cranberry ['krænbərɪ] n canneberge f.
crane [kreɪn] n grue f ♦ vt, vi: **to ~ forward, to ~ one's neck** allonger le cou.
cranium, pl **crania** ['kreɪnɪəm, 'kreɪnɪə] n boîte crânienne.
crank [kræŋk] n manivelle f; (person) excentrique m/f.
crankshaft ['kræŋkʃɑ:ft] n vilebrequin m.
cranky ['kræŋkɪ] adj excentrique, loufoque; (bad-tempered) grincheux(euse), revêche.
cranny ['krænɪ] n see **nook**.
crap [kræp] n (col!) conneries fpl (!); **to have a ~** chier (!).
crappy ['kræpɪ] adj (col) merdique (!).
crash [kræʃ] n fracas m; (of car, plane) collision f; (of business) faillite f; (STOCK EXCHANGE) krach m ♦ vt (plane) écraser ♦ vi (plane) s'écraser; (two cars) se percuter, s'emboutir; (fig) s'effondrer; **to ~ into** se jeter or se fracasser contre; **he ~ed the car into a wall** il s'est écrasé contre un mur avec sa voiture.
crash barrier n (BRIT AUT) rail m de sécurité.
crash course n cours intensif.
crash helmet n casque (protecteur).
crash landing n atterrissage forcé or en catastrophe.
crass [kræs] adj grossier(ière), crasse.
crate [kreɪt] n cageot m.
crater ['kreɪtə*] n cratère m.
cravat [krə'væt] n foulard (noué autour du cou).
crave [kreɪv] vt, vi: **to ~ for** désirer violemment, avoir un besoin physiologique de, avoir une envie irrésistible de.
craving ['kreɪvɪŋ] n: ~ **(for)** (for food, cigarettes etc) envie f irrésistible (de).
crawl [krɔ:l] vi ramper; (vehicle) avancer au pas ♦ n (SWIMMING) crawl m; **to ~ on one's hands and knees** aller à quatre pattes; **to ~**

to sb (col) faire de la lèche à qn.
crawler lane ['krɔ:lə-] n (BRIT AUT) file f or voie f pour véhicules lents.
crayfish ['kreɪfɪʃ] n (pl inv) (freshwater) écrevisse f; (saltwater) langoustine f.
crayon ['kreɪən] n crayon m (de couleur).
craze [kreɪz] n engouement m.
crazed [kreɪzd] adj (look, person) affolé(e); (pottery, glaze) craquelé(e).
crazy ['kreɪzɪ] adj fou(folle); **to go ~** devenir fou; **to be ~ about sb** (col) aimer qn à la folie; **he's ~ about skiing** (col) c'est un fana(tique) de ski.
crazy paving n (BRIT) dallage irrégulier (en pierres plates).
creak [kri:k] vi (hinge) grincer; (floor, shoes) craquer.
cream [kri:m] n crème f ♦ adj (colour) crème inv; **whipped ~** crème fouettée.
▶**cream off** vt (fig) prélever.
cream cake n (petit) gâteau à la crème.
cream cheese n fromage m à la crème, fromage blanc.
creamery ['kri:mərɪ] n (shop) crémerie f; (factory) laiterie f.
creamy ['kri:mɪ] adj crémeux(euse).
crease [kri:s] n pli m ♦ vt froisser, chiffonner ♦ vi se froisser, se chiffonner.
crease-resistant ['kri:srɪzɪstənt] adj infroissable.
create [kri:'eɪt] vt créer; (impression, fuss) faire.
creation [kri:'eɪʃən] n création f.
creative [kri:'eɪtɪv] adj créateur(trice).
creativity [kri:eɪ'tɪvɪtɪ] n créativité f.
creator [kri:'eɪtə*] n créateur/trice.
creature ['kri:tʃə*] n créature f.
creature comforts npl petit confort.
crèche [krɛʃ] n garderie f, crèche f.
credence ['kri:dns] n croyance f, foi f.
credentials [krɪ'dɛnʃlz] npl (papers) références fpl; (letters of reference) pièces justificatives.
credibility [krɛdɪ'bɪlɪtɪ] n crédibilité f.
credible ['krɛdɪbl] adj digne de foi, crédible.
credit ['krɛdɪt] n crédit m; (SCOL) unité f de valeur ♦ vt (COMM) créditer; (believe: also: **give ~ to**) ajouter foi à, croire; **to ~ sb with** (fig) prêter or attribuer à qn; **to ~ £5 to sb** créditer (le compte de) qn de 5 livres; **to be in ~** (person, bank account) être créditeur(trice); **on ~** à crédit; **to one's ~** à son honneur; à son actif; **to take the ~ for** s'attribuer le mérite de; **it does him ~** cela lui fait honneur.
creditable ['krɛdɪtəbl] adj honorable, estimable.
credit account n compte m client.
credit agency n (BRIT) agence f de renseignements commerciaux.
credit balance n solde créditeur.
credit bureau n (US) agence f de renseigne-

ments commerciaux.
credit card *n* carte *f* de crédit.
credit control *n* suivi *m* des factures.
credit facilities *npl* facilités *fpl* de paiement.
credit limit *n* limite *f* de crédit.
credit note *n* (*BRIT*) avoir *m*.
creditor ['krɛdɪtə*] *n* créancier/ière.
credits ['krɛdɪts] *npl* (*CINE*) générique *m*.
credit transfer *n* virement *m*.
creditworthy ['krɛdɪtwəːðɪ] *adj* solvable.
credulity [krɪ'djuːlɪtɪ] *n* crédulité *f*.
creed [kriːd] *n* croyance *f*; credo *m*, principes *mpl*.
creek [kriːk] *n* crique *f*, anse *f*; (*US*) ruisseau *m*, petit cours d'eau.
creel ['kriːl] *n* panier *m* de pêche; (*also*: **lobster** ~) panier à homards.
creep, *pt, pp* **crept** [kriːp, krɛpt] *vi* ramper; (*fig*) se faufiler, se glisser; (*plant*) grimper ♦ *n* (*col*) saligaud *m*; **he's a** ~ c'est un type puant; **it gives me the** ~**s** cela me fait froid dans le dos; **to** ~ **up on sb** s'approcher furtivement de qn.
creeper ['kriːpə*] *n* plante grimpante.
creepers ['kriːpəz] *npl* (*US: for baby*) barboteuse *f*.
creepy ['kriːpɪ] *adj* (*frightening*) qui fait frissonner, qui donne la chair de poule.
creepy-crawly ['kriːpɪ'krɔːlɪ] *n* (*col*) bestiole *f*.
cremate [krɪ'meɪt] *vt* incinérer.
cremation [krɪ'meɪʃən] *n* incinération *f*.
crematorium, *pl* **crematoria** [krɛmə'tɔːrɪəm, -'tɔːrɪə] *n* four *m* crématoire.
creosote ['krɪəsəut] *n* créosote *f*.
crepe [kreɪp] *n* crêpe *m*.
crepe bandage *n* (*BRIT*) bande *f* Velpeau ®.
crepe paper *n* papier *m* crépon.
crepe sole *n* semelle *f* de crêpe.
crept [krɛpt] *pt, pp of* **creep**.
crescendo [krɪ'ʃɛndəu] *n* crescendo *m*.
crescent ['krɛsnt] *n* croissant *m*; (*street*) rue *f* (*en arc de cercle*).
cress [krɛs] *n* cresson *m*.
crest [krɛst] *n* crête *f*; (*of helmet*) cimier *m*; (*of coat of arms*) timbre *m*.
crestfallen ['krɛstfɔːlən] *adj* déconfit(e), découragé(e).
Crete ['kriːt] *n* Crète *f*.
crevasse [krɪ'væs] *n* crevasse *f*.
crevice ['krɛvɪs] *n* fissure *f*, lézarde *f*, fente *f*.
crew [kruː] *n* équipage *m*; (*CINE*) équipe *f* (de tournage); (*gang*) bande *f*.
crew-cut ['kruːkʌt] *n*: **to have a** ~ avoir les cheveux en brosse.
crew-neck ['kruːnɛk] *n* col ras.
crib [krɪb] *n* lit *m* d'enfant ♦ *vt* (*col*) copier.
cribbage ['krɪbɪdʒ] *n sorte de jeu de cartes*.
crick [krɪk] *n* crampe *f*; ~ **in the neck** torticolis *m*.
cricket ['krɪkɪt] *n* (*insect*) grillon *m*, cri-cri *m inv*; (*game*) cricket *m*.
cricketer ['krɪkɪtə*] *n* joueur *m* de cricket.

crime [kraɪm] *n* crime *m*; **minor** ~ délit *m or* infraction *f* mineur(e).
crime wave *n* poussée *f* de la criminalité.
criminal ['krɪmɪnl] *adj*, *n* criminel(le).
crimp [krɪmp] *vt* friser, frisotter.
crimson ['krɪmzn] *adj* cramoisi(e).
cringe [krɪndʒ] *vi* avoir un mouvement de recul; (*fig*) s'humilier, ramper.
crinkle ['krɪŋkl] *vt* froisser, chiffonner.
cripple ['krɪpl] *n* boiteux/euse, infirme *m/f* ♦ *vt* estropier, paralyser; (*ship, plane*) immobiliser; (*production, exports*) paralyser; ~**d with rheumatism** perclus(e) de rhumatismes.
crippling ['krɪplɪŋ] *adj* (*disease*) handicapant(e); (*taxation, debts*) écrasant(e).
crisis, *pl* **crises** ['kraɪsɪs, -siːz] *n* crise *f*.
crisp [krɪsp] *adj* croquant(e); (*fig*) vif(vive); brusque.
crisps [krɪsps] *npl* (*BRIT*) (pommes) chips *fpl*.
crisscross ['krɪskrɔs] *adj* entrecroisé(e), en croisillons ♦ *vt* sillonner; ~ **pattern** croisillons *mpl*.
criterion, *pl* **criteria** [kraɪ'tɪərɪən, -'tɪərɪə] *n* critère *m*.
critic ['krɪtɪk] *n* critique *m/f*.
critical ['krɪtɪkl] *adj* critique; **to be** ~ **of sb/sth** critiquer qn/qch.
critically ['krɪtɪklɪ] *adv* (*examine*) d'un œil critique; (*speak*) sévèrement; ~ **ill** gravement malade.
criticism ['krɪtɪsɪzəm] *n* critique *f*.
criticize ['krɪtɪsaɪz] *vt* critiquer.
croak [krəuk] *vi* (*frog*) coasser; (*raven*) croasser.
Croat ['krəuæt] *adj*, *n* = **Croatian**.
Croatia [krəu'eɪʃə] *n* Croatie *f*.
Croatian [krəu'eɪʃən] *adj* croate ♦ *n* Croate *m/f*; (*LING*) croate *m*.
crochet ['krəuʃeɪ] *n* travail *m* au crochet.
crock [krɔk] *n* cruche *f*; (*col: also*: **old** ~) épave *f*.
crockery ['krɔkərɪ] *n* vaisselle *f*.
crocodile ['krɔkədaɪl] *n* crocodile *m*.
crocus ['krəukəs] *n* crocus *m*.
croft [krɔft] *n* (*BRIT*) petite ferme.
crofter ['krɔftə*] *n* (*BRIT*) fermier *m*.
crone [krəun] *n* vieille bique, (vieille) sorcière.
crony ['krəunɪ] *n* copain/copine.
crook [kruk] *n* escroc *m*; (*of shepherd*) houlette *f*.
crooked ['krukɪd] *adj* courbé(e), tordu(e); (*action*) malhonnête.
crop [krɔp] *n* (*produce*) culture *f*; (*amount produced*) récolte *f*; (*riding* ~) cravache *f*; (*of bird*) jabot *m* ♦ *vt* (*hair*) tondre; (*subj: animals: grass*) brouter.
▶**crop up** *vi* surgir, se présenter, survenir.
cropper ['krɔpə*] *n*: **to come a** ~ (*col*) faire une culbute, s'étaler.
crop spraying [-spreɪɪŋ] *n* pulvérisation *f* des cultures.
croquet ['krəukeɪ] *n* croquet *m*.

croquette [krɔ'kɛt] *n* croquette *f*.

cross [krɔs] *n* croix *f*; (*BIOL*) croisement *m* ♦ *vt* (*street etc*) traverser; (*arms, legs, BIOL*) croiser; (*cheque*) barrer; (*thwart: person, plan*) contrarier ♦ *vi*: **the boat ~es from ... to ...** le bateau fait la traversée de ... à ... ♦ *adj* en colère, fâché(e); **to ~ o.s.** se signer, faire le signe de (la) croix; **we have a ~ed line** (*BRIT: on telephone*) il y a des interférences; **they've got their lines ~ed** (*fig*) il y a un malentendu entre eux; **to be/get ~ with sb (about sth)** être en colère/se fâcher contre qn (à propos de qch).

▶**cross out** *vt* barrer, biffer.

▶**cross over** *vi* traverser.

crossbar ['krɔsbɑː*] *n* barre transversale.

crossbow ['krɔsbəu] *n* arbalète *f*.

crossbreed ['krɔsbriːd] *n* hybride *m*, métis/se.

cross-Channel ferry ['krɔs'tʃænl-] *n* ferry *m* qui fait la traversée de la Manche.

cross-check ['krɔstʃɛk] *n* recoupement *m* ♦ *vi* vérifier par recoupement.

cross-country (race) ['krɔs'kʌntrɪ-] *n* cross(-country) *m*.

cross-dressing [krɔs'drɛsɪŋ] *n* travestisme *m*.

cross-examination ['krɔsɪgzæmɪ'neɪʃən] *n* (*LAW*) examen *m* contradictoire (*d'un témoin*).

cross-examine ['krɔsɪg'zæmɪn] *vt* (*LAW*) faire subir un examen contradictoire à.

cross-eyed ['krɔsaɪd] *adj* qui louche.

crossfire ['krɔsfaɪə*] *n* feux croisés.

crossing ['krɔsɪŋ] *n* croisement *m*, carrefour *m*; (*sea passage*) traversée *f*; (*also: pedestrian ~*) passage clouté.

crossing point *n* poste frontalier.

cross-purposes ['krɔs'pəːpəsɪz] *npl*: **to be at ~ with sb** comprendre qn de travers; **we're (talking) at ~** on ne parle pas de la même chose.

cross-question ['krɔs'kwɛstʃən] *vt* faire subir un interrogatoire à.

cross-reference ['krɔs'rɛfrəns] *n* renvoi *m*, référence *f*.

crossroads ['krɔsrəudz] *n* carrefour *m*.

cross section *n* (*BIOL*) coupe transversale; (*in population*) échantillon *m*.

crosswalk ['krɔswɔːk] *n* (*US*) passage clouté.

crosswind ['krɔswɪnd] *n* vent *m* de travers.

crosswise ['krɔswaɪz] *adv* en travers.

crossword ['krɔswəːd] *n* mots *mpl* croisés.

crotch [krɔtʃ] *n* (*of garment*) entre-jambes *m inv*.

crotchet ['krɔtʃɪt] *n* (*MUS*) noire *f*.

crotchety ['krɔtʃɪtɪ] *adj* (*person*) grognon(ne), grincheux(euse).

crouch [krautʃ] *vi* s'accroupir; se tapir; se ramasser.

croup [kruːp] *n* (*MED*) croup *m*.

crouton ['kruːtɔn] *n* croûton *m*.

crow [krəu] *n* (*bird*) corneille *f*; (*of cock*) chant *m* du coq, cocorico *m* ♦ *vi* (*cock*) chanter; (*fig*) pavoiser, chanter victoire.

crowbar ['krəubɑː*] *n* levier *m*.

crowd [kraud] *n* foule *f* ♦ *vt* bourrer, remplir ♦ *vi* affluer, s'attrouper, s'entasser; **~s of people** une foule de gens.

crowded ['kraudɪd] *adj* bondé(e), plein(e); **~ with** plein de.

crowd scene *n* (*CINE, THEAT*) scène *f* de foule.

crown [kraun] *n* couronne *f*; (*of head*) sommet *m* de la tête, calotte crânienne; (*of hat*) fond *m*; (*of hill*) sommet *m* ♦ *vt* (*also tooth*) couronner.

crown court *n* (*BRIT*) ≈ Cour *f* d'assises.

En Angleterre et au Pays de Galles, une **crown court** *est une cour de justice où sont jugées les affaires très graves, telles que le meurtre, l'homicide, le viol et le vol, en présence d'un jury. Tous les crimes et délits, quel que soit leur degré de gravité, doivent d'abord passer devant une* **magistrates' court**. *Il existe environ 90 crown courts.*

---

crowning ['kraunɪŋ] *adj* (*achievement, glory*) suprême.

crown jewels *npl* joyaux *mpl* de la Couronne.

crown prince *n* prince héritier.

crow's-feet ['krəuzfiːt] *npl* pattes *fpl* d'oie (*fig*).

crow's-nest ['krəuznɛst] *n* (*on sailing-ship*) nid *m* de pie.

crucial ['kruːʃl] *adj* crucial(e), décisif(ive); **~ to** essentiel(le) à.

crucifix ['kruːsɪfɪks] *n* crucifix *m*.

crucifixion [kruːsɪ'fɪkʃən] *n* crucifiement *m*, crucifixion *f*.

crucify ['kruːsɪfaɪ] *vt* crucifier, mettre en croix; (*fig*) crucifier.

crude [kruːd] *adj* (*materials*) brut(e); non raffiné(e); (*basic*) rudimentaire, sommaire; (*vulgar*) cru(e), grossier(ière).

crude (oil) *n* (pétrole) brut *m*.

cruel ['kruəl] *adj* cruel(le).

cruelty ['kruəltɪ] *n* cruauté *f*.

cruet ['kruːɪt] *n* huilier *m*; vinaigrier *m*.

cruise [kruːz] *n* croisière *f* ♦ *vi* (*ship*) croiser; (*car*) rouler; (*aircraft*) voler; (*taxi*) être en maraude.

cruise missile *n* missile *m* de croisière.

cruiser ['kruːzə*] *n* croiseur *m*.

cruising speed ['kruːzɪŋ-] *n* vitesse *f* de croisière.

crumb [krʌm] *n* miette *f*.

crumble ['krʌmbl] *vt* émietter ♦ *vi* s'émietter; (*plaster etc*) s'effriter; (*land, earth*) s'ébouler; (*building*) s'écrouler, crouler; (*fig*) s'effondrer.

crumbly ['krʌmblɪ] *adj* friable.

crummy ['krʌmɪ] *adj* (*col*) minable; (: *unwell*) mal fichu(e), patraque.

crumpet ['krʌmpɪt] *n* petite crêpe (épaisse).

crumple ['krʌmpl] *vt* froisser, friper.

crunch [krʌntʃ] *vt* croquer; (*underfoot*) faire craquer, écraser; faire crisser ♦ *n* (*fig*) instant *m or* moment *m* critique, moment de vérité.

crunchy ['krʌntʃɪ] *adj* croquant(e), croustillant(e).

crusade [kruːˈseɪd] *n* croisade *f* ♦ *vi* (*fig*): **to ~ for/against** partir en croisade pour/contre.

crusader [kruːˈseɪdə*] *n* croisé *m*; (*fig*): **~ (for)** champion *m* (de).

crush [krʌʃ] *n* foule *f*, cohue *f*; (*love*): **to have a ~ on sb** avoir le béguin pour qn; (*drink*): **lemon ~** citron pressé ♦ *vt* écraser; (*crumple*) froisser; (*grind, break up: garlic, ice*) piler; (*: grapes*) presser.

crush barrier *n* (*BRIT*) barrière *f* de sécurité.

crushing ['krʌʃɪŋ] *adj* écrasant(e).

crust [krʌst] *n* croûte *f*.

crustacean [krʌsˈteɪʃən] *n* crustacé *m*.

crusty ['krʌstɪ] *adj* (*bread*) croustillant(e); (*col: person*) revêche, bourru(e); (*: remark*) irrité(e).

crutch [krʌtʃ] *n* béquille *f*; (*TECH*) support *m*; (*also*: **crotch**) entrejambe *m*.

crux [krʌks] *n* point crucial.

cry [kraɪ] *vi* pleurer; (*shout: also*: **~ out**) crier ♦ *n* cri *m*; **what are you ~ing about?** pourquoi pleures-tu?; **to ~ for help** appeler à l'aide; **she had a good ~** elle a pleuré un bon coup; **it's a far ~ from ...** (*fig*) on est loin de ....
▸**cry off** *vi* se dédire; se décommander.

crying ['kraɪɪŋ] *adj* (*fig*) criant(e), flagrant(e).

crypt [krɪpt] *n* crypte *f*.

cryptic ['krɪptɪk] *adj* énigmatique.

crystal ['krɪstl] *n* cristal *m*.

crystal-clear ['krɪstl'klɪə*] *adj* clair(e) comme de l'eau de roche.

crystallize ['krɪstəlaɪz] *vt* cristalliser ♦ *vi* (se) cristalliser; **~d fruits** (*BRIT*) fruits confits.

CSA *n abbr* = *Confederate States of America*; (*BRIT*: = *Child Support Agency*) *organisme pour la protection des enfants de parents séparés, qui contrôle le versement des pensions alimentaires.*

CSC *n abbr* (= *Civil Service Commission*) *commission de recrutement des fonctionnaires.*

CSE *n abbr* (*BRIT*: = *Certificate of Secondary Education*) ≈ BEPC *m*.

CS gas *n* (*BRIT*) gaz *m* C.S.

CST *abbr* (*US*: = *Central Standard Time*) *fuseau horaire.*

CT *abbr* (*US*) = *Connecticut*.

ct *abbr* = *carat*.

CTC *n abbr* (*BRIT*) = **city technology college**.

CT scanner *n abbr* (*MED*: = *computerized tomography scanner*) scanner *m*, tomodensitomètre *m*.

cu. *abbr* = **cubic**.

cub [kʌb] *n* petit *m* (*d'un animal*); (*also*: **~ scout**) louveteau *m*.

Cuba ['kjuːbə] *n* Cuba *m*.

Cuban ['kjuːbən] *adj* cubain(e) ♦ *n* Cubain/e.

cubbyhole ['kʌbɪhəʊl] *n* cagibi *m*.

cube [kjuːb] *n* cube *m* ♦ *vt* (*MATH*) élever au cube.

cube root *n* racine *f* cubique.

cubic ['kjuːbɪk] *adj* cubique; **~ metre** *etc* mètre *m etc* cube; **~ capacity** (*AUT*) cylindrée *f*.

cubicle ['kjuːbɪkl] *n* box *m*, cabine *f*.

cuckoo ['kʊkuː] *n* coucou *m*.

cuckoo clock *n* (*pendule f à*) coucou *m*.

cucumber ['kjuːkʌmbə*] *n* concombre *m*.

cud [kʌd] *n*: **to chew the ~** ruminer.

cuddle ['kʌdl] *vt* câliner, caresser ♦ *vi* se blottir l'un contre l'autre.

cuddly ['kʌdlɪ] *adj* câlin(e).

cudgel ['kʌdʒl] *n* gourdin *m* ♦ *vt*: **to ~ one's brains** se creuser la tête.

cue [kjuː] *n* queue *f* de billard; (*THEAT etc*) signal *m*.

cuff [kʌf] *n* (*of shirt, coat etc*) poignet *m*, manchette *f*; (*US: on trousers*) revers *m*; (*blow*) gifle *f* ♦ *vt* gifler; **off the ~** *adv* de chic, à l'improviste.

cufflink ['kʌflɪŋk] *n* bouton *m* de manchette.

cu. in. *abbr* = *cubic inches*.

cuisine [kwɪˈziːn] *n* cuisine *f*, art *m* culinaire.

cul-de-sac ['kʌldəsæk] *n* cul-de-sac *m*, impasse *f*.

culinary ['kʌlɪnərɪ] *adj* culinaire.

cull [kʌl] *vt* sélectionner; (*kill selectively*) pratiquer l'abattage sélectif de.

culminate ['kʌlmɪneɪt] *vi*: **to ~ in** finir *or* se terminer par; (*lead to*) mener à.

culmination [kʌlmɪˈneɪʃən] *n* point culminant.

culottes [kjuːˈlɒts] *npl* jupe-culotte *f*.

culpable ['kʌlpəbl] *adj* coupable.

culprit ['kʌlprɪt] *n* coupable *m/f*.

cult [kʌlt] *n* culte *m*.

cult figure *n* idole *f*.

cultivate ['kʌltɪveɪt] *vt* (*also fig*) cultiver.

cultivation [kʌltɪˈveɪʃən] *n* culture *f*.

cultural ['kʌltʃərəl] *adj* culturel(le).

culture ['kʌltʃə*] *n* (*also fig*) culture *f*.

cultured ['kʌltʃəd] *adj* cultivé(e) (*fig*).

cumbersome ['kʌmbəsəm] *adj* encombrant(e), embarrassant(e).

cumin ['kʌmɪn] *n* (*spice*) cumin *m*.

cumulative ['kjuːmjʊlətɪv] *adj* cumulatif(ive).

cunning ['kʌnɪŋ] *n* ruse *f*, astuce *f* ♦ *adj* rusé(e), malin(igne); (*clever: device, idea*) astucieux(euse).

cunt [kʌnt] *n* (*col!*) chatte *f* (*!*); (*insult*) salaud *m* (*!*), salope *f* (*!*).

cup [kʌp] *n* tasse *f*; (*prize, event*) coupe *f*; (*of bra*) bonnet *m*; **a ~ of tea** une tasse de thé.

cupboard ['kʌbəd] *n* placard *m*.

cup final *n* (*BRIT FOOTBALL*) finale *f* de la coupe.

Cupid ['kjuːpɪd] *n* Cupidon *m*; (*figurine*) amour *m*.

cupidity [kjuːˈpɪdɪtɪ] *n* cupidité *f*.

cupola ['kjuːpələ] *n* coupole *f*.

cuppa ['kʌpə] n (BRIT col) tasse f de thé.
cup-tie ['kʌptaɪ] n (BRIT FOOTBALL) match m de coupe.
curable ['kjuərəbl] adj guérissable, curable.
curate ['kjuərɪt] n vicaire m.
curator [kjuə'reɪtə*] n conservateur m (d'un musée etc).
curb [kə:b] vt refréner, mettre un frein à; (expenditure) limiter, juguler ♦ n frein m (fig); (US) = **kerb**.
curd cheese n ≈ fromage blanc.
curdle ['kə:dl] vi (se) cailler.
curds [kə:dz] npl lait caillé.
cure [kjuə*] vt guérir; (CULIN) saler; fumer; sécher ♦ n remède m; **to be ~d of sth** être guéri de qch.
cure-all ['kjuərɔ:l] n (also fig) panacée f.
curfew ['kə:fju:] n couvre-feu m.
curio ['kjuərɪəu] n bibelot m, curiosité f.
curiosity [kjuərɪ'ɒsɪtɪ] n curiosité f.
curious ['kjuərɪəs] adj curieux(euse); **I'm ~ about him** il m'intrigue.
curiously ['kjuərɪəslɪ] adv curieusement; (inquisitively) avec curiosité; **~ enough,** ... bizarrement ....
curl [kə:l] n boucle f (de cheveux); (of smoke etc) volute f ♦ vt, vi boucler; (tightly) friser.
▶**curl up** vi s'enrouler; se pelotonner.
curler ['kə:lə*] n bigoudi m, rouleau m; (SPORT) joueur/euse de curling.
curlew ['kə:lu:] n courlis m.
curling ['kə:lɪŋ] n (sport) curling m.
curling tongs, (US) **curling irons** npl fer m à friser.
curly ['kə:lɪ] adj bouclé(e); (tightly curled) frisé(e).
currant ['kʌrnt] n raisin m de Corinthe, raisin sec.
currency ['kʌrnsɪ] n monnaie f; **foreign ~** devises étrangères, monnaie étrangère; **to gain ~** (fig) s'accréditer.
current ['kʌrnt] n courant m ♦ adj courant(e); (tendency, price, event) actuel(le); **direct/ alternating ~** (ELEC) courant continu/ alternatif; **the ~ issue of a magazine** le dernier numéro d'un magazine; **in ~ use** d'usage courant.
current account n (BRIT) compte courant.
current affairs npl (questions fpl d')actualité f.
current assets npl (COMM) actif m disponible.
current liabilities npl (COMM) passif m exigible.
currently ['kʌrntlɪ] adv actuellement.
curriculum, pl **~s** or **curricula** [kə'rɪkjuləm, -lə] n programme m d'études.
curriculum vitae (CV) [-'vi:taɪ] n curriculum vitae (CV) m.
curry ['kʌrɪ] n curry m ♦ vt: **to ~ favour with** chercher à gagner la faveur or à s'attirer les bonnes grâces de; **chicken ~** curry de poulet, poulet m au curry.

curry powder n poudre f de curry.
curse [kə:s] vi jurer, blasphémer ♦ vt maudire ♦ n malédiction f; fléau m; (swearword) juron m.
cursor ['kə:sə*] n (COMPUT) curseur m.
cursory ['kə:sərɪ] adj superficiel(le), hâtif(ive).
curt [kə:t] adj brusque, sec(sèche).
curtail [kə:'teɪl] vt (visit etc) écourter; (expenses etc) réduire.
curtain ['kə:tn] n rideau m; **to draw the ~s** (together) fermer or tirer les rideaux; (apart) ouvrir les rideaux.
curtain call n (THEAT) rappel m.
curts(e)y ['kə:tsɪ] n révérence f ♦ vi faire une révérence.
curvature ['kə:vətʃə*] n courbure f.
curve [kə:v] n courbe f; (in the road) tournant m, virage m ♦ vt courber ♦ vi se courber; (road) faire une courbe.
curved [kə:vd] adj courbe.
cushion ['kuʃən] n coussin m ♦ vt (seat) rembourrer; (shock) amortir.
cushy ['kuʃɪ] adj (col): **a ~ job** un boulot de tout repos; **to have a ~ time** se la couler douce.
custard ['kʌstəd] n (for pouring) crème anglaise.
custard powder n (BRIT) ≈ crème pâtissière instantanée.
custodial sentence [kʌs'təudɪəl-] n peine f de prison.
custodian [kʌs'təudɪən] n gardien/ne; (of collection etc) conservateur/trice.
custody ['kʌstədɪ] n (of child) garde f; (for offenders) détention préventive; **to take sb into ~** placer qn en détention préventive; **in the ~ of** sous la garde de.
custom ['kʌstəm] n coutume f, usage m; (LAW) droit coutumier, coutume; (COMM) clientèle f.
customary ['kʌstəmərɪ] adj habituel(le); **it is ~ to do it** l'usage veut qu'on le fasse.
custom-built ['kʌstəm'bɪlt] adj see **custom-made**.
customer ['kʌstəmə*] n client/e; **he's an awkward ~** (col) ce n'est pas quelqu'un de facile.
customer profile n profil m du client.
customized ['kʌstəmaɪzd] adj personnalisé(e).
custom-made ['kʌstəm'meɪd] adj (clothes) fait(e) sur mesure; (other goods: also: **custom-built**) hors série, fait(e) sur commande.
customs ['kʌstəmz] npl douane f; **to go through (the) ~** passer la douane.
Customs and Excise n (BRIT) administration f des douanes.
customs officer n douanier m.
cut [kʌt] vb (pt, pp **cut**) vt couper; (meat) découper; (shape, make) tailler; couper; creuser; graver; (reduce) réduire; (col: lecture, ap-

pointment) manquer ♦ *vi* couper; (*intersect*) se couper ♦ *n* (*gen*) coupure *f*; (*of clothes*) coupe *f*; (*of jewel*) taille *f*; (*in salary etc*) réduction *f*; (*of meat*) morceau *m*; **cold ~s** *npl* (*US*) viandes froides; **to ~ teeth** (*baby*) faire ses dents; **to ~ a tooth** percer une dent; **to ~ one's finger** se couper le doigt; **to get one's hair ~** se faire couper les cheveux; **to ~ sth short** couper court à qch; **to ~ sb dead** ignorer (complètement) qn.

►**cut back** *vt* (*plants*) tailler; (*production, expenditure*) réduire.

►**cut down** *vt* (*tree*) abattre; (*reduce*) réduire; **to ~ sb down to size** (*fig*) remettre qn à sa place.

►**cut down on** *vt fus* réduire.

►**cut in** *vi* (*interrupt: conversation*): **to ~ in (on)** couper la parole (à); (*AUT*) faire une queue de poisson.

►**cut off** *vt* couper; (*fig*) isoler; **we've been ~ off** (*TEL*) nous avons été coupés.

►**cut out** *vt* (*picture etc*) découper; (*remove*) ôter; supprimer.

►**cut up** *vt* découper.

cut-and-dried ['kʌtən'draɪd] *adj* (*also*: **cut-and-dry**) tout(e) fait(e), tout(e) décidé(e).

cutaway ['kʌtəweɪ] *adj, n*: **~ (drawing)** écorché *m*.

cutback ['kʌtbæk] *n* réduction *f*.

cute [kjuːt] *adj* mignon(ne), adorable; (*clever*) rusé(e), astucieux(euse).

cut glass *n* cristal taillé.

cuticle ['kjuːtɪkl] *n* (*on nail*): **~ remover** repousse-peaux *m inv*.

cutlery ['kʌtlərɪ] *n* couverts *mpl*; (*trade*) coutellerie *f*.

cutlet ['kʌtlɪt] *n* côtelette *f*.

cutoff ['kʌtɔf] *n* (*also*: **~ point**) seuil-limite *m*.

cutoff switch *n* interrupteur *m*.

cutout ['kʌtaut] *n* coupe-circuit *m inv*; (*paper figure*) découpage *m*.

cut-price ['kʌt'praɪs], (*US*) **cut-rate** ['kʌt'reɪt] *adj* au rabais, à prix réduit.

cutthroat ['kʌtθrəut] *n* assassin *m* ♦ *adj*: **~ competition** concurrence *f* sauvage.

cutting ['kʌtɪŋ] *adj* tranchant(e), coupant(e); (*fig*) cinglant(e), mordant(e) ♦ *n* (*BRIT: from newspaper*) coupure *f* (de journal); (: *RAIL*) tranchée *f*; (*CINE*) montage *m*.

cutting edge *n* (*of knife*) tranchant *m*; **on** *or* **at the ~ of** à la pointe de.

cuttlefish ['kʌtlfɪʃ] *n* seiche *f*.

cut-up ['kʌtʌp] *adj* affecté(e), démoralisé(e).

CV *n abbr* = **curriculum vitae**.

cwo *abbr* (*COMM*) = **cash with order**.

cwt. *abbr* = **hundredweight**.

cyanide ['saɪənaɪd] *n* cyanure *m*.

cybernetics [saɪbə'netɪks] *n* cybernétique *f*.

cyclamen ['sɪkləmən] *n* cyclamen *m*.

cycle ['saɪkl] *n* cycle *m* ♦ *vi* faire de la bicyclette.

cycle race *n* course *f* cycliste.

cycle rack *n* râtelier *m* à bicyclette.

cycling ['saɪklɪŋ] *n* cyclisme *m*; **to go on a ~ holiday** (*BRIT*) faire du cyclotourisme.

cyclist ['saɪklɪst] *n* cycliste *m/f*.

cyclone ['saɪkləun] *n* cyclone *m*.

cygnet ['sɪgnɪt] *n* jeune cygne *m*.

cylinder ['sɪlɪndə*] *n* cylindre *m*.

cylinder block *n* bloc-cylindres *m*.

cylinder capacity *n* cylindrée *f*.

cylinder head *n* culasse *f*.

cylinder-head gasket ['sɪlɪndəhɛd-] *n* joint *m* de culasse.

cymbals ['sɪmblz] *npl* cymbales *fpl*.

cynic ['sɪnɪk] *n* cynique *m/f*.

cynical ['sɪnɪkl] *adj* cynique.

cynicism ['sɪnɪsɪzəm] *n* cynisme *m*.

CYO *n abbr* (*US*: = *Catholic Youth Organization*) ≈ JC *f*.

cypress ['saɪprɪs] *n* cyprès *m*.

Cypriot ['sɪprɪət] *adj* cypriote, chypriote ♦ *n* Cypriote *m/f*, Chypriote *m/f*.

Cyprus ['saɪprəs] *n* Chypre *f*.

cyst [sɪst] *n* kyste *m*.

cystitis [sɪs'taɪtɪs] *n* cystite *f*.

CZ *n abbr* (*US*: = *Central Zone*) zone du canal de Panama.

czar [zɑː*] *n* tsar *m*.

Czech [tʃɛk] *adj* tchèque ♦ *n* Tchèque *m/f*; (*LING*) tchèque *m*; **the ~ Republic** la République tchèque.

Czechoslovak [tʃɛkə'sləuvæk] *adj, n* = **Czechoslovakian**.

Czechoslovakia [tʃɛkəslə'vækɪə] *n* Tchécoslovaquie *f*.

Czechoslovakian [tʃɛkəslə'vækɪən] *adj* tchécoslovaque ♦ *n* Tchécoslovaque *m/f*.

D d

D, d [diː] *n* (*letter*) D, d *m*; (*MUS*): **D** ré *m*; **D for David**, (*US*) **D for Dog** D comme Désirée.

D *abbr* (*US POL*) = **democrat(ic)**.

d *abbr* (*BRIT*: *old*) = **penny**.

d. *abbr* = **died**.

DA *n abbr* (*US*) = **district attorney**.

dab [dæb] *vt* (*eyes, wound*) tamponner; (*paint, cream*) appliquer par petites touches *or* rapidement); **a ~ of paint** un petit coup de peinture.

dabble ['dæbl] *vi*: **to ~ in** faire *or* se mêler *or* s'occuper un peu de.

Dacca ['dækə] *n* Dacca.

dachshund ['dækshund] *n* teckel *m*.

dad, daddy [dæd, 'dædɪ] *n* papa *m*.

daddy-long-legs [dædɪ'lɒŋlegz] *n* tipule *f*;

faucheux m.

daffodil ['dæfədɪl] n jonquille f.

daft [dɑ:ft] adj (col) idiot(e), stupide; **to be ~ about** être toqué(e) or mordu(e) de.

dagger ['dægə*] n poignard m; **to be at ~s drawn with sb** être à couteaux tirés avec qn; **to look ~s at sb** foudroyer qn du regard.

dahlia ['deɪljə] n dahlia m.

daily ['deɪlɪ] adj quotidien(ne), journalier(ière) ♦ n quotidien m; (BRIT: servant) femme f de ménage (à la journée) ♦ adv tous les jours; **twice ~** deux fois par jour.

dainty ['deɪntɪ] adj délicat(e), mignon(ne).

dairy ['dɛərɪ] n (shop) crémerie f, laiterie f; (on farm) laiterie ♦ adj laitier(ière).

dairy cow n vache laitière.

dairy farm n exploitation f pratiquant l'élevage laitier.

dairy produce n produits laitiers.

dais ['deɪɪs] n estrade f.

daisy ['deɪzɪ] n pâquerette f.

daisy wheel n (on printer) marguerite f.

daisy-wheel printer ['deɪzɪwi:l-] n imprimante f à marguerite.

Dakar ['dækə] n Dakar.

dale [deɪl] n vallon m.

dally ['dælɪ] vi musarder, flâner.

dalmatian [dæl'meɪʃən] n (dog) dalmatien/ne.

dam [dæm] n barrage m; (reservoir) réservoir m, lac m de retenue ♦ vt endiguer.

damage ['dæmɪdʒ] n dégâts mpl, dommages mpl; (fig) tort m ♦ vt endommager, abîmer; (fig) faire du tort à; **~ to property** dégâts matériels.

damages ['dæmɪdʒɪz] npl (LAW) dommages-intérêts mpl; **to pay £5000 in ~** payer 5000 livres de dommages-intérêts.

damaging ['dæmɪdʒɪŋ] adj: **~ (to)** préjudiciable (à), nuisible (à).

Damascus [də'mɑːskəs] n Damas.

dame [deɪm] n (title) titre porté par une femme décorée de l'ordre de l'Empire Britannique ou d'un ordre de chevalerie; titre porté par la femme ou la veuve d'un chevalier ou baronnet; (US col) nana f; (THEAT) vieille dame (rôle comique joué par un homme).

damn [dæm] vt condamner; (curse) maudire ♦ n (col): **I don't give a ~** je m'en fous ♦ adj (col): **this ~ ...** ce sacré or foutu ...; **~ (it)!** zut!

damnable ['dæmnəbl] adj (col: behaviour) odieux(euse), détestable; (: weather) épouvantable, abominable.

damnation [dæm'neɪʃən] n (REL) damnation f ♦ excl (col) malédiction!, merde!

damning ['dæmɪŋ] adj (evidence) accablant(e).

damp [dæmp] adj humide ♦ n humidité f ♦ vt (also: **~en**: cloth, rag) humecter; (: enthusiasm etc) refroidir.

dampcourse ['dæmpkɔːs] n couche isolante

(contre l'humidité).

damper ['dæmpə*] n (MUS) étouffoir m; (of fire) registre m; **to put a ~ on** (fig: atmosphere, enthusiasm) refroidir.

dampness ['dæmpnɪs] n humidité f.

damson ['dæmzən] n prune f de Damas.

dance [dɑ:ns] n danse f; (ball) bal m ♦ vi danser; **to ~ about** sautiller, gambader.

dance hall n salle f de bal, dancing m.

dancer ['dɑ:nsə*] n danseur/euse.

dancing ['dɑ:nsɪŋ] n danse f.

D and C n abbr (MED: = dilation and curettage) curetage m.

dandelion ['dændɪlaɪən] n pissenlit m.

dandruff ['dændrəf] n pellicules fpl.

dandy ['dændɪ] n dandy m, élégant m ♦ adj (US col) fantastique, super.

Dane [deɪn] n Danois/e.

danger ['deɪndʒə*] n danger m; **there is a ~ of fire** il y a (un) risque d'incendie; **in ~** en danger; **he was in ~ of falling** il risquait de tomber; **out of ~** hors de danger.

danger list n (MED): **on the ~** dans un état critique.

danger money n (BRIT) prime f de risque.

dangerous ['deɪndʒrəs] adj dangereux(euse).

dangerously ['deɪndʒrəslɪ] adv dangereusement; **~ ill** très gravement malade, en danger de mort.

danger zone n zone dangereuse.

dangle ['dæŋgl] vt balancer; (fig) faire miroiter ♦ vi pendre, se balancer.

Danish ['deɪnɪʃ] adj danois(e) ♦ n (LING) danois m.

Danish pastry n feuilleté m (recouvert d'un glaçage et fourré aux fruits etc).

dank [dæŋk] adj froid(e) et humide.

Danube ['dænjuːb] n: **the ~** le Danube.

dapper ['dæpə*] adj pimpant(e).

Dardanelles [dɑːdə'nɛlz] npl Dardanelles fpl.

dare [dɛə*] vt: **to ~ sb to do** défier qn or mettre qn au défi de faire ♦ vi: **to ~ (to) do sth** oser faire qch; **I ~n't tell him** (BRIT) je n'ose pas le lui dire; **I ~ say he'll turn up** il est probable qu'il viendra.

daredevil ['dɛədɛvl] n casse-cou m inv.

Dar-es-Salaam ['dɑːrɛssə'lɑːm] n Dar-es-Salaam, Dar-es-Salam.

daring ['dɛərɪŋ] adj hardi(e), audacieux(euse) ♦ n audace f, hardiesse f.

dark [dɑːk] adj (night, room) obscur(e), sombre; (colour, complexion) foncé(e), sombre; (fig) sombre ♦ n: **in the ~** dans le noir; **in the ~ about** (fig) ignorant tout de; **after ~** après la tombée de la nuit; **it is/is getting ~** il fait nuit/commence à faire nuit.

darken [dɑːkn] vt obscurcir, assombrir ♦ vi s'obscurcir, s'assombrir.

dark glasses npl lunettes noires.

dark horse n (fig): **he's a ~** on ne sait pas grand-chose de lui.

darkly ['dɑːklɪ] adv (gloomily) mélancolique-

ment; (*in a sinister way*) lugubrement.
darkness ['dɑːknɪs] *n* obscurité *f*.
darkroom ['dɑːkrum] *n* chambre noire.
darling ['dɑːlɪŋ] *adj, n* chéri(e).
darn [dɑːn] *vt* repriser.
dart [dɑːt] *n* fléchette *f* ♦ *vi*: **to ~ towards** (*also*: **make a ~ towards**) se précipiter *or* s'élancer vers; **to ~ away/along** partir/ passer comme une flèche.
dartboard ['dɑːtbɔːd] *n* cible *f* (de jeu de fléchettes).
darts [dɑːts] *n* jeu *m* de fléchettes.
dash [dæʃ] *n* (*sign*) tiret *m*; (*small quantity*) goutte *f*, larme *f* ♦ *vt* (*missile*) jeter *or* lancer violemment; (*hopes*) anéantir ♦ *vi*: **to ~ towards** (*also*: **make a ~ towards**) se précipiter *or* se ruer vers; **a ~ of soda** un peu d'eau gazeuse.
▶**dash away** *vi* partir à toute allure.
dashboard ['dæʃbɔːd] *n* (*AUT*) tableau *m* de bord.
dashing ['dæʃɪŋ] *adj* fringant(e).
dastardly ['dæstədlɪ] *adj* lâche.
DAT *n abbr* (= *digital audio tape*) cassette *f* audio digitale.
data ['deɪtə] *npl* données *fpl*.
database ['deɪtəbeɪs] *n* base *f* de données.
data capture *n* saisie *f* de données.
data processing *n* traitement *m* (électronique) de l'information.
data transmission *n* transmission *f* de données.
date [deɪt] *n* date *f*; (*appointment*) rendez-vous *m*; (*fruit*) datte *f* ♦ *vt* dater; (*col: girl etc*) sortir avec; **what's the ~ today?** quelle date sommes-nous aujourd'hui?; **~ of birth** date de naissance; **closing ~** date de clôture; **to ~** *adv* à ce jour; **out of ~** périmé(e); **up to ~** à la page; mis(e) à jour; moderne; **to bring up to ~** (*correspondence, information*) mettre à jour; (*method*) moderniser; (*person*) mettre au courant; **letter ~d 5th July** *or* (*US*) **July 5th** lettre (datée) du 5 juillet.
dated ['deɪtɪd] *adj* démodé(e).
dateline ['deɪtlaɪn] *n* ligne *f* de changement de date.
date rape *n* viol *m* (à l'issue d'un rendez-vous galant).
date stamp *n* timbre-dateur *m*.
daub [dɔːb] *vt* barbouiller.
daughter ['dɔːtə*] *n* fille *f*.
daughter-in-law ['dɔːtərɪnlɔː] *n* belle-fille *f*, bru *f*.
daunt [dɔːnt] *vt* intimider, décourager.
daunting ['dɔːntɪŋ] *adj* décourageant(e), intimidant(e).
dauntless ['dɔːntlɪs] *adj* intrépide.
dawdle ['dɔːdl] *vi* traîner, lambiner; **to ~ over one's work** traînasser *or* lambiner sur son travail.
dawn [dɔːn] *n* aube *f*, aurore *f* ♦ *vi* (*day*) se lever, poindre; (*fig*) naître, se faire jour; **at ~**

à l'aube; **from ~ to dusk** du matin au soir; **it ~ed on him that** ... il lui vint à l'esprit que ....
dawn chorus *n* (*BRIT*) chant *m* des oiseaux à l'aube.
day [deɪ] *n* jour *m*; (*as duration*) journée *f*; (*period of time, age*) époque *f*, temps *m*; **the ~ before** la veille, le jour précédent; **the ~ after, the following ~** le lendemain, le jour suivant; **the ~ before yesterday** avant-hier; **the ~ after tomorrow** après-demain; **(on) the ~ that ...** le jour où ...; **~ by ~** jour après jour; **by ~** de jour; **paid by the ~** payé(e) à la journée; **these ~s, in the present ~** de nos jours, à l'heure actuelle.
daybook ['deɪbuk] *n* (*BRIT*) main courante, brouillard *m*, journal *m*.
day boy *n* (*SCOL*) externe *m*.
daybreak ['deɪbreɪk] *n* point *m* du jour.
daycare centre ['deɪkeə-] *n* garderie *f*.
daydream ['deɪdriːm] *n* rêverie *f* ♦ *vi* rêver (tout éveillé).
day girl *n* (*SCOL*) externe *f*.
daylight ['deɪlaɪt] *n* (lumière *f* du) jour *m*.
daylight robbery *n*: **it's ~** (*fig, col*) c'est du vol caractérisé *or* manifeste.
daylight saving time *n* (*US*) heure *f* d'été.
day release *n*: **to be on ~** avoir une journée de congé pour formation professionnelle.
day return (ticket) *n* (*BRIT*) billet *m* d'aller-retour (valable pour la journée).
day shift *n* équipe *f* de jour.
daytime ['deɪtaɪm] *n* jour *m*, journée *f*.
day-to-day ['deɪtə'deɪ] *adj* (*routine, expenses*) journalier(ière); **on a ~ basis** au jour le jour.
day trip *n* excursion *f* (d'une journée).
day tripper *n* excursionniste *m/f*.
daze [deɪz] *vt* (*subj: drug*) hébéter; (*: blow*) étourdir ♦ *n*: **in a ~** hébété(e); étourdi(e).
dazzle ['dæzl] *vt* éblouir, aveugler.
dazzling ['dæzlɪŋ] *adj* (*light*) aveuglant(e), éblouissant(e); (*fig*) éblouissant(e).
DC *abbr* (*ELEC*) = **direct current**; (*US*) = **District of Columbia**.
DCC *n abbr* ® (= *digital compact cassette*) DCC ®.
DD *n abbr* (= *Doctor of Divinity*) titre universitaire.
dd. *abbr* (*COMM*) = **delivered**.
D/D *abbr* = **direct debit**.
D-day ['diːdeɪ] *n* le jour J.
DDS *n abbr* (*US*: = *Doctor of Dental Science, Doctor of Dental Surgery*) titres universitaires.
DDT *n abbr* (= *dichlorodiphenyl trichloroethane*) DDT *m*.
DE *abbr* (*US*) = **Delaware**.
DEA *n abbr* (*US*: = *Drug Enforcement Administration*) ≈ brigade *f* des stupéfiants.
deacon ['diːkən] *n* diacre *m*.
dead [ded] *adj* mort(e); (*numb*) engourdi(e), insensible ♦ *adv* absolument, complètement;

the ~ *npl* les morts; **he was shot** ~ il a été tué d'un coup de revolver; ~ **on time** à l'heure pile; ~ **tired** éreinté(e), complètement fourbu(e); **to stop** ~ s'arrêter pile *or* net; **the line has gone** ~ (*TEL*) on n'entend plus rien.

dead beat *adj* (*col*) claqué(e), crevé(e).

deaden ['dɛdn] *vt* (*blow, sound*) amortir; (*make numb*) endormir, rendre insensible.

dead end *n* impasse *f*.

dead-end ['dɛdɛnd] *adj*: **a** ~ **job** un emploi *or* poste sans avenir.

dead heat *n* (*SPORT*): **to finish in a** ~ terminer ex aequo.

dead-letter office [dɛd'lɛtər-] *n* ≈ centre *m* de recherche du courrier.

deadline ['dɛdlaɪn] *n* date *f or* heure *f* limite; **to work to a** ~ avoir des délais stricts à respecter.

deadlock ['dɛdlɔk] *n* impasse *f* (*fig*).

dead loss *n* (*col*): **to be a** ~ (*person*) n'être bon(bonne) à rien; (*thing*) ne rien valoir.

deadly ['dɛdlɪ] *adj* mortel(le); (*weapon*) meurtrier(ière); ~ **dull** ennuyeux(euse) à mourir, mortellement ennuyeux.

deadpan ['dɛdpæn] *adj* impassible; (*humour*) pince-sans-rire *inv*.

Dead Sea *n*: **the** ~ la mer Morte.

dead season *n* (*TOURISM*) morte saison.

deaf [dɛf] *adj* sourd(e); **to turn a** ~ **ear to sth** faire la sourde oreille à qch.

deaf-aid ['dɛfeɪd] *n* (*BRIT*) appareil auditif.

deaf-and-dumb ['dɛfən'dʌm] *adj* sourd(e)-muet(te); ~ **alphabet** alphabet *m* des sourds-muets.

deafen ['dɛfn] *vt* rendre sourd(e); (*fig*) assourdir.

deafening ['dɛfnɪŋ] *adj* assourdissant(e).

deaf-mute ['dɛfmjuːt] *n* sourd/e-muet/te.

deafness ['dɛfnɪs] *n* surdité *f*.

deal [diːl] *n* affaire *f*, marché *m* ♦ *vt* (*pt, pp* **dealt** [dɛlt]) (*blow*) porter; (*cards*) donner, distribuer; **to strike a** ~ **with sb** faire *or* conclure un marché avec qn; **it's a** ~! (*col*) marché conclu!, tope-là!, topez-là!; **he got a bad** ~ **from them** ils ont mal agi envers lui; **he got a fair** ~ **from them** ils ont agi loyalement envers lui; **a good** ~ (*a lot*) beaucoup; **a good** ~ **of, a great** ~ **of** beaucoup de, énormément de.

►**deal in** *vt fus* (*COMM*) faire le commerce de, être dans le commerce de.

►**deal with** *vt fus* (*COMM*) traiter avec; (*handle*) s'occuper *or* se charger de; (*be about: book etc*) traiter de.

dealer ['diːlə*] *n* marchand *m*.

dealership ['diːləʃɪp] *n* concession *f*.

dealings ['diːlɪŋz] *npl* (*in goods, shares*) opérations *fpl*, transactions *fpl*; (*relations*) relations *fpl*, rapports *mpl*.

dealt [dɛlt] *pt, pp of* **deal**.

dean [diːn] *n* (*REL, BRIT SCOL*) doyen *m*; (*US*

SCOL) conseiller/ère (principal(e)) d'éducation.

dear [dɪə*] *adj* cher(chère); (*expensive*) cher, coûteux(euse) ♦ *n*: **my** ~ mon cher/ma chère; ~ **me!** mon Dieu!; **D~ Sir/Madam** (*in letter*) Monsieur/Madame; **D~ Mr/Mrs X** Cher Monsieur/Chère Madame X.

dearly ['dɪəlɪ] *adv* (*love*) tendrement; (*pay*) cher.

dearth [dəːθ] *n* disette *f*, pénurie *f*.

death [dɛθ] *n* mort *f*; (*ADMIN*) décès *m*.

deathbed ['dɛθbɛd] *n* lit *m* de mort.

death certificate *n* acte *m* de décès.

death duties *npl* (*BRIT*) droits *mpl* de succession.

deathly ['dɛθlɪ] *adj* de mort ♦ *adv* comme la mort.

death penalty *n* peine *f* de mort.

death rate *n* taux *m* de mortalité.

death row [-'rəu] *n* (*US*) quartier *m* des condamnés à mort; **to be on** ~ être condamné à la peine de mort.

death sentence *n* condamnation *f* à mort.

death squad *n* escadron *m* de la mort.

deathtrap ['dɛθtræp] *n* endroit (*or* véhicule *etc*) dangereux.

deb [dɛb] *n abbr* (*col*) = **debutante**.

debar [dɪ'bɑː*] *vt*: **to** ~ **sb from a club** *etc* exclure qn d'un club *etc*; **to** ~ **sb from doing** interdire à qn de faire.

debase [dɪ'beɪs] *vt* (*currency*) déprécier, dévaloriser; (*person*) abaisser, avilir.

debatable [dɪ'beɪtəbl] *adj* discutable, contestable; **it is** ~ **whether** ... il est douteux que ....

debate [dɪ'beɪt] *n* discussion *f*, débat *m* ♦ *vt* discuter, débattre ♦ *vi* (*consider*): **to** ~ **whether** se demander si.

debauchery [dɪ'bɔːtʃərɪ] *n* débauche *f*.

debenture [dɪ'bɛntʃə*] *n* (*COMM*) obligation *f*.

debilitate [dɪ'bɪlɪteɪt] *vt* débiliter.

debit ['dɛbɪt] *n* débit *m* ♦ *vt*: **to** ~ **a sum to sb** *or* **to sb's account** porter une somme au débit de qn, débiter qn d'une somme.

debit balance *n* solde débiteur.

debit note *n* note *f* de débit.

debrief [diː'briːf] *vt* demander un compte rendu de fin de mission à.

debriefing [diː'briːfɪŋ] *n* compte rendu *m*.

debris ['dɛbriː] *n* débris *mpl*, décombres *mpl*.

debt [dɛt] *n* dette *f*; **to be in** ~ avoir des dettes, être endetté(e); **bad** ~ créance *f* irrécouvrable.

debt collector *n* agent *m* de recouvrements.

debtor ['dɛtə*] *n* débiteur/trice.

debug [diː'bʌg] *vt* (*COMPUT*) déverminer.

debunk [diː'bʌŋk] *vt* (*theory, claim*) montrer le ridicule de.

debut ['deɪbjuː] *n* début(s) *m(pl)*.

debutante ['dɛbjutænt] *n* débutante *f*.

Dec. *abbr* (= *December*) déc.

decade ['dɛkeɪd] *n* décennie *f*, décade *f*.

decadence ['dɛkədəns] *n* décadence *f*.

decadent ['dɛkədənt] *adj* décadent(e).
de-caff ['diːkæf] *n* (*col*) déca *m*.
decaffeinated [dɪ'kæfɪneɪtɪd] *adj* décaféiné(e).
decamp [dɪ'kæmp] *vi* (*col*) décamper, filer.
decant [dɪ'kænt] *vt* (*wine*) décanter.
decanter [dɪ'kæntə*] *n* carafe *f*.
decarbonize [diː'kɑːbənaɪz] *vt* (*AUT*) décalaminer.
decathlon [dɪ'kæθlən] *n* décathlon *m*.
decay [dɪ'keɪ] *n* décomposition *f*, pourrissement *m*; (*fig*) déclin *m*, délabrement *m*; (*also*: **tooth ~**) carie *f* (dentaire) ♦ *vi* (*rot*) se décomposer, pourrir; (*fig*) se délabrer; décliner; se détériorer.
decease [dɪ'siːs] *n* décès *m*.
deceased [dɪ'siːst] *n*: **the ~** le/la défunt/e.
deceit [dɪ'siːt] *n* tromperie *f*, supercherie *f*.
deceitful [dɪ'siːtful] *adj* trompeur(euse).
deceive [dɪ'siːv] *vt* tromper; **to ~ o.s.** s'abuser.
decelerate [diː'sɛləreɪt] *vt, vi* ralentir.
December [dɪ'sɛmbə*] *n* décembre *m*; *for phrases see also* **July**.
decency ['diːsənsɪ] *n* décence *f*.
decent ['diːsənt] *adj* décent(e), convenable; **they were very ~ about it** ils se sont montrés très chics.
decently ['diːsəntlɪ] *adv* (*respectably*) décemment, convenablement; (*kindly*) décemment.
decentralization [diːsɛntrəlaɪ'zeɪʃən] *n* décentralisation *f*.
decentralize [diː'sɛntrəlaɪz] *vt* décentraliser.
deception [dɪ'sɛpʃən] *n* tromperie *f*.
deceptive [dɪ'sɛptɪv] *adj* trompeur(euse).
decibel ['dɛsɪbɛl] *n* décibel *m*.
decide [dɪ'saɪd] *vt* (*person*) décider; (*question, argument*) trancher, régler ♦ *vi* se décider, décider; **to ~ to do/that** décider de faire/que; **to ~ on** décider, se décider pour; **to ~ on doing** décider de faire; **to ~ against doing** décider de ne pas faire.
decided [dɪ'saɪdɪd] *adj* (*resolute*) résolu(e), décidé(e); (*clear, definite*) net(te), marqué(e).
decidedly [dɪ'saɪdɪdlɪ] *adv* résolument; incontestablement, nettement.
deciding [dɪ'saɪdɪŋ] *adj* décisif(ive).
deciduous [dɪ'sɪdjuəs] *adj* à feuilles caduques.
decimal ['dɛsɪməl] *adj* décimal(e) ♦ *n* décimale *f*; **to three ~ places** (jusqu')à la troisième décimale.
decimalize ['dɛsɪmələɪz] *vt* (*BRIT*) décimaliser.
decimal point *n* ≈ virgule *f*.
decimate ['dɛsɪmeɪt] *vt* décimer.
decipher [dɪ'saɪfə*] *vt* déchiffrer.
decision [dɪ'sɪʒən] *n* décision *f*; **to make a ~** prendre une décision.
decisive [dɪ'saɪsɪv] *adj* décisif(ive); (*influence*) décisif, déterminant(e); (*manner, person*) décidé(e), catégorique; (*reply*) ferme, catégorique.
deck [dɛk] *n* (*NAUT*) pont *m*; (*of bus*): **top ~** impériale *f*; (*of cards*) jeu *m*; **to go up on ~** monter sur le pont; **below ~** dans l'entrepont; **record/cassette ~** platine-disques/-cassettes *f*.
deckchair ['dɛktʃɛə*] *n* chaise longue.
deck hand *n* matelot *m*.
declaration [dɛklə'reɪʃən] *n* déclaration *f*.
declare [dɪ'klɛə*] *vt* déclarer.
declassify [diː'klæsɪfaɪ] *vt* rendre accessible au public *or* à tous.
decline [dɪ'klaɪn] *n* (*decay*) déclin *m*; (*lessening*) baisse *f* ♦ *vt* refuser, décliner ♦ *vi* décliner; être en baisse, baisser; **~ in living standards** baisse du niveau de vie; **to ~ to do sth** refuser (poliment) de faire qch.
declutch ['diː'klʌtʃ] *vi* (*BRIT*) débrayer.
decode ['diː'kəud] *vt* décoder.
decoder [diː'kəudə*] *n* (*COMPUT, TV*) décodeur *m*.
decompose [diːkəm'pəuz] *vi* se décomposer.
decomposition [diːkɔmpə'zɪʃən] *n* décomposition *f*.
decompression [diːkəm'prɛʃən] *n* décompression *f*.
decompression chamber *n* caisson *m* de décompression.
decongestant [diːkən'dʒɛstənt] *n* décongestif *m*.
decontaminate [diːkən'tæmɪneɪt] *vt* décontaminer.
decontrol [diːkən'trəul] *vt* (*prices etc*) libérer.
décor ['deɪkɔː*] *n* décor *m*.
decorate ['dɛkəreɪt] *vt* (*adorn, give a medal to*) décorer; (*paint and paper*) peindre et tapisser.
decoration [dɛkə'reɪʃən] *n* (*medal etc, adornment*) décoration *f*.
decorative ['dɛkərətɪv] *adj* décoratif(ive).
decorator ['dɛkəreɪtə*] *n* peintre *m* en bâtiment.
decorum [dɪ'kɔːrəm] *n* décorum *m*, bienséance *f*.
decoy ['diːkɔɪ] *n* piège *m*; **they used him as a ~ for the enemy** ils se sont servis de lui pour attirer l'ennemi.
decrease *n* ['diːkriːs] diminution *f* ♦ *vt, vi* [diː'kriːs] diminuer; **to be on the ~** diminuer, être en diminution.
decreasing [diː'kriːsɪŋ] *adj* en voie de diminution.
decree [dɪ'kriː] *n* (*POL, REL*) décret *m*; (*LAW*) arrêt *m*, jugement *m* ♦ *vt*: **to ~ (that)** décréter (que), ordonner (que); **~ absolute** jugement définitif (de divorce); **~ nisi** jugement provisoire de divorce.
decrepit [dɪ'krɛpɪt] *adj* (*person*) décrépit(e); (*building*) délabré(e).
decry [dɪ'kraɪ] *vt* condamner ouvertement, déplorer; (*disparage*) dénigrer, décrier.
dedicate ['dɛdɪkeɪt] *vt* consacrer; (*book etc*) dédier.
dedicated ['dɛdɪkeɪtɪd] *adj* (*person*) dévoué(e);

(*COMPUT*) spécialisé(e), dédié(e); ~ **word processor** station *f* de traitement de texte.

dedication [dɛdɪ'keɪʃən] *n* (*devotion*) dévouement *m*; (*in book*) dédicace *f*.

deduce [dɪ'djuːs] *vt* déduire, conclure.

deduct [dɪ'dʌkt] *vt*: **to ~ sth (from)** déduire qch (de), retrancher qch (de); (*from wage etc*) prélever qch (sur), retenir qch (sur).

deduction [dɪ'dʌkʃən] *n* (*deducting*) déduction *f*; (*from wage etc*) prélèvement *m*, retenue *f*; (*deducing*) déduction, conclusion *f*.

deed [diːd] *n* action *f*, acte *m*; (*LAW*) acte notarié, contrat *m*; ~ **of covenant** (acte *m* de) donation *f*.

deem [diːm] *vt* (*formal*) juger, estimer; **to ~ it wise to do** juger bon de faire.

deep [diːp] *adj* (*water, sigh, sorrow, thoughts*) profond(e); (*voice*) grave ♦ *adv*: ~ **in snow** recouvert(e) d'une épaisse couche de neige; **spectators stood 20** ~ il y avait 20 rangs de spectateurs; **knee-~ in water** dans l'eau jusqu'aux genoux; **4 metres** ~ de 4 mètres de profondeur; **he took a ~ breath** il inspira profondément, il prit son souffle.

deepen [diːpn] *vt* (*hole*) approfondir ♦ *vi* s'approfondir; (*darkness*) s'épaissir.

deep-freeze ['diːp'friːz] *n* congélateur *m* ♦ *vt* surgeler.

deep-fry ['diːp'fraɪ] *vt* faire frire (dans une friteuse).

deeply ['diːplɪ] *adv* profondément; (*dig*) en profondeur; (*regret, interest*) vivement.

deep-rooted ['diːp'ruːtɪd] *adj* (*prejudice*) profondément enraciné(e); (*affection*) profond(e); (*habit*) invétéré(e).

deep-sea ['diːp'siː] *adj*: ~ **diver** plongeur sous-marin; ~ **diving** plongée sous-marine; ~ **fishing** pêche hauturière.

deep-seated ['diːp'siːtɪd] *adj* (*beliefs*) profondément enraciné(e).

deep-set ['diːpsɛt] *adj* (*eyes*) enfoncé(e).

deer [dɪə*] *n* (*pl inv*): **the** ~ les cervidés *mpl* (*ZOOL*); (**red**) ~ cerf *m*; (**fallow**) ~ daim *m*; (**roe**) ~ chevreuil *m*.

deerskin ['dɪəskɪn] *n* peau *f* de daim.

deerstalker ['dɪəstɔːkə*] *n* (*person*) chasseur *m* de cerf; (*hat*) casquette *f* à la Sherlock Holmes.

deface [dɪ'feɪs] *vt* dégrader; barbouiller; rendre illisible.

defamation [dɛfə'meɪʃən] *n* diffamation *f*.

defamatory [dɪ'fæmətrɪ] *adj* diffamatoire, diffamant(e).

default [dɪ'fɔːlt] *vi* (*LAW*) faire défaut; (*gen*) manquer à ses engagements ♦ *n* (*COMPUT*: *also*: ~ **value**) valeur *f* par défaut; **by** ~ (*LAW*) par défaut, par contumace; (*SPORT*) par forfait; **to ~ on a debt** ne pas s'acquitter d'une dette.

defaulter [dɪ'fɔːltə*] *n* (*on debt*) débiteur défaillant.

default option *n* (*COMPUT*) option *f* par dé-

faut.

defeat [dɪ'fiːt] *n* défaite *f* ♦ *vt* (*team, opponents*) battre; (*fig: plans, efforts*) faire échouer.

defeatism [dɪ'fiːtɪzəm] *n* défaitisme *m*.

defeatist [dɪ'fiːtɪst] *adj, n* défaitiste (*m/f*).

defecate ['dɛfəkeɪt] *vi* déféquer.

defect *n* ['diːfɛkt] défaut *m* ♦ *vi* [dɪ'fɛkt]: **to ~ to the enemy/the West** passer à l'ennemi/ l'Ouest; **physical** ~ malformation *f*, vice *m* de conformation; **mental** ~ anomalie *or* déficience mentale.

defective [dɪ'fɛktɪv] *adj* défectueux(euse).

defector [dɪ'fɛktə*] *n* transfuge *m/f*.

defence, (*US*) **defense** [dɪ'fɛns] *n* défense *f*; **in** ~ **of** pour défendre; **witness for the** ~ témoin *m* à décharge; **the Ministry of D~**, (*US*) **the Department of Defense** le ministère de la Défense nationale.

defenceless [dɪ'fɛnslɪs] *adj* sans défense.

defend [dɪ'fɛnd] *vt* défendre; (*decision, action, opinion*) justifier, défendre.

defendant [dɪ'fɛndənt] *n* défendeur/deresse; (*in criminal case*) accusé/e, prévenu/e.

defender [dɪ'fɛndə*] *n* défenseur *m*.

defending champion [dɪ'fɛndɪŋ-] *n* (*SPORT*) champion/ne en titre.

defending counsel [dɪ'fɛndɪŋ-] *n* (*LAW*) avocat *m* de la défense.

defense [dɪ'fɛns] *n* (*US*) = **defence**.

defensive [dɪ'fɛnsɪv] *adj* défensif(ive) ♦ *n* défensive *f*; **on the** ~ sur la défensive.

defer [dɪ'fɜː*] *vt* (*postpone*) différer, ajourner ♦ *vi* (*submit*): **to ~ to sb/sth** déférer à qn/ qch, s'en remettre à qn/qch.

deference ['dɛfərəns] *n* déférence *f*, égards *mpl*; **out of** *or* **in** ~ **to** par déférence *or* égards pour.

defiance [dɪ'faɪəns] *n* défi *m*; **in** ~ **of** au mépris de.

defiant [dɪ'faɪənt] *adj* provocant(e), de défi.

defiantly [dɪ'faɪəntlɪ] *adv* d'un air (*or* d'un ton) de défi.

deficiency [dɪ'fɪʃənsɪ] *n* insuffisance *f*, déficience *f*; carence *f*; (*COMM*) déficit *m*, découvert *m*.

deficiency disease *n* maladie *f* de carence.

deficient [dɪ'fɪʃənt] *adj* insuffisant(e); défectueux(euse); déficient(e); **to be** ~ **in** manquer de.

deficit ['dɛfɪsɪt] *n* déficit *m*.

defile [dɪ'faɪl] *vt* souiller ♦ *vi* défiler ♦ *n* ['diːfaɪl] défilé *m*.

define [dɪ'faɪn] *vt* définir.

definite ['dɛfɪnɪt] *adj* (*fixed*) défini(e), (bien) déterminé(e); (*clear, obvious*) net(te), manifeste; (*LING*) défini(e); **he was** ~ **about it** il a été catégorique; il était sûr de son fait.

definitely ['dɛfɪnɪtlɪ] *adv* sans aucun doute.

definition [dɛfɪ'nɪʃən] *n* définition *f*.

definitive [dɪ'fɪnɪtɪv] *adj* définitif(ive).

deflate [diː'fleɪt] *vt* dégonfler; (*pompous person*) rabattre le caquet à; (*ECON*) provoquer la déflation de; (: *prices*) faire tomber *or* baisser.

deflation [diːˈfleɪʃən] *n* (*ECON*) déflation *f*.

deflationary [diːˈfleɪʃənrɪ] *adj* (*ECON*) déflationniste.

deflect [dɪˈflɛkt] *vt* détourner, faire dévier.

defog [ˈdiːˈfɔg] *vt* (*US AUT*) désembuer.

defogger [ˈdiːˈfɔgə*] *n* (*US AUT*) dispositif *m* anti-buée *inv*.

deform [dɪˈfɔːm] *vt* déformer.

deformed [dɪˈfɔːmd] *adj* difforme.

deformity [dɪˈfɔːmɪtɪ] *n* difformité *f*.

defraud [dɪˈfrɔːd] *vt* frauder; **to ~ sb of sth** soutirer qch malhonnêtement à qn; escroquer qch à qn; frustrer qn de qch.

defray [dɪˈfreɪ] *vt*: **to ~ sb's expenses** défrayer qn (de ses frais), rembourser *or* payer à qn ses frais.

defrost [diːˈfrɔst] *vt* (*fridge*) dégivrer; (*frozen food*) décongeler.

deft [dɛft] *adj* adroit(e), preste.

defunct [dɪˈfʌŋkt] *adj* défunt(e).

defuse [diːˈfjuːz] *vt* désamorcer.

defy [dɪˈfaɪ] *vt* défier; (*efforts etc*) résister à.

degenerate *vi* [dɪˈdʒɛnəreɪt] dégénérer ♦ *adj* [dɪˈdʒɛnərɪt] dégénéré(e).

degradation [dɛgrəˈdeɪʃən] *n* dégradation *f*.

degrade [dɪˈgreɪd] *vt* dégrader.

degrading [dɪˈgreɪdɪŋ] *adj* dégradant(e).

degree [dɪˈgriː] *n* degré *m*; (*SCOL*) diplôme *m* (universitaire); **10 ~s below (zero)** 10 degrés au-dessous de zéro; **a (first) ~ in maths** (*BRIT*) une licence en maths; **a considerable ~ of risk** un considérable facteur *or* élément de risque; **by ~s** (*gradually*) par degrés; **to some ~, to a certain ~** jusqu'à un certain point, dans une certaine mesure.

dehydrated [diːhaɪˈdreɪtɪd] *adj* déshydraté(e); (*milk, eggs*) en poudre.

dehydration [diːhaɪˈdreɪʃən] *n* déshydratation *f*.

de-ice [ˈdiːˈaɪs] *vt* (*windscreen*) dégivrer.

de-icer [ˈdiːˈaɪsə*] *n* dégivreur *m*.

deign [deɪn] *vi*: **to ~ to do** daigner faire.

deity [ˈdiːɪtɪ] *n* divinité *f*; dieu *m*, déesse *f*.

déjà vu [deɪʒɑːˈvuː] *n*: **I had a sense of ~** j'ai eu une impression de déjà-vu.

dejected [dɪˈdʒɛktɪd] *adj* abattu(e), déprimé(e).

dejection [dɪˈdʒɛkʃən] *n* abattement *m*, découragement *m*.

Del. *abbr* (*US*) = *Delaware*.

del. *abbr* = *delete*.

delay [dɪˈleɪ] *vt* (*journey, operation*) retarder, différer; (*travellers, trains*) retarder; (*payment*) différer ♦ *vi* s'attarder ♦ *n* délai *m*, retard *m*; **without ~** sans délai, sans tarder.

delayed-action [dɪˈleɪdˈækʃən] *adj* à retardement.

delectable [dɪˈlɛktəbl] *adj* délicieux(euse).

delegate *n* [ˈdɛlɪgɪt] délégué/e ♦ *vt* [ˈdɛlɪgeɪt] déléguer; **to ~ sth to sb/sb to do sth** délé-

guer qch à qn/qn pour faire qch.

delegation [dɛlɪˈgeɪʃən] *n* délégation *f*.

delete [dɪˈliːt] *vt* rayer, supprimer; (*COMPUT*) effacer.

Delhi [ˈdɛlɪ] *n* Delhi.

deli [ˈdɛlɪ] *n* épicerie fine.

deliberate *adj* [dɪˈlɪbərɪt] (*intentional*) délibéré(e); (*slow*) mesuré(e) ♦ *vi* [dɪˈlɪbəreɪt] délibérer, réfléchir.

deliberately [dɪˈlɪbərɪtlɪ] *adv* (*on purpose*) exprès, délibérément.

deliberation [dɪlɪbəˈreɪʃən] *n* délibération *f*, réflexion *f*; (*gen pl: discussion*) délibérations, débats *mpl*.

delicacy [ˈdɛlɪkəsɪ] *n* délicatesse *f*; (*choice food*) mets fin *or* délicat, friandise *f*.

delicate [ˈdɛlɪkɪt] *adj* délicat(e).

delicately [ˈdɛlɪkɪtlɪ] *adv* délicatement; (*act, express*) avec délicatesse, avec tact.

delicatessen [dɛlɪkəˈtɛsn] *n* épicerie fine.

delicious [dɪˈlɪʃəs] *adj* délicieux(euse), exquis(e).

delight [dɪˈlaɪt] *n* (grande) joie, grand plaisir ♦ *vt* enchanter; **a ~ to the eyes** un régal *or* plaisir pour les yeux; **to take ~ in** prendre grand plaisir à; **to be the ~ of** faire les délices *or* la joie de.

delighted [dɪˈlaɪtɪd] *adj*: **~ (at *or* with sth)** ravi(e) (de qch); **to be ~ to do sth/that** être enchanté(e) *or* ravi(e) de faire qch/que; **I'd be ~** j'en serais enchanté *or* ravi.

delightful [dɪˈlaɪtful] *adj* (*person, child*) absolument charmant(e), adorable; (*evening, view*) merveilleux(euse); (*meal*) délicieux(euse).

delimit [diːˈlɪmɪt] *vt* délimiter.

delineate [dɪˈlɪnɪeɪt] *vt* tracer, esquisser; (*fig*) dépeindre, décrire.

delinquency [dɪˈlɪŋkwənsɪ] *n* délinquance *f*.

delinquent [dɪˈlɪŋkwənt] *adj*, *n* délinquant(e).

delirious [dɪˈlɪrɪəs] *adj* (*MED, fig*) délirant(e); **to be ~** délirer.

delirium [dɪˈlɪrɪəm] *n* délire *m*.

deliver [dɪˈlɪvə*] *vt* (*mail*) distribuer; (*goods*) livrer; (*message*) remettre; (*speech*) prononcer; (*warning, ultimatum*) lancer; (*free*) délivrer; (*MED*) accoucher; **to ~ the goods** (*fig*) tenir ses promesses.

deliverance [dɪˈlɪvrəns] *n* délivrance *f*, libération *f*.

delivery [dɪˈlɪvərɪ] *n* (*of mail*) distribution *f*; (*of goods*) livraison *f*; (*of speaker*) élocution *f*; (*MED*) accouchement *m*; **to take ~ of** prendre livraison de.

delivery note *n* bon *m* de livraison.

delivery van, (*US*) **delivery truck** *n* fourgonnette *f or* camionnette *f* de livraison.

delouse [ˈdiːˈlaus] *vt* épouiller, débarrasser de sa (*or* leur *etc*) vermine.

delta [ˈdɛltə] *n* delta *m*.

delude [dɪˈluːd] *vt* tromper, leurrer; **to ~ o.s.** se leurrer, se faire des illusions.

deluge [ˈdɛljuːdʒ] *n* déluge *m* ♦ *vt* (*fig*): **to ~**

(with) inonder (de).
delusion [dɪ'luːʒən] n illusion f; **to have ~s of grandeur** être un peu mégalomane.
de luxe [də'lʌks] adj de luxe.
delve [dɛlv] vi: ~ **into** fouiller dans.
Dem. abbr (US POL) = **democrat(ic)**.
demagogue ['dɛməgɔg] n démagogue m/f.
demand [dɪ'mɑːnd] vt réclamer, exiger; (need) exiger, requérir ♦ n exigence f; (claim) revendication f; (ECON) demande f; **to ~ sth (from** or **of sb)** exiger qch (de qn), réclamer qch (à qn); **in ~** demandé(e), recherché(e); **on ~** sur demande.
demanding [dɪ'mɑːndɪŋ] adj (person) exigeant(e); (work) astreignant(e).
demarcation [diːmɑː'keɪʃən] n démarcation f.
demarcation dispute n (INDUSTRY) conflit m d'attributions.
demean [dɪ'miːn] vt: **to ~ o.s.** s'abaisser.
demeanour, (US) **demeanor** [dɪ'miːnə*] n comportement m; maintien m.
demented [dɪ'mɛntɪd] adj dément(e), fou(folle).
demilitarized zone [diː'mɪlɪtəraɪzd-] n zone démilitarisée.
demise [dɪ'maɪz] n décès m.
demist [diː'mɪst] vt (BRIT AUT) désembuer.
demister [diː'mɪstə*] n (BRIT AUT) dispositif m anti-buée inv.
demo ['dɛməu] n abbr (col: = demonstration) manif f.
demobilize [diː'məubɪlaɪz] vt démobiliser.
democracy [dɪ'mɔkrəsɪ] n démocratie f.
democrat ['dɛməkræt] n démocrate m/f.
democratic [dɛmə'krætɪk] adj démocratique; **the D~ Party** (US) le parti démocrate.
demography [dɪ'mɔgrəfɪ] n démographie f.
demolish [dɪ'mɔlɪʃ] vt démolir.
demolition [dɛmə'lɪʃən] n démolition f.
demon ['diːmən] n démon m ♦ cpd: **a ~ squash player** un crack en squash; **a ~ driver** un fou du volant.
demonstrate ['dɛmənstreɪt] vt démontrer, prouver ♦ vi: **to ~ (for/against)** manifester (en faveur de/contre).
demonstration [dɛmən'streɪʃən] n démonstration f; (POL etc) manifestation f; **to hold a ~** (POL etc) organiser une manifestation, manifester.
demonstrative [dɪ'mɔnstrətɪv] adj démonstratif(ive).
demonstrator ['dɛmənstreɪtə*] n (POL etc) manifestant/e; (COMM: sales person) vendeur/euse; (: car, computer etc) modèle m de démonstration.
demoralize [dɪ'mɔrəlaɪz] vt démoraliser.
demote [dɪ'məut] vt rétrograder.
demotion [dɪ'məuʃən] n rétrogradation f.
demur [dɪ'məː*] vi: **to ~ (at sth)** hésiter (devant qch); (object) élever des objections (contre qch) ♦ n: **without ~** sans hésiter; sans faire de difficultés.

demure [dɪ'mjuə*] adj sage, réservé(e); d'une modestie affectée.
demurrage [dɪ'mʌrɪdʒ] n droits mpl de magasinage; surestarie f.
den [dɛn] n tanière f, antre m.
denationalization [diːnæʃnəlaɪ'zeɪʃən] n dénationalisation f.
denationalize [diː'næʃnəlaɪz] vt dénationaliser.
denial [dɪ'naɪəl] n (of accusation) démenti m; (of rights, guilt, truth) dénégation f.
denier ['dɛnɪə*] n denier m; **15 ~ stockings** bas de 15 deniers.
denigrate ['dɛnɪgreɪt] vt dénigrer.
denim ['dɛnɪm] n coton émerisé.
denim jacket n veste f en jean.
denims ['dɛnɪmz] npl (blue-)jeans mpl.
denizen ['dɛnɪzn] n (inhabitant) habitant/e; (foreigner) étranger/ère.
Denmark ['dɛnmɑːk] n Danemark m.
denomination [dɪnɔmɪ'neɪʃən] n (money) valeur f; (REL) confession f; culte m.
denominator [dɪ'nɔmɪneɪtə*] n dénominateur m.
denote [dɪ'nəut] vt dénoter.
denounce [dɪ'nauns] vt dénoncer.
dense [dɛns] adj dense; (col: stupid) obtus(e), dur(e) or lent(e) à la comprenette.
densely ['dɛnslɪ] adv: **~ wooded** couvert(e) d'épaisses forêts; **~ populated** à forte densité (de population), très peuplé(e).
density ['dɛnsɪtɪ] n densité f; **single/double ~ disk** (COMPUT) disquette f (à) simple/double densité.
dent [dɛnt] n bosse f ♦ vt (also: **make a ~ in**) cabosser; **to make a ~ in** (fig) entamer.
dental ['dɛntl] adj dentaire.
dental floss [-flɔs] n fil m dentaire.
dental surgeon n (chirurgien/ne) dentiste.
dentifrice ['dɛntɪfrɪs] n dentifrice m.
dentist ['dɛntɪst] n dentiste m/f; **~'s surgery** (BRIT) cabinet m de dentiste.
dentistry ['dɛntɪstrɪ] n art m dentaire.
denture(s) ['dɛntʃə(z)] n(pl) dentier m.
denunciation [dɪnʌnsɪ'eɪʃən] n dénonciation f.
deny [dɪ'naɪ] vt nier; (refuse) refuser; (disown) renier; **he denies having said it** il nie l'avoir dit.
deodorant [diː'əudərənt] n désodorisant m, déodorant m.
depart [dɪ'pɑːt] vi partir; **to ~ from** (leave) quitter, partir de; (fig: differ from) s'écarter de.
departed [dɪ'pɑːtɪd] adj (dead) défunt(e); **the (dear) ~** le défunt/la défunte/les défunts.
department [dɪ'pɑːtmənt] n (COMM) rayon m; (SCOL) section f; (POL) ministère m, département m; **that's not my ~** (fig) ce n'est pas mon domaine or ma compétence, ce n'est pas mon rayon; **D~ of State** (US) Département d'État.
departmental [diːpɑːt'mɛntl] adj d'une or de

la section; d'un or du ministère, d'un or du département; ~ **manager** chef *m* de service; (*in shop*) chef de rayon.

department store *n* grand magasin.

departure [dɪ'pɑːtʃə*] *n* départ *m*; (*fig*): ~ **from** écart *m* par rapport à; **a new** ~ une nouvelle voie.

departure lounge *n* salle *f* de départ.

depend [dɪ'pɛnd] *vi*: **to** ~ **(up)on** dépendre de; (*rely on*) compter sur; (*financially*) dépendre (financièrement) de, être à la charge de; **it** ~**s** cela dépend; ~**ing on the result** ... selon le résultat ....

dependable [dɪ'pɛndəbl] *adj* sûr(e), digne de confiance.

dependant [dɪ'pɛndənt] *n* personne *f* à charge.

dependence [dɪ'pɛndəns] *n* dépendance *f*.

dependent [dɪ'pɛndənt] *adj*: **to be** ~ **(on)** dépendre (de) ♦ *n* = **dependant**.

depict [dɪ'pɪkt] *vt* (*in picture*) représenter; (*in words*) (dé)peindre, décrire.

depilatory [dɪ'pɪlətrɪ] *n* (*also*: ~ **cream**) dépilatoire *m*, crème *f* à épiler.

depleted [dɪ'pliːtɪd] *adj* (considérablement) réduit(e) or diminué(e).

deplorable [dɪ'plɔːrəbl] *adj* déplorable, lamentable.

deplore [dɪ'plɔː*] *vt* déplorer.

deploy [dɪ'plɔɪ] *vt* déployer.

depopulate [diː'pɒpjuleɪt] *vt* dépeupler.

depopulation ['diːpɒpju'leɪʃən] *n* dépopulation *f*, dépeuplement *m*.

deport [dɪ'pɔːt] *vt* déporter, expulser.

deportation [diːpɔː'teɪʃən] *n* déportation *f*, expulsion *f*.

deportation order *n* arrêté *m* d'expulsion.

deportee [diːpɔː'tiː] *n* déporté/e.

deportment [dɪ'pɔːtmənt] *n* maintien *m*, tenue *f*.

depose [dɪ'pəuz] *vt* déposer.

deposit [dɪ'pɒzɪt] *n* (*CHEM, COMM, GEO*) dépôt *m*; (*of ore, oil*) gisement *m*; (*part payment*) arrhes *fpl*, acompte *m*; (*on bottle etc*) consigne *f*; (*for hired goods etc*) cautionnement *m*, garantie *f* ♦ *vt* déposer; (*valuables*) mettre or laisser en dépôt; **to put down a** ~ **of £50** verser 50 livres d'arrhes or d'acompte; laisser 50 livres en garantie.

deposit account *n* compte *m* de dépôt.

depositor [dɪ'pɒzɪtə*] *n* déposant/e.

depository [dɪ'pɒzɪtərɪ] *n* (*person*) dépositaire *m/f*; (*place*) dépôt *m*.

depot ['dɛpəu] *n* dépôt *m*.

depraved [dɪ'preɪvd] *adj* dépravé(e), perverti(e).

depravity [dɪ'prævɪtɪ] *n* dépravation *f*.

deprecate ['dɛprɪkeɪt] *vt* désapprouver.

deprecating ['dɛprɪkeɪtɪŋ] *adj* (*disapproving*) désapprobateur(trice); (*apologetic*): **a** ~ **smile** un sourire d'excuse.

depreciate [dɪ'priːʃɪeɪt] *vt* déprécier ♦ *vi* se déprécier, se dévaloriser.

depreciation [dɪpriːʃɪ'eɪʃən] *n* dépréciation *f*.

depress [dɪ'prɛs] *vt* déprimer; (*press down*) appuyer sur, abaisser.

depressant [dɪ'prɛsnt] *n* (*MED*) dépresseur *m*.

depressed [dɪ'prɛst] *adj* (*person*) déprimé(e), abattu(e); (*area*) en déclin, touché(e) par le sous-emploi; (*COMM: market, trade*) maussade; **to get** ~ se démoraliser, se laisser abattre.

depressing [dɪ'prɛsɪŋ] *adj* déprimant(e).

depression [dɪ'prɛʃən] *n* (*also ECON*) dépression *f*.

deprivation [dɛprɪ'veɪʃən] *n* privation *f*; (*loss*) perte *f*.

deprive [dɪ'praɪv] *vt*: **to** ~ **sb of** priver qn de; enlever à qn.

deprived [dɪ'praɪvd] *adj* déshérité(e).

dept. *abbr* (= *department*) dép., dépt.

depth [dɛpθ] *n* profondeur *f*; **in the** ~**s of** au fond de; au cœur de; au plus profond de; **at a** ~ **of 3 metres** à 3 mètres de profondeur; **to be out of one's** ~ (*BRIT: swimmer*) ne plus avoir pied; (*fig*) être dépassé(e), nager; **to study sth in** ~ étudier qch en profondeur.

depth charge *n* grenade sous-marine.

deputation [dɛpju'teɪʃən] *n* députation *f*, délégation *f*.

deputize ['dɛpjutaɪz] *vi*: **to** ~ **for** assurer l'intérim de.

deputy ['dɛpjutɪ] *n* (*replacement*) suppléant/e, intérimaire *m/f*; (*second in command*) adjoint/e ♦ *adj*: ~ **chairman** vice-président *m*; ~ **head** (*SCOL*) directeur/trice adjoint(e), sous-directeur/trice; ~ **leader** (*BRIT POL*) vice-président/e, secrétaire adjoint(e).

derail [dɪ'reɪl] *vt* faire dérailler; **to be** ~**ed** dérailler.

derailment [dɪ'reɪlmənt] *n* déraillement *m*.

deranged [dɪ'reɪndʒd] *adj*: **to be (mentally)** ~ avoir le cerveau dérangé.

derby ['dəːrbɪ] *n* (*US*) (chapeau *m*) melon *m*.

Derbys *abbr* (*BRIT*) = *Derbyshire*.

deregulate [dɪ'rɛgjuleɪt] *vt* libérer, dérégler.

deregulation [dɪrɛgju'leɪʃən] *n* libération *f*, dérèglement *m*.

derelict ['dɛrɪlɪkt] *adj* abandonné(e), à l'abandon.

deride [dɪ'raɪd] *vt* railler.

derision [dɪ'rɪʒən] *n* dérision *f*.

derisive [dɪ'raɪsɪv] *adj* moqueur(euse), railleur(euse).

derisory [dɪ'raɪsərɪ] *adj* (*sum*) dérisoire; (*smile, person*) moqueur(euse), railleur(euse).

derivation [dɛrɪ'veɪʃən] *n* dérivation *f*.

derivative [dɪ'rɪvətɪv] *n* dérivé *m* ♦ *adj* dérivé(e).

derive [dɪ'raɪv] *vt*: **to** ~ **sth from** tirer qch de; trouver qch dans ♦ *vi*: **to** ~ **from** provenir de, dériver de.

dermatitis [dəːmə'taɪtɪs] *n* dermatite *f*.

dermatology [dəːmə'tɔlədʒɪ] *n* dermatologie

f.

derogatory [dɪ'rɔgətərɪ] *adj* désobligeant(e); péjoratif(ive).

derrick ['dɛrɪk] *n* mât *m* de charge; derrick *m*.

derv [dəːv] *n (BRIT)* gas-oil *m*, diesel *m*.

DES *n abbr (BRIT: = Department of Education and Science)* ministère *de l'éducation nationale et des sciences.*

desalination [diːsælɪ'neɪʃən] *n* dessalement *m*, dessalage *m*.

descend [dɪ'sɛnd] *vt, vi* descendre; **to ~ from** descendre de, être issu(e) de; **in ~ing order of importance** par ordre d'importance décroissante.

▶**descend on** *vt fus (subj: enemy, angry person)* tomber *or* sauter sur; *(: misfortune)* s'abattre sur; *(: gloom, silence)* envahir; **visitors ~ed (up)on us** des gens sont arrivés chez nous à l'improviste.

descendant [dɪ'sɛndənt] *n* descendant/e.

descent [dɪ'sɛnt] *n* descente *f; (origin)* origine *f.*

describe [dɪs'kraɪb] *vt* décrire.

description [dɪs'krɪpʃən] *n* description *f; (sort)* sorte *f,* espèce *f;* **of every ~** de toutes sortes.

descriptive [dɪs'krɪptɪv] *adj* descriptif(ive).

desecrate ['dɛsɪkreɪt] *vt* profaner.

desert *n* ['dɛzət] désert *m* ♦ *vb* [dɪ'zəːt] *vt* déserter, abandonner ♦ *vi (MIL)* déserter.

deserter [dɪ'zəːtə*] *n* déserteur *m.*

desertion [dɪ'zəːʃən] *n* désertion *f.*

desert island *n* île déserte.

deserts [dɪ'zəːts] *npl:* **to get one's just ~** n'avoir que ce qu'on mérite.

deserve [dɪ'zəːv] *vt* mériter.

deservedly [dɪ'zəːvɪdlɪ] *adv* à juste titre, à bon droit.

deserving [dɪ'zəːvɪŋ] *adj (person)* méritant(e); *(action, cause)* méritoire.

desiccated ['dɛsɪkeɪtɪd] *adj* séché(e).

design [dɪ'zaɪn] *n (sketch)* plan *m*, dessin *m; (layout, shape)* conception *f,* ligne *f; (pattern)* dessin, motif(s) *m(pl); (of dress, car)* modèle *m; (art)* design *m*, stylisme *m; (intention)* dessein *m* ♦ *vt* dessiner; *(plan)* concevoir; **to have ~s on** avoir des visées sur; **well-~ed** *adj* bien conçu(e); **industrial ~** esthétique industrielle.

designate *vt* ['dɛzɪgneɪt] désigner ♦ *adj* ['dɛzɪgnɪt] désigné(e).

designation [dɛzɪg'neɪʃən] *n* désignation *f.*

designer [dɪ'zaɪnə*] *n (ARCHIT, ART)* dessinateur/trice; *(INDUSTRY)* concepteur *m*, designer *m; (FASHION)* modéliste *m/f.*

desirability [dɪzaɪərə'bɪlɪtɪ] *n* avantage *m*; attrait *m.*

desirable [dɪ'zaɪərəbl] *adj* désirable; **it is ~ that** il est souhaitable que.

desire [dɪ'zaɪə*] *n* désir *m* ♦ *vt* désirer, vouloir; **to ~ to do sth/that** désirer faire qch/que.

desirous [dɪ'zaɪərəs] *adj:* **~ of** désireux(euse) de.

desk [dɛsk] *n (in office)* bureau *m; (for pupil)* pupitre *m; (BRIT: in shop, restaurant)* caisse *f; (in hotel, at airport)* réception *f.*

desktop computer ['dɛsktɔp-] *n* ordinateur *m* de bureau *or* de table.

desktop publishing ['dɛsktɔp-] *n* publication assistée par ordinateur, PAO *f.*

desolate ['dɛsəlɪt] *adj* désolé(e).

desolation [dɛsə'leɪʃən] *n* désolation *f.*

despair [dɪs'pɛə*] *n* désespoir *m* ♦ *vi:* **to ~ of** désespérer de; **to be in ~** être au désespoir.

despatch [dɪs'pætʃ] *n, vt =* **dispatch**.

desperate ['dɛspərɪt] *adj* désespéré(e); *(fugitive)* prêt(e) à tout; *(measures)* désespéré, extrême; **we are getting ~** nous commençons à désespérer.

desperately ['dɛspərɪtlɪ] *adv* désespérément; *(very)* terriblement, extrêmement; **~ ill** très gravement malade.

desperation [dɛspə'reɪʃən] *n* désespoir *m*; **in ~** en désespoir de cause.

despicable [dɪs'pɪkəbl] *adj* méprisable.

despise [dɪs'paɪz] *vt* mépriser, dédaigner.

despite [dɪs'paɪt] *prep* malgré, en dépit de.

despondent [dɪs'pɔndənt] *adj* découragé(e), abattu(e).

despot ['dɛspɔt] *n* despote *m/f.*

dessert [dɪ'zəːt] *n* dessert *m.*

dessertspoon [dɪ'zəːtspuːn] *n* cuiller *f* à dessert.

destabilize [diː'steɪbɪlaɪz] *vt* déstabiliser.

destination [dɛstɪ'neɪʃən] *n* destination *f.*

destine ['dɛstɪn] *vt* destiner.

destined ['dɛstɪnd] *adj:* **to be ~ to do sth** être destiné(e) à faire qch; **~ for London** à destination de Londres.

destiny ['dɛstɪnɪ] *n* destinée *f*, destin *m.*

destitute ['dɛstɪtjuːt] *adj* indigent(e), dans le dénuement; **~ of** dépourvu(e) *or* dénué(e) de.

destroy [dɪs'trɔɪ] *vt* détruire.

destroyer [dɪs'trɔɪə*] *n (NAUT)* contre-torpilleur *m.*

destruction [dɪs'trʌkʃən] *n* destruction *f.*

destructive [dɪs'trʌktɪv] *adj* destructeur(trice).

desultory ['dɛsəltərɪ] *adj (reading, conversation)* décousu(e); *(contact)* irrégulier(ière).

detach [dɪ'tætʃ] *vt* détacher.

detachable [dɪ'tætʃəbl] *adj* amovible, détachable.

detached [dɪ'tætʃt] *adj (attitude)* détaché(e).

detached house *n* pavillon *m*, maison(nette) (individuelle).

detachment [dɪ'tætʃmənt] *n (MIL)* détachement *m; (fig)* détachement, indifférence *f.*

detail ['diːteɪl] *n* détail *m; (MIL)* détachement *m* ♦ *vt* raconter en détail, énumérer; *(MIL):* **to ~ sb (for)** affecter qn (à), détacher qn (pour); **in ~** en détail; **to go into ~(s)** entrer dans les détails.

detailed ['diːteɪld] *adj* détaillé(e).

detain [dɪ'teɪn] *vt* retenir; (*in captivity*) détenir; (*in hospital*) hospitaliser.

detainee [di:teɪ'ni:] *n* détenu/e.

detect [dɪ'tɛkt] *vt* déceler, percevoir; (*MED, POLICE*) dépister; (*MIL, RADAR, TECH*) détecter.

detection [dɪ'tɛkʃən] *n* découverte *f*; (*MED, POLICE*) dépistage *m*; (*MIL, RADAR, TECH*) détection *f*; **to escape** ~ échapper aux recherches, éviter d'être découvert(e); (*mistake*) passer inaperçu(e); **crime** ~ le dépistage des criminels.

detective [dɪ'tɛktɪv] *n* agent *m* de la sûreté, policier *m*; **private** ~ détective privé.

detective story *n* roman policier.

detector [dɪ'tɛktə*] *n* détecteur *m*.

détente [deɪ'tɑːnt] *n* détente *f*.

detention [dɪ'tɛnʃən] *n* détention *f*; (*SCOL*) retenue *f*, consigne *f*.

deter [dɪ'tə:*] *vt* dissuader.

detergent [dɪ'tə:dʒənt] *n* détersif *m*, détergent *m*.

deteriorate [dɪ'tɪərɪəreɪt] *vi* se détériorer, se dégrader.

deterioration [dɪtɪərɪə'reɪʃən] *n* détérioration *f*.

determination [dɪtə:mɪ'neɪʃən] *n* détermination *f*.

determine [dɪ'tə:mɪn] *vt* déterminer; **to** ~ **to do** résoudre de faire, se déterminer à faire.

determined [dɪ'tə:mɪnd] *adj* (*person*) déterminé(e), décidé(e); (*quantity*) déterminé, établi(e); (*effort*) très gros(se).

deterrence [dɪ'tɛrns] *n* dissuasion *f*.

deterrent [dɪ'tɛrənt] *n* effet *m* de dissuasion; **force** *f* de dissuasion; **to act as a** ~ avoir un effet dissuasif.

detest [dɪ'tɛst] *vt* détester, avoir horreur de.

detestable [dɪ'tɛstəbl] *adj* détestable, odieux(euse).

detonate ['dɛtəneɪt] *vi* exploser ♦ *vt* faire exploser *or* détoner.

detonator ['dɛtəneɪtə*] *n* détonateur *m*.

detour ['di:tuə*] *n* détour *m*; (*US AUT: diversion*) déviation *f*.

detract [dɪ'trækt] *vt*: **to** ~ **from** (*quality, pleasure*) diminuer; (*reputation*) porter atteinte à.

detractor [dɪ'træktə*] *n* détracteur/trice.

detriment [dɪ'trɪmənt] *n*: **to the** ~ **of** au détriment de, au préjudice de; **without** ~ **to** sans porter atteinte *or* préjudice à, sans conséquences fâcheuses pour.

detrimental [dɛtrɪ'mɛntl] *adj*: ~ **to** préjudiciable *or* nuisible à.

deuce [dju:s] *n* (*TENNIS*) égalité *f*.

devaluation [dɪvælju'eɪʃən] *n* dévaluation *f*.

devalue ['di:'vælju:] *vt* dévaluer.

devastate ['dɛvəsteɪt] *vt* dévaster; **he was** ~**d by the news** cette nouvelle lui a porté un coup terrible.

devastating ['dɛvəsteɪtɪŋ] *adj* dévasta-

teur(trice).

devastation [dɛvəs'teɪʃən] *n* dévastation *f*.

develop [dɪ'vɛləp] *vt* (*gen*) développer; (*habit*) contracter; (*resources*) mettre en valeur, exploiter; (*land*) aménager ♦ *vi* se développer; (*situation, disease: evolve*) évoluer; (*facts, symptoms: appear*) se manifester, se produire; **to** ~ **a taste for sth** prendre goût à qch; **to** ~ **into** devenir.

developer [dɪ'vɛləpə*] *n* (*PHOT*) révélateur *m*; (*of land*) promoteur *m*; (*also*: **property** ~) promoteur immobilier.

developing country [dɪ'vɛləpɪŋ-] *n* pays *m* en voie de développement.

development [dɪ'vɛləpmənt] *n* développement *m*; (*of affair, case*) rebondissement *m*, fait(s) nouveau(x).

development area *n* zone *f* à urbaniser.

deviate ['di:vɪeɪt] *vi*: **to** ~ **(from)** dévier (de).

deviation [di:vɪ'eɪʃən] *n* déviation *f*.

device [dɪ'vaɪs] *n* (*scheme*) moyen *m*, expédient *m*; (*apparatus*) engin *m*, dispositif *m*; **explosive** ~ engin explosif.

devil ['dɛvl] *n* diable *m*; démon *m*.

devilish ['dɛvlɪʃ] *adj* diabolique.

devil-may-care ['dɛvlmeɪ'kɛə*] *adj* je-m'en-foutiste.

devil's advocate *n*: **to play** ~ se faire avocat du diable.

devious ['di:vɪəs] *adj* (*means*) détourné(e); (*person*) sournois(e), dissimulé(e).

devise [dɪ'vaɪz] *vt* imaginer, concevoir.

devoid [dɪ'vɔɪd] *adj*: ~ **of** dépourvu(e) de, dénué(e) de.

devolution [di:və'lu:ʃən] *n* (*POL*) décentralisation *f*.

devolve [dɪ'vɔlv] *vi*: **to** ~ **(up)on** retomber sur.

devote [dɪ'vəut] *vt*: **to** ~ **sth to** consacrer qch à.

devoted [dɪ'vəutɪd] *adj* dévoué(e); **to be** ~ **to** être dévoué(e) *or* très attaché(e) à; (*subj: book etc*) être consacré(e) à.

devotee [dɛvəu'ti:] *n* (*REL*) adepte *m/f*; (*MUS, SPORT*) fervent/e.

devotion [dɪ'vəuʃən] *n* dévouement *m*, attachement *m*; (*REL*) dévotion *f*, piété *f*.

devour [dɪ'vauə*] *vt* dévorer.

devout [dɪ'vaut] *adj* pieux(euse), dévot(e).

dew [dju:] *n* rosée *f*.

dexterity [dɛks'tɛrɪtɪ] *n* dextérité *f*, adresse *f*.

dext(e)rous ['dɛkstrəs] *adj* adroit(e).

dg *abbr* (= *decigram*) dg.

diabetes [daɪə'bi:ti:z] *n* diabète *m*.

diabetic [daɪə'bɛtɪk] *n* diabétique *m/f* ♦ *adj* (*person*) diabétique; (*chocolate, jam*) pour diabétiques.

diabolical [daɪə'bɔlɪkl] *adj* diabolique; (*col: dreadful*) infernal(e), atroce.

diaeresis [daɪ'ɛrɪsɪs] *n* tréma *m*.

diagnose [daɪəg'nəuz] *vt* diagnostiquer.

diagnosis, *pl* **diagnoses** [daɪəg'nəusɪs, -si:z]

diagnostic *m*.

diagonal [daɪˈægənl] *adj* diagonal(e) ♦ *n* diagonale *f*.

diagram ['daɪəgræm] *n* diagramme *m*, schéma *m*.

dial ['daɪəl] *n* cadran *m* ♦ *vt* (*number*) faire, composer; **to ~ a wrong number** faire un faux numéro; **can I ~ London direct?** puis-je *or* est-ce-que je peux avoir Londres par l'automatique?

dial. *abbr* = **dialect**.

dialect ['daɪəlɛkt] *n* dialecte *m*.

dialling code ['daɪəlɪŋ-] *n* indicatif *m* (téléphonique).

dialling tone ['daɪəlɪŋ-], (*US*) **dial tone** *n* tonalité *f*.

dialogue ['daɪəlɔg] *n* dialogue *m*.

dialysis [daɪˈælɪsɪs] *n* dialyse *f*.

diameter [daɪˈæmɪtə*] *n* diamètre *m*.

diametrically [daɪəˈmɛtrɪklɪ] *adv*: **~ opposed (to)** diamétralement opposé(e) (à).

diamond ['daɪəmənd] *n* diamant *m*; (*shape*) losange *m*; **~s** *npl* (*CARDS*) carreau *m*.

diamond ring *n* bague *f* de diamant(s).

diaper ['daɪəpə*] *n* (*US*) couche *f*.

diaphragm ['daɪəfræm] *n* diaphragme *m*.

diarrhoea, (*US*) **diarrhea** [daɪəˈriːə] *n* diarrhée *f*.

diary ['daɪərɪ] *n* (*daily account*) journal *m*; (*book*) agenda *m*; **to keep a ~** tenir un journal.

diatribe ['daɪətraɪb] *n* diatribe *f*.

dice [daɪs] *n* (*pl inv*) dé *m* ♦ *vt* (*CULIN*) couper en dés *or* en cubes.

dicey ['daɪsɪ] *adj* (*col*): **it's a bit ~** c'est un peu risqué.

dichotomy [daɪˈkɔtəmɪ] *n* dichotomie *f*.

dickhead ['dɪkhɛd] *n* (*BRIT col!*) tête *f* de nœud (*!*).

Dictaphone ['dɪktəfəʊn] *n* ® Dictaphone *m* ®.

dictate *vt* [dɪkˈteɪt] dicter ♦ *vi*: **to ~ to** (*person*) imposer sa volonté à, régenter; **I won't be ~d to** je n'ai d'ordres à recevoir de personne ♦ *n* ['dɪkteɪt] injonction *f*.

dictation [dɪkˈteɪʃən] *n* dictée *f*; **at ~ speed** à une vitesse de dictée.

dictator [dɪkˈteɪtə*] *n* dictateur *m*.

dictatorship [dɪkˈteɪtəʃɪp] *n* dictature *f*.

diction ['dɪkʃən] *n* diction *f*, élocution *f*.

dictionary ['dɪkʃənrɪ] *n* dictionnaire *m*.

did [dɪd] *pt of* **do**.

didactic [daɪˈdæktɪk] *adj* didactique.

didn't ['dɪdnt] = **did not**.

die [daɪ] *n* (*pl*: **dice**) dé *m*; (*pl*: **dies**) coin *m*; matrice *f*; étampe *f* ♦ *vi*: **to ~ (of** *or* **from)** mourir (de); **to be dying** être mourant(e); **to be dying for sth** avoir une envie folle de qch; **to be dying to do sth** mourir d'envie de faire qch.

▶**die away** *vi* s'éteindre.

▶**die down** *vi* se calmer, s'apaiser.

▶**die out** *vi* disparaître, s'éteindre.

diehard ['daɪhɑːd] *n* réactionnaire *m/f*, jusqu'au-boutiste *m/f*.

diesel ['diːzl] *n* diesel *m*.

diesel engine *n* moteur *m* diesel.

diesel fuel, diesel oil *n* carburant *m* diesel.

diet ['daɪət] *n* alimentation *f*; (*restricted food*) régime *m* ♦ *vi* (*also:* **be on a ~**) suivre un régime; **to live on a ~ of** se nourrir de.

dietician [daɪəˈtɪʃən] *n* diététicien/ne.

differ ['dɪfə*] *vi*: **to ~ from sth** être différent(e) de; différer de; **to ~ from sb over sth** ne pas être d'accord avec qn au sujet de qch.

difference ['dɪfrəns] *n* différence *f*; (*quarrel*) différend *m*, désaccord *m*; **it makes no ~ to me** cela m'est égal, cela m'est indifférent; **to settle one's ~s** résoudre la situation.

different ['dɪfrənt] *adj* différent(e).

differential [dɪfəˈrɛnʃəl] *n* (*AUT, wages*) différentiel *m*.

differentiate [dɪfəˈrɛnʃɪeɪt] *vt* différencier ♦ *vi* se différencier; **to ~ between** faire une différence entre.

differently ['dɪfrəntlɪ] *adv* différemment.

difficult ['dɪfɪkəlt] *adj* difficile; **~ to understand** difficile à comprendre.

difficulty ['dɪfɪkəltɪ] *n* difficulté *f*; **to have difficulties with** avoir des ennuis *or* problèmes avec; **to be in ~** avoir des difficultés, avoir des problèmes.

diffidence ['dɪfɪdəns] *n* manque *m* de confiance en soi, manque d'assurance.

diffident ['dɪfɪdənt] *adj* qui manque de confiance *or* d'assurance, peu sûr(e) de soi.

diffuse *adj* [dɪˈfjuːs] diffus(e) ♦ *vt* [dɪˈfjuːz] diffuser, répandre.

dig [dɪg] *vt* (*pt, pp* **dug**) (*hole*) creuser; (*garden*) bêcher ♦ *n* (*prod*) coup *m* de coude; (*fig*) coup de griffe *or* de patte; (*ARCHAEOLOGY*) fouille *f*; **to ~ into** (*snow, soil*) creuser; **to ~ into one's pockets for sth** fouiller dans ses poches pour chercher *or* prendre qch; **to ~ one's nails into** enfoncer ses ongles dans.

▶**dig in** *vi* (*also:* **~ o.s. in:** *MIL*) se retrancher; (*: fig*) tenir bon, se braquer; (*col: eat*) attaquer (un repas *or* un plat *etc*) ♦ *vt* (*compost*) bien mélanger à la bêche; (*knife, claw*) enfoncer; **to ~ in one's heels** (*fig*) se braquer, se buter.

▶**dig out** *vt* (*survivors, car from snow*) sortir *or* dégager (à coups de pelles *or* pioches).

▶**dig up** *vt* déterrer.

digest *vt* [daɪˈdʒɛst] digérer ♦ *n* ['daɪdʒɛst] sommaire *m*, résumé *m*.

digestible [dɪˈdʒɛstəbl] *adj* digestible.

digestion [dɪˈdʒɛstʃən] *n* digestion *f*.

digestive [dɪˈdʒɛstɪv] *adj* digestif(ive).

digit ['dɪdʒɪt] *n* chiffre *m* (*de 0 à 9*); (*finger*) doigt *m*.

digital ['dɪdʒɪtl] *adj* digital(e); (*watch*) à affichage numérique *or* digital.

digital compact cassette _n_ cassette _f_ numérique.
dignified ['dɪgnɪfaɪd] _adj_ digne.
dignitary ['dɪgnɪtərɪ] _n_ dignitaire _m_.
dignity ['dɪgnɪtɪ] _n_ dignité _f_.
digress [daɪ'grɛs] _vi_: **to ~ from** s'écarter de, s'éloigner de.
digression [daɪ'grɛʃən] _n_ digression _f_.
digs [dɪgz] _npl_ (_BRIT col_) piaule _f_, chambre meublée.
dilapidated [dɪ'læpɪdeɪtɪd] _adj_ délabré(e).
dilate [daɪ'leɪt] _vt_ dilater ♦ _vi_ se dilater.
dilatory ['dɪlətərɪ] _adj_ dilatoire.
dilemma [daɪ'lɛmə] _n_ dilemme _m_; **to be in a ~** être pris dans un dilemme.
diligent ['dɪlɪdʒənt] _adj_ appliqué(e), assidu(e).
dill [dɪl] _n_ aneth _m_.
dilly-dally ['dɪlɪ'dælɪ] _vi_ hésiter, tergiverser; traînasser, lambiner.
dilute [daɪ'luːt] _vt_ diluer ♦ _adj_ dilué(e).
dim [dɪm] _adj_ (_light, eyesight_) faible; (_memory, outline_) vague, indécis(e); (_stupid_) borné(e), obtus(e) ♦ _vt_ (_light_) réduire, baisser; (_US AUT_) mettre en code, baisser; **to take a ~ view of sth** voir qch d'un mauvais œil.
dime [daɪm] _n_ (_US_) = 10 cents.
dimension [daɪ'mɛnʃən] _n_ dimension _f_.
-dimensional [dɪ'mɛnʃənl] _adj suffix_: **two~** à deux dimensions.
diminish [dɪ'mɪnɪʃ] _vt, vi_ diminuer.
diminished [dɪ'mɪnɪʃt] _adj_: **~ responsibility** (_LAW_) responsabilité atténuée.
diminutive [dɪ'mɪnjutɪv] _adj_ minuscule, tout(e) petit(e) ♦ _n_ (_LING_) diminutif _m_.
dimly ['dɪmlɪ] _adv_ faiblement; vaguement.
dimmer ['dɪmə*] _n_ (_also_: **~ switch**) variateur _m_; **~s** _npl_ (_US AUT_: dipped headlights) phares _mpl_ code _inv_; (: _parking lights_) feux _mpl_ de position.
dimple ['dɪmpl] _n_ fossette _f_.
dim-witted ['dɪm'wɪtɪd] _adj_ (_col_) stupide, borné(e).
din [dɪn] _n_ vacarme _m_ ♦ _vt_: **to ~ sth into sb** (_col_) enfoncer qch dans la tête _or_ la caboche de qn.
dine [daɪn] _vi_ dîner.
diner ['daɪnə*] _n_ (_person_) dîneur/euse; (_RAIL_) = **dining car**; (_US: eating place_) petit restaurant.
dinghy ['dɪŋgɪ] _n_ youyou _m_; (_inflatable_) canot _m_ pneumatique; (_also_: **sailing ~**) voilier _m_, dériveur _m_.
dingy ['dɪndʒɪ] _adj_ miteux(euse), minable.
dining car ['daɪnɪŋ-] _n_ voiture-restaurant _f_, wagon-restaurant _m_.
dining room ['daɪnɪŋ-] _n_ salle _f_ à manger.
dinner ['dɪnə*] _n_ dîner _m_; (_public_) banquet _m_; **~'s ready!** à table!
dinner jacket _n_ smoking _m_.
dinner party _n_ dîner _m_.
dinner time _n_ heure _f_ du dîner.
dinosaur ['daɪnəsɔ:*] _n_ dinosaure _m_.
dint [dɪnt] _n_: **by ~ of (doing) sth** à force de

(faire) qch.
diocese ['daɪəsɪs] _n_ diocèse _m_.
dioxide [daɪ'ɔksaɪd] _n_ dioxyde _m_.
Dip. _abbr_ (_BRIT_) = **diploma**.
dip [dɪp] _n_ déclivité _f_; (_in sea_) baignade _f_, bain _m_ ♦ _vt_ tremper, plonger; (_BRIT AUT_: lights) mettre en code, baisser ♦ _vi_ plonger.
diphtheria [dɪf'θɪərɪə] _n_ diphtérie _f_.
diphthong ['dɪfθɔŋ] _n_ diphtongue _f_.
diploma [dɪ'pləumə] _n_ diplôme _m_.
diplomacy [dɪ'pləuməsɪ] _n_ diplomatie _f_.
diplomat ['dɪpləmæt] _n_ diplomate _m_.
diplomatic [dɪplə'mætɪk] _adj_ diplomatique; **to break off ~ relations (with)** rompre les relations diplomatiques (avec).
diplomatic corps _n_ corps _m_ diplomatique.
diplomatic immunity _n_ immunité _f_ diplomatique.
dipstick ['dɪpstɪk] _n_ (_AUT_) jauge _f_ de niveau d'huile.
dipswitch ['dɪpswɪtʃ] _n_ (_BRIT AUT_) commutateur _m_ de code.
dire [daɪə*] _adj_ extrême, affreux(euse).
direct [daɪ'rɛkt] _adj_ direct(e); (_manner, person_) direct, franc(franche) ♦ _vt_ diriger, orienter; **can you ~ me to ...?** pouvez-vous m'indiquer le chemin de ...?; **to ~ sb to do sth** ordonner à qn de faire qch.
direct cost _n_ (_COMM_) coût _m_ variable.
direct current _n_ (_ELEC_) courant continu.
direct debit _n_ (_BANKING_) prélèvement _m_ automatique.
direct dialling _n_ (_TEL_) automatique _m_.
direct hit _n_ (_MIL_) coup _m_ au but, touché _m_.
direction [dɪ'rɛkʃən] _n_ direction _f_; (_THEAT_) mise _f_ en scène; (_CINE, TV_) réalisation _f_; **~s** _npl_ (_instructions: to a place_) indications _fpl_; **~s for use** mode _m_ d'emploi; **to ask for ~s** demander sa route _or_ son chemin; **sense of ~** sens _m_ de l'orientation; **in the ~ of** dans la direction de, vers.
directive [dɪ'rɛktɪv] _n_ directive _f_; **a government ~** une directive du gouvernement.
direct labour _n_ main-d'œuvre directe; employés municipaux.
directly [dɪ'rɛktlɪ] _adv_ (_in straight line_) directement, tout droit; (_at once_) tout de suite, immédiatement.
direct mail _n_ vente _f_ par publicité directe.
direct mailshot _n_ (_BRIT_) publicité postale.
directness [daɪ'rɛktnɪs] _n_ (_of person, speech_) franchise _f_.
director [dɪ'rɛktə*] _n_ directeur _m_; (_board member_) administrateur _m_; (_THEAT_) metteur _m_ en scène; (_CINE, TV_) réalisateur/trice; **D~ of Public Prosecutions** (_BRIT_) ≈ procureur général.
directory [dɪ'rɛktərɪ] _n_ annuaire _m_; (_also_: **street ~**) indicateur _m_ de rues; (_also_: **trade ~**) annuaire du commerce; (_COMPUT_) répertoire _m_.
directory enquiries, (_US_) **directory assis-**

tance n (TEL: service) renseignements mpl.

dirt [dɔːt] n saleté f; (mud) boue f; **to treat sb like** ~ traiter qn comme un chien.

dirt-cheap ['dɔːt'tʃiːp] adj (ne) coûtant presque rien.

dirt road n chemin non macadamisé or non revêtu.

dirty ['dɔːtɪ] adj sale ♦ vt salir; ~ **story** histoire cochonne; ~ **trick** coup tordu.

disability [dɪsə'bɪlɪtɪ] n invalidité f, infirmité f.

disability allowance n allocation f d'invalidité or d'infirmité.

disable [dɪs'eɪbl] vt (subj: illness, accident) rendre or laisser infirme; (tank, gun) mettre hors d'action.

disabled [dɪs'eɪbld] adj infirme, invalide; (maimed) mutilé(e); (through illness, old age) impotent(e).

disadvantage [dɪsəd'vɑːntɪdʒ] n désavantage m, inconvénient m.

disadvantaged [dɪsəd'vɑːntɪdʒd] adj (person) désavantagé(e).

disadvantageous [dɪsædvɑːn'teɪdʒəs] adj désavantageux(euse).

disaffected [dɪsə'fɛktɪd] adj: ~ **(to or towards)** mécontent(e) (de).

disaffection [dɪsə'fɛkʃən] n désaffection f, mécontentement m.

disagree [dɪsə'griː] vi (differ) ne pas concorder; (be against, think otherwise): **to** ~ **(with)** ne pas être d'accord (avec); **garlic** ~**s with me** l'ail ne me convient pas, je ne supporte pas l'ail.

disagreeable [dɪsə'griːəbl] adj désagréable.

disagreement [dɪsə'griːmənt] n désaccord m, différend m.

disallow ['dɪsə'lau] vt rejeter, désavouer; (BRIT FOOTBALL: goal) refuser.

disappear [dɪsə'pɪə*] vi disparaître.

disappearance [dɪsə'pɪərəns] n disparition f.

disappoint [dɪsə'pɔɪnt] vt décevoir.

disappointed [dɪsə'pɔɪntɪd] adj déçu(e).

disappointing [dɪsə'pɔɪntɪŋ] adj décevant(e).

disappointment [dɪsə'pɔɪntmənt] n déception f.

disapproval [dɪsə'pruːvəl] n désapprobation f.

disapprove [dɪsə'pruːv] vi: **to** ~ **of** désapprouver.

disapproving [dɪsə'pruːvɪŋ] adj désapprobateur(trice), de désapprobation.

disarm [dɪs'ɑːm] vt désarmer.

disarmament [dɪs'ɑːməmənt] n désarmement m.

disarming [dɪs'ɑːmɪŋ] adj (smile) désarmant(e).

disarray [dɪsə'reɪ] n désordre m, confusion f; **in** ~ (troops) en déroute; (thoughts) embrouillé(e); (clothes) en désordre; **to throw into** ~ semer la confusion or le désordre dans (or parmi).

disaster [dɪ'zɑːstə*] n catastrophe f, désastre m.

disastrous [dɪ'zɑːstrəs] adj désastreux(euse).

disband [dɪs'bænd] vt démobiliser; disperser ♦ vi se séparer; se disperser.

disbelief ['dɪsbə'liːf] n incrédulité f; **in** ~ avec incrédulité.

disbelieve ['dɪsbə'liːv] vt (person) ne pas croire; (story) mettre en doute; **I don't** ~ **you** je veux bien vous croire.

disc [dɪsk] n disque m.

disc. abbr (COMM) = **discount.**

discard [dɪs'kɑːd] vt (old things) se défaire de, mettre au rencart or au rebut; (fig) écarter, renoncer à.

disc brake n frein m à disque.

discern [dɪ'sɜːn] vt discerner, distinguer.

discernible [dɪ'sɜːnəbl] adj discernable, perceptible; (object) visible.

discerning [dɪ'sɜːnɪŋ] adj judicieux(euse), perspicace.

discharge vt [dɪs'tʃɑːdʒ] (duties) s'acquitter de; (settle: debt) s'acquitter de, régler; (waste etc) déverser; décharger; (ELEC, MED) émettre; (patient) renvoyer (chez lui); (employee, soldier) congédier, licencier; (defendant) relaxer, élargir ♦ n [ˈdɪstʃɑːdʒ] (ELEC, MED etc) émission f; (also: **vaginal** ~) pertes blanches; (dismissal) renvoi m; licenciement m; élargissement m; **to** ~ **one's gun** faire feu; ~**d bankrupt** failli/e réhabilité(e).

disciple [dɪ'saɪpl] n disciple m.

disciplinary ['dɪsɪplɪnərɪ] adj disciplinaire; **to take** ~ **action against sb** prendre des mesures disciplinaires à l'encontre de qn.

discipline ['dɪsɪplɪn] n discipline f ♦ vt discipliner; (punish) punir; **to** ~ **o.s. to do sth** s'imposer or s'astreindre à une discipline pour faire qch.

disc jockey (DJ) n disque-jockey m (DJ).

disclaim [dɪs'kleɪm] vt désavouer, dénier.

disclaimer [dɪs'kleɪmə*] n démenti m, dénégation f; **to issue a** ~ publier un démenti.

disclose [dɪs'kləuz] vt révéler, divulguer.

disclosure [dɪs'kləuʒə*] n révélation f, divulgation f.

disco ['dɪskəu] n abbr = **discothèque.**

discolour, (US) **discolor** [dɪs'kʌlə*] vt décolorer; (sth white) jaunir ♦ vi se décolorer; jaunir.

discolo(u)ration [dɪskʌlə'reɪʃən] n décoloration f; jaunissement m.

discolo(u)red [dɪs'kʌləd] adj décoloré(e); jauni(e).

discomfort [dɪs'kʌmfət] n malaise m, gêne f; (lack of comfort) manque m de confort.

disconcert [dɪskən'sɜːt] vt déconcerter, décontenancer.

disconnect [dɪskə'nɛkt] vt détacher; (ELEC, RADIO) débrancher; (gas, water) couper.

disconnected [dɪskə'nɛktɪd] adj (speech, thoughts) décousu(e), peu cohérent(e).

disconsolate [dɪs'kɔnsəlɪt] adj inconsolable.

discontent [dɪskən'tɛnt] n mécontentement

m.

discontented [dɪskən'tɛntɪd] *adj* mécontent(e).

discontinue [dɪskən'tɪnjuː] *vt* cesser, interrompre; "~d" (*COMM*) "fin de série".

discord ['dɪskɔːd] *n* discorde *f*, dissension *f*; (*MUS*) dissonance *f*.

discordant [dɪs'kɔːdənt] *adj* discordant(e), dissonant(e).

discotheque ['dɪskəutɛk] *n* discothèque *f*.

discount *n* ['dɪskaunt] remise *f*, rabais *m* ♦ *vt* [dɪs'kaunt] (*report etc*) ne pas tenir compte de; **to give sb a ~ on sth** faire une remise *or* un rabais à qn sur qch; **~ for cash** escompte *f* au comptant; **at a ~** avec une remise *or* réduction, au rabais.

discount house *n* (*FINANCE*) banque *f* d'escompte; (*COMM: also*: **discount store**) magasin *m* de discount.

discount rate *n* taux *m* de remise.

discourage [dɪs'kʌrɪdʒ] *vt* décourager; (*dissuade, deter*) dissuader, décourager.

discouragement [dɪs'kʌrɪdʒmənt] *n* (*depression*) découragement *m*; **to act as a ~ to sb** dissuader qn.

discouraging [dɪs'kʌrɪdʒɪŋ] *adj* décourageant(e).

discourteous [dɪs'kəːtɪəs] *adj* incivil(e), discourtois(e).

discover [dɪs'kʌvə*] *vt* découvrir.

discovery [dɪs'kʌvərɪ] *n* découverte *f*.

discredit [dɪs'krɛdɪt] *vt* mettre en doute; discréditer ♦ *n* discrédit *m*.

discreet [dɪ'skriːt] *adj* discret(ète).

discreetly [dɪ'skriːtlɪ] *adv* discrètement.

discrepancy [dɪ'skrɛpənsɪ] *n* divergence *f*, contradiction *f*.

discretion [dɪ'skrɛʃən] *n* discrétion *f*; **use your own ~** à vous de juger.

discretionary [dɪ'skrɛʃənrɪ] *adj* (*powers*) discrétionnaire.

discriminate [dɪ'skrɪmɪneɪt] *vi*: **to ~ between** établir une distinction entre, faire la différence entre; **to ~ against** pratiquer une discrimination contre.

discriminating [dɪ'skrɪmɪneɪtɪŋ] *adj* qui a du discernement.

discrimination [dɪskrɪmɪ'neɪʃən] *n* discrimination *f*; (*judgment*) discernement *m*; **racial/sexual ~** discrimination raciale/sexuelle.

discus ['dɪskəs] *n* disque *m*.

discuss [dɪ'skʌs] *vt* discuter de; (*debate*) discuter.

discussion [dɪ'skʌʃən] *n* discussion *f*; **under ~** en discussion.

disdain [dɪs'deɪn] *n* dédain *m*.

disease [dɪ'ziːz] *n* maladie *f*.

diseased [dɪ'ziːzd] *adj* malade.

disembark [dɪsɪm'bɑːk] *vt, vi* débarquer.

disembarkation [dɪsɛmbɑː'keɪʃən] *n* débarquement *m*.

disembodied ['dɪsɪm'bɔdɪd] *adj* désincar-

né(e).

disembowel ['dɪsɪm'bauəl] *vt* éviscérer, étriper.

disenchanted ['dɪsɪn'tʃɑːntɪd] *adj*: **~ (with)** désenchanté(e) (de), désabusé(e) (de).

disenfranchise ['dɪsɪn'fræntʃaɪz] *vt* priver du droit de vote; (*COMM*) retirer la franchise à.

disengage [dɪsɪn'geɪdʒ] *vt* dégager; (*TECH*) déclencher; **to ~ the clutch** (*AUT*) débrayer.

disentangle [dɪsɪn'tæŋgl] *vt* démêler.

disfavour, (US) disfavor [dɪs'feɪvə*] *n* défaveur *f*; disgrâce *f*.

disfigure [dɪs'fɪgə*] *vt* défigurer.

disgorge [dɪs'gɔːdʒ] *vt* déverser.

disgrace [dɪs'greɪs] *n* honte *f*; (*disfavour*) disgrâce *f* ♦ *vt* déshonorer, couvrir de honte.

disgraceful [dɪs'greɪsful] *adj* scandaleux(euse), honteux(euse).

disgruntled [dɪs'grʌntld] *adj* mécontent(e).

disguise [dɪs'gaɪz] *n* déguisement *m* ♦ *vt* déguiser; (*voice*) déguiser, contrefaire; (*feelings etc*) masquer, dissimuler; **in ~** déguisé(e); **to ~ o.s. as** se déguiser en; **there's no disguising the fact that ...** on ne peut pas se dissimuler que ....

disgust [dɪs'gʌst] *n* dégoût *m*, aversion *f* ♦ *vt* dégoûter, écœurer.

disgusting [dɪs'gʌstɪŋ] *adj* dégoûtant(e), révoltant(e).

dish [dɪʃ] *n* plat *m*; **to do** *or* **wash the ~es** faire la vaisselle.

▶**dish out** *vt* distribuer.

▶**dish up** *vt* servir; (*facts, statistics*) sortir, débiter.

dishcloth ['dɪʃklɔθ] *n* (*for drying*) torchon *m*; (*for washing*) lavette *f*.

dishearten [dɪs'hɑːtn] *vt* décourager.

dishevelled, (US) disheveled [dɪ'ʃɛvəld] *adj* ébouriffé(e); décoiffé(e); débraillé(e).

dishonest [dɪs'ɔnɪst] *adj* malhonnête.

dishonesty [dɪs'ɔnɪstɪ] *n* malhonnêteté *f*.

dishonour, (US) dishonor [dɪs'ɔnə*] *n* déshonneur *m*.

dishono(u)rable [dɪs'ɔnərəbl] *adj* déshonorant(e).

dish soap *n* (*US*) produit *m* pour la vaisselle.

dishtowel ['dɪʃtauəl] *n* torchon *m* (à vaisselle).

dishwasher ['dɪʃwɔʃə*] *n* lave-vaisselle *m*; (*person*) plongeur/euse.

dishy ['dɪʃɪ] *adj* (*BRIT col*) séduisant(e), sexy *inv*.

disillusion [dɪsɪ'luːʒən] *vt* désabuser, désenchanter ♦ *n* désenchantement *m*; **to become ~ed (with)** perdre ses illusions (en ce qui concerne).

disillusionment [dɪsɪ'luːʒənmənt] *n* désillusionnement *m*, désillusion *f*.

disincentive [dɪsɪn'sɛntɪv] *n*: **it's a ~** c'est démotivant; **to be a ~ to sb** démotiver qn.

disinclined ['dɪsɪn'klaɪnd] *adj*: **to be ~ to do sth** être peu disposé(e) *or* peu enclin(e) à faire qch.

disinfect [dısın'fɛkt] vt désinfecter.

disinfectant [dısın'fɛktənt] n désinfectant m.

disinflation [dısın'fleıʃən] n désinflation f.

disinformation [dısınfə'meıʃən] n désinformation f.

disinherit [dısın'hɛrıt] vt déshériter.

disintegrate [dıs'ıntıgreıt] vi se désintégrer.

disinterested [dıs'ıntrəstıd] adj désintéressé(e).

disjointed [dıs'dʒɔıntıd] adj décousu(e), incohérent(e).

disk [dısk] n (COMPUT) disquette f; **single-/double-sided ~** disquette une face/double face.

disk drive n lecteur m de disquette.

diskette [dıs'kɛt] n (COMPUT) disquette f.

disk operating system (DOS) n système m d'exploitation à disques (DOS).

dislike [dıs'laık] n aversion f, antipathie f ♦ vt ne pas aimer; **to take a ~ to sb/sth** prendre qn/qch en grippe; **I ~ the idea** l'idée me déplaît.

dislocate ['dısləkeıt] vt disloquer, déboîter; (services etc) désorganiser; **he has ~d his shoulder** il s'est disloqué l'épaule.

dislodge [dıs'lɔdʒ] vt déplacer, faire bouger; (enemy) déloger.

disloyal [dıs'lɔıəl] adj déloyal(e).

dismal ['dızməl] adj lugubre, maussade.

dismantle [dıs'mæntl] vt démonter; (fort, warship) démanteler.

dismast [dıs'mɑːst] vt démâter.

dismay [dıs'meı] n consternation f ♦ vt consterner; **much to my ~** à ma grande consternation, à ma grande inquiétude.

dismiss [dıs'mıs] vt congédier, renvoyer; (idea) écarter; (LAW) rejeter ♦ vi (MIL) rompre les rangs.

dismissal [dıs'mısl] n renvoi m.

dismount [dıs'maunt] vi mettre pied à terre.

disobedience [dısə'biːdıəns] n désobéissance f.

disobedient [dısə'biːdıənt] adj désobéissant(e), indiscipliné(e).

disobey [dısə'beı] vt désobéir à; (rule) transgresser, enfreindre.

disorder [dıs'ɔːdə*] n désordre m; (rioting) désordres mpl; (MED) troubles mpl.

disorderly [dıs'ɔːdəlı] adj (room) en désordre; (behaviour, retreat, crowd) désordonné(e).

disorderly conduct n (LAW) conduite f contraire aux bonnes mœurs.

disorganized [dıs'ɔːgənaızd] adj désorganisé(e).

disorientated [dıs'ɔːrıɛnteıtıd] adj désorienté(e).

disown [dıs'əun] vt renier.

disparaging [dıs'pærıdʒıŋ] adj désobligeant(e); **to be ~ about sb/sth** faire des remarques désobligeantes sur qn/qch.

disparate ['dıspərıt] adj disparate.

disparity [dıs'pærıtı] n disparité f.

dispassionate [dıs'pæʃənət] adj calme, froid(e); impartial(e), objectif(ive).

dispatch [dıs'pætʃ] vt expédier, envoyer; (deal with: business) régler, en finir avec ♦ n envoi m, expédition f; (MIL, PRESS) dépêche f.

dispatch department n service m des expéditions.

dispatch rider n (MIL) estafette f.

dispel [dıs'pɛl] vt dissiper, chasser.

dispensary [dıs'pɛnsərı] n pharmacie f; (in chemist's) officine f.

dispense [dıs'pɛns] vt distribuer, administrer; (medicine) préparer (et vendre); **to ~ sb from** dispenser qn de.

▶**dispense with** vt fus se passer de; (make unnecessary) rendre superflu(e).

dispenser [dıs'pɛnsə*] n (device) distributeur m.

dispensing chemist [dıs'pɛnsıŋ-] n (BRIT) pharmacie f.

dispersal [dıs'pəːsl] n dispersion f; (ADMIN) déconcentration f.

disperse [dıs'pəːs] vt disperser; (knowledge) disséminer ♦ vi se disperser.

dispirited [dıs'pırıtıd] adj découragé(e), déprimé(e).

displace [dıs'pleıs] vt déplacer.

displaced person [dıs'pleıst-] n (POL) personne déplacée.

displacement [dıs'pleısmənt] n déplacement m.

display [dıs'pleı] n (of goods) étalage m; affichage m; (computer ~: information) visualisation f; (: device) visuel m; (of feeling) manifestation f; (pej) ostentation f; (show, spectacle) spectacle m; (military ~) parade f militaire ♦ vt montrer; (goods) mettre à l'étalage, exposer; (results, departure times) afficher; (pej) faire étalage de; **on ~** (exhibits) exposé(e), exhibé(e); (goods) à l'étalage.

display advertising n publicité rédactionnelle.

displease [dıs'pliːz] vt mécontenter, contrarier; **~d with** mécontent(e) de.

displeasure [dıs'plɛʒə*] n mécontentement m.

disposable [dıs'pəuzəbl] adj (pack etc) jetable; (income) disponible; **~ nappy** (BRIT) couche f à jeter, couche-culotte f.

disposal [dıs'pəuzl] n (availability, arrangement) disposition f; (of property etc: by selling) vente f; (: by giving away) cession f; (of rubbish) évacuation f, destruction f; **at one's ~** à sa disposition; **to put sth at sb's ~** mettre qch à la disposition de qn.

dispose [dıs'pəuz] vt disposer.

▶**dispose of** vt fus (time, money) disposer de; (unwanted goods) se débarrasser de, se défaire de; (COMM: stock) écouler, vendre; (problem) expédier.

disposed [dıs'pəuzd] adj: **~ to do** disposé(e) à faire.

disposition [dɪspəˈzɪʃən] n disposition f; (*temperament*) naturel m.

dispossess [ˈdɪspəˈzɛs] vt: **to ~ sb (of)** déposséder qn (de).

disproportion [dɪsprəˈpɔːʃən] n disproportion f.

disproportionate [dɪsprəˈpɔːʃənət] adj disproportionné(e).

disprove [dɪsˈpruːv] vt réfuter.

dispute [dɪsˈpjuːt] n discussion f; (*also*: **industrial ~**) conflit m ♦ vt contester; (*matter*) discuter; (*victory*) disputer; **to be in** *or* **under ~** (*matter*) être en discussion; (*territory*) être contesté(e).

disqualification [dɪskwɔlɪfɪˈkeɪʃən] n disqualification f; **~ (from driving)** (*BRIT*) retrait m du permis (de conduire).

disqualify [dɪsˈkwɔlɪfaɪ] vt (*SPORT*) disqualifier; **to ~ sb for sth/from doing** (*status, situation*) rendre qn inapte à qch/à faire; (*authority*) signifier à qn l'interdiction de faire; **to ~ sb (from driving)** (*BRIT*) retirer à qn son permis (de conduire).

disquiet [dɪsˈkwaɪət] n inquiétude f, trouble m.

disquieting [dɪsˈkwaɪətɪŋ] adj inquiétant(e), alarmant(e).

disregard [dɪsrɪˈgɑːd] vt ne pas tenir compte de ♦ n (*indifference*): **~ (for)** (*feelings*) indifférence f (pour), insensibilité f (à); (*danger, money*) mépris m (pour).

disrepair [ˈdɪsrɪˈpɛə*] n mauvais état; **to fall into ~** (*building*) tomber en ruine; (*street*) se dégrader.

disreputable [dɪsˈrɛpjutəbl] adj (*person*) de mauvaise réputation, peu recommandable; (*behaviour*) déshonorant(e); (*area*) mal famé(e), louche.

disrepute [ˈdɪsrɪˈpjuːt] n déshonneur m, discrédit m; **to bring into ~** faire tomber dans le discrédit.

disrespectful [dɪsrɪˈspɛktful] adj irrespectueux(euse).

disrupt [dɪsˈrʌpt] vt (*plans, meeting, lesson*) perturber, déranger.

disruption [dɪsˈrʌpʃən] n perturbation f, dérangement m.

disruptive [dɪsˈrʌptɪv] adj perturbateur (trice).

dissatisfaction [dɪssætɪsˈfækʃən] n mécontentement m, insatisfaction f.

dissatisfied [dɪsˈsætɪsfaɪd] adj: **~ (with)** mécontent(e) *or* insatisfait(e) (de).

dissect [dɪˈsɛkt] vt disséquer; (*fig*) disséquer, éplucher.

disseminate [dɪˈsɛmɪneɪt] vt disséminer.

dissent [dɪˈsɛnt] n dissentiment m, différence f d'opinion.

dissenter [dɪˈsɛntə*] n (*REL, POL etc*) dissident/e.

dissertation [dɪsəˈteɪʃən] n (*SCOL*) mémoire m.

disservice [dɪsˈsəːvɪs] n: **to do sb a ~** rendre

un mauvais service à qn; desservir qn.

dissident [ˈdɪsɪdnt] adj, n dissident(e).

dissimilar [dɪˈsɪmɪlə*] adj: **~ (to)** dissemblable (à), différent(e) (de).

dissipate [ˈdɪsɪpeɪt] vt dissiper; (*energy, efforts*) disperser.

dissipated [ˈdɪsɪpeɪtɪd] adj dissolu(e); débauché(e).

dissociate [dɪˈsəuʃɪeɪt] vt dissocier; **to ~ o.s. from** se désolidariser de.

dissolute [ˈdɪsəluːt] adj débauché(e), dissolu(e).

dissolution [dɪsəˈluːʃən] n dissolution f.

dissolve [dɪˈzɔlv] vt dissoudre ♦ vi se dissoudre, fondre; (*fig*) disparaître.

dissuade [dɪˈsweɪd] vt: **to ~ sb (from)** dissuader qn (de).

distaff [ˈdɪstɑːf] n: **~ side** côté maternel.

distance [ˈdɪstns] n distance f; **what's the ~ to London?** à quelle distance se trouve Londres?; **it's within walking ~** on peut y aller à pied; **in the ~** au loin.

distant [ˈdɪstnt] adj lointain(e), éloigné(e); (*manner*) distant(e), froid(e).

distaste [dɪsˈteɪst] n dégoût m.

distasteful [dɪsˈteɪstful] adj déplaisant(e), désagréable.

Dist. Atty. abbr (*US*) = **district attorney**.

distemper [dɪsˈtɛmpə*] n (*paint*) détrempe f, badigeon m; (*of dogs*) maladie f de Carré.

distended [dɪsˈtɛndɪd] adj (*stomach*) dilaté(e).

distil, (*US*) **distill** [dɪsˈtɪl] vt distiller.

distillery [dɪsˈtɪlərɪ] n distillerie f.

distinct [dɪsˈtɪŋkt] adj distinct(e); (*preference, progress*) marqué(e); **as ~ from** par opposition à, en contraste avec.

distinction [dɪsˈtɪŋkʃən] n distinction f; (*in exam*) mention f très bien; **to draw a ~ between** faire une distinction entre; **a writer of ~** un écrivain réputé.

distinctive [dɪsˈtɪŋktɪv] adj distinctif(ive).

distinctly [dɪsˈtɪŋktlɪ] adv distinctement; (*specify*) expressément.

distinguish [dɪsˈtɪŋgwɪʃ] vt distinguer ♦ vi: **to ~ between** (*concepts*) distinguer entre, faire une distinction entre; **to ~ o.s.** se distinguer.

distinguished [dɪsˈtɪŋgwɪʃt] adj (*eminent, refined*) distingué(e); (*career*) remarquable, brillant(e).

distinguishing [dɪsˈtɪŋgwɪʃɪŋ] adj (*feature*) distinctif(ive), caractéristique.

distort [dɪsˈtɔːt] vt déformer.

distortion [dɪsˈtɔːʃən] n déformation f.

distract [dɪsˈtrækt] vt distraire, déranger.

distracted [dɪsˈtræktɪd] adj (*look etc*) éperdu(e), égaré(e).

distraction [dɪsˈtrækʃən] n distraction f, dérangement m; **to drive sb to ~** rendre qn fou(folle).

distraught [dɪsˈtrɔːt] adj éperdu(e).

distress [dɪsˈtrɛs] n détresse f; (*pain*) douleur f

♦ *vt* affliger; **in** ~ (*ship*) en perdition; (*plane*) en détresse; **~ed area** (*BRIT*) zone sinistrée.

distressing [dɪs'tresɪŋ] *adj* douloureux(euse), pénible, affligeant(e).

distress signal *n* signal *m* de détresse.

distribute [dɪs'trɪbju:t] *vt* distribuer.

distribution [dɪstrɪ'bju:ʃən] *n* distribution *f*.

distribution cost *n* coût *m* de distribution.

distributor [dɪs'trɪbjutə*] *n* (*gen*, *TECH*) distributeur *m*; (*COMM*) concessionnaire *m/f*.

district ['dɪstrɪkt] *n* (*of country*) région *f*; (*of town*) quartier *m*; (*ADMIN*) district *m*.

district attorney *n* (*US*) ≈ procureur *m* de la République.

district council *n* (*BRIT*) ≈ conseil municipal.

En Grande-Bretagne, un **district council** est une administration locale qui gère un **district**. Les conseillers ("**councillors**") sont élus au niveau local, en général tous les 4 ans. Le district council est financé par des impôts locaux et par des subventions du gouvernement.

district nurse *n* (*BRIT*) infirmière visiteuse.

distrust [dɪs'trʌst] *n* méfiance *f*, doute *m* ♦ *vt* se méfier de.

distrustful [dɪs'trʌstful] *adj* méfiant(e).

disturb [dɪs'tə:b] *vt* troubler; (*inconvenience*) déranger; **sorry to** ~ **you** excusez-moi de vous déranger.

disturbance [dɪs'tə:bəns] *n* dérangement *m*; (*political etc*) troubles *mpl*; (*by drunks etc*) tapage *m*; **to cause a** ~ troubler l'ordre public; ~ **of the peace** (*LAW*) tapage injurieux *or* nocturne.

disturbed [dɪs'tə:bd] *adj* agité(e), troublé(e); **to be mentally/emotionally** ~ avoir des problèmes psychologiques/affectifs.

disturbing [dɪs'tə:bɪŋ] *adj* troublant(e), inquiétant(e).

disuse [dɪs'ju:s] *n*: **to fall into** ~ tomber en désuétude.

disused [dɪs'ju:zd] *adj* désaffecté(e).

ditch [dɪtʃ] *n* fossé *m* ♦ *vt* (*col*) abandonner.

dither ['dɪðə*] *vi* hésiter.

ditto ['dɪtəu] *adv* idem.

divan [dɪ'væn] *n* divan *m*.

divan bed *n* divan-lit *m*.

dive [daɪv] *n* plongeon *m*; (*of submarine*) plongée *f*; (*AVIAT*) piqué *m*; (*pej: café, bar etc*) bouge *m* ♦ *vi* plonger.

diver ['daɪvə*] *n* plongeur *m*.

diverge [daɪ'və:dʒ] *vi* diverger.

divergent [daɪ'və:dʒənt] *adj* divergent(e).

diverse [daɪ'və:s] *adj* divers(e).

diversification [daɪvə:sɪfɪ'keɪʃən] *n* diversification *f*.

diversify [daɪ'və:sɪfaɪ] *vt* diversifier.

diversion [daɪ'və:ʃən] *n* (*BRIT AUT*) déviation *f*; (*distraction*, *MIL*) diversion *f*.

diversionary tactics [daɪ'və:ʃənrɪ-] *npl* tactique *fsg* de diversion.

diversity [daɪ'və:sɪtɪ] *n* diversité *f*, variété *f*.

divert [daɪ'və:t] *vt* (*BRIT: traffic*) dévier; (*plane*) dérouter; (*train, river*) détourner; (*amuse*) divertir.

divest [daɪ'vest] *vt*: **to** ~ **sb of** dépouiller qn de.

divide [dɪ'vaɪd] *vt* diviser; (*separate*) séparer ♦ *vi* se diviser; **to** ~ (**between** *or* **among**) répartir *or* diviser (entre); **40** ~**d by 5** 40 divisé *or* par 5.

▶**divide out** *vt*: **to** ~ **out (between** *or* **among)** distribuer *or* répartir (entre).

divided [dɪ'vaɪdɪd] *adj* (*fig: country, couple*) désuni(e); (*opinions*) partagé(e).

divided skirt *n* jupe-culotte *f*.

dividend ['dɪvɪdend] *n* dividende *m*.

dividend cover *n* rapport *m* dividendes-résultat.

dividers [dɪ'vaɪdəz] *npl* compas *m* à pointes sèches; (*between pages*) feuillets *mpl* intercalaires.

divine [dɪ'vaɪn] *adj* divin(e) ♦ *vt* (*future*) prédire; (*truth*) deviner, entrevoir; (*water, metal*) détecter la présence de (*par l'intermédiaire de la radiesthésie*).

diving ['daɪvɪŋ] *n* plongée (*sous-marine*).

diving board *n* plongeoir *m*.

diving suit *n* scaphandre *m*.

divinity [dɪ'vɪnɪtɪ] *n* divinité *f*; (*as study*) théologie *f*.

division [dɪ'vɪʒən] *n* (*also BRIT FOOTBALL*) division *f*; (*separation*) séparation *f*; (*BRIT POL*) vote *m*; ~ **of labour** division du travail.

divisive [dɪ'vaɪsɪv] *adj* qui entraîne la division, qui crée des dissensions.

divorce [dɪ'vɔ:s] *n* divorce *m* ♦ *vt* divorcer d'avec.

divorced [dɪ'vɔ:st] *adj* divorcé(e).

divorcee [dɪvɔ:'si:] *n* divorcé/e.

divot ['dɪvət] *n* (*GOLF*) motte *f* de gazon.

divulge [daɪ'vʌldʒ] *vt* divulguer, révéler.

DIY *adj, n abbr* (*BRIT*) = **do-it-yourself**.

dizziness ['dɪzɪnɪs] *n* vertige *m*, étourdissement *m*.

dizzy ['dɪzɪ] *adj* (*height*) vertigineux(euse); **to make sb** ~ donner le vertige à qn; **I feel** ~ la tête me tourne, j'ai la tête qui tourne.

DJ *n abbr* = **disc jockey**.

d.j. *n abbr* = **dinner jacket**.

Djakarta [dʒə'ka:tə] *n* Djakarta.

DJIA *n abbr* (*US STOCK EXCHANGE*) = *Dow-Jones Industrial Average*.

dl *abbr* (= *decilitre*) dl.

DLit(t) *n abbr* (= *Doctor of Literature, Doctor of Letters*) *titre universitaire*.

DLO *n abbr* = **dead-letter office**.

dm *abbr* (= *decimetre*) dm.

DMus *n abbr* (= *Doctor of Music*) *titre universitaire*.

DMZ *n abbr* = **demilitarized zone**.

DNA *n abbr* (= *deoxyribonucleic acid*) ADN *m*.

do *abbr* (= *ditto*) d°.

=============== *KEYWORD*

do [duː] (*pt* **did,** *pp* **done**) *n* (*inf:* party etc) soirée *f*, fête *f*; (*: formal gathering*) réception *f*

♦ *vb* **1** (*in negative constructions*) *non traduit*; **I don't understand** je ne comprends pas

2 (*to form questions*) *non traduit*; **didn't you know?** vous ne le saviez pas?; **why didn't you come?** pourquoi n'êtes-vous pas venu?

3 (*for emphasis, in polite expressions*): **she does seem rather late** je trouve qu'elle est bien en retard; ~ **sit down/help yourself** asseyez-vous/servez-vous je vous en prie; **I DO wish I could go** j'aimerais tant y aller; **but I DO like it!** mais si, je l'aime!

4 (*used to avoid repeating vb*): **she swims better than I** ~ elle nage mieux que moi; ~ **you agree?** — **yes, I** ~**/no, I don't** vous êtes d'accord? — oui/non; **she lives in Glasgow** — **so** ~ **I** elle habite Glasgow — moi aussi; **who broke it?** — **I did** qui l'a cassé? — c'est moi

5 (*in question tags*): **he laughed, didn't he?** il a ri, n'est-ce pas?; **I don't know him,** ~ **I?** je ne crois pas le connaître

♦ *vt* (*gen: carry out, perform etc*) faire; (*visit: city, museum*) faire, visiter; **what are you** ~**ing tonight?** qu'est-ce que vous faites ce soir?; **what did he** ~ **with the cat?** qu'a t'il fait du chat?; **to** ~ **the cooking/washing-up** faire la cuisine/la vaisselle; **to** ~ **one's teeth/hair/nails** se brosser les dents/se coiffer/se faire les ongles; **the car was** ~**ing 100** la voiture faisait du 100 (à l'heure)

♦ *vi* **1** (*act, behave*) faire; ~ **as I** ~ faites comme moi

2 (*get on, fare*) marcher; **the firm is** ~**ing well** l'entreprise marche bien; **how** ~ **you** ~**?** comment allez-vous?; (*on being introduced*) enchanté(e)!

3 (*suit*) aller; **will it** ~**?** est-ce que ça ira?

4 (*be sufficient*) suffire, aller; **will £10** ~**?** est-ce que 10 livres suffiront?; **that'll** ~ ça suffit, ça ira; **that'll** ~**!** (*in annoyance*) ça va *or* suffit comme ça!; **to make** ~ **(with)** se contenter (de)

▶**do away with** *vt fus* abolir; (*kill*) supprimer

▶**do for** *vt fus* (*BRIT col: clean for*) faire le ménage chez

▶**do up** *vt* (*laces, dress*) attacher; (*buttons*) boutonner; (*zip*) fermer; (*renovate: room*) refaire; (*: house*) remettre à neuf; **to** ~ **o.s. up** se faire beau(belle)

▶**do with** *vt fus* (*need*): **I could** ~ **with a drink/some help** quelque chose à boire/un peu d'aide ne serait pas de refus; **it could** ~ **with a wash** ça ne lui ferait pas de mal d'être lavé; (*be connected*): **that has nothing to** ~ **with you** cela ne vous concerne pas; **I won't have anything to** ~ **with it** je ne veux pas m'en mêler; **what has that got to** ~ **with it?** quel est le rapport?, qu'est-ce que cela

vient faire là-dedans?

▶**do without** *vi* s'en passer ♦ *vt fus* se passer de.

─────────────────────

DOA *abbr* (= *dead on arrival*) décédé(e) à l'admission.

d.o.b. *abbr* = **date of birth**.

doc [dɔk] *n* (*col*) toubib *m*.

docile ['dəʊsaɪl] *adj* docile.

dock [dɔk] *n* dock *m*; (*wharf*) quai *m*; (*LAW*) banc *m* des accusés ♦ *vi* se mettre à quai ♦ *vt*: **they** ~**ed a third of his wages** ils lui ont retenu *or* décompté un tiers de son salaire.

dock dues *npl* droits *mpl* de bassin.

docker ['dɔkə*] *n* docker *m*.

docket ['dɔkɪt] *n* bordereau *m*; (*on parcel etc*) étiquette *f or* fiche *f* (*décrivant le contenu d'un paquet etc*).

dockyard ['dɔkjɑːd] *n* chantier *m* de construction navale.

doctor ['dɔktə*] *n* médecin *m*, docteur *m*; (*PhD etc*) docteur *m* ♦ *vt* (*cat*) couper; (*interfere with: food*) altérer; (*: drink*) frelater; (*: text, document*) arranger; ~**'s office** (*US*) cabinet *m* de consultation; **D**~ **of Philosophy (PhD)** doctorat *m*; titulaire *m/f* d'un doctorat.

doctorate ['dɔktərɪt] *n* doctorat *m*.

─────────────────────

Le **doctorate** *est le diplôme universitaire le plus prestigieux. Il est le résultat d'au minimum trois années de recherches et est accordé après soutenance d'une thèse devant un jury. Le doctorat le plus courant est le PhD (Doctor of Philosophy), accordé en lettres, en sciences et en ingénierie, bien qu'il existe également d'autres doctorats spécialisés (en musique, en droit, etc); voir* **Bachelor's degree, Master's degree**

─────────────────────

doctrine ['dɔktrɪn] *n* doctrine *f*.

docudrama ['dɔkjudrɑːmə] *n* (*TV*) docudrame *m*.

document *n* ['dɔkjʊmənt] document *m* ♦ *vt* ['dɔkjʊmɛnt] documenter.

documentary [dɔkju'mɛntərɪ] *adj, n* documentaire (*m*).

documentation [dɔkjumən'teɪʃən] *n* documentation *f*.

DOD *n abbr* (*US*) = **Department of Defense**.

doddering ['dɔdərɪŋ] *adj* (*senile*) gâteux(euse).

doddery ['dɔdərɪ] *adj* branlant(e).

doddle ['dɔdl] *n*: **it's a** ~ (*col*) c'est simple comme bonjour, c'est du gâteau.

Dodecanese (Islands) [dəʊdɪkə'niːz-] *n(pl)* Dodécanèse *m*.

dodge [dɔdʒ] *n* truc *m*; combine *f* ♦ *vt* esquiver, éviter ♦ *vi* faire un saut de côté; (*SPORT*) faire une esquive; **to** ~ **out of the way** s'esquiver; **to** ~ **through the traffic** se faufiler *or* faire de savantes manœuvres entre les voitures.

dodgems ['dɔdʒəmz] *npl* (*BRIT*) autos tamponneuses.

dodgy ['dɔdʒɪ] *adj* (*col: uncertain*) douteux(euse); (*: shady*) louche.

DOE *n abbr* (*BRIT*) = Department of the Environment; (*US*) = Department of Energy.

doe [dəʊ] *n* (*deer*) biche *f*; (*rabbit*) lapine *f*.

does [dʌz] *see* do.

doesn't ['dʌznt] = does not.

dog [dɔg] *n* chien/ne ♦ *vt* (*follow closely*) suivre de près, ne pas lâcher d'une semelle; (*fig: memory etc*) poursuivre, harceler; **to go to the ~s** (*nation etc*) aller à vau-l'eau.

dog biscuits *npl* biscuits *mpl* pour chien.

dog collar *n* collier *m* de chien; (*fig*) faux-col *m* d'ecclésiastique.

dog-eared ['dɔgɪəd] *adj* corné(e).

dog food *n* nourriture *f* pour les chiens *or* le chien.

dogged ['dɔgɪd] *adj* obstiné(e), opiniâtre.

doggy ['dɔgɪ] *n* (*col*) toutou *m*.

doggy bag *n petit sac pour emporter les restes.*

dogma ['dɔgmə] *n* dogme *m*.

dogmatic [dɔg'mætɪk] *adj* dogmatique.

do-gooder [du:'gʊdə*] *n* (*pej*) faiseur/euse de bonnes œuvres.

dogsbody ['dɔgzbɔdɪ] *n* (*BRIT*) bonne *f* à tout faire, tâcheron *m*.

doily ['dɔɪlɪ] *n* dessus *m* d'assiette.

doing ['duɪŋ] *n*: **this is your ~** c'est votre travail, c'est vous qui avez fait ça.

doings ['duɪŋz] *npl* activités *fpl*.

do-it-yourself ['du:ɪtjɔː'sɛlf] *n* bricolage *m*.

doldrums ['dɔldrəmz] *npl*: **to be in the ~** avoir le cafard; être dans le marasme.

dole [dəʊl] *n* (*BRIT: payment*) allocation *f* de chômage; **on the ~** au chômage.

▶**dole out** *vt* donner au compte-gouttes.

doleful ['dəʊlfʊl] *adj* triste, lugubre.

doll [dɔl] *n* poupée *f*.

▶**doll up** *vt*: **to ~ o.s. up** se faire beau(belle).

dollar ['dɔlə*] *n* dollar *m*.

dollop ['dɔləp] *n* (*of butter, cheese*) bon morceau, (*of cream*) bonne cuillerée.

dolly ['dɔlɪ] *n* poupée *f*.

dolphin ['dɔlfɪn] *n* dauphin *m*.

domain [də'meɪn] *n* (*also fig*) domaine *m*.

dome [dəʊm] *n* dôme *m*.

domestic [də'mɛstɪk] *adj* (*duty, happiness*) familial(e); (*policy, affairs, flights*) intérieur(e); (*news*) national(e); (*animal*) domestique.

domesticated [də'mɛstɪkeɪtɪd] *adj* domestiqué(e); (*pej*) d'intérieur; **he's very ~** il participe volontiers aux tâches ménagères; question ménage, il est très organisé.

domesticity [dəʊmɛs'tɪsɪtɪ] *n* vie *f* de famille.

domestic servant *n* domestique *m/f*.

domicile ['dɔmɪsaɪl] *n* domicile *m*.

dominant ['dɔmɪnənt] *adj* dominant(e).

dominate ['dɔmɪneɪt] *vt* dominer.

domination [dɔmɪ'neɪʃən] *n* domination *f*.

domineering [dɔmɪ'nɪərɪŋ] *adj* domina-

teur(trice), autoritaire.

Dominican Republic [də'mɪnɪkən-] *n* République Dominicaine.

dominion [də'mɪnɪən] *n* domination *f*; territoire *m*; dominion *m*.

domino, ~es ['dɔmɪnəʊ] *n* domino *m*; **~es** *n* (*game*) dominos *mpl*.

don [dɔn] *n* (*BRIT*) professeur *m* d'université ♦ *vt* revêtir.

donate [də'neɪt] *vt* faire don de, donner.

donation [də'neɪʃən] *n* donation *f*, don *m*.

done [dʌn] *pp of* do.

donkey ['dɔŋkɪ] *n* âne *m*.

donkey-work ['dɔŋkɪwɔːk] *n* (*BRIT col*) le gros du travail, le plus dur (du travail).

donor ['dəʊnə*] *n* (*of blood etc*) donneur/euse; (*to charity*) donateur/trice.

donor card *n* carte *f* de don d'organes.

don't [dəʊnt] = do not.

doodle ['du:dl] *n* griffonnage *m*, gribouillage *m* ♦ *vi* griffonner, gribouiller.

doom [du:m] *n* (*fate*) destin *m*; (*ruin*) ruine *f* ♦ *vt*: **to be ~ed (to failure)** être voué(e) à l'échec.

doomsday ['du:mzdeɪ] *n* le Jugement dernier.

door [dɔː*] *n* porte *f*; (*of vehicle*) portière *f*, porte; **to go from ~ to ~** aller de porte en porte.

doorbell ['dɔːbɛl] *n* sonnette *f*.

door handle *n* poignée *f* de porte.

doorman ['dɔːmən] *n* (*in hotel*) portier *m*; (*in block of flats*) concierge *m*.

doormat ['dɔːmæt] *n* paillasson *m*.

doorpost ['dɔːpəʊst] *n* montant *m* de porte.

doorstep ['dɔːstɛp] *n* pas *m* de (la) porte, seuil *m*.

door-to-door ['dɔːtə'dɔː*] *adj*: **~ selling** vente *f* à domicile.

doorway ['dɔːweɪ] *n* (*embrasure f de*) porte *f*.

dope [dəʊp] *n* (*col*) drogue *f*; (*: information*) tuyaux *mpl*, rancards *mpl* ♦ *vt* (*horse etc*) doper.

dopey ['dəʊpɪ] *adj* (*col*) à moitié endormi(e).

dormant ['dɔːmənt] *adj* assoupi(e), en veilleuse; (*rule, law*) inappliqué(e).

dormer ['dɔːmə*] *n* (*also: ~ window*) lucarne *f*.

dormice ['dɔːmaɪs] *npl of* dormouse.

dormitory ['dɔːmɪtrɪ] *n* dortoir *m*; (*US: hall of residence*) foyer *m* d'étudiants.

dormouse, pl dormice ['dɔːmaʊs, -maɪs] *n* loir *m*.

Dors *abbr* (*BRIT*) = Dorset.

DOS [dɔs] *n abbr* = disk operating system.

dosage ['dəʊsɪdʒ] *n* dose *f*; dosage *m*; (*on label*) posologie *f*.

dose [dəʊs] *n* dose *f*; (*BRIT: bout*) attaque *f* ♦ *vt*: **to ~ o.s.** se bourrer de médicaments; **a ~ of flu** une belle *or* bonne grippe.

dosser ['dɔsə*] *n* (*BRIT col*) clochard/e.

doss house ['dɔs-] *n* (*BRIT*) asile *m* de nuit.

dossier ['dɔsɪeɪ] *n* dossier *m*.

DOT *n abbr* (*US*) = Department of Transportation.

dot [dɔt] *n* point *m* ♦ *vt*: ~**ted with** parsemé(e) de; **on the** ~ à l'heure tapante.

dot command *n* (*COMPUT*) commande précédée d'un point.

dote [dəut]: **to** ~ **on** *vt fus* être fou(folle) de.

dot-matrix printer [dɔt'meɪtrɪks-] *n* imprimante matricielle.

dotted line ['dɔtɪd-] *n* ligne pointillée; (*AUT*) ligne discontinue; **to sign on the** ~ signer à l'endroit indiqué or sur la ligne pointillée; (*fig*) donner son consentement.

dotty ['dɔtɪ] *adj* (*col*) loufoque, farfelu(e).

double ['dʌbl] *adj* double ♦ *adv* (*fold*) en deux; (*twice*): **to cost** ~ (**sth**) coûter le double (de qch) or deux fois plus (que qch) ♦ *n* double *m*; (*CINE*) doublure *f* ♦ *vt* doubler; (*fold*) plier en deux ♦ *vi* doubler; (*have two uses*): **to** ~ **as** servir aussi de; ~ **five two six (5526)** (*BRIT TEL*) cinquante-cinq - vingt-six; **it's spelt with a** ~ **"l"** ça s'écrit avec deux "l"; **on the** ~, (*BRIT*) **at the** ~ au pas de course.

▶**double back** *vi* (*person*) revenir sur ses pas.

▶**double up** *vi* (*bend over*) se courber, se plier; (*share room*) partager la chambre.

double bass *n* contrebasse *f*.

double bed *n* grand lit.

double-breasted ['dʌbl'brestɪd] *adj* croisé(e).

double-check ['dʌbl'tʃek] *vt*, *vi* revérifier.

double-clutch ['dʌbl'klʌtʃ] *vi* (*US*) faire un double débrayage.

double cream *n* (*BRIT*) crème fraîche épaisse.

doublecross ['dʌbl'krɔs] *vt* doubler, trahir.

doubledecker ['dʌbl'dekə*] *n* autobus *m* à impériale.

double declutch *vi* (*BRIT*) faire un double débrayage.

double exposure *n* (*PHOT*) surimpression *f*.

double glazing *n* (*BRIT*) double vitrage *m*.

double-page ['dʌblpeɪdʒ] *adj*: ~ **spread** publicité *f* en double page.

double parking *n* stationnement *m* en double file.

double room *n* chambre *f* pour deux.

doubles ['dʌblz] *n* (*TENNIS*) double *m*.

double whammy [-'wæmɪ] *n* (*col*) double contretemps *m*.

doubly ['dʌblɪ] *adv* doublement, deux fois plus.

doubt [daut] *n* doute *m* ♦ *vt* douter de; **without (a)** ~ sans aucun doute; **beyond** ~ *adv* indubitablement ♦ *adj* indubitable; **to** ~ **that** douter que; **I** ~ **it very much** j'en doute fort.

doubtful ['dautful] *adj* douteux(euse); (*person*) incertain(e); **to be** ~ **about sth** avoir des doutes sur qch, ne pas être convaincu de qch; **I'm a bit** ~ je n'en suis pas certain or sûr.

doubtless ['dautlɪs] *adv* sans doute, sûrement.

dough [dəu] *n* pâte *f*; (*col: money*) fric *m*, pognon *m*.

doughnut ['dəunʌt] *n* beignet *m*.

dour [duə*] *adj* austère.

douse [dauz] *vt* (*with water*) tremper, inonder; (*flames*) éteindre.

dove [dʌv] *n* colombe *f*.

Dover ['dəuvə*] *n* Douvres.

dovetail ['dʌvteɪl] *n*: ~ **joint** assemblage *m* à queue d'aronde ♦ *vi* (*fig*) concorder.

dowager ['dauədʒə*] *n* douairière *f*.

dowdy ['daudɪ] *adj* démodé(e); mal fagoté(e).

Dow-Jones average ['dau'dʒəunz-] *n* (*US*) indice *m* Dow-Jones.

down [daun] *n* (*fluff*) duvet *m*; (*hill*) colline (dénudée) ♦ *adv* en bas ♦ *prep* en bas de ♦ *vt* (*enemy*) abattre; (*col: drink*) siffler; ~ **there** là-bas (en bas), là au fond; ~ **here** ici en bas; **the price of meat is** ~ le prix de la viande a baissé; **I've got it** ~ **in my diary** c'est inscrit dans mon agenda; **to pay £2** ~ verser 2 livres d'arrhes or en acompte; **England is two goals** ~ l'Angleterre a deux buts de retard; **to** ~ **tools** (*BRIT*) cesser le travail; ~ **with X!** à bas X!

down-and-out ['daunəndaut] *n* (*tramp*) clochard/e.

down-at-heel ['daunət'hi:l] *adj* (*fig*) miteux(euse).

downbeat ['daunbi:t] *n* (*MUS*) temps frappé ♦ *adj* sombre, négatif(ive).

downcast ['daunkɑ:st] *adj* démoralisé(e).

downer ['daunə*] *n* (*col: drug*) tranquillisant *m*; **to be on a** ~ (*depressed*) flipper.

downfall ['daunfɔ:l] *n* chute *f*; ruine *f*.

downgrade ['daungreɪd] *vt* déclasser.

downhearted ['daun'hɑ:tɪd] *adj* découragé(e).

downhill ['daun'hɪl] *adv* (*face, look*) en aval, vers l'aval; (*roll, go*) vers le bas, en bas ♦ *n* (*SKI: also*: ~ **race**) descente *f*; **to go** ~ descendre; (*business*) péricliter, aller à vau-l'eau.

Downing Street ['daunɪŋ-] *n* (*BRIT*): **10** ~ *résidence du Premier ministre*.

Downing Street *est une rue de Westminster (à Londres) où se trouvent la résidence officielle du Premier ministre (numéro 10) et celle du ministre des Finances (numéro 11). Le nom* **"Downing Street"** *est souvent utilisé pour désigner le gouvernement britannique.*

---

download ['daunləud] *vt* télécharger.

down-market ['daun'mɑ:kɪt] *adj* (*product*) bas de gamme *inv*.

down payment *n* acompte *m*.

downplay ['daunpleɪ] *vt* (*US*) minimiser (l'importance de).

downpour ['daunpɔ:*] *n* pluie torrentielle, déluge *m*.

downright ['daunraɪt] *adj* franc(franche); (*refusal*) catégorique.

Downs [daunz] *npl* (*BRIT*): **the ~** *collines crayeuses du sud-est de l'Angleterre.*

downsize [daun'saɪz] *vt* réduire l'effectif de.

Down's syndrome [daunz-] *n* mongolisme *m*, trisomie *f*; **a ~ baby** un bébé mongolien *or* trisomique.

downstairs ['daun'stɛəz] *adv* (*on or to ground floor*) au rez-de-chaussée; (*on or to floor below*) à l'étage inférieur; **to come ~, to go ~** descendre (l'escalier).

downstream ['daunstri:m] *adv* en aval.

downtime ['dauntaɪm] *n* (*of machine etc*) temps mort; (*of person*) temps d'arrêt.

down-to-earth ['dauntu'ə:θ] *adj* terre à terre *inv*.

downtown ['daun'taun] *adv* en ville ♦ *adj* (*US*): **~ Chicago** le centre commerçant de Chicago.

downtrodden ['dauntrɔdn] *adj* opprimé(e).

down under *adv* en Australie (*or* Nouvelle Zélande).

downward ['daunwəd] *adj* vers le bas; **a ~ trend** une tendance à la baisse, une diminution progressive.

downward(s) ['daunwəd(z)] *adv* vers le bas.

dowry ['dauri] *n* dot *f*.

doz. *abbr* (= *dozen*) douz.

doze [dəuz] *vi* sommeiller.

▶**doze off** *vi* s'assoupir.

dozen ['dʌzn] *n* douzaine *f*; **a ~ books** une douzaine de livres; **80p a ~** 80p la douzaine; **~s of times** des centaines de fois.

DPh, DPhil *n abbr* (= *Doctor of Philosophy*) *titre universitaire.*

DPP *n abbr* (*BRIT*) = **Director of Public Prosecutions.**

DPT *n abbr* (*MED*: = *diphtheria, pertussis, tetanus*) DCT *m*.

DPW *n abbr* (*US*) = *Department of Public Works.*

Dr *abbr* (= *doctor*) Dr.

Dr. *abbr* (= *doctor*) Dr; (*in street names*) = **drive**.

dr *abbr* (*COMM*) = **debtor**.

drab [dræb] *adj* terne, morne.

draft [drɑ:ft] *n* brouillon *m*; (*of contract, document*) version *f* préliminaire; (*COMM*) traite *f*; (*US MIL*) contingent *m*; (: *call-up*) conscription *f* ♦ *vt* faire le brouillon de; (*document, report*) rédiger une version préliminaire de; *see also* **draught**.

drag [dræg] *vt* traîner; (*river*) draguer ♦ *vi* traîner ♦ *n* (*AVIAT, NAUT*) résistance *f*; (*col: person*) raseur/euse; (: *task etc*) corvée *f*; (*women's clothing*): **in ~** (en) travesti.

▶**drag away** *vt*: **to ~ away (from)** arracher *or* emmener de force (de).

▶**drag on** *vi* s'éterniser.

dragnet ['drægnɛt] *n* drège *f*; (*fig*) piège *m*, filets *mpl*.

dragon ['drægn] *n* dragon *m*.

dragonfly ['drægənflaɪ] *n* libellule *f*.

dragoon [drə'gu:n] *n* (*cavalryman*) dragon *m* ♦ *vt*: **to ~ sb into doing sth** (*BRIT*) forcer qn à faire qch.

drain [dreɪn] *n* égout *m*; (*on resources*) saignée *f* ♦ *vt* (*land, marshes*) drainer, assécher; (*vegetables*) égoutter; (*reservoir etc*) vider ♦ *vi* (*water*) s'écouler; **to feel ~ed (of energy or emotion)** être miné(e).

drainage ['dreɪnɪdʒ] *n* système *m* d'égouts.

draining board ['dreɪnɪŋ-], (*US*) **drainboard** ['dreɪnbɔːd] *n* égouttoir *m*.

drainpipe ['dreɪnpaɪp] *n* tuyau *m* d'écoulement.

drake [dreɪk] *n* canard *m* (mâle).

dram [dræm] *n* petit verre.

drama ['drɑːmə] *n* (*art*) théâtre *m*, art *m* dramatique; (*play*) pièce *f*; (*event*) drame *m*.

dramatic [drə'mætɪk] *adj* (*THEAT*) dramatique; (*impressive*) spectaculaire.

dramatically [drə'mætɪklɪ] *adv* de façon spectaculaire.

dramatist ['dræmətɪst] *n* auteur *m* dramatique.

dramatize ['dræmətaɪz] *vt* (*events etc*) dramatiser; (*adapt*) adapter pour la télévision (*or* pour l'écran).

drank [dræŋk] *pt of* drink.

drape [dreɪp] *vt* draper.

draper ['dreɪpə*] *n* (*BRIT*) marchand/e de nouveautés.

drapes [dreɪps] *npl* (*US*) rideaux *mpl*.

drastic ['dræstɪk] *adj* (*measures*) d'urgence, énergique; (*change*) radical(e).

drastically ['dræstɪklɪ] *adv* radicalement.

draught, (*US*) **draft** [drɑːft] *n* courant *m* d'air; (*of chimney*) tirage *m*; (*NAUT*) tirant *m* d'eau; **on ~** (*beer*) à la pression.

draught beer *n* bière *f* (à la) pression.

draughtboard ['drɑːftbɔːd] *n* (*BRIT*) damier *m*.

draughts [drɑːfts] *n* (*BRIT*) (jeu *m* de) dames *fpl*.

draughtsman, (*US*) **draftsman** ['drɑːftsmən] *n* dessinateur/trice (industriel(le)).

draughtsmanship, (*US*) **draftsmanship** ['drɑːftsmənʃɪp] *n* (*technique*) dessin industriel; (*art*) graphisme *m*.

draw [drɔː] *vb* (*pt* **drew**, *pp* **drawn** [druː, drɔːn]) *vt* tirer; (*attract*) attirer; (*picture*) dessiner; (*line, circle*) tracer; (*money*) retirer; (*comparison, distinction*): **to ~ (between)** faire (entre) ♦ *vi* (*SPORT*) faire match nul ♦ *n* match nul; (*lottery*) loterie *f*; (: *picking of ticket*) tirage *m* au sort; **to ~ to a close** toucher à *or* tirer à sa fin; **to ~ near** *vi* s'approcher; approcher.

▶**draw back** *vi* (*move back*): **to ~ back (from)** reculer (de).

▶**draw in** *vi* (*BRIT*: *car*) s'arrêter le long du trottoir; (: *train*) entrer en gare *or* dans la station.

▶**draw on** *vt* (*resources*) faire appel à; (*imagination, person*) avoir recours à, faire appel à.

▶**draw out** *vi* (*lengthen*) s'allonger ♦ *vt* (*money*) retirer.

▶**draw up** *vi* (*stop*) s'arrêter ♦ *vt* (*document*) établir, dresser; (*plans*) formuler, dessiner.

drawback ['drɔːbæk] *n* inconvénient *m*, désavantage *m*.

drawbridge ['drɔːbrɪdʒ] *n* pont-levis *m*.

drawee [drɔː'iː] *n* tiré *m*.

drawer [drɔː*] *n* tiroir *m*; ['drɔːə*] (*of cheque*) tireur *m*.

drawing ['drɔːɪŋ] *n* dessin *m*.

drawing board *n* planche *f* à dessin.

drawing pin *n* (*BRIT*) punaise *f*.

drawing room *n* salon *m*.

drawl [drɔːl] *n* accent traînant.

drawn [drɔːn] *pp of* draw ♦ *adj* (*haggard*) tiré(e), crispé(e).

drawstring ['drɔːstrɪŋ] *n* cordon *m*.

dread [drɛd] *n* épouvante *f*, effroi *m* ♦ *vt* redouter, appréhender.

dreadful ['drɛdful] *adj* épouvantable, affreux(euse).

dream [driːm] *n* rêve *m* ♦ *vt, vi* (*pt, pp* **dreamed** *or* **dreamt** [drɛmt]) rêver; **to have a ~ about sb/sth** rêver à qn/qch; **sweet ~s!** faites de beaux rêves!

▶**dream up** *vt* inventer.

dreamer ['driːmə*] *n* rêveur/euse.

dream world *n* monde *m* imaginaire.

dreamy ['driːmɪ] *adj* (*absent-minded*) rêveur(euse).

dreary ['drɪərɪ] *adj* triste; monotone.

dredge [drɛdʒ] *vt* draguer.

▶**dredge up** *vt* draguer; (*fig: unpleasant facts*) (faire) ressortir.

dredger ['drɛdʒə*] *n* (*ship*) dragueur *m*; (*machine*) drague *f*; (*BRIT: also*: **sugar ~**) saupoudreuse *f*.

dregs [drɛgz] *npl* lie *f*.

drench [drɛntʃ] *vt* tremper; **~ed to the skin** trempé(e) jusqu'aux os.

dress [drɛs] *n* robe *f*; (*clothing*) habillement *m*, tenue *f* ♦ *vt* habiller; (*wound*) panser; (*food*) préparer ♦ *vi*: **she ~es very well** elle s'habille très bien; **to ~ o.s., to get ~ed** s'habiller; **to ~ a shop window** faire l'étalage *or* la vitrine.

▶**dress up** *vi* s'habiller; (*in fancy dress*) se déguiser.

dress circle *n* premier balcon.

dress designer *n* modéliste *m/f*, dessinateur/trice de mode.

dresser ['drɛsə*] *n* (*THEAT*) habilleur/euse; (*also*: **window ~**) étalagiste *m/f*; (*furniture*) vaisselier *m*.

dressing ['drɛsɪŋ] *n* (*MED*) pansement *m*; (*CULIN*) sauce *f*, assaisonnement *m*.

dressing gown *n* (*BRIT*) robe *f* de chambre.

dressing room *n* (*THEAT*) loge *f*; (*SPORT*) vestiaire *m*.

dressing table *n* coiffeuse *f*.

dressmaker ['drɛsmeɪkə*] *n* couturière *f*.

dressmaking ['drɛsmeɪkɪŋ] *n* couture *f*; travaux *mpl* de couture.

dress rehearsal *n* (répétition *f*) générale *f*.

dress shirt *n* chemise *f* à plastron.

dressy ['drɛsɪ] *adj* (*col: clothes*) (qui fait) habillé(e).

drew [druː] *pt of* draw.

dribble ['drɪbl] *vi* tomber goutte à goutte; (*baby*) baver ♦ *vt* (*ball*) dribbler.

dried [draɪd] *adj* (*fruit, beans*) sec(sèche); (*eggs, milk*) en poudre.

drier ['draɪə*] *n* = dryer.

drift [drɪft] *n* (*of current etc*) force *f*; direction *f*; (*of sand etc*) amoncellement *m*; (*of snow*) rafale *f*; coulée *f*; (*: on ground*) congère *f*; (*general meaning*) sens général ♦ *vi* (*boat*) aller à la dérive, dériver; (*sand, snow*) s'amonceler, s'entasser; **to let things ~** laisser les choses aller à la dérive; **to ~ apart** (*friends, lovers*) s'éloigner l'un de l'autre; **I get** *or* **catch your ~** je vois en gros ce que vous voulez dire.

drifter ['drɪftə*] *n* personne *f* sans but dans la vie.

driftwood ['drɪftwud] *n* bois flotté.

drill [drɪl] *n* perceuse *f*; (*bit*) foret *m*; (*of dentist*) roulette *f*, fraise *f*; (*MIL*) exercice *m* ♦ *vt* percer; (*soldiers*) faire faire l'exercice à; (*pupils: in grammar*) faire faire des exercices à ♦ *vi* (*for oil*) faire un *or* des forage(s).

drilling ['drɪlɪŋ] *n* (*for oil*) forage *m*.

drilling rig *n* (*on land*) tour *f* (de forage), derrick *m*; (*at sea*) plate-forme *f* de forage.

drily ['draɪlɪ] *adv* = dryly.

drink [drɪŋk] *n* boisson *f* ♦ *vt, vi* (*pt* **drank**, *pp* **drunk** [dræŋk, drʌŋk]) boire; **to have a ~** boire quelque chose, boire un verre; **a ~ of water** un verre d'eau; **would you like something to ~?** aimeriez-vous boire quelque chose?; **we had ~s before lunch** on a pris l'apéritif.

▶**drink in** *vt* (*fresh air*) inspirer profondément; (*story*) avaler, ne pas perdre une miette de; (*sight*) se remplir la vue de.

drinkable ['drɪŋkəbl] *adj* (*not dangerous*) potable; (*palatable*) buvable.

drink-driving ['drɪŋk'draɪvɪŋ] *n* conduite *f* en état d'ivresse.

drinker ['drɪŋkə*] *n* buveur/euse.

drinking ['drɪŋkɪŋ] *n* (*drunkenness*) boisson *f*, alcoolisme *m*.

drinking fountain *n* (*in park etc*) fontaine publique; (*in building*) jet *m* d'eau potable.

drinking water *n* eau *f* potable.

drip [drɪp] *n* goutte *f*; (*sound: of water etc*) bruit *m* de l'eau qui tombe goutte à goutte; (*MED*) goutte-à-goutte *m inv*, perfusion *f*; (*col: person*) lavette *f*, nouille *f* ♦ *vi* tomber goutte à goutte; (*washing*) s'égoutter; (*wall*) suinter.

drip-dry ['drɪp'draɪ] *adj* (*shirt*) sans repassage.

drip-feed ['drɪpfiːd] *vt* alimenter au goutte-à-goutte *or* par perfusion.

dripping ['drɪpɪŋ] *n* graisse *f* de rôti ♦ *adj*: **~ wet** trempé(e).

drive [draɪv] *n* promenade *f or* trajet *m* en voiture; (*also*: **~way**) allée *f*; (*energy*) dynamisme *m*, énergie *f*; (*PSYCH*) besoin *m*; pulsion *f*; (*push*) effort (concerté); campagne *f*; (*SPORT*) drive *m*; (*TECH*) entraînement *m*; traction *f*; transmission *f*; (*COMPUT*: *also*: **disk ~**) lecteur *m* de disquette ♦ *vb* (*pt* **drove**, *pp* **driven** [drəuv, 'drɪvn]) *vt* conduire; (*nail*) enfoncer; (*push*) chasser, pousser; (*TECH*: *motor*) actionner; entraîner ♦ *vi* (*be at the wheel*) conduire; (*travel by car*) aller en voiture; **to go for a ~** aller faire une promenade en voiture; **it's 3 hours' ~ from London** Londres est à 3 heures de route; **left-/right-hand ~** (*AUT*) conduite *f* à gauche/droite; **front-/rear-wheel ~** (*AUT*) traction *f* avant/arrière; **to ~ sb to (do) sth** pousser *or* conduire qn à (faire) qch; **to ~ sb mad** rendre qn fou(folle).

▶**drive at** *vt fus* (*fig*: *intend*, *mean*) vouloir dire, en venir à.

▶**drive on** *vi* poursuivre sa route, continuer; (*after stopping*) reprendre sa route, repartir ♦ *vt* (*incite*, *encourage*) inciter.

drive-by ['draɪvbaɪ] *n* (*also*: ~ **shooting**) (*tentative d'*)assassinat par coups de feu tirés d'une voiture.

drive-in ['draɪvɪn] *adj*, *n* (*esp US*) drive-in (*m*).

drive-in window *n* (*US*) guichet-auto *m*.

drivel ['drɪvl] *n* (*col*) idioties *fpl*, imbécillités *fpl*.

driven ['drɪvn] *pp of* **drive**.

driver ['draɪvə*] *n* conducteur/trice; (*of taxi*, *bus*) chauffeur *m*.

driver's license *n* (*US*) permis *m* de conduire.

driveway ['draɪvweɪ] *n* allée *f*.

driving ['draɪvɪŋ] *adj*: ~ **rain** *n* pluie battante ♦ *n* conduite *f*.

driving force *n* locomotive *f*, élément *m* dynamique.

driving instructor *n* moniteur *m* d'auto-école.

driving lesson *n* leçon *f* de conduite.

driving licence *n* (*BRIT*) permis *m* de conduire.

driving school *n* auto-école *f*.

driving test *n* examen *m* du permis de conduire.

drizzle ['drɪzl] *n* bruine *f*, crachin *m* ♦ *vi* bruiner.

droll [drəul] *adj* drôle.

dromedary ['drɒmədərɪ] *n* dromadaire *m*.

drone [drəun] *vi* (*bee*) bourdonner; (*engine etc*) ronronner; (*also*: ~ **on**) parler d'une voix monocorde ♦ *n* bourdonnement *m*; ronronnement *m*; (*male bee*) faux-bourdon *m*.

drool [dru:l] *vi* baver; **to ~ over sb/sth** (*fig*) baver d'admiration *or* être en extase devant qn/qch.

droop [dru:p] *vi* s'affaisser; tomber.

drop [drɒp] *n* goutte *f*; (*fall*: *also in price*) baisse *f*; (: *in salary*) réduction *f*; (*also*: **parachute ~**) saut *m*; (*of cliff*) dénivellation *f*, à-pic *m* ♦ *vt*

laisser tomber; (*voice*, *eyes*, *price*) baisser; (*set down from car*) déposer ♦ *vi* (*wind*, *temperature*, *price*, *voice*) tomber; (*numbers*, *attendance*) diminuer; ~**s** *npl* (*MED*) gouttes; **cough ~s** pastilles *fpl* pour la toux; **a ~ of 10%** une baisse (*or* réduction) de 10%; **to ~ anchor** jeter l'ancre; **to ~ sb a line** mettre un mot à qn.

▶**drop in** *vi* (*col*: *visit*): **to ~ in (on)** faire un saut (chez), passer (chez).

▶**drop off** *vi* (*sleep*) s'assoupir ♦ *vt*: **to ~ sb off** déposer qn.

▶**drop out** *vi* (*withdraw*) se retirer; (*student etc*) abandonner, décrocher.

droplet ['drɒplɪt] *n* gouttelette *f*.

dropout ['drɒpaut] *n* (*from society*) marginal/e; (*from university*) drop-out *m/f*, dropé/e.

dropper ['drɒpə*] *n* (*MED etc*) compte-gouttes *m inv*.

droppings ['drɒpɪŋz] *npl* crottes *fpl*.

dross [drɒs] *n* déchets *mpl*; rebut *m*.

drought [draut] *n* sécheresse *f*.

drove [drəuv] *pt of* **drive** ♦ *n*: ~**s of people** une foule de gens.

drown [draun] *vt* noyer; (*also*: ~ **out**: *sound*) couvrir, étouffer ♦ *vi* se noyer.

drowse [drauz] *vi* somnoler.

drowsy ['drauzɪ] *adj* somnolent(e).

drudge [drʌdʒ] *n* bête *f* de somme (*fig*).

drudgery ['drʌdʒərɪ] *n* corvée *f*.

drug [drʌg] *n* médicament *m*; (*narcotic*) drogue *f* ♦ *vt* droguer; **he's on ~s** il se drogue; (*MED*) il est sous médication.

drug addict *n* toxicomane *m/f*.

druggist ['drʌgɪst] *n* (*US*) pharmacien/ne-droguiste.

drug peddler *n* revendeur/euse de drogue.

drugstore ['drʌgstɔ:*] *n* (*US*) pharmacie-droguerie *f*, drugstore *m*.

drum [drʌm] *n* tambour *m*; (*for oil*, *petrol*) bidon *m* ♦ *vt*: **to ~ one's fingers on the table** pianoter *or* tambouriner sur la table; ~**s** *npl* (*MUS*) batterie *f*.

▶**drum up** *vt* (*enthusiasm*, *support*) susciter, rallier.

drummer ['drʌmə*] *n* (joueur *m* de) tambour *m*.

drum roll *n* roulement *m* de tambour.

drumstick ['drʌmstɪk] *n* (*MUS*) baguette *f* de tambour; (*of chicken*) pilon *m*.

drunk [drʌŋk] *pp of* **drink** ♦ *adj* ivre, soûl(e) ♦ *n* soûlard/e; homme/femme soûl(e); **to get ~** s'enivrer, se soûler.

drunkard ['drʌŋkəd] *n* ivrogne *m/f*.

drunken ['drʌŋkən] *adj* ivre, soûl(e); (*habitual*) ivrogne, d'ivrogne; ~ **driving** conduite *f* en état d'ivresse.

drunkenness ['drʌŋkənnɪs] *n* ivresse *f*; ivrognerie *f*.

dry [draɪ] *adj* sec(sèche); (*day*) sans pluie; (*humour*) pince-sans-rire; (*uninteresting*) aride, rébarbatif(ive) ♦ *vt* sécher; (*clothes*) faire sécher ♦ *vi* sécher; **on ~ land** sur la terre ferme; **to ~ one's hands/hair/eyes** se sécher les mains/les cheveux/les yeux.

▶**dry up** *vi* (*also fig: source of supply, imagination*) se tarir; (*: speaker*) sécher, rester sec.

dry-clean ['draɪ'kliːn] *vt* nettoyer à sec.

dry-cleaner ['draɪ'kliːnə*] *n* teinturier *m*.

dry-cleaner's ['draɪ'kliːnəz] *n* teinturerie *f*.

dry-cleaning ['draɪ'kliːnɪŋ] *n* nettoyage *m* à sec.

dry dock *n* (*NAUT*) cale sèche, bassin *m* de radoub.

dryer ['draɪə*] *n* séchoir *m*; (*spin-~*) essoreuse *f*.

dry goods *npl* (*COMM*) textiles *mpl*, mercerie *f*.

dry goods store *n* (*US*) magasin *m* de nouveautés.

dry ice *n* neige *f* carbonique.

dryly ['draɪlɪ] *adv* sèchement, d'un ton sec.

dryness ['draɪnɪs] *n* sécheresse *f*.

dry rot *n* pourriture sèche (*du bois*).

dry run *n* (*fig*) essai *m*.

dry ski slope *n* piste (de ski) artificielle.

DSc *n abbr* (= *Doctor of Science*) titre universitaire.

DSS *n abbr* (*BRIT*) = *Department of Social Security*.

DST *abbr* (*US*: = *Daylight Saving Time*) heure d'été.

DT *n abbr* (*COMPUT*) = **data transmission**.

DTI *n abbr* (*BRIT*) = *Department of Trade and Industry*.

DTP *n abbr* = **desktop publishing**.

DT's [diː'tiːz] *n abbr* (*col*: = *delirium tremens*) delirium tremens *m*.

dual ['djuəl] *adj* double.

dual carriageway *n* (*BRIT*) route *f* à quatre voies.

dual-control ['djuəlkən'trəul] *adj* à doubles commandes.

dual nationality *n* double nationalité *f*.

dual-purpose ['djuəl'pəːpəs] *adj* à double emploi.

dubbed [dʌbd] *adj* (*CINE*) doublé(e); (*nicknamed*) surnommé(e).

dubious ['djuːbɪəs] *adj* hésitant(e), incertain(e); (*reputation, company*) douteux(euse); **I'm very ~ about it** j'ai des doutes sur la question, je n'en suis pas sûr du tout.

Dublin ['dʌblɪn] *n* Dublin.

Dubliner ['dʌblɪnə*] *n* habitant/e de Dublin; originaire *m/f* de Dublin.

duchess ['dʌtʃɪs] *n* duchesse *f*.

duck [dʌk] *n* canard *m* ♦ *vi* se baisser vivement, baisser subitement la tête ♦ *vt* plonger dans l'eau.

duckling ['dʌklɪŋ] *n* caneton *m*.

duct [dʌkt] *n* conduite *f*, canalisation *f*; (*ANAT*) conduit *m*.

dud [dʌd] *n* (*shell*) obus non éclaté; (*object, tool*): **it's a ~** c'est de la camelote, ça ne marche pas ♦ *adj* (*BRIT: cheque*) sans provi-

sion; (*: note, coin*) faux(fausse).

due [djuː] *adj* dû(due); (*expected*) attendu(e); (*fitting*) qui convient ♦ *n* dû *m* ♦ *adv*: **~ north** droit vers le nord; **~s** *npl* (*for club, union*) cotisation *f*; (*in harbour*) droits *mpl* (de port); **in ~ course** en temps utile *or* voulu; (*in the end*) finalement; **~ to** dû à; causé par; **the rent is ~ on the 30th** il faut payer le loyer le 30; **the train is ~ at 8** le train est attendu à 8 h; **she is ~ back tomorrow** elle doit rentrer demain; **I am ~ 6 days' leave** j'ai droit à 6 jours de congé.

due date *n* date *f* d'échéance.

duel ['djuəl] *n* duel *m*.

duet [djuː'ɛt] *n* duo *m*.

duff [dʌf] *adj* (*BRIT col*) nullard(e), nul(le).

duffelbag, duffle bag ['dʌflbæg] *n* sac marin.

duffelcoat, duffle coat ['dʌflkəut] *n* duffel-coat *m*.

duffer ['dʌfə*] *n* (*col*) nullard/e.

dug [dʌg] *pt*, *pp* of **dig**.

dugout ['dʌgaut] *n* (*SPORT*) banc *m* de touche.

duke [djuːk] *n* duc *m*.

dull [dʌl] *adj* (*boring*) ennuyeux(euse); (*slow*) borné(e); (*lacklustre*) morne, terne; (*sound, pain*) sourd(e); (*weather, day*) gris(e), maussade; (*blade*) émoussé(e) ♦ *vt* (*pain, grief*) atténuer; (*mind, senses*) engourdir.

duly ['djuːlɪ] *adv* (*on time*) en temps voulu; (*as expected*) comme il se doit.

dumb [dʌm] *adj* muet(te); (*stupid*) bête; **to be struck ~** (*fig*) rester abasourdi(e), être sidéré(e).

dumbbell ['dʌmbɛl] *n* (*SPORT*) haltère *m*.

dumbfounded [dʌm'faundɪd] *adj* sidéré(e).

dummy ['dʌmɪ] *n* (*tailor's model*) mannequin *m*; (*SPORT*) feinte *f*; (*BRIT: for baby*) tétine *f* ♦ *adj* faux(fausse), factice.

dummy run *n* essai *m*.

dump [dʌmp] *n* tas *m* d'ordures; (*place*) décharge (publique); (*MIL*) dépôt *m*; (*COMPUT*) listage *m* (de la mémoire) ♦ *vt* (*put down*) déposer; déverser; (*get rid of*) se débarrasser de; (*COMPUT*) lister; (*COMM: goods*) vendre à perte (*sur le marché extérieur*); **to be (down) in the ~s** (*col*) avoir le cafard, broyer du noir.

dumping ['dʌmpɪŋ] *n* (*ECON*) dumping *m*; (*of rubbish*): **"no ~"** "décharge interdite".

dumpling ['dʌmplɪŋ] *n* boulette *f* (de pâte).

dumpy ['dʌmpɪ] *adj* courtaud(e), boulot(te).

dunce [dʌns] *n* âne *m*, cancre *m*.

dune [djuːn] *n* dune *f*.

dung [dʌŋ] *n* fumier *m*.

dungarees [dʌŋgə'riːz] *npl* bleu(s) *m(pl)*; (*for child, woman*) salopette *f*.

dungeon ['dʌndʒən] *n* cachot *m*.

dunk [dʌŋk] *vt* tremper.

Dunkirk [dʌn'kəːk] *n* Dunkerque *f*.

duo ['djuːəu] *n* (*gen, MUS*) duo *m*.

duodenal [djuːəu'diːnl] *adj* duodénal(e); **~ ulcer** ulcère *m* du duodénum.

dupe [dju:p] *n* dupe *f* ♦ *vt* duper, tromper.
duplex ['dju:plɛks] *n* (*US*: *also*: ~ **apartment**) duplex *m*.
duplicate *n* ['dju:plɪkət] double *m*, copie exacte; (*copy of letter etc*) duplicata *m* ♦ *adj* (*copy*) en double ♦ *vt* ['dju:plɪkeɪt] faire un double de; (*on machine*) polycopier; **in** ~ en deux exemplaires, en double; ~ **key** double *m* de la (*or* d'une) clé.
duplicating machine ['dju:plɪkeɪtɪŋ-], **duplicator** ['dju:plɪkeɪtə*] *n* duplicateur *m*.
duplicity [dju:'plɪsɪtɪ] *n* duplicité *f*, fausseté *f*.
Dur *abbr* (*BRIT*) = Durham.
durability [djuərə'bɪlɪtɪ] *n* solidité *f*; durabilité *f*.
durable ['djuərəbl] *adj* durable; (*clothes, metal*) résistant(e), solide.
duration [djuə'reɪʃən] *n* durée *f*.
duress [djuə'rɛs] *n*: **under** ~ sous la contrainte.
Durex ['djuərɛks] *n* ® (*BRIT*) préservatif (masculin).
during ['djuərɪŋ] *prep* pendant, au cours de.
dusk [dʌsk] *n* crépuscule *m*.
dusky ['dʌskɪ] *adj* sombre.
dust [dʌst] *n* poussière *f* ♦ *vt* (*furniture*) essuyer, épousseter; (*cake etc*): **to** ~ **with** saupoudrer de.
▶**dust off** *vt* (*also fig*) dépoussiérer.
dustbin ['dʌstbɪn] *n* (*BRIT*) poubelle *f*.
duster ['dʌstə*] *n* chiffon *m*.
dust jacket *n* jacquette *f*.
dustman ['dʌstmən] *n* (*BRIT*) boueux *m*, éboueur *m*.
dustpan ['dʌstpæn] *n* pelle *f* à poussière.
dusty ['dʌstɪ] *adj* poussiéreux(euse).
Dutch [dʌtʃ] *adj* hollandais(e), néerlandais(e) ♦ *n* (*LING*) hollandais *m*, néerlandais *m* ♦ *adv*: **to go** ~ *or* **d**~ partager les frais; **the** ~ *npl* les Hollandais, les Néerlandais.
Dutch auction *n* enchères *fpl* à la baisse.
Dutchman ['dʌtʃmən], **Dutchwoman** ['dʌtʃwumən] *n* Hollandais/e.
dutiable ['dju:tɪəbl] *adj* taxable; soumis(e) à des droits de douane.
dutiful ['dju:tɪful] *adj* (*child*) respectueux(euse); (*husband, wife*) plein(e) d'égards, prévenant(e); (*employee*) consciencieux(euse).
duty ['dju:tɪ] *n* devoir *m*; (*tax*) droit *m*, taxe *f*; **duties** *npl* fonctions *fpl*; **to make it one's** ~ **to do sth** se faire un devoir de faire qch; **to pay** ~ **on sth** payer un droit *or* une taxe sur qch; **on** ~ de service; (*at night etc*) de garde; **off** ~ libre, pas de service *or* de garde.
duty-free ['dju:tɪ'fri:] *adj* exempté(e) de douane, hors-taxe; ~ **shop** boutique *f* hors-taxe.
duty officer *n* (*MIL etc*) officier *m* de permanence.
duvet ['du:veɪ] *n* (*BRIT*) couette *f*.
DV *abbr* (= *Deo volente*) si Dieu le veut.

DVLA *n abbr* (*BRIT*: = *Driver and Vehicle Licensing Agency*) *service qui délivre les cartes grises et les permis de conduire.*
DVM *n abbr* (*US*: = *Doctor of Veterinary Medicine*) *titre universitaire.*
dwarf [dwɔ:f] *n* nain/e ♦ *vt* écraser.
dwell, *pt, pp* **dwelt** [dwɛl, dwɛlt] *vi* demeurer.
▶**dwell on** *vt fus* s'étendre sur.
dweller ['dwɛlə*] *n* habitant/e.
dwelling ['dwɛlɪŋ] *n* habitation *f*, demeure *f*.
dwindle ['dwɪndl] *vi* diminuer, décroître.
dwindling ['dwɪndlɪŋ] *adj* décroissant(e), en diminution.
dye [daɪ] *n* teinture *f* ♦ *vt* teindre; **hair** ~ teinture pour les cheveux.
dyestuffs ['daɪstʌfs] *npl* colorants *mpl*.
dying ['daɪɪŋ] *adj* mourant(e), agonisant(e).
dyke [daɪk] *n* (*embankment*) digue *f*.
dynamic [daɪ'næmɪk] *adj* dynamique.
dynamics [daɪ'næmɪks] *n or npl* dynamique *f*.
dynamite ['daɪnəmaɪt] *n* dynamite *f* ♦ *vt* dynamiter, faire sauter à la dynamite.
dynamo ['daɪnəməu] *n* dynamo *f*.
dynasty ['dɪnəstɪ] *n* dynastie *f*.
dysentery ['dɪsntrɪ] *n* dysenterie *f*.
dyslexia [dɪs'lɛksɪə] *n* dyslexie *f*.
dyslexic [dɪs'lɛksɪk] *adj*, *n* dyslexique *m/f*.
dyspepsia [dɪs'pɛpsɪə] *n* dyspepsie *f*.
dystrophy ['dɪstrəfɪ] *n* dystrophie *f*; **muscular** ~ dystrophie musculaire.

E e

E, e [i:] *n* (*letter*) E, e *m*; (*MUS*): **E** mi *m*; **E for Edward**, (*US*) **E for Easy** E comme Eugène.
E *abbr* (= *east*) E ♦ *n abbr* (*DRUGS*) = **ecstasy.**
E111 ['i:wʌnɪ'lɛvn] *n abbr* (*also*: **form** ~) formulaire *m* E111.
ea. *abbr* = **each.**
E.A. *n abbr* (*US*: = *educational age*) *niveau scolaire.*
each [i:tʃ] *adj* chaque ♦ *pron* chacun(e); ~ **one** chacun(e); ~ **other** se (*or* nous *etc*); **they hate** ~ **other** ils se détestent (mutuellement); **you are jealous of** ~ **other** vous êtes jaloux l'un de l'autre; ~ **day** chaque jour, tous les jours; **they have 2 books** ~ ils ont 2 livres chacun; **they cost £5** ~ ils coûtent 5 livres (la) pièce; ~ **of us** chacun(e) de nous.
eager ['i:gə*] *adj* impatient(e); avide; ardent(e), passionné(e); (*keen: pupil*) plein(e) d'enthousiasme, qui se passionne pour les études; **to be** ~ **to do sth** être impatient de faire qch, brûler de faire qch; désirer vivement faire qch; **to be** ~ **for** désirer vive-

ment, être avide de.

eagle ['i:gl] *n* aigle *m*.

E and OE *abbr* = **errors and omissions excepted**.

ear [ɪə*] *n* oreille *f*; (*of corn*) épi *m*; **up to one's ~s in debt** endetté(e) jusqu'au cou.

earache ['ɪəreɪk] *n* douleurs *fpl* aux oreilles.

eardrum ['ɪədrʌm] *n* tympan *m*.

earful ['ɪəful] *n* (*col*): **to give sb an ~** passer un savon à qn.

earl [ə:l] *n* comte *m*.

earlier ['ə:lɪə*] *adj* (*date etc*) plus rapproché(e); (*edition etc*) plus ancien(ne), antérieur(e) ♦ *adv* plus tôt.

early ['ə:lɪ] *adv* tôt, de bonne heure; (*ahead of time*) en avance ♦ *adj* précoce; qui se manifeste (*or* se fait) tôt *or* de bonne heure; (*Christians, settlers*) premier(ière); **have an ~ night/start** couchez-vous/partez tôt *or* de bonne heure; **take the ~ train** prenez le premier train; **in the ~** *or* **~ in the spring/19th century** au début *or* commencement du printemps/19ème siècle; **you're ~!** tu es en avance!; **~ in the morning** tôt le matin; **she's in her ~ forties** elle a un peu plus de quarante ans *or* de la quarantaine; **at your earliest convenience** (*COMM*) dans les meilleurs délais.

early retirement *n* retraite anticipée.

early warning system *n* système *m* de première alerte.

earmark ['ɪəmɑ:k] *vt*: **to ~ sth for** réserver *or* destiner qch à.

earn [ə:n] *vt* gagner; (*COMM: yield*) rapporter; **to ~ one's living** gagner sa vie; **this ~ed him much praise, he ~ed much praise for this** ceci lui a valu de nombreux éloges; **he's ~ed his rest/reward** il mérite *or* a bien mérité *or* a bien gagné son repos/sa récompense.

earned income [ə:nd-] *n* revenu *m* du travail.

earnest ['ə:nɪst] *adj* sérieux(euse) ♦ *n* (*also:* **~ money**) acompte *m*, arrhes *fpl*; **in ~** *adv* sérieusement, pour de bon.

earnings ['ə:nɪŋz] *npl* salaire *m*; gains *mpl*; (*of company etc*) profits *mpl*, bénéfices *mpl*.

ear, nose and throat specialist *n* oto-rhino-laryngologiste *m/f*.

earphones ['ɪəfəunz] *npl* écouteurs *mpl*.

earplugs ['ɪəplʌgz] *npl* boules *fpl* Quiès ®; (*to keep out water*) protège-tympans *mpl*.

earring ['ɪərɪŋ] *n* boucle *f* d'oreille.

earshot ['ɪəʃɔt] *n*: **out of/within ~** hors de portée/à portée de voix.

earth [ə:θ] *n* (*gen, also BRIT ELEC*) terre *f*; (*of fox etc*) terrier *m* ♦ *vt* (*BRIT ELEC*) relier à la terre.

earthenware ['ə:θnwɛə*] *n* poterie *f*; faïence *f* ♦ *adj* de *or* en faïence.

earthly ['ə:θlɪ] *adj* terrestre; **~ paradise** paradis *m* terrestre; **there is no ~ reason to think** ... il n'y a absolument aucune raison *or* pas

la moindre raison de penser ....

earthquake ['ə:θkweɪk] *n* tremblement *m* de terre, séisme *m*.

earth-shattering ['ə:θʃætərɪŋ] *adj* stupéfiant(e).

earth tremor *n* secousse *f* sismique.

earthworks ['ə:θwə:ks] *npl* travaux *mpl* de terrassement.

earthworm ['ə:θwə:m] *n* ver *m* de terre.

earthy ['ə:θɪ] *adj* (*fig*) terre à terre *inv*; truculent(e).

earwax ['ɪəwæks] *n* cérumen *m*.

earwig ['ɪəwɪg] *n* perce-oreille *m*.

ease [i:z] *n* facilité *f*, aisance *f* ♦ *vt* (*soothe*) calmer; (*loosen*) relâcher, détendre; (*help pass*): **to ~ sth in/out** faire pénétrer/sortir qch délicatement *or* avec douceur; faciliter la pénétration/la sortie de qch ♦ *vi* (*situation*) se détendre; **with ~** sans difficulté, aisément; **life of ~** vie oisive; **at ~** à l'aise; (*MIL*) au repos.

▶**ease off, ease up** *vi* diminuer; (*slow down*) ralentir; (*relax*) se détendre.

easel ['i:zl] *n* chevalet *m*.

easily ['i:zɪlɪ] *adv* facilement.

easiness ['i:zɪnɪs] *n* facilité *f*; (*of manner*) aisance *f*; nonchalance *f*.

east [i:st] *n* est *m* ♦ *adj* d'est ♦ *adv* à l'est, vers l'est; **the E~** l'Orient *m*; (*POL*) les pays *mpl* de l'Est.

Easter ['i:stə*] *n* Pâques *fpl* ♦ *adj* (*holidays*) de Pâques, pascal(e).

Easter egg *n* œuf *m* de Pâques.

Easter Island *n* île *f* de Pâques.

easterly ['i:stəlɪ] *adj* d'est.

Easter Monday *n* le lundi de Pâques.

eastern ['i:stən] *adj* de l'est, oriental(e); **E~ Europe** l'Europe de l'Est; **the E~ bloc** (*POL*) les pays *mpl* de l'est.

Easter Sunday *n* le dimanche de Pâques.

East Germany *n* (*formerly*) Allemagne *f* de l'Est.

eastward(s) ['i:stwəd(z)] *adv* vers l'est, à l'est.

easy ['i:zɪ] *adj* facile; (*manner*) aisé(e) ♦ *adv*: **to take it** *or* **things ~** ne pas se fatiguer; (*not worry*) ne pas (trop) s'en faire; **payment on ~ terms** (*COMM*) facilités *fpl* de paiement; **that's easier said than done** c'est plus facile à dire qu'à faire, c'est vite dit; **I'm ~** (*col*) ça m'est égal.

easy chair *n* fauteuil *m*.

easy-going ['i:zɪ'gəuɪŋ] *adj* accommodant(e), facile à vivre.

easy touch *n* (*col*): **he's an ~** c'est une bonne poire.

eat, *pt* **ate**, *pp* **eaten** [i:t, eɪt, 'i:tn] *vt, vi* manger.

▶**eat away** *vt* (*subj: sea*) saper, éroder; (: *acid*) ronger, corroder.

▶**eat away at, eat into** *vt fus* ronger, attaquer.

▶**eat out** *vi* manger au restaurant.

▶**eat up** *vt* (*food*) finir (de manger); **it ~s up electricity** ça bouffe du courant, ça consomme beaucoup d'électricité.

eatable ['i:təbl] *adj* mangeable; (*safe to eat*) comestible.

eau de Cologne ['əudəkə'ləun] *n* eau *f* de Cologne.

eaves [i:vz] *npl* avant-toit *m*.

eavesdrop ['i:vzdrɔp] *vi*: **to ~ (on)** écouter de façon indiscrète.

ebb [ɛb] *n* reflux *m* ♦ *vi* refluer; (*fig: also*: ~ **away**) décliner; **the ~ and flow** le flux et le reflux; **to be at a low ~** (*fig*) être bien bas(se), ne pas aller bien fort.

ebb tide *n* marée descendante, reflux *m*.

ebony ['ɛbənɪ] *n* ébène *f*.

ebullient [ɪ'bʌlɪənt] *adj* exubérant(e).

EC *n abbr* (= *European Community*) CE *f* (= *Communauté européenne*).

eccentric [ɪk'sɛntrɪk] *adj*, *n* excentrique (*m/f*).

ecclesiastic(al) [ɪkli:zɪ'æstɪk(l)] *adj* ecclésiastique.

ECG *n abbr* = **electrocardiogram**.

ECGD *n abbr* (= *Export Credits Guarantee Department*) *service de garantie financière à l'exportation*.

echo, ~es ['ɛkəu] *n* écho *m* ♦ *vt* répéter; faire chorus avec ♦ *vi* résonner; faire écho.

éclair ['eɪklɛə*] *n* éclair *m* (*CULIN*).

eclipse [ɪ'klɪps] *n* éclipse *f* ♦ *vt* éclipser.

ECM *n abbr* (*US*) = *European Common Market*.

eco- ['i:kəu] *prefix* éco-.

eco-friendly [i:kəu'frɛndlɪ] *adj* non nuisible à *or* qui ne nuit pas à l'environnement.

ecological [i:kə'lɔdʒɪkəl] *adj* écologique.

ecologist [ɪ'kɔlədʒɪst] *n* écologiste *m/f*.

ecology [ɪ'kɔlədʒɪ] *n* écologie *f*.

economic [i:kə'nɔmɪk] *adj* économique; (*profitable*) rentable.

economical [i:kə'nɔmɪkl] *adj* économique; (*person*) économe.

economically [i:kə'nɔmɪklɪ] *adv* économiquement.

economics [i:kə'nɔmɪks] *n* économie *f* politique ♦ *npl* côté *m or* aspect *m* économique.

economist [ɪ'kɔnəmɪst] *n* économiste *m/f*.

economize [ɪ'kɔnəmaɪz] *vi* économiser, faire des économies.

economy [ɪ'kɔnəmɪ] *n* économie *f*; **economies of scale** économies d'échelle.

economy class *n* (*AVIAT etc*) classe *f* touriste.

economy size *n* taille *f* économique.

ecosystem ['i:kəusɪstəm] *n* écosystème *m*.

eco-tourism [i:kəu'tuərɪzəm] *n* écotourisme *m*.

ECSC *n abbr* (= *European Coal & Steel Community*) CECA *f* (= *Communauté européenne du charbon et de l'acier*).

ecstasy ['ɛkstəsɪ] *n* extase *f*; (*DRUGS*) ecstasy *m*; **to go into ecstasies over** s'extasier sur.

ecstatic [ɛks'tætɪk] *adj* extatique, en extase.

ECT *n abbr* = **electroconvulsive therapy**.

ECU, ecu ['eɪkju:] *n abbr* (= *European Currency Unit*) ECU *m*, écu *m*.

Ecuador ['ɛkwədɔ:*] *n* Équateur *m*.

ecumenical [i:kju'mɛnɪkl] *adj* œcuménique.

eczema ['ɛksɪmə] *n* eczéma *m*.

eddy ['ɛdɪ] *n* tourbillon *m*.

edge [ɛdʒ] *n* bord *m*; (*of knife etc*) tranchant *m*, fil *m* ♦ *vt* border ♦ *vi*: **to ~ forward** avancer petit à petit; **to ~ away from** s'éloigner furtivement de; **on ~** (*fig*) = **edgy**; **to have the ~ on** (*fig*) l'emporter (de justesse) sur, être légèrement meilleur que.

edgeways ['ɛdʒweɪz] *adv* latéralement; **he couldn't get a word in ~** il ne pouvait pas placer un mot.

edging ['ɛdʒɪŋ] *n* bordure *f*.

edgy ['ɛdʒɪ] *adj* crispé(e), tendu(e).

edible ['ɛdɪbl] *adj* comestible; (*meal*) mangeable.

edict ['i:dɪkt] *n* décret *m*.

edifice ['ɛdɪfɪs] *n* édifice *m*.

edifying ['ɛdɪfaɪɪŋ] *adj* édifiant(e).

Edinburgh ['ɛdɪnbərə] *n* Édimbourg.

edit ['ɛdɪt] *vt* éditer; (*magazine*) diriger; (*newspaper*) être le rédacteur *or* la rédactrice en chef de.

edition [ɪ'dɪʃən] *n* édition *f*.

editor ['ɛdɪtə*] *n* (*in newspaper*) rédacteur/trice; rédacteur/trice en chef; (*of sb's work*) éditeur/trice; (*also*: **film ~**) monteur/euse.

editorial [ɛdɪ'tɔ:rɪəl] *adj* de la rédaction, éditorial(e) ♦ *n* éditorial *m*; **the ~ staff** la rédaction.

EDP *n abbr* = **electronic data processing**.

EDT *abbr* (*US*: = *Eastern Daylight Time*) heure d'été de New York.

educate ['ɛdjukeɪt] *vt* instruire; éduquer; **~d at ...** qui a fait ses études à ....

educated guess ['ɛdjukeɪtɪd-] *n* supposition éclairée.

education [ɛdju'keɪʃən] *n* éducation *f*; (*schooling*) enseignement *m*, instruction *f*; (*at university: subject etc*) pédagogie *f*; **primary** *or* (*US*) **elementary/secondary ~** instruction *f* primaire/secondaire.

educational [ɛdju'keɪʃənl] *adj* pédagogique, scolaire; (*useful*) instructif(ive); (*games, toys*) éducatif(ive); **~ technology** technologie *f* de l'enseignement.

Edwardian [ɛd'wɔ:dɪən] *adj* de l'époque du roi Édouard VII, des années 1900.

EE *abbr* = **electrical engineer**.

EEC *n abbr* (= *European Economic Community*) C.E.E. *f* (= *Communauté économique européenne*).

EEG *n abbr* = **electroencephalogram**.

eel [i:l] *n* anguille *f*.

EENT *n abbr* (*US MED*) = *eye, ear, nose and throat*.

EEOC *n abbr* (*US*) = **Equal Employment Opportunity Commission**.

eerie ['ɪərɪ] *adj* inquiétant(e), spectral(e), surnaturel(le).

EET *abbr* (= *Eastern European Time*) HEO (= *heure d'Europe orientale*).

effect [ɪ'fɛkt] *n* effet *m* ♦ *vt* effectuer; **to take ~** (*LAW*) entrer en vigueur, prendre effet; (*drug*) agir, faire son effet; **to put into ~** (*plan*) mettre en application *or* à exécution; **to have an ~ on sb/sth** avoir *or* produire un effet sur qn/qch; **in ~** en fait; **his letter is to the ~ that** ... sa lettre nous apprend que ....

effective [ɪ'fɛktɪv] *adj* efficace; (*striking: display, outfit*) frappant(e), qui produit *or* fait de l'effet; **to become ~** (*LAW*) entrer en vigueur, prendre effet; **~ date** date *f* d'effet *or* d'entrée en vigueur.

effectively [ɪ'fɛktɪvlɪ] *adv* efficacement; (*strikingly*) d'une manière frappante, avec beaucoup d'effet; (*in reality*) effectivement, en fait.

effectiveness [ɪ'fɛktɪvnɪs] *n* efficacité *f*.

effects [ɪ'fɛkts] *npl* (*THEAT*) effets *mpl*; (*property*) effets, affaires *fpl*.

effeminate [ɪ'fɛmɪnɪt] *adj* efféminé(e).

effervescent [ɛfə'vɛsnt] *adj* effervescent(e).

efficacy ['ɛfɪkəsɪ] *n* efficacité *f*.

efficiency [ɪ'fɪʃənsɪ] *n* efficacité *f*; rendement *m*.

efficiency apartment *n* (*US*) studio *m* avec coin cuisine.

efficient [ɪ'fɪʃənt] *adj* efficace; (*machine, car*) d'un bon rendement.

efficiently [ɪ'fɪʃəntlɪ] *adv* efficacement.

effigy ['ɛfɪdʒɪ] *n* effigie *f*.

effluent ['ɛfluənt] *n* effluent *m*.

effort ['ɛfət] *n* effort *m*; **to make an ~ to do sth** faire *or* fournir un effort pour faire qch.

effortless ['ɛfətlɪs] *adj* sans effort, aisé(e).

effrontery [ɪ'frʌntərɪ] *n* effronterie *f*.

effusive [ɪ'fjuːsɪv] *adj* (*person*) expansif(ive); (*welcome*) chaleureux(euse).

EFL *n abbr* (*SCOL*) = *English as a Foreign Language.*

EFTA ['ɛftə] *n abbr* (= *European Free Trade Association*) AELE *f* (= *Association européenne de libre-échange*).

e.g. *adv abbr* (= *exempli gratia*) par exemple, p. ex.

egalitarian [ɪgælɪ'tɛərɪən] *adj* égalitaire.

egg [ɛg] *n* œuf *m*.
▶**egg on** *vt* pousser.

eggcup ['ɛgkʌp] *n* coquetier *m*.

eggplant ['ɛgplɑːnt] *n* aubergine *f*.

eggshell ['ɛgʃɛl] *n* coquille *f* d'œuf ♦ *adj* (*colour*) blanc cassé *inv*.

egg-timer ['ɛgtaɪmə*] *n* sablier *m*.

egg white *n* blanc *m* d'œuf.

egg yolk *n* jaune *m* d'œuf.

ego ['iːgəu] *n* moi *m*.

egoism ['ɛgəuɪzəm] *n* égoïsme *m*.

egoist ['ɛgəuɪst] *n* égoïste *m/f*.

egotism ['ɛgəutɪzəm] *n* égotisme *m*.

egotist ['ɛgəutɪst] *n* égocentrique *m/f*.

ego trip *n*: **to be on an ~** être en plein délire d'autosatisfaction.

Egypt ['iːdʒɪpt] *n* Égypte *f*.

Egyptian [ɪ'dʒɪpʃən] *adj* égyptien(ne) ♦ *n* Égyptien/ne.

eiderdown ['aɪdədaun] *n* édredon *m*.

eight [eɪt] *num* huit.

eighteen [eɪ'tiːn] *num* dix-huit.

eighth [eɪtθ] *num* huitième.

eighty ['eɪtɪ] *num* quatre-vingt(s).

Eire ['ɛərə] *n* République *f* d'Irlande.

EIS *n abbr* (= *Educational Institute of Scotland*) syndicat enseignant.

either ['aɪðə*] *adj* l'un ou l'autre; (*both, each*) chaque; **on ~ side** de chaque côté ♦ *pron*: **~ (of them)** l'un ou l'autre; **I don't like ~** je n'aime ni l'un ni l'autre ♦ *adv* non plus; **no, I don't ~** moi non plus ♦ *conj*: **~ good or bad** ou bon ou mauvais, soit bon soit mauvais; **I haven't seen ~ one or the other** je n'ai vu ni l'un ni l'autre.

ejaculation [ɪdʒækju'leɪʃən] *n* (*PHYSIOL*) éjaculation *f*.

eject [ɪ'dʒɛkt] *vt* expulser; éjecter ♦ *vi* (*pilot*) s'éjecter.

ejector seat [ɪ'dʒɛktə-] *n* siège *m* éjectable.

eke [iːk]: **to ~ out** *vt* faire durer; augmenter.

EKG *n abbr* (*US*) = **electrocardiogram**.

el [ɛl] *n abbr* (*US col*) = **elevated railroad**.

elaborate *adj* [ɪ'læbərɪt] compliqué(e), recherché(e), minutieux(euse) ♦ *vb* [ɪ'læbəreɪt] *vt* élaborer ♦ *vi* entrer dans les détails.

elapse [ɪ'læps] *vi* s'écouler, passer.

elastic [ɪ'læstɪk] *adj, n* élastique (*m*).

elastic band *n* (*BRIT*) élastique *m*.

elasticity [ɪlæs'tɪsɪtɪ] *n* élasticité *f*.

elated [ɪ'leɪtɪd] *adj* transporté(e) de joie.

elation [ɪ'leɪʃən] *n* (grande) joie, allégresse *f*.

elbow ['ɛlbəu] *n* coude *m* ♦ *vt*: **to ~ one's way through the crowd** se frayer un passage à travers la foule (en jouant des coudes).

elbow grease *n*: **to use a bit of ~** mettre de l'huile de coude.

elder ['ɛldə*] *adj* aîné(e) ♦ *n* (*tree*) sureau *m*; **one's ~s** ses aînés.

elderly ['ɛldəlɪ] *adj* âgé(e) ♦ *npl*: **the ~** les personnes âgées.

elder statesman *n* vétéran *m* de la politique.

eldest ['ɛldɪst] *adj, n*: **the ~ (child)** l'aîné(e) (des enfants).

elect [ɪ'lɛkt] *vt* élire; (*choose*): **to ~ to do** choisir de faire ♦ *adj*: **the president ~** le président désigné.

election [ɪ'lɛkʃən] *n* élection *f*; **to hold an ~** procéder à une élection.

election campaign *n* campagne électorale.

electioneering [ɪlɛkʃə'nɪərɪŋ] *n* propagande électorale, manœuvres électorales.

elector [ɪ'lɛktə*] *n* électeur/trice.

electoral [ɪ'lɛktərəl] *adj* électoral(e).

electoral college n collège électoral.
electoral roll n (BRIT) liste électorale.
electorate [ɪˈlɛktərɪt] n électorat m.
electric [ɪˈlɛktrɪk] adj électrique.
electrical [ɪˈlɛktrɪkl] adj électrique.
electrical engineer n ingénieur électricien.
electrical failure n panne d'électricité or de courant.
electric blanket n couverture chauffante.
electric chair n chaise f électrique.
electric cooker n cuisinière f électrique.
electric current n courant m électrique.
electric fire n (BRIT) radiateur m électrique.
electrician [ɪlɛkˈtrɪʃən] n électricien m.
electricity [ɪlɛkˈtrɪsɪtɪ] n électricité f; **to switch on/off the** ~ rétablir/couper le courant.
electricity board n (BRIT) ≈ agence régionale de l'E.D.F.
electric light n lumière f électrique.
electric shock n choc m or décharge f électrique.
electrify [ɪˈlɛktrɪfaɪ] vt (RAIL) électrifier; (audience) électriser.
electro... [ɪˈlɛktrəu] prefix électro....
electrocardiogram (ECG) [ɪˈlɛktrə ˈkɑːdɪəgræm] n électrocardiogramme m (ECG).
electro-convulsive therapy [ɪˈlɛktrə kənˈvʌlsɪv-] n électrochocs mpl.
electrocute [ɪˈlɛktrəkjuːt] vt électrocuter.
electrode [ɪˈlɛktrəud] n électrode f.
electroencephalogram (EEG) [ɪˈlɛktrəu ɛnˈsɛfələgræm] n électroencéphalogramme m (EEG).
electrolysis [ɪlɛkˈtrɒlɪsɪs] n électrolyse f.
electromagnetic [ɪˈlɛktrəmægˈnɛtɪk] adj électromagnétique.
electron [ɪˈlɛktrɒn] n électron m.
electronic [ɪlɛkˈtrɒnɪk] adj électronique.
electronic data processing (EDP) n traitement m électronique des données.
electronic mail n courrier m électronique.
electronics [ɪlɛkˈtrɒnɪks] n électronique f.
electronics engineer n électronicien/ne.
electron microscope n microscope m électronique.
electroplated [ɪˈlɛktrəˈpleɪtɪd] adj plaqué(e) or doré(e) or argenté(e) par galvanoplastie.
electrotherapy [ɪˈlɛktrəˈθɛrəpɪ] n électrothérapie f.
elegance [ˈɛlɪgəns] n élégance f.
elegant [ˈɛlɪgənt] adj élégant(e).
element [ˈɛlɪmənt] n (gen) élément m; (of heater, kettle etc) résistance f.
elementary [ɛlɪˈmɛntərɪ] adj élémentaire; (school, education) primaire.

Aux États-Unis et au Canada, une **elementary school** (également appelée "grade school" ou "grammar school" aux États-Unis) est une

école publique où les enfants passent les six à huit premières années de leur scolarité.

elephant [ˈɛlɪfənt] n éléphant m.
elevate [ˈɛlɪveɪt] vt élever.
elevated railroad [ˈɛlɪveɪtɪd-] n (US) métro aérien.
elevation [ɛlɪˈveɪʃən] n élévation f; (height) altitude f.
elevator [ˈɛlɪveɪtə*] n élévateur m, montecharge m inv; (US: lift) ascenseur m.
eleven [ɪˈlɛvn] num onze.
elevenses [ɪˈlɛvnzɪz] npl (BRIT) ≈ pause-café f.
eleventh [ɪˈlɛvnθ] adj onzième; **at the** ~ **hour** (fig) à la dernière minute.
elf, pl **elves** [ɛlf, ɛlvz] n lutin m.
elicit [ɪˈlɪsɪt] vt: **to** ~ (**from**) obtenir (de); tirer (de).
eligible [ˈɛlɪdʒəbl] adj éligible; (for membership) admissible; ~ **for a pension** ayant droit à la retraite.
eliminate [ɪˈlɪmɪneɪt] vt éliminer.
elimination [ɪlɪmɪˈneɪʃən] n élimination f; **by process of** ~ par élimination.
élite [eɪˈliːt] n élite f.
élitist [eɪˈliːtɪst] adj (pej) élitiste.
elixir [ɪˈlɪksə*] n élixir m.
Elizabethan [ɪlɪzəˈbiːθən] adj élisabéthain(e).
ellipse [ɪˈlɪps] n ellipse f.
elliptical [ɪˈlɪptɪkl] adj elliptique.
elm [ɛlm] n orme m.
elocution [ɛləˈkjuːʃən] n élocution f.
elongated [ˈiːlɒŋgeɪtɪd] adj étiré(e), allongé(e).
elope [ɪˈləup] vi (lovers) s'enfuir (ensemble).
elopement [ɪˈləupmənt] n fugue amoureuse.
eloquence [ˈɛləkwəns] n éloquence f.
eloquent [ˈɛləkwənt] adj éloquent(e).
else [ɛls] adv d'autre; **something** ~ quelque chose d'autre, autre chose; **somewhere** ~ ailleurs, autre part; **everywhere** ~ partout ailleurs; **everyone** ~ tous les autres; **nothing** ~ rien d'autre; **is there anything** ~ **I can do?** est-ce que je peux faire quelque chose d'autre?; **where** ~? à quel autre endroit?; **little** ~ pas grand-chose d'autre.
elsewhere [ɛlsˈwɛə*] adv ailleurs, autre part.
ELT n abbr (SCOL) = English Language Teaching.
elucidate [ɪˈluːsɪdeɪt] vt élucider.
elude [ɪˈluːd] vt échapper à; (question) éluder.
elusive [ɪˈluːsɪv] adj insaisissable; (answer) évasif(ive).
elves [ɛlvz] npl of **elf**.
emaciated [ɪˈmeɪsɪeɪtɪd] adj émacié(e), décharné(e).
E-mail, e-mail [ˈiːmeɪl] n abbr (= electronic mail) courrier m électronique ♦ vt: **to** ~ **sb** envoyer un message électronique à qn.
emanate [ˈɛməneɪt] vi: **to** ~ **from** émaner de.
emancipate [ɪˈmænsɪpeɪt] vt émanciper.
emancipation [ɪmænsɪˈpeɪʃən] n émancipation f.

emasculate [ɪ'mæskjuleɪt] vt émasculer.

embalm [ɪm'bɑ:m] vt embaumer.

embankment [ɪm'bæŋkmənt] n (of road, railway) remblai m, talus m; (riverside) berge f, quai m; (dyke) digue f.

embargo, **~es** [ɪm'bɑ:gəu] n (COMM, NAUT) embargo m ♦ vt frapper d'embargo, mettre l'embargo sur; **to put an ~ on sth** mettre l'embargo sur qch.

embark [ɪm'bɑ:k] vi: **to ~ (on)** (s')embarquer (à bord de or sur) ♦ vt embarquer; **to ~ on** (journey etc) commencer, entreprendre; (fig) se lancer or s'embarquer dans.

embarkation [ɛmbɑ:'keɪʃən] n embarquement m.

embarkation card n carte f d'embarquement.

embarrass [ɪm'bærəs] vt embarrasser, gêner; **to be ~ed** être gêné(e).

embarrassing [ɪm'bærəsɪŋ] adj gênant(e), embarrassant(e).

embarrassment [ɪm'bærəsmənt] n embarras m, gêne f.

embassy ['ɛmbəsɪ] n ambassade f; **the French E~** l'ambassade de France.

embed [ɪm'bɛd] vt enfoncer; sceller.

embellish [ɪm'bɛlɪʃ] vt embellir; enjoliver.

embers ['ɛmbəz] npl braise f.

embezzle [ɪm'bɛzl] vt détourner.

embezzlement [ɪm'bɛzlmənt] n détournement m (de fonds).

embezzler [ɪm'bɛzlə*] n escroc m.

embitter [ɪm'bɪtə*] vt aigrir; envenimer.

emblem ['ɛmbləm] n emblème m.

embodiment [ɪm'bɔdɪmənt] n personification f, incarnation f.

embody [ɪm'bɔdɪ] vt (features) réunir, comprendre; (ideas) formuler, exprimer.

embolden [ɪm'bəuldn] vt enhardir.

embolism ['ɛmbəlɪzəm] n embolie f.

embossed [ɪm'bɔst] adj repoussé(e); gaufré(e); **~ with** où figure(nt) en relief.

embrace [ɪm'breɪs] vt embrasser, étreindre; (include) embrasser, couvrir, comprendre ♦ vi s'embrasser, s'étreindre ♦ n étreinte f.

embroider [ɪm'brɔɪdə*] vt broder; (fig: story) enjoliver.

embroidery [ɪm'brɔɪdərɪ] n broderie f.

embroil [ɪm'brɔɪl] vt: **to become ~ed (in sth)** se retrouver mêlé(e) (à qch), se laisser entraîner (dans qch).

embryo ['ɛmbrɪəu] n (also fig) embryon m.

emend [ɪ'mɛnd] vt (text) corriger.

emerald ['ɛmərəld] n émeraude f.

emerge [ɪ'mə:dʒ] vi apparaître, surgir; **it ~s that** (BRIT) il ressort que.

emergence [ɪ'mə:dʒəns] n apparition f, (of nation) naissance f.

emergency [ɪ'mə:dʒənsɪ] n urgence f; **in an ~** en cas d'urgence; **state of ~** état m d'urgence.

emergency exit n sortie f de secours.

emergency landing n atterrissage forcé.

emergency lane n (US AUT) accotement stabilisé.

emergency road service n (US) service m de dépannage.

emergency service n service m d'urgence.

emergency stop n (BRIT AUT) arrêt m d'urgence.

emergent [ɪ'mə:dʒənt] adj: **~ nation** pays m en voie de développement.

emery board ['ɛmərɪ-] n lime f à ongles (en carton émerisé).

emery paper ['ɛmərɪ-] n papier m (d')émeri.

emetic [ɪ'mɛtɪk] n vomitif m, émétique m.

emigrant ['ɛmɪgrənt] n émigrant/e.

emigrate ['ɛmɪgreɪt] vi émigrer.

emigration [ɛmɪ'greɪʃən] n émigration f.

émigré ['ɛmɪgreɪ] n émigré/e.

eminence ['ɛmɪnəns] n éminence f.

eminent ['ɛmɪnənt] adj éminent(e).

eminently ['ɛmɪnəntlɪ] adv éminemment, admirablement.

emission [ɪ'mɪʃən] n émission f.

emit [ɪ'mɪt] vt émettre.

emolument [ɪ'mɔljumənt] n (often pl: formal) émoluments mpl; (fee) honoraires mpl; (salary) traitement m.

emotion [ɪ'məuʃən] n sentiment m; (as opposed to reason) émotion f, sentiments.

emotional [ɪ'məuʃənl] adj (person) émotif(ive), très sensible; (scene) émouvant(e); (tone, speech) qui fait appel aux sentiments.

emotionally [ɪ'məuʃnəlɪ] adv (behave) émotivement; (be involved) affectivement; (speak) avec émotion; **~ disturbed** qui souffre de troubles de l'affectivité.

emotive [ɪ'məutɪv] adj émotif(ive); **~ power** capacité f d'émouvoir or de toucher.

empathy ['ɛmpəθɪ] n communion f d'idées or de sentiments; empathie f; **to feel ~ with sb** se mettre à la place de qn.

emperor ['ɛmpərə*] n empereur m.

emphasis, pl **-ases** ['ɛmfəsɪs, -siːz] n accent m; force f, insistance f; **to lay** or **place ~ on sth** (fig) mettre l'accent sur, insister sur; **the ~ is on reading** la lecture tient une place primordiale, on accorde une importance particulière à la lecture.

emphasize ['ɛmfəsaɪz] vt (syllable, word, point) appuyer or insister sur; (feature) souligner, accentuer.

emphatic [ɛm'fætɪk] adj (strong) énergique, vigoureux(euse); (unambiguous, clear) catégorique.

emphatically [ɛm'fætɪklɪ] adv avec vigueur or énergie; catégoriquement.

empire ['ɛmpaɪə*] n empire m.

empirical [ɛm'pɪrɪkl] adj empirique.

employ [ɪm'plɔɪ] vt employer; **he's ~ed in a bank** il est employé de banque, il travaille dans une banque.

employee [ɪmplɔɪ'iː] n employé/e.

employer [ɪmˈplɔɪə*] n employeur/euse.

employment [ɪmˈplɔɪmənt] n emploi m; **to find** ~ trouver un emploi or du travail; **without** ~ au chômage, sans emploi; **place of** ~ lieu m de travail.

employment agency n agence f or bureau m de placement.

employment exchange n (BRIT) agence f pour l'emploi.

empower [ɪmˈpauə*] vt: **to** ~ **sb to do** autoriser or habiliter qn à faire.

empress [ˈɛmprɪs] n impératrice f.

emptiness [ˈɛmptɪnɪs] n vide m.

empty [ˈɛmptɪ] adj vide; (street, area) désert(e); (threat, promise) en l'air, vain(e) ♦ n (bottle) bouteille f vide ♦ vt vider ♦ vi se vider; (liquid) s'écouler; **on an** ~ **stomach** à jeun; **to** ~ **into** (river) se jeter dans, se déverser dans.

empty-handed [ˈɛmptɪˈhændɪd] adj les mains vides.

empty-headed [ˈɛmptɪˈhɛdɪd] adj écervelé(e), qui n'a rien dans la tête.

EMS n abbr (= European Monetary System) SME m.

EMT n abbr = emergency medical technician.

EMU n abbr (= European Monetary Union) UME f.

emulate [ˈɛmjuleɪt] vt rivaliser avec, imiter.

emulsion [ɪˈmʌlʃən] n émulsion f; (also: ~ **paint**) peinture mate.

enable [ɪˈneɪbl] vt: **to** ~ **sb to do** permettre à qn de faire, donner à qn la possibilité de faire.

enact [ɪˈnækt] vt (LAW) promulguer; (play, scene) jouer, représenter.

enamel [ɪˈnæməl] n émail m.

enamel paint n peinture émaillée.

enamoured [ɪˈnæməd] adj: ~ **of** amoureux(euse) de; (idea) enchanté(e) par.

encampment [ɪnˈkæmpmənt] n campement m.

encased [ɪnˈkeɪst] adj: ~ **in** enfermé(e) dans, recouvert(e) de.

enchant [ɪnˈtʃɑːnt] vt enchanter.

enchanting [ɪnˈtʃɑːntɪŋ] adj ravissant(e), enchanteur(eresse).

encircle [ɪnˈsɜːkl] vt entourer, encercler.

enc(l). abbr (on letters etc: = enclosed, enclosure) PJ.

enclose [ɪnˈkləuz] vt (land) clôturer; (letter etc): **to** ~ **(with)** joindre (à); **please find** ~**d** veuillez trouver ci-joint.

enclosure [ɪnˈkləuʒə*] n enceinte f; (in letter etc) annexe f.

encoder [ɪnˈkəudə*] n (COMPUT) encodeur m.

encompass [ɪnˈkʌmpəs] vt encercler, entourer; (include) contenir, inclure.

encore [ɒŋˈkɔː*] excl, n bis (m).

encounter [ɪnˈkauntə*] n rencontre f ♦ vt rencontrer.

encourage [ɪnˈkʌrɪdʒ] vt encourager; (industry, growth) favoriser; **to** ~ **sb to do sth** encourager qn à faire qch.

encouragement [ɪnˈkʌrɪdʒmənt] n encouragement m.

encouraging [ɪnˈkʌrɪdʒɪŋ] adj encourageant(e).

encroach [ɪnˈkrəutʃ] vi: **to** ~ **(up)on** empiéter sur.

encrust [ɪnˈkrʌst] vt encroûter; (with jewels etc) incruster.

encrusted [ɪnˈkrʌstɪd] adj: ~ **(with)** incrusté(e) (de).

encumber [ɪnˈkʌmbə*] vt: **to be** ~**ed with** (luggage) être encombré(e) de; (debts) être grevé(e) de.

encyclop(a)edia [ɛnsaɪkləuˈpiːdɪə] n encyclopédie f.

end [ɛnd] n (gen, also: aim) fin f; (of table, street, line, rope etc) bout m, extrémité f; (of pointed object) pointe f; (of town) bout m ♦ vt terminer; (also: **bring to an** ~, **put an** ~ **to**) mettre fin à ♦ vi se terminer, finir; **from** ~ **to** ~ d'un bout à l'autre; **to come to an** ~ prendre fin; **to be at an** ~ être fini(e), être terminé(e); **in the** ~ finalement; **on** ~ (object) debout, dressé(e); **to stand on** ~ (hair) se dresser sur la tête; **for 5 hours on** ~ durant 5 heures d'affilée or de suite; **for hours on** ~ pendant des heures (et des heures); **at the** ~ **of the day** (BRIT fig) en fin de compte; **to this** ~, **with this** ~ **in view** à cette fin, dans ce but.

▶**end up** vi: **to** ~ **up in** finir or se terminer par; (place) finir or aboutir à.

endanger [ɪnˈdeɪndʒə*] vt mettre en danger; **an** ~**ed species** une espèce en voie de disparition.

endear [ɪnˈdɪə*] vt: **to** ~ **o.s. to sb** se faire aimer de qn.

endearing [ɪnˈdɪərɪŋ] adj attachant(e).

endearment [ɪnˈdɪəmənt] n: **to whisper** ~**s** murmurer des mots or choses tendres; **term of** ~ terme m d'affection.

endeavour, (US) **endeavor** [ɪnˈdɛvə*] n tentative f, effort m ♦ vi: **to** ~ **to do** tenter or s'efforcer de faire.

endemic [ɛnˈdɛmɪk] adj endémique.

ending [ˈɛndɪŋ] n dénouement m, conclusion f; (LING) terminaison f.

endive [ˈɛndaɪv] n (curly) chicorée f; (smooth, flat) endive f.

endless [ˈɛndlɪs] adj sans fin, interminable; (patience, resources) inépuisable, sans limites; (possibilities) illimité(e).

endorse [ɪnˈdɔːs] vt (cheque) endosser; (approve) appuyer, approuver, sanctionner.

endorsee [ɪndɔːˈsiː] n bénéficiaire m/f, endossataire m/f.

endorsement [ɪnˈdɔːsmənt] n (approval) caution f, aval m; (signature) endossement m; (BRIT: on driving licence) contravention f (portée au permis de conduire).

endorser [ɪnˈdɔːsə*] n avaliste m, endosseur m.

endow [ɪn'dau] _vt_ (_provide with money_) faire une donation à, doter; (_equip_): **to ~ with** gratifier de, doter de.

endowment [ɪn'daumənt] _n_ dotation _f_.

endowment mortgage _n_ hypothèque liée à _une assurance-vie_.

endowment policy _n_ assurance _f_ à capital différé.

end product _n_ (INDUSTRY) produit fini; (_fig_) résultat _m_, aboutissement _m_.

end result _n_ résultat final.

endurable [ɪn'djuərəbl] _adj_ supportable.

endurance [ɪn'djuərəns] _n_ endurance _f_, résistance _f_; patience _f_.

endurance test _n_ test _m_ d'endurance.

endure [ɪn'djuə*] _vt_ supporter, endurer ♦ _vi_ durer.

end user _n_ (COMPUT) utilisateur final.

enema ['ɛnɪmə] _n_ (MED) lavement _m_.

enemy ['ɛnəmɪ] _adj, n_ ennemi(e); **to make an ~ of sb** se faire un(e) ennemi(e) de qn, se mettre qn à dos.

energetic [ɛnə'dʒɛtɪk] _adj_ énergique; (_activity_) très actif(ive), qui fait se dépenser (physiquement).

energy ['ɛnədʒɪ] _n_ énergie _f_; **Department of E~** ministère _m_ de l'Énergie.

energy crisis _n_ crise _f_ de l'énergie.

energy-saving ['ɛnədʒɪ'seɪvɪŋ] _adj_ (_policy_) d'économie d'énergie; (_device_) qui permet de réaliser des économies d'énergie.

enervating ['ɛnəveɪtɪŋ] _adj_ débilitant(e), affaiblissant(e).

enforce [ɪn'fɔːs] _vt_ (LAW) appliquer, faire respecter.

enforced [ɪn'fɔːst] _adj_ forcé(e).

enfranchise [ɪn'fræntʃaɪz] _vt_ accorder le droit de vote à; (_set free_) affranchir.

engage [ɪn'ɡeɪdʒ] _vt_ engager; (MIL) engager le combat avec; (_lawyer_) prendre ♦ _vi_ (TECH) s'enclencher, s'engrener; **to ~ in** se lancer dans; **to ~ sb in conversation** engager la conversation avec qn.

engaged [ɪn'ɡeɪdʒd] _adj_ (BRIT: _busy, in use_) occupé(e); (_betrothed_) fiancé(e); **to get ~** se fiancer; **he is ~ in research/a survey** il fait de la recherche/une enquête.

engaged tone _n_ (BRIT TEL) tonalité _f_ occupé _inv_.

engagement [ɪn'ɡeɪdʒmənt] _n_ obligation _f_, engagement _m_; (_appointment_) rendez-vous _m inv_; (_to marry_) fiançailles _fpl_; (MIL) combat _m_; **I have a previous ~** j'ai déjà un rendez-vous, je suis déjà prise(e).

engagement ring _n_ bague _f_ de fiançailles.

engaging [ɪn'ɡeɪdʒɪŋ] _adj_ engageant(e), attirant(e).

engender [ɪn'dʒɛndə*] _vt_ produire, causer.

engine ['ɛndʒɪn] _n_ (AUT) moteur _m_; (RAIL) locomotive _f_.

engine driver _n_ (BRIT: _of train_) mécanicien _m_.

engineer [ɛndʒɪ'nɪə*] _n_ ingénieur _m_; (BRIT: _for domestic appliances_) réparateur _m_; (US RAIL) mécanicien _m_; **civil/mechanical ~** ingénieur des Travaux Publics _or_ des Ponts et Chaussées/mécanicien.

engineering [ɛndʒɪ'nɪərɪŋ] _n_ engineering _m_, ingénierie _f_; (_of bridges, ships_) génie _m_; (_of machine_) mécanique _f_ ♦ _cpd_: **~ works** _or_ **factory** atelier _m_ de construction mécanique.

engine failure _n_ panne _f_.

engine trouble _n_ ennuis _mpl_ mécaniques.

England ['ɪŋɡlənd] _n_ Angleterre _f_.

English ['ɪŋɡlɪʃ] _adj_ anglais(e) ♦ _n_ (LING) anglais _m_; **the ~** _npl_ les Anglais; **an ~ speaker** un anglophone.

English Channel _n_: **the ~** la Manche.

Englishman ['ɪŋɡlɪʃmən], **Englishwoman** ['ɪŋɡlɪʃwumən] _n_ Anglais/e.

English-speaking ['ɪŋɡlɪʃ'spiːkɪŋ] _adj_ qui parle anglais; anglophone.

engrave [ɪn'ɡreɪv] _vt_ graver.

engraving [ɪn'ɡreɪvɪŋ] _n_ gravure _f_.

engrossed [ɪn'ɡrəust] _adj_: **~ in** absorbé(e) par, plongé(e) dans.

engulf [ɪn'ɡʌlf] _vt_ engloutir.

enhance [ɪn'hɑːns] _vt_ rehausser, mettre en valeur; (_position_) améliorer; (_reputation_) accroître.

enigma [ɪ'nɪɡmə] _n_ énigme _f_.

enigmatic [ɛnɪɡ'mætɪk] _adj_ énigmatique.

enjoy [ɪn'dʒɔɪ] _vt_ aimer, prendre plaisir à; (_have benefit of: health, fortune_) jouir de; (: _success_) connaître; **to ~ o.s.** s'amuser.

enjoyable [ɪn'dʒɔɪəbl] _adj_ agréable.

enjoyment [ɪn'dʒɔɪmənt] _n_ plaisir _m_.

enlarge [ɪn'lɑːdʒ] _vt_ accroître; (PHOT) agrandir ♦ _vi_: **to ~ on** (_subject_) s'étendre sur.

enlarged [ɪn'lɑːdʒd] _adj_ (_edition_) augmenté(e); (MED: _organ, gland_) anormalement gros(se), hypertrophié(e).

enlargement [ɪn'lɑːdʒmənt] _n_ (PHOT) agrandissement _m_.

enlighten [ɪn'laɪtn] _vt_ éclairer.

enlightened [ɪn'laɪtnd] _adj_ éclairé(e).

enlightening [ɪn'laɪtnɪŋ] _adj_ instructif(ive), révélateur(trice).

enlightenment [ɪn'laɪtnmənt] _n_ édification _f_; éclaircissements _mpl_; (HISTORY): **the E~** ≈ le Siècle des lumières.

enlist [ɪn'lɪst] _vt_ recruter; (_support_) s'assurer ♦ _vi_ s'engager; **~ed man** (US MIL) simple soldat _m_.

enliven [ɪn'laɪvn] _vt_ animer, égayer.

enmity ['ɛnmɪtɪ] _n_ inimitié _f_.

ennoble [ɪ'nəubl] _vt_ (_with title_) anoblir.

enormity [ɪ'nɔːmɪtɪ] _n_ énormité _f_.

enormous [ɪ'nɔːməs] _adj_ énorme.

enormously [ɪ'nɔːməslɪ] _adv_ (_increase_) dans des proportions énormes; (_rich_) extrêmement.

enough [ɪ'nʌf] _adj, n_: **~ time/books** assez _or_ suffisamment de temps/livres ♦ _adv_: **big ~** assez _or_ suffisamment grand; **have you got**

~? (en) avez-vous assez?; **will 5 be** ~? est-ce que 5 suffiront?, est-ce qu'il y en aura assez avec 5?; **that's** ~! ça suffit!, assez!; **that's** ~, **thanks** cela suffit *or* c'est assez, merci; **I've had** ~! je n'en peux plus!; **he has not worked** ~ il n'a pas assez *or* suffisamment travaillé, il n'a pas travaillé assez *or* suffisamment; ~! assez!, ça suffit!; **it's hot** ~ **(as it is)**! il fait assez chaud comme ça!; **he was kind** ~ **to lend me the money** il a eu la gentillesse de me prêter l'argent; ... **which, funnily** ~ ... qui, chose curieuse.

enquire [ɪn'kwaɪə*] *vt, vi* = inquire.

enrage [ɪn'reɪdʒ] *vt* mettre en fureur *or* en rage, rendre furieux(euse).

enrich [ɪn'rɪtʃ] *vt* enrichir.

enrol, *(US)* **enroll** [ɪn'rəul] *vt* inscrire ♦ *vi* s'inscrire.

enrol(l)ment [ɪn'rəulmənt] *n* inscription *f.*

en route [ɔn'ru:t] *adv* en route, en chemin; ~ **for** *or* **to** en route vers, à destination de.

ensconced [ɪn'skɔnst] *adj*: ~ **in** bien calé(e) dans.

enshrine [ɪn'ʃraɪn] *vt (fig)* préserver.

ensign *n (NAUT)* ['ɛnsən] enseigne *f*, pavillon *m; (MIL)* ['ɛnsaɪn] porte-étendard *m.*

enslave [ɪn'sleɪv] *vt* asservir.

ensue [ɪn'sju:] *vi* s'ensuivre, résulter.

ensure [ɪn'ʃuə*] *vt* assurer, garantir; **to** ~ **that** s'assurer que.

ENT *n abbr (= Ear, Nose and Throat)* ORL *f.*

entail [ɪn'teɪl] *vt* entraîner, nécessiter.

entangle [ɪn'tæŋgl] *vt* emmêler, embrouiller; **to become** ~**d in sth** *(fig)* se laisser entraîner *or* empêtrer dans qch.

enter ['ɛntə*] *vt (room)* entrer dans, pénétrer dans; *(club, army)* entrer à; *(profession)* embrasser; *(competition)* s'inscrire à *or* pour; *(sb for a competition)* (faire) inscrire; *(write down)* inscrire, noter; *(COMPUT)* entrer, introduire ♦ *vi* entrer.

►**enter for** *vt fus* s'inscrire à, se présenter pour *or* à.

►**enter into** *vt fus (explanation)* se lancer dans; *(negotiations)* entamer; *(debate)* prendre part à; *(agreement)* conclure.

►**enter up** *vt* inscrire.

►**enter (up)on** *vt fus* commencer.

enteritis [ɛntə'raɪtɪs] *n* entérite *f.*

enterprise ['ɛntəpraɪz] *n (company, undertaking)* entreprise *f; (initiative)* (esprit *m* d')initiative *f.*

enterprising ['ɛntəpraɪzɪŋ] *adj* entreprenant(e), dynamique.

entertain [ɛntə'teɪn] *vt* amuser, distraire; *(invite)* recevoir (à dîner); *(idea, plan)* envisager.

entertainer [ɛntə'teɪnə*] *n* artiste *m/f* de variétés.

entertaining [ɛntə'teɪnɪŋ] *adj* amusant(e), distrayant(e) ♦ *n*: **to do a lot of** ~ beaucoup recevoir.

entertainment [ɛntə'teɪnmənt] *n (amusement)* distraction *f*, divertissement *m*, amusement *m; (show)* spectacle *m.*

entertainment allowance *n* frais *mpl* de représentation.

enthral [ɪn'θrɔːl] *vt* captiver, passionner.

enthralling [ɪn'θrɔːlɪŋ] *adj* captivant(e); enchanteur(eresse).

enthuse [ɪn'θuːz] *vi*: **to** ~ **about** *or* **over** parler avec enthousiasme de.

enthusiasm [ɪn'θuːzɪæzəm] *n* enthousiasme *m.*

enthusiast [ɪn'θuːzɪæst] *n* enthousiaste *m/f*; **a jazz** *etc* ~ un fervent *or* passionné du jazz *etc.*

enthusiastic [ɪnθuːzɪ'æstɪk] *adj* enthousiaste; **to be** ~ **about** être enthousiasmé(e) par.

entice [ɪn'taɪs] *vt* attirer, séduire.

enticing [ɪn'taɪsɪŋ] *adj (person, offer)* séduisant(e); *(food)* alléchant(e).

entire [ɪn'taɪə*] *adj* (tout) entier(ère).

entirely [ɪn'taɪəlɪ] *adv* entièrement, complètement.

entirety [ɪn'taɪərətɪ] *n*: **in its** ~ dans sa totalité.

entitle [ɪn'taɪtl] *vt (allow)*: **to** ~ **sb to do** donner (le) droit à qn de faire; **to** ~ **sb to sth** donner droit à qch à qn.

entitled [ɪn'taɪtld] *adj (book)* intitulé(e); **to be** ~ **to sth/to do sth** avoir droit à qch/le droit de faire qch.

entity ['ɛntɪtɪ] *n* entité *f.*

entrails ['ɛntreɪlz] *npl* entrailles *fpl.*

entrance *n* ['ɛntrns] entrée *f* ♦ *vt* [ɪn'trɑːns] enchanter, ravir; **to gain** ~ **to** *(university etc)* être admis à.

entrance examination *n* examen *m* d'entrée *or* d'admission.

entrance fee *n* droit *m* d'inscription; *(to museum etc)* prix *m* d'entrée.

entrance ramp *n (US AUT)* bretelle *f* d'accès.

entrancing [ɪn'trɑːnsɪŋ] *adj* enchanteur(teresse), ravissant(e).

entrant ['ɛntrnt] *n (in race etc)* participant/e, concurrent/e; *(BRIT: in exam)* candidat/e.

entreat [ɛn'triːt] *vt* supplier.

entreaty [ɛn'triːtɪ] *n* supplication *f*, prière *f.*

entrée ['ɔntreɪ] *n (CULIN)* entrée *f.*

entrenched [ɛn'trɛntʃt] *adj* retranché(e).

entrepreneur ['ɔntrəprə'nə:*] *n* entrepreneur *m.*

entrepreneurial ['ɔntrəprə'nə:rɪəl] *adj* animé(e) d'un esprit d'entreprise.

entrust [ɪn'trʌst] *vt*: **to** ~ **sth to** confier qch à.

entry ['ɛntrɪ] *n* entrée *f; (in register, diary)* inscription *f; (in ledger)* écriture *f*; **"no** ~**"** "défense d'entrer", "entrée interdite"; *(AUT)* "sens interdit"; **single/double** ~ **book-keeping** comptabilité *f* en partie simple/ double.

entry form *n* feuille *f* d'inscription.

entry phone *n (BRIT)* interphone *m (à l'entrée d'un immeuble).*

entwine [ɪn'twaɪn] *vt* entrelacer.

E-number ['iːnʌmbə*] *n* additif *m* (alimentaire).

enumerate [ɪ'njuːməreɪt] *vt* énumérer.

enunciate [ɪ'nʌnsɪeɪt] *vt* énoncer; prononcer.

envelop [ɪn'vɛləp] *vt* envelopper.

envelope ['ɛnvələup] *n* enveloppe *f*.

enviable ['ɛnvɪəbl] *adj* enviable.

envious ['ɛnvɪəs] *adj* envieux(euse).

environment [ɪn'vaɪərnmənt] *n* milieu *m*; environnement *m*; **Department of the E~** (*BRIT*) *ministère de l'équipement et de l'aménagement du territoire.*

environmental [ɪnvaɪərn'mɛntl] *adj* écologique, relatif(ive) à l'environnement; ~ **studies** (*in school etc*) écologie *f*.

environmentalist [ɪnvaɪərn'mɛntlɪst] *n* écologiste *m/f*.

environmentally [ɪnvaɪərn'mɛntlɪ] *adv:* ~ **sound/friendly** qui ne nuit pas à l'environnement.

Environmental Protection Agency (EPA) *n* (*US*) ≈ ministère *m* de l'Environnement.

envisage [ɪn'vɪzɪdʒ] *vt* envisager; prévoir.

envision [ɪn'vɪʒən] *vt* envisager, concevoir.

envoy ['ɛnvɔɪ] *n* envoyé/e.

envy ['ɛnvɪ] *n* envie *f* ♦ *vt* envier; **to ~ sb sth** envier qch à qn.

enzyme ['ɛnzaɪm] *n* enzyme *m*.

EPA *n abbr* (*US*) = **Environmental Protection Agency.**

ephemeral [ɪ'fɛmərl] *adj* éphémère.

epic ['ɛpɪk] *n* épopée *f* ♦ *adj* épique.

epicentre, (*US*) **epicenter** ['ɛpɪsɛntə*] *n* épicentre *m*.

epidemic [ɛpɪ'dɛmɪk] *n* épidémie *f*.

epilepsy ['ɛpɪlɛpsɪ] *n* épilepsie *f*.

epileptic [ɛpɪ'lɛptɪk] *adj, n* épileptique (*m/f*).

epilogue ['ɛpɪlɔg] *n* épilogue *m*.

episcopal [ɪ'pɪskəpl] *adj* épiscopal(e).

episode ['ɛpɪsəud] *n* épisode *m*.

epistle [ɪ'pɪsl] *n* épître *f*.

epitaph ['ɛpɪtɑːf] *n* épitaphe *f*.

epithet ['ɛpɪθɛt] *n* épithète *f*.

epitome [ɪ'pɪtəmɪ] *n* (*fig*) quintessence *f*, type *m*.

epitomize [ɪ'pɪtəmaɪz] *vt* (*fig*) illustrer, incarner.

epoch ['iːpɔk] *n* époque *f*, ère *f*.

epoch-making ['iːpɔkmeɪkɪŋ] *adj* qui fait époque.

eponymous [ɪ'pɔnɪməs] *adj* de ce *or* du même nom, éponyme.

equable ['ɛkwəbl] *adj* égal(e); de tempérament égal.

equal ['iːkwl] *adj* égal(e) ♦ *n* égal/e ♦ *vt* égaler; ~ **to** (*task*) à la hauteur de; ~ **to doing** de taille à *or* capable de faire.

equality [iː'kwɔlɪtɪ] *n* égalité *f*.

equalize ['iːkwəlaɪz] *vt, vi* égaliser.

equalizer ['iːkwəlaɪzə*] *n* but égalisateur.

equally ['iːkwəlɪ] *adv* également; (*just as*) tout aussi; **they are ~ clever** ils sont tout aussi intelligents.

Equal Opportunities Commission, (*US*) **Equal Employment Opportunity Commission** *n commission pour la non discrimination dans l'emploi.*

equal(s) sign *n* signe *m* d'égalité.

equanimity [ɛkwə'nɪmɪtɪ] *n* égalité *f* d'humeur.

equate [ɪ'kweɪt] *vt:* **to ~ sth with** comparer qch à; assimiler qch à; **to ~ sth to** mettre qch en équation avec; égaler qch à.

equation [ɪ'kweɪʃən] *n* (*MATH*) équation *f*.

equator [ɪ'kweɪtə*] *n* équateur *m*.

equatorial [ɛkwə'tɔːrɪəl] *adj* équatorial(e).

Equatorial Guinea *n* Guinée équatoriale.

equestrian [ɪ'kwɛstrɪən] *adj* équestre ♦ *n* écuyer/ère, cavalier/ère.

equilibrium [iːkwɪ'lɪbrɪəm] *n* équilibre *m*.

equinox ['iːkwɪnɔks] *n* équinoxe *m*.

equip [ɪ'kwɪp] *vt* équiper; **to ~ sb/sth with** équiper *or* munir qn/qch de; **he is well ~ped for the job** il a les compétences *or* les qualités requises pour ce travail.

equipment [ɪ'kwɪpmənt] *n* équipement *m*; (*electrical etc*) appareillage *m*, installation *f*.

equitable ['ɛkwɪtəbl] *adj* équitable.

equities ['ɛkwɪtɪz] *npl* (*BRIT COMM*) actions cotées en Bourse.

equity ['ɛkwɪtɪ] *n* équité *f*.

equity capital *n* capitaux *mpl* propres.

equivalent [ɪ'kwɪvəlnt] *adj* équivalent(e) ♦ *n* équivalent *m*; **to be ~ to** équivaloir à, être équivalent(e) à.

equivocal [ɪ'kwɪvəkl] *adj* équivoque; (*open to suspicion*) douteux(euse).

equivocate [ɪ'kwɪvəkeɪt] *vi* user de faux-fuyants; éviter de répondre.

equivocation [ɪkwɪvə'keɪʃən] *n* équivoque *f*.

ER *abbr* (*BRIT*: = *Elizabeth Regina*) *la reine Élisabeth.*

ERA *n abbr* (*US POL*: = *Equal Rights Amendment*) *amendement sur l'égalité des droits des femmes.*

era ['ɪərə] *n* ère *f*, époque *f*.

eradicate [ɪ'rædɪkeɪt] *vt* éliminer.

erase [ɪ'reɪz] *vt* effacer.

eraser [ɪ'reɪzə*] *n* gomme *f*.

erect [ɪ'rɛkt] *adj* droit(e) ♦ *vt* construire; (*monument*) ériger, élever; (*tent etc*) dresser.

erection [ɪ'rɛkʃən] *n* (*PHYSIOL*) érection *f*; (*of building*) construction *f*; (*of machinery etc*) installation *f*.

ergonomics [əːgə'nɔmɪks] *n* ergonomie *f*.

ERISA *n abbr* (*US*: = *Employee Retirement Income Security Act*) *loi sur les pensions de retraite.*

Eritrea [ɛrɪ'treɪə] *n* Érythrée *f*.

ERM *n abbr* (= *Exchange Rate Mechanism*) mécanisme *m* des taux de change.

ermine ['əːmɪn] *n* hermine *f*.

ERNIE ['əːnɪ] *n abbr* (*BRIT*: = *Electronic Random*

Number Indicator Equipment) ordinateur servant au tirage des bons à lots gagnants.

erode [ɪ'rəud] *vt* éroder; (*metal*) ronger.

erogenous zone [ɪ'rɔdʒənəs-] *n* zone *f* érogène.

erosion [ɪ'rəuʒən] *n* érosion *f*.

erotic [ɪ'rɔtɪk] *adj* érotique.

eroticism [ɪ'rɔtɪsɪzəm] *n* érotisme *m*.

err [əː*] *vi* se tromper; (*REL*) pécher.

errand ['ɛrnd] *n* course *f*, commission *f*; **to run ~s** faire des courses; **~ of mercy** mission *f* de charité, acte *m* charitable.

errand boy *n* garçon *m* de courses.

erratic [ɪ'rætɪk] *adj* irrégulier(ière); inconstant(e).

erroneous [ɪ'rəunɪəs] *adj* erroné(e).

error ['ɛrə*] *n* erreur *f*; **typing/spelling ~** faute *f* de frappe/d'orthographe; **in ~** par erreur, par méprise; **~s and omissions excepted** sauf erreur ou omission.

error message *n* (*COMPUT*) message *m* d'erreur.

erstwhile ['əːstwaɪl] *adj* précédent(e), d'autrefois.

erudite ['ɛrjudaɪt] *adj* savant(e).

erupt [ɪ'rʌpt] *vi* entrer en éruption; (*fig*) éclater, exploser.

eruption [ɪ'rʌpʃən] *n* éruption *f*; (*of anger, violence*) explosion *f*.

ESA *n abbr* (= *European Space Agency*) ASE *f* (= *Agence spatiale européenne*).

escalate ['ɛskəleɪt] *vi* s'intensifier; (*costs*) monter en flèche.

escalation [ɛskə'leɪʃən] *n* escalade *f*.

escalation clause *n* clause *f* d'indexation.

escalator ['ɛskəleɪtə*] *n* escalier roulant.

escapade [ɛskə'peɪd] *n* fredaine *f*; équipée *f*.

escape [ɪ'skeɪp] *n* évasion *f*, fuite *f*; (*of gas etc*) fuite; (: *TECH*) échappement *m* ♦ *vi* s'échapper, fuir; (*from jail*) s'évader; (*fig*) s'en tirer, en réchapper; (*leak*) fuir; s'échapper ♦ *vt* échapper à; **to ~ from** (*person*) échapper à; (*place*) s'échapper de; (*fig*) fuir; **to ~ to** (*another place*) fuir à, s'enfuir à; **to ~ to safety** se réfugier dans *or* gagner un endroit sûr; **to ~ notice** passer inaperçu(e).

escape artist *n* virtuose *m/f* de l'évasion.

escape clause *n* clause *f* dérogatoire.

escapee [ɪskeɪ'piː] *n* évadé/e.

escape key *n* (*COMPUT*) touche *f* d'échappement.

escape route *n* (*from fire*) issue *f* de secours; (*of prisoners etc*) voie empruntée pour s'échapper.

escapism [ɪ'skeɪpɪzəm] *n* évasion *f* (*fig*).

escapist [ɪ'skeɪpɪst] *adj* (*literature*) d'évasion ♦ *n* personne *f* qui se réfugie hors de la réalité.

escapologist [ɛskə'pɔlədʒɪst] *n* (*BRIT*) = **escape artist**.

escarpment [ɪs'kɑːpmənt] *n* escarpement *m*.

eschew [ɪs'tʃuː] *vt* éviter.

escort *vt* [ɪ'skɔːt] escorter ♦ *n* ['ɛskɔːt] escorte *f*; (*to dance etc*): **her ~** son compagnon *or* cavalier; **his ~** sa compagne.

escort agency *n* bureau *m* d'hôtesses.

Eskimo ['ɛskɪməu] *adj* esquimau(de), eskimo ♦ *n* Esquimau/de; (*LING*) esquimau *m*.

ESL *n abbr* (*SCOL*) = *English as a Second Language*.

esophagus [iː'sɔfəgəs] *n* (*US*) = **oesophagus**.

esoteric [ɛsə'tɛrɪk] *adj* ésotérique.

ESP *n abbr* = **extrasensory perception**; (*SCOL*) = *English for Special Purposes*.

esp. *abbr* = **especially**.

especially [ɪ'spɛʃlɪ] *adv* (*specifically*) spécialement, exprès; (*more than usually*) particulièrement; (*above all*) particulièrement, surtout.

espionage ['ɛspɪənɑːʒ] *n* espionnage *m*.

esplanade [ɛsplə'neɪd] *n* esplanade *f*.

espouse [ɪ'spauz] *vt* épouser, embrasser.

Esquire [ɪ'skwaɪə*] *n* (*BRIT*: *abbr* **Esq.**): J. Brown, ~ Monsieur J. Brown.

essay ['ɛseɪ] *n* (*SCOL*) dissertation *f*; (*LITERATURE*) essai *m*; (*attempt*) tentative *f*.

essence ['ɛsns] *n* essence *f*; **in ~** en substance; **speed is of the ~** l'essentiel, c'est la rapidité.

essential [ɪ'sɛnʃl] *adj* essentiel(le); (*basic*) fondamental(e) ♦ *n* élément essentiel; **it is ~ that** il est essentiel *or* primordial que.

essentially [ɪ'sɛnʃlɪ] *adv* essentiellement.

EST *abbr* (*US*: = *Eastern Standard Time*) heure d'hiver de New York.

est. *abbr* = **established, estimate(d)**.

establish [ɪ'stæblɪʃ] *vt* établir; (*business*) fonder, créer; (*one's power etc*) asseoir, affermir.

establishment [ɪ'stæblɪʃmənt] *n* établissement *m*; création *f*; (*institution*) établissement *m*; **the E~** les pouvoirs établis; l'ordre établi.

estate [ɪ'steɪt] *n* (*land*) domaine *m*, propriété *f*; (*LAW*) biens *mpl*, succession *f*; (*BRIT*: *also*: **housing ~**) lotissement *m*.

estate agency *n* (*BRIT*) agence immobilière.

estate agent *n* (*BRIT*) agent immobilier.

estate car *n* (*BRIT*) break *m*.

esteem [ɪ'stiːm] *n* estime *f* ♦ *vt* estimer; apprécier; **to hold sb in high ~** tenir qn en haute estime.

esthetic [ɪs'θɛtɪk] *adj* (*US*) = **aesthetic**.

estimate *n* ['ɛstɪmət] estimation *f*; (*COMM*) devis *m* ♦ *vt* ['ɛstɪmeɪt] estimer ♦ *vi* (*BRIT COMM*): **to ~ for** estimer, faire une estimation de; (*bid for*) faire un devis pour; **to give sb an ~ of** faire *or* donner un devis à qn pour; **at a rough ~** approximativement.

estimation [ɛstɪ'meɪʃən] *n* opinion *f*; estime *f*; **in my ~** à mon avis, selon moi.

Estonia [ɛ'stəunɪə] *n* Estonie *f*.

Estonian [ɛ'stəunɪən] *adj* estonien(ne) ♦ *n* Estonien/ne; (*LING*) estonien *m*.

estranged [ɪs'treɪndʒd] *adj* (*couple*) séparé(e); (*husband, wife*) dont on s'est séparé(e).

estrangement [ɪs'treɪndʒmənt] *n* (*from wife, family*) séparation *f*.

estrogen ['iːstrəudʒən] *n* (*US*) = **oestrogen**.

estuary ['ɛstjuərɪ] *n* estuaire *m*.

ET *n abbr* (*BRIT*: = *Employment Training*) formation professionnelle pour les demandeurs d'emploi ♦ *abbr* (*US*: = *Eastern Time*) *heure de New York*.

ETA *n abbr* (= *estimated time of arrival*) HPA *f* (= *heure probable d'arrivée*).

et al. *abbr* (= *et alii: and others*) et coll.

etc. *abbr* (= *et cetera*) etc.

etch [ɛtʃ] *vt* graver à l'eau forte.

etching ['ɛtʃɪŋ] *n* eau-forte *f*.

ETD *n abbr* (= *estimated time of departure*) HPD *f* (= *heure probable de départ*).

eternal [ɪ'təːnl] *adj* éternel(le).

eternity [ɪ'təːnɪtɪ] *n* éternité *f*.

ether ['iːθə*] *n* éther *m*.

ethereal [ɪ'θɪərɪəl] *adj* éthéré(e).

ethical ['ɛθɪkl] *adj* moral(e).

ethics ['ɛθɪks] *n* éthique *f* ♦ *npl* moralité *f*.

Ethiopia [iːθɪ'əupɪə] *n* Éthiopie *f*.

Ethiopian [iːθɪ'əupɪən] *adj* éthiopien(ne) ♦ *n* Éthiopien/ne.

ethnic ['ɛθnɪk] *adj* ethnique; (*clothes, food*) folklorique, exotique; *propre aux minorités ethniques non-occidentales*.

ethnic cleansing [-'klɛnzɪŋ] *n* purification *f* ethnique.

ethnology [ɛθ'nɔlədʒɪ] *n* ethnologie *f*.

ethos ['iːθɔs] *n* (système *m* de) valeurs *fpl*.

etiquette ['ɛtɪkɛt] *n* convenances *fpl*, étiquette *f*.

ETV *n abbr* (*US*: = *Educational Television*) télévision scolaire.

etymology [ɛtɪ'mɔlədʒɪ] *n* étymologie *f*.

EU *n abbr* (= *European Union*) UE *f*.

eucalyptus [juːkə'lɪptəs] *n* eucalyptus *m*.

eulogy ['juːlədʒɪ] *n* éloge *m*.

euphemism ['juːfəmɪzəm] *n* euphémisme *m*.

euphemistic [juːfə'mɪstɪk] *adj* euphémique.

euphoria [juː'fɔːrɪə] *n* euphorie *f*.

Eurasia [juə'reɪʃə] *n* Eurasie *f*.

Eurasian [juə'reɪʃən] *adj* eurasien(ne); (*continent*) eurasiatique ♦ *n* Eurasien/ne.

Euratom [juə'rætəm] *n abbr* (= *European Atomic Energy Community*) EURATOM *f*.

Euro- ['juərəu] *prefix* euro-.

Eurocheque ['juərəutʃɛk] *n* eurochèque *m*.

Eurocrat ['juərəukræt] *n* eurocrate *m/f*.

Eurodollar ['juərəudɔlə*] *n* eurodollar *m*.

Europe ['juərəp] *n* Europe *f*.

European [juərə'piːən] *adj* européen(ne) ♦ *n* Européen/ne.

European Court of Justice *n* Cour *f* de Justice de la CEE.

Euro-sceptic ['juərəuskɛptɪk] *n* eurosceptique *m/f*.

euthanasia [juːθə'neɪzɪə] *n* euthanasie *f*.

evacuate [ɪ'vækjueɪt] *vt* évacuer.

evacuation [ɪvækju'eɪʃən] *n* évacuation *f*.

evacuee [ɪvækju'iː] *n* évacué/e.

evade [ɪ'veɪd] *vt* échapper à; (*question etc*) éluder; (*duties*) se dérober à.

evaluate [ɪ'væljueɪt] *vt* évaluer.

evangelist [ɪ'vændʒəlɪst] *n* évangéliste *m*.

evangelize [ɪ'vændʒəlaɪz] *vt* évangéliser, prêcher l'Évangile à.

evaporate [ɪ'væpəreɪt] *vi* s'évaporer ♦ *vt* faire évaporer.

evaporated milk [ɪ'væpəreɪtɪd-] *n* lait condensé (non sucré).

evaporation [ɪvæpə'reɪʃən] *n* évaporation *f*.

evasion [ɪ'veɪʒən] *n* dérobade *f*; (*excuse*) faux-fuyant *m*.

evasive [ɪ'veɪsɪv] *adj* évasif(ive).

eve [iːv] *n*: **on the ~ of** à la veille de.

even ['iːvn] *adj* régulier(ière), égal(e); (*number*) pair(e) ♦ *adv* même; **~ if** même si + *indicative*; **~ though** quand (bien) même + *conditional*, alors même que + *conditional*; **~ more** encore plus; **~ faster** encore plus vite; **~ so** quand même; **not ~** pas même; **to break ~** s'y retrouver, équilibrer ses comptes; **to get ~ with sb** prendre sa revanche sur qn.

▶**even out** *vi* s'égaliser.

even-handed [iːvn'hændɪd] *adj* équitable.

evening ['iːvnɪŋ] *n* soir *m*; (*as duration, event*) soirée *f*; **in the ~** le soir; **this ~** ce soir; **tomorrow/yesterday ~** demain/hier soir.

evening class *n* cours *m* du soir.

evening dress *n* (*man's*) habit *m* de soirée, smoking *m*; (*woman's*) robe *f* de soirée.

evenly ['iːvnlɪ] *adv* uniformément, également; (*space*) régulièrement.

evensong ['iːvnsɔŋ] *n* office *m* du soir.

event [ɪ'vɛnt] *n* événement *m*; (*SPORT*) épreuve *f*; **in the course of ~s** par la suite; **in the ~ of** en cas de; **in the ~** en réalité, en fait; **at all ~s** (*BRIT*), **in any ~** en tout cas, de toute manière.

eventful [ɪ'vɛntful] *adj* mouvementé(e).

eventing [ɪ'vɛntɪŋ] *n* (*HORSE-RIDING*) concours complet (*équitation*).

eventual [ɪ'vɛntʃuəl] *adj* final(e).

eventuality [ɪvɛntʃu'ælɪtɪ] *n* possibilité *f*, éventualité *f*.

eventually [ɪ'vɛntʃuəlɪ] *adv* finalement.

ever ['ɛvə*] *adv* jamais; (*at all times*) toujours; **the best ~** le meilleur qu'on ait jamais vu; **did you ~ meet him?** est-ce qu'il vous est arrivé de le rencontrer?; **have you ~ been there?** y êtes-vous déjà allé?; **for ~** pour toujours; **hardly ~** ne ... presque jamais; **~ since** *adv* depuis ♦ *conj* depuis que; **so pretty** si joli; **thank you ~ so much** merci mille fois;

Everest ['ɛvərɪst] *n* (*also*: **Mount ~**) le mont Everest, l'Everest *m*.

evergreen ['ɛvəgriːn] *n* arbre *m* à feuilles persistantes.

everlasting [ɛvəˈlɑːstɪŋ] *adj* éternel(le).
every [ˈɛvrɪ] *adj* chaque; ~ **day** tous les jours, chaque jour; ~ **other/third day** tous les deux/trois jours; ~ **other car** une voiture sur deux; ~ **now and then** de temps en temps; **I have** ~ **confidence in him** j'ai entièrement *or* pleinement confiance en lui.
everybody [ˈɛvrɪbɔdɪ] *pron* tout le monde, tous *pl*; ~ **knows about it** tout le monde le sait; ~ **else** tous les autres.
everyday [ˈɛvrɪdeɪ] *adj* (*expression*) courant(e), d'usage courant; (*use*) courant; (*occurrence, experience*) de tous les jours, ordinaire.
everyone [ˈɛvrɪwʌn] = **everybody**.
everything [ˈɛvrɪθɪŋ] *pron* tout; ~ **is ready** tout est prêt; **he did** ~ **possible** il a fait tout son possible.
everywhere [ˈɛvrɪwɛə*] *adv* partout; ~ **you go you meet …** où qu'on aille, on rencontre ….
evict [ɪˈvɪkt] *vt* expulser.
eviction [ɪˈvɪkʃən] *n* expulsion *f*.
eviction notice *n* préavis *m* d'expulsion.
evidence [ˈɛvɪdns] *n* (*proof*) preuve(s) *f(pl)*; (*of witness*) témoignage *m*; (*sign*): **to show** ~ **of** donner des signes de; **to give** ~ témoigner, déposer; **in** ~ (*obvious*) en évidence; en vue.
evident [ˈɛvɪdnt] *adj* évident(e).
evidently [ˈɛvɪdntlɪ] *adv* de toute évidence.
evil [ˈiːvl] *adj* mauvais(e) ♦ *n* mal *m*.
evince [ɪˈvɪns] *vt* manifester.
evocative [ɪˈvɔkətɪv] *adj* évocateur(trice).
evoke [ɪˈvəuk] *vt* évoquer; (*admiration*) susciter.
evolution [iːvəˈluːʃən] *n* évolution *f*.
evolve [ɪˈvɔlv] *vt* élaborer ♦ *vi* évoluer, se transformer.
ewe [juː] *n* brebis *f*.
ewer [ˈjuːə*] *n* broc *m*.
ex- [ɛks] *prefix* (*former: husband, president etc*) ex-; (*out of*): **the price** ~ **works** le prix départ usine.
exacerbate [ɛksˈæsəbeɪt] *vt* (*pain*) exacerber, accentuer; (*fig*) aggraver.
exact [ɪgˈzækt] *adj* exact(e) ♦ *vt*: **to** ~ **sth (from)** extorquer qch (à); exiger qch (de).
exacting [ɪgˈzæktɪŋ] *adj* exigeant(e); (*work*) fatigant(e).
exactitude [ɪgˈzæktɪtjuːd] *n* exactitude *f*, précision *f*.
exactly [ɪgˈzæktlɪ] *adv* exactement; ~! parfaitement!, précisément!
exaggerate [ɪgˈzædʒəreɪt] *vt, vi* exagérer.
exaggeration [ɪgzædʒəˈreɪʃən] *n* exagération *f*.
exalted [ɪgˈzɔːltɪd] *adj* (*rank*) élevé(e); (*person*) haut placé(e); (*elated*) exalté(e).
exam [ɪgˈzæm] *n abbr* (*SCOL*) = **examination**.
examination [ɪgzæmɪˈneɪʃən] *n* (*SCOL, MED*) examen *m*; **to take** *or* (*BRIT*) **sit an** ~ passer un examen; **the matter is under** ~ la question est à l'examen.

examine [ɪgˈzæmɪn] *vt* (*gen*) examiner; (*SCOL, LAW: person*) interroger; (*inspect: machine, premises*) inspecter; (*passport*) contrôler; (*luggage*) fouiller.
examiner [ɪgˈzæmɪnə*] *n* examinateur/trice.
example [ɪgˈzɑːmpl] *n* exemple *m*; **for** ~ par exemple; **to set a good/bad** ~ donner le bon/mauvais exemple.
exasperate [ɪgˈzɑːspəreɪt] *vt* exaspérer, agacer.
exasperation [ɪgzɑːspəˈreɪʃən] *n* exaspération *f*, irritation *f*.
excavate [ˈɛkskəveɪt] *vt* excaver; (*object*) mettre au jour.
excavation [ɛkskəˈveɪʃən] *n* excavation *f*.
excavator [ˈɛkskəveɪtə*] *n* excavateur *m*, excavatrice *f*.
exceed [ɪkˈsiːd] *vt* dépasser; (*one's powers*) outrepasser.
exceedingly [ɪkˈsiːdɪŋlɪ] *adv* excessivement.
excel [ɪkˈsɛl] *vi* exceller ♦ *vt* surpasser; **to** ~ **o.s.** (*BRIT*) se surpasser.
excellence [ˈɛksələns] *n* excellence *f*.
Excellency [ˈɛksələnsɪ] *n*: **His** ~ son Excellence *f*.
excellent [ˈɛksələnt] *adj* excellent(e).
except [ɪkˈsɛpt] *prep* (*also*: ~ **for**, ~**ing**) sauf, excepté, à l'exception de ♦ *vt* excepter; ~ **if/when** sauf si/quand; ~ **that** excepté que, si ce n'est que.
exception [ɪkˈsɛpʃən] *n* exception *f*; **to take** ~ **to** s'offusquer de; **with the** ~ **of** à l'exception de.
exceptional [ɪkˈsɛpʃənl] *adj* exceptionnel(le).
excerpt [ˈɛksəːpt] *n* extrait *m*.
excess [ɪkˈsɛs] *n* excès *m*; **in** ~ **of** plus de.
excess baggage *n* excédent *m* de bagages.
excess fare *n* supplément *m*.
excessive [ɪkˈsɛsɪv] *adj* excessif(ive).
excess supply *n* suroffre *f*, offre *f* excédentaire.
exchange [ɪksˈtʃeɪndʒ] *n* échange *m*; (*also*: **telephone** ~) central *m* ♦ *vt*: **to** ~ **(for)** échanger (contre); **in** ~ **for** en échange de; **foreign** ~ (*COMM*) change *m*.
exchange control *n* contrôle *m* des changes.
exchange market *n* marché *m* des changes.
exchange rate *n* taux *m* de change.
exchequer [ɪksˈtʃɛkə*] *n* (*BRIT*) Echiquier *m*, ≈ ministère *m* des Finances.
excisable [ɪkˈsaɪzəbl] *adj* taxable.
excise *n* [ˈɛksaɪz] taxe *f* ♦ *vt* [ɛkˈsaɪz] exciser.
excise duties *npl* impôts indirects.
excitable [ɪkˈsaɪtəbl] *adj* excitable, nerveux(euse).
excite [ɪkˈsaɪt] *vt* exciter; **to get** ~**d** s'exciter.
excitement [ɪkˈsaɪtmənt] *n* excitation *f*.
exciting [ɪkˈsaɪtɪŋ] *adj* passionnant(e).
excl. *abbr* = **excluding, exclusive (of)**.
exclaim [ɪkˈskleɪm] *vi* s'exclamer.
exclamation [ɛkskləˈmeɪʃən] *n* exclamation *f*.
exclamation mark *n* point *m* d'exclamation.

exclude [ɪkˈskluːd] *vt* exclure.
excluding [ɪkˈskluːdɪŋ] *prep*: ~ **VAT** la TVA non comprise.
exclusion [ɪkˈskluːʒən] *n* exclusion *f*; **to the ~ of** à l'exclusion de.
exclusion clause *n* clause *f* d'exclusion.
exclusion zone *n* zone interdite.
exclusive [ɪkˈskluːsɪv] *adj* exclusif(ive); (*club, district*) sélect(e); (*item of news*) en exclusivité ♦ *adv* (*COMM*) exclusivement, non inclus; ~ **of VAT** TVA non comprise; ~ **of postage** (les) frais de poste non compris; **from 1st to 15th March** ~ du 1er au 15 mars exclusivement *or* exclu; ~ **rights** (*COMM*) exclusivité *f*.
exclusively [ɪkˈskluːsɪvlɪ] *adv* exclusivement.
excommunicate [ɛkskəˈmjuːnɪkeɪt] *vt* excommunier.
excrement [ˈɛkskrəmənt] *n* excrément *m*.
excruciating [ɪkˈskruːʃɪeɪtɪŋ] *adj* atroce, déchirant(e).
excursion [ɪkˈskəːʃən] *n* excursion *f*.
excursion ticket *n* billet *m* tarif excursion.
excusable [ɪkˈskjuːzəbl] *adj* excusable.
excuse *n* [ɪkˈskjuːs] excuse *f* ♦ *vt* [ɪkˈskjuːz] excuser; (*justify*) excuser, justifier; **to ~ sb from** (*activity*) dispenser qn de; ~ **me!** excusez-moi!, pardon!; **now if you will ~ me, ...** maintenant, si vous (le) permettez ...; **to make ~s for sb** trouver des excuses à qn; **to ~ o.s. for sth/for doing sth** s'excuser de/d'avoir fait qch.
ex-directory [ˈɛksdɪˈrɛktərɪ] *adj* (*BRIT*): ~ **(phone) number** numéro *m* (de téléphone) sur la liste rouge.
execute [ˈɛksɪkjuːt] *vt* exécuter.
execution [ɛksɪˈkjuːʃən] *n* exécution *f*.
executioner [ɛksɪˈkjuːʃnə*] *n* bourreau *m*.
executive [ɪgˈzɛkjutɪv] *n* (*COMM*) cadre *m*; (*POL*) exécutif *m* ♦ *adj* exécutif(ive); (*position, job*) de cadre; (*secretary*) de direction; (*offices*) de la direction; (*car, plane*) de fonction.
executive director *n* administrateur/trice.
executor [ɪgˈzɛkjutə*] *n* exécuteur/trice testamentaire.
exemplary [ɪgˈzɛmplərɪ] *adj* exemplaire.
exemplify [ɪgˈzɛmplɪfaɪ] *vt* illustrer.
exempt [ɪgˈzɛmpt] *adj*: ~ **from** exempté(e) *or* dispensé(e) de ♦ *vt*: **to ~ sb from** exempter *or* dispenser qn de.
exemption [ɪgˈzɛmpʃən] *n* exemption *f*, dispense *f*.
exercise [ˈɛksəsaɪz] *n* exercice *m* ♦ *vt* exercer; (*patience etc*) faire preuve de; (*dog*) promener ♦ *vi* (*also*: **to take** ~) prendre de l'exercice.
exercise bike *n* vélo *m* d'appartement.
exercise book *n* cahier *m*.
exert [ɪgˈzəːt] *vt* exercer, employer; (*strength, force*) employer; **to ~ o.s.** se dépenser.
exertion [ɪgˈzəːʃən] *n* effort *m*.

ex gratia [ˈɛksˈɡreɪʃə] *adj*: ~ **payment** gratification *f*.
exhale [ɛksˈheɪl] *vt* expirer; exhaler ♦ *vi* expirer.
exhaust [ɪgˈzɔːst] *n* (*also*: ~ **fumes**) gaz *mpl* d'échappement; (*also*: ~ **pipe**) tuyau *m* d'échappement ♦ *vt* épuiser; **to ~ o.s.** s'épuiser.
exhausted [ɪgˈzɔːstɪd] *adj* épuisé(e).
exhausting [ɪgˈzɔːstɪŋ] *adj* épuisant(e).
exhaustion [ɪgˈzɔːstʃən] *n* épuisement *m*; **nervous ~** fatigue nerveuse.
exhaustive [ɪgˈzɔːstɪv] *adj* très complet(ète).
exhibit [ɪgˈzɪbɪt] *n* (*ART*) pièce *f or* objet *m* exposé(e); (*LAW*) pièce à conviction ♦ *vt* exposer; (*courage, skill*) faire preuve de.
exhibition [ɛksɪˈbɪʃən] *n* exposition *f*; ~ **of temper** manifestation *f* de colère.
exhibitionist [ɛksɪˈbɪʃənɪst] *n* exhibitionniste *m/f*.
exhibitor [ɪgˈzɪbɪtə*] *n* exposant/e.
exhilarating [ɪgˈzɪləreɪtɪŋ] *adj* grisant(e); stimulant(e).
exhilaration [ɪgzɪləˈreɪʃən] *n* euphorie *f*, ivresse *f*.
exhort [ɪgˈzɔːt] *vt* exhorter.
exile [ˈɛksaɪl] *n* exil *m*; (*person*) exilé/e ♦ *vt* exiler; **in ~** en exil.
exist [ɪgˈzɪst] *vi* exister.
existence [ɪgˈzɪstəns] *n* existence *f*; **to be in ~** exister.
existentialism [ɛgzɪsˈtɛnʃlɪzəm] *n* existentialisme *m*.
existing [ɪgˈzɪstɪŋ] *adj* (*laws*) existant(e); (*system, regime*) actuel(le).
exit [ˈɛksɪt] *n* sortie *f* ♦ *vi* (*COMPUT, THEAT*) sortir.
exit poll *n* sondage *m* (*fait à la sortie de l'isoloir*).
exit ramp *n* (*US AUT*) bretelle *f* d'accès.
exit visa *n* visa *m* de sortie.
exodus [ˈɛksədəs] *n* exode *m*.
ex officio [ˈɛksəˈfɪʃɪəu] *adj*, *adv* d'office, de droit.
exonerate [ɪgˈzɔnəreɪt] *vt*: **to ~ from** disculper de.
exorbitant [ɪgˈzɔːbɪtnt] *adj* (*price*) exorbitant(e), excessif(ive); (*demands*) exorbitant, démesuré(e).
exorcize [ˈɛksɔːsaɪz] *vt* exorciser.
exotic [ɪgˈzɔtɪk] *adj* exotique.
expand [ɪkˈspænd] *vt* (*area*) agrandir; (*quantity*) accroître; (*influence etc*) étendre ♦ *vi* (*population, production*) s'accroître; (*trade, influence etc*) se développer, s'étendre; (*gas, metal*) se dilater; **to ~ on** (*notes, story etc*) développer.
expanse [ɪkˈspæns] *n* étendue *f*.
expansion [ɪkˈspænʃən] *n* (*see expand*) développement *m*; accroissement *m*; extension *f*; dilatation *f*.
expansionism [ɪkˈspænʃənɪzəm] *n* expansion-

nisme *m*.

expansionist [ɪk'spænʃənɪst] *adj* expansionniste.

expatriate *n* [ɛks'pætrɪət] expatrié/e ♦ *vt* [ɛks'pætrɪeɪt] expatrier, exiler.

expect [ɪk'spɛkt] *vt* (*anticipate*) s'attendre à, s'attendre à ce que + *sub*; (*count on*) compter sur, escompter; (*hope for*) espérer; (*require*) demander, exiger; (*suppose*) supposer; (*await, also baby*) attendre ♦ *vi*: **to be ~ing** être enceinte; **to ~ sb to do** (*anticipate*) s'attendre à ce que qn fasse; (*demand*) attendre de qn qu'il fasse; **to ~ to do sth** penser *or* compter faire qch, s'attendre à faire qch; **as ~ed** comme prévu; **I ~ so** je crois que oui, je crois bien.

expectancy [ɪk'spɛktənsɪ] *n* attente *f*; **life ~** espérance *f* de vie.

expectant [ɪk'spɛktənt] *adj* qui attend (quelque chose); **~ mother** future maman.

expectantly [ɪk'spɛktəntlɪ] *adv* (*look, listen*) avec l'air d'attendre quelque chose.

expectation [ɛkspɛk'teɪʃən] *n* attente *f*, prévisions *fpl*; espérance(s) *f(pl)*; **in ~ of** dans l'attente de, en prévision de; **against** *or* **contrary to all ~(s)** contre toute attente, contrairement à ce qu'on attendait; **to come** *or* **live up to sb's ~s** répondre à l'attente *or* aux espérances de qn.

expedience, expediency [ɪk'spiːdɪəns, ɪk'spiːdɪənsɪ] *n* opportunité *f*; convenance *f* (du moment); **for the sake of ~** parce que c'est (*or* c'était) plus simple *or* plus commode.

expedient [ɪk'spiːdɪənt] *adj* indiqué(e), opportun(e); commode ♦ *n* expédient *m*.

expedite ['ɛkspədaɪt] *vt* hâter; expédier.

expedition [ɛkspə'dɪʃən] *n* expédition *f*.

expeditionary force [ɛkspə'dɪʃənrɪ-] *n* corps *m* expéditionnaire.

expeditious [ɛkspə'dɪʃəs] *adj* expéditif(ive), prompt(e).

expel [ɪk'spɛl] *vt* chasser, expulser; (*SCOL*) renvoyer, exclure.

expend [ɪk'spɛnd] *vt* consacrer; (*use up*) dépenser.

expendable [ɪk'spɛndəbl] *adj* remplaçable.

expenditure [ɪk'spɛndɪtʃə*] *n* dépense *f*; dépenses *fpl*.

expense [ɪk'spɛns] *n* (*cost*) coût *m*; (*spending*) dépense *f*, frais *mpl*; **~s** *npl* frais *mpl*; dépenses; **to go to the ~ of** faire la dépense de; **at great/little ~** à grands/peu de frais; **at the ~ of** aux frais de; (*fig*) aux dépens de.

expense account *n* (note *f* de) frais *mpl*.

expensive [ɪk'spɛnsɪv] *adj* cher(chère), coûteux(euse); **to be ~** coûter cher; **~ tastes** goûts *mpl* de luxe.

experience [ɪk'spɪərɪəns] *n* expérience *f* ♦ *vt* connaître; éprouver; **to know by ~** savoir par expérience.

experienced [ɪk'spɪərɪənst] *adj* expérimenté(e).

experiment [ɪk'spɛrɪmənt] *n* expérience *f* ♦ *vi* faire une expérience; **to ~ with** expérimenter; **to perform** *or* **carry out an ~** faire une expérience; **as an ~** à titre d'expérience.

experimental [ɪkspɛrɪ'mɛntl] *adj* expérimental(e).

expert ['ɛkspəːt] *adj* expert(e) ♦ *n* expert *m*; **~ in** *or* **at doing sth** spécialiste de qch; **an ~ on sth** un spécialiste de qch; **~ witness** (*LAW*) expert *m*,

expertise [ɛkspəː'tiːz] *n* (grande) compétence.

expire [ɪk'spaɪə*] *vi* expirer.

expiry [ɪk'spaɪərɪ] *n* expiration *f*.

explain [ɪk'spleɪn] *vt* expliquer.

▸**explain away** *vt* justifier, excuser.

explanation [ɛksplə'neɪʃən] *n* explication *f*; **to find an ~ for sth** trouver une explication à qch.

explanatory [ɪk'splænətrɪ] *adj* explicatif(ive).

expletive [ɪk'spliːtɪv] *n* juron *m*.

explicit [ɪk'splɪsɪt] *adj* explicite; (*definite*) formel(le).

explode [ɪk'spləʊd] *vi* exploser ♦ *vt* faire exploser; (*fig: theory*) démolir; **to ~ a myth** détruire un mythe.

exploit *n* ['ɛksplɔɪt] exploit *m* ♦ *vt* [ɪk'splɔɪt] exploiter.

exploitation [ɛksplɔɪ'teɪʃən] *n* exploitation *f*.

exploration [ɛksplə'reɪʃən] *n* exploration *f*.

exploratory [ɪk'splɔrətrɪ] *adj* (*fig: talks*) préliminaire; **~ operation** (*MED*) intervention *f* (à visée) exploratrice.

explore [ɪk'splɔː*] *vt* explorer; (*possibilities*) étudier, examiner.

explorer [ɪk'splɔːrə*] *n* explorateur/trice.

explosion [ɪk'spləʊʒən] *n* explosion *f*.

explosive [ɪk'spləʊsɪv] *adj* explosif(ive) ♦ *n* explosif *m*.

exponent [ɪk'spəʊnənt] *n* (*of school of thought etc*) interprète *m*, représentant *m*; (*MATH*) exposant *m*.

export *vt* [ɛk'spɔːt] exporter ♦ *n* ['ɛkspɔːt] exportation *f* ♦ *cpd* d'exportation.

exportation [ɛkspɔː'teɪʃən] *n* exportation *f*.

exporter [ɛk'spɔːtə*] *n* exportateur *m*.

export licence *n* licence *f* d'exportation.

expose [ɪk'spəʊz] *vt* exposer; (*unmask*) démasquer, dévoiler; **to ~ o.s.** (*LAW*) commettre un outrage à la pudeur.

exposed [ɪk'spəʊzd] *adj* (*land, house*) exposé(e); (*ELEC: wire*) à nu; (*pipe, beam*) apparent(e).

exposition [ɛkspə'zɪʃən] *n* exposition *f*.

exposure [ɪk'spəʊʒə*] *n* exposition *f*; (*PHOT*) (temps *m* de) pose *f*; (: *shot*) pose; **suffering from ~** (*MED*) souffrant des effets du froid et de l'épuisement; **to die of ~** (*MED*) mourir de froid.

exposure meter *n* posemètre *m*.

expound [ɪk'spaʊnd] *vt* exposer, expliquer.

express [ɪk'sprɛs] *adj* (*definite*) formel(le), exprès(esse); (*BRIT: letter etc*) exprès *inv* ♦ *n* (*train*) rapide *m* ♦ *adv* (*send*) exprès ♦ *vt* exprimer; **to ~ o.s.** s'exprimer.
expression [ɪk'sprɛʃən] *n* expression *f*.
expressionism [ɪk'sprɛʃənɪzəm] *n* expressionnisme *m*.
expressive [ɪk'sprɛsɪv] *adj* expressif(ive).
expressly [ɪk'sprɛslɪ] *adv* expressément, formellement.
expressway [ɪk'sprɛsweɪ] *n* (*US*) voie *f* express (à plusieurs files).
expropriate [ɛks'prəʊprɪeɪt] *vt* exproprier.
expulsion [ɪk'spʌlʃən] *n* expulsion *f*; renvoi *m*.
exquisite [ɛk'skwɪzɪt] *adj* exquis(e).
ex-serviceman ['ɛks'sə:vɪsmən] *n* ancien combattant.
ext. *abbr* (*TEL*) = extension.
extemporize [ɪk'stɛmpəraɪz] *vi* improviser.
extend [ɪk'stɛnd] *vt* (*visit, street*) prolonger; (*deadline*) reporter, remettre; (*building*) agrandir; (*offer*) présenter, offrir; (*COMM: credit*) accorder ♦ *vi* (*land*) s'étendre.
extension [ɪk'stɛnʃən] *n* (*see extend*) prolongation *f*; agrandissement *m*; (*building*) annexe *f*; (*to wire, table*) rallonge *f*; (*telephone: in offices*) poste *m*; (*: in private house*) téléphone *m* supplémentaire; **~ 3718** (*TEL*) poste 3718.
extension cable *n* (*ELEC*) rallonge *f*.
extensive [ɪk'stɛnsɪv] *adj* étendu(e), vaste; (*damage, alterations*) considérable; (*inquiries*) approfondi(e); (*use*) largement répandu(e).
extensively [ɪk'stɛnsɪvlɪ] *adv* (*altered, damaged etc*) considérablement; **he's travelled ~** il a beaucoup voyagé.
extent [ɪk'stɛnt] *n* étendue *f*; (*degree: of damage, loss*) importance *f*; **to some ~** dans une certaine mesure; **to a certain ~** dans une certaine mesure, jusqu'à un certain point; **to a large ~** en grande partie; **to what ~?** dans quelle mesure?, jusqu'à quel point?; **to such an ~ that ...** à tel point que ....
extenuating [ɪk'stɛnjʊeɪtɪŋ] *adj*: **~ circumstances** circonstances atténuantes.
exterior [ɛk'stɪərɪə*] *adj* extérieur(e), du dehors ♦ *n* extérieur *m*; dehors *m*.
exterminate [ɪk'stə:mɪneɪt] *vt* exterminer.
extermination [ɪkstə:mɪ'neɪʃən] *n* extermination *f*.
external [ɛk'stə:nl] *adj* externe ♦ *n*: **the ~s** les apparences *fpl*; **for ~ use only** (*MED*) à usage externe.
externally [ɛk'stə:nəlɪ] *adv* extérieurement.
extinct [ɪk'stɪŋkt] *adj* éteint(e).
extinction [ɪk'stɪŋkʃən] *n* extinction *f*.
extinguish [ɪk'stɪŋgwɪʃ] *vt* éteindre.
extinguisher [ɪk'stɪŋgwɪʃə*] *n* extincteur *m*.
extol, (*US*) **extoll** [ɪk'stəʊl] *vt* (*merits*) chanter, prôner; (*person*) chanter les louanges de.
extort [ɪk'stɔ:t] *vt*: **to ~ sth (from)** extorquer qch (à).

extortion [ɪk'stɔ:ʃən] *n* extorsion *f*.
extortionate [ɪk'stɔ:ʃnɪt] *adj* exorbitant(e).
extra ['ɛkstrə] *adj* supplémentaire, de plus ♦ *adv* (*in addition*) en plus ♦ *n* supplément *m*; (*THEAT*) figurant/e; **wine will cost ~** le vin sera en supplément; **~ large sizes** très grandes tailles.
extra... ['ɛkstrə] *prefix* extra....
extract *vt* [ɪk'strækt] extraire; (*tooth*) arracher; (*money, promise*) soutirer ♦ *n* ['ɛkstrækt] extrait *m*.
extraction [ɪk'strækʃən] *n* (*also descent*) extraction *f*.
extractor fan [ɪk'stræktə-] *n* exhausteur *m*, ventilateur *m* extracteur.
extracurricular ['ɛkstrəkə'rɪkjulə*] *adj* (*SCOL*) parascolaire.
extradite ['ɛkstrədaɪt] *vt* extrader.
extradition [ɛkstrə'dɪʃən] *n* extradition *f*.
extramarital ['ɛkstrə'mærɪtl] *adj* extraconjugal(e).
extramural ['ɛkstrə'mjuərl] *adj* hors-faculté *inv*.
extraneous [ɛk'streɪnɪəs] *adj*: **~ to** étranger(ère) à.
extraordinary [ɪk'strɔ:dnrɪ] *adj* extraordinaire; **the ~ thing is that ...** le plus étrange *or* étonnant c'est que ....
extraordinary general meeting *n* assemblée générale extraordinaire.
extrapolation [ɛkstræpə'leɪʃən] *n* extrapolation *f*.
extrasensory perception (ESP) ['ɛkstrə'sɛnsərɪ-] *n* perception extrasensorielle.
extra time *n* (*FOOTBALL*) prolongations *fpl*.
extravagance [ɪk'strævəgəns] *n* (*excessive spending*) prodigalités *fpl*; (*thing bought*) folie *f*, dépense excessive *or* exagérée.
extravagant [ɪk'strævəgənt] *adj* extravagant(e); (*in spending: person*) prodigue, dépensier(ière); (*: tastes*) dispendieux(euse).
extreme [ɪk'stri:m] *adj, n* extrême (*m*); **the ~ left/right** (*POL*) l'extrême gauche *f*/droite *f*; **~s of temperature** différences *fpl* extrêmes de température.
extremely [ɪk'stri:mlɪ] *adv* extrêmement.
extremist [ɪk'stri:mɪst] *adj, n* extrémiste (*m/f*).
extremity [ɪk'strɛmɪtɪ] *n* extrémité *f*.
extricate ['ɛkstrɪkeɪt] *vt*: **to ~ sth (from)** dégager qch (de).
extrovert ['ɛkstrəvə:t] *n* extraverti/e.
exuberance [ɪg'zju:bərns] *n* exubérance *f*.
exuberant [ɪg'zju:bərnt] *adj* exubérant(e).
exude [ɪg'zju:d] *vt* exsuder; (*fig*) respirer; **the charm *etc* he ~s** le charme *etc* qui émane de lui.
exult [ɪg'zʌlt] *vi* exulter, jubiler.
exultant [ɪg'zʌltənt] *adj* (*shout, expression*) de triomphe; **to be ~** jubiler, triompher.
exultation [ɛgzʌl'teɪʃən] *n* exultation *f*, jubilation *f*.

eye [aɪ] n œil m (pl yeux); (of needle) trou m, chas m ♦ vt examiner; **as far as the ~ can see** à perte de vue; **to keep an ~ on** surveiller; **to have an ~ for sth** avoir l'œil pour qch; **in the public ~** en vue; **with an ~ to doing sth** (BRIT) en vue de faire qch; **there's more to this than meets the ~** ce n'est pas aussi simple que cela paraît.

eyeball ['aɪbɔːl] n globe m oculaire.

eyebath ['aɪbɑːθ] n (BRIT) œillère f (pour bains d'œil).

eyebrow ['aɪbrau] n sourcil m.

eyebrow pencil n crayon m à sourcils.

eye-catching ['aɪkætʃɪŋ] adj voyant(e), accrocheur(euse).

eye cup n (US) = eyebath.

eyedrops ['aɪdrɔps] npl gouttes fpl pour les yeux.

eyeful ['aɪful] n: **to get an ~ (of sth)** se rincer l'œil (en voyant qch).

eyeglass ['aɪglɑːs] n monocle m.

eyelash ['aɪlæʃ] n cil m.

eyelet ['aɪlɪt] n œillet m.

eye-level ['aɪlɛvl] adj en hauteur.

eyelid ['aɪlɪd] n paupière f.

eyeliner ['aɪlaɪnə*] n eye-liner m.

eye-opener ['aɪəupnə*] n révélation f.

eyeshadow ['aɪʃædəu] n ombre f à paupières.

eyesight ['aɪsaɪt] n vue f.

eyesore ['aɪsɔː*] n horreur f, chose f qui dépare or enlaidit.

eyestrain ['aɪstreɪn] adj: **to get ~** se fatiguer la vue or les yeux.

eyetooth, pl **-teeth** ['aɪtuːθ, -tiːθ] n canine supérieure; **to give one's eyeteeth for sth/to do sth** (fig) donner n'importe quoi pour qch/pour faire qch.

eyewash ['aɪwɔʃ] n bain m d'œil; (fig) frime f.

eye witness n témoin m oculaire.

eyrie ['ɪərɪ] n aire f.

F f

F, f [ɛf] n (letter) F, f m; (MUS): **F** fa m; **F for Frederick**, (US) **F for Fox** F comme François.

F abbr (= Fahrenheit) F.

FA n abbr (BRIT: = Football Association) fédération de football.

FAA n abbr (US) = Federal Aviation Administration.

fable ['feɪbl] n fable f.

fabric ['fæbrɪk] n tissu m ♦ cpd: **~ ribbon** n (for typewriter) ruban m (en) tissu.

fabricate ['fæbrɪkeɪt] vt fabriquer, inventer.

fabrication [fæbrɪ'keɪʃən] n fabrication f, invention f.

fabulous ['fæbjuləs] adj fabuleux(euse); (col: super) formidable, sensationnel(le).

façade [fə'sɑːd] n façade f.

face [feɪs] n visage m, figure f; expression f; grimace f; (of clock) cadran m; (of building) façade f; (side, surface) face f ♦ vt faire face à; (facts etc) accepter; **~ down** (person) à plat ventre; (card) face en dessous; **to lose/save ~** perdre/sauver la face; **to pull a ~** faire une grimace; **in the ~ of** (difficulties etc) face à, devant; **on the ~ of it** à première vue.

▶**face up to** vt fus faire face à, affronter.

face cloth n (BRIT) gant m de toilette.

face cream n crème f pour le visage.

face lift n lifting m; (of façade etc) ravalement m, retapage m.

face powder n poudre f (pour le visage).

face-saving ['feɪsseɪvɪŋ] adj qui sauve la face.

facet ['fæsɪt] n facette f.

facetious [fə'siːʃəs] adj facétieux(euse).

face-to-face ['feɪstə'feɪs] adv face à face.

face value ['feɪs'væljuː] n (of coin) valeur nominale; **to take sth at ~** (fig) prendre qch pour argent comptant.

facia ['feɪʃə] n = fascia.

facial ['feɪʃl] adj facial(e) ♦ n soin complet du visage.

facile ['fæsaɪl] adj facile.

facilitate [fə'sɪlɪteɪt] vt faciliter.

facility [fə'sɪlɪtɪ] n facilité f; **facilities** npl installations fpl, équipement m; **credit facilities** facilités de paiement.

facing ['feɪsɪŋ] prep face à, en face de ♦ n (of wall etc) revêtement m; (SEWING) revers m.

facsimile [fæk'sɪmɪlɪ] n (exact replica) facsimilé m; (also: **~ machine**) télécopieur m; (transmitted document) télécopie f.

fact [fækt] n fait m; **in ~** en fait; **to know for a ~ that** ... savoir pertinemment que ....

fact-finding ['fæktfaɪndɪŋ] adj: **a ~ tour** or **mission** une mission d'enquête.

faction ['fækʃən] n faction f.

factional ['fækʃənl] adj de factions.

factor ['fæktə*] n facteur m; (COMM) factor m, société f d'affacturage; (: agent) dépositaire m/f ♦ vi faire du factoring; **safety ~** facteur de sécurité.

factory ['fæktərɪ] n usine f, fabrique f.

factory farming n (BRIT) élevage industriel.

factory floor n: **the ~** (workers) les ouvriers mpl; (workshop) l'usine f; **on the ~** dans les ateliers.

factory ship n navire-usine m.

factual ['fæktjuəl] adj basé(e) sur les faits.

faculty ['fækəltɪ] n faculté f; (US: teaching staff) corps enseignant.

fad [fæd] n (col) manie f; engouement m.

fade [feɪd] vi se décolorer, passer; (light, sound, hope) s'affaiblir, disparaître; (flower) se faner.

▶**fade in** vt (*picture*) ouvrir en fondu; (*sound*) monter progressivement.

▶**fade out** vt (*picture*) fermer en fondu; (*sound*) baisser progressivement.

faeces, (US) **feces** ['fiːsiːz] npl fèces fpl.

fag [fæg] n (BRIT col: *cigarette*) sèche f; (: *chore*): **what a** ~! quelle corvée!; (US col: *homosexual*) pédé m.

fag end n (BRIT col) mégot m.

fagged out [fægd-] adj (BRIT col) crevé(e).

fail [feɪl] vt (*exam*) échouer à; (*candidate*) recaler; (*subj: courage, memory*) faire défaut à ♦ vi échouer; (*supplies*) manquer; (*eyesight, health, light: also:* **be** ~**ing**) baisser, s'affaiblir; (*brakes*) lâcher; **to** ~ **to do sth** (*neglect*) négliger de or ne pas faire qch; (*be unable*) ne pas arriver or parvenir à faire qch; **without** ~ à coup sûr; sans faute.

failing ['feɪlɪŋ] n défaut m ♦ prep faute de; ~ **that** à défaut, sinon.

failsafe ['feɪlseɪf] adj (*device etc*) à sûreté intégrée.

failure ['feɪljə*] n échec m; (*person*) raté/e; (*mechanical etc*) défaillance f; **his** ~ **to turn up** le fait de n'être pas venu or qu'il ne soit pas venu.

faint [feɪnt] adj faible; (*recollection*) vague; (*mark*) à peine visible; (*smell, breeze, trace*) léger(ère) ♦ n évanouissement m ♦ vi s'évanouir; **to feel** ~ défaillir.

faintest ['feɪntɪst] adj: **I haven't the** ~ **idea** je n'en ai pas la moindre idée.

faint-hearted ['feɪnt'hɑːtɪd] adj pusillanime.

faintly ['feɪntlɪ] adv faiblement; vaguement.

faintness ['feɪntnɪs] n faiblesse f.

fair [feə*] adj équitable, juste; (*reasonable*) correct(e), honnête; (*hair*) blond(e); (*skin, complexion*) pâle, blanc(blanche); (*weather*) beau(belle); (*good enough*) assez bon(ne) ♦ adv: **to play** ~ jouer franc jeu ♦ n foire f; (BRIT: *funfair*) fête (foraine) f; (*also:* **trade** ~) foire(-exposition) f commerciale; **it's not** ~! ce n'est pas juste!; **a** ~ **amount of** une quantité considérable de.

fair copy n copie f au propre; corrigé m.

fair game n: **to be** ~ (**for**) être une cible légitime (pour).

fairground ['feəgraund] n champ m de foire.

fair-haired [feə'heəd] adj (*person*) aux cheveux clairs, blond(e).

fairly ['feəlɪ] adv équitablement; (*quite*) assez; **I'm** ~ **sure** j'en suis quasiment or presque sûr.

fairness ['feənɪs] n (*of trial etc*) justice f, équité f; (*of person*) sens m de la justice; **in all** ~ en toute justice.

fair play n fair play m.

fairy ['feərɪ] n fée f.

fairy godmother n bonne fée.

fairy lights npl (BRIT) guirlande f électrique.

fairy tale n conte m de fées.

faith [feɪθ] n foi f; (*trust*) confiance f; (*sect*) culte m, religion f; **to have** ~ **in sb/sth** avoir confiance en qn/qch.

faithful ['feɪθful] adj fidèle.

faithfully ['feɪθfəlɪ] adv fidèlement; **yours** ~ (BRIT: *in letters*) veuillez agréer l'expression de mes salutations les plus distinguées.

faith healer [-hiːlə*] n guérisseur/euse.

fake [feɪk] n (*painting etc*) faux m; (*photo*) trucage m; (*person*) imposteur m ♦ adj faux(fausse) ♦ vt (*emotions*) simuler; (*photo*) truquer; (*story*) fabriquer; **his illness is a** ~ sa maladie est une comédie or de la simulation.

falcon ['fɔːlkən] n faucon m.

Falkland Islands ['fɔːlklənd-] npl: **the** ~ les Malouines fpl, les îles fpl Falkland.

fall [fɔːl] n chute f; (*decrease*) baisse f; (US: *autumn*) automne m ♦ vi (pt **fell**, pp **fallen** [fɛl, 'fɔːlən]) tomber; ~**s** npl (*waterfall*) chute f d'eau, cascade f; **to** ~ **flat** vi (*on one's face*) tomber de tout son long, s'étaler; (*joke*) tomber à plat; (*plan*) échouer; **to** ~ **short of** (*sb's expectations*) ne pas répondre à; **a** ~ **of snow** (BRIT) une chute de neige.

▶**fall apart** vi tomber en morceaux; (*col: emotionally*) craquer.

▶**fall back** vi reculer, se retirer.

▶**fall back on** vt fus se rabattre sur; **to have something to** ~ **back on** (*money etc*) avoir quelque chose en réserve; (*job etc*) avoir une solution de rechange.

▶**fall behind** vi prendre du retard.

▶**fall down** vi (*person*) tomber; (*building, hopes*) s'effondrer, s'écrouler.

▶**fall for** vt fus (*trick*) se laisser prendre à; (*person*) tomber amoureux(euse) de.

▶**fall in** vi s'effondrer; (MIL) se mettre en rangs.

▶**fall in with** vt fus (*sb's plans etc*) accepter.

▶**fall off** vi tomber; (*diminish*) baisser, diminuer.

▶**fall out** vi (*friends etc*) se brouiller.

▶**fall over** vi tomber (par terre).

▶**fall through** vi (*plan, project*) tomber à l'eau.

fallacy ['fæləsɪ] n erreur f, illusion f.

fallback ['fɔːlbæk] adj: ~ **position** position f de repli.

fallen ['fɔːlən] pp of **fall**.

fallible ['fæləbl] adj faillible.

fallopian tube [fə'ləupɪən-] n (ANAT) trompe f de Fallope.

fallout ['fɔːlaut] n retombées (radioactives).

fallout shelter n abri m anti-atomique.

fallow ['fæləu] adj en jachère; en friche.

false [fɔːls] adj faux(fausse); **under** ~ **pretences** sous un faux prétexte.

false alarm n fausse alerte.

falsehood ['fɔːlshud] n mensonge m.

falsely ['fɔːlslɪ] adv (*accuse*) à tort.

false teeth npl (BRIT) fausses dents.

falsify ['fɔːlsɪfaɪ] vt falsifier; (*accounts*) maquiller.

falter ['fɔːltə*] vi chanceler, vaciller.
fame [feɪm] n renommée f, renom m.
familiar [fə'mɪlɪə*] adj familier(ière); **to be ~ with sth** connaître qch; **to make o.s. ~ with sth** se familiariser avec qch; **to be on ~ terms with sb** bien connaître qn.
familiarity [fəmɪlɪ'ærɪtɪ] n familiarité f.
familiarize [fə'mɪlɪəraɪz] vt familiariser.
family ['fæmɪlɪ] n famille f.
family allowance n (BRIT) allocations familiales.
family business n entreprise familiale.
family credit n (BRIT) complément familial.
family doctor n médecin m de famille.
family life n vie f de famille.
family man n père m de famille.
family planning clinic n centre m de planning familial.
family tree n arbre m généalogique.
famine ['fæmɪn] n famine f.
famished ['fæmɪʃt] adj affamé(e); **I'm ~!** (col) je meurs de faim!
famous ['feɪməs] adj célèbre.
famously ['feɪməslɪ] adv (get on) fameusement, à merveille.
fan [fæn] n (folding) éventail m; (ELEC) ventilateur m; (person) fan m, admirateur/trice; (: SPORT) supporter m/f ♦ vt éventer; (fire, quarrel) attiser.
▶**fan out** vi se déployer (en éventail).
fanatic [fə'nætɪk] n fanatique m/f.
fanatical [fə'nætɪkl] adj fanatique.
fan belt n courroie f de ventilateur.
fancied ['fænsɪd] adj imaginaire.
fanciful ['fænsɪful] adj fantaisiste.
fan club n fan-club m.
fancy ['fænsɪ] n fantaisie f, envie f, imagination f ♦ cpd (de) fantaisie inv ♦ vt (feel like, want) avoir envie de; (imagine) imaginer; **to take a ~ to** se prendre d'affection pour; s'enticher de; **it took** or **caught my ~** ça m'a plu; **when the ~ takes him** quand ça lui prend; **to ~ that ...** se figurer or s'imaginer que ...; **he fancies her** elle lui plaît.
fancy dress n déguisement m, travesti m.
fancy-dress ball [fænsɪ'drɛs-] n bal masqué or costumé.
fancy goods npl articles mpl (de) fantaisie.
fanfare ['fænfɛə*] n fanfare f (musique).
fanfold paper ['fænfəuld-] n papier m à pliage accordéon.
fang [fæŋ] n croc m; (of snake) crochet m.
fan heater n (BRIT) radiateur soufflant.
fanlight ['fænlaɪt] n imposte f.
fanny ['fænɪ] n (BRIT col!) chatte f (!); (US col) cul m (!).
fantasize ['fæntəsaɪz] vi fantasmer.
fantastic [fæn'tæstɪk] adj fantastique.
fantasy ['fæntəsɪ] n imagination f, fantaisie f; fantasme m.
fanzine ['fænziːn] n fanzine m.
FAO n abbr (= Food and Agriculture Organization)

FAO f.
FAQ abbr (= free alongside quay) FLQ.
far [fɑː*] adj: **the ~ side/end** l'autre côté/bout; **the ~ left/right** (POL) l'extrême gauche f/ droite f ♦ adv loin; **is it ~ to London?** est-ce qu'on est loin de Londres?; **it's not ~ (from here)** ce n'est pas loin (d'ici); **~ away, ~ off** au loin, dans le lointain; **~ better** beaucoup mieux; **~ from** loin de; **by ~** de loin, de beaucoup; **as ~ back as the 13th century** dès le 13e siècle; **go as ~ as the farm** allez jusqu'à la ferme; **as ~ as I know** pour autant que je sache; **as ~ as possible** dans la mesure du possible; **how ~ have you got with your work?** où en êtes-vous dans votre travail?
faraway ['fɑːrəweɪ] adj lointain(e); (look) absent(e).
farce [fɑːs] n farce f.
farcical ['fɑːsɪkl] adj grotesque.
fare [fɛə*] n (on trains, buses) prix m du billet; (in taxi) prix de la course; (passenger in taxi) client m; (food) table f, chère f ♦ vi se débrouiller.
Far East n: **the ~** l'Extrême-Orient m.
farewell [fɛə'wɛl] excl, n adieu (m) ♦ cpd (party etc) d'adieux.
far-fetched ['fɑː'fɛtʃt] adj exagéré(e), poussé(e).
farm [fɑːm] n ferme f ♦ vt cultiver.
▶**farm out** vt (work etc) distribuer.
farmer ['fɑːmə*] n fermier/ière; cultivateur/ trice.
farmhand ['fɑːmhænd] n ouvrier/ière agricole.
farmhouse ['fɑːmhaus] n (maison f de) ferme f.
farming ['fɑːmɪŋ] n agriculture f; **intensive ~** culture intensive; **sheep ~** élevage m du mouton.
farm labourer n = farmhand.
farmland ['fɑːmlænd] n terres cultivées or arables.
farm produce n produits mpl agricoles.
farm worker n = farmhand.
farmyard ['fɑːmjɑːd] n cour f de ferme.
Faroe Islands ['fɛərəu-] npl, **Faroes** ['fɛərəuz] npl: **the ~** les îles fpl Féroé or Faeroe.
far-reaching ['fɑː'riːtʃɪŋ] adj d'une grande portée.
far-sighted ['fɑː'saɪtɪd] adj presbyte; (fig) prévoyant(e), qui voit loin.
fart [fɑːt] (col!) n pet m ♦ vi péter.
farther ['fɑːðə*] adv plus loin ♦ adj plus eloigné(e), plus lointain(e).
farthest ['fɑːðɪst] superlative of far.
FAS abbr (BRIT: = free alongside ship) FLB.
fascia ['feɪʃə] n (AUT) (garniture f du) tableau m de bord.
fascinate ['fæsɪneɪt] vt fasciner, captiver.
fascinating ['fæsɪneɪtɪŋ] adj fascinant(e).
fascination [fæsɪ'neɪʃən] n fascination f.

fascism ['fæʃɪzəm] n fascisme m.
fascist ['fæʃɪst] adj, n fasciste (m/f).
fashion ['fæʃən] n mode f; (manner) façon f, manière f ♦ vt façonner; **in ~** à la mode; **out of ~** démodé(e); **in the Greek ~** à la grecque; **after a ~** (finish, manage etc) tant bien que mal.
fashionable ['fæʃnəbl] adj à la mode.
fashion designer n (grand(e)) couturier/ière.
fashion show n défilé m de mannequins or de mode.
fast [fɑːst] adj rapide; (clock): **to be ~** avancer; (dye, colour) grand or bon teint inv ♦ adv vite, rapidement; (stuck, held) solidement ♦ n jeûne m ♦ vi jeûner; **my watch is 5 minutes ~** ma montre avance de 5 minutes; **~ asleep** profondément endormi; **as ~ as I can** aussi vite que je peux; **to make a boat ~** (BRIT) amarrer un bateau.
fasten ['fɑːsn] vt attacher, fixer; (coat) attacher, fermer ♦ vi se fermer, s'attacher.
►**fasten (up)on** vt fus (idea) se cramponner à.
fastener ['fɑːsnə*], **fastening** ['fɑːsnɪŋ] n fermeture f, attache f; (BRIT: zip ~) fermeture éclair inv ® or à glissière.
fast food n fast food m, restauration f rapide.
fastidious [fæs'tɪdɪəs] adj exigeant(e), difficile.
fast lane n (AUT: in Britain) voie f de droite.
fat [fæt] adj gros(se) ♦ n graisse f; (on meat) gras m; **to live off the ~ of the land** vivre grassement.
fatal ['feɪtl] adj fatal(e); (leading to death) mortel(le).
fatalism ['feɪtlɪzəm] n fatalisme m.
fatality [fə'tælɪtɪ] n (road death etc) victime f, décès m.
fatally ['feɪtəlɪ] adv fatalement; mortellement.
fate [feɪt] n destin m; (of person) sort m; **to meet one's ~** trouver la mort.
fated ['feɪtɪd] adj (person) condamné(e); (project) voué(e) à l'échec.
fateful ['feɪtful] adj fatidique.
fat-free ['fæt'friː] adj sans matières grasses.
father ['fɑːðə*] n père m.
Father Christmas n le Père Noël.
fatherhood ['fɑːðəhud] n paternité f.
father-in-law ['fɑːðərənlɔː] n beau-père m.
fatherland ['fɑːðəlænd] n (mère f) patrie f.
fatherly ['fɑːðəlɪ] adj paternel(le).
fathom ['fæðəm] n brasse f (= 1828 mm) ♦ vt (mystery) sonder, pénétrer.
fatigue [fə'tiːg] n fatigue f; (MIL) corvée f; **metal ~** fatigue du métal.
fatness ['fætnɪs] n corpulence f, grosseur f.
fatten ['fætn] vt, vi engraisser; **chocolate is ~ing** le chocolat fait grossir.
fatty ['fætɪ] adj (food) gras(se) ♦ n (col) gros/grosse.
fatuous ['fætjuəs] adj stupide.
faucet ['fɔːsɪt] n (US) robinet m.

fault [fɔːlt] n faute f; (defect) défaut m; (GEO) faille f ♦ vt trouver des défauts à, prendre en défaut; **it's my ~** c'est de ma faute; **to find ~ with** trouver à redire or à critiquer à; **at ~** fautif(ive), coupable; **to a ~** à l'excès.
faultless ['fɔːltlɪs] adj impeccable; irréprochable.
faulty ['fɔːltɪ] adj défectueux(euse).
fauna ['fɔːnə] n faune f.
faux pas ['fəu'pɑː] n impair m, bévue f, gaffe f.
favour, (US) **favor** ['feɪvə*] n faveur f; (help) service m ♦ vt (proposition) être en faveur de; (pupil etc) favoriser; (team, horse) donner gagnant; **to do sb a ~** rendre un service à qn; **in ~ of** en faveur de; **to be in ~ of sth/of doing sth** être partisan de qch/de faire qch; **to find ~ with sb** trouver grâce aux yeux de qn.
favo(u)rable ['feɪvrəbl] adj favorable; (price) avantageux(euse).
favo(u)rably ['feɪvrəblɪ] adv favorablement.
favo(u)rite ['feɪvrɪt] adj, n favori(te).
favo(u)ritism ['feɪvrɪtɪzəm] n favoritisme m.
fawn [fɔːn] n faon m ♦ adj (also: ~-coloured) fauve ♦ vi: **to ~ (up)on** flatter servilement.
fax [fæks] n (document) télécopie f; (machine) télécopieur m ♦ vt envoyer par télécopie.
FBI n abbr (US: = Federal Bureau of Investigation) FBI m.
FCC n abbr (US) = Federal Communications Commission.
FCO n abbr (BRIT: = Foreign and Commonwealth Office) ministère m des Affaires étrangères et du Commonwealth.
FD n abbr (US) = fire department.
FDA n abbr (US: = Food and Drug Administration) office m de contrôle des produits pharmaceutiques et alimentaires.
FE n abbr = further education.
fear [fɪə*] n crainte f, peur f ♦ vt craindre ♦ vi: **to ~ for** craindre pour; **to ~ that** craindre que; **~ of heights** vertige m; **for ~ of** de peur que + sub or de + infinitive.
fearful ['fɪəful] adj (timid) craintif(ive); (sight, noise) affreux(euse), épouvantable; **to be ~ of** avoir peur de, craindre.
fearfully ['fɪəfəlɪ] adv (timidly) craintivement; (col: very) affreusement.
fearless ['fɪəlɪs] adj intrépide, sans peur.
fearsome ['fɪəsəm] adj (opponent) redoutable; (sight) épouvantable.
feasibility [fiːzə'bɪlɪtɪ] n (of plan) possibilité f de réalisation, faisabilité f.
feasibility study n étude f de faisabilité.
feasible ['fiːzəbl] adj faisable, réalisable.
feast [fiːst] n festin m, banquet m; (REL: also: ~ day) fête f ♦ vi festoyer; **to ~ on** se régaler de.
feat [fiːt] n exploit m, prouesse f.
feather ['feðə*] n plume f ♦ vt: **to ~ one's nest**

(*fig*) faire sa pelote ♦ *cpd* (*bed etc*) de plumes.

feather-weight ['fɛðəweɪt] *n* poids *m* plume *inv*.

feature ['fiːtʃə*] *n* caractéristique *f*; (*article*) chronique *f*, rubrique *f* ♦ *vt* (*subj: film*) avoir pour vedette(s) ♦ *vi* figurer (en bonne place); ~s *npl* (*of face*) traits *mpl*; **a (special)** ~ **on sth/sb** un reportage sur qch/qn; **it** ~**d prominently in** ... cela a figuré en bonne place sur *or* dans ....

feature film *n* long métrage.

featureless ['fiːtʃəlɪs] *adj* anonyme, sans traits distinctifs.

Feb. *abbr* (= *February*) fév.

February ['fɛbruərɪ] *n* février *m*; *for phrases see also* **July**.

feces ['fiːsiːz] *npl* (*US*) = **faeces**.

feckless ['fɛklɪs] *adj* inepte.

Fed *abbr* (*US*) = **federal; federation**.

fed [fɛd] *pt, pp of* **feed; to be** ~ **up** en avoir marre *or* plein le dos.

Fed. [fɛd] *n abbr* (*US col*) = **Federal Reserve Board**.

federal ['fɛdərəl] *adj* fédéral(e).

Federal Reserve Board *n* (*US*) organe de contrôle de la banque centrale américaine.

Federal Trade Commission (FTC) *n* (*US*) organisme de protection contre les pratiques commerciales abusives.

federation [fɛdə'reɪʃən] *n* fédération *f*.

fee [fiː] *n* rémunération *f*; (*of doctor, lawyer*) honoraires *mpl*; (*of school, college etc*) frais *mpl* de scolarité; (*for examination*) droits *mpl*; **entrance/membership** ~ droit d'entrée/d'inscription; **for a small** ~ pour une somme modique.

feeble ['fiːbl] *adj* faible.

feeble-minded ['fiːbl'maɪndɪd] *adj* faible d'esprit.

feed [fiːd] *n* (*of baby*) tétée *f*; (*of animal*) fourrage *m*; pâture *f*; (*on printer*) mécanisme *m* d'alimentation ♦ *vt* (*pt, pp* **fed** [fɛd]) nourrir; (*horse etc*) donner à manger à; (*machine*) alimenter; (*data etc*): **to** ~ **sth into** fournir qch à, introduire qch dans.

▶**feed back** *vt* (*results*) donner en retour.

▶**feed on** *vt fus* se nourrir de.

feedback ['fiːdbæk] *n* feed-back *m*; (*from person*) réactions *fpl*.

feeder ['fiːdə*] *n* (*bib*) bavette *f*.

feeding bottle ['fiːdɪŋ-] *n* (*BRIT*) biberon *m*.

feel [fiːl] *n* sensation *f* ♦ *vt* (*pt, pp* **felt** [fɛlt]) (*touch*) toucher; tâter, palper; (*cold, pain*) sentir; (*grief, anger*) ressentir, éprouver; (*think, believe*): **to** ~ (**that**) trouver que; **I** ~ **that you ought to do it** il me semble que vous devriez le faire; **to** ~ **hungry/cold** avoir faim/froid; **to** ~ **lonely/better** se sentir seul/mieux; **I don't** ~ **well** je ne me sens pas bien; **to** ~ **sorry for** avoir pitié de; **it** ~**s soft** c'est doux au toucher; **it** ~**s colder here**

je trouve qu'il fait plus froid ici; **it** ~**s like velvet** on dirait du velours, ça ressemble au velours; **to** ~ **like** (*want*) avoir envie de; **to** ~ **about** *or* **around** fouiller, tâtonner; **to get the** ~ **of sth** (*fig*) s'habituer à qch.

feeler ['fiːlə*] *n* (*of insect*) antenne *f*; (*fig*): **to put out a** ~ *or* ~**s** tâter le terrain.

feeling ['fiːlɪŋ] *n* sensation *f*, sentiment *m*; (*impression*) sentiment *m*; **to hurt sb's** ~**s** froisser qn; ~**s ran high about it** cela a déchaîné les passions; **what are your** ~**s about the matter?** quel est votre sentiment sur cette question?; **my** ~ **is that** ... j'estime que ...; **I have a** ~ **that** ... j'ai l'impression que ....

fee-paying school ['fiːpeɪɪŋ-] *n* établissement (d'enseignement) privé.

feet [fiːt] *npl of* **foot**.

feign [feɪn] *vt* feindre, simuler.

felicitous [fɪ'lɪsɪtəs] *adj* heureux(euse).

fell [fɛl] *pt of* **fall** ♦ *vt* (*tree*) abattre ♦ *n* (*BRIT: mountain*) montagne *f*; (: *moorland*): **the** ~**s** la lande ♦ *adj*: **with one** ~ **blow** d'un seul coup.

fellow ['fɛləu] *n* type *m*; (*comrade*) compagnon *m*; (*of learned society*) membre *m*; (*of university*) universitaire *m/f* (*membre du conseil*) ♦ *cpd*: **their** ~ **prisoners/students** leurs camarades prisonniers/étudiants; **his** ~ **workers** ses collègues *mpl* (de travail).

fellow citizen *n* concitoyen/ne.

fellow countryman *n* compatriote *m*.

fellow feeling *n* sympathie *f*.

fellow men *npl* semblables *mpl*.

fellowship ['fɛləuʃɪp] *n* (*society*) association *f*; (*comradeship*) amitié *f*, camaraderie *f*; (*SCOL*) sorte de bourse universitaire.

fellow traveller *n* compagnon/compagne de route; (*POL*) communisant/e.

fell-walking ['fɛlwɔːkɪŋ] *n* (*BRIT*) randonnée *f* en montagne.

felon ['fɛlən] *n* (*LAW*) criminel/le.

felony ['fɛlənɪ] *n* (*LAW*) crime *m*, forfait *m*.

felt [fɛlt] *pt, pp of* **feel** ♦ *n* feutre *m*.

felt-tip pen ['fɛlttɪp-] *n* stylo-feutre *m*.

female ['fiːmeɪl] *n* (*ZOOL*) femelle *f*; (*pej: woman*) bonne femme ♦ *adj* (*BIOL, ELEC*) femelle; (*sex, character*) féminin(e); (*vote etc*) des femmes; (*child etc*) du sexe féminin; **male and** ~ **students** étudiants et étudiantes.

female impersonator *n* (*THEAT*) travesti *m*.

feminine ['fɛmɪnɪn] *adj* féminin(e) ♦ *n* féminin *m*.

femininity [fɛmɪ'nɪnɪtɪ] *n* féminité *f*.

feminism ['fɛmɪnɪzəm] *n* féminisme *m*.

feminist ['fɛmɪnɪst] *n* féministe *m/f*.

fen [fɛn] *n* (*BRIT*): **the F**~**s** les plaines *fpl* du Norfolk (*anciennement marécageuses*).

fence [fɛns] *n* barrière *f*; (*SPORT*) obstacle *m*; (*col: person*) receleur/euse ♦ *vt* (*also:* ~ **in**) clôturer ♦ *vi* faire de l'escrime; **to sit on the** ~ (*fig*) ne pas se mouiller.

fencing ['fɛnsɪŋ] *n* (*sport*) escrime *m*.

fend [fɛnd] *vi*: **to ~ for o.s.** se débrouiller (tout seul).

▶**fend off** *vt (attack etc)* parer.

fender ['fɛndə*] *n (of fireplace)* garde-feu *m inv*; *(on boat)* défense *f*; *(US: of car)* aile *f*.

fennel ['fɛnl] *n* fenouil *m*.

ferment *vi* [fə'mɛnt] fermenter ♦ *n* ['fə:mɛnt] agitation *f*, effervescence *f*.

fermentation [fə:mɛn'teɪʃən] *n* fermentation *f*.

fern [fə:n] *n* fougère *f*.

ferocious [fə'rəuʃəs] *adj* féroce.

ferocity [fə'rɔsɪtɪ] *n* férocité *f*.

ferret ['fɛrɪt] *n* furet *m*.

▶**ferret about, ferret around** *vi* fureter.

▶**ferret out** *vt* dénicher.

ferry ['fɛrɪ] *n (small)* bac *m*; *(large: also: ~boat)* ferry(-boat *m*) *m* ♦ *vt* transporter; **to ~ sth/ sb across** *or* **over** faire traverser qch/qn.

ferryman ['fɛrɪmən] *n* passeur *m*.

fertile ['fə:taɪl] *adj* fertile; *(BIOL)* fécond(e); **~ period** période *f* de fécondité.

fertility [fə'tɪlɪtɪ] *n* fertilité *f*; fécondité *f*.

fertility drug *n* médicament *m* contre la stérilité.

fertilize ['fə:tɪlaɪz] *vt* fertiliser; féconder.

fertilizer ['fə:tɪlaɪzə*] *n* engrais *m*.

fervent ['fə:vənt] *adj* fervent(e), ardent(e).

fervour, (US) fervor ['fə:və*] *n* ferveur *f*.

fester ['fɛstə*] *vi* suppurer.

festival ['fɛstɪvəl] *n (REL)* fête *f*; *(ART, MUS)* festival *m*.

festive ['fɛstɪv] *adj* de fête; **the ~ season** *(BRIT: Christmas)* la période des fêtes.

festivities [fɛs'tɪvɪtɪz] *npl* réjouissances *fpl*.

festoon [fɛs'tu:n] *vt*: **to ~ with** orner de.

fetch [fɛtʃ] *vt* aller chercher; *(BRIT: sell for)* se vendre; **how much did it ~?** ça a atteint quel prix?

▶**fetch up** *vi (BRIT)* se retrouver.

fetching ['fɛtʃɪŋ] *adj* charmant(e).

fête [feɪt] *n* fête *f*, kermesse *f*.

fetid ['fɛtɪd] *adj* fétide.

fetish ['fɛtɪʃ] *n* fétiche *m*.

fetter ['fɛtə*] *vt* entraver.

fetters ['fɛtəz] *npl* chaînes *fpl*.

fettle ['fɛtl] *n (BRIT)*: **in fine ~** en bonne forme.

fetus ['fi:təs] *n (US)* = **foetus**.

feud [fju:d] *n* dispute *f*, dissension *f* ♦ *vi* se disputer, se quereller; **a family ~** une querelle de famille.

feudal ['fju:dl] *adj* féodal(e).

feudalism ['fju:dlɪzəm] *n* féodalité *f*.

fever ['fi:və*] *n* fièvre *f*; **he has a ~** il a de la fièvre.

feverish ['fi:vərɪʃ] *adj* fiévreux(euse), fébrile.

few [fju:] *adj* peu de ♦ *pron*: **~ succeed** il y en a peu qui réussissent, (bien) peu réussissent; **they were ~** ils étaient peu (nombreux), il y en avait peu; **a ~ ...** quelques ...; **I know a ~** j'en connais quelques-uns; **quite a ~ ...** un certain nombre de ..., pas mal de ...; **in the**

next ~ days dans les jours qui viennent; **in the past ~ days** ces derniers jours; **every ~ days/months** tous les deux ou trois jours/ mois; **a ~ more ...** encore quelques ..., quelques ... de plus.

fewer ['fju:ə*] *adj* moins de ♦ *pron* moins; **they are ~ now** il y en a moins maintenant, ils sont moins (nombreux) maintenant.

fewest ['fju:ɪst] *adj* le moins nombreux.

FFA *n abbr* = *Future Farmers of America*.

FH *abbr (BRIT)* = **fire hydrant**.

FHA *n abbr (US:* = *Federal Housing Administration)* office fédéral du logement.

fiancé [fɪ'ɑ̃:ŋseɪ] *n* fiancé *m*.

fiancée [fɪ'ɑ̃:ŋseɪ] *n* fiancée *f*.

fiasco [fɪ'æskəu] *n* fiasco *m*.

fib [fɪb] *n* bobard *m*.

fibre, (US) fiber ['faɪbə*] *n* fibre *f*.

fibreboard, (US) fiberboard ['faɪbəbɔ:d] *n* panneau *m* de fibres.

fibre-glass, (US) fiber-glass ['faɪbəglɑ:s] *n* fibre de verre.

fibrositis [faɪbrə'saɪtɪs] *n* aponévrosite *f*.

FICA *n abbr (US)* = *Federal Insurance Contributions Act*.

fickle ['fɪkl] *adj* inconstant(e), volage, capricieux(euse).

fiction ['fɪkʃən] *n* romans *mpl*, littérature *f* romanesque; *(invention)* fiction *f*.

fictional ['fɪkʃənl] *adj* fictif(ive).

fictionalize ['fɪkʃnəlaɪz] *vt* romancer.

fictitious [fɪk'tɪʃəs] *adj* fictif(ive), imaginaire.

fiddle ['fɪdl] *n (MUS)* violon *m*; *(cheating)* combine *f*; escroquerie *f* ♦ *vt (BRIT: accounts)* falsifier, maquiller; **tax ~** fraude fiscale, combine *f* pour échapper au fisc; **to work a ~** traficoter.

▶**fiddle with** *vt fus* tripoter.

fiddler ['fɪdlə*] *n* violoniste *m/f*.

fiddly ['fɪdlɪ] *adj (task)* minutieux(euse).

fidelity [fɪ'dɛlɪtɪ] *n* fidélité *f*.

fidget ['fɪdʒɪt] *vi* se trémousser, remuer.

fidgety ['fɪdʒɪtɪ] *adj* agité(e), qui a la bougeotte.

fiduciary [fɪ'dju:ʃɪərɪ] *n* agent *m* fiduciaire.

field [fi:ld] *n* champ *m*; *(fig)* domaine *m*, champ; *(SPORT: ground)* terrain *m*; *(COMPUT)* champ, zone *f*; **to lead the ~** *(SPORT, COMM)* dominer; **the children had a ~ day** *(fig)* c'était un grand jour pour les enfants.

field glasses *npl* jumelles *fpl*.

field hospital *n* antenne chirurgicale.

field marshal *n* maréchal *m*.

fieldwork ['fi:ldwə:k] *n* travaux *mpl* pratiques *(or* recherches *fpl)* sur le terrain.

fiend [fi:nd] *n* démon *m*.

fiendish ['fi:ndɪʃ] *adj* diabolique.

fierce [fɪəs] *adj (look)* féroce, sauvage; *(wind, attack)* (très) violent(e); *(fighting, enemy)* acharné(e).

fiery ['faɪərɪ] *adj* ardent(e), brûlant(e); fougueux(euse).

FIFA ['fiːfə] n abbr (= Fédération internationale de Football Association) FIFA f.

fifteen [fɪf'tiːn] num quinze.

fifth [fɪfθ] num cinquième.

fiftieth ['fɪftɪɪθ] num cinquantième.

fifty ['fɪftɪ] num cinquante.

fifty-fifty ['fɪftɪ'fɪftɪ] adv: **to share ~ with sb** partager moitié-moitié avec qn ♦ adj: **to have a ~ chance (of success)** avoir une chance sur deux (de réussir).

fig [fɪg] n figue f.

fight [faɪt] n bagarre f; (MIL) combat m; (against cancer etc) lutte f ♦ vb (pt, pp **fought** [fɔːt]) vt se battre contre; (cancer, alcoholism) combattre, lutter contre; (LAW: case) défendre ♦ vi se battre; (fig): **to ~ (for/against)** lutter (pour/contre).

fighter ['faɪtə*] n lutteur m (fig); (plane) chasseur m.

fighter pilot n pilote m de chasse.

fighting ['faɪtɪŋ] n combats mpl; (brawls) bagarres fpl.

figment ['fɪgmənt] n: **a ~ of the imagination** une invention.

figurative ['fɪgjurətɪv] adj figuré(e).

figure ['fɪgə*] n (DRAWING, GEOM) figure f; (number, cipher) chiffre m; (body, outline) silhouette f, ligne f, formes fpl; (person) personnage m ♦ vt (US) supposer ♦ vi (appear) figurer; (US: make sense) s'expliquer; **public ~ personnalité f**; **~ of speech** figure f de rhétorique.

▶**figure on** vt fus (US): **to ~ on doing** compter faire.

▶**figure out** vt arriver à comprendre; calculer.

figurehead ['fɪgəhɛd] n (NAUT) figure f de proue; (pej) prête-nom m.

figure skating n figures imposées (en patinage); patinage m artistique.

Fiji (Islands) ['fiːdʒiː-] n(pl) (îles fpl) Fi(d)ji fpl.

filament ['fɪləmənt] n filament m.

filch [fɪltʃ] vt (col: steal) voler, chiper.

file [faɪl] n (tool) lime f; (dossier) dossier m; (folder) dossier, chemise f; (: binder) classeur m; (COMPUT) fichier m; (row) file f ♦ vt (nails, wood) limer; (papers) classer; (LAW: claim) faire enregistrer; déposer ♦ vi: **to ~ in/out** entrer/sortir l'un derrière l'autre; **to ~ past** défiler devant; **to ~ a suit against sb** (LAW) intenter un procès à qn.

file name n (COMPUT) nom m de fichier.

filibuster ['fɪlɪbʌstə*] (esp US POL) n (also: ~er) obstructionniste m/f ♦ vi faire de l'obstructionnisme.

filing ['faɪlɪŋ] n (travaux mpl de) classement m; **~s** npl limaille f.

filing cabinet n classeur m (meuble).

filing clerk n documentaliste m/f.

Filipino [fɪlɪ'piːnəu] n (person) Philippin/e; (LING) tagalog m.

fill [fɪl] vt remplir; (vacancy) pourvoir à ♦ n: **to**

eat one's ~ manger à sa faim.

▶**fill in** vt (hole) boucher; (form) remplir; (details, report) compléter.

▶**fill out** vt (form, receipt) remplir.

▶**fill up** vt remplir ♦ vi (AUT) faire le plein; **~ it up, please** (AUT) le plein, s'il vous plaît.

fillet ['fɪlɪt] n filet m ♦ vt préparer en filets.

fillet steak n filet m de bœuf, tournedos m.

filling ['fɪlɪŋ] n (CULIN) garniture f, farce f; (for tooth) plombage m.

filling station n station f d'essence.

fillip ['fɪlɪp] n coup m de fouet (fig).

filly ['fɪlɪ] n pouliche f.

film [fɪlm] n film m; (PHOT) pellicule f, film ♦ vt (scene) filmer.

film star n vedette f de cinéma.

filmstrip ['fɪlmstrɪp] n (film m pour) projection f fixe.

film studio n studio m (de cinéma).

Filofax ['faɪləufæks] n ® Filofax m ®.

filter ['fɪltə*] n filtre m ♦ vt filtrer.

filter coffee n café m filtre.

filter lane n (BRIT AUT: at traffic lights) voie f de dégagement; (: on motorway) voie de sortie.

filter tip n bout m filtre.

filth [fɪlθ] n saleté f.

filthy ['fɪlθɪ] adj sale, dégoûtant(e); (language) ordurier(ière), grossier(ière).

fin [fɪn] n (of fish) nageoire f.

final ['faɪnl] adj final(e), dernier(ière); (decision, answer) définitif(ive) ♦ n (SPORT) finale f, **~s** npl (SCOL) examens mpl de dernière année; **~ demand** (on invoice etc) dernier rappel.

finale [fɪ'nɑːlɪ] n finale m.

finalist ['faɪnəlɪst] n (SPORT) finaliste m/f.

finalize ['faɪnəlaɪz] vt mettre au point.

finally ['faɪnəlɪ] adv (lastly) en dernier lieu; (eventually) enfin, finalement; (irrevocably) définitivement.

finance [faɪ'næns] n finance f ♦ vt financer; **~s** npl finances fpl.

financial [faɪ'nænʃəl] adj financier(ière); **~ statement** bilan m, exercice financier.

financially [faɪ'nænʃəlɪ] adv financièrement.

financial year n année f budgétaire.

financier [faɪ'nænsɪə*] n financier m.

find [faɪnd] vt (pt, pp **found** [faund]) trouver; (lost object) retrouver ♦ n trouvaille f, découverte f; **to ~ sb guilty** (LAW) déclarer qn coupable; **to ~ (some) difficulty in doing sth** avoir du mal à faire qch.

▶**find out** vt se renseigner sur; (truth, secret) découvrir; (person) démasquer ♦ vi: **to ~ out about** se renseigner sur; (by chance) apprendre.

findings ['faɪndɪŋz] npl (LAW) conclusions fpl, verdict m; (of report) constatations fpl.

fine [faɪn] adj beau(belle); excellent(e); (subtle, not coarse) fin(e) ♦ adv (well) très bien; (small) fin, finement ♦ n (LAW) amende f; contravention f ♦ vt (LAW) condamner à une amende; donner une contravention à; **he's ~** il va bien; **the weather is ~** il fait beau; **you're doing ~** c'est bien, vous vous débrouillez bien; **to cut it ~** calculer un peu juste.

fine arts *npl* beaux-arts *mpl*.

fine print *n*: **the ~** ce qui est imprimé en tout petit.

finery ['faɪnərɪ] *n* parure *f*.

finesse [fɪ'nɛs] *n* finesse *f*, élégance *f*.

fine-tooth comb ['faɪntu:θ-] *n*: **to go through sth with a ~** *(fig)* passer qch au peigne fin *or* au crible.

finger ['fɪŋgə*] *n* doigt *m* ♦ *vt* palper, toucher.

fingernail ['fɪŋgəneɪl] *n* ongle *m* (de la main).

fingerprint ['fɪŋgəprɪnt] *n* empreinte digitale ♦ *vt (person)* prendre les empreintes digitales de.

fingerstall ['fɪŋgəstɔːl] *n* doigtier *m*.

fingertip ['fɪŋgətɪp] *n* bout *m* du doigt; *(fig)*: **to have sth at one's ~s** avoir qch à sa disposition; *(knowledge)* savoir qch sur le bout du doigt.

finicky ['fɪnɪkɪ] *adj* tatillon(ne), méticuleux(euse); minutieux(euse).

finish ['fɪnɪʃ] *n* fin *f*; *(SPORT)* arrivée *f*; *(polish etc)* finition *f* ♦ *vt* finir, terminer ♦ *vi* finir, se terminer; *(session)* s'achever; **to ~ doing sth** finir de faire qch; **to ~ third** arriver *or* terminer troisième.

►**finish off** *vt* finir, terminer; *(kill)* achever.

►**finish up** *vi, vt* finir.

finished product ['fɪnɪʃt-] *n* produit fini.

finishing line ['fɪnɪʃɪŋ-] *n* ligne *f* d'arrivée.

finishing school ['fɪnɪʃɪŋ-] *n* institution privée *(pour jeunes filles)*.

finite ['faɪnaɪt] *adj* fini(e); *(verb)* conjugué(e).

Finland ['fɪnlənd] *n* Finlande *f*.

Finn [fɪn] *n* Finnois/e; Finlandais/e.

Finnish ['fɪnɪʃ] *adj* finnois(e); finlandais(e) ♦ *n (LING)* finnois *m*.

fiord [fjɔːd] *n* fjord *m*.

fir [fəː*] *n* sapin *m*.

fire ['faɪə*] *n* feu *m*; incendie *m* ♦ *vt (discharge)*: **to ~ a gun** tirer un coup de feu; *(fig)* enflammer, animer; *(dismiss)* mettre à la porte, renvoyer ♦ *vi* tirer, faire feu ♦ *cpd*: **~ hazard, ~ risk: that's a ~ hazard** *or* **risk** cela présente un risque d'incendie; **on ~** en feu; **to set ~ to sth, set sth on ~** mettre le feu à qch; **insured against ~** assuré contre l'incendie.

fire alarm *n* avertisseur *m* d'incendie.

firearm ['faɪərɑːm] *n* arme *f* à feu.

fire brigade *n (BRIT)* (régiment *m* de sapeurs-)pompiers *mpl*.

fire chief *n (US)* = **fire master**.

fire department *n (US)* = **fire brigade**.

fire door *n* porte *f* coupe-feu.

fire engine *n* pompe *f* à incendie.

fire escape *n* escalier *m* de secours.

fire extinguisher *n* extincteur *m*.

fireguard ['faɪəgɑːd] *n (BRIT)* garde-feu *m inv*.

fire insurance *n* assurance *f* incendie.

fireman ['faɪəmən] *n* pompier *m*.

fire master *n (BRIT)* capitaine *m* des pompiers.

fireplace ['faɪəpleɪs] *n* cheminée *f*.

fireproof ['faɪəpruːf] *adj* ignifuge.

fire regulations *npl* consignes *fpl* en cas d'incendie.

fire screen *n (decorative)* écran *m* de cheminée; *(for protection)* garde-feu *m inv*.

fireside ['faɪəsaɪd] *n* foyer *m*, coin *m* du feu.

fire station *n* caserne *f* de pompiers.

firewood ['faɪəwud] *n* bois *m* de chauffage.

firework ['faɪəwəːk] *n* feu *m* d'artifice; **~s** *npl (display)* feu(x) d'artifice.

firing ['faɪərɪŋ] *n (MIL)* feu *m*, tir *m*.

firing squad *n* peloton *m* d'exécution.

firm [fəːm] *adj* ferme ♦ *n* compagnie *f*, firme *f*.

firmly ['fəːmlɪ] *adv* fermement.

firmness ['fəːmnɪs] *n* fermeté *f*.

first [fəːst] *adj* premier(ière) ♦ *adv (before others)* le premier, la première; *(before other things)* en premier, d'abord; *(when listing reasons etc)* en premier lieu, premièrement ♦ *n (person: in race)* premier/ière; *(BRIT SCOL)* mention *f* très bien; *(AUT)* première *f*; **the ~ of January** le premier janvier; **at ~** au commencement, au début; **~ of all** tout d'abord, pour commencer; **in the ~ instance** en premier lieu; **I'll do it ~ thing tomorrow** je le ferai tout de suite demain matin.

first aid *n* premiers secours *or* soins.

first-aid kit [fəːst'eɪd-] *n* trousse *f* à pharmacie.

first-class ['fəːst'klɑːs] *adj* de première classe.

first-class mail *n* courrier *m* rapide.

first-hand ['fəːst'hænd] *adj* de première main.

first lady *n (US)* femme *f* du président.

firstly ['fəːstlɪ] *adv* premièrement, en premier lieu.

first name *n* prénom *m*.

first night *n (THEAT)* première *f*.

first-rate ['fəːst'reɪt] *adj* excellent(e).

first-time buyer ['fəːsttaɪm-] *n personne achetant une maison ou un appartement pour la première fois.*

fir tree *n* sapin *m*.

FIS *n abbr (BRIT: = Family Income Supplement)* complément familial.

fiscal ['fɪskl] *adj* fiscal(e); **~ year** exercice financier.

fish [fɪʃ] *n (pl inv)* poisson *m*; poissons *mpl* ♦ *vt, vi* pêcher; **to ~** a river pêcher dans une rivière; **to go ~ing** aller à la pêche.

fisherman ['fɪʃəmən] *n* pêcheur *m*.

fishery ['fɪʃərɪ] *n* pêcherie *f*.

fish factory *n (BRIT)* conserverie *f* de poissons.

fish farm *n* établissement *m* piscicole.

fish fingers *npl (BRIT)* bâtonnets de poisson (congelés).

fish hook *n* hameçon *m*.

fishing boat ['fɪʃɪŋ-] n barque f de pêche.
fishing industry ['fɪʃɪŋ-] n industrie f de la pêche.
fishing line ['fɪʃɪŋ-] n ligne f (de pêche).
fishing rod ['fɪʃɪŋ-] n canne f à pêche.
fishing tackle ['fɪʃɪŋ-] n attirail m de pêche.
fish market n marché m au poisson.
fishmonger ['fɪʃmʌŋgə*] n marchand m de poisson; ~'s **(shop)** poissonnerie f.
fish slice n (BRIT) pelle f à poisson.
fish sticks npl (US) = **fish fingers.**
fishy ['fɪʃɪ] adj (fig) suspect(e), louche.
fission ['fɪʃən] n fission f; **atomic** or **nuclear** ~ fission nucléaire.
fissure ['fɪʃə*] n fissure f.
fist [fɪst] n poing m.
fistfight ['fɪstfaɪt] n pugilat m, bagarre f (à coups de poing).
fit [fɪt] adj (MED, SPORT) en (bonne) forme; (proper) convenable; approprié(e) ♦ vt (subj: clothes) aller à; (adjust) ajuster; (put in, attach) installer, poser; adapter; (equip) équiper, garnir, munir ♦ vi (clothes) aller; (parts) s'adapter; (in space, gap) entrer, s'adapter ♦ n (MED) accès m, crise f; (of coughing) quinte f; ~ **to** en état de; ~ **for** digne de, apte à; **to keep** ~ se maintenir en forme; **this dress is a tight/good** ~ cette robe est un peu juste/(me) va très bien; **a** ~ **of anger** un accès de colère; **to have a** ~ (MED) faire or avoir une crise; (col) piquer une crise; **by** ~s **and starts** par à-coups.
▶**fit in** vi s'accorder; (person) s'adapter.
▶**fit out** vt (BRIT: also: **fit up**) équiper.
fitful ['fɪtful] adj intermittent(e).
fitment ['fɪtmənt] n meuble encastré, élément m.
fitness ['fɪtnɪs] n (MED) forme f physique; (of remark) à-propos m, justesse f.
fitted kitchen ['fɪtɪd-] n (BRIT) cuisine équipée.
fitter ['fɪtə*] n monteur m; (DRESSMAKING) essayeur/euse.
fitting ['fɪtɪŋ] adj approprié(e) ♦ n (of dress) essayage m; (of piece of equipment) pose f, installation f.
fitting room n (in shop) cabine f d'essayage.
fittings ['fɪtɪŋz] npl installations fpl.
five [faɪv] num cinq.
five-day week ['faɪvdeɪ-] n semaine f de cinq jours.
fiver ['faɪvə*] n (col: BRIT) billet m de cinq livres; (: US) billet de cinq dollars.
fix [fɪks] vt fixer; (sort out) arranger; (mend) réparer; (make ready: meal, drink) préparer; (col: game etc) truquer ♦ n: **to be in a** ~ être dans le pétrin.
▶**fix up** vt (meeting) arranger; **to** ~ **sb up with sth** faire avoir qch à qn.
fixation [fɪk'seɪʃən] n (PSYCH) fixation f; (fig) obsession f.
fixed [fɪkst] adj (prices etc) fixe; **there's a** ~

charge il y a un prix forfaitaire; **how are you** ~ **for money?** (col) question fric, ça va?
fixed assets npl immobilisations fpl.
fixture ['fɪkstʃə*] n installation f (fixe); (SPORT) rencontre f (au programme).
fizz [fɪz] vi pétiller.
fizzle ['fɪzl] vi pétiller.
▶**fizzle out** vi rater.
fizzy ['fɪzɪ] adj pétillant(e); gazeux(euse).
fjord [fjɔːd] n = **fiord.**
FL, Fla. abbr (US) = Florida.
flabbergasted ['flæbəgɑːstɪd] adj sidéré(e), ahuri(e).
flabby ['flæbɪ] adj mou(molle).
flag [flæg] n drapeau m; (also: ~**stone**) dalle f ♦ vi faiblir; fléchir; ~ **of convenience** pavillon m de complaisance.
▶**flag down** vt héler, faire signe (de s'arrêter) à.
flagon ['flægən] n bonbonne f.
flagpole ['flægpəʊl] n mât m.
flagrant ['fleɪgrənt] adj flagrant(e).
flag stop n (US: for bus) arrêt facultatif.
flair [flɛə*] n flair m.
flak [flæk] n (MIL) tir antiaérien; (col: criticism) critiques fpl.
flake [fleɪk] n (of rust, paint) écaille f; (of snow, soap powder) flocon m ♦ vi (also: ~ **off**) s'écailler.
flaky ['fleɪkɪ] adj (paintwork) écaillé(e); (skin) desquamé(e); (pastry) feuilleté(e).
flamboyant [flæm'bɔɪənt] adj flamboyant(e), éclatant(e); (person) haut(e) en couleur.
flame [fleɪm] n flamme f.
flamingo [flə'mɪŋgəʊ] n flamant m (rose).
flammable ['flæməbl] adj inflammable.
flan [flæn] n (BRIT) tarte f.
Flanders ['flɑːndəz] n Flandre(s) f(pl).
flange [flændʒ] n boudin m; collerette f.
flank [flæŋk] n flanc m ♦ vt flanquer.
flannel ['flænl] n (BRIT: also: **face** ~) gant m de toilette; (fabric) flanelle f; (BRIT col) baratin m; ~**s** npl pantalon m de flanelle.
flap [flæp] n (of pocket, envelope) rabat m ♦ vt (wings) battre (de) ♦ vi (sail, flag) claquer; (col: also: **be in a** ~) paniquer.
flapjack ['flæpdʒæk] n (US: pancake) ≈ crêpe f; (BRIT: biscuit) galette f.
flare [flɛə*] n fusée éclairante; (in skirt etc) évasement m.
▶**flare up** vi s'embraser; (fig: person) se mettre en colère, s'emporter; (: revolt) éclater.
flared ['flɛəd] adj (trousers) à jambes évasées; (skirt) évasé(e).
flash [flæʃ] n éclair m; (also: **news** ~) flash m (d'information); (PHOT) flash ♦ vt (switch on) allumer (brièvement); (direct): **to** ~ **sth at** braquer qch sur; (flaunt) étaler, exhiber; (send: message) câbler ♦ vi briller; jeter des éclairs; (light on ambulance etc) clignoter; **in a** ~ en un clin d'œil; **to** ~ **one's headlights**

faire un appel de phares; **he** ~**ed by** _or_ **past** il passa (devant nous) comme un éclair.

flashback ['flæʃbæk] _n_ flashback _m_, retour _m_ en arrière.

flashbulb ['flæʃbʌlb] _n_ ampoule _f_ de flash.

flash card _n_ (_SCOL_) carte _f_ (_support visuel_).

flashcube ['flæʃkjuːb] _n_ cube-flash _m_.

flasher ['flæʃə*] _n_ (_AUT_) clignotant _m_.

flashlight ['flæʃlaɪt] _n_ lampe _f_ de poche.

flashpoint ['flæʃpɔɪnt] _n_ point _m_ d'ignition; (_fig_): **to be at** ~ être sur le point d'exploser.

flashy ['flæʃɪ] _adj_ (_pej_) tape-à-l'œil _inv_, tapageur(euse).

flask [flɑːsk] _n_ flacon _m_, bouteille _f_; (_CHEM_) ballon _m_; (_also_: **vacuum** ~) bouteille _f_ thermos ®.

flat [flæt] _adj_ plat(e); (_tyre_) dégonflé(e), à plat; (_denial_) catégorique; (_MUS_) bémolisé(e); (: _voice_) faux(fausse) ♦ _n_ (_BRIT_: _rooms_) appartement _m_; (_AUT_) crevaison _f_, pneu crevé; (_MUS_) bémol _m_; ~ **out** (_work_) sans relâche; (_race_) à fond; ~ **rate of pay** (_COMM_) (salaire _m_) fixe.

flat-footed ['flæt'futɪd] _adj_: **to be** ~ avoir les pieds plats.

flatly ['flætlɪ] _adv_ catégoriquement.

flatmate ['flætmeɪt] _n_ (_BRIT_): **he's my** ~ il partage l'appartement avec moi.

flatness ['flætnɪs] _n_ (_of land_) absence _f_ de relief, aspect plat.

flat-screen ['flætskriːn] _adj_ à écran plat.

flatten ['flætn] _vt_ (_also_: ~ **out**) aplatir; (_house, city_) raser.

flatter ['flætə*] _vt_ flatter.

flatterer ['flætərə*] _n_ flatteur _m_.

flattering ['flætərɪŋ] _adj_ flatteur(euse); (_clothes etc_) seyant(e).

flattery ['flætərɪ] _n_ flatterie _f_.

flatulence ['flætjuləns] _n_ flatulence _f_.

flaunt [flɔːnt] _vt_ faire étalage de.

flavour, (_US_**) flavor** ['fleɪvə*] _n_ goût _m_, saveur _f_; (_of ice cream etc_) parfum _m_ ♦ _vt_ parfumer, aromatiser; **vanilla-**~**ed** à l'arôme de vanille, vanillé(e); **to give** _or_ **add** ~ **to** donner du goût à, relever.

flavo(u)ring ['fleɪvərɪŋ] _n_ arôme _m_ (synthétique).

flaw [flɔː] _n_ défaut _m_.

flawless ['flɔːlɪs] _adj_ sans défaut.

flax [flæks] _n_ lin _m_.

flaxen ['flæksən] _adj_ blond(e).

flea [fliː] _n_ puce _f_.

flea market _n_ marché _m_ aux puces.

fleck [flɛk] _n_ (_of dust_) particule _f_; (_of mud, paint, colour_) tacheture _f_, moucheture _f_ ♦ _vt_ tacher, éclabousser; **brown** ~**ed with white** brun moucheté de blanc.

fledg(e)ling ['flɛdʒlɪŋ] _n_ oisillon _m_.

flee, _pt, pp_ **fled** [fliː, flɛd] _vt_ fuir, s'enfuir de ♦ _vi_ fuir, s'enfuir.

fleece [fliːs] _n_ toison _f_ ♦ _vt_ (_col_) voler, filouter.

fleecy ['fliːsɪ] _adj_ (_blanket_) moelleux(euse);

(_cloud_) floconneux(euse).

fleet [fliːt] _n_ flotte _f_; (_of lorries, cars etc_) parc _m_; convoi _m_.

fleeting ['fliːtɪŋ] _adj_ fugace, fugitif(ive); (_visit_) très bref(brève).

Flemish ['flɛmɪʃ] _adj_ flamand(e) ♦ _n_ (_LING_) flamand _m_; **the** ~ _npl_ les Flamands.

flesh [flɛʃ] _n_ chair _f_.

flesh wound [-wuːnd] _n_ blessure superficielle.

flew [fluː] _pt of_ **fly**.

flex [flɛks] _n_ fil _m_ _or_ câble _m_ électrique (souple) ♦ _vt_ fléchir; (_muscles_) tendre.

flexibility [flɛksɪ'bɪlɪtɪ] _n_ flexibilité _f_.

flexible ['flɛksəbl] _adj_ flexible; (_person, schedule_) souple.

flexitime ['flɛksɪtaɪm] _n_ horaire _m_ variable _or_ à la carte.

flick [flɪk] _n_ petite tape; chiquenaude _f_; sursaut _m_.

▶**flick through** _vt fus_ feuilleter.

flicker ['flɪkə*] _vi_ vaciller ♦ _n_ vacillement _m_; **a** ~ **of light** une brève lueur.

flick knife _n_ (_BRIT_) couteau _m_ à cran d'arrêt.

flicks [flɪks] _npl_ (_col_) ciné _m_.

flier ['flaɪə*] _n_ aviateur _m_.

flight [flaɪt] _n_ vol _m_; (_escape_) fuite _f_; (_also_: ~ **of steps**) escalier _m_; **to take** ~ prendre la fuite; **to put to** ~ mettre en fuite.

flight attendant _n_ (_US_) steward _m_, hôtesse _f_ de l'air.

flight crew _n_ équipage _m_.

flight deck _n_ (_AVIAT_) poste _m_ de pilotage; (_NAUT_) pont _m_ d'envol.

flight path _n_ trajectoire _f_ (de vol).

flight recorder _n_ enregistreur _m_ de vol.

flimsy ['flɪmzɪ] _adj_ (_partition, fabric_) peu solide, mince; (_excuse_) pauvre, mince.

flinch [flɪntʃ] _vi_ tressaillir; **to** ~ **from** se dérober à, reculer devant.

fling [flɪŋ] _vt_ (_pt, pp_ **flung** [flʌŋ]) jeter, lancer ♦ _n_ (_love affair_) brève liaison, passade _f_.

flint [flɪnt] _n_ silex _m_; (_in lighter_) pierre _f_ (à briquet).

flip [flɪp] _n_ chiquenaude _f_ ♦ _vt_ donner une chiquenaude à; (_US_: _pancake_) faire sauter ♦ _vi_: **to** ~ **for sth** (_US_) jouer qch à pile ou face.

▶**flip through** _vt fus_ feuilleter.

flippant ['flɪpənt] _adj_ désinvolte, irrévérencieux(euse).

flipper ['flɪpə*] _n_ (_of animal_) nageoire _f_; (_for swimmer_) palme _f_.

flip side _n_ (_of record_) deuxième face _f_.

flirt [flɜːt] _vi_ flirter ♦ _n_ flirteuse _f_.

flirtation [flɜː'teɪʃən] _n_ flirt _m_.

flit [flɪt] _vi_ voleter.

float [fləut] _n_ flotteur _m_; (_in procession_) char _m_; (_sum of money_) réserve _f_ ♦ _vi_ flotter; (_bather_) flotter, faire la planche ♦ _vt_ faire flotter; (_loan, business, idea_) lancer.

floating ['fləutɪŋ] _adj_ flottant(e); ~ **vote** voix flottante; ~ **voter** électeur indécis.

flock [flɔk] n troupeau m; (of birds) vol m; (of people) foule f.

floe [fləu] n (also: **ice** ~) iceberg m.

flog [flɔg] vt fouetter.

flood [flʌd] n inondation f; (of words, tears etc) flot m, torrent m ♦ vt inonder; (AUT: carburettor) noyer; to ~ **the market** (COMM) inonder le marché; **in** ~ en crue.

flooding ['flʌdɪŋ] n inondation f.

floodlight ['flʌdlaɪt] n projecteur m ♦ vt éclairer aux projecteurs, illuminer.

floodlit ['flʌdlɪt] pt, pp of **floodlight** ♦ adj illuminé(e).

flood tide n marée montante.

floodwater ['flʌdwɔːtə*] n eau f de la crue.

floor [flɔː*] n sol m; (storey) étage m; (of sea, valley) fond m; (fig: at meeting): **the** ~ l'assemblée f, les membres mpl de l'assemblée ♦ vt terrasser; (baffle) désorienter; **on the** ~ par terre; **ground** ~, (US) **first** ~ rez-de-chaussée m; **first** ~, (US) **second** ~ premier étage; **top** ~ dernier étage; **to have the** ~ (speaker) avoir la parole.

floorboard ['flɔːbɔːd] n planche f (du plancher).

flooring ['flɔːrɪŋ] n sol m; (wooden) plancher m; (material to make floor) matériau(x) m(pl) pour planchers; (covering) revêtement m de sol.

floor lamp n (US) lampadaire m.

floor show n spectacle m de variétés.

floorwalker ['flɔːwɔːkə*] n (esp US) surveillant m (de grand magasin).

flop [flɔp] n fiasco m ♦ vi (fail) faire fiasco.

floppy ['flɔpɪ] adj lâche, flottant(e); ~ **hat** chapeau m à bords flottants.

floppy disk n disquette f, disque m souple.

flora ['flɔːrə] n flore f.

floral ['flɔːrl] adj floral(e).

Florence ['flɔrəns] n Florence.

florid ['flɔrɪd] adj (complexion) fleuri(e); (style) plein(e) de fioritures.

florist ['flɔrɪst] n fleuriste m/f; ~'s **(shop)** magasin m or boutique f de fleuriste.

flotation [fləu'teɪʃən] n (of shares) émission f; (of company) lancement m (en Bourse).

flounce [flauns] n volant m.

►**flounce out** vi sortir dans un mouvement d'humeur.

flounder ['flaundə*] n (ZOOL) flet m ♦ vi patauger.

flour ['flauə*] n farine f.

flourish ['flʌrɪʃ] vi prospérer ♦ vt brandir ♦ n fioriture f; (of trumpets) fanfare f.

flourishing ['flʌrɪʃɪŋ] adj prospère, florissant(e).

flout [flaut] vt se moquer de, faire fi de.

flow [fləu] n (of water, traffic etc) écoulement m; (tide, influx) flux m; (of orders, letters etc) flot m; (of blood, ELEC) circulation f; (of river) courant m ♦ vi couler; (traffic) s'écouler; (robes, hair) flotter.

flow chart, flow diagram n organigramme

m.

flower ['flauə*] n fleur f ♦ vi fleurir; **in** ~ en fleur.

flower bed n plate-bande f.

flowerpot ['flauəpɔt] n pot m (à fleurs).

flowery ['flauərɪ] adj fleuri(e).

flown [fləun] pp of **fly**.

flu [fluː] n grippe f.

fluctuate ['flʌktjueɪt] vi varier, fluctuer.

fluctuation [flʌktju'eɪʃən] n fluctuation f, variation f.

flue [fluː] n conduit m.

fluency ['fluːənsɪ] n facilité f, aisance f.

fluent ['fluːənt] adj (speech, style) coulant(e), aisé(e); **he's a** ~ **speaker/reader** il s'exprime/lit avec aisance or facilité; **he speaks** ~ **French, he's** ~ **in French** il parle le français couramment.

fluently ['fluːəntlɪ] adv couramment; avec aisance or facilité.

fluff [flʌf] n duvet m; peluche f.

fluffy ['flʌfɪ] adj duveteux(euse), pelucheux(euse); ~ **toy** jouet m en peluche.

fluid ['fluːɪd] n fluide m; (in diet) liquide m ♦ adj fluide.

fluid ounce n (BRIT) = 0.028 l; 0.05 pints.

fluke [fluːk] n (col) coup m de veine.

flummox ['flʌməks] vt dérouter, déconcerter.

flung [flʌŋ] pt, pp of **fling**.

flunky ['flʌŋkɪ] n larbin m.

fluorescent [fluə'rɛsnt] adj fluorescent(e).

fluoride ['fluəraɪd] n fluor m.

fluorine ['fluəriːn] n fluor m.

flurry ['flʌrɪ] n (of snow) rafale f, bourrasque f; ~ **of activity/excitement** affairement m/ excitation f soudain(e).

flush [flʌʃ] n rougeur f; (fig) éclat m; afflux m ♦ vt nettoyer à grande eau; (also: ~ **out**) débusquer ♦ vi rougir ♦ adj (col) en fonds; (level): ~ **with** au ras de, de niveau avec; **to** ~ **the toilet** tirer la chasse (d'eau); **hot** ~**es** (MED) bouffées fpl de chaleur.

flushed ['flʌʃt] adj (tout(e)) rouge.

fluster ['flʌstə*] n agitation f, trouble m.

flustered ['flʌstəd] adj énervé(e).

flute [fluːt] n flûte f.

fluted ['fluːtɪd] adj cannelé(e).

flutter ['flʌtə*] n agitation f; (of wings) battement m ♦ vi battre des ailes, voleter; (person) aller et venir dans une grande agitation.

flux [flʌks] n: **in a state of** ~ fluctuant sans cesse.

fly [flaɪ] n (insect) mouche f; (on trousers: also: **flies**) braguette f ♦ vb (pt **flew**, pp **flown** [fluː, fləun]) vt (plane) piloter; (passengers, cargo) transporter (par avion); (distances) parcourir ♦ vi voler; (passengers) aller en avion; (escape) s'enfuir, fuir; (flag) se déployer; **to** ~ **open** s'ouvrir brusquement; **to** ~ **off the handle** s'énerver, s'emporter.

►**fly away** vi s'envoler.

▶**fly in** *vi* (*plane*) atterrir; (*person*): **he flew in yesterday** il est arrivé hier (par avion).

▶**fly off** *vi* s'envoler.

▶**fly out** *vi* (*see* fly in) s'envoler; partir (par avion).

fly-fishing ['flaɪfɪʃɪŋ] *n* pêche *f* à la mouche.

flying ['flaɪɪŋ] *n* (*activity*) aviation *f* ♦ *adj*: ~ **visit** visite *f* éclair *inv*; **with** ~ **colours** haut la main; **he doesn't like** ~ il n'aime pas voyager en avion.

flying buttress *n* arc-boutant *m*.

flying picket *n* piquet *m* de grève volant.

flying saucer *n* soucoupe volante.

flying squad *n* (*POLICE*) brigade volante.

flying start *n*: **to get off to a** ~ faire un excellent départ.

flyleaf ['flaɪliːf] *n* page *f* de garde.

flyover ['flaɪəʊvə*] *n* (*BRIT: overpass*) saut-de-mouton *m*, pont autoroutier.

flypast ['flaɪpɑːst] *n* défilé aérien.

flysheet ['flaɪʃiːt] *n* (*for tent*) double toit *m*.

flyweight ['flaɪweɪt] *n* (*SPORT*) poids *m* mouche.

flywheel ['flaɪwiːl] *n* volant *m* (de commande).

FM *abbr* (*BRIT MIL*) = **field marshal**; (*RADIO*) = **frequency modulation**.

FMB *n abbr* (*US*) = Federal Maritime Board.

FMCS *n abbr* (*US: = Federal Mediation and Conciliation Services*) *organisme de conciliation en cas de conflits du travail*.

FO *n abbr* (*BRIT*) = **Foreign Office**.

foal [fəʊl] *n* poulain *m*.

foam [fəʊm] *n* écume *f*; (*on beer*) mousse *f*; (*also*: **plastic** ~) mousse cellulaire or de plastique ♦ *vi* écumer; (*soapy water*) mousser.

foam rubber *n* caoutchouc *m* mousse.

FOB *abbr* (= *free on board*) fob.

fob [fɒb] *n* (*also*: **watch** ~) chaîne *f*, ruban *m* ♦ *vt*: **to** ~ **sb off with** refiler à qn; se débarrasser de qn avec.

foc *abbr* (*BRIT*) = **free of charge**.

focal ['fəʊkl] *adj* (*also fig*) focal(e).

focal point *n* foyer *m*; (*fig*) centre *m* de l'attention, point focal.

focus ['fəʊkəs] *n* (*pl*: ~**es**) foyer *m*; (*of interest*) centre *m* ♦ *vt* (*field glasses etc*) mettre au point; (*light rays*) faire converger ♦ *vi*: **to** ~ (**on**) (*with camera*) régler la mise au point (sur); (*person*) fixer son regard (sur); **in** ~ au point; **out of** ~ pas au point.

fodder ['fɒdə*] *n* fourrage *m*.

FOE *n abbr* (= *Friends of the Earth*) AT *mpl* (= *Amis de la Terre*); (*US*: = *Fraternal Order of Eagles*) *organisation charitable*.

foe [fəʊ] *n* ennemi *m*.

foetus, (*US*) **fetus** ['fiːtəs] *n* fœtus *m*.

fog [fɒg] *n* brouillard *m*.

fogbound ['fɒgbaʊnd] *adj* bloqué(e) par le brouillard.

foggy ['fɒgɪ] *adj*: **it's** ~ il y a du brouillard.

fog lamp, (*US*) **fog light** *n* (*AUT*) phare *m* anti-brouillard.

foible ['fɔɪbl] *n* faiblesse *f*.

foil [fɔɪl] *vt* déjouer, contrecarrer ♦ *n* feuille *f* de métal; (*kitchen* ~) papier *m* alu(minium); (*FENCING*) fleuret *m*; **to act as a** ~ **to** (*fig*) servir de repoussoir or de faire-valoir à.

foist [fɔɪst] *vt*: **to** ~ **sth on sb** imposer qch à qn.

fold [fəʊld] *n* (*bend, crease*) pli *m*; (*AGR*) parc *m* à moutons; (*fig*) bercail *m* ♦ *vt* plier; **to** ~ **one's arms** croiser les bras.

▶**fold up** *vi* (*map etc*) se plier, se replier; (*business*) fermer boutique ♦ *vt* (*map etc*) plier, replier.

folder ['fəʊldə*] *n* (*for papers*) chemise *f*; (: *binder*) classeur *m*; (*brochure*) dépliant *m*.

folding ['fəʊldɪŋ] *adj* (*chair, bed*) pliant(e).

foliage ['fəʊlɪɪdʒ] *n* feuillage *m*.

folk [fəʊk] *npl* gens *mpl* ♦ *cpd* folklorique; ~**s** *npl* famille *f*, parents *mpl*.

folklore ['fəʊklɔː*] *n* folklore *m*.

folksong ['fəʊksɒŋ] *n* chanson *f* folklorique; (*contemporary*) chanson folk *inv*.

follow ['fɒləʊ] *vt* suivre ♦ *vi* suivre; (*result*) s'ensuivre; **to** ~ **sb's advice** suivre les conseils de qn; **I don't quite** ~ **you** je ne vous suis plus; **to** ~ **in sb's footsteps** emboîter le pas à qn; (*fig*) suivre les traces de qn; **it** ~**s that** ... de ce fait, il s'ensuit que ...; **he** ~**ed suit** il fit de même.

▶**follow out** *vt* (*idea, plan*) poursuivre, mener à terme.

▶**follow through** *vt* = follow out.

▶**follow up** *vt* (*victory*) tirer parti de; (*letter, offer*) donner suite à; (*case*) suivre.

follower ['fɒləʊə*] *n* disciple *m/f*, partisan/e.

following ['fɒləʊɪŋ] *adj* suivant(e) ♦ *n* partisans *mpl*, disciples *mpl*.

follow-up ['fɒləʊʌp] *n* suite *f*; suivi *m*.

folly ['fɒlɪ] *n* inconscience *f*; sottise *f*; (*building*) folie *f*.

fond [fɒnd] *adj* (*memory, look*) tendre, affectueux(euse); **to be** ~ **of** aimer beaucoup.

fondle ['fɒndl] *vt* caresser.

fondly ['fɒndlɪ] *adv* (*lovingly*) tendrement; (*naïvely*) naïvement.

fondness ['fɒndnɪs] *n* (*for things*) attachement *m*; (*for people*) sentiments affectueux; **a special** ~ **for** une prédilection pour.

font [fɒnt] *n* (*REL*) fonts baptismaux; (*TYP*) police *f* de caractères.

food [fuːd] *n* nourriture *f*.

food chain *n* chaîne *f* alimentaire.

food mixer *n* mixeur *m*.

food poisoning *n* intoxication *f* alimentaire.

food processor *n* robot *m* de cuisine.

food stamp *n* (*US*) bon *m* de nourriture (*pour indigents*).

foodstuffs ['fuːdstʌfs] *npl* denrées *fpl* alimentaires.

fool [fuːl] *n* idiot/e; (*HISTORY: of king*) bouffon *m*, fou *m*; (*CULIN*) purée *f* de fruits à la crème

♦ vt berner, duper ♦ vi (also: ~ **around**) faire l'idiot or l'imbécile; **to make a ~ of sb** (ridicule) ridiculiser qn; (trick) avoir or duper qn; **to make a ~ of o.s.** se couvrir de ridicule; **you can't ~ me** vous (ne) me la ferez pas, on (ne) me la fait pas.

►**fool about, fool around** vi (pej: waste time) traînailler, glandouiller; (: behave foolishly) faire l'imbécile.

foolhardy ['fu:lhɑːdɪ] adj téméraire, imprudent(e).

foolish ['fu:lɪʃ] adj idiot(e), stupide; (rash) imprudent(e).

foolishly ['fu:lɪʃlɪ] adv stupidement.

foolishness ['fu:lɪʃnɪs] n idiotie f, stupidité f.

foolproof ['fu:lpru:f] adj (plan etc) infaillible.

foolscap ['fu:lskæp] n ≈ papier m ministre.

foot [fut] n (pl: **feet** [fi:t]) pied m; (measure) pied (= 304 mm; 12 inches); (of animal) patte f ♦ vt (bill) casquer, payer; **on ~** à pied; **to find one's feet** (fig) s'acclimater; **to put one's ~ down** (AUT) appuyer sur le champignon; (say no) s'imposer.

footage ['futɪdʒ] n (CINE: length) ≈ métrage m; (: material) séquences fpl.

foot and mouth (disease) n fièvre aphteuse.

football ['futbɔːl] n ballon m (de football); (sport: BRIT) football m foot m; (: US) football américain.

footballer ['futbɔːlə*] n (BRIT) = football player.

football game n match m de football.

football ground n terrain m de football.

football match n (BRIT) match m de foot(ball).

football player n footballeur m, joueur m de football.

Les **football pools** - ou plus familièrement les "**pools**" - sont une sorte de loto sportif britannique où l'on parie sur les matches de football qui se jouent tous les samedis. L'expression consacrée en anglais est "to do the pools". Les parieurs envoient à l'avance les fiches qu'ils ont complétées à l'organisme qui gère les paris et ils attendent les résultats, qui sont annoncés à 17 h le samedi. Les sommes gagnées se comptent parfois en milliers (ou même en millions) de livres sterling.

---

footbrake ['futbreɪk] n frein m à pied.

footbridge ['futbrɪdʒ] n passerelle f.

foothills ['futhɪlz] npl contreforts mpl.

foothold ['futhəuld] n prise f (de pied).

footing ['futɪŋ] n (fig) position f; **to lose one's ~** perdre pied; **on an equal ~** sur pied d'égalité.

footlights ['futlaɪts] npl rampe f.

footman ['futmən] n laquais m.

footnote ['futnəut] n note f (en bas de page).

footpath ['futpɑːθ] n sentier m; (in street) trot-

toir m.

footprint ['futprɪnt] n trace f (de pied).

footrest ['futrɛst] n marchepied m.

footsie ['futsɪ] n (col): **to play ~ with sb** faire du pied à qn.

footsore ['futsɔː*] adj: **to be ~** avoir mal aux pieds.

footstep ['futstɛp] n pas m.

footwear ['futwɛə*] n chaussure(s) f(pl) (terme générique en anglais).

FOR abbr (= free on rail) franco wagon.

====================================== KEYWORD

for [fɔː*] prep **1** (indicating destination, intention, purpose) pour; **the train ~ London** le train pour or (à destination) de Londres; **he went ~ the paper** il est allé chercher le journal; **it's time ~ lunch** c'est l'heure du déjeuner; **what's it ~?** ça sert à quoi?; **what ~?** (why) pourquoi?; (to what end) pour quoi faire?, à quoi bon?; **~ sale** à vendre

2 (on behalf of, representing) pour; **the MP ~ Hove** le député de Hove; **to work ~ sb/sth** travailler pour qn/qch; **G ~ George** G comme Georges

3 (because of) pour; **~ this reason** pour cette raison; **~ fear of being criticized** de peur d'être critiqué

4 (with regard to) pour; **it's cold ~ July** il fait froid pour juillet; **a gift ~ languages** un don pour les langues

5 (in exchange for): **I sold it ~ £5** je l'ai vendu 5 livres; **to pay 50 pence ~ a ticket** payer un billet 50 pence

6 (in favour of) pour; **are you ~ or against us?** êtes-vous pour ou contre nous?

7 (referring to distance) pendant, sur; **there are roadworks ~ 5 km** il y a des travaux sur 5 km; **we walked ~ miles** nous avons marché pendant des kilomètres

8 (referring to time) pendant; depuis; pour; **he was away ~ 2 years** il a été absent pendant 2 ans; **she will be away ~ a month** elle sera absente (pendant) un mois; **I have known her ~ years** je la connais depuis des années; **can you do it ~ tomorrow?** est-ce que tu peux le faire pour demain?

9 (with infinitive clauses): **it is not ~ me to decide** ce n'est pas à moi de décider; **it would be best ~ you to leave** le mieux serait que vous partiez; **there is still time ~ you to do it** vous avez encore le temps de le faire; **~ this to be possible** ... pour que cela soit possible ...

10 (in spite of): **~ all that** malgré cela, néanmoins; **~ all his work/efforts** malgré tout son travail/tous ses efforts; **~ all his complaints, he's very fond of her** il a beau se plaindre, il l'aime beaucoup

♦ conj (since, as: rather formal) car.

forage ['fɔrɪdʒ] n fourrage m ♦ vi fourrager,

fouiller.

forage cap *n* calot *m*.

foray ['fɔreɪ] *n* incursion *f*.

forbad(e) [fə'bæd] *pt of* **forbid**.

forbearing [fɔ:'bɛərɪŋ] *adj* patient(e), tolérant(e).

forbid, *pt* **forbad(e)**, *pp* **forbidden** [fə'bɪd, -'bæd, -'bɪdn] *vt* défendre, interdire; **to ~ sb to do** défendre *or* interdire à qn de faire.

forbidden [fə'bɪdn] *adj* défendu(e).

forbidding [fə'bɪdɪŋ] *adj* d'aspect *or* d'allure sévère *or* sombre.

force [fɔ:s] *n* force *f* ♦ *vt* forcer; **the F~s** *npl* (*BRIT*) l'armée *f*; **to ~ sb to do sth** forcer qn à faire qch; **in ~** en force; **to come into ~** entrer en vigueur; **a ~ 5 wind** un vent de force 5; **the sales ~** (*COMM*) la force de vente; **to join ~s** unir ses forces.

▶**force back** *vt* (*crowd, enemy*) repousser; (*tears*) refouler.

▶**force down** *vt* (*food*) se forcer à manger.

forced [fɔ:st] *adj* forcé(e).

force-feed ['fɔ:sfi:d] *vt* nourrir de force.

forceful ['fɔ:sful] *adj* énergique, volontaire.

forcemeat ['fɔ:smi:t] *n* (*BRIT CULIN*) farce *f*.

forceps ['fɔ:sɛps] *npl* forceps *m*.

forcibly ['fɔ:səblɪ] *adv* par la force, de force; (*vigorously*) énergiquement.

ford [fɔ:d] *n* gué *m* ♦ *vt* passer à gué.

fore [fɔ:*] *n*: **to the ~** en évidence.

forearm ['fɔ:rɑ:m] *n* avant-bras *m inv*.

forebear ['fɔ:bɛə*] *n* ancêtre *m*.

foreboding [fɔ:'bəudɪŋ] *n* pressentiment *m* (néfaste).

forecast ['fɔ:kɑ:st] *n* prévision *f*; (*also:* **weather ~**) prévisions météorologiques, météo *f* ♦ *vt* (*irreg: like* **cast**) prévoir.

foreclose [fɔ:'kləuz] *vt* (*LAW: also:* **~ on**) saisir.

foreclosure [fɔ:'kləuʒə*] *n* saisie *f* du bien hypothéqué.

forecourt ['fɔ:kɔ:t] *n* (*of garage*) devant *m*.

forefathers ['fɔ:fɑ:ðəz] *npl* ancêtres *mpl*.

forefinger ['fɔ:fɪŋgə*] *n* index *m*.

forefront ['fɔ:frʌnt] *n*: **in the ~ of** au premier rang *or* plan de.

forego, *pt* **forewent**, *pp* **foregone** [fɔ:'gəu, -'wɛnt, -'gɔn] *vt* renoncer à.

foregoing ['fɔ:gəuɪŋ] *adj* susmentionné(e) ♦ *n*: **the ~** ce qui précède.

foregone ['fɔ:gɔn] *adj*: **it's a ~ conclusion** c'est à prévoir, c'est couru d'avance.

foreground ['fɔ:graund] *n* premier plan ♦ *cpd* (*COMPUT*) prioritaire.

forehand ['fɔ:hænd] *n* (*TENNIS*) coup droit.

forehead ['fɔrɪd] *n* front *m*.

foreign ['fɔrɪn] *adj* étranger(ère); (*trade*) extérieur(e).

foreign body *n* corps étranger.

foreign currency *n* devises étrangères.

foreigner ['fɔrɪnə*] *n* étranger/ère.

foreign exchange *n* (*system*) change *m*; (*money*) devises *fpl*.

foreign exchange market *n* marché *m* des devises.

foreign exchange rate *n* cours *m* des devises.

foreign investment *n* investissement *m* à l'étranger.

Foreign Office *n* (*BRIT*) ministère *m* des Affaires étrangères.

foreign secretary *n* (*BRIT*) ministre *m* des Affaires étrangères.

foreleg ['fɔ:lɛg] *n* patte *f* de devant; jambe antérieure.

foreman ['fɔ:mən] *n* contremaître *m*; (*LAW: of jury*) président *m* (du jury).

foremost ['fɔ:məust] *adj* le(la) plus en vue; premier(ière) ♦ *adv*: **first and ~** avant tout, tout d'abord.

forename ['fɔ:neɪm] *n* prénom *m*.

forensic [fə'rɛnsɪk] *adj*: **~ medicine** médecine légale; **~ expert** expert *m* de la police, expert légiste.

foreplay ['fɔ:pleɪ] *n* stimulation *f* érotique, prélude *m*.

forerunner ['fɔ:rʌnə*] *n* précurseur *m*.

foresee, *pt* **foresaw**, *pp* **foreseen** [fɔ:'si:, -'sɔ:, -'si:n] *vt* prévoir.

foreseeable [fɔ:'si:əbl] *adj* prévisible.

foreshadow [fɔ:'ʃædəu] *vt* présager, annoncer, laisser prévoir.

foreshorten [fɔ:'ʃɔ:tn] *vt* (*figure, scene*) réduire, faire en raccourci.

foresight ['fɔ:saɪt] *n* prévoyance *f*.

foreskin ['fɔ:skɪn] *n* (*ANAT*) prépuce *m*.

forest ['fɔrɪst] *n* forêt *f*.

forestall [fɔ:'stɔ:l] *vt* devancer.

forestry ['fɔrɪstrɪ] *n* sylviculture *f*.

foretaste ['fɔ:teɪst] *n* avant-goût *m*.

foretell, *pt, pp* **foretold** [fɔ:'tɛl, -'təuld] *vt* prédire.

forethought ['fɔ:θɔ:t] *n* prévoyance *f*.

forever [fə'rɛvə*] *adv* pour toujours; (*fig*) continuellement.

forewarn [fɔ:'wɔ:n] *vt* avertir.

forewent [fɔ:'wɛnt] *pt of* **forego**.

foreword ['fɔ:wə:d] *n* avant-propos *m inv*.

forfeit ['fɔ:fɪt] *n* prix *m*, rançon *f* ♦ *vt* perdre; (*one's life, health*) payer de.

forgave [fə'geɪv] *pt of* **forgive**.

forge [fɔ:dʒ] *n* forge *f* ♦ *vt* (*signature*) contrefaire; (*wrought iron*) forger; **to ~ documents/a will** fabriquer de faux papiers/un faux testament; **to ~ money** (*BRIT*) fabriquer de la fausse monnaie.

▶**forge ahead** *vi* pousser de l'avant, prendre de l'avance.

forger ['fɔ:dʒə*] *n* faussaire *m*.

forgery ['fɔ:dʒərɪ] *n* faux *m*, contrefaçon *f*.

forget, *pt* **forgot**, *pp* **forgotten** [fə'gɛt, -'gɔt, -'gɔtn] *vt, vi* oublier.

forgetful [fə'gɛtful] *adj* distrait(e), étourdi(e); **~ of** oublieux(euse) de.

forgetfulness [fə'gɛtfulnɪs] *n* tendance *f* aux

oublis; (*oblivion*) oubli *m*.

forget-me-not [fə'gɛtmɪnɒt] *n* myosotis *m*.

forgive, *pt* **forgave,** *pp* **forgiven** [fə'gɪv, -'geɪv, -'gɪvn] *vt* pardonner; **to ~ sb for sth/ for doing sth** pardonner qch à qn/à qn de faire qch.

forgiveness [fə'gɪvnɪs] *n* pardon *m*.

forgiving [fə'gɪvɪŋ] *adj* indulgent(e).

forgo, *pt* **forwent,** *pp* **forgone** [fɔː'gəu, -'wɛnt, -'gɒn] *vt* = **forego**.

forgot [fə'gɒt] *pt of* **forget**.

forgotten [fə'gɒtn] *pp of* **forget**.

fork [fɔːk] *n* (*for eating*) fourchette *f*; (*for gardening*) fourche *f*; (*of roads*) bifurcation *f*; (*of railways*) embranchement *m* ♦ *vi* (*road*) bifurquer.

▶**fork out** (*col: pay*) *vt* allonger, se fendre de ♦ *vi* casquer.

forked [fɔːkt] *adj* (*lightning*) en zigzags, ramifié(e).

fork-lift truck ['fɔːklɪft-] *n* chariot élévateur.

forlorn [fə'lɔːn] *adj* abandonné(e), délaissé(e); (*hope, attempt*) désespéré(e).

form [fɔːm] *n* forme *f*; (*SCOL*) classe *f*; (*questionnaire*) formulaire *m* ♦ *vt* former; **in the ~ of** sous forme de; **to ~ part of sth** faire partie de qch; **to be in good ~** (*SPORT, fig*) être en forme; **in top ~** en pleine forme.

formal ['fɔːməl] *adj* (*offer, receipt*) en bonne et due forme; (*person*) cérémonieux(euse), à cheval sur les convenances; (*occasion, dinner*) officiel(le); (*ART, PHILOSOPHY*) formel(le); **~ dress** tenue *f* de cérémonie; (*evening dress*) tenue de soirée.

formality [fɔː'mælɪtɪ] *n* formalité *f*; cérémonie(s) *f(pl)*.

formalize ['fɔːməlaɪz] *vt* officialiser.

formally ['fɔːməlɪ] *adv* officiellement; formellement; cérémonieusement.

format ['fɔːmæt] *n* format *m* ♦ *vt* (*COMPUT*) formater.

formation [fɔː'meɪʃən] *n* formation *f*.

formative ['fɔːmətɪv] *adj*: **~ years** années *fpl* d'apprentissage (*fig*) *or* de formation (*d'un enfant, d'un adolescent*).

former ['fɔːmə*] *adj* ancien(ne) (*before n*), précédent(e); **the ~ ... the latter** le premier ... le second, celui-là ... celui-ci; **the ~ president** l'ex-président; **the ~ Yugoslavia/Soviet Union** l'ex Yougoslavie/Union Soviétique.

formerly ['fɔːməlɪ] *adv* autrefois.

form feed *n* (*on printer*) alimentation *f* en feuilles.

formidable ['fɔːmɪdəbl] *adj* redoutable.

formula ['fɔːmjulə] *n* formule *f*; **F~ One** (*AUT*) Formule un.

formulate ['fɔːmjuleɪt] *vt* formuler.

fornicate ['fɔːnɪkeɪt] *vi* forniquer.

forsake, *pt* **forsook,** *pp* **forsaken** [fə'seɪk, -'suk, -'seɪkən] *vt* abandonner.

fort [fɔːt] *n* fort *m*; **to hold the ~** (*fig*) assurer la permanence.

forte ['fɔːtɪ] *n* (*point*) fort *m*.

forth [fɔːθ] *adv* en avant; **to go back and ~** aller et venir; **and so ~** et ainsi de suite.

forthcoming [fɔːθ'kʌmɪŋ] *adj* qui va paraître *or* avoir lieu prochainement; (*character*) ouvert(e), communicatif(ive).

forthright ['fɔːθraɪt] *adj* franc(franche), direct(e).

forthwith ['fɔːθ'wɪθ] *adv* sur le champ.

fortieth ['fɔːtɪɪθ] *num* quarantième.

fortification [fɔːtɪfɪ'keɪʃən] *n* fortification *f*.

fortified wine ['fɔːtɪfaɪd-] *n* vin liquoreux *or* de liqueur.

fortify ['fɔːtɪfaɪ] *vt* fortifier.

fortitude ['fɔːtɪtjuːd] *n* courage *m*, force *f* d'âme.

fortnight ['fɔːtnaɪt] *n* (*BRIT*) quinzaine *f*, quinze jours *mpl*; **it's a ~ since** ... il y a quinze jours que ....

fortnightly ['fɔːtnaɪtlɪ] *adj* bimensuel(le) ♦ *adv* tous les quinze jours.

FORTRAN ['fɔːtræn] *n* FORTRAN *m*.

fortress ['fɔːtrɪs] *n* forteresse *f*.

fortuitous [fɔː'tjuːɪtəs] *adj* fortuit(e).

fortunate ['fɔːtʃənɪt] *adj*: **to be ~** avoir de la chance; **it is ~ that** c'est une chance que, il est heureux que.

fortunately ['fɔːtʃənɪtlɪ] *adv* heureusement, par bonheur.

fortune ['fɔːtʃən] *n* chance *f*; (*wealth*) fortune *f*; **to make a ~** faire fortune.

fortuneteller ['fɔːtʃəntɛlə*] *n* diseuse *f* de bonne aventure.

forty ['fɔːtɪ] *num* quarante.

forum ['fɔːrəm] *n* forum *m*, tribune *f*.

forward ['fɔːwəd] *adj* (*movement, position*) en avant, vers l'avant; (*not shy*) effronté(e); (*COMM: delivery, sales, exchange*) à terme ♦ *adv* en avant ♦ *n* (*SPORT*) avant *m* ♦ *vt* (*letter*) faire suivre; (*parcel, goods*) expédier; (*fig*) promouvoir, contribuer au développement *or* à l'avancement de; **to move ~** avancer; **"please ~"** "prière de faire suivre"; **~ planning** planification *f* à long terme.

forwards ['fɔːwədz] *adv* en avant.

forwent [fɔː'wɛnt] *pt of* **forgo**.

fossil ['fɒsl] *adj, n* fossile (*m*); **~ fuel** combustible *m* fossile.

foster ['fɒstə*] *vt* encourager, favoriser.

foster brother *n* frère adoptif; frère de lait.

foster child *n* enfant adopté.

foster mother *n* mère adoptive; mère nourricière.

fought [fɔːt] *pt, pp of* **fight**.

foul [faul] *adj* (*weather, smell, food*) infect(e); (*language*) ordurier(ière); (*deed*) infâme ♦ *n* (*FOOTBALL*) faute *f* ♦ *vt* salir, encrasser; (*football player*) commettre une faute sur; (*entangle: anchor, propeller*) emmêler.

foul play *n* (*SPORT*) jeu déloyal; **~ is not suspected** la mort (*or* l'incendie *etc*) n'a pas de causes suspectes, on écarte l'hypothèse d'un meurtre (*or* d'un acte criminel).

found [faund] *pt, pp of* **find ♦** *vt* (*establish*) fonder.

foundation [faun'deɪʃən] *n* (*act*) fondation *f*; (*base*) fondement *m*; (*also*: ~ **cream**) fond *m* de teint; ~**s** *npl* (*of building*) fondations *fpl*; **to lay the** ~**s** (*fig*) poser les fondements.

foundation stone *n* première pierre.

founder ['faundə*] *n* fondateur *m* ♦ *vi* couler, sombrer.

founding ['faundɪŋ] *adj*: ~ **fathers** (*esp US*) pères *mpl* fondateurs; ~ **member** membre *m* fondateur.

foundry ['faundrɪ] *n* fonderie *f*.

fount [faunt] *n* source *f*; (*TYP*) fonte *f*.

fountain ['fauntɪn] *n* fontaine *f*.

fountain pen *n* stylo *m* (à encre).

four [fɔ:*] *num* quatre; **on all** ~**s** à quatre pattes.

four-letter word ['fɔ:lɛtə-] *n* obscénité *f*, gros mot.

four-poster ['fɔ:'pəustə*] *n* (*also*: ~ **bed**) lit *m* à baldaquin.

foursome ['fɔ:səm] *n* partie *f* à quatre; sortie *f* à quatre.

fourteen ['fɔ:'ti:n] *num* quatorze.

fourth ['fɔ:θ] *num* quatrième ♦ *n* (*AUT: also*: ~ **gear**) quatrième *f*.

four-wheel drive ['fɔ:wi:l-] *n* (*AUT*): **with** ~ à quatre roues motrices.

fowl [faul] *n* volaille *f*.

fox [fɔks] *n* renard *m* ♦ *vt* mystifier.

fox fur *n* renard *m*.

foxglove ['fɔksglʌv] *n* (*BOT*) digitale *f*.

fox-hunting ['fɔkshʌntɪŋ] *n* chasse *f* au renard.

foyer ['fɔɪeɪ] *n* vestibule *m*; (*THEAT*) foyer *m*.

FP *n abbr* (*BRIT*) = *former pupil*; (*US*) = *fireplug*.

FPA *n abbr* (*BRIT*) = *Family Planning Association*.

Fr. *abbr* (= *father*: *REL*) P; (= *friar*) F.

fr. *abbr* (= *franc*) F.

fracas ['fræka:] *n* bagarre *f*.

fraction ['frækʃən] *n* fraction *f*.

fractionally ['frækʃnəlɪ] *adv*: ~ **smaller** *etc* un poil plus petit *etc*.

fractious ['frækʃəs] *adj* grincheux(euse).

fracture ['fræktʃə*] *n* fracture *f* ♦ *vt* fracturer.

fragile ['frædʒaɪl] *adj* fragile.

fragment ['frægmənt] *n* fragment *m*.

fragmentary ['frægməntərɪ] *adj* fragmentaire.

fragrance ['freɪgrəns] *n* parfum *m*.

fragrant ['freɪgrənt] *adj* parfumé(e), odorant(e).

frail [freɪl] *adj* fragile, délicat(e).

frame [freɪm] *n* (*of building*) charpente *f*; (*of human, animal*) charpente, ossature *f*; (*of picture*) cadre *m*; (*of door, window*) encadrement *m*, chambranle *m*; (*of spectacles: also*: ~**s**) monture *f* ♦ *vt* encadrer; (*theory, plan*) construire, élaborer; **to** ~ **sb** (*col*) monter un coup contre qn; ~ **of mind** disposition *f* d'esprit.

framework ['freɪmwə:k] *n* structure *f*.

France [fra:ns] *n* la France; **in** ~ en France.

franchise ['fræntʃaɪz] *n* (*POL*) droit *m* de vote; (*COMM*) franchise *f*.

franchisee [fræntʃaɪ'zi:] *n* franchisé *m*.

franchiser ['fræntʃaɪzə*] *n* franchiseur *m*.

frank [fræŋk] *adj* franc(franche) ♦ *vt* (*letter*) affranchir.

Frankfurt ['fræŋkfə:t] *n* Francfort.

franking machine ['fræŋkɪŋ-] *n* machine *f* à affranchir.

frankly ['fræŋklɪ] *adv* franchement.

frankness ['fræŋknɪs] *n* franchise *f*.

frantic ['fræntɪk] *adj* frénétique; (*desperate: need, desire*) effréné(e); (*person*) hors de soi.

frantically ['fræntɪklɪ] *adv* frénétiquement.

fraternal [frə'tə:nl] *adj* fraternel(le).

fraternity [frə'tə:nɪtɪ] *n* (*club*) communauté *f*, confrérie *f*; (*spirit*) fraternité *f*.

fraternize ['frætənaɪz] *vi* fraterniser.

fraud [frɔ:d] *n* supercherie *f*, fraude *f*, tromperie *f*; (*person*) imposteur *m*.

fraudulent ['frɔ:djulənt] *adj* frauduleux(euse).

fraught [frɔ:t] *adj* (*tense: person*) très tendu(e); (*: situation*) pénible; ~ **with** (*difficulties etc*) chargé(e) de, plein(e) de.

fray [freɪ] *n* bagarre *f*; (*MIL*) combat *m* ♦ *vt* effilocher ♦ *vi* s'effilocher; **tempers were** ~**ed** les gens commençaient à s'énerver; **her nerves were** ~**ed** elle était à bout de nerfs.

FRB *n abbr* (*US*) = *Federal Reserve Board*.

FRCM *n abbr* (*BRIT*) = *Fellow of the Royal College of Music*.

FRCO *n abbr* (*BRIT*) = *Fellow of the Royal College of Organists*.

FRCP *n abbr* (*BRIT*) = *Fellow of the Royal College of Physicians*.

FRCS *n abbr* (*BRIT*) = *Fellow of the Royal College of Surgeons*.

freak [fri:k] *n* (*also cpd*) phénomène *m*, créature ou événement exceptionnel par sa rareté, son caractère d'anomalie; (*pej: fanatic*): **health** ~ fana *m/f* *or* obsédé/e de l'alimentation saine (*or* de la forme physique).

▶**freak out** *vi* (*col: drop out*) se marginaliser; (*: on drugs*) se défoncer.

freakish ['fri:kɪʃ] *adj* insolite; anormal(e).

freckle ['frɛkl] *n* tache *f* de rousseur.

free [fri:] *adj* libre; (*gratis*) gratuit(e); (*liberal*) généreux(euse), large ♦ *vt* (*prisoner etc*) libérer; (*jammed object or person*) dégager; **to give sb a** ~ **hand** donner carte blanche à qn; ~ **and easy** sans façon, décontracté(e); **admission** ~ entrée libre; ~ (**of charge**) *adv* gratuitement.

freebie ['fri:bɪ] *n* (*col*): **it's a** ~ c'est gratuit.

freedom ['fri:dəm] *n* liberté *f*.

freedom fighter *n* combattant *m* de la liberté.

free enterprise *n* libre entreprise *f*.

Freefone ['fri:fəun] *n* ® numéro vert.

free-for-all ['fri:fərɔ:l] n mêlée générale.
free gift n prime f.
freehold ['fri:həuld] n propriété foncière libre.
free kick n (SPORT) coup franc.
freelance ['fri:lɑ:ns] adj (journalist etc) indépendant(e); (work) à la pige, à la tâche.
freeloader ['fri:ləudə*] n (pej) parasite m.
freely ['fri:lɪ] adv librement; (liberally) libéralement.
free-market economy [fri:'mɑ:kɪt-] n économie f de marché.
freemason ['fri:meɪsn] n franc-maçon m.
freemasonry ['fri:meɪsnrɪ] n franc-maçonnerie f.
freepost ['fri:pəust] n franchise postale.
free-range ['fri:'reɪndʒ] adj (eggs) de ferme.
free sample n échantillon gratuit.
free speech n liberté f d'expression.
free trade n libre-échange m.
freeway ['fri:weɪ] n (US) autoroute f.
freewheel [fri:'wi:l] vi descendre en roue libre.
freewheeling [fri:'wi:lɪŋ] adj indépendant(e), libre.
free will n libre arbitre m; **of one's own** ~ de son plein gré.
freeze [fri:z] vb (pt **froze**, pp **frozen** [frəuz, 'frəuzn]) vi geler ♦ vt geler; (food) congeler; (prices, salaries) bloquer, geler ♦ n gel m; blocage m.
▶**freeze over** vi (river) geler; (windscreen) se couvrir de givre or de glace.
▶**freeze up** vi geler.
freeze-dried ['fri:zdraɪd] adj lyophilisé(e).
freezer ['fri:zə*] n congélateur m.
freezing ['fri:zɪŋ] adj: ~ **(cold)** (room etc) glacial(e); (person, hands) gelé(e), glacé(e) ♦ n: **3 degrees below** ~ 3 degrés au-dessous de zéro.
freezing point n point m de congélation.
freight [freɪt] n (goods) fret m, cargaison f; (money charged) fret, prix m du transport; ~ **forward** port dû; ~ **inward** port payé par le destinataire.
freighter ['freɪtə*] n (NAUT) cargo m.
freight forwarder [-fɔ:wədə*] n transitaire m.
freight train n (US) train m de marchandises.
French [frɛntʃ] adj français(e) ♦ n (LING) français m; **the** ~ npl les Français.
French bean n (BRIT) haricot vert.
French bread n pain m (français).
French Canadian adj canadien(ne) français(e) ♦ n Canadien/ne français(e).
French dressing n (CULIN) vinaigrette f.
French fried potatoes, (US) **French fries** npl (pommes de terre fpl) frites fpl.
French Guiana [-gaɪ'ænə] n Guyane française.
French loaf n ≈ pain m, ≈ parisien m.
Frenchman ['frɛntʃmən] n Français m.
French Riviera n: **the** ~ la Côte d'Azur.

French stick n ≈ baguette f.
French window n porte-fenêtre f.
Frenchwoman ['frɛntʃwumən] n Française f.
frenetic [frə'nɛtɪk] adj frénétique.
frenzy ['frɛnzɪ] n frénésie f.
frequency ['fri:kwənsɪ] n fréquence f.
frequency modulation (FM) n modulation f de fréquence (FM, MF).
frequent adj ['fri:kwənt] fréquent(e) ♦ vt [frɪ'kwɛnt] fréquenter.
frequently ['fri:kwəntlɪ] adv fréquemment.
fresco ['frɛskəu] n fresque f.
fresh [frɛʃ] adj frais(fraîche); (new) nouveau(nouvelle); (cheeky) familier(ière), culotté(e); **to make a** ~ **start** prendre un nouveau départ.
freshen ['frɛʃən] vi (wind, air) fraîchir.
▶**freshen up** vi faire un brin de toilette.
freshener ['frɛʃnə*] n: **skin** ~ astringent m; **air** ~ désodorisant m.
fresher ['frɛʃə*] n (BRIT SCOL: col) = **freshman**.
freshly ['frɛʃlɪ] adv nouvellement, récemment.
freshman ['frɛʃmən] n (SCOL) bizuth m, étudiant/e de première année.
freshness ['frɛʃnɪs] n fraîcheur f.
freshwater ['frɛʃwɔ:tə*] adj (fish) d'eau douce.
fret [frɛt] vi s'agiter, se tracasser.
fretful ['frɛtful] adj (child) grincheux(euse).
Freudian ['frɔɪdɪən] adj freudien(ne); ~ **slip** lapsus m.
FRG n abbr (= Federal Republic of Germany) RFA f.
Fri. abbr (= Friday) ve.
friar ['fraɪə*] n moine m, frère m.
friction ['frɪkʃən] n friction f, frottement m.
friction feed n (on printer) entraînement m par friction.
Friday ['fraɪdɪ] n vendredi m; for phrases see also **Tuesday**.
fridge [frɪdʒ] n (BRIT) frigo m, frigidaire m ®.
fridge-freezer ['frɪdʒ'fri:zə*] n réfrigérateur-congélateur m.
fried [fraɪd] pt, pp of **fry** ♦ adj frit(e); ~ **egg** œuf m sur le plat.
friend [frɛnd] n ami/e; **to make** ~**s with** se lier (d'amitié) avec.
friendliness ['frɛndlɪnɪs] n attitude amicale.
friendly ['frɛndlɪ] adj amical(e); (kind) sympathique, gentil(le); (POL: country, government) ami(e) ♦ n (also: ~ **match**) match amical; **to be** ~ **with** être ami(e) avec; **to be** ~ **to** être bien disposé(e) à l'égard de.
friendly fire n: **they were killed by** ~ ils sont morts sous les tirs de leur propre camp.
friendly society n société f mutualiste.
friendship ['frɛndʃɪp] n amitié f.
frieze [fri:z] n frise f, bordure f.
frigate ['frɪgɪt] n (NAUT: modern) frégate f.
fright [fraɪt] n peur f, effroi m; **to take** ~ prendre peur, s'effrayer; **she looks a** ~ elle a l'air d'un épouvantail.

frighten ['fraɪtn] *vt* effrayer, faire peur à.
▶**frighten away**, **frighten off** *vt* (*birds, children etc*) faire fuir, effaroucher.
frightened ['fraɪtnd] *adj*: **to be ~ (of)** avoir peur (de).
frightening ['fraɪtnɪŋ] *adj* effrayant(e).
frightful ['fraɪtful] *adj* affreux(euse).
frightfully ['fraɪtfəlɪ] *adv* affreusement.
frigid ['frɪdʒɪd] *adj* (*woman*) frigide.
frigidity [frɪ'dʒɪdɪtɪ] *n* frigidité *f*.
frill [frɪl] *n* (*of dress*) volant *m*; (*of shirt*) jabot *m*; **without ~s** (*fig*) sans manières.
frilly ['frɪlɪ] *adj* à fanfreluches.
fringe [frɪndʒ] *n* frange *f*; (*edge: of forest etc*) bordure *f*; (*fig*): **on the ~** en marge.
fringe benefits *npl* avantages sociaux *or* en nature.
fringe theatre *n* théâtre *m* d'avant-garde.
Frisbee ['frɪzbɪ] *n* ® Frisbee *m* ®.
frisk [frɪsk] *vt* fouiller.
frisky ['frɪskɪ] *adj* vif(vive), sémillant(e).
fritter ['frɪtə*] *n* beignet *m*.
▶**fritter away** *vt* gaspiller.
frivolity [frɪ'vɔlɪtɪ] *n* frivolité *f*.
frivolous ['frɪvələs] *adj* frivole.
frizzy ['frɪzɪ] *adj* crépu(e).
fro [frəu] *see* **to**.
frock [frɔk] *n* robe *f*.
frog [frɔg] *n* grenouille *f*; **to have a ~ in one's throat** avoir un chat dans la gorge.
frogman ['frɔgmən] *n* homme-grenouille *m*.
frogmarch ['frɔgmɑːtʃ] *vt* (*BRIT*): **to ~ sb in/out** faire entrer/sortir qn de force.
frolic ['frɔlɪk] *n* ébats *mpl* ♦ *vi* folâtrer, batifoler.

============================= *KEYWORD*

from [frɔm] *prep* **1** (*indicating starting place, origin etc*) de; **where do you come ~?**, **where are you ~?** d'où venez-vous?; **where has he come ~?** d'où arrive-t-il?; **~ London to Paris** de Londres à Paris; **a letter/telephone call ~ my sister** une lettre/un appel de ma sœur; **to drink ~ the bottle** boire à (même) la bouteille
2 (*indicating time*) (à partir) de; **~ one o'clock to** *or* **until** *or* **till two** d'une heure à deux heures; **~ January (on)** à partir de janvier
3 (*indicating distance*) de; **the hotel is one kilometre ~ the beach** l'hôtel est à un kilomètre de la plage
4 (*indicating price, number etc*) de; **the interest rate was increased ~ 9% to 10%** le taux d'intérêt est passé de 9 à 10%
5 (*indicating difference*) de; **he can't tell red ~ green** il ne peut pas distinguer le rouge du vert
6 (*because of, on the basis of*): **~ what he says** d'après ce qu'il dit; **weak ~ hunger** affaibli par la faim

frond [frɔnd] *n* fronde *f*.
front [frʌnt] *n* (*of house, dress*) devant *m*; (*of coach, train*) avant *m*; (*of book*) couverture *f*; (*promenade: also*: **sea ~**) bord *m* de mer; (*MIL, POL, METEOROLOGY*) front *m*; (*fig: appearances*) contenance *f*, façade *f* ♦ *adj* de devant; premier(ière) ♦ *vi*: **to ~ onto sth** donner sur qch; **in ~ (of)** devant.
frontage ['frʌntɪdʒ] *n* façade *f*; (*of shop*) devanture *f*.
frontal ['frʌntl] *adj* frontal(e).

Le **front bench** *est le banc du gouvernement, placé à la droite du Speaker, ou celui du cabinet fantôme, placé à sa gauche. Ils se font face dans l'enceinte de la Chambre des communes. Par extension,* **front bench** *désigne les dirigeants des groupes parlementaires de la majorité et de l'opposition, qui sont appelés "frontbenchers" par opposition aux autres députés qui sont appelés "backbenchers".*

---

front desk *n* (*US: in hotel, at doctor's*) réception *f*.
front door *n* porte *f* d'entrée; (*of car*) portière *f* avant.
frontier ['frʌntɪə*] *n* frontière *f*.
frontispiece ['frʌntɪspiːs] *n* frontispice *m*.
front page *n* première page.
front room *n* (*BRIT*) pièce *f* de devant, salon *m*.
front runner *n* (*fig*) favori/te.
front-wheel drive ['frʌntwiːl-] *n* traction *f* avant.
frost [frɔst] *n* gel *m*, gelée *f*; (*also*: **hoar~**) givre *m*.
frostbite ['frɔstbaɪt] *n* gelures *fpl*.
frosted ['frɔstɪd] *adj* (*glass*) dépoli(e); (*esp US: cake*) glacé(e).
frosting ['frɔstɪŋ] *n* (*esp US: on cake*) glaçage *m*.
frosty ['frɔstɪ] *adj* (*window*) couvert(e) de givre; (*welcome*) glacial(e).
froth [frɔθ] *n* mousse *f*; écume *f*.
frown [fraun] *n* froncement *m* de sourcils ♦ *vi* froncer les sourcils.
▶**frown on** *vt* (*fig*) désapprouver.
froze [frəuz] *pt of* **freeze**.
frozen ['frəuzn] *pp of* **freeze** ♦ *adj* (*food*) congelé(e); (*COMM: assets*) gelé(e).
FRS *n abbr* (*BRIT*: = *Fellow of the Royal Society*) membre de l'Académie des sciences; (*US*: = *Federal Reserve System*) banque centrale américaine.
frugal ['fruːgl] *adj* frugal(e).
fruit [fruːt] *n* (*pl inv*) fruit *m*.
fruiterer ['fruːtərə*] *n* fruitier *m*, marchand/e de fruits; **~'s (shop)** fruiterie *f*.
fruit fly *n* mouche *f* du vinaigre, drosophile *f*.
fruitful ['fruːtful] *adj* fructueux(euse); (*plant, soil*) fécond(e).
fruition [fruː'ɪʃən] *n*: **to come to ~** se réaliser.

fruit juice *n* jus *m* de fruit.
fruitless ['fru:tlɪs] *adj* (*fig*) vain(e), infructueux(euse).
fruit machine *n* (*BRIT*) machine *f* à sous.
fruit salad *n* salade *f* de fruits.
frump [frʌmp] *n* mocheté *f*.
frustrate [frʌs'treɪt] *vt* frustrer; (*plot, plans*) faire échouer.
frustrated [frʌs'treɪtɪd] *adj* frustré(e).
frustrating [frʌs'treɪtɪŋ] *adj* (*job*) frustrant(e); (*day*) démoralisant(e).
frustration [frʌs'treɪʃən] *n* frustration *f*.
fry, *pt, pp* **fried** [fraɪ, -d] *vt* (faire) frire; **the small ~** le menu fretin.
frying pan ['fraɪɪŋ-] *n* poêle *f* (à frire).
FT *n abbr* (*BRIT*: = *Financial Times*) *journal financier.*
ft. *abbr* = **foot, feet.**
FTC *n abbr* (*US*) = **Federal Trade Commission.**
FTSE 100 (Share) Index *n abbr* (= *Financial Times Stock Exchange 100 (Share) Index*) indice *m* Footsie *m* des cent grandes valeurs.
fuchsia ['fju:ʃə] *n* fuchsia *m*.
fuck [fʌk] *vt, vi* (*col!*) baiser (*!*); ~ **off!** fous le camp! (*!*).
fuddled ['fʌdld] *adj* (*muddled*) embrouillé(e), confus(e).
fuddy-duddy ['fʌdɪdʌdɪ] *adj* (*pej*) vieux jeu *inv*, ringard(e).
fudge [fʌdʒ] *n* (*CULIN*) sorte de confiserie à base de sucre, de beurre et de lait ♦ *vt* (*issue, problem*) esquiver.
fuel [fjuəl] *n* (*for heating*) combustible *m*; (*for propelling*) carburant *m*.
fuel oil *n* mazout *m*.
fuel pump *n* (*AUT*) pompe *f* d'alimentation.
fuel tank *n* cuve *f* à mazout, citerne *f*; (*in vehicle*) réservoir *m* de *or* à carburant.
fug [fʌg] *n* (*BRIT*) puanteur *f*, odeur *f* de renfermé.
fugitive ['fju:dʒɪtɪv] *n* fugitif/ive.
fulfil, (*US*) **fulfill** [ful'fɪl] *vt* (*function*) remplir; (*order*) exécuter; (*wish, desire*) satisfaire, réaliser.
fulfilled [ful'fɪld] *adj* (*person*) comblé(e), épanoui(e).
fulfil(l)ment [ful'fɪlmənt] *n* (*of wishes*) réalisation *f*.
full [ful] *adj* plein(e); (*details, information*) complet(ète); (*price*) fort(e), normal(e); (*skirt*) ample, large ♦ *adv*: **to know ~ well that** savoir fort bien que; ~ (**up**) (*hotel etc*) complet(ète); **I'm ~ (up)** j'ai bien mangé; ~ **employment/fare** plein emploi/tarif; **a ~ two hours** deux bonnes heures; **at ~ speed** à toute vitesse; **in ~** (*reproduce, quote, pay*) intégralement; (*write name etc*) en toutes lettres.
fullback ['fulbæk] *n* (*RUGBY, FOOTBALL*) arrière *m*.
full-blooded ['ful'blʌdɪd] *adj* (*vigorous*) vigoureux(euse).

full-cream ['ful'kri:m] *adj*: ~ **milk** (*BRIT*) lait entier.
full-grown ['ful'grəun] *adj* arrivé(e) à maturité, adulte.
full-length ['ful'leŋθ] *adj* (*portrait*) en pied; ~ **film** long métrage.
full moon *n* pleine lune.
full-scale ['fulskeɪl] *adj* (*model*) grandeur nature *inv*; (*search, retreat*) complet(ète), total(e).
full-sized ['ful'saɪzd] *adj* (*portrait etc*) grandeur nature *inv*.
full stop *n* point *m*.
full-time ['ful'taɪm] *adj* (*work*) à plein temps ♦ *n* (*SPORT*) fin *f* du match.
fully ['fulɪ] *adv* entièrement, complètement; (*at least*): ~ **as big** au moins aussi grand.
fully-fledged ['fulɪ'fledʒd] *adj* (*teacher, barrister*) diplômé(e); (*citizen, member*) à part entière.
fulsome ['fulsəm] *adj* (*pej*: *praise*) excessif(ive); (: *manner*) exagéré(e).
fumble ['fʌmbl] *vi* fouiller, tâtonner ♦ *vt* (*ball*) mal réceptionner, cafouiller.
▶**fumble with** *vt fus* tripoter.
fume [fju:m] *vi* rager; ~**s** *npl* vapeurs *fpl*, émanations *fpl*, gaz *mpl*.
fumigate ['fju:mɪgeɪt] *vt* désinfecter (par fumigation).
fun [fʌn] *n* amusement *m*, divertissement *m*; **to have ~** s'amuser; **for ~** pour rire; **it's not much ~** ce n'est pas très drôle *or* amusant; **to make ~ of** se moquer de.
function ['fʌŋkʃən] *n* fonction *f*; (*reception, dinner*) cérémonie *f*, soirée officielle ♦ *vi* fonctionner; **to ~ as** faire office de.
functional ['fʌŋkʃənl] *adj* fonctionnel(le).
function key *n* (*COMPUT*) touche *f* de fonction.
fund [fʌnd] *n* caisse *f*, fonds *m*; (*source, store*) source *f*, mine *f*; ~**s** *npl* fonds *mpl*.
fundamental [fʌndə'mentl] *adj* fondamental(e); ~**s** *npl* principes *mpl* de base.
fundamentalism [fʌndə'mentəlizəm] *n* intégrisme *m*.
fundamentalist [fʌndə'mentəlist] *n* intégriste *m/f*.
fundamentally [fʌndə'mentəlɪ] *adv* fondamentalement.
funding ['fʌndɪŋ] *n* financement *m*.
fund-raising ['fʌndreɪzɪŋ] *n* collecte *f* de fonds.
funeral ['fju:nərəl] *n* enterrement *m*, obsèques *fpl* (*more formal occasion*).
funeral director *n* entrepreneur *m* des pompes funèbres.
funeral parlour *n* dépôt *m* mortuaire.
funeral service *n* service *m* funèbre.
funereal [fju:'nɪərɪəl] *adj* lugubre, funèbre.
fun fair *n* (*BRIT*) fête (foraine).
fungus, *pl* **fungi** ['fʌŋgəs, -gaɪ] *n* champignon *m*; (*mould*) moisissure *f*.

funicular [fju:'nɪkjʊlə*] n (also: ~ **railway**) funiculaire m.

funky ['fʌŋkɪ] adj (music) funky inv; (col: excellent) super inv.

funnel ['fʌnl] n entonnoir m; (of ship) cheminée f.

funnily ['fʌnɪlɪ] adv (see funny) drôlement; curieusement.

funny ['fʌnɪ] adj amusant(e), drôle; (strange) curieux(euse), bizarre.

funny bone n endroit sensible du coude.

fun run n course f de fond (pour amateurs).

fur [fə:*] n fourrure f; (BRIT: in kettle etc) (dépôt m de) tartre m.

fur coat n manteau m de fourrure.

furious ['fjʊərɪəs] adj furieux(euse); (effort) acharné(e); **to be ~ with sb** être dans une fureur noire contre qn.

furiously ['fjʊərɪəslɪ] adv furieusement; avec acharnement.

furl [fə:l] vt rouler; (NAUT) ferler.

furlong ['fə:lɔŋ] n = 201.17 m (terme d'hippisme).

furlough ['fə:ləʊ] n permission f, congé m.

furnace ['fə:nɪs] n fourneau m.

furnish ['fə:nɪʃ] vt meubler; (supply) fournir; **~ed flat** or (US) **apartment** meublé m.

furnishings ['fə:nɪʃɪŋz] npl mobilier m, articles mpl d'ameublement.

furniture ['fə:nɪtʃə*] n meubles mpl, mobilier m; **piece of ~** meuble m.

furniture polish n encaustique f.

furore [fjʊə'rɔ:rɪ] n (protests) protestations fpl.

furrier ['fʌrɪə*] n fourreur m.

furrow ['fʌrəʊ] n sillon m.

furry ['fə:rɪ] adj (animal) à fourrure; (toy) en peluche.

further ['fə:ðə*] adj supplémentaire, autre; nouveau(nouvelle) ♦ adv plus loin; (more) davantage; (moreover) de plus ♦ vt faire avancer or progresser, promouvoir; **how much ~ is it?** quelle distance or combien reste-t-il à parcourir?; **until ~ notice** jusqu'à nouvel ordre or avis; **~ to your letter of ...** (COMM) suite à votre lettre du ...

further education n enseignement m postscolaire (recyclage, formation professionnelle).

furthermore [fə:ðə'mɔ:*] adv de plus, en outre.

furthermost ['fə:ðəməʊst] adj le(la) plus éloigné(e).

furthest ['fə:ðɪst] superlative of **far**.

furtive ['fə:tɪv] adj furtif(ive).

furtively ['fə:tɪvlɪ] adv furtivement.

fury ['fjʊərɪ] n fureur f.

fuse, (US) **fuze** [fju:z] n fusible m; (for bomb etc) amorce f, détonateur m ♦ vt, vi (metal) fondre; (fig) fusionner; (ELEC): **to ~ the lights** faire sauter les fusibles or les plombs; **a ~ has blown** un fusible a sauté.

fuse box n boîte f à fusibles.

fuselage ['fju:zəlɑ:ʒ] n fuselage m.

fuse wire n fusible m.

fusillade [fju:zɪ'leɪd] n fusillade f; (fig) feu roulant.

fusion ['fju:ʒən] n fusion f.

fuss [fʌs] n (anxiety, excitement) chichis mpl, façons fpl; (commotion) tapage m; (complaining, trouble) histoire(s) f(pl) ♦ vi faire des histoires ♦ vt (person) embêter; **to make a ~** faire des façons (or des histoires); **to make a ~ of sb** dorloter qn.

▶**fuss over** vt fus (person) dorloter.

fusspot ['fʌspɔt] n (col): **don't be such a ~!** ne fais pas tant d'histoires!

fussy ['fʌsɪ] adj (person) tatillon(ne), difficile; chichiteux(euse); (dress, style) tarabis coté(e); **I'm not ~** (col) ça m'est égal.

fusty ['fʌstɪ] adj (old-fashioned) vieillot(te); (smell) de renfermé or moisi.

futile ['fju:taɪl] adj futile.

futility [fju:'tɪlɪtɪ] n futilité f.

futon ['fu:tɒn] n futon m.

future ['fju:tʃə*] adj futur(e) ♦ n avenir m; (LING) futur m; **in (the) ~** à l'avenir; **in the near/immediate ~** dans un avenir proche/immédiat.

futures ['fju:tʃəz] npl (COMM) opérations fpl à terme.

futuristic [fju:tʃə'rɪstɪk] adj futuriste.

fuze [fju:z] n, vt, vi (US) = **fuse**.

fuzzy ['fʌzɪ] adj (PHOT) flou(e); (hair) crépu(e).

fwd. abbr = forward.

fwy abbr (US) = freeway.

FY abbr = fiscal year.

FYI abbr = for your information.

G g

G, g [dʒi:] n (letter) G, g m; (MUS): **G** sol m; **G for George** G comme Gaston.

G n abbr (BRIT SCOL: = good) b (= bien); (US CINE: = general (audience)) ≈ tous publics; **G7** (POL) G7 m.

g abbr (= gram, gravity) g.

GA abbr (US) = Georgia.

gab [gæb] n (col): **to have the gift of the ~** avoir la langue bien pendue.

gabble ['gæbl] vi bredouiller; jacasser.

gaberdine [gæbə'di:n] n gabardine f.

gable ['geɪbl] n pignon m.

Gabon [gə'bɒn] n Gabon m.

gad about ['gædə'baʊt] vi (col) se balader.

gadget ['gædʒɪt] n gadget m.

Gaelic ['geɪlɪk] adj, n gaélique (m).

gaffe [gæf] n gaffe f.

gaffer ['gæfə*] n (BRIT: foreman) contremaître m; (BRIT col: boss) patron m.

gag [gæg] *n* bâillon *m*; (*joke*) gag *m* ♦ *vt* (*prisoner etc*) bâillonner ♦ *vi* (*choke*) étouffer.

gaga ['gɑːgɑː] *adj*: **to go** ~ devenir gaga *or* gâteux(euse).

gaiety ['geɪtɪ] *n* gaieté *f*.

gaily ['geɪlɪ] *adv* gaiement.

gain [geɪn] *n* gain *m*, profit *m* ♦ *vt* gagner ♦ *vi* (*watch*) avancer; **to** ~ **in/by** gagner en/à; **to** ~ **3lbs (in weight)** prendre 3 livres; **to** ~ **ground** gagner du terrain.
▶**gain (up)on** *vt fus* rattraper.

gainful ['geɪnful] *adj* profitable, lucratif(ive).

gainfully ['geɪnfəlɪ] *adv*: **to be** ~ **employed** avoir un emploi rémunéré.

gainsay [geɪn'seɪ] *vt* (*irreg*: *like* **say**) contredire; nier.

gait [geɪt] *n* démarche *f*.

gal. *abbr* = **gallon**.

gala ['gɑːlə] *n* gala *m*; **swimming** ~ grand concours de natation.

Galápagos (Islands) [gə'læpəgəs-] *npl*: **the** ~ les (îles *fpl*) Galapagos *fpl*.

galaxy ['gæləksɪ] *n* galaxie *f*.

gale [geɪl] *n* coup *m* de vent; ~ **force 10** vent *m* de force 10.

gall [gɔːl] *n* (*ANAT*) bile *f*; (*fig*) effronterie *f* ♦ *vt* ulcérer, irriter.

gall. *abbr* = **gallon**.

gallant ['gælənt] *adj* vaillant(e), brave; (*towards ladies*) empressé(e), galant(e).

gallantry ['gæləntrɪ] *n* bravoure *f*, vaillance *f*; empressement *m*, galanterie *f*.

gall-bladder ['gɔːlblædə*] *n* vésicule *f* biliaire.

galleon ['gælɪən] *n* galion *m*.

gallery ['gælərɪ] *n* galerie *f*; (*for spectators*) tribune *f*; (: *in theatre*) dernier balcon; (*also*: **art** ~) musée *m*; (: *private*) galerie.

galley ['gælɪ] *n* (*ship's kitchen*) cambuse *f*; (*ship*) galère *f*; (*also*: ~ **proof**) placard *m*, galée *f*.

Gallic ['gælɪk] *adj* (*of Gaul*) gaulois(e); (*French*) français(e).

galling ['gɔːlɪŋ] *adj* irritant(e).

gallon ['gælən] *n* gallon *m* (= *8 pints; BRIT* = 4.543 l; *US* = 3.785 l).

gallop ['gæləp] *n* galop *m* ♦ *vi* galoper; ~**ing in-flation** inflation galopante.

gallows ['gæləuz] *n* potence *f*.

gallstone ['gɔːlstəun] *n* calcul *m* (biliaire).

Gallup Poll ['gæləp-] *n* sondage *m* Gallup.

galore [gə'lɔː*] *adv* en abondance, à gogo.

galvanize ['gælvənaɪz] *vt* galvaniser; (*fig*): **to** ~ **sb into action** galvaniser qn.

Gambia ['gæmbɪə] *n* Gambie *f*.

gambit ['gæmbɪt] *n* (*fig*): **(opening)** ~ manœuvre *f* stratégique.

gamble ['gæmbl] *n* pari *m*, risque calculé ♦ *vt*, *vi* jouer; **to** ~ **on the Stock Exchange** jouer en *or* à la Bourse; **to** ~ **on** (*fig*) miser sur.

gambler ['gæmblə*] *n* joueur *m*.

gambling ['gæmblɪŋ] *n* jeu *m*.

gambol ['gæmbl] *vi* gambader.

game [geɪm] *n* jeu *m*; (*event*) match *m*; (*HUNTING*) gibier *m* ♦ *adj* brave; (*ready*): **to be** ~ **(for sth/to do)** être prêt(e) (à qch/à faire), se sentir de taille (à faire); **a** ~ **of football/tennis** une partie de football/tennis; ~**s** (*SCOL*) sport *m*; **big** ~ gros gibier.

game bird *n* gibier *m* à plume.

gamekeeper ['geɪmkiːpə*] *n* garde-chasse *m*.

gamely ['geɪmlɪ] *adv* vaillamment.

game reserve *n* réserve animalière.

games console ['geɪmz-] *n* console *f* de jeux vidéo.

gameshow ['geɪmʃəu] *n* jeu télévisé.

gamesmanship ['geɪmzmənʃɪp] *n* roublardise *f*.

gaming ['geɪmɪŋ] *n* jeu *m*, jeux *mpl* d'argent.

gammon ['gæmən] *n* (*bacon*) quartier *m* de lard fumé; (*ham*) jambon fumé.

gamut ['gæmət] *n* gamme *f*.

gang [gæŋ] *n* bande *f*, groupe *m*.
▶**gang up** *vi*: **to** ~ **up on sb** se liguer contre qn.

Ganges ['gændʒiːz] *n*: **the** ~ le Gange.

gangland ['gæŋlænd] *adj*: ~ **killer** tueur professionnel du milieu; ~ **boss** chef *m* de gang.

gangling ['gæŋglɪŋ], **gangly** ['gæŋglɪ] *adj* dégingandé(e).

gangplank ['gæŋplæŋk] *n* passerelle *f*.

gangrene ['gæŋgriːn] *n* gangrène *f*.

gangster ['gæŋstə*] *n* gangster *m*, bandit *m*.

gangway ['gæŋweɪ] *n* passerelle *f*; (*BRIT*: *of bus*) couloir central.

gantry ['gæntrɪ] *n* portique *m*; (*for rocket*) tour *f* de lancement.

GAO *n abbr* (*US*: = *General Accounting Office*) ≈ Cour *f* des comptes.

gaol [dʒeɪl] *n*, *vt* (*BRIT*) = **jail**.

gap [gæp] *n* trou *m*; (*in time*) intervalle *m*; (*fig*) lacune *f*, vide *m*.

gape [geɪp] *vi* être *or* rester bouche bée.

gaping ['geɪpɪŋ] *adj* (*hole*) béant(e).

garage ['gærɑːʒ] *n* garage *m*.

garb [gɑːb] *n* tenue *f*, costume *m*.

garbage ['gɑːbɪdʒ] *n* ordures *fpl*, détritus *mpl*; (*fig*: *col*) conneries *fpl*.

garbage can *n* (*US*) poubelle *f*, boîte *f* à ordures.

garbage collector *n* (*US*) éboueur *m*.

garbage disposal (unit) *n* (*US*) broyeur *m* d'ordures.

garbage truck *n* (*US*) camion *m* (du ramassage) des ordures, benne *f* à ordures.

garbled ['gɑːbld] *adj* déformé(e); faussé(e).

garden ['gɑːdn] *n* jardin *m* ♦ *vi* jardiner; ~**s** *npl* (*public*) jardin public; (*private*) parc *m*.

garden centre *n* garden-centre *m*, pépinière *f*.

garden city *n* (*BRIT*) cité-jardin *f*.

gardener ['gɑːdnə*] *n* jardinier *m*.

gardening ['gɑːdnɪŋ] *n* jardinage *m*.

gargle ['gɑːgl] *vi* se gargariser ♦ *n* gargarisme

m.

gargoyle ['gɑːgɔɪl] *n* gargouille *f.*

garish ['gɛərɪʃ] *adj* criard(e), voyant(e).

garland ['gɑːlənd] *n* guirlande *f*; couronne *f.*

garlic ['gɑːlɪk] *n* ail *m.*

garment ['gɑːmənt] *n* vêtement *m.*

garner ['gɑːnə*] *vt* engranger, amasser.

garnish ['gɑːnɪʃ] *vt* garnir.

garret ['gærɪt] *n* mansarde *f.*

garrison ['gærɪsn] *n* garnison *f* ♦ *vt* mettre en garnison, stationner.

garrulous ['gærjuləs] *adj* volubile, loquace.

garter ['gɑːtə*] *n* jarretière *f*, (*US: suspender*) jarretelle *f.*

garter belt *n* (*US*) porte-jarretelles *m inv.*

gas [gæs] *n* gaz *m*; (*used as anaesthetic*): **to be given** ~ se faire endormir; (*US: gasoline*) essence *f* ♦ *vt* asphyxier; (*MIL*) gazer.

Gascony ['gæskənɪ] *n* Gascogne *f.*

gas cooker *n* (*BRIT*) cuisinière *f* à gaz.

gas cylinder *n* bouteille *f* de gaz.

gaseous ['gæsɪəs] *adj* gazeux(euse).

gas fire *n* (*BRIT*) radiateur *m* à gaz.

gas-fired ['gæsfaɪəd] *adj* au gaz.

gash [gæʃ] *n* entaille *f*; (*on face*) balafre *f* ♦ *vt* tailler; balafrer.

gasket ['gæskɪt] *n* (*AUT*) joint *m* de culasse.

gas mask *n* masque *m* à gaz.

gas meter *n* compteur *m* à gaz.

gasoline ['gæsəliːn] *n* (*US*) essence *f.*

gasp [gɑːsp] *vi* haleter; (*fig*) avoir le souffle coupé.

▶**gasp out** *vt* (*say*) dire dans un souffle *or* d'une voix entrecoupée.

gas ring *n* brûleur *m.*

gas station *n* (*US*) station-service *f.*

gas stove *n* réchaud *m* à gaz; (*cooker*) cuisinière *f* à gaz.

gassy ['gæsɪ] *adj* gazeux(euse).

gas tank *n* (*US AUT*) réservoir *m* d'essence.

gas tap *n* bouton *m* (de cuisinière à gaz); (*on pipe*) robinet *m* à gaz.

gastric ['gæstrɪk] *adj* gastrique.

gastric ulcer *n* ulcère *m* de l'estomac.

gastroenteritis ['gæstrəuɛntə'raɪtɪs] *n* gastroentérite *f.*

gastronomy [gæs'trɔnəmɪ] *n* gastronomie *f.*

gasworks ['gæswəːks] *n, npl* usine *f* à gaz.

gate [geɪt] *n* (*of garden*) portail *m*; (*of farm, at level crossing*) barrière *f*; (*of building, town, at airport*) porte *f*; (*of lock*) vanne *f.*

gâteau, *pl* ~**x** ['gætəu, -z] *n* gros gâteau à la crème.

gatecrash ['geɪtkræʃ] *vt* s'introduire sans invitation dans.

gatecrasher ['geɪtkræʃə*] *n* intrus/e.

gatehouse ['geɪthaus] *n* loge *f.*

gateway ['geɪtweɪ] *n* porte *f.*

gather ['gæðə*] *vt* (*flowers, fruit*) cueillir; (*pick up*) ramasser; (*assemble*) rassembler, réunir; (*understand*) comprendre ♦ *vi* (*assemble*) se rassembler; (*dust*) s'amasser; (*clouds*) s'amonceler; **to** ~ **(from/that)** conclure *or* déduire (de/que); **as far as I can** ~ d'après ce que je comprends; **to** ~ **speed** prendre de la vitesse.

gathering ['gæðərɪŋ] *n* rassemblement *m.*

GATT [gæt] *n abbr* (= *General Agreement on Tariffs and Trade*) GATT *m.*

gauche [gəuʃ] *adj* gauche, maladroit(e).

gaudy ['gɔːdɪ] *adj* voyant(e).

gauge [geɪdʒ] *n* (*standard measure*) calibre *m*; (*RAIL*) écartement *m*; (*instrument*) jauge *f* ♦ *vt* jauger; (*fig: sb's capabilities, character*) juger de; **to** ~ **the right moment** calculer le moment propice; **petrol** ~, (*US*) **gas** ~ jauge d'essence.

Gaul [gɔːl] *n* (*country*) Gaule *f*; (*person*) Gaulois/e.

gaunt [gɔːnt] *adj* décharné(e); (*grim, desolate*) désolé(e).

gauntlet ['gɔːntlɪt] *n* (*fig*): **to throw down the** ~ jeter le gant; **to run the** ~ **through an angry crowd** se frayer un passage à travers une foule hostile *or* entre deux haies de manifestants *etc* hostiles.

gauze [gɔːz] *n* gaze *f.*

gave [geɪv] *pt of* **give.**

gavel ['gævl] *n* marteau *m.*

gawky ['gɔːkɪ] *adj* dégingandé(e), godiche.

gawp [gɔːp] *vi*: **to** ~ **at** regarder bouche bée.

gay [geɪ] *adj* (*homosexual*) homosexuel(le); (*slightly old-fashioned: cheerful*) gai(e), réjoui(e); (*colour*) gai, vif(vive).

gaze [geɪz] *n* regard *m* fixe ♦ *vi*: **to** ~ **at** *vt* fixer du regard.

gazelle [gə'zɛl] *n* gazelle *f.*

gazette [gə'zɛt] *n* (*newspaper*) gazette *f*; (*official publication*) journal officiel.

gazetteer [gæzə'tɪə*] *n* dictionnaire *m* géographique.

gazump [gə'zʌmp] *vi* (*BRIT*) revenir sur une promesse de vente pour accepter un prix plus élevé.

gazumping [gə'zʌmpɪŋ] *n* le fait de revenir sur une promesse de vente pour accepter un prix plus élevé.

GB *abbr* = **Great Britain.**

GBH *n abbr* (*BRIT LAW: col*) = **grievous bodily harm.**

GC *n abbr* (*BRIT*: = *George Cross*) distinction honorifique.

GCE *n abbr* (*BRIT*) = *General Certificate of Education.*

GCHQ *n abbr* (*BRIT*: = *Government Communications Headquarters*) centre d'interception des télécommunications étrangères.

GCSE *n abbr* (*BRIT*: = *General Certificate of Secondary Education*) examen passé à l'âge de 16 ans sanctionnant les connaissances de l'élève; **she's got eight** ~**s** elle a réussi dans huit matières aux épreuves du GCSE.

Gdns. *abbr* = *gardens.*

GDP *n abbr* = **gross domestic product.**

GDR n abbr (old: = German Democratic Republic) RDA f.

gear [gɪə*] n matériel m, équipement m; (TECH) engrenage m; (AUT) vitesse f ♦ vt (fig: adapt) adapter; **top** or (US) **high/low/bottom** ~ quatrième (or cinquième)/deuxième/première vitesse; **in** ~ en prise; **out of** ~ au point mort; **our service is** ~**ed to meet the needs of the disabled** notre service répond de façon spécifique aux besoins des handicapés.

▶**gear up** vi: **to** ~ **up (to do)** se préparer (à faire).

gear box n boîte f de vitesse.

gear lever, (US) **gear shift** n levier m de vitesse.

GED n abbr (US SCOL) = general educational development.

geese [giːs] npl of **goose.**

geezer ['giːzə*] n (BRIT col) mec m.

Geiger counter ['gaɪgə-] n compteur m Geiger.

gel [dʒɛl] n gelée f; (CHEMISTRY) colloïde m.

gelatin(e) ['dʒɛlətiːn] n gélatine f.

gelignite ['dʒɛlɪgnaɪt] n plastic m.

gem [dʒɛm] n pierre précieuse.

Gemini ['dʒɛmɪnaɪ] n les Gémeaux mpl; **to be** ~ être des Gémeaux.

gen [dʒɛn] n (BRIT col): **to give sb the** ~ **on sth** mettre qn au courant de qch.

Gen. abbr (MIL: = general) Gal.

gen. abbr (= general, generally) gén.

gender ['dʒɛndə*] n genre m.

gene [dʒiːn] n (BIOL) gène m.

genealogy [dʒiːnɪ'ælədʒɪ] n généalogie f.

general ['dʒɛnərl] n général m ♦ adj général(e); **in** ~ en général; **the** ~ **public** le grand public; ~ **audit** (COMM) vérification annuelle.

general anaesthetic n anesthésie générale.

general election n élection(s) législative(s).

generalization ['dʒɛnrəlaɪ'zeɪʃən] n généralisation f.

generalize ['dʒɛnrəlaɪz] vi généraliser.

generally ['dʒɛnrəlɪ] adv généralement.

general manager n directeur général.

general practitioner (GP) n généraliste m/f; **who's your GP?** qui est votre médecin traitant?

general strike n grève générale.

generate ['dʒɛnəreɪt] vt engendrer; (electricity) produire.

generation [dʒɛnə'reɪʃən] n génération f; (of electricity etc) production f.

generator ['dʒɛnəreɪtə*] n générateur m.

generic [dʒɪ'nɛrɪk] adj générique.

generosity [dʒɛnə'rɔsɪtɪ] n générosité f.

generous ['dʒɛnərəs] adj généreux(euse); (copious) copieux(euse).

genesis ['dʒɛnɪsɪs] n genèse f.

genetic [dʒɪ'nɛtɪk] adj génétique.

genetic engineering n génie m génétique.

genetic fingerprinting [-'fɪŋgəprɪntɪŋ] n système m d'empreinte génétique.

genetics [dʒɪ'nɛtɪks] n génétique f.

Geneva [dʒɪ'niːvə] n Genève; **Lake** ~ le lac Léman.

genial ['dʒiːnɪəl] adj cordial(e), chaleureux(euse); (climate) clément(e).

genitals ['dʒɛnɪtlz] npl organes génitaux.

genitive ['dʒɛnɪtɪv] n génitif m.

genius ['dʒiːnɪəs] n génie m.

Genoa ['dʒɛnəuə] n Gênes.

genocide ['dʒɛnəusaɪd] n génocide m.

gent [dʒɛnt] n abbr (BRIT col) = gentleman.

genteel [dʒɛn'tiːl] adj de bon ton, distingué(e).

gentle ['dʒɛntl] adj doux(douce).

gentleman ['dʒɛntlmən] n monsieur m; (wellbred man) gentleman m; ~'**s agreement** gentleman's agreement m.

gentlemanly ['dʒɛntlmənlɪ] adj bien élevé(e).

gentleness ['dʒɛntlnɪs] n douceur f.

gently ['dʒɛntlɪ] adv doucement.

gentry ['dʒɛntrɪ] n petite noblesse.

gents [dʒɛnts] n W.-C. mpl (pour hommes).

genuine ['dʒɛnjuɪn] adj véritable, authentique; (person, emotion) sincère.

genuinely ['dʒɛnjuɪnlɪ] adv sincèrement, vraiment.

geographer [dʒɪ'ɔgrəfə*] n géographe m/f.

geographic(al) [dʒɪə'græfɪk(l)] adj géographique.

geography [dʒɪ'ɔgrəfɪ] n géographie f.

geological [dʒɪə'lɔdʒɪkl] adj géologique.

geologist [dʒɪ'ɔlədʒɪst] n géologue m/f.

geology [dʒɪ'ɔlədʒɪ] n géologie f.

geometric(al) [dʒɪə'mɛtrɪk(l)] adj géométrique.

geometry [dʒɪ'ɔmətrɪ] n géométrie f.

Geordie ['dʒɔːdɪ] n (col) habitant/e de Tyneside; originaire m/f de Tyneside.

Georgia ['dʒɔːdʒə] n Géorgie f.

Georgian ['dʒɔːdʒən] adj (GEO) géorgien(ne) ♦ n Géorgien/ne; (LING) géorgien m.

geranium [dʒɪ'reɪnɪəm] n géranium m.

geriatric [dʒɛrɪ'ætrɪk] adj gériatrique.

germ [dʒəːm] n (MED) microbe m; (BIO, fig) germe m.

German ['dʒəːmən] adj allemand(e) ♦ n Allemand/e; (LING) allemand m.

germane [dʒəː'meɪn] adj (formal): ~ **(to)** se rapportant (à).

German measles n rubéole f.

Germany ['dʒəːmənɪ] n Allemagne f.

germination [dʒəːmɪ'neɪʃən] n germination f.

germ warfare n guerre f bactériologique.

gerrymandering ['dʒɛrɪmændərɪŋ] n tripotage m du découpage électoral.

gestation [dʒɛs'teɪʃən] n gestation f.

gesticulate [dʒɛs'tɪkjuleɪt] vi gesticuler.

gesture ['dʒɛstjə*] n geste m; **as a** ~ **of friendship** en témoignage d'amitié.

=========================== *KEYWORD*

get [gɛt] (*pt, pp* **got**, *pp* **gotten** (*US*)) *vi* **1** (*become, be*) devenir; **to ~ old/tired** devenir vieux/fatigué, vieillir/se fatiguer; **to ~ drunk** s'enivrer; **to ~ ready/washed/shaved** *etc* se préparer/laver/raser *etc*; **to ~ killed** se faire tuer; **when do I ~ paid?** quand est-ce que je serai payé?; **it's ~ting late** il se fait tard

2 (*go*): **to ~ to/from** aller à/de; **to ~ home** rentrer chez soi; **how did you ~ here?** comment es-tu arrivé ici?; **he got across the bridge/under the fence** il a traversé le pont/est passé au-dessous de la barrière

3 (*begin*) commencer *or* se mettre à; **I'm ~ting to like him** je commence à l'apprécier; **let's ~ going** *or* **started** allons-y

4 (*modal aux vb*): **you've got to do it** il faut que vous le fassiez; **I've got to tell the police** je dois le dire à la police

♦ *vt* **1**: **to ~ sth done** (*do*) faire qch; (*have done*) faire faire qch; **to ~ sth/sb ready** préparer qch/qn; **to ~ one's hair cut** se faire couper les cheveux; **to ~ sb to do sth** faire faire qch à qn; **to ~ sb drunk** enivrer qn

2 (*obtain: money, permission, results*) obtenir, avoir; (*find: job, flat*) trouver; (*fetch: person, doctor, object*) aller chercher; **to ~ sth for sb** procurer qch à qn; **~ me Mr Jones, please** (*on phone*) passez-moi Mr Jones, s'il vous plaît; **can I ~ you a drink?** est-ce que je peux vous servir à boire?

3 (*receive: present, letter*) recevoir, avoir; (*acquire: reputation*) avoir; (*: prize*) obtenir; **what did you ~ for your birthday?** qu'est-ce que tu as eu pour ton anniversaire?

4 (*catch*) prendre, saisir, attraper; (*hit: target etc*) atteindre; **to ~ sb by the arm/throat** prendre *or* saisir *or* attraper qn par le bras/à la gorge; **~ him!** arrête-le!; **he really ~s me!** il me porte sur les nerfs!

5 (*take, move*) faire parvenir; **do you think we'll ~ it through the door?** on arrivera à le faire passer par la porte?; **I'll ~ you there somehow** je me débrouillerai pour t'y emmener

6 (*catch, take: plane, bus etc*) prendre

7 (*understand*) comprendre, saisir; (*hear*) entendre; **I've got it!** j'ai compris!; **I didn't ~ your name** je n'ai pas entendu votre nom

8 (*have, possess*): **to have got** avoir; **how many have you got?** vous en avez combien?

▶**get about** *vi* se déplacer; (*news*) se répandre

▶**get across** *vt*: **to ~ across (to)** (*message, meaning*) faire passer à ♦ *vi*: **to ~ across to** (*subj: speaker*) se faire comprendre (par)

▶**get along** *vi* (*agree*) s'entendre; (*depart*) s'en aller; (*manage*) = **get by**

▶**get at** *vt fus* (*attack*) s'en prendre à; (*reach*) attraper, atteindre; **what are you ~ting at?** à quoi voulez-vous en venir?

▶**get away** *vi* partir, s'en aller; (*escape*) s'échapper

▶**get away with** *vt fus* en être quitte pour; se faire passer *or* pardonner

▶**get back** *vi* (*return*) rentrer ♦ *vt* récupérer, recouvrer; **to ~ back to** (*start again*) retourner *or* revenir à; (*contact again*) recontacter

▶**get back at** *vt fus* (*col*): **to ~ back at sb** rendre la monnaie de sa pièce à qn

▶**get by** *vi* (*pass*) passer; (*manage*) se débrouiller; **I can ~ by in Dutch** je me débrouille en hollandais

▶**get down** *vi, vt fus* descendre ♦ *vt* descendre; (*depress*) déprimer

▶**get down to** *vt fus* (*work*) se mettre à (faire); **to ~ down to business** passer aux choses sérieuses

▶**get in** *vi* entrer; (*arrive home*) rentrer; (*train*) arriver ♦ *vt* (*bring in: harvest*) rentrer; (*: coal*) faire rentrer; (*: supplies*) faire des provisions de

▶**get into** *vt fus* entrer dans; (*car, train etc*) monter dans; (*clothes*) mettre, enfiler, endosser; **to ~ into bed/a rage** se mettre au lit/en colère

▶**get off** *vi* (*from train etc*) descendre; (*depart: person, car*) s'en aller; (*escape*) s'en tirer ♦ *vt* (*remove: clothes, stain*) enlever; (*send off*) expédier; (*have as leave: day, time*) **we got 2 days off** nous avons eu 2 jours de congé ♦ *vt fus* (*train, bus*) descendre de; **to ~ off to a good start** (*fig*) prendre un bon départ

▶**get on** *vi* (*at exam etc*) se débrouiller; (*agree*): **to ~ on (with)** s'entendre (avec); **how are you ~ting on?** comment ça va? ♦ *vt fus* monter dans; (*horse*) monter sur

▶**get on to** *vt fus* (*BRIT: deal with: problem*) s'occuper de; (*contact: person*) contacter

▶**get out** *vi* sortir; (*of vehicle*) descendre; (*news etc*) s'ébruiter ♦ *vt* sortir

▶**get out of** *vt fus* sortir de; (*duty etc*) échapper à, se soustraire à

▶**get over** *vt fus* (*illness*) se remettre de ♦ *vt* (*communicate: idea etc*) communiquer; (*finish*): **let's ~ it over (with)** finissons-en

▶**get round** *vi*: **to ~ round to doing sth** se mettre (finalement) à faire qch ♦ *vt fus* contourner; (*fig: person*) entortiller

▶**get through** *vi* (*TEL*) avoir la communication; **to ~ through to sb** atteindre qn ♦ *vt fus* (*finish: work, book*) finir, terminer

▶**get together** *vi* se réunir ♦ *vt* rassembler

▶**get up** *vi* (*rise*) se lever ♦ *vt fus* monter

▶**get up to** *vt fus* (*reach*) arriver à; (*prank etc*) faire.

getaway ['gɛtəweɪ] *n* fuite *f*.

getaway car *n* voiture prévue pour prendre la fuite.

get-together ['gɛttəgɛðə*] *n* petite réunion, petite fête.

get-up ['gɛtʌp] n (col: outfit) accoutrement m.
get-well card [gɛt'wɛl-] n carte f de vœux de bon rétablissement.
geyser ['giːzə*] n chauffe-eau m inv; (GEO) geyser m.
Ghana ['gɑːnə] n Ghana m.
Ghanaian [gɑːˈneɪən] adj ghanéen(ne) ♦ n Ghanéen/ne.
ghastly ['gɑːstlɪ] adj atroce, horrible; (pale) livide, blême.
gherkin ['gəːkɪn] n cornichon m.
ghetto ['gɛtəu] n ghetto m.
ghetto blaster [-blɑːstə*] n (col) gros radio-cassette.
ghost [gəust] n fantôme m, revenant m ♦ vt (sb else's book) écrire.
ghostly ['gəustlɪ] adj fantomatique.
ghostwriter ['gəustraɪtə*] n nègre m (fig).
ghoul [guːl] n (ghost) vampire m.
ghoulish ['guːlɪʃ] adj (tastes etc) morbide.
GHQ n abbr (MIL: = general headquarters) GQG m.
GI n abbr (US col: = government issue) soldat de l'armée américaine, GI m.
giant ['dʒaɪənt] n géant/e ♦ adj géant(e), énorme; ~ **(size) packet** paquet géant.
giant killer n (SPORT) équipe inconnue qui remporte un match contre une équipe renommée.
gibber ['dʒɪbə*] vi émettre des sons inintelligibles.
gibberish ['dʒɪbərɪʃ] n charabia m.
gibe [dʒaɪb] n sarcasme m ♦ vi: **to ~ at** railler.
giblets ['dʒɪblɪts] npl abats mpl.
Gibraltar [dʒɪˈbrɔːltə*] n Gibraltar m.
giddiness ['gɪdɪnɪs] n vertige m.
giddy ['gɪdɪ] adj (dizzy): **to be** (or **feel**) ~ avoir le vertige; (height) vertigineux(euse); (thoughtless) sot(te), étourdi(e).
gift [gɪft] n cadeau m, présent m; (donation) don m; (COMM: also: **free** ~) cadeau(-réclame) m; (talent): **to have a ~ for sth** avoir des dons pour or le don de qch.
gifted ['gɪftɪd] adj doué(e).
gift token, gift voucher n bon m d'achat.
gig [gɪg] n (col: of musician) gig f.
gigabyte ['dʒɪgəbaɪt] n gigaoctet m.
gigantic [dʒaɪˈgæntɪk] adj gigantesque.
giggle ['gɪgl] vi pouffer, ricaner sottement ♦ n petit rire sot, ricanement m.
GIGO ['gaɪgəu] abbr (COMPUT: col: = garbage in, garbage out) qualité d'entrée = qualité de sortie.
gild [gɪld] vt dorer.
gill [dʒɪl] n (measure) = 0.25 pints (BRIT = 0.148 l; US = 0.118 l).
gills [gɪlz] npl (of fish) ouïes fpl, branchies fpl.
gilt [gɪlt] n dorure f ♦ adj doré(e).
gilt-edged ['gɪltɛdʒd] adj (stocks, securities) de premier ordre.
gimlet ['gɪmlɪt] n vrille f.
gimmick ['gɪmɪk] n truc m; **sales** ~ offre pro-

motionnelle.
gin [dʒɪn] n gin m.
ginger ['dʒɪndʒə*] n gingembre m.
▶**ginger up** vt secouer; animer.
ginger ale, ginger beer n boisson gazeuse au gingembre.
gingerbread ['dʒɪndʒəbrɛd] n pain m d'épices.
ginger group n (BRIT) groupe m de pression.
ginger-haired ['dʒɪndʒə'hɛəd] adj roux (rousse).
gingerly ['dʒɪndʒəlɪ] adv avec précaution.
gingham ['gɪŋəm] n vichy m.
ginseng ['dʒɪnsɛŋ] n ginseng m.
gipsy ['dʒɪpsɪ] n gitan/e, bohémien/ne ♦ cpd: ~ **caravan** n roulotte f.
giraffe [dʒɪˈrɑːf] n girafe f.
girder ['gəːdə*] n poutrelle f.
girdle ['gəːdl] n (corset) gaine f ♦ vt ceindre.
girl [gəːl] n fille f, fillette f; (young unmarried woman) jeune fille; (daughter) fille; **an English** ~ une jeune Anglaise; **a little English** ~ une petite Anglaise.
girlfriend ['gəːlfrɛnd] n (of girl) amie f; (of boy) petite amie.
girlish ['gəːlɪʃ] adj de jeune fille.
Girl Scout n (US) guide f.
Giro ['dʒaɪrəu] n: **the National** ~ (BRIT) ≈ les comptes chèques postaux.
giro ['dʒaɪrəu] n (bank ~) virement m bancaire; (post office ~) mandat m.
girth [gəːθ] n circonférence f; (of horse) sangle f.
gist [dʒɪst] n essentiel m.
give [gɪv] n (of fabric) élasticité f ♦ vb (pt **gave**, pp **given**) [geɪv, 'gɪvn]) vt donner ♦ vi (break) céder; (stretch: fabric) se prêter; **to ~ sb sth**, ~ **sth to sb** donner qch à qn; **to ~ a cry/sigh** pousser un cri/un soupir; **how much did you** ~ **for it?** combien (l')avez-vous payé?; **12 o'clock,** ~ **or take a few minutes** midi, à quelques minutes près; **to ~ way** vi céder; (BRIT AUT) donner la priorité.
▶**give away** vt donner; (give free) faire cadeau de; (betray) donner, trahir; (disclose) révéler; (bride) conduire à l'autel.
▶**give back** vt rendre.
▶**give in** vi céder ♦ vt donner.
▶**give off** vt dégager.
▶**give out** vt (food etc) distribuer; (news) annoncer ♦ vi (be exhausted: supplies) s'épuiser; (fail) lâcher.
▶**give up** vi renoncer ♦ vt renoncer à; **to ~ up smoking** arrêter de fumer; **to ~ o.s. up** se rendre.
give-and-take ['gɪvənd'teɪk] n concessions mutuelles.
giveaway ['gɪvəweɪ] n (col): **her expression was a** ~ son expression la trahissait; **the exam was a** ~! cet examen, c'était du gâteau! ♦ cpd: ~ **prices** prix sacrifiés.
given ['gɪvn] pp of **give** ♦ adj (fixed: time, amount) donné(e), déterminé(e) ♦ conj: ~ **the**

circumstances ... étant donné les circonstances ..., vu les circonstances ...; ~ **that** ... étant donné que ....

glacial ['gleɪsɪəl] *adj* (GEO) glaciaire; (*wind, weather*) glacial(e).

glacier ['glæsɪə*] *n* glacier *m*.

glad [glæd] *adj* content(e); **to be ~ about sth/ that** être heureux(euse) *or* bien content de qch/que; **I was ~ of his help** j'étais bien content de (pouvoir compter sur) son aide *or* qu'il m'aide.

gladden ['glædn] *vt* réjouir.

glade [gleɪd] *n* clairière *f*.

gladioli [glædɪ'əʊlaɪ] *npl* glaïeuls *mpl*.

gladly ['glædlɪ] *adv* volontiers.

glamorous ['glæmərəs] *adj* séduisant(e).

glamour ['glæmə*] *n* éclat *m*, prestige *m*.

glance [glɑːns] *n* coup *m* d'œil ♦ *vi*: **to ~ at** jeter un coup d'œil à.

▶**glance off** *vt fus* (*bullet*) ricocher sur.

glancing ['glɑːnsɪŋ] *adj* (*blow*) oblique.

gland [glænd] *n* glande *f*.

glandular ['glændjʊlə*] *adj*: ~ **fever** (BRIT) mononucléose infectieuse.

glare [glɛə*] *n* lumière éblouissante ♦ *vi* briller d'un éclat aveuglant; **to ~ at** lancer un *or* des regard(s) furieux à.

glaring ['glɛərɪŋ] *adj* (*mistake*) criant(e), qui saute aux yeux.

glasnost ['glæznɒst] *n* glasnost *f*.

glass [glɑːs] *n* verre *m*; (*also*: **looking ~**) miroir *m*.

glass-blowing ['glɑːsbləʊɪŋ] *n* soufflage *m* (du verre).

glass ceiling *n* (*fig*) plafond dans l'échelle hiérarchique au-dessus duquel les femmes ou les membres d'une minorité ethnique ne semblent pouvoir s'élever.

glasses ['glɑːsəs] *npl* lunettes *fpl*.

glass fibre *n* fibre *f* de verre.

glasshouse ['glɑːshaʊs] *n* serre *f*.

glassware ['glɑːswɛə*] *n* verrerie *f*.

glassy ['glɑːsɪ] *adj* (*eyes*) vitreux(euse).

Glaswegian [glæs'wiːdʒən] *adj* de Glasgow ♦ *n* habitant/e de Glasgow; natif/ive de Glasgow.

glaze [gleɪz] *vt* (*door*) vitrer; (*pottery*) vernir; (CULIN) glacer ♦ *n* vernis *m*; (CULIN) glaçage *m*.

glazed [gleɪzd] *adj* (*eye*) vitreux(euse); (*pottery*) verni(e); (*tiles*) vitrifié(e).

glazier ['gleɪzɪə*] *n* vitrier *m*.

gleam [gliːm] *n* lueur *f* ♦ *vi* luire, briller; **a ~ of hope** une lueur d'espoir.

gleaming ['gliːmɪŋ] *adj* luisant(e).

glean [gliːn] *vt* (*information*) recueillir.

glee [gliː] *n* joie *f*.

gleeful ['gliːfʊl] *adj* joyeux(euse).

glen [glɛn] *n* vallée *f*.

glib [glɪb] *adj* qui a du bagou; facile.

glide [glaɪd] *vi* glisser; (AVIAT, *bird*) planer ♦ *n* glissement *m*; vol plané.

glider ['glaɪdə*] *n* (AVIAT) planeur *m*.

gliding ['glaɪdɪŋ] *n* (AVIAT) vol *m* à voile.

glimmer ['glɪmə*] *vi* luire ♦ *n* lueur *f*.

glimpse [glɪmps] *n* vision passagère, aperçu *m* ♦ *vt* entrevoir, apercevoir; **to catch a ~ of** entrevoir.

glint [glɪnt] *n* éclair *m* ♦ *vi* étinceler.

glisten ['glɪsn] *vi* briller, luire.

glitter ['glɪtə*] *vi* scintiller, briller ♦ *n* scintillement *m*.

glitz [glɪts] *n* (*col*) clinquant *m*.

gloat [gləʊt] *vi*: **to ~ (over)** jubiler (à propos de).

global ['gləʊbl] *adj* (*world-wide*) mondial(e); (*overall*) global(e).

global warming [-'wɔːmɪŋ] *n* réchauffement *m* de la planète.

globe [gləʊb] *n* globe *m*.

globe-trotter ['gləʊbtrɒtə*] *n* globe-trotter *m*.

globule ['glɒbjuːl] *n* (ANAT) globule *m*; (*of water etc*) gouttelette *f*.

gloom [gluːm] *n* obscurité *f*; (*sadness*) tristesse *f*, mélancolie *f*.

gloomy ['gluːmɪ] *adj* sombre, triste, mélancolique; **to feel ~** avoir *or* se faire des idées noires.

glorification [glɔːrɪfɪ'keɪʃən] *n* glorification *f*.

glorify ['glɔːrɪfaɪ] *vt* glorifier.

glorious ['glɔːrɪəs] *adj* glorieux(euse); (*beautiful*) splendide.

glory ['glɔːrɪ] *n* gloire *f*; splendeur *f* ♦ *vi*: **to ~ in** se glorifier de.

glory hole *n* (*col*) capharnaüm *m*.

Glos *abbr* (BRIT) = *Gloucestershire*.

gloss [glɒs] *n* (*shine*) brillant *m*, vernis *m*; (*also*: ~ **paint**) peinture brillante *or* laquée.

▶**gloss over** *vt fus* glisser sur.

glossary ['glɒsərɪ] *n* glossaire *m*, lexique *m*.

glossy ['glɒsɪ] *adj* brillant(e), luisant(e) ♦ *n* (*also*: ~ **magazine**) revue *f* de luxe.

glove [glʌv] *n* gant *m*.

glove compartment *n* (AUT) boîte *f* à gants, vide-poches *m inv*.

glow [gləʊ] *vi* rougeoyer; (*face*) rayonner ♦ *n* rougeoiement *m*.

glower ['glaʊə*] *vi* lancer des regards mauvais.

glowing ['gləʊɪŋ] *adj* (*fire*) rougeoyant(e); (*complexion*) éclatant(e); (*report, description etc*) dithyrambique.

glow-worm ['gləʊwəːm] *n* ver luisant.

glucose ['gluːkəʊs] *n* glucose *m*.

glue [gluː] *n* colle *f* ♦ *vt* coller.

glue-sniffing ['gluːsnɪfɪŋ] *n* inhalation *f* de colle.

glum [glʌm] *adj* maussade, morose.

glut [glʌt] *n* surabondance *f* ♦ *vt* rassasier; (*market*) encombrer.

glutinous ['gluːtɪnəs] *adj* visqueux(euse).

glutton ['glʌtn] *n* glouton/ne; **a ~ for work** un bourreau de travail.

gluttonous ['glʌtənəs] *adj* glouton(ne).

gluttony ['glʌtənɪ] n gloutonnerie f; (sin) gourmandise f.

glycerin(e) ['glɪsəriːn] n glycérine f.

gm abbr (= gram) g.

GMAT n abbr (US: = Graduate Management Admissions Test) examen d'admission dans le 2e cycle de l'enseignement supérieur.

GMB n abbr (BRIT) = General Municipal and Boilermakers (Union).

GMT abbr (= Greenwich Mean Time) GMT.

gnarled [nɑːld] adj noueux(euse).

gnash [næʃ] vt: to ~ one's teeth grincer des dents.

gnat [næt] n moucheron m.

gnaw [nɔː] vt ronger.

gnome [nəum] n gnome m, lutin m.

GNP n abbr = gross national product.

go [gəu] vb (pt **went**, pp **gone** [wɛnt, gɔn]) vi aller; (depart) partir, s'en aller; (work) marcher; (be sold): to ~ **for £10** se vendre 10 livres; (fit, suit): to ~ **with** aller avec; (become): to ~ **pale/mouldy** pâlir/moisir; (break etc) céder ♦ n (pl: ~**es**): to **have a** ~ **(at)** essayer (de faire); to **be on the** ~ être en mouvement; **whose** ~ **is it?** à qui est-ce de jouer?; to ~ **by car/on foot** aller en voiture/à pied; **he's** ~**ing to do** il va faire, il est sur le point de faire; to ~ **for a walk** aller se promener; to ~ **dancing/shopping** aller danser/faire les courses; to ~ **looking for sb/sth** aller or partir à la recherche de qn/qch; to ~ **to sleep** s'endormir; to ~ **and see sb, to** ~ **to see sb** aller voir qn; **how is it** ~**ing?** comment ça marche?; **how did it** ~**?** comment est-ce que ça s'est passé?; to ~ **round the back/by the shop** passer par derrière/devant le magasin; **my voice has gone** j'ai une extinction de voix; **the cake is all gone** il n'y a plus de gâteau; **I'll take whatever is** ~**ing** (BRIT) je prendrai ce qu'il y a (or ce que vous avez); ... **to** ~ (US: food) ... à emporter.

►**go about** vi (also: ~ **around**) aller çà et là; (: rumour) se répandre ♦ vt fus: **how do I** ~ **about this?** comment dois-je m'y prendre (pour faire ceci)?; to ~ **about one's business** s'occuper de ses affaires.

►**go after** vt fus (pursue) poursuivre, courir après; (job, record etc) essayer d'obtenir.

►**go against** vt fus (be unfavourable to) être défavorable à; (be contrary to) être contraire à.

►**go ahead** vi (make progress) avancer; (get going) y aller.

►**go along** vi aller, avancer ♦ vt fus longer, parcourir; **as you** ~ **along (with your work)** au fur et à mesure (de votre travail); to ~ **along with** (accompany) accompagner; (agree with: idea) être d'accord sur; (: person) suivre.

►**go away** vi partir, s'en aller.

►**go back** vi rentrer; revenir; (go again) retourner.

►**go back on** vt fus (promise) revenir sur.

►**go by** vi (years, time) passer, s'écouler ♦ vt fus s'en tenir à; (believe) en croire.

►**go down** vi descendre; (ship) couler; (sun) se coucher ♦ vt fus descendre; **that should** ~ **down well with him** (fig) ça devrait lui plaire.

►**go for** vt fus (fetch) aller chercher; (like) aimer; (attack) s'en prendre à; attaquer.

►**go in** vi entrer.

►**go in for** vt fus (competition) se présenter à; (like) aimer.

►**go into** vt fus entrer dans; (investigate) étudier, examiner; (embark on) se lancer dans.

►**go off** vi partir, s'en aller; (food) se gâter; (bomb) sauter; (lights etc) s'éteindre; (event) se dérouler ♦ vt fus ne plus aimer, ne plus avoir envie de; **the gun went off** le coup est parti; to ~ **off to sleep** s'endormir; **the party went off well** la fête s'est bien passée or était très réussie.

►**go on** vi continuer; (happen) se passer; (lights) s'allumer ♦ vt fus (be guided by: evidence etc) se fonder sur; to ~ **on doing** continuer à faire; **what's** ~**ing on here?** qu'est-ce qui se passe ici?

►**go on at** vt fus (nag) tomber sur le dos de.

►**go on with** vt fus poursuivre, continuer.

►**go out** vi sortir; (fire, light) s'éteindre; (tide) descendre; to ~ **out with sb** sortir avec qn.

►**go over** vi (ship) chavirer ♦ vt fus (check) revoir, vérifier; to ~ **over sth in one's mind** repasser qch dans son esprit.

►**go round** vi (circulate: news, rumour) circuler; (revolve) tourner; (visit): to ~ **round to sb's** passer chez qn; aller chez qn; (make a detour): to ~ **round (by)** faire un détour (par); (suffice) suffire (pour tout le monde).

►**go through** vt fus (town etc) traverser; (search through) fouiller; (examine: list, book) lire or regarder en détail, éplucher; (perform: lesson) réciter; (: formalities) remplir; (: programme) exécuter.

►**go through with** vt fus (plan, crime) aller jusqu'au bout de.

►**go under** vi (sink: also fig) couler; (: person) succomber.

►**go up** vi monter; (price) augmenter ♦ vt fus gravir; to ~ **up in flames** flamber, s'enflammer brusquement.

►**go without** vt fus se passer de.

goad [gəud] vt aiguillonner.

go-ahead ['gəuəhɛd] adj dynamique, entreprenant(e) ♦ n feu vert.

goal [gəul] n but m.

goal difference n différence f de buts.

goalie ['gəulɪ] n (col) goal m.

goalkeeper ['gəulkiːpə*] n gardien m de but.

goal post n poteau m de but.

goat [gəut] n chèvre f.

gobble ['gɔbl] vt (also: ~ **down**, ~ **up**) engloutir.

go-between ['gǝubɪtwiːn] n médiateur m.
Gobi Desert ['gǝubɪ-] n désert m de Gobi.
goblet ['gɔblɪt] n goblet m.
goblin ['gɔblɪn] n lutin m.
go-cart ['gǝukɑːt] n kart m ♦ cpd: ~ **racing** n karting m.
god [gɔd] n dieu m; **G~** Dieu.
god-awful [gɔd'ɔːfǝl] adj (col) franchement atroce.
godchild ['gɔdtʃaɪld] n filleul/e.
goddamn(ed) ['gɔddæm(d)] excl (esp US col): **goddamn (it)!** nom de Dieu! ♦ adj satané(e), sacré(e) ♦ adv sacrément.
goddaughter ['gɔddɔːtǝ*] n filleule f.
goddess ['gɔdɪs] n déesse f.
godfather ['gɔdfɑːðǝ*] n parrain m.
god-fearing ['gɔdfɪǝrɪŋ] adj croyant(e).
god-forsaken ['gɔdfǝseɪkǝn] adj maudit(e).
godmother ['gɔdmʌðǝ*] n marraine f.
godparents ['gɔdpɛǝrǝnts] npl: **the** ~ le parrain et la marraine.
godsend ['gɔdsend] n aubaine f.
godson ['gɔdsʌn] n filleul m.
goes [gǝuz] vb see **go**.
gofer ['gǝufǝ*] n coursier/ière.
go-getter ['gǝugetǝ*] n arriviste m/f.
goggle ['gɔgl] vi: **to** ~ **at** regarder avec des yeux ronds.
goggles ['gɔglz] npl lunettes (protectrices) (de motocycliste etc).
going ['gǝuɪŋ] n (conditions) état m du terrain ♦ adj: **the** ~ **rate** le tarif (en vigueur); **a** ~ **concern** une affaire prospère; **it was slow** ~ les progrès étaient lents, ça n'avançait pas vite.
going-over [gǝuɪŋ'ǝuvǝ*] n vérification f, révision f; (col: beating) passage m à tabac.
goings-on ['gǝuɪŋz'ɔn] npl (col) manigances fpl.
go-kart ['gǝukɑːt] n = **go-cart**.
gold [gǝuld] n or m ♦ adj en or; (reserves) d'or.
golden ['gǝuldǝn] adj (made of gold) en or; (gold in colour) doré(e).
golden age n âge m d'or.
golden handshake n (BRIT) prime f de départ.
golden rule n règle f d'or.
goldfish ['gǝuldfɪʃ] n poisson m rouge.
gold leaf n or m en feuille.
gold medal n (SPORT) médaille f d'or.
goldmine ['gǝuldmaɪn] n mine f d'or.
gold-plated ['gǝuld'pleɪtɪd] adj plaqué(e) or inv.
goldsmith ['gǝuldsmɪθ] n orfèvre m.
gold standard n étalon-or m.
golf [gɔlf] n golf m.
golf ball n balle f de golf; (on typewriter) boule f.
golf club n club m de golf; (stick) club m, crosse f de golf.
golf course n terrain m de golf.
golfer ['gɔlfǝ*] n joueur/euse de golf.

golfing ['gɔlfɪŋ] n golf m.
gondola ['gɔndǝlǝ] n gondole f.
gondolier [gɔndǝ'lɪǝ*] n gondolier m.
gone [gɔn] pp of **go** ♦ adj parti(e).
goner ['gɔnǝ*] n (col): **to be a** ~ être fichu(e) or foutu(e).
gong [gɔŋ] n gong m.
good [gud] adj bon(ne); (kind) gentil(le); (child) sage ♦ n bien m; ~! bon!, très bien!; **to be** ~ **at** être bon en; **it's** ~ **for you** c'est bon pour vous; **it's a** ~ **thing you were there** heureusement que vous étiez là; **she is** ~ **with children/her hands** elle sait bien s'occuper des enfants/sait se servir de ses mains; **to feel** ~ se sentir bien; **it's** ~ **to see you** ça me fait plaisir de vous voir, je suis content de vous voir; **he's up to no** ~ il prépare quelque mauvais coup; **it's no** ~ **complaining** cela ne sert à rien de se plaindre; **for the common** ~ dans l'intérêt commun; **for** ~ (for ever) pour de bon, une fois pour toutes; **would you be** ~ **enough to ...?** auriez-vous la bonté or l'amabilité de ...?; **that's very** ~ **of you** c'est très gentil de votre part; **is this any** ~? (will it do?) est-ce que ceci fera l'affaire?, est-ce que cela peut vous rendre service?; (what's it like?) qu'est-ce que ça vaut?; **a** ~ **deal (of)** beaucoup (de); **a** ~ **many** beaucoup (de); ~ **morning/afternoon!** bonjour!; ~ **evening!** bonsoir!; ~ **night!** bonsoir!; (on going to bed) bonne nuit!
goodbye [gud'baɪ] excl au revoir!; **to say** ~ **to** dire au revoir à.
good faith n bonne foi.
good-for-nothing ['gudfǝnʌθɪŋ] adj bon(ne) or propre à rien.
Good Friday n Vendredi saint.
good-humoured ['gud'hjuːmǝd] adj (person) jovial(e); (remark, joke) sans malice.
good-looking ['gud'lukɪŋ] adj bien inv.
good-natured ['gud'neɪtʃǝd] adj (person) qui a un bon naturel; (discussion) enjoué(e).
goodness ['gudnɪs] n (of person) bonté f; **for** ~ **sake!** je vous en prie!; ~ **gracious!** mon Dieu!
goods [gudz] npl marchandise f, articles mpl; (COMM etc) marchandises; ~ **and chattels** biens mpl et effets mpl.
goods train n (BRIT) train m de marchandises.
goodwill [gud'wɪl] n bonne volonté; (COMM) réputation f (auprès de la clientèle).
goody-goody ['gudɪgudɪ] n (pej) petit saint, sainte nitouche.
gooey ['guːɪ] adj (BRIT col) gluant(e).
goose, pl **geese** [guːs, giːs] n oie f.
gooseberry ['guzbǝrɪ] n groseille f à maquereau; **to play** ~ (BRIT) tenir la chandelle.
gooseflesh ['guːsfleʃ] n, **goosepimples** ['guːspɪmplz] npl chair f de poule.
goose step n (MIL) pas m de l'oie.
GOP n abbr (US POL: col: = Grand Old Party) parti

républicain.

gopher ['gəufə*] n = **gofer.**

gore [gɔː*] vt encorner ♦ n sang m.

gorge [gɔːdʒ] n gorge f ♦ vt: **to ~ o.s. (on)** se gorger (de).

gorgeous ['gɔːdʒəs] adj splendide, superbe.

gorilla [gə'rɪlə] n gorille m.

gormless ['gɔːmlɪs] adj (BRIT col) lourdaud(e).

gorse [gɔːs] n ajoncs mpl.

gory ['gɔːrɪ] adj sanglant(e).

go-slow ['gəu'sləu] n (BRIT) grève perlée.

gospel ['gɔspl] n évangile m.

gossamer ['gɔsəmə*] n (cobweb) fils mpl de la vierge; (light fabric) étoffe très légère.

gossip ['gɔsɪp] n bavardages mpl; (malicious) commérage m, cancans mpl; (person) commère f ♦ vi bavarder; cancaner, faire des commérages; **a piece of ~** un ragot, un racontar.

gossip column n (PRESS) échos mpl.

got [gɔt] pt, pp of **get.**

Gothic ['gɔθɪk] adj gothique.

gotten ['gɔtn] (US) pp of **get.**

gouge [gaudʒ] vt (also: ~ **out:** hole etc) évider; (: initials) tailler; **to ~ sb's eyes out** crever les yeux à qn.

gourd [guəd] n calebasse f, gourde f.

gourmet ['guəmeɪ] n gourmet m, gastronome m/f.

gout [gaut] n goutte f.

govern ['gʌvən] vt (gen, LING) gouverner.

governess ['gʌvənɪs] n gouvernante f.

governing ['gʌvənɪŋ] adj (POL) au pouvoir, au gouvernement; ~ **body** conseil m d'administration.

government ['gʌvnmənt] n gouvernement m; (BRIT: ministers) ministère m ♦ cpd de l'État; **local ~** administration locale.

governmental [gʌvn'mɛntl] adj gouvernemental(e).

government housing n (US) logements sociaux.

government stock n titres mpl d'État.

governor ['gʌvənə*] n (of colony, state, bank) gouverneur m; (of school, hospital etc) administrateur/trice; (BRIT: of prison) directeur/trice.

Govt abbr (= government) gvt.

gown [gaun] n robe f; (of teacher, BRIT: of judge) toge f.

GP n abbr (MED) = **general practitioner.**

GPMU n abbr (BRIT) = Graphical, Paper and Media Union.

GPO n abbr (BRIT: old) = General Post Office; (US) = Government Printing Office.

gr. abbr (COMM) = **gross.**

grab [græb] vt saisir, empoigner; (property, power) se saisir de ♦ vi: **to ~ at** essayer de saisir.

grace [greɪs] n grâce f ♦ vt honorer; **5 days' ~** répit m de 5 jours; **to say ~** dire le bénédicité; (after meal) dire les grâces; **with a**

good/bad ~ de bonne/mauvaise grâce; **his sense of humour is his saving ~** il se rachète par son sens de l'humour.

graceful ['greɪsful] adj gracieux(euse), élégant(e).

gracious ['greɪʃəs] adj (kind) charmant(e), bienveillant(e); (elegant) plein(e) d'élégance, d'une grande élégance; (formal: pardon etc) miséricordieux(euse) ♦ excl: **(good) ~!** mon Dieu!

gradation [grə'deɪʃən] n gradation f.

grade [greɪd] n (COMM) qualité f; calibre m; catégorie f; (in hierarchy) grade m, échelon m; (US: SCOL) note f, classe f; (: gradient) pente f ♦ vt classer; calibrer; graduer; **to make the ~** (fig) réussir.

grade crossing n (US) passage m à niveau.

grade school n (US) école f primaire.

gradient ['greɪdɪənt] n inclinaison f, pente f; (GEOM) gradient m.

gradual ['grædjuəl] adj graduel(le), progressif(ive).

gradually ['grædjuəlɪ] adv peu à peu, graduellement.

graduate n ['grædjuɪt] diplômé/e d'université; (US) diplômé/e de fin d'études ♦ vi ['grædjueɪt] obtenir un diplôme d'université (or de fin d'études).

graduated pension ['grædjueɪtɪd-] n retraite calculée en fonction des derniers salaires.

graduation [grædju'eɪʃən] n cérémonie f de remise des diplômes.

graffiti [grə'fiːtɪ] npl graffiti mpl.

graft [grɑːft] n (AGR, MED) greffe f; (bribery) corruption f ♦ vt greffer; **hard ~** (col) boulot acharné.

grain [greɪn] n grain m; (no pl: cereals) céréales fpl; (US: corn) blé m; **it goes against the ~** cela va à l'encontre de sa (or ma etc) nature.

gram [græm] n gramme m.

grammar ['græmə*] n grammaire f.

grammar school n (BRIT) ≈ lycée m.

grammatical [grə'mætɪkl] adj grammatical(e).

gramme [græm] n = **gram.**

gramophone ['græməfəun] n (BRIT) gramophone m.

granary ['grænərɪ] n grenier m.

grand [grænd] adj splendide, imposant(e); (terrific) magnifique, formidable; (also humorous: gesture etc) noble ♦ n (col: thousand) mille livres fpl (or dollars mpl).

grandchildren ['græntʃɪldrən] npl petits-enfants mpl.

granddad ['grændæd] n grand-papa m.

granddaughter ['grændɔːtə*] n petite-fille f.

grandeur ['grændjə*] n magnificence f, splendeur f; (of position etc) éminence f.

grandfather ['grændfɑːðə*] n grand-père m.

grandiose ['grændɪəus] adj grandiose; (pej) pompeux(euse).

grand jury n (US) jury m d'accusation (formé

de 12 à 23 jurés).

grandma ['grænmɑː] *n* grand-maman *f*.

grandmother ['grænmʌðə*] *n* grand-mère *f*.

grandpa ['grænpɑː] *n* = **granddad**.

grandparent ['grændpɛərənt] *n* grand-père/grand-mère.

grand piano *n* piano *m* à queue.

Grand Prix ['grɑː'priː] *n* (*AUT*) grand prix automobile.

grandson ['grænsʌn] *n* petit-fils *m*.

grandstand ['grændstænd] *n* (*SPORT*) tribune *f*.

grand total *n* total général.

granite ['grænɪt] *n* granit *m*.

granny ['grænɪ] *n* grand-maman *f*.

grant [grɑːnt] *vt* accorder; (*a request*) accéder à; (*admit*) concéder ♦ *n* (*SCOL*) bourse *f*; (*ADMIN*) subside *m*, subvention *f*; **to take sth for** ~**ed** considérer qch comme acquis; **to** ~ **that** admettre que.

granulated ['grænjuleɪtɪd] *adj*: ~ **sugar** sucre *m* en poudre.

granule ['grænjuːl] *n* granule *m*.

grape [greɪp] *n* raisin *m*; **a bunch of** ~**s** une grappe de raisin.

grapefruit ['greɪpfruːt] *n* pamplemousse *m*.

grapevine ['greɪpvaɪn] *n* vigne *f*; **I heard it on the** ~ (*fig*) je l'ai appris par le téléphone arabe.

graph [grɑːf] *n* graphique *m*, courbe *f*.

graphic ['græfɪk] *adj* graphique; (*vivid*) vivant(e).

graphic designer *n* graphiste *m/f*.

graphic equalizer *n* égaliseur *m* graphique.

graphics ['græfɪks] *n* (*art*) arts *mpl* graphiques; (*process*) graphisme *m*; (*pl: drawings*) illustrations *fpl*.

graphite ['græfaɪt] *n* graphite *m*.

graph paper *n* papier millimétré.

grapple ['græpl] *vi*: **to** ~ **with** être aux prises avec.

grappling iron ['græplɪŋ-] *n* (*NAUT*) grappin *m*.

grasp [grɑːsp] *vt* saisir, empoigner; (*understand*) saisir, comprendre ♦ *n* (*grip*) prise *f*; (*fig*) compréhension *f*, connaissance *f*; **to have sth within one's** ~ avoir qch à sa portée; **to have a good** ~ **of sth** (*fig*) bien comprendre qch.

▶**grasp at** *vt fus* (*rope etc*) essayer de saisir; (*fig: opportunity*) sauter sur.

grasping ['grɑːspɪŋ] *adj* avide.

grass [grɑːs] *n* herbe *f*; (*BRIT col: informer*) mouchard/e; (: *ex-terrorist*) balanceur/euse.

grasshopper ['grɑːshɔpə*] *n* sauterelle *f*.

grassland ['grɑːslænd] *n* prairie *f*.

grass roots *npl* (*fig*) base *f*.

grass snake *n* couleuvre *f*.

grassy ['grɑːsɪ] *adj* herbeux(euse).

grate [greɪt] *n* grille *f* de cheminée ♦ *vi* grincer ♦ *vt* (*CULIN*) râper.

grateful ['greɪtful] *adj* reconnaissant(e).

gratefully ['greɪtfəlɪ] *adv* avec reconnais-

sance.

grater ['greɪtə*] *n* râpe *f*.

gratification [grætɪfɪ'keɪʃən] *n* satisfaction *f*.

gratify ['grætɪfaɪ] *vt* faire plaisir à; (*whim*) satisfaire.

gratifying ['grætɪfaɪɪŋ] *adj* agréable; satisfaisant(e).

grating ['greɪtɪŋ] *n* (*iron bars*) grille *f* ♦ *adj* (*noise*) grinçant(e).

gratitude ['grætɪtjuːd] *n* gratitude *f*.

gratuitous [grə'tjuːɪtəs] *adj* gratuit(e).

gratuity [grə'tjuːɪtɪ] *n* pourboire *m*.

grave [greɪv] *n* tombe *f* ♦ *adj* grave, sérieux(euse).

gravedigger ['greɪvdɪgə*] *n* fossoyeur *m*.

gravel ['grævl] *n* gravier *m*.

gravely ['greɪvlɪ] *adv* gravement, sérieusement; ~ **ill** gravement malade.

gravestone ['greɪvstəun] *n* pierre tombale.

graveyard ['greɪvjɑːd] *n* cimetière *m*.

gravitate ['grævɪteɪt] *vi* graviter.

gravity ['grævɪtɪ] *n* (*PHYSICS*) gravité *f*; pesanteur *f*; (*seriousness*) gravité, sérieux *m*.

gravy ['greɪvɪ] *n* jus *m* (de viande); sauce *f* (au jus de viande).

gravy boat *n* saucière *f*.

gravy train *n* (*col*): **to ride the** ~ avoir une bonne planque.

gray [greɪ] *adj* (*US*) = **grey**.

graze [greɪz] *vi* paître, brouter ♦ *vt* (*touch lightly*) frôler, effleurer; (*scrape*) écorcher ♦ *n* écorchure *f*.

grazing ['greɪzɪŋ] *n* (*pasture*) pâturage *m*.

grease [griːs] *n* (*fat*) graisse *f*; (*lubricant*) lubrifiant *m* ♦ *vt* graisser; lubrifier; **to** ~ **the skids** (*US: fig*) huiler les rouages.

grease gun *n* graisseur *m*.

greasepaint ['griːspeɪnt] *n* produits *mpl* de maquillage.

greaseproof paper ['griːspruːf-] *n* (*BRIT*) papier sulfurisé.

greasy ['griːsɪ] *adj* gras(se), graisseux(euse); (*hands, clothes*) graisseux; (*BRIT: road, surface*) glissant(e).

great [greɪt] *adj* grand(e); (*heat, pain etc*) très fort(e), intense; (*col*) formidable; **they're** ~ **friends** ils sont très amis, ce sont de grands amis; **we had a** ~ **time** nous nous sommes bien amusés; **it was** ~! c'était fantastique or super!; **the** ~ **thing is that** ... ce qu'il y a de vraiment bien c'est que ....

Great Barrier Reef *n*: **the** ~ la Grande Barrière.

Great Britain *n* Grande-Bretagne *f*.

great-grandchild, *pl* **-children** [greɪt'græntʃaɪld, -tʃɪldrən] *n* arrière-petit(e)-enfant.

great-grandfather [greɪt'grænfɑːðə*] *n* arrière-grand-père *m*.

great-grandmother [greɪt'grænmʌðə*] *n* arrière-grand-mère *f*.

Great Lakes *npl*: **the** ~ les Grands Lacs.

greatly ['greɪtlɪ] *adv* très, grandement; (*with verbs*) beaucoup.

greatness ['greɪtnɪs] *n* grandeur *f*.

Grecian ['griːʃən] *adj* grec(grecque).

Greece [griːs] *n* Grèce *f*.

greed [griːd] *n* (*also*: ~iness) avidité *f*; (*for food*) gourmandise *f*.

greedily ['griːdɪlɪ] *adv* avidement; avec gourmandise.

greedy ['griːdɪ] *adj* avide; gourmand(e).

Greek [griːk] *adj* grec(grecque) ♦ *n* Grec/ Grecque; (*LING*) grec *m*; **ancient/modern** ~ grec classique/moderne.

green [griːn] *adj* vert(e); (*inexperienced*) (bien) jeune, naïf(ïve); (*ecological: product etc*) écologique ♦ *n* (*colour, of golf course*) vert *m*; (*stretch of grass*) pelouse *f*; (*also*: **village** ~) ≈ place *f* du village; ~**s** *npl* légumes verts; **to have** ~ **fingers** *or* (*US*) **a** ~ **thumb** (*fig*) avoir le pouce vert; **G**~ (*POL*) écologiste (*m/f*); **the G**~ **Party** le parti écologiste.

green belt *n* (*round town*) ceinture verte.

green card *n* (*AUT*) carte verte.

greenery ['griːnərɪ] *n* verdure *f*.

greenfly ['griːnflaɪ] *n* (*BRIT*) puceron *m*.

greengage ['griːngeɪdʒ] *n* reine-claude *f*.

greengrocer ['griːngrəʊsə*] *n* (*BRIT*) marchand *m* de fruits et légumes.

greenhouse ['griːnhaʊs] *n* serre *f*.

greenhouse effect *n*: **the** ~ l'effet *m* de serre.

greenhouse gas *n* gaz *m* contribuant à l'effet de serre.

greenish ['griːnɪʃ] *adj* verdâtre.

Greenland ['griːnlənd] *n* Groenland *m*.

Greenlander ['griːnləndə*] *n* Groenlandais/e.

green light *n*: **to give sb/sth the** ~ donner le feu vert à qn/qch.

green pepper *n* poivron (vert).

green pound *n* (*ECON*) livre verte.

greet [griːt] *vt* accueillir.

greeting ['griːtɪŋ] *n* salutation *f*; **Christmas/ birthday** ~**s** souhaits *mpl* de Noël/de bon anniversaire.

greeting(s) card *n* carte *f* de vœux.

gregarious [grə'gɛərɪəs] *adj* grégaire; sociable.

grenade [grə'neɪd] *n* (*also*: **hand** ~) grenade *f*.

grew [gruː] *pt of* **grow**.

grey [greɪ] *adj* gris(e); (*dismal*) sombre; **to go** ~ (commencer à) grisonner.

grey-haired [greɪ'hɛəd] *adj* aux cheveux gris.

greyhound ['greɪhaʊnd] *n* lévrier *m*.

grid [grɪd] *n* grille *f*; (*ELEC*) réseau *m*; (*US AUT*) intersection *f* (*matérialisée par des marques au sol*).

griddle [grɪdl] *n* (*on cooker*) plaque chauffante.

gridiron ['grɪdaɪən] *n* gril *m*.

gridlock ['grɪdlɔk] *n* (*traffic jam*) embouteillage *m*.

grief [griːf] *n* chagrin *m*, douleur *f*; **to come to**

~ (*plan*) échouer; (*person*) avoir un malheur.

grievance ['griːvəns] *n* doléance *f*, grief *m*; (*cause for complaint*) grief.

grieve [griːv] *vi* avoir du chagrin; se désoler ♦ *vt* faire de la peine à, affliger; **to** ~ **at** se désoler de; pleurer.

grievous ['griːvəs] *adj* grave; cruel(le); ~ **bodily harm** (*LAW*) coups *mpl* et blessures *fpl*.

grill [grɪl] *n* (*on cooker*) gril *m* ♦ *vt* (*BRIT*) griller; (*question*) interroger longuement, cuisiner.

grille [grɪl] *n* grillage *m*; (*AUT*) calandre *f*.

grill(room) ['grɪl(rum)] *n* rôtisserie *f*.

grim [grɪm] *adj* sinistre, lugubre.

grimace [grɪ'meɪs] *n* grimace *f* ♦ *vi* grimacer, faire une grimace.

grime [graɪm] *n* crasse *f*.

grimy ['graɪmɪ] *adj* crasseux(euse).

grin [grɪn] *n* large sourire *m* ♦ *vi* sourire; **to** ~ (**at**) faire un grand sourire (à).

grind [graɪnd] *vb* (*pt, pp* **ground** [graund]) *vt* écraser; (*coffee, pepper etc*) moudre; (*US: meat*) hacher; (*make sharp*) aiguiser; (*polish: gem, lens*) polir ♦ *vi* (*car gears*) grincer ♦ *n* (*work*) corvée *f*; **to** ~ **one's teeth** grincer des dents; **to** ~ **to a halt** (*vehicle*) s'arrêter dans un grincement de freins; (*fig*) s'arrêter, s'immobiliser; **the daily** ~ (*col*) le train-train quotidien.

grinder ['graɪndə*] *n* (*machine: for coffee*) moulin *m* (à café); (: *for waste disposal etc*) broyeur *m*.

grindstone ['graɪndstəʊn] *n*: **to keep one's nose to the** ~ travailler sans relâche.

grip [grɪp] *n* (*control, grasp*) étreinte *f*; (*hold*) prise *f*; (*handle*) poignée *f*; (*holdall*) sac *m* de voyage ♦ *vt* saisir, empoigner; étreindre; **to come to** ~**s with** se colleter avec, en venir aux prises avec; **to** ~ **the road** (*AUT*) adhérer à la route; **to lose one's** ~ lâcher prise; (*fig*) perdre les pédales, être dépassé(e).

gripe [graɪp] *n* (*MED*) coliques *fpl*; (*col: complaint*) ronchonnement *m*, rouspétance *f* ♦ *vi* (*col*) râler.

gripping ['grɪpɪŋ] *adj* prenant(e), palpitant(e).

grisly ['grɪzlɪ] *adj* sinistre, macabre.

grist [grɪst] *n* (*fig*): **it's** (**all**) ~ **to his mill** ça l'arrange, ça apporte de l'eau à son moulin.

gristle ['grɪsl] *n* cartilage *m* (*de poulet etc*).

grit [grɪt] *n* gravillon *m*; (*courage*) cran *m* ♦ *vt* (*road*) sabler; **to** ~ **one's teeth** serrer les dents; **to have a piece of** ~ **in one's eye** avoir une poussière *or* saleté dans l'œil.

grits [grɪts] *npl* (*US*) gruau *m* de maïs.

grizzle ['grɪzl] *vi* (*BRIT*) pleurnicher.

grizzly ['grɪzlɪ] *n* (*also*: ~ **bear**) grizzli *m*, ours gris.

groan [grəʊn] *n* gémissement *m*; grognement *m* ♦ *vi* gémir; grogner.

grocer ['grəʊsə*] *n* épicier *m*; **at the** ~**'s** à l'épicerie, chez l'épicier.

groceries ['grəʊsərɪz] *npl* provisions *fpl*.

grocery ['grəʊsərɪ] *n* (*shop*) épicerie *f*.

grog [grɔg] *n* grog *m*.

groggy ['grɔgɪ] *adj* groggy *inv*.

groin [grɔɪn] *n* aine *f*.

groom [gruːm] *n* palefrenier *m*; (*also:* **bride~**) marié *m* ♦ *vt* (*horse*) panser; (*fig*): **to ~ sb for** former qn pour.

groove [gruːv] *n* sillon *m*, rainure *f*.

grope [grəup] *vi* tâtonner; **to ~ for** *vt fus* chercher à tâtons.

gross [grəus] *adj* grossier(ière); (*COMM*) brut(e) ♦ *n* (*pl inv*) (*twelve dozen*) grosse *f* ♦ *vt* (*COMM*): **to ~ £500,000** gagner 500 000 livres avant impôt.

gross domestic product (GDP) *n* produit brut intérieur (PIB).

grossly ['grəuslɪ] *adv* (*greatly*) très, grandement.

gross national product (GNP) *n* produit national brut (PNB).

grotesque [grə'tɛsk] *adj* grotesque.

grotto ['grɔtəu] *n* grotte *f*.

grotty ['grɔtɪ] *adj* (*BRIT col*) minable.

grouch [grautʃ] (*col*) *vi* rouspéter ♦ *n* (*person*) rouspéteur/euse.

ground [graund] *pt, pp of* grind ♦ *n* sol *m*, terre *f*; (*land*) terrain *m*, terres *fpl*; (*SPORT*) terrain; (*reason: gen pl*) raison *f*; (*US: also:* **~ wire**) terre *f* ♦ *vt* (*plane*) empêcher de décoller, retenir au sol; (*US ELEC*) équiper d'une prise de terre, mettre à la terre ♦ *vi* (*ship*) s'échouer ♦ *adj* (*coffee etc*) moulu(e); (*US: meat*) haché(e); **~s** *npl* (*gardens etc*) parc *m*, domaine *m*; (*of coffee*) marc *m*; **on the ~, to the ~** par terre; **below ~** sous terre; **to gain/lose ~** gagner/perdre du terrain; **common ~** terrain d'entente; **he covered a lot of ~ in his lecture** sa conférence a traité un grand nombre de questions *or* la question en profondeur.

ground cloth *n* (*US*) = **groundsheet**.

ground control *n* (*AVIAT, SPACE*) centre *m* de contrôle (au sol).

ground floor *n* (*BRIT*) rez-de-chaussée *m*.

grounding ['graundɪŋ] *n* (*in education*) connaissances *fpl* de base.

groundless ['graundlɪs] *adj* sans fondement.

groundnut ['graundnʌt] *n* arachide *f*.

ground rent *n* (*BRIT*) fermage *m*.

ground rules *npl*: **the ~** les principes *mpl* de base.

groundsheet ['graundʃiːt] *n* (*BRIT*) tapis *m* de sol.

groundsman ['graundzmən], (*US*) **groundskeeper** ['graundzkiːpə*] *n* (*SPORT*) gardien *m* de stade.

ground staff *n* équipage *m* au sol.

groundswell ['graundswɛl] *n* lame *f or* vague *f* de fond.

ground-to-air ['grauntu'ɛə*] *adj* (*MIL*) sol-air *inv*.

ground-to-ground ['grauntə'graund] *adj* (*MIL*) sol-sol *inv*.

groundwork ['graundwəːk] *n* préparation *f*.

group [gruːp] *n* groupe *m* ♦ *vt* (*also:* **~ together**) grouper ♦ *vi* (*also:* **~ together**) se grouper.

groupie ['gruːpɪ] *n* groupie *f*.

group therapy *n* thérapie *f* de groupe.

grouse [graus] *n* (*pl inv*) (*bird*) grouse *f* (*sorte de coq de bruyère*) ♦ *vi* (*complain*) rouspéter, râler.

grove [grəuv] *n* bosquet *m*.

grovel ['grɔvl] *vi* (*fig*): **to ~ (before)** ramper (devant).

grow, pt grew, pp grown [grəu, gruː, grəun] *vi* (*plant*) pousser, croître; (*person*) grandir; (*increase*) augmenter, se développer; (*become*): **to ~ rich/weak** s'enrichir/s'affaiblir ♦ *vt* cultiver, faire pousser.

►**grow apart** *vi* (*fig*) se détacher (l'un de l'autre).

►**grow away from** *vt fus* (*fig*) s'éloigner de.

►**grow on** *vt fus*: **that painting is ~ing on me** je finirai par aimer ce tableau.

►**grow out of** *vt fus* (*clothes*) devenir trop grand pour; (*habit*) perdre (avec le temps); **he'll ~ out of it** ça lui passera.

►**grow up** *vi* grandir.

grower ['grəuə*] *n* producteur *m*; (*AGR*) cultivateur/trice.

growing ['grəuɪŋ] *adj* (*fear, amount*) croissant(e), grandissant(e); **~ pains** (*MED*) fièvre *f* de croissance; (*fig*) difficultés *fpl* de croissance.

growing pains *npl* (*fig*) difficultés *fpl* de croissance.

growl [graul] *vi* grogner.

grown [grəun] *pp of* grow ♦ *adj* adulte.

grown-up [grəun'ʌp] *n* adulte *m/f*, grande personne.

growth [grəuθ] *n* croissance *f*, développement *m*; (*what has grown*) pousse *f*; poussée *f*; (*MED*) grosseur *f*, tumeur *f*.

growth rate *n* taux *m* de croissance.

GRSM *n abbr* (*BRIT*) = Graduate of the Royal Schools of Music.

grub [grʌb] *n* larve *f*; (*col: food*) bouffe *f*.

grubby ['grʌbɪ] *adj* crasseux(euse).

grudge [grʌdʒ] *n* rancune *f* ♦ *vt*: **to ~ sb sth** donner qch à qn à contre-cœur; reprocher qch à qn; **to bear sb a ~** (**for**) garder rancune *or* en vouloir à qn (de); **he ~s spending** il rechigne à dépenser.

grudgingly ['grʌdʒɪŋlɪ] *adv* à contre-cœur, de mauvaise grâce.

gruelling ['gruəlɪŋ] *adj* exténuant(e).

gruesome ['gruːsəm] *adj* horrible.

gruff [grʌf] *adj* bourru(e).

grumble ['grʌmbl] *vi* rouspéter, ronchonner.

grumpy ['grʌmpɪ] *adj* grincheux(euse).

grunge [grʌndʒ] *n* (*MUS, style*) grunge *m*.

grunt [grʌnt] *vi* grogner ♦ *n* grognement *m*.

G-string ['dʒiːstrɪŋ] *n* (*garment*) cache-sexe *m inv*.

GSUSA n abbr = Girl Scouts of the United States of America.

GU abbr (US) = Guam.

guarantee [gærən'tiː] n garantie f ♦ vt garantir; **he can't ~ (that) he'll come** il n'est pas absolument certain de pouvoir venir.

guarantor [gærən'tɔː*] n garant/e.

guard [gɑːd] n garde f, surveillance f; (squad, BOXING, FENCING) garde f; (one man) garde m; (BRIT RAIL) chef m de train; (safety device: on machine) dispositif m de sûreté; (also: **fire~**) garde-feu m inv ♦ vt garder, surveiller; (protect): **to ~ (against or from)** protéger (contre); **to be on one's ~** (fig) être sur ses gardes.

▶**guard against** vi: **to ~ against doing sth** se garder de faire qch.

guard dog n chien m de garde.

guarded ['gɑːdɪd] adj (fig) prudent(e).

guardian ['gɑːdɪən] n gardien/ne; (of minor) tuteur/trice.

guard's van ['gɑːdz-] n (BRIT RAIL) fourgon m.

Guatemala [gwɑːtɪ'mɑːlə] n Guatémala m.

Guernsey ['gɜːnzɪ] n Guernesey m or f.

guerrilla [gə'rɪlə] n guérillero m.

guerrilla warfare n guérilla f.

guess [gɛs] vi deviner ♦ vt deviner; (US) croire, penser ♦ n supposition f, hypothèse f; **to take or have a ~** essayer de deviner; **to keep sb ~ing** laisser qn dans le doute or l'incertitude, tenir qn en haleine.

guesstimate ['gɛstɪmɪt] n (col) estimation f.

guesswork ['gɛswɜːk] n hypothèse f, **I got the answer by ~** j'ai deviné la réponse.

guest [gɛst] n invité/e; (in hotel) client/e; **be my ~** faites comme chez vous.

guest-house ['gɛsthaus] n pension f.

guest room n chambre f d'amis.

guff [gʌf] n (col) bêtises fpl.

guffaw [gʌ'fɔː] n gros rire ♦ vi pouffer de rire.

guidance ['gaɪdəns] n conseils mpl; **under the ~ of** conseillé(e) or encadré(e) par, sous la conduite de; **vocational ~** orientation professionnelle; **marriage ~** conseils conjugaux.

guide [gaɪd] n (person, book etc) guide m; (also: **girl ~**) guide f ♦ vt guider; **to be ~d by sb/sth** se laisser guider par qn/qch.

guidebook ['gaɪdbuk] n guide m.

guided missile ['gaɪdɪd-] n missile téléguidé.

guide dog n chien m d'aveugle.

guide lines npl (fig) instructions générales, conseils mpl.

guild [gɪld] n corporation f; cercle m, association f.

guildhall ['gɪldhɔːl] n (BRIT) hôtel m de ville.

guile [gaɪl] n astuce f.

guileless ['gaɪllɪs] adj candide.

guillotine ['gɪlətiːn] n guillotine f; (for paper) massicot m.

guilt [gɪlt] n culpabilité f.

guilty ['gɪltɪ] adj coupable; **to plead ~/not ~** plaider coupable/non coupable; **to feel ~ about doing sth** avoir mauvaise conscience à faire qch.

Guinea ['gɪnɪ] n: **Republic of ~** (République f de) Guinée f.

guinea ['gɪnɪ] n (BRIT) guinée f (= 21 shillings: cette monnaie de compte ne s'emploie plus).

guinea pig n cobaye m.

guise [gaɪz] n aspect m, apparence f.

guitar [gɪ'tɑː*] n guitare f.

guitarist [gɪ'tɑːrɪst] n guitariste m/f.

gulch [gʌltʃ] n (US) ravin m.

gulf [gʌlf] n golfe m; (abyss) gouffre m; **the (Persian) G~** le golfe Persique.

Gulf States npl: **the ~** (in Middle East) les pays mpl du Golfe.

Gulf Stream n: **the ~** le Gulf Stream.

gull [gʌl] n mouette f.

gullet ['gʌlɪt] n gosier m.

gullibility [gʌlɪ'bɪlɪtɪ] n crédulité f.

gullible ['gʌlɪbl] adj crédule.

gully ['gʌlɪ] n ravin m; ravine f, couloir m.

gulp [gʌlp] vi avaler sa salive; (from emotion) avoir la gorge serrée, s'étrangler ♦ vt (also: **~ down**) avaler ♦ n (of drink) gorgée f; **at one ~** d'un seul coup.

gum [gʌm] n (ANAT) gencive f; (glue) colle f; (sweet) boule f de gomme; (also: **chewing-~**) chewing-gum m ♦ vt coller.

▶**gum up** vt: **to ~ up the works** (col) bousiller tout.

gumboil ['gʌmbɔɪl] n abcès m dentaire.

gumboots ['gʌmbuːts] npl (BRIT) bottes fpl en caoutchouc.

gumption ['gʌmpʃən] n bon sens, jugeote f.

gun [gʌn] n (small) revolver m, pistolet m; (rifle) fusil m, carabine f; (cannon) canon m ♦ vt (also: **~ down**) abattre; **to stick to one's ~s** (fig) ne pas en démordre.

gunboat ['gʌnbəut] n canonnière f.

gun dog n chien m de chasse.

gunfire ['gʌnfaɪə*] n fusillade f.

gunk [gʌŋk] n (col) saleté f.

gunman ['gʌnmən] n bandit armé.

gunner ['gʌnə*] n artilleur m.

gunpoint ['gʌnpɔɪnt] n: **at ~** sous la menace du pistolet (or fusil).

gunpowder ['gʌnpaudə*] n poudre f à canon.

gunrunner ['gʌnrʌnə*] n trafiquant m d'armes.

gunrunning ['gʌnrʌnɪŋ] n trafic m d'armes.

gunshot ['gʌnʃɔt] n coup m de feu; **within ~** à portée de fusil.

gunsmith ['gʌnsmɪθ] n armurier m.

gurgle ['gɜːgl] n gargouillis m ♦ vi gargouiller.

guru ['guruː] n gourou m.

gush [gʌʃ] n jaillissement m, jet m ♦ vi jaillir; (fig) se répandre en effusions.

gushing ['gʌʃɪŋ] adj (person) trop exubérant(e) or expansif(ive); (compliments) exagéré(e).

gusset ['gʌsɪt] *n* gousset *m*, soufflet *m*; (*in tights, pants*) entre-jambes *m*.

gust [gʌst] *n* (*of wind*) rafale *f*; (*of smoke*) bouffée *f*.

gusto ['gʌstəu] *n* enthousiasme *m*.

gusty ['gʌstɪ] *adj* venteux(euse); ~ **winds** des rafales de vent.

gut [gʌt] *n* intestin *m*, boyau *m*; (*MUS etc*) boyau ♦ *vt* (*poultry, fish*) vider; (*building*) ne laisser que les murs de; ~**s** *npl* boyaux *mpl*; (*col: courage*) cran *m*; **to hate sb's** ~**s** ne pas pouvoir voir qn en peinture *or* sentir qn.

gut reaction *n* réaction instinctive.

gutsy ['gʌtsɪ] *adj* (*person*) qui a du cran; (*style*) qui a du punch.

gutted ['gʌtɪd] *adj*: **I was** ~ (*col: disappointed*) j'étais carrément dégoûté.

gutter ['gʌtə*] *n* (*of roof*) gouttière *f*; (*in street*) caniveau *m*; (*fig*) ruisseau *m*.

gutter press *n*: **the** ~ la presse de bas étage *or* à scandale.

guttural ['gʌtərl] *adj* guttural(e).

guy [gaɪ] *n* (*also*: ~**rope**) corde *f*; (*col: man*) type *m*; (*figure*) effigie de Guy Fawkes.

Guyana [gaɪ'ænə] *n* Guyane *f*.

Guy Fawkes' Night, *que l'on appelle également "bonfire night", commémore l'échec du complot (le "Gunpowder Plot") contre James Ist et son parlement le 5 novembre 1605. L'un des conspirateurs, Guy Fawkes, avait été surpris dans les caves du parlement alors qu'il s'apprêtait à y mettre le feu. Chaque année pour le 5 novembre, les enfants préparent à l'avance une effigie de Guy Fawkes et ils demandent aux passants "un penny pour le guy" avec lequel ils pourront s'acheter des fusées de feu d'artifice. Beaucoup de gens font encore un feu dans leur jardin sur lequel ils brûlent le "guy".*

---

guzzle ['gʌzl] *vi* s'empiffrer ♦ *vt* avaler gloutonnement.

gym [dʒɪm] *n* (*also*: **gymnasium**) gymnase *m*; (*also*: **gymnastics**) gym *f*.

gymkhana [dʒɪm'kɑːnə] *n* gymkhana *m*.

gymnasium [dʒɪm'neɪzɪəm] *n* gymnase *m*.

gymnast ['dʒɪmnæst] *n* gymnaste *m/f*.

gymnastics [dʒɪm'næstɪks] *n*, *npl* gymnastique *f*.

gym shoes *npl* chaussures *fpl* de gym(nastique).

gym slip *n* (*BRIT*) tunique *f* (d'écolière).

gynaecologist, (*US*) **gynecologist** [gaɪnɪ-'kɔlədʒɪst] *n* gynécologue *m/f*.

gynaecology, (*US*) **gynecology** [gaɪnə-'kɔlədʒɪ] *n* gynécologie *f*.

gypsy ['dʒɪpsɪ] *n* = **gipsy**.

gyrate [dʒaɪ'reɪt] *vi* tournoyer.

gyroscope ['dʒaɪərəskəup] *n* gyroscope *m*.

H h

H, h [eɪtʃ] *n* (*letter*) H, h *m*; **H for Harry**, (*US*) **H for How** H comme Henri.

habeas corpus ['heɪbɪəs'kɔːpəs] *n* (*LAW*) habeas corpus *m*.

haberdashery [hæbə'dæʃərɪ] *n* (*BRIT*) mercerie *f*.

habit ['hæbɪt] *n* habitude *f*; (*costume*) habit *m*, tenue *f*; **to get out of/into the** ~ **of doing sth** perdre/prendre l'habitude de faire qch.

habitable ['hæbɪtəbl] *adj* habitable.

habitat ['hæbɪtæt] *n* habitat *m*.

habitation [hæbɪ'teɪʃən] *n* habitation *f*.

habitual [hə'bɪtjuəl] *adj* habituel(le); (*drinker, liar*) invétéré(e).

habitually [hə'bɪtjuəlɪ] *adv* habituellement, d'habitude.

hack [hæk] *vt* hacher, tailler ♦ *n* (*cut*) entaille *f*; (*blow*) coup *m*; (*pej: writer*) nègre *m*; (*old horse*) canasson *m*.

hackles ['hæklz] *npl*: **to make sb's** ~ **rise** (*fig*) mettre qn hors de soi.

hackney cab ['hæknɪ-] *n* fiacre *m*.

hackneyed ['hæknɪd] *adj* usé(e), rebattu(e).

hacksaw ['hæksɔː] *n* scie *f* à métaux.

had [hæd] *pt, pp of* **have**.

haddock, *pl* ~ *or* ~**s** ['hædək] *n* églefin *m*; **smoked** ~ haddock *m*.

hadn't ['hædnt] = **had not**.

haematology, (*US*) **hematology** ['hiːmə-'tɔlədʒɪ] *n* hématologie *f*.

haemoglobin, (*US*) **hemoglobin** ['hiːmə-'gləubɪn] *n* hémoglobine *f*.

haemophilia, (*US*) **hemophilia** ['hiːmə'fɪlɪə] *n* hémophilie *f*.

haemorrhage, (*US*) **hemorrhage** ['hɛmə-rɪdʒ] *n* hémorragie *f*.

haemorrhoids, (*US*) **hemorrhoids** ['hɛmə-rɔɪdz] *npl* hémorroïdes *fpl*.

hag [hæg] *n* (*ugly*) vieille sorcière; (*nasty*) chameau *m*, harpie *f*; (*witch*) sorcière.

haggard ['hægəd] *adj* hagard(e), égaré(e).

haggis ['hægɪs] *n* haggis *m*.

haggle ['hægl] *vi* marchander; **to** ~ **over** chicaner sur.

haggling ['hæglɪŋ] *n* marchandage *m*.

Hague [heɪg] *n*: **The** ~ La Haye.

hail [heɪl] *n* grêle *f* ♦ *vt* (*call*) héler; (*greet*) acclamer ♦ *vi* grêler; (*originate*): **he** ~**s from Scotland** il est originaire d'Écosse.

hailstone ['heɪlstəun] *n* grêlon *m*.

hailstorm ['heɪlstɔːm] *n* averse *f* de grêle.

hair [hɛə*] *n* cheveux *mpl*; (*on body*) poils *mpl*,

pilosité f; (single hair: on head) cheveu m; (: on body) poil m; **to do one's** ~ se coiffer.

hairbrush ['hɛəbrʌʃ] n brosse f à cheveux.

haircut ['hɛəkʌt] n coupe f (de cheveux).

hairdo ['hɛədu:] n coiffure f.

hairdresser ['hɛədrɛsə*] n coiffeur/euse.

hair-dryer ['hɛədraɪə*] n sèche-cheveux m.

-haired [hɛəd] suffix: **fair/long**~ aux cheveux blonds/longs.

hair gel n gel m pour cheveux.

hairgrip ['hɛəgrɪp] n pince f à cheveux.

hairline ['hɛəlaɪn] n naissance f des cheveux.

hairline fracture n fêlure f.

hairnet ['hɛənɛt] n résille f.

hair oil n huile f capillaire.

hairpiece ['hɛəpiːs] n postiche m.

hairpin ['hɛəpɪn] n épingle f à cheveux.

hairpin bend, (US**) hairpin curve** n virage m en épingle à cheveux.

hairraising ['hɛəreɪzɪŋ] adj à (vous) faire dresser les cheveux sur la tête.

hair remover n dépilateur m.

hair spray n laque f (pour les cheveux).

hairstyle ['hɛəstaɪl] n coiffure f.

hairy ['hɛərɪ] adj poilu(e); chevelu(e); (fig) effrayant(e).

Haiti ['heɪtɪ] n Haïti m.

hake [heɪk] n colin m, merlu m.

halcyon ['hælsɪən] adj merveilleux(euse).

hale [heɪl] adj: ~ **and hearty** robuste, en pleine santé.

half [hɑːf] n (pl **halves** [hɑːvz]) moitié f; (SPORT: of match) mi-temps f; (: of ground) moitié (du terrain) ♦ adj demi(e) ♦ adv (à) moitié, à demi; ~-**an-hour** une demi-heure; ~ **a dozen** une demi-douzaine; ~ **a pound** une demi-livre, ≈ 250 g; **two and a** ~ deux et demi; **a week and a** ~ une semaine et demie; ~ **(of it)** la moitié; ~ **(of)** la moitié de; ~ **the amount of** la moitié de; **to cut sth in** ~ couper qch en deux; ~ **past three** trois heures et demie; ~ **empty/closed** à moitié vide/fermé; **to go halves (with sb)** se mettre de moitié avec qn.

half-back ['hɑːfbæk] n (SPORT) demi m.

half-baked ['hɑːf'beɪkt] adj (col: idea, scheme) qui ne tient pas debout.

half-breed ['hɑːfbriːd] n = **halfcaste**.

half-brother ['hɑːfbrʌðə*] n demi-frère m.

half-caste ['hɑːfkɑːst] n métis/se.

half-hearted ['hɑːf'hɑːtɪd] adj tiède, sans enthousiasme.

half-hour [hɑːf'auə*] n demi-heure f.

half-mast ['hɑːf'mɑːst] n: **at** ~ (flag) en berne, à mi-mât.

halfpenny ['heɪpnɪ] n demi-penny m.

half-price ['hɑːf'praɪs] adj à moitié prix ♦ adv (also: **at** ~) à moitié prix.

half term n (BRIT SCOL) congé m de demi-trimestre.

half-time [hɑːf'taɪm] n mi-temps f.

halfway ['hɑːf'weɪ] adv à mi-chemin; **to meet**

sb ~ (fig) parvenir à un compromis avec qn.

halfway house n (hostel) centre m de réadaptation (pour anciens prisonniers, malades mentaux etc); (fig): **a** ~ **(between)** une étape intermédiaire (entre).

half-wit ['hɑːfwɪt] n (col) idiot/e, imbécile m/f.

half-yearly [hɑːf'jɪəlɪ] adv deux fois par an ♦ adj semestriel(le).

halibut ['hælɪbət] n (pl inv) flétan m.

halitosis [hælɪ'təʊsɪs] n mauvaise haleine.

hall [hɔːl] n salle f; (entrance way) hall m, entrée f; (corridor) couloir m; (mansion) château m, manoir m; ~ **of residence** n (BRIT) pavillon m or résidence f universitaire.

hallmark ['hɔːlmɑːk] n poinçon m; (fig) marque f.

hallo [hə'ləʊ] excl = **hello**.

Hallowe'en ['hæləʊ'iːn] n veille f de la Toussaint.

Selon la tradition, **Hallowe'en** est la nuit des fantômes et des sorcières. En Écosse et aux États-Unis surtout (beaucoup moins en Angleterre) les enfants, pour fêter Hallowe'en, se déguisent ce soir-là et ils vont ainsi de porte en porte en demandant de petits cadeaux (du chocolat, une pomme etc).

---

hallucination [həluːsɪ'neɪʃən] n hallucination f.

hallucinogenic [həluːsɪnəʊ'dʒɛnɪk] adj hallucinogène.

hallway ['hɔːlweɪ] n vestibule m; couloir m.

halo ['heɪləʊ] n (of saint etc) auréole f; (of sun) halo m.

halt [hɔːlt] n halte f, arrêt m ♦ vt faire arrêter ♦ vi faire halte, s'arrêter; **to call a** ~ **to sth** (fig) mettre fin à qch.

halter ['hɔːltə*] n (for horse) licou m.

halterneck ['hɔːltənɛk] adj (dress) (avec) dos nu inv.

halve [hɑːv] vt (apple etc) partager or diviser en deux; (reduce by half) réduire de moitié.

halves [hɑːvz] npl of **half**.

ham [hæm] n jambon m; (col: also: **radio** ~) radio-amateur m; (: also: ~ **actor**) cabotin/e.

Hamburg ['hæmbɜːg] n Hambourg.

hamburger ['hæmbɜːgə*] n hamburger m.

ham-fisted ['hæm'fɪstɪd], (US) **ham-handed** ['hæm'hændɪd] adj maladroit(e).

hamlet ['hæmlɪt] n hameau m.

hammer ['hæmə*] n marteau m ♦ vt (fig) éreinter, démolir ♦ vi (at door) frapper à coups redoublés; **to** ~ **a point home to sb** faire rentrer qch dans la tête de qn.

▶**hammer out** vt (metal) étendre au marteau; (fig: solution) élaborer.

hammock ['hæmək] n hamac m.

hamper ['hæmpə*] vt gêner ♦ n panier m (d'osier).

hamster ['hæmstə*] n hamster m.

hamstring ['hæmstrɪŋ] n (ANAT) tendon m du

jarret.

hand [hænd] _n_ main _f_; (_of clock_) aiguille _f_; (_handwriting_) écriture _f_; (_at cards_) jeu _m_; (_measurement: of horse_) paume _f_; (_worker_) ouvrier/ière ♦ _vt_ passer, donner; **to give sb a ~** donner un coup de main à qn; **at ~** à portée de la main; **in ~** en main; (_work_) en cours; **we have the situation in ~** nous avons la situation bien en main; **to be on ~** (_person_) être disponible; (_emergency services_) se tenir prêt(e) (à intervenir); **to ~** (_information etc_) sous la main, à portée de la main; **to force sb's ~** forcer la main à qn; **to have a free ~** avoir carte blanche; **to have sth in one's ~** tenir qch à la main; **on the one ~ ..., on the other ~** d'une part ..., d'autre part.

►**hand down** _vt_ passer; (_tradition, heirloom_) transmettre; (_US: sentence, verdict_) prononcer.

►**hand in** _vt_ remettre.

►**hand out** _vt_ distribuer.

►**hand over** _vt_ remettre; (_powers etc_) transmettre.

►**hand round** _vt_ (_BRIT: information_) faire circuler; (_: chocolates etc_) faire passer.

handbag ['hændbæg] _n_ sac _m_ à main.

hand baggage _n_ bagages _mpl_ à main; **one item of ~** un bagage à main.

handball ['hændbɔːl] _n_ handball _m_.

handbasin ['hændbeɪsn] _n_ lavabo _m_.

handbook ['hændbuk] _n_ manuel _m_.

handbrake ['hændbreɪk] _n_ frein _m_ à main.

h & c _abbr_ (_BRIT_) = hot and cold (water).

hand cream _n_ crème _f_ pour les mains.

handcuffs ['hændkʌfs] _npl_ menottes _fpl_.

handful ['hændful] _n_ poignée _f_.

hand-held ['hænd'held] _adj_ à main.

handicap ['hændɪkæp] _n_ handicap _m_ ♦ _vt_ handicaper; **mentally/physically ~ped** handicapé(e) mentalement/physiquement.

handicraft ['hændɪkrɑːft] _n_ travail _m_ d'artisanat, technique artisanale.

handiwork ['hændɪwəːk] _n_ ouvrage _m_; **this looks like his ~** (_pej_) ça a tout l'air d'être son œuvre.

handkerchief ['hæŋkətʃɪf] _n_ mouchoir _m_.

handle ['hændl] _n_ (_of door etc_) poignée _f_; (_of cup etc_) anse _f_; (_of knife etc_) manche _m_; (_of saucepan_) queue _f_; (_for winding_) manivelle _f_ ♦ _vt_ toucher, manier; (_deal with_) s'occuper de; (_treat: people_) prendre; **"~ with care"** "fragile".

handlebar(s) ['hændlbɑː(z)] _n(pl)_ guidon _m_.

handling ['hændlɪŋ] _n_ (_AUT_) maniement _m_; (_treatment_): **his ~ of the matter** la façon dont il a traité l'affaire.

handling charges _npl_ frais _mpl_ de manutention; (_BANKING_) agios _mpl_.

hand-luggage ['hændlʌgɪdʒ] _n_ bagages _mpl_ à main.

handmade ['hænd'meɪd] _adj_ fait(e) à la main.

handout ['hændaut] _n_ documentation _f_, prospectus _m_; (_press ~_) communiqué _m_ de presse.

hand-picked ['hænd'pɪkt] _adj_ (_produce_) cueilli(e) à la main; (_staff etc_) trié(e) sur le volet.

handrail ['hændreɪl] _n_ (_on staircase etc_) rampe _f_, main courante.

handset ['hændset] _n_ (_TEL_) combiné _m_.

handshake ['hændʃeɪk] _n_ poignée _f_ de main; (_COMPUT_) établissement _m_ de la liaison.

handsome ['hænsəm] _adj_ beau(belle); (_gift_) généreux(euse); (_profit_) considérable.

hands-on [hændz'ɔn] _adj_ (_training, experience_) sur le tas; **she has a very ~ approach** sa politique est de mettre la main à la pâte.

handstand ['hændstænd] _n_: **to do a ~** faire l'arbre droit.

hand-to-mouth ['hændtə'mauθ] _adj_ (_existence_) au jour le jour.

handwriting ['hændraɪtɪŋ] _n_ écriture _f_.

handwritten ['hændrɪtn] _adj_ manuscrit(e), écrit(e) à la main.

handy ['hændɪ] _adj_ (_person_) adroit(e); (_close at hand_) sous la main; (_convenient_) pratique; **to come in ~** être (_or_ s'avérer) utile.

handyman ['hændɪmæn] _n_ bricoleur _m_; (_servant_) homme _m_ à tout faire.

hang, _pt, pp_ **hung** [hæŋ, hʌŋ] _vt_ accrocher; (_criminal: pt, pp_ **hanged**) pendre ♦ _vi_ pendre; (_hair, drapery_) tomber ♦ _n_: **to get the ~ of (doing) sth** (_col_) attraper le coup pour faire qch.

►**hang about** _vi_ flâner, traîner.

►**hang back** _vi_ (_hesitate_): **to ~ back (from doing)** être réticent(e) (pour faire).

►**hang on** _vi_ (_wait_) attendre ♦ _vt fus_ (_depend on_) dépendre de; **to ~ on to** (_keep hold of_) ne pas lâcher; (_keep_) garder.

►**hang out** _vt_ (_washing_) étendre (dehors) ♦ _vi_ pendre; (_col: live_) habiter, percher.

►**hang together** _vi_ (_argument etc_) se tenir, être cohérent(e).

►**hang up** _vi_ (_TEL_) raccrocher ♦ _vt_ accrocher, suspendre; **to ~ up on sb** (_TEL_) raccrocher au nez de qn.

hangar ['hæŋə*] _n_ hangar _m_.

hangdog ['hæŋdɔg] _adj_ (_look, expression_) de chien battu.

hanger ['hæŋə*] _n_ cintre _m_, portemanteau _m_.

hanger-on [hæŋər'ɔn] _n_ parasite _m_.

hang-glider ['hæŋglaɪdə*] _n_ deltaplane _m_.

hang-gliding ['hæŋglaɪdɪŋ] _n_ vol _m_ libre _or_ sur aile delta.

hanging ['hæŋɪŋ] _n_ (_execution_) pendaison _f_.

hangman ['hæŋmən] _n_ bourreau _m_.

hangover ['hæŋəuvə*] _n_ (_after drinking_) gueule _f_ de bois.

hang-up ['hæŋʌp] _n_ complexe _m_.

hank [hæŋk] _n_ écheveau _m_.

hanker ['hæŋkə*] _vi_: **to ~ after** avoir envie de.

hankering ['hæŋkərɪŋ] _n_: **to have a ~ for/to do sth** avoir une grande envie de/de faire qch.

hankie, hanky ['hæŋkɪ] *n abbr* = **handkerchief**.

Hants *abbr* (*BRIT*) = Hampshire.

haphazard [hæp'hæzəd] *adj* fait(e) au hasard, fait(e) au petit bonheur.

hapless ['hæplɪs] *adj* malheureux(euse).

happen ['hæpən] *vi* arriver, se passer, se produire; **what's ~ing?** que se passe-t-il?; **she ~ed to be free** il s'est trouvé (*or* se trouvait) qu'elle était libre; **if anything ~ed to him** s'il lui arrivait quoi que ce soit; **as it ~s** justement.

►**happen (up)on** *vt fus* tomber sur.

happening ['hæpnɪŋ] *n* événement *m*.

happily ['hæpɪlɪ] *adv* heureusement.

happiness ['hæpɪnɪs] *n* bonheur *m*.

happy ['hæpɪ] *adj* heureux(euse); **~ with** (*arrangements etc*) satisfait(e) de; **yes, I'd be ~ to** oui, avec plaisir *or* (bien) volontiers; **~ birthday!** bon anniversaire!; **~ Christmas/New Year!** joyeux Noël/bonne année!

happy-go-lucky ['hæpɪɡəʊ'lʌkɪ] *adj* insouciant(e).

happy hour *n* l'heure *f* de l'apéritif, *heure pendant laquelle les consommations sont à prix réduit.*

harangue [hə'ræŋ] *vt* haranguer.

harass ['hærəs] *vt* accabler, tourmenter.

harassed ['hærəst] *adj* tracassé(e).

harassment ['hærəsmənt] *n* tracasseries *fpl*.

harbour, (*US*) **harbor** ['hɑ:bə*] *n* port *m* ♦ *vt* héberger, abriter; (*hopes, suspicions*) entretenir; **to ~ a grudge against sb** en vouloir à qn.

harbo(u)r dues *npl* droits *mpl* de port.

harbo(u)r master *n* capitaine *m* du port.

hard [hɑ:d] *adj* dur(e) ♦ *adv* (*work*) dur; (*think, try*) sérieusement; **to look ~ at** regarder fixement; regarder de près; **to drink ~** boire sec; **~ luck!** pas de veine!; **no ~ feelings!** sans rancune!; **to be ~ of hearing** être dur(e) d'oreille; **to be ~ done by** être traité(e) injustement; **to be ~ on sb** être dur(e) avec qn; **I find it ~ to believe that ...** je n'arrive pas à croire que ....

hard-and-fast ['hɑ:dən'fɑ:st] *adj* strict(e), absolu(e).

hardback ['hɑ:dbæk] *n* livre relié.

hardboard ['hɑ:dbɔ:d] *n* Isorel *m* ®.

hard-boiled egg ['hɑ:d'bɔɪld-] *n* œuf dur.

hard cash *n* espèces *fpl*.

hard copy *n* (*COMPUT*) sortie *f* or copie *f* papier.

hard-core ['hɑ:d'kɔ:*] *adj* (*pornography*) (dit(e)) dur(e); (*supporters*) inconditionnel(le).

hard court *n* (*TENNIS*) court *m* en dur.

hard disk *n* (*COMPUT*) disque dur.

harden ['hɑ:dn] *vt* durcir; (*steel*) tremper; (*fig*) endurcir ♦ *vi* (*substance*) durcir.

hardened ['hɑ:dnd] *adj* (*criminal*) endurci(e); **to be ~ to sth** s'être endurci(e) à qch, être (devenu(e)) insensible à qch.

hardening ['hɑ:dnɪŋ] *n* durcissement *m*.

hard-headed ['hɑ:d'hedɪd] *adj* réaliste; décidé(e).

hard-hearted ['hɑ:d'hɑ:tɪd] *adj* dur(e), impitoyable.

hard-hitting ['hɑ:d'hɪtɪŋ] *adj* (*speech, article*) sans complaisances.

hard labour *n* travaux forcés.

hardliner [hɑ:d'laɪnə*] *n* intransigeant/e, dur/e.

hard-luck story [hɑ:d'lʌk-] *n* histoire larmoyante.

hardly ['hɑ:dlɪ] *adv* (*scarcely*) à peine; (*harshly*) durement; **it's ~ the case** ce n'est guère le cas; **~ anywhere/ever** presque nulle part/jamais; **I can ~ believe it** j'ai du mal à le croire.

hardness ['hɑ:dnɪs] *n* dureté *f*.

hard-nosed ['hɑ:d'nəʊzd] *adj* impitoyable, dur(e).

hard-pressed ['hɑ:d'prest] *adj* sous pression.

hard sell *n* vente agressive.

hardship ['hɑ:dʃɪp] *n* épreuves *fpl*; privations *fpl*.

hard shoulder *n* (*BRIT AUT*) accotement stabilisé.

hard-up [hɑ:d'ʌp] *adj* (*col*) fauché(e).

hardware ['hɑ:dwɛə*] *n* quincaillerie *f*; (*COMPUT*) matériel *m*.

hardware shop *n* quincaillerie *f*.

hard-wearing [hɑ:d'wɛərɪŋ] *adj* solide.

hard-won ['hɑ:d'wʌn] *adj* (si) durement gagné(e).

hard-working [hɑ:d'wə:kɪŋ] *adj* travailleur(euse), consciencieux(euse).

hardy ['hɑ:dɪ] *adj* robuste; (*plant*) résistant(e) au gel.

hare [hɛə*] *n* lièvre *m*.

hare-brained ['hɛəbreɪnd] *adj* farfelu(e); écervelé(e).

harelip ['hɛəlɪp] *n* (*MED*) bec-de-lièvre *m*.

harem [hɑ:'ri:m] *n* harem *m*.

hark back [hɑ:k-] *vi*: **to ~ to** (en) revenir toujours à.

harm [hɑ:m] *n* mal *m*; (*wrong*) tort *m* ♦ *vt* (*person*) faire du mal *or* du tort à; (*thing*) endommager; **to mean no ~** ne pas avoir de mauvaises intentions; **there's no ~ in trying** on peut toujours essayer; **out of ~'s way** à l'abri du danger, en lieu sûr.

harmful ['hɑ:mful] *adj* nuisible.

harmless [hɑ:mlɪs] *adj* inoffensif(ive); sans méchanceté.

harmonic [hɑ:'mɒnɪk] *adj* harmonique.

harmonica [hɑ:'mɒnɪkə] *n* harmonica *m*.

harmonics [hɑ:'mɒnɪks] *npl* harmoniques *mpl or fpl*.

harmonious [hɑ:'məʊnɪəs] *adj* harmonieux(euse).

harmonium [hɑ:'məʊnɪəm] *n* harmonium *m*.

harmonize [hɑ:mənaɪz] *vt* harmoniser ♦ *vi* s'harmoniser.

harmony ['hɑːmənɪ] *n* harmonie *f*.
harness ['hɑːnɪs] *n* harnais *m* ♦ *vt* (*horse*) harnacher; (*resources*) exploiter.
harp [hɑːp] *n* harpe *f* ♦ *vi*: **to ~ on about** parler tout le temps de.
harpist ['hɑːpɪst] *n* harpiste *m/f*.
harpoon [hɑːˈpuːn] *n* harpon *m*.
harpsichord ['hɑːpsɪkɔːd] *n* clavecin *m*.
harrow ['hærəʊ] *n* (*AGR*) herse *f*.
harrowing ['hærəʊɪŋ] *adj* déchirant(e).
harry ['hærɪ] *vt* (*MIL*, *fig*) harceler.
harsh [hɑːʃ] *adj* (*hard*) dur(e), sévère; (*rough: surface*) rugueux(euse); (*: sound*) discordant(e); (*: taste*) âpre.
harshly ['hɑːʃlɪ] *adv* durement, sévèrement.
harshness ['hɑːʃnɪs] *n* dureté *f*, sévérité *f*.
harvest ['hɑːvɪst] *n* (*of corn*) moisson *f*; (*of fruit*) récolte *f*; (*of grapes*) vendange *f* ♦ *vi*, *vt* moissonner; récolter; vendanger.
harvester ['hɑːvɪstə*] *n* (*machine*) moissonneuse *f*; (*also*: **combine ~**) moissonneuse-batteuse(-lieuse *f*) *f*; (*person*) moissonneur/euse.
has [hæz] *vb see* **have**.
has-been ['hæzbiːn] *n* (*col: person*): **he/she's a ~** il/elle a fait son temps *or* est fini(e).
hash [hæʃ] *n* (*CULIN*) hachis *m*; (*fig: mess*) gâchis *m* ♦ *n abbr* (*col*) = **hashish**.
hashish ['hæʃɪʃ] *n* haschisch *m*.
hasn't ['hæznt] = **has not**.
hassle ['hæsl] *n* (*col: fuss*) histoire(s) *f(pl)*.
haste [heɪst] *n* hâte *f*, précipitation *f*; **in ~** à la hâte, précipitamment.
hasten ['heɪsn] *vt* hâter, accélérer ♦ *vi* se hâter, s'empresser; **I ~ to add that** ... je m'empresse d'ajouter que ....
hastily ['heɪstɪlɪ] *adv* à la hâte, précipitamment.
hasty ['heɪstɪ] *adj* hâtif(ive), précipité(e).
hat [hæt] *n* chapeau *m*.
hatbox ['hætbɔks] *n* carton *m* à chapeau.
hatch [hætʃ] *n* (*NAUT: also*: **~way**) écoutille *f*; (*BRIT: also*: **service ~**) passe-plats *m inv* ♦ *vi* éclore ♦ *vt* faire éclore; (*fig: scheme*) tramer, ourdir.
hatchback ['hætʃbæk] *n* (*AUT*) modèle *m* avec hayon arrière.
hatchet ['hætʃɪt] *n* hachette *f*.
hatchet job *n* (*col*) démolissage *m*.
hatchet man *n* (*col*) homme *m* de main.
hate [heɪt] *vt* haïr, détester ♦ *n* haine *f*; **to ~ to do** *or* **doing** détester faire; **I ~ to trouble you, but** ... désolé de vous déranger, mais ....
hateful ['heɪtful] *adj* odieux(euse), détestable.
hatred ['heɪtrɪd] *n* haine *f*.
hat trick *n* (*BRIT SPORT, also fig*): **to get a ~** réussir trois coups (*or* gagner trois matchs *etc*) consécutifs.
haughty ['hɔːtɪ] *adj* hautain(e), arrogant(e).
haul [hɔːl] *vt* traîner, tirer; (*by lorry*) camionner; (*NAUT*) haler ♦ *n* (*of fish*) prise *f*; (*of stolen goods etc*) butin *m*.
haulage ['hɔːlɪdʒ] *n* transport routier.
haulage contractor *n* (*BRIT: firm*) entreprise *f* de transport (routier); (*: person*) transporteur routier.
haulier ['hɔːlɪə*], (*US*) **hauler** ['hɔːlə*] *n* transporteur (routier), camionneur *m*.
haunch [hɔːntʃ] *n* hanche *f*; **~ of venison** cuissot *m* de chevreuil.
haunt [hɔːnt] *vt* (*subj: ghost, fear*) hanter; (*: person*) fréquenter ♦ *n* repaire *m*.
haunted ['hɔːntɪd] *adj* (*castle etc*) hanté(e); (*look*) égaré(e), hagard(e).
haunting ['hɔːntɪŋ] *adj* (*sight, music*) obsédant(e).
Havana [həˈvænə] *n* La Havane.

═══════════════════════════════ *KEYWORD*

have [hæv] (*pt*, *pp* **had**) *aux vb* **1** (*gen*) avoir; être; **to ~ arrived/gone** être arrivé(e)/allé(e); **to ~ eaten/slept** avoir mangé/dormi; **he has been promoted** il a eu une promotion
2 (*in tag questions*): **you've done it, ~n't you?** vous l'avez fait, n'est-ce pas?
3 (*in short answers and questions*): **no I ~n't!/yes we ~!** mais non!/mais si!; **so I ~!** ah oui!, oui c'est vrai!; **I've been there before, ~ you?** j'y suis déjà allé, et vous?
♦ *modal aux vb* (*be obliged*): **to ~ (got) to do sth** devoir faire qch; être obligé(e) de faire qch; **she has (got) to do it** elle doit le faire, il faut qu'elle le fasse; **you ~n't to tell her** vous n'êtes pas obligé de le lui dire; (*must not*) ne le lui dites surtout pas
♦ *vt* **1** (*possess, obtain*) avoir; **he has (got) blue eyes/dark hair** il a les yeux bleus/les cheveux bruns; **may I ~ your address?** puis-je avoir votre adresse?
2 (*+noun: take, hold etc*): **to ~ breakfast/a bath/a shower** prendre le petit déjeuner/un bain/une douche; **to ~ dinner/lunch** dîner/déjeuner; **to ~ a swim** nager; **to ~ a meeting** se réunir; **to ~ a party** organiser une fête; **let me ~ a try** laissez-moi essayer
3: **to ~ sth done** faire faire qch; **to ~ one's hair cut** se faire couper les cheveux; **to ~ sb do sth** faire faire qch à qn
4 (*experience, suffer*) avoir; **to ~ a cold/flu** avoir un rhume/la grippe; **to ~ an operation** se faire opérer; **I won't ~ it** cela ne se passera pas ainsi
5 (*inf: dupe*) avoir; **he's been had** il s'est fait avoir *or* rouler
▶**have out** *vt*: **to ~ it out with sb** (*settle a problem etc*) s'expliquer (franchement) avec qn.

═══════════════════════════════════════

haven ['heɪvn] *n* port *m*; (*fig*) havre *m*.
haversack ['hævəsæk] *n* sac *m* à dos.
haves [hævz] *npl* (*col*): **the ~ and have-nots** les riches et les pauvres.
havoc ['hævək] *n* ravages *mpl*, dégâts *mpl*;

to play ~ **with** (fig) désorganiser complètement; détraquer.

Hawaii [hə'waɪiː] n (îles fpl) Hawaii m.

Hawaiian [hə'waɪjən] adj hawaïen(ne) ♦ n Hawaïen/ne; (LING) hawaïen m.

hawk [hɔːk] n faucon m ♦ vt (goods for sale) colporter.

hawker ['hɔːkə*] n colporteur m.

hawkish ['hɔːkɪʃ] adj belliciste.

hawthorn ['hɔːθɔːn] n aubépine f.

hay [heɪ] n foin m.

hay fever n rhume m des foins.

haystack ['heɪstæk] n meule f de foin.

haywire ['heɪwaɪə*] adj (col): **to go** ~ perdre la tête; mal tourner.

hazard ['hæzəd] n (chance) hasard m, chance f; (risk) danger m, risque m ♦ vt risquer, hasarder; **to be a health/fire** ~ présenter un risque d'incendie/pour la santé; **to** ~ **a guess** émettre or hasarder une hypothèse.

hazardous ['hæzədəs] adj hasardeux(euse), risqué(e).

hazard pay n (US) prime f de risque.

hazard warning lights npl (AUT) feux mpl de détresse.

haze [heɪz] n brume f.

hazel [heɪzl] n (tree) noisetier m ♦ adj (eyes) noisette inv.

hazelnut ['heɪzlnʌt] n noisette f.

hazy ['heɪzɪ] adj brumeux(euse); (idea) vague; (photograph) flou(e).

H-bomb ['eɪtʃbɔm] n bombe f H.

HE abbr = high explosive; (REL, DIPLOMACY) = His (or Her) Excellency.

he [hiː] pron il; **it is** ~ **who** ... c'est lui qui ...; **here** ~ **is** le voici; ~**-bear** etc ours etc mâle.

head [hɛd] n tête f; (leader) chef m ♦ vt (list) être en tête de; (group) être à la tête de; ~**s** (on coin) (le côté) face; ~**s or tails** pile ou face; ~ **over heels in love** follement or éperdument amoureux(euse); **to** ~ **the ball** faire une tête; **10 francs a or per** ~ 10 F par personne; **to sit at the** ~ **of the table** présider la tablée; **to have a** ~ **for business** avoir des dispositions pour les affaires; **to have no** ~ **for heights** être sujet(te) au vertige; **to come to a** ~ (fig: situation etc) devenir critique.

► **head for** vt fus se diriger vers.

► **head off** vt (threat, danger) détourner.

headache ['hɛdeɪk] n mal m de tête; **to have a** ~ avoir mal à la tête.

headband ['hɛdbænd] n bandeau m.

headboard ['hɛdbɔːd] n dosseret m.

head cold n rhume m de cerveau.

headdress ['hɛddrɛs] n coiffure f.

headed notepaper ['hɛdɪd-] n papier m à lettres m en-tête.

header ['hɛdə*] n (BRIT col: FOOTBALL) (coup m de) tête f; (: fall) chute f (or plongeon m) la tête la première.

head-first ['hɛd'fɜːst] adv (lit) la tête la pre-

mière.

headhunt ['hɛdhʌnt] vt: **she was** ~**ed** elle a été recrutée par un chasseur de têtes.

headhunter ['hɛdhʌntə*] n chasseur m de têtes.

heading ['hɛdɪŋ] n titre m; (subject title) rubrique f.

headlamp ['hɛdlæmp] n = **headlight**.

headland ['hɛdlənd] n promontoire m, cap m.

headlight ['hɛdlaɪt] n phare m.

headline ['hɛdlaɪn] n titre m.

headlong ['hɛdlɔŋ] adv (fall) la tête la première; (rush) tête baissée.

headmaster [hɛd'mɑːstə*] n directeur m, proviseur m.

headmistress [hɛd'mɪstrɪs] n directrice f.

head office n siège m, direction f (générale).

head-on [hɛd'ɔn] adj (collision) de plein fouet.

headphones ['hɛdfəunz] npl casque m (à écouteurs).

headquarters (HQ) ['hɛdkwɔːtəz] npl (of business) siège m, direction f (générale); (MIL) quartier général.

head-rest ['hɛdrɛst] n appui-tête m.

headroom ['hɛdrum] n (in car) hauteur f de plafond; (under bridge) hauteur limite; dégagement m.

headscarf ['hɛdskɑːf] n foulard m.

headset ['hɛdsɛt] n = **headphones**.

headstone ['hɛdstəun] n (on grave) pierre tombale.

headstrong ['hɛdstrɔŋ] adj têtu(e), entêté(e).

head waiter n maître m d'hôtel.

headway ['hɛdweɪ] n: **to make** ~ avancer, faire des progrès.

headwind ['hɛdwɪnd] n vent m contraire.

heady ['hɛdɪ] adj capiteux(euse); enivrant(e).

heal [hiːl] vt, vi guérir.

health [hɛlθ] n santé f; **Department of H**~ (US) ≈ ministère m de la Santé; **Department of H**~ **(DH)** (BRIT) ≈ ministère m de la Santé.

health care n services médicaux.

health centre n (BRIT) centre m de santé.

health food(s) n(pl) aliment(s) naturel(s).

health food shop n magasin m diététique.

health hazard n risque m pour la santé.

Health Service n: **the** ~ (BRIT) ≈ la Sécurité Sociale.

healthy ['hɛlθɪ] adj (person) en bonne santé; (climate, food, attitude etc) sain(e).

heap [hiːp] n tas m, monceau m ♦ vt entasser, amonceler; ~**s (of)** (col: lots) des tas (de); **to** ~ **favours/praise/gifts** etc **on sb** combler qn de faveurs/d'éloges/de cadeaux etc.

hear, pt, pp **heard** [hɪə*, hɜːd] vt entendre; (news) apprendre; (lecture) assister à, écouter ♦ vi entendre; **to** ~ **about** entendre parler de; (have news of) avoir des nouvelles de; **did you** ~ **about the move?** tu es au courant du déménagement?; **to** ~ **from sb** recevoir des nouvelles de qn; **I've never heard of that book** je n'ai jamais entendu parler de ce livre.

▶**hear out** *vt* écouter jusqu'au bout.

hearing ['hɪərɪŋ] *n* (*sense*) ouïe *f*; (*of witnesses*) audition *f*; (*of a case*) audience *f*; (*of committee*) séance *f*; **to give sb a ~** (*BRIT*) écouter ce que qn a à dire.

hearing aid *n* appareil *m* acoustique.

hearsay ['hɪəseɪ] *n* on-dit *mpl*, rumeurs *fpl*; **by ~** *adv* par ouï-dire.

hearse [hɜːs] *n* corbillard *m*.

heart [hɑːt] *n* cœur *m*; **~s** *npl* (*CARDS*) cœur; **at ~** au fond; **by ~** (*learn, know*) par cœur; **to have a weak ~** avoir le cœur malade, avoir des problèmes de cœur; **to lose ~** perdre courage, se décourager; **to take ~** prendre courage; **to set one's ~ on sth/on doing sth** vouloir absolument qch/faire qch; **the ~ of the matter** le fond du problème.

heartache ['hɑːteɪk] *n* chagrin *m*, douleur *f*.

heart attack *n* crise *f* cardiaque.

heartbeat ['hɑːtbiːt] *n* battement *m* de cœur.

heartbreak ['hɑːtbreɪk] *n* immense chagrin *m*.

heartbreaking ['hɑːtbreɪkɪŋ] *adj* navrant(e), déchirant(e).

heartbroken ['hɑːtbrəukən] *adj*: **to be ~** avoir beaucoup de chagrin.

heartburn ['hɑːtbəːn] *n* brûlures *fpl* d'estomac.

-hearted ['hɑːtɪd] *suffix*: **kind~** généreux(euse), qui a bon cœur.

heartening ['hɑːtnɪŋ] *adj* encourageant(e), réconfortant(e).

heart failure *n* (*MED*) arrêt *m* du cœur.

heartfelt ['hɑːtfɛlt] *adj* sincère.

hearth [hɑːθ] *n* foyer *m*, cheminée *f*.

heartily ['hɑːtɪlɪ] *adv* chaleureusement; (*laugh*) de bon cœur; (*eat*) de bon appétit; **to agree ~** être entièrement d'accord; **to be ~ sick of** (*BRIT*) en avoir ras le bol de.

heartland ['hɑːtlænd] *n* centre *m*, cœur *m*; **France's ~s** la France profonde.

heartless ['hɑːtlɪs] *adj* sans cœur, insensible, cruel(le).

heartstrings ['hɑːtstrɪŋz] *npl*: **to tug (at) sb's ~** toucher *or* faire vibrer les cordes sensibles de qn.

heartthrob ['hɑːtθrɔb] *n* idole *f*.

heart-to-heart ['hɑːt'tə'hɑːt] *adj, adv* à cœur ouvert.

heart transplant *n* greffe *f* du cœur.

heartwarming ['hɑːtwɔːmɪŋ] *adj* réconfortant(e).

hearty ['hɑːtɪ] *adj* chaleureux(euse); robuste, vigoureux(euse).

heat [hiːt] *n* chaleur *f*; (*fig*) ardeur *f*; feu *m*; (*SPORT*: *also*: **qualifying ~**) éliminatoire *f*; (*ZOOL*): **in** *or* (*BRIT*) **on ~** en chaleur ♦ *vt* chauffer.

▶**heat up** *vi* (*liquids*) chauffer; (*room*) se réchauffer ♦ *vt* réchauffer.

heated ['hiːtɪd] *adj* chauffé(e); (*fig*) passionné(e); échauffé(e), excité(e).

heater ['hiːtə*] *n* appareil *m* de chauffage; radiateur *m*.

heath [hiːθ] *n* (*BRIT*) lande *f*.

heathen ['hiːðn] *adj*, *n* païen(ne).

heather ['hɛðə*] *n* bruyère *f*.

heating ['hiːtɪŋ] *n* chauffage *m*.

heat-resistant ['hiːtrɪzɪstənt] *adj* résistant(e) à la chaleur.

heat-seeking ['hiːtsiːkɪŋ] *adj* guidé(e) par infrarouge.

heatstroke ['hiːtstrəuk] *n* coup *m* de chaleur.

heatwave ['hiːtweɪv] *n* vague *f* de chaleur.

heave [hiːv] *vt* soulever (avec effort) ♦ *vi* se soulever; (*retch*) avoir des haut-le-cœur ♦ *n* (*push*) poussée *f*; **to ~ a sigh** pousser un gros soupir.

heaven ['hɛvn] *n* ciel *m*, paradis *m*; **~ forbid!** surtout pas!; **thank ~!** Dieu merci!; **for ~'s sake!** (*pleading*) je vous en prie!; (*protesting*) mince alors!

heavenly ['hɛvnlɪ] *adj* céleste, divin(e).

heavily ['hɛvɪlɪ] *adv* lourdement; (*drink, smoke*) beaucoup; (*sleep, sigh*) profondément.

heavy ['hɛvɪ] *adj* lourd(e); (*work, rain, user, eater*) gros(se); (*drinker, smoker*) grand(e); **it's ~ going** ça ne va pas tout seul, c'est pénible.

heavy cream *n* (*US*) crème fraîche épaisse.

heavy-duty ['hɛvɪ'djuːtɪ] *adj* à usage intensif.

heavy goods vehicle (HGV) *n* (*BRIT*) poids lourd *m* (P.L.).

heavy-handed ['hɛvɪ'hændɪd] *adj* (*fig*) maladroit(e), qui manque de tact.

heavy metal *n* (*MUS*) heavy metal *m*.

heavy-set ['hɛvɪ'sɛt] *adj* (*esp US*) costaud(e).

heavyweight ['hɛvɪweɪt] *n* (*SPORT*) poids lourd.

Hebrew ['hiːbruː] *adj* hébraïque ♦ *n* (*LING*) hébreu *m*.

Hebrides ['hɛbrɪdiːz] *n*: **the ~** les Hébrides *fpl*.

heck [hɛk] *n* (*col*): **why the ~ ...?** pourquoi diable ...?; **a ~ of a lot** une sacrée quantité; **he has done a ~ of a lot for us** il a vraiment beaucoup fait pour nous.

heckle ['hɛkl] *vt* interpeller (*un orateur*).

heckler ['hɛklə*] *n* interrupteur *m*; élément perturbateur.

hectare ['hɛktɑː*] *n* (*BRIT*) hectare *m*.

hectic ['hɛktɪk] *adj* agité(e), trépidant(e); (*busy*) trépidant(e).

hector ['hɛktə*] *vt* rudoyer, houspiller.

he'd [hiːd] = **he would**, **he had**.

hedge [hɛdʒ] *n* haie *f* ♦ *vi* se défiler ♦ *vt*: **to ~ one's bets** (*fig*) se couvrir; **as a ~ against inflation** pour se prémunir contre l'inflation.

▶**hedge in** *vt* entourer d'une haie.

hedgehog ['hɛdʒhɔg] *n* hérisson *m*.

hedgerow ['hɛdʒrəu] *n* haie(s) *f(pl)*.

hedonism ['hiːdənɪzəm] *n* hédonisme *m*.

heed [hiːd] *vt* (*also*: **take ~ of**) tenir compte de, prendre garde à.

heedless ['hiːdlɪs] *adj* insouciant(e).

heel [hi:l] n talon m ♦ vt (shoe) retalonner; **to bring to** ~ (dog) faire venir à ses pieds; (fig: person) rappeler à l'ordre; **to take to one's** ~s prendre ses jambes à son cou.

hefty ['hɛftɪ] adj (person) costaud(e); (parcel) lourd(e); (piece, price) gros(se).

heifer ['hɛfə*] n génisse f.

height [haɪt] n (of person) taille f, grandeur f; (of object) hauteur f; (of plane, mountain) altitude f; (high ground) hauteur, éminence f; (fig: of glory) sommet m; (: of stupidity) comble m; **what** ~ **are you?** combien mesurez-vous?, quelle est votre taille?; **of average** ~ de taille moyenne; **to be afraid of** ~s être sujet(te) au vertige; **it's the** ~ **of fashion** c'est le dernier cri.

heighten ['haɪtn] vt hausser, surélever; (fig) augmenter.

heinous ['heɪnəs] adj odieux(euse), atroce.

heir [ɛə*] n héritier m.

heir apparent n héritier présomptif.

heiress ['ɛərɛs] n héritière f.

heirloom ['ɛəlu:m] n meuble m (or bijou m or tableau m) de famille.

heist [haɪst] n (US col: hold-up) casse m.

held [hɛld] pt, pp of **hold**.

helicopter ['hɛlɪkɔptə*] n hélicoptère m.

heliport ['hɛlɪpɔ:t] n (AVIAT) héliport m.

helium ['hi:lɪəm] n hélium m.

hell [hɛl] n enfer m; **a** ~ **of a ...** (col) un(e) sacré(e) ...; **oh** ~! (col) merde!

he'll [hi:l] = **he will, he shall**.

hell-bent [hɛl'bɛnt] adj (col): **to be** ~ **on doing sth** vouloir à tout prix faire qch.

hellish ['hɛlɪʃ] adj infernal(e).

hello [hə'ləu] excl bonjour!; salut! (to sb one addresses as "tu"); (surprise) tiens!

helm [hɛlm] n (NAUT) barre f.

helmet ['hɛlmɪt] n casque m.

helmsman ['hɛlmzmən] n timonier m.

help [hɛlp] n aide f; (charwoman) femme f de ménage; (assistant etc) employé/e ♦ vt aider; ~! au secours!; ~ **yourself (to bread)** servez-vous (de pain); **can I** ~ **you?** (in shop) vous désirez?; **with the** ~ **of** (person) avec l'aide de; (tool etc) à l'aide de; **to be of** ~ **to sb** être utile à qn; **to** ~ **sb (to) do sth** aider qn à faire qch; **I can't** ~ **saying** je ne peux pas m'empêcher de dire; **he can't** ~ **it** il ne peut pas s'en empêcher.

helper ['hɛlpə*] n aide m/f, assistant/e.

helpful ['hɛlpful] adj serviable, obligeant(e); (useful) utile.

helping ['hɛlpɪŋ] n portion f.

helping hand n coup m de main; **to give sb a** ~ prêter main-forte à qn.

helpless ['hɛlplɪs] adj impuissant(e); (baby) sans défense.

helplessly ['hɛlplɪslɪ] adv (watch) sans pouvoir rien faire.

helpline ['hɛlplaɪn] n numéro téléphonique que l'on peut appeler pour obtenir une as-

sistance sociale, médicale, judiciaire etc ou des renseignements sur un produit commercial.

Helsinki ['hɛlsɪŋkɪ] n Helsinki.

helter-skelter ['hɛltə'skɛltə*] n (BRIT: at amusement park) toboggan m.

hem [hɛm] n ourlet m ♦ vt ourler.

▶**hem in** vt cerner; **to feel** ~**med in** (fig) avoir l'impression d'étouffer, se sentir oppressé(e) or écrasé(e).

he-man ['hi:mæn] n (col) macho m.

hematology ['hi:mə'tɔlədʒɪ] n (US) = **haematology**.

hemisphere ['hɛmɪsfɪə*] n hémisphère m.

hemlock ['hɛmlɔk] n ciguë f.

hemoglobin ['hi:mə'gləubɪn] n (US) = **haemoglobin**.

hemophilia ['hi:mə'fɪlɪə] n (US) = **haemophilia**.

hemorrhage ['hɛmərɪdʒ] n (US) = **haemorrhage**.

hemorrhoids ['hɛmərɔɪdz] npl (US) = **haemorrhoids**.

hemp [hɛmp] n chanvre m.

hen [hɛn] n poule f; (female bird) femelle f.

hence [hɛns] adv (therefore) d'où, de là; **2 years** ~ d'ici 2 ans.

henceforth [hɛns'fɔ:θ] adv dorénavant.

henchman ['hɛntʃmən] n (pej) acolyte m, séide m.

henna ['hɛnə] n henné m.

hen party n (col) réunion f or fête f entre femmes.

henpecked ['hɛnpɛkt] adj dominé par sa femme.

hepatitis [hɛpə'taɪtɪs] n hépatite f.

her [hə:*] pron (direct) la, l' + vowel or h mute; (indirect) lui; (stressed, after prep) elle; see note at **she** ♦ adj son(sa), ses pl; **I see** ~ je la vois; **give** ~ **a book** donne-lui un livre; **after** ~ après elle.

herald ['hɛrəld] n héraut m ♦ vt annoncer.

heraldic [hɛ'rældɪk] adj héraldique.

heraldry ['hɛrəldrɪ] n héraldique f; (coat of arms) blason m.

herb [hə:b] n herbe f; ~s npl (CULIN) fines herbes.

herbaceous [hə:'beɪʃəs] adj herbacé(e).

herbal ['hə:bl] adj à base de plantes; ~ **tea** tisane f.

herbicide ['hə:bɪsaɪd] n herbicide m.

herd [hə:d] n troupeau m; (of wild animals, swine) troupeau, troupe f ♦ vt (drive: animals, people) mener, conduire; (gather) rassembler; ~**ed together** parqués (comme du bétail).

here [hɪə*] adv ici ♦ excl tiens!, tenez!; ~! présent!; ~ **is,** ~ **are** voici; ~**'s my sister** voici ma sœur; ~ **he/she is** le/la voici; ~ **she comes** la voici qui vient; **come** ~! viens ici!; ~ **and there** ici et là.

hereabouts ['hɪərə'bauts] adv par ici, dans les parages.

hereafter [hɪərˈɑːftəʳ] *adv* après, plus tard; ci-après ♦ *n:* **the ~** l'au-delà *m.*

hereby [hɪəˈbaɪ] *adv* (*in letter*) par la présente.

hereditary [hɪˈrɛdɪtrɪ] *adj* héréditaire.

heredity [hɪˈrɛdɪtɪ] *n* hérédité *f.*

heresy [ˈhɛrəsɪ] *n* hérésie *f.*

heretic [ˈhɛrətɪk] *n* hérétique *m/f.*

heretical [hɪˈrɛtɪkl] *adj* hérétique.

herewith [hɪəˈwɪθ] *adv* avec ceci, ci-joint.

heritage [ˈhɛrɪtɪdʒ] *n* héritage *m,* patrimoine *m;* **our national ~** notre patrimoine national.

hermetically [həːˈmɛtɪklɪ] *adv* hermétiquement; **~ sealed** hermétiquement fermé *or* clos.

hermit [ˈhəːmɪt] *n* ermite *m.*

hernia [ˈhəːnɪə] *n* hernie *f.*

hero, *pl* **~es** [ˈhɪərəu] *n* héros *m.*

heroic [hɪˈrəuɪk] *adj* héroïque.

heroin [ˈhɛrəuɪn] *n* héroïne *f.*

heroin addict *n* héroïnomane *m/f.*

heroine [ˈhɛrəuɪn] *n* héroïne *f* (*femme*).

heroism [ˈhɛrəuɪzəm] *n* héroïsme *m.*

heron [ˈhɛrən] *n* héron *m.*

hero worship *n* culte *m* (du héros).

herring [ˈhɛrɪŋ] *n* hareng *m.*

hers [həːz] *pron* le(la) sien(ne), les siens(siennes); **a friend of ~** un(e) ami(e) à elle, un(e) de ses ami(e)s; **this is ~** c'est à elle, c'est le sien.

herself [həːˈsɛlf] *pron* (*reflexive*) se; (*emphatic*) elle-même; (*after prep*) elle.

Herts [hɑːts] *abbr* (*BRIT*) = Hertfordshire.

he's [hiːz] = **he is, he has.**

hesitant [ˈhɛzɪtənt] *adj* hésitant(e), indécis(e); **to be ~ about doing sth** hésiter à faire qch.

hesitate [ˈhɛzɪteɪt] *vi:* **to ~ (about/to do)** hésiter (sur/à faire).

hesitation [hɛzɪˈteɪʃən] *n* hésitation *f;* **I have no ~ in saying (that)** ... je n'hésiterai pas à dire (que) ....

hessian [ˈhɛsɪən] *n* (toile *f* de) jute *m.*

heterogeneous [hɛtərəˈdʒiːnɪəs] *adj* hétérogène.

heterosexual [hɛtərəuˈsɛksjuəl] *adj, n* hétérosexuel(le).

het up [hɛtˈʌp] *adj* (*col*) agité(e), excité(e).

HEW *n abbr* (*US:* = Department of Health, Education and Welfare*) ministère de la santé publique, de l'enseignement et du bien-être.

hew [hjuː] *vt* tailler (*à la hache*).

hex [hɛks] (*US*) *n* sort *m* ♦ *vt* jeter un sort sur.

hexagon [ˈhɛksəgən] *n* hexagone *m.*

hexagonal [hɛkˈsægənl] *adj* hexagonal(e).

hey [heɪ] *excl* hé!

heyday [ˈheɪdeɪ] *n:* **the ~ of** l'âge *m* d'or de, les beaux jours de.

HF *n abbr* (= high frequency) HF *f.*

HGV *n abbr* = **heavy goods vehicle.**

HI *abbr* (*US*) = Hawaii.

hi [haɪ] *excl* salut!

hiatus [haɪˈeɪtəs] *n* trou *m,* lacune *f;* (*LING*) hiatus *m.*

hibernate [ˈhaɪbəneɪt] *vi* hiberner.

hibernation [haɪbəˈneɪʃən] *n* hibernation *f.*

hiccough, hiccup [ˈhɪkʌp] *vi* hoqueter ♦ *n* hoquet *m;* **to have (the) ~s** avoir le hoquet.

hick [hɪk] *n* (*US col*) plouc *m,* péquenaud/e.

hid [hɪd] *pt of* **hide.**

hidden [ˈhɪdn] *pp of* **hide** ♦ *adj:* **there are no ~ extras** absolument tout est compris dans le prix; **~ agenda** intentions non déclarées.

hide [haɪd] *n* (*skin*) peau *f* ♦ *vb* (*pt* **hid,** *pp* **hidden** [hɪd, 'hɪdn]) *vt:* **to ~ sth (from sb)** cacher qch (à qn); (*feelings, truth*) dissimuler qch (à qn) ♦ *vi:* **to ~ (from sb)** se cacher de qn.

hide-and-seek [ˈhaɪdənˈsiːk] *n* cache-cache *m.*

hideaway [ˈhaɪdəweɪ] *n* cachette *f.*

hideous [ˈhɪdɪəs] *adj* hideux(euse); atroce.

hide-out [ˈhaɪdaut] *n* cachette *f.*

hiding [ˈhaɪdɪŋ] *n* (*beating*) correction *f,* volée *f* de coups; **to be in ~** (*concealed*) se tenir caché(e).

hiding place *n* cachette *f.*

hierarchy [ˈhaɪərɑːkɪ] *n* hiérarchie *f.*

hieroglyphic [haɪərəˈglɪfɪk] *adj* hiéroglyphique; **~s** *npl* hiéroglyphes *mpl.*

hi-fi [ˈhaɪfaɪ] *adj, n abbr* (= high fidelity) hi-fi (*f*) *inv.*

higgledy-piggledy [ˈhɪgldɪˈpɪgldɪ] *adv* pêle-mêle, dans le plus grand désordre.

high [haɪ] *adj* haut(e); (*speed, respect, number*) grand(e); (*price*) élevé(e); (*wind*) fort(e), violent(e); (*voice*) aigu(aiguë); (*col: person: on drugs*) défoncé(e), fait(e); (*: on drink*) soûl(e), bourré(e); (*BRIT CULIN: meat, game*) faisandé(e); (*: spoilt*) avarié(e) ♦ *adv* en haut ♦ *n:* **exports have reached a new ~** les exportations ont atteint un nouveau record; **20 m ~** haut(e) de 20 m; **to pay a ~ price for sth** payer cher pour qch.

highball [ˈhaɪbɔːl] *n* (*US*) whisky *m* à l'eau avec des glaçons.

highboy [ˈhaɪbɔɪ] *n* (*US*) grande commode.

highbrow [ˈhaɪbrau] *adj, n* intellectuel(le).

highchair [ˈhaɪtʃɛəʳ] *n* chaise haute (*pour enfant*).

high-class [ˈhaɪˈklɑːs] *adj* (*neighbourhood, hotel*) chic *inv,* de grand standing; (*performance etc*) de haut niveau.

High Court *n* (*LAW*) cour *f* suprême.

> La **High Court** en Grande-Bretagne est la plus haute cour de justice à laquelle les affaires les plus graves telles que le meurtre et le viol sont soumises et où elles sont jugées devant un jury.

higher [ˈhaɪəʳ] *adj* (*form of life, study etc*) supérieur(e) ♦ *adv* plus haut.

higher education *n* études supérieures.

highfalutin [haɪfəˈluːtɪn] *adj* (*col*) affecté(e).

high finance *n* la haute finance.

high-flier, high-flyer [haɪˈflaɪəʳ] *n* (*fig: ambitious*) ambitieux/euse; (*: gifted*) personne particulièrement douée et promise à un *avenir brillant.*

high-flying [haɪˈflaɪɪŋ] *adj* (*fig*) ambitieux(euse), de haut niveau.

high-handed [haɪˈhændɪd] *adj* très autoritaire; très cavalier(ière).

high-heeled [haɪˈhiːld] *adj* à hauts talons.

highjack [ˈhaɪdʒæk] *n, vt* = **hijack**.

high jump *n* (*SPORT*) saut *m* en hauteur.

highlands [ˈhaɪləndz] *npl* région montagneuse; **the H~** (*in Scotland*) les Highlands *mpl*.

high-level [ˈhaɪlɛvl] *adj* (*talks etc*) à un haut niveau; **~ language** (*COMPUT*) langage évolué.

highlight [ˈhaɪlaɪt] *n* (*fig: of event*) point culminant ♦ *vt* faire ressortir, souligner; **~s** *npl* (*hairstyle*) reflets *mpl*.

highlighter [ˈhaɪlaɪtə*] *n* (*pen*) surligneur (lumineux).

highly [ˈhaɪlɪ] *adv* très, fort, hautement; **~ paid** très bien payé(e); **to speak ~ of** dire beaucoup de bien de.

highly-strung [ˈhaɪlɪˈstrʌŋ] *adj* nerveux(euse), toujours tendu(e).

High Mass *n* grand-messe *f*.

highness [ˈhaɪnɪs] *n* hauteur *f*; **Her H~** son Altesse *f*.

high-pitched [haɪˈpɪtʃt] *adj* aigu(ë).

high point *n*: **the ~ (of)** le clou (de), le point culminant (de).

high-powered [ˈhaɪˈpauəd] *adj* (*engine*) performant(e); (*fig: person*) dynamique; (*: job, businessman*) très important(e).

high-pressure [ˈhaɪprɛʃə*] *adj* à haute pression.

high-rise block [ˈhaɪraɪz-] *n* tour *f* (d'habitation).

high school *n* lycée *m*; (*US*) établissement *m* d'enseignement supérieur.

---

*Une **high school** est un établissement d'enseignement secondaire. Aux États-Unis, il y a la Junior High School, qui correspond au collège, et la Senior High School, qui correspond au lycée. En Grande-Bretagne, c'est un nom que l'on donne parfois aux écoles secondaires; voir **elementary school***

---

high season *n* (*BRIT*) haute saison.

high spirits *npl* pétulance *f*; **to be in ~** être plein(e) d'entrain.

high street *n* (*BRIT*) grand-rue *f*.

highway [ˈhaɪweɪ] *n* grand'route *f*, route nationale; **the information ~** l'autoroute *f* de l'information.

Highway Code *n* (*BRIT*) code *m* de la route.

highwayman [ˈhaɪweɪmən] *n* voleur *m* de grand chemin.

hijack [ˈhaɪdʒæk] *vt* détourner (*par la force*) ♦ *n* (*also*: **~ing**) détournement *m* (d'avion).

hijacker [ˈhaɪdʒækə*] *n* auteur *m* d'un détournement d'avion, pirate *m* de l'air.

hike [haɪk] *vi* aller à pied ♦ *n* excursion *f* à

pied, randonnée *f*; (*col: in prices etc*) augmentation *f* ♦ *vt* (*col*) augmenter.

hiker [ˈhaɪkə*] *n* promeneur/euse, excursionniste *m/f*.

hiking [ˈhaɪkɪŋ] *n* excursions *fpl* à pied, randonnée *f*.

hilarious [hɪˈlɛərɪəs] *adj* (*behaviour, event*) désopilant(e).

hilarity [hɪˈlærɪtɪ] *n* hilarité *f*.

hill [hɪl] *n* colline *f*; (*fairly high*) montagne *f*; (*on road*) côte *f*.

hillbilly [ˈhɪlbɪlɪ] *n* (*US*) montagnard/e du sud des USA; (*pej*) péquenaud *m*.

hillock [ˈhɪlək] *n* petite colline, butte *f*.

hillside [ˈhɪlsaɪd] *n* (flanc *m* de) coteau *m*.

hill start *n* (*AUT*) démarrage *m* en côte.

hilly [ˈhɪlɪ] *adj* vallonné(e); montagneux(euse); (*road*) à fortes côtes.

hilt [hɪlt] *n* (*of sword*) garde *f*; **to the ~** (*fig: support*) à fond.

him [hɪm] *pron* (*direct*) le, l' + *vowel or h mute*; (*stressed, indirect, after prep*) lui; **I see ~** je le vois; **give ~ a book** donne-lui un livre; **after ~ après lui.**

Himalayas [hɪməˈleɪəz] *npl*: **the ~** l'Himalaya *m*.

himself [hɪmˈsɛlf] *pron* (*reflexive*) se; (*emphatic*) lui-même; (*after prep*) lui.

hind [haɪnd] *adj* de derrière ♦ *n* biche *f*.

hinder [ˈhɪndə*] *vt* gêner; (*delay*) retarder; (*prevent*): **to ~ sb from doing** empêcher qn de faire.

hindquarters [ˈhaɪndˈkwɔːtəz] *npl* (*ZOOL*) arrière-train *m*.

hindrance [ˈhɪndrəns] *n* gêne *f*, obstacle *m*.

hindsight [ˈhaɪndsaɪt] *n* bon sens après coup; **with the benefit of ~** avec du recul, rétrospectivement.

Hindu [ˈhɪnduː] *n* Hindou/e.

hinge [hɪndʒ] *n* charnière *f* ♦ *vi* (*fig*): **to ~ on** dépendre de.

hint [hɪnt] *n* allusion *f*; (*advice*) conseil *m* ♦ *vt*: **to ~ that** insinuer que ♦ *vi*: **to ~ at** faire une allusion à; **to drop a ~** faire une allusion *or* insinuation; **give me a ~** (*clue*) mettez-moi sur la voie, donnez-moi une indication.

hip [hɪp] *n* hanche *f*; (*BOT*) fruit *m* de l'églantier *or* du rosier.

hip flask *n* flacon *m* (pour la poche).

hip hop *n* hip hop *m*.

hippie, hippy [ˈhɪpɪ] *n* hippie *m/f*.

hip pocket *n* poche-revolver *f*.

hippopotamus, *pl* **~es** *or* **hippopotami** [hɪpəˈpɔtəməs, -ˈpɔtəmaɪ] *n* hippopotame *m*.

hippy [ˈhɪpɪ] *n* = **hippie**.

hire [ˈhaɪə*] *vt* (*BRIT: car, equipment*) louer; (*worker*) embaucher, engager ♦ *n* location *f*; **for ~** à louer; (*taxi*) libre; **on ~** en location.

▶**hire out** *vt* louer.

hire(d) car [ˈhaɪəd(-)] *n* (*BRIT*) voiture louée.

hire purchase (H.P.) *n* (*BRIT*) achat *m* (*or* vente *f*) à tempérament *or* crédit; **to buy sth**

on ~ acheter qch en location-vente.

his [hɪz] *pron* le(la) sien(ne), les siens(siennes) ♦ *adj* son(sa), ses *pl*; **this is** ~ c'est à lui, c'est le sien.

hiss [hɪs] *vi* siffler ♦ *n* sifflement *m*.

histogram ['hɪstəgræm] *n* histogramme *m*.

historian [hɪ'stɔːrɪən] *n* historien/ne.

historic(al) [hɪ'stɔrɪk(l)] *adj* historique.

history ['hɪstərɪ] *n* histoire *f*; **medical** ~ (*of patient*) passé médical.

histrionics [hɪstrɪ'ɒnɪks] *n* gestes *mpl* dramatiques, cinéma *m* (*fig*).

hit [hɪt] *vt* (*pt, pp* **hit**) frapper; (*knock against*) cogner; (*reach: target*) atteindre, toucher; (*collide with: car*) entrer en collision avec, heurter; (*fig: affect*) toucher; (*find*) tomber sur ♦ *n* coup *m*; (*success*) coup réussi; succès *m*; (*song*) chanson *f* à succès, tube *m*; **to ~ it off with sb** bien s'entendre avec qn; **to ~ the headlines** être à la une des journaux; **to ~ the road** (*col*) se mettre en route.

▶**hit back** *vi*: **to ~ back at sb** prendre sa revanche sur qn.

▶**hit out at** *vt fus* envoyer un coup à; (*fig*) attaquer.

▶**hit (up)on** *vt fus* (*answer*) trouver (par hasard); (*solution*) tomber sur (par hasard).

hit-and-miss ['hɪtænd'mɪs] *adj* au petit bonheur (la chance).

hit-and-run driver ['hɪtænd'rʌn-] *n* chauffard *m*.

hitch [hɪtʃ] *vt* (*fasten*) accrocher, attacher; (*also*: ~ **up**) remonter d'une saccade ♦ *n* (*knot*) nœud *m*; (*difficulty*) anicroche *f*, contretemps *m*; **to ~ a lift** faire du stop; **technical** ~ incident *m* technique.

▶**hitch up** *vt* (*horse, cart*) atteler; *see also* **hitch**.

hitch-hike ['hɪtʃhaɪk] *vi* faire de l'auto-stop.

hitch-hiker ['hɪtʃhaɪkə*] *n* auto-stoppeur/euse.

hi-tech ['haɪ'tek] *adj* de pointe ♦ *n* high-tech *m*.

hitherto [hɪðə'tuː] *adv* jusqu'ici, jusqu'à présent.

hit list *n* liste noire.

hitman ['hɪtmæn] *n* (*col*) tueur *m* à gages.

hit-or-miss ['hɪtə'mɪs] *adj* au petit bonheur (la chance); **it's ~ whether ...** il est loin d'être certain que ... + *sub*.

hit parade *n* hit parade *m*.

HIV *n abbr* (= *human immunodeficiency virus*) HIV *m*, VIH *m*; ~-**negative/-positive** séronégatif(ive)/séropositif(ive).

hive [haɪv] *n* ruche *f*; **the shop was a ~ of activity** (*fig*) le magasin était une véritable ruche.

▶**hive off** *vt* (*col*) mettre à part, séparer.

hl *abbr* (= *hectolitre*) hl.

HM *abbr* (= *His (or Her) Majesty*) SM.

HMG *abbr* (*BRIT*) = *His (or Her) Majesty's Government*.

HMI *n abbr* (*BRIT SCOL*) = *His (or Her) Majesty's Inspector*.

HMO *n abbr* (*US*: = *health maintenance organization*) *organisme médical assurant un forfait entretien de santé*.

HMS *abbr* (*BRIT*) = *His (or Her) Majesty's Ship*.

HMSO *n abbr* (*BRIT*: = *His (or Her) Majesty's Stationery Office*) ≈ Imprimerie nationale.

HNC *n abbr* (*BRIT*: = *Higher National Certificate*) ≈ DUT *m*.

HND *n abbr* (*BRIT*: = *Higher National Diploma*) ≈ licence *f* de sciences et techniques.

hoard [hɔːd] *n* (*of food*) provisions *fpl*, réserves *fpl*; (*of money*) trésor *m* ♦ *vt* amasser.

hoarding ['hɔːdɪŋ] *n* (*BRIT*) panneau *m* d'affichage *or* publicitaire.

hoarfrost ['hɔːfrɒst] *n* givre *m*.

hoarse [hɔːs] *adj* enroué(e).

hoax [həuks] *n* canular *m*.

hob [hɒb] *n* plaque chauffante.

hobble ['hɒbl] *vi* boitiller.

hobby ['hɒbɪ] *n* passe-temps favori.

hobby-horse ['hɒbɪhɔːs] *n* cheval *m* à bascule; (*fig*) dada *m*.

hobnail(ed) boot ['hɒbneɪl(d)-] *n* chaussure (à semelle) cloutée.

hobnob ['hɒbnɒb] *vi*: **to ~ with** frayer avec, fréquenter.

hobo ['həubəu] *n* (*US*) vagabond *m*.

hock [hɒk] *n* (*BRIT: wine*) vin *m* du Rhin; (*of animal, CULIN*) jarret *m*; (*col*): **to be in** ~ (*person*) avoir des dettes; (*object*) être en gage *or* au clou.

hockey ['hɒkɪ] *n* hockey *m*.

hocus-pocus ['həukəs'pəukəs] *n* (*trickery*) supercherie *f*; (*words of magician*) formules *fpl* magiques; (: *jargon*) galimatias *m*.

hod [hɒd] *n* oiseau *m*, hotte *f*.

hodgepodge ['hɒdʒpɒdʒ] *n* = **hotchpotch**.

hoe [həu] *n* houe *f*, binette *f* ♦ *vt* (*ground*) biner; (*plants etc*) sarcler.

hog [hɒg] *n* porc (châtré) ♦ *vt* (*fig*) accaparer; **to go the whole** ~ aller jusqu'au bout.

Hogmanay [hɒgmə'neɪ] *n* (*Scottish*) réveillon *m* du jour de l'An, Saint-Sylvestre *f*.

hogwash ['hɒgwɒʃ] *n* (*col*) foutaises *fpl*.

hoist [hɔɪst] *n* palan *m* ♦ *vt* hisser.

hoity-toity [hɔɪtɪ'tɔɪtɪ] *adj* (*col*) prétentieux(euse), qui se donne de grands airs.

hold [həuld] *vb* (*pt, pp* **held** [held]) *vt* tenir; (*contain*) contenir; (*keep back*) retenir; (*believe*) maintenir; considérer; (*possess*) avoir; détenir ♦ *vi* (*withstand pressure*) tenir (bon); (*be valid*) valoir ♦ *n* prise *f*; (*fig*) influence *f*; (*NAUT*) cale *f*; **to catch** *or* **get (a)** ~ **of** saisir; **to get** ~ **of** (*fig*) trouver; **to get** ~ **of o.s.** se contrôler; ~ **the line!** (*TEL*) ne quittez pas!; **to** ~ **one's own** (*fig*) (bien) se défendre; **to** ~ **office** (*POL*) avoir un portefeuille; **to** ~ **firm** *or* **fast** tenir bon; **he ~s the view that ...** il pense *or* estime que ..., d'après lui ...; **to** ~ **sb responsible for sth** tenir qn pour responsable de qch.

▶**hold back** *vt* retenir; (*secret*) cacher; **to ~**

sb back from doing sth empêcher qn de faire qch.

▶**hold down** vt (person) maintenir à terre; (job) occuper.

▶**hold forth** vi pérorer.

▶**hold off** vt tenir à distance ♦ vi (rain): **if the rain ~s off** s'il ne pleut pas, s'il ne se met pas à pleuvoir.

▶**hold on** vi tenir bon; (wait) attendre; **~ on!** (TEL) ne quittez pas!

▶**hold on to** vt fus se cramponner à; (keep) conserver, garder.

▶**hold out** vt offrir ♦ vi (resist): **to ~ out (against)** résister (devant), tenir bon (devant).

▶**hold over** vt (meeting etc) ajourner, reporter.

▶**hold up** vt (raise) lever; (support) soutenir; (delay) retarder; (: traffic) ralentir; (rob) braquer.

holdall ['həʊldɔːl] n (BRIT) fourre-tout m inv.

holder ['həʊldə*] n (of ticket, record) détenteur/trice; (of office, title, passport etc) titulaire m/f.

holding ['həʊldɪŋ] n (share) intérêts mpl; (farm) ferme f.

holding company n holding m.

holdup ['həʊldʌp] n (robbery) hold-up m; (delay) retard m; (BRIT: in traffic) embouteillage m.

hole [həʊl] n trou m ♦ vt trouer, faire un trou dans; **~ in the heart** (MED) communication f interventriculaire; **to pick ~s (in)** (fig) chercher des poux (dans).

▶**hole up** vi se terrer.

holiday ['hɔlədɪ] n (BRIT: vacation) vacances fpl; (day off) jour m de congé; (public) jour férié; **to be on ~** être en congé; **tomorrow is a ~** demain c'est fête, on a congé demain.

holiday camp n (BRIT: for children) colonie f de vacances; (: also: **holiday centre**) camp m de vacances.

holidaymaker ['hɔlədɪmeɪkə*] n (BRIT) vacancier/ière.

holiday pay n paie f des vacances.

holiday resort n centre m de villégiature or de vacances.

holiday season n période f des vacances.

holiness ['həʊlɪnɪs] n sainteté f.

holistic [həʊ'lɪstɪk] adj holiste, holistique.

Holland ['hɔlənd] n Hollande f.

holler ['hɔlə*] vi (col) brailler.

hollow ['hɔləʊ] adj creux(euse); (fig) faux(fausse) ♦ n creux m; (in land) dépression f (de terrain), cuvette f ♦ vt: **to ~ out** creuser, évider.

holly ['hɔlɪ] n houx m.

hollyhock ['hɔlɪhɔk] n rose trémière.

holocaust ['hɔləkɔːst] n holocauste m.

hologram ['hɔləgræm] n hologramme m.

hols [hɔlz] npl (col) vacances fpl.

holster ['həʊlstə*] n étui m de revolver.

holy ['həʊlɪ] adj saint(e); (bread, water) bénit(e); (ground) sacré(e).

Holy Communion n la (sainte) communion.

Holy Ghost, Holy Spirit n Saint-Esprit m.

Holy Land n: **the ~** la Terre Sainte.

holy orders npl ordres (majeurs).

homage ['hɔmɪdʒ] n hommage m; **to pay ~ to** rendre hommage à.

home [həʊm] n foyer m, maison f; (country) pays natal, patrie f; (institution) maison ♦ adj de famille; (ECON, POL) national(e), intérieur(e); (SPORT: team) qui reçoit; (: match, win) sur leur (or notre) terrain ♦ adv chez soi, à la maison; au pays natal; (right in: nail etc) à fond; **at ~** chez soi, à la maison; **to go** (or **come**) **~** rentrer (chez soi), rentrer à la maison (or au pays); **make yourself at ~** faites comme chez vous; **near my ~** près de chez moi.

▶**home in on** vt fus (missiles) se diriger automatiquement vers or sur.

home address n domicile permanent.

home-brew [həʊm'bruː] n vin m (or bière f) maison.

homecoming ['həʊmkʌmɪŋ] n retour m (au bercail).

home computer n ordinateur m domestique.

Home Counties npl les comtés autour de Londres.

home economics n économie f domestique.

home ground n: **to be on ~** être sur son terrain.

home-grown ['həʊmgrəʊn] adj (not foreign) du pays; (from garden) du jardin.

home help n (BRIT) aide-ménagère f.

homeland ['həʊmlænd] n patrie f.

homeless ['həʊmlɪs] adj sans foyer, sans abri; **the ~** npl les sans-abri mpl.

home loan n prêt m sur hypothèque.

homely ['həʊmlɪ] adj simple, sans prétention; accueillant(e).

home-made [həʊm'meɪd] adj fait(e) à la maison.

Home Office n (BRIT) ministère m de l'Intérieur.

homeopathy etc [həʊmɪ'ɔpəθɪ] (US) = **homoeopathy** etc.

homeowner ['həʊməʊnə*] n propriétaire occupant.

home rule n autonomie f.

Home Secretary n (BRIT) ministre m de l'Intérieur.

homesick ['həʊmsɪk] adj: **to be ~** avoir le mal du pays; (missing one's family) s'ennuyer de sa famille.

homestead ['həʊmstɛd] n propriété f; (farm) ferme f.

home town n ville natale.

home truth n: **to tell sb a few ~s** dire ses quatre vérités à qn.

homeward ['həʊmwəd] adj (journey) du retour ♦ adv = **homewards**.

homewards ['həʊmwədz] *adv* vers la maison.
homework ['həʊmwɜːk] *n* devoirs *mpl*.
homicidal [hɒmɪ'saɪdl] *adj* homicide.
homicide ['hɒmɪsaɪd] *n* (*US*) homicide *m*.
homily ['hɒmɪlɪ] *n* homélie *f*.
homing ['həʊmɪŋ] *adj* (*device, missile*) à tête chercheuse; ~ **pigeon** pigeon voyageur.
homoeopath, (*US*) **homeopath** ['həʊmɪəʊpæθ] *n* homéopathe *m/f*.
homoeopathy, (*US*) **homeopathy** [həʊmɪ-'ɒpəθɪ] *n* homéopathie *f*.
homogeneous [hɒməʊ'dʒiːnɪəs] *adj* homogène.
homogenize [hə'mɒdʒənaɪz] *vt* homogénéiser.
homosexual [hɒməʊ'sɛksjʊəl] *adj*, *n* homosexuel(le).
Hon. *abbr* (= *honourable, honorary*) dans un titre.
Honduras [hɒn'djʊərəs] *n* Honduras *m*.
hone [həʊn] *n* pierre *f* à aiguiser ♦ *vt* affûter, aiguiser.
honest ['ɒnɪst] *adj* honnête; (*sincere*) franc(franche); **to be quite ~ with you** ... à dire vrai ....
honestly ['ɒnɪstlɪ] *adv* honnêtement; franchement.
honesty ['ɒnɪstɪ] *n* honnêteté *f*.
honey ['hʌnɪ] *n* miel *m*; (*US col: darling*) chéri/e.
honeycomb ['hʌnɪkəʊm] *n* rayon *m* de miel; (*pattern*) nid *m* d'abeilles, motif alvéolé ♦ *vt* (*fig*): **to ~ with** cribler de.
honeymoon ['hʌnɪmuːn] *n* lune *f* de miel, voyage *m* de noces.
honeysuckle ['hʌnɪsʌkl] *n* chèvrefeuille *m*.
Hong Kong ['hɒŋ'kɒŋ] *n* Hong Kong.
honk [hɒŋk] *n* (*AUT*) coup *m* de klaxon ♦ *vi* klaxonner.
Honolulu [hɒnə'luːluː] *n* Honolulu.
honorary ['ɒnərərɪ] *adj* honoraire; (*duty, title*) honorifique.
honour, (*US*) **honor** ['ɒnə*] *vt* honorer ♦ *n* honneur *m*; **in ~ of** en l'honneur de.
hono(u)rable ['ɒnərəbl] *adj* honorable.
hono(u)r-bound ['ɒnə'baʊnd] *adj*: **to be ~ to do** se devoir de faire.
hono(u)rs degree ['ɒnəz-] *n* (*SCOL*) ≈ licence *f*.

Un **honours degree** est un diplôme universitaire que l'on reçoit après trois années d'études en Angleterre et quatre années en Écosse. Les mentions qui l'accompagnent sont, par ordre décroissant: "first class" (très bien/bien), "upper second class" (assez bien), "lower second class" (passable), et "third class" (diplôme sans mention). Le titulaire d'un honours degree a un titre qu'il peut mettre à la suite de son nom, par exemple: Peter Jones BA Hons; voir **ordinary degree**

---

honours list *n* (*BRIT*): **the ~** la liste des per-

sonnes auxquelles une distinction honorifique est conférée par le souverain.

L'**honours list** est la liste des citoyens du Royaume-Uni et du Commonwealth auxquels le souverain confère un titre ou une décoration. Cette liste est préparée par le Premier ministre et paraît deux fois par an, au Nouvel An et lors de l'anniversaire officiel du règne du souverain. Des personnes qui se sont distinguées dans le monde des affaires, des sports et des médias, ainsi que dans les forces armées, mais également des citoyens "ordinaires" qui se consacrent à des œuvres de charité sont ainsi récompensées.

Hons. *abbr* (*SCOL*) = **hono(u)rs degree**.
hood [hʊd] *n* capuchon *m*; (*BRIT AUT*) capote *f*; (*US AUT*) capot *m*; (*col*) truand *m*.
hoodlum ['huːdləm] *n* truand *m*.
hoodwink ['hʊdwɪŋk] *vt* tromper.
hoof, *pl* ~**s** *or* **hooves** [huːf, huːvz] *n* sabot *m*.
hook [hʊk] *n* crochet *m*; (*on dress*) agrafe *f*; (*for fishing*) hameçon *m* ♦ *vt* accrocher; (*dress*) agrafer; ~ **and eye** agrafe; **by ~ or by crook** de gré ou de force, coûte que coûte; **to be ~ed (on)** (*col*) être accroché(e) (par); (*person*) être dingue (de).
▶**hook up** *vt* (*RADIO, TV etc*) faire un duplex entre.
hooligan ['huːlɪgən] *n* voyou *m*.
hoop [huːp] *n* cerceau *m*; (*of barrel*) cercle *m*.
hoot [huːt] *vi* (*AUT*) klaxonner; (*siren*) mugir; (*owl*) hululer ♦ *vt* (*jeer at*) huer ♦ *n* huée *f*; coup *m* de klaxon; mugissement *m*; hululement *m*; **to ~ with laughter** rire aux éclats.
hooter ['huːtə*] *n* (*BRIT AUT*) klaxon *m*; (*NAUT, factory*) sirène *f*.
hoover ['huːvə*] *n* ® (*BRIT*) aspirateur *m* ♦ *vt* (*room*) passer l'aspirateur dans; (*carpet*) passer l'aspirateur sur.
hooves [huːvz] *npl of* **hoof**.
hop [hɒp] *vi* sauter; (*on one foot*) sauter à cloche-pied ♦ *n* saut *m*.
hope [həʊp] *vt, vi* espérer ♦ *n* espoir *m*; **I ~ so** je l'espère; **I ~ not** j'espère que non.
hopeful ['həʊpful] *adj* (*person*) plein(e) d'espoir; (*situation*) prometteur(euse), encourageant(e); **I'm ~ that she'll manage to come** j'ai bon espoir qu'elle pourra venir.
hopefully ['həʊpfulɪ] *adv* avec espoir, avec optimisme; ~, **they'll come back** espérons bien qu'ils reviendront.
hopeless ['həʊplɪs] *adj* désespéré(e), sans espoir; (*useless*) nul(le).
hopelessly ['həʊplɪslɪ] *adv* (*live etc*) sans espoir; ~ **confused** *etc* complètement désorienté *etc*.
hopper ['hɒpə*] *n* (*chute*) trémie *f*.
hops [hɒps] *npl* houblon *m*.
horde [hɔːd] *n* horde *f*.
horizon [hə'raɪzn] *n* horizon *m*.

horizontal [hɔrɪ'zɔntl] adj horizontal(e).
hormone ['hɔːməun] n hormone f.
hormone replacement therapy n hormonothérapie substitutive, traitement hormono-supplétif.
horn [hɔːn] n corne f; (MUS) cor m; (AUT) klaxon m.
horned [hɔːnd] adj (animal) à cornes.
hornet ['hɔːnɪt] n frelon m.
horny ['hɔːnɪ] adj corné(e); (hands) calleux(euse); (col: aroused) excité(e).
horoscope ['hɔrəskəup] n horoscope m.
horrendous [hə'rɛndəs] adj horrible, affreux(euse).
horrible ['hɔrɪbl] adj horrible, affreux(euse).
horrid ['hɔrɪd] adj méchant(e), désagréable.
horrific [hɔ'rɪfɪk] adj horrible.
horrify ['hɔrɪfaɪ] vt horrifier.
horrifying ['hɔrɪfaɪŋ] adj horrifiant(e).
horror ['hɔrə*] n horreur f.
horror film n film m d'épouvante.
horror-struck ['hɔrəstrʌk], **horror-stricken** ['hɔrəstrɪkn] adj horrifié(e).
hors d'œuvre [ɔː'dəːvrə] n hors d'œuvre m.
horse [hɔːs] n cheval m.
horseback ['hɔːsbæk]: **on** ~ adj, adv à cheval.
horsebox ['hɔːsbɔks] n van m.
horse chestnut n marron m (d'Inde).
horse-drawn ['hɔːsdrɔːn] adj tiré(e) par des chevaux.
horsefly ['hɔːsflaɪ] n taon m.
horseman ['hɔːsmən] n cavalier m.
horsemanship ['hɔːsmənʃɪp] n talents mpl de cavalier.
horseplay ['hɔːspleɪ] n chahut m (blagues etc).
horsepower (hp) ['hɔːspauə*] n puissance f (en chevaux); cheval-vapeur m (CV).
horse-racing ['hɔːsreɪsɪŋ] n courses fpl de chevaux.
horseradish ['hɔːsrædɪʃ] n raifort m.
horseshoe ['hɔːsʃuː] n fer m à cheval.
horse show n concours m hippique.
horse-trading ['hɔːstreɪdɪŋ] n maquignonage m.
horse trials npl = **horse show**.
horsewhip ['hɔːswɪp] vt cravacher.
horsewoman ['hɔːswumən] n cavalière f.
horsey ['hɔːsɪ] adj féru(e) d'équitation or de cheval; (appearance) chevalin(e).
horticulture ['hɔːtɪkʌltʃə*] n horticulture f.
hose [həuz] n tuyau m; (also: garden ~) tuyau d'arrosage.
▶**hose down** vt laver au jet.
hosepipe ['həuzpaɪp] n tuyau m; (in garden) tuyau d'arrosage; (for fire) tuyau d'incendie.
hosiery ['həuzɪərɪ] n (in shop) (rayon m des) bas mpl.
hospice ['hɔspɪs] n hospice m.
hospitable ['hɔspɪtəbl] adj hospitalier(ière).
hospital ['hɔspɪtl] n hôpital m; **in** ~, (US) **in the** ~ à l'hôpital.
hospitality [hɔspɪ'tælɪtɪ] n hospitalité f.

hospitalize ['hɔspɪtəlaɪz] vt hospitaliser.
host [həust] n hôte m; (in hotel etc) patron m; (TV, RADIO) présentateur/trice, animateur/trice; (large number): **a** ~ **of** une foule de; (REL) hostie f ♦ vt (TV programme) présenter, animer.
hostage ['hɔstɪdʒ] n otage m.
host country n pays m d'accueil, pays-hôte m.
hostel ['hɔstl] n foyer m; (also: **youth** ~) auberge f de jeunesse.
hostelling ['hɔstlɪŋ] n: **to go (youth)** ~ faire une virée or randonnée en séjournant dans des auberges de jeunesse.
hostess ['həustɪs] n hôtesse f; (AVIAT) hôtesse de l'air; (in nightclub) entraîneuse f.
hostile ['hɔstaɪl] adj hostile.
hostility [hɔ'stɪlɪtɪ] n hostilité f.
hot [hɔt] adj chaud(e); (as opposed to only warm) très chaud; (spicy) fort(e); (fig) acharné(e); brûlant(e); violent(e), passionné(e); **to be** ~ (person) avoir chaud; (thing) être (très) chaud; (weather) faire chaud.
▶**hot up** (BRIT col) vi (situation) devenir tendu(e); (party) s'animer ♦ vt (pace) accélérer, forcer; (engine) gonfler.
hot-air balloon [hɔt'ɛə-] n montgolfière f, ballon m.
hotbed ['hɔtbɛd] n (fig) foyer m, pépinière f.
hotchpotch ['hɔtʃpɔtʃ] n (BRIT) mélange m hétéroclite.
hot dog n hot-dog m.
hotel [həu'tɛl] n hôtel m.
hotelier [həu'tɛlɪə*] n hôtelier/ière.
hotel industry n industrie hôtelière.
hotel room n chambre f d'hôtel.
hot flush n (BRIT) bouffée f de chaleur.
hotfoot ['hɔtfut] adv à toute vitesse.
hothead ['hɔthɛd] n (fig) tête brûlée.
hotheaded [hɔt'hɛdɪd] adj impétueux(euse).
hothouse ['hɔthaus] n serre chaude.
hot line n (POL) téléphone m rouge, ligne directe.
hotly ['hɔtlɪ] adv passionnément, violemment.
hotplate ['hɔtpleɪt] n (on cooker) plaque chauffante.
hotpot ['hɔtpɔt] n (BRIT CULIN) ragoût m.
hot potato n (BRIT col) sujet brûlant; **to drop sb/sth like a** ~ laisser tomber qn/qch brusquement.
hot seat n (fig) poste chaud.
hot spot n point chaud.
hot spring n source thermale.
hot-tempered ['hɔt'tɛmpəd] adj emporté(e).
hot-water bottle [hɔt'wɔːtə-] n bouillotte f.
hot-wire ['hɔtwaɪə*] vt (col: car) démarrer en faisant se toucher les fils de contact.
hound [haund] vt poursuivre avec acharnement ♦ n chien courant; **the** ~**s** la meute.
hour ['auə*] n heure f; **at 30 miles an** ~ ≈ à 50 km à l'heure; **lunch** ~ heure du déjeuner; **to pay sb by the** ~ payer qn à l'heure.

hourly ['auəlı] *adj* toutes les heures; (*rate*) horaire; ~ **paid** *adj* payé(e) à l'heure.

house *n* [haus] (*pl:* ~s ['hauzız]) maison *f*; (*POL*) chambre *f*; (*THEAT*) salle *f*; auditoire *m* ♦ *vt* [hauz] (*person*) loger, héberger; **at** (*or* **to**) **my** ~ chez moi; **the H~ of Commons/of Lords** (*BRIT*) la Chambre des communes/des lords; **the H~ (of Representatives)** (*US*) la Chambre des représentants; **on the** ~ (*fig*) aux frais de la maison.

Le parlement en Grande-Bretagne est constitué de deux assemblées:

-La **House of Lords***, présidée par le Lord Chancellor et composée de membres du haut clergé et de lords séculiers dont le titre est, soit héréditaire, soit attribué par le souverain (dans ce dernier cas, il peut être héréditaire ou à vie); elle peut amender certains projets de loi votés par la Chambre des communes, mais elle n'est pas habilitée à débattre des projets de lois de finances. La Chambre des lords fait également office de la juridiction suprême en Angleterre et au Pays de Galles.*

-La **House of Commons***, présidée par le* **Speaker** *et composée de plus de 600 députés (les* **MP***) élus au suffrage universel direct. Ceux-ci reçoivent tous un salaire. La Chambre des communes siège environ 175 jours par an.*

Aux États-Unis, le parlement, appelé le **Congress***, est constitué du* **Senate** *et de la* **House of Représentatives***. Cette dernière comprend actuellement 435 membres, le nombre de représentants par État étant proportionnel à la densité de population de cet État. Ils sont élus pour deux ans au suffrage universel direct et siègent au* **Capitol***, à Washington D.C.*

---

house arrest *n* assignation *f* à domicile.

houseboat ['hausbəut] *n* bateau (aménagé en habitation).

housebound ['hausbaund] *adj* confiné(e) chez soi.

housebreaking ['hausbreıkıŋ] *n* cambriolage *m* (avec effraction).

house-broken ['hausbrəukn] *adj* (*US*) = **house-trained**.

housecoat ['hauskəut] *n* peignoir *m*.

household ['haushəuld] *n* ménage *m*; (*people*) famille *f*, maisonnée *f*; ~ **name** nom connu de tout le monde.

householder ['haushəuldə*] *n* propriétaire *m/f*; (*head of house*) chef *m* de ménage *or* de famille.

househunting ['haushʌntıŋ] *n*: **to go** ~ se mettre en quête d'une maison (*or* d'un appartement).

housekeeper ['hauski:pə*] *n* gouvernante *f*.

housekeeping ['hauski:pıŋ] *n* (*work*) ménage *m*; (*also:* ~ **money**) argent *m* du ménage; (*COMPUT*) gestion *f* (des disques).

houseman ['hausmən] *n* (*BRIT MED*) ≈ interne *m*.

house-owner ['hausəunə*] *n* propriétaire *m/f* (*de maison ou d'appartement*).

house-proud ['hauspraud] *adj* qui tient à avoir une maison impeccable.

house-to-house ['haustə'haus] *adj* (*enquiries etc*) chez tous les habitants (du quartier *etc*).

house-train ['haustreın] *vt* (*pet*) apprendre à être propre à.

house-trained ['haustreınd] *adj* (*BRIT: animal*) propre.

house-warming ['hauswɔ:mıŋ] *n* (*also:* ~ **party**) pendaison *f* de crémaillère.

housewife ['hauswaıf] *n* ménagère *f*; femme *f* du foyer.

housework ['hauswə:k] *n* (travaux *mpl* du) ménage *m*.

housing ['hauzıŋ] *n* logement *m* ♦ *cpd* (*problem, shortage*) de *or* du logement.

housing association *n* fondation *f* charitable fournissant des logements.

housing benefit *n* (*BRIT*) ≈ allocations *fpl* logement.

housing conditions *npl* conditions *fpl* de logement.

housing development, (*BRIT*) **housing estate** *n* cité *f*; lotissement *m*.

hovel ['hɔvl] *n* taudis *m*.

hover ['hɔvə*] *vi* planer; **to** ~ **round sb** rôder *or* tourner autour de qn.

hovercraft ['hɔvəkrɑ:ft] *n* aéroglisseur *m*.

hoverport ['hɔvəpɔ:t] *n* hoverport *m*.

how [hau] *adv* comment; ~ **are you?** comment allez-vous?; ~ **do you do?** bonjour; (*on being introduced*) enchanté(e); ~ **far is it to ...?** combien y a-t-il jusqu'à ...?; ~ **long have you been here?** depuis combien de temps êtes-vous là?; ~ **lovely!** que *or* comme c'est joli!; ~ **many/much?** combien?; ~ **many people/much milk** combien de gens/lait; ~ **old are you?** quel âge avez-vous?; ~**'s life?** (*col*) comment ça va?; ~ **about a drink?** si on buvait quelque chose?; ~ **is it that ...?** comment se fait-il que ... + *sub*?

however [hau'ɛvə*] *conj* pourtant, cependant ♦ *adv* de quelque façon *or* manière que + *sub*; (+ *adjective*) quelque *or* si ... que + *sub*; (*in questions*) comment.

howitzer ['hauıtsə*] *n* (*MIL*) obusier *m*.

howl [haul] *n* hurlement *m* ♦ *vi* hurler.

howler ['haulə*] *n* gaffe *f*, bourde *f*.

howling ['haulıŋ] *adj*: **a** ~ **wind** *or* **gale** un vent à décorner les bœufs.

HP *n abbr* (*BRIT*) = **hire purchase**.

hp *abbr* (*AUT*) = **horsepower**.

HQ *n abbr* (= *headquarters*) QG *m*.

HR *n abbr* (*US*) = **House of Representatives**.

HRH *abbr* (= *His (or Her) Royal Highness*) SAR.

hr(s) *abbr* (= *hour(s)*) h.

HRT *n abbr* = **hormone replacement therapy**.

HS *abbr* (*US*) = **high school**.
HST *abbr* (*US*: = *Hawaiian Standard Time*) *heure de Hawaii*.
hub [hʌb] *n* (*of wheel*) moyeu *m*; (*fig*) centre *m*, foyer *m*.
hubbub ['hʌbʌb] *n* brouhaha *m*.
hub cap *n* (*AUT*) enjoliveur *m*.
HUD *n abbr* (*US*: = *Department of Housing and Urban Development*) *ministère de l'urbanisme et du logement*.
huddle ['hʌdl] *vi*: **to ~ together** se blottir les uns contre les autres.
hue [hju:] *n* teinte *f*, nuance *f*; **~ and cry** *n* tollé (*général*), clameur *f*.
huff [hʌf] *n*: **in a ~** fâché(e); **to take the ~** prendre la mouche.
huffy ['hʌfɪ] *adj* (*col*) froissé(e).
hug [hʌg] *vt* serrer dans ses bras; (*shore, kerb*) serrer ♦ *n* étreinte *f*; **to give sb a ~** serrer qn dans ses bras.
huge [hju:dʒ] *adj* énorme, immense.
hulk [hʌlk] *n* (*ship*) vieux rafiot; (*car, building*) carcasse *f*; (*person*) mastodonte *m*, malabar *m*.
hulking ['hʌlkɪŋ] *adj* balourd(e).
hull [hʌl] *n* (*of ship, nuts*) coque *f*; (*of peas*) cosse *f*.
hullabaloo ['hʌləbə'lu:] *n* (*col: noise*) tapage *m*, raffut *m*.
hullo [hə'ləu] *excl* = **hello**.
hum [hʌm] *vt* (*tune*) fredonner ♦ *vi* fredonner; (*insect*) bourdonner; (*plane, tool*) vrombir ♦ *n* fredonnement *m*; bourdonnement *m*; vrombissement *m*.
human ['hju:mən] *adj* humain(e) ♦ *n* (*also*: **~ being**) être humain.
humane [hju:'meɪn] *adj* humain(e), humanitaire.
humanism ['hju:mənɪzəm] *n* humanisme *m*.
humanitarian [hju:mænɪ'tɛərɪən] *adj* humanitaire.
humanity [hju:'mænɪtɪ] *n* humanité *f*.
humanly ['hju:mənlɪ] *adv* humainement.
humanoid ['hju:mənɔɪd] *adj*, *n* humanoïde (*m/f*).
human rights *npl* droits *mpl* de l'homme.
humble ['hʌmbl] *adj* humble, modeste ♦ *vt* humilier.
humbly ['hʌmblɪ] *adv* humblement, modestement.
humbug ['hʌmbʌg] *n* fumisterie *f*; (*BRIT: sweet*) bonbon *m* à la menthe.
humdrum ['hʌmdrʌm] *adj* monotone, routinier(ière).
humid ['hju:mɪd] *adj* humide.
humidifier [hju:'mɪdɪfaɪə*] *n* humidificateur *m*.
humidity [hju:'mɪdɪtɪ] *n* humidité *f*.
humiliate [hju:'mɪlɪeɪt] *vt* humilier.
humiliation [hju:mɪlɪ'eɪʃən] *n* humiliation *f*.
humility [hju:'mɪlɪtɪ] *n* humilité *f*.
humorist ['hju:mərɪst] *n* humoriste *m/f*.

humorous ['hju:mərəs] *adj* humoristique; (*person*) plein(e) d'humour.
humour, (*US*) **humor** ['hju:mə*] *n* humour *m*; (*mood*) humeur *f* ♦ *vt* (*person*) faire plaisir à; se prêter aux caprices de; **sense of ~** sens *m* de l'humour; **to be in a good/bad ~** être de bonne/mauvaise humeur.
humo(u)rless ['hu:məlɪs] *adj* dépourvu(e) d'humour.
hump [hʌmp] *n* bosse *f*.
humpback ['hʌmpbæk] *n* bossu/e; (*BRIT: also*: **~ bridge**) dos-d'âne *m*.
humus ['hju:məs] *n* humus *m*.
hunch [hʌntʃ] *n* bosse *f*; (*premonition*) intuition *f*; **I have a ~ that** j'ai (comme une vague) idée que.
hunchback ['hʌntʃbæk] *n* bossu/e.
hunched [hʌntʃt] *adj* arrondi(e), voûté(e).
hundred ['hʌndrəd] *num* cent; **about a ~ people** une centaine de personnes; **~s of people** des centaines de gens; **I'm a ~ per cent sure** j'en suis absolument certain.
hundredweight ['hʌndrɪdweɪt] *n* (*BRIT*) = 50.8 *kg; 112 lb;* (*US*) = 45.3 *kg; 100 lb.*
hung [hʌŋ] *pt, pp of* **hang**.
Hungarian [hʌŋ'gɛərɪən] *adj* hongrois(e) ♦ *n* Hongrois/e; (*LING*) hongrois *m*.
Hungary ['hʌŋgərɪ] *n* Hongrie *f*.
hunger ['hʌŋgə*] *n* faim *f* ♦ *vi*: **to ~ for** avoir faim de, désirer ardemment.
hunger strike *n* grève *f* de la faim.
hungover [hʌŋ'əuvə*] *adj* (*col*): **to be ~** avoir la gueule de bois.
hungrily ['hʌŋgrəlɪ] *adv* voracement; (*fig*) avidement.
hungry ['hʌŋgrɪ] *adj* affamé(e); **to be ~** avoir faim; **~ for** (*fig*) avide de.
hung up *adj* (*col*) complexé(e), bourré(e) de complexes.
hunk [hʌŋk] *n* gros morceau; (*col: man*) beau mec.
hunt [hʌnt] *vt* (*seek*) chercher; (*SPORT*) chasser ♦ *vi* chasser ♦ *n* chasse *f*.
► **hunt down** *vt* pourchasser.
hunter ['hʌntə*] *n* chasseur *m*; (*BRIT: horse*) cheval *m* de chasse.
hunting ['hʌntɪŋ] *n* chasse *f*.
hurdle ['hə:dl] *n* (*for fences*) claie *f*; (*SPORT*) haie *f*; (*fig*) obstacle *m*.
hurl [hə:l] *vt* lancer (avec violence).
hurling ['hə:lɪŋ] *n* (*SPORT*) *genre de hockey joué en Irlande*.
hurly-burly ['hə:lɪ'bə:lɪ] *n* tohu-bohu *m inv*; brouhaha *m*.
hurrah, hurray [hu'rɑ:, hu'reɪ] *n* hourra *m*.
hurricane ['hʌrɪkən] *n* ouragan *m*.
hurried ['hʌrɪd] *adj* pressé(e), précipité(e); (*work*) fait(e) à la hâte.
hurriedly ['hʌrɪdlɪ] *adv* précipitamment, à la hâte.
hurry ['hʌrɪ] *n* hâte *f*, précipitation *f* ♦ *vi* se presser, se dépêcher ♦ *vt* (*person*) faire

presser, faire se dépêcher; (*work*) presser; **to be in a ~** être pressé(e); **to do sth in a ~** faire qch en vitesse; **to ~ in/out** entrer/ sortir précipitamment; **to ~ home** se dépêcher de rentrer.

▶**hurry along** *vi* marcher d'un pas pressé.

▶**hurry away**, **hurry off** *vi* partir précipitamment.

▶**hurry up** *vi* se dépêcher.

hurt [həːt] *vb* (*pt, pp* **hurt**) *vt* (*cause pain to*) faire mal à; (*injure, fig*) blesser; (*damage: business, interests etc*) nuire à, faire du tort à ♦ *vi* faire mal ♦ *adj* blessé(e); **I ~ my arm** je me suis fait mal au bras; **where does it ~?** où avez-vous mal?, où est-ce que ça vous fait mal?

hurtful ['həːtful] *adj* (*remark*) blessant(e).

hurtle ['həːtl] *vt* lancer (de toutes ses forces) ♦ *vi*: **to ~ past** passer en trombe; **to ~ down** dégringoler.

husband ['hʌzbənd] *n* mari *m*.

hush [hʌʃ] *n* calme *m*, silence *m* ♦ *vt* faire taire; **~!** chut!

▶**hush up** *vt* (*fact*) étouffer.

hush-hush [hʌʃ'hʌʃ] *adj* (*col*) ultra-secret(ète).

husk [hʌsk] *n* (*of wheat*) balle *f*; (*of rice, maize*) enveloppe *f*; (*of peas*) cosse *f*.

husky ['hʌskɪ] *adj* rauque; (*burly*) costaud(e) ♦ *n* chien *m* esquimau *or* de traîneau.

hustings ['hʌstɪŋz] *npl* (*BRIT POL*) plate-forme électorale.

hustle ['hʌsl] *vt* pousser, bousculer ♦ *n* bousculade *f*; **~ and bustle** *n* tourbillon *m* (d'activité).

hut [hʌt] *n* hutte *f*; (*shed*) cabane *f*.

hutch [hʌtʃ] *n* clapier *m*.

hyacinth ['haɪəsɪnθ] *n* jacinthe *f*.

hybrid ['haɪbrɪd] *adj*, *n* hybride (*m*).

hydrant ['haɪdrənt] *n* prise *f* d'eau; (*also*: **fire ~**) bouche *f* d'incendie.

hydraulic [haɪ'drɔːlɪk] *adj* hydraulique.

hydraulics [haɪ'drɔːlɪks] *n* hydraulique *f*.

hydrochloric ['haɪdrəu'klɔrɪk] *adj*: **~ acid** acide *m* chlorhydrique.

hydroelectric ['haɪdrəuɪ'lɛktrɪk] *adj* hydro-électrique.

hydrofoil ['haɪdrəfɔɪl] *n* hydrofoil *m*.

hydrogen ['haɪdrədʒən] *n* hydrogène *m*.

hydrogen bomb *n* bombe *f* à hydrogène.

hydrophobia ['haɪdrə'fəubɪə] *n* hydrophobie *f*.

hydroplane ['haɪdrəpleɪn] *n* (*seaplane*) hydravion *m*; (*jetfoil*) hydroglisseur *m*.

hyena [haɪ'iːnə] *n* hyène *f*.

hygiene ['haɪdʒiːn] *n* hygiène *f*.

hygienic [haɪ'dʒiːnɪk] *adj* hygiénique.

hymn [hɪm] *n* hymne *m*; cantique *m*.

hype [haɪp] *n* (*col*) matraquage *m* publicitaire *or* médiatique.

hyperactive ['haɪpər'æktɪv] *adj* hyperactif(ive).

hypermarket ['haɪpəmɑːkɪt] *n* (*BRIT*) hypermarché *m*.

hypertension ['haɪpə'tɛnʃən] *n* (*MED*) hypertension *f*.

hyphen ['haɪfn] *n* trait *m* d'union.

hypnosis [hɪp'nəusɪs] *n* hypnose *f*.

hypnotic [hɪp'nɔtɪk] *adj* hypnotique.

hypnotism ['hɪpnətɪzəm] *n* hypnotisme *m*.

hypnotist ['hɪpnətɪst] *n* hypnotiseur/euse.

hypnotize ['hɪpnətaɪz] *vt* hypnotiser.

hypoallergenic ['haɪpəuæle'dʒɛnɪk] *adj* hypoallergique.

hypochondriac [haɪpə'kɔndrɪæk] *n* hypocondriaque *m/f*.

hypocrisy [hɪ'pɔkrɪsɪ] *n* hypocrisie *f*.

hypocrite ['hɪpəkrɪt] *n* hypocrite *m/f*.

hypocritical [hɪpə'krɪtɪkl] *adj* hypocrite.

hypodermic [haɪpə'dəːmɪk] *adj* hypodermique ♦ *n* (*syringe*) seringue *f* hypodermique.

hypotenuse [haɪ'pɔtɪnjuːz] *n* hypoténuse *f*.

hypothermia [haɪpə'θəːmɪə] *n* hypothermie *f*.

hypothesis, *pl* **hypotheses** [haɪ'pɔθɪsɪs, -siːz] *n* hypothèse *f*.

hypothetic(al) [haɪpəu'θɛtɪk(l)] *adj* hypothétique.

hysterectomy [hɪstə'rɛktəmɪ] *n* hystérectomie *f*.

hysteria [hɪ'stɪərɪə] *n* hystérie *f*.

hysterical [hɪ'stɛrɪkl] *adj* hystérique; **to become ~** avoir une crise de nerfs.

hysterics [hɪ'stɛrɪks] *npl* (violente) crise de nerfs; (*laughter*) crise de rire; **to have ~** avoir une crise de nerfs; attraper un fou rire.

Hz *abbr* (= *hertz*) Hz.

I i

I, i [aɪ] *n* (*letter*) I, i *m*; **I for Isaac**, (*US*) **I for Item** I comme Irma.

I [aɪ] *pron* je; (*before vowel*) j'; (*stressed*) moi ♦ *abbr* (= *island, isle*) I.

IA, Ia. *abbr* (*US*) = Iowa.

IAEA *n abbr* = **International Atomic Energy Agency**.

IBA *n abbr* (*BRIT*: = *Independent Broadcasting Authority*) ≈ CNCL *f* (= *Commission nationale de la communication audio-visuelle*).

Iberian [aɪ'bɪərɪən] *adj* ibérique, ibérien(ne).

Iberian Peninsula *n*: **the ~** la péninsule Ibérique.

IBEW *n abbr* (*US*: = *International Brotherhood of Electrical Workers*) *syndicat international des électriciens*.

i/c *abbr* (*BRIT*) = **in charge**.

ICBM *n abbr* (= *intercontinental ballistic missile*) ICBM *m*, engin *m* balistique à portée intercontinentale.

ICC *n abbr* (= *International Chamber of Commerce*) CCI *f*; (*US*) = *Interstate Commerce Commission*.

ice [aɪs] *n* glace *f*; (*on road*) verglas *m* ♦ *vt* (*cake*) glacer; (*drink*) faire rafraîchir ♦ *vi* (*also*: ~ **over**) geler; (*also*: ~ **up**) se givrer; **to put sth on** ~ (*fig*) mettre qch en attente.

Ice Age *n* ère *f* glaciaire.

ice axe *n* piolet *m*.

iceberg ['aɪsbəːg] *n* iceberg *m*; **the tip of the** ~ (*also fig*) la partie émergée de l'iceberg.

icebox ['aɪsbɔks] *n* (*US*) réfrigérateur *m*; (*BRIT*) compartiment *m* à glace; (*insulated box*) glacière *f*.

icebreaker ['aɪsbreɪkə*] *n* brise-glace *m*.

ice bucket *n* seau *m* à glace.

ice-cap ['aɪskæp] *n* calotte *f* glaciaire.

ice-cold [aɪs'kəuld] *adj* glacé(e).

ice cream *n* glace *f*.

ice cube *n* glaçon *m*.

iced [aɪst] *adj* (*drink*) frappé(e); (*coffee, tea, also cake*) glacé(e).

ice hockey *n* hockey *m* sur glace.

Iceland ['aɪslənd] *n* Islande *f*.

Icelander ['aɪsləndə*] *n* Islandais/e.

Icelandic [aɪs'lændɪk] *adj* islandais(e) ♦ *n* (*LING*) islandais *m*.

ice lolly [-'lɔlɪ] *n* (*BRIT*) esquimau *m*.

ice pick *n* pic *m* à glace.

ice rink *n* patinoire *f*.

ice-skate ['aɪsskeɪt] *n* patin *m* à glace ♦ *vi* faire du patin à glace.

ice-skating ['aɪsskeɪtɪŋ] *n* patinage *m* (sur glace).

icicle ['aɪsɪkl] *n* glaçon *m* (*naturel*).

icing ['aɪsɪŋ] *n* (*AVIAT etc*) givrage *m*; (*CULIN*) glaçage *m*.

icing sugar *n* (*BRIT*) sucre *m* glace.

ICJ *n abbr* = **International Court of Justice**.

icon ['aɪkɔn] *n* icône *f*.

ICR *n abbr* (*US*) = *Institute for Cancer Research*.

ICRC *n abbr* (= *International Committee of the Red Cross*) CICR *m*.

ICU *n abbr* = **intensive care unit**.

icy ['aɪsɪ] *adj* glacé(e); (*road*) verglacé(e); (*weather, temperature*) glacial(e).

ID *abbr* (*US*) = *Idaho*.

I'd [aɪd] = **I would, I had**.

Ida. *abbr* (*US*) = *Idaho*.

ID card *n* = **identity card**.

IDD *n abbr* (*BRIT TEL*: = *international direct dialling*) automatique international.

idea [aɪ'dɪə] *n* idée *f*; **good** ~! bonne idée!; **to have an** ~ **that** ... avoir idée que ...; **I haven't the least** ~ je n'ai pas la moindre idée.

ideal [aɪ'dɪəl] *n* idéal *m* ♦ *adj* idéal(e).

idealist [aɪ'dɪəlɪst] *n* idéaliste *m/f*.

ideally [aɪ'dɪəlɪ] *adv* idéalement, dans l'idéal; ~ **the book should have** ... l'idéal serait que le livre ait ....

identical [aɪ'dentɪkl] *adj* identique.

identification [aɪdentɪfɪ'keɪʃən] *n* identification *f*; **means of** ~ pièce *f* d'identité.

identify [aɪ'dentɪfaɪ] *vt* identifier ♦ *vi*: **to** ~ **with** s'identifier à.

Identikit [aɪ'dentɪkɪt] *n* ®: ~ **(picture)** portrait-robot *m*.

identity [aɪ'dentɪtɪ] *n* identité *f*.

identity card *n* carte *f* d'identité.

identity parade *n* (*BRIT*) parade *f* d'identification.

ideological [aɪdɪə'lɔdʒɪkl] *adj* idéologique.

ideology [aɪdɪ'ɔlədʒɪ] *n* idéologie *f*.

idiocy ['ɪdɪəsɪ] *n* idiotie *f*, stupidité *f*.

idiom ['ɪdɪəm] *n* langue *f*, idiome *m*; (*phrase*) expression *f* idiomatique.

idiomatic [ɪdɪə'mætɪk] *adj* idiomatique.

idiosyncrasy [ɪdɪəu'sɪŋkrəsɪ] *n* particularité *f*, caractéristique *f*.

idiot ['ɪdɪət] *n* idiot/e, imbécile *m/f*.

idiotic [ɪdɪ'ɔtɪk] *adj* idiot(e), bête, stupide.

idle ['aɪdl] *adj* sans occupation, désœuvré(e); (*lazy*) oisif(ive), paresseux(euse); (*unemployed*) au chômage; (*machinery*) au repos; (*question, pleasures*) vain(e), futile ♦ *vi* (*engine*) tourner au ralenti; **to lie** ~ être arrêté, ne pas fonctionner.

▸**idle away** *vt*: **to** ~ **away one's time** passer son temps à ne rien faire.

idleness ['aɪdlnɪs] *n* désœuvrement *m*; oisiveté *f*.

idler ['aɪdlə*] *n* désœuvré/e; oisif/ive.

idle time *n* (*COMM*) temps mort.

idol ['aɪdl] *n* idole *f*.

idolize ['aɪdəlaɪz] *vt* idolâtrer, adorer.

idyllic [ɪ'dɪlɪk] *adj* idyllique.

i.e. *abbr* (= *id est: that is*) c. à d., c'est-à-dire.

if [ɪf] *conj* si ♦ *n*: **there are a lot of** ~**s and buts** il y a beaucoup de si *mpl* et de mais *mpl*; **I'd be pleased** ~ **you could do it** je serais très heureux si vous pouviez le faire; ~ **necessary** si nécessaire, le cas échéant; ~ **only he were here** si seulement il était là; ~ **only to show him my gratitude** ne serait-ce que pour lui témoigner ma gratitude.

iffy ['ɪfɪ] *adj* (*col*) douteux(euse).

igloo ['ɪgluː] *n* igloo *m*.

ignite [ɪg'naɪt] *vt* mettre le feu à, enflammer ♦ *vi* s'enflammer.

ignition [ɪg'nɪʃən] *n* (*AUT*) allumage *m*; **to switch on/off the** ~ mettre/couper le contact.

ignition key *n* (*AUT*) clé *f* de contact.

ignoble [ɪg'nəubl] *adj* ignoble, indigne.

ignominious [ɪgnə'mɪnɪəs] *adj* honteux(euse), ignominieux(euse).

ignoramus [ɪgnə'reɪməs] *n* personne *f* ignare.

ignorance ['ɪgnərəns] *n* ignorance *f*; **to keep sb in** ~ **of sth** tenir qn dans l'ignorance de qch.

ignorant ['ɪgnərənt] *adj* ignorant(e); **to be** ~ **of** (*subject*) ne rien connaître en; (*events*) ne pas être au courant de.

ignore [ɪgˈnɔː*] *vt* ne tenir aucun compte de, ne pas relever; (*person*) faire semblant de ne pas reconnaître, ignorer; (*fact*) méconnaître.
ikon [ˈaɪkɔn] *n* = **icon.**
IL *abbr* (*US*) = *Illinois.*
ILA *n abbr* (*US*: = *International Longshoremen's Association*) syndicat international des dockers.
ill [ɪl] *adj* (*sick*) malade; (*bad*) mauvais(e) ♦ *n* mal *m* ♦ *adv*: **to speak/think ~ of sb** dire/penser du mal de qn; **to take** *or* **be taken ~** tomber malade.
Ill. *abbr* (*US*) = *Illinois.*
I'll [aɪl] = **I will, I shall.**
ill-advised [ɪləd'vaɪzd] *adj* (*decision*) peu judicieux(euse); (*person*) malavisé(e).
ill-at-ease [ɪlət'iːz] *adj* mal à l'aise.
ill-considered [ɪlkən'sɪdəd] *adj* (*plan*) inconsidéré(e), irréfléchi(e).
ill-disposed [ɪldɪs'pəuzd] *adj*: **to be ~ towards sb/sth** être mal disposé(e) envers qn/qch.
illegal [ɪ'liːgl] *adj* illégal(e).
illegally [ɪ'liːgəlɪ] *adv* illégalement.
illegible [ɪ'lɛdʒɪbl] *adj* illisible.
illegitimate [ɪlɪ'dʒɪtɪmət] *adj* illégitime.
ill-fated [ɪl'feɪtɪd] *adj* malheureux(euse); (*day*) néfaste.
ill-favoured, (*US*) **ill-favored** [ɪl'feɪvəd] *adj* déplaisant(e).
ill feeling *n* ressentiment *m*, rancune *f*.
ill-gotten [ˈɪlgɔtn] *adj* (*gains etc*) mal acquis(e).
ill health *n* mauvaise santé.
illicit [ɪ'lɪsɪt] *adj* illicite.
ill-informed [ɪlɪn'fɔːmd] *adj* (*judgment*) erroné(e); (*person*) mal renseigné(e).
illiterate [ɪ'lɪtərət] *adj* illettré(e); (*letter*) plein(e) de fautes.
ill-mannered [ɪl'mænəd] *adj* impoli(e), grossier(ière).
illness [ˈɪlnɪs] *n* maladie *f*.
illogical [ɪ'lɔdʒɪkl] *adj* illogique.
ill-suited [ɪl'suːtɪd] *adj* (*couple*) mal assorti(e); **he is ~ to the job** il n'est pas vraiment fait pour ce travail.
ill-timed [ɪl'taɪmd] *adj* inopportun(e).
ill-treat [ɪl'triːt] *vt* maltraiter.
ill-treatment [ɪl'triːtmənt] *n* mauvais traitement.
illuminate [ɪ'luːmɪneɪt] *vt* (*room, street*) éclairer; (*building*) illuminer; **~d sign** enseigne lumineuse.
illuminating [ɪ'luːmɪneɪtɪŋ] *adj* éclairant(e).
illumination [ɪluːmɪ'neɪʃən] *n* éclairage *m*; illumination *f*.
illusion [ɪ'luːʒən] *n* illusion *f*; **to be under the ~ that** avoir l'illusion que.
illusive, illusory [ɪ'luːsɪv, ɪ'luːsərɪ] *adj* illusoire.
illustrate [ˈɪləstreɪt] *vt* illustrer.
illustration [ɪlə'streɪʃən] *n* illustration *f*.

illustrator [ˈɪləstreɪtə*] *n* illustrateur/trice.
illustrious [ɪ'lʌstrɪəs] *adj* illustre.
ill will *n* malveillance *f*.
ILO *n abbr* (= *International Labour Organization*) OIT *f*.
ILWU *n abbr* (*US*: = *International Longshoremen's and Warehousemen's Union*) syndicat international des dockers et des magaziniers.
I'm [aɪm] = **I am.**
image [ˈɪmɪdʒ] *n* image *f*; (*public face*) image de marque.
imagery [ˈɪmɪdʒərɪ] *n* images *fpl*.
imaginable [ɪ'mædʒɪnəbl] *adj* imaginable.
imaginary [ɪ'mædʒɪnərɪ] *adj* imaginaire.
imagination [ɪmædʒɪ'neɪʃən] *n* imagination *f*.
imaginative [ɪ'mædʒɪnətɪv] *adj* imaginatif(ive), plein(e) d'imagination.
imagine [ɪ'mædʒɪn] *vt* s'imaginer; (*suppose*) imaginer, supposer.
imbalance [ɪm'bæləns] *n* déséquilibre *m*.
imbecile [ˈɪmbəsiːl] *n* imbécile *m/f*.
imbue [ɪm'bjuː] *vt*: **to ~ sth with** imprégner qch de.
IMF *n abbr* = **International Monetary Fund.**
imitate [ˈɪmɪteɪt] *vt* imiter.
imitation [ɪmɪ'teɪʃən] *n* imitation *f*.
imitator [ˈɪmɪteɪtə*] *n* imitateur/trice.
immaculate [ɪ'mækjulət] *adj* impeccable; (*REL*) immaculé(e).
immaterial [ɪmə'tɪərɪəl] *adj* sans importance, insignifiant(e).
immature [ɪmə'tjuə*] *adj* (*fruit*) qui n'est pas mûr(e); (*person*) qui manque de maturité.
immaturity [ɪmə'tjuərɪtɪ] *n* immaturité *f*.
immeasurable [ɪ'mɛʒrəbl] *adj* incommensurable.
immediacy [ɪ'miːdɪəsɪ] *n* (*of events etc*) caractère *or* rapport immédiat; (*of needs*) urgence *f*.
immediate [ɪ'miːdɪət] *adj* immédiat(e).
immediately [ɪ'miːdɪətlɪ] *adv* (*at once*) immédiatement; **~ next to** juste à côté de.
immense [ɪ'mɛns] *adj* immense; énorme.
immensity [ɪ'mɛnsɪtɪ] *n* immensité *f*.
immerse [ɪ'məːs] *vt* immerger, plonger; **to ~ sth in** plonger qch dans.
immersion heater [ɪ'məːʃən-] *n* (*BRIT*) chauffe-eau *m* électrique.
immigrant [ˈɪmɪgrənt] *n* immigrant/e; (*already established*) immigré/e.
immigration [ɪmɪ'greɪʃən] *n* immigration *f*.
immigration authorities *npl* service *m* de l'immigration.
immigration laws *npl* lois *fpl* sur l'immigration.
imminent [ˈɪmɪnənt] *adj* imminent(e).
immobile [ɪ'məubaɪl] *adj* immobile.
immobilize [ɪ'məubɪlaɪz] *vt* immobiliser.
immoderate [ɪ'mɔdərət] *adj* immodéré(e), démesuré(e).
immodest [ɪ'mɔdɪst] *adj* (*indecent*) indécent(e); (*boasting*) pas modeste, présomp-

immoral [ɪˈmɔrl] *adj* immoral(e).

immorality [ɪmɔˈrælɪtɪ] *n* immoralité *f*.

immortal [ɪˈmɔːtl] *adj, n* immortel(le).

immortalize [ɪˈmɔːtlaɪz] *vt* immortaliser.

immovable [ɪˈmuːvəbl] *adj* (*object*) fixe; immobilier(ière); (*person*) inflexible; (*opinion*) immuable.

immune [ɪˈmjuːn] *adj*: ~ **(to)** immunisé(e) (contre).

immune system *n* système *m* immunitaire.

immunity [ɪˈmjuːnɪtɪ] *n* immunité *f*; **diplomatic** ~ immunité diplomatique.

immunization [ɪmjunaɪˈzeɪʃən] *n* immunisation *f*.

immunize [ˈɪmjunaɪz] *vt* immuniser.

imp [ɪmp] *n* (*small devil*) lutin *m*; (*child*) petit diable.

impact [ˈɪmpækt] *n* choc *m*, impact *m*; (*fig*) impact.

impair [ɪmˈpɛə*] *vt* détériorer, diminuer.

impaired [ɪmˈpɛəd] *adj* (*organ, vision*) abîmé(e), détérioré(e); **his memory/circulation is** ~ il a des problèmes de mémoire/circulation; **visually** ~ malvoyant(e); **hearing** ~ malentendant(e); **mentally/physically** ~ intellectuellement/physiquement diminué(e).

impale [ɪmˈpeɪl] *vt* empaler.

impart [ɪmˈpɑːt] *vt* (*make known*) communiquer, transmettre; (*bestow*) confier, donner.

impartial [ɪmˈpɑːʃl] *adj* impartial(e).

impartiality [ɪmpɑːʃɪˈælɪtɪ] *n* impartialité *f*.

impassable [ɪmˈpɑːsəbl] *adj* infranchissable; (*road*) impraticable.

impasse [æmˈpɑːs] *n* (*fig*) impasse *f*.

impassioned [ɪmˈpæʃənd] *adj* passionné(e).

impassive [ɪmˈpæsɪv] *adj* impassible.

impatience [ɪmˈpeɪʃəns] *n* impatience *f*.

impatient [ɪmˈpeɪʃənt] *adj* impatient(e); **to get** *or* **grow** ~ s'impatienter.

impeach [ɪmˈpiːtʃ] *vt* accuser, attaquer; (*public official*) mettre en accusation.

impeachment [ɪmˈpiːtʃmənt] *n* (*LAW*) (mise *f* en) accusation *f*.

impeccable [ɪmˈpɛkəbl] *adj* impeccable, parfait(e).

impecunious [ɪmpɪˈkjuːnɪəs] *adj* sans ressources.

impede [ɪmˈpiːd] *vt* gêner.

impediment [ɪmˈpɛdɪmənt] *n* obstacle *m*; (*also*: **speech** ~) défaut *m* d'élocution.

impel [ɪmˈpɛl] *vt* (*force*): **to** ~ **sb (to do sth)** forcer qn (à faire qch).

impending [ɪmˈpɛndɪŋ] *adj* imminent(e).

impenetrable [ɪmˈpɛnɪtrəbl] *adj* impénétrable.

imperative [ɪmˈpɛrətɪv] *adj* nécessaire; urgent(e), pressant(e); (*tone*) impérieux(euse) ♦ *n* (*LING*) impératif *m*.

imperceptible [ɪmpəˈsɛptɪbl] *adj* imperceptible.

imperfect [ɪmˈpəːfɪkt] *adj* imparfait(e); (*goods etc*) défectueux(euse) ♦ *n* (*LING*: *also*: ~ **tense**) imparfait *m*.

imperfection [ɪmpəːˈfɛkʃən] *n* imperfection *f*; défectuosité *f*.

imperial [ɪmˈpɪərɪəl] *adj* impérial(e); (*BRIT*: *measure*) légal(e).

imperialism [ɪmˈpɪərɪəlɪzəm] *n* impérialisme *m*.

imperil [ɪmˈpɛrɪl] *vt* mettre en péril.

imperious [ɪmˈpɪərɪəs] *adj* impérieux(euse).

impersonal [ɪmˈpəːsənl] *adj* impersonnel(le).

impersonate [ɪmˈpəːsəneɪt] *vt* se faire passer pour; (*THEAT*) imiter.

impersonation [ɪmpəːsəˈneɪʃən] *n* (*LAW*) usurpation *f* d'identité; (*THEAT*) imitation *f*.

impersonator [ɪmˈpəːsəneɪtə*] *n* imposteur *m*; (*THEAT*) imitateur/trice.

impertinence [ɪmˈpəːtɪnəns] *n* impertinence *f*, insolence *f*.

impertinent [ɪmˈpəːtɪnənt] *adj* impertinent(e), insolent(e).

imperturbable [ɪmpəˈtəːbəbl] *adj* imperturbable.

impervious [ɪmˈpəːvɪəs] *adj* imperméable; (*fig*): ~ **to** insensible à; inaccessible à.

impetuous [ɪmˈpɛtjuəs] *adj* impétueux(euse), fougueux(euse).

impetus [ˈɪmpətəs] *n* impulsion *f*; (*of runner*) élan *m*.

impinge [ɪmˈpɪndʒ]: **to** ~ **on** *vt fus* (*person*) affecter, toucher; (*rights*) empiéter sur.

impish [ˈɪmpɪʃ] *adj* espiègle.

implacable [ɪmˈplækəbl] *adj* implacable.

implant [ɪmˈplɑːnt] *vt* (*MED*) implanter; (*fig*) inculquer.

implausible [ɪmˈplɔːzɪbl] *adj* peu plausible.

implement *n* [ˈɪmplɪmənt] outil *m*, instrument *m*; (*for cooking*) ustensile *m* ♦ *vt* [ˈɪmplɪment] exécuter, mettre à effet.

implicate [ˈɪmplɪkeɪt] *vt* impliquer, compromettre.

implication [ɪmplɪˈkeɪʃən] *n* implication *f*; **by** ~ indirectement.

implicit [ɪmˈplɪsɪt] *adj* implicite; (*complete*) absolu(e), sans réserve.

implicitly [ɪmˈplɪsɪtlɪ] *adv* implicitement; absolument, sans réserve.

implore [ɪmˈplɔː*] *vt* implorer, supplier.

imply [ɪmˈplaɪ] *vt* (*hint*) suggérer, laisser entendre; (*mean*) indiquer, supposer.

impolite [ɪmpəˈlaɪt] *adj* impoli(e).

imponderable [ɪmˈpɒndərəbl] *adj* impondérable.

import *vt* [ɪmˈpɔːt] importer ♦ *n* [ˈɪmpɔːt] (*COMM*) importation *f*; (*meaning*) portée *f*, signification *f* ♦ *cpd* (*duty, licence etc*) d'importation.

importance [ɪmˈpɔːtns] *n* importance *f*; **to be of great/little** ~ avoir beaucoup/peu d'importance.

important [ɪmˈpɔːtnt] *adj* important(e); **it is** ~ **that** il importe que, il est important que; **it's**

not ~ c'est sans importance, ce n'est pas important.

importantly [ɪmˈpɔːtntlɪ] *adv* (*with an air of importance*) d'un air important; (*essentially*): **but, more** ~ ... mais, (ce qui est) plus important encore ....

importation [ˌɪmpɔːˈteɪʃən] *n* importation *f*.

imported [ɪmˈpɔːtɪd] *adj* importé(e), d'importation.

importer [ɪmˈpɔːtə*] *n* importateur/trice.

impose [ɪmˈpəuz] *vt* imposer ♦ *vi*: **to** ~ **on sb** abuser de la gentillesse de qn.

imposing [ɪmˈpəuzɪŋ] *adj* imposant(e), impressionnant(e).

imposition [ˌɪmpəˈzɪʃən] *n* (*of tax etc*) imposition *f*; **to be an** ~ **on** (*person*) abuser de la gentillesse *or* la bonté de.

impossibility [ɪmpɔsəˈbɪlɪtɪ] *n* impossibilité *f*.

impossible [ɪmˈpɔsɪbl] *adj* impossible; **it is** ~ **for me to leave** il m'est impossible de partir.

impostor [ɪmˈpɔstə*] *n* imposteur *m*.

impotence [ˈɪmpətns] *n* impuissance *f*.

impotent [ˈɪmpətnt] *adj* impuissant(e).

impound [ɪmˈpaund] *vt* confisquer, saisir.

impoverished [ɪmˈpɔvərɪʃt] *adj* pauvre, appauvri(e).

impracticable [ɪmˈpræktɪkəbl] *adj* impraticable.

impractical [ɪmˈpræktɪkl] *adj* pas pratique; (*person*) qui manque d'esprit pratique.

imprecise [ˌɪmprɪˈsaɪs] *adj* imprécis(e).

impregnable [ɪmˈprɛgnəbl] *adj* (*fortress*) imprenable; (*fig*) inattaquable; irréfutable.

impregnate [ˈɪmprɛgneɪt] *vt* imprégner; (*fertilize*) féconder.

impresario [ɪmprɪˈsɑːrɪəu] *n* impresario *m*.

impress [ɪmˈprɛs] *vt* impressionner, faire impression sur; (*mark*) imprimer, marquer; **to** ~ **sth on sb** faire bien comprendre qch à qn.

impression [ɪmˈprɛʃən] *n* impression *f*; (*of stamp, seal*) empreinte *f*; **to make a good/bad** ~ **on sb** faire bonne/mauvaise impression sur qn; **to be under the** ~ **that** avoir l'impression que.

impressionable [ɪmˈprɛʃnəbl] *adj* impressionnable, sensible.

impressionist [ɪmˈprɛʃənɪst] *n* impressionniste *m/f*.

impressive [ɪmˈprɛsɪv] *adj* impressionnant(e).

imprint [ˈɪmprɪnt] *n* empreinte *f*; (*PUBLISHING*) notice *f*; (*: label*) nom *m* (de collection *or* d'éditeur).

imprinted [ɪmˈprɪntɪd] *adj*: ~ **on** imprimé(e) sur; (*fig*) imprimé(e) *or* gravé(e) dans.

imprison [ɪmˈprɪzn] *vt* emprisonner, mettre en prison.

imprisonment [ɪmˈprɪznmənt] *n* emprisonnement *m*.

improbable [ɪmˈprɔbəbl] *adj* improbable; (*excuse*) peu plausible.

impromptu [ɪmˈprɔmptjuː] *adj* impromptu(e) ♦ *adv* impromptu.

improper [ɪmˈprɔpə*] *adj* (*wrong*) incorrect(e); (*unsuitable*) déplacé(e), de mauvais goût; indécent(e).

impropriety [ˌɪmprəˈpraɪətɪ] *n* inconvenance *f*; (*of expression*) impropriété *f*.

improve [ɪmˈpruːv] *vt* améliorer ♦ *vi* s'améliorer; (*pupil etc*) faire des progrès.

▶**improve (up)on** *vt fus* (*offer*) enchérir sur.

improvement [ɪmˈpruːvmənt] *n* amélioration *f*; (*of pupil etc*) progrès *m*; **to make ~s to** apporter des améliorations à.

improvisation [ˌɪmprəvaɪˈzeɪʃən] *n* improvisation *f*.

improvise [ˈɪmprəvaɪz] *vt, vi* improviser.

imprudence [ɪmˈpruːdns] *n* imprudence *f*.

imprudent [ɪmˈpruːdnt] *adj* imprudent(e).

impudent [ˈɪmpjudnt] *adj* impudent(e).

impugn [ɪmˈpjuːn] *vt* contester, attaquer.

impulse [ˈɪmpʌls] *n* impulsion *f*; **on** ~ impulsivement, sur un coup de tête.

impulse buy *n* achat *m* d'impulsion.

impulsive [ɪmˈpʌlsɪv] *adj* impulsif(ive).

impunity [ɪmˈpjuːnɪtɪ] *n*: **with** ~ impunément.

impure [ɪmˈpjuə*] *adj* impur(e).

impurity [ɪmˈpjuərɪtɪ] *n* impureté *f*.

IN *abbr* (*US*) = Indiana.

================================== *KEYWORD*

in [ɪn] *prep* **1** (*indicating place, position*) dans; ~ **the house/the fridge** dans la maison/le frigo; ~ **the garden** dans le *or* au jardin; ~ **town** en ville; ~ **the country** à la campagne; ~ **school** à l'école; ~ **here/there** ici/là

2 (*with place names: of town, region, country*): ~ **London** à Londres; ~ **England** en Angleterre; ~ **Japan** au Japon; ~ **the United States** aux États-Unis

3 (*indicating time: during*): ~ **spring** au printemps; ~ **summer** en été; ~ **May/1992** en mai/1992; ~ **the afternoon** (dans) l'après-midi; **at 4 o'clock** ~ **the afternoon** à 4 heures de l'après-midi

4 (*indicating time: in the space of*) en; (*: future*) dans; **I did it** ~ **3 hours/days** je l'ai fait en 3 heures/jours; **I'll see you** ~ **2 weeks** *or* ~ **2 weeks' time** je te verrai dans 2 semaines; **once** ~ **a hundred years** une fois tous les cent ans

5 (*indicating manner etc*) à; ~ **a loud/soft voice** à voix haute/basse; ~ **pencil** au crayon; ~ **writing** par écrit; ~ **French** en français; **to pay** ~ **dollars** payer en dollars; **the boy** ~ **the blue shirt** le garçon à *or* avec la chemise bleue

6 (*indicating circumstances*): ~ **the sun** au soleil; ~ **the shade** à l'ombre; ~ **the rain** sous la pluie

7 (*indicating mood, state*): ~ **tears** en larmes; ~ **anger** sous le coup de la colère; ~ **despair** au désespoir; ~ **good condition** en bon état;

to live ~ luxury vivre dans le luxe
8 (with ratios, numbers): 1 ~ 10 (households),
1 (household) ~ 10 1 (ménage) sur 10; 20
pence ~ the pound 20 pence par livre sterling; they lined up ~ twos ils se mirent en
rangs (deux) par deux; ~ hundreds par centaines
9 (referring to people, works) chez; the disease is common ~ children c'est une maladie courante chez les enfants; ~ (the
works of) Dickens chez Dickens, dans
(l'œuvre de) Dickens
10 (indicating profession etc) dans; to be ~
teaching être dans l'enseignement
11 (after superlative) de; the best pupil ~ the
class le meilleur élève de la classe
12 (with present participle): ~ saying this en
disant ceci
♦ adv: to be ~ (person: at home, work) être là;
(train, ship, plane) être arrivé(e); (in fashion)
être à la mode; to ask sb ~ inviter qn à entrer; to run/limp etc ~ entrer en courant/
boitant etc; their party is ~ leur parti est au
pouvoir
♦ n: the ~s and outs (of) (of proposal, situation
etc) les tenants et aboutissants (de).

in. abbr = **inch(es)**.
inability [ɪnə'bɪlɪtɪ] n incapacité f; ~ to pay incapacité de payer.
inaccessible [ɪnək'sɛsɪbl] adj inaccessible.
inaccuracy [ɪn'ækjurəsɪ] n inexactitude f;
manque m de précision.
inaccurate [ɪn'ækjurət] adj inexact(e); (person) qui manque de précision.
inaction [ɪn'ækʃən] n inaction f, inactivité f.
inactivity [ɪnæk'tɪvɪtɪ] n inactivité f.
inadequacy [ɪn'ædɪkwəsɪ] n insuffisance f.
inadequate [ɪn'ædɪkwət] adj insuffisant(e),
inadéquat(e).
inadmissible [ɪnəd'mɪsəbl] adj (behaviour)
inadmissible; (LAW: evidence) irrecevable.
inadvertent [ɪnəd'vəːtnt] adj (mistake) com-
mis(e) par inadvertance.
inadvertently [ɪnəd'vəːtntlɪ] adv par mégarde.
inadvisable [ɪnəd'vaɪzəbl] adj à déconseiller;
it is ~ to il est déconseillé de.
inane [ɪ'neɪn] adj inepte, stupide.
inanimate [ɪn'ænɪmət] adj inanimé(e).
inapplicable [ɪn'æplɪkəbl] adj inapplicable.
inappropriate [ɪnə'prəuprɪət] adj inoppor-
tun(e), mal à propos; (word, expression) impropre.
inapt [ɪn'æpt] adj inapte; peu approprié(e).
inaptitude [ɪn'æptɪtjuːd] n inaptitude f.
inarticulate [ɪnaː'tɪkjulət] adj (person) qui
s'exprime mal; (speech) indistinct(e).
inasmuch [ɪnəz'mʌtʃ] adv: ~ as vu que, en ce
sens que.
inattention [ɪnə'tɛnʃən] n manque m
d'attention.
inattentive [ɪnə'tɛntɪv] adj inattentif(ive), dis-

trait(e); négligent(e).
inaudible [ɪn'ɔːdɪbl] adj inaudible.
inaugural [ɪ'nɔːgjurəl] adj inaugural(e).
inaugurate [ɪ'nɔːgjureɪt] vt inaugurer; (president, official) investir de ses fonctions.
inauguration [ɪnɔːgju'reɪʃən] n inauguration f;
investiture f.
inauspicious [ɪnɔːs'pɪʃəs] adj peu propice.
in-between [ɪnbɪ'twiːn] adj entre les deux.
inborn [ɪn'bɔːn] adj (feeling) inné(e); (defect)
congénital(e).
inbred [ɪn'brɛd] adj inné(e), naturel(le);
(family) consanguin(e).
inbreeding [ɪn'briːdɪŋ] n croisement m
d'animaux de même souche; unions consanguines.
Inc. abbr = **incorporated**.
Inca ['ɪŋkə] adj (also: ~n) inca inv ♦ n Inca m/f.
incalculable [ɪn'kælkjuləbl] adj incalculable.
incapability [ɪnkeɪpə'bɪlɪtɪ] n incapacité f.
incapable [ɪn'keɪpəbl] adj: ~ (of) incapable
(de).
incapacitate [ɪnkə'pæsɪteɪt] vt: to ~ sb from
doing rendre qn incapable de faire.
incapacitated [ɪnkə'pæsɪteɪtɪd] adj (LAW) frap-
pé(e) d'incapacité.
incapacity [ɪnkə'pæsɪtɪ] n incapacité f.
incarcerate [ɪn'kaːsəreɪt] vt incarcérer.
incarnate adj [ɪn'kaːnɪt] incarné(e) ♦ vt
['ɪnkaːneɪt] incarner.
incarnation [ɪnkaː'neɪʃən] n incarnation f.
incendiary [ɪn'sɛndɪərɪ] adj incendiaire ♦ n
(bomb) bombe f incendiaire.
incense n ['ɪnsɛns] encens m ♦ vt [ɪn'sɛns] (anger) mettre en colère.
incense burner n encensoir m.
incentive [ɪn'sɛntɪv] n encouragement m, raison f de se donner de la peine.
incentive scheme n système m de primes
d'encouragement.
inception [ɪn'sɛpʃən] n commencement m, début m.
incessant [ɪn'sɛsnt] adj incessant(e).
incessantly [ɪn'sɛsntlɪ] adv sans cesse, constamment.
incest ['ɪnsɛst] n inceste m.
inch [ɪntʃ] n pouce m (= 25 mm; 12 in a foot);
within an ~ of à deux doigts de; he wouldn't
give an ~ (fig) il n'a pas voulu céder d'un
pouce or faire la plus petite concession.
▶**inch forward** vi avancer petit à petit.
inch tape n (BRIT) centimètre m (de couturière).
incidence ['ɪnsɪdns] n (of crime, disease) fréquence f.
incident ['ɪnsɪdnt] n incident m; (in book) péri-
pétie f.
incidental [ɪnsɪ'dɛntl] adj accessoire; (unplanned) accidentel(le); ~ to qui accompagne; ~ expenses faux frais mpl.
incidentally [ɪnsɪ'dɛntəlɪ] adv (by the way) à
propos.

incidental music *n* musique *f* de fond.
incident room *n* (*POLICE*) salle *f* d'opérations.
incinerate [ɪn'sɪnəreɪt] *vt* incinérer.
incinerator [ɪn'sɪnəreɪtə*] *n* incinérateur *m*.
incipient [ɪn'sɪpɪənt] *adj* naissant(e).
incision [ɪn'sɪʒən] *n* incision *f*.
incisive [ɪn'saɪsɪv] *adj* incisif(ive); mordant(e).
incisor [ɪn'saɪzə*] *n* incisive *f*.
incite [ɪn'saɪt] *vt* inciter, pousser.
incl. *abbr* = **including, inclusive (of)**.
inclement [ɪn'klɛmənt] *adj* inclément(e), rigoureux(euse).
inclination [ɪnklɪ'neɪʃən] *n* inclination *f*.
incline *n* ['ɪnklaɪn] pente *f*, plan incliné ♦ *vb* [ɪn'klaɪn] *vt* incliner ♦ *vi*: **to ~ to** avoir tendance à; **to be ~d to do** être enclin(e) à faire; (*have a tendency to do*) avoir tendance à faire; **to be well ~d towards sb** être bien disposé(e) à l'égard de qn.
include [ɪn'kluːd] *vt* inclure, comprendre; **the tip is/is not ~d** le service est compris/n'est pas compris.
including [ɪn'kluːdɪŋ] *prep* y compris; **~ tip** service compris.
inclusion [ɪn'kluːʒən] *n* inclusion *f*.
inclusive [ɪn'kluːsɪv] *adj* inclus(e), compris(e); **£50 ~ of all surcharges** 50 livres tous frais compris.
inclusive terms *npl* (*BRIT*) prix tout compris.
incognito [ɪnkɔg'niːtəʊ] *adv* incognito.
incoherent [ɪnkəʊ'hɪərənt] *adj* incohérent(e).
income ['ɪnkʌm] *n* revenu *m*; **gross/net ~** revenu brut/net; **~ and expenditure account** compte *m* de recettes et de dépenses.
income support *n* (*BRIT*) ≈ revenu *m* minimum d'insertion, RMI *m*.
income tax *n* impôt *m* sur le revenu.
income tax inspector *n* inspecteur *m* des contributions directes.
income tax return *n* déclaration *f* des revenus.
incoming ['ɪnkʌmɪŋ] *adj* (*passengers, mail*) à l'arrivée; (*government, tenant*) nouveau(nouvelle); **~ tide** marée montante.
incommunicado ['ɪnkəmjunɪ'kɑːdəʊ] *adj*: **to hold sb ~** tenir qn au secret.
incomparable [ɪn'kɔmpərəbl] *adj* incomparable.
incompatible [ɪnkəm'pætɪbl] *adj* incompatible.
incompetence [ɪn'kɔmpɪtns] *n* incompétence *f*, incapacité *f*.
incompetent [ɪn'kɔmpɪtnt] *adj* incompétent(e), incapable.
incomplete [ɪnkəm'pliːt] *adj* incomplet(ète).
incomprehensible [ɪnkɔmprɪ'hɛnsɪbl] *adj* incompréhensible.
inconceivable [ɪnkən'siːvəbl] *adj* inconcevable.
inconclusive [ɪnkən'kluːsɪv] *adj* peu concluant(e); (*argument*) peu convaincant(e).
incongruous [ɪn'kɔŋgruəs] *adj* peu appro-

prié(e); (*remark, act*) incongru(e), déplacé(e).
inconsequential [ɪnkɔnsɪ'kwɛnʃl] *adj* sans importance.
inconsiderable [ɪnkən'sɪdərəbl] *adj*: **not ~** non négligeable.
inconsiderate [ɪnkən'sɪdərət] *adj* (*action*) inconsidéré(e); (*person*) qui manque d'égards.
inconsistency [ɪnkən'sɪstənsɪ] *n* (*of actions etc*) inconséquence *f*; (*of work*) irrégularité *f*; (*of statement etc*) incohérence *f*.
inconsistent [ɪnkən'sɪstnt] *adj* inconséquent(e); irregulier(ière); peu cohérent(e); **~ with** en contradiction avec.
inconsolable [ɪnkən'səuləbl] *adj* inconsolable.
inconspicuous [ɪnkən'spɪkjuəs] *adj* qui passe inaperçu(e); (*colour, dress*) discret(ète); **to make o.s. ~** ne pas se faire remarquer.
inconstant [ɪn'kɔnstnt] *adj* inconstant(e); variable.
incontinence [ɪn'kɔntɪnəns] *n* incontinence *f*.
incontinent [ɪn'kɔntɪnənt] *adj* incontinent(e).
incontrovertible [ɪnkɔntrə'vəːtəbl] *adj* irréfutable.
inconvenience [ɪnkən'viːnjəns] *n* inconvénient *m*; (*trouble*) dérangement *m* ♦ *vt* déranger; **don't ~ yourself** ne vous dérangez pas.
inconvenient [ɪnkən'viːnjənt] *adj* malcommode; (*time, place*) mal choisi(e), qui ne convient pas; **that time is very ~ for me** c'est un moment qui ne me convient pas du tout.
incorporate [ɪn'kɔːpəreɪt] *vt* incorporer; (*contain*) contenir ♦ *vi* fusionner; (*two firms*) se constituer en société.
incorporated [ɪn'kɔːpəreɪtɪd] *adj*: **~ company** (*US: abbr* **Inc.**) ≈ société *f* anonyme (S.A.).
incorrect [ɪnkə'rɛkt] *adj* incorrect(e); (*opinion, statement*) inexact(e).
incorrigible [ɪn'kɔrɪdʒɪbl] *adj* incorrigible.
incorruptible [ɪnkə'rʌptɪbl] *adj* incorruptible.
increase *n* ['ɪnkriːs] augmentation *f* ♦ *vi, vt* [ɪn'kriːs] augmenter; **an ~ of 5%** une augmentation de 5%; **to be on the ~** être en augmentation.
increasing [ɪn'kriːsɪŋ] *adj* croissant(e).
increasingly [ɪn'kriːsɪŋlɪ] *adv* de plus en plus.
incredible [ɪn'krɛdɪbl] *adj* incroyable.
incredulous [ɪn'krɛdjuləs] *adj* incrédule.
increment ['ɪnkrɪmənt] *n* augmentation *f*.
incriminate [ɪn'krɪmɪneɪt] *vt* incriminer, compromettre.
incriminating [ɪn'krɪmɪneɪtɪŋ] *adj* compromettant(e).
incrust [ɪn'krʌst] *vt* = **encrust**.
incubate ['ɪnkjubeɪt] *vt* (*egg*) couver, incuber ♦ *vi* (*eggs*) couver; (*disease*) couver.
incubation [ɪnkju'beɪʃən] *n* incubation *f*.
incubation period *n* période *f* d'incubation.
incubator ['ɪnkjubeɪtə*] *n* incubateur *m*; (*for babies*) couveuse *f*.
inculcate ['ɪnkʌlkeɪt] *vt*: **to ~ sth in sb** inculquer qch à qn.

incumbent [ɪn'kʌmbənt] *adj*: it is ~ on him to ... il lui incombe *or* appartient de ... ♦ *n* titulaire *m/f*.

incur [ɪn'kə:*] *vt* (*expenses*) encourir; (*anger*, *risk*) s'exposer à; (*debt*) contracter; (*loss*) subir.

incurable [ɪn'kjuərəbl] *adj* incurable.

incursion [ɪn'kə:ʃən] *n* incursion *f*.

Ind. *abbr* (*US*) = *Indiana*.

indebted [ɪn'dɛtɪd] *adj*: to be ~ to sb (for) être redevable à qn (de).

indecency [ɪn'di:snsɪ] *n* indécence *f*.

indecent [ɪn'di:snt] *adj* indécent(e), inconvenant(e).

indecent assault *n* (*BRIT*) attentat *m* à la pudeur.

indecent exposure *n* outrage *m* public à la pudeur.

indecipherable [ɪndɪ'saɪfərəbl] *adj* indéchiffrable.

indecision [ɪndɪ'sɪʒən] *n* indécision *f*.

indecisive [ɪndɪ'saɪsɪv] *adj* indécis(e); (*discussion*) peu concluant(e).

indeed [ɪn'di:d] *adv* en effet, effectivement; (*furthermore*) d'ailleurs; **yes ~!** certainement!

indefatigable [ɪndɪ'fætɪgəbl] *adj* infatigable.

indefensible [ɪndɪ'fɛnsɪbl] *adj* (*conduct*) indéfendable.

indefinable [ɪndɪ'faɪnəbl] *adj* indéfinissable.

indefinite [ɪn'dɛfɪnɪt] *adj* indéfini(e); (*answer*) vague; (*period, number*) indéterminé(e).

indefinitely [ɪn'dɛfɪnɪtlɪ] *adv* (*wait*) indéfiniment; (*speak*) vaguement, avec imprécision.

indelible [ɪn'dɛlɪbl] *adj* indélébile.

indelicate [ɪn'dɛlɪkɪt] *adj* (*tactless*) indélicat(e), grossier(ière); (*not polite*) inconvenant(e), malséant(e).

indemnify [ɪn'dɛmnɪfaɪ] *vt* indemniser, dédommager.

indemnity [ɪn'dɛmnɪtɪ] *n* (*insurance*) assurance *f*, garantie *f*; (*compensation*) indemnité *f*.

indent [ɪn'dɛnt] *vt* (*text*) commencer en retrait.

indentation [ɪndɛn'teɪʃən] *n* découpure *f*; (*TYP*) alinéa *m*; (*on metal*) bosse *f*.

indenture [ɪn'dɛntʃə*] *n* contrat *m* d'emploi-formation.

independence [ɪndɪ'pɛndns] *n* indépendance *f*.

> L'**Independence Day** *est la fête nationale aux États-Unis, le 4 juillet. Il commémore l'adoption de la déclaration d'Indépendance, en 1776, écrite par Thomas Jefferson et proclamant la séparation des 13 colonies américaines de la Grande-Bretagne.*

independent [ɪndɪ'pɛndnt] *adj* indépendant(e); **to become ~** s'affranchir.

independently [ɪndɪ'pɛndntlɪ] *adv* de façon indépendante; ~ **of** indépendamment de.

in-depth ['ɪndɛpθ] *adj* approfondi(e).

indescribable [ɪndɪ'skraɪbəbl] *adj* indescriptible.

indeterminate [ɪndɪ'tə:mɪnɪt] *adj* indéterminé(e).

index ['ɪndɛks] *n* (*pl*: ~**es**: *in book*) index *m*; (: *in library etc*) catalogue *m*; (*pl*: **indices** ['ɪndɪsi:z]) (*ratio, sign*) indice *m*.

index card *n* fiche *f*.

index finger *n* index *m*.

index-linked ['ɪndɛks'lɪŋkt], (*US*) **indexed** ['ɪndɛkst] *adj* indexé(e) (sur le coût de la vie *etc*).

India ['ɪndɪə] *n* Inde *f*.

Indian ['ɪndɪən] *adj* indien(ne) ♦ *n* Indien/ne.

Indian ink *n* encre *f* de Chine.

Indian Ocean *n*: the ~ l'océan Indien.

Indian summer *n* (*fig*) été indien, beaux jours en automne.

India paper *n* papier *m* bible.

India rubber *n* gomme *f*.

indicate ['ɪndɪkeɪt] *vt* indiquer ♦ *vi* (*BRIT AUT*): to ~ **left/right** mettre son clignotant à gauche/à droite.

indication [ɪndɪ'keɪʃən] *n* indication *f*, signe *m*.

indicative [ɪn'dɪkətɪv] *adj* indicatif(ive) ♦ *n* (*LING*) indicatif *m*; to be ~ **of sth** être symptomatique de qch.

indicator ['ɪndɪkeɪtə*] *n* (*sign*) indicateur *m*; (*AUT*) clignotant *m*.

indices ['ɪndɪsi:z] *npl of* **index**.

indict [ɪn'daɪt] *vt* accuser.

indictable [ɪn'daɪtəbl] *adj* (*person*) passible de poursuites; ~ **offence** délit *m* tombant sous le coup de la loi.

indictment [ɪn'daɪtmənt] *n* accusation *f*.

indifference [ɪn'dɪfrəns] *n* indifférence *f*.

indifferent [ɪn'dɪfrənt] *adj* indifférent(e); (*poor*) médiocre, quelconque.

indigenous [ɪn'dɪdʒɪnəs] *adj* indigène.

indigestible [ɪndɪ'dʒɛstɪbl] *adj* indigeste.

indigestion [ɪndɪ'dʒɛstʃən] *n* indigestion *f*, mauvaise digestion.

indignant [ɪn'dɪgnənt] *adj*: ~ **(at sth/with sb)** indigné(e) (de qch/contre qn).

indignation [ɪndɪg'neɪʃən] *n* indignation *f*.

indignity [ɪn'dɪgnɪtɪ] *n* indignité *f*, affront *m*.

indigo ['ɪndɪgəʊ] *adj* indigo *inv* ♦ *n* indigo *m*.

indirect [ɪndɪ'rɛkt] *adj* indirect(e).

indirectly [ɪndɪ'rɛktlɪ] *adv* indirectement.

indiscreet [ɪndɪ'skri:t] *adj* indiscret(ète); (*rash*) imprudent(e).

indiscretion [ɪndɪ'skrɛʃən] *n* (*see indiscreet*) indiscrétion *f*; imprudence *f*.

indiscriminate [ɪndɪ'skrɪmɪnət] *adj* (*person*) qui manque de discernement; (*admiration*) aveugle; (*killings*) commis(e) au hasard.

indispensable [ɪndɪ'spɛnsəbl] *adj* indispensable.

indisposed [ɪndɪ'spəʊzd] *adj* (*unwell*) indisposé(e), souffrant(e).

indisposition [ɪndɪspə'zɪʃən] *n* (*illness*) indisposition *f*, malaise *m*.
indisputable [ɪndɪ'spjuːtəbl] *adj* incontestable, indiscutable.
indistinct [ɪndɪ'stɪŋkt] *adj* indistinct(e); (*memory, noise*) vague.
indistinguishable [ɪndɪ'stɪŋgwɪʃəbl] *adj* impossible à distinguer.
individual [ɪndɪ'vɪdjuəl] *n* individu *m* ♦ *adj* individuel(le); (*characteristic*) particulier(ière), original(e).
individualist [ɪndɪ'vɪdjuəlɪst] *n* individualiste *m/f*.
individuality [ɪndɪvɪdju'ælɪtɪ] *n* individualité *f*.
individually [ɪndɪ'vɪdjuəlɪ] *adv* individuellement.
indivisible [ɪndɪ'vɪzɪbl] *adj* indivisible; (*MATH*) insécable.
Indo-China ['ɪndəu'tʃaɪnə] *n* Indochine *f*.
indoctrinate [ɪn'dɔktrɪneɪt] *vt* endoctriner.
indoctrination [ɪndɔktrɪ'neɪʃən] *n* endoctrinement *m*.
indolent ['ɪndələnt] *adj* indolent(e), nonchalant(e).
Indonesia [ɪndə'niːzɪə] *n* Indonésie *f*.
Indonesian [ɪndə'niːzɪən] *adj* indonésien(ne) ♦ *n* Indonésien/ne; (*LING*) indonésien *m*.
indoor ['ɪndɔː*] *adj* d'intérieur; (*plant*) d'appartement; (*swimming pool*) couvert(e); (*sport, games*) pratiqué(e) en salle.
indoors [ɪn'dɔːz] *adv* à l'intérieur; (*at home*) à la maison.
indubitable [ɪn'djuːbɪtəbl] *adj* indubitable, incontestable.
induce [ɪn'djuːs] *vt* persuader; (*bring about*) provoquer; **to ~ sb to do sth** inciter *or* pousser qn à faire qch.
inducement [ɪn'djuːsmənt] *n* incitation *f*; (*incentive*) but *m*; (*pej: bribe*) pot-de-vin *m*.
induct [ɪn'dʌkt] *vt* établir dans ses fonctions; (*fig*) initier.
induction [ɪn'dʌkʃən] *n* (*MED: of birth*) accouchement provoqué.
induction course *n* (*BRIT*) stage *m* de mise au courant.
indulge [ɪn'dʌldʒ] *vt* (*whim*) céder à, satisfaire; (*child*) gâter ♦ *vi*: **to ~ in sth** s'offrir qch, se permettre qch; se livrer à qch.
indulgence [ɪn'dʌldʒəns] *n* fantaisie *f* (que l'on s'offre); (*leniency*) indulgence *f*.
indulgent [ɪn'dʌldʒənt] *adj* indulgent(e).
industrial [ɪn'dʌstrɪəl] *adj* industriel(le); (*injury*) du travail; (*dispute*) ouvrier(ière).
industrial action *n* action revendicative.
industrial estate *n* (*BRIT*) zone industrielle.
industrialist [ɪn'dʌstrɪəlɪst] *n* industriel *m*.
industrialize [ɪn'dʌstrɪəlaɪz] *vt* industrialiser.
industrial park *n* (*US*) zone industrielle.
industrial relations *npl* relations *fpl* dans l'entreprise.
industrial tribunal *n* (*BRIT*) ≈ conseil *m* de prud'hommes.

industrial unrest *n* (*BRIT*) agitation sociale, conflits sociaux.
industrious [ɪn'dʌstrɪəs] *adj* travailleur(euse).
industry ['ɪndəstrɪ] *n* industrie *f*; (*diligence*) zèle *m*, application *f*.
inebriated [ɪ'niːbrɪeɪtɪd] *adj* ivre.
inedible [ɪn'ɛdɪbl] *adj* immangeable; (*plant etc*) non comestible.
ineffective [ɪnɪ'fɛktɪv], **ineffectual** [ɪnɪ'fɛktʃuəl] *adj* inefficace; incompétent(e).
inefficiency [ɪnɪ'fɪʃənsɪ] *n* inefficacité *f*.
inefficient [ɪnɪ'fɪʃənt] *adj* inefficace.
inelegant [ɪn'ɛlɪgənt] *adj* peu élégant(e), inélégant(e).
ineligible [ɪn'ɛlɪdʒɪbl] *adj* (*candidate*) inéligible; **to be ~ for sth** ne pas avoir droit à qch.
inept [ɪ'nɛpt] *adj* inepte.
ineptitude [ɪ'nɛptɪtjuːd] *n* ineptie *f*.
inequality [ɪnɪ'kwɔlɪtɪ] *n* inégalité *f*.
inequitable [ɪn'ɛkwɪtəbl] *adj* inéquitable, inique.
ineradicable [ɪnɪ'rædɪkəbl] *adj* indéracinable, tenace.
inert [ɪ'nɜːt] *adj* inerte.
inertia [ɪ'nɜːʃə] *n* inertie *f*.
inertia-reel seat belt [ɪ'nɜːʃə'riːl-] *n* ceinture *f* de sécurité à enrouleur.
inescapable [ɪnɪ'skeɪpəbl] *adj* inéluctable, inévitable.
inessential [ɪnɪ'sɛnʃl] *adj* superflu(e).
inestimable [ɪn'ɛstɪməbl] *adj* inestimable, incalculable.
inevitable [ɪn'ɛvɪtəbl] *adj* inévitable.
inevitably [ɪn'ɛvɪtəblɪ] *adv* inévitablement, fatalement.
inexact [ɪnɪg'zækt] *adj* inexact(e).
inexcusable [ɪnɪks'kjuːzəbl] *adj* inexcusable.
inexhaustible [ɪnɪg'zɔːstɪbl] *adj* inépuisable.
inexorable [ɪn'ɛksərəbl] *adj* inexorable.
inexpensive [ɪnɪk'spɛnsɪv] *adj* bon marché *inv*.
inexperience [ɪnɪk'spɪərɪəns] *n* inexpérience *f*, manque *m* d'expérience.
inexperienced [ɪnɪk'spɪərɪənst] *adj* inexpérimenté(e); **to be ~ in sth** manquer d'expérience dans qch.
inexplicable [ɪnɪk'splɪkəbl] *adj* inexplicable.
inexpressible [ɪnɪk'sprɛsɪbl] *adj* inexprimable; indicible.
inextricable [ɪnɪk'strɪkəbl] *adj* inextricable.
infallibility [ɪnfælə'bɪlɪtɪ] *n* infaillibilité *f*.
infallible [ɪn'fælɪbl] *adj* infaillible.
infamous ['ɪnfəməs] *adj* infâme, abominable.
infamy ['ɪnfəmɪ] *n* infamie *f*.
infancy ['ɪnfənsɪ] *n* petite enfance, bas âge; (*fig*) enfance, débuts *mpl*.
infant ['ɪnfənt] *n* (*baby*) nourrisson *m*; (*young child*) petit(e) enfant.
infantile ['ɪnfəntaɪl] *adj* infantile.
infant mortality *n* mortalité *f* infantile.
infantry ['ɪnfəntrɪ] *n* infanterie *f*.
infantryman ['ɪnfəntrɪmən] *n* fantassin *m*.

infant school n (BRIT) classes fpl préparatoires (entre 5 et 7 ans).

infatuated [ɪn'fætjueɪtɪd] adj: ~ **with** entiché(e) de; **to become** ~ **(with sb)** s'enticher (de qn).

infatuation [ɪnfætju'eɪʃən] n toquade f; engouement m.

infect [ɪn'fɛkt] vt infecter, contaminer; (fig: pej) corrompre; ~**ed with** (illness) atteint(e) de; **to become** ~**ed** (wound) s'infecter.

infection [ɪn'fɛkʃən] n infection f; contagion f.

infectious [ɪn'fɛkʃəs] adj infectieux(euse); (also fig) contagieux(euse).

infer [ɪn'fəː*] vt: **to** ~ **(from)** conclure (de), déduire (de).

inference ['ɪnfərəns] n conclusion f, déduction f.

inferior [ɪn'fɪərɪə*] adj inférieur(e); (goods) de qualité inférieure ♦ n inférieur/e; (in rank) subalterne m/f; **to feel** ~ avoir un sentiment d'infériorité.

inferiority [ɪnfɪərɪ'ɔrɪtɪ] n infériorité f.

inferiority complex n complexe m d'infériorité.

infernal [ɪn'fəːnl] adj infernal(e).

infernally [ɪn'fəːnəlɪ] adv abominablement.

inferno [ɪn'fəːnəʊ] n enfer m; brasier m.

infertile [ɪn'fəːtaɪl] adj stérile.

infertility [ɪnfəː'tɪlɪtɪ] n infertilité f, stérilité f.

infested [ɪn'fɛstɪd] adj: ~ **(with)** infesté(e) (de).

infidelity [ɪnfɪ'dɛlɪtɪ] n infidélité f.

in-fighting ['ɪnfaɪtɪŋ] n querelles fpl internes.

infiltrate ['ɪnfɪltreɪt] vt (troops etc) faire s'infiltrer; (enemy line etc) s'infiltrer dans ♦ vi s'infiltrer.

infinite ['ɪnfɪnɪt] adj infini(e); (time, money) illimité(e).

infinitely ['ɪnfɪnɪtlɪ] adv infiniment.

infinitesimal [ɪnfɪnɪ'tɛsɪməl] adj infinitésimal(e).

infinitive [ɪn'fɪnɪtɪv] n infinitif m.

infinity [ɪn'fɪnɪtɪ] n infinité f; (also MATH) infini m.

infirm [ɪn'fəːm] adj infirme.

infirmary [ɪn'fəːmərɪ] n hôpital m; (in school, factory) infirmerie f.

infirmity [ɪn'fəːmɪtɪ] n infirmité f.

inflamed [ɪn'fleɪmd] adj enflammé(e).

inflammable [ɪn'flæməbl] adj (BRIT) inflammable.

inflammation [ɪnflə'meɪʃən] n inflammation f.

inflammatory [ɪn'flæmətərɪ] adj (speech) incendiaire.

inflatable [ɪn'fleɪtəbl] adj gonflable.

inflate [ɪn'fleɪt] vt (tyre, balloon) gonfler; (fig) grossir; gonfler; faire monter.

inflated [ɪn'fleɪtɪd] adj (style) enflé(e); (value) exagéré(e).

inflation [ɪn'fleɪʃən] n (ECON) inflation f.

inflationary [ɪn'fleɪʃənərɪ] adj inflationniste.

inflection [ɪn'flɛkʃən] n inflexion f; (ending) désinence f.

inflexible [ɪn'flɛksɪbl] adj inflexible, rigide.

inflict [ɪn'flɪkt] vt: **to** ~ **on** infliger à.

infliction [ɪn'flɪkʃən] n infliction f; affliction f.

in-flight ['ɪnflaɪt] adj (refuelling) en vol; (service etc) à bord.

inflow ['ɪnfləʊ] n afflux m.

influence ['ɪnfluəns] n influence f ♦ vt influencer; **under the** ~ **of** sous l'effet de; **under the** ~ **of drink** en état d'ébriété.

influential [ɪnflu'ɛnʃl] adj influent(e).

influenza [ɪnflu'ɛnzə] n grippe f.

influx ['ɪnflʌks] n afflux m.

inform [ɪn'fɔːm] vt: **to** ~ **sb (of)** informer or avertir qn (de) ♦ vi: **to** ~ **on sb** dénoncer qn, informer contre qn; **to** ~ **sb about** renseigner qn sur, mettre qn au courant de.

informal [ɪn'fɔːml] adj (person, manner) simple, sans cérémonie; (announcement, visit) non officiel(le); **"dress** ~**"** "tenue de ville".

informality [ɪnfɔː'mælɪtɪ] n simplicité f, absence f de cérémonie; caractère non officiel.

informal language n langage m de la conversation.

informally [ɪn'fɔːməlɪ] adv sans cérémonie, en toute simplicité; non officiellement.

informant [ɪn'fɔːmənt] n informateur/trice.

information [ɪnfə'meɪʃən] n information(s) f(pl); renseignements mpl; (knowledge) connaissances fpl; **to get** ~ **on** se renseigner sur; **a piece of** ~ un renseignement; **for your** ~ à titre d'information.

information bureau n bureau m de renseignements.

information processing n traitement m de l'information.

information retrieval n recherche f (informatique) de renseignements.

information technology (IT) n informatique f.

informative [ɪn'fɔːmətɪv] adj instructif(ive).

informed [ɪn'fɔːmd] adj (bien) informé(e); **an** ~ **guess** une hypothèse fondée sur la connaissance des faits.

informer [ɪn'fɔːmə*] n dénonciateur/trice; (also: **police** ~) indicateur/trice.

infra dig ['ɪnfrə'dɪg] adj abbr (col: = infra dignitatem) au-dessous de ma (or sa etc) dignité.

infra-red [ɪnfrə'rɛd] adj infrarouge.

infrastructure ['ɪnfrəstrʌktʃə*] n infrastructure f.

infrequent [ɪn'friːkwənt] adj peu fréquent(e), rare.

infringe [ɪn'frɪndʒ] vt enfreindre ♦ vi: **to** ~ **on** empiéter sur.

infringement [ɪn'frɪndʒmənt] n: ~ **(of)** infraction f (à).

infuriate [ɪn'fjuərɪeɪt] vt mettre en fureur.

infuriating [ɪn'fjuərɪeɪtɪŋ] adj exaspérant(e).

infuse [ɪn'fjuːz] vt: **to** ~ **sb with sth** (fig) insuffler qch à qn.

infusion [ɪnˈfjuːʒən] n (tea etc) infusion f.
ingenious [ɪnˈdʒiːnjəs] adj ingénieux(euse).
ingenuity [ɪndʒɪˈnjuːɪtɪ] n ingéniosité f.
ingenuous [ɪnˈdʒɛnjuəs] adj franc(franche), ouvert(e).
ingot [ˈɪŋgət] n lingot m.
ingrained [ɪnˈgreɪnd] adj enraciné(e).
ingratiate [ɪnˈgreɪʃɪeɪt] vt: **to ~ o.s. with** s'insinuer dans les bonnes grâces de, se faire bien voir de.
ingratiating [ɪnˈgreɪʃɪeɪtɪŋ] adj (smile, speech) insinuant(e); (person) patelin(e).
ingratitude [ɪnˈgrætɪtjuːd] n ingratitude f.
ingredient [ɪnˈgriːdɪənt] n ingrédient m; élément m.
ingrowing [ˈɪŋgrəʊɪŋ], **ingrown** [ˈɪŋgrəʊn] adj: **~ toenail** ongle incarné.
inhabit [ɪnˈhæbɪt] vt habiter.
inhabitable [ɪnˈhæbɪtəbl] adj habitable.
inhabitant [ɪnˈhæbɪtnt] n habitant/e.
inhale [ɪnˈheɪl] vt inhaler; (perfume) respirer ♦ vi (in smoking) avaler la fumée.
inhaler [ɪnˈheɪlə*] n inhalateur m.
inherent [ɪnˈhɪərənt] adj: **~ (in or to)** inhérent(e) (à).
inherently [ɪnˈhɪərəntlɪ] adv (easy, difficult) en soi; (lazy) fondamentalement.
inherit [ɪnˈhɛrɪt] vt hériter (de).
inheritance [ɪnˈhɛrɪtəns] n héritage m; **law of ~** droit m de la succession.
inhibit [ɪnˈhɪbɪt] vt (PSYCH) inhiber; **to ~ sb from doing** empêcher or retenir qn de faire.
inhibited [ɪnˈhɪbɪtɪd] adj (person) inhibé(e).
inhibiting [ɪnˈhɪbɪtɪŋ] adj gênant(e).
inhibition [ɪnhɪˈbɪʃən] n inhibition f.
inhospitable [ɪnhɔsˈpɪtəbl] adj inhospitalier(ière).
in-house [ˈɪnˈhaʊs] adj (system) interne; (training) effectué(e) sur place or dans le cadre de la compagnie ♦ adv (train, produce) sur place.
inhuman [ɪnˈhjuːmən] adj inhumain(e).
inhumane [ɪnhjuːˈmeɪn] adj inhumain(e).
inimitable [ɪˈnɪmɪtəbl] adj inimitable.
iniquity [ɪˈnɪkwɪtɪ] n iniquité f.
initial [ɪˈnɪʃl] adj initial(e) ♦ n initiale f ♦ vt parafer; **~s** npl initiales fpl; (as signature) parafe m.
initialize [ɪˈnɪʃəlaɪz] vt (COMPUT) initialiser.
initially [ɪˈnɪʃəlɪ] adv initialement, au début.
initiate [ɪˈnɪʃɪeɪt] vt (start) entreprendre; amorcer; lancer; (person) initier; **to ~ sb into a secret** initier qn à un secret; **to ~ proceedings against sb** (LAW) intenter une action à qn, engager des poursuites contre qn.
initiation [ɪnɪʃɪˈeɪʃən] n (into secret etc) initiation f.
initiative [ɪˈnɪʃətɪv] n initiative f; **to take the ~** prendre l'initiative.
inject [ɪnˈdʒɛkt] vt (liquid, fig: money) injecter; (person) faire une piqûre à.
injection [ɪnˈdʒɛkʃən] n injection f, piqûre f; **to**

have an ~ se faire faire une piqûre.
injudicious [ɪndʒuˈdɪʃəs] adj peu judicieux(euse).
injunction [ɪnˈdʒʌŋkʃən] n (LAW) injonction f, ordre m.
injure [ˈɪndʒə*] vt blesser; (wrong) faire du tort à; (damage: reputation etc) compromettre; (feelings) heurter; **to ~ o.s.** se blesser.
injured [ˈɪndʒəd] adj (person, leg etc) blessé(e); (tone, feelings) offensé(e); **~ party** (LAW) partie lésée.
injurious [ɪnˈdʒuərɪəs] adj: **~ (to)** préjudiciable (à).
injury [ˈɪndʒərɪ] n blessure f; (wrong) tort m; **to escape without ~** s'en sortir sain et sauf.
injury time n (SPORT) arrêts mpl de jeu.
injustice [ɪnˈdʒʌstɪs] n injustice f; **you do me an ~** vous êtes injuste envers moi.
ink [ɪŋk] n encre f.
ink-jet printer [ˈɪŋkdʒɛt-] n imprimante f à jet d'encre.
inkling [ˈɪŋklɪŋ] n soupçon m, vague idée f.
inkpad [ˈɪŋkpæd] n tampon m encreur.
inky [ˈɪŋkɪ] adj taché(e) d'encre.
inlaid [ˈɪnleɪd] adj incrusté(e); (table etc) marqueté(e).
inland adj [ˈɪnlənd] intérieur(e) ♦ adv [ɪnˈlænd] à l'intérieur, dans les terres; **~ waterways** canaux mpl et rivières fpl.
Inland Revenue n (BRIT) fisc m.
in-laws [ˈɪnlɔːz] npl beaux-parents mpl; belle famille.
inlet [ˈɪnlɛt] n (GEO) crique f.
inlet pipe n (TECH) tuyau m d'arrivée.
inmate [ˈɪnmeɪt] n (in prison) détenu/e; (in asylum) interné/e.
inmost [ˈɪnməʊst] adj le(la) plus profond(e).
inn [ɪn] n auberge f.
innards [ˈɪnədz] npl (col) entrailles fpl.
innate [ɪˈneɪt] adj inné(e).
inner [ˈɪnə*] adj intérieur(e).
inner city n (vieux quartiers du) centre urbain (souffrant souvent de délabrement, d'embouteillages etc).
innermost [ˈɪnəməʊst] adj le(la) plus profond(e).
inner tube n (of tyre) chambre f à air.
innings [ˈɪnɪŋz] n (CRICKET) tour m de batte; (BRIT fig): **he has had a good ~** il (en) a bien profité.
innocence [ˈɪnəsns] n innocence f.
innocent [ˈɪnəsnt] adj innocent(e).
innocuous [ɪˈnɔkjuəs] adj inoffensif(ive).
innovation [ɪnəʊˈveɪʃən] n innovation f.
innuendo, ~es [ɪnjuˈɛndəʊ] n insinuation f, allusion (malveillante).
innumerable [ɪˈnjuːmrəbl] adj innombrable.
inoculate [ɪˈnɔkjuleɪt] vt: **to ~ sb with sth** inoculer qch à qn; **to ~ sb against sth** vacciner qn contre qch.
inoculation [ɪnɔkjuˈleɪʃən] n inoculation f.
inoffensive [ɪnəˈfɛnsɪv] adj inoffensif(ive).

inopportune [ɪn'ɔpətjuːn] *adj* inopportun(e).
inordinate [ɪ'nɔːdɪnət] *adj* démesuré(e).
inordinately [ɪ'nɔːdɪnətlɪ] *adv* démesurément.
inorganic [ɪnɔː'gænɪk] *adj* inorganique.
in-patient ['ɪnpeɪʃənt] *n* malade hospitalisé(e).
input ['ɪnput] *n* (ELEC) énergie *f*, puissance *f*; (*of machine*) consommation *f*; (*of computer*) information fournie ♦ *vt* (COMPUT) introduire, entrer.
inquest ['ɪnkwɛst] *n* enquête (criminelle).
inquire [ɪn'kwaɪə*] *vi* demander ♦ *vt* demander, s'informer de; **to ~ about** s'informer de, se renseigner sur; **to ~ when/where/whether** demander quand/où/si.
▶**inquire after** *vt fus* demander des nouvelles de.
▶**inquire into** *vt fus* faire une enquête sur.
inquiring [ɪn'kwaɪərɪŋ] *adj* (*mind*) curieux(euse), investigateur(trice).
inquiry [ɪn'kwaɪərɪ] *n* demande *f* de renseignements; (LAW) enquête *f*, investigation *f*; **to hold an ~ into sth** enquêter sur qch.
inquiry desk *n* (BRIT) guichet *m* de renseignements.
inquiry office *n* (BRIT) bureau *m* de renseignements.
inquisition [ɪnkwɪ'zɪʃən] *n* enquête *f*, investigation *f*; (REL): **the I~** l'Inquisition *f*.
inquisitive [ɪn'kwɪzɪtɪv] *adj* curieux(euse).
inroads ['ɪnrəudz] *npl*: **to make ~ into** (*savings, supplies*) entamer.
ins *abbr* = **inches**.
insane [ɪn'seɪn] *adj* fou(folle); (MED) aliéné(e).
insanitary [ɪn'sænɪtərɪ] *adj* insalubre.
insanity [ɪn'sænɪtɪ] *n* folie *f*; (MED) aliénation (mentale).
insatiable [ɪn'seɪʃəbl] *adj* insatiable.
inscribe [ɪn'skraɪb] *vt* inscrire; (*book etc*): **to ~ (to sb)** dédicacer (à qn).
inscription [ɪn'skrɪpʃən] *n* inscription *f*; (*in book*) dédicace *f*.
inscrutable [ɪn'skruːtəbl] *adj* impénétrable.
inseam ['ɪnsiːm] *n* (US): **~ measurement** hauteur *f* d'entre-jambe.
insect ['ɪnsɛkt] *n* insecte *m*.
insect bite *n* piqûre *f* d'insecte.
insecticide [ɪn'sɛktɪsaɪd] *n* insecticide *m*.
insect repellent *n* crème *f* anti-insectes.
insecure [ɪnsɪ'kjuə*] *adj* peu solide; peu sûr(e); (*person*) anxieux(euse).
insecurity [ɪnsɪ'kjuərɪtɪ] *n* insécurité *f*.
insensible [ɪn'sɛnsɪbl] *adj* insensible; (*unconscious*) sans connaissance.
insensitive [ɪn'sɛnsɪtɪv] *adj* insensible.
insensitivity [ɪnsɛnsɪ'tɪvɪtɪ] *n* insensibilité *f*.
inseparable [ɪn'sɛprəbl] *adj* inséparable.
insert *vt* [ɪn'səːt] insérer ♦ *n* ['ɪnsəːt] insertion *f*.
insertion [ɪn'səːʃən] *n* insertion *f*.
in-service ['ɪn'səːvɪs] *adj* (*training*) continu(e); (*course*) d'initiation; de perfectionnement;

de recyclage.
inshore [ɪn'ʃɔː*] *adj* côtier(ière) ♦ *adv* près de la côte; vers la côte.
inside ['ɪn'saɪd] *n* intérieur *m*; (*of road*: BRIT) côté *m* gauche (*de la route*); (: *US, Europe etc*) côté droit (*de la route*) ♦ *adj* intérieur(e) ♦ *adv* à l'intérieur, dedans ♦ *prep* à l'intérieur de; (*of time*): **~ 10 minutes** en moins de 10 minutes; **~s** *npl* (*col*) intestins *mpl*; **~ out** *adv* à l'envers; **to turn sth ~ out** retourner qch; **to know sth ~ out** connaître qch à fond *or* comme sa poche; **~ information** renseignements *mpl* à la source; **~ story** histoire racontée par un témoin.
inside forward *n* (SPORT) intérieur *m*.
inside lane *n* (AUT: *in Britain*) voie *f* de gauche; (: *in US, Europe*) voie *f* de droite.
inside leg measurement *n* (BRIT) hauteur *f* d'entre-jambe.
insider [ɪn'saɪdə*] *n* initié/e.
insider dealing, insider trading *n* (STOCK EXCHANGE) délit *m* d'initiés.
insidious [ɪn'sɪdɪəs] *adj* insidieux(euse).
insight ['ɪnsaɪt] *n* perspicacité *f*; (*glimpse, idea*) aperçu *m*; **to gain (an) ~ into** parvenir à comprendre.
insignia [ɪn'sɪgnɪə] *npl* insignes *mpl*.
insignificant [ɪnsɪg'nɪfɪknt] *adj* insignifiant(e).
insincere [ɪnsɪn'sɪə*] *adj* hypocrite.
insincerity [ɪnsɪn'sɛrɪtɪ] *n* manque *m* de sincérité, hypocrisie *f*.
insinuate [ɪn'sɪnjueɪt] *vt* insinuer.
insinuation [ɪnsɪnju'eɪʃən] *n* insinuation *f*.
insipid [ɪn'sɪpɪd] *adj* insipide, fade.
insist [ɪn'sɪst] *vi* insister; **to ~ on doing** insister pour` faire; **to ~ that** insister pour que; (*claim*) maintenir *or* soutenir que.
insistence [ɪn'sɪstəns] *n* insistance *f*.
insistent [ɪn'sɪstənt] *adj* insistant(e), pressant(e).
insofar [ɪnsəu'fɑː*]: **~ as** *conj* dans la mesure où.
insole ['ɪnsəul] *n* semelle intérieure; (*fixed part of shoe*) première *f*.
insolence ['ɪnsələns] *n* insolence *f*.
insolent ['ɪnsələnt] *adj* insolent(e).
insoluble [ɪn'sɔljubl] *adj* insoluble.
insolvency [ɪn'sɔlvənsɪ] *n* insolvabilité *f*; faillite *f*.
insolvent [ɪn'sɔlvənt] *adj* insolvable; (*bankrupt*) en faillite.
insomnia [ɪn'sɔmnɪə] *n* insomnie *f*.
insomniac [ɪn'sɔmnɪæk] *n* insomniaque *m/f*.
inspect [ɪn'spɛkt] *vt* inspecter; (BRIT: *ticket*) contrôler.
inspection [ɪn'spɛkʃən] *n* inspection *f*; contrôle *m*.
inspector [ɪn'spɛktə*] *n* inspecteur/trice; contrôleur/euse.
inspiration [ɪnspə'reɪʃən] *n* inspiration *f*.
inspire [ɪn'spaɪə*] *vt* inspirer.
inspired [ɪn'spaɪəd] *adj* (*writer, book etc*) inspi-

ré(e); **in an ~ moment** dans un moment d'inspiration.

inspiring [in'spaiəriŋ] *adj* inspirant(e).

inst. *abbr (BRIT COMM: = instant)*: **of the 16th ~** du 16 courant.

instability [instə'biliti] *n* instabilité *f*.

install [in'stɔːl] *vt* installer.

installation [instə'leiʃən] *n* installation *f*.

installment plan *n (US)* achat *m (or* vente *f)* à tempérament *or* crédit.

instalment, *(US)* **installment** [in'stɔːlmənt] *n* acompte *m*, versement partiel; *(of TV serial etc)* épisode *m*; **in ~s** *(pay)* à tempérament; *(receive)* en plusieurs fois.

instance ['instəns] *n* exemple *m*; **for ~** par exemple; **in many ~s** dans bien des cas; **in that ~** dans ce cas; **in the first ~** tout d'abord, en premier lieu.

instant ['instənt] *n* instant *m* ♦ *adj* immédiat(e); urgent(e); *(coffee, food)* instantané(e), en poudre; **the 10th ~** le 10 courant.

instantaneous [instən'teiniəs] *adj* instantané(e).

instantly ['instəntli] *adv* immédiatement, tout de suite.

instant replay *n (US TV)* retour *m* sur une séquence.

instead [in'sted] *adv* au lieu de cela; **~ of** au lieu de; **~ of sb** à la place de qn.

instep ['instep] *n* cou-de-pied *m*; *(of shoe)* cambrure *f*.

instigate ['instigeit] *vt (rebellion, strike, crime)* inciter à; *(new ideas etc)* susciter.

instigation [insti'geiʃən] *n* instigation *f*; **at sb's ~** à l'instigation de qn.

instil [in'stil] *vt*: **to ~ (into)** inculquer (à); *(courage)* insuffler (à).

instinct ['instiŋkt] *n* instinct *m*.

instinctive [in'stiŋktiv] *adj* instinctif(ive).

instinctively [in'stiŋktivli] *adv* instinctivement.

institute ['institjuːt] *n* institut *m* ♦ *vt* instituer, établir; *(inquiry)* ouvrir; *(proceedings)* entamer.

institution [insti'tjuːʃən] *n* institution *f*; *(school)* établissement *m* (scolaire); *(for care)* établissement (psychiatrique *etc*).

institutional [insti'tjuːʃənl] *adj* institutionnel(le); **~ care** soins fournis par un établissement médico-social.

instruct [in'strʌkt] *vt* instruire, former; **to ~ sb in sth** enseigner qch à qn; **to ~ sb to do** charger qn *or* ordonner à qn de faire.

instruction [in'strʌkʃən] *n* instruction *f*; **~s** *npl* directives *fpl*; **~s for use** mode *m* d'emploi.

instruction book *n* manuel *m* d'instructions.

instructive [in'strʌktiv] *adj* instructif(ive).

instructor [in'strʌktə*] *n* professeur *m*; *(for skiing, driving)* moniteur *m*.

instrument ['instrumənt] *n* instrument *m*.

instrumental [instru'mentl] *adj (MUS)* instrumental(e); **to be ~ in sth/in doing sth** con-

tribuer à qch/à faire qch.

instrumentalist [instru'mentəlist] *n* instrumentiste *m/f*.

instrument panel *n* tableau *m* de bord.

insubordinate [insə'bɔːdənit] *adj* insubordonné(e).

insubordination [insəbɔːdə'neiʃən] *n* insubordination *f*.

insufferable [in'sʌfrəbl] *adj* insupportable.

insufficient [insə'fiʃənt] *adj* insuffisant(e).

insufficiently [insə'fiʃəntli] *adv* insuffisamment.

insular ['insjulə*] *adj* insulaire; *(outlook)* étroit(e); *(person)* aux vues étroites.

insulate ['insjuleit] *vt* isoler; *(against sound)* insonoriser.

insulating tape ['insjuleitiŋ-] *n* ruban isolant.

insulation [insju'leiʃən] *n* isolation *f*; insonorisation *f*.

insulin ['insjulin] *n* insuline *f*.

insult *n* ['insʌlt] insulte *f*, affront *m* ♦ *vt* [in'sʌlt] insulter, faire un affront à.

insulting [in'sʌltiŋ] *adj* insultant(e), injurieux(euse).

insuperable [in'sjuːprəbl] *adj* insurmontable.

insurance [in'ʃuərəns] *n* assurance *f*; **fire/life ~** assurance-incendie/-vie; **to take out ~ (against)** s'assurer (contre).

insurance agent *n* agent *m* d'assurances.

insurance broker *n* courtier *m* en assurances.

insurance policy *n* police *f* d'assurance.

insurance premium *n* prime *f* d'assurance.

insure [in'ʃuə*] *vt* assurer; **to ~ sb/sb's life** assurer qn/la vie de qn; **to be ~d for £5000** être assuré(e) pour 5 000 livres.

insured [in'ʃuəd] *n*: **the ~** l'assuré/e.

insurer [in'ʃuərə*] *n* assureur *m*.

insurgent [in'sɔːdʒənt] *adj*, *n* insurgé(e).

insurmountable [insə'mauntəbl] *adj* insurmontable.

insurrection [insə'rekʃən] *n* insurrection *f*.

intact [in'tækt] *adj* intact(e).

intake ['inteik] *n (TECH)* admission *f*; adduction *f*; *(of food)* consommation *f*; *(BRIT SCOL)*: **an ~ of 200 a year** 200 admissions par an.

intangible [in'tændʒibl] *adj* intangible; *(assets)* immatériel(le).

integral ['intigrəl] *adj* intégral(e); *(part)* intégrant(e).

integrate ['intigreit] *vt* intégrer ♦ *vi* s'intégrer.

integrated circuit ['intigreitid-] *n (COMPUT)* circuit intégré.

integration [inti'greiʃən] *n* intégration *f*; **racial ~** intégration raciale.

integrity [in'tegriti] *n* intégrité *f*.

intellect ['intəlekt] *n* intelligence *f*.

intellectual [intə'lektjuəl] *adj*, *n* intellectuel(le).

intelligence [in'telidʒəns] *n* intelligence *f*; *(MIL etc)* informations *fpl*, renseignements *mpl*.

intelligence quotient (IQ) n quotient intellectuel (QI).

Intelligence Service n services mpl de renseignements.

intelligence test n test m d'intelligence.

intelligent [ɪn'tɛlɪdʒənt] adj intelligent(e).

intelligently [ɪn'tɛlɪdʒəntlɪ] adv intelligemment.

intelligible [ɪn'tɛlɪdʒɪbl] adj intelligible.

intemperate [ɪn'tɛmpərət] adj immodéré(e); (drinking too much) adonné(e) à la boisson.

intend [ɪn'tɛnd] vt (gift etc): **to ~ sth for** destiner qch à; **to ~ to do** avoir l'intention de faire.

intended [ɪn'tɛndɪd] adj (insult) intentionnel(le); (journey) projeté(e); (effect) voulu(e).

intense [ɪn'tɛns] adj intense; (person) véhément(e).

intensely [ɪn'tɛnslɪ] adv intensément; (moving) profondément.

intensify [ɪn'tɛnsɪfaɪ] vt intensifier.

intensity [ɪn'tɛnsɪtɪ] n intensité f.

intensive [ɪn'tɛnsɪv] adj intensif(ive).

intensive care n: **to be in ~** être en réanimation; **~ unit** n service m de réanimation.

intent [ɪn'tɛnt] n intention f ♦ adj attentif(ive), absorbé(e); **to all ~s and purposes** en fait, pratiquement; **to be ~ on doing sth** être (bien) décidé à faire qch.

intention [ɪn'tɛnʃən] n intention f.

intentional [ɪn'tɛnʃənl] adj intentionnel(le), délibéré(e).

intently [ɪn'tɛntlɪ] adv attentivement.

inter [ɪn'tə:*] vt enterrer.

interact [ɪntər'ækt] vi avoir une action réciproque.

interaction [ɪntər'ækʃən] n interaction f.

interactive [ɪntər'æktɪv] adj (group) interactif(ive); (COMPUT) interactif, conversationnel(le).

intercede [ɪntə'si:d] vi: **to ~ with sb/on behalf of sb** intercéder auprès de qn/en faveur de qn.

intercept [ɪntə'sɛpt] vt intercepter; (person) arrêter au passage.

interception [ɪntə'sɛpʃən] n interception f.

interchange n ['ɪntətʃeɪndʒ] (exchange) échange m; (on motorway) échangeur m ♦ vt [ɪntə'tʃeɪndʒ] échanger; mettre à la place l'un(e) de l'autre.

interchangeable [ɪntə'tʃeɪndʒəbl] adj interchangeable.

intercity [ɪntə'sɪtɪ] adj: **~ (train)** train m rapide.

intercom ['ɪntəkɔm] n interphone m.

interconnect [ɪntəkə'nɛkt] vi (rooms) communiquer.

intercontinental ['ɪntəkɔntɪ'nɛntl] adj intercontinental(e).

intercourse ['ɪntəkɔːs] n rapports mpl; **sexual ~** rapports sexuels.

interdependent [ɪntədɪ'pɛndənt] adj interdépendant(e).

interest ['ɪntrɪst] n intérêt m; (COMM: stake, share) participation f, intérêts mpl ♦ vt intéresser; **compound/simple ~** intérêt composé/simple; **British ~s in the Middle East** les intérêts britanniques au Moyen-Orient; **his main ~ is ...** ce qui l'intéresse le plus est ....

interested ['ɪntrɪstɪd] adj intéressé(e); **to be ~ in** s'intéresser à.

interest-free ['ɪntrɪst'friː] adj sans intérêt.

interesting ['ɪntrɪstɪŋ] adj intéressant(e).

interest rate n taux m d'intérêt.

interface ['ɪntəfeɪs] n (COMPUT) interface f.

interfere [ɪntə'fɪə*] vi: **to ~ in** (quarrel, other people's business) se mêler à; **to ~ with** (object) tripoter, toucher à; (plans) contrecarrer; (duty) être en conflit avec; **don't ~** mêlez-vous de vos affaires.

interference [ɪntə'fɪərəns] n (gen) intrusion f; (PHYSICS) interférence f; (RADIO, TV) parasites mpl.

interfering [ɪntə'fɪərɪŋ] adj importun(e).

interim ['ɪntərɪm] adj provisoire; (post) intérimaire ♦ n: **in the ~** dans l'intérim.

interior [ɪn'tɪərɪə*] n intérieur m ♦ adj intérieur(e).

interior decorator, interior designer n décorateur/trice d'intérieur.

interjection [ɪntə'dʒɛkʃən] n interjection f.

interlock [ɪntə'lɔk] vi s'enclencher ♦ vt enclencher.

interloper ['ɪntələupə*] n intrus/e.

interlude ['ɪntəluːd] n intervalle m; (THEAT) intermède m.

intermarry [ɪntə'mærɪ] vi former des alliances entre familles (or tribus); former des unions consanguines.

intermediary [ɪntə'miːdɪərɪ] n intermédiaire m/f.

intermediate [ɪntə'miːdɪət] adj intermédiaire; (SCOL: course, level) moyen(ne).

interment [ɪn'tə:mənt] n inhumation f, enterrement m.

interminable [ɪn'tə:mɪnəbl] adj sans fin, interminable.

intermission [ɪntə'mɪʃən] n pause f; (THEAT, CINE) entracte m.

intermittent [ɪntə'mɪtnt] adj intermittent(e).

intermittently [ɪntə'mɪtntlɪ] adv par intermittence, par intervalles.

intern vt [ɪn'tə:n] interner ♦ n ['ɪntə:n] (US) interne m/f.

internal [ɪn'tə:nl] adj interne; (dispute, reform etc) intérieur(e); **~ injuries** lésions fpl internes.

internally [ɪn'tə:nəlɪ] adv intérieurement; **"not to be taken ~"** "pour usage externe".

Internal Revenue (Service) (IRS) n (US) fisc m.

international [ɪntə'næʃənl] adj international(e) ♦ n (BRIT SPORT) international m.

International Atomic Energy Agency (IAEA) *n* Agence Internationale de l'Énergie Atomique (AIEA).

International Court of Justice (ICJ) *n* Cour internationale de justice (CIJ).

international date line *n* ligne *f* de changement de date.

internationally [ɪntəˈnæʃnəlɪ] *adv* dans le monde entier.

International Monetary Fund (IMF) *n* Fonds monétaire international (FMI).

international relations *npl* relations internationales.

internecine [ɪntəˈniːsaɪn] *adj* mutuellement destructeur(trice).

internee [ɪntəːˈniː] *n* interné/e.

internment [ɪnˈtɔːnmənt] *n* internement *m*.

interplay [ˈɪntəpleɪ] *n* effet *m* réciproque, jeu *m*.

Interpol [ˈɪntəpɒl] *n* Interpol *m*.

interpret [ɪnˈtɔːprɪt] *vt* interpréter ♦ *vi* servir d'interprète.

interpretation [ɪntəːprɪˈteɪʃən] *n* interprétation *f*.

interpreter [ɪnˈtɔːprɪtə*] *n* interprète *m/f*.

interpreting [ɪnˈtɔːprɪtɪŋ] *n* (*profession*) interprétariat *m*.

interrelated [ɪntərɪˈleɪtɪd] *adj* en corrélation, en rapport étroit.

interrogate [ɪnˈtɛrəʊgeɪt] *vt* interroger; (*suspect etc*) soumettre à un interrogatoire.

interrogation [ɪntɛrəʊˈgeɪʃən] *n* interrogation *f*; interrogatoire *m*.

interrogative [ɪntəˈrɒgətɪv] *adj* interrogateur(trice) ♦ *n* (*LING*) interrogatif *m*.

interrogator [ɪnˈtɛrəgeɪtə*] *n* interrogateur/trice.

interrupt [ɪntəˈrʌpt] *vt* interrompre.

interruption [ɪntəˈrʌpʃən] *n* interruption *f*.

intersect [ɪntəˈsɛkt] *vt* couper, croiser; (*MATH*) intersecter ♦ *vi* se croiser, se couper; s'intersecter.

intersection [ɪntəˈsɛkʃən] *n* intersection *f*; (*of roads*) croisement *m*.

intersperse [ɪntəˈspɔːs] *vt*: **to ~ with** parsemer de.

intertwine [ɪntəˈtwaɪn] *vt* entrelacer ♦ *vi* s'entrelacer.

interval [ˈɪntəvl] *n* intervalle *m*; (*BRIT: THEAT*) entracte *m*; (: *SPORT*) mi-temps *f*; **bright ~s** (*in weather*) éclaircies *fpl*; **at ~s** par intervalles.

intervene [ɪntəˈviːn] *vi* (*time*) s'écouler (entre-temps); (*event*) survenir; (*person*) intervenir.

intervention [ɪntəˈvɛnʃən] *n* intervention *f*.

interview [ˈɪntəvjuː] *n* (*RADIO, TV etc*) interview *f*; (*for job*) entrevue *f* ♦ *vt* interviewer; avoir une entrevue avec.

interviewee [ɪntəvjuˈiː] *n* (*for job*) candidat *m* (*qui passe un entretien*); (*TV etc*) invité/e, personne interviewée.

interviewer [ˈɪntəvjuə*] *n* interviewer *m*.

intestate [ɪnˈtɛsteɪt] *adj* intestat *f inv*.

intestinal [ɪnˈtɛstɪnl] *adj* intestinal(e).

intestine [ɪnˈtɛstɪn] *n* intestin *m*; **large ~** gros intestin; **small ~** intestin grêle.

intimacy [ˈɪntɪməsɪ] *n* intimité *f*.

intimate *adj* [ˈɪntɪmət] intime; (*knowledge*) approfondi(e) ♦ *vt* [ˈɪntɪmeɪt] suggérer, laisser entendre; (*announce*) faire savoir.

intimately [ˈɪntɪmətlɪ] *adv* intimement.

intimation [ɪntɪˈmeɪʃən] *n* annonce *f*.

intimidate [ɪnˈtɪmɪdeɪt] *vt* intimider.

intimidation [ɪntɪmɪˈdeɪʃən] *n* intimidation *f*.

into [ˈɪntu] *prep* dans; **~ pieces/French** en morceaux/français; **to change pounds ~ dollars** changer des livres en dollars.

intolerable [ɪnˈtɒlərəbl] *adj* intolérable.

intolerance [ɪnˈtɒlərns] *n* intolérance *f*.

intolerant [ɪnˈtɒlərnt] *adj*: **~ (of)** intolérant(e) (de); (*MED*) intolérant (à).

intonation [ɪntəʊˈneɪʃən] *n* intonation *f*.

intoxicate [ɪnˈtɒksɪkeɪt] *vt* enivrer.

intoxicated [ɪnˈtɒksɪkeɪtɪd] *adj* ivre.

intoxication [ɪntɒksɪˈkeɪʃən] *n* ivresse *f*.

intractable [ɪnˈtræktəbl] *adj* (*child, temper*) indocile, insoumis(e); (*problem*) insoluble; (*illness*) incurable.

intransigent [ɪnˈtrænsɪdʒənt] *adj* intransigeant(e).

intransitive [ɪnˈtrænsɪtɪv] *adj* intransitif(ive).

intra-uterine device (IUD) [ˈɪntrəˈjuːtəraɪn-] *n* dispositif intra-utérin (DIU), stérilet *m*.

intravenous [ɪntrəˈviːnəs] *adj* intraveineux(euse).

in-tray [ˈɪntreɪ] *n* courrier *m* "arrivée".

intrepid [ɪnˈtrɛpɪd] *adj* intrépide.

intricacy [ˈɪntrɪkəsɪ] *n* complexité *f*.

intricate [ˈɪntrɪkət] *adj* complexe, compliqué(e).

intrigue [ɪnˈtriːg] *n* intrigue *f* ♦ *vt* intriguer ♦ *vi* intriguer, comploter.

intriguing [ɪnˈtriːgɪŋ] *adj* fascinant(e).

intrinsic [ɪnˈtrɪnsɪk] *adj* intrinsèque.

introduce [ɪntrəˈdjuːs] *vt* introduire; **to ~ sb (to sb)** présenter qn (à qn); **to ~ sb to** (*pastime, technique*) initier qn à; **may I ~ ...?** je vous présente ....

introduction [ɪntrəˈdʌkʃən] *n* introduction *f*; (*of person*) présentation *f*; **a letter of ~** une lettre de recommandation.

introductory [ɪntrəˈdʌktərɪ] *adj* préliminaire, introductif(ive); **~ remarks** remarques *fpl* liminaires; **an ~ offer** une offre de lancement.

introspection [ɪntrəʊˈspɛkʃən] *n* introspection *f*.

introspective [ɪntrəʊˈspɛktɪv] *adj* introspectif(ive).

introvert [ˈɪntrəʊvɔːt] *adj, n* introverti(e).

intrude [ɪnˈtruːd] *vi* (*person*) être importun(e); **to ~ on** *or* **into** (*conversation etc*) s'immiscer dans; **am I intruding?** est-ce que je vous dérange?

intruder [ɪn'truːdə*] n intrus/e.

intrusion [ɪn'truːʒən] n intrusion f.

intrusive [ɪn'truːsɪv] adj importun(e), gênant(e).

intuition [ɪntjuː'ɪʃən] n intuition f.

intuitive [ɪn'tjuːɪtɪv] adj intuitif(ive).

inundate ['ɪnʌndeɪt] vt: **to ~ with** inonder de.

inure [ɪn'juə*] vt: **to ~ (to)** habituer (à).

invade [ɪn'veɪd] vt envahir.

invader [ɪn'veɪdə*] n envahisseur m.

invalid n ['ɪnvəlɪd] malade m/f; (with disability) invalide m/f ♦ adj [ɪn'vælɪd] (not valid) invalide, non valide.

invalidate [ɪn'vælɪdeɪt] vt invalider, annuler.

invalid chair ['ɪnvəlɪd-] n (BRIT) fauteuil m d'infirme.

invaluable [ɪn'væljuəbl] adj inestimable, inappréciable.

invariable [ɪn'vɛərɪəbl] adj invariable; (fig) immanquable.

invariably [ɪn'vɛərɪəblɪ] adv invariablement; **she is ~ late** elle est toujours en retard.

invasion [ɪn'veɪʒən] n invasion f.

invective [ɪn'vɛktɪv] n invective f.

inveigle [ɪn'viːgl] vt: **to ~ sb into (doing) sth** amener qn à (faire) qch (par la ruse or la flatterie).

invent [ɪn'vɛnt] vt inventer.

invention [ɪn'vɛnʃən] n invention f.

inventive [ɪn'vɛntɪv] adj inventif(ive).

inventiveness [ɪn'vɛntɪvnɪs] n esprit inventif or d'invention.

inventor [ɪn'vɛntə*] n inventeur/trice.

inventory ['ɪnvəntrɪ] n inventaire m.

inventory control n (COMM) contrôle m des stocks.

inverse [ɪn'vəːs] adj inverse ♦ n inverse m, contraire m; **in ~ proportion (to)** inversement proportionel(le) (à).

inversely [ɪn'vəːslɪ] adv inversement.

invert [ɪn'vəːt] vt intervertir; (cup, object) retourner.

invertebrate [ɪn'vəːtɪbrət] n invertébré m.

inverted commas [ɪn'vəːtɪd-] npl (BRIT) guillemets mpl.

invest [ɪn'vɛst] vt investir; (endow): **to ~ sb with sth** conférer qch à qn ♦ vi faire un investissement, investir; **to ~ in** placer de l'argent or investir dans; (acquire) s'offrir, faire l'acquisition de.

investigate [ɪn'vɛstɪgeɪt] vt étudier, examiner; (crime) faire une enquête sur.

investigation [ɪnvɛstɪ'geɪʃən] n examen m; (of crime) enquête f, investigation f.

investigative [ɪn'vɛstɪgeɪtɪv] adj: **~ journalism** enquête-reportage f, journalisme m d'enquête.

investigator [ɪn'vɛstɪgeɪtə*] n investigateur/trice; **private ~** détective privé.

investiture [ɪn'vɛstɪtʃə*] n investiture f.

investment [ɪn'vɛstmənt] n investissement m, placement m.

investment income n revenu m de placement.

investment trust n société f d'investissements.

investor [ɪn'vɛstə*] n épargnant/e; (shareholder) actionnaire m/f.

inveterate [ɪn'vɛtərət] adj invétéré(e).

invidious [ɪn'vɪdɪəs] adj injuste; (task) déplaisant(e).

invigilate [ɪn'vɪdʒɪleɪt] (BRIT) vt surveiller ♦ vi être de surveillance.

invigilator [ɪn'vɪdʒɪleɪtə*] n surveillant m (d'examen).

invigorating [ɪn'vɪgəreɪtɪŋ] adj vivifiant(e); stimulant(e).

invincible [ɪn'vɪnsɪbl] adj invincible.

inviolate [ɪn'vaɪələt] adj inviolé(e).

invisible [ɪn'vɪzɪbl] adj invisible.

invisible assets npl (BRIT) actif incorporel.

invisible ink n encre f sympathique.

invisible mending n stoppage m.

invitation [ɪnvɪ'teɪʃən] n invitation f; **by ~ only** sur invitation; **at sb's ~** à la demande de qn.

invite [ɪn'vaɪt] vt inviter; (opinions etc) demander; (trouble) chercher; **to ~ sb (to do)** inviter qn (à faire); **to ~ sb to dinner** inviter qn à dîner.

▶**invite out** vt inviter (à sortir).

▶**invite over** vt inviter (chez soi).

inviting [ɪn'vaɪtɪŋ] adj engageant(e), attrayant(e); (gesture) encourageant(e).

invoice ['ɪnvɔɪs] n facture f ♦ vt facturer; **to ~ sb for goods** facturer des marchandises à qn.

invoke [ɪn'vəuk] vt invoquer.

involuntary [ɪn'vɔləntrɪ] adj involontaire.

involve [ɪn'vɔlv] vt (entail) impliquer; (concern) concerner; (require) nécessiter; **to ~ sb in** (theft etc) impliquer qn dans; (activity, meeting) faire participer qn à.

involved [ɪn'vɔlvd] adj complexe; **to feel ~** se sentir concerné(e); **to become ~ (in love etc)** s'engager.

involvement [ɪn'vɔlvmənt] n (personal role) participation f; (of resources, funds) mise f en jeu.

invulnerable [ɪn'vʌlnərəbl] adj invulnérable.

inward ['ɪnwəd] adj (movement) vers l'intérieur; (thought, feeling) profond(e), intime ♦ adv = **inwards**.

inwardly ['ɪnwədlɪ] adv (feel, think etc) secrètement, en son for intérieur.

inwards ['ɪnwədz] adv vers l'intérieur.

I/O abbr (COMPUT: = input/output) E/S.

IOC n abbr (= International Olympic Committee) CIO m (= Comité international olympique).

iodine ['aɪəudiːn] n iode m.

ion ['aɪən] n ion m.

Ionian Sea [aɪ'əunɪən-] n: **the ~** la mer Ionienne.

ioniser ['aɪənaɪzə*] *n* ioniseur *m*.
iota [aɪ'əutə] *n* (*fig*) brin *m*, grain *m*.
IOU *n abbr* (= *I owe you*) reconnaissance *f* de dette.
IOW *abbr* (*BRIT*) = *Isle of Wight*.
IPA *n abbr* (= *International Phonetic Alphabet*) A.P.I. *m*.
IQ *n abbr* = **intelligence quotient**.
IRA *n abbr* (= *Irish Republican Army*) IRA *f*; (*US*) = *individual retirement account*.
Iran [ɪ'rɑ:n] *n* Iran *m*.
Iranian [ɪ'reɪnɪən] *adj* iranien(ne) ♦ *n* Iranien/ne; (*LING*) iranien *m*.
Iraq [ɪ'rɑ:k] *n* Irak *m*.
Iraqi [ɪ'rɑ:kɪ] *adj* irakien(ne) ♦ *n* Irakien/ne.
irascible [ɪ'ræsɪbl] *adj* irascible.
irate [aɪ'reɪt] *adj* courroucé(e).
Ireland ['aɪələnd] *n* Irlande *f*; **Republic of ~** République *f* d'Irlande.
iris, **~es** ['aɪrɪs, -ɪz] *n* iris *m*.
Irish ['aɪrɪʃ] *adj* irlandais(e) ♦ *n* (*LING*) irlandais *m*; **the ~** *npl* les Irlandais.
Irishman ['aɪrɪʃmən] *n* Irlandais *m*.
Irish Sea *n*: **the ~** la mer d'Irlande.
Irishwoman ['aɪrɪʃwumən] *n* Irlandaise *f*.
irk [ə:k] *vt* ennuyer.
irksome ['ə:ksəm] *adj* ennuyeux(euse).
IRN *n abbr* (= *Independent Radio News*) *agence de presse radiophonique*.
IRO *n abbr* (*US*) = *International Refugee Organization*.
iron ['aɪən] *n* fer *m*; (*for clothes*) fer *m* à repasser ♦ *adj* de *or* en fer ♦ *vt* (*clothes*) repasser; **~s** *npl* (*chains*) fers *mpl*, chaînes *fpl*.
▶**iron out** *vt* (*crease*) faire disparaître au fer; (*fig*) aplanir; faire disparaître.
Iron Curtain *n*: **the ~** le rideau de fer.
iron foundry *n* fonderie *f* de fonte.
ironic(al) [aɪ'rɔnɪk(l)] *adj* ironique.
ironically [aɪ'rɔnɪklɪ] *adv* ironiquement.
ironing ['aɪənɪŋ] *n* repassage *m*.
ironing board *n* planche *f* à repasser.
ironmonger ['aɪənmʌŋgə*] *n* (*BRIT*) quincaillier *m*; **~'s (shop)** quincaillerie *f*.
iron ore *n* minerai *m* de fer.
ironworks ['aɪənwə:ks] *n* usine *f* sidérurgique.
irony ['aɪrənɪ] *n* ironie *f*.
irrational [ɪ'ræʃənl] *adj* irrationnel(le); déraisonnable; qui manque de logique.
irreconcilable [ɪrɛkən'saɪləbl] *adj* irréconciliable; (*opinion*): **~ with** inconciliable avec.
irredeemable [ɪrɪ'di:məbl] *adj* (*COMM*) non remboursable.
irrefutable [ɪrɪ'fju:təbl] *adj* irréfutable.
irregular [ɪ'rɛgjulə*] *adj* irrégulier(ière).
irregularity [ɪrɛgju'lærɪtɪ] *n* irrégularité *f*.
irrelevance [ɪ'rɛləvəns] *n* manque *m* de rapport *or* d'à-propos.
irrelevant [ɪ'rɛləvənt] *adj* sans rapport, hors de propos.
irreligious [ɪrɪ'lɪdʒəs] *adj* irréligieux(euse).

irreparable [ɪ'rɛprəbl] *adj* irréparable.
irreplaceable [ɪrɪ'pleɪsəbl] *adj* irremplaçable.
irrepressible [ɪrɪ'prɛsəbl] *adj* irrépressible.
irreproachable [ɪrɪ'prəutʃəbl] *adj* irréprochable.
irresistible [ɪrɪ'zɪstɪbl] *adj* irrésistible.
irresolute [ɪ'rɛzəlu:t] *adj* irrésolu(e), indécis(e).
irrespective [ɪrɪ'spɛktɪv]: **~ of** *prep* sans tenir compte de.
irresponsible [ɪrɪ'spɔnsɪbl] *adj* (*act*) irréfléchi(e); (*person*) qui n'a pas le sens des responsabilités.
irretrievable [ɪrɪ'tri:vəbl] *adj* irréparable, irrémédiable; (*object*) introuvable.
irreverent [ɪ'rɛvərnt] *adj* irrévérencieux(euse).
irrevocable [ɪ'rɛvəkəbl] *adj* irrévocable.
irrigate ['ɪrɪgeɪt] *vt* irriguer.
irrigation [ɪrɪ'geɪʃən] *n* irrigation *f*.
irritable ['ɪrɪtəbl] *adj* irritable.
irritate ['ɪrɪteɪt] *vt* irriter.
irritation [ɪrɪ'teɪʃən] *n* irritation *f*.
IRS *n abbr* (*US*) = **Internal Revenue Service**.
is [ɪz] *vb see* **be**.
ISBN *n abbr* (= *International Standard Book Number*) ISBN *m*.
Islam ['ɪzlɑ:m] *n* Islam *m*.
island ['aɪlənd] *n* île *f*; (*also*: **traffic ~**) refuge *m* (pour piétons).
islander ['aɪləndə*] *n* habitant/e d'une île, insulaire *m/f*.
isle [aɪl] *n* île *f*.
isn't ['ɪznt] = **is not**.
isolate ['aɪsəleɪt] *vt* isoler.
isolated ['aɪsəleɪtɪd] *adj* isolé(e).
isolation [aɪsə'leɪʃən] *n* isolement *m*.
isolationism [aɪsə'leɪʃənɪzəm] *n* isolationnisme *m*.
isotope ['aɪsəutəup] *n* isotope *m*.
Israel ['ɪzreɪl] *n* Israël *m*.
Israeli [ɪz'reɪlɪ] *adj* israélien(ne) ♦ *n* Israélien/ne.
issue ['ɪʃu:] *n* question *f*, problème *m*; (*outcome*) résultat *m*, issue *f*; (*of banknotes etc*) émission *f*; (*of newspaper etc*) numéro *m*; (*offspring*) descendance *f* ♦ *vt* (*rations, equipment*) distribuer; (*orders*) donner; (*book*) faire paraître, publier; (*banknotes, cheques, stamps*) émettre, mettre en circulation ♦ *vi*: **to ~ from** provenir de; **at ~** en jeu, en cause; **to avoid the ~** éluder le problème; **to take ~ with sb (over sth)** exprimer son désaccord avec qn (sur qch); **to make an ~ of sth** faire de qch un problème; **to confuse** *or* **obscure the ~** embrouiller la question.
Istanbul [ɪstæn'bu:l] *n* Istamboul, Istanbul.
isthmus ['ɪsməs] *n* isthme *m*.
IT *n abbr* = **information technology**.

=================================== KEYWORD

it [ɪt] *pron* **1** (*specific: subject*) il(elle); (: *direct object*) le(la, l'); (: *indirect object*) lui; ~**'s on the table** c'est *or* il (*or* elle) est sur la table; **about/from/of** ~ en; **I spoke to him about** ~ je lui en ai parlé; **what did you learn from** ~**?** qu'est-ce que vous en avez retiré?; **I'm proud of** ~ j'en suis fier; **I've come from** ~ j'en viens; **in/to** ~ y; **put the book in** ~ mettez-y le livre; **it's on** ~ c'est dessus; **he agreed to** ~ il y a consenti; **did you go to** ~**?** (*party, concert etc*) est-ce que vous y êtes allé(s)?; **above** ~, **over** ~ (au-)dessus; **below** ~, **under** ~ (en-)dessous; **in front of/behind** ~ devant/derrière
2 (*impersonal*) il; ce, cela, ça; ~**'s raining** il pleut; ~**'s Friday tomorrow** demain c'est vendredi *or* nous sommes vendredi; ~**'s 6 o'clock** il est 6 heures; ~**'s 2 hours by train** c'est à 2 heures de train; **who is** ~**?** — ~**'s me** qui est-ce? — c'est moi.

ITA *n abbr* (*BRIT*: = *initial teaching alphabet*) alphabet en partie phonétique utilisé pour l'enseignement de la lecture.
Italian [ɪ'tæljən] *adj* italien(ne) ♦ *n* Italien/ne; (*LING*) italien *m*.
italic [ɪ'tælɪk] *adj* italique; ~**s** *npl* italique *m*.
Italy ['ɪtəlɪ] *n* Italie *f*.
itch [ɪtʃ] *n* démangeaison *f* ♦ *vi* (*person*) éprouver des démangeaisons; (*part of body*) démanger; **I'm** ~**ing to do** l'envie me démange de faire.
itching ['ɪtʃɪŋ] *n* démangeaison *f*.
itchy ['ɪtʃɪ] *adj* qui démange; **my back is** ~ j'ai le dos qui me démange.
it'd ['ɪtd] = **it would, it had**.
item ['aɪtəm] *n* (*gen*) article *m*; (*on agenda*) question *f*, point *m*; (*in programme*) numéro *m*; (*also*: **news** ~) nouvelle *f*; ~**s of clothing** articles vestimentaires.
itemize ['aɪtəmaɪz] *vt* détailler, spécifier.
itemized bill ['aɪtəmaɪzd-] *n* facture détaillée.
itinerant [ɪ'tɪnərənt] *adj* itinérant(e); (*musician*) ambulant(e).
itinerary [aɪ'tɪnərərɪ] *n* itinéraire *m*.
it'll ['ɪtl] = **it will, it shall**.
ITN *n abbr* (*BRIT*: = *Independent Television News*) chaîne de télévision commerciale.
its [ɪts] *adj* son(sa), ses *pl* ♦ *pron* le(la) sien(ne), les siens(siennes).
it's [ɪts] = **it is, it has**.
itself [ɪt'sɛlf] *pron* (*emphatic*) lui-même(elle-même); (*reflexive*) se.
ITV *n abbr* (*BRIT*: = *Independent Television*) chaîne de télévision commerciale.

ITV *est une chaîne de télévision britannique financée par la publicité. Les actualités, documentaires, débats, etc, constituent environ un tiers des émissions de ITV, le reste étant par-* tagé *entre les sports, les films, les feuilletons, les jeux, les séries, etc. Des compagnies indépendantes fournissent des émissions au niveau régional.*

IUD *n abbr* = **intra-uterine device**.
I've [aɪv] = **I have**.
ivory ['aɪvərɪ] *n* ivoire *m*.
Ivory Coast *n* Côte *f* d'Ivoire.
ivory tower *n* (*fig*) tour *f* d'ivoire.
ivy ['aɪvɪ] *n* lierre *m*.

L'**Ivy League** *regroupe les huit universités les plus prestigieuses du nord-est des États-Unis, ainsi surnommées à cause de leurs murs recouverts de lierre. Elles organisent des compétitions sportives entre elles. Ces universités sont: Brown, Columbia, Cornell, Dartmouth College, Harvard, Princeton, l'université de Pennsylvanie et Yale.*

J j

===================================

J, j [dʒeɪ] *n* (*letter*) J, j *m*; **J for Jack**, (*US*) **J for Jig** J comme Joseph.
JA *n abbr* = **judge advocate**.
J/A *abbr* = **joint account**.
jab [dʒæb] *vt*: **to** ~ **sth into** enfoncer *or* planter qch dans ♦ *n* coup *m*; (*MED: col*) piqûre *f*.
jabber ['dʒæbə*] *vt*, *vi* bredouiller, baragouiner.
jack [dʒæk] *n* (*AUT*) cric *m*; (*BOWLS*) cochonnet *m*; (*CARDS*) valet *m*.
▶**jack in** *vt* (*col*) laisser tomber.
▶**jack up** *vt* soulever (au cric).
jackal ['dʒækl] *n* chacal *m*.
jackass ['dʒækæs] *n* (*also fig*) âne *m*.
jackdaw ['dʒækdɔː] *n* choucas *m*.
jacket ['dʒækɪt] *n* veste *f*, veston *m*; (*of boiler etc*) enveloppe *f*; (*of book*) couverture *f*, jaquette *f*.
jacket potato *n* pomme *f* de terre en robe des champs.
jack-in-the-box ['dʒækɪnðəbɔks] *n* diable *m* à ressort.
jack-knife ['dʒæknaɪf] *n* couteau *m* de poche ♦ *vi*: **the lorry** ~**d** la remorque (du camion) s'est mise en travers.
jack-of-all-trades ['dʒækəv'ɔːltreɪdz] *n* bricoleur *m*.
jack plug *n* (*BRIT*) jack *m*.
jackpot ['dʒækpɔt] *n* gros lot.
Jacuzzi [dʒə'kuːzɪ] *n* ® jacuzzi *m* ®.
jade [dʒeɪd] *n* (*stone*) jade *m*.

jaded ['dʒeɪdɪd] *adj* éreinté(e), fatigué(e).

JAG *n abbr* = **Judge Advocate General**.

jagged ['dʒægɪd] *adj* dentelé(e).

jaguar ['dʒægjuə*] *n* jaguar *m*.

jail [dʒeɪl] *n* prison *f* ♦ *vt* emprisonner, mettre en prison.

jailbird ['dʒeɪlbəːd] *n* récidiviste *m/f*.

jailbreak ['dʒeɪlbreɪk] *n* évasion *f*.

jailer ['dʒeɪlə*] *n* geôlier/ière.

jalopy [dʒə'lɒpɪ] *n* (*col*) vieux clou.

jam [dʒæm] *n* confiture *f*; (*of shoppers etc*) cohue *f*; (*also*: **traffic** ~) embouteillage *m* ♦ *vt* (*passage etc*) encombrer, obstruer; (*mechanism, drawer etc*) bloquer, coincer; (*RADIO*) brouiller ♦ *vi* (*mechanism, sliding part*) se coincer, se bloquer; (*gun*) s'enrayer; **to get sb out of a** ~ (*col*) sortir qn du pétrin; **to** ~ **sth into** entasser *or* comprimer qch dans; enfoncer qch dans; **the telephone lines are** ~**med** les lignes (téléphoniques) sont encombrées.

Jamaica [dʒə'meɪkə] *n* Jamaïque *f*.

Jamaican [dʒə'meɪkən] *adj* jamaïquain(e) ♦ *n* Jamaïquain/e.

jamb ['dʒæm] *n* jambage *m*.

jam-packed [dʒæm'pækt] *adj*: ~ **(with)** bourré(e) (de).

jam session *n* jam session *f*.

Jan. *abbr* (= *January*) janv.

jangle ['dʒæŋgl] *vi* cliqueter.

janitor ['dʒænɪtə*] *n* (*caretaker*) huissier *m*; concierge *m*.

January ['dʒænjuərɪ] *n* janvier *m*; *for phrases see also* **July**.

Japan [dʒə'pæn] *n* Japon *m*.

Japanese [dʒæpə'niːz] *adj* japonais(e) ♦ *n* (*pl inv*) Japonais/e; (*LING*) japonais *m*.

jar [dʒɑː*] *n* (*container*) pot *m*, bocal *m* ♦ *vi* (*sound*) produire un son grinçant *or* discordant; (*colours etc*) détonner, jurer ♦ *vt* (*shake*) ébranler, secouer.

jargon ['dʒɑːgən] *n* jargon *m*.

jarring ['dʒɑːrɪŋ] *adj* (*sound, colour*) discordant(e).

Jas. *abbr* = **James**.

jasmin(e) ['dʒæzmɪn] *n* jasmin *m*.

jaundice ['dʒɔːndɪs] *n* jaunisse *f*.

jaundiced ['dʒɔːndɪst] *adj* (*fig*) envieux(euse), désapprobateur(trice).

jaunt [dʒɔːnt] *n* balade *f*.

jaunty ['dʒɔːntɪ] *adj* enjoué(e); désinvolte.

Java ['dʒɑːvə] *n* Java *f*.

javelin ['dʒævlɪn] *n* javelot *m*.

jaw [dʒɔː] *n* mâchoire *f*.

jawbone ['dʒɔːbəun] *n* maxillaire *m*.

jay [dʒeɪ] *n* geai *m*.

jaywalker ['dʒeɪwɔːkə*] *n* piéton indiscipliné.

jazz [dʒæz] *n* jazz *m*.

▶**jazz up** *vt* animer, égayer.

jazz band *n* orchestre *m or* groupe *m* de jazz.

jazzy ['dʒæzɪ] *adj* bariolé(e), tapageur(euse); (*beat*) de jazz.

JCB *n* ® excavatrice *f*.

JCS *n abbr* (*US*) = *Joint Chiefs of Staff*.

JD *n abbr* (*US*: = *Doctor of Laws*) titre universitaire; (: = *Justice Department*) ministère de la Justice.

jealous ['dʒɛləs] *adj* jaloux(ouse).

jealously ['dʒɛləslɪ] *adv* jalousement.

jealousy ['dʒɛləsɪ] *n* jalousie *f*.

jeans [dʒiːnz] *npl* (blue-)jean *m*.

Jeep [dʒiːp] *n* ® jeep *f*.

jeer [dʒɪə*] *vi*: **to** ~ **(at)** huer; se moquer cruellement (de), railler.

jeering ['dʒɪərɪŋ] *adj* railleur(euse), moqueur(euse) ♦ *n* huées *fpl*.

jeers ['dʒɪəz] *npl* huées *fpl*; sarcasmes *mpl*.

jelly ['dʒɛlɪ] *n* gelée *f*.

jellyfish ['dʒɛlɪfɪʃ] *n* méduse *f*.

jeopardize ['dʒɛpədaɪz] *vt* mettre en danger *or* péril.

jeopardy ['dʒɛpədɪ] *n*: **in** ~ en danger *or* péril.

jerk [dʒəːk] *n* secousse *f*; saccade *f*; sursaut *m*, spasme *m*; (*col*) pauvre type *m* ♦ *vt* donner une secousse à ♦ *vi* (*vehicles*) cahoter.

jerkin ['dʒəːkɪn] *n* blouson *m*.

jerky ['dʒəːkɪ] *adj* saccadé(e); cahotant(e).

jerry-built ['dʒɛrɪbɪlt] *adj* de mauvaise qualité.

jerry can ['dʒɛrɪ-] *n* bidon *m*.

Jersey ['dʒəːzɪ] *n* Jersey *f*.

jersey ['dʒəːzɪ] *n* tricot *m*; (*fabric*) jersey *m*.

Jerusalem [dʒə'ruːsləm] *n* Jérusalem.

jest [dʒɛst] *n* plaisanterie *f*; **in** ~ en plaisantant.

jester ['dʒɛstə*] *n* (*HIST*) plaisantin *m*.

Jesus ['dʒiːzəs] *n* Jésus; ~ **Christ** Jésus-Christ.

jet [dʒɛt] *n* (*of gas, liquid*) jet *m*; (*AUT*) gicleur *m*; (*AVIAT*) avion *m* à réaction, jet *m*.

jet-black ['dʒɛt'blæk] *adj* (d'un noir) de jais.

jet engine *n* moteur *m* à réaction.

jet lag *n* décalage *m* horaire.

jetsam ['dʒɛtsəm] *n* objets jetés à la mer (et rejetés sur la côte).

jet-setter ['dʒɛtsɛtə*] *n* membre *m* du *or* de la jet set.

jettison ['dʒɛtɪsn] *vt* jeter par-dessus bord.

jetty ['dʒɛtɪ] *n* jetée *f*, digue *f*.

Jew [dʒuː] *n* Juif *m*.

jewel ['dʒuːəl] *n* bijou *m*, joyau *m*.

jeweller ['dʒuːələ*] *n* bijoutier/ière, joaillier *m*; ~**'s (shop)** *n* bijouterie *f*, joaillerie *f*.

jewellery ['dʒuːəlrɪ] *n* bijoux *mpl*.

Jewess ['dʒuːɪs] *n* Juive *f*.

Jewish ['dʒuːɪʃ] *adj* juif(juive).

JFK *n abbr* (*US*) = *John Fitzgerald Kennedy International Airport*.

jib [dʒɪb] *n* (*NAUT*) foc *m*; (*of crane*) flèche *f* ♦ *vi* (*horse*) regimber; **to** ~ **at doing sth** rechigner à faire qch.

jibe [dʒaɪb] *n* sarcasme *m*.

jiffy ['dʒɪfɪ] *n* (*col*): **in a** ~ en un clin d'œil.

jig [dʒɪg] *n* (*dance, tune*) gigue *f*.

jigsaw ['dʒɪgsɔː] *n* (*also*: ~ **puzzle**) puzzle *m*;

(*tool*) scie sauteuse.

jilt [dʒɪlt] *vt* laisser tomber, plaquer.

jingle ['dʒɪŋgl] *n* (*advertising* ~) couplet *m* publicitaire ♦ *vi* cliqueter, tinter.

jingoism ['dʒɪŋgəʊɪzəm] *n* chauvinisme *m*.

jinx [dʒɪŋks] *n* (*col*) (mauvais) sort.

jitters ['dʒɪtəz] *npl* (*col*): **to get the** ~ avoir la trouille *or* la frousse.

jittery ['dʒɪtərɪ] *adj* (*col*) nerveux(euse); **to be** ~ avoir les nerfs en pelote.

jiujitsu [dʒuː'dʒɪtsuː] *n* jiu-jitsu *m*.

job [dʒɔb] *n* travail *m*; (*employment*) emploi *m*, poste *m*, place *f*; **a part-time/full-time** ~ un emploi à temps partiel/à plein temps; **he's only doing his** ~ il fait son boulot; **it's a good** ~ **that** ... c'est heureux *or* c'est une chance que ...; **just the** ~! (c'est) juste *or* exactement ce qu'il faut!

jobber ['dʒɔbə*] *n* (*BRIT STOCK EXCHANGE*) négociant *m* en titres.

jobbing ['dʒɔbɪŋ] *adj* (*BRIT: workman*) à la tâche, à la journée.

Jobcentre ['dʒɔbsɛntə*] *n* agence *f* pour l'emploi.

job creation scheme *n* plan *m* pour la création d'emplois.

job description *n* description *f* du poste.

jobless ['dʒɔblɪs] *adj* sans travail, au chômage ♦ *npl*: **the** ~ les sans-emploi *m inv*, les chômeurs *mpl*.

job lot *n* lot *m* (d'articles divers).

job satisfaction *n* satisfaction professionnelle.

job security *n* sécurité *f* de l'emploi.

job specification *n* caractéristiques *fpl* du poste.

Jock [dʒɔk] *n* (*col: Scotsman*) Écossais *m*.

jockey ['dʒɔkɪ] *n* jockey *m* ♦ *vi*: **to** ~ **for position** manœuvrer pour être bien placé.

jockey box *n* (*US AUT*) boîte *f* à gants, videpoches *m inv*.

jockstrap ['dʒɔkstræp] *n* slip *m* de sport.

jocular ['dʒɔkjʊlə*] *adj* jovial(e), enjoué(e); facétieux(euse).

jog [dʒɔg] *vt* secouer ♦ *vi* (*SPORT*) faire du jogging; **to** ~ **along** cahoter; trotter; **to** ~ **sb's memory** rafraîchir la mémoire de qn.

jogger ['dʒɔgə*] *n* jogger *m/f*.

jogging ['dʒɔgɪŋ] *n* jogging *m*.

john [dʒɔn] *n* (*US col*): **the** ~ (*toilet*) les cabinets *mpl*.

join [dʒɔɪn] *vt* unir, assembler; (*become member of*) s'inscrire à; (*meet*) rejoindre, retrouver; se joindre à ♦ *vi* (*roads, rivers*) se rejoindre, se rencontrer ♦ *n* raccord *m*; **will you** ~ **us for dinner?** vous dînerez bien avec nous?; **I'll** ~ **you later** je vous rejoindrai plus tard; **to** ~ **forces (with)** s'associer (à).

▶**join in** *vi* se mettre de la partie ♦ *vt* se mêler à.

▶**join up** *vi* s'engager.

joiner ['dʒɔɪnə*] *n* menuisier *m*.

joinery ['dʒɔɪnərɪ] *n* menuiserie *f*.

joint [dʒɔɪnt] *n* (*TECH*) jointure *f*; joint *m*; (*ANAT*) articulation *f*, jointure; (*BRIT: CULIN*) rôti *m*; (*col: place*) boîte *f* ♦ *adj* commun(e); (*committee*) mixte, paritaire; ~ **responsibility** coresponsabilité *f*.

joint account (J/A) *n* compte joint.

jointly ['dʒɔɪntlɪ] *adv* ensemble, en commun.

joint ownership *n* copropriété *f*.

joint-stock company ['dʒɔɪntstɔk-] *n* société *f* par actions.

joint venture *n* entreprise commune.

joist [dʒɔɪst] *n* solive *f*.

joke [dʒəʊk] *n* plaisanterie *f*; (*also*: **practical** ~) farce *f* ♦ *vi* plaisanter; **to play a** ~ **on** jouer un tour à, faire une farce à.

joker ['dʒəʊkə*] *n* plaisantin *m*, blagueur/euse; (*CARDS*) joker *m*.

joking ['dʒəʊkɪŋ] *n* plaisanterie *f*.

jollity ['dʒɔlɪtɪ] *n* réjouissances *fpl*, gaieté *f*.

jolly ['dʒɔlɪ] *adj* gai(e), enjoué(e) ♦ *adv* (*BRIT col*) rudement, drôlement ♦ *vt* (*BRIT*): **to** ~ **sb along** amadouer qn, convaincre *or* entraîner qn à force d'encouragements; ~ **good!** (*BRIT*) formidable!

jolt [dʒəʊlt] *n* cahot *m*, secousse *f* ♦ *vt* cahoter, secouer.

Jordan [dʒɔːdən] *n* (*country*) Jordanie *f*; (*river*) Jourdain *m*.

Jordanian [dʒɔː'deɪnɪən] *adj* jordanien(ne) ♦ *n* Jordanien/ne.

joss stick ['dʒɔsstɪk] *n* bâton *m* d'encens.

jostle ['dʒɔsl] *vt* bousculer, pousser ♦ *vi* jouer des coudes.

jot [dʒɔt] *n*: **not one** ~ pas un brin.

▶**jot down** *vt* inscrire rapidement, noter.

jotter ['dʒɔtə*] *n* (*BRIT*) cahier *m* (de brouillon); bloc-notes *m*.

journal ['dʒəːnl] *n* journal *m*.

journalese [dʒəːnə'liːz] *n* (*pej*) style *m* journalistique.

journalism ['dʒəːnəlɪzəm] *n* journalisme *m*.

journalist ['dʒəːnəlɪst] *n* journaliste *m/f*.

journey ['dʒəːnɪ] *n* voyage *m*; (*distance covered*) trajet *m*; **a 5-hour** ~ un voyage de 5 heures ♦ *vi* voyager.

jovial ['dʒəʊvɪəl] *adj* jovial(e).

jowl [dʒaʊl] *n* mâchoire *f* (*inférieure*); bajoue *f*.

joy [dʒɔɪ] *n* joie *f*.

joyful ['dʒɔɪfʊl], **joyous** ['dʒɔɪəs] *adj* joyeux(euse).

joyride ['dʒɔɪraɪd] *vi*: **to go joyriding** faire une virée dans une voiture volée.

joyrider ['dʒɔɪraɪdə*] *n* voleur/euse de voiture (*qui fait une virée dans le véhicule volé*).

joystick ['dʒɔɪstɪk] *n* (*AVIAT*) manche *m* à balai; (*COMPUT*) manche à balai, manette *f* (de jeu).

JP *n abbr* = **Justice of the Peace**.

Jr. *abbr* = **junior**.

JTPA *n abbr* (*US: = Job Training Partnership Act*) *programme gouvernemental de formation*.

jubilant ['dʒu:bɪlnt] *adj* triomphant(e); réjoui(e).

jubilation [dʒu:bɪ'leɪʃən] *n* jubilation *f*.

jubilee ['dʒu:bɪli:] *n* jubilé *m*; **silver ~** (jubilé du) vingt-cinquième anniversaire.

judge [dʒʌdʒ] *n* juge *m* ♦ *vt* juger; (*estimate: weight, size etc*) apprécier; (*consider*) estimer ♦ *vi*: **judging *or* to ~ by his expression** d'après son expression; **as far as I can ~** autant que je puisse en juger; **I ~d it necessary to inform him** j'ai jugé nécessaire de l'informer.

judge advocate (JA) *n* (*MIL*) magistrat *m* militaire.

judg(e)ment ['dʒʌdʒmənt] *n* jugement *m*; (*punishment*) châtiment *m*; **in my ~** à mon avis; **to pass ~ on** (*LAW*) prononcer un jugement (sur).

judicial [dʒu:'dɪʃl] *adj* judiciaire; (*fair*) impartial(e).

judiciary [dʒu:'dɪʃɪərɪ] *n* (pouvoir *m*) judiciaire *m*.

judicious [dʒu:'dɪʃəs] *adj* judicieux(euse).

judo ['dʒu:dəu] *n* judo *m*.

jug [dʒʌg] *n* pot *m*, cruche *f*.

jugged hare ['dʒʌgd-] *n* (*BRIT*) civet *m* de lièvre.

juggernaut ['dʒʌgənɔ:t] *n* (*BRIT: huge truck*) mastodonte *m*.

juggle ['dʒʌgl] *vi* jongler.

juggler ['dʒʌglə*] *n* jongleur *m*.

Jugoslav ['ju:gəu'slɑ:v] *adj, n* = **Yugoslav**.

jugular ['dʒʌgjulə*] *adj*: **~ (vein)** veine *f* jugulaire.

juice [dʒu:s] *n* jus *m*; (*col: petrol*): **we've run out of ~** c'est la panne sèche.

juicy ['dʒu:sɪ] *adj* juteux(euse).

jukebox ['dʒu:kbɔks] *n* juke-box *m*.

Jul. *abbr* (= *July*) juil.

July [dʒu:'laɪ] *n* juillet *m*; **the first of ~** le premier juillet; **(on) the eleventh of ~** le onze juillet; **in the month of ~** au mois de juillet; **at the beginning/end of ~** au début/à la fin (du mois) de juillet, début/fin juillet; **in the middle of ~** au milieu (du mois) de juillet, à la mi-juillet; **during ~** pendant le mois de juillet; **in ~ of next year** en juillet de l'année prochaine; **each *or* every ~** tous les ans *or* chaque année en juillet; **~ was wet this year** il a beaucoup plu cette année en juillet.

jumble ['dʒʌmbl] *n* fouillis *m* ♦ *vt* (*also: ~ up, ~ together*) mélanger, brouiller.

jumble sale *n* (*BRIT*) vente *f* de charité.

> *Les **jumble sales** ont lieu dans les églises, salles des fêtes ou halls d'écoles, et l'on y vend des articles de toutes sortes, en général bon marché et surtout d'occasion, pour collecter des fonds pour une œuvre de charité, une école (par exemple, pour acheter un ordinateur), ou encore une église (pour réparer un toit etc).*

jumbo ['dʒʌmbəu] *adj*: **~ jet** (avion) gros porteur (à réaction); **~ size** format maxi *or* extra-grand.

jump [dʒʌmp] *vi* sauter, bondir; (*start*) sursauter; (*increase*) monter en flèche ♦ *vt* sauter, franchir ♦ *n* saut *m*, bond *m*; sursaut *m*; (*fence*) obstacle *m*; **to ~ the queue** (*BRIT*) passer avant son tour.

▶**jump about** *vi* sautiller.

▶**jump at** *vt fus* (*fig*) sauter sur; **he ~ed at the offer** il s'est empressé d'accepter la proposition.

▶**jump down** *vi* sauter (pour descendre).

▶**jump up** *vi* se lever (d'un bond).

jumped-up ['dʒʌmptʌp] *adj* (*BRIT pej*) parvenu(e).

jumper ['dʒʌmpə*] *n* (*BRIT: pullover*) pull-over *m*; (*US: pinafore dress*) robe-chasuble *f*; (*SPORT*) sauteur/euse.

jump leads, (*US*) **jumper cables** *npl* câbles *mpl* de démarrage.

jump-start ['dʒʌmpstɑ:t] *vt* (*car: push*) démarrer en poussant; (: *with jump leads*) démarrer avec des câbles (de démarrage); (*fig: project, situation*) faire redémarrer promptement.

jumpy ['dʒʌmpɪ] *adj* nerveux(euse), agité(e).

Jun. *abbr* = **June**; **junior**.

Junr *abbr* = **junior**.

junction ['dʒʌŋkʃən] *n* (*BRIT: of roads*) carrefour *m*; (*of rails*) embranchement *m*.

juncture ['dʒʌŋktʃə*] *n*: **at this ~** à ce moment-là, sur ces entrefaites.

June [dʒu:n] *n* juin *m*; *for phrases see also* **July**.

jungle ['dʒʌŋgl] *n* jungle *f*.

junior ['dʒu:nɪə*] *adj, n*: **he's ~ to me (by 2 years), he's my ~ (by 2 years)** il est mon cadet (de 2 ans), il est plus jeune que moi (de 2 ans); **he's ~ to me** (*seniority*) il est en dessous de moi (dans la hiérarchie), j'ai plus d'ancienneté que lui.

junior executive *n* cadre moyen.

junior high school *n* (*US*) ≈ collège *m* d'enseignement secondaire.

junior minister *n* (*BRIT*) ministre *m* sous tutelle.

junior partner *n* associé(-adjoint) *m*.

junior school *n* (*BRIT*) école *f* primaire, cours moyen.

junior sizes *npl* (*COMM*) tailles *fpl* fillettes/garçonnets.

juniper ['dʒu:nɪpə*] *n*: **~ berry** baie *f* de genièvre.

junk [dʒʌŋk] *n* (*rubbish*) bric-à-brac *m inv*; (*ship*) jonque *f* ♦ *vt* (*col*) abandonner, mettre au rancart.

junk bond *n* (*COMM*) obligation hautement spéculative utilisée dans les OPA agressives.

junk dealer *n* brocanteur/euse.

junket ['dʒʌŋkɪt] *n* (*CULIN*) lait caillé; (*BRIT col*): **to go on a ~, go ~ing** voyager aux

frais de la princesse.
junk food *n* snacks vite prêts (*sans valeur nutritive*).
junkie ['dʒʌŋkɪ] *n* (*col*) junkie *m*, drogué/e.
junk mail *n* prospectus *mpl*.
junk room *n* (*US*) débarras *m*.
junk shop *n* (*boutique f de*) brocanteur *m*.
junta ['dʒʌntə] *n* junte *f*.
Jupiter ['dʒuːpɪtə*] *n* (*planet*) Jupiter *f*.
jurisdiction [dʒuərɪs'dɪkʃən] *n* juridiction *f*; **it falls** *or* **comes within/outside our** ~ cela est/n'est pas de notre compétence *or* ressort.
jurisprudence [dʒuərɪs'pruːdəns] *n* jurisprudence *f*.
juror ['dʒuərə*] *n* juré *m*.
jury ['dʒuərɪ] *n* jury *m*.
jury box *n* banc *m* des jurés.
juryman ['dʒuərɪmən] *n* = **juror.**
just [dʒʌst] *adj* juste ♦ *adv*: **he's** ~ **done it/left it** il vient de le faire/partir; ~ **as I expected** exactement *or* précisément comme je m'y attendais; ~ **right/two o'clock** exactement *or* juste ce qu'il faut/deux heures; **we were** ~ **going** nous partions; **I was** ~ **about to phone** j'allais téléphoner; ~ **as he was leaving** au moment *or* à l'instant précis où il partait; **it's** ~ **before/enough/here** juste avant/assez/là; **it's** ~ **me/a mistake** ce n'est que moi/(rien) qu'une erreur; ~ **missed/caught** manqué/attrapé de justesse; ~ **listen to this!** écoutez un peu ça!; ~ **ask someone the way** vous n'avez qu'à demander votre chemin à quelqu'un; **it's** ~ **as good** c'est (vraiment) aussi bon; **it's** ~ **as well that you ...** heureusement que vous ...; **not** ~ **now** pas tout de suite; ~ **a minute!**, ~ **one moment!** un instant (s'il vous plaît)!
justice ['dʒʌstɪs] *n* justice *f*; **Lord Chief J~** (*BRIT*) premier président de la cour d'appel; **this photo doesn't do you** ~ cette photo ne vous avantage pas.
Justice of the Peace (JP) *n* juge *m* de paix.
justifiable [dʒʌstɪ'faɪəbl] *adj* justifiable.
justifiably [dʒʌstɪ'faɪəblɪ] *adv* légitimement, à juste titre.
justification [dʒʌstɪfɪ'keɪʃən] *n* justification *f*.
justify ['dʒʌstɪfaɪ] *vt* justifier; **to be justified in doing sth** être en droit de faire qch.
justly ['dʒʌstlɪ] *adv* avec raison, justement.
justness ['dʒʌstnɪs] *n* justesse *f*.
jut [dʒʌt] *vi* (*also:* ~ **out**) dépasser, faire saillie.
jute [dʒuːt] *n* jute *m*.
juvenile ['dʒuːvənaɪl] *adj* juvénile; (*court, books*) pour enfants ♦ *n* adolescent/e.
juvenile delinquency *n* délinquance *f* juvénile.
juxtapose ['dʒʌkstəpəuz] *vt* juxtaposer.
juxtaposition ['dʒʌkstəpə'zɪʃən] *n* juxtaposition *f*.

K k

K, k [keɪ] *n* (*letter*) K, k *m*; **K for King** K comme Kléber.
K *abbr* (= *kilobyte*) Ko; (*BRIT*: = *Knight*) titre honorifique ♦ *n abbr* (= *one thousand*) K.
kaftan ['kæftæn] *n* cafetan *m*.
Kalahari Desert [kælə'hɑːrɪ-] *n* désert *m* de Kalahari.
kale [keɪl] *n* chou frisé.
kaleidoscope [kə'laɪdəskəup] *n* kaléidoscope *m*.
kamikaze [kæmɪ'kɑːzɪ] *adj* kamikaze.
Kampala [kæm'pɑːlə] *n* Kampala.
Kampuchea [kæmpu'tʃɪə] *n* Kampuchéa *m*.
kangaroo [kæŋgə'ruː] *n* kangourou *m*.
Kans. *abbr* (*US*) = **Kansas.**
kaput [kə'put] *adj* (*col*) kapout, capout.
karaoke [kɑːrə'əukɪ] *n* karaoke *m*.
karate [kə'rɑːtɪ] *n* karaté *m*.
Kashmir [kæʃ'mɪə*] *n* Cachemire *m*.
Kazakhstan [kɑːzɑːk'stæn] *n* Kazakhstan *m*.
KC *n abbr* (*BRIT LAW*: = *King's Counsel*) titre donné à certains avocats; see also **QC.**
kd *abbr* (*US*: = *knocked down*) en pièces détachées.
kebab [kə'bæb] *n* kébab *m*.
keel [kiːl] *n* quille *f*; **on an even** ~ (*fig*) à flot.
▶**keel over** *vi* (*NAUT*) chavirer, dessaler; (*person*) tomber dans les pommes.
keen [kiːn] *adj* (*interest, desire, competition*) vif(vive); (*eye, intelligence*) pénétrant(e); (*edge*) effilé(e); (*eager*) plein(e) d'enthousiasme; **to be** ~ **to do** *or* **on doing sth** désirer vivement faire qch, tenir beaucoup à faire qch; **to be** ~ **on sth/sb** aimer beaucoup qch/qn; **I'm not** ~ **on going** je ne suis pas chaud pour aller, je n'ai pas très envie d'y aller.
keenly ['kiːnlɪ] *adv* (*enthusiastically*) avec enthousiasme; (*feel*) vivement, profondément; (*look*) intensément.
keenness ['kiːnnɪs] *n* (*eagerness*) enthousiasme *m*; ~ **to do** vif désir de faire.
keep [kiːp] *vb* (*pt, pp* **kept** [kept]) *vt* (*retain, preserve*) garder; (*hold back*) retenir; (*a shop, the books, a diary*) tenir; (*feed: one's family etc*) entretenir, assurer la subsistance de; (*a promise*) tenir; (*chickens, bees, pigs etc*) élever ♦ *vi* (*food*) se conserver; (*remain: in a certain state or place*) rester ♦ *n* (*of castle*) donjon *m*; (*food etc*): **enough for his** ~ assez pour (assurer) sa subsistance; **to** ~ **doing sth** continuer à faire qch; faire qch continuelle-

ment; **to ~ sb from doing/sth from happening** empêcher qn de faire *or* que qn (ne)
fasse/que qch (n')arrive; **to ~ sb happy/a
place tidy** faire que qn soit content/qu'un
endroit reste propre; **to ~ sb waiting** faire
attendre qn; **to ~ an appointment** ne pas
manquer un rendez-vous; **to ~ a record of
sth** prendre note de qch; **to ~ sth to o.s.**
garder qch pour soi, tenir qch secret; **to ~
sth (back) from sb** cacher qch à qn; **to ~
time** (*clock*) être à l'heure, ne pas retarder.

▶**keep away** *vt:* **to ~ sth/sb away from sb** tenir qch/qn éloigné de qn ♦ *vi:* **to ~ away
(from)** ne pas s'approcher (de).

▶**keep back** *vt* (*crowds, tears, money*) retenir
♦ *vi* rester en arrière.

▶**keep down** *vt* (*control: prices, spending*) empêcher d'augmenter, limiter; (*retain: food*)
garder ♦ *vi* (*person*) rester assis(e); rester
par terre.

▶**keep in** *vt* (*invalid, child*) garder à la maison;
(*SCOL*) consigner ♦ *vi* (*col*): **to ~ in with sb**
rester en bons termes avec qn.

▶**keep off** *vi* ne pas s'approcher; "~ **off the
grass**" "pelouse interdite".

▶**keep on** *vi* continuer; **to ~ on doing** continuer à faire.

▶**keep out** *vt* empêcher d'entrer ♦ *vi* rester
en dehors; "~ **out**" "défense d'entrer".

▶**keep up** *vi* se maintenir; (*fig: in comprehension*) suivre ♦ *vt* continuer, maintenir; **to ~
up with** se maintenir au niveau de; **to ~ up
with sb** (*in race etc*) aller aussi vite que qn,
être du même niveau que qn.

keeper ['ki:pə*] *n* gardien/ne.

keep-fit [ki:p'fɪt] *n* gymnastique *f* de maintien.

keeping ['ki:pɪŋ] *n* (*care*) garde *f*; **in ~ with** à
l'avenant de; en accord avec.

keeps [ki:ps] *n*: **for ~** (*col*) pour de bon, pour
toujours.

keepsake ['ki:pseɪk] *n* souvenir *m*.

keg [kɛg] *n* barrique *f*, tonnelet *m*.

Ken. *abbr* (*US*) = Kentucky.

kennel ['kɛnl] *n* niche *f*; **~s** *npl* chenil *m*.

Kenya ['kɛnjə] *n* Kenya *m*.

Kenyan ['kɛnjən] *adj* kenyen(ne) ♦ *n* Kenyen/
ne.

kept [kɛpt] *pt, pp of* **keep**.

kerb [kə:b] *n* (*BRIT*) bordure *f* du trottoir.

kerb crawler [-krɔ:lə*] *n personne qui ac-
coste les prostitué(e)s en voiture.*

kernel ['kə:nl] *n* amande *f*; (*fig*) noyau *m*.

kerosene ['kɛrəsi:n] *n* kérosène *m*.

ketchup ['kɛtʃəp] *n* ketchup *m*.

kettle ['kɛtl] *n* bouilloire *f*.

kettle drums *npl* timbales *fpl*.

key [ki:] *n* (*gen, MUS*) clé *f*; (*of piano, typewriter*)
touche *f*; (*on map*) légende *f* ♦ *cpd* (-)clé.

▶**key in** *vt* (*text*) introduire au clavier.

keyboard ['ki:bɔ:d] *n* clavier *m* ♦ *vt* (*text*) saisir.

keyboarder ['ki:bɔ:də*] *n* claviste *m/f*.

keyed up [ki:d'ʌp] *adj:* **to be (all) ~** être su-
rexcité(e).

keyhole ['ki:həul] *n* trou *m* de la serrure.

keyhole surgery *n chirurgie très minutieuse
où l'incision est minimale.*

keynote ['ki:nəut] *n* (*MUS*) tonique *f*; (*fig*) note
dominante.

keypad ['ki:pæd] *n* pavé *m* numérique.

key ring *n* porte-clés *m*.

keystroke ['ki:strəuk] *n* frappe *f*.

kg *abbr* (= *kilogram*) K.

KGB *n abbr* KGB *m*.

khaki ['kɑ:kɪ] *adj, n* kaki (*m*).

kibbutz [kɪ'buts] *n* kibboutz *m*.

kick [kɪk] *vt* donner un coup de pied à ♦ *vi*
(*horse*) ruer ♦ *n* coup *m* de pied; (*of rifle*) recul *m*; (*col: thrill*): **he does it for ~s** il le fait
parce que ça l'excite, il le fait pour le plaisir.

▶**kick around** *vi* (*col*) traîner.

▶**kick off** *vi* (*SPORT*) donner le coup d'envoi.

kick-off ['kɪkɔf] *n* (*SPORT*) coup *m* d'envoi.

kick-start ['kɪkstɑ:t] *n* (*also:* **~er**) lanceur *m* au
pied.

kid [kɪd] *n* (*col: child*) gamin/e, gosse *m/f*; (*animal, leather*) chevreau *m* ♦ *vi* (*col*) plaisanter,
blaguer.

kid gloves *npl:* **to treat sb with ~** traiter qn
avec ménagement.

kidnap ['kɪdnæp] *vt* enlever, kidnapper.

kidnapper ['kɪdnæpə*] *n* ravisseur/euse.

kidnapping ['kɪdnæpɪŋ] *n* enlèvement *m*.

kidney ['kɪdnɪ] *n* (*ANAT*) rein *m*; (*CULIN*) rognon *m*.

kidney bean *n* haricot *m* rouge.

kidney machine *n* (*MED*) rein artificiel.

Kilimanjaro [kɪlɪmən'dʒɑ:rəu] *n*: **Mount ~** Kilimandjaro *m*.

kill [kɪl] *vt* tuer; (*fig*) faire échouer; détruire;
supprimer ♦ *n* mise *f* à mort; **to ~ time** tuer
le temps.

▶**kill off** *vt* exterminer; (*fig*) éliminer.

killer ['kɪlə*] *n* tueur/euse; meurtrier/ière.

killer instinct *n* combativité *f*; **to have the ~**
avoir un tempérament de battant.

killing ['kɪlɪŋ] *n* meurtre *m*; tuerie *f*, massacre
m; (*col*): **to make a ~** se remplir les poches,
réussir un beau coup ♦ *adj* (*col*) tordant(e).

kill-joy ['kɪldʒɔɪ] *n* rabat-joie *m inv*.

kiln [kɪln] *n* four *m*.

kilo ['ki:ləu] *n abbr* (= *kilogram*) kilo *m*.

kilobyte ['ki:ləubaɪt] *n* kilo-octet *m*.

kilogram(me) ['kɪləugræm] *n* kilogramme *m*.

kilometre, (*US*) **kilometer** ['kɪləmi:tə*] *n* kilomètre *m*.

kilowatt ['kɪləuwɔt] *n* kilowatt *m*.

kilt [kɪlt] *n* kilt *m*.

kilter ['kɪltə*] *n:* **out of ~** déréglé(e), détra-
qué(e).

kimono [kɪ'məunəu] *n* kimono *m*.

kin [kɪn] *n see* **next-of-kin, kith**.

kind [kaɪnd] *adj* gentil(le), aimable ♦ *n* sorte *f*, espèce *f*; (*species*) genre *m*; **to be two of a ~** se ressembler; **would you be ~ enough to ...?, would you be so ~ as to ...?** auriez-vous la gentillesse *or* l'obligeance de ...?; **it's very ~ of you (to do)** c'est très aimable à vous (de faire); **in ~** (*COMM*) en nature; (*fig*): **to repay sb in ~** rendre la pareille à qn.

kindergarten ['kɪndəgɑːtn] *n* jardin *m* d'enfants.

kind-hearted [kaɪnd'hɑːtɪd] *adj* bon(bonne).

kindle ['kɪndl] *vt* allumer, enflammer.

kindling ['kɪndlɪŋ] *n* petit bois.

kindly ['kaɪndlɪ] *adj* bienveillant(e), plein(e) de gentillesse ♦ *adv* avec bonté; **will you ~ ...** auriez-vous la bonté *or* l'obligeance de ...; **he didn't take it ~** il l'a mal pris.

kindness ['kaɪndnɪs] *n* bonté *f*, gentillesse *f*.

kindred ['kɪndrɪd] *adj* apparenté(e); **~ spirit** âme *f* sœur.

kinetic [kɪ'nɛtɪk] *adj* cinétique.

king [kɪŋ] *n* roi *m*.

kingdom ['kɪŋdəm] *n* royaume *m*.

kingfisher ['kɪŋfɪʃə*] *n* martin-pêcheur *m*.

kingpin ['kɪŋpɪn] *n* (*TECH*) pivot *m*; (*fig*) cheville ouvrière.

king-size(d) ['kɪŋsaɪz(d)] *adj* (*cigarette*) (format) extra-long(longue).

kink [kɪŋk] *n* (*of rope*) entortillement *m*; (*in hair*) ondulation *f*; (*col: fig*) aberration *f*.

kinky ['kɪŋkɪ] *adj* (*fig*) excentrique; (*pej*) aux goûts spéciaux.

kinship ['kɪnʃɪp] *n* parenté *f*.

kinsman ['kɪnzmən] *n* parent *m*.

kinswoman ['kɪnzwumən] *n* parente *f*.

kiosk ['kiːɔsk] *n* kiosque *m*; (*BRIT: also*: **telephone ~**) cabine *f* (téléphonique); (: *also*: **newspaper ~**) kiosque à journaux.

kipper ['kɪpə*] *n* hareng fumé et salé.

Kirghizia [kəː'gɪzɪə] *n* Kirghizistan *m*.

kiss [kɪs] *n* baiser *m* ♦ *vt* embrasser; **to ~ (each other)** s'embrasser; **to ~ sb goodbye** dire au revoir à qn en l'embrassant; **~ of life** *n* (*BRIT*) bouche à bouche *m*.

kissagram ['kɪsəgræm] *n* baiser envoyé à l'occasion d'une célébration par l'intermédiaire d'une personne employée à cet effet.

kit [kɪt] *n* équipement *m*, matériel *m*; (*set of tools etc*) trousse *f*; (*for assembly*) kit *m*; **tool ~** nécessaire *m* à outils.

▶**kit out** *vt* (*BRIT*) équiper.

kitbag ['kɪtbæg] *n* sac *m* de voyage *or* de marin.

kitchen ['kɪtʃɪn] *n* cuisine *f*.

kitchen garden *n* jardin *m* potager.

kitchen sink *n* évier *m*.

kitchen unit *n* (*BRIT*) élément *m* de cuisine.

kitchenware ['kɪtʃɪnwɛə*] *n* vaisselle *f*; ustensiles *mpl* de cuisine.

kite [kaɪt] *n* (*toy*) cerf-volant *m*; (*ZOOL*) milan *m*.

kith [kɪθ] *n*: **~ and kin** parents et amis *mpl*.

kitten ['kɪtn] *n* petit chat, chaton *m*.

kitty ['kɪtɪ] *n* (*money*) cagnotte *f*.

kiwi ['kiːwiː] *n*: **~ (fruit)** kiwi *m*.

KKK *n abbr* (*US*) = **Ku Klux Klan**.

Kleenex ['kliːnɛks] *n* ® Kleenex *m* ®.

kleptomaniac [klɛptəu'meɪnɪæk] *n* kleptomane *m/f*.

km *abbr* (= *kilometre*) km.

km/h *abbr* (= *kilometres per hour*) km/h.

knack [næk] *n*: **to have the ~ (of doing)** avoir le coup (pour faire); **there's a ~** il y a un coup à prendre *or* une combine.

knackered ['nækəd] *adj* (*col*) crevé(e), nase.

knapsack ['næpsæk] *n* musette *f*.

knave [neɪv] *n* (*CARDS*) valet *m*.

knead [niːd] *vt* pétrir.

knee [niː] *n* genou *m*.

kneecap ['niːkæp] *n* rotule *f* ♦ *vt* tirer un coup de feu dans la rotule de.

knee-deep ['niːdiːp] *adj*: **the water was ~** l'eau arrivait aux genoux.

kneel [niːl], *pt*, *pp* **knelt** [niːl, nɛlt] *vi* (*also*: **~ down**) s'agenouiller.

kneepad ['niːpæd] *n* genouillère *f*.

knell [nɛl] *n* glas *m*.

knelt [nɛlt] *pt*, *pp of* **kneel**.

knew [njuː] *pt of* **know**.

knickers ['nɪkəz] *npl* (*BRIT*) culotte *f* (de femme).

knick-knack ['nɪknæk] *n* colifichet *m*.

knife [naɪf] *n* (*pl* **knives**) couteau *m* ♦ *vt* poignarder, frapper d'un coup de couteau; **~, fork and spoon** couvert *m*.

knife-edge ['naɪfɛdʒ] *n*: **to be on a ~** être sur le fil du rasoir.

knight [naɪt] *n* chevalier *m*; (*CHESS*) cavalier *m*.

knighthood ['naɪthud] *n* chevalerie *f*; (*title*): **to get a ~** être fait chevalier.

knit [nɪt] *vt* tricoter; (*fig*): **to ~ together** unir ♦ *vi* (*broken bones*) se ressouder.

knitted ['nɪtɪd] *adj* en tricot.

knitting ['nɪtɪŋ] *n* tricot *m*.

knitting machine *n* machine *f* à tricoter.

knitting needle *n* aiguille *f* à tricoter.

knitting pattern *n* modèle *m* (pour tricot).

knitwear ['nɪtwɛə*] *n* tricots *mpl*, lainages *mpl*.

knives [naɪvz] *npl of* **knife**.

knob [nɔb] *n* bouton *m*; (*BRIT*): **a ~ of butter** une noix de beurre.

knobbly ['nɔblɪ], (*US*) **knobby** ['nɔbɪ] *adj* (*wood, surface*) noueux(euse); (*knees*) noueux.

knock [nɔk] *vt* frapper; (*make: hole etc*): **to ~ a hole in** faire un trou dans, trouer; (*force: nail etc*): **to ~ a nail into** enfoncer un clou dans; (*fig: col*) dénigrer ♦ *vi* (*engine*) cogner; (*at door etc*): **to ~ at/on** frapper à/sur ♦ *n* coup *m*; **he ~ed at the door** il frappa à la porte.

▶**knock down** *vt* renverser; (*price*) réduire.

▶**knock off** *vi* (*col: finish*) s'arrêter (de travailler) ♦ vt (*vase, object*) faire tomber; (*col: steal*) piquer; (*fig: from price etc*): **to ~ off £10** faire une remise de 10 livres.

►**knock out** vt assommer; (*BOXING*) mettre k.-o.

►**knock over** vt (*object*) faire tomber; (*pedestrian*) renverser.

knockdown ['nɔkdaun] adj (*price*) sacrifié(e).

knocker ['nɔkə*] n (*on door*) heurtoir m.

knocking ['nɔkɪŋ] n coups mpl.

knock-kneed [nɔk'niːd] adj aux genoux cagneux.

knockout ['nɔkaut] n (*BOXING*) knock-out m, K.-O. m.

knockout competition n (*BRIT*) compétition f avec épreuves éliminatoires.

knock-up ['nɔkʌp] n (*TENNIS*): **to have a ~** faire des balles.

knot [nɔt] n (*gen*) nœud m ♦ vt nouer; **to tie a ~** faire un nœud.

knotty ['nɔtɪ] adj (*fig*) épineux(euse).

know [nəu] vt (*pt* **knew**, *pp* **known** [njuː, nəun]) savoir; (*person, place*) connaître; **to ~ that** savoir que; **to ~ how to do** savoir faire; **to ~ about/of sth** être au courant de/connaître qch; **to get to ~ sth** (*fact*) apprendre qch; (*place*) apprendre à connaître qch; **I don't ~ him** je ne le connais pas; **to ~ right from wrong** savoir distinguer le bon du mauvais; **as far as I ~ ...** à ma connaissance ..., autant que je sache ....

know-all ['nəuɔːl] n (*BRIT pej*) je-sais-tout m/f.

know-how ['nəuhau] n savoir-faire m, technique f, compétence f.

knowing ['nəuɪŋ] adj (*look etc*) entendu(e).

knowingly ['nəuɪŋlɪ] adv sciemment; d'un air entendu.

know-it-all ['nəuɪtɔːl] n (*US*) = **know-all**.

knowledge ['nɔlɪdʒ] n connaissance f; (*learning*) connaissances, savoir m; **to have no ~ of** ignorer; **not to my ~** pas à ma connaissance; **without my ~** à mon insu; **to have a working ~ of French** se débrouiller en français; **it is common ~ that ...** chacun sait que ...; **it has come to my ~ that ...** j'ai appris que ....

knowledgeable ['nɔlɪdʒəbl] adj bien informé(e).

known [nəun] pp of **know** ♦ adj (*thief, facts*) notoire; (*expert*) célèbre.

knuckle ['nʌkl] n articulation f (des phalanges), jointure f.

►**knuckle down** vi (*col*) s'y mettre.

►**knuckle under** vi (*col*) céder.

knuckleduster ['nʌkldʌstə*] n coup-de-poing américain.

KO abbr (= *knock out*) n K.-O. m ♦ vt mettre K.-O.

koala [kəu'ɑːlə] n (*also:* ~ **bear**) koala m.

kook [kuːk] n (*US col*) loufoque m/f.

Koran [kɔ'rɑːn] n Coran m.

Korea [kə'rɪə] n Corée f; **North/South ~** Corée du Nord/Sud.

Korean [kə'rɪən] adj coréen(ne) ♦ n Coréen/ne.

kosher ['kəuʃə*] adj kascher inv.

kowtow ['kau'tau] vi: **to ~ to sb** s'aplatir devant qn.

Kremlin ['krɛmlɪn] n: **the ~** le Kremlin.

KS abbr (*US*) = Kansas.

Kt abbr (*BRIT*: = *Knight*) titre honorifique.

Kuala Lumpur ['kwɑːlə'lumpuə*] n Kuala Lumpur.

kudos ['kjuːdɔs] n gloire f, lauriers mpl.

Kurd [kəːd] n Kurde m/f.

Kuwait [ku'weɪt] n Koweït f, Kuweit f.

Kuwaiti [ku'weɪtɪ] adj koweïtien(ne) ♦ n Koweïtien/ne.

kW abbr (= *kilowatt*) kW.

KY, Ky. abbr (*US*) = Kentucky.

L l

L, l [ɛl] n (*letter*) L, l m; **L for Lucy,** (*US*) **L for Love** L comme Louis.

L abbr (= *lake, large*) L; (= *left*) g; (*BRIT AUT*: = *learner*) signale un conducteur débutant.

l abbr (= *litre*) l.

LA n abbr (*US*) = Los Angeles ♦ abbr (*US*) = Louisiana.

La. abbr (*US*) = Louisiana.

lab [læb] n abbr (= *laboratory*) labo m.

Lab. abbr (*Canada*) = Labrador.

label ['leɪbl] n étiquette f; (*brand: of record*) marque f ♦ vt étiqueter; **to ~ sb a ...** qualifier qn de ....

labor etc ['leɪbə*] (*US*) = **labour** etc.

laboratory [lə'bɔrətərɪ] n laboratoire m.

Labor Day n (*US, Canada*) fête f du travail (*le premier lundi de septembre*).

laborious [lə'bɔːrɪəs] adj laborieux(euse).

labor union n (*US*) syndicat m.

Labour ['leɪbə*] n (*BRIT POL: also:* **the ~ Party**) le parti travailliste, les travaillistes mpl.

labour, (*US*) **labor** ['leɪbə*] n (*task*) travail m; (*workmen*) main-d'œuvre f; (*MED*) travail, accouchement m ♦ vi: **to ~ (at)** travailler dur (à), peiner (sur); **in ~** (*MED*) en travail.

labo(u)r camp n camp m de travaux forcés.

labo(u)r cost n coût m de la main-d'œuvre; coût de la façon.

labo(u)red ['leɪbəd] adj lourd(e), laborieux(euse); (*breathing*) difficile, pénible; (*style*) lourd, embarrassé(e).

labo(u)rer ['leɪbərə*] n manœuvre m; (*on farm*) ouvrier m agricole.

labo(u)r force n main-d'œuvre f.

labo(u)r-intensive [leɪbərɪn'tɛnsɪv] adj intensif(ive) en main-d'œuvre.

labo(u)r market n marché m du travail.

labo(u)r pains npl douleurs fpl de l'accouchement.

labo(u)r relations npl relations fpl dans l'entreprise.

labo(u)r-saving ['leɪbəseɪvɪŋ] adj qui simplifie le travail.

labo(u)r unrest n agitation sociale.

labyrinth ['læbɪrɪnθ] n labyrinthe m, dédale m.

lace [leɪs] n dentelle f; (of shoe etc) lacet m ♦ vt (shoe) lacer; (drink) arroser, corser.

lacemaking ['leɪsmeɪkɪŋ] n fabrication f de dentelle.

laceration [læsə'reɪʃən] n lacération f.

lace-up ['leɪsʌp] adj (shoes etc) à lacets.

lack [læk] n manque m ♦ vt manquer de; **through** or **for** ~ **of** faute de, par manque de; **to be** ~**ing** manquer, faire défaut; **to be** ~**ing in** manquer de.

lackadaisical [lækə'deɪzɪkl] adj nonchalant(e), indolent(e).

lackey ['lækɪ] n (also fig) laquais m.

lacklustre ['læklʌstə*] adj terne.

laconic [lə'kɒnɪk] adj laconique.

lacquer ['lækə*] n laque f.

lacy ['leɪsɪ] adj comme de la dentelle, qui ressemble à de la dentelle.

lad [læd] n garçon m, gars m; (BRIT: in stable etc) lad m.

ladder ['lædə*] n échelle f; (BRIT: in tights) maille filée ♦ vt, vi (BRIT: tights) filer.

laden ['leɪdn] adj: ~ **(with)** chargé(e) (de); **fully** ~ (truck, ship) en pleine charge.

ladle ['leɪdl] n louche f.

lady ['leɪdɪ] n dame f; L~ **Smith** lady Smith; **the ladies' (room)** les toilettes fpl des dames; **a** ~ **doctor** une doctoresse, une femme médecin.

ladybird ['leɪdɪbɜːd], (US) **ladybug** ['leɪdɪbʌg] n coccinelle f.

lady-in-waiting ['leɪdɪɪn'weɪtɪŋ] n dame f d'honneur.

ladykiller ['leɪdɪkɪlə*] n don Juan m.

ladylike ['leɪdɪlaɪk] adj distingué(e).

ladyship ['leɪdɪʃɪp] n: **your L~** Madame la comtesse (or la baronne etc).

lag [læg] n = **time** ~ ♦ vi (also: ~ **behind**) rester en arrière, traîner ♦ vt (pipes) calorifuger.

lager ['lɑːgə*] n bière blonde.

lager lout n (BRIT col) jeune voyou m (porté sur la boisson).

lagging ['lægɪŋ] n enveloppe isolante, calorifuge m.

lagoon [lə'guːn] n lagune f.

Lagos ['leɪgɒs] n Lagos.

laid [leɪd] pt, pp of **lay**.

laid-back [leɪd'bæk] adj (col) relaxe, décontracté(e).

lain [leɪn] pp of **lie**.

lair [lɛə*] n tanière f, gîte m.

laissez-faire [lɛseɪ'fɛə*] n libéralisme m.

laity ['leɪətɪ] n laïques mpl.

lake [leɪk] n lac m.

Lake District n: **the** ~ (BRIT) la région des lacs.

lamb [læm] n agneau m.

lamb chop n côtelette f d'agneau.

lambskin ['læmskɪn] n (peau f d')agneau m.

lambswool ['læmzwul] n laine f d'agneau.

lame [leɪm] adj boiteux(euse); ~ **duck** (fig) canard boiteux.

lamely ['leɪmlɪ] adv (fig) sans conviction.

lament [lə'ment] n lamentation f ♦ vt pleurer, se lamenter sur.

lamentable ['læməntəbl] adj déplorable, lamentable.

laminated ['læmɪneɪtɪd] adj laminé(e); (windscreen) (en verre) feuilleté.

lamp [læmp] n lampe f.

lamplight ['læmplaɪt] n: **by** ~ à la lumière de la (or d'une) lampe.

lampoon [læm'puːn] n pamphlet m.

lamppost ['læmppəust] n (BRIT) réverbère m.

lampshade ['læmpʃeɪd] n abat-jour m inv.

lance [lɑːns] n lance f ♦ vt (MED) inciser.

lance corporal n (BRIT) (soldat m de) première classe m.

lancet ['lɑːnsɪt] n (MED) bistouri m.

Lancs [læŋks] abbr (BRIT) = Lancashire.

land [lænd] n (as opposed to sea) terre f (ferme); (country) pays m; (soil) terre; terrain m; (estate) terre(s), domaine(s) m(pl) ♦ vi (from ship) débarquer; (AVIAT) atterrir; (fig: fall) (re)tomber ♦ vt (passengers, goods) débarquer; (obtain) décrocher; **to go/travel by** ~ se déplacer par voie de terre; **to own** ~ être propriétaire foncier; **to** ~ **on one's feet** (also fig) retomber sur ses pieds.

▶**land up** vi atterrir, (finir par) se retrouver.

landed gentry ['lændɪd-] n (BRIT) propriétaires terriens or fonciers.

landfill site ['lændfɪl-] n centre m d'enfouissement des déchets.

landing ['lændɪŋ] n (from ship) débarquement m; (AVIAT) atterrissage m; (of staircase) palier m.

landing card n carte f de débarquement.

landing craft n péniche f de débarquement.

landing gear n train m d'atterrissage.

landing stage n (BRIT) débarcadère m, embarcadère m.

landing strip n piste f d'atterrissage.

landlady ['lændleɪdɪ] n propriétaire f, logeuse f.

landlocked ['lændlɒkt] adj entouré(e) de terre(s), sans accès à la mer.

landlord ['lændlɔːd] n propriétaire m, logeur m; (of pub etc) patron m.

landlubber ['lændlʌbə*] n terrien/ne.

landmark ['lændmɑːk] n (point m de) repère m; **to be a** ~ (fig) faire date or époque.

landowner ['lændəunə*] n propriétaire foncier or terrien.

landscape ['lænskeɪp] n paysage m.
landscape architect, landscape gardener n paysagiste m/f.
landscape painting n (ART) paysage m.
landslide ['lændslaɪd] n (GEO) glissement m (de terrain); (fig: POL) raz-de-marée (électoral).
lane [leɪn] n (in country) chemin m; (in town) ruelle f; (AUT) voie f; file f; (in race) couloir m; **shipping ~ route** f maritime or de navigation.
language ['læŋgwɪdʒ] n langue f; (way one speaks) langage m; **bad ~** grossièretés fpl, langage grossier.
language laboratory n laboratoire m de langues.
languid ['læŋgwɪd] adj languissant(e); langoureux(euse).
languish ['læŋgwɪʃ] vi languir.
lank [læŋk] adj (hair) raide et terne.
lanky ['læŋkɪ] adj grand(e) et maigre, efflanqué(e).
lanolin(e) ['lænəlɪn] n lanoline f.
lantern ['læntn] n lanterne f.
Laos [laus] n Laos m.
lap [læp] n (of track) tour m (de piste); (of body): **in** or **on one's ~** sur les genoux ♦ vt (also: ~ **up**) laper ♦ vi (waves) clapoter.
▶**lap up** vt (fig) boire comme du petit-lait, se gargariser de; (: lies etc) gober.
La Paz [læ'pæz] n La Paz.
lapdog ['læpdɔg] n chien m d'appartement.
lapel [lə'pɛl] n revers m.
Lapland ['læplænd] n Laponie f.
lapse [læps] n défaillance f; (in behaviour) écart m (de conduite) ♦ vi (LAW) cesser d'être en vigueur; se périmer; **to ~ into bad habits** prendre de mauvaises habitudes; **~ of time** laps m de temps, intervalle m; **a ~ of memory** un trou de mémoire.
laptop ['læptɔp] n (also: ~ **computer**) ordinateur portatif.
larceny ['lɑːsənɪ] n vol m.
lard [lɑːd] n saindoux m.
larder ['lɑːdə*] n garde-manger m inv.
large [lɑːdʒ] adj grand(e); (person, animal) gros(grosse); **to make ~r** agrandir; **a ~ number of people** beaucoup de gens; **by and ~** en général; **on a ~ scale** sur une grande échelle; **at ~** (free) en liberté; (generally) en général; pour la plupart.
largely ['lɑːdʒlɪ] adv en grande partie.
large-scale ['lɑːdʒ'skeɪl] adj (map, drawing etc) à grande échelle; (fig) important(e).
lark [lɑːk] n (bird) alouette f; (joke) blague f, farce f.
▶**lark about** vi faire l'idiot, rigoler.
larva, pl **larvae** ['lɑːvə, -iː] n larve f.
laryngitis [lærɪn'dʒaɪtɪs] n laryngite f.
larynx ['lærɪŋks] n larynx m.
lasagne [lə'zænjə] n lasagne f.
lascivious [lə'sɪvɪəs] adj lascif(ive).

laser ['leɪzə*] n laser m.
laser beam n rayon m laser.
laser printer n imprimante f laser.
lash [læʃ] n coup m de fouet; (also: **eye~**) cil m ♦ vt fouetter; (tie) attacher;
▶**lash down** vt attacher; amarrer; arrimer ♦ vi (rain) tomber avec violence.
▶**lash out** vi: **to ~ out (at** or **against sb/sth)** attaquer violemment (qn/qch); **to ~ out (on sth)** (col: spend) se fendre (de qch).
lashing ['læʃɪŋ] n: **~s of** (BRIT col: cream etc) des masses de.
lass [læs] n (jeune) fille f.
lasso [læ'suː] n lasso m ♦ vt prendre au lasso.
last [lɑːst] adj dernier(ière) ♦ adv en dernier ♦ vi durer; **~ week** la semaine dernière; **~ night** hier soir; la nuit dernière; **at ~** enfin; **~ but one** avant-dernier(ière); **the ~ time** la dernière fois; **it ~s (for) 2 hours** ça dure 2 heures.
last-ditch ['lɑːst'dɪtʃ] adj ultime, désespéré(e).
lasting ['lɑːstɪŋ] adj durable.
lastly ['lɑːstlɪ] adv en dernier lieu, pour finir.
last-minute ['lɑːstmɪnɪt] adj de dernière minute.
latch [lætʃ] n loquet m.
▶**latch on to** vt (cling to: person) s'accrocher à; (: idea) trouver bon(ne).
latchkey ['lætʃkiː] n clé f (de la porte d'entrée).
late [leɪt] adj (not on time) en retard; (far on in day etc) dernier(ière); tardif(ive); (recent) récent(e), dernier; (former) ancien(ne); (dead) défunt(e) ♦ adv tard; (behind time, schedule) en retard; **to be ~** avoir du retard; **to be 10 minutes ~** avoir 10 minutes de retard; **to work ~** travailler tard; **~ in life** sur le tard, à un âge avancé; **of ~** dernièrement; **in ~ May** vers la fin (du mois) de mai, fin mai; **the ~ Mr X** feu M. X.
latecomer ['leɪtkʌmə*] n retardataire m/f.
lately ['leɪtlɪ] adv récemment.
lateness ['leɪtnɪs] n (of person) retard m; (of event) heure tardive.
latent ['leɪtnt] adj latent(e); **~ defect** vice caché.
later ['leɪtə*] adj (date etc) ultérieur(e); (version etc) plus récent(e) ♦ adv plus tard; **~ on today** plus tard dans la journée.
lateral ['lætərl] adj latéral(e).
latest ['leɪtɪst] adj tout(e) dernier(ière); **the ~ news** les dernières nouvelles; **at the ~** au plus tard.
latex ['leɪtɛks] n latex m.
lath, **~s** [læθ, læðz] n latte f.
lathe [leɪð] n tour m.
lather ['lɑːðə*] n mousse f (de savon) ♦ vt savonner ♦ vi mousser.
Latin ['lætɪn] n latin m ♦ adj latin(e).
Latin America n Amérique latine.
Latin American adj latino-américain(e), d'Amérique latine ♦ n Latino-Américain/e.

latitude ['lætɪtjuːd] n (also fig) latitude f.
latrine [lə'triːn] n latrines fpl.
latter ['lætə*] adj deuxième, dernier(ière) ♦ n: **the ~** ce dernier, celui-ci.
latterly ['lætəlɪ] adv dernièrement, récemment.
lattice ['lætɪs] n treillis m; treillage m.
lattice window n fenêtre treillissée, fenêtre à croisillons.
Latvia ['lætvɪə] n Lettonie f.
Latvian ['lætvɪən] adj letton(ne) ♦ n Letton/ne; (LING) letton m.
laudable ['lɔːdəbl] adj louable.
laudatory ['lɔːdətrɪ] adj élogieux(euse).
laugh [lɑːf] n rire m ♦ vi rire.
►**laugh at** vt fus se moquer de; (joke) rire de.
►**laugh off** vt écarter or rejeter par une plaisanterie or par une boutade.
laughable ['lɑːfəbl] adj risible, ridicule.
laughing ['lɑːfɪŋ] adj rieur(euse); **this is no ~ matter** il n'y a pas de quoi rire, ça n'a rien d'amusant.
laughing gas n gaz hilarant.
laughing stock n: **the ~ of** la risée de.
laughter ['lɑːftə*] n rire m; (people laughing) rires mpl.
launch [lɔːntʃ] n lancement m; (boat) chaloupe f; (also: **motor ~**) vedette f ♦ vt (ship, rocket, plan) lancer.
►**launch out** vi: **to ~ out (into)** se lancer (dans).
launching ['lɔːntʃɪŋ] n lancement m.
launch(ing) pad n rampe f de lancement.
launder ['lɔːndə*] vt blanchir.
Launderette [lɔːn'drɛt], (US) **Laundromat** ['lɔːndrəmæt] n ® laverie f (automatique).
laundry ['lɔːndrɪ] n blanchisserie f; (clothes) linge m; **to do the ~** faire la lessive.
laureate ['lɔːrɪət] adj see **poet laureate**.
laurel ['lɔrl] n laurier m; **to rest on one's ~s** se reposer sur ses lauriers.
lava ['lɑːvə] n lave f.
lavatory ['lævətərɪ] n toilettes fpl.
lavatory paper n (BRIT) papier m hygiénique.
lavender ['lævəndə*] n lavande f.
lavish ['lævɪʃ] adj copieux(euse); somptueux(euse); (giving freely): **~ with** prodigue de ♦ vt: **to ~ sth on sb** prodiguer qch à qn.
lavishly ['lævɪʃlɪ] adv (give, spend) sans compter; (furnished) luxueusement.
law [lɔː] n loi f; (science) droit m; **against the ~** contraire à la loi; **to study ~** faire du droit; **to go to ~** (BRIT) avoir recours à la justice; **~ and order** n l'ordre public.
law-abiding ['lɔːəbaɪdɪŋ] adj respectueux(euse) des lois.
lawbreaker ['lɔːbreɪkə*] n personne f qui transgresse la loi.
law court n tribunal m, cour f de justice.
lawful ['lɔːful] adj légal(e); permis(e).
lawfully ['lɔːfəlɪ] adv légalement.
lawless ['lɔːlɪs] adj sans loi.

Law Lord n (BRIT) juge siégant à la Chambre des Lords.
lawmaker ['lɔːmeɪkə*] n législateur/trice.
lawn [lɔːn] n pelouse f.
lawnmower ['lɔːnməuə*] n tondeuse f à gazon.
lawn tennis n tennis m.
law school n faculté f de droit.
law student n étudiant/e en droit.
lawsuit ['lɔːsuːt] n procès m; **to bring a ~ against** engager des poursuites contre.
lawyer ['lɔːjə*] n (consultant, with company) juriste m; (for sales, wills etc) ≈ notaire m; (partner, in court) ≈ avocat m.
lax [læks] adj relâché(e).
laxative ['læksətɪv] n laxatif m.
laxity ['læksɪtɪ] n relâchement m.
lay [leɪ] pt of **lie** ♦ adj laïque; profane ♦ vt (pt, pp **laid** [leɪd]) poser, mettre; (eggs) pondre; (trap) tendre; (plans) élaborer; **to ~ the table** mettre la table; **to ~ the facts/one's proposals before sb** présenter les faits/ses propositions à qn; **to get laid** (col!) baiser (!); se faire baiser (!).
►**lay aside**, **lay by** vt mettre de côté.
►**lay down** vt poser; **to ~ down the law** (fig) faire la loi.
►**lay in** vt accumuler, s'approvisionner en.
►**lay into** vi (col: attack) tomber sur; (: scold) passer une engueulade à.
►**lay off** vt (workers) licencier.
►**lay on** vt (water, gas) mettre, installer; (provide: meal etc) fournir; (paint) étaler.
►**lay out** vt (design) dessiner, concevoir; (display) disposer; (spend) dépenser.
►**lay up** vt (to store) amasser; (car) remiser; (ship) désarmer; (subj: illness) forcer à s'aliter.
layabout ['leɪəbaut] n fainéant/e.
lay-by ['leɪbaɪ] n (BRIT) aire f de stationnement (sur le bas-côté).
lay days npl (NAUT) estarie f.
layer ['leɪə*] n couche f.
layette [leɪ'ɛt] n layette f.
layman ['leɪmən] n laïque m; profane m.
lay-off ['leɪɔf] n licenciement m.
layout ['leɪaut] n disposition f, plan m, agencement m; (PRESS) mise f en page.
laze [leɪz] vi paresser.
laziness ['leɪzɪnɪs] n paresse f.
lazy ['leɪzɪ] adj paresseux(euse).
LB abbr (Canada) = Labrador.
lb. abbr (= libra: pound) unité de poids.
lbw abbr (CRICKET: = leg before wicket) faute dans laquelle le joueur a la jambe devant le guichet.
LC n abbr (US) = Library of Congress.
lc abbr (TYP: = lower case) b.d.c.
L/C abbr = **letter of credit**.
LCD n abbr = **liquid crystal display**.
Ld abbr (BRIT: = lord) titre honorifique.
LDS n abbr (= Licentiate in Dental Surgery) di-

plôme universitaire; (= *Latter-day Saints*) Église de Jésus-Christ des Saints du dernier jour.

LEA *n abbr* (*BRIT*: = *local education authority*) services locaux de l'enseignement.

lead¹ [li:d] *n* (*front position*) tête *f*; (*distance, time ahead*) avance *f*; (*clue*) piste *f*; (*to battery*) raccord *m*; (*ELEC*) fil *m*; (*for dog*) laisse *f*; (*THEAT*) rôle principal ♦ *vb* (*pt, pp* **led** [lɛd]) *vt* mener, conduire; (*induce*) amener; (*be leader of*) être à la tête de; (*SPORT*) être en tête de; (*orchestra: BRIT*) être le premier violon de; (: *US*) diriger ♦ *vi* mener, être en tête; **to ~ to** mener à; (*result in*) conduire à; aboutir à; **to ~sb astray** détourner qn du droit chemin; **to be in the ~** (*SPORT: in race*) mener, être en tête; (: *match*) mener (à la marque); **to take the ~** (*SPORT*) passer en tête, prendre la tête; mener; (*fig*) prendre l'initiative; **to ~ sb to believe that ...** amener qn à croire que ...; **to ~ sb to do sth** amener qn à faire qch.
► **lead away** *vt* emmener.
► **lead back** *vt* ramener.
► **lead off** *vi* (*in game etc*) commencer.
► **lead on** *vt* (*tease*) faire marcher; **to ~ sb on to** (*induce*) amener qn à.
► **lead up to** *vt* conduire à.
lead² [lɛd] *n* (*chemical*) plomb *m*; (*in pencil*) mine *f*.
leaded ['lɛdɪd] *adj* (*windows*) à petits carreaux.
leaden ['lɛdn] *adj* de *or* en plomb.
leader ['liːdə*] *n* (*of team*) chef *m*; (*of party etc*) dirigeant/e, leader *m*; (*in newspaper*) éditorial *m*; **they are ~s in their field** (*fig*) ils sont à la pointe du progrès dans leur domaine; **the L~ of the House** (*BRIT*) le chef de la majorité ministérielle.
leadership ['liːdəʃɪp] *n* direction *f*; **under the ~ of ...** sous la direction de ...; **qualities of ~** qualités *fpl* de chef *or* de meneur.
lead-free ['lɛdfriː] *adj* sans plomb.
leading ['liːdɪŋ] *adj* de premier plan; (*main*) principal(e); **a ~ question** une question tendancieuse; **~ role** rôle prépondérant *or* de premier plan.
leading lady *n* (*THEAT*) vedette (féminine).
leading light *n* (*person*) sommité *f*, personnalité *f* de premier plan.
leading man *n* (*THEAT*) vedette (masculin).
lead pencil [lɛd-] *n* crayon noir *or* à papier.
lead poisoning [lɛd-] *n* saturnisme *m*.
lead time [liːd-] *n* (*COMM*) délai *m* de livraison.
lead weight [lɛd-] *n* plomb *m*.
leaf, *pl* **leaves** [liːf, liːvz] *n* feuille *f*; (*of table*) rallonge *f*; **to turn over a new ~** (*fig*) changer de conduite *or* d'existence; **to take a ~ out of sb's book** (*fig*) prendre exemple sur qn.
► **leaf through** *vt* (*book*) feuilleter.
leaflet ['liːflɪt] *n* prospectus *m*, brochure *f*;

(*POL, REL*) tract *m*.
leafy ['liːfɪ] *adj* feuillu(e).
league [liːg] *n* ligue *f*; (*FOOTBALL*) championnat *m*; (*measure*) lieue *f*; **to be in ~ with** avoir partie liée avec, être de mèche avec.
league table *n* classement *m*.
leak [liːk] *n* (*out, also fig*) fuite *f*; (*in*) infiltration *f* ♦ *vi* (*pipe, liquid etc*) fuir; (*shoes*) prendre l'eau ♦ *vt* (*liquid*) répandre; (*information*) divulguer.
► **leak out** *vi* fuir; (*information*) être divulgué(e).
leakage ['liːkɪdʒ] *n* (*also fig*) fuite *f*.
leaky ['liːkɪ] *adj* (*pipe, bucket*) qui fuit, percé(e); (*roof*) qui coule; (*shoe*) qui prend l'eau; (*boat*) qui fait eau.
lean [liːn] *adj* maigre ♦ *n* (*of meat*) maigre *m* ♦ *vb* (*pt, pp* **leaned** *or* **leant** [lɛnt]) *vt*: **to ~ sth on** appuyer qch sur ♦ *vi* (*slope*) pencher; (*rest*): **to ~ against** s'appuyer contre; être appuyé(e) contre; **to ~ on** s'appuyer sur.
► **lean back** *vi* se pencher en arrière.
► **lean forward** *vi* se pencher en avant.
► **lean out** *vi*: **to ~ out (of)** se pencher au dehors (de).
► **lean over** *vi* se pencher.
leaning ['liːnɪŋ] *adj* penché(e) ♦ *n*: ~ **(towards)** penchant *m* (pour); **the L~ Tower of Pisa** la tour penchée de Pise.
leant [lɛnt] *pt, pp of* **lean**.
lean-to ['liːntuː] *n* appentis *m*.
leap [liːp] *n* bond *m*, saut *m* ♦ *vi* (*pt, pp* **leaped** *or* **leapt** [lɛpt]) bondir, sauter; **to ~ at an offer** saisir une offre.
► **leap up** *vi* (*person*) faire un bond; se lever d'un bond.
leapfrog ['liːpfrɒg] *n* jeu *m* de saute-mouton.
leapt [lɛpt] *pt, pp of* **leap**.
leap year *n* année *f* bissextile.
learn, *pt, pp* **learned** *or* **learnt** [ləːn, -t] *vt, vi* apprendre; **to ~ how to do sth** apprendre à faire qch; **we were sorry to ~ that ...** nous apprenons avec regret que ...; **to ~ about sth** (*SCOL*) étudier qch; (*hear*) apprendre qch.
learned ['ləːnɪd] *adj* érudit(e), savant(e).
learner ['ləːnə*] *n* débutant/e; (*BRIT: also*: ~ **driver**) (conducteur/trice) débutant(e).
learning ['ləːnɪŋ] *n* savoir *m*.
lease [liːs] *n* bail *m* ♦ *vt* louer à bail; **on ~** en location.
► **lease back** *vt* vendre en cession-bail.
leaseback ['liːsbæk] *n* cession-bail *f*.
leasehold ['liːshəʊld] *n* (*contract*) bail *m* ♦ *adj* loué(e) à bail.
leash [liːʃ] *n* laisse *f*.
least [liːst] *adj*: **the ~ +** *noun* le(la) plus petit(e), le(la) moindre; (*smallest amount of*) le moins de; **the ~ +** *adjective* le(la) moins; **the ~ money** le moins d'argent; **the ~ expensive** le moins cher; **at ~** au moins; **not in the ~** pas le moins du monde.

leather ['lɛðə*] n cuir m ♦ cpd en or de cuir; ~ **goods** maroquinerie f.

leave [liːv] vb (pt, pp **left** [lɛft]) vt laisser; (go away from) quitter ♦ vi partir, s'en aller ♦ n (time off) congé m; (MIL, also: consent) permission f; **to be left** rester; **there's some milk left over** il reste du lait; **to ~ school** quitter l'école, terminer sa scolarité; ~ **it to me!** laissez-moi faire!, je m'en occupe!; **on ~** en permission; **to take one's ~ of** prendre congé de; ~ **of absence** n congé exceptionnel; (MIL) permission spéciale.

▶**leave behind** vt (also fig) laisser; (opponent in race) distancer; (forget) laisser, oublier.

▶**leave off** vt (cover, lid, heating) ne pas (re)mettre; (light) ne pas (r)allumer, laisser éteint(e); (BRIT col: stop): **to ~ off (doing sth)** s'arrêter (de faire qch).

▶**leave on** vt (coat etc) garder, ne pas enlever; (lid) laisser dessus; (light, fire, cooker) laisser allumé(e).

▶**leave out** vt oublier, omettre.

leaves [liːvz] npl of **leaf**.

leavetaking ['liːvteɪkɪŋ] n adieux mpl.

Lebanese [lɛbə'niːz] adj libanais(e) ♦ n (pl inv) Libanais/e.

Lebanon ['lɛbənən] n Liban m.

lecherous ['lɛtʃərəs] adj lubrique.

lectern ['lɛktəːn] n lutrin m, pupitre m.

lecture ['lɛktʃə*] n conférence f; (SCOL) cours (magistral) ♦ vi donner des cours; enseigner ♦ vt (reprove) sermonner, réprimander; **to ~ on** faire un cours (or son cours) sur; **to give a ~ (on)** faire une conférence (sur); faire un cours (sur).

lecture hall n amphithéâtre m.

lecturer ['lɛktʃərə*] n (speaker) conférencier/ière; (BRIT: at university) professeur m (d'université), ≈ maître assistant, maître de conférences; **assistant ~** (BRIT) ≈ assistant/e; **senior ~** (BRIT) ≈ chargé/e d'enseignement.

lecture theatre n = **lecture hall**.

LED n abbr (= light-emitting diode) LED f, diode électroluminescente.

led [lɛd] pt, pp of **lead**[1].

ledge [lɛdʒ] n (of window, on wall) rebord m; (of mountain) saillie f, corniche f.

ledger ['lɛdʒə*] n registre m, grand livre.

lee [liː] n côté m sous le vent; **in the ~ of** à l'abri de.

leech [liːtʃ] n sangsue f.

leek [liːk] n poireau m.

leer [lɪə*] vi: **to ~ at sb** regarder qn d'un air mauvais or concupiscent, lorgner qn.

leeward ['liːwəd] adj, adv sous le vent ♦ n côté m sous le vent; **to ~** sous le vent.

leeway ['liːweɪ] n (fig): **to make up ~** rattraper son retard; **to have some ~** avoir une certaine liberté d'action.

left [lɛft] pt, pp of **leave** ♦ adj gauche ♦ adv à gauche ♦ n gauche f; **on the ~, to the ~** à

gauche; **the L~** (POL) la gauche.

left-hand drive ['lɛfthænd-] n (BRIT) conduite f à gauche.

left-handed [lɛft'hændɪd] adj gaucher(ère); (scissors etc) pour gauchers.

left-hand side ['lɛfthænd-] n gauche f, côté m gauche.

leftie ['lɛftɪ] n (col) gaucho m/f, gauchiste m/f.

leftist ['lɛftɪst] adj (POL) gauchiste, de gauche.

left-luggage (office) [lɛft'lʌgɪdʒ(-)] n (BRIT) consigne f.

left-overs ['lɛftəʊvəz] npl restes mpl.

left wing n (MIL, SPORT) aile f gauche; (POL) gauche f ♦ adj: **left-wing** (POL) de gauche.

left-winger ['lɛft'wɪŋgə*] n (POL) membre m de la gauche; (SPORT) ailier m gauche.

lefty ['lɛftɪ] n (col) = **leftie**.

leg [lɛg] n jambe f; (of animal) patte f; (of furniture) pied m; (CULIN: of chicken) cuisse f; **1st/ 2nd ~** (SPORT) match m aller/retour; (of journey) 1ère/2ème étape; ~ **of lamb** (CULIN) gigot m d'agneau; **to stretch one's ~s** se dégourdir les jambes.

legacy ['lɛgəsɪ] n (also fig) héritage m, legs m.

legal ['liːgl] adj légal(e); **to take ~ action** or **proceedings against sb** poursuivre qn en justice.

legal adviser n conseiller/ère juridique.

legality [lɪ'gælɪtɪ] n légalité f.

legalize ['liːgəlaɪz] vt légaliser.

legally ['liːgəlɪ] adv légalement; ~ **binding** juridiquement contraignant(e).

legal tender n monnaie légale.

legation [lɪ'geɪʃən] n légation f.

legend ['lɛdʒənd] n légende f.

legendary ['lɛdʒəndərɪ] adj légendaire.

-legged ['lɛgɪd] suffix: **two~** à deux pattes (or jambes or pieds).

leggings ['lɛgɪŋz] npl jambières fpl, guêtres fpl.

leggy ['lɛgɪ] adj aux longues jambes.

legibility [lɛdʒɪ'bɪlɪtɪ] n lisibilité f.

legible ['lɛdʒəbl] adj lisible.

legibly ['lɛdʒəblɪ] adv lisiblement.

legion ['liːdʒən] n légion f.

legionnaire [liːdʒə'nɛə*] n légionnaire m; ~**'s disease** maladie f du légionnaire.

legislate ['lɛdʒɪsleɪt] vi légiférer.

legislation [lɛdʒɪs'leɪʃən] n législation f; **a piece of ~** un texte de loi.

legislative ['lɛdʒɪslətɪv] adj législatif(ive).

legislator ['lɛdʒɪsleɪtə*] n législateur/trice.

legislature ['lɛdʒɪslətʃə*] n corps législatif.

legitimacy [lɪ'dʒɪtɪməsɪ] n légitimité f.

legitimate [lɪ'dʒɪtɪmət] adj légitime.

legitimize [lɪ'dʒɪtɪmaɪz] vt légitimer.

legless ['lɛglɪs] adj (BRIT col) bourré(e).

leg-room ['lɛgruːm] n place f pour les jambes.

Leics abbr (BRIT) = **Leicestershire**.

leisure ['lɛʒə*] n (time) loisir m, temps m; (free time) temps libre, loisirs mpl; **at ~** (tout) à loisir; à tête reposée.

leisure centre n centre m de loisirs.
leisurely ['lɛʒəlɪ] adj tranquille; fait(e) sans se presser.
leisure suit n (BRIT) survêtement m (mode).
lemon ['lɛmən] n citron m.
lemonade [lɛmə'neɪd] n limonade f.
lemon cheese n, **lemon curd** n crème f de citron.
lemon juice n jus m de citron.
lemon squeezer [-skwiːzə*] n presse-citron m inv.
lemon tea n thé m au citron.
lend, pt, pp **lent** [lɛnd, lɛnt] vt: to ~ sth (to sb) prêter qch (à qn); to ~ a hand donner un coup de main.
lender ['lɛndə*] n prêteur/euse.
lending library ['lɛndɪŋ-] n bibliothèque f de prêt.
length [lɛŋθ] n longueur f; (section: of road, pipe etc) morceau m, bout m; ~ of time durée f; what ~ is it? quelle longueur fait-il?; it is 2 metres in ~ cela fait 2 mètres de long; to fall full ~ tomber de tout son long; at ~ (at last) enfin, à la fin; (lengthily) longuement; to go to any ~(s) to do sth faire n'importe quoi pour faire qch, ne reculer devant rien pour faire qch.
lengthen ['lɛŋθn] vt allonger, prolonger ♦ vi s'allonger.
lengthways ['lɛŋθweɪz] adv dans le sens de la longueur, en long.
lengthy ['lɛŋθɪ] adj (très) long(longue).
leniency ['liːnɪənsɪ] n indulgence f, clémence f.
lenient ['liːnɪənt] adj indulgent(e), clément(e).
leniently ['liːnɪəntlɪ] adv avec indulgence or clémence.
lens [lɛnz] n lentille f; (of spectacles) verre m; (of camera) objectif m.
Lent [lɛnt] n carême m.
lent [lɛnt] pt, pp of **lend**.
lentil ['lɛntl] n lentille f.
Leo ['liːəu] n le Lion; to be ~ être du Lion.
leopard ['lɛpəd] n léopard m.
leotard ['liːətɑːd] n maillot m (de danseur etc).
leper ['lɛpə*] n lépreux/euse.
leper colony n léproserie f.
leprosy ['lɛprəsɪ] n lèpre f.
lesbian ['lɛzbɪən] n lesbienne f ♦ adj lesbien(ne).
lesion ['liːʒən] n (MED) lésion f.
Lesotho [lɪ'suːtuː] n Lesotho m.
less [lɛs] adj moins de ♦ pron, adv moins; ~ than that/you moins que cela/vous; ~ than half moins de la moitié; ~ than one/a kilo/3 metres moins de un/d'un kilo/de 3 mètres; ~ and ~ de moins en moins; the ~ he works ... moins il travaille ....
lessee [lɛ'siː] n locataire m/f (à bail), preneur/euse du bail.
lessen ['lɛsn] vi diminuer, s'amoindrir, s'atténuer ♦ vt diminuer, réduire, atténuer.

lesser ['lɛsə*] adj moindre; to a ~ extent or degree à un degré moindre.
lesson ['lɛsn] n leçon f; a maths ~ une leçon or un cours de maths; to give ~s in donner des cours de; it taught him a ~ (fig) cela lui a servi de leçon.
lessor ['lɛsɔː*, lɛ'sɔː*] n bailleur/eresse.
lest [lɛst] conj de peur de + infinitive, de peur que + sub.
let, pt, pp **let** [lɛt] vt laisser; (BRIT: lease) louer; to ~ sb do sth laisser qn faire qch; to ~ sb know sth faire savoir qch à qn, prévenir qn de qch; he ~ me go il m'a laissé partir; ~ the water boil and ... faites bouillir l'eau et ...; ~'s go allons-y; ~ him come qu'il vienne; "to ~" (BRIT) "à louer".
►**let down** vt (lower) baisser; (dress) rallonger; (hair) défaire; (BRIT: tyre) dégonfler; (disappoint) décevoir.
►**let go** vi lâcher prise ♦ vt lâcher.
►**let in** vt laisser entrer; (visitor etc) faire entrer; what have you ~ yourself in for? à quoi t'es-tu engagé?
►**let off** vt (allow to leave) laisser partir; (not punish) ne pas punir; (subj: taxi driver, bus driver) déposer; (firework etc) faire partir; (smell etc) dégager; to ~ off steam (fig: col) se défouler, décharger sa rate or bile.
►**let on** vi (col): to ~ on that ... révéler que ..., dire que ....
►**let out** vt laisser sortir; (dress) élargir; (scream) laisser échapper; (rent out) louer.
►**let up** vi diminuer, s'arrêter.
let-down ['lɛtdaun] n (disappointment) déception f.
lethal ['liːθl] adj mortel(le), fatal(e).
lethargic [lɛ'θɑːdʒɪk] adj léthargique.
lethargy ['lɛθədʒɪ] n léthargie f.
letter ['lɛtə*] n lettre f; ~s npl (LITERATURE) lettres; small/capital ~ minuscule f/majuscule f; ~ of credit lettre f de crédit.
letter bomb n lettre piégée.
letterbox ['lɛtəbɔks] n (BRIT) boîte f aux or à lettres.
letterhead ['lɛtəhɛd] n en-tête m.
lettering ['lɛtərɪŋ] n lettres fpl; caractères mpl.
letter opener n coupe-papier m.
letterpress ['lɛtəprɛs] n (method) typographie f.
letter quality n qualité f "courrier".
letters patent npl brevet m d'invention.
lettuce ['lɛtɪs] n laitue f, salade f.
let-up ['lɛtʌp] n répit m, détente f.
leukaemia, (US) **leukemia** [luː'kiːmɪə] n leucémie f.
level ['lɛvl] adj plat(e), plan(e), uni(e); horizontal(e) ♦ n niveau m; (flat place) terrain plat; (also: spirit ~) niveau à bulle ♦ vt niveler, aplanir; (gun) pointer, braquer; (accusation): to ~ (against) lancer or porter (contre) ♦ vi (col): to ~ with sb être franc(franche) avec qn; "A" ~s npl (BRIT: for-

merly) ≈ baccalauréat *m*; *"O"* ~**s** *npl* (*BRIT: formerly*) *examens passés à l'âge de 16 ans sanctionnant les connaissances de l'élève*, ≈ brevet *m* des collèges; **a** ~ **spoonful** (*CULIN*) une cuillerée à raser; **to be** ~ **with** être au même niveau que; **to draw** ~ **with** (*team*) arriver à égalité de points avec, égaliser avec; arriver au même classement que; (*runner, car*) arriver à la hauteur de, rattraper; **on the** ~ à l'horizontale; (*fig: honest*) régulier(ière).

▶**level off, level out** *vi* (*prices etc*) se stabiliser ♦ *vt* (*ground*) aplanir, niveler.

level crossing *n* (*BRIT*) passage *m* à niveau.

level-headed [lɛvlˈhɛdɪd] *adj* équilibré(e).

levelling, (*US*) **leveling** [ˈlɛvlɪŋ] *adj* (*process, effect*) de nivellement.

level playing field *n*: **to compete on a** ~ jouer sur un terrain d'égalité.

lever [ˈliːvə*] *n* levier *m* ♦ *vt*: **to** ~ **up/out** soulever/extraire au moyen d'un levier.

leverage [ˈliːvərɪdʒ] *n*: ~ (**on** *or* **with**) prise *f* (sur).

levity [ˈlɛvɪtɪ] *n* manque *m* de sérieux, légèreté *f*.

levy [ˈlɛvɪ] *n* taxe *f*, impôt *m* ♦ *vt* prélever, imposer; percevoir.

lewd [luːd] *adj* obscène, lubrique.

lexicographer [lɛksɪˈkɔgrəfə*] *n* lexicographe *m/f*.

lexicography [lɛksɪˈkɔgrəfɪ] *n* lexicographie *f*.

LGV *n abbr* (= *Large Goods Vehicle*) poids lourd.

LI *abbr* (*US*) = *Long Island*.

liabilities [laɪəˈbɪlətɪz] *npl* (*COMM*) obligations *fpl*, engagements *mpl*; (*on balance sheet*) passif *m*.

liability [laɪəˈbɪlətɪ] *n* responsabilité *f*; (*handicap*) handicap *m*.

liable [ˈlaɪəbl] *adj* (*subject*): ~ **to** sujet(te) à; passible de; (*responsible*): ~ **(for)** responsable (de); (*likely*): ~ **to do** susceptible de faire; **to be** ~ **to a fine** être passible d'une amende.

liaise [liːˈeɪz] *vi*: **to** ~ **with** rester en liaison avec.

liaison [liːˈeɪzɔn] *n* liaison *f*.

liar [ˈlaɪə*] *n* menteur/euse.

libel [ˈlaɪbl] *n* écrit *m* diffamatoire; diffamation *f* ♦ *vt* diffamer.

libellous [ˈlaɪbləs] *adj* diffamatoire.

liberal [ˈlɪbərl] *adj* libéral(e); (*generous*): ~ **with** prodigue de, généreux(euse) avec ♦ *n*: **L~** (*POL*) libéral/e.

Liberal Democrat *n* démocrate *m/f*.

liberality [lɪbəˈrælɪtɪ] *n* (*generosity*) générosité *f*, libéralité *f*.

liberalize [ˈlɪbərəlaɪz] *vt* libéraliser.

liberal-minded [ˈlɪbərlˈmaɪndɪd] *adj* libéral(e), tolérant(e).

liberate [ˈlɪbəreɪt] *vt* libérer.

liberation [lɪbəˈreɪʃən] *n* libération *f*.

liberation theology *n* théologie *f* de libé-

ration.

Liberia [laɪˈbɪərɪə] *n* Libéria *m*, Liberia *m*.

Liberian [laɪˈbɪərɪən] *adj* libérien(ne) ♦ *n* Libérien/ne.

liberty [ˈlɪbətɪ] *n* liberté *f*; **at** ~ **to do** libre de faire; **to take the** ~ **of** prendre la liberté de, se permettre de.

libido [lɪˈbiːdəu] *n* libido *f*.

Libra [ˈliːbrə] *n* la Balance; **to be** ~ être de la Balance.

librarian [laɪˈbrɛərɪən] *n* bibliothécaire *m/f*.

library [ˈlaɪbrərɪ] *n* bibliothèque *f*.

library book *n* livre *m* de bibliothèque.

libretto [lɪˈbrɛtəu] *n* livret *m*.

Libya [ˈlɪbɪə] *n* Libye *f*.

Libyan [ˈlɪbɪən] *adj* libyen(ne), de Libye ♦ *n* Libyen/ne.

lice [laɪs] *npl of* **louse**.

licence, (*US*) **license** [ˈlaɪsns] *n* autorisation *f*, permis *m*; (*COMM*) licence *f*; (*RADIO, TV*) redevance *f*; (*also*: **driving** ~, (*US*) **driver's** ~) permis *m* (de conduire); (*excessive freedom*) licence; **import** ~ licence d'importation; **produced under** ~ fabriqué(e) sous licence.

licence number *n* (*BRIT AUT*) numéro *m* d'immatriculation.

license [ˈlaɪsns] *n* (*US*) = **licence** ♦ *vt* donner une licence à; (*car*) acheter la vignette de; délivrer la vignette de.

licensed [ˈlaɪsnst] *adj* (*for alcohol*) patenté(e) pour la vente des spiritueux, qui a une patente de débit de boissons.

licensee [laɪsənˈsiː] *n* (*BRIT: of pub*) patron/ne, gérant/e.

license plate *n* (*esp US AUT*) plaque *f* minéralogique.

licentious [laɪˈsɛnʃəs] *adj* licentieux(euse).

lichen [ˈlaɪkən] *n* lichen *m*.

lick [lɪk] *vt* lécher; (*col: defeat*) écraser, flanquer une piquette *or* raclée à ♦ *n* coup *m* de langue; **a** ~ **of paint** un petit coup de peinture.

licorice [ˈlɪkərɪs] *n* = **liquorice**.

lid [lɪd] *n* couvercle *m*; **to take the** ~ **off sth** (*fig*) exposer *or* étaler qch au grand jour.

lido [ˈlaɪdəu] *n* piscine *f* en plein air; complexe *m* balnéaire.

lie [laɪ] *n* mensonge *m* ♦ *vi* mentir; (*pt* **lay,** *pp* **lain** [leɪ, leɪn]) (*rest*) être étendu(e) *or* allongé(e) *or* couché(e); (*in grave*) être enterré(e), reposer; (*of object: be situated*) se trouver, être; **to** ~ **low** (*fig*) se cacher, rester caché(e); **to tell** ~**s** mentir.

▶**lie about, lie around** *vi* (*things*) traîner; (*person*) traînasser, flemmarder.

▶**lie back** *vi* se renverser en arrière.

▶**lie down** *vi* se coucher, s'étendre.

▶**lie up** *vi* (*hide*) se cacher.

Liechtenstein [ˈlɪktənstaɪn] *n* Liechtenstein *m*.

lie detector *n* détecteur *m* de mensonges.

lie-down [ˈlaɪdaun] *n* (*BRIT*): **to have a** ~

s'allonger, se reposer.

lie-in ['laɪɪn] *n* (*BRIT*): **to have a** ~ faire la grasse matinée.

lieu [luː]: **in** ~ **of** *prep* au lieu de, à la place de.

Lieut. *abbr* (= *lieutenant*) Lt.

lieutenant [lɛf'tɛnənt, (*US*) luː'tɛnənt] *n* lieutenant *m*.

lieutenant-colonel [lɛf'tɛnənt'kəːnl, (*US*) luː'tɛnənt'kəːnl] *n* lieutenant-colonel *m*.

life, *pl* **lives** [laɪf, laɪvz] *n* vie *f* ♦ *cpd* de vie; de la vie; à vie; **true to** ~ réaliste, fidèle à la réalité; **to paint from** ~ peindre d'après nature; **to be sent to prison for** ~ être condamné(e) (à la réclusion criminelle) à perpétuité; **country/city** ~ la vie à la campagne/à la ville.

life annuity *n* pension *f*, rente viagère.

life assurance *n* (*BRIT*) = **life insurance**.

lifebelt ['laɪfbɛlt] *n* (*BRIT*) bouée *f* de sauvetage.

lifeblood ['laɪfblʌd] *n* (*fig*) élément moteur.

lifeboat ['laɪfbəut] *n* canot *m* or chaloupe *f* de sauvetage.

lifebuoy ['laɪfbɔɪ] *n* bouée *f* de sauvetage.

life expectancy *n* espérance *f* de vie.

lifeguard ['laɪfgɑːd] *n* surveillant *m* de baignade.

life imprisonment *n* prison *f* à vie; (*LAW*) réclusion *f* à perpétuité.

life insurance *n* assurance-vie *f*.

life jacket *n* gilet *m* or ceinture *f* de sauvetage.

lifeless ['laɪflɪs] *adj* sans vie, inanimé(e); (*dull*) qui manque de vie or de vigueur.

lifelike ['laɪflaɪk] *adj* qui semble vrai(e) or vivant(e); ressemblant(e).

lifeline ['laɪflaɪn] *n* corde *f* de sauvetage.

lifelong ['laɪflɔŋ] *adj* de toute une vie, de toujours.

life preserver [-prɪ'zəːvə*] *n* (*US*) gilet *m* or ceinture *f* de sauvetage.

lifer ['laɪfə*] *n* (*col*) condamné/e à perpète.

life-raft ['laɪfrɑːft] *n* radeau *m* de sauvetage.

life-saver ['laɪfseɪvə*] *n* surveillant *m* de baignade.

life sentence *n* condamnation *f* à vie or à perpétuité.

life-sized ['laɪfsaɪzd] *adj* grandeur nature *inv*.

life span *n* (durée *f* de) vie *f*.

life style *n* style *m* de vie.

life support system *n* (*MED*) respirateur artificiel.

lifetime ['laɪftaɪm] *n*: **in his** ~ de son vivant; **the chance of a** ~ la chance de ma (or sa *etc*) vie, une occasion unique.

lift [lɪft] *vt* soulever, lever; (*steal*) prendre, voler ♦ *vi* (*fog*) se lever ♦ *n* (*BRIT*: *elevator*) ascenseur *m*; **to give sb a** ~ (*BRIT*) emmener or prendre qn en voiture.

▶**lift off** *vi* (*rocket, helicopter*) décoller.

▶**lift out** *vt* sortir; (*troops, evacuees etc*) évacuer par avion or hélicoptère.

▶**lift up** *vt* soulever.

lift-off ['lɪftɔf] *n* décollage *m*.

ligament ['lɪgəmənt] *n* ligament *m*.

light [laɪt] *n* lumière *f*; (*daylight*) lumière, jour *m*; (*lamp*) lampe *f*; (*AUT*: *traffic* ~, *rear* ~) feu *m*; (*: headlamp*) phare *m*; (*for cigarette etc*): **have you got a** ~? avez-vous du feu? ♦ *vt* (*pt, pp* **lighted** *or* **lit** [lɪt]) (*candle, cigarette, fire*) allumer; (*room*) éclairer ♦ *adj* (*room, colour*) clair(e); (*not heavy, also fig*) léger(ère) ♦ *adv* (*travel*) avec peu de bagages; **to turn the** ~ **on/off** allumer/éteindre; **to cast** *or* **shed** *or* **throw** ~ **on** éclaircir; **to come to** ~ être dévoilé(e) *or* découvert(e); **in the** ~ **of** à la lumière de; étant donné; **to make** ~ **of sth** (*fig*) prendre qch à la légère, faire peu de cas de qch.

▶**light up** *vi* s'allumer; (*face*) s'éclairer ♦ *vt* (*illuminate*) éclairer, illuminer.

light bulb *n* ampoule *f*.

lighten ['laɪtn] *vi* s'éclairer ♦ *vt* (*give light to*) éclairer; (*make lighter*) éclaircir; (*make less heavy*) alléger.

lighter ['laɪtə*] *n* (*also*: **cigarette** ~) briquet *m*; (*: in car*) allume-cigare *m inv*; (*boat*) péniche *f*.

light-fingered [laɪt'fɪŋgəd] *adj* chapardeur(euse).

light-headed [laɪt'hɛdɪd] *adj* étourdi(e), écervelé(e).

light-hearted [laɪt'hɑːtɪd] *adj* gai(e), joyeux(euse), enjoué(e).

lighthouse ['laɪthaus] *n* phare *m*.

lighting ['laɪtɪŋ] *n* (*on road*) éclairage *m*; (*in theatre*) éclairages.

lighting-up time [laɪtɪŋ'ʌp-] *n* (*BRIT*) heure officielle de la tombée du jour.

lightly ['laɪtlɪ] *adv* légèrement; **to get off** ~ s'en tirer à bon compte.

light meter *n* (*PHOT*) photomètre *m*, cellule *f*.

lightness ['laɪtnɪs] *n* clarté *f*; (*in weight*) légèreté *f*.

lightning ['laɪtnɪŋ] *n* éclair *m*, foudre *f*.

lightning conductor, (*US*) **lightning rod** *n* paratonnerre *m*.

lightning strike *n* (*BRIT*) grève *f* surprise.

light pen *n* crayon *m* optique.

lightship ['laɪtʃɪp] *n* bateau-phare *m*.

lightweight ['laɪtweɪt] *adj* (*suit*) léger(ère); (*boxer*) poids léger *inv*.

light year ['laɪtjɪə*] *n* année-lumière *f*.

like [laɪk] *vt* aimer (bien) ♦ *prep* comme ♦ *adj* semblable, pareil(le) ♦ *n*: **the** ~ un(e) pareil(le) *or* semblable; **le**(la) pareil(le); (*pej*) (d')autres du même genre or acabit; **his** ~**s and dislikes** ses goûts *mpl* or préférences *fpl*; **I would** ~, **I'd** ~ je voudrais, j'aimerais; **would you** ~ **a coffee?** voulez-vous du café?; **to be/look** ~ **sb/sth** ressembler à qn/qch; **what's he** ~? comment est-il?; **what's the weather** ~? quel temps fait-il?; **that's just** ~ **him** c'est bien de lui, ça lui ressemble; **something** ~ **that** quelque chose comme ça;

I feel ~ a drink je boirais bien quelque chose; if you ~ si vous voulez; there's nothing ~ ... il n'y a rien de tel que ....

likeable ['laɪkəbl] adj sympathique, agréable.

likelihood ['laɪklɪhud] n probabilité f; in all ~ selon toute vraisemblance.

likely ['laɪklɪ] adj (result, outcome) probable; (excuse) plausible; he's ~ to leave il va sûrement partir, il risque fort de partir; not ~! (col) pas de danger!

like-minded ['laɪk'maɪndɪd] adj de même opinion.

liken ['laɪkən] vt: to ~ sth to comparer qch à.

likeness ['laɪknɪs] n ressemblance f.

likewise ['laɪkwaɪz] adv de même, pareillement.

liking ['laɪkɪŋ] n affection f, penchant m; goût m; to take a ~ to sb se prendre d'amitié pour qn; to be to sb's ~ être au goût de qn, plaire à qn.

lilac ['laɪlək] n lilas m ♦ adj lilas inv.

Lilo ['laɪləu] n ® matelas m pneumatique.

lilt [lɪlt] n rythme m, cadence f.

lilting ['lɪltɪŋ] adj aux cadences mélodieuses; chantant(e).

lily ['lɪlɪ] n lis m; ~ of the valley muguet m.

Lima ['liːmə] n Lima.

limb [lɪm] n membre m; to be out on a ~ (fig) être isolé(e).

limber ['lɪmbə*]: to ~ up vi se dégourdir, se mettre en train.

limbo ['lɪmbəu] n: to be in ~ (fig) être tombé(e) dans l'oubli.

lime [laɪm] n (tree) tilleul m; (fruit) citron vert, lime f; (GEO) chaux f.

lime juice n jus m de citron vert.

limelight ['laɪmlaɪt] n: in the ~ (fig) en vedette, au premier plan.

limerick ['lɪmərɪk] n petit poème humoristique.

limestone ['laɪmstəun] n pierre f à chaux; (GEO) calcaire m.

limit ['lɪmɪt] n limite f ♦ vt limiter; weight/speed ~ limite de poids/de vitesse.

limitation [lɪmɪ'teɪʃən] n limitation f, restriction f.

limited ['lɪmɪtɪd] adj limité(e), restreint(e); ~ edition édition f à tirage limité.

limited (liability) company (Ltd) n (BRIT) ≈ société f anonyme (SA).

limitless ['lɪmɪtlɪs] adj illimité(e).

limousine ['lɪməziːn] n limousine f.

limp [lɪmp] n: to have a ~ boiter ♦ vi boiter ♦ adj mou(molle).

limpet ['lɪmpɪt] n patelle f; like a ~ (fig) comme une ventouse.

limpid ['lɪmpɪd] adj limpide.

linchpin ['lɪntʃpɪn] n esse f; (fig) pivot m.

Lincs [lɪŋks] abbr (BRIT) = Lincolnshire.

line [laɪn] n (gen) ligne f; (rope) corde f; (wire) fil m; (of poem) vers m; (row, series) rangée f; file f, queue f; (COMM: series of goods) arti-

cle(s) m(pl), ligne de produits ♦ vt (clothes): to ~ (with) doubler (de); (box): to ~ (with) garnir or tapisser (de); (subj: trees, crowd) border; to cut in ~ (US) passer avant son tour; in his ~ of business dans sa partie, dans son rayon; on the right ~s sur la bonne voie; a new ~ in cosmetics une nouvelle ligne de produits de beauté; hold the ~ please (BRIT TEL) ne quittez pas; to be in ~ for sth (fig) être en lice pour qch; in ~ with en accord avec, en conformité avec; to bring sth into ~ with sth aligner qch sur qch; to draw the ~ at (doing) sth (fig) se refuser à (faire) qch; ne pas tolérer or admettre (qu'on fasse) qch; to take the ~ that ... être d'avis or de l'opinion que ....

▶**line up** vi s'aligner, se mettre en rang(s) ♦ vt aligner; (set up, have ready) prévoir; trouver; to have sb/sth ~d up avoir qn/qch en vue or de prévu(e).

linear ['lɪnɪə*] adj linéaire.

lined [laɪnd] adj (paper) réglé(e); (face) marqué(e), ridé(e); (clothes) doublé(e).

line feed n (COMPUT) interligne m.

lineman ['laɪnmən] n (US: RAIL) poseur m de rails; (: TEL) ouvrier m de ligne; (: FOOTBALL) avant m.

linen ['lɪnɪn] n linge m (de corps or de maison); (cloth) lin m.

line printer n imprimante f (ligne par) ligne.

liner ['laɪnə*] n paquebot m de ligne.

linesman ['laɪnzmən] n (TENNIS) juge m de ligne; (FOOTBALL) juge m de touche.

line-up ['laɪnʌp] n file f; (also: police ~) parade f d'identification; (SPORT) (composition f de l')équipe f.

linger ['lɪŋgə*] vi s'attarder; traîner; (smell, tradition) persister.

lingerie ['lænʒəriː] n lingerie f.

lingering ['lɪŋgərɪŋ] adj persistant(e); qui subsiste; (death) lent(e).

lingo, ~es ['lɪŋgəu] n (pej) jargon m.

linguist ['lɪŋgwɪst] n linguiste m/f; personne douée pour les langues.

linguistic [lɪŋ'gwɪstɪk] adj linguistique.

linguistics [lɪŋ'gwɪstɪks] n linguistique f.

lining ['laɪnɪŋ] n doublure f; (TECH) revêtement m; (: of brakes) garniture f.

link [lɪŋk] n (of a chain) maillon m; (connection) lien m, rapport m ♦ vt relier, lier, unir; rail ~ liaison f ferroviaire.

▶**link up** vt relier ♦ vi se rejoindre; s'associer.

links [lɪŋks] npl (terrain m de) golf m.

link-up ['lɪŋkʌp] n lien m, rapport m; (of roads) jonction f, raccordement m; (of spaceships) arrimage m; (RADIO, TV) liaison f; (: programme) duplex m.

linoleum [lɪ'nəuliəm] n linoléum m.

linseed oil ['lɪnsiːd-] n huile f de lin.

lint [lɪnt] n tissu ouaté (pour pansements).

lintel ['lɪntl] n linteau m.

lion ['laɪən] n lion m.

lion cub *n* lionceau *m*.

lioness ['laɪənɪs] *n* lionne *f*.

lip [lɪp] *n* lèvre *f*; (*of cup etc*) rebord *m*; (*insolence*) insolences *fpl*.

liposuction ['lɪpəusʌkʃən] *n* liposuccion *f*.

lipread ['lɪpriːd] *vi* lire sur les lèvres.

lip salve [-sælv] *n* pommade *f* pour les lèvres, pommade rosat.

lip service *n*: **to pay ~ to sth** ne reconnaître le mérite de qch que pour la forme *or* qu'en paroles.

lipstick ['lɪpstɪk] *n* rouge *m* à lèvres.

liquefy ['lɪkwɪfaɪ] *vt* liquéfier ♦ *vi* se liquéfier.

liqueur [lɪ'kjuə*] *n* liqueur *f*.

liquid ['lɪkwɪd] *n* liquide *m* ♦ *adj* liquide.

liquid assets *npl* liquidités *fpl*, disponibilités *fpl*.

liquidate ['lɪkwɪdeɪt] *vt* liquider.

liquidation [lɪkwɪ'deɪʃən] *n* liquidation *f*; **to go into ~** déposer son bilan.

liquidator ['lɪkwɪdeɪtə*] *n* liquidateur *m*.

liquid crystal display (LCD) *n* affichage *m* à cristaux liquides.

liquidize ['lɪkwɪdaɪz] *vt* (*BRIT CULIN*) passer au mixer.

liquidizer ['lɪkwɪdaɪzə*] *n* (*BRIT CULIN*) mixer *m*.

liquor ['lɪkə*] *n* spiritueux *m*, alcool *m*.

liquorice ['lɪkərɪs] *n* (*BRIT*) réglisse *m*.

Lisbon ['lɪzbən] *n* Lisbonne *f*.

lisp [lɪsp] *n* zézaiement *m*.

lissom ['lɪsəm] *adj* souple, agile.

list [lɪst] *n* liste *f*; (*of ship*) inclinaison *f* ♦ *vt* (*write down*) inscrire; faire la liste de; (*enumerate*) énumérer; (*COMPUT*) lister ♦ *vi* (*ship*) gîter, donner de la bande; **shopping ~** liste des courses.

listed building ['lɪstɪd-] *n* (*ARCHIT*) monument classé.

listed company ['lɪstɪd-] *n* société cotée en Bourse.

listen ['lɪsn] *vi* écouter; **to ~ to** écouter.

listener ['lɪsnə*] *n* auditeur/trice.

listeria [lɪs'tɪərɪə] *n* listéria *f*.

listing ['lɪstɪŋ] *n* (*COMPUT*) listage *m*; (: *hard copy*) liste *f*, listing *m*.

listless ['lɪstlɪs] *adj* indolent(e), apathique.

listlessly ['lɪstlɪslɪ] *adv* avec indolence *or* apathie.

list price *n* prix *m* de catalogue.

lit [lɪt] *pt, pp of* **light**.

litany ['lɪtənɪ] *n* litanie *f*.

liter ['liːtə*] *n* (*US*) = **litre**.

literacy ['lɪtərəsɪ] *n* degré *m* d'alphabétisation, fait *m* de savoir lire et écrire.

literal ['lɪtərl] *adj* littéral(e).

literally ['lɪtrəlɪ] *adv* littéralement.

literary ['lɪtərərɪ] *adj* littéraire.

literate ['lɪtərət] *adj* qui sait lire et écrire, instruit(e).

literature ['lɪtrɪtʃə*] *n* littérature *f*; (*brochures etc*) copie *f* publicitaire, prospectus *mpl*.

lithe [laɪð] *adj* agile, souple.

lithography [lɪ'θɔgrəfɪ] *n* lithographie *f*.

Lithuania [lɪθju'eɪnɪə] *n* Lituanie *f*.

Lithuanian [lɪθju'eɪnɪən] *adj* lituanien(ne) ♦ *n* Lituanien/ne; (*LING*) lituanien *m*.

litigate ['lɪtɪgeɪt] *vt* mettre en litige ♦ *vi* plaider.

litigation [lɪtɪ'geɪʃən] *n* litige *m*; contentieux *m*.

litmus ['lɪtməs] *n*: **~ paper** papier *m* de tournesol.

litre, (*US*) **liter** ['liːtə*] *n* litre *m*.

litter ['lɪtə*] *n* (*rubbish*) détritus *mpl*, ordures *fpl*; (*young animals*) portée *f* ♦ *vt* éparpiller; laisser des détritus dans; **~ed with** jonché(e) de, couvert(e) de.

litter bin *n* (*BRIT*) boîte *f* à ordures, poubelle *f*.

litter lout, (*US*) **litterbug** ['lɪtəbʌg] *n* personne qui jette des détritus par terre.

little ['lɪtl] *adj* (*small*) petit(e); (*not much*): **it's ~** c'est peu ♦ *adv* peu; **~ milk** peu de lait; **a ~** un peu (de); **a ~ milk** un peu de lait; **for a ~ while** pendant un petit moment; **with ~ difficulty** sans trop de difficulté; **as ~ as possible** le moins possible; **~ by ~** petit à petit, peu à peu; **to make ~ of** faire peu de cas de.

little-known ['lɪtl'nəun] *adj* peu connu(e).

liturgy ['lɪtədʒɪ] *n* liturgie *f*.

live *vi* [lɪv] vivre; (*reside*) vivre, habiter ♦ *adj* [laɪv] (*animal*) vivant(e), en vie; (*wire*) sous tension; (*broadcast*) (transmis(e)) en direct; (*issue*) d'actualité, brûlant(e); (*unexploded*) non explosé(e); **to ~ in London** habiter (à) Londres; **to ~ together** vivre ensemble, cohabiter; **~ ammunition** munitions *fpl* de combat.

▶**live down** *vt* faire oublier (avec le temps).

▶**live in** *vi* être logé(e) et nourri(e); être interne.

▶**live off** *vt* (*land, fish etc*) vivre de; (*pej: parents etc*) vivre aux crochets de.

▶**live on** *vt fus* (*food*) vivre de ♦ *vi* survivre; **to ~ on £50 a week** vivre avec 50 livres par semaine.

▶**live out** *vi* (*BRIT: students*) être externe ♦ *vt*: **to ~ out one's days** *or* **life** passer sa vie.

▶**live up** *vt*: **to ~ it up** (*col*) faire la fête; mener la grande vie.

▶**live up to** *vt fus* se montrer à la hauteur de.

live-in ['lɪvɪn] *adj* (*nanny*) à demeure; **~ partner** concubin/e.

livelihood ['laɪvlɪhud] *n* moyens *mpl* d'existence.

liveliness ['laɪvlɪnəs] *n* vivacité *f*, entrain *m*.

lively ['laɪvlɪ] *adj* vif(vive), plein(e) d'entrain.

liven up ['laɪvn-] *vt* (*room etc*) égayer; (*discussion, evening*) animer.

liver ['lɪvə*] *n* foie *m*.

liverish ['lɪvərɪʃ] *adj* qui a mal au foie; (*fig*) grincheux(euse).

Liverpudlian [lɪvə'pʌdlɪən] *adj* de Liverpool

♦ *n* habitant/e de Liverpool; natif/ive de Liverpool.

livery ['lɪvərɪ] *n* livrée *f*.

lives [laɪvz] *npl of* **life**.

livestock ['laɪvstɔk] *n* cheptel *m*, bétail *m*.

live wire [laɪv-] *n* (*col, fig*): **to be a (real)** ~ péter le feu.

livid ['lɪvɪd] *adj* livide, blafard(e); (*furious*) furieux(euse), furibond(e).

living ['lɪvɪŋ] *adj* vivant(e), en vie ♦ *n*: **to earn** *or* **make a** ~ gagner sa vie; **cost of** ~ coût *m* de la vie; **within** ~ **memory** de mémoire d'homme.

living conditions *npl* conditions *fpl* de vie.

living expenses *npl* dépenses courantes.

living room *n* salle *f* de séjour.

living wage *n* salaire *m* permettant de vivre (décemment).

lizard ['lɪzəd] *n* lézard *m*.

llama ['lɑːmə] *n* lama *m*.

LLB *n abbr* (= *Bachelor of Laws*) titre universitaire.

LLD *n abbr* (= *Doctor of Laws*) titre universitaire.

LMT *abbr* (*US*: = *Local Mean Time*) heure locale.

load [ləud] *n* (*weight*) poids *m*; (*thing carried*) chargement *m*, charge *f*; (*ELEC, TECH*) charge ♦ *vt* (*lorry, ship*): **to** ~ **(with)** charger (de); (*gun, camera*): **to** ~ **(with)** charger (avec); (*COMPUT*) charger; **a** ~ **of**, ~**s of** (*fig*) un *or* des tas de, des masses de.

loaded ['ləudɪd] *adj* (*dice*) pipé(e); (*question*) insidieux(euse); (*col: rich*) bourré(e) de fric; (*: drunk*) bourré.

loading bay ['ləudɪŋ-] *n* aire *f* de chargement.

loaf, loaves [ləuf, ləuvz] *n* pain *m*, miche *f* ♦ *vi* (*also:* ~ **about**, ~ **around**) fainéanter, traîner.

loam [ləum] *n* terreau *m*.

loan [ləun] *n* prêt *m* ♦ *vt* prêter; **on** ~ prêté(e), en prêt; **public** ~ emprunt public.

loan account *n* compte *m* de prêt.

loan capital *n* capital-obligations *m*.

loan shark *n* (*col, pej*) usurier *m*.

loath [ləuθ] *adj*: **to be** ~ **to do** répugner à faire.

loathe [ləuð] *vt* détester, avoir en horreur.

loathing ['ləuðɪŋ] *n* dégoût *m*, répugnance *f*.

loathsome ['ləuðsəm] *adj* répugnant(e), détestable.

loaves [ləuvz] *npl of* **loaf**.

lob [lɔb] *vt* (*ball*) lober.

lobby ['lɔbɪ] *n* hall *m*, entrée *f*; (*POL*) groupe *m* de pression, lobby *m* ♦ *vt* faire pression sur.

lobbyist ['lɔbɪɪst] *n* membre *m/f* d'un groupe de pression.

lobe [ləub] *n* lobe *m*.

lobster ['lɔbstə*] *n* homard *m*.

lobster pot *n* casier *m* à homards.

local ['ləukl] *adj* local(e) ♦ *n* (*BRIT: pub*) pub *m* *or* café *m* du coin; **the** ~**s** *npl* les gens *mpl* du pays *or* du coin.

local anaesthetic *n* anesthésie locale.

local authority *n* collectivité locale, municipalité *f*.

local call *n* (*TEL*) communication urbaine.

local government *n* administration locale *or* municipale.

locality [ləu'kælɪtɪ] *n* région *f*, environs *mpl*; (*position*) lieu *m*.

localize ['ləukəlaɪz] *vt* localiser.

locally ['ləukəlɪ] *adv* localement; dans les environs *or* la région.

locate [ləu'keɪt] *vt* (*find*) trouver, repérer; (*situate*) situer.

location [ləu'keɪʃən] *n* emplacement *m*; **on** ~ (*CINE*) en extérieur.

loch [lɔx] *n* lac *m*, loch *m*.

lock [lɔk] *n* (*of door, box*) serrure *f*; (*of canal*) écluse *f*; (*of hair*) mèche *f*, boucle *f* ♦ *vt* (*with key*) fermer à clé; (*immobilize*) bloquer ♦ *vi* (*door etc*) fermer à clé; (*wheels*) se bloquer; ~ **stock and barrel** (*fig*) en bloc; **on full** ~ (*BRIT AUT*) le volant tourné à fond.

▶**lock away** *vt* (*valuables*) mettre sous clé; (*criminal*) mettre sous les verrous, enfermer.

▶**lock out** *vt* enfermer dehors; (*on purpose*) mettre à la porte; (*: workers*) lock-outer.

▶**lock up** *vi* tout fermer (à clé).

locker ['lɔkə*] *n* casier *m*.

locket ['lɔkɪt] *n* médaillon *m*.

lockjaw ['lɔkdʒɔː] *n* tétanos *m*.

lockout ['lɔkaut] *n* (*INDUSTRY*) lock-out *m*, grève patronale.

locksmith ['lɔksmɪθ] *n* serrurier *m*.

lock-up ['lɔkʌp] *n* (*prison*) prison *f*; (*cell*) cellule *f* provisoire; (*also:* ~ **garage**) box *m*.

locomotive [ləukə'məutɪv] *n* locomotive *f*.

locum ['ləukəm] *n* (*MED*) suppléant/e (de médecin).

locust ['ləukəst] *n* locuste *f*, sauterelle *f*.

lodge [lɔdʒ] *n* pavillon *m* (de gardien); (*FREEMASONRY*) loge *f* ♦ *vi* (*person*): **to** ~ **with** être logé(e) chez, être en pension chez ♦ *vt* (*appeal etc*) présenter; déposer; **to** ~ **a complaint** porter plainte; **to** ~ **(itself) in/between** se loger dans/entre.

lodger ['lɔdʒə*] *n* locataire *m/f*; (*with room and meals*) pensionnaire *m/f*.

lodging ['lɔdʒɪŋ] *n* logement *m*; *see also* **board**.

lodging house *n* (*BRIT*) pension *f* de famille.

lodgings ['lɔdʒɪŋz] *npl* chambre *f*, meublé *m*.

loft [lɔft] *n* grenier *m*; (*US*) grenier aménagé (en appartement) (*gén dans ancien entrepôt ou fabrique*).

lofty ['lɔftɪ] *adj* élevé(e); (*haughty*) hautain(e); (*sentiments, aims*) noble.

log [lɔg] *n* (*of wood*) bûche *f*; (*book*) = **logbook** ♦ *n abbr* (= *logarithm*) log *m* ♦ *vt* enregistrer.

▶**log in, log on** *vi* (*COMPUT*) ouvrir une session, entrer dans le système.

▶**log off, log out** *vi* (*COMPUT*) clore une session, sortir du système.

logarithm ['lɒgərɪðm] *n* logarithme *m*.

logbook ['lɒgbʊk] *n* (*NAUT*) livre *m or* journal *m* de bord; (*AVIAT*) carnet *m* de vol; (*of lorry driver*) carnet de route; (*of events, movement of goods etc*) registre *m*; (*of car*) ≈ carte grise.

log cabin *n* cabane *f* en rondins.

log fire *n* feu *m* de bois.

logger ['lɒgə*] *n* bûcheron *m*.

loggerheads ['lɒgəhɛdz] *npl*: **at ~ (with)** à couteaux tirés (avec).

logic ['lɒdʒɪk] *n* logique *f*.

logical ['lɒdʒɪkl] *adj* logique.

logically ['lɒdʒɪkəlɪ] *adv* logiquement.

logistics [lɒ'dʒɪstɪks] *n* logistique *f*.

logjam ['lɒgdʒæm] *n*: **to break the ~** créer une ouverture dans l'impasse.

logo ['ləʊgəʊ] *n* logo *m*.

loin [lɔɪn] *n* (*CULIN*) filet *m*, longe *f*; **~s** *npl* reins *mpl*.

loin cloth *n* pagne *m*.

loiter ['lɔɪtə*] *vi* s'attarder; **to ~ (about)** traîner, musarder; (*pej*) rôder.

loll [lɒl] *vi* (*also*: **~ about**) se prélasser, fainéanter.

lollipop ['lɒlɪpɒp] *n* sucette *f*.

Les **lollipop men/ladies** *sont employés pour aider les enfants à traverser la rue à proximité des écoles à l'heure où ils entrent en classe et à la sortie. On les repère facilement à cause de leur long ciré blanc et ils portent une pancarte ronde pour faire signe aux automobilistes de s'arrêter. On les appelle ainsi car la forme circulaire de cette pancarte rappelle une sucette.*

---

lollop ['lɒləp] *vi* (*BRIT*) avancer (*or* courir) maladroitement.

lolly ['lɒlɪ] *n* (*col: ice*) esquimau *m*; (*: lollipop*) sucette *f*; (*: money*) fric *m*.

Lombardy ['lɒmbədɪ] *n* Lombardie *f*.

London ['lʌndən] *n* Londres.

Londoner ['lʌndənə*] *n* Londonien/ne.

lone [ləʊn] *adj* solitaire.

loneliness ['ləʊnlɪnɪs] *n* solitude *f*, isolement *m*.

lonely ['ləʊnlɪ] *adj* seul(e); (*childhood etc*) solitaire; (*place*) solitaire, isolé(e); **to feel ~** se sentir seul.

lonely hearts *adj*: **~ ad** petite annonce (personnelle); **~ club** club *m* de rencontres (*pour personnes seules*).

lone parent *n* parent *m* unique.

loner ['ləʊnə*] *n* solitaire *m/f*.

lonesome ['ləʊnsəm] *adj* seul(e); solitaire.

long [lɒŋ] *adj* long(longue) ♦ *adv* longtemps ♦ *n*: **the ~ and the short of it is that ...** (*fig*) le fin mot de l'histoire c'est que ... ♦ *vi*: **to ~ for sth/to do** avoir très envie de qch/de faire; attendre qch avec impatience/impatience de faire; **he had ~ understood that ...** il avait compris depuis longtemps que ...; **how ~ is this river/course?** quelle est la

longueur de ce fleuve/la durée de ce cours?; **6 metres ~ (long)** de 6 mètres; **6 months ~** qui dure 6 mois, de 6 mois; **all night ~** toute la nuit; **he no ~er comes** il ne vient plus; **~ before** longtemps avant; **before ~ (+ future)** avant peu, dans peu de temps; (*+ past*) peu de temps après; **~ ago** il y a longtemps; **don't be ~!** fais vite!, dépêche-toi!; **I shan't be ~** je n'en ai pas pour longtemps; **at ~ last** enfin; **in the ~ run** à la longue; finalement; **so** *or* **as ~ as** pourvu que.

long-distance [lɒŋ'dɪstəns] *adj* (*race*) de fond; (*call*) interurbain(e).

long-haired ['lɒŋ'hɛəd] *adj* (*person*) aux cheveux longs; (*animal*) aux longs poils.

longhand ['lɒŋhænd] *n* écriture normale *or* courante.

longing ['lɒŋɪŋ] *n* désir *m*, envie *f*, nostalgie *f* ♦ *adj* plein(e) d'envie *or* de nostalgie.

longingly ['lɒŋɪŋlɪ] *adv* avec désir *or* nostalgie.

longitude ['lɒŋgɪtjuːd] *n* longitude *f*.

long johns [-dʒɒnz] *npl* caleçons longs.

long jump *n* saut *m* en longueur.

long-lost ['lɒŋlɒst] *adj* perdu(e) depuis longtemps.

long-playing ['lɒŋpleɪɪŋ] *adj*: **~ record (LP)** (disque *m*) 33 tours *m inv*.

long-range ['lɒŋ'reɪndʒ] *adj* à longue portée, à long terme; (*weather forecast*) à long terme.

longshoreman ['lɒŋʃɔːmən] *n* (*US*) docker *m*, débardeur *m*.

long-sighted ['lɒŋ'saɪtɪd] *adj* (*BRIT*) presbyte; (*fig*) prévoyant(e).

long-standing ['lɒŋ'stændɪŋ] *adj* de longue date.

long-suffering [lɒŋ'sʌfərɪŋ] *adj* empreint(e) d'une patience résignée; extrêmement patient(e).

long-term ['lɒŋtəːm] *adj* à long terme.

long wave *n* (*RADIO*) grandes ondes, ondes longues.

long-winded [lɒŋ'wɪndɪd] *adj* intarissable, interminable.

loo [luː] *n* (*BRIT col*) w.-c. *mpl*, petit coin.

loofah ['luːfə] *n* sorte d'éponge végétale.

look [lʊk] *vi* regarder; (*seem*) sembler, paraître, avoir l'air; (*building etc*): **to ~ south/on to the sea** donner au sud/sur la mer ♦ *n* regard *m*; (*appearance*) air *m*, allure *f*, aspect *m*; **~s** *npl* physique *m*, beauté *f*; **to ~ like** ressembler à; **it ~s like him** on dirait que c'est lui; **it ~s about 4 metres long** je dirais que ça fait 4 mètres de long, à vue de nez, ça fait 4 mètres de long; **it ~s all right to me** ça me paraît bien; **to have a ~ at sth** jeter un coup d'œil à qch; **to have a ~ for sth** chercher qch; **to ~ ahead** regarder devant soi; (*fig*) envisager l'avenir.

►**look after** *vt fus* s'occuper de, prendre soin de; (*luggage etc: watch over*) garder, surveiller.

►**look around** *vi* regarder autour de soi.

►**look at** *vt fus* regarder.

►**look back** *vi*: to ~ **back at sth/sb** se retourner pour regarder qch/qn; **to look back on** (*event, period*) évoquer, repenser à.

►**look down on** *vt fus* (*fig*) regarder de haut, dédaigner.

►**look for** *vt fus* chercher.

►**look forward to** *vt fus* attendre avec impatience; **I'm not** ~**ing forward to it** cette perspective ne me réjouit guère; ~**ing forward to hearing from you** (*in letter*) dans l'attente de vous lire.

►**look in** *vi*: to ~ **in on sb** passer voir qn.

►**look into** *vt fus* (*matter, possibility*) examiner, étudier.

►**look on** *vi* regarder (en spectateur).

►**look out** *vi* (*beware*): **to ~ out (for)** prendre garde (à), faire attention (à).

►**look out for** *vt fus* être à la recherche de; guetter.

►**look over** *vt* (*essay*) jeter un coup d'œil à; (*town, building*) visiter (rapidement); (*person*) jeter un coup d'œil à; examiner de la tête aux pieds.

►**look round** *vi* (*turn*) regarder derrière soi, se retourner; **to ~ round for sth** chercher qch.

►**look through** *vt fus* (*papers, book*) examiner; (*: briefly*) parcourir; (*telescope*) regarder à travers.

►**look to** *vt fus* veiller à; (*rely on*) compter sur.

►**look up** *vi* lever les yeux; (*improve*) s'améliorer ♦ *vt* (*word*) chercher; (*friend*) passer voir.

►**look up to** *vt fus* avoir du respect pour.

look-out ['lukaut] *n* poste *m* de guet; guetteur *m*; **to be on the ~ (for)** guetter.

look-up table ['lukʌp-] *n* (*COMPUT*) table *f* à consulter.

LOOM *n abbr* (*US*: = *Loyal Order of Moose*) *association charitable*.

loom [luːm] *n* métier *m* à tisser ♦ *vi* surgir; (*fig*) menacer, paraître imminent(e).

loony ['luːnɪ] *adj, n* (*col*) timbré(e), cinglé(e) (*m/f*).

loop [luːp] *n* boucle *f*; (*contraceptive*) stérilet *m*.

loophole ['luːphəʊl] *n* porte *f* de sortie (*fig*); échappatoire *f*.

loose [luːs] *adj* (*knot, screw*) desserré(e); (*stone*) branlant(e); (*clothes*) vague, ample, lâche; (*animal*) en liberté, échappé(e); (*life*) dissolu(e); (*morals, discipline*) relâché(e); (*thinking*) peu rigoureux(euse), vague; (*translation*) approximatif(ive) ♦ *vt* (*free: animal*) lâcher; (*: prisoner*) relâcher, libérer; (*slacken*) détendre, relâcher, desserrer; défaire; donner du mou à; donner du ballant à; (*BRIT: arrow*) tirer; ~ **connection** (*ELEC*) mauvais contact; **to be at a ~ end** *or* (*US*) **at ~ ends** (*fig*) ne pas trop savoir quoi faire; **to tie up ~ ends** (*fig*) mettre au point *or* régler

les derniers détails.

loose change *n* petite monnaie.

loose-fitting ['luːsfɪtɪŋ] *adj* (*clothes*) ample.

loose-leaf ['luːsliːf] *adj*: ~ **binder** *or* **folder** classeur *m* à feuilles *or* feuillets mobiles.

loose-limbed [luːs'lɪmd] *adj* agile, souple.

loosely ['luːslɪ] *adv* sans serrer; approximativement.

loosely-knit ['luːslɪ'nɪt] *adj* élastique.

loosen ['luːsn] *vt* desserrer, relâcher, défaire.

►**loosen up** *vi* (*before game*) s'échauffer; (*col: relax*) se détendre, se laisser aller.

loot [luːt] *n* butin *m* ♦ *vt* piller.

looter ['luːtə*] *n* pillard *m*, casseur *m*.

looting ['luːtɪŋ] *n* pillage *m*.

lop [lɔp]: **to ~ off** *vt* couper, trancher.

lop-sided ['lɔp'saɪdɪd] *adj* de travers, asymétrique.

lord [lɔːd] *n* seigneur *m*; **L~ Smith** lord Smith; **the L~** (*REL*) le Seigneur; **the (House of) L~s** (*BRIT*) la Chambre des Lords.

lordly ['lɔːdlɪ] *adj* noble, majestueux(euse); (*arrogant*) hautain(e).

lordship ['lɔːdʃɪp] *n* (*BRIT*): **your L~** Monsieur le comte (*or* le baron *or* le Juge).

lore [lɔː*] *n* tradition(s) *f(pl)*.

lorry ['lɔrɪ] *n* (*BRIT*) camion *m*.

lorry driver *n* (*BRIT*) camionneur *m*, routier *m*.

lose [luːz], *pt, pp* **lost** [luːz, lɔst] *vt* perdre; (*opportunity*) manquer, perdre; (*pursuers*) distancer, semer ♦ *vi* perdre; **to ~ (time)** (*clock*) retarder; **to ~ no time (in doing sth)** ne pas perdre de temps (à faire qch); **to get lost** *vi* (*person*) se perdre; **my watch has got lost** ma montre est perdue.

loser ['luːzə*] *n* perdant/e; **to be a good/bad ~** être beau/mauvais joueur.

loss [lɔs] *n* perte *f*; **to cut one's ~es** limiter les dégâts; **to make a ~** enregistrer une perte; **to sell sth at a ~** vendre qch à perte; **to be at a ~** être perplexe *or* embarrassé(e); **to be at a ~ to do** se trouver incapable de faire.

loss adjuster *n* (*INSURANCE*) responsable *m/f* de l'évaluation des dommages.

loss leader *n* (*COMM*) article sacrifié.

lost [lɔst] *pt, pp of* **lose** ♦ *adj* perdu(e); ~ **in thought** perdu dans ses pensées; ~ **and found property** (*US*) objets trouvés; ~ **and found** *n* (*US*) (bureau *m* des) objets trouvés.

lost property *n* (*BRIT*) objets trouvés; ~ **office** *or* **department** (bureau *m* des) objets trouvés.

lot [lɔt] *n* (*at auctions*) lot *m*; (*destiny*) sort *m*, destinée *f*; **the ~** le tout; tous *mpl*, toutes *fpl*; **a ~** beaucoup; **a ~ of** beaucoup de; ~**s of** des tas de; **to draw ~s (for sth)** tirer (qch) au sort.

lotion ['ləʊʃən] *n* lotion *f*.

lottery ['lɔtərɪ] *n* loterie *f*.

loud [laud] *adj* bruyant(e), sonore, fort(e); (*gaudy*) voyant(e), tapageur(euse) ♦ *adv* (*speak etc*) fort; **out** ~ tout haut.

loudhailer [laud'heɪlə*] *n* (*BRIT*) porte-voix *m inv*.

loudly ['laudlɪ] *adv* fort, bruyamment.

loudspeaker [laud'spiːkə*] *n* haut-parleur *m*.

lounge [laundʒ] *n* salon *m*; (*of airport*) salle *f* ♦ *vi* se prélasser, paresser.

lounge bar *n* (salle *f* de) bar *m*.

lounge suit *n* (*BRIT*) complet *m*; (*: on invitation*) "tenue de ville".

louse, *pl* **lice** [laus, laɪs] *n* pou *m*.

▶**louse up** *vt* (*col*) gâcher.

lousy ['lauzɪ] *adj* (*fig*) infect(e), moche.

lout [laut] *n* rustre *m*, butor *m*.

louvre, (*US*) **louver** ['luːvə*] *adj* (*door, window*) à claire-voie.

lovable ['lʌvəbl] *adj* très sympathique; adorable.

love [lʌv] *n* amour *m* ♦ *vt* aimer; aimer beaucoup; **to** ~ **to do** aimer beaucoup *or* adorer faire; **I'd** ~ **to come** cela me ferait très plaisir (de venir); **"15** ~**"** (*TENNIS*) "15 à rien *or* zéro"; **to be/fall in** ~ **with** être/tomber amoureux(euse) de; **to make** ~ faire l'amour; ~ **at first sight** le coup de foudre; **to send one's** ~ **to sb** adresser ses amitiés à qn; ~ **from Anne,** ~**, Anne** affectueusement, Anne.

love affair *n* liaison (amoureuse).

love child *n* enfant *m/f* illégitime *or* naturel(le).

loved ones ['lʌvdwʌnz] *npl* proches *mpl* et amis chers.

love-hate relationship [lʌv'heɪt-] *n* rapport ambigu; **they have a** ~ ils s'aiment et se détestent à la fois.

love letter *n* lettre *f* d'amour.

love life *n* vie sentimentale.

lovely ['lʌvlɪ] *adj* (*pretty: girl, house, garden*) ravissant(e); (*friend, wife*) charmant(e); (*holiday, surprise*) très agréable, merveilleux(euse); **we had a** ~ **time** c'était vraiment très bien, nous avons eu beaucoup de plaisir.

lover ['lʌvə*] *n* amant *m*; (*amateur*): **a** ~ **of** un(e) ami(e) de, un(e) amoureux(euse) de.

lovesick ['lʌvsɪk] *adj* qui se languit d'amour.

lovesong ['lʌvsɔŋ] *n* chanson *f* d'amour.

loving ['lʌvɪŋ] *adj* affectueux(euse), tendre, aimant(e).

low [ləu] *adj* bas(basse) ♦ *adv* bas ♦ *n* (*METEOROLOGY*) dépression *f* ♦ *vi* (*cow*) mugir; **to feel** ~ se sentir déprimé(e); **he's very** ~ (*ill*) il est bien bas *or* très affaibli; **to turn (down)** ~ *vt* baisser; **to reach a new** *or* **an all-time** ~ tomber au niveau le plus bas.

low-alcohol [ləu'ælkəhɔl] *adj* à faible teneur en alcool, peu alcoolisé(e).

lowbrow ['ləubrau] *adj* sans prétentions intellectuelles.

low-calorie ['ləu'kælərɪ] *adj* hypocalorique.

low-cut ['ləukʌt] *adj* (*dress*) décolleté(e).

low-down ['ləudaun] *n* (*col*): **he gave me the** ~ **(on it)** il m'a mis au courant ♦ *adj* (*mean*) méprisable.

lower ['ləuə*] *adj, adv comparative of* **low** ♦ *vt* baisser; (*resistance*) diminuer ♦ *vi* ['lauə*] (*person*): **to** ~ **at sb** jeter un regard mauvais *or* noir à qn; (*sky, clouds*) être menaçant.

low-fat ['ləu'fæt] *adj* maigre.

low-key ['ləu'kiː] *adj* modéré(e); discret(ète).

lowland ['ləulənd] *n* plaine *f*.

low-level ['ləulɛvl] *adj* bas(basse); (*flying*) à basse altitude.

low-loader ['ləuləudə*] *n* semi-remorque *f* à plate-forme surbaissée.

lowly ['ləulɪ] *adj* humble, modeste.

low-lying [ləu'laɪɪŋ] *adj* à faible altitude.

low-paid [ləu'peɪd] *adj* mal payé(e), aux salaires bas.

low-rise ['ləuraɪz] *adj* bas(se), de faible hauteur.

low-tech ['ləutɛk] *adj* sommaire.

loyal ['lɔɪəl] *adj* loyal(e), fidèle.

loyalist ['lɔɪəlɪst] *n* loyaliste *m/f*.

loyalty ['lɔɪəltɪ] *n* loyauté *f*, fidélité *f*.

lozenge ['lɔzɪndʒ] *n* (*MED*) pastille *f*; (*GEOM*) losange *m*.

LP *n abbr* = **long-playing record**.

L-plates ['ɛlpleɪts] *npl* (*BRIT*) plaques *fpl* (obligatoires) d'apprenti conducteur.

Les **L-plates** *sont des carrés blancs portant un "L" rouge que l'on met à l'avant et à l'arrière de sa voiture pour montrer qu'on n'a pas encore son permis de conduire. Jusqu'à l'obtention du permis, l'apprenti conducteur a un permis provisoire et n'a le droit de conduire que si un conducteur qualifié est assis à côté de lui. Il est interdit aux apprentis conducteurs de circuler sur les autoroutes, même s'ils sont accompagnés.*

LPN *n abbr* (*US: = Licensed Practical Nurse*) infirmier/ière diplômé(e).

LRAM *n abbr* (*BRIT*) = *Licentiate of the Royal Academy of Music.*

LSAT *n abbr* (*US*) = *Law School Admissions Test.*

LSD *n abbr* (= *lysergic acid diethylamide*) LSD *m*; (*BRIT: = pounds, shillings and pence*) système monétaire en usage en GB jusqu'en 1971.

LSE *n abbr* = *London School of Economics.*

LT *abbr* (*ELEC: = low tension*) BT.

Lt. *abbr* (= *lieutenant*) Lt.

Ltd *abbr* (*COMM*) = **limited**.

lubricant ['luːbrɪkənt] *n* lubrifiant *m*.

lubricate ['luːbrɪkeɪt] *vt* lubrifier, graisser.

lucid ['luːsɪd] *adj* lucide.

lucidity [luː'sɪdɪtɪ] *n* lucidité *f*.

luck [lʌk] *n* chance *f*; **bad** ~ malchance *f*, malheur *m*; **to be in** ~ avoir de la chance; **to be out of** ~ ne pas avoir de chance; **good** ~! bonne chance!

luckily ['lʌkɪlɪ] *adv* heureusement, par bonheur.

luckless ['lʌklɪs] *adj* (*person*) malchanceux(euse); (*trip*) marqué(e) par la malchance.

lucky ['lʌkɪ] *adj* (*person*) qui a de la chance; (*coincidence*) heureux(euse); (*number etc*) qui porte bonheur.

lucrative ['lu:krətɪv] *adj* lucratif(ive), rentable, qui rapporte.

ludicrous ['lu:dɪkrəs] *adj* ridicule, absurde.

ludo ['lu:dəu] *n* jeu *m* des petits chevaux.

lug [lʌg] *vt* traîner, tirer.

luggage ['lʌgɪdʒ] *n* bagages *mpl*.

luggage lockers *npl* consigne *f* automatique.

luggage rack *n* (*in train*) porte-bagages *m inv*; (: *made of string*) filet *m* à bagages; (*on car*) galerie *f*.

luggage van, (*US*) **luggage car** *n* (*RAIL*) fourgon *m* (à bagages).

lugubrious [lu'gu:brɪəs] *adj* lugubre.

lukewarm ['lu:kwɔ:m] *adj* tiède.

lull [lʌl] *n* accalmie *f* ♦ *vt* (*child*) bercer; (*person, fear*) apaiser, calmer.

lullaby ['lʌləbaɪ] *n* berceuse *f*.

lumbago [lʌm'beɪgəu] *n* lumbago *m*.

lumber ['lʌmbə*] *n* bric-à-brac *m inv* ♦ *vt* (*BRIT col*): **to ~ sb with sth/sb** coller *or* refiler qch/qn à qn ♦ *vi* (*also*: ~ **about**, ~ **along**) marcher pesamment.

lumberjack ['lʌmbədʒæk] *n* bûcheron *m*.

lumber room *n* (*BRIT*) débarras *m*.

lumber yard *n* entrepôt *m* de bois.

luminous ['lu:mɪnəs] *adj* lumineux(euse).

lump [lʌmp] *n* morceau *m*; (*in sauce*) grumeau *m*; (*swelling*) grosseur *f* ♦ *vt* (*also*: ~ **together**) réunir, mettre en tas.

lump sum *n* somme globale *or* forfaitaire.

lumpy ['lʌmpɪ] *adj* (*sauce*) qui a des grumeaux.

lunacy ['lu:nəsɪ] *n* démence *f*, folie *f*.

lunar ['lu:nə*] *adj* lunaire.

lunatic ['lu:nətɪk] *n* fou/folle, dément/e ♦ *adj* fou(folle), dément(e).

lunatic asylum *n* asile *m* d'aliénés.

lunch [lʌntʃ] *n* déjeuner *m* ♦ *vi* déjeuner; **it is his ~ hour** c'est l'heure où il déjeune; **to invite sb to** *or* **for ~** inviter qn à déjeuner.

luncheon ['lʌntʃən] *n* déjeuner *m*.

luncheon meat *n* sorte de saucisson.

luncheon voucher *n* chèque-repas *m*, ticket-repas *m*.

lunchtime ['lʌntʃtaɪm] *n* l'heure *f* du déjeuner.

lung [lʌŋ] *n* poumon *m*.

lung cancer *n* cancer *m* du poumon.

lunge [lʌndʒ] *vi* (*also*: ~ **forward**) faire un mouvement brusque en avant; **to ~ at sb** envoyer *or* assener un coup à qn.

lupin ['lu:pɪn] *n* lupin *m*.

lurch [lə:tʃ] *vi* vaciller, tituber ♦ *n* écart *m* brusque, embardée *f*; **to leave sb in the ~** laisser qn se débrouiller *or* se dépêtrer

tout(e) seul(e).

lure [luə*] *n* appât *m*, leurre *m* ♦ *vt* attirer *or* persuader par la ruse.

lurid ['luərɪd] *adj* affreux(euse), atroce.

lurk [lə:k] *vi* se tapir, se cacher.

luscious ['lʌʃəs] *adj* succulent(e); appétissant(e).

lush [lʌʃ] *adj* luxuriant(e).

lust [lʌst] *n* luxure *f*; lubricité *f*; désir *m*; (*fig*): ~ **for** soif *f* de.

▶**lust after** *vt fus* convoiter, désirer.

luster ['lʌstə*] *n* (*US*) = **lustre**.

lustful ['lʌstful] *adj* lascif(ive).

lustre, (*US*) **luster** ['lʌstə*] *n* lustre *m*, brillant *m*.

lusty ['lʌstɪ] *adj* vigoureux(euse), robuste.

lute [lu:t] *n* luth *m*.

Luxembourg ['lʌksəmbə:g] *n* Luxembourg *m*.

luxuriant [lʌg'zjuərɪənt] *adj* luxuriant(e).

luxurious [lʌg'zjuərɪəs] *adj* luxueux(euse).

luxury ['lʌkʃərɪ] *n* luxe *m* ♦ *cpd* de luxe.

LV *n abbr* (*BRIT*) = **luncheon voucher**.

LW *abbr* (*RADIO*: = *long wave*) GO.

Lycra ['laɪkrə] *n* ® Lycra *m* ®.

lying ['laɪɪŋ] *n* mensonge(s) *m(pl)* ♦ *adj* (*statement, story*) mensonger(ère), faux(fausse); (*person*) menteur(euse).

lynch [lɪntʃ] *vt* lyncher.

lynx [lɪŋks] *n* lynx *m inv*.

Lyons ['laɪənz] *n* Lyon *m*.

lyre ['laɪə*] *n* lyre *f*.

lyric ['lɪrɪk] *adj* lyrique; ~**s** *npl* (*of song*) paroles *fpl*.

lyrical ['lɪrɪkl] *adj* lyrique.

lyricism ['lɪrɪsɪzəm] *n* lyrisme *m*.

M m

M, m [ɛm] *n* (*letter*) M, m *m*; **M for Mary**, (*US*) **M for Mike** M comme Marcel.

M *n abbr* (*BRIT*: = *motorway*): **the M8** ≈ l'A8 ♦ *abbr* (= *medium*) M.

m *abbr* (= *metre*) m; (= *million*) M; (= *mile*) mi.

MA *n abbr* (*SCOL*) = **Master of Arts** ♦ *abbr* (*US*) = *military academy*; (*US*) = *Massachusetts*.

mac [mæk] *n* (*BRIT*) imper(méable *m*) *m*.

macabre [mə'kɑ:brə] *adj* macabre.

macaroni [mækə'rəunɪ] *n* macaronis *mpl*.

macaroon [mækə'ru:n] *n* macaron *m*.

mace [meɪs] *n* masse *f*; (*spice*) macis *m*.

Macedonia [mæsɪ'dəunɪə] *n* Macédoine *f*.

Macedonian [mæsɪ'dəunɪən] *adj* macédonien(ne) ♦ *n* Macédonien/ne; (*LING*) macédonien *m*.

machinations [mækɪ'neɪʃənz] *npl* machina-

tions *fpl*, intrigues *fpl*.
machine [mə'ʃiːn] *n* machine *f* ♦ *vt* (*dress etc*) coudre à la machine; (*TECH*) usiner.
machine code *n* (*COMPUT*) code *m* machine.
machine gun *n* mitrailleuse *f*.
machine language *n* (*COMPUT*) langage *m* machine.
machine-readable [mə'ʃiːnriːdəbl] *adj* (*COMPUT*) exploitable par une machine.
machinery [mə'ʃiːnərɪ] *n* machinerie *f*, machines *fpl*; (*fig*) mécanisme(s) *m(pl)*.
machine shop *n* atelier *m* d'usinage.
machine tool *n* machine-outil *f*.
machine washable *adj* (*garment*) lavable en machine.
machinist [mə'ʃiːnɪst] *n* machiniste *m/f*.
macho ['mætʃəu] *adj* macho *inv*.
mackerel ['mækrl] *n* (*pl inv*) maquereau *m*.
mackintosh ['mækɪntɔʃ] *n* (*BRIT*) imperméable *m*.
macro... ['mækrəu] *prefix* macro....
macro-economics ['mækrəuiːkə'nɔmɪks] *n* macro-économie *f*.
mad [mæd] *adj* fou(folle); (*foolish*) insensé(e); (*angry*) furieux(euse); **to go** ~ devenir fou; **to be** ~ **(keen) about** *or* **on sth** (*col*) être follement passionné de qch, être fou de qch.
madam ['mædəm] *n* madame *f*; **yes** ~ oui Madame; **M**~ **Chairman** Madame la Présidente.
madcap ['mædkæp] *adj* (*col*) écervelé(e).
mad cow disease *n* maladie *f* des vaches folles.
madden ['mædn] *vt* exaspérer.
maddening ['mædnɪŋ] *adj* exaspérant(e).
made [meɪd] *pt, pp of* **make**.
Madeira [mə'dɪərə] *n* (*GEO*) Madère *f*; (*wine*) madère *m*.
made-to-measure ['meɪdtə'mɛʒə*] *adj* (*BRIT*) fait(e) sur mesure.
madhouse ['mædhaus] *n* (*also fig*) maison *f* de fous.
madly ['mædlɪ] *adv* follement.
madman ['mædmən] *n* fou *m*, aliéné *m*.
madness ['mædnɪs] *n* folie *f*.
Madrid [mə'drɪd] *n* Madrid.
Mafia ['mæfɪə] *n* maf(f)ia *f*.
mag. [mæg] *n abbr* (*BRIT col*) = **magazine** (*PRESS*).
magazine [mægə'ziːn] *n* (*PRESS*) magazine *m*, revue *f*; (*MIL: store*) dépôt *m*, arsenal *m*; (*of firearm*) magasin *m*.
maggot ['mægət] *n* ver *m*, asticot *m*.
magic ['mædʒɪk] *n* magie *f* ♦ *adj* magique.
magical ['mædʒɪkl] *adj* magique.
magician [mə'dʒɪʃən] *n* magicien/ne.
magistrate ['mædʒɪstreɪt] *n* magistrat *m*; juge *m*; ~**'s court** (*BRIT*) ≈ tribunal *m* d'instance.
magnanimous [mæg'nænɪməs] *adj* magnanime.
magnate ['mægneɪt] *n* magnat *m*.
magnesium [mæg'niːzɪəm] *n* magnésium *m*.
magnet ['mægnɪt] *n* aimant *m*.

magnetic [mæg'nɛtɪk] *adj* magnétique.
magnetic disk *n* (*COMPUT*) disque *m* magnétique.
magnetic tape *n* bande *f* magnétique.
magnetism ['mægnɪtɪzəm] *n* magnétisme *m*.
magnification [mægnɪfɪ'keɪʃən] *n* grossissement *m*.
magnificence [mæg'nɪfɪsns] *n* magnificence *f*.
magnificent [mæg'nɪfɪsnt] *adj* superbe, magnifique.
magnify ['mægnɪfaɪ] *vt* grossir; (*sound*) amplifier.
magnifying glass ['mægnɪfaɪɪŋ-] *n* loupe *f*.
magnitude ['mægnɪtjuːd] *n* ampleur *f*.
magnolia [mæg'nəulɪə] *n* magnolia *m*.
magpie ['mægpaɪ] *n* pie *f*.
mahogany [mə'hɔgənɪ] *n* acajou *m* ♦ *cpd* en (bois d')acajou.
maid [meɪd] *n* bonne *f*; **old** ~ (*pej*) vieille fille.
maiden ['meɪdn] *n* jeune fille *f* ♦ *adj* (*aunt etc*) non mariée; (*speech, voyage*) inaugural(e).
maiden name *n* nom *m* de jeune fille.
mail [meɪl] *n* poste *f*; (*letters*) courrier *m* ♦ *vt* envoyer (par la poste); **by** ~ par la poste.
mailbag ['meɪlbæg] *n* (*US*) sac postal; (*postman's*) sacoche *f*.
mailbox ['meɪlbɔks] *n* (*US: for letters etc*; *COMPUT*) boîte *f* aux lettres.
mailing list ['meɪlɪŋ-] *n* liste *f* d'adresses.
mailman ['meɪlmæn] *n* (*US*) facteur *m*.
mail-order ['meɪlɔːdə*] *n* vente *f* *or* achat *m* par correspondance ♦ *cpd*: ~ **firm** *or* **house** maison *f* de vente par correspondance.
mailshot ['meɪlʃɔt] *n* (*BRIT*) mailing *m*.
mail train *n* train postal.
mail truck *n* (*US AUT*) = **mail van**.
mail van *n* (*BRIT: AUT*) voiture *f* *or* fourgonnette *f* des postes; (: *RAIL*) wagon-poste *m*.
maim [meɪm] *vt* mutiler.
main [meɪn] *adj* principal(e) ♦ *n* (*pipe*) conduite principale, canalisation *f*; **the** ~**s** (*ELEC*) le secteur; **the** ~ **thing** l'essentiel *m*; **in the** ~ dans l'ensemble.
main course *n* (*CULIN*) plat *m* de résistance.
mainframe ['meɪnfreɪm] *n* (*also*: ~ **computer**) (gros) ordinateur, unité centrale.
mainland ['meɪnlənd] *n* continent *m*.
mainline ['meɪnlaɪn] *adj* (*RAIL*) de grande ligne ♦ *vb* (*drugs slang*) *vt* se shooter à ♦ *vi* se shooter.
main line *n* (*RAIL*) grande ligne.
mainly ['meɪnlɪ] *adv* principalement, surtout.
main road *n* grand axe, route nationale.
mainstay ['meɪnsteɪ] *n* (*fig*) pilier *m*.
mainstream ['meɪnstriːm] *n* (*fig*) courant principal.
maintain [meɪn'teɪn] *vt* entretenir; (*continue*) maintenir, préserver; (*affirm*) soutenir; **to** ~ **that** ... soutenir que ....
maintenance ['meɪntənəns] *n* entretien *m*; (*LAW: alimony*) pension *f* alimentaire.
maintenance contract *n* contrat *m*

d'entretien.

maintenance order n (LAW) obligation f alimentaire.

maisonette [meɪzə'nɛt] n (BRIT) appartement m en duplex.

maize [meɪz] n maïs m.

Maj. abbr (MIL) = **major**.

majestic [mə'dʒɛstɪk] adj majestueux(euse).

majesty ['mædʒɪstɪ] n majesté f.

major ['meɪdʒə*] n (MIL) commandant m ♦ adj important(e), principal(e); (MUS) majeur(e) ♦ vi (US SCOL): **to ~ (in)** se spécialiser (en); **a ~ operation** (MED) une grosse opération.

Majorca [mə'jɔːkə] n Majorque f.

major general n (MIL) général m de division.

majority [mə'dʒɔrɪtɪ] n majorité f ♦ cpd (verdict, holding) majoritaire.

make [meɪk] vt (pt, pp **made** [meɪd]) faire; (manufacture) faire, fabriquer; (cause to be): **to ~ sb sad** etc rendre qn triste etc; (force): **to ~ sb do sth** obliger qn à faire qch, faire faire qch à qn; (equal): **2 and 2 ~ 4** 2 et 2 font 4 ♦ n fabrication f; (brand) marque f; **to ~ it** (in time etc) y arriver; (succeed) réussir; **what time do you ~ it?** quelle heure avez-vous?; **to ~ good** vi (succeed) faire son chemin, réussir ♦ vt (deficit) combler; (losses) compenser; **to ~ do with** se contenter de; se débrouiller avec.

▶**make for** vt fus (place) se diriger vers.

▶**make off** vi filer.

▶**make out** vt (write out) écrire; (understand) comprendre; (see) distinguer; (claim, imply) prétendre, vouloir faire croire; **to ~ out a case for sth** présenter des arguments solides en faveur de qch.

▶**make over** vt (assign): **to ~ over (to)** céder (à), transférer (au nom de).

▶**make up** vt (invent) inventer, imaginer; (parcel) faire ♦ vi se réconcilier; (with cosmetics) se maquiller, se farder; **to be made up of** se composer de.

▶**make up for** vt fus compenser; racheter.

make-believe ['meɪkbɪliːv] n: **a world of ~** un monde de chimères or d'illusions; **it's just ~** c'est de la fantaisie; c'est une illusion.

maker ['meɪkə*] n fabricant m.

makeshift ['meɪkʃɪft] adj provisoire, improvisé(e).

make-up ['meɪkʌp] n maquillage m.

make-up bag n trousse f de maquillage.

make-up remover n démaquillant m.

making ['meɪkɪŋ] n (fig): **in the ~** en formation or gestation; **he has the ~s of an actor** il a l'étoffe d'un acteur.

maladjusted [mælə'dʒʌstɪd] adj inadapté(e).

malaise [mæ'leɪz] n malaise m.

malaria [mə'lɛərɪə] n malaria f, paludisme m.

Malawi [mə'lɑːwɪ] n Malawi m.

Malay [mə'leɪ] adj malais(e) ♦ n (person) Malais/e; (language) malais m.

Malaya [mə'leɪə] n Malaisie f.

Malayan [mə'leɪən] adj, n = **Malay**.

Malaysia [mə'leɪzɪə] n Malaisie f.

Malaysian [mə'leɪzɪən] adj malaisien(ne) ♦ n Malaisien/ne.

Maldives ['mɔːldaɪvz] npl: **the ~** les Maldives fpl.

male [meɪl] n (BIOL, ELEC) mâle m ♦ adj (sex, attitude) masculin(e); mâle; (child.etc) du sexe masculin; **~ and female students** étudiants et étudiantes.

male chauvinist n phallocrate m.

male nurse n infirmier m.

malevolence [mə'lɛvələns] n malveillance f.

malevolent [mə'lɛvələnt] adj malveillant(e).

malfunction [mæl'fʌŋkʃən] n fonctionnement défectueux.

malice ['mælɪs] n méchanceté f, malveillance f.

malicious [mə'lɪʃəs] adj méchant(e), malveillant(e); (LAW) avec intention criminelle.

malign [mə'laɪn] vt diffamer, calomnier.

malignant [mə'lɪgnənt] adj (MED) malin(igne).

malingerer [mə'lɪŋgərə*] n simulateur/trice.

mall [mɔːl] n (also: **shopping ~**) centre commercial.

malleable ['mælɪəbl] adj malléable.

mallet ['mælɪt] n maillet m.

malnutrition [mælnjuː'trɪʃən] n malnutrition f.

malpractice [mæl'præktɪs] n faute professionnelle; négligence f.

malt [mɔːlt] n malt m ♦ cpd (whisky) pur malt.

Malta ['mɔːltə] n Malte f.

Maltese [mɔːl'tiːz] adj maltais(e) ♦ n (pl inv) Maltais/e; (LING) maltais m.

maltreat [mæl'triːt] vt maltraiter.

mammal ['mæml] n mammifère m.

mammoth ['mæməθ] n mammouth m ♦ adj géant(e), monstre.

man, pl **men** [mæn, mɛn] n homme m; (CHESS) pièce f; (DRAUGHTS) pion m ♦ vt garnir d'hommes; servir, assurer le fonctionnement de; être de service à; **an old ~** un vieillard; **~ and wife** mari et femme.

Man. abbr (Canada) = **Manitoba**.

manacles ['mænəklz] npl menottes fpl.

manage ['mænɪdʒ] vi se débrouiller; y arriver, réussir ♦ vt (business) gérer; (team, operation) diriger; (device, things to do, carry etc) arriver à se débrouiller avec, s'en tirer avec; **to ~ to do** se débrouiller pour faire; (succeed) réussir à faire.

manageable ['mænɪdʒəbl] adj maniable; (task etc) faisable.

management ['mænɪdʒmənt] n administration f, direction f; (persons: of business, firm) dirigeants mpl; cadres mpl; (: of hotel, shop, theatre) direction; **"under new ~"** "changement de gérant", "changement de propriétaire".

management accounting n comptabilité f de gestion.

management consultant n conseiller/ère

de direction.

manager ['mænɪdʒə*] n (*of business*) directeur m; (*of institution etc*) administrateur m; (*of department, unit*) responsable m/f, chef m; (*of hotel etc*) gérant m; (*of artist*) impresario m; **sales** ~ responsable *or* chef des ventes.

manageress [mænɪdʒə'rɛs] n directrice f; (*of hotel etc*) gérante f.

managerial [mænɪ'dʒɪərɪəl] adj directorial(e); ~ **staff** cadres mpl.

managing director (MD) ['mænɪdʒɪŋ-] n directeur général.

Mancunian [mæŋ'kjuːnɪən] adj de Manchester ♦ n habitant/e de Manchester; natif/ive de Manchester.

mandarin ['mændərɪn] n (*also*: ~ **orange**) mandarine f; (*person*) mandarin m.

mandate ['mændeɪt] n mandat m.

mandatory ['mændətərɪ] adj obligatoire; (*powers etc*) mandataire.

mandolin(e) ['mændəlɪn] n mandoline f.

mane [meɪn] n crinière f.

maneuver etc [mə'nuːvə*] (*US*) = **manoeuvre** etc.

manfully ['mænfəlɪ] adv vaillamment.

manganese [mæŋgə'niːz] n manganèse m.

mangetout ['mɔnʒ'tuː] n mange-tout m inv.

mangle ['mæŋgl] vt déchiqueter; mutiler ♦ n essoreuse f; calandre f.

mango, ~**es** ['mæŋgəu] n mangue f.

mangrove ['mæŋgrəuv] n palétuvier m.

mangy ['meɪndʒɪ] adj galeux(euse).

manhandle ['mænhændl] vt (*mistreat*) maltraiter, malmener; (*move by hand*) manutentionner.

manhole ['mænhəul] n trou m d'homme.

manhood ['mænhud] n âge m d'homme; virilité f.

man-hour ['mænauə*] n heure-homme f, heure f de main-d'œuvre.

manhunt ['mænhʌnt] n chasse f à l'homme.

mania ['meɪnɪə] n manie f.

maniac ['meɪnɪæk] n maniaque m/f.

manic ['mænɪk] adj maniaque.

manic-depressive ['mænɪkdɪ'prɛsɪv] adj, n (*PSYCH*) maniaco-dépressif(ive).

manicure ['mænɪkjuə*] n manucure f ♦ vt (*person*) faire les mains à.

manicure set n trousse f à ongles.

manifest ['mænɪfɛst] vt manifester ♦ adj manifeste, évident(e) ♦ n (*AVIAT, NAUT*) manifeste m.

manifestation [mænɪfɛs'teɪʃən] n manifestation f.

manifesto [mænɪ'fɛstəu] n manifeste m (*POL*).

manifold ['mænɪfəuld] adj multiple, varié(e) ♦ n (*AUT etc*): **exhaust** ~ collecteur m d'échappement.

Manila [mə'nɪlə] n Manille, Manila.

manila [mə'nɪlə] adj: ~ **paper** papier m bulle.

manipulate [mə'nɪpjuleɪt] vt manipuler.

manipulation [mənɪpju'leɪʃən] n manipulation

f.

mankind [mæn'kaɪnd] n humanité f, genre humain.

manliness ['mænlɪnɪs] n virilité f.

manly ['mænlɪ] adj viril(e); courageux(euse).

man-made ['mæn'meɪd] adj artificiel(le).

manna ['mænə] n manne f.

mannequin ['mænɪkɪn] n mannequin m.

manner ['mænə*] n manière f, façon f; (**good**) ~**s** (bonnes) manières; **bad** ~**s** mauvaises manières; **all** ~ **of** toutes sortes de.

mannerism ['mænərɪzəm] n particularité f de langage (*or* de comportement), tic m.

mannerly ['mænəlɪ] adj poli(e), courtois(e).

manoeuvrable, (*US*) **maneuverable** [mə'nuːvrəbl] adj facile à manœuvrer.

manoeuvre, (*US*) **maneuver** [mə'nuːvə*] vt, vi manœuvrer ♦ n manœuvre f; **to** ~ **sb into doing sth** manipuler qn pour lui faire faire qch.

manor ['mænə*] n (*also*: ~ **house**) manoir m.

manpower ['mænpauə*] n main-d'œuvre f.

manservant, pl **menservants** ['mænsə:vənt, 'mɛn-] n domestique m.

mansion ['mænʃən] n château m, manoir m.

manslaughter ['mænslɔːtə*] n homicide m involontaire.

mantelpiece ['mæntlpiːs] n cheminée f.

mantle ['mæntl] n cape f; (*fig*) manteau m.

man-to-man ['mæntə'mæn] adj, adv d'homme à homme.

manual ['mænjuəl] adj manuel(le) ♦ n manuel m.

manual worker n travailleur manuel.

manufacture [mænju'fæktʃə*] vt fabriquer ♦ n fabrication f.

manufactured goods [mænju'fæktʃəd-] npl produits manufacturés.

manufacturer [mænju'fæktʃərə*] n fabricant m.

manufacturing industries [mænju'fæktʃərɪŋ-] npl industries fpl de transformation.

manure [mə'njuə*] n fumier m; (*artificial*) engrais m.

manuscript ['mænjuskrɪpt] n manuscrit m.

many ['mɛnɪ] adj beaucoup de, de nombreux(euses) ♦ pron beaucoup, un grand nombre; **how** ~? combien?; **a great** ~ un grand nombre (de); **too** ~ **difficulties** trop de difficultés; **twice as** ~ deux fois plus; ~ **a** ... bien des ..., plus d'un(e) ....

Maori ['mauri] n Maori/e ♦ adj maori(e).

map [mæp] n carte f ♦ vt dresser la carte de.

▶**map out** vt tracer; (*fig: career, holiday*) organiser, préparer (à l'avance); (*: essay*) faire le plan de.

maple ['meɪpl] n érable m.

Mar. abbr = **March**.

mar [mɑː*] vt gâcher, gâter.

marathon ['mærəθən] n marathon m ♦ adj: **a** ~ **session** une séance-marathon.

marathon runner n coureur/euse de marathon, marathonien/ne.

marauder [mə'rɔːdə*] n maraudeur/euse.

marble ['mɑːbl] n marbre m; (toy) bille f; ~**s** n (game) billes.

March [mɑːtʃ] n mars m; for phrases see also **July**.

march [mɑːtʃ] vi marcher au pas; (demonstrators) défiler ♦ n marche f; (demonstration) rallye m; **to ~ out of/into** etc sortir de/entrer dans etc (de manière décidée ou impulsive).

marcher ['mɑːtʃə*] n (demonstrator) manifestant/e, marcheur/euse.

marching ['mɑːtʃɪŋ] n: **to give sb his ~ orders** (fig) renvoyer qn; envoyer promener qn.

march-past ['mɑːtʃpɑːst] n défilé m.

mare [mɛə*] n jument f.

marg. [mɑːdʒ] n abbr (col) = **margarine**.

margarine [mɑːdʒə'riːn] n margarine f.

margin ['mɑːdʒɪn] n marge f.

marginal ['mɑːdʒɪnl] adj marginal(e); ~ **seat** (POL) siège disputé.

marginally ['mɑːdʒɪnəlɪ] adv très légèrement, sensiblement.

marigold ['mærɪɡəʊld] n souci m.

marijuana [mærɪ'wɑːnə] n marijuana f.

marina [mə'riːnə] n marina f.

marinade n [mærɪ'neɪd] marinade f ♦ vt ['mærɪneɪd] = **marinate**.

marinate ['mærɪneɪt] vt (faire) mariner.

marine [mə'riːn] adj marin(e) ♦ n fusilier marin; (US) marine m.

marine insurance n assurance f maritime.

marital ['mærɪtl] adj matrimonial(e); ~ **status** situation f de famille.

maritime ['mærɪtaɪm] adj maritime.

maritime law n droit m maritime.

marjoram ['mɑːdʒərəm] n marjolaine f.

mark [mɑːk] n marque f; (of skid etc) trace f; (BRIT SCOL) note f; (SPORT) cible f; (currency) mark m; (BRIT TECH): **M~ 2/3** 2ème/3ème série f or version f ♦ vt (also SPORT: player) marquer; (stain) tacher; (BRIT SCOL) noter; corriger; **punctuation ~s** signes mpl de ponctuation; **to ~ time** marquer le pas; **to be quick off the ~ (in doing)** (fig) ne pas perdre de temps (pour faire); **up to the ~** (in efficiency) à la hauteur.

▸**mark down** vt (prices, goods) démarquer, réduire le prix de.

▸**mark off** vt (tick off) cocher, pointer.

▸**mark out** vt désigner.

▸**mark up** vt (price) majorer.

marked [mɑːkt] adj marqué(e), net(te).

markedly ['mɑːkɪdlɪ] adv visiblement, manifestement.

marker ['mɑːkə*] n (sign) jalon m; (bookmark) signet m.

market ['mɑːkɪt] n marché m ♦ vt (COMM) commercialiser; **to be on the ~** être sur le marché; **on the open ~** en vente libre; **to play the ~** jouer à la or spéculer en Bourse.

marketable ['mɑːkɪtəbl] adj commercialisable.

market analysis n analyse f de marché.

market day n jour m de marché.

market demand n besoins mpl du marché.

market economy n économie f de marché.

market forces npl tendances fpl du marché.

market garden n (BRIT) jardin maraîcher.

marketing ['mɑːkɪtɪŋ] n marketing m.

marketplace ['mɑːkɪtpleɪs] n place f du marché; (COMM) marché m.

market price n prix marchand.

market research n étude f de marché.

market value n valeur marchande; valeur du marché.

marking ['mɑːkɪŋ] n (on animal) marque f, tache f; (on road) signalisation f.

marksman ['mɑːksmən] n tireur m d'élite.

marksmanship ['mɑːksmənʃɪp] n adresse f au tir.

mark-up ['mɑːkʌp] n (COMM: margin) marge f (bénéficiaire); (: increase) majoration f.

marmalade ['mɑːməleɪd] n confiture f d'oranges.

maroon [mə'ruːn] vt (fig): **to be ~ed (in** or **at)** être bloqué(e) (à) ♦ adj bordeaux inv.

marquee [mɑː'kiː] n chapiteau m.

marquess, marquis ['mɑːkwɪs] n marquis m.

Marrakech, Marrakesh [mærə'kɛʃ] n Marrakech.

marriage ['mærɪdʒ] n mariage m.

marriage bureau n agence matrimoniale.

marriage certificate n extrait m d'acte de mariage.

marriage guidance, (US) **marriage counseling** n conseils conjugaux.

marriage of convenience n mariage m de convenance.

married ['mærɪd] adj marié(e); (life, love) conjugal(e).

marrow ['mærəʊ] n moelle f; (vegetable) courge f.

marry ['mærɪ] vt épouser, se marier avec; (subj: father, priest etc) marier ♦ vi (also: **get married**) se marier.

Mars [mɑːz] n (planet) Mars f.

Marseilles [mɑː'seɪlz] n Marseille.

marsh [mɑːʃ] n marais m, marécage m.

marshal ['mɑːʃl] n maréchal m; (US: fire, police) ≈ capitaine m; (for demonstration, meeting) membre m du service d'ordre ♦ vt rassembler.

marshalling yard ['mɑːʃlɪŋ-] n (RAIL) gare f de triage.

marshmallow [mɑːʃ'mæləʊ] n (BOT) guimauve f; (sweet) (pâte f de) guimauve.

marshy ['mɑːʃɪ] adj marécageux(euse).

marsupial [mɑː'suːpɪəl] adj marsupial(e) ♦ n marsupial m.

martial ['mɑːʃl] adj martial(e).

martial arts npl arts martiaux.

martial law n loi martiale.

Martian ['mɑːʃən] n Martien/ne.

martin ['mɑːtɪn] *n* (*also*: **house** ~) martinet *m*.
martyr ['mɑːtə*] *n* martyr/e ♦ *vt* martyriser.
martyrdom ['mɑːtədəm] *n* martyre *m*.
marvel ['mɑːvl] *n* merveille *f* ♦ *vi*: **to** ~ **(at)** s'émerveiller (de).
marvellous, (*US*) **marvelous** ['mɑːvləs] *adj* merveilleux(euse).
Marxism ['mɑːksɪzəm] *n* marxisme *m*.
Marxist ['mɑːksɪst] *adj*, *n* marxiste (*m/f*).
marzipan ['mɑːzɪpæn] *n* pâte *f* d'amandes.
mascara [mæs'kɑːrə] *n* mascara *m*.
mascot ['mæskət] *n* mascotte *f*.
masculine ['mæskjulɪn] *adj* masculin(e) ♦ *n* masculin *m*.
masculinity [mæskju'lɪnɪtɪ] *n* masculinité *f*.
MASH [mæʃ] *n abbr* (*US MIL*) = *mobile army surgical hospital*.
mash [mæʃ] *vt* (*CULIN*) faire une purée de.
mashed [mæʃt] *adj*: ~ **potatoes** purée *f* de pommes de terre.
mask [mɑːsk] *n* masque *m* ♦ *vt* masquer.
masochism ['mæsəʊkɪzəm] *n* masochisme *m*.
masochist ['mæsəʊkɪst] *n* masochiste *m/f*.
mason ['meɪsn] *n* (*also*: **stone**~) maçon *m*; (*also*: **free**~) franc-maçon *m*.
masonic [mə'sɒnɪk] *adj* maçonnique.
masonry ['meɪsnrɪ] *n* maçonnerie *f*.
masquerade [mæskə'reɪd] *n* bal masqué; (*fig*) mascarade *f* ♦ *vi*: **to** ~ **as** se faire passer pour.
mass [mæs] *n* multitude *f*, masse *f*; (*PHYSICS*) masse; (*REL*) messe *f* ♦ *vi* se masser; **the** ~**es** les masses; **to go to** ~ aller à la messe.
Mass. *abbr* (*US*) = *Massachusetts*.
massacre ['mæsəkə*] *n* massacre *m* ♦ *vt* massacrer.
massage ['mæsɑːʒ] *n* massage *m* ♦ *vt* masser.
masseur [mæ'sɜː*] *n* masseur *m*.
masseuse [mæ'sɜːz] *n* masseuse *f*.
massive ['mæsɪv] *adj* énorme, massif(ive).
mass market *n* marché *m* grand public.
mass media *npl* mass-media *mpl*.
mass meeting *n* rassemblement *m* de masse.
mass-produce ['mæsprə'djuːs] *vt* fabriquer en série.
mass production *n* fabrication *f* en série.
mast [mɑːst] *n* mât *m*; (*RADIO*, *TV*) pylône *m*.
mastectomy [mæs'tɛktəmɪ] *n* mastectomie *f*.
master ['mɑːstə*] *n* maître *m*; (*in secondary school*) professeur *m*; (*title for boys*): **M**~ **X** Monsieur X ♦ *vt* maîtriser; (*learn*) apprendre à fond; (*understand*) posséder parfaitement *or* à fond; ~ **of ceremonies (MC)** *n* maître des cérémonies; **M**~ **of Arts/Science (MA/MSc)** *n* ≈ titulaire *m/f* d'une maîtrise (en lettres/science); **M**~ **of Arts/Science degree (MA/MSc)** *n* ≈ maîtrise *f*; **M**~**'s degree** *n* ≈ maîtrise.

Le **Master's degree** est un diplôme que l'on prépare en général après le **Bachelor's degree**, bien que certaines universités décernent un Master's au lieu d'un Bachelor's. Pour l'obtenir, il faut soit suivre des cours, soit rédiger un mémoire à partir d'une recherche personnelle, soit encore les deux. Les principaux masters sont le MA (Master of Arts), et le MSc (Master of Science), qui comprennent cours et mémoire, et le MLitt (Master of Letters) et le MPhil (Master of Philosophy), qui reposent uniquement sur le mémoire; *voir* **doctorate**

---

master disk *n* (*COMPUT*) disque original.
masterful ['mɑːstəful] *adj* autoritaire, impérieux(euse).
master key *n* passe-partout *m inv*.
masterly ['mɑːstəlɪ] *adj* magistral(e).
mastermind ['mɑːstəmaɪnd] *n* esprit supérieur ♦ *vt* diriger, être le cerveau de.
masterpiece ['mɑːstəpiːs] *n* chef-d'œuvre *m*.
master plan *n* stratégie *f* d'ensemble.
master stroke *n* coup *m* de maître.
mastery ['mɑːstərɪ] *n* maîtrise *f*; connaissance parfaite.
mastiff ['mæstɪf] *n* mastiff *m*.
masturbate ['mæstəbeɪt] *vi* se masturber.
masturbation [mæstə'beɪʃən] *n* masturbation *f*.
mat [mæt] *n* petit tapis; (*also*: **door**~) paillasson *m* ♦ *adj* = **matt**.
match [mætʃ] *n* allumette *f*; (*game*) match *m*, partie *f*; (*fig*) égal/e; mariage *m*; parti *m* ♦ *vt* assortir; (*go well with*) aller bien avec, s'assortir à; (*equal*) égaler, valoir ♦ *vi* être assorti(e); **to be a good** ~ être bien assorti(e).
►**match up** *vt* assortir.
matchbox ['mætʃbɒks] *n* boîte *f* d'allumettes.
matching ['mætʃɪŋ] *adj* assorti(e).
matchless ['mætʃlɪs] *adj* sans égal.
mate [meɪt] *n* camarade *m/f* de travail; (*col*) copain/copine; (*animal*) partenaire *m/f*, mâle/femelle; (*in merchant navy*) second *m* ♦ *vi* s'accoupler ♦ *vt* accoupler.
material [mə'tɪərɪəl] *n* (*substance*) matière *f*, matériau *m*; (*cloth*) tissu *m*, étoffe *f* ♦ *adj* matériel(le); (*important*) essentiel(le); ~**s** *npl* matériaux *mpl*; **reading** ~ de quoi lire, de la lecture.
materialistic [mətɪərɪə'lɪstɪk] *adj* matérialiste.
materialize [mə'tɪərɪəlaɪz] *vi* se matérialiser, se réaliser.
materially [mə'tɪərɪəlɪ] *adv* matériellement; essentiellement.
maternal [mə'tɜːnl] *adj* maternel(le).
maternity [mə'tɜːnɪtɪ] *n* maternité *f* ♦ *cpd* de maternité, de grossesse.
maternity benefit *n* prestation *f* de maternité.
maternity hospital *n* maternité *f*.
matey ['meɪtɪ] *adj* (*BRIT col*) copain-copain *inv*.
math. [mæθ] *n abbr* (*US*: = *mathematics*) maths *fpl*.
mathematical [mæθə'mætɪkl] *adj* mathémati-

que.

mathematician [mæθəmə'tɪʃən] n mathématicien/ne.

mathematics [mæθə'mætɪks] n mathématiques fpl.

maths [mæθs] n abbr (BRIT: = mathematics) maths fpl.

matinée ['mætɪneɪ] n matinée f.

mating ['meɪtɪŋ] n accouplement m.

mating call n appel m du mâle.

mating season n saison f des amours.

matriarchal [meɪtrɪ'ɑːkl] adj matriarcal(e).

matrices ['meɪtrɪsiːz] npl of **matrix**.

matriculation [mətrɪkju'leɪʃən] n inscription f.

matrimonial [mætrɪ'məunɪəl] adj matrimonial(e), conjugal(e).

matrimony ['mætrɪmənɪ] n mariage m.

matrix, pl **matrices** ['meɪtrɪks, 'meɪtrɪsiːz] n matrice f.

matron ['meɪtrən] n (in hospital) infirmière-chef f; (in school) infirmière f.

matronly ['meɪtrənlɪ] adj de matrone; imposant(e).

matt [mæt] adj mat(e).

matted ['mætɪd] adj emmêlé(e).

matter ['mætə*] n (question f, (PHYSICS) matière f, substance f; (content) contenu m, fond m; (MED: pus) pus m ♦ vi importer; **it doesn't** ~ cela n'a pas d'importance; (I don't mind) cela ne fait rien; **what's the** ~? qu'est-ce qu'il y a?, qu'est-ce qui ne va pas?; **no** ~ **what** quoiqu'il arrive; **that's another** ~ c'est une autre affaire; **as a** ~ **of course** tout naturellement; **as a** ~ **of fact** en fait; **it's a** ~ **of habit** c'est une question d'habitude; **printed** ~ imprimés mpl; **reading** ~ (BRIT) de quoi lire, de la lecture.

matter-of-fact ['mætərəv'fækt] adj terre à terre, neutre.

matting ['mætɪŋ] n natte f.

mattress ['mætrɪs] n matelas m.

mature [mə'tjuə*] adj mûr(e); (cheese) fait(e) ♦ vi mûrir; se faire.

mature student n étudiant/e plus âgé(e) que la moyenne.

maturity [mə'tjuərɪtɪ] n maturité f.

maudlin ['mɔːdlɪn] adj larmoyant(e).

maul [mɔːl] vt lacérer.

Mauritania [mɔːrɪ'teɪnɪə] n Mauritanie f.

Mauritius [mə'rɪʃəs] n l'île f Maurice.

mausoleum [mɔːsə'lɪəm] n mausolée m.

mauve [məuv] adj mauve.

maverick ['mævrɪk] n (fig) franc-tireur m, non-conformiste m/f.

mawkish ['mɔːkɪʃ] adj mièvre; fade.

max. abbr = **maximum**.

maxim ['mæksɪm] n maxime f.

maxima ['mæksɪmə] npl of **maximum**.

maximize ['mæksɪmaɪz] vt (profits etc, chances) maximiser.

maximum ['mæksɪməm] adj maximum ♦ n (pl **maxima** ['mæksɪmə]) maximum m.

May [meɪ] n mai m; for phrases see also **July**.

may [meɪ] vi (conditional: **might**) (indicating possibility): **he** ~ **come** il se peut qu'il vienne; (be allowed to): ~ **I smoke?** puis-je fumer?; (wishes): ~ **God bless you!** (que) Dieu vous bénisse!; ~ **I sit here?** vous permettez que je m'assoie ici?; **he might be there** il pourrait bien y être, il se pourrait qu'il y soit; **I might as well go** je ferais aussi bien d'y aller, autant y aller; **you might like to try** vous pourriez (peut-être) essayer.

maybe ['meɪbiː] adv peut-être; ~ **he'll** ... peut-être qu'il ...; ~ **not** peut-être pas.

May Day n le Premier mai.

mayday ['meɪdeɪ] n S.O.S. m.

mayhem ['meɪhɛm] n grabuge m.

mayonnaise [meɪə'neɪz] n mayonnaise f.

mayor [mɛə*] n maire m.

mayoress ['mɛərɛs] n maire m; épouse f du maire.

maypole ['meɪpəul] n mât enrubanné (autour duquel on danse).

maze [meɪz] n labyrinthe m, dédale m.

MB abbr (COMPUT) = **megabyte**; (Canada) = Manitoba.

MBA n abbr (= Master of Business Administration) titre universitaire.

MBBS, MBChB n abbr (BRIT: = Bachelor of Medicine and Surgery) titre universitaire.

MBE n abbr (BRIT: = Member of the Order of the British Empire) titre honorifique.

MC n abbr = **master of ceremonies**.

MCAT n abbr (US) = Medical College Admissions Test.

MCP n abbr (BRIT col: = male chauvinist pig) phallocrate m.

MD n abbr (= Doctor of Medicine) titre universitaire; (COMM) = **managing director** ♦ abbr (US) = Maryland.

Md. abbr (US) = Maryland.

MDT abbr (US: = Mountain Daylight Time) heure d'été des Montagnes Rocheuses.

ME n abbr (US: = medical examiner) médecin légiste m/f; (MED: = myalgic encephalomyelitis) encéphalomyélite f myalgique ♦ abbr (US) = Maine.

me [miː] pron me, m' + vowel; (stressed, after prep) moi; **it's** ~ c'est moi; **it's for** ~ c'est pour moi.

meadow ['mɛdəu] n prairie f, pré m.

meagre, (US) **meager** ['miːgə*] adj maigre.

meal [miːl] n repas m; (flour) farine f; **to go out for a** ~ sortir manger.

meals on wheels npl (BRIT) repas livrés à domicile aux personnes âgées ou handicapées.

mealtime ['miːltaɪm] n heure f du repas.

mealy-mouthed ['miːlɪmauðd] adj mielleux(euse).

mean [miːn] adj (with money) avare, radin(e); (unkind) mesquin(e), méchant(e); (US col: animal) méchant, vicieux(euse); (: person) vache; (*average*) moyen(ne) ♦ *vt* (*pt, pp* **meant** [mɛnt]) (*signify*) signifier, vouloir dire; (*intend*): **to ~ to do** avoir l'intention de faire ♦ *n* moyenne *f*; **to be meant for** être destiné(e) à; **do you ~ it?** vous êtes sérieux?; **what do you ~?** que voulez-vous dire?

meander [mɪ'ændə*] *vi* faire des méandres; (*fig*) flâner.

meaning ['miːnɪŋ] *n* signification *f*, sens *m*.

meaningful ['miːnɪŋful] *adj* significatif(ive); (*relationship*) valable.

meaningless ['miːnɪŋlɪs] *adj* dénué(e) de sens.

meanness ['miːnnɪs] *n* avarice *f*; mesquinerie *f*.

means [miːnz] *npl* moyens *mpl*; **by ~ of** par l'intermédiaire de; au moyen de; **by all ~** je vous en prie.

means test *n* (*ADMIN*) contrôle *m* des conditions de ressources.

meant [mɛnt] *pt, pp of* **mean**.

meantime ['miːntaɪm] *adv*, **meanwhile** ['miːnwaɪl] *adv* (*also*: **in the ~**) pendant ce temps.

measles ['miːzlz] *n* rougeole *f*.

measly ['miːzlɪ] *adj* (*col*) minable.

measurable ['mɛʒərəbl] *adj* mesurable.

measure ['mɛʒə*] *vt, vi* mesurer ♦ *n* mesure *f*; (*ruler*) règle (graduée); **a litre ~** un litre; **some ~ of success** un certain succès; **to take ~s to do sth** prendre des mesures pour faire qch.

▶**measure up** *vi*: **to ~ up (to)** être à la hauteur (de).

measured ['mɛʒəd] *adj* mesuré(e).

measurement ['mɛʒəmənt] *n*: **chest/hip ~** tour *m* de poitrine/hanches; **~s** *npl* mesures *fpl*; **to take sb's ~s** prendre les mesures de qn.

meat [miːt] *n* viande *f*; **cold ~s** (*BRIT*) viandes froides; **crab ~** crabe *f*.

meatball ['miːtbɔːl] *n* boulette *f* de viande.

meat pie *n* pâté *m* en croûte.

meaty ['miːtɪ] *adj* (*flavour*) de viande; (*fig: argument, book*) étoffé(e), substantiel(le).

Mecca ['mɛkə] *n* La Mecque; (*fig*): **a ~ (for)** la Mecque (de).

mechanic [mɪ'kænɪk] *n* mécanicien *m*.

mechanical [mɪ'kænɪkl] *adj* mécanique.

mechanical engineering *n* (*science*) mécanique *f*; (*industry*) construction *f* mécanique.

mechanics [mə'kænɪks] *n* mécanique *f* ♦ *npl* mécanisme *m*.

mechanism ['mɛkənɪzəm] *n* mécanisme *m*.

mechanization [mɛkənaɪ'zeɪʃən] *n* mécanisation *f*.

MEd *n abbr* (= *Master of Education*) titre universitaire.

medal ['mɛdl] *n* médaille *f*.

medallion [mɪ'dælɪən] *n* médaillon *m*.

medallist, (*US*) **medalist** ['mɛdlɪst] *n* (*SPORT*) médaillé/e.

meddle ['mɛdl] *vi*: **to ~ in** se mêler de,

s'occuper de; **to ~ with** toucher à.

meddlesome ['mɛdlsəm], **meddling** ['mɛdlɪŋ] *adj* indiscret(ète), qui se mêle de ce qui ne le (*or* la) regarde pas; touche-à-tout *inv*.

media ['miːdɪə] *npl* media *mpl*.

media circus *n* (*event*) battage *m* médiatique; (*group of journalists*) cortège *m* médiatique.

mediaeval [mɛdɪ'iːvl] *adj* = **medieval**.

median ['miːdɪən] *n* (*US: also*: **~ strip**) bande médiane.

media research *n* étude *f* de l'audience.

mediate ['miːdɪeɪt] *vi* s'interposer; servir d'intermédiaire.

mediation [miːdɪ'eɪʃən] *n* médiation *f*.

mediator ['miːdɪeɪtə*] *n* médiateur/trice.

Medicaid ['mɛdɪkeɪd] *n* (*US*) *assistance médicale aux indigents*.

medical ['mɛdɪkl] *adj* médical(e) ♦ *n* (*also*: **~ examination**) visite médicale; examen médical.

medical certificate *n* certificat médical.

medical student *n* étudiant/e en médecine.

Medicare ['mɛdɪkeə*] *n* (*US*) *régime d'assurance maladie*.

medicated ['mɛdɪkeɪtɪd] *adj* traitant(e), médicamenteux(euse).

medication [mɛdɪ'keɪʃən] *n* (*drugs etc*) médication *f*.

medicinal [mɛ'dɪsɪnl] *adj* médicinal(e).

medicine ['mɛdsɪn] *n* médecine *f*; (*drug*) médicament *m*.

medicine chest *n* pharmacie *f* (*murale ou portative*).

medicine man *n* sorcier *m*.

medieval [mɛdɪ'iːvl] *adj* médiéval(e).

mediocre [miːdɪ'əukə*] *adj* médiocre.

mediocrity [miːdɪ'ɔkrɪtɪ] *n* médiocrité *f*.

meditate ['mɛdɪteɪt] *vi*: **to ~ (on)** méditer (sur).

meditation [mɛdɪ'teɪʃən] *n* méditation *f*.

Mediterranean [mɛdɪtə'reɪnɪən] *adj* méditerranéen(ne); **the ~ (Sea)** la (mer) Méditerranée.

medium ['miːdɪəm] *adj* moyen(ne) ♦ *n* (*pl* **media**) (*means*) moyen *m*; (*pl* **mediums**) (*person*) médium *m*; **the happy ~** le juste milieu.

medium-dry ['miːdɪəm'draɪ] *adj* demi-sec.

medium-sized ['miːdɪəm'saɪzd] *adj* de taille moyenne.

medium wave *n* (*RADIO*) ondes moyennes, petites ondes.

medley ['mɛdlɪ] *n* mélange *m*.

meek [miːk] *adj* doux(douce), humble.

meet, *pt, pp* **met** [miːt, mɛt] *vt* rencontrer; (*by arrangement*) retrouver, rejoindre; (*for the first time*) faire la connaissance de; (*go and fetch*): **I'll ~ you at the station** j'irai te chercher à la gare; (*problem*) faire face à; (*requirements*) satisfaire à, répondre à; (*bill, expenses*) régler, honorer ♦ *vi* se rencontrer; se retrouver; (*in session*) se réunir; (*join: objects*) se joindre ♦ *n* (*BRIT: HUNTING*) rendez-vous *m* de chasse; (*US SPORT*) rencontre *f*, meeting *m*; **pleased to** ~ **you!** enchanté!

▶**meet up** *vi*: **to** ~ **up with sb** rencontrer qn.

▶**meet with** *vt fus* rencontrer.

meeting ['miːtɪŋ] *n* rencontre *f*; (*session: of club etc*) réunion *f*; (*formal*) assemblée *f*; (*SPORT: rally*) rencontre, meeting *m*; (*interview*) entrevue *f*; **she's at a** ~ (*COMM*) elle est en conférence; **to call a** ~ convoquer une réunion.

meeting place *n* lieu *m* de (la) réunion; (*for appointment*) lieu de rendez-vous.

megabyte ['mɛgəbaɪt] *n* (*COMPUT*) méga-octet *m*.

megalomaniac [mɛgələ'meɪnɪæk] *n* mégalomane *m/f*.

megaphone ['mɛgəfəun] *n* porte-voix *m inv*.

megawatt ['mɛgəwɔt] *n* mégawatt *m*.

melancholy ['mɛlənkəlɪ] *n* mélancolie *f* ♦ *adj* mélancolique.

mellow ['mɛləu] *adj* velouté(e); doux(douce); (*colour*) riche et profond(e); (*fruit*) mûr(e) ♦ *vi* (*person*) s'adoucir.

melodious [mɪ'ləudɪəs] *adj* mélodieux(euse).

melodrama ['mɛləudrɑːmə] *n* mélodrame *m*.

melodramatic [mɛlədrə'mætɪk] *adj* mélodramatique.

melody ['mɛlədɪ] *n* mélodie *f*.

melon ['mɛlən] *n* melon *m*.

melt [mɛlt] *vi* fondre; (*become soft*) s'amollir; (*fig*) s'attendrir ♦ *vt* faire fondre.

▶**melt away** *vi* fondre complètement.

▶**melt down** *vt* fondre.

meltdown ['mɛltdaun] *n* fusion *f* (du cœur d'un réacteur nucléaire).

melting point ['mɛltɪŋ-] *n* point *m* de fusion.

melting pot ['mɛltɪŋ-] *n* (*fig*) creuset *m*; **to be in the** ~ être encore en discussion.

member ['mɛmbə*] *n* membre *m*; (*of club, political party*) membre, adhérent/e ♦ *cpd*: ~ **country/state** *n* pays *m*/état *m* membre; **M~ of Parliament (MP)** *n* (*BRIT*) député *m*; **M~ of the European Parliament (MEP)** *n* Eurodéputé *m*; **M~ of the House of Representatives (MHR)** *n* (*US*) membre de la Chambre des représentants.

membership ['mɛmbəʃɪp] *n* (*becoming a member*) adhésion *f*; admission *f*; (*being a member*) qualité *f* de membre, fait *m* d'être membre; (*the members*) membres *mpl*, adhérents *mpl*; (*number of members*) nombre *m* des membres *or* adhérents.

membership card *n* carte *f* de membre.

membrane ['mɛmbreɪn] *n* membrane *f*.

memento [mə'mɛntəu] *n* souvenir *m*.

memo ['mɛməu] *n* note *f* (de service).

memoir ['mɛmwɑː*] *n* mémoire *m*, étude *f*; ~**s** *npl* mémoires.

memo pad *n* bloc-notes *m*.

memorable ['mɛmərəbl] *adj* mémorable.

memorandum, *pl* **memoranda** [mɛmə'rændəm, -də] *n* note *f* (de service); (*DIPLOMACY*) mémorandum *m*.

memorial [mɪ'mɔːrɪəl] *n* mémorial *m* ♦ *adj* commémoratif(ive).

> **Memorial Day** est un jour férié aux États-Unis, le dernier lundi de mai dans la plupart des États, à la mémoire des soldats américains morts au combat.

memorize ['mɛməraɪz] *vt* apprendre *or* retenir par cœur.

memory ['mɛmərɪ] *n* mémoire *f*; (*recollection*) souvenir *m*; **to have a good/bad** ~ avoir une bonne/mauvaise mémoire; **loss of** ~ perte *f* de mémoire; **in** ~ **of** à la mémoire de.

men [mɛn] *npl of* **man**.

menace ['mɛnɪs] *n* menace *f*; (*col: nuisance*) peste *f*, plaie *f* ♦ *vt* menacer; **a public** ~ un danger public.

menacing ['mɛnɪsɪŋ] *adj* menaçant(e).

menagerie [mɪ'nædʒərɪ] *n* ménagerie *f*.

mend [mɛnd] *vt* réparer; (*darn*) raccommoder, repriser ♦ *n* reprise *f*; **on the** ~ en voie de guérison.

mending ['mɛndɪŋ] *n* raccommodages *mpl*.

menial ['miːnɪəl] *adj* de domestique, inférieur(e); subalterne.

meningitis [mɛnɪn'dʒaɪtɪs] *n* méningite *f*.

menopause ['mɛnəupɔːz] *n* ménopause *f*.

menservants ['mɛnsəːvənts] *npl of* **manservant**.

men's room *n*: **the** ~ (*esp US*) les toilettes *fpl* pour hommes.

menstruate ['mɛnstrueɪt] *vi* avoir ses règles.

menstruation [mɛnstru'eɪʃən] *n* menstruation *f*.

menswear ['mɛnzwɛə*] *n* vêtements *mpl* d'hommes.

mental ['mɛntl] *adj* mental(e); ~ **illness** maladie mentale.

mental hospital *n* hôpital *m* psychiatrique.

mentality [mɛn'tælɪtɪ] *n* mentalité *f*.

mentally ['mɛntlɪ] *adv*: **to be** ~ **handicapped** être handicapé/e mental(e).

menthol ['mɛnθɒl] *n* menthol *m*.

mention ['mɛnʃən] *n* mention *f* ♦ *vt* mentionner, faire mention de; **don't** ~ **it!** je vous en prie, il n'y a pas de quoi!; **I need hardly** ~ **that** ... est-il besoin de rappeler que ...?; **not to** ~ ..., **without** ~**ing** ... sans parler de ..., sans compter ....

mentor ['mɛntɔː*] *n* mentor *m*.

menu ['mɛnjuː] *n* (*in restaurant, COMPUT*) menu *m*; (*printed*) carte *f*.

menu-driven ['mɛnjuːdrɪvn] *adj* (*COMPUT*) piloté(e) par menu.

MEP *n abbr* = **Member of the European Parliament**.

mercantile ['məːkəntaɪl] *adj* marchand(e); (*law*) commercial(e).

mercenary ['məːsɪnərɪ] *adj* mercantile ♦ *n* mercenaire *m*.

merchandise ['mɜːtʃəndaɪz] n marchandises fpl ♦ vt commercialiser.

merchandiser ['mɜːtʃəndaɪzə*] n marchandiseur m.

merchant ['mɜːtʃənt] n négociant m, marchand m; **timber/wine** ~ négociant en bois/vins, marchand de bois/vins.

merchant bank n (BRIT) banque f d'affaires.

merchantman ['mɜːtʃəntmən] n navire marchand.

merchant navy, (US) **merchant marine** n marine marchande.

merciful ['mɜːsɪful] adj miséricordieux(euse), clément(e).

mercifully ['mɜːsɪflɪ] adv avec clémence; (fortunately) par bonheur, Dieu merci.

merciless ['mɜːsɪlɪs] adj impitoyable, sans pitié.

mercurial [mɜː'kjuərɪəl] adj changeant(e); (lively) vif(vive).

mercury ['mɜːkjurɪ] n mercure m.

mercy ['mɜːsɪ] n pitié f, merci f; (REL) miséricorde f; **to have** ~ **on sb** avoir pitié de qn; **at the** ~ **of** à la merci de.

mercy killing n euthanasie f.

mere [mɪə*] adj simple.

merely ['mɪəlɪ] adv simplement, purement.

merge [mɜːdʒ] vt unir; (COMPUT) fusionner, interclasser ♦ vi se fondre; (COMM) fusionner.

merger ['mɜːdʒə*] n (COMM) fusion f.

meridian [mə'rɪdɪən] n méridien m.

meringue [mə'ræŋ] n meringue f.

merit ['mɛrɪt] n mérite m, valeur f ♦ vt mériter.

meritocracy [mɛrɪ'tɔkrəsɪ] n méritocratie f.

mermaid ['mɜːmeɪd] n sirène f.

merrily ['mɛrɪlɪ] adv joyeusement, gaiement.

merriment ['mɛrɪmənt] n gaieté f.

merry ['mɛrɪ] adj gai(e); **M~ Christmas!** joyeux Noël!

merry-go-round ['mɛrɪgəuraund] n manège m.

mesh [mɛʃ] n maille f; filet m ♦ vi (gears) s'engrener; **wire** ~ grillage m (métallique), treillis m (métallique).

mesmerize ['mɛzməraɪz] vt hypnotiser; fasciner.

mess [mɛs] n désordre m, fouillis m, pagaille f; (MIL) mess m, cantine f; **to be (in) a** ~ être en désordre; **to be/get o.s. in a** ~ (fig) être/se mettre dans le pétrin.

▶**mess about**, **mess around** vi (col) perdre son temps.

▶**mess about** or **around with** vt fus (col) chambarder, tripoter.

▶**mess up** vt salir; chambarder; gâcher.

message ['mɛsɪdʒ] n message m; **to get the** ~ (fig: col) saisir, piger.

message switching [-swɪtʃɪŋ] n (COMPUT) commutation f de messages.

messenger ['mɛsɪndʒə*] n messager m.

Messiah [mɪ'saɪə] n Messie m.

Messrs, Messrs. ['mɛsəz] abbr (on letters: = messieurs) MM.

messy ['mɛsɪ] adj sale; en désordre.

Met [mɛt] n abbr (US) = Metropolitan Opera.

met [mɛt] pt, pp of **meet** ♦ adj abbr (= meteorological) météo inv.

metabolism [mɛ'tæbəlɪzəm] n métabolisme m.

metal ['mɛtl] n métal m ♦ vt empierrer.

metallic [mɛ'tælɪk] adj métallique.

metallurgy [mɛ'tælədʒɪ] n métallurgie f.

metalwork ['mɛtlwɜːk] n (craft) ferronnerie f.

metamorphosis, pl **-ses** [mɛtə'mɔːfəsɪs, -siːz] n métamorphose f.

metaphor ['mɛtəfə*] n métaphore f.

metaphysics [mɛtə'fɪzɪks] n métaphysique f.

mete [miːt]: **to** ~ **out** vt fus infliger.

meteor ['miːtɪə*] n météore m.

meteoric [miːtɪ'ɔrɪk] adj (fig) fulgurant(e).

meteorite ['miːtɪəraɪt] n météorite m or f.

meteorological [miːtɪərə'lɔdʒɪkl] adj météorologique.

meteorology [miːtɪə'rɔlədʒɪ] n météorologie f.

meter ['miːtə*] n (instrument) compteur m; (also: **parking** ~) parc(o)mètre m; (US) = **metre**.

methane ['miːθeɪn] n méthane m.

method ['mɛθəd] n méthode f; ~ **of payment** mode m or modalité f de paiement.

methodical [mɪ'θɔdɪkl] adj méthodique.

Methodist ['mɛθədɪst] adj, n méthodiste (m/f).

methylated spirit ['mɛθɪleɪtɪd-] n (BRIT: also: **meths**) alcool m à brûler.

meticulous [mɛ'tɪkjuləs] adj méticuleux(euse).

metre, (US) **meter** ['miːtə*] n mètre m.

metric ['mɛtrɪk] adj métrique; **to go** ~ adopter le système métrique.

metrical ['mɛtrɪkl] adj métrique.

metrication [mɛtrɪ'keɪʃən] n conversion f au système métrique.

metric system n système m métrique.

metric ton n tonne f.

metronome ['mɛtrənəum] n métronome m.

metropolis [mɪ'trɔpəlɪs] n métropole f.

metropolitan [mɛtrə'pɔlɪtən] adj métropolitain(e).

Metropolitan Police n (BRIT): **the** ~ la police londonienne.

mettle ['mɛtl] n courage m.

mew [mjuː] vi (cat) miauler.

mews [mjuːz] n (BRIT): ~ **cottage** maisonnette aménagée dans une ancienne écurie ou remise.

Mexican ['mɛksɪkən] adj mexicain(e) ♦ n Mexicain/e.

Mexico ['mɛksɪkəu] n Mexique m.

Mexico City n Mexico.

mezzanine ['mɛtsəniːn] n mezzanine f; (of shops, offices) entresol m.

MFA n abbr (US: = Master of Fine Arts) titre universitaire.

mfr abbr = **manufacture, manufacturer**.

mg abbr (= milligram) mg.

Mgr abbr (= Monseigneur, Monsignor) Mgr; (= manager) dir.

MHR n abbr (US) = **Member of the House of Representatives**.

MHz abbr (= megahertz) MHz.

MI abbr (US) = Michigan.

MI5 n abbr (BRIT: = Military Intelligence 5) ≈ DST f.

MI6 n abbr (BRIT: = Military Intelligence 6) ≈ DGSE f.

MIA abbr (= missing in action) disparu au combat.

miaow [miː'au] vi miauler.

mice [maɪs] npl of **mouse**.

Mich. abbr (US) = Michigan.

microbe ['maɪkrəub] n microbe m.

microbiology [maɪkrəbaɪ'ɒlədʒɪ] n microbiologie f.

microchip ['maɪkrəutʃɪp] n (ELEC) puce f.

micro(computer) ['maɪkrəu(kəm'pjuːtə*)] n micro(-ordinateur m) m.

microcosm ['maɪkrəukɔzəm] n microcosme m.

microeconomics ['maɪkrəuiːkə'nɔmɪks] n micro-économie f.

microfiche ['maɪkrəufiːʃ] n microfiche f.

microfilm ['maɪkrəufɪlm] n microfilm m ♦ vt microfilmer.

microlight ['maɪkrəulaɪt] n ULM m.

micrometer [maɪ'krɔmɪtə*] n palmer m, micromètre m.

microphone ['maɪkrəfəun] n microphone m.

microprocessor ['maɪkrəu'prəusɛsə*] n microprocesseur m.

microscope ['maɪkrəskəup] n microscope m; **under the** ~ au microscope.

microscopic [maɪkrə'skɒpɪk] adj microscopique.

microwave ['maɪkrəuweɪv] n (also: ~ **oven**) four m à micro-ondes.

mid [mɪd] adj: ~ **May** la mi-mai; ~ **afternoon** le milieu de l'après-midi; **in** ~ **air** en plein ciel; **he's in his** ~ **thirties** il a dans les trente-cinq ans.

midday [mɪd'deɪ] n midi m.

middle ['mɪdl] n milieu m; (waist) ceinture f, taille f ♦ adj du milieu; **in the** ~ **of the night** au milieu de la nuit; **I'm in the** ~ **of reading it** je suis (justement) en train de le lire.

middle age n tranche d'âge aux limites floues, entre la quarantaine et le début du troisième âge.

middle-aged [mɪdl'eɪdʒd] adj (people: see middle age) d'un certain âge, ni vieux ni jeune; (pej: values, outlook) conventionnel(le), rassis(e).

Middle Ages npl: **the** ~ le moyen âge.

middle class n: **the** ~**(es)** ≈ les classes moyennes ♦ adj (also: **middle-class**) ≈ (petit(e)-)bourgeois(e).

Middle East n: **the** ~ le Proche-Orient, le Moyen-Orient.

middleman ['mɪdlmæn] n intermédiaire m.

middle management n cadres moyens.

middle name n second prénom.

middle-of-the-road ['mɪdləvðə'rəud] adj (policy) modéré(e), du juste milieu; (music etc) plutôt classique, assez traditionnel(le).

middleweight ['mɪdlweɪt] n (BOXING) poids moyen.

middling ['mɪdlɪŋ] adj moyen(ne).

Middx abbr (BRIT) = Middlesex.

midge [mɪdʒ] n moucheron m.

midget ['mɪdʒɪt] n nain/e ♦ adj minuscule.

midi system ['mɪdɪ-] n chaîne f midi.

Midlands ['mɪdləndz] npl comtés du centre de l'Angleterre.

midnight ['mɪdnaɪt] n minuit m; **at** ~ à minuit.

midriff ['mɪdrɪf] n estomac m, taille f.

midst [mɪdst] n: **in the** ~ **of** au milieu de.

midsummer [mɪd'sʌmə*] n milieu m de l'été.

midway [mɪd'weɪ] adj, adv: ~ **(between)** à mi-chemin (entre).

midweek [mɪd'wiːk] adj du milieu de la semaine ♦ adv au milieu de la semaine, en pleine semaine.

midwife, midwives ['mɪdwaɪf, -vz] n sage-femme f.

midwifery ['mɪdwɪfərɪ] n obstétrique f.

midwinter [mɪd'wɪntə*] n milieu m de l'hiver.

miffed [mɪft] adj (col) fâché(e), vexé(e).

might [maɪt] vb see **may** ♦ n puissance f, force f.

mighty ['maɪtɪ] adj puissant(e) ♦ adv (col) rudement.

migraine ['miːgreɪn] n migraine f.

migrant ['maɪgrənt] n (bird, animal) migrateur m; (person) migrant/e; nomade m/f ♦ adj migrateur(trice); migrant(e); nomade; (worker) saisonnier(ière).

migrate [maɪ'greɪt] vi émigrer.

migration [maɪ'greɪʃən] n migration f.

mike [maɪk] n abbr (= microphone) micro m.

Milan [mɪ'læn] n Milan.

mild [maɪld] adj doux(douce); (reproach) léger(ère); (illness) bénin(igne) ♦ n bière légère.

mildew ['mɪldjuː] n mildiou m.

mildly ['maɪldlɪ] adv doucement; légèrement; **to put it** ~ (col) c'est le moins qu'on puisse dire.

mildness ['maɪldnɪs] n douceur f.

mile [maɪl] n mil(l)e m (= 1609 m); **to do 30** ~**s per gallon** ≈ faire 9,4 litres aux cent.

mileage ['maɪlɪdʒ] n distance f en milles, ≈ kilométrage m.

mileage allowance n ≈ indemnité f kilométrique.

mileometer [maɪ'lɔmɪtə*] n (BRIT) = **milometer**.

milestone ['maɪlstəun] n borne f; (fig) jalon m.

milieu ['miːljəː] n milieu m.

militant ['mɪlɪtnt] adj, n militant(e).

militarism ['mɪlɪtərɪzəm] n militarisme m.

militaristic [mɪlɪtə'rɪstɪk] *adj* militariste.
military ['mɪlɪtərɪ] *adj* militaire ♦ *n*: **the ~**
l'armée *f*, les militaires *mpl*.
military service *n* service *m* (militaire *ou* national).
militate ['mɪlɪteɪt] *vi*: **to ~ against** militer contre.
militia [mɪ'lɪʃə] *n* milice *f*.
milk [mɪlk] *n* lait *m* ♦ *vt* (*cow*) traire; (*fig*) dépouiller, plumer.
milk chocolate *n* chocolat *m* au lait.
milk float *n* (*BRIT*) voiture *f or* camionnette *f*
du *or* de laitier.
milking ['mɪlkɪŋ] *n* traite *f*.
milkman ['mɪlkmən] *n* laitier *m*.
milk shake *n* milk-shake *m*.
milk tooth *n* dent *f* de lait.
milk truck *n* (*US*) = **milk float**.
milky ['mɪlkɪ] *adj* lacté(e); (*colour*) laiteux(euse).
Milky Way *n* Voie lactée.
mill [mɪl] *n* moulin *m*; (*factory*) usine *f*, fabrique *f*; (*spinning ~*) filature *f*; (*flour ~*) minoterie *f* ♦ *vt* moudre, broyer ♦ *vi* (*also: ~ about*) grouiller.
millennium, *pl* **~s** *or* **millennia** [mɪ'lɛnɪəm, -'lɛnɪə] *n* millénaire *m*.
miller ['mɪlə*] *n* meunier *m*.
millet ['mɪlɪt] *n* millet *m*.
milli... ['mɪlɪ] *prefix* milli....
milligram(me) ['mɪlɪgræm] *n* milligramme *m*.
millilitre, (*US*) **milliliter** ['mɪlɪli:tə*] *n* millilitre *m*.
millimetre, (*US*) **millimeter** ['mɪlɪmi:tə*] *n* millimètre *m*.
milliner ['mɪlɪnə*] *n* modiste *f*.
millinery ['mɪlɪnərɪ] *n* modes *fpl*.
million ['mɪljən] *n* million *m*.
millionaire [mɪljə'nɛə*] *n* millionnaire *m*.
millipede ['mɪlɪpi:d] *n* mille-pattes *m inv*.
millstone ['mɪlstəun] *n* meule *f*.
millwheel ['mɪlwi:l] *n* roue *f* de moulin.
milometer [maɪ'lɒmɪtə*] *n* (*BRIT*) ≈ compteur *m* kilométrique.
mime [maɪm] *n* mime *m* ♦ *vt*, *vi* mimer.
mimic ['mɪmɪk] *n* imitateur/trice ♦ *vt*, *vi* imiter, contrefaire.
mimicry ['mɪmɪkrɪ] *n* imitation *f*; (*ZOOL*) mimétisme *m*.
Min. *abbr* (*BRIT POL*) = **ministry**.
min. *abbr* (= *minute*) mn.; (= *minimum*) min.
minaret [mɪnə'rɛt] *n* minaret *m*.
mince [mɪns] *vt* hacher ♦ *vi* (*in walking*)
marcher à petits pas maniérés ♦ *n* (*BRIT CULIN*) viande hachée, hachis *m*; **he does not ~ (his) words** il ne mâche pas ses mots.
mincemeat ['mɪnsmi:t] *n hachis de fruits secs utilisés en pâtisserie*.
mince pie *n sorte de tarte aux fruits secs*.
mincer ['mɪnsə*] *n* hachoir *m*.
mincing ['mɪnsɪŋ] *adj* affecté(e).
mind [maɪnd] *n* esprit *m* ♦ *vt* (*attend to, look

after) s'occuper de; (*be careful*) faire attention à; (*object to*): **I don't ~ the noise** je ne crains pas le bruit, le bruit ne me dérange pas; **do you ~ if ...?** est-ce que cela vous gêne si ...?; **I don't ~** cela ne me dérange pas; **~ you, ...** remarquez, ...; **never ~** peu importe, ça ne fait rien; **it is on my ~** cela me préoccupe; **to change one's ~** changer d'avis; **to be in two ~s about sth** (*BRIT*) être indécis(e) *or* irrésolu(e) en ce qui concerne qch; **to my ~** à mon avis, selon moi; **to be out of one's ~** ne plus avoir toute sa raison; **to keep sth in ~** ne pas oublier qch; **to bear sth in ~** tenir compte de qch; **to have sb/sth in ~** avoir qn/qch en tête; **to have in ~ to do** avoir l'intention de faire; **it went right out of my ~** ça m'est complètement sorti de la tête; **to bring** *or* **call sth to ~** se rappeler qch; **to make up one's ~** se décider; **"~ the step"** "attention à la marche".
mind-boggling ['maɪndbɒglɪŋ] *adj* (*col*)
époustouflant(e), ahurissant(e).
-minded ['maɪndɪd] *adj*: **fair~** impartial(e); **an industrially~ nation** une nation orientée vers l'industrie.
minder ['maɪndə*] *n* (*child ~*) gardienne *f*;
(*bodyguard*) ange gardien (*fig*).
mindful ['maɪndful] *adj*: **~ of** attentif(ive) à, soucieux(euse) de.
mindless ['maɪndlɪs] *adj* irréfléchi(e); (*violence, crime*) insensé(e).
mine [maɪn] *pron* le(la) mien(ne), les miens(miennes); **this book is ~** ce livre est à moi ♦ *n* mine *f* ♦ *vt* (*coal*) extraire; (*ship, beach*) miner.
mine detector *n* détecteur *m* de mines.
minefield ['maɪnfi:ld] *n* champ *m* de mines.
miner ['maɪnə*] *n* mineur *m*.
mineral ['mɪnərəl] *adj* minéral(e) ♦ *n* minéral *m*; **~s** *npl* (*BRIT*: *soft drinks*) boissons gazeuses (sucrées).
mineralogy [mɪnə'rælədʒɪ] *n* minéralogie *f*.
mineral water *n* eau minérale.
minesweeper ['maɪnswi:pə*] *n* dragueur *m* de mines.
mingle ['mɪŋgl] *vt* mêler, mélanger ♦ *vi*: **to ~ with** se mêler à.
mingy ['mɪndʒɪ] *adj* (*col*) radin(e).
miniature ['mɪnətʃə*] *adj* (en) miniature ♦ *n* miniature *f*.
minibus ['mɪnɪbʌs] *n* minibus *m*.
minicab ['mɪnɪkæb] *n* (*BRIT*) minitaxi *m*.
minicomputer ['mɪnɪkəm'pju:tə*] *n* mini-ordinateur *m*.
minim ['mɪnɪm] *n* (*MUS*) blanche *f*.
minima ['mɪnɪmə] *npl of* **minimum**.
minimal ['mɪnɪml] *adj* minimal(e).
minimalist ['mɪnɪməlɪst] *adj*, *n* minimaliste (*m/f*).
minimize ['mɪnɪmaɪz] *vt* minimiser.
minimum ['mɪnɪməm] *n* (*pl*: **minima** ['mɪnɪmə])
minimum *m* ♦ *adj* minimum; **to reduce to a ~**

réduire au minimum.

minimum lending rate (MLR) n (ECON) taux m de crédit minimum.

mining ['maɪnɪŋ] n exploitation minière ♦ adj minier(ière); de mineurs.

minion ['mɪnjən] n (pej) laquais m; favori/te.

mini-series ['mɪnɪsɪəriːz] n téléfilm m en plusieurs parties.

miniskirt ['mɪnɪskəːt] n mini-jupe f.

minister ['mɪnɪstə*] n (BRIT POL) ministre m; (REL) pasteur m ♦ vi: **to ~ to sb** donner ses soins à qn; **to ~ to sb's needs** pourvoir aux besoins de qn.

ministerial [mɪnɪs'tɪərɪəl] adj (BRIT POL) ministériel(le).

ministry ['mɪnɪstrɪ] n (BRIT POL) ministère m; (REL): **to go into the ~** devenir pasteur.

mink [mɪŋk] n vison m.

mink coat n manteau m de vison.

Minn. abbr (US) = Minnesota.

minnow ['mɪnəu] n vairon m.

minor ['maɪnə*] adj petit(e), de peu d'importance; (MUS) mineur(e) ♦ n (LAW) mineur/e.

Minorca [mɪ'nɔːkə] n Minorque f.

minority [maɪ'nɔrɪtɪ] n minorité f; **to be in a ~** être en minorité.

minster ['mɪnstə*] n église abbatiale.

minstrel ['mɪnstrəl] n trouvère m, ménestrel m.

mint [mɪnt] n (plant) menthe f; (sweet) bonbon m à la menthe ♦ vt (coins) battre; **the (Royal) M~**, (US) **the (US) M~** ≈ l'hôtel m de la Monnaie; **in ~ condition** à l'état de neuf.

mint sauce n sauce f à la menthe.

minuet [mɪnju'ɛt] n menuet m.

minus ['maɪnəs] n (also: ~ **sign**) signe m moins ♦ prep moins.

minuscule ['mɪnəskjuːl] adj minuscule.

minute adj [maɪ'njuːt] minuscule; (detailed) minutieux(euse) ♦ n ['mɪnɪt] minute f; (official record) procès-verbal m, compte rendu; ~**s** npl procès-verbal; **it is 5 ~s past 3** il est 3 heures 5; **wait a ~!** (attendez) un instant!; **at the last ~** à la dernière minute; **up to the ~** (fashion) dernier cri; (news) de dernière minute; (machine, technology) de pointe; **in ~ detail** par le menu.

minute book n registre m des procès-verbaux.

minute hand n aiguille f des minutes.

minutely [maɪ'njuːtlɪ] adv (by a small amount) de peu, de manière infime; (in detail) minutieusement, dans les moindres détails.

minutiae [mɪ'njuːʃiː] npl menus détails.

miracle ['mɪrəkl] n miracle m.

miraculous [mɪ'rækjuləs] adj miraculeux(euse).

mirage ['mɪrɑːʒ] n mirage m.

mire ['maɪə*] n bourbe f, boue f.

mirror ['mɪrə*] n miroir m, glace f ♦ vt refléter.

mirror image n image inversée.

mirth [məːθ] n gaieté f.

misadventure [mɪsəd'ventʃə*] n mésaventure f; **death by ~** (BRIT) décès accidentel.

misanthropist [mɪ'zænθrəpɪst] n misanthrope m/f.

misapply [mɪsə'plaɪ] vt mal employer.

misapprehension ['mɪsæprɪ'hɛnʃən] n malentendu m, méprise f.

misappropriate [mɪsə'prəuprɪeɪt] vt détourner.

misappropriation ['mɪsəprəuprɪ'eɪʃən] n escroquerie f, détournement m.

misbehave [mɪsbɪ'heɪv] vi mal se conduire.

misbehaviour, (US) misbehavior [mɪsbɪ'heɪvjə*] n mauvaise conduite.

misc. abbr = miscellaneous.

miscalculate [mɪs'kælkjuleɪt] vt mal calculer.

miscalculation ['mɪskælkju'leɪʃən] n erreur f de calcul.

miscarriage ['mɪskærɪdʒ] n (MED) fausse couche; ~ **of justice** erreur f judiciaire.

miscarry [mɪs'kærɪ] vi (MED) faire une fausse couche; (fail: plans) échouer, mal tourner.

miscellaneous [mɪsɪ'leɪnɪəs] adj (items, expenses) divers(es); (selection) varié(e).

miscellany [mɪ'sɛlənɪ] n recueil m.

mischance [mɪs'tʃɑːns] n malchance f; **by (some) ~** par malheur.

mischief ['mɪstʃɪf] n (naughtiness) sottises fpl; (harm) mal m, dommage m; (maliciousness) méchanceté f.

mischievous ['mɪstʃɪvəs] adj (naughty) coquin(e), espiègle; (harmful) méchant(e).

misconception ['mɪskən'sɛpʃən] n idée fausse.

misconduct [mɪs'kɔndʌkt] n inconduite f; **professional ~** faute professionnelle.

misconstrue [mɪskən'struː] vt mal interpréter.

miscount [mɪs'kaunt] vt, vi mal compter.

misdeed ['mɪs'diːd] n méfait m.

misdemeanour, (US) misdemeanor [mɪsdɪ'miːnə*] n écart m de conduite; infraction f.

misdirect [mɪsdɪ'rɛkt] vt (person) mal renseigner; (letter) mal adresser.

miser ['maɪzə*] n avare m/f.

miserable ['mɪzərəbl] adj malheureux(euse); (wretched) misérable; **to feel ~** avoir le cafard.

miserably ['mɪzərəblɪ] adv (smile, answer) tristement; (live, pay) misérablement; (fail) lamentablement.

miserly ['maɪzəlɪ] adj avare.

misery ['mɪzərɪ] n (unhappiness) tristesse f; (pain) souffrances fpl; (wretchedness) misère f.

misfire [mɪs'faɪə*] vi rater; (car engine) avoir des ratés.

misfit ['mɪsfɪt] n (person) inadapté/e.

misfortune [mɪs'fɔːtʃən] n malchance f, malheur m.

misgiving(s) [mɪs'gɪvɪŋ(z)] *n(pl)* craintes *fpl*, soupçons *mpl*; **to have ~s about sth** avoir des doutes quant à qch.

misguided [mɪs'gaɪdɪd] *adj* malavisé(e).

mishandle [mɪs'hændl] *vt* (*treat roughly*) malmener; (*mismanage*) mal s'y prendre pour faire *or* résoudre *etc*.

mishap ['mɪshæp] *n* mésaventure *f*.

mishear [mɪs'hɪə*] *vt*, *vi irreg* mal entendre.

mishmash ['mɪʃmæʃ] *n* (*col*) fatras *m*, méli-mélo *m*.

misinform [mɪsɪn'fɔːm] *vt* mal renseigner.

misinterpret [mɪsɪn'tɜːprɪt] *vt* mal interpréter.

misinterpretation ['mɪsɪntɜːprɪ'teɪʃən] *n* interprétation erronée, contresens *m*.

misjudge [mɪs'dʒʌdʒ] *vt* méjuger, se méprendre sur le compte de.

mislay [mɪs'leɪ] *vt irreg* égarer.

mislead [mɪs'liːd] *vt irreg* induire en erreur.

misleading [mɪs'liːdɪŋ] *adj* trompeur(euse).

misled [mɪs'lɛd] *pt, pp of* **mislead.**

mismanage [mɪs'mænɪdʒ] *vt* mal gérer; mal s'y prendre pour faire *or* résoudre *etc*.

mismanagement [mɪs'mænɪdʒmənt] *n* mauvaise gestion.

misnomer [mɪs'nəumə*] *n* terme *or* qualificatif trompeur *or* peu approprié.

misogynist [mɪ'sɔdʒɪnɪst] *n* misogyne *m/f*.

misplace [mɪs'pleɪs] *vt* égarer; **to be ~d** (*trust etc*) être mal placé(e).

misprint ['mɪsprɪnt] *n* faute *f* d'impression.

mispronounce [mɪsprə'nauns] *vt* mal prononcer.

misquote ['mɪs'kwəut] *vt* citer erronément *or* inexactement.

misread [mɪs'riːd] *vt irreg* mal lire.

misrepresent [mɪsrɛprɪ'zɛnt] *vt* présenter sous un faux jour.

Miss [mɪs] *n* Mademoiselle; **Dear ~ Smith** Chère Mademoiselle Smith.

miss [mɪs] *vt* (*fail to get*) manquer, rater; (*appointment, class*) manquer; (*escape, avoid*) échapper à, éviter; (*notice loss of: money etc*) s'apercevoir de l'absence de; (*regret the absence of*): **I ~ him/it** il/cela me manque ♦ *vi* manquer ♦ *n* (*shot*) coup manqué; **the bus just ~ed the wall** le bus a évité le mur de justesse; **you're ~ing the point** vous êtes à côté de la question.

▶**miss out** *vt* (*BRIT*) oublier.

▶**miss out on** *vt fus* (*fun, party*) rater, manquer; (*chance, bargain*) laisser passer.

Miss. *abbr* (*US*) = Mississippi.

missal ['mɪsl] *n* missel *m*.

misshapen [mɪs'ʃeɪpən] *adj* difforme.

missile ['mɪsaɪl] *n* (*AVIAT*) missile *m*; (*object thrown*) projectile *m*.

missile base *n* base *f* de missiles.

missile launcher [-lɔːntʃə*] *n* lance-missiles *m*.

missing ['mɪsɪŋ] *adj* manquant(e); (*after escape, disaster: person*) disparu(e); **to go ~** disparaître; **~ person** personne disparue, disparu/e.

mission ['mɪʃən] *n* mission *f*; **on a ~ to sb** en mission auprès de qn.

missionary ['mɪʃənrɪ] *n* missionnaire *m/f*.

missive ['mɪsɪv] *n* missive *f*.

misspell ['mɪs'spɛl] *vt* (*irreg: like* **spell**) mal orthographier.

misspent ['mɪs'spɛnt] *adj:* **his ~ youth** sa folle jeunesse.

mist [mɪst] *n* brume *f* ♦ *vi* (*also: ~ over, ~ up*) devenir brumeux(euse); (*BRIT: windows*) s'embuer.

mistake [mɪs'teɪk] *n* erreur *f*, faute *f* ♦ *vt* (*irreg: like* **take**) (*meaning*) mal comprendre; (*intentions*) se méprendre sur; **to ~ for** prendre pour; **by ~** par erreur, par inadvertance; **to make a ~** (*in writing*) faire une faute; (*in calculating etc*) faire une erreur; **to make a ~ about sb/sth** se tromper sur le compte de qn/sur qch.

mistaken [mɪs'teɪkən] *pp of* **mistake** ♦ *adj* (*idea etc*) erroné(e); **to be ~** faire erreur, se tromper.

mistaken identity *n* erreur *f* d'identité.

mistakenly [mɪs'teɪkənlɪ] *adv* par erreur, par mégarde.

mister ['mɪstə*] *n* (*col*) Monsieur *m*; *see* **Mr.**

mistletoe ['mɪsltəu] *n* gui *m*.

mistook [mɪs'tuk] *pt of* **mistake.**

mistranslation [mɪstræns'leɪʃən] *n* erreur *f* de traduction, contresens *m*.

mistreat [mɪs'triːt] *vt* maltraiter.

mistress ['mɪstrɪs] *n* maîtresse *f*; (*BRIT: in primary school*) institutrice *f*; *see* **Mrs.**

mistrust [mɪs'trʌst] *vt* se méfier de ♦ *n:* **~ (of)** méfiance *f* (à l'égard de).

mistrustful [mɪs'trʌstful] *adj:* **~ (of)** méfiant(e) (à l'égard de).

misty ['mɪstɪ] *adj* brumeux(euse).

misty-eyed ['mɪstɪ'aɪd] *adj* les yeux embués de larmes; (*fig*) sentimental(e).

misunderstand [mɪsʌndə'stænd] *vt*, *vi irreg* mal comprendre.

misunderstanding ['mɪsʌndə'stændɪŋ] *n* méprise *f*, malentendu *m*.

misunderstood [mɪsʌndə'stud] *pt, pp of* **misunderstand.**

misuse *n* [mɪs'juːs] mauvais emploi; (*of power*) abus *m* ♦ *vt* [mɪs'juːz] mal employer; abuser de.

MIT *n abbr* (*US*) = Massachusetts Institute of Technology.

mite [maɪt] *n* (*small quantity*) grain *m*, miette *f*; (*BRIT: small child*) petit/e.

mitigate ['mɪtɪgeɪt] *vt* atténuer; **mitigating circumstances** circonstances atténuantes.

mitigation [mɪtɪ'geɪʃən] *n* atténuation *f*.

mitre, (*US*) **miter** ['maɪtə*] *n* mitre *f*; (*CARPENTRY*) onglet *m*.

mitt(en) ['mɪt(n)] *n* mitaine *f*; moufle *f*.

mix [mɪks] *vt* mélanger ♦ *vi* se mélanger ♦ *n* mélange *m*; dosage *m*; **to ~ sth with sth** mélanger qch à qch; **to ~ business with pleasure** unir l'utile à l'agréable; **cake ~** préparation *f* pour gâteau.
▶**mix in** *vt* incorporer, mélanger.
▶**mix up** *vt* mélanger; (*confuse*) confondre; **to be ~ed up in sth** être mêlé(e) à qch *or* impliqué(e) dans qch.
mixed [mɪkst] *adj* (*assorted*) assortis(ies); (*school etc*) mixte.
mixed-ability ['mɪkstə'bɪlɪtɪ] *adj* (*class etc*) sans groupes de niveaux.
mixed bag *n*: **it's a (bit of a) ~** il y a (un peu) de tout.
mixed blessing *n*: **it's a ~** cela a du bon et du mauvais.
mixed doubles *npl* (*SPORT*) double *m* mixte.
mixed economy *n* économie *f* mixte.
mixed grill *n* (*BRIT*) assortiment *m* de grillades.
mixed marriage *n* mariage *m* mixte.
mixed-up [mɪkst'ʌp] *adj* (*person*) désorienté(e) (*fig*).
mixer ['mɪksə*] *n* (*for food*) batteur *m*, mixeur *m*; (*person*): **he is a good ~** il est très sociable.
mixer tap *n* (robinet *m*) mélangeur *m*.
mixture ['mɪkstʃə*] *n* assortiment *m*, mélange *m*; (*MED*) préparation *f*.
mix-up ['mɪksʌp] *n* confusion *f*.
MK *abbr* (*BRIT TECH*) = **mark**.
mk *abbr* = **mark** (*currency*).
mkt *abbr* = **market**.
MLitt *n abbr* (= *Master of Literature, Master of Letters*) *titre universitaire*.
MLR *n abbr* (*BRIT*) = **minimum lending rate**.
mm *abbr* (= *millimetre*) mm.
MN *abbr* (*BRIT*) = **Merchant Navy**; (*US*) = *Minnesota*.
MO *n abbr* (*MED*) = *medical officer*, (*US col*: = *modus operandi*) méthode *f* ♦ *abbr* (*US*) = *Missouri*.
Mo. *abbr* (*US*) = *Missouri*.
m.o. *abbr* = **money order**.
moan [məun] *n* gémissement *m* ♦ *vi* gémir; (*col*: *complain*): **to ~ (about)** se plaindre (de).
moaner ['məunə*] *n* (*col*) rouspéteur/euse, râleur/euse.
moaning ['məunɪŋ] *n* gémissements *mpl*.
moat [məut] *n* fossé *m*, douves *fpl*.
mob [mɔb] *n* foule *f*; (*disorderly*) cohue *f*; (*pej*): **the ~** la populace ♦ *vt* assaillir.
mobile ['məubaɪl] *adj* mobile ♦ *n* (*ART*) mobile *m*; **applicants must be ~** (*BRIT*) les candidats devront être prêts à accepter tout déplacement.
mobile home *n* caravane *f*.
mobile phone *n* téléphone portatif.
mobile shop *n* (*BRIT*) camion *m* magasin.
mobility [məu'bɪlɪtɪ] *n* mobilité *f*.
mobilize ['məubɪlaɪz] *vt*, *vi* mobiliser.

moccasin ['mɔkəsɪn] *n* mocassin *m*.
mock [mɔk] *vt* ridiculiser, se moquer de ♦ *adj* faux(fausse).
mockery ['mɔkərɪ] *n* moquerie *f*, raillerie *f*; **to make a ~ of** ridiculiser, tourner en dérision.
mocking ['mɔkɪŋ] *adj* moqueur(euse).
mockingbird ['mɔkɪŋbɜːd] *n* moqueur *m*.
mock-up ['mɔkʌp] *n* maquette *f*.
MOD *n abbr* (*BRIT*) = **Ministry of Defence**; *see* **defence**.
mod cons ['mɔd'kɔnz] *npl abbr* (*BRIT*) = **modern conveniences**; *see* **convenience**.
mode [məud] *n* mode *m*; (*of transport*) moyen *m*.
model ['mɔdl] *n* modèle *m*; (*person: for fashion*) mannequin *m*; (*: for artist*) modèle ♦ *vt* modeler ♦ *vi* travailler comme mannequin ♦ *adj* (*railway: toy*) modèle réduit *inv*; (*child, factory*) modèle; **to ~ clothes** présenter des vêtements; **to ~ sb/sth on** modeler qn/qch sur.
modeller, (*US*) **modeler** ['mɔdlə*] *n* modeleur *m*; (*model maker*) maquettiste *m/f*; fabricant *m* de modèles réduits.
modem ['məudɛm] *n* modem *m*.
moderate *adj*, *n* ['mɔdərət] *adj* modéré(e) ♦ *n* (*POL*) modéré/e ♦ *vb* ['mɔdəreɪt] *vi* se modérer, se calmer ♦ *vt* modérer.
moderately ['mɔdərətlɪ] *adv* (*act*) avec modération *or* mesure; (*expensive, difficult*) moyennement; (*pleased, happy*) raisonnablement, assez; **~ priced** à un prix raisonnable.
moderation [mɔdə'reɪʃən] *n* modération *f*, mesure *f*; **in ~** à dose raisonnable, pris(e) *or* pratiqué(e) modérément.
moderator ['mɔdəreɪtə*] *n* (*REL*): **M~** président *m* (*de l'Assemblée générale de l'Église presbytérienne*); (*POL*) modérateur *m*.
modern ['mɔdən] *adj* moderne; **~ languages** langues vivantes.
modernization [mɔdənaɪ'zeɪʃən] *n* modernisation *f*.
modernize ['mɔdənaɪz] *vt* moderniser.
modest ['mɔdɪst] *adj* modeste.
modesty ['mɔdɪstɪ] *n* modestie *f*.
modicum ['mɔdɪkəm] *n*: **a ~ of** un minimum de.
modification [mɔdɪfɪ'keɪʃən] *n* modification *f*; **to make ~s** faire *or* apporter des modifications.
modify ['mɔdɪfaɪ] *vt* modifier.
modish ['məudɪʃ] *adj* à la mode.
Mods [mɔdz] *n abbr* (*BRIT*: = (*Honour*) *Moderations*) *premier examen universitaire (à Oxford)*.
modular ['mɔdjulə*] *adj* (*filing, unit*) modulaire.
modulate ['mɔdjuleɪt] *vt* moduler.
modulation [mɔdju'leɪʃən] *n* modulation *f*.
module ['mɔdjuːl] *n* module *m*.
mogul ['məugl] *n* (*fig*) nabab *m*; (*SKI*) bosse *f*.

MOH *n abbr* (*BRIT*) = *Medical Officer of Health*.
mohair ['məuheə*] *n* mohair *m*.
Mohammed [mə'hæmed] *n* Mahomet *m*.
moist [mɔɪst] *adj* humide, moite.
moisten ['mɔɪsn] *vt* humecter, mouiller légèrement.
moisture ['mɔɪstʃə*] *n* humidité *f*; (*on glass*) buée *f*.
moisturize ['mɔɪstʃəraɪz] *vt* (*skin*) hydrater.
moisturizer ['mɔɪstʃəraɪzə*] *n* produit hydratant.
molar ['məulə*] *n* molaire *f*.
molasses [məu'læsɪz] *n* mélasse *f*.
mold [məuld] *n*, *vt* (*US*) = **mould**.
Moldavia [mɔl'deɪvɪə], **Moldova** [mɔl'dəuvə] *n* Moldavie *f*.
Moldavian [mɔl'deɪvɪən], **Moldovan** [mɔl'dəuvən] *adj* moldave.
mole [məul] *n* (*animal*) taupe *f*; (*spot*) grain *m* de beauté.
molecule ['mɔlɪkjuːl] *n* molécule *f*.
molehill ['məulhɪl] *n* taupinière *f*.
molest [məu'lɛst] *vt* tracasser; molester.
mollusc ['mɔləsk] *n* mollusque *m*.
mollycoddle ['mɔlɪkɔdl] *vt* chouchouter, couver.
Molotov cocktail ['mɔlətɔf-] *n* cocktail *m* Molotov.
molt [məult] *vi* (*US*) = **moult**.
molten ['məultən] *adj* fondu(e).
mom [mɔm] *n* (*US*) = **mum**.
moment ['məumənt] *n* moment *m*, instant *m*; (*importance*) importance *f*; **at the** ~ en ce moment; **for the** ~ pour l'instant; **in a** ~ dans un instant; **"one** ~ **please"** (*TEL*) "ne quittez pas".
momentarily ['məuməntrɪlɪ] *adv* momentanément; (*US: soon*) bientôt.
momentary ['məuməntərɪ] *adj* momentané(e), passager(ère).
momentous [məu'mɛntəs] *adj* important(e), capital(e).
momentum [məu'mɛntəm] *n* élan *m*, vitesse acquise; **to gather** ~ prendre de la vitesse.
mommy ['mɔmɪ] *n* (*US: mother*) maman *f*.
Mon. *abbr* (= *Monday*) l.
Monaco ['mɔnəkəu] *n* Monaco *f*.
monarch ['mɔnək] *n* monarque *m*.
monarchist ['mɔnəkɪst] *n* monarchiste *m/f*.
monarchy ['mɔnəkɪ] *n* monarchie *f*.
monastery ['mɔnəstərɪ] *n* monastère *m*.
monastic [mə'næstɪk] *adj* monastique.
Monday ['mʌndɪ] *n* lundi *m*; *for phrases see also* **Tuesday**.
monetarist ['mʌnɪtərɪst] *n* monétariste *m/f*.
monetary ['mʌnɪtərɪ] *adj* monétaire.
money ['mʌnɪ] *n* argent *m*; **to make** ~ (*person*) gagner de l'argent; (*business*) rapporter; **I've got no** ~ **left** je n'ai plus d'argent, je n'ai plus un sou.
moneyed ['mʌnɪd] *adj* riche.
moneylender ['mʌnɪlɛndə*] *n* prêteur/euse.

moneymaker ['mʌnɪmeɪkə*] *n* (*BRIT col: business*) affaire lucrative.
moneymaking ['mʌnɪmeɪkɪŋ] *adj* lucratif(ive), qui rapporte (de l'argent).
money market *n* marché financier.
money order *n* mandat *m*.
money-spinner ['mʌnɪspɪnə*] *n* (*col*) mine *f* d'or (*fig*).
money supply *n* masse *f* monétaire.
Mongol ['mɔŋgəl] *n* Mongol/e; (*LING*) mongol *m*.
mongol ['mɔŋgəl] *adj*, *n* (*MED*) mongolien(ne).
Mongolia [mɔŋ'gəulɪə] *n* Mongolie *f*.
Mongolian [mɔŋ'gəulɪən] *adj* mongol(e) ♦ *n* Mongol/e; (*LING*) mongol *m*.
mongoose ['mɔŋguːs] *n* mangouste *f*.
mongrel ['mʌŋgrəl] *n* (*dog*) bâtard *m*.
monitor ['mɔnɪtə*] *n* (*BRIT SCOL*) chef *m* de classe; (*US SCOL*) surveillant *m* (d'examen); (*TV*, *COMPUT*) écran *m*, moniteur *m* ♦ *vt* contrôler; (*foreign station*) être à l'écoute de.
monk [mʌŋk] *n* moine *m*.
monkey ['mʌŋkɪ] *n* singe *m*.
monkey nut *n* (*BRIT*) cacahuète *f*.
monkey wrench *n* clé *f* à molette.
mono ['mɔnəu] *adj* mono *inv*.
mono... ['mɔnəu] *prefix* mono....
monochrome ['mɔnəkrəum] *adj* monochrome.
monocle ['mɔnəkl] *n* monocle *m*.
monogamous [mɔ'nɔgəməs] *adj* monogame.
monogamy [mɔ'nɔgəmɪ] *n* monogamie *f*.
monogram ['mɔnəgræm] *n* monogramme *m*.
monolith ['mɔnəlɪθ] *n* monolithe *m*.
monologue ['mɔnəlɔg] *n* monologue *m*.
monoplane ['mɔnəpleɪn] *n* monoplan *m*.
monopolize [mə'nɔpəlaɪz] *vt* monopoliser.
monopoly [mə'nɔpəlɪ] *n* monopole *m*; **Monopolies and Mergers Commission** (*BRIT*) *commission britannique d'enquête sur les monopoles*.
monorail ['mɔnəureɪl] *n* monorail *m*.
monosodium glutamate [mɔnə'səudɪəm 'gluːtəmeɪt] *n* glutamate *m* de sodium.
monosyllabic [mɔnəsɪ'læbɪk] *adj* monosyllabique; (*person*) laconique.
monosyllable ['mɔnəsɪləbl] *n* monosyllabe *m*.
monotone ['mɔnətəun] *n* ton *m* (*or* voix *f*) monocorde; **to speak in a** ~ parler sur un ton monocorde.
monotonous [mə'nɔtənəs] *adj* monotone.
monotony [mə'nɔtənɪ] *n* monotonie *f*.
monoxide [mɔ'nɔksaɪd] *n*: **carbon** ~ oxyde *m* de carbone.
monsoon [mɔn'suːn] *n* mousson *f*.
monster ['mɔnstə*] *n* monstre *m*.
monstrosity [mɔns'trɔsɪtɪ] *n* monstruosité *f*, atrocité *f*.
monstrous ['mɔnstrəs] *adj* (*huge*) gigantesque; (*atrocious*) monstrueux(euse), atroce.
Mont. *abbr* (*US*) = *Montana*.
montage [mɔn'tɑːʒ] *n* montage *m*.
Mont Blanc [mɔblɑ̃] *n* Mont Blanc *m*.

month [mʌnθ] n mois m; **every** ~ tous les mois; **300 dollars a** ~ 300 dollars par mois.

monthly ['mʌnθlı] adj mensuel(le) ♦ adv mensuellement ♦ n (magazine) mensuel m, publication mensuelle; **twice** ~ deux fois par mois.

Montreal [mɔntrı'ɔːl] n Montréal.

monument ['mɔnjumənt] n monument m.

monumental [mɔnju'mɛntl] adj monumental(e).

monumental mason n marbrier m.

moo [muː] vi meugler, beugler.

mood [muːd] n humeur f, disposition f; **to be in a good/bad** ~ être de bonne/mauvaise humeur; **to be in the** ~ **for** être d'humeur à, avoir envie de.

moody ['muːdı] adj (variable) d'humeur changeante, lunatique; (sullen) morose, maussade.

moon [muːn] n lune f.

moonbeam ['muːnbiːm] n rayon m de lune.

moon landing n alunissage m.

moonlight ['muːnlaıt] n clair m de lune ♦ vi travailler au noir.

moonlighting ['muːnlaıtıŋ] n travail m au noir.

moonlit ['muːnlıt] adj éclairé(e) par la lune; **a** ~ **night** une nuit de lune.

moonshot ['muːnʃɔt] n (SPACE) tir m lunaire.

moonstruck ['muːnstrʌk] adj fou(folle), dérangé(e).

moony ['muːnı] adj: **to have** ~ **eyes** avoir l'air dans la lune or rêveur.

Moor [muə*] n Maure/Mauresque.

moor [muə*] n lande f ♦ vt (ship) amarrer ♦ vi mouiller.

moorings ['muərıŋz] npl (chains) amarres fpl; (place) mouillage m.

Moorish ['muərıʃ] adj maure(mauresque).

moorland ['muələnd] n lande f.

moose [muːs] n (pl inv) élan m.

moot [muːt] vt soulever ♦ adj: ~ **point** point m discutable.

mop [mɔp] n balai m à laver ♦ vt éponger, essuyer; ~ **of hair** tignasse f.

▶**mop up** vt éponger.

mope [məup] vi avoir le cafard, se morfondre.

▶**mope about, mope around** vi broyer du noir, se morfondre.

moped ['məupɛd] n cyclomoteur m.

moquette [mɔ'kɛt] n moquette f.

MOR adj abbr (MUS: = middle-of-the-road) tous publics.

moral ['mɔrl] adj moral(e) ♦ n morale f; ~**s** npl moralité f.

morale [mɔ'rɑːl] n moral m.

morality [mə'rælıtı] n moralité f.

moralize ['mɔrəlaız] vi: **to** ~ **(about)** moraliser (sur).

morally ['mɔrəlı] adv moralement.

moral victory n victoire morale.

morass [mə'ræs] n marais m, marécage m.

moratorium [mɔrə'tɔːrıəm] n moratoire m.

morbid ['mɔːbıd] adj morbide.

KEYWORD

more [mɔː*] adj **1** (greater in number etc) plus (de), davantage; ~ **people/work (than)** plus de gens/de travail (que)

2 (additional) encore (de); **do you want (some)** ~ **tea?** voulez-vous encore du thé?; **I have no** or **I don't have any** ~ **money** je n'ai plus d'argent; **it'll take a few** ~ **weeks** ça prendra encore quelques semaines

♦ pron plus, davantage; ~ **than 10** plus de 10; **it cost** ~ **than we expected** cela a coûté plus que prévu; **I want** ~ j'en veux plus or davantage; **is there any** ~? est-ce qu'il en reste?; **there's no** ~ il n'y en a plus; **a little** ~ un peu plus; **many/much** ~ beaucoup plus, bien davantage

♦ adv: ~ **dangerous/easily (than)** plus dangereux/facilement (que); ~ **and** ~ **expensive** de plus en plus cher; ~ **or less** plus ou moins; ~ **than ever** plus que jamais; **once** ~ encore une fois, une fois de plus; **and what's** ~ … et de plus …, et qui plus est …

moreover [mɔː'rəuvə*] adv de plus.

morgue [mɔːg] n morgue f.

MORI ['mɔːrı] n abbr (BRIT: = Market & Opinion Research Institute) institut de sondage.

moribund ['mɔrıbʌnd] adj moribond(e).

morning ['mɔːnıŋ] n matin m; (as duration) matinée f; **in the** ~ le matin; **7 o'clock in the** ~ 7 heures du matin; **this** ~ ce matin.

morning-after pill ['mɔːnıŋ'ɑːftə-] n pilule f du lendemain.

morning sickness n nausées matinales.

Moroccan [mə'rɔkən] adj marocain(e) ♦ n Marocain/e.

Morocco [mə'rɔkəu] n Maroc m.

moron ['mɔːrɔn] n idiot/e, minus m/f.

moronic [mə'rɔnık] adj idiot(e), imbécile.

morose [mə'rəus] adj morose, maussade.

morphine ['mɔːfiːn] n morphine f.

morris dancing ['mɔrıs-] n (BRIT) danses folkloriques anglaises.

Morse [mɔːs] n (also: ~ **code**) morse m.

morsel ['mɔːsl] n bouchée f.

mortal ['mɔːtl] adj, n mortel(le).

mortality [mɔː'tælıtı] n mortalité f.

mortality rate n (taux m de) mortalité f.

mortar ['mɔːtə*] n mortier m.

mortgage ['mɔːgıdʒ] n hypothèque f; (loan) prêt m (or crédit m) hypothécaire ♦ vt hypothéquer; **to take out a** ~ prendre une hypothèque, faire un emprunt.

mortgage company n (US) société f de crédit immobilier.

mortgagee [mɔːgə'dʒiː] n prêteur/euse (sur hypothèque).

mortgagor ['mɔːgədʒə*] n emprunteur/euse

(sur hypothèque).

mortician [mɔːˈtɪʃən] *n* (*US*) entrepreneur *m* de pompes funèbres.

mortified [ˈmɔːtɪfaɪd] *adj* mortifié(e).

mortise lock [ˈmɔːtɪs-] *n* serrure encastrée.

mortuary [ˈmɔːtjuərɪ] *n* morgue *f*.

mosaic [məʊˈzeɪɪk] *n* mosaïque *f*.

Moscow [ˈmɔskəʊ] *n* Moscou.

Moslem [ˈmɔzləm] *adj*, *n* = **Muslim**.

mosque [mɔsk] *n* mosquée *f*.

mosquito, ~**es** [mɔsˈkiːtəʊ] *n* moustique *m*.

mosquito net *n* moustiquaire *f*.

moss [mɔs] *n* mousse *f*.

mossy [ˈmɔsɪ] *adj* moussu(e).

most [məʊst] *adj* la plupart de; le plus de ♦ *pron* la plupart ♦ *adv* le plus; (*very*) très, extrêmement; **the** ~ (*also: + adjective*) le plus; ~ **fish** la plupart des poissons; ~ **of** la plus grande partie de; ~ **of them** la plupart d'entre eux; **I saw** ~ j'en ai vu la plupart; c'est moi qui en ai vu le plus; **at the (very)** ~ au plus; **to make the** ~ **of** profiter au maximum de.

mostly [ˈməʊstlɪ] *adv* surtout, principalement.

MOT *n abbr* (*BRIT*: = *Ministry of Transport*): **the** ~ **(test)** visite technique (annuelle) obligatoire des véhicules à moteur.

motel [məʊˈtɛl] *n* motel *m*.

moth [mɔθ] *n* papillon *m* de nuit; mite *f*.

mothball [ˈmɔθbɔːl] *n* boule *f* de naphtaline.

moth-eaten [ˈmɔθiːtn] *adj* mité(e).

mother [ˈmʌðə*] *n* mère *f* ♦ *vt* (*care for*) dorloter.

mother board *n* (*COMPUT*) carte-mère *f*.

motherhood [ˈmʌðəhud] *n* maternité *f*.

mother-in-law [ˈmʌðərɪnlɔː] *n* belle-mère *f*.

motherly [ˈmʌðəlɪ] *adj* maternel(le).

mother-of-pearl [ˈmʌðərəvˈpɜːl] *n* nacre *f*.

mother's help *n* aide *f* or auxiliaire *f* familiale.

mother-to-be [ˈmʌðətəˈbiː] *n* future maman *f*.

mother tongue *n* langue maternelle.

mothproof [ˈmɔθpruːf] *adj* traité(e) à l'antimite.

motif [məʊˈtiːf] *n* motif *m*.

motion [ˈməʊʃən] *n* mouvement *m*; (*gesture*) geste *m*; (*at meeting*) motion *f*; (*BRIT: also:* **bowel** ~) selles *fpl* ♦ *vt*, *vi:* **to** ~ (**to**) **sb to do** faire signe à qn de faire; **to be in** ~ (*vehicle*) être en marche; **to set in** ~ mettre en marche; **to go through the** ~**s of doing sth** (*fig*) faire qch machinalement *or* sans conviction.

motionless [ˈməʊʃənlɪs] *adj* immobile, sans mouvement.

motion picture *n* film *m*.

motivate [ˈməʊtɪveɪt] *vt* motiver.

motivated [ˈməʊtɪveɪtɪd] *adj* motivé(e).

motivation [məʊtɪˈveɪʃən] *n* motivation *f*.

motive [ˈməʊtɪv] *n* motif *m*, mobile *m* ♦ *adj* moteur(trice); **from the best (of)** ~**s** avec les meilleures intentions (du monde).

motley [ˈmɔtlɪ] *adj* hétéroclite; bigarré(e), bariolé(e).

motor [ˈməʊtə*] *n* moteur *m*; (*BRIT col: vehicle*) auto *f* ♦ *adj* moteur(trice).

motorbike [ˈməʊtəbaɪk] *n* moto *f*.

motorboat [ˈməʊtəbəʊt] *n* bateau *m* à moteur.

motorcade [ˈməʊtəkeɪd] *n* cortège *m* d'automobiles *or* de voitures.

motorcar [ˈməʊtəkɑː] *n* (*BRIT*) automobile *f*.

motorcoach [ˈməʊtəkəʊtʃ] *n* (*BRIT*) car *m*.

motorcycle [ˈməʊtəsaɪkl] *n* vélomoteur *m*.

motorcyclist [ˈməʊtəsaɪklɪst] *n* motocycliste *m/f*.

motoring [ˈməʊtərɪŋ] (*BRIT*) *n* tourisme *m* automobile ♦ *adj* (*accident*) de voiture, de la route; ~ **holiday** vacances *fpl* en voiture; ~ **offence** infraction *f* au code de la route.

motorist [ˈməʊtərɪst] *n* automobiliste *m/f*.

motorize [ˈməʊtəraɪz] *vt* motoriser.

motor oil *n* huile *f* de graissage.

motor racing *n* (*BRIT*) course *f* automobile.

motor scooter *n* scooter *m*.

motor vehicle *n* véhicule *m* automobile.

motorway [ˈməʊtəweɪ] *n* (*BRIT*) autoroute *f*.

mottled [ˈmɔtld] *adj* tacheté(e), marbré(e).

motto, ~**es** [ˈmɔtəʊ] *n* devise *f*.

mould, (*US*) **mold** [məʊld] *n* moule *m*; (*mildew*) moisissure *f* ♦ *vt* mouler, modeler; (*fig*) façonner.

mo(u)lder [ˈməʊldə*] *vi* (*decay*) moisir.

mo(u)lding [ˈməʊldɪŋ] *n* (*ARCHIT*) moulure *f*.

mo(u)ldy [ˈməʊldɪ] *adj* moisi(e).

moult, (*US*) **molt** [məʊlt] *vi* muer.

mound [maund] *n* monticule *m*, tertre *m*.

mount [maunt] *n* mont *m*, montagne *f*; (*horse*) monture *f*; (*for jewel etc*) monture ♦ *vt* monter; (*exhibition*) organiser, monter; (*picture*) monter sur carton; (*stamp*) coller dans un album ♦ *vi* (*also:* ~ **up**) s'élever, monter.

mountain [ˈmauntɪn] *n* montagne *f* ♦ *cpd* de (la) montagne; **to make a** ~ **out of a molehill** (*fig*) se faire une montagne d'un rien.

mountain bike *n* VTT *m*, vélo *m* tout terrain.

mountaineer [mauntɪˈnɪə*] *n* alpiniste *m/f*.

mountaineering [mauntɪˈnɪərɪŋ] *n* alpinisme *m*; **to go** ~ faire de l'alpinisme.

mountainous [ˈmauntɪnəs] *adj* montagneux(euse).

mountain range *n* chaîne *f* de montagnes.

mountain rescue team *n* colonne *f* de secours.

mountainside [ˈmauntɪnsaɪd] *n* flanc *m* *or* versant *m* de la montagne.

mounted [ˈmauntɪd] *adj* monté(e).

Mount Everest *n* le mont Everest.

mourn [mɔːn] *vt* pleurer ♦ *vi:* **to** ~ **(for)** se lamenter (sur).

mourner [ˈmɔːnə*] *n* parent/e *or* ami/e du défunt; personne *f* en deuil *or* venue rendre hommage au défunt.

mournful [ˈmɔːnful] *adj* triste, lugubre.

mourning [ˈmɔːnɪŋ] *n* deuil *m* ♦ *cpd* (*dress*) de

deuil; **in** ~ en deuil.
mouse, pl **mice** [maus, maɪs] n (also COMPUT) souris f.
mousetrap ['maustræp] n souricière f.
moussaka [mu'sɑ:kə] n moussaka f.
mousse [mu:s] n mousse f.
moustache [məs'tɑ:ʃ] n moustache(s) f(pl).
mousy ['mausɪ] adj (person) effacé(e); (hair) d'un châtain terne.
mouth, ~**s** [mauθ, -ðz] n bouche f; (of dog, cat) gueule f; (of river) embouchure f; (of bottle) goulot m; (opening) orifice m.
mouthful ['mauθful] n bouchée f.
mouth organ n harmonica m.
mouthpiece ['mauθpi:s] n (of musical instrument) bec m, embouchure f; (spokesman) porte-parole m inv.
mouth-to-mouth ['mauθtə'mauθ] adj: ~ **resuscitation** bouche à bouche m.
mouthwash ['mauθwɔʃ] n eau f dentifrice.
mouth-watering ['mauθwɔ:tərɪŋ] adj qui met l'eau à la bouche.
movable ['mu:vəbl] adj mobile.
move [mu:v] n (movement) mouvement m; (in game) coup m; (: turn to play) tour m; (change of house) déménagement m ♦ vt déplacer, bouger; (emotionally) émouvoir f; (POL: resolution etc) proposer ♦ vi (gen) bouger, remuer; (traffic) circuler; (also: ~ **house**) déménager; **to** ~ **towards** se diriger vers; **to** ~ **sb to do sth** pousser or inciter qn à faire qch; **to get a** ~ **on** se dépêcher, se remuer.
▶**move about, move around** vi (fidget) remuer; (travel) voyager, se déplacer.
▶**move along** vi se pousser.
▶**move away** vi s'en aller, s'éloigner.
▶**move back** vi revenir, retourner.
▶**move forward** vi avancer ♦ vt avancer; (people) faire avancer.
▶**move in** vi (to a house) emménager.
▶**move off** vi s'éloigner, s'en aller.
▶**move on** vi se remettre en route ♦ vt (onlookers) faire circuler.
▶**move out** vi (of house) déménager.
▶**move over** vi se pousser, se déplacer.
▶**move up** vi avancer; (employee) avoir de l'avancement.
movement ['mu:vmənt] n mouvement m; ~ **(of the bowels)** (MED) selles fpl.
mover ['mu:və*] n auteur m d'une proposition.
movie ['mu:vɪ] n film m; **the** ~**s** le cinéma.
movie camera n caméra f.
moviegoer ['mu:vɪɡəuə*] n (US) cinéphile m/f.
moving ['mu:vɪŋ] adj en mouvement; (touching) émouvant(e) ♦ n (US) déménagement m.
mow, pt **mowed,** pp **mowed** or **mown** [məu, -n] vt faucher; (lawn) tondre.
▶**mow down** vt faucher.
mower ['məuə*] n (also: **lawn**~) tondeuse f à gazon.
Mozambique [məuzəm'bi:k] n Mozambique

m.
MP n abbr (= Military Police) PM; (BRIT) = **Member of Parliament**; (Canada) = Mounted Police.
mpg n abbr = miles per gallon (30 mpg = 9,4 l. aux 100 km).
mph abbr = miles per hour (60 mph = 96 km/h).
MPhil n abbr (US: = Master of Philosophy) titre universitaire.
MPS n abbr (BRIT) = Member of the Pharmaceutical Society.
Mr, Mr. ['mɪstə*] n: ~ **X** Monsieur X, M. X.
MRC n abbr (BRIT: = Medical Research Council) conseil de la recherche médicale.
MRCP n abbr (BRIT) = Member of the Royal College of Physicians.
MRCS n abbr (BRIT) = Member of the Royal College of Surgeons.
MRCVS n abbr (BRIT) = Member of the Royal College of Veterinary Surgeons.
Mrs, Mrs. ['mɪsɪz] n: ~ **X** Madame X, Mme X.
MS n abbr (= manuscript) ms; (= multiple sclerosis) SEP f; (US: = Master of Science) titre universitaire ♦ abbr (US) = Mississippi.
Ms, Ms. [mɪz] n (= Miss or Mrs): ~ **X** Madame X, Mme X.
MSA n abbr (US: = Master of Science in Agriculture) titre universitaire.
MSc n abbr = Master of Science.
MSG n abbr = monosodium glutamate.
MST abbr (US: = Mountain Standard Time) heure d'hiver des Montagnes Rocheuses.
MSW n abbr (US: = Master of Social Work) titre universitaire.
MT n abbr (= machine translation) TM ♦ abbr (US) = Montana.
Mt abbr (GEO: = mount) Mt.
MTV n abbr = music television.
much [mʌtʃ] adj beaucoup de ♦ adv, n or pron beaucoup; ~ **milk** beaucoup de lait; **how** ~ **is it?** combien est-ce que ça coûte?; **it's not** ~ ce n'est pas beaucoup; **too** ~ trop (de); **so** ~ tant (de); **I like it very/so** ~ j'aime beaucoup/tellement ça; **thank you very** ~ merci beaucoup; ~ **to my amazement** ... à mon grand étonnement ....
muck [mʌk] n (mud) boue f; (dirt) ordures fpl.
▶**muck about** vi (col) faire l'imbécile; (: waste time) traînasser; (: tinker) bricoler; tripoter.
▶**muck in** vi (BRIT col) donner un coup de main.
▶**muck out** vt (stable) nettoyer.
▶**muck up** vt (col: ruin) gâcher, esquinter; (: dirty) salir.
muckraking ['mʌkreɪkɪŋ] n (fig: col) déterrement m d'ordures.
mucky ['mʌkɪ] adj (dirty) boueux(euse), sale.
mucus ['mju:kəs] n mucus m.
mud [mʌd] n boue f.
muddle ['mʌdl] n pagaille f; désordre m, fouillis m ♦ vt (also: ~ **up**) brouiller, embrouiller; **to be in a** ~ (person) ne plus savoir ou l'on

en est; **to get in a** ~ (*while explaining etc*) s'embrouiller.

▶**muddle along** *vi* aller son chemin tant bien que mal.

▶**muddle through** *vi* se débrouiller.

muddle-headed [mʌdl'hɛdɪd] *adj* (*person*) à l'esprit embrouillé *or* confus, dans le brouillard.

muddy ['mʌdɪ] *adj* boueux(euse).

mud flats *npl* plage *f* de vase.

mudguard ['mʌdgɑːd] *n* garde-boue *m inv*.

mudpack ['mʌdpæk] *n* masque *m* de beauté.

mud-slinging ['mʌdslɪŋɪŋ] *n* médisance *f*, dénigrement *m*.

muesli ['mjuːzlɪ] *n* muesli *m*.

muff [mʌf] *n* manchon *m* ♦ *vt* (*col: shot, catch etc*) rater, louper; **to** ~ **it** rater *or* louper son coup.

muffin ['mʌfɪn] *n petit pain rond et plat*.

muffle ['mʌfl] *vt* (*sound*) assourdir, étouffer; (*against cold*) emmitoufler.

muffled ['mʌfld] *adj* étouffé(e), voilé(e).

muffler ['mʌflə*] *n* (*scarf*) cache-nez *m inv*; (*US AUT*) silencieux *m*.

mufti ['mʌftɪ] *n*: **in** ~ en civil.

mug [mʌg] *n* (*cup*) tasse *f* (*sans soucoupe*); (: *for beer*) chope *f*; (*col: face*) bouille *f*; (: *fool*) poire *f* ♦ *vt* (*assault*) agresser; **it's a** ~**'s game** (*BRIT*) c'est bon pour les imbéciles.

▶**mug up** *vt* (*BRIT col: also:* ~ **up on**) bosser, bûcher.

mugger ['mʌgə*] *n* agresseur *m*.

mugging ['mʌgɪŋ] *n* agression *f*.

muggins ['mʌgɪnz] *n* (*col*) ma pomme.

muggy ['mʌgɪ] *adj* lourd(e), moite.

mug shot *n* (*col: POLICE*) photo *f* de criminel; (: *gen: photo*) photo d'identité.

mulatto, ~es [mjuːˈlætəu] *n* mulâtre/esse.

mulberry ['mʌlbrɪ] *n* (*fruit*) mûre *f*; (*tree*) mûrier *m*.

mule [mjuːl] *n* mule *f*.

mull [mʌl]: **to** ~ **over** *vt* réfléchir à, ruminer.

mulled [mʌld] *adj*: ~ **wine** vin chaud.

multi... ['mʌltɪ] *prefix* multi....

multi-access ['mʌltɪ'æksɛs] *adj* (*COMPUT*) à accès multiple.

multicoloured, (*US*) **multicolored** ['mʌltɪkʌləd] *adj* multicolore.

multifarious [mʌltɪ'fɛərɪəs] *adj* divers(es); varié(e).

multilateral [mʌltɪ'lætərl] *adj* (*POL*) multilatéral(e).

multi-level ['mʌltɪlɛvl] *adj* (*US*) = **multistorey**.

multimillionaire [mʌltɪmɪljə'nɛə*] *n* milliardaire *m/f*.

multinational [mʌltɪ'næʃənl] *n* multinationale *f* ♦ *adj* multinational(e).

multiple ['mʌltɪpl] *adj* multiple ♦ *n* multiple *m*; (*BRIT: also:* ~ **store**) magasin *m* à succursales (multiples).

multiple choice *adj* à choix multiple.

multiple crash *n* carambolage *m*.

multiple sclerosis *n* sclérose *f* en plaques.

multiplex ['mʌltɪplɛks] *n* (*also:* ~ **cinema**) (cinéma *m*) multisalles *m*.

multiplication [mʌltɪplɪ'keɪʃən] *n* multiplication *f*.

multiplication table *n* table *f* de multiplication.

multiplicity [mʌltɪ'plɪsɪtɪ] *n* multiplicité *f*.

multiply ['mʌltɪplaɪ] *vt* multiplier ♦ *vi* se multiplier.

multiracial [mʌltɪ'reɪʃl] *adj* multiracial(e).

multistorey ['mʌltɪ'stɔːrɪ] *adj* (*BRIT: building*) à étages; (: *car park*) à étages *or* niveaux multiples.

multitude ['mʌltɪtjuːd] *n* multitude *f*.

mum [mʌm] *n* (*BRIT*) maman *f* ♦ *adj*: **to keep** ~ ne pas souffler mot; ~**'s the word!** motus et bouche cousue!

mumble ['mʌmbl] *vt, vi* marmotter, marmonner.

mumbo jumbo ['mʌmbəu-] *n* (*col*) baragouin *m*, charabia *m*.

mummify ['mʌmɪfaɪ] *vt* momifier.

mummy ['mʌmɪ] *n* (*BRIT: mother*) maman *f*; (*embalmed*) momie *f*.

mumps [mʌmps] *n* oreillons *mpl*.

munch [mʌntʃ] *vt, vi* mâcher.

mundane [mʌn'deɪn] *adj* banal(e), terre à terre *inv*.

municipal [mjuː'nɪsɪpl] *adj* municipal(e).

municipality [mjuːnɪsɪ'pælɪtɪ] *n* municipalité *f*.

munitions [mjuː'nɪʃənz] *npl* munitions *fpl*.

mural ['mjuərl] *n* peinture murale.

murder ['məːdə*] *n* meurtre *m*, assassinat *m* ♦ *vt* assassiner; **to commit** ~ commettre un meurtre.

murderer ['məːdərə*] *n* meurtrier *m*, assassin *m*.

murderess ['məːdərɪs] *n* meurtrière *f*.

murderous ['məːdərəs] *adj* meurtrier(ière).

murk [məːk] *n* obscurité *f*.

murky ['məːkɪ] *adj* sombre, ténébreux(euse).

murmur ['məːmə*] *n* murmure *m* ♦ *vt, vi* murmurer; **heart** ~ (*MED*) souffle *m* au cœur.

MusB(ac) *n abbr* (= *Bachelor of Music*) titre universitaire.

muscle ['mʌsl] *n* muscle *m*.

▶**muscle in** *vi* s'imposer, s'immiscer.

muscular ['mʌskjulə*] *adj* musculaire; (*person, arm*) musclé(e).

muscular dystrophy *n* dystrophie *f* musculaire.

MusD(oc) *n abbr* (= *Doctor of Music*) titre universitaire.

muse [mjuːz] *vi* méditer, songer ♦ *n* muse *f*.

museum [mjuː'zɪəm] *n* musée *m*.

mush [mʌʃ] *n* bouillie *f*; (*pej*) sentimentalité *f* à l'eau de rose.

mushroom ['mʌʃrum] *n* champignon *m* ♦ *vi* (*fig*) pousser comme un (*or* des) champignon(s).

mushy ['mʌʃɪ] *adj* (*vegetables, fruit*) en bouillie; (*movie etc*) à l'eau de rose.

music ['mjuːzɪk] *n* musique *f*.

musical ['mjuːzɪkl] *adj* musical(e); (*person*) musicien(ne) ♦ *n* (*show*) comédie musicale.

music(al) box *n* boîte *f* à musique.

musical chairs *npl* chaises musicales; (*fig*) **to play** ~ faire des permutations.

musical instrument *n* instrument *m* de musique.

music centre *n* chaîne compacte.

music hall *n* music-hall *m*.

musician [mjuː'zɪʃən] *n* musicien/ne.

music stand *n* pupitre *m* à musique.

musk [mʌsk] *n* musc *m*.

musket ['mʌskɪt] *n* mousquet *m*.

muskrat ['mʌskræt] *n* rat musqué.

musk rose *n* (*BOT*) rose *f* muscade.

Muslim ['mʌzlɪm] *adj*, *n* musulman(e).

muslin ['mʌzlɪn] *n* mousseline *f*.

musquash ['mʌskwɔʃ] *n* loutre *f*; (*fur*) rat *m* d'Amérique, ondatra *m*.

mussel ['mʌsl] *n* moule *f*.

must [mʌst] *aux vb* (*obligation*): I ~ **do it** je dois le faire, il faut que je le fasse; (*probability*): **he** ~ **be there by now** il doit y être maintenant, il y est probablement maintenant; **I** ~ **have made a mistake** j'ai dû me tromper ♦ *n* nécessité *f*, impératif *m*; **it's a** ~ c'est indispensable.

mustache ['mʌstæʃ] *n* (*US*) = **moustache**.

mustard ['mʌstəd] *n* moutarde *f*.

mustard gas *n* ypérite *f*, gaz *m* moutarde.

muster ['mʌstə*] *vt* rassembler; (*also*: ~ **up**: *strength, courage*) rassembler.

mustiness ['mʌstɪnɪs] *n* goût *m* de moisi; odeur *f* de moisi *or* de renfermé.

mustn't ['mʌsnt] = **must not**.

musty ['mʌstɪ] *adj* qui sent le moisi *or* le renfermé.

mutant ['mjuːtənt] *adj* mutant(e) ♦ *n* mutant *m*.

mutate [mjuː'teɪt] *vi* subir une mutation.

mutation [mjuː'teɪʃən] *n* mutation *f*.

mute [mjuːt] *adj*, *n* muet(te).

muted ['mjuːtɪd] *adj* (*noise*) sourd(e), assourdi(e); (*criticism*) voilé(e); (*MUS*) en sourdine; (: *trumpet*) bouché(e).

mutilate ['mjuːtɪleɪt] *vt* mutiler.

mutilation [mjuːtɪ'leɪʃən] *n* mutilation *f*.

mutinous ['mjuːtɪnəs] *adj* (*troops*) mutiné(e); (*attitude*) rebelle.

mutiny ['mjuːtɪnɪ] *n* mutinerie *f* ♦ *vi* se mutiner.

mutter ['mʌtə*] *vt*, *vi* marmonner, marmotter.

mutton ['mʌtn] *n* mouton *m*.

mutual ['mjuːtʃuəl] *adj* mutuel(le), réciproque.

mutually ['mjuːtʃuəlɪ] *adv* mutuellement, réciproquement.

Muzak ['mjuːzæk] *n* ® (*often pej*) musique *f* d'ambiance.

muzzle ['mʌzl] *n* museau *m*; (*protective device*) muselière *f*; (*of gun*) gueule *f* ♦ *vt* museler.

MVP *n abbr* (*US SPORT*) = *most valuable player*.

MW *abbr* (= *medium wave*) PO.

my [maɪ] *adj* mon(ma), mes *pl*.

Myanmar ['maɪænmɑ:*] *n* Myanmar *m*.

myopic [maɪ'ɔpɪk] *adj* myope.

myriad ['mɪrɪəd] *n* myriade *f*.

myself [maɪ'self] *pron* (*reflexive*) me; (*emphatic*) moi-même; (*after prep*) moi.

mysterious [mɪs'tɪərɪəs] *adj* mystérieux(euse).

mystery ['mɪstərɪ] *n* mystère *m*.

mystery story *n* roman *m* à suspense.

mystic ['mɪstɪk] *n* mystique *m/f* ♦ *adj* (*mysterious*) ésotérique.

mystical ['mɪstɪkl] *adj* mystique.

mystify ['mɪstɪfaɪ] *vt* mystifier; (*puzzle*) ébahir.

mystique [mɪs'tiːk] *n* mystique *f*.

myth [mɪθ] *n* mythe *m*.

mythical ['mɪθɪkl] *adj* mythique.

mythological [mɪθə'lɔdʒɪkl] *adj* mythologique.

mythology [mɪ'θɔlədʒɪ] *n* mythologie *f*.

N n

N, n [ɛn] *n* (*letter*) N, n *m*; **N for Nellie,** (*US*) **N for Nan** N comme Nicolas.

N *abbr* (= *north*) N.

NA *n abbr* (*US*: = *Narcotics Anonymous*) *association d'aide aux drogués*; (*US*) = *National Academy*.

n/a *abbr* (= *not applicable*) n.a.; (*COMM etc*) = *no account*.

NAACP *n abbr* (*US*) = *National Association for the Advancement of Colored People*.

NAAFI ['næfɪ] *n abbr* (*BRIT*: = *Navy, Army & Air Force Institute*) *organisme responsable des magasins et cantines de l'armée*.

nab [næb] *vt* (*col*) pincer, attraper.

NACU *n abbr* (*US*) = *National Association of Colleges and Universities*.

nadir ['neɪdɪə*] *n* (*ASTRONOMY*) nadir *m*; (*fig*) fond *m*, point *m* extrême.

nag [næg] *vt* (*person*) être toujours après, reprendre sans arrêt ♦ *n* (*pej*: *horse*) canasson *m*; (*person*): **she's an awful** ~ elle est constamment après lui (*or* eux *etc*), elle est terriblement casse-pieds.

nagging ['nægɪŋ] *adj* (*doubt, pain*) persistant(e) ♦ *n* remarques continuelles.

nail [neɪl] *n* (*human*) ongle *m*; (*metal*) clou *m* ♦ *vt* clouer; **to** ~ **sb down to a date/price** contraindre qn à accepter *or* donner une date/un prix; **to pay cash on the ~** (*BRIT*) payer rubis sur l'ongle.

nailbrush ['neɪlbrʌʃ] *n* brosse *f* à ongles.

nailfile ['neɪlfaɪl] *n* lime *f* à ongles.

nail polish *n* vernis *m* à ongles.

nail polish remover *n* dissolvant *m*.

nail scissors *npl* ciseaux *mpl* à ongles.

nail varnish *n* (*BRIT*) = **nail polish**.

Nairobi [naɪˈrəubɪ] *n* Nairobi.

naïve [naɪˈiːv] *adj* naïf(ïve).

naïveté [naɪˈiːvteɪ], **naivety** [naɪˈiːvɪtɪ] *n* naïveté *f*.

naked ['neɪkɪd] *adj* nu(e); **with the ~ eye** à l'œil nu.

nakedness ['neɪkɪdnɪs] *n* nudité *f*.

NAM *n abbr* (*US*) = *National Association of Manufacturers*.

name [neɪm] *n* nom *m*; (*reputation*) réputation *f* ♦ *vt* nommer; citer; (*price, date*) fixer, donner; **by ~** par son nom; de nom; **in the ~ of** au nom de; **what's your ~?** quel est votre nom?; **my ~ is Peter** je m'appelle Peter; **to take sb's ~ and address** relever l'identité de qn *or* les nom et adresse de qn; **to make a ~ for o.s.** se faire un nom; **to get (o.s.) a bad ~** se faire une mauvaise réputation; **to call sb ~s** traiter qn de tous les noms.

name dropping *n* mention (*pour se faire valoir*) *du nom de personnalités qu'on connaît (ou prétend connaître)*.

nameless ['neɪmlɪs] *adj* sans nom; (*witness, contributor*) anonyme.

namely ['neɪmlɪ] *adv* à savoir.

nameplate ['neɪmpleɪt] *n* (*on door etc*) plaque *f*.

namesake ['neɪmseɪk] *n* homonyme *m*.

nan bread [nɑː-] *n* nan *m*.

nanny ['nænɪ] *n* bonne *f* d'enfants.

nanny goat *n* chèvre *f*.

nap [næp] *n* (*sleep*) (petit) somme ♦ *vi:* **to be caught ~ping** être pris(e) à l'improviste *or* en défaut.

NAPA *n abbr* (*US*: = *National Association of Performing Artists*) *syndicat des gens du spectacle.*

napalm ['neɪpɑːm] *n* napalm *m*.

nape [neɪp] *n:* **~ of the neck** nuque *f*.

napkin ['næpkɪn] *n* serviette *f* (de table).

Naples ['neɪplz] *n* Naples.

Napoleonic [nəpəulɪˈɔnɪk] *adj* napoléonien(ne).

nappy ['næpɪ] *n* (*BRIT*) couche *f* (*gen pl*).

nappy liner *n* (*BRIT*) protège-couche *m*.

narcissistic [nɑːsɪˈsɪstɪk] *adj* narcissique.

narcissus, *pl* **narcissi** [nɑːˈsɪsəs, -saɪ] *n* narcisse *m*.

narcotic [nɑːˈkɔtɪk] *n* (*MED*) narcotique *m*; **~s** *npl* (*drugs*) stupéfiants *mpl*.

nark [nɑːk] *vt* (*BRIT col*) mettre en rogne.

narrate [nəˈreɪt] *vt* raconter, narrer.

narration [nəˈreɪʃən] *n* narration *f*.

narrative ['nærətɪv] *n* récit *m* ♦ *adj* narra-

tif(ive).

narrator [nəˈreɪtə*] *n* narrateur/trice.

narrow ['nærəu] *adj* étroit(e); (*fig*) restreint(e), limité(e) ♦ *vi* devenir plus étroit, se rétrécir; **to have a ~ escape** l'échapper belle; **to ~ sth down to** réduire qch à.

narrow gauge *n* (*RAIL*) à voie étroite.

narrowly ['nærəulɪ] *adv:* **he ~ missed injury/the tree** il a failli se blesser/rentrer dans l'arbre; **he only ~ missed the target** il a manqué la cible de peu *or* de justesse.

narrow-minded [nærəuˈmaɪndɪd] *adj* à l'esprit étroit, borné(e).

NAS *n abbr* (*US*) = *National Academy of Sciences*.

NASA ['næsə] *n abbr* (*US:* = *National Aeronautics and Space Administration*) NASA *f*.

nasal ['neɪzl] *adj* nasal(e).

Nassau ['næsɔː] *n* (*in Bahamas*) Nassau.

nastily ['nɑːstɪlɪ] *adv* (*say, act*) méchamment.

nastiness ['nɑːstɪnɪs] *n* (*of person, remark*) méchanceté *f*.

nasturtium [nəsˈtəːʃəm] *n* capucine *f*.

nasty ['nɑːstɪ] *adj* (*person*) méchant(e); très désagréable; (*smell*) dégoûtant(e); (*wound, situation*) mauvais(e), vilain(e); (*weather*) affreux(euse); **to turn ~** (*situation*) mal tourner; (*weather*) se gâter; (*person*) devenir méchant; **it's a ~ business** c'est une sale affaire.

NAS/UWT *n abbr* (*BRIT:* = *National Association of Schoolmasters/Union of Women Teachers*) *syndicat enseignant.*

nation ['neɪʃən] *n* nation *f*.

national ['næʃənl] *adj* national(e) ♦ *n* (*abroad*) ressortissant/e; (*when home*) national/e.

national anthem *n* hymne national.

National Curriculum *n* (*BRIT*) *programme scolaire commun à toutes les écoles publiques en Angleterre et au Pays de Galles comprenant dix disciplines.*

national debt *n* dette publique.

national dress *n* costume national.

National Guard *n* (*US*) milice *f* (*de volontaires dans chaque État*).

National Health Service (NHS) *n* (*BRIT*) *service national de santé,* ≈ Sécurité Sociale.

National Insurance *n* (*BRIT*) ≈ Sécurité Sociale.

nationalism ['næʃnəlɪzəm] *n* nationalisme *m*.

nationalist ['næʃnəlɪst] *adj, n* nationaliste (*m/f*).

nationality [næʃəˈnælɪtɪ] *n* nationalité *f*.

nationalization [næʃnəlaɪˈzeɪʃən] *n* nationalisation *f*.

nationalize ['næʃnəlaɪz] *vt* nationaliser.

nationally ['næʃnəlɪ] *adv* du point de vue national; dans le pays entier.

national park *n* parc national.

national press *n* presse nationale.

National Security Council *n* (*US*) conseil national de sécurité.

national service *n* (*MIL*) service *m* militaire.

> Le **National Trust** est un organisme indépendant, à but non lucratif, dont la mission est de protéger et de mettre en valeur les monuments et les sites britanniques en raison de leur intérêt historique ou de leur beauté naturelle.

nation-wide ['neɪʃənwaɪd] adj s'étendant à l'ensemble du pays; (problem) à l'échelle du pays entier ♦ adv à travers or dans tout le pays.

native ['neɪtɪv] n habitant/e du pays, autochtone m/f; (in colonies) indigène m/f ♦ adj du pays, indigène; (country) natal(e); (language) maternel(le); (ability) inné(e); **a ~ of Russia** une personne originaire de Russie; **a ~ speaker of French** une personne de langue maternelle française.

Native American n Indien/ne d'Amérique.

Nativity [nə'tɪvɪtɪ] n (REL): **the ~** la Nativité.

nativity play n mystère m or miracle m de la Nativité.

NATO ['neɪtəu] n abbr (= North Atlantic Treaty Organization) OTAN f.

natter ['nætə*] vi (BRIT) bavarder.

natural ['nætʃrəl] adj naturel(le); **to die of ~ causes** mourir d'une mort naturelle.

natural childbirth n accouchement m sans douleur.

natural gas n gaz naturel.

natural history n histoire naturelle.

naturalist ['nætʃrəlɪst] n naturaliste m/f.

naturalization ['nætʃrəlaɪ'zeɪʃən] n naturalisation f; acclimatation f.

naturalize ['nætʃrəlaɪz] vt naturaliser; (plant) acclimater; **to become ~d** (person) se faire naturaliser.

naturally ['nætʃrəlɪ] adv naturellement.

naturalness ['nætʃrəlnɪs] n naturel m.

natural resources npl ressources naturelles.

natural selection n sélection naturelle.

natural wastage n (INDUSTRY) départs naturels et volontaires.

nature ['neɪtʃə*] n nature f; **by ~** par tempérament, de nature; **documents of a confidential ~** documents à caractère confidentiel.

-natured ['neɪtʃəd] suffix: **ill~** qui a un mauvais caractère.

nature reserve n (BRIT) réserve naturelle.

nature trail n sentier de découverte de la nature.

naturist ['neɪtʃərɪst] n naturiste m/f.

naught [nɔːt] n = **nought**.

naughtiness ['nɔːtɪnɪs] n (of child) désobéissance f; (of story etc) grivoiserie f.

naughty ['nɔːtɪ] adj (child) vilain(e), pas sage; (story, film) grivois(e).

nausea ['nɔːsɪə] n nausée f.

nauseate ['nɔːsɪeɪt] vt écœurer, donner la nausée à.

nauseating ['nɔːsɪeɪtɪŋ] adj écœurant(e), dégoûtant(e).

nauseous ['nɔːsɪəs] adj nauséabond(e), écœurant(e); (feeling sick): **to be ~** avoir des nausées.

nautical ['nɔːtɪkl] adj nautique.

nautical mile n mille marin (= 1853 m).

naval ['neɪvl] adj naval(e).

naval officer n officier m de marine.

nave [neɪv] n nef f.

navel ['neɪvl] n nombril m.

navigable ['nævɪgəbl] adj navigable.

navigate ['nævɪgeɪt] vt diriger, piloter ♦ vi naviguer; (AUT) indiquer la route à suivre.

navigation [nævɪ'geɪʃən] n navigation f.

navigator ['nævɪgeɪtə*] n navigateur m.

navvy ['nævɪ] n (BRIT) terrassier m.

navy ['neɪvɪ] n marine f; **Department of the N~** (US) ministère m de la Marine.

navy(-blue) ['neɪvɪ('bluː)] adj bleu marine inv.

Nazareth ['næzərɪθ] n Nazareth.

Nazi ['nɑːtsɪ] adj nazi(e) ♦ n Nazi/e.

NB abbr (= nota bene) NB; (Canada) = New Brunswick.

NBA n abbr (US) = National Basketball Association, National Boxing Association.

NBC n abbr (US: = National Broadcasting Company) chaîne de télévision.

NBS n abbr (US: = National Bureau of Standards) office de normalisation.

NC abbr (COMM etc) = no charge; (US) = North Carolina.

NCC n abbr (BRIT: = Nature Conservancy Council) organisme de protection de la nature; (US) = National Council of Churches.

NCCL n abbr (BRIT: = National Council for Civil Liberties) association de défense des libertés publiques.

NCO n abbr = **non-commissioned officer.**

ND, N. Dak. abbr (US) = North Dakota.

NE abbr (US) = Nebraska, New England.

NEA n abbr (US) = National Education Association.

neap [niːp] n (also: ~tide) mortes-eaux fpl.

Neapolitan [nɪə'pɒlɪtən] adj napolitain(e) ♦ n Napolitain/e.

near [nɪə*] adj proche ♦ adv près ♦ prep (also: ~ to) près de ♦ vt approcher de; ~ **here/there** près d'ici/non loin de là; **£25,000 or ~est offer** (BRIT) 25 000 livres à débattre; **in the ~ future** dans un proche avenir; **the building is ~ing completion** le bâtiment est presque terminé; **to come ~** vi s'approcher.

nearby [nɪə'baɪ] adj proche ♦ adv tout près, à proximité.

Near East n: **the ~** le Proche-Orient.

nearer ['nɪərə*] adj plus proche ♦ adv plus près.

nearly ['nɪəlɪ] adv presque; **I ~ fell** j'ai failli tomber; **it's not ~ big enough** ce n'est vraiment pas assez grand, c'est loin d'être assez grand.

near miss n collision évitée de justesse; (when aiming) coup manqué de peu or de justesse.

nearness ['nɪənɪs] *n* proximité *f*.

nearside ['nɪəsaɪd] (*AUT*) *n* (*right-hand drive*) côté *m* gauche; (*left-hand drive*) côté droit ♦ *adj* de gauche; de droite.

near-sighted [nɪə'saɪtɪd] *adj* myope.

neat [niːt] *adj* (*person, work*) soigné(e); (*room etc*) bien tenu(e) *or* rangé(e); (*solution, plan*) habile; (*spirits*) pur(e); **I drink it** ~ je le bois sec *or* sans eau.

neatly ['niːtlɪ] *adv* avec soin *or* ordre; habilement.

neatness ['niːtnɪs] *n* (*tidiness*) netteté *f*; (*skilfulness*) habileté *f*.

Nebr. *abbr* (*US*) = Nebraska.

nebulous ['nɛbjuləs] *adj* nébuleux(euse).

necessarily ['nɛsɪsrɪlɪ] *adv* nécessairement; **not** ~ pas nécessairement *or* forcément.

necessary ['nɛsɪsrɪ] *adj* nécessaire; **if** ~ si besoin est, le cas échéant.

necessitate [nɪ'sɛsɪteɪt] *vt* nécessiter.

necessity [nɪ'sɛsɪtɪ] *n* nécessité *f*; chose nécessaire *or* essentielle; **in case of** ~ en cas d'urgence.

neck [nɛk] *n* cou *m*; (*of horse, garment*) encolure *f*; (*of bottle*) goulot *m* ♦ *vi* (*col*) se peloter; ~ **and** ~ à égalité; **to stick one's** ~ **out** (*col*) se mouiller.

necklace ['nɛklɪs] *n* collier *m*.

neckline ['nɛklaɪn] *n* encolure *f*.

necktie ['nɛktaɪ] *n* (*esp US*) cravate *f*.

nectar ['nɛktə*] *n* nectar *m*.

nectarine ['nɛktərɪn] *n* brugnon *m*, nectarine *f*.

NEDC *n abbr* (*BRIT*: = National Economic Development Council*) conseil national pour le développement économique.

Neddy ['nɛdɪ] *n abbr* (*BRIT col*) = NEDC.

née [neɪ] *adj*: ~ **Scott** née Scott.

need [niːd] *n* besoin *m* ♦ *vt* avoir besoin de; **to** ~ **to do** devoir faire; avoir besoin de faire; **you don't** ~ **to go** vous n'avez pas besoin *or* vous n'êtes pas obligé de partir; **a signature is** ~**ed** il faut une signature; **to be in** ~ **of** *or* **have** ~ **of** avoir besoin de; **£10 will meet my immediate** ~**s** 10 livres suffiront pour mes besoins immédiats; **in case of** ~ en cas de besoin, au besoin; **there's no** ~ **to do** ... il n'y a pas lieu de faire ..., il n'est pas nécessaire de faire ...; **there's no** ~ **for that** ce n'est pas la peine, cela n'est pas nécessaire.

needle ['niːdl] *n* aiguille *f*; (*on record player*) saphir *m* ♦ *vt* (*col*) asticoter, tourmenter.

needlecord ['niːdlkɔːd] *n* (*BRIT*) velours *m* milleraies.

needless ['niːdlɪs] *adj* inutile; ~ **to say,** ... inutile de dire que ....

needlessly ['niːdlɪslɪ] *adv* inutilement.

needlework ['niːdlwɜːk] *n* (*activity*) travaux *mpl* d'aiguille; (*object*) ouvrage *m*.

needn't ['niːdnt] = need not.

needy ['niːdɪ] *adj* nécessiteux(euse).

negation [nɪ'geɪʃən] *n* négation *f*.

negative ['nɛgətɪv] *n* (*PHOT, ELEC*) négatif *m*; (*LING*) terme *m* de négation ♦ *adj* négatif(ive); **to answer in the** ~ répondre par la négative.

negative equity *n* situation dans laquelle la valeur d'une maison est inférieure à celle de l'emprunt-logement contracté pour la payer.

neglect [nɪ'glɛkt] *vt* négliger ♦ *n* (*of person, duty, garden*) le fait de négliger; (*state of*) ~ abandon *m*; **to** ~ **to do sth** négliger *or* omettre de faire qch.

neglected [nɪ'glɛktɪd] *adj* négligé(e), à l'abandon.

neglectful [nɪ'glɛktful] *adj* (*gen*) négligent(e); **to be** ~ **of sb/sth** négliger qn/qch.

negligee ['nɛglɪʒeɪ] *n* déshabillé *m*.

negligence ['nɛglɪdʒəns] *n* négligence *f*.

negligent ['nɛglɪdʒənt] *adj* négligent(e).

negligently ['nɛglɪdʒəntlɪ] *adv* par négligence; (*offhandedly*) négligemment.

negligible ['nɛglɪdʒɪbl] *adj* négligeable.

negotiable [nɪ'gəuʃɪəbl] *adj* négociable; **not** ~ (*cheque*) non négociable.

negotiate [nɪ'gəuʃɪeɪt] *vi* négocier ♦ *vt* (*COMM*) négocier; (*obstacle*) franchir; négocier; (*bend in road*) négocier; **to** ~ **with sb for sth** négocier avec qn en vue d'obtenir qch.

negotiating table [nɪ'gəuʃɪeɪtɪŋ-] *n* table *f* des négociations.

negotiation [nɪgəuʃɪ'eɪʃən] *n* négociation *f*, pourparlers *mpl*; **to enter into** ~**s with sb** engager des négociations avec qn.

negotiator [nɪ'gəuʃɪeɪtə*] *n* négociateur/trice *f*.

Negress ['niːgrɪs] *n* négresse *f*.

Negro ['niːgrəu] *adj* (*gen*) noir(e); (*music, arts*) nègre, noir ♦ *n* (*pl*: ~**es**) Noir/e.

neigh [neɪ] *vi* hennir.

neighbour, (*US*) **neighbor** ['neɪbə*] *n* voisin/e.

neighbo(u)rhood ['neɪbəhud] *n* quartier *m*; voisinage *m*.

neighbourhood watch *n* (*BRIT*: also: ~ **scheme**) système de surveillance, assuré par les habitants d'un même quartier.

neighbo(u)ring ['neɪbərɪŋ] *adj* voisin(e), avoisinant(e).

neighbo(u)rly ['neɪbəlɪ] *adj* obligeant(e); (*relations*) de bon voisinage.

neither ['naɪðə*] *adj, pron* aucun(e) (des deux), ni l'un(e) ni l'autre ♦ *conj*: **I didn't move and** ~ **did Claude** je n'ai pas bougé, (et) Claude non plus ♦ *adv*: ~ **good nor bad** ni bon ni mauvais; ..., ~ **did I refuse** ..., (et *or* mais) je n'ai pas non plus refusé.

neo... ['niːəu] *prefix* néo-.

neolithic [niːəu'lɪθɪk] *adj* néolithique.

neologism [nɪ'ɔlədʒɪzəm] *n* néologisme *m*.

neon ['niːɔn] *n* néon *m*.

neon light *n* lampe *f* au néon.

neon sign *n* enseigne (lumineuse) au néon.

Nepal [nɪ'pɔːl] *n* Népal *m*.

nephew ['nɛvjuː] n neveu m.

nepotism ['nɛpətɪzəm] n népotisme m.

nerd [nɜːd] n (col) pauvre mec m, ballot m.

nerve [nɜːv] n nerf m; (bravery) sang-froid m, courage m; (cheek) aplomb m, toupet m; **he gets on my ~s** il m'énerve; **to have a fit of ~s** avoir le trac; **to lose one's ~** (self-confidence) perdre son sang-froid.

nerve centre n (ANAT) centre nerveux; (fig) centre névralgique.

nerve gas n gaz m neuroplégique.

nerve-racking ['nɜːvrækɪŋ] adj angoissant(e).

nervous ['nɜːvəs] adj nerveux(euse); (apprehensive) inquiet(ète), plein(e) d'appréhension.

nervous breakdown n dépression nerveuse.

nervously ['nɜːvəslɪ] adv nerveusement.

nervousness ['nɜːvəsnɪs] n nervosité f; inquiétude f, appréhension f.

nervous wreck n: **to be a ~** être une boule de nerfs.

nervy ['nɜːvɪ] adj: **he's very ~** il a les nerfs à fleur de peau or à vif.

nest [nɛst] n nid m ♦ vi (se) nicher, faire son nid; **~ of tables** table f gigogne.

nest egg n (fig) bas m de laine, magot m.

nestle ['nɛsl] vi se blottir.

nestling ['nɛstlɪŋ] n oisillon m.

net [nɛt] n (also fabric) filet m ♦ adj net(te) ♦ vt (fish etc) prendre au filet; (money: subj: person) toucher; (: deal, sale) rapporter; **~ of tax** net d'impôt; **he earns £10,000 ~ per year** il gagne 10 000 livres net par an.

netball ['nɛtbɔːl] n netball m.

net curtains npl voilages mpl.

Netherlands ['nɛðələndz] npl: **the ~** les Pays-Bas mpl.

net profit n bénéfice net.

nett [nɛt] adj = **net**.

netting ['nɛtɪŋ] n (for fence etc) treillis m, grillage m; (fabric) voile m.

nettle ['nɛtl] n ortie f.

network ['nɛtwɜːk] n réseau m ♦ vt (RADIO, TV) diffuser sur l'ensemble du réseau; (computers) interconnecter.

neuralgia [njuə'ræld3ə] n névralgie f.

neurological [njuərə'lɔdʒɪkl] adj neurologique.

neurosis, pl **neuroses** [njuə'rəusɪs, -siːz] n névrose f.

neurotic [njuə'rɔtɪk] adj, n névrosé(e).

neuter ['njuːtə*] adj, n neutre (m) ♦ vt (cat etc) châtrer, couper.

neutral ['njuːtrəl] adj neutre ♦ n (AUT) point mort.

neutrality [njuː'trælɪtɪ] n neutralité f.

neutralize ['njuːtrəlaɪz] vt neutraliser.

neutron bomb ['njuːtrɔn-] n bombe f à neutrons.

Nev. abbr (US) = Nevada.

never ['nɛvə*] adv (ne ...) jamais; **~ again** plus jamais; **~ in my life** jamais de ma vie; see also **mind**.

never-ending [nɛvər'ɛndɪŋ] adj interminable.

nevertheless [nɛvəðə'lɛs] adv néanmoins, malgré tout.

new [njuː] adj nouveau(nouvelle); (brand new) neuf(neuve); **as good as ~** comme neuf.

New Age n New Age m.

newborn ['njuːbɔːn] adj nouveau-né(e).

newcomer ['njuːkʌmə*] n nouveau venu/nouvelle venue.

new-fangled ['njuːfæŋgld] adj (pej) ultramoderne (et farfelu(e)).

new-found ['njuːfaund] adj de fraîche date; (friend) nouveau(nouvelle).

Newfoundland ['njuːfənlənd] n Terre-Neuve f.

New Guinea n Nouvelle-Guinée f.

newly ['njuːlɪ] adv nouvellement, récemment.

newly-weds ['njuːlɪwɛdz] npl jeunes mariés mpl.

new moon n nouvelle lune.

newness ['njuːnɪs] n nouveauté f; (of fabric, clothes etc) état neuf.

New Orleans [-'ɔːliːənz] n la Nouvelle-Orléans.

news [njuːz] n nouvelle(s) f(pl); (RADIO, TV) informations fpl; **a piece of ~** une nouvelle; **good/bad ~** bonne/mauvaise nouvelle; **financial ~** (PRESS, RADIO, TV) page financière.

news agency n agence f de presse.

newsagent ['njuːzeɪdʒənt] n (BRIT) marchand m de journaux.

news bulletin n (RADIO, TV) bulletin m d'informations.

newscaster ['njuːzkɑːstə*] n (RADIO, TV) présentateur/trice.

newsdealer ['njuːzdiːlə*] n (US) = **newsagent**.

news flash n flash m d'information.

newsletter ['njuːzlɛtə*] n bulletin m.

newspaper ['njuːzpeɪpə*] n journal m; **daily ~** quotidien m; **weekly ~** hebdomadaire m.

newsprint ['njuːzprɪnt] n papier m (de) journal.

newsreader ['njuːzriːdə*] n = **newscaster**.

newsreel ['njuːzriːl] n actualités (filmées).

newsroom ['njuːzruːm] n (PRESS) salle f de rédaction; (RADIO, TV) studio m.

news stand n kiosque m à journaux.

newsworthy ['njuːzwɜːðɪ] adj: **to be ~** valoir la peine d'être publié.

newt [njuːt] n triton m.

new town n (BRIT) ville nouvelle.

New Year n Nouvel An; **Happy ~!** Bonne Année!; **to wish sb a happy ~** souhaiter la Bonne Année à qn.

New Year's Day n le jour de l'An.

New Year's Eve n la Saint-Sylvestre.

New York [-'jɔːk] n New York; (also: **~ State**) New York m.

New Zealand [-'ziːlənd] n Nouvelle-Zélande f ♦ adj néo-zélandais(e).

New Zealander [-'zi:ləndə*] *n* Néo-Zélandais/e.

next [nɛkst] *adj* (*seat, room*) voisin(e), d'à côté; (*meeting, bus stop*) suivant(e); prochain(e) ♦ *adv* la fois suivante; la prochaine fois; (*afterwards*) ensuite; ~ **to** *prep* à côté de; ~ **to nothing** presque rien; ~ **time** *adv* la prochaine fois; **the** ~ **day** le lendemain, le jour suivant *or* d'après; ~ **week** la semaine prochaine; **the** ~ **week** la semaine suivante; ~ **year** l'année prochaine; "**turn to the** ~ **page**" "voir page suivante"; **who's** ~? c'est à qui?; **the week after** ~ dans deux semaines; **when do we meet** ~? quand nous revoyons-nous?

next door *adv* à côté.

next-of-kin ['nɛkstəv'kın] *n* parent *m* le plus proche.

NF *n abbr* (*BRIT POL*: = *National Front*) ≈ FN ♦ *abbr* (*Canada*) = *Newfoundland*.

NFL *n abbr* (*US*) = *National Football League*.

Nfld. *abbr* (*Canada*) = *Newfoundland*.

NG *abbr* (*US*) = **National Guard**.

NGO *n abbr* (*US*: = *non-governmental organization*) ONG *f*.

NH *abbr* (*US*) = *New Hampshire*.

NHL *n abbr* (*US*) = *National Hockey League*.

NHS *n abbr* (*BRIT*) = **National Health Service**.

NI *abbr* = **Northern Ireland**; (*BRIT*) = **National Insurance**.

Niagara Falls [naɪ'æɡərə-] *npl*: **the** ~ les chutes *fpl* du Niagara.

nib [nɪb] *n* (*of pen*) (bec *m* de) plume *f*.

nibble ['nɪbl] *vt* grignoter.

Nicaragua [nɪkə'ræɡjuə] *n* Nicaragua *m*.

Nicaraguan [nɪkə'ræɡjuən] *adj* nicaraguayen(ne) ♦ *n* Nicaraguayen/ne.

nice [naɪs] *adj* (*holiday, trip, taste*) agréable; (*flat, picture*) joli(e); (*person*) gentil(le); (*distinction, point*) subtil(e).

nice-looking ['naɪslukɪŋ] *adj* joli(e).

nicely ['naɪslɪ] *adv* agréablement; joliment; gentiment; subtilement; **that will do** ~ ce sera parfait.

niceties ['naɪsɪtɪz] *npl* subtilités *fpl*.

niche [ni:ʃ] *n* (*ARCHIT*) niche *f*.

nick [nɪk] *n* encoche *f*; (*BRIT col*): **in good** ~ en bon état ♦ *vt* (*cut*): **to** ~ **o.s.** se couper; (*col: steal*) faucher, piquer; (: *BRIT: arrest*) choper, pincer; **in the** ~ **of time** juste à temps.

nickel ['nɪkl] *n* nickel *m*; (*US*) pièce *f* de 5 cents.

nickname ['nɪkneɪm] *n* surnom *m* ♦ *vt* surnommer.

Nicosia [nɪkə'si:ə] *n* Nicosie.

nicotine ['nɪkəti:n] *n* nicotine *f*.

nicotine patch *n* timbre *m* anti-tabac, patch *m*.

niece [ni:s] *n* nièce *f*.

nifty ['nɪftɪ] *adj* (*col: car, jacket*) qui a du chic *or* de la classe; (: *gadget, tool*) astucieux(euse).

Niger ['naɪdʒə*] *n* (*country, river*) Niger *m*.

Nigeria [naɪ'dʒɪərɪə] *n* Nigéria *m or f*.

Nigerian [naɪ'dʒɪərɪən] *adj* nigérien(ne) ♦ *n* Nigérien/ne.

niggardly ['nɪɡədlɪ] *adj* (*person*) parcimonieux(euse), pingre; (*allowance, amount*) misérable.

nigger ['nɪɡə*] *n* (*col!: highly offensive*) nègre/négresse.

niggle ['nɪɡl] *vt* tracasser ♦ *vi* (*find fault*) trouver toujours à redire; (*fuss*) n'être jamais content(e).

niggling ['nɪɡlɪŋ] *adj* tatillon(ne); (*detail*) insignifiant(e); (*doubt, pain*) persistant(e).

night [naɪt] *n* nuit *f*; (*evening*) soir *m*; **at** ~ la nuit; **by** ~ de nuit; **in the** ~, **during the** ~ pendant la nuit; **the** ~ **before last** avant-hier soir.

night-bird ['naɪtbə:d] *n* oiseau *m* nocturne; (*fig*) couche-tard *m inv*, noctambule *m/f*.

nightcap ['naɪtkæp] *n* boisson prise avant le coucher.

night club *n* boîte *f* de nuit.

nightdress ['naɪtdrɛs] *n* chemise *f* de nuit.

nightfall ['naɪtfɔ:l] *n* tombée *f* de la nuit.

nightie ['naɪtɪ] *n* chemise *f* de nuit.

nightingale ['naɪtɪŋɡeɪl] *n* rossignol *m*.

night life *n* vie *f* nocturne.

nightly ['naɪtlɪ] *adj* de chaque nuit *or* soir; (*by night*) nocturne ♦ *adv* chaque nuit *or* soir; nuitamment.

nightmare ['naɪtmɛə*] *n* cauchemar *m*.

night porter *n* gardien *m* de nuit, concierge *m* de service la nuit.

night safe *n* coffre *m* de nuit.

night school *n* cours *mpl* du soir.

nightshade ['naɪtʃeɪd] *n*: **deadly** ~ (*BOT*) belladone *f*.

nightshift ['naɪtʃɪft] *n* équipe *f* de nuit.

night-time ['naɪttaɪm] *n* nuit *f*.

night watchman *n* veilleur *m* de nuit; poste *m* de nuit.

nihilism ['naɪɪlɪzəm] *n* nihilisme *m*.

nil [nɪl] *n* rien *m*; (*BRIT SPORT*) zéro *m*.

Nile [naɪl] *n*: **the** ~ le Nil.

nimble ['nɪmbl] *adj* agile.

nine [naɪn] *num* neuf.

nineteen [naɪn'ti:n] *num* dix-neuf.

ninety ['naɪntɪ] *num* quatre-vingt-dix.

ninth [naɪnθ] *num* neuvième.

nip [nɪp] *vt* pincer ♦ *vi* (*BRIT col*): **to** ~ **out/down/up** sortir/descendre/monter en vitesse ♦ *n* pincement *m*; (*drink*) petit verre; **to** ~ **into a shop** faire un saut dans un magasin.

nipple ['nɪpl] *n* (*ANAT*) mamelon *m*, bout *m* du sein.

nippy ['nɪpɪ] *adj* (*BRIT: person*) alerte, leste; (: *car*) nerveux(euse).

nit [nɪt] *n* (*in hair*) lente *f*; (*col: idiot*) imbécile *m/f*, crétin/e.

nit-pick ['nɪtpɪk] *vi* (*col*) être tatillon(ne).

nitrogen ['naɪtrədʒən] *n* azote *m*.

nitroglycerin(e) ['naɪtrəu'glɪsəriːn] n nitroglycérine f.

nitty-gritty ['nɪtɪ'grɪtɪ] n (fam): **to get down to the** ~ en venir au fond du problème.

nitwit ['nɪtwɪt] n (col) nigaud/e.

NJ abbr (US) = New Jersey.

NLF n abbr (= National Liberation Front) FLN m.

NLQ abbr (= near letter quality) qualité f courrier.

NLRB n abbr (US: = National Labor Relations Board) organisme de protection des travailleurs.

NM, N. Mex. abbr (US) = New Mexico.

══════════════ KEYWORD ══════════════

no [nəu] (pl ~**es**) adv (opposite of "yes") non; **are you coming?** — ~ **(I'm not)** est-ce que vous venez? — non; **would you like some more?** — ~ **thank you** vous en voulez encore? — non merci

♦ adj (not any) pas de, aucun(e) (used with "ne"); **I have** ~ **money/books** je n'ai pas d'argent/de livres; ~ **student would have done it** aucun étudiant ne l'aurait fait; "~ **smoking**" "défense de fumer"; "~ **dogs**" "les chiens ne sont pas admis"

♦ n non m; **I won't take** ~ **for an answer** n'est pas question de refuser.

no. abbr (= number) nº.

nobble ['nɔbl] vt (BRIT col: bribe: person) soudoyer, acheter; (: person: to speak to) mettre le grappin sur; (RACING: horse, dog) droguer (pour l'empêcher de gagner).

Nobel prize [nəu'bɛl-] n prix m Nobel.

nobility [nəu'bɪlɪtɪ] n noblesse f.

noble ['nəubl] adj noble.

nobleman ['nəublmən] n noble m.

nobly ['nəublɪ] adv noblement.

nobody ['nəubədɪ] pron personne (with negative).

no-claims bonus ['nəukleɪmz-] n bonus m.

nocturnal [nɔk'tɜːnl] adj nocturne.

nod [nɔd] vi faire un signe de (la) tête (affirmatif ou amical); (sleep) somnoler ♦ vt: **to** ~ **one's head** faire un signe de (la) tête; (in agreement) faire signe que oui ♦ n signe m de (la) tête; **they** ~**ded their agreement** ils ont acquiescé d'un signe de la tête.

▶**nod off** vi s'assoupir.

no-fly zone [nəu'flaɪ-] n zone interdite (aux avions et hélicoptères).

noise [nɔɪz] n bruit m.

noiseless ['nɔɪzlɪs] adj silencieux(euse).

noisily ['nɔɪzɪlɪ] adv bruyamment.

noisy ['nɔɪzɪ] adj bruyant(e).

nomad ['nəumæd] n nomade m/f.

nomadic [nəu'mædɪk] adj nomade.

no man's land n no man's land m.

nominal ['nɔmɪnl] adj (rent, fee) symbolique; (value) nominal(e).

nominate ['nɔmɪneɪt] vt (propose) proposer; (elect) nommer.

nomination [nɔmɪ'neɪʃən] n nomination f.

nominee [nɔmɪ'niː] n candidat agréé; personne nommée.

non- [nɔn] prefix non-.

nonalcoholic [nɔnælkə'hɔlɪk] adj nonalcoolisé(e).

nonbreakable [nɔn'breɪkəbl] adj incassable.

nonce word ['nɔns-] n mot créé pour l'occasion.

nonchalant ['nɔnʃələnt] adj nonchalant(e).

noncommissioned [nɔnkə'mɪʃənd] adj: ~ **officer** sous-officier m.

noncommittal [nɔnkə'mɪtl] adj évasif(ive).

nonconformist [nɔnkən'fɔːmɪst] n nonconformiste m/f ♦ adj non-conformiste, dissident(e).

noncontributory [nɔnkən'trɪbjutərɪ] adj: ~ **pension scheme** or (US) **plan** régime de retraite payée par l'employeur.

noncooperation ['nɔnkəuɔpə'reɪʃən] n refus m de coopérer, non-coopération f.

nondescript ['nɔndɪskrɪpt] adj quelconque, indéfinissable.

none [nʌn] pron aucun/e; ~ **of you** aucun d'entre vous, personne parmi vous; **I have** ~ je n'en ai pas; **I have** ~ **left** je n'en ai plus; ~ **at all** (not one) aucun(e); **how much milk?** — ~ **at all** combien de lait? — pas du tout; **he's** ~ **the worse for it** il ne s'en porte pas plus mal.

nonentity [nɔ'nɛntɪtɪ] n personne insignifiante.

nonessential [nɔnɪ'sɛnʃl] adj accessoire, superflu(e) ♦ n: ~**s** le superflu.

nonetheless ['nʌnðə'lɛs] adv néanmoins.

nonevent [nɔnɪ'vɛnt] n événement manqué.

nonexecutive [nɔnɪg'zɛkjutɪv] adj: ~ **director** administrateur/trice, conseiller/ère de direction.

nonexistent [nɔnɪg'zɪstənt] adj inexistant(e).

nonfiction [nɔn'fɪkʃən] n littérature f non-romanesque.

nonflammable [nɔn'flæməbl] adj ininflammable.

nonintervention ['nɔnɪntə'vɛnʃən] n non-intervention f.

no-no ['nəunəu] n (col): **it's a** ~ il n'en est pas question.

non obst. abbr (= non obstante: notwithstanding) nonobstant.

no-nonsense [nəu'nɔnsəns] adj (manner, person) plein(e) de bon sens.

nonpayment [nɔn'peɪmənt] n non-paiement m.

nonplussed [nɔn'plʌst] adj perplexe.

non-profit-making [nɔn'prɔfɪtmeɪkɪŋ] adj à but non lucratif.

nonsense ['nɔnsəns] n absurdités fpl, idioties fpl; ~! ne dites pas d'idioties!; **it is** ~ **to say that** ... il est absurde de dire que ....

nonsensical [nɔn'sɛnsɪkl] adj absurde, qui n'a

pas de sens.

nonshrink [nɔn'ʃrɪŋk] *adj* (*BRIT*) irrétrécissable.

nonskid [nɔn'skɪd] *adj* antidérapant(e).

nonsmoker ['nɔn'sməukə*] *n* non-fumeur *m*.

nonstarter [nɔn'stɑːtə*] *n*: **it's a ~** c'est voué à l'échec.

nonstick ['nɔn'stɪk] *adj* qui n'attache pas.

nonstop ['nɔn'stɔp] *adj* direct(e), sans arrêt (*or* escale) ♦ *adv* sans arrêt.

nontaxable [nɔn'tæksəbl] *adj*: **~ income** revenu *m* non imposable.

non-U ['nɔnjuː] *adj abbr* (*BRIT col*: = *non-upper class*) qui ne se dit (*or* se fait) pas.

nonvolatile [nɔn'vɔlətaɪl] *adj*: **~ memory** (*COMPUT*) mémoire rémanente *or* non volatile.

nonvoting [nɔn'vəutɪŋ] *adj*: **~ shares** actions *fpl* sans droit de vote.

non-white ['nɔn'waɪt] *adj* de couleur ♦ *n* personne *f* de couleur.

no-win situation [nəu'wɪn-] *n* impasse *f*; **we're in a ~** nous sommes dans l'impasse.

noodles ['nuːdlz] *npl* nouilles *fpl*.

nook [nuk] *n*: **~s and crannies** recoins *mpl*.

noon [nuːn] *n* midi *m*.

no one ['nəuwʌn] *pron* = **nobody**.

noose [nuːs] *n* nœud coulant; (*hangman's*) corde *f*.

nor [nɔː*] *conj* = **neither** ♦ *adv see* **neither**.

Norf *abbr* (*BRIT*) = **Norfolk**.

norm [nɔːm] *n* norme *f*.

normal ['nɔːml] *adj* normal(e) ♦ *n*: **to return to ~** redevenir normal(e).

normality [nɔː'mælɪtɪ] *n* normalité *f*.

normally ['nɔːməlɪ] *adv* normalement.

Normandy ['nɔːməndɪ] *n* Normandie *f*.

north [nɔːθ] *n* nord *m* ♦ *adj* du nord, nord *inv* ♦ *adv* au *or* vers le nord.

North Africa *n* Afrique *f* du Nord.

North African *adj* nord-africain(e), d'Afrique du Nord ♦ *n* Nord-Africain/e.

North America *n* Amérique *f* du Nord.

North American *n* Nord-Américain/e ♦ *adj* nord-américain(e), d'Amérique du Nord.

Northants [nɔː'θænts] *abbr* (*BRIT*) = **Northamptonshire**.

northbound ['nɔːθbaund] *adj* (*traffic*) en direction du nord; (*carriageway*) nord *inv*.

Northd *abbr* (*BRIT*) = **Northumberland**.

north-east [nɔːθ'iːst] *n* nord-est *m*.

northerly ['nɔːðəlɪ] *adj* (*wind, direction*) du nord.

northern ['nɔːðən] *adj* du nord, septentrional(e).

Northern Ireland *n* Irlande *f* du Nord.

North Pole *n*: **the ~** le pôle Nord.

North Sea *n*: **the ~** la mer du Nord.

North Sea oil *n* pétrole *m* de la mer du Nord.

northward(s) ['nɔːθwəd(z)] *adv* vers le nord.

north-west [nɔːθ'wɛst] *n* nord-ouest *m*.

Norway ['nɔːweɪ] *n* Norvège *f*.

Norwegian [nɔː'wiːdʒən] *adj* norvégien(ne). ♦ *n* Norvégien/ne; (*LING*) norvégien *m*.

nos. *abbr* (= *numbers*) nᵒˢ.

nose [nəuz] *n* nez *m*; (*fig*) flair *m* ♦ *vi* (*also*: **~ one's way**) avancer précautionneusement; **to pay through the ~ (for sth)** (*col*) payer un prix excessif (pour qch).

▶**nose about, nose around** *vi* fouiner *or* fureter (partout).

nosebleed ['nəuzbliːd] *n* saignement *m* de nez.

nose-dive ['nəuzdaɪv] *n* (descente *f* en) piqué *m*.

nose drops *npl* gouttes *fpl* pour le nez.

nosey ['nəuzɪ] *adj* curieux(euse).

nostalgia [nɔs'tældʒɪə] *n* nostalgie *f*.

nostalgic [nɔs'tældʒɪk] *adj* nostalgique.

nostril ['nɔstrɪl] *n* narine *f*; (*of horse*) naseau *m*.

nosy ['nəuzɪ] *adj* = **nosey**.

not [nɔt] *adv* (ne ...) pas; **I hope ~** j'espère que non; **~ at all** pas du tout; (*after thanks*) de rien; **you must ~** *or* **mustn't do this** tu ne dois pas faire ça; **he isn't** ... il n'est pas ....

notable ['nəutəbl] *adj* notable.

notably ['nəutəblɪ] *adv* en particulier.

notary ['nəutərɪ] *n* (*also*: **~ public**) notaire *m*.

notation [nəu'teɪʃən] *n* notation *f*.

notch [nɔtʃ] *n* encoche *f*.

▶**notch up** *vt* (*score*) marquer; (*victory*) remporter.

note [nəut] *n* note *f*; (*letter*) mot *m*; (*banknote*) billet *m* ♦ *vt* (*also*: **~ down**) noter; (*notice*) constater; **just a quick ~ to let you know** ... juste un mot pour vous dire ...; **to take ~s** prendre des notes; **to compare ~s** (*fig*) échanger des (*or* leurs *etc*) impressions; **to take ~ of** prendre note de; **a person of ~** une personne éminente.

notebook ['nəutbuk] *n* carnet *m*; (*for shorthand etc*) bloc-notes *m*.

note-case ['nəutkeɪs] *n* (*BRIT*) porte-feuille *m*.

noted ['nəutɪd] *adj* réputé(e).

notepad ['nəutpæd] *n* bloc-notes *m*.

notepaper ['nəutpeɪpə*] *n* papier *m* à lettres.

noteworthy ['nəutwəːðɪ] *adj* remarquable.

nothing ['nʌθɪŋ] *n* rien *m*; **he does ~** il ne fait rien; **~ new** rien de nouveau; **for ~** (*free*) pour rien, gratuitement; **~ at all** rien du tout.

notice ['nəutɪs] *n* avis *m*; (*of leaving*) congé *m*; (*BRIT: review: of play etc*) critique *f*, compte rendu *m* ♦ *vt* remarquer, s'apercevoir de; **without ~** sans préavis; **advance ~** préavis *m*; **to give sb ~ of sth** notifier qn de qch; **at short ~** dans un délai très court; **until further ~** jusqu'à nouvel ordre; **to give ~,** **hand in one's ~** (*subj: employee*) donner sa démission, démissionner; **to take ~ of** prêter attention à; **to bring sth to sb's ~** porter qch à la connaissance de qn; **it has come to my ~ that** ... on m'a signalé que ...; **to escape** *or* **avoid ~** (essayer de) passer inaperçu *or* ne pas se faire remarquer.

noticeable ['nəutɪsəbl] *adj* visible.
notice board *n* (*BRIT*) panneau *m* d'affichage.
notification [nəutɪfɪ'keɪʃən] *n* notification *f*.
notify ['nəutɪfaɪ] *vt*: **to ~ sth to sb** notifier qch
à qn; **to ~ sb of sth** avertir qn de qch.
notion ['nəuʃən] *n* idée *f*; (*concept*) notion *f*.
notions ['nəuʃənz] *npl* (*US: haberdashery*) mercerie *f*.
notoriety [nəutə'raɪətɪ] *n* notoriété *f*.
notorious [nəu'tɔːrɪəs] *adj* notoire (*souvent en
mal*).
notoriously [nəu'tɔːrɪəslɪ] *adj* notoirement.
Notts [nɔts] *abbr* (*BRIT*) = Nottinghamshire.
notwithstanding [nɔtwɪθ'stændɪŋ] *adv* néanmoins ♦ *prep* en dépit de.
nougat ['nuːgɑː] *n* nougat *m*.
nought [nɔːt] *n* zéro *m*.
noun [naun] *n* nom *m*.
nourish ['nʌrɪʃ] *vt* nourrir.
nourishing ['nʌrɪʃɪŋ] *adj* nourrissant(e).
nourishment ['nʌrɪʃmənt] *n* nourriture *f*.
Nov. *abbr* (= *November*) nov.
Nova Scotia ['nəuvə'skəuʃə] *n* Nouvelle-
Écosse *f*.
novel ['nɔvl] *n* roman *m* ♦ *adj* nou-
veau(nouvelle), original(e).
novelist ['nɔvəlɪst] *n* romancier *m*.
novelty ['nɔvəltɪ] *n* nouveauté *f*.
November [nəu'vɛmbə*] *n* novembre *m*; *for
phrases see also* **July**.
novice ['nɔvɪs] *n* novice *m/f*.
NOW [nau] *n abbr* (*US*) = National Organization
for Women.
now [nau] *adv* maintenant ♦ *conj*: ~ **(that)**
maintenant (que); **right ~** tout de suite; **by
~** à l'heure qu'il est; **just ~**: **that's the fashion just ~** c'est la mode en ce moment *or*
maintenant; **I saw her just ~** je viens de la
voir, je l'ai vue à l'instant; **I'll read it just ~**
je vais le lire à l'instant *or* dès maintenant;
~ and then, **~ and again** de temps en temps;
from ~ on dorénavant; **in 3 days from ~**
dans *or* d'ici trois jours; **be-
tween ~ and Monday** d'ici (à) lundi; **that's all
for ~** c'est tout pour l'instant.
nowadays ['nauədeɪz] *adv* de nos jours.
nowhere ['nəuwɛə*] *adv* nulle part; **~ else**
nulle part ailleurs.
noxious ['nɔkʃəs] *adj* toxique.
nozzle ['nɔzl] *n* (*of hose*) jet *m*, lance *f*.
NP *n abbr* = **notary public.**
NS *abbr* (*Canada*) = Nova Scotia.
NSC *n abbr* (*US*) = **National Security Council.**
NSF *n abbr* (*US*) = National Science Foundation.
NSPCC *n abbr* (*BRIT*) = National Society for the
Prevention of Cruelty to Children.
NSW *abbr* (*Australia*) = New South Wales.
NT *n abbr* (= *New Testament*) NT *m* ♦ *abbr* (*Cana-
da*) = Northwest Territories.
nth [ɛnθ] *adj*: **for the ~ time** (*col*) pour la
énième fois.
nuance ['njuːɑːns] *n* nuance *f*.

nubile ['njuːbaɪl] *adj* nubile; (*attractive*) jeune
et désirable.
nuclear ['njuːklɪə*] *adj* nucléaire.
nuclear disarmament *n* désarmement *m* nucléaire.
nuclear family *n* famille *f* nucléaire.
nuclear-free zone ['njuːklɪə'friː-] *n* zone *f* où
le nucléaire est interdit.
nucleus, *pl* **nuclei** ['njuːklɪəs, 'njuːklɪaɪ] *n*
noyau *m*.
NUCPS *n abbr* (*BRIT*: = National Union of Civil
and Public Servants*) syndicat des fonctionnaires.
nude [njuːd] *adj* nu(e) ♦ *n* (*ART*) nu *m*; **in the ~**
(tout(e)) nu(e).
nudge [nʌdʒ] *vt* donner un (petit) coup de
coude à.
nudist ['njuːdɪst] *n* nudiste *m/f*.
nudist colony *n* colonie *f* de nudistes.
nudity ['njuːdɪtɪ] *n* nudité *f*.
nugget ['nʌgɪt] *n* pépite *f*.
nuisance ['njuːsns] *n*: **it's a ~** c'est (très) ennuyeux *or* gênant; **he's a ~** il est assom-
mant *or* casse-pieds; **what a ~!** quelle
barbe!
NUJ *n abbr* (*BRIT*: = National Union of Journalists*) syndicat des journalistes.
nuke [njuːk] *n* (*col*) bombe *f* atomique.
null [nʌl] *adj*: **~ and void** nul(le) et non ave-
nu(e).
nullify ['nʌlɪfaɪ] *vt* invalider.
NUM *n abbr* (*BRIT*: = National Union of Mineworkers*) syndicat des mineurs.
numb [nʌm] *adj* engourdi(e) ♦ *vt* engourdir; **~
with cold** engourdi(e) par le froid, transi(e)
(de froid); **~ with fear** transi de peur, para-
lysé(e) par la peur.
number ['nʌmbə*] *n* nombre *m*; (*numeral*)
chiffre *m*; (*of house, car, telephone, newspaper*) numéro *m* ♦ *vt* numéroter; (*include*)
compter; **a ~ of** un certain nombre de; **to be
~ed among** compter parmi; **the staff ~s 20**
le nombre d'employés s'élève à *or* est de 20;
wrong ~ (*TEL*) mauvais numéro.
numbered account ['nʌmbəd-] *n* (*in bank*)
compte numéroté.
number plate *n* (*BRIT AUT*) plaque *f* minéralogique *or* d'immatriculation.
Number Ten *n* (*BRIT*: = 10 Downing Street*) résidence du Premier ministre.
numbness ['nʌmnɪs] *n* torpeur *f*; (*due to cold*)
engourdissement *m*.
numbskull ['nʌmskʌl] *n* (*col*) gourde *f*.
numeral ['njuːmərəl] *n* chiffre *m*.
numerate ['njuːmərɪt] *adj* (*BRIT*): **to be ~** avoir
des notions d'arithmétique.
numerical [njuː'mɛrɪkl] *adj* numérique.
numerous ['njuːmərəs] *adj* nombreux(euse).
nun [nʌn] *n* religieuse *f*, sœur *f*.
nunnery ['nʌnərɪ] *n* couvent *m*.
nuptial ['nʌpʃəl] *adj* nuptial(e).
nurse [nəːs] *n* infirmière *f*; (*also*: **~maid**)

bonne *f* d'enfants ♦ *vt* (*patient, cold*) soigner; (*baby: BRIT*) bercer (dans ses bras); (*: US*) allaiter, nourrir; (*hope*) nourrir *m*.

nursery ['nəːsərɪ] *n* (*room*) nursery *f*; (*institution*) pouponnière *f*; (*for plants*) pépinière *f*.

nursery rhyme *n* comptine *f*, chansonnette *f* pour enfants.

nursery school *n* école maternelle.

nursery slope *n* (*BRIT SKI*) piste *f* pour débutants.

nursing ['nəːsɪŋ] *n* (*profession*) profession *f* d'infirmière ♦ *adj* (*mother*) qui allaite.

nursing home *n* clinique *f*; maison *f* de convalescence.

nurture ['nəːtʃə*] *vt* élever.

NUS *n abbr* (*BRIT*: = National Union of Students) *syndicat des étudiants*.

NUT *n abbr* (*BRIT*: = National Union of Teachers) *syndicat enseignant*.

nut [nʌt] *n* (*of metal*) écrou *m*; (*fruit*) noix *f*, noisette *f*, cacahuète *f* (*terme générique en anglais*) ♦ *adj* (*chocolate etc*) aux noisettes; **he's ~s** (*col*) il est dingue.

nutcase ['nʌtkeɪs] *n* (*col*) dingue *m/f*.

nutcrackers ['nʌtkrækəz] *npl* casse-noix *m inv*, casse-noisette(s) *m*.

nutmeg ['nʌtmeg] *n* (noix *f*) muscade *f*.

nutrient ['njuːtrɪənt] *adj* nutritif(ive) ♦ *n* substance nutritive.

nutrition [njuː'trɪʃən] *n* nutrition *f*, alimentation *f*.

nutritionist [njuː'trɪʃənɪst] *n* nutritionniste *m/f*.

nutritious [njuː'trɪʃəs] *adj* nutritif(ive), nourrissant(e).

nutshell ['nʌtʃel] *n* coquille *f* de noix; **in a ~** en un mot.

nutty ['nʌtɪ] *adj* (*flavour*) à la noisette; (*col: person*) cinglé(e), dingue.

nuzzle ['nʌzl] *vi*: **to ~ up to** fourrer son nez contre.

NV *abbr* (*US*) = Nevada.

NWT *abbr* (*Canada*) = Northwest Territories.

NY *abbr* (*US*) = New York.

NYC *abbr* (*US*) = New York City.

nylon ['naɪlɔn] *n* nylon *m* ♦ *adj* de *or* en nylon; **~s** *npl* bas *mpl* nylon.

nymph [nɪmf] *n* nymphe *f*.

nymphomaniac ['nɪmfəu'meɪnɪæk] *adj, n* nymphomane (*f*).

NYSE *n abbr* (*US*) = New York Stock Exchange.

NZ *abbr* = New Zealand.

O o

O, o [əu] *n* (*letter*) O, o *m*; (*US SCOL*: = *outstanding*) tb (= très bien); **O for Oliver**, (*US*) **O for Oboe** O comme Oscar.

oaf [əuf] *n* balourd *m*.

oak [əuk] *n* chêne *m* ♦ *cpd* de *or* en (bois de) chêne.

O&M *n abbr* = organization and method.

OAP *n abbr* (*BRIT*) = old age pensioner.

oar [ɔː*] *n* aviron *m*, rame *f*; **to put** *or* **shove one's ~ in** (*fig: col*) mettre son grain de sel.

oarsman ['ɔːzmən], **oarswoman** ['ɔːzwumən] *n* rameur/euse; (*NAUT, SPORT*) nageur/euse.

OAS *n abbr* (= Organization of American States) OEA *f* (= Organisation des États américains).

oasis, *pl* **oases** [əu'eɪsɪs, əu'eɪsiːz] *n* oasis *f*.

oath [əuθ] *n* serment *m*; (*swear word*) juron *m*; **to take the ~** prêter serment; **on** (*BRIT*) *or* **under ~** sous serment; assermenté(e).

oatmeal ['əutmiːl] *n* flocons *mpl* d'avoine.

oats [əuts] *n* avoine *f*.

OAU *n abbr* (= Organization of African Unity) OUA *f* (= Organisation de l'unité africaine).

obdurate ['ɔbdjurɪt] *adj* obstiné(e); impénitent(e); intraitable.

OBE *n abbr* (*BRIT*: = Order of the British Empire) *distinction honorifique*.

obedience [ə'biːdɪəns] *n* obéissance *f*; **in ~ to** conformément à.

obedient [ə'biːdɪənt] *adj* obéissant(e); **to be ~ to sb/sth** obéir à qn/qch.

obelisk ['ɔbɪlɪsk] *n* obélisque *m*.

obese [əu'biːs] *adj* obèse.

obesity [əu'biːsɪtɪ] *n* obésité *f*.

obey [ə'beɪ] *vt* obéir à; (*instructions, regulations*) se conformer à ♦ *vi* obéir.

obituary [ə'bɪtjuərɪ] *n* nécrologie *f*.

object *n* ['ɔbdʒɪkt] objet *m*; (*purpose*) but *m*, objet; (*LING*) complément *m* d'objet ♦ *vi* [əb'dʒɛkt]: **to ~ to** (*attitude*) désapprouver; (*proposal*) protester contre, élever une objection contre; **I ~!** je proteste!; **he ~ed that** ... il a fait valoir *or* a objecté que ...; **do you ~ to my smoking?** est-ce que cela vous gêne si je fume?; **what's the ~ of doing that?** quel est l'intérêt de faire cela?; **money is no ~** l'argent n'est pas un problème.

objection [əb'dʒɛkʃən] *n* objection *f*; (*drawback*) inconvénient *m*; **if you have no ~** si vous n'y voyez pas d'inconvénient; **to make** *or* **raise an ~** élever une objection.

objectionable [əb'dʒɛkʃənəbl] *adj* très désagréable; choquant(e).

objective [əb'dʒɛktɪv] *n* objectif *m* ♦ *adj* objectif(ive).

objectivity [ɔbdʒɪk'tɪvɪtɪ] *n* objectivité *f*.

object lesson *n* (*fig*) (bonne) illustration.

objector [əb'dʒɛktə*] *n* opposant/e.

obligation [ɔblɪ'geɪʃən] *n* obligation *f*, devoir *m*; (*debt*) dette *f* (de reconnaissance); "**without** ~" "sans engagement".

obligatory [ə'blɪɡətərɪ] *adj* obligatoire.

oblige [ə'blaɪdʒ] *vt* (*force*): **to** ~ **sb to do** obliger *or* forcer qn à faire; (*do a favour*) rendre service à, obliger; **to be** ~**d to sb for sth** être obligé(e) à qn de qch; **anything to** ~! (*col*) (toujours) prêt à rendre service!

obliging [ə'blaɪdʒɪŋ] *adj* obligeant(e), serviable.

oblique [ə'bliːk] *adj* oblique; (*allusion*) indirect(e) ♦ *n* (*BRIT TYP*): ~ (**stroke**) barre *f* oblique.

obliterate [ə'blɪtəreɪt] *vt* effacer.

oblivion [ə'blɪvɪən] *n* oubli *m*.

oblivious [ə'blɪvɪəs] *adj*: ~ **of** oublieux(euse) de.

oblong ['ɔblɔŋ] *adj* oblong(ue) ♦ *n* rectangle *m*.

obnoxious [əb'nɔkʃəs] *adj* odieux(euse); (*smell*) nauséabond(e).

o.b.o. *abbr* (*US*: = *or best offer. in classified ads*) ≈ à débattre.

oboe ['əubəu] *n* hautbois *m*.

obscene [əb'siːn] *adj* obscène.

obscenity [əb'sɛnɪtɪ] *n* obscénité *f*.

obscure [əb'skjuə*] *adj* obscur(e) ♦ *vt* obscurcir; (*hide: sun*) cacher.

obscurity [əb'skjuərɪtɪ] *n* obscurité *f*.

obsequious [əb'siːkwɪəs] *adj* obséquieux(euse).

observable [əb'zɔːvəbl] *adj* observable; (*appreciable*) notable.

observance [əb'zɔːvns] *n* observance *f*, observation *f*; **religious** ~**s** observances religieuses.

observant [əb'zɔːvnt] *adj* observateur(trice).

observation [ɔbzə'veɪʃən] *n* observation *f*; (*by police etc*) surveillance *f*.

observation post *n* (*MIL*) poste *m* d'observation.

observatory [əb'zɔːvətrɪ] *n* observatoire *m*.

observe [əb'zɔːv] *vt* observer; (*remark*) faire observer *or* remarquer.

observer [əb'zɔːvə*] *n* observateur/trice.

obsess [əb'sɛs] *vt* obséder; **to be** ~**ed by** *or* **with sb/sth** être obsédé(e) par qn/qch.

obsession [əb'sɛʃən] *n* obsession *f*.

obsessive [əb'sɛsɪv] *adj* obsédant(e).

obsolescence [ɔbsə'lɛsns] *n* vieillissement *m*; obsolescence *f*; **built-in** *or* **planned** ~ (*COMM*) désuétude calculée.

obsolescent [ɔbsə'lɛsnt] *adj* obsolescent(e), en voie d'être périmé(e).

obsolete ['ɔbsəliːt] *adj* dépassé(e), périmé(e).

obstacle ['ɔbstəkl] *n* obstacle *m*.

obstacle race *n* course *f* d'obstacles.

obstetrician [ɔbstə'trɪʃən] *n* obstétricien/ne.

obstetrics [ɔb'stɛtrɪks] *n* obstétrique *f*.

obstinacy ['ɔbstɪnəsɪ] *n* obstination *f*.

obstinate ['ɔbstɪnɪt] *adj* obstiné(e); (*pain, cold*) persistant(e).

obstreperous [əb'strɛpərəs] *adj* turbulent(e).

obstruct [əb'strʌkt] *vt* (*block*) boucher, obstruer; (*halt*) arrêter; (*hinder*) entraver.

obstruction [əb'strʌkʃən] *n* obstruction *f*; obstacle *m*.

obstructive [əb'strʌktɪv] *adj* obstructionniste.

obtain [əb'teɪn] *vt* obtenir ♦ *vi* avoir cours.

obtainable [əb'teɪnəbl] *adj* qu'on peut obtenir.

obtrusive [əb'truːsɪv] *adj* (*person*) importun(e); (*smell*) pénétrant(e); (*building etc*) trop en évidence.

obtuse [əb'tjuːs] *adj* obtus(e).

obverse ['ɔbvɔːs] *n* (*of medal, coin*) côté *m* face; (*fig*) contrepartie *f*.

obviate ['ɔbvɪeɪt] *vt* parer à, obvier à.

obvious ['ɔbvɪəs] *adj* évident(e), manifeste.

obviously ['ɔbvɪəslɪ] *adv* manifestement; (*of course*): ~, **he** ... *or* **he** ~ ... il est bien évident qu'il ...; ~! bien sûr!; ~ **not**! évidemment pas!, bien sûr que non!

OCAS *n abbr* (= *Organization of Central American States*) ODEAC *f* (= *Organisation des États d'Amérique centrale*).

occasion [ə'keɪʒən] *n* occasion *f*; (*event*) événement *m* ♦ *vt* occasionner, causer; **on that** ~ à cette occasion; **to rise to the** ~ se montrer à la hauteur de la situation.

occasional [ə'keɪʒənl] *adj* pris(e) (*or* fait(e) *etc*) de temps en temps; occasionnel(le).

occasionally [ə'keɪʒənəlɪ] *adv* de temps en temps; **very** ~ (assez) rarement.

occasional table *n* table décorative.

occult [ɔ'kʌlt] *adj* occulte ♦ *n*: **the** ~ le surnaturel.

occupancy ['ɔkjupənsɪ] *n* occupation *f*.

occupant ['ɔkjupənt] *n* occupant *m*.

occupation [ɔkju'peɪʃən] *n* occupation *f*; (*job*) métier *m*, profession *f*; **unfit for** ~ (*house*) impropre à l'habitation.

occupational [ɔkju'peɪʃənl] *adj* (*accident, disease*) du travail; (*hazard*) du métier.

occupational guidance *n* (*BRIT*) orientation professionnelle.

occupational pension *n* retraite professionnelle.

occupational therapy *n* ergothérapie *f*.

occupier ['ɔkjupaɪə*] *n* occupant/e.

occupy ['ɔkjupaɪ] *vt* occuper; **to** ~ **o.s. with** *or* **by doing** s'occuper à faire; **to be occupied with sth** être occupé(e) avec qch.

occur [ə'kɔː*] *vi* se produire; (*difficulty, opportunity*) se présenter; (*phenomenon, error*) se rencontrer; **to** ~ **to sb** venir à l'esprit de qn.

occurrence [ə'kʌrəns] *n* présence *f*, existence *f*; cas *m*, fait *m*.

ocean ['əuʃən] *n* océan *m*; ~**s of** (*col*) des masses de.

ocean bed *n* fond (sous-)marin.

ocean-going ['əʊʃəngəʊɪŋ] *adj* de haute mer.

Oceania [əʊʃɪ'eɪnɪə] *n* Océanie *f*.

ocean liner *n* paquebot *m*.

ochre ['əʊkə*] *adj* ocre.

o'clock [ə'klɔk] *adv*: **it is 5 ~** il est 5 heures.

OCR *n abbr* = **optical character reader, optical character recognition**.

Oct. *abbr* (= *October*) oct.

octagonal [ɔk'tægənl] *adj* octogonal(e).

octane ['ɔkteɪn] *n* octane *m*; **high-~** **petrol** *or* (*US*) **gas** essence *f* à indice d'octane élevé.

octave ['ɔktɪv] *n* octave *f*.

October [ɔk'təʊbə*] *n* octobre *m*; *for phrases see also* **July**.

octogenarian ['ɔktəʊdʒɪ'nɛərɪən] *n* octogénaire *m/f*.

octopus ['ɔktəpəs] *n* pieuvre *f*.

odd [ɔd] *adj* (*strange*) bizarre, curieux(euse); (*number*) impair(e); (*left over*) qui reste, en plus; (*not of a set*) dépareillé(e); **60-~** 60 et quelques; **at ~ times** de temps en temps; **the ~ one out** l'exception *f*.

oddball ['ɔdbɔːl] *n* (*col*) excentrique *m/f*.

oddity ['ɔdɪtɪ] *n* bizarrerie *f*; (*person*) excentrique *m/f*.

odd-job man [ɔd'dʒɔb-] *n* homme *m* à tout faire.

odd jobs *npl* petits travaux divers.

oddly ['ɔdlɪ] *adv* bizarrement, curieusement.

oddments ['ɔdmənts] *npl* (*BRIT COMM*) fins *fpl* de série.

odds [ɔdz] *npl* (*in betting*) cote *f*; **the ~ are against his coming** il y a peu de chances qu'il vienne; **it makes no ~** cela n'a pas d'importance; **to succeed against all the ~** réussir contre toute attente; **~ and ends** de petites choses; **at ~** en désaccord.

odds-on [ɔdz'ɔn] *adj*: **the ~ favourite** le grand favori; **it's ~ that he'll come** il y a toutes les chances *or* gros à parier qu'il vienne.

ode [əʊd] *n* ode *f*.

odious ['əʊdɪəs] *adj* odieux(euse), détestable.

odometer [ɔ'dɔmɪtə*] *n* odomètre *m*.

odour, (*US*) **odor** ['əʊdə*] *n* odeur *f*.

odo(u)rless ['əʊdəlɪs] *adj* inodore.

OECD *n abbr* (= *Organization for Economic Co-operation and Development*) OCDE *f* (= *Organisation de coopération et de développement économique*).

oesophagus, (*US*) **esophagus** [iː'sɔfəgəs] *n* œsophage *m*.

oestrogen, (*US*) **estrogen** ['iːstrəʊdʒən] *n* œstrogène *m*.

========================= *KEYWORD*

of [ɔv, əv] *prep* **1** (*gen*) de; **a friend ~ ours** un de nos amis; **a boy ~ 10** un garçon de 10 ans; **that was kind ~ you** c'était gentil de votre part

2 (*expressing quantity, amount, dates etc*) de;

a kilo ~ flour un kilo de farine; **how much ~ this do you need?** combien vous en faut-il?; **there were 3 ~ them** (*people*) ils étaient 3; (*objects*) il y en avait 3; **3 ~ us went** 3 d'entre nous y sont allé(e)s; **the 5th ~ July** le 5 juillet; **a quarter ~ 4** (*US*) 4 heures moins le quart

3 (*from, out of*) en, de; **a statue ~ marble** une statue de *or* en marbre; **made ~ wood** (fait) en bois.

off [ɔf] *adj, adv* (*engine*) coupé(e); (*tap*) fermé(e); (*BRIT: food*) mauvais(e), avancé(e); (: *milk*) tourné(e); (*absent*) absent(e); (*cancelled*) annulé(e); (*removed*): **the lid was ~** le couvercle était retiré *or* n'était pas mis ♦ *prep* de; sur; **to be ~** (*to leave*) partir, s'en aller; **I must be ~** il faut que je file; **to be ~ sick** être absent pour cause de maladie; **a day ~** un jour de congé; **to have an ~ day** n'être pas en forme; **he had his coat ~** il avait enlevé son manteau; **the hook is ~** le crochet s'est détaché; le crochet n'est pas mis; **10% ~** (*COMM*) 10% de rabais; **5 km ~ (the road)** à 5 km (de la route); **~ the coast** au large de la côte; **a house ~ the main road** une maison à l'écart de la grand-route; **it's a long way ~** c'est loin (d'ici); **I'm ~ meat** je ne mange plus de viande; je n'aime plus la viande; **on the ~ chance** à tout hasard; **to be well/badly ~** être bien/mal loti; (*financially*) être aisé/dans la gêne; **~ and on, on and ~** de temps à autre; **I'm afraid the chicken is ~** (*BRIT: not available*) je regrette, il n'y a plus de poulet; **that's a bit ~** (*fig: col*) c'est un peu fort.

offal ['ɔfl] *n* (*CULIN*) abats *mpl*.

offbeat ['ɔfbiːt] *adj* excentrique.

off-centre [ɔf'sɛntə*] *adj* décentré(e), excentré(e).

off-colour ['ɔf'kʌlə*] *adj* (*BRIT: ill*) malade, mal fichu(e); **to feel ~** être mal fichu.

offence, (*US*) **offense** [ə'fɛns] *n* (*crime*) délit *m*, infraction *f*; **to give ~ to** blesser, offenser; **to take ~ at** se vexer de, s'offenser de; **to commit an ~** commettre une infraction.

offend [ə'fɛnd] *vt* (*person*) offenser, blesser ♦ *vi*: **to ~ against** (*law, rule*) contrevenir à, enfreindre.

offender [ə'fɛndə*] *n* délinquant/e; (*against regulations*) contrevenant/e.

offending [ə'fɛndɪŋ] *adj* incriminé(e).

offense [ə'fɛns] *n* (*US*) = **offence**.

offensive [ə'fɛnsɪv] *adj* offensant(e), choquant(e); (*smell etc*) très déplaisant(e); (*weapon*) offensif(ive) ♦ *n* (*MIL*) offensive *f*.

offer ['ɔfə*] *n* offre *f*, proposition *f* ♦ *vt* offrir, proposer; **to make an ~ for sth** faire une offre pour qch; **to ~ sth to sb, ~ sb sth** offrir qch à qn; **to ~ to do sth** proposer de faire qch; **"on special ~"** (*COMM*) "en promotion".

offering [ˈɔfərɪŋ] n offrande f.
offhand [ɔfˈhænd] adj désinvolte ♦ adv spontanément; **I can't tell you** ~ je ne peux pas vous le dire comme ça.
office [ˈɔfɪs] n (place) bureau m; (position) charge f, fonction f; **doctor's** ~ (US) cabinet (médical); **to take** ~ entrer en fonctions; **through his good** ~**s** (fig) grâce à ses bons offices; **O**~ **of Fair Trading** (BRIT) organisme de protection contre les pratiques commerciales abusives.
office automation n bureautique f.
office bearer n (of club etc) membre m du bureau.
office block, (US) **office building** n immeuble m de bureaux.
office boy n garçon m de bureau.
office hours npl heures fpl de bureau; (US MED) heures de consultation.
office manager n responsable administratif(ive).
officer [ˈɔfɪsə*] n (MIL etc) officier m; (of organization) membre m du bureau directeur; (also: **police** ~) agent m (de police).
office work n travail m de bureau.
office worker n employé/e de bureau.
official [əˈfɪʃl] adj (authorized) officiel(le) ♦ n officiel m; (civil servant) fonctionnaire m/f; employé/e.
officialdom [əˈfɪʃldəm] n bureaucratie f.
officially [əˈfɪʃəlɪ] adv officiellement.
official receiver n administrateur m judiciaire, syndic m de faillite.
officiate [əˈfɪʃɪeɪt] vi (REL) officier; **to** ~ **as Mayor** exercer les fonctions de maire; **to** ~ **at a marriage** célébrer un mariage.
officious [əˈfɪʃəs] adj trop empressé(e).
offing [ˈɔfɪŋ] n: **in the** ~ (fig) en perspective.
off-key [ɔfˈkiː] adj faux(fausse) ♦ adv faux.
off-licence [ˈɔflaɪsns] n (BRIT: shop) débit m de vins et de spiritueux.

Un **off-licence** est un magasin où l'on vend de l'alcool (à emporter) aux heures où les pubs sont fermés. On peut également y acheter des boissons non alcoolisées, des cigarettes, des chips, des bonbons, des chocolats etc.

---

off-limits [ɔfˈlɪmɪts] adj (esp US) dont l'accès est interdit.
off line adj (COMPUT) (en mode) autonome; (: switched off) non connecté(e).
off-load [ˈɔfləud] vt: **to** ~ **sth (onto)** (goods) décharger qch (sur); (job) se décharger de qch (sur).
off-peak [ˈɔfˈpiːk] adj aux heures creuses.
off-putting [ˈɔfputɪŋ] adj (BRIT) rébarbatif(ive); rebutant(e), peu engageant(e).
off-season [ˈɔfˈsiːzn] adj, adv hors-saison (inv).
offset [ˈɔfsɛt] vt irreg (counteract) contrebalancer, compenser ♦ n (also: ~ **printing**) offset m.

offshoot [ˈɔfʃuːt] n (fig) ramification f, antenne f; (: of discussion etc) conséquence f.
offshore [ɔfˈʃɔː*] adj (breeze) de terre; (island) proche du littoral; (fishing) côtier(ière); ~ **oilfield** gisement m pétrolifère en mer.
offside [ˈɔfˈsaɪd] n (AUT: with right-hand drive) côté droit; (: with left-hand drive) côté gauche ♦ adj (AUT) de droite; de gauche; (SPORT) hors jeu.
offspring [ˈɔfsprɪŋ] n progéniture f.
offstage [ɔfˈsteɪdʒ] adv dans les coulisses.
off-the-cuff [ɔfðəˈkʌf] adv au pied levé; de chic.
off-the-job [ˈɔfðəˈdʒɔb] adj: ~ **training** formation professionnelle extérieure.
off-the-peg [ˈɔfðəˈpɛg], (US) **off-the-rack** [ˈɔfðəˈræk] adv en prêt-à-porter.
off-the-record [ˈɔfðəˈrɛkɔːd] adj (remark) confidentiel(le), sans caractère officiel ♦ adv officieusement.
off-white [ˈɔfwaɪt] adj blanc cassé inv.
Ofgas [ˈɔfgæs] n (BRIT: = Office of Gas Supply) organisme qui surveille les activités des compagnies de gaz.
Oftel [ˈɔftɛl] n (BRIT: = Office of Telecommunications) organisme qui supervise les télécommunications.
often [ˈɔfn] adv souvent; **how** ~ **do you go?** vous y allez tous les combien?; **how** ~ **have you been there?** vous y êtes allé combien de fois?; **as** ~ **as not** la plupart du temps.
Ofwat [ˈɔfwɔt] n (BRIT: = Office of Water Services) organisme qui surveille les activités des compagnies des eaux.
ogle [ˈəugl] vt lorgner.
ogre [ˈəugə*] n ogre m.
OH abbr (US) = Ohio.
oh [əu] excl ô!, oh!, ah!
OHMS abbr (BRIT) = On His (or Her) Majesty's Service.
oil [ɔɪl] n huile f; (petroleum) pétrole m; (for central heating) mazout m ♦ vt (machine) graisser.
oilcan [ˈɔɪlkæn] n burette f de graissage; (for storing) bidon m à huile.
oil change n vidange f.
oilfield [ˈɔɪlfiːld] n gisement m de pétrole.
oil filter n (AUT) filtre m à huile.
oil-fired [ˈɔɪlfaɪəd] adj au mazout.
oil gauge n jauge f de niveau d'huile.
oil industry n industrie pétrolière.
oil level n niveau m d'huile.
oil painting n peinture f à l'huile.
oil refinery n raffinerie f de pétrole.
oil rig n derrick m; (at sea) plate-forme pétrolière.
oilskins [ˈɔɪlskɪnz] npl ciré m.
oil slick n nappe f de mazout.
oil tanker n pétrolier m.
oil well n puits m de pétrole.
oily [ˈɔɪlɪ] adj huileux(euse); (food) gras(se).
ointment [ˈɔɪntmənt] n onguent m.

OK *abbr* (*US*) = Oklahoma.

O.K., okay ['əu'keı] (*col*) *excl* d'accord! ♦ *vt* approuver, donner son accord à ♦ *n*: **to give sth one's** ~ donner son accord à qch ♦ *adj* en règle; en bon état; sain et sauf; acceptable; **is it** ~?, **are you** ~? ça va?; **are you** ~ **for money?** ça va *or* ira question argent?; **it's** ~ **with** *or* **by me** ça me va, c'est d'accord en ce qui me concerne.

Okla. *abbr* (*US*) = Oklahoma.

old [əuld] *adj* vieux(vieille); (*person*) vieux, âgé(e); (*former*) ancien(ne), vieux; **how** ~ **are you?** quel âge avez-vous?; **he's 10 years** ~ il a 10 ans, il est âgé de 10 ans; **~er brother/sister** frère/sœur aîné(e); **any** ~ **thing will do** n'importe quoi fera l'affaire.

old age *n* vieillesse *f*.

old age pensioner (OAP) *n* (*BRIT*) retraité/e.

old-fashioned ['əuld'fæʃnd] *adj* démodé(e); (*person*) vieux jeu *inv*.

old maid *n* vieille fille.

old people's home *n* maison *f* de retraite.

old-style ['əuldstaıl] *adj* à l'ancienne (mode).

old-time ['əuld'taım] *adj* du temps jadis, d'autrefois.

old-timer [əuld'taımə*] *n* ancien *m*.

old wives' tale *n* conte *m* de bonne femme.

O-level ['əulevl] *n* (*in England and Wales: formerly*) *examen passé à l'âge de 16 ans sanctionnant les connaissances de l'élève*, ≈ brevet *m* des collèges.

olive ['ɔlıv] *n* (*fruit*) olive *f*; (*tree*) olivier *m* ♦ *adj* (*also*: ~**-green**) (vert) olive *inv*.

olive oil *n* huile *f* d'olive.

Olympic [əu'lımpık] *adj* olympique; **the** ~ **Games, the** ~**s** les Jeux *mpl* olympiques.

OM *n abbr* (*BRIT*: = Order of Merit) *titre honorifique*.

Oman [əu'ma:n] *n* Oman *m*.

OMB *n abbr* (*US*: = Office of Management and Budget*) *service conseillant le président en matière budgétaire*.

omelet(te) ['ɔmlıt] *n* omelette *f*; **ham/cheese** ~ omelette au jambon/fromage.

omen ['əumən] *n* présage *m*.

ominous ['ɔmınəs] *adj* menaçant(e), inquiétant(e); (*event*) de mauvais augure.

omission [əu'mıʃən] *n* omission *f*.

omit [əu'mıt] *vt* omettre; **to** ~ **to do sth** négliger de faire qch.

omnivorous [ɔm'nıvrəs] *adj* omnivore.

ON *abbr* (*Canada*) = Ontario.

─────────── *KEYWORD*

on [ɔn] *prep* **1** (*indicating position*) sur; ~ **the table** sur la table; ~ **the wall** sur le *or* au mur; ~ **the left** à gauche; **I haven't any money** ~ **me** je n'ai pas d'argent sur moi

2 (*indicating means, method, condition etc*): ~ **foot** à pied; ~ **the train/plane** (*be*) dans le train/l'avion; (*go*) en train/avion; ~ **the telephone/radio/television** au téléphone/à la

radio/à la télévision; **to be** ~ **drugs** se droguer; ~ **holiday**, (*US*) ~ **vacation** en vacances; ~ **the continent** sur le continent

3 (*referring to time*): ~ **Friday** vendredi; ~ **Fridays** le vendredi; ~ **June 20th** le 20 juin; **a week** ~ **Friday** vendredi en huit; ~ **arrival** à l'arrivée; ~ **seeing this** en voyant cela

4 (*about, concerning*) sur, de; **a book** ~ **Balzac/physics** un livre sur Balzac/de physique

5 (*at the expense of*): **this round is** ~ **me** c'est ma tournée

♦ *adv* **1** (*referring to dress, covering*): **to have one's coat** ~ avoir (mis) son manteau; **to put one's coat** ~ mettre son manteau; **what's she got** ~? qu'est-ce qu'elle porte?; **screw the lid** ~ **tightly** vissez bien le couvercle

2 (*further, continuously*): **to walk** *etc* ~ continuer à marcher *etc*; ~ **and off** de temps à autre; **from that day** ~ depuis ce jour

♦ *adj* **1** (*in operation: machine*) en marche; (: *radio, TV, light*) allumé(e); (: *tap, gas*) ouvert(e); (: *brakes*) mis(e); **is the meeting still** ~? (*not cancelled*) est-ce que la réunion a bien lieu?; (*in progress*) la réunion dure-t-elle encore?; **it was well** ~ **in the evening** c'était tard dans la soirée; **when is this film** ~? quand passe ce film?

2 (*col*): **that's not** ~! (*not acceptable*) cela ne se fait pas!; (*not possible*) pas question!

ONC *n abbr* (*BRIT*: = Ordinary National Certificate) ≈ BT *m*.

once [wʌns] *adv* une fois; (*formerly*) autrefois ♦ *conj* une fois que; ~ **he had left/it was done** une fois qu'il fut parti/que ce fut terminé; **at** ~ tout de suite, immédiatement; (*simultaneously*) à la fois; **all at** ~ *adv* tout d'un coup; ~ **a week** une fois par semaine; ~ **more** encore une fois; **I knew him** ~ je l'ai connu autrefois; ~ **and for all** une fois pour toutes; ~ **upon a time there was** ... il y avait une fois ..., il était une fois ....

oncoming ['ɔnkʌmıŋ] *adj* (*traffic*) venant en sens inverse.

OND *n abbr* (*BRIT*: = Ordinary National Diploma) ≈ BTS *m*.

─────────── *KEYWORD*

one [wʌn] *num* un(e); ~ **hundred and fifty** cent cinquante; ~ **day** un jour

♦ *adj* **1** (*sole*) seul(e), unique; **the** ~ **book which** l'unique *or* le seul livre qui; **the** ~ **man who** le seul (homme) qui

2 (*same*) même; **they came in the** ~ **car** ils sont venus dans la même voiture

♦ *pron* **1**: **this** ~ celui-ci(celle-ci); **that** ~ celui-là(celle-là); **I've already got** ~/**a red** ~ j'en ai déjà un(e)/un(e) rouge; ~ **by** ~ un(e) à *or* par un(e); **which** ~ **do you want?** lequel voulez-vous?

2: ~ **another** l'un(e) l'autre; **to look at** ~ **another** se regarder

3 (*impersonal*) on; ~ **never knows** on ne sait jamais; **to cut** ~**'s finger** se couper le doigt

4 (*phrases*): **to be** ~ **up on sb** avoir l'avantage sur qn; **to be at** ~ **(with sb)** être d'accord (avec qn).

one-armed bandit ['wʌnɑ:md-] *n* machine *f* à sous.

one-day excursion ['wʌndeɪ-] *n* (*US*) billet *m* d'aller-retour (valable pour la journée).

One-hundred share index ['wʌnhʌndrəd-] *n* indice *m* Footsie des cent grandes valeurs.

one-man ['wʌn'mæn] *adj* (*business*) dirigé(e) *etc* par un seul homme.

one-man band *n* homme-orchestre *m*.

one-off [wʌn'ɔf] (*BRIT col*) *n* exemplaire *m* unique ♦ *adj* unique.

one-parent family ['wʌnpɛərənt-] *n* famille monoparentale.

one-piece ['wʌnpi:s] *adj*: ~ **bathing suit** maillot *m* une pièce.

onerous ['ɔnərəs] *adj* (*task, duty*) pénible; (*responsibility*) lourd(e).

oneself [wʌn'sɛlf] *pron* se; (*after prep, also emphatic*) soi-même; **by** ~ tout seul.

one-sided [wʌn'saɪdɪd] *adj* (*decision*) unilatéral(e); (*judgment, account*) partial(e); (*contest*) inégal(e).

one-time ['wʌntaɪm] *adj* d'autrefois.

one-to-one ['wʌntəwʌn] *adj* (*relationship*) univoque.

one-upmanship [wʌn'ʌpmənʃɪp] *n*: **the art of** ~ l'art de faire mieux que les autres.

one-way ['wʌnweɪ] *adj* (*street, traffic*) à sens unique.

ongoing ['ɔngəʊɪŋ] *adj* en cours; suivi(e).

onion ['ʌnjən] *n* oignon *m*.

on line *adj* (*COMPUT*) en ligne; (: *switched on*) connecté(e).

onlooker ['ɔnlʊkə*] *n* spectateur/trice.

only ['əʊnlɪ] *adv* seulement ♦ *adj* seul(e), unique ♦ *conj* seulement, mais; **an** ~ **child** un enfant unique; **not** ~ non seulement; **I** ~ **took one** j'en ai seulement pris un, je n'en ai pris qu'un; **I saw her** ~ **yesterday** je l'ai vue hier encore; **I'd be** ~ **too pleased to help** je ne serais que trop content de vous aider; **I would come,** ~ **I'm very busy** je viendrais bien mais j'ai beaucoup à faire.

ono *abbr* (*BRIT*: = *or nearest offer: in classified ads*) ≈ à débattre.

onset ['ɔnsɛt] *n* début *m*; (*of winter, old age*) approche *f*.

onshore ['ɔnʃɔ:*] *adj* (*wind*) du large.

onslaught ['ɔnslɔ:t] *n* attaque *f*, assaut *m*.

Ont. *abbr* (*Canada*) = Ontario.

on-the-job ['ɔnðə'dʒɔb] *adj*: ~ **training** formation *f* sur place.

onto ['ɔntu] *prep* = on to.

onus ['əʊnəs] *n* responsabilité *f*; **the** ~ **is upon** him **to prove it** c'est à lui de le prouver.

onward(s) ['ɔnwəd(z)] *adv* (*move*) en avant.

onyx ['ɔnɪks] *n* onyx *m*.

oops [ʊps] *excl* houp!; ~**-a-daisy!** houp-là!

ooze [u:z] *vi* suinter.

opacity [əʊ'pæsɪtɪ] *n* opacité *f*.

opal ['əʊpl] *n* opale *f*.

opaque [əʊ'peɪk] *adj* opaque.

OPEC ['əʊpɛk] *n abbr* (= *Organization of Petroleum-Exporting Countries*) OPEP *f* (= *Organisation des pays exportateurs de pétrole*).

open ['əʊpn] *adj* ouvert(e); (*car*) découvert(e); (*road, view*) dégagé(e); (*meeting*) public(ique); (*admiration*) manifeste; (*question*) non résolu(e); (*enemy*) déclaré(e) ♦ *vt* ouvrir ♦ *vi* (*flower, eyes, door, debate*) s'ouvrir; (*shop, bank, museum*) ouvrir; (*book etc: commence*) commencer, débuter; **in the** ~ **(air)** en plein air; **the** ~ **sea** le large; ~ **ground** (*among trees*) clairière *f*; (*waste ground*) terrain *m* vague; **to have an** ~ **mind (on sth)** avoir l'esprit ouvert (sur qch).

▶**open on to** *vt fus* (*subj: room, door*) donner sur.

▶**open out** *vt* ouvrir ♦ *vi* s'ouvrir.

▶**open up** *vt* ouvrir; (*blocked road*) dégager ♦ *vi* s'ouvrir.

open-air [əʊpn'ɛə*] *adj* en plein air.

open-and-shut ['əʊpnən'ʃʌt] *adj*: ~ **case** cas *m* limpide.

open day *n* journée *f* portes ouvertes.

open-ended [əʊpn'ɛndɪd] *adj* (*fig*) non limité(e).

opener ['əʊpnə*] *n* (*also*: **can** ~, **tin** ~) ouvre-boîtes *m*.

open-heart surgery [əʊpn'hɑ:t-] *n* chirurgie *f* à cœur ouvert.

opening ['əʊpnɪŋ] *n* ouverture *f*; (*opportunity*) occasion *f*; débouché *m*; (*job*) poste vacant.

opening night *n* (*THEAT*) première *f*.

open learning centre *n centre ouvert à tous où l'on dispense un enseignement général à temps partiel.*

openly ['əʊpnlɪ] *adv* ouvertement.

open-minded [əʊpn'maɪndɪd] *adj* à l'esprit ouvert.

open-necked ['əʊpnnɛkt] *adj* à col ouvert.

openness ['əʊpnnɪs] *n* (*frankness*) franchise *f*.

open-plan ['əʊpn'plæn] *adj* sans cloisons.

open prison *n* prison ouverte.

open sandwich *n* canapé *m*.

open shop *n entreprise qui admet les travailleurs non syndiqués.*

Open University *n* (*BRIT*) *cours universitaires par correspondance.*

---

*L'**Open University** a été fondée en 1969. L'enseignement comprend des cours (certaines plages horaires sont réservées à cet effet à la télévision et à la radio), des devoirs qui sont envoyés par l'étudiant à son directeur ou sa directrice d'études, et un stage obligatoire en* *université d'été. Il faut préparer un certain nombre d'unités de valeur pendant une période de temps déterminée et obtenir la moyenne à un certain nombre d'entre elles pour recevoir le diplôme visé.*

opera ['ɔpərə] *n* opéra *m*.

opera glasses *npl* jumelles *fpl* de théâtre.

opera house *n* opéra *m*.

opera singer *n* chanteur/euse d'opéra.

operate ['ɔpəreit] *vt* (*machine*) faire marcher, faire fonctionner; (*system*) pratiquer ♦ *vi* fonctionner; (*drug*) faire effet; **to ~ on sb (for)** (*MED*) opérer qn (de).

operatic [ɔpə'rætik] *adj* d'opéra.

operating ['ɔpəreitiŋ] *adj* (*COMM: costs, profit*) d'exploitation; (*MED*): **~ table/theatre** table *f*/salle *f* d'opération.

operating room *n* (*US*) salle *f* d'opération.

operating system *n* (*COMPUT*) système *m* d'exploitation.

operation [ɔpə'reiʃən] *n* opération *f*; (*of machine*) fonctionnement *m*; **to have an ~ (for)** se faire opérer (de); **to be in ~** (*machine*) être en service; (*system*) être en vigueur.

operational [ɔpə'reiʃənl] *adj* opérationnel(le); (*ready for use or action*) en état de marche; **when the service is fully ~** lorsque le service fonctionnera pleinement.

operative ['ɔpərətiv] *adj* (*measure*) en vigueur ♦ *n* (*in factory*) ouvrier/ière; **the ~ word** le mot clef.

operator ['ɔpəreitə*] *n* (*of machine*) opérateur/trice; (*TEL*) téléphoniste *m/f*.

operetta [ɔpə'rɛtə] *n* opérette *f*.

ophthalmologist [ɔfθæl'mɔlədʒist] *n* ophtalmologiste *m/f*, ophthalmologue *m/f*.

opinion [ə'pinjən] *n* opinion *f*, avis *m*; **in my ~** à mon avis; **to seek a second ~** demander un deuxième avis.

opinionated [ə'pinjəneitid] *adj* aux idées bien arrêtées.

opinion poll *n* sondage *m* d'opinion.

opium ['əupiəm] *n* opium *m*.

opponent [ə'pəunənt] *n* adversaire *m/f*.

opportune ['ɔpətjuːn] *adj* opportun(e).

opportunist [ɔpə'tjuːnist] *n* opportuniste *m/f*.

opportunity [ɔpə'tjuːniti] *n* occasion *f*; **to take the ~ to do** *or* **of doing** profiter de l'occasion pour faire.

oppose [ə'pəuz] *vt* s'opposer à; **~d to** *adj* opposé(e) à; **as ~d to** par opposition à.

opposing [ə'pəuziŋ] *adj* (*side*) opposé(e).

opposite ['ɔpəzit] *adj* opposé(e); (*house etc*) d'en face ♦ *adv* en face ♦ *prep* en face de ♦ *n* opposé *m*, contraire *m*; (*of word*) contraire; **"see ~ page"** "voir ci-contre".

opposite number *n* (*BRIT*) homologue *m/f*.

opposite sex *n*: **the ~** l'autre sexe.

opposition [ɔpə'ziʃən] *n* opposition *f*.

oppress [ə'prɛs] *vt* opprimer.

oppression [ə'prɛʃən] *n* oppression *f*.

oppressive [ə'prɛsiv] *adj* oppressif(ive).

opprobrium [ə'prəubriəm] *n* (*formal*) opprobre *m*.

opt [ɔpt] *vi*: **to ~ for** opter pour; **to ~ to do** choisir de faire.

▶**opt out** *vi* (*school, hospital*) devenir autonome; (*health service*) devenir privé(e); **to ~ out of** choisir de quitter.

optical ['ɔptikl] *adj* optique; (*instrument*) d'optique.

optical character reader/recognition (OCR) *n* lecteur *m*/lecture *f* optique.

optical fibre *n* fibre *f* optique.

optician [ɔp'tiʃən] *n* opticien/ne.

optics ['ɔptiks] *n* optique *f*.

optimism ['ɔptimizəm] *n* optimisme *m*.

optimist ['ɔptimist] *n* optimiste *m/f*.

optimistic [ɔpti'mistik] *adj* optimiste.

optimum ['ɔptiməm] *adj* optimum.

option ['ɔpʃən] *n* choix *m*, option *f*; (*SCOL*) matière *f* à option; (*COMM*) option; **to keep one's ~s open** (*fig*) ne pas s'engager; **I have no ~** je n'ai pas le choix.

optional ['ɔpʃənl] *adj* facultatif(ive); (*COMM*) en option; **~ extras** accessoires *mpl* en option, options *fpl*.

opulence ['ɔpjuləns] *n* opulence *f*, abondance *f*.

opulent ['ɔpjulənt] *adj* opulent(e); abondant(e).

OR *abbr* (*US*) = *Oregon*.

or [ɔː*] *conj* ou; (*with negative*): **he hasn't seen ~ heard anything** il n'a rien vu ni entendu; **~ else** sinon; ou bien, ou alors.

oracle ['ɔrəkl] *n* oracle *m*.

oral ['ɔːrəl] *adj* oral(e) ♦ *n* oral *m*.

orange ['ɔrindʒ] *n* (*fruit*) orange *f* ♦ *adj* orange *inv*.

orangeade [ɔrindʒ'eid] *n* orangeade *f*.

oration [ɔː'reiʃən] *n* discours solennel.

orator ['ɔrətə*] *n* orateur/trice.

oratorio [ɔrə'tɔːriəu] *n* oratorio *m*.

orb [ɔːb] *n* orbe *m*.

orbit ['ɔːbit] *n* orbite *f* ♦ *vt* décrire une *or* des orbite(s) autour de; **to be in/go into ~ (round)** être/entrer en orbite (autour de).

orbital ['ɔːbitl] *n* (*also: ~ motorway*) périphérique *f*.

orchard ['ɔːtʃəd] *n* verger *m*; **apple ~** verger de pommiers.

orchestra ['ɔːkistrə] *n* orchestre *m*; (*US: seating*) (fauteuils *mpl* d')orchestre.

orchestral [ɔː'kɛstrəl] *adj* orchestral(e); (*concert*) symphonique.

orchestrate ['ɔːkistreit] *vt* (*MUS, fig*) orchestrer.

orchid ['ɔːkid] *n* orchidée *f*.

ordain [ɔː'dein] *vt* (*REL*) ordonner; (*decide*) décréter.

ordeal [ɔː'diːl] *n* épreuve *f*.

order ['ɔːdə*] *n* ordre *m*; (*COMM*) commande *f*

♦ *vt* ordonner; (*COMM*) commander; **in** ~ en ordre; (*of document*) en règle; **out of** ~ hors service; (*telephone*) en dérangement; **a machine in working** ~ une machine en état de marche; **in** ~ **of size** par ordre de grandeur; **in** ~ **to do/that** pour faire/que + *sub*; **to** ~ **sb to do** ordonner à qn de faire; **to place an** ~ **for sth with sb** commander qch auprès de qn, passer commande de qch à qn; **to be on** ~ être en commande; **made to** ~ fait sur commande; **to be under** ~**s to do sth** avoir ordre de faire qch; **a point of** ~ un point de procédure; **to the** ~ **of** (*BANKING*) à l'ordre de.

order book *n* carnet *m* de commandes.

order form *n* bon *m* de commande.

orderly ['ɔːdəlɪ] *n* (*MIL*) ordonnance *f* ♦ *adj* (*room*) en ordre; (*mind*) méthodique; (*person*) qui a de l'ordre.

order number *n* numéro *m* de commande.

ordinal ['ɔːdɪnl] *adj* (*number*) ordinal(e).

ordinary ['ɔːdnrɪ] *adj* ordinaire, normal(e); (*pej*) ordinaire, quelconque; **out of the** ~ exceptionnel(le).

ordinary degree *n* (*SCOL*) ≈ licence *f* libre.

Un **ordinary degree** *est un diplôme inférieur à* l'**honours degree** *que l'on obtient en général après trois années d'études universitaires. Il peut aussi être décerné en cas d'échec à* l'honours degree.

---

ordinary seaman (OS) *n* (*BRIT*) matelot *m*.

ordinary shares *npl* actions *fpl* ordinaires.

ordination [ɔːdɪ'neɪʃən] *n* ordination *f*.

ordnance ['ɔːdnəns] *n* (*MIL: unit*) service *m* du matériel.

Ordnance Survey map *n* (*BRIT*) ≈ carte *f* d'État-major.

ore [ɔː*] *n* minerai *m*.

Ore(g). *abbr* (*US*) = Oregon.

organ ['ɔːgən] *n* organe *m*; (*MUS*) orgue *m*, orgues *fpl*.

organic [ɔː'gænɪk] *adj* organique; (*crops etc*) biologique, naturel(le).

organism ['ɔːgənɪzəm] *n* organisme *m*.

organist ['ɔːgənɪst] *n* organiste *m/f*.

organization [ɔːgənaɪ'zeɪʃən] *n* organisation *f*.

organization chart *n* organigramme *m*.

organize ['ɔːgənaɪz] *vt* organiser; **to get** ~**d** s'organiser.

organized crime ['ɔːgənaɪzd-] *n* crime organisé, grand banditisme.

organized labour ['ɔːgənaɪzd-] *n* main-d'œuvre syndiquée.

organizer ['ɔːgənaɪzə*] *n* organisateur/trice.

orgasm ['ɔːgæzəm] *n* orgasme *m*.

orgy ['ɔːdʒɪ] *n* orgie *f*.

Orient ['ɔːrɪənt] *n*: **the** ~ l'Orient *m*.

oriental [ɔːrɪ'entl] *adj* oriental(e) ♦ *n* Oriental/e.

orientate ['ɔːrɪənteɪt] *vt* orienter.

orifice ['ɔrɪfɪs] *n* orifice *m*.

origin ['ɔrɪdʒɪn] *n* origine *f*; **country of** ~ pays *m* d'origine.

original [ə'rɪdʒɪnl] *adj* original(e); (*earliest*) originel(le) ♦ *n* original *m*.

originality [ərɪdʒɪ'nælɪtɪ] *n* originalité *f*.

originally [ə'rɪdʒɪnəlɪ] *adv* (*at first*) à l'origine.

originate [ə'rɪdʒɪneɪt] *vi*: **to** ~ **from** être originaire de; (*suggestion*) provenir de; **to** ~ **in** prendre naissance dans; avoir son origine dans.

originator [ə'rɪdʒɪneɪtə*] *n* auteur *m*.

Orkneys ['ɔːknɪz] *npl*: **the** ~ (*also*: **the Orkney Islands**) les Orcades *fpl*.

ornament ['ɔːnəmənt] *n* ornement *m*; (*trinket*) bibelot *m*.

ornamental [ɔːnə'mentl] *adj* décoratif(ive); (*garden*) d'agrément.

ornamentation [ɔːnəmen'teɪʃən] *n* ornementation *f*.

ornate [ɔː'neɪt] *adj* très orné(e).

ornithologist [ɔːnɪ'θɔlədʒɪst] *n* ornithologue *m/f*.

ornithology [ɔːnɪ'θɔlədʒɪ] *n* ornithologie *f*.

orphan ['ɔːfn] *n* orphelin/e ♦ *vt*: **to be** ~**ed** devenir orphelin.

orphanage ['ɔːfənɪdʒ] *n* orphelinat *m*.

orthodox ['ɔːθədɔks] *adj* orthodoxe.

orthopaedic, (*US*) **orthopedic** [ɔːθə'piːdɪk] *adj* orthopédique.

OS *abbr* (*BRIT*: = Ordnance Survey*) ≈ IGN *m* (= *Institut géographique national*); (: *NAUT*) = **ordinary seaman**; (: *DRESS*) = **outsize**.

O/S *abbr* = **out of stock**.

Oscar ['ɔskə*] *n* oscar *m*.

oscillate ['ɔsɪleɪt] *vi* osciller.

OSHA *n* *abbr* (*US*: = Occupational Safety and Health Administration*) office de l'hygiène et de la sécurité au travail.

Oslo ['ɔzləu] *n* Oslo.

ostensible [ɔs'tensɪbl] *adj* prétendu(e); apparent(e).

ostensibly [ɔs'tensɪblɪ] *adv* en apparence.

ostentation [ɔsten'teɪʃən] *n* ostentation *f*.

ostentatious [ɔsten'teɪʃəs] *adj* prétentieux(euse); ostentatoire.

osteopath ['ɔstɪəpæθ] *n* ostéopathe *m/f*.

ostracize ['ɔstrəsaɪz] *vt* frapper d'ostracisme.

ostrich ['ɔstrɪtʃ] *n* autruche *f*.

OT *n* *abbr* (= Old Testament*) AT *m*.

OTB *n* *abbr* (*US*: = off-track betting*) paris pris en dehors du champ de course.

O.T.E. *abbr* (= on-target earnings*) primes *fpl* sur objectifs inclus.

other ['ʌðə*] *adj* autre ♦ *pron*: **the** ~ **(one)** l'autre; ~**s** (~ *people*) d'autres; **some** ~ **people have still to arrive** on attend encore quelques personnes; **the** ~ **day** l'autre jour; ~ **than** autrement que; à part; **some actor or** ~ un certain acteur, je ne sais quel acteur; **somebody or** ~ quelqu'un; **the car was none** ~ **than John's** la voiture n'était autre que celle de John.

otherwise ['ʌðəwaɪz] *adv, conj* autrement; **an** ~ **good piece of work** par ailleurs, un beau travail.

OTT *abbr* (*col*) = **over the top**; *see* **top**.

otter ['ɔtə*] *n* loutre *f*.

OU *n abbr* (*BRIT*) = **Open University**.

ouch [autʃ] *excl* aïe!

ought, *pt* **ought** [ɔːt] *aux vb*: **I** ~ **to do it** je devrais le faire, il faudrait que je le fasse; **this** ~ **to have been corrected** cela aurait dû être corrigé; **he** ~ **to win** il devrait gagner; **you** ~ **to go and see it** vous devriez aller le voir.

ounce [auns] *n* once *f* (= 28.35g; 16 in a pound).

our ['auə*] *adj* notre, nos *pl*.

ours [auəz] *pron* le(la) nôtre, les nôtres.

ourselves [auə'sɛlvz] *pron pl* (*reflexive, after preposition*) nous; (*emphatic*) nous-mêmes; **we did it (all) by** ~ nous avons fait ça tout seuls.

oust [aust] *vt* évincer.

out [aut] *adv* dehors; (*published, not at home etc*) sorti(e); (*light, fire*) éteint(e); (*on strike*) en grève ♦ *vt*: **to** ~ **sb** révéler l'homosexualité de qn; ~ **here** ici; ~ **there** là-bas; **he's** ~ (*absent*) il est sorti; (*unconscious*) il est sans connaissance; **to be** ~ **in one's calculations** s'être trompé dans ses calculs; **to run/back** *etc* ~ sortir en courant/en reculant *etc*; **to be** ~ **and about** *or* (*US*) **around again** être de nouveau sur pied; **before the week was** ~ avant la fin de la semaine; **the journey** ~ l'aller *m*; **the boat was 10 km** ~ le bateau était à 10 km du rivage; ~ **loud** *adv* à haute voix; ~ **of** *prep* (*outside*) en dehors de; (*because of: anger etc*) par; (*from among*): ~ **of 10** sur 10; (*without*): ~ **of petrol** sans essence, à court d'essence; **made** ~ **of wood** en *or* de bois; ~ **of order** (*machine*) en panne; (*TEL*: *line*) en dérangement; ~ **of stock** (*COMM*: *article*) épuisé(e); (: *shop*) en rupture de stock.

outage ['autɪdʒ] *n* (*esp US: power failure*) panne *f or* coupure *f* de courant.

out-and-out ['autəndaut] *adj* véritable.

outback ['autbæk] *n* campagne isolée; (*in Australia*) intérieur *m*.

outbid [aut'bɪd] *irreg vt* surenchérir.

outboard ['autbɔːd] *n*: ~ **(motor)** (moteur *m*) hors-bord *m*.

outbound ['autbaund] *adj*: ~ **(from/for)** en partance (de/pour).

outbreak ['autbreɪk] *n* éruption *f*, explosion *f*; (*start*) déclenchement *m*.

outbuilding ['autbɪldɪŋ] *n* dépendance *f*.

outburst ['autbəːst] *n* explosion *f*, accès *m*.

outcast ['autkɑːst] *n* exilé(e); (*socially*) paria *m*.

outclass [aut'klɑːs] *vt* surclasser.

outcome ['autkʌm] *n* issue *f*, résultat *m*.

outcrop ['autkrɔp] *n* affleurement *m*.

outcry ['autkraɪ] *n* tollé (général).

outdated [aut'deɪtɪd] *adj* démodé(e).

outdistance [aut'dɪstəns] *vt* distancer.

outdo [aut'duː] *vt irreg* surpasser.

outdoor [aut'dɔː*] *adj* de *or* en plein air.

outdoors [aut'dɔːz] *adv* dehors; au grand air.

outer ['autə*] *adj* extérieur(e); ~ **suburbs** grande banlieue.

outer space *n* espace *m* cosmique.

outfit ['autfɪt] *n* équipement *m*; (*clothes*) tenue *f*; (*col*: *COMM*) organisation *f*, boîte *f*.

outfitter ['autfɪtə*] *n* (*BRIT*): **"(gent's)** ~'s" "confection pour hommes".

outgoing ['autgəuɪŋ] *adj* (*president, tenant*) sortant(e); (*character*) ouvert(e), extraverti(e).

outgoings ['autgəuɪŋz] *npl* (*BRIT*: *expenses*) dépenses *fpl*.

outgrow [aut'grəu] *vt irreg* (*clothes*) devenir trop grand(e) pour.

outhouse ['authaus] *n* appentis *m*, remise *f*.

outing ['autɪŋ] *n* sortie *f*; excursion *f*.

outlandish [aut'lændɪʃ] *adj* étrange.

outlast [aut'lɑːst] *vt* survivre à.

outlaw ['autlɔː] *n* hors-la-loi *m inv* ♦ *vt* (*person*) mettre hors la loi; (*practice*) proscrire.

outlay ['autleɪ] *n* dépenses *fpl*; (*investment*) mise *f* de fonds.

outlet ['autlɛt] *n* (*for liquid etc*) issue *f*, sortie *f*; (*for emotion*) exutoire *m*; (*for goods*) débouché *m*; (*also*: **retail** ~) point *m* de vente; (*US: ELEC*) prise *f* de courant.

outline ['autlaɪn] *n* (*shape*) contour *m*; (*summary*) esquisse *f*, grandes lignes.

outlive [aut'lɪv] *vt* survivre à.

outlook ['autluk] *n* perspective *f*.

outlying ['autlaɪɪŋ] *adj* écarté(e).

outmanoeuvre [autmə'nuːvə*] *vt* (*rival etc*) avoir au tournant.

outmoded [aut'məudɪd] *adj* démodé(e); dépassé(e).

outnumber [aut'nʌmbə*] *vt* surpasser en nombre.

out-of-court [autəv'kɔːt] *adj, adv* à l'aimable.

out-of-date [autəv'deɪt] *adj* (*passport, ticket*) périmé(e); (*theory, idea*) dépassé(e); (*custom*) désuet(ète); (*clothes*) démodé(e).

out-of-the-way ['autəvðə'weɪ] *adj* loin de tout; (*fig*) insolite.

outpatient ['autpeɪʃənt] *n* malade *m/f* en consultation externe.

outpost ['autpəust] *n* avant-poste *m*.

outpouring ['autpɔːrɪŋ] *n* (*fig*) épanchement(s) *m(pl)*.

output ['autput] *n* rendement *m*, production *f* ♦ *vt* (*COMPUT*) sortir.

outrage ['autreɪdʒ] *n* atrocité *f*, acte *m* de violence; scandale *m* ♦ *vt* outrager.

outrageous [aut'reɪdʒəs] *adj* atroce; scandaleux(euse).

outrider ['autraɪdə*] *n* (*on motorcycle*) motard *m*.

outright *adv* [aut'raɪt] complètement; catégoriquement; carrément; sur le coup ♦ *adj* ['autraɪt] complet(ète); catégorique.

outrun [aut'rʌn] *vt irreg* dépasser.

outset ['autsɛt] *n* début *m*.

outshine [aut'ʃaın] *vt irreg* (*fig*) éclipser.

outside [aut'saıd] *n* extérieur *m* ♦ *adj* extérieur(e); (*remote*, *unlikely*): **an ~ chance** une (très) faible chance ♦ *adv* (au) dehors, à l'extérieur ♦ *prep* hors de, à l'extérieur de; **at the ~** (*fig*) au plus or maximum; **~ left/right** *n* (*FOOTBALL*) ailier gauche/droit.

outside broadcast *n* (*RADIO*, *TV*) reportage *m*.

outside lane *n* (*AUT*: *in Britain*) voie *f* de droite; (: *in US, Europe*) voie de gauche.

outside line *n* (*TEL*) ligne extérieure.

outsider [aut'saıdə*] *n* (*in race etc*) outsider *m*; (*stranger*) étranger/ère.

outsize ['autsaız] *adj* énorme; (*clothes*) grande taille *inv*.

outskirts ['autskə:ts] *npl* faubourgs *mpl*.

outsmart [aut'smɑ:t] *vt* se montrer plus malin(igne) *or* futé(e) que.

outspoken [aut'spəukən] *adj* très franc(franche).

outspread [aut'sprɛd] *adj* (*wings*) déployé(e).

outstanding [aut'stændıŋ] *adj* remarquable, exceptionnel(le); (*unfinished*) en suspens; en souffrance; non réglé(e); **your account is still ~** vous n'avez pas encore tout remboursé.

outstay [aut'steı] *vt*: **to ~ one's welcome** abuser de l'hospitalité de son hôte.

outstretched [aut'strɛtʃt] *adj* (*hand*) tendu(e); (*body*) étendu(e).

outstrip [aut'strıp] *vt* (*also fig*) dépasser.

out-tray ['auttreı] *n* courrier *m* "départ".

outvote [aut'vəut] *vt*: **to ~ sb (by)** mettre qn en minorité (par); **to ~ sth (by)** rejeter qch (par).

outward ['autwəd] *adj* (*sign, appearances*) extérieur(e); (*journey*) (d')aller.

outwardly ['autwədlı] *adv* extérieurement; en apparence.

outweigh [aut'weı] *vt* l'emporter sur.

outwit [aut'wıt] *vt* se montrer plus malin que.

oval ['əuvl] *adj*, *n* ovale (*m*).

> L'**Oval Office** *est le bureau personnel du président des États-Unis à la Maison-Blanche, ainsi appelé du fait de sa forme ovale. Par extension, ce terme désigne la présidence elle-même.*

ovarian [əu'vɛərıən] *adj* ovarien(ne); (*cancer*) des ovaires.

ovary ['əuvərı] *n* ovaire *m*.

ovation [əu'veıʃən] *n* ovation *f*.

oven ['ʌvn] *n* four *m*.

ovenproof ['ʌvnpru:f] *adj* allant au four.

oven-ready ['ʌvnrɛdı] *adj* prêt(e) à cuire.

ovenware ['ʌvnwɛə*] *n* plats *mpl* allant au four.

over ['əuvə*] *adv* (par-)dessus; (*excessively*) trop ♦ *adj (or adv)* (*finished*) fini(e), terminé(e); (*too much*) en plus ♦ *prep* sur; par-dessus; (*above*) au-dessus de; (*on the other side of*) de l'autre côté de; (*more than*) plus de; (*during*) pendant; (*about, concerning*): **they fell out ~ money/her** ils se sont brouillés pour des questions d'argent/à cause d'elle; **~ here** ici; **~ there** là-bas; **all ~** (*everywhere*) partout; (*finished*) fini(e); **~ and ~ (again)** à plusieurs reprises; **~ and above** en plus de; **to ask sb ~** inviter qn (à passer); **to go ~ to sb's** passer chez qn; **now ~ to our Paris correspondent** nous passons l'antenne à notre correspondant à Paris; **the world ~** dans le monde entier; **she's not ~ intelligent** (*BRIT*) elle n'est pas particulièrement intelligente.

over... ['əuvə*] *prefix*: **~abundant** surabondant(e).

overact [əuvər'ækt] *vi* (*THEAT*) outrer son rôle.

overall *adj*, *n* ['əuvərɔ:l] *adj* (*length*) total(e); (*study*) d'ensemble ♦ *n* (*BRIT*) blouse *f* ♦ *adv* [əuvər'ɔ:l] dans l'ensemble, en général; **~s** *npl* bleus *mpl* (de travail).

overall majority *n* majorité absolue.

overanxious [əuvər'æŋkʃəs] *adj* trop anxieux(euse).

overawe [əuvər'ɔ:] *vt* impressionner.

overbalance [əuvə'bæləns] *vi* basculer.

overbearing [əuvə'bɛərıŋ] *adj* impérieux(euse), autoritaire.

overboard ['əuvəbɔ:d] *adv* (*NAUT*) par-dessus bord; **to go ~ for sth** (*fig*) s'emballer (pour qch).

overbook [əuvə'buk] *vi* faire du surbooking.

overcapitalize [əuvə'kæpıtəlaız] *vt* surcapitaliser.

overcast ['əuvəkɑ:st] *adj* couvert(e).

overcharge [əuvə'tʃɑ:dʒ] *vt*: **to ~ sb for sth** faire payer qch trop cher à qn.

overcoat ['əuvəkəut] *n* pardessus *m*.

overcome [əuvə'kʌm] *vt irreg* triompher de; surmonter ♦ *adj* (*emotionally*) bouleversé(e); **~ with grief** accablé(e) de douleur.

overconfident [əuvə'kɔnfıdənt] *adj* trop sûr(e) de soi.

overcrowded [əuvə'kraudıd] *adj* bondé(e).

overcrowding [əuvə'kraudıŋ] *n* surpeuplement *m*; (*in bus*) encombrement *m*.

overdo [əuvə'du:] *vt irreg* exagérer; (*overcook*) trop cuire; **to ~ it, to ~ things** (*work too hard*) en faire trop, se surmener.

overdose ['əuvədəus] *n* dose excessive.

overdraft ['əuvədrɑ:ft] *n* découvert *m*.

overdrawn [əuvə'drɔ:n] *adj* (*account*) à découvert.

overdrive ['əuvədraıv] *n* (*AUT*) (vitesse *f*) surmultipliée *f*.

overdue [əuvə'dju:] *adj* en retard; (*bill*) impayé(e); (*recognition*) tardif(ive); **that change was long ~** ce changement n'avait que trop tardé.

overemphasis [əuvər'ɛmfəsıs] *n*: **to put an ~ on** accorder trop d'importance à.

overestimate [əuvər'ɛstımeıt] *vt* surestimer.

overexcited [əuvərɪk'saɪtɪd] *adj* surexcité(e).

overexertion [əuvərɪg'zəːʃən] *n* surmenage *m* (physique).

overexpose [əuvərɪk'spəuz] *vt* (*PHOT*) surexposer.

overflow *vi* [əuvə'fləu] déborder ♦ *n* ['əuvəfləu] trop-plein *m*; (*also:* ~ **pipe**) tuyau *m* d'écoulement, trop-plein *m*.

overfly [əuvə'flaɪ] *vt irreg* survoler.

overgenerous [əuvə'dʒɛnərəs] *adj* (*person*) prodigue; (*offer*) excessif(ive).

overgrown [əuvə'grəun] *adj* (*garden*) envahi(e) par la végétation; **he's just an ~ schoolboy** (*fig*) c'est un écolier attardé.

overhang ['əuvə'hæŋ] *irreg vt* surplomber ♦ *vi* faire saillie.

overhaul *vt* [əuvə'hɔːl] réviser ♦ *n* ['əuvəhɔːl] révision *f*.

overhead *adv* [əuvə'hɛd] au-dessus ♦ *adj*, *n* ['əuvəhɛd] *adj* aérien(ne); (*lighting*) vertical(e) ♦ *n* (*US*) = **overheads**.

overheads ['əuvəhɛdz] *npl* (*BRIT*) frais généraux.

overhear [əuvə'hɪə*] *vt irreg* entendre (par hasard).

overheat [əuvə'hiːt] *vi* devenir surchauffé(e); (*engine*) chauffer.

overjoyed [əuvə'dʒɔɪd] *adj* ravi(e), enchanté(e).

overkill ['əuvəkɪl] *n* (*fig*): **it would be** ~ ce serait de trop.

overland ['əuvəlænd] *adj*, *adv* par voie de terre.

overlap *vi* [əuvə'læp] se chevaucher ♦ *n* ['əuvəlæp] chevauchement *m*.

overleaf [əuvə'liːf] *adv* au verso.

overload [əuvə'ləud] *vt* surcharger.

overlook [əuvə'luk] *vt* (*have view of*) donner sur; (*miss*) oublier, négliger; (*forgive*) fermer les yeux sur.

overlord ['əuvəlɔːd] *n* chef *m* suprême.

overmanning [əuvə'mænɪŋ] *n* sureffectif *m*, main-d'œuvre *f* pléthorique.

overnight *adv* [əuvə'naɪt] (*happen*) durant la nuit; (*fig*) soudain ♦ *adj* ['əuvənaɪt] d'une (*or* de) nuit; soudain(e); **he stayed there** ~ il y a passé la nuit; **if you travel** ~ ... si tu fais le voyage de nuit ...; **he'll be away** ~ il ne rentrera pas ce soir.

overpass ['əuvəpɑːs] *n* pont autoroutier; (*US*) passerelle *f*, pont *m*.

overpay [əuvə'peɪ] *vt*: **to** ~ **sb by £50** donner à qn 50 livres de trop.

overplay [əuvə'pleɪ] *vt* exagérer; **to** ~ **one's hand** trop présumer de sa situation.

overpower [əuvə'pauə*] *vt* vaincre; (*fig*) accabler.

overpowering [əuvə'pauərɪŋ] *adj* irrésistible; (*heat, stench*) suffocant(e).

overproduction ['əuvəprə'dʌkʃən] *n* surproduction *f*.

overrate [əuvə'reɪt] *vt* surestimer.

overreact [əuvəriː'ækt] *vi* réagir de façon excessive.

override [əuvə'raɪd] *vt* (*irreg: like* **ride**) (*order, objection*) passer outre à; (*decision*) annuler.

overriding [əuvə'raɪdɪŋ] *adj* prépondérant(e).

overrule [əuvə'ruːl] *vt* (*decision*) annuler; (*claim*) rejeter.

overrun [əuvə'rʌn] *irreg vt* (*MIL: country etc*) occuper; (*time limit etc*) dépasser ♦ *vi* dépasser le temps imparti; **the town is** ~ **with tourists** la ville est envahie de touristes.

overseas [əuvə'siːz] *adv* outre-mer; (*abroad*) à l'étranger ♦ *adj* (*trade*) extérieur(e); (*visitor*) étranger(ère).

oversee [əuvə'siː] *vt irreg* surveiller.

overseer ['əuvəsɪə*] *n* (*in factory*) contremaître *m*.

overshadow [əuvə'ʃædəu] *vt* (*fig*) éclipser.

overshoot [əuvə'ʃuːt] *vt irreg* dépasser.

oversight ['əuvəsaɪt] *n* omission *f*, oubli *m*; **due to an** ~ par suite d'une inadvertance.

oversimplify [əuvə'sɪmplɪfaɪ] *vt* simplifier à l'excès.

oversleep [əuvə'sliːp] *vi irreg* se réveiller (trop) tard.

overspend [əuvə'spɛnd] *vi irreg* dépenser de trop; **we have overspent by 5,000 dollars** nous avons dépassé notre budget de 5 000 dollars, nous avons dépensé 5 000 dollars de trop.

overspill ['əuvəspɪl] *n* excédent *m* de population.

overstaffed [əuvə'stɑːft] *adj*: **to be** ~ avoir trop de personnel, être en surnombre.

overstate [əuvə'steɪt] *vt* exagérer.

overstatement [əuvə'steɪtmənt] *n* exagération *f*.

overstay [əuvə'steɪ] *vt*: **to** ~ **one's welcome (at sb's)** abuser de l'hospitalité de qn.

overstep [əuvə'stɛp] *vt*: **to** ~ **the mark** dépasser la mesure.

overstock [əuvə'stɔk] *vt* stocker en surabondance.

overstretched [əuvə'strɛtʃt] *adj* (*person*) débordé(e); **my budget is** ~ j'ai atteint les limites de mon budget.

overstrike *n* ['əuvəstraɪk] (*on printer*) superposition *f*, double frappe *f* ♦ *vt irreg* [əuvə'straɪk] surimprimer.

overt [əu'vɔːt] *adj* non dissimulé(e).

overtake [əuvə'teɪk] *vt irreg* dépasser; (*AUT*) dépasser, doubler.

overtaking [əuvə'teɪkɪŋ] *n* (*AUT*) dépassement *m*.

overtax [əuvə'tæks] *vt* (*ECON*) surimposer; (*fig: strength, patience*) abuser de; **to** ~ **o.s.** se surmener.

overthrow [əuvə'θrəu] *vt irreg* (*government*) renverser.

overtime ['əuvətaɪm] *n* heures *fpl* supplémentaires; **to do** *or* **work** ~ faire des heures supplémentaires.

overtime ban n refus m de faire des heures supplémentaires.

overtone ['əuvətəun] n (also: ~s) note f, sous-entendus mpl.

overture ['əuvətʃuə*] n (MUS, fig) ouverture f.

overturn [əuvə'tɜ:n] vt renverser ♦ vi se retourner.

overview ['əuvəvju:] n vue f d'ensemble.

overweight [əuvə'weit] adj (person) trop gros(se); (luggage) trop lourd(e).

overwhelm [əuvə'welm] vt accabler; submerger; écraser.

overwhelming [əuvə'welmiŋ] adj (victory, defeat) écrasant(e); (desire) irrésistible; **one's ~ impression is of heat** on a une impression dominante de chaleur.

overwhelmingly [əuvə'welmiŋli] adv (vote) en masse; (win) d'une manière écrasante.

overwork [əuvə'wɜ:k] n surmenage m ♦ vt surmener ♦ vi se surmener.

overwrite [əuvə'rait] vt irreg (COMPUT) écraser.

overwrought [əuvə'rɔ:t] adj excédé(e).

ovulation [ɔvju'leiʃən] n ovulation f.

owe [əu] vt devoir; **to ~ sb sth, to ~ sth to sb** devoir qch à qn.

owing to ['əuiŋtu:] prep à cause de, en raison de.

owl [aul] n hibou m.

own [əun] vt posséder ♦ vi (BRIT): **to ~ to sth** reconnaître or avouer qch; **to ~ to having done sth** avouer avoir fait qch ♦ adj propre; **a room of my ~** une chambre à moi, ma propre chambre; **can I have it for my (very) ~?** puis-je l'avoir pour moi (tout) seul?; **to get one's ~ back** prendre sa revanche; **on one's ~** tout(e) seul(e); **to come into one's ~** trouver sa voie; trouver sa justification.

▶**own up** vi avouer.

own brand n (COMM) marque f de distributeur.

owner ['əunə*] n propriétaire m/f.

owner-occupier ['əunər'ɔkjupaiə*] n propriétaire occupant.

ownership ['əunəʃip] n possession f; **it's under new ~** (shop etc) il y a eu un changement de propriétaire.

own goal n: **he scored an ~** (SPORT) il a marqué un but contre son camp; (fig) cela s'est retourné contre lui.

ox, pl **oxen** [ɔks, 'ɔksn] n bœuf m.

Oxbridge, nom formé à partir des mots Ox(ford) et (Cam)bridge, s'utilise pour parler de ces deux universités comme formant un tout, dans la mesure où elles sont toutes deux les universités britanniques les plus prestigieuses et mondialement connues.

Oxfam ['ɔksfæm] n abbr (BRIT: = Oxford Committee for Famine Relief) association humanitaire.

oxide ['ɔksaid] n oxyde m.

Oxon. ['ɔksn] abbr (BRIT: = Oxoniensis) = of Oxford.

oxtail ['ɔksteil] n: **~ soup** soupe f à la queue de bœuf.

oxyacetylene ['ɔksiə'sɛtili:n] adj oxyacétylénique; **~ burner, ~ lamp** chalumeau m oxyacétylénique.

oxygen ['ɔksidʒən] n oxygène m.

oxygen mask n masque m à oxygène.

oxygen tent n tente f à oxygène.

oyster ['ɔistə*] n huître f.

oz. abbr = **ounce.**

ozone ['əuzəun] n ozone m.

P p

P, p [pi:] n (letter) P, p m; **P for Peter** P comme Pierre.

P abbr = **president, prince.**

p abbr (= page) p; (BRIT) = **penny, pence.**

PA n abbr = **personal assistant, public address system** ♦ abbr (US) = Pennsylvania.

pa [pɑ:] n (col) papa m.

Pa. abbr (US) = Pennsylvania.

p.a. abbr = per annum.

PAC n abbr (US) = political action committee.

pace [peis] n pas m; (speed) allure f; vitesse f ♦ vi: **to ~ up and down** faire les cent pas; **to keep ~ with** aller à la même vitesse que; (events) se tenir au courant de; **to set the ~** (running) donner l'allure; (fig) donner le ton; **to put sb through his ~s** (fig) mettre qn à l'épreuve.

pacemaker ['peismeikə*] n (MED) stimulateur m cardiaque.

pacific [pə'sifik] adj pacifique ♦ n: **the P~ (Ocean)** le Pacifique, l'océan m Pacifique.

pacification [pæsifi'keiʃən] n pacification f.

pacifier ['pæsifaiə*] n (US: dummy) tétine f.

pacifist ['pæsifist] n pacifiste m/f.

pacify ['pæsifai] vt pacifier; (soothe) calmer.

pack [pæk] n paquet m; ballot m; (of hounds) meute f; (of thieves, wolves etc) bande f; (of cards) jeu m ♦ vt (goods) empaqueter, emballer; (in suitcase etc) emballer; (box) remplir; (cram) entasser; (press down) tasser; damer; (COMPUT) grouper, tasser ♦ vi: **to ~ (one's bags)** faire ses bagages; **to ~ into** (room, stadium) s'entasser dans; **to send sb ~ing** (col) envoyer promener qn.

▶**pack in** (BRIT col) vi (machine) tomber en panne ♦ vt (boyfriend) plaquer; **~ it in!** laisse tomber!

▶**pack off** vt (person) envoyer (promener),

expédier.

►**pack up** vi (BRIT col: machine) tomber en panne; (: person) se tirer ♦ vt (belongings) ranger; (goods, presents) empaqueter, emballer.

package ['pækɪdʒ] n paquet m; (of goods) emballage m, conditionnement m; (also: ~ **deal**) marché global; forfait m; (COMPUT) progiciel m ♦ vt (goods) conditionner.

package holiday n (BRIT) vacances organisées.

package tour n voyage organisé.

packaging ['pækɪdʒɪŋ] n conditionnement m.

packed [pækt] adj (crowded) bondé(e); ~ **lunch** (BRIT) repas froid.

packer ['pækə*] n (person) emballeur/euse; conditionneur/euse.

packet ['pækɪt] n paquet m.

packet switching [-swɪtʃɪŋ] n (COMPUT) commutation f de paquets.

pack ice ['pækaɪs] n banquise f.

packing ['pækɪŋ] n emballage m.

packing case n caisse f (d'emballage).

pact [pækt] n pacte m, traité m.

pad [pæd] n bloc(-notes m) m; (for inking) tampon m encreur; (col: flat) piaule f ♦ vt rembourrer ♦ vi: **to ~ in/about** etc entrer/aller et venir etc à pas feutrés.

padded cell ['pædɪd-] n cellule capitonnée.

padding ['pædɪŋ] n rembourrage m; (fig) délayage m.

paddle ['pædl] n (oar) pagaie f ♦ vi barboter, faire trempette ♦ vt: **to ~ a canoe** etc pagayer.

paddle steamer n bateau m à aubes.

paddling pool ['pædlɪŋ-] n petit bassin.

paddock ['pædək] n enclos m; paddock m.

paddy ['pædɪ] n (also: ~ **field**) rizière f.

padlock ['pædlɒk] n cadenas m ♦ vt cadenasser.

padre ['pɑːdrɪ] n aumônier m.

paediatrician, (US) **pediatrician** [piːdɪə-'trɪʃən] n pédiatre m/f.

paediatrics, (US) **pediatrics** [piːdɪ'ætrɪks] n pédiatrie f.

paedophile, (US) **pedophile** ['piːdəufaɪl] n pédophile m.

pagan ['peɪɡən] adj, n païen(ne).

page [peɪdʒ] n (of book) page f; (also: ~ **boy**) groom m, chasseur m; (at wedding) garçon m d'honneur ♦ vt (in hotel etc) (faire) appeler.

pageant ['pædʒənt] n spectacle m historique; grande cérémonie.

pageantry ['pædʒəntrɪ] n apparat m, pompe f.

page break n fin f or saut m de page.

pager ['peɪdʒə*] n système m de téléappel, bip m.

paginate ['pædʒɪneɪt] vt paginer.

pagination [pædʒɪ'neɪʃən] n pagination f.

pagoda [pə'ɡəudə] n pagode f.

paid [peɪd] pt, pp of **pay** ♦ adj (work, official) rémunéré(e); **to put ~ to** (BRIT) mettre fin à,

mettre par terre.

paid-up ['peɪdʌp], (US) **paid-in** ['peɪdɪn] adj (member) à jour de sa cotisation; (shares) libéré(e); ~ **capital** capital versé.

pail [peɪl] n seau m.

pain [peɪn] n douleur f; **to be in ~** souffrir, avoir mal; **to have a ~ in** avoir mal à or une douleur à or dans; **to take ~s to do** se donner du mal pour faire; **on ~ of death** sous peine de mort.

pained ['peɪnd] adj peiné(e), chagrin(e).

painful ['peɪnful] adj douloureux(euse); (difficult) difficile, pénible.

painfully ['peɪnfəlɪ] adv (fig: very) terriblement.

painkiller ['peɪnkɪlə*] n calmant m.

painless ['peɪnlɪs] adj indolore.

painstaking ['peɪnzteɪkɪŋ] adj (person) soigneux(euse); (work) soigné(e).

paint [peɪnt] n peinture f ♦ vt peindre; (fig) dépeindre; **to ~ the door blue** peindre la porte en bleu; **to ~ in oils** faire de la peinture à l'huile.

paintbox ['peɪntbɒks] n boîte f de couleurs.

paintbrush ['peɪntbrʌʃ] n pinceau m.

painter ['peɪntə*] n peintre m.

painting ['peɪntɪŋ] n peinture f; (picture) tableau m.

paint-stripper ['peɪntstrɪpə*] n décapant m.

paintwork ['peɪntwɜːk] n (BRIT) peintures fpl; (: of car) peinture f.

pair [pɛə*] n (of shoes, gloves etc) paire f; (couple) couple m; (twosome) duo m; ~ **of scissors** (paire de) ciseaux mpl; ~ **of trousers** pantalon m.

►**pair off** vi se mettre par deux.

pajamas [pə'dʒɑːməz] npl (US) pyjama(s) m(pl).

Pakistan [pɑːkɪ'stɑːn] n Pakistan m.

Pakistani [pɑːkɪ'stɑːnɪ] adj pakistanais(e) ♦ n Pakistanais/e.

PAL [pæl] n abbr (TV: = phase alternation line) PAL m.

pal [pæl] n (col) copain/copine.

palace ['pæləs] n palais m.

palatable ['pælɪtəbl] adj bon(bonne), agréable au goût.

palate ['pælɪt] n palais m (ANAT).

palatial [pə'leɪʃəl] adj grandiose, magnifique.

palaver [pə'lɑːvə*] n palabres fpl or mpl; histoire(s) f(pl).

pale [peɪl] adj pâle ♦ vi pâlir ♦ n: **to be beyond the ~** être au ban de la société; **to grow** or **turn ~** (person) pâlir; ~ **blue** adj bleu pâle inv; **to ~ into insignificance (beside)** perdre beaucoup d'importance (par rapport à).

paleness ['peɪlnɪs] n pâleur f.

Palestine ['pælɪstaɪn] n Palestine f.

Palestinian [pælɪs'tɪnɪən] adj palestinien(ne) ♦ n Palestinien/ne.

palette ['pælɪt] n palette f.

paling ['peɪlɪŋ] n (stake) palis m; (fence) palissade f.

palisade [pælɪ'seɪd] n palissade f.
pall [pɔːl] n (of smoke) voile m ♦ vi: **to ~ (on)** devenir lassant (pour).
pallet ['pælɪt] n (for goods) palette f.
pallid ['pælɪd] adj blême.
pallor ['pælə*] n pâleur f.
pally ['pælɪ] (col) copain(copine).
palm [pɑːm] n (ANAT) paume f; (also: ~ **tree**) palmier m; (leaf, symbol) palme f ♦ vt: **to ~ sth off on sb** (col) refiler qch à qn.
palmist ['pɑːmɪst] n chiromancien/ne.
Palm Sunday n le dimanche des Rameaux.
palpable ['pælpəbl] adj évident(e), manifeste.
palpitation [pælpɪ'teɪʃən] n palpitation f.
paltry ['pɔːltrɪ] adj dérisoire; piètre.
pamper ['pæmpə*] vt gâter, dorloter.
pamphlet ['pæmflət] n brochure f; (political etc) tract m.
pan [pæn] n (also: **sauce**~) casserole f; (also: **frying** ~) poêle f; (of lavatory) cuvette f ♦ vi (CINE) faire un panoramique ♦ vt (col: book, film) éreinter; **to ~ for gold** laver du sable aurifère.
panacea [pænə'sɪə] n panacée f.
Panama ['pænəmɑː] n Panama m.
Panama canal n canal m de Panama.
pancake ['pænkeɪk] n crêpe f.
Pancake Day n (BRIT) mardi gras.
pancake roll n rouleau m de printemps.
pancreas ['pæŋkrɪəs] n pancréas m.
panda ['pændə] n panda m.
panda car n (BRIT) ≈ voiture f pie inv.
pandemonium [pændɪ'məʊnɪəm] n tohu-bohu m.
pander ['pændə*] vi: **to ~ to** flatter bassement; obéir servilement à.
p&h abbr (US: = postage and handling) frais mpl de port.
P&L abbr = profit and loss.
p&p abbr (BRIT: = postage and packing) frais mpl de port.
pane [peɪn] n carreau m (de fenêtre).
panel ['pænl] n (of wood, cloth etc) panneau m; (RADIO, TV) panel m, invités mpl; (of experts) table ronde, comité m.
panel game n (BRIT) jeu m (radiophonique/ télévisé).
panelling, (US) **paneling** ['pænəlɪŋ] n boiseries fpl.
panellist, (US) **panelist** ['pænəlɪst] n invité/e (d'un panel), membre d'un panel.
pang [pæŋ] n: **~s of remorse** pincements mpl de remords; **~s of hunger/conscience** tiraillements mpl d'estomac/de la conscience.
panhandler ['pænhændlə*] n (US col) mendiant/e.
panic ['pænɪk] n panique f, affolement m ♦ vi s'affoler, paniquer.
panic buying [-baɪɪŋ] n achats mpl de précaution.
panicky ['pænɪkɪ] adj (person) qui panique or s'affole facilement.

panic-stricken ['pænɪkstrɪkən] adj affolé(e).
pannier ['pænɪə*] n (on animal) bât m; (on bicycle) sacoche f.
panorama [pænə'rɑːmə] n panorama m.
panoramic [pænə'ræmɪk] adj panoramique.
pansy ['pænzɪ] n (BOT) pensée f; (col) tapette f, pédé m.
pant [pænt] vi haleter.
pantechnicon [pæn'teknɪkən] n (BRIT) (grand) camion de déménagement.
panther ['pænθə*] n panthère f.
panties ['pæntɪz] npl slip m, culotte f.
pantihose ['pæntɪhəʊz] n (US) collant m.
panto ['pæntəʊ] n = **pantomime.**
pantomime ['pæntəmaɪm] n (BRIT) spectacle m de Noël.

Une **pantomime** (à ne pas confondre avec le mot tel qu'on l'utilise en français), que l'on appelle également de façon familière "panto", est un genre de farce où le personnage principal est souvent un jeune garçon et où il y a toujours une **dame**, c'est-à-dire une vieille femme jouée par un homme, et un méchant. La plupart du temps, l'histoire est basée sur un conte de fées comme Cendrillon ou Le Chat botté, et le public est encouragé à participer en prévenant le héros d'un danger imminent. Ce genre de spectacle, qui s'adresse surtout aux enfants, vise également un public d'adultes au travers des nombreuses plaisanteries faisant allusion à des faits d'actualité.

---

pantry ['pæntrɪ] n garde-manger m inv; (room) office m.
pants [pænts] n (BRIT: woman's) culotte f, slip m; (: man's) slip m, caleçon m; (US: trousers) pantalon m.
pantsuit ['pæntsuːt] n (US) tailleur-pantalon m.
papacy ['peɪpəsɪ] n papauté f.
papal ['peɪpəl] adj papal(e), pontifical(e).
paparazzi [pæpə'rætsiː] npl paparazzi mpl.
paper ['peɪpə*] n papier m; (also: **wall**~) papier peint; (also: **news**~) journal m; (study, article) article m; (exam) épreuve écrite ♦ adj en or de papier ♦ vt tapisser (de papier peint); **a piece of ~** (odd bit) un bout de papier; (sheet) une feuille de papier; **to put sth down on ~** mettre qch par écrit.
paper advance n (on printer) avance f (du) papier.
paperback ['peɪpəbæk] n livre m de poche; livre broché or non relié ♦ adj: **~ edition** édition brochée.
paper bag n sac m en papier.
paperboy ['peɪpəbɔɪ] n (selling) vendeur m de journaux; (delivering) livreur m de journaux.
paper clip n trombone m.
paper handkerchief n mouchoir m en papier.
paper mill n papeterie f.
paper money n papier-monnaie m.

paper profit *n* profit *m* théorique.
papers ['peɪpəz] *npl* (*also*: **identity** ~) papiers *mpl* (d'identité).
paper shop *n* (*BRIT*) marchand *m* de journaux.
paperweight ['peɪpəweɪt] *n* presse-papiers *m inv*.
paperwork ['peɪpəwɔːk] *n* paperasserie *f*.
papier-mâché ['pæpɪeɪ'mæʃeɪ] *n* papier mâché.
paprika ['pæprɪkə] *n* paprika *m*.
Pap test, Pap smear ['pæp-] *n* (*MED*) frottis *m*.
par [pɑː*] *n* pair *m*; (*GOLF*) normale *f* du parcours; **on a** ~ **with** à égalité avec, au même niveau que; **at** ~ au pair; **above/below** ~ au-dessus/au-dessous du pair; **to feel below** *or* **under** *or* **not up to** ~ ne pas se sentir en forme.
parable ['pærəbl] *n* parabole *f* (*REL*).
parabola [pə'ræbələ] *n* parabole *f* (*MATH*).
parachute ['pærəʃuːt] *n* parachute *m* ♦ *vi* sauter en parachute.
parachute jump *n* saut *m* en parachute.
parachutist ['pærəʃuːtɪst] *n* parachutiste *m/f*.
parade [pə'reɪd] *n* défilé *m*; (*inspection*) revue *f*; (*street*) boulevard *m* ♦ *vt* (*fig*) faire étalage de ♦ *vi* défiler; **a fashion** ~ (*BRIT*) un défilé de mode.
parade ground *n* terrain *m* de manœuvre.
paradise ['pærədaɪs] *n* paradis *m*.
paradox ['pærədɔks] *n* paradoxe *m*.
paradoxical [pærə'dɔksɪkl] *adj* paradoxal(e).
paradoxically [pærə'dɔksɪklɪ] *adv* paradoxalement.
paraffin ['pærəfɪn] *n* (*BRIT*): ~ **(oil)** pétrole (lampant); **liquid** ~ huile *f* de paraffine.
paraffin heater *n* (*BRIT*) poêle *m* à mazout.
paraffin lamp *n* (*BRIT*) lampe *f* à pétrole.
paragon ['pærəgən] *n* parangon *m*.
paragraph ['pærəgrɑːf] *n* paragraphe *m*; **to begin a new** ~ aller à la ligne.
Paraguay ['pærəgwaɪ] *n* Paraguay *m*.
Paraguayan [pærə'gwaɪən] *adj* paraguayen(ne) ♦ *n* Paraguayen/ne.
parallel ['pærəlɛl] *adj*: ~ **(with** *or* **to)** parallèle (à); (*fig*) analogue (à) ♦ *n* (*line*) parallèle *f*; (*fig, GEO*) parallèle *m*.
paralysis [pə'rælɪsɪs], *pl* **paralyses** [pə'rælɪsɪs, -siːz] *n* paralysie *f*.
paralytic [pærə'lɪtɪk] *adj* paralytique; (*BRIT col*: *drunk*) ivre mort(e).
paralyze ['pærəlaɪz] *vt* paralyser.
paramedic [pærə'mɛdɪk] *n* auxiliaire *m/f* médical(e).
parameter [pə'ræmɪtə*] *n* paramètre *m*.
paramilitary [pærə'mɪlɪtərɪ] *adj* paramilitaire.
paramount ['pærəmaunt] *adj*: **of** ~ **importance** de la plus haute *or* grande importance.
paranoia [pærə'nɔɪə] *n* paranoïa *f*.
paranoid ['pærənɔɪd] *adj* (*PSYCH*) paranoïaque; (*neurotic*) paranoïde.

paranormal [pærə'nɔːml] *adj* paranormal(e).
paraphernalia [pærəfə'neɪlɪə] *n* attirail *m*, affaires *fpl*.
paraphrase ['pærəfreɪz] *vt* paraphraser.
paraplegic [pærə'pliːdʒɪk] *n* paraplégique *m/f*.
parapsychology [pærəsaɪ'kɔlədʒɪ] *n* parapsychologie *f*.
parasite ['pærəsaɪt] *n* parasite *m*.
parasol ['pærəsɔl] *n* ombrelle *f*; (*at café etc*) parasol *m*.
paratrooper ['pærətruːpə*] *n* parachutiste *m* (*soldat*).
parcel ['pɑːsl] *n* paquet *m*, colis *m* ♦ *vt* (*also*: ~ **up**) empaqueter.
►**parcel out** *vt* répartir.
parcel bomb *n* (*BRIT*) colis piégé.
parcel post *n* service *m* de colis postaux.
parch [pɑːtʃ] *vt* dessécher.
parched [pɑːtʃt] *adj* (*person*) assoiffé(e).
parchment ['pɑːtʃmənt] *n* parchemin *m*.
pardon ['pɑːdn] *n* pardon *m*; grâce *f* ♦ *vt* pardonner à; (*LAW*) gracier; ~! pardon!; ~ **me!** excusez-moi!; **I beg your** ~! pardon!, je suis désolé!; **(I beg your)** ~?, (*US*) ~ **me?** pardon?
pare [pɛə*] *vt* (*BRIT*: *nails*) couper; (*fruit etc*) peler; (*fig: costs etc*) réduire.
parent ['pɛərənt] *n* père *m* *or* mère *f*; ~**s** *npl* parents *mpl*.
parentage ['pɛərəntɪdʒ] *n* naissance *f*; **of unknown** ~ de parents inconnus.
parental [pə'rɛntl] *adj* parental(e), des parents.
parent company *n* société *f* mère.
parenthesis, *pl* **parentheses** [pə'rɛnθɪsɪs, -siːz] *n* parenthèse *f*; **in parentheses** entre parenthèses.
parenthood ['pɛərənthud] *n* paternité *f* *or* maternité *f*.
parenting ['pɛərəntɪŋ] *n* le métier de parent, le travail d'un parent.
Paris ['pærɪs] *n* Paris.
parish ['pærɪʃ] *n* paroisse *f*; (*civil*) ≈ commune *f* ♦ *adj* paroissial(e).
parish council *n* (*BRIT*) ≈ conseil municipal.
parishioner [pə'rɪʃənə*] *n* paroissien/ne.
Parisian [pə'rɪzɪən] *adj* parisien(ne) ♦ *n* Parisien/ne.
parity ['pærɪtɪ] *n* parité *f*.
park [pɑːk] *n* parc *m*, jardin public ♦ *vt* garer ♦ *vi* se garer.
parka ['pɑːkə] *n* parka *m*.
parking ['pɑːkɪŋ] *n* stationnement *m*; "**no** ~" "stationnement interdit".
parking lights *npl* feux *mpl* de stationnement.
parking lot *n* (*US*) parking *m*, parc *m* de stationnement.
parking meter *n* parc(o)mètre *m*.
parking offence, (*US*) **parking violation** *n* infraction *f* au stationnement.
parking place *n* place *f* de stationnement.
parking ticket *n* P.-V. *m*.
Parkinson's ['pɑːkɪnsənz] *n* (*also*: ~ **disease**)

maladie *f* de Parkinson, parkinson *m*.

parkway ['pɑːkweɪ] *n* (US) route *f* express (*en site vert ou aménagé*).

parlance ['pɑːləns] *n*: **in common/modern** ~ dans le langage courant/actuel.

parliament ['pɑːləmənt] *n* parlement *m*.

Le **Parliament** *est l'assemblée législative britannique; elle est composée de deux chambres: la* **House of Commons** *et la* **House of Lords**. *Ses bureaux sont les "Houses of Parliament" au palais de Westminster à Londres. Chaque Parliament est en général élu pour cinq ans. Les débats du Parliament sont maintenant retransmis à la télévision.*

---

parliamentary [pɑːlə'mɛntərɪ] *adj* parlementaire.

parlour, (US) **parlor** ['pɑːlə*] *n* salon *m*.

parlous ['pɑːləs] *adj* (*formal*) précaire.

Parmesan [pɑːmɪ'zæn] *n* (*also:* ~ **cheese**) Parmesan *m*.

parochial [pə'rəukɪəl] *adj* paroissial(e); (*pej*) à l'esprit de clocher.

parody ['pærədɪ] *n* parodie *f*.

parole [pə'rəul] *n*: **on** ~ en liberté conditionnelle.

paroxysm ['pærəksɪzəm] *n* (*MED, of grief*) paroxysme *m*; (*of anger*) accès *m*.

parquet ['pɑːkeɪ] *n*: ~ **floor(ing)** parquet *m*.

parrot ['pærət] *n* perroquet *m*.

parrot fashion *adv* comme un perroquet.

parry ['pærɪ] *vt* esquiver, parer à.

parsimonious [pɑːsɪ'məunɪəs] *adj* parcimonieux(euse).

parsley ['pɑːslɪ] *n* persil *m*.

parsnip ['pɑːsnɪp] *n* panais *m*.

parson ['pɑːsn] *n* ecclésiastique *m*; (*Church of England*) pasteur *m*.

parsonage ['pɑːsnɪdʒ] *n* presbytère *m*.

part [pɑːt] *n* partie *f*; (*of machine*) pièce *f*; (*THEAT etc*) rôle *m*; (*MUS*) voix *f*; partie ♦ *adj* partiel(le) ♦ *adv* = **partly** ♦ *vt* séparer ♦ *vi* (*people*) se séparer; (*roads*) se diviser; **to take** ~ **in** participer à, prendre part à; **to take sb's** ~ prendre le parti de qn, prendre parti pour qn; **on his** ~ de sa part; **for my** ~ en ce qui me concerne; **for the most** ~ en grande partie; dans la plupart des cas; **for the better** ~ **of the day** pendant la plus grande partie de la journée; **to be** ~ **and parcel of** faire partie de; **to take sth in good/bad** ~ prendre qch du bon/mauvais côté; ~ **of speech** (*LING*) partie *f* du discours.

►**part with** *vt fus* se séparer de; se défaire de.

partake [pɑː'teɪk] *vi irreg* (*formal*): **to** ~ **of sth** prendre part à qch, partager qch.

part exchange *n* (*BRIT*): **in** ~ en reprise.

partial ['pɑːʃl] *adj* partiel(le); (*unjust*) partial(e); **to be** ~ **to** aimer, avoir un faible pour.

partially ['pɑːʃəlɪ] *adv* en partie, partiellement;

partialement.

participant [pɑː'tɪsɪpənt] *n*: ~ **(in)** participant/e (à).

participate [pɑː'tɪsɪpeɪt] *vi*: **to** ~ **(in)** participer (à), prendre part (à).

participation [pɑːtɪsɪ'peɪʃən] *n* participation *f*.

participle ['pɑːtɪsɪpl] *n* participe *m*.

particle ['pɑːtɪkl] *n* particule *f*.

particular [pə'tɪkjulə*] *adj* (*specific*) particulier(ière); (*special*) particulier, spécial(e); (*fussy*) difficile, exigeant(e); méticuleux(euse); ~**s** *npl* détails *mpl*; (*information*) renseignements *mpl*; **in** ~ surtout, en particulier.

particularly [pə'tɪkjuləlɪ] *adv* particulièrement; (*in particular*) en particulier.

parting ['pɑːtɪŋ] *n* séparation *f*; (*BRIT: in hair*) raie *f* ♦ *adj* d'adieu; **his** ~ **shot was** ... il lança en partant ....

partisan [pɑːtɪ'zæn] *n* partisan/e ♦ *adj* partisan(e); de parti.

partition [pɑː'tɪʃən] *n* (*POL*) partition *f*, division *f*; (*wall*) cloison *f*.

partly ['pɑːtlɪ] *adv* en partie, partiellement.

partner ['pɑːtnə*] *n* (*COMM*) associé/e; (*SPORT*) partenaire *m/f*; (*at dance*) cavalier/ière ♦ *vt* être l'associé *or* le partenaire *or* le cavalier de.

partnership ['pɑːtnəʃɪp] *n* association *f*; **to go into** ~ **(with)**, **form a** ~ **(with)** s'associer (avec).

part payment *n* acompte *m*.

partridge ['pɑːtrɪdʒ] *n* perdrix *f*.

part-time ['pɑːt'taɪm] *adj*, *adv* à mi-temps, à temps partiel.

part-timer [pɑːt'taɪmə*] *n* (*also:* **part-time worker**) travailleur/euse à temps partiel.

party ['pɑːtɪ] *n* (*POL*) parti *m*; (*team*) équipe *f*; groupe *m*; (*LAW*) partie *f*; (*celebration*) réception *f*; soirée *f*; réunion *f*, fête *f*; **dinner** ~ dîner *m*; **to give** *or* **throw a** ~ donner une réception; **we're having a** ~ **next Saturday** nous organisons une soirée *or* réunion entre amis samedi prochain; **it's for our son's birthday** ~ c'est pour la fête (*or* le goûter) d'anniversaire de notre garçon; **to be a** ~ **to a crime** être impliqué(e) dans un crime.

party line *n* (*POL*) ligne *f* politique; (*TEL*) ligne partagée.

party piece *n* numéro habituel.

party political broadcast *n* émission réservée à un parti politique.

pass [pɑːs] *vt* (*time, object*) passer; (*place*) passer devant; (*car, friend*) croiser; (*exam*) être reçu(e) à, réussir; (*candidate*) admettre; (*overtake, surpass*) dépasser; (*approve*) approuver, accepter; (*law*) promulguer ♦ *vi* passer; (*SCOL*) être reçu(e) *or* admis(e), réussir ♦ *n* (*permit*) laissez-passer *m inv*; carte *f* d'accès *or* d'abonnement; (*in mountains*) col *m*; (*SPORT*) passe *f*; (*SCOL: also:* ~ **mark**): **to get a** ~ être reçu(e) (sans mention); **she**

could ~ **for 25** on lui donnerait 25 ans; **to ~ sth through a ring** *etc* (faire) passer qch dans un anneau *etc*; **could you ~ the vegetables round?** pourriez-vous faire passer les légumes?; **things have come to a pretty ~** (*BRIT*) voilà où on en est!; **to make a ~ at sb** (*col*) faire des avances à qn.

▶**pass away** *vi* mourir.

▶**pass by** *vi* passer ♦ *vt* négliger.

▶**pass down** *vt* (*customs, inheritance*) transmettre.

▶**pass on** *vi* (*die*) s'éteindre, décéder ♦ *vt* (*hand on*): **to ~ on (to)** transmettre (à); (: *illness*) passer (à); (: *price rises*) répercuter (sur).

▶**pass out** *vi* s'évanouir; (*BRIT MIL*) sortir (*d'une école militaire*).

▶**pass over** *vt* (*ignore*) passer sous silence.

▶**pass up** *vt* (*opportunity*) laisser passer.

passable ['pɑːsəbl] *adj* (*road*) praticable; (*work*) acceptable.

passage ['pæsɪdʒ] *n* (*also:* ~**way**) couloir *m*; (*gen, in book*) passage *m*; (*by boat*) traversée *f*.

passenger ['pæsɪndʒə*] *n* passager/ère.

passer-by ['pɑːsə'baɪ] *n* passant/e.

passing ['pɑːsɪŋ] *adj* (*fig*) passager(ère); **in ~** en passant.

passing place *n* (*AUT*) aire *f* de croisement.

passion ['pæʃən] *n* passion *f*; **to have a ~ for sth** avoir la passion de qch.

passionate ['pæʃənɪt] *adj* passionné(e).

passion fruit *n* fruit *m* de la passion.

passion play *n* mystère *m* de la Passion.

passive ['pæsɪv] *adj* (*also LING*) passif(ive).

passive smoking *n* tabagisme passif.

passkey ['pɑːskiː] *n* passe *m*.

Passover ['pɑːsəuvə*] *n* Pâque juive.

passport ['pɑːspɔːt] *n* passeport *m*.

passport control *n* contrôle *m* des passeports.

password ['pɑːswɜːd] *n* mot *m* de passe.

past [pɑːst] *prep* (*further than*) au delà de, plus loin que; après; (*later than*) après ♦ *adj* passé(e); (*president etc*) ancien(ne) ♦ *n* passé *m*; **quarter/half ~ four** quatre heures et quart/ demie; **ten/twenty ~ four** quatre heures dix/vingt; **he's ~ forty** il a dépassé la quarantaine, il a plus de *or* passé quarante ans; **it's ~ midnight** il est plus de minuit, il est passé minuit; **for the ~ few/3 days** depuis quelques/3 jours; ces derniers/3 derniers jours; **to run ~** passer en courant; **he ran ~ me** il m'a dépassé en courant; il a passé devant moi en courant; **in the ~** (*gen*) dans le temps, autrefois; (*LING*) au passé; **I'm ~ caring** je ne m'en fais plus; **to be ~ it** (*BRIT col: person*) avoir passé l'âge.

pasta ['pæstə] *n* pâtes *fpl*.

paste [peɪst] *n* (*glue*) colle *f* (de pâte); (*jewellery*) strass *m*; (*CULIN*) pâté *m* (à tartiner); pâte *f* ♦ *vt* coller; **tomato ~** concentré *m* de tomate, purée *f* de tomate.

pastel ['pæstl] *adj* pastel *inv*.

pasteurized ['pæstəraɪzd] *adj* pasteurisé(e).

pastille ['pæstl] *n* pastille *f*.

pastime ['pɑːstaɪm] *n* passe-temps *m inv*, distraction *f*.

past master *n* (*BRIT*): **to be a ~ at** être expert en.

pastor ['pɑːstə*] *n* pasteur *m*.

pastoral ['pɑːstərl] *adj* pastoral(e).

pastry ['peɪstrɪ] *n* pâte *f*; (*cake*) pâtisserie *f*.

pasture ['pɑːstʃə*] *n* pâturage *m*.

pasty *n* ['pæstɪ] petit pâté (en croûte) ♦ *adj* ['peɪstɪ] pâteux(euse); (*complexion*) terreux(euse).

pat [pæt] *vt* donner une petite tape à ♦ *n*: **a ~ of butter** une noisette de beurre; **to give sb/o.s. a ~ on the back** (*fig*) congratuler qn/ se congratuler; **he knows it (off) ~**, (*US*) **he has it down ~** il sait cela sur le bout des doigts.

patch [pætʃ] *n* (*of material*) pièce *f*; (*spot*) tache *f*; (*of land*) parcelle *f* ♦ *vt* (*clothes*) rapiécer; **a bad ~** (*BRIT*) une période difficile.

▶**patch up** *vt* réparer.

patchwork ['pætʃwɜːk] *n* patchwork *m*.

patchy ['pætʃɪ] *adj* inégal(e).

pate [peɪt] *n*: **a bald ~** un crâne chauve *or* dégarni.

pâté ['pæteɪ] *n* pâté *m*, terrine *f*.

patent ['peɪtnt, (*US*) 'pætənt] *n* brevet *m* (d'invention) ♦ *vt* faire breveter ♦ *adj* patent(e), manifeste.

patent leather *n* cuir verni.

patently ['peɪtntlɪ] *adv* manifestement.

patent medicine *n* spécialité *f* pharmaceutique.

patent office *n* bureau *m* des brevets.

paternal [pə'tɜːnl] *adj* paternel(le).

paternity [pə'tɜːnɪtɪ] *n* paternité *f*.

paternity suit *n* (*LAW*) action *f* en recherche de paternité.

path [pɑːθ] *n* chemin *m*, sentier *m*; allée *f*; (*of planet*) course *f*; (*of missile*) trajectoire *f*.

pathetic [pə'θetɪk] *adj* (*pitiful*) pitoyable; (*very bad*) lamentable, minable; (*moving*) pathétique.

pathological [pæθə'lɒdʒɪkl] *adj* pathologique.

pathologist [pə'θɒlədʒɪst] *n* pathologiste *m/f*.

pathology [pə'θɒlədʒɪ] *n* pathologie *f*.

pathos ['peɪθɒs] *n* pathétique *m*.

pathway ['pɑːθweɪ] *n* chemin *m*, sentier *m*.

patience ['peɪʃns] *n* patience *f*; (*BRIT: CARDS*) réussite *f*; **to lose (one's) ~** perdre patience.

patient ['peɪʃnt] *n* patient/e; (*in hospital*) malade *m/f* ♦ *adj* patient(e).

patiently ['peɪʃntlɪ] *adv* patiemment.

patio ['pætɪəu] *n* patio *m*.

patriot ['peɪtrɪət] *n* patriote *m/f*.

patriotic [pætrɪ'ɒtɪk] *adj* patriotique; (*person*) patriote.

patriotism ['pætrɪətɪzəm] *n* patriotisme *m*.

patrol [pə'trəul] *n* patrouille *f* ♦ *vt* patrouiller

dans; **to be on** ~ être de patrouille.
patrol boat *n* patrouilleur *m*.
patrol car *n* voiture *f* de police.
patrolman [pə'trəulmən] *n* (*US*) agent *m* de police.
patron ['peɪtrən] *n* (*in shop*) client/e; (*of charity*) patron/ne; ~ **of the arts** mécène *m*.
patronage ['pætrənɪdʒ] *n* patronage *m*, appui *m*.
patronize ['pætrənaɪz] *vt* être (un) client *or* un habitué de; (*fig*) traiter avec condescendance.
patronizing ['pætrənaɪzɪŋ] *adj* condescendant(e).
patron saint *n* saint(e) patron/ne.
patter ['pætə*] *n* crépitement *m*, tapotement *m*; (*sales talk*) boniment *m* ♦ *vi* crépiter, tapoter.
pattern ['pætən] *n* modèle *m*; (*SEWING*) patron *m*; (*design*) motif *m*; (*sample*) échantillon *m*; **behaviour** ~ mode *m* de comportement.
patterned ['pætənd] *adj* à motifs.
paucity ['pɔːsɪtɪ] *n* pénurie *f*, carence *f*.
paunch [pɔːntʃ] *n* gros ventre, bedaine *f*.
pauper ['pɔːpə*] *n* indigent/e; ~**'s grave** fosse commune.
pause [pɔːz] *n* pause *f*, arrêt *m*; (*MUS*) silence *m* ♦ *vi* faire une pause, s'arrêter; **to** ~ **for breath** reprendre son souffle; (*fig*) faire une pause.
pave [peɪv] *vt* paver, daller; **to** ~ **the way for** ouvrir la voie à.
pavement ['peɪvmənt] *n* (*BRIT*) trottoir *m*; (*US*) chaussée *f*.
pavilion [pə'vɪlɪən] *n* pavillon *m*; tente *f*; (*SPORT*) stand *m*.
paving ['peɪvɪŋ] *n* pavage *m*, dallage *m*.
paving stone *n* pavé *m*.
paw [pɔː] *n* patte *f* ♦ *vt* donner un coup de patte à; (*subj: person: pej*) tripoter.
pawn [pɔːn] *n* gage *m*; (*CHESS, also fig*) pion *m* ♦ *vt* mettre en gage.
pawnbroker ['pɔːnbrəukə*] *n* prêteur *m* sur gages.
pawnshop ['pɔːnʃɔp] *n* mont-de-piété *m*.
pay [peɪ] *n* salaire *m*; (*of manual worker*) paie *f* ♦ *vb* (*pt, pp* **paid** [peɪd]) *vt* payer; (*be profitable to: also fig*) rapporter à ♦ *vi* payer; (*be profitable*) être rentable; **how much did you** ~ **for it?** combien l'avez-vous payé?, vous l'avez payé combien?; **I paid £5 for that record** j'ai payé ce disque 5 livres; **to** ~ **one's way** payer sa part; (*company*) couvrir ses frais; **to** ~ **dividends** (*fig*) porter ses fruits, s'avérer rentable; **it won't** ~ **you to do that** vous ne gagnerez rien à faire cela; **to** ~ **attention (to)** prêter attention (à).
►**pay back** *vt* rembourser.
►**pay in** *vt* verser.
►**pay off** *vt* (*debts*) régler, acquitter; (*creditor, mortgage*) rembourser; (*workers*) licencier ♦ *vi* (*plan, patience*) se révéler payant(e); **to**

~ **sth off in instalments** payer qch à tempérament.
►**pay out** *vt* (*money*) payer, sortir de sa poche; (*rope*) laisser filer.
►**pay up** *vt* (*debts*) régler; (*amount*) payer.
payable ['peɪəbl] *adj* payable; **to make a cheque** ~ **to sb** établir un chèque à l'ordre de qn.
pay award *n* augmentation *f*.
pay day *n* jour *m* de paie.
PAYE *n abbr* (*BRIT*: = *pay as you earn*) système de retenue des impôts à la source.
payee [peɪ'iː] *n* bénéficiaire *m/f*.
pay envelope *n* (*US*) (enveloppe *f* de) paie *f*.
paying ['peɪɪŋ] *adj* payant(e); ~ **guest** hôte payant.
payload ['peɪləud] *n* charge *f* utile.
payment ['peɪmənt] *n* paiement *m*; (*of bill*) règlement *m*; (*of deposit, cheque*) versement *m*; **advance** ~ (*part sum*) acompte *m*; (*total sum*) paiement anticipé; **deferred** ~, ~ **by instalments** paiement par versements échelonnés; **monthly** ~ mensualité *f*; **in** ~ **for, in** ~ **of** en règlement de; **on** ~ **of £5** pour 5 livres.
pay packet *n* (*BRIT*) paie *f*.
payphone ['peɪfəun] *n* cabine *f* téléphonique, téléphone public.
payroll ['peɪrəul] *n* registre *m* du personnel; **to be on a firm's** ~ être employé par une entreprise.
pay slip *n* (*BRIT*) bulletin *m* de paie, feuille *f* de paie.
pay station *n* (*US*) cabine *f* téléphonique.
PBS *n abbr* (*US*: = *Public Broadcasting Service*) groupement d'aide à la réalisation d'émissions pour la TV publique.
PC *n abbr* = **personal computer**; (*BRIT*) = **police constable** ♦ *adj abbr* = **politically correct** ♦ *abbr* (*BRIT*) = *Privy Councillor*.
pc *abbr* = **per cent, postcard**.
p/c *abbr* = **petty cash**.
PCB *n abbr* = **printed circuit board**.
PD *n abbr* (*US*) = **police department**.
pd *abbr* = **paid**.
PDSA *n abbr* (*BRIT*) = *People's Dispensary for Sick Animals*.
PDT *abbr* (*US*: = *Pacific Daylight Time*) heure d'été du Pacifique.
PE *n abbr* (= *physical education*) EPS *f* ♦ *abbr* (*Canada*) = *Prince Edward Island*.
pea [piː] *n* (petit) pois.
peace [piːs] *n* paix *f*; (*calm*) calme *m*, tranquillité *f*; **to be at** ~ **with sb/sth** être en paix avec qn/qch; **to keep the** ~ (*subj: policeman*) assurer le maintien de l'ordre; (: *citizen*) ne pas troubler l'ordre.
peaceable ['piːsəbl] *adj* paisible, pacifique.
peaceful ['piːsful] *adj* paisible, calme.
peacekeeper ['piːskiːpə*] *n* (*force*) force gardienne de la paix.
peacekeeping ['piːskiːpɪŋ] *n* maintien *m* de la

paix.

peacekeeping force n forces fpl qui assurent le maintien de la paix.

peace offering n gage m de réconciliation; (*humorous*) gage de paix.

peach [piːtʃ] n pêche f.

peacock ['piːkɔk] n paon m.

peak [piːk] n (*mountain*) pic m, cime f; (*fig: highest level*) maximum m; (: *of career, fame*) apogée m.

peak-hour ['piːkauə*] adj (*traffic etc*) de pointe.

peak hours npl heures fpl d'affluence.

peak period n période f de pointe.

peak rate n plein tarif.

peaky ['piːkɪ] adj (*BRIT col*) fatigué(e).

peal [piːl] n (*of bells*) carillon m; ~s of laughter éclats mpl de rire.

peanut ['piːnʌt] n arachide f, cacahuète f.

peanut butter n beurre m de cacahuète.

pear [pɛə*] n poire f.

pearl [pɜːl] n perle f.

peasant ['pɛznt] n paysan/ne.

peat [piːt] n tourbe f.

pebble ['pɛbl] n galet m, caillou m.

peck [pɛk] vt (*also:* ~ *at*) donner un coup de bec à; (*food*) picorer ♦ n coup m de bec; (*kiss*) bécot m.

pecking order ['pɛkɪŋ-] n ordre m hiérarchique.

peckish ['pɛkɪʃ] adj (*BRIT col*): **I feel** ~ je mangerais bien quelque chose, j'ai la dent.

peculiar [pɪ'kjuːlɪə*] adj (*odd*) étrange, bizarre, curieux(euse); (*particular*) particulier(ière); ~ **to** particulier à.

peculiarity [pɪkjuːlɪ'ærɪtɪ] n bizarrerie f, particularité f.

pecuniary [pɪ'kjuːnɪərɪ] adj pécuniaire.

pedal ['pɛdl] n pédale f ♦ vi pédaler.

pedal bin n (*BRIT*) poubelle f à pédale.

pedantic [pɪ'dæntɪk] adj pédant(e).

peddle ['pɛdl] vt colporter; (*drugs*) faire le trafic de.

peddler ['pɛdlə*] n colporteur m; camelot m.

pedestal ['pɛdəstl] n piédestal m.

pedestrian [pɪ'dɛstrɪən] n piéton m ♦ adj piétonnier(ière); (*fig*) prosaïque, terre à terre inv.

pedestrian crossing n (*BRIT*) passage clouté.

pedestrian precinct n (*BRIT*) zone piétonne.

pediatrics [piːdɪ'ætrɪks] n (*US*) = **paediatrics**.

pedigree ['pɛdɪgriː] n ascendance f; (*of animal*) pedigree m ♦ cpd (*animal*) de race.

pedlar ['pɛdlə*] n = **peddler**.

pee [piː] vi (*col*) faire pipi, pisser.

peek [piːk] vi jeter un coup d'œil (furtif).

peel [piːl] n pelure f, épluchure f; (*of orange, lemon*) écorce f ♦ vt peler, éplucher ♦ vi (*paint etc*) s'écailler; (*wallpaper*) se décoller.

►**peel back** vt décoller.

peeler ['piːlə*] n (*potato etc* ~) éplucheur m.

peelings ['piːlɪŋz] npl pelures fpl, épluchures fpl.

peep [piːp] n (*BRIT: look*) coup d'œil furtif; (*sound*) pépiement m ♦ vi (*BRIT*) jeter un coup d'œil (furtif).

►**peep out** vi (*BRIT*) se montrer (furtivement).

peephole ['piːphəul] n judas m.

peer [pɪə*] vi: **to** ~ **at** regarder attentivement, scruter ♦ n (*noble*) pair m; (*equal*) pair, égal/e.

peerage ['pɪərɪdʒ] n pairie f.

peerless ['pɪəlɪs] adj incomparable, sans égal.

peeved [piːvd] adj irrité(e), ennuyé(e).

peevish ['piːvɪʃ] adj grincheux(euse), maussade.

peg [pɛg] n cheville f, (*for coat etc*) patère f, (*BRIT: also:* **clothes** ~) pince f à linge ♦ vt (*clothes*) accrocher; (*BRIT: groundsheet*) fixer (avec des piquets); (*fig: prices, wages*) contrôler, stabiliser.

pejorative [pɪ'dʒɔrətɪv] adj péjoratif(ive).

Pekin [piː'kɪn] n, **Peking** [piː'kɪŋ] n Pékin.

pekingese [piːkɪ'niːz] n pékinois m.

pelican ['pɛlɪkən] n pélican m.

pelican crossing n (*BRIT AUT*) feu m à commande manuelle.

pellet ['pɛlɪt] n boulette f; (*of lead*) plomb m.

pell-mell ['pɛl'mɛl] adv pêle-mêle.

pelmet ['pɛlmɪt] n cantonnière f; lambrequin m.

pelt [pɛlt] vt: **to** ~ **sb** (**with**) bombarder qn (de) ♦ vi (*rain*) tomber à seaux ♦ n peau f.

pelvis ['pɛlvɪs] n bassin m.

pen [pɛn] n (*for writing*) stylo m; (*for sheep*) parc m; (*US col: prison*) taule f; **to put** ~ **to paper** prendre la plume.

penal ['piːnl] adj pénal(e).

penalize ['piːnəlaɪz] vt pénaliser; (*fig*) désavantager.

penal servitude [-'səːvɪtjuːd] n travaux forcés.

penalty ['pɛnltɪ] n pénalité f; sanction f; (*fine*) amende f; (*SPORT*) pénalisation f; (*FOOTBALL: also:* ~ **kick**) penalty m.

penalty area n (*BRIT SPORT*) surface f de réparation.

penalty clause n clause pénale.

penalty kick n (*FOOTBALL*) penalty m.

penalty shoot-out [-'ʃuːtaut] n (*FOOTBALL*) épreuve f des penalties.

penance ['pɛnəns] n pénitence f.

pence [pɛns] npl (*BRIT*) see **penny**.

penchant ['pɑ̃ːʃɑ̃ːŋ] n penchant m.

pencil ['pɛnsl] n crayon m ♦ vt: **to** ~ **sth in** noter qch provisoirement.

pencil case n trousse f (d'écolier).

pencil sharpener n taille-crayon(s) m inv.

pendant ['pɛndnt] n pendentif m.

pending ['pɛndɪŋ] prep en attendant ♦ adj en suspens.

pendulum ['pɛndjuləm] n pendule m; (*of clock*) balancier m.

penetrate ['pɛnɪtreɪt] vt pénétrer dans; pénétrer.

penetrating ['pɛnɪtreɪtɪŋ] *adj* pénétrant(e).

penetration [pɛnɪ'treɪʃən] *n* pénétration *f*.

penfriend ['pɛnfrɛnd] *n* (*BRIT*) correspondant/e.

penguin ['pɛŋgwɪn] *n* pingouin *m*.

penicillin [pɛnɪ'sɪlɪn] *n* pénicilline *f*.

peninsula [pə'nɪnsjulə] *n* péninsule *f*.

penis ['pi:nɪs] *n* pénis *m*, verge *f*.

penitence ['pɛnɪtns] *n* repentir *m*.

penitent ['pɛnɪtnt] *adj* repentant(e).

penitentiary [pɛnɪ'tɛnʃərɪ] *n* (*US*) prison *f*.

penknife ['pɛnnaɪf] *n* canif *m*.

Penn(a). *abbr* (*US*) = Pennsylvania.

pen name *n* nom *m* de plume, pseudonyme *m*.

pennant ['pɛnənt] *n* flamme *f*, banderole *f*.

penniless ['pɛnɪlɪs] *adj* sans le sou.

Pennines ['pɛnaɪnz] *npl*: **the** ~ les Pennines *fpl*.

penny, *pl* **pennies** *or* **pence** (*BRIT*) ['pɛnɪ, 'pɛnɪz, pɛns] *n* penny *m* (*pl* pennies) (*new:* 100 in a pound; *old:* 12 in a shilling; on tend à employer "pennies" ou "two-pence piece" etc pour les pièces, "pence" pour la valeur).

penpal ['pɛnpæl] *n* correspondant/e.

penpusher ['pɛnpuʃɛ*] *n* (*pej*) gratte-papier *m* inv.

pension ['pɛnʃən] *n* retraite *f*; (*MIL*) pension *f*.

▶**pension off** *vt* mettre à la retraite.

pensionable ['pɛnʃnəbl] *adj* qui a droit à une retraite.

pensioner ['pɛnʃənə*] *n* (*BRIT*) retraité/e.

pension fund *n* caisse *f* de retraite.

pensive ['pɛnsɪv] *adj* pensif(ive).

pentagon ['pɛntəgən] *n* pentagone *m*; **the P~** (*US POL*) le Pentagone.

Le **Pentagon** est le nom donné aux bureaux du ministère de la Défense américain, situés à Arlington en Virginie, à cause de la forme pentagonale du bâtiment dans lequel ils se trouvent. Par extension, ce terme est également utilisé en parlant du ministère lui-même.

Pentecost ['pɛntɪkɔst] *n* Pentecôte *f*.

penthouse ['pɛnthaus] *n* appartement *m* (de luxe) en attique.

pent-up ['pɛntʌp] *adj* (*feelings*) refoulé(e).

penultimate [pɪ'nʌltɪmət] *adj* pénultième, avant-dernier(ière).

penury ['pɛnjurɪ] *n* misère *f*.

people ['pi:pl] *npl* gens *mpl*; personnes *fpl*; (*citizens*) peuple *m* ♦ *n* (*nation, race*) peuple *m* ♦ *vt* peupler; **several** ~ **came** plusieurs personnes sont venues; **I know** ~ **who ...** je connais des gens qui ...; **the room was full of** ~ la salle était pleine de monde *or* de gens; ~ **say that ...** on dit *or* les gens disent que ...; **old** ~ les personnes âgées; **young** ~ les jeunes; **a man of the** ~ un homme du peuple.

PEP [pɛp] *n* (= *personal equity plan*) ≈ CEA *m* (= compte d'épargne en actions)

pep [pɛp] *n* (*col*) entrain *m*, dynamisme *m*.

▶**pep up** *vt* (*col*) remonter.

pepper ['pɛpə*] *n* poivre *m*; (*vegetable*) poivron *m* ♦ *vt* poivrer.

peppermint ['pɛpəmɪnt] *n* (*plant*) menthe poivrée; (*sweet*) pastille *f* de menthe.

pepperoni [pɛpə'rəunɪ] *n* saucisson sec de porc et de bœuf très poivré.

pepperpot ['pɛpəpɔt] *n* poivrière *f*.

peptalk ['pɛptɔ:k] *n* (*col*) (petit) discours d'encouragement.

per [pɔ:*] *prep* par; ~ **hour** (*miles etc*) à l'heure; (*fee*) (de) l'heure; ~ **kilo** *etc* le kilo *etc*; ~ **day/person** par jour/personne; **as** ~ **your instructions** conformément à vos instructions.

per annum *adv* par an.

per capita *adj, adv* par habitant, par personne.

perceive [pə'si:v] *vt* percevoir; (*notice*) remarquer, s'apercevoir de.

per cent *adv* pour cent; **a 20** ~ **discount** une réduction de 20 pour cent.

percentage [pə'sɛntɪdʒ] *n* pourcentage *m*; **on a** ~ **basis** au pourcentage.

percentage point *n*: **ten** ~**s** dix pour cent.

perceptible [pə'sɛptɪbl] *adj* perceptible.

perception [pə'sɛpʃən] *n* perception *f*; (*insight*) sensibilité *f*.

perceptive [pə'sɛptɪv] *adj* (*remark, person*) perspicace.

perch [pɔ:tʃ] *n* (*fish*) perche *f*; (*for bird*) perchoir *m* ♦ *vi* (se) percher.

percolate ['pɔ:kəleɪt] *vt, vi* passer.

percolator ['pɔ:kəleɪtə*] *n* percolateur *m*; cafetière *f* électrique.

percussion [pə'kʌʃən] *n* percussion *f*.

peremptory [pə'rɛmptərɪ] *adj* péremptoire.

perennial [pə'rɛnɪəl] *adj* perpétuel(le); (*BOT*) vivace ♦ *n* plante *f* vivace.

perfect *adj, n* ['pɔ:fɪkt] *adj* parfait(e) ♦ *n* (*also:* ~ **tense**) parfait *m* ♦ *vt* [pə'fɛkt] parfaire; mettre au point; **he's a** ~ **stranger to me** il m'est totalement inconnu.

perfection [pə'fɛkʃən] *n* perfection *f*.

perfectionist [pə'fɛkʃənɪst] *n* perfectionniste *m/f*.

perfectly ['pɔ:fɪktlɪ] *adv* parfaitement; **I'm** ~ **happy with the situation** cette situation me convient parfaitement; **you know** ~ **well** vous le savez très bien.

perforate ['pɔ:fəreɪt] *vt* perforer, percer.

perforated ulcer ['pɔ:fəreɪtɪd-] *n* (*MED*) ulcère perforé.

perforation [pɔ:fə'reɪʃən] *n* perforation *f*; (*line of holes*) pointillé *m*.

perform [pə'fɔ:m] *vt* (*carry out*) exécuter, remplir; (*concert etc*) jouer, donner ♦ *vi* jouer.

performance [pə'fɔ:məns] *n* représentation *f*, spectacle *m*; (*of an artist*) interprétation *f*; (*of player etc*) prestation *f*; (*of car, engine*) performance *f*; **the team put up a good** ~

l'équipe a bien joué.

performer [pə'fɔːmə*] *n* artiste *m/f*.

performing [pə'fɔːmɪŋ] *adj* (*animal*) savant(e).

performing arts *npl*: **the** ~ les arts *mpl* du spectacle.

perfume ['pɜːfjuːm] *n* parfum *m* ♦ *vt* parfumer.

perfunctory [pə'fʌŋktərɪ] *adj* négligent(e), pour la forme.

perhaps [pə'hæps] *adv* peut-être; ~ **he'll** ... peut-être qu'il ...; ~ **so/not** peut-être que oui/que non.

peril ['perɪl] *n* péril *m*.

perilous ['perɪləs] *adj* périlleux(euse).

perilously ['perɪləslɪ] *adv*: **they came** ~ **close to being caught** ils ont été à deux doigts de se faire prendre.

perimeter [pə'rɪmɪtə*] *n* périmètre *m*.

perimeter wall *n* mur *m* d'enceinte.

period ['pɪərɪəd] *n* période *f*; (*HISTORY*) époque *f*; (*SCOL*) cours *m*; (*full stop*) point *m*; (*MED*) règles *fpl* ♦ *adj* (*costume, furniture*) d'époque; **for a** ~ **of three weeks** pour (une période de) trois semaines; **the holiday** ~ (*BRIT*) la période des vacances.

periodic [pɪərɪ'ɔdɪk] *adj* périodique.

periodical [pɪərɪ'ɔdɪkl] *adj* périodique ♦ *n* périodique *m*.

periodically [pɪərɪ'ɔdɪklɪ] *adv* périodiquement.

period pains *npl* (*BRIT*) douleurs menstruelles.

peripatetic [perɪpə'tɛtɪk] *adj* (*salesman*) ambulant; (*BRIT*: *teacher*) qui travaille dans plusieurs établissements.

peripheral [pə'rɪfərəl] *adj* périphérique ♦ *n* (*COMPUT*) périphérique *m*.

periphery [pə'rɪfərɪ] *n* périphérie *f*.

periscope ['perɪskəup] *n* périscope *m*.

perish ['perɪʃ] *vi* périr, mourir; (*decay*) se détériorer.

perishable ['perɪʃəbl] *adj* périssable.

perishables ['perɪʃəblz] *npl* denrées *fpl* périssables.

perishing ['perɪʃɪŋ] *adj* (*BRIT col*: *cold*) glacial(e).

peritonitis [perɪtə'naɪtɪs] *n* péritonite *f*.

perjure ['pɜːdʒə*] *vt*: **to** ~ **o.s.** se parjurer.

perjury ['pɜːdʒərɪ] *n* (*LAW*: *in court*) faux témoignage; (*breach of oath*) parjure *m*.

perk [pɜːk] *n* (*col*) avantage *m*, à-côté *m*.

▶**perk up** *vi* (*col*: *cheer up*) se ragaillardir.

perky ['pɜːkɪ] *adj* (*cheerful*) guilleret(te), gai(e).

perm [pɜːm] *n* (*for hair*) permanente *f* ♦ *vt*: **to have one's hair** ~**ed** se faire faire une permanente.

permanence ['pɜːmənəns] *n* permanence *f*.

permanent ['pɜːmənənt] *adj* permanent(e); (*job, position*) permanent, fixe; (*dye, ink*) indélébile; **I'm not** ~ **here** je ne suis pas ici à titre définitif; ~ **address** adresse habituelle.

permanently ['pɜːmənəntlɪ] *adv* de façon permanente.

permeable ['pɜːmɪəbl] *adj* perméable.

permeate ['pɜːmɪeɪt] *vi* s'infiltrer ♦ *vt* s'infiltrer dans; pénétrer.

permissible [pə'mɪsɪbl] *adj* permis(e), acceptable.

permission [pə'mɪʃən] *n* permission *f*, autorisation *f*; **to give sb** ~ **to do sth** donner à qn la permission de faire qch.

permissive [pə'mɪsɪv] *adj* tolérant(e); **the** ~ **society** la société de tolérance.

permit *n* ['pɜːmɪt] permis *m*; (*entrance pass*) autorisation *f*, laisser-passer *m*; (*for goods*) licence *f* ♦ *vt* [pə'mɪt] permettre; **to** ~ **sb to do** autoriser qn à faire, permettre à qn de faire; **weather** ~**ting** si le temps le permet.

permutation [pɜːmju'teɪʃən] *n* permutation *f*.

pernicious [pɜː'nɪʃəs] *adj* pernicieux(euse), nocif(ive).

pernickety [pə'nɪkɪtɪ] *adj* (*col*) pointilleux(euse), tatillon(ne); (*task*) minutieux(euse).

perpendicular [pɜːpən'dɪkjulə*] *adj*, *n* perpendiculaire (*f*).

perpetrate ['pɜːpɪtreɪt] *vt* perpétrer, commettre.

perpetual [pə'pɛtjuəl] *adj* perpétuel(le).

perpetuate [pə'pɛtjueɪt] *vt* perpétuer.

perpetuity [pɜːpɪ'tjuːɪtɪ] *n*: **in** ~ à perpétuité.

perplex [pə'plɛks] *vt* rendre perplexe; (*complicate*) embrouiller.

perplexing [pɜː'plɛksɪŋ] *adj* embarrassant(e).

perquisites ['pɜːkwɪzɪts] *npl* (*also*: **perks**) avantages *mpl* annexes.

persecute ['pɜːsɪkjuːt] *vt* persécuter.

persecution [pɜːsɪ'kjuːʃən] *n* persécution *f*.

perseverance [pɜːsɪ'vɪərns] *n* persévérance *f*, ténacité *f*.

persevere [pɜːsɪ'vɪə*] *vi* persévérer.

Persia ['pɜːʃə] *n* Perse *f*.

Persian ['pɜːʃən] *adj* persan(e) ♦ *n* (*LING*) persan *m*; **the** (~) **Gulf** le golfe Persique.

Persian cat *n* chat persan.

persist [pə'sɪst] *vi*: **to** ~ (**in doing**) persister (à faire), s'obstiner (à faire).

persistence [pə'sɪstəns] *n* persistance *f*, obstination *f*; opiniâtreté *f*.

persistent [pə'sɪstənt] *adj* persistant(e), tenace; (*lateness, rain*) persistant; ~ **offender** (*LAW*) multirécidiviste *m/f*.

persnickety [pə'snɪkɪtɪ] *adj* (*US col*) = **pernickety**.

person ['pɜːsn] *n* personne *f*; **in** ~ en personne; **on** *or* **about one's** ~ sur soi; ~ **to call** (*TEL*) appel *m* avec préavis.

personable ['pɜːsnəbl] *adj* de belle prestance, au physique attrayant.

personal ['pɜːsnl] *adj* personnel(le); ~ **belongings**, ~ **effects** effets personnels; ~ **hygiene** hygiène *f* intime; **a** ~ **interview** un entretien.

personal allowance *n* (*TAX*) part *f* du revenu non imposable.

personal assistant (PA) *n* secrétaire personnel(le).

personal call *n* (*TEL*) communication *f* avec préavis.

personal column *n* annonces personnelles.

personal computer (PC) *n* ordinateur individuel, PC *m*.

personal details *npl* (*on form etc*) coordonnées *fpl*.

personal identification number (PIN) *n* (*COMPUT, BANKING*) numéro *m* d'identification personnel.

personality [pɔːsəˈnælɪtɪ] *n* personnalité *f*.

personally [ˈpɔːsnəlɪ] *adv* personnellement.

personal organizer *n* agenda (personnel) (*style Filofax*); (*electronic*) agenda électronique.

personal property *n* biens personnels.

personal stereo *n* walkman *m* ®, baladeur *m*.

personify [pɔːˈsɔnɪfaɪ] *vt* personnifier.

personnel [pɔːsəˈnɛl] *n* personnel *m*.

personnel department *n* service *m* du personnel.

personnel manager *n* chef *m* du personnel.

perspective [pɔˈspɛktɪv] *n* perspective *f*; **to get sth into ~** ramener qch à sa juste mesure.

perspex [ˈpɔːspɛks] *n* ® (*BRIT*) Plexiglas *m* ®.

perspicacity [pɔːspɪˈkæsɪtɪ] *n* perspicacité *f*.

perspiration [pɔːspɪˈreɪʃən] *n* transpiration *f*.

perspire [pɔˈspaɪə*] *vi* transpirer.

persuade [pɔˈsweɪd] *vt*: **to ~ sb to do sth** persuader qn de faire qch, amener *or* décider qn à faire qch; **to ~ sb of sth/that** persuader qn de qch/que.

persuasion [pɔˈsweɪʒən] *n* persuasion *f*; (*creed*) conviction *f*.

persuasive [pɔˈsweɪsɪv] *adj* persuasif(ive).

pert [pɔːt] *adj* coquin(e), mutin(e).

pertaining [pɔːˈteɪnɪŋ]: **~ to** *prep* relatif(ive) à.

pertinent [ˈpɔːtɪnənt] *adj* pertinent(e).

perturb [pɔˈtɔːb] *vt* troubler, inquiéter.

perturbing [pɔˈtɔːbɪŋ] *adj* troublant(e).

Peru [pɔˈruː] *n* Pérou *m*.

perusal [pɔˈruːzl] *n* lecture (attentive).

Peruvian [pɔˈruːvjən] *adj* péruvien(ne) ♦ *n* Péruvien/ne.

pervade [pɔˈveɪd] *vt* se répandre dans, envahir.

pervasive [pɔˈveɪsɪv] *adj* (*smell*) pénétrant(e); (*influence*) insidieux(euse); (*gloom, ideas*) diffus(e).

perverse [pɔˈvɔːs] *adj* pervers(e); (*stubborn*) entêté(e), contrariant(e).

perversion [pɔˈvɔːʃən] *n* perversion *f*.

perversity [pɔˈvɔːsɪtɪ] *n* perversité *f*.

pervert *n* [ˈpɔːvɔːt] perverti/e ♦ *vt* [pɔˈvɔːt] pervertir.

pessimism [ˈpɛsɪmɪzəm] *n* pessimisme *m*.

pessimist [ˈpɛsɪmɪst] *n* pessimiste *m/f*.

pessimistic [pɛsɪˈmɪstɪk] *adj* pessimiste.

pest [pɛst] *n* animal *m* (*or* insecte *m*) nuisible; (*fig*) fléau *m*.

pest control *n* lutte *f* contre les nuisibles.

pester [ˈpɛstə*] *vt* importuner, harceler.

pesticide [ˈpɛstɪsaɪd] *n* pesticide *m*.

pestilence [ˈpɛstɪləns] *n* peste *f*.

pestle [ˈpɛsl] *n* pilon *m*.

pet [pɛt] *n* animal familier; (*favourite*) chouchou *m* ♦ *vt* choyer ♦ *vi* (*col*) se peloter; **~ lion** *etc* lion *etc* apprivoisé.

petal [ˈpɛtl] *n* pétale *m*.

peter [ˈpiːtə*]: **to ~ out** *vi* s'épuiser; s'affaiblir.

petite [pɔˈtiːt] *adj* menu(e).

petition [pɔˈtɪʃən] *n* pétition *f* ♦ *vt* adresser une pétition à ♦ *vi*: **to ~ for divorce** demander le divorce.

pet name *n* (*BRIT*) petit nom.

petrified [ˈpɛtrɪfaɪd] *adj* (*fig*) mort(e) de peur.

petrify [ˈpɛtrɪfaɪ] *vt* pétrifier.

petrochemical [pɛtrəˈkɛmɪkl] *adj* pétrochimique.

petrodollars [ˈpɛtrəudɔləz] *npl* pétrodollars *mpl*.

petrol [ˈpɛtrəl] *n* (*BRIT*) essence *f*.

petrol bomb *n* cocktail *m* Molotov.

petrol can *n* (*BRIT*) bidon *m* à essence.

petrol engine *n* (*BRIT*) moteur *m* à essence.

petroleum [pɔˈtrəuliəm] *n* pétrole *m*.

petroleum jelly *n* vaseline *f*.

petrol pump *n* (*BRIT*: *in car, at garage*) pompe *f* à essence.

petrol station *n* (*BRIT*) station-service *f*.

petrol tank *n* (*BRIT*) réservoir *m* d'essence.

petticoat [ˈpɛtɪkəut] *n* jupon *m*.

pettifogging [ˈpɛtɪfɔgɪŋ] *adj* chicanier(ière).

pettiness [ˈpɛtɪnɪs] *n* mesquinerie *f*.

petty [ˈpɛtɪ] *adj* (*mean*) mesquin(e); (*unimportant*) insignifiant(e), sans importance.

petty cash *n* caisse *f* des dépenses courantes, petite caisse.

petty officer *n* second-maître *m*.

petulant [ˈpɛtjulənt] *adj* irritable.

pew [pjuː] *n* banc *m* (d'église).

pewter [ˈpjuːtə*] *n* étain *m*.

Pfc *abbr* (*US MIL*) = private first class.

PG *n abbr* (*CINE*: = *parental guidance*) *avis des parents recommandé*.

PGA *n abbr* = *Professional Golfers Association*.

PH *n abbr* (*US MIL*: = *Purple Heart*) *décoration accordée aux blessés de guerre*.

PHA *n abbr* (*US*: = *Public Housing Administration*) *organisme d'aide à la construction*.

phallic [ˈfælɪk] *adj* phallique.

phantom [ˈfæntəm] *n* fantôme *m*; (*vision*) fantasme *m*.

Pharaoh [ˈfɛərəu] *n* pharaon *m*.

pharmaceutical [fɑːməˈsjuːtɪkl] *adj* pharmaceutique ♦ *n*: **~s** produits *mpl* pharmaceutiques.

pharmacist [ˈfɑːməsɪst] *n* pharmacien/ne.

pharmacy [ˈfɑːməsɪ] *n* pharmacie *f*.

phase [feɪz] *n* phase *f*, période *f* ♦ *vt*: **to ~ sth in/out** introduire/supprimer qch progressivement.

PhD *abbr* (= *Doctor of Philosophy*) *title* ≈ Docteur *m* en Droit *or* Lettres *etc* ♦ *n* ≈ doctorat *m*; titulaire *m* d'un doctorat; *see also* **doctorate**.

pheasant ['fɛznt] *n* faisan *m*.

phenomenon, *pl* **phenomena** [fə'nɔmɪnən, -nə] *n* phénomène *m*.

phew [fjuː] *excl* ouf!

phial ['faɪəl] *n* fiole *f*.

philanderer [fɪ'lændərə*] *n* don Juan *m*.

philanthropic [fɪlən'θrɔpɪk] *adj* philanthropique.

philanthropist [fɪ'lænθrəpɪst] *n* philanthrope *m/f*.

philatelist [fɪ'lætəlɪst] *n* philatéliste *m/f*.

philately [fɪ'lætəlɪ] *n* philatélie *f*.

Philippines ['fɪlɪpiːnz] *npl* (*also*: **Philippine Islands**): **the ~** les Philippines *fpl*.

philosopher [fɪ'lɔsəfə*] *n* philosophe *m*.

philosophical [fɪlə'sɔfɪkl] *adj* philosophique.

philosophy [fɪ'lɔsəfɪ] *n* philosophie *f*.

phlegm [flɛm] *n* flegme *m*.

phlegmatic [flɛg'mætɪk] *adj* flegmatique.

phobia ['fəubjə] *n* phobie *f*.

phone [fəun] *n* téléphone *m* ♦ *vt* téléphoner à ♦ *vi* téléphoner; **to be on the ~** avoir le téléphone; (*be calling*) être au téléphone.

►**phone back** *vt*, *vi* rappeler.

phone book *n* annuaire *m*.

phone box, phone booth *n* cabine *f* téléphonique.

phone call *n* coup *m* de fil *or* de téléphone.

phonecard ['fəunkɑːd] *n* télécarte *f*.

phone-in ['fəunɪn] *n* (*BRIT RADIO, TV*) programme *m* à ligne ouverte.

phone tapping [-tæpɪŋ] *n* mise *f* sur écoutes téléphoniques.

phonetics [fə'nɛtɪks] *n* phonétique *f*.

phoney ['fəunɪ] *adj* faux(fausse), factice ♦ *n* (*person*) charlatan *m*; fumiste *m/f*.

phonograph ['fəunəgrɑːf] *n* (*US*) électrophone *m*.

phony ['fəunɪ] *adj*, *n* = **phoney**.

phosphate ['fɔsfeɪt] *n* phosphate *m*.

phosphorus ['fɔsfərəs] *n* phosphore *m*.

photo ['fəutəu] *n* photo *f*.

photo... ['fəutəu] *prefix* photo....

photocall ['fəutəukɔːl] *n* séance *f* de photos pour la presse.

photocopier ['fəutəukɔpɪə*] *n* copieur *m*.

photocopy ['fəutəukɔpɪ] *n* photocopie *f* ♦ *vt* photocopier.

photoelectric [fəutəuɪ'lɛktrɪk] *adj* photoélectrique; **~ cell** cellule *f* photoélectrique.

Photofit ['fəutəufɪt] *n* ® portrait-robot *m*.

photogenic [fəutəu'dʒɛnɪk] *adj* photogénique.

photograph ['fəutəgrɑːf] *n* photographie *f* ♦ *vt* photographier; **to take a ~ of sb** prendre qn en photo.

photographer [fə'tɔgrəfə*] *n* photographe *m/f*.

photographic [fəutə'græfɪk] *adj* photographique.

photography [fə'tɔgrəfɪ] *n* photographie *f*.

photo opportunity *n* occasion, souvent arrangée, pour prendre des photos d'une personnalité.

Photostat ['fəutəustæt] *n* ® photocopie *f*, photostat *m*.

photosynthesis [fəutəu'sɪnθəsɪs] *n* photosynthèse *f*.

phrase [freɪz] *n* expression *f*; (*LING*) locution *f* ♦ *vt* exprimer; (*letter*) rédiger.

phrasebook ['freɪzbuk] *n* recueil *m* d'expressions (pour touristes).

physical ['fɪzɪkl] *adj* physique; **~ examination** examen médical; **~ education** éducation physique; **~ exercises** gymnastique *f*.

physically ['fɪzɪklɪ] *adv* physiquement.

physician [fɪ'zɪʃən] *n* médecin *m*.

physicist ['fɪzɪsɪst] *n* physicien/ne.

physics ['fɪzɪks] *n* physique *f*.

physiological [fɪzɪə'lɔdʒɪkl] *adj* physiologique.

physiology [fɪzɪ'ɔlədʒɪ] *n* physiologie *f*.

physiotherapist [fɪzɪəu'θɛrəpɪst] *n* kinésithérapeute *m/f*.

physiotherapy [fɪzɪəu'θɛrəpɪ] *n* kinésithérapie *f*.

physique [fɪ'ziːk] *n* (*appearance*) physique *m*; (*health etc*) constitution *f*.

pianist ['piːənɪst] *n* pianiste *m/f*.

piano [pɪ'ænəu] *n* piano *m*.

piano accordion *n* (*BRIT*) accordéon *m* à touches.

Picardy ['pɪkədɪ] *n* Picardie *f*.

piccolo ['pɪkələu] *n* piccolo *m*.

pick [pɪk] *n* (*tool: also*: **~-axe**) pic *m*, pioche *f* ♦ *vt* choisir; (*gather*) cueillir; (*scab, spot*) gratter, écorcher; **take your ~** faites votre choix; **the ~ of** le(la) meilleur(e) de; **to ~ a bone** ronger un os; **to ~ one's nose** se mettre le doigt dans le nez; **to ~ one's teeth** se curer les dents; **to ~ sb's brains** faire appel aux lumières de qn; **to ~ pockets** pratiquer le vol à la tire; **to ~ a quarrel/fight with sb** chercher querelle à/la bagarre avec qn.

►**pick off** *vt* (*kill*) (viser soigneusement et) abattre.

►**pick on** *vt fus* (*person*) harceler.

►**pick out** *vt* choisir; (*distinguish*) distinguer.

►**pick up** *vi* (*improve*) remonter, s'améliorer ♦ *vt* ramasser; (*telephone*) décrocher; (*collect*) passer prendre; (*AUT: give lift to*) prendre; (*learn*) apprendre; (*RADIO, TV, TEL*) capter; **to ~ up speed** prendre de la vitesse; **to ~ o.s. up** se relever; **to ~ up where one left off** reprendre là où l'on s'est arrêté.

pickaxe, (*US*) **pickax** ['pɪkæks] *n* pioche *f*.

picket ['pɪkɪt] *n* (*in strike*) gréviste *m/f* participant à un piquet de grève; piquet *m* de grève ♦ *vt* mettre un piquet de grève devant.

picket line *n* piquet *m* de grève.

pickings ['pɪkɪŋz] *npl*: **there are rich ~ to be had in ...** il y a gros à gagner dans ....

pickle ['pɪkl] *n* (*also*: **~s**: *as condiment*) pickles *mpl*; (*fig*): **in a ~** dans le pétrin ♦ *vt* conserver dans du vinaigre *or* dans de la saumure.

pick-me-up ['pɪkmiːʌp] *n* remontant *m*.

pickpocket ['pɪkpɔkɪt] *n* pickpocket *m*.

pickup ['pɪkʌp] *n* (*BRIT*: *on record player*) bras *m* pick-up; (*small truck*: *also*: **~ truck**, **~ van**) camionnette *f*.

picnic ['pɪknɪk] *n* pique-nique *m* ♦ *vi* pique-niquer.

picnicker ['pɪknɪkə*] *n* pique-niqueur/euse.

pictorial [pɪk'tɔːrɪəl] *adj* illustré(e).

picture ['pɪktʃə*] *n* (*also TV*) image *f*; (*painting*) peinture *f*, tableau *m*; (*photograph*) photo(graphie) *f*; (*drawing*) dessin *m*; (*film*) film *m* ♦ *vt* se représenter; (*describe*) dépeindre, représenter; **the ~s** (*BRIT*) le cinéma; **to take a ~ of sb/sth** prendre qn/qch en photo; **the overall ~** le tableau d'ensemble; **to put sb in the ~** mettre qn au courant.

picture book *n* livre *m* d'images.

picturesque [pɪktʃə'rɛsk] *adj* pittoresque.

picture window *n* baie vitrée, fenêtre *f* panoramique.

piddling ['pɪdlɪŋ] *adj* (*col*) insignifiant(e).

pidgin ['pɪdʒɪn] *adj*: **~ English** pidgin *m*.

pie [paɪ] *n* tourte *f*; (*of meat*) pâté *m* en croûte.

piebald ['paɪbɔːld] *adj* pie *inv*.

piece [piːs] *n* morceau *m*; (*of land*) parcelle *f*; (*item*): **a ~ of furniture/advice** un meuble/conseil; (*DRAUGHTS etc*) pion *m* ♦ *vt*: **to ~ together** rassembler; **in ~s** (*broken*) en morceaux, en miettes; (*not yet assembled*) en pièces détachées; **to take to ~s** démonter; **in one ~** (*object*) intact(e); **to get back all in one ~** (*person*) rentrer sain et sauf; **a 10p ~** (*BRIT*) une pièce de 10p; **~ by ~** morceau par morceau; **a six-~ band** un orchestre de six musiciens; **to say one's ~** réciter son morceau.

piecemeal ['piːsmiːl] *adv* par bouts.

piece rate *n* taux *m or* tarif *m* à la pièce.

piecework ['piːswəːk] *n* travail *m* aux pièces *or* à la pièce.

pie chart *n* graphique *m* à secteurs, camembert *m*.

Piedmont ['piːdmɔnt] *n* Piémont *m*.

pier [pɪə*] *n* jetée *f*; (*of bridge etc*) pile *f*.

pierce [pɪəs] *vt* percer, transpercer; **to have one's ears ~d** se faire percer les oreilles.

piercing ['pɪəsɪŋ] *adj* (*cry*) perçant(e).

piety ['paɪətɪ] *n* piété *f*.

piffling ['pɪflɪŋ] *adj* insignifiant(e).

pig [pɪg] *n* cochon *m*, porc *m*.

pigeon ['pɪdʒən] *n* pigeon *m*.

pigeonhole ['pɪdʒənhəul] *n* casier *m*.

pigeon-toed ['pɪdʒəntəud] *adj* marchant les pieds en dedans.

piggy bank ['pɪgɪ-] *n* tirelire *f*.

pigheaded ['pɪg'hɛdɪd] *adj* entêté(e), têtu(e).

piglet ['pɪglɪt] *n* petit cochon, porcelet *m*.

pigment ['pɪgmənt] *n* pigment *m*.

pigmentation [pɪgmən'teɪʃən] *n* pigmentation *f*.

pigmy ['pɪgmɪ] *n* = **pygmy**.

pigskin ['pɪgskɪn] *n* (peau *f* de) porc *m*.

pigsty ['pɪgstaɪ] *n* porcherie *f*.

pigtail ['pɪgteɪl] *n* natte *f*, tresse *f*.

pike [paɪk] *n* (*spear*) pique *f*; (*fish*) brochet *m*.

pilchard ['pɪltʃəd] *n* pilchard *m* (*sorte de sardine*).

pile [paɪl] *n* (*pillar, of books*) pile *f*; (*heap*) tas *m*; (*of carpet*) épaisseur *f* ♦ *vb* (*also*: **~ up**) *vt* empiler, entasser ♦ *vi* s'entasser; **in a ~** en tas.

▶**pile on** *vt*: **to ~ it on** (*col*) exagérer.

piles [paɪlz] *npl* hémorroïdes *fpl*.

pileup ['paɪlʌp] *n* (*AUT*) télescopage *m*, collision *f* en série.

pilfer ['pɪlfə*] *vt* chaparder ♦ *vi* commettre des larcins.

pilfering ['pɪlfərɪŋ] *n* chapardage *m*.

pilgrim ['pɪlgrɪm] *n* pèlerin *m*.

pilgrimage ['pɪlgrɪmɪdʒ] *n* pèlerinage *m*.

pill [pɪl] *n* pilule *f*; **the ~** la pilule; **to be on the ~** prendre la pilule.

pillage ['pɪlɪdʒ] *vt* piller.

pillar ['pɪlə*] *n* pilier *m*.

pillar box *n* (*BRIT*) boîte *f* aux lettres (*publique*).

pillion ['pɪljən] *n* (*of motor cycle*) siège *m* arrière; **to ride ~** être derrière; (*on horse*) être en croupe.

pillory ['pɪlərɪ] *n* pilori *m* ♦ *vt* mettre au pilori.

pillow ['pɪləu] *n* oreiller *m*.

pillowcase ['pɪləukeɪs], **pillowslip** ['pɪləuslɪp] *n* taie *f* d'oreiller.

pilot ['paɪlət] *n* pilote *m* ♦ *cpd* (*scheme etc*) pilote, expérimental(e) ♦ *vt* piloter.

pilot boat *n* bateau-pilote *m*.

pilot light *n* veilleuse *f*.

pimento [pɪ'mɛntəu] *n* piment *m*.

pimp [pɪmp] *n* souteneur *m*, maquereau *m*.

pimple ['pɪmpl] *n* bouton *m*.

pimply ['pɪmplɪ] *adj* boutonneux(euse).

PIN *n abbr* = **personal identification number**.

pin [pɪn] *n* épingle *f*; (*TECH*) cheville *f*; (*BRIT*: *drawing ~*) punaise *f*; (*in grenade*) goupille *f*; (*BRIT ELEC*: *of plug*) broche *f* ♦ *vt* épingler; **~s and needles** fourmis *fpl*; **to ~ sb against/to** clouer qn contre/à; **to ~ sth on sb** (*fig*) mettre qch sur le dos de qn.

▶**pin down** *vt* (*fig*): **to ~ sb down** obliger qn à répondre; **there's something strange here but I can't quite ~ it down** il y a quelque chose d'étrange ici, mais je n'arrive pas exactement à savoir quoi.

pinafore ['pɪnəfɔː*] *n* tablier *m*.

pinafore dress *n* robe-chasuble *f*.

pinball ['pɪnbɔːl] *n* flipper *m*.

pincers ['pɪnsəz] *npl* tenailles *fpl*.

pinch [pɪntʃ] n pincement m; (of salt etc) pincée f ♦ vt pincer; (col: steal) piquer, chiper ♦ vi (shoe) serrer; **at a ~** à la rigueur; **to feel the ~** (fig) se ressentir des restrictions (or de la récession etc).

pinched [pɪntʃt] adj (drawn) tiré(e); **~ with cold** transi(e) de froid; **~ for** (short of): **~ for money** à court d'argent; **~ for space** à l'étroit.

pincushion ['pɪnkuʃən] n pelote f à épingles.

pine [paɪn] n (also: **~ tree**) pin m ♦ vi: **to ~ for** aspirer à, désirer ardemment.

▶**pine away** vi dépérir.

pineapple ['paɪnæpl] n ananas m.

pine cone n pomme f de pin.

pine needle n aiguille f de pin.

ping [pɪŋ] n (noise) tintement m.

Ping-Pong ['pɪŋpɒŋ] n ® ping-pong m ®.

pink [pɪŋk] adj rose ♦ n (colour) rose m; (BOT) œillet m, mignardise f.

pinking shears ['pɪŋkɪŋ-] npl ciseaux mpl à denteler.

pin money n (BRIT) argent m de poche.

pinnacle ['pɪnəkl] n pinacle m.

pinpoint ['pɪnpɔɪnt] vt indiquer (avec précision).

pinstripe ['pɪnstraɪp] n rayure très fine.

pint [paɪnt] n pinte f (BRIT = 0.57 l; US = 0.47 l); (BRIT col) ≈ demi m, ≈ pot m.

pinup ['pɪnʌp] n pin-up f inv.

pioneer [paɪə'nɪə*] n explorateur/trice; (early settler) pionnier m; (fig) pionnier, précurseur m ♦ vt être un pionnier de.

pious ['paɪəs] adj pieux(euse).

pip [pɪp] n (seed) pépin m; (BRIT: time signal on radio) top m.

pipe [paɪp] n tuyau m, conduite f; (for smoking) pipe f; (MUS) pipeau m ♦ vt amener par tuyau; **~s** npl (also: **bag~s**) cornemuse f.

▶**pipe down** vi (col) se taire.

pipe cleaner n cure-pipe m.

piped music [paɪpt-] n musique f de fond.

pipe dream n chimère f, utopie f.

pipeline ['paɪplaɪn] n (for gas) gazoduc m, pipeline m; (for oil) oléoduc m, pipeline; **it is in the ~** (fig) c'est en route, ça va se faire.

piper ['paɪpə*] n joueur/euse de pipeau (or de cornemuse).

pipe tobacco n tabac m pour la pipe.

piping ['paɪpɪŋ] adv: **~ hot** très chaud(e).

piquant ['piːkənt] adj piquant(e).

pique [piːk] n dépit m.

piracy ['paɪərəsɪ] n piraterie f.

pirate ['paɪərət] n pirate m ♦ vt (record, video, book) pirater.

pirate radio n (BRIT) radio f pirate.

pirouette [pɪru'et] n pirouette f ♦ vi faire une or des pirouette(s).

Pisces ['paɪsiːz] n les Poissons mpl; **to be ~** être des Poissons.

piss [pɪs] vi (col!) pisser (!); **~ off!** tire-toi! (!).

pissed [pɪst] adj (BRIT col: drunk) bourré(e).

pistol ['pɪstl] n pistolet m.

piston ['pɪstən] n piston m.

pit [pɪt] n trou m, fosse f; (also: **coal ~**) puits m de mine; (also: **orchestra ~**) fosse d'orchestre ♦ vt: **to ~ sb against sb** opposer qn à qn; **to ~ o.s. against** se mesurer à; **~s** npl (in motor racing) aire f de service.

pitapat ['pɪtə'pæt] adv (BRIT): **to go ~** (heart) battre la chamade; (rain) tambouriner.

pitch [pɪtʃ] n (throw) lancement m; (MUS) ton m; (of voice) hauteur f; (fig: degree) degré m; (also: **sales ~**) baratin m, boniment m; (BRIT SPORT) terrain m; (NAUT) tangage m; (tar) poix f ♦ vt (throw) lancer; (tent) dresser; (set: price, message) adapter, positionner ♦ vi (NAUT) tanguer; (fall): **to ~ into/off** tomber dans/de; **to be ~ed forward** être projeté(e) en avant; **at this ~** à ce rythme.

pitch-black ['pɪtʃ'blæk] adj noir(e) comme poix.

pitched battle [pɪtʃt-] n bataille rangée.

pitcher ['pɪtʃə*] n cruche f.

pitchfork ['pɪtʃfɔːk] n fourche f.

piteous ['pɪtɪəs] adj pitoyable.

pitfall ['pɪtfɔːl] n trappe f, piège m.

pith [pɪθ] n (of plant) moelle f; (of orange) intérieur m de l'écorce; (fig) essence f, vigueur f.

pithead ['pɪthed] n (BRIT) bouche f de puits.

pithy ['pɪθɪ] adj piquant(e); vigoureux(euse).

pitiable ['pɪtɪəbl] adj pitoyable.

pitiful ['pɪtɪful] adj (touching) pitoyable; (contemptible) lamentable.

pitifully ['pɪtɪfəlɪ] adv pitoyablement; lamentablement.

pitiless ['pɪtɪlɪs] adj impitoyable.

pittance ['pɪtns] n salaire m de misère.

pitted ['pɪtɪd] adj: **~ with** (chickenpox) grêlé(e) par; (rust) piqué(e) de.

pity ['pɪtɪ] n pitié f ♦ vt plaindre; **what a ~!** quel dommage!; **it is a ~ that you can't come** c'est dommage que vous ne puissiez venir; **to have** or **take ~ on sb** avoir pitié de qn.

pitying ['pɪtɪɪŋ] adj compatissant(e).

pivot ['pɪvət] n pivot m ♦ vi pivoter.

pixel ['pɪksl] n (COMPUT) pixel m.

pixie ['pɪksɪ] n lutin m.

pizza ['piːtsə] n pizza f.

placard ['plækɑːd] n affiche f.

placate [plə'keɪt] vt apaiser, calmer.

placatory [plə'keɪtərɪ] adj d'apaisement, lénifiant(e).

place [pleɪs] n endroit m, lieu m; (proper position, rank, seat) place f; (house) maison f, logement m; (in street names): **Laurel ~** ≈ rue des Lauriers; (home): **at/to his ~** chez lui ♦ vt (position) placer, mettre; (identify) situer; reconnaître; **to take ~** avoir lieu; (occur) se produire; **from ~ to ~** d'un endroit à l'autre; **all over the ~** partout; **out of ~** (not suitable) déplacé(e), inopportun(e); **I feel out of ~ here** je ne me sens pas à ma place ici;

in the first ~ d'abord, en premier; **to put sb in his** ~ (fig) remettre qn à sa place; **he's going** ~**s** (fig: col) il fait son chemin; **it is not my** ~ **to do it** ce n'est pas à moi de le faire; **to** ~ **an order with sb (for)** (COMM) passer commande à qn (de); **to be** ~**d** (in race, exam) se placer; **how are you** ~**d next week?** comment ça se présente pour la semaine prochaine?

placebo [plə'siːbəu] n placebo m.

place mat n set m de table; (in linen etc) napperon m.

placement ['pleɪsmənt] n placement m; poste m.

place name n nom m de lieu.

placenta [plə'sɛntə] n placenta m.

placid ['plæsɪd] adj placide.

placidity [plə'sɪdɪtɪ] n placidité f.

plagiarism ['pleɪdʒjərɪzəm] n plagiat m.

plagiarist ['pleɪdʒjərɪst] n plagiaire m/f.

plagiarize ['pleɪdʒjəraɪz] vt plagier.

plague [pleɪg] n fléau m; (MED) peste f ♦ vt (fig) tourmenter; **to** ~ **sb with questions** harceler qn de questions.

plaice [pleɪs] n (pl inv) carrelet m.

plaid [plæd] n tissu écossais.

plain [pleɪn] adj (clear) clair(e), évident(e); (simple) simple, ordinaire; (frank) franc(franche); (not handsome) quelconque, ordinaire; (cigarette) sans filtre; (without seasoning etc) nature inv; (in one colour) uni(e) ♦ adv franchement, carrément ♦ n plaine f; **in** ~ **clothes** (police) en civil; **to make sth** ~ **to sb** faire clairement comprendre qch à qn.

plain chocolate n chocolat m à croquer.

plainly ['pleɪnlɪ] adv clairement; (frankly) carrément, sans détours.

plainness ['pleɪnnɪs] n simplicité f.

plain speaking n propos mpl sans équivoque; **she has a reputation for** ~ elle est bien connue pour son franc parler or sa franchise.

plaintiff ['pleɪntɪf] n plaignant/e.

plaintive ['pleɪntɪv] adj plaintif(ive).

plait [plæt] n tresse f, natte f ♦ vt tresser, natter.

plan [plæn] n plan m; (scheme) projet m ♦ vt (think in advance) projeter; (prepare) organiser ♦ vi faire des projets; **to** ~ **to do** projeter de faire; **how long do you** ~ **to stay?** combien de temps comptez-vous rester?

plane [pleɪn] n (AVIAT) avion m; (tree) platane m; (tool) rabot m; (ART, MATH etc) plan m ♦ adj plan(e), plat(e); plate(e) ♦ vt (with tool) raboter.

planet ['plænɪt] n planète f.

planetarium [plænɪ'tɛərɪəm] n planétarium m.

plank [plæŋk] n planche f; (POL) point m d'un programme.

plankton ['plæŋktən] n plancton m.

planned economy [plænd-] n économie planifiée.

planner ['plænə*] n planificateur/trice; (chart) planning m; **town** or (US) **city** ~ urbaniste m/f.

planning ['plænɪŋ] n planification f; **family** ~ planning familial.

planning permission n (BRIT) permis m de construire.

plant [plɑːnt] n plante f; (machinery) matériel m; (factory) usine f ♦ vt planter; (bomb) déposer, poser.

plantation [plæn'teɪʃən] n plantation f.

plant pot n (BRIT) pot m de fleurs.

plaque [plæk] n plaque f.

plasma ['plæzmə] n plasma m.

plaster ['plɑːstə*] n plâtre m; (BRIT: also: **sticking** ~) pansement adhésif ♦ vt plâtrer; (cover): **to** ~ **with** couvrir de; **in** ~ (BRIT: leg etc) dans le plâtre; ~ **of Paris** plâtre à mouler.

plasterboard ['plɑːstəbɔːd] n Placoplâtre m ®.

plaster cast n (MED) plâtre m; (model, statue) moule m.

plastered ['plɑːstəd] adj (col) soûl(e).

plasterer ['plɑːstərə*] n plâtrier m.

plastic ['plæstɪk] n plastique m ♦ adj (made of plastic) en plastique; (flexible) plastique, malléable; (art) plastique.

plastic bag n sac m en plastique.

plastic bullet n balle f de plastique.

plastic explosive n plastic m.

plasticine ['plæstɪsiːn] n ® pâte f à modeler.

plastic surgery n chirurgie f esthétique.

plate [pleɪt] n (dish) assiette f; (sheet of metal, on door, PHOT) plaque f; (TYP) cliché m; (in book) gravure f; (AUT: number ~) plaque minéralogique; **gold/silver** ~ (dishes) vaisselle f d'or/d'argent.

plateau, ~**s** or ~**x** ['plætəu, -z] n plateau m.

plateful ['pleɪtful] n assiette f, assiettée f.

plate glass n verre m à vitre, vitre f.

platen ['plætən] n (on typewriter, printer) rouleau m.

plate rack n égouttoir m.

platform ['plætfɔːm] n (at meeting) tribune f; (BRIT: of bus) plate-forme f; (stage) estrade f; (RAIL) quai m; **the train leaves from** ~ **7** le train part de la voie 7.

platform ticket n (BRIT) billet m de quai.

platinum ['plætɪnəm] n platine m.

platitude ['plætɪtjuːd] n platitude f, lieu commun.

platoon [plə'tuːn] n peloton m.

platter ['plætə*] n plat m.

plaudits ['plɔːdɪts] npl applaudissements mpl.

plausible ['plɔːzɪbl] adj plausible; (person) convaincant(e).

play [pleɪ] n jeu m; (THEAT) pièce f (de théâtre) ♦ vt (game) jouer à; (team, opponent) jouer contre; (instrument) jouer de; (part, piece of music, note) jouer ♦ vi jouer; **to bring** or **call into** ~ faire entrer en jeu; ~ **on words** jeu de mots; **to** ~ **a trick on sb** jouer un tour à qn; **they're** ~**ing at soldiers** ils jouent aux soldats; **to** ~ **for time** (fig) chercher à gagner du temps; **to** ~ **into sb's hands** (fig) faire le jeu de qn.

▶**play about, play around** *vi* (*person*) s'amuser.

▶**play along** *vi* (*fig*): **to ~ along with** (*person*) entrer dans le jeu de ♦ *vt* (*fig*): **to ~ sb along** faire marcher qn.

▶**play back** *vt* repasser, réécouter.

▶**play down** *vt* minimiser.

▶**play on** *vt fus* (*sb's feelings, credulity*) jouer sur; **to ~ on sb's nerves** porter sur les nerfs de qn.

▶**play up** *vi* (*cause trouble*) faire des siennes.

playact ['pleɪækt] *vi* jouer la comédie.

playboy ['pleɪbɔɪ] *n* playboy *m*.

played-out ['pleɪd'aut] *adj* épuisé(e).

player ['pleɪə*] *n* joueur/euse; (*THEAT*) acteur/trice; (*MUS*) musicien/ne.

playful ['pleɪful] *adj* enjoué(e).

playgoer ['pleɪɡəuə*] *n* amateur/trice de théâtre, habitué/e des théâtres.

playground ['pleɪɡraund] *n* cour *f* de récréation.

playgroup ['pleɪɡru:p] *n* garderie *f*.

playing card ['pleɪɪŋ-] *n* carte *f* à jouer.

playing field ['pleɪɪŋ-] *n* terrain *m* de sport.

playmaker ['pleɪmeɪkə*] *n* (*SPORT*) *joueur qui crée des occasions de marquer des buts pour ses coéquipiers.*

playmate ['pleɪmeɪt] *n* camarade *m/f*, copain/copine.

play-off ['pleɪɔf] *n* (*SPORT*) belle *f*.

playpen ['pleɪpen] *n* parc *m* (pour bébé).

playroom ['pleɪru:m] *n* salle *f* de jeux.

plaything ['pleɪθɪŋ] *n* jouet *m*.

playtime ['pleɪtaɪm] *n* (*SCOL*) récréation *f*.

playwright ['pleɪraɪt] *n* dramaturge *m*.

plc *abbr* (*BRIT*) = **public limited company**.

plea [pli:] *n* (*request*) appel *m*; (*excuse*) excuse *f*; (*LAW*) défense *f*.

plea bargaining *n* (*LAW*) *négociations entre le procureur, l'avocat de la défense et parfois le juge, pour réduire la gravité des charges.*

plead [pli:d] *vt* plaider; (*give as excuse*) invoquer ♦ *vi* (*LAW*) plaider; (*beg*): **to ~ with sb** (**for sth**) implorer qn (d'accorder qch); **to ~ for sth** implorer qch; **to ~ guilty/not guilty** plaider coupable/non coupable.

pleasant ['pleznt] *adj* agréable.

pleasantly ['plezntlɪ] *adv* agréablement.

pleasantry ['plezntrɪ] *n* (*joke*) plaisanterie *f*; **pleasantries** *npl* (*polite remarks*) civilités *fpl*.

please [pli:z] *vt* plaire à ♦ *vi* (*think fit*): **do as you ~** faites comme il vous plaira; **~!** s'il te (*or* vous) plaît; **my bill, ~** l'addition, s'il vous plaît; **~ don't cry!** je t'en prie, ne pleure pas!; **~ yourself!** (faites) comme vous voulez!

pleased [pli:zd] *adj*: **~ (with)** content(e) (de); **~ to meet you** enchanté (de faire votre connaissance); **we are ~ to inform you that ...** nous sommes heureux de vous annoncer que ....

pleasing ['pli:zɪŋ] *adj* plaisant(e), qui fait plaisir.

pleasurable ['pleʒərəbl] *adj* très agréable.

pleasure ['pleʒə*] *n* plaisir *m*; **"it's a ~"** "je vous en prie"; **with ~** avec plaisir; **is this trip for business or ~?** est-ce un voyage d'affaires ou d'agrément?

pleasure cruise *n* croisière *f*.

pleat [pli:t] *n* pli *m*.

plebiscite ['plebɪsɪt] *n* plébiscite *m*.

plebs [plebz] *npl* (*pej*) bas peuple.

plectrum ['plektrəm] *n* plectre *m*.

pledge [pledʒ] *n* gage *m*; (*promise*) promesse *f* ♦ *vt* engager; promettre; **to ~ support for sb** s'engager à soutenir qn; **to ~ sb to secrecy** faire promettre à qn de garder le secret.

plenary ['pli:nərɪ] *adj*: **in ~ session** en séance plénière.

plentiful ['plentɪful] *adj* abondant(e), copieux(euse).

plenty ['plentɪ] *n* abondance *f*; **~ of** beaucoup de; (*sufficient*) (bien) assez de; **we've got ~ of time** nous avons largement le temps.

pleurisy ['pluərɪsɪ] *n* pleurésie *f*.

Plexiglas ['pleksɪɡlɑːs] *n* ® (*US*) Plexiglas *m* ®.

pliable ['plaɪəbl] *adj* flexible; (*person*) malléable.

pliers ['plaɪəz] *npl* pinces *fpl*.

plight [plaɪt] *n* situation *f* critique.

plimsolls ['plɪmsəlz] *npl* (*BRIT*) (chaussures *fpl*) tennis *fpl*.

plinth [plɪnθ] *n* socle *m*.

PLO *n abbr* (= *Palestine Liberation Organization*) OLP *f*.

plod [plɔd] *vi* avancer péniblement; (*fig*) peiner.

plodder ['plɔdə*] *n* bûcheur/euse.

plodding ['plɔdɪŋ] *adj* pesant(e).

plonk [plɔŋk] (*col*) *n* (*BRIT*: *wine*) pinard *m*, piquette *f* ♦ *vt*: **to ~ sth down** poser brusquement qch.

plot [plɔt] *n* complot *m*, conspiration *f*; (*of story, play*) intrigue *f*; (*of land*) lot *m* de terrain, lopin *m* ♦ *vt* (*mark out*) pointer; relever; (*conspire*) comploter ♦ *vi* comploter; **a vegetable ~** (*BRIT*) un carré de légumes.

plotter ['plɔtə*] *n* conspirateur/trice; (*COMPUT*) traceur *m*.

plough, (*US*) **plow** [plau] *n* charrue *f* ♦ *vt* (*earth*) labourer.

▶**plough back** *vt* (*COMM*) réinvestir.

▶**plough through** *vt fus* (*snow etc*) avancer péniblement dans.

ploughing, (*US*) **plowing** ['plauɪŋ] *n* labourage *m*.

ploughman, (*US*) **plowman** ['plaumən] *n* laboureur *m*; **~'s lunch** (*BRIT*) *repas sommaire de pain et de fromage.*

ploy [plɔɪ] *n* stratagème *m*.

pluck [plʌk] *vt* (*fruit*) cueillir; (*musical instru-*

ment) pincer; (*bird*) plumer ♦ *n* courage *m*, cran *m*; **to ~ one's eyebrows** s'épiler les sourcils; **to ~ up courage** prendre son courage à deux mains.

plucky ['plʌkɪ] *adj* courageux(euse).

plug [plʌg] *n* bouchon *m*, bonde *f*; (*ELEC*) prise *f* de courant; (*AUT*: *also*: **spark(ing) ~**) bougie *f* ♦ *vt* (*hole*) boucher; (*col*: *advertise*) faire du battage pour, matraquer; **to give sb/sth a ~** (*col*) faire de la pub pour qn/qch.

▶**plug in** (*ELEC*) *vt* brancher ♦ *vi* se brancher.

plughole ['plʌghəul] *n* (*BRIT*) trou *m* (d'écoulement).

plum [plʌm] *n* (*fruit*) prune *f* ♦ *adj*: **~ job** (*col*) travail *m* en or.

plumage ['plu:mɪdʒ] *n* plumage *m*.

plumb [plʌm] *adj* vertical(e) ♦ *n* plomb *m* ♦ *adv* (*exactly*) en plein ♦ *vt* sonder.

▶**plumb in** *vt* (*washing machine*) faire le raccordement de.

plumber ['plʌmə*] *n* plombier *m*.

plumbing ['plʌmɪŋ] *n* (*trade*) plomberie *f*; (*piping*) tuyauterie *f*.

plumbline ['plʌmlaɪn] *n* fil *m* à plomb.

plume [plu:m] *n* plume *f*, plumet *m*.

plummet ['plʌmɪt] *vi* plonger, dégringoler.

plump [plʌmp] *adj* rondelet(te), dodu(e), bien en chair ♦ *vt*: **to ~ sth (down) on** laisser tomber qch lourdement sur.

▶**plump for** *vt fus* (*col*: *choose*) se décider pour.

▶**plump up** *vt* (*cushion*) battre (pour lui redonner forme).

plunder ['plʌndə*] *n* pillage *m* ♦ *vt* piller.

plunge [plʌndʒ] *n* plongeon *m* ♦ *vt* plonger ♦ *vi* (*fall*) tomber, dégringoler; **to take the ~** se jeter à l'eau; **to ~ a room into darkness** plonger une pièce dans l'obscurité.

plunger ['plʌndʒə*] *n* piston *m*; (*for blocked sink*) (débouchoir *m* à) ventouse *f*.

plunging ['plʌndʒɪŋ] *adj* (*neckline*) plongeant(e).

pluperfect [plu:'pə:fɪkt] *n* plus-que-parfait *m*.

plural ['pluərl] *adj* pluriel(le) ♦ *n* pluriel *m*.

plus [plʌs] *n* (*also*: **~ sign**) signe *m* plus ♦ *prep* plus; **ten/twenty ~** plus de dix/vingt; **it's a ~** c'est un atout.

plus fours *npl* pantalon *m* (de) golf.

plush [plʌʃ] *adj* somptueux(euse) ♦ *n* peluche *f*.

plutonium [plu:'təunɪəm] *n* plutonium *m*.

ply [plaɪ] *n* (*of wool*) fil *m*; (*of wood*) feuille *f*, épaisseur *f* ♦ *vt* (*tool*) manier; (*a trade*) exercer ♦ *vi* (*ship*) faire la navette; **three ~ (wool)** *n* laine *f* trois fils; **to ~ sb with drink** donner continuellement à boire à qn.

plywood ['plaɪwud] *n* contreplaqué *m*.

PM *n abbr* (*BRIT*) = **prime minister**.

p.m. *adv abbr* (= *post meridiem*) de l'après-midi.

PMS *n abbr* (= *premenstrual syndrome*) syndrome prémenstruel.

PMT *n abbr* = **premenstrual tension**.

pneumatic [nju:'mætɪk] *adj* pneumatique; **~ drill** marteau-piqueur *m*.

pneumonia [nju:'məunɪə] *n* pneumonie *f*.

PO *n abbr* (= *Post Office*) PTT *fpl*; (*MIL*) = **petty officer**.

po *abbr* = **postal order**.

POA *n abbr* (*BRIT*) = *Prison Officers' Association*.

poach [pəutʃ] *vt* (*cook*) pocher; (*steal*) pêcher (*or* chasser) sans permis ♦ *vi* braconner.

poached [pəutʃt] *adj* (*egg*) poché(e).

poacher ['pəutʃə*] *n* braconnier *m*.

poaching ['pəutʃɪŋ] *n* braconnage *m*.

PO box *n abbr* = **post office box**.

pocket ['pɔkɪt] *n* poche *f* ♦ *vt* empocher; **to be (£5) out of ~** (*BRIT*) en être de sa poche (pour 5 livres).

pocketbook ['pɔkɪtbuk] *n* (*wallet*) portefeuille *m*; (*notebook*) carnet *m*; (*US*: *handbag*) sac *m* à main.

pocket knife *n* canif *m*.

pocket money *n* argent *m* de poche.

pockmarked ['pɔkmɑ:kt] *adj* (*face*) grêlé(e).

pod [pɔd] *n* cosse *f* ♦ *vt* écosser.

podgy ['pɔdʒɪ] *adj* rondelet(te).

podiatrist [pɔ'di:ətrɪst] *n* (*US*) pédicure *m/f*.

podiatry [pɔ'di:ətrɪ] *n* (*US*) pédicurie *f*.

podium ['pəudɪəm] *n* podium *m*.

POE *n abbr* = *port of embarkation, port of entry*.

poem ['pəuɪm] *n* poème *m*.

poet ['pəuɪt] *n* poète *m*.

poetic [pəu'etɪk] *adj* poétique.

poet laureate *n* poète lauréat.

En Grande-Bretagne, le **poet laureate** est un poète qui reçoit un traitement en tant que poète de la cour et qui est officier de la maison royale à vie. Le premier d'entre eux fut Ben Jonson, en 1616. Jadis, le poète lauréat écrivait des poèmes lors des grandes occasions, mais cette tradition n'est plus guère observée.

poetry ['pəuɪtrɪ] *n* poésie *f*.

poignant ['pɔɪnjənt] *adj* poignant(e); (*sharp*) vif(vive).

point [pɔɪnt] *n* (*tip*) pointe *f*; (*in time*) moment *m*; (*in space*) endroit *m*; (*GEOM*, *SCOL*, *SPORT*, *on scale*) point *m*; (*subject*, *idea*) point, sujet *m*; (*also*: **decimal ~**): **2 ~ 3 (2.3)** 2 virgule 3 (2,3); (*BRIT ELEC*: *also*: **power ~**) prise *f* (de courant) ♦ *vt* (*show*) indiquer; (*wall*, *window*) jointoyer; (*gun etc*): **to ~ sth at** braquer *or* diriger qch sur ♦ *vi* montrer du doigt; **to ~ to** montrer du doigt; (*fig*) signaler; **~s** *npl* (*AUT*) vis platinées; (*RAIL*) aiguillage *m*; **good ~s** qualités *fpl*; **the train stops at Carlisle and all ~s south** le train dessert Carlisle et toutes les gares vers le sud; **to make a ~** faire une remarque; **to make a ~ of doing sth** ne pas manquer de faire qch; **to make one's ~** se faire comprendre; **to get the ~** comprendre, saisir; **to come to the ~** en venir au fait; **when it comes to the ~** le moment venu; **there's no** ~ **(in doing)** cela ne sert à rien (de faire); **to be on the** ~ **of doing sth** être sur le point de faire qch; **that's the whole** ~! précisément!; **to be beside the** ~ être à côté de la question; **you've got a** ~ **there!** (c'est) juste!; **in** ~ **of fact** en fait, en réalité; ~ **of departure** (*also fig*) point de départ; ~ **of order** point de procédure; ~ **of sale** (*COMM*) point de vente; ~ **of view** point de vue.

▶**point out** *vt* faire remarquer, souligner.

point-blank ['pɔɪnt'blæŋk] *adv* (*also*: **at** ~ **range**) à bout portant ♦ *adj* (*fig*) catégorique.

point duty *n* (*BRIT*): **to be on** ~ diriger la circulation.

pointed ['pɔɪntɪd] *adj* (*shape*) pointu(e); (*remark*) plein(e) de sous-entendus.

pointedly ['pɔɪntɪdlɪ] *adv* d'une manière significative.

pointer ['pɔɪntə*] *n* (*stick*) baguette *f*; (*needle*) aiguille *f*; (*dog*) chien *m* d'arrêt; (*clue*) indication *f*; (*advice*) tuyau *m*.

pointless ['pɔɪntlɪs] *adj* inutile, vain(e).

poise [pɔɪz] *n* (*balance*) équilibre *m*; (*of head, body*) port *m*; (*calmness*) calme *m* ♦ *vt* placer en équilibre; **to be** ~**d for** (*fig*) être prêt à.

poison ['pɔɪzn] *n* poison *m* ♦ *vt* empoisonner.

poisoning ['pɔɪznɪŋ] *n* empoisonnement *m*.

poisonous ['pɔɪznəs] *adj* (*snake*) venimeux(euse); (*substance etc*) vénéneux(euse); (*fumes*) toxique; (*fig*) pernicieux(euse).

poke [pəʊk] *vt* (*fire*) tisonner; (*jab with finger, stick etc*) piquer; pousser du doigt; (*put*): **to** ~ **sth into** fourrer *or* enfoncer qch dans ♦ *n* (*jab*) (petit) coup; (*to fire*) coup *m* de tisonnier; **to** ~ **one's head out of the window** passer la tête par la fenêtre; **to** ~ **fun at sb** se moquer de qn.

▶**poke about** *vi* fureter.

poker ['pəʊkə*] *n* tisonnier *m*; (*CARDS*) poker *m*.

poker-faced ['pəʊkə'feɪst] *adj* au visage impassible.

poky ['pəʊkɪ] *adj* exigu(ë).

Poland ['pəʊlənd] *n* Pologne *f*.

polar ['pəʊlə*] *adj* polaire.

polar bear *n* ours blanc.

polarize ['pəʊləraɪz] *vt* polariser.

Pole [pəʊl] *n* Polonais/e.

pole [pəʊl] *n* (*of wood*) mât *m*, perche *f*; (*ELEC*) poteau *m*; (*GEO*) pôle *m*.

poleaxe ['pəʊlæks] *vt* (*fig*) terrasser.

pole bean *n* (*US*) haricot *m* (à rames).

polecat ['pəʊlkæt] *n* putois *m*.

Pol. Econ. ['pɔlɪkɔn] *n abbr* = *political economy*.

polemic [pɔ'lemɪk] *n* polémique *f*.

pole star ['pəʊlstɑ:*] *n* étoile *f* polaire.

pole vault ['pəʊlvɔ:lt] *n* saut *m* à la perche.

police [pə'li:s] *npl* police *f* ♦ *vt* maintenir l'ordre dans; **a large number of** ~ **were hurt** de nombreux policiers ont été blessés.

police car *n* voiture *f* de police.

police constable *n* (*BRIT*) agent *m* de police.

police department *n* (*US*) services *mpl* de police.

police force *n* police *f*, forces *fpl* de l'ordre.

policeman [pə'li:smən] *n* agent *m* de police, policier *m*.

police officer *n* agent *m* de police.

police record *n* casier *m* judiciaire.

police state *n* état policier.

police station *n* commissariat *m* de police.

policewoman [pə'li:swʊmən] *n* femme-agent *f*.

policy ['pɔlɪsɪ] *n* politique *f*; (*also*: **insurance** ~) police *f* (d'assurance); (*of newspaper, company*) politique générale; **to take out a** ~ (*INSURANCE*) souscrire une police d'assurance.

policy holder *n* assuré/e.

policy-making ['pɔlɪsɪmeɪkɪŋ] *n* élaboration *f* de nouvelles lignes d'action.

polio ['pəʊlɪəʊ] *n* polio *f*.

Polish ['pəʊlɪʃ] *adj* polonais(e) ♦ *n* (*LING*) polonais *m*.

polish ['pɔlɪʃ] *n* (*for shoes*) cirage *m*; (*for floor*) cire *f*, encaustique *f*; (*for nails*) vernis *m*; (*shine*) éclat *m*, poli *m*; (*fig: refinement*) raffinement *m* ♦ *vt* (*put polish on: shoes, wood*) cirer; (*make shiny*) astiquer, faire briller; (*fig: improve*) perfectionner.

▶**polish off** *vt* (*work*) expédier; (*food*) liquider.

polished ['pɔlɪʃt] *adj* (*fig*) raffiné(e).

polite [pə'laɪt] *adj* poli(e); **it's not** ~ **to do that** ça ne se fait pas.

politely [pə'laɪtlɪ] *adv* poliment.

politeness [pə'laɪtnɪs] *n* politesse *f*.

politic ['pɔlɪtɪk] *adj* diplomatique.

political [pə'lɪtɪkl] *adj* politique.

political asylum *n* asile *m* politique.

politically [pə'lɪtɪklɪ] *adv* politiquement.

politically correct *adj* politiquement correct(e).

politician [pɔlɪ'tɪʃən] *n* homme/femme politique, politicien/ne.

politics ['pɔlɪtɪks] *n* politique *f*.

polka ['pɔlkə] *n* polka *f*.

polka dot *n* pois *m*.

poll [pəʊl] *n* scrutin *m*, vote *m*; (*also*: **opinion** ~) sondage *m* (d'opinion) ♦ *vt* obtenir; **to go to the** ~**s** (*voters*) aller aux urnes; (*government*) tenir des élections.

pollen ['pɔlən] *n* pollen *m*.

pollen count *n* taux *m* de pollen.

pollination [pɔlɪ'neɪʃən] *n* pollinisation *f*.

polling ['pəʊlɪŋ] *n* (*BRIT POL*) élections *fpl*; (*TEL*) invitation *f* à émettre.

polling booth *n* (*BRIT*) isoloir *m*.

polling day *n* (*BRIT*) jour *m* des élections.

polling station *n* (*BRIT*) bureau *m* de vote.

pollster ['pəʊlstə*] *n* sondeur *m*, enquêteur/euse.

poll tax *n* (*BRIT: formerly*) ≈ impôts locaux.

pollutant [pə'lu:tənt] *n* polluant *m*.

pollute [pə'lu:t] *vt* polluer.
pollution [pə'lu:ʃən] *n* pollution *f*.
polo ['pəuləu] *n* polo *m*.
poloneck ['pəuləunɛk] *n* col roulé ♦ *adj* à col roulé.
poly ['pɔlɪ] *n abbr* (BRIT) = **polytechnic**.
poly bag *n* (BRIT col) sac *m* en plastique.
polyester [pɔlɪ'ɛstə*] *n* polyester *m*.
polygamy [pə'lɪgəmɪ] *n* polygamie *f*.
polygraph ['pɔlɪgrɑːf] *n* détecteur *m* de mensonges.
Polynesia [pɔlɪ'niːzɪə] *n* Polynésie *f*.
Polynesian [pɔlɪ'niːzɪən] *adj* polynésien(ne) ♦ *n* Polynésien/ne.
polyp ['pɔlɪp] *n* (MED) polype *m*.
polystyrene [pɔlɪ'staɪriːn] *n* polystyrène *m*.
polytechnic [pɔlɪ'tɛknɪk] *n* (college) IUT *m*, Institut *m* universitaire de technologie.
polythene ['pɔlɪθiːn] *n* polyéthylène *m*.
polythene bag *n* sac *m* en plastique.
polyurethane [pɔlɪ'juərɪθeɪn] *n* polyuréthane *m*.
pomegranate ['pɔmɪgrænɪt] *n* grenade *f*.
pommel ['pɔml] *n* pommeau *m* ♦ *vt* = **pummel**.
pomp [pɔmp] *n* pompe *f*, faste *f*, apparat *m*.
pompom ['pɔmpɔm] *n* pompon *m*.
pompous ['pɔmpəs] *adj* pompeux(euse).
pond [pɔnd] *n* étang *m*; (stagnant) mare *f*.
ponder ['pɔndə*] *vi* réfléchir ♦ *vt* considérer, peser.
ponderous ['pɔndərəs] *adj* pesant(e), lourd(e).
pong [pɔŋ] (BRIT col) *n* puanteur *f* ♦ *vi* schlinguer.
pontiff ['pɔntɪf] *n* pontife *m*.
pontificate [pɔn'tɪfɪkeɪt] *vi* (fig): **to ~ (about)** pontifier (sur).
pontoon [pɔn'tuːn] *n* ponton *m*; (BRIT: CARDS) vingt-et-un *m*.
pony ['pəunɪ] *n* poney *m*.
ponytail ['pəunɪteɪl] *n* queue *f* de cheval.
pony trekking [-trɛkɪŋ] *n* (BRIT) randonnée *f* équestre or à cheval.
poodle ['puːdl] *n* caniche *m*.
pooh-pooh ['puː'puː] *vt* dédaigner.
pool [puːl] *n* (of rain) flaque *f*; (pond) mare *f*; (artificial) bassin *m*; (also: **swimming ~**) piscine *f*; (sth shared) fonds commun; (money at cards) cagnotte *f*; (billiards) poule *f*; (COMM: consortium) pool *m*; (US: monopoly trust) trust *m* ♦ *vt* mettre en commun; **typing ~**, (US) **secretary ~** pool *m* dactylographique; **to do the (football) ~s** (BRIT) ≈ jouer au loto sportif; see also **football pools**.
poor [puə*] *adj* pauvre; (mediocre) médiocre, faible, mauvais(e) ♦ *npl*: **the ~** les pauvres *mpl*.
poorly ['puəlɪ] *adv* pauvrement; médiocrement ♦ *adj* souffrant(e), malade.
pop [pɔp] *n* (noise) bruit sec; (MUS) musique *f* pop; (col: drink) soda *m*; (US col: father) papa *m* ♦ *vt* (put) fourrer, mettre (rapidement) ♦ *vi* éclater; (cork) sauter; **she ~ped her head**

out of the window elle passa la tête par la fenêtre.
▶**pop in** *vi* entrer en passant.
▶**pop out** *vi* sortir.
▶**pop up** *vi* apparaître, surgir.
pop concert *n* concert *m* pop.
popcorn ['pɔpkɔːn] *n* pop-corn *m*.
pope [pəup] *n* pape *m*.
poplar ['pɔplə*] *n* peuplier *m*.
poplin ['pɔplɪn] *n* popeline *f*.
popper ['pɔpə*] *n* (BRIT) bouton-pression *m*.
poppy ['pɔpɪ] *n* coquelicot *m*; pavot *m*.
poppycock ['pɔpɪkɔk] *n* (col) balivernes *fpl*.
Popsicle ['pɔpsɪkl] *n* ® (US) esquimau *m* (glace).
populace ['pɔpjuləs] *n* peuple *m*.
popular ['pɔpjulə*] *adj* populaire; (fashionable) à la mode; **to be ~ (with)** (person) avoir du succès (auprès de); (decision) être bien accueilli(e) (par).
popularity [pɔpju'lærɪtɪ] *n* popularité *f*.
popularize ['pɔpjuləraɪz] *vt* populariser; (science) vulgariser.
populate ['pɔpjuleɪt] *vt* peupler.
population [pɔpju'leɪʃən] *n* population *f*.
population explosion *n* explosion *f* démographique.
populous ['pɔpjuləs] *adj* populeux(euse).
porcelain ['pɔːslɪn] *n* porcelaine *f*.
porch [pɔːtʃ] *n* porche *m*.
porcupine ['pɔːkjupaɪn] *n* porc-épic *m*.
pore [pɔː*] *n* pore *m* ♦ *vi*: **to ~ over** s'absorber dans, être plongé(e) dans.
pork [pɔːk] *n* porc *m*.
pork chop *n* côte *f* de porc.
porn [pɔːn] *adj*, *n* (col) porno (*m*).
pornographic [pɔːnə'græfɪk] *adj* pornographique.
pornography [pɔː'nɔgrəfɪ] *n* pornographie *f*.
porous ['pɔːrəs] *adj* poreux(euse).
porpoise ['pɔːpəs] *n* marsouin *m*.
porridge ['pɔrɪdʒ] *n* porridge *m*.
port [pɔːt] *n* (harbour) port *m*; (opening in ship) sabord *m*; (NAUT: left side) bâbord *m*; (wine) porto *m*; (COMPUT) port *m*, accès *m* ♦ *cpd* portuaire, du port; **to ~** (NAUT) à bâbord; **~ of call** (port d')escale *f*.
portable ['pɔːtəbl] *adj* portatif(ive).
portal ['pɔːtl] *n* portail *m*.
portcullis [pɔːt'kʌlɪs] *n* herse *f*.
portend [pɔː'tɛnd] *vt* présager, annoncer.
portent ['pɔːtɛnt] *n* présage *m*.
porter ['pɔːtə*] *n* (for luggage) porteur *m*; (doorkeeper) gardien/ne; portier *m*.
portfolio [pɔːt'fəulɪəu] *n* portefeuille *m*; (of artist) portfolio *m*.
porthole ['pɔːthəul] *n* hublot *m*.
portico ['pɔːtɪkəu] *n* portique *m*.
portion ['pɔːʃən] *n* portion *f*, part *f*.
portly ['pɔːtlɪ] *adj* corpulent(e).
portrait ['pɔːtreɪt] *n* portrait *m*.
portray [pɔː'treɪ] *vt* faire le portrait de; (in

writing) dépeindre, représenter.

portrayal [pɔːˈtreɪəl] _n_ portrait _m_, représentation _f._

Portugal [ˈpɔːtjugl] _n_ Portugal _m._

Portuguese [pɔːtjuˈgiːz] _adj_ portugais(e) ♦ _n_ (_pl inv_) Portugais/e; (_LING_) portugais _m._

Portuguese man-of-war [-mænəvˈwɔː*] _n_ (_jellyfish_) galère _f._

pose [pəuz] _n_ pose _f_; (_pej_) affectation _f_ ♦ _vi_ poser; (_pretend_): **to ~ as** se poser en ♦ _vt_ poser, créer; **to strike a ~** poser (pour la galerie).

poser [ˈpəuzə*] _n_ question difficile _or_ embarrassante; (_person_) = **poseur.**

poseur [pəuˈzəː*] _n_ (_pej_) poseur/euse.

posh [pɔʃ] _adj_ (_col_) chic _inv_; **to talk ~** parler d'une manière affectée.

position [pəˈzɪʃən] _n_ position _f_; (_job_) situation _f_ ♦ _vt_ mettre en place _or_ en position; **to be in a ~ to do sth** être en mesure de faire qch.

positive [ˈpɔzɪtɪv] _adj_ positif(ive); (_certain_) sûr(e), certain(e); (_definite_) formel(le), catégorique; (_clear_) indéniable, réel(le).

posse [ˈpɔsɪ] _n_ (_US_) détachement _m._

possess [pəˈzɛs] _vt_ posséder; **like one ~ed** comme un fou; **whatever can have ~ed you?** qu'est-ce qui vous a pris?

possession [pəˈzɛʃən] _n_ possession _f_; **to take ~ of sth** prendre possession de qch.

possessive [pəˈzɛsɪv] _adj_ possessif(ive).

possessiveness [pəˈzɛsɪvnɪs] _n_ possessivité _f._

possessor [pəˈzɛsə*] _n_ possesseur _m._

possibility [pɔsɪˈbɪlɪtɪ] _n_ possibilité _f_; éventualité _f_; **he's a ~ for the part** c'est un candidat possible pour le rôle.

possible [ˈpɔsɪbl] _adj_ possible; (_solution_) envisageable, éventuel(le); **it is ~ to do it** il est possible de le faire; **as far as ~** dans la mesure du possible, autant que possible; **if ~** si possible; **as big as ~** aussi gros que possible.

possibly [ˈpɔsɪblɪ] _adv_ (_perhaps_) peut-être; **if you ~ can** si cela vous est possible; **I cannot ~ come** il m'est impossible de venir.

post [pəust] _n_ (_BRIT: mail_) poste _f_; (_: collection_) levée _f_; (_: letters, delivery_) courrier _m_; (_job, situation_) poste _m_; (_pole_) poteau _m_; (_trading ~_) comptoir (commercial) ♦ _vt_ (_BRIT: send by post, MIL_) poster; (_BRIT: appoint_): **to ~ to** affecter à; (_notice_) afficher; **by ~** (_BRIT_) par la poste; **by return of ~** (_BRIT_) par retour du courrier; **to keep sb ~ed** tenir qn au courant.

post... [pəust] _prefix_ post...; **~ 1990** _adj_ d'après 1990 ♦ _adv_ après 1990.

postage [ˈpəustɪdʒ] _n_ affranchissement _m_; **~ paid** port payé; **~ prepaid** (_US_) franco (de port).

postage stamp _n_ timbre-poste _m._

postal [ˈpəustl] _adj_ postal(e).

postal order _n_ mandat(-poste _m_) _m._

postbag [ˈpəustbæg] _n_ (_BRIT_) sac postal; (_postman's_) sacoche _f._

postbox [ˈpəustbɔks] _n_ (_BRIT_) boîte _f_ aux lettres (_publique_).

postcard [ˈpəustkɑːd] _n_ carte postale.

postcode [ˈpəustkəud] _n_ (_BRIT_) code postal.

postdate [ˈpəustˈdeɪt] _vt_ (_cheque_) postdater.

poster [ˈpəustə*] _n_ affiche _f._

poste restante [pəustˈrɛstɑːnt] _n_ (_BRIT_) poste restante.

posterior [pɔsˈtɪərɪə*] _n_ (_col_) postérieur _m_, derrière _m._

posterity [pɔsˈtɛrɪtɪ] _n_ postérité _f._

poster paint _n_ gouache _f._

post exchange (PX) _n_ (_US MIL_) magasin _m_ de l'armée.

post-free [pəustˈfriː] _adj_ (_BRIT_) franco (de port).

postgraduate [ˈpəustˈgrædjuət] _n_ ≈ étudiant/e de troisième cycle.

posthumous [ˈpɔstjuməs] _adj_ posthume.

posthumously [ˈpɔstjuməslɪ] _adv_ après la mort de l'auteur, à titre posthume.

posting [ˈpəustɪŋ] _n_ (_BRIT_) affectation _f._

postman [ˈpəustmən] _n_ facteur _m._

postmark [ˈpəustmɑːk] _n_ cachet _m_ (de la poste).

postmaster [ˈpəustmɑːstə*] _n_ receveur _m_ des postes.

Postmaster General _n_ ≈ ministre _m_ des Postes et Télécommunications.

postmistress [ˈpəustmɪstrɪs] _n_ receveuse _f_ des postes.

post-mortem [pəustˈmɔːtəm] _n_ autopsie _f._

postnatal [ˈpəustˈneɪtl] _adj_ post-natal(e).

post office _n_ (_building_) poste _f_; (_organization_) postes _fpl._

post office box (PO box) _n_ boîte postale (B.P.).

post-paid [ˈpəustˈpeɪd] _adj_ (_BRIT_) port payé.

postpone [pəsˈpəun] _vt_ remettre (à plus tard), reculer.

postponement [pəsˈpəunmənt] _n_ ajournement _m_, renvoi _m._

postscript [ˈpəustskrɪpt] _n_ post-scriptum _m._

postulate [ˈpɔstjuleɪt] _vt_ postuler.

posture [ˈpɔstʃə*] _n_ posture _f_, attitude _f_ ♦ _vi_ poser.

postwar [pəustˈwɔː*] _adj_ d'après-guerre.

posy [ˈpəuzɪ] _n_ petit bouquet.

pot [pɔt] _n_ (_for cooking_) marmite _f_; casserole _f_; (_for plants, jam_) pot _m_; (_piece of pottery_) poterie _f_; (_col: marijuana_) herbe _f_ ♦ _vt_ (_plant_) mettre en pot; **to go to ~** aller à vau-l'eau; **~s of** (_BRIT col_) beaucoup de, plein de.

potash [ˈpɔtæʃ] _n_ potasse _f._

potassium [pəˈtæsɪəm] _n_ potassium _m._

potato, ~es [pəˈteɪtəu] _n_ pomme _f_ de terre.

potato crisps, (_US_) **potato chips** _npl_ chips _mpl._

potato flour _n_ fécule _f._

potato peeler _n_ épluche-légumes _m._

potbellied [ˈpɔtbɛlɪd] _adj_ (_from overeating_) bedonnant(e); (_from malnutrition_) au ventre ballonné.

potency ['pəʊtnsɪ] *n* puissance *f*, force *f*; (*of drink*) degré *m* d'alcool.

potent ['pəʊtnt] *adj* puissant(e); (*drink*) fort(e), très alcoolisé(e).

potentate ['pəʊtnteɪt] *n* potentat *m*.

potential [pə'tɛnʃl] *adj* potentiel(le) ♦ *n* potentiel *m*; **to have** ~ être prometteur(euse); ouvrir des possibilités.

potentially [pə'tɛnʃəlɪ] *adv* potentiellement; **it's** ~ **dangerous** ça pourrait se révéler dangereux, il y a possibilité de danger.

pothole ['pɒthəʊl] *n* (*in road*) nid *m* de poule; (*BRIT: underground*) gouffre *m*, caverne *f*.

potholer ['pɒthəʊlə*] *n* (*BRIT*) spéléologue *m/f*.

potholing ['pɒthəʊlɪŋ] *n* (*BRIT*): **to go** ~ faire de la spéléologie.

potion ['pəʊʃən] *n* potion *f*.

potluck [pɒt'lʌk] *n*: **to take** ~ tenter sa chance.

potpourri [pəʊ'pʊriː] *n* pot-pourri *m*.

pot roast *n* rôti *m* à la cocotte.

potshot ['pɒtʃɒt] *n*: **to take** ~**s at** canarder.

potted ['pɒtɪd] *adj* (*food*) en conserve; (*plant*) en pot; (*fig: shortened*) abrégé(e).

potter ['pɒtə*] *n* potier *m* ♦ *vi* (*BRIT*): **to** ~ **around,** ~ **about** bricoler; ~**'s wheel** tour *m* de potier.

pottery ['pɒtərɪ] *n* poterie *f*; **a piece of** ~ une poterie.

potty ['pɒtɪ] *adj* (*BRIT col: mad*) dingue ♦ *n* (*child's*) pot *m*.

potty-training ['pɒtɪtreɪnɪŋ] *n* apprentissage *m* de la propreté.

pouch [paʊtʃ] *n* (*ZOOL*) poche *f*; (*for tobacco*) blague *f*.

pouf(fe) [puːf] *n* (*stool*) pouf *m*.

poultice ['pəʊltɪs] *n* cataplasme *m*.

poultry ['pəʊltrɪ] *n* volaille *f*.

poultry farm *n* élevage *m* de volaille.

poultry farmer *n* aviculteur *m*.

pounce [paʊns] *vi*: **to** ~ **(on)** bondir (sur), fondre (sur) ♦ *n* bond *m*, attaque *f*.

pound [paʊnd] *n* livre *f* (*weight* = 453g, *16 ounces; money* = 100 *pence*); (*for dogs, cars*) fourrière *f* ♦ *vt* (*beat*) bourrer de coups, marteler; (*crush*) piler, pulvériser; (*with guns*) pilonner ♦ *vi* (*beat*) battre violemment, taper; **half a** ~ **(of)** une demi-livre (de); **a five-** ~ **note** un billet de cinq livres.

pounding ['paʊndɪŋ] *n*: **to take a** ~ (*fig*) prendre une râclée.

pound sterling *n* livre *f* sterling.

pour [pɔː*] *vt* verser ♦ *vi* couler à flots; (*rain*) pleuvoir à verse; **to come** ~**ing in** (*water*) entrer à flots; (*letters*) arriver par milliers; (*cars, people*) affluer.

▶**pour away, pour off** *vt* vider.

▶**pour in** *vi* (*people*) affluer, se précipiter.

▶**pour out** *vi* (*people*) sortir en masse ♦ *vt* vider; déverser; (*serve: a drink*) verser.

pouring ['pɔːrɪŋ] *adj*: ~ **rain** pluie torrentielle.

pout [paʊt] *n* moue *f* ♦ *vi* faire la moue.

poverty ['pɒvətɪ] *n* pauvreté *f*, misère *f*.

poverty line *n* seuil *m* de pauvreté.

poverty-stricken ['pɒvətɪstrɪkn] *adj* pauvre, déshérité(e).

poverty trap *n* (*BRIT*) piège *m* de la pauvreté.

POW *n abbr* = **prisoner of war**.

powder ['paʊdə*] *n* poudre *f* ♦ *vt* poudrer; **to** ~ **one's nose** se poudrer; (*euphemism*) aller à la salle de bain; ~**ed milk** lait *m* en poudre.

powder compact *n* poudrier *m*.

powder keg *n* (*fig*) poudrière *f*.

powder puff *n* houppette *f*.

powder room *n* toilettes *fpl* (pour dames).

powdery ['paʊdərɪ] *adj* poudreux(euse).

power ['paʊə*] *n* (*strength*) puissance *f*, force *f*; (*ability, POL: of party, leader*) pouvoir *m*; (*MATH*) puissance; (*of speech, thought*) faculté *f*; (*ELEC*) courant *m* ♦ *vt* faire marcher, actionner; **to do all in one's** ~ **to help sb** faire tout ce qui est en son pouvoir pour aider qn; **the world** ~**s** les grandes puissances; **to be in** ~ être au pouvoir.

powerboat ['paʊəbəʊt] *n* (*BRIT*) hors-bord *m*.

power cut *n* (*BRIT*) coupure *f* de courant.

powered ['paʊəd] *adj*: ~ **by** actionné(e) par, fonctionnant à; **nuclear-** ~ **submarine** sous-marin *m* (à propulsion) nucléaire.

power failure *n* panne *f* de courant.

powerful ['paʊəful] *adj* puissant(e).

powerhouse ['paʊəhaʊs] *n* (*fig: person*) fonceur *m*; **a** ~ **of ideas** une mine d'idées.

powerless ['paʊəlɪs] *adj* impuissant(e).

power line *n* ligne *f* électrique.

power of attorney *n* procuration *f*.

power point *n* (*BRIT*) prise *f* de courant.

power station *n* centrale *f* électrique.

power steering *n* direction assistée.

powwow ['paʊwaʊ] *n* conciliabule *m*.

pox [pɒks] *n see* **chickenpox**.

pp *abbr* (= *per procurationem: by proxy*) p.p.

PPE *n abbr* (*BRIT SCOL*) = philosophy, politics and economics.

PPS *n abbr* (= *post postscriptum*) PPS; (*BRIT*: = *parliamentary private secretary*) parlementaire chargé de mission auprès d'un ministre.

PQ *abbr* (*Canada*: = *Province of Quebec*) PQ.

PR *n abbr* = **proportional representation, public relations** ♦ *abbr* (*US*) = *Puerto Rico*.

Pr. *abbr* (= *prince*) Pce.

practicability [præktɪkə'bɪlɪtɪ] *n* possibilité *f* de réalisation.

practicable ['præktɪkəbl] *adj* (*scheme*) réalisable.

practical ['præktɪkl] *adj* pratique.

practicality [præktɪ'kælɪtɪ] *n* (*of plan*) aspect *m* pratique; (*of person*) sens *m* pratique; **practicalities** *npl* détails *mpl* pratiques.

practical joke *n* farce *f*.

practically ['præktɪklɪ] *adv* (*almost*) pratiquement.

practice ['præktɪs] *n* pratique *f*; (*of profession*)

exercice *m*; (*at football etc*) entraînement *m*; (*business*) cabinet *m*; clientèle *f* ♦ *vt, vi* (*US*) = **practise; in** ~ (*in reality*) en pratique; **out of** ~ rouillé(e); (*in reality*) en pratique; **out of** ~ rouillé(e); **2 hours' piano** ~ 2 heures de travail *or* d'exercices au piano; **target** ~ exercices de tir; **it's common** ~ c'est courant, ça se fait couramment; **to put sth into** ~ mettre qch en pratique.

practice match *n* match *m* d'entraînement.

practise, (*US*) **practice** ['præktɪs] *vt* (*work at: piano, one's backhand etc*) s'exercer à, travailler; (*train for: skiing, running etc*) s'entraîner à; (*a sport, religion, method*) pratiquer; (*profession*) exercer ♦ *vi* s'exercer, travailler; (*train*) s'entraîner; **to** ~ **for a match** s'entraîner pour un match.

practised, (*US*) **practiced** ['præktɪst] *adj* (*person*) expérimenté(e); (*performance*) impeccable; (*liar*) invétéré(e); **with a** ~ **eye** d'un œil exercé.

practising, (*US*) **practicing** ['præktɪsɪŋ] *adj* (*Christian etc*) pratiquant(e); (*lawyer*) en exercice; (*homosexual*) déclaré.

practitioner [præk'tɪʃənə*] *n* praticien/ne.

pragmatic [præg'mætɪk] *adj* pragmatique.

Prague [prɑ:g] *n* Prague.

prairie ['prɛərɪ] *n* savane *f*; (*US*): **the** ~**s** la Prairie.

praise [preɪz] *n* éloge(s) *m(pl)*, louange(s) *f(pl)* ♦ *vt* louer, faire l'éloge de.

praiseworthy ['preɪzwə:ðɪ] *adj* digne de louanges.

pram [præm] *n* (*BRIT*) landau *m*, voiture *f* d'enfant.

prance [prɑ:ns] *vi* (*horse*) caracoler.

prank [præŋk] *n* farce *f*.

prat [præt] *n* (*BRIT col*) imbécile *m*, andouille *f*.

prattle ['prætl] *vi* jacasser.

prawn [prɔ:n] *n* crevette *f* (rose).

pray [preɪ] *vi* prier.

prayer [prɛə*] *n* prière *f*.

prayer book *n* livre *m* de prières.

pre... ['pri:] *prefix* pré...; ~**-1970** *adj* d'avant 1970 ♦ *adv* avant 1970.

preach [pri:tʃ] *vt, vi* prêcher; **to** ~ **at sb** faire la morale à qn.

preacher ['pri:tʃə*] *n* prédicateur *m*; (*US: clergyman*) pasteur *m*.

preamble ['pri:æmbl] *n* préambule *m*.

prearranged [pri:ə'reɪndʒd] *adj* organisé(e) *or* fixé(e) à l'avance.

precarious [prɪ'kɛərɪəs] *adj* précaire.

precaution [prɪ'kɔ:ʃən] *n* précaution *f*.

precautionary [prɪ'kɔ:ʃənrɪ] *adj* (*measure*) de précaution.

precede [prɪ'si:d] *vt, vi* précéder.

precedence ['prɛsɪdəns] *n* préséance *f*.

precedent ['prɛsɪdənt] *n* précédent *m*; **to establish** *or* **set a** ~ créer un précédent.

preceding [prɪ'si:dɪŋ] *adj* qui précède (*or* précédait).

precept ['pri:sɛpt] *n* précepte *m*.

precinct ['pri:sɪŋkt] *n* (*round cathedral*) pourtour *m*, enceinte *f*; (*US: district*) circonscription *f*, arrondissement *m*; ~**s** *npl* (*neighbourhood*) alentours *mpl*, environs *mpl*; **pedestrian** ~ zone piétonne; **shopping** ~ (*BRIT*) centre commercial.

precious ['prɛʃəs] *adj* précieux(euse) ♦ *adv* (*col*): ~ **little** *or* **few** fort peu; **your** ~ **dog** (*ironic*) ton chien chéri, ton chéri chien.

precipice ['prɛsɪpɪs] *n* précipice *m*.

precipitate *adj* [prɪ'sɪpɪtɪt] (*hasty*) précipité(e) ♦ *vt* [prɪ'sɪpɪteɪt] précipiter.

precipitation [prɪsɪpɪ'teɪʃən] *n* précipitation *f*.

precipitous [prɪ'sɪpɪtəs] *adj* (*steep*) abrupt(e), à pic.

précis, *pl* **précis** ['preɪsi:, -z] *n* résumé *m*.

precise [prɪ'saɪs] *adj* précis(e).

precisely [prɪ'saɪslɪ] *adv* précisément.

precision [prɪ'sɪʒən] *n* précision *f*.

preclude [prɪ'klu:d] *vt* exclure, empêcher; **to** ~ **sb from doing** empêcher qn de faire.

precocious [prɪ'kəʊʃəs] *adj* précoce.

preconceived [pri:kən'si:vd] *adj* (*idea*) préconçu(e).

preconception [pri:kən'sɛpʃən] *n* idée préconçue.

precondition [pri:kən'dɪʃən] *n* condition *f* nécessaire.

precursor [pri:'kə:sə*] *n* précurseur *m*.

predate [pri:'deɪt] *vt* (*precede*) antidater.

predator ['prɛdətə*] *n* prédateur *m*, rapace *m*.

predatory ['prɛdətərɪ] *adj* rapace.

predecessor ['pri:dɪsɛsə*] *n* prédécesseur *m*.

predestination [pri:dɛstɪ'neɪʃən] *n* prédestination *f*.

predetermine [pri:dɪ'tə:mɪn] *vt* déterminer à l'avance.

predicament [prɪ'dɪkəmənt] *n* situation *f* difficile.

predicate ['prɛdɪkɪt] *n* (*LING*) prédicat *m*.

predict [prɪ'dɪkt] *vt* prédire.

predictable [prɪ'dɪktəbl] *adj* prévisible.

predictably [prɪ'dɪktəblɪ] *adv* (*behave, react*) de façon prévisible; ~ **she didn't arrive** comme on pouvait s'y attendre, elle n'est pas venue.

prediction [prɪ'dɪkʃən] *n* prédiction *f*.

predispose [pri:dɪs'pəʊz] *vt* prédisposer.

predominance [prɪ'dɒmɪnəns] *n* prédominance *f*.

predominant [prɪ'dɒmɪnənt] *adj* prédominant(e).

predominantly [prɪ'dɒmɪnəntlɪ] *adv* en majeure partie; surtout.

predominate [prɪ'dɒmɪneɪt] *vi* prédominer.

pre-eminent [prɪ'ɛmɪnənt] *adj* prééminent(e).

pre-empt [prɪ'ɛmt] *vt* (*BRIT*) acquérir par droit de préemption; (*fig*) anticiper sur; **to** ~ **the issue** conclure avant même d'ouvrir les débats.

pre-emptive [prɪ'ɛmtɪv] *adj*: ~ **strike** attaque (*or* action) préventive.

preen [priːn] *vt*: **to ~ itself** (*bird*) se lisser les plumes; **to ~ o.s.** s'admirer.

prefab ['priːfæb] *n* bâtiment préfabriqué.

prefabricated [priː'fæbrɪkeɪtɪd] *adj* préfabriqué(e).

preface ['prɛfəs] *n* préface *f*.

prefect ['priːfɛkt] *n* (*BRIT*: *in school*) élève chargé de certaines fonctions de discipline; (*in France*) préfet *m*.

prefer [prɪ'fəː*] *vt* préférer; (*LAW*): **to ~ charges** procéder à une inculpation; **to ~ coffee to tea** préférer le café au thé.

preferable ['prɛfrəbl] *adj* préférable.

preferably ['prɛfrəblɪ] *adv* de préférence.

preference ['prɛfrəns] *n* préférence *f*; **in ~ to sth** plutôt que qch, de préférence à qch.

preference shares *npl* (*BRIT*) actions privilégiées.

preferential [prɛfə'rɛnʃəl] *adj* préférentiel(le); **~ treatment** traitement *m* de faveur.

preferred stock [prɪ'fəːd-] *npl* (*US*) = **preference shares**.

prefix ['priːfɪks] *n* préfixe *m*.

pregnancy ['prɛgnənsɪ] *n* grossesse *f*.

pregnancy test *n* test *m* de grossesse.

pregnant ['prɛgnənt] *adj* enceinte *adj f*; **3 months ~** enceinte de 3 mois.

prehistoric ['priːhɪs'tɔrɪk] *adj* préhistorique.

prehistory [priː'hɪstərɪ] *n* préhistoire *f*.

prejudge [priː'dʒʌdʒ] *vt* préjuger de.

prejudice ['prɛdʒudɪs] *n* préjugé *m*; (*harm*) tort *m*, préjudice *m* ♦ *vt* porter préjudice à; (*bias*): **to ~ sb in favour of/against** prévenir qn en faveur de/contre.

prejudiced ['prɛdʒudɪst] *adj* (*person*) plein(e) de préjugés; (*view*) préconçu(e), partial(e); **to be ~ against sb/sth** avoir un parti-pris contre qn/qch.

prelate ['prɛlət] *n* prélat *m*.

preliminaries [prɪ'lɪmɪnərɪz] *npl* préliminaires *mpl*.

preliminary [prɪ'lɪmɪnərɪ] *adj* préliminaire.

prelude ['prɛljuːd] *n* prélude *m*.

premarital ['priː'mærɪtl] *adj* avant le mariage.

premature ['prɛmətʃuə*] *adj* prématuré(e); **to be ~ (in doing sth)** aller un peu (trop) vite (en faisant qch).

premeditated [priː'mɛdɪteɪtɪd] *adj* prémédité(e).

premeditation [priːmɛdɪ'teɪʃən] *n* préméditation *f*.

premenstrual [priː'mɛnstruəl] *adj* prémenstruel(le).

premenstrual tension *n* irritabilité *f* avant les règles.

premier ['prɛmɪə*] *adj* premier(ière), principal(e) ♦ *n* (*POL*) premier ministre.

premiere ['prɛmɪɛə*] *n* première *f*.

premise ['prɛmɪs] *n* prémisse *f*.

premises ['prɛmɪsɪz] *npl* locaux *mpl*; **on the ~** sur les lieux; sur place; **business ~** locaux commerciaux.

premium ['priːmɪəm] *n* prime *f*; **to be at a ~** (*fig: housing etc*) être très demandé(e), être rarissime; **to sell at a ~** (*shares*) vendre au-dessus du pair.

premium bond *n* (*BRIT*) bon *m* à lots.

> Les **premium bonds** *sont des bons du Trésor que le public peut acheter. Les intérêts ne sont pas versés, mais il y a chaque mois un tirage au sort par ordinateur. Les personnes dont le bon a été sélectionné gagnent une somme d'argent pouvant aller de quelques livres à plusieurs milliers de livres.*

premium deal *n* (*COMM*) offre spéciale.

premium gasoline *n* (*US*) super *m*.

premonition [prɛmə'nɪʃən] *n* prémonition *f*.

preoccupation [priːɔkju'peɪʃən] *n* préoccupation *f*.

preoccupied [priː'ɔkjupaɪd] *adj* préoccupé(e).

prep [prɛp] *adj abbr*: **~ school** = **preparatory school** ♦ *n abbr* (*SCOL*: = *preparation*) étude *f*.

prepackaged [priː'pækɪdʒd] *adj* préempaqueté(e).

prepaid [priː'peɪd] *adj* payé(e) d'avance.

preparation [prɛpə'reɪʃən] *n* préparation *f*; **~s** (*for trip, war*) préparatifs *mpl*; **in ~ for** en vue de.

preparatory [prɪ'pærətərɪ] *adj* préparatoire; **~ to sth/to doing sth** en prévision de qch/avant de faire qch.

preparatory school *n* école primaire privée; (*US*) lycée privé.

> *En Grande-Bretagne, une* **preparatory school** *- ou, plus familièrement, une* **prep school** *- est une école payante qui prépare les enfants de 7 à 13 ans aux* **public schools**.

prepare [prɪ'pɛə*] *vt* préparer ♦ *vi*: **to ~ for** se préparer à.

prepared [prɪ'pɛəd] *adj*: **~ for** préparé(e) à; **~ to** prêt(e) à.

preponderance [prɪ'pɔndərns] *n* prépondérance *f*.

preposition [prɛpə'zɪʃən] *n* préposition *f*.

prepossessing [priːpə'zɛsɪŋ] *adj* avenant(e), engageant(e).

preposterous [prɪ'pɔstərəs] *adj* absurde.

prep school *n* = **preparatory school**.

prerecord ['priːrɪ'kɔːd] *vt*: **~ed broadcast** émission *f* en différé; **~ed cassette** cassette enregistrée.

prerequisite [priː'rɛkwɪzɪt] *n* condition *f* préalable.

prerogative [prɪ'rɔgətɪv] *n* prérogative *f*.

presbyterian [prɛzbɪ'tɪərɪən] *adj, n* presbytérien(ne).

presbytery ['prɛzbɪtərɪ] *n* presbytère *m*.

preschool ['priː'skuːl] *adj* préscolaire; (*child*) d'âge préscolaire.

prescribe [prɪ'skraɪb] *vt* prescrire; **~d books**

(*BRIT SCOL*) œuvres *fpl* au programme.

prescription [prɪ'skrɪpʃən] *n* prescription *f*; (*MED*) ordonnance *f*; **to make up** *or* (*US*) **fill a** ~ faire une ordonnance; **"only available on** ~" "uniquement sur ordonnance".

prescription charges *npl* (*BRIT*) participation *f* fixe au coût de l'ordonnance.

prescriptive [prɪ'skrɪptɪv] *adj* normatif(ive).

presence ['prɛzns] *n* présence *f*; ~ **of mind** présence d'esprit.

present ['prɛznt] *adj* présent(e) ♦ *n* cadeau *m*; (*also*: ~ **tense**) présent *m* ♦ *vt* [prɪ'zɛnt] présenter; (*give*): **to** ~ **sb with sth** offrir qch à qn; **to be** ~ **at** assister à; **those** ~ les présents; **at** ~ en ce moment; **to give sb a** ~ offrir un cadeau à qn; **to** ~ **sb (to sb)** présenter qn (à qn).

presentable [prɪ'zɛntəbl] *adj* présentable.

presentation [prɛzn'teɪʃən] *n* présentation *f*; (*gift*) cadeau *m*, présent *m*; (*ceremony*) remise *f* du cadeau; **on** ~ **of** (*voucher etc*) sur présentation de.

present-day ['prɛzntdeɪ] *adj* contemporain(e), actuel(le).

presenter [prɪ'zɛntə*] *n* (*BRIT RADIO, TV*) présentateur/trice.

presently ['prɛzntlɪ] *adv* (*soon*) tout à l'heure, bientôt; (*at present*) en ce moment; (*US: now*) maintenant.

preservation [prɛzə'veɪʃən] *n* préservation *f*, conservation *f*.

preservative [prɪ'zə:vətɪv] *n* agent *m* de conservation.

preserve [prɪ'zə:v] *vt* (*keep safe*) préserver, protéger; (*maintain*) conserver, garder; (*food*) mettre en conserve ♦ *n* (*for game, fish*) réserve *f*; (*often pl: jam*) confiture *f*; (: *fruit*) fruits *mpl* en conserve.

preshrunk [pri:'ʃrʌŋk] *adj* irrétrécissable.

preside [prɪ'zaɪd] *vi* présider.

presidency ['prɛzɪdənsɪ] *n* présidence *f*.

president ['prɛzɪdənt] *n* président/e; (*US: of company*) président-directeur général, PDG *m*.

presidential [prɛzɪ'dɛnʃl] *adj* présidentiel(le).

press [prɛs] *n* (*tool, machine, newspapers*) presse *f*; (*for wine*) pressoir *m*; (*crowd*) cohue *f*, foule *f* ♦ *vt* (*push*) appuyer sur; (*squeeze*) presser, serrer; (*clothes: iron*) repasser; (*pursue*) talonner; (*insist*): **to** ~ **sth on sb** presser qn d'accepter qch; (*urge, entreat*): **to** ~ **sb to do** *or* **into doing sth** pousser qn à faire qch ♦ *vi* appuyer, peser; se presser; **we are** ~**ed for time** le temps nous manque; **to** ~ **for sth** faire pression pour obtenir qch; **to** ~ **sb for an answer** presser qn de répondre; **to** ~ **charges against sb** (*LAW*) engager des poursuites contre qn; **to go to** ~ (*newspaper*) aller à l'impression; **to be in the** ~ (*being printed*) être sous presse; (*in the newspapers*) être dans le journal.

▶**press ahead** *vi* = **press on**.

▶**press on** *vi* continuer.

press agency *n* agence *f* de presse.

press clipping *n* coupure *f* de presse.

press conference *n* conférence *f* de presse.

press cutting *n* = **press clipping**.

press-gang ['prɛsgæŋ] *vt* (*fig*): **to** ~ **sb into doing sth** faire pression sur qn pour qu'il fasse qch.

pressing ['prɛsɪŋ] *adj* urgent(e), pressant(e) ♦ *n* repassage *m*.

press officer *n* attaché/e de presse.

press release *n* communiqué *m* de presse.

press stud *n* (*BRIT*) bouton-pression *m*.

press-up ['prɛsʌp] *n* (*BRIT*) traction *f*.

pressure ['prɛʃə*] *n* pression *f*; (*stress*) tension *f* ♦ *vt* = **to put** ~ **on**; **to put** ~ **on sb (to do sth)** faire pression sur qn (pour qu'il fasse qch).

pressure cooker *n* cocotte-minute *f*.

pressure gauge *n* manomètre *m*.

pressure group *n* groupe *m* de pression.

pressurize ['prɛʃəraɪz] *vt* pressuriser; (*BRIT fig*): **to** ~ **sb (into doing sth)** faire pression sur qn (pour qu'il fasse qch).

pressurized ['prɛʃəraɪzd] *adj* pressurisé(e).

Prestel ['prɛstɛl] *n* ® ≈ Minitel *m* ®.

prestige [prɛs'ti:ʒ] *n* prestige *m*.

prestigious [prɛs'tɪdʒəs] *adj* prestigieux(euse).

presumably [prɪ'zju:məblɪ] *adv* vraisemblablement; ~ **he did it** c'est sans doute lui (qui a fait cela).

presume [prɪ'zju:m] *vt* présumer, supposer; **to** ~ **to do** (*dare*) se permettre de faire.

presumption [prɪ'zʌmpʃən] *n* supposition *f*, présomption *f*; (*boldness*) audace *f*.

presumptuous [prɪ'zʌmpʃəs] *adj* présomptueux(euse).

presuppose [pri:sə'pəuz] *vt* présupposer.

pre-tax [pri:'tæks] *adj* avant impôt(s).

pretence, (*US*) **pretense** [prɪ'tɛns] *n* (*claim*) prétention *f*; (*pretext*) prétexte *m*; **she is devoid of all** ~ elle n'est pas du tout prétentieuse; **to make a** ~ **of doing** faire semblant de faire; **on** *or* **under the** ~ **of doing sth** sous prétexte de faire qch.

pretend [prɪ'tɛnd] *vt* (*feign*) feindre, simuler ♦ *vi* (*feign*) faire semblant; (*claim*): **to** ~ **to sth** prétendre à qch; **to** ~ **to do** faire semblant de faire.

pretense [prɪ'tɛns] *n* (*US*) = **pretence**.

pretension [prɪ'tɛnʃən] *n* (*claim*) prétention *f*; **to have no** ~**s to sth/to being sth** n'avoir aucune prétention à qch/à être qch.

pretentious [prɪ'tɛnʃəs] *adj* prétentieux(euse).

preterite ['prɛtərɪt] *n* prétérit *m*.

pretext ['pri:tɛkst] *n* prétexte *m*; **on** *or* **under the** ~ **of doing sth** sous prétexte de faire qch.

pretty ['prɪtɪ] *adj* joli(e) ♦ *adv* assez.

prevail [prɪ'veɪl] *vi* (*win*) l'emporter, prévaloir; (*be usual*) avoir cours; (*persuade*): **to** ~ **(up)on sb to do** persuader qn de faire.

prevailing [prɪ'veɪlɪŋ] *adj* dominant(e).

prevalent ['prɛvələnt] *adj* répandu(e), courant(e); (*fashion*) en vogue.
prevarication [prɪværɪ'keɪʃən] *n* (usage *m* de) faux-fuyants *mpl*.
prevent [prɪ'vɛnt] *vt*: **to ~ (from doing)** empêcher (de faire).
preventable [prɪ'vɛntəbl] *adj* évitable.
preventative [prɪ'vɛntətɪv] *adj* préventif(ive).
prevention [prɪ'vɛnʃən] *n* prévention *f*.
preventive [prɪ'vɛntɪv] *adj* préventif(ive).
preview ['priːvjuː] *n* (*of film*) avant-première *f*; (*fig*) aperçu *m*.
previous ['priːvɪəs] *adj* (*last*) précédent(e); (*earlier*) antérieur(e); (*question, experience*) préalable; **I have a ~ engagement** je suis déjà pris(e); **~ to doing** avant de faire.
previously ['priːvɪəslɪ] *adv* précédemment, auparavant.
prewar [priː'wɔː*] *adj* d'avant-guerre.
prey [preɪ] *n* proie *f* ♦ *vi*: **to ~ on** s'attaquer à; **it was ~ing on his mind** ça le rongeait *or* minait.
price [praɪs] *n* prix *m*; (*BETTING: odds*) cote *f* ♦ *vt* (*goods*) fixer le prix de; tarifer; **what is the ~ of ...?** combien coûte ...?, quel est le prix de ...?; **to go up** *or* **rise in ~** augmenter; **to put a ~ on sth** chiffrer qch; **to be ~d out of the market** (*article*) être trop cher pour soutenir la concurrence; (*producer, nation*) ne pas pouvoir soutenir la concurrence; **what ~ his promises now?** (*BRIT*) que valent maintenant toutes ses promesses?; **he regained his freedom, but at a ~** il a retrouvé sa liberté, mais cela lui a coûté cher.
price control *n* contrôle *m* des prix.
price-cutting ['praɪskʌtɪŋ] *n* réductions *fpl* de prix.
priceless ['praɪslɪs] *adj* sans prix, inestimable; (*col: amusing*) impayable.
price list *n* tarif *m*.
price range *n* gamme *f* de prix; **it's within my ~** c'est dans mes prix.
price tag *n* étiquette *f*.
price war *n* guerre *f* des prix.
pricey ['praɪsɪ] *adj* (*col*) chérot *inv*.
prick [prɪk] *n* piqûre *f*; (*col!*) bitte *f* (*!*); connard *m* (*!*) ♦ *vt* piquer; **to ~ up one's ears** dresser *or* tendre l'oreille.
prickle ['prɪkl] *n* (*of plant*) épine *f*; (*sensation*) picotement *m*.
prickly ['prɪklɪ] *adj* piquant(e), épineux(euse); (*fig: person*) irritable.
prickly heat *n* fièvre *f* miliaire.
prickly pear *n* figue *f* de Barbarie.
pride [praɪd] *n* (*feeling proud*) fierté *f*; (*: pej*) orgueil *m*; (*self-esteem*) amour-propre *m* ♦ *vt*: **to ~ o.s. on** se flatter de; s'enorgueillir de; **to take (a) ~ in** être (très) fier(ère) de; **to take a ~ in doing** mettre sa fierté à faire; **to have ~ of place** (*BRIT*) avoir la place d'honneur.
priest [priːst] *n* prêtre *m*.

priestess ['priːstɪs] *n* prêtresse *f*.
priesthood ['priːsthud] *n* prêtrise *f*, sacerdoce *m*.
prig [prɪg] *n* poseur/euse, fat *m*.
prim [prɪm] *adj* collet monté *inv*, guindé(e).
primacy ['praɪməsɪ] *n* primauté *f*.
prima facie ['praɪmə'feɪʃɪ] *adj*: **to have a ~ case** (*LAW*) avoir une affaire qui paraît fondée.
primal ['praɪməl] *adj* (*first in time*) primitif(ive); (*first in importance*) primordial(e).
primarily ['praɪmərɪlɪ] *adv* principalement, essentiellement.
primary ['praɪmərɪ] *adj* primaire; (*first in importance*) premier(ière), primordial(e) ♦ *n* (*US: election*) (élection *f*) primaire *f*.

> *Aux États-Unis, les* **primaries** *constituent un processus de sélection préliminaire des candidats qui seront choisis par les principaux partis lors de la campagne électorale pour l'élection présidentielle. Elles ont lieu dans 35 États, de février à juin, l'année de l'élection. Chaque État envoie en juillet - août des* **delegates** *aux conventions démocrate et républicaine chargées de désigner leur candidat à la présidence. Ces* **delegates** *sont généralement choisis en fonction du nombre de voix obtenu par les candidats lors des* **primaries***.*

primary colour *n* couleur fondamentale.
primary school *n* (*BRIT*) école *f* primaire.

> *Les* **primary schools** *en Grande-Bretagne accueillent les enfants de 5 à 11 ans. Elles marquent le début du cycle scolaire obligatoire et elles comprennent deux sections: la section des petits ("infant school") et la section des grands ("junior school"); voir* **secondary school**

primate *n* (*REL*) ['praɪmɪt] primat *m*; (*ZOOL*) ['praɪmeɪt] primate *m*.
prime [praɪm] *adj* primordial(e), fondamental(e); (*excellent*) excellent(e) ♦ *vt* (*gun, pump*) amorcer; (*fig*) mettre au courant; **in the ~ of life** dans la fleur de l'âge.
prime minister *n* Premier ministre.
primer ['praɪmə*] *n* (*book*) premier livre, manuel *m* élémentaire; (*paint*) apprêt *m*; (*of gun*) amorce *f*.
prime time *n* (*RADIO, TV*) heure(s) *f(pl)* de grande écoute.
primeval [praɪ'miːvl] *adj* primitif(ive).
primitive ['prɪmɪtɪv] *adj* primitif(ive).
primrose ['prɪmrəuz] *n* primevère *f*.
primus (stove) ['praɪməs-] *n ®* (*BRIT*) réchaud *m* de camping.
prince [prɪns] *n* prince *m*.
princess [prɪn'sɛs] *n* princesse *f*.
principal ['prɪnsɪpl] *adj* principal(e) ♦ *n* (*headmaster*) directeur *m*, principal *m*; (*in play*) rôle principal; (*money*) principal *m*.

principality [prɪnsɪ'pælɪtɪ] *n* principauté *f*.
principally ['prɪnsɪplɪ] *adv* principalement.
principle ['prɪnsɪpl] *n* principe *m*; **in ~** en principe; **on ~** par principe.
print [prɪnt] *n* (*mark*) empreinte *f*; (*letters*) caractères *mpl*; (*fabric*) imprimé *m*; (*ART*) gravure *f*, estampe *f*; (*PHOT*) épreuve *f* ♦ *vt* imprimer; (*publish*) publier; (*write in capitals*) écrire en majuscules; **out of ~** épuisé(e).
▶**print out** *vt* (*COMPUT*) imprimer.
printed circuit board (PCB) ['prɪntɪd-] *n* carte *f* à circuit imprimé.
printed matter ['prɪntɪd-] *n* imprimés *mpl*.
printer ['prɪntə*] *n* imprimeur *m*; (*machine*) imprimante *f*.
printhead ['prɪnthɛd] *n* tête *f* d'impression.
printing ['prɪntɪŋ] *n* impression *f*.
printing press *n* presse *f* typographique.
print-out ['prɪntaʊt] *n* copie *f* papier, tirage *m*.
print wheel *n* marguerite *f*.
prior ['praɪə*] *adj* antérieur(e), précédent(e) ♦ *n* (*REL*) prieur *m*; **~ to doing** avant de faire; **without ~ notice** sans préavis; **to have a ~ claim to sth** avoir priorité pour qch.
priority [praɪ'ɒrɪtɪ] *n* priorité *f*; **to have** *or* **take ~ over sth/sb** avoir la priorité sur qch/qn.
priory ['praɪərɪ] *n* prieuré *m*.
prise [praɪz] *vt*: **to ~ open** forcer.
prism ['prɪzəm] *n* prisme *m*.
prison ['prɪzn] *n* prison *f*.
prison camp *n* camp *m* de prisonniers.
prisoner ['prɪznə*] *n* prisonnier/ière; **the ~ at the bar** l'accusé/e; **to take sb ~** faire qn prisonnier; **~ of war** prisonnier de guerre.
prissy ['prɪsɪ] *adj* bégueule.
pristine ['prɪstiːn] *adj* virginal(e).
privacy ['prɪvəsɪ] *n* intimité *f*, solitude *f*.
private ['praɪvɪt] *adj* (*not public*) privé(e); (*personal*) personnel(le); (*house, car, lesson*) particulier(ière) ♦ *n* soldat *m* de deuxième classe; **"~"** (*on envelope*) "personnelle"; **in ~** en privé; **in (his) ~ life** dans sa vie privée; **he is a very ~ person** il est très secret; **to be in ~ practice** être médecin (*or* dentiste *etc*) non conventionné; **~ hearing** (*LAW*) audience *f* à huis-clos.
private enterprise *n* entreprise privée.
private eye *n* détective privé.
private limited company *n* (*BRIT*) société *f* à participation restreinte (*non cotée en Bourse*).
privately ['praɪvɪtlɪ] *adv* en privé; (*within oneself*) intérieurement.
private parts *npl* parties (*génitales*).
private property *n* propriété privée.
private school *n* école privée.
privation [praɪ'veɪʃən] *n* privation *f*.
privatize ['praɪvɪtaɪz] *vt* privatiser.
privet ['prɪvɪt] *n* troène *m*.
privilege ['prɪvɪlɪdʒ] *n* privilège *m*.
privileged ['prɪvɪlɪdʒd] *adj* privilégié(e); **to be ~ to do sth** avoir le privilège de faire qch.

privy ['prɪvɪ] *adj*: **to be ~ to** être au courant de.
privy council *n* conseil privé.

*Le **privy council** existe en Angleterre depuis l'avènement des Normands. À l'époque, ses membres étaient les conseillers privés du roi, mais en 1688 le cabinet les a supplantés. Les ministres du cabinet sont aujourd'hui automatiquement conseillers du roi, et ce titre est également accordé aux personnes qui ont occupé de hautes fonctions en politique, dans le clergé ou dans les milieux juridiques. Les pouvoirs de ces conseillers en tant que tels sont maintenant limités.*

prize [praɪz] *n* prix *m* ♦ *adj* (*example, idiot*) parfait(e); (*bull, novel*) primé(e) ♦ *vt* priser, faire grand cas de.
prize-fighter ['praɪzfaɪtə*] *n* boxeur professionnel.
prize giving *n* distribution *f* des prix.
prize money *n* argent *m* du prix.
prizewinner ['praɪzwɪnə*] *n* gagnant/e.
prizewinning ['praɪzwɪnɪŋ] *adj* gagnant(e); (*novel, essay etc*) primé(e).
PRO *n abbr* = **public relations officer**.
pro [prəʊ] *n* (*SPORT*) professionnel/le; **the ~s and cons** le pour et le contre.
pro- [prəʊ] *prefix* (*in favour of*) pro-.
pro-active [prəʊ'æktɪv] *adj* dynamique.
probability [prɒbə'bɪlɪtɪ] *n* probabilité *f*; **in all ~** très probablement.
probable ['prɒbəbl] *adj* probable; **it is ~/hardly ~ that ...** il est probable/peu probable que ....
probably ['prɒbəblɪ] *adv* probablement.
probate ['prəʊbɪt] *n* (*LAW*) validation *f*, homologation *f*.
probation [prə'beɪʃən] *n* (*in employment*) (période *f* d')essai *m*; (*LAW*) liberté surveillée; (*REL*) noviciat *m*, probation *f*; **on ~** (*employee*) à l'essai; (*LAW*) en liberté surveillée.
probationary [prə'beɪʃənrɪ] *adj* (*period*) d'essai.
probe [prəʊb] *n* (*MED, SPACE*) sonde *f*; (*enquiry*) enquête *f*, investigation *f* ♦ *vt* sonder, explorer.
probity ['prəʊbɪtɪ] *n* probité *f*.
problem ['prɒbləm] *n* problème *m*; **to have ~s with the car** avoir des ennuis avec la voiture; **what's the ~?** qu'y a-t-il?, quel est le problème?; **I had no ~ in finding her** je n'ai pas eu de mal à la trouver; **no ~!** pas de problème!
problematic [prɒblə'mætɪk] *adj* problématique.
problem-solving ['prɒbləmsɒlvɪŋ] *n* résolution *f* de problèmes; **an approach to ~** une approche en matière de résolution de problèmes.
procedure [prə'siːdʒə*] *n* (*ADMIN, LAW*) procé-

dure *f*; (*method*) marche *f* à suivre, façon *f* de procéder.

proceed [prə'siːd] *vi* (*go forward*) avancer; (*go about it*) procéder; (*continue*): **to ~ (with)** continuer, poursuivre; **to ~ to** aller à; passer à; **to ~ to do** se mettre à faire; **I am not sure how to ~** je ne sais pas exactement comment m'y prendre; **to ~ against sb** (*LAW*) intenter des poursuites contre qn.

proceedings [prə'siːdɪŋz] *npl* mesures *fpl*; (*LAW*) poursuites *fpl*; (*meeting*) réunion *f*, séance *f*; (*records*) compte rendu; actes *mpl*.

proceeds ['prəusiːdz] *npl* produit *m*, recette *f*.

process ['prəusɛs] *n* processus *m*; (*method*) procédé *m* ♦ *vt* traiter ♦ *vi* [prə'sɛs] (*BRIT formal: go in procession*) défiler; **in ~** en cours; **we are in the ~ of doing** nous sommes en train de faire.

processed cheese ['prəusɛst-] *n* ≈ fromage fondu.

processing ['prəusɛsɪŋ] *n* traitement *m*.

procession [prə'sɛʃən] *n* défilé *m*, cortège *m*; **funeral ~** cortège funèbre, convoi *m* mortuaire.

pro-choice [prəu'tʃɔɪs] *adj* en faveur de l'avortement.

proclaim [prə'kleɪm] *vt* déclarer, proclamer.

proclamation [prɔklə'meɪʃən] *n* proclamation *f*.

proclivity [prə'klɪvɪtɪ] *n* inclination *f*.

procrastination [prəukræstɪ'neɪʃən] *n* procrastination *f*.

procreation [prəukrɪ'eɪʃən] *n* procréation *f*.

Procurator Fiscal ['prɔkjureɪtə-] *n* (*Scottish*) ≈ procureur *m* (*de la République*).

procure [prə'kjuə*] *vt* (*for o.s.*) se procurer; (*for sb*) procurer.

procurement [prə'kjuəmənt] *n* achat *m*, approvisionnement *m*.

prod [prɔd] *vt* pousser ♦ *n* (*push, jab*) petit coup, poussée *f*.

prodigal ['prɔdɪgl] *adj* prodigue.

prodigious [prə'dɪdʒəs] *adj* prodigieux(euse).

prodigy ['prɔdɪdʒɪ] *n* prodige *m*.

produce *n* ['prɔdjuːs] (*AGR*) produits *mpl* ♦ *vt* [prə'djuːs] produire; (*to show*) présenter; (*cause*) provoquer, causer; (*THEAT*) monter, mettre en scène.

producer [prə'djuːsə*] *n* (*THEAT*) metteur *m* en scène; (*AGR, CINE*) producteur *m*.

product ['prɔdʌkt] *n* produit *m*.

production [prə'dʌkʃən] *n* production *f*; (*THEAT*) mise *f* en scène; **to put into ~** (*goods*) entreprendre la fabrication de.

production agreement *n* (*US*) accord *m* de productivité.

production line *n* chaîne *f* (de fabrication).

production manager *n* directeur/trice de la production.

productive [prə'dʌktɪv] *adj* productif(ive).

productivity [prɔdʌk'tɪvɪtɪ] *n* productivité *f*.

productivity agreement *n* (*BRIT*) accord *m* de productivité.

productivity bonus *n* prime *f* de rendement.

Prof. [prɔf] *abbr* (= *professor*) Prof.

profane [prə'feɪn] *adj* sacrilège; (*lay*) profane.

profess [prə'fɛs] *vt* professer; **I do not ~ to be an expert** je ne prétends pas être spécialiste.

professed [prə'fɛst] *adj* (*self-declared*) déclaré(e).

profession [prə'fɛʃən] *n* profession *f*; **the ~s** les professions libérales.

professional [prə'fɛʃənl] *n* (*SPORT*) professionnel/le ♦ *adj* professionnel(le); (*work*) de professionnel; **he's a ~ man** il exerce une profession libérale; **to take ~ advice** consulter un spécialiste.

professionalism [prə'fɛʃnəlɪzəm] *n* professionnalisme *m*.

professionally [prə'fɛʃnəlɪ] *adv* professionnellement; (*SPORT: play*) en professionnel; **I only know him ~** je n'ai avec lui que des relations de travail.

professor [prə'fɛsə*] *n* professeur *m* (*titulaire d'une chaire*); (*US: teacher*) professeur *m*.

professorship [prə'fɛsəʃɪp] *n* chaire *f*.

proffer ['prɔfə*] *vt* (*hand*) tendre; (*remark*) faire; (*apologies*) présenter.

proficiency [prə'fɪʃənsɪ] *n* compétence *f*, aptitude *f*.

proficient [prə'fɪʃənt] *adj* compétent(e), capable.

profile ['prəufaɪl] *n* profil *m*; **to keep a high/low ~** (*fig*) rester *or* être très en évidence/discret(ète).

profit ['prɔfɪt] *n* (*from trading*) bénéfice *m*; (*advantage*) profit *m* ♦ *vi*: **to ~ (by *or* from)** profiter (de); **~ and loss account** compte *m* de profits et pertes; **to make a ~** faire un *or* des bénéfice(s); **to sell sth at a ~** vendre qch à profit.

profitability [prɔfɪtə'bɪlɪtɪ] *n* rentabilité *f*.

profitable ['prɔfɪtəbl] *adj* lucratif(ive), rentable; (*fig: beneficial*) avantageux(euse); (*: meeting*) fructueux(euse).

profit centre *n* centre *m* de profit.

profiteering [prɔfɪ'tɪərɪŋ] *n* (*pej*) mercantilisme *m*.

profit-making ['prɔfɪtmeɪkɪŋ] *adj* à but lucratif.

profit margin *n* marge *f* bénéficiaire.

profit-sharing ['prɔfɪtʃɛərɪŋ] *n* intéressement *m* aux bénéfices.

profits tax *n* (*BRIT*) impôt *m* sur les bénéfices.

profligate ['prɔflɪgɪt] *adj* (*behaviour, act*) dissolu(e); (*person*) débauché(e); (*extravagant*): **~ (with)** prodigue (de).

pro forma ['prəu'fɔːmə] *adj*: **~ invoice** facture *f* pro-forma.

profound [prə'faund] *adj* profond(e).

profuse [prə'fjuːs] *adj* abondant(e).

profusely [prə'fjuːslɪ] *adv* abondamment; (*thank etc*) avec effusion.

profusion [prə'fjuːʒən] *n* profusion *f*, abondance *f*.

progeny ['prɒdʒɪnɪ] *n* progéniture *f*; descendants *mpl*.

programme, (*US, also:* BRIT COMPUT) **program** ['prəugræm] *n* programme *m*; (*RADIO, TV*) émission *f* ♦ *vt* programmer.

program(m)er ['prəugræmə*] *n* programmeur/euse.

program(m)ing ['prəugræmɪŋ] *n* programmation *f*.

program(m)ing language *n* langage *m* de programmation.

progress *n* ['prəugrɛs] progrès *m* ♦ *vi* [prə'grɛs] progresser, avancer; **in** ~ en cours; **to make** ~ progresser, faire des progrès, être en progrès; **as the match** ~ed au fur et à mesure que la partie avançait.

progression [prə'grɛʃən] *n* progression *f*.

progressive [prə'grɛsɪv] *adj* progressif(ive); (*person*) progressiste.

progressively [prə'grɛsɪvlɪ] *adv* progressivement.

progress report *n* (MED) bulletin *m* de santé; (ADMIN) rapport *m* d'activité; rapport sur l'état (d'avancement) des travaux.

prohibit [prə'hɪbɪt] *vt* interdire, défendre; **to** ~ **sb from doing sth** défendre *or* interdire à qn de faire qch; **"smoking** ~**ed"** "défense de fumer".

prohibition [prəuɪ'bɪʃən] *n* prohibition *f*.

prohibitive [prə'hɪbɪtɪv] *adj* (*price etc*) prohibitif(ive).

project *n* ['prɒdʒɛkt] (*plan*) projet *m*, plan *m*; (*venture*) opération *f*, entreprise *f*; (*gen* SCOL: *research*) étude *f*, dossier *m* ♦ *vb* [prə'dʒɛkt] *vt* projeter ♦ *vi* (*stick out*) faire saillie, s'avancer.

projectile [prə'dʒɛktaɪl] *n* projectile *m*.

projection [prə'dʒɛkʃən] *n* projection *f*; (*overhang*) saillie *f*.

projectionist [prə'dʒɛkʃənɪst] *n* (CINE) projectionniste *m/f*.

projection room *n* (CINE) cabine *f* de projection.

projector [prə'dʒɛktə*] *n* (CINE etc) projecteur *m*.

proletarian [prəulɪ'tɛərɪən] *adj* prolétarien(ne) ♦ *n* prolétaire *m/f*.

proletariat [prəulɪ'tɛərɪət] *n* prolétariat *m*.

pro-life [prəu'laɪf] *adj* contre l'avortement.

proliferate [prə'lɪfəreɪt] *vi* proliférer.

proliferation [prəlɪfə'reɪʃən] *n* prolifération *f*.

prolific [prə'lɪfɪk] *adj* prolifique.

prologue ['prəulɒg] *n* prologue *m*.

prolong [prə'lɒŋ] *vt* prolonger.

prom [prɒm] *n abbr* = **promenade, promenade concert**; (*US: ball*) bal *m* d'étudiants.

promenade [prɒmə'nɑːd] *n* (*by sea*) esplanade *f*, promenade *f*.

promenade concert *n* concert *m* (de musique classique).

En Grande-Bretagne, un **promenade concert** *(ou* **prom***) est un concert de musique classique, ainsi appelé car, à l'origine, le public restait debout et se promenait au lieu de rester assis. De nos jours, une partie du public reste debout, mais il y a également des places assises (plus chères). Les Proms les plus connus sont les Proms londoniens. La dernière séance (the Last Night of the Proms) est un grand événement médiatique où se jouent des airs traditionnels et patriotiques.*

Aux États-Unis et au Canada, le **prom** *ou* **promenade** *est un bal organisé par le lycée.*

---

promenade deck *n* (NAUT) pont *m* promenade.

prominence ['prɒmɪnəns] *n* proéminence *f*; importance *f*.

prominent ['prɒmɪnənt] *adj* (*standing out*) proéminent(e); (*important*) important(e); **he is** ~ **in the field of** ... il est très connu dans le domaine de ....

prominently ['prɒmɪnəntlɪ] *adv* (*display, set*) bien en évidence; **he figured** ~ **in the case** il a joué un rôle important dans l'affaire.

promiscuity [prɒmɪs'kjuːɪtɪ] *n* (*sexual*) légèreté *f* de mœurs.

promiscuous [prə'mɪskjuəs] *adj* (*sexually*) de mœurs légères.

promise ['prɒmɪs] *n* promesse *f* ♦ *vt*, *vi* promettre; **to make sb a** ~ faire une promesse à qn; **to** ~ **(sb) to do sth** promettre (à qn) de faire qch; **a young man of** ~ un jeune homme plein d'avenir; **to** ~ **well** *vi* promettre.

promising ['prɒmɪsɪŋ] *adj* prometteur(euse).

promissory note ['prɒmɪsərɪ-] *n* billet *m* à ordre.

promontory ['prɒməntrɪ] *n* promontoire *m*.

promote [prə'məut] *vt* promouvoir; (*venture, event*) organiser, mettre sur pied; (*new product*) lancer; **the team was** ~**d to the second division** (BRIT FOOTBALL) l'équipe est montée en 2e division.

promoter [prə'məutə*] *n* (*of event*) organisateur/trice; (*of cause etc*) partisan/e, défenseur *m*.

promotion [prə'məuʃən] *n* promotion *f*.

prompt [prɒmpt] *adj* rapide ♦ *n* (COMPUT) message *m* (de guidage) ♦ *vt* inciter; (*cause*) entraîner, provoquer; (THEAT) souffler (son rôle *or* ses répliques) à; **they're very** ~ (*punctual*) ils sont ponctuels; **at 8 o'clock** ~ à 8 heures précises; **he was** ~ **to accept** il a tout de suite accepté; **to** ~ **sb to do** inciter *or* pousser qn à faire.

prompter ['prɒmptə*] *n* (THEAT) souffleur *m*.

promptly ['prɒmptlɪ] *adv* rapidement, sans délai; ponctuellement.

promptness ['prɒmptnɪs] *n* rapidité *f*; promptitude *f*; ponctualité *f*.

promulgate ['prɔməlgeɪt] *vt* promulguer.

prone [prəun] *adj* (*lying*) couché(e) (face contre terre); (*liable*): ~ **to** enclin(e) à; **to be ~ to illness** être facilement malade; **to be ~ to an illness** être sujet à une maladie; **she is ~ to burst into tears if** ... elle a tendance à tomber en larmes si ....

prong [prɔŋ] *n* pointe *f*; (*of fork*) dent *f*.

pronoun ['prəunaun] *n* pronom *m*.

pronounce [prə'nauns] *vt* prononcer ♦ *vi*: **to ~ (up)on** se prononcer sur; **they ~d him unfit to drive** ils l'ont déclaré inapte à la conduite.

pronounced [prə'naunst] *adj* (*marked*) prononcé(e).

pronouncement [prə'naunsmənt] *n* déclaration *f*.

pronunciation [prənʌnsɪ'eɪʃən] *n* prononciation *f*.

proof [pru:f] *n* preuve *f*; (*test, of book*, PHOT) épreuve *f*; (*of alcohol*) degré *m* ♦ *adj*: ~ **against** à l'épreuve de ♦ *vt* (BRIT: *tent, anorak*) imperméabiliser; **to be 70° ~** ≈ titrer 40 degrés.

proofreader ['pru:fri:də*] *n* correcteur/trice (d'épreuves).

prop [prɔp] *n* support *m*, étai *m* ♦ *vt* (*also*: ~ **up**) étayer, soutenir; (*lean*): **to ~ sth against** appuyer qch contre *or* à.

Prop. *abbr* (COMM) = **proprietor**.

propaganda [prɔpə'gændə] *n* propagande *f*.

propagation [prɔpə'geɪʃən] *n* propagation *f*.

propel [prə'pɛl] *vt* propulser, faire avancer.

propeller [prə'pɛlə*] *n* hélice *f*.

propelling pencil [prə'pɛlɪŋ-] *n* (BRIT) portemine *m inv*.

propensity [prə'pɛnsɪtɪ] *n* propension *f*.

proper ['prɔpə*] *adj* (*suited, right*) approprié(e), bon(bonne); (*seemly*) correct(e), convenable; (*authentic*) vrai(e), véritable; (*col: real*) fini(e), vrai(e); **to go through the ~ channels** (ADMIN) passer par la voie officielle.

properly ['prɔpəlɪ] *adv* correctement, convenablement; (*really*) bel et bien.

proper noun *n* nom *m* propre.

property ['prɔpətɪ] *n* (*possessions*) biens *mpl*; (*house etc*) propriété *f*; (*land*) terres *fpl*, domaine *m*; (CHEM *etc: quality*) propriété *f*; **it's their ~** cela leur appartient, c'est leur propriété.

property developer *n* (BRIT) promoteur immobilier.

property owner *n* propriétaire *m*.

property tax *n* impôt foncier.

prophecy ['prɔfɪsɪ] *n* prophétie *f*.

prophesy ['prɔfɪsaɪ] *vt* prédire ♦ *vi* prophétiser.

prophet ['prɔfɪt] *n* prophète *m*.

prophetic [prə'fɛtɪk] *adj* prophétique.

proportion [prə'pɔːʃən] *n* proportion *f*; (*share*) part *f*; partie *f* ♦ *vt* proportionner; **to be in/**

out of ~ to *or* **with sth** être à la mesure de/ hors de proportion avec qch; **to see sth in ~** (*fig*) ramener qch à de justes proportions.

proportional [prə'pɔːʃənl], **proportionate** [prə'pɔːʃənɪt] *adj* proportionnel(le).

proportional representation (PR) *n* (POL) représentation proportionnelle.

proposal [prə'pəuzl] *n* proposition *f*, offre *f*; (*plan*) projet *m*; (*of marriage*) demande *f* en mariage.

propose [prə'pəuz] *vt* proposer, suggérer; (*have in mind*): **to ~ sth/to do** *or* **doing sth** envisager qch/de faire qch ♦ *vi* faire sa demande en mariage; **to ~ to do** avoir l'intention de faire.

proposer [prə'pəuzə*] *n* (BRIT: *of motion etc*) auteur *m*.

proposition [prɔpə'zɪʃən] *n* proposition *f*; **to make sb a ~** faire une proposition à qn.

propound [prə'paund] *vt* proposer, soumettre.

proprietary [prə'praɪətərɪ] *adj* de marque déposée; ~ **article** article *m* *or* produit *m* de marque; ~ **brand** marque déposée.

proprietor [prə'praɪətə*] *n* propriétaire *m/f*.

propriety [prə'praɪətɪ] *n* (*seemliness*) bienséance *f*, convenance *f*.

propulsion [prə'pʌlʃən] *n* propulsion *f*.

pro rata [prəu'rɑːtə] *adv* au prorata.

prosaic [prəu'zeɪɪk] *adj* prosaïque.

Pros. Atty. *abbr* (US) = **prosecuting attorney**.

proscribe [prə'skraɪb] *vt* proscrire.

prose [prəuz] *n* prose *f*; (SCOL: *translation*) thème *m*.

prosecute ['prɔsɪkju:t] *vt* poursuivre.

prosecuting attorney (Pros. Atty.) ['prɔsɪkju:tɪŋ-] *n* (US) procureur *m*.

prosecution [prɔsɪ'kju:ʃən] *n* poursuites *fpl* judiciaires; (*accusing side*) accusation *f*.

prosecutor ['prɔsɪkju:tə*] *n* procureur *m*; (*also*: **public ~**) ministère public.

prospect *n* ['prɔspɛkt] perspective *f*; (*hope*) espoir *m*, chances *fpl* ♦ *vt, vi* [prə'spɛkt] prospecter; **we are faced with the ~ of leaving** nous risquons de devoir partir; **there is every ~ of an early victory** tout laisse prévoir une victoire rapide.

prospecting [prə'spɛktɪŋ] *n* prospection *f*.

prospective [prə'spɛktɪv] *adj* (*possible*) éventuel(le); (*future*) futur(e).

prospector [prə'spɛktə*] *n* prospecteur *m*; **gold ~** chercheur *m* d'or.

prospects ['prɔspɛkts] *npl* (*for work etc*) possibilités *fpl* d'avenir, débouchés *mpl*.

prospectus [prə'spɛktəs] *n* prospectus *m*.

prosper ['prɔspə*] *vi* prospérer.

prosperity [prɔ'spɛrɪtɪ] *n* prospérité *f*.

prosperous ['prɔspərəs] *adj* prospère.

prostate ['prɔsteɪt] *n* (*also*: ~ **gland**) prostate *f*.

prostitute ['prɔstɪtju:t] *n* prostituée *f*; **male ~** prostitué *m*.

prostitution [prɔstɪ'tju:ʃən] *n* prostitution *f*.

prostrate *adj* ['prɒstreɪt] prosterné(e); (*fig*) prostré(e) ♦ *vt* [prɒ'streɪt]: **to ~ o.s. (before sb)** se prosterner (devant qn).

protagonist [prə'tægənɪst] *n* protagoniste *m.*

protect [prə'tɛkt] *vt* protéger.

protection [prə'tɛkʃən] *n* protection *f*; **to be under sb's ~** être sous la protection de qn.

protectionism [prə'tɛkʃənɪzəm] *n* protectionnisme *m.*

protection racket *n* racket *m.*

protective [prə'tɛktɪv] *adj* protecteur(trice); **~ custody** (*LAW*) détention préventive.

protector [prə'tɛktə*] *n* protecteur/trice.

protégé ['prəʊtɛʒeɪ] *n* protégé *m.*

protégée ['prəʊtɛʒeɪ] *n* protégée *f.*

protein ['prəʊtiːn] *n* protéine *f.*

pro tem [prəʊ'tɛm] *adv abbr* (= *pro tempore: for the time being*) provisoirement.

protest *n* ['prəʊtɛst] protestation *f* ♦ *vb* [prə'tɛst] *vi*: **to ~ against/about** protester contre/à propos de ♦ *vt* protester de.

Protestant ['prɒtɪstənt] *adj*, *n* protestant(e).

protester, protestor [prə'tɛstə*] *n* (*in demonstration*) manifestant/e.

protest march *n* manifestation *f.*

protocol ['prəʊtəkɒl] *n* protocole *m.*

prototype ['prəʊtətaɪp] *n* prototype *m.*

protracted [prə'træktɪd] *adj* prolongé(e).

protractor [prə'træktə*] *n* (*GEOM*) rapporteur *m.*

protrude [prə'truːd] *vi* avancer, dépasser.

protuberance [prə'tjuːbərəns] *n* protubérance *f.*

proud [praʊd] *adj* fier(ère); (*pej*) orgueilleux(euse); **to be ~ to do sth** être fier de faire qch; **to do sb ~** (*col*) faire honneur à qn; **to do o.s. ~** (*col*) ne se priver de rien.

proudly ['praʊdlɪ] *adv* fièrement.

prove [pruːv] *vt* prouver, démontrer ♦ *vi*: **to ~ correct** *etc* s'avérer juste *etc*; **to ~ o.s.** montrer ce dont on est capable; **to ~ o.s./itself (to be) useful** *etc* se montrer *or* se révéler utile *etc*; **he was ~d right in the end** il s'est avéré qu'il avait raison.

proverb ['prɒvəːb] *n* proverbe *m.*

proverbial [prə'vəːbɪəl] *adj* proverbial(e).

provide [prə'vaɪd] *vt* fournir; **to ~ sb with sth** fournir qch à qn; **to be ~d with** (*person*) disposer de; (*thing*) être équipé(e) *or* muni(e) de.

▶**provide for** *vt fus* (*person*) subvenir aux besoins de; (*emergency*) prévoir.

provided [prə'vaɪdɪd] *conj*: **~ (that)** à condition que + *sub*.

Providence ['prɒvɪdəns] *n* la Providence.

providing [prə'vaɪdɪŋ] *conj* à condition que + *sub*.

province ['prɒvɪns] *n* province *f.*

provincial [prə'vɪnʃəl] *adj* provincial(e).

provision [prə'vɪʒən] *n* (*supply*) provision *f*; (*supplying*) fourniture *f*; approvisionnement *m*; (*stipulation*) disposition *f*; **~s** *npl* (*food*)

provisions *fpl*; **to make ~ for** (*one's future*) assurer; (*one's family*) assurer l'avenir de; **there's no ~ for this in the contract** le contrat ne prévoit pas cela.

provisional [prə'vɪʒənl] *adj* provisoire ♦ *n*: **P~** (*Irish POL*) Provisional *m* (*membre de la tendance activiste de l'IRA*).

provisional licence *n* (*BRIT AUT*) permis *m* provisoire.

provisionally [prə'vɪʒnəlɪ] *adv* provisoirement.

proviso [prə'vaɪzəʊ] *n* condition *f*; **with the ~ that** à la condition (expresse) que.

Provo ['prɒvəʊ] *n abbr* (*col*) = **Provisional**.

provocation [prɒvə'keɪʃən] *n* provocation *f.*

provocative [prə'vɒkətɪv] *adj* provocateur(trice), provocant(e).

provoke [prə'vəʊk] *vt* provoquer; **to ~ sb sth/to do** *or* **into doing sth** pousser qn à qch/à faire qch.

provoking [prə'vəʊkɪŋ] *adj* énervant(e), exaspérant(e).

provost ['prɒvəst] *n* (*BRIT*: *of university*) principal *m*; (*Scottish*) maire *m.*

prow [praʊ] *n* proue *f.*

prowess ['praʊɪs] *n* prouesse *f.*

prowl [praʊl] *vi* (*also*: **~ about**, **~ around**) rôder ♦ *n*: **to be on the ~** rôder.

prowler ['praʊlə*] *n* rôdeur/euse.

proximity [prɒk'sɪmɪtɪ] *n* proximité *f.*

proxy ['prɒksɪ] *n* procuration *f*; **by ~** par procuration.

PRP *n abbr* (= *performance related pay*) salaire *m* au rendement.

prude [pruːd] *n* prude *f.*

prudence ['pruːdns] *n* prudence *f.*

prudent ['pruːdnt] *adj* prudent(e).

prudish ['pruːdɪʃ] *adj* prude, pudibond(e).

prune [pruːn] *n* pruneau *m* ♦ *vt* élaguer.

pry [praɪ] *vi*: **to ~ into** fourrer son nez dans.

PS *n abbr* (= *postscript*) PS *m.*

psalm [sɑːm] *n* psaume *m.*

PSAT *n abbr* (*US*) = *Preliminary Scholastic Aptitude Test.*

PSBR *n abbr* (*BRIT*: = *public sector borrowing requirement*) besoins *mpl* d'emprunts des pouvoirs publics.

pseud [sjuːd] *n* (*BRIT col*: *intellectually*) pseudo-intello *m*; (*: socially*) snob *m/f.*

pseudo- ['sjuːdəʊ] *prefix* pseudo-.

pseudonym ['sjuːdənɪm] *n* pseudonyme *m.*

PST *abbr* (*US*: = *Pacific Standard Time*) heure d'hiver du Pacifique.

PSV *n abbr* (*BRIT*) = **public service vehicle**.

psyche ['saɪkɪ] *n* psychisme *m.*

psychiatric [saɪkɪ'ætrɪk] *adj* psychiatrique.

psychiatrist [saɪ'kaɪətrɪst] *n* psychiatre *m/f.*

psychiatry [saɪ'kaɪətrɪ] *n* psychiatrie *f.*

psychic ['saɪkɪk] *adj* (*also*: **~al**) (méta)psychique; (*person*) doué(e) de télépathie *or* d'un sixième sens.

psycho ['saɪkəʊ] *n* (*col*) psychopathe *m/f.*

psychoanalyse [saɪkəu'ænəlaɪz] *vt* psychanalyser.

psychoanalysis, *pl* **-ses** [saɪkəuə'nælɪsɪs, -siːz] *n* psychanalyse *f*.

psychoanalyst [saɪkəu'ænəlɪst] *n* psychanalyste *m/f*.

psychological [saɪkə'lɔdʒɪkl] *adj* psychologique.

psychologist [saɪ'kɔlədʒɪst] *n* psychologue *m/f*.

psychology [saɪ'kɔlədʒɪ] *n* psychologie *f*.

psychopath ['saɪkəupæθ] *n* psychopathe *m/f*.

psychosis, *pl* **psychoses** [saɪ'kəusɪs, -siːz] *n* psychose *f*.

psychosomatic [saɪkəusə'mætɪk] *adj* psychosomatique.

psychotherapy [saɪkəu'θɛrəpɪ] *n* psychothérapie *f*.

psychotic [saɪ'kɔtɪk] *adj*, *n* psychotique (*m/f*).

PT *n abbr* (*BRIT*: = *physical training*) EPS *f*.

Pt. *abbr* (*in place names*: = *Point*) Pte.

pt *abbr* = **pint, point.**

PTA *n abbr* = *Parent-Teacher Association*.

Pte. *abbr* (*BRIT MIL*) = **private**.

PTO *abbr* (= *please turn over*) TSVP (= *tournez s'il vous plaît*).

PTV *n abbr* (*US*) = *pay television, public television*.

pub [pʌb] *n abbr* (= *public house*) pub *m*.

> *Un* **pub** *comprend en général deux salles: l'une ("the lounge") est plutôt confortable, avec des fauteuils et des bancs capitonnés, tandis que l'autre ("the public bar") est simplement un bar où les consommations sont en général moins chères. Cette dernière est souvent aussi une salle de jeux, les jeux les plus courants étant les fléchettes, les dominos et le billard. Il y a parfois aussi une petite arrière-salle douillette appelée "the snug". Beaucoup de pubs servent maintenant des repas, surtout à l'heure du déjeuner, et c'est alors le seul moment où les enfants sont acceptés, à condition d'être accompagnés. Les pubs sont en général ouverts de 11 h à 23 h, mais cela peut varier selon leur licence; certains pubs ferment l'après-midi.*

pub crawl *n* (*BRIT col*): **to go on a** ~ faire la tournée des bars.

puberty ['pjuːbətɪ] *n* puberté *f*.

pubic ['pjuːbɪk] *adj* pubien(ne), du pubis.

public ['pʌblɪk] *adj* public(ique) ♦ *n* public *m*; **in** ~ en public; **the general** ~ le grand public; **to be** ~ **knowledge** être de notoriété publique; **to go** ~ (*COMM*) être coté(e) en Bourse.

public address system (PA) *n* (système *m* de) sonorisation *f*, sono *f* (*col*).

publican ['pʌblɪkən] *n* patron *m* or gérant *m* de pub.

publication [pʌblɪ'keɪʃən] *n* publication *f*.

public company *n* société *f* anonyme (*cotée en Bourse*).

public convenience *n* (*BRIT*) toilettes *fpl*.

public holiday *n* (*BRIT*) jour férié.

public house *n* (*BRIT*) pub *m*.

publicity [pʌb'lɪsɪtɪ] *n* publicité *f*.

publicize ['pʌblɪsaɪz] *vt* faire connaître, rendre public.

public limited company (plc) *n* ≈ société *f* anonyme (SA) (*cotée en Bourse*).

publicly ['pʌblɪklɪ] *adv* publiquement, en public.

public opinion *n* opinion publique.

public ownership *n*: **to be taken into** ~ être nationalisé(e), devenir propriété de l'État.

public prosecutor *n* ≈ procureur *m* (*de la République*); ~**'s office** parquet *m*.

public relations (PR) *n or npl* relations publiques (RP).

public relations officer *n* responsable *m/f* des relations publiques.

public school *n* (*BRIT*) école privée; (*US*) école publique.

> *Une* **public school** *est un établissement d'enseignement secondaire privé. Bon nombre d'entre elles sont des pensionnats. Beaucoup ont également une école primaire qui leur est rattachée (une* **prep** *ou* **preparatory school***) pour préparer les élèves au cycle secondaire. Ces écoles sont en général prestigieuses, et les frais de scolarité sont très élevés dans les plus connues (Westminster, Eton, Harrow). Beaucoup d'élèves vont ensuite à l'université, et un grand nombre entre à Oxford ou à Cambridge. Les grands industriels, les députés et les hauts fonctionnaires sortent souvent de ces écoles.*
> *En Écosse et aux États-Unis, le terme "public school" désigne tout simplement une école publique gratuite.*

public sector *n* secteur public.

public service vehicle (PSV) *n* (*BRIT*) véhicule affecté au transport de personnes.

public-spirited [pʌblɪk'spɪrɪtɪd] *adj* qui fait preuve de civisme.

public transport, (*US*) **public transportation** *n* transports *mpl* en commun.

public utility *n* service public.

public works *npl* travaux publics.

publish ['pʌblɪʃ] *vt* publier.

publisher ['pʌblɪʃə*] *n* éditeur *m*.

publishing ['pʌblɪʃɪŋ] *n* (*industry*) édition *f*; (*of a book*) publication *f*.

publishing company *n* maison *f* d'édition.

puce [pjuːs] *adj* puce.

puck [pʌk] *n* (*elf*) lutin *m*; (*ICE HOCKEY*) palet *m*.

pucker ['pʌkə*] *vt* plisser.

pudding ['pudɪŋ] *n* (*BRIT: sweet*) dessert *m*, entremets *m*; (*sausage*) boudin *m*; **rice** ~ ≈ riz *m* au lait; **black** ~, (*US*) **blood** ~ boudin (noir).

puddle ['pʌdl] *n* flaque *f* d'eau.
puerile ['pjuəraɪl] *adj* puéril(e).
Puerto Rico ['pwɜːtəu'riːkəu] *n* Porto Rico *f*.
puff [pʌf] *n* bouffée *f* ♦ *vt*: **to ~ one's pipe** tirer sur sa pipe; (*also*: ~ **out**: *sails, cheeks*) gonfler ♦ *vi* sortir par bouffées; (*pant*) haleter; **to ~ out smoke** envoyer des bouffées de fumée.
puffed [pʌft] *adj* (*col*: *out of breath*) tout(e) essouflé(e).
puffin ['pʌfɪn] *n* macareux *m*.
puff pastry, (*US*) **puff paste** *n* pâte feuilletée.
puffy ['pʌfɪ] *adj* bouffi(e), boursouflé(e).
pugnacious [pʌg'neɪʃəs] *adj* pugnace, batailleur(euse).
pull [pul] *n* (*of moon, magnet, the sea etc*) attraction *f*; (*fig*) influence *f* ♦ *vt* tirer; (*strain: muscle, tendon*) se claquer ♦ *vi* tirer; **to give sth a ~** (*tug*) tirer sur qch; **to ~ a face** faire une grimace; **to ~ to pieces** mettre en morceaux; **to ~ one's punches** (*also fig*) ménager son adversaire; **to ~ one's weight** y mettre du sien; **to ~ o.s. together** se ressaisir; **to ~ sb's leg** (*fig*) faire marcher qn; **to ~ strings (for sb)** intervenir (en faveur de qn).
▶**pull about** *vt* (*BRIT: handle roughly: object*) maltraiter; (*: person*) malmener.
▶**pull apart** *vt* séparer; (*break*) mettre en pièces, démantibuler.
▶**pull down** *vt* baisser, abaisser; (*house*) démolir; (*tree*) abattre.
▶**pull in** *vi* (*AUT*) se ranger; (*RAIL*) entrer en gare.
▶**pull off** *vt* enlever, ôter; (*deal etc*) conclure.
▶**pull out** *vi* démarrer, partir; (*withdraw*) se retirer; (*AUT: come out of line*) déboîter ♦ *vt* sortir; arracher; (*withdraw*) retirer.
▶**pull over** *vi* (*AUT*) se ranger.
▶**pull round** *vi* (*unconscious person*) revenir à soi; (*sick person*) se rétablir.
▶**pull through** *vi* s'en sortir.
▶**pull up** *vi* (*stop*) s'arrêter ♦ *vt* remonter; (*uproot*) déraciner, arracher; (*stop*) arrêter.
pulley ['pulɪ] *n* poulie *f*.
pull-out ['pulaut] *n* (*of forces etc*) retrait *m* ♦ *cpd* (*magazine, pages*) détachable.
pullover ['puləuvə*] *n* pull-over *m*, tricot *m*.
pulp [pʌlp] *n* (*of fruit*) pulpe *f*; (*for paper*) pâte *f* à papier; (*pej: also*: ~ **magazines** *etc*) presse *f* à sensation *or* de bas étage; **to reduce sth to (a) ~** réduire qch en purée.
pulpit ['pulpɪt] *n* chaire *f*.
pulsate [pʌl'seɪt] *vi* battre, palpiter; (*music*) vibrer.
pulse [pʌls] *n* (*of blood*) pouls *m*; (*of heart*) battement *m*; (*of music, engine*) vibrations *fpl*; **to feel** *or* **take sb's ~** prendre le pouls à qn.
pulses ['pʌlsəz] *npl* (*CULIN*) légumineuses *fpl*.
pulverize ['pʌlvəraɪz] *vt* pulvériser.
puma ['pjuːmə] *n* puma *m*.
pumice ['pʌmɪs] *n* (*also*: ~ **stone**) pierre *f*

ponce.
pummel ['pʌml] *vt* rouer de coups.
pump [pʌmp] *n* pompe *f*; (*shoe*) escarpin *m* ♦ *vt* pomper; (*fig: col*) faire parler; **to ~ sb for information** essayer de soutirer des renseignements à qn.
▶**pump up** *vt* gonfler.
pumpkin ['pʌmpkɪn] *n* potiron *m*, citrouille *f*.
pun [pʌn] *n* jeu *m* de mots, calembour *m*.
punch [pʌntʃ] *n* (*blow*) coup *m* de poing; (*fig: force*) vivacité *f*, mordant *m*; (*tool*) poinçon *m*; (*drink*) punch *m* ♦ *vt* (*make a hole*) poinçonner, perforer; (*hit*): **to ~ sb/sth** donner un coup de poing à qn/sur qch; **to ~ a hole (in)** faire un trou (dans).
▶**punch in** *vi* (*US*) pointer (en arrivant).
▶**punch out** *vi* (*US*) pointer (en partant).
punch-drunk ['pʌntʃdrʌŋk] *adj* (*BRIT*) sonné(e).
punch(ed) card [pʌntʃ(t)-] *n* carte perforée.
punch line *n* (*of joke*) conclusion *f*.
punch-up ['pʌntʃʌp] *n* (*BRIT col*) bagarre *f*.
punctual ['pʌŋktjuəl] *adj* ponctuel(le).
punctuality [pʌŋktju'ælɪtɪ] *n* ponctualité *f*.
punctually ['pʌŋktjuəlɪ] *adv* ponctuellement; **it will start ~ at 6** cela commencera à 6 heures précises.
punctuate ['pʌŋktjueɪt] *vt* ponctuer.
punctuation [pʌŋktju'eɪʃən] *n* ponctuation *f*.
punctuation mark *n* signe *m* de ponctuation.
puncture ['pʌŋktʃə*] *n* (*BRIT*) crevaison *f* ♦ *vt* crever; **I have a ~** (*AUT*) j'ai (un pneu) crevé.
pundit ['pʌndɪt] *n* individu *m* qui pontifie, pontife *m*.
pungent ['pʌndʒənt] *adj* piquant(e); (*fig*) mordant(e), caustique.
punish ['pʌnɪʃ] *vt* punir; **to ~ sb for sth/for doing sth** punir qn de qch/d'avoir fait qch.
punishable ['pʌnɪʃəbl] *adj* punissable.
punishing ['pʌnɪʃɪŋ] *adj* (*fig: exhausting*) épuisant(e) ♦ *n* punition *f*.
punishment ['pʌnɪʃmənt] *n* punition *f*, châtiment *m*; (*fig: col*): **to take a lot of ~** (*boxer*) encaisser; (*car, person etc*) être mis(e) à dure épreuve.
punk [pʌŋk] *n* (*person: also*: ~ **rocker**) punk *m/f*; (*music: also*: ~ **rock**) le punk; (*US col: hoodlum*) voyou *m*.
punt [pʌnt] *n* (*boat*) bachot *m*; (*IRELAND*) livre irlandaise ♦ *vi* (*BRIT: bet*) parier.
punter ['pʌntə*] *n* (*BRIT: gambler*) parieur/euse; (*: col*) Monsieur *m* tout le monde; type *m*.
puny ['pjuːnɪ] *adj* chétif(ive).
pup [pʌp] *n* chiot *m*.
pupil ['pjuːpl] *n* élève *m/f*; (*of eye*) pupille *f*.
puppet ['pʌpɪt] *n* marionnette *f*, pantin *m*.
puppet government *n* gouvernement *m* fantoche.
puppy ['pʌpɪ] *n* chiot *m*, petit chien.
purchase ['pɜːtʃɪs] *n* achat *m*; (*grip*) prise *f* ♦ *vt*

acheter; **to get a ~ on** trouver appui sur.
purchase order n ordre m d'achat.
purchase price n prix m d'achat.
purchaser ['pɔːtʃɪsə*] n acheteur/euse.
purchase tax n (BRIT) taxe f à l'achat.
purchasing power ['pɔːtʃɪsɪŋ-] n pouvoir m d'achat.
pure [pjuə*] adj pur(e); **a ~ wool jumper** un pull en pure laine; **~ and simple** pur(e) et simple.
purebred ['pjuəbrɛd] adj de race.
purée ['pjuəreɪ] n purée f.
purely ['pjuəlɪ] adv purement.
purge [pɔːdʒ] n (MED) purge f; (POL) épuration f, purge ♦ vt purger; (fig) épurer, purger.
purification [pjuərɪfɪ'keɪʃən] n purification f.
purify ['pjuərɪfaɪ] vt purifier, épurer.
purist ['pjuərɪst] n puriste m/f.
puritan ['pjuərɪtən] n puritain/e.
puritanical [pjuərɪ'tænɪkl] adj puritain(e).
purity ['pjuərɪtɪ] n pureté f.
purl [pɔːl] n maille f à l'envers ♦ vt tricoter à l'envers.
purloin [pɔː'lɔɪn] vt dérober.
purple ['pɔːpl] adj violet(te); cramoisi(e).
purport [pɔː'pɔːt] vi: **to ~ to be/do** prétendre être/faire.
purpose ['pɔːpəs] n intention f, but m; **on ~** exprès; **for illustrative ~s** à titre d'illustration; **for teaching ~s** dans un but pédagogique; **for the ~s of this meeting** pour cette réunion; **to no ~** en pure perte.
purpose-built ['pɔːpəs'bɪlt] adj (BRIT) fait(e) sur mesure.
purposeful ['pɔːpəsful] adj déterminé(e), résolu(e).
purposely ['pɔːpəslɪ] adv exprès.
purr [pɔː*] n ronronnement m ♦ vi ronronner.
purse [pɔːs] n porte-monnaie m inv, bourse f; (US: handbag) sac m (à main) ♦ vt serrer, pincer.
purser ['pɔːsə*] n (NAUT) commissaire m du bord.
purse snatcher [-'snætʃə*] n (US) voleur m à l'arraché.
pursue [pə'sjuː] vt poursuivre; (pleasures) rechercher; (inquiry, matter) approfondir.
pursuer [pə'sjuːə*] n poursuivant/e.
pursuit [pə'sjuːt] n poursuite f; (occupation) occupation f, activité f; **scientific ~s** recherches fpl scientifiques; **in (the) ~ of sth** à la recherche de qch.
purveyor [pə'veɪə*] n fournisseur m.
pus [pʌs] n pus m.
push [puʃ] n poussée f; (effort) gros effort; (drive) énergie f ♦ vt pousser; (button) appuyer sur; (thrust): **to ~ sth (into)** enfoncer qch (dans); (fig) mettre en avant, faire de la publicité pour ♦ vi pousser; appuyer; **to ~ a door open/shut** pousser une porte (pour l'ouvrir/pour la fermer); "**~**" (on door) "pousser"; (on bell) "appuyer"; **to ~ for** (bet-

ter pay, conditions) réclamer; **to be ~ed for time/money** être à court de temps/d'argent; **she is ~ing fifty** (col) elle frise la cinquantaine; **at a ~** (BRIT col) à la limite, à la rigueur.
►**push aside** vt écarter.
►**push in** vi s'introduire de force.
►**push off** vi (col) filer, ficher le camp.
►**push on** vi (continue) continuer.
►**push over** vt renverser.
►**push through** vt (measure) faire voter.
►**push up** vt (total, prices) faire monter.
push-bike ['puʃbaɪk] n (BRIT) vélo m.
push-button ['puʃbʌtn] n bouton(-poussoir m) m.
pushchair ['puʃtʃɛə*] n (BRIT) poussette f.
pusher ['puʃə*] n (also: drug ~) revendeur/euse (de drogue), ravitailleur/euse (en drogue).
pushover ['puʃəuvə*] n (col): **it's a ~** c'est un jeu d'enfant.
push-up ['puʃʌp] n (US) traction f.
pushy ['puʃɪ] adj (pej) arriviste.
puss, pussy(-cat) [pus, pusɪ(kæt)] n minet m.
put, pt, pp **put** [put] vt mettre; (place) poser, placer; (say) dire, exprimer; (a question) poser; (estimate) estimer; **to ~ sb in a good/bad mood** mettre qn de bonne/mauvaise humeur; **to ~ sb to bed** mettre qn au lit, coucher qn; **to ~ sb to a lot of trouble** déranger qn; **how shall I ~ it?** comment dirais-je?, comment dire?; **to ~ a lot of time into sth** passer beaucoup de temps à qch; **to ~ money on a horse** miser sur un cheval; **I ~ it to you that ...** (BRIT) je (vous) suggère que ..., je suis d'avis que ...; **to stay ~** ne pas bouger.
►**put about** vi (NAUT) virer de bord ♦ vt (rumour) faire courir.
►**put across** vt (ideas etc) communiquer; faire comprendre.
►**put aside** vt mettre de côté.
►**put away** vt (store) ranger.
►**put back** vt (replace) remettre, replacer; (postpone) remettre; (delay, also: watch, clock) retarder; **this will ~ us back ten years** cela nous ramènera dix ans en arrière.
►**put by** vt (money) mettre de côté, économiser.
►**put down** vt (parcel etc) poser, déposer; (pay) verser; (in writing) mettre par écrit, inscrire; (suppress: revolt etc) réprimer, écraser; (attribute) attribuer.
►**put forward** vt (ideas) avancer, proposer; (date, watch, clock) avancer.
►**put in** vt (gas, electricity) installer; (application, complaint) faire.
►**put in for** vt fus (job) poser sa candidature pour; (promotion) solliciter.
►**put off** vt (light etc) éteindre; (postpone) remettre à plus tard, ajourner; (discourage) dissuader.

▶**put on** *vt* (*clothes, lipstick etc*) mettre; (*light etc*) allumer; (*play etc*) monter; (*extra bus, train etc*) mettre en service; (*food, meal*) servir; (*weight*) prendre; (*assume: accent, manner*) prendre; (*: airs*) se donner, prendre; (*brake*) mettre; (*col: tease*) faire marcher; (*inform, indicate*): **to ~ sb on to sb/sth** indiquer qn/qch à qn.

▶**put out** *vt* mettre dehors; (*one's hand*) tendre; (*news, rumour*) faire courir, répandre; (*light etc*) éteindre; (*person: inconvenience*) déranger, gêner; (*BRIT: dislocate*) se démettre ♦ *vi* (*NAUT*): **to ~ out to sea** prendre le large; **to ~ out from Plymouth** quitter Plymouth.

▶**put through** *vt* (*caller*) mettre en communication; (*call*) passer; **~ me through to Miss Blair** passez-moi Miss Blair.

▶**put together** *vt* mettre ensemble; (*assemble: furniture, toy etc*) monter, assembler; (*meal*) préparer.

▶**put up** *vt* (*raise*) lever, relever, remonter; (*pin up*) afficher; (*hang*) accrocher; (*build*) construire, ériger; (*a tent*) monter; (*increase*) augmenter; (*accommodate*) loger; (*incite*): **to ~ sb up to doing sth** pousser qn à faire qch; **to ~ sth up for sale** mettre qch en vente.

▶**put upon** *vt fus*: **to be ~ upon** (*imposed on*) se laisser faire.

▶**put up with** *vt fus* supporter.

putrid ['pjuːtrɪd] *adj* putride.

putt [pʌt] *vt, vi* putter ♦ *n* putt *m*.

putter ['pʌtə*] *n* (*GOLF*) putter *m*.

putting green ['pʌtɪŋ-] *n* green *m*.

putty ['pʌtɪ] *n* mastic *m*.

put-up ['putʌp] *adj*: **~ job** coup monté.

puzzle ['pʌzl] *n* énigme *f*, mystère *m*; (*jigsaw*) puzzle *m*; (*also: crossword ~*) problème *m* de mots croisés ♦ *vt* intriguer, rendre perplexe ♦ *vi* se creuser la tête; **to ~ over** chercher à comprendre; **to be ~d about sth** être perplexe au sujet de qch.

puzzling ['pʌzlɪŋ] *adj* déconcertant(e), inexplicable.

PVC *n abbr* (= *polyvinyl chloride*) PVC *m*.

Pvt. *abbr* (*US MIL*) = **private**.

pw *abbr* (= *per week*) p.sem.

PX *n abbr* (*US MIL*) = **post exchange**.

pygmy ['pɪgmɪ] *n* pygmée *m/f*.

pyjamas [pɪ'dʒɑːməz] *npl* (*BRIT*) pyjama *m*; **a pair of ~** un pyjama.

pylon ['paɪlən] *n* pylône *m*.

pyramid ['pɪrəmɪd] *n* pyramide *f*.

Pyrenean [pɪrə'niːən] *adj* pyrénéen(ne), des Pyrénées.

Pyrenees [pɪrə'niːz] *npl*: **the ~** les Pyrénées *fpl*.

Pyrex ['paɪrɛks] *n* ® Pyrex *m* ® ♦ *cpd*: **~ dish** plat *m* en Pyrex.

python ['paɪθən] *n* python *m*.

Q q

Q, q [kjuː] *n* (*letter*) Q, q *m*; **Q for Queen** Q comme Quintal.

Qatar [kæ'tɑː*] *n* Qatar *m*, Katar *m*.

> En Angleterre, un **QC** *ou* **Queen's Counsel** (*ou* **KC** *pour* **King's Counsel**, *sous le règne d'un roi*) *est un avocat qui reçoit un poste de haut fonctionnaire sur recommandation du Lord Chancellor. Il fait alors souvent suivre son nom des lettres QC, et lorsqu'il a au tribunal, il est toujours accompagné par un autre avocat (un "junior barrister").*

QED *abbr* (= *quod erat demonstrandum*) CQFD.

QM *n abbr* = **quartermaster**.

q.t. *n abbr* (*col: = quiet*): **on the ~** discrètement.

qty *abbr* (= *quantity*) qté.

quack [kwæk] *n* (*of duck*) coin-coin *m inv*; (*pej: doctor*) charlatan *m* ♦ *vi* faire coin-coin.

quad [kwɔd] *n abbr* = **quadruple, quadruplet, quadrangle**.

quadrangle ['kwɔdræŋgl] *n* (*MATH*) quadrilatère *m*; (*courtyard: abbr:* **quad**) cour *f*.

quadruped ['kwɔdrupɛd] *n* quadrupède *m*.

quadruple [kwɔ'druːpl] *adj, n* quadruple (*m*) ♦ *vt, vi* quadrupler.

quadruplet [kwɔ'druːplɪt] *n* un/une des quadruplé(e)s.

quagmire ['kwægmaɪə*] *n* bourbier *m*.

quail [kweɪl] *n* (*ZOOL*) caille *f* ♦ *vi*: **to ~ at** *or* **before** se décourager devant.

quaint [kweɪnt] *adj* bizarre; (*old-fashioned*) désuet(ète); au charme vieillot, pittoresque.

quake [kweɪk] *vi* trembler ♦ *n abbr* = **earthquake**.

Quaker ['kweɪkə*] *n* quaker/esse.

qualification [kwɔlɪfɪ'keɪʃən] *n* (*degree etc*) diplôme *m*; (*ability*) compétence *f*, qualification *f*; (*limitation*) réserve *f*, restriction *f*; **what are your ~s?** qu'avez-vous comme diplômes?; quelles sont vos qualifications?

qualified ['kwɔlɪfaɪd] *adj* diplômé(e); (*able*) compétent(e), qualifié(e); (*limited*) conditionnel(le); **it was a ~ success** ce fut un succès mitigé; **~ for/to do** qui a les diplômes requis pour/pour faire; qualifié pour/pour faire.

qualify ['kwɔlɪfaɪ] *vt* qualifier; (*limit: statement*) apporter des réserves à ♦ *vi*: **to ~ (as)** obtenir son diplôme (de); **to ~ (for)** remplir les conditions requises (pour); (*SPORT*) se qualifier (pour).

qualifying ['kwɔlɪfaɪɪŋ] adj: ~ **exam** examen m d'entrée; ~ **round** éliminatoires fpl.
qualitative ['kwɔlɪtətɪv] adj qualitatif(ive).
quality ['kwɔlɪtɪ] n qualité f ♦ cpd de qualité; **of good/poor** ~ de bonne/mauvaise qualité.
quality control n contrôle m de qualité.
quality of life n qualité f de la vie.
quality papers npl (BRIT): **the** ~ la presse d'information.

> Les **quality (news)papers** (ou la **quality press**) englobent les journaux sérieux, quotidiens ou hebdomadaires, par opposition aux journaux populaires (**tabloid press**). Ces journaux visent un public qui souhaite des informations détaillées sur un éventail très vaste de sujets et qui est prêt à consacrer beaucoup de temps à leur lecture. Les quality newspapers sont en général de grand format.

qualm [kwɑ:m] n doute m; scrupule m; **to have** ~**s about sth** avoir des doutes sur qch; éprouver des scrupules à propos de qch.
quandary ['kwɔndrɪ] n: **in a** ~ devant un dilemme, dans l'embarras.
quango ['kwæŋgəu] n abbr (BRIT: = quasi-autonomous non-governmental organization) commission nommée par le gouvernement.
quantifiable [kwɔntɪ'faɪəbl] adj quantifiable.
quantitative ['kwɔntɪtətɪv] adj quantitatif(ive).
quantity ['kwɔntɪtɪ] n quantité f; **in** ~ en grande quantité.
quantity surveyor n (BRIT) métreur vérificateur.
quantum leap ['kwɔntəm-] n (fig) bond m en avant.
quarantine ['kwɔrntiːn] n quarantaine f.
quark [kwɑ:k] n quark m.
quarrel ['kwɔrl] n querelle f, dispute f ♦ vi se disputer, se quereller; **to have a** ~ **with sb** se quereller avec qn; **I've no** ~ **with him** je n'ai rien contre lui; **I can't** ~ **with that** je ne vois rien à redire à cela.
quarrelsome ['kwɔrəlsəm] adj querelleur(euse).
quarry ['kwɔrɪ] n (for stone) carrière f; (animal) proie f, gibier m ♦ vt (marble etc) extraire.
quart [kwɔ:t] n ≈ litre m.
quarter ['kwɔ:tə*] n quart m; (of year) trimestre m; (district) quartier m; (US, Canada: 25 cents) (pièce f de) vingt-cinq cents mpl ♦ vt partager en quartiers or en quatre; (MIL) caserner, cantonner; ~**s** npl logement m; (MIL) quartiers mpl, cantonnement m; **a** ~ **of an hour** un quart d'heure; **it's a** ~ **to 3**, (US) **it's a** ~ **of 3** il est 3 heures moins le quart; **it's a** ~ **past 3**, (US) **it's a** ~ **after 3** il est 3 heures et quart; **from all** ~**s** de tous côtés; **at close** ~**s** tout près.
quarterback ['kwɔ:təbæk] n (US FOOTBALL) quarterback m/f.

quarter-deck ['kwɔ:tədɛk] n (NAUT) plage f arrière.
quarter final n quart m de finale.
quarterly ['kwɔ:təlɪ] adj trimestriel(le) ♦ adv tous les trois mois ♦ n (PRESS) revue trimestrielle.
quartermaster ['kwɔ:təmɑ:stə*] n (MIL) intendant m militaire de troisième classe; (NAUT) maître m de manœuvre.
quartet(te) [kwɔ:'tɛt] n quatuor m; (jazz players) quartette m.
quarto ['kwɔ:təu] adj, n in-quarto (m) inv.
quartz [kwɔ:ts] n quartz m ♦ cpd de or en quartz; (watch, clock) à quartz.
quash [kwɔʃ] vt (verdict) annuler, casser.
quasi- ['kweɪzaɪ] prefix quasi- + noun; quasi, presque + adjective.
quaver ['kweɪvə*] n (BRIT MUS) croche f ♦ vi trembler.
quay [ki:] n (also: ~**side**) quai m.
Que. abbr (Canada) = Quebec.
queasy ['kwi:zɪ] adj (stomach) délicat(e); **to feel** ~ avoir mal au cœur.
Quebec [kwɪ'bɛk] n Québec m.
queen [kwi:n] n (gen) reine f; (CARDS etc) dame f.
queen mother n reine mère f.

> Le **Queen's speech** (ou **King's speech**) est le discours lu par le souverain à l'ouverture du **Parliament**, dans la **House of Lords**, en présence des lords et des députés. Il contient le programme de politique générale que propose le gouvernement pour la session, et il est préparé par le Premier ministre en consultation avec le cabinet.

queer [kwɪə*] adj étrange, curieux(euse); (suspicious) louche; (BRIT: sick): **I feel** ~ je ne me sens pas bien ♦ n (col) homosexuel m.
quell [kwɛl] vt réprimer, étouffer.
quench [kwɛntʃ] vt (flames) éteindre; **to** ~ **one's thirst** se désaltérer.
querulous ['kwɛruləs] adj (person) récriminateur(trice); (voice) plaintif(ive).
query ['kwɪərɪ] n question f; (doubt) doute m; (question mark) point m d'interrogation ♦ vt (disagree with, dispute) mettre en doute, questionner.
quest [kwɛst] n recherche f, quête f.
question ['kwɛstʃən] n question f ♦ vt (person) interroger; (plan, idea) mettre en question or en doute; **to ask sb a** ~, **to put a** ~ **to sb** poser une question à qn; **to bring** or **call sth into** ~ remettre qch en question; **the** ~ **is** ... la question est de savoir ...; **it's a** ~ **of doing** il s'agit de faire; **there's some** ~ **of doing** il est question de faire; **beyond** ~ sans aucun doute; **out of the** ~ hors de question.
questionable ['kwɛstʃənəbl] adj discutable.
questioner ['kwɛstʃənə*] n personne f qui pose une question (or qui a posé la question

etc).

questioning ['kwɛstʃənɪŋ] *adj* interrogateur(trice) ♦ *n* interrogatoire *m*.

question mark *n* point *m* d'interrogation.

questionnaire [kwɛstʃə'nɛə*] *n* questionnaire *m*.

queue [kjuː] (*BRIT*) *n* queue *f*, file *f* ♦ *vi* faire la queue; **to jump the** ~ passer avant son tour.

quibble ['kwɪbl] *vi* ergoter, chicaner.

quick [kwɪk] *adj* rapide; (*reply*) prompt(e), rapide; (*mind*) vif(vive) ♦ *n*: **cut to the** ~ (*fig*) touché(e) au vif; **be** ~!; dépêche-toi!; **to be** ~ **to act** agir tout de suite.

quicken ['kwɪkən] *vt* accélérer, presser; (*rouse*) stimuler ♦ *vi* s'accélérer, devenir plus rapide.

quick fix *n* solution *f* de fortune.

quicklime ['kwɪklaɪm] *n* chaux vive.

quickly ['kwɪklɪ] *adv* (*fast*) vite, rapidement; (*immediately*) tout de suite.

quickness ['kwɪknɪs] *n* rapidité *f*, promptitude *f*; (*of mind*) vivacité *f*.

quicksand ['kwɪksænd] *n* sables mouvants.

quickstep ['kwɪkstɛp] *n* fox-trot *m*.

quick-tempered [kwɪk'tɛmpəd] *adj* emporté(e).

quick-witted [kwɪk'wɪtɪd] *adj* à l'esprit vif.

quid [kwɪd] *n* (*pl inv*: *BRIT col*) livre *f*.

quid pro quo ['kwɪdprəu'kwəu] *n* contrepartie *f*.

quiet ['kwaɪət] *adj* tranquille, calme; (*not noisy: engine*) silencieux(euse); (*reserved*) réservé(e); (*not busy: day, business*) calme; (*ceremony, colour*) discret(ète) ♦ *n* tranquillité *f*, calme *m* ♦ *vt, vi* (*US*) = **quieten**; **keep** ~!; tais-toi!; **on the** ~ en secret, discrètement; **I'll have a** ~ **word with him** je lui en parlerai discrètement.

quieten ['kwaɪətn] (*also*: ~ **down**) *vi* se calmer, s'apaiser ♦ *vt* calmer, apaiser.

quietly ['kwaɪətlɪ] *adv* tranquillement, calmement; discrètement.

quietness ['kwaɪətnɪs] *n* tranquillité *f*, calme *m*; silence *m*.

quill [kwɪl] *n* plume *f* (d'oie).

quilt [kwɪlt] *n* édredon *m*; (*continental* ~) couette *f*.

quin [kwɪn] *n abbr* = **quintuplet**.

quince [kwɪns] *n* coing *m*; (*tree*) cognassier *m*.

quinine [kwɪ'niːn] *n* quinine *f*.

quintet(te) [kwɪn'tɛt] *n* quintette *m*.

quintuplet [kwɪn'tjuːplɪt] *n* quintuplé/e.

quip [kwɪp] *n* remarque piquante *or* spirituelle, pointe *f* ♦ *vt*: ... **he** ~**ped** ... lança-t-il.

quire ['kwaɪə*] *n* ≈ main *f* (de papier).

quirk [kwəːk] *n* bizarrerie *f*; **by some** ~ **of fate** par un caprice du hasard.

quit [kwɪt], *pt, pp* **quit** *or* **quitted** [kwɪt] *vt* quitter ♦ *vi* (*give up*) abandonner, renoncer; (*resign*) démissionner; **to** ~ **doing** arrêter de faire; ~ **stalling!** (*US col*) arrête de te dérober!;

notice to ~ (*BRIT*) congé *m* (*signifié au locataire*).

quite [kwaɪt] *adv* (*rather*) assez, plutôt; (*entirely*) complètement, tout à fait; ~ **new** plutôt neuf; tout à fait neuf; **she's** ~ **pretty** elle est plutôt jolie; **I** ~ **understand** je comprends très bien; ~ **a few of them** un assez grand nombre d'entre eux; **that's not** ~ **right** ce n'est pas tout à fait juste; **not** ~ **as many as last time** pas tout à fait autant que la dernière fois; ~ (**so**)! exactement!

Quito ['kiːtəu] *n* Quito.

quits [kwɪts] *adj*: ~ (**with**) quitte (envers); **let's call it** ~ restons-en là.

quiver ['kwɪvə*] *vi* trembler, frémir ♦ *n* (*for arrows*) carquois *m*.

quiz [kwɪz] *n* (*on TV*) jeu-concours *m* (télévisé); (*in magazine etc*) test *m* de connaissances ♦ *vt* interroger.

quizzical ['kwɪzɪkl] *adj* narquois(e).

quoits [kwɔɪts] *npl* jeu *m* du palet.

quorum ['kwɔːrəm] *n* quorum *m*.

quota ['kwəutə] *n* quota *m*.

quotation [kwəu'teɪʃən] *n* citation *f*; (*of shares etc*) cote *f*, cours *m*; (*estimate*) devis *m*.

quotation marks *npl* guillemets *mpl*.

quote [kwəut] *n* citation *f* ♦ *vt* (*sentence, author*) citer; (*price*) donner, soumettre; (*shares*) coter ♦ *vi*: **to** ~ **from** citer; **to** ~ **for a job** établir un devis pour des travaux; ~**s** *npl* (*col*) = **quotation marks**; **in** ~**s** entre guillemets; ~ ... **unquote** (*in dictation*) ouvrez les guillemets ... fermez les guillemets.

quotient ['kwəuʃənt] *n* quotient *m*.

qv *abbr* (= *quod vide: which see*) voir.

qwerty keyboard ['kwəːtɪ-] *n* clavier *m* QWERTY.

R r

R, r [ɑː*] *n* (*letter*) R, r *m*; **R for Robert**, (*US*) **R for Roger** R comme Raoul.

R *abbr* (= *right*) dr; (= *river*) riv., fl.; (= *Réaumur (scale)*) R; (*US CINE*: = *restricted*) *interdit aux moins de 17 ans*; (*US POL*) = **republican**; (*BRIT*) = *Rex, Regina*.

RA *abbr* = **rear admiral** ♦ *n abbr* (*BRIT*) = **Royal Academy**, *Royal Academician*.

RAAF *n abbr* = *Royal Australian Air Force*.

Rabat [rə'bɑːt] *n* Rabat.

rabbi ['ræbaɪ] *n* rabbin *m*.

rabbit ['ræbɪt] *n* lapin *m* ♦ *vi*: **to** ~ (**on**) (*BRIT*) parler à n'en plus finir.

rabbit hole *n* terrier *m* (de lapin).

rabbit hutch *n* clapier *m*.

rabble ['ræbl] n (pej) populace f.
rabid ['ræbɪd] adj enragé(e).
rabies ['reɪbiːz] n rage f.
RAC n abbr (BRIT: = Royal Automobile Club) ≈ ACF m.
raccoon [rə'kuːn] n raton m laveur.
race [reɪs] n race f; (competition, rush) course f ♦ vt (person) faire la course avec; (horse) faire courir; (engine) emballer ♦ vi courir; (engine) s'emballer; **the human ~** la race humaine; **to ~ in/out** etc entrer/sortir etc à toute vitesse.
race car n (US) = **racing car**.
race car driver n (US) = **racing driver**.
racecourse ['reɪskɔːs] n champ m de courses.
racehorse ['reɪshɔːs] n cheval m de course.
race relations npl rapports mpl entre les races.
racetrack ['reɪstræk] n piste f.
racial ['reɪʃl] adj racial(e).
racialism ['reɪʃlɪzəm] n racisme m.
racialist ['reɪʃlɪst] adj, n raciste (m/f).
racing ['reɪsɪŋ] n courses fpl.
racing car n (BRIT) voiture f de course.
racing driver n (BRIT) pilote m de course.
racism ['reɪsɪzəm] n racisme m.
racist ['reɪsɪst] adj, n (pej) raciste (m/f).
rack [ræk] n (also: **luggage ~**) filet m à bagages; (also: **roof ~**) galerie f ♦ vt tourmenter; **magazine ~** porte-revues m inv; **shoe ~** étagère f à chaussures; **toast ~** porte-toast m; **to ~ one's brains** se creuser la cervelle; **to go to ~ and ruin** (building) tomber en ruine; (business) péricliter.
▶**rack up** vt accumuler.
racket ['rækɪt] n (for tennis) raquette f; (noise) tapage m, vacarme m; (swindle) escroquerie f; (organized crime) racket m.
racketeer [rækɪ'tɪə*] n (esp US) racketteur m.
racoon [rə'kuːn] n = **raccoon**.
racquet ['rækɪt] n raquette f.
racy ['reɪsɪ] adj plein(e) de verve; osé(e).
RADA [rɑːdə] n abbr (BRIT) = Royal Academy of Dramatic Art.
radar ['reɪdɑː*] n radar m ♦ cpd radar inv.
radar trap n contrôle m radar.
radial ['reɪdɪəl] adj (also: **~-ply**) à carcasse radiale.
radiance ['reɪdɪəns] n éclat m, rayonnement m.
radiant ['reɪdɪənt] adj rayonnant(e); (PHYSICS) radiant(e).
radiate ['reɪdɪeɪt] vt (heat) émettre, dégager ♦ vi (lines) rayonner.
radiation [reɪdɪ'eɪʃən] n rayonnement m; (radioactive) radiation f.
radiation sickness n mal m des rayons.
radiator ['reɪdɪeɪtə*] n radiateur m.
radiator cap n bouchon m de radiateur.
radiator grill n (AUT) calandre f.
radical ['rædɪkl] adj radical(e).
radii ['reɪdɪaɪ] npl of **radius**.
radio ['reɪdɪəu] n radio f ♦ vi: **to ~ to sb** en-

voyer un message radio à qn ♦ vt (information) transmettre par radio; (one's position) signaler par radio; (person) appeler par radio; **on the ~** à la radio.
radioactive ['reɪdɪəu'æktɪv] adj radioactif(ive).
radioactivity ['reɪdɪəuæk'tɪvɪtɪ] n radioactivité f.
radio announcer n annonceur m.
radio-controlled ['reɪdɪəukən'trəuld] adj radioguidé(e).
radiographer [reɪdɪ'ɔgrəfə*] n radiologue m/f (technicien).
radiography [reɪdɪ'ɔgrəfɪ] n radiographie f.
radiologist [reɪdɪ'ɔlədʒɪst] n radiologue m/f (médecin).
radiology [reɪdɪ'ɔlədʒɪ] n radiologie f.
radio station n station f de radio.
radio taxi n radio-taxi m.
radiotelephone ['reɪdɪəu'tɛlɪfəun] n radiotéléphone m.
radiotherapist ['reɪdɪəu'θɛrəpɪst] n radiothérapeute m/f.
radiotherapy ['reɪdɪəu'θɛrəpɪ] n radiothérapie f.
radish ['rædɪʃ] n radis m.
radium ['reɪdɪəm] n radium m.
radius, pl **radii** ['reɪdɪəs, -ɪaɪ] n rayon m; (ANAT) radius m; **within a ~ of 50 miles** dans un rayon de 50 milles.
RAF n abbr (BRIT) = **Royal Air Force**.
raffia ['ræfɪə] n raphia m.
raffish ['ræfɪʃ] adj dissolu(e); canaille.
raffle ['ræfl] n tombola f ♦ vt mettre comme lot dans une tombola.
raft [rɑːft] n (craft; also: **life ~**) radeau m; (logs) train m de flottage.
rafter ['rɑːftə*] n chevron m.
rag [ræg] n chiffon m; (pej: newspaper) feuille f, torchon m; (for charity) attractions organisées par les étudiants au profit d'œuvres de charité ♦ vt (BRIT) chahuter, mettre en boîte; **~s** npl haillons mpl; **in ~s** (person) en haillons; (clothes) en lambeaux.
rag-and-bone man [rægən'bəunmæn] n chiffonnier m.
ragbag ['rægbæg] n (fig) ramassis m.

Rag Day ou plus communément **Rag Week**, est un jour, ou une semaine, où les étudiants se déguisent et collectent de l'argent pour des œuvres de charité. Toutes sortes d'animations sont organisées à cette occasion (marches sponsorisées, spectacles de rue etc). Des magazines (les "rag mags") contenant des plaisanteries osées sont vendus dans les rues, également au profit des œuvres. Enfin, la plupart des universités organisent un bal (le "rag ball").

---

rag doll n poupée f de chiffon.
rage [reɪdʒ] n (fury) rage f, fureur f ♦ vi (per-

son) être fou(folle) de rage; (*storm*) faire rage, être déchaîné(e); **to fly into a** ~ se mettre en rage; **it's all the** ~ cela fait fureur.

ragged ['rægɪd] *adj* (*edge*) inégal(e), qui accroche; (*cuff*) effiloché(e); (*appearance*) déguenillé(e).

raging ['reɪdʒɪŋ] *adj* (*sea, storm*) en furie; (*fever, pain*) violent(e); ~ **toothache** rage *f* de dents; **in a** ~ **temper** dans une rage folle.

rag trade *n* (*col*): **the** ~ la confection.

raid [reɪd] *n* (*MIL*) raid *m*; (*criminal*) hold-up *m inv*; (*by police*) descente *f*, rafle *f* ♦ *vt* faire un raid sur *or* un hold-up dans *or* une descente dans.

raider ['reɪdə*] *n* malfaiteur *m*.

rail [reɪl] *n* (*on stair*) rampe *f*; (*on bridge, balcony*) balustrade *f*; (*of ship*) bastingage *m*; (*for train*) rail *m*; ~**s** *npl* rails *mpl*, voie ferrée; **by** ~ par chemin de fer, par le train.

railcard ['reɪlkɑːd] *n* (*BRIT*) carte *f* de chemin de fer; **young person's** ~ carte *f* jeune.

railing(s) ['reɪlɪŋ(z)] *n(pl)* grille *f*.

railway ['reɪlweɪ], (*US*) **railroad** ['reɪlrəud] *n* chemin *m* de fer.

railway engine *n* locomotive *f*.

railway line *n* ligne *f* de chemin de fer; (*track*) voie ferrée.

railwayman ['reɪlweɪmən] *n* cheminot *m*.

railway station *n* gare *f*.

rain [reɪn] *n* pluie *f* ♦ *vi* pleuvoir; **in the** ~ sous la pluie; **it's** ~**ing** il pleut; **it's** ~**ing cats and dogs** il pleut à torrents.

rainbow ['reɪnbəu] *n* arc-en-ciel *m*.

raincoat ['reɪnkəut] *n* imperméable *m*.

raindrop ['reɪndrɔp] *n* goutte *f* de pluie.

rainfall ['reɪnfɔːl] *n* chute *f* de pluie; (*measurement*) hauteur *f* des précipitations.

rainforest ['reɪnfɔrɪst] *n* forêt tropicale.

rainproof ['reɪnpruːf] *adj* imperméable.

rainstorm ['reɪnstɔːm] *n* pluie torrentielle.

rainwater ['reɪnwɔːtə*] *n* eau *f* de pluie.

rainy ['reɪnɪ] *adj* pluvieux(euse).

raise [reɪz] *n* augmentation *f* ♦ *vt* (*lift*) lever; hausser; (*end: siege, embargo*) lever; (*build*) ériger; (*increase*) augmenter; (*a protest, doubt*) provoquer, causer; (*a question*) soulever; (*cattle, family*) élever; (*crop*) faire pousser; (*army, funds*) rassembler; (*loan*) obtenir; **to** ~ **one's glass to sb/sth** porter un toast en l'honneur de qn/qch; **to** ~ **one's voice** élever la voix; **to** ~ **sb's hopes** donner de l'espoir à qn; **to** ~ **a laugh/a smile** faire rire/sourire.

raisin ['reɪzn] *n* raisin sec.

Raj [rɑːdʒ] *n*: **the** ~ l'empire *m* (*aux Indes*).

rajah ['rɑːdʒə] *n* radja(h) *m*.

rake [reɪk] *n* (*tool*) râteau *m*; (*person*) débauché *m* ♦ *vt* (*garden*) ratisser; (*fire*) tisonner; (*with machine gun*) balayer ♦ *vi*: **to** ~ **through** (*fig: search*) fouiller (dans).

rake-off ['reɪkɔf] *n* (*col*) pourcentage *m*.

rakish ['reɪkɪʃ] *adj* dissolu(e); cavalier(ière).

rally ['rælɪ] *n* (*POL etc*) meeting *m*, rassemblement *m*; (*AUT*) rallye *m*; (*TENNIS*) échange *m* ♦ *vt* rassembler, rallier ♦ *vi* se rallier; (*sick person*) aller mieux; (*Stock Exchange*) reprendre.

▶**rally round** *vi* venir en aide ♦ *vt fus* se rallier à; venir en aide à.

rallying point ['rælɪŋ-] *n* (*MIL*) point *m* de ralliement.

RAM [ræm] *n abbr* (*COMPUT*) = **random access memory**.

ram [ræm] *n* bélier *m* ♦ *vt* enfoncer; (*soil*) tasser; (*crash into*) emboutir; percuter; éperonner.

ramble ['ræmbl] *n* randonnée *f* ♦ *vi* (*pej: also:* ~ **on**) discourir, pérorer.

rambler ['ræmblə*] *n* promeneur/euse, randonneur/euse; (*BOT*) rosier grimpant.

rambling ['ræmblɪŋ] *adj* (*speech*) décousu(e); (*house*) plein(e) de coins et de recoins; (*BOT*) grimpant(e).

RAMC *n abbr* (*BRIT*) = **Royal Army Medical Corps**.

ramification [ræmɪfɪ'keɪʃən] *n* ramification *f*.

ramp [ræmp] *n* (*incline*) rampe *f*; dénivellation *f*; (*in garage*) pont *m*.

rampage [ræm'peɪdʒ] *n*: **to be on the** ~ se déchaîner ♦ *vi*: **they went rampaging through the town** ils ont envahi les rues et ont tout saccagé sur leur passage.

rampant ['ræmpənt] *adj* (*disease etc*) qui sévit.

ram raiding [-reɪdɪŋ] *n* pillage d'un magasin en enfonçant la vitrine avec une voiture volée.

ramshackle ['ræmʃækl] *adj* (*house*) délabré(e); (*car etc*) déglingué(e).

RAN *n abbr* = **Royal Australian Navy**.

ran [ræn] *pt of* **run**.

ranch [rɑːntʃ] *n* ranch *m*.

rancher ['rɑːntʃə*] *n* (*owner*) propriétaire *m* de ranch; (*ranch hand*) cowboy *m*.

rancid ['rænsɪd] *adj* rance.

rancour, (*US*) **rancor** ['ræŋkə*] *n* rancune *f*, rancœur *f*.

R&B *n abbr* = **rhythm and blues**.

R&D *n abbr* (= *research and development*) R-D *f*.

random ['rændəm] *adj* fait(e) *or* établi(e) au hasard; (*COMPUT, MATH*) aléatoire ♦ *n*: **at** ~ au hasard.

random access memory (RAM) *n* (*COMPUT*) mémoire vive, RAM *f*.

R&R *n abbr* (*US MIL*) = **rest and recreation**.

randy ['rændɪ] *adj* (*BRIT col*) excité(e); lubrique.

rang [ræŋ] *pt of* **ring**.

range [reɪndʒ] *n* (*of mountains*) chaîne *f*; (*of missile, voice*) portée *f*; (*of products*) choix *m*, gamme *f*; (*also:* **shooting** ~) champ *m* de tir; (*: indoor*) stand *m* de tir; (*also:* **kitchen** ~) fourneau *m* (de cuisine) ♦ *vt* (*place*) mettre en rang, placer; (*roam*) parcourir ♦ *vi*: **to** ~ **over** couvrir; **to** ~ **from ... to** aller de ... à

price ~ éventail *m* des prix; **do you have anything else in this price** ~? avez-vous autre chose dans ces prix?; **within (firing)** ~ à portée (de tir); ~**d left/right** (*text*) justifié à gauche/à droite.

ranger ['reɪndʒə*] *n* garde *m* forestier.

Rangoon [ræŋ'guːn] *n* Rangoon.

rank [ræŋk] *n* rang *m*; (*MIL*) grade *m*; (*BRIT: also:* **taxi** ~) station *f* de taxis ♦ *vi:* **to** ~ **among** compter *or* se classer parmi ♦ *vt:* **I** ~ **him sixth** je le place sixième ♦ *adj* (*smell*) nauséabond(e); (*hypocrisy, injustice etc*) flagrant(e); **he's a** ~ **outsider** il n'est vraiment pas dans la course; **the** ~**s** (*MIL*) la troupe; **the** ~ **and file** (*fig*) la masse, la base; **to close** ~**s** (*MIL, fig*) serrer les rangs.

rankle ['ræŋkl] *vi* (*insult*) rester sur le cœur.

ransack ['rænsæk] *vt* fouiller (à fond); (*plunder*) piller.

ransom ['rænsəm] *n* rançon *f*; **to hold sb to** ~ (*fig*) exercer un chantage sur qn.

rant [rænt] *vi* fulminer.

ranting ['ræntɪŋ] *n* invectives *fpl.*

rap [ræp] *n* petit coup sec; tape *f* ♦ *vt* frapper sur *or* à; taper sur.

rape [reɪp] *n* viol *m*; (*BOT*) colza *m* ♦ *vt* violer.

rape(seed) oil ['reɪp(siːd)-] *n* huile *f* de colza.

rapid ['ræpɪd] *adj* rapide.

rapidity [rə'pɪdɪtɪ] *n* rapidité *f.*

rapidly ['ræpɪdlɪ] *adv* rapidement.

rapids ['ræpɪdz] *npl* (*GEO*) rapides *mpl.*

rapist ['reɪpɪst] *n* auteur *m* d'un viol.

rapport [ræ'pɔː*] *n* entente *f.*

rapt [ræpt] *adj* (*attention*) extrême; **to be** ~ **in contemplation** être perdu(e) dans la contemplation.

rapture ['ræptʃə*] *n* extase *f*, ravissement *m*; **to go into** ~**s over** s'extasier sur.

rapturous ['ræptʃərəs] *adj* extasié(e); frénétique.

rare [rɛə*] *adj* rare; (*CULIN: steak*) saignant(e).

rarebit ['rɛəbɪt] *n see* **Welsh rarebit**.

rarefied ['rɛərɪfaɪd] *adj* (*air, atmosphere*) raréfié(e).

rarely ['rɛəlɪ] *adv* rarement.

raring ['rɛərɪŋ] *adj:* **to be** ~ **to go** (*col*) être très impatient(e) de commencer.

rarity ['rɛərɪtɪ] *n* rareté *f.*

rascal ['rɑːskl] *n* vaurien *m.*

rash [ræʃ] *adj* imprudent(e), irréfléchi(e) ♦ *n* (*MED*) rougeur *f*, éruption *f*; **to come out in a** ~ avoir une éruption.

rasher ['ræʃə*] *n* fine tranche (de lard).

rasp [rɑːsp] *n* (*tool*) lime *f* ♦ *vt* (*speak: also:* ~ **out**) dire d'une voix grinçante.

raspberry ['rɑːzbərɪ] *n* framboise *f.*

raspberry bush *n* framboisier *m.*

rasping ['rɑːspɪŋ] *adj:* ~ **noise** grincement *m.*

Rastafarian [ræstə'fɛərɪən] *adj, n* rastafari (*m/f*).

rat [ræt] *n* rat *m.*

ratable ['reɪtəbl] *adj* = **rateable**.

ratchet ['rætʃɪt] *n:* ~ **wheel** roue *f* à rochet.

rate [reɪt] *n* (*ratio*) taux *m*, pourcentage *m*; (*speed*) vitesse *f*, rythme *m*; (*price*) tarif *m* ♦ *vt* classer; évaluer; **to** ~ **sb/sth as** considérer qn/qch comme; **to** ~ **sb/sth among** classer qn/qch parmi; **to** ~ **sb/sth highly** avoir une haute opinion de qn/qch; **at a** ~ **of 60 kph** à une vitesse de 60 km/h; ~ **of exchange** taux *or* cours *m* du change; ~ **of flow** débit *m*; ~ **of return** (taux de) rendement *m*; **pulse** ~ fréquence *f* des pulsations.

rateable value ['reɪtəbl-] *n* (*BRIT*) valeur locative imposable.

ratepayer ['reɪtpeɪə*] *n* (*BRIT*) contribuable *m/f* (*payant les impôts locaux*).

rates ['reɪts] *npl* (*BRIT*) impôts locaux.

rather ['rɑːðə*] *adv* (*somewhat*) assez, plutôt; (*to some extent*) un peu; **it's** ~ **expensive** c'est assez cher; (*too much*) c'est un peu cher; **there's** ~ **a lot** il y en a beaucoup; **I would** *or* **I'd** ~ **go** j'aimerais mieux *or* je préférerais partir; **I had** ~ **go** il vaudrait mieux que je parte; **I'd** ~ **not leave** j'aimerais mieux ne pas partir; **or** ~ (*more accurately*) ou plutôt; **I** ~ **think he won't come** je crois bien qu'il ne viendra pas.

ratification [rætɪfɪ'keɪʃən] *n* ratification *f.*

ratify ['rætɪfaɪ] *vt* ratifier.

rating ['reɪtɪŋ] *n* classement *m*; cote *f*; (*NAUT: category*) classe *f*; (: *sailor: BRIT*) matelot *m*; ~**s** *npl* (*RADIO, TV*) indice(s) *m(pl)* d'écoute.

ratio ['reɪʃɪəu] *n* proportion *f*; **in the** ~ **of 100 to 1** dans la proportion de 100 contre 1.

ration ['ræʃən] *n* (*gen pl*) ration(s) *f(pl)* ♦ *vt* rationner.

rational ['ræʃnl] *adj* raisonnable, sensé(e); (*solution, reasoning*) logique; (*MED*) lucide.

rationale [ræʃə'nɑːl] *n* raisonnement *m*; justification *f.*

rationalization [ræʃnəlaɪ'zeɪʃən] *n* rationalisation *f.*

rationalize ['ræʃnəlaɪz] *vt* rationaliser; (*conduct*) essayer d'expliquer *or* de motiver.

rationally ['ræʃnəlɪ] *adv* raisonnablement; logiquement.

rationing ['ræʃnɪŋ] *n* rationnement *m.*

ratpack ['rætpæk] *n* (*BRIT col*) journalistes *mpl* de la presse à sensation.

rat poison *n* mort-aux-rats *f inv.*

rat race *n* foire *f* d'empoigne.

rattan [ræ'tæn] *n* rotin *m.*

rattle ['rætl] *n* cliquetis *m*; (*louder*) bruit *m* de ferraille; (*object: of baby*) hochet *m*; (: *of sports fan*) crécelle *f* ♦ *vi* cliqueter; faire un bruit de ferraille *or* du bruit ♦ *vt* agiter (bruyamment); (*col: disconcert*) décontenancer; (: *annoy*) embêter.

rattlesnake ['rætlsneɪk] *n* serpent *m* à sonnettes.

ratty ['rætɪ] *adj* (*col*) en rogne.

raucous ['rɔːkəs] *adj* rauque.

raucously ['rɔːkəslɪ] *adv* d'une voix rauque.

raunchy ['rɔːntʃɪ] *adj* (*col: voice, image, act*)

sexy; (:*scenes, film*) lubrique.
ravage ['rævɪdʒ] *vt* ravager.
ravages ['rævɪdʒɪz] *npl* ravages *mpl*.
rave [reɪv] *vi* (*in anger*) s'emporter; (*with enthusiasm*) s'extasier; (*MED*) délirer ♦ *n*: **a** ~ **(party)** une rave, une soirée techno ♦ *adj* (*scene, culture, music*) rave, techno ♦ *cpd*: ~ **review** (*col*) critique *f* dithyrambique.
raven ['reɪvən] *n* grand corbeau.
ravenous ['rævənəs] *adj* affamé(e).
ravine [rə'viːn] *n* ravin *m*.
raving ['reɪvɪŋ] *adj*: ~ **lunatic** *n* fou furieux/folle furieuse.
ravings ['reɪvɪŋz] *npl* divagations *fpl*.
ravioli [rævɪ'əʊlɪ] *n* ravioli *mpl*.
ravish ['rævɪʃ] *vt* ravir.
ravishing ['rævɪʃɪŋ] *adj* enchanteur(eresse).
raw [rɔː] *adj* (*uncooked*) cru(e); (*not processed*) brut(e); (*sore*) à vif, irrité(e); (*inexperienced*) inexpérimenté(e); ~ **deal** (*col: bad bargain*) sale coup *m*; (: *unfair treatment*): **to get a** ~ **deal** être traité(e) injustement.
Rawalpindi [rɔːl'pɪndɪ] *n* Rawalpindi.
raw material *n* matière première.
ray [reɪ] *n* rayon *m*; ~ **of hope** lueur *f* d'espoir.
rayon ['reɪɒn] *n* rayonne *f*.
raze [reɪz] *vt* (*also:* ~ **to the ground**) raser.
razor ['reɪzə*] *n* rasoir *m*.
razor blade *n* lame *f* de rasoir.
razzle(-dazzle) ['ræzl('dæzl)] *n* (*BRIT col*): **to go on the** ~ faire la bringue.
razzmatazz ['ræzmə'tæz] *n* (*col*) tralala *m*, tapage *m*.
RC *abbr* = **Roman Catholic**.
RCAF *n abbr* = *Royal Canadian Air Force*.
RCMP *n abbr* = *Royal Canadian Mounted Police*.
RCN *n abbr* = *Royal Canadian Navy*.
RD *abbr* (*US*) = *rural delivery*.
Rd *abbr* = *road*.
RDC *n abbr* (*BRIT*) = *rural district council*.
RE *n abbr* (*BRIT*) = *religious education*; (*BRIT MIL*) = *Royal Engineers*.
re [riː] *prep* concernant.
reach [riːtʃ] *n* portée *f*, atteinte *f*; (*of river etc*) étendue *f* ♦ *vt* atteindre, arriver à ♦ *vi* s'étendre; (*stretch out hand*): **to** ~ **up/down/out etc (for sth)** lever/baisser/allonger etc le bras (pour prendre qch); **to** ~ **sb by phone** joindre qn par téléphone; **out of/within** ~ (*object*) hors de/à portée; **within easy** ~ (**of**) (*place*) à proximité (de), proche (de).
react [riː'ækt] *vi* réagir.
reaction [riː'ækʃən] *n* réaction *f*.
reactionary [riː'ækʃənrɪ] *adj*, *n* réactionnaire (*m/f*).
reactor [riː'æktə*] *n* réacteur *m*.
read, *pt, pp* **read** [riːd, rɛd] *vi* lire ♦ *vt* lire; (*understand*) comprendre, interpréter; (*study*) étudier; (*subj: instrument etc*) indiquer, marquer; **to take sth as read** (*fig*) considérer qch comme accepté; **do you** ~ **me?** (*TEL*) est-ce que vous me recevez?

▸**read out** *vt* lire à haute voix.
▸**read over** *vt* relire.
▸**read through** *vt* (*quickly*) parcourir; (*thoroughly*) lire jusqu'au bout.
▸**read up** *vt*, **read up on** *vt fus* étudier.
readable ['riːdəbl] *adj* facile *or* agréable à lire.
reader ['riːdə*] *n* lecteur/trice; (*book*) livre *m* de lecture; (*BRIT: at university*) maître *m* de conférences.
readership ['riːdəʃɪp] *n* (*of paper etc*) (nombre *m* de) lecteurs *mpl*.
readily ['rɛdɪlɪ] *adv* volontiers, avec empressement; (*easily*) facilement.
readiness ['rɛdɪnɪs] *n* empressement *m*; **in** ~ (*prepared*) prêt(e).
reading ['riːdɪŋ] *n* lecture *f*; (*understanding*) interprétation *f*; (*on instrument*) indications *fpl*.
reading lamp *n* lampe *f* de bureau.
reading room *n* salle *f* de lecture.
readjust [riːə'dʒʌst] *vt* rajuster; (*instrument*) régler de nouveau ♦ *vi* (*person*): **to** ~ **(to)** se réadapter (à).
ready ['rɛdɪ] *adj* prêt(e); (*willing*) prêt, disposé(e); (*quick*) prompt(e); (*available*) disponible ♦ *n*: **at the** ~ (*MIL*) prêt à faire feu; (*fig*) tout(e) prêt(e); **for use** prêt à l'emploi; **to be** ~ **to do sth** être prêt à faire qch; **to get** ~ *vi* se préparer ♦ *vt* préparer.
ready cash *n* (argent *m*) liquide *m*.
ready-made ['rɛdɪ'meɪd] *adj* tout(e) fait(e).
ready-mix ['rɛdɪmɪks] *n* (*for cakes etc*) préparation *f* en sachet.
ready reckoner [-'rɛknə*] *n* (*BRIT*) barème *m*.
ready-to-wear ['rɛdɪtə'wɛə*] *adj* (en) prêt-à-porter.
reagent [riː'eɪdʒənt] *n* réactif *m*.
real [rɪəl] *adj* réel(le); (*genuine*) véritable; (*proper*) vrai(e); (*US col: very*) vraiment; **in** ~ **life** dans la réalité.
real ale *n* bière traditionnelle.
real estate *n* biens fonciers *or* immobiliers.
realism ['rɪəlɪzəm] *n* réalisme *m*.
realist ['rɪəlɪst] *n* réaliste *m/f*.
realistic [rɪə'lɪstɪk] *adj* réaliste.
reality [riː'ælɪtɪ] *n* réalité *f*; **in** ~ en réalité, en fait.
realization [rɪəlaɪ'zeɪʃən] *n* prise *f* de conscience; réalisation *f*.
realize ['rɪəlaɪz] *vt* (*understand*) se rendre compte de, prendre conscience de; (*a project, COMM: asset*) réaliser.
really ['rɪəlɪ] *adv* vraiment.
realm [rɛlm] *n* royaume *m*.
real-time ['riːltaɪm] *adj* (*COMPUT*) en temps réel.
Realtor ['rɪəltɔː*] *n* ® (*US*) agent immobilier.
ream [riːm] *n* rame *f* (*de papier*); ~**s** *npl* (*fig: col*) des pages et des pages.
reap [riːp] *vt* moissonner; (*fig*) récolter.
reaper ['riːpə*] *n* (*machine*) moissonneuse *f*.
reappear [riːə'pɪə*] *vi* réapparaître, reparaître.

reappearance [riːəˈpɪərəns] n réapparition f.
reapply [riːəˈplaɪ] vi: **to ~ for** (job) faire une nouvelle demande d'emploi concernant; reposer sa candidature à; (loan, grant) faire une nouvelle demande de.
reappraisal [riːəˈpreɪzl] n réévaluation f.
rear [rɪə*] adj de derrière, arrière inv; (AUT: wheel etc) arrière ♦ n arrière m, derrière m ♦ vt (cattle, family) élever ♦ vi (also: ~ **up**: animal) se cabrer.
rear admiral (RA) n vice-amiral m.
rear-engined [ˈrɪərˈɛndʒɪnd] adj (AUT) avec moteur à l'arrière.
rearguard [ˈrɪəɡɑːd] n arrière-garde f.
rearm [riːˈɑːm] vt, vi réarmer.
rearmament [riːˈɑːməmənt] n réarmement m.
rearrange [riːəˈreɪndʒ] vt réarranger.
rear-view [ˈrɪəvjuː]: ~ **mirror** n (AUT) rétroviseur m.
reason [ˈriːzn] n raison f ♦ vi: **to ~ with sb** raisonner qn, faire entendre raison à qn; **the ~ for/why** la raison de/pour laquelle; **to have ~ to think** avoir lieu de penser; **it stands to ~ that** il va sans dire que; **she claims with good ~ that** ... elle affirme à juste titre que ...; **all the more ~ why** raison de plus pour + infinitive or **pour que** + sub.
reasonable [ˈriːznəbl] adj raisonnable; (not bad) acceptable.
reasonably [ˈriːznəblɪ] adv (to behave) raisonnablement; (fairly) assez; **one can ~ assume that** ... on est fondé à or il est permis de supposer que ....
reasoned [ˈriːznd] adj (argument) raisonné(e).
reasoning [ˈriːznɪŋ] n raisonnement m.
reassemble [riːəˈsɛmbl] vt rassembler; (machine) remonter.
reassert [riːəˈsɜːt] vt réaffirmer.
reassurance [riːəˈʃʊərəns] n assurance f, garantie f, (comfort) réconfort m.
reassure [riːəˈʃʊə*] vt rassurer; **to ~ sb of** donner à qn l'assurance répétée de.
reassuring [riːəˈʃʊərɪŋ] adj rassurant(e).
reawakening [riːəˈweɪknɪŋ] n réveil m.
rebate [ˈriːbeɪt] n (on product) rabais m; (on tax etc) dégrèvement m; (repayment) remboursement m.
rebel n [ˈrɛbl] rebelle m/f ♦ vi [rɪˈbɛl] se rebeller, se révolter.
rebellion [rɪˈbɛljən] n rébellion f, révolte f.
rebellious [rɪˈbɛljəs] adj rebelle.
rebirth [riːˈbɜːθ] n renaissance f.
rebound vi [rɪˈbaund] (ball) rebondir ♦ n [ˈriːbaund] rebond m.
rebuff [rɪˈbʌf] n rebuffade f ♦ vt repousser.
rebuild [riːˈbɪld] vt irreg reconstruire.
rebuke [rɪˈbjuːk] n réprimande f, reproche m ♦ vt réprimander.
rebut [rɪˈbʌt] vt réfuter.
rebuttal [rɪˈbʌtl] n réfutation f.
recalcitrant [rɪˈkælsɪtrənt] adj récalcitrant(e).
recall [rɪˈkɔːl] vt rappeler; (remember) se rappeler, se souvenir de ♦ n rappel m; **beyond ~** adj irrévocable.
recant [rɪˈkænt] vi se rétracter; (REL) abjurer.
recap [ˈriːkæp] n récapitulation f ♦ vt, vi récapituler.
recapitulate [riːkəˈpɪtjuleɪt] vt, vi récapituler.
recapture [riːˈkæptʃə*] vt reprendre; (atmosphere) recréer.
recd. abbr = **received**.
recede [rɪˈsiːd] vi s'éloigner; reculer; redescendre.
receding [rɪˈsiːdɪŋ] adj (forehead, chin) fuyant(e); ~ **hairline** front dégarni.
receipt [rɪˈsiːt] n (document) reçu m; (for parcel etc) accusé m de réception; (act of receiving) réception f; ~**s** npl (COMM) recettes fpl; **to acknowledge ~ of** accuser réception de; **we are in ~ of** ... nous avons reçu ....
receivable [rɪˈsiːvəbl] adj (COMM) recevable; (: owing) à recevoir.
receive [rɪˈsiːv] vt recevoir; (guest) recevoir, accueillir; **"~d with thanks"** (COMM) "pour acquit".

En Grande-Bretagne, la **received pronunciation** ou **RP** est une prononciation de la langue anglaise qui, notamment encore, était surtout associée à l'aristocratie et à la bourgeoisie, mais qui maintenant est en général considérée comme la prononciation correcte.

---

receiver [rɪˈsiːvə*] n (TEL) récepteur m, combiné m; (RADIO) récepteur; (of stolen goods) receleur m; (COMM) administrateur m judiciaire.
receivership [rɪˈsiːvəʃɪp] n: **to go into ~** être placé sous administration judiciaire.
recent [ˈriːsnt] adj récent(e); **in ~ years** au cours de ces dernières années.
recently [ˈriːsntlɪ] adv récemment; **as ~ as** pas plus tard que; **until ~** jusqu'à il y a peu de temps encore.
receptacle [rɪˈsɛptɪkl] n récipient m.
reception [rɪˈsɛpʃən] n réception f; (welcome) accueil m, réception.
reception centre n (BRIT) centre m d'accueil.
reception desk n réception f.
receptionist [rɪˈsɛpʃənɪst] n réceptionniste m/f.
receptive [rɪˈsɛptɪv] adj réceptif(ive).
recess [rɪˈsɛs] n (in room) renfoncement m; (for bed) alcôve f; (secret place) recoin m; (POL etc: holiday) vacances fpl; (US: LAW: short break) suspension f d'audience; (SCOL: esp US) récréation f.
recession [rɪˈsɛʃən] n (ECON) récession f.
recharge [riːˈtʃɑːdʒ] vt (battery) recharger.
rechargeable [riːˈtʃɑːdʒəbl] adj rechargeable.
recipe [ˈrɛsɪpɪ] n recette f.
recipient [rɪˈsɪpɪənt] n bénéficiaire m/f; (of letter) destinataire m/f.
reciprocal [rɪˈsɪprəkl] adj réciproque.

reciprocate [rɪ'sɪprəkeɪt] *vt* retourner, offrir en retour ♦ *vi* en faire autant.

recital [rɪ'saɪtl] *n* récital *m*.

recite [rɪ'saɪt] *vt* (*poem*) réciter; (*complaints etc*) énumérer.

reckless ['rɛkləs] *adj* (*driver etc*) imprudent(e); (*spender etc*) insouciant(e).

recklessly ['rɛkləslɪ] *adv* imprudemment; avec insouciance.

reckon ['rɛkən] *vt* (*count*) calculer, compter; (*consider*) considérer, estimer; (*think*): I ~ (that) ... je pense (que) ..., j'estime (que) ... ♦ *vi*: he is somebody to be ~ed with il ne faut pas le sous-estimer; to ~ without sb/sth ne pas tenir compte de qn/qch.
▶**reckon on** *vt fus* compter sur, s'attendre à.

reckoning ['rɛknɪŋ] *n* compte *m*, calcul *m*; estimation *f*; the day of ~ le jour du Jugement.

reclaim [rɪ'kleɪm] *vt* (*land*) amender; (: *from sea*) assécher; (: *from forest*) défricher; (*demand back*) réclamer (le remboursement *or* la restitution de).

reclamation [rɛklə'meɪʃən] *n* (*of land*) amendement *m*; assèchement *m*; défrichement *m*.

recline [rɪ'klaɪn] *vi* être allongé(e) *or* étendu(e).

reclining [rɪ'klaɪnɪŋ] *adj* (*seat*) à dossier réglable.

recluse [rɪ'kluːs] *n* reclus/e, ermite *m*.

recognition [rɛkəg'nɪʃən] *n* reconnaissance *f*; in ~ of en reconnaissance de; to gain ~ être reconnu(e); transformed beyond ~ méconnaissable.

recognizable ['rɛkəgnaɪzəbl] *adj*: ~ (by) reconnaissable (à).

recognize ['rɛkəgnaɪz] *vt*: to ~ (by/as) reconnaître (à/comme étant).

recoil [rɪ'kɔɪl] *vi* (*person*): to ~ (from) reculer (devant) ♦ *n* (*of gun*) recul *m*.

recollect [rɛkə'lɛkt] *vt* se rappeler, se souvenir de.

recollection [rɛkə'lɛkʃən] *n* souvenir *m*; to the best of my ~ autant que je m'en souvienne.

recommend [rɛkə'mɛnd] *vt* recommander; she has a lot to ~ her elle a beaucoup de choses en sa faveur.

recommendation [rɛkəmɛn'deɪʃən] *n* recommandation *f*.

recommended retail price (RRP) [rɛkə'mɛndɪd-] *n* (*BRIT*) prix conseillé.

recompense ['rɛkəmpɛns] *vt* récompenser; (*compensate*) dédommager ♦ *n* récompense *f*; dédommagement *m*.

reconcilable ['rɛkənsaɪləbl] *adj* (*ideas*) conciliable.

reconcile ['rɛkənsaɪl] *vt* (*two people*) réconcilier; (*two facts*) concilier, accorder; to ~ o.s. to se résigner à.

reconciliation [rɛkənsɪlɪ'eɪʃən] *n* réconciliation *f*; conciliation *f*.

recondite [rɪ'kɔndaɪt] *adj* abstrus(e), obscur(e).

recondition [riːkən'dɪʃən] *vt* remettre à neuf; réviser entièrement.

reconnaissance [rɪ'kɔnɪsns] *n* (*MIL*) reconnaissance *f*.

reconnoitre, (*US*) **reconnoiter** [rɛkə'nɔɪtə*] (*MIL*) *vt* reconnaître ♦ *vi* faire une reconnaissance.

reconsider [riːkən'sɪdə*] *vt* reconsidérer.

reconstitute [riː'kɔnstɪtjuːt] *vt* reconstituer.

reconstruct [riːkən'strʌkt] *vt* (*building*) reconstruire; (*crime*) reconstituer.

reconstruction [riːkən'strʌkʃən] *n* reconstruction *f*; reconstitution *f*.

reconvene [riːkən'viːn] *vt* reconvoquer ♦ *vi* se réunir *or* s'assembler de nouveau.

record *n* ['rɛkɔːd] rapport *m*, récit *m*; (*of meeting etc*) procès-verbal *m*; (*register*) registre *m*; (*file*) dossier *m*; (*COMPUT*) article *m*; (*also*: police ~) casier *m* judiciaire; (*MUS*: *disc*) disque *m*; (*SPORT*) record *m* ♦ *vt* [rɪ'kɔːd] (*set down*) noter; (*relate*) rapporter; (*MUS*: *song etc*) enregistrer; in ~ time dans un temps record *inv*; public ~s archives *fpl*; to keep a ~ of noter; to keep the ~ straight (*fig*) mettre les choses au point; he is on ~ as saying that ... il a déclaré en public que ...; Italy's excellent ~ les excellents résultats obtenus par l'Italie; off the ~ *adj* officieux(euse) ♦ *adv* officieusement.

record card *n* (*in file*) fiche *f*.

recorded delivery letter [rɪ'kɔːdɪd-] *n* (*BRIT POST*) ≈ lettre recommandée.

recorder [rɪ'kɔːdə*] *n* (*LAW*) avocat nommé à la fonction de juge; (*MUS*) flûte *f* à bec.

record holder *n* (*SPORT*) détenteur/trice du record.

recording [rɪ'kɔːdɪŋ] *n* (*MUS*) enregistrement *m*.

recording studio *n* studio *m* d'enregistrement.

record library *n* discothèque *f*.

record player *n* électrophone *m*.

recount [rɪ'kaunt] *vt* raconter.

re-count *n* ['riːkaunt] (*POL*: *of votes*) nouveau décompte (des suffrages) ♦ *vt* [riː'kaunt] recompter.

recoup [rɪ'kuːp] *vt*: to ~ one's losses récupérer ce qu'on a perdu, se refaire.

recourse [rɪ'kɔːs] *n* recours *m*; expédient *m*; to have ~ to recourir à, avoir recours à.

recover [rɪ'kʌvə*] *vt* récupérer ♦ *vi* (*from illness*) se rétablir; (*from shock*) se remettre; (*country*) se redresser.

re-cover [riː'kʌvə*] *vt* (*chair etc*) recouvrir.

recovery [rɪ'kʌvərɪ] *n* récupération *f*; rétablissement *m*; redressement *m*.

recreate [riːkrɪ'eɪt] *vt* recréer.

recreation [rɛkrɪ'eɪʃən] *n* récréation *f*, détente *f*.

recreational [rɛkrɪ'eɪʃənl] *adj* pour la détente, récréatif(ive).

recreational drug n drogue que l'on prend pour le plaisir et non pour des raisons médicales ou par dépendance.

recreational vehicle (RV) n (US) camping-car m.

recrimination [rɪkrɪmɪ'neɪʃən] n récrimination f.

recruit [rɪ'kruːt] n recrue f ♦ vt recruter.

recruiting office [rɪ'kruːtɪŋ-] n bureau m de recrutement.

recruitment [rɪ'kruːtmənt] n recrutement m.

rectangle ['rɛktæŋgl] n rectangle m.

rectangular [rɛk'tæŋgjulə*] adj rectangulaire.

rectify ['rɛktɪfaɪ] vt (error) rectifier, corriger; (omission) réparer.

rector ['rɛktə*] n (REL) pasteur m; (in Scottish universities) personnalité élue par les étudiants pour les représenter.

rectory ['rɛktərɪ] n presbytère m.

rectum ['rɛktəm] n (ANAT) rectum m.

recuperate [rɪ'kjuːpəreɪt] vi (from illness) se rétablir.

recur [rɪ'kə:*] vi se reproduire; (idea, opportunity) se retrouver; (symptoms) réapparaître.

recurrence [rɪ'kə:rns] n répétition f; réapparition f.

recurrent [rɪ'kə:rnt] adj périodique, fréquent(e).

recurring [rɪ'kə:rɪŋ] adj (MATH) périodique.

recycle [riː'saɪkl] vt, vi recycler.

red [rɛd] n rouge m; (POL: pej) rouge m/f ♦ adj rouge; **in the ~** (account) à découvert; (business) en déficit.

red alert n alerte f rouge.

red-blooded [rɛd'blʌdɪd] adj (col) viril, vigoureux(euse).

Une **redbrick university**, ainsi nommée à cause du matériau de construction répandu à l'époque (la brique), est une université britannique provinciale construite assez récemment, en particulier fin XIXe-début XXe siècle. Il y en a notamment une à Manchester, une à Liverpool et une à Bristol. Ce terme est utilisé pour établir une distinction avec les universités les plus anciennes et traditionnelles.

red carpet treatment n réception f en grande pompe.

Red Cross n Croix-Rouge f.

redcurrant ['rɛdkʌrənt] n groseille f (rouge).

redden ['rɛdn] vt, vi rougir.

reddish ['rɛdɪʃ] adj rougeâtre; (hair) plutôt roux(rousse).

redecorate [riː'dɛkəreɪt] vt refaire à neuf, repeindre et retapisser.

redecoration [riːdɛkə'reɪʃən] n remise f à neuf.

redeem [rɪ'diːm] vt (debt) rembourser; (sth in pawn) dégager; (fig, also REL) racheter.

redeemable [rɪ'diːməbl] adj rachetable; remboursable, amortissable.

redeeming [rɪ'diːmɪŋ] adj (feature) qui sauve, qui rachète (le reste).

redefine [riːdɪ'faɪn] vt redéfinir.

redemption [rɪ'dɛmʃən] n (REL) rédemption f; **past or beyond ~** (situation) irrémédiable; (place) qui ne peut plus être sauvé(e); (person) irrécupérable.

redeploy [riːdɪ'plɔɪ] vt (MIL) redéployer; (staff, resources) reconvertir.

redeployment [riːdɪ'plɔɪmənt] n redéploiement m; reconversion f.

redevelop [riːdɪ'vɛləp] vt rénover.

redevelopment [riːdɪ'vɛləpmənt] n rénovation f, reconstruction f.

red-handed [rɛd'hændɪd] adj: **to be caught ~** être pris(e) en flagrant délit or la main dans le sac.

redhead ['rɛdhɛd] n roux/rousse.

red herring n (fig) diversion f, fausse piste.

red-hot [rɛd'hɒt] adj chauffé(e) au rouge, brûlant(e).

redirect [riːdaɪ'rɛkt] vt (mail) faire suivre.

redistribute [riːdɪ'strɪbjuːt] vt redistribuer.

red-letter day ['rɛdlɛtə-] n grand jour, jour mémorable.

red light n: **to go through a ~** (AUT) brûler un feu rouge.

red-light district ['rɛdlaɪt-] n quartier réservé.

red meat n viande f rouge.

redness ['rɛdnɪs] n rougeur f; (of hair) rousseur f.

redo [riː'duː] vt irreg refaire.

redolent ['rɛdələnt] adj: **~ of** qui sent; (fig) qui évoque.

redouble [riː'dʌbl] vt: **to ~ one's efforts** redoubler d'efforts.

redraft [riː'drɑːft] vt remanier.

redress [rɪ'drɛs] n réparation f ♦ vt redresser; **to ~ the balance** rétablir l'équilibre.

Red Sea n: **the ~** la mer Rouge.

redskin ['rɛdskɪn] n Peau-Rouge m/f.

red tape n (fig) paperasserie (administrative).

reduce [rɪ'djuːs] vt réduire; (lower) abaisser; **"~ speed now"** (AUT) "ralentir"; **to ~ sth by/to** réduire qch de/à; **to ~ sb to tears** faire pleurer qn.

reduced [rɪ'djuːst] adj réduit(e); **"greatly ~ prices"** "gros rabais"; **at a ~ price** (goods) au rabais; (ticket etc) à prix réduit.

reduction [rɪ'dʌkʃən] n réduction f; (of price) baisse f; (discount) rabais m; réduction.

redundancy [rɪ'dʌndənsɪ] n (BRIT) licenciement m, mise f au chômage; **compulsory ~** licenciement; **voluntary ~** départ m volontaire.

redundancy payment n (BRIT) indemnité f de licenciement.

redundant [rɪ'dʌndnt] adj (BRIT: worker) licencié(e), mis(e) au chômage; (detail, object) superflu(e); **to be made ~** (worker) être li-

cencié, être mis au chômage.
reed [riːd] *n* (*BOT*) roseau *m*; (*MUS: of clarinet etc*) anche *f*.
re-educate [riːˈedjukeɪt] *vt* rééduquer.
reedy [ˈriːdɪ] *adj* (*voice, instrument*) ténu(e).
reef [riːf] *n* (*at sea*) récif *m*, écueil *m*.
reek [riːk] *vi*: **to ~ (of)** puer, empester.
reel [riːl] *n* bobine *f*; (*TECH*) dévidoir *m*; (*FISHING*) moulinet *m*; (*CINE*) bande *f* ♦ *vt* (*TECH*) bobiner; (*also:* **~ up**) enrouler ♦ *vi* (*sway*) chanceler; **my head is ~ing** j'ai la tête qui tourne.
▶**reel off** *vt* (*say*) énumérer, débiter.
re-election [riːɪˈlekʃən] *n* réélection *f*.
re-enter [riːˈentə*] *vt* (*also SPACE*) rentrer dans.
re-entry [riːˈentrɪ] *n* (*also SPACE*) rentrée *f*.
re-export *vt* [ˈriːɪksˈpɔːt] réexporter ♦ *n* [riːˈekspɔːt] marchandise réexportée; (*act*) réexportation *f*.
ref [ref] *n abbr* (*col: = referee*) arbitre *m*.
ref. *abbr* (*COMM: = with reference to*) réf.
refectory [rɪˈfektərɪ] *n* réfectoire *m*.
refer [rɪˈfəː*] *vt*: **to ~ sth to** (*dispute, decision*) soumettre qch à; **to ~ sb to** (*inquirer: for information*) adresser *or* envoyer qn à; (*reader: to text*) renvoyer qn à; **he ~red me to the manager** il m'a dit de m'adresser au directeur.
▶**refer to** *vt fus* (*allude to*) parler de, faire allusion à; (*apply to*) s'appliquer à; (*consult*) se reporter à; **~ring to your letter** (*COMM*) en réponse à votre lettre.
referee [refəˈriː] *n* arbitre *m*; (*TENNIS*) juge-arbitre *m*; (*BRIT: for job application*) répondant/e ♦ *vt* arbitrer.
reference [ˈrefrəns] *n* référence *f*, renvoi *m*; (*mention*) allusion *f*, mention *f*; (*for job application: letter*) références; lettre *f* de recommandation; (*: person*) répondant/e; **with ~ to** en ce qui concerne; (*COMM: in letter*) me référant à; **"please quote this ~"** (*COMM*) "prière de rappeler cette référence".
reference book *n* ouvrage *m* de référence.
reference library *n* bibliothèque *f* d'ouvrages à consulter.
reference number *n* (*COMM*) numéro *m* de référence.
referendum, *pl* **referenda** [refəˈrendəm, -də] *n* référendum *m*.
referral [rɪˈfəːrəl] *n* soumission *f*; **she got a ~ to a specialist** elle a été adressée à un spécialiste.
refill *vt* [riːˈfɪl] remplir à nouveau; (*pen, lighter etc*) recharger ♦ *n* [ˈriːfɪl] (*for pen etc*) recharge *f*.
refine [rɪˈfaɪn] *vt* (*sugar, oil*) raffiner; (*taste*) affiner.
refined [rɪˈfaɪnd] *adj* (*person, taste*) raffiné(e).
refinement [rɪˈfaɪnmənt] *n* (*of person*) raffinement *m*.
refinery [rɪˈfaɪnərɪ] *n* raffinerie *f*.

refit (*NAUT*) *n* [ˈriːfɪt] remise *f* en état ♦ *vt* [riːˈfɪt] remettre en état.
reflate [riːˈfleɪt] *vt* (*economy*) relancer.
reflation [riːˈfleɪʃən] *n* relance *f*.
reflationary [riːˈfleɪʃənrɪ] *adj* de relance.
reflect [rɪˈflekt] *vt* (*light, image*) réfléchir, refléter; (*fig*) refléter ♦ *vi* (*think*) réfléchir, méditer.
▶**reflect on** *vt fus* (*discredit*) porter atteinte à, faire tort à.
reflection [rɪˈflekʃən] *n* réflexion *f*; (*image*) reflet *m*; (*criticism*): **~ on** critique *f* de; atteinte *f* à; **on ~** réflexion faite.
reflector [rɪˈflektə*] *n* (*also AUT*) réflecteur *m*.
reflex [ˈriːfleks] *adj*, *n* réflexe (*m*).
reflexive [rɪˈfleksɪv] *adj* (*LING*) réfléchi(e).
reform [rɪˈfɔːm] *n* réforme *f* ♦ *vt* réformer.
reformat [riːˈfɔːmæt] *vt* (*COMPUT*) reformater.
Reformation [refəˈmeɪʃən] *n*: **the ~** la Réforme.
reformatory [rɪˈfɔːmətərɪ] *n* (*US*) centre *m* d'éducation surveillée.
reformed [rɪˈfɔːmd] *adj* amendé(e), assagi(e).
reformer [rɪˈfɔːmə*] *n* réformateur/trice.
refrain [rɪˈfreɪn] *vi*: **to ~ from doing** s'abstenir de faire ♦ *n* refrain *m*.
refresh [rɪˈfreʃ] *vt* rafraîchir; (*subj: food, sleep etc*) redonner des forces à.
refresher course [rɪˈfreʃə-] *n* (*BRIT*) cours *m* de recyclage.
refreshing [rɪˈfreʃɪŋ] *adj* rafraîchissant(e); (*sleep*) réparateur(trice); (*fact, idea etc*) qui réjouit par son originalité *or* sa rareté.
refreshment [rɪˈfreʃmənt] *n*: **for some ~** (*eating*) pour se restaurer *or* sustenter; **in need of ~** (*resting etc*) ayant besoin de refaire ses forces; **~(s)** rafraîchissement(s) *m(pl)*.
refrigeration [rɪfrɪdʒəˈreɪʃən] *n* réfrigération *f*.
refrigerator [rɪˈfrɪdʒəreɪtə*] *n* réfrigérateur *m*, frigidaire *m*.
refuel [riːˈfjuəl] *vt* ravitailler en carburant ♦ *vi* se ravitailler en carburant.
refuge [ˈrefjuːdʒ] *n* refuge *m*; **to take ~ in** se réfugier dans.
refugee [refjuˈdʒiː] *n* réfugié/e.
refugee camp *n* camp *m* de réfugiés.
refund *n* [ˈriːfʌnd] remboursement *m* ♦ *vt* [rɪˈfʌnd] rembourser.
refurbish [riːˈfəːbɪʃ] *vt* remettre à neuf.
refurnish [riːˈfəːnɪʃ] *vt* remeubler.
refusal [rɪˈfjuːzəl] *n* refus *m*; **to have first ~ on sth** avoir droit de préemption sur qch.
refuse *n* [ˈrefjuːs] ordures *fpl*, détritus *mpl* ♦ *vt*, *vi* [rɪˈfjuːz] refuser; **to ~ to do sth** refuser de faire qch.
refuse collection *n* ramassage *m* d'ordures.
refuse disposal *n* élimination *f* des ordures.
refusenik [rɪˈfjuːznɪk] *n* refuznik *m/f*.
refute [rɪˈfjuːt] *vt* réfuter.
regain [rɪˈgeɪn] *vt* regagner; retrouver.
regal [ˈriːgl] *adj* royal(e).

regale [rɪ'geɪl] *vt:* **to ~ sb with sth** régaler qn de qch.

regalia [rɪ'geɪlɪə] *n* insignes *mpl* de la royauté.

regard [rɪ'gɑːd] *n* respect *m*, estime *f*, considération *f* ♦ *vt* considérer; **to give one's ~s to** faire ses amitiés à; **"with kindest ~s"** "bien amicalement"; **as ~s, with ~ to** en ce qui concerne.

regarding [rɪ'gɑːdɪŋ] *prep* en ce qui concerne.

regardless [rɪ'gɑːdlɪs] *adv* quand même; **~ of** sans se soucier de.

regatta [rɪ'gætə] *n* régate *f.*

regency ['riːdʒənsɪ] *n* régence *f.*

regenerate [rɪ'dʒɛnəreɪt] *vt* régénérer ♦ *vi* se régénérer.

regent ['riːdʒənt] *n* régent/e.

reggae ['rɛgeɪ] *n* reggae *m.*

régime [reɪ'ʒiːm] *n* régime *m.*

regiment *n* ['rɛdʒɪmənt] régiment *m* ♦ *vt* ['rɛdʒɪment] imposer une discipline trop stricte à.

regimental [rɛdʒɪ'mɛntl] *adj* d'un *or* du régiment.

regimentation [rɛdʒɪmɛn'teɪʃən] *n* réglementation excessive.

region ['riːdʒən] *n* région *f*; **in the ~ of** (*fig*) aux alentours de.

regional ['riːdʒənl] *adj* régional(e).

En Écosse, le **regional council** est une assemblée délibérante régionale dont les membres sont élus tous les quatre ans. Elle est responsable, entre autres, de l'urbanisme, des transports, de l'éducation, de la police et des pompiers; *voir* **district council**

regional development *n* aménagement *m* du territoire.

register ['rɛdʒɪstə*] *n* registre *m*; (*also:* **electoral ~**) liste électorale ♦ *vt* enregistrer, inscrire; (*birth*) déclarer; (*vehicle*) immatriculer; (*luggage*) enregistrer; (*letter*) envoyer en recommandé; (*subj: instrument*) marquer ♦ *vi* se faire inscrire; (*at hotel*) signer le registre; (*make impression*) être (bien) compris(e); **to ~ for a course** s'inscrire à un cours; **to ~ a protest** protester.

registered ['rɛdʒɪstəd] *adj* (*design*) déposé(e); (*BRIT: letter*) recommandé(e); (*student, voter*) inscrit(e).

registered company *n* société immatriculée.

registered nurse *n* (*US*) infirmier/ière diplômé(e) d'État.

registered office *n* siège social.

registered trademark *n* marque déposée.

registrar ['rɛdʒɪstrɑː*] *n* officier *m* de l'état civil; secrétaire (général).

registration [rɛdʒɪs'treɪʃən] *n* (*act*) enregistrement *m*; inscription *f*; (*BRIT AUT: also:* **~ number**) numéro *m* d'immatriculation.

registry ['rɛdʒɪstrɪ] *n* bureau *m* de l'enregistrement.

registry office *n* (*BRIT*) bureau *m* de l'état civil; **to get married in a ~** ≈ se marier à la mairie.

regret [rɪ'grɛt] *n* regret *m* ♦ *vt* regretter; **to ~ that** regretter que + *sub*; **we ~ to inform you that** ... nous sommes au regret de vous informer que ....

regretfully [rɪ'grɛtfəlɪ] *adv* à *or* avec regret.

regrettable [rɪ'grɛtəbl] *adj* regrettable, fâcheux(euse).

regrettably [rɪ'grɛtəblɪ] *adv* (*drunk, late*) fâcheusement; **~, he** ... malheureusement, il ....

regroup [riː'gruːp] *vt* regrouper ♦ *vi* se regrouper.

regt *abbr* = **regiment**.

regular ['rɛgjulə*] *adj* régulier(ière); (*usual*) habituel(le), normal(e); (*listener, reader*) fidèle; (*soldier*) de métier; (*COMM: size*) ordinaire ♦ *n* (*client etc*) habitué/e.

regularity [rɛgju'lærɪtɪ] *n* régularité *f.*

regularly ['rɛgjuləlɪ] *adv* régulièrement.

regulate ['rɛgjuleɪt] *vt* régler.

regulation [rɛgju'leɪʃən] *n* (*rule*) règlement *m*; (*adjustment*) réglage *m* ♦ *cpd* réglementaire.

rehabilitate [riːə'bɪlɪteɪt] *vt* (*criminal*) réinsérer; (*drug addict*) désintoxiquer; (*invalid*) rééduquer.

rehabilitation ['riːəbɪlɪ'teɪʃən] *n* (*of offender*) réhabilitation *f*; (*of disabled*) rééducation *f*, réadaptation *f.*

rehash [riː'hæʃ] *vt* (*col*) remanier.

rehearsal [rɪ'həːsəl] *n* répétition *f*; **dress ~** (*répétition*) générale *f.*

rehearse [rɪ'həːs] *vt* répéter.

rehouse [riː'hauz] *vt* reloger.

reign [reɪn] *n* règne *m* ♦ *vi* régner.

reigning ['reɪnɪŋ] *adj* (*monarch*) régnant(e); (*champion*) actuel(le).

reimburse [riːɪm'bəːs] *vt* rembourser.

rein [reɪn] *n* (*for horse*) rêne *f*; **to give sb free ~** (*fig*) donner carte blanche à qn.

reincarnation [riːɪnkɑː'neɪʃən] *n* réincarnation *f.*

reindeer ['reɪndɪə*] *n* (*pl inv*) renne *m.*

reinforce [riːɪn'fɔːs] *vt* renforcer.

reinforced concrete [riːɪn'fɔst-] *n* béton armé.

reinforcement [riːɪn'fɔːsmənt] *n* (*action*) renforcement *m*; **~s** *npl* (*MIL*) renfort(s) *m(pl)*.

reinstate [riːɪn'steɪt] *vt* rétablir, réintégrer.

reinstatement [riːɪn'steɪtmənt] *n* réintégration *f.*

reissue [riː'ɪʃjuː] *vt* (*book*) rééditer; (*film*) ressortir.

reiterate [riː'ɪtəreɪt] *vt* réitérer, répéter.

reject *n* ['riːdʒɛkt] (*COMM*) article *m* de rebut ♦ *vt* [rɪ'dʒɛkt] refuser; (*COMM: goods*) mettre au rebut; (*idea*) rejeter.

rejection [rɪ'dʒɛkʃən] *n* rejet *m*, refus *m.*

rejoice [rɪ'dʒɔɪs] *vi:* **to ~ (at *or* over)** se réjouir (de).

rejoinder [rɪ'dʒɔɪndə*] *n* (*retort*) réplique *f*.

rejuvenate [rɪ'dʒuːvəneɪt] *vt* rajeunir.

rekindle [riː'kɪndl] *vt* rallumer; (*fig*) raviver.

relapse [rɪ'læps] *n* (*MED*) rechute *f*.

relate [rɪ'leɪt] *vt* (*tell*) raconter; (*connect*) établir un rapport entre ♦ *vi*: **to ~ to** (*connect*) se rapporter à; (*interact*) établir un rapport *or* une entente avec.

related [rɪ'leɪtɪd] *adj* apparenté(e).

relating [rɪ'leɪtɪŋ]: **~ to** *prep* concernant.

relation [rɪ'leɪʃən] *n* (*person*) parent/e; (*link*) rapport *m*, lien *m*; **diplomatic/international ~s** relations diplomatiques/internationales; **in ~ to** en ce qui concerne; par rapport à; **to bear no ~ to** être sans rapport avec.

relationship [rɪ'leɪʃənʃɪp] *n* rapport *m*, lien *m*; (*personal ties*) relations *fpl*, rapports; (*also:* **family ~**) lien de parenté; (*affair*) liaison *f*; **they have a good ~** ils s'entendent bien.

relative ['rɛlətɪv] *n* parent/e ♦ *adj* relatif(ive); (*respective*) respectif(ive); **all her ~s** toute sa famille.

relatively ['rɛlətɪvlɪ] *adv* relativement.

relax [rɪ'læks] *vi* se relâcher; (*person: unwind*) se détendre; (*calm down*) se calmer ♦ *vt* relâcher; (*mind, person*) détendre.

relaxation [riːlæk'seɪʃən] *n* relâchement *m*; détente *f*; (*entertainment*) distraction *f*.

relaxed [rɪ'lækst] *adj* relâché(e); détendu(e).

relaxing [rɪ'læksɪŋ] *adj* délassant(e).

relay ['riːleɪ] *n* (*SPORT*) course *f* de relais ♦ *vt* (*message*) retransmettre, relayer.

release [rɪ'liːs] *n* (*from prison, obligation*) libération *f*; (*of gas etc*) émission *f*; (*of film etc*) sortie *f*; (*record*) disque *m*; (*device*) déclencheur *m* ♦ *vt* (*prisoner*) libérer; (*book, film*) sortir; (*report, news*) rendre public, publier; (*gas etc*) émettre, dégager; (*free: from wreckage etc*) dégager; (*TECH: catch, spring etc*) déclencher; (*let go*) relâcher; lâcher; desserrer; **to ~ one's grip** *or* **hold** lâcher prise; **to ~ the clutch** (*AUT*) débrayer.

relegate ['rɛləgeɪt] *vt* reléguer; (*SPORT*): **to be ~d** descendre dans une division inférieure.

relent [rɪ'lɛnt] *vi* se laisser fléchir.

relentless [rɪ'lɛntlɪs] *adj* implacable.

relevance ['rɛləvəns] *n* pertinence *f*; **~ of sth to sth** rapport *m* entre qch et qch.

relevant ['rɛləvənt] *adj* approprié(e); (*fact*) significatif(ive); (*information*) utile, pertinent(e); **~ to** ayant rapport à, approprié à.

reliability [rɪlaɪə'bɪlɪtɪ] *n* sérieux *m*; fiabilité *f*.

reliable [rɪ'laɪəbl] *adj* (*person, firm*) sérieux(euse), fiable; (*method, machine*) fiable.

reliably [rɪ'laɪəblɪ] *adv*: **to be ~ informed** savoir de source sûre.

reliance [rɪ'laɪəns] *n*: **~ (on)** (*trust*) confiance *f* (en); (*dependence*) besoin *m* (de), dépendance *f* (de).

reliant [rɪ'laɪənt] *adj*: **to be ~ on sth/sb** dé-

relic ['rɛlɪk] *n* (*REL*) relique *f*; (*of the past*) vestige *m*.

relief [rɪ'liːf] *n* (*from pain, anxiety*) soulagement *m*; (*help, supplies*) secours *m(pl)*; (*of guard*) relève *f*; (*ART, GEO*) relief *m*; **by way of light ~** pour faire diversion.

relief map *n* carte *f* en relief.

relief road *n* (*BRIT*) route *f* de délestage.

relieve [rɪ'liːv] *vt* (*pain, patient*) soulager; (*bring help*) secourir; (*take over from: gen*) relayer; (*: guard*) relever; **to ~ sb of sth** débarrasser qn de qch; **to ~ sb of his command** (*MIL*) relever qn de ses fonctions; **to ~ o.s.** (*euphemism*) se soulager, faire ses besoins.

relieved [rɪ'liːvd] *adj* soulagé(e); **to be ~ that ...** être soulagé que ...; **I'm ~ to hear it** je suis soulagé de l'entendre.

religion [rɪ'lɪdʒən] *n* religion *f*.

religious [rɪ'lɪdʒəs] *adj* religieux(euse); (*book*) de piété.

religious education *n* instruction religieuse.

relinquish [rɪ'lɪŋkwɪʃ] *vt* abandonner; (*plan, habit*) renoncer à.

relish ['rɛlɪʃ] *n* (*CULIN*) condiment *m*; (*enjoyment*) délectation *f* ♦ *vt* (*food etc*) savourer; **to ~ doing** se délecter à faire.

relive [riː'lɪv] *vt* revivre.

reload [riː'ləud] *vt* recharger.

relocate [riːləu'keɪt] *vt* (*business*) transférer ♦ *vi* se transférer, s'installer *or* s'établir ailleurs; **to ~ in** (déménager et) s'installer *or* s'établir à, se transférer à.

reluctance [rɪ'lʌktəns] *n* répugnance *f*.

reluctant [rɪ'lʌktənt] *adj* peu disposé(e), qui hésite; **to be ~ to do sth** hésiter à faire qch.

reluctantly [rɪ'lʌktəntlɪ] *adv* à contrecœur, sans enthousiasme.

rely [rɪ'laɪ]: **to ~ on** *vt fus* compter sur; (*be dependent*) dépendre de.

remain [rɪ'meɪn] *vi* rester; **to ~ silent** garder le silence; **I ~, yours faithfully** (*BRIT: in letters*) je vous prie d'agréer, Monsieur (*etc*), l'assurance de mes sentiments distingués.

remainder [rɪ'meɪndə*] *n* reste *m*; (*COMM*) fin *f* de série.

remaining [rɪ'meɪnɪŋ] *adj* qui reste.

remains [rɪ'meɪnz] *npl* restes *mpl*.

remand [rɪ'mɑːnd] *n*: **on ~** en détention préventive ♦ *vt*: **to ~ in custody** écrouer; renvoyer en détention provisoire.

remand home *n* (*BRIT*) centre *m* d'éducation surveillée.

remark [rɪ'mɑːk] *n* remarque *f*, observation *f* ♦ *vt* (faire) remarquer, dire; (*notice*) remarquer; **to ~ on sth** faire une *or* des remarque(s) sur qch.

remarkable [rɪ'mɑːkəbl] *adj* remarquable.

remarry [riː'mærɪ] *vi* se remarier.

remedial [rɪ'miːdɪəl] *adj* (*tuition, classes*) de rattrapage.

remedy ['rɛmədɪ] *n*: **~ (for)** remède *m* (contre

or à). ♦ *vt* remédier à.

remember [rɪ'mɛmbə*] *vt* se rappeler, se souvenir de; **I ~ seeing it, I ~ having seen it** je me rappelle l'avoir vu *or* que je l'ai vu; **she ~ed to do it** elle a pensé à le faire; **~ me to your wife** rappelez-moi au bon souvenir de votre femme.

remembrance [rɪ'mɛmbrəns] *n* souvenir *m*; mémoire *f*.

> **Remembrance Sunday** *ou* **Remembrance Day** *est le dimanche le plus proche du 11 novembre, jour où la Première Guerre mondiale a officiellement pris fin. Il rend hommage aux victimes des deux guerres mondiales. À cette occasion, on observe deux minutes de silence à 11 h, heure de la signature de l'armistice avec l'Allemagne en 1918; certains membres de la famille royale et du gouvernement déposent des gerbes de coquelicots au cénotaphe de Whitehall, et des couronnes sont placées sur les monuments aux morts dans toute la Grande-Bretagne; par ailleurs, les gens portent des coquelicots artificiels fabriqués et vendus par des membres de la légion britannique blessés au combat, au profit des blessés de guerre et de leur famille.*

remind [rɪ'maɪnd] *vt*: **to ~ sb of sth** rappeler qch à qn; **to ~ sb to do** faire penser à qn à faire, rappeler à qn qu'il doit faire; **that ~s me!** j'y pense!

reminder [rɪ'maɪndə*] *n* rappel *m*; (*note etc*) pense-bête *m*.

reminisce [rɛmɪ'nɪs] *vi*: **to ~ (about)** évoquer ses souvenirs (de).

reminiscences [rɛmɪ'nɪsnsɪz] *npl* réminiscences *fpl*, souvenirs *mpl*.

reminiscent [rɛmɪ'nɪsnt] *adj*: **~ of** qui rappelle, qui fait penser à.

remiss [rɪ'mɪs] *adj* négligent(e); **it was ~ of me** c'était une négligence de ma part.

remission [rɪ'mɪʃən] *n* rémission *f*; (*of debt, sentence*) remise *f*; (*of fee*) exemption *f*.

remit [rɪ'mɪt] *vt* (*send: money*) envoyer.

remittance [rɪ'mɪtns] *n* envoi *m*, paiement *m*.

remnant ['rɛmnənt] *n* reste *m*, restant *m*; **~s** *npl* (*COMM*) coupons *mpl*; fins *fpl* de série.

remonstrate ['rɛmənstreɪt] *vi*: **to ~ (with sb about sth)** se plaindre (à qn de qch).

remorse [rɪ'mɔːs] *n* remords *m*.

remorseful [rɪ'mɔːsful] *adj* plein(e) de remords.

remorseless [rɪ'mɔːslɪs] *adj* (*fig*) impitoyable.

remote [rɪ'məut] *adj* éloigné(e), lointain(e); (*person*) distant(e); **there is a ~ possibility that ...** il est tout juste possible que ....

remote control *n* télécommande *f*.

remote-controlled [rɪ'məutkən'trəuld] *adj* téléguidé(e).

remotely [rɪ'məutlɪ] *adv* au loin; (*slightly*) très vaguement.

remoteness [rɪ'məutnɪs] *n* éloignement *m*.

remould ['riːməuld] *n* (*BRIT: tyre*) pneu rechapé.

removable [rɪ'muːvəbl] *adj* (*detachable*) amovible.

removal [rɪ'muːvəl] *n* (*taking away*) enlèvement *m*; suppression *f*; (*BRIT: from house*) déménagement *m*; (*from office: dismissal*) renvoi *m*; (*MED*) ablation *f*.

removal man *n* (*BRIT*) déménageur *m*.

removal van *n* (*BRIT*) camion *m* de déménagement.

remove [rɪ'muːv] *vt* enlever, retirer; (*employee*) renvoyer; (*stain*) faire partir; (*doubt, abuse*) supprimer; **first cousin once ~d** cousin/e au deuxième degré.

remover [rɪ'muːvə*] *n* (*for paint*) décapant *m*; (*for varnish*) dissolvant *m*; **make-up ~** démaquillant *m*.

remunerate [rɪ'mjuːnəreɪt] *vt* rémunérer.

remuneration [rɪmjuːnə'reɪʃən] *n* rémunération *f*.

rename [riː'neɪm] *vt* rebaptiser.

rend, *pt, pp* rent [rɛnd, rɛnt] *vt* déchirer.

render ['rɛndə*] *vt* rendre; (*CULIN: fat*) clarifier.

rendering ['rɛndərɪŋ] *n* (*MUS etc*) interprétation *f*.

rendez-vous ['rɔndɪvuː] *n* rendez-vous *m inv* ♦ *vi* opérer une jonction, se rejoindre; (*spaceship*) effectuer un rendez-vous (dans l'espace); **to ~ with sb** rejoindre qn.

renegade ['rɛnɪgeɪd] *n* rénégat/e.

renew [rɪ'njuː] *vt* renouveler; (*negotiations*) reprendre; (*acquaintance*) renouer.

renewable [rɪ'njuːəbl] *adj* renouvelable; **~ energy, ~s** énergies renouvelables.

renewal [rɪ'njuːəl] *n* renouvellement *m*; reprise *f*.

renounce [rɪ'nauns] *vt* renoncer à; (*disown*) renier.

renovate ['rɛnəveɪt] *vt* rénover; (*work of art*) restaurer.

renovation [rɛnə'veɪʃən] *n* rénovation *f*; restauration *f*.

renown [rɪ'naun] *n* renommée *f*.

renowned [rɪ'naund] *adj* renommé(e).

rent [rɛnt] *pt, pp of* **rend** ♦ *n* loyer *m* ♦ *vt* louer; (*car, TV*) louer, prendre en location; (*also: ~ out: car, TV*) louer, donner en location.

rental ['rɛntl] *n* (*for television, car*) (prix *m* de) location *f*.

rent boy *n* (*BRIT col*) jeune prostitué.

renunciation [rɪnʌnsɪ'eɪʃən] *n* renonciation *f*; (*self-denial*) renoncement *m*.

reopen [riː'əupən] *vt* rouvrir.

reopening [riː'əupnɪŋ] *n* réouverture *f*.

reorder [riː'ɔːdə*] *vt* commander de nouveau; (*rearrange*) réorganiser.

reorganize [riː'ɔːgənaɪz] *vt* réorganiser.

rep [rɛp] *n abbr* (*COMM*) = **representative**; (*THEAT*) = **repertory**.

Rep. *abbr* (*US POL*) = **representative, republi-**

can.

repair [rɪ'pɛə*] *n* réparation *f* ♦ *vt* réparer; **in good/bad** ~ en bon/mauvais état; **under** ~ en réparation.

repair kit *n* trousse *f* de réparations.

repair man *n* réparateur *m*.

repair shop *n* (*AUT etc*) atelier *m* de réparations.

repartee [rɛpɑː'tiː] *n* repartie *f*.

repast [rɪ'pɑːst] *n* (*formal*) repas *m*.

repatriate [riː'pætrɪeɪt] *vt* rapatrier.

repay [riː'peɪ] *vt irreg* (*money, creditor*) rembourser; (*sb's efforts*) récompenser.

repayment [riː'peɪmənt] *n* remboursement *m*; récompense *f*.

repeal [rɪ'piːl] *n* (*of law*) abrogation *f*; (*of sentence*) annulation *f* ♦ *vt* abroger; annuler.

repeat [rɪ'piːt] *n* (*RADIO, TV*) reprise *f* ♦ *vt* répéter; (*pattern*) reproduire; (*promise, attack, also COMM: order*) renouveler; (*SCOL: a class*) redoubler ♦ *vi* répéter.

repeatedly [rɪ'piːtɪdlɪ] *adv* souvent, à plusieurs reprises.

repel [rɪ'pɛl] *vt* repousser.

repellent [rɪ'pɛlənt] *adj* repoussant(e) ♦ *n*: **insect** ~ insectifuge *m*; **moth** ~ produit *m* antimite(s).

repent [rɪ'pɛnt] *vi*: **to** ~ **(of)** se repentir (de).

repentance [rɪ'pɛntəns] *n* repentir *m*.

repercussion [riːpə'kʌʃən] *n* (*consequence*) répercussion *f*.

repertoire ['rɛpətwɑː*] *n* répertoire *m*.

repertory ['rɛpətərɪ] *n* (*also:* ~ **theatre**) théâtre *m* de répertoire.

repertory company *n* troupe théâtrale permanente.

repetition [rɛpɪ'tɪʃən] *n* répétition *f*.

repetitious [rɛpɪ'tɪʃəs] *adj* (*speech*) plein(e) de redites.

repetitive [rɪ'pɛtɪtɪv] *adj* (*movement, work*) répétitif(ive); (*speech*) plein(e) de redites.

replace [rɪ'pleɪs] *vt* (*put back*) remettre, replacer; (*take the place of*) remplacer; (*TEL*): "~ **the receiver**" "raccrochez".

replacement [rɪ'pleɪsmənt] *n* replacement *m*; remplacement *m*; (*person*) remplaçant/e.

replacement part *n* pièce *f* de rechange.

replay ['riːpleɪ] *n* (*of match*) match rejoué; (*of tape, film*) répétition *f*.

replenish [rɪ'plɛnɪʃ] *vt* (*glass*) remplir (de nouveau); (*stock etc*) réapprovisionner.

replete [rɪ'pliːt] *adj* rempli(e); (*well-fed*): ~ **(with)** rassasié(e).

replica ['rɛplɪkə] *n* réplique *f*, copie exacte.

reply [rɪ'plaɪ] *n* réponse *f* ♦ *vi* répondre; **in** ~ **(to)** en réponse (à); **there's no** ~ (*TEL*) ça ne répond pas.

reply coupon *n* coupon-réponse *m*.

report [rɪ'pɔːt] *n* rapport *m*; (*PRESS etc*) reportage *m*; (*BRIT: also:* **school** ~) bulletin *m* (scolaire); (*of gun*) détonation *f* ♦ *vt* rapporter, faire un compte rendu de; (*PRESS etc*) faire un reportage sur; (*bring to notice: occurrence*) signaler; (: *person*) dénoncer ♦ *vi* (*make a report*): **to** ~ **(on)** faire un rapport (sur); (*for newspaper*) faire un reportage (sur); (*present o.s.*): **to** ~ **(to sb)** se présenter (chez qn); **it is** ~**ed that** on dit *or* annonce que; **it is** ~**ed from Berlin that** on nous apprend de Berlin que.

report card *n* (*US, Scottish*) bulletin *m* (scolaire).

reportedly [rɪ'pɔːtɪdlɪ] *adv*: **she is** ~ **living in Spain** elle habiterait en Espagne; **he** ~ **ordered them to ...** il leur aurait ordonné de ....

reported speech *n* (*LING*) discours indirect.

reporter [rɪ'pɔːtə*] *n* reporter *m*.

repose [rɪ'pəuz] *n*: **in** ~ *en or* au repos.

repossess [riːpə'zɛs] *vt* saisir.

repossession order [riːpə'zɛʃən-] *n* ordre *m* de reprise de possession.

reprehensible [rɛprɪ'hɛnsɪbl] *adj* répréhensible.

represent [rɛprɪ'zɛnt] *vt* représenter; (*explain*): **to** ~ **to sb that** expliquer à qn que.

representation [rɛprɪzɛn'teɪʃən] *n* représentation *f*; ~**s** *npl* (*protest*) démarche *f*.

representative [rɛprɪ'zɛntətɪv] *n* représentant/e; (*COMM*) représentant/e (de commerce); (*US POL*) député *m* ♦ *adj*: ~ **(of)** représentatif(ive) (de), caractéristique (de).

repress [rɪ'prɛs] *vt* réprimer.

repression [rɪ'prɛʃən] *n* répression *f*.

repressive [rɪ'prɛsɪv] *adj* répressif(ive).

reprieve [rɪ'priːv] *n* (*LAW*) grâce *f*; (*fig*) sursis *m*, délai *m* ♦ *vt* gracier; accorder un sursis *or* un délai à.

reprimand ['rɛprɪmɑːnd] *n* réprimande *f* ♦ *vt* réprimander.

reprint *n* ['riːprɪnt] réimpression *f* ♦ *vt* [riː'prɪnt] réimprimer.

reprisal [rɪ'praɪzl] *n* représailles *fpl*; **to take** ~**s** user de représailles.

reproach [rɪ'prəutʃ] *n* reproche *m* ♦ *vt*: **to** ~ **sb with sth** reprocher qch à qn; **beyond** ~ irréprochable.

reproachful [rɪ'prəutʃful] *adj* de reproche.

reproduce [riːprə'djuːs] *vt* reproduire ♦ *vi* se reproduire.

reproduction [riːprə'dʌkʃən] *n* reproduction *f*.

reproductive [riːprə'dʌktɪv] *adj* repro- ducteur(trice).

reproof [rɪ'pruːf] *n* reproche *m*.

reprove [rɪ'pruːv] *vt* (*action*) réprouver; (*person*): **to** ~ **(for)** blâmer (de).

reproving [rɪ'pruːvɪŋ] *adj* réprobateur(trice).

reptile ['rɛptaɪl] *n* reptile *m*.

Repub. *abbr* (*US POL*) = **republican**.

republic [rɪ'pʌblɪk] *n* république *f*.

republican [rɪ'pʌblɪkən] *adj, n* républicain(e).

repudiate [rɪ'pjuːdɪeɪt] *vt* (*ally, behaviour*) désavouer; (*accusation*) rejeter; (*wife*) répu-

dier.
repugnant [rɪˈpʌgnənt] *adj* répugnant(e).
repulse [rɪˈpʌls] *vt* repousser.
repulsion [rɪˈpʌlʃən] *n* répulsion *f*.
repulsive [rɪˈpʌlsɪv] *adj* repoussant(e), répulsif(ive).
reputable [ˈrɛpjutəbl] *adj* de bonne réputation; (*occupation*) honorable.
reputation [rɛpjuˈteɪʃən] *n* réputation *f*; **to have a ~ for** être réputé(e) pour; **he has a ~ for being awkward** il a la réputation de ne pas être commode.
repute [rɪˈpjuːt] *n* (bonne) réputation.
reputed [rɪˈpjuːtɪd] *adj* réputé(e); **he is ~ to be rich/intelligent** *etc* on dit qu'il est riche/intelligent *etc*.
reputedly [rɪˈpjuːtɪdlɪ] *adv* d'après ce qu'on dit.
request [rɪˈkwɛst] *n* demande *f*; (*formal*) requête *f* ♦ *vt*: **to ~ (of** *or* **from sb)** demander (à qn); **at the ~ of** à la demande de.
request stop *n* (*BRIT: for bus*) arrêt facultatif.
requiem [ˈrɛkwɪəm] *n* requiem *m*.
require [rɪˈkwaɪə*] *vt* (*need: subj: person*) avoir besoin de; (*: thing, situation*) nécessiter, demander; (*demand*) exiger, requérir; (*order*): **to ~ sb to do sth/sth of sb** exiger que qn fasse qch/qch de qn; **if ~d** s'il le faut; **what qualifications are ~d?** quelles sont les qualifications requises?; **~d by law** requis par la loi.
required [rɪˈkwaɪəd] *adj* requis(e), voulu(e).
requirement [rɪˈkwaɪəmənt] *n* exigence *f*; besoin *m*; condition *f* (requise).
requisite [ˈrɛkwɪzɪt] *n* chose *f* nécessaire ♦ *adj* requis(e), nécessaire; **toilet ~s** accessoires *mpl* de toilette.
requisition [rɛkwɪˈzɪʃən] *n*: **~ (for)** demande *f* (de) ♦ *vt* (*MIL*) réquisitionner.
reroute [riːˈruːt] *vt* (*train etc*) dérouter.
resale [ˈriːˈseɪl] *n* revente *f*.
resale price maintenance (RPM) *n* vente *au détail à prix imposé.*
rescind [rɪˈsɪnd] *vt* annuler; (*law*) abroger; (*judgment*) rescinder.
rescue [ˈrɛskjuː] *n* sauvetage *m*; (*help*) secours *mpl* ♦ *vt* sauver; **to come to sb's ~** venir au secours de qn.
rescue party *n* équipe *f* de sauvetage.
rescuer [ˈrɛskjuə*] *n* sauveteur *m*.
research [rɪˈsəːtʃ] *n* recherche(s) *f(pl)* ♦ *vt* faire des recherches sur ♦ *vi*: **to ~ (into sth)** faire des recherches (sur qch); **a piece of ~** un travail de recherche; **~ and development (R & D)** recherche-développement (R-D).
researcher [rɪˈsəːtʃə*] *n* chercheur/euse.
research work *n* recherches *fpl*.
resell [riːˈsɛl] *vt irreg* revendre.
resemblance [rɪˈzɛmbləns] *n* ressemblance *f*; **to bear a strong ~ to** ressembler beaucoup à.

resemble [rɪˈzɛmbl] *vt* ressembler à.
resent [rɪˈzɛnt] *vt* éprouver du ressentiment de, être contrarié(e) par.
resentful [rɪˈzɛntful] *adj* irrité(e), plein(e) de ressentiment.
resentment [rɪˈzɛntmənt] *n* ressentiment *m*.
reservation [rɛzəˈveɪʃən] *n* (*booking*) réservation *f*; (*doubt; protected area*) réserve *f*; (*BRIT AUT: also*: **central ~**) bande médiane; **to make a ~ (in an hotel/a restaurant/on a plane)** réserver *or* retenir une chambre/une table/une place; **with ~s** (*doubts*) avec certaines réserves.
reservation desk *n* (*US: in hotel*) réception *f*.
reserve [rɪˈzəːv] *n* réserve *f*; (*SPORT*) remplaçant/e ♦ *vt* (*seats etc*) réserver, retenir; **~s** *npl* (*MIL*) réservistes *mpl*; **in ~** en réserve.
reserve currency *n* monnaie *f* de réserve.
reserved [rɪˈzəːvd] *adj* réservé(e).
reserve price *n* (*BRIT*) mise *f* à prix, prix *m* de départ.
reserve team *n* (*BRIT SPORT*) deuxième équipe *f*.
reservist [rɪˈzəːvɪst] *n* (*MIL*) réserviste *m*.
reservoir [ˈrɛzəvwɑː*] *n* réservoir *m*.
reset [riːˈsɛt] *vt irreg* remettre; (*clock, watch*) mettre à l'heure; (*COMPUT*) remettre à zéro.
reshape [riːˈʃeɪp] *vt* (*policy*) réorganiser.
reshuffle [riːˈʃʌfl] *n*: **Cabinet ~** (*POL*) remaniement ministériel.
reside [rɪˈzaɪd] *vi* résider.
residence [ˈrɛzɪdəns] *n* résidence *f*; **to take up ~** s'installer; **in ~** (*queen etc*) en résidence; (*doctor*) résidant(e).
residence permit *n* (*BRIT*) permis *m* de séjour.
resident [ˈrɛzɪdənt] *n* résident/e ♦ *adj* résidant(e).
residential [rɛzɪˈdɛnʃəl] *adj* de résidence; (*area*) résidentiel(le).
residue [ˈrɛzɪdjuː] *n* reste *m*; (*CHEM, PHYSICS*) résidu *m*.
resign [rɪˈzaɪn] *vt* (*one's post*) se démettre de ♦ *vi*: **to ~ (from)** démissionner (de); **to ~ o.s. to** (*endure*) se résigner à.
resignation [rɛzɪgˈneɪʃən] *n* démission *f*; résignation *f*; **to tender one's ~** donner sa démission.
resigned [rɪˈzaɪnd] *adj* résigné(e).
resilience [rɪˈzɪlɪəns] *n* (*of material*) élasticité *f*; (*of person*) ressort *m*.
resilient [rɪˈzɪlɪənt] *adj* (*person*) qui réagit, qui a du ressort.
resin [ˈrɛzɪn] *n* résine *f*.
resist [rɪˈzɪst] *vt* résister à.
resistance [rɪˈzɪstəns] *n* résistance *f*.
resistant [rɪˈzɪstənt] *adj*: **~ (to)** résistant(e) (à).
resolute [ˈrɛzəluːt] *adj* résolu(e).
resolution [rɛzəˈluːʃən] *n* résolution *f*; **to make a ~** prendre une résolution.

resolve [rɪ'zɔlv] n résolution f ♦ vt (decide): **to ~ to do** résoudre or décider de faire; (problem) résoudre.

resolved [rɪ'zɔlvd] adj résolu(e).

resonance ['rɛzənəns] n résonance f.

resonant ['rɛzənənt] adj résonnant(e).

resort [rɪ'zɔːt] n (town) station f (de vacances); (recourse) recours m ♦ vi: **to ~ to** avoir recours à; **seaside/winter sports ~** station balnéaire/de sports d'hiver; **in the last ~** en dernier ressort.

resound [rɪ'zaund] vi: **to ~ (with)** retentir (de).

resounding [rɪ'zaundɪŋ] adj retentissant(e).

resource [rɪ'sɔːs] n ressource f, **~s** npl ressources; **natural ~s** ressources naturelles; **to leave sb to his** (or her) **own ~s** (fig) livrer qn à lui-même (or elle-même).

resourceful [rɪ'sɔːsful] adj plein(e) de ressource, débrouillard(e).

resourcefulness [rɪ'sɔːsfəlnɪs] n ressource f.

respect [rɪs'pɛkt] n respect m; (point, detail): **in some ~s** à certains égards ♦ vt respecter; **~s** npl respects, hommages mpl; **to have** or **show ~ for sb/sth** respecter qn/qch; **out of ~ for** par respect pour; **with ~ to** en ce qui concerne; **in ~ of** sous le rapport de, quant à; **in this ~** sous ce rapport, à cet égard; **with due ~ I** ... malgré le respect que je vous dois, je ....

respectability [rɪspɛktə'bɪlɪt] n respectabilité f.

respectable [rɪs'pɛktəbl] adj respectable; (quite good: result etc) honorable; (player) assez bon(bonne).

respectful [rɪs'pɛktful] adj respectueux(euse).

respective [rɪs'pɛktɪv] adj respectif(ive).

respectively [rɪs'pɛktɪvlɪ] adv respectivement.

respiration [rɛspɪ'reɪʃən] n respiration f.

respirator ['rɛspɪreɪtə*] n respirateur m.

respiratory ['rɛspərətərɪ] adj respiratoire.

respite ['rɛspaɪt] n répit m.

resplendent [rɪs'plɛndənt] adj resplendissant(e).

respond [rɪs'pɔnd] vi répondre; (to treatment) réagir.

respondent [rɪs'pɔndənt] n (LAW) défendeur/deresse.

response [rɪs'pɔns] n réponse f; (to treatment) réaction f; **in ~ to** en réponse à.

responsibility [rɪspɔnsɪ'bɪlɪtɪ] n responsabilité f; **to take ~ for sth/sb** accepter la responsabilité de qch/d'être responsable de qn.

responsible [rɪs'pɔnsɪbl] adj (liable): **~ (for)** responsable (de); (person) digne de confiance; (job) qui comporte des responsabilités; **to be ~ to sb (for sth)** être responsable devant qn (de qch).

responsibly [rɪs'pɔnsɪblɪ] adv avec sérieux.

responsive [rɪs'pɔnsɪv] adj qui n'est pas réservé(e) or indifférent(e).

rest [rɛst] n repos m; (stop) arrêt m, pause f; (MUS) silence m; (support) support m, appui m; (remainder) reste m, restant m ♦ vi se reposer; (be supported): **to ~ on** appuyer or reposer sur; (remain) rester ♦ vt (lean): **to ~ sth on/against** appuyer qch sur/contre; **the ~ of them** les autres; **to set sb's mind at ~** tranquilliser qn; **it ~s with him to** c'est à lui de; **~ assured that ...** soyez assuré que ....

restart [riː'stɑːt] vt (engine) remettre en marche; (work) reprendre.

restaurant ['rɛstərɔŋ] n restaurant m.

restaurant car n (BRIT) wagon-restaurant m.

rest cure n cure f de repos.

restful ['rɛstful] adj reposant(e).

rest home n maison f de repos.

restitution [rɛstɪ'tjuːʃən] n (act) restitution f; (reparation) réparation f.

restive ['rɛstɪv] adj agité(e), impatient(e); (horse) rétif(ive).

restless ['rɛstlɪs] adj agité(e); **to get ~** s'impatienter.

restlessly ['rɛstlɪslɪ] adv avec agitation.

restock [riː'stɔk] vt réapprovisionner.

restoration [rɛstə'reɪʃən] n restauration f; restitution f.

restorative [rɪ'stɔrətɪv] adj reconstituant(e) ♦ n reconstituant m.

restore [rɪ'stɔː*] vt (building) restaurer; (sth stolen) restituer; (peace, health) rétablir.

restorer [rɪ'stɔrə*] n (ART etc) restaurateur/trice (d'œuvres d'art).

restrain [rɪs'treɪn] vt (feeling) contenir; (person): **to ~ (from doing)** retenir (de faire).

restrained [rɪs'treɪnd] adj (style) sobre; (manner) mesuré(e).

restraint [rɪs'treɪnt] n (restriction) contrainte f; (moderation) retenue f; (of style) sobriété f; **wage ~** limitations salariales.

restrict [rɪs'trɪkt] vt restreindre, limiter.

restricted area [rɪs'trɪktɪd-] n (AUT) zone f à vitesse limitée.

restriction [rɪs'trɪkʃən] n restriction f, limitation f.

restrictive [rɪs'trɪktɪv] adj restrictif(ive).

restrictive practices npl (INDUSTRY) pratiques fpl entravant la libre concurrence.

rest room n (US) toilettes fpl.

restructure [riː'strʌktʃə*] vt restructurer.

result [rɪ'zʌlt] n résultat m ♦ vi: **to ~ (from)** résulter (de); **to ~ in** aboutir à, se terminer par; **as a ~ it is too expensive** il en résulte que c'est trop cher; **as a ~ of** à la suite de.

resultant [rɪ'zʌltənt] adj résultant(e).

resume [rɪ'zjuːm] vt (work, journey) reprendre; (sum up) résumer ♦ vi (work etc) reprendre.

résumé ['reɪzjuːmeɪ] n (summary) résumé m; (US: curriculum vitae) curriculum vitae m inv.

resumption [rɪ'zʌmpʃən] n reprise f.

resurgence [rɪ'sɔːdʒəns] n réapparition f.

resurrection [rɛzə'rɛkʃən] n résurrection f.

resuscitate - reverie

resuscitate [rɪ'sʌsɪteɪt] vt (MED) réanimer.
resuscitation [rɪsʌsɪ'teɪʃən] n réanimation f.
retail ['riːteɪl] n (vente f au) détail m ♦ cpd de or au détail ♦ vt vendre au détail ♦ vi: **to ~ at 10 francs** se vendre au détail à 10 francs.
retailer ['riːteɪlə*] n détaillant/e.
retail outlet n point m de vente.
retail price n prix m de détail.
retail price index n ≈ indice m des prix.
retain [rɪ'teɪn] vt (keep) garder, conserver; (employ) engager.
retainer [rɪ'teɪnə*] n (servant) serviteur m; (fee) acompte m, provision f.
retaliate [rɪ'tælɪeɪt] vi: **to ~ (against)** se venger (de); **to ~ (on sb)** rendre la pareille (à qn).
retaliation [rɪtælɪ'eɪʃən] n représailles fpl, vengeance f; **in ~ for** par représailles pour.
retaliatory [rɪ'tælɪətərɪ] adj de représailles.
retarded [rɪ'tɑːdɪd] adj retardé(e).
retch [retʃ] vi avoir des haut-le-cœur.
retentive [rɪ'tentɪv] adj: **~ memory** excellente mémoire.
rethink ['riː'θɪŋk] vt repenser.
reticence ['retɪsns] n réticence f.
reticent ['retɪsnt] adj réticent(e).
retina ['retɪnə] n rétine f.
retinue ['retɪnjuː] n suite f, cortège m.
retire [rɪ'taɪə*] vi (give up work) prendre sa retraite; (withdraw) se retirer, partir; (go to bed) (aller) se coucher.
retired [rɪ'taɪəd] adj (person) retraité(e).
retirement [rɪ'taɪəmənt] n retraite f.
retirement age n âge m de la retraite.
retiring [rɪ'taɪərɪŋ] adj (person) réservé(e); (chairman etc) sortant(e).
retort [rɪ'tɔːt] n (reply) riposte f; (container) cornue f ♦ vi riposter.
retrace [riː'treɪs] vt reconstituer; **to ~ one's steps** revenir sur ses pas.
retract [rɪ'trækt] vt (statement, claws) rétracter; (undercarriage, aerial) rentrer, escamoter ♦ vi se rétracter; rentrer.
retractable [rɪ'træktəbl] adj escamotable.
retrain [riː'treɪn] vt recycler ♦ vi se recycler.
retraining [riː'treɪnɪŋ] n recyclage m.
retread vt [riː'tred] (AUT: tyre) rechaper ♦ n ['riːtred] pneu rechapé.
retreat [rɪ'triːt] n retraite f ♦ vi battre en retraite; (flood) reculer; **to beat a hasty ~** (fig) partir avec précipitation.
retrial [riː'traɪəl] n nouveau procès.
retribution [retrɪ'bjuːʃən] n châtiment m.
retrieval [rɪ'triːvəl] n récupération f; réparation f; recherche f et extraction f.
retrieve [rɪ'triːv] vt (sth lost) récupérer; (situation, honour) sauver; (error, loss) réparer; (COMPUT) rechercher.
retriever [rɪ'triːvə*] n chien m d'arrêt.
retroactive [retrəʊ'æktɪv] adj rétroactif(ive).
retrograde ['retrəgreɪd] adj rétrograde.
retrospect ['retrəspekt] n: **in ~** rétrospective-

ment, après coup.
retrospective [retrə'spektɪv] adj (law) rétroactif(ive) ♦ n (ART) rétrospective f.
return [rɪ'təːn] n (going or coming back) retour m; (of sth stolen etc) restitution f; (recompense) récompense f; (FINANCE: from land, shares) rapport m; (report) relevé m, rapport ♦ cpd (journey) de retour; (BRIT: ticket) aller et retour; (match) retour ♦ vi (person etc: come back) revenir; (: go back) retourner ♦ vt rendre; (bring back) rapporter; (send back) renvoyer; (put back) remettre; (POL: candidate) élire; **~s** npl (COMM) recettes fpl; bénéfices mpl; (: ~ed goods) marchandises renvoyées; **many happy ~s (of the day)!** bon anniversaire!; **by ~ (of post)** par retour (du courrier); **in ~ (for)** en échange (de).
returnable [rɪ'təːnəbl] adj (bottle etc) consigné(e).
returner [rɪ'təːnə*] n femme qui reprend un travail après avoir élevé ses enfants.
returning officer [rɪ'təːnɪŋ-] n (BRIT POL) président m de bureau de vote.
return key n (COMPUT) touche f de retour.
reunion [riː'juːnɪən] n réunion f.
reunite [riːjuː'naɪt] vt réunir.
rev [rev] n abbr (= revolution: AUT) tour m ♦ vb (also: **~ up**) vt emballer ♦ vi s'emballer.
Rev. abbr = **reverend**.
revaluation [riːvæljuː'eɪʃən] n réévaluation f.
revamp [riː'væmp] vt (house) retaper; (firm) réorganiser.
rev counter n (BRIT) compte-tours m inv.
Revd. abbr = **reverend**.
reveal [rɪ'viːl] vt (make known) révéler; (display) laisser voir.
revealing [rɪ'viːlɪŋ] adj révélateur(trice); (dress) au décolleté généreux or suggestif.
reveille [rɪ'vælɪ] n (MIL) réveil m.
revel ['revl] vi: **to ~ in sth/in doing** se délecter de qch/à faire.
revelation [revə'leɪʃən] n révélation f.
reveller ['revlə*] n fêtard m.
revelry ['revlrɪ] n festivités fpl.
revenge [rɪ'vendʒ] n vengeance f; (in game etc) revanche f ♦ vt venger; **to take ~** se venger.
revengeful [rɪ'vendʒful] adj vengeur(eresse); vindicatif(ive).
revenue ['revənjuː] n revenu m.
reverberate [rɪ'vəːbəreɪt] vi (sound) retentir, se répercuter; (light) se réverbérer.
reverberation [rɪvəːbə'reɪʃən] n répercussion f; réverbération f.
revere [rɪ'vɪə*] vt vénérer, révérer.
reverence ['revərəns] n vénération f, révérence f.
reverend ['revərənd] adj vénérable; **the R~ John Smith** (Anglican) le révérend John Smith; (Catholic) l'abbé John Smith; (Protestant) le pasteur John Smith.
reverent ['revərənt] adj respectueux(euse).
reverie ['revərɪ] n rêverie f.

reversal [rɪ'vɜːsl] *n* (*of opinion*) revirement *m*.

reverse [rɪ'vɜːs] *n* contraire *m*, opposé *m*; (*back*) dos *m*, envers *m*; (*AUT: also:* ~ **gear**) marche *f* arrière ♦ *adj* (*order, direction*) opposé(e), inverse ♦ *vt* (*turn*) renverser, retourner; (*change*) renverser, changer complètement; (*LAW: judgment*) réformer ♦ *vi* (*BRIT AUT*) faire marche arrière; **to go into** ~ faire marche arrière; **in** ~ **order** en ordre inverse.

reversed charge call [rɪ'vɜːst-] *n* (*BRIT TEL*) communication *f* en PCV.

reverse video *n* vidéo *m* inverse.

reversible [rɪ'vɜːsəbl] *adj* (*garment*) réversible; (*procedure*) révocable.

reversing lights [rɪ'vɜːsɪŋ-] *npl* (*BRIT AUT*) feux *mpl* de marche arrière *or* de recul.

reversion [rɪ'vɜːʃən] *n* retour *m*.

revert [rɪ'vɜːt] *vi:* **to** ~ **to** revenir à, retourner à.

review [rɪ'vjuː] *n* revue *f*; (*of book, film*) critique *f* ♦ *vt* passer en revue; faire la critique de; **to come under** ~ être révisé(e).

reviewer [rɪ'vjuːə*] *n* critique *m*.

revile [rɪ'vaɪl] *vt* injurier.

revise [rɪ'vaɪz] *vt* (*manuscript*) revoir, corriger; (*opinion*) réviser, modifier; (*study: subject, notes*) réviser; ~**d edition** édition revue et corrigée.

revision [rɪ'vɪʒən] *n* révision *f*; (*revised version*) version corrigée.

revitalize [riː'vaɪtəlaɪz] *vt* revitaliser.

revival [rɪ'vaɪvəl] *n* reprise *f*; rétablissement *m*; (*of faith*) renouveau *m*.

revive [rɪ'vaɪv] *vt* (*person*) ranimer; (*custom*) rétablir; (*hope, courage*) redonner; (*play, fashion*) reprendre ♦ *vi* (*person*) reprendre connaissance; (*hope*) renaître; (*activity*) reprendre.

revoke [rɪ'vəuk] *vt* révoquer; (*promise, decision*) revenir sur.

revolt [rɪ'vəult] *n* révolte *f* ♦ *vi* se révolter, se rebeller.

revolting [rɪ'vəultɪŋ] *adj* dégoûtant(e).

revolution [rɛvə'luːʃən] *n* révolution *f*; (*of wheel etc*) tour *m*, révolution.

revolutionary [rɛvə'luːʃənrɪ] *adj, n* révolutionnaire (*m/f*).

revolutionize [rɛvə'luːʃənaɪz] *vt* révolutionner.

revolve [rɪ'vɒlv] *vi* tourner.

revolver [rɪ'vɒlvə*] *n* revolver *m*.

revolving [rɪ'vɒlvɪŋ] *adj* (*chair*) pivotant(e); (*light*) tournant(e).

revolving door *n* (porte *f* à) tambour *m*.

revue [rɪ'vjuː] *n* (*THEAT*) revue *f*.

revulsion [rɪ'vʌlʃən] *n* dégoût *m*, répugnance *f*.

reward [rɪ'wɔːd] *n* récompense *f* ♦ *vt:* **to** ~ **(for)** récompenser (de).

rewarding [rɪ'wɔːdɪŋ] *adj* (*fig*) qui (en) vaut la peine, gratifiant(e); **financially** ~ finan-

cièrement intéressant(e).

rewind [riː'waɪnd] *vt irreg* (*watch*) remonter; (*ribbon etc*) réembobiner.

rewire [riː'waɪə*] *vt* (*house*) refaire l'installation électrique de.

reword [riː'wɜːd] *vt* formuler *or* exprimer différemment.

rewrite [riː'raɪt] *vt irreg* récrire.

Reykjavik ['reɪkjəviːk] *n* Reykjavik.

RFD *abbr* (*US POST*) = rural free delivery.

Rh *abbr* (= *rhesus*) Rh.

rhapsody ['ræpsədɪ] *n* (*MUS*) rhapsodie *f*; (*fig*) éloge délirant.

rhesus negative ['riːsəs-] *adj* (*MED*) de rhésus négatif.

rhesus positive ['riːsəs-] *adj* (*MED*) de rhésus positif.

rhetoric ['rɛtərɪk] *n* rhétorique *f*.

rhetorical [rɪ'tɒrɪkl] *adj* rhétorique.

rheumatic [ruː'mætɪk] *adj* rhumatismal(e).

rheumatism ['ruːmətɪzəm] *n* rhumatisme *m*.

rheumatoid arthritis ['ruːmətɔɪd-] *n* polyarthrite *f* chronique.

Rhine [raɪn] *n:* **the** ~ le Rhin.

rhinestone ['raɪnstəun] *n* faux diamant.

rhinoceros [raɪ'nɒsərəs] *n* rhinocéros *m*.

Rhodes [rəudz] *n* Rhodes *f*.

Rhodesia [rəu'diːʒə] *n* Rhodésie *f*.

Rhodesian [rəu'diːʒən] *adj* rhodésien(ne) ♦ *n* Rhodésien/ne.

rhododendron [rəudə'dɛndrn] *n* rhododendron *m*.

Rhône [rəun] *n:* **the** ~ le Rhône.

rhubarb ['ruːbɑːb] *n* rhubarbe *f*.

rhyme [raɪm] *n* rime *f*; (*verse*) vers *mpl* ♦ *vi:* **to** ~ **(with)** rimer (avec); **without** ~ **or reason** sans rime ni raison.

rhythm ['rɪðm] *n* rythme *m*.

rhythmic(al) ['rɪðmɪk(l)] *adj* rythmique.

rhythmically ['rɪðmɪklɪ] *adv* avec rythme.

rhythm method *n* méthode *f* des températures.

RI *n abbr* (*BRIT*) = religious instruction ♦ *abbr* (*US*) = Rhode Island.

rib [rɪb] *n* (*ANAT*) côte *f* ♦ *vt* (*mock*) taquiner.

ribald ['rɪbəld] *adj* paillard(e).

ribbed [rɪbd] *adj* (*knitting*) à côtes; (*shell*) strié(e).

ribbon ['rɪbən] *n* ruban *m*; **in** ~**s** (*torn*) en lambeaux.

rice [raɪs] *n* riz *m*.

ricefield ['raɪsfiːld] *n* rizière *f*.

rice pudding *n* riz *m* au lait.

rich [rɪtʃ] *adj* riche; (*gift, clothes*) somptueux(euse); **the** ~ *npl* les riches *mpl*; ~**es** *npl* richesses *fpl*; **to be** ~ **in sth** être riche en qch.

richly ['rɪtʃlɪ] *adv* richement; (*deserved, earned*) largement, grandement.

richness ['rɪtʃnɪs] *n* richesse *f*.

rickets ['rɪkɪts] *n* rachitisme *m*.

rickety ['rɪkɪtɪ] *adj* branlant(e).

rickshaw ['rɪkʃɔː] n pousse(-pousse) m inv.
ricochet ['rɪkəʃeɪ] n ricochet m ♦ vi ricocher.
rid, pt, pp **rid** [rɪd] vt: **to ~ sb of** débarrasser qn de; **to get ~ of** se débarrasser de.
riddance ['rɪdns] n: **good ~!** bon débarras!
ridden ['rɪdn] pp of **ride**.
riddle ['rɪdl] n (puzzle) énigme f ♦ vt: **to be ~d with** être criblé(e) de.
ride [raɪd] n promenade f, tour m; (distance covered) trajet m ♦ vb (pt **rode**, pp **ridden** [raʊd, 'rɪdn]) vi (as sport) monter (à cheval), faire du cheval; (go somewhere: on horse, bicycle) aller (à cheval or bicyclette etc); (journey: on bicycle, motor cycle, bus) rouler ♦ vt (a certain horse) monter; (distance) parcourir, faire; **we rode all day/all the way** nous sommes restés toute la journée en selle/ avons fait tout le chemin en selle or à cheval; **to ~ a horse/bicycle/camel** monter à cheval/à bicyclette/à dos de chameau; **can you ~ a bike?** est-ce que tu sais monter à bicyclette?; **to ~ at anchor** (NAUT) être à l'ancre; **horse/car ~** promenade or tour à cheval/en voiture; **to go for a ~** faire une promenade (en voiture or à bicyclette etc); **to take sb for a ~** (fig) faire marcher qn; rouler qn.
▶**ride out** vt: **to ~ out the storm** (fig) surmonter les difficultés.
rider ['raɪdə*] n cavalier/ière; (in race) jockey m; (on bicycle) cycliste m/f; (on motorcycle) motocycliste m/f; (in document) annexe f, clause additionnelle.
ridge [rɪdʒ] n (of hill) faîte m; (of roof, mountain) arête f; (on object) strie f.
ridicule ['rɪdɪkjuːl] n ridicule m; dérision f ♦ vt ridiculiser, tourner en dérision; **to hold sb/ sth up to ~** tourner qn/qch en ridicule.
ridiculous [rɪ'dɪkjuləs] adj ridicule.
riding ['raɪdɪŋ] n équitation f.
riding school n manège m, école f d'équitation.
rife [raɪf] adj répandu(e); **~ with** abondant(e) en.
riffraff ['rɪfræf] n racaille f.
rifle ['raɪfl] n fusil m (à canon rayé) ♦ vt vider, dévaliser.
▶**rifle through** vt fus fouiller dans.
rifle range n champ m de tir; (indoor) stand m de tir.
rift [rɪft] n fente f, fissure f; (fig: disagreement) désaccord m.
rig [rɪg] n (also: **oil ~**: on land) derrick m; (: at sea) plate-forme pétrolière ♦ vt (election etc) truquer.
▶**rig out** vt (BRIT) habiller; (: pej) fringuer, attifer.
▶**rig up** vt arranger, faire avec des moyens de fortune.
rigging ['rɪgɪŋ] n (NAUT) gréement m.
right [raɪt] adj (true) juste, exact(e); (correctly chosen: answer, road etc) bon(bonne); (suit-

able) approprié(e), convenable; (just) juste, équitable; (morally good) bien inv; (not left) droit(e) ♦ n (title, claim) droit m; (not left) droite f ♦ adv (answer) correctement; (not on the left) à droite ♦ vt redresser ♦ excl bon!; **the ~ time** (precise) l'heure exacte; (not wrong) la bonne heure; **to be ~** (person) avoir raison; (answer) être juste or correct(e); **to get sth ~** ne pas se tromper sur qch; **let's get it ~ this time!** essayons de ne pas nous tromper cette fois-ci!; **you did the ~ thing** vous avez bien fait; **to put a mistake ~** (BRIT) rectifier une erreur; **~ now** en ce moment même; tout de suite; **~ before/after** juste avant/après; **~ against the wall** tout contre le mur; **~ ahead** tout droit; droit devant; **~ in the middle** en plein milieu; **~ away** immédiatement; **to go ~ to the end of sth** aller jusqu'au bout de qch; **by ~s** en toute justice; **on the ~** à droite; **~ and wrong** le bien et le mal; **to be in the ~** avoir raison; **film ~s** droits d'adaptation cinématographique; **~ of way** droit m de passage; (AUT) priorité f.
right angle n angle droit.
righteous ['raɪtʃəs] adj droit(e), vertueux(euse); (anger) justifié(e).
righteousness ['raɪtʃəsnɪs] n droiture f, vertu f.
rightful ['raɪtful] adj (heir) légitime.
rightfully ['raɪtfəlɪ] adv à juste titre, légitimement.
right-handed [raɪt'hændɪd] adj (person) droitier(ière).
right-hand man ['raɪthænd-] n bras droit (fig).
right-hand side ['raɪthænd-] n côté droit.
rightly ['raɪtlɪ] adv bien, correctement; (with reason) à juste titre; **if I remember ~** (BRIT) si je me souviens bien.
right-minded ['raɪt'maɪndɪd] adj sensé(e), sain(e) d'esprit.
rights issue n (STOCK EXCHANGE) émission préférentielle or de droit de souscription.
right wing n (MIL, SPORT) aile droite; (POL) droite f ♦ adj: **right-wing** (POL) de droite.
right-winger [raɪt'wɪŋə*] n (POL) membre m de la droite; (SPORT) ailier droit.
rigid ['rɪdʒɪd] adj rigide; (principle) strict(e).
rigidity [rɪ'dʒɪdɪtɪ] n rigidité f.
rigidly ['rɪdʒɪdlɪ] adv rigidement; (behave) inflexiblement.
rigmarole ['rɪgmərəul] n galimatias m, comédie f.
rigor ['rɪgə*] n (US) = **rigour**.
rigor mortis ['rɪgə'mɔːtɪs] n rigidité f cadavérique.
rigorous ['rɪgərəs] adj rigoureux(euse).
rigorously ['rɪgərəslɪ] adv rigoureusement.
rigour, (US) **rigor** ['rɪgə*] n rigueur f.
rig-out ['rɪgaut] n (BRIT col) tenue f.
rile [raɪl] vt agacer.

rim [rɪm] *n* bord *m*; (*of spectacles*) monture *f*; (*of wheel*) jante *f*.

rimless ['rɪmlɪs] *adj* (*spectacles*) à monture invisible.

rind [raɪnd] *n* (*of bacon*) couenne *f*; (*of lemon etc*) écorce *f*.

ring [rɪŋ] *n* anneau *m*; (*on finger*) bague *f*; (*also*: **wedding** ~) alliance *f*; (*for napkin*) rond *m*; (*of people, objects*) cercle *m*; (*of spies*) réseau *m*; (*of smoke etc*) rond; (*arena*) piste *f*, arène *f*; (*for boxing*) ring *m*; (*sound of bell*) sonnerie *f*; (*telephone call*) coup *m* de téléphone ♦ *vb* (*pt* **rang**, *pp* **rung** [ræŋ, rʌŋ]) *vi* (*person, bell*) sonner; (*also*: ~ **out**: *voice, words*) retentir; (*TEL*) téléphoner ♦ *vt* (*BRIT TEL*: *also*: ~ **up**) téléphoner à; **to** ~ **the bell** sonner; **to give sb a** ~ (*TEL*) passer un coup de téléphone *or* de fil à qn; **that has the** ~ **of truth about it** cela sonne vrai; **the name doesn't** ~ **a bell (with me)** ce nom ne me dit rien.

▶**ring back** *vt, vi* (*BRIT TEL*) rappeler.

▶**ring off** *vi* (*BRIT TEL*) raccrocher.

ring binder *n* classeur *m* à anneaux.

ring finger *n* annulaire *m*.

ringing ['rɪŋɪŋ] *n* (*of bell*) tintement *m*; (*louder, also of telephone*) sonnerie *f*; (*in ears*) bourdonnement *m*.

ringing tone *n* (*BRIT TEL*) sonnerie *f*.

ringleader ['rɪŋliːdə*] *n* (*of gang*) chef *m*, meneur *m*.

ringlets ['rɪŋlɪts] *npl* anglaises *fpl*.

ring road *n* (*BRIT*) route *f* de ceinture.

rink [rɪŋk] *n* (*also*: **ice** ~) patinoire *f*; (*for rollerskating*) skating *m*.

rinse [rɪns] *n* rinçage *m* ♦ *vt* rincer.

Rio (de Janeiro) ['riːəu(dədʒə'nɪərəu)] *n* Rio de Janeiro.

riot ['raɪət] *n* émeute *f*, bagarres *fpl* ♦ *vi* manifester avec violence; **a** ~ **of colours** une débauche *or* orgie de couleurs; **to run** ~ se déchaîner.

rioter ['raɪətə*] *n* émeutier/ière, manifestant/e.

riot gear *n*: **in** ~ casqué et portant un bouclier.

riotous ['raɪətəs] *adj* tapageur(euse); tordant(e).

riotously ['raɪətəslɪ] *adv*: ~ **funny** tordant(e).

riot police *n* forces *fpl* de police intervenant en cas d'émeute; **hundreds of** ~ des centaines de policiers casqués et armés.

RIP *abbr* (= *rest in peace*) RIP.

rip [rɪp] *n* déchirure *f* ♦ *vt* déchirer ♦ *vi* se déchirer.

▶**rip up** *vt* déchirer.

ripcord ['rɪpkɔːd] *n* poignée *f* d'ouverture.

ripe [raɪp] *adj* (*fruit*) mûr(e); (*cheese*) fait(e).

ripen ['raɪpn] *vt* mûrir ♦ *vi* mûrir; se faire.

ripeness ['raɪpnɪs] *n* maturité *f*.

rip-off ['rɪpɔf] *n* (*col*): **it's a** ~! c'est du vol manifeste!

riposte [rɪ'pɔst] *n* riposte *f*.

ripple ['rɪpl] *n* ride *f*, ondulation *f*; égrènement *m*, cascade *f* ♦ *vi* se rider, onduler ♦ *vt* rider, faire onduler.

rise [raɪz] *n* (*slope*) côte *f*, pente *f*; (*hill*) élévation *f*; (*increase: in wages: BRIT*) augmentation *f*; (*: in prices, temperature*) hausse *f*, augmentation; (*fig*) ascension *f* ♦ *vi* (*pt* **rose**, *pp* **risen** [rəuz, rɪzn]) s'élever, monter; (*prices*) augmenter, monter; (*waters, river*) monter; (*sun, wind, person: from chair, bed*) se lever; (*also*: ~ **up**: *rebel*) se révolter; se rebeller; ~ **to power** montée *f* au pouvoir; **to give** ~ **to** donner lieu à; **to** ~ **to the occasion** se montrer à la hauteur.

rising ['raɪzɪŋ] *adj* (*increasing: number, prices*) en hausse; (*tide*) montant(e); (*sun, moon*) levant(e) ♦ *n* (*uprising*) soulèvement *m*, insurrection *f*.

rising damp *n* humidité *f* (montant des fondations).

rising star *n* (*also fig*) étoile montante.

risk [rɪsk] *n* risque *m*, danger *m*; (*deliberate*) risque ♦ *vt* risquer; **to take** *or* **run the** ~ **of doing** courir le risque de faire; **at** ~ en danger; **at one's own** ~ à ses risques et périls; **it's a fire/health** ~ cela présente un risque d'incendie/pour la santé; **I'll** ~ **it** je vais risquer le coup.

risk capital *n* capital-risques *m*.

risky ['rɪskɪ] *adj* risqué(e).

risqué ['riːskeɪ] *adj* (*joke*) risqué(e).

rissole ['rɪsəul] *n* croquette *f*.

rite [raɪt] *n* rite *m*; **the last** ~s les derniers sacrements.

ritual ['rɪtjuəl] *adj* rituel(le) ♦ *n* rituel *m*.

rival ['raɪvl] *n* rival/e; (*in business*) concurrent/e ♦ *adj* rival(e); qui fait concurrence *f* ♦ *vt* être en concurrence avec; **to** ~ **sb/sth** rivaliser avec qn/qch de.

rivalry ['raɪvlrɪ] *n* rivalité *f*; concurrence *f*.

river ['rɪvə*] *n* rivière *f*; (*major, also fig*) fleuve *m* ♦ *cpd* (*port, traffic*) fluvial(e); **up/down** ~ en amont/aval.

riverbank ['rɪvəbæŋk] *n* rive *f*, berge *f*.

riverbed ['rɪvəbed] *n* lit *m* (de rivière *or* de fleuve).

riverside ['rɪvəsaɪd] *n* bord *m* de la rivière *or* du fleuve.

rivet ['rɪvɪt] *n* rivet *m* ♦ *vt* riveter; (*fig*) river, fixer.

riveting ['rɪvɪtɪŋ] *adj* (*fig*) fascinant(e).

Riviera [rɪvɪ'ɛərə] *n*: **the (French)** ~ la Côte d'Azur; **the Italian** ~ la Riviera (italienne).

Riyadh [rɪ'jɑːd] *n* Riyad.

RMT *n abbr* (= *Rail, Maritime and Transport*) syndicat des transports.

RN *n abbr* (*BRIT*) = **Royal Navy**; (*US*) = **registered nurse**.

RNA *n abbr* (= *ribonucleic acid*) ARN *m*.

RNLI *n abbr* (*BRIT*: = *Royal National Lifeboat Institution*) ≈ SNSM *f*.

RNZAF *n abbr* = *Royal New Zealand Air Force*.

RNZN *n abbr* = Royal New Zealand Navy.

road [rəʊd] *n* route *f*; (*in town*) rue *f*; (*fig*) chemin, voie *f*; **main ~** grande route; **major ~** route principale *or* à priorité; **minor ~** voie secondaire; **it takes four hours by ~** il y a quatre heures de route; **"~ up"** (*BRIT*) "attention travaux".

roadblock ['rəʊdblɔk] *n* barrage routier.

road haulage *n* transports routiers.

roadhog ['rəʊdhɔg] *n* chauffard *m*.

road map *n* carte routière.

road safety *n* sécurité routière.

roadside ['rəʊdsaɪd] *n* bord *m* de la route, bas-côté *m* ♦ *cpd* (situé(e) *etc*) au bord de la route; **by the ~** au bord de la route.

roadsign ['rəʊdsaɪn] *n* panneau *m* de signalisation.

roadsweeper ['rəʊdswiːpə*] *n* (*BRIT*: *person*) balayeur/euse.

road user *n* usager *m* de la route.

roadway ['rəʊdweɪ] *n* chaussée *f*.

roadworks ['rəʊdwəːks] *npl* travaux *mpl* (de réfection des routes).

roadworthy ['rəʊdwəːðɪ] *adj* en bon état de marche.

roam [rəʊm] *vi* errer, vagabonder ♦ *vt* parcourir, errer par.

roar [rɔː*] *n* rugissement *m*; (*of crowd*) hurlements *mpl*; (*of vehicle, thunder, storm*) grondement *m* ♦ *vi* rugir; hurler; gronder; **to ~ with laughter** rire à gorge déployée.

roaring ['rɔːrɪŋ] *adj*: **a ~ fire** une belle flambée; **a ~ success** un succès fou; **to do a ~ trade** faire des affaires d'or.

roast [rəʊst] *n* rôti *m* ♦ *vt* (*meat*) (faire) rôtir.

roast beef *n* rôti *m* de bœuf, rosbif *m*.

roasting ['rəʊstɪŋ] *n* (*col*): **to give sb a ~** sonner les cloches à qn.

rob [rɔb] *vt* (*person*) voler; (*bank*) dévaliser; **to ~ sb of sth** voler *or* dérober qch à qn; (*fig*: *deprive*) priver qn de qch.

robber ['rɔbə*] *n* bandit *m*, voleur *m*.

robbery ['rɔbərɪ] *n* vol *m*.

robe [rəʊb] *n* (*for ceremony etc*) robe *f*; (*also*: **bath~**) peignoir *m* ♦ *vt* revêtir (d'une robe).

robin ['rɔbɪn] *n* rouge-gorge *m*.

robot ['rəʊbɔt] *n* robot *m*.

robotics [rə'bɔtɪks] *n* robotique *m*.

robust [rəʊ'bʌst] *adj* robuste; (*material, appetite*) solide.

rock [rɔk] *n* (*substance*) roche *f*, roc *m*; (*boulder*) rocher *m*; roche; (*BRIT*: *sweet*) ≈ sucre *m* d'orge ♦ *vt* (*swing gently*: *cradle*) balancer; (: *child*) bercer; (*shake*) ébranler, secouer ♦ *vi* (se) balancer; être ébranlé(e) *or* secoué(e); **on the ~s** (*drink*) avec des glaçons; (*ship*) sur les écueils; (*marriage etc*) en train de craquer; **to ~ the boat** (*fig*) jouer les trouble-fête.

rock and roll *n* rock (and roll) *m*, rock'n'roll *m*.

rock bottom ['rɔk'bɔtəm] *n* (*fig*) niveau le plus bas ♦ *adj*: **rock-bottom** (*fig*: *prices*) sacrifié(e); **to reach** *or* **touch rock bottom** (*price, person*) tomber au plus bas.

rock climber *n* varappeur/euse.

rock climbing *n* varappe *f*.

rockery ['rɔkərɪ] *n* (jardin *m* de) rocaille *f*.

rocket ['rɔkɪt] *n* fusée *f*; (*MIL*) fusée, roquette *f* ♦ *vi* (*prices*) monter en flèche.

rocket launcher [-lɔːnʃə*] *n* lance-roquettes *m inv*.

rock face *n* paroi rocheuse.

rock fall *n* chute *f* de pierres.

rocking chair ['rɔkɪŋ-] *n* fauteuil *m* à bascule.

rocking horse ['rɔkɪŋ-] *n* cheval *m* à bascule.

rocky ['rɔkɪ] *adj* (*hill*) rocheux(euse); (*path*) rocailleux(euse); (*unsteady*: *table*) branlant(e).

Rocky Mountains *npl*: **the ~** les (montagnes *fpl*) Rocheuses *fpl*.

rod [rɔd] *n* (*metallic*) tringle *f*; (*TECH*) tige *f*; (*wooden*) baguette *f*; (*also*: **fishing ~**) canne *f* à pêche.

rode [rəʊd] *pt of* **ride**.

rodent ['rəʊdnt] *n* rongeur *m*.

rodeo ['rəʊdɪəʊ] *n* rodéo *m*.

roe [rəʊ] *n* (*species*: *also*: **~ deer**) chevreuil *m*; (*of fish*: *also*: **hard ~**) œufs *mpl* de poisson; **soft ~** laitance *f*.

roe deer *n* chevreuil *m*; chevreuil femelle.

rogue [rəʊg] *n* coquin/e.

roguish ['rəʊgɪʃ] *adj* coquin(e).

role [rəʊl] *n* rôle *m*.

role model *n* modèle *m* à émuler.

role play, role playing *n* jeu *m* de rôle.

roll [rəʊl] *n* rouleau *m*; (*of banknotes*) liasse *f*; (*also*: **bread ~**) petit pain; (*register*) liste *f*; (*sound*: *of drums etc*) roulement *m*; (*movement*: *of ship*) roulis *m* ♦ *vt* rouler; (*also*: **~ up**: *string*) enrouler; (*also*: **~ out**: *pastry*) étendre au rouleau ♦ *vi* rouler; (*wheel*) tourner; **cheese ~** ≈ sandwich *m* au fromage (*dans un petit pain*).

▶**roll about, roll around** *vi* rouler çà et là; (*person*) se rouler par terre.

▶**roll by** *vi* (*time*) s'écouler, passer.

▶**roll in** *vi* (*mail, cash*) affluer.

▶**roll over** *vi* se retourner.

▶**roll up** *vi* (*col*: *arrive*) arriver, s'amener ♦ *vt* (*carpet, cloth, map*) rouler; (*sleeves*) retrousser; **to ~ o.s. up into a ball** se rouler en boule.

roll call *n* appel *m*.

rolled-gold ['rəʊldgəʊld] *adj* plaqué or *inv*.

roller ['rəʊlə*] *n* rouleau *m*; (*wheel*) roulette *f*.

roller blind *n* (*BRIT*) store *m*.

roller coaster *n* montagnes *fpl* russes.

roller skates *npl* patins *mpl* à roulettes.

rollicking ['rɔlɪkɪŋ] *adj* bruyant(e) et joyeux(euse); (*play*) bouffon(ne); **to have a ~ time** s'amuser follement.

rolling ['rəʊlɪŋ] *adj* (*landscape*) onduleux(euse).

rolling mill *n* laminoir *m*.

rolling pin *n* rouleau *m* à pâtisserie.
rolling stock *n* (*RAIL*) matériel roulant.
roll-on-roll-off ['rəulɔn'rəulɔf] *adj* (*BRIT: ferry*) transroulier(ière).
roly-poly ['rəulɪ'pəulɪ] *n* (*BRIT CULIN*) roulé *m* à la confiture.
ROM [rɔm] *n abbr* (*COMPUT*: = *read-only memory*) mémoire morte, ROM *f*.
Roman ['rəumən] *adj* romain(e) ♦ *n* Romain/e.
Roman Catholic *adj, n* catholique (*m/f*).
romance [rə'mæns] *n* histoire *f* (*or* film *m or* aventure *f*) romanesque; (*charm*) poésie *f*; (*love affair*) idylle *f*.
Romanesque [rəumə'nɛsk] *adj* roman(e).
Romania [rəu'meɪnɪə] *n* Roumanie *f*.
Romanian [rəu'meɪnɪən] *adj* roumain(e) ♦ *n* Roumain/e; (*LING*) roumain *m*.
Roman numeral *n* chiffre romain.
romantic [rə'mæntɪk] *adj* romantique; (*play, attachment*) sentimental(e).
romanticism [rə'mæntɪsɪzəm] *n* romantisme *m*.
Romany ['rɔmənɪ] *adj* de bohémien ♦ *n* bohémien/ne; (*LING*) romani *m*.
Rome [rəum] *n* Rome.
romp [rɔmp] *n* jeux bruyants ♦ *vi* (*also:* ~ **about**) s'ébattre, jouer bruyamment; **to** ~ **home** (*horse*) arriver bon premier.
rompers ['rɔmpəz] *npl* barboteuse *f*.
rondo ['rɔndəu] *n* (*MUS*) rondeau *m*.
roof [ru:f] *n* toit *m*; (*of tunnel, cave*) plafond *m* ♦ *vt* couvrir (d'un toit); **the** ~ **of the mouth** la voûte du palais.
roof garden *n* toit-terrasse *m*.
roofing ['ru:fɪŋ] *n* toiture *f*.
roof rack *n* (*AUT*) galerie *f*.
rook [ruk] *n* (*bird*) freux *m*; (*CHESS*) tour *f* ♦ *vt* (*col: cheat*) rouler, escroquer.
rookie ['rukɪ] *n* (*col: esp MIL*) bleu *m*.
room [ru:m] *n* (*in house*) pièce *f*; (*also:* **bed**~) chambre *f* (à coucher); (*in school etc*) salle *f*; (*space*) place *f*; ~**s** *npl* (*lodging*) meublé *m*; "~**s to let**", (*US*) "~**s for rent**" "chambres à louer"; **is there** ~ **for this?** est-ce qu'il y a de la place pour ceci?; **to make** ~ **for sb** faire de la place à qn; **there is** ~ **for improvement** on peut faire mieux.
rooming house ['ru:mɪŋ-] *n* (*US*) maison *f* de rapport.
roommate ['ru:mmeɪt] *n* camarade *m/f* de chambre.
room service *n* service *m* des chambres (*dans un hôtel*).
room temperature *n* température ambiante; "**serve at** ~" (*wine*) "servir chambré".
roomy ['ru:mɪ] *adj* spacieux(euse); (*garment*) ample.
roost [ru:st] *n* juchoir *m* ♦ *vi* se jucher.
rooster ['ru:stə*] *n* coq *m*.
root [ru:t] *n* (*BOT, MATH*) racine *f*; (*fig: of problem*) origine *f*, fond *m* ♦ *vi* (*plant*)

s'enraciner; **to take** ~ (*plant, idea*) prendre racine.
▶**root about** *vi* (*fig*) fouiller.
▶**root for** *vt fus* (*col*) applaudir.
▶**root out** *vt* extirper.
root beer *n* (*US*) sorte de limonade à base d'extraits végétaux.
rope [rəup] *n* corde *f*; (*NAUT*) cordage *m* ♦ *vt* (*box*) corder; (*climbers*) encorder; **to** ~ **sb in** (*fig*) embringuer qn; **to know the** ~**s** (*fig*) être au courant, connaître les ficelles.
rope ladder *n* échelle *f* de corde.
ropey ['rəupɪ] *adj* (*col*) pas fameux(euse) *or* brillant(e); **I feel a bit** ~ **today** c'est pas la forme aujourd'hui.
rosary ['rəuzərɪ] *n* chapelet *m*.
rose [rəuz] *pt of* **rise** ♦ *n* rose *f*; (*also:* ~**bush**) rosier *m*; (*on watering can*) pomme *f* ♦ *adj* rose.
rosé ['rəuzeɪ] *n* rosé *m*.
rosebed ['rəuzbɛd] *n* massif *m* de rosiers.
rosebud ['rəuzbʌd] *n* bouton *m* de rose.
rosebush ['rəuzbuʃ] *n* rosier *m*.
rosemary ['rəuzmərɪ] *n* romarin *m*.
rosette [rəu'zɛt] *n* rosette *f*; (*larger*) cocarde *f*.
ROSPA ['rɔspə] *n abbr* (*BRIT*) = *Royal Society for the Prevention of Accidents*.
roster ['rɔstə*] *n*: **duty** ~ tableau *m* de service.
rostrum ['rɔstrəm] *n* tribune *f* (*pour un orateur etc*).
rosy ['rəuzɪ] *adj* rose; **a** ~ **future** un bel avenir.
rot [rɔt] *n* (*decay*) pourriture *f*; (*fig: pej*) idioties *fpl*, balivernes *fpl* ♦ *vt, vi* pourrir; **to stop the** ~ (*BRIT fig*) rétablir la situation; **dry** ~ pourriture sèche (*du bois*); **wet** ~ pourriture (du bois).
rota ['rəutə] *n* liste *f*, tableau *m* de service; **on a** ~ **basis** par roulement.
rotary ['rəutərɪ] *adj* rotatif(ive).
rotate [rəu'teɪt] *vt* (*revolve*) faire tourner; (*change round: crops*) alterner; (*: jobs*) faire à tour de rôle ♦ *vi* (*revolve*) tourner.
rotating [rəu'teɪtɪŋ] *adj* (*movement*) tournant(e).
rotation [rəu'teɪʃən] *n* rotation *f*; **in** ~ à tour de rôle.
rote [rəut] *n*: **by** ~ machinalement, par cœur.
rotor ['rəutə*] *n* rotor *m*.
rotten ['rɔtn] *adj* (*decayed*) pourri(e); (*dishonest*) corrompu(e); (*col: bad*) mauvais(e), moche; **to feel** ~ (*ill*) être mal fichu(e).
rotting ['rɔtɪŋ] *adj* pourrissant(e).
rotund [rəu'tʌnd] *adj* rondelet(te); arrondi(e).
rouble, (*US*) **ruble** ['ru:bl] *n* rouble *m*.
rouge [ru:ʒ] *n* rouge *m* (à joues).
rough [rʌf] *adj* (*cloth, skin*) rêche, rugueux(euse); (*terrain*) accidenté(e); (*path*) rocailleux(euse); (*voice*) rauque, rude; (*person, manner: coarse*) rude, fruste; (*: violent*) brutal(e); (*district, weather*) mauvais(e); (*plan*) ébauché(e); (*guess*) approximatif(ive) ♦ *n* (*GOLF*) rough *m* ♦ *vt*: **to** ~ **it** vivre à la

dure; **the sea is ~ today** la mer est agitée aujourd'hui; **to have a ~ time (of it)** en voir de dures; **~ estimate** approximation *f*; **to play ~** jouer avec brutalité; **to sleep ~** (*BRIT*) coucher à la dure; **to feel ~** (*BRIT*) être mal fichu(e).

▶**rough out** *vt* (*draft*) ébaucher.

roughage ['rʌfɪdʒ] *n* fibres *fpl* diététiques.

rough-and-ready ['rʌfən'rɛdɪ] *adj* (*accommodation, method*) rudimentaire.

rough-and-tumble ['rʌfən'tʌmbl] *n* agitation *f*.

roughcast ['rʌfkɑːst] *n* crépi *m*.

rough copy, rough draft *n* brouillon *m*.

roughen ['rʌfn] *vt* (*a surface*) rendre rude *or* rugueux(euse).

rough justice *n* justice *f* sommaire.

roughly ['rʌflɪ] *adv* (*handle*) rudement, brutalement; (*make*) grossièrement; (*approximately*) à peu près, en gros; **~ speaking** en gros.

roughness ['rʌfnɪs] *n* (*of cloth, skin*) rugosité *f*; (*of person*) rudesse *f*; brutalité *f*.

roughshod ['rʌfʃɔd] *adv*: **to ride ~ over** ne tenir aucun compte de.

rough work *n* (*at school etc*) brouillon *m*.

roulette [ruːˈlɛt] *n* roulette *f*.

Roumania *etc* [ruːˈmeɪnɪə] = **Romania** *etc*.

round [raund] *adj* rond(e) ♦ *n* rond *m*, cercle *m*; (*BRIT*: *of toast*) tranche *f*; (*duty: of policeman, milkman etc*) tournée *f*; (*: of doctor*) visites *fpl*; (*game: of cards, in competition*) partie *f*; (*BOXING*) round *m*; (*of talks*) série *f* ♦ *vt* (*corner*) tourner; (*bend*) prendre; (*cape*) doubler ♦ *prep* autour de ♦ *adv*: **right ~, all ~** tout autour; **the long way ~** (par) le chemin le plus long; **all the year ~** toute l'année; **in ~ figures** en chiffres ronds; **it's just ~ the corner** c'est juste après le coin; (*fig*) c'est tout près; **to ask sb ~** inviter qn (chez soi); **I'll be ~ at 6 o'clock** je serai là à 6 heures; **to go ~** faire le tour *or* un détour; **to go ~ to sb's (house)** aller chez qn; **to go ~ an obstacle** contourner un obstacle; **go ~ the back** passez par derrière; **to go ~ a house** visiter une maison, faire le tour d'une maison; **enough to go ~** assez pour tout le monde; **she arrived ~ (about) noon** (*BRIT*) elle est arrivée vers midi; **~ the clock** 24 heures sur 24; **to go the ~s** (*disease, story*) circuler; **the daily ~** (*fig*) la routine quotidienne; **~ of ammunition** cartouche *f*; **~ of applause** ban *m*, applaudissements *mpl*; **~ of drinks** tournée *f*; **~ of sandwiches** (*BRIT*) sandwich de pain de mie.

▶**round off** *vt* (*speech etc*) terminer.

▶**round up** *vt* rassembler; (*criminals*) effectuer une rafle de; (*prices*) arrondir (au chiffre supérieur).

roundabout ['raundəbaut] *n* (*BRIT AUT*) rond-point *m* (à sens giratoire); (*at fair*) manège *m* (de chevaux de bois) ♦ *adj* (*route, means*) dé-

tourné(e).

rounded ['raundɪd] *adj* arrondi(e); (*style*) harmonieux(euse).

rounders ['raundəz] *npl* (*game*) ≈ balle *f* au camp.

roundly ['raundlɪ] *adv* (*fig*) tout net, carrément.

round-robin ['raundrɔbɪn] *n* (*SPORT: also:* **~ tournament**) tournoi où tous les joueurs se rencontrent.

round-shouldered ['raund'ʃəuldəd] *adj* au dos rond.

round trip *n* (*voyage m*) aller et retour *m*.

roundup ['raundʌp] *n* rassemblement *m*; (*of criminals*) rafle *f*; **a ~ of the latest news** un rappel des derniers événements.

rouse [rauz] *vt* (*wake up*) réveiller; (*stir up*) susciter; provoquer; éveiller.

rousing ['rauzɪŋ] *adj* (*welcome*) enthousiaste.

rout [raut] *n* (*MIL*) déroute *f* ♦ *vt* mettre en déroute.

route [ruːt] *n* itinéraire *m*; (*of bus*) parcours *m*; (*of trade, shipping*) route *f*; **"all ~s"** (*AUT*) "toutes directions"; **the best ~ to London** le meilleur itinéraire pour aller à Londres; **en ~ for** en route pour.

route map *n* (*BRIT: for journey*) croquis *m* d'itinéraire; (*for trains etc*) carte *f* du réseau.

routine [ruːˈtiːn] *adj* (*work*) ordinaire, courant(e); (*procedure*) d'usage ♦ *n* routine *f*; (*THEAT*) numéro *m*; **daily ~** occupations journalières.

roving ['rəuvɪŋ] *adj* (*life*) vagabond(e).

roving reporter *n* reporter volant.

row[1] [rəu] *n* (*line*) rangée *f*; (*of people, seats, KNITTING*) rang *m*; (*behind one another: of cars, people*) file *f* ♦ *vi* (*in boat*) ramer; (*as sport*) faire de l'aviron ♦ *vt* (*boat*) faire aller à la rame *or* à l'aviron; **in a ~** (*fig*) d'affilée.

row[2] [rau] *n* (*noise*) vacarme *m*; (*dispute*) dispute *f*, querelle *f*; (*scolding*) réprimande *f*, savon *m* ♦ *vi* (*also:* **to have a ~**) se disputer, se quereller.

rowboat ['rəubəut] *n* (*US*) canot *m* (à rames).

rowdiness ['raudɪnɪs] *n* tapage *m*, chahut *m*; (*fighting*) bagarre *f*.

rowdy ['raudɪ] *adj* chahuteur(euse); bagarreur(euse) ♦ *n* voyou *m*.

rowdyism ['raudɪɪzəm] *n* tendances *fpl* à la violence; actes *mpl* de violence.

rowing ['rəuɪŋ] *n* canotage *m*; (*as sport*) aviron *m*.

rowing boat *n* (*BRIT*) canot *m* (à rames).

rowlock ['rɔlək] *n* (*BRIT*) dame *f* de nage, tolet *m*.

royal ['rɔɪəl] *adj* royal(e).

La **Royal Academy** *ou* **Royal Academy of Arts**, *fondée en 1768 par George III pour encourager la peinture, la sculpture et l'architecture, est située à Burlington House, sur Piccadilly. Une exposition des œuvres d'artistes contempo-*

rains a lieu tous les étés. L'Académie dispense également des cours en peinture, sculpture et architecture.

Royal Air Force (RAF) *n* (*BRIT*) *armée de l'air britannique.*

royal blue *adj* bleu roi *inv.*

royalist ['rɔɪəlɪst] *adj*, *n* royaliste *(m/f).*

Royal Navy (RN) *n* (*BRIT*) *marine de guerre britannique.*

royalty ['rɔɪəltɪ] *n* (*royal persons*) (membres *mpl* de la) famille royale; (*payment: to author*) droits *mpl* d'auteur; (*: to inventor*) royalties *fpl.*

RP *n abbr* (*BRIT*: = *received pronunciation*) prononciation *f* standard.

rpm *abbr* (= *revolutions per minute*) t/mn (= *tours/minute*).

RR *abbr* (*US*) = **railroad.**

RSA *n abbr* (*BRIT*) = Royal Society of Arts, Royal Scottish Academy.

RSI *n abbr* (*MED*: = *repetitive strain injury*) microtraumatisme permanent.

RSPB *n abbr* (*BRIT*: = *Royal Society for the Protection of Birds*) ≈ LPO *f.*

RSPCA *n abbr* (*BRIT*: = *Royal Society for the Prevention of Cruelty to Animals*) ≈ SPA *f.*

RSVP *abbr* (= *répondez s'il vous plaît*) RSVP.

RTA *n abbr* (= *road traffic accident*) accident *m* de la route.

Rt Hon. *abbr* (*BRIT*: = *Right Honourable*) titre donné aux députés de la Chambre des communes.

Rt Rev. *abbr* (= *Right Reverend*) très révérend.

rub [rʌb] *n* (*with cloth*) coup *m* de chiffon *or* de torchon; (*on person*) friction *f* ♦ *vt* frotter; frictionner; **to ~ sb up** *or* (*US*) **~ sb the wrong way** prendre qn à rebrousse-poil.

▶**rub down** *vt* (*body*) frictionner; (*horse*) bouchonner.

▶**rub in** *vt* (*ointment*) faire pénétrer.

▶**rub off** *vi* partir; **to ~ off on** déteindre sur.

▶**rub out** *vt* effacer ♦ *vi* s'effacer.

rubber ['rʌbə*] *n* caoutchouc *m*; (*BRIT*: *eraser*) gomme *f* (à effacer).

rubber band *n* élastique *m.*

rubber bullet *n* balle *f* en caoutchouc.

rubber plant *n* caoutchouc *m* (*plante verte*).

rubber ring *n* (*for swimming*) bouée *f* (de natation).

rubber stamp *n* tampon *m.*

rubber-stamp [rʌbə'stæmp] *vt* (*fig*) approuver sans discussion.

rubbery ['rʌbərɪ] *adj* caoutchouteux(euse).

rubbish ['rʌbɪʃ] *n* (*from household*) ordures *fpl*; (*fig: pej*) choses *fpl* sans valeur; camelote *f*; (*nonsense*) bêtises *fpl*, idioties *fpl* ♦ *vt* (*BRIT col*) dénigrer, rabaisser; **what you've just said is ~** tu viens de dire une bêtise.

rubbish bin *n* (*BRIT*) boîte *f* à ordures, poubelle *f.*

rubbish dump *n* (*in town*) décharge publi-

que, dépotoir *m.*

rubbishy ['rʌbɪʃɪ] *adj* (*BRIT col*) qui ne vaut rien, moche.

rubble ['rʌbl] *n* décombres *mpl*; (*smaller*) gravats *mpl.*

ruble ['ruːbl] *n* (*US*) = **rouble.**

ruby ['ruːbɪ] *n* rubis *m.*

RUC *n abbr* (*BRIT*) = Royal Ulster Constabulary.

rucksack ['rʌksæk] *n* sac *m* à dos.

ructions ['rʌkʃənz] *npl* grabuge *m.*

rudder ['rʌdə*] *n* gouvernail *m.*

ruddy ['rʌdɪ] *adj* (*face*) coloré(e); (*col: damned*) sacré(e), fichu(e).

rude [ruːd] *adj* (*impolite: person*) impoli(e); (*: word, manners*) grossier(ière); (*shocking*) indécent(e), inconvenant(e); **to be ~ to sb** être grossier envers qn.

rudely ['ruːdlɪ] *adv* impoliment; grossièrement.

rudeness ['ruːdnɪs] *n* impolitesse *f*; grossièreté *f.*

rudiment ['ruːdɪmənt] *n* rudiment *m.*

rudimentary [ruːdɪ'mɛntərɪ] *adj* rudimentaire.

rue [ruː] *vt* se repentir de, regretter amèrement.

rueful ['ruːful] *adj* triste.

ruff [rʌf] *n* fraise *f*, collerette *f.*

ruffian ['rʌfɪən] *n* brute *f*, voyou *m.*

ruffle ['rʌfl] *vt* (*hair*) ébouriffer; (*clothes*) chiffonner; (*water*) agiter; (*fig: person*) émouvoir, faire perdre son flegme à.

rug [rʌg] *n* petit tapis; (*BRIT*: *for knees*) couverture *f.*

rugby ['rʌgbɪ] *n* (*also*: **~ football**) rugby *m.*

rugged ['rʌgɪd] *adj* (*landscape*) accidenté(e); (*features, kindness, character*) rude; (*determination*) farouche.

rugger ['rʌgə*] *n* (*BRIT col*) rugby *m.*

ruin ['ruːɪn] *n* ruine *f* ♦ *vt* ruiner; (*spoil: clothes*) abîmer; **~s** *npl* ruine(s); **in ~s** en ruine.

ruination [ruːɪ'neɪʃən] *n* ruine *f.*

ruinous ['ruːɪnəs] *adj* ruineux(euse).

rule [ruːl] *n* règle *f*; (*regulation*) règlement *m*; (*government*) autorité *f*, gouvernement *m*; (*dominion etc*): **under British ~** sous l'autorité britannique ♦ *vt* (*country*) gouverner; (*person*) dominer; (*decide*) décider ♦ *vi* commander; décider; (*LAW*): **to ~ against/in favour of/on** statuer contre/en faveur de/sur; **to ~ that** (*umpire, judge etc*) décider que; **it's against the ~s** c'est contraire au règlement; **by ~ of thumb** à vue de nez; **as a ~** normalement, en règle générale.

▶**rule out** *vt* exclure; **murder cannot be ~d out** l'hypothèse d'un meurtre ne peut être exclue.

ruled [ruːld] *adj* (*paper*) réglé(e).

ruler ['ruːlə*] *n* (*sovereign*) souverain/e; (*leader*) chef *m* (d'État); (*for measuring*) règle *f.*

ruling ['ruːlɪŋ] *adj* (*party*) au pouvoir; (*class*) dirigeant(e) ♦ *n* (*LAW*) décision *f.*

rum [rʌm] *n* rhum *m* ♦ *adj* (*BRIT col*) bizarre.

Rumania *etc* [ruːˈmeɪnɪə] = **Romania** *etc.*

rumble [ˈrʌmbl] *n* grondement *m*; gargouillement *m* ♦ *vi* gronder; (*stomach, pipe*) gargouiller.

rumbustious [rʌmˈbʌstʃəs], (*US*) **rumbunctious** [rʌmˈbʌŋkʃəs] *adj* (*person*) exubérant(e).

rummage [ˈrʌmɪdʒ] *vi* fouiller.

rumour, (*US*) **rumor** [ˈruːmə*] *n* rumeur *f*, bruit *m* (qui court) ♦ *vt*: **it is ~ed that** le bruit court que.

rump [rʌmp] *n* (*of animal*) croupe *f*; (*also*: ~ **steak**) romsteck *m*.

rumple [ˈrʌmpl] *vt* (*hair*) ébouriffer; (*clothes*) chiffonner, friper.

rumpus [ˈrʌmpəs] *n* (*col*) tapage *m*, chahut *m*; (*quarrel*) prise *f* de bec; **to kick up a ~** faire toute une histoire.

run [rʌn] *n* (*race etc*) course *f*; (*outing*) tour *m* or promenade *f* (en voiture); (*journey*) parcours *m*, trajet *m*; (*series*) suite *f*, série *f*; (*THEAT*) série de représentations; (*SKI*) piste *f*; (*in tights, stockings*) maille filée, échelle *f* ♦ *vb* (*pt* **ran**, *pp* **run** [ræn, rʌn]) *vt* (*business*) diriger; (*competition, course*) organiser; (*hotel, house*) tenir; (*COMPUT: program*) exécuter; (*force through: rope, pipe*): **to ~ sth through** faire passer qch à travers; (*to pass: hand, finger*): **to ~ sth over** promener or passer qch sur; (*water, bath*) faire couler ♦ *vi* courir; (*pass: road etc*) passer; (*work: machine, factory*) marcher; (*bus, train*) circuler; (*continue: play*) se jouer, être à l'affiche; (*: contract*) être valide or en vigueur; (*slide: drawer etc*) glisser; (*flow: river, bath*) couler; (*colours, washing*) déteindre; (*in election*) être candidat, se présenter; **to go for a ~** aller courir or faire un peu de course à pied; (*in car*) faire un tour or une promenade (en voiture); **to break into a ~** se mettre à courir; **a ~ of luck** une série de coups de chance; **to have the ~ of sb's house** avoir la maison de qn à sa disposition; **there was a ~ on** (*meat, tickets*) les gens se sont rués sur; **in the long ~** à longue échéance; à la longue; en fin de compte; **in the short ~** à brève échéance, à court terme; **on the ~** en fuite; **to make a ~ for it** s'enfuir; **I'll ~ you to the station** je vais vous emmener or conduire à la gare; **to ~ errands** faire des commissions; **the train ~s between Gatwick and Victoria** le train assure le service entre Gatwick et Victoria; **the bus ~s every 20 minutes** il y a un autobus toutes les 20 minutes; **it's very cheap to ~** (*car, machine*) c'est très économique; **to ~ on petrol** or (*US*) **gas/on diesel/off batteries** marcher à l'essence/au diesel/sur piles; **to ~ for president** être candidat à la présidence; **their losses ran into millions** leurs pertes se sont élevées à plusieurs millions; **to be ~ off one's feet** (*BRIT*) ne plus savoir où donner de la tête.

▶**run about** *vi* (*children*) courir çà et là.

▶**run across** *vt fus* (*find*) trouver par hasard.

▶**run away** *vi* s'enfuir.

▶**run down** *vi* (*clock*) s'arrêter (faute d'avoir été remonté) ♦ *vt* (*AUT*) renverser; (*BRIT: reduce: production*) réduire progressivement; (*: factory/shop*) réduire progressivement la production/l'activité de; (*criticize*) critiquer, dénigrer; **to be ~ down** être fatigué(e) or à plat.

▶**run in** *vt* (*BRIT: car*) roder.

▶**run into** *vt fus* (*meet: person*) rencontrer par hasard; (*: trouble*) se heurter à; (*collide with*) heurter; **to ~ into debt** contracter des dettes.

▶**run off** *vi* s'enfuir ♦ *vt* (*water*) laisser s'écouler.

▶**run out** *vi* (*person*) sortir en courant; (*liquid*) couler; (*lease*) expirer; (*money*) être épuisé(e).

▶**run out of** *vt fus* se trouver à court de; **I've ~ out of petrol** or (*US*) **gas** je suis en panne d'essence.

▶**run over** *vt* (*AUT*) écraser ♦ *vt fus* (*revise*) revoir, reprendre.

▶**run through** *vt fus* (*instructions*) reprendre, revoir.

▶**run up** *vt* (*debt*) laisser accumuler; **to ~ up against** (*difficulties*) se heurter à.

runaround [ˈrʌnəraund] *n* (*col*): **to give sb the ~** rester très évasif.

runaway [ˈrʌnəweɪ] *adj* (*horse*) emballé(e); (*truck*) fou(folle); (*inflation*) galopant(e).

rundown [ˈrʌndaun] *n* (*BRIT: of industry etc*) réduction progressive.

rung [rʌŋ] *pp of* **ring** ♦ *n* (*of ladder*) barreau *m*.

run-in [ˈrʌnɪn] *n* (*col*) accrochage *m*, prise *f* de bec.

runner [ˈrʌnə*] *n* (*in race: person*) coureur/euse; (*: horse*) partant *m*; (*on sledge*) patin *m*; (*for drawer etc*) coulisseau *m*; (*carpet: in hall etc*) chemin *m*.

runner bean *n* (*BRIT*) haricot *m* (à rames).

runner-up [rʌnərˈʌp] *n* second/e.

running [ˈrʌnɪŋ] *n* (*in race etc*) course *f*; (*of business*) direction *f*; (*of event*) organisation *f*; (*of machine etc*) marche *f*, fonctionnement *m* ♦ *adj* (*water*) courant(e); (*commentary*) suivi(e); **6 days ~** 6 jours de suite; **to be in/out of the ~ for sth** être/ne pas être sur les rangs pour qch.

running costs *npl* (*of business*) frais *mpl* de gestion; (*of car*): **the ~ are high** elle revient cher.

running head *n* (*TYP, WORD PROCESSING*) titre courant.

running mate *n* (*US POL*) *candidat à la vice-présidence.*

runny [ˈrʌnɪ] *adj* qui coule.

run-off [ˈrʌnɔf] *n* (*in contest, election*) deuxième tour *m*; (*extra race etc*) épreuve *f* supplémentaire.

run-of-the-mill ['rʌnəvðə'mɪl] *adj* ordinaire, banal(e).

runt [rʌnt] *n* (*also pej*) avorton *m*.

run-through ['rʌnθruː] *n* répétition *f*, essai *m*.

run-up ['rʌnʌp] *n* (*BRIT*): ~ **to sth** période *f* précédant qch.

runway ['rʌnweɪ] *n* (*AVIAT*) piste *f* (d'envol *or* d'atterrissage).

rupee [ruː'piː] *n* roupie *f*.

rupture ['rʌptʃə*] *n* (*MED*) hernie *f* ♦ *vt*: **to ~ o.s.** se donner une hernie.

rural ['ruərl] *adj* rural(e).

ruse [ruːz] *n* ruse *f*.

rush [rʌʃ] *n* course précipitée; (*of crowd*) ruée *f*, bousculade *f*; (*hurry*) hâte *f*, bousculade; (*current*) flot *m*; (*BOT*) jonc *m*; (*for chair*) paille *f* ♦ *vt* transporter *or* envoyer d'urgence; (*attack: town etc*) prendre d'assaut; (*BRIT col: overcharge*) estamper; faire payer ♦ *vi* se précipiter; **don't ~ me!** laissez-moi le temps de souffler!; **to ~ sth off** (*do quickly*) faire qch à la hâte; (*send*) envoyer d'urgence; **is there any ~ for this?** est-ce urgent?; **we've had a ~ of orders** nous avons reçu une avalanche de commandes; **I'm in a ~ (to do)** je suis vraiment pressé (de faire); **gold ~** ruée vers l'or.

▶**rush through** *vt fus* (*work*) exécuter à la hâte ♦ *vt* (*COMM: order*) exécuter d'urgence.

rush hour *n* heures *fpl* de pointe *or* d'affluence.

rush job *n* travail urgent.

rush matting *n* natte *f* de paille.

rusk [rʌsk] *n* biscotte *f*.

Russia ['rʌʃə] *n* Russie *f*.

Russian ['rʌʃən] *adj* russe ♦ *n* Russe *m/f*; (*LING*) russe *m*.

rust [rʌst] *n* rouille *f* ♦ *vi* rouiller.

rustic ['rʌstɪk] *adj* rustique ♦ *n* (*pej*) rustaud/e.

rustle ['rʌsl] *vi* bruire, produire un bruissement ♦ *vt* (*paper*) froisser; (*US: cattle*) voler.

rustproof ['rʌstpruːf] *adj* inoxydable.

rustproofing ['rʌstpruːfɪŋ] *n* traitement *m* antirouille.

rusty ['rʌstɪ] *adj* rouillé(e).

rut [rʌt] *n* ornière *f*; (*ZOOL*) rut *m*; **to be in a ~** (*fig*) suivre l'ornière, s'encroûter.

rutabaga [ruːtə'beɪgə] *n* (*US*) rutabaga *m*.

ruthless ['ruːθlɪs] *adj* sans pitié, impitoyable.

ruthlessness ['ruːθlɪsnɪs] *n* dureté *f*, cruauté *f*.

RV *abbr* (= *revised version*) *traduction anglaise de la Bible de 1885* ♦ *n abbr* (*US*) = **recreational vehicle**.

rye [raɪ] *n* seigle *m*.

rye bread *n* pain *m* de seigle.

S s

S, s [ɛs] *n* (*letter*) S, s *m*; (*US SCOL*: = *satisfactory*) ≈ assez bien; **S for Sugar** S comme Suzanne.

S *abbr* (= *south, small*) S; (= *saint*) St.

SA *n abbr* = **South Africa, South America**.

Sabbath ['sæbəθ] *n* (*Jewish*) sabbat *m*; (*Christian*) dimanche *m*.

sabbatical [sə'bætɪkl] *adj*: ~ **year** année *f* sabbatique.

sabotage ['sæbətɑːʒ] *n* sabotage *m* ♦ *vt* saboter.

saccharin(e) ['sækərɪn] *n* saccharine *f*.

sachet ['sæʃeɪ] *n* sachet *m*.

sack [sæk] *n* (*bag*) sac *m* ♦ *vt* (*dismiss*) renvoyer, mettre à la porte; (*plunder*) piller, mettre à sac; **to give sb the ~** renvoyer qn, mettre qn à la porte; **to get the ~** être renvoyé(e) *or* mis(e) à la porte.

sackful ['sækful] *n*: **a ~ of** un (plein) sac de.

sacking ['sækɪŋ] *n* toile *f* à sac; (*dismissal*) renvoi *m*.

sacrament ['sækrəmənt] *n* sacrement *m*.

sacred ['seɪkrɪd] *adj* sacré(e).

sacred cow *n* (*fig*) chose sacro-sainte.

sacrifice ['sækrɪfaɪs] *n* sacrifice *m* ♦ *vt* sacrifier; **to make ~s (for sb)** se sacrifier *or* faire des sacrifices (pour qn).

sacrilege ['sækrɪlɪdʒ] *n* sacrilège *m*.

sacrosanct ['sækrəusæŋkt] *adj* sacro-saint(e).

sad [sæd] *adj* (*unhappy*) triste; (*deplorable*) triste, fâcheux(euse).

sadden ['sædn] *vt* attrister, affliger.

saddle ['sædl] *n* selle *f* ♦ *vt* (*horse*) seller; **to be ~d with sth** (*col*) avoir qch sur les bras.

saddlebag ['sædlbæg] *n* sacoche *f*.

sadism ['seɪdɪzəm] *n* sadisme *m*.

sadist ['seɪdɪst] *n* sadique *m/f*.

sadistic [sə'dɪstɪk] *adj* sadique.

sadly ['sædlɪ] *adv* tristement; (*regrettably*) malheureusement.

sadness ['sædnɪs] *n* tristesse *f*.

sado-masochism [seɪdəu'mæsəkɪzəm] *n* sado-masochisme *m*.

sae *abbr* (*BRIT*: = *stamped addressed envelope*) *enveloppe affranchie pour la réponse*.

safari [sə'fɑːrɪ] *n* safari *m*.

safari park *n* réserve *f*.

safe [seɪf] *adj* (*out of danger*) hors de danger, en sécurité; (*not dangerous*) sans danger; (*cautious*) prudent(e); (*sure: bet etc*) assuré(e) ♦ *n* coffre-fort *m*; ~ **from** à l'abri de; ~ **and sound** sain(e) et sauf(sauve); **(just) to**

be on the ~ side pour plus de sûreté, par précaution; to play ~ ne prendre aucun risque; it is ~ to say that ... on peut dire sans crainte que ...; ~ journey! bon voyage!

safe bet n: it was a ~ ça ne comportait pas trop de risques; it's a ~ that he'll be late il y a toutes les chances pour qu'il soit en retard.

safe-breaker ['seɪfbreɪkə*] n (BRIT) perceur m de coffre-fort.

safe-conduct [seɪf'kɔndʌkt] n sauf-conduit m.

safe-cracker ['seɪfkrækə*] n = safe-breaker.

safe-deposit ['seɪfdɪpɔzɪt] n (vault) dépôt m de coffres-forts; (box) coffre-fort m.

safeguard ['seɪfgɑːd] n sauvegarde f, protection f ♦ vt sauvegarder, protéger.

safe haven n zone f de sécurité.

safekeeping ['seɪf'kiːpɪŋ] n bonne garde.

safely ['seɪflɪ] adv sans danger, sans risque; (without mishap) sans accident; I can ~ say ... je peux dire à coup sûr ....

safe passage n: to grant sb ~ accorder un laissez-passer à qn.

safe sex n rapports sexuels protégés.

safety ['seɪftɪ] n sécurité f; ~ first! la sécurité d'abord!

safety belt n ceinture f de sécurité.

safety catch n cran m de sûreté or sécurité.

safety net n filet m de sécurité.

safety pin n épingle f de sûreté or de nourrice.

safety valve n soupape f de sûreté.

saffron ['sæfrən] n safran m.

sag [sæg] vi s'affaisser, fléchir; pendre.

saga ['sɑːgə] n saga f; (fig) épopée f.

sage [seɪdʒ] n (herb) sauge f; (man) sage m.

Sagittarius [sædʒɪ'tɛərɪəs] n le Sagittaire; to be ~ être du Sagittaire.

sago ['seɪgəu] n sagou m.

Sahara [sə'hɑːrə] n: the ~ (Desert) le (désert du) Sahara m.

Sahel [sæ'hɛl] n Sahel m.

said [sɛd] pt, pp of say.

Saigon [saɪ'gɔn] n Saigon m.

sail [seɪl] n (on boat) voile f; (trip): to go for a ~ faire un tour en bateau ♦ vt (boat) manœuvrer, piloter ♦ vi (travel: ship) avancer, naviguer; (: passenger) aller or se rendre (en bateau); (set off) partir, prendre la mer; (SPORT) faire de la voile; they ~ed into Le Havre ils sont entrés dans le port du Havre.

▶sail through vi, vt fus (fig) réussir haut la main.

sailboat ['seɪlbəut] n (US) bateau m à voiles, voilier m.

sailing ['seɪlɪŋ] n (SPORT) voile f; to go ~ faire de la voile.

sailing boat n bateau m à voiles, voilier m.

sailing ship n grand voilier.

sailor ['seɪlə*] n marin m, matelot m.

saint [seɪnt] n saint/e.

saintly ['seɪntlɪ] adj saint(e), plein(e) de bonté.

sake [seɪk] n: for the ~ of (out of concern for) pour, dans l'intérêt de; (out of consideration for) par égard pour; (in order to achieve) pour plus de, par souci de; arguing for arguing's ~ discuter pour (le plaisir de) discuter; for the ~ of argument à titre d'exemple; for heaven's ~! pour l'amour du ciel!

salad ['sæləd] n salade f; tomato ~ salade de tomates.

salad bowl n saladier m.

salad cream n (BRIT) (sorte f de) mayonnaise f.

salad dressing n vinaigrette f.

salad oil n huile f de table.

salami [sə'lɑːmɪ] n salami m.

salaried ['sælərɪd] adj (staff) salarié(e), qui touche un traitement.

salary ['sælərɪ] n salaire m, traitement m.

salary scale n échelle f des traitements.

sale [seɪl] n vente f; (at reduced prices) soldes mpl; "for ~" "à vendre"; on ~ en vente; on ~ or return vendu(e) avec faculté de retour; closing-down or (US) liquidation ~ liquidation f (avant fermeture); ~ and lease back n cession-bail f.

saleroom ['seɪlruːm] n salle f des ventes.

sales assistant n (BRIT) vendeur/euse.

sales clerk n (US) vendeur/euse.

sales conference n réunion f de vente.

sales drive n campagne commerciale, animation f des ventes.

sales force n (ensemble m du) service des ventes.

salesman ['seɪlzmən] n vendeur m; (representative) représentant m de commerce.

sales manager n directeur commercial.

salesmanship ['seɪlzmənʃɪp] n art m de la vente.

sales tax n (US) taxe f à l'achat.

saleswoman ['seɪlzwumən] n vendeuse f.

salient ['seɪlɪənt] adj saillant(e).

saline ['seɪlaɪn] adj salin(e).

saliva [sə'laɪvə] n salive f.

sallow ['sæləu] adj cireux(euse).

sally forth, sally out ['sælɪ-] vi partir plein(e) d'entrain.

salmon ['sæmən] n (pl inv) saumon m.

salmon trout n truite saumonée.

saloon [sə'luːn] n (US) bar m; (BRIT AUT) berline f; (ship's lounge) salon m.

SALT [sɔːlt] n abbr (= Strategic Arms Limitation Talks/Treaty) SALT m.

salt [sɔːlt] n sel m ♦ vt saler ♦ cpd de sel; (CULIN) salé(e); an old ~ un vieux loup de mer.

▶salt away vt mettre de côté.

salt cellar n salière f.

salt-free ['sɔːlt'friː] adj sans sel.

saltwater ['sɔːlt'wɔːtə*] adj (fish etc) (d'eau) de mer.

salty ['sɔːltɪ] adj salé(e).

salubrious [sə'luːbrɪəs] adj salubre.

salutary ['sæljutərɪ] adj salutaire.

salute [səˈluːt] *n* salut *m* ♦ *vt* saluer.

salvage [ˈsælvɪdʒ] *n* (*saving*) sauvetage *m*; (*things saved*) biens sauvés *or* récupérés ♦ *vt* sauver, récupérer.

salvage vessel *n* bateau *m* de sauvetage.

salvation [sælˈveɪʃən] *n* salut *m*.

Salvation Army *n* Armée *f* du Salut.

salver [ˈsælvə*] *n* plateau *m* de métal.

salvo [ˈsælvəʊ] *n* salve *f*.

Samaritan [səˈmærɪtən] *n*: **the ~s** (*organization*) ≈ S.O.S. Amitié.

same [seɪm] *adj* même ♦ *pron*: **the ~** le(la) même, les mêmes; **the ~ book as** le même livre que; **on the ~ day** le même jour; **at the ~ time** en même temps; **all** *or* **just the ~** tout de même, quand même; **they're one and the ~** (*person/thing*) c'est une seule et même personne/chose; **to do the ~** faire de même, en faire autant; **to do the ~ as sb** faire comme qn; **and the ~ to you!** et à vous de même!; (*after insult*) toi-même!; **~ here!** moi aussi!; **the ~ again!** (*in bar etc*) la même chose!

sample [ˈsɑːmpl] *n* échantillon *m*; (*MED*) prélèvement *m* ♦ *vt* (*food, wine*) goûter; **to take a ~** prélever un échantillon; **free ~** échantillon gratuit.

sanatorium, *pl* **sanatoria** [sænəˈtɔːrɪəm, -rɪə] *n* sanatorium *m*.

sanctify [ˈsæŋktɪfaɪ] *vt* sanctifier.

sanctimonious [sæŋktɪˈməʊnɪəs] *adj* moralisateur(trice).

sanction [ˈsæŋkʃən] *n* sanction *f* ♦ *vt* cautionner, sanctionner; **to impose economic ~s on** *or* **against** prendre des sanctions économiques contre.

sanctity [ˈsæŋktɪtɪ] *n* sainteté *f*, caractère sacré.

sanctuary [ˈsæŋktjʊərɪ] *n* (*holy place*) sanctuaire *m*; (*refuge*) asile *m*; (*for wild life*) réserve *f*.

sand [sænd] *n* sable *m* ♦ *vt* sabler; (*also:* ~ **down:** *wood etc*) poncer.

sandal [ˈsændl] *n* sandale *f*.

sandbag [ˈsændbæg] *n* sac *m* de sable.

sandblast [ˈsændblɑːst] *vt* décaper à la sableuse.

sandbox [ˈsændbɒks] *n* (*US: for children*) tas *m* de sable.

sandcastle [ˈsændkɑːsl] *n* château *m* de sable.

sand dune *n* dune *f* de sable.

sander [ˈsændə*] *n* ponceuse *f*.

S&M *n abbr* (= *sadomasochism*) sadomasochisme *m*.

sandpaper [ˈsændpeɪpə*] *n* papier *m* de verre.

sandpit [ˈsændpɪt] *n* (*BRIT: for children*) tas *m* de sable.

sands [sændz] *npl* plage *f* (de sable).

sandstone [ˈsændstəʊn] *n* grès *m*.

sandstorm [ˈsændstɔːm] *n* tempête *f* de sable.

sandwich [ˈsændwɪtʃ] *n* sandwich *m* ♦ *vt* (*also:* ~ **in**) intercaler; **~ed between** pris en sandwich entre; **cheese/ham ~** sandwich au fromage/jambon.

sandwich board *n* panneau *m* publicitaire (porté par un homme-sandwich).

sandwich course *n* (*BRIT*) cours *m* de formation professionnelle.

sandy [ˈsændɪ] *adj* sablonneux(euse); couvert(e) de sable; (*colour*) sable *inv*, blond roux *inv*.

sane [seɪn] *adj* (*person*) sain(e) d'esprit; (*outlook*) sensé(e), sain(e).

sang [sæŋ] *pt of* **sing**.

sanguine [ˈsæŋgwɪn] *adj* optimiste.

sanitarium, *pl* **sanitaria** [sænɪˈtɛərɪəm, -rɪə] *n* (*US*) = **sanatorium**.

sanitary [ˈsænɪtərɪ] *adj* (*system, arrangements*) sanitaire; (*clean*) hygiénique.

sanitary towel, (*US*) **sanitary napkin** *n* serviette *f* hygiénique.

sanitation [sænɪˈteɪʃən] *n* (*in house*) installations *fpl* sanitaires; (*in town*) système *m* sanitaire.

sanitation department *n* (*US*) service *m* de voirie.

sanity [ˈsænɪtɪ] *n* santé mentale; (*common sense*) bon sens.

sank [sæŋk] *pt of* **sink**.

San Marino [ˈsænməˈriːnəʊ] *n* Saint-Marin *m*.

Santa Claus [sæntəˈklɔːz] *n* le Père Noël.

Santiago [sæntɪˈɑːgəʊ] *n* (*also:* ~ **de Chile**) Santiago (du Chili).

sap [sæp] *n* (*of plants*) sève *f* ♦ *vt* (*strength*) saper, miner.

sapling [ˈsæplɪŋ] *n* jeune arbre *m*.

sapphire [ˈsæfaɪə*] *n* saphir *m*.

sarcasm [ˈsɑːkæzm] *n* sarcasme *m*, raillerie *f*.

sarcastic [sɑːˈkæstɪk] *adj* sarcastique.

sarcophagus, *pl* **sarcophagi** [sɑːˈkɒfəgəs, -gaɪ] *n* sarcophage *m*.

sardine [sɑːˈdiːn] *n* sardine *f*.

Sardinia [sɑːˈdɪnɪə] *n* Sardaigne *f*.

Sardinian [sɑːˈdɪnɪən] *adj* sarde ♦ *n* Sarde *m/f*; (*LING*) sarde *m*.

sardonic [sɑːˈdɒnɪk] *adj* sardonique.

sari [ˈsɑːrɪ] *n* sari *m*.

sartorial [sɑːˈtɔːrɪəl] *adj* vestimentaire.

SAS *n abbr* (*BRIT MIL*: = *Special Air Service*) ≈ GIGN *m*.

SASE *n abbr* (*US*: = *self-addressed stamped envelope*) enveloppe affranchie pour la réponse.

sash [sæʃ] *n* écharpe *f*.

sash window *n* fenêtre *f* à guillotine.

Sask. *abbr* (*Canada*) = Saskatchewan.

SAT *n abbr* (*US*) = Scholastic Aptitude Test.

sat [sæt] *pt, pp of* **sit**.

Sat. *abbr* (= *Saturday*) sa.

Satan [ˈseɪtn] *n* Satan *m*.

satanic [səˈtænɪk] *adj* satanique, démoniaque.

satchel [ˈsætʃl] *n* cartable *m*.

sated [ˈseɪtɪd] *adj* repu(e); blasé(e).

satellite [ˈsætəlaɪt] *adj, n* satellite (*m*).

satellite television *n* télévision *f* par satellite.

satiate ['seɪʃɪeɪt] vt rassasier.

satin ['sætɪn] n satin m ♦ adj en or de satin, satiné(e); **with a ~ finish** satiné(e).

satire ['sætaɪə*] n satire f.

satirical [sə'tɪrɪkl] adj satirique.

satirist ['sætɪrɪst] n (writer) auteur m satirique; (cartoonist) caricaturiste m/f.

satirize ['sætɪraɪz] vt faire la satire de, satiriser.

satisfaction [sætɪs'fækʃən] n satisfaction f.

satisfactory [sætɪs'fæktərɪ] adj satisfaisant(e).

satisfied ['sætɪsfaɪd] adj satisfait(e); **to be ~ with sth** être satisfait de qch.

satisfy ['sætɪsfaɪ] vt satisfaire, contenter; (convince) convaincre, persuader; **to ~ the requirements** remplir les conditions; **to ~ sb (that)** convaincre qn (que); **to ~ o.s. of sth** vérifier qch, s'assurer de qch.

satisfying ['sætɪsfaɪɪŋ] adj satisfaisant(e).

satsuma [sæt'suːmə] n satsuma f.

saturate ['sætʃəreɪt] vt: **to ~ (with)** saturer (de).

saturated fat ['sætʃəreɪtɪd-] n graisse saturée.

saturation [sætʃə'reɪʃən] n saturation f.

Saturday ['sætədɪ] n samedi m; for phrases see also **Tuesday**.

sauce [sɔːs] n sauce f.

saucepan ['sɔːspən] n casserole f.

saucer ['sɔːsə*] n soucoupe f.

saucy ['sɔːsɪ] adj impertinent(e).

Saudi Arabia ['saudɪ-] n Arabie f Saoudite or Séoudite.

Saudi (Arabian) ['saudɪ-] adj saoudien(ne) ♦ n Saoudien/ne.

sauna ['sɔːnə] n sauna m.

saunter ['sɔːntə*] vi: **to ~ to** aller en flânant or se balader jusqu'à.

sausage ['sɔsɪdʒ] n saucisse f; (salami etc) saucisson m.

sausage roll n friand m.

sauté ['səuteɪ] adj (CULIN: potatoes) sauté(e); (: onions) revenu(e) ♦ vt faire sauter; faire revenir.

savage ['sævɪdʒ] adj (cruel, fierce) brutal(e), féroce; (primitive) primitif(ive), sauvage ♦ n sauvage m/f ♦ vt attaquer férocement.

savagery ['sævɪdʒrɪ] n sauvagerie f, brutalité f, férocité f.

save [seɪv] vt (person, belongings) sauver; (money) mettre de côté, économiser; (time) (faire) gagner; (food) garder; (COMPUT) sauvegarder; (avoid: trouble) éviter ♦ vi (also: ~ up) mettre de l'argent de côté ♦ n (SPORT) arrêt m (du ballon) ♦ prep sauf, à l'exception de; **it will ~ me an hour** ça me fera gagner une heure; **to ~ face** sauver la face; **God ~ the Queen!** vive la Reine!

saving ['seɪvɪŋ] n économie f ♦ adj: **the ~ grace of** ce qui rachète; **~s** npl économies fpl; **to make ~s** faire des économies.

savings account n compte m d'épargne.

savings bank n caisse f d'épargne.

saviour, (US) **savior** ['seɪvjə*] n sauveur m.

savour, (US) **savor** ['seɪvə*] n saveur f, goût m ♦ vt savourer.

savo(u)ry ['seɪvərɪ] adj savoureux(euse); (dish: not sweet) salé(e).

savvy ['sævɪ] n (col) jugeote f.

saw [sɔː] pt of see ♦ n (tool) scie f ♦ vt (pt sawed, pp sawed or sawn [sɔːn]) scier; **to ~ sth up** débiter qch à la scie.

sawdust ['sɔːdʌst] n sciure f.

sawmill ['sɔːmɪl] n scierie f.

sawn-off ['sɔːnɔf], (US) **sawed-off** ['sɔːdɔf] adj: **~ shotgun** carabine f à canon scié.

saxophone ['sæksəfəun] n saxophone m.

say [seɪ] n: **to have one's ~** dire ce qu'on a à dire ♦ vt (pt, pp said [sɛd]) dire; **to have a ~** avoir voix au chapitre; **could you ~ that again?** pourriez-vous répéter ceci?; **to ~ yes/no** dire oui/non; **she said (that) I was to give you this** elle m'a chargé de vous remettre ceci; **my watch ~s 3 o'clock** ma montre indique 3 heures, il est 3 heures à ma montre; **shall we ~ Tuesday?** disons mardi?; **that doesn't ~ much for him** ce n'est pas vraiment à son honneur; **when all is said and done** en fin de compte, en définitive; **there is something or a lot to be said for it** cela a des avantages; **that is to ~** c'est-à-dire; **to ~ nothing of** sans compter; **~ that ...** mettons or disons que ...; **that goes without ~ing** cela va sans dire, cela va de soi.

saying ['seɪɪŋ] n dicton m, proverbe m.

SBA n abbr (US: = Small Business Administration) organisme d'aide aux PME.

SC n abbr (US) = **supreme court** ♦ abbr (US) = South Carolina.

s/c abbr = **self-contained**.

scab [skæb] n croûte f; (pej) jaune m.

scabby ['skæbɪ] adj croûteux(euse).

scaffold ['skæfəld] n échafaud m.

scaffolding ['skæfəldɪŋ] n échafaudage m.

scald [skɔːld] n brûlure f ♦ vt ébouillanter.

scalding ['skɔːldɪŋ] adj (also: ~ hot) brûlant(e), bouillant(e).

scale [skeɪl] n (of fish) écaille f; (MUS) gamme f; (of ruler, thermometer etc) graduation f, échelle (graduée); (of salaries, fees etc) barème m; (of map, also size, extent) échelle ♦ vt (mountain) escalader; (fish) écailler; **pay ~** échelle des salaires; **~ of charges** tarif m (des consultations or prestations etc); **on a large ~** sur une grande échelle, en grand; **to draw sth to ~** dessiner qch à l'échelle; **small-~ model** modèle réduit.

▶**scale down** vt réduire.

scaled-down [skeɪl'daun] adj à échelle réduite.

scale drawing n dessin m à l'échelle.

scale model n modèle m à l'échelle.

scales [skeɪlz] *npl* balance *f*; (*larger*) bascule *f*.

scallion ['skæljən] *n* oignon *m*; (*US: shallot*) échalote *f*; (: *leek*) poireau *m*.

scallop ['skɔləp] *n* coquille *f* Saint-Jacques.

scalp [skælp] *n* cuir chevelu ♦ *vt* scalper.

scalpel ['skælpl] *n* scalpel *m*.

scalper ['skælpə*] *n* (*US col: of tickets*) revendeur *m* de billets.

scam [skæm] *n* (*col*) arnaque *f*.

scamp [skæmp] *vt* bâcler.

scamper ['skæmpə*] *vi*: **to ~ away, ~ off** détaler.

scampi ['skæmpɪ] *npl* langoustines (frites), scampi *mpl*.

scan [skæn] *vt* scruter, examiner; (*glance at quickly*) parcourir; (*poetry*) scander; (*TV, RADAR*) balayer ♦ *n* (*MED*) scanographie *f*.

scandal ['skændl] *n* scandale *m*; (*gossip*) ragots *mpl*.

scandalize ['skændəlaɪz] *vt* scandaliser, indigner.

scandalous ['skændələs] *adj* scandaleux(euse).

Scandinavia [skændɪ'neɪvɪə] *n* Scandinavie *f*.

Scandinavian [skændɪ'neɪvɪən] *adj* scandinave ♦ *n* Scandinave *m/f*.

scanner ['skænə*] *n* (*RADAR, MED*) scanner *m*, scanographe *m*.

scant [skænt] *adj* insuffisant(e).

scantily ['skæntɪlɪ] *adv*: **~ clad** *or* **dressed** vêtu(e) du strict minimum.

scanty ['skæntɪ] *adj* peu abondant(e), insuffisant(e), maigre.

scapegoat ['skeɪpgəʊt] *n* bouc *m* émissaire.

scar [skɑː] *n* cicatrice *f* ♦ *vt* laisser une cicatrice *or* une marque à.

scarce [skɛəs] *adj* rare, peu abondant(e).

scarcely ['skɛəslɪ] *adv* à peine, presque pas; **~ anybody** pratiquement personne; **I can ~ believe it** j'ai du mal à le croire.

scarcity ['skɛəsɪtɪ] *n* rareté *f*, manque *m*, pénurie *f*.

scarcity value *n* valeur *f* de rareté.

scare [skɛə*] *n* peur *f*, panique *f* ♦ *vt* effrayer, faire peur à; **to ~ sb stiff** faire une peur bleue à qn; **bomb ~** alerte *f* à la bombe.

▶**scare away, scare off** *vt* faire fuir.

scarecrow ['skɛəkrəʊ] *n* épouvantail *m*.

scared ['skɛəd] *adj*: **to be ~** avoir peur.

scaremonger ['skɛəmʌŋgə*] *n* alarmiste *m/f*.

scarf, *pl* **scarves** [skɑːf, skɑːvz] *n* (*long*) écharpe *f*; (*square*) foulard *m*.

scarlet ['skɑːlɪt] *adj* écarlate.

scarlet fever *n* scarlatine *f*.

scarper ['skɑːpə*] *vi* (*BRIT col*) ficher le camp.

scarves [skɑːvz] *npl of* **scarf**.

scary ['skɛərɪ] *adj* (*col*) qui fiche la frousse.

scathing ['skeɪðɪŋ] *adj* cinglant(e), acerbe; **to be ~ about sth** être très critique vis-à-vis de qch.

scatter ['skætə*] *vt* éparpiller, répandre; (*crowd*) disperser ♦ *vi* se disperser.

scatterbrained ['skætəbreɪnd] *adj* écervelé(e), étourdi(e).

scattered ['skætəd] *adj* épars(e), dispersé(e).

scatty ['skætɪ] *adj* (*BRIT col*) loufoque.

scavenge ['skævəndʒ] *vi* (*person*): **to ~ (for)** faire les poubelles (pour trouver); **to ~ for food** (*hyenas etc*) se nourrir de charognes.

scavenger ['skævəndʒə*] *n* éboueur *m*.

SCE *n abbr* = *Scottish Certificate of Education*.

scenario [sɪ'nɑːrɪəʊ] *n* scénario *m*.

scene [siːn] *n* (*THEAT, fig etc*) scène *f*; (*of crime, accident*) lieu(x) *m(pl)*, endroit *m*; (*sight, view*) spectacle *m*, vue *f*; **behind the ~s** (*also fig*) dans les coulisses; **to make a ~** (*col: fuss*) faire une scène *or* toute une histoire; **to appear on the ~** (*also fig*) faire son apparition, arriver; **the political ~** la situation politique.

scenery ['siːnərɪ] *n* (*THEAT*) décor(s) *m(pl)*; (*landscape*) paysage *m*.

scenic ['siːnɪk] *adj* scénique; offrant de beaux paysages *or* panoramas.

scent [sɛnt] *n* parfum *m*, odeur *f*; (*fig: track*) piste *f*; (*sense of smell*) odorat *m* ♦ *vt* parfumer; (*smell, also fig*) flairer; **to put** *or* **throw sb off the ~** (*fig*) mettre *or* lancer qn sur une mauvaise piste.

sceptic, (*US*) **skeptic** ['skɛptɪk] *n* sceptique *m/f*.

sceptical, (*US*) **skeptical** ['skɛptɪkl] *adj* sceptique.

scepticism, (*US*) **skepticism** ['skɛptɪsɪzəm] *n* scepticisme *m*.

sceptre, (*US*) **scepter** ['sɛptə*] *n* sceptre *m*.

schedule ['ʃɛdjuːl, (*US*) 'skɛdjuːl] *n* programme *m*, plan *m*; (*of trains*) horaire *m*; (*of prices etc*) barème *m*, tarif *m* ♦ *vt* prévoir; **as ~d** comme prévu; **on ~** à l'heure (prévue); **to be ahead of/behind ~** avoir de l'avance/du retard; **we are working to a very tight ~** notre programme de travail est très serré *or* intense; **everything went according to ~** tout s'est passé comme prévu.

scheduled ['ʃɛdjuːld, (*US*) 'skɛdjuːld] *adj* (*date, time*) prévu(e), indiqué(e); (*visit, event*) programmé(e), prévu(e); (*train, bus, stop, flight*) régulier(ière).

schematic [skɪ'mætɪk] *adj* schématique.

scheme [skiːm] *n* plan *m*, projet *m*; (*method*) procédé *m*; (*dishonest plan, plot*) complot *m*, combine *f*; (*arrangement*) arrangement *m*, classification *f*; (*pension ~ etc*) régime *m* ♦ *vt*, *vi* comploter, manigancer; **colour ~** combinaison *f* de(s) couleurs.

scheming ['skiːmɪŋ] *adj* rusé(e), intrigant(e) ♦ *n* manigances *fpl*, intrigues *fpl*.

schism ['skɪzəm] *n* schisme *m*.

schizophrenia [skɪtsə'friːnɪə] *n* schizophrénie *f*.

schizophrenic [skɪtsə'frɛnɪk] *adj* schizophrène.

scholar ['skɔlə*] n érudit/e.
scholarly ['skɔləlı] adj érudit(e), savant(e).
scholarship ['skɔləʃɪp] n érudition f; (grant) bourse f (d'études).
school [sku:l] n (gen) école f; (in university) faculté f; (secondary school) collège m, lycée m; (of fish) banc m ♦ cpd scolaire ♦ vt (animal) dresser.
school age n âge m scolaire.
schoolbook ['sku:lbuk] n livre m scolaire or de classe.
schoolboy ['sku:lbɔı] n écolier m; collégien m, lycéen m.
schoolchild, pl **-children** ['sku:ltʃaıld, -'tʃıldrən] n écolier/ière, collégien/ne, lycéen/ne.
schooldays ['sku:ldeız] npl années fpl de scolarité.
schoolgirl ['sku:lgə:l] n écolière f; collégienne f, lycéenne f.
schooling ['sku:lıŋ] n instruction f, études fpl.
school-leaver ['sku:lli:və*] n (BRIT) jeune qui vient de terminer ses études secondaires.
schoolmaster ['sku:lmɑ:stə*] n (primary) instituteur m; (secondary) professeur m.
schoolmistress ['sku:lmıstrıs] n (primary) institutrice f; (secondary) professeur m.
school report n (BRIT) bulletin m (scolaire).
schoolroom ['sku:lru:m] n (salle f de) classe f.
schoolteacher ['sku:lti:tʃə*] n (primary) instituteur/trice; (secondary) professeur m.
schoolyard ['sku:ljɑ:d] n (US) cour f de récréation.
schooner ['sku:nə*] n (ship) schooner m, goélette f; (glass) grand verre (à xérès).
sciatica [saı'ætıkə] n sciatique f.
science ['saıəns] n science f; the ~s les sciences; (SCOL) les matières fpl scientifiques.
science fiction n science-fiction f.
scientific [saıən'tıfık] adj scientifique.
scientist ['saıəntıst] n scientifique m/f.
sci-fi ['saıfaı] n abbr (col: = science fiction) SF f.
Scilly Isles ['sılı'aılz] npl, **Scillies** ['sılız] npl: the ~ les Sorlingues fpl, les îles fpl Scilly.
scintillating ['sıntıleıtıŋ] adj scintillant(e), étincelant(e); (wit etc) brillant(e).
scissors ['sızəz] npl ciseaux mpl; **a pair of ~** une paire de ciseaux.
sclerosis [sklı'rəusıs] n sclérose f.
scoff [skɔf] vt (BRIT col: eat) avaler, bouffer ♦ vi: **to ~ (at)** (mock) se moquer (de).
scold [skəuld] vt gronder, attraper, réprimander.
scolding ['skəuldıŋ] n réprimande f.
scone [skɔn] n sorte de petit pain rond au lait.
scoop [sku:p] n pelle f (à main); (for ice cream) boule f à glace; (PRESS) reportage exclusif or à sensation.
▶**scoop out** vt évider, creuser.
▶**scoop up** vt ramasser.
scooter ['sku:tə*] n (motor cycle) scooter m;

(toy) trottinette f.
scope [skəup] n (capacity: of plan, undertaking) portée f, envergure f; (: of person) compétence f, capacités fpl; (opportunity) possibilités fpl; **within the ~ of** dans les limites de; **there is plenty of ~ for improvement** (BRIT) cela pourrait être beaucoup mieux.
scorch [skɔ:tʃ] vt (clothes) brûler (légèrement), roussir; (earth, grass) dessécher, brûler.
scorched earth policy ['skɔ:tʃt-] n politique f de la terre brûlée.
scorcher ['skɔ:tʃə*] n (col: hot day) journée f torride.
scorching ['skɔ:tʃıŋ] adj torride, brûlant(e).
score [skɔ:*] n score m, décompte m des points; (MUS) partition f; (twenty) vingt ♦ vt (goal, point) marquer; (success) remporter; (cut: leather, wood, card) entailler, inciser ♦ vi marquer des points; (FOOTBALL) marquer un but; (keep score) compter les points; **on that ~** sur ce chapitre, à cet égard; **to have an old ~ to settle with sb** (fig) avoir un (vieux) compte à régler avec qn; **~s of** (fig) des tas de; **to ~ well/6 out of 10** obtenir un bon résultat/6 sur 10.
▶**score out** vt rayer, barrer, biffer.
scoreboard ['skɔ:bɔ:d] n tableau m.
scorecard ['skɔ:kɑ:d] n (SPORT) carton m, feuille f de marque.
scoreline ['skɔ:laın] n (SPORT) score m.
scorer ['skɔ:rə*] n (FOOTBALL) auteur m du but; buteur m; (keeping score) marqueur m.
scorn [skɔ:n] n mépris m, dédain m ♦ vt mépriser, dédaigner.
scornful ['skɔ:nful] adj méprisant(e), dédaigneux(euse).
Scorpio ['skɔ:pıəu] n le Scorpion; **to be ~** être du Scorpion.
scorpion ['skɔ:pıən] n scorpion m.
Scot [skɔt] n Écossais/e.
Scotch [skɔtʃ] n whisky m, scotch m.
scotch [skɔtʃ] vt faire échouer; enrayer; étouffer.
Scotch tape n ® scotch m ®, ruban adhésif.
scot-free ['skɔt'fri:] adj: **to get off ~** s'en tirer sans être puni(e) (or sans payer); s'en sortir indemne.
Scotland ['skɔtlənd] n Écosse f.
Scots [skɔts] adj écossais(e).
Scotsman ['skɔtsmən] n Écossais m.
Scotswoman ['skɔtswumən] n Écossaise f.
Scottish ['skɔtıʃ] adj écossais(e); **the ~ National Party** le parti national écossais.
scoundrel ['skaundrl] n vaurien m.
scour ['skauə*] vt (clean) récurer; frotter; décaper; (search) battre, parcourir.
scourer ['skauərə*] n tampon abrasif or à récurer; (powder) poudre f à récurer.
scourge [skə:dʒ] n fléau m.
scouring pad ['skauərıŋ-] n tampon abrasif or à récurer.

scout [skaut] *n* (*MIL*) éclaireur *m*; (*also*: **boy ~**) scout *m*.

▶**scout around** *vi* chercher.

scowl [skaul] *vi* se renfrogner, avoir l'air maussade; **to ~ at** regarder de travers.

scrabble ['skræbl] *vi* (*claw*): **to ~ (at)** gratter; **to ~ about** *or* **around for sth** chercher qch à tâtons ♦ *n*: **S~** ® Scrabble *m* ®.

scraggy ['skrægɪ] *adj* décharné(e), efflanqué(e), famélique.

scram [skræm] *vi* (*col*) ficher le camp.

scramble ['skræmbl] *n* bousculade *f*, ruée *f* ♦ *vi* avancer tant bien que mal (à quatre pattes *or* en grimpant); **to ~ for** se bousculer *or* se disputer pour (avoir); **to go scrambling** (*SPORT*) faire du trial.

scrambled eggs ['skræmbld-] *npl* œufs brouillés.

scrap [skræp] *n* bout *m*, morceau *m*; (*fight*) bagarre *f*; (*also*: **~ iron**) ferraille *f* ♦ *vt* jeter, mettre au rebut; (*fig*) abandonner, laisser tomber; **~s** *npl* (*waste*) déchets *mpl*; **to sell sth for ~** vendre qch à la casse *or* à la ferraille.

scrapbook ['skræpbuk] *n* album *m*.

scrap dealer *n* marchand *m* de ferraille.

scrape [skreɪp] *vt*, *vi* gratter, racler ♦ *n*: **to get into a ~** s'attirer des ennuis.

▶**scrape through** *vi* (*in exam etc*) réussir de justesse.

scraper ['skreɪpə*] *n* grattoir *m*, racloir *m*.

scrap heap *n* tas *m* de ferraille; (*fig*): **on the ~** au rancart *or* rebut.

scrap merchant *n* (*BRIT*) marchand *m* de ferraille.

scrap metal *n* ferraille *f*.

scrap paper *n* papier *m* brouillon.

scrappy ['skræpɪ] *adj* fragmentaire, décousu(e).

scrap yard *n* parc *m* à ferrailles; (*for cars*) cimetière *m* de voitures.

scratch [skrætʃ] *n* égratignure *f*, rayure *f*; éraflure *f*; (*from claw*) coup *m* de griffe ♦ *adj*: **~ team** équipe de fortune *or* improvisée ♦ *vt* (*record*) rayer; (*paint etc*) érafler; (*with claw, nail*) griffer; (*COMPUT*) effacer ♦ *vi* (se) gratter; **to start from ~** partir de zéro; **to be up to ~** être à la hauteur.

scrawl [skrɔːl] *n* gribouillage *m* ♦ *vi* gribouiller.

scrawny ['skrɔːnɪ] *adj* décharné(e).

scream [skriːm] *n* cri perçant, hurlement *m* ♦ *vi* crier, hurler; **to be a ~** (*col*) être impayable; **to ~ at sb to do sth** crier *or* hurler à qn de faire qch.

scree [skriː] *n* éboulis *m*.

screech [skriːtʃ] *n* cri strident, hurlement *m*; (*of tyres, brakes*) crissement *m*, grincement *m* ♦ *vi* hurler; crisser, grincer.

screen [skriːn] *n* écran *m*, paravent *m*; (*CINE, TV*) écran; (*fig*) écran, rideau *m* ♦ *vt* masquer, cacher; (*from the wind etc*) abriter,

protéger; (*film*) projeter; (*candidates etc*) filtrer; (*for illness*): **to ~ sb for sth** faire subir un test de dépistage de qch à qn.

screen editing [-'edɪtɪŋ] *n* (*COMPUT*) édition *f or* correction *f* sur écran.

screening ['skriːnɪŋ] *n* (*of film*) projection *f*; (*MED*) test *m* (*or* tests) de dépistage; (*for security*) filtrage *m*.

screen memory *n* (*COMPUT*) mémoire *f* écran.

screenplay ['skriːnpleɪ] *n* scénario *m*.

screen test *n* bout *m* d'essai.

screw [skruː] *n* vis *f*; (*propeller*) hélice *f* ♦ *vt* visser; (*col!: woman*) baiser (*!*); **to ~ sth to the wall** visser qch au mur; **to have one's head ~ed on** (*fig*) avoir la tête sur les épaules.

▶**screw up** *vt* (*paper, material*) froisser; (*col: ruin*) bousiller; **to ~ up one's face** faire la grimace.

screwdriver ['skruːdraɪvə*] *n* tournevis *m*.

screwed-up ['skruːd'ʌp] *adj* (*col*): **to be ~** être paumé(e).

screwy ['skruːɪ] *adj* (*col*) dingue, cinglé(e).

scribble ['skrɪbl] *n* gribouillage *m* ♦ *vt* gribouiller, griffonner; **to ~ sth down** griffonner qch.

scribe [skraɪb] *n* scribe *m*.

script [skrɪpt] *n* (*CINE etc*) scénario *m*, texte *m*; (*in exam*) copie *f*; (*writing*) (écriture *f*) script *m*.

scripted ['skrɪptɪd] *adj* (*RADIO, TV*) préparé(e) à l'avance.

Scripture ['skrɪptʃə*] *n* Écriture sainte.

scriptwriter ['skrɪptraɪtə*] *n* scénariste *m/f*, dialoguiste *m/f*.

scroll [skrəul] *n* rouleau *m* ♦ *vt* (*COMPUT*) faire défiler (sur l'écran).

scrotum ['skrəutəm] *n* scrotum *m*.

scrounge [skraundʒ] (*col*) *vt*: **to ~ sth (off** *or* **from sb)** se faire payer qch (par qn), emprunter qch (à qn) ♦ *vi*: **to ~ on sb** vivre aux crochets de qn.

scrounger ['skraundʒə*] *n* parasite *m*.

scrub [skrʌb] *n* (*clean*) nettoyage *m* (à la brosse); (*land*) broussailles *fpl* ♦ *vt* (*floor*) nettoyer à la brosse; (*pan*) récurer; (*washing*) frotter; (*reject*) annuler.

scrubbing brush ['skrʌbɪŋ-] *n* brosse dure.

scruff [skrʌf] *n*: **by the ~ of the neck** par la peau du cou.

scruffy ['skrʌfɪ] *adj* débraillé(e).

scrum(mage) ['skrʌm(ɪdʒ)] *n* mêlée *f*.

scruple ['skruːpl] *n* scrupule *m*; **to have no ~s about doing sth** n'avoir aucun scrupule à faire qch.

scrupulous ['skruːpjuləs] *adj* scrupuleux(euse).

scrupulously ['skruːpjuləslɪ] *adv* scrupuleusement; **to be ~ honest** être d'une honnêteté scrupuleuse.

scrutinize ['skruːtɪnaɪz] *vt* scruter, examiner

minutieusement.

scrutiny ['skruːtɪnɪ] n examen minutieux; **under the ~ of sb** sous la surveillance de qn.

scuba ['skuːbə] n scaphandre m (autonome).

scuba diving n plongée sous-marine (autonome).

scuff [skʌf] vt érafler.

scuffle ['skʌfl] n échauffourée f, rixe f.

scull [skʌl] n aviron m.

scullery ['skʌlərɪ] n arrière-cuisine f.

sculptor ['skʌlptə*] n sculpteur m.

sculpture ['skʌlptʃə*] n sculpture f.

scum [skʌm] n écume f, mousse f; (pej: people) rebut m, lie f.

scupper ['skʌpə*] vt (BRIT) saborder.

scurrilous ['skʌrɪləs] adj haineux(euse), virulent(e); calomnieux(euse).

scurry ['skʌrɪ] vi filer à toute allure; **to ~ off** détaler, se sauver.

scurvy ['skəːvɪ] n scorbut m.

scuttle ['skʌtl] n (NAUT) écoutille f; (also: **coal ~**) seau m (à charbon) ♦ vt (ship) saborder ♦ vi (scamper): **to ~ away, ~ off** détaler.

scythe [saɪð] n faux f.

SD, S. Dak. abbr (US) = **South Dakota.**

SDI n abbr (= Strategic Defense Initiative) IDS f.

SDLP n abbr (BRIT POL) = Social Democratic and Labour Party.

SDP n abbr (BRIT POL) = Social Democratic Party.

sea [siː] n mer f ♦ cpd marin(e), de (la) mer, maritime; **on the ~** (boat) en mer; (town) au bord de la mer; **by** or **beside the ~** (holiday) au bord de la mer; (village) près de la mer; **by ~** par mer, en bateau; **out to ~** au large; **(out) at ~** en mer; **heavy** or **rough ~(s)** grosse mer, mer agitée; **a ~ of faces** (fig) une multitude de visages; **to be all at ~** (fig) nager complètement.

sea bed n fond m de la mer.

sea bird n oiseau m de mer.

seaboard ['siːbɔːd] n côte f.

sea breeze n brise f de mer.

seafarer ['siːfɛərə*] n marin m.

seafaring ['siːfɛərɪŋ] adj (life) de marin; **~ people** les gens mpl de mer.

seafood ['siːfuːd] n fruits mpl de mer.

sea front n bord m de mer.

seagoing ['siːɡəʊɪŋ] adj (ship) de haute mer.

seagull ['siːɡʌl] n mouette f.

seal [siːl] n (animal) phoque m; (stamp) sceau m, cachet m; (impression) cachet, estampille f ♦ vt sceller; (envelope) coller; (: with seal) cacheter; (decide: sb's fate) décider (de); (: bargain) conclure; **~ of approval** approbation f.

▶**seal off** vt (close) condamner; (forbid entry to) interdire l'accès de.

sea level n niveau m de la mer.

sealing wax ['siːlɪŋ-] n cire f à cacheter.

sea lion n lion m de mer.

sealskin ['siːlskɪn] n peau f de phoque.

seam [siːm] n couture f; (of coal) veine f, filon

m; **the hall was bursting at the ~s** la salle était pleine à craquer.

seaman ['siːmən] n marin m.

seamanship ['siːmənʃɪp] n qualités fpl de marin.

seamless ['siːmlɪs] adj sans couture(s).

seamy ['siːmɪ] adj louche, mal famé(e).

seance ['seɪɒns] n séance f de spiritisme.

seaplane ['siːpleɪn] n hydravion m.

seaport ['siːpɔːt] n port m de mer.

search [səːtʃ] n (for person, thing) recherche(s) f(pl); (of drawer, pockets) fouille f; (LAW: at sb's home) perquisition f ♦ vt fouiller; (examine) examiner minutieusement; scruter ♦ vi: **to ~ for** chercher; **in ~ of** à la recherche de; **"~ and replace"** (COMPUT) "rechercher et remplacer".

▶**search through** vt fus fouiller.

searcher ['səːtʃə*] n chercheur/euse.

searching ['səːtʃɪŋ] adj (look, question) pénétrant(e); (examination) minutieux(euse).

searchlight ['səːtʃlaɪt] n projecteur m.

search party n expédition f de secours.

search warrant n mandat m de perquisition.

searing ['sɪərɪŋ] adj (heat) brûlant(e); (pain) aigu(ë).

seashore ['siːʃɔː*] n rivage m, plage f, bord m de (la) mer; **on the ~** sur le rivage.

seasick ['siːsɪk] adj: **to be ~** avoir le mal de mer.

seaside ['siːsaɪd] n bord m de la mer.

seaside resort n station f balnéaire.

season ['siːzn] n saison f ♦ vt assaisonner, relever; **to be in/out of ~** être/ne pas être de saison; **the busy ~** (for shops) la période de pointe; (for hotels etc) la pleine saison; **the open ~** (HUNTING) la saison de la chasse.

seasonal ['siːzənl] adj saisonnier(ière).

seasoned ['siːznd] adj (wood) séché(e); (fig: worker, actor, troops) expérimenté(e); **a ~ campaigner** un vieux militant, un vétéran.

seasoning ['siːznɪŋ] n assaisonnement m.

season ticket n carte f d'abonnement.

seat [siːt] n siège m; (in bus, train: place) place f; (PARLIAMENT) siège; (buttocks) postérieur m; (of trousers) fond m ♦ vt faire asseoir, placer; (have room for) avoir des places assises pour, pouvoir accueillir; **are there any ~s left?** est-ce qu'il reste des places?; **to take one's ~** prendre place; **to be ~ed** être assis; **please be ~ed** veuillez vous asseoir.

seat belt n ceinture f de sécurité.

seating capacity ['siːtɪŋ-] n nombre m de places assises.

SEATO ['siːtəʊ] n abbr (= Southeast Asia Treaty Organization) OTASE f (= Organisation du traité de l'Asie du Sud-Est).

sea urchin n oursin m.

sea water n eau f de mer.

seaweed ['siːwiːd] n algues fpl.

seaworthy ['siːwəːðɪ] adj en état de naviguer.

SEC n abbr (US: = Securities and Exchange Commission) ≈ COB *f* (= *Commission des opérations de Bourse*).

sec. *abbr* (= *second*) sec.

secateurs [sɛkə'təːz] *npl* sécateur *m*.

secede [sɪ'siːd] *vi* faire sécession.

secluded [sɪ'kluːdɪd] *adj* retiré(e), à l'écart.

seclusion [sɪ'kluːʒən] *n* solitude *f*.

second[1] ['sɛkənd] *num* deuxième, second(e) ♦ *adv* (*in race etc*) en seconde position ♦ *n* (*unit of time*) seconde *f*; (*in series, position*) deuxième *m/f*, second/e; (*BRIT SCOL*) ≈ licence *f* avec mention bien *or* assez bien; (*AUT: also*: ~ **gear**) seconde *f*; (*COMM: imperfect*) article *m* de second choix ♦ *vt* (*motion*) appuyer; **Charles the S**~ Charles II; **just a** ~! une seconde!, un instant!; (*stopping sb*) pas si vite!; ~ **floor** (*BRIT*) deuxième (étage) *m*; (*US*) premier (étage) *m*; **to ask for a** ~ **opinion** (*MED*) demander l'avis d'un autre médecin; **to have** ~ **thoughts (about doing sth)** changer d'avis (à propos de faire qch); **on** ~ **thoughts** *or* (*US*) **thought** à la réflexion.

second[2] [sɪ'kɔnd] *vt* (*employee*) détacher, mettre en détachement.

secondary ['sɛkəndərɪ] *adj* secondaire.

secondary school *n* collège *m*, lycée *m*.

Une **secondary school** *est un établissement d'enseignement pour les élèves de 11 à 18 ans, certains d'entre eux pouvant décider d'arrêter leurs études à 16 ans. La plupart de ces écoles sont des* **comprehensive schools** *sans examen d'entrée; mais certaines sont encore à recrutement sélectif; voir* **primary school**

second-best [sɛkənd'bɛst] *n* deuxième choix *m*; **as a** ~ faute de mieux.

second-class ['sɛkənd'klɑːs] *adj* de deuxième classe ♦ *adv*: **to send sth** ~ envoyer qch à tarif réduit; **to travel** ~ voyager en seconde; ~ **citizen** citoyen/ne de deuxième classe.

second cousin *n* cousin/e issu(e) de germains.

seconder ['sɛkəndə*] *n* personne *f* qui appuie une motion.

second-guess ['sɛkənd'gɛs] *vt* (*predict*) (essayer d')anticiper; **they're still trying to** ~ **his motives** ils essaient toujours de comprendre ses raisons.

second hand *n* (*on clock*) trotteuse *f*.

secondhand ['sɛkənd'hænd] *adj* d'occasion ♦ *adv* (*buy*) d'occasion; **to hear sth** ~ apprendre qch indirectement.

second-in-command ['sɛkəndɪnkə'mɑːnd] *n* (*MIL*) commandant *m* en second; (*ADMIN*) adjoint/e, sous-chef *m*.

secondly ['sɛkəndlɪ] *adv* deuxièmement; **firstly** ... ~ ... d'abord ... ensuite ... *or* de plus ...

secondment [sɪ'kɔndmənt] *n* (*BRIT*) détachement *m*.

second-rate ['sɛkənd'reɪt] *adj* de deuxième ordre, de qualité inférieure.

Second World War *n* Deuxième *or* Seconde Guerre mondiale.

secrecy ['siːkrəsɪ] *n* secret *m*; **in** ~ en secret, dans le secret.

secret ['siːkrɪt] *adj* secret(ète) ♦ *n* secret *m*; **in** ~ *adv* en secret, secrètement, en cachette; **to keep sth** ~ **from sb** cacher qch à qn, ne pas révéler qch à qn; **keep it** ~ n'en parle à personne; **to make no** ~ **of sth** ne pas cacher qch.

secret agent *n* agent secret.

secretarial [sɛkrɪ'tɛərɪəl] *adj* de secrétaire, de secrétariat.

secretariat [sɛkrɪ'tɛərɪət] *n* secrétariat *m*.

secretary ['sɛkrətrɪ] *n* secrétaire *m/f*; (*COMM*) secrétaire général; **S**~ **of State** (*US POL*) ≈ ministre *m* des Affaires étrangères; **S**~ **of State (for)** (*BRIT POL*) ministre *m* (de).

secretary-general ['sɛkrətrɪ'dʒɛnərl] *n* secrétaire général.

secrete [sɪ'kriːt] *vt* (*ANAT*, *BIOL*, *MED*) sécréter; (*hide*) cacher.

secretion [sɪ'kriːʃən] *n* sécrétion *f*.

secretive ['siːkrətɪv] *adj* réservé(e); (*pej*) cachottier(ière), dissimulé(e).

secretly ['siːkrɪtlɪ] *adv* en secret, secrètement, en cachette.

secret police *n* police secrète.

secret service *n* services secrets.

sect [sɛkt] *n* secte *f*.

sectarian [sɛk'tɛərɪən] *adj* sectaire.

section ['sɛkʃən] *n* coupe *f*, section *f*; (*department*) section; (*COMM*) rayon *m*; (*of document*) section, article *m*, paragraphe *m* ♦ *vt* sectionner; **the business** *etc* ~ (*PRESS*) la page des affaires *etc*.

sectional ['sɛkʃənl] *adj* (*drawing*) en coupe.

sector ['sɛktə*] *n* secteur *m*.

secular ['sɛkjulə*] *adj* profane; laïque; séculier(ière).

secure [sɪ'kjuə*] *adj* (*free from anxiety*) sans inquiétude, sécurisé(e); (*firmly fixed*) solide, bien attaché(e) (*or* fermé(e) *etc*); (*in safe place*) en lieu sûr, en sûreté ♦ *vt* (*fix*) fixer, attacher; (*get*) obtenir, se procurer; (*COMM*: *loan*) garantir; **to make sth** ~ bien fixer *or* attacher qch; **to** ~ **sth for sb** obtenir qch pour qn, procurer qch à qn.

secured creditor [sɪ'kjuəd-] *n* créancier/ière privilégié(e).

security [sɪ'kjuərɪtɪ] *n* sécurité *f*, mesures *fpl* de sécurité; (*for loan*) caution *f*, garantie *f*; **securities** *npl* (*STOCK EXCHANGE*) valeurs *fpl*, titres *mpl*; **to increase** *or* **tighten** ~ renforcer les mesures de sécurité; ~ **of tenure** stabilité *f* d'un emploi, titularisation *f*.

Security Council *n*: **the** ~ le Conseil de sécurité.

security forces *npl* forces *fpl* de sécurité.

security guard *n* garde chargé de la sécurité; (*transporting money*) convoyeur *m* de fonds.

security risk *n* menace *f* pour la sécurité de l'état (*or* d'une entreprise *etc*).
secy *abbr* (= *secretary*) secr.
sedan [sə'dæn] *n* (*US AUT*) berline *f*.
sedate [sɪ'deɪt] *adj* calme; posé(e) ♦ *vt* donner des sédatifs à.
sedation [sɪ'deɪʃən] *n* (*MED*) sédation *f*; **to be under** ~ être sous calmants.
sedative ['sɛdɪtɪv] *n* calmant *m*, sédatif *m*.
sedentary ['sɛdntrɪ] *adj* sédentaire.
sediment ['sɛdɪmənt] *n* sédiment *m*, dépôt *m*.
sedition [sɪ'dɪʃən] *n* sédition *f*.
seduce [sɪ'djuːs] *vt* séduire.
seduction [sɪ'dʌkʃən] *n* séduction *f*.
seductive [sɪ'dʌktɪv] *adj* séduisant(e), séducteur(trice).
see [siː] *vb* (*pt* **saw**, *pp* **seen** [sɔː, siːn]) *vt* (*gen*) voir; (*accompany*): **to** ~ **sb to the door** reconduire *or* raccompagner qn jusqu'à la porte ♦ *vi* voir ♦ *n* évêché *m*; **to** ~ **that** (*ensure*) veiller à ce que + *sub*, faire en sorte que + *sub*, s'assurer que; **there was nobody to be** ~**n** il n'y avait pas un chat; **let me** ~ (*show me*) fais(-moi) voir; (*let me think*) voyons (un peu); **to go and** ~ **sb** aller voir qn; ~ **for yourself** voyez vous-même; **I don't know what she** ~**s in him** je ne sais pas ce qu'elle lui trouve; **as far as I can** ~ pour autant que je puisse en juger; ~ **you!** au revoir!, à bientôt!; ~ **you soon/later/tomorrow!** à bientôt/plus tard/demain!
▶**see about** *vt fus* (*deal with*) s'occuper de.
▶**see off** *vt* accompagner (à la gare *or* à l'aéroport *etc*).
▶**see through** *vt* mener à bonne fin ♦ *vt fus* voir clair dans.
▶**see to** *vt fus* s'occuper de, se charger de.
seed [siːd] *n* graine *f*; (*fig*) germe *m*; (*TENNIS etc*) tête *f* de série; **to go to** ~ monter en graine; (*fig*) se laisser aller.
seedless ['siːdlɪs] *adj* sans pépins.
seedling ['siːdlɪŋ] *n* jeune plant *m*, semis *m*.
seedy ['siːdɪ] *adj* (*shabby*) minable, miteux(euse).
seeing ['siːɪŋ] *conj*: ~ (**that**) vu que, étant donné que.
seek, · *pt, pp* **sought** [siːk, sɔːt] *vt* chercher, rechercher; **to** ~ **advice/help from sb** demander conseil/de l'aide à qn.
▶**seek out** *vt* (*person*) chercher.
seem [siːm] *vi* sembler, paraître; **there** ~**s to be** ... il semble qu'il y a ..., on dirait qu'il y a ...; **it** ~**s (that)** ... il semble que ...; **what** ~**s to be the trouble?** qu'est-ce qui ne va pas?
seemingly ['siːmɪŋlɪ] *adv* apparemment.
seen [siːn] *pp of* **see**.
seep [siːp] *vi* suinter, filtrer.
seer [sɪə*] *n* prophète/prophétesse, voyant/e.
seersucker ['sɪəsʌkə*] *n* cloqué *m*, étoffe cloquée.
seesaw ['siːsɔː] *n* (jeu *m* de) bascule *f*.
seethe [siːð] *vi* être en effervescence; **to** ~ **with anger** bouillir de colère.
see-through ['siːθruː] *adj* transparent(e).
segment ['sɛgmənt] *n* segment *m*.
segregate ['sɛgrɪgeɪt] *vt* séparer, isoler.
segregation [sɛgrɪ'geɪʃən] *n* ségrégation *f*.
Seine [seɪn] *n*: **the** ~ la Seine.
seismic ['saɪzmɪk] *adj* sismique.
seize [siːz] *vt* (*grasp*) saisir, attraper; (*take possession of*) s'emparer de; (*LAW*) saisir.
▶**seize up** *vi* (*TECH*) se gripper.
▶**seize (up)on** *vt fus* saisir, sauter sur.
seizure ['siːʒə*] *n* (*MED*) crise *f*, attaque *f*; (*LAW*) saisie *f*.
seldom ['sɛldəm] *adv* rarement.
select [sɪ'lɛkt] *adj* choisi(e), d'élite; (*hotel, restaurant, club*) chic *inv*, sélect *inv* ♦ *vt* sélectionner, choisir; **a** ~ **few** quelques privilégiés.
selection [sɪ'lɛkʃən] *n* sélection *f*, choix *m*.
selection committee *n* comité *m* de sélection.
selective [sɪ'lɛktɪv] *adj* sélectif(ive); (*school*) à recrutement sélectif.
selector [sɪ'lɛktə*] *n* (*person*) sélectionneur/euse; (*TECH*) sélecteur *m*.
self [sɛlf] *n* (*pl* **selves** [sɛlvz]): **the** ~ le moi *inv* ♦ *prefix* auto-.
self-addressed ['sɛlfə'drɛst] *adj*: ~ **envelope** enveloppe *f* à mon (*or* votre *etc*) nom.
self-adhesive [sɛlfəd'hiːzɪv] *adj* autocollant(e).
self-assertive [sɛlfə'səːtɪv] *adj* autoritaire.
self-assurance [sɛlfə'ʃuərəns] *n* assurance *f*.
self-assured [sɛlfə'ʃuəd] *adj* sûr(e) de soi, plein(e) d'assurance.
self-catering [sɛlf'keɪtərɪŋ] *adj* (*BRIT: flat*) avec cuisine, où l'on peut faire sa cuisine; (: *holiday*) en appartement (*or* chalet *etc*) loué.
self-centred, (*US*) **self-centered** [sɛlf'sɛntəd] *adj* égocentrique.
self-cleaning [sɛlf'kliːnɪŋ] *adj* autonettoyant(e).
self-confessed [sɛlfkən'fɛst] *adj* (*alcoholic etc*) déclaré(e), qui ne s'en cache pas.
self-confidence [sɛlf'kɔnfɪdns] *n* confiance *f* en soi.
self-conscious [sɛlf'kɔnʃəs] *adj* timide, qui manque d'assurance.
self-contained [sɛlfkən'teɪnd] *adj* (*BRIT: flat*) avec entrée particulière, indépendant(e).
self-control [sɛlfkən'trəul] *n* maîtrise *f* de soi.
self-defeating [sɛlfdɪ'fiːtɪŋ] *adj* qui a un effet contraire à l'effet recherché.
self-defence, (*US*) **self-defense** [sɛlfdɪ'fɛns] *n* légitime défense *f*.
self-discipline [sɛlf'dɪsɪplɪn] *n* discipline personnelle.
self-employed [sɛlfɪm'plɔɪd] *adj* qui travaille à son compte.
self-esteem [sɛlfɪ'stiːm] *n* amour-propre *m*.
self-evident [sɛlf'ɛvɪdnt] *adj* évident(e), qui va de soi.
self-explanatory [sɛlfɪk'splænətrɪ] *adj* qui se

passe d'explication.

self-governing [sɛlf'gʌvənɪŋ] *adj* autonome.

self-help ['sɛlf'hɛlp] *n* initiative personnelle, efforts personnels.

self-importance [sɛlfɪm'pɔːtns] suffisance *f*.

self-indulgent [sɛlfɪn'dʌldʒənt] *adj* qui ne se refuse rien.

self-inflicted [sɛlfɪn'flɪktɪd] *adj* volontaire.

self-interest [sɛlf'ɪntrɪst] *n* intérêt personnel.

selfish ['sɛlfɪʃ] *adj* égoïste.

selfishness ['sɛlfɪʃnɪs] *n* égoïsme *m*.

selfless ['sɛlflɪs] *adj* désintéressé(e).

selflessly ['sɛlflɪslɪ] *adv* sans penser à soi.

self-made man ['sɛlfmeɪd-] *n* self-made man *m*.

self-pity [sɛlf'pɪtɪ] *n* apitoiement *m* sur soi-même.

self-portrait [sɛlf'pɔːtreɪt] *n* autoportrait *m*.

self-possessed [sɛlfpə'zɛst] *adj* assuré(e).

self-preservation [sɛlfprɛzə'veɪʃən] *n* instinct *m* de conservation.

self-raising [sɛlf'reɪzɪŋ], (*US*) **self-rising** [sɛlf'raɪzɪŋ] *adj*: ~ **flour** farine *f* pour gâteaux (*avec levure incorporée*).

self-reliant [sɛlfrɪ'laɪənt] *adj* indépendant(e).

self-respect [sɛlfrɪs'pɛkt] *n* respect *m* de soi, amour-propre *m*.

self-respecting [sɛlfrɪs'pɛktɪŋ] *adj* qui se respecte.

self-righteous [sɛlf'raɪtʃəs] *adj* satisfait(e) de soi, pharisaïque.

self-rising [sɛlf'raɪzɪŋ] *adj* (*US*) = **self-raising**.

self-sacrifice [sɛlf'sækrɪfaɪs] *n* abnégation *f*.

self-same ['sɛlfseɪm] *adj* même.

self-satisfied [sɛlf'sætɪsfaɪd] *adj* content(e) de soi, suffisant(e).

self-sealing [sɛlf'siːlɪŋ] *adj* (*envelope*) autocollant(e).

self-service [sɛlf'sɔːvɪs] *adj*, *n* libre-service (*m*), self-service (*m*).

self-styled ['sɛlfstaɪld] *adj* soi-disant *inv*.

self-sufficient [sɛlfsə'fɪʃənt] *adj* indépendant(e).

self-supporting [sɛlfsə'pɔːtɪŋ] *adj* financièrement indépendant(e).

self-taught [sɛlf'tɔːt] *adj* autodidacte.

self-test ['sɛlftɛst] *n* (*COMPUT*) test *m* automatique.

sell, *pt, pp* **sold** [sɛl, səuld] *vt* vendre ♦ *vi* se vendre; **to** ~ **at** *or* **for 10 F** se vendre 10 F; **to** ~ **sb an idea** (*fig*) faire accepter une idée à qn.

►**sell off** *vt* liquider.

►**sell out** *vi*: **to** ~ **out (to)** (*COMM*) vendre son fonds *or* son affaire (à) ♦ *vt* vendre tout son stock de; **the tickets are all sold out** il ne reste plus de billets.

►**sell up** *vi* vendre son fonds *or* son affaire.

sell-by date ['sɛlbaɪ-] *n* date *f* limite de vente.

seller ['sɛlə*] *n* vendeur/euse, marchand/e; ~'**s market** marché *m* à la hausse.

selling price ['sɛlɪŋ-] *n* prix *m* de vente.

Sellotape ['sɛləuteɪp] *n* ® (*BRIT*) papier collant, scotch *m* ®.

sellout ['sɛlaut] *n* trahison *f*, capitulation *f*; (*of tickets*): **it was a** ~ tous les billets ont été vendus.

selves [sɛlvz] *npl of* **self**.

semantic [sɪ'mæntɪk] *adj* sémantique.

semantics [sɪ'mæntɪks] *n* sémantique *f*.

semaphore ['sɛməfɔː*] *n* signaux *mpl* à bras; (*RAIL*) sémaphore *m*.

semblance ['sɛmblns] *n* semblant *m*.

semen ['siːmən] *n* sperme *m*.

semester [sɪ'mɛstə*] *n* (*esp US*) semestre *m*.

semi... ['sɛmɪ] *prefix* semi-, demi-; à demi, à moitié ♦ *n*: **semi** = **semidetached** (**house**).

semi-breve ['sɛmɪbriːv] *n* (*BRIT*) ronde *f*.

semicircle ['sɛmɪsəːkl] *n* demi-cercle *m*.

semicircular ['sɛmɪ'səːkjulə*] *adj* en demi-cercle, semi-circulaire.

semicolon [sɛmɪ'kəulən] *n* point-virgule *m*.

semiconductor [sɛmɪkən'dʌktə*] *n* semiconducteur *m*.

semiconscious [sɛmɪ'kɔnʃəs] *adj* à demi conscient(e).

semidetached (house) [sɛmɪdɪ'tætʃt-] *n* (*BRIT*) maison jumelée *or* jumelle.

semifinal [sɛmɪ'faɪnl] *n* demi-finale *f*.

seminar ['sɛmɪnɑː*] *n* séminaire *m*.

seminary ['sɛmɪnərɪ] *n* (*REL: for priests*) séminaire *m*.

semiprecious [sɛmɪ'prɛʃəs] *adj* semi-précieux(euse).

semiquaver ['sɛmɪkweɪvə*] *n* (*BRIT*) double croche *f*.

semiskilled [sɛmɪ'skɪld] *adj*: ~ **worker** ouvrier/ière spécialisé(e).

semi-skimmed ['sɛmɪ'skɪmd] *adj* demi-écrémé(e).

semitone ['sɛmɪtəun] *n* (*MUS*) demi-ton *m*.

semolina [sɛmə'liːnə] *n* semoule *f*.

SEN *n abbr* (*BRIT*) = *State Enrolled Nurse*.

Sen., sen. *abbr* = *senator, senior*.

senate ['sɛnɪt] *n* sénat *m*.

Le **Senate** *est la chambre haute du* **Congress**, *le parlement des États-Unis. Il est composé de 100 sénateurs, 2 par État, élus au suffrage universel direct tous les 6 ans, un tiers d'entre eux étant renouvelé tous les 2 ans.*

---

senator ['sɛnɪtə*] *n* sénateur *m*.

send, *pt, pp* **sent** [sɛnd, sɛnt] *vt* envoyer; **to** ~ **by post** *or* (*US*) **mail** envoyer *or* expédier par la poste; **to** ~ **sb for sth** envoyer qn chercher qch; **to** ~ **word that ...** faire dire que ...; **she** ~**s (you) her love** elle vous adresse ses amitiés; **to** ~ **sb to Coventry** (*BRIT*) mettre qn en quarantaine; **to** ~ **sb to sleep** endormir qn; **to** ~ **sb into fits of laughter** faire rire qn aux éclats; **to** ~ **sth flying** envoyer valser qch.

►**send away** *vt* (*letter, goods*) envoyer, expédier.

▶**send away for** vt fus commander par correspondance, se faire envoyer.

▶**send back** vt renvoyer.

▶**send for** vt fus envoyer chercher; faire venir; (by post) se faire envoyer, commander par correspondance.

▶**send in** vt (report, application, resignation) remettre.

▶**send off** vt (goods) envoyer, expédier; (BRIT SPORT: player) expulser or renvoyer du terrain.

▶**send on** vt (BRIT: letter) faire suivre; (luggage etc: in advance) (faire) expédier à l'avance.

▶**send out** vt (invitation) envoyer (par la poste); (emit: light, heat, signals) émettre.

▶**send round** vt (letter, document etc) faire circuler.

▶**send up** vt (person, price) faire monter; (BRIT: parody) mettre en boîte, parodier.

sender ['sɛndə*] n expéditeur/trice.

send-off ['sɛndɔf] n: **a good** ~ des adieux chaleureux.

Senegal [sɛnɪ'gɔːl] n Sénégal m.

Senegalese [sɛnɪgə'liːz] adj sénégalais(e) ♦ n (pl inv) Sénégalais/e.

senile ['siːnaɪl] adj sénile.

senility [sɪ'nɪlɪtɪ] n sénilité f.

senior ['siːnɪə*] adj (older) aîné(e), plus âgé(e); (of higher rank) supérieur(e) ♦ n aîné/e; (in service) personne f qui a plus d'ancienneté; **P. Jones** ~ P. Jones père.

senior citizen n personne âgée.

senior high school n (US) ≈ lycée m.

seniority [siːnɪ'ɔrɪtɪ] n priorité f d'âge, ancienneté f; (in rank) supériorité f (hiérarchique).

sensation [sɛn'seɪʃən] n sensation f; **to create a** ~ faire sensation.

sensational [sɛn'seɪʃənl] adj qui fait sensation; (marvellous) sensationnel(le).

sense [sɛns] n sens m; (feeling) sentiment m; (meaning) signification f; (wisdom) bon sens ♦ vt sentir, pressentir; ~**s** npl raison f; **it makes** ~ c'est logique; ~ **of humour** sens de l'humour; **there is no** ~ **in (doing)** that cela n'a pas de sens; **to come to one's** ~**s** (regain consciousness) reprendre conscience; (become reasonable) revenir à la raison; **to take leave of one's** ~**s** perdre la tête.

senseless ['sɛnslɪs] adj insensé(e), stupide; (unconscious) sans connaissance.

sensibility [sɛnsɪ'bɪlɪtɪ] n sensibilité f; **sensibilities** npl susceptibilité f.

sensible ['sɛnsɪbl] adj sensé(e), raisonnable; (shoes etc) pratique.

sensitive ['sɛnsɪtɪv] adj: ~ **(to)** sensible (à); **he is very** ~ **about it** c'est un point très sensible (chez lui).

sensitivity [sɛnsɪ'tɪvɪtɪ] n sensibilité f.

sensual ['sɛnsjuəl] adj sensuel(le).

sensuous ['sɛnsjuəs] adj voluptueux(euse),

sensuel(le).

sent [sɛnt] pt, pp of **send**.

sentence ['sɛntns] n (LING) phrase f; (LAW: judgment) condamnation f, sentence f; (: punishment) peine f ♦ vt: **to** ~ **sb to death/to 5 years** condamner qn à mort/à 5 ans; **to pass** ~ **on sb** prononcer une peine contre qn.

sentiment ['sɛntɪmənt] n sentiment. m; (opinion) opinion f, avis m.

sentimental [sɛntɪ'mɛntl] adj sentimental(e).

sentimentality [sɛntɪmɛn'tælɪtɪ] n sentimentalité f, sensiblerie f.

sentry ['sɛntrɪ] n sentinelle f, factionnaire m.

sentry duty n: **to be on** ~ être de faction.

Seoul [səul] n Séoul.

separable ['sɛprəbl] adj séparable.

separate adj ['sɛprɪt] séparé(e), indépendant(e), différent(e) ♦ vb ['sɛpəreɪt] vt séparer ♦ vi se séparer; ~ **from** distinct(e) de; **under** ~ **cover** (COMM) sous pli séparé; **to** ~ **into** diviser en.

separately ['sɛprɪtlɪ] adv séparément.

separates ['sɛprɪts] npl (clothes) coordonnés mpl.

separation [sɛpə'reɪʃən] n séparation f.

Sept. abbr (= September) sept.

September [sɛp'tɛmbə*] n septembre m; for phrases see also **July**.

septic ['sɛptɪk] adj septique; (wound) infecté(e); **to go** ~ s'infecter.

septicaemia [sɛptɪ'siːmɪə] n septicémie f.

septic tank n fosse f septique.

sequel ['siːkwl] n conséquence f; séquelles fpl; (of story) suite f.

sequence ['siːkwəns] n ordre m, suite f; **in** ~ par ordre, dans l'ordre, les uns après les autres; ~ **of tenses** concordance f des temps.

sequential [sɪ'kwɛnʃəl] adj: ~ **access** (COMPUT) accès séquentiel.

sequin ['siːkwɪn] n paillette f.

Serb [sɔːb] adj, n = **Serbian**.

Serbia ['sɔːbɪə] n Serbie f.

Serbian ['sɔːbɪən] adj serbe ♦ n Serbe m/f; (LING) serbe m.

Serbo-Croat ['sɔːbəu'krəuæt] n (LING) serbo-croate m.

serenade [sɛrə'neɪd] n sérénade f ♦ vt donner une sérénade à.

serene [sɪ'riːn] adj serein(e), calme, paisible.

serenity [sə'rɛnɪtɪ] n sérénité f, calme m.

sergeant ['sɑːdʒənt] n sergent m; (POLICE) brigadier m.

sergeant major n sergent-major m.

serial ['sɪərɪəl] n feuilleton m ♦ adj (COMPUT: interface, printer) série inv; (: access) séquentiel(le).

serialize ['sɪərɪəlaɪz] vt publier (or adapter) en feuilleton.

serial killer n meurtrier m tuant en série.

serial number n numéro m de série.

series ['sɪərɪz] n série f; (PUBLISHING) collection *f*.

serious ['sɪərɪəs] *adj* sérieux(euse); (*accident etc*) grave; **are you ~ (about it?)** parlez-vous sérieusement?

seriously ['sɪərɪəslɪ] *adv* sérieusement, gravement; **~ rich/difficult** (*col: extremely*) drôlement riche/difficile; **to take sth/sb ~** prendre qch/qn au sérieux.

seriousness ['sɪərɪəsnɪs] *n* sérieux *m*, gravité *f*.

sermon ['sə:mən] *n* sermon *m*.

serrated [sɪ'reɪtɪd] *adj* en dents de scie.

serum ['sɪərəm] *n* sérum *m*.

servant ['sə:vənt] *n* domestique *m/f*; (*fig*) serviteur/servante.

serve [sə:v] *vt* (*employer etc*) servir, être au service de; (*purpose*) servir à; (*customer, food, meal*) servir; (*apprenticeship*) faire, accomplir; (*prison term*) faire; purger ♦ *vi* (*also TENNIS*) servir; (*be useful*): **to ~ as/for/to do** servir de/à/à faire ♦ *n* (*TENNIS*) service *m*; **are you being ~d?** est-ce qu'on s'occupe de vous?; **to ~ on a committee/jury** faire partie d'un comité/jury; **it ~s him right** c'est bien fait pour lui; **it ~s my purpose** cela fait mon affaire.

►**serve out, serve up** *vt* (*food*) servir.

service ['sə:vɪs] *n* (*gen*) service *m*; (*AUT: maintenance*) révision *f*; (*REL*) office *m* ♦ *vt* (*car, washing machine*) réviser; **the S~s** *npl* les forces armées; **to be of ~ to sb, to do sb a ~** rendre service à qn; **to put one's car in for ~** donner sa voiture à réviser; **dinner ~** service de table.

serviceable ['sə:vɪsəbl] *adj* pratique, commode.

service area *n* (*on motorway*) aire *f* de services.

service charge *n* (*BRIT*) service *m*.

service industries *npl* les industries *fpl* de service, les services *mpl*.

serviceman ['sə:vɪsmən] *n* militaire *m*.

service station *n* station-service *f*.

serviette [sə:vɪ'ɛt] *n* (*BRIT*) serviette *f* (de table).

servile ['sə:vaɪl] *adj* servile.

session ['sɛʃən] *n* (*sitting*) séance *f*; (*SCOL*) année *f* scolaire (*or* universitaire); **to be in ~** siéger, être en session *or* en séance.

session musician *n* musicien/ne de studio.

set [sɛt] *n* série *f*, assortiment *m*; (*of tools etc*) jeu *m*; (*RADIO, TV*) poste *m*; (*TENNIS*) set *m*; (*group of people*) cercle *m*, milieu *m*; (*CINE*) plateau *m*; (*THEAT: stage*) scène *f*; (: *scenery*) décor *m*; (*MATH*) ensemble *m*; (*HAIRDRESSING*) mise *f* en plis ♦ *adj* (*fixed*) fixe, déterminé(e); (*ready*) prêt(e) ♦ *vb* (*pt, pp* **set**) *vt* (*place*) mettre, poser, placer; (*fix, establish*) fixer; (: *record*) établir; (*assign: task, homework*) donner; (*adjust*) régler; (*decide: rules etc*) fixer, choisir; (*TYP*) composer ♦ *vi* (*sun*) se coucher; (*jam, jelly, concrete*) prendre; **to be**

~ on doing être résolu(e) à faire; **to be all ~ to do** être (fin) prêt(e) pour faire; **to be (dead) ~ against** être (totalement) opposé à; **he's ~ in his ways** il n'est pas très souple, il tient à ses habitudes; **to ~ to music** mettre en musique; **to ~ on fire** mettre le feu à; **~ free** libérer; **to ~ sth going** déclencher qch; **to ~ the alarm clock for 7 o'clock** mettre le réveil à sonner à sept heures; **to ~ sail** partir, prendre la mer; **a ~ phrase** une expression toute faite, une locution; **a ~ of false teeth** un dentier; **a ~ of dining-room furniture** une salle à manger.

►**set about** *vt fus* (*task*) entreprendre, se mettre à; **to ~ about doing sth** se mettre à faire qch.

►**set aside** *vt* mettre de côté.

►**set back** *vt* (*in time*): **to ~ back (by)** retarder (de); (*place*): **a house ~ back from the road** une maison située en retrait de la route.

►**set in** *vi* (*infection, bad weather*) s'installer; (*complications*) survenir, surgir; **the rain has ~ in for the day** c'est parti pour qu'il pleuve toute la journée.

►**set off** *vi* se mettre en route, partir ♦ *vt* (*bomb*) faire exploser; (*cause to start*) déclencher; (*show up well*) mettre en valeur, faire valoir.

►**set out** *vi*: **to ~ out to do** entreprendre de faire; avoir pour but *or* intention de faire ♦ *vt* (*arrange*) disposer; (*state*) présenter, exposer; **to ~ out (from)** partir (de).

►**set up** *vt* (*organization*) fonder, constituer; (*monument*) ériger; **to ~ up shop** (*fig*) s'établir, s'installer.

setback ['sɛtbæk] *n* (*hitch*) revers *m*, contretemps *m*; (*in health*) rechute *f*.

set menu *n* menu *m*.

set square *n* équerre *f*.

settee [sɛ'ti:] *n* canapé *m*.

setting ['sɛtɪŋ] *n* cadre *m*; (*of jewel*) monture *f*.

setting lotion *n* lotion *f* pour mise en plis.

settle ['sɛtl] *vt* (*argument, matter, account*) régler; (*problem*) résoudre; (*MED: calm*) calmer; (*colonize: land*) coloniser ♦ *vi* (*bird, dust etc*) se poser; (*sediment*) se déposer; (*also:* **~ down**) s'installer, se fixer; (: *become calmer*) se calmer; se ranger; **to ~ to sth** se mettre sérieusement à qch; **to ~ for sth** accepter qch, se contenter de qch; **to ~ on sth** opter *or* se décider pour qch; **that's ~d then** alors, c'est d'accord!; **to ~ one's stomach** calmer des maux d'estomac.

►**settle in** *vi* s'installer.

►**settle up** *vi*: **to ~ up with sb** régler (ce que l'on doit à) qn.

settlement ['sɛtlmənt] *n* (*payment*) règlement *m*; (*agreement*) accord *m*; (*colony*) colonie *f*; (*village etc*) établissement *m*; hameau *m*; **in ~ of our account** (*COMM*) en règlement de notre compte.

settler ['sɛtlə*] *n* colon *m*.

setup ['sɛtʌp] n (arrangement) manière f dont les choses sont organisées; (situation) situation f, allure f des choses.

seven ['sɛvn] num sept.

seventeen [sɛvn'tiːn] num dix-sept.

seventh ['sɛvnθ] num septième.

seventy ['sɛvntɪ] num soixante-dix.

sever ['sɛvə*] vt couper, trancher; (relations) rompre.

several ['sɛvrl] adj, pron plusieurs (m/fpl); ~ **of us** plusieurs d'entre nous; ~ **times** plusieurs fois.

severance ['sɛvərəns] n (of relations) rupture f.

severance pay n indemnité f de licenciement.

severe [sɪ'vɪə*] adj sévère, strict(e); (serious) grave, sérieux(euse); (hard) rigoureux(euse), dur(e); (plain) sévère, austère.

severely [sɪ'vɪəlɪ] adv sévèrement; (wounded, ill) gravement.

severity [sɪ'vɛrɪtɪ] n sévérité f; gravité f; rigueur f.

sew, pt **sewed**, pp **sewn** [səu, səud, səun] vt, vi coudre.

▶**sew up** vt (re)coudre; **it is all sewn up** (fig) c'est dans le sac or dans la poche.

sewage ['suːɪdʒ] n vidange(s) f(pl).

sewage works n champ m d'épandage.

sewer ['suːə*] n égout m.

sewing ['səuɪŋ] n couture f.

sewing machine n machine f à coudre.

sewn [səun] pp of **sew**.

sex [sɛks] n sexe m; **to have ~ with** avoir des rapports (sexuels) avec.

sex act n acte sexuel.

sex appeal n sex-appeal m.

sex education n éducation sexuelle.

sexism ['sɛksɪzəm] n sexisme m.

sexist ['sɛksɪst] adj sexiste.

sex life n vie sexuelle.

sex object n femme-objet f, objet sexuel.

sextet [sɛks'tɛt] n sextuor m.

sexual ['sɛksjuəl] adj sexuel(le); ~ **assault** attentat m à la pudeur; ~ **harassment** harcèlement sexuel; ~ **intercourse** rapports sexuels.

sexy ['sɛksɪ] adj sexy inv.

Seychelles [seɪ'ʃɛl(z)] npl: **the** ~ les Seychelles fpl.

SF n abbr (= science fiction) SF f.

SG n abbr (US) = **Surgeon General**.

Sgt abbr (= sergeant) Sgt.

shabbiness ['ʃæbɪnɪs] n aspect miteux; mesquinerie f.

shabby ['ʃæbɪ] adj miteux(euse); (behaviour) mesquin(e), méprisable.

shack [ʃæk] n cabane f, hutte f.

shackles ['ʃæklz] npl chaînes fpl, entraves fpl.

shade [ʃeɪd] n ombre f; (for lamp) abat-jour m inv; (of colour) nuance f, ton m; (US: window ~) store m; (small quantity): **a** ~ **of** un soupçon de ♦ vt abriter du soleil, ombrager; ~**s** npl (US: sunglasses) lunettes fpl de soleil; **in the** ~ à l'ombre; **a** ~ **smaller** un tout petit peu plus petit.

shadow ['ʃædəu] n ombre f ♦ vt (follow) filer; **without** or **beyond a** ~ **of doubt** sans l'ombre d'un doute.

shadow cabinet n (BRIT POL) cabinet parallèle formé par le parti qui n'est pas au pouvoir.

shadowy ['ʃædəuɪ] adj ombragé(e); (dim) vague, indistinct(e).

shady ['ʃeɪdɪ] adj ombragé(e); (fig: dishonest) louche, véreux(euse).

shaft [ʃɑːft] n (of arrow, spear) hampe f; (AUT, TECH) arbre m; (of mine) puits m; (of lift) cage f; (of light) rayon m, trait m; **ventilator** ~ conduit m d'aération or de ventilation.

shaggy ['ʃægɪ] adj hirsute; en broussaille.

shake [ʃeɪk] vb (pt **shook**, pp **shaken** [ʃuk, 'ʃeɪkn]) vt secouer; (bottle, cocktail) agiter; (house, confidence) ébranler ♦ vi trembler ♦ n secousse f; **to** ~ **one's head** (in refusal etc) dire or faire non de la tête; (in dismay) secouer la tête; **to** ~ **hands with sb** serrer la main à qn.

▶**shake off** vt secouer; (fig) se débarrasser de.

▶**shake up** vt secouer.

shake-up ['ʃeɪkʌp] n grand remaniement.

shakily ['ʃeɪkɪlɪ] adv (reply) d'une voix tremblante; (walk) d'un pas mal assuré; (write) d'une main tremblante.

shaky ['ʃeɪkɪ] adj (hand, voice) tremblant(e); (building) branlant(e), peu solide; (memory) chancelant(e); (knowledge) incertain(e).

shale [ʃeɪl] n schiste argileux.

shall [ʃæl] aux vb: **I** ~ **go** j'irai.

shallot [ʃə'lɔt] n (BRIT) échalote f.

shallow ['ʃæləu] adj peu profond(e); (fig) superficiel(le), qui manque de profondeur.

sham [ʃæm] n frime f; (jewellery, furniture) imitation f ♦ adj feint(e), simulé(e) ♦ vt feindre, simuler.

shambles ['ʃæmblz] n confusion f, pagaïe f, fouillis m; **the economy is (in) a complete** ~ l'économie est dans la confusion la plus totale.

shambolic [ʃæm'bɔlɪk] adj (col) bordélique.

shame [ʃeɪm] n honte f ♦ vt faire honte à; **it is a** ~ **(that/to do)** c'est dommage (que + sub/de faire); **what a** ~! quel dommage!; **to put sb/sth to** ~ (fig) faire honte à qn/qch.

shamefaced ['ʃeɪmfeɪst] adj honteux(euse), penaud(e).

shameful ['ʃeɪmful] adj honteux(euse), scandaleux(euse).

shameless ['ʃeɪmlɪs] adj éhonté(e), effronté(e); (immodest) impudique.

shampoo [ʃæm'puː] n shampooing m ♦ vt faire un shampooing à; ~ **and set** shampooing et mise f en plis.

shamrock ['ʃæmrɔk] n trèfle m (emblème natio-

nal de l'Irlande).

shandy ['ʃændɪ] *n* bière panachée.

shan't [ʃɑːnt] = **shall not**.

shantytown ['ʃæntɪtaun] *n* bidonville *m*.

SHAPE [ʃeɪp] *n abbr* (= *Supreme Headquarters Allied Powers, Europe*) *quartier général des forces alliées en Europe.*

shape [ʃeɪp] *n* forme *f* ♦ *vt* façonner, modeler; (*clay, stone*) donner forme à; (*statement*) formuler; (*sb's ideas, character*) former; (*sb's life*) déterminer; (*course of events*) influer sur le cours de ♦ *vi* (*also:* ~ **up**: *events*) prendre tournure; (: *person*) faire des progrès, s'en sortir; **to take** ~ prendre forme *or* tournure; **in the** ~ **of a heart** en forme de cœur; **I can't bear gardening in any** ~ **or form** je déteste le jardinage sous quelque forme que ce soit; **to get o.s. into** ~ (re)trouver la forme.

-shaped [ʃeɪpt] *suffix:* **heart-**~ en forme de cœur.

shapeless ['ʃeɪplɪs] *adj* informe, sans forme.

shapely ['ʃeɪplɪ] *adj* bien proportionné(e), beau(belle).

share [ʃɛə*] *n* (*thing received, contribution*) part *f*; (*COMM*) action *f* ♦ *vt* partager; (*have in common*) avoir en commun; **to** ~ **out** (*among or between*) partager (entre); **to** ~ **in** (*joy, sorrow*) prendre part à; (*profits*) participer à, avoir part à; (*work*) partager.

share capital *n* capital social.

share certificate *n* certificat *m or* titre *m* d'action.

shareholder ['ʃɛəhəuldə*] *n* actionnaire *m/f*.

share index *n* indice *m* de la Bourse.

shark [ʃɑːk] *n* requin *m*.

sharp [ʃɑːp] *adj* (*razor, knife*) tranchant(e), bien aiguisé(e); (*point*) aigu(ë); (*nose, chin*) pointu(e); (*outline*) net(te); (*curve, bend*) brusque; (*cold, pain*) vif(vive); (*MUS*) dièse; (*voice*) coupant(e); (*person: quick-witted*) vif(vive), éveillé(e); (: *unscrupulous*) malhonnête ♦ *n* (*MUS*) dièse *m* ♦ *adv:* **at 2 o'clock** ~ à 2 heures pile *or* tapantes; **turn** ~ **left** tournez immédiatement à gauche; **to be** ~ **with sb** être brusque avec qn; **look** ~! dépêche-toi!

sharpen ['ʃɑːpn] *vt* aiguiser; (*pencil*) tailler; (*fig*) aviver.

sharpener ['ʃɑːpnə*] *n* (*also:* **pencil** ~) taille-crayon(s) *m inv*; (*also:* **knife** ~) aiguisoir *m*.

sharp-eyed [ʃɑːp'aɪd] *adj* à qui rien n'échappe.

sharpish ['ʃɑːpɪʃ] *adv* (*BRIT col: quickly*) en vitesse.

sharply ['ʃɑːplɪ] *adv* (*abruptly*) brusquement; (*clearly*) nettement; (*harshly*) sèchement, vertement.

sharp-tempered [ʃɑːp'tɛmpəd] *adj* prompt(e) à se mettre en colère.

sharp-witted [ʃɑːp'wɪtɪd] *adj* à l'esprit vif, malin(igne).

shatter ['ʃætə*] *vt* fracasser, briser, faire voler en éclats; (*fig: upset*) bouleverser; (: *ruin*) briser, ruiner ♦ *vi* voler en éclats, se briser, se fracasser.

shattered ['ʃætəd] *adj* (*overwhelmed, grief-stricken*) bouleversé(e); (*col: exhausted*) éreinté(e).

shatterproof ['ʃætəpruːf] *adj* incassable.

shave [ʃeɪv] *vt* raser ♦ *vi* se raser ♦ *n:* **to have a** ~ se raser.

shaven ['ʃeɪvn] *adj* (*head*) rasé(e).

shaver ['ʃeɪvə*] *n* (*also:* **electric** ~) rasoir *m* électrique.

shaving ['ʃeɪvɪŋ] *n* (*action*) rasage *m*; ~**s** *npl* (*of wood etc*) copeaux *mpl*.

shaving brush *n* blaireau *m*.

shaving cream *n* crème *f* à raser.

shaving soap *n* savon *m* à barbe.

shawl [ʃɔːl] *n* châle *m*.

she [ʃiː] *pron* elle; **there** ~ **is** la voilà; ~- **elephant** *etc* éléphant *m etc* femelle; *NB: for ships, countries follow the gender of your translation.*

sheaf, *pl* **sheaves** [ʃiːf, ʃiːvz] *n* gerbe *f*.

shear [ʃɪə*] *vt* (*pt* ~**ed**, *pp* ~**ed** *or* **shorn** [ʃɔːn]) (*sheep*) tondre.

▶**shear off** *vt* tondre; (*branch*) élaguer.

shears ['ʃɪəz] *npl* (*for hedge*) cisaille(s) *f(pl)*.

sheath [ʃiːθ] *n* gaine *f*, fourreau *m*, étui *m*; (*contraceptive*) préservatif *m*.

sheathe [ʃiːð] *vt* gainer; (*sword*) rengainer.

sheath knife *n* couteau *m* à gaine.

sheaves [ʃiːvz] *npl of* **sheaf**.

shed [ʃɛd] *n* remise *f*, resserre *f*; (*INDUSTRY, RAIL*) hangar *m* ♦ *vt* (*pt, pp* **shed**) (*leaves, fur etc*) perdre; (*tears*) verser, répandre; **to** ~ **light on** (*problem, mystery*) faire la lumière sur.

she'd [ʃiːd] = **she had, she would**.

sheen [ʃiːn] *n* lustre *m*.

sheep [ʃiːp] *n* (*pl inv*) mouton *m*.

sheepdog ['ʃiːpdɔg] *n* chien *m* de berger.

sheep farmer *n* éleveur *m* de moutons.

sheepish ['ʃiːpɪʃ] *adj* penaud(e), timide.

sheepskin ['ʃiːpskɪn] *n* peau *f* de mouton.

sheepskin jacket *n* canadienne *f*.

sheer [ʃɪə*] *adj* (*utter*) pur(e), pur et simple; (*steep*) à pic, abrupt(e); (*almost transparent*) extrêmement fin(e) ♦ *adv* à pic, abruptement; **by** ~ **chance** par pur hasard.

sheet [ʃiːt] *n* (*on bed*) drap *m*; (*of paper*) feuille *f*; (*of glass, metal*) feuille, plaque *f*.

sheet feed *n* (*on printer*) alimentation *f* en papier (feuille à feuille).

sheet lightning *n* éclair *m* en nappe(s).

sheet metal *n* tôle *f*.

sheet music *n* partition(s) *f(pl)*.

sheik(h) [ʃeɪk] *n* cheik *m*.

shelf, *pl* **shelves** [ʃɛlf, ʃɛlvz] *n* étagère *f*, rayon *m*; **set of shelves** rayonnage *m*.

shelf life *n* (*COMM*) durée *f* de conservation (avant la vente).

shell [ʃɛl] *n* (*on beach*) coquillage *m*; (*of egg,*

nut etc) coquille f; (explosive) obus m; (of building) carcasse f ♦ vt (crab, prawn etc) décortiquer; (peas) écosser; (MIL) bombarder (d'obus).

▶**shell out** vi (col): **to ~ out (for)** casquer (pour).

she'll [ʃiːl] = **she will, she shall**.

shellfish ['ʃɛlfɪʃ] n (pl inv) (crab etc) crustacé m; (scallop etc) coquillage m; (pl: as food) crustacés; coquillages.

shellsuit ['ʃɛlsuːt] n survêtement m.

shelter ['ʃɛltə*] n abri m, refuge m ♦ vt abriter, protéger; (give lodging to) donner asile à ♦ vi s'abriter, se mettre à l'abri; **to take ~ (from)** s'abriter (de).

sheltered ['ʃɛltəd] adj (life) retiré(e), à l'abri des soucis; (spot) abrité(e).

shelve [ʃɛlv] vt (fig) mettre en suspens or en sommeil.

shelves ['ʃɛlvz] npl of **shelf**.

shelving ['ʃɛlvɪŋ] n (shelves) rayonnage(s) m(pl).

shepherd ['ʃɛpəd] n berger m ♦ vt (guide) guider, escorter.

shepherdess ['ʃɛpədɪs] n bergère f.

shepherd's pie ['ʃɛpədz-] n ≈ hachis m Parmentier.

sherbet ['ʃəːbət] n (BRIT: powder) poudre acidulée; (US: water ice) sorbet m.

sheriff ['ʃɛrɪf] n shérif m.

sherry ['ʃɛrɪ] n xérès m, sherry m.

she's [ʃiːz] = **she is, she has**.

Shetland ['ʃɛtlənd] n (also: **the ~s, the ~ Isles** or **Islands**) les îles fpl Shetland.

Shetland pony n poney m des îles Shetland.

shield [ʃiːld] n bouclier m ♦ vt: **to ~ (from)** protéger (de or contre).

shift [ʃɪft] n (change) changement m; (of workers) équipe f, poste m ♦ vt déplacer, changer de place; (remove) enlever ♦ vi changer de place, bouger; **the wind has ~ed to the south** le vent a tourné au sud; **a ~ in demand** (COMM) un déplacement de la demande.

shift key n (on typewriter) touche f de majuscule.

shiftless ['ʃɪftlɪs] adj fainéant(e).

shift work n travail m par roulement; **to do ~** travailler par roulement.

shifty ['ʃɪftɪ] adj sournois(e); (eyes) fuyant(e).

Shiite ['ʃiːaɪt] n Chiite m/f ♦ adj chiite.

shilling ['ʃɪlɪŋ] n (BRIT) shilling m (= 12 old pence; 20 in a pound).

shilly-shally ['ʃɪlɪʃælɪ] vi tergiverser, atermoyer.

shimmer ['ʃɪmə*] n miroitement m, chatoiement m ♦ vi miroiter, chatoyer.

shin [ʃɪn] n tibia m ♦ vi: **to ~ up/down a tree** grimper dans un/descendre d'un arbre.

shindig ['ʃɪndɪg] n (col) bamboula f.

shine [ʃaɪn] n éclat m, brillant m ♦ vb (pt, pp **shone** [ʃɔn]) vi briller ♦ vt faire briller or re-

luire; (torch): **to ~ on** braquer sur.

shingle ['ʃɪŋgl] n (on beach) galets mpl; (on roof) bardeau m.

shingles ['ʃɪŋglz] n (MED) zona m.

shining ['ʃaɪnɪŋ] adj brillant(e).

shiny ['ʃaɪnɪ] adj brillant(e).

ship [ʃɪp] n bateau m; (large) navire m ♦ vt transporter (par mer); (send) expédier (par mer); (load) charger, embarquer; **on board ~** à bord.

shipbuilder ['ʃɪpbɪldə*] n constructeur m de navires.

shipbuilding ['ʃɪpbɪldɪŋ] n construction navale.

ship canal n canal m maritime or de navigation.

ship chandler [-'tʃɑːndlə*] n fournisseur m maritime, shipchandler m.

shipment ['ʃɪpmənt] n cargaison f.

shipowner ['ʃɪpəunə*] n armateur m.

shipper ['ʃɪpə*] n affréteur m, expéditeur m.

shipping ['ʃɪpɪŋ] n (ships) navires mpl; (traffic) navigation f.

shipping agent n agent m maritime.

shipping company n compagnie f de navigation.

shipping lane n couloir m de navigation.

shipping line n = **shipping company**.

shipshape ['ʃɪpʃeɪp] adj en ordre impeccable.

shipwreck ['ʃɪprɛk] n épave f; (event) naufrage m ♦ vt: **to be ~ed** faire naufrage.

shipyard ['ʃɪpjɑːd] n chantier naval.

shire ['ʃaɪə*] n (BRIT) comté m.

shirk [ʃəːk] vt esquiver, se dérober à.

shirt [ʃəːt] n chemise f; **in ~ sleeves** en bras de chemise.

shirty ['ʃəːtɪ] adj (BRIT col) de mauvais poil.

shit [ʃɪt] excl (col!) merde (!).

shiver ['ʃɪvə*] n frisson m ♦ vi frissonner.

shoal [ʃəul] n (of fish) banc m.

shock [ʃɔk] n (impact) choc m, heurt m; (ELEC) secousse f, décharge f; (emotional) choc; (MED) commotion f, choc ♦ vt (scandalize) choquer, scandaliser; (upset) bouleverser; **suffering from ~** (MED) commotionné(e); **it gave us a ~** ça nous a fait un choc; **it came as a ~ to hear that ...** nous avons appris avec stupeur que ....

shock absorber [-əbzɔːbə*] n amortisseur m.

shocker ['ʃɔkə*] n (col): **the news was a real ~ to him** il a vraiment été choqué par cette nouvelle.

shocking ['ʃɔkɪŋ] adj choquant(e), scandaleux(euse); (weather, handwriting) épouvantable.

shockproof ['ʃɔkpruːf] adj anti-choc inv.

shock therapy, shock treatment n (MED) (traitement m par) électrochoc(s) m(pl).

shock wave n (also fig) onde f de choc.

shod [ʃɔd] pt, pp of **shoe**; **well-~** bien chaussé(e).

shoddy ['ʃɔdɪ] adj de mauvaise qualité, mal

fait(e).

shoe [ʃuː] _n_ chaussure _f_, soulier _m_; (_also:_ **horse**~) fer _m_ à cheval; (_also:_ **brake** ~) mâchoire _f_ de frein ♦ _vt_ (_pt, pp_ **shod** [ʃɔd]) (_horse_) ferrer.

shoebrush ['ʃuːbrʌʃ] _n_ brosse _f_ à chaussures.

shoehorn ['ʃuːhɔːn] _n_ chausse-pied _m_.

shoelace ['ʃuːleɪs] _n_ lacet _m_ (de soulier).

shoemaker ['ʃuːmeɪkə*] _n_ cordonnier _m_, fabricant _m_ de chaussures.

shoe polish _n_ cirage _m_.

shoeshop ['ʃuːʃɔp] _n_ magasin _m_ de chaussures.

shoestring ['ʃuːstrɪŋ] _n_: **on a** ~ (_fig_) avec un budget dérisoire; avec des moyens très restreints.

shoetree ['ʃuːtriː] _n_ embauchoir _m_.

shone [ʃɔn] _pt, pp of_ **shine**.

shoo [ʃuː] _excl_ (allez,) ouste! ♦ _vt_ (_also:_ ~ **away,** ~ **off**) chasser.

shook [ʃuk] _pt of_ **shake**.

shoot [ʃuːt] _n_ (on branch, seedling) pousse _f_; (_shooting party_) partie _f_ de chasse ♦ _vb_ (_pt, pp_ **shot** [ʃɔt]) _vt_ (_game: BRIT_) chasser; tirer; abattre; (_person_) blesser (_or_ tuer) d'un coup de fusil (_or_ de revolver); (_execute_) fusiller; (_CINE_) tourner ♦ _vi_ (with gun, bow): **to** ~ (**at**) tirer (sur); (_FOOTBALL_) shooter, tirer; **to** ~ **past sb** passer en flèche devant qn; **to** ~ **in/out** entrer/sortir comme une flèche.
▶**shoot down** _vt_ (_plane_) abattre.
▶**shoot up** _vi_ (_fig_) monter en flèche.

shooting ['ʃuːtɪŋ] _n_ (_shots_) coups _mpl_ de feu; (_attack_) fusillade _f_; (: _murder_) homicide _m_ (à l'aide d'une arme à feu); (_HUNTING_) chasse _f_; (_CINE_) tournage _m_.

shooting range _n_ stand _m_ de tir.

shooting star _n_ étoile filante.

shop [ʃɔp] _n_ magasin _m_; (_workshop_) atelier _m_ ♦ _vi_ (_also:_ **go** ~**ping**) faire ses courses _or_ ses achats; **repair** ~ atelier de réparations; **to talk** ~ (_fig_) parler boutique.
▶**shop around** _vi_ faire le tour des magasins (pour comparer les prix); (_fig_) se renseigner avant de choisir _or_ décider.

shopaholic [ʃɔpə'hɔlɪk] _n_ (_col_) personne qui achète sans pouvoir s'arrêter.

shop assistant _n_ (_BRIT_) vendeur/euse.

shop floor _n_ (_BRIT: fig_) ouvriers _mpl_.

shopkeeper ['ʃɔpkiːpə*] _n_ marchand/e, commerçant/e.

shoplift ['ʃɔplɪft] _vi_ voler à l'étalage.

shoplifter ['ʃɔplɪftə*] _n_ voleur/euse à l'étalage.

shoplifting ['ʃɔplɪftɪŋ] _n_ vol _m_ à l'étalage.

shopper ['ʃɔpə*] _n_ personne _f_ qui fait ses courses, acheteur/euse.

shopping ['ʃɔpɪŋ] _n_ (_goods_) achats _mpl_, provisions _fpl_.

shopping bag _n_ sac _m_ (à provisions).

shopping centre _n_ centre commercial.

shopping mall _n_ centre commercial.

shop-soiled ['ʃɔpsɔɪld] _adj_ défraîchi(e), qui a fait la vitrine.

shop steward _n_ (_BRIT INDUSTRY_) délégué/e syndical(e).

shop window _n_ vitrine _f_.

shore [ʃɔː*] _n_ (of sea, lake) rivage _m_, rive _f_ ♦ _vt_: **to** ~ (**up**) étayer; **on** ~ à terre.

shore leave _n_ (_NAUT_) permission _f_ à terre.

shorn [ʃɔːn] _pp of_ **shear** ♦ _adj_: ~ **of** dépouillé(e) de.

short [ʃɔːt] _adj_ (not long) court(e); (soon finished) court, bref(brève); (person, step) petit(e); (curt) brusque, sec(sèche); (insufficient) insuffisant(e) ♦ _n_ (also: ~ **film**) court métrage; **to be** ~ **of sth** être à court de _or_ manquer de qch; **to be in** ~ **supply** manquer, être difficile à trouver; **I'm 3** ~ il m'en manque 3; **in** ~ bref; en bref; ~ **of doing** à moins de faire; **everything** ~ **of** tout sauf; **it is** ~ **for** c'est l'abréviation _or_ le diminutif de; **a** ~ **time ago** il y a peu de temps; **in the** ~ **term** à court terme; **to cut** ~ (speech, visit) abréger, écourter; (person) couper la parole à; **to fall** ~ **of** ne pas être à la hauteur de; **to stop** ~ s'arrêter net; **to stop** ~ **of** ne pas aller jusqu'à.

shortage ['ʃɔːtɪdʒ] _n_ manque _m_, pénurie _f_.

shortbread ['ʃɔːtbrɛd] _n_ ≈ sablé _m_.

short-change [ʃɔːt'tʃeɪndʒ] _vt_: **to** ~ **sb** ne pas rendre assez à qn.

short-circuit [ʃɔːt'səːkɪt] _n_ court-circuit _m_ ♦ _vt_ court-circuiter ♦ _vi_ se mettre en court-circuit.

shortcoming ['ʃɔːtkʌmɪŋ] _n_ défaut _m_.

short(crust) pastry ['ʃɔːt(krʌst)-] _n_ (_BRIT_) pâte brisée.

shortcut ['ʃɔːtkʌt] _n_ raccourci _m_.

shorten ['ʃɔːtn] _vt_ raccourcir; (text, visit) abréger.

shortening ['ʃɔːtnɪŋ] _n_ (_CULIN_) matière grasse.

shortfall ['ʃɔːtfɔːl] _n_ déficit _m_.

shorthand ['ʃɔːthænd] _n_ (_BRIT_) sténo(graphie) _f_; **to take sth down in** ~ prendre qch en sténo.

shorthand notebook _n_ bloc _m_ sténo.

shorthand typist _n_ (_BRIT_) sténodactylo _m/f_.

short list _n_ (_BRIT: for job_) liste _f_ des candidats sélectionnés.

short-lived ['ʃɔːt'lɪvd] _adj_ de courte durée.

shortly ['ʃɔːtlɪ] _adv_ bientôt, sous peu.

shortness ['ʃɔːtnɪs] _n_ brièveté _f_.

shorts [ʃɔːts] _npl_ (also: **a pair of** ~) un short.

short-sighted [ʃɔːt'saɪtɪd] _adj_ (_BRIT_) myope; (fig) qui manque de clairvoyance.

short-staffed [ʃɔːt'stɑːft] _adj_ à court de personnel.

short story _n_ nouvelle _f_.

short-tempered [ʃɔːt'tɛmpəd] _adj_ qui s'emporte facilement.

short-term ['ʃɔːttəːm] _adj_ (effect) à court terme.

short time n: **to work** ~, **to be on** ~ (IN-DUSTRY) être en chômage partiel, travailler à horaire réduit.

short wave n (RADIO) ondes courtes.

shot [ʃɔt] pt, pp of **shoot** ♦ n coup m (de feu); (shotgun pellets) plombs mpl; (person) tireur m; (try) coup, essai m; (injection) piqûre f; (PHOT) photo f; **to fire a** ~ **at sb/sth** tirer sur qn/qch; **to have a** ~ **at (doing) sth** essayer de faire qch; **like a** ~ comme une flèche; (very readily) sans hésiter; **to get** ~ **of sb/sth** (col) se débarrasser de qn/qch; **a big** ~ (col) un gros bonnet.

shotgun [ʃɔtɡʌn] n fusil m de chasse.

should [ʃud] aux vb: **I** ~ **go now** je devrais partir maintenant; **he** ~ **be there now** il devrait être arrivé maintenant; **I** ~ **go if I were you** si j'étais vous j'irais; **I** ~ **like to** j'aimerais bien, volontiers; ~ **he phone ...** si jamais il téléphone ....

shoulder [ʃəuldə*] n épaule f, (BRIT: of road): **hard** ~ accotement m ♦ vt (fig) endosser, se charger de; **to look over one's** ~ regarder derrière soi (en tournant la tête); **to rub** ~s **with sb** (fig) côtoyer qn; **to give sb the cold** ~ (fig) battre froid à qn.

shoulder bag n sac m à bandoulière.

shoulder blade n omoplate f.

shoulder strap n bretelle f.

shouldn't [ʃudnt] = **should not**.

shout [ʃaut] n cri m ♦ vt crier ♦ vi crier, pousser des cris; **to give sb a** ~ appeler qn.

▶**shout down** vt huer.

shouting [ʃautɪŋ] n cris mpl.

shouting match n (col) engueulade f, empoignade f.

shove [ʃʌv] vt pousser; (col: put): **to** ~ **sth in** fourrer or ficher qch dans ♦ n poussée f; **he** ~d **me out of the way** il m'a écarté en me poussant.

▶**shove off** vi (NAUT) pousser au large; (fig: col) ficher le camp.

shovel [ʃʌvl] n pelle f ♦ vt pelleter, enlever (or enfourner) à la pelle.

show [ʃəu] n (of emotion) manifestation f, démonstration f; (semblance) semblant m, apparence f; (exhibition) exposition f, salon m; (THEAT) spectacle m, représentation f; (CINE) séance f ♦ vb (pt ~ed, pp shown [ʃəun]) vt montrer; (courage etc) faire preuve de, manifester; (exhibit) exposer ♦ vi se voir, être visible; **to ask for a** ~ **of hands** demander que l'on vote à main levée; **to be on** ~ être exposé(e); **it's just for** ~ c'est juste pour l'effet; **who's running the** ~ **here?** (col) qui est-ce qui commande ici?; **to** ~ **sb to his seat/to the door** conduire qn jusqu'à sa place/la porte; **to** ~ **a profit/ loss** (COMM) indiquer un bénéfice/une perte; **it just goes to** ~ **that ...** ça prouve bien que ....

▶**show in** vt faire entrer.

▶**show off** vi (pej) crâner ♦ vt (display) faire valoir; (pej) faire étalage de.

▶**show out** vt reconduire à la porte.

▶**show up** vi (stand out) ressortir; (col: turn up) se montrer ♦ vt démontrer; (unmask) démasquer, dénoncer.

showbiz [ʃəubɪz] n (col) showbiz m.

show business n le monde du spectacle.

showcase [ʃəukeɪs] n vitrine f.

showdown [ʃəudaun] n épreuve f de force.

shower [ʃauə*] n (also: ~ **bath**) douche f; (rain) averse f; (of stones etc) pluie f, grêle f; (US: party) réunion organisée pour la remise de cadeaux ♦ vi prendre une douche, se doucher ♦ vt: **to** ~ **sb with** (gifts etc) combler qn de; (abuse etc) accabler qn de; (missiles) bombarder qn de; **to have** or **take a** ~ prendre une douche, se doucher.

shower cap n bonnet m de douche.

showerproof [ʃauəpru:f] adj imperméable.

showery [ʃauərɪ] adj (weather) pluvieux(euse).

showground [ʃəuɡraund] n champ m de foire.

showing [ʃəuɪŋ] n (of film) projection f.

show jumping [-dʒʌmpɪŋ] n concours m hippique.

showman [ʃəumən] n (at fair, circus) forain m; (fig) comédien m.

showmanship [ʃəumənʃɪp] n art m de la mise en scène.

shown [ʃəun] pp of **show**.

show-off [ʃəuɔf] n (col: person) crâneur/euse, m'as-tu-vu/e.

showpiece [ʃəupi:s] n (of exhibition etc) joyau m, clou m; **that hospital is a** ~ cet hôpital est un modèle du genre.

showroom [ʃəurum] n magasin m or salle f d'exposition.

show trial n grand procès m médiatique (qui fait un exemple).

showy [ʃəuɪ] adj tapageur(euse).

shrank [ʃræŋk] pt of **shrink**.

shrapnel [ʃræpnl] n éclats mpl d'obus.

shred [ʃred] n (gen pl) lambeau m, petit morceau; (fig: of truth, evidence) parcelle f ♦ vt mettre en lambeaux, déchirer; (documents) détruire; (CULIN) râper; couper en lanières.

shredder [ʃredə*] n (for vegetables) râpeur m; (for documents, papers) déchiqueteuse f.

shrewd [ʃru:d] adj astucieux(euse), perspicace.

shrewdness [ʃru:dnɪs] n perspicacité f.

shriek [ʃri:k] n cri perçant or aigu, hurlement m ♦ vt, vi hurler, crier.

shrift [ʃrɪft] n: **to give sb short** ~ expédier qn sans ménagements.

shrill [ʃrɪl] adj perçant(e), aigu(ë), strident(e).

shrimp [ʃrɪmp] n crevette grise.

shrine [ʃraɪn] n châsse f; (place) lieu m de pèlerinage.

shrink pt **shrank**, pp **shrunk** [ʃrɪŋk, ʃræŋk, ʃrʌŋk] vi rétrécir; (fig) se réduire; se contracter ◆ *vt* (*wool*) (faire) rétrécir ◆ *n* (*col: pej*) psychanalyste *m/f*; **to ~ from (doing) sth** reculer devant (la pensée de faire) qch.

shrinkage ['ʃrɪŋkɪdʒ] *n* (*of clothes*) rétrécissement *m*.

shrink-wrap ['ʃrɪŋkræp] *vt* emballer sous film plastique.

shrivel ['ʃrɪvl] (*also: ~ up*) *vt* ratatiner, flétrir ◆ *vi* se ratatiner, se flétrir.

shroud [ʃraud] *n* linceul *m* ◆ *vt*: **~ed in mystery** enveloppé(e) de mystère.

Shrove Tuesday ['ʃrəuv-] *n* (le) Mardi gras.

shrub [ʃrʌb] *n* arbuste *m*.

shrubbery ['ʃrʌbərɪ] *n* massif *m* d'arbustes.

shrug [ʃrʌg] *n* haussement *m* d'épaules ◆ *vt, vi*: **to ~ (one's shoulders)** hausser les épaules.

▶**shrug off** *vt* faire fi de; (*cold, illness*) se débarrasser de.

shrunk [ʃrʌŋk] *pp of* **shrink**.

shrunken ['ʃrʌŋkn] *adj* ratatiné(e).

shudder ['ʃʌdə*] *n* frisson *m*, frémissement *m* ◆ *vi* frissonner, frémir.

shuffle ['ʃʌfl] *vt* (*cards*) battre; **to ~ (one's feet)** traîner les pieds.

shun [ʃʌn] *vt* éviter, fuir.

shunt [ʃʌnt] *vt* (*RAIL: direct*) aiguiller; (: *divert*) détourner ◆ *vi*: **to ~ (to and fro)** faire la navette.

shunting yard ['ʃʌntɪŋ-] *n* voies *fpl* de garage *or* de triage.

shush [ʃuʃ] *excl* chut!

shut, *pt, pp* **shut** [ʃʌt] *vt* fermer ◆ *vi* (se) fermer.

▶**shut down** *vt* fermer définitivement; (*machine*) arrêter ◆ *vi* fermer définitivement.

▶**shut off** *vt* couper, arrêter.

▶**shut out** *vt* (*person, cold*) empêcher d'entrer; (*noise*) éviter d'entendre; (*block: view*) boucher; (: *memory of sth*) chasser de son esprit.

▶**shut up** *vi* (*col: keep quiet*) se taire ◆ *vt* (*close*) fermer; (*silence*) faire taire.

shutdown ['ʃʌtdaun] *n* fermeture *f*.

shutter ['ʃʌtə*] *n* volet *m*; (*PHOT*) obturateur *m*.

shuttle ['ʃʌtl] *n* navette *f*; (*also: ~ service*) (service *m* de) navette *f* ◆ *vi* (*vehicle, person*) faire la navette ◆ *vt* (*passengers*) transporter par un système de navette.

shuttlecock ['ʃʌtlkɔk] *n* volant *m* (*de badminton*).

shuttle diplomacy *n* navettes *fpl* diplomatiques.

shy [ʃaɪ] *adj* timide; **to fight ~ of** se dérober devant; **to be ~ of doing sth** hésiter à faire qch, ne pas oser faire qch ◆ *vi*: **to ~ away from doing sth** (*fig*) craindre de faire qch.

shyness ['ʃaɪnɪs] *n* timidité *f*.

Siam [saɪ'æm] *n* Siam *m*.

Siamese [saɪə'miːz] *adj*: **~ cat** chat siamois *mpl*; **~ twins** (frères *mpl*) siamois *mpl*, (sœurs

fpl) siamoises *fpl*.

Siberia [saɪ'bɪərɪə] *n* Sibérie *f*.

siblings ['sɪblɪŋz] *npl* (*formal*) enfants *mpl* d'un même couple.

Sicilian [sɪ'sɪlɪən] *adj* sicilien(ne) ◆ *n* Sicilien/ne.

Sicily ['sɪsɪlɪ] *n* Sicile *f*.

sick [sɪk] *adj* (*ill*) malade; (*vomiting*): **to be ~** vomir; (*humour*) noir(e), macabre; **to feel ~** avoir envie de vomir, avoir mal au cœur; **to fall ~** tomber malade; **to be (off)** ~ être absent(e) pour cause de maladie; **a ~ person** un(e) malade; **to be ~ of** (*fig*) en avoir assez de.

sickbag ['sɪkbæg] *n* sac *m* vomitoire.

sick bay *n* infirmerie *f*.

sick building syndrome *n maladie dûe à la climatisation, l'éclairage artificiel etc des bureaux.*

sicken ['sɪkn] *vt* écœurer ◆ *vi*: **to be ~ing for** **sth** (*cold, flu etc*) couver qch.

sickening ['sɪknɪŋ] *adj* (*fig*) écœurant(e), révoltant(e), répugnant(e).

sickle ['sɪkl] *n* faucille *f*.

sick leave *n* congé *m* de maladie.

sickle-cell anaemia ['sɪklsɛl-] *n* anémie *f* à hématies falciformes, drépanocytose *f*.

sickly ['sɪklɪ] *adj* maladif(ive), souffreteux(euse); (*causing nausea*) écœurant(e).

sickness ['sɪknɪs] *n* maladie *f*; (*vomiting*) vomissement(s) *m(pl)*.

sickness benefit *n* (prestations *fpl* de l')assurance-maladie *f*.

sick pay *n* indemnité *f* de maladie (*versée par l'employeur*).

sickroom ['sɪkruːm] *n* infirmerie *f*.

side [saɪd] *n* côté *m*; (*of animal*) flanc *m*; (*of lake, road*) bord *m*; (*of mountain*) versant *m*; (*fig: aspect*) côté, aspect *m*; (*team: SPORT*) équipe *f* ◆ *cpd* (*door, entrance*) latéral(e) ◆ *vi*: **to ~ with** **sb** prendre le parti de qn, se ranger du côté de qn; **by the ~ of** au bord de; **~ by ~** côte à côte; **the right/ wrong ~** le bon/mauvais côté, l'endroit/l'envers *m*; **they are on our ~** ils sont avec nous; **from all ~s** de tous côtés; **to take ~s (with)** prendre parti (pour); **a ~ of beef** ≈ un quartier de bœuf.

sideboard ['saɪdbɔːd] *n* buffet *m*.

sideboards ['saɪdbɔːdz] (*BRIT*), **sideburns** ['saɪdbəːnz] *npl* (*whiskers*) pattes *fpl*.

sidecar ['saɪdkɑː*] *n* side-car *m*.

side dish *n* (plat *m* d')accompagnement *m*.

side drum *n* (*MUS*) tambour plat, caisse claire.

side effect *n* (*MED*) effet *m* secondaire.

sidekick ['saɪdkɪk] *n* (*col*) sous-fifre *m*.

sidelight ['saɪdlaɪt] *n* (*AUT*) veilleuse *f*.

sideline ['saɪdlaɪn] *n* (*SPORT*) (ligne *f* de) touche *f*; (*fig*) activité *f* secondaire.

sidelong ['saɪdlɔŋ] *adj*: **to give sb a ~ glance** regarder qn du coin de l'œil.

side plate *n* petite assiette.

side road n petite route, route transversale.
sidesaddle ['saɪdsædl] adv en amazone.
side show n attraction f.
sidestep ['saɪdstɛp] vt (question) éluder; (problem) éviter ♦ vi (BOXING etc) esquiver.
side street n rue transversale.
sidetrack ['saɪdtræk] vt (fig) faire dévier de son sujet.
sidewalk ['saɪdwɔːk] n (US) trottoir m.
sideways ['saɪdweɪz] adv de côté.
siding ['saɪdɪŋ] n (RAIL) voie f de garage.
sidle ['saɪdl] vi: **to ~ up (to)** s'approcher furtivement (de).
SIDS [sɪdz] n abbr (= sudden infant death syndrome) mort subite du nourrisson, mort f au berceau.
siege [siːdʒ] n siège m; **to lay ~ to** assiéger.
siege economy n économie f de (temps de) siège.
Sierra Leone [sɪˈɛrəlɪˈəun] n Sierra Leone f.
sieve [sɪv] n tamis m, passoire f ♦ vt tamiser, passer (au tamis).
sift [sɪft] vt passer au tamis or au crible; (fig) passer au crible ♦ vi (fig): **to ~ through** passer en revue.
sigh [saɪ] n soupir m ♦ vi soupirer, pousser un soupir.
sight [saɪt] n (faculty) vue f; (spectacle) spectacle m; (on gun) mire f ♦ vt apercevoir; **in ~** visible; (fig) en vue; **out of ~** hors de vue; **at ~** (COMM) à vue; **at first ~** à première vue, au premier abord; **I know her by ~** je la connais de vue; **to catch ~ of sb/sth** apercevoir qn/qch; **to lose ~ of sb/sth** perdre qn/qch de vue; **to set one's ~s on sth** jeter son dévolu sur qch.
sighted ['saɪtɪd] adj qui voit; **partially ~** qui a un certain degré de vision.
sightseeing ['saɪtsiːɪŋ] n tourisme m; **to go ~** faire du tourisme.
sightseer ['saɪtsiːə*] n touriste m/f.
sign [saɪn] n (gen) signe m; (with hand etc) signe, geste m; (notice) panneau m, écriteau m; (also: road ~) panneau de signalisation ♦ vt signer; **as a ~ of** en signe de; **it's a good/bad ~** c'est bon/mauvais signe; **plus/minus ~** signe plus/moins; **there's no ~ of a change of mind** rien ne laisse présager un revirement; **he was showing ~s of improvement** il commençait visiblement à faire des progrès; **to ~ one's name** signer.
▸**sign away** vt (rights etc) renoncer officiellement à.
▸**sign in** vi signer le registre (en arrivant).
▸**sign off** vi (RADIO, TV) terminer l'émission.
▸**sign on** vi (MIL) s'engager; (as unemployed) s'inscrire au chômage; (enrol): **to ~ on for a course** s'inscrire pour un cours ♦ vt (MIL) engager; (employee) embaucher.
▸**sign out** vi signer le registre (en partant).
▸**sign over** vt: **to ~ sth over to sb** céder qch par écrit à qn.
▸**sign up** (MIL) vt engager ♦ vi s'engager.
signal ['sɪgnl] n signal m ♦ vi (AUT) mettre son clignotant ♦ vt (person) faire signe à; (message) communiquer par signaux; **to ~ a left/right turn** (AUT) indiquer or signaler que l'on tourne à gauche/droite; **to ~ to sb (to do sth)** faire signe à qn (de faire qch).
signal box n (RAIL) poste m d'aiguillage.
signalman [sɪgnlmən] n (RAIL) aiguilleur m.
signatory ['sɪgnətərɪ] n signataire m/f.
signature ['sɪgnətʃə*] n signature f.
signature tune n indicatif musical.
signet ring ['sɪgnət-] n chevalière f.
significance [sɪgˈnɪfɪkəns] n signification f; importance f; **that is of no ~** ceci n'a pas d'importance.
significant [sɪgˈnɪfɪkənt] adj significatif(ive); (important) important(e), considérable.
significantly [sɪgˈnɪfɪkəntlɪ] adv (improve, increase) sensiblement; (smile) d'un air entendu, éloquemment; **~, ...** fait significatif, ...
signify ['sɪgnɪfaɪ] vt signifier.
sign language n langage m par signes.
signpost ['saɪnpəust] n poteau indicateur.
silage ['saɪlɪdʒ] n (fodder) fourrage vert; (method) ensilage m.
silence ['saɪləns] n silence m ♦ vt faire taire, réduire au silence.
silencer ['saɪlənsə*] n (on gun, BRIT AUT) silencieux m.
silent ['saɪlnt] adj silencieux(euse); (film) muet(te); **to keep** or **remain ~** garder le silence, ne rien dire.
silently ['saɪlntlɪ] adv silencieusement.
silent partner n (COMM) bailleur m de fonds, commanditaire m.
silhouette [sɪluːˈɛt] n silhouette f ♦ vt: **~d against** se profilant sur, se découpant contre.
silicon ['sɪlɪkən] n silicium m.
silicon chip n puce f électronique.
silicone ['sɪlɪkəun] n silicone f.
silk [sɪlk] n soie f ♦ cpd de or en soie.
silky ['sɪlkɪ] adj soyeux(euse).
sill [sɪl] n (also: **window~**) rebord m (de la fenêtre); (of door) seuil m; (AUT) bas m de marche.
silly ['sɪlɪ] adj stupide, sot(te), bête; **to do something ~** faire une bêtise.
silo ['saɪləu] n silo m.
silt [sɪlt] n vase f; limon m.
silver ['sɪlvə*] n argent m; (money) monnaie f (en pièces d'argent); (also: **~ware**) argenterie f ♦ cpd d'argent, en argent.
silver paper (BRIT), **silver foil** n papier m d'argent or d'étain.
silver-plated [sɪlvəˈpleɪtɪd] adj plaqué(e) argent.
silversmith ['sɪlvəsmɪθ] n orfèvre m/f.
silverware ['sɪlvəwɛə*] n argenterie f.
silver wedding (anniversary) n noces fpl d'argent.

silvery ['sɪlvrɪ] adj argenté(e).
similar ['sɪmɪlə*] adj: ~ **(to)** semblable (à).
similarity [sɪmɪ'lærɪtɪ] n ressemblance f, similarité f.
similarly ['sɪmɪləlɪ] adv de la même façon, de même.
simile ['sɪmɪlɪ] n comparaison f.
simmer ['sɪmə*] vi cuire à feu doux, mijoter.
▶**simmer down** vi (fig: col) se calmer.
simper ['sɪmpə*] vi minauder.
simpering ['sɪmprɪŋ] adj stupide.
simple ['sɪmpl] adj simple; **the** ~ **truth** la vérité pure et simple.
simple interest n (MATH, COMM) intérêts mpl simples.
simple-minded [sɪmpl'maɪndɪd] adj simplet(te), simple d'esprit.
simpleton ['sɪmpltən] n nigaud/e, niais/e.
simplicity [sɪm'plɪsɪtɪ] n simplicité f.
simplification [sɪmplɪfɪ'keɪʃən] n simplification f.
simplify ['sɪmplɪfaɪ] vt simplifier.
simply ['sɪmplɪ] adv simplement; (without fuss) avec simplicité.
simulate ['sɪmjuleɪt] vt simuler, feindre.
simulation [sɪmju'leɪʃən] n simulation f.
simultaneous [sɪməl'teɪnɪəs] adj simultané(e).
simultaneously [sɪməl'teɪnɪəslɪ] adv simultanément.
sin [sɪn] n péché m ♦ vi pécher.
Sinai ['saɪneɪaɪ] n Sinaï m.
since [sɪns] adv, prep depuis ♦ conj (time) depuis que; (because) puisque, étant donné que, comme; ~ **then** depuis ce moment-là; ~ **Monday** depuis lundi; (ever) ~ **I arrived** depuis mon arrivée, depuis que je suis arrivé.
sincere [sɪn'sɪə*] adj sincère.
sincerely [sɪn'sɪəlɪ] adv sincèrement; **Yours** ~ (at end of letter) veuillez agréer, Monsieur (or Madame), l'expression de mes sentiments distingués or les meilleurs.
sincerity [sɪn'sɛrɪtɪ] n sincérité f.
sine [saɪn] n (MATH) sinus m.
sinew ['sɪnjuː] n tendon m; ~s npl muscles mpl.
sinful ['sɪnful] adj coupable.
sing, pt **sang**, pp **sung** [sɪŋ, sæŋ, sʌŋ] vt, vi chanter.
Singapore [sɪŋgə'pɔː*] n Singapour m.
singe [sɪndʒ] vt brûler légèrement; (clothes) roussir.
singer ['sɪŋə*] n chanteur/euse.
Singhalese [sɪŋə'liːz] adj = **Sinhalese**.
singing ['sɪŋɪŋ] n (of person, bird) chant m; façon f de chanter; (of kettle, bullet, in ears) sifflement m.
single ['sɪŋgl] adj seul(e), unique; (unmarried) célibataire; (not double) simple ♦ n (BRIT: also: ~ **ticket**) aller m (simple); (record) 45 tours m; **not a** ~ **one was left** il n'en est pas resté un(e) seul(e); **every** ~ **day** chaque jour sans exception.
▶**single out** vt choisir; distinguer.

single bed n lit m à une place.
single-breasted ['sɪŋglbrɛstɪd] adj droit(e).
Single European Market n: **the** ~ le marché unique européen.
single file n: **in** ~ en file indienne.
single-handed [sɪŋgl'hændɪd] adv tout(e) seul(e), sans (aucune) aide.
single-minded [sɪŋgl'maɪndɪd] adj résolu(e), tenace.
single parent n parent unique (or célibataire).
single room n chambre f à un lit or pour une personne.
singles ['sɪŋglz] npl (TENNIS) simple m; (US: single people) célibataires m/fpl.
singles bar n (esp US) bar m de rencontres pour célibataires.
single-sex school [sɪŋgl'sɛks-] n école f non mixte.
singlet ['sɪŋglɪt] n tricot m de corps.
singly ['sɪŋglɪ] adv séparément.
singsong ['sɪŋsɔŋ] adj (tone) chantant(e) ♦ n (songs): **to have a** ~ chanter quelque chose (ensemble).
singular ['sɪŋgjulə*] adj singulier(ière); (odd) singulier, étrange; (LING) (au) singulier, du singulier ♦ n (LING) singulier m; **in the feminine** ~ au féminin singulier.
singularly ['sɪŋgjuləlɪ] adv singulièrement; étrangement.
Sinhalese [sɪnhə'liːz] adj cingalais(e).
sinister ['sɪnɪstə*] adj sinistre.
sink [sɪŋk] n évier m ♦ vb (pt **sank**, pp **sunk** [sæŋk, sʌŋk]) vt (ship) (faire) couler, faire sombrer; (foundations) creuser; (piles etc): **to** ~ **sth into** enfoncer qch dans ♦ vi couler, sombrer; (ground etc) s'affaisser; **he sank into a chair/the mud** il s'est enfoncé dans un fauteuil/la boue; **a** ~**ing feeling** un serrement de cœur.
▶**sink in** vi s'enfoncer, pénétrer; (explanation): **it took a long time to** ~ **in** il a fallu longtemps pour que ça rentre.
sinking ['sɪŋkɪŋ] adj: **that** ~ **feeling** un serrement de cœur.
sinking fund n fonds mpl d'amortissement.
sink unit n bloc-évier m.
sinner ['sɪnə*] n pécheur/eresse.
Sinn Féin [ʃɪn'feɪn] n Sinn Féin m (parti politique irlandais qui soutient l'IRA).
Sino- ['saɪnəu] prefix sino-.
sinuous ['sɪnjuəs] adj sinueux(euse).
sinus ['saɪnəs] n (ANAT) sinus m inv.
sip [sɪp] n petite gorgée ♦ vt boire à petites gorgées.
siphon ['saɪfən] n siphon m ♦ vt (also: ~ **off**) siphonner; (: fig: funds) transférer; (: illegally) détourner.
sir [sə*] n monsieur m; **S**~ **John Smith** sir John Smith; **yes** ~ oui Monsieur; **Dear S**~ (in letter) Monsieur.
siren ['saɪərn] n sirène f.

sirloin ['sə:lɔɪn] n aloyau m.
sirloin steak n bifteck m dans l'aloyau.
sirocco [sɪ'rɔkəu] n sirocco m.
sisal ['saɪsəl] n sisal m.
sissy ['sɪsɪ] n (col: coward) poule mouillée.
sister ['sɪstə*] n sœur f; (nun) religieuse f, (bonne) sœur; (BRIT: nurse) infirmière f en chef ♦ cpd: ~ **organization** organisation f sœur; ~ **ship** sister(-)ship m.
sister-in-law ['sɪstərɪnlɔː] n belle-sœur f.
sit, pt, pp **sat** [sɪt, sæt] vi s'asseoir; (assembly) être en séance, siéger; (for painter) poser; (dress etc) tomber ♦ vt (exam) passer, se présenter à; **to ~ on a committee** faire partie d'un comité; **to ~ tight** ne pas bouger.
▶**sit about, sit around** vi être assis(e) or rester à ne rien faire.
▶**sit back** vi (in seat) bien s'installer, se carrer.
▶**sit down** vi s'asseoir; **to be ~ting down** être assis(e).
▶**sit in** vi: **to ~ in on a discussion** assister à une discussion.
▶**sit up** vi s'asseoir; (not go to bed) rester debout, ne pas se coucher.
sitcom ['sɪtkɔm] n abbr (TV: = situation comedy) série f comique.
sit-down ['sɪtdaun] adj: **a ~ strike** une grève sur le tas; **a ~ meal** un repas assis.
site [saɪt] n emplacement m, site m; (also: **building ~**) chantier m ♦ vt placer.
sit-in ['sɪtɪn] n (demonstration) sit-in m inv, occupation f de locaux.
siting ['saɪtɪŋ] n (location) emplacement m.
sitter ['sɪtə*] n (for painter) modèle m; (also: **baby~**) baby-sitter m/f.
sitting ['sɪtɪŋ] n (of assembly etc) séance f; (in canteen) service m.
sitting member n (POL) parlementaire m/f en exercice.
sitting room n salon m.
sitting tenant n (BRIT) locataire occupant(e).
situate ['sɪtjueɪt] vt situer.
situated ['sɪtjueɪtɪd] adj situé(e).
situation [sɪtju'eɪʃən] n situation f; **"~s vacant/wanted"** (BRIT) "offres/demandes d'emploi".
situation comedy n (THEAT) comédie f de situation.
six [sɪks] num six.
six-pack ['sɪkspæk] n (esp US) pack m de six canettes.
sixteen [sɪks'tiːn] num seize.
sixth ['sɪksθ] adj sixième; **the upper/lower ~** (BRIT SCOL) la terminale/la première.
sixty ['sɪkstɪ] num soixante.
size [saɪz] n dimensions fpl; (of person) taille f; (of estate, area) étendue f; (of problem) ampleur f; (of company) importance f; (of clothing) taille f; (of shoes) pointure f; (glue) colle f; **I take ~ 14** (of dress etc) ≈ je prends du 42 or la taille 42; **the small/large ~** (of soap pow-

der etc) le petit/grand modèle; **it's the ~ of ...** c'est de la taille (or grosseur) de ..., c'est grand (or gros) comme ...; **cut to ~** découpé(e) aux dimensions voulues.
▶**size up** vt juger, jauger.
sizeable ['saɪzəbl] adj assez grand(e) or gros(se); assez important(e).
sizzle ['sɪzl] vi grésiller.
SK abbr (Canada) = Saskatchewan.
skate [skeɪt] n patin m; (fish: pl inv) raie f ♦ vi patiner.
▶**skate over, skate around** vt (problem, issue) éluder.
skateboard ['skeɪtbɔːd] n skateboard m, planche f à roulettes.
skater ['skeɪtə*] n patineur/euse.
skating ['skeɪtɪŋ] n patinage m.
skating rink n patinoire f.
skeleton ['skelɪtn] n squelette m; (outline) schéma m.
skeleton key n passe-partout m.
skeleton staff n effectifs réduits.
skeptic etc ['skeptɪk] (US) = **sceptic** etc.
sketch [sketʃ] n (drawing) croquis m, esquisse f; (THEAT) sketch m, saynète f ♦ vt esquisser, faire un croquis or une esquisse de.
sketch book n carnet m à dessin.
sketch pad n bloc m à dessin.
sketchy ['sketʃɪ] adj incomplet(ète), fragmentaire.
skew [skjuː] n (BRIT): **on the ~** de travers, en biais.
skewer ['skjuːə*] n brochette f.
ski [skiː] n ski m ♦ vi skier, faire du ski.
ski boot n chaussure f de ski.
skid [skɪd] n dérapage m ♦ vi déraper; **to go into a ~** déraper.
skid mark n trace f de dérapage.
skier ['skiːə*] n skieur/euse.
skiing ['skiːɪŋ] n ski m; **to go ~** (aller) faire du ski.
ski instructor n moniteur/trice de ski.
ski jump n (ramp) tremplin m; (event) saut m à skis.
skilful, (US) **skillful** ['skɪlful] adj habile, adroit(e).
ski lift n remonte-pente m inv.
skill [skɪl] n (ability) habileté f, adresse f, talent m; (art, craft) technique(s) f(pl), compétences fpl.
skilled [skɪld] adj habile, adroit(e); (worker) qualifié(e).
skillet ['skɪlɪt] n poêlon m.
skillful etc ['skɪlful] (US) = **skilful** etc.
skil(l)fully ['skɪlfəlɪ] adv habilement, adroitement.
skim [skɪm] vt (milk) écrémer; (soup) écumer; (glide over) raser, effleurer ♦ vi: **to ~ through** (fig) parcourir.
skimmed milk [skɪmd-] n lait écrémé.
skimp [skɪmp] vt (work) bâcler, faire à la vavite; (cloth etc) lésiner sur.

skimpy ['skɪmpɪ] *adj* étriqué(e); maigre.
skin [skɪn] *n* peau *f* ♦ *vt* (*fruit etc*) éplucher; (*animal*) écorcher; **wet** *or* **soaked to the** ~ trempé(e) jusqu'aux os.
skin cancer *n* cancer *m* de la peau.
skin-deep ['skɪn'diːp] *adj* superficiel(le).
skin diver *n* plongeur/euse sous-marin(e).
skin diving *n* plongée sous-marine.
skinflint ['skɪnflɪnt] *n* grippe-sou *m*.
skin graft *n* greffe *f* de peau.
skinhead ['skɪnhɛd] *n* skinhead *m*.
skinny ['skɪnɪ] *adj* maigre, maigrichon(ne).
skin test *n* cuti(-réaction *f*) *f*.
skintight ['skɪntaɪt] *adj* (*dress etc*) collant(e), ajusté(e).
skip [skɪp] *n* petit bond *or* saut; (*container*) benne *f* ♦ *vi* gambader, sautiller; (*with rope*) sauter à la corde ♦ *vt* (*pass over*) sauter; **to ~ school** (*esp US*) faire l'école buissonnière.
ski pants *npl* pantalon *m* de ski.
ski pole *n* bâton *m* de ski.
skipper ['skɪpə*] *n* (*NAUT*, *SPORT*) capitaine *m* ♦ *vt* (*boat*) commander; (*team*) être le chef de.
skipping rope ['skɪpɪŋ-] *n* (*BRIT*) corde *f* à sauter.
ski resort *n* station *f* de sports d'hiver.
skirmish ['skəːmɪʃ] *n* escarmouche *f*, accrochage *m*.
skirt [skəːt] *n* jupe *f* ♦ *vt* longer, contourner.
skirting board ['skəːtɪŋ-] *n* (*BRIT*) plinthe *f*.
ski run *n* piste *f* de ski.
ski suit *n* combinaison *f* de ski.
skit [skɪt] *n* sketch *m* satirique.
ski tow *n* = **ski lift**.
skittle ['skɪtl] *n* quille *f*, ~**s** (*game*) (jeu *m* de) quilles *fpl*.
skive [skaɪv] *vi* (*BRIT col*) tirer au flanc.
skulk [skʌlk] *vi* rôder furtivement.
skull [skʌl] *n* crâne *m*.
skullcap ['skʌlkæp] *n* calotte *f*.
skunk [skʌŋk] *n* mouffette *f*; (*fur*) sconse *m*.
sky [skaɪ] *n* ciel *m*; **to praise sb to the skies** porter qn aux nues.
sky-blue [skaɪ'bluː] *adj* bleu ciel *inv*.
skydiving ['skaɪdaɪvɪŋ] *n* parachutisme *m* (*en chute libre*).
sky-high ['skaɪ'haɪ] *adv* très haut ♦ *adj* exorbitant(e); **prices are** ~ les prix sont exorbitants.
skylark ['skaɪlɑːk] *n* (*bird*) alouette *f* (*des champs*).
skylight ['skaɪlaɪt] *n* lucarne *f*.
skyline ['skaɪlaɪn] *n* (*horizon*) (ligne *f* d')horizon *m*; (*of city*) ligne des toits.
skyscraper ['skaɪskreɪpə*] *n* gratte-ciel *m inv*.
slab [slæb] *n* plaque *f*; dalle *f*; (*of wood*) bloc *m*; (*of meat, cheese*) tranche épaisse.
slack [slæk] *adj* (*loose*) lâche, desserré(e); (*slow*) stagnant(e); (*careless*) négligent(e), peu sérieux(euse) *or* conscientieux(euse); (*COMM: market*) peu actif(ive); (*: demand*) faible; (*period*) creux(euse) ♦ *n* (*in rope etc*) mou *m*; **business is** ~ les affaires vont mal.
slacken ['slækn] (*also*: ~ **off**) *vi* ralentir, diminuer ♦ *vt* relâcher.
slacks [slæks] *npl* pantalon *m*.
slag [slæg] *n* scories *fpl*.
slag heap *n* crassier *m*.
slain [sleɪn] *pp of* **slay**.
slake [sleɪk] *vt* (*one's thirst*) étancher.
slalom ['slɑːləm] *n* slalom *m*.
slam [slæm] *vt* (*door*) (faire) claquer; (*throw*) jeter violemment, flanquer; (*criticize*) éreinter, démolir ♦ *vi* claquer.
slammer ['slæmə*] *n* (*col*): **the** ~ la taule.
slander ['slɑːndə*] *n* calomnie *f*; (*LAW*) diffamation *f* ♦ *vt* calomnier; diffamer.
slanderous ['slɑːndrəs] *adj* calomnieux(euse); diffamatoire.
slang [slæŋ] *n* argot *m*.
slanging match ['slæŋɪŋ-] *n* (*BRIT col*) engueulade *f*, empoignade *f*.
slant [slɑːnt] *n* inclinaison *f*; (*fig*) angle *m*, point *m* de vue.
slanted ['slɑːntɪd] *adj* tendancieux(euse).
slanting ['slɑːntɪŋ] *adj* en pente, incliné(e); couché(e).
slap [slæp] *n* claque *f*, gifle *f*; (*on the back*) tape *f* ♦ *vt* donner une claque *or* une gifle (*or* une tape) à ♦ *adv* (*directly*) tout droit, en plein.
slapdash ['slæpdæʃ] *adj* (*work*) fait(e) sans soin *or* à la va-vite; (*person*) insouciant(e), négligent(e).
slaphead ['slæphɛd] *n* (*BRIT col*) abruti/e, taré/e.
slapstick ['slæpstɪk] *n* (*comedy*) grosse farce (*style tarte à la crème*).
slap-up ['slæpʌp] *adj* (*BRIT*): **a** ~ **meal** un repas extra *or* fameux.
slash [slæʃ] *vt* entailler, taillader; (*fig: prices*) casser.
slat [slæt] *n* (*of wood*) latte *f*, lame *f*.
slate [sleɪt] *n* ardoise *f* ♦ *vt* (*fig: criticize*) éreinter, démolir.
slaughter ['slɔːtə*] *n* carnage *m*, massacre *m*; (*of animals*) abattage *m* ♦ *vt* (*animal*) abattre; (*people*) massacrer.
slaughterhouse ['slɔːtəhaus] *n* abattoir *m*.
Slav [slɑːv] *adj* slave.
slave [sleɪv] *n* esclave *m/f* ♦ *vi* (*also*: ~ **away**) trimer, travailler comme un forçat; **to ~ (away) at sth/at doing sth** se tuer à qch/à faire qch.
slave driver *n* (*col, pej*) négrier/ière.
slave labour *n* travail *m* d'esclave; **it's just** ~ (*fig*) c'est de l'esclavage.
slaver ['slævə*] *vi* (*dribble*) baver.
slavery ['sleɪvərɪ] *n* esclavage *m*.
Slavic ['slævɪk] *adj* slave.
slavish ['sleɪvɪʃ] *adj* servile.
slavishly ['sleɪvɪʃlɪ] *adv* (*copy*) servilement.
Slavonic [slə'vɔnɪk] *adj* slave.
slay, *pt* **slew**, *pp* **slain** [sleɪ, sluː, sleɪn] *vt* (*liter-*

ary) tuer.

sleazy ['sli:zɪ] *adj* miteux(euse), minable.

sledge [slɛdʒ] *n* luge *f*.

sledgehammer ['slɛdʒhæmə*] *n* marteau *m* de forgeron.

sleek [sli:k] *adj* (*hair, fur*) brillant(e), luisant(e); (*car, boat*) aux lignes pures *or* élégantes.

sleep [sli:p] *n* sommeil *m* ♦ *vi* (*pt, pp* **slept** [slɛpt]) dormir; (*spend night*) dormir, coucher ♦ *vt*: **we can ~ 4** on peut coucher *or* loger 4 personnes; **to go to ~** s'endormir; **to have a good night's ~** passer une bonne nuit; **to put to ~** (*patient*) endormir; (*animal: euphemism: kill*) piquer; **to ~ lightly** avoir le sommeil léger; **to ~ with sb** (*euphemism*) coucher avec qn.

▶**sleep in** *vi* (*lie late*) faire la grasse matinée; (*oversleep*) se réveiller trop tard.

sleeper ['sli:pə*] *n* (*person*) dormeur/euse; (*BRIT RAIL: on track*) traverse *f*; (: *train*) train *m* de voitures-lits; (: *carriage*) wagon-lits *m*, voiture-lits *f*; (: *berth*) couchette *f*.

sleepily ['sli:pɪlɪ] *adv* d'un air endormi.

sleeping ['sli:pɪŋ] *adj* qui dort, endormi(e).

sleeping bag *n* sac *m* de couchage.

sleeping car *n* wagon-lits *m*, voiture-lits *f*.

sleeping partner *n* (*BRIT COMM*) = **silent partner.**

sleeping pill *n* somnifère *m*.

sleeping sickness *n* maladie *f* du sommeil.

sleepless ['sli:plɪs] *adj*: **a ~ night** une nuit blanche.

sleeplessness ['sli:plɪsnɪs] *n* insomnie *f*.

sleepwalk ['sli:pwɔ:k] *vi* marcher en dormant.

sleepwalker ['sli:pwɔ:kə*] *n* somnambule *m/f*.

sleepy ['sli:pɪ] *adj* qui a envie de dormir; (*fig*) endormi(e); **to be** *or* **feel ~** avoir sommeil, avoir envie de dormir.

sleet [sli:t] *n* neige fondue.

sleeve [sli:v] *n* manche *f*; (*of record*) pochette *f*.

sleeveless ['sli:vlɪs] *adj* (*garment*) sans manches.

sleigh [sleɪ] *n* traîneau *m*.

sleight [slaɪt] *n*: **~ of hand** tour *m* de passe-passe.

slender ['slɛndə*] *adj* svelte, mince; (*fig*) faible, ténu(e).

slept [slɛpt] *pt, pp of* **sleep.**

sleuth [slu:θ] *n* (*col*) détective (privé).

slew [slu:] *vi* (*also*: **~ round**) virer, pivoter ♦ *pt of* **slay.**

slice [slaɪs] *n* tranche *f*; (*round*) rondelle *f* ♦ *vt* couper en tranches (*or* en rondelles); **~d bread** pain *m* en tranches.

slick [slɪk] *adj* brillant(e) en apparence; mielleux(euse) ♦ *n* (*also*: **oil ~**) nappe *f* de pétrole, marée noire.

slid [slɪd] *pt, pp of* **slide.**

slide [slaɪd] *n* (*in playground*) toboggan *m*; (*PHOT*) diapositive *f*; (*BRIT: also*: **hair ~**) bar-

rette *f*; (*microscope ~*) (lame *f*) porte-objet *m*; (*in prices*) chute *f*, baisse *f* ♦ *vb* (*pt, pp* **slid** [slɪd]) *vt* (faire) glisser ♦ *vi* glisser; **to let things ~** (*fig*) laisser les choses aller à la dérive.

slide projector *n* (*PHOT*) projecteur *m* de diapositives.

slide rule *n* règle *f* à calcul.

sliding ['slaɪdɪŋ] *adj* (*door*) coulissant(e); **~ roof** (*AUT*) toit ouvrant.

sliding scale *n* échelle *f* mobile.

slight [slaɪt] *adj* (*slim*) mince, menu(e); (*frail*) frêle; (*trivial*) faible, insignifiant(e); (*small*) petit(e), léger(ère) (*before n*) ♦ *n* offense *f*, affront *m* ♦ *vt* (*offend*) blesser, offenser; **the ~est** le (*or* la) moindre; **not in the ~est** pas le moins du monde, pas du tout.

slightly ['slaɪtlɪ] *adv* légèrement, un peu; **~ built** fluet(te).

slim [slɪm] *adj* mince ♦ *vi* maigrir, suivre un régime amaigrissant.

slime [slaɪm] *n* vase *f*; substance visqueuse.

slimming [slɪmɪŋ] *n* amaigrissement *m* ♦ *adj* (*diet, pills*) amaigrissant(e), pour maigrir.

slimy ['slaɪmɪ] *adj* visqueux(euse), gluant(e); (*covered with mud*) vaseux(euse).

sling [slɪŋ] *n* (*MED*) écharpe *f* ♦ *vt* (*pt, pp* **slung** [slʌŋ]) lancer, jeter; **to have one's arm in a ~** avoir le bras en écharpe.

slink [slɪŋk], *pt, pp* **slunk** [slʌŋk, slʌŋk] *vi*: **to ~ away** *or* **off** s'en aller furtivement.

slinky ['slɪŋkɪ] *adj* (*clothes*) moulant(e).

slip [slɪp] *n* faux pas; (*mistake*) erreur *f*, bévue *f*; (*underskirt*) combinaison *f*; (*of paper*) petite feuille, fiche *f* ♦ *vt* (*slide*) glisser ♦ *vi* (*slide*) glisser; (*move smoothly*): **to ~ into/out of** se glisser *or* se faufiler dans/hors de; (*decline*) baisser; **to let a chance ~ by** laisser passer une occasion; **to ~ sth on/off** enfiler/enlever qch; **it ~ped from her hand** cela lui a glissé des mains; **to give sb the ~** fausser compagnie à qn; **a ~ of the tongue** un lapsus.

▶**slip away** *vi* s'esquiver.

▶**slip in** *vt* glisser.

▶**slip out** *vi* sortir.

slip-on ['slɪpɔn] *adj* facile à enfiler; **~ shoes** mocassins *mpl*.

slipped disc [slɪpt-] *n* hernie discale.

slipper ['slɪpə*] *n* pantoufle *f*.

slippery ['slɪpərɪ] *adj* glissant(e); (*fig: person*) insaisissable.

slip road *n* (*BRIT: to motorway*) bretelle *f* d'accès.

slipshod ['slɪpʃɔd] *adj* négligé(e), peu soigné(e).

slip-up ['slɪpʌp] *n* bévue *f*.

slipway ['slɪpweɪ] *n* cale *f* (de construction *or* de lancement).

slit [slɪt] *n* fente *f*; (*cut*) incision *f*; (*tear*) déchirure *f* ♦ *vt* (*pt, pp* **slit**) fendre; couper; inciser; déchirer; **to ~ sb's throat** trancher la gorge à qn.

slither ['slɪðə*] *vi* glisser, déraper.

sliver ['slɪvə*] *n* (*of glass, wood*) éclat *m*; (*of cheese, sausage*) petit morceau.

slob [slɔb] *n* (*col*) rustaud/e.

slog [slɔg] *n* (*BRIT*) gros effort; tâche fastidieuse ♦ *vi* travailler très dur.

slogan ['sləʊgən] *n* slogan *m*.

slop [slɔp] *vi* (*also:* ~ **over**) se renverser; déborder ♦ *vt* répandre; renverser.

slope [sləʊp] *n* pente *f*; (*side of mountain*) versant *m*; (*slant*) inclinaison *f* ♦ *vi*: **to** ~ **down** être *or* descendre en pente; **to** ~ **up** monter.

sloping ['sləʊpɪŋ] *adj* en pente, incliné(e); (*handwriting*) penché(e).

sloppy ['slɔpɪ] *adj* (*work*) peu soigné(e), bâclé(e); (*appearance*) négligé(e), débraillé(e); (*film etc*) sentimental(e).

slosh [slɔʃ] *vi* (*col*): **to** ~ **about** *or* **around** (*children*) patauger; (*liquid*) clapoter.

sloshed [slɔʃt] *adj* (*col: drunk*) bourré(e).

slot [slɔt] *n* fente *f*; (*fig: in timetable, RADIO, TV*) créneau *m*, plage *f* ♦ *vt*: **to** ~ **into** encastrer *or* insérer dans ♦ *vi*: **to** ~ **into** s'encastrer *or* s'insérer dans.

sloth [sləʊθ] *n* (*vice*) paresse *f*; (*ZOOL*) paresseux *m*.

slot machine *n* (*BRIT: vending machine*) distributeur *m* (automatique), machine *f* à sous; (*for gambling*) appareil *m* *or* machine à sous.

slot meter *n* (*BRIT*) compteur *m* à pièces.

slouch [slaʊtʃ] *vi* avoir le dos rond, être voûté(e).

▸**slouch about**, **slouch around** *vi* traîner à ne rien faire.

Slovak ['sləʊvæk] *adj* slovaque ♦ *n* Slovaque *m/f*; (*LING*) slovaque *m*; **the** ~ **Republic** la République slovaque.

Slovakia [sləʊ'vækɪə] *n* Slovaquie *f*.

Slovakian [sləʊ'vækɪən] *adj, n* = **Slovak**.

Slovene [sləʊ'viːn] *adj* slovène ♦ *n* Slovène *m/f*; (*LING*) slovène *m*.

Slovenia [sləʊ'viːnɪə] *n* Slovénie *f*.

Slovenian [sləʊ'viːnɪən] *adj, n* = **Slovene**.

slovenly ['slʌvənlɪ] *adj* sale, débraillé(e), négligé(e).

slow [sləʊ] *adj* lent(e); (*watch*): **to be** ~ retarder ♦ *adv* lentement ♦ *vt, vi* (*also:* ~ **down**, ~ **up**) ralentir; " ~ " (*road sign*) "ralentir"; **at a** ~ **speed** à petite vitesse; **to be** ~ **to act/ decide** être lent à agir/décider; **my watch is 20 minutes** ~ ma montre retarde de 20 minutes; **business is** ~ les affaires marchent au ralenti; **to go** ~ (*driver*) rouler lentement; (*in industrial dispute*) faire la grève perlée.

slow-acting [sləʊ'æktɪŋ] *adj* qui agit lentement, à action lente.

slowcoach ['sləʊkəʊtʃ] *n* (*BRIT col*) lambin/e.

slowly ['sləʊlɪ] *adv* lentement.

slow motion *n*: **in** ~ au ralenti.

slowness ['sləʊnɪs] *n* lenteur *f*.

slowpoke ['sləʊpəʊk] *n* (*US col*) = **slowcoach**.

sludge [slʌdʒ] *n* boue *f*.

slug [slʌg] *n* limace *f*; (*bullet*) balle *f*.

sluggish ['slʌgɪʃ] *adj* mou(molle), lent(e); (*business, sales*) stagnant(e).

sluice [sluːs] *n* écluse *f*; (*also:* ~ **gate**) vanne *f* ♦ *vt*: **to** ~ **down** *or* **out** laver à grande eau.

slum [slʌm] *n* taudis *m*.

slumber ['slʌmbə*] *n* sommeil *m*.

slump [slʌmp] *n* baisse soudaine, effondrement *m*; crise *f* ♦ *vi* s'effondrer, s'affaisser.

slung [slʌŋ] *pt, pp of* **sling**.

slunk [slʌŋk] *pt, pp of* **slink**.

slur [slɜː*] *n* bredouillement *m*; (*smear*): ~ (**on**) atteinte *f* (à); insinuation *f* (contre) ♦ *vt* mal articuler; **to be a** ~ **on** porter atteinte à.

slurp [slɜːp] *vt, vi* boire à grand bruit.

slurred [slɜːd] *adj* (*pronunciation*) inarticulé(e), indistinct(e).

slush [slʌʃ] *n* neige fondue.

slush fund *n* caisse noire, fonds secrets.

slushy ['slʌʃɪ] *adj* (*snow*) fondu(e); (*street*) couvert(e) de neige fondue; (*BRIT: fig*) à l'eau de rose.

slut [slʌt] *n* souillon *f*.

sly [slaɪ] *adj* rusé(e); sournois(e); **on the** ~ en cachette.

smack [smæk] *n* (*slap*) tape *f*; (*on face*) gifle *f* ♦ *vt* donner une tape à; gifler; (*child*) donner la fessée à ♦ *vi*: **to** ~ **of** avoir des relents de, sentir ♦ *adv* (*col*): **it fell** ~ **in the middle** c'est tombé en plein milieu *or* en plein dedans; **to** ~ **one's lips** se lécher les babines.

smacker ['smækə*] *n* (*col: kiss*) bisou *m* *or* bise *f* sonore; (*: BRIT: pound note*) livre *f*; (*: US: dollar bill*) dollar *m*.

small [smɔːl] *adj* petit(e); (*letter*) minuscule ♦ *n*: **the** ~ **of the back** le creux des reins; **to get** *or* **grow** ~**er** diminuer; **to make** ~**er** (*amount, income*) diminuer; (*object, garment*) rapetisser; **a** ~ **shopkeeper** un petit commerçant.

small ads *npl* (*BRIT*) petites annonces.

small arms *npl* armes individuelles.

small business *n* petit commerce, petite affaire.

small change *n* petite *or* menue monnaie.

smallholder ['smɔːlhəʊldə*] *n* (*BRIT*) petit cultivateur.

smallholding ['smɔːlhəʊldɪŋ] *n* (*BRIT*) petite ferme.

small hours *npl*: **in the** ~ au petit matin.

smallish ['smɔːlɪʃ] *adj* plutôt *or* assez petit(e).

small-minded [smɔːl'maɪndɪd] *adj* mesquin(e).

smallpox ['smɔːlpɔks] *n* variole *f*.

small print *n* (*in contract etc*) clause(s) imprimée(s) en petits caractères.

small-scale ['smɔːlskeɪl] *adj* (*map, model*) à échelle réduite, à petite échelle; (*business, farming*) peu important(e), modeste.

small talk *n* menus propos.

small-time ['smɔːltaɪm] *adj* (*farmer etc*) petit(e); **a** ~ **thief** un voleur à la petite semaine.

small-town ['smɔːltaun] *adj* provincial(e).

smarmy ['smɑːmɪ] *adj* (*BRIT pej*) flagorneur(euse), lécheur(euse).

smart [smɑːt] *adj* élégant(e), chic *inv*; (*clever*) intelligent(e); (*pej*) futé(e); (*quick*) vif(vive), prompt(e) ♦ *vi* faire mal, brûler; **the ~ set** le beau monde; **to look ~** être élégant(e); **my eyes are ~ing** j'ai les yeux irrités *or* qui me piquent.

smartcard ['smɑːtkɑːd] *n* carte *f* à puce.

smarten up ['smɑːtn-] *vi* devenir plus élégant(e), se faire beau(belle) ♦ *vt* rendre plus élégant(e).

smash [smæʃ] *n* (*also*: ~-**up**) collision *f*, accident *m*; (*sound*) fracas *m* ♦ *vt* casser, briser, fracasser; (*opponent*) écraser; (*hopes*) ruiner, détruire; (*SPORT: record*) pulvériser ♦ *vi* se briser, se fracasser; s'écraser.

▶**smash up** *vt* (*car*) bousiller; (*room*) tout casser dans.

smash hit *n* (grand) succès.

smashing ['smæʃɪŋ] *adj* (*col*) formidable.

smattering ['smætərɪŋ] *n*: **a ~ of** quelques notions de.

smear [smɪə*] *n* tache *f*, salissure *f*; trace *f*; (*MED*) frottis *m*; (*insult*) calomnie *f* ♦ *vt* enduire; (*fig*) porter atteinte à; **his hands were ~ed with oil/ink** il avait les mains maculées de cambouis/d'encre.

smear campaign *n* campagne *f* de dénigrement.

smear test *n* (*BRIT MED*) frottis *m*.

smell [smɛl] *n* odeur *f*; (*sense*) odorat *m* ♦ *vb* (*pt, pp* **smelt** *or* **smelled** [smɛlt, smɛld]) *vt* sentir ♦ *vi* (*food etc*): **to ~ (of)** sentir; (*pej*) sentir mauvais; **it ~s good** ça sent bon.

smelly ['smɛlɪ] *adj* qui sent mauvais, malodorant(e).

smelt [smɛlt] *pt, pp of* **smell** ♦ *vt* (*ore*) fondre.

smile [smaɪl] *n* sourire *m* ♦ *vi* sourire.

smiling ['smaɪlɪŋ] *adj* souriant(e).

smirk [smɜːk] *n* petit sourire suffisant *or* affecté.

smith [smɪθ] *n* maréchal-ferrant *m*; forgeron *m*.

smithy ['smɪðɪ] *n* forge *f*.

smitten ['smɪtn] *adj*: ~ **with** pris(e) de; frappé(e) de.

smock [smɔk] *n* blouse *f*, sarrau *m*.

smog [smɔg] *n* brouillard mêlé de fumée.

smoke [sməuk] *n* fumée *f* ♦ *vt, vi* fumer; **to have a ~** fumer une cigarette; **do you ~?** est-ce que vous fumez?; **to go up in ~** (*house etc*) brûler; (*fig*) partir en fumée.

smoked ['sməukt] *adj* (*bacon, glass*) fumé(e).

smokeless fuel ['sməuklɪs-] *n* combustible non polluant.

smokeless zone ['sməuklɪs-] *n* (*BRIT*) zone *f* où l'usage du charbon est réglementé.

smoker ['sməukə*] *n* (*person*) fumeur/euse; (*RAIL*) wagon *m* fumeurs.

smoke screen *n* rideau *m* or écran *m* de fumée; (*fig*) paravent *m*.

smoke shop *n* (*US*) (bureau *m* de) tabac *m*.

smoking ['sməukɪŋ] *n*: "**no ~**" (*sign*) "défense de fumer"; **he's given up ~** il a arrêté de fumer.

smoking compartment, (*US*) **smoking car** *n* wagon *m* fumeurs.

smoking room *n* fumoir *m*.

smoky ['sməukɪ] *adj* enfumé(e).

smolder ['sməuldə*] *vi* (*US*) = **smoulder**.

smoochy ['smuːtʃɪ] *adj* (*col*) langoureux(euse).

smooth [smuːð] *adj* lisse; (*sauce*) onctueux(euse); (*flavour, whisky*) moelleux(euse); (*cigarette*) doux(douce); (*movement*) régulier(ière), sans à-coups *or* heurts; (*landing, takeoff*) en douceur; (*flight*) sans secousses; (*person*) doucereux(euse), mielleux(euse) ♦ *vt* lisser, défroisser; (*also*: ~ **out**: *creases, difficulties*) faire disparaître.

▶**smooth over** *vt*: **to ~ things over** (*fig*) arranger les choses.

smoothly ['smuːðlɪ] *adv* (*easily*) facilement, sans difficulté(s); **everything went ~** tout s'est bien passé.

smother ['smʌðə*] *vt* étouffer.

smoulder, (*US*) **smolder** ['sməuldə*] *vi* couver.

smudge [smʌdʒ] *n* tache *f*, bavure *f* ♦ *vt* salir, maculer.

smug [smʌg] *adj* suffisant(e), content(e) de soi.

smuggle ['smʌgl] *vt* passer en contrebande *or* en fraude; **to ~ in/out** (*goods etc*) faire entrer/sortir clandestinement *or* en fraude.

smuggler ['smʌglə*] *n* contrebandier/ière.

smuggling ['smʌglɪŋ] *n* contrebande *f*.

smut [smʌt] *n* (*grain of soot*) grain *m* de suie; (*mark*) tache *f* de suie; (*in conversation etc*) obscénités *fpl*.

smutty ['smʌtɪ] *adj* (*fig*) grossier(ière), obscène.

snack [snæk] *n* casse-croûte *m inv*; **to have a ~** prendre un en-cas, manger quelque chose (de léger).

snack bar *n* snack(-bar) *m*.

snag [snæg] *n* inconvénient *m*, difficulté *f*.

snail [sneɪl] *n* escargot *m*.

snake [sneɪk] *n* serpent *m*.

snap [snæp] *n* (*sound*) claquement *m*, bruit sec; (*photograph*) photo *f*, instantané *m*; (*game*) sorte de jeu de bataille ♦ *adj* subit(e); fait(e) sans réflechir ♦ *vt* faire claquer; (*break*) casser net; (*photograph*) prendre un instantané de ♦ *vi* se casser net *or* avec un bruit sec; (*fig: person*) craquer; **to ~ at sb** (*subj: person*) parler d'un ton brusque à qn; (: *dog*) essayer de mordre qn; **to ~ open/ shut** s'ouvrir/se refermer brusquement; **to ~ one's fingers at** (*fig*) se moquer de; **a cold ~** (*of weather*) un refroidissement soudain de la température.

▶**snap off** *vt* (*break*) casser net.

▶**snap up** *vt* sauter sur, saisir.

snap fastener *n* bouton-pression *m*.

snappy ['snæpɪ] *adj* prompt(e); (*slogan*) qui a du punch; **make it ~!** (*col: hurry up*) grouille-toi!, magne-toi!

snapshot ['snæpʃɒt] *n* photo *f*, instantané *m*.

snare [snɛə*] *n* piège *m* ♦ *vt* attraper, prendre au piège.

snarl [snɑːl] *n* grondement *m or* grognement *m* féroce ♦ *vi* gronder ♦ *vt*: **to get ~ed up** (*wool, plans*) s'emmêler; (*traffic*) se bloquer.

snatch [snætʃ] *n* (*fig*) vol *m*; (*BRIT: small amount*): **~es of** des fragments *mpl or* bribes *fpl* de ♦ *vt* saisir (*d'un geste vif*); (*steal*) voler ♦ *vi*: **don't ~!** doucement!; **to ~ a sandwich** manger *or* avaler un sandwich à la hâte; **to ~ some sleep** arriver à dormir un peu.

▶**snatch up** *vt* saisir, s'emparer de.

snazzy ['snæzɪ] *adj* (*col: clothes*) classe *inv*, chouette.

sneak [sniːk] *vi*: **to ~ in/out** entrer/sortir furtivement *or* à la dérobée ♦ *vt*: **to ~ a look at sth** regarder furtivement qch.

sneakers ['sniːkəz] *npl* chaussures *fpl* de tennis *or* basket.

sneaking ['sniːkɪŋ] *adj*: **to have a ~ feeling or suspicion that ...** avoir la vague impression que ....

sneaky ['sniːkɪ] *adj* sournois(e).

sneer [snɪə*] *n* ricanement *m* ♦ *vi* ricaner, sourire d'un air sarcastique; **to ~ at sb/sth** se moquer de qn/qch avec mépris.

sneeze [sniːz] *n* éternuement *m* ♦ *vi* éternuer.

snide [snaɪd] *adj* sarcastique, narquois(e).

sniff [snɪf] *n* reniflement *m* ♦ *vi* renifler ♦ *vt* renifler, flairer; (*glue, drug*) sniffer, respirer.

▶**sniff at** *vt fus*: **it's not to be ~ed at** il ne faut pas cracher dessus, ce n'est pas à dédaigner.

sniffer dog ['snɪfə-] *n* (*POLICE*) *chien dressé pour la recherche d'explosifs et de stupéfiants.*

snigger ['snɪgə*] *n* ricanement *m*; rire moqueur ♦ *vi* ricaner; pouffer de rire.

snip [snɪp] *n* petit bout; (*bargain*) (bonne) occasion *or* affaire ♦ *vt* couper.

sniper ['snaɪpə*] *n* (*marksman*) tireur embusqué.

snippet ['snɪpɪt] *n* bribes *fpl*.

snivelling ['snɪvlɪŋ] *adj* larmoyant(e), pleurnicheur(euse).

snob [snɒb] *n* snob *m/f*.

snobbery ['snɒbərɪ] *n* snobisme *m*.

snobbish ['snɒbɪʃ] *adj* snob *inv*.

snog [snɒg] *vi* (*col*) se bécoter.

snooker ['snuːkə*] *n* sorte de jeu de billard.

snoop [snuːp] *vi*: **to ~ on sb** espionner qn; **to ~ about somewhere** fourrer son nez quelque part.

snooper ['snuːpə*] *n* fureteur/euse.

snooty ['snuːtɪ] *adj* snob *inv*, prétentieux(euse).

snooze [snuːz] *n* petit somme ♦ *vi* faire un petit somme.

snore [snɔː*] *vi* ronfler ♦ *n* ronflement *m*.

snoring ['snɔːrɪŋ] *n* ronflement(s) *m(pl)*.

snorkel ['snɔːkl] *n* (*of swimmer*) tuba *m*.

snort [snɔːt] *n* grognement *m* ♦ *vi* grogner; (*horse*) renâcler ♦ *vt* (*col: drugs*) sniffer.

snotty ['snɒtɪ] *adj* morveux(euse).

snout [snaut] *n* museau *m*.

snow [snəu] *n* neige *f* ♦ *vi* neiger ♦ *vt*: **to be ~ed under with work** être débordé(e) de travail.

snowball ['snəubɔːl] *n* boule *f* de neige.

snowbound ['snəubaund] *adj* enneigé(e), bloqué(e) par la neige.

snow-capped ['snəukæpt] *adj* (*peak, mountain*) couvert(e) de neige.

snowdrift ['snəudrɪft] *n* congère *f*.

snowdrop ['snəudrɒp] *n* perce-neige *m*.

snowfall ['snəufɔːl] *n* chute *f* de neige.

snowflake ['snəufleɪk] *n* flocon *m* de neige.

snowman ['snəumæn] *n* bonhomme *m* de neige.

snowplough, (*US*) **snowplow** ['snəuplau] *n* chasse-neige *m inv*.

snowshoe ['snəuʃuː] *n* raquette *f* (*pour la neige*).

snowstorm ['snəustɔːm] *n* tempête *f* de neige.

snowy ['snəuɪ] *adj* neigeux(euse); (*covered with snow*) enneigé(e).

SNP *n abbr* (*BRIT POL*) = **Scottish National Party**.

snub [snʌb] *vt* repousser, snober ♦ *n* rebuffade *f*.

snub-nosed [snʌb'nəuzd] *adj* au nez retroussé.

snuff [snʌf] *n* tabac *m* à priser ♦ *vt* (*also: ~ out: candle*) moucher.

snuff movie *n* (*col*) *film pornographique qui se termine par le meurtre réel de l'un des acteurs.*

snug [snʌg] *adj* douillet(te), confortable; **it's a ~ fit** c'est bien ajusté(e).

snuggle ['snʌgl] *vi*: **to ~ down in bed/up to sb** se pelotonner dans son lit/contre qn.

SO *abbr* (*BANKING*) = **standing order**.

= *KEYWORD*

so [səu] *adv* **1** (*thus, likewise*) ainsi, de cette façon; **if ~** si oui; **~ do or have I** moi aussi; **it's 5 o'clock — ~ it is!** il est 5 heures — en effet! *or* c'est vrai!; **I hope/think ~** je l'espère/le crois; **~ far** jusqu'ici, jusqu'à maintenant; (*in past*) jusque-là; **quite ~!** exactement!, c'est bien ça!; **even ~** quand même, tout de même

2 (*in comparisons etc: to such a degree*) si, tellement; **~ big (that)** si *or* tellement grand (que); **she's not ~ clever as her brother** elle n'est pas aussi intelligente que son frère

3: **~ much** *adj, adv* tant (de); **I've got ~ much**

work j'ai tant de travail; **I love you ~ much** je vous aime tant; ~ **many** tant (de)
4 (*phrases*): **10 or ~** à peu près *or* environ 10; ~ **long!** (*inf: goodbye*) au revoir!, à un de ces jours!; ~ **to speak** pour ainsi dire; ~ **(what)?** (*col*) (bon) et alors?, et après?
♦ *conj* **1** (*expressing purpose*): ~ **as to do** pour faire, afin de faire; ~ **(that)** pour que *or* afin que +*sub*
2 (*expressing result*) donc, par conséquent; ~ **that** si bien que, de (telle) sorte que; ~ **that's the reason!** c'est donc (pour) ça!

soak [səuk] *vt* faire *or* laisser tremper ♦ *vi* tremper; **to be ~ed through** être trempé jusqu'aux os.
▶**soak in** *vi* pénétrer, être absorbé(e).
▶**soak up** *vt* absorber.
soaking ['səukɪŋ] *adj* (*also*: ~ **wet**) trempé(e).
so and so *n* un tel/une telle.
soap [səup] *n* savon *m*.
soapbox ['səupbɔks] *n* tribune improvisée (en plein air).
soapflakes ['səupfleɪks] *npl* paillettes *fpl* de savon.
soap opera *n* feuilleton télévisé (*quotidienneté réaliste ou embellie*).
soap powder *n* lessive *f*, détergent *m*.
soapsuds ['səupsʌds] *npl* mousse *f* de savon.
soapy ['səupɪ] *adj* savonneux(euse).
soar [sɔ:*] *vi* monter (en flèche), s'élancer; ~**ing prices** prix qui grimpent.
sob [sɔb] *n* sanglot *m* ♦ *vi* sangloter.
s.o.b. *n* *abbr* (*US col!*: = *son of a bitch*) salaud *m* (*!*).
sober ['səubə*] *adj* qui n'est pas (*or* plus) ivre; (*sedate*) sérieux(euse), sensé(e); (*moderate*) mesuré(e); (*colour, style*) sobre, discret(ète).
▶**sober up** *vt* dégriser ♦ *vi* se dégriser.
sobriety [sə'braɪətɪ] *n* (*not being drunk*) sobriété *f*; (*seriousness, sedateness*) sérieux *m*.
sob story *n* (*col, pej*) histoire larmoyante.
Soc. *abbr* (= *society*) Soc.
so-called ['səu'kɔ:ld] *adj* soi-disant *inv*.
soccer ['sɔkə*] *n* football *m*.
soccer pitch *n* terrain *m* de football.
soccer player *n* footballeur *m*.
sociable ['səuʃəbl] *adj* sociable.
social ['səuʃl] *adj* social(e) ♦ *n* (petite) fête.
social climber *n* arriviste *m/f*.
social club *n* amicale *f*, foyer *m*.
Social Democrat *n* social-démocrate *m/f*.
social insurance *n* (*US*) sécurité sociale.
socialism ['səuʃəlɪzəm] *n* socialisme *m*.
socialist ['səuʃəlɪst] *adj, n* socialiste (*m/f*).
socialite ['səuʃəlaɪt] *n* personnalité mondaine.
socialize ['səuʃəlaɪz] *vi* voir *or* rencontrer des gens, se faire des amis; **to ~ with** fréquenter; lier connaissance *or* parler avec.
social life *n* vie sociale; **how's your ~?** est-ce que tu sors beaucoup?
socially ['səuʃəlɪ] *adv* socialement, en société.

social science *n* sciences humaines.
social security *n* aide sociale.
social services *npl* services sociaux.
social welfare *n* sécurité sociale.
social work *n* assistance sociale.
social worker *n* assistant/e social(e).
society [sə'saɪətɪ] *n* société *f*; (*club*) société, association *f*; (*also*: **high ~**) (haute) société, grand monde ♦ *cpd* (*party*) mondain(e).
socio-economic ['səusɪəui:kə'nɔmɪk] *adj* socioéconomique.
sociological [səusɪə'lɔdʒɪkl] *adj* sociologique.
sociologist [səusɪ'ɔlədʒɪst] *n* sociologue *m/f*.
sociology [səusɪ'ɔlədʒɪ] *n* sociologie *f*.
sock [sɔk] *n* chaussette *f* ♦ *vt* (*col: hit*) flanquer un coup à; **to pull one's ~s up** (*fig*) se secouer (les puces).
socket ['sɔkɪt] *n* cavité *f*; (*ELEC: also*: **wall ~**) prise *f* de courant; (*: for light bulb*) douille *f*.
sod [sɔd] *n* (*of earth*) motte *f*; (*BRIT col!*) con *m* (*!*); salaud *m* (*!*).
▶**sod off** *vi*: ~ **off!** (*BRIT col!*) fous le camp!, va te faire foutre! (*!*).
soda ['səudə] *n* (*CHEM*) soude *f*; (*also*: ~ **water**) eau *f* de Seltz; (*US: also*: ~ **pop**) soda *m*.
sodden ['sɔdn] *adj* trempé(e); détrempé(e).
sodium ['səudɪəm] *n* sodium *m*.
sodium chloride *n* chlorure *m* de sodium.
sofa ['səufə] *n* sofa *m*, canapé *m*.
Sofia ['səufɪə] *n* Sofia.
soft [sɔft] *adj* (*not rough*) doux(douce); (*not hard*) doux; mou(molle); (*not loud*) doux, léger(ère); (*kind*) doux, gentil(le); (*weak*) indulgent(e); (*stupid*) stupide, débile.
soft-boiled ['sɔftbɔɪld] *adj* (*egg*) à la coque.
soft drink *n* boisson non alcoolisée.
soft drugs *npl* drogues douces.
soften ['sɔfn] *vt* (r)amollir; adoucir; atténuer ♦ *vi* se ramollir; s'adoucir; s'atténuer.
softener ['sɔfnə*] *n* (*water* ~) adoucisseur *m*; (*fabric* ~) produit assouplissant.
soft fruit *n* (*BRIT*) baies *fpl*.
soft furnishings *npl* tissus *mpl* d'ameublement.
soft-hearted [sɔft'ha:tɪd] *adj* au cœur tendre.
softly ['sɔftlɪ] *adv* doucement; légèrement; gentiment.
softness ['sɔftnɪs] *n* douceur *f*.
soft option *n* solution *f* de facilité.
soft sell *n* promotion *f* de vente discrète.
soft target *n* cible *f* facile.
soft toy *n* jouet *m* en peluche.
software ['sɔftwɛə*] *n* logiciel *m*, software *m*.
software package *n* progiciel *m*.
soggy ['sɔgɪ] *adj* trempé(e); détrempé(e).
soil [sɔɪl] *n* (*earth*) sol *m*, terre *f* ♦ *vt* salir; (*fig*) souiller.
soiled [sɔɪld] *adj* sale; (*COMM*) défraîchi(e).
sojourn ['sɔdʒə:n] *n* (*formal*) séjour *m*.
solace ['sɔlɪs] *n* consolation *f*, réconfort *m*.
solar ['səulə*] *adj* solaire.
solarium, *pl* **solaria** [sə'lɛərɪəm, -rɪə] *n* sola-

rium *m*.

solar panel *n* panneau *m* solaire.

solar plexus [-'plɛksəs] *n* (*ANAT*) plexus *m* solaire.

solar power *n* énergie *f* solaire.

sold [səuld] *pt, pp of* **sell**.

solder ['səuldə*] *vt* souder (*au fil à souder*) ♦ *n* soudure *f*.

soldier ['səuldʒə*] *n* soldat *m*, militaire *m* ♦ *vi*: **to ~ on** persévérer, s'accrocher; **toy ~** petit soldat.

sold out *adj* (*COMM*) épuisé(e).

sole [səul] *n* (*of foot*) plante *f*; (*of shoe*) semelle *f*; (*fish: pl inv*) sole *f* ♦ *adj* seul(e), unique; **the ~ reason** la seule et unique raison.

solely ['səulli] *adv* seulement, uniquement; **I will hold you ~ responsible** je vous en tiendrai pour seul responsable.

solemn ['sɔləm] *adj* solennel(le); sérieux(euse), grave.

sole trader *n* (*COMM*) chef *m* d'entreprise individuelle.

solicit [sə'lɪsɪt] *vt* (*request*) solliciter ♦ *vi* (*prostitute*) racoler.

solicitor [sə'lɪsɪtə*] *n* (*BRIT: for wills etc*) ≈ notaire *m*; (*: in court*) ≈ avocat *m*.

solid ['sɔlɪd] *adj* (*not hollow*) plein(e), compact(e), massif(ive); (*strong, sound, reliable, not liquid*) solide; (*meal*) consistant(e), substantiel(le); (*vote*) unanime ♦ *n* solide *m*; **to be on ~ ground** être sur la terre ferme; (*fig*) être en terrain sûr; **we waited 2 ~ hours** nous avons attendu deux heures entières.

solidarity [sɔlɪ'dærɪtɪ] *n* solidarité *f*.

solid fuel *n* combustible *m* solide.

solidify [sə'lɪdɪfaɪ] *vi* se solidifier ♦ *vt* solidifier.

solidity [sə'lɪdɪtɪ] *n* solidité *f*.

solid-state ['sɔlɪdsteɪt] *adj* (*ELEC*) à circuits intégrés.

soliloquy [sə'lɪləkwɪ] *n* monologue *m*.

solitaire [sɔlɪ'tɛə*] *n* (*gem, BRIT: game*) solitaire *m*; (*US: card game*) réussite *f*.

solitary ['sɔlɪtərɪ] *adj* solitaire.

solitary confinement *n* (*LAW*) isolement *m* (cellulaire).

solitude ['sɔlɪtjuːd] *n* solitude *f*.

solo ['səuləu] *n* solo *m*.

soloist ['səuləuɪst] *n* soliste *m/f*.

Solomon Islands ['sɔləmən-] *npl*: **the ~** les (îles *fpl*) Salomon *fpl*.

solstice ['sɔlstɪs] *n* solstice *m*.

soluble ['sɔljubl] *adj* soluble.

solution [sə'luːʃən] *n* solution *f*.

solve [sɔlv] *vt* résoudre.

solvency ['sɔlvənsɪ] *n* (*COMM*) solvabilité *f*.

solvent ['sɔlvənt] *adj* (*COMM*) solvable ♦ *n* (*CHEM*) (dis)solvant *m*.

solvent abuse *n* usage *m* de solvants hallucinogènes.

Som. *abbr* (*BRIT*) = **Somerset**.

Somali [səu'mɑːlɪ] *adj* somali(e), somalien(ne)

♦ *n* Somali/e, Somalien/ne.

Somalia [səu'mɑːlɪə] *n* (République *f* de) Somalie *f*.

Somaliland [səu'mɑːlɪlænd] *n* Somaliland *m*.

sombre, (*US*) **somber** ['sɔmbə*] *adj* sombre, morne.

===================================== *KEYWORD*

some [sʌm] *adj* **1** (*a certain amount or number of*): **~ tea/water/ice cream** du thé/de l'eau/de la glace; **~ children/apples** des enfants/pommes

2 (*certain: in contrasts*): **~ people say that ...** il y a des gens qui disent que ...; **~ films were excellent, but most ...** certains films étaient excellents, mais la plupart ...

3 (*unspecified*): **~ woman was asking for you** il y avait une dame qui vous demandait; **he was asking for ~ book (or other)** il demandait un livre quelconque; **~ day** un de ces jours; **~ day next week** un jour la semaine prochaine; **after ~ time** après un certain temps; **at ~ length** assez longuement; **in ~ form or other** sous une forme ou une autre, sous une forme quelconque

♦ *pron* **1** (*a certain number*) quelques-un(e)s, certain(e)s; **I've got ~** (*books etc*) j'en ai (quelques-uns); **~ (of them) have been sold** certains ont été vendus

2 (*a certain amount*) un peu; **I've got ~** (*money, milk*) j'en ai (un peu); **would you like ~?** est-ce que vous en voulez?, en voulez-vous?

♦ *adv*: **~ 10 people** quelque 10 personnes, 10 personnes environ.

somebody ['sʌmbədɪ] *pron* quelqu'un; **~ or other** quelqu'un, je ne sais qui.

someday ['sʌmdeɪ] *adv* un de ces jours, un jour ou l'autre.

somehow ['sʌmhau] *adv* d'une façon ou d'une autre; (*for some reason*) pour une raison ou une autre.

someone ['sʌmwʌn] *pron* = **somebody**.

someplace ['sʌmpleɪs] *adv* (*US*) = **somewhere**.

somersault ['sʌməsɔːlt] *n* culbute *f*, saut périlleux ♦ *vi* faire la culbute *or* un saut périlleux; (*car*) faire un tonneau.

something ['sʌmθɪŋ] *pron* quelque chose *m*; **~ interesting** quelque chose d'intéressant; **~ to do** quelque chose à faire; **he's ~ like me** il est un peu comme moi; **it's ~ of a problem** il y a là un problème.

sometime ['sʌmtaɪm] *adv* (*in future*) un de ces jours, un jour ou l'autre; (*in past*): **~ last month** au cours du mois dernier.

sometimes ['sʌmtaɪmz] *adv* quelquefois, parfois.

somewhat ['sʌmwɔt] *adv* quelque peu, un peu.

somewhere ['sʌmwɛə*] *adv* quelque part; **~ else** ailleurs, autre part.

son [sʌn] n fils m.
sonar ['səunɑ:*] n sonar m.
sonata [sə'nɑːtə] n sonate f.
song [sɒŋ] n chanson f.
songbook ['sɒŋbuk] n chansonnier m.
songwriter ['sɒŋraɪtə*] n auteur-compositeur m.
sonic ['sɒnɪk] adj (boom) supersonique.
son-in-law ['sʌnɪnlɔː] n gendre m, beau-fils m.
sonnet ['sɒnɪt] n sonnet m.
sonny ['sʌnɪ] n (col) fiston m.
soon [suːn] adv bientôt; (early) tôt; ~ afterwards peu après; quite ~ sous peu; how ~ can you do it? combien de temps vous faut-il pour le faire, au plus pressé?; how ~ can you come back? quand ou dans combien de temps pouvez-vous revenir, au plus tôt; see you ~! à bientôt!; see also as.
sooner ['suːnə*] adv (time) plus tôt; (preference): I would ~ do j'aimerais autant or je préférerais faire; ~ or later tôt ou tard; no ~ said than done sitôt dit, sitôt fait; the ~ the better le plus tôt sera le mieux; no ~ had we left than ... à peine étions-nous partis que ....
soot [sut] n suie f.
soothe [suːð] vt calmer, apaiser.
soothing ['suːðɪŋ] adj (ointment etc) lénitif(ive), lénifiant(e); (tone, words etc) apaisant(e); (drink, bath) relaxant(e).
SOP n abbr = standard operating procedure.
sop [sɒp] n: that's only a ~ c'est pour nous (or les etc) amadouer.
sophisticated [sə'fɪstɪkeɪtɪd] adj raffiné(e), sophistiqué(e); (system etc) très perfectionné(e), sophistiqué.
sophistication [səfɪstɪ'keɪʃən] n raffinement m; (niveau m de) perfectionnement m.
sophomore ['sɒfəmɔː*] n (US) étudiant/e de seconde année.
soporific [sɒpə'rɪfɪk] adj soporifique ♦ n somnifère m.
sopping ['sɒpɪŋ] adj (also: ~ wet) tout(e) trempé(e).
soppy ['sɒpɪ] adj (pej) sentimental(e).
soprano [sə'prɑːnəu] n (voice) soprano m; (singer) soprano m/f.
sorbet ['sɔːbeɪ] n sorbet m.
sorcerer ['sɔːsərə*] n sorcier m.
sordid ['sɔːdɪd] adj sordide.
sore [sɔː*] adj (painful) douloureux(euse), sensible; (offended) contrarié(e), vexé(e) ♦ n plaie f; to have a ~ throat avoir mal à la gorge; it's a ~ point (fig) c'est un point délicat.
sorely ['sɔːlɪ] adv (tempted) fortement.
sorrel ['sɒrəl] n oseille f.
sorrow ['sɒrəu] n peine f, chagrin m.
sorrowful ['sɒrəuful] adj triste.
sorry ['sɒrɪ] adj désolé(e); (condition, excuse, tale) triste, déplorable; (sight) désolant(e); ~! pardon!, excusez-moi!; to feel ~ for sb plaindre qn; I'm ~ to hear that ... je suis désolé(e) or navré(e) d'apprendre que ...; to be ~ about sth regretter qch.
sort [sɔːt] n genre m, espèce f, sorte f; (make: of coffee, car etc) marque f ♦ vt (also: ~ out: papers) trier; classer; ranger; (: letters etc) trier; (: problems) résoudre, régler; (COMPUT) trier; what ~ do you want? quelle sorte or quel genre voulez-vous?; what ~ of car? quelle marque de voiture?; I'll do nothing of the ~! je ne ferai rien de tel!; it's ~ of awkward (col) c'est plutôt gênant.
sortie ['sɔːtɪ] n sortie f.
sorting office ['sɔːtɪŋ-] n (POST) bureau m de tri.
SOS n abbr (= save our souls) SOS m.
so-so ['səusəu] adv comme ci comme ça.
soufflé ['suːfleɪ] n soufflé m.
sought [sɔːt] pt, pp of **seek**.
sought-after ['sɔːtɑːftə*] adj recherché(e).
soul [səul] n âme f; the poor ~ had nowhere to sleep le pauvre n'avait nulle part où dormir; I didn't see a ~ je n'ai vu (absolument) personne.
soul-destroying ['səuldɪstrɔɪŋ] adj démoralisant(e).
soulful ['səulful] adj plein(e) de sentiment.
soulless ['səullɪs] adj sans cœur, inhumain(e).
soul mate n âme f sœur.
soul-searching ['səulsɜːtʃɪŋ] n: after much ~, I decided ... j'ai longuement réfléchi avant de décider ....
sound [saund] adj (healthy) en bonne santé, sain(e); (safe, not damaged) solide, en bon état; (reliable, not superficial) sérieux(euse), solide; (sensible) sensé(e) ♦ adv: ~ asleep dormant d'un profond sommeil ♦ n (noise) son m; bruit m; (GEO) détroit m, bras m de mer ♦ vt (alarm) sonner; (also: ~ out: opinions) sonder ♦ vi sonner, retentir; (fig: seem) sembler (être); to be of ~ mind être sain(e) d'esprit; I don't like the ~ of it ça ne me dit rien qui vaille; to ~ one's horn (AUT) klaxonner, actionner son avertisseur; to ~ like ressembler à; it ~s as if ... il semblerait que ..., j'ai l'impression que ....
▶**sound off** vi (col): to ~ off (about) la ramener (sur).
sound barrier n mur m du son.
soundbite ['saundbaɪt] n phrase toute faite (pour être citée dans les médias).
sound effects npl bruitage m.
sound engineer n ingénieur m du son.
sounding ['saundɪŋ] n (NAUT etc) sondage m.
sounding board n (MUS) table f d'harmonie; (fig): to use sb as a ~ for one's ideas essayer ses idées sur qn.
soundly ['saundlɪ] adv (sleep) profondément; (beat) complètement, à plate couture.
soundproof ['saundpruːf] vt insonoriser ♦ adj insonorisé(e).
sound system n sono(risation) f.

soundtrack ['saundtræk] *n* (*of film*) bande *f* sonore.

sound wave *n* (*PHYSICS*) onde *f* sonore.

soup [su:p] *n* soupe *f*, potage *m*; **in the** ~ (*fig*) dans le pétrin.

soup course *n* potage *m*.

soup kitchen *n* soupe *f* populaire.

soup plate *n* assiette creuse *or* à soupe.

soupspoon ['su:pspu:n] *n* cuiller *f* à soupe.

sour ['sauə*] *adj* aigre, acide; (*milk*) tourné(e), aigre; (*fig*) acerbe, aigre; revêche; **to go** *or* **turn** ~ (*milk, wine*) tourner; (*fig: relationship, plans*) mal tourner; **it's** ~ **grapes** c'est du dépit.

source [sɔ:s] *n* source *f*; **I have it from a reliable** ~ **that** je sais de source sûre que.

south [sauθ] *n* sud *m* ♦ *adj* sud *inv*, du sud ♦ *adv* au sud, vers le sud; **(to the)** ~ **of** au sud de; **to travel** ~ aller en direction du sud; **the S~ of France** le Sud de la France, le Midi.

South Africa *n* Afrique *f* du Sud.

South African *adj* sud-africain(e) ♦ *n* Sud-Africain/e.

South America *n* Amérique *f* du Sud.

South American *adj* sud-américain(e) ♦ *n* Sud-Américain/e.

southbound ['sauθbaund] *adj* en direction du sud; (*carriageway*) sud *inv*.

south-east [sauθ'i:st] *n* sud-est *m*.

South-East Asia *n* le Sud-Est asiatique.

southerly ['sʌðəlɪ] *adj* du sud; au sud.

southern ['sʌðən] *adj* (du) sud; méridional(e); **with a** ~ **aspect** orienté(e) *or* exposé(e) au sud; **the** ~ **hemisphere** l'hémisphère sud *or* austral.

South Pole *n* Pôle *m* Sud.

South Sea Islands *npl*: **the** ~ l'Océanie *f*.

South Seas *npl*: **the** ~ les mers *fpl* du Sud.

South Vietnam *n* Viêt-Nam *m* du Sud.

southward(s) ['sauθwəd(z)] *adv* vers le sud.

south-west [sauθ'wɛst] *n* sud-ouest *m*.

souvenir [su:və'nɪə*] *n* souvenir *m* (*objet*).

sovereign ['sɔvrɪn] *adj, n* souverain(e).

sovereignty ['sɔvrɪntɪ] *n* souveraineté *f*.

soviet ['səuvɪət] *adj* soviétique.

Soviet Union *n*: **the** ~ l'Union *f* soviétique.

sow *n* [sau] truie *f* ♦ *vt* [səu] (*pt* ~**ed**, *pp* **sown** [səun]) semer.

soya ['sɔɪə], (*US*) **soy** [sɔɪ] *n*: ~ **bean** graine *f* de soja; ~ **sauce** sauce *f* au soja.

sozzled ['sɔzld] *adj* (*BRIT col*) paf *inv*.

spa [spɑ:] *n* (*town*) station thermale; (*US: also*: **health** ~) établissement *m* de cure de rajeunissement.

space [speɪs] *n* (*gen*) espace *m*; (*room*) place *f*; espace; (*length of time*) laps *m* de temps ♦ *cpd* spatial(e) ♦ *vt* (*also*: ~ **out**) espacer; **to clear a** ~ **for sth** faire de la place pour qch; **in a confined** ~ dans un espace réduit *or* restreint; **in a short** ~ **of time** dans peu de temps; **(with)in the** ~ **of an hour** en l'espace d'une heure.

space bar *n* (*on typewriter*) barre *f* d'espacement.

spacecraft ['speɪskrɑ:ft] *n* engin spatial.

spaceman ['speɪsmæn] *n* astronaute *m*, cosmonaute *m*.

spaceship ['speɪsʃɪp] *n* engin *or* vaisseau spatial.

space shuttle *n* navette spatiale.

spacesuit ['speɪssu:t] *n* combinaison spatiale.

spacewoman ['speɪswumən] *n* astronaute *f*, cosmonaute *f*.

spacing ['speɪsɪŋ] *n* espacement *m*; **single/double** ~ (*TYP etc*) interligne *m* simple/double.

spacious ['speɪʃəs] *adj* spacieux(euse), grand(e).

spade [speɪd] *n* (*tool*) bêche *f*, pelle *f*; (*child's*) pelle; ~**s** *npl* (*CARDS*) pique *m*.

spadework ['speɪdwə:k] *n* (*fig*) gros *m* du travail.

spaghetti [spə'gɛtɪ] *n* spaghetti *mpl*.

Spain [speɪn] *n* Espagne *f*.

span [spæn] *n* (*of bird, plane*) envergure *f*; (*of arch*) portée *f*; (*in time*) espace *m* de temps, durée *f* ♦ *vt* enjamber, franchir; (*fig*) couvrir, embrasser.

Spaniard ['spænjəd] *n* Espagnol/e.

spaniel ['spænjəl] *n* épagneul *m*.

Spanish ['spænɪʃ] *adj* espagnol(e), d'Espagne ♦ *n* (*LING*) espagnol *m*; **the** ~ *npl* les Espagnols; ~ **omelette** omelette *f* à l'espagnole.

spank [spæŋk] *vt* donner une fessée à.

spanner ['spænə*] *n* (*BRIT*) clé *f* (de mécanicien).

spar [spɑ:*] *n* espar *m* ♦ *vi* (*BOXING*) s'entraîner.

spare [spɛə*] *adj* de réserve, de rechange; (*surplus*) de or en trop, de reste ♦ *n* (*part*) pièce *f* de rechange, pièce détachée ♦ *vt* (*do without*) se passer de; (*afford to give*) donner, accorder, passer; (*refrain from hurting*) épargner; (*refrain from using*) ménager; **to** ~ (*surplus*) en surplus, de trop; **there are 2 going** ~ (*BRIT*) il y en a 2 de disponible; **to** ~ **no expense** ne pas reculer devant la dépense; **can you** ~ **the time?** est-ce que vous avez le temps?; **there is no time to** ~ il n'y a pas de temps à perdre; **I've a few minutes to** ~ je dispose de quelques minutes.

spare part *n* pièce *f* de rechange, pièce détachée.

spare room *n* chambre *f* d'ami.

spare time *n* moments *mpl* de loisir.

spare tyre *n* (*AUT*) pneu *m* de rechange.

spare wheel *n* (*AUT*) roue *f* de secours.

sparing ['spɛərɪŋ] *adj*: **to be** ~ **with** ménager.

sparingly ['spɛərɪŋlɪ] *adv* avec modération.

spark [spɑ:k] *n* étincelle *f*; (*fig*) étincelle, lueur *f*.

spark(ing) plug ['spɑ:k(ɪŋ)-] *n* bougie *f*.

sparkle ['spɑ:kl] *n* scintillement *m*, étincellement *m*, éclat *m* ♦ *vi* étinceler, scintiller;

(*bubble*) pétiller.
sparkler ['spɑːklə*] n cierge m magique.
sparkling ['spɑːklɪŋ] adj étincelant(e), scintillant(e); (*wine*) mousseux(euse), pétillant(e).
sparring partner ['spɑːrɪŋ-] n sparring-partner m; (*fig*) vieil(le) ennemi/e.
sparrow ['spærəu] n moineau m.
sparse [spɑːs] adj clairsemé(e).
spartan ['spɑːtən] adj (*fig*) spartiate.
spasm ['spæzəm] n (*MED*) spasme m; (*fig*) accès m.
spasmodic [spæz'mɔdɪk] adj (*fig*) intermittent(e).
spastic ['spæstɪk] n handicapé/e moteur.
spat [spæt] pt, pp of **spit** ♦ n (*US*) prise f de bec.
spate [speɪt] n (*fig*): ~ **of** avalanche f or torrent m de; **in** ~ (*river*) en crue.
spatial ['speɪʃl] adj spatial(e).
spatter ['spætə*] n éclaboussure(s) f(pl) ♦ vt éclabousser ♦ vi gicler.
spatula ['spætjulə] n spatule f.
spawn [spɔːn] vt pondre; (*pej*) engendrer ♦ vi frayer ♦ n frai m.
SPCA n abbr (*US*: = Society for the Prevention of Cruelty to Animals*) ≈ SPA f.
SPCC n abbr (*US*: = Society for the Prevention of Cruelty to Children*).
speak, pt **spoke,** pp **spoken** [spiːk, spəuk, 'spəukn] vt (*language*) parler; (*truth*) dire ♦ vi parler; (*make a speech*) prendre la parole; **to** ~ **to sb/of** or **about sth** parler à qn/de qch; ~**ing!** (*on telephone*) c'est moi-même!; **to** ~ **one's mind** dire ce que l'on pense; **it** ~**s for itself** c'est évident; ~ **up!** parle plus fort!; **he has no money to** ~ **of** il n'a pas d'argent.
▶**speak for** vt fus: **to** ~ **for sb** parler pour qn; **that picture is already spoken for** (*in shop*) ce tableau est déjà réservé.
speaker ['spiːkə*] n (*in public*) orateur m; (*also:* **loud**~) haut-parleur m; (*POL*): **the S**~ *le président de la Chambre des communes* (*BRIT*) or *des représentants* (*US*); **are you a Welsh** ~? parlez-vous gallois?
speaking ['spiːkɪŋ] adj parlant(e); **French-**~ **people** les francophones; **to be on** ~ **terms** se parler.
spear [spɪə*] n lance f ♦ vt transpercer.
spearhead ['spɪəhɛd] n fer m de lance; (*MIL*) colonne f d'attaque ♦ vt (*attack etc*) mener.
spearmint ['spɪəmɪnt] n (*BOT etc*) menthe verte.
spec [spɛk] n (*BRIT col*): **on** ~ à tout hasard; **to buy on** ~ acheter avec l'espoir de faire une bonne affaire.
special ['spɛʃl] adj spécial(e) ♦ n (*train*) train spécial; **take** ~ **care** soyez particulièrement prudents; **nothing** ~ rien de spécial; **today's** ~ (*at restaurant*) le plat du jour.
special agent n agent secret.
special correspondent n envoyé spécial.
special delivery n (*POST*): **by** ~ en exprès.
special effects npl (*CINE*) effets spéciaux.

specialist ['spɛʃəlɪst] n spécialiste m/f; **heart** ~ cardiologue m/f.
speciality [spɛʃɪ'ælɪtɪ] n spécialité f.
specialize ['spɛʃəlaɪz] vi: **to** ~ **(in)** se spécialiser (dans).
specially ['spɛʃlɪ] adv spécialement, particulièrement.
special offer n (*COMM*) réclame f.
specialty ['spɛʃəltɪ] n (*US*) = **speciality**.
species ['spiːʃiːz] n (pl inv) espèce f.
specific [spə'sɪfɪk] adj (*not vague*) précis(e), explicite; (*particular*) particulier(ière); (*BOT, CHEM etc*) spécifique; **to be** ~ **to** être particulier à, être le or un caractère (or les caractères) spécifique(s) de.
specifically [spə'sɪfɪklɪ] adv explicitement, précisément; (*intend, ask, design*) expressément, spécialement; (*exclusively*) exclusivement, spécifiquement.
specification [spɛsɪfɪ'keɪʃən] n spécification f; stipulation f; ~**s** npl (*of car, building etc*) spécification.
specify ['spɛsɪfaɪ] vt spécifier, préciser; **unless otherwise specified** sauf indication contraire.
specimen ['spɛsɪmən] n spécimen m, échantillon m; (*MED*) prélèvement m.
specimen copy n spécimen m.
specimen signature n spécimen m de signature.
speck [spɛk] n petite tache, petit point; (*particle*) grain m.
speckled ['spɛkld] adj tacheté(e), moucheté(e).
specs [spɛks] npl (*col*) lunettes fpl.
spectacle ['spɛktəkl] n spectacle m.
spectacle case n (*BRIT*) étui m à lunettes.
spectacles ['spɛktəklz] npl (*BRIT*) lunettes fpl.
spectacular [spɛk'tækjulə*] adj spectaculaire ♦ n (*CINE etc*) superproduction f.
spectator [spɛk'teɪtə*] n spectateur/trice.
spectator sport n: **football is a great** ~ le football est un sport qui passionne les foules.
spectra ['spɛktrə] npl of **spectrum**.
spectre, (*US*) **specter** ['spɛktə*] n spectre m, fantôme m.
spectrum, pl **spectra** ['spɛktrəm, -rə] n spectre m; (*fig*) gamme f.
speculate ['spɛkjuleɪt] vi spéculer; (*try to guess*): **to** ~ **about** s'interroger sur.
speculation [spɛkju'leɪʃən] n spéculation f; conjectures fpl.
speculative ['spɛkjulətɪv] adj spéculatif(ive).
speculator ['spɛkjuleɪtə*] n spéculateur/trice.
speech [spiːtʃ] n (*faculty*) parole f; (*talk*) discours m, allocution f; (*manner of speaking*) façon f de parler, langage m; (*language*) langage m; (*enunciation*) élocution f.
speech day n (*BRIT SCOL*) distribution f des prix.
speech impediment n défaut m d'élocution.

speechless ['spiːtʃlɪs] *adj* muet(te).
speech therapy *n* orthophonie *f*.
speed [spiːd] *n* vitesse *f*; (*promptness*) rapidité *f* ♦ *vi* (*pt, pp* **sped** [spɛd]): **to ~ along/by** *etc* aller/passer *etc* à toute vitesse; (*AUT: exceed ~ limit*) faire un excès de vitesse; **at ~** (*BRIT*) rapidement; **at full** *or* **top ~** à toute vitesse *or* allure; **at a ~ of 70 km/h** à une vitesse de 70 km/h; **shorthand/typing ~s** nombre *m* de mots à la minute en sténographie/dactylographie; **a five-~ gearbox** une boîte cinq vitesses.
►**speed up**, *pt, pp* **~ed up** *vi* aller plus vite, accélérer ♦ *vt* accélérer.
speedboat ['spiːdbəut] *n* vedette *f*, hors-bord *m inv*.
speedily ['spiːdɪlɪ] *adv* rapidement, promptement.
speeding ['spiːdɪŋ] *n* (*AUT*) excès *m* de vitesse.
speed limit *n* limitation *f* de vitesse, vitesse maximale permise.
speedometer [spɪ'dɔmɪtə*] *n* compteur *m* (de vitesse).
speed trap *n* (*AUT*) piège *m* de police pour contrôle de vitesse.
speedway *n* (*SPORT*) piste *f* de vitesse pour motos; (*: also: ~ racing*) épreuve(s) *f(pl)* de vitesse de motos.
speedy [spiːdɪ] *adj* rapide, prompt(e).
speleologist [spɛlɪ'ɔladʒɪst] *n* spéléologue *m/f*.
spell [spɛl] *n* (*also: magic ~*) sortilège *m*, charme *m*; (*period of time*) (courte) période ♦ *vt* (*pt, pp* **spelt** *or* **~ed** [spɛlt, spɛld]) (*in writing*) écrire, orthographier; (*aloud*) épeler; (*fig*) signifier; **to cast a ~ on sb** jeter un sort à qn; **he can't ~** il fait des fautes d'orthographe; **how do you ~ your name?** comment écrivez-vous votre nom?; **can you ~ it for me?** pouvez-vous me l'épeler?
spellbound ['spɛlbaund] *adj* envoûté(e), subjugué(e).
spelling ['spɛlɪŋ] *n* orthographe *f*.
spelt [spɛlt] *pt, pp of* **spell**.
spend, *pt, pp* **spent** [spɛnd, spɛnt] *vt* (*money*) dépenser; (*time, life*) passer; (*devote*): **to ~ time/money/effort on sth** consacrer du temps/de l'argent/de l'énergie à qch.
spending ['spɛndɪŋ] *n* dépenses *fpl*; **government ~** les dépenses publiques.
spending money *n* argent *m* de poche.
spending power *n* pouvoir *m* d'achat.
spendthrift ['spɛndθrɪft] *n* dépensier/ière.
spent [spɛnt] *pt, pp of* **spend** ♦ *adj* (*patience*) épuisé(e), à bout; (*cartridge, bullets*) vide; **~ matches** vieilles allumettes.
sperm [spəːm] *n* spermatozoïde *m*; (*semen*) sperme *m*.
sperm bank *n* banque *f* du sperme.
sperm whale *n* cachalot *m*.
spew [spjuː] *vt* vomir.
sphere [sfɪə*] *n* sphère *f*; (*fig*) sphère, domaine *m*.

spherical ['sfɛrɪkl] *adj* sphérique.
sphinx [sfɪŋks] *n* sphinx *m*.
spice [spaɪs] *n* épice *f* ♦ *vt* épicer.
spick-and-span ['spɪkən'spæn] *adj* impeccable.
spicy ['spaɪsɪ] *adj* épicé(e), relevé(e); (*fig*) piquant(e).
spider ['spaɪdə*] *n* araignée *f*; **~'s web** toile *f* d'araignée.
spiel [spiːl] *n* laïus *m inv*.
spike [spaɪk] *n* pointe *f*; (*ELEC*) pointe de tension; **~s** *npl* (*SPORT*) chaussures *fpl* à pointes.
spike heel *n* (*US*) talon *m* aiguille.
spiky ['spaɪkɪ] *adj* (*bush, branch*) épineux(euse); (*animal*) plein(e) de piquants.
spill, *pt, pp* **spilt** *or* **~ed** [spɪl, -t, -d] *vt* renverser; répandre ♦ *vi* se répandre; **to ~ the beans** (*col*) vendre la mèche; (*: confess*) lâcher le morceau.
►**spill out** *vi* sortir à flots, se répandre.
►**spill over** *vi* déborder.
spillage ['spɪlɪdʒ] *n* (*of oil*) déversement *m* (accidentel).
spin [spɪn] *n* (*revolution of wheel*) tour *m*; (*AVIAT*) (chute *f* en) vrille *f*; (*trip in car*) petit tour, balade *f* ♦ *vb* (*pt, pp* **spun** [spʌn]) *vt* (*wool etc*) filer; (*wheel*) faire tourner; (*BRIT: clothes*) essorer ♦ *vi* tourner, tournoyer; **to ~ a yarn** débiter une longue histoire; **to ~ a coin** (*BRIT*) jouer à pile ou face.
►**spin out** *vt* faire durer.
spina bifida ['spaɪnə'bɪfɪdə] *n* spina-bifida *m inv*.
spinach ['spɪnɪtʃ] *n* épinard *m*; (*as food*) épinards.
spinal ['spaɪnl] *adj* vertébral(e), spinal(e).
spinal column *n* colonne vertébrale.
spinal cord *n* moelle épinière.
spindly ['spɪndlɪ] *adj* grêle, filiforme.
spin doctor *n* (*col*) personne employée pour présenter un parti politique sous un jour favorable.
spin-dry ['spɪn'draɪ] *vt* essorer.
spin-dryer [spɪn'draɪə*] *n* (*BRIT*) essoreuse *f*.
spine [spaɪn] *n* colonne vertébrale; (*thorn*) épine *f*, piquant *m*.
spine-chilling ['spaɪntʃɪlɪŋ] *adj* terrifiant(e).
spineless ['spaɪnlɪs] *adj* invertébré(e); (*fig*) mou(molle), sans caractère.
spinner ['spɪnə*] *n* (*of thread*) fileur/euse.
spinning ['spɪnɪŋ] *n* (*of thread*) filage *m*; (*by machine*) filature *f*.
spinning top *n* toupie *f*.
spinning wheel *n* rouet *m*.
spin-off ['spɪnɔf] *n* sous-produit *m*; avantage inattendu.
spinster ['spɪnstə*] *n* célibataire *f*; vieille fille.
spiral ['spaɪərl] *n* spirale *f* ♦ *adj* en spirale ♦ *vi* (*fig: prices etc*) monter en flèche; **the inflationary ~** la spirale inflationniste.
spiral staircase *n* escalier *m* en colimaçon.
spire ['spaɪə*] *n* flèche *f*, aiguille *f*.

spirit ['spɪrɪt] n (*soul*) esprit m, âme f; (*ghost*) esprit, revenant m; (*mood*) esprit, état m d'esprit; (*courage*) courage m, énergie f; ~s npl (*drink*) spiritueux mpl, alcool m; **in good ~s** de bonne humeur; **in low ~s** démoralisé(e); **community ~** solidarité f; **public ~** civisme m.

spirit duplicator n duplicateur m à alcool.

spirited ['spɪrɪtɪd] adj vif(vive), fougueux(euse), plein(e) d'allant.

spirit level n niveau m à bulle.

spiritual ['spɪrɪtjuəl] adj spirituel(le); religieux(euse) ♦ n (*also*: **Negro ~**) spiritual m.

spiritualism ['spɪrɪtjuəlɪzəm] n spiritisme m.

spit [spɪt] n (*for roasting*) broche f; (*spittle*) crachat m; (*saliva*) salive f ♦ vi (pt, pp **spat** [spæt]) cracher; (*sound*) crépiter.

spite [spaɪt] n rancune f, dépit m ♦ vt contrarier, vexer; **in ~ of** en dépit de, malgré.

spiteful ['spaɪtful] adj malveillant(e), rancunier(ière).

spitroast ['spɪt'rəust] vt faire rôtir à la broche.

spitting ['spɪtɪŋ] n: "**~ prohibited**" "défense de cracher" ♦ adj: **to be the ~ image of sb** être le portrait tout craché de qn.

spittle ['spɪtl] n salive f; bave f; crachat m.

spiv [spɪv] n (*BRIT col*) chevalier m d'industrie, aigrefin m.

splash [splæʃ] n éclaboussement m; (*of colour*) tache f ♦ excl (*sound*) plouf! ♦ vt éclabousser ♦ vi (*also*: **~ about**) barboter, patauger.

splashdown ['splæʃdaun] n amerrissage m.

splay [spleɪ] adj: **~footed** marchant les pieds en dehors.

spleen [spliːn] n (*ANAT*) rate f.

splendid ['splendɪd] adj splendide, superbe, magnifique.

splendour, (*US*) **splendor** ['splendə*] n splendeur f, magnificence f.

splice [splaɪs] vt épisser.

splint [splɪnt] n attelle f, éclisse f.

splinter ['splɪntə*] n (*wood*) écharde f; (*metal*) éclat m ♦ vi se fragmenter.

splinter group n groupe dissident.

split [splɪt] n fente f, déchirure f; (*fig: POL*) scission f ♦ vb (pt, pp **split**) vt fendre, déchirer; (*party*) diviser; (*work, profits*) partager, répartir ♦ vi (*break*) se fendre, se briser; (*divide*) se diviser; **let's ~ the difference** coupons la poire en deux; **to do the ~s** faire le grand écart.

▶**split up** vi (*couple*) se séparer, rompre; (*meeting*) se disperser.

split-level ['splɪtlevl] adj (*house*) à deux or plusieurs niveaux.

split peas npl pois cassés.

split personality n double personnalité f.

split second n fraction f de seconde.

splitting ['splɪtɪŋ] adj: **a ~ headache** un mal de tête atroce.

splutter ['splʌtə*] vi bafouiller; postillonner.

spoil, pt, pp **spoilt** or **~ed** [spɔɪl, -t, -d] vt (*damage*) abîmer; (*mar*) gâcher; (*child*) gâter; (*ballot paper*) rendre nul ♦ vi: **to be ~ing for a fight** chercher la bagarre.

spoils [spɔɪlz] npl butin m.

spoilsport ['spɔɪlspɔːt] n trouble-fête m/f inv, rabat-joie m inv.

spoilt [spɔɪlt] pt, pp of **spoil** ♦ adj (*child*) gâté(e); (*ballot paper*) nul(le).

spoke [spəuk] pt of **speak** ♦ n rayon m.

spoken ['spəukn] pp of **speak**.

spokesman ['spəuksmən], **spokeswoman** [-wumən] n porte-parole m inv.

spokesperson ['spəukspəːsn] n porte-parole m inv.

sponge [spʌndʒ] n éponge f; (*CULIN: also*: **~ cake**) ≈ biscuit m de Savoie ♦ vt éponger ♦ vi: **to ~ on** or (*US*) **off of** vivre aux crochets de.

sponge bag n (*BRIT*) trousse f de toilette.

sponge cake n ≈ biscuit m de Savoie.

sponger ['spʌndʒə*] n (*pej*) parasite m.

spongy ['spʌndʒɪ] adj spongieux(euse).

sponsor ['spɔnsə*] n sponsor m, personne f (or organisme m) qui assure le parrainage; (*of new member*) parrain m/marraine f ♦ vt (*programme, competition etc*) parrainer, patronner, sponsoriser; (*POL: bill*) présenter; (*new member*) parrainer; **I ~ed him at 3p a mile** (*in fund-raising race*) je me suis engagé à lui donner 3p par mile.

sponsorship ['spɔnsəʃɪp] n patronage m, parrainage m.

spontaneity [spɔntə'neɪtɪ] n spontanéité f.

spontaneous [spɔn'teɪnɪəs] adj spontané(e).

spoof [spuːf] n (*parody*) parodie f; (*trick*) canular m.

spooky ['spuːkɪ] adj qui donne la chair de poule.

spool [spuːl] n bobine f.

spoon [spuːn] n cuiller f.

spoon-feed ['spuːnfiːd] vt nourrir à la cuiller; (*fig*) mâcher le travail à.

spoonful ['spuːnful] n cuillerée f.

sporadic [spə'rædɪk] adj sporadique.

sport [spɔːt] n sport m; (*amusement*) divertissement m; (*person*) chic type/chic fille ♦ vt arborer; **indoor/outdoor ~s** sports en salle/ de plein air; **to say sth in ~** dire qch pour rire.

sporting ['spɔːtɪŋ] adj sportif(ive); **to give sb a ~ chance** donner sa chance à qn.

sport jacket n (*US*) = **sports jacket**.

sports car n voiture f de sport.

sports ground n terrain m de sport.

sports jacket n veste f de sport.

sportsman ['spɔːtsmən] n sportif m.

sportsmanship ['spɔːtsmənʃɪp] n esprit sportif, sportivité f.

sports page n page f des sports.

sportswear ['spɔːtsweə*] n vêtements mpl de sport.

sportswoman ['spɔːtswumən] *n* sportive *f*.
sporty ['spɔːtɪ] *adj* sportif(ive).
spot [spɔt] *n* tache *f*; (*dot: on pattern*) pois *m*; (*pimple*) bouton *m*; (*place*) endroit *m*, coin *m*; (*also*: ~ **advertisement**) message *m* publicitaire; (*small amount*): **a** ~ **of** un peu de ♦ *vt* (*notice*) apercevoir, repérer; **on the** ~ sur place, sur les lieux; (*immediately*) sur le champ; **to put sb on the** ~ (*fig*) mettre qn dans l'embarras; **to come out in** ~s se couvrir de boutons, avoir une éruption de boutons.
spot check *n* contrôle intermittent.
spotless ['spɔtlɪs] *adj* immaculé(e).
spotlight ['spɔtlaɪt] *n* projecteur *m*; (*AUT*) phare *m* auxiliaire.
spot-on [spɔt'ɔn] *adj* (*BRIT col*) en plein dans le mille.
spot price *n* prix *m* sur place.
spotted ['spɔtɪd] *adj* tacheté(e), moucheté(e); à pois; ~ **with** tacheté(e) de.
spotty ['spɔtɪ] *adj* (*face*) boutonneux(euse).
spouse [spauz] *n* époux/épouse.
spout [spaut] *n* (*of jug*) bec *m*; (*of liquid*) jet *m* ♦ *vi* jaillir.
sprain [spreɪn] *n* entorse *f*, foulure *f* ♦ *vt*: **to** ~ **one's ankle** se fouler *or* se tordre la cheville.
sprang [spræŋ] *pt of* **spring**.
sprawl [sprɔːl] *vi* s'étaler ♦ *n*: **urban** ~ expansion urbaine; **to send sb** ~**ing** envoyer qn rouler par terre.
spray [spreɪ] *n* jet *m* (en fines gouttelettes); (*container*) vaporisateur *m*, bombe *f*; (*of flowers*) petit bouquet ♦ *vt* vaporiser, pulvériser; (*crops*) traiter ♦ *cpd* (*deodorant etc*) en bombe *or* atomiseur.
spread [spred] *n* (*distribution*) répartition *f*; (*CULIN*) pâte *f* à tartiner; (*PRESS, TYP: two pages*) double page *f* ♦ *vb* (*pt, pp* **spread**) *vt* (*paste, contents*) étendre, étaler; (*rumour, disease*) répandre, propager; (*repayments*) échelonner, étaler; (*wealth*) répartir ♦ *vi* s'étendre; se répandre; se propager; **middle-age** ~ embonpoint *m* (pris avec l'âge).
spread-eagled ['spredi:gld] *adj*: **to be** *or* **lie** ~ être étendu(e) bras et jambes écartés.
spreadsheet ['spredʃiːt] *n* (*COMPUT*) tableur *m*.
spree [spriː] *n*: **to go on a** ~ faire la fête.
sprig [sprɪg] *n* rameau *m*.
sprightly ['spraɪtlɪ] *adj* alerte.
spring [sprɪŋ] *n* (*leap*) bond *m*, saut *m*; (*coiled metal*) ressort *m*; (*bounciness*) élasticité *f*; (*season*) printemps *m*; (*of water*) source *f* ♦ *vb* (*pt* **sprang**, *pp* **sprung** [spræŋ, sprʌŋ]) *vi* bondir, sauter ♦ *vt*: **to** ~ **a leak** (*pipe etc*) se mettre à fuir; **he sprang the news on me** il m'a annoncé la nouvelle de but en blanc; **in** ~, **in the** ~ au printemps; **to** ~ **from** provenir de; **to** ~ **into action** passer à l'action; **to**

walk with a ~ **in one's step** marcher d'un pas souple.
▶**spring up** *vi* (*problem*) se présenter, surgir.
springboard ['sprɪŋbɔːd] *n* tremplin *m*.
spring-clean [sprɪŋ'kliːn] *n* (*also*: ~**ing**) grand nettoyage de printemps.
spring onion *n* (*BRIT*) ciboule *f*, cive *f*.
spring roll *n* rouleau *m* de printemps.
springtime ['sprɪŋtaɪm] *n* printemps *m*.
springy ['sprɪŋɪ] *adj* élastique, souple.
sprinkle ['sprɪŋkl] *vt* (*pour*) répandre; verser; **to** ~ **water** *etc* **on**, ~ **with water** *etc* asperger d'eau *etc*; **to** ~ **sugar** *etc* **on**, ~ **with sugar** *etc* saupoudrer de sucre *etc*; ~**d with** (*fig*) parsemé(e) de.
sprinkler ['sprɪŋklə*] *n* (*for lawn etc*) arroseur *m*; (*to put out fire*) diffuseur *m* d'extincteur automatique d'incendie.
sprinkling ['sprɪŋklɪŋ] *n* (*of water*) quelques gouttes *fpl*; (*of salt*) pincée *f*; (*of sugar*) légère couche.
sprint [sprɪnt] *n* sprint *m* ♦ *vi* sprinter.
sprinter ['sprɪntə*] *n* sprinteur/euse.
sprite [spraɪt] *n* lutin *m*.
spritzer ['sprɪtsə*] *n* boisson à base de vin blanc et d'eau de Seltz.
sprocket ['sprɔkɪt] *n* (*on printer etc*) picot *m*.
sprout [spraut] *vi* germer, pousser.
sprouts [sprauts] *npl* (*also*: **Brussels** ~) choux *mpl* de Bruxelles.
spruce [spruːs] *n* épicéa *m* ♦ *adj* net(te), pimpant(e).
▶**spruce up** *vt* (*smarten up: room etc*) apprêter; **to** ~ **o.s.** se faire beau(belle).
sprung [sprʌŋ] *pp of* **spring**.
spry [spraɪ] *adj* alerte, vif(vive).
SPUC *n abbr* = *Society for the Protection of Unborn Children*.
spud [spʌd] *n* (*col: potato*) patate *f*.
spun [spʌn] *pt, pp of* **spin**.
spur [spəː*] *n* éperon *m*; (*fig*) aiguillon *m* ♦ *vt* (*also*: ~ **on**) éperonner; aiguillonner; **on the** ~ **of the moment** sous l'impulsion du moment.
spurious ['spjuərɪəs] *adj* faux(fausse).
spurn [spəːn] *vt* repousser avec mépris.
spurt [spəːt] *n* jet *m*; (*of energy*) sursaut *m* ♦ *vi* jaillir, gicler; **to put in** *or* **on a** ~ (*runner*) piquer un sprint; (*fig: in work etc*) donner un coup de collier.
sputter ['spʌtə*] *vi* = **splutter**.
spy [spaɪ] *n* espion/ne ♦ *vi*: **to** ~ **on** espionner, épier ♦ *vt* (*see*) apercevoir ♦ *cpd* (*film, story*) d'espionnage.
spying ['spaɪɪŋ] *n* espionnage *m*.
Sq. *abbr* (*in address*) = **square**.
sq. *abbr* (*MATH etc*) = **square**.
squabble ['skwɔbl] *n* querelle *f*, chamaillerie *f* ♦ *vi* se chamailler.
squad [skwɔd] *n* (*MIL, POLICE*) escouade *f*, groupe *m*; (*FOOTBALL*) contingent *m*; **flying** ~ (*POLICE*) brigade volante.

squad car n (BRIT POLICE) voiture f de police.
squaddie ['skwɔdɪ] n (MIL col) troufion m, bidasse m.
squadron ['skwɔdrn] n (MIL) escadron m; (AVIAT, NAUT) escadrille f.
squalid ['skwɔlɪd] adj sordide, ignoble.
squall [skwɔːl] n rafale f, bourrasque f.
squalor ['skwɔlə*] n conditions fpl sordides.
squander ['skwɔndə*] vt gaspiller, dilapider.
square [skwɛə*] n carré m; (in town) place f; (US: block of houses) îlot m, pâté m de maisons; (instrument) équerre f ♦ adj carré(e); (honest) honnête, régulier(ière); (col: ideas, tastes) vieux jeu inv, qui retarde ♦ vt (arrange) régler; arranger; (MATH) élever au carré; (reconcile) concilier ♦ vi (agree) cadrer, s'accorder; **all ~** quitte; à égalité; **a ~ meal** un repas convenable; **2 metres ~** (de) 2 mètres sur 2; **1 ~ metre** 1 mètre carré; **we're back to ~ one** (fig) on se retrouve à la case départ.
▶**square up** vi (BRIT: settle) régler; **to ~ up with sb** régler ses comptes avec qn.
square bracket n (TYP) crochet m.
squarely ['skwɛəlɪ] adv carrément; (honestly, fairly) honnêtement, équitablement.
square root n racine carrée.
squash [skwɔʃ] n (BRIT: drink): **lemon/orange ~** citronnade/orangeade f; (SPORT) squash m; (vegetable) courge f ♦ vt écraser.
squat [skwɔt] adj petit(e) et épais(se), ramassé(e) ♦ vi s'accroupir; (on property) squatter, squattériser.
squatter ['skwɔtə*] n squatter m.
squawk [skwɔːk] vi pousser un or des gloussement(s).
squeak [skwiːk] n (of hinge, wheel etc) grincement m; (of shoes) craquement m; (of mouse etc) petit cri aigu ♦ vi grincer, crier.
squeaky ['skwiːkɪ] adj grinçant(e); **to be ~ clean** (fig) être au-dessus de tout soupçon.
squeal [skwiːl] vi pousser un or des cri(s) aigu(s) or perçant(s).
squeamish ['skwiːmɪʃ] adj facilement dégoûté(e), facilement scandalisé(e).
squeeze [skwiːz] n pression f; (also: **credit ~**) encadrement m du crédit, restrictions fpl de crédit ♦ vt presser; (hand, arm) serrer ♦ vi: **to ~ past/under sth** se glisser avec (beaucoup de) difficulté devant/sous qch; **a ~ of lemon** quelques gouttes de citron.
▶**squeeze out** vt exprimer; (fig) soutirer.
squelch [skwɛltʃ] vi faire un bruit de succion; patauger.
squib [skwɪb] n pétard m.
squid [skwɪd] n calmar m.
squiggle ['skwɪgl] n gribouillis m.
squint [skwɪnt] vi loucher ♦ n: **he has a ~** il louche, il souffre de strabisme; **to ~ at sth** regarder qch du coin de l'œil; (quickly) jeter un coup d'œil à qch.
squire ['skwaɪə*] n (BRIT) propriétaire terrien.

squirm [skwəːm] vi se tortiller.
squirrel ['skwɪrəl] n écureuil m.
squirt [skwəːt] n jet m ♦ vi jaillir, gicler.
Sr abbr = **senior, sister** (REL).
SRC n abbr (BRIT: = Students' Representative Council) ≈ CROUS m.
Sri Lanka [srɪˈlæŋkə] n Sri Lanka m or f.
SRN n abbr (BRIT) = State Registered Nurse.
SRO abbr (US) = standing room only.
SS abbr (= steamship) S/S.
SSA n abbr (US: = Social Security Administration) organisme de sécurité sociale.
SST n abbr (US) = supersonic transport.
ST abbr (US: = Standard Time) heure officielle.
St abbr (= saint) St; (= street) R.
stab [stæb] n (with knife etc) coup m (de couteau etc); (col: try): **to have a ~ at (doing) sth** s'essayer à (faire) qch ♦ vt poignarder; **to ~ sb to death** tuer qn à coups de couteau.
stabbing ['stæbɪŋ] n: **there's been a ~** quelqu'un a été attaqué à coups de couteau ♦ adj (pain, ache) lancinant(e).
stability [stəˈbɪlɪtɪ] n stabilité f.
stabilization [steɪbəlaɪˈzeɪʃən] n stabilisation f.
stabilize ['steɪbəlaɪz] vt stabiliser ♦ vi se stabiliser.
stabilizer ['steɪbəlaɪzə*] n stabilisateur m.
stable ['steɪbl] n écurie f ♦ adj stable; **riding ~s** centre m d'équitation.
staccato [stəˈkɑːtəu] adv staccato ♦ adj (MUS) piqué(e); (noise, voice) saccadé(e).
stack [stæk] n tas m, pile f ♦ vt empiler, entasser; **there's ~s of time** (BRIT col) on a tout le temps.
stadium ['steɪdɪəm] n stade m.
staff [stɑːf] n (work force) personnel m; (BRIT SCOL: also: **teaching ~**) professeurs mpl, enseignants mpl, personnel enseignant; (servants) domestiques mpl; (MIL) état-major m; (stick) perche f, bâton m ♦ vt pourvoir en personnel.
staffroom ['stɑːfruːm] n salle f des professeurs.
Staffs abbr (BRIT) = Staffordshire.
stag [stæg] n cerf m; (BRIT STOCK EXCHANGE) loup m.
stage [steɪdʒ] n scène f; (profession): **the ~** le théâtre; (point) étape f, stade m; (platform) estrade f ♦ vt (play) monter, mettre en scène; (demonstration) organiser; (fig: recovery etc) effectuer; **in ~s** par étapes, par degrés; **to go through a difficult ~** traverser une période difficile; **in the early ~s** au début; **in the final ~s** à la fin.
stagecoach ['steɪdʒkəutʃ] n diligence f.
stage door n entrée f des artistes.
stage fright n trac m.
stagehand ['steɪdʒhænd] n machiniste m.
stage-manage ['steɪdʒmænɪdʒ] vt (fig) orchestrer.
stage manager n régisseur m.

stagger ['stægə*] *vi* chanceler, tituber ♦ *vt* (*person*) stupéfier; bouleverser; (*hours, holidays*) étaler, échelonner.

staggering ['stægərɪŋ] *adj* (*amazing*) stupéfiant(e), renversant(e).

staging post ['steɪdʒɪŋ-] *n* relais *m*.

stagnant ['stægnənt] *adj* stagnant(e).

stagnate [stæg'neɪt] *vi* stagner, croupir.

stagnation [stæg'neɪʃən] *n* stagnation *f*.

stag night, stag party *n* enterrement *m* de vie de garçon.

staid [steɪd] *adj* posé(e), rassis(e).

stain [steɪn] *n* tache *f*; (*colouring*) colorant *m* ♦ *vt* tacher; (*wood*) teindre.

stained glass window [steɪnd-] *n* vitrail *m*.

stainless ['steɪnlɪs] *adj* (*steel*) inoxydable.

stain remover *n* détachant *m*.

stair [stɛə*] *n* (*step*) marche *f*; ~s *npl* escalier *m*; **on the ~s** dans l'escalier.

staircase ['stɛəkeɪs], **stairway** ['stɛəweɪ] *n* escalier *m*.

stairwell ['stɛəwɛl] *n* cage *f* d'escalier.

stake [steɪk] *n* pieu *m*, poteau *m*; (*BETTING*) enjeu *m* ♦ *vt* risquer, jouer; (*also*: ~ **out**: *area*) marquer, délimiter; **to be at** ~ être en jeu; **to have a** ~ **in sth** avoir des intérêts (en jeu) dans qch; **to** ~ **a claim (to sth)** revendiquer (qch).

stakeout ['steɪkaut] *n* surveillance *f*; **to be on a** ~ effectuer une surveillance.

stalactite ['stæləktaɪt] *n* stalactite *f*.

stalagmite ['stæləgmaɪt] *n* stalagmite *f*.

stale [steɪl] *adj* (*bread*) rassis(e); (*beer*) éventé(e); (*smell*) de renfermé.

stalemate ['steɪlmeɪt] *n* pat *m*; (*fig*) impasse *f*.

stalk [stɔːk] *n* tige *f* ♦ *vt* traquer ♦ *vi*: **to** ~ **in/ out** *etc* entrer/sortir *etc* avec raideur.

stall [stɔːl] *n* (*BRIT*: *in street, market etc*) éventaire *m*, étal *m*; (*in stable*) stalle *f* ♦ *vt* (*AUT*) caler ♦ *vi* (*AUT*) caler; (*fig*) essayer de gagner du temps; ~s *npl* (*BRIT*: *in cinema, theatre*) orchestre *m*; **a newspaper/flower** ~ un kiosque à journaux/de fleuriste.

stallholder ['stɔːlhəuldə*] *n* (*BRIT*) marchand/e en plein air.

stallion ['stæljən] *n* étalon *m* (*cheval*).

stalwart ['stɔːlwət] *n* partisan *m* fidèle.

stamen ['steɪmɛn] *n* étamine *f*.

stamina ['stæmɪnə] *n* vigueur *f*, endurance *f*.

stammer ['stæmə*] *n* bégaiement *m* ♦ *vi* bégayer.

stamp [stæmp] *n* timbre *m*; (*mark, also fig*) empreinte *f*; (*on document*) cachet *m* ♦ *vi* (*also*: ~ **one's foot**) taper du pied ♦ *vt* tamponner, estamper; (*letter*) timbrer; ~**ed addressed envelope (s.a.e.)** enveloppe affranchie pour la réponse.

▶**stamp out** *vt* (*fire*) piétiner; (*crime*) éradiquer; (*opposition*) éliminer.

stamp album *n* album *m* de timbres(-poste).

stamp collecting [-kəlɛktɪŋ] *n* philatélie *f*.

stamp duty *n* (*BRIT*) droit *m* de timbre.

stampede [stæm'piːd] *n* ruée *f*; (*of cattle*) débandade *f*.

stamp machine *n* distributeur *m* de timbres-poste.

stance [stæns] *n* position *f*.

stand [stænd] *n* (*position*) position *f*; (*MIL*) résistance *f*; (*structure*) guéridon *m*; support *m*; (*COMM*) étalage *m*, stand *m*; (*SPORT*) tribune *f*; (*also*: **music** ~) pupitre *m* ♦ *vb* (*pt, pp* **stood** [stud]) *vi* être *or* se tenir (debout); (*rise*) se lever, se mettre debout; (*be placed*) se trouver ♦ *vt* (*place*) mettre, poser; (*tolerate, withstand*) supporter; **to make a** ~ prendre position; **to take a** ~ **on an issue** prendre position sur un problème; **to** ~ **for parliament** (*BRIT*) se présenter aux élections (*comme candidat à la députation*); **to** ~ **guard** *or* **watch** (*MIL*) monter la garde; **it** ~**s to reason** c'est logique; **cela va de soi;** **as things** ~ dans l'état actuel des choses; **to** ~ **sb a drink/ meal** payer à boire/à manger à qn; **I can't** ~ **him** je ne peux pas le voir.

▶**stand aside** *vi* s'écarter.

▶**stand by** *vi* (*be ready*) se tenir prêt(e) ♦ *vt fus* (*opinion*) s'en tenir à.

▶**stand down** *vi* (*withdraw*) se retirer; (*LAW*) renoncer à ses droits.

▶**stand for** *vt fus* (*signify*) représenter, signifier; (*tolerate*) supporter, tolérer.

▶**stand in for** *vt fus* remplacer.

▶**stand out** *vi* (*be prominent*) ressortir.

▶**stand up** *vi* (*rise*) se lever, se mettre debout.

▶**stand up for** *vt fus* défendre.

▶**stand up to** *vt fus* tenir tête à, résister à.

stand-alone ['stændələun] *adj* (*COMPUT*) autonome.

standard ['stændəd] *n* (*reference*) norme *f*; (*level*) niveau *m*; (*flag*) étendard *m* ♦ *adj* (*size etc*) ordinaire, normal(e); (*model, feature*) standard *inv*; (*practice*) courant(e); (*text*) de base; ~s *npl* (*morals*) morale *f*, principes *mpl*; **to be** *or* **come up to** ~ être du niveau voulu *or* à la hauteur; **to apply a double** ~ avoir *or* appliquer deux poids deux mesures; ~ **of living** niveau de vie.

standardization [stændədaɪ'zeɪʃən] *n* standardisation *f*.

standardize ['stændədaɪz] *vt* standardiser.

standard lamp *n* (*BRIT*) lampadaire *m*.

standard time *n* heure légale.

stand-by ['stændbaɪ] *n* remplaçant/e ♦ *adj* (*provisions*) de réserve; **to be on** ~ se tenir prêt(e) (à intervenir); (*doctor*) être de garde.

stand-by generator *n* générateur *m* de secours.

stand-by passenger *n* passager/ère en stand-by *or* en attente.

stand-by ticket *n* billet *m* stand-by.

stand-in ['stændɪn] *n* remplaçant/e; (*CINE*) doublure *f*.

standing ['stændɪŋ] *adj* debout *inv*; (*permanent: rule*) immuable; (*army*) de métier; (*grievance*) constant(e), de longue date ♦ *n* réputation *f*, rang *m*, standing *m*; (*duration*): **of 6 months'** ~ qui dure depuis 6 mois; **of many years'** ~ qui dure *or* existe depuis longtemps; **he was given a** ~ **ovation** on s'est levé pour l'acclamer; **it's a** ~ **joke** c'est un vieux sujet de plaisanterie; **a man of some** ~ un homme estimé.

standing committee *n* commission permanente.

standing order *n* (*BRIT: at bank*) virement permanent; ~**s** *npl* (*MIL*) règlement *m*.

standing room *n* places *fpl* debout.

stand-off ['stændɔf] *n* (*esp US: stalemate*) impasse *f*.

stand-offish [stænd'ɔfɪʃ] *adj* distant(e), froid(e).

standpat ['stændpæt] *adj* (*US*) inflexible, rigide.

standpipe ['stændpaɪp] *n* colonne *f* d'alimentation.

standpoint ['stændpɔɪnt] *n* point *m* de vue.

standstill ['stændstɪl] *n*: **at a** ~ à l'arrêt; (*fig*) au point mort; **to come to a** ~ s'immobiliser, s'arrêter.

stank [stæŋk] *pt of* **stink**.

stanza ['stænzə] *n* strophe *f*; couplet *m*.

staple ['steɪpl] *n* (*for papers*) agrafe *f*; (*chief product*) produit *m* de base ♦ *adj* (*food, crop, industry etc*) de base, principal(e) ♦ *vt* agrafer.

stapler ['steɪplə*] *n* agrafeuse *f*.

star [stɑ:*] *n* étoile *f*; (*celebrity*) vedette *f* ♦ *vi*: **to** ~ **(in)** être la vedette (de) ♦ *vt* (*CINE*) avoir pour vedette; **4-~ hotel** hôtel *m* 4 étoiles; **2-~ petrol** (*BRIT*) essence *f* ordinaire; **4-~ petrol** (*BRIT*) super *m*.

star attraction *n* grande attraction.

starboard ['stɑ:bəd] *n* tribord *m*; **to** ~ à tribord.

starch [stɑ:tʃ] *n* amidon *m*.

starched ['stɑ:tʃt] *adj* (*collar*) amidonné(e), empesé(e).

starchy ['stɑ:tʃɪ] *adj* riche en féculents; (*person*) guindé(e).

stardom ['stɑ:dəm] *n* célébrité *f*.

stare [stɛə*] *n* regard *m* fixe ♦ *vi*: **to** ~ **at** regarder fixement.

starfish ['stɑ:fɪʃ] *n* étoile *f* de mer.

stark [stɑ:k] *adj* (*bleak*) désolé(e), morne; (*simplicity, colour*) austère; (*reality, poverty*) nu(e) ♦ *adv*: ~ **naked** complètement nu(e).

starkers ['stɑ:kəz] *adj*: **to be** ~ (*BRIT col*) être à poil.

starlet ['stɑ:lɪt] *n* (*CINE*) starlette *f*.

starlight ['stɑ:laɪt] *n*: **by** ~ à la lumière des étoiles.

starling ['stɑ:lɪŋ] *n* étourneau *m*.

starlit ['stɑ:lɪt] *adj* étoilé(e); illuminé(e) par les étoiles.

starry ['stɑ:rɪ] *adj* étoilé(e).

starry-eyed [stɑ:rɪ'aɪd] *adj* (*innocent*) ingénu(e).

Stars and Stripes *npl*: **the** ~ la bannière étoilée.

star sign *n* signe zodiacal *or* du zodiaque.

star-studded ['stɑ:stʌdɪd] *adj*: **a** ~ **cast** une distribution prestigieuse.

start [stɑ:t] *n* commencement *m*, début *m*; (*of race*) départ *m*; (*sudden movement*) sursaut *m*; (*advantage*) avance *f* ♦ *vt* commencer; (*found: business, newspaper*) lancer, créer ♦ *vi* partir, se mettre en route; (*jump*) sursauter; **at the** ~ au début; **for a** ~ d'abord, pour commencer; **to make an early** ~ partir *or* commencer de bonne heure; **to** ~ **doing** *sth* se mettre à faire qch; **to** ~ **(off) with ...** (*firstly*) d'abord ...; (*at the beginning*) au commencement ....

▶**start off** *vi* commencer; (*leave*) partir.

▶**start over** *vi* (*US*) recommencer.

▶**start up** *vi* commencer; (*car*) démarrer ♦ *vt* déclencher; (*car*) mettre en marche.

starter ['stɑ:tə*] *n* (*AUT*) démarreur *m*; (*SPORT: official*) starter *m*; (*: runner, horse*) partant *m*; (*BRIT CULIN*) entrée *f*.

starting handle ['stɑ:tɪŋ-] *n* (*BRIT*) manivelle *f*.

starting point ['stɑ:tɪŋ-] *n* point *m* de départ.

starting price ['stɑ:tɪŋ-] *n* prix initial.

startle ['stɑ:tl] *vt* faire sursauter; donner un choc à.

startling ['stɑ:tlɪŋ] *adj* surprenant(e), saisissant(e).

star turn *n* (*BRIT*) vedette *f*.

starvation [stɑ:'veɪʃən] *n* faim *f*, famine *f*; **to die of** ~ mourir de faim *or* d'inanition.

starve [stɑ:v] *vi* mourir de faim; être affamé(e) ♦ *vt* affamer; **I'm starving** je meurs de faim.

stash [stæʃ] *vt* (*col*): **to** ~ *sth* **away** planquer qch.

state [steɪt] *n* état *m*; (*pomp*): **in** ~ en grande pompe ♦ *vt* (*declare*) déclarer, affirmer; (*specify*) indiquer, spécifier; **to be in a** ~ être dans tous ses états; ~ **of emergency** état d'urgence; ~ **of mind** état d'esprit; **the** ~ **of the art** l'état actuel de la technologie (*or* des connaissances).

state control *n* contrôle *m* de l'État.

stated ['steɪtɪd] *adj* fixé(e), prescrit(e).

State Department *n* (*US*) Département *m* d'État, ≈ ministère *m* des Affaires étrangères.

state education *n* (*BRIT*) enseignement public.

stateless ['steɪtlɪs] *adj* apatride.

stately ['steɪtlɪ] *adj* majestueux(euse), imposant(e).

statement ['steɪtmənt] *n* déclaration *f*; (*LAW*) déposition *f*; (*ECON*) relevé *m*; **official** ~ communiqué officiel; ~ **of account, bank** ~ relevé de compte.

state-owned ['steɪtəʊnd] *adj* étatisé(e).

States [steɪts] *npl*: **the** ~ les États-Unis *mpl*.

state school *n* école publique.

state secret *n* secret *m* d'État.

statesman ['steɪtsmən] *n* homme *m* d'État.

statesmanship ['steɪtsmənʃɪp] *n* qualités *fpl* d'homme d'État.

static ['stætɪk] *n* (*RADIO*) parasites *mpl*; (*also*: ~ **electricity**) électricité *f* statique ♦ *adj* statique.

station ['steɪʃən] *n* gare *f*; (*MIL, POLICE*) poste *m* (militaire *or* de police *etc*); (*rank*) condition *f*, rang *m* ♦ *vt* placer, poster; **action** ~**s** postes de combat; **to be** ~**ed in** (*MIL*) être en garnison à.

stationary ['steɪʃnərɪ] *adj* à l'arrêt, immobile.

stationer ['steɪʃənə*] *n* papetier/ière; ~**'s** (**shop**) papeterie *f*.

stationery ['steɪʃnərɪ] *n* papier *m* à lettres, petit matériel de bureau.

station master *n* (*RAIL*) chef *m* de gare.

station wagon *n* (*US*) break *m*.

statistic [stə'tɪstɪk] *n* statistique *f*.

statistical [stə'tɪstɪkl] *adj* statistique.

statistics [stə'tɪstɪks] *n* (*science*) statistique *f*.

statue ['stætjuː] *n* statue *f*.

statuesque [stætju'ɛsk] *adj* sculptural(e).

statuette [stætju'ɛt] *n* statuette *f*.

stature ['stætʃə*] *n* stature *f*; (*fig*) envergure *f*.

status ['steɪtəs] *n* position *f*, situation *f*; (*prestige*) prestige *m*; (*ADMIN, official position*) statut *m*.

status quo [-'kwəʊ] *n*: **the** ~ le statu quo.

status symbol *n* marque *f* de standing, signe extérieur de richesse.

statute ['stætjuːt] *n* loi *f*; ~**s** *npl* (*of club etc*) statuts *mpl*.

statute book *n* ≈ code *m*, textes *mpl* de loi.

statutory ['stætjutrɪ] *adj* statutaire, prévu(e) par un article de loi; ~ **meeting** assemblée constitutive *or* statutaire.

staunch [stɔːntʃ] *adj* sûr(e), loyal(e) ♦ *vt* étancher.

stave [steɪv] *n* (*MUS*) portée *f* ♦ *vt*: **to** ~ **off** (*attack*) parer; (*threat*) conjurer.

stay [steɪ] *n* (*period of time*) séjour *m*; (*LAW*): ~ **of execution** sursis *m* à statuer ♦ *vi* rester; (*reside*) loger; (*spend some time*) séjourner; **to** ~ **put** ne pas bouger; **to** ~ **with friends** loger chez des amis; **to** ~ **the night** passer la nuit.

▶**stay behind** *vi* rester en arrière.

▶**stay in** *vi* (*at home*) rester à la maison.

▶**stay on** *vi* rester.

▶**stay out** *vi* (*of house*) ne pas rentrer; (*strikers*) rester en grève.

▶**stay up** *vi* (*at night*) ne pas se coucher.

staying power ['steɪɪŋ-] *n* endurance *f*.

STD *n abbr* (*BRIT*: = *subscriber trunk dialling*) l'automatique *m*; (= *sexually transmitted disease*) MST *f*.

stead [stɛd] *n* (*BRIT*): **in sb's** ~ à la place de qn; **to stand sb in good** ~ être très utile *or* servir beaucoup à qn.

steadfast ['stɛdfɑːst] *adj* ferme, résolu(e).

steadily ['stɛdɪlɪ] *adv* régulièrement; fermement; d'une voix *etc* ferme.

steady ['stɛdɪ] *adj* stable, solide, ferme; (*regular*) constant(e), régulier(ière); (*person*) calme, pondéré(e) ♦ *vt* assurer, stabiliser; (*voice*) assurer; **to** ~ **oneself** reprendre son aplomb.

steak [steɪk] *n* (*meat*) bifteck *m*, steak *m*; (*fish*) tranche *f*.

steakhouse ['steɪkhaʊs] *n* ≈ grill-room *m*.

steal [stiːl], *pt* **stole**, *pp* **stolen** [stiːl, stəʊl, 'stəʊln] *vt, vi* voler.

▶**steal away**, **steal off** *vi* s'esquiver.

stealth [stɛlθ] *n*: **by** ~ furtivement.

stealthy ['stɛlθɪ] *adj* furtif(ive).

steam [stiːm] *n* vapeur *f* ♦ *vt* passer à la vapeur; (*CULIN*) cuire à la vapeur ♦ *vi* fumer; (*ship*): **to** ~ **along** filer; **under one's own** ~ (*fig*) par ses propres moyens; **to run out of** ~ (*fig: person*) caler; être à bout; **to let off** ~ (*fig: col*) se défouler.

▶**steam up** *vi* (*window*) se couvrir de buée; **to get** ~**ed up about sth** (*fig: col*) s'exciter à propos de qch.

steam engine *n* locomotive *f* à vapeur.

steamer ['stiːmə*] *n* (bateau *m* à) vapeur *m*; (*CULIN*) couscoussier *m*.

steam iron *n* fer *m* à repasser à vapeur.

steamroller ['stiːmrəʊlə*] *n* rouleau compresseur.

steamy ['stiːmɪ] *adj* embué(e), humide.

steed [stiːd] *n* (*literary*) coursier *m*.

steel [stiːl] *n* acier *m* ♦ *cpd* d'acier.

steel band *n* steel band *m*.

steel industry *n* sidérurgie *f*.

steel mill *n* aciérie *f*, usine *f* sidérurgique.

steelworks ['stiːlwɜːks] *n* aciérie *f*.

steely ['stiːlɪ] *adj* (*determination*) inflexible; (*eyes, gaze*) d'acier.

steep [stiːp] *adj* raide, escarpé(e); (*price*) très élevé(e), excessif(ive) ♦ *vt* (faire) tremper.

steeple ['stiːpl] *n* clocher *m*.

steeplechase ['stiːpltʃeɪs] *n* steeple(-chase) *m*.

steeplejack ['stiːpldʒæk] *n* réparateur *m* de clochers et de hautes cheminées.

steeply ['stiːplɪ] *adv* en pente raide.

steer [stɪə*] *n* bœuf *m* ♦ *vt* diriger, gouverner; (*lead*) guider ♦ *vi* tenir le gouvernail; **to** ~ **clear of sb/sth** (*fig*) éviter qn/qch.

steering ['stɪərɪŋ] *n* (*AUT*) conduite *f*.

steering column *n* (*AUT*) colonne *f* de direction.

steering committee *n* comité *m* d'organisation.

steering wheel *n* volant *m*.

stellar ['stɛlə*] *adj* stellaire.

stem [stɛm] *n* (*of plant*) tige *f*; (*of leaf, fruit*) queue *f*; (*of glass*) pied *m* ♦ *vt* contenir, endiguer; juguler.

▶**stem from** *vt fus* provenir de, découler de.

stench [stɛntʃ] *n* puanteur *f*.

stencil ['stɛnsl] *n* stencil *m*; pochoir *m* ♦ *vt* polycopier.

stenographer [stɛ'nɔgrəfə*] *n* (*US*) sténographe *m/f*.

stenography [stɛ'nɔgrəfɪ] *n* (*US*) sténo(graphie) *f*.

step [stɛp] *n* pas *m*; (*stair*) marche *f*; (*action*) mesure *f*, disposition *f* ♦ *vi*: **to ~ forward** faire un pas en avant, avancer; **~s** *npl* (*BRIT*) = **stepladder**; **~ by ~** pas à pas; (*fig*) petit à petit; **to be in ~ (with)** (*fig*) aller dans le sens (de); **to be out of ~ (with)** (*fig*) être déphasé(e) (par rapport à).

▶**step down** *vi* (*fig*) se retirer, se désister.

▶**step in** *vi* (*fig*) intervenir.

▶**step off** *vt fus* descendre de.

▶**step over** *vt fus* enjamber.

▶**step up** *vt* augmenter; intensifier.

step aerobics *npl* ® step *m* ®.

stepbrother ['stɛpbrʌðə*] *n* demi-frère *m*.

stepchild ['stɛptʃaɪld] *n* beau-fils/belle-fille.

stepdaughter ['stɛpdɔːtə*] *n* belle-fille *f*.

stepfather ['stɛpfɑːðə*] *n* beau-père *m*.

stepladder ['stɛplædə*] *n* (*BRIT*) escabeau *m*.

stepmother ['stɛpmʌðə*] *n* belle-mère *f*.

stepping stone ['stɛpɪŋ-] *n* pierre *f* de gué; (*fig*) tremplin *m*.

step Reebok [-'riːbɔk] *n* ® step *m* ®.

stepsister ['stɛpsɪstə*] *n* demi-sœur *f*.

stepson ['stɛpsʌn] *n* beau-fils *m*.

stereo ['stɛrɪəu] *n* (*system*) stéréo *f*; (*record player*) chaîne *f* stéréo ♦ *adj* (*also*: **~phonic**) stéréophonique; **in ~** en stéréo.

stereotype ['stɪərɪətaɪp] *n* stéréotype *m* ♦ *vt* stéréotyper.

sterile ['stɛraɪl] *adj* stérile.

sterility [stɛ'rɪlɪtɪ] *n* stérilité *f*.

sterilization [stɛrɪlaɪ'zeɪʃən] *n* stérilisation *f*.

sterilize ['stɛrɪlaɪz] *vt* stériliser.

sterling ['stəːlɪŋ] *adj* sterling *inv*; (*silver*) de bon aloi, fin(e); (*fig*) à toute épreuve, excellent(e) ♦ *n* (*currency*) livre *f* sterling *inv*; **a pound ~** une livre sterling.

sterling area *n* zone *f* sterling *inv*.

stern [stəːn] *adj* sévère ♦ *n* (*NAUT*) arrière *m*, poupe *f*.

sternum ['stəːnəm] *n* sternum *m*.

steroid ['stɪərɔɪd] *n* stéroïde *m*.

stethoscope ['stɛθəskəup] *n* stéthoscope *m*.

stevedore ['stiːvədɔː*] *n* docker *m*, débardeur *m*.

stew [stjuː] *n* ragoût *m* ♦ *vt*, *vi* cuire à la casserole; **~ed tea** le thé trop infusé; **~ed fruit** fruits cuits *or* en compote.

steward ['stjuːəd] *n* (*AVIAT, NAUT, RAIL*) steward *m*; (*in club etc*) intendant *m*; (*also*: **shop ~**) délégué syndical.

stewardess ['stjuːədɛs] *n* hôtesse *f*.

stewardship ['stjuːədʃɪp] *n* intendance *f*.

stewing steak ['stjuːɪŋ-], (*US*) **stew meat** *n* bœuf *m* à braiser.

St. Ex. *abbr* = **stock exchange**.

stg *abbr* = **sterling**.

stick [stɪk] *n* bâton *m*; (*of chalk etc*) morceau *m* ♦ *vb* (*pt*, *pp* **stuck** [stʌk]) *vt* (*glue*) coller; (*thrust*): **to ~ sth into** piquer *or* planter *or* enfoncer qch dans; (*col: put*) mettre, fourrer; (*: tolerate*) supporter ♦ *vi* (*adhere*) coller; (*remain*) rester; (*get jammed: door, lift*) se bloquer; **to get hold of the wrong end of the ~** (*BRIT fig*) comprendre de travers; **to ~ to** (*one's word, promise*) s'en tenir à; (*principles*) rester fidèle à.

▶**stick around** *vi* (*col*) rester (dans les parages).

▶**stick out** *vi* dépasser, sortir ♦ *vt*: **to ~ it out** (*col*) tenir le coup.

▶**stick up** *vi* dépasser, sortir.

▶**stick up for** *vt fus* défendre.

sticker ['stɪkə*] *n* auto-collant *m*.

sticking plaster ['stɪkɪŋ-] *n* sparadrap *m*, pansement adhésif.

sticking point ['stɪkɪŋ-] *n* (*fig*) point *m* de friction.

stickleback ['stɪklbæk] *n* épinoche *f*.

stickler ['stɪklə*] *n*: **to be a ~ for** être pointilleux(euse) sur.

stick shift *n* (*US AUT*) levier *m* de vitesses.

stick-up ['stɪkʌp] *n* (*col*) braquage *m*, hold-up *m*.

sticky ['stɪkɪ] *adj* poisseux(euse); (*label*) adhésif(ive).

stiff [stɪf] *adj* (*gen*) raide, rigide; (*door, brush*) dur(e); (*difficult*) difficile, ardu(e); (*cold*) froid(e), distant(e); (*strong, high*) fort(e), élevé(e); **to be or feel ~** (*person*) avoir des courbatures; **to have a ~ back** avoir mal au dos; **~ upper lip** (*BRIT: fig*) flegme *m* (*typiquement britannique*).

stiffen ['stɪfn] *vt* raidir, renforcer ♦ *vi* se raidir; se durcir.

stiffness ['stɪfnɪs] *n* raideur *f*.

stifle ['staɪfl] *vt* étouffer, réprimer.

stifling ['staɪflɪŋ] *adj* (*heat*) suffocant(e).

stigma, *pl* (*BOT, MED, REL*) **~ta**, (*fig*) **~s** ['stɪgmə, stɪg'mɑːtə] *n* stigmate *m*.

stile [staɪl] *n* échalier *m*.

stiletto [stɪ'lɛtəu] *n* (*BRIT: also*: **~ heel**) talon *m* aiguille.

still [stɪl] *adj* (*motionless*) immobile; (*calm*) calme, tranquille; (*BRIT: orange drink etc*) non gazeux(euse) ♦ *adv* (*up to this time*) encore, toujours; (*even*) encore; (*nonetheless*) quand même, tout de même ♦ *n* (*CINE*) photo *f*; **to stand ~** rester immobile, ne pas bouger; **keep ~!** ne bouge pas!; **he ~ hasn't arrived** il n'est pas encore arrivé, il n'est toujours pas arrivé.

stillborn ['stɪlbɔːn] *adj* mort-né(e).

still life *n* nature morte.

stilt [stɪlt] *n* échasse *f*; (*pile*) pilotis *m*.
stilted ['stɪltɪd] *adj* guindé(e), emprunté(e).
stimulant ['stɪmjulənt] *n* stimulant *m*.
stimulate ['stɪmjuleɪt] *vt* stimuler.
stimulating ['stɪmjuleɪtɪŋ] *adj* stimulant(e).
stimulation [stɪmju'leɪʃən] *n* stimulation *f*.
stimulus, pl stimuli ['stɪmjuləs, 'stɪmjulaɪ] *n* stimulant *m*; (*BIOL, PSYCH*) stimulus *m*.
sting [stɪŋ] *n* piqûre *f*; (*organ*) dard *m*; (*col: confidence trick*) arnaque *m* ♦ *vt* (*pt, pp* **stung** [stʌŋ]) piquer ♦ *vi* piquer; **my eyes are ~ing** j'ai les yeux qui piquent.
stingy ['stɪndʒɪ] *adj* avare, pingre, chiche.
stink [stɪŋk] *n* puanteur *f* ♦ *vi* (*pt* **stank**, *pp* **stunk** [stæŋk, stʌŋk]) puer, empester.
stinker ['stɪŋkə*] *n* (*col: problem, exam*) vacherie *f*; (: *person*) dégueulasse *m/f*.
stinking ['stɪŋkɪŋ] *adj* (*fig: col*) infect(e); **~ rich** bourré(e) de pognon.
stint [stɪnt] *n* part *f* de travail ♦ *vi*: **to ~ on** lésiner sur, être chiche de.
stipend ['staɪpɛnd] *n* (*of vicar etc*) traitement *m*.
stipendiary [staɪ'pɛndɪərɪ] *adj*: **~ magistrate** juge *m* de tribunal d'instance.
stipulate ['stɪpjuleɪt] *vt* stipuler.
stipulation [stɪpju'leɪʃən] *n* stipulation *f*, condition *f*.
stir [stə:*] *n* agitation *f*, sensation *f* ♦ *vt* remuer ♦ *vi* remuer, bouger; **to give sth a ~** remuer qch; **to cause a ~** faire sensation.
►**stir up** *vt* exciter.
stir-fry ['stə:'fraɪ] *vt* faire sauter ♦ *n*: **vegetable ~** légumes sautés à la poêle.
stirring ['stə:rɪŋ] *adj* excitant(e); émouvant(e).
stirrup ['stɪrəp] *n* étrier *m*.
stitch [stɪtʃ] *n* (*SEWING*) point *m*; (*KNITTING*) maille *f*; (*MED*) point de suture; (*pain*) point de côté ♦ *vt* coudre, piquer; suturer.
stoat [stəut] *n* hermine *f* (*avec son pelage d'été*).
stock [stɔk] *n* réserve *f*, provision *f*; (*COMM*) stock *m*; (*AGR*) cheptel *m*, bétail *m*; (*CULIN*) bouillon *m*; (*FINANCE*) valeurs *fpl*, titres *mpl*; (*RAIL: also:* **rolling ~**) matériel roulant; (*descent, origin*) souche *f* ♦ *adj* (*fig: reply etc*) courant(e); classique ♦ *vt* (*have in stock*) avoir, vendre; **well-~ed** bien approvisionné(e) *or* fourni(e); **in ~** en stock, en magasin; **out of ~** épuisé(e); **to take ~** (*fig*) faire le point; **~s and shares** valeurs (mobilières), titres; **government ~** fonds publics.
►**stock up** *vi*: **to ~ up (with)** s'approvisionner (en).
stockade [stɔ'keɪd] *n* palissade *f*.
stockbroker ['stɔkbrəukə*] *n* agent *m* de change.
stock control *n* (*COMM*) gestion *f* des stocks.
stock cube *n* (*BRIT CULIN*) bouillon-cube *m*.
stock exchange *n* Bourse *f* (des valeurs).
stockholder ['stɔkhəuldə*] *n* actionnaire *m/f*.
Stockholm ['stɔkhəum] *n* Stockholm.

stocking ['stɔkɪŋ] *n* bas *m*.
stock-in-trade ['stɔkɪn'treɪd] *n* (*fig*): **it's his ~** c'est sa spécialité.
stockist ['stɔkɪst] *n* (*BRIT*) stockiste *m*.
stock market *n* (*BRIT*) Bourse *f*, marché financier.
stock phrase *n* cliché *m*.
stockpile ['stɔkpaɪl] *n* stock *m*, réserve *f* ♦ *vt* stocker, accumuler.
stockroom ['stɔkru:m] *n* réserve *f*, magasin *m*.
stocktaking ['stɔkteɪkɪŋ] *n* (*BRIT COMM*) inventaire *m*.
stocky ['stɔkɪ] *adj* trapu(e), râblé(e).
stodgy ['stɔdʒɪ] *adj* bourratif(ive), lourd(e).
stoic ['stəuɪk] *n* stoïque *m/f*.
stoical ['stəuɪkl] *adj* stoïque.
stoke [stəuk] *vt* garnir, entretenir; chauffer.
stoker ['stəukə*] *n* (*RAIL, NAUT etc*) chauffeur *m*.
stole [stəul] *pt of* **steal** ♦ *n* étole *f*.
stolen ['stəuln] *pp of* **steal**.
stolid ['stɔlɪd] *adj* impassible, flegmatique.
stomach ['stʌmək] *n* estomac *m*; (*abdomen*) ventre *m* ♦ *vt* supporter, digérer.
stomach ache *n* mal *m* à l'estomac *or* au ventre.
stomach pump *n* pompe stomacale.
stomach ulcer *n* ulcère *m* à l'estomac.
stomp [stɔmp] *vi*: **to ~ in/out** entrer/sortir d'un pas bruyant.
stone [stəun] *n* pierre *f*; (*pebble*) caillou *m*, galet *m*; (*in fruit*) noyau *m*; (*MED*) calcul *m*; (*BRIT: weight*) = 6.348 *kg*; 14 *pounds* ♦ *cpd* de *or* en pierre ♦ *vt* dénoyauter; **within a ~'s throw of the station** à deux pas de la gare.
Stone Age *n*: **the ~** l'âge *m* de pierre.
stone-cold ['stəun'kəuld] *adj* complètement froid(e).
stoned [stəund] *adj* (*col: drunk*) bourré(e); (: *on drugs*) défoncé(e).
stone-deaf ['stəun'dɛf] *adj* sourd(e) comme un pot.
stonemason ['stəunmeɪsn] *n* tailleur *m* de pierre(s).
stonewall [stəun'wɔ:l] *vi* faire de l'obstruction ♦ *vt* faire obstruction à.
stonework ['stəunwə:k] *n* maçonnerie *f*.
stony ['stəunɪ] *adj* pierreux(euse), rocailleux(euse).
stood [stud] *pt, pp of* **stand**.
stooge [stu:dʒ] *n* (*col*) larbin *m*.
stool [stu:l] *n* tabouret *m*.
stoop [stu:p] *vi* (*also:* **have a ~**) être voûté(e); (*bend*) se baisser, se courber; (*fig*): **to ~ to sth/doing sth** s'abaisser jusqu'à qch/jusqu'à faire qch.
stop [stɔp] *n* arrêt *m*; (*short stay*) halte *f*; (*in punctuation*) point *m* ♦ *vt* arrêter; (*break off*) interrompre; (*also:* **put a ~ to**) mettre fin à; (*prevent*) empêcher ♦ *vi* s'arrêter; (*rain, noise etc*) cesser, s'arrêter; **to ~ doing sth** cesser

or arrêter de faire qch; **to ~ sb (from) doing sth** empêcher qn de faire qch; **to ~ dead** *vi* s'arrêter net; **~ it!** arrête!

▶**stop by** *vi* s'arrêter (au passage).

▶**stop off** *vi* faire une courte halte.

▶**stop up** *vt* (*hole*) boucher.

stopcock ['stɔpkɔk] *n* robinet *m* d'arrêt.

stopgap ['stɔpgæp] *n* (*person*) bouche-trou *m*; (*also*: **~ measure**) mesure *f* intérimaire.

stoplights ['stɔplaɪts] *npl* (*AUT*) signaux *mpl* de stop, feux *mpl* arrière.

stopover ['stɔpəʊvə*] *n* halte *f*; (*AVIAT*) escale *f*.

stoppage ['stɔpɪdʒ] *n* arrêt *m*; (*of pay*) retenue *f*; (*strike*) arrêt de travail.

stopper ['stɔpə*] *n* bouchon *m*.

stop press *n* nouvelles *fpl* de dernière heure.

stopwatch ['stɔpwɔtʃ] *n* chronomètre *m*.

storage ['stɔːrɪdʒ] *n* emmagasinage *m*; (*of nuclear waste etc*) stockage *m*; (*in house*) rangement *m*; (*COMPUT*) mise *f* en mémoire *or* réserve.

storage heater *n* (*BRIT*) radiateur *m* électrique par accumulation.

store [stɔː*] *n* provision *f*, réserve *f*; (*depot*) entrepôt *m*; (*BRIT: large shop*) grand magasin; (*US: shop*) magasin *m* ♦ *vt* emmagasiner; (*nuclear waste etc*) stocker; (*in filing system*) classer, ranger; (*COMPUT*) mettre en mémoire; **~s** *npl* provisions; **who knows what is in ~ for us?** qui sait ce que l'avenir nous réserve *or* ce qui nous attend?; **to set great/ little ~ by sth** faire grand cas/peu de cas de qch.

▶**store up** *vt* mettre en réserve, emmagasiner.

storehouse ['stɔːhaus] *n* entrepôt *m*.

storekeeper ['stɔːkiːpə*] *n* (*US*) commerçant/ e.

storeroom ['stɔːruːm] *n* réserve *f*, magasin *m*.

storey, (*US*) **story** ['stɔːrɪ] *n* étage *m*.

stork [stɔːk] *n* cigogne *f*.

storm [stɔːm] *n* tempête *f*; (*also*: **electric ~**) orage *m* ♦ *vi* (*fig*) fulminer ♦ *vt* prendre d'assaut.

storm cloud *n* nuage *m* d'orage.

storm door *n* double-porte (extérieure).

stormy ['stɔːmɪ] *adj* orageux(euse).

story ['stɔːrɪ] *n* histoire *f*; récit *m*; (*PRESS: article*) article *m*; (*: subject*) affaire *f*; (*US*) = **storey**.

storybook ['stɔːrɪbuk] *n* livre *m* d'histoires *or* de contes.

storyteller ['stɔːrɪtelə*] *n* conteur/euse.

stout [staut] *adj* solide; (*brave*) intrépide; (*fat*) gros(se), corpulent(e) ♦ *n* bière brune.

stove [stəʊv] *n* (*for cooking*) fourneau *m*; (*: small*) réchaud *m*; (*for heating*) poêle *m*; **gas/electric ~** (*cooker*) cuisinière *f* à gaz/ électrique.

stow [stəʊ] *vt* ranger; cacher.

stowaway ['stəʊəweɪ] *n* passager/ère clan-

destin(e).

straddle ['strædl] *vt* enjamber, être à cheval sur.

strafe [strɑːf] *vt* mitrailler.

straggle ['strægl] *vi* être (*or* marcher) en désordre; **~d along the coast** disséminé(e) tout au long de la côte.

straggler ['stræglə*] *n* traînard/e.

straggling ['stræglɪŋ], **straggly** ['strægli] *adj* (*hair*) en désordre.

straight [streɪt] *adj* droit(e); (*frank*) honnête, franc(franche); (*plain, uncomplicated*) simple; (*THEAT: part, play*) sérieux(euse); (*col: heterosexual*) hétéro *inv* ♦ *adv* (*tout*) droit; (*drink*) sec, sans eau ♦ *n*: **the ~** (*SPORT*) la ligne droite; **to put** *or* **get ~** mettre en ordre, mettre de l'ordre dans; **let's get this ~** mettons les choses au point; **10 ~ wins** 10 victoires d'affilée; **to go ~ home** rentrer directement à la maison; **~ away**, **~ off** (*at once*) tout de suite; **~ off**, **~ out** sans hésiter.

straighten ['streɪtn] *vt* (*also*: **~ out**) redresser; **to ~ things out** arranger les choses.

straight-faced [streɪt'feɪst] *adj* impassible ♦ *adv* en gardant son sérieux.

straightforward [streɪt'fɔːwəd] *adj* simple; (*frank*) honnête, direct(e).

strain [streɪn] *n* (*TECH*) tension *f*; pression *f*; (*physical*) effort *m*; (*mental*) tension (nerveuse); (*MED*) entorse *f*; (*streak, trace*) tendance *f*; élément *m*; (*breed*) variété *f*; (*of virus*) souche *f*; **~s** *npl* (*of music*) accents *mpl*, accords *mpl* ♦ *vt* tendre fortement; mettre à l'épreuve; (*filter*) passer, filtrer ♦ *vi* peiner, fournir un gros effort; **he's been under a lot of ~** il a traversé des moments très difficiles, il est très éprouvé nerveusement.

strained [streɪnd] *adj* (*laugh etc*) forcé(e), contraint(e); (*relations*) tendu(e).

strainer ['streɪnə*] *n* passoire *f*.

strait [streɪt] *n* (*GEO*) détroit *m*; **to be in dire ~s** (*fig*) être dans une situation désespérée.

straitjacket ['streɪtdʒækɪt] *n* camisole *f* de force.

strait-laced [streɪt'leɪst] *adj* collet monté *inv*.

strand [strænd] *n* (*of thread*) fil *m*, brin *m* ♦ *vt* (*boat*) échouer.

stranded ['strændɪd] *adj* en rade, en plan.

strange [streɪndʒ] *adj* (*not known*) inconnu(e); (*odd*) étrange, bizarre.

strangely ['streɪndʒlɪ] *adv* étrangement, bizarrement.

stranger ['streɪndʒə*] *n* (*unknown*) inconnu/e; (*from somewhere else*) étranger/ère; **I'm a ~ here** je ne suis pas d'ici.

strangle ['stræŋgl] *vt* étrangler.

stranglehold ['stræŋglhəʊld] *n* (*fig*) emprise totale, mainmise *f*.

strangulation [stræŋgju'leɪʃən] *n* strangulation *f*.

strap [stræp] *n* lanière *f*, courroie *f*, sangle *f*;

(of slip, dress) bretelle f ♦ vt attacher (avec une courroie etc).

straphanging ['stræphæŋɪŋ] n (fait m de) voyager debout (dans le métro etc).

strapless ['stræplɪs] adj (bra, dress) sans bretelles.

strapped [stræpt] adj: **to be ~ for cash** (col) être à court d'argent.

strapping ['stræpɪŋ] adj bien découplé(e), costaud(e).

Strasbourg ['stræzbɔːg] n Strasbourg.

strata ['strɑːtə] npl of **stratum**.

stratagem ['strætɪdʒəm] n stratagème m.

strategic [strə'tiːdʒɪk] adj stratégique.

strategist ['strætɪdʒɪst] n stratège m.

strategy ['strætɪdʒɪ] n stratégie f.

stratosphere ['strætəsfɪə*] n stratosphère f.

stratum, pl **strata** ['strɑːtəm, 'strɑːtə] n strate f, couche f.

straw [strɔː] n paille f; **that's the last ~!** ça c'est le comble!

strawberry ['strɔːbərɪ] n fraise f; (plant) fraisier m.

stray [streɪ] adj (animal) perdu(e), errant(e) ♦ vi s'égarer; **~ bullet** balle perdue.

streak [striːk] n raie f, bande f, filet m; (fig: of madness etc): **a ~ of** une or des tendance(s) à ♦ vt zébrer, strier ♦ vi: **to ~ past** passer à toute allure; **to have ~s in one's hair** s'être fait faire des mèches; **a winning/losing ~** une bonne/mauvaise série or période.

streaker ['striːkə*] n personne qui traverse une foule en courant toute nue.

streaky ['striːkɪ] adj zébré(e), strié(e).

streaky bacon n (BRIT) ≈ lard m (maigre).

stream [striːm] n (brook) ruisseau m; (current) courant m, flot m; (of people) défilé ininterrompu, flot ♦ vt (SCOL) répartir par niveau ♦ vi ruisseler; **to ~ in/out** entrer/sortir à flots; **against the ~** à contre courant; **on ~** (new power plant etc) en service.

streamer ['striːmə*] n serpentin m, banderole f.

stream feed n (on photocopier etc) alimentation f en continu.

streamline ['striːmlaɪn] vt donner un profil aérodynamique à; (fig) rationaliser.

streamlined ['striːmlaɪnd] adj (AVIAT) fuselé(e), profilé(e); (AUT) aérodynamique; (fig) rationalisé(e).

street [striːt] n rue f; **the back ~s** les quartiers pauvres; **to be on the ~s** (homeless) être à la rue or sans abri; (as prostitute) faire le trottoir.

streetcar ['striːtkɑː*] n (US) tramway m.

street cred [-krɛd] n (col): **to have ~** être branché(e).

street lamp n réverbère m.

street lighting n éclairage public.

street map, street plan n plan m des rues.

street market n marché m à ciel ouvert.

streetwise ['striːtwaɪz] adj (col) futé(e), réaliste.

strength [strɛŋθ] n force f; (of girder, knot etc) solidité f; (of chemical solution) titre m; (of wine) degré m d'alcool; **on the ~ of** en vertu de; **at full ~** au grand complet; **below ~** à effectifs réduits.

strengthen ['strɛŋθn] vt renforcer; (muscle) fortifier.

strenuous ['strɛnjuəs] adj vigoureux(euse), énergique; (tiring) ardu(e), fatigant(e).

stress [strɛs] n (force, pressure) pression f; (mental strain) tension (nerveuse); (accent) accent m; (emphasis) insistance f ♦ vt insister sur, souligner; **to lay great ~ on sth** insister beaucoup sur qch; **to be under ~** être stressé(e).

stressful ['strɛsful] adj (job) stressant(e).

stretch [strɛtʃ] n (of sand etc) étendue f; (of time) période f ♦ vi s'étirer; (extend): **to ~ to** or **as far as** s'étendre jusqu'à; (be enough: money, food): **to ~ to** aller pour ♦ vt tendre, étirer; (spread) étendre; (fig) pousser (au maximum); **at a ~** sans discontinuer, sans interruption; **to ~ a muscle** se distendre un muscle; **to ~ one's legs** se dégourdir les jambes.

►**stretch out** vi s'étendre ♦ vt (arm etc) allonger, tendre; (to spread) étendre; **to ~ out for sth** allonger la main pour prendre qch.

stretcher ['strɛtʃə*] n brancard m, civière f.

stretcher-bearer ['strɛtʃəbɛərə*] n brancardier m.

stretch marks npl (on skin) vergetures fpl.

strewn [struːn] adj: **~ with** jonché(e) de.

stricken ['strɪkən] adj très éprouvé(e); dévasté(e); (ship) très endommagé(e); **~ with** frappé(e) or atteint(e) de.

strict [strɪkt] adj strict(e); **in ~ confidence** tout à fait confidentiellement.

strictly ['strɪktlɪ] adv strictement; **~ confidential** strictement confidentiel(le); **~ speaking** à strictement parler.

strictness ['strɪktnɪs] n sévérité f.

stride [straɪd] n grand pas, enjambée f ♦ vi (pt **strode**, pp **stridden** [strəud, 'strɪdn]) marcher à grands pas; **to take in one's ~** (fig: changes etc) accepter sans sourciller.

strident ['straɪdnt] adj strident(e).

strife [straɪf] n conflit m, dissensions fpl.

strike [straɪk] n grève f; (of oil etc) découverte f; (attack) raid m ♦ vb (pt, pp **struck** [strʌk]) vt frapper; (oil etc) trouver, découvrir; (make: agreement, deal) conclure ♦ vi faire grève; (attack) attaquer; (clock) sonner; **to go on** or **come out on ~** se mettre en grève, faire grève; **to ~ a match** frotter une allumette; **to ~ a balance** (fig) trouver un juste milieu.

►**strike back** vi (MIL, fig) contre-attaquer.

►**strike down** vt (fig) terrasser.

►**strike off** vt (from list) rayer; (: doctor etc) radier.

►**strike out** vt rayer.

▶**strike up** vt (MUS) se mettre à jouer; **to ~ up a friendship with** se lier d'amitié avec.

strikebreaker ['straɪkbreɪkə*] n briseur m de grève.

striker ['straɪkə*] n gréviste m/f; (SPORT) buteur m.

striking ['straɪkɪŋ] adj frappant(e), saisissant(e).

strimmer ['strɪmə*] n ® (BRIT) coupe-bordures m.

string [strɪŋ] n ficelle f, fil m; (row: of beads) rang m; (: of onions, excuses) chapelet m; (: of people, cars) file f; (MUS) corde f; (COMPUT) châine f ♦ vt (pt, pp **strung** [strʌŋ]): **to ~ out** échelonner; **to ~ together** enchaîner; **the ~s** (MUS) les instruments mpl à cordes; **to get a job by pulling ~s** obtenir un emploi en faisant jouer le piston; **with no ~s attached** (fig) sans conditions.

string bean n haricot vert.

string(ed) instrument [strɪŋ(d)-] n (MUS) instrument m à cordes.

stringent ['strɪndʒənt] adj rigoureux(euse); (need) impérieux(euse).

string quartet n quatuor m à cordes.

strip [strɪp] n bande f; (SPORT: **wearing the Celtic ~** en tenue du Celtic ♦ vt déshabiller; (fig) dégarnir, dépouiller; (also: ~ **down**: machine) démonter ♦ vi se déshabiller.

strip cartoon n bande dessinée.

stripe [straɪp] n raie f, rayure f.

striped ['straɪpt] adj rayé(e), à rayures.

strip light n (BRIT) (tube m au) néon m.

stripper ['strɪpə*] n strip-teaseuse f.

strip-search ['strɪpsə:tʃ] n fouille corporelle (en faisant se déshabiller la personne) ♦ vt: **to ~ sb** fouiller qn (en le faisant se déshabiller).

striptease ['strɪptiːz] n strip-tease m.

strive, pt **strove,** pp **striven** [straɪv, strəuv, 'strɪvn] vi: **to ~ to do** s'efforcer de faire.

strobe [strəub] n (also: ~ **light**) stroboscope m.

strode [strəud] pt of **stride**.

stroke [strəuk] n coup m; (MED) attaque f; (caress) caresse f; (SWIMMING: style) (sorte f de) nage f; (of piston) course f ♦ vt caresser; **at a ~** d'un (seul) coup; **on the ~ of 5** à 5 heures sonnantes; **a ~ of luck** un coup de chance; **a 2-~ engine** un moteur à 2 temps.

stroll [strəul] n petite promenade ♦ vi flâner, se promener nonchalamment; **to go for a ~** aller se promener or faire un tour.

stroller ['strəulə*] n (US) poussette f.

strong [strɒŋ] adj (gen) fort(e); (healthy) vigoureux(euse); (object, material) solide; (distaste, desire) vif(vive); (drugs, chemicals) puissant(e) ♦ adv: **to be going ~** (company) marcher bien; (person) être toujours solide; **they are 50 ~** ils sont au nombre de 50.

strong-arm ['strɒŋɑːm] adj (tactics, methods) musclé(e).

strongbox ['strɒŋbɒks] n coffre-fort m.

stronghold ['strɒŋhəuld] n bastion m.

strongly ['strɒŋlɪ] adv fortement, avec force; vigoureusement; solidement; **I feel ~ about it** c'est une question qui me tient particulièrement à cœur; (negatively) j'y suis profondément opposé(e).

strongman ['strɒŋmæn] n hercule m, colosse m; (fig) homme m à poigne.

strongroom ['strɒŋruːm] n chambre forte.

stroppy ['strɒpɪ] adj (BRIT col) contrariant(e), difficile.

strove [strəuv] pt of **strive**.

struck [strʌk] pt, pp of **strike**.

structural ['strʌktʃrəl] adj structural(e); (CONSTR) de construction; affectant les parties portantes.

structurally ['strʌktʃrəlɪ] adv du point de vue de la construction.

structure ['strʌktʃə*] n structure f; (building) construction f.

struggle ['strʌgl] n lutte f ♦ vi lutter, se battre; **to have a ~ to do sth** avoir beaucoup de mal à faire qch.

strum [strʌm] vt (guitar) gratter de.

strung [strʌŋ] pt, pp of **string**.

strut [strʌt] n étai m, support m ♦ vi se pavaner.

strychnine ['strɪkniːn] n strychnine f.

stub [stʌb] n bout m; (of ticket etc) talon m ♦ vt: **to ~ one's toe (on sth)** se heurter le doigt de pied (contre qch).

▶**stub out** vt écraser.

stubble ['stʌbl] n chaume m; (on chin) barbe f de plusieurs jours.

stubborn ['stʌbən] adj têtu(e), obstiné(e), opiniâtre.

stubby ['stʌbɪ] adj trapu(e); gros(se) et court(e).

stucco ['stʌkəu] n stuc m.

stuck [stʌk] pt, pp of **stick** ♦ adj (jammed) bloqué(e), coincé(e); **to get ~** se bloquer or coincer.

stuck-up [stʌk'ʌp] adj prétentieux(euse).

stud [stʌd] n clou m (à grosse tête); (collar ~) bouton m de col; (of horses) écurie f, haras m; (also: ~ **horse**) étalon m ♦ vt (fig): ~**ded with** parsemé(e) or criblé(e) de.

student ['stjuːdənt] n étudiant/e ♦ cpd estudiantin(e); universitaire; d'étudiant; **law/ medical ~** étudiant en droit/médecine.

student driver n (US) (conducteur/trice) débutant(e).

students' union n (BRIT: association) ≈ union f des étudiants; (: building) ≈ foyer m des étudiants.

studied ['stʌdɪd] adj étudié(e), calculé(e).

studio ['stjuːdɪəu] n studio m, atelier m.

studio flat, (US) studio apartment n studio m.

studious ['stjuːdɪəs] adj studieux(euse), appliqué(e); (studied) étudié(e).

studiously ['stjuːdɪəslɪ] adv (carefully) soigneusement.

study ['stʌdɪ] *n* étude *f*; (*room*) bureau *m* ♦ *vt* étudier ♦ *vi* étudier, faire ses études; **to make a ~ of sth** étudier qch, faire une étude de qch; **to ~ for an exam** préparer un examen.

stuff [stʌf] *n* (*gen*) chose(s) *f(pl)*, truc *m*; (*belongings*) affaires *fpl*, trucs; (*substance*) substance *f* ♦ *vt* rembourrer; (*CULIN*) farcir; (*animal: for exhibition*) empailler; **my nose is ~ed up** j'ai le nez bouché; **get ~ed!** (*col!*) va te faire foutre! (*!*); **~ed toy** jouet *m* en peluche.

stuffing ['stʌfɪŋ] *n* bourre *f*, rembourrage *m*; (*CULIN*) farce *f*.

stuffy ['stʌfɪ] *adj* (*room*) mal ventilé(e) *or* aéré(e); (*ideas*) vieux jeu *inv*.

stumble ['stʌmbl] *vi* trébucher.
►**stumble across** *vt fus* (*fig*) tomber sur.

stumbling block ['stʌmblɪŋ-] *n* pierre *f* d'achoppement.

stump [stʌmp] *n* souche *f*; (*of limb*) moignon *m* ♦ *vt*: **to be ~ed** sécher, ne pas savoir que répondre.

stun [stʌn] *vt* (*subj: blow*) étourdir; (: *news*) abasourdir, stupéfier.

stung [stʌŋ] *pt, pp of* **sting**.

stunk [stʌŋk] *pp of* **stink**.

stunning ['stʌnɪŋ] *adj* étourdissant(e); (*fabulous*) stupéfiant(e), sensationnel(le).

stunt [stʌnt] *n* tour *m* de force; truc *m* publicitaire; (*AVIAT*) acrobatie *f* ♦ *vt* retarder, arrêter.

stunted ['stʌntɪd] *adj* rabougri(e).

stuntman ['stʌntmæn] *n* cascadeur *m*.

stupefaction [stjuːpɪ'fækʃən] *n* stupéfaction *f*, stupeur *f*.

stupefy ['stjuːpɪfaɪ] *vt* étourdir; abrutir; (*fig*) stupéfier.

stupendous [stjuː'pɛndəs] *adj* prodigieux(euse), fantastique.

stupid ['stjuːpɪd] *adj* stupide, bête.

stupidity [stjuː'pɪdɪtɪ] *n* stupidité *f*, bêtise *f*.

stupidly ['stjuːpɪdlɪ] *adv* stupidement, bêtement.

stupor ['stjuːpə*] *n* stupeur *f*.

sturdy ['stɜːdɪ] *adj* robuste, vigoureux(euse), solide.

sturgeon ['stɜːdʒən] *n* esturgeon *m*.

stutter ['stʌtə*] *n* bégaiement *m* ♦ *vi* bégayer.

sty [staɪ] *n* (*of pigs*) porcherie *f*.

stye [staɪ] *n* (*MED*) orgelet *m*.

style [staɪl] *n* style *m*; (*of dress etc*) genre *m*; (*distinction*) allure *f*, cachet *m*, style *m*; **in the latest ~** à la dernière mode; **hair ~** coiffure *f*.

stylish ['staɪlɪʃ] *adj* élégant(e), chic *inv*.

stylist ['staɪlɪst] *n* (*hair ~*) coiffeur/euse; (*literary ~*) styliste *m/f*.

stylized ['staɪlaɪzd] *adj* stylisé(e).

stylus, *pl* **styli** *or* **styluses** ['staɪləs, -laɪ] *n* (*of record player*) pointe *f* de lecture.

Styrofoam ['staɪrəfəum] *n* ® (*US*) polystyrène expansé ♦ *adj* en polystyrène.

suave [swɑːv] *adj* doucereux(euse), onctueux(euse).

sub [sʌb] *n abbr* = **submarine, subscription**.

sub... [sʌb] *prefix* sub..., sous-.

subcommittee ['sʌbkəmɪtɪ] *n* sous-comité *m*.

subconscious [sʌb'kɔnʃəs] *adj* subconscient(e) ♦ *n* subconscient *m*.

subcontinent [sʌb'kɔntɪnənt] *n*: **the (Indian) ~** le sous-continent indien.

subcontract *n* ['sʌb'kɔntrækt] contrat *m* de sous-traitance ♦ *vt* [sʌbkən'trækt] sous-traiter.

subcontractor ['sʌbkən'træktə*] *n* sous-traitant *m*.

subdivide [sʌbdɪ'vaɪd] *vt* subdiviser.

subdivision ['sʌbdɪvɪʒən] *n* subdivision *f*.

subdue [səb'djuː] *vt* subjuguer, soumettre.

subdued [səb'djuːd] *adj* contenu(e), atténué(e); (*light*) tamisé(e); (*person*) qui a perdu de son entrain.

sub-editor ['sʌb'ɛdɪtə*] *n* (*BRIT*) secrétaire *m/f* de (la) rédaction.

subject *n* ['sʌbdʒɪkt] sujet *m*; (*SCOL*) matière *f* ♦ *vt* [səb'dʒɛkt]: **to ~ to** soumettre à; exposer à; **to be ~ to** (*law*) être soumis(e) à; (*disease*) être sujet(te) à; **~ to confirmation in writing** sous réserve de confirmation écrite; **to change the ~** changer de conversation.

subjection [səb'dʒɛkʃən] *n* soumission *f*, sujétion *f*.

subjective [səb'dʒɛktɪv] *adj* subjectif(ive).

subject matter *n* sujet *m*; contenu *m*.

sub judice [sʌb'djuːdɪsɪ] *adj* (*LAW*) devant les tribunaux.

subjugate ['sʌbdʒugeɪt] *vt* subjuguer.

subjunctive [səb'dʒʌŋktɪv] *adj* subjonctif(ive) ♦ *n* subjonctif *m*.

sublet [sʌb'lɛt] *vt* sous-louer.

sublime [sə'blaɪm] *adj* sublime.

subliminal [sʌb'lɪmɪnl] *adj* subliminal(e).

submachine gun ['sʌbmə'ʃiːn-] *n* mitraillette *f*.

submarine [sʌbmə'riːn] *n* sous-marin *m*.

submerge [səb'mɜːdʒ] *vt* submerger; immerger ♦ *vi* plonger.

submersion [səb'mɜːʃən] *n* submersion *f*; immersion *f*.

submission [səb'mɪʃən] *n* soumission *f*; (*to committee etc*) présentation *f*.

submissive [səb'mɪsɪv] *adj* soumis(e).

submit [səb'mɪt] *vt* soumettre ♦ *vi* se soumettre.

subnormal [sʌb'nɔːml] *adj* au-dessous de la normale; (*person*) arriéré(e).

subordinate [sə'bɔːdɪnət] *adj, n* subordonné(e).

subpoena [səb'piːnə] (*LAW*) *n* citation *f*, assignation *f* ♦ *vt* citer *or* assigner (à comparaître).

subroutine [sʌbruː'tiːn] *n* (*COMPUT*) sous-programme *m*.

subscribe [səb'skraɪb] *vi* cotiser; **to ~ to** (*opin-*

ion, fund) souscrire à; (newspaper) s'abonner à; être abonné(e) à.

subscriber [səb'skraɪbə*] n (to periodical, telephone) abonné/e.

subscript ['sʌbskrɪpt] n (TYP) indice inférieur.

subscription [səb'skrɪpʃən] n (to fund) souscription f; (to magazine etc) abonnement m; (membership dues) cotisation f; **to take out a ~ to** s'abonner à.

subsequent ['sʌbsɪkwənt] adj ultérieur(e), suivant(e); **~ to** prep à la suite de.

subsequently ['sʌbsɪkwəntlɪ] adv par la suite.

subservient [səb'sə:vɪənt] adj obséquieux(euse).

subside [səb'saɪd] vi s'affaisser; (flood) baisser; (wind) tomber.

subsidence [səb'saɪdns] n affaissement m.

subsidiarity [səbsɪdɪ'ærɪtɪ] n (POL) subsidiarité f.

subsidiary [səb'sɪdɪərɪ] adj subsidiaire; accessoire; (BRIT SCOL: subject) complémentaire ♦ n filiale f.

subsidize ['sʌbsɪdaɪz] vt subventionner.

subsidy ['sʌbsɪdɪ] n subvention f.

subsist [səb'sɪst] vi: **to ~ on sth** (arriver à) vivre avec or subsister avec qch.

subsistence [səb'sɪstəns] n existence f, subsistance f.

subsistence allowance n indemnité f de séjour.

subsistence level n niveau m de vie minimum.

substance ['sʌbstəns] n substance f; (fig) essentiel m; **a man of ~** un homme jouissant d'une certaine fortune; **to lack ~** être plutôt mince (fig).

substance abuse n abus m de substances toxiques.

substandard [sʌb'stændəd] adj (goods) de qualité inférieure, qui laisse à désirer; (housing) inférieur(e) aux normes requises.

substantial [səb'stænʃl] adj substantiel(le); (fig) important(e).

substantially [səb'stænʃəlɪ] adv considérablement; en grande partie.

substantiate [səb'stænʃɪeɪt] vt étayer, fournir des preuves à l'appui de.

substitute ['sʌbstɪtjuːt] n (person) remplaçant/e; (thing) succédané m ♦ vt: **to ~ sth/sb for** substituer qch/qn à, remplacer par qch/qn.

substitute teacher n (US) suppléant/e.

substitution [sʌbstɪ'tjuːʃən] n substitution f.

subterfuge ['sʌbtəfjuːdʒ] n subterfuge m.

subterranean [sʌbtə'reɪnɪən] adj souterrain(e).

subtitle ['sʌbtaɪtl] n (CINE) sous-titre m.

subtle ['sʌtl] adj subtil(e).

subtlety ['sʌtltɪ] n subtilité f.

subtly ['sʌtlɪ] adv subtilement.

subtotal [sʌb'təutl] n total partiel.

subtract [səb'trækt] vt soustraire, retrancher.

subtraction [səb'trækʃən] n soustraction f.

subtropical [sʌb'trɔpɪkl] adj subtropical(e).

suburb ['sʌbəːb] n faubourg m; **the ~s** la banlieue.

suburban [sə'bəːbən] adj de banlieue, suburbain(e).

suburbia [sə'bəːbɪə] n la banlieue.

subvention [səb'vɛnʃən] n (subsidy) subvention f.

subversion [səb'vəːʃən] n subversion f.

subversive [səb'vəːsɪv] adj subversif(ive).

subway ['sʌbweɪ] n (US) métro m; (BRIT) passage souterrain.

sub-zero [sʌb'zɪərəu] adj au-dessous de zéro.

succeed [sək'siːd] vi réussir ♦ vt succéder à; **to ~ in doing** réussir à faire.

succeeding [sək'siːdɪŋ] adj suivant(e), qui suit (or suivent or suivront etc).

success [sək'sɛs] n succès m; réussite f.

successful [sək'sɛsful] adj qui a du succès; (candidate) choisi(e), agréé(e); (business) prospère, qui réussit; (attempt) couronné(e) de succès; **to be ~ (in doing)** réussir (à faire).

successfully [sək'sɛsfəlɪ] adv avec succès.

succession [sək'sɛʃən] n succession f; **in ~** successivement; **3 years in ~** 3 ans de suite.

successive [sək'sɛsɪv] adj successif(ive); **on 3 ~ days** 3 jours de suite or consécutifs.

successor [sək'sɛsə*] n successeur m.

succinct [sək'sɪŋkt] adj succinct(e), bref(brève).

succulent ['sʌkjulənt] adj succulent(e) ♦ n (BOT): **~s** plantes grasses.

succumb [sə'kʌm] vi succomber.

such [sʌtʃ] adj tel(telle); (of that kind): **~ a book** un livre de ce genre or pareil, un tel livre ♦ adv si; **~ books** des livres de ce genre or pareils, de tels livres; (so much): **~ courage** un tel courage; **~ a long trip** un si long voyage; **~ good books** de si bons livres; **~ a long trip that** un voyage si or tellement long que; **~ a lot of** tellement or tant de; **making ~ a noise that** faisant un tel bruit que or tellement de bruit que; **~ a long time ago** il y a si or tellement longtemps; **~ as** (like) tel(telle) que, comme; **a noise ~ as to** un bruit de nature à; **~ books as I have** les quelques livres que j'ai; **as ~** adv en tant que tel(telle), à proprement parler.

such-and-such ['sʌtʃənsʌtʃ] adj tel(telle) ou tel(telle).

suchlike ['sʌtʃlaɪk] pron (col): **and ~** et le reste.

suck [sʌk] vt sucer; (breast, bottle) téter; (subj: pump, machine) aspirer.

sucker ['sʌkə*] n (BOT, ZOOL, TECH) ventouse f; (col) naïf/ive, poire f.

suckle ['sʌkl] vt allaiter.

sucrose ['suːkrəuz] n saccharose m.

suction ['sʌkʃən] n succion f.

suction pump *n* pompe aspirante.
Sudan [su'dɑːn] *n* Soudan *m*.
Sudanese [suːdə'niːz] *adj* soudanais(e) ♦ *n* Soudanais/e.
sudden ['sʌdn] *adj* soudain(e), subit(e); **all of a** ~ soudain, tout à coup.
sudden-death [sʌdn'dεθ] *n*: ~ **play-off** *partie supplémentaire pour départager les adversaires.*
suddenly ['sʌdnlɪ] *adv* brusquement, tout à coup, soudain.
suds [sʌdz] *npl* eau savonneuse.
sue [suː] *vt* poursuivre en justice, intenter un procès à ♦ *vi*: **to** ~ **(for)** intenter un procès (pour); **to** ~ **for divorce** engager une procédure de divorce; **to** ~ **sb for damages** poursuivre qn en dommages-intérêts.
suede [sweɪd] *n* daim *m*, cuir suédé ♦ *cpd* de daim.
suet ['suɪt] *n* graisse *f* de rognon *or* de bœuf.
Suez Canal ['suːɪz-] *n* canal *m* de Suez.
Suff. *abbr* (*BRIT*) = *Suffolk.*
suffer ['sʌfə*] *vt* souffrir, subir; (*bear*) tolérer, supporter, subir ♦ *vi* souffrir; **to** ~ **from** (*illness*) souffrir de, avoir; **to** ~ **from the effects of alcohol/a fall** se ressentir des effets de l'alcool/des conséquences d'une chute.
sufferance ['sʌfərns] *n*: **he was only there on** ~ sa présence était seulement tolérée.
sufferer ['sʌfərə*] *n* malade *m/f*; victime *m/f*.
suffering ['sʌfərɪŋ] *n* souffrance(s) *f(pl)*.
suffice [sə'faɪs] *vi* suffire.
sufficient [sə'fɪʃənt] *adj* suffisant(e); ~ **money** suffisamment d'argent.
sufficiently [sə'fɪʃəntlɪ] *adv* suffisamment, assez.
suffix ['sʌfɪks] *n* suffixe *m*.
suffocate ['sʌfəkeɪt] *vi* suffoquer; étouffer.
suffocation [sʌfə'keɪʃən] *n* suffocation *f*, (*MED*) asphyxie *f*.
suffrage ['sʌfrɪdʒ] *n* suffrage *m*; droit *m* de suffrage *or* de vote.
suffuse [sə'fjuːz] *vt* baigner, imprégner; **the room was** ~**d with light** la pièce baignait dans la lumière *or* était imprégnée de lumière.
sugar ['ʃugə*] *n* sucre *m* ♦ *vt* sucrer.
sugar beet *n* betterave sucrière.
sugar bowl *n* sucrier *m*.
sugar cane *n* canne *f* à sucre.
sugar-coated ['ʃugə'kəʊtɪd] *adj* dragéifié(e).
sugar lump *n* morceau *m* de sucre.
sugar refinery *n* raffinerie *f* de sucre.
sugary ['ʃugərɪ] *adj* sucré(e).
suggest [sə'dʒεst] *vt* suggérer, proposer; (*indicate*) laisser supposer, suggérer; **what do you** ~ **I do?** que vous me suggérez de faire?
suggestion [sə'dʒεstʃən] *n* suggestion *f*.
suggestive [sə'dʒεstɪv] *adj* suggestif(ive).
suicidal [suɪ'saɪdl] *adj* suicidaire.
suicide ['suɪsaɪd] *n* suicide *m*; **to commit** ~ se suicider.

suicide attempt, suicide bid *n* tentative *f* de suicide.
suit [suːt] *n* (*man's*) costume *m*, complet *m*; (*woman's*) tailleur *m*, ensemble *m*; (*CARDS*) couleur *f*; (*law~*) procès *m* ♦ *vt* aller à; convenir à; (*adapt*): **to** ~ **sth to** adapter *or* approprier qch à; **to be** ~**ed to sth** (*suitable for*) être adapté(e) *or* approprié(e) à qch; **well** ~**ed** (*couple*) faits l'un pour l'autre, très bien assortis; **to bring a** ~ **against sb** intenter un procès contre qn; **to follow** ~ (*fig*) faire de même.
suitable ['suːtəbl] *adj* qui convient; approprié(e), adéquat(e); **would tomorrow be** ~? est-ce que demain vous convien- drait?; **we found somebody** ~ nous avons trouvé la personne qu'il nous faut.
suitably ['suːtəblɪ] *adv* comme il se doit (*or* se devait *etc*), convenablement.
suitcase ['suːtkeɪs] *n* valise *f*.
suite [swiːt] *n* (*of rooms, also MUS*) suite *f*; (*furniture*): **bedroom/dining room** ~ (ensemble *m* de) chambre *f* à coucher/salle *f* à manger; **a three-piece** ~ un salon (canapé et deux fauteuils).
suitor ['suːtə*] *n* soupirant *m*, prétendant *m*.
sulfate ['sʌlfeɪt] *n* (*US*) = **sulphate**.
sulfur *etc* ['sʌlfə*] (*US*) = **sulphur** *etc*.
sulk [sʌlk] *vi* bouder.
sulky ['sʌlkɪ] *adj* boudeur(euse), maussade.
sullen ['sʌlən] *adj* renfrogné(e), maussade; morne.
sulphate, (*US*) **sulfate** ['sʌlfeɪt] *n* sulfate *m*; **copper** ~ sulfate de cuivre.
sulphur, (*US*) **sulfur** ['sʌlfə*] *n* soufre *m*.
sulphur dioxide *n* anhydride sulfureux.
sulphuric, (*US*) **sulfuric** [sʌl'fjuərɪk] *adj*: ~ **acid** acide *m* sulfurique.
sultan ['sʌltən] *n* sultan *m*.
sultana [sʌl'tɑːnə] *n* (*fruit*) raisin (sec) de Smyrne.
sultry ['sʌltrɪ] *adj* étouffant(e).
sum [sʌm] *n* somme *f*; (*SCOL etc*) calcul *m*.
▶**sum up** *vt* résumer; (*evaluate rapidly*) récapituler ♦ *vi* résumer.
Sumatra [su'mɑːtrə] *n* Sumatra *m*.
summarize ['sʌməraɪz] *vt* résumer.
summary ['sʌmərɪ] *n* résumé *m* ♦ *adj* (*justice*) sommaire.
summer ['sʌmə*] *n* été *m* ♦ *cpd* d'été, estival(e); **in (the)** ~ en été, pendant l'été.
summer camp *n* (*US*) colonie *f* de vacances.
summerhouse ['sʌməhaus] *n* (*in garden*) pavillon *m*.
summertime ['sʌmətaɪm] *n* (*season*) été *m*.
summer time *n* (*by clock*) heure *f* d'été.
summery ['sʌmərɪ] *adj* estival(e); d'été.
summing-up [sʌmɪŋ'ʌp] *n* résumé *m*, récapitulation *f*.
summit ['sʌmɪt] *n* sommet *m*; (*also*: ~ **conference**) (conférence *f* au) sommet *m*.
summon ['sʌmən] *vt* appeler, convoquer; **to**

~ **a witness** citer or assigner un témoin.

▶**summon up** vt rassembler, faire appel à.

summons ['sʌmənz] n citation f, assignation f ♦ vt citer, assigner; **to serve a** ~ **on sb** remettre une assignation à qn.

sumo ['suːməu] n: ~ **wrestling** sumo m.

sump [sʌmp] n (BRIT AUT) carter m.

sumptuous ['sʌmptjuəs] adj somptueux(euse).

sun [sʌn] n soleil m; **in the** ~ au soleil; **to catch the** ~ prendre le soleil; **everything under the** ~ absolument tout.

Sun. abbr (= Sunday) dim.

sunbathe ['sʌnbeɪð] vi prendre un bain de soleil.

sunbeam ['sʌnbiːm] n rayon m de soleil.

sunbed ['sʌnbɛd] n lit pliant; (with sun lamp) lit à ultra-violets.

sunburn ['sʌnbəːn] n coup m de soleil.

sunburnt ['sʌnbəːnt], **sunburned** ['sʌnbəːnd] adj bronzé(e), hâlé(e); (painfully) brûlé(e) par le soleil.

sun cream n crème f (anti-)solaire.

sundae ['sʌndeɪ] n sundae m, coupe glacée.

Sunday ['sʌndɪ] n dimanche m; for phrases see also **Tuesday**.

Sunday paper n journal m du dimanche.

Les **Sunday papers** sont une véritable institution en Grande-Bretagne. Il y a des "quality" Sunday papers et des "popular" Sunday papers, et la plupart des quotidiens ont un journal du dimanche qui leur est associé, bien que leurs équipes de rédacteurs soient différentes. Les quality Sunday papers ont plusieurs suppléments et magazines; voir **quality press** et **tabloid press**

Sunday school n ≈ catéchisme m.

sundial ['sʌndaɪəl] n cadran m solaire.

sundown ['sʌndaun] n coucher m du soleil.

sundries ['sʌndrɪz] npl articles divers.

sundry ['sʌndrɪ] adj divers(e), différent(e); **all and** ~ tout le monde, n'importe qui.

sunflower ['sʌnflauə*] n tournesol m.

sung [sʌŋ] pp of **sing**.

sunglasses ['sʌnglaːsɪz] npl lunettes fpl de soleil.

sunk [sʌŋk] pp of **sink**.

sunken ['sʌŋkn] adj (rock, ship) submergé(e); (eyes, cheeks) creux(euse); (bath) encastré(e).

sunlamp ['sʌnlæmp] n lampe f à rayons ultra-violets.

sunlight ['sʌnlaɪt] n (lumière f du) soleil m.

sunlit ['sʌnlɪt] adj ensoleillé(e).

sunny ['sʌnɪ] adj ensoleillé(e); (fig) épanoui(e), radieux(euse); **it is** ~ il fait (du) soleil, il y a du soleil.

sunrise ['sʌnraɪz] n lever m du soleil.

sun roof n (AUT) toit ouvrant.

sunscreen ['sʌnskriːn] n crème f solaire.

sunset ['sʌnsɛt] n coucher m du soleil.

sunshade ['sʌnʃeɪd] n (lady's) ombrelle f; (over table) parasol m.

sunshine ['sʌnʃaɪn] n (lumière f du) soleil m.

sunspot ['sʌnspɔt] n tache f solaire.

sunstroke ['sʌnstrəuk] n insolation f, coup m de soleil.

suntan ['sʌntæn] n bronzage m.

suntanned ['sʌntænd] adj bronzé(e).

suntan oil n huile f solaire.

suntrap ['sʌntræp] n coin très ensoleillé.

super ['suːpə*] adj (col) formidable.

superannuation [suːpərænjuˈeɪʃən] n cotisations fpl pour la pension.

superb [suːˈpəːb] adj superbe, magnifique.

Super Bowl n (US SPORT) Super Bowl m.

supercilious [suːpəˈsɪlɪəs] adj hautain(e), dédaigneux(euse).

superconductor [suːpəkənˈdʌktə*] n supraconducteur m.

superficial [suːpəˈfɪʃəl] adj superficiel(le).

superficially [suːpəˈfɪʃəlɪ] adv superficiellement.

superfluous [suˈpəːfluəs] adj superflu(e).

superglue ['suːpəgluː] n colle forte.

superhighway ['suːpəhaɪweɪ] n (US) voie f express (à plusieurs files); **the information** ~ la super-autoroute de l'information.

superhuman [suːpəˈhjuːmən] adj surhumain(e).

superimpose ['suːpərɪmˈpəuz] vt superposer.

superintend [suːpərɪnˈtɛnd] vt surveiller.

superintendent [suːpərɪnˈtɛndənt] n directeur/trice; (POLICE) ≈ commissaire m.

superior [suˈpɪərɪə*] adj supérieur(e); (COMM: goods, quality) de qualité supérieure; (smug) condescendant(e), méprisant(e) ♦ n supérieur/e; **Mother S**~ (REL) Mère supérieure.

superiority [supɪərɪˈɔrɪtɪ] n supériorité f.

superlative [suˈpəːlətɪv] adj sans pareil(le), suprême ♦ n (LING) superlatif m.

superman ['suːpəmæn] n surhomme m.

supermarket ['suːpəmaːkɪt] n supermarché m.

supermodel ['suːpəmɔdl] n top model m.

supernatural [suːpəˈnætʃərəl] adj surnaturel(le).

supernova [suːpəˈnəuvə] n supernova f.

superpower ['suːpəpauə*] n (POL) superpuissance f.

supersede [suːpəˈsiːd] vt remplacer, supplanter.

supersonic ['suːpəˈsɔnɪk] adj supersonique.

superstar ['suːpəstaː*] n (CINE etc) superstar f; (SPORT) superchampion/ne ♦ adj (status, lifestyle) de superstar.

superstition [suːpəˈstɪʃən] n superstition f.

superstitious [suːpəˈstɪʃəs] adj superstitieux(euse).

superstore ['suːpəstɔː*] n (BRIT) hypermarché m, grand surface.

supertanker ['suːpətæŋkə*] *n* pétrolier géant, superpétrolier *m*.

supertax ['suːpətæks] *n* tranche supérieure de l'impôt.

supervise ['suːpəvaɪz] *vt* (*children etc*) surveiller; (*organization, work*) diriger.

supervision [suːpə'vɪʒən] *n* surveillance *f*; direction *f*; **under medical** ~ sous contrôle du médecin.

supervisor ['suːpəvaɪzə*] *n* surveillant/e; (*in shop*) chef *m* de rayon; (*SCOL*) directeur/ trice de thèse.

supervisory ['suːpəvaɪzərɪ] *adj* de surveillance.

supine ['suːpaɪn] *adj* couché(e) *or* étendu(e) sur le dos.

supper ['sʌpə*] *n* dîner *m*; (*late*) souper *m*; **to have** ~ dîner; souper.

supplant [sə'plɑːnt] *vt* supplanter.

supple ['sʌpl] *adj* souple.

supplement *n* ['sʌplɪmənt] supplément *m* ♦ *vt* [sʌplɪ'ment] ajouter à, compléter.

supplementary [sʌplɪ'mentərɪ] *adj* supplémentaire.

supplementary benefit *n* (*BRIT*) allocation *f* supplémentaire d'aide sociale.

supplier [sə'plaɪə*] *n* fournisseur *m*.

supply [sə'plaɪ] *vt* (*goods*): **to** ~ **sth** (**to sb**) fournir qch (à qn); (*people, organization*): **to** ~ **sb** (**with sth**) approvisionner *or* ravitailler qn (en qch); fournir qn (en qch), fournir qch à qn; (*system, machine*): **to** ~ **sth** (**with sth**) alimenter qch (en qch); (*a need*) répondre à ♦ *n* provision *f*, réserve *f*; (*supplying*) approvisionnement *m*; (*TECH*) alimentation *f*; **supplies** *npl* (*food*) vivres *mpl*; (*MIL*) subsistances *fpl*; **office supplies** fournitures *fpl* de bureau; **to be in short** ~ être rare, manquer; **the electricity/water/gas** ~ l'alimentation en électricité/eau/gaz; ~ **and demand** l'offre *f* et la demande; **it comes supplied with an adaptor** il (*or* elle) est pourvu(e) d'un adaptateur.

supply teacher *n* (*BRIT*) suppléant/e.

support [sə'pɔːt] *n* (*moral, financial etc*) soutien *m*, appui *m*; (*TECH*) support *m*, soutien ♦ *vt* soutenir, supporter; (*financially*) subvenir aux besoins de; (*uphold*) être pour, être partisan de, appuyer; (*SPORT: team*) être pour; **to** ~ **o.s.** (*financially*) gagner sa vie.

supporter [sə'pɔːtə*] *n* (*POL etc*) partisan/e; (*SPORT*) supporter *m*.

supporting [sə'pɔːtɪŋ] *adj* (*wall*) d'appui.

supporting actor/actress *n* second rôle *m/f*.

supporting role *n* second rôle *m*.

supportive [sə'pɔːtɪv] *adj*: **my family were very** ~ ma famille m'a été d'un grand soutien.

suppose [sə'pəʊz] *vt*, *vi* supposer; imaginer; **to be** ~**d to do/be** être censé(e) faire/être; **I don't** ~ **she'll come** je suppose qu'elle ne viendra pas, cela m'étonnerait qu'elle

vienne.

supposedly [sə'pəʊzɪdlɪ] *adv* soi-disant.

supposing [sə'pəʊzɪŋ] *conj* si, à supposer que + *sub*.

supposition [sʌpə'zɪʃən] *n* supposition *f*, hypothèse *f*.

suppository [sə'pɒzɪtrɪ] *n* suppositoire *m*.

suppress [sə'pres] *vt* (*revolt, feeling*) réprimer; (*publication*) supprimer; (*scandal*) étouffer.

suppression [sə'preʃən] *n* suppression *f*, répression *f*.

suppressor [sə'presə*] *n* (*ELEC etc*) dispositif *m* antiparasite.

supremacy [su'preməsɪ] *n* suprématie *f*.

supreme [su'priːm] *adj* suprême.

Supreme Court *n* (*US*) Cour *f* suprême.

supremo [su'priːməu] *n* grand chef.

Supt. *abbr* (*POLICE*) = **superintendent**.

surcharge ['sɜːtʃɑːdʒ] *n* surcharge *f*; (*extra tax*) surtaxe *f*.

sure [ʃuə*] *adj* (*gen*) sûr(e); (*definite, convinced*) sûr, certain(e) ♦ *adv* (*col: esp US*): **that** ~ **is pretty, that's** ~ **pretty** c'est drôlement joli(e); ~! (*of course*) bien sûr!; ~ **enough** effectivement; **I'm not** ~ **how/why/ when** je ne sais pas très bien comment/ pourquoi/quand; **to be** ~ **of o.s.** être sûr de soi; **to make** ~ **of** s'assurer de; vérifier.

sure-fire ['ʃuəfaɪə*] *adj* (*col*) certain(e), infaillible.

sure-footed [ʃuə'futɪd] *adj* au pied sûr.

surely ['ʃuəlɪ] *adv* sûrement; certainement; ~ **you don't mean that!** vous ne parlez pas sérieusement!

surety ['ʃuərətɪ] *n* caution *f*; **to go** *or* **stand** ~ **for sb** se porter caution pour qn.

surf [sɜːf] *n* ressac *m*.

surface ['sɜːfɪs] *n* surface *f* ♦ *vt* (*road*) poser le revêtement de ♦ *vi* remonter à la surface; faire surface; **on the** ~ (*fig*) au premier abord.

surface area *n* superficie *f*, aire *f*.

surface mail *n* courrier *m* par voie de terre (*or* maritime).

surface-to-surface ['sɜːfɪstə'sɜːfɪs] *adj* (*MIL*) sol-sol *inv*.

surfboard ['sɜːfbɔːd] *n* planche *f* de surf.

surfeit ['sɜːfɪt] *n*: **a** ~ **of** un excès de; une indigestion de.

surfer ['sɜːfə*] *n* surfiste *m/f*.

surfing ['sɜːfɪŋ] *n* surf *m*.

surge [sɜːdʒ] *n* vague *f*, montée *f*; (*ELEC*) pointe *f* de courant ♦ *vi* déferler; **to** ~ **forward** se précipiter (en avant).

surgeon ['sɜːdʒən] *n* chirurgien *m*.

Surgeon General *n* (*US*) chef *m* du service fédéral de la santé publique.

surgery ['sɜːdʒərɪ] *n* chirurgie *f*; (*BRIT: room*) cabinet *m* (de consultation); (: *session*) consultation *f*; (: *of MP etc*) permanence *f* (*où le député etc reçoit les électeurs etc*); **to undergo** ~ être opéré(e).

surgery hours npl (BRIT) heures fpl de consultation.

surgical ['sɜːdʒɪkl] adj chirurgical(e).

surgical spirit n (BRIT) alcool m à 90°.

surly ['sɜːlɪ] adj revêche, maussade.

surmise [sə'maɪz] vt présumer, conjecturer.

surmount [sə'maunt] vt surmonter.

surname ['sɜːneɪm] n nom m de famille.

surpass [sɔː'pɑːs] vt surpasser, dépasser.

surplus ['sɜːpləs] n surplus m, excédent m ♦ adj en surplus, de trop; **it is ~ to our requirements** cela dépasse nos besoins; **~ stock** surplus m.

surprise [sə'praɪz] n (gen) surprise f; (astonishment) étonnement m ♦ vt surprendre; étonner; **to take by ~** (person) prendre au dépourvu; (MIL: town, fort) prendre par surprise.

surprising [sə'praɪzɪŋ] adj surprenant(e), étonnant(e).

surprisingly [sə'praɪzɪŋlɪ] adv (easy, helpful) étonnamment, étrangement; (somewhat) ~, **he agreed** curieusement, il a accepté.

surrealism [sə'rɪəlɪzəm] n surréalisme m.

surrealist [sə'rɪəlɪst] adj, n surréaliste (m/f).

surrender [sə'rɛndə*] n reddition f, capitulation f ♦ vi se rendre, capituler ♦ vt (claim, right) renoncer à.

surrender value n valeur f de rachat.

surreptitious [sʌrəp'tɪʃəs] adj subreptice, furtif(ive).

surrogate ['sʌrəgɪt] n (BRIT: substitute) substitut m ♦ adj de substitution, de remplacement; **a food ~** un succédané alimentaire; ~ **coffee** ersatz m or succédané m de café.

surrogate mother n mère porteuse or de substitution.

surround [sə'raund] vt entourer; (MIL etc) encercler.

surrounding [sə'raundɪŋ] adj environnant(e).

surroundings [sə'raundɪŋz] npl environs mpl, alentours mpl.

surtax ['sɜːtæks] n surtaxe f.

surveillance [sɜː'veɪləns] n surveillance f.

survey n ['sɜːveɪ] enquête f, étude f; (in house buying etc) inspection f, (rapport m d')expertise f; (of land) levé m; (comprehensive view: of situation etc) vue f d'ensemble ♦ vt [sɜː'veɪ] passer en revue; enquêter sur; inspecter; (building) expertiser; (land) faire le levé de.

surveying [sə'veɪɪŋ] n arpentage m.

surveyor [sə'veɪə*] n (of building) expert m; (of land) (arpenteur m) géomètre m.

survival [sə'vaɪvl] n survie f; (relic) vestige m ♦ cpd (course, kit) de survie.

survive [sə'vaɪv] vi survivre; (custom etc) subsister ♦ vt survivre à, réchapper de; (person) survivre à.

survivor [sə'vaɪvə*] n survivant/e.

susceptible [sə'sɛptəbl] adj: ~ **(to)** sensible (à); (disease) prédisposé(e) (à).

suspect adj, n ['sʌspɛkt] suspect(e) ♦ vt [səs'pɛkt] soupçonner, suspecter.

suspected [səs'pɛktɪd] adj: **a ~ terrorist** personne soupçonnée de terrorisme; **he had a ~ broken arm** il avait une supposée fracture du bras.

suspend [səs'pɛnd] vt suspendre.

suspended animation [səs'pɛndɪd-] n: **in a state of ~** en hibernation.

suspended sentence [səs'pɛndɪd-] n condamnation f avec sursis.

suspender belt [səs'pɛndə-] n (BRIT) porte-jarretelles m inv.

suspenders [səs'pɛndəz] npl (BRIT) jarretelles fpl; (US) bretelles fpl.

suspense [səs'pɛns] n attente f; (in film etc) suspense m.

suspension [səs'pɛnʃən] n (gen, AUT) suspension f; (of driving licence) retrait m provisoire.

suspension bridge n pont suspendu.

suspicion [səs'pɪʃən] n soupçon(s) m(pl); **to be under ~** être considéré(e) comme suspect(e), être suspecté(e); **arrested on ~ of murder** arrêté sur présomption de meurtre.

suspicious [səs'pɪʃəs] adj (suspecting) soupçonneux(euse), méfiant(e); (causing suspicion) suspect(e); **to be ~ of or about sb/sth** avoir des doutes à propos de qn/sur qch, trouver qn/qch suspect(e).

suss out ['sʌs'aut] vt (BRIT col: discover) suppu ter; (: understand) piger.

sustain [səs'teɪn] vt supporter; soutenir; corroborer; (suffer) subir; recevoir.

sustainable [səs'teɪnəbl] adj (rate, growth) qui peut être maintenu(e); (agriculture, development) durable.

sustained [səs'teɪnd] adj (effort) soutenu(e), prolongé(e).

sustenance ['sʌstɪnəns] n nourriture f; moyens mpl de subsistance.

suture ['suːtʃə*] n suture f.

SW abbr (= short wave) OC.

swab [swɔb] n (MED) tampon m; prélèvement m ♦ vt (NAUT: also: ~ **down**) nettoyer.

swagger ['swægə*] vi plastronner, parader.

swallow ['swɔləu] n (bird) hirondelle f; (of food etc) gorgée f ♦ vt avaler; (fig) gober.

▶**swallow up** vt engloutir.

swam [swæm] pt of **swim**.

swamp [swɔmp] n marais m, marécage m ♦ vt submerger.

swampy ['swɔmpɪ] adj marécageux(euse).

swan [swɔn] n cygne m.

swank [swæŋk] vi (col) faire de l'épate.

swan song n (fig) chant m du cygne.

swap [swɔp] n échange m, troc m ♦ vt: **to ~ (for)** échanger (contre), troquer (contre).

SWAPO ['swɑːpəu] n abbr (= South-West Africa People's Organization) SWAPO f.

swarm [swɔːm] n essaim m ♦ vi essaimer; fourmiller, grouiller.

swarthy ['swɔːðɪ] _adj_ basané(e), bistré(e).
swashbuckling ['swɔʃbʌklɪŋ] _adj_ (_film_) de cape et d'épée.
swastika ['swɒstɪkə] _n_ croix gammée.
SWAT _n abbr_ (_US:_ = _Special Weapons and Tactics_) ≈ CRS _f_.
swat [swɔt] _vt_ écraser ♦ _n_ (_BRIT:_ _also:_ **fly ~**) tapette _f_.
swathe [sweɪð] _vt:_ **to ~ in** (_bandages, blankets_) embobiner de.
swatter ['swɔtə*] _n_ (_also:_ **fly ~**) tapette _f_.
sway [sweɪ] _vi_ se balancer, osciller; tanguer ♦ _vt_ (_influence_) influencer ♦ _n_ (_rule, power_): **~ (over)** emprise _f_ (sur); **to hold ~ over sb** avoir de l'emprise sur qn.
Swaziland ['swɑːzɪlænd] _n_ Swaziland _m_.
swear, _pt_ **swore,** _pp_ **sworn** [sweə*, swɔː*, swɔːn] _vi_ jurer; **to ~ to sth** jurer de qch; **to ~ an oath** prêter serment.
▶**swear in** _vt_ assermenter.
swearword ['sweəwɜːd] _n_ gros mot, juron _m_.
sweat [swɛt] _n_ sueur _f_, transpiration _f_ ♦ _vi_ suer; **in a ~** en sueur.
sweatband ['swɛtbænd] _n_ (_SPORT_) bandeau _m_.
sweater ['swɛtə*] _n_ tricot _m_, pull _m_.
sweatshirt ['swɛtʃɜːt] _n_ sweat-shirt _m_.
sweatshop ['swɛtʃɔp] _n_ atelier _m_ où les ouvriers sont exploités.
sweaty ['swɛtɪ] _adj_ en sueur, moite _or_ mouillé(e) de sueur.
Swede [swiːd] _n_ Suédois/e.
swede [swiːd] _n_ (_BRIT_) rutabaga _m_.
Sweden ['swiːdn] _n_ Suède _f_.
Swedish ['swiːdɪʃ] _adj_ suédois(e) ♦ _n_ (_LING_) suédois _m_.
sweep [swiːp] _n_ coup _m_ de balai; (_curve_) grande courbe; (_range_) champ _m_; (_also:_ **chimney ~**) ramoneur _m_ ♦ _vb_ (_pt, pp_ **swept** [swɛpt]) _vt_ balayer; (_fashion, craze_) se répandre dans ♦ _vi_ avancer majestueusement _or_ rapidement; s'élancer; s'étendre.
▶**sweep away** _vt_ balayer; entraîner; emporter.
▶**sweep past** _vi_ passer majestueusement _or_ rapidement.
▶**sweep up** _vt, vi_ balayer.
sweeper ['swiːpə*] _n_ (_person_) balayeur _m_; (_machine_) balayeuse _f_; (_FOOTBALL_) libéro _m_.
sweeping ['swiːpɪŋ] _adj_ (_gesture_) large; circulaire; (_changes, reforms_) radical(e); **a ~ statement** une généralisation hâtive.
sweepstake ['swiːpsteɪk] _n_ sweepstake _m_.
sweet [swiːt] _n_ (_BRIT_) dessert _m_; (_candy_) bonbon _m_ ♦ _adj_ doux(douce); (_not savoury_) sucré(e); (_fresh_) frais(fraîche), pur(e); (_kind_) gentil(le); (_cute_) mignon(ne) ♦ _adv:_ **to smell ~** sentir bon; **to taste ~** avoir un goût sucré; **~ and sour** _adj_ aigre-doux(douce).
sweetbread ['swiːtbrɛd] _n_ ris _m_ de veau.
sweetcorn ['swiːtkɔːn] _n_ maïs doux.
sweeten ['swiːtn] _vt_ sucrer; (_fig_) adoucir.
sweetener ['swiːtnə*] _n_ (_CULIN_) édulcorant _m_.

sweetheart ['swiːthɑːt] _n_ amoureux/euse.
sweetly ['swiːtlɪ] _adv_ (_smile_) gentiment; (_sing, play_) mélodieusement.
sweetness ['swiːtnɪs] _n_ douceur _f_; (_of taste_) goût sucré.
sweet pea _n_ pois _m_ de senteur.
sweet potato _n_ patate douce.
sweetshop ['swiːtʃɔp] _n_ (_BRIT_) confiserie _f_.
sweet tooth _n:_ **to have a ~** aimer les sucreries.
swell [swɛl] _n_ (_of sea_) houle _f_ ♦ _adj_ (_col: excellent_) chouette ♦ _vb_ (_pt_ **~ed,** _pp_ **swollen** _or_ **~ed** ['swəulən]) _vt_ augmenter; grossir ♦ _vi_ grossir, augmenter; (_sound_) s'enfler; (_MED_) enfler.
swelling ['swɛlɪŋ] _n_ (_MED_) enflure _f_, grosseur _f_.
sweltering ['swɛltərɪŋ] _adj_ étouffant(e), oppressant(e).
swept [swɛpt] _pt, pp of_ **sweep.**
swerve [swɜːv] _vi_ faire une embardée _or_ un écart; dévier.
swift [swɪft] _n_ (_bird_) martinet _m_ ♦ _adj_ rapide, prompt(e).
swiftly ['swɪftlɪ] _adv_ rapidement, vite.
swiftness ['swɪftnɪs] _n_ rapidité _f_.
swig [swɪg] _n_ (_col: drink_) lampée _f_.
swill [swɪl] _n_ pâtée _f_ ♦ _vt_ (_also:_ **~ out, ~ down**) laver à grande eau.
swim [swɪm] _n:_ **to go for a ~** aller nager _or_ se baigner ♦ _vb_ (_pt_ **swam,** _pp_ **swum** [swæm, swʌm]) _vi_ nager; (_SPORT_) faire de la natation; (_fig: head, room_) tourner ♦ _vt_ traverser (à la nage); (_distance_) faire (à la nage); **to ~ a length** nager une longueur; **to go ~ming** aller nager.
swimmer ['swɪmə*] _n_ nageur/euse.
swimming ['swɪmɪŋ] _n_ nage _f_, natation _f_.
swimming baths _npl_ (_BRIT_) piscine _f_.
swimming cap _n_ bonnet _m_ de bain.
swimming costume _n_ (_BRIT_) maillot _m_ (de bain).
swimmingly ['swɪmɪŋlɪ] _adv:_ **to go ~** (_wonderfully_) se dérouler à merveille.
swimming pool _n_ piscine _f_.
swimming trunks _npl_ maillot _m_ de bain.
swimsuit ['swɪmsuːt] _n_ maillot _m_ (de bain).
swindle ['swɪndl] _n_ escroquerie _f_ ♦ _vt_ escroquer.
swindler ['swɪndlə*] _n_ escroc _m_.
swine [swaɪn] _n_ (_pl inv_) pourceau _m_, porc _m_; (_col!_) salaud _m_ (_!_).
swing [swɪŋ] _n_ balançoire _f_; (_movement_) balancement _m_, oscillations _fpl_; (_MUS_) swing _m_; rythme _m_ ♦ _vb_ (_pt, pp_ **swung** [swʌŋ]) _vt_ balancer, faire osciller; (_also:_ **~ round**) tourner, faire virer ♦ _vi_ se balancer, osciller; (_also:_ **~ round**) virer, tourner; **a ~ to the left** (_POL_) un revirement en faveur de la gauche; **to be in full ~** battre son plein; **to get into the ~ of things** se mettre dans le bain; **the road ~s south** la route prend la direction sud.

swing bridge *n* pont tournant.
swing door *n* (*BRIT*) porte battante.
swingeing ['swɪndʒɪŋ] *adj* (*BRIT*) écrasant(e); considérable.
swinging ['swɪŋɪŋ] *adj* rythmé(e); entraînant(e); (*fig*) dans le vent; ~ **door** (*US*) porte battante.
swipe [swaɪp] *n* grand coup; gifle *f* ♦ *vt* (*hit*) frapper à toute volée; gifler; (*col: steal*) piquer; (*credit card etc*) faire passer (dans la machine).
swirl [swəːl] *n* tourbillon *m* ♦ *vi* tourbillonner, tournoyer.
swish [swɪʃ] *adj* (*BRIT col: smart*) rupin(e) ♦ *vi* (*whip*) siffler; (*skirt, long grass*) bruire.
Swiss [swɪs] *adj* suisse ♦ *n* (*pl inv*) Suisse/esse.
Swiss French *adj* suisse romand(e).
Swiss German *adj* suisse-allemand(e).
Swiss roll *n* gâteau roulé.
switch [swɪtʃ] *n* (*for light, radio etc*) bouton *m*; (*change*) changement *m*, revirement *m* ♦ *vt* (*change*) changer; (*exchange*) intervertir; (*invert*): **to ~** (**round** *or* **over**) changer de place.
▶**switch off** *vt* éteindre; (*engine*) arrêter.
▶**switch on** *vt* allumer; (*engine, machine*) mettre en marche; (*BRIT: water supply*) ouvrir.
switchback ['swɪtʃbæk] *n* (*BRIT*) montagnes *fpl* russes.
switchblade ['swɪtʃbleɪd] *n* (*also:* ~ **knife**) couteau *m* à cran d'arrêt.
switchboard ['swɪtʃbɔːd] *n* (*TEL*) standard *m*.
switchboard operator *n* (*TEL*) standardiste *m/f*.
Switzerland ['swɪtsələnd] *n* Suisse *f*.
swivel ['swɪvl] *vi* (*also:* ~ **round**) pivoter, tourner.
swollen ['swəulən] *pp of* **swell** ♦ *adj* (*ankle etc*) enflé(e).
swoon [swuːn] *vi* se pâmer.
swoop [swuːp] *n* (*by police etc*) rafle *f*, descente *f*; (*of bird etc*) descente *f* en piqué ♦ *vi* (*also:* ~ **down**) descendre en piqué, piquer.
swop [swɔp] *n*, *vt* = **swap**.
sword [sɔːd] *n* épée *f*.
swordfish ['sɔːdfɪʃ] *n* espadon *m*.
swore [swɔː*] *pt of* **swear**.
sworn [swɔːn] *pp of* **swear**.
swot [swɔt] *vt*, *vi* bûcher, potasser.
swum [swʌm] *pp of* **swim**.
swung [swʌŋ] *pt*, *pp of* **swing**.
sycamore ['sɪkəmɔː*] *n* sycomore *m*.
sycophant ['sɪkəfænt] *n* flagorneur/euse.
sycophantic [sɪkə'fæntɪk] *adj* flagorneur(euse).
Sydney ['sɪdnɪ] *n* Sydney.
syllable ['sɪləbl] *n* syllabe *f*.
syllabus ['sɪləbəs] *n* programme *m*; **on the ~** au programme.
symbol ['sɪmbl] *n* symbole *m*.
symbolic(al) [sɪm'bɔlɪk(l)] *adj* symbolique.

symbolism ['sɪmbəlɪzəm] *n* symbolisme *m*.
symbolize ['sɪmbəlaɪz] *vt* symboliser.
symmetrical [sɪ'mɛtrɪkl] *adj* symétrique.
symmetry ['sɪmɪtrɪ] *n* symétrie *f*.
sympathetic [sɪmpə'θɛtɪk] *adj* (*showing pity*) compatissant(e); (*understanding*) bienveillant(e), compréhensif(ive); ~ **towards** bien disposé(e) envers.
sympathetically [sɪmpə'θɛtɪklɪ] *adv* avec compassion (*or* bienveillance).
sympathize ['sɪmpəθaɪz] *vi*: **to ~ with sb** (*in grief*) être de tout cœur avec qn, compatir à la douleur de qn; (*in predicament*) partager les sentiments de qn; **to ~ with** (*sb's feelings*) comprendre.
sympathizer ['sɪmpəθaɪzə*] *n* (*POL*) sympathisant/e.
sympathy ['sɪmpəθɪ] *n* compassion *f*; **in ~ with** en accord avec; (*strike*) en *or* par solidarité avec; **with our deepest ~** en vous priant d'accepter nos sincères condoléances.
symphonic [sɪm'fɔnɪk] *adj* symphonique.
symphony ['sɪmfənɪ] *n* symphonie *f*.
symphony orchestra *n* orchestre *m* symphonique.
symposium [sɪm'pəuzɪəm] *n* symposium *m*.
symptom ['sɪmptəm] *n* symptôme *m*; indice *m*.
symptomatic [sɪmptə'mætɪk] *adj* symptomatique.
synagogue ['sɪnəgɔg] *n* synagogue *f*.
sync [sɪŋk] *n* (*col*): **in/out of ~** bien/mal synchronisé(e); **they're in ~ with each other** (*fig*) le courant passe bien entre eux.
synchromesh [sɪŋkrəu'mɛʃ] *n* (*AUT*) synchronisation *f*.
synchronize ['sɪŋkrənaɪz] *vt* synchroniser ♦ *vi*: **to ~ with** se produire en même temps que.
synchronized swimming ['sɪŋkrənaɪzd-] *n* natation synchronisée.
syncopated ['sɪŋkəpeɪtɪd] *adj* syncopé(e).
syndicate ['sɪndɪkɪt] *n* syndicat *m*, coopérative *f*; (*PRESS*) agence *f* de presse.
syndrome ['sɪndrəum] *n* syndrome *m*.
synonym ['sɪnənɪm] *n* synonyme *m*.
synonymous [sɪ'nɔnɪməs] *adj*: ~ (**with**) synonyme (de).
synopsis, *pl* **synopses** [sɪ'nɔpsɪs, -siːz] *n* résumé *m*, synopsis *m or f*.
syntax ['sɪntæks] *n* syntaxe *f*.
synthesis, *pl* **syntheses** ['sɪnθəsɪs, -siːz] *n* synthèse *f*.
synthesizer ['sɪnθəsaɪzə*] *n* (*MUS*) synthétiseur *m*.
synthetic [sɪn'θɛtɪk] *adj* synthétique ♦ *n* matière *f* synthétique; ~**s** *npl* textiles artificiels.
syphilis ['sɪfɪlɪs] *n* syphilis *f*.
syphon ['saɪfən] *n*, *vb* = **siphon**.
Syria ['sɪrɪə] *n* Syrie *f*.
Syrian ['sɪrɪən] *adj* syrien(ne) ♦ *n* Syrien/ne.
syringe [sɪ'rɪndʒ] *n* seringue *f*.

syrup ['sɪrəp] n sirop m; (*BRIT: also*: **golden ~**) mélasse raffinée.
syrupy ['sɪrəpɪ] adj sirupeux(euse).
system ['sɪstəm] n système m; (*order*) méthode f; (*ANAT*) organisme m.
systematic [sɪstə'mætɪk] adj systématique; méthodique.
system disk n (*COMPUT*) disque m système.
systems analyst n analyste-programmeur m/f.

T t

T, t [tiː] n (*letter*) T, t m; **T for Tommy** T comme Thérèse.
TA n abbr (*BRIT*) = Territorial Army.
ta [tɑː] excl (*BRIT col*) merci!
tab [tæb] n abbr = **tabulator** ♦ n (*loop on coat etc*) attache f; (*label*) étiquette f; **to keep ~s on** (*fig*) surveiller.
tabby ['tæbɪ] n (*also*: ~ **cat**) chat/te tigré(e).
tabernacle ['tæbənækl] n tabernacle m.
table ['teɪbl] n table f ♦ vt (*BRIT: motion etc*) présenter; **to lay** or **set the ~** mettre le couvert or la table; **to clear the ~** débarrasser la table; **league ~** (*BRIT FOOTBALL, RUGBY*) classement m (du championnat); **~ of contents** table des matières.
tablecloth ['teɪblklɔθ] n nappe f.
table d'hôte [tɑːbl'dəut] adj (*meal*) à prix fixe.
table football n baby-foot m.
table lamp n lampe décorative.
tablemat ['teɪblmæt] n (*for plate*) napperon m, set m; (*for hot dish*) dessous-de-plat m inv.
table salt n sel fin or de table.
tablespoon ['teɪblspuːn] n cuiller f de service; (*also*: ~**ful**: *as measurement*) cuillerée f à soupe.
tablet ['tæblɪt] n (*MED*) comprimé m; (*: for sucking*) pastille f; (*for writing*) bloc m; (*of stone*) plaque f, ~ **of soap** (*BRIT*) savonnette f.
table tennis n ping-pong m, tennis m de table.
table wine n vin m de table.
tabloid ['tæblɔɪd] n (*newspaper*) tabloïde m; **the ~s** les journaux mpl populaires.

> Le terme **tabloid press** désigne les journaux populaires de demi-format où l'on trouve beaucoup de photos et qui adoptent un style très concis. Ce type de journaux vise des lecteurs s'intéressant aux faits divers ayant un parfum de scandale; voir **quality press**

taboo [tə'buː] adj, n tabou (m).

tabulate ['tæbjuleɪt] vt (*data, figures*) mettre sous forme de table(s).
tabulator ['tæbjuleɪtə*] n tabulateur m.
tachograph ['tækəgrɑːf] n tachygraphe m.
tachometer [tæ'kɔmɪtə*] n tachymètre m.
tacit ['tæsɪt] adj tacite.
taciturn ['tæsɪtɜːn] adj taciturne.
tack [tæk] n (*nail*) petit clou; (*stitch*) point m de bâti; (*NAUT*) bord m, bordée f ♦ vt clouer; bâtir ♦ vi tirer un or des bord(s); **to change ~** virer de bord; **on the wrong ~** (*fig*) sur la mauvaise voie; **to ~ sth on to (the end of) sth** (*of letter, book*) rajouter qch à la fin de qch.
tackle ['tækl] n matériel m, équipement m; (*for lifting*) appareil m de levage; (*FOOTBALL, RUGBY*) plaquage m ♦ vt (*difficulty*) s'attaquer à; (*FOOTBALL, RUGBY*) plaquer.
tacky ['tækɪ] adj collant(e); pas sec(sèche); (*col: shabby*) moche.
tact [tækt] n tact m.
tactful ['tæktful] adj plein(e) de tact.
tactfully ['tæktfəlɪ] adv avec tact.
tactical ['tæktɪkl] adj tactique; ~ **error** erreur f de tactique.
tactical voting n vote m tactique.
tactician [tæk'tɪʃən] n tacticien/ne.
tactics ['tæktɪks] n, npl tactique f.
tactless ['tæktlɪs] adj qui manque de tact.
tactlessly ['tæktlɪslɪ] adv sans tact.
tadpole ['tædpəul] n têtard m.
Tadzhikistan [tædʒɪkɪ'stɑːn] n = Tajikistan.
taffy ['tæfɪ] n (*US*) (bonbon m au) caramel m.
tag [tæg] n étiquette f; **price/name** ~ étiquette (portant le prix/le nom).
▶**tag along** vi suivre.
Tahiti [tɑː'hiːtɪ] n Tahiti m.
tail [teɪl] n queue f; (*of shirt*) pan m ♦ vt (*follow*) suivre, filer; **to turn ~** se sauver à toutes jambes; *see also* **head**.
▶**tail away, tail off** vi (*in size, quality etc*) baisser peu à peu.
tailback ['teɪlbæk] n (*BRIT*) bouchon m.
tail coat n habit m.
tail end n bout m, fin f.
tailgate ['teɪlgeɪt] n (*AUT*) hayon m arrière.
tail light n (*AUT*) feu m arrière.
tailor ['teɪlə*] n tailleur m (*artisan*) ♦ vt: **to ~ sth (to)** adapter qch exactement (à); ~**'s (shop)** (boutique f de) tailleur m.
tailoring ['teɪlərɪŋ] n (*cut*) coupe f.
tailor-made ['teɪlə'meɪd] adj fait(e) sur mesure; (*fig*) conçu(e) spécialement.
tailwind ['teɪlwɪnd] n vent m arrière inv.
taint [teɪnt] vt (*meat, food*) gâter; (*fig: reputation*) salir.
tainted ['teɪntɪd] adj (*food*) gâté(e); (*water, air*) infecté(e); (*fig*) souillé(e).
Taiwan ['taɪ'wɑːn] n Taiwan (*no article*).
Tajikistan [tædʒɪkɪ'stɑːn] n Tadjikistan m/f.
take [teɪk] vb (*pt* **took**, *pp* **taken** [tuk, 'teɪkn]) vt prendre; (*gain: prize*) remporter; (*require: ef-*

fort, courage) demander; (*tolerate*) accepter, supporter; (*hold: passengers etc*) contenir; (*accompany*) emmener, accompagner; (*bring, carry*) apporter, emporter; (*exam*) passer, se présenter à; (*conduct: meeting*) présider ♦ *vi* (*dye, fire etc*) prendre ♦ *n* (*CINE*) prise *f* de vues; **to ~ sth from** (*drawer etc*) prendre qch dans; (*person*) prendre qch à; **I ~ it that** je suppose que; **I took him for a doctor** je l'ai pris pour un docteur; **to ~ sb's hand** prendre qn par la main; **to ~ for a walk** (*child, dog*) emmener promener; **to be taken ill** tomber malade; **to ~ it upon o.s. to do sth** prendre sur soi de faire qch; **~ the first (street) on the left** prenez la première à gauche; **it won't ~ long** ça ne prendra pas longtemps; **I was quite taken with her/it** elle/cela m'a beaucoup plu.

▶**take after** *vt fus* ressembler à.
▶**take apart** *vt* démonter.
▶**take away** *vt* emporter; (*remove*) enlever; (*subtract*) soustraire ♦ *vi*: **to ~ away from** diminuer.
▶**take back** *vt* (*return*) rendre, rapporter; (*one's words*) retirer.
▶**take down** *vt* (*building*) démolir; (*dismantle: scaffolding*) démonter; (*letter etc*) prendre, écrire.
▶**take in** *vt* (*deceive*) tromper, rouler; (*understand*) comprendre, saisir; (*include*) couvrir, inclure; (*lodger*) prendre; (*orphan, stray dog*) recueillir; (*dress, waistband*) reprendre.
▶**take off** *vi* (*AVIAT*) décoller ♦ *vt* (*remove*) enlever; (*imitate*) imiter, pasticher.
▶**take on** *vt* (*work*) accepter, se charger de; (*employee*) prendre, embaucher; (*opponent*) accepter de se battre contre.
▶**take out** *vt* sortir; (*remove*) enlever; (*licence*) prendre, se procurer; **to ~ sth out of** enlever qch de; prendre qch dans; **don't ~ it out on me!** ne t'en prends pas à moi!
▶**take over** *vt* (*business*) reprendre ♦ *vi*: **to ~ over from sb** prendre la relève de qn.
▶**take to** *vt fus* (*person*) se prendre d'amitié pour; (*activity*) prendre goût à; **to ~ to doing sth** prendre l'habitude de faire qch.
▶**take up** *vt* (*one's story, a dress*) reprendre; (*occupy: time, space*) prendre, occuper; (*engage in: hobby etc*) se mettre à; (*accept: offer, challenge*) accepter; (*absorb: liquids*) absorber ♦ *vi*: **to ~ up with sb** se lier d'amitié avec qn.

takeaway ['teɪkəweɪ] (*BRIT*) *adj* (*food*) à emporter ♦ *n* (*shop, restaurant*) ≈ traiteur *m* (*qui vend des plats à emporter*).
take-home pay ['teɪkhəum-] *n* salaire net.
taken ['teɪkən] *pp of* **take**.
takeoff ['teɪkɔf] *n* (*AVIAT*) décollage *m*.
takeout ['teɪkaut] *adj* (*US*) = **takeaway**.
takeover ['teɪkəuvə*] *n* (*COMM*) rachat *m*.
takeover bid *n* offre publique d'achat, OPA *f*.
takings ['teɪkɪŋz] *npl* (*COMM*) recette *f*.

talc [tælk] *n* (*also*: **~um powder**) talc *m*.
tale [teɪl] *n* (*story*) conte *m*, histoire *f*; (*account*) récit *m*; (*pej*) histoire; **to tell ~s** (*fig*) rapporter.
talent ['tælnt] *n* talent *m*, don *m*.
talented ['tæləntɪd] *adj* doué(e), plein(e) de talent.
talent scout *n* découvreur *m* de vedettes (*or* joueurs *etc*).
talisman ['tælɪzmən] *n* talisman *m*.
talk [tɔːk] *n* propos *mpl*; (*gossip*) racontars *mpl* (*pej*); (*conversation*) discussion *f*; (*interview*) entretien *m*; (*a speech*) causerie *f*, exposé *m* ♦ *vi* (*chatter*) bavarder; **~s** *npl* (*POL etc*) entretiens *mpl*; conférence *f*; **to give a ~** faire un exposé; **to ~ about** parler de; (*converse*) s'entretenir *or* parler de; **~ing of films, have you seen ...?** à propos de films, avez-vous vu ...?; **to ~ sb out of/into doing** persuader qn de ne pas faire/de faire; **to ~ shop** parler métier *or* affaires.
▶**talk over** *vt* discuter (de).
talkative ['tɔːkətɪv] *adj* bavard(e).
talker ['tɔːkə*] *n* causeur/euse; (*pej*) bavard/e.
talking point ['tɔːkɪŋ-] *n* sujet *m* de conversation.
talking-to ['tɔːkɪŋtu] *n*: **to give sb a good ~** passer un savon à qn.
talk show *n* (*TV, RADIO*) causerie (télévisée *or* radiodiffusée).
tall [tɔːl] *adj* (*person*) grand(e); (*building, tree*) haut(e); **to be 6 feet ~** ≈ mesurer 1 mètre 80; **how ~ are you?** combien mesurez-vous?
tallboy ['tɔːlbɔɪ] *n* (*BRIT*) grande commode.
tallness ['tɔːlnɪs] *n* grande taille; hauteur *f*.
tall story *n* histoire *f* invraisemblable.
tally ['tælɪ] *n* compte *m* ♦ *vi*: **to ~ (with)** correspondre (à); **to keep a ~ of sth** tenir le compte de qch.
talon ['tælən] *n* griffe *f*; (*of eagle*) serre *f*.
tambourine [tæmbə'riːn] *n* tambourin *m*.
tame [teɪm] *adj* apprivoisé(e); (*fig: story, style*) insipide.
Tamil ['tæmɪl] *adj* tamoul(e) *or* tamil(e) ♦ *n* Tamoul/e *or* Tamil/e; (*LING*) tamoul *m or* tamil *m*.
tamper ['tæmpə*] *vi*: **to ~ with** toucher à (*en cachette ou sans permission*).
tampon ['tæmpən] *n* tampon *m* hygiénique *or* périodique.
tan [tæn] *n* (*also*: **sun~**) bronzage *m* ♦ *vt, vi* bronzer, brunir ♦ *adj* (*colour*) brun roux *inv*; **to get a ~** bronzer.
tandem ['tændəm] *n* tandem *m*.
tandoori [tæn'duərɪ] *adj* tandouri.
tang [tæŋ] *n* odeur (*or* saveur) piquante.
tangent ['tændʒənt] *n* (*MATH*) tangente *f*; **to go off at a ~** (*fig*) changer complètement de direction.
tangerine [tændʒə'riːn] *n* mandarine *f*.
tangible ['tændʒəbl] *adj* tangible; **~ assets** biens réels.

Tangier [tæn'dʒɪə*] *n* Tanger.
tangle ['tæŋgl] *n* enchevêtrement *m* ♦ *vt* enchevêtrer; **to get in(to) a ~** s'emmêler.
tango ['tæŋgəu] *n* tango *m*.
tank [tæŋk] *n* réservoir *m*; (*for processing*) cuve *f*; (*for fish*) aquarium *m*; (*MIL*) char *m* d'assaut, tank *m*.
tankard ['tæŋkəd] *n* chope *f*.
tanker ['tæŋkə*] *n* (*ship*) pétrolier *m*, tanker *m*; (*truck*) camion-citerne *m*; (*RAIL*) wagon-citerne *m*.
tanned [tænd] *adj* bronzé(e).
tannin ['tænɪn] *n* tanin *m*.
tanning ['tænɪŋ] *n* (*of leather*) tannage *m*.
tannoy ['tænɔɪ] *n* ® (*BRIT*) haut-parleur *m*; **over the ~** par haut-parleur.
tantalizing ['tæntəlaɪzɪŋ] *adj* (*smell*) extrêmement appétissant(e); (*offer*) terriblement tentant(e).
tantamount ['tæntəmaunt] *adj*: **~ to** qui équivaut à.
tantrum ['tæntrəm] *n* accès *m* de colère; **to throw a ~** piquer une colère.
Tanzania [tænzə'nɪə] *n* Tanzanie *f*.
Tanzanian [tænzə'nɪən] *adj* tanzanien(ne) ♦ *n* Tanzanien/ne.
tap [tæp] *n* (*on sink etc*) robinet *m*; (*gentle blow*) petite tape ♦ *vt* frapper *or* taper légèrement; (*resources*) exploiter, utiliser; (*telephone*) mettre sur écoute; **on ~** (*beer*) en tonneau; (*fig: resources*) disponible.
tap-dancing ['tæpdɑːnsɪŋ] *n* claquettes *fpl*.
tape [teɪp] *n* ruban *m*; (*also:* **magnetic ~**) bande *f* (magnétique) ♦ *vt* (*record*) enregistrer (au magnétophone *or* sur bande); **on ~** (*song etc*) enregistré(e).
tape deck *n* platine *f* d'enregistrement.
tape measure *n* mètre *m* à ruban.
taper ['teɪpə*] *n* cierge *m* ♦ *vi* s'effiler.
tape-record ['teɪprɪkɔːd] *vt* enregistrer (au magnétophone *or* sur bande).
tape recorder *n* magnétophone *m*.
tape recording *n* enregistrement *m* (au magnétophone).
tapered ['teɪpəd], **tapering** ['teɪpərɪŋ] *adj* fuselé(e), effilé(e).
tapestry ['tæpɪstrɪ] *n* tapisserie *f*.
tape-worm ['teɪpwəːm] *n* ver *m* solitaire, ténia *m*.
tapioca [tæpɪ'əukə] *n* tapioca *m*.
tappet ['tæpɪt] *n* (*AUT*) poussoir *m* (de soupape).
tar [tɑː] *n* goudron *m*; **low-/middle-~** cigarettes cigarettes *fpl* à faible/moyenne teneur en goudron.
tarantula [tə'ræntjulə] *n* tarentule *f*.
tardy ['tɑːdɪ] *adj* tardif(ive).
target ['tɑːgɪt] *n* cible *f*; (*fig: objective*) objectif *m*; **to be on ~** (*project*) progresser comme prévu.
target practice *n* exercices *mpl* de tir (à la cible).

tariff ['tærɪf] *n* (*COMM*) tarif *m*; (*taxes*) tarif douanier.
tariff barrier *n* barrière douanière.
tarmac ['tɑːmæk] *n* (*BRIT: on road*) macadam *m*; (*AVIAT*) aire *f* d'envol ♦ *vt* (*BRIT*) goudronner.
tarnish ['tɑːnɪʃ] *vt* ternir.
tarot ['tærəu] *n* tarot *m*.
tarpaulin [tɑː'pɔːlɪn] *n* bâche goudronnée.
tarragon ['tærəgən] *n* estragon *m*.
tart [tɑːt] *n* (*CULIN*) tarte *f*; (*BRIT col: pej: woman*) poule *f* ♦ *adj* (*flavour*) âpre, aigrelet(te).
▶**tart up** *vt* (*col*): **to ~ o.s. up** se faire beau(belle); (: *pej*) s'attifer.
tartan ['tɑːtn] *n* tartan *m* ♦ *adj* écossais(e).
tartar ['tɑːtə*] *n* (*on teeth*) tartre *m*.
tartar sauce *n* sauce *f* tartare.
task [tɑːsk] *n* tâche *f*; **to take to ~** prendre à partie.
task force *n* (*MIL, POLICE*) détachement spécial.
taskmaster ['tɑːskmɑːstə*] *n*: **he's a hard ~** il est très exigeant dans le travail.
Tasmania [tæz'meɪnɪə] *n* Tasmanie *f*.
tassel ['tæsl] *n* gland *m*; pompon *m*.
taste [teɪst] *n* goût *m*; (*fig: glimpse, idea*) idée *f*, aperçu *m* ♦ *vt* goûter ♦ *vi*: **to ~ of** (*fish etc*) avoir le *or* un goût de; **it ~s like fish** ça a un *or* le goût de poisson, on dirait du poisson; **what does it ~ like?** quel goût ça a?; **you can ~ the garlic (in it)** on sent bien l'ail; **can I have a ~ of this wine?** puis-je goûter un peu de ce vin?; **to have a ~ of sth** goûter (à) qch; **to have a ~ for sth** aimer qch, avoir un penchant pour qch; **to be in good/bad** *or* **poor ~** être de bon/mauvais goût.
taste bud *n* papille *f*.
tasteful ['teɪstful] *adj* de bon goût.
tastefully ['teɪstfəlɪ] *adv* avec goût.
tasteless ['teɪstlɪs] *adj* (*food*) qui n'a aucun goût; (*remark*) de mauvais goût.
tasty ['teɪstɪ] *adj* savoureux(euse), délicieux(euse).
tattered ['tætəd] *adj see* **tatters**.
tatters ['tætəz] *npl*: **in ~** (*also:* **tattered**) en lambeaux.
tattoo [tə'tuː] *n* tatouage *m*; (*spectacle*) parade *f* militaire ♦ *vt* tatouer.
tatty ['tætɪ] *adj* (*BRIT col*) défraîchi(e), en piteux état.
taught [tɔːt] *pt, pp of* **teach**.
taunt [tɔːnt] *n* raillerie *f* ♦ *vt* railler.
Taurus ['tɔːrəs] *n* le Taureau; **to be ~** être du Taureau.
taut [tɔːt] *adj* tendu(e).
tavern ['tævən] *n* taverne *f*.
tawdry ['tɔːdrɪ] *adj* (d'un mauvais goût) criard.
tawny ['tɔːnɪ] *adj* fauve (*couleur*).
tax [tæks] *n* (*on goods etc*) taxe *f*; (*on income*) impôts *mpl*, contributions *fpl* ♦ *vt* taxer; imposer; (*fig: strain: patience etc*) mettre à

l'épreuve; **before/after** ~ avant/après l'impôt; **free of** ~ exonéré(e) d'impôt.

taxable ['tæksəbl] *adj* (*income*) imposable.

tax allowance *n* part *f* du revenu non imposable, abattement *m* à la base.

taxation [tæk'seɪʃən] *n* taxation *f*; impôts *mpl*, contributions *fpl*; **system of** ~ système fiscal.

tax avoidance *n* évasion fiscale.

tax collector *n* percepteur *m*.

tax disc *n* (*BRIT AUT*) vignette *f* (automobile).

tax evasion *n* fraude fiscale.

tax exemption *n* exonération fiscale, exemption *f* d'impôts.

tax exile *n personne qui s'expatrie pour raisons fiscales.*

tax-free ['tæksfriː] *adj* exempt(e) d'impôts.

tax haven *n* paradis fiscal.

taxi ['tæksɪ] *n* taxi *m* ♦ *vi* (*AVIAT*) rouler (lentement) au sol.

taxidermist ['tæksɪdəːmɪst] *n* empailleur/euse (*d'animaux*).

taxi driver *n* chauffeur *m* de taxi.

tax inspector *n* (*BRIT*) percepteur *m*.

taxi rank (*BRIT*), **taxi stand** *n* station *f* de taxis.

tax payer [-peɪə*] *n* contribuable *m/f*.

tax rebate *n* ristourne *f* d'impôt.

tax relief *n* dégrèvement *or* allègement fiscal, réduction *f* d'impôt.

tax return *n* déclaration *f* d'impôts *or* de revenus.

tax year *n* année fiscale.

TB *n abbr* = **tuberculosis**.

TD *n abbr* (*US*) = **Treasury Department**; (*: FOOTBALL*) = **touchdown**.

tea [tiː] *n* thé *m*; (*BRIT: snack: for children*) goûter *m*; **high** ~ (*BRIT*) *collation combinant goûter et dîner*.

tea bag *n* sachet *m* de thé.

tea break *n* (*BRIT*) pause-thé *f*.

teacake ['tiːkeɪk] *n* (*BRIT*) ≈ petit pain aux raisins.

teach, *pt, pp* **taught** [tiːtʃ, tɔːt] *vt*: **to** ~ **sb sth,** ~ **sth to sb** apprendre qch à qn; (*in school etc*) enseigner qch à qn ♦ *vi* enseigner; **it taught him a lesson** (*fig*) ça lui a servi de leçon.

teacher ['tiːtʃə*] *n* (*in secondary school*) professeur *m*; (*in primary school*) instituteur/trice; **French** ~ professeur de français.

teacher training college *n* (*for primary schools*) ≈ école normale d'instituteurs; (*for secondary schools*) collège *m* de formation pédagogique (*pour l'enseignement secondaire*).

teaching ['tiːtʃɪŋ] *n* enseignement *m*.

teaching aids *npl* supports *mpl* pédagogiques.

teaching hospital *n* (*BRIT*) C.H.U. *m*, centre *m* hospitalo-universitaire.

teaching staff *n* (*BRIT*) enseignants *mpl*.

tea cosy *n* couvre-théière *m*.

teacup ['tiːkʌp] *n* tasse *f* à thé.

teak [tiːk] *n* teck *m* ♦ *adj* en *or* de teck.

tea leaves *npl* feuilles *fpl* de thé.

team [tiːm] *n* équipe *f*; (*of animals*) attelage *m*.

►**team up** *vi*: **to** ~ **up (with)** faire équipe (avec).

team games *npl* jeux *mpl* d'équipe.

teamwork ['tiːmwəːk] *n* travail *m* d'équipe.

tea party *n* thé *m* (*réception*).

teapot ['tiːpɔt] *n* théière *f*.

tear¹ *n* [tɛə*] déchirure *f* ♦ *vb* (*pt* **tore** [tɔː*, toːn]) *vt* se déchirer; **to** ~ **to pieces** *or* **to bits** *or* **to shreds** mettre en pièces; (*fig*) démolir.

►**tear along** *vi* (*rush*) aller à toute vitesse.

►**tear apart** *vt* (*also fig*) déchirer.

►**tear away** *vt*: **to** ~ **o.s. away (from sth)** (*fig*) s'arracher (de qch).

►**tear out** *vt* (*sheet of paper, cheque*) arracher.

►**tear up** *vt* (*sheet of paper etc*) déchirer, mettre en morceaux *or* pièces.

tear² ['tɪə*] *n* larme *f*; **in** ~**s** en larmes; **to burst into** ~**s** fondre en larmes.

tearaway ['tɛərəweɪ] *n* (*col*) casse-cou *m inv*.

teardrop ['tɪədrɔp] *n* larme *f*.

tearful ['tɪəful] *adj* larmoyant(e).

tear gas ['tɪə-] *n* gaz *m* lacrymogène.

tearoom ['tiːruːm] *n* salon *m* de thé.

tease [tiːz] *n* taquin/e ♦ *vt* taquiner; (*unkindly*) tourmenter.

tea set *n* service *m* à thé.

teashop ['tiːʃɔp] *n* (*BRIT*) pâtisserie-salon de thé *f*.

Teasmade ['tiːzmeɪd] *n* ® machine *f* à faire le thé.

teaspoon ['tiːspuːn] *n* petite cuiller; (*also: ~ful: as measurement*) ≈ cuillerée *f* à café.

tea strainer *n* passoire *f* (à thé).

teat [tiːt] *n* tétine *f*.

teatime ['tiːtaɪm] *n* l'heure *f* du thé.

tea towel *n* (*BRIT*) torchon *m* (à vaisselle).

tea urn *n* fontaine *f* à thé.

tech [tɛk] *n abbr* (*col*) = **technology**, **technical college**.

technical ['tɛknɪkl] *adj* technique.

technical college *n* C.E.T. *m*, collège *m* d'enseignement technique.

technicality [tɛknɪ'kælɪtɪ] *n* technicité *f*; (*detail*) détail *m* technique; **on a legal** ~ à cause de (*or* grâce à) l'application à la lettre d'une subtilité juridique; pour vice de forme.

technically ['tɛknɪklɪ] *adv* techniquement; (*strictly speaking*) en théorie, en principe.

technician [tɛk'nɪʃən] *n* technicien/ne.

technique [tɛk'niːk] *n* technique *f*.

techno ['tɛknəu] *n* (*MUS*) techno *f*.

technocrat ['tɛknəkræt] *n* technocrate *m/f*.

technological [tɛknə'lɔdʒɪkl] *adj* technologique.

technologist [tɛk'nɔlədʒɪst] *n* technologue *m/f*.

technology [tɛk'nɔlədʒɪ] *n* technologie *f*.

teddy (bear) ['tɛdɪ-] *n* ours *m* (en peluche).

tedious ['tiːdɪəs] *adj* fastidieux(euse).

tedium ['tiːdɪəm] *n* ennui *m*.

tee [tiː] *n* (*GOLF*) tee *m*.

teem [tiːm] *vi*: **to ~ (with)** grouiller (de); **it is ~ing (with rain)** il pleut à torrents.

teenage ['tiːneɪdʒ] *adj* (*fashions etc*) pour jeunes, pour adolescents.

teenager ['tiːneɪdʒə*] *n* jeune *m/f*, adolescent/e.

teens [tiːnz] *npl*: **to be in one's ~** être adolescent(e).

tee-shirt ['tiːʃəːt] *n* = **T-shirt**.

teeter ['tiːtə*] *vi* chanceler, vaciller.

teeth [tiːθ] *npl of* **tooth**.

teethe [tiːð] *vi* percer ses dents.

teething ring ['tiːðɪŋ-] *n* anneau *m* (*pour bébé qui perce ses dents*).

teething troubles ['tiːðɪŋ-] *npl* (*fig*) difficultés initiales.

teetotal ['tiːˈtəutl] *adj* (*person*) qui ne boit jamais d'alcool.

teetotaller, (*US*) **teetotaler** ['tiːˈtəutlə*] *n* personne *f* qui ne boit jamais d'alcool.

TEFL ['tɛfl] *n abbr* = *Teaching of English as a Foreign Language*.

Teflon ['tɛflɔn] *n* ® Téflon *m* ®.

Teheran [tɛəˈrɑːn] *n* Téhéran.

tel. *abbr* (= *telephone*) tél.

Tel Aviv ['tɛləˈviːv] *n* Tel Aviv.

telecast ['tɛlɪkɑːst] *vt* télédiffuser, téléviser.

telecommunications ['tɛlɪkəmjuːnɪ'keɪʃənz] *n* télécommunications *fpl*.

telegram ['tɛlɪgræm] *n* télégramme *m*.

telegraph ['tɛlɪgrɑːf] *n* télégraphe *m*.

telegraphic [tɛlɪ'græfɪk] *adj* télégraphique.

telegraph pole *n* poteau *m* télégraphique.

telegraph wire *n* fil *m* télégraphique.

telepathic [tɛlɪ'pæθɪk] *adj* télépathique.

telepathy [tə'lɛpəθɪ] *n* télépathie *f*.

telephone ['tɛlɪfəun] *n* téléphone *m* ♦ *vt* (*person*) téléphoner à; (*message*) téléphoner; **to have a ~,** (*BRIT*) **to be on the ~** (*subscriber*) être abonné(e) au téléphone; **to be on the ~** (*be speaking*) être au téléphone.

telephone booth, (*BRIT*) **telephone box** *n* cabine *f* téléphonique.

telephone call *n* appel *m* téléphonique, communication *f* téléphonique.

telephone directory *n* annuaire *m* (du téléphone).

telephone exchange *n* central *m* (téléphonique).

telephone number *n* numéro *m* de téléphone.

telephone operator *n* téléphoniste *m/f*, standardiste *m/f*.

telephone tapping [-tæpɪŋ] *n* mise *f* sur écoute.

telephonist [tə'lɛfənɪst] *n* (*BRIT*) téléphoniste *m/f*.

telephoto ['tɛlɪfəutəu] *adj*: **~ lens** téléobjectif *m*.

teleprinter ['tɛlɪprɪntə*] *n* téléscripteur *m*.

Teleprompter ['tɛlɪprɔmptə*] *n* ® (*US*) prompteur *m*.

telesales ['tɛlɪseɪlz] *npl* télévente *f*.

telescope ['tɛlɪskəup] *n* télescope *m* ♦ *vi* se télescoper ♦ *vt* télescoper.

telescopic [tɛlɪ'skɔpɪk] *adj* télescopique; (*umbrella*) à manche télescopique.

Teletext ['tɛlɪtɛkst] *n* ® télétexte *m*.

telethon ['tɛlɪθɔn] *n* téléthon *m*.

televise ['tɛlɪvaɪz] *vt* téléviser.

television ['tɛlɪvɪʒən] *n* télévision *f*.

television licence *n* (*BRIT*) redevance *f* (de l'audio-visuel).

television programme *n* émission *f* de télévision.

television set *n* poste *m* de télévision, téléviseur *m*.

telex ['tɛlɛks] *n* télex *m* ♦ *vt* (*message*) envoyer par télex; (*person*) envoyer un télex à ♦ *vi* envoyer un télex.

tell, *pt, pp* **told** [tɛl, təuld] *vt* dire; (*relate: story*) raconter; (*distinguish*): **to ~ sth from** distinguer qch de ♦ *vi* (*talk*): **to ~ (of)** parler (de); (*have effect*) se faire sentir, se voir; **to ~ sb to do** dire à qn de faire; **to ~ sb about sth** (*place, object etc*) parler de qch à qn; (*what happened etc*) raconter qch à qn; **to ~ the time** (*know how to*) savoir lire l'heure; **can you ~ me the time?** pourriez-vous me dire l'heure?; **(I) ~ you what ...** écoute, ...; **I can't ~ them apart** je n'arrive pas à les distinguer.

▶**tell off** *vt* réprimander, gronder.

▶**tell on** *vt fus* (*inform against*) dénoncer, rapporter contre.

teller ['tɛlə*] *n* (*in bank*) caissier/ière.

telling ['tɛlɪŋ] *adj* (*remark, detail*) révélateur(trice).

telltale ['tɛlteɪl] *n* rapporteur/euse ♦ *adj* (*sign*) éloquent(e), révélateur(trice).

telly ['tɛlɪ] *n abbr* (*BRIT col*: = *television*) télé *f*.

temerity [tə'mɛrɪtɪ] *n* témérité *f*.

temp [tɛmp] *abbr* (*BRIT col*: = *temporary*) *n* intérimaire *m/f* ♦ *vi* travailler comme intérimaire.

temper ['tɛmpə*] *n* (*nature*) caractère *m*; (*mood*) humeur *f*; (*fit of anger*) colère *f* ♦ *vt* (*moderate*) tempérer, adoucir; **to be in a ~** être en colère; **to lose one's ~** se mettre en colère; **to keep one's ~** rester calme.

temperament ['tɛmprəmənt] *n* (*nature*) tempérament *m*.

temperamental [tɛmprə'mɛntl] *adj* capricieux(euse).

temperance ['tɛmpərns] *n* modération *f*; (*in drinking*) tempérance *f*.

temperate ['tɛmprət] *adj* modéré(e); (*climate*) tempéré(e).

temperature ['tɛmprətʃə*] *n* température *f*; **to have** *or* **run a ~** avoir de la fièvre.

temperature chart *n* (*MED*) feuille *f* de tem-

pérature.
tempered ['tɛmpəd] *adj* (*steel*) trempé(e).
tempest ['tɛmpɪst] *n* tempête *f*.
tempestuous [tɛm'pɛstjʊəs] *adj* (*fig*) orageux(euse); (*: person*) passionné(e).
tempi ['tɛmpiː] *npl of* **tempo**.
template ['tɛmplɪt] *n* patron *m*.
temple ['tɛmpl] *n* (*building*) temple *m*; (*ANAT*) tempe *f*.
templet ['tɛmplɪt] *n* = **template**.
tempo, ~**s** *or* **tempi** ['tɛmpəʊ, 'tɛmpiː] *n* tempo *m*; (*fig: of life etc*) rythme *m*.
temporal ['tɛmpərl] *adj* temporel(le).
temporarily ['tɛmpərərɪlɪ] *adv* temporairement; provisoirement.
temporary ['tɛmpərərɪ] *adj* temporaire, provisoire; (*job, worker*) temporaire; ~ **secretary** (secrétaire *f*) intérimaire *f*; **a** ~ **teacher** un professeur remplaçant *or* suppléant.
temporize ['tɛmpəraɪz] *vi* atermoyer; transiger.
tempt [tɛmpt] *vt* tenter; **to** ~ **sb into doing** induire qn à faire; **to be** ~**ed to do sth** être tenté(e) de faire qch.
temptation [tɛmp'teɪʃən] *n* tentation *f*.
tempting ['tɛmptɪŋ] *adj* tentant(e).
ten [tɛn] *num* dix ♦ *n*: ~**s of thousands** des dizaines *fpl* de milliers.
tenable ['tɛnəbl] *adj* défendable.
tenacious [tə'neɪʃəs] *adj* tenace.
tenacity [tə'næsɪtɪ] *n* ténacité *f*.
tenancy ['tɛnənsɪ] *n* location *f*; état *m* de locataire.
tenant ['tɛnənt] *n* locataire *m/f*.
tend [tɛnd] *vt* s'occuper de; (*sick etc*) soigner ♦ *vi*: **to** ~ **to do** avoir tendance à faire; (*colour*): **to** ~ **to** tirer sur.
tendency ['tɛndənsɪ] *n* tendance *f*.
tender ['tɛndə*] *adj* tendre; (*delicate*) délicat(e); (*sore*) sensible; (*affectionate*) tendre, doux(douce) ♦ *n* (*COMM: offer*) soumission *f*; (*money*): **legal** ~ **cours légal** ♦ *vt* offrir; **to** ~ **one's resignation** donner *or* remettre sa démission; **to put in a** ~ **(for)** faire une soumission (pour); **to put work out to** ~ (*BRIT*) mettre un contrat en adjudication.
tenderize ['tɛndəraɪz] *vt* (*CULIN*) attendrir.
tenderly ['tɛndəlɪ] *adv* tendrement.
tenderness ['tɛndənɪs] *n* tendresse *f*; (*of meat*) tendreté *f*.
tendon ['tɛndən] *n* tendon *m*.
tenement ['tɛnəmənt] *n* immeuble *m* (de rapport).
Tenerife [tɛnə'riːf] *n* Ténérife *f*.
tenet ['tɛnət] *n* principe *m*.
Tenn. *abbr* (*US*) = *Tennessee*.
tenner ['tɛnə*] *n* (*BRIT col*) billet *m* de dix livres.
tennis ['tɛnɪs] *n* tennis *m* ♦ *cpd* (*club, match, racket, player*) de tennis.
tennis ball *n* balle *f* de tennis.
tennis court *n* (court *m* de) tennis *m*.

tennis elbow *n* (*MED*) synovite *f* du coude.
tennis shoes *npl* (chaussures *fpl* de) tennis *mpl*.
tenor ['tɛnə*] *n* (*MUS*) ténor *m*; (*of speech etc*) sens général.
tenpin bowling ['tɛnpɪn-] *n* (*BRIT*) bowling *m* (à 10 quilles).
tense [tɛns] *adj* tendu(e); (*person*) tendu, crispé(e) ♦ *n* (*LING*) temps *m* ♦ *vt* (*tighten: muscles*) tendre.
tenseness ['tɛnsnɪs] *n* tension *f*.
tension ['tɛnʃən] *n* tension *f*.
tent [tɛnt] *n* tente *f*.
tentacle ['tɛntəkl] *n* tentacule *m*.
tentative ['tɛntətɪv] *adj* timide, hésitant(e); (*conclusion*) provisoire.
tenterhooks ['tɛntəhʊks] *npl*: **on** ~ sur des charbons ardents.
tenth [tɛnθ] *num* dixième.
tent peg *n* piquet *m* de tente.
tent pole *n* montant *m* de tente.
tenuous ['tɛnjʊəs] *adj* ténu(e).
tenure ['tɛnjʊə*] *n* (*of property*) bail *m*; (*of job*) période *f* de jouissance; statut *m* de titulaire.
tepid ['tɛpɪd] *adj* tiède.
Ter. *abbr* = **terrace**.
term [təːm] *n* (*limit*) terme *m*; (*word*) terme, mot *m*; (*SCOL*) trimestre *m*; (*LAW*) session *f* ♦ *vt* appeler; ~**s** *npl* (*conditions*) conditions *fpl*; (*COMM*) tarif *m*; ~ **of imprisonment** peine *f* de prison; **his** ~ **of office** la période où il était en fonction; **in the short/long** ~ à court/long terme; "**easy** ~**s**" (*COMM*) "facilités de paiement"; **to come to** ~**s with** (*problem*) faire face à; **to be on good** ~**s with** bien s'entendre avec, être en bons termes avec.
terminal ['təːmɪnl] *adj* terminal(e); (*disease*) dans sa phase terminale ♦ *n* (*ELEC*) borne *f*; (*for oil, ore etc, also COMPUT*) terminal *m*; (*also: air* ~) aérogare *f*; (*BRIT: also: coach* ~) gare routière.
terminate ['təːmɪneɪt] *vt* mettre fin à ♦ *vi*: **to** ~ **in** finir en *or* par.
termination [təːmɪ'neɪʃən] *n* fin *f*; cessation *f*; (*of contract*) résiliation *f*; ~ **of pregnancy** (*MED*) interruption *f* de grossesse.
termini ['təːmɪnaɪ] *npl of* **terminus**.
terminology [təːmɪ'nɔlədʒɪ] *n* terminologie *f*.
terminus, *pl* **termini** ['təːmɪnəs, 'təːmɪnaɪ] *n* terminus *m inv*.
termite ['təːmaɪt] *n* termite *m*.
term paper *n* (*US UNIVERSITY*) dissertation trimestrielle.
Terr. *abbr* = **terrace**.
terrace ['tɛrəs] *n* terrasse *f*; (*BRIT: row of houses*) rangée *f* de maisons (*attenantes les unes aux autres*); **the** ~**s** (*BRIT SPORT*) les gradins *mpl*.
terraced ['tɛrəst] *adj* (*garden*) en terrasses; (*in a row: house, cottage etc*) attenant(e) aux

maisons voisines.

terracotta ['tɛrə'kɔtə] *n* terre cuite.

terrain [tɛ'reɪn] *n* terrain *m* (*sol*).

terrible ['tɛrɪbl] *adj* terrible, atroce; (*weather, work*) affreux(euse), épouvantable.

terribly ['tɛrɪblɪ] *adv* terriblement; (*very badly*) affreusement mal.

terrier ['tɛrɪə*] *n* terrier *m* (*chien*).

terrific [tə'rɪfɪk] *adj* fantastique, incroyable, terrible; (*wonderful*) formidable, sensationnel(le).

terrify ['tɛrɪfaɪ] *vt* terrifier.

territorial [tɛrɪ'tɔːrɪəl] *adj* territorial(e).

territorial waters *npl* eaux territoriales.

territory ['tɛrɪtərɪ] *n* territoire *m*.

terror ['tɛrə*] *n* terreur *f*.

terrorism ['tɛrərɪzəm] *n* terrorisme *m*.

terrorist ['tɛrərɪst] *n* terroriste *m/f*.

terrorize ['tɛrəraɪz] *vt* terroriser.

terse [tɜːs] *adj* (*style*) concis(e); (*reply*) laconique.

tertiary ['tɜːʃərɪ] *adj* tertiaire; ~ **education** (*BRIT*) enseignement *m* postscolaire.

Terylene ['tɛrɪliːn] *n* ® (*BRIT*) tergal *m* ®.

TESL ['tɛsl] *n abbr* = Teaching of English as a Second Language.

TESSA ['tɛsə] *n abbr* (*BRIT*: = Tax Exempt Special Savings Account*) *compte de dépôt aux intérêts exempts d'impôts si le capital reste bloqué*.

test [tɛst] *n* (*trial, check*) essai *m*; (*: of goods in factory*) contrôle *m*; (*of courage etc*) épreuve *f*; (*MED*) examens *mpl*; (*CHEM*) analyses *fpl*; (*exam: of intelligence etc*) test *m* (d'aptitude*; (*: in school*) interrogation *f* de contrôle; (*also:* **driving** ◊ ~) (examen du) permis *m* de conduire ◊ *vt* essayer; contrôler; mettre à l'épreuve; examiner; analyser; tester; faire subir une interrogation (de contrôle) à; **to put sth to the** ~ mettre qch à l'épreuve.

testament ['tɛstəmənt] *n* testament *m*; **the Old/New T**~ l'Ancien/le Nouveau Testament.

test ban *n* (*also:* **nuclear** ~) interdiction *f* des essais nucléaires.

test case *n* (*LAW, fig*) affaire-test *f*.

testes ['tɛstiːz] *npl* testicules *mpl*.

test flight *n* vol *m* d'essai.

testicle ['tɛstɪkl] *n* testicule *m*.

testify ['tɛstɪfaɪ] *vi* (*LAW*) témoigner, déposer; **to** ~ **to sth** (*LAW*) attester qch; (*gen*) témoigner de qch.

testimonial [tɛstɪ'məunɪəl] *n* (*BRIT: reference*) recommandation *f*; (*gift*) témoignage *m* d'estime.

testimony ['tɛstɪmənɪ] *n* (*LAW*) témoignage *m*, déposition *f*.

testing ['tɛstɪŋ] *adj* (*situation, period*) difficile.

test match *n* (*CRICKET, RUGBY*) match international.

testosterone [tɛs'tɔstərəun] *n* testostérone *f*.

test paper *n* (*SCOL*) interrogation écrite.

test pilot *n* pilote *m* d'essai.

test tube *n* éprouvette *f*.

test-tube baby ['tɛsttjuːb-] *n* bébé-éprouvette *m*.

testy ['tɛstɪ] *adj* irritable.

tetanus ['tɛtənəs] *n* tétanos *m*.

tetchy ['tɛtʃɪ] *adj* hargneux(euse).

tether ['tɛðə*] *vt* attacher ◊ *n*: **at the end of one's** ~ à bout (de patience).

Tex. *abbr* (*US*) = Texas.

text [tɛkst] *n* texte *m*.

textbook ['tɛkstbuk] *n* manuel *m*.

textile ['tɛkstaɪl] *n* textile *m*.

textual ['tɛkstjuəl] *adj* textuel(le).

texture ['tɛkstʃə*] *n* texture *f*; (*of skin, paper etc*) grain *m*.

TGIF *abbr* (*col*) = thank God it's Friday.

TGWU *n abbr* (*BRIT*: = Transport and General Workers' Union*) syndicat de transporteurs.

Thai [taɪ] *adj* thaïlandais(e) ◊ *n* Thaïlandais/e; (*LING*) thaï *m*.

Thailand ['taɪlænd] *n* Thaïlande *f*.

thalidomide [θə'lɪdəmaɪd] *n* ® thalidomide *f* ®.

Thames [tɛmz] *n*: **the** ~ la Tamise.

than [ðæn, ðən] *conj* que; (*with numerals*): **more** ~ **10/once** plus de 10/d'une fois; **I have more/less** ~ **you** j'en ai plus/moins que toi; **she has more apples** ~ **pears** elle a plus de pommes que de poires; **it is better to phone** ~ **to write** il vaut mieux téléphoner (plutôt) qu'écrire; **no sooner did he leave** ~ **the phone rang** il venait de partir quand le téléphone a sonné.

thank [θæŋk] *vt* remercier, dire merci à; ~ **you (very much)** merci (beaucoup); ~ **heavens**, ~ **God** Dieu merci.

thankful ['θæŋkful] *adj*: ~ **(for)** reconnaissant(e) (de); ~ **for/that** (*relieved*) soulagé(e) de/que.

thankfully ['θæŋkfəlɪ] *adv* avec reconnaissance; avec soulagement; ~ **there were few victims** il y eut fort heureusement peu de victimes.

thankless ['θæŋklɪs] *adj* ingrat(e).

thanks [θæŋks] *npl* remerciements *mpl* ◊ *excl* merci!; ~ **to** *prep* grâce à.

Thanksgiving (Day) ['θæŋksgɪvɪŋ-] *n* jour *m* d'action de grâce.

Thanksgiving Day *est un jour de congé aux États-Unis, le quatrième jeudi du mois de novembre, commémorant la bonne récolte que les Pélerins venus de Grande-Bretagne ont eue en 1621; traditionnellement, c'était un jour où l'on remerciait Dieu et où l'on organisait un grand festin.*
Une fête semblable, mais qui n'a aucun rapport avec les Pères Pélerins, a lieu au Canada le deuxième lundi d'octobre.

=============================== *KEYWORD*

that [ðæt] *adj* (*demonstrative:* pl **those**) ce, cet
+vowel or h mute, f cette; ~ **man/woman/book**
cet homme/cette femme/ce livre; (*not this*)
cet homme-là/cette femme-là/ce livre-là; ~
one celui-là(celle-là)

♦ *pron* **1** (*demonstrative:* pl **those**) ce; (*not this
one*) cela, ça; (*the one*) celui(celle); **who's**
~? qui est-ce?; **what's** ~? qu'est-ce que
c'est?; **is** ~ **you?** c'est toi?; **I prefer this to** ~
je préfère ceci à cela *or* ça; ~**'s what he
said** c'est *or* voilà ce qu'il a dit; **all** ~ tout
cela, tout ça; ~ **is (to say)** c'est-à-dire, à savoir; **at** *or* **with** ~, **she ...** là-dessus, elle ...;
do it like ~ fais-le comme ça

2 (*relative: subject*) qui; (: *object*) que; (: *indirect*) lequel(laquelle), lesquels(lesquelles)
pl; **the book** ~ **I read** le livre que j'ai lu; **the
books** ~ **are in the library** les livres qui sont
dans la bibliothèque; **all** ~ **I have** tout ce que
j'ai; **the box** ~ **I put it in** la boîte dans laquelle je l'ai mis; **the people** ~ **I spoke to** les
gens auxquels *or* à qui j'ai parlé; **not** ~ **I
know of** pas à ma connaissance

3 (*relative: of time*) où; **the day** ~ **he came** le
jour où il est venu

♦ *conj* que; **he thought** ~ **I was ill** il pensait
que j'étais malade

♦ *adv* (*demonstrative*): **I can't work** ~ **much** je
ne peux pas travailler autant que cela; **I
didn't know it was** ~ **bad** je ne savais pas
que c'était si *or* aussi mauvais; ~ **high** aussi
haut; si haut; **it's about** ~ **high** c'est à peu
près de cette hauteur.

thatched [θætʃt] *adj* (*roof*) de chaume; ~ **cottage** chaumière f.
Thatcherism ['θætʃərɪzəm] *n* thatchérisme *m*.
thaw [θɔː] *n* dégel *m* ♦ *vi* (*ice*) fondre; (*food*)
dégeler ♦ *vt* (*food*) (faire) dégeler; **it's** ~**ing**
(*weather*) il dégèle.

=============================== *KEYWORD*

the [ðiː, ðə] *def art* **1** (*gen*) le, la f, l' *+vowel or h
mute,* les *pl*; (NB: *à +le(s)* = au(x); *de + le* = du;
de +les = des); ~ **boy/girl/ink** le garçon/la
fille/l'encre; ~ **children** les enfants; ~ **history of** ~ **world** l'histoire du monde; **give it
to** ~ **postman** donne-le au facteur; **to play** ~
piano/flute jouer du piano/de la flûte; ~ **rich
and** ~ **poor** les riches et les pauvres

2 (*in titles*): **Elizabeth** ~ **First** Elisabeth première; **Peter** ~ **Great** Pierre le Grand

3 (*in comparisons*): ~ **more he works,** ~
more he earns plus il travaille, plus il gagne
de l'argent; ~ **sooner** ~ **better** le plus tôt
sera le mieux.

theatre, (*US*) **theater** ['θɪətə*] *n* théâtre *m*.
theatre-goer ['θɪətəgəuə*] *n* habitué/e du
théâtre.

theatrical [θɪˈætrɪkl] *adj* théâtral(e); ~ **company** troupe f de théâtre.
theft [θɛft] *n* vol *m* (*larcin*).
their [ðɛə*] *adj* leur, leurs *pl*.
theirs [ðɛəz] *pron* le(la) leur, les leurs; **it is** ~
c'est à eux; **a friend of** ~ un de leurs amis.
them [ðɛm, ðəm] *pron* (*direct*) les; (*indirect*)
leur; (*stressed, after prep*) eux(elles); **I see** ~
je les vois; **give** ~ **the book** donne-leur le
livre; **give me a few of** ~ donnez m'en quelques uns (*or* quelques unes).
theme [θiːm] *n* thème *m*.
theme park *n* parc *m* à thème.
theme song *n* chanson principale.
themselves [ðəmˈsɛlvz] *pl pron* (*reflexive*) se;
(*emphatic*) eux-mêmes(elles-mêmes); **between** ~ entre eux(elles).
then [ðɛn] *adv* (*at that time*) alors, à ce
moment-là; (*next*) puis, ensuite; (*and also*) et
puis ♦ *conj* (*therefore*) alors, dans ce cas ♦ *adj*:
the ~ **president** le président d'alors *or* de
l'époque; **by** ~ (*past*) à ce moment-là; (*future*) d'ici là; **from** ~ **on** dès lors; **before** ~
avant; **until** ~ jusqu'à ce moment-là,
jusque-là; **and** ~ **what?** et puis après?; **what
do you want me to do** ~? (*afterwards*) que
veux-tu que je fasse ensuite?; (*in that case*)
bon alors, qu'est-ce que je fais?
theologian [θɪəˈləudʒən] *n* théologien/ne.
theological [θɪəˈlɒdʒɪkl] *adj* théologique.
theology [θɪˈɒlədʒɪ] *n* théologie f.
theorem ['θɪərəm] *n* théorème *m*.
theoretical [θɪəˈrɛtɪkl] *adj* théorique.
theorize ['θɪəraɪz] *vi* élaborer une théorie;
(*pej*) faire des théories.
theory ['θɪərɪ] *n* théorie f.
therapeutic(al) [θɛrəˈpjuːtɪk(l)] *adj* thérapeutique.
therapist ['θɛrəpɪst] *n* thérapeute *m/f*.
therapy ['θɛrəpɪ] *n* thérapie f.

=============================== *KEYWORD*

there [ðɛə*] *adv* **1**: ~ **is,** ~ **are** il y a; ~ **are 3 of
them** (*people, things*) il y en a 3; ~ **has been
an accident** il y a eu un accident

2 (*referring to place*) là, là-bas; **it's** ~ c'est
là(-bas). **in/on/up/down** ~ là-dedans/là-
dessus/là-haut/en bas; **he went** ~ **on Friday**
il y est allé vendredi; **to go** ~ **and back** faire
l'aller-retour; **I want that book** ~ je veux ce
livre-là; ~ **he is!** le voilà!

3: ~, ~ (*esp to child*) allons, allons!

thereabouts ['ðɛərə'bauts] *adv* (*place*) par là,
près de là; (*amount*) environ, à peu près.
thereafter [ðɛərˈɑːftə*] *adv* par la suite.
thereby ['ðɛəbaɪ] *adv* ainsi.
therefore ['ðɛəfɔː*] *adv* donc, par conséquent.
there's ['ðɛəz] = **there is, there has**.
thereupon [ðɛərəˈpɒn] *adv* (*at that point*) sur
ce; (*formal: on that subject*) à ce sujet.
thermal ['θəːml] *adj* thermique; ~ **paper/**

printer papier *m*/imprimante *f* thermique.
thermodynamics ['θə:mədaɪ'næmɪks] *n* thermodynamique *f*.
thermometer [θə'mɒmɪtə*] *n* thermomètre *m*.
thermonuclear ['θə:məʊ'njuːklɪə*] *adj* thermonucléaire.
Thermos ['θə:məs] *n* ® (*also:* ~ **flask**) thermos *m or f inv* ®.
thermostat ['θə:məʊstæt] *n* thermostat *m*.
thesaurus [θɪ'sɔːrəs] *n* dictionnaire *m* synonymique.
these [ðiːz] *pl pron* ceux-ci(celles-ci) ♦ *pl adj* ces; (*not those*): ~ **books** ces livres-ci.
thesis, *pl* **theses** ['θiːsɪs, 'θiːsiːz] *n* thèse *f*.
they [ðeɪ] *pl pron* ils(elles); (*stressed*) eux(elles); ~ **say that** ... (*it is said that*) on dit que ....
they'd [ðeɪd] = **they had, they would.**
they'll [ðeɪl] = **they shall, they will.**
they're [ðɛə*] = **they are.**
they've [ðeɪv] = **they have.**
thick [θɪk] *adj* épais(se); (*crowd*) dense; (*stupid*) bête, borné(e) ♦ *n*: **in the** ~ **of** au beau milieu de, en plein cœur de; **it's 20 cm** ~ ça a 20 cm d'épaisseur.
thicken ['θɪkn] *vi* s'épaissir ♦ *vt* (*sauce etc*) épaissir.
thicket ['θɪkɪt] *n* fourré *m*, hallier *m*.
thickly ['θɪklɪ] *adv* (*spread*) en couche épaisse; (*cut*) en tranches épaisses; ~ **populated** à forte densité de population.
thickness ['θɪknɪs] *n* épaisseur *f*.
thickset [θɪk'sɛt] *adj* trapu(e), costaud(e).
thickskinned [θɪk'skɪnd] *adj* (*fig*) peu sensible.
thief, *pl* **thieves** [θiːf, θiːvz] *n* voleur/euse.
thieving ['θiːvɪŋ] *n* vol *m* (*larcin*).
thigh [θaɪ] *n* cuisse *f*.
thighbone ['θaɪbəʊn] *n* fémur *m*.
thimble ['θɪmbl] *n* dé *m* (à coudre).
thin [θɪn] *adj* mince; (*person*) maigre; (*soup*) peu épais(se); (*hair, crowd*) clairsemé(e); (*fog*) léger(ère) ♦ *vt* (*hair*) éclaircir; (*also:* ~ **down**: *sauce, paint*) délayer ♦ *vi* (*fog*) s'éclaircir; (*also:* ~ **out**: *crowd*) se disperser; **his hair is** ~**ning** il se dégarnit.
thing [θɪŋ] *n* chose *f*; (*object*) objet *m*; (*contraption*) truc *m*; ~**s** *npl* (*belongings*) affaires *fpl*; **first** ~ (**in the morning**) à la première heure, tout de suite (le matin); **last** ~ (**at night**), **he** ... juste avant de se coucher, il ...; **the** ~ **is** ... c'est que ...; **for one** ~ d'abord; **the best** ~ **would be to** le mieux serait de; **how are** ~**s?** comment ça va?; **she's got a** ~ **about** ... elle déteste ...; **poor** ~! le (*or* la) pauvre!
think, *pt, pp* **thought** [θɪŋk, θɔːt] *vi* penser, réfléchir ♦ *vt* penser, croire; (*imagine*) s'imaginer; **to** ~ **of** penser à; **what do you** ~ **of it?** qu'en pensez-vous?; **what did you** ~ **of them?** qu'avez-vous pensé d'eux?; **to** ~ **about sth/sb** penser à qch/qn; **I'll** ~ **about it** je vais y réfléchir; **to** ~ **of doing** avoir l'idée de faire; **I** ~ **so/not** je crois *or* pense que

oui/non; **to** ~ **well of** avoir une haute opinion de; ~ **again!** attention, réfléchis bien!; **to** ~ **aloud** penser tout haut.
►**think out** *vt* (*plan*) bien réfléchir à; (*solution*) trouver.
►**think over** *vt* bien réfléchir à; **I'd like to** ~ **things over** (*offer, suggestion*) j'aimerais bien y réfléchir un peu.
►**think through** *vt* étudier dans tous les détails.
►**think up** *vt* inventer, trouver.
thinking ['θɪŋkɪŋ] *n*: **to my (way of)** ~ selon moi.
think tank *n* groupe *m* de réflexion.
thinly ['θɪnlɪ] *adv* (*cut*) en tranches fines; (*spread*) en couche mince.
thinness ['θɪnnɪs] *n* minceur *f*; maigreur *f*.
third [θə:d] *num* troisième ♦ *n* troisième *m/f*; (*fraction*) tiers *m*; (*BRIT SCOL: degree*) ≈ licence *f* avec mention passable; **a** ~ **of** le tiers de.
third-degree burns ['θə:ddɪgriː-] *npl* brûlures *fpl* au troisième degré.
thirdly ['θə:dlɪ] *adv* troisièmement.
third party insurance *n* (*BRIT*) assurance *f* au tiers.
third-rate ['θə:d'reɪt] *adj* de qualité médiocre.
Third World *n*: **the** ~ le Tiers-Monde.
thirst [θə:st] *n* soif *f*.
thirsty ['θə:stɪ] *adj* qui a soif, assoiffé(e); **to be** ~ avoir soif.
thirteen [θə:'tiːn] *num* treize.
thirtieth ['θə:tɪɪθ] *num* trentième.
thirty ['θə:tɪ] *num* trente.

==================================== *KEYWORD*

this [ðɪs] *adj* (*demonstrative*: *pl* **these**) ce, *+vowel or h mute*, cette *f*; ~ **man/woman/book** cet homme/cette femme/ce livre; (*not that*) cet homme-ci/cette femme-ci/ce livre-ci; ~ **one** celui-ci(celle-ci); ~ **time** cette fois-ci; ~ **time last year** l'année dernière à la même époque; ~ **way** (*in this direction*) par ici; (*in this fashion*) de cette façon, ainsi
♦ *pron* (*demonstrative*: *pl* **these**) ce; (*not that one*) celui-ci(celle-ci), ceci; **who's** ~? qui est-ce?; **what's** ~? qu'est-ce que c'est?; **I prefer** ~ **to that** je préfère ceci à cela; **they were talking of** ~ **and that** ils parlaient de choses et d'autres; ~ **is what he said** voici ce qu'il a dit; ~ **is Mr Brown** (*in introductions*) je vous présente Mr Brown; (*in photo*) c'est Mr Brown; (*on telephone*) ici Mr Brown
♦ *adv* (*demonstrative*): **it was about** ~ **big** c'était à peu près de cette grandeur *or* grand comme ça; **I didn't know it was** ~ **bad** je ne savais pas que c'était si *or* aussi mauvais.

thistle ['θɪsl] *n* chardon *m*.
thong [θɒŋ] *n* lanière *f*.
thorn [θɔːn] *n* épine *f*.

thorny ['θɔːnɪ] *adj* épineux(euse).
thorough ['θʌrə] *adj* (*search*) minutieux(euse); (*knowledge, research*) approfondi(e); (*work*) consciencieux(euse); (*cleaning*) à fond.
thoroughbred ['θʌrəbrɛd] *n* (*horse*) pur-sang *m inv*.
thoroughfare ['θʌrəfɛə*] *n* rue *f*; "**no ~**" (*BRIT*) "passage interdit".
thoroughgoing ['θʌrəgəuɪŋ] *adj* (*analysis*) approfondi(e); (*reform*) profond(e).
thoroughly ['θʌrəlɪ] *adv* minutieusement; en profondeur; à fond; **he ~ agreed** il était tout à fait d'accord.
thoroughness ['θʌrənɪs] *n* soin (méticuleux).
those [ðəuz] *pl pron* ceux-là(celles-là) ♦ *pl adj* ces; (*not these*): ~ **books** ces livres-là.
though [ðəu] *conj* bien que + *sub*, quoique + *sub* ♦ *adv* pourtant; **even ~** quand bien même + *conditional*; **it's not easy, ~** pourtant, ce n'est pas facile.
thought [θɔːt] *pt, pp of* **think** ♦ *n* pensée *f*; (*opinion*) avis *m*; (*intention*) intention *f*; **after much ~** après mûre réflexion; **I've just had a ~** je viens de penser à quelque chose; **to give sth some ~** réfléchir à qch.
thoughtful ['θɔːtful] *adj* pensif(ive); (*considerate*) prévenant(e).
thoughtfully ['θɔːtfəlɪ] *adv* pensivement; avec prévenance.
thoughtless ['θɔːtlɪs] *adj* étourdi(e); qui manque de considération.
thoughtlessly ['θɔːtlɪslɪ] *adv* inconsidérément.
thought-provoking ['θɔːtprəvəukɪŋ] *adj* stimulant(e).
thousand ['θauzənd] *num* mille; **one ~** mille; **~s of** des milliers de.
thousandth ['θauzəntθ] *num* millième.
thrash [θræʃ] *vt* rouer de coups; donner une correction à; (*defeat*) battre à plate(s) couture(s).
▶**thrash about** *vi* se débattre.
▶**thrash out** *vt* débattre de.
thrashing ['θræʃɪŋ] *n*: **to give sb a ~** = **to thrash sb**.
thread [θrɛd] *n* fil *m*; (*of screw*) pas *m*, filetage *m* ♦ *vt* (*needle*) enfiler; **to ~ one's way between** se faufiler entre.
threadbare ['θrɛdbɛə*] *adj* râpé(e), élimé(e).
threat [θrɛt] *n* menace *f*; **to be under ~ of** être menacé(e) de.
threaten ['θrɛtn] *vi* (*storm*) menacer ♦ *vt*: **to ~ sb with sth/to do** menacer qn de qch/de faire.
threatening ['θrɛtnɪŋ] *adj* menaçant(e).
three [θriː] *num* trois.
three-dimensional [θriːdɪ'mɛnʃənl] *adj* à trois dimensions; (*film*) en relief.
threefold ['θriːfəuld] *adv*: **to increase ~** tripler.
three-piece ['θriːpiːs]: **~ suit** *n* complet *m* (avec gilet); **~ suite** *n* salon *m* comprenant un canapé et deux fauteuils assortis.

three-ply [θriː'plaɪ] *adj* (*wood*) à trois épaisseurs; (*wool*) trois fils *inv*.
three-quarters [θriː'kwɔːtəz] *npl* trois-quarts *mpl*; ~ **full** aux trois-quarts plein.
three-wheeler [θriː'wiːlə*] *n* (*car*) voiture *f* à trois roues.
thresh [θrɛʃ] *vt* (*AGR*) battre.
threshing machine ['θrɛʃɪŋ-] *n* batteuse *f*.
threshold ['θrɛʃhəuld] *n* seuil *m*; **to be on the ~ of** (*fig*) être au seuil de.
threshold agreement *n* (*ECON*) accord *m* d'indexation des salaires.
threw [θruː] *pt of* **throw**.
thrift [θrɪft] *n* économie *f*.
thrifty ['θrɪftɪ] *adj* économe.
thrill [θrɪl] *n* frisson *m*, émotion *f* ♦ *vi* tressaillir, frissonner ♦ *vt* (*audience*) électriser; **to be ~ed** (*with gift etc*) être ravi(e).
thriller ['θrɪlə*] *n* film *m* (*or* roman *m or* pièce *f*) à suspense.
thrilling ['θrɪlɪŋ] *adj* (*book, play etc*) saisissant(e); (*news, discovery*) excitant(e).
thrive, *pt* thrived, throve, *pp* thrived, thriven [θraɪv, θrəuv, 'θrɪvn] *vi* pousser *or* se développer bien; (*business*) prospérer; **he ~s on it** cela lui réussit.
thriving ['θraɪvɪŋ] *adj* vigoureux(euse); (*industry etc*) prospère.
throat [θrəut] *n* gorge *f*; **to have a sore ~** avoir mal à la gorge.
throb [θrɔb] *n* (*of heart*) pulsation *f*; (*of engine*) vibration *f*; (*of pain*) élancement *m* ♦ *vi* (*heart*) palpiter; (*engine*) vibrer; (*pain*) lanciner; (*wound*) causer des élancements; **my head is ~bing** j'ai des élancements dans la tête.
throes [θrəuz] *npl*: **in the ~ of** au beau milieu de; en proie à; **in the ~ of death** à l'agonie.
thrombosis [θrɔm'bəusɪs] *n* thrombose *f*.
throne [θrəun] *n* trône *m*.
throng ['θrɔŋ] *n* foule *f* ♦ *vt* se presser dans.
throttle ['θrɔtl] *n* (*AUT*) accélérateur *m* ♦ *vt* étrangler.
through [θruː] *prep* à travers; (*time*) pendant, durant; (*by means of*) par, par l'intermédiaire de; (*owing to*) à cause de ♦ *adj* (*ticket, train, passage*) direct(e) ♦ *adv* à travers; **(from) Monday ~ Friday** (*US*) de lundi à vendredi; **to let sb ~** laisser passer qn; **to put sb ~ to sb** (*TEL*) passer qn à qn; **to be ~** (*TEL*) avoir la communication; (*have finished*) avoir fini; "**no ~ traffic**" (*US*) "passage interdit"; "**no ~ way**" (*BRIT*) "impasse".
throughout [θruː'aut] *prep* (*place*) partout dans; (*time*) durant tout(e) le(la) ♦ *adv* partout.
throughput ['θruːput] *n* (*of goods, materials*) quantité de matières premières utilisée; (*COMPUT*) débit *m*.
throve [θrəuv] *pt of* **thrive**.
throw [θrəu] *n* jet *m*; (*SPORT*) lancer *m* ♦ *vt* (*pt* **threw**, *pp* **thrown** [θruː, θrəun]) lancer, jeter;

(*SPORT*) lancer; (*rider*) désarçonner; (*fig*) décontenancer; (*pottery*) tourner; **to ~ a party** donner une réception.
▶**throw about, throw around** *vt* (*litter etc*) éparpiller.
▶**throw away** *vt* jeter.
▶**throw off** *vt* se débarrasser de.
▶**throw out** *vt* jeter dehors; (*reject*) rejeter.
▶**throw together** *vt* (*clothes, meal etc*) assembler à la hâte; (*essay*) bâcler.
▶**throw up** *vi* vomir.
throwaway ['θrəuəweɪ] *adj* à jeter.
throwback ['θrəubæk] *n*: **it's a ~ to** ça nous *etc* ramène à.
throw-in ['θrəuɪn] *n* (*SPORT*) remise *f* en jeu.
thru [θru:] *prep, adj, adv* (*US*) = **through**.
thrush [θrʌʃ] *n* (*ZOOL*) grive *f*; (*MED*: *esp in children*) muguet *m*; (*: BRIT*: *in women*) muguet vaginal.
thrust [θrʌst] *n* (*TECH*) poussée *f* ♦ *vt* (*pt, pp* **thrust**) pousser brusquement; (*push in*) enfoncer.
thrusting ['θrʌstɪŋ] *adj* dynamique; qui se met trop en avant.
thud [θʌd] *n* bruit sourd.
thug [θʌg] *n* voyou *m*.
thumb [θʌm] *n* (*ANAT*) pouce *m* ♦ *vt* (*book*) feuilleter; **to ~ a lift** faire de l'auto-stop, arrêter une voiture; **to give sb/sth the ~s up/ ~s down** donner/refuser de donner le feu vert à qn/qch.
thumb index *n* répertoire *m* (à onglets).
thumbnail ['θʌmneɪl] *n* ongle *m* du pouce.
thumbnail sketch *n* croquis *m*.
thumbtack ['θʌmtæk] *n* (*US*) punaise *f* (*clou*).
thump [θʌmp] *n* grand coup *m*; (*sound*) bruit sourd ♦ *vt* cogner sur ♦ *vi* cogner, frapper.
thunder ['θʌndə*] *n* tonnerre *m* ♦ *vi* tonner; (*train etc*): **to ~ past** passer dans un grondement *or* un bruit de tonnerre.
thunderbolt ['θʌndəbəult] *n* foudre *f*.
thunderclap ['θʌndəklæp] *n* coup *m* de tonnerre.
thunderous ['θʌndrəs] *adj* étourdissant(e).
thunderstorm ['θʌndəstɔːm] *n* orage *m*.
thunderstruck ['θʌndəstrʌk] *adj* (*fig*) abasourdi(e).
thundery ['θʌndərɪ] *adj* orageux(euse).
Thur(s). *abbr* (= *Thursday*) jeu.
Thursday ['θəːzdɪ] *n* jeudi *m*; *for phrases see also* **Tuesday**.
thus [ðʌs] *adv* ainsi.
thwart [θwɔːt] *vt* contrecarrer.
thyme [taɪm] *n* thym *m*.
thyroid ['θaɪrɔɪd] *n* thyroïde *f*.
tiara [tɪ'ɑːrə] *n* (*woman's*) diadème *m*.
Tibet [tɪ'bɛt] *n* Tibet *m*.
Tibetan [tɪ'bɛtən] *adj* tibétain(e) ♦ *n* Tibétain/ e; (*LING*) tibétain *m*.
tibia ['tɪbɪə] *n* tibia *m*.
tic [tɪk] *n* tic (nerveux).
tick [tɪk] *n* (*sound: of clock*) tic-tac *m*; (*mark*)

coche *f*; (*ZOOL*) tique *f*; (*BRIT col*): **in a ~** dans un instant; (*BRIT col*: *credit*): **to buy sth on ~** acheter qch à crédit ♦ *vi* faire tic-tac ♦ *vt* cocher; **to put a ~ against sth** cocher qch.
▶**tick off** *vt* cocher; (*person*) réprimander, attraper.
▶**tick over** *vi* (*BRIT*: *engine*) tourner au ralenti; (*: fig*) aller *or* marcher doucettement.
ticker tape ['tɪkə-] *n* bande *f* de téléscripteur; (*US*: *in celebrations*) ≈ serpentin *m*.
ticket ['tɪkɪt] *n* billet *m*; (*for bus, tube*) ticket *m*; (*in shop: on goods*) étiquette *f*; (*: from cash register*) reçu *m*, ticket; (*for library*) carte *f*; (*US POL*) liste électorale (*soutenue par un parti*); **to get a (parking) ~** (*AUT*) attraper une contravention (*pour stationnement illégal*).
ticket agency *n* (*THEAT*) agence *f* de spectacles.
ticket collector *n* contrôleur/euse.
ticket holder *n* personne munie d'un billet.
ticket inspector *n* contrôleur/euse.
ticket office *n* guichet *m*, bureau *m* de vente des billets.
tickle ['tɪkl] *n* chatouillement *m* ♦ *vt* chatouiller; (*fig*) plaire à; faire rire.
ticklish ['tɪklɪʃ] *adj* (*person*) chatouilleux(euse); (*which tickles: blanket*) qui chatouille; (*: cough*) qui irrite.
tidal ['taɪdl] *adj* à marée.
tidal wave *n* raz-de-marée *m inv*.
tidbit ['tɪdbɪt] *n* (*esp US*) = **titbit**.
tiddlywinks ['tɪdlɪwɪŋks] *n* jeu *m* de puce.
tide [taɪd] *n* marée *f*; (*fig: of events*) cours *m* ♦ *vt*: **to ~ sb over** dépanner qn; **high/low ~** marée haute/basse.
tidily ['taɪdɪlɪ] *adv* avec soin, soigneusement.
tidiness ['taɪdɪnɪs] *n* bon ordre; goût *m* de l'ordre.
tidy ['taɪdɪ] *adj* (*room*) bien rangé(e); (*dress, work*) net(nette), soigné(e); (*person*) ordonné(e), qui a de l'ordre; (*: in character*) soigneux(euse); (*mind*) méthodique ♦ *vt* (*also*: ~ **up**) ranger; **to ~ o.s. up** s'arranger.
tie [taɪ] *n* (*string etc*) cordon *m*; (*BRIT*: *also*: **neck~**) cravate *f*; (*fig: link*) lien *m*; (*SPORT*: *draw*) égalité *f* de points; match nul; (*: match*) rencontre *f*; (*US RAIL*) traverse *f* ♦ *vt* (*parcel*) attacher; (*ribbon*) nouer ♦ *vi* (*SPORT*) faire match nul; finir à égalité de points; **"black/white ~"** "smoking/habit de rigueur"; **family ~s** liens de famille; **to ~ sth in a bow** faire un nœud à *or* avec qch; **to ~ a knot in sth** faire un nœud à qch.
▶**tie down** *vt* attacher; (*fig*): **to ~ sb down to** contraindre qn à accepter.
▶**tie in** *vi*: **to ~ in (with)** (*correspond*) correspondre (à).
▶**tie on** *vt* (*BRIT*: *label etc*) attacher (avec une ficelle).
▶**tie up** *vt* (*parcel*) ficeler; (*dog, boat*) attacher; (*arrangements*) conclure; **to be ~d up** (*busy*) être pris *or* occupé.

tie-break(er) ['taɪbreɪk(ə*)] n (TENNIS) tie-break m; (in quiz) question f subsidiaire.

tie-on ['taɪɔn] adj (BRIT: label) qui s'attache.

tie-pin ['taɪpɪn] n (BRIT) épingle f de cravate.

tier [tɪə*] n gradin m; (of cake) étage m.

Tierra del Fuego [tɪˈɛrədɛlˈfweɪgəu] n Terre f de Feu.

tie tack n (US) épingle f de cravate.

tiff [tɪf] n petite querelle.

tiger ['taɪgə*] n tigre m.

tight [taɪt] adj (rope) tendu(e), raide; (clothes) étroit(e), très juste; (budget, programme, bend) serré(e); (control) strict(e), sévère; (col: drunk) ivre, rond(e) ♦ adv (squeeze) très fort; (shut) à bloc, hermétiquement; **to be packed** ~ (suitcase) être bourré(e); (people) être serré(e); **everybody hold** ~! accrochez-vous bien!

tighten ['taɪtn] vt (rope) tendre; (screw) resserrer; (control) renforcer ♦ vi se tendre; se resserrer.

tight-fisted [taɪtˈfɪstɪd] adj avare.

tight-lipped ['taɪtˈlɪpt] adj: **to be** ~ (about sth) (silent) ne pas desserrer les lèvres or les dents (au sujet de qch); **she was** ~ **with anger** elle pinçait les lèvres de colère.

tightly ['taɪtlɪ] adv (grasp) bien, très fort.

tight-rope ['taɪtrəup] n corde f raide.

tight-rope walker n funambule m/f.

tights [taɪts] npl (BRIT) collant m.

tigress ['taɪgrɪs] n tigresse f.

tilde ['tɪldə] n tilde m.

tile [taɪl] n (on roof) tuile f; (on wall or floor) carreau m ♦ vt (floor, bathroom etc) carreler.

tiled [taɪld] adj en tuiles; carrelé(e).

till [tɪl] n caisse (enregistreuse) ♦ vt (land) cultiver ♦ prep, conj = **until**.

tiller ['tɪlə*] n (NAUT) barre f (du gouvernail).

tilt [tɪlt] vt pencher, incliner ♦ vi pencher, être incliné(e) ♦ n (slope) inclinaison f; **to wear one's hat at a** ~ porter son chapeau incliné sur le côté; **(at) full** ~ à toute vitesse.

timber ['tɪmbə*] n (material) bois m de construction; (trees) arbres mpl.

time [taɪm] n temps m; (epoch: often pl) époque f, temps m; (by clock) heure f; (moment) moment m; (occasion, also MATH) fois f; (MUS) mesure f ♦ vt (race) chronométrer; (programme) minuter; (remark etc) choisir le moment de; **a long** ~ un long moment, longtemps; **for the** ~ **being** pour le moment; **from** ~ **to** ~ de temps en temps; ~ **after** ~, ~ **and again** bien des fois; **in** ~ (soon enough) à temps; (after some time) avec le temps, à la longue; (MUS) en mesure; **in a week's** ~ dans une semaine; **in no** ~ en un rien de temps; **on** ~ à l'heure; **to be 30 minutes behind/ahead of** ~ avoir 30 minutes de retard/d'avance; **by the** ~ **he arrived** quand il est arrivé, le temps qu'il arrive sub; **5** ~ **s 5** 5 fois 5; **what** ~ **is it?** quelle heure est-il?; **what** ~ **do you make it?** quelle heure avez-

vous?; **to have a good** ~ bien s'amuser; **we** (or they etc) **had a hard** ~ ça a été difficile or pénible; ~ **'s up!** c'est l'heure!; **I've no** ~ **for it** (fig) cela m'agace; **he'll do it in his own (good)** ~ (without being hurried) il le fera quand il en aura le temps; **he'll do it in** or (US) **on his own** ~ (out of working hours) il le fera à ses heures perdues; **to be behind the** ~ **s** retarder (sur son temps).

time-and-motion study ['taɪmənd'məuʃən-] n étude f des cadences.

time bomb n bombe f à retardement.

time clock n horloge pointeuse.

time-consuming ['taɪmkənsjuːmɪŋ] adj qui prend beaucoup de temps.

time difference n décalage m horaire.

time frame n délais mpl.

time-honoured, (US) **time-honored** ['taɪmɔnəd] adj consacré(e).

timekeeper ['taɪmkiːpə*] n (SPORT) chronomètre m.

time lag n (BRIT) décalage m; (: in travel) décalage f horaire.

timeless ['taɪmlɪs] adj éternel(le).

time limit n limite f de temps, délai m.

timely ['taɪmlɪ] adj opportun(e).

time off n temps m libre.

timer ['taɪmə*] n (in kitchen) compte-minutes m inv; (TECH) minuteur m.

time-saving ['taɪmseɪvɪŋ] adj qui fait gagner du temps.

time scale n délais mpl.

time-sharing ['taɪmʃeərɪŋ] n (COMPUT) temps partagé.

time sheet n feuille f de présence.

time signal n signal m horaire.

time switch n (BRIT) minuteur m; (: for lighting) minuterie f.

timetable ['taɪmteɪbl] n (RAIL) (indicateur m) horaire m; (SCOL) emploi m du temps; (programme of events etc) programme m.

time zone n fuseau m horaire.

timid ['tɪmɪd] adj timide; (easily scared) peureux(euse).

timidity [tɪˈmɪdɪtɪ] n timidité f.

timing ['taɪmɪŋ] n minutage m; chronométrage m; **the** ~ **of his resignation** le moment choisi pour sa démission.

timing device n (on bomb) mécanisme m de retardement.

timpani ['tɪmpənɪ] npl timbales fpl.

tin [tɪn] n étain m; (also: ~ **plate**) fer-blanc m; (BRIT: can) boîte f (de conserve); (: for baking) moule m (à gâteau); **a** ~ **of paint** un pot de peinture.

tin foil n papier m d'étain.

tinge [tɪndʒ] n nuance f ♦ vt: ~**d with** teinté(e) de.

tingle ['tɪŋgl] n picotement m; frisson m ♦ vi picoter.

tinker ['tɪŋkə*] n rétameur ambulant; (gipsy) romanichel m.

▶**tinker with** *vt fus* bricoler, rafistoler.
tinkle ['tɪŋkl] *vi* tinter ♦ *n* (*col*): **to give sb a ~** passer un coup de fil à qn.
tin mine *n* mine *f* d'étain.
tinned [tɪnd] *adj* (*BRIT*: *food*) en boîte, en conserve.
tinnitus ['tɪnɪtəs] *n* (*MED*) acouphène *m*.
tinny ['tɪnɪ] *adj* métallique.
tin opener [-'əʊpnə*] *n* (*BRIT*) ouvre-boîte(s) *m*.
tinsel ['tɪnsl] *n* guirlandes *fpl* de Noël (*argentées*).
tint [tɪnt] *n* teinte *f*; (*for hair*) shampooing colorant ♦ *vt* (*hair*) faire un shampooing colorant à.
tinted ['tɪntɪd] *adj* (*hair*) teint(e); (*spectacles, glass*) teinté(e).
tiny ['taɪnɪ] *adj* minuscule.
tip [tɪp] *n* (*end*) bout *m*; (*protective: on umbrella etc*) embout *m*; (*gratuity*) pourboire *m*; (*BRIT: for coal*) terril *m*; (: *for rubbish*) décharge *f*; (*advice*) tuyau *m* ♦ *vt* (*waiter*) donner un pourboire à; (*tilt*) incliner; (*overturn: also: ~ over*) renverser; (*empty: also: ~ out*) déverser; (*predict: winner etc*) pronostiquer; **he ~ped out the contents of the box** il a vidé le contenu de la boîte.
▶**tip off** *vt* prévenir, avertir.
tip-off ['tɪpɔf] *n* (*hint*) tuyau *m*.
tipped ['tɪpt] *adj* (*BRIT: cigarette*) (à bout) filtre *inv*; **steel-~** à bout métallique, à embout de métal.
Tipp-Ex ['tɪpɛks] *n* ® (*BRIT*) Tipp-Ex *m* ®.
tipple ['tɪpl] (*BRIT*) *vi* picoler ♦ *n*: **to have a ~** boire un petit coup.
tipster ['tɪpstə*] *n* (*RACING*) pronostiqueur *m*.
tipsy ['tɪpsɪ] *adj* un peu ivre, éméché(e).
tiptoe ['tɪptəʊ] *n*: **on ~** sur la pointe des pieds.
tiptop ['tɪptɔp] *adj*: **in ~ condition** en excellent état.
tirade [taɪ'reɪd] *n* diatribe *f*.
tire ['taɪə*] *n* (*US*) = **tyre** ♦ *vt* fatiguer ♦ *vi* se fatiguer.
▶**tire out** *vt* épuiser.
tired ['taɪəd] *adj* fatigué(e); **to be/feel/look ~** être/se sentir/avoir l'air fatigué; **to be ~ of** en avoir assez de, être las(lasse) de.
tiredness ['taɪədnɪs] *n* fatigue *f*.
tireless ['taɪəlɪs] *adj* infatigable, inlassable.
tiresome ['taɪsəm] *adj* ennuyeux(euse).
tiring ['taɪərɪŋ] *adj* fatigant(e).
tissue ['tɪʃuː] *n* tissu *m*; (*paper handkerchief*) mouchoir *m* en papier, kleenex *m* ®.
tissue paper *n* papier *m* de soie.
tit [tɪt] *n* (*bird*) mésange *f*; (*col: breast*) nichon *m*; **to give ~ for tat** rendre coup pour coup.
titanium [tɪ'teɪnɪəm] *n* titane *m*.
titbit ['tɪtbɪt] *n* (*food*) friandise *f*; (*before meal*) amuse-gueule *m inv*; (*news*) potin *m*.
titillate ['tɪtɪleɪt] *vt* titiller, exciter.
titivate ['tɪtɪveɪt] *vt* pomponner.

title ['taɪtl] *n* titre *m*; (*LAW*: *right*): **~ (to)** droit *m* (à).
title deed *n* (*LAW*) titre (constitutif) de propriété.
title page *n* page *f* de titre.
title role *n* rôle principal.
titter ['tɪtə*] *vi* rire (bêtement).
tittle-tattle ['tɪtltætl] *n* bavardages *mpl*.
titular ['tɪtjʊlə*] *adj* (*in name only*) nominal(e).
tizzy ['tɪzɪ] *n*: **to be in a ~** être dans tous ses états.
T-junction ['tiː'dʒʌŋkʃən] *n* croisement *m* en T.
TM *n abbr* = **trademark, transcendental meditation**.
TN *abbr* (*US*) = *Tennessee*.
TNT *n abbr* (= *trinitrotoluene*) TNT *m*.

================================= *KEYWORD*

to [tuː, tə] *prep* **1** (*direction*) à; (*towards*) vers; envers; **to go ~ France/Portugal/London/ school** aller en France/au Portugal/à Londres/à l'école; **to go ~ Claude's/the doctor's** aller chez Claude/le docteur; **the road ~ Edinburgh** la route d'Édimbourg
2 (*as far as*) (jusqu')à; **to count ~ 10** compter jusqu'à 10; **from 40 ~ 50 people** de 40 à 50 personnes
3 (*with expressions of time*): **a quarter ~ 5** 5 heures moins le quart; **it's twenty ~ 3** il est 3 heures moins vingt
4 (*for, of*) de; **the key ~ the front door** la clé de la porte d'entrée; **a letter ~ his wife** une lettre (adressée) à sa femme
5 (*expressing indirect object*) à; **to give sth ~ sb** donner qch à qn; **to talk ~ sb** parler à qn; **it belongs ~ him** cela lui appartient, c'est à lui
6 (*in relation to*) à; **3 goals ~ 2** 3 (buts) à 2; **30 miles ~ the gallon** ≈ 9,4 litres aux cent (km)
7 (*purpose, result*): **to come ~ sb's aid** venir au secours de qn, porter secours à qn; **to sentence sb ~ death** condamner qn à mort; **~ my surprise** à ma grande surprise
♦ *with vb* **1** (*simple infinitive*): **~ go/eat** aller/ manger
2 (*following another vb*): **to want/try/start ~ do** vouloir/essayer de/commencer à faire
3 (*with vb omitted*): **I don't want ~** je ne veux pas
4 (*purpose, result*) pour; **I did it ~ help you** je l'ai fait pour vous aider
5 (*equivalent to relative clause*): **I have things ~ do** j'ai des choses à faire; **the main thing is ~ try** l'important est d'essayer
6 (*after adjective etc*): **ready ~ go** prêt(e) à partir; **too old/young ~ ...** trop vieux/jeune pour ...
♦ *adv*: **push/pull the door ~** tirez/poussez la porte; **to go ~ and fro** aller et venir.

toad [təud] n crapaud m.

toadstool ['təudstu:l] n champignon (vénéneux).

toady ['təudɪ] vi flatter bassement.

toast [təust] n (CULIN) pain grillé, toast m; (drink, speech) toast ♦ vt (CULIN) faire griller; (drink to) porter un toast à; **a piece** or **slice of** ~ un toast.

toaster ['təustə*] n grille-pain m inv.

toastmaster ['təustmɑ:stə*] n animateur m pour réceptions.

toast rack n porte-toast m inv.

tobacco [tə'bækəu] n tabac m; **pipe** ~ tabac à pipe.

tobacconist [tə'bækənɪst] n marchand/e de tabac; ~'s **(shop)** (bureau m de) tabac m.

Tobago [tə'beɪgəu] n see **Trinidad and Tobago**.

toboggan [tə'bɔgən] n toboggan m; (child's) luge f.

today [tə'deɪ] adv, n (also fig) aujourd'hui (m); **what day is it** ~? quel jour sommes-nous aujourd'hui?; **what date is it** ~? quelle est la date aujourd'hui?; ~ **is the 4th of March** aujourd'hui nous sommes le 4 mars; **a week ago** ~ il y a huit jours aujourd'hui.

toddler ['tɔdlə*] n enfant m/f qui commence à marcher, bambin m.

toddy ['tɔdɪ] n grog m.

to-do [tə'du:] n (fuss) histoire f, affaire f.

toe [təu] n doigt m de pied, orteil m; (of shoe) bout m ♦ vt: **to** ~ **the line** (fig) obéir, se conformer; **big** ~ gros orteil; **little** ~ petit orteil.

TOEFL n abbr = Test(ing) of English as a Foreign Language.

toehold ['təuhəuld] n prise f.

toenail ['təuneɪl] n ongle m de l'orteil.

toffee ['tɔfɪ] n caramel m.

toffee apple n (BRIT) pomme caramélisée.

tofu ['təufu:] n fromage m de soja.

toga ['təugə] n toge f.

together [tə'gɛðə*] adv ensemble; (at same time) en même temps; ~ **with** prep avec.

togetherness [tə'gɛðənɪs] n camaraderie f; intimité f.

toggle switch ['tɔgl-] n (COMPUT) interrupteur m à bascule.

Togo ['təugəu] n Togo m.

togs [tɔgz] npl (col: clothes) fringues fpl.

toil [tɔɪl] n dur travail, labeur m ♦ vi travailler dur; peiner.

toilet ['tɔɪlət] n (BRIT: lavatory) toilettes fpl, cabinets mpl ♦ cpd (bag, soap etc) de toilette; **to go to the** ~ aller aux toilettes.

toilet bag n (BRIT) nécessaire m de toilette.

toilet bowl n cuvette f des W.-C.

toilet paper n papier m hygiénique.

toiletries ['tɔɪlətrɪz] npl articles mpl de toilette.

toilet roll n rouleau m de papier hygiénique.

toilet water n eau f de toilette.

to-ing and fro-ing ['tu:ɪŋən'frəuɪŋ] n (BRIT) allées et venues fpl.

token ['təukən] n (sign) marque f, témoignage m; (voucher) bon m, coupon m ♦ cpd (fee, strike) symbolique; **by the same** ~ (fig) de même; **book/record** ~ (BRIT) chèque-livre/-disque m.

tokenism ['təukənɪzəm] n (POL): **it's just** ~ c'est une politique de pure forme.

Tokyo ['təukjəu] n Tokyo.

told [təuld] pt, pp of **tell**.

tolerable ['tɔlərəbl] adj (bearable) tolérable; (fairly good) passable.

tolerably ['tɔlərəblɪ] adv: ~ **good** tolérable.

tolerance ['tɔlərns] n (also TECH) tolérance f.

tolerant ['tɔlərnt] adj: ~ **(of)** tolérant(e) (à l'égard de).

tolerate ['tɔləreɪt] vt supporter; (MED, TECH) tolérer.

toleration [tɔlə'reɪʃən] n tolérance f.

toll [təul] n (tax, charge) péage m ♦ vi (bell) sonner; **the accident** ~ **on the roads** le nombre des victimes de la route.

tollbridge ['təulbrɪdʒ] n pont m à péage.

toll call n (US TEL) appel m (à) longue distance.

toll-free ['təul'fri:] adj (US) gratuit(e) ♦ adv gratuitement.

tomato, ~es [tə'mɑ:təu] n tomate f.

tomb [tu:m] n tombe f.

tombola [tɔm'bəulə] n tombola f.

tomboy ['tɔmbɔɪ] n garçon manqué.

tombstone ['tu:mstəun] n pierre tombale.

tomcat ['tɔmkæt] n matou m.

tomorrow [tə'mɔrəu] adv, n (also fig) demain (m); **the day after** ~ après-demain; **a week** ~ demain en huit; ~ **morning** demain matin.

ton [tʌn] n tonne f (Brit: = 1016 kg; US = 907 kg; metric = 1000 kg); (NAUT: also: **register** ~) tonneau m (= 2.83 cu.m); ~s of (col) des tas de.

tonal ['təunl] adj tonal(e).

tone [təun] n ton m; (of radio, BRIT TEL) tonalité f ♦ vi s'harmoniser.

▶**tone down** vt (colour, criticism) adoucir; (sound) baisser.

▶**tone up** vt (muscles) tonifier.

tone-deaf [təun'dɛf] adj qui n'a pas d'oreille.

toner ['təunə*] n (for photocopier) encre f.

Tonga [tɔŋə] n îles fpl Tonga.

tongs [tɔŋz] npl pinces fpl; (for coal) pincettes fpl; (for hair) fer m à friser.

tongue [tʌŋ] n langue f; ~ **in cheek** adv ironiquement.

tongue-tied ['tʌŋtaɪd] adj (fig) muet(te).

tongue-twister ['tʌŋtwɪstə*] n phrase f très difficile à prononcer.

tonic ['tɔnɪk] n (MED) tonique m; (MUS) tonique f; (also: ~ **water**) tonic m.

tonight [tə'naɪt] adv, n cette nuit; (this evening) ce soir; **(I'll) see you** ~! à ce soir!

tonnage ['tʌnɪdʒ] n (NAUT) tonnage m.

tonne [tʌn] n (BRIT: metric ton) tonne f.

tonsil ['tɔnsl] n amygdale f; **to have one's** ~s

out se faire opérer des amygdales.

tonsillitis [tɒnsɪ'laɪtɪs] *n* amygdalite *f*; **to have ~** avoir une angine *or* une amygdalite.

too [tuː] *adv* (*excessively*) trop; (*also*) aussi; **it's ~ sweet** c'est trop sucré; **I went ~** moi aussi, j'y suis allé; **~ much** *adv* trop ♦ *adj* trop de; **~ many** *adj* trop de; **~ bad!** tant pis!

took [tuk] *pt of* **take**.

tool [tuːl] *n* outil *m*; (*fig*) instrument *m* ♦ *vt* travailler, ouvrager.

tool box *n* boîte *f* à outils.

tool kit *n* trousse *f* à outils.

toot [tuːt] *n* coup *m* de sifflet (*or* de klaxon) ♦ *vi* siffler; (*with car-horn*) klaxonner.

tooth, *pl* **teeth** [tuːθ, tiːθ] *n* (*ANAT*, *TECH*) dent *f*; **to have a ~ out** *or* (*US*) **pulled** se faire arracher une dent; **to brush one's teeth** se laver les dents; **by the skin of one's teeth** (*fig*) de justesse.

toothache ['tuːθeɪk] *n* mal *m* de dents; **to have ~** avoir mal aux dents.

toothbrush ['tuːθbrʌʃ] *n* brosse *f* à dents.

toothpaste ['tuːθpeɪst] *n* (*pâte f*) dentifrice *m*.

toothpick ['tuːθpɪk] *n* cure-dent *m*.

tooth powder *n* poudre *f* dentifrice.

top [tɒp] *n* (*of mountain, head*) sommet *m*; (*of page, ladder*) haut *m*; (*of list, queue*) commencement *m*; (*of box, cupboard, table*) dessus *m*; (*lid: of box, jar*) couvercle *m*; (*: of bottle*) bouchon *m*; (*toy*) toupie *f*; (*DRESS: blouse etc*) haut *m*; (*of pyjamas*) veste *f* ♦ *adj* du haut; (*in rank*) premier(ière); (*best*) meilleur(e) ♦ *vt* (*exceed*) dépasser; (*be first in*) être en tête de; **the ~ of the milk** (*BRIT*) la crème du lait; **at the ~ of the stairs/ page/street** en haut de l'escalier/de la page/de la rue; **on ~ of** sur; (*in addition to*) en plus de; **from ~ to toe** (*BRIT*) de la tête aux pieds; **at the ~ of the list** en tête de liste; **at the ~ of one's voice** à tue-tête; **at ~ speed** à toute vitesse; **over the ~** (*col: behaviour etc*) qui dépasse les limites.

▶**top up**, (*US*) **top off** *vt* remplir.

topaz ['təʊpæz] *n* topaze *f*.

top-class ['tɒp'klɑːs] *adj* de première classe; (*SPORT*) de haute compétition.

topcoat ['tɒpkəʊt] *n* pardessus *m*.

topflight ['tɒpflaɪt] *adj* excellent(e).

top floor *n* dernier étage.

top hat *n* haut-de-forme *m*.

top-heavy [tɒp'hɛvɪ] *adj* (*object*) trop lourd(e) du haut.

topic ['tɒpɪk] *n* sujet *m*, thème *m*.

topical ['tɒpɪkl] *adj* d'actualité.

topless ['tɒplɪs] *adj* (*bather etc*) aux seins nus; **~ swimsuit** monokini *m*.

top-level ['tɒplɛvl] *adj* (*talks*) à l'échelon le plus élevé.

topmost ['tɒpməʊst] *adj* le(la) plus haut(e).

top-notch ['tɒp'nɒtʃ] *adj* (*col*) de premier ordre.

topography [tə'pɒɡrəfɪ] *n* topographie *f*.

topping ['tɒpɪŋ] *n* (*CULIN*) couche *f* de crème,

fromage etc qui recouvre un plat.

topple ['tɒpl] *vt* renverser, faire tomber ♦ *vi* basculer; tomber.

top-ranking ['tɒpræŋkɪŋ] *adj* très haut placé(e).

top-secret ['tɒp'siːkrɪt] *adj* ultra-secret(ète).

top-security ['tɒpsə'kjuərɪtɪ] *adj* (*BRIT*) de haute sécurité.

topsy-turvy ['tɒpsɪ'tɜːvɪ] *adj*, *adv* sens dessus-dessous.

top-up ['tɒpʌp] *n*: **would you like a ~?** je vous en remets *or* rajoute?

top-up loan *n* (*BRIT*) prêt *m* complémentaire.

torch [tɔːtʃ] *n* torche *f*; (*BRIT: electric*) lampe *f* de poche.

tore [tɔː*] *pt of* **tear**.

torment *n* ['tɔːmɛnt] tourment *m* ♦ *vt* [tɔː'mɛnt] tourmenter; (*fig: annoy*) agacer.

torn [tɔːn] *pp of* **tear** ♦ *adj*: **~ between** (*fig*) tiraillé(e) entre.

tornado, **~es** [tɔː'neɪdəʊ] *n* tornade *f*.

torpedo, **~es** [tɔː'piːdəʊ] *n* torpille *f*.

torpedo boat *n* torpilleur *m*.

torpor ['tɔːpə*] *n* torpeur *f*.

torrent ['tɒrnt] *n* torrent *m*.

torrential [tɒ'rɛnʃl] *adj* torrentiel(le).

torrid ['tɒrɪd] *adj* torride; (*fig*) ardent(e).

torso ['tɔːsəʊ] *n* torse *m*.

tortoise ['tɔːtəs] *n* tortue *f*.

tortoiseshell ['tɔːtəʃɛl] *adj* en écaille.

tortuous ['tɔːtjʊəs] *adj* tortueux(euse).

torture ['tɔːtʃə*] *n* torture *f* ♦ *vt* torturer.

torturer ['tɔːtʃərə*] *n* tortionnaire *m*.

Tory ['tɔːrɪ] *adj* (*BRIT POL*) tory (*pl* tories), conservateur(trice) ♦ *n* tory *m/f*, conservateur/trice.

toss [tɒs] *vt* lancer, jeter; (*BRIT: pancake*) faire sauter; (*head*) rejeter en arrière ♦ *vi*: **to ~ up for sth** (*BRIT*) jouer qch à pile ou face ♦ *n* (*movement: of head etc*) mouvement soudain; (*of coin*) tirage *m* à pile ou face; **to ~ a coin** jouer à pile ou face; **to ~ and turn** (*in bed*) se tourner et se retourner; **to win/lose the ~** gagner/perdre à pile ou face; (*SPORT*) gagner/perdre le tirage au sort.

tot [tɒt] *n* (*BRIT: drink*) petit verre; (*child*) bambin *m*.

▶**tot up** *vt* (*BRIT: figures*) additionner.

total ['təʊtl] *adj* total(e) ♦ *n* total *m* ♦ *vt* (*add up*) faire le total de, totaliser; (*amount to*) s'élever à; **in ~** au total.

totalitarian [təʊtælɪ'tɛərɪən] *adj* totalitaire.

totality [təʊ'tælɪtɪ] *n* totalité *f*.

totally ['təʊtəlɪ] *adv* totalement.

tote bag [təʊt-] *n* fourre-tout *m inv*.

totem pole ['təʊtəm-] *n* mât *m* totémique.

totter ['tɒtə*] *vi* chanceler; (*object, government*) être chancelant(e).

touch [tʌtʃ] *n* contact *m*, toucher *m*; (*sense, also skill: of pianist etc*) toucher; (*fig: note, also FOOTBALL*) touche *f* ♦ *vt* (*gen*) toucher; (*tamper with*) toucher à; **the personal ~** la petite note personnelle; **to put the finishing ~es to sth** mettre la dernière main à qch; **a ~ of** (*fig*) un petit peu de; une touche de; **in ~ with** en contact *or* rapport avec; **to get in ~ with** prendre contact avec; **I'll be in ~** je resterai en contact; **to lose ~** (*friends*) se perdre de vue; **to be out of ~ with events** ne pas être au courant de ce qui se passe.

▶**touch on** *vt fus* (*topic*) effleurer, toucher.

▶**touch up** *vt* (*paint*) retoucher.

touch-and-go ['tʌtʃən'gəu] *adj* incertain(e); **it was ~ whether we did it** nous avons failli ne pas le faire.

touchdown ['tʌtʃdaun] *n* atterrissage *m*; (*on sea*) amerrissage *m*; (*US FOOTBALL*) essai *m*.

touched [tʌtʃt] *adj* touché(e); (*col*) cinglé(e).

touching ['tʌtʃɪŋ] *adj* touchant(e), attendrissant(e).

touchline ['tʌtʃlaɪn] *n* (*SPORT*) (ligne *f* de) touche *f*.

touch-sensitive ['tʌtʃsɛnsɪtɪv] *adj* (*keypad*) à effleurement; (*screen*) tactile.

touch-type ['tʌtʃtaɪp] *vi* taper au toucher.

touchy ['tʌtʃɪ] *adj* (*person*) susceptible.

tough [tʌf] *adj* dur(e); (*resistant*) résistant(e), solide; (*meat*) dur, coriace; (*journey*) pénible; (*task, problem, situation*) difficile; (*rough*) dur ♦ *n* (*gangster etc*) dur *m*; **~ luck!** pas de chance!; tant pis!

toughen ['tʌfn] *vt* rendre plus dur(e) (*or* plus résistant(e) *or* plus solide).

toughness ['tʌfnɪs] *n* dureté *f*; résistance *f*; solidité *f*.

toupee ['tuːpeɪ] *n* postiche *m*.

tour ['tuə*] *n* voyage *m*; (*also:* **package ~**) voyage organisé; (*of town, museum*) tour *m*, visite *f*; (*by artist*) tournée *f* ♦ *vt* visiter; **to go on a ~ of** (*museum, region*) visiter; **to go on ~** partir en tournée.

touring ['tuərɪŋ] *n* voyages *mpl* touristiques, tourisme *m*.

tourism ['tuərɪzm] *n* tourisme *m*.

tourist ['tuərɪst] *n* touriste *m/f* ♦ *adv* (*travel*) en classe touriste ♦ *cpd* touristique; **the ~ trade** le tourisme.

tourist class *n* (*AVIAT*) classe *f* touriste.

tourist office *n* syndicat *m* d'initiative.

tournament ['tuənəmənt] *n* tournoi *m*.

tourniquet ['tuənɪkeɪ] *n* (*MED*) garrot *m*.

tour operator *n* (*BRIT*) organisateur *m* de voyages, tour-opérateur *m*.

tousled ['tauzld] *adj* (*hair*) ébouriffé(e).

tout [taut] *vi*: **to ~ for** essayer de raccrocher, racoler; **to ~ sth (around)** (*BRIT*) essayer de placer *or* (re)vendre qch ♦ *n* (*BRIT*: **ticket ~**) revendeur *m* de billets.

tow [təu] *n*: **to give sb a ~** (*AUT*) remorquer qn ♦ *vt* remorquer; **"on ~"**, (*US*) **"in ~"** (*AUT*) "véhicule en remorque".

toward(s) [tə'wɔːd(z)] *prep* vers; (*of attitude*) envers, à l'égard de; (*of purpose*) pour; **~ noon/the end of the year** vers midi/la fin de

l'année; **to feel friendly ~ sb** être bien disposé envers qn.

towel ['tauəl] *n* serviette *f* (de toilette); (*also:* **tea ~**) torchon *m*; **to throw in the ~** (*fig*) jeter l'éponge.

towelling ['tauəlɪŋ] *n* (*fabric*) tissu-éponge *m*.

towel rail, (*US*) **towel rack** *n* porte-serviettes *m inv*.

tower ['tauə*] *n* tour *f* ♦ *vi* (*building, mountain*) se dresser (majestueusement); **to ~ above** *or* **over sb/sth** dominer qn/qch.

tower block *n* (*BRIT*) tour *f* (d'habitation).

towering ['tauərɪŋ] *adj* très haut(e), imposant(e).

towline ['təulaɪn] *n* (*câble m* de) remorque *f*.

town [taun] *n* ville *f*; **to go to ~** aller en ville; (*fig*) y mettre le paquet; **in the ~** dans la ville, en ville; **to be out of ~** (*person*) être en déplacement.

town centre *n* centre *m* de la ville, centre-ville *m*.

town clerk *n* ≈ secrétaire *m/f* de mairie.

town council *n* conseil municipal.

town crier [-'kraɪə*] *n* (*BRIT*) crieur public.

town hall *n* ≈ mairie *f*.

townie ['taunɪ] *n* (*BRIT col*) citadin/e.

town plan *n* plan *m* de ville.

town planner *n* urbaniste *m/f*.

town planning *n* urbanisme *m*.

township ['taunʃɪp] *n* banlieue noire (*établie sous le régime de l'apartheid*).

townspeople ['taunzpiːpl] *npl* citadins *mpl*.

towpath ['təupɑːθ] *n* (chemin *m* de) halage *m*.

towrope ['təurəup] *n* (câble *m* de) remorque *f*.

tow truck *n* (*US*) dépanneuse *f*.

toxic ['tɔksɪk] *adj* toxique.

toxin ['tɔksɪn] *n* toxine *f*.

toy [tɔɪ] *n* jouet *m*.

▶**toy with** *vt fus* jouer avec; (*idea*) caresser.

toyshop ['tɔɪʃɔp] *m* magasin *m* de jouets.

trace [treɪs] *n* trace *f* ♦ *vt* (*draw*) tracer, dessiner; (*follow*) suivre la trace de; (*locate*) retrouver; **without ~** (*disappear*) sans laisser de traces; **there was no ~ of it** il n'y en avait pas trace.

trace element *n* oligo-élément *m*.

trachea [trə'kɪə] *n* (*ANAT*) trachée *f*.

tracing paper ['treɪsɪŋ-] *n* papier-calque *m*.

track [træk] *n* (*mark*) trace *f*; (*path: gen*) chemin *m*, piste *f*; (: *of bullet etc*) trajectoire *f*; (: *of suspect, animal*) piste *f*; (*RAIL*) voie ferrée, rails *mpl*; (*on tape, COMPUT, SPORT*) piste *f*; (*on record*) plage *f* ♦ *vt* suivre la trace *or* la piste de; **to keep ~ of** suivre; **to be on the right ~** (*fig*) être sur la bonne voie.

▶**track down** *vt* (*prey*) trouver et capturer; (*sth lost*) finir par retrouver.

tracked [trækt] *adj* (*AUT*) à chenille.

tracker dog ['trækə-] *n* (*BRIT*) chien dressé pour suivre une piste.

track events *npl* (*SPORT*) épreuves *fpl* sur piste.

tracking station ['trækɪŋ-] n (*SPACE*) centre m d'observation de satellites.

track meet n (*US*) réunion sportive sur piste.

track record n: **to have a good ~** (*fig*) avoir fait ses preuves.

track suit n survêtement m.

tract [trækt] n (*GEO*) étendue f, zone f; (*pamphlet*) tract m; **respiratory ~** (*ANAT*) système m respiratoire.

traction ['trækʃən] n traction f.

tractor ['træktə*] n tracteur m.

trade [treɪd] n commerce m; (*skill, job*) métier m ♦ vi faire du commerce; **to ~ with/in** faire du commerce avec/le commerce de; **foreign ~** commerce extérieur; **Department of T~ and Industry (DTI)** (*BRIT*) ministère m du Commerce et de l'Industrie.

▶**trade in** vt (*old car etc*) faire reprendre.

trade barrier n barrière commerciale.

trade deficit n déficit extérieur.

Trade Descriptions Act n (*BRIT*) *loi contre les appellations et la publicité mensongères.*

trade discount n remise f au détaillant.

trade fair n foire(-exposition) commerciale.

trade-in ['treɪdɪn] n reprise f.

trade-in price n prix m à la reprise.

trademark ['treɪdmɑːk] n marque f de fabrique.

trade mission n mission commerciale.

trade name n marque déposée.

trade-off ['treɪdɔf] n (*exchange*) échange f; (*balancing*) équilibre m.

trader ['treɪdə*] n commerçant/e, négociant/e.

trade secret n secret m de fabrication.

tradesman ['treɪdzmən] n (*shopkeeper*) commerçant m; (*skilled worker*) ouvrier qualifié.

trade union n syndicat m.

trade unionist [-'juːnjənɪst] n syndicaliste m/f.

trade wind n alizé m.

trading ['treɪdɪŋ] n affaires fpl, commerce m.

trading estate n (*BRIT*) zone industrielle.

trading stamp n timbre-prime m.

tradition [trə'dɪʃən] n tradition f; **~s** npl coutumes fpl, traditions.

traditional [trə'dɪʃənl] adj traditionnel(le).

traffic ['træfɪk] n trafic m; (*cars*) circulation f ♦ vi: **to ~ in** (*pej: liquor, drugs*) faire le trafic de.

traffic calming [-'kɑːmɪŋ] n ralentissement m de la circulation.

traffic circle n (*US*) rond-point m.

traffic island n refuge m (pour piétons).

traffic jam n embouteillage m.

trafficker ['træfɪkə*] n trafiquant/e.

traffic lights npl feux mpl (de signalisation).

traffic offence n (*BRIT*) infraction f au code de la route.

traffic sign n panneau m de signalisation.

traffic violation n (*US*) = **traffic offence**.

traffic warden n contractuel/le.

tragedy ['trædʒədɪ] n tragédie f.

tragic ['trædʒɪk] adj tragique.

trail [treɪl] n (*tracks*) trace f, piste f; (*path*) chemin m, piste; (*of smoke etc*) traînée f ♦ vt traîner, tirer; (*follow*) suivre ♦ vi traîner; **to be on sb's ~** être sur la piste de qn.

▶**trail away, trail off** vi (*sound, voice*) s'évanouir; (*interest*) disparaître.

▶**trail behind** vi traîner, être à la traîne.

trailer ['treɪlə*] n (*AUT*) remorque f; (*US*) caravane f; (*CINE*) bande-annonce f.

trailer truck n (*US*) (camion m) semi-remorque m.

train [treɪn] n train m; (*in underground*) rame f; (*of dress*) traîne f; (*BRIT: series*): **~ of events** série f d'événements ♦ vt (*apprentice, doctor etc*) former; (*sportsman*) entraîner; (*dog*) dresser; (*memory*) exercer; (*point: gun etc*): **to ~ sth on** braquer qch sur ♦ vi recevoir sa formation; s'entraîner; **one's ~ of thought** le fil de sa pensée; **to go by ~** voyager par le train *or* en train; **to ~ sb to do sth** apprendre à qn à faire qch; (*employee*) former qn à faire qch.

train attendant n (*US*) employé/e des wagons-lits.

trained [treɪnd] adj qualifié(e), qui a reçu une formation; dressé(e).

trainee [treɪ'niː] n stagiaire m/f; (*in trade*) apprenti/e.

trainer ['treɪnə*] n (*SPORT*) entraîneur/euse; (*of dogs etc*) dresseur/euse; **~s** npl (*shoes*) chaussures fpl de sport.

training ['treɪnɪŋ] n formation f; entraînement m; dressage m; **in ~** (*SPORT*) à l'entraînement; (*fit*) en forme.

training college n école professionnelle; (*for teachers*) ≈ école normale.

training course n cours m de formation professionnelle.

traipse [treɪps] vi (se) traîner, déambuler.

trait [treɪt] n trait m (de caractère).

traitor ['treɪtə*] n traître m.

trajectory [trə'dʒɛktərɪ] n trajectoire f.

tram [træm] n (*BRIT: also: ~car*) tram(way) m.

tramline ['træmlaɪn] n ligne f de tram(way).

tramp [træmp] n (*person*) vagabond/e, clochard/e; (*col: pej: woman*): **to be a ~** être coureuse ♦ vi marcher d'un pas lourd ♦ vt (*walk through: town, streets*) parcourir à pied.

trample ['træmpl] vt: **to ~ (underfoot)** piétiner; (*fig*) bafouer.

trampoline ['træmpəliːn] n trampolino m.

trance [trɑːns] n transe f; (*MED*) catalepsie f; **to go into a ~** entrer en transe.

tranquil ['træŋkwɪl] adj tranquille.

tranquillity [træŋ'kwɪlɪtɪ] n tranquillité f.

tranquillizer ['træŋkwɪlaɪzə*] n (*MED*) tranquillisant m.

transact [træn'zækt] vt (*business*) traiter.

transaction [træn'zækʃən] n transaction f; **~s** npl (*minutes*) actes mpl; **cash ~** transaction au comptant.

transatlantic ['trænzət'læntɪk] *adj* transatlantique.

transcend [træn'sɛnd] *vt* transcender; (*excel over*) surpasser.

transcendental [trænsɛn'dɛntl] *adj*: ~ **meditation** méditation transcendantale.

transcribe [træn'skraɪb] *vt* transcrire.

transcript ['trænskrɪpt] *n* transcription *f* (*texte*).

transcription [træn'skrɪpʃən] *n* transcription *f*.

transept ['trænsɛpt] *n* transept *m*.

transfer *n* ['trænsfə*] (*gen, also SPORT*) transfert *m*; (*POL: of power*) passation *f*; (*of money*) virement *m*; (*picture, design*) décalcomanie *f*; (: *stick-on*) autocollant *m* ♦ *vt* [træns'fə:*] transférer; passer; virer; décalquer; **to ~ the charges** (*BRIT TEL*) téléphoner en P.C.V.; **by bank ~** par virement bancaire.

transferable [træns'fə:rəbl] *adj* transmissible, transférable; "**not ~**" "**personnel**".

transfix [træns'fɪks] *vt* transpercer; (*fig*): **~ed with fear** paralysé(e) par la peur.

transform [træns'fɔ:m] *vt* transformer.

transformation [trænsfə'meɪʃən] *n* transformation *f*.

transformer [træns'fɔ:mə*] *n* (*ELEC*) transformateur *m*.

transfusion [træns'fju:ʒən] *n* transfusion *f*.

transgress [træns'grɛs] *vt* transgresser.

transient ['trænzɪənt] *adj* transitoire, éphémère.

transistor [træn'zɪstə*] *n* (*ELEC; also*: ~ **radio**) transistor *m*.

transit ['trænzɪt] *n*: **in ~** en transit.

transit camp *n* camp *m* de transit.

transition [træn'zɪʃən] *n* transition *f*.

transitional [træn'zɪʃənl] *adj* transitoire.

transitive ['trænzɪtɪv] *adj* (*LING*) transitif(ive).

transit lounge *n* (*AVIAT*) salle *f* de transit.

transitory ['trænzɪtəri] *adj* transitoire.

translate [trænz'leɪt] *vt*: **to ~ (from/into)** traduire (du/en).

translation [trænz'leɪʃən] *n* traduction *f*; (*SCOL: as opposed to prose*) version *f*.

translator [trænz'leɪtə*] *n* traducteur/trice.

translucent [trænz'lu:snt] *adj* translucide.

transmission [trænz'mɪʃən] *n* transmission *f*.

transmit [trænz'mɪt] *vt* transmettre; (*RADIO, TV*) émettre.

transmitter [trænz'mɪtə*] *n* émetteur *m*.

transparency [træns'pɛərnsɪ] *n* (*BRIT PHOT*) diapositive *f*.

transparent [træns'pærnt] *adj* transparent(e).

transpire [træns'paɪə*] *vi* (*become known*): **it finally ~d that ...** on a finalement appris que ...; (*happen*) arriver.

transplant *vt* [træns'plɑ:nt] transplanter; (*seedlings*) repiquer ♦ *n* ['trænsplɑ:nt] (*MED*) transplantation *f*; **to have a heart ~** subir une greffe du cœur.

transport *n* ['trænspɔ:t] transport *m* ♦ *vt* [træns'pɔ:t] transporter; **public ~** transports en commun; **Department of T~** (*BRIT*) ministère *m* des Transports.

transportation [trænspɔ:'teɪʃən] *n* (*moyen m de*) transport *m*; (*of prisoners*) transportation *f*; **Department of T~** (*US*) ministère *m* des Transports.

transport café *n* (*BRIT*) ≈ routier *m*.

transpose [træns'pəuz] *vt* transposer.

transsexual [trænz'sɛksjuəl] *adj, n* transsexuel(le).

transverse ['trænzvə:s] *adj* transversal(e).

transvestite [trænz'vɛstaɪt] *n* travesti/e.

trap [træp] *n* (*snare, trick*) piège *m*; (*carriage*) cabriolet *m* ♦ *vt* prendre au piège; (*immobilize*) bloquer; (*jam*) coincer; **to set** *or* **lay a ~ (for sb)** tendre un piège (à qn); **to shut one's ~** (*col*) la fermer.

trap door *n* trappe *f*.

trapeze [trə'pi:z] *n* trapèze *m*.

trapper ['træpə*] *n* trappeur *m*.

trappings ['træpɪŋz] *npl* ornements *mpl*; attributs *mpl*.

trash [træʃ] *n* (*pej: goods*) camelote *f*; (: *nonsense*) sottises *fpl*; (*US: rubbish*) ordures *fpl*.

trash can *n* (*US*) boîte *f* à ordures.

trashy ['træʃɪ] *adj* (*col*) de camelote, qui ne vaut rien.

trauma ['trɔ:mə] *n* traumatisme *m*.

traumatic [trɔ:'mætɪk] *adj* traumatisant(e).

travel ['trævl] *n* voyage(s) *m(pl)* ♦ *vi* voyager; (*move*) aller, se déplacer ♦ *vt* (*distance*) parcourir; **this wine doesn't ~ well** ce vin voyage mal.

travel agency *n* agence *f* de voyages.

travel agent *n* agent *m* de voyages.

travel brochure *n* brochure *f* touristique.

traveller, (*US*) **traveler** ['trævlə*] *n* voyageur/euse; (*COMM*) représentant *m* de commerce.

traveller's cheque, (*US*) **traveler's check** *n* chèque *m* de voyage.

travelling, (*US*) **traveling** ['trævlɪŋ] *n* voyage(s) *m(pl)* ♦ *adj* (*circus, exhibition*) ambulant(e) ♦ *cpd* (*bag, clock*) de voyage; (*expenses*) de déplacement.

travel(l)ing salesman *n* voyageur *m* de commerce.

travelogue ['trævəlɔg] *n* (*book, talk*) récit *m* de voyage; (*film*) documentaire *m* de voyage.

travel sickness *n* mal *m* de la route (*or* de mer *or* de l'air).

traverse ['trævəs] *vt* traverser.

travesty ['trævəstɪ] *n* parodie *f*.

trawler ['trɔ:lə*] *n* chalutier *m*.

tray [treɪ] *n* (*for carrying*) plateau *m*; (*on desk*) corbeille *f*.

treacherous ['trɛtʃərəs] *adj* traître(sse); **road conditions are ~** l'état des routes est dangereux.

treachery ['trɛtʃərɪ] *n* traîtrise *f*.

treacle ['tri:kl] *n* mélasse *f*.

tread [trɛd] *n* pas *m*; (*sound*) bruit *m* de pas; (*of tyre*) chape *f*, bande *f* de roulement ♦ *vi* (*pt* **trod**, *pp* **trodden** [trɔd, 'trɔdn]) marcher.
▶**tread on** *vt fus* marcher sur.
treadle ['trɛdl] *n* pédale *f* (*de machine*).
treas. *abbr* = **treasurer**.
treason ['triːzn] *n* trahison *f*.
treasure ['trɛʒə*] *n* trésor *m* ♦ *vt* (*value*) tenir beaucoup à; (*store*) conserver précieusement.
treasure hunt *n* chasse *f* au trésor.
treasurer ['trɛʒərə*] *n* trésorier/ière.
treasury ['trɛʒərɪ] *n* trésorerie *f*; **the T~**, (*US*) **the T~ Department** ≈ le ministère des Finances.
treasury bill *n* bon *m* du Trésor.
treat [triːt] *n* petit cadeau, petite surprise ♦ *vt* traiter; **it was a ~** ça m'a (*or* nous a *etc*) vraiment fait plaisir; **to ~ sb to sth** offrir qch à qn; **to ~ sth as a joke** prendre qch à la plaisanterie.
treatise ['triːtɪz] *n* traité *m* (*ouvrage*).
treatment ['triːtmənt] *n* traitement *m*; **to have ~ for sth** (*MED*) suivre un traitement pour qch.
treaty ['triːtɪ] *n* traité *m*.
treble ['trɛbl] *adj* triple ♦ *n* (*MUS*) soprano *m* ♦ *vt*, *vi* tripler.
treble clef *n* clé *f* de sol.
tree [triː] *n* arbre *m*.
tree-lined ['triːlaɪnd] *adj* bordé(e) d'arbres.
treetop ['triːtɔp] *n* cime *f* d'un arbre.
tree trunk *n* tronc *m* d'arbre.
trek [trɛk] *n* voyage *m*; randonnée *f*; (*tiring walk*) tirée *f* ♦ *vi* (*as holiday*) faire de la randonnée.
trellis ['trɛlɪs] *n* treillis *m*, treillage *m*.
tremble ['trɛmbl] *vi* trembler.
trembling ['trɛmblɪŋ] *n* tremblement *m* ♦ *adj* tremblant(e).
tremendous [trɪ'mɛndəs] *adj* énorme, formidable; (*excellent*) fantastique, formidable.
tremendously [trɪ'mɛndəslɪ] *adv* énormément, extrêmement + *adjective*; formidablement.
tremor ['trɛmə*] *n* tremblement *m*; (*also:* **earth ~**) secousse *f* sismique.
trench [trɛntʃ] *n* tranchée *f*.
trench coat *n* trench-coat *m*.
trench warfare *n* guerre *f* de tranchées.
trend [trɛnd] *n* (*tendency*) tendance *f*; (*of events*) cours *m*; (*fashion*) mode *f*; **~ towards/away from doing** tendance à faire/à ne pas faire; **to set the ~** donner le ton; **to set a ~** lancer une mode.
trendy ['trɛndɪ] *adj* (*idea*) dans le vent; (*clothes*) dernier cri *inv*.
trepidation [trɛpɪ'deɪʃən] *n* vive agitation.
trespass ['trɛspəs] *vi*: **to ~ on** s'introduire sans permission dans; (*fig*) empiéter sur; **"no ~ing"** "propriété privée", "défense d'entrer".

trespasser ['trɛspəsə*] *n* intrus/e; **"~s will be prosecuted"** "interdiction d'entrer sous peine de poursuites".
tress [trɛs] *n* boucle *f* de cheveux.
trestle ['trɛsl] *n* tréteau *m*.
trestle table *n* table *f* à tréteaux.
trial ['traɪəl] *n* (*LAW*) procès *m*, jugement *m*; (*test: of machine etc*) essai *m*; (*hardship*) épreuve *f*; (*worry*) souci *m*; **~s** *npl* (*SPORT*) épreuves éliminatoires; **horse ~s** concours *m* hippique; **~ by jury** jugement par jury; **to be sent for ~** être traduit(e) en justice; **to be on ~** passer en jugement; **by ~ and error** par tâtonnements.
trial balance *n* (*COMM*) balance *f* de vérification.
trial basis *n*: **on a ~** pour une période d'essai.
trial run *n* essai *m*.
triangle ['traɪæŋgl] *n* (*MATH*, *MUS*) triangle *m*.
triangular [traɪ'æŋgjulə*] *adj* triangulaire.
triathlon [traɪ'æθlən] *n* triathlon *m*.
tribal ['traɪbl] *adj* tribal(e).
tribe [traɪb] *n* tribu *f*.
tribesman ['traɪbzmən] *n* membre *m* de la tribu.
tribulation [trɪbju'leɪʃən] *n* tribulation *f*, malheur *m*.
tribunal [traɪ'bjuːnl] *n* tribunal *m*.
tributary ['trɪbjutərɪ] *n* (*river*) affluent *m*.
tribute ['trɪbjuːt] *n* tribut *m*, hommage *m*; **to pay ~ to** rendre hommage à.
trice [traɪs] *n*: **in a ~** en un clin d'œil.
trick [trɪk] *n* ruse *f*; (*clever act*) astuce *f*; (*joke*) tour *m*; (*CARDS*) levée *f* ♦ *vt* attraper, rouler; **to play a ~ on sb** jouer un tour à qn; **to ~ sb into doing sth** persuader qn par la ruse de faire qch; **to ~ sb out of sth** obtenir qch de qn par la ruse; **it's a ~ of the light** c'est une illusion d'optique causée par la lumière; **that should do the ~** (*col*) ça devrait faire l'affaire.
trickery ['trɪkərɪ] *n* ruse *f*.
trickle ['trɪkl] *n* (*of water etc*) filet *m* ♦ *vi* couler en un filet *or* goutte à goutte; **to ~ in/out** (*people*) entrer/sortir par petits groupes.
trick question *n* question-piège *f*.
trickster ['trɪkstə*] *n* arnaqueur/euse, filou *m*.
tricky ['trɪkɪ] *adj* difficile, délicat(e).
tricycle ['traɪsɪkl] *n* tricycle *m*.
trifle ['traɪfl] *n* bagatelle *f*; (*CULIN*) ≈ diplomate *m* ♦ *adv*: **a ~ long** un peu long ♦ *vi*: **to ~ with** traiter à la légère.
trifling ['traɪflɪŋ] *adj* insignifiant(e).
trigger ['trɪgə*] *n* (*of gun*) gâchette *f*.
▶**trigger off** *vt* déclencher.
trigonometry [trɪgə'nɔmətrɪ] *n* trigonométrie *f*.
trilby ['trɪlbɪ] *n* (*BRIT: also:* **~ hat**) chapeau mou, feutre *m*.
trill [trɪl] *n* (*of bird*, *MUS*) trille *m*.
trilogy ['trɪlədʒɪ] *n* trilogie *f*.
trim [trɪm] *adj* net(te); (*house, garden*) bien

tenu(e); (*figure*) svelte ♦ *n* (*haircut etc*) légère coupe; (*embellishment*) finitions *fpl*; (*on car*) garnitures *fpl* ♦ *vt* couper légèrement; (*decorate*): **to ~ (with)** décorer (de); (*NAUT: a sail*) gréer; **to keep in (good) ~** maintenir en (bon) état.

trimmings ['trɪmɪŋz] *npl* décorations *fpl*; (*extras: gen CULIN*) garniture *f*.

Trinidad and Tobago ['trɪnɪdæd-] *n* Trinité et Tobago *f*.

Trinity ['trɪnɪtɪ] *n*: **the ~** la Trinité.

trinket ['trɪŋkɪt] *n* bibelot *m*; (*piece of jewellery*) colifichet *m*.

trio ['triːəu] *n* trio *m*.

trip [trɪp] *n* voyage *m*; (*excursion*) excursion *f*; (*stumble*) faux pas ♦ *vi* faire un faux pas, trébucher; (*go lightly*) marcher d'un pas léger; **on a ~** en voyage.

▶**trip up** *vi* trébucher ♦ *vt* faire un croc-en-jambe à.

tripartite [traɪˈpɑːtaɪt] *adj* triparti(e).

tripe [traɪp] *n* (*CULIN*) tripes *fpl*; (*pej: rubbish*) idioties *fpl*.

triple ['trɪpl] *adj* triple ♦ *adv*: **~ the distance/the speed** trois fois la distance/la vitesse.

triple jump *n* triple saut *m*.

triplets ['trɪplɪts] *npl* triplés/ées.

triplicate ['trɪplɪkət] *n*: **in ~** en trois exemplaires.

tripod ['traɪpɔd] *n* trépied *m*.

Tripoli ['trɪpəlɪ] *n* Tripoli.

tripper ['trɪpə*] *n* (*BRIT*) touriste *m/f*; excursionniste *m/f*.

tripwire ['trɪpwaɪə*] *n* fil *m* de déclenchement.

trite [traɪt] *adj* banal(e).

triumph ['traɪʌmf] *n* triomphe *m* ♦ *vi*: **to ~ (over)** triompher (de).

triumphal [traɪˈʌmfl] *adj* triomphal(e).

triumphant [traɪˈʌmfənt] *adj* triomphant(e).

trivia ['trɪvɪə] *npl* futilités *fpl*.

trivial ['trɪvɪəl] *adj* insignifiant(e); (*commonplace*) banal(e).

triviality [trɪvɪˈælɪtɪ] *n* caractère insignifiant; banalité *f*.

trivialize ['trɪvɪəlaɪz] *vt* rendre banal(e).

trod [trɔd] *pt of* **tread**.

trodden ['trɔdn] *pp of* **tread**.

trolley ['trɔlɪ] *n* chariot *m*.

trolley bus *n* trolleybus *m*.

trollop ['trɔləp] *n* prostituée *f*.

trombone [trɔmˈbəun] *n* trombone *m*.

troop [truːp] *n* bande *f*, groupe *m* ♦ *vi*: **to ~ in/out** entrer/sortir en groupe; **~ing the colour** (*BRIT: ceremony*) le salut au drapeau.

troop carrier *n* (*plane*) avion *m* de transport de troupes; (*NAUT: also*: **troopship**) transport *m* (*navire*).

trooper ['truːpə*] *n* (*MIL*) soldat *m* de cavalerie; (*US: policeman*) ≈ gendarme *m*.

troops [truːps] *npl* (*MIL*) troupes *fpl*; (: *men*) hommes *mpl*, soldats *mpl*.

troopship ['truːpʃɪp] *n* transport *m* (*navire*).

trophy ['trəufɪ] *n* trophée *m*.

tropic ['trɔpɪk] *n* tropique *m*; **in the ~s** sous les tropiques; **T~ of Cancer/Capricorn** tropique du Cancer/Capricorne.

tropical ['trɔpɪkl] *adj* tropical(e).

trot [trɔt] *n* trot *m* ♦ *vi* trotter; **on the ~** (*BRIT: fig*) d'affilée.

▶**trot out** *vt* (*excuse, reason*) débiter; (*names, facts*) réciter les uns après les autres.

trouble ['trʌbl] *n* difficulté(s) *f(pl)*, problème(s) *m(pl)*; (*worry*) ennuis *mpl*, soucis *mpl*; (*bother, effort*) peine *f*; (*POL*) conflit(s) *m(pl)*, troubles *mpl*; (*MED*): **stomach** *etc* **~** troubles gastriques *etc* ♦ *vt* déranger, gêner; (*worry*) inquiéter ♦ *vi*: **to ~ to do** prendre la peine de faire; **~s** *npl* (*POL etc*) troubles; **to be in ~** avoir des ennuis; (*ship, climber etc*) être en difficulté; **to have ~ doing sth** avoir du mal à faire qch; **to go to the ~ of doing** se donner le mal de faire; **it's no ~!** je vous en prie!; **please don't ~ yourself** je vous en prie, ne vous dérangez pas!; **the ~ is ...** le problème, c'est que ...; **what's the ~?** qu'est-ce qui ne va pas?

troubled [trʌbld] *adj* (*person*) inquiet(ète); (*epoch, life*) agité(e).

trouble-free ['trʌblfriː] *adj* sans problèmes *or* ennuis.

troublemaker ['trʌblmeɪkə*] *n* élément perturbateur, fauteur *m* de troubles.

troubleshooter ['trʌblʃuːtə*] *n* (*in conflict*) conciliateur *m*.

troublesome ['trʌblsəm] *adj* ennuyeux(euse), gênant(e).

trouble spot *n* point chaud (*fig*).

troubling ['trʌblɪŋ] *adj* (*times, thought*) inquiétant(e).

trough [trɔf] *n* (*also*: **drinking ~**) abreuvoir *m*; (*also*: **feeding ~**) auge *f*; (*channel*) chenal *m*; **~ of low pressure** (*METEOROLOGY*) dépression *f*.

trounce [trauns] *vt* (*defeat*) battre à plates coutures.

troupe [truːp] *n* troupe *f*.

trouser press *n* presse-pantalon *m inv*.

trousers ['trauzəz] *npl* pantalon *m*; **short ~** (*BRIT*) culottes courtes.

trouser suit *n* (*BRIT*) tailleur-pantalon *m*.

trousseau, *pl* **~x** *or* **~s** ['truːsəu, -z] *n* trousseau *m*.

trout [traut] *n* (*pl inv*) truite *f*.

trowel ['trauəl] *n* truelle *f*.

truant ['truənt] *n*: **to play ~** (*BRIT*) faire l'école buissonnière.

truce [truːs] *n* trêve *f*.

truck [trʌk] *n* camion *m*; (*RAIL*) wagon *m* à plate-forme; (*for luggage*) chariot *m* (à bagages).

truck driver *n* camionneur *m*.

trucker ['trʌkə*] *n* (*esp US*) camionneur *m*.

truck farm *n* (*US*) jardin maraîcher.

trucking ['trʌkɪŋ] *n* (*esp US*) transport routier.

trucking company n (*US*) entreprise f de transport (routier).

truck stop (*US*) routier m, restaurant m de routiers.

truculent ['trʌkjulənt] adj agressif(ive).

trudge [trʌdʒ] vi marcher lourdement, se traîner.

true [truː] adj vrai(e); (*accurate*) exact(e); (*genuine*) vrai, véritable; (*faithful*) fidèle; (*wall*) d'aplomb; (*beam*) droit(e); (*wheel*) dans l'axe; **to come** ~ se réaliser; ~ **to life** réaliste.

truffle ['trʌfl] n truffe f.

truly ['truːlɪ] adv vraiment, réellement; (*truthfully*) sans mentir; (*faithfully*) fidèlement; **yours** ~ (*in letter*) je vous prie d'agréer, Monsieur (*or* Madame *etc*), l'expression de mes sentiments respectueux.

trump [trʌmp] n atout m; **to turn up ~s** (*fig*) faire des miracles.

trump card n atout m; (*fig*) carte maîtresse f.

trumped-up [trʌmpt'ʌp] adj inventé(e) (de toutes pièces).

trumpet ['trʌmpɪt] n trompette f.

truncated [trʌŋ'keɪtɪd] adj tronqué(e).

truncheon ['trʌntʃən] n bâton m (d'agent de police); matraque f.

trundle ['trʌndl] vt, vi: **to ~ along** rouler bruyamment.

trunk [trʌŋk] n (*of tree, person*) tronc m; (*of elephant*) trompe f; (*case*) malle f; (*US AUT*) coffre m.

trunk call n (*BRIT TEL*) communication interurbaine.

trunk road n (*BRIT*) ≈ (route f) nationale f.

trunks [trʌŋks] npl (*also:* **swimming ~**) maillot m *or* slip m de bain.

truss [trʌs] n (*MED*) bandage m herniaire ♦ vt: **to ~ (up)** (*CULIN*) brider.

trust [trʌst] n confiance f; (*LAW*) fidéicommis m; (*COMM*) trust m ♦ vt (*rely on*) avoir confiance en; (*entrust*): **to ~ sth to sb** confier qch à qn; (*hope*): **to ~ (that)** espérer (que); **to take sth on ~** accepter qch sans garanties (*or* sans preuves); **in ~** (*LAW*) par fidéicommis.

trust company n société f fiduciaire.

trusted ['trʌstɪd] adj en qui l'on a confiance.

trustee [trʌs'tiː] n (*LAW*) fidéicommissaire m/f; (*of school etc*) administrateur/trice.

trustful ['trʌstful] adj confiant(e).

trust fund n fonds m en fidéicommis.

trusting ['trʌstɪŋ] adj confiant(e).

trustworthy ['trʌstwəːðɪ] adj digne de confiance.

trusty ['trʌstɪ] adj fidèle.

truth, ~**s** [truːθ, truːðz] n vérité f.

truthful ['truːθful] adj (*person*) qui dit la vérité; (*description*) exact(e), vrai(e).

truthfully ['truːθfəlɪ] adv sincèrement, sans mentir.

truthfulness ['truːθfəlnɪs] n véracité f.

try [traɪ] n essai m, tentative f; (*RUGBY*) essai ♦ vt (*LAW*) juger; (*test: sth new*) essayer, tester; (*strain*) éprouver ♦ vi essayer; **to ~ to do** essayer *or* chercher à faire; (*seek*) chercher à faire; **to ~ one's (very) best** *or* one's (very) hardest faire de son mieux; **to give sth a ~** essayer qch.

▶**try on** vt (*clothes*) essayer; **to ~ it on** (*fig*) tenter le coup, bluffer.

▶**try out** vt essayer, mettre à l'essai.

trying ['traɪɪŋ] adj pénible.

tsar [zɑː*] n tsar m.

T-shirt ['tiːʃəːt] n tee-shirt m.

T-square ['tiːskwɛə*] n équerre f en T.

TT adj abbr (*BRIT col*) = **teetotal** ♦ abbr (*US*) = Trust Territory.

tub [tʌb] n cuve f; baquet m; (*bath*) baignoire f.

tuba ['tjuːbə] n tuba m.

tubby ['tʌbɪ] adj rondelet(te).

tube [tjuːb] n tube m; (*BRIT: underground*) métro m; (*for tyre*) chambre f à air; (*col: television*): **the** ~ la télé.

tubeless ['tjuːblɪs] adj (*tyre*) sans chambre à air.

tuber ['tjuːbə*] n (*BOT*) tubercule m.

tuberculosis [tjubəːkjuˈləusɪs] n tuberculose f.

tube station n (*BRIT*) station f de métro.

tubing ['tjuːbɪŋ] n tubes mpl; **a piece of** ~ un tube.

tubular ['tjuːbjulə*] adj tubulaire.

TUC n abbr (*BRIT*: = Trades Union Congress) confédération f des syndicats britanniques.

tuck [tʌk] n (*SEWING*) pli m, rempli m ♦ vt (*put*) mettre.

▶**tuck away** vt cacher, ranger.

▶**tuck in** vt rentrer; (*child*) border ♦ vi (*eat*) manger de bon appétit; attaquer le repas.

▶**tuck up** vt (*child*) border.

tuck shop n (*BRIT SCOL*) boutique f à provisions.

Tue(s). abbr (= Tuesday) ma.

Tuesday ['tjuːzdɪ] n mardi m; **(the date) today is** ~ **23rd March** nous sommes aujourd'hui le mardi 23 mars; **on** ~ mardi; **on ~s** le mardi; **every** ~ tous les mardis, chaque mardi; **every other** ~ un mardi sur deux; **last/next** ~ mardi dernier/prochain; ~ **next** mardi qui vient; **the following** ~ le mardi suivant; **a week/fortnight on** ~, ~ **week/fortnight** mardi en huit/quinze; **the** ~ **before last** l'autre mardi; **the** ~ **after next** mardi en huit; ~ **morning/lunchtime/afternoon/evening** mardi matin/midi/après-midi/soir; ~ **night** mardi soir; (*overnight*) la nuit de mardi (à mercredi); ~**'s newspaper** le journal de mardi.

tuft [tʌft] n touffe f.

tug [tʌg] n (*ship*) remorqueur m ♦ vt tirer (sur).

tug-of-love [tʌgəvˈlʌv] n lutte acharnée entre parents divorcés pour avoir la garde d'un enfant.

tug-of-war [tʌgəv'wɔ:*] n lutte f à la corde.
tuition [tjuː'ɪʃən] n (BRIT: lessons) leçons fpl; (US: fees) frais mpl de scolarité.
tulip ['tjuːlɪp] n tulipe f.
tumble ['tʌmbl] n (fall) chute f, culbute f ♦ vi tomber, dégringoler; (somersault) faire une or des culbute(s) ♦ vt renverser, faire tomber; **to ~ to sth** (col) réaliser qch.
tumbledown ['tʌmbldaun] adj délabré(e).
tumble dryer n (BRIT) séchoir m (à linge) à air chaud.
tumbler ['tʌmblə*] n verre (droit), gobelet m.
tummy ['tʌmɪ] n (col) ventre m.
tumour, (US) **tumor** ['tjuːmə*] n tumeur f.
tumult ['tjuːmʌlt] n tumulte m.
tumultuous [tjuː'mʌltjuəs] adj tumultueux(euse).
tuna ['tjuːnə] n (pl inv) (also: ~ **fish**) thon m.
tune [tjuːn] n (melody) air m ♦ vt (MUS) accorder; (RADIO, TV, AUT) régler, mettre au point; **to be in/out of ~** (instrument) être accordé/désaccordé; (singer) chanter juste/faux; **to be in/out of ~ with** (fig) être en accord/désaccord avec; **she was robbed to the ~ of £10,000** (fig) on lui a volé la jolie somme de 10 000 livres.
▶**tune in** vi (RADIO, TV): **to ~ in (to)** se mettre à l'écoute (de).
▶**tune up** vi (musician) accorder son instrument.
tuneful ['tjuːnful] adj mélodieux(euse).
tuner ['tjuːnə*] n (radio set) radio-préamplificateur m; **piano ~** accordeur m de pianos.
tuner amplifier n radio-ampli m.
tungsten ['tʌŋstn] n tungstène m.
tunic ['tjuːnɪk] n tunique f.
tuning ['tjuːnɪŋ] n réglage m.
tuning fork n diapason m.
Tunis ['tjuːnɪs] n Tunis.
Tunisia [tjuː'nɪzɪə] n Tunisie f.
Tunisian [tjuː'nɪzɪən] adj tunisien(ne) ♦ n Tunisien/ne.
tunnel ['tʌnl] n tunnel m; (in mine) galerie f ♦ vi creuser un tunnel (or une galerie).
tunnel vision n (MED) rétrécissement m du champ visuel; (fig) vision étroite des choses.
tunny ['tʌnɪ] n thon m.
turban ['tɜːbən] n turban m.
turbid ['tɜːbɪd] adj boueux(euse).
turbine ['tɜːbaɪn] n turbine f.
turbo ['tɜːbəu] n turbo m.
turbojet [tɜːbəu'dʒɛt] n turboréacteur m.
turboprop [tɜːbəu'prɔp] n (engine) turbopropulseur m.
turbot ['tɜːbət] n (pl inv) turbot m.
turbulence ['tɜːbjuləns] n (AVIAT) turbulence f.
turbulent ['tɜːbjulənt] adj turbulent(e); (sea) agité(e).
tureen [tə'riːn] n soupière f.

turf [tɜːf] n gazon m; (clod) motte f (de gazon) ♦ vt gazonner; **the T~** le turf, les courses fpl.
▶**turf out** vt (col) jeter; jeter dehors.
turf accountant n (BRIT) bookmaker m.
turgid ['tɜːdʒɪd] adj (speech) pompeux(euse).
Turin [tjuə'rɪn] n Turin.
Turk [tɜːk] n Turc/Turque.
Turkey ['tɜːkɪ] n Turquie f.
turkey ['tɜːkɪ] n dindon m, dinde f.
Turkish ['tɜːkɪʃ] adj turc(turque) ♦ n (LING) turc m.
Turkish bath n bain turc.
Turkish delight n loukoum m.
turmeric ['tɜːmərɪk] n curcuma m.
turmoil ['tɜːmɔɪl] n trouble m, bouleversement m.
turn [tɜːn] n tour m; (in road) tournant m; (tendency: of mind, events) tournure f; (performance) numéro m; (MED) crise f, attaque f ♦ vt tourner; (collar, steak) retourner; (milk) faire tourner; (change): **to ~ sth into** changer qch en; (shape: wood, metal) tourner ♦ vi tourner; (person: look back) se (re)tourner; (reverse direction) faire demi-tour; (change) changer; (become) devenir; **to ~ into** se changer en, se transformer en; **a good ~** un service; **a bad ~** un mauvais tour; **it gave me quite a ~** ça m'a fait un coup; **"no left ~"** (AUT) "défense de tourner à gauche"; **it's your ~** c'est (à) votre tour; **in ~** à tour de rôle; **to take ~s** se relayer; **to take ~s at** faire à tour de rôle; **at the ~ of the year/ century** à la fin de l'année/du siècle; **to take a ~ for the worse** (situation, events) empirer; **his health or he has taken a ~ for the worse** son état s'est aggravé.
▶**turn about** vi faire demi-tour; faire un demi-tour.
▶**turn away** vi se détourner, tourner la tête ♦ vt (reject: person) renvoyer; (: business) refuser.
▶**turn back** vi revenir, faire demi-tour.
▶**turn down** vt (refuse) rejeter, refuser; (reduce) baisser; (fold) rabattre.
▶**turn in** vi (col: go to bed) aller se coucher ♦ vt (fold) rentrer.
▶**turn off** vi (from road) tourner ♦ vt (light, radio etc) éteindre; (engine) arrêter.
▶**turn on** vi (light, radio etc) allumer; (engine) mettre en marche.
▶**turn out** vt (light, gas) éteindre; (produce: goods, novel, good pupils) produire ♦ vi (appear, attend: troops, doctor etc) être présent(e); **to ~ out to be ...** s'avérer ..., se révéler ....
▶**turn over** vi (person) se retourner ♦ vt (object) retourner; (page) tourner.
▶**turn round** vi faire demi-tour; (rotate) tourner.
▶**turn up** vi (person) arriver, se pointer; (lost object) être retrouvé(e) ♦ vt (collar) remonter; (increase: sound, volume etc) mettre plus

fort.

turnabout ['tɜːnəbaut], **turnaround** ['tɜːnəraund] n volte-face f inv.

turncoat ['tɜːnkəut] n rénégat/e.

turned-up ['tɜːndʌp] adj (nose) retroussé(e).

turning ['tɜːnɪŋ] n (in road) tournant m; **the first ~ on the right** la première (rue or route) à droite.

turning circle n (BRIT) rayon m de braquage.

turning point n (fig) tournant m, moment décisif.

turning radius n (US) = **turning circle**.

turnip ['tɜːnɪp] n navet m.

turnout ['tɜːnaut] n (nombre m de personnes dans l')assistance f.

turnover ['tɜːnəuvə*] n (COMM: amount of money) chiffre m d'affaires; (: of goods) roulement m; (CULIN) sorte de chausson; **there is a rapid ~ in staff** le personnel change souvent.

turnpike ['tɜːnpaɪk] n (US) autoroute f à péage.

turnstile ['tɜːnstaɪl] n tourniquet m (d'entrée).

turntable ['tɜːnteɪbl] n (on record player) platine f.

turn-up ['tɜːnʌp] n (BRIT: on trousers) revers m.

turpentine ['tɜːpəntaɪn] n (also: **turps**) (essence f de) térébenthine f.

turquoise ['tɜːkwɔɪz] n (stone) turquoise f ♦ adj turquoise inv.

turret ['tʌrɪt] n tourelle f.

turtle ['tɜːtl] n tortue marine.

turtleneck (sweater) ['tɜːtlnɛk-] n pullover m à col montant.

Tuscany ['tʌskənɪ] n Toscane f.

tusk [tʌsk] n défense f (d'éléphant).

tussle ['tʌsl] n bagarre f, mêlée f.

tutor ['tjuːtə*] n (BRIT SCOL) directeur/trice d'études; (private teacher) précepteur/trice.

tutorial [tjuː'tɔːrɪəl] n (SCOL) (séance f de) travaux mpl pratiques.

tuxedo [tʌk'siːdəu] n (US) smoking m.

TV [tiː'viː] n abbr (= television) télé f, TV f.

TV dinner n plateau-repas surgelé.

twaddle ['twɔdl] n balivernes fpl.

twang [twæŋ] n (of instrument) son vibrant; (of voice) ton nasillard ♦ vi vibrer ♦ vt (guitar) pincer les cordes de.

tweak [twiːk] vt (nose) tordre; (ear, hair) tirer.

tweed [twiːd] n tweed m.

tweezers ['twiːzəz] npl pince f à épiler.

twelfth [twɛlfθ] num douzième.

Twelfth Night n la fête des Rois.

twelve [twɛlv] num douze; **at ~ (o'clock)** à midi; (midnight) à minuit.

twentieth ['twɛntɪɪθ] num vingtième.

twenty ['twɛntɪ] num vingt.

twerp [twəːp] n (col) imbécile m/f.

twice [twaɪs] adv deux fois; **~ as much** deux fois plus; **~ a week** deux fois par semaine; **she is ~ your age** elle a deux fois ton âge.

twiddle ['twɪdl] vt, vi: **to ~ (with) sth** tripoter

qch; **to ~ one's thumbs** (fig) se tourner les pouces.

twig [twɪg] n brindille f ♦ vt, vi (col) piger.

twilight ['twaɪlaɪt] n crépuscule m; (morning) aube f; **in the ~** dans la pénombre.

twill [twɪl] n serge m.

twin [twɪn] adj, n jumeau(elle) ♦ vt jumeler.

twin(-bedded) room ['twɪn('bɛdɪd)-] n chambre f à deux lits.

twin beds npl lits mpl jumeaux.

twin-carburettor ['twɪnkɑːbjuˈrɛtə*] adj à double carburateur.

twine [twaɪn] n ficelle f ♦ vi (plant) s'enrouler.

twin-engined [twɪn'ɛndʒɪnd] adj bimoteur; **~ aircraft** bimoteur m.

twinge [twɪndʒ] n (of pain) élancement m; (of conscience) remords m.

twinkle ['twɪŋkl] n scintillement m; pétillement m ♦ vi scintiller; (eyes) pétiller.

twin town n ville jumelée.

twirl [twəːl] n tournoiement m ♦ vt faire tournoyer ♦ vi tournoyer.

twist [twɪst] n torsion f, tour m; (in wire, flex) tortillon m; (bend: in road) tournant m; (in story) coup m de théâtre ♦ vt tordre; (weave) entortiller; (roll around) enrouler; (fig) déformer ♦ vi s'entortiller; s'enrouler; (road) serpenter; **to ~ one's ankle/wrist** (MED) tordre la cheville/le poignet.

twisted ['twɪstɪd] adj (wire, rope) entortillé(e); (ankle, wrist) tordu(e), foulé(e); (fig: logic, mind) tordu.

twit [twɪt] n (col) crétin/e.

twitch [twɪtʃ] n saccade f; (nervous) tic m ♦ vi se convulser; avoir un tic.

two [tuː] num deux; **~ by ~**, **in ~s** par deux; **to put ~ and ~ together** (fig) faire le rapport.

two-bit [tuː'bɪt] adj (esp US col, pej) de pacotille.

two-door [tuː'dɔː*] adj (AUT) à deux portes.

two-faced [tuː'feɪst] adj (pej: person) faux(fausse).

twofold ['tuːfəuld] adv: **to increase ~** doubler ♦ adj (increase) de cent pour cent; (reply) en deux parties.

two-piece ['tuːpiːs] n (also: **~ suit**) (costume m) deux-pièces m inv; (also: **~ swimsuit**) (maillot m de bain) deux-pièces.

two-seater [tuː'siːtə*] n (plane) (avion m) biplace m; (car) voiture f à deux places.

twosome ['tuːsəm] n (people) couple m.

two-stroke ['tuːstrəuk] n (also: **~ engine**) moteur m à deux temps ♦ adj à deux temps.

two-tone ['tuːtəun] adj (in colour) à deux tons.

two-way ['tuːweɪ] adj (traffic) dans les deux sens; **~ radio** émetteur-récepteur m.

TX abbr (US) = Texas.

tycoon [taɪ'kuːn] n: **(business) ~** gros homme d'affaires.

type [taɪp] n (category) genre m, espèce f; (model) modèle m; (example) type m; (TYP)

type, caractère *m* ♦ *vt* (*letter etc*) taper (à la machine); **what ~ do you want?** quel genre voulez-vous?; **in bold/italic ~** en caractères gras/en italiques.

typecast ['taɪpkɑːst] *adj* condamné(e) à toujours jouer le même rôle.

typeface ['taɪpfeɪs] *n* police *f* (de caractères).

typescript ['taɪpskrɪpt] *n* texte dactylographié.

typeset ['taɪpset] *vt* composer (*en imprimerie*).

typesetter ['taɪpsetə*] *n* compositeur *m*.

typewriter ['taɪpraɪtə*] *n* machine *f* à écrire.

typewritten ['taɪprɪtn] *adj* dactylographié(e).

typhoid ['taɪfɔɪd] *n* typhoïde *f*.

typhoon [taɪ'fuːn] *n* typhon *m*.

typhus ['taɪfəs] *n* typhus *m*.

typical ['tɪpɪkl] *adj* typique, caractéristique.

typify ['tɪpɪfaɪ] *vt* être caractéristique de.

typing ['taɪpɪŋ] *n* dactylo(graphie) *f*.

typing error *n* faute *f* de frappe.

typing pool *n* pool *m* de dactylos.

typist ['taɪpɪst] *n* dactylo *m/f*.

typo ['taɪpəu] *n abbr* (*col: = typographical error*) coquille *f*.

typography [taɪ'pɒɡrəfɪ] *n* typographie *f*.

tyranny ['tɪrənɪ] *n* tyrannie *f*.

tyrant ['taɪərnt] *n* tyran *m*.

tyre, (*US*) **tire** ['taɪə*] *n* pneu *m*.

tyre pressure *n* pression *f* (de gonflage).

Tyrol [tɪ'rəul] *n* Tyrol *m*.

Tyrolean [tɪrə'liːən], **Tyrolese** [tɪrə'liːz] *adj* tyrolien(ne) ♦ *n* Tyrolien/ne.

Tyrrhenian Sea [tɪ'riːnɪən-] *n*: **the ~** la mer Tyrrhénienne.

tzar [zɑː*] *n* = **tsar**.

U u

U, u [juː] *n* (*letter*) U, u *m*; **U for Uncle** U comme Ursule.

U *n abbr* (*BRIT CINE: = universal*) ≈ tous publics.

UAW *n abbr* (*US: = United Automobile Workers*) syndicat des ouvriers de l'automobile.

UB40 *n abbr* (*BRIT: = unemployment benefit form 40*) numéro de référence d'un formulaire d'inscription au chômage: par extension, le bénéficiaire.

U-bend ['juːbend] *n* (*BRIT AUT*) coude *m*, virage *m* en épingle à cheveux; (*in pipe*) coude.

ubiquitous [juː'bɪkwɪtəs] *adj* doué(e) d'ubiquité, omniprésent(e).

UCAS ['juːkæs] *n abbr* (*BRIT*) = Universities and Colleges Admissions Service.

UDA *n abbr* (*BRIT*) = Ulster Defence Association.

UDC *n abbr* (*BRIT*) = Urban District Council.

udder ['ʌdə*] *n* pis *m*, mamelle *f*.

UDI *n abbr* (*BRIT POL*) = unilateral declaration of independence.

UDR *n abbr* (*BRIT*) = Ulster Defence Regiment.

UEFA [juː'eɪfə] *n abbr* (*= Union of European Football Associations*) UEFA *f*.

UFO ['juːfəu] *n abbr* (*= unidentified flying object*) ovni *m* (*= objet volant non identifié*).

Uganda [juː'ɡændə] *n* Ouganda *m*.

Ugandan [juː'ɡændən] *adj* ougandais(e) ♦ *n* Ougandais/e.

UGC *n abbr* (*BRIT: = University Grants Committee*) commission d'attribution des dotations aux universités.

ugh [əːh] *excl* pouah!

ugliness ['ʌɡlɪnɪs] *n* laideur *f*.

ugly ['ʌɡlɪ] *adj* laid(e), vilain(e); (*fig*) répugnant(e).

UHF *abbr* (*= ultra-high frequency*) UHF.

UHT *adj abbr* (*= ultra-heat treated*): **~ milk** lait *m* UHT *or* longue conservation.

UK *n abbr* = **United Kingdom**.

Ukraine [juː'kreɪn] *n* Ukraine *f*.

Ukrainian [juː'kreɪnɪən] *adj* ukrainien(ne) ♦ *n* Ukrainien/ne; (*LING*) ukrainien *m*.

ulcer ['ʌlsə*] *n* ulcère *m*; **mouth ~** aphte *f*.

Ulster ['ʌlstə*] *n* Ulster *m*.

ulterior [ʌl'tɪərɪə*] *adj* ultérieur(e); **~ motive** arrière-pensée *f*.

ultimate ['ʌltɪmət] *adj* ultime, final(e); (*authority*) suprême ♦ *n*: **the ~ in luxury** le summum du luxe.

ultimately ['ʌltɪmətlɪ] *adv* (*in the end*) en fin de compte; (*at last*) finalement; (*eventually*) par la suite.

ultimatum, *pl* **~s** *or* **ultimata** [ʌltɪ'meɪtəm, -tə] *n* ultimatum *m*.

ultrasonic [ʌltrə'sɒnɪk] *adj* ultrasonique.

ultrasound ['ʌltrəsaund] *n* (*MED*) ultrason *m*.

ultraviolet ['ʌltrə'vaɪəlɪt] *adj* ultraviolet(te).

umbilical [ʌmbɪ'laɪkl] *adj*: **~ cord** cordon ombilical.

umbrage ['ʌmbrɪdʒ] *n*: **to take ~** prendre ombrage, se froisser.

umbrella [ʌm'brelə] *n* parapluie *m*; (*fig*): **under the ~ of** sous les auspices de; chapeauté(e) par.

umlaut ['umlaut] *n* tréma *m*.

umpire ['ʌmpaɪə*] *n* arbitre *m*; (*TENNIS*) juge *m* de chaise ♦ *vt* arbitrer.

umpteen [ʌmp'tiːn] *adj* je ne sais combien de; **for the ~th time** pour la nième fois.

UMW *n abbr* (*= United Mineworkers of America*) syndicat des mineurs.

UN *n abbr* = **United Nations**.

unabashed [ʌnə'bæʃt] *adj* nullement intimidé(e).

unabated [ʌnə'beɪtɪd] *adj* non diminué(e).

unable [ʌn'eɪbl] *adj*: **to be ~ to** ne (pas) pouvoir, être dans l'impossibilité de; (*not capable*) être incapable de.

unabridged [ʌnə'brɪdʒd] *adj* complet(ète), intégral(e).

unacceptable [ʌnək'sɛptəbl] *adj* (*behaviour*) inadmissible; (*price, proposal*) inacceptable.

unaccompanied [ʌnə'kʌmpənɪd] *adj* (*child, lady*) non accompagné(e); (*singing, song*) sans accompagnement.

unaccountably [ʌnə'kauntəblɪ] *adv* inexplicablement.

unaccounted [ʌnə'kauntɪd] *adj*: **two passengers are** ~ **for** on est sans nouvelles de deux passagers.

unaccustomed [ʌnə'kʌstəmd] *adj* inaccoutumé(e), inhabituel(le); **to be** ~ **to sth** ne pas avoir l'habitude de qch.

unacquainted [ʌnə'kweɪntɪd] *adj*: **to be** ~ **with** ne pas connaître.

unadulterated [ʌnə'dʌltəreɪtɪd] *adj* pur(e), naturel(le).

unaffected [ʌnə'fɛktɪd] *adj* (*person, behaviour*) naturel(le); (*emotionally*): **to be** ~ **by** ne pas être touché(e) par.

unafraid [ʌnə'freɪd] *adj*: **to be** ~ ne pas avoir peur.

unaided [ʌn'eɪdɪd] *adj* sans aide, tout(e) seul(e).

unanimity [juːnə'nɪmɪtɪ] *n* unanimité *f*.

unanimous [juː'nænɪməs] *adj* unanime.

unanimously [juː'nænɪməslɪ] *adv* à l'unanimité.

unanswered [ʌn'ɑːnsəd] *adj* (*question, letter*) sans réponse.

unappetizing [ʌn'æpɪtaɪzɪŋ] *adj* peu appétissant(e).

unappreciative [ʌnə'priːʃɪətɪv] *adj* indifférent(e).

unarmed [ʌn'ɑːmd] *adj* (*person*) non armé(e); (*combat*) sans armes.

unashamed [ʌnə'ʃeɪmd] *adj* sans honte; impudent(e).

unassisted [ʌnə'sɪstɪd] *adj* non assisté(e) ♦ *adv* sans aide, tout(e) seul(e).

unassuming [ʌnə'sjuːmɪŋ] *adj* modeste, sans prétentions.

unattached [ʌnə'tætʃt] *adj* libre, sans attaches.

unattended [ʌnə'tɛndɪd] *adj* (*car, child, luggage*) sans surveillance.

unattractive [ʌnə'træktɪv] *adj* peu attrayant(e).

unauthorized [ʌn'ɔːθəraɪzd] *adj* non autorisé(e), sans autorisation.

unavailable [ʌnə'veɪləbl] *adj* (*article, room, book*) (qui n'est) pas disponible; (*person*) (qui n'est) pas libre.

unavoidable [ʌnə'vɔɪdəbl] *adj* inévitable.

unavoidably [ʌnə'vɔɪdəblɪ] *adv* inévitablement.

unaware [ʌnə'wɛə*] *adj*: **to be** ~ **of** ignorer, ne pas savoir, être inconscient(e) de.

unawares [ʌnə'wɛəz] *adv* à l'improviste, au dépourvu.

unbalanced [ʌn'bælənst] *adj* déséquilibré(e).

unbearable [ʌn'bɛərəbl] *adj* insupportable.

unbeatable [ʌn'biːtəbl] *adj* imbattable.

unbeaten [ʌn'biːtn] *adj* invaincu(e); (*record*) non battu(e).

unbecoming [ʌnbɪ'kʌmɪŋ] *adj* (*unseemly: language, behaviour*) malséant(e), inconvenant(e); (*unflattering: garment*) peu seyant(e).

unbeknown(st) [ʌnbɪ'nəun(st)] *adv*: ~ **to** à l'insu de.

unbelief [ʌnbɪ'liːf] *n* incrédulité *f*.

unbelievable [ʌnbɪ'liːvəbl] *adj* incroyable.

unbelievingly [ʌnbɪ'liːvɪŋlɪ] *adv* avec incrédulité.

unbend [ʌn'bɛnd] *vb* (*irreg*) *vi* se détendre ♦ *vt* (*wire*) redresser, détordre.

unbending [ʌn'bɛndɪŋ] *adj* (*fig*) inflexible.

unbias(s)ed [ʌn'baɪəst] *adj* impartial(e).

unblemished [ʌn'blɛmɪʃt] *adj* impeccable.

unblock [ʌn'blɔk] *vt* (*pipe*) déboucher; (*road*) dégager.

unborn [ʌn'bɔːn] *adj* à naître.

unbounded [ʌn'baundɪd] *adj* sans bornes, illimité(e).

unbreakable [ʌn'breɪkəbl] *adj* incassable.

unbridled [ʌn'braɪdld] *adj* débridé(e), déchaîné(e).

unbroken [ʌn'brəukn] *adj* intact(e); (*line*) continu(e); (*record*) non battu(e).

unbuckle [ʌn'bʌkl] *vt* déboucler.

unburden [ʌn'bəːdn] *vt*: **to** ~ **o.s.** s'épancher, se livrer.

unbutton [ʌn'bʌtn] *vt* déboutonner.

uncalled-for [ʌn'kɔːldfɔː*] *adj* déplacé(e), injustifié(e).

uncanny [ʌn'kænɪ] *adj* étrange, troublant(e).

unceasing [ʌn'siːsɪŋ] *adj* incessant(e), continu(e).

unceremonious [ʌnsɛrɪ'məunɪəs] *adj* (*abrupt, rude*) brusque.

uncertain [ʌn'səːtn] *adj* incertain(e); **we were** ~ **whether ...** nous ne savions pas vraiment si ...; **in no** ~ **terms** sans équivoque possible.

uncertainty [ʌn'səːtntɪ] *n* incertitude *f*, doutes *mpl*.

unchallenged [ʌn'tʃælɪndʒd] *adj* (*gen*) incontesté(e); (*information*) non contesté(e); **to go** ~ ne pas être contesté.

unchanged [ʌn'tʃeɪndʒd] *adj* inchangé(e).

uncharitable [ʌn'tʃærɪtəbl] *adj* peu charitable.

uncharted [ʌn'tʃɑːtɪd] *adj* inexploré(e).

unchecked [ʌn'tʃɛkt] *adj* non réprimé(e).

uncivilized [ʌn'sɪvɪlaɪzd] *adj* non civilisé(e); (*fig*) barbare.

uncle ['ʌŋkl] *n* oncle *m*.

unclear [ʌn'klɪə*] *adj* (qui n'est) pas clair(e) or évident(e); **I'm still** ~ **about what I'm supposed to do** je ne sais pas encore exactement ce que je dois faire.

uncoil [ʌn'kɔɪl] *vt* dérouler ♦ *vi* se dérouler.

uncomfortable [ʌn'kʌmfətəbl] *adj* inconfortable; (*uneasy*) mal à l'aise, gêné(e); (*situation*) désagréable.

uncomfortably [ʌn'kʌmfətəblɪ] adv inconfortablement; d'un ton etc gêné or embarrassé; désagréablement.

uncommitted [ʌnkə'mɪtɪd] adj (attitude, country) non engagé(e).

uncommon [ʌn'kɔmən] adj rare, singulier(ière), peu commun(e).

uncommunicative [ʌnkə'mjuːnɪkətɪv] adj réservé(e).

uncomplicated [ʌn'kɔmplɪkeɪtɪd] adj simple, peu compliqué(e).

uncompromising [ʌn'kɔmprəmaɪzɪŋ] adj intransigeant(e), inflexible.

unconcerned [ʌnkən'səːnd] adj (unworried): **to be ~ (about)** ne pas s'inquiéter (de).

unconditional [ʌnkən'dɪʃənl] adj sans conditions.

uncongenial [ʌnkən'dʒiːnɪəl] adj peu agréable.

unconnected [ʌnkə'nɛktɪd] adj (unrelated): ~ **(with)** sans rapport (avec).

unconscious [ʌn'kɔnʃəs] adj sans connaissance, évanoui(e); (unaware) inconscient(e) ♦ n: **the ~** l'inconscient m; **to knock sb ~** assommer qn.

unconsciously [ʌn'kɔnʃəslɪ] adv inconsciemment.

unconstitutional [ʌnkɔnstɪ'tjuːʃənl] adj anticonstitutionnel(le).

uncontested [ʌnkən'tɛstɪd] adj (champion) incontesté(e); (POL: seat) non disputé(e).

uncontrollable [ʌnkən'trəuləbl] adj (child, dog) indiscipliné(e); (emotion) irrépressible.

uncontrolled [ʌnkən'trəuld] adj (laughter, price rises) incontrôlé(e).

unconventional [ʌnkən'vɛnʃənl] adj non conventionnel(le).

unconvinced [ʌnkən'vɪnst] adj: **to be ~** ne pas être convaincu(e).

unconvincing [ʌnkən'vɪnsɪŋ] adj peu convaincant(e).

uncork [ʌn'kɔːk] vt déboucher.

uncorroborated [ʌnkə'rɔbəreɪtɪd] adj non confirmé(e).

uncouth [ʌn'kuːθ] adj grossier(ière), fruste.

uncover [ʌn'kʌvə*] vt découvrir.

unctuous ['ʌŋktjuəs] adj onctueux(euse), mielleux(euse).

undamaged [ʌn'dæmɪdʒd] adj (goods) intact(e), en bon état; (fig: reputation) intact(e).

undaunted [ʌn'dɔːntɪd] adj non intimidé(e), inébranlable.

undecided [ʌndɪ'saɪdɪd] adj indécis(e), irrésolu(e).

undelivered [ʌndɪ'lɪvəd] adj non remis(e), non livré(e).

undeniable [ʌndɪ'naɪəbl] adj indéniable, incontestable.

under ['ʌndə*] prep sous; (less than) (de) moins de; au-dessous de; (according to) selon, en vertu de ♦ adv au-dessous; en dessous; **from ~ sth** de dessous or de sous qch; ~ **there** là-

dessous; **in ~ 2 hours** en moins de 2 heures; ~ **anaesthetic** sous anesthésie; ~ **discussion** en discussion; ~ **the circumstances** étant donné les circonstances; ~ **repair** en (cours de) réparation.

under... ['ʌndə*] prefix sous-.

under-age [ʌndər'eɪdʒ] adj qui n'a pas l'âge réglementaire.

underarm ['ʌndərɑːm] adv par en-dessous ♦ adj (throw) par en-dessous; (deodorant) pour les aisselles.

undercapitalized [ʌndə'kæpɪtəlaɪzd] adj sous-capitalisé(e).

undercarriage ['ʌndəkærɪdʒ] n (BRIT AVIAT) train m d'atterrissage.

undercharge [ʌndə'tʃɑːdʒ] vt ne pas faire payer assez à.

underclass ['ʌndəklɑːs] n ≈ quart-monde m.

underclothes ['ʌndəkləuðz] npl sous-vêtements mpl; (women's only) dessous mpl.

undercoat ['ʌndəkəut] n (paint) couche f de fond.

undercover [ʌndə'kʌvə*] adj secret(ète), clandestin(e).

undercurrent ['ʌndəkʌrnt] n courant sous-jacent.

undercut [ʌndə'kʌt] vt irreg vendre moins cher que.

underdeveloped ['ʌndədɪ'vɛləpt] adj sous-développé(e).

underdog ['ʌndədɔg] n opprimé m.

underdone [ʌndə'dʌn] adj (food) pas assez cuit(e).

underemployment [ʌndərɪm'plɔɪmənt] n sous-emploi m.

underestimate ['ʌndər'ɛstɪmeɪt] vt sous-estimer, mésestimer.

underexposed ['ʌndərɪks'pəuzd] adj (PHOT) sous-exposé(e).

underfed [ʌndə'fɛd] adj sous-alimenté(e).

underfoot [ʌndə'fut] adv sous les pieds.

under-funded ['ʌndə'fʌndɪd] adj: **to be ~** (organization) ne pas être doté(e) de fonds suffisants.

undergo [ʌndə'gəu] vt irreg subir; (treatment) suivre; **the car is ~ing repairs** la voiture est en réparation.

undergraduate [ʌndə'grædjuɪt] n étudiant/e (qui prépare la licence) ♦ cpd: ~ **courses** cours mpl préparant à la licence.

underground ['ʌndəgraund] adj souterrain(e); (fig) clandestin(e) ♦ n (BRIT) métro m; (POL) clandestinité f.

undergrowth ['ʌndəgrəuθ] n broussailles fpl, sous-bois m.

underhand(ed) [ʌndə'hænd(ɪd)] adj (fig) sournois(e), en dessous.

underinsured [ʌndərɪn'ʃuəd] adj sous-assuré(e).

underlie [ʌndə'laɪ] vt irreg être à la base de; **the underlying cause** la cause sous-jacente.

underline [ʌndə'laɪn] vt souligner.

underling ['ʌndəlɪŋ] *n* (*pej*) sous-fifre *m*, subalterne *m*.

undermanning [ʌndə'mænɪŋ] *n* pénurie *f* de main-d'œuvre.

undermentioned [ʌndə'mɛnʃənd] *adj* mentionné(e) ci-dessous.

undermine [ʌndə'maɪn] *vt* saper, miner.

underneath [ʌndə'niːθ] *adv* (en) dessous ♦ *prep* sous, au-dessous de.

undernourished [ʌndə'nʌrɪʃt] *adj* sous-alimenté(e).

underpaid [ʌndə'peɪd] *adj* sous-payé(e).

underpants ['ʌndəpænts] *npl* caleçon *m*, slip *m*.

underpass ['ʌndəpɑːs] *n* (*BRIT*) passage souterrain; (: *on motorway*) passage inférieur.

underpin [ʌndə'pɪn] *vt* (*argument, case*) étayer.

underplay [ʌndə'pleɪ] *vt* (*BRIT*) minimiser.

underpopulated [ʌndə'pɒpjuleɪtɪd] *adj* sous-peuplé(e).

underprice [ʌndə'praɪs] *vt* vendre à un prix trop bas.

underprivileged [ʌndə'prɪvɪlɪdʒd] *adj* défavorisé(e), déshérité(e).

underrate [ʌndə'reɪt] *vt* sous-estimer, mésestimer.

underscore [ʌndə'skɔː*] *vt* souligner.

underseal [ʌndə'siːl] *vt* (*BRIT*) traiter contre la rouille.

undersecretary ['ʌndə'sɛkrətrɪ] *n* sous-secrétaire *m*.

undersell [ʌndə'sɛl] *vt* (*competitors*) vendre moins cher que.

undershirt ['ʌndəʃəːt] *n* (*US*) tricot *m* de corps.

undershorts ['ʌndəʃɔːts] *npl* (*US*) caleçon *m*, slip *m*.

underside ['ʌndəsaɪd] *n* dessous *m*.

undersigned ['ʌndə'saɪnd] *adj, n* soussigné(e) (*m/f*).

underskirt ['ʌndəskəːt] *n* (*BRIT*) jupon *m*.

understaffed [ʌndə'stɑːft] *adj* qui manque de personnel.

understand [ʌndə'stænd] *vb* (*irreg: like* **stand**) *vt, vi* comprendre; **I ~ that ...** je me suis laissé dire que ...; je crois comprendre que ...; **to make o.s. understood** se faire comprendre.

understandable [ʌndə'stændəbl] *adj* compréhensible.

understanding [ʌndə'stændɪŋ] *adj* compréhensif(ive) ♦ *n* compréhension *f*; (*agreement*) accord *m*; **to come to an ~ with sb** s'entendre avec qn; **on the ~ that ...** à condition que ....

understate [ʌndə'steɪt] *vt* minimiser.

understatement ['ʌndəsteɪtmənt] *n*: **that's an ~** c'est (bien) peu dire, le terme est faible.

understood [ʌndə'stud] *pt, pp of* **understand** ♦ *adj* entendu(e); (*implied*) sous-entendu(e).

understudy ['ʌndəstʌdɪ] *n* doublure *f*.

undertake [ʌndə'teɪk] *vt irreg* (*job, task*) entreprendre; (*duty*) se charger de; **to ~ to do sth** s'engager à faire qch.

undertaker ['ʌndəteɪkə*] *n* entrepreneur *m* des pompes funèbres, croque-mort *m*.

undertaking ['ʌndəteɪkɪŋ] *n* entreprise *f*; (*promise*) promesse *f*.

undertone ['ʌndətəun] *n* (*low voice*): **in an ~** à mi-voix; (*of criticism etc*) nuance cachée.

undervalue [ʌndə'væljuː] *vt* sous-estimer.

underwater [ʌndə'wɔːtə*] *adv* sous l'eau ♦ *adj* sous-marin(e).

underwear ['ʌndəwɛə*] *n* sous-vêtements *mpl*; (*women's only*) dessous *mpl*.

underweight [ʌndə'weɪt] *adj* d'un poids insuffisant; (*person*) trop maigre.

underworld ['ʌndəwəːld] *n* (*of crime*) milieu *m*, pègre *f*.

underwrite [ʌndə'raɪt] *vt* (*FINANCE*) garantir; (*INSURANCE*) souscrire.

underwriter ['ʌndəraɪtə*] *n* (*INSURANCE*) souscripteur *m*.

undeserving [ʌndɪ'zəːvɪŋ] *adj*: **to be ~ of** ne pas mériter.

undesirable [ʌndɪ'zaɪərəbl] *adj* peu souhaitable; indésirable.

undeveloped [ʌndɪ'vɛləpt] *adj* (*land, resources*) non exploité(e).

undies ['ʌndɪz] *npl* (*col*) dessous *mpl*, lingerie *f*.

undiluted ['ʌndaɪ'luːtɪd] *adj* pur(e), non dilué(e).

undiplomatic ['ʌndɪplə'mætɪk] *adj* peu diplomatique, maladroit(e).

undischarged ['ʌndɪs'tʃɑːdʒd] *adj*: **~ bankrupt** failli(e) non réhabilité(e).

undisciplined [ʌn'dɪsɪplɪnd] *adj* indiscipliné(e).

undisguised ['ʌndɪs'gaɪzd] *adj* (*dislike, amusement etc*) franc(franche).

undisputed ['ʌndɪs'pjuːtɪd] *adj* incontesté(e).

undistinguished ['ʌndɪs'tɪŋgwɪʃt] *adj* médiocre, quelconque.

undisturbed [ʌndɪs'təːbd] *adj* (*sleep*) tranquille, paisible; **to leave ~** ne pas déranger.

undivided [ʌndɪ'vaɪdɪd] *adj*: **can I have your ~ attention?** puis-je avoir toute votre attention?

undo [ʌn'duː] *vt irreg* défaire.

undoing [ʌn'duːɪŋ] *n* ruine *f*, perte *f*.

undone [ʌn'dʌn] *pp of* **undo**; **to come ~** se défaire.

undoubted [ʌn'dautɪd] *adj* indubitable, certain(e).

undoubtedly [ʌn'dautɪdlɪ] *adv* sans aucun doute.

undress [ʌn'drɛs] *vi* se déshabiller ♦ *vt* déshabiller.

undrinkable [ʌn'drɪŋkəbl] *adj* (*unpalatable*) imbuvable; (*poisonous*) non potable.

undue [ʌn'djuː] *adj* indu(e), excessif(ive).

undulating ['ʌndjuleɪtɪŋ] *adj* ondoyant(e), onduleux(euse).

unduly [ʌn'djuːlɪ] *adv* trop, excessivement.

undying [ʌn'daɪɪŋ] adj éternel(le).

unearned [ʌn'ɜːnd] adj (praise, respect) immérité(e); ~ **income** rentes fpl.

unearth [ʌn'ɜːθ] vt déterrer; (fig) dénicher.

unearthly [ʌn'ɜːθlɪ] adj surnaturel(le); (hour) indu(e), impossible.

uneasy [ʌn'iːzɪ] adj mal à l'aise, gêné(e); (worried) inquiet(ète); **to feel** ~ **about doing sth** se sentir mal à l'aise à l'idée de faire qch.

uneconomic(al) ['ʌniːkə'nɒmɪk(l)] adj peu économique; peu rentable.

uneducated [ʌn'ɛdjukeɪtɪd] adj sans éducation.

unemployed [ʌnɪm'plɔɪd] adj sans travail, au chômage ♦ n: **the** ~ les chômeurs mpl.

unemployment [ʌnɪm'plɔɪmənt] n chômage m.

unemployment benefit, (US) **unemployment compensation** n allocation f de chômage.

unending [ʌn'ɛndɪŋ] adj interminable.

unenviable [ʌn'ɛnvɪəbl] adj peu enviable.

unequal [ʌn'iːkwəl] adj inégal(e).

unequalled, (US) **unequaled** [ʌn'iːkwəld] adj inégalé(e).

unequivocal [ʌnɪ'kwɪvəkl] adj (answer) sans équivoque; (person) catégorique.

unerring [ʌn'ɜːrɪŋ] adj infaillible, sûr(e).

UNESCO [juː'nɛskəu] n abbr (= United Nations Educational, Scientific and Cultural Organization) UNESCO f.

unethical [ʌn'ɛθɪkl] adj (methods) immoral(e); (doctor's behaviour) qui ne respecte pas l'éthique.

uneven [ʌn'iːvn] adj inégal(e); irrégulier(ière).

uneventful [ʌnɪ'vɛntful] adj tranquille, sans histoires.

unexceptional [ʌnɪk'sɛpʃənl] adj banal(e), quelconque.

unexciting [ʌnɪk'saɪtɪŋ] adj pas passionnant(e).

unexpected [ʌnɪk'spɛktɪd] adj inattendu(e), imprévu(e).

unexpectedly [ʌnɪk'spɛktɪdlɪ] adv contre toute attente; (arrive) à l'improviste.

unexplained [ʌnɪk'spleɪnd] adj inexpliqué(e).

unexploded [ʌnɪk'spləudɪd] adj non explosé(e) or éclaté(e).

unfailing [ʌn'feɪlɪŋ] adj inépuisable; infaillible.

unfair [ʌn'fɛə*] adj: ~ **(to)** injuste (envers); **it's** ~ **that** ... il n'est pas juste que ....

unfair dismissal n licenciement abusif.

unfairly [ʌn'fɛəlɪ] adv injustement.

unfaithful [ʌn'feɪθful] adj infidèle.

unfamiliar [ʌnfə'mɪlɪə*] adj étrange, inconnu(e); **to be** ~ **with sth** mal connaître qch.

unfashionable [ʌn'fæʃnəbl] adj (clothes) démodé(e); (district) déshérité(e), pas à la mode.

unfasten [ʌn'fɑːsn] vt défaire; détacher.

unfathomable [ʌn'fæðəməbl] adj insondable.

unfavourable, (US) **unfavorable** [ʌn'feɪvrəbl] adj défavorable.

unfavo(u)rably [ʌn'feɪvrəblɪ] adv: **to look** ~ **upon** ne pas être favorable à.

unfeeling [ʌn'fiːlɪŋ] adj insensible, dur(e).

unfinished [ʌn'fɪnɪʃt] adj inachevé(e).

unfit [ʌn'fɪt] adj (physically) pas en forme; (incompetent): ~ **(for)** impropre (à); (work, service) inapte (à).

unflagging [ʌn'flægɪŋ] adj infatigable, inlassable.

unflappable [ʌn'flæpəbl] adj imperturbable.

unflattering [ʌn'flætərɪŋ] adj (dress, hairstyle) qui n'avantage pas; (remark) peu flatteur(euse).

unflinching [ʌn'flɪntʃɪŋ] adj stoïque.

unfold [ʌn'fəuld] vt déplier; (fig) révéler, exposer ♦ vi se dérouler.

unforeseeable [ʌnfɔː'siːəbl] adj imprévisible.

unforeseen ['ʌnfɔː'siːn] adj imprévu(e).

unforgettable [ʌnfə'gɛtəbl] adj inoubliable.

unforgivable [ʌnfə'gɪvəbl] adj impardonnable.

unformatted [ʌn'fɔːmætɪd] adj (disk, text) non formaté(e).

unfortunate [ʌn'fɔːtʃnət] adj malheureux(euse); (event, remark) malencontreux(euse).

unfortunately [ʌn'fɔːtʃnətlɪ] adv malheureusement.

unfounded [ʌn'faundɪd] adj sans fondement.

unfriendly [ʌn'frɛndlɪ] adj froid(e), inamical(e).

unfulfilled [ʌnful'fɪld] adj (ambition, prophecy) non réalisé(e); (desire) insatisfait(e); (promise) non tenu(e); (terms of contract) non rempli(e); (person) qui n'a pas su se réaliser.

unfurl [ʌn'fɜːl] vt déployer.

unfurnished [ʌn'fɜːnɪʃt] adj non meublé(e).

ungainly [ʌn'geɪnlɪ] adj gauche, dégingandé(e).

ungodly [ʌn'gɒdlɪ] adj impie; **at an** ~ **hour** à une heure indue.

ungrateful [ʌn'greɪtful] adj qui manque de reconnaissance, ingrat(e).

unguarded [ʌn'gɑːdɪd] adj: ~ **moment** moment m d'inattention.

unhappily [ʌn'hæpɪlɪ] adv tristement; (unfortunately) malheureusement.

unhappiness [ʌn'hæpɪnɪs] n tristesse f, peine f.

unhappy [ʌn'hæpɪ] adj triste, malheureux(euse); (unfortunate: remark etc) malheureux(euse); (not pleased): ~ **with** mécontent(e) de, peu satisfait(e) de.

unharmed [ʌn'hɑːmd] adj indemne, sain(e) et sauf(sauve).

UNHCR n abbr (= United Nations High Commission for Refugees) HCR m.

unhealthy [ʌn'hɛlθɪ] adj (gen) malsain(e); (person) maladif(ive).

unheard-of [ʌn'hɜːdɒv] adj inouï(e), sans précédent.

unhelpful [ʌnˈhɛlpful] *adj* (*person*) peu serviable; (*advice*) peu utile.

unhesitating [ʌnˈhɛzɪteɪtɪŋ] *adj* (*loyalty*) spontané(e); (*reply, offer*) immédiat(e).

unholy [ʌnˈhəʊlɪ] *adj*: **an ~ alliance** une alliance contre nature; **he got home at an ~ hour** il est rentré à une heure impossible.

unhook [ʌnˈhʊk] *vt* décrocher; dégrafer.

unhurt [ʌnˈhɜːt] *adj* indemne, sain(e) et sauf(sauve).

unhygienic [ˈʌnhaɪˈdʒiːnɪk] *adj* antihygiénique.

UNICEF [ˈjuːnɪsɛf] *n abbr* (= *United Nations Children's Fund*) UNICEF *m*, FISE *m*.

unicorn [ˈjuːnɪkɔːn] *n* licorne *f*.

unidentified [ʌnaɪˈdɛntɪfaɪd] *adj* non identifié(e).

uniform [ˈjuːnɪfɔːm] *n* uniforme *m* ♦ *adj* uniforme.

uniformity [juːnɪˈfɔːmɪtɪ] *n* uniformité *f*.

unify [ˈjuːnɪfaɪ] *vt* unifier.

unilateral [juːnɪˈlætərəl] *adj* unilatéral(e).

unimaginable [ʌnɪˈmædʒɪnəbl] *adj* inimaginable, inconcevable.

unimaginative [ʌnɪˈmædʒɪnətɪv] *adj* sans imagination.

unimpaired [ʌnɪmˈpɛəd] *adj* intact(e).

unimportant [ʌnɪmˈpɔːtənt] *adj* sans importance.

unimpressed [ʌnɪmˈprɛst] *adj* pas impressionné(e).

uninhabited [ʌnɪnˈhæbɪtɪd] *adj* inhabité(e).

uninhibited [ʌnɪnˈhɪbɪtɪd] *adj* sans inhibitions; sans retenue.

uninjured [ʌnˈɪndʒəd] *adj* indemne.

uninspiring [ʌnɪnˈspaɪərɪŋ] *adj* peu inspirant(e).

unintelligent [ʌnɪnˈtɛlɪdʒənt] *adj* inintelligent(e).

unintentional [ʌnɪnˈtɛnʃənəl] *adj* involontaire.

unintentionally [ʌnɪnˈtɛnʃnəlɪ] *adv* sans le vouloir.

uninvited [ʌnɪnˈvaɪtɪd] *adj* (*guest*) qui n'a pas été invité(e).

uninviting [ʌnɪnˈvaɪtɪŋ] *adj* (*place*) peu attirant(e); (*food*) peu appétissant(e).

union [ˈjuːnjən] *n* union *f*; (*also: **trade** ~*) syndicat *m* ♦ *cpd* du syndicat, syndical(e).

unionize [ˈjuːnjənaɪz] *vt* syndiquer.

Union Jack *n* drapeau du *Royaume-Uni*.

Union of Soviet Socialist Republics (USSR) *n* (*formerly*) Union *f* des républiques socialistes soviétiques (URSS).

union shop *n* entreprise où tous les travailleurs doivent être syndiqués.

unique [juːˈniːk] *adj* unique.

unisex [ˈjuːnɪsɛks] *adj* unisexe.

UNISON [ˈjuːnɪsn] *n* (*trade union*) grand syndicat des services publics en Grande-Bretagne.

unison [ˈjuːnɪsn] *n*: **in ~** à l'unisson, en chœur.

unit [ˈjuːnɪt] *n* unité *f*; (*section: of furniture etc*)

élément *m*, bloc *m*; (*team, squad*) groupe *m*, service *m*; **production** ~ atelier *m* de fabrication; **sink** ~ bloc-évier *m*.

unit cost *n* coût *m* unitaire.

unite [juːˈnaɪt] *vt* unir ♦ *vi* s'unir.

united [juːˈnaɪtɪd] *adj* uni(e); unifié(e); (*efforts*) conjugué(e).

United Arab Emirates *npl* Émirats Arabes Unis.

United Kingdom (UK) *n* Royaume-Uni *m* (R.U.).

United Nations (Organization) (UN, UNO) *n* (Organisation *f* des) Nations unies (ONU).

United States (of America) (US, USA) *n* États-Unis *mpl*.

unit price *n* prix *m* unitaire.

unit trust *n* (*BRIT COMM*) fonds commun de placement, FCP *m*.

unity [ˈjuːnɪtɪ] *n* unité *f*.

Univ. *abbr* = **university**.

universal [juːnɪˈvɜːsl] *adj* universel(le).

universe [ˈjuːnɪvɜːs] *n* univers *m*.

university [juːnɪˈvɜːsɪtɪ] *n* université *f* ♦ *cpd* (*student, professor*) d'université; (*education, year, degree*) universitaire.

unjust [ʌnˈdʒʌst] *adj* injuste.

unjustifiable [ˈʌndʒʌstɪˈfaɪəbl] *adj* injustifiable.

unjustified [ʌnˈdʒʌstɪfaɪd] *adj* injustifié(e); (*text*) non justifié(e).

unkempt [ʌnˈkɛmpt] *adj* mal tenu(e), débraillé(e); mal peigné(e).

unkind [ʌnˈkaɪnd] *adj* peu gentil(le), méchant(e).

unkindly [ʌnˈkaɪndlɪ] *adv* (*treat, speak*) avec méchanceté.

unknown [ʌnˈnəʊn] *adj* inconnu(e); **~ to me** sans que je le sache; **~ quantity** (*MATH, fig*) inconnue *f*.

unladen [ʌnˈleɪdn] *adj* (*ship, weight*) à vide.

unlawful [ʌnˈlɔːful] *adj* illégal(e).

unleaded [ʌnˈlɛdɪd] *n* (*also:* ~ **petrol**) essence *f* sans plomb.

unleash [ʌnˈliːʃ] *vt* détacher; (*fig*) déchaîner, déclencher.

unleavened [ʌnˈlɛvnd] *adj* sans levain.

unless [ʌnˈlɛs] *conj*: **~ he leaves** à moins qu'il (ne) parte; **~ we leave** à moins de partir, à moins que nous (ne) partions; **~ otherwise stated** sauf indication contraire; **~ I am mistaken** si je ne me trompe.

unlicensed [ʌnˈlaɪsnst] *adj* (*BRIT*) non patenté(e) pour la vente des spiritueux.

unlike [ʌnˈlaɪk] *adj* dissemblable, différent(e) ♦ *prep* à la différence de, contrairement à.

unlikelihood [ʌnˈlaɪklɪhʊd] *adj* improbabilité *f*.

unlikely [ʌnˈlaɪklɪ] *adj* (*result, event*) improbable; (*explanation*) invraisemblable.

unlimited [ʌnˈlɪmɪtɪd] *adj* illimité(e).

unlisted [ˈʌnˈlɪstɪd] *adj* (*US TEL*) sur la liste rouge; (*STOCK EXCHANGE*) non coté(e) en

Bourse.

unlit [ʌn'lɪt] *adj* (*room*) non éclairé(e).

unload [ʌn'ləud] *vt* décharger.

unlock [ʌn'lɔk] *vt* ouvrir.

unlucky [ʌn'lʌkɪ] *adj* malchanceux(euse); (*object, number*) qui porte malheur; **to be ~** (*person*) ne pas avoir de chance.

unmanageable [ʌn'mænɪdʒəbl] *adj* (*unwieldy: tool, vehicle*) peu maniable; (: *situation*) inextricable.

unmanned [ʌn'mænd] *adj* sans équipage.

unmannerly [ʌn'mænəlɪ] *adj* mal élevé(e), impoli(e).

unmarked [ʌn'mɑːkt] *adj* (*unstained*) sans marque; **~ police car** voiture de police banalisée.

unmarried [ʌn'mærɪd] *adj* célibataire.

unmask [ʌn'mɑːsk] *vt* démasquer.

unmatched [ʌn'mætʃt] *adj* sans égal(e).

unmentionable [ʌn'menʃnəbl] *adj* (*topic*) dont on ne parle pas; (*word*) qui ne se dit pas.

unmerciful [ʌn'məːsɪful] *adj* sans pitié.

unmistakable [ʌnmɪs'teɪkəbl] *adj* indubitable; qu'on ne peut pas ne pas reconnaître.

unmitigated [ʌn'mɪtɪgeɪtɪd] *adj* non mitigé(e), absolu(e), pur(e).

unnamed [ʌn'neɪmd] *adj* (*nameless*) sans nom; (*anonymous*) anonyme.

unnatural [ʌn'nætʃrəl] *adj* non naturel(le); contre nature.

unnecessary [ʌn'nesəsərɪ] *adj* inutile, superflu(e).

unnerve [ʌn'nəːv] *vt* faire perdre son sang-froid à.

unnoticed [ʌn'nəutɪst] *adj* inaperçu(e); **to go ~** passer inaperçu.

UNO ['juːnəu] *n abbr* = **United Nations Organization**.

unobservant [ʌnəb'zəːvnt] *adj* pas observateur(trice).

unobtainable [ʌnəb'teɪnəbl] *adj* (*TEL*) impossible à obtenir.

unobtrusive [ʌnəb'truːsiv] *adj* discret(ète).

unoccupied [ʌn'ɔkjupaɪd] *adj* (*seat, table, also MIL*) libre; (*house*) inoccupé(e).

unofficial [ʌnə'fɪʃl] *adj* non officiel(le); (*strike*) ≈ non sanctionné(e) par la centrale.

unopposed [ʌnə'pəuzd] *adj* sans opposition.

unorthodox [ʌn'ɔːθədɔks] *adj* peu orthodoxe.

unpack [ʌn'pæk] *vi* défaire sa valise, déballer ses affaires.

unpaid [ʌn'peɪd] *adj* (*bill*) impayé(e); (*holiday*) non-payé(e), sans salaire; (*work*) non rétribué(e); (*worker*) bénévole.

unpalatable [ʌn'pælətəbl] *adj* (*truth*) désagréable (à entendre).

unparalleled [ʌn'pærəleld] *adj* incomparable, sans égal.

unpatriotic ['ʌnpætrɪ'ɔtɪk] *adj* (*person*) manquant de patriotisme; (*speech, attitude*) antipatriotique.

unplanned [ʌn'plænd] *adj* (*visit*) imprévu(e);

(*baby*) non prévu(e).

unpleasant [ʌn'pleznt] *adj* déplaisant(e), désagréable.

unplug [ʌn'plʌg] *vt* débrancher.

unpolluted [ʌnpə'luːtɪd] *adj* non pollué(e).

unpopular [ʌn'pɔpjulə*] *adj* impopulaire; **to make o.s. ~ (with)** se rendre impopulaire (auprès de).

unprecedented [ʌn'presɪdentɪd] *adj* sans précédent.

unpredictable [ʌnprɪ'dɪktəbl] *adj* imprévisible.

unprejudiced [ʌn'predʒudɪst] *adj* (*not biased*) impartial(e); (*having no prejudices*) qui n'a pas de préjugés.

unprepared [ʌnprɪ'peəd] *adj* (*person*) qui n'est pas suffisamment préparé(e); (*speech*) improvisé(e).

unprepossessing ['ʌnpriːpə'zesɪŋ] *adj* peu avenant(e).

unpretentious [ʌnprɪ'tenʃəs] *adj* sans prétention(s).

unprincipled [ʌn'prɪnsɪpld] *adj* sans principes.

unproductive [ʌnprə'dʌktɪv] *adj* improductif(ive); (*discussion*) stérile.

unprofessional [ʌnprə'feʃənl] *adj* (*conduct*) contraire à la déontologie.

unprofitable [ʌn'prɔfɪtəbl] *adj* non rentable.

UNPROFOR [ʌn'prəufɔː*] *n abbr* (= *United Nations Protection Force*) FORPRONU *f*.

unprotected ['ʌnprə'tektɪd] *adj* (*sex*) non protégé(e).

unprovoked [ʌnprə'vəukt] *adj* (*attack*) sans provocation.

unpunished [ʌn'pʌnɪʃt] *adj* impuni(e); **to go ~** rester impuni.

unqualified [ʌn'kwɔlɪfaɪd] *adj* (*teacher*) non diplômé(e), sans titres; (*success*) sans réserve, total(e).

unquestionably [ʌn'kwestʃənəblɪ] *adv* incontestablement.

unquestioning [ʌn'kwestʃənɪŋ] *adj* (*obedience, acceptance*) inconditionnel(le).

unravel [ʌn'rævl] *vt* démêler.

unreal [ʌn'rɪəl] *adj* irréel(le).

unrealistic ['ʌnrɪə'lɪstɪk] *adj* (*idea*) irréaliste; (*estimate*) peu réaliste.

unreasonable [ʌn'riːznəbl] *adj* qui n'est pas raisonnable; **to make ~ demands on sb** exiger trop de qn.

unrecognizable [ʌn'rekəgnaɪzəbl] *adj* pas reconnaissable.

unrecognized [ʌn'rekəgnaɪzd] *adj* (*talent, genius*) méconnu(e); (*POL: régime*) non reconnu(e).

unrecorded [ʌnrɪ'kɔːdɪd] *adj* non enregistré(e).

unrefined [ʌnrɪ'faɪnd] *adj* (*sugar, petroleum*) non raffiné(e).

unrehearsed [ʌnrɪ'həːst] *adj* (*THEAT etc*) qui n'a pas été répété(e); (*spontaneous*) spontané(e).

unrelated [ʌnrɪ'leɪtɪd] *adj* sans rapport; sans lien de parenté.

unrelenting [ʌnrɪ'lentɪŋ] *adj* implacable; acharné(e).

unreliable [ʌnrɪ'laɪəbl] *adj* sur qui (*or* quoi) on ne peut pas compter, peu fiable.

unrelieved [ʌnrɪ'liːvd] *adj* (*monotony*) constant(e), uniforme.

unremitting [ʌnrɪ'mɪtɪŋ] *adj* inlassable, infatigable, acharné(e).

unrepeatable [ʌnrɪ'piːtəbl] *adj* (*offer*) unique, exceptionnel(le).

unrepentant [ʌnrɪ'pentənt] *adj* impénitent(e).

unrepresentative ['ʌnrɛprɪ'zentətɪv] *adj*: ~ (of) peu représentatif(ive) (de).

unreserved [ʌnrɪ'zɜːvd] *adj* (*seat*) non réservé(e); (*approval, admiration*) sans réserve.

unresponsive [ʌnrɪs'pɒnsɪv] *adj* insensible.

unrest [ʌn'rɛst] *n* agitation *f*, troubles *mpl*.

unrestricted [ʌnrɪ'strɪktɪd] *adj* illimité(e); **to have ~ access** to avoir librement accès *or* accès en tout temps à.

unrewarded [ʌnrɪ'wɔːdɪd] *adj* pas récompensé(e).

unripe [ʌn'raɪp] *adj* pas mûr(e).

unrivalled, (*US*) **unrivaled** [ʌn'raɪvəld] *adj* sans égal, incomparable.

unroll [ʌn'rəul] *vt* dérouler.

unruffled [ʌn'rʌfld] *adj* (*person*) imperturbable; (*hair*) qui n'est pas ébouriffé(e).

unruly [ʌn'ruːlɪ] *adj* indiscipliné(e).

unsafe [ʌn'seɪf] *adj* (*machine, wiring*) dangereux(euse); (*method*) hasardeux(euse); ~ **to drink/eat** non potable/comestible.

unsaid [ʌn'sɛd] *adj*: **to leave sth ~** passer qch sous silence.

unsaleable, (*US*) **unsalable** [ʌn'seɪləbl] *adj* invendable.

unsatisfactory ['ʌnsætɪs'fæktərɪ] *adj* qui laisse à désirer.

unsavoury, (*US*) **unsavory** [ʌn'seɪvərɪ] *adj* (*fig*) peu recommandable, répugnant(e).

unscathed [ʌn'skeɪðd] *adj* indemne.

unscientific ['ʌnsaɪən'tɪfɪk] *adj* non scientifique.

unscrew [ʌn'skruː] *vt* dévisser.

unscrupulous [ʌn'skruːpjuləs] *adj* sans scrupules.

unseat [ʌn'siːt] *vt* (*rider*) désarçonner; (*fig: official*) faire perdre son siège à.

unsecured ['ʌnsɪ'kjuəd] *adj*: ~ **creditor** créancier/ière sans garantie.

unseeded [ʌn'siːdɪd] *adj* (*SPORT*) non classé(e).

unseemly [ʌn'siːmlɪ] *adj* inconvenant(e).

unseen [ʌn'siːn] *adj* (*person*) invisible; (*danger*) imprévu(e).

unselfish [ʌn'sɛlfɪʃ] *adj* désintéressé(e).

unsettled [ʌn'sɛtld] *adj* (*restless*) perturbé(e); (*unpredictable*) instable; incertain(e); (*not finalized*) non résolu(e).

unsettling [ʌn'sɛtlɪŋ] *adj* qui a un effet perturbateur.

unshak(e)able [ʌn'ʃeɪkəbl] *adj* inébranlable.

unshaven [ʌn'ʃeɪvn] *adj* non *or* mal rasé(e).

unsightly [ʌn'saɪtlɪ] *adj* disgracieux(euse), laid(e).

unskilled [ʌn'skɪld] *adj*: ~ **worker** manœuvre *m*.

unsociable [ʌn'səuʃəbl] *adj* (*person*) peu sociable; (*behaviour*) qui manque de sociabilité.

unsocial [ʌn'səuʃl] *adj* (*hours*) en dehors de l'horaire normal.

unsold [ʌn'səuld] *adj* invendu(e), non vendu(e).

unsolicited [ʌnsə'lɪsɪtɪd] *adj* non sollicité(e).

unsophisticated [ʌnsə'fɪstɪkeɪtɪd] *adj* simple, naturel(le).

unsound [ʌn'saund] *adj* (*health*) chancelant(e); (*floor, foundations*) peu solide; (*policy, advice*) peu judicieux(euse).

unspeakable [ʌn'spiːkəbl] *adj* indicible; (*awful*) innommable.

unspoken [ʌn'spəukn] *adj* (*word*) qui n'est pas prononcé(e); (*agreement, approval*) tacite.

unsteady [ʌn'stɛdɪ] *adj* mal assuré(e), chancelant(e), instable.

unstinting [ʌn'stɪntɪŋ] *adj* (*support*) total(e), sans réserve; (*generosity*) sans limites.

unstuck [ʌn'stʌk] *adj*: **to come ~** se décoller; (*fig*) faire fiasco.

unsubstantiated ['ʌnsəb'stænʃɪeɪtɪd] *adj* (*rumour*) qui n'est pas confirmé(e); (*accusation*) sans preuve.

unsuccessful [ʌnsək'sɛsful] *adj* (*attempt*) infructueux(euse); (*writer, proposal*) qui n'a pas de succès; (*marriage*) malheureux(euse), qui ne réussit pas; **to be ~** (*in attempting sth*) ne pas réussir; ne pas avoir de succès; (*application*) ne pas être retenu(e).

unsuccessfully [ʌnsək'sɛsfəlɪ] *adv* en vain.

unsuitable [ʌn'suːtəbl] *adj* qui ne convient pas, peu approprié(e); inopportun(e).

unsuited [ʌn'suːtɪd] *adj*: **to be ~ for** *or* **to** être inapte *or* impropre à.

unsung ['ʌnsʌŋ] *adj*: **an ~ hero** un héros méconnu.

unsupported [ʌnsə'pɔːtɪd] *adj* (*claim*) non soutenu(e); (*theory*) qui n'est pas corroboré(e).

unsure [ʌn'ʃuə*] *adj* pas sûr(e); **to be ~ of o.s.** ne pas être sûr de soi, manquer de confiance en soi.

unsuspecting [ʌnsə'spɛktɪŋ] *adj* qui ne se méfie pas.

unsweetened [ʌn'swiːtnd] *adj* non sucré(e).

unswerving [ʌn'swɜːvɪŋ] *adj* inébranlable.

unsympathetic ['ʌnsɪmpə'θɛtɪk] *adj* hostile; (*unpleasant*) antipathique; ~ **to** indifférent(e) à.

untangle [ʌn'tæŋgl] *vt* démêler, débrouiller.

untapped [ʌn'tæpt] *adj* (*resources*) inexploité(e).

untaxed [ʌn'tækst] *adj* (*goods*) non taxé(e); (*income*) non imposé(e).

unthinkable [ʌn'θɪŋkəbl] *adj* impensable, inconcevable.

unthinkingly [ʌn'θɪŋkɪŋlɪ] *adv* sans réfléchir.

untidy [ʌn'taɪdɪ] *adj* (*room*) en désordre; (*appearance*) désordonné(e), débraillé(e); (*person*) sans ordre, désordonné; débraillé; (*work*) peu soigné(e).

untie [ʌn'taɪ] *vt* (*knot, parcel*) défaire; (*prisoner, dog*) détacher.

until [ən'tɪl] *prep* jusqu'à; (*after negative*) avant ♦ *conj* jusqu'à ce que + *sub*, en attendant que + *sub*; (*in past, after negative*) avant que + *sub*; ~ **now** jusqu'à présent, jusqu'ici; ~ **then** jusque-là; **from morning** ~ **night** du matin au soir *or* jusqu'au soir.

untimely [ʌn'taɪmlɪ] *adj* inopportun(e); (*death*) prématuré(e).

untold [ʌn'təʊld] *adj* incalculable; indescriptible.

untouched [ʌn'tʌtʃt] *adj* (*not used etc*) tel(le) quel(le), intact(e); (*safe: person*) indemne; (*unaffected*): ~ **by** indifférent(e) à.

untoward [ʌntə'wɔːd] *adj* fâcheux(euse), malencontreux(euse).

untrained ['ʌn'treɪnd] *adj* (*worker*) sans formation; (*troops*) sans entraînement; **to the** ~ **eye** à l'œil non exercé.

untrammelled [ʌn'træmld] *adj* sans entraves.

untranslatable [ʌntrænz'leɪtəbl] *adj* intraduisible.

untrue [ʌn'truː] *adj* (*statement*) faux(fausse).

untrustworthy [ʌn'trʌstwəːðɪ] *adj* (*person*) pas digne de confiance, peu sûr(e).

unusable [ʌn'juːzəbl] *adj* inutilisable.

unused *adj* [ʌn'juːzd] (*new*) neuf(neuve); [ʌn'juːst]: **to be** ~ **to sth/to doing sth** ne pas avoir l'habitude de qch/de faire qch.

unusual [ʌn'juːʒuəl] *adj* insolite, exceptionnel(le), rare.

unusually [ʌn'juːʒuəlɪ] *adv* exceptionnellement, particulièrement.

unveil [ʌn'veɪl] *vt* dévoiler.

unwanted [ʌn'wɒntɪd] *adj* non désiré(e).

unwarranted [ʌn'wɒrəntɪd] *adj* injustifié(e).

unwary [ʌn'wɛərɪ] *adj* imprudent(e).

unwavering [ʌn'weɪvərɪŋ] *adj* inébranlable.

unwelcome [ʌn'wɛlkəm] *adj* importun(e); **to feel** ~ se sentir de trop.

unwell [ʌn'wɛl] *adj* indisposé(e), souffrant(e); **to feel** ~ ne pas se sentir bien.

unwieldy [ʌn'wiːldɪ] *adj* difficile à manier.

unwilling [ʌn'wɪlɪŋ] *adj*: **to be** ~ **to do** ne pas vouloir faire.

unwillingly [ʌn'wɪlɪŋlɪ] *adv* à contrecœur, contre son gré.

unwind [ʌn'waɪnd] *vb* (*irreg*) *vt* dérouler ♦ *vi* (*relax*) se détendre.

unwise [ʌn'waɪz] *adj* imprudent(e), peu judicieux(euse).

unwitting [ʌn'wɪtɪŋ] *adj* involontaire.

unworkable [ʌn'wəːkəbl] *adj* (*plan etc*) inexploitable.

unworthy [ʌn'wəːðɪ] *adj* indigne.

unwrap [ʌn'ræp] *vt* défaire; ouvrir.

unwritten [ʌn'rɪtn] *adj* (*agreement*) tacite.

unzip [ʌn'zɪp] *vt* ouvrir (la fermeture éclair de).

=========== *KEYWORD*

up [ʌp] *prep*: **he went** ~ **the stairs/the hill** il a monté l'escalier/la colline; **the cat was** ~ **a tree** le chat était dans un arbre; **they live further** ~ **the street** ils habitent plus haut dans la rue
♦ *vi* (*col*): **she** ~**ped and left** elle a fichu le camp sans plus attendre
♦ *adv* **1** en haut; en l'air; (*upwards, higher*): ~ **in the sky/the mountains** (là-haut) dans le ciel/les montagnes; **put it a bit higher** ~ mettez-le un peu plus haut; ~ **there** là-haut; ~ **above** au-dessus; **"this side** ~**" "haut"**
2: **to be** ~ (*out of bed*) être levé(e); (*prices*) avoir augmenté *or* monté; (*finished*): **when the year was** ~ à la fin de l'année; **time's** ~ c'est l'heure
3: ~ **to** (*as far as*) jusqu'à; ~ **to now** jusqu'à présent
4: **to be** ~ **to** (*depending on*): **it's** ~ **to you** c'est à vous de décider; (*equal to*): **he's not** ~ **to it** (*job, task etc*) il n'en est pas capable; (*inf: be doing*): **what is he** ~ **to?** qu'est-ce qu'il peut bien faire?
5 (*phrases*): **he's well** ~ **in** *or* **on ...** (*BRIT: knowledgeable*) il s'y connaît en ...; ~ **with Leeds United!** vive Leeds United!; **what's** ~**?** (*col*) qu'est-ce qui ne va pas?; **what's** ~ **with him?** (*col*) qu'est-ce qui lui arrive?
♦ *n*: ~**s and downs** hauts et bas *mpl*.

up-and-coming [ʌpənd'kʌmɪŋ] *adj* plein(e) d'avenir *or* de promesses.

upbeat ['ʌpbiːt] *n* (*MUS*) levé *m*; (*in economy, prosperity*) amélioration *f* ♦ *adj* (*optimistic*) optimiste.

upbraid [ʌp'breɪd] *vt* morigéner.

upbringing ['ʌpbrɪŋɪŋ] *n* éducation *f*.

upcoming ['ʌpkʌmɪŋ] *adj* tout(e) prochain(e).

update [ʌp'deɪt] *vt* mettre à jour.

upend [ʌp'ɛnd] *vt* mettre debout.

up-front [ʌp'frʌnt] *adj* franc(franche) ♦ *adv* (*pay*) d'avance.

upgrade [ʌp'greɪd] *vt* (*person*) promouvoir; (*job*) revaloriser; (*property, equipment*) moderniser.

upheaval [ʌp'hiːvl] *n* bouleversement *m*; branle-bas *m*; crise *f*.

uphill [ʌp'hɪl] *adj* qui monte; (*fig: task*) difficile, pénible ♦ *adv* (*face, look*) en amont, vers l'amont; (*go, move*) vers le haut, en haut; **to go** ~ monter.

uphold [ʌp'həʊld] *vt irreg* maintenir; soutenir.

upholstery [ʌp'həʊlstərɪ] *n* rembourrage *m*; (*of car*) garniture *f*.

upkeep ['ʌpkiːp] *n* entretien *m*.

up-market [ˌʌpˈmɑːkɪt] *adj* (*product*) haut de gamme *inv.*

upon [əˈpɒn] *prep* sur.

upper [ˈʌpə*] *adj* supérieur(e); du dessus ♦ *n* (*of shoe*) empeigne *f.*

upper class *n*: **the** ~ ≈ la haute bourgeoisie ♦ *adj*: **upper-class** (*district*) élégant(e), huppé(e); (*accent, attitude*) caractéristique des classes supérieures.

uppercut [ˈʌpəkʌt] *n* uppercut *m.*

upper hand *n*: **to have the** ~ avoir le dessus.

Upper House *n*: **the** ~ (*in Britain*) la Chambre des Lords, la Chambre haute; (*in France, in the US etc*) le Sénat.

uppermost [ˈʌpəmoʊst] *adj* le(la) plus haut(e); en dessus; **it was** ~ **in my mind** j'y pensais avant tout autre chose.

Upper Volta [-ˈvɒltə] *n* Haute Volta.

upright [ˈʌpraɪt] *adj* droit(e); vertical(e); (*fig*) droit, honnête ♦ *n* montant *m.*

uprising [ˈʌpraɪzɪŋ] *n* soulèvement *m*, insurrection *f.*

uproar [ˈʌprɔː*] *n* tumulte *m*, vacarme *m.*

uproarious [ʌpˈrɔːrɪəs] *adj* (*event etc*) désopilant(e); ~ **laughter** un brouhaha de rires.

uproot [ʌpˈruːt] *vt* déraciner.

upset *n* [ˈʌpsɛt] dérangement *m* ♦ *vt* [ʌpˈsɛt] (*irreg: like* **set**) (*glass etc*) renverser; (*plan*) déranger; (*person: offend*) contrarier; (*: grieve*) faire de la peine à; bouleverser ♦ *adj* [ʌpˈsɛt] contrarié(e); peiné(e); (*stomach*) détraqué(e), dérangé(e); **to get** ~ (*sad*) devenir triste; (*offended*) se vexer; **to have a stomach** ~ (*BRIT*) avoir une indigestion.

upset price *n* (*US, Scottish*) mise *f* à prix, prix *m* de départ.

upsetting [ʌpˈsɛtɪŋ] *adj* (*offending*) vexant(e); (*annoying*) ennuyeux(euse).

upshot [ˈʌpʃɒt] *n* résultat *m*; **the** ~ **of it all was that** ... il a résulté de tout cela que ....

upside down [ˈʌpsaɪd-] *adv* à l'envers.

upstage [ˈʌpˈsteɪdʒ] *vt*: **to** ~ **sb** souffler la vedette à qn.

upstairs [ʌpˈstɛəz] *adv* en haut ♦ *adj* (*room*) du dessus, d'en haut ♦ *n*: **there's no** ~ il n'y a pas d'étage.

upstart [ˈʌpstɑːt] *n* parvenu/e.

upstream [ʌpˈstriːm] *adv* en amont.

upsurge [ˈʌpsɜːdʒ] *n* (*of enthusiasm etc*) vague *f.*

uptake [ˈʌpteɪk] *n*: **he is quick/slow on the** ~ il comprend vite/est lent à comprendre.

uptight [ʌpˈtaɪt] *adj* (*col*) très tendu(e), crispé(e).

up-to-date [ˈʌptəˈdeɪt] *adj* moderne; très récent(e).

upturn [ˈʌptɜːn] *n* (*in economy*) reprise *f.*

upturned [ˈʌptɜːnd] *adj* (*nose*) retroussé(e).

upward [ˈʌpwəd] *adj* ascendant(e); vers le haut ♦ *adv see* **upwards**.

upwardly-mobile [ˈʌpwədlɪˈmoʊbaɪl] *adj* à mobilité sociale ascendante.

upwards [ˈʌpwədz] *adv* vers le haut; **and** ~ et plus, et au-dessus.

URA *n abbr* (*US*) = *Urban Renewal Administration.*

Ural Mountains [ˈjuərəl-] *npl*: **the** ~ (*also*: **the Urals**) les monts *mpl* Oural, l'Oural *m.*

uranium [juəˈreɪnɪəm] *n* uranium *m.*

Uranus [juəˈreɪnəs] *n* Uranus *f.*

urban [ˈɜːbən] *adj* urbain(e).

urbane [ɜːˈbeɪn] *adj* urbain(e), courtois(e).

urbanization [ɜːbənaɪˈzeɪʃən] *n* urbanisation *f.*

urchin [ˈɜːtʃɪn] *n* gosse *m*, garnement *m.*

Urdu [ˈuəduː] *n* ourdou *m.*

urge [ɜːdʒ] *n* besoin (impératif), envie (pressante) ♦ *vt* (*caution etc*) recommander avec insistance; (*person*): **to** ~ **sb to do** presser qn de faire, recommander avec insistance à qn de faire.

▶**urge on** *vt* pousser, presser.

urgency [ˈɜːdʒənsɪ] *n* urgence *f*; (*of tone*) insistance *f.*

urgent [ˈɜːdʒənt] *adj* urgent(e); (*plea, tone*) pressant(e).

urgently [ˈɜːdʒəntlɪ] *adv* d'urgence, de toute urgence; (*need*) sans délai.

urinal [ˈjuərɪnl] *n* (*BRIT*) urinoir *m.*

urinate [ˈjuərɪneɪt] *vi* uriner.

urine [ˈjuərɪn] *n* urine *f.*

urn [ɜːn] *n* urne *f*; (*also*: **tea** ~) fontaine *f* à thé.

Uruguay [ˈjuərəgwaɪ] *n* Uruguay *m.*

Uruguayan [juərəˈgwaɪən] *adj* uruguayen(ne) ♦ *n* Uruguayen/ne.

US *n abbr* = *United States.*

us [ʌs] *pron* nous.

USA *n abbr* = *United States of America*; (*MIL*) = *United States Army.*

usable [ˈjuːzəbl] *adj* utilisable.

USAF *n abbr* = *United States Air Force.*

usage [ˈjuːzɪdʒ] *n* usage *m.*

USCG *n abbr* = *United States Coast Guard.*

USDA *n abbr* = *United States Department of Agriculture.*

USDAW [ˈʌzdɔː] *n abbr* (*BRIT*: = *Union of Shop, Distributive and Allied Workers*) syndicat du commerce de détail et de la distribution.

USDI *n abbr* = *United States Department of the Interior.*

use *n* [juːs] emploi *m*, utilisation *f*; usage *m* ♦ *vt* [juːz] se servir de, utiliser, employer; **in** ~ en usage; **out of** ~ hors d'usage; **to be of** ~ servir, être utile; **to make** ~ **of sth** utiliser qch; **ready for** ~ prêt à l'emploi; **it's no** ~ ça ne sert à rien; **to have the** ~ **of** avoir l'usage de; **what's this** ~**d for?** à quoi est-ce que ça sert?; **she** ~**d to do it** elle le faisait (autrefois), elle avait coutume de le faire; **to be** ~**d to** avoir l'habitude de, être habitué(e) à; **to get** ~**d to** s'habituer à.

▶**use up** *vt* finir, épuiser; (*food*) consommer.

used [juːzd] *adj* (*car*) d'occasion.

useful ['juːsful] *adj* utile; **to come in** ~ être utile.
usefulness ['juːsfəlnɪs] *n* utilité *f*.
useless ['juːslɪs] *adj* inutile.
user ['juːzə*] *n* utilisateur/trice, usager *m*.
user-friendly ['juːzə'frendlɪ] *adj* convivial(e), facile d'emploi.
USES *n abbr* = *United States Employment Service*.
usher ['ʌʃə*] *n* placeur *m* ♦ *vt*: **to** ~ **sb in** faire entrer qn.
usherette [ʌʃə'rɛt] *n* (*in cinema*) ouvreuse *f*.
USIA *n abbr* = *United States Information Agency*.
USM *n abbr* = *United States Mail, United States Mint*.
USN *n abbr* = *United States Navy*.
USPHS *n abbr* = *United States Public Health Service*.
USPO *n abbr* = *United States Post Office*.
USS *abbr* = *United States Ship (or Steamer)*.
USSR *n abbr* = **Union of Soviet Socialist Republics**.
usu. *abbr* = **usually**.
usual ['juːʒuəl] *adj* habituel(le); **as** ~ comme d'habitude.
usually ['juːʒuəlɪ] *adv* d'habitude, d'ordinaire.
usurer ['juːʒərə*] *n* usurier/ière.
usurp [juː'zəːp] *vt* usurper.
UT *abbr* (*US*) = *Utah*.
utensil [juː'tɛnsl] *n* ustensile *m*; **kitchen** ~**s** batterie *f* de cuisine.
uterus ['juːtərəs] *n* utérus *m*.
utilitarian [juːtɪlɪ'tɛərɪən] *adj* utilitaire.
utility [juː'tɪlɪtɪ] *n* utilité *f*; (*also*: **public** ~) service public.
utility room *n* buanderie *f*.
utilization [juːtɪlaɪ'zeɪʃən] *n* utilisation *f*.
utilize ['juːtɪlaɪz] *vt* utiliser; exploiter.
utmost ['ʌtməust] *adj* extrême, le(la) plus grand(e) ♦ *n*: **to do one's** ~ faire tout son possible; **of the** ~ **importance** d'une importance capitale, de la plus haute importance.
utter ['ʌtə*] *adj* total(e), complet(ète) ♦ *vt* prononcer, proférer; émettre.
utterance ['ʌtrns] *n* paroles *fpl*.
utterly ['ʌtəlɪ] *adv* complètement, totalement.
U-turn ['juː'təːn] *n* demi-tour *m*; (*fig*) volteface *f inv*.
Uzbekistan [ʌzbɛkɪ'stɑːn] *n* Ouzbékistan *m*.

V v

V, v [viː] *n* (*letter*) V, v *m*; **V for Victor** V comme Victor.
v *abbr* (= *verse*, = *vide: see*) v.; (= *versus*) c.; (= *volt*) V.
VA, Va. *abbr* (*US*) = *Virginia*.
vac [væk] *n abbr* (*BRIT col*) = **vacation**.
vacancy ['veɪkənsɪ] *n* (*BRIT: job*) poste vacant; (*room*) chambre *f* disponible; **"no vacancies"** "complet".
vacant ['veɪkənt] *adj* (*post*) vacant(e); (*seat etc*) libre, disponible; (*expression*) distrait(e).
vacant lot *n* terrain inoccupé; (*for sale*) terrain à vendre.
vacate [və'keɪt] *vt* quitter.
vacation [və'keɪʃən] *n* (*esp US*) vacances *fpl*; **to take a** ~ prendre des vacances; **on** ~ en vacances.
vacation course *n* cours *mpl* de vacances.
vaccinate ['væksɪneɪt] *vt* vacciner.
vaccination [væksɪ'neɪʃən] *n* vaccination *f*.
vaccine ['væksiːn] *n* vaccin *m*.
vacuum ['vækjum] *n* vide *m*.
vacuum bottle *n* (*US*) = **vacuum flask**.
vacuum cleaner *n* aspirateur *m*.
vacuum flask *n* (*BRIT*) bouteille *f* thermos ®.
vacuum-packed ['vækjumpækt] *adj* emballé(e) sous vide.
vagabond ['vægəbɔnd] *n* vagabond/e; (*tramp*) chemineau *m*, clochard/e.
vagary ['veɪgərɪ] *n* caprice *m*.
vagina [və'dʒaɪnə] *n* vagin *m*.
vagrancy ['veɪgrənsɪ] *n* vagabondage *m*.
vagrant ['veɪgrənt] *n* vagabond/e, mendiant/e.
vague [veɪg] *adj* vague, imprécis(e); (*blurred: photo, memory*) flou(e); **I haven't the** ~**st idea** je n'en ai pas la moindre idée.
vaguely ['veɪglɪ] *adv* vaguement.
vain [veɪn] *adj* (*useless*) vain(e); (*conceited*) vaniteux(euse); **in** ~ en vain.
valance ['væləns] *n* (*of bed*) tour *m* de lit.
valedictory [vælɪ'dɪktərɪ] *adj* d'adieu.
valentine ['væləntaɪn] *n* (*also*: ~ **card**) carte *f* de la Saint-Valentin.
valet ['vælɪt] *n* valet *m* de chambre.
valet parking *n* parcage *m* par les soins du personnel (de l'hôtel *etc*).
valet service *n* (*for clothes*) pressing *m*; (*for car*) nettoyage complet.
valiant ['vælɪənt] *adj* vaillant(e), courageux(euse).
valid ['vælɪd] *adj* valide, valable; (*excuse*) valable.

validate ['vælɪdeɪt] *vt* (*contract, document*) valider; (*argument, claim*) prouver la justesse de, confirmer.

validity [və'lɪdɪtɪ] *n* validité *f*.

valise [və'liːz] *n* sac *m* de voyage.

valley ['vælɪ] *n* vallée *f*.

valour, (*US*) **valor** ['vælə*] *n* courage *m*.

valuable ['væljuəbl] *adj* (*jewel*) de grande valeur; (*time*) précieux(euse); ~s *npl* objets *mpl* de valeur.

valuation [vælju'eɪʃən] *n* évaluation *f*, expertise *f*.

value ['væljuː] *n* valeur *f* ♦ *vt* (*fix price*) évaluer, expertiser; (*cherish*) tenir à; **you get good ~ (for money) in that shop** vous en avez pour votre argent dans ce magasin; **to lose (in)** ~ (*currency*) baisser; (*property*) se déprécier; **to gain (in)** ~ (*currency*) monter; (*property*) prendre de la valeur; **to be of great ~ to sb** (*fig*) être très utile à qn.

value added tax (VAT) [-'ædɪd-] *n* (*BRIT*) taxe *f* à la valeur ajoutée (TVA).

valued ['væljuːd] *adj* (*appreciated*) estimé(e).

valuer ['væljuə*] *n* expert *m* (en estimations).

valve [vælv] *n* (*in machine*) soupape *f*; (*on tyre*) valve *f*; (*in radio*) lampe *f*.

vampire ['væmpaɪə*] *n* vampire *m*.

van [væn] *n* (*AUT*) camionnette *f*; (*BRIT RAIL*) fourgon *m*.

V and A *n abbr* (*BRIT*) = *Victoria and Albert Museum.*

vandal ['vændl] *n* vandale *m/f*.

vandalism ['vændəlɪzəm] *n* vandalisme *m*.

vandalize ['vændəlaɪz] *vt* saccager.

vanguard ['væŋgɑːd] *n* avant-garde *m*.

vanilla [və'nɪlə] *n* vanille *f* ♦ *cpd* (*ice cream*) à la vanille.

vanish ['vænɪʃ] *vi* disparaître.

vanity ['vænɪtɪ] *n* vanité *f*.

vanity case *n* sac *m* de toilette.

vantage ['vɑːntɪdʒ] *n*: ~ **point** bonne position.

vaporize ['veɪpəraɪz] *vt* vaporiser ♦ *vi* se vaporiser.

vapour, (*US*) **vapor** ['veɪpə*] *n* vapeur *f*; (*on window*) buée *f*.

vapo(u)r trail *n* (*AVIAT*) traînée *f* de condensation.

variable ['vɛərɪəbl] *adj* variable; (*mood*) changeant(e) ♦ *n* variable *f*.

variance ['vɛərɪəns] *n*: **to be at** ~ **(with)** être en désaccord (avec); (*facts*) être en contradiction (avec).

variant ['vɛərɪənt] *n* variante *f*.

variation [vɛərɪ'eɪʃən] *n* variation *f*; (*in opinion*) changement *m*.

varicose ['værɪkəus] *adj*: ~ **veins** varices *fpl*.

varied ['vɛərɪd] *adj* varié(e), divers(e).

variety [və'raɪətɪ] *n* variété *f*; (*quantity*): **a wide** ~ **of** ... une quantité *or* un grand nombre de ... (différent(e)s *or* divers(es)); **for a** ~ **of reasons** pour diverses raisons.

variety show *n* (spectacle *m* de) variétés *fpl*.

various ['vɛərɪəs] *adj* divers(e), différent(e); (*several*) divers, plusieurs; **at** ~ **times** (*different*) en diverses occasions; (*several*) à plusieurs reprises.

varnish ['vɑːnɪʃ] *n* vernis *m*; (*for nails*) vernis (à ongles) ♦ *vt* vernir; **to** ~ **one's nails** se vernir les ongles.

vary ['vɛərɪ] *vt, vi* varier, changer; **to** ~ **with** *or* **according to** varier selon.

varying ['vɛərɪŋ] *adj* variable.

vase [vɑːz] *n* vase *m*.

vasectomy [væ'sɛktəmɪ] *n* vasectomie *f*.

Vaseline ['væsɪliːn] *n* ® vaseline *f*.

vast [vɑːst] *adj* vaste, immense; (*amount, success*) énorme.

vastly ['vɑːstlɪ] *adv* infiniment, extrêmement.

vastness ['vɑːstnɪs] *n* immensité *f*.

VAT [væt] *n abbr* (*BRIT*) = **value added tax.**

vat [væt] *n* cuve *f*.

Vatican ['vætɪkən] *n*: **the** ~ le Vatican.

vatman ['vætmæn] *n* (*BRIT col*) contrôleur *m* de la T.V.A.

vault [vɔːlt] *n* (*of roof*) voûte *f*; (*tomb*) caveau *m*; (*in bank*) salle *f* des coffres; chambre forte; (*jump*) saut *m* ♦ *vt* (*also*: ~ **over**) sauter (d'un bond).

vaunted ['vɔːntɪd] *adj*: **much-**~ tant célébré(e).

VC *n abbr* = **vice-chairman**; (*BRIT*: = *Victoria Cross*) distinction militaire.

VCR *n abbr* = **video cassette recorder.**

VD *n abbr* = **venereal disease.**

VDU *n abbr* = **visual display unit.**

veal [viːl] *n* veau *m*.

veer [vɪə*] *vi* tourner; virer.

veg. [vɛdʒ] *n abbr* (*BRIT col*) = **vegetable(s).**

vegan ['viːgən] *n* végétalien/ne.

vegeburger ['vɛdʒɪbəːgə*] *n* burger végétarien.

vegetable ['vɛdʒtəbl] *n* légume *m* ♦ *adj* végétal(e).

vegetable garden *n* (jardin *m*) potager *m*.

vegetarian [vɛdʒɪ'tɛərɪən] *adj, n* végétarien(ne).

vegetate ['vɛdʒɪteɪt] *vi* végéter.

vegetation [vɛdʒɪ'teɪʃən] *n* végétation *f*.

vegetative ['vɛdʒɪtətɪv] *adj* (*lit*) végétal(e); (*fig*) végétatif(ive).

veggieburger ['vɛdʒɪbəːgə*] *n* = **vegeburger.**

vehemence ['viːɪməns] *n* véhémence *f*, violence *f*.

vehement ['viːɪmənt] *adj* violent(e), impétueux(euse); (*impassioned*) ardent(e).

vehicle ['viːɪkl] *n* véhicule *m*.

vehicular [vɪ'hɪkjulə*] *adj*: **"no** ~ **traffic"** "interdit à tout véhicule".

veil [veɪl] *n* voile *m* ♦ *vt* voiler; **under a** ~ **of secrecy** (*fig*) dans le plus grand secret.

veiled [veɪld] *adj* voilé(e).

vein [veɪn] *n* veine *f*; (*on leaf*) nervure *f*; (*fig: mood*) esprit *m*.

Velcro ['vɛlkrəu] *n* ® velcro *m* ®.

vellum ['vɛləm] n (writing paper) vélin m.
velocity [vɪ'lɒsɪtɪ] n vitesse f, vélocité f.
velour(s) [və'luə*] n velours m.
velvet ['vɛlvɪt] n velours m.
vending machine ['vɛndɪŋ-] n distributeur m automatique.
vendor ['vɛndə*] n vendeur/euse; **street** ~ marchand ambulant.
veneer [və'nɪə*] n placage m de bois; (fig) vernis m.
venerable ['vɛnərəbl] adj vénérable.
venereal [vɪ'nɪərɪəl] adj: ~ **disease (VD)** maladie vénérienne.
Venetian [vɪ'niːʃən] adj: ~ **blind** store vénitien.
Venezuela [vɛnɛ'zweɪlə] n Venezuela m.
Venezuelan [vɛnɛ'zweɪlən] adj vénézuélien(ne) ♦ n Vénézuélien/ne.
vengeance ['vɛndʒəns] n vengeance f; **with a** ~ (fig) vraiment, pour de bon.
vengeful ['vɛndʒful] adj vengeur(geresse).
Venice ['vɛnɪs] n Venise.
venison ['vɛnɪsn] n venaison f.
venom ['vɛnəm] n venin m.
venomous ['vɛnəməs] adj venimeux(euse).
vent [vɛnt] n conduit m d'aération; (in dress, jacket) fente f ♦ vt (fig: one's feelings) donner libre cours à.
ventilate ['vɛntɪleɪt] vt (room) ventiler, aérer.
ventilation [vɛntɪ'leɪʃən] n ventilation f, aération f.
ventilation shaft n conduit m de ventilation or d'aération.
ventilator ['vɛntɪleɪtə*] n ventilateur m.
ventriloquist [vɛn'trɪləkwɪst] n ventriloque m/f.
venture ['vɛntʃə*] n entreprise f ♦ vt risquer, hasarder ♦ vi s'aventurer, se risquer; **a business** ~ une entreprise commerciale; **to** ~ **to do sth** se risquer à faire qch.
venture capital n capital-risques m.
venue ['vɛnjuː] n (of conference etc) lieu m de la réunion (or manifestation etc); (of match) lieu de la rencontre.
Venus ['viːnəs] n (planet) Vénus f.
veracity [və'ræsɪtɪ] n véracité f.
veranda(h) [və'rændə] n véranda f.
verb [vɜːb] n verbe m.
verbal ['vɜːbl] adj verbal(e); (translation) littéral(e).
verbally ['vɜːbəlɪ] adv verbalement.
verbatim [vɜː'beɪtɪm] adj, adv mot pour mot.
verbose [vɜː'bəus] adj verbeux(euse).
verdict ['vɜːdɪkt] n verdict m; ~ **of guilty/not guilty** verdict de culpabilité/de non-culpabilité.
verge [vɜːdʒ] n bord m; "**soft ~s**" (BRIT) "accotements non stabilisés"; **on the** ~ **of doing** sur le point de faire.
►**verge on** vt fus approcher de.
verger ['vɜːdʒə*] n (REL) bedeau m.
verification [vɛrɪfɪ'keɪʃən] n vérification f.

verify ['vɛrɪfaɪ] vt vérifier.
veritable ['vɛrɪtəbl] adj véritable.
vermin ['vɜːmɪn] npl animaux mpl nuisibles; (insects) vermine f.
vermouth ['vɜːməθ] n vermouth m.
vernacular [və'nækjulə*] n langue f vernaculaire, dialecte m.
versatile ['vɜːsətaɪl] adj polyvalent(e).
verse [vɜːs] n vers mpl; (stanza) strophe f; (in bible) verset m; **in** ~ en vers.
versed [vɜːst] adj: **(well-)~ in** versé(e) dans.
version ['vɜːʃən] n version f.
versus ['vɜːsəs] prep contre.
vertebra, pl ~**e** ['vɜːtɪbrə, -briː] n vertèbre f.
vertebrate ['vɜːtɪbrɪt] n vertébré m.
vertical ['vɜːtɪkl] adj vertical(e) ♦ n verticale f.
vertically ['vɜːtɪklɪ] adv verticalement.
vertigo ['vɜːtɪgəu] n vertige m; **to suffer from** ~ avoir des vertiges.
verve [vɜːv] n brio m; enthousiasme m.
very ['vɛrɪ] adv très ♦ adj: **the** ~ **book which** le livre même que; **the** ~ **thought (of it)** ... rien que d'y penser ...; **at the** ~ **end** tout à la fin; **the** ~ **last** le tout dernier; **at the** ~ **least** au moins; ~ **well** très bien; ~ **little** très peu; ~ **much** beaucoup.
vespers ['vɛspəz] npl vêpres fpl.
vessel ['vɛsl] n (ANAT, NAUT) vaisseau m; (container) récipient m.
vest [vɛst] n (BRIT) tricot m de corps; (US) gilet m ♦ vt: **to** ~ **sb with sth, to** ~ **sth in sb** investir qn de qch.
vested interest n: **to have a** ~ **in doing** avoir tout intérêt à faire; ~**s** npl (COMM) droits acquis.
vestibule ['vɛstɪbjuːl] n vestibule m.
vestige ['vɛstɪdʒ] n vestige m.
vestry ['vɛstrɪ] n sacristie f.
Vesuvius [vɪ'suːvɪəs] n Vésuve m.
vet [vɛt] n abbr (= veterinary surgeon) vétérinaire m/f ♦ vt examiner minutieusement; (text) revoir; (candidate) se renseigner soigneusement sur, soumettre à une enquête approfondie.
veteran ['vɛtərn] n vétéran m; (also: **war** ~) ancien combattant ♦ adj: **she's a** ~ **campaigner for** ... cela fait très longtemps qu'elle lutte pour ....
veteran car n voiture f d'époque.
veterinarian [vɛtrɪ'nɛərɪən] n (US) = **veterinary surgeon**.
veterinary ['vɛtrɪnərɪ] adj vétérinaire.
veterinary surgeon n (BRIT) vétérinaire m/f.
veto ['viːtəu] n (pl ~**es**) veto m ♦ vt opposer son veto à; **to put a** ~ **on** mettre (or opposer) son veto à.
vetting ['vɛtɪŋ] n: **positive** ~ enquête f de sécurité.
vex [vɛks] vt fâcher, contrarier.
vexed [vɛkst] adj (question) controversé(e).
VFD n abbr (US) = voluntary fire department.
VG n abbr (BRIT: SCOL etc: = very good) tb (= très

bien).

VHF *abbr* (= *very high frequency*) VHF.

VI *abbr* (*US*) = Virgin Islands.

via ['vaɪə] *prep* par, via.

viability [vaɪə'bɪlɪtɪ] *n* viabilité *f*.

viable ['vaɪəbl] *adj* viable.

viaduct ['vaɪədʌkt] *n* viaduc *m*.

vial ['vaɪəl] *m* fiole *f*.

vibes [vaɪbz] *npl* (*col*): **I get good/bad ~ about it** je le sens bien/ne le sens pas; **there are good/bad ~ between us** entre nous le courant passe bien/ne passe pas.

vibrant ['vaɪbrnt] *adj* (*sound, colour*) vibrant(e).

vibraphone ['vaɪbrəfəun] *n* vibraphone *m*.

vibrate [vaɪ'breɪt] *vi*: **to ~ (with)** vibrer (de); (*resound*) retentir (de).

vibration [vaɪ'breɪʃən] *n* vibration *f*.

vibrator [vaɪ'breɪtə*] *n* vibromasseur *m*.

vicar ['vɪkə*] *n* pasteur *m* (*de l'Église anglicane*).

vicarage ['vɪkərɪdʒ] *n* presbytère *m*.

vicarious [vɪ'kɛərɪəs] *adj* (*pleasure, experience*) indirect(e).

vice [vaɪs] *n* (*evil*) vice *m*; (*TECH*) étau *m*.

vice- [vaɪs] *prefix* vice-.

vice-chairman [vaɪs'tʃɛəmən] *n* vice-président/e.

vice-chancellor [vaɪs'tʃɑːnsələ*] *n* (*BRIT*) ≈ président/e d'université.

vice-president [vaɪs'prezɪdənt] *n* vice-président/e.

viceroy ['vaɪsrɔɪ] *n* vice-roi *m*.

vice squad *n* ≈ brigade mondaine.

vice versa ['vaɪsɪ'vəːsə] *adv* vice versa.

vicinity [vɪ'sɪnɪtɪ] *n* environs *mpl*, alentours *mpl*.

vicious ['vɪʃəs] *adj* (*remark*) cruel(le), méchant(e); (*blow*) brutal(e); **a ~ circle** un cercle vicieux.

viciousness ['vɪʃəsnɪs] *n* méchanceté *f*, cruauté *f*; brutalité *f*.

vicissitudes [vɪ'sɪsɪtjuːdz] *npl* vicissitudes *fpl*.

victim ['vɪktɪm] *n* victime *f*; **to be the ~ of** être victime de.

victimization [vɪktɪmaɪ'zeɪʃən] *n* brimades *fpl*; représailles *fpl*.

victimize ['vɪktɪmaɪz] *vt* brimer; exercer des représailles sur.

victor ['vɪktə*] *n* vainqueur *m*.

Victorian [vɪk'tɔːrɪən] *adj* victorien(ne).

victorious [vɪk'tɔːrɪəs] *adj* victorieux(euse).

victory ['vɪktərɪ] *n* victoire *f*; **to win a ~ over sb** remporter une victoire sur qn.

video ['vɪdɪəu] *n* (~ *film*) vidéo *f*; (*also:* ~ **cassette**) vidéocassette *f*; (*also:* ~ **cassette recorder**) magnétoscope *m* ♦ *vt* (*with recorder*) enregistrer; (*with camera*) filmer ♦ *cpd* vidéo *inv*.

video camera *n* caméra *f* vidéo *inv*.

video cassette *n* vidéocassette *f*.

video (cassette) recorder *n* magnétoscope *m*.

videodisc ['vɪdɪəudɪsk] *n* vidéodisque *m*.

video game *n* jeu *m* vidéo *inv*.

video nasty *n* vidéo à caractère violent ou pornographique.

videophone ['vɪdɪəufəun] *n* visiophone *m*, vidéophone *m*.

video recording *n* enregistrement *m* (en) vidéo *inv*.

video tape *n* bande *f* vidéo *inv*; (*cassette*) vidéocassette *f*.

vie [vaɪ] *vi*: **to ~ with** lutter avec, rivaliser avec.

Vienna [vɪ'ɛnə] *n* Vienne.

Vietnam, Viet Nam ['vjɛt'næm] *n* Viêt-nam *or* Vietnam *m*.

Vietnamese [vjɛtnə'miːz] *adj* vietnamien(ne) ♦ *n* (*pl inv*) Vietnamien/ne; (*LING*) vietnamien *m*.

view [vjuː] *n* vue *f*; (*opinion*) avis *m*, vue ♦ *vt* (*situation*) considérer; (*house*) visiter; **on ~** (*in museum etc*) exposé(e); **in full ~ of sb** sous les yeux de qn; **to be within ~ (of sth)** être à portée de vue (de qch); **an overall ~ of the situation** une vue d'ensemble de la situation; **in my ~** à mon avis; **in ~ of the fact that** étant donné que; **with a ~ to doing sth** dans l'intention de faire qch.

viewdata ['vjuːdeɪtə] *n* (*BRIT*) télétexte *m* (*version téléphonique*).

viewer ['vjuːə*] *n* (*viewfinder*) viseur *m*; (*small projector*) visionneuse *f*; (*TV*) téléspectateur/trice.

viewfinder ['vjuːfaɪndə*] *n* viseur *m*.

viewpoint ['vjuːpɔɪnt] *n* point *m* de vue.

vigil ['vɪdʒɪl] *n* veille *f*; **to keep ~** veiller.

vigilance ['vɪdʒɪləns] *n* vigilance *f*.

vigilance committee *n* comité *m* d'autodéfense.

vigilant ['vɪdʒɪlənt] *adj* vigilant(e).

vigilante [vɪdʒɪ'læntɪ] *n* justicier *ou* membre *m* d'un groupe d'autodéfense.

vigorous ['vɪgərəs] *adj* vigoureux(euse).

vigour, (*US*) vigor ['vɪgə*] *n* vigueur *f*.

vile [vaɪl] *adj* (*action*) vil(e); (*smell*) abominable; (*temper*) massacrant(e).

vilify ['vɪlɪfaɪ] *vt* calomnier, vilipender.

villa ['vɪlə] *n* villa *f*.

village ['vɪlɪdʒ] *n* village *m*.

villager ['vɪlɪdʒə*] *n* villageois/e.

villain ['vɪlən] *n* (*scoundrel*) scélérat *m*; (*criminal*) bandit *m*; (*in novel etc*) traître *m*.

VIN *n abbr* (*US*) = vehicle identification number.

vinaigrette [vɪneɪ'grɛt] *n* vinaigrette *f*.

vindicate ['vɪndɪkeɪt] *vt* défendre avec succès; justifier.

vindication [vɪndɪ'keɪʃən] *n*: **in ~ of** pour justifier.

vindictive [vɪn'dɪktɪv] *adj* vindicatif(ive), rancunier(ière).

vine [vaɪn] *n* vigne *f*; (*climbing plant*) plante grimpante.

vinegar ['vɪnɪgə*] *n* vinaigre *m*.

vine grower n viticulteur m.
vine-growing ['vaɪngrəʊɪŋ] adj viticole ♦ n viticulture f.
vineyard ['vɪnjɑːd] n vignoble m.
vintage ['vɪntɪdʒ] n (year) année f, millésime m; **the 1970** ~ le millésime 1970.
vintage car n voiture ancienne.
vintage wine n vin m de grand cru.
vinyl ['vaɪnl] n vinyle m.
viola [vɪ'əʊlə] n alto m.
violate ['vaɪəleɪt] vt violer.
violation [vaɪə'leɪʃən] n violation f; **in** ~ **of** (rule, law) en infraction à, en violation de.
violence ['vaɪələns] n violence f; (POL etc) incidents violents.
violent ['vaɪələnt] adj violent(e); **a** ~ **dislike of sb/sth** une aversion profonde pour qn/qch.
violently ['vaɪələntlɪ] adv violemment; (ill, angry) terriblement.
violet ['vaɪələt] adj (colour) violet(te) ♦ n (plant) violette f.
violin [vaɪə'lɪn] n violon m.
violinist [vaɪə'lɪnɪst] n violoniste m/f.
VIP n abbr (= very important person) VIP m.
viper ['vaɪpə*] n vipère f.
viral ['vaɪərəl] adj viral(e).
virgin ['vəːdʒɪn] n vierge f ♦ adj vierge; **she is a** ~ elle est vierge; **the Blessed V**~ la Sainte Vierge.
virginity [vəː'dʒɪnɪtɪ] n virginité f.
Virgo ['vəːgəʊ] n la Vierge; **to be** ~ être de la Vierge.
virile ['vɪraɪl] adj viril(e).
virility [vɪ'rɪlɪtɪ] n virilité f.
virtual ['vəːtjuəl] adj (COMPUT, PHYSICS) virtuel(le); (in effect): **it's a** ~ **impossibility** c'est quasiment impossible; **the** ~ **leader** le chef dans la pratique.
virtually ['vəːtjuəlɪ] adv (almost) pratiquement; **it is** ~ **impossible** c'est quasiment impossible.
virtual reality n réalité virtuelle.
virtue ['vəːtjuː] n vertu f; (advantage) mérite m, avantage m; **by** ~ **of** par le fait de.
virtuosity [vəːtju'ɒsɪtɪ] n virtuosité f.
virtuoso [vəːtju'əʊzəʊ] n virtuose m/f.
virtuous ['vəːtjuəs] adj vertueux(euse).
virulent ['vɪrulənt] adj virulent(e).
virus ['vaɪərəs] n virus m.
visa ['viːzə] n visa m.
vis-à-vis [viːzə'viː] prep vis-à-vis de.
viscount ['vaɪkaunt] n vicomte m.
viscous ['vɪskəs] adj visqueux(euse), gluant(e).
vise [vaɪs] n (US TECH) = **vice**.
visibility [vɪzɪ'bɪlɪtɪ] n visibilité f.
visible ['vɪzəbl] adj visible; ~ **exports/imports** exportations/importations fpl visibles.
visibly ['vɪzəblɪ] adv visiblement.
vision ['vɪʒən] n (sight) vue f, vision f; (foresight, in dream) vision.
visionary ['vɪʒənrɪ] n visionnaire m/f.

visit ['vɪzɪt] n visite f; (stay) séjour m ♦ vt (person) rendre visite à; (place) visiter; **on a private/official** ~ en visite privée/officielle.
visiting ['vɪzɪtɪŋ] adj (speaker, team) invité(e), de l'extérieur.
visiting card n carte f de visite.
visiting hours npl heures fpl de visite.
visiting professor n ≈ professeur associé.
visitor ['vɪzɪtə*] n visiteur/euse; (in hotel) client/e.
visitors' book n livre m d'or; (in hotel) registre m.
visor ['vaɪzə*] n visière f.
VISTA ['vɪstə] n abbr (= Volunteers in Service to America) programme d'assistance bénévole aux régions pauvres.
vista ['vɪstə] n vue f, perspective f.
visual ['vɪzjuəl] adj visuel(le).
visual aid n support visuel (pour l'enseignement).
visual arts npl arts mpl plastiques.
visual display unit (VDU) n console f de visualisation, visuel m.
visualize ['vɪzjuəlaɪz] vt se représenter; (foresee) prévoir.
visually ['vɪzjuəlɪ] adv visuellement; ~ **handicapped** handicapé(e) visuel(le).
vital ['vaɪtl] adj vital(e); **of** ~ **importance (to sb/sth)** d'une importance capitale (pour qn/qch).
vitality [vaɪ'tælɪtɪ] n vitalité f.
vitally ['vaɪtəlɪ] adv extrêmement.
vital statistics npl (of population) statistiques fpl démographiques; (col: woman's) mensurations fpl.
vitamin ['vɪtəmɪn] n vitamine f.
vitiate ['vɪʃɪeɪt] vt vicier.
vitreous ['vɪtrɪəs] adj (china) vitreux(euse); (enamel) vitrifié(e).
vitriolic [vɪtrɪ'ɒlɪk] adj (fig) venimeux(euse).
viva ['vaɪvə] n (also: ~ **voce**) (examen) oral.
vivacious [vɪ'veɪʃəs] adj animé(e), qui a de la vivacité.
vivacity [vɪ'væsɪtɪ] n vivacité f.
vivid ['vɪvɪd] adj (account) frappant(e); (light, imagination) vif(vive).
vividly ['vɪvɪdlɪ] adv (describe) d'une manière vivante; (remember) de façon précise.
vivisection [vɪvɪ'sɛkʃən] n vivisection f.
vixen ['vɪksn] n renarde f, (pej: woman) mégère f.
viz [vɪz] abbr (= vide licet: namely) à savoir, c. à d.
VLF abbr = very low frequency.
V-neck ['viːnɛk] n décolleté m en V.
VOA n abbr (= Voice of America) voix f de l'Amérique (émissions de radio à destination de l'étranger).
vocabulary [vəʊ'kæbjulərɪ] n vocabulaire m.
vocal ['vəʊkl] adj vocal(e); (articulate) qui n'hésite pas à s'exprimer, qui sait faire entendre ses opinions; ~**s** npl voix fpl.

vocal cords *npl* cordes vocales.
vocalist ['vəʊkəlɪst] *n* chanteur/euse.
vocation [vəʊ'keɪʃən] *n* vocation *f*.
vocational [vəʊ'keɪʃənl] *adj* professionnel(le); ~ **guidance/training** orientation/formation professionnelle.
vociferous [və'sɪfərəs] *adj* bruyant(e).
vodka ['vɒdkə] *n* vodka *f*.
vogue [vəʊg] *n* mode *f*; (*popularity*) vogue *f*; **to be in** ~ être en vogue *or* à la mode.
voice [vɔɪs] *n* voix *f*, (*opinion*) avis *m* ♦ *vt* (*opinion*) exprimer, formuler; **in a loud/soft** ~ à voix haute/basse; **to give** ~ **to** exprimer.
voice-over ['vɔɪsəʊvə*] *n* voix off *f*.
void [vɔɪd] *n* vide *m* ♦ *adj* (*invalid*) nul(le); (*empty*): ~ **of** vide de, dépourvu(e) de.
voile [vɔɪl] *n* voile *m* (*tissu*).
vol. *abbr* (= *volume*) vol.
volatile ['vɒlətaɪl] *adj* volatil(e); (*fig*) versatile.
volcanic [vɒl'kænɪk] *adj* volcanique.
volcano, ~**es** [vɒl'keɪnəʊ] *n* volcan *m*.
volition [və'lɪʃən] *n*: **of one's own** ~ de son propre gré.
volley ['vɒlɪ] *n* (*of gunfire*) salve *f*; (*of stones etc*) pluie *f*, volée *f*; (*TENNIS etc*) volée.
volleyball ['vɒlɪbɔːl] *n* volley(-ball) *m*.
volt [vəʊlt] *n* volt *m*.
voltage ['vəʊltɪdʒ] *n* tension *f*, voltage *m*; **high/low** ~ haute/basse tension.
voluble ['vɒljʊbl] *adj* volubile.
volume ['vɒljuːm] *n* volume *m*; (*of tank*) capacité *f*; ~ **one/two** (*of book*) tome un/deux; **his expression spoke** ~**s** son expression en disait long.
volume control *n* (*RADIO, TV*) bouton *m* de réglage du volume.
volume discount *n* (*COMM*) remise *f* sur la quantité.
voluminous [və'luːmɪnəs] *adj* volumineux(euse).
voluntarily ['vɒləntrɪlɪ] *adv* volontairement; bénévolement.
voluntary ['vɒləntərɪ] *adj* volontaire; (*unpaid*) bénévole.
voluntary liquidation *n* (*COMM*) dépôt *m* de bilan.
voluntary redundancy *n* (*BRIT*) départ *m* volontaire (*en cas de licenciements*).
volunteer [vɒlən'tɪə*] *n* volontaire *m/f* ♦ *vi* (*MIL*) s'engager comme volontaire; **to** ~ **to do** se proposer pour faire.
voluptuous [və'lʌptjʊəs] *adj* voluptueux(euse).
vomit ['vɒmɪt] *n* vomissure *f* ♦ *vt*, *vi* vomir.
voracious [və'reɪʃəs] *adj* vorace; (*reader*) avide.
vote [vəʊt] *n* vote *m*, suffrage *m*; (*cast*) voix *f*, vote; (*franchise*) droit *m* de vote ♦ *vt* (*bill*) voter; (*chairman*) élire ♦ *vi* voter; **to put sth to the** ~, **to take a** ~ **on sth** mettre qch aux voix, procéder à un vote sur qch; ~ **for** *or* **in favour of/against** vote pour/contre; **to** ~ **to**

do sth voter en faveur de faire qch; ~ **of censure** motion *f* de censure; ~ **of thanks** discours *m* de remerciement.
voter ['vəʊtə*] *n* électeur/trice.
voting ['vəʊtɪŋ] *n* scrutin *m*.
voting paper *n* (*BRIT*) bulletin *m* de vote.
voting right *n* droit *m* de vote.
vouch [vaʊtʃ]: **to** ~ **for** *vt fus* se porter garant de.
voucher ['vaʊtʃə*] *n* (*for meal, petrol*) bon *m*; (*receipt*) reçu *m*; **travel** ~ bon *m* de transport.
vow [vaʊ] *n* vœu *m*, serment *m* ♦ *vi* jurer; **to take** *or* **make a** ~ **to do sth** faire le vœu de faire qch.
vowel ['vaʊəl] *n* voyelle *f*.
voyage ['vɔɪɪdʒ] *n* voyage *m* par mer, traversée *f*.
voyeur [vwɑː'jə:*] *n* voyeur *m*.
VP *n abbr* = **vice-president**.
vs *abbr* (= *versus*) c.
VSO *n abbr* (*BRIT*: = *Voluntary Service Overseas*) ≈ coopération civile.
VT, Vt. *abbr* (*US*) = *Vermont*.
vulgar ['vʌlgə*] *adj* vulgaire.
vulgarity [vʌl'gærɪtɪ] *n* vulgarité *f*.
vulnerability [vʌlnərə'bɪlɪtɪ] *n* vulnérabilité *f*.
vulnerable ['vʌlnərəbl] *adj* vulnérable.
vulture ['vʌltʃə*] *n* vautour *m*.

W w

W, w ['dʌblju:] *n* (*letter*) W, w *m*; **W for William** W comme William.
W *abbr* (= *west*) O; (*ELEC*: = *watt*) W.
WA *abbr* (*US*) = *Washington*.
wad [wɒd] *n* (*of cotton wool, paper*) tampon *m*; (*of banknotes etc*) liasse *f*.
wadding ['wɒdɪŋ] *n* rembourrage *m*.
waddle ['wɒdl] *vi* se dandiner.
wade [weɪd] *vi*: **to** ~ **through** marcher dans, patauger dans ♦ *vt* passer à gué.
wafer ['weɪfə*] *n* (*CULIN*) gaufrette *f*; (*REL*) pain *m* d'hostie; (*COMPUT*) tranche *f* (de silicium).
wafer-thin ['weɪfə'θɪn] *adj* ultra-mince, mince comme du papier à cigarette.
waffle ['wɒfl] *n* (*CULIN*) gaufre *f*; (*col*) rabâchage *m*; remplissage *m* ♦ *vi* parler pour ne rien dire; faire du remplissage.
waffle iron *n* gaufrier *m*.
waft [wɒft] *vt* porter ♦ *vi* flotter.
wag [wæg] *vt* agiter, remuer ♦ *vi* remuer; **the dog** ~**ged its tail** le chien a remué la queue.
wage [weɪdʒ] *n* (*also*: ~**s**) salaire *m*, paye *f* ♦ *vt*: **to** ~ **war** faire la guerre; **a day's** ~**s** un

jour de salaire.

wage claim n demande f d'augmentation de salaire.

wage differential n éventail m des salaires.

wage earner [-ɔːnə*] n salarié/e; (*bread-winner*) soutien m de famille.

wage freeze n blocage m des salaires.

wage packet n (*BRIT*) (enveloppe f de) paye f.

wager ['weɪdʒə*] n pari m ♦ vt parier.

waggle ['wægl] vt, vi remuer.

wag(g)on ['wægən] n (*horse-drawn*) chariot m; (*BRIT RAIL*) wagon m (de marchandises).

wail [weɪl] n gémissement m; (*of siren*) hurlement m ♦ vi gémir; hurler.

waist [weɪst] n taille f, ceinture f.

waistcoat ['weɪskəut] n (*BRIT*) gilet m.

waistline ['weɪstlaɪn] n (tour m de) taille f.

wait [weɪt] n attente f ♦ vi attendre; **to ~ for sb/sth** attendre qn/qch; **to keep sb ~ing** faire attendre qn; **~ a minute!** un instant!; **"repairs while you ~"** "réparations minute"; **I can't ~ to ...** (*fig*) je meurs d'envie de ...; **to lie in ~ for** guetter.

▶**wait behind** vi rester (à attendre).

▶**wait on** vt fus servir.

▶**wait up** vi attendre, ne pas se coucher; **don't ~ up for me** ne m'attendez pas pour aller vous coucher.

waiter ['weɪtə*] n garçon m (de café), serveur m.

waiting ['weɪtɪŋ] n: **"no ~"** (*BRIT AUT*) "stationnement interdit".

waiting list n liste f d'attente.

waiting room n salle f d'attente.

waitress ['weɪtrɪs] n serveuse f.

waive [weɪv] vt renoncer à, abandonner.

waiver ['weɪvə*] n dispense f.

wake [weɪk] vb (*pt* **woke**, **~d**, *pp* **woken**, **~d** [wəuk, 'wəukn]) vt (*also*: ~ **up**) réveiller ♦ vi (*also*: ~ **up**) se réveiller ♦ n (*for dead person*) veillée f mortuaire; (*NAUT*) sillage m; **to ~ up to sth** (*fig*) se rendre compte de qch; **in the ~ of** (*fig*) à la suite de; **to follow in sb's ~** (*fig*) marcher sur les traces de qn.

waken ['weɪkn] vt, vi = **wake**.

Wales [weɪlz] n pays m de Galles.

walk [wɔːk] n promenade f; (*short*) petit tour; (*gait*) démarche f; (*pace*): **at a quick ~** d'un pas rapide; (*path*) chemin m; (*in park etc*) allée f ♦ vi marcher; (*for pleasure, exercise*) se promener ♦ vt (*distance*) faire à pied; (*dog*) promener; **10 minutes' ~ from** à 10 minutes de marche de; **to go for a ~** se promener; faire un tour; **I'll ~ you home** je vais vous raccompagner chez vous; **from all ~s of life** de toutes conditions sociales.

▶**walk out** vi (*go out*) sortir; (*as protest*) partir (en signe de protestation); (*strike*) se mettre en grève; **to ~ out on sb** quitter qn.

walkabout ['wɔːkəbaut] n: **to go (on a) ~** (*VIP*) prendre un bain de foule.

walker ['wɔːkə*] n (*person*) marcheur/euse.

walkie-talkie ['wɔːkɪ'tɔːkɪ] n talkie-walkie m.

walking ['wɔːkɪŋ] n marche f à pied; **it's within ~ distance** on peut y aller à pied.

walking holiday n vacances passées à faire de la randonnée.

walking shoes npl chaussures fpl de marche.

walking stick n canne f.

Walkman ['wɔːkmən] n ® Walkman m ®.

walk-on ['wɔːkɔn] adj (*THEAT: part*) de figurant/e.

walkout ['wɔːkaut] n (*of workers*) grève-surprise f.

walkover ['wɔːkəuvə*] n (*col*) victoire f or examen m etc facile.

walkway ['wɔːkweɪ] n promenade f, cheminement piéton.

wall [wɔːl] n mur m; (*of tunnel, cave*) paroi f; **to go to the ~** (*fig: firm etc*) faire faillite.

▶**wall in** vt (*garden etc*) entourer d'un mur.

wall cupboard n placard mural.

walled [wɔːld] adj (*city*) fortifié(e).

wallet ['wɔlɪt] n portefeuille m.

wallflower ['wɔːlflauə*] n giroflée f; **to be a ~** (*fig*) faire tapisserie.

wall hanging n tenture (murale), tapisserie f.

wallop ['wɔləp] vt (*BRIT col*) taper sur, cogner.

wallow ['wɔləu] vi se vautrer; **to ~ in one's grief** se complaire à sa douleur.

wallpaper ['wɔːlpeɪpə*] n papier peint.

wall-to-wall ['wɔːltə'wɔːl] adj: **~ carpeting** moquette f.

wally ['wɔlɪ] n (*col*) imbécile m/f.

walnut ['wɔːlnʌt] n noix f; (*tree*) noyer m.

walrus, *pl* **~** *or* **~es** ['wɔːlrəs] n morse m.

waltz [wɔːlts] n valse f ♦ vi valser.

wan [wɔn] adj pâle; triste.

wand [wɔnd] n (*also*: **magic ~**) baguette f (magique).

wander ['wɔndə*] vi (*person*) errer, aller sans but; (*thoughts*) vagabonder; (*river*) serpenter ♦ vt errer dans.

wanderer ['wɔndərə*] n vagabond/e.

wandering ['wɔndrɪŋ] adj (*tribe*) nomade; (*minstrel, actor*) ambulant/e.

wane [weɪn] vi (*moon*) décroître; (*reputation*) décliner.

wangle ['wæŋgl] (*BRIT col*) vt se débrouiller pour avoir; carotter ♦ n combine f, magouille f.

wanker ['wæŋkə*] n (*col!*) branleur m (!).

want [wɔnt] vt vouloir; (*need*) avoir besoin de; (*lack*) manquer de ♦ n (*poverty*) pauvreté f, besoin m; **~s** npl (*needs*) besoins mpl; **for ~ of** par manque de, faute de; **to ~ to do** vouloir faire; **to ~ sb to do** vouloir que qn fasse; **you're ~ed on the phone** on vous demande au téléphone; **"cook ~ed"** "on demande un cuisinier".

want ads npl (*US*) petites annonces.

wanting ['wɔntɪŋ] adj: **to be ~ (in)** manquer (de); **to be found ~** ne pas être à la hauteur.

wanton ['wɒntn] *adj* capricieux(euse); déver-
gondé(e).

war [wɔː*] *n* guerre *f*; **to go to** ~ se mettre en
guerre.

warble ['wɔːbl] *n* (*of bird*) gazouillis *m* ♦ *vi* gazouiller.

war cry *n* cri *m* de guerre.

ward [wɔːd] *n* (*in hospital*) salle *f*; (*POL*) section
électorale; (*LAW: child*) pupille *m/f*.

►**ward off** *vt* parer, éviter.

warden ['wɔːdn] *n* (*BRIT: of institution*)
directeur/trice; (*of park, game reserve*)
gardien/ne; (*BRIT: also:* **traffic** ~)
contractuel/le.

warder ['wɔːdə*] *n* (*BRIT*) gardien *m* de prison.

wardrobe ['wɔːdrəub] *n* (*cupboard*) armoire *f*;
(*clothes*) garde-robe *f*; (*THEAT*) costumes *mpl*.

warehouse ['wɛəhaus] *n* entrepôt *m*.

wares [wɛəz] *npl* marchandises *fpl*.

warfare ['wɔːfɛə*] *n* guerre *f*.

war game *n* jeu *m* de stratégie militaire.

warhead ['wɔːhɛd] *n* (*MIL*) ogive *f*.

warily ['wɛərɪlɪ] *adv* avec prudence, avec précaution.

warlike ['wɔːlaɪk] *adj* guerrier(ière).

warm [wɔːm] *adj* chaud(e); (*person, greeting,
welcome, applause*) chaleureux(euse); (*supporter*) ardent(e), enthousiaste; **it's** ~ il fait
chaud; **I'm** ~ j'ai chaud; **to keep sth** ~ tenir
qch au chaud; **with my** ~**est thanks/con-
gratulations** avec mes remerciements/mes
félicitations les plus sincères.

►**warm up** *vi* (*person, room*) se réchauffer;
(*water*) chauffer; (*athlete, discussion*)
s'échauffer ♦ *vt* réchauffer; chauffer; (*engine*) faire chauffer.

warm-blooded ['wɔːm'blʌdɪd] *adj* (*ZOOL*) à
sang chaud.

war memorial *n* monument *m* aux morts.

warm-hearted [wɔːm'hɑːtɪd] *adj* affec-
tueux(euse).

warmly ['wɔːmlɪ] *adv* chaudement; chaleureusement.

warmonger ['wɔːmʌŋgə*] *n* belliciste *m/f*.

warmongering ['wɔːmʌŋgrɪŋ] *n* propagande *f*
belliciste, bellicisme *m*.

warmth [wɔːmθ] *n* chaleur *f*.

warm-up ['wɔːmʌp] *n* (*SPORT*) période *f*
d'échauffement.

warn [wɔːn] *vt* avertir, prévenir; **to** ~ **sb not
to do sth** *or* **against doing sth** prévenir qn
de ne pas faire qch.

warning ['wɔːnɪŋ] *n* avertissement *m*; (*notice*)
avis *m*; **without (any)** ~ (*suddenly*) inopinément; (*without notifying*) sans prévenir; **gale**
~ (*METEOROLOGY*) avis de grand vent.

warning light *n* avertisseur lumineux.

warning triangle *n* (*AUT*) triangle *m* de pré-
signalisation.

warp [wɔːp] *n* (*TEXTILES*) chaîne *f* ♦ *vi* (*wood*)
travailler, se voiler *or* gauchir ♦ *vt* voiler;

(*fig*) pervertir.

warpath ['wɔːpɑːθ] *n*: **to be on the** ~ (*fig*) être
sur le sentier de la guerre.

warped [wɔːpt] *adj* (*wood*) gauchi(e); (*fig*) per-
verti(e).

warrant ['wɔrnt] *n* (*guarantee*) garantie *f*;
(*LAW: to arrest*) mandat *m* d'arrêt; (: *to search*)
mandat de perquisition ♦ *vt* (*justify, merit*)
justifier.

warrant officer *n* (*MIL*) adjudant *m*; (*NAUT*)
premier-maître *m*.

warranty ['wɒrəntɪ] *n* garantie *f*; **under** ~
(*COMM*) sous garantie.

warren ['wɒrən] *n* (*of rabbits*) terriers *mpl*, garenne *f*.

warring ['wɔːrɪŋ] *adj* (*nations*) en guerre; (*interests etc*) contradictoire, opposé(e).

warrior ['wɒrɪə*] *n* guerrier/ière.

Warsaw ['wɔːsɔː] *n* Varsovie.

warship ['wɔːʃɪp] *n* navire *m* de guerre.

wart [wɔːt] *n* verrue *f*.

wartime ['wɔːtaɪm] *n*: **in** ~ en temps de
guerre.

wary ['wɛərɪ] *adj* prudent(e); **to be** ~ **about** *or*
of doing sth hésiter beaucoup à faire qch.

was [wɒz] *pt of* **be**.

wash [wɒʃ] *vt* laver; (*sweep, carry: sea etc*) emporter, entraîner; (: *ashore*) rejeter ♦ *vi* se
laver ♦ *n* (*paint*) badigeon *m*; (*washing programme*) lavage *m*; (*of ship*) sillage *m*; **to give
sth a** ~ laver qch; **to have a** ~ se laver,
faire sa toilette; **he was** ~**ed overboard** il a
été emporté par une vague.

►**wash away** *vt* (*stain*) enlever au lavage;
(*subj: river etc*) emporter.

►**wash down** *vt* laver; laver à grande eau.

►**wash off** *vi* partir au lavage.

►**wash up** *vi* faire la vaisselle; (*US: have a
wash*) se débarbouiller.

Wash. *abbr* (*US*) = *Washington*.

washable ['wɒʃəbl] *adj* lavable.

washbasin ['wɒʃbeɪsn] *n* lavabo *m*.

washcloth ['wɒʃklɒθ] *n* (*US*) gant *m* de toilette.

washer ['wɒʃə*] *n* (*TECH*) rondelle *f*, joint *m*.

washing ['wɒʃɪŋ] *n* (*BRIT: linen etc*) lessive *f*.

washing line *n* (*BRIT*) corde *f* à linge.

washing machine *n* machine *f* à laver.

washing powder *n* (*BRIT*) lessive *f* (en
poudre).

Washington ['wɒʃɪŋtən] *n* (*city, state*) Washington *m*.

washing-up [wɒʃɪŋ'ʌp] *n* (*BRIT*) vaisselle *f*.

washing-up liquid *n* (*BRIT*) produit *m* pour la
vaisselle.

wash-out ['wɒʃaut] *n* (*col*) désastre *m*.

washroom ['wɒʃrum] *n* toilettes *fpl*.

wasn't ['wɒznt] = **was not**.

Wasp, WASP [wɒsp] *n abbr* (*US col*: = *White
Anglo-Saxon Protestant*) *surnom, souvent péjoratif, donné à l'américain de souche
anglo-saxonne, aisé et de tendance conser-*

vatrice.
wasp [wɔsp] *n* guêpe *f.*
waspish ['wɔspɪʃ] *adj* irritable.
wastage ['weɪstɪdʒ] *n* gaspillage *m*; (*in manufacturing, transport etc*) déchet *m.*
waste [weɪst] *n* gaspillage *m*; (*of time*) perte *f*; (*rubbish*) déchets *mpl*; (*also:* **household ~**) ordures *fpl* ♦ *adj* (*material*) de rebut; (*energy, heat*) perdu(e); (*food*) inutilisé(e); (*land, ground: in city*) à l'abandon; (*: in country*) inculte, en friche ♦ *vt* gaspiller; (*time, opportunity*) perdre; **~s** *npl* étendue *f* désertique; **it's a ~ of money** c'est de l'argent jeté en l'air; **to go to ~** être gaspillé(e); **to lay ~** (*destroy*) dévaster.
▶**waste away** *vi* dépérir.
wastebasket ['weɪstbɑːskɪt] *n* = **wastepaper basket**.
waste disposal (unit) *n* (*BRIT*) broyeur *m* d'ordures.
wasteful ['weɪstful] *adj* gaspilleur(euse); (*process*) peu économique.
waste ground *n* (*BRIT*) terrain *m* vague.
wasteland ['weɪstlənd] *n* terres *fpl* à l'abandon; (*in town*) terrain(s) *m(pl)* vague(s).
wastepaper basket ['weɪstpeɪpə-] *n* corbeille *f* à papier.
waste pipe *n* (tuyau *m* de) vidange *f.*
waste products *npl* (*INDUSTRY*) déchets *mpl* (de fabrication).
waster ['weɪstə*] *n* (*col*) bon/ne à rien.
watch [wɔtʃ] *n* montre *f*; (*act of watching*) surveillance *f*; guet *m*; (*guard: MIL*) sentinelle *f*; (*: NAUT*) homme *m* de quart; (*NAUT: spell of duty*) quart *m* ♦ *vt* (*look at*) observer; (*: match, programme*) regarder; (*spy on, guard*) surveiller; (*be careful of*) faire attention à ♦ *vi* regarder; (*keep guard*) monter la garde; **to keep a close ~ on sb/sth** surveiller qn/qch de près; **~ what you're doing** fais attention à ce que tu fais.
▶**watch out** *vi* faire attention.
watchband ['wɔtʃbænd] *n* (*US*) bracelet *m* de montre.
watchdog ['wɔtʃdɔg] *n* chien *m* de garde; (*fig*) gardien/ne.
watchful ['wɔtʃful] *adj* attentif(ive), vigilant(e).
watchmaker ['wɔtʃmeɪkə*] *n* horloger/ère.
watchman ['wɔtʃmən] *n* gardien *m*; (*also:* **night ~**) veilleur *m* de nuit.
watch stem *n* (*US*) remontoir *m.*
watch strap *n* bracelet *m* de montre.
watchword ['wɔtʃwəːd] *n* mot *m* de passe.
water ['wɔːtə*] *n* eau *f* ♦ *vt* (*plant*) arroser ♦ *vi* (*eyes*) larmoyer; **a drink of ~** un verre d'eau; **in British ~s** dans les eaux territoriales Britanniques; **to pass ~** uriner; **to make sb's mouth ~** mettre l'eau à la bouche de qn.
▶**water down** *vt* (*milk*) couper d'eau; (*fig: story*) édulcorer.

water closet *n* (*BRIT*) w.-c. *mpl*, waters *mpl.*
watercolour, (*US*) **watercolor** ['wɔːtəkʌlə*] *n* aquarelle *f*; **~s** *npl* couleurs *fpl* pour aquarelle.
water-cooled ['wɔːtəkuːld] *adj* à refroidissement par eau.
watercress ['wɔːtəkrɛs] *n* cresson *m* (de fontaine).
waterfall ['wɔːtəfɔːl] *n* chute *f* d'eau.
waterfront ['wɔːtəfrʌnt] *n* (*seafront*) front *m* de mer; (*at docks*) quais *mpl.*
water heater *n* chauffe-eau *m.*
water hole *n* mare *f.*
water ice *n* (*BRIT*) sorbet *m.*
watering can ['wɔːtərɪŋ-] *n* arrosoir *m.*
water level *n* niveau *m* de l'eau; (*of flood*) niveau des eaux.
water lily *n* nénuphar *m.*
waterline ['wɔːtəlaɪn] *n* (*NAUT*) ligne *f* de flottaison.
waterlogged ['wɔːtəlɔgd] *adj* détrempé(e); imbibé(e) d'eau.
water main *n* canalisation *f* d'eau.
watermark ['wɔːtəmɑːk] *n* (*on paper*) filigrane *m.*
watermelon ['wɔːtəmɛlən] *n* pastèque *f.*
water polo *n* water-polo *m.*
waterproof ['wɔːtəpruːf] *adj* imperméable.
water-repellent ['wɔːtərɪ'pɛlnt] *adj* hydrofuge.
watershed ['wɔːtəʃɛd] *n* (*GEO*) ligne *f* de partage des eaux; (*fig*) moment *m* critique, point décisif.
water-skiing ['wɔːtəskiːɪŋ] *n* ski *m* nautique.
water softener *n* adoucisseur *m* d'eau.
water tank *n* réservoir *m* d'eau.
watertight ['wɔːtətaɪt] *adj* étanche.
water vapour *n* vapeur *f* d'eau.
waterway ['wɔːtəweɪ] *n* cours *m* d'eau navigable.
waterworks ['wɔːtəwəːks] *npl* station *f* hydraulique.
watery ['wɔːtərɪ] *adj* (*colour*) délavé(e); (*coffee*) trop faible.
watt [wɔt] *n* watt *m.*
wattage ['wɔtɪdʒ] *n* puissance *f* or consommation *f* en watts.
wattle ['wɔtl] *n* clayonnage *m.*
wave [weɪv] *n* vague *f*; (*of hand*) geste *m*, signe *m*; (*RADIO*) onde *f*; (*in hair*) ondulation *f*; (*fig: of enthusiasm, strikes etc*) vague ♦ *vi* faire signe de la main; (*flag*) flotter au vent ♦ *vt* (*handkerchief*) agiter; (*stick*) brandir; (*hair*) onduler; **to ~ goodbye to sb** dire au revoir de la main à qn; **short/medium ~** (*RADIO*) ondes courtes/moyennes; **long ~** (*RADIO*) grandes ondes; **the new ~** (*CINE, MUS*) la nouvelle vague.
▶**wave aside, wave away** *vt* (*person*): **to ~ sb aside** faire signe à qn de s'écarter;. (*fig: suggestion, objection*) rejeter, repousser; (*: doubts*) chasser.

waveband ['weɪvbænd] *n* bande *f* de fréquences.

wavelength ['weɪvlɛŋθ] *n* longueur *f* d'ondes.

waver ['weɪvə*] *vi* vaciller; (*voice*) trembler; (*person*) hésiter.

wavy ['weɪvɪ] *adj* ondulé(e); onduleux(euse).

wax [wæks] *n* cire *f*; (*for skis*) fart *m* ♦ *vt* cirer; (*car*) lustrer ♦ *vi* (*moon*) croître.

waxen [wæksn] *adj* cireux(euse).

waxworks ['wækswɔːks] *npl* personnages *mpl* de cire; musée *m* de cire.

way [weɪ] *n* chemin *m*, voie *f*; (*path, access*) passage *m*; (*distance*) distance *f*; (*direction*) chemin, direction *f*; (*manner*) façon *f*, manière *f*; (*habit*) habitude *f*, façon; (*condition*) état *m*; **which** ~? — **this** ~ par où *or* de quel côté? — par ici; **to crawl one's** ~ **to ...** ramper jusqu'à ...; **to lie one's** ~ **out of it** s'en sortir par un mensonge; **to lose one's** ~ perdre son chemin; **on the** ~ **(to)** en route (pour); **to be on one's** ~ être en route; **to be in the** ~ bloquer le passage; (*fig*) gêner; **to keep out of sb's** ~ éviter qn; **it's a long** ~ **away** c'est loin d'ici; **the village is rather out of the** ~ le village est plutôt à l'écart *or* isolé; **to go out of one's** ~ **to do** (*fig*) se donner beaucoup de mal pour faire; **to be under** ~ (*work, project*) être en cours; **to make** ~ **(for sb/sth)** faire place (à qn/qch), s'écarter pour laisser passer (qn/qch); **to get one's own** ~ arriver à ses fins; **put it the right** ~ **up** (*BRIT*) mettez-le dans le bon sens; **to be the wrong** ~ **round** être à l'envers, ne pas être dans le bon sens; **he's in a bad** ~ il va mal; **in a** ~ d'un côté; **in some** ~s à certains égards; d'un côté; **in the** ~ **of** en fait de, comme; **by** ~ **of** (*through*) en passant par, via; (*as a sort of*) en guise de; "~ **in**" (*BRIT*) "entrée"; "~ **out**" (*BRIT*) "sortie"; **the** ~ **back** le chemin du retour; **this** ~ **and that** par-ci par-là; "**give** ~" (*BRIT AUT*) "cédez la priorité"; **no** ~! (*col*) pas question!

waybill ['weɪbɪl] *n* (*COMM*) récépissé *m*.

waylay ['weɪ'leɪ] *vt irreg* attaquer; (*fig*): **I got waylaid** quelqu'un m'a accroché.

wayside ['weɪsaɪd] *n* bord *m* de la route; **to fall by the** ~ (*fig*) abandonner; (*morally*) quitter le droit chemin.

way station *n* (*US RAIL*) petite gare; (: *fig*) étape *f*.

wayward ['weɪwəd] *adj* capricieux(euse), entêté(e).

WC *n abbr* (*BRIT*: = *water closet*) w.-c. *mpl*, waters *mpl*.

WCC *n abbr* (= *World Council of Churches*) COE *m* (= *Conseil œcuménique des Églises*).

we [wiː] *pl pron* nous.

weak [wiːk] *adj* faible; (*health*) fragile; (*beam etc*) peu solide; (*tea, coffee*) léger(ère); **to grow** ~(**er**) s'affaiblir, faiblir.

weaken ['wiːkn] *vi* faiblir ♦ *vt* affaiblir.

weak-kneed ['wiːk'niːd] *adj* (*fig*) lâche, faible.

weakling ['wiːklɪŋ] *n* gringalet *m*; faible *m/f*.

weakly ['wiːklɪ] *adj* chétif(ive) ♦ *adv* faiblement.

weakness ['wiːknɪs] *n* faiblesse *f*; (*fault*) point *m* faible.

wealth [wɛlθ] *n* (*money, resources*) richesse(s) *f(pl)*; (*of details*) profusion *f*.

wealth tax *n* impôt *m* sur la fortune.

wealthy ['wɛlθɪ] *adj* riche.

wean [wiːn] *vt* sevrer.

weapon ['wɛpən] *n* arme *f*.

wear [wɛə*] *n* (*use*) usage *m*; (*deterioration through use*) usure *f*; (*clothing*): **sports/baby**~ vêtements *mpl* de sport/pour bébés; **town/ evening** ~ tenue *f* de ville/de soirée ♦ *vb* (*pt wore, pp worn* [wɔː*, wɔːn]) *vt* (*clothes*) porter; (*beard etc*) avoir; (*damage: through use*) user ♦ *vi* (*last*) faire de l'usage; (*rub etc through*) s'user; ~ **and tear** usure *f*; **to** ~ **a hole in sth** faire (à la longue) un trou dans qch.

►**wear away** *vt* user, ronger ♦ *vi* s'user, être rongé(e).

►**wear down** *vt* user; (*strength*) épuiser.

►**wear off** *vi* disparaître.

►**wear on** *vi* se poursuivre; passer.

►**wear out** *vt* user; (*person, strength*) épuiser.

wearable ['wɛərəbl] *adj* mettable.

wearily ['wɪərɪlɪ] *adv* avec lassitude.

weariness ['wɪərɪnɪs] *n* épuisement *m*, lassitude *f*.

wearisome ['wɪərɪsəm] *adj* (*tiring*) fatigant(e); (*boring*) ennuyeux(euse).

weary ['wɪərɪ] *adj* (*tired*) épuisé(e); (*dispirited*) las(lasse); abattu(e) ♦ *vt* lasser ♦ *vi*: **to** ~ **of** se lasser de.

weasel ['wiːzl] *n* (*ZOOL*) belette *f*.

weather ['wɛðə*] *n* temps *m* ♦ *vt* (*wood*) faire mûrir; (*tempest, crisis*) essuyer, être pris(e) dans; survivre à, tenir le coup durant; **what's the** ~ **like?** quel temps fait-il?; **under the** ~ (*fig: ill*) mal fichu(e).

weather-beaten ['wɛðəbiːtn] *adj* (*person*) hâlé(e); (*building*) dégradé(e) par les intempéries.

weather cock *n* girouette *f*.

weather forecast *n* prévisions *fpl* météorologiques, météo *f*.

weatherman ['wɛðəmæn] *n* météorologue *m*.

weatherproof ['wɛðəpruːf] *adj* (*garment*) imperméable; (*building*) étanche.

weather report *n* bulletin *m* météo, météo *f*.

weather vane [-veɪn] *n* = **weather cock**.

weave [wiːv], *pt* **wove**, *pp* **woven** [wiːv, wəuv, 'wəuvn] *vt* (*cloth*) tisser; (*basket*) tresser ♦ *vi* (*fig: pt, pp* ~**d**: *move in and out*) se faufiler.

weaver ['wiːvə*] *n* tisserand/e.

weaving ['wiːvɪŋ] *n* tissage *m*.

web [wɛb] *n* (*of spider*) toile *f*; (*on foot*) palmure *f*; (*fabric, also fig*) tissu *m*.

webbed [wɛbd] *adj* (*foot*) palmé(e).

webbing ['wɛbɪŋ] *n* (*on chair*) sangles *fpl*.

wed [wɛd] vt (pt, pp **wedded**) épouser ♦ n: **the newly-~s** les jeunes mariés.

Wed. abbr (= Wednesday) me.

we'd [wi:d] = we had, we would.

wedded ['wɛdɪd] pt, pp of **wed**.

wedding ['wɛdɪŋ] n mariage m.

wedding anniversary n anniversaire m de mariage; **silver/golden** ~ noces fpl d'argent/ d'or.

wedding day n jour m du mariage.

wedding dress n robe f de mariée.

wedding present n cadeau m de mariage.

wedding ring n alliance f.

wedge [wɛdʒ] n (of wood etc) coin m; (under door etc) cale f; (of cake) part f ♦ vt (fix) caler; (push) enfoncer, coincer.

wedge-heeled shoes ['wɛdʒhi:ld-] npl chaussures fpl à semelles compensées.

wedlock ['wɛdlɔk] n (union f du) mariage m.

Wednesday ['wɛdnzdɪ] n mercredi m; for phrases see also **Tuesday**.

wee [wi:] adj (Scottish) petit(e); tout(e) petit(e).

weed [wi:d] n mauvaise herbe ♦ vt désherber.

▶**weed out** vt éliminer.

weed-killer ['wi:dkɪlə*] n désherbant m.

weedy ['wi:dɪ] adj (man) gringalet.

week [wi:k] n semaine f; **once/twice a** ~ une fois/deux fois par semaine; **in two ~s' time** dans quinze jours; **Tuesday** ~, **a** ~ **on Tuesday** mardi en huit.

weekday ['wi:kdeɪ] n jour m de semaine; (COMM) jour ouvrable; **on ~s** en semaine.

weekend [wi:k'ɛnd] n week-end m.

weekend case n sac m de voyage.

weekly ['wi:klɪ] adv une fois par semaine, chaque semaine ♦ adj, n hebdomadaire (m).

weep, pt, pp **wept** [wi:p, wɛpt] vi (person) pleurer; (MED: wound etc) suinter.

weeping willow ['wi:pɪŋ-] n saule pleureur.

weepy ['wi:pɪ] n (col: film) mélo m.

weft [wɛft] n (TEXTILES) trame f.

weigh [weɪ] vt, vi peser; **to** ~ **anchor** lever l'ancre; **to** ~ **the pros and cons** peser le pour et le contre.

▶**weigh down** vt (branch) faire plier; (fig: with worry) accabler.

▶**weigh out** vt (goods) peser.

▶**weigh up** vt examiner.

weighbridge ['weɪbrɪdʒ] n pont-bascule m.

weighing machine ['weɪɪŋ-] n balance f, bascule f.

weight [weɪt] n poids m ♦ vt alourdir; (fig: factor) pondérer; **sold by** ~ vendu au poids; **to put on/lose** ~ grossir/maigrir; **~s and measures** poids et mesures.

weighting ['weɪtɪŋ] n: ~ **allowance** indemnité f de résidence.

weightlessness ['weɪtlɪsnɪs] n apesanteur f.

weightlifter ['weɪtlɪftə*] n haltérophile m.

weight training n musculation f.

weighty ['weɪtɪ] adj lourd(e).

weir [wɪə*] n barrage m.

weird [wɪəd] adj bizarre; (eerie) surnaturel(le).

weirdo ['wɪədəu] n (col) type m bizarre.

welcome ['wɛlkəm] adj bienvenu(e) ♦ n accueil m ♦ vt accueillir; (also: **bid** ~) souhaiter la bienvenue à; (be glad of) se réjouir de; **to be** ~ être le(la) bienvenu(e); **to make sb** ~ faire bon accueil à qn; **you're** ~ **to try** vous pouvez essayer si vous voulez; **you're** ~! (after thanks) de rien, il n'y a pas de quoi.

welcoming ['wɛlkəmɪŋ] adj accueillant(e); (speech) d'accueil.

weld [wɛld] n soudure f ♦ vt souder.

welder ['wɛldə*] n (person) soudeur m.

welding ['wɛldɪŋ] n soudure f (autogène).

welfare ['wɛlfɛə*] n bien-être m.

welfare state n État-providence m.

welfare work n travail social.

well [wɛl] n puits m ♦ adv bien ♦ adj: **to be** ~ aller bien ♦ excl eh bien!; bon!; enfin!; ~ **done!** bravo!; **I don't feel** ~ je ne me sens pas bien; **get** ~ **soon!** remets-toi vite!; **to do** ~ **in sth** bien réussir en or dans qch; **to think** ~ **of sb** penser du bien de qn; **as** ~ (in addition) aussi, également; **you might as** ~ **tell me** tu ferais aussi bien de me le dire; **as** ~ **as** aussi bien que or de; en plus de; ~, **as I was saying** ... donc, comme je disais ....

▶**well up** vi (tears, emotions) monter.

we'll [wi:l] = we will, we shall.

well-behaved ['wɛlbɪ'heɪvd] adj sage, obéissant(e).

well-being ['wɛl'bi:ɪŋ] n bien-être m.

well-bred ['wɛl'brɛd] adj bien élevé(e).

well-built ['wɛl'bɪlt] adj (house) bien construit(e); (person) bien bâti(e).

well-chosen ['wɛl'tʃəuzn] adj (remarks, words) bien choisi(e), pertinent(e).

well-developed ['wɛldɪ'vɛləpt] adj (girl) bien fait(e).

well-disposed ['wɛldɪs'pəuzd] adj: ~ **to(wards)** bien disposé(e) envers.

well-dressed ['wɛl'drɛst] adj bien habillé(e), bien vêtu(e).

well-earned ['wɛl'ə:nd] adj (rest) bien mérité(e).

well-groomed ['wɛl'gru:md] adj très soigné(e) de sa personne.

well-heeled ['wɛl'hi:ld] adj (col: wealthy) fortuné(e), riche.

well-informed ['wɛlɪn'fɔ:md] adj (having knowledge of sth) bien renseigné(e); (having general knowledge) cultivé(e).

Wellington ['wɛlɪŋtən] n Wellington.

wellingtons ['wɛlɪŋtənz] npl (also: **wellington boots**) bottes fpl de caoutchouc.

well-kept ['wɛl'kɛpt] adj (house, grounds) bien tenu(e), bien entretenu(e); (secret) bien gardé(e); (hair, hands) soigné(e).

well-known ['wɛl'nəun] adj (person) bien connu(e).

well-mannered ['wɛl'mænəd] *adj* bien élevé(e).

well-meaning ['wɛl'miːnɪŋ] *adj* bien intentionné(e).

well-nigh ['wɛl'naɪ] *adv:* ~ **impossible** pratiquement impossible.

well-off ['wɛl'ɔf] *adj* aisé(e), assez riche.

well-read ['wɛl'rɛd] *adj* cultivé(e).

well-spoken ['wɛl'spəukn] *adj* (*person*) qui parle bien; (*words*) bien choisi(e).

well-stocked ['wɛl'stɔkt] *adj* bien approvisionné(e).

well-timed ['wɛl'taɪmd] *adj* opportun(e).

well-to-do ['wɛltə'duː] *adj* aisé(e), assez riche.

well-wisher ['wɛlwɪʃə*] *n* ami/e, admirateur/trice; **scores of** ~**s had gathered** de nombreux amis et admirateurs s'étaient rassemblés; **letters from** ~**s** des lettres d'encouragement.

well-woman clinic ['wɛlwumən-] *n service de check-up pour les femmes dans un cabinet médical.*

Welsh [wɛlʃ] *adj* gallois(e) ♦ *n* (*LING*) gallois *m*; **the** ~ *npl* les Gallois.

Welshman, Welshwoman ['wɛlʃmən, -wumən] *n* Gallois/e.

Welsh rarebit *n* croûte *f* au fromage.

welter ['wɛltə*] *n* fatras *m*.

went [wɛnt] *pt of* **go**.

wept [wɛpt] *pt, pp of* **weep**.

were [wəː*] *pt of* **be**.

we're [wɪə*] = **we are**.

weren't [wəːnt] = **were not**.

werewolf, *pl* **-wolves** ['wɪəwulf, -wulvz] *n* loup-garou *m*.

west [wɛst] *n* ouest *m* ♦ *adj* ouest *inv*, de *or* à l'ouest ♦ *adv* à *or* vers l'ouest; **the W**~ l'Occident *m*, l'Ouest.

westbound ['wɛstbaund] *adj* (*traffic*) en direction de l'ouest; (*carriageway*) ouest *inv*.

West Country *n:* **the** ~ le sud-ouest de l'Angleterre.

westerly ['wɛstəlɪ] *adj* (*situation*) à l'ouest; (*wind*) d'ouest.

western ['wɛstən] *adj* occidental(e), de *or* à l'ouest ♦ *n* (*CINE*) western *m*.

westerner ['wɛstənə*] *n* occidental/e.

westernized ['wɛstənaɪzd] *adj* occidentalisé(e).

West German (*formerly*) *adj* ouest-allemand(e) ♦ *n* Allemand/e de l'Ouest.

West Germany *n* (*formerly*) Allemagne *f* de l'Ouest.

West Indian *adj* antillais(e) ♦ *n* Antillais/e.

West Indies [-'ɪndɪz] *npl:* **the** ~ les Antilles *fpl*.

Westminster ['wɛstmɪnstə*] *n* (*BRIT PARLIAMENT*) Westminster *m*.

westward(s) ['wɛstwəd(z)] *adv* vers l'ouest.

wet [wɛt] *adj* mouillé(e); (*damp*) humide; (*soaked*) trempé(e); (*rainy*) pluvieux(euse) ♦ *vt:* **to** ~ **one's pants** *or* **o.s.** mouiller sa culotte, faire pipi dans sa culotte; **to get** ~ se

mouiller; *"*~ **paint"** "attention peinture fraîche".

wet blanket *n* (*fig*) rabat-joie *m inv*.

wetness ['wɛtnɪs] *n* humidité *f*.

wet suit *n* combinaison *f* de plongée.

we've [wiːv] = **we have**.

whack [wæk] *vt* donner un grand coup à.

whacked [wækt] *adj* (*BRIT col*: tired) crevé(e).

whale [weɪl] *n* (*ZOOL*) baleine *f*.

whaler ['weɪlə*] *n* (*ship*) baleinier *m*.

whaling ['weɪlɪŋ] *n* pêche *f* à la baleine.

wharf, *pl* **wharves** [wɔːf, wɔːvz] *n* quai *m*.

═══════════════════════ *KEYWORD*

what [wɔt] *adj* quel(le); ~ **size is he?** quelle taille fait-il?; ~ **colour is it?** de quelle couleur est-ce?; ~ **books do you need?** quels livres vous faut-il?; ~ **a mess!** quel désordre!

♦ *pron* **1** (*interrogative*) que, *prep* +quoi; ~ **are you doing?** que faites-vous?, qu'est-ce que vous faites?; ~ **is happening?** qu'est-ce qui se passe?, que se passe-t-il?; ~ **are you talking about?** de quoi parlez-vous?; ~ **is it called?** comment est-ce que ça s'appelle?; ~ **about me?** et moi?; ~ **about doing ...?** et si on faisait ...?

2 (*relative: subject*) ce qui; (*: direct object*) ce que; (*: indirect object*) ce +*prep* +quoi, ce dont; **I saw** ~ **you did/was on the table** j'ai vu ce que vous avez fait/ce qui était sur la table; **tell me** ~ **you remember** dites-moi ce dont vous vous souvenez; ~ **I want is a cup of tea** ce que je veux, c'est une tasse de thé

♦ *excl* (*disbelieving*) quoi!, comment!

whatever [wɔt'ɛvə*] *adj:* ~ **book** quel que soit le livre que (*or* qui) + *sub*; n'importe quel livre ♦ *pron:* **do** ~ **is necessary** faites (tout) ce qui est nécessaire; ~ **happens** quoi qu'il arrive; **no reason** ~ *or* **whatsoever** pas la moindre raison; **nothing** ~ *or* **whatsoever** rien du tout.

whatsoever [wɔtsəu'ɛvə*] *adj see* **whatever**.

wheat [wiːt] *n* blé *m*, froment *m*.

wheatgerm ['wiːtdʒəːm] *n* germe *m* de blé.

wheatmeal ['wiːtmiːl] *n* farine bise.

wheedle ['wiːdl] *vt:* **to** ~ **sb into doing sth** cajoler *or* enjôler qn pour qu'il fasse qch; **to** ~ **sth out of sb** obtenir qch de qn par des cajoleries.

wheel [wiːl] *n* roue *f*; (*AUT: also:* **steering** ~) volant *m*; (*NAUT*) gouvernail *m* ♦ *vt* pousser, rouler ♦ *vi* (*also:* ~ **round**) tourner.

wheelbarrow ['wiːlbærəu] *n* brouette *f*.

wheelbase ['wiːlbeɪs] *n* empattement *m*.

wheelchair ['wiːltʃɛə*] *n* fauteuil roulant.

wheel clamp *n* (*AUT*) sabot *m* (de Denver).

wheeler-dealer ['wiːlə'diːlə*] *n* (*pej*) combinard/e, affairiste *m/f*.

wheelie-bin ['wiːlɪbɪn] *n* (*BRIT*) poubelle *f* à roulettes.

wheeling ['wi:lɪŋ] n: ~ **and dealing** (pej) manigances fpl, magouilles fpl.

wheeze [wi:z] n respiration bruyante (d'asthmatique) ♦ vi respirer bruyamment.

wheezy ['wi:zɪ] adj sifflant(e).

═══════════════════════════════ KEYWORD

when [wen] adv quand; ~ **did he go?** quand est-ce qu'il est parti?

♦ conj **1** (at, during, after the time that) quand, lorsque; **she was reading** ~ **I came in** elle lisait quand or lorsque je suis entré

2 (on, at which): **on the day** ~ **I met him** le jour où je l'ai rencontré

3 (whereas) alors que; **I thought I was wrong** ~ **in fact I was right** j'ai cru que j'avais tort alors qu'en fait j'avais raison.

whenever [wɛn'ɛvə*] adv quand donc ♦ conj quand; (every time that) chaque fois que; **I go** ~ **I can** j'y vais quand or chaque fois que je le peux.

where [wɛə*] adv, conj où; **this is** ~ c'est là que; ~ **are you from?** d'où venez vous?

whereabouts ['wɛərəbauts] adv où donc ♦ n: **sb's** ~ l'endroit où se trouve qn.

whereas [wɛər'æz] conj alors que.

whereby [wɛə'baɪ] adv (formal) par lequel (or laquelle etc).

whereupon [wɛərə'pɔn] adv sur quoi, et sur ce.

wherever [wɛər'ɛvə*] adv où donc ♦ conj où que + sub; **sit** ~ **you like** asseyez-vous (là) où vous voulez.

wherewithal ['wɛəwɪðɔ:l] n: **the** ~ **(to do sth)** les moyens mpl (de faire qch).

whet [wɛt] vt aiguiser.

whether ['wɛðə*] conj si; **I don't know** ~ **to accept or not** je ne sais pas si je dois accepter ou non; **it's doubtful** ~ il est peu probable que; ~ **you go or not** que vous y alliez ou non.

whey [weɪ] n petit-lait m.

═══════════════════════════════ KEYWORD

which [wɪtʃ] adj **1** (interrogative: direct, indirect) quel(le); ~ **picture do you want?** quel tableau voulez-vous?; ~ **one?** lequel(laquelle)?

2: **in** ~ **case** auquel cas

♦ pron **1** (interrogative) lequel(laquelle), lesquels(lesquelles) pl; **I don't mind** ~ peu importe lequel; ~ **(of these) are yours?** lesquels sont à vous?; **tell me** ~ **you want** dites-moi lesquels or ceux que vous voulez

2 (relative: subject) qui; (: object) que, prep +lequel(laquelle); (NB: à + lequel = auquel; de + lequel = duquel); **the apple** ~ **you ate/**~ **is on the table** la pomme que vous avez mangée/qui est sur la table; **the chair on** ~ **you are sitting** la chaise sur laquelle vous êtes assis; **the book of** ~ **you spoke** le livre dont vous avez parlé; **he knew,** ~ **is true/I**

feared il le savait, ce qui est vrai/ce que je craignais; **after** ~ après quoi.

whichever [wɪtʃ'ɛvə*] adj: **take** ~ **book you prefer** prenez le livre que vous préférez, peu importe lequel; ~ **book you take** quel que soit le livre que vous preniez; ~ **way you go** de quelque façon que vous + sub.

whiff [wɪf] n bouffée f; **to catch a** ~ **of sth** sentir l'odeur de qch.

while [waɪl] n moment m ♦ conj pendant que; (as long as) tant que; (as, whereas) alors que; (though) quoique + sub; **for a** ~ pendant quelque temps; **in a** ~ dans un moment; **all the** ~ pendant tout ce temps-là; **we'll make it worth your** ~ nous vous récompenserons de votre peine.

▶**while away** vt (time) (faire) passer.

whilst [waɪlst] conj = **while**.

whim [wɪm] n caprice m.

whimper ['wɪmpə*] n geignement m ♦ vi geindre.

whimsical ['wɪmzɪkl] adj (person) capricieux(euse); (look) étrange.

whine [waɪn] n gémissement m ♦ vi gémir, geindre; pleurnicher.

whip [wɪp] n fouet m; (for riding) cravache f; (POL: person) chef m de file (assurant la discipline dans son groupe parlementaire) ♦ vt fouetter; (snatch) enlever (or sortir) brusquement.

▶**whip up** vt (cream) fouetter; (col: meal) préparer en vitesse; (stir up: support) stimuler; (: feeling) attiser, aviver.

Un **whip** est un député dont le rôle est, entre autres, de s'assurer que les membres de son parti sont régulièrement présents à la **House of Commons**, surtout lorsque les votes ont lieu. Les convocations que les whips envoient se distinguent, selon leur degré d'importance, par le fait qu'elles sont soulignées 1, 2 ou 3 fois (les "1-, 2-, ou 3-line whips").

---

whiplash ['wɪplæʃ] n (MED: also: ~ **injury**) coup m du lapin.

whipped cream [wɪpt-] n crème fouettée.

whipping boy ['wɪpɪŋ-] n (fig) bouc m émissaire.

whip-round ['wɪpraund] n (BRIT) collecte f.

whirl [wə:l] n tourbillon m ♦ vt faire tourbillonner; faire tournoyer ♦ vi tourbillonner.

whirlpool ['wə:lpu:l] n tourbillon m.

whirlwind ['wə:lwɪnd] n tornade f.

whirr [wə:*] vi bruire; ronronner; vrombir.

whisk [wɪsk] n (CULIN) fouet m ♦ vt fouetter, battre; **to** ~ **sb away** or **off** emmener qn rapidement.

whiskers ['wɪskəz] npl (of animal) moustaches fpl; (of man) favoris mpl.

whisky, (Irish, US) **whiskey** ['wɪskɪ] n whisky m.

whisper ['wɪspə*] *n* chuchotement *m*; (*fig: of leaves*) bruissement *m*; (*rumour*) rumeur *f* ♦ *vt, vi* chuchoter; **to ~ sth to sb** chuchoter qch à (l'oreille de) qn.

whispering ['wɪspərɪŋ] *n* chuchotement(s) *m(pl)*.

whist [wɪst] *n* (*BRIT*) whist *m*.

whistle ['wɪsl] *n* (*sound*) sifflement *m*; (*object*) sifflet *m* ♦ *vi* siffler ♦ *vt* siffler, siffloter.

whistle-stop ['wɪslstɔp] *adj*: **to make a ~ tour of** (*POL*) faire la tournée électorale des petits patelins de.

Whit [wɪt] *n* la Pentecôte.

white [waɪt] *adj* blanc(blanche); (*with fear*) blême ♦ *n* blanc *m*; (*person*) blanc/blanche; **to turn** *or* **go ~** (*person*) pâlir, blêmir; (*hair*) blanchir; **the ~s** (*washing*) le linge blanc; **tennis ~s** tenue *f* de tennis.

whitebait ['waɪtbeɪt] *n* blanchaille *f*.

white coffee *n* (*BRIT*) café *m* au lait, (café) crème *m*.

white-collar worker ['waɪtkɔlə-] *n* employé/e de bureau.

white elephant *n* (*fig*) objet dispendieux et superflu.

white goods *npl* (*appliances*) (gros) électroménager *m*; (*linen etc*) linge *m* de maison.

white-hot [waɪt'hɔt] *adj* (*metal*) incandescent(e).

White House *n* (*US*): **the ~** la Maison-Blanche.

La **White House** *est un grand bâtiment blanc situé à Washington D.C. où réside le président des États-Unis. Par extension, ce terme désigne l'exécutif américain.*

white lie *n* pieux mensonge.

whiteness ['waɪtnɪs] *n* blancheur *f*.

white noise *n* son *m* blanc.

whiteout ['waɪtaʊt] *n* jour blanc.

white paper *n* (*POL*) livre blanc.

whitewash ['waɪtwɔʃ] *n* (*paint*) lait *m* de chaux ♦ *vt* blanchir à la chaux; (*fig*) blanchir.

whiting ['waɪtɪŋ] *n* (*pl inv*) (*fish*) merlan *m*.

Whit Monday *n* le lundi de Pentecôte.

Whitsun ['wɪtsn] *n* la Pentecôte.

whittle ['wɪtl] *vt*: **to ~ away, ~ down** (*costs*) réduire, rogner.

whizz [wɪz] *vi* aller (*or* passer) à toute vitesse.

whizz kid *n* (*col*) petit prodige.

WHO *n abbr* (= World Health Organization) OMS *f* (= Organisation mondiale de la Santé).

who [huː] *pron* qui.

whodunit [huː'dʌnɪt] *n* (*col*) roman policier.

whoever [huː'evə*] *pron*: **~ finds it** celui(celle) qui le trouve (, qui que ce soit), quiconque le trouve; **ask ~ you like** demandez à qui vous voulez; **~ he marries** qui que ce soit *or* quelle que soit la personne qu'il épouse; **~**

told you that? qui a bien pu vous dire ça?, qui donc vous a dit ça?

whole [həʊl] *adj* (*complete*) entier(ière), tout(e); (*not broken*) intact(e), complet(ète) ♦ *n* (*total*) totalité *f*; (*sth not broken*) tout *m*; **the ~ lot (of it)** tout; **the ~ lot (of them)** tous (sans exception); **the ~ of the time** tout le temps; **the ~ of the town** la ville tout entière; **~ villages were destroyed** des villages entiers ont été détruits; **on the ~, as a ~** dans l'ensemble.

wholehearted [həʊl'hɑːtɪd] *adj* sans réserve(s), sincère.

wholemeal ['həʊlmiːl] *adj* (*BRIT: flour, bread*) complet(ète).

whole note *n* (*US*) ronde *f*.

wholesale ['həʊlseɪl] *n* (vente *f* en) gros *m* ♦ *adj* de gros; (*destruction*) systématique.

wholesaler ['həʊlseɪlə*] *n* grossiste *m/f*.

wholesome ['həʊlsəm] *adj* sain(e); (*advice*) salutaire.

wholewheat ['həʊlwiːt] *adj* = **wholemeal**.

wholly ['həʊlɪ] *adv* entièrement, tout à fait.

========================== *KEYWORD*

whom [huːm] *pron* **1** (*interrogative*) qui; **~ did you see?** qui avez-vous vu?; **to ~ did you give it?** à qui l'avez-vous donné?

2 (*relative*) que, *prep* + qui; **the man ~ I saw/to ~ I spoke** l'homme que j'ai vu/à qui j'ai parlé.

whooping cough ['huːpɪŋ-] *n* coqueluche *f*.

whoops [wuːps] *excl* (*also: ~-a-daisy*) oups!, houp-là!

whoosh [wuːʃ] *n, vi*: **the skiers ~ed past, the skiers came by with a ~** les skieurs passèrent dans un glissement rapide.

whopper ['wɔpə*] *n* (*col: lie*) gros bobard; (*: large thing*) monstre *m*, phénomène *m*.

whopping ['wɔpɪŋ] *adj* (*col: big*) énorme.

whore [hɔː*] *n* (*col: pej*) putain *f*.

========================== *KEYWORD*

whose [huːz] *adj* **1** (*possessive: interrogative*): **~ book is this?** à qui est ce livre?; **~ pencil have you taken?** à qui est le crayon que vous avez pris?, c'est le crayon de qui que vous avez pris?; **~ daughter are you?** de qui êtes-vous la fille?

2 (*possessive: relative*): **the man ~ son you rescued** l'homme dont *or* de qui vous avez sauvé le fils; **the girl ~ sister you were speaking to** la fille à la sœur de qui *or* de laquelle vous parliez; **the woman ~ car was stolen** la femme dont la voiture a été volée ♦ *pron* à qui; **~ is this?** à qui est ceci?; **I know ~ it is** je sais à qui c'est.

Who's Who ['huːz'huː] *n* ≈ Bottin Mondain.

why [waɪ] *adv* pourquoi ♦ *excl* eh bien!, tiens!; **the reason ~** la raison pour laquelle; **~ is he**

late? pourquoi est-il en retard?

whyever [waɪˈɛvə*] *adv* pourquoi donc, mais pourquoi.

WI *n abbr* (*BRIT*: = *Women's Institute*) amicale de femmes au foyer ♦ *abbr* (*GEO*) = **West Indies**; (*US*) = *Wisconsin*.

wick [wɪk] *n* mèche *f* (*de bougie*).

wicked [ˈwɪkɪd] *adj* foncièrement mauvais(e), inique; (*mischievous: grin, look*) espiègle, malicieux(euse); (*terrible: prices, weather*) épouvantable.

wicker [ˈwɪkə*] *n* osier *m*; (*also:* ~**work**) vannerie *f*.

wicket [ˈwɪkɪt] *n* (*CRICKET*) guichet *m*; espace compris entre les deux guichets.

wicket keeper *n* (*CRICKET*) gardien *m* de guichet.

wide [waɪd] *adj* large; (*region, knowledge*) vaste, très étendu(e); (*choice*) grand(e) ♦ *adv*: **to open** ~ ouvrir tout grand; **to shoot** ~ tirer à côté; **it is 3 metres** ~ cela fait 3 mètres de large.

wide-angle lens [ˈwaɪdæŋgl-] *n* objectif *m* grand-angulaire.

wide-awake [waɪdəˈweɪk] *adj* bien éveillé(e).

wide-eyed [waɪdˈaɪd] *adj* aux yeux écarquillés; (*fig*) naïf(ïve), crédule.

widely [ˈwaɪdlɪ] *adv* (*different*) radicalement; (*spaced*) sur une grande étendue; (*believed*) généralement; **to be** ~ **read** (*author*) être beaucoup lu(e); (*reader*) avoir beaucoup lu, être cultivé(e).

widen [ˈwaɪdn] *vt* élargir.

wideness [ˈwaɪdnɪs] *n* largeur *f*.

wide open *adj* grand(e) ouvert(e).

wide-ranging [waɪdˈreɪndʒɪŋ] *adj* (*survey, report*) vaste; (*interests*) divers(e).

widespread [ˈwaɪdsprɛd] *adj* (*belief etc*) très répandu(e).

widow [ˈwɪdəu] *n* veuve *f*.

widowed [ˈwɪdəud] *adj* (qui est devenu(e)) veuf(veuve).

widower [ˈwɪdəuə*] *n* veuf *m*.

width [wɪdθ] *n* largeur *f*; **it's 7 metres in** ~ cela fait 7 mètres de large.

widthways [ˈwɪdθweɪz] *adv* en largeur.

wield [wiːld] *vt* (*sword*) manier; (*power*) exercer.

wife, *pl* **wives** [waɪf, waɪvz] *n* femme (mariée), épouse *f*.

wig [wɪg] *n* perruque *f*.

wigging [ˈwɪgɪŋ] *n* (*BRIT col*) savon *m*, engueulade *f*.

wiggle [ˈwɪgl] *vt* agiter, remuer ♦ *vi* (*loose screw etc*) branler; (*worm*) se tortiller.

wiggly [ˈwɪglɪ] *adj* (*line*) ondulé(e).

wild [waɪld] *adj* sauvage; (*sea*) déchaîné(e); (*idea, life*) fou(folle); extravagant(e); (*col: angry*) hors de soi, furieux(euse); (*: enthusiastic*): **to be** ~ **about** être fou(folle) *or* dingue de ♦ *n*: **the** ~ la nature; ~**s** *npl* régions *fpl* sauvages.

wild card *n* (*COMPUT*) caractère *m* de remplacement.

wildcat [ˈwaɪldkæt] *n* chat *m* sauvage.

wildcat strike *n* grève *f* sauvage.

wilderness [ˈwɪldənɪs] *n* désert *m*, région *f* sauvage.

wildfire [ˈwaɪldfaɪə*] *n*: **to spread like** ~ se répandre comme une traînée de poudre.

wild-goose chase [waɪldˈguːs-] *n* (*fig*) fausse piste.

wildlife [ˈwaɪldlaɪf] *n* faune *f* (et flore *f*) sauvage(s).

wildly [ˈwaɪldlɪ] *adv* (*applaud*) frénétiquement; (*hit, guess*) au hasard; (*happy*) follement.

wiles [waɪlz] *npl* ruses *fpl*, artifices *mpl*.

wilful, (*US*) **willful** [ˈwɪlful] *adj* (*person*) obstiné(e); (*action*) délibéré(e); (*crime*) prémédité(e).

will [wɪl] (*vt: pt, pp* **willed**) *aux vb* **1** (*forming future tense*): **I** ~ **finish it tomorrow** je le finirai demain; **I** ~ **have finished it by tomorrow** je l'aurai fini d'ici demain; ~ **you do it? — yes I** ~/**no I won't** le ferez-vous? — oui/non; **you won't lose it,** ~ **you?** vous ne le perdrez pas, n'est-ce pas?

2 (*in conjectures, predictions*): **he** ~ *or* **he'll be there by now** il doit être arrivé à l'heure qu'il est; **that** ~ **be the postman** ça doit être le facteur

3 (*in commands, requests, offers*): ~ **you be quiet!** voulez-vous bien vous taire!; ~ **you help me?** est-ce que vous pouvez m'aider?; ~ **you have a cup of tea?** voulez-vous une tasse de thé?; **I won't put up with it!** je ne le tolérerai pas!

♦ *vt*: **to** ~ **sb to do** souhaiter ardemment que qn fasse; **he** ~**ed himself to go on** par un suprême effort de volonté, il continua

♦ *n* volonté *f*; testament *m*; **to do sth of one's own free** ~ faire qch de son propre gré; **against one's** ~ à contre-cœur.

willful [ˈwɪlful] *adj* (*US*) = **wilful.**

willing [ˈwɪlɪŋ] *adj* de bonne volonté, serviable ♦ *n*: **to show** ~ faire preuve de bonne volonté; **he's** ~ **to do it** il est disposé à le faire, il veut bien le faire.

willingly [ˈwɪlɪŋlɪ] *adv* volontiers.

willingness [ˈwɪlɪŋnɪs] *n* bonne volonté.

will-o'-the-wisp [ˈwɪləðəˈwɪsp] *n* (*also fig*) feu follet *m*.

willow [ˈwɪləu] *n* saule *m*.

will power *n* volonté *f*.

willy-nilly [ˈwɪlɪˈnɪlɪ] *adv* bon gré mal gré.

wilt [wɪlt] *vi* dépérir.

Wilts [wɪlts] *abbr* (*BRIT*) = **Wiltshire.**

wily [ˈwaɪlɪ] *adj* rusé(e).

wimp [wɪmp] *n* (*col*) mauviette *f*.

win [wɪn] *n* (*in sports etc*) victoire *f* ♦ *vb* (*pt, pp* **won** [wʌn]) *vt* (*battle, money*) gagner; (*prize,* *contract*) remporter; (*popularity*) acquérir ♦ *vi* gagner.

►**win over**, (*BRIT*) **win round** *vt* gagner, se concilier.

wince [wɪns] *n* tressaillement *m* ♦ *vi* tressaillir.

winch [wɪntʃ] *n* treuil *m*.

Winchester disk ['wɪntʃɪstə-] *n* (*COMPUT*) disque *m* Winchester.

wind¹ [wɪnd] *n* (*also MED*) vent *m* ♦ *vt* (*take breath away*) couper le souffle à; **the ~(s)** (*MUS*) les instruments *mpl* à vent; **into** *or* **against the ~** contre le vent; **to get ~ of sth** (*fig*) avoir vent de qch; **to break ~** avoir des gaz.

wind², *pt, pp* **wound** [waɪnd, waʊnd] *vt* enrouler; (*wrap*) envelopper; (*clock, toy*) remonter ♦ *vi* (*road, river*) serpenter.

►**wind down** *vt* (*car window*) baisser; (*fig: production, business*) réduire progressivement.

►**wind up** *vt* (*clock*) remonter; (*debate*) terminer, clôturer.

windbreak ['wɪndbreɪk] *n* brise-vent *m inv*.

windcheater ['wɪndtʃiːtə*], (*US*) **windbreaker** ['wɪndbreɪkə*] *n* anorak *m*.

winder ['waɪndə*] *n* (*BRIT: on watch*) remontoir *m*.

windfall ['wɪndfɔːl] *n* coup *m* de chance.

winding ['waɪndɪŋ] *adj* (*road*) sinueux(euse); (*staircase*) tournant(e).

wind instrument *n* (*MUS*) instrument *m* à vent.

windmill ['wɪndmɪl] *n* moulin *m* à vent.

window ['wɪndəʊ] *n* fenêtre *f*; (*in car, train, also:* ~**pane**) vitre *f*; (*in shop etc*) vitrine *f*.

window box *n* jardinière *f*.

window cleaner *n* (*person*) laveur/euse de vitres.

window dressing *n* arrangement *m* de la vitrine.

window envelope *n* enveloppe *f* à fenêtre.

window frame *n* châssis *m* de fenêtre.

window ledge *n* rebord *m* de la fenêtre.

window pane *n* vitre *f*, carreau *m*.

window-shopping ['wɪndəʊʃɔpɪŋ] *n*: **to go ~** faire du lèche-vitrines.

windowsill ['wɪndəʊsɪl] *n* (*inside*) appui *m* de la fenêtre; (*outside*) rebord *m* de la fenêtre.

windpipe ['wɪndpaɪp] *n* gosier *m*.

wind power *n* énergie éolienne.

windscreen ['wɪndskriːn], (*US*) **windshield** ['wɪndʃiːld] *n* pare-brise *m inv*.

windscreen washer *n* lave-glace *m inv*.

windscreen wiper [-waɪpə*] *n* essuie-glace *m inv*.

windsurfing ['wɪndsəːfɪŋ] *n* planche *f* à voile.

windswept ['wɪndswept] *adj* balayé(e) par le vent.

wind tunnel *n* soufflerie *f*.

windy ['wɪndɪ] *adj* venté(e), venteux(euse); **it's ~** il y a du vent.

wine [waɪn] *n* vin *m* ♦ *vt*: **to ~ and dine sb** offrir un dîner bien arrosé à qn.

wind bar *n* bar *m* à vin.

wine cellar *n* cave *f* à vins.

wine glass *n* verre *m* à vin.

wine list *n* carte *f* des vins.

wine merchant *n* marchand/e de vins.

wine tasting [-teɪstɪŋ] *n* dégustation *f* (de vins).

wine waiter *n* sommelier *m*.

wing [wɪŋ] *n* aile *f*; (*in air force*) groupe *m* d'escadrilles; **~s** *npl* (*THEAT*) coulisses *fpl*.

winger ['wɪŋə*] *n* (*SPORT*) ailier *m*.

wing mirror *n* (*BRIT*) rétroviseur latéral.

wing nut *n* papillon *m*, écrou *m* à ailettes.

wingspan ['wɪŋspæn] *n*, **wingspread** ['wɪŋspred] *n* envergure *f*.

wink [wɪŋk] *n* clin *m* d'œil ♦ *vi* faire un clin d'œil; (*blink*) cligner des yeux.

winkle ['wɪŋkl] *n* bigorneau *m*.

winner ['wɪnə*] *n* gagnant/e.

winning ['wɪnɪŋ] *adj* (*team*) gagnant(e); (*goal*) décisif(ive); (*charming*) charmeur(euse).

winning post *n* poteau *m* d'arrivée.

winnings ['wɪnɪŋz] *npl* gains *mpl*.

winsome ['wɪnsəm] *adj* avenant(e), engageant(e).

winter ['wɪntə*] *n* hiver *m* ♦ *vi* hiverner.

winter sports *npl* sports *mpl* d'hiver.

wintry ['wɪntrɪ] *adj* hivernal(e).

wipe [waɪp] *n* coup *m* de torchon (*or* de chiffon *or* d'éponge) ♦ *vt* essuyer; **to give sth a ~** donner un coup de torchon à qch; **to ~ one's nose** se moucher.

►**wipe off** *vt* essuyer.

►**wipe out** *vt* (*debt*) régler; (*memory*) oublier; (*destroy*) anéantir.

►**wipe up** *vt* essuyer.

wire ['waɪə*] *n* fil *m* (de fer); (*ELEC*) fil électrique; (*TEL*) télégramme *m* ♦ *vt* (*fence*) grillager; (*house*) faire l'installation électrique de; (*also:* ~ **up**) brancher.

wire brush *n* brosse *f* métallique.

wire cutters [-kʌtəz] *npl* cisaille *f*.

wireless ['waɪəlɪs] *n* (*BRIT*) télégraphie *f* sans fil; (*set*) T.S.F. *f*.

wire netting *n* treillis *m* métallique, grillage *m*.

wire service *n* (*US*) revue *f* de presse (*par téléscripteur*).

wire-tapping ['waɪə'tæpɪŋ] *n* écoute *f* téléphonique.

wiring ['waɪərɪŋ] *n* (*ELEC*) installation *f* électrique.

wiry ['waɪərɪ] *adj* noueux(euse), nerveux(euse).

Wis. *abbr* (*US*) = Wisconsin.

wisdom ['wɪzdəm] *n* sagesse *f*; (*of action*) prudence *f*.

wisdom tooth *n* dent *f* de sagesse.

wise [waɪz] *adj* sage, prudent(e), judicieux(euse); **I'm none the ~r** je ne suis pas plus avancé(e) pour autant.

▶**wise up** *vi* (*col*)**: to ~ up to** commencer à se rendre compte de.

...wise [waɪz] *suffix*: **time~** en ce qui concerne le temps, question temps.

wisecrack ['waɪzkræk] *n* sarcasme *m*.

wish [wɪʃ] *n* (*desire*) désir *m*; (*specific desire*) souhait *m*, vœu *m* ♦ *vt* souhaiter, désirer, vouloir; **best ~es** (*on birthday etc*) meilleurs vœux; **with best ~es** (*in letter*) bien amicalement; **give her my best ~es** faites-lui mes amitiés; **to ~ sb goodbye** dire au revoir à qn; **he ~ed me well** il me souhaitait de réussir; **to ~ to do/sb to do** désirer *or* vouloir faire/que qn fasse; **to ~ for** souhaiter; **to ~ sth on sb** souhaiter qch à qn.

wishbone ['wɪʃbəʊn] *n* fourchette *f*.

wishful ['wɪʃfʊl] *adj*: **it's ~ thinking** c'est prendre ses désirs pour des réalités.

wishy-washy ['wɪʃɪ'wɔʃɪ] *adj* (*col: person*) qui manque de caractère, falot(e); (*: ideas, thinking*) faiblard(e).

wisp [wɪsp] *n* fine mèche (*de cheveux*); (*of smoke*) mince volute *f*; **a ~ of straw** un fétu de paille.

wistful ['wɪstfʊl] *adj* mélancolique.

wit [wɪt] *n* (*gen pl: intelligence*) intelligence *f*, esprit *m*; (*presence of mind*) présence *f* d'esprit; (*wittiness*) esprit; (*person*) homme/femme d'esprit; **to be at one's ~s' end** (*fig*) ne plus savoir que faire; **to have one's ~s about one** avoir toute sa présence d'esprit, ne pas perdre la tête; **to ~** *adv* à savoir.

witch [wɪtʃ] *n* sorcière *f*.

witchcraft ['wɪtʃkrɑːft] *n* sorcellerie *f*.

witch doctor *n* sorcier *m*.

witch-hunt ['wɪtʃhʌnt] *n* chasse *f* aux sorcières.

════════ *KEYWORD*

with [wɪð, wɪθ] *prep* **1** (*in the company of*) avec; (*at the home of*) chez; **we stayed ~ friends** nous avons logé chez des amis; **I'll be ~ you in a minute** je suis à vous dans un instant

2 (*descriptive*)**: a room ~ a view** une chambre avec vue; **the man ~ the grey hat/blue eyes** l'homme au chapeau gris/aux yeux bleus

3 (*indicating manner, means, cause*)**: ~ tears in her eyes** les larmes aux yeux; **to walk ~ a stick** marcher avec une canne; **red ~ anger** rouge de colère; **to shake ~ fear** trembler de peur; **to fill sth ~ water** remplir qch d'eau

4: I'm ~ you (*I understand*) je vous suis; **to be ~ it** (*col: up-to-date*) être dans le vent.

withdraw [wɪθ'drɔː] *irreg vt* retirer ♦ *vi* se retirer; (*go back on promise*) se rétracter; **to ~ into o.s.** se replier sur soi-même.

withdrawal [wɪθ'drɔːəl] *n* retrait *m*; (*MED*) état *m* de manque.

withdrawal symptoms *npl*: **to have ~** être en état de manque, présenter les symptômes *mpl* de sevrage.

withdrawn [wɪθ'drɔːn] *pp of* **withdraw** ♦ *adj* (*person*) renfermé(e).

wither ['wɪðə*] *vi* se faner.

withered ['wɪðəd] *adj* fané(e), flétri(e); (*limb*) atrophié(e).

withhold [wɪθ'həʊld] *vt irreg* (*money*) retenir; (*decision*) remettre; (*permission*): **to ~ (from)** refuser (à); (*information*): **to ~ (from)** cacher (à).

within [wɪð'ɪn] *prep* à l'intérieur de ♦ *adv* à l'intérieur; **~ sight of** en vue de; **~ a mile of** à moins d'un mille de; **~ the week** avant la fin de la semaine; **~ an hour from now** d'ici une heure; **to be ~ the law** être légal(e) *or* dans les limites de la légalité.

without [wɪð'aʊt] *prep* sans; **~ anybody knowing** sans que personne ne sache; **to go** *or* **do ~ sth** se passer de qch.

withstand [wɪθ'stænd] *vt irreg* résister à.

witness ['wɪtnɪs] *n* (*person*) témoin *m*; (*evidence*) témoignage *m* ♦ *vt* (*event*) être témoin de; (*document*) attester l'authenticité de; **to bear ~ to sth** témoigner de qch; **~ for the prosecution/defence** témoin à charge/à décharge; **to ~ to sth/having seen sth** témoigner de qch/d'avoir vu qch.

witness box, (*US*) **witness stand** *n* barre *f* des témoins.

witticism ['wɪtɪsɪzəm] *n* mot *m* d'esprit.

witty ['wɪtɪ] *adj* spirituel(le), plein(e) d'esprit.

wives [waɪvz] *npl of* **wife**.

wizard ['wɪzəd] *n* magicien *m*.

wizened ['wɪznd] *adj* ratatiné(e).

wk *abbr* = **week**.

Wm. *abbr* = **William**.

WO *n abbr* = **warrant officer**.

wobble ['wɔbl] *vi* trembler; (*chair*) branler.

wobbly ['wɔblɪ] *adj* tremblant(e); branlant(e).

woe [wəʊ] *n* malheur *m*.

woeful ['wəʊfʊl] *adj* (*sad*) malheureux(euse); (*terrible*) affligeant(e).

wok [wɔk] *n* wok *m*.

woke [wəʊk] *pt of* **wake**.

woken ['wəʊkn] *pp of* **wake**.

wolf, *pl* **wolves** [wʊlf, wʊlvz] *n* loup *m*.

woman, *pl* **women** ['wʊmən, 'wɪmɪn] *n* femme *f* ♦ *cpd*: **~ doctor** femme *f* médecin; **~ friend** amie *f*; **~ teacher** professeur *m* femme; **young ~** jeune femme; **women's page** (*PRESS*) page *f* des lectrices.

womanize ['wʊmənaɪz] *vi* jouer les séducteurs.

womanly ['wʊmənlɪ] *adj* féminin(e).

womb [wuːm] *n* (*ANAT*) utérus *m*.

women ['wɪmɪn] *npl of* **woman**.

Women's (Liberation) Movement *n* (*also:* **women's lib**) mouvement *m* de libération de la femme, MLF *m*.

won [wʌn] *pt*, *pp of* **win**.

wonder ['wʌndə*] *n* merveille *f*, miracle *m*; (*feeling*) émerveillement *m* ♦ *vi*: **to ~ whether** se demander si; **to ~ at** s'étonner de; **s'émerveiller de; to ~ about** songer à; **it's no ~ that** il n'est pas étonnant que + *sub*.

wonderful ['wʌndəful] *adj* merveilleux(euse).

wonderfully ['wʌndəfəlɪ] *adv* (+ *adj*) merveilleusement; (+ *vb*) à merveille.

wonky ['wɔŋkɪ] *adj* (*BRIT col*) qui ne va *or* ne marche pas très bien.

wont [wəunt] *n*: **as is his/her ~** comme de coutume.

won't [wəunt] = **will not**.

woo [wu:] *vt* (*woman*) faire la cour à.

wood [wud] *n* (*timber, forest*) bois *m* ♦ *cpd* de bois, en bois.

wood carving *n* sculpture *f* en *or* sur bois.

wooded ['wudɪd] *adj* boisé(e).

wooden ['wudn] *adj* en bois; (*fig*) raide; inexpressif(ive).

woodland ['wudlənd] *n* forêt *f*, région boisée.

woodpecker ['wudpɛkə*] *n* pic *m* (*oiseau*).

wood pigeon *n* ramier *m*.

woodwind ['wudwɪnd] *n* (*MUS*) bois *m*; **the ~** (*MUS*) les bois.

woodwork ['wudwə:k] *n* menuiserie *f*.

woodworm ['wudwə:m] *n* ver *m* du bois; **the table has got ~** la table est piquée des vers.

woof [wuf] *n* (*of dog*) aboiement *m* ♦ *vi* aboyer; **~, ~!** oua, oua!

wool [wul] *n* laine *f*; **to pull the ~ over sb's eyes** (*fig*) en faire accroire à qn.

woollen, (*US*) **woolen** ['wulən] *adj* de laine; (*industry*) lainier(ière) ♦ *n*: **~s** lainages *mpl*.

woolly, (*US*) **wooly** ['wulɪ] *adj* laineux(euse); (*fig: ideas*) confus(e).

woozy ['wu:zɪ] *adj* (*col*) dans les vapes.

word [wə:d] *n* mot *m*; (*spoken*) parole *f*; (*promise*) parole; (*news*) nouvelles *fpl* ♦ *vt* rédiger, formuler; **~ for ~** (*repeat*) mot pour mot; (*translate*) mot à mot; **what's the ~ for "pen" in French?** comment dit-on "pen" en français?; **to put sth into ~s** exprimer qch; **in other ~s** en d'autres termes; **to have a ~ with sb** toucher un mot à qn; **to have ~s with sb** (*quarrel with*) avoir des mots avec qn; **to break/keep one's ~** manquer à/tenir sa parole; **I'll take your ~ for it** je vous crois sur parole; **to send ~ of** prévenir de; **to leave ~ (with sb/for sb) that** ... laisser un mot (à qn/pour qn) disant que ....

wording ['wə:dɪŋ] *n* termes *mpl*, langage *m*; libellé *m*.

word of mouth *n*: **by** *or* **through ~** de bouche à oreille.

word-perfect ['wə:d'pə:fɪkt] *adj*: **he was ~ (in his speech** *etc*), **his speech** *etc* **was ~** il savait son discours *etc* sur le bout du doigt.

word processing *n* traitement *m* de texte.

word processor [-prəusɛsə*] *n* machine *f* de traitement de texte.

wordwrap ['wə:dræp] *n* (*COMPUT*) retour *m* (automatique) à la ligne.

wordy ['wə:dɪ] *adj* verbeux(euse).

wore [wɔ:*] *pt of* **wear**.

work [wə:k] *n* travail *m*; (*ART, LITERATURE*) œuvre *f* ♦ *vi* travailler; (*mechanism*) marcher, fonctionner; (*plan etc*) marcher; (*medicine*) agir ♦ *vt* (*clay, wood etc*) travailler; (*mine etc*) exploiter; (*machine*) faire marcher *or* fonctionner; **to go to ~** aller travailler; **to set to ~, to start ~** se mettre à l'œuvre; **to be at ~ (on sth)** travailler (sur qch); **to be out of ~** être au chômage; **to ~ hard** travailler dur; **to ~ loose** se défaire, se desserrer.

▶**work on** *vt fus* travailler à; (*principle*) se baser sur.

▶**work out** *vi* (*plans etc*) marcher; (*SPORT*) s'entraîner ♦ *vt* (*problem*) résoudre; (*plan*) élaborer; **it ~s out at £100** ça fait 100 livres.

workable ['wə:kəbl] *adj* (*solution*) réalisable.

workaholic [wə:kə'hɔlɪk] *n* bourreau *m* de travail.

workbench ['wə:kbɛntʃ] *n* établi *m*.

worked up [wə:kt-] *adj*: **to get ~** se mettre dans tous ses états.

worker ['wə:kə*] *n* travailleur/euse, ouvrier/ière; **office ~** employé/e de bureau.

work force *n* main-d'œuvre *f*.

work-in ['wə:kɪn] *n* (*BRIT*) occupation *f* d'usine *etc* (*sans arrêt de la production*).

working ['wə:kɪŋ] *adj* (*day, tools etc, conditions*) de travail; (*wife*) qui travaille; (*partner, population*) actif(ive); **in ~ order** en état de marche; **a ~ knowledge of English** une connaissance toute pratique de l'anglais.

working capital *n* (*COMM*) fonds *mpl* de roulement.

working class *n* classe ouvrière ♦ *adj*: **working-class** ouvrier(ière), de la classe ouvrière.

working man *n* travailleur *m*.

working party *n* (*BRIT*) groupe *m* de travail.

working week *n* semaine *f* de travail.

work-in-progress ['wə:kɪn'prəugrɛs] *n* (*COMM*) en-cours *m inv*; (*: value*) valeur *f* des en-cours.

workload ['wə:kləud] *n* charge *f* de travail.

workman ['wə:kmən] *n* ouvrier *m*.

workmanship ['wə:kmənʃɪp] *n* métier *m*, habileté *f*; facture *f*.

workmate ['wə:kmeɪt] *n* collègue *m/f*.

workout ['wə:kaut] *n* (*SPORT*) séance *f* d'entraînement.

work permit *n* permis *m* de travail.

works [wə:ks] *n* (*BRIT: factory*) usine *f* ♦ *npl* (*of clock, machine*) mécanisme *m*; **road ~** travaux *mpl* (d'entretien des routes).

works council *n* comité *m* d'entreprise.

work sheet *n* (*COMPUT*) feuille *f* de programmation.

workshop ['wə:kʃɔp] *n* atelier *m*.

work station *n* poste *m* de travail.

work study n étude f du travail.

worktop ['wɔːktɔp] n plan m de travail.

work-to-rule ['wɔːktə'ruːl] n (BRIT) grève f du zèle.

world [wɔːld] n monde m ♦ cpd (champion) du monde; (power, war) mondial(e); **all over the ~** dans le monde entier, partout dans le monde; **to think the ~ of sb** (fig) ne jurer que par qn; **what in the ~ is he doing?** qu'est-ce qu'il peut bien être en train de faire?; **to do sb a ~ of good** faire le plus grand bien à qn; **W~ War One/Two, the First/Second W~ War** la Première/Deuxième Guerre mondiale; **out of this ~** adj extraordinaire.

World Cup n: **the ~** (FOOTBALL) la Coupe du monde.

world-famous [wɔːld'feɪməs] adj de renommée mondiale.

worldly ['wɔːldlɪ] adj de ce monde.

world music n world music f.

World Series n: **the ~** (US: BASEBALL) le championnat national de baseball.

world-wide ['wɔːld'waɪd] adj universel(le) ♦ adv dans le monde entier.

worm [wɔːm] n ver m.

worn [wɔːn] pp of **wear** ♦ adj usé(e).

worn-out ['wɔːnaut] adj (object) complètement usé(e); (person) épuisé(e).

worried ['wʌrɪd] adj inquiet(ète); **to be ~ about sth** être inquiet au sujet de qch.

worrier ['wʌrɪə*] n inquiet/ète.

worrisome ['wʌrɪsəm] adj inquiétant(e).

worry ['wʌrɪ] n souci m ♦ vt inquiéter ♦ vi s'inquiéter, se faire du souci; **to ~ about** or **over sth/sb** se faire du souci pour or à propos de qch/qn.

worrying ['wʌrɪɪŋ] adj inquiétant(e).

worse [wɔːs] adj pire, plus mauvais(e) ♦ adv plus mal ♦ n pire m; **to get ~** (condition, situation) empirer, se dégrader; **a change for the ~** une détérioration; **he is none the ~ for it** il ne s'en porte pas plus mal; **so much the ~ for you!** tant pis pour vous!

worsen ['wɔːsn] vt, vi empirer.

worse off adj moins à l'aise financièrement; (fig): **you'll be ~ this way** ça ira moins bien de cette façon; **he is now ~ than before** il se retrouve dans une situation pire qu'auparavant.

worship ['wɔːʃɪp] n culte m ♦ vt (God) rendre un culte à; (person) adorer; **Your W~** (BRIT: to mayor) Monsieur le Maire; (: to judge) Monsieur le Juge.

worshipper ['wɔːʃɪpə*] n adorateur/trice; (in church) fidèle m/f.

worst [wɔːst] adj le(la) pire, le(la) plus mauvais(e) ♦ adv le plus mal ♦ n pire m; **at ~** au pis aller; **if the ~ comes to the ~** si le pire doit arriver.

worst-case ['wɔːstkeɪs] adj: **the ~ scenario** le pire scénario or cas de figure.

worsted ['wustɪd] n: (**wool**) ~ laine peignée.

worth [wɔːθ] n valeur f ♦ adj: **to be ~** valoir; **how much is it ~?** ça vaut combien?; **it's ~ it** cela en vaut la peine; **50 pence ~ of apples** (pour) 50 pence de pommes.

worthless ['wɔːθlɪs] adj qui ne vaut rien.

worthwhile ['wɔːθ'waɪl] adj (activity) qui en vaut la peine; (cause) louable; **a ~ book** un livre qui vaut la peine d'être lu.

worthy ['wɔːðɪ] adj (person) digne; (motive) louable; ~ **of** digne de.

━━━━━━━━━━━━━━━━━━━━━ KEYWORD

would [wud] aux vb **1** (conditional tense): **if you asked him he ~ do it** si vous le lui demandiez, il le ferait; **if you had asked him he ~ have done it** si vous le lui aviez demandé, il l'aurait fait

2 (in offers, invitations, requests): **~ you like a biscuit?** voulez-vous un biscuit?; **~ you close the door please?** voulez-vous fermer la porte, s'il vous plaît?

3 (in indirect speech): **I said I ~ do it** j'ai dit que je le ferais

4 (emphatic): **it WOULD have to snow today!** naturellement il neige aujourd'hui! or il fallait qu'il neige aujourd'hui!

5 (insistence): **she ~n't do it** elle n'a pas voulu or elle a refusé de le faire

6 (conjecture): **it ~ have been midnight** il devait être minuit

7 (indicating habit): **he ~ go there on Mondays** il y allait le lundi.

would-be ['wudbiː] adj (pej) soi-disant.

wound vb [waund] pt, pp of **wind** ♦ n, vt [wuːnd] n blessure f ♦ vt blesser; **~ed in the leg** blessé à la jambe.

wove [wəuv] pt of **weave**.

woven ['wəuvn] pp of **weave**.

WP n abbr = **word processing, word processor** ♦ abbr (BRIT col) = **weather permitting**.

WPC n abbr (BRIT) = **woman police constable**.

wpm abbr (= words per minute) mots/minute.

WRAC n abbr (BRIT: = Women's Royal Army Corps) auxiliaires féminines de l'armée de terre.

WRAF n abbr (BRIT: = Women's Royal Air Force) auxiliaires féminines de l'armée de l'air.

wrangle ['ræŋgl] n dispute f ♦ vi se disputer.

wrap [ræp] n (stole) écharpe f; (cape) pèlerine f ♦ vt (also: ~ up) envelopper; **under ~s** (fig: plan, scheme) secret(ète).

wrapper ['ræpə*] n (BRIT: of book) couverture f; (on chocolate etc) papier m.

wrapping paper ['ræpɪŋ-] n papier m d'emballage; (for gift) papier cadeau.

wrath [rɔθ] n courroux m.

wreak [riːk] vt (destruction) entraîner; **to ~ havoc** faire des ravages; **to ~ vengeance on** se venger de, exercer sa vengeance sur.

wreath, ~s [riːθ, riːðz] n couronne f.

wreck [rɛk] n (*sea disaster*) naufrage m; (*ship*) épave f; (*pej: person*) loque (humaine) ♦ vt démolir; (*ship*) provoquer le naufrage de; (*fig*) briser, ruiner.

wreckage ['rɛkɪdʒ] n débris mpl; (*of building*) décombres mpl; (*of ship*) naufrage m.

wrecker ['rɛkə*] n (*US: breakdown van*) dépanneuse f.

WREN [rɛn] n abbr (*BRIT*) membre du WRNS.

wren [rɛn] n (*ZOOL*) troglodyte m.

wrench [rɛntʃ] n (*TECH*) clé f (à écrous); (*tug*) violent mouvement de torsion; (*fig*) arrachement m ♦ vt tirer violemment sur, tordre; **to ~ sth from** arracher qch (violemment) à or de.

wrest [rɛst] vt: **to ~ sth from sb** arracher or ravir qch à qn.

wrestle ['rɛsl] vi: **to ~ (with sb)** lutter (avec qn); **to ~ with** (*fig*) se débattre avec, lutter contre.

wrestler ['rɛslə*] n lutteur/euse.

wrestling ['rɛslɪŋ] n lutte f; (*also:* **all-in ~**: *BRIT*) catch m.

wrestling match n rencontre f de lutte (or de catch).

wretch [rɛtʃ] n pauvre malheureux/euse; **little ~!** (*often humorous*) petit(e) misérable!

wretched ['rɛtʃɪd] adj misérable; (*col*) maudit(e).

wriggle ['rɪgl] n tortillement m ♦ vi se tortiller.

wring, pt, pp **wrung** [rɪŋ, rʌŋ] vt tordre; (*wet clothes*) essorer; (*fig*): **to ~ sth out of** arracher qch à.

wringer ['rɪŋə*] n essoreuse f.

wringing ['rɪŋɪŋ] adj (*also:* **~ wet**) tout mouillé(e), trempé(e).

wrinkle ['rɪŋkl] n (*on skin*) ride f; (*on paper etc*) pli m ♦ vt rider, plisser ♦ vi se plisser.

wrinkled ['rɪŋkld] adj, **wrinkly** ['rɪŋklɪ] adj (*fabric, paper*) froissé(e), plissé(e); (*surface*) plissé; (*skin*) ridé(e), plissé.

wrist [rɪst] n poignet m.

wristband ['rɪstbænd] n (*BRIT: of shirt*) poignet m; (: *of watch*) bracelet m.

wrist watch n montre-bracelet f.

writ [rɪt] n acte m judiciaire; **to issue a ~ against sb, serve a ~ on sb** assigner qn en justice.

write, pt **wrote**, pp **written** [raɪt, rəut, 'rɪtn] vt, vi écrire; **to ~ sb a letter** écrire une lettre à qn.

▶**write away** vi: **to ~ away for** (*information*) (écrire pour) demander; (*goods*) (écrire pour) commander.

▶**write down** vt noter; (*put in writing*) mettre par écrit.

▶**write off** vt (*debt*) passer aux profits et pertes; (*depreciate*) amortir; (*smash up: car etc*) démolir complètement.

▶**write out** vt écrire; (*copy*) recopier.

▶**write up** vt rédiger.

write-off ['raɪtɔf] n perte totale; **the car is a ~** la voiture est bonne pour la casse.

write-protect ['raɪtprə'tɛkt] vt (*COMPUT*) protéger contre l'écriture.

writer ['raɪtə*] n auteur m, écrivain m.

write-up ['raɪtʌp] n (*review*) critique f.

writhe [raɪð] vi se tordre.

writing ['raɪtɪŋ] n écriture f; (*of author*) œuvres fpl; **in ~** par écrit; **in my own ~** écrit(e) de ma main.

writing case n nécessaire m de correspondance.

writing desk n secrétaire m.

writing paper n papier m à lettres.

written ['rɪtn] pp of **write**.

WRNS n abbr (*BRIT: = Women's Royal Naval Service*) auxiliaires féminines de la marine.

wrong [rɔŋ] adj faux(fausse); (*incorrectly chosen: number, road etc*) mauvais(e); (*not suitable*) qui ne convient pas; (*wicked*) mal; (*unfair*) injuste ♦ adv faux ♦ n tort m ♦ vt faire du tort à, léser; **to be ~** (*answer*) être faux(fausse); (*in doing/saying*) avoir tort (de dire/faire); **you are ~ to do it** tu as tort de le faire; **it's ~ to steal, stealing is ~** c'est mal de voler; **you are ~ about that, you've got it ~** tu te trompes; **to be in the ~** avoir tort; **what's ~?** qu'est-ce qui ne va pas?; **there's nothing ~** tout va bien; **what's ~ with the car?** qu'est-ce qu'elle a, la voiture?; **to go ~** (*person*) se tromper; (*plan*) mal tourner; (*machine*) se détraquer.

wrongdoer ['rɔŋduːə*] n malfaiteur m.

wrong-foot [rɔŋ'fut] vt (*SPORT*) prendre à contre-pied; (*fig*) prendre au dépourvu.

wrongful ['rɔŋful] adj injustifié(e); **~ dismissal** (*INDUSTRY*) licenciement abusif.

wrongly ['rɔŋlɪ] adv à tort; (*answer, do, count*) mal, incorrectement; (*treat*) injustement.

wrong number n (*TEL*): **you have the ~** vous vous êtes trompé de numéro.

wrong side n (*of cloth*) envers m.

wrote [rəut] pt of **write**.

wrought [rɔːt] adj: **~ iron** fer forgé.

wrung [rʌŋ] pt, pp of **wring**.

WRVS n abbr (*BRIT: = Women's Royal Voluntary Service*) auxiliaires féminines bénévoles au service de la collectivité.

wry [raɪ] adj désabusé(e).

wt. abbr (= *weight*) pds.

WV, W. Va. abbr (*US*) = West Virginia.

WY, Wyo. abbr (*US*) = Wyoming.

WYSIWYG ['wɪzɪwɪg] abbr (*COMPUT: = what you see is what you get*) ce que vous voyez est ce que vous aurez.

X x

X, x [ɛks] n (letter) X, x m; (BRIT CINE: formerly) film interdit aux moins de 18 ans; **X for Xmas** X comme Xavier.

Xerox ['zɪərɔks] n ® (also: ~ **machine**) photocopieuse f; (photocopy) photocopie f ♦ vt photocopier.

XL abbr (= extra large) XL.

Xmas ['ɛksməs] n abbr = **Christmas**.

X-rated ['ɛks'reɪtɪd] adj (US: film) interdit(e) aux moins de 18 ans.

X-ray ['ɛksreɪ] n rayon m X; (photograph) radio(graphie) f ♦ vt radiographier.

xylophone ['zaɪləfəun] n xylophone m.

Y y

Y, y [waɪ] n (letter) Y, y m; **Y for Yellow**, (US) **Y for Yoke** Y comme Yvonne.

yacht [jɔt] n voilier m; (motor, luxury ~) yacht m.

yachting ['jɔtɪŋ] n yachting m, navigation f de plaisance.

yachtsman ['jɔtsmən] n yacht(s)man m.

yam [jæm] n igname f.

Yank [jæŋk], **Yankee** ['jæŋkɪ] n (pej) Amerloque m/f, Ricain/e.

yank [jæŋk] vt tirer d'un coup sec.

yap [jæp] vi (dog) japper.

yard [jɑːd] n (of house etc) cour f; (US: garden) jardin m; (measure) yard m (= 914 mm; 3 feet); **builder's ~** chantier m.

yardstick ['jɑːdstɪk] n (fig) mesure f, critère m.

yarn [jɑːn] n fil m; (tale) longue histoire.

yawn [jɔːn] n bâillement m ♦ vi bâiller.

yawning ['jɔːnɪŋ] adj (gap) béant(e).

yd abbr = **yard**.

yeah [jɛə] adv (col) ouais.

year [jɪə*] n an m, année f; (SCOL etc) année; **every ~** tous les ans, chaque année; **this ~** cette année; **a or per ~** par an; **~ in, ~ out** année après année; **to be 8 ~s old** avoir 8 ans; **an eight-~-old child** un enfant de huit ans.

yearbook ['jɪəbuk] n annuaire m.

yearly ['jɪəlɪ] adj annuel(le) ♦ adv annuellement; **twice ~** deux fois par an.

yearn [jəːn] vi: **to ~ for sth/to do** aspirer à qch/à faire, languir après qch.

yearning ['jəːnɪŋ] n désir ardent, envie f.

yeast [jiːst] n levure f.

yell [jɛl] n hurlement m, cri m ♦ vi hurler.

yellow ['jɛləu] adj, n jaune (m).

yellow fever n fièvre f jaune.

yellowish ['jɛləuɪʃ] adj qui tire sur le jaune, jaunâtre (pej).

Yellow Pages npl ® pages fpl jaunes.

Yellow Sea n: **the ~** la mer Jaune.

yelp [jɛlp] n jappement m; glapissement m ♦ vi japper; glapir.

Yemen ['jɛmən] n Yémen m.

yen [jɛn] n (currency) yen m; (craving): **~ for/to do** grand(e) envie f or désir m de/de faire.

yeoman ['jəumən] n: **Y~ of the Guard** hallebardier m de la garde royale.

yes [jɛs] adv oui; (answering negative question) si ♦ n oui m; **to say ~ (to)** dire oui (à).

yesterday ['jɛstədɪ] adv, n hier (m); **~ morning/evening** hier matin/soir; **the day before ~** avant-hier; **all day ~** toute la journée d'hier.

yet [jɛt] adv encore; déjà ♦ conj pourtant, néanmoins; **it is not finished ~** ce n'est pas encore fini or toujours pas fini; **must you go just ~?** dois-tu déjà partir?; **the best ~** le meilleur jusqu'ici or jusque-là; **as ~** jusqu'ici, encore; **a few days ~** encore quelques jours; **~ again** une fois de plus.

yew [juː] n if m.

Y-fronts ['waɪfrʌnts] npl ® (BRIT) slip m kangourou.

YHA n abbr (BRIT) = Youth Hostels Association.

Yiddish ['jɪdɪʃ] n yiddish m.

yield [jiːld] n production f, rendement m; (FINANCE) rapport m ♦ vt produire, rendre, rapporter; (surrender) céder ♦ vi céder; (US AUT) céder la priorité; **a ~ of 5%** un rendement de 5%.

YMCA n abbr (= Young Men's Christian Association) ≈ union chrétienne de jeunes gens (UCJG).

yob(bo) ['jɔb(əu)] n (BRIT col) loubar(d) m.

yodel ['jəudl] vi faire des tyroliennes, jodler.

yoga ['jəugə] n yoga m.

yog(h)ourt, yog(h)urt ['jəugət] n yaourt m.

yoke [jəuk] n joug m ♦ vt (also: ~ **together**: oxen) accoupler.

yolk [jəuk] n jaune m (d'œuf).

yonder ['jɔndə*] adv là(-bas).

yonks [jɔŋks] npl (col): **for ~** très longtemps; **we've been here for ~** ça fait une éternité qu'on est ici; **we were there for ~** on est resté là pendant des lustres.

Yorks [jɔːks] abbr (BRIT) = Yorkshire.

══════════════════ KEYWORD

you [ju:] *pron* **1** (*subject*) tu; (*polite form*) vous; (*plural*) vous; ~ **French enjoy your food** vous autres Français, vous aimez bien manger; ~ **and I will go** toi et moi *or* vous et moi, nous irons

2 (*object: direct, indirect*) te, t' +*vowel*; vous; **I know** ~ je te *or* vous connais; **I gave it to** ~, je vous l'ai donné, je te l'ai donné

3 (*stressed*) toi; vous; **I told YOU to do it** c'est à toi *or* vous que j'ai dit de le faire

4 (*after prep, in comparisons*) toi; vous; **it's for** ~ c'est pour toi *or* vous; **she's younger than** ~ elle est plus jeune que toi *or* vous

5 (*impersonal: one*) on; **fresh air does** ~ **good** l'air frais fait du bien; ~ **never know** on ne sait jamais

──────────────────

you'd [ju:d] = **you had, you would.**
you'll [ju:l] = **you will, you shall.**
young [jʌŋ] *adj* jeune ♦ *npl* (*of animal*) petits *mpl*; (*people*): **the** ~ les jeunes, la jeunesse; **a** ~ **man** un jeune homme; **a** ~ **lady** (*unmarried*) une jeune fille, une demoiselle; (*married*) une jeune femme *or* dame; **my** ~**er brother** mon frère cadet; **the** ~**er generation** la jeune génération.
youngish ['jʌŋɪʃ] *adj* assez jeune.
youngster ['jʌŋstə*] *n* jeune *m/f*; (*child*) enfant *m/f*.
your [jɔ:*] *adj* ton(ta), tes *pl*; (*polite form, pl*) votre, vos *pl*.
you're [juə*] = **you are.**
yours [jɔ:z] *pron* le(la) tien(ne), les tiens(tiennes); (*polite form, pl*) le(la) vôtre, les vôtres; **is it** ~? c'est à toi (*or* à vous)?; **a friend of** ~ un(e) de tes (*or* de vos) amis.
yourself [jɔ:'sɛlf] *pron* (*reflexive*) te; (*: polite form*) vous; (*after prep*) toi; vous; (*emphatic*) toi-même; vous-même; **you** ~ **told me** c'est vous qui me l'avez dit, vous me l'avez dit vous-même.
yourselves [jɔ:'sɛlvz] *pl pron* vous; (*emphatic*) vous-mêmes.
youth [ju:θ] *n* jeunesse *f*; (*young man: pl* ~**s** [ju:ðz]) jeune homme *m*; **in my** ~ dans ma jeunesse, quand j'étais jeune.
youth club *n* centre *m* de jeunes.
youthful ['ju:θful] *adj* jeune; (*enthusiasm etc*) juvénile; (*misdemeanour*) de jeunesse.
youthfulness ['ju:θfəlnɪs] *n* jeunesse *f*.
youth hostel *n* auberge *f* de jeunesse.
youth movement *n* mouvement *m* de jeunes.
you've [ju:v] = **you have.**
yowl [jaul] *n* hurlement *m*; miaulement *m* ♦ *vi* hurler; miauler.
YT *abbr* (*Canada*) = Yukon Territory.
Yugoslav ['ju:gəuslɑ:v] *adj* yougoslave ♦ *n* Yougoslave *m/f*.
Yugoslavia [ju:gəu'slɑ:vɪə] *n* Yougoslavie *f*.

Yugoslavian [ju:gəu'slɑ:vɪən] *adj* yougoslave.
Yule [ju:l]: ~ **log** *n* bûche *f* de Noël.
yuppie ['jʌpɪ] *n* yuppie *m/f*.
YWCA *n abbr* (= *Young Women's Christian Association*) union chrétienne féminine.

══════════════════

Z z

══════════════════

Z, z [zɛd, (*US*) zi:] *n* (*letter*) Z, z *m*; **Z for Zebra** Z comme Zoé.
Zaïre [zɑː'iːə*] *n* Zaïre *m*.
Zambia ['zæmbɪə] *n* Zambie *f*.
Zambian ['zæmbɪən] *adj* zambien(ne) ♦ *n* Zambien/ne.
zany ['zeɪnɪ] *adj* farfelu(e), loufoque.
zap [zæp] *vt* (*COMPUT*) effacer.
zeal [zi:l] *n* (*revolutionary etc*) ferveur *f*, (*keenness*) ardeur *f*, zèle *m*.
zealot ['zɛlət] *n* fanatique *m/f*.
zealous ['zɛləs] *adj* fervent(e); ardent(e), zélé(e).
zebra ['zi:brə] *n* zèbre *m*.
zebra crossing *n* (*BRIT*) passage *m* pour piétons.
zenith ['zɛnɪθ] *n* (*ASTRONOMY*) zénith *m*; (*fig*) zénith, apogée *m*.
zero ['zɪərəu] *n* zéro *m* ♦ *vi*: **to** ~ **in on** (*target*) se diriger droit sur; **5° below** ~ 5 degrés au-dessous de zéro.
zero hour *n* l'heure *f* H.
zero option *n* (*POL*): **the** ~ l'option *f* zéro.
zero-rated ['zi:rəureɪtɪd] *adj* (*BRIT*) exonéré(e) de TVA.
zest [zɛst] *n* entrain *m*, élan *m*; (*of lemon etc*) zeste *m*.
zigzag ['zɪgzæg] *n* zigzag *m* ♦ *vi* zigzaguer, faire des zigzags.
Zimbabwe [zɪm'bɑ:bwɪ] *n* Zimbabwe *m*.
Zimbabwean [zɪm'bɑ:bwɪən] *adj* zimbabwéen(ne) ♦ *n* Zimbabwéen/ne.
Zimmer ['zɪmə*] *n* ® (*also:* ~ **frame**) déambulateur *m*.
zinc [zɪŋk] *n* zinc *m*.
Zionism ['zaɪənɪzəm] *n* sionisme *m*.
Zionist ['zaɪənɪst] *adj* sioniste ♦ *n* Sioniste *m/f*.
zip [zɪp] *n* (*also:* ~ **fastener**, (*US*) ~**per**) fermeture *f* éclair ® *or* à glissière; (*energy*) entrain *m* ♦ *vt* (*also:* ~ **up**) fermer (avec une fermeture éclair ®).
zip code *n* (*US*) code postal.
zither ['zɪðə*] *n* cithare *f*.
zodiac ['zəudɪæk] *n* zodiaque *m*.
zombie ['zɒmbɪ] *n* (*fig*): **like a** ~ avec l'air d'un zombie, comme un automate.
zone [zəun] *n* zone *f*.

zonked [zɔŋkt] *adj* (*col*) crevé(e), claqué(e).
zoo [zuː] *n* zoo *m*.
zoological [zuə'lɔdʒɪkl] *adj* zoologique.
zoologist [zu'ɔlədʒɪst] *n* zoologiste *m/f*.
zoology [zuː'ɔlədʒɪ] *n* zoologie *f*.
zoom [zuːm] *vi*: **to ~ past** passer en trombe;
  to ~ in (on sb/sth) (*PHOT, CINE*) zoomer (sur
  qn/qch).
zoom lens *n* zoom *m*, objectif *m* à focale variable.
zucchini [zuː'kiːnɪ] *n(pl)* (*US*) courgette(s)
  f(pl).
Zulu ['zuːluː] *adj* zoulou ♦ *n* Zoulou *m/f*.
Zürich ['zjuərɪk] *n* Zurich.

Grammar
Grammaire

Using the Grammar

The Grammar section deals systematically and comprehensively with all the information you will need in order to communicate accurately in French. The user-friendly layout explains the grammar point on a left-hand page, leaving the facing page free for illustrative examples. The bracketed numbers, (→1) etc, direct you to the relevant example in every case.

The Grammar section also provides invaluable guidance on the danger of translating English structures by identical structures in French. Use of Numbers and Punctuation are important areas covered towards the end of the section. Finally, the index lists the main words and grammatical terms in both English and French.

Abbreviations

ctd.	continued	**p(p)**	page(s)	**qu**	quelqu'un
fem.	feminine	**perf.**	perfect	**sb**	somebody
infin.	infinitive	**plur.**	plural	**sing.**	singular
masc.	masculine	**qch**	quelque chose	**sth**	something

4 CONTENTS

VERBS

NOUNS

ARTICLES

ADJECTIVES

Simple Tenses: formation

In French the simple tenses are:

Present	(→ **1**)
Imperfect	(→ **2**)
Future	(→ **3**)
Conditional	(→ **4**)
Past Historic	(→ **5**)
Present Subjunctive	(→ **6**)
Imperfect Subjunctive	(→ **7**)

They are formed by adding endings to a verb stem. The endings show the number and person of the subject of the verb (→ **8**)

The stem and endings of regular verbs are totally predictable. The following sections show all the patterns for regular verbs. For irregular verbs see pp. 74 ff.

Regular Verbs

There are three regular verb patterns (called conjugations), each identifiable by the ending of the infinitive:

● First conjugation verbs end in **-er** e.g. **donner** to give

● Second conjugation verbs end in **-ir** e.g. **finir** to finish

● Third conjugation verbs end in **-re** e.g. **vendre** to sell

These three conjugations are treated in order on the following pages.

Continued

1 **je donne**
  I give, I am giving, I do give

2 **je donnais**
  I gave, I was giving, I used to give

3 **je donnerai**
  I shall give, I shall be giving

4 **je donnerais**
  I should/would give, I should/would be giving

5 **je donnai**
  I gave

6 **(que) je donne**
  (that) I give/gave

7 **(que) je donnasse**
  (that) I gave

8 **je donne**   I give
  nous donnons   we give
  je donnerais   I would give
  nous donnerions   we would give

Simple Tenses: First Conjugation

● The stem is formed as follows:

TENSE	FORMATION	EXAMPLE
Present		
Imperfect		
Past Historic	infinitive minus **-er**	**donn-**
Present Subjunctive		
Imperfect Subjunctive		
Future	infinitive	**donner-**
Conditional		

● To the appropriate stem add the following endings:

		PRESENT (→**1**)	IMPERFECT (→**2**)	PAST HISTORIC (→**3**)
sing.	1st person	-e	-ais	-ai
	2nd person	-es	-ais	-as
	3rd person	-e	-ait	-a
plur.	1st person	-ons	-ions	-âmes
	2nd person	-ez	-iez	-âtes
	3rd person	-ent	-aient	-èrent

		PRESENT SUBJUNCTIVE (→**4**)	IMPERFECT SUBJUNCTIVE (→**5**)
sing.	1st person	-e	-asse
	2nd person	-es	-asses
	3rd person	-e	-ât
plur.	1st person	-ions	-assions
	2nd person	-iez	-assiez
	3rd person	-ent	-assent

		FUTURE (→**6**)	CONDITIONAL (→**7**)
sing.	1st person	-ai	-ais
	2nd person	-as	-ais
	3rd person	-a	-ait
plur.	1st person	-ons	-ions
	2nd person	-ez	-iez
	3rd person	-ont	-aient

1 *PRESENT*		**2** *IMPERFECT*		**3** *PAST HISTORIC*	
je	donne	je	donnais	je	donnai
tu	donnes	tu	donnais	tu	donnas
il	donne	il	donnait	il	donna
elle	donne	elle	donnait	elle	donna
nous	donnons	nous	donnions	nous	donnâmes
vous	donnez	vous	donniez	vous	donnâtes
ils	donnent	ils	donnaient	ils	donnèrent
elles	donnent	elles	donnaient	elles	donnèrent

4 *PRESENT SUBJUNCTIVE*		**5** *IMPERFECT SUBJUNCTIVE*	
je	donne	je	donnasse
tu	donnes	tu	donnasses
il	donne	il	donnât
elle	donne	elle	donnât
nous	donnions	nous	donnassions
vous	donniez	vous	donnassiez
ils	donnent	ils	donnassent
elles	donnent	elles	donnassent

6 *FUTURE*		**7** *CONDITIONAL*	
je	donnerai	je	donnerais
tu	donneras	tu	donnerais
il	donnera	il	donnerait
elle	donnera	elle	donnerait
nous	donnerons	nous	donnerions
vous	donnerez	vous	donneriez
ils	donneront	ils	donneraient
elles	donneront	elles	donneraient

Simple Tenses: Second Conjugation

● The stem is formed as follows:

TENSE	FORMATION	EXAMPLE
Present		
Imperfect		
Past Historic	infinitive minus -ir	fin-
Present Subjunctive		
Imperfect Subjunctive		
Future	infinitive	finir-
Conditional		

● To the appropriate stem add the following endings:

		PRESENT (→1)	IMPERFECT (→2)	PAST HISTORIC (→3)
sing.	1st person	-is	-issais	-is
	2nd person	-is	-issais	-is
	3rd person	-it	-issait	-it
plur.	1st person	-issons	-issions	-îmes
	2nd person	-issez	-issiez	-îtes
	3rd person	-issent	-issaient	-irent

		PRESENT SUBJUNCTIVE (→4)	IMPERFECT SUBJUNCTIVE (→5)
sing.	1st person	-isse	-isse
	2nd person	-isses	-isses
	3rd person	-isse	-ît
plur.	1st person	-issions	-issions
	2nd person	-issiez	-issiez
	3rd person	-issent	-issent

		FUTURE (→6)	CONDITIONAL (→7)
sing.	1st person	-ai	-ais
	2nd person	-as	-ais
	3rd person	-a	-ait
plur.	1st person	-ons	-ions
	2nd person	-ez	-iez
	3rd person	-ont	-aient

1 *PRESENT*		**2** *IMPERFECT*		**3** *PAST HISTORIC*	
je	fin**is**	je	fin**issais**	je	fin**is**
tu	fin**is**	tu	fin**issais**	tu	fin**is**
il	fin**it**	il	fin**issait**	il	fin**it**
elle	fin**it**	elle	fin**issait**	elle	fin**it**
nous	fin**issons**	nous	fin**issions**	nous	fin**îmes**
vous	fin**issez**	vous	fin**issiez**	vous	fin**îtes**
ils	fin**issent**	ils	fin**issaient**	ils	fin**irent**
elles	fin**issent**	elles	fin**issaient**	elles	fin**irent**

4 *PRESENT SUBJUNCTIVE*		**5** *IMPERFECT SUBJUNCTIVE*	
je	fin**isse**	je	fin**isse**
tu	fin**isses**	tu	fin**isses**
il	fin**isse**	il	fin**ît**
elle	fin**isse**	elle	fin**ît**
nous	fin**issions**	nous	fin**issions**
vous	fin**issiez**	vous	fin**issiez**
ils	fin**issent**	ils	fin**issent**
elles	fin**issent**	elles	fin**issent**

6 *FUTURE*		**7** *CONDITIONAL*	
je	fin**irai**	je	fin**irais**
tu	fin**iras**	tu	fin**irais**
il	fin**ira**	il	fin**irait**
elle	fin**ira**	elle	fin**irait**
nous	fin**irons**	nous	fin**irions**
vous	fin**irez**	vous	fin**iriez**
ils	fin**iront**	ils	fin**iraient**
elles	fin**iront**	elles	fin**iraient**

Simple Tenses: Third Conjugation

● The stem is formed as follows:

TENSE	FORMATION	EXAMPLE
Present		
Imperfect		
Past Historic	infinitive minus **-re**	**vend-**
Present Subjunctive		
Imperfect Subjunctive		
Future	infinitive minus **-e**	**vendr-**
Conditional		

● To the appropriate stem add the following endings:

		PRESENT (→**1**)	IMPERFECT (→**2**)	PAST HISTORIC (→**3**)
sing.	1st person	-s	-ais	-is
	2nd person	-s	-ais	-is
	3rd person	–	-ait	-it
plur.	1st person	-ons	-ions	-îmes
	2nd person	-ez	-iez	-îtes
	3rd person	-ent	-aient	-irent

		PRESENT SUBJUNCTIVE (→**4**)	IMPERFECT SUBJUNCTIVE (→**5**)
sing.	1st person	-e	-isse
	2nd person	-es	-isses
	3rd person	-e	-ît
plur.	1st person	-ions	-issions
	2nd person	-iez	-issiez
	3rd person	-ent	-issent

		FUTURE (→**6**)	CONDITIONAL (→**7**)
sing.	1st person	-ai	-ais
	2nd person	-as	-ais
	3rd person	-a	-ait
plur.	1st person	-ons	-ions
	2nd person	-ez	-iez
	3rd person	-ont	-aient

1 PRESENT		**2** IMPERFECT		**3** PAST HISTORIC	
je	vend**s**	je	vend**ais**	je	vend**is**
tu	vend**s**	tu	vend**ais**	tu	vend**is**
il	vend	il	vend**ait**	il	vend**it**
elle	vend	elle	vend**ait**	elle	vend**it**
nous	vend**ons**	nous	vend**ions**	nous	vend**îmes**
vous	vend**ez**	vous	vend**iez**	vous	vend**îtes**
ils	vend**ent**	ils	vend**aient**	ils	vend**irent**
elles	vend**ent**	elles	vend**aient**	elles	vend**irent**

4 PRESENT SUBJUNCTIVE		**5** IMPERFECT SUBJUNCTIVE	
je	vend**e**	je	vend**isse**
tu	vend**es**	tu	vend**isses**
il	vend**e**	il	vend**ît**
elle	vend**e**	elle	vend**ît**
nous	vend**ions**	nous	vend**issions**
vous	vend**iez**	vous	vend**issiez**
ils	vend**ent**	ils	vend**issent**
elles	vend**ent**	elles	vend**issent**

6 FUTURE		**7** CONDITIONAL	
je	vend**rai**	je	vend**rais**
tu	vend**ras**	tu	vend**rais**
il	vend**ra**	il	vend**rait**
elle	vend**ra**	elle	vend**rait**
nous	vend**rons**	nous	vend**rions**
vous	vend**rez**	vous	vend**riez**
ils	vend**ront**	ils	vend**raient**
elles	vend**ront**	elles	vend**raient**

First Conjugation Spelling Irregularities

Before certain endings, the stems of some '-er' verbs may change slightly.

Below, and on subsequent pages, the verb types are identified, and the changes described are illustrated by means of a representative verb.

Verbs ending:	**-cer**
Change:	**c** becomes **ç** before **a** or **o**
Tenses affected:	Present, Imperfect, Past Historic, Imperfect Subjunctive, Present Participle
Model:	**lancer** *to throw* (→ **1**)

● Why the change occurs:
   A cedilla is added to the **c** to retain its soft [s] pronunciation before the vowels **a** and **o**

Verbs ending:	**-ger**
Change:	**g** becomes **ge** before **a** or **o**
Tenses affected:	Present, Imperfect, Past Historic, Imperfect Subjunctive, Present Participle
Model:	**manger** *to eat* (→ **2**)

● Why the change occurs:
   An **e** is added after the **g** to retain its soft [ʒ] pronunciation before the vowels **a** and **o**

Continued

1

INFINITIVE
lancer

PRESENT PARTICIPLE
lançant

PRESENT
je lance
tu lances
il/elle lance
nous lançons
vous lancez
ils/elles lancent

IMPERFECT
je lançais
tu lançais
il/elle lançait
nous lancions
vous lanciez
ils/elles lançaient

PAST HISTORIC
je lançai
tu lanças
il/elle lança
nous lançâmes
vous lançâtes
ils/elles lancèrent

IMPERFECT SUBJUNCTIVE
je lançasse
tu lançasses
il/elle lançât
nous lançassions
vous lançassiez
ils/elles lançassent

2

INFINITIVE
manger

PRESENT PARTICIPLE
mangeant

PRESENT
je mange
tu manges
il/elle mange
nous mangeons
vous mangez
ils/elles mangent

IMPERFECT
je mangeais
tu mangeais
il/elle mangeait
nous mangions
vous mangiez
ils/elles mangeaient

PAST HISTORIC
je mangeai
tu mangeas
il/elle mangea
nous mangeâmes
vous mangeâtes
ils/elles mangèrent

IMPERFECT SUBJUNCTIVE
je mangeasse
tu mangeasses
il/elle mangeât
nous mangeassions
vous mangeassiez
ils/elles mangeassent

First Conjugation Spelling Irregularities (ctd.)

Verbs ending   **-eler**
Change: **-l** doubles before **-e**, **-es**, **-ent** and throughout the
                    Future and Conditional tenses
Tenses affected: Present, Present Subjunctive, Future, Conditional
Model: **appeler** *to call* (→ **1**)

● Exceptions: **geler** *to freeze* ⎫ like **mener** (p. 18)
              peler *to peel*   ⎭

Verbs ending   **-eter**
Change: **-t** doubles before **-e**, **es**, **-ent** and throughout the
                    Future and Conditional tenses
Tenses affected: Present, Present Subjunctive, Future, Conditional
Model: **jeter** *to throw* (→ **2**)

● Exceptions: **acheter** *to buy* ⎫ like **mener** (p. 18)
              haleter *to pant* ⎭

Verbs ending   **-yer**
Change: **y** changes to **i** before **-e**, **-es**, **-ent** and throughout
                    the Future and Conditional tenses
Tenses affected: Present, Present Subjunctive, Future, Conditional
Model: **essuyer** *to wipe* (→ **3**)

● The change described is optional for verbs ending in **-ayer** e.g.
  payer *to pay*, **essayer** *to try*

Continued

1 *PRESENT (+ SUBJUNCTIVE)*

   j'appelle
  tu appelles
 il/elle appelle
  nous appelons
    (appelions)
  vous appelez
    (appeliez)
 ils/elles appellent

FUTURE

   j'appellerai
  tu appelleras
  il appellera *etc.*

CONDITIONAL

   j'appellerais
  tu appellerais
  il appellerait *etc.*

2 *PRESENT (+ SUBJUNCTIVE)*

   je jette
  tu jettes
 il/elle jette
  nous jetons
    (jetions)
  vous jetez
    (jetiez)
 ils/elles jettent

FUTURE

   je jetterai
  tu jetteras
  il jettera *etc.*

CONDITIONAL

   je jetterais
  tu jetterais
  il jetterait *etc.*

3 *PRESENT (+ SUBJUNCTIVE)*

   j'essuie
  tu essuies
 il/elle essuie
  nous essuyons
    (essuyions)
  vous essuyez
    (essuyiez)
 ils/elles essuient

FUTURE

   j'essuierai
  tu essuieras
  il essuiera *etc.*

CONDITIONAL

   j'essuierais
  tu essuierais
  il essuierait *etc.*

First Conjugation Spelling Irregularities (ctd.)

Verbs ending	**mener**, **peser**, **lever** etc
Change:	**e** changes to **è**, before **-e**, **-es**, **-ent** and throughout the Future and Conditional tenses
Tenses affected:	Present, Present Subjunctive, Future, Conditional
Model:	**mener** *to lead* (→ **1**)

Verbs like:	**céder**, **régler**, **espérer** etc
Change:	**é** changes to **è** before **-e**, **-es**, **-ent**
Tenses affected:	Present, Present Subjunctive
Model:	**céder** *to yield* (→ **2**)

1 *PRESENT (+ SUBJUNCTIVE)*   *FUTURE*
      je mène   **je mènerai**
      tu mènes   **tu mèneras**
    il/elle mène   **il mènera** *etc.*
    nous menons
      (menions)   *CONDITIONAL*
    vous menez   **je mènerais**
      (meniez)   **tu mènerais**
  ils/elles mènent   **il mènerait** *etc.*

2 *PRESENT (+ SUBJUNCTIVE)*
      je cède
      tu cèdes
    il/elle cède
    nous cédons
      (cédions)
    vous cédez
      (cédiez)
  ils/elles cèdent

The Imperative

The imperative is the form of the verb used to give commands or orders. It can be used politely, as in English 'Shut the door, please'.

The imperative is the same as the present tense **tu**, **nous** and **vous** forms without the subject pronouns:

donne*	**finis**	**vends**
give	*finish*	*sell*

*The final 's' of the present tense of first conjugation verbs is dropped, except before **y** and **en** (→ **1**)

donnons	**finissons**	**vendons**
let's give	*let's finish*	*let's sell*

donnez	**finissez**	**vendez**
give	*finish*	*sell*

● The imperative of irregular verbs is given in the verb tables, pp. 74 ff.

● Position of object pronouns with the imperative:
in POSITIVE commands: they follow the verb and are attached to it by hyphens (→ **2**)
in NEGATIVE commands: they precede the verb and are not attached to it (→ **3**)

● For the order of object pronouns, see p. 170

● For reflexive verbs – e.g. **se lever** *to get up* – the object pronoun is the reflexive pronoun (→ **4**)

1 Compare: **Tu donnes de l'argent à Paul**
          You give (some) money to Paul
   and: **Donne de l'argent à Paul**
          Give (some) money to Paul

2 **Excusez-moi**   **Envoyons-les-leur**
   Excuse me   Let's send them to them
   Crois-nous   **Expliquez-le-moi**
   Believe us   Explain it to me
   Attendons-la   **Rends-la-lui**
   Let's wait for her/it   Give it back to him/her

3 **Ne me dérange pas**   **Ne leur en parlons pas**
   Don't disturb me   Let's not speak to them about it
   Ne les négligeons pas   **N'y pense plus**
   Let's not neglect them   Don't think about it any more
   Ne leur répondez pas   **Ne la lui rends pas**
   Don't answer them   Don't give it back to him/her

4 **Lève-toi**   **Ne te lève pas**
   Get up   Don't get up
   Dépêchons-nous   **Ne nous affolons pas**
   Let's hurry   Let's not panic
   Levez-vous   **Ne vous levez pas**
   Get up   Don't get up

Compound Tenses: formation

In French the compound tenses are:

Perfect	(→ **1**)
Pluperfect	(→ **2**)
Future Perfect	(→ **3**)
Conditional Perfect	(→ **4**)
Past Anterior	(→ **5**)
Perfect Subjunctive	(→ **6**)
Pluperfect Subjunctive	(→ **7**)

They consist of the past participle of the verb together with an auxiliary verb. Most verbs take the auxiliary **avoir**, but some take **être** (see p. 28).

Compound tenses are formed in exactly the same way for both regular and irregular verbs, the only difference being that irregular verbs may have an irregular past participle.

The Past Participle

For all compound tenses you need to know how to form the past participle of the verb. For regular verbs this is as follows:
● 1st conjugation: replace the **-er** of the infinitive by **-é** (→ **8**)
● 2nd conjugation: replace the **-ir** of the infinitive by **-i** (→ **9**)
● 3rd conjugation: replace the **-re** of the infinitive by **-u** (→ **10**)

● See p. 50 for agreement of past participles.

Continued

with **avoir**   with **être**

1 **j'ai donné**   **je suis tombé**
I gave, have given   I fell, have fallen

2 **j'avais donné**   **j'étais tombé**
I had given   I had fallen

3 **j'aurai donné**   **je serai tombé**
I shall have given   I shall have fallen

4 **j'aurais donné**   **je serais tombé**
I should/would have given I should/would have fallen

5 **j'eus donné**   **je fus tombé**
I had given   I had fallen

6 **(que) j'aie donné**   **(que) je sois tombé**
(that) I gave, have given (that) I fell, have fallen

7 **(que) j'eusse donné**   **(que) je fusse tombé**
(that) I had given   (that) I had fallen

8 **donner → donné**
to give   given

9 **finir → fini**
to finish finished

10 **vendre → vendu**
to sell   sold

Compound Tenses: formation (ctd.)

Verbs taking the auxiliary avoir

Perfect tense: the present tense of **avoir** plus the past participle (→ **1**)

Pluperfect tense: the imperfect tense of **avoir** plus the past participle (→ **2**)

Future Perfect: the future tense of **avoir** plus the past participle (→ **3**)

Conditional Perfect: the conditional of **avoir** plus the past participle (→ **4**)

Past Anterior: the past historic of **avoir** plus the past participle (→ **5**)

Perfect Subjunctive: the present subjunctive of **avoir** plus the past participle (→ **6**)

Pluperfect Subjunctive: the imperfect subjunctive of **avoir** plus the past participle (→ **7**)

● For how to form the past participle of regular verbs see p. 22. The past participle of irregular verbs is given for each verb in the verb tables, pp. 74 ff.

● The past participle must agree in number and in gender with any preceding direct object (see p. 50)

Continued

1 *PERFECT*
j'ai donné   nous avons donné
tu as donné   vous avez donné
il/elle a donné   ils/elles ont donné

2 *PLUPERFECT*
j'avais donné   nous avions donné
tu avais donné   vous aviez donné
il/elle avait donné   ils/elles avaient donné

3 *FUTURE PERFECT*
j'aurai donné   nous aurons donné
tu auras donné   vous aurez donné
il/elle aura donné   ils/elles auront donné

4 *CONDITIONAL PERFECT*
j'aurais donné   nous aurions donné
tu aurais donné   vous auriez donné
il/elle aurait donné   ils/elles auraient donné

5 *PAST ANTERIOR*
j'eus donné   nous eûmes donné
tu eus donné   vous eûtes donné
il/elle eut donné   ils/elles eurent donné

6 *PERFECT SUBJUNCTIVE*
j'aie donné   nous ayons donné
tu aies donné   vous ayez donné
il/elle ait donné   ils/elles aient donné

7 *PLUPERFECT SUBJUNCTIVE*
j'eusse donné   nous eussions donné
tu eusses donné   vous eussiez donné
il/elle eût donné   ils/elles eussent donné

Compound Tenses: formation (ctd.)

Verbs taking the auxiliary être

Perfect tense: the present tense of **être** plus the past participle (→ **1**)

Pluperfect tense: the imperfect tense of **être** plus the past participle (→ **2**)

Future Perfect: the future tense of **être** plus the past participle (→ **3**)

Conditional Perfect: the conditional of **être** plus the past participle (→ **4**)

Past Anterior: the past historic of **être** plus the past participle (→ **5**)

Perfect Subjunctive: the present subjunctive of **être** plus the past participle (→ **6**)

Pluperfect Subjunctive: the imperfect subjunctive of **être** plus the past participle (→ **7**)

- For how to form the past participle of regular verbs see p. 22. The past participle of irregular verbs is given for each verb in the verb tables, pp. 74 ff.

- For agreement of past participles, see p. 50

- For a list of verbs and verb types that take the auxiliary **être**, see p. 28

Continued

1 *PERFECT*

je suis tombé(e)	nous sommes tombé(e)s
tu es tombé(e)	vous êtes tombé(e)(s)
il est tombé	ils sont tombés
elle est tombée	elles sont tombées

2 *PLUPERFECT*

j'étais tombé(e)	nous étions tombé(e)s
tu étais tombé(e)	vous étiez tombé(e)(s)
il était tombé	ils étaient tombés
elle était tombée	elles étaient tombées

3 *FUTURE PERFECT*

je serai tombé(e)	nous serons tombé(e)s
tu seras tombé(e)	vous serez tombé(e)(s)
il sera tombé	ils seront tombés
elle sera tombée	elles seront tombées

4 *CONDITIONAL PERFECT*

je serais tombé(e)	nous serions tombé(e)s
tu serais tombé(e)	vous seriez tombé(e)(s)
il serait tombé	ils seraient tombés
elle serait tombée	elles seraient tombées

5 *PAST ANTERIOR*

je fus tombé(e)	nous fûmes tombé(e)s
tu fus tombé(e)	vous fûtes tombé(e)(s)
il fut tombé	ils furent tombés
elle fut tombée	elles furent tombées

6 *PERFECT SUBJUNCTIVE*

je sois tombé(e)	nous soyons tombé(e)s
tu sois tombé(e)	vous soyez tombé(e)(s)
il soit tombé	ils soient tombés
elle soit tombée	elles soient tombées

7 *PLUPERFECT SUBJUNCTIVE*

je fusse tombé(e)	nous fussions tombé(e)s
tu fusses tombé(e)	vous fussiez tombé(e)(s)
il fût tombé	ils fussent tombés
elle fût tombée	elles fussent tombées

Compound Tenses (ctd.)

The following verbs take the auxiliary être

● Reflexive verbs (see p. 30) (→ **1**)

● The following intransitive verbs (i.e. verbs which cannot take a direct object), largely expressing motion or a change of state:

aller	to go (→ **2**)	**passer**	to pass
arriver	to arrive; to happen	**rentrer**	to go back/in
descendre	to go/come down	**rester**	to stay (→ **5**)
devenir	to become	**retourner**	to go back
entrer	to go/come in	**revenir**	to come back
monter	to go/come up	**sortir**	to go/come out
mourir	to die (→ **3**)	**tomber**	to fall
naître	to be born	**venir**	to come (→ **6**)
partir	to leave (→ **4**)		

● Of these, the following are conjugated with **avoir** when used transitively (i.e. with a direct object):

descendre	to bring/take down
entrer	to bring/take in
monter	to bring/take up (→ **7**)
passer	to pass; to spend (→ **8**)
rentrer	to bring/take in
retourner	to turn over
sortir	to bring/take out (→ **9**)

● Note that the past participle must show an agreement in number and gender whenever the auxiliary is **être** EXCEPT FOR REFLEXIVE VERBS WHERE THE REFLEXIVE PRONOUN IS THE INDIRECT OBJECT (see p. 50)

1 je me suis arrêté(e)
I stopped
tu t'es levé(e)
you got up

elle s'est trompée
she made a mistake
ils s'étaient battus
they had fought (one another)

2 elle est allée
she went

3 ils sont morts
they died

4 vous êtes partie
you left (*addressing a female person*)
vous êtes parties
you left (*addressing more than one female person*)

5 nous sommes resté(e)s
we stayed

6 elles étaient venues
they [female] had come

7 Il a monté les valises
He's taken up the cases

8 Nous avons passé trois semaines chez elle
We spent three weeks at her place

9 Avez-vous sorti la voiture?
Have you taken the car out?

Reflexive Verbs

A reflexive verb is one accompanied by a reflexive pronoun, e.g. **se lever** *to get up*; **se laver** *to wash (oneself)*. The pronouns are:

PERSON	SINGULAR	PLURAL
1st	**me (m')**	**nous**
2nd	**te (t')**	**vous**
3rd	**se (s')**	**se (s')**

The forms shown in brackets are used before a vowel, an **h** 'mute', or the pronoun **y** (→ **1**)

● In positive commands, **te** changes to **toi** (→ **2**)

● The reflexive pronoun 'reflects back' to the subject, but it is not always translated in English (→ **3**)
The plural pronouns are sometimes translated as *one another, each other* (the 'reciprocal' meaning) (→ **4**)
The reciprocal meaning may be emphasised by **l'un(e) l'autre (les un(e)s les autres)** (→ **5**)

● Simple tenses of reflexive verbs are conjugated in exactly the same way as those of non-reflexive verbs except that the reflexive pronoun is always used. Compound tenses are formed with the auxiliary **être**. A sample reflexive verb is conjugated in full on pp. 34 and 35.

For agreement of past participles, see p. 32

Position of Reflexive Pronouns

● In constructions other than the imperative affirmative the pronoun comes before the verb (→ **6**)

● In the imperative affirmative, the pronoun follows the verb and is attached to it by a hyphen (→ **7**)

Continued

1 Je m'ennuie
I'm bored
Elle s'habille
She's getting dressed
Ils s'y intéressent
They are interested in it
2 Assieds-toi
Sit down
Tais-toi
Be quiet
3 Je me prépare
I'm getting (myself) ready
Nous nous lavons
We're washing (ourselves)
Elle se lève
She gets up
4 Nous nous parlons
We speak to each other
Ils se ressemblent
They resemble one another
5 Ils se regardent l'un l'autre
They are looking at each other
6 Je me couche tôt
I go to bed early
Comment vous appelez-vous?
What is your name?
Il ne s'est pas rasé
He hasn't shaved
Ne te dérange pas pour nous
Don't put yourself out on our account
7 Dépêche-toi
Hurry (up)
Renseignons-nous
Let's find out
Asseyez-vous
Sit down

Reflexive Verbs (ctd.)

Past Participle Agreement

● In most reflexive verbs the reflexive pronoun is a DIRECT object pronoun (→ **1**)

● When a direct object accompanies the reflexive verb the pronoun is then the INDIRECT object (→ **2**)

● The past participle of a reflexive verb agrees in number and gender with a direct object which *precedes* the verb (usually, but not always, the reflexive pronoun) (→ **3**)
The past participle does not change if the direct object follows the verb (→ **4**)

Here are some common reflexive verbs:

s'en aller	*to go away*	**se hâter**	*to hurry*
s'amuser	*to enjoy oneself*	**se laver**	*to wash (oneself)*
s'appeler	*to be called*	**se lever**	*to get up*
s'arrêter	*to stop*	**se passer**	*to happen*
s'asseoir	*to sit (down)*	**se promener**	*to go for a walk*
se baigner	*to go swimming*	**se rappeler**	*to remember*
se blesser	*to hurt oneself*	**se ressembler**	*to resemble each other*
se coucher	*to go to bed*	**se retourner**	*to turn round*
se demander	*to wonder*	**se réveiller**	*to wake up*
se dépêcher	*to hurry*	**se sauver**	*to run away*
se diriger	*to make one's way*	**se souvenir de**	*to remember*
s'endormir	*to fall asleep*	**se taire**	*to be quiet*
s'ennuyer	*to be/get bored*	**se tromper**	*to be mistaken*
se fâcher	*to get angry*	**se trouver**	*to be (situated)*
s'habiller	*to dress (oneself)*		

Continued

1 Je m'appelle
I'm called (*literally: I call myself*)
Asseyez-vous
Sit down (*literally: Seat yourself*)
Ils se lavent
They wash (themselves)

2 Elle se lave les mains
She's washing her hands (*literally: She's washing to herself the hands*)
Je me brosse les dents
I brush my teeth
Nous nous envoyons des cadeaux à Noël
We send presents to each other at Christmas

3 'Je me suis endormi' s'est-il excusé
'I fell asleep', he apologized
Pauline s'est dirigée vers la sortie
Pauline made her way towards the exit
Ils se sont levés vers dix heures
They got up around ten o'clock
Elles se sont excusées de leur erreur
They apologised for their mistake
Est-ce que tu t'es blessée, Cécile?
Have you hurt yourself, Cécile?

4 Elle s'est lavé les cheveux
She (has) washed her hair
Nous nous sommes serré la main
We shook hands
Christine s'est cassé la jambe
Christine has broken her leg

Reflexive Verbs (ctd.)

Conjugation of: **se laver** *to wash (oneself)*

I *SIMPLE TENSES*

PRESENT

je me lave	nous nous lavons
tu te laves	vous vous lavez
il/elle se lave	ils/elles se lavent

IMPERFECT

je me lavais	nous nous lavions
tu te lavais	vous vous laviez
il/elle se lavait	ils/elles se lavaient

FUTURE

je me laverai	nous nous laverons
tu te laveras	vous vous laverez
il/elle se lavera	ils/elles se laveront

CONDITIONAL

je me laverais	nous nous laverions
tu te laverais	vous vous laveriez
il/elle se laverait	ils/elles se laveraient

PAST HISTORIC

je me lavai	nous nous lavâmes
tu te lavas	vous vous lavâtes
il/elle se lava	ils/elles se lavèrent

PRESENT SUBJUNCTIVE

je me lave	nous nous lavions
tu te laves	vous vous laviez
il/elle se lave	ils/elles se lavent

IMPERFECT SUBJUNCTIVE

je me lavasse	nous nous lavassions
tu te lavasses	vous vous lavassiez
il/elle se lavât	ils/elles se lavassent

Reflexive Verbs (ctd.)

Conjugation of: **se laver** *to wash (oneself)*

II *COMPOUND TENSES*

PERFECT
je me suis lavé(e)	**nous nous sommes lavé(e)s**
tu t'es lavé(e)	**vous vous êtes lavé(e)(s)**
il/elle s'est lavé(e)	**ils/elles se sont lavé(e)s**

PLUPERFECT
je m'étais lavé(e)	**nous nous étions lavé(e)s**
tu t'étais lavé(e)	**vous vous étiez lavé(e)(s)**
il/elle s'était lavé(e)	**ils/elles s'étaient lavé(e)s**

FUTURE PERFECT
je me serai lavé(e)	**nous nous serons lavé(e)s**
tu te seras lavé(e)	**vous vous serez lavé(e)(s)**
il/elle se sera lavé(e)	**ils/elles se seront lavé(e)s**

CONDITIONAL PERFECT
je me serais lavé(e)	**nous nous serions lavé(e)s**
tu te serais lavé(e)	**vous vous seriez lavé(e)(s)**
il/elle se serait lavé(e)	**ils/elles se seraient lavé(e)s**

PAST ANTERIOR
je me fus lavé(e)	**nous nous fûmes lavé(e)s**
tu te fus lavé(e)	**vous vous fûtes lavé(e)(s)**
il/elle se fut lavé(e)	**ils/elles se furent lavé(e)s**

PERFECT SUBJUNCTIVE
je me sois lavé(e)	**nous nous soyons lavé(e)s**
tu te sois lavé(e)	**vous vous soyez lavé(e)(s)**
il/elle se soit lavé(e)	**ils/elles se soient lavé(e)s**

PLUPERFECT SUBJUNCTIVE
je me fusse lavé(e)	**nous nous fussions lavé(e)s**
tu te fusses lavé(e)	**vous vous fussiez lavé(e)(s)**
il/elle se fût lavé(e)	**ils/elles se fussent lavé(e)s**

The Passive

In the passive, the subject *receives* the action (e.g. *I was hit*) as opposed to *performing* it (e.g. *I hit him*). In English the verb 'to be' is used with the past participle. In French the passive is formed in exactly the same way, i.e.:

a tense of **être** + past participle

The past participle agrees in number and gender with the subject (→**1**)

A sample verb is conjugated in the passive voice on pp. 38 and 39.

● The indirect object in French cannot become the subject in the passive:

in **quelqu'un m'a donné un livre** the indirect object **m'** cannot become the subject of a passive verb (unlike English: *someone gave me a book→I was given a book*)

● The passive meaning is often expressed in French by:
– **on** plus a verb in the active voice (→**2**)
– a reflexive verb (see p. 30) (→**3**)

Continued

1 **Philippe a été récompensé**
  Phillip has been rewarded
  Cette peinture est très admirée
  This painting is greatly admired
  Ils le feront pourvu qu'ils soient payés
  They'll do it provided they're paid
  Les enfants seront félicités
  The children will be congratulated
  Cette mesure aurait été critiquée si ...
  This measure would have been criticized if ...
  Les portes avaient été fermées
  The doors had been closed

2 **On leur a envoyé une lettre**
  They were sent a letter
  On nous a montré le jardin
  We were shown the garden
  On m'a dit que ...
  I was told that ...

3 **Ils se vendent 30 francs (la) pièce**
  They are sold for 30 francs each
  Ce mot ne s'emploie plus
  This word is no longer used

The Passive (ctd.)

Conjugation of: **être aimé** *to be liked*

PRESENT

je suis aimé(e)	nous sommes aimé(e)s
tu es aimé(e)	vous êtes aimé(e)(s)
il/elle est aimé(e)	ils/elles sont aimé(e)s

IMPERFECT

j'étais aimé(e)	nous étions aimé(e)s
tu étais aimé(e)	vous étiez aimé(e)(s)
il/elle était aimé(e)	ils/elles étaient aimé(e)s

FUTURE

je serai aimé(e)	nous serons aimé(e)s
tu seras aimé(e)	vous serez aimé(e)(s)
il/elle sera aimé(e)	ils/elles seront aimé(e)s

CONDITIONAL

je serais aimé(e)	nous serions aimé(e)s
tu serais aimé(e)	vous seriez aimé(e)(s)
il/elle serait aimé(e)	ils/elles seraient aimé(e)s

PAST HISTORIC

je fus aimé(e)	nous fûmes aimé(e)s
tu fus aimé(e)	vous fûtes aimé(e)(s)
il/elle fut aimé(e)	ils/elles furent aimé(e)s

PRESENT SUBJUNCTIVE

je sois aimé(e)	nous soyons aimé(e)s
tu sois aimé(e)	vous soyez aimé(e)(s)
il/elle soit aimé(e)	ils/elles soient aimé(e)s

IMPERFECT SUBJUNCTIVE

je fusse aimé(e)	nous fussions aimé(e)s
tu fusses aimé(e)	vous fussiez aimé(e)(s)
il/elle fût aimé(e)	ils/elles fussent aimé(e)s

The Passive (ctd.)

Conjugation of: **être aimé** *to be liked*

PERFECT
  j'ai été aimé(e)   **nous avons été aimé(e)s**
  tu as été aimé(e)   **vous avez été aimé(e)(s)**
  il/elle a été aimé(e)   **ils/elles ont été aimé(e)s**

PLUPERFECT
  j'avais été aimé(e)   **nous avions été aimé(e)s**
  tu avais été aimé(e)   **vous aviez été aimé(e)(s)**
  il/elle avait été aimé(e)   **ils/elles avaient été aimé(e)s**

FUTURE PERFECT
  j'aurai été aimé(e)   **nous aurons été aimé(e)s**
  tu auras été aimé(e)   **vous aurez été aimé(e)(s)**
  il/elle aura été aimé(e)   **ils/elles auront été aimé(e)s**

CONDITIONAL PERFECT
  j'aurais été aimé(e)   **nous aurions été aimé(e)s**
  tu aurais été aimé(e)   **vous auriez été aimé(e)(s)**
  il/elle aurait été aimé(e)   **ils/elles auraient été aimé(e)s**

PAST ANTERIOR
  j'eus été aimé(e)   **nous eûmes été aimé(e)s**
  tu eus été aimé(e)   **vous eûtes été aimé(e)(s)**
  il/elle eut été aimé(e)   **ils/elles eurent été aimé(e)s**

PERFECT SUBJUNCTIVE
  j'aie été aimé(e)   **nous ayons été aimé(e)s**
  tu aies été aimé(e)   **vous ayez été aimé(e)(s)**
  il/elle ait été aimé(e)   **ils/elles aient été aimé(e)s**

PLUPERFECT SUBJUNCTIVE
  j'eusse été aimé(e)   **nous eussions été aimé(e)s**
  tu eusses été aimé(e)   **vous eussiez été aimé(e)(s)**
  il/elle eût été aimé(e)   **ils/elles eussent été aimé(e)s**

Impersonal Verbs

Impersonal verbs are used only in the infinitive and in the third person singular with the subject pronoun **il**, generally translated *it*.

    e.g. **il pleut**
    it's raining
    il est facile de dire que ...
    it's easy to say that ...

The most common impersonal verbs are:

INFINITIVE	CONSTRUCTIONS
s'agir	**il s'agit de** + noun (→**1**)
	it's a question/matter of something,
	it's about something
	il s'agit de + infinitive (→**2**)
	it's a question/matter of doing; somebody must do
falloir	**il faut** + noun object (+ indirect object) (→**3**)
	(somebody) needs something, something is necessary (to somebody)
	il faut + infinitive (+ indirect object) (→**4**)
	it is necessary to do
	il faut que + subjunctive (→**5**)
	it is necessary to do, somebody must do
grêler	**il grêle**
	it's hailing
neiger	**il neige**
	it's snowing
pleuvoir	**il pleut** }(→**6**)
	it's raining
tonner	**il tonne**
	it's thundering
valoir mieux	**il vaut mieux** + infinitive (→**7**)
	it's better to do
	il vaut mieux que + subjunctive (→**8**)
	it's better to do/that somebody does

Continued

1 Il ne s'agit pas d'argent
It isn't a question/matter of money
De quoi s'agit-il?
What is it about?
Il s'agit de la vie d'une famille au début du siècle
It's about the life of a family at the turn of the century

2 Il s'agit de faire vite
We must act quickly

3 Il faut du courage pour faire ça
One needs courage to do that; Courage is needed to do that
Il me faut une chaise de plus
I need an extra chair

4 Il faut partir
It is necessary to leave; We/I/You must leave*
Il me fallait prendre une décision
I had to make a decision

5 Il faut que vous partiez
You have to leave/You must leave
Il faudrait que je fasse mes valises
I should have to/ought to pack my cases

6 Il pleuvait à verse
It was raining heavily/It was pouring

7 Il vaut mieux refuser
It's better to refuse; You/He/I had better refuse*
Il vaudrait mieux rester
You/We/She had better stay*

8 Il vaudrait mieux que nous ne venions pas
It would be better if we didn't come; We'd better not come

The translation here obviously depends on context

Impersonal Verbs (ctd.)

The following verbs are also commonly used in impersonal constructions:

INFINITIVE	*CONSTRUCTIONS*
avoir	**il y a** + noun (→**1**)
	there is/are
être	**il est** + noun (→**2**)
	it is; there are (very literary style)
	il est + adjective + **de** + infinitive (→**3**)
	it is
faire	**il fait** + adjective of weather (→**4**)
	it is
	il fait + noun depicting weather/dark/light etc.
	it is (→**5**)
manquer	**il manque** + noun (+ indirect object) (→**6**)
	there is/are ... missing, something is
	missing/lacking
paraître	**il paraît que** + subjunctive (→**7**)
	it seems/appears that
	il paraît + indirect object + **que** + indicative (→**8**)
	it seems/appears to somebody that
rester	**il reste** + noun (+ indirect object) (→**9**)
	there is/are ... left, (somebody) has something left
sembler	**il semble que** + subjunctive (→**10**)
	it seems/appears that
	il semble + indirect object + **que** + indicative (→**11**)
	it seems/appears to somebody that
suffire	**il suffit de** + infinitive (→**12**)
	it is enough to do
	il suffit de + noun (→**13**)
	something is enough, it only takes something

Continued

1 Il y a du pain (qui reste)
There is some bread (left)
Il n'y avait pas de lettres ce matin
There were no letters this morning

2 Il est dix heures
It's ten o'clock
Il est des gens qui ...
There are (some) people who ...

3 Il était inutile de protester
It was useless to protest
Il est facile de critiquer
Criticizing is easy

4 Il fait beau/mauvais
It's lovely/horrible weather

5 Il faisait du soleil/du vent
It was sunny/windy
Il fait jour/nuit
It's light/dark

6 Il manque deux tasses
There are two cups missing; Two cups are missing
Il manquait un bouton à sa chemise
His shirt had a button missing

7 Il paraît qu'ils partent demain
It appears they are leaving tomorrow

8 Il nous paraît certain qu'il aura du succès
It seems certain to us that he'll be successful

9 Il reste deux miches de pain
There are two loaves left
Il lui restait cinquante francs
He/She had fifty francs left

10 Il semble que vous ayez raison
It seems that you are right

11 Il me semblait qu'il conduisait trop vite
It seemed to me (that) he was driving too fast

12 Il suffit de téléphoner pour réserver une place
You need only phone to reserve a seat

13 Il suffit d'une seule erreur pour tout gâcher
One single error is enough to ruin everything

The Infinitive

The infinitive is the form of the verb found in dictionary entries meaning 'to ...', e.g. **donner** *to give*, **vivre** *to live*.

There are three main types of verbal construction involving the infinitive:

- with no linking preposition (→**1**)
- with the linking preposition **à** (→**2**)
  (see also p. 64)
- with the linking preposition **de** (→**3**)
  (see also p. 64)

Verbs followed by an infinitive with no linking preposition

- **devoir, pouvoir, savoir, vouloir** and **falloir** (i.e. modal auxiliary verbs: p. 52) (→**1**)
- **valoir mieux:** see Impersonal Verbs, p. 40
- verbs of seeing or hearing e.g. **voir** *to see*, **entendre** *to hear* (→**4**)
- intransitive verbs of motion e.g. **aller** *to go*, **descendre** *to come/go down* (→**5**)
- **envoyer** *to send* (→**6**)
- **faillir** (→**7**)
- **faire** (→**8**)
- **laisser** *to let, allow* (→**9**)
- The following common verbs:

adorer	*to love*	
aimer	*to like, love*	(→**10**)
aimer mieux	*to prefer*	(→**11**)
compter	*to expect*	
désirer	*to wish, want*	(→**12**)
détester	*to hate*	(→**13**)
espérer	*to hope*	(→**14**)
oser	*to dare*	(→**15**)
préférer	*to prefer*	
sembler	*to seem*	(→**16**)
souhaiter	*to wish*	

Continued

1 **Voulez-vous attendre?**
Would you like to wait?

2 **J'apprends à nager**
I'm learning to swim

3 **Essayez de venir**
Try to come

4 **Il nous a vus arriver**
He saw us arriving

On les entend chanter
You can hear them singing

5 **Allez voir Nicolas**
Go and see Nicolas
Descends leur demander
Go down and ask them

6 **Je l'ai envoyé les voir**
I sent him to see them

7 **J'ai failli tomber**
I almost fell

8 **Ne me faites pas rire!**
Don't make me laugh!
J'ai fait réparer ma valise
I've had my case repaired

9 **Laissez-moi passer**
Let me pass

10 **Il aime nous accompagner**
He likes to come with us

11 **J'aimerais mieux le choisir moi-même**
I'd rather choose it myself

12 **Elle ne désire pas venir**
She doesn't wish to come

13 **Je déteste me lever le matin**
I hate getting up in the morning

14 **Espérez-vous aller en vacances?**
Are you hoping to go on holiday?

15 **Nous n'avons pas osé y retourner**
We haven't dared go back

16 **Vous semblez être inquiet**
You seem to be worried

The Infinitive: Set Expressions

The following are set in French with the meaning shown:

aller chercher	*to go for, to go and get*	(→**1**)
envoyer chercher	*to send for*	(→**2**)
entendre dire que	*to hear it said that*	(→**3**)
entendre parler de	*to hear of/about*	(→**4**)
faire entrer	*to show in*	(→**5**)
faire sortir	*to let out*	(→**6**)
faire venir	*to send for*	(→**7**)
laisser tomber	*to drop*	(→**8**)
vouloir dire	*to mean*	(→**9**)

The Perfect Infinitive

● The perfect infinitive is formed using the auxiliary verb **avoir** or **être** as appropriate with the past participle of the verb (→**10**)

● The perfect infinitive is found:
– following the preposition **après** *after* (→**11**)
– following certain verbal constructions (→**12**)

1 **Va chercher tes photos**
   Go and get your photos
   Il est allé chercher Alexandre
   He's gone to get Alexander

2 **J'ai envoyé chercher un médecin**
   I've sent for a doctor

3 **J'ai entendu dire qu'il est malade**
   I've heard it said that he's ill

4 **Je n'ai plus entendu parler de lui**
   I didn't hear anything more (said) of him

5 **Fais entrer nos invités**
   Show our guests in

6 **J'ai fait sortir le chat**
   I've let the cat out

7 **Je vous ai fait venir parce que ...**
   I sent for you because ...

8 **Il a laissé tomber le vase**
   He dropped the vase

9 **Qu'est-ce que cela veut dire?**
   What does that mean?

10 **avoir fini**
    to have finished
    être allé   **s'être levé**
    to have gone   to have got up

11 **Après avoir pris cette décision, il nous a appelé**
    After making/having made that decision, he called us
    Après être sorties, elles se sont dirigées vers le parking
    After leaving/having left, they headed for the car park
    Après nous être levé(e)s, nous avons lu les journaux
    After getting up/having got up, we read the papers

12 **pardonner à qn d'avoir fait**
    to forgive sb for doing/having done
    remercier qn d'avoir fait
    to thank sb for doing/having done
    regretter d'avoir fait
    to be sorry for doing/having done

The Present Participle

Formation

● 1st conjugation
Replace the **-er** of the infinitive by **-ant** (→**1**)

 – Verbs ending in **-cer**: **c** changes to **ç** (→**2**)
 – Verbs ending in **-ger**: **g** changes to **ge** (→**3**)

● 2nd conjugation
Replace the **-ir** of the infinitive by **-issant** (→**4**)

● 3rd conjugation
Replace the **-re** of the infinitive by **-ant** (→**5**)

● For irregular present participles, see irregular verbs, p. 74 ff.

Uses

The present participle has a more restricted use in French than in English.

● Used as a verbal form, the present participle is invariable. It is found:
 – on its own, where it corresponds to the English present participle (→**6**)
 – following the preposition **en** (→**7**)
 Note, in particular, the construction:
 verb + **en** + present participle
 which is often translated by an English phrasal verb, i.e. one followed by a preposition like *to run down, to bring up* (→**8**)

● Used as an adjective, the present participle agrees in number and gender with the noun or pronoun (→**9**)

● Note, in particular, the use of **ayant** and **étant** – the present participles of the auxiliary verbs **avoir** and **être** – with a past participle (→**10**)

Continued

1 **donner** → **donnant**
   to give   giving

2 **lancer** → **lançant**
   to throw   throwing

3 **manger** → **mangeant**
   to eat   eating

4 **finir**   → **finissant**
   to finish   finishing

5 **vendre** → **vendant**
   to sell   selling

6 **David, habitant près de Paris, a la possibilité de ...**
   David, living near Paris, has the opportunity of ...
   Elle, pensant que je serais fâché, a dit '...'
   She, thinking that I would be angry, said '...'
   Ils m'ont suivi, criant à tue-tête
   They followed me, shouting at the top of their voices

7 **En attendant sa sœur, Richard s'est endormi**
   While waiting for his sister, Richard fell asleep
   Téléphone-nous en arrivant chez toi
   Telephone us when you get home
   En appuyant sur ce bouton, on peut ...
   By pressing this button, you can ...
   Il s'est blessé en essayant de sauver un chat
   He hurt himself trying to rescue a cat

8 **sortir en courant**
   to run out (*literally: to go out running*)
   avancer en boîtant
   to limp along (*literally: to go forward limping*)

9 **le soleil couchant**   **une lumière éblouissante**
   the setting sun   a dazzling light
   ils sont déroutants   **elles étaient étonnantes**
   they are disconcerting   they were surprising

10 **Ayant mangé plus tôt, il a pu ...**
    Having eaten earlier, he was able to ...
    Etant arrivée en retard, elle a dû ...
    Having arrived late, she had to ...

Past Participle Agreement

Like adjectives, a past participle must sometimes agree in number and gender with a noun or pronoun. For the rules of agreement, see below. Example: **donné**

	MASCULINE	FEMININE
SING.	donné	donnée
PLUR.	donnés	données

● When the masculine singular form already ends in **-s**, no further **s** is added in the masculine plural, e.g. **pris** *taken*

Rules of Agreement in Compound Tenses

● When the auxiliary verb is **avoir**
The past participle remains in the masculine singular form, unless a direct object precedes the verb. The past participle then agrees in number and gender with the preceding direct object (→**1**)

● When the auxiliary verb is **être**
The past participle of a non-reflexive verb agrees in number and gender with the subject (→**2**)
The past participle of a reflexive verb agrees in number and gender with the reflexive pronoun, if the pronoun is a direct object (→**3**)
No agreement is made if the reflexive pronoun is an indirect object (→**4**)

The Past Participle as an adjective

The past participle agrees in number and gender with the noun or pronoun (→**5**)

1 **Voici le livre que vous avez demandé**
Here's the book you asked for
Laquelle avaient-elles choisie?
Which one had they chosen?
Ces amis? Je les ai rencontrés à Edimbourg
Those friends? I met them in Edinburgh
Il a gardé toutes les lettres qu'elle a écrites
He has kept all the letters she wrote

2 **Est-ce que ton frère est allé à l'étranger?**
Did your brother go abroad?
Elle était restée chez elle
She had stayed at home
Ils sont partis dans la matinée
They left in the morning
Mes cousines sont revenues hier
My cousins came back yesterday

3 **Tu t'es rappelé d'acheter du pain, Georges?**
Did you remember to buy bread, George?
Martine s'est demandée pourquoi il l'appelait
Martine wondered why he was calling her
'Lui et moi nous nous sommes cachés' a-t-elle dit
'He and I hid,' she said
Les vendeuses se sont mises en grève
Shop assistants have gone on strike
Vous vous êtes brouillés?
Have you fallen out with each other?
Les ouvrières s'étaient entraidées
The workers had helped one another

4 **Elle s'est lavé les mains**
She washed her hands
Ils se sont parlé pendant des heures
They talked to each other for hours

5 **à un moment donné**   **la porte ouverte**
at a given time   the open door
ils sont bien connus   **elles semblent fatiguées**
they are well-known   they seem tired

Modal Auxiliary Verbs

● In French, the modal auxiliary verbs are: **devoir**, **pouvoir**, **savoir**, **vouloir** and **falloir**.

● They are followed by a verb in the infinitive and have the following meanings:

devoir   *to have to, must* (→**1**)
to be due to (→**2**)
in the conditional/conditional perfect:
should/should have, ought/ought to have (→**3**)

pouvoir   *to be able to, can* (→**4**)
to be allowed to, can, may (→**5**)
indicating possibility: *may/might/could* (→**6**)

savoir   *to know how to, can* (→**7**)

vouloir   *to want/wish to* (→**8**)
to be willing to, will (→**9**)
in polite phrases (→**10**)

falloir   *to be necessary:* see Impersonal Verbs, p. 40

1 **Je dois leur rendre visite**
   I must visit them
   Elle a dû partir
   She (has) had to leave
   Il a dû regretter d'avoir parlé
   He must have been sorry he spoke

2 **Vous devez revenir demain**
   You're due (to come) back tomorrow
   Je devais attraper le train de neuf heures mais ...
   I was (supposed) to catch the nine o'clock train but ...

3 **Je devrais le faire**
   I ought to do it
   J'aurais dû m'excuser
   I ought to have apologised

4 **Il ne peut pas lever le bras**
   He can't raise his arm
   Pouvez-vous réparer cette montre?
   Can you mend this watch?

5 **Puis-je les accompagner?**
   May I go with them?

6 **Il peut encore changer d'avis**
   He may change his mind yet
   Cela pourrait être vrai
   It could/might be true

7 **Savez-vous conduire?**
   Can you drive?
   Je ne sais pas faire une omelette
   I don't know how to make an omelette

8 **Elle veut rester encore un jour**
   She wants to stay another day

9 **Ils ne voulaient pas le faire**
   They wouldn't do it/They weren't willing to do it
   Ma voiture ne veut pas démarrer
   My car won't start

10 **Voulez-vous boire quelque chose?**
   Would you like something to drink?

Use of Tenses

The Present

● Unlike English, French does not distinguish between the simple present (e.g. *I smoke, he reads, we live*) and the continuous present (e.g. *I am smoking, he is reading, we are living*) (→ 1)

● To emphasise continuity, the following constructions may be used:

être en train de faire
être à faire } *to be doing* (→ 2)

● French uses the present tense where English uses the perfect in the following cases:
  – with certain prepositions of time – notably **depuis** *for/since* – when an action begun in the past is continued in the present (→ 3)
    Note, however, that the perfect is used as in English when the verb is negative or the action has been completed (→ 4)
  – in the construction **venir de faire** *to have just done* (→ 5)

The Future

The future is generally used as in English, but note the following:

● Immediate future time is often expressed by means of the present tense of **aller** plus an infinitive (→ 6)

● In time clauses expressing future action, French uses the future where English uses the present (→ 7)

The Future Perfect

● Used as in English to mean *shall/will have done* (→ 8)

● In time clauses expressing future action, where English uses the perfect tense (→ 9)

Continued

1 **Je fume**   I smoke OR I am smoking
  Il lit   He reads OR He is reading
  Nous habitons   We live OR We are living

2 **Il est en train de travailler**
  He's (busy) working

3 **Paul apprend à nager depuis six mois**
  Paul's been learning to swim for six months (*and still is*)
  Je suis debout depuis sept heures
  I've been up since seven
  Il y a longtemps que vous attendez?
  Have you been waiting long?
  Voilà deux semaines que nous sommes ici
  That's two weeks we've been here (now)

4 **Ils ne se sont pas vus depuis des mois**
  They haven't seen each other for months
  Elle est revenue il y a un an
  She came back a year ago

5 **Elisabeth vient de partir**
  Elizabeth has just left

6 **Tu vas tomber si tu ne fais pas attention**
  You'll fall if you're not careful
  Il va manquer le train
  He's going to miss the train
  Ça va prendre une demi-heure
  It'll take half an hour

7 **Quand il viendra vous serez en vacances**
  When he comes you'll be on holiday
  Faites-nous savoir aussitôt qu'elle arrivera
  Let us know as soon as she arrives

8 **J'aurai fini dans une heure**
  I shall have finished in an hour

9 **Quand tu auras lu ce roman, rends-le-moi**
  When you've read the novel, give it back to me
  Je partirai dès que j'aurai fini
  I'll leave as soon as I've finished

Use of Tenses (ctd.)

The Imperfect

● The imperfect describes:
- an action (or state) in the past without definite limits in time (→ **1**)
- habitual action(s) in the past (often translated by means of *would* or *used to*) (→ **2**)

● French uses the imperfect tense where English uses the pluperfect in the following cases:
- with certain prepositions of time – notably **depuis** *for/ since* – when an action begun in the remoter past was continued in the more recent past (→ **3**)

  Note, however, that the pluperfect *is* used as in English, when the verb is negative or the action has been completed (→ **4**)
- in the construction **venir de faire** *to have just done* (→ **5**)

The Perfect

● The perfect is used to recount a completed action or event in the past. Note that this corresponds to a perfect tense or a simple past tense in English (→ **6**)

The Past Historic

● Only ever used in *written, literary* French, the past historic recounts a completed action in the past, corresponding to a simple past tense in English (→ **7**)

The Past Anterior

This tense is used instead of the pluperfect when a verb in another part of the sentence is in the past historic. That is

● in time clauses, after conjunctions like: **quand**, **lorsque** *when*, **dès que**, **aussitôt que** *as soon as*, **après que** *after* (→ **8**)
● after **à peine** *hardly, scarcely* (→ **9**)

The Subjunctive

● In spoken French, the present subjunctive generally replaces the imperfect subjunctive. See also pp. 58 ff.

1 **Elle regardait par la fenêtre**
She was looking out of the window
Il pleuvait quand je suis sorti de chez moi
It was raining when I left the house
Nos chambres donnaient sur la plage
Our rooms overlooked the beach

2 **Dans sa jeunesse il se levait à l'aube**
In his youth he got up at dawn
Nous causions des heures entières
We would talk for hours on end
Elle te taquinait, n'est-ce pas?
She used to tease you, didn't she?

3 **Nous habitions à Londres depuis deux ans**
We had been living in London for two years (*and still were*)
Il était malade depuis 1985
He had been ill since 1985
Il y avait assez longtemps qu'il le faisait
He had been doing it for quite a long time

4 **Voilà un an que je ne l'avais pas vu**
I hadn't seen him for a year
Il y avait une heure qu'elle était arrivée
She had arrived one hour before

5 **Je venais de les rencontrer**
I had just met them

6 **Nous sommes allés au bord de la mer**
We went/have been to the seaside
Il a refusé de nous aider
He (has) refused to help us
La voiture ne s'est pas arrêtée
The car didn't stop/hasn't stopped

7 **Le roi mourut en 1592**
The king died in 1592

8 **Quand il eut fini, il se leva**
When he had finished, he got up

9 **A peine eut-il parlé qu'on frappa à la porte**
He had scarcely spoken when there was a knock at the door

The Subjunctive: when to use it

(For how to form the subjunctive see pp. 6 ff.)

● After certain conjunctions

quoique **bien que**	*although* (→ **1**)
pour que **afin que**	*so that* (→ **2**)

pourvu que   *provided that* (→ **3**)
jusqu'à ce que   *until* (→ **4**)
avant que (... ne)   *before* (→ **5**)
à moins que (... ne)   *unless* (→ **6**)

de peur que (... ne) **de crainte que (... ne)**	*for fear that, lest* (→ **7**)

Note that the **ne** following the conjunctions in examples **5** to **7** has no translation value. It is often omitted in spoken informal French.

● After the conjunctions

de sorte que **de façon que** **de manière que**	*so that* (indicating a *purpose*) (→ **8**)

When these conjunctions introduce a *result* and not a *purpose*, the subjunctive is not used (→ **9**)

● After impersonal constructions which express necessity, possibility etc

il faut que **il est nécessaire que**	*it is necessary that* (→ **10**)

il est possible que   *it is possible that* (→ **11**)
il semble que   *it seems that* (→ **12**)
il vaut mieux que   *it is better that* (→ **13**)
il est dommage que   *it's a pity that* (→ **14**)

Continued

1 **Bien qu'il fasse beaucoup d'efforts, il est peu récompensé**
Although he makes a lot of effort, he isn't rewarded for it

2 **Demandez un reçu afin que vous puissiez être remboursé**
Ask for a receipt so that you can get a refund

3 **Nous partirons ensemble pourvu que Sylvie soit d'accord**
We'll leave together provided Sylvie agrees

4 **Reste ici jusqu'à ce que nous revenions**
Stay here until we come back

5 **Je le ferai avant que tu ne partes**
I'll do it before you leave

6 **Ce doit être Paul, à moins que je ne me trompe**
That must be Paul, unless I'm mistaken

7 **Parlez bas de peur qu'on ne vous entende**
Speak softly lest anyone hears you

8 **Retournez-vous de sorte que je vous voie**
Turn round so that I can see you

9 **Il refuse de le faire de sorte que je dois le faire moi-même**
He refuses to do it so that I have to do it myself

10 **Il faut que je vous parle immédiatement**
I must speak to you right away/It is necessary that I speak …

11 **Il est possible qu'ils aient raison**
They may be right/It's possible that they are right

12 **Il semble qu'elle ne soit pas venue**
It appears that she hasn't come

13 **Il vaut mieux que vous restiez chez vous**
It's better that you stay at home

14 **Il est dommage qu'elle ait perdu cette adresse**
It's a shame/a pity that she's lost the address

The Subjunctive: when to use it (ctd.)

● After verbs of:
 – 'wishing'

 vouloir que
 désirer que } *to wish that, want* (→ **1**)
 souhaiter que

 – 'fearing'

 craindre que
 avoir peur que } *to be afraid that* (→ **2**)

Note that **ne** in the first phrase of example 2 has no translation value. It is often omitted in spoken informal French.

 – 'ordering', 'forbidding', 'allowing'

 ordonner que *to order that* (→ **3**)
 défendre que *to forbid that* (→ **4**)
 permettre que *to allow that* (→ **5**)

 – opinion, expressing uncertainty

 croire que
 penser que } *to think that* (→ **6**)
 douter que *to doubt that* (→ **7**)

 – emotion (e.g. regret, shame, pleasure)

 regretter que *to be sorry that* (→ **8**)
 être content/surpris etc **que**
 to be pleased/ surprised etc *that* (→ **9**)

● After a superlative (→ **10**)

● After certain adjectives expressing some sort of 'uniqueness'

 dernier ... qui/que *last ... who/that*
 premier ... qui/que *first ... who/that*
 meilleur ... qui/que *best ... who/that* } (→ **11**)
 seul }
 unique } **... qui/que** *only ... who/that*

Continued

1　**Nous voulons qu'elle soit contente**
　　We want her to be happy (*literally: We want that she is happy*)
　　Désirez-vous que je le fasse?
　　Do you want me to do it?

2　**Il craint qu'il ne soit trop tard**
　　He's afraid it may be too late
　　Avez-vous peur qu'il ne revienne pas?
　　Are you afraid that he won't come back?

3　**Il a ordonné qu'ils soient désormais à l'heure**
　　He has ordered that they be on time from now on

4　**Elle défend que vous disiez cela**
　　She forbids you to say that

5　**Permettez que nous vous aidions**
　　Allow us to help you

6　**Je ne pense pas qu'ils soient venus**
　　I don't think they came

7　**Nous doutons qu'il ait dit la vérité**
　　We doubt that he told the truth

8　**Je regrette que vous ne puissiez pas venir**
　　I'm sorry that you cannot come

9　**Je suis content que vous les aimiez**
　　I'm pleased that you like them

10　**la personne la plus sympathique que je connaisse**
　　the nicest person I know
　　l'article le moins cher que j'aie jamais acheté
　　the cheapest item I have ever bought

11　**Voici la dernière lettre qu'elle m'ait écrite**
　　This is the last letter she wrote to me
　　David est la seule personne qui puisse me conseiller
　　David is the only person who can advise me

The Subjunctive: when to use it (ctd.)

● After   **si (...) que**   *however (...)*   (→ **1**)
            qui que   *whoever*   (→ **2**)
            quoi que   *whatever*   (→ **3**)

   ● After **que** in the following:
     – to form the 3rd person imperative or to express a wish (→ **4**)
     – when **que** has the meaning *if*, replacing **si** in a clause (→ **5**)
     – when **que** has the meaning *whether* (→ **6**)

● In relative clauses following certain types of indefinite and negative construction (→ **7/8**)

● In set expressions (→ **9**)

1 **si courageux qu'il soit**
however brave he may be
si peu que ce soit
however little it is

2 **Qui que vous soyez, allez-vous-en!**
Whoever you are, go away!

3 **Quoi que nous fassions, ...**
Whatever we do, ...

4 **Qu'il entre!**
Let him come in!
Que cela vous serve de leçon!
Let that be a lesson to you!

5 **S'il fait beau et que tu te sentes mieux, nous irons ...**
If it's nice and you're feeling better, we'll go ...

6 **Que tu viennes ou non, je ...**
Whether you come or not, I ...

7 **Il cherche une maison qui ait deux caves**
He's looking for a house which has two cellars
(*subjunctive used since such a house may or may not exist*)
J'ai besoin d'un livre qui décrive l'art du mime
I need a book which describes the art of mime
(*subjunctive used since such a book may or may not exist*)

8 **Je n'ai rencontré personne qui la connaisse**
I haven't met anyone who knows her
Il n'y a rien qui puisse vous empêcher de ...
There's nothing that can prevent you from ...

9 **Vive le roi!**
Long live the king!
Que Dieu vous bénisse!
God bless you!

Verbs governing à and de

The following lists (pp. 64 to 72) contain common verbal constructions using the prepositions **à** and **de**

Note the following abbreviations:

infin.	infinitive
perf. infin.	perfect infinitive*
qch	quelque chose
qn	quelqu'un
sb	somebody
sth	something

*For formation see p. 46

accuser qn de qch/de + perf. infin.	to accuse sb of sth/of doing, having done (→**1**)
accoutumer qn à qch/à + infin.	to accustom sb to sth/to doing
acheter qch à qn	to buy sth from sb/for sb (→**2**)
achever de + infin.	to end up doing
aider qn à + infin.	to help sb to do (→**3**)
s'amuser à + infin.	to have fun doing
s'apercevoir de qch	to notice sth (→**4**)
apprendre qch à qn	to teach sb sth
apprendre à + infin.	to learn to do (→**5**)
apprendre à qn à + infin.	to teach sb to do (→**6**)
s'approcher de qn/qch	to approach sb/sth (→**7**)
arracher qch à qn	to snatch sth from sb (→**8**)
(s')arrêter de + infin.	to stop doing (→**9**)
arriver à + infin.	to manage to do (→**10**)
assister à qch	to attend sth, be at sth
s'attendre à + infin.	to expect to do (→**11**)
blâmer qn de qch/de + perf. infin.	to blame sb for sth/for having done (→**12**)
cacher qch à qn	to hide sth from sb (→**13**)
cesser de + infin.	to stop doing (→**14**)

Continued

1 **Il m'a accusé d'avoir menti**
He accused me of lying

2 **Marie-Christine leur a acheté deux billets**
Marie-Christine bought two tickets from/for them

3 **Aidez-moi à porter ces valises**
Help me to carry these cases

4 **Il ne s'est pas aperçu de son erreur**
He didn't notice his mistake

5 **Elle apprend à lire**
She's learning to read

6 **Je lui apprends à nager**
I'm teaching him/her to swim

7 **Elle s'est approchée de moi, en disant '...'**
She came up to me, saying '...'

8 **Le voleur lui a arraché l'argent**
The thief snatched the money from him/her

9 **Arrêtez de faire du bruit!**
Stop being (so) noisy!

10 **Je n'arrive pas à le comprendre**
I can't understand it

11 **Est-ce qu'elle s'attendait à le voir?**
Was she expecting to see him?

12 **Je ne la blâme pas de l'avoir fait**
I don't blame her for doing it

13 **Cache-les-leur!**
Hide them from them!

14 **Est-ce qu'il a cessé de pleuvoir?**
Has it stopped raining?

Verbs governing à and de (ctd.)

changer de qch	*to change sth* (→ **1**)
se charger de qch/**de** + infin.	*to see to sth/undertake to do*
chercher à + infin.	*to try to do*
commander à qn **de** + infin.	*to order sb to do* (→ **2**)
commencer à/de + infin.	*to begin to do* (→ **3**)
conseiller à qn **de** + infin.	*to advise sb to do* (→ **4**)
consentir à qch/**à** + infin.	*to agree to sth/to do* (→ **5**)
continuer à/de + infin.	*to continue to do*
craindre de + infin.	*to be afraid to do/of doing*
décider de + infin.	*to decide to* (→ **6**)
se décider à + infin.	*to make up one's mind to do*
défendre à qn **de** + infin.	*to forbid sb to do* (→ **7**)
demander qch **à** qn	*to ask sb sth/for sth* (→ **8**)
demander à qn **de** + infin.	*to ask sb to do* (→ **9**)
se dépêcher de + infin.	*to hurry to do*
dépendre de qn/qch	*to depend on sb/sth*
déplaire à qn	*to displease sb* (→ **10**)
désobéir à qn	*to disobey sb* (→ **11**)
dire à qn **de** + infin.	*to tell sb to do* (→ **12**)
dissuader qn **de** + infin.	*to dissuade sb from doing*
douter de qch	*to doubt sth*
se douter de qch	*to suspect sth*
s'efforcer de + infin.	*to strive to do*
empêcher qn **de** + infin.	*to prevent sb from doing* (→ **13**)
emprunter qch **à** qn	*to borrow sth from sb* (→ **14**)
encourager qn **à** + infin.	*to encourage sb to do* (→ **15**)
enlever qch **à** qn	*to take sth away from sb*
enseigner qch **à** qn	*to teach sb sth*
enseigner à qn **à** + infin.	*to teach sb to do*
entreprendre de + infin.	*to undertake to do*
essayer de + infin.	*to try to do* (→ **16**)
éviter de + infin.	*to avoid doing* (→ **17**)

Continued

1 **J'ai changé d'avis/de robe**
I changed my mind/my dress
Il faut changer de train à Toulouse
You have to change trains at Toulouse

2 **Il leur a commandé de tirer**
He ordered them to shoot

3 **Il commence à neiger**
It's starting to snow

4 **Il leur a conseillé d'attendre**
He advised them to wait

5 **Je n'ai pas consenti à l'aider**
I haven't agreed to help him/her

6 **Qu'est-ce que vous avez décidé de faire?**
What have you decided to do?

7 **Je leur ai défendu de sortir**
I've forbidden them to go out

8 **Je lui ai demandé l'heure**
I asked him/her the time
Il lui a demandé un livre
He asked him/her for a book

9 **Demande à Alain de le faire**
Ask Alan to do it

10 **Leur attitude lui déplaît**
He/She doesn't like their attitude

11 **Ils lui désobéissent souvent**
They often disobey him/her

12 **Dites-leur de se taire**
Tell them to be quiet

13 **Le bruit m'empêche de travailler**
The noise is preventing me from working

14 **Puis-je vous emprunter ce stylo?**
May I borrow this pen from you?

15 **Elle encourage ses enfants à être indépendants**
She encourages her children to be independent

16 **Essayez d'arriver à l'heure**
Try to arrive on time

17 **Il évite de lui parler**
He avoids speaking to him/her

Verbs governing à and de (ctd.)

s'excuser de qch / de + (perf.) infin.	*to apologise for sth/for doing, having done (→ 1)*
exceller à + infin.	*to excel at doing*
se fâcher de qch	*to be annoyed at sth*
feindre de + infin.	*to pretend to do (→ 2)*
féliciter qn de qch / de + (perf.) infin.	*to congratulate sb on sth/on doing, having done (→ 3)*
se fier à qn	*to trust sb (→ 4)*
finir de + infin.	*to finish doing (→ 5)*
forcer qn à + infin.	*to force sb to do*
habituer qn à + infin.	*to accustom sb to doing*
s'habituer à + infin.	*to get/be used to doing (→ 6)*
se hâter de + infin.	*to hurry to do*
hésiter à + infin.	*to hesitate to do*
interdire à qn de + infin.	*to forbid sb to do (→ 7)*
s'intéresser à qn / qch / à + infin.	*to be interested in sb/sth/in doing (→ 8)*
inviter qn à + infin.	*to invite sb to do (→ 9)*
jouer à (+ sports, games)	*to play (→ 10)*
jouer de (+ musical instruments)	*to play (→ 11)*
jouir de qch	*to enjoy sth (→ 12)*
jurer de + infin.	*to swear to do*
louer qn de qch	*to praise sb for sth*
manquer à qn	*to be missed by sb (→ 13)*
manquer de qch	*to lack sth*
manquer de + infin.	*to fail to do (→ 14)*
se marier à qn	*to marry sb*
se méfier de qn	*to distrust sb*
menacer de + infin.	*to threaten to do (→ 15)*
mériter de + infin.	*to deserve to do (→ 16)*
se mettre à + infin.	*to begin to do*
se moquer de qn / qch	*to make fun of sb/sth*
négliger de + infin.	*to fail to do*

Continued

1 **Je m'excuse d'être (arrivé) en retard**
I apologise for being (arriving) late

2 **Elle feint de dormir**
She's pretending to be asleep

3 **Je l'ai félicitée d'avoir gagné**
I congratulated her on winning

4 **Je ne me fie pas à ces gens-là**
I don't trust those people

5 **Avez-vous fini de lire ce journal?**
Have you finished reading this newspaper?

6 **Il s'est habitué à boire moins de café**
He got used to drinking less coffee

7 **Il a interdit aux enfants de jouer avec des allumettes**
He's forbidden the children to play with matches

8 **Elle s'intéresse beaucoup au sport**
She's very interested in sport

9 **Il m'a invitée à danser**
He asked me to dance

10 **Elle joue au tennis et au hockey**
She plays tennis and hockey

11 **Il joue du piano et de la guitare**
He plays the piano and the guitar

12 **Il jouit d'une santé solide**
He enjoys good health

13 **Tu manques à tes parents**
Your parents miss you

14 **Je ne manquerai pas de le lui dire**
I'll be sure to tell him/her about it

15 **Elle a menacé de démissionner tout de suite**
She threatened to resign at once

16 **Ils méritent d'être promus**
They deserve to be promoted

Verbs governing à and de (ctd.)

nuire à qch	*to harm sth* (→ **1**)
obéir à qn	*to obey sb*
obliger qn **à** + infin.	*to oblige sb to do* (→ **2**)
s'occuper de qch / qn	*to look after sth/sb* (→ **3**)
offrir de + infin.	*to offer to do* (→ **4**)
omettre de + infin.	*to fail to do*
ordonner à qn **de** + infin.	*to order sb to do* (→ **5**)
ôter qch **à** qn	*to take sth away from sb*
oublier de + infin.	*to forget to do*
pardonner qch **à** qn	*to forgive sb for sth*
pardonner à qn **de** + perf. infin.	*to forgive sb for having done* (→ **6**)
parvenir à + infin.	*to manage to do*
se passer de qch	*to do/go without sth* (→ **7**)
penser à qn / qch	*to think about sb/sth* (→ **8**)
permettre qch **à** qn	*to allow sb sth*
permettre à qn **de** + infin.	*to allow sb to do* (→ **9**)
persister à + infin.	*to persist in doing*
persuader qn **de** + infin.	*to persuade sb to do* (→ **10**)
se plaindre de qch	*to complain about sth*
plaire à qn	*to please sb* (→ **11**)
pousser qn **à** + infin.	*to urge sb to do*
prendre qch **à** qn	*to take sth from sb* (→ **12**)
préparer qn **à** + infin.	*to prepare sb to do*
se préparer à + infin.	*to get ready to do*
prier qn **de** + infin.	*to beg sb to do*
profiter de qch / **de** + infin.	*to take advantage of sth/of doing*
promettre à qn **de** + infin.	*to promise sb to do* (→ **13**)
proposer de + infin.	*to suggest doing* (→ **14**)
punir qn **de** qch	*to punish sb for sth* (→ **15**)
récompenser qn **de** qch	*to reward sb for sth*
réfléchir à qch	*to think about sth*
refuser de + infin.	*to refuse to do* (→ **16**)

Continued

1 **Ce mode de vie va nuire à sa santé**
This lifestyle will damage her health

2 **Il les a obligés à faire la vaisselle**
He made them do the washing-up

3 **Je m'occupe de ma nièce**
I'm looking after my niece

4 **Stuart a offert de nous accompagner**
Stuart has offered to go with us

5 **Les soldats leur ont ordonné de se rendre**
The soldiers ordered them to give themselves up

6 **Est-ce que tu as pardonné à Charles de t'avoir menti?**
Have you forgiven Charles for lying to you?

7 **Nous nous sommes passés d'électricité pendant plusieurs jours**
We did without electricity for several days

8 **Je pense souvent à toi**
I often think about you

9 **Permettez-moi de continuer, s'il vous plaît**
Allow me to go on, please

10 **Elle nous a persuadés de rester**
She persuaded us to stay

11 **Est-ce que ce genre de film lui plaît?**
Does he/she like this kind of film?

12 **Je lui ai pris son baladeur**
I took his personal stereo from him

13 **Ils ont promis à Pascale de venir**
They promised Pascale that they would come

14 **J'ai proposé de les inviter**
I suggested inviting them

15 **Il a été puni de sa malhonnêteté**
He has been punished for his dishonesty

16 **Il a refusé de coopérer**
He has refused to cooperate

Verbs governing à and de (ctd.)

regretter de + perf. infin.	*to regret doing, having done* (→ **1**)
remercier qn de qch/de + perf. infin.	*to thank sb for sth/for doing, having done* (→ **2**)
renoncer à qch/à + infin.	*to give sth up/give up doing*
reprocher qch à qn	*to reproach sb with/for sth* (→ **3**)
résister à qch	*to resist sth* (→ **4**)
résoudre de + infin.	*to resolve to do*
ressembler à qn/qch	*to look/be like sb/sth* (→ **5**)
réussir à + infin.	*to manage to do* (→ **6**)
rire de qn/qch	*to laugh at sb/sth*
risquer de + infin.	*to risk doing* (→ **7**)
servir à qch/à + infin.	*to be used for sth/for doing* (→ **8**)
se servir de qch	*to use sth; to help oneself to sth* (→ **9**)
songer à + infin.	*to think of doing*
se souvenir de qn/qch/de + perf. infin.	*to remember sb/sth/doing, having done* (→ **10**)
succéder à qn	*to succeed sb*
survivre à qn	*to outlive sb* (→ **11**)
tâcher de + infin.	*to try to do* (→ **12**)
tarder à + infin.	*to delay doing* (→ **13**)
tendre à + infin.	*to tend to do*
tenir à + infin.	*to be keen to do* (→ **14**)
tenter de + infin.	*to try to do* (→ **15**)
se tromper de qch	*to be wrong about sth* (→ **16**)
venir de* + infin.	*to have just done* (→ **17**)
vivre de qch	*to live on sth*
voler qch à qn	*to steal sth from sb*

*See also Use of Tenses, pp. 54 and 56

1 **Je regrette de ne pas vous avoir écrit plus tôt**
   I'm sorry for not writing to you sooner

2 **Nous les avons remerciés de leur gentillesse**
   We thanked them for their kindness

3 **On lui reproche son manque d'enthousiasme**
   They're reproaching him for his lack of enthusiasm

4 **Comment résistez-vous à la tentation?**
   How do you resist temptation?

5 **Elles ressemblent beaucoup à leur mère**
   They look very like their mother

6 **Vous avez réussi à me convaincre**
   You've managed to convince me

7 **Vous risquez de tomber en faisant cela**
   You risk falling doing that

8 **Ce bouton sert à régler le volume**
   This knob is (used) for adjusting the volume

9 **Il s'est servi d'un tournevis pour l'ouvrir**
   He used a screwdriver to open it

10 **Vous vous souvenez de Lucienne?**
   Do you remember Lucienne?
   Il ne se souvient pas de l'avoir perdu
   He doesn't remember losing it

11 **Elle a survécu à son mari**
   She outlived her husband

12 **Tâchez de ne pas être en retard!**
   Try not to be late!

13 **Il n'a pas tardé à prendre une décision**
   He was not long in taking a decision

14 **Elle tient à le faire elle-même**
   She's keen to do it herself

15 **J'ai tenté de la comprendre**
   I've tried to understand her

16 **Je me suis trompé de route**
   I took the wrong road

17 **Mon père vient de téléphoner**   **Nous venions d'arriver**
   My father's just phoned   We had just arrived

Irregular Verbs

The verbs listed opposite and conjugated on pp. 76 to 131 provide the main patterns for irregular verbs. The verbs are grouped opposite according to their infinitive ending (except **avoir** and **être**), and are shown in the following tables in alphabetical order.

In the tables, the most important irregular verbs are given in their most common simple tenses, together with the imperative and the present participle.

The auxiliary (**avoir** or **être**) is also shown for each verb, together with the past participle, to enable you to form all the compound tenses, as on pp. 24 and 26.

● For a fuller list of irregular verbs, the reader is referred to Collins Gem French Verb Tables, which shows you how to conjugate some 2000 French verbs.

Continued

avoir
être

'-er':   aller
          envoyer

'-ir':   acquérir
          bouillir
          courir
          cueillir
          dormir
          fuir
          haïr
          mourir
          ouvrir
          partir
          sentir
          servir
          sortir
          tenir
          venir
          vêtir

'-oir':   s'asseoir
          devoir
          falloir
          pleuvoir
          pouvoir
          recevoir
          savoir
          valoir
          voir
          vouloir

'-re':   battre
          boire
          connaître
          coudre
          craindre
          croire
          croître
          cuire
          dire
          écrire
          faire
          lire
          mettre
          moudre
          naître
          paraître
          plaire
          prendre
          résoudre
          rire
          rompre
          suffire
          suivre
          se taire
          vaincre
          vivre

acquérir *to acquire*   Auxiliary: **avoir**

PAST PARTICIPLE
acquis

PRESENT PARTICIPLE
acquérant

IMPERATIVE
acquiers
acquérons
acquérez

PRESENT
    j'acquiers
tu **acquiers**
il **acquiert**
nous **acquérons**
vous **acquérez**
ils **acquièrent**

FUTURE
    j'acquerrai
tu **acquerras**
il **acquerra**
nous **acquerrons**
vous **acquerrez**
ils **acquerront**

PRESENT SUBJUNCTIVE
    j'acquière
tu **acquières**
il **acquière**
nous **acquérions**
vous **acquériez**
ils **acquièrent**

IMPERFECT
    j'acquérais
tu **acquérais**
il **acquérait**
nous **acquérions**
vous **acquériez**
ils **acquéraient**

CONDITIONAL
    j'acquerrais
tu **acquerrais**
il **acquerrait**
nous **acquerrions**
vous **acquerriez**
ils **acquerraient**

PAST HISTORIC
    j'acquis
tu **acquis**
il **acquit**
nous **acquîmes**
vous **acquîtes**
ils **acquirent**

aller *to go*

Auxiliary: **être**

PAST PARTICIPLE
allé

PRESENT PARTICIPLE
allant

IMPERATIVE
va
allons
allez

PRESENT

je	**vais**
tu	**vas**
il	**va**
nous	allons
vous	allez
ils	**vont**

FUTURE

	j'irai
tu	**iras**
il	**ira**
nous	**irons**
vous	**irez**
ils	**iront**

PRESENT SUBJUNCTIVE

	j'aille
tu	**ailles**
il	**aille**
nous	allions
vous	alliez
ils	**aillent**

IMPERFECT

	j'allais
tu	allais
il	allait
nous	allions
vous	alliez
ils	allaient

CONDITIONAL

	j'irais
tu	**irais**
il	**irait**
nous	**irions**
vous	**iriez**
ils	**iraient**

PAST HISTORIC

	j'allai
tu	allas
il	alla
nous	allâmes
vous	allâtes
ils	allèrent

s'asseoir to sit down · Auxiliary: être

PAST PARTICIPLE
assis

PRESENT PARTICIPLE
s'asseyant

IMPERATIVE
assieds-toi
asseyons-nous
asseyez-vous

PRESENT

je	m'assieds or assois
tu	t'assieds or assois
il	s'assied or assoit
nous	nous asseyons or assoyons
vous	vous asseyez or assoyez
ils	s'asseyent or assoient

IMPERFECT

je	m'asseyais
tu	t'asseyais
il	s'asseyait
nous	nous asseyions
vous	vous asseyiez
ils	s'asseyaient

FUTURE

je	m'assiérai
tu	t'assiéras
il	s'assiéra
nous	nous assiérons
vous	vous assiérez
ils	s'assiéront

CONDITIONAL

je	m'assiérais
tu	t'assiérais
il	s'assiérait
nous	nous assiérions
vous	vous assiériez
ils	s'assiéraient

PRESENT SUBJUNCTIVE

je	m'asseye
tu	t'asseyes
il	s'asseye
nous	nous asseyions
vous	vous asseyiez
ils	s'asseyent

PAST HISTORIC

je	m'assis
tu	t'assis
il	s'assit
nous	nous assîmes
vous	vous assîtes
ils	s'assirent

avoir *to have*　　　　　　　Auxiliary: **avoir**

PAST PARTICIPLE
eu

IMPERATIVE
aie
ayons
ayez

PRESENT PARTICIPLE
ayant

PRESENT
　　　j'**ai**
　tu　**as**
　il　**a**
nous　**avons**
vous　**avez**
　ils　**ont**

IMPERFECT
　　　j'**avais**
　tu　**avais**
　il　**avait**
nous　**avions**
vous　**aviez**
　ils　**avaient**

FUTURE
　　　j'**aurai**
　tu　**auras**
　il　**aura**
nous　**aurons**
vous　**aurez**
　ils　**auront**

CONDITIONAL
　　　j'**aurais**
　tu　**aurais**
　il　**aurait**
nous　**aurions**
vous　**auriez**
　ils　**auraient**

PRESENT SUBJUNCTIVE
　　　j'**aie**
　tu　**aies**
　il　**ait**
nous　**ayons**
vous　**ayez**
　ils　**aient**

PAST HISTORIC
　　　j'**eus**
　tu　**eus**
　il　**eut**
nous　**eûmes**
vous　**eûtes**
　ils　**eurent**

battre *to beat*   Auxiliary: **avoir**

PAST PARTICIPLE
battu

IMPERATIVE
bats
battons
battez

PRESENT PARTICIPLE
battant

PRESENT
je	**bats**
tu	**bats**
il	**bat**
nous	battons
vous	battez
ils	battent

IMPERFECT
je	battais
tu	battais
il	battait
nous	battions
vous	battiez
ils	battaient

FUTURE
je	battrai
tu	battras
il	battra
nous	battrons
vous	battrez
ils	battront

CONDITIONAL
je	battrais
tu	battrais
il	battrait
nous	battrions
vous	battriez
ils	battraient

PRESENT SUBJUNCTIVE
je	batte
tu	battes
il	batte
nous	battions
vous	battiez
ils	battent

PAST HISTORIC
je	battis
tu	battis
il	battit
nous	battîmes
vous	battîtes
ils	battirent

boire *to drink*   Auxiliary: **avoir**

PAST PARTICIPLE
bu

PRESENT PARTICIPLE
buvant

IMPERATIVE
bois
buvons
buvez

PRESENT
je	bois
tu	bois
il	boit
nous	**buvons**
vous	**buvez**
ils	**boivent**

IMPERFECT
je	**buvais**
tu	**buvais**
il	**buvait**
nous	**buvions**
vous	**buviez**
ils	**buvaient**

FUTURE
je	boirai
tu	boiras
il	boira
nous	boirons
vous	boirez
ils	boiront

CONDITIONAL
je	boirais
tu	boirais
il	boirait
nous	boirions
vous	boiriez
ils	boiraient

PRESENT SUBJUNCTIVE
je	**boive**
tu	**boives**
il	**boive**
nous	**buvions**
vous	**buviez**
ils	**boivent**

PAST HISTORIC
je	**bus**
tu	**bus**
il	**but**
nous	**bûmes**
vous	**bûtes**
ils	**burent**

bouillir *to boil*   Auxiliary: **avoir**

PAST PARTICIPLE
bouilli

PRESENT PARTICIPLE
bouillant

IMPERATIVE
bous
bouillons
bouillez

PRESENT		IMPERFECT	
je	**bous**	je	**bouillais**
tu	**bous**	tu	**bouillais**
il	**bout**	il	**bouillait**
nous	**bouillons**	nous	**bouillions**
vous	**bouillez**	vous	**bouilliez**
ils	**bouillent**	ils	**bouillaient**

FUTURE		CONDITIONAL	
je	bouillirai	je	bouillirais
tu	bouilliras	tu	bouillirais
il	bouillira	il	bouillirait
nous	bouillirons	nous	bouillirions
vous	bouillirez	vous	bouilliriez
ils	bouilliront	ils	bouilliraient

PRESENT SUBJUNCTIVE		PAST HISTORIC	
je	**bouille**	je	bouillis
tu	**bouilles**	tu	bouillis
il	**bouille**	il	bouillit
nous	**bouillions**	nous	bouillîmes
vous	**bouilliez**	vous	bouillîtes
ils	**bouillent**	ils	bouillirent

connaître *to know*   Auxiliary: **avoir**

PAST PARTICIPLE
connu

PRESENT PARTICIPLE
connaissant

IMPERATIVE
connais
connaissons
connaissez

PRESENT

je	**connais**
tu	**connais**
il	connaît
nous	**connaissons**
vous	**connaissez**
ils	**connaissent**

IMPERFECT

je	**connaissais**
tu	**connaissais**
il	**connaissait**
nous	**connaissions**
vous	**connaissiez**
ils	**connaissaient**

FUTURE

je	connaîtrai
tu	connaîtras
il	connaîtra
nous	connaîtrons
vous	connaîtrez
ils	connaîtront

CONDITIONAL

je	connaîtrais
tu	connaîtrais
il	connaîtrait
nous	connaîtrions
vous	connaîtriez
ils	connaîtraient

PRESENT SUBJUNCTIVE

je	**connaisse**
tu	**connaisses**
il	**connaisse**
nous	**connaissions**
vous	**connaissiez**
ils	**connaissent**

PAST HISTORIC

je	**connus**
tu	**connus**
il	**connut**
nous	**connûmes**
vous	**connûtes**
ils	**connurent**

coudre *to sew* Auxiliary: **avoir**

PAST PARTICIPLE
cousu

PRESENT PARTICIPLE
cousant

IMPERATIVE
couds
cousons
cousez

PRESENT
je couds
tu couds
il coud
nous cousons
vous cousez
ils cousent

IMPERFECT
je cousais
tu cousais
il cousait
nous cousions
vous cousiez
ils cousaient

FUTURE
je coudrai
tu coudras
il coudra
nous coudrons
vous coudrez
ils coudront

CONDITIONAL
je coudrais
tu coudrais
il coudrait
nous coudrions
vous coudriez
ils coudraient

PRESENT SUBJUNCTIVE
je couse
tu couses
il couse
nous cousions
vous cousiez
ils cousent

PAST HISTORIC
je cousis
tu cousis
il cousit
nous cousîmes
vous cousîtes
ils cousirent

courir *to run*   Auxiliary: **avoir**

PAST PARTICIPLE
couru

PRESENT PARTICIPLE
courant

IMPERATIVE
cours
courons
courez

PRESENT

je	**cours**
tu	**cours**
il	**court**
nous	**courons**
vous	**courez**
ils	**courent**

IMPERFECT

je	**courais**
tu	**courais**
il	**courait**
nous	**courions**
vous	**couriez**
ils	**couraient**

FUTURE

je	**courrai**
tu	**courras**
il	**courra**
nous	**courrons**
vous	**courrez**
ils	**courront**

CONDITIONAL

je	**courrais**
tu	**courrais**
il	**courrait**
nous	**courrions**
vous	**courriez**
ils	**courraient**

PRESENT SUBJUNCTIVE

je	**coure**
tu	**coures**
il	**coure**
nous	**courions**
vous	**couriez**
ils	**courent**

PAST HISTORIC

je	**courus**
tu	**courus**
il	**courut**
nous	**courûmes**
vous	**courûtes**
ils	**coururent**

craindre *to fear*　　　　　　　Auxiliary: **avoir**

PAST PARTICIPLE
craint

IMPERATIVE
crains
craignons
craignez

PRESENT PARTICIPLE
craignant

PRESENT		*IMPERFECT*	
je	**crains**	je	**craignais**
tu	**crains**	tu	**craignais**
il	**craint**	il	**craignait**
nous	**craignons**	nous	**craignions**
vous	**craignez**	vous	**craigniez**
ils	**craignent**	ils	**craignaient**

FUTURE		*CONDITIONAL*	
je	craindrai	je	craindrais
tu	craindras	tu	craindrais
il	craindra	il	craindrait
nous	craindrons	nous	craindrions
vous	craindrez	vous	craindriez
ils	craindront	ils	craindraient

PRESENT SUBJUNCTIVE		*PAST HISTORIC*	
je	**craigne**	je	**craignis**
tu	**craignes**	tu	**craignis**
il	**craigne**	il	**craignit**
nous	**craignions**	nous	**craignîmes**
vous	**craigniez**	vous	**craignîtes**
ils	**craignent**	ils	**craignirent**

Verbs ending in **-eindre** and **-oindre** are conjugated similarly

croire *to believe*   Auxiliary: **avoir**

PAST PARTICIPLE
cru

PRESENT PARTICIPLE
croyant

IMPERATIVE
crois
croyons
croyez

PRESENT
je	crois
tu	crois
il	**croit**
nous	**croyons**
vous	**croyez**
ils	croient

IMPERFECT
je	**croyais**
tu	**croyais**
il	**croyait**
nous	**croyions**
vous	**croyiez**
ils	**croyaient**

FUTURE
je	croirai
tu	croiras
il	croira
nous	croirons
vous	croirez
ils	croiront

CONDITIONAL
je	croirais
tu	croirais
il	croirait
nous	croirions
vous	croiriez
ils	croiraient

PRESENT SUBJUNCTIVE
je	croie
tu	croies
il	croie
nous	**croyions**
vous	**croyiez**
ils	croient

PAST HISTORIC
je	**crus**
tu	**crus**
il	**crut**
nous	**crûmes**
vous	**crûtes**
ils	**crurent**

croître *to grow* Auxiliary: **avoir**

PAST PARTICIPLE
crû

PRESENT PARTICIPLE
croissant

IMPERATIVE
croîs
croissons
croissez

PRESENT
je	**croîs**
tu	**croîs**
il	croît
nous	**croissons**
vous	**croissez**
ils	**croissent**

IMPERFECT
je	**croissais**
tu	**croissais**
il	**croissait**
nous	**croissions**
vous	**croissiez**
ils	**croissaient**

FUTURE
je	croîtrai
tu	croîtras
il	croîtra
nous	croîtrons
vous	croîtrez
ils	croîtront

CONDITIONAL
je	croîtrais
tu	croîtrais
il	croîtrait
nous	croîtrions
vous	croîtriez
ils	croîtraient

PRESENT SUBJUNCTIVE
je	**croisse**
tu	**croisses**
il	**croisse**
nous	**croissions**
vous	**croissiez**
ils	**croissent**

PAST HISTORIC
je	**crûs**
tu	**crûs**
il	**crût**
nous	**crûmes**
vous	**crûtes**
ils	**crûrent**

cueillir *to pick*

Auxiliary: **avoir**

PAST PARTICIPLE
cueilli

PRESENT PARTICIPLE
cueillant

IMPERATIVE
cueille
cueillons
cueillez

PRESENT
je	cueille
tu	cueilles
il	cueille
nous	cueillons
vous	cueillez
ils	cueillent

IMPERFECT
je	cueillais
tu	cueillais
il	cueillait
nous	cueillions
vous	cueilliez
ils	cueillaient

FUTURE
je	cueillerai
tu	cueilleras
il	cueillera
nous	cueillerons
vous	cueillerez
ils	cueilleront

CONDITIONAL
je	cueillerais
tu	cueillerais
il	cueillerait
nous	cueillerions
vous	cueilleriez
ils	cueilleraient

PRESENT SUBJUNCTIVE
je	cueille
tu	cueilles
il	cueille
nous	cueillions
vous	cueilliez
ils	cueillent

PAST HISTORIC
je	cueillis
tu	cueillis
il	cueillit
nous	cueillîmes
vous	cueillîtes
ils	cueillirent

cuire *to cook*   Auxiliary: **avoir**

PAST PARTICIPLE
  cuit

IMPERATIVE
  cuis
  cuisons
  cuisez

PRESENT PARTICIPLE
  cuisant

PRESENT
  je   cuis
  tu   cuis
  il   **cuit**
  nous **cuisons**
  vous **cuisez**
  ils **cuisent**

IMPERFECT
  je   cuisais
  tu   cuisais
  il   cuisait
  nous cuisions
  vous cuisiez
  ils cuisaient

FUTURE
  je   cuirai
  tu   cuiras
  il   cuira
  nous cuirons
  vous cuirez
  ils cuiront

CONDITIONAL
  je   cuirais
  tu   cuirais
  il   cuirait
  nous cuirions
  vous cuiriez
  ils cuiraient

PRESENT SUBJUNCTIVE
  je   cuise
  tu   cuises
  il   cuise
  nous cuisions
  vous cuisiez
  ils cuisent

PAST HISTORIC
  je   cuisis
  tu   cuisis
  il   cuisit
  nous cuisîmes
  vous cuisîtes
  ils cuisirent

---

nuire *to harm*, conjugated similarly, but past participle **nui**

devoir *to have to; to owe*   Auxiliary: **avoir**

PAST PARTICIPLE
dû

PRESENT PARTICIPLE
devant

IMPERATIVE
dois
devons
devez

PRESENT

je	dois
tu	dois
il	doit
nous	devons
vous	devez
ils	doivent

IMPERFECT

je	devais
tu	devais
il	devait
nous	devions
vous	deviez
ils	devaient

FUTURE

je	devrai
tu	devras
il	devra
nous	devrons
vous	devrez
ils	devront

CONDITIONAL

je	devrais
tu	devrais
il	devrait
nous	devrions
vous	devriez
ils	devraient

PRESENT SUBJUNCTIVE

je	doive
tu	doives
il	doive
nous	devions
vous	deviez
ils	doivent

PAST HISTORIC

je	dus
tu	dus
il	dut
nous	dûmes
vous	dûtes
ils	durent

dire *to say, tell*   Auxiliary: **avoir**

PAST PARTICIPLE
dit

PRESENT PARTICIPLE
disant

IMPERATIVE
dis
disons
dites

PRESENT		IMPERFECT	
je	dis	**je**	**disais**
tu	dis	**tu**	**disais**
il	**dit**	**il**	**disait**
nous	**disons**	**nous**	**disions**
vous	**dites**	**vous**	**disiez**
ils	**disent**	**ils**	**disaient**

FUTURE		CONDITIONAL	
je	dirai	je	dirais
tu	diras	tu	dirais
il	dira	il	dirait
nous	dirons	nous	dirions
vous	direz	vous	diriez
ils	diront	ils	diraient

PRESENT SUBJUNCTIVE		PAST HISTORIC	
je	**dise**	**je**	**dis**
tu	**dises**	**tu**	**dis**
il	**dise**	**il**	**dit**
nous	**disions**	**nous**	**dîmes**
vous	**disiez**	**vous**	**dîtes**
ils	**disent**	**ils**	**dirent**

---

interdire *to forbid*, conjugated similarly, but 2nd person plural of the present tense is **vous interdisez**

dormir *to sleep*   Auxiliary: **avoir**

PAST PARTICIPLE	IMPERATIVE
dormi	**dors**
	dormons
PRESENT PARTICIPLE	**dormez**
dormant	

PRESENT		IMPERFECT	
je	**dors**	je	**dormais**
tu	**dors**	tu	**dormais**
il	**dort**	il	**dormait**
nous	**dormons**	nous	**dormions**
vous	**dormez**	vous	**dormiez**
ils	**dorment**	ils	**dormaient**

FUTURE		CONDITIONAL	
je	dormirai	je	dormirais
tu	dormiras	tu	dormirais
il	dormira	il	dormirait
nous	dormirons	nous	dormirions
vous	dormirez	vous	dormiriez
ils	dormiront	ils	dormiraient

PRESENT SUBJUNCTIVE		PAST HISTORIC	
je	**dorme**	je	dormis
tu	**dormes**	tu	dormis
il	**dorme**	il	dormit
nous	**dormions**	nous	dormîmes
vous	**dormiez**	vous	dormîtes
ils	**dorment**	ils	dormirent

écrire *to write*　　　　Auxiliary: **avoir**

PAST PARTICIPLE
écrit

PRESENT PARTICIPLE
écrivant

IMPERATIVE
écris
écrivons
écrivez

PRESENT
j'	écris
tu	écris
il	écrit
nous	**écrivons**
vous	**écrivez**
ils	**écrivent**

IMPERFECT
	j'écrivais
tu	**écrivais**
il	**écrivait**
nous	**écrivions**
vous	**écriviez**
ils	**écrivaient**

FUTURE
	j'écrirai
tu	écriras
il	écrira
nous	écrirons
vous	écrirez
ils	écriront

CONDITIONAL
	j'écrirais
tu	écrirais
il	écrirait
nous	écririons
vous	écririez
ils	écriraient

PRESENT SUBJUNCTIVE
	j'écrive
tu	**écrives**
il	**écrive**
nous	**écrivions**
vous	**écriviez**
ils	**écrivent**

PAST HISTORIC
	j'écrivis
tu	**écrivis**
il	**écrivit**
nous	**écrivîmes**
vous	**écrivîtes**
ils	**écrivirent**

envoyer *to send*   Auxiliary: **avoir**

PAST PARTICIPLE
envoyé

IMPERATIVE
envoie
envoyons
envoyez

PRESENT PARTICIPLE
envoyant

PRESENT

	j'envoie
tu	envoies
il	envoie
nous	envoyons
vous	envoyez
ils	envoient

IMPERFECT

	j'envoyais
tu	envoyais
il	envoyait
nous	envoyions
vous	envoyiez
ils	envoyaient

FUTURE

	j'enverrai
tu	**enverras**
il	**enverra**
nous	**enverrons**
vous	**enverrez**
ils	**enverront**

CONDITIONAL

	j'enverrais
tu	**enverrais**
il	**enverrait**
nous	**enverrions**
vous	**enverriez**
ils	**enverraient**

PRESENT SUBJUNCTIVE

	j'envoie
tu	envoies
il	envoie
nous	envoyions
vous	envoyiez
ils	envoient

PAST HISTORIC

	j'envoyai
tu	envoyas
il	envoya
nous	envoyâmes
vous	envoyâtes
ils	envoyèrent

être *to be*   Auxiliary: **avoir**

PAST PARTICIPLE
été

PRESENT PARTICIPLE
étant

IMPERATIVE
sois
soyons
soyez

PRESENT		*IMPERFECT*	
je	**suis**		**j'étais**
tu	**es**	tu	**étais**
il	**est**	il	**était**
nous	**sommes**	nous	**étions**
vous	**êtes**	vous	**étiez**
ils	**sont**	ils	**étaient**

FUTURE		*CONDITIONAL*	
je	**serai**	je	**serais**
tu	**seras**	tu	**serais**
il	**sera**	il	**serait**
nous	**serons**	nous	**serions**
vous	**serez**	vous	**seriez**
ils	**seront**	ils	**seraient**

PRESENT SUBJUNCTIVE		*PAST HISTORIC*	
je	**sois**	je	**fus**
tu	**sois**	tu	**fus**
il	**soit**	il	**fut**
nous	**soyons**	nous	**fûmes**
vous	**soyez**	vous	**fûtes**
ils	**soient**	ils	**furent**

faire *to do; to make*   Auxiliary: **avoir**

PAST PARTICIPLE
fait

IMPERATIVE
fais
faisons
faites

PRESENT PARTICIPLE
faisant

PRESENT

je	fais
tu	fais
il	**fait**
nous	**faisons**
vous	**faites**
ils	**font**

IMPERFECT

je	**faisais**
tu	**faisais**
il	**faisait**
nous	**faisions**
vous	**faisiez**
ils	**faisaient**

FUTURE

je	**ferai**
tu	**feras**
il	**fera**
nous	**ferons**
vous	**ferez**
ils	**feront**

CONDITIONAL

je	**ferais**
tu	**ferais**
il	**ferait**
nous	**ferions**
vous	**feriez**
ils	**feraient**

PRESENT SUBJUNCTIVE

je	**fasse**
tu	**fasses**
il	**fasse**
nous	**fassions**
vous	**fassiez**
ils	**fassent**

PAST HISTORIC

je	**fis**
tu	**fis**
il	**fit**
nous	**fîmes**
vous	**fîtes**
ils	**firent**

falloir *to be necessary*   Auxiliary: **avoir**

PAST PARTICIPLE
  fallu

IMPERATIVE
  not used

PRESENT PARTICIPLE
  not used

PRESENT
  il faut

IMPERFECT
  il fallait

FUTURE
  il faudra

CONDITIONAL
  il faudrait

PRESENT SUBJUNCTIVE
  il faille

PAST HISTORIC
  il fallut

fuir *to flee*   Auxiliary: **avoir**

PAST PARTICIPLE
fui

PRESENT PARTICIPLE
fuyant

IMPERATIVE
fuis
fuyons
fuyez

PRESENT		*IMPERFECT*	
je	fuis	**je**	**fuyais**
tu	fuis	**tu**	**fuyais**
il	fuit	**il**	**fuyait**
nous	**fuyons**	**nous**	**fuyions**
vous	**fuyez**	**vous**	**fuyiez**
ils	**fuient**	**ils**	**fuyaient**

FUTURE		*CONDITIONAL*	
je	fuirai	je	fuirais
tu	fuiras	tu	fuirais
il	fuira	il	fuirait
nous	fuirons	nous	fuirions
vous	fuirez	vous	fuiriez
ils	fuiront	ils	fuiraient

PRESENT SUBJUNCTIVE		*PAST HISTORIC*	
je	**fuie**	je	fuis
tu	**fuies**	tu	fuis
il	**fuie**	il	fuit
nous	**fuyions**	nous	fuîmes
vous	**fuyiez**	vous	fuîtes
ils	**fuient**	ils	fuirent

haïr *to hate*   Auxiliary: **avoir**

PAST PARTICIPLE
haï

PRESENT PARTICIPLE
haïssant

IMPERATIVE
hais
haïssons
haïssez

PRESENT
je	hais
tu	hais
il	hait
nous	**haïssons**
vous	**haïssez**
ils	**haïssent**

IMPERFECT
je	**haïssais**
tu	**haïssais**
il	**haïssait**
nous	**haïssions**
vous	**haïssiez**
ils	**haïssaient**

FUTURE
je	haïrai
tu	haïras
il	haïra
nous	haïrons
vous	haïrez
ils	haïront

CONDITIONAL
je	haïrais
tu	haïrais
il	haïrait
nous	haïrions
vous	haïriez
ils	haïraient

PRESENT SUBJUNCTIVE
je	**haïsse**
tu	**haïsses**
il	**haïsse**
nous	**haïssions**
vous	**haïssiez**
ils	**haïssent**

PAST HISTORIC
je	**haïs**
tu	**haïs**
il	**haït**
nous	**haïmes**
vous	**haïtes**
ils	**haïrent**

lire *to read*　　　　　　　　　　　Auxiliary: **avoir**

PAST PARTICIPLE
lu

PRESENT PARTICIPLE
lisant

IMPERATIVE
lis
lisons
lisez

PRESENT		IMPERFECT	
je	lis	**je**	**lisais**
tu	lis	**tu**	**lisais**
il	**lit**	**il**	**lisait**
nous	**lisons**	**nous**	**lisions**
vous	**lisez**	**vous**	**lisiez**
ils	**lisent**	**ils**	**lisaient**

FUTURE		CONDITIONAL	
je	lirai	je	lirais
tu	liras	tu	lirais
il	lira	il	lirait
nous	lirons	nous	lirions
vous	lirez	vous	liriez
ils	liront	ils	liraient

PRESENT SUBJUNCTIVE		PAST HISTORIC	
je	**lise**	**je**	**lus**
tu	**lises**	**tu**	**lus**
il	**lise**	**il**	**lut**
nous	**lisions**	**nous**	**lûmes**
vous	**lisiez**	**vous**	**lûtes**
ils	**lisent**	**ils**	**lurent**

mettre *to put*   Auxiliary: **avoir**

PAST PARTICIPLE
  mis

PRESENT PARTICIPLE
  mettant

IMPERATIVE
  mets
  mettons
  mettez

PRESENT
  je **mets**
  tu **mets**
  il **met**
  nous mettons
  vous mettez
  ils mettent

IMPERFECT
  je mettais
  tu mettais
  il mettait
  nous mettions
  vous mettiez
  ils mettaient

FUTURE
  je mettrai
  tu mettras
  il mettra
  nous mettrons
  vous mettrez
  ils mettront

CONDITIONAL
  je mettrais
  tu mettrais
  il mettrait
  nous mettrions
  vous mettriez
  ils mettraient

PRESENT SUBJUNCTIVE
  je mette
  tu mettes
  il mette
  nous mettions
  vous mettiez
  ils mettent

PAST HISTORIC
  je **mis**
  tu **mis**
  il **mit**
  nous **mîmes**
  vous **mîtes**
  ils **mirent**

moudre *to grind*   Auxiliary: **avoir**

PAST PARTICIPLE
moulu

PRESENT PARTICIPLE
moulant

IMPERATIVE
mouds
moulons
moulez

PRESENT
- je mouds
- tu mouds
- il moud
- **nous moulons**
- **vous moulez**
- **ils moulent**

IMPERFECT
- **je moulais**
- **tu moulais**
- **il moulait**
- **nous moulions**
- **vous mouliez**
- **ils moulaient**

FUTURE
- je moudrai
- tu moudras
- il moudra
- nous moudrons
- vous moudrez
- ils moudront

CONDITIONAL
- je moudrais
- tu moudrais
- il moudrait
- nous moudrions
- vous moudriez
- ils moudraient

PRESENT SUBJUNCTIVE
- **je moule**
- **tu moules**
- **il moule**
- **nous moulions**
- **vous mouliez**
- **ils moulent**

PAST HISTORIC
- **je moulus**
- **tu moulus**
- **il moulut**
- **nous moulûmes**
- **vous moulûtes**
- **ils moulurent**

mourir *to die*

Auxiliary: **être**

PAST PARTICIPLE
mort

PRESENT PARTICIPLE
mourant

IMPERATIVE
meurs
mourons
mourez

PRESENT

je	meurs
tu	meurs
il	meurt
nous	mourons
vous	mourez
ils	meurent

IMPERFECT

je	mourais
tu	mourais
il	mourait
nous	mourions
vous	mouriez
ils	mouraient

FUTURE

je	mourrai
tu	mourras
il	mourra
nous	mourrons
vous	mourrez
ils	mourront

CONDITIONAL

je	mourrais
tu	mourrais
il	mourrait
nous	mourrions
vous	mourriez
ils	mourraient

PRESENT SUBJUNCTIVE

je	meure
tu	meures
il	meure
nous	mourions
vous	mouriez
ils	meurent

PAST HISTORIC

je	mourus
tu	mourus
il	mourut
nous	mourûmes
vous	mourûtes
ils	moururent

naître *to be born* Auxiliary: **être**

PAST PARTICIPLE
né

PRESENT PARTICIPLE
naissant

IMPERATIVE
nais
naissons
naissez

PRESENT
je	nais
tu	nais
il	naît
nous	naissons
vous	naissez
ils	naissent

IMPERFECT
je	naissais
tu	naissais
il	naissait
nous	naissions
vous	naissiez
ils	naissaient

FUTURE
je	naîtrai
tu	naîtras
il	naîtra
nous	naîtrons
vous	naîtrez
ils	naîtront

CONDITIONAL
je	naîtrais
tu	naîtrais
il	naîtrait
nous	naîtrions
vous	naîtriez
ils	naîtraient

PRESENT SUBJUNCTIVE
je	naisse
tu	naisses
il	naisse
nous	naissions
vous	naissiez
ils	naissent

PAST HISTORIC
je	naquis
tu	naquis
il	naquit
nous	naquîmes
vous	naquîtes
ils	naquirent

ouvrir *to open*   Auxiliary: **avoir**

PAST PARTICIPLE
ouvert

PRESENT PARTICIPLE
ouvrant

IMPERATIVE
ouvre
ouvrons
ouvrez

PRESENT		*IMPERFECT*	
j'ouvre		**j'ouvrais**	
tu	**ouvres**	**tu**	**ouvrais**
il	**ouvre**	**il**	**ouvrait**
nous	**ouvrons**	**nous**	**ouvrions**
vous	**ouvrez**	**vous**	**ouvriez**
ils	**ouvrent**	**ils**	**ouvraient**

FUTURE		*CONDITIONAL*	
j'ouvrirai		j'ouvrirais	
tu	ouvriras	tu	ouvrirais
il	ouvrira	il	ouvrirait
nous	ouvrirons	nous	ouvririons
vous	ouvrirez	vous	ouvririez
ils	ouvriront	ils	ouvriraient

PRESENT SUBJUNCTIVE		*PAST HISTORIC*	
j'ouvre		j'ouvris	
tu	**ouvres**	tu	ouvris
il	**ouvre**	il	ouvrit
nous	**ouvrions**	nous	ouvrîmes
vous	**ouvriez**	vous	ouvrîtes
ils	**ouvrent**	ils	ouvrirent

---

offrir *to offer*, **souffrir** *to suffer* are conjugated similarly

paraître *to appear*   Auxiliary: **avoir**

PAST PARTICIPLE
paru

PRESENT PARTICIPLE
paraissant

IMPERATIVE
parais
paraissons
paraissez

PRESENT

je	**parais**
tu	**parais**
il	paraît
nous	**paraissons**
vous	**paraissez**
ils	**paraissent**

IMPERFECT

je	**paraissais**
tu	**paraissais**
il	**paraissait**
nous	**paraissions**
vous	**paraissiez**
ils	**paraissaient**

FUTURE

je	paraîtrai
tu	paraîtras
il	paraîtra
nous	paraîtrons
vous	paraîtrez
ils	paraîtront

CONDITIONAL

je	paraîtrais
tu	paraîtrais
il	paraîtrait
nous	paraîtrions
vous	paraîtriez
ils	paraîtraient

PRESENT SUBJUNCTIVE

je	**paraisse**
tu	**paraisses**
il	**paraisse**
nous	**paraissions**
vous	**paraissiez**
ils	**paraissent**

PAST HISTORIC

je	**parus**
tu	**parus**
il	**parut**
nous	**parûmes**
vous	**parûtes**
ils	**parurent**

partir *to leave* Auxiliary: **être**

PAST PARTICIPLE	IMPERATIVE
parti	**pars**
	partons
PRESENT PARTICIPLE	**partez**
partant	

PRESENT

je	**pars**
tu	**pars**
il	**part**
nous	**partons**
vous	**partez**
ils	**partent**

IMPERFECT

je	**partais**
tu	**partais**
il	**partait**
nous	**partions**
vous	**partiez**
ils	**partaient**

FUTURE

je	partirai
tu	partiras
il	partira
nous	partirons
vous	partirez
ils	partiront

CONDITIONAL

je	partirais
tu	partirais
il	partirait
nous	partirions
vous	partiriez
ils	partiraient

PRESENT SUBJUNCTIVE

je	**parte**
tu	**partes**
il	**parte**
nous	**partions**
vous	**partiez**
ils	**partent**

PAST HISTORIC

je	partis
tu	partis
il	partit
nous	partîmes
vous	partîtes
ils	partirent

plaire to please   Auxiliary: **avoir**

PAST PARTICIPLE
plu

IMPERATIVE
plais
plaisons
plaisez

PRESENT PARTICIPLE
plaisant

PRESENT		IMPERFECT	
je	plais	**je**	**plaisais**
tu	plais	**tu**	**plaisais**
il	**plaît**	**il**	**plaisait**
nous	**plaisons**	**nous**	**plaisions**
vous	**plaisez**	**vous**	**plaisiez**
ils	**plaisent**	**ils**	**plaisaient**

FUTURE		CONDITIONAL	
je	plairai	je	plairais
tu	plairas	tu	plairais
il	plaira	il	plairait
nous	plairons	nous	plairions
vous	plairez	vous	plairiez
ils	plairont	ils	plairaient

PRESENT SUBJUNCTIVE		PAST HISTORIC	
je	**plaise**	**je**	**plus**
tu	**plaises**	**tu**	**plus**
il	**plaise**	**il**	**plut**
nous	**plaisions**	**nous**	**plûmes**
vous	**plaisiez**	**vous**	**plûtes**
ils	**plaisent**	**ils**	**plurent**

pleuvoir *to rain*　　　　　　　Auxiliary: **avoir**

PAST PARTICIPLE
plu

IMPERATIVE
not used

PRESENT PARTICIPLE
pleuvant

PRESENT
　　il　**pleut**

IMPERFECT
　　il　**pleuvait**

FUTURE
　　il　**pleuvra**

CONDITIONAL
　　il　**pleuvrait**

PRESENT SUBJUNCTIVE
　　il　**pleuve**

PAST HISTORIC
　　il　**plut**

pouvoir *to be able to*   Auxiliary: **avoir**

PAST PARTICIPLE	IMPERATIVE
pu	*not used*

PRESENT PARTICIPLE
pouvant

PRESENT		IMPERFECT	
je	**peux***	je	**pouvais**
tu	**peux**	tu	**pouvais**
il	**peut**	il	**pouvait**
nous	**pouvons**	nous	**pouvions**
vous	**pouvez**	vous	**pouviez**
ils	**peuvent**	ils	**pouvaient**

FUTURE		CONDITIONAL	
je	**pourrai**	je	**pourrais**
tu	**pourras**	tu	**pourrais**
il	**pourra**	il	**pourrait**
nous	**pourrons**	nous	**pourrions**
vous	**pourrez**	vous	**pourriez**
ils	**pourront**	ils	**pourraient**

PRESENT SUBJUNCTIVE		PAST HISTORIC	
je	**puisse**	je	**pus**
tu	**puisses**	tu	**pus**
il	**puisse**	il	**put**
nous	**puissions**	nous	**pûmes**
vous	**puissiez**	vous	**pûtes**
ils	**puissent**	ils	**purent**

*In questions: **puis-je?**

prendre *to take*   Auxiliary: **avoir**

PAST PARTICIPLE
pris

IMPERATIVE
prends
prenons
prenez

PRESENT PARTICIPLE
prenant

PRESENT		IMPERFECT	
je	prends	**je**	**prenais**
tu	prends	**tu**	**prenais**
il	prend	**il**	**prenait**
nous	**prenons**	**nous**	**prenions**
vous	**prenez**	**vous**	**preniez**
ils	**prennent**	**ils**	**prenaient**

FUTURE		CONDITIONAL	
je	prendrai	je	prendrais
tu	prendras	tu	prendrais
il	prendra	il	prendrait
nous	prendrons	nous	prendrions
vous	prendrez	vous	prendriez
ils	prendront	ils	prendraient

PRESENT SUBJUNCTIVE		PAST HISTORIC	
je	**prenne**	**je**	**pris**
tu	**prennes**	**tu**	**pris**
il	**prenne**	**il**	**prit**
nous	**prenions**	**nous**	**prîmes**
vous	**preniez**	**vous**	**prîtes**
ils	**prennent**	**ils**	**prirent**

recevoir *to receive*　　　Auxiliary: **avoir**

PAST PARTICIPLE	IMPERATIVE
reçu	reçois
	recevons
PRESENT PARTICIPLE	recevez
recevant	

PRESENT		IMPERFECT	
je	reçois	je	recevais
tu	reçois	tu	recevais
il	reçoit	il	recevait
nous	recevons	nous	recevions
vous	recevez	vous	receviez
ils	reçoivent	ils	recevaient

FUTURE		CONDITIONAL	
je	recevrai	je	recevrais
tu	recevras	tu	recevrais
il	recevra	il	recevrait
nous	recevrons	nous	recevrions
vous	recevrez	vous	recevriez
ils	recevront	ils	recevraient

PRESENT SUBJUNCTIVE		PAST HISTORIC	
je	reçoive	je	reçus
tu	reçoives	tu	reçus
il	reçoive	il	reçut
nous	recevions	nous	reçûmes
vous	receviez	vous	reçûtes
ils	reçoivent	ils	reçurent

résoudre to solve   Auxiliary: **avoir**

PAST PARTICIPLE
résolu

IMPERATIVE
résous
résolvons
résolvez

PRESENT PARTICIPLE
résolvant

PRESENT

je	résous
tu	résous
il	résout
nous	résolvons
vous	résolvez
ils	résolvent

IMPERFECT

je	résolvais
tu	résolvais
il	résolvait
nous	résolvions
vous	résolviez
ils	résolvaient

FUTURE

je	résoudrai
tu	résoudras
il	résoudra
nous	résoudrons
vous	résoudrez
ils	résoudront

CONDITIONAL

je	résoudrais
tu	résoudrais
il	résoudrait
nous	résoudrions
vous	résoudriez
ils	résoudraient

PRESENT SUBJUNCTIVE

je	résolve
tu	résolves
il	résolve
nous	résolvions
vous	résolviez
ils	résolvent

PAST HISTORIC

je	résolus
tu	résolus
il	résolut
nous	résolûmes
vous	résolûtes
ils	résolurent

rire to laugh | Auxiliary: **avoir**

PAST PARTICIPLE	IMPERATIVE
ri	ris
	rions
PRESENT PARTICIPLE	riez
riant	

PRESENT		IMPERFECT	
je	ris	je	riais
tu	ris	tu	riais
il	**rit**	il	riait
nous	rions	nous	riions
vous	riez	vous	riiez
ils	rient	ils	riaient

FUTURE		CONDITIONAL	
je	rirai	je	rirais
tu	riras	tu	rirais
il	rira	il	rirait
nous	rirons	nous	ririons
vous	rirez	vous	ririez
ils	riront	ils	riraient

PRESENT SUBJUNCTIVE		PAST HISTORIC	
je	rie	**je**	**ris**
tu	ries	**tu**	**ris**
il	rie	**il**	**rit**
nous	riions	**nous**	**rîmes**
vous	riiez	**vous**	**rîtes**
ils	rient	**ils**	**rirent**

rompre *to break*   Auxiliary: **avoir**

PAST PARTICIPLE
rompu

IMPERATIVE
romps
rompons
rompez

PRESENT PARTICIPLE
rompant

PRESENT
je	romps
tu	romps
il	**rompt**
nous	rompons
vous	rompez
ils	rompent

IMPERFECT
je	rompais
tu	rompais
il	rompait
nous	rompions
vous	rompiez
ils	rompaient

FUTURE
je	romprai
tu	rompras
il	rompra
nous	romprons
vous	romprez
ils	rompront

CONDITIONAL
je	romprais
tu	romprais
il	romprait
nous	romprions
vous	rompriez
ils	rompraient

PRESENT SUBJUNCTIVE
je	rompe
tu	rompes
il	rompe
nous	rompions
vous	rompiez
ils	rompent

PAST HISTORIC
je	rompis
tu	rompis
il	rompit
nous	rompîmes
vous	rompîtes
ils	rompirent

savoir *to know*   Auxiliary: **avoir**

PAST PARTICIPLE
su

PRESENT PARTICIPLE
sachant

IMPERATIVE
sache
sachons
sachez

PRESENT

je	sais
tu	sais
il	sait
nous	savons
vous	savez
ils	savent

FUTURE

je	saurai
tu	sauras
il	saura
nous	saurons
vous	saurez
ils	sauront

PRESENT SUBJUNCTIVE

je	sache
tu	saches
il	sache
nous	sachions
vous	sachiez
ils	sachent

IMPERFECT

je	savais
tu	savais
il	savait
nous	savions
vous	saviez
ils	savaient

CONDITIONAL

je	saurais
tu	saurais
il	saurait
nous	saurions
vous	sauriez
ils	sauraient

PAST HISTORIC

je	sus
tu	sus
il	sut
nous	sûmes
vous	sûtes
ils	surent

sentir *to feel; to smell*   Auxiliary: **avoir**

PAST PARTICIPLE
senti

IMPERATIVE
sens
sentons
sentez

PRESENT PARTICIPLE
sentant

PRESENT

je	**sens**
tu	**sens**
il	**sent**
nous	**sentons**
vous	**sentez**
ils	**sentent**

IMPERFECT

je	**sentais**
tu	**sentais**
il	**sentait**
nous	**sentions**
vous	**sentiez**
ils	**sentaient**

FUTURE

je	sentirai
tu	sentiras
il	sentira
nous	sentirons
vous	sentirez
ils	sentiront

CONDITIONAL

je	sentirais
tu	sentirais
il	sentirait
nous	sentirions
vous	sentiriez
ils	sentiraient

PRESENT SUBJUNCTIVE

je	**sente**
tu	**sentes**
il	**sente**
nous	**sentions**
vous	**sentiez**
ils	**sentent**

PAST HISTORIC

je	sentis
tu	sentis
il	sentit
nous	sentîmes
vous	sentîtes
ils	sentirent

servir *to serve* Auxiliary: **avoir**

PAST PARTICIPLE
servi

PRESENT PARTICIPLE
servant

IMPERATIVE
sers
servons
servez

PRESENT
je	**sers**
tu	**sers**
il	**sert**
nous	**servons**
vous	**servez**
ils	**servent**

IMPERFECT
je	**servais**
tu	**servais**
il	**servait**
nous	**servions**
vous	**serviez**
ils	**servaient**

FUTURE
je	servirai
tu	serviras
il	servira
nous	servirons
vous	servirez
ils	serviront

CONDITIONAL
je	servirais
tu	servirais
il	servirait
nous	servirions
vous	serviriez
ils	serviraient

PRESENT SUBJUNCTIVE
je	**serve**
tu	**serves**
il	**serve**
nous	**servions**
vous	**serviez**
ils	**servent**

PAST HISTORIC
je	servis
tu	servis
il	servit
nous	servîmes
vous	servîtes
ils	servirent

sortir *to go/come out*   Auxiliary: **être**

PAST PARTICIPLE
sorti

PRESENT PARTICIPLE
sortant

IMPERATIVE
sors
sortons
sortez

PRESENT

je	**sors**
tu	**sors**
il	**sort**
nous	**sortons**
vous	**sortez**
ils	**sortent**

IMPERFECT

je	**sortais**
tu	**sortais**
il	**sortait**
nous	**sortions**
vous	**sortiez**
ils	**sortaient**

FUTURE

je	sortirai
tu	sortiras
il	sortira
nous	sortirons
vous	sortirez
ils	sortiront

CONDITIONAL

je	sortirais
tu	sortirais
il	sortirait
nous	sortirions
vous	sortiriez
ils	sortiraient

PRESENT SUBJUNCTIVE

je	**sorte**
tu	**sortes**
il	**sorte**
nous	**sortions**
vous	**sortiez**
ils	**sortent**

PAST HISTORIC

je	sortis
tu	sortis
il	sortit
nous	sortîmes
vous	sortîtes
ils	sortirent

suffire *to be enough*   Auxiliary: **avoir**

PAST PARTICIPLE
suffi

PRESENT PARTICIPLE
suffisant

IMPERATIVE
suffis
suffisons
suffisez

PRESENT
je	suffis
tu	suffis
il	suffit
nous	**suffisons**
vous	**suffisez**
ils	**suffisent**

IMPERFECT
je	**suffisais**
tu	**suffisais**
il	**suffisait**
nous	**suffisions**
vous	**suffisiez**
ils	**suffisaient**

FUTURE
je	suffirai
tu	suffiras
il	suffira
nous	suffirons
vous	suffirez
ils	suffiront

CONDITIONAL
je	suffirais
tu	suffirais
il	suffirait
nous	suffirions
vous	suffiriez
ils	suffiraient

PRESENT SUBJUNCTIVE
je	**suffise**
tu	**suffises**
il	**suffise**
nous	**suffisions**
vous	**suffisiez**
ils	**suffisent**

PAST HISTORIC
je	**suffis**
tu	**suffis**
il	**suffit**
nous	**suffîmes**
vous	**suffîtes**
ils	**suffirent**

suivre *to follow*   Auxiliary: **avoir**

PAST PARTICIPLE
suivi

IMPERATIVE
suis
suivons
suivez

PRESENT PARTICIPLE
suivant

PRESENT
je **suis**
tu **suis**
il **suit**
nous suivons
vous suivez
ils suivent

IMPERFECT
je suivais
tu suivais
il suivait
nous suivions
vous suiviez
ils suivaient

FUTURE
je suivrai
tu suivras
il suivra
nous suivrons
vous suivrez
ils suivront

CONDITIONAL
je suivrais
tu suivrais
il suivrait
nous suivrions
vous suivriez
ils suivraient

PRESENT SUBJUNCTIVE
je suive
tu suives
il suive
nous suivions
vous suiviez
ils suivent

PAST HISTORIC
je suivis
tu suivis
il suivit
nous suivîmes
vous suivîtes
ils suivirent

se taire *to stop talking*   Auxiliary: **être**

PAST PARTICIPLE
tu

PRESENT PARTICIPLE
se taisant

IMPERATIVE
tais-toi
taisons-nous
taisez-vous

PRESENT

je	me tais
tu	te tais
il	se tait
nous	**nous taisons**
vous	**vous taisez**
ils	**se taisent**

IMPERFECT

je	**me taisais**
tu	**te taisais**
il	**se taisait**
nous	**nous taisions**
vous	**vous taisiez**
ils	**se taisaient**

FUTURE

je	me tairai
tu	te tairas
il	se taira
nous	nous tairons
vous	vous tairez
ils	se tairont

CONDITIONAL

je	me tairais
tu	te tairais
il	se tairait
nous	nous tairions
vous	vous tairiez
ils	se tairaient

PRESENT SUBJUNCTIVE

je	**me taise**
tu	**te taises**
il	**se taise**
nous	**nous taisions**
vous	**vous taisiez**
ils	**se taisent**

PAST HISTORIC

je	**me tus**
tu	**te tus**
il	**se tut**
nous	**nous tûmes**
vous	**vous tûtes**
ils	**se turent**

tenir *to hold*   Auxiliary: **avoir**

PAST PARTICIPLE
tenu

PRESENT PARTICIPLE
tenant

IMPERATIVE
tiens
tenons
tenez

PRESENT
je	**tiens**
tu	**tiens**
il	**tient**
nous	**tenons**
vous	**tenez**
ils	**tiennent**

IMPERFECT
je	**tenais**
tu	**tenais**
il	**tenait**
nous	**tenions**
vous	**teniez**
ils	**tenaient**

FUTURE
je	**tiendrai**
tu	**tiendras**
il	**tiendra**
nous	**tiendrons**
vous	**tiendrez**
ils	**tiendront**

CONDITIONAL
je	**tiendrais**
tu	**tiendrais**
il	**tiendrait**
nous	**tiendrions**
vous	**tiendriez**
ils	**tiendraient**

PRESENT SUBJUNCTIVE
je	**tienne**
tu	**tiennes**
il	**tienne**
nous	**tenions**
vous	**teniez**
ils	**tiennent**

PAST HISTORIC
je	**tins**
tu	**tins**
il	**tint**
nous	**tînmes**
vous	**tîntes**
ils	**tinrent**

vaincre *to defeat*   Auxiliary: **avoir**

PAST PARTICIPLE
vaincu

IMPERATIVE
vaincs
vainquons
vainquez

PRESENT PARTICIPLE
vainquant

PRESENT			*IMPERFECT*	
je	vaincs		**je**	**vainquais**
tu	vaincs		**tu**	**vainquais**
il	vainc		**il**	**vainquait**
nous	**vainquons**		**nous**	**vainquions**
vous	**vainquez**		**vous**	**vainquiez**
ils	**vainquent**		**ils**	**vainquaient**

FUTURE			*CONDITIONAL*	
je	vaincrai		je	vaincrais
tu	vaincras		tu	vaincrais
il	vaincra		il	vaincrait
nous	vaincrons		nous	vaincrions
vous	vaincrez		vous	vaincriez
ils	vaincront		ils	vaincraient

PRESENT SUBJUNCTIVE			*PAST HISTORIC*	
je	**vainque**		**je**	**vainquis**
tu	**vainques**		**tu**	**vainquis**
il	**vainque**		**il**	**vainquit**
nous	**vainquions**		**nous**	**vainquîmes**
vous	**vainquiez**		**vous**	**vainquîtes**
ils	**vainquent**		**ils**	**vainquirent**

valoir *to be worth*　　　　Auxiliary: **avoir**

PAST PARTICIPLE
valu

PRESENT PARTICIPLE
valant

IMPERATIVE
vaux
valons
valez

PRESENT
je	vaux
tu	vaux
il	vaut
nous	valons
vous	valez
ils	valent

IMPERFECT
je	valais
tu	valais
il	valait
nous	valions
vous	valiez
ils	valaient

FUTURE
je	vaudrai
tu	vaudras
il	vaudra
nous	vaudrons
vous	vaudrez
ils	vaudront

CONDITIONAL
je	vaudrais
tu	vaudrais
il	vaudrait
nous	vaudrions
vous	vaudriez
ils	vaudraient

PRESENT SUBJUNCTIVE
je	vaille
tu	vailles
il	vaille
nous	valions
vous	valiez
ils	vaillent

PAST HISTORIC
je	valus
tu	valus
il	valut
nous	valûmes
vous	valûtes
ils	valurent

venir *to come* Auxiliary: **être**

PAST PARTICIPLE
venu

PRESENT PARTICIPLE
venant

IMPERATIVE
viens
venons
venez

PRESENT		*IMPERFECT*	
je	viens	je	venais
tu	viens	tu	venais
il	vient	il	venait
nous	venons	nous	venions
vous	venez	vous	veniez
ils	viennent	ils	venaient

FUTURE		*CONDITIONAL*	
je	viendrai	je	viendrais
tu	viendras	tu	viendrais
il	viendra	il	viendrait
nous	viendrons	nous	viendrions
vous	viendrez	vous	viendriez
ils	viendront	ils	viendraient

PRESENT SUBJUNCTIVE		*PAST HISTORIC*	
je	vienne	je	vins
tu	viennes	tu	vins
il	vienne	il	vint
nous	venions	nous	vînmes
vous	veniez	vous	vîntes
ils	viennent	ils	vinrent

vêtir *to dress*   Auxiliary: **avoir**

PAST PARTICIPLE	IMPERATIVE
vêtu	**vêts**
	vêtons
PRESENT PARTICIPLE	**vêtez**
vêtant	

PRESENT		IMPERFECT	
je	**vêts**	je	**vêtais**
tu	**vêts**	tu	**vêtais**
il	**vêt**	il	**vêtait**
nous	**vêtons**	nous	**vêtions**
vous	**vêtez**	vous	**vêtiez**
ils	**vêtent**	ils	**vêtaient**

FUTURE		CONDITIONAL	
je	vêtirai	je	vêtirais
tu	vêtiras	tu	vêtirais
il	vêtira	il	vêtirait
nous	vêtirons	nous	vêtirions
vous	vêtirez	vous	vêtiriez
ils	vêtiront	ils	vêtiraient

PRESENT SUBJUNCTIVE		PAST HISTORIC	
je	**vête**	je	vêtis
tu	**vêtes**	tu	vêtis
il	**vête**	il	vêtit
nous	**vêtions**	nous	vêtîmes
vous	**vêtiez**	vous	vêtîtes
ils	**vêtent**	ils	vêtirent

vivre *to live*　　　　　　　　Auxiliary: **avoir**

PAST PARTICIPLE	IMPERATIVE
vécu	**vis**
	vivons
PRESENT PARTICIPLE	vivez
vivant	

PRESENT		IMPERFECT	
je	**vis**	je	vivais
tu	**vis**	tu	vivais
il	**vit**	il	vivait
nous	vivons	nous	vivions
vous	vivez	vous	viviez
ils	vivent	ils	vivaient

FUTURE		CONDITIONAL	
je	vivrai	je	vivrais
tu	vivras	tu	vivrais
il	vivra	il	vivrait
nous	vivrons	nous	vivrions
vous	vivrez	vous	vivriez
ils	vivront	ils	vivraient

PRESENT SUBJUNCTIVE		PAST HISTORIC	
je	vive	je	**vécus**
tu	vives	tu	**vécus**
il	vive	il	**vécut**
nous	vivions	nous	**vécûmes**
vous	viviez	vous	**vécûtes**
ils	vivent	ils	**vécurent**

voir *to see*   Auxiliary: **avoir**

PAST PARTICIPLE
vu

IMPERATIVE
vois
voyons
voyez

PRESENT PARTICIPLE
voyant

PRESENT
je **vois**
tu **vois**
il **voit**
nous **voyons**
vous **voyez**
ils **voient**

IMPERFECT
je **voyais**
tu **voyais**
il **voyait**
nous **voyions**
vous **voyiez**
ils **voyaient**

FUTURE
je **verrai**
tu **verras**
il **verra**
nous **verrons**
vous **verrez**
ils **verront**

CONDITIONAL
je **verrais**
tu **verrais**
il **verrait**
nous **verrions**
vous **verriez**
ils **verraient**

PRESENT SUBJUNCTIVE
je **voie**
tu **voies**
il **voie**
nous **voyions**
vous **voyiez**
ils **voient**

PAST HISTORIC
je **vis**
tu **vis**
il **vit**
nous **vîmes**
vous **vîtes**
ils **virent**

vouloir *to wish, want*

Auxiliary: **avoir**

PAST PARTICIPLE	IMPERATIVE
voulu	veuille
	veuillons
PRESENT PARTICIPLE	veuillez
voulant	

PRESENT

je	veux
tu	veux
il	veut
nous	voulons
vous	voulez
ils	veulent

IMPERFECT

je	voulais
tu	voulais
il	voulait
nous	voulions
vous	vouliez
ils	voulaient

FUTURE

je	voudrai
tu	voudras
il	voudra
nous	voudrons
vous	voudrez
ils	voudront

CONDITIONAL

je	voudrais
tu	voudrais
il	voudrait
nous	voudrions
vous	voudriez
ils	voudraient

PRESENT SUBJUNCTIVE

je	veuille
tu	veuilles
il	veuille
nous	voulions
vous	vouliez
ils	veuillent

PAST HISTORIC

je	voulus
tu	voulus
il	voulut
nous	voulûmes
vous	voulûtes
ils	voulurent

The Gender of Nouns

In French, all nouns are either masculine or feminine, whether denoting people, animals or things. Unlike English, there is no neuter gender for inanimate objects and abstract nouns.

Gender is largely unpredictable and has to be learnt for each noun. However, the following guidelines will help you determine the gender for certain types of nouns.

- Nouns denoting male people and animals are usually – but not always – masculine, e.g.

  un homme   **un taureau**
  a man   *a bull*
  un infirmier   **un cheval**
  a (male) nurse   *a horse*

- Nouns denoting female people and animals are usually – but not always – feminine, e.g.

  une fille   **une vache**
  a girl   *a cow*
  une infirmière   **une brebis**
  a nurse   *a ewe*

- Some nouns are masculine OR feminine depending on the sex of the person to whom they refer, e.g.

  un camarade   **une camarade**
  a (male) friend   *a (female) friend*
  un Belge   **une Belge**
  a Belgian (man)   *a Belgian (woman)*

- Other nouns referring to either men or women have only one gender which applies to both, e.g.

  un professeur   **une personne**   **une sentinelle**
  a teacher   *a person*   *a sentry*
  un témoin   **une victime**   **une recrue**
  a witness   *a victim*   *a recruit*

● Sometimes the ending of the noun indicates its gender. Shown below are some of the most important to guide you:

Masculine endings

-age	**le courage** *courage*, **le rinçage** *rinsing*
	EXCEPTIONS: **une cage** *a cage*, **une image** *a picture*, **la nage** *swimming*, **une page** *a page*, **une plage** *a beach*, **une rage** *a rage*
-ment	**le commencement** *the beginning*
	EXCEPTION: **une jument** *a mare*
-oir	**un couloir** *a corridor*, **un miroir** *a mirror*
-sme	**le pessimisme** *pessimism*, **l'enthousiasme** *enthusiasm*

Feminine endings

-ance, anse	**la confiance** *confidence*, **la danse** *dancing*
-ence, -ense	**la prudence** *caution*, **la défense** *defence*
	EXCEPTION: **le silence** *silence*
-ion	**une région** *a region*, **une addition** *a bill*
	EXCEPTIONS: **un pion** *a pawn*, **un espion** *a spy*
-oire	**une baignoire** *a bath(tub)*
-té, -tié	**la beauté** *beauty*, **la moitié** *half*

● Suffixes which differentiate between male and female are shown on pp. 134 and 136

● The following words have different meanings depending on gender:

le crêpe	*crêpe*	**la crêpe**	*pancake*
le livre	*book*	**la livre**	*pound*
le manche	*handle*	**la manche**	*sleeve*
le mode	*method*	**la mode**	*fashion*
le moule	*mould*	**la moule**	*mussel*
le page	*page(boy)*	**la page**	*page (in book)*
le physique	*physique*	**la physique**	*physics*
le poêle	*stove*	**la poêle**	*frying pan*
le somme	*nap*	**la somme**	*sum*
le tour	*turn*	**la tour**	*tower*
le voile	*veil*	**la voile**	*sail*

Gender: the formation of feminines

As in English, male and female are sometimes differentiated by the use of two quite separate words, e.g.

mon oncle	**ma tante**
my uncle	*my aunt*
un taureau	**une vache**
a bull	*a cow*

There are, however, some words in French which show this distinction by the form of their ending

● Some nouns add an **e** to the masculine singular form to form the feminine (→ **1**)

● If the masculine singular form already ends in **-e**, no further **e** is added in the feminine (→ **2**)

● Some nouns undergo a further change when **e** is added. These changes occur regularly and are shown on p. 136

Feminine forms to note

MASCULINE	FEMININE	
un âne	**une ânesse**	*donkey*
le comte	**la comtesse**	*count/countess*
le duc	**la duchesse**	*duke/duchess*
un Esquimau	**une Esquimaude**	*Eskimo*
le fou	**la folle**	*madman/madwoman*
le Grec	**la Grecque**	*Greek*
un hôte	**une hôtesse**	*host/hostess*
le jumeau	**la jumelle**	*twin*
le maître	**la maîtresse**	*master/mistress*
le prince	**la princesse**	*prince/princess*
le tigre	**la tigresse**	*tiger/tigress*
le traître	**la traîtresse**	*traitor*
le Turc	**la Turque**	*Turk*
le vieux	**la vieille**	*old man/old woman*

Continued

1 **un ami**
   a (male) friend
   un employé
   a (male) employee
   un Français
   a Frenchman

                    une amie
                    a (female) friend
                    une employée
                    a (female) employee
                    une Française
                    a Frenchwoman

2 **un élève**
   a (male) pupil
   un collègue
   a (male) colleague
   un camarade
   a (male) friend

                    une élève
                    a (female) pupil
                    une collègue
                    a (female) colleague
                    une camarade
                    a (female) friend

Regular feminine endings

MASC. SING.	FEM. SING.	
-f	-ve	(→ 1)
-x	-se	(→ 2)
-eur	-euse	(→ 3)
-teur	-teuse	(→ 4)
	-trice	(→ 5)

Some nouns double the final consonant before adding **e**:

MASC. SING.	FEM. SING.	
-an	-anne	(→ 6)
-en	-enne	(→ 7)
-on	-onne	(→ 8)
-et	-ette	(→ 9)
-el	-elle	(→ 10)

Some nouns add an accent to the final syllable before adding **e**:

MASC. SING.	FEM. SING.	
-er	-ère	(→ 11)

Pronunciation and feminine endings

This is dealt with on p. 244.

1 **un sportif**
   a sportsman
   un veuf
   a widower

   une sportive
   a sportswoman
   une veuve
   a widow

2 **un époux**
   a husband
   un amoureux
   a man in love

   une épouse
   a wife
   une amoureuse
   a woman in love

3 **un danseur**
   a dancer
   un voleur
   a thief

   une danseuse
   a dancer
   une voleuse
   a thief

4 **un menteur**
   a liar
   un chanteur
   a singer

   une menteuse
   a liar
   une chanteuse
   a singer

5 **un acteur**
   an actor
   un conducteur
   a driver

   une actrice
   an actress
   une conductrice
   a driver

6 **un paysan**
   a countryman

   une paysanne
   a countrywoman

7 **un Parisien**
   a Parisian

   une Parisienne
   a Parisian (woman)

8 **un baron**
   a baron

   une baronne
   a baroness

9 **le cadet**
   the youngest (child)

   la cadette
   the youngest (child)

10 **un intellectuel**
   an intellectual

   une intellectuelle
   an intellectual

11 **un étranger**
   a foreigner
   le dernier
   the last (one)

   une étrangère
   a foreigner
   la dernière
   the last (one)

The formation of plurals

● Most nouns add **s** to the singular form (→ **1**)

● When the singular form already ends in **-s**, **-x** or **-z**, no further **s** is added (→ **2**)

● For nouns ending in **-au**, **-eau** or **-eu**, the plural ends in **-aux**, **-eaux** or **-eux** (→ **3**)

Exceptions:	**pneu**	*tyre*	(plur: **pneus**)
	bleu	*bruise*	(plur: **bleus**)

● For nouns ending in **-al** or **-ail**, the plural ends in **-aux** (→ **4**)

Exceptions:	**bal**	*ball*	(plur: **bals**)
	festival	*festival*	(plur: **festivals**)
	chandail	*sweater*	(plur: **chandails**)
	détail	*detail*	(plur: **détails**)

● Forming the plural of compound nouns is complicated and you are advised to check each one individually in a dictionary

Irregular plural forms

● Some masculine nouns ending in **-ou** add **x** in the plural. These are:

bijou	*jewel*	**genou**	*knee*	**joujou**	*toy*
caillou	*pebble*	**hibou**	*owl*	**pou**	*louse*
chou	*cabbage*				

● Some other nouns are totally unpredictable. Chief among these are:

SINGULAR	*PLURAL*
œil *eye*	**yeux**
ciel *sky*	**cieux**
Monsieur *Mr.*	**Messieurs**
Madame *Mrs.*	**Mesdames**
Mademoiselle *Miss*	**Mesdemoiselles**

Pronunciation of plural forms
This is dealt with on p. 244

1 le jardin   **les jardins**
the garden   the gardens
une voiture   **des voitures**
a car   (some) cars
l'hôtel   **les hôtels**
the hotel   the hotels

2 un tas   **des tas**
a heap   (some) heaps
une voix   **des voix**
a voice   (some) voices
le gaz   **les gaz**
the gas   the gases

3 un tuyau   **des tuyaux**
a pipe   (some) pipes
le chapeau   **les chapeaux**
the hat   the hats
le feu   **les feux**
the fire   the fires

4 le journal   **les journaux**
the newspaper   the newspapers
un travail   **des travaux**
a job   (some) jobs

The Definite Article

	WITH MASC. NOUN	WITH FEM. NOUN	
SING.	le (l')	la (l')	the
PLUR.	les	les	the

● The gender and number of the noun determines the form of the article (→ 1)

● le and la change to l' before a vowel or an h 'mute' (→ 2)

● For uses of the definite article see p. 142

● à + le/la (l'), à + les

	WITH MASC. NOUN	WITH FEM. NOUN	
SING.	au (à l')	à la (à l')	(→ 3)
PLUR.	aux	aux	

● The definite article combines with the preposition à, as shown above. You should pay particular attention to the masculine singular form au, and both plural forms aux, since these are not visually the sum of their parts

● de + le/la (l'), de + les

	WITH MASC. NOUN	WITH FEM. NOUN	
SING.	du (de l')	de la (de l')	(→ 4)
PLUR.	des	des	

● The definite article combines with the preposition de, as shown above. You should pay particular attention to the masculine singular form du, and both plural forms des, since these are not visually the sum of their parts

Continued

MASCULINE	FEMININE
1 le train	**la gare**
the train	the station
le garçon	**la fille**
the boy	the girl
les hôtels	**les écoles**
the hotels	the schools
les professeurs	**les femmes**
the teachers	the women
2 l'acteur	**l'actrice**
the actor	the actress
l'effet	**l'eau**
the effect	the water
l'ingrédient	**l'idée**
the ingredient	the idea
l'objet	**l'ombre**
the object	the shadow
l'univers	**l'usine**
the universe	the factory
l'hôpital	**l'heure**
the hospital	the time
3 au cinéma	**à la bibliothèque**
at/to the cinema	at/to the library
à l'employé	**à l'infirmière**
to the employee	to the nurse
à l'hôpital	**à l'hôtesse**
at/to the hospital	to the hostess
aux étudiants	**aux maisons**
to the students	to the houses
4 du bureau	**de la réunion**
from/of the office	from/of the meeting
de l'auteur	**de l'Italienne**
from/of the author	from/of the Italian woman
de l'hôte	**de l'horloge**
from/of the host	of the clock
des Etats-Unis	**des vendeuses**
from/of the United States	from/of the saleswomen

Uses of the definite article

While the definite article is used in much the same way in French as it is in English, its use is more widespread in French. Unlike English the definite article is also used:

● with abstract nouns, except when following certain prepositions (→ **1**)

● in generalisations, especially with plural or uncountable* nouns (→ **2**)

● with names of countries (→ **3**)
Exceptions: no article with countries following **en** *to/in* (→ **4**)

● with parts of the body (→ **5**)
'Ownership' is often indicated by an indirect object pronoun or a reflexive pronoun (→ **6**)

● in expressions of quantity/rate/price (→ **7**)

● with titles/ranks/professions followed by a proper name (→ **8**)

● The definite article is NOT used with nouns in apposition (→ **9**)

*An uncountable noun is one which cannot be used in the plural or with an indefinite article, e.g. **l'acier** *steel*, **le lait** *milk*

1 Les prix montent
   Prices are rising
   L'amour rayonne dans ses yeux
   Love shines in his eyes
   BUT   **avec plaisir   sans espoir**
              with pleasure   without hope
2 Je n'aime pas le café
   I don't like coffee
   Les enfants ont besoin d'être aimés
   Children need to be loved
3 le Japon   la France   l'Italie   les Pays-Bas
   Japan   France   Italy   The Netherlands
4 aller en Ecosse   Il travaille en Allemagne
   to go to Scotland   He works in Germany
5 Tournez la tête à gauche
   Turn your head to the left
   J'ai mal à la gorge
   My throat is sore, I have a sore throat
6 La tête me tourne
   My head is spinning
   Elle s'est brossé les dents
   She brushed her teeth
7 40 francs le mètre/le kilo/la douzaine/la pièce
   40 francs a metre/a kilo/a dozen/each
   rouler à 80 km à l'heure
   to go at 50 m.p.h.
   payé à l'heure/au jour/au mois
   paid by the hour/by the day/by the month
8 le roi Georges III   le capitaine Darbeau
   King George III   Captain Darbeau
   le docteur Rousseau   Monsieur le président
   Dr. Rousseau   Mr. Chairman/President
9 Victor Hugo, grand écrivain du dix-neuvième siècle
   Victor Hugo, a great author of the nineteenth century
   Joseph Leblanc, inventeur et entrepreneur, a été le premier ...
   Joseph Leblanc, an inventor and entrepreneur, was the first ...

The Partitive Article

The partitive article has the sense of *some* or *any*, although the French is not always translated in English.

Forms of the partitive

	WITH MASC. NOUN	WITH FEM. NOUN	
SING.	**du (de l')**	**de la (de l')**	*some, any*
PLUR.	**des**	**des**	*some, any*

● The gender and number of the noun determines the form of the partitive (→ **1**)

● The forms shown in brackets are used before a vowel or an **h** 'mute' (→ **2**)

● **des** becomes **de** (**d'** + vowel) before an adjective (→ **3**), unless the adjective and noun are seen as forming one unit (→ **4**)

● In negative sentences **de** (**d'** + vowel) is used for both genders, singular and plural (→ **5**)
Exception: after **ne ... que** *only*, the positive forms above are used (→ **6**)

1 **Avez-vous du sucre?**
   Have you any sugar?
   J'ai acheté de la farine et de la margarine
   I bought (some) flour and margarine
   Il a mangé des gâteaux
   He ate some cakes
   Est-ce qu'il y a des lettres pour moi?
   Are there (any) letters for me?

2 **Il me doit de l'argent**   **C'est de l'histoire ancienne**
   He owes me (some) money   That's ancient history

3 **Il a fait de gros efforts pour nous aider**
   He made a great effort to help us
   Cette région a de belles églises
   This region has some beautiful churches

4 **des grandes vacances**   **des jeunes gens**
   summer holidays   young people

5 **Je n'ai pas de nourriture/d'argent**
   I don't have any food/money
   Vous n'avez pas de timbres/d'œufs?
   Have you no stamps/eggs?
   Je ne mange jamais de viande/d'omelettes
   I never eat meat/omelettes
   Il ne veut plus de visiteurs/d'eau
   He doesn't want any more visitors/water

6 **Il ne boit que du thé/de la bière/de l'eau**
   He only drinks tea/beer/water
   Je n'ai que des problèmes avec cette machine
   I have nothing but problems with this machine

The Indefinite Article

	WITH MASC. NOUN	WITH FEM. NOUN	
SING.	**un**	**une**	*a*
PLUR.	**des**	**des**	*some*

● **des** is also the plural of the partitive article (see p. 144)

● In negative sentences, **de** (**d'** + vowel) is used for both singular and plural (→ **1**)

● The indefinite article is used in French largely as it is in English EXCEPT:

– there is no article when a person's profession is being stated (→ **2**)
The article *is* present however, following **ce** (**c'** + vowel) (→ **3**)

– the English article is not translated by **un**/**une** in constructions like *what a surprise, what an idiot* (→ **4**)

– in structures of the type given in example **5** the article **un**/**une** is used in French and not translated in English (→ **5**)

1 Je n'ai pas de livre/d'enfants
I don't have a book/(any) children

2 Il est professeur   **Ma mère est infirmière**
He's a teacher   My mother's a nurse

3 C'est un médecin
He's/She's a doctor
Ce sont des acteurs
They're actors

4 Quelle surprise!   **Quel dommage!**
What a surprise!   What a shame!

5 avec une grande sagesse/un courage admirable
with great wisdom/admirable courage
Il a fait preuve d'un sang-froid incroyable
He showed incredible coolness
Un produit d'une qualité incomparable
A product of incomparable quality

Adjectives

Most adjectives agree in number and in gender with the noun or pronoun.

The formation of feminines

● Most adjectives add an **e** to the masculine singular form (→ **1**)

● If the masculine singular form already ends in **-e**, no further **e** is added (→ **2**)

● Some adjectives undergo a further change when **e** is added. These changes occur regularly and are shown on p. 150

● Irregular feminine forms are shown on p. 152

The formation of plurals

● The plural of both regular and irregular adjectives is formed by adding an **s** to the masculine or feminine singular form, as appropriate (→ **3**)

● When the masculine singular form already ends in **-s** or **-x**, no further **s** is added (→ **4**)

● For masculine singulars ending in **-au** and **-eau**, the masculine plural is **-aux** and **-eaux** (→ **5**)

● For masculine singulars ending in **-al**, the masculine plural is **-aux** (→ **6**)

> Exceptions: **final** (masculine plural **finals**)
> **fatal** (masculine plural **fatals**)
> **naval** (masculine plural **navals**)

Pronunciation of feminine and plural adjectives
This is dealt with on p. 244

1   **mon frère aîné**   **ma sœur aînée**
my elder brother   my elder sister
le petit garçon   **la petite fille**
the little boy   the little girl
un sac gris   **une chemise grise**
a grey bag   a grey shirt
un bruit fort   **une voix forte**
a loud noise   a loud voice

2   **un jeune homme**   **une jeune femme**
a young man   a young woman
l'autre verre   **l'autre assiette**
the other glass   the other plate

3   **le dernier train**   **les derniers trains**
the last train   the last trains
une vieille maison   **de vieilles maisons**
an old house   old houses
un long voyage   **de longs voyages**
a long journey   long journeys
la rue étroite   **les rues étroites**
the narrow street   the narrow streets

4   **un diplomate français**   **des diplomates français**
a French diplomat   French diplomats
un homme dangereux   **des hommes dangereux**
a dangerous man   dangerous men

5   **le nouveau professeur**   **les nouveaux professeurs**
the new teacher   the new teachers
un chien esquimau   **des chiens esquimaux**
a husky (Fr. = an Eskimo dog)   huskies (Fr. = Eskimo dogs)

6   **un ami loyal**   **des amis loyaux**
a loyal friend   loyal friends
un geste amical   **des gestes amicaux**
a friendly gesture   friendly gestures

Regular feminine endings

MASC. SING.	FEM. SING.	EXAMPLES	
-f	-ve	neuf, vif	(→ **1**)
-x	-se	heureux, jaloux	(→ **2**)
-eur	-euse	travailleur, flâneur	(→ **3**)
-teur	⎰ -teuse	flatteur, menteur	(→ **4**)
	⎱ -trice	destructeur, séducteur	(→ **5**)

Exceptions:

bref: see p. 152

doux, faux, roux, vieux: see p. 152

extérieur, inférieur, intérieur, meilleur, supérieur: all add **e** to the masculine

enchanteur: fem. = **enchanteresse**

MASC. SING.	FEM. SING.	EXAMPLES	
-an	-anne	paysan	(→ **6**)
-en	-enne	ancien, parisien	(→ **7**)
-on	-onne	bon, breton	(→ **8**)
-as	-asse	bas, las	(→ **9**)
-et*	-ette	muet, violet	(→ **10**)
-el	-elle	annuel, mortel	(→ **11**)
-eil	-eille	pareil, vermeil	(→ **12**)

Exception:

ras: fem. = **rase**

MASC. SING.	FEM. SING.	EXAMPLES	
-et*	-ète	secret, complet	(→ **13**)
-er	-ère	étranger, fier	(→ **14**)

*Note that there are two feminine endings for masculine adjectives ending in **-et**.

1 **un résultat positif**
a positive result

   une attitude positive
   a positive attitude

2 **d'un ton sérieux**
in a serious tone (of voice)

   une voix sérieuse
   a serious voice

3 **un enfant trompeur**
a deceitful child

   une déclaration trompeuse
   a misleading statement

4 **un tableau flatteur**
a flattering picture

   une comparaison flatteuse
   a flattering comparison

5 **un geste protecteur**
a protective gesture

   une couche protectrice
   a protective layer

6 **un problème paysan**
a farming problem

   la vie paysanne
   country life

7 **un avion égyptien**
an Egyptian plane

   une statue égyptienne
   an Egyptian statue

8 **un bon repas**
a good meal

   de bonne humeur
   in a good mood

9 **un plafond bas**
a low ceiling

   à voix basse
   in a low voice

10 **un travail net**
a clean piece of work

   une explication nette
   a clear explanation

11 **un homme cruel**
a cruel man

   une remarque cruelle
   a cruel remark

12 **un livre pareil**
such a book

   en pareille occasion
   on such an occasion

13 **un regard inquiet**
an anxious look

   une attente inquiète
   an anxious wait

14 **un goût amer**
a bitter taste

   une amère déception
   a bitter disappointment

Adjectives with irregular feminine forms

MASC. SING.	FEM. SING.		
aigu	aiguë	*sharp; high-pitched*	(→ **1**)
ambigu	ambiguë	*ambiguous*	
beau (bel)*	belle	*beautiful*	
bénin	bénigne	*benign*	
blanc	blanche	*white*	
bref	brève	*brief, short*	(→ **2**)
doux	douce	*soft; sweet*	
épais	épaisse	*think*	
esquimau	esquimaude	*Eskimo*	
faux	fausse	*wrong*	
favori	favorite	*favourite*	(→ **3**)
fou (fol)*	folle	*mad*	
frais	fraîche	*fresh*	(→ **4**)
franc	franche	*frank*	
gentil	gentille	*kind*	
grec	grecque	*Greek*	
gros	grosse	*big*	
jumeau	jumelle	*twin*	(→ **5**)
long	longue	*long*	
malin	maligne	*malignant*	
mou (mol)*	molle	*soft*	
nouveau (nouvel)*	nouvelle	*new*	
nul	nulle	*no*	
public	publique	*public*	(→ **6**)
roux	rousse	*red-haired*	
sec	sèche	*dry*	
sot	sotte	*foolish*	
turc	turque	*Turkish*	
vieux (vieil)*	vieille	*old*	

*This form is used when the following word begins with a vowel or an **h** 'mute' (→ **7**)

1 **un son aigu**
   a high-pitched sound

   une douleur aiguë
   a sharp pain

2 **un bref discours**
   a short speech

   une brève rencontre
   a short meeting

3 **mon sport favori**
   my favourite sport

   ma chanson favorite
   my favourite song

4 **du pain frais**
   fresh bread

   de la crème fraîche
   fresh cream

5 **mon frère jumeau**
   my twin brother

   ma sœur jumelle
   my twin sister

6 **un jardin public**
   a (public) park

   l'opinion publique
   public opinion

7 **un bel appartement**
   a beautiful flat
   le nouvel inspecteur
   the new inspector
   un vieil arbre
   an old tree

   un bel habit
   a beautiful outfit
   un nouvel harmonica
   a new harmonica
   un vieil hôtel
   an old hotel

Comparatives and Superlatives

Comparatives
These are formed using the following constructions:

plus ... (que)	*more ... (than)*	(→ **1**)
moins ... (que)	*less ... (than)*	(→ **2**)
aussi ... que	*as ... as*	(→ **3**)
si ... que*	*as ... as*	(→ **4**)

*used mainly after a negative

Superlatives
These are formed using the following constructions:

le/la/les plus ... (que)	*the most ... (that)*	(→ **5**)
le/la/les moins ... (que)	*the least ... (that)*	(→ **6**)

● When the possessive adjective is present, two constructions are possible (→ **7**)
● After a superlative the preposition **de** is often translated as *in* (→ **8**)
● If a clause follows a superlative, the verb is in the subjunctive (→ **9**)

Adjectives with irregular comparatives/superlatives

ADJECTIVE	COMPARATIVE	SUPERLATIVE
bon	**meilleur**	**le meilleur**
good	*better*	*the best*
mauvais	**pire** OR	**le pire** OR
bad	**plus mauvais**	**le plus mauvais**
	worse	*the worst*
petit	**moindre*** OR	**le moindre*** OR
small	**plus petit**	**le plus petit**
	smaller;	*the smallest;*
	lesser	*the least*

*used only with abstract nouns

● Comparative and superlative adjectives agree in number and in gender with the noun, just like any other adjective (→ **10**)

1 **une raison plus grave**
a more serious reason
Elle est plus petite que moi
She is smaller than me
2 **un film moins connu**
a less well-known film
C'est moins cher qu'il ne pense
It's cheaper than he thinks
3 **Robert était aussi inquiet que moi**
Robert was as worried as I was
Cette ville n'est pas aussi grande que Bordeaux
This town isn't as big as Bordeaux
4 **Ils ne sont pas si contents que ça**
They aren't as happy as all that
5 **le guide le plus utile**   **la voiture la plus petite**
the most useful guidebook   the smallest car
les plus grandes maisons
the biggest houses
6 **le mois le moins agréable**   **la fille la moins forte**
the least pleasant month   the weakest girl
les moins belles peintures
the least attractive paintings
7 **Mon désir le plus cher** ⎱
Mon plus cher désir   ⎰ **est de voyager**
My dearest wish is to travel
8 **la plus grande gare de Londres**
the biggest station in London
l'habitant le plus âgé du village/de la région
the oldest inhabitant in the village/in the area
9 **la personne la plus gentille que je connaisse**
the nicest person I know
10 **les moindres difficultés**
the least difficulties
la meilleure qualité
the best quality

Demonstrative Adjectives

	MASCULINE	*FEMININE*	
SING.	**ce (cet)**	**cette**	*this; that*
PLUR.	**ces**	**ces**	*these; those*

● Demonstrative adjectives agree in number and gender with the noun (→ **1**)

● **cet** is used when the following word begins with a vowel or an **h** 'mute' (→ **2**)

● For emphasis or in order to distinguish between people or objects, **-ci** or **-là** is added to the noun: **-ci** indicates proximity (usually translated *this*) and **là** distance (*that*) (→ **3**)

1 **Ce stylo ne marche pas**
   This/That pen isn't working
   Comment s'appelle cette entreprise?
   What's this/that company called?
   Ces livres sont les miens
   These/Those books are mine
   Ces couleurs sont plus jolies
   These/Those colours are nicer

2 **cet oiseau**
   this/that bird
   cet article
   this/that article
   cet homme
   this/that man

3 **Combien coûte ce manteau-ci?**
   How much is this coat?
   Je voudrais cinq de ces pommes-là
   I'd like five of those apples
   Est-ce que tu reconnais cette personne-là?
   Do you recognize that person?
   Mettez ces vêtements-ci dans cette valise-là
   Put these clothes in that case
   Ce garçon-là appartient à ce groupe-ci
   That boy belongs to this group

Interrogative Adjectives

	MASCULINE	FEMININE	
SING.	quel?	quelle?	what?; which?
PLUR.	quels?	quelles?	what?; which?

● Interrogative adjectives agree in number and gender with the noun (→ 1)

● The forms shown above are also used in indirect questions (→ 2)

Exclamatory Adjectives

	MASCULINE	FEMININE	
SING.	quel!	quelle!	what (a)!
PLUR.	quels!	quelles!	what!

● Exclamatory adjectives agree in number and gender with the noun (→ 3)

● For other exclamations, see p. 214

1 **Quel genre d'homme est-ce?**
What type of man is he?
Quelle est leur décision?
What is their decision?
Vous jouez de quels instruments?
What instruments do you play?
Quelles offres avez-vous reçues?
What offers have you received?
Quel vin recommandez-vous?
Which wine do you recommend?
Quelles couleurs préférez-vous?
Which colours do you prefer?

2 **Je ne sais pas à quelle heure il est arrivé**
I don't know what time he arrived
Dites-moi quels sont les livres les plus intéressants
Tell me which books are the most interesting

3 **Quel dommage!**
What a pity!
Quelle idée!
What an idea!
Quels beaux livres vous avez!
What fine books you have!
Quelles jolies fleurs!
What nice flowers!

Possessive Adjectives

WITH SING. NOUN		WITH PLUR. NOUN	
MASC.	FEM.	MASC./FEM.	
mon	ma (mon)	mes	my
ton	ta (ton)	tes	your
son	sa (son)	ses	his; her; its
notre	notre	nos	our
votre	votre	vos	your
leur	leur	leurs	their

● Possessive adjectives agree in number and gender with the noun, NOT WITH THE OWNER (→ **1**)

● The forms shown in brackets are used when the following word begins with a vowel or an **h** 'mute' (→ **2**)

● **son**, **sa**, **ses** have the additional meaning of *one's* (→ **3**)

1 Catherine a oublié son parapluie
Catherine has left her umbrella
Paul cherche sa montre
Paul's looking for his watch
Mon frère et ma sœur habitent à Glasgow
My brother and sister live in Glasgow
Est-ce que tes voisins ont vendu leur voiture?
Did your neighbours sell their car?
Rangez vos affaires
Put your things away

2 mon appareil-photo
my camera
ton histoire
your story
son erreur
his/her mistake
mon autre sœur
my other sister

3 perdre son équilibre
to lose one's balance
présenter ses excuses
to offer one's apologies

Position of Adjectives

● French adjectives usually follow the noun (→ **1**)

● Adjectives of colour or nationality *always* follow the noun (→ **2**)

● As in English, demonstrative, possessive, numerical and interrogative adjectives precede the noun (→ **3**)

● The adjectives **autre** *other* and **chaque** *each, every* precede the noun (→ **4**)

● The following common adjectives can precede the noun:

beau	*beautiful*	**jeune**	*young*
bon	*good*	**joli**	*pretty*
court	*short*	**long**	*long*
dernier	*last*	**mauvais**	*bad*
grand	*great*	**petit**	*small*
gros	*big*	**tel**	*such (a)*
haut	*high*	**vieux**	*old*

● The meaning of the following adjectives varies according to their position:

	BEFORE NOUN	AFTER NOUN	
ancien	*former*	*old, ancient*	(→ **5**)
brave	*good*	*brave*	(→ **6**)
cher	*dear (beloved)*	*expensive*	(→ **7**)
grand	*great*	*tall*	(→ **8**)
même	*same*	*very*	(→ **9**)
pauvre	*poor* (wretched)	*poor* (not rich)	(→ **10**)
propre	*own*	*clean*	(→ **11**)
seul	*single, sole*	*on one's own*	(→ **12**)
simple	*mere, simple*	*simple, easy*	(→ **13**)
vrai	*real*	*true*	(→ **14**)

● Adjectives following the noun are linked by **et** (→ **15**)

1 **le chapitre suivant**
the following chapter

l'heure exacte
the right time

2 **une cravate rouge**
a red tie

un mot français
a French word

3 **ce dictionnaire**
this dictionary

mon père
my father

le premier étage
the first floor

deux exemples
two examples

quel homme?
which man?

4 **une autre fois**
another time

chaque jour
every day

5 **un ancien collègue**
a former colleague

l'histoire ancienne
ancient history

6 **un brave homme**
a good man

un homme brave
a brave man

7 **mes chers amis**
my dear friends

une robe chère
an expensive dress

8 **un grand peintre**
a great painter

un homme grand
a tall man

9 **la même réponse**
the same answer

vos paroles mêmes
your very words

10 **cette pauvre femme**
that poor woman

une nation pauvre
a poor nation

11 **ma propre vie**
my own life

une chemise propre
a clean shirt

12 **une seule réponse**
a single reply

une femme seule
a woman on her own

13 **un simple regard**
a mere look

un problème simple
a simple problem

14 **la vraie raison**
the real reason

les faits vrais
the true facts

15 **un acte lâche et trompeur**
a cowardly, deceitful act

un acte lâche, trompeur et ignoble
a cowardly, deceitful and ignoble act

Personal Pronouns

SUBJECT PRONOUNS

PERSON	SINGULAR	PLURAL
1st	**je (j')**	**nous**
	I	*we*
2nd	**tu**	**vous**
	you	*you*
3rd (masc.)	**il**	**ils**
	he; it	*they*
(fem.)	**elle**	**elles**
	she; it	*they*

je changes to **j'** before a vowel, an **h** 'mute', or the pronoun **y** (→ **1**)

● **tu/vous**

Vous, as well as being the second person plural, is also used when addressing one person. As a general rule, use **tu** only when addressing a friend, a child, a relative, someone you know very well, or when invited to do so. In all other cases use **vous**. For singular and plural uses of **vous**, see example **2**.

● **il/elle; ils/elles**

The form of the 3rd person pronouns reflects the number and gender of the noun(s) they replace, referring to animals and things as well as to people. **Ils** also replaces a combination of masculine and feminine nouns (→ **3**)

● Sometimes stressed pronouns replace the subject pronouns, see p. 172

Continued

1 J'arrive!
I'm just coming!
J'en ai trois
I've got 3 of them
J'hésite à le déranger
I hesitate to disturb him
J'y pense souvent
I often think about it

2 Compare: **Vous êtes certain, Monsieur Leclerc?**
                    Are you sure, Mr Leclerc?
   and: **Vous êtes certains, les enfants?**
                    Are you sure, children?
   Compare: **Vous êtes partie quand, Estelle?**
                    When did you leave, Estelle?
   and: **Estelle et Sophie – vous êtes parties quand?**
                    Estelle and Sophie – when did you leave?

3 Où logent ton père et ta mère quand ils vont à Rome?
Where do your father and mother stay when they go to Rome?
Donne-moi le journal et les lettres quand ils arriveront
Give me the newspaper and the letters when they arrive

Personal Pronouns (ctd.)

DIRECT OBJECT PRONOUNS

PERSON	SINGULAR	PLURAL
1st	**me (m')**	**nous**
	me	*us*
2nd	**te (t')**	**vous**
	you	*you*
3rd (masc.)	**le (l')**	**les**
	him; it	*them*
(fem.)	**la (l')**	**les**
	her; it	*them*

The forms shown in brackets are used before a vowel, an **h** 'mute', or the pronoun **y** (→ **1**)

● In positive commands **me** and **te** change to **moi** and **toi** except before **en** or **y** (→ **2**)

● **le** sometimes functions as a 'neuter' pronoun, referring to an idea or information contained in a previous statement or question. It is often not translated (→ **3**)

Position of direct object pronouns
● In constructions other than the imperative affirmative the pronoun comes before the verb (→ **4**)
The same applies when the verb is in the infinitive (→ **5**)
In the imperative affirmative, the pronoun follows the verb and is attached to it by a hyphen (→ **6**)

● For further information, see Order of Object Pronouns, p. 170

Reflexive Pronouns
These are dealt with under reflexive verbs, p. 30

Continued

1 **Il m'a vu**
He saw me
Je ne t'oublierai jamais
I'll never forget you
Ça l'habitue à travailler seul
That gets him/her used to working on his/her own
Je veux l'y accoutumer
I want to accustom him/her to it

2 **Avertis-moi de ta décision** → **Avertis-m'en**
Inform me of your decision   Inform me of it

3 **Il n'est pas là. – Je le sais bien.**
He isn't there. – I know that.
Aidez-moi si vous le pouvez
Help me if you can
Elle viendra demain. – Je l'espère bien.
She'll come tomorrow. – I hope so.

4 **Je t'aime**
I love you
Les voyez-vous?
Can you see them?
Elle ne nous connaît pas
She doesn't know us
Est-ce que tu ne les aimes pas?
Don't you like them?
Ne me faites pas rire
Don't make me laugh

5 **Puis-je vous aider?**
May I help you?

6 **Aidez-moi**   **Suivez-nous**
Help me   Follow us

Personal Pronouns (ctd.)

INDIRECT OBJECT PRONOUNS

PERSON	SINGULAR	PLURAL
1st	me (m')	nous
2nd	te (t')	vous
3rd (masc.)	lui	leur
(fem.)	lui	leur

me and te change to m' and t' before a vowel or an h 'mute'
(→1)

● In positive commands, me and te change to moi and toi except
before en (→2)

● The pronouns shown in the above table replace the preposition à +
noun, where the noun is a person or an animal (→3)

● The verbal construction affects the translation of the pronoun (→4)

Position of indirect object pronouns

● In constructions other than the imperative affirmative, the pronoun
comes before the verb (→5)
The same applies when the verb is in the infinitive (→6)
In the imperative affirmative, the pronoun follows the verb and is
attached to it by a hyphen (→7)

● For further information, see Order of Object Pronouns, p. 170

Reflexive Pronouns
These are dealt with under reflexive verbs, p. 30

Continued

1 Tu m'as donné ce livre
You gave me this book
Ils t'ont caché les faits
They hid the facts from you

2 Donnez-moi du sucre   → **Donnez-m'en**
Give me some sugar   Give me some
Garde-toi assez d'argent   → **Garde-t'en assez**
Keep enough money for   Keep enough for yourself
yourself

3 J'écris à Suzanne   → **Je lui écris**
I'm writing to Suzanne   I'm writing to her
Donne du lait au chat   → **Donne-lui du lait**
Give the cat some milk   Give it some milk

4 arracher qch à qn   to snatch sth from sb:
    Un voleur m'a arraché mon porte-monnaie
    A thief snatched my purse from me
promettre qch à qn   to promise sb sth:
    Il leur a promis un cadeau
    He promised them a present
demander à qn de faire   to ask sb to do:
    Elle nous avait demandé de revenir
    She had asked us to come back

5 Elle vous a écrit   **Vous a-t-elle écrit?**
She's written to you   Has she written to you?
Il ne nous parle pas
He doesn't speak to us
Est-ce que cela ne vous intéresse pas?
Doesn't it interest you?
Ne leur répondez pas
Don't answer them

6 Voulez-vous leur envoyer l'adresse?
Do you want to send them the address?

7 Répondez-moi   **Donnez-nous la réponse**
Answer me   Tell us the answer

Personal Pronouns (ctd.)

Order of object pronouns

● When two object pronouns of different persons come before the verb, the order is: indirect before direct, i.e.

$$\left.\begin{array}{l}\textbf{me}\\\textbf{te}\\\textbf{nous}\\\textbf{vous}\end{array}\right\}\text{ before }\left\{\begin{array}{l}\textbf{le}\\\textbf{la}\\\textbf{les}\end{array}\right.\quad(\rightarrow \textbf{1})$$

● When two 3rd person object pronouns come before the verb, the order is: direct before indirect, i.e.

$$\left.\begin{array}{l}\textbf{le}\\\textbf{la}\\\textbf{les}\end{array}\right\}\text{ before }\left\{\begin{array}{l}\textbf{lui}\\\textbf{leur}\end{array}\right.\quad(\rightarrow \textbf{2})$$

● When two object pronouns come after the verb (i.e. in the imperative affirmative), the order is: direct before indirect, i.e.

$$\left.\begin{array}{l}\textbf{le}\\\textbf{la}\\\textbf{les}\end{array}\right\}\text{ before }\left\{\begin{array}{l}\textbf{moi}\\\textbf{toi}\\\textbf{lui}\\\textbf{nous}\\\textbf{vous}\\\textbf{leur}\end{array}\right.\quad(\rightarrow \textbf{3})$$

● The pronouns **y** and **en** (see pp. 176 and 174) always come last (→ **4**)

1 **Dominique vous l'envoie demain**
   Dominique's sending it to you tomorrow
   Est-ce qu'il te les a montrés?
   Has he shown them to you?
   Ne me le dis pas
   Don't tell me (it)
   Il ne veut pas nous la prêter
   He won't lend it to us

2 **Elle le leur a emprunté**
   She borrowed it from them
   Je les lui ai lus
   I read them to him/her
   Ne la leur donne pas
   Don't give it to them
   Je voudrais les lui rendre
   I'd like to give them back to him/her

3 **Rends-les-moi**
   Give them back to me
   Donnez-le-nous
   Give it to us
   Apportons-les-leur
   Let's take them to them

4 **Donnez-leur-en**
   Give them some
   Je l'y ai déposé
   I dropped him there
   Ne nous en parlez plus
   Don't speak to us about it any more

Personal Pronouns (ctd.)

STRESSED OR DISJUNCTIVE PRONOUNS

PERSON	SINGULAR	PLURAL
1st	**moi**	**nous**
	me	*us*
2nd	**toi**	**vous**
	you	*you*
3rd (masc.)	**lui**	**eux**
	him; it	*them*
(fem.)	**elle**	**elles**
	her; it	*them*
('reflexive')	**soi**	
	oneself	

● These pronouns are used:
  – after prepositions (→ **1**)
  – on their own (→ **2**)
  – following **c'est**, **ce sont** *it is* (→ **3**)
  – for emphasis, especially where contrast is involved (→ **4**)
  – when the subject consists of two or more pronouns (→ **5**)
  – when the subject consists of a pronoun and a noun (→ **6**)
  – in comparisons (→ **7**)
  – before relative pronouns (→ **8**)

● For particular emphasis **-même** (singular) or **-mêmes** (plural) is added to the pronoun (→ **9**)

moi-même	*myself*	**nous-mêmes**	*ourselves*
toi-même	*yourself*	**vous-même**	*yourself*
lui-même	*himself; itself*	**vous-mêmes**	*yourselves*
elle-même	*herself; itself*	**eux-mêmes**	*themselves*
soi-même	*oneself*	**elles-mêmes**	*themselves*

1 **Je pense à toi**
   I think about you
   C'est pour elle
   This is for her
   Venez avec moi
   Come with me

   Partez sans eux
   Leave without them
   Assieds-toi à côté de lui
   Sit beside him
   Il a besoin de nous
   He needs us

2 **Qui a fait cela? – Lui.**
   Who did that? – He did.
   Qui est-ce qui gagne? – Moi
   Who's winning? – Me

3 **C'est toi, Simon? – Non, c'est moi, David.**
   Is that you, Simon? – No, it's me, David
   Qui est-ce? – Ce sont eux.
   Who is it? – It's them.

4 **Ils voyagent séparément: lui par le train, elle en autobus**
   They travel separately: he by train and she by bus
   Toi, tu ressembles à ton père, eux pas
   You look like your father, *they* don't
   Il n'a pas l'air de s'ennuyer, lui!
   He doesn't look bored!

5 **Lui et moi partons demain**
   He and I are leaving tomorrow
   Ni vous ni elles ne pouvez rester
   Neither you nor they can stay

6 **Mon père et elle ne s'entendent pas**
   My father and she don't get on

7 plus jeune que moi
   younger than me

   Il est moins grand que toi
   He's smaller than you (are)

8 **Moi, qui étais malade, je n'ai pas pu les accompagner**
   I, who was ill, couldn't go with them
   Ce sont eux qui font du bruit, pas nous
   They're the ones making the noise, not us

9 **Je l'ai fait moi-même**
   I did it myself

The pronoun en

● **en** replaces the preposition **de** + noun (→ **1**)
The verbal construction can affect the translation (→ **2**)

● **en** also replaces the partitive article (*English* = *some, any*) + noun
(→ **3**)

In expressions of quantity **en** represents the noun (→ **4**)

● Position:
en comes before the verb, except in positive commands when it
follows and is attached to the verb by a hyphen (→ **5**)

● **en** follows other object pronouns (→ **6**)

1 **Il est fier de son succès**   → **Il en est fier**
   He's proud of his success   He's proud of it
   Elle est sortie du cinéma   → **Elle en est sortie**
   She came out of the cinema   She came out (of it)
   Je suis couvert de peinture → **J'en suis couvert**
   I'm covered in paint   I'm covered in it
   Il a beaucoup d'amis   → **Il en a beaucoup**
   He has lots of friends   He has lots (of them)
2 **avoir besoin de qch**   to need sth:
      J'en ai besoin
      I need it/them
   avoir peur de qch   to be afraid of sth:
      J'en ai peur
      I'm afraid of it/them
3 **Avez-vous de l'argent?** → **En avez-vous?**
   Have you any money?   Do you have any?
   Je veux acheter des timbres → **Je veux en acheter**
   I want to buy some stamps   I want to buy some
4 **J'ai deux crayons**   → **J'en ai deux**
   I've two pencils   I've two (of them)
   Combien de sœurs as-tu? – J'en ai trois.
   How many sisters do you have? – I have three.
5 **Elle en a discuté avec moi**
   She discussed it with me
   En êtes-vous content?
   Are you pleased with
   it/them?
   Je veux en garder trois
   I want to keep three of them
   N'en parlez plus
   Don't talk about it any more
   Prenez-en   **Soyez-en fier**
   Take some   Be proud of it/them
6 **Donnez-leur-en**   **Il m'en a parlé**
   Give them some   He spoke to me about it

The pronoun y

● **y** replaces the preposition **à** + noun (→ **1**)
  The verbal construction can affect the translation (→ **2**)

● **y** also replaces the prepositions **dans** and **sur** + noun (→ **3**)

● **y** can also mean *there* (→ **4**)

● Position:
  y comes before the verb, except in positive commands when it
  follows and is attached to the verb by a hyphen (→ **5**)

● **y** follows other object pronouns (→ **6**)

1 **Ne touchez pas à ce bouton** → **N'y touchez pas**
Don't touch this switch   Don't touch it
Il participe aux concerts → **Il y participe**
He takes part in the concerts   He takes part (in them)

2 **penser à qch**   to think about sth:
  J'y pense souvent
  I often think about it
consentir à qch   to agree to sth:
  Tu y as consenti?
  Have you agreed to it?

3 **Mettez-les dans la boîte** → **Mettez-les-y**
Put them in the box   Put them in it
Il les a mis sur les étagères → **Il les y a mis**
He put them on the shelves   He put them on them
J'ai placé de l'argent sur ce
compte → **J'y ai placé de l'argent**
I've put money into this   I've put money into it
account

4 **Elle y passe tout l'été**
She spends the whole summer there

5 **Il y a ajouté du sucre**
He added sugar to it
Elle n'y a pas écrit son nom
She hasn't written her name on it
Comment fait-on pour y aller?
How do you get there?
N'y pense plus!
Don't give it another thought!
Restez-y **Réfléchissez-y**
Stay there Think it over

6 **Elle m'y a conduit** **Menez-nous-y**
She drove me there Take us there

Indefinite Pronouns

aucun(e)	none, not any	(→1)
certain(e)s	some, certain	(→2)
chacun(e)	each (one) everybody	(→3)
on	one, you somebody they, people we (informal use)	(→4)
personne	nobody	(→5)
plusieurs	several	(→6)
quelque chose	something; anything	(→7)
quelques-un(e)s	some, a few	(→8)
quelqu'un	somebody; anybody	(→9)
rien	nothing	(→10)
tout	all; everything	(→11)
tous (toutes)	all	(→12)
l'un(e) ... l'autre	(the) one ... the other	
les un(e)s ... les autres	some ... others	(→13)

● **aucun(e), personne, rien**

When used as subject or object of the verb, these require the word **ne** placed immediately before the verb. Note that **aucun** further needs the pronoun **en** when used as an object (→14)

● **quelque chose, rien**

When qualified by an adjective, these pronouns require the preposition **de** before the adjective (→15)

1 **Combien en avez-vous? – Aucun**
  How many have you got? – None

2 **Certains pensent que ...**
  Some (people) think that ...

3 **Chacune de ces boîtes est pleine**   **Chacun son tour!**
  Each of these boxes is full   Everybody in turn!

4 **On voit l'église de cette fenêtre**
  You can see the church from this window
  À la campagne on se couche tôt
  In the country they/we go to bed early
  Est-ce qu'on lui a permis de rester?
  Was he/she allowed to stay?

5 **Qui voyez-vous? – Personne**
  Who can you see? – Nobody

6 **Ils sont plusieurs**
  There are several of them

7 **Mange donc quelque chose!**   **Tu as vu quelque chose?**
  Eat something!   Did you see anything?

8 **Je connais quelques-uns de ses amis**
  I know some of his/her friends

9 **Quelqu'un a appelé**   **Tu as vu quelqu'un?**
  Somebody called (out)   Did you see anybody?

10 **Qu'est-ce que tu as dans la main? – Rien**
   What have you got in your hand? – Nothing

11 **Il a tout gâché**   **Tout va bien**
   He has spoiled everything   All's well

12 **Tu les as tous?**   **Elles sont toutes venues**
   Do you have all of them?   They all came

13 **Les uns sont satisfaits, les autres pas**
   Some are satisfied, (the) others aren't

14 **Je ne vois personne**   **Rien ne lui plaît**
   I can't see anyone   Nothing pleases him/her
   Aucune des entreprises ne veut ... **Il n'en a aucun**
   None of the companies wants ...   He hasn't any (of them)

15 **quelque chose de grand**   **rien d'intéressant**
   something big   nothing interesting

Relative Pronouns

qui   *who; which*
que   *who(m); which*

These are subject and direct object pronouns that introduce a clause and refer to people or things.

	PEOPLE	THINGS
SUBJECT	**qui** (→1)	**qui** (→3)
	who, that	*which, that*
DIRECT OBJECT	**que (qu')** (→2)	**que (qu')** (→4)
	who(m), that	*which, that*

● **que** changes to **qu'** before a vowel (→2/4)
● You cannot omit the object relative pronoun in French as you can in English (→2/4)

After a preposition:
● When referring to people, use **qui** (→5)
    Exceptions: after **parmi** *among* and **entre** *between* use
    lesquels/lesquelles (see below) (→6)
● When referring to things, use forms of **lequel**:

	MASCULINE	FEMININE	
SING.	**lequel**	**laquelle**	*which*
PLUR.	**lesquels**	**lesquelles**	*which*

The pronoun agrees in number and gender with the noun (→7)

● After the prepositions **à** and **de, lequel** and **lesquel(le)s** contract as follows:

　　　　à + lequel → auquel
　　　　à + lesquels → auxquels　　　(→8)
　　　　à + lesquelles → auxquelles

　　　　de + lequel → duquel
　　　　de + lesquels → desquels　　　(→9)
　　　　de + lesquelles → desquelles

Continued

1 **Mon frère, qui a vingt ans, est à l'université**
My brother, who's twenty, is at university

2 **Les amis que je vois le plus sont ...**
The friends (that) I see most are ...
Lucienne, qu'il connaît depuis longtemps, est ...
Lucienne, whom he has known for a long time, is ...

3 **Il y a un escalier qui mène au toit**
There's a staircase which leads to the roof

4 **La maison que nous avons achetée a ...**
The house (which) we've bought has ...
Voici le cadeau qu'elle m'a envoyé
This is the present (that) she sent me

5 **la personne à qui il parle**
the person he's talking to
la personne avec qui je voyage
the person with whom I travel
les enfants pour qui je l'ai acheté
the children for whom I bought it

6 **Il y avait des jeunes, parmi lesquels Robert**
There were some young people, Robert among them
les filles entre lesquelles j'étais assis
the girls between whom I was sitting

7 **le torchon avec lequel il l'essuie**
the cloth he's wiping it with
la table sur laquelle je l'ai mis
the table on which I put it
les moyens par lesquels il l'accomplit
the means by which he achieves it
les pièces pour lesquelles elle est connue
the plays for which she is famous

8 **le magasin auquel il livre ces marchandises**
the shop to which he delivers these goods

9 **les injustices desquelles il se plaint**
the injustices he's complaining about

Relative Pronouns (ctd.)

quoi   *which, what*

● When the relative pronoun does not refer to a specific noun, **quoi** is used after a preposition (→**1**)

dont   *whose, of whom, of which*

● **dont** often (but not always) replaces **de qui, duquel**, **de laquelle**, and **desquel(le)s** (→**2**)

● It cannot replace **de qui, duquel** etc in the construction preposition + noun + **de qui/duquel** (→**3**)

Continued

1 **C'est en quoi vous vous trompez**
That's where you're wrong
A quoi, j'ai répondu '…'
To which I replied, '…'

2 **la femme dont (= de qui) la voiture est garée en face**
the woman whose car is parked opposite
un prix dont (= de qui) je suis fier
an award I am proud of
un ami dont (= de qui) je connais le frère
a friend whose brother I know
les enfants dont (= de qui) vous vous occupez
the children you look after
le film dont (= duquel) il a parlé
the film of which he spoke
la fenêtre dont (= de laquelle) les rideaux sont tirés
the window whose curtains are drawn
des livres dont (= desquels) j'ai oublié les titres
books whose titles I've forgotten
les maladies dont (= desquelles) il souffre
the illnesses he suffers from

3 **une personne sur l'aide de qui on peut compter**
a person whose help one can rely on
les enfants aux parents de qui j'écris
the children to whose parents I'm writing
la maison dans le jardin de laquelle il y a …
the house in whose garden there is …

Relative Pronouns (ctd.)

ce qui, ce que *that which, what*
These are used when the relative pronoun does not refer to a specific noun, and they are often translated as *what* (literally: *that which*)

> **ce qui**   is used as the subject (→**1**)
> **ce que***   is used as the direct object (→**2**)
>
> ***que** changes to **qu'** before a vowel (→**2**)

● Note the construction

> **tout ce qui** ⎫
> **tout ce que** ⎬ *everything/all that* (→**3**)

● **de + ce que → ce dont** (→**4**)

● preposition + **ce que → ce** + preposition + **quoi** (→**5**)

● When **ce qui**, **ce que** etc, refers to a previous CLAUSE the translation is *which* (→**6**)

Continued

1 **Ce qui m'intéresse ne l'intéresse pas forcément**
What interests me doesn't necessarily interest him
Je n'ai pas vu ce qui s'est passé
I didn't see what happened

2 **Ce que j'aime c'est la musique classique**
What I like is classical music
Montrez-moi ce qu'il vous a donné
Show me what he gave you

3 **Tout ce qui reste c'est ...**
All that's left is ...
Donnez-moi tout ce que vous avez
Give me everything you have

4 **Il risque de perdre ce dont il est si fier**
He risks losing what he's so proud of
Voilà ce dont il s'agit
That's what it's about

5 **Ce n'est pas ce à quoi je m'attendais**
It's not what I was expecting
Ce à quoi je m'intéresse particulièrement c'est ...
What I'm particularly interested in is ...

6 **Il est d'accord, ce qui m'étonne**
He agrees, which surprises me
Il a dit qu'elle ne venait pas, ce que nous savions déjà
He said she wasn't coming, which we already knew

Interrogative Pronouns

qui?   *who?; whom?*
que?   *what?*
quoi?   *what?*

These pronouns are used in direct questions.

The form of the pronoun depends on:

- whether it refers to people or to things
- whether it is the subject or object of the verb, or if it comes after a preposition

Qui and **que** have longer forms, as shown in the tables below.

● Referring to people:

SUBJECT	**qui?**	
	qui est-ce qui?	(→**1**)
	who?	
OBJECT	**qui?**	
	qui est-ce que*?	(→**2**)
	who(m)?	
AFTER PREPOSITIONS	**qui?**	
	who(m)?	(→**3**)

● Referring to things:

SUBJECT	**qu'est-ce qui?**	(→**4**)
	what?	
OBJECT	**que*?**	
	qu'est-ce que*?	(→**5**)
	what?	
AFTER PREPOSITIONS	**quoi?**	(→**6**)
	what?	

***que** changes to **qu'** before a vowel (→**2, 5**)

Continued

1 **Qui vient?**
   Qui est-ce qui vient?
   Who's coming?

2 **Qui vois-tu?**
   Qui est-ce que tu vois?
   Who(m) can you see?
   Qui a-t-elle rencontré?
   Qui est-ce qu'elle a rencontré?
   Who(m) did she meet?

3 **De qui parle-t-il?**
   Who's he talking about?
   Pour qui est ce livre?
   Who's this book for?
   A qui avez-vous écrit?
   To whom did you write?

4 **Qu'est-ce qui se passe?**
   What's happening?
   Qu'est-ce qui a vexé Paul?
   What upset Paul?

5 **Que faites-vous?**
   Qu'est-ce que vous faites?
   What are you doing?
   Qu'a-t-il dit?
   Qu'est-ce qu'il a dit?
   What did he say?

6 **A quoi cela sert-il?**
   What's that used for?
   De quoi a-t-on parlé?
   What was the discussion about?
   Sur quoi vous basez-vous?
   What do you base it on?

Interrogative Pronouns (ctd.)

qui   *who; whom*
ce qui   *what*
ce que   *what*
quoi   *what*

These pronouns are used in indirect questions.
The form of the pronoun depends on:

- whether it refers to people or to things
- whether it is the subject or object of the verb, or if it comes
  after a preposition

● Referring to people: use **qui** in all instances (→**1**)

● Referring to things:

SUBJECT	**ce qui** *what*	(→**2**)
OBJECT	**ce que*** *what*	(→**3**)
AFTER PREPOSITIONS	**quoi** *what*	(→**4**)

***que** changes to **qu'** before a vowel (→**3**)

Continued

1 **Demande-lui qui est venu**
Ask him who came
Je me demande qui ils ont vu
I wonder who they saw
Dites-moi qui vous préférez
Tell me who you prefer
Elle ne sait pas à qui s'adresser
She doesn't know who to apply to
Demandez-leur pour qui elles travaillent
Ask them who they work for

2 **Il se demande ce qui se passe**
He's wondering what's happening
Je ne sais pas ce qui vous fait croire que ...
I don't know what makes you think that ...

3 **Raconte-nous ce que tu as fait**
Tell us what you did
Je me demande ce qu'elle pense
I wonder what she's thinking

4 **On ne sait pas de quoi vivent ces animaux**
We don't know what these animals live on
Je vais lui demander à quoi il fait allusion
I'm going to ask him what he's hinting at

Interrogative Pronouns (ctd.)

lequel?, laquelle?; lesquels?, lesquelles?

	MASCULINE	FEMININE	
SING.	**lequel?**	**laquelle?**	which (one)?
PLUR.	**lesquels?**	**lesquelles?**	which (ones)?

● The pronoun agrees in number and gender with the noun it refers to
(→**1**)

● The same forms are used in indirect questions (→**2**)

● After the prepositions **à** and **de**, **lequel** and **lesquel(le)s** contract as
follows:

> **à + lequel? → auquel?**
> **à + lesquels? → auxquels?**
> **à + lesquelles? → auxquelles?**
>
> **de + lequel? → duquel?**
> **de + lesquels? → desquels?**
> **de + lesquelles? → desquelles?**

1 **J'ai choisi un livre. – Lequel?**
  I've chosen a book. – Which one?
  Laquelle de ces valises est la vôtre?
  Which of these cases is yours?
  Amenez quelques amis. – Lesquels?
  Bring some friends. – Which ones?
  Lesquelles de vos sœurs sont mariées?
  Which of your sisters are married?

2 **Je me demande laquelle des maisons est la leur**
  I wonder which is their house
  Dites-moi lesquels d'entre eux étaient là
  Tell me which of them were there

Possessive Pronouns

SINGULAR

MASCULINE	FEMININE	
le mien	la mienne	*mine*
le tien	la tienne	*yours*
le sien	la sienne	*his; hers; its*
le nôtre	la nôtre	*ours*
le vôtre	la vôtre	*yours*
le leur	la leur	*theirs*

PLURAL

MASCULINE	FEMININE	
les miens	les miennes	*mine*
les tiens	les tiennes	*yours*
les siens	les siennes	*his; hers; its*
les nôtres	les nôtres	*ours*
les vôtres	les vôtres	*yours*
les leurs	les leurs	*theirs*

● The pronoun agrees in number and gender with the noun it replaces, NOT WITH THE OWNER (→**1**)

● Alternative translations are *my own, your own* etc; **le sien, la sienne** etc. may also mean *one's own* (→**2**)

● After the prepositions **à** and **de** the articles **le** and **les** are contracted in the normal way (see p. 140):

> à + le mien → au mien
> à + les miens → aux miens   (→**3**)
> à + les miennes → aux miennes
>
> de + le mien → du mien
> de + les miens → des miens   (→**4**)
> de + les miennes → des miennes

1 Demandez à Carole si ce stylo est le sien
Ask Carol if this pen is hers
Quelle équipe a gagné – la leur ou la nôtre?
Which team won – theirs or ours?
Mon stylo marche mieux que le tien
My pen writes better than yours
Richard a pris mes affaires pour les siennes
Richard mistook my belongings for his
Si tu n'as pas de disques, emprunte les miens
If you don't have any records, borrow mine
Nos maisons sont moins grandes que les vôtres
Our houses are smaller than yours

2 Est-ce que leur entreprise est aussi grande que la vôtre?
Is their company as big as your own?
Leurs prix sont moins élevés que les nôtres
Their prices are lower than our own
Le bonheur des autres importe plus que le sien
Other people's happiness matters more than one's own

3 Pourquoi préfères-tu ce manteau au mien?
Why do you prefer this coat to mine?
Quelles maisons ressemblent aux leurs?
Which houses resemble theirs?

4 Leur car est garé
Their coach is parked
Vos livres sont au-dessus des miens
Your books are on top of mine

Demonstrative Pronouns

celui, celle; ceux, celles

	MASCULINE	FEMININE	
SING.	**celui**	**celle**	*the one*
PLUR.	**ceux**	**celles**	*the ones*

● The pronoun agrees in number and gender with the noun it replaces
  (→**1**)

● Uses:
  - preceding a relative pronoun, meaning *the one(s) who/which*
    (→**1**)
  - preceding the preposition **de**, meaning *the one(s) belonging to,
    the one(s) of* (→**2**)
  - with **-ci** and **-là**, for emphasis or to distinguish between two things:

	MASCULINE	FEMININE		
SING.	**celui-ci**	**celle-ci**	*this (one)*	(→**3**)
PLUR.	**ceux-ci**	**celles-ci**	*these (ones)*	

	MASCULINE	FEMININE		
SING.	**celui-là**	**celle-là**	*that (one)*	(→**3**)
PLUR.	**ceux-là**	**celles-là**	*those (ones)*	

  - an additional meaning of **celui-ci / celui-là** etc. is *the former/the
    latter*

Continued

1 **Lequel? – Celui qui parle à Anne**
  Which man? – The one who's talking to Anne
  Quelle robe désirez-vous? – Celle qui est en vitrine
  Which dress do you want? – The one which is in the window
  Est-ce que ces livres sont ceux qu'il t'a donnés?
  Are these the books that he gave you?
  Quelles filles? – Celles que nous avons vues hier
  Which girls? – The ones we saw yesterday
  Cet article n'est pas celui dont vous m'avez parlé
  This article isn't the one you spoke to me about

2 **Ce jardin est plus grand que celui de mes parents**
  This garden is bigger than my parents' (garden)
  Est-ce que ta fille est plus âgée que celle de Gabrielle?
  Is your daughter older than Gabrielle's (daughter)?
  Je préfère les enfants de Paul à ceux de Roger
  I prefer Paul's children to Roger's (children)
  Comparez vos réponses à celles de votre voisin
  Compare your answers with your neighbours (answers)
  les montagnes d'Écosse et celles du pays de Galles
  the mountains of Scotland and those of Wales

3 **Quel tailleur préférez-vous: celui-ci ou celui-là?**
  Which suit do you prefer: this one or that one?
  Cette chemise a deux poches mais celle-la n'en a pas
  This shirt has two pockets but that one has none
  Quels œufs choisirais-tu: ceux-ci ou ceux-là?
  Which eggs would you choose: these (ones) or those (ones)?
  De toutes mes jupes, celle-ci me va le mieux
  Of all my skirts, this one fits me best

Demonstrative Pronouns (ctd.)

ce (c')   *it, that*

● Usually used with **être**, in the expressions **c'est**, **c'était**, **ce sont** etc. (→**1**)

● Note the spelling **ç** when followed by the letter **a** (→**2**)

● Uses:
  – to identify a person or object (→**3**)
  – for emphasis (→**4**)
  – as a neuter pronoun, referring to a statement, idea etc. (→**5**)

ce qui, ce que, ce dont   etc.: see Relative Pronouns (p. 184), Interrogative Pronouns (p. 188)

cela, ça   *it, that*

● **cela** and **ça** are used as 'neuter' pronouns, referring to a statement, an idea, an object (→**6**)

● In everyday spoken language **ça** is used in preference to **cela**

ceci   *this* (→**7**)

● **ceci** is not used as often as 'this' in English; **cela**, **ça** are often used where we use 'this'

1 C'est ...
It's/That's ...

C'était moi
It was me

2 Ça a été la cause de ...
It has been cause of ...

3 Qui est-ce?
Who is it?; Who's this/that?; Who's he/she?
C'est lui/mon frère/nous
It's/That's him/my brother/us
C'est une infirmière*
She's a nurse
Qu'est-ce que c'est?
What's this/that?
C'est une agrafeuse
It's a stapler

Ce sont eux
It's them
Ce sont des professeurs*
They're teachers
Qu'est-ce que c'est que ça?
What's that?
Ce sont des trombones
They're paper clips

4 C'est moi qui ai téléphoné
It was me who phoned
Ce sont les enfants qui importent le plus
It's the children who matter most

5 C'est très intéressant
That's/It's very interesting
Ce serait dangereux
That/It would be dangerous

6 Ça ne fait rien
It doesn't matter
A quoi bon faire ça?
What's the use of doing that?
Cela ne compte pas
That doesn't count
Cela demande du temps
It/That takes time

7 A qui est ceci?
Whose is this?

Ouvrez-le comme ceci
Open it like this

*See pp. 146 and 147 for the use of the article when stating a person's profession

Adverbs

Formation

● Most adverbs are formed by adding **-ment** to the feminine form of the adjective (→**1**)

● **-ment** is added to the *masculine* form when the masculine form ends in **-é**, **-i** or **-u** (→**2**)
Exception: **gai** (→**3**)
Occasionally the **u** changes to **û** before **-ment** is added (→**4**)

● If the adjective ends in **-ant** or **-ent**, the adverb ends in **-amment** or **-emment** (→**5**)
Exceptions: **lent**, **présent** (→**6**)

Irregular Adverbs

ADJECTIVE		ADVERB		
aveugle	blind	aveuglément	blindly	
bon	good	bien	well	(→**7**)
bref	brief	brièvement	briefly	
énorme	enormous	énormément	enormously	
exprès	express	expressément	expressly	(→**8**)
gentil	kind	gentiment	kindly	
mauvais	bad	mal	badly	(→**9**)
meilleur	better	mieux	better	
pire	worse	pis	worse	
précis	precise	précisément	precisely	
profond	deep	profondément	deeply	(→**10**)
traître	treacherous	traîtreusement	treacherously	

Adjectives used as adverbs

Certain adjectives are used adverbially. These include: **bas**, **bon**, **cher**, **clair**, **court**, **doux**, **droit**, **dur**, **faux**, **ferme**, **fort**, **haut**, **mauvais** and **net** (→**11**)

1 *MASC/FEM. ADJECTIVE* — *ADVERB*
heureux/heureuse fortunate — **heureusement** fortunately
franc/franche frank — **franchement** frankly
extrême/extrême extreme — **extrêmement** extremely

2 *MASC. ADJECTIVE* — *ADVERB*
désespéré desperate — **désespérément** desperately
vrai true — **vraiment** truly
résolu resolute — **résolument** resolutely

3 **gai** cheerful — **gaiement** OR **gaîment** cheerfully

4 **continu** continuous — **continûment** continuously

5 **constant** constant — **constamment** constantly
courant fluent — **couramment** fluently
évident obvious — **évidemment** obviously
fréquent frequent — **fréquemment** frequently

6 **lent** slow — **lentement** slowly
présent present — **présentement** presently

7 **Elle travaille bien**
She works well

8 **Il a expressément défendu qu'on parte**
He has expressly forbidden us to leave

9 **Un emploi mal payé**
A badly paid job

10 **J'ai été profondément ému**
I was deeply moved

11 **parler bas/haut**
to speak softly/loudly
coûter cher
to be expensive
voir clair
to see clearly
travailler dur
to work hard
chanter faux
to sing off key
sentir bon/mauvais
to smell nice/horrible

Position of Adverbs

● When the adverb accompanies a verb in a simple tense, it generally follows the verb (→ **1**)
● When the adverb accompanies a verb in a compound tense, it generally comes between the auxiliary verb and the past participle (→ **2**)
  Some adverbs, however, follow the past participle (→ **3**)
● When the adverb accompanies an adjective or another adverb it generally precedes the adjective/adverb (→ **4**)

Comparatives of Adverbs

These are formed using the following constructions:

plus ... (que)	*more ... (than)*	(→ **5**)
moins ... (que)	*less ... (than)*	(→ **6**)
aussi ... que	*as ... as*	(→ **7**)
si ... que*	*as ... as*	(→ **8**)

*used mainly after a negative

Superlatives of Adverbs

These are formed using the following constructions:

le plus ... (que)	*the most ... (that)*	(→ **9**)
le moins ... (que)	*the least ... (that)*	(→ **10**)

Adverbs with irregular comparatives/superlatives

ADVERB	COMPARATIVE	SUPERLATIVE
beaucoup	**plus**	**le plus**
a lot	*more*	*(the) most*
bien	**mieux**	**le mieux**
well	*better*	*(the) best*
mal	**pis** OR	**le pis** OR
	plus mal	**le plus mal**
badly	*worse*	*(the) worst*
peu	**moins**	**le moins**
little	*less*	*(the) least*

1 **Il dort encore**
He's still asleep

  Je pense souvent à toi
  I often think about you

2 **Ils sont déjà partis**
They've already gone
J'ai presque fini
I'm almost finished

  J'ai toujours cru que ...
  I've always thought that ...
  Il a trop mangé
  He's eaten too much

3 **On les a vus partout**
We saw them everywhere

  Elle est revenue hier
  She came back yesterday

4 **un très beau chemisier**
a very nice blouse
beaucoup plus vite
much faster

  une femme bien habillée
  a well-dressed woman
  peu souvent
  not very often

5 **plus vite**
more quickly
Elle chante plus fort que moi
She sings louder than I do

  plus régulièrement
  more regularly

6 **moins facilement**
less easily

  moins souvent
  less often

  Nous nous voyons moins fréquemment qu'auparavant
  We see each other less frequently than before

7 **Faites-le aussi vite que possible**
Do it as quickly as possible
Il en sait aussi long que nous
He knows as much about it as we do

8 **Ce n'est pas si loin que je pensais**
It's not as far as I thought

9 **Marianne court le plus vite**
Marianne runs fastest
Le plus tôt que je puisse venir c'est samedi
The earliest that I can come is Saturday

10 **C'est l'auteur que je connais le moins bien**
It's the writer I'm least familiar with

Common adverbs and their usage

assez	*enough; quite*	(→ **1**) See also below
aussi	*also, too; as*	(→ **2**)
autant	*as much*	(→ **3**) See also below
beaucoup	*a lot; much*	(→ **4**) See also below
bien	*well; very* *very much; 'indeed'*	(→ **5**) See also below
combien	*how much; how many*	(→ **6**) See also below
comme	*how; what*	(→ **7**)
déjà	*already; before*	(→ **8**)
encore	*still; yet* *more; even*	(→ **9**)
moins	*less*	(→ **10**) See also below
peu	*little, not much; not very*	(→ **11**) See also below
plus	*more*	(→ **12**) See also below
si	*so; such*	(→ **13**)
tant	*so much*	(→ **14**) See also below
toujours	*always; still*	(→ **15**)
trop	*too much; too*	(→ **16**) See also below

● **assez, autant, beaucoup, combien** etc. are used in the construction *adverb* + **de** + *noun* with the following meanings:

assez de	*enough*	(→**17**)
autant de	*as much; as many* *so much; so many*	
beaucoup de	*a lot of*	
combien de	*how much; how many*	
moins de	*less; fewer*	(→**17**)
peu de	*little, not much; few,* *not many*	
plus de	*more*	
tant de	*so much; so many*	
trop de	*too much; too many*	

● **bien** can be followed by a partitive article (see p. 144) plus a noun to mean *a lot of; a good many* (→ **18**)

1 **Avez-vous assez chaud?**
  Are you warm enough?
  Il est assez tard
  It's quite late

2 **Je préfère ça aussi**
  I prefer it too
  Elle est aussi grande que moi
  She is as tall as I am

3 **Je voyage autant que lui**
  I have as much as him

4 **Tu lis beaucoup?**
  Do you read a lot?
  C'est beaucoup plus loin?
  Is it much further?

5 **Bien joué!**
  Well played!
  Je suis bien content que ...
  I'm very pleased that ...
  Il s'est bien amusé
  He enjoyed himself very much
  Je l'ai bien fait
  I DID do it

6 **Combien coûte ce livre?**
  How much is this book?
  Vous êtes combien?
  How many of you are there?

7 **Comme tu es jolie!**
  How pretty you look!
  Comme il fait beau!
  What lovely weather!

8 **Je l'ai déjà fait**
  I've already done it
  Êtes-vous déjà allé en France?
  Have you been to France before?

9 **J'en ai encore deux**
  I've still got two
  Elle n'est pas encore là
  She isn't there yet
  Encore du café, Alain?
  More coffee, Alan?
  Encore mieux!
  Even better!

10 **Travaillez moins**
  Work less
  Je suis moins étonné que toi
  I'm less surprised than you are

11 **Elle mange peu**
  She doesn't eat very much
  C'est peu important
  It's not very important

12 **Il se détend plus**
  He relaxes more
  Elle est plus timide que Sophie
  She is shyer than Sophie

13 **Simon est si charmant**
  Simon is so charming
  une si belle vue
  such a lovely view

14 **Elle l'aime tant** She loves him so much

15 **Il dit toujours ça!**
  He always says that!
  Tu le vois toujours?
  Do you still see him?

16 **J'ai trop mangé**
  I've eaten too much
  C'est trop cher
  It's too expensive

17 **assez d'argent/de livres**
  enough money/books
  moins de temps/d'amis
  less time/fewer friends

18 **bien du mal/des gens** a lot of harm/a good many people

On the following pages you will find some of the most frequent uses of prepositions in French. Particular attention is paid to cases where usage differs markedly from English. It is often difficult to give an English equivalent for French prepositions, since usage *does* vary so much between the two languages.

In the list below, the broad meaning of the preposition is given on the left, with examples of usage following.

Prepositions are dealt with in alphabetical order, except **à**, **de** and **en** which are shown first.

à

at	**lancer qch à qn**	*to throw sth at sb*
	il habite à St. Pierre	*he lives at St. Pierre*
	à 5 francs (la) pièce	*(at) 5 francs each*
	à 100 km à l'heure	*at 100 km per hour*
in	**à la campagne**	*in the country*
	à Londres	*in London*
	au lit	*in bed* (also *to bed*)
	un livre à la main	*with a book in his/her hand*
on	**un tableau au mur**	*a picture on the wall*
to	**aller au cinéma**	*to go to the cinema*
	donner qch à qn	*to give sth to sb*
	le premier/dernier à faire	*the first/last to do*
	demander qch à qn	*to ask sb sth*
from	**arracher qch à qn**	*to snatch sth from sb*
	acheter qch à qn	*to buy sth from sb*
	cacher qch à qn	*to hide sth from sb*
	emprunter qch à qn	*to borrow sth from sb*
	prendre qch à qn	*to take sth from sb*
	voler qch à qn	*to steal sth from sb*

descriptive	**la femme au chapeau vert**	*the woman with the green hat*
	un garçon aux yeux bleus	*a boy with blue eyes*
manner, means	**à l'anglaise**	*in the English manner*
	fait à la main	*handmade*
	à bicyclette/cheval	*by bicycle/on horseback* (BUT note other forms of transport used with **en** and **par**)
	à pied	*on foot*
	chauffer au gaz	*to heat with/by gas*
	à pas lents	*with slow steps*
	cuisiner au beurre	*to cook with butter*
time, date: *at, in*	**à minuit**	*at midnight*
	à trois heures cinq	*at five past three*
	au 20ème siècle	*in the 20th century*
	à Noël/Pâques	*at Christmas/Easter*
distance	**à 6 km d'ici**	*(at a distance of) 6 km from here*
	à deux pas de chez moi	*just a step from my place*
destined for	**une tasse à thé**	*a teacup* (compare **une tasse de thé**)
	un service à café	*a coffee service*
after certain adjectives	**son écriture est difficile à lire**	*his writing is difficult to read* (compare the usage with **de**, p. 206)
	prêt à tout	*ready for anything*
after certain verbs *Continued*	see p. 64	

de

from	**venir de Londres**	to come from London
	du matin au soir	from morning till night
	du 21 juin au 5 juillet	from 21st June till 5th July
	de 10 à 15	from 10 to 15
belonging to, *of*	**un ami de la famille**	a family friend
	les vents d'automne	the autumn winds
contents, composition, material	**une boîte d'allumettes**	a box of matches
	une tasse de thé	a cup of tea (compare **une tasse à thé**)
	une robe de soie	a silk dress
manner	**d'une façon irrégulière**	in an irregular way
	d'un coup de couteau	with the blow of a knife
quality	**la société de consommation**	the consumer society
	des objets de valeur	valuable items
comparative + a number	**il y avait plus/moins de cent personnes**	there were more/fewer than a hundred people
after superlatives: *in*	**la plus/moins belle ville du monde**	the most/least beautiful city in the world
after certain adjectives	**surpris de voir**	surprised to see
	il est difficile d'y accéder	access is difficult (compare the usage with **à**, p. 205)
after certain verbs	see p. 64	

en

place: *to, in, on*	**en ville**	*in/to town*
	en pleine mer	*on the open sea*
	en France	*in/to France* (note that masculine countries use **à**)
dates, months: *in*	**en 1923**	*in 1923*
	en janvier	*in January*
transport	**en voiture**	*by car*
	en avion	*by plane* (but note usage of **à** and **par** in other expressions)
language	**en français**	*in French*
duration	**je le ferai en trois jours**	*I'll do it in three days* (i.e. *I'll take 3 days to do it.* compare **dans trois jours**)
material	**un bracelet en or**	*a bracelet made of gold* (note that the use of **en** stresses the material more than the use of **de**)
	consister en	*to consist of*
in the manner of, like a	**parler en vrai connaisseur**	*to speak like a real connoisseur*
	déguisé en cowboy	*dressed up as a cowboy*
+ present participle	**il l'a vu en passant devant la porte**	*he saw it as he came past the door*

Continued

avant

before	**il est arrivé avant toi**	he arrived before you
+ infinitive (add **de**)	**je vais finir ça avant de manger**	I'm going to finish this before eating
preference	**la santé avant tout**	health above all things

chez

at the home of	**chez lui/moi** **être chez soi** **venez chez nous**	at his/my house to be at home come round to our place
at/to a shop	**chez le boucher**	at/to the butcher's
in a person, among a group of people or animals	**ce que je n'aime pas chez lui c'est son ...** **chez les fourmis**	what I don't like in him is his ... among ants

dans

position	**dans une boîte**	in(to) a box
circumstance	**dans son enfance**	in his childhood
future time	**dans trois jours**	in three days' time (compare **en trois jours**, p. 207)

depuis

since: time place	**depuis mardi** **il pleut depuis Paris**	since Tuesday it's been raining since Paris
for	**il habite cette maison depuis 3 ans**	he's been living in this house for 3 years (NOTE TENSE)

dès

past time	**dès mon enfance**	*since my childhood*
future time	**je le ferai dès mon retour**	*I'll do it as soon as I get back*

entre

between	**entre 8 et 10**	*between 8 and 10*
among	**Jean et Pierre, entre autres**	*Jean and Pierre, among others*
reciprocal	**s'aider entre eux**	*to help each other (out)*

d'entre

of, among	**trois d'entre eux**	*three of them*

par

agent of passive: by	**renversé par une voiture**	*knocked down by a car*
	tué par la foudre	*killed by lightning*
weather conditions	**par un beau jour d'été**	*on a lovely summer's day*
by (means of)	**par un couloir/sentier**	*by a corridor/path*
	par le train	*by train (but see also à and en)*
	par l'intermédiaire de M. Duval	*through Mr. Duval*
distribution	**deux par deux**	*two by two*
	par groupes de dix	*in groups of ten*
	deux fois par jour	*twice a day*

Continued

pour

for	c'est pour vous	it's for you
	c'est pour demain	it's for tomorrow
	une chambre pour 2 nuits	a room for 2 nights
	pour un enfant, il se débrouille bien	for a child he manages very well
	il part pour l'Espagne	he's leaving for Spain
	il l'a fait pour vous	he did it for you
	il lui a donné 50 francs pour ce livre	he gave him 50 francs for this book
	je ne suis pas pour cette idée	I'm not for that idea
	pour qui me prends-tu?	who do you take me for?
	il passe pour un idiot	he's taken for a fool
+ infinitive: (in order) to	elle se pencha pour le ramasser	she bent down to pick it up
	c'est trop fragile pour servir de siège	it's too fragile to be used as a seat
to(wards)	être bon/gentil pour qn	to be kind to sb
with prices, time	pour 200 francs d'essence	200 francs' worth of petrol
	j'en ai encore pour une heure	I'll be another hour (at it) yet

sans

without	sans eau	without water
	sans ma femme	without my wife
+ infinitive	sans compter les autres	without counting the others

sauf

except (for)	**tous sauf lui**	*all except him*
	sauf quand il pleut	*except when its raining*
barring	**sauf imprévu**	*barring the unexpected*
	sauf avis contraire	*unless you hear to the contrary*

sur

on	**sur le siège**	*on the seat*
	sur l'armoire	*on top of the wardrobe*
	sur le mur	*on (top of) the wall (if the meaning is hanging on the wall use à, p. 204)*
	sur votre gauche	*on your left*
	être sur le point de faire	*to be on the point of doing*
on (to)	**mettez-le sur la table**	*put it on the table*
proportion: out of, by	**8 sur 10**	*8 out of 10*
	un automobiliste sur 5	*one motorist in 5*
	la pièce fait 2 mètres sur 3	*the room measures 2 metres by 3*

Conjunctions

There are conjunctions which introduce a main clause, such as **et** *and*, **mais** *but*, **si** *if*, **ou** *or* etc., and those which introduce subordinate clauses like **parce que** *because*, **pendant que** *while*, **après que** *after* etc. They are all used in much the same way as in English, but the following points are of note:

● Some conjunctions in French require a following subjunctive, see p. 58

● Some conjunctions are 'split' in French like *both ... and*, *either ... or* in English:

et ... et	*both ... and*	(→ **1**)
ni ... ni ... ne	*neither ... nor*	(→ **2**)
ou (bien) .. ou (bien)	*either ... or (else)*	(→ **3**)
soit ... soit	*either ... or*	(→ **4**)

● **si** + **il(s)** → **s'il(s)** (→ **5**)

● **que**
– meaning *that* (→ **6**)
– replacing another conjunction (→ **7**)
– replacing **si**, see p. 62
– in comparisons, meaning *as*, *than* (→ **8**)
– followed by the subjunctive, see p. 62

● **aussi** *so*, *therefore*: the subject and verb are inverted if the subject is a pronoun (→ **9**)

1 Ces fleurs poussent et en été et en hiver
These flowers grow in both summer and winter

2 Ni lui ni elle ne sont venus
Neither he nor she came
Ils n'ont ni argent ni nourriture
They have neither money nor food

3 Elle doit être ou naïve ou stupide
She must be either naïve or stupid
Ou bien il m'évite ou bien il ne me reconnaît pas
Either he's avoiding me or else he doesn't recognise me

4 Il faut choisir soit l'un soit l'autre
You have to choose either one or the other

5 Je ne sais pas s'il vient/s'ils viennent
I don't know if he's coming/if they're coming
Dis-moi s'il y a des erreurs
Tell me if there are any mistakes
Votre passeport, s'il vous plaît
Your passport, please

6 Il dit qu'il t'a vu
He says (that) he saw you
Est-ce qu'elle sait que vous êtes là?
Does she know that you're here?

7 Quand tu seras plus grand et que tu auras une maison à toi, ...
When you're older and you have a house of your own, ...
Comme il pleuvait et que je n'avais pas de parapluie, ...
As it was raining and I didn't have an umbrella, ...

8 Ils n'y vont pas aussi souvent que nous
They don't go there as often as we do
Il les aime plus que jamais
He likes them more than ever
L'argent est moins lourd que le plomb
Silver is lighter than lead

9 Ceux-ci sont plus rares, aussi coûtent-ils cher
These ones are rarer, so they're expensive

Word Order

Word order in French is largely the same as in English, except for the following. Most of these have already been dealt with under the appropriate part of speech, but are summarised here along with other instances not covered elsewhere.

● Object pronouns nearly always come before the verb (→ **1**)
  For details, see pp. 166 to 170

● Certain adjectives come after the noun (→ **2**)
  For details, see p. 162

● Adverbs accompanying a verb in a simple tense usually follow the verb (→ **3**)
  For details, see p. 200

● After **aussi** *so, therefore*, **à peine** *hardly*, **peut-être** *perhaps*, the verb and subject are inverted (→ **4**)

● After the relative pronoun **dont** *whose* (→ **5**)
  For details, see p. 182

● In exclamations, **que** and **comme** do not affect the normal word order (→ **6**)

● Following direct speech:
  – the *verb* + *subject* order is inverted to become *subject* + *verb* (→ **7**)
  – with a pronoun subject, the verb and pronoun are linked by a hyphen (→ **8**)
  – when the verb ends in a vowel in the 3rd person singular, **-t-** is inserted between the pronoun and the verb (→ **9**)

For word order in negative sentences, see p. 216
For word order in interrogative sentences, see pp. 220 and 222

1 **Je les vois!**
   I can see them!

   Il me l'a donné
   He gave it to me

2 **une ville française**
   a French town

   du vin rouge
   some red wine

3 **Il pleut encore**
   It's still raining

   Elle m'aide quelquefois
   She sometimes helps me

4 **Il vit tout seul, aussi fait-il ce qu'il veut**
   He lives alone, so he does what he likes

   A peine la pendule avait-elle sonné trois heures que ...
   Hardly had the clock struck three when ...

   Peut-être avez-vous raison
   Perhaps you're right

5 Compare: **un homme dont je connais la fille**
             a man whose daughter I know

   and: **un homme dont la fille me connaît**
          a man whose daughter knows me

   If the person (or object) 'owned' is the *object* of the verb, the order is:
   dont + verb + noun (1st sentence)
   If the person (or object) 'owned' is the *subject* of the verb, the order is:
   dont + noun + verb (2nd sentence)

   Note also: **l'homme dont elle est la fille**
                the man whose daughter she is

6 **Qu'il fait chaud!**
   How warm it is!

   Que je suis content de vous voir!
   How pleased I am to see you!

   Comme c'est cher
   How expensive it is!

   Que tes voisins sont gentils!
   How kind your neighbours are!

7 **'Je pense que oui' a dit Luc**
   'I think so,' said Luke

   'Ça ne fait rien' répondit Jean
   'It doesn't matter,' John replied

8 **'Quelle horreur!' me suis-je exclamé**
   'How awful!' I exclaimed

9 **'Pourquoi pas?' a-t-elle demandé**
   'Why not?' she asked

   'Si c'est vrai,' continua-t-il '...'
   'If it's true,' he went on '...'

Negatives

ne ... pas	*not*
ne ... point (literary)	*not*
ne ... rien	*nothing*
ne ... personne	*nobody*
ne ... plus	*no longer, no more*
ne ... jamais	*never*
ne ... que	*only*
ne ... aucun(e)	*no*
ne ... nul(le)	*no*
ne ... nulle part	*nowhere*
ne ... ni	*neither ... nor*
ne ... ni ... ni	*neither ... nor*

● **Word order**

– In simple tenses and the imperative:
  ne precedes the verb (and any object pronouns) and the second
  element follows the verb (→ **1**)

– In compound tenses:
  i **ne ... pas, ne ... point, ne ... rien, ne ... plus, ne ...
     jamais, ne ... guère** follow the pattern:
     ne + auxiliary verb + **pas** + past participle (→ **2**)
  ii **ne ... personne, ne ... que, ne ... aucun(e), ne ... nul(le),
     ne ... nulle part, ne ... ni (... ni)** follow the pattern:
     ne + auxiliary verb + past participle + **personne** (→ **3**)

– With a verb in the infinitive:
  ne ... pas, ne ... point (etc. see i above) come together (→ **4**)

● For use of **rien**, **personne** and **aucun** as pronouns, see p. 178

1 **Je ne fume pas**
I don't smoke
Ne changez rien
Don't change anything
Je ne vois personne
I can't see anybody
Nous ne nous verrons plus
We won't see each other any more
Il n'arrive jamais à l'heure
He never arrives on time
Il n'avait qu'une valise
He only had one suitcase
Je n'ai reçu aucune réponse
I have received no reply
Il ne boit ni ne fume
He neither drinks nor smokes
Ni mon fils ni ma fille ne les connaissaient
Neither my son nor my daughter knew them

2 **Elle n'a pas fait ses devoirs**
She hasn't done her homework
Ne vous a-t-il rien dit?
Didn't he say anything to you?
Ils n'avaient jamais vu une si belle maison
They had never seen such a beautiful house
Tu n'as guère changé
You've hardly changed

3 **Je n'ai parlé à personne**
I haven't spoken to anybody
Il n'avait mangé que la moitié du repas
He had only eaten half the meal
Elle ne les a trouvés nulle part
She couldn't find them anywhere
Il ne l'avait ni vu ni entendu
He had neither seen nor heard him

4 **Il essayait de ne pas rire**
He was trying not to laugh

Negatives (ctd.)

● Combination of negatives.
  These are the most common combinations of negative particles:

ne ... plus jamais	(→ 1)
ne ... plus personne	(→ 2)
ne ... plus rien	(→ 3)
ne ... plus ni ... ni ...	(→ 4)
ne ... jamais personne	(→ 5)
ne ... jamais rien	(→ 6)
ne ... jamais que	(→ 7)
ne ... jamais ni ... ni ...	(→ 8)
(ne ... pas) non plus	(→ 9)

non and **pas**

● **non** *no* is the usual negative response to a question (→ **10**)
  It is often translated as *not* (→ **11**)
● **pas** is generally used when a distinction is being made, or for emphasis (→ **12**)
  It is often translated as *not* (→ **13**)

1 **Je ne le ferai plus jamais**
I'll never do it again

2 **Je ne connais plus personne à Rouen**
I don't know anybody in Rouen any more

3 **Ces marchandises ne valaient plus rien**
Those goods were no longer worth anything

4 **Ils n'ont plus ni chats ni chiens**
They no longer have either cats or dogs

5 **On n'y voit jamais personne**
You never see anybody there

6 **Ils ne font jamais rien d'intéressant**
They never do anything interesting

7 **Je n'ai jamais parlé qu'à sa femme**
I've only ever spoken to his wife

8 **Il ne m'a jamais ni écrit ni téléphoné**
He has never either written to me or phoned me

9 **Ils n'ont pas d'enfants et nous non plus**
They don't have any children and neither do we
Je ne les aime pas – Moi non plus
I don't like them – Neither do I; I don't either

10 **Vous voulez nous accompagner? – Non**
Do you want to come with us? – No (I don't)

11 **Tu viens ou non?**
Are you coming or not?
J'espère que non
I hope not

12 **Ma sœur aime le ski, moi pas**
My sister likes skiing, I don't

13 **Qui a fait ça? – Pas moi!**
Who did that? – Not me!
Est-il de retour? – Pas encore
Is he back? – Not yet
Tu as froid? – Pas du tout
Are you cold? – Not at all

Question forms: direct

There are four ways of forming direct questions in French:

- by inverting the normal word order so that
  pronoun subject + verb → verb + pronoun subject.
  A hyphen links the verb and pronoun (→ **1**)

  - When the subject is a noun, a pronoun is inserted after the verb and linked to it by a hyphen (→ **2**)

  - When the verb ends in a vowel in the third person singular, **-t-** is inserted before the pronoun (→ **3**)

- by maintaining the word order *subject + verb*, but by using a rising intonation at the end of the sentence (→ **4**)

- by inserting **est-ce que** before the construction *subject + verb* (→ **5**)

- by using an interrogative word at the beginning of the sentence, together with inversion *or* the **est-ce que** form above (→ **6**)

1 **Aimez-vous la France?**
Do you like France?
Est-ce possible?
Is it possible?
Part-on tout de suite?
Are we leaving right away?

Avez-vous fini?
Have you finished?
Est-elle restée?
Did she stay?

2 **Tes parents sont-ils en vacances?**
Are your parents on holiday?
Jean-Benoît est-il parti?
Has Jean-Benoît left?

3 **A-t-elle de l'argent?**
Has she any money?
La pièce dure-t-elle longtemps?
Does the play last long?
Mon père a-t-il téléphoné?
Has my father phoned?

4 **Il l'a fini**
He's finished it
Robert va venir
Robert's coming

Il l'a fini?
Has he finished it?
Robert va venir?
Is Robert coming?

5 **Est-ce que tu la connais?**
Do you know her?
Est-ce que tes parents sont revenus d'Italie?
Have your parents come back from Italy?

6 **Quel train** { **prends-tu?**
             { **est-ce que tu prends?**
What train are you getting?
Lequel { **est-ce que ta sœur préfère?**
        { **ta sœur préfère-t-elle?**
Which one does your sister prefer?
Quand { **êtes-vous arrivé?**
        { **est-ce que vous êtes arrivé?**
When did you arrive?
Pourquoi { **ne sont-ils pas venus?**
           { **est-ce qu'ils ne sont pas venus?**
Why haven't they come?

Question forms: indirect

An indirect question is one that is 'reported', e.g. he asked me *what the time was*, tell me *which way to go*. Word order in indirect questions is as follows:

● *interrogative word* + *subject* + *verb* (→ **1**)

● when the subject is a noun, and not a pronoun, the subject and verb are often inverted (→ **2**)

n'est-ce pas

This is used wherever English would use *isn't it?*, *don't they?*, *weren't we?*, *is it?* etc. tagged on to the end of a sentence (→ **3**)

oui and si

Oui is the word for *yes* in answer to a question put in the affirmative (→ **4**)
Si is the word for *yes* in answer to a question put in the negative or to contradict a negative statement (→ **5**)

1 **Je me demande s'il viendra**
   I wonder if he'll come
   Je ne sais pas à quoi ça sert
   I don't know what it's for
   Dites-moi quel autobus va à la gare
   Tell me which bus goes to the station
   Il m'a demandé combien d'argent j'avais
   He asked me how much money I had

2 **Elle ne sait pas à quelle heure commence le film**
   She doesn't know what time the film starts
   Je me demande où sont mes clés
   I wonder where my keys are
   Elle nous a demandé comment allait notre père
   She asked us how our father was
   je ne sais pas ce que veulent dire ces mots
   I don't know what these words mean

3 **Il fait chaud, n'est-ce pas?**
   It's warm, isn't it?
   Vous n'oublierez pas, n'est-ce pas?
   You won't forget, will you?

4 **Tu l'as fait? – Oui**
   Have you done it? – Yes (I have)

5 **Tu ne l'as pas fait? – Si**
   Haven't you done it? – Yes (I have)

Numbers

Cardinal (*one, two etc.*)		**Ordinal** (*first, second etc.*)	
zéro	0		
un (une)	1	premier (première)	1er, 1ère
deux	2	deuxième, second(e)	2ème
trois	3	troisième	3ème
quatre	4	quatrième	4ème
cinq	5	cinquième	5ème
six	6	sixième	6ème
sept	7	septième	7ème
huit	8	huitième	8ème
neuf	9	neuvième	9ème
dix	10	dixième	10ème
onze	11	onzième	11ème
douze	12	douzième	12ème
treize	13	treizième	13ème
quatorze	14	quatorzième	14ème
quinze	15	quinzième	15ème
seize	16	seizième	16ème
dix-sept	17	dix-septième	17ème
dix-huit	18	dix-huitième	18ème
dix-neuf	19	dix-neuvième	19ème
vingt	20	vingtième	20ème
vingt et un (une)	21	vingt et unième	21ème
vingt-deux	22	vingt-deuxième	22ème
vingt-trois	23	vingt-troisième	23ème
trente	30	trentième	30ème
quarante	40	quarantième	40ème
cinquante	50	cinquantième	50ème
soixante	60	soixantième	60ème
soixante-dix	70	soixante-dixième	70ème
soixante et onze	71	soixante-onzième	71ème
soixante-douze	72	soixante-douzième	72ème
quatre-vingts	80	quatre-vingtième	80ème
quatre-vingt-un (une)	81	quatre-vingt-unième	81ème
quatre-vingt-dix	90	quatre-vingt-dixième	90ème
quatre-vingt-onze	91	quatre-vingt-onzième	91ème

Numbers (ctd.)

Cardinal		Ordinal	
cent	100	centième	100ème
cent un (une)	101	cent unième	101ème
cent deux	102	cent deuxième	102ème
cent dix	110	cent dixième	110ème
cent quarante-deux	142	cent quarante-deuxième	142ème
deux cents	200	deux centième	200ème
duex cent un (une)	201	deux cent unième	201ème
duex cent deux	202	deux cent-deuxième	202ème
trois cents	300	trois centième	300ème
quatre cents	400	quatre centième	400ème
cinq cents	500	cinq centième	500ème
six cents	600	six centième	600ème
sept cents	700	sept centième	700ème
huit cents	800	huit centième	800ème
neuf cents	900	neuf centième	900ème
mille	1000	millième	1000ème
mille un (une)	1001	mille unième	1001ème
mille deux	1002	mille deuxième	1002ème
deux mille	2000	deux millième	2000ème
cent mille	100.000	cent millième	100.000ème
un million	1.000.000	millionième	1.000.000ème
deux millions	2.000.000	deux millionième	2.000.000ème

Fractions		Others	
un demi, une demie	½	zéro virgule cinq	0,5
un tiers	⅓	un virgule trois	1,3
deux tiers	⅔	dix pour cent	10%
un quart	¼	deux plus deux	2 + 2
trois quarts	¾	deux moins deux	2 − 2
un cinquième	⅕	deux fois deux	2 × 2
cinq et trois quarts	5¾	deux divisé par deux	2 ÷ 2

Note the use of points with large numbers and commas with fractions, i.e. the opposite of English usage.

Numbers: Other Uses

● **-aine** denoting approximate numbers:

une douzaine (de pommes)	about a dozen (apples)
une quinzaine (d'hommes)	about fifteen (men)
des centaines de personnes	hundreds of people
BUT: **un millier (de voitures)**	about a thousand (cars)

● measurements:

vingt mètres carrés	20 square metres
vingt mètres cubes	20 cubic metres
un pont long de quarante mètres	a bridge 40 metres long
avoir trois mètres de large/de haut	to be 3 metres wide/high

● miscellaneous:

Il habite au dix	He lives at number 10
C'est au chapitre sept	It's in chapter 7
(C'est) à la page 17	(It's) on page 17
(Il habite) au septième étage	(He lives) on the 7th floor
Il est arrivé le septième	He came in 7th
échelle au vingt-cinq millième	scale 1:25,000

Telephone numbers

Je voudrais Edimbourg trois cent trente, vingt-deux, dix
I would like Edinburgh 330 22 10

Je voudrais le soixante-cinq, treize, vingt-deux, zéro deux
Could you get me 65 13 22 02

Poste trois cent trente-cinq
Extension number 335

Poste vingt-deux, trente-trois
Extension number 22 33

N.B. In French, telephone numbers are broken down into groups of two or three numbers (never four), and are not spoken separately as in English. They are also written in groups of two or three numbers.

The calendar

Dates

Quelle est la date d'aujourd'hui?
Quel jour sommes-nous? } What's the date today?

C'est ...
Nous sommes ... } It's the ...

le premier février	1st of February
le deux février	2nd of February
le vingt-huit février	28th of February

Il vient le sept mars   He's coming on the 7th of March

N.B. Use cardinal numbers except for the first of the month.

Years

Je suis né en 1971
I was born in 1971

le douze février { **dix-neuf cent soixante et onze**
                       mil neuf cent soixante et onze
(on) 12th February 1971

N.B. There are two ways of expressing the year (see last example).
Note the spelling of **mil** *one thousand* in dates.

Other expressions

dans les années cinquante	during the fifties
au vingtième siècle	in the twentieth century
en mai	in May
lundi (quinze)	on Monday (the 15th)
le lundi	on Mondays
dans dix jours	in 10 days' time
il y a dix jours	10 days ago

The Time

Quelle heure est-il?	*What time is it?*
Il est ...	*It's ...*

00.00	**minuit** *midnight, twelve o'clock*
00.10	**minuit dix, zéro heure dix**
00.15	**minuit et quart, zéro heure quinze**
00.30	**minuit et demi, zéro heure trente**
00.45	**une heure moins (le) quart, zéro heure quarante-cinq**
01.00	**une heure du matin** *one a.m., one o'clock in the morning*
01.10	**une heure dix (du matin)**
01.15	**une heure et quart, une heure quinze**
01.30	**une heure et demie, une heure trente**
01.45	**deux heures moins (le) quart, une heure quarante-cinq**
01.50	**deux heures moins dix, une heure cinquante**
01.59	**deux heures moins une, une heure cinquante-neuf**
12.00	**midi, douze heures** *noon, twelve o'clock*
12.30	**midi et demi, douze heures trente**
13.00	**une heure de l'après-midi, treize heures** *one p.m., one o'clock in the afternoon*
01.30	**une heure et demie (de l'après-midi), treize heures trente**
19.00	**sept heures du soir, dix-neuf heures** *seven p.m., seven o'clock in the evening*
19.30	**sept heures et demie (du soir), dix-neuf heures trente**

A quelle heure venez-vous? – A sept heures
What time are you coming? – At seven o'clock
Les bureaux sont fermés de midi à quatorze heures
The offices are closed from twelve until two
à deux heures du matin/de l'après-midi
at two o'clock in the morning/afternoon, at two a.m./p.m.
à sept heures du soir
at seven o'clock in the evening, at seven p.m.
à cinq heures précises *or* **pile**
at five o'clock sharp
vers neuf heures
about nine o'clock
peu avant/après midi
shortly before/after noon
entre huit et neuf heures
between eight and nine o'clock
Il est plus de trois heures et demie
It's after half past three
Il faut y être à dix heures au plus tard/au plus tôt
You have to be there by ten o'clock at the latest/earliest
Ne venez pas plus tard que onze heures moins le quart
Come no later than a quarter to eleven
Il en a pour une demi-heure
He'll be half an hour (at it)
Elle est restée sans connaissance pendant un quart d'heure
She was unconscious for a quarter of an hour
Je les attends depuis une heure
I've been waiting for them for an hour/since one o'clock
Ils sont partis il y a quelques minutes
They left a few minutes ago
Je l'ai fait en vingt minutes
I did it in twenty minutes
Le train arrive dans une heure
The train arrives in an hour('s time)
Combien de temps dure ce film?
How long does this film last?

230 TRANSLATION PROBLEMS

Beware of translating word for word. While on occasion this is quite possible, quite often it is not. The need for caution is illustrated by the following:

● English phrasal verbs (i.e. verbs followed by a preposition) e.g. *to run away*, *to fall down* are often translated by one word in French (→ **1**)

● English verbal constructions often contain a preposition where none exists in French, or vice versa (→ **2**)

● Two or more prepositions in English may have a single rendering in French (→ **3**)

● A word which is singular in English may be plural in French, or vice versa (→ **4**)

● French has no equivalent of the possessive construction denoted by *--'s/--'s* (→ **5**)
See also *at/in/to*, p. 234

Specific problems

-ing

This is translated in a variety of ways in French:

● *to be ...-ing* is translated by a simple verb (→ **6**)
Exception: when a physical position is denoted, a past participle is used (→ **7**)

● in the construction *to see/hear sb ...-ing*, use an infinitive or **qui** + verb (→ **8**)

-ing can also be translated by:
  – an infinitive (→ **9**)
    (see p. 44)
  – a perfect infinitive (→ **10**)
    (see p. 46)
  – a present participle (→ **11**)
    (see p. 48)
  – a noun (→ **12**)

Continued

1 **s'enfuir**
to run away

tomber
to fall down

céder
to give in

2 **payer**
to pay for

regarder
to look at

écouter
to listen to

obéir à
to obey

nuire à
to harm

manquer de
to lack

3 **s'étonner de**
to be surprised at

satisfait de
satisfied with

voler qch à
to steal sth from

apte à
capable of; fit for

4 **les bagages**
the luggage

ses cheveux
his/her hair

le bétail
the cattle

mon pantalon
my trousers

5 **la voiture de mon frère**
my brother's car
(*literally: ... of my brother*)

la chambre des enfants
the children's bedroom
(*literally: ... of the children*)

6 **Il part demain**
He's leaving tomorrow

Je lisais un roman
I was reading a novel

7 **Elle est assise là-bas**
She's sitting over there

Il était couché par terre
He was lying on the ground

8 **Je les vois** { **venir** / **qui viennent** } I can see them coming

Je l'ai entendue { **chanter** / **qui chantait** } I heard her singing

9 **J'aime aller au cinéma**
I like going to the cinema

Arrêtez de parler!
Stop talking!

Au lieu de répondre
Instead of answering

Avant de partir
Before leaving

10 **Après avoir ouvert la boîte, il ...**
After opening the box, he ...

11 **Etant plus timide que moi, elle ...**
Being shyer than me, she ...

12 **Le ski me maintient en forme**
Skiing keeps me fit

to be

- Generally translated by **être** (→ **1**)
  When physical location is implied, **se trouver** may be used (→ **2**)

- In set expressions, describing physical and emotional conditions,
  avoir is used:
avoir chaud/froid	*to be warm/cold*
avoir faim/soif	*to be hungry/thirsty*
avoir peur/honte	*to be afraid/ashamed*
avoir tort/raison	*to be wrong/right*

- Describing the weather, e.g. *what's the weather like?*, *it's windy/sunny*, use **faire** (→ **3**)

- For ages, e.g. *he is 6*, use **avoir** (→ **4**)

- For state of health, e.g. *he's unwell*, *how are you?*, use **aller** (→ **5**)

it is, it's

- Usually **il/elle est**, when referring to a noun (→ **6**)

- For expressions of time, also use **il est** (→ **7**)

- To describe the weather, e.g. *it's windy*, see above

- In the construction: *it is difficult/easy to do sth*, use **il est** (→ **8**)

- In all other constructions, use **c'est** (→ **9**)

there is/there are

- Both are translated by **il y a** (→ **10**)

can, be able

- Physical ability is expressed by **pouvoir** (→ **11**)

- If the meaning is *to know how to*, use **savoir** (→ **12**)

- *Can* + a 'verb of hearing or seeing etc.' in English is not translated in French (→ **13**)

1 **Il est tard**   **C'est peu probable**
It's late   It's not very likely

2 **Où se trouve la gare?**
Where's the station?

3 **Quel temps fait-il?**   **Il fait beau/mauvais/du vent**
What's the weather like?   It's lovely/miserable/windy

4 **Quel âge avez-vous?**   **J'ai quinze ans**
How old are you?   I'm fifteen

5 **Comment allez-vous?**   **Je vais très bien**
How are you?   I'm very well

6 **Où est mon parapluie? – Il est là, dans le coin**
Where's my umbrella? – It's there, in the corner
Descends la valise si elle n'est pas trop lourde
Bring down the case if it isn't too heavy

7 **Quelle heure est-il? – Il est sept heures et demie**
What's the time? – It's half past seven

8 **Il est difficile de répondre à cette question**
It's difficult to reply to this question

9 **C'est moi qui ne l'aime pas**
It's me who doesn't like him
C'est Charles/ma mère qui l'a dit
It's Charles/my mother who said so
C'est ici que je les ai achetés
It's here that I bought them
C'est parce que la poste est fermée que …
It's because the post office is closed that …

10 **Il y a quelqu'un à la porte**
There's somebody at the door
Il y a cinq livres sur la table
There are five books on the table

11 **Pouvez-vous atteindre cette étagère?**
Can you reach up to that shelf?

12 **Elle ne sait pas nager**
She can't swim

13 **Je ne vois rien**   **Il les entendait**
I can't see anything   He could hear them

to (see also below)

● Generally translated by **à** (→ **1**)
(See p. 204)

● In time expressions, e.g. *10 to 6*, use **moins** (→ **2**)

● When the meaning is *in order to*, use **pour** (→ **3**)

● Following a verb, as in *to try to do, to like to do*, see pp. 44 and 64

● *easy/difficult/impossible* etc. *to do*:
The preposition used depends on whether a specific noun is referred to (→ **4**) or not (→ **5**)

at/in/to

● With feminine countries, use **en** (→ **6**)
With masculine countries, use **au** (**aux** with plural countries) (→ **7**)

● With towns, use **à** (→ **8**)

● *at/to the butcher's/grocer's* etc.: use **à** + noun designating the shop, or **chez** + noun designating the shopkeeper (→ **9**)

● *at/to the dentist's/doctor's* etc.: use **chez** (→ **10**)

● *at/to ...'s/...s' house*: use **chez** (→ **11**)

1 **Donne le livre à Patrick**
Give the book to Patrick

2 **dix heures moins cinq**   **à sept heures moins le quart**
five to ten   at a quarter to seven

3 **Je l'ai fait pour vous aider**
I did it to help you
Il se pencha pour nouer son lacet
He bent down to tie his shoelace

4 **Ce livre est difficile à lire**
This book is difficult to read

5 **Il est difficile de comprendre leurs raisons**
It's difficult to understand their reasons

6 **Il est allé en France/en Suisse**
He has gone to France/to Switzerland
un village en Norvège/en Belgique
a village in Norway/in Belgium

7 **Etes-vous allé au Canada/au Danemark/aux Etats-Unis?**
Have you been to Canada/to Denmark/to the United States?
une ville au Japon/au Brésil
a town in Japan/in Brazil

8 **Il est allé à Vienne/à Bruxelles**
He has gone to Vienna/to Brussels
Il habite à Londres/à Genève
He lives in London/in Geneva
Ils logent dans un hôtel à St. Pierre
They're staying in a hotel at St. Pierre

9 **Je l'ai acheté** { **à l'épicerie** / **chez l'épicier** } I bought it at the grocer's
Elle est allée { **à la boulangerie** / **chez le boulanger** } She's gone to the baker's

10 **J'ai un rendez-vous chez le dentiste**
I've an appointment at the dentist's
Il est allé chez le médecin
He has gone to the doctor's

11 **chez Christian**   **chez les Pagot**
at/to Christian's house   at/to the Pagots' house

General Points

● Activity of the lips

The lips play a very important part in French. When a vowel is described as having 'rounded' lips, the lips are slightly drawn together and pursed, as when an English speaker expresses exaggerated surprise with the vowel 'ooh!'. Equally, if the lips are said to be 'spread', the corners are pulled firmly back towards the cheeks, tendng to reveal the front teeth.

In English, lip position is not important, and vowel sounds tend to merge because of this. In French, the activity of the lips means that every vowel sound is clearly distinct from every other.

● No diphthongs

A diphthong is a glide between two vowel sounds in the same syllable. In English, there are few 'pure' vowel sounds, but largely diphthongs instead. Although speakers of English may *think* they produce one vowel sound in the word 'day', in fact they use a diphthong, which in this instance is a glide between the vowels [e] and [ɪ]: [deɪ]. In French the tension maintained in the lips, tongue and the mouth in general prevents diphthongs occurring, as the vowel sound is kept constant throughout. Hence the French word corresponding to the above example, 'dé', is pronounced with no final [ɪ] sound, but is phonetically represented thus: [de].

● Consonants

In English, consonants are often pronounced with a degree of laxness that can result in their practically disappearing altogether although not strictly 'silent'. In a relaxed pronunciation of a word such as 'hat', the 't' is often scarcely heard, or is replaced by a 'glottal stop' (a sort of jerk in the throat). This never occurs in French, where consonants are always given their full value.

Pronunciation of Consonants

Some consonants are pronounced almost exactly as in English: [b, p, f, v, g, k, m, w].

Most others are similar to English, but slight differences should be noted.

EXAMPLES	HINTS ON PRONUNCIATION
[d] **d**in**d**e	
[t] **t**en**t**e	The tip of the tongue touches the upper front teeth and not the roof of the mouth as in English
[n] **n**o**nn**e	
[l] **L**i**ll**e	
[s] tou**s ç**a	The tip of the tongue is down behind the bottom front teeth, lower than in English
[z] **z**éro ro**s**e	
[ʃ] **ch**ose ta**ch**e	Like the *sh* of English *shout*
[ʒ] **j**e **g**ilet bei**g**e	Like the *s* of English *measure*
[j] **y**eux pai**ll**e	Like the *y* of English *yes*

Three consonants are not heard in English:

[ʀ] **r**a**r**e veni**r**	*R* is often silent in English, e.g. fa*r*m. In French the [ʀ] is never silent, unless it follows an **e** at the end of a word e.g. cherch**er**. To pronounce it, try to make a short sound like gargling. Similar, too, to the Scottish pronunciation of lo*ch*
[ɲ] vi**gn**e a**gn**eau	Similar to the *ni* of Spa*ni*ard
[ɥ] h**u**ile l**u**eur	Like a very rapid [y] (see p. 239) followed immediately by the next vowel of the word

Pronunciation of Vowels

EXAMPLES	HINTS ON PRONUNCIATION
[a] patte plat amour	Similar to the vowel in English *pat*
[ɑ] bas pâte	Longer than the sound above, it resembles the English exclamation of surprise *ah!* Similar, too, to the English vowel in *car* without the final *r* sound
[ɛ] lait jouet merci	Similar to the English vowel in *pet*. Beware of using the English diphthong [eɪ] as in *pay*
[e] été jouer	A pure vowel, again quite different from the diphthong in English *pay*
[ə] le premier	Similar to the English sound in butt*er* when the *r* is not pronounced
[i] ici vie lycée	The lips are well spread towards the cheeks while uttering this sound. Shorter than the English vowel in *see*
[ɔ] mort homme	The lips are well rounded while producing a sound similar to the *o* of English *cot*
[o] mot dôme eau	A pure vowel with strongly rounded lips; quite different from the diphthong in English *bone, low*

[u] gen**ou roue**   A pure vowel with strongly rounded lips. Similar to the English *ooh!* of surprise

[y] **rue** vê**tu**   Often the most difficult for English speakers to produce: round your lips and try to pronounce [i] (see above). There is no [j] sound (see p. 237) as there is in English *pure*

[œ] s**œu**r b**eu**rre   Similar to the vowel in English *fir* or *murmur*, but without the *r* sound and with the lips more strongly rounded

[ø] p**eu** d**eux**   To pronounce this, try to say [e] (see above) with the lips strongly rounded

Nasal Vowels

These are spelt with a vowel followed by a 'nasal' consonant – **n** or **m**. The production of nasal vowels really requires the help of a teacher or a recording of the sound. However, to help you, the vowel is pronounced by allowing the air from the lungs to come partly down the nose and partly through the mouth, and the **n** or **m** is not pronounced at all.

[ɑ̃] l**en**t s**an**g d**an**s

[ɛ̃] mat**in** pl**ein**

[ɔ̃] n**on** p**on**t

[œ̃] br**un un** parf**um**

In each case, the vowel shown in the phonetic symbol is pronounced as described above, but air is allowed to come through the nose as well as the mouth

From Spelling to Sounds

Although it may not seem so at first sight, there are some fairly precise 'rules' which can help you to know how to pronounce French words from their spelling.

Vowels

SPELLING	PRONOUNCED	EXAMPLES
a, à	[a]	chatte, table
a, â	[ɑ]	pâte, pas
e, é	[e]	été, marcher
e, é, ê	[ɛ]	fenêtre, fermer, chère
e	[ɔ]	double, fenêtre
i, î, y	[i]	lit. abîmer, lycée
o, ô	[o]	pot, trop, dôme
o	[ɔ]	sotte, orange
u, û	[y]	battu, fût, pur

Vowel Groups

There are several groups of vowels in French spelling which are regularly pronounced in the same way:

ai	[ɛ] or [e]	maison, marchai, faire
ail	[aj]	portail
ain, aim, (c)in, im	[ɛ̃]	pain, faim, frein, impair
au	[o]	auberge, landau
an, am, en, em	[ɑ̃]	plan, ample, entrer, temps
eau	[o]	bateau, eau
eu	[œ] or [ø]	feu, peur
euil(le), ueil	[œj]	feuille, recueil
oi, oy	[wa]	voire, voyage
on, om	[ɔ̃]	ton, compter
ou	[u]	hibou, outil
œu	[œ]	sœur, cœur
ue	[y]	rue
un, um	[œ̃]	brun, parfum

Added to these are the many groups of letters occurring at the end of words, where their pronunciation is predictable, bearing in mind the tendency (see p. 242) of final consonants to remain silent:

TYPICAL WORDS	PRONUNCIATION OF FINAL SYLLABLE
pas, mât, chat	[ɑ] or [a]
marcher, marchez marchais, marchait, baie, valet, mes, fumée	[e] or [ɛ]
nid	[i]
chaud, vaut, faux, sot, tôt, Pernod, dos, croc	[o]
bout, bijoux, sous, boue	[u]
fut, fût, crus, crûs	[y]
queue, heureux, bleus	[ø]
en, vend, vent, an, sang, grand, dans	[ɑ̃]
fin, feint, frein, vain	[ɛ̃]
on, pont, fond, avons	[ɔ̃]
brun, parfum	[œ̃]

Continued

From Spelling to Sounds (ctd.)

Consonants

● Final consonants are usually silent (→**1**)

● **n** or **m** at the end of a syllable or word are silent, but they have the effect of 'nasalizing' the preceding vowel(s) (see p. 239 on Nasal Vowels)

● The letter **h** is either 'silent' ('mute') or 'aspirate' when it begins a word. When silent, the word behaves as though it started with a vowel and takes a liaison with the preceding word where appropriate.
When the **h** is aspirate, no liaison is made (→**2**)
There is no way of predicting which words start with which sort of **h** – this simply has to be learnt with each word

● The following consonants in spelling have predictable pronunciations: b, d, f, k, l, p, r, t, v, w, x, y, z. Others vary:

SPELLING	PRONOUNCED	ENGLISH EXAMPLES	
c + **a, o, u**	[k]	**c**an, **c**ot, **c**ut	
+ **l, r**		**c**lass, **c**ram	(→**3**)
c + **e, i, y**	[s]	**c**eiling, i**c**e	(→**4**)
ç + **a, o, u**	[s]	**c**eiling, i**c**e	(→**5**)
ch	[ʃ]	**sh**op, la**sh**	(→**6**)
g + **a, o, u**	[g]	**g**ate, **g**ot, **g**un	
+ **l, r**		**g**lass, **g**ramme	(→**7**)
g + **e, i, y**	[ʒ]	lei**s**ure	(→**8**)
gn	[ɲ]	compa**ni**on, o**ni**on	(→**9**)
j	[ʒ]	mea**s**ure	(→**10**)
q, qu	[k]	**qu**ay, **k**it	(→**11**)
s between vowels:	[z]	ro**s**e	
elsewhere	[s]	**s**it	(→**12**)
th	[t]	**Th**omas	(→**13**)
t in **-tion**	[s]	**s**it	(→**14**)

1 éclat
[ekla]

nez
[ne]

chaud
[ʃo]

aider
[ɛde]

2 silent **h**:
des hôtels
[de zotɛl]

aspirate **h**:
des haricots
[de aʀiko]

3 café
[kafe]

côte
[kot]

culture
[kyltyʀ]

classe
[klas]

croûte
[kʀut]

4 ceci
[səsi]

cil
[sil]

cycliste
[siklist]

5 ça
[sɑ]

garçon
[gaʀsɔ̃]

déçu
[desy]

6 chat
[ʃa]

riche
[ʀiʃ]

7 gare
[gaʀ]

gourde
[guʀd]

aigu
[ɛgy]

glaise
[glɛz]

gramme
[gʀam]

8 gemme
[ʒɛm]

gilet
[ʒilɛ]

gymnaste
[ʒimnast]

9 vigne
[viɲ]

oignon
[ɔɲɔ̃]

10 joli
[ʒɔli]

Jules
[ʒyl]

11 quiche
[kiʃ]

quitter
[kite]

12 sable
[sablə]

maison
[mɛzɔ̃]

13 théâtre
[teɑtʀ]

Thomas
[tɔma]

14 nation
[nasjɔ̃]

action
[aksjɔ̃]

Feminine Forms and Pronunciation

● For adjectives and nouns ending in a vowel in the masculine, the addition of an **e** to form the feminine does not alter the pronunciation (→**1**)

● If the masculine ends with a silent consonant, generally **-d**, **-s**, **-r** or **-t**, the consonant is sounded in the feminine (→**2**)
This also applies when the final consonant is doubled before the addition of the feminine **e** (→**3**)

● If the masculine ends in a nasal vowel and a silent **n**, e.g. **-an**, **-on**, **-in**, the vowel is no longer nasalized and the **-n** is pronounced in the feminine (→**4**)
This also applies when the final **-n** is doubled before the addition of the feminine **e** (→**5**)

● Where the masculine and feminine forms have totally different endings (see pp. 136 and 150), the pronunciation of course varies accordingly (→**6**)

Plural Forms and Pronunciation

● The addition of **s** or **x** to form regular plurals generally does not affect pronunciation (→**7**)

● Where liaison has to be made, the final **-s** or **-x** of the plural form is pronounced (→**8**)

● Where the masculine singular and plural forms have totally different endings (see pp. 138 and 148), the pronunciation of course varies accordingly (→**9**)

● Note the change in pronunciation in the following nouns:

SINGULAR		PLURAL		
bœuf	[bœf]	**bœufs**	[bø]	*ox/oxen*
œuf	[œf]	**œufs**	[ø]	*egg/eggs*
os	[ɔs]	**os**	[o]	*bone/bones*

ADJECTIVES		NOUNS	
1 joli [ʒɔli]	→ **jolie** [ʒɔli]	**un ami** [ami]	→ **une amie** [ami]
déçu [desy]	→ **déçue** [desy]	**un employé** [ãplwaje]	→ **une employée** [ãplwaje]
2 chaud [ʃo]	→ **chaude** [ʃod]	**un étudiant** [etydjã]	→ **une étudiante** [etydjãt]
français [fRãsɛ]	→ **française** [fRãsɛz]	**un Anglais** [ãglɛ]	→ **une Anglaise** [ãglɛz]
inquiet [ɛ̃kjɛ]	→ **inquiète** [ɛ̃kjɛt]	**un étranger** [etRãʒe]	→ **une étrangère** [etRãʒɛR]
3 violet [vjɔlɛ]	→ **violette** [vjɔlɛt]	**le cadet** [kadɛ]	→ **la cadette** [kadɛt]
gras [gRɑ]	→ **grasse** [gRɑs]		→
4 plein [plɛ̃]	→ **pleine** [plɛn]	**le souverain** [suvRɛ̃]	→ **la souveraine** [suvRɛn]
fin [fɛ̃]	→ **fine** [fin]	**Le Persan** [pɛRsã]	→ **la Persane** [pɛRsan]
brun [bRœ̃]	→ **brune** [bRyn]	**le voisin** [vwazɛ̃]	→ **la voisine** [vwazin]
5 canadien [kanadjɛ̃]	→ **canadienne** [kanadjɛn]	**le paysan** [peizã]	→ **la paysanne** [peizan]
breton [bRətɔ̃]	→ **bretonne** [bRətɔn]	**le baron** [baRɔ̃]	→ **la baronne** [baRɔn]
6 vif [vif]	→ **vive** [viv]	**le veuf** [vœf]	→ **la veuve** [vœv]
traître [tRɛtRɛ]	→ **traîtresse** [tRɛtRɛs]	**le maître** [mɛtRə]	→ **la maîtresse** [mɛtRɛs]
7 beau [bo]	→ **beaux** [bo]	**la maison** [mɛzɔ̃]	→ **les maisons** [mɛzɔ̃]
8 des anciens élèves [de zãsjɛ̃ zelɛv] **de beaux arbres** [də bo zaRbR(ə)]			
9 amical [amikal]	→ **amicaux** [amiko]	**un journal** [ʒuRnal]	→ **des journaux** [ʒuRno]

The Alphabet

A, a	[ɑ]	**J, j**	[ʒi]	**S, s**	[ɛs]
B, b	[be]	**K, k**	[ka]	**T, t**	[te]
C, c	[se]	**L, l**	[ɛl]	**U, u**	[y]
D, d	[de]	**M, m**	[ɛm]	**V, v**	[ve]
E, e	[ə]	**N, n**	[ɛn]	**W, w**	[dubləve]
F, f	[ɛf]	**O, o**	[o]	**X, x**	[iks]
G, g	[ʒe]	**P, p**	[pe]	**Y, y**	[igRɛk]
H, h	[aʃ]	**Q, q**	[ky]	**Z, z**	[zɛd]
I, i	[i]	**R, r**	[ɛr]		

Capital letters are used as in English *except* for the following:

● adjectives of nationality

    e.g. **une ville espagnole**   **un auteur français**
         a Spanish town   a French author

● languages

    e.g. **Parlez-vous anglais?**   **Il parle français et allemand**
         Do you speak English?   He speaks French and German

● days of the week:

lundi	Monday
mardi	Tuesday
mercredi	Wednesday
jeudi	Thursday
vendredi	Friday
samedi	Saturday
dimanche	Sunday

● months of the year:

janvier	January	**juillet**	July
février	February	**août**	August
mars	March	**septembre**	September
avril	April	**octobre**	October
mai	May	**novembre**	November
juin	June	**décembre**	December

The following index lists comprehensively both grammatical terms and key words in French and English contained in this book.